Oxford Dictionary of
National Biography

Volume 36

Oxford Dictionary of National Biography

IN ASSOCIATION WITH

The British Academy

From the earliest times to the year 2000

Edited by

H. C. G. Matthew

and

Brian Harrison

Volume 36

Macquarie–Martin

OXFORD

UNIVERSITY PRESS

OXFORD
UNIVERSITY PRESS

Great Clarendon Street, Oxford OX2 6DP

Oxford University Press is a department of the University of Oxford.
It furthers the University's objective of excellence in research, scholarship,
and education by publishing worldwide in

Oxford New York

Auckland Bangkok Buenos Aires Cape Town
Chennai Dar es Salaam Delhi Hong Kong Istanbul Karachi
Kolkata Kuala Lumpur Madrid Melbourne Mexico City Mumbai Nairobi
São Paulo Shanghai Taipei Tokyo Toronto

Oxford is a registered trade mark of Oxford University Press
in the UK and in certain other countries

Published in the United States
by Oxford University Press Inc., New York

British Library Cataloguing in Publication Data
Data available

Library of Congress Cataloging in Publication Data
Data available: for details see volume 1, p. iv

ISBN 0-19-861386-5 (this volume)
ISBN 0-19-861411-X (set of sixty volumes)

Text captured by Alliance Phototypesetters, Pondicherry
Illustrations reproduced and archived by
Alliance Graphics Ltd, UK
Typeset in OUP Swift by Interactive Sciences Limited, Gloucester
Printed in Great Britain on acid-free paper by
Butler and Tanner Ltd,
Frome, Somerset

LIST OF ABBREVIATIONS

1 General abbreviations

AB	bachelor of arts
ABC	Australian Broadcasting Corporation
ABC TV	ABC Television
act.	active
A$	Australian dollar
AD	*anno domini*
AFC	Air Force Cross
AIDS	acquired immune deficiency syndrome
AK	Alaska
AL	Alabama
A level	advanced level [examination]
ALS	associate of the Linnean Society
AM	master of arts
AMICE	associate member of the Institution of Civil Engineers
ANZAC	Australian and New Zealand Army Corps
appx *pl.* appxs	appendix(es)
AR	Arkansas
ARA	associate of the Royal Academy
ARCA	associate of the Royal College of Art
ARCM	associate of the Royal College of Music
ARCO	associate of the Royal College of Organists
ARIBA	associate of the Royal Institute of British Architects
ARP	air-raid precautions
ARRC	associate of the Royal Red Cross
ARSA	associate of the Royal Scottish Academy
art.	article / item
ASC	Army Service Corps
Asch	Austrian Schilling
ASDIC	Antisubmarine Detection Investigation Committee
ATS	Auxiliary Territorial Service
ATV	Associated Television
Aug	August
AZ	Arizona
b.	born
BA	bachelor of arts
BA (Admin.)	bachelor of arts (administration)
BAFTA	British Academy of Film and Television Arts
BAO	bachelor of arts in obstetrics
bap.	baptized
BBC	British Broadcasting Corporation / Company
BC	before Christ
BCE	before the common (*or* Christian) era
BCE	bachelor of civil engineering
BCG	bacillus of Calmette and Guérin [inoculation against tuberculosis]
BCh	bachelor of surgery
BChir	bachelor of surgery
BCL	bachelor of civil law

BCnL	bachelor of canon law
BCom	bachelor of commerce
BD	bachelor of divinity
BEd	bachelor of education
BEng	bachelor of engineering
bk *pl.* bks	book(s)
BL	bachelor of law / letters / literature
BLitt	bachelor of letters
BM	bachelor of medicine
BMus	bachelor of music
BP	before present
BP	British Petroleum
Bros.	Brothers
BS	(1) bachelor of science; (2) bachelor of surgery; (3) British standard
BSc	bachelor of science
BSc (Econ.)	bachelor of science (economics)
BSc (Eng.)	bachelor of science (engineering)
bt	baronet
BTh	bachelor of theology
bur.	buried
C.	command [identifier for published parliamentary papers]
c.	*circa*
c.	*capitulum pl. capitula*: chapter(s)
CA	California
Cantab.	Cantabrigiensis
cap.	*capitulum pl. capitula*: chapter(s)
CB	companion of the Bath
CBE	commander of the Order of the British Empire
CBS	Columbia Broadcasting System
cc	cubic centimetres
C$	Canadian dollar
CD	compact disc
Cd	command [identifier for published parliamentary papers]
CE	Common (*or* Christian) Era
cent.	century
cf.	compare
CH	Companion of Honour
chap.	chapter
ChB	bachelor of surgery
CI	Imperial Order of the Crown of India
CIA	Central Intelligence Agency
CID	Criminal Investigation Department
CIE	companion of the Order of the Indian Empire
Cie	Compagnie
CLit	companion of literature
CM	master of surgery
cm	centimetre(s)

Cmd	command [identifier for published parliamentary papers]
CMG	companion of the Order of St Michael and St George
Cmnd	command [identifier for published parliamentary papers]
CO	Colorado
Co.	company
co.	county
col. *pl.* cols.	column(s)
Corp.	corporation
CSE	certificate of secondary education
CSI	companion of the Order of the Star of India
CT	Connecticut
CVO	commander of the Royal Victorian Order
cwt	hundredweight
$	(American) dollar
d.	(1) penny (pence); (2) died
DBE	dame commander of the Order of the British Empire
DCH	diploma in child health
DCh	doctor of surgery
DCL	doctor of civil law
DCnL	doctor of canon law
DCVO	dame commander of the Royal Victorian Order
DD	doctor of divinity
DE	Delaware
Dec	December
dem.	demolished
DEng	doctor of engineering
des.	destroyed
DFC	Distinguished Flying Cross
DipEd	diploma in education
DipPsych	diploma in psychiatry
diss.	dissertation
DL	deputy lieutenant
DLitt	doctor of letters
DLittCelt	doctor of Celtic letters
DM	(1) Deutschmark; (2) doctor of medicine; (3) doctor of musical arts
DMus	doctor of music
DNA	dioxyribonucleic acid
doc.	document
DOL	doctor of oriental learning
DPH	diploma in public health
DPhil	doctor of philosophy
DPM	diploma in psychological medicine
DSC	Distinguished Service Cross
DSc	doctor of science
DSc (Econ.)	doctor of science (economics)
DSc (Eng.)	doctor of science (engineering)
DSM	Distinguished Service Medal
DSO	companion of the Distinguished Service Order
DSocSc	doctor of social science
DTech	doctor of technology
DTh	doctor of theology
DTM	diploma in tropical medicine
DTMH	diploma in tropical medicine and hygiene
DU	doctor of the university
DUniv	doctor of the university
dwt	pennyweight
EC	European Community
ed. *pl.* eds.	edited / edited by / editor(s)
Edin.	Edinburgh
edn	edition
EEC	European Economic Community
EFTA	European Free Trade Association
EICS	East India Company Service
EMI	Electrical and Musical Industries (Ltd)
Eng.	English
enl.	enlarged
ENSA	Entertainments National Service Association
ep. *pl.* epp.	*epistola(e)*
ESP	extra-sensory perception
esp.	especially
esq.	esquire
est.	estimate / estimated
EU	European Union
ex	sold by (*lit.* out of)
excl.	excludes / excluding
exh.	exhibited
exh. cat.	exhibition catalogue
f. *pl.* ff.	following [pages]
FA	Football Association
FACP	fellow of the American College of Physicians
facs.	facsimile
FANY	First Aid Nursing Yeomanry
FBA	fellow of the British Academy
FBI	Federation of British Industries
FCS	fellow of the Chemical Society
Feb	February
FEng	fellow of the Fellowship of Engineering
FFCM	fellow of the Faculty of Community Medicine
FGS	fellow of the Geological Society
fig.	figure
FIMechE	fellow of the Institution of Mechanical Engineers
FL	Florida
fl.	*floruit*
FLS	fellow of the Linnean Society
FM	frequency modulation
fol. *pl.* fols.	folio(s)
Fr	French francs
Fr.	French
FRAeS	fellow of the Royal Aeronautical Society
FRAI	fellow of the Royal Anthropological Institute
FRAM	fellow of the Royal Academy of Music
FRAS	(1) fellow of the Royal Asiatic Society; (2) fellow of the Royal Astronomical Society
FRCM	fellow of the Royal College of Music
FRCO	fellow of the Royal College of Organists
FRCOG	fellow of the Royal College of Obstetricians and Gynaecologists
FRCP(C)	fellow of the Royal College of Physicians of Canada
FRCP (Edin.)	fellow of the Royal College of Physicians of Edinburgh
FRCP (Lond.)	fellow of the Royal College of Physicians of London
FRCPath	fellow of the Royal College of Pathologists
FRCPsych	fellow of the Royal College of Psychiatrists
FRCS	fellow of the Royal College of Surgeons
FRGS	fellow of the Royal Geographical Society
FRIBA	fellow of the Royal Institute of British Architects
FRICS	fellow of the Royal Institute of Chartered Surveyors
FRS	fellow of the Royal Society
FRSA	fellow of the Royal Society of Arts

FRSCM	fellow of the Royal School of Church Music
FRSE	fellow of the Royal Society of Edinburgh
FRSL	fellow of the Royal Society of Literature
FSA	fellow of the Society of Antiquaries
ft	foot *pl.* feet
FTCL	fellow of Trinity College of Music, London
ft-lb per min.	foot-pounds per minute [unit of horsepower]
FZS	fellow of the Zoological Society
GA	Georgia
GBE	knight or dame grand cross of the Order of the British Empire
GCB	knight grand cross of the Order of the Bath
GCE	general certificate of education
GCH	knight grand cross of the Royal Guelphic Order
GCHQ	government communications headquarters
GCIE	knight grand commander of the Order of the Indian Empire
GCMG	knight or dame grand cross of the Order of St Michael and St George
GCSE	general certificate of secondary education
GCSI	knight grand commander of the Order of the Star of India
GCStJ	bailiff or dame grand cross of the order of St John of Jerusalem
GCVO	knight or dame grand cross of the Royal Victorian Order
GEC	General Electric Company
Ger.	German
GI	government (*or* general) issue
GMT	Greenwich mean time
GP	general practitioner
GPU	[Soviet special police unit]
GSO	general staff officer
Heb.	Hebrew
HEICS	Honourable East India Company Service
HI	Hawaii
HIV	human immunodeficiency virus
HK$	Hong Kong dollar
HM	his / her majesty('s)
HMAS	his / her majesty's Australian ship
HMNZS	his / her majesty's New Zealand ship
HMS	his / her majesty's ship
HMSO	His / Her Majesty's Stationery Office
HMV	His Master's Voice
Hon.	Honourable
hp	horsepower
hr	hour(s)
HRH	his / her royal highness
HTV	Harlech Television
IA	Iowa
ibid.	*ibidem*: in the same place
ICI	Imperial Chemical Industries (Ltd)
ID	Idaho
IL	Illinois
illus.	illustration
illustr.	illustrated
IN	Indiana
in.	inch(es)
Inc.	Incorporated
incl.	includes / including
IOU	I owe you
IQ	intelligence quotient
Ir£	Irish pound
IRA	Irish Republican Army

ISO	companion of the Imperial Service Order
It.	Italian
ITA	Independent Television Authority
ITV	Independent Television
Jan	January
JP	justice of the peace
jun.	junior
KB	knight of the Order of the Bath
KBE	knight commander of the Order of the British Empire
KC	king's counsel
kcal	kilocalorie
KCB	knight commander of the Order of the Bath
KCH	knight commander of the Royal Guelphic Order
KCIE	knight commander of the Order of the Indian Empire
KCMG	knight commander of the Order of St Michael and St George
KCSI	knight commander of the Order of the Star of India
KCVO	knight commander of the Royal Victorian Order
keV	kilo-electron-volt
KG	knight of the Order of the Garter
KGB	[Soviet committee of state security]
KH	knight of the Royal Guelphic Order
KLM	Koninklijke Luchtvaart Maatschappij (Royal Dutch Air Lines)
km	kilometre(s)
KP	knight of the Order of St Patrick
KS	Kansas
KT	knight of the Order of the Thistle
kt	knight
KY	Kentucky
£	pound(s) sterling
£E	Egyptian pound
L	lira *pl.* lire
l. *pl.* ll.	line(s)
LA	Lousiana
LAA	light anti-aircraft
LAH	licentiate of the Apothecaries' Hall, Dublin
Lat.	Latin
lb	pound(s), unit of weight
LDS	licence in dental surgery
lit.	literally
LittB	bachelor of letters
LittD	doctor of letters
LKQCPI	licentiate of the King and Queen's College of Physicians, Ireland
LLA	lady literate in arts
LLB	bachelor of laws
LLD	doctor of laws
LLM	master of laws
LM	licentiate in midwifery
LP	long-playing record
LRAM	licentiate of the Royal Academy of Music
LRCP	licentiate of the Royal College of Physicians
LRCPS (Glasgow)	licentiate of the Royal College of Physicians and Surgeons of Glasgow
LRCS	licentiate of the Royal College of Surgeons
LSA	licentiate of the Society of Apothecaries
LSD	lysergic acid diethylamide
LVO	lieutenant of the Royal Victorian Order
M. *pl.* MM.	Monsieur *pl.* Messieurs
m	metre(s)

m. *pl.* mm.	membrane(s)
MA	(1) Massachusetts; (2) master of arts
MAI	master of engineering
MB	bachelor of medicine
MBA	master of business administration
MBE	member of the Order of the British Empire
MC	Military Cross
MCC	Marylebone Cricket Club
MCh	master of surgery
MChir	master of surgery
MCom	master of commerce
MD	(1) doctor of medicine; (2) Maryland
MDMA	methylenedioxymethamphetamine
ME	Maine
MEd	master of education
MEng	master of engineering
MEP	member of the European parliament
MG	Morris Garages
MGM	Metro-Goldwyn-Mayer
Mgr	Monsignor
MI	(1) Michigan; (2) military intelligence
MI1c	[secret intelligence department]
MI5	[military intelligence department]
MI6	[secret intelligence department]
MI9	[secret escape service]
MICE	member of the Institution of Civil Engineers
MIEE	member of the Institution of Electrical Engineers
min.	minute(s)
Mk	mark
ML	(1) licentiate of medicine; (2) master of laws
MLitt	master of letters
Mlle	Mademoiselle
mm	millimetre(s)
Mme	Madame
MN	Minnesota
MO	Missouri
MOH	medical officer of health
MP	member of parliament
m.p.h.	miles per hour
MPhil	master of philosophy
MRCP	member of the Royal College of Physicians
MRCS	member of the Royal College of Surgeons
MRCVS	member of the Royal College of Veterinary Surgeons
MRIA	member of the Royal Irish Academy
MS	(1) master of science; (2) Mississippi
MS *pl.* MSS	manuscript(s)
MSc	master of science
MSc (Econ.)	master of science (economics)
MT	Montana
MusB	bachelor of music
MusBac	bachelor of music
MusD	doctor of music
MV	motor vessel
MVO	member of the Royal Victorian Order
n. *pl.* nn.	note(s)
NAAFI	Navy, Army, and Air Force Institutes
NASA	National Aeronautics and Space Administration
NATO	North Atlantic Treaty Organization
NBC	National Broadcasting Corporation
NC	North Carolina
NCO	non-commissioned officer
ND	North Dakota
n.d.	no date
NE	Nebraska
nem. con.	*nemine contradicente*: unanimously
new ser.	new series
NH	New Hampshire
NHS	National Health Service
NJ	New Jersey
NKVD	[Soviet people's commissariat for internal affairs]
NM	New Mexico
nm	nanometre(s)
no. *pl.* nos.	number(s)
Nov	November
n.p.	no place [of publication]
NS	new style
NV	Nevada
NY	New York
NZBS	New Zealand Broadcasting Service
OBE	officer of the Order of the British Empire
obit.	obituary
Oct	October
OCTU	officer cadets training unit
OECD	Organization for Economic Co-operation and Development
OEEC	Organization for European Economic Co-operation
OFM	order of Friars Minor [Franciscans]
OFMCap	Ordine Frati Minori Cappucini: member of the Capuchin order
OH	Ohio
OK	Oklahoma
O level	ordinary level [examination]
OM	Order of Merit
OP	order of Preachers [Dominicans]
op. *pl.* opp.	opus *pl.* opera
OPEC	Organization of Petroleum Exporting Countries
OR	Oregon
orig.	original
OS	old style
OSB	Order of St Benedict
OTC	Officers' Training Corps
OWS	Old Watercolour Society
Oxon.	Oxoniensis
p. *pl.* pp.	page(s)
PA	Pennsylvania
p.a.	per annum
para.	paragraph
PAYE	pay as you earn
pbk *pl.* pbks	paperback(s)
per.	[during the] period
PhD	doctor of philosophy
pl.	(1) plate(s); (2) plural
priv. coll.	private collection
pt *pl.* pts	part(s)
pubd	published
PVC	polyvinyl chloride
q. *pl.* qq.	(1) question(s); (2) quire(s)
QC	queen's counsel
R	rand
R.	Rex / Regina
r	recto
r.	reigned / ruled
RA	Royal Academy / Royal Academician

RAC	Royal Automobile Club
RAF	Royal Air Force
RAFVR	Royal Air Force Volunteer Reserve
RAM	[member of the] Royal Academy of Music
RAMC	Royal Army Medical Corps
RCA	Royal College of Art
RCNC	Royal Corps of Naval Constructors
RCOG	Royal College of Obstetricians and Gynaecologists
RDI	royal designer for industry
RE	Royal Engineers
repr. *pl.* reprs.	reprint(s) / reprinted
repro.	reproduced
rev.	revised / revised by / reviser / revision
Revd	Reverend
RHA	Royal Hibernian Academy
RI	(1) Rhode Island; (2) Royal Institute of Painters in Water-Colours
RIBA	Royal Institute of British Architects
RIN	Royal Indian Navy
RM	Reichsmark
RMS	Royal Mail steamer
RN	Royal Navy
RNA	ribonucleic acid
RNAS	Royal Naval Air Service
RNR	Royal Naval Reserve
RNVR	Royal Naval Volunteer Reserve
RO	Record Office
r.p.m.	revolutions per minute
RRS	royal research ship
Rs	rupees
RSA	(1) Royal Scottish Academician; (2) Royal Society of Arts
RSPCA	Royal Society for the Prevention of Cruelty to Animals
Rt Hon.	Right Honourable
Rt Revd	Right Reverend
RUC	Royal Ulster Constabulary
Russ.	Russian
RWS	Royal Watercolour Society
S4C	Sianel Pedwar Cymru
s.	shilling(s)
s.a.	*sub anno*: under the year
SABC	South African Broadcasting Corporation
SAS	Special Air Service
SC	South Carolina
ScD	doctor of science
S$	Singapore dollar
SD	South Dakota
sec.	second(s)
sel.	selected
sen.	senior
Sept	September
ser.	series
SHAPE	supreme headquarters allied powers, Europe
SIDRO	Société Internationale d'Énergie Hydro-Électrique
sig. *pl.* sigs.	signature(s)
sing.	singular
SIS	Secret Intelligence Service
SJ	Society of Jesus
Skr	Swedish krona
Span.	Spanish
SPCK	Society for Promoting Christian Knowledge
SS	(1) Santissimi; (2) Schutzstaffel; (3) steam ship
STB	bachelor of theology
STD	doctor of theology
STM	master of theology
STP	doctor of theology
supp.	supposedly
suppl. *pl.* suppls.	supplement(s)
s.v.	*sub verbo* / *sub voce*: under the word / heading
SY	steam yacht
TA	Territorial Army
TASS	[Soviet news agency]
TB	tuberculosis (*lit.* tubercle bacillus)
TD	(1) *teachtaí dála* (member of the Dáil); (2) territorial decoration
TN	Tennessee
TNT	trinitrotoluene
trans.	translated / translated by / translation / translator
TT	tourist trophy
TUC	Trades Union Congress
TX	Texas
U-boat	*Unterseeboot*: submarine
Ufa	Universum-Film AG
UMIST	University of Manchester Institute of Science and Technology
UN	United Nations
UNESCO	United Nations Educational, Scientific, and Cultural Organization
UNICEF	United Nations International Children's Emergency Fund
unpubd	unpublished
USS	United States ship
UT	Utah
v	verso
v.	versus
VA	Virginia
VAD	Voluntary Aid Detachment
VC	Victoria Cross
VE-day	victory in Europe day
Ven.	Venerable
VJ-day	victory over Japan day
vol. *pl.* vols.	volume(s)
VT	Vermont
WA	Washington [state]
WAAC	Women's Auxiliary Army Corps
WAAF	Women's Auxiliary Air Force
WEA	Workers' Educational Association
WHO	World Health Organization
WI	Wisconsin
WRAF	Women's Royal Air Force
WRNS	Women's Royal Naval Service
WV	West Virginia
WVS	Women's Voluntary Service
WY	Wyoming
¥	yen
YMCA	Young Men's Christian Association
YWCA	Young Women's Christian Association

2 Institution abbreviations

All Souls Oxf.	All Souls College, Oxford
AM Oxf.	Ashmolean Museum, Oxford
Balliol Oxf.	Balliol College, Oxford
BBC WAC	BBC Written Archives Centre, Reading
Beds. & Luton ARS	Bedfordshire and Luton Archives and Record Service, Bedford
Berks. RO	Berkshire Record Office, Reading
BFI	British Film Institute, London
BFI NFTVA	British Film Institute, London, National Film and Television Archive
BGS	British Geological Survey, Keyworth, Nottingham
Birm. CA	Birmingham Central Library, Birmingham City Archives
Birm. CL	Birmingham Central Library
BL	British Library, London
BL NSA	British Library, London, National Sound Archive
BL OIOC	British Library, London, Oriental and India Office Collections
BLPES	London School of Economics and Political Science, British Library of Political and Economic Science
BM	British Museum, London
Bodl. Oxf.	Bodleian Library, Oxford
Bodl. RH	Bodleian Library of Commonwealth and African Studies at Rhodes House, Oxford
Borth. Inst.	Borthwick Institute of Historical Research, University of York
Boston PL	Boston Public Library, Massachusetts
Bristol RO	Bristol Record Office
Bucks. RLSS	Buckinghamshire Records and Local Studies Service, Aylesbury
CAC Cam.	Churchill College, Cambridge, Churchill Archives Centre
Cambs. AS	Cambridgeshire Archive Service
CCC Cam.	Corpus Christi College, Cambridge
CCC Oxf.	Corpus Christi College, Oxford
Ches. & Chester ALSS	Cheshire and Chester Archives and Local Studies Service
Christ Church Oxf.	Christ Church, Oxford
Christies	Christies, London
City Westm. AC	City of Westminster Archives Centre, London
CKS	Centre for Kentish Studies, Maidstone
CLRO	Corporation of London Records Office
Coll. Arms	College of Arms, London
Col. U.	Columbia University, New York
Cornwall RO	Cornwall Record Office, Truro
Courtauld Inst.	Courtauld Institute of Art, London
CUL	Cambridge University Library
Cumbria AS	Cumbria Archive Service
Derbys. RO	Derbyshire Record Office, Matlock
Devon RO	Devon Record Office, Exeter
Dorset RO	Dorset Record Office, Dorchester
Duke U.	Duke University, Durham, North Carolina
Duke U., Perkins L.	Duke University, Durham, North Carolina, William R. Perkins Library
Durham Cath. CL	Durham Cathedral, chapter library
Durham RO	Durham Record Office
DWL	Dr Williams's Library, London
Essex RO	Essex Record Office
E. Sussex RO	East Sussex Record Office, Lewes
Eton	Eton College, Berkshire
FM Cam.	Fitzwilliam Museum, Cambridge
Folger	Folger Shakespeare Library, Washington, DC
Garr. Club	Garrick Club, London
Girton Cam.	Girton College, Cambridge
GL	Guildhall Library, London
Glos. RO	Gloucestershire Record Office, Gloucester
Gon. & Caius Cam.	Gonville and Caius College, Cambridge
Gov. Art Coll.	Government Art Collection
GS Lond.	Geological Society of London
Hants. RO	Hampshire Record Office, Winchester
Harris Man. Oxf.	Harris Manchester College, Oxford
Harvard TC	Harvard Theatre Collection, Harvard University, Cambridge, Massachusetts, Nathan Marsh Pusey Library
Harvard U.	Harvard University, Cambridge, Massachusetts
Harvard U., Houghton L.	Harvard University, Cambridge, Massachusetts, Houghton Library
Herefs. RO	Herefordshire Record Office, Hereford
Herts. ALS	Hertfordshire Archives and Local Studies, Hertford
Hist. Soc. Penn.	Historical Society of Pennsylvania, Philadelphia
HLRO	House of Lords Record Office, London
Hult. Arch.	Hulton Archive, London and New York
Hunt. L.	Huntington Library, San Marino, California
ICL	Imperial College, London
Inst. CE	Institution of Civil Engineers, London
Inst. EE	Institution of Electrical Engineers, London
IWM	Imperial War Museum, London
IWM FVA	Imperial War Museum, London, Film and Video Archive
IWM SA	Imperial War Museum, London, Sound Archive
JRL	John Rylands University Library of Manchester
King's AC Cam.	King's College Archives Centre, Cambridge
King's Cam.	King's College, Cambridge
King's Lond.	King's College, London
King's Lond., Liddell Hart C.	King's College, London, Liddell Hart Centre for Military Archives
Lancs. RO	Lancashire Record Office, Preston
L. Cong.	Library of Congress, Washington, DC
Leics. RO	Leicestershire, Leicester, and Rutland Record Office, Leicester
Lincs. Arch.	Lincolnshire Archives, Lincoln
Linn. Soc.	Linnean Society of London
LMA	London Metropolitan Archives
LPL	Lambeth Palace, London
Lpool RO	Liverpool Record Office and Local Studies Service
LUL	London University Library
Magd. Cam.	Magdalene College, Cambridge
Magd. Oxf.	Magdalen College, Oxford
Man. City Gall.	Manchester City Galleries
Man. CL	Manchester Central Library
Mass. Hist. Soc.	Massachusetts Historical Society, Boston
Merton Oxf.	Merton College, Oxford
MHS Oxf.	Museum of the History of Science, Oxford
Mitchell L., Glas.	Mitchell Library, Glasgow
Mitchell L., NSW	State Library of New South Wales, Sydney, Mitchell Library
Morgan L.	Pierpont Morgan Library, New York
NA Canada	National Archives of Canada, Ottawa
NA Ire.	National Archives of Ireland, Dublin
NAM	National Army Museum, London
NA Scot.	National Archives of Scotland, Edinburgh
News Int. RO	News International Record Office, London
NG Ire.	National Gallery of Ireland, Dublin

NG Scot.	National Gallery of Scotland, Edinburgh
NHM	Natural History Museum, London
NL Aus.	National Library of Australia, Canberra
NL Ire.	National Library of Ireland, Dublin
NL NZ	National Library of New Zealand, Wellington
NL NZ, Turnbull L.	National Library of New Zealand, Wellington, Alexander Turnbull Library
NL Scot.	National Library of Scotland, Edinburgh
NL Wales	National Library of Wales, Aberystwyth
NMG Wales	National Museum and Gallery of Wales, Cardiff
NMM	National Maritime Museum, London
Norfolk RO	Norfolk Record Office, Norwich
Northants. RO	Northamptonshire Record Office, Northampton
Northumbd RO	Northumberland Record Office
Notts. Arch.	Nottinghamshire Archives, Nottingham
NPG	National Portrait Gallery, London
NRA	National Archives, London, Historical Manuscripts Commission, National Register of Archives
Nuffield Oxf.	Nuffield College, Oxford
N. Yorks. CRO	North Yorkshire County Record Office, Northallerton
NYPL	New York Public Library
Oxf. UA	Oxford University Archives
Oxf. U. Mus. NH	Oxford University Museum of Natural History
Oxon. RO	Oxfordshire Record Office, Oxford
Pembroke Cam.	Pembroke College, Cambridge
PRO	National Archives, London, Public Record Office
PRO NIre.	Public Record Office for Northern Ireland, Belfast
Pusey Oxf.	Pusey House, Oxford
RA	Royal Academy of Arts, London
Ransom HRC	Harry Ransom Humanities Research Center, University of Texas, Austin
RAS	Royal Astronomical Society, London
RBG Kew	Royal Botanic Gardens, Kew, London
RCP Lond.	Royal College of Physicians of London
RCS Eng.	Royal College of Surgeons of England, London
RGS	Royal Geographical Society, London
RIBA	Royal Institute of British Architects, London
RIBA BAL	Royal Institute of British Architects, London, British Architectural Library
Royal Arch.	Royal Archives, Windsor Castle, Berkshire [by gracious permission of her majesty the queen]
Royal Irish Acad.	Royal Irish Academy, Dublin
Royal Scot. Acad.	Royal Scottish Academy, Edinburgh
RS	Royal Society, London
RSA	Royal Society of Arts, London
RS Friends, Lond.	Religious Society of Friends, London
St Ant. Oxf.	St Antony's College, Oxford
St John Cam.	St John's College, Cambridge
S. Antiquaries, Lond.	Society of Antiquaries of London
Sci. Mus.	Science Museum, London
Scot. NPG	Scottish National Portrait Gallery, Edinburgh
Scott Polar RI	University of Cambridge, Scott Polar Research Institute
Sheff. Arch.	Sheffield Archives
Shrops. RRC	Shropshire Records and Research Centre, Shrewsbury
SOAS	School of Oriental and African Studies, London
Som. ARS	Somerset Archive and Record Service, Taunton
Staffs. RO	Staffordshire Record Office, Stafford
Suffolk RO	Suffolk Record Office
Surrey HC	Surrey History Centre, Woking
TCD	Trinity College, Dublin
Trinity Cam.	Trinity College, Cambridge
U. Aberdeen	University of Aberdeen
U. Birm.	University of Birmingham
U. Birm. L.	University of Birmingham Library
U. Cal.	University of California
U. Cam.	University of Cambridge
UCL	University College, London
U. Durham	University of Durham
U. Durham L.	University of Durham Library
U. Edin.	University of Edinburgh
U. Edin., New Coll.	University of Edinburgh, New College
U. Edin., New Coll. L.	University of Edinburgh, New College Library
U. Edin. L.	University of Edinburgh Library
U. Glas.	University of Glasgow
U. Glas. L.	University of Glasgow Library
U. Hull	University of Hull
U. Hull, Brynmor Jones L.	University of Hull, Brynmor Jones Library
U. Leeds	University of Leeds
U. Leeds, Brotherton L.	University of Leeds, Brotherton Library
U. Lond.	University of London
U. Lpool	University of Liverpool
U. Lpool L.	University of Liverpool Library
U. Mich.	University of Michigan, Ann Arbor
U. Mich., Clements L.	University of Michigan, Ann Arbor, William L. Clements Library
U. Newcastle	University of Newcastle upon Tyne
U. Newcastle, Robinson L.	University of Newcastle upon Tyne, Robinson Library
U. Nott.	University of Nottingham
U. Nott. L.	University of Nottingham Library
U. Oxf.	University of Oxford
U. Reading	University of Reading
U. Reading L.	University of Reading Library
U. St Andr.	University of St Andrews
U. St Andr. L.	University of St Andrews Library
U. Southampton	University of Southampton
U. Southampton L.	University of Southampton Library
U. Sussex	University of Sussex, Brighton
U. Texas	University of Texas, Austin
U. Wales	University of Wales
U. Warwick Mod. RC	University of Warwick, Coventry, Modern Records Centre
V&A	Victoria and Albert Museum, London
V&A NAL	Victoria and Albert Museum, London, National Art Library
Warks. CRO	Warwickshire County Record Office, Warwick
Wellcome L.	Wellcome Library for the History and Understanding of Medicine, London
Westm. DA	Westminster Diocesan Archives, London
Wilts. & Swindon RO	Wiltshire and Swindon Record Office, Trowbridge
Worcs. RO	Worcestershire Record Office, Worcester
W. Sussex RO	West Sussex Record Office, Chichester
W. Yorks. AS	West Yorkshire Archive Service
Yale U.	Yale University, New Haven, Connecticut
Yale U., Beinecke L.	Yale University, New Haven, Connecticut, Beinecke Rare Book and Manuscript Library
Yale U. CBA	Yale University, New Haven, Connecticut, Yale Center for British Art

3 Bibliographic abbreviations

Adams, *Drama* W. D. Adams, *A dictionary of the drama*, 1: *A–G* (1904); 2: *H–Z* (1956) [vol. 2 microfilm only]

AFM J O'Donovan, ed. and trans., *Annala rioghachta Eireann | Annals of the kingdom of Ireland by the four masters*, 7 vols. (1848–51); 2nd edn (1856); 3rd edn (1990)

Allibone, *Dict.* S. A. Allibone, *A critical dictionary of English literature and British and American authors*, 3 vols. (1859–71); suppl. by J. F. Kirk, 2 vols. (1891)

ANB J. A. Garraty and M. C. Carnes, eds., *American national biography*, 24 vols. (1999)

Anderson, *Scot. nat.* W. Anderson, *The Scottish nation, or, The surnames, families, literature, honours, and biographical history of the people of Scotland*, 3 vols. (1859–63)

Ann. mon. H. R. Luard, ed., *Annales monastici*, 5 vols., Rolls Series, 36 (1864–9)

Ann. Ulster S. Mac Airt and G. Mac Niocaill, eds., *Annals of Ulster (to AD 1131)* (1983)

APC *Acts of the privy council of England*, new ser., 46 vols. (1890–1964)

APS *The acts of the parliaments of Scotland*, 12 vols. in 13 (1814–75)

Arber, *Regs. Stationers* F. Arber, ed., *A transcript of the registers of the Company of Stationers of London, 1554–1640 AD*, 5 vols. (1875–94)

ArchR *Architectural Review*

ASC D. Whitelock, D. C. Douglas, and S. I. Tucker, ed. and trans., *The Anglo-Saxon Chronicle: a revised translation* (1961)

AS chart. P. H. Sawyer, *Anglo-Saxon charters: an annotated list and bibliography*, Royal Historical Society Guides and Handbooks (1968)

AusDB D. Pike and others, eds., *Australian dictionary of biography*, 16 vols. (1966–2002)

Baker, *Serjeants* J. H. Baker, *The order of serjeants at law*, SeldS, suppl. ser., 5 (1984)

Bale, *Cat.* J. Bale, *Scriptorum illustrium Maioris Brytannie, quam nunc Angliam et Scotiam vocant: catalogus*, 2 vols. in 1 (Basel, 1557–9); facs. edn (1971)

Bale, *Index* J. Bale, *Index Britanniae scriptorum*, ed. R. L. Poole and M. Bateson (1902); facs. edn (1990)

BBCS *Bulletin of the Board of Celtic Studies*

BDMBR J. O. Baylen and N. J. Gossman, eds., *Biographical dictionary of modern British radicals*, 3 vols. in 4 (1979–88)

Bede, *Hist. eccl.* *Bede's Ecclesiastical history of the English people*, ed. and trans. B. Colgrave and R. A. B. Mynors, OMT (1969); repr. (1991)

Bénézit, *Dict.* E. Bénézit, *Dictionnaire critique et documentaire des peintres, sculpteurs, dessinateurs et graveurs*, 3 vols. (Paris, 1911–23); new edn, 8 vols. (1948–66), repr. (1966); 3rd edn, rev. and enl., 10 vols. (1976); 4th edn, 14 vols. (1999)

BIHR *Bulletin of the Institute of Historical Research*

Birch, *Seals* W. de Birch, *Catalogue of seals in the department of manuscripts in the British Museum*, 6 vols. (1887–1900)

Bishop Burnet's History *Bishop Burnet's History of his own time*, ed. M. J. Routh, 2nd edn, 6 vols. (1833)

Blackwood *Blackwood's [Edinburgh] Magazine*, 328 vols. (1817–1980)

Blain, Clements & Grundy, *Feminist comp.* V. Blain, P. Clements, and I. Grundy, eds., *The feminist companion to literature in English* (1990)

BL cat. *The British Library general catalogue of printed books* [in 360 vols. with suppls., also CD-ROM and online]

BMJ *British Medical Journal*

Boase & Courtney, *Bibl. Corn.* G. C. Boase and W. P. Courtney, *Bibliotheca Cornubiensis: a catalogue of the writings … of Cornishmen*, 3 vols. (1874–82)

Boase, *Mod. Eng. biog.* F. Boase, *Modern English biography: containing many thousand concise memoirs of persons who have died since the year 1850*, 6 vols. (privately printed, Truro, 1892–1921); repr. (1965)

Boswell, *Life* *Boswell's Life of Johnson: together with Journal of a tour to the Hebrides and Johnson's Diary of a journey into north Wales*, ed. G. B. Hill, enl. edn, rev. L. F. Powell, 6 vols. (1934–50); 2nd edn (1964); repr. (1971)

Brown & Stratton, *Brit. mus.* J. D. Brown and S. S. Stratton, *British musical biography* (1897)

Bryan, *Painters* M. Bryan, *A biographical and critical dictionary of painters and engravers*, 2 vols. (1816); new edn, ed. G. Stanley (1849); new edn, ed. R. E. Graves and W. Armstrong, 2 vols. (1886–9); [4th edn], ed. G. C. Williamson, 5 vols. (1903–5) [various reprs.]

Burke, *Gen. GB* J. Burke, *A genealogical and heraldic history of the commoners of Great Britain and Ireland*, 4 vols. (1833–8); new edn as *A genealogical and heraldic dictionary of the landed gentry of Great Britain and Ireland*, 3 vols. [1843–9] [many later edns]

Burke, *Gen. Ire.* J. B. Burke, *A genealogical and heraldic history of the landed gentry of Ireland* (1899); 2nd edn (1904); 3rd edn (1912); 4th edn (1958); 5th edn as *Burke's Irish family records* (1976)

Burke, *Peerage* J. Burke, *A general [later edns A genealogical] and heraldic dictionary of the peerage and baronetage of the United Kingdom [later edns the British empire]* (1829–)

Burney, *Hist. mus.* C. Burney, *A general history of music, from the earliest ages to the present period*, 4 vols. (1776–89)

Burtchaell & Sadleir, *Alum. Dubl.* G. D. Burtchaell and T. U. Sadleir, *Alumni Dublinenses: a register of the students, graduates, and provosts of Trinity College* (1924); [2nd edn], with suppl., in 2 pts (1935)

Calamy rev. A. G. Matthews, *Calamy revised* (1934); repr. (1988)

CCI *Calendar of confirmations and inventories granted and given up in the several commissariots of Scotland* (1876–)

CClR *Calendar of the close rolls preserved in the Public Record Office*, 47 vols. (1892–1963)

CDS J. Bain, ed., *Calendar of documents relating to Scotland*, 4 vols., PRO (1881–8); suppl. vol. 5, ed. G. G. Simpson and J. D. Galbraith [1986]

CEPR letters W. H. Bliss, C. Johnson, and J. Twemlow, eds., *Calendar of entries in the papal registers relating to Great Britain and Ireland: papal letters* (1893–)

CGPLA *Calendars of the grants of probate and letters of administration [in 4 ser.: England & Wales, Northern Ireland, Ireland, and Éire]*

Chambers, *Scots.* R. Chambers, ed., *A biographical dictionary of eminent Scotsmen*, 4 vols. (1832–5)

Chancery records chancery records pubd by the PRO

Chancery records (RC) chancery records pubd by the Record Commissions

CIPM	*Calendar of inquisitions post mortem*, [20 vols.], PRO (1904–); also *Henry VII*, 3 vols. (1898–1955)
Clarendon, *Hist. rebellion*	E. Hyde, earl of Clarendon, *The history of the rebellion and civil wars in England*, 6 vols. (1888); repr. (1958) and (1992)
Cobbett, *Parl. hist.*	W. Cobbett and J. Wright, eds., *Cobbett's Parliamentary history of England*, 36 vols. (1806–1820)
Colvin, *Archs.*	H. Colvin, *A biographical dictionary of British architects, 1600–1840*, 3rd edn (1995)
Cooper, *Ath. Cantab.*	C. H. Cooper and T. Cooper, *Athenae Cantabrigienses*, 3 vols. (1858–1913); repr. (1967)
CPR	*Calendar of the patent rolls preserved in the Public Record Office* (1891–)
Crockford	*Crockford's Clerical Directory*
CS	Camden Society
CSP	*Calendar of state papers* [in 11 ser.: *domestic, Scotland, Scottish series, Ireland, colonial, Commonwealth, foreign, Spain* [at Simancas], *Rome, Milan,* and *Venice*]
CYS	Canterbury and York Society
DAB	*Dictionary of American biography*, 21 vols. (1928–36), repr. in 11 vols. (1964); 10 suppls. (1944–96)
DBB	D. J. Jeremy, ed., *Dictionary of business biography*, 5 vols. (1984–6)
DCB	G. W. Brown and others, *Dictionary of Canadian biography*, [14 vols.] (1966–)
Debrett's Peerage	*Debrett's Peerage* (1803–) [sometimes *Debrett's Illustrated peerage*]
Desmond, *Botanists*	R. Desmond, *Dictionary of British and Irish botanists and horticulturists* (1977); rev. edn (1994)
Dir. Brit. archs.	A. Felstead, J. Franklin, and L. Pinfield, eds., *Directory of British architects, 1834–1900* (1993); 2nd edn, ed. A. Brodie and others, 2 vols. (2001)
DLB	J. M. Bellamy and J. Saville, eds., *Dictionary of labour biography*, [10 vols.] (1972–)
DLitB	Dictionary of Literary Biography
DNB	*Dictionary of national biography*, 63 vols. (1885–1900), suppl., 3 vols. (1901); repr. in 22 vols. (1908–9); 10 further suppls. (1912–96); *Missing persons* (1993)
DNZB	W. H. Oliver and C. Orange, eds., *The dictionary of New Zealand biography*, 5 vols. (1990–2000)
DSAB	W. J. de Kock and others, eds., *Dictionary of South African biography*, 5 vols. (1968–87)
DSB	C. C. Gillispie and F. L. Holmes, eds., *Dictionary of scientific biography*, 16 vols. (1970–80); repr. in 8 vols. (1981); 2 vol. suppl. (1990)
DSBB	A. Slaven and S. Checkland, eds., *Dictionary of Scottish business biography, 1860–1960*, 2 vols. (1986–90)
DSCHT	N. M. de S. Cameron and others, eds., *Dictionary of Scottish church history and theology* (1993)
Dugdale, *Monasticon*	W. Dugdale, *Monasticon Anglicanum*, 3 vols. (1655–72); 2nd edn, 3 vols. (1661–82); new edn, ed. J. Caley, J. Ellis, and B. Bandinel, 6 vols. in 8 pts (1817–30); repr. (1846) and (1970)
DWB	J. E. Lloyd and others, eds., *Dictionary of Welsh biography down to 1940* (1959) [Eng. trans. of *Y bywgraffiadur Cymreig hyd 1940*, 2nd edn (1954)]
EdinR	*Edinburgh Review, or, Critical Journal*
EETS	Early English Text Society
Emden, *Cam.*	A. B. Emden, *A biographical register of the University of Cambridge to 1500* (1963)
Emden, *Oxf.*	A. B. Emden, *A biographical register of the University of Oxford to AD 1500*, 3 vols. (1957–9); also *A biographical register of the University of Oxford, AD 1501 to 1540* (1974)
EngHR	*English Historical Review*
Engraved Brit. ports.	F. M. O'Donoghue and H. M. Hake, *Catalogue of engraved British portraits preserved in the department of prints and drawings in the British Museum*, 6 vols. (1908–25)
ER	The English Reports, 178 vols. (1900–32)
ESTC	*English short title catalogue, 1475–1800* [CD-ROM and online]
Evelyn, *Diary*	*The diary of John Evelyn*, ed. E. S. De Beer, 6 vols. (1955); repr. (2000)
Farington, *Diary*	*The diary of Joseph Farington*, ed. K. Garlick and others, 17 vols. (1978–98)
Fasti Angl. (Hardy)	J. Le Neve, *Fasti ecclesiae Anglicanae*, ed. T. D. Hardy, 3 vols. (1854)
Fasti Angl., 1066–1300	[J. Le Neve], *Fasti ecclesiae Anglicanae, 1066–1300*, ed. D. E. Greenway and J. S. Barrow, [8 vols.] (1968–)
Fasti Angl., 1300–1541	[J. Le Neve], *Fasti ecclesiae Anglicanae, 1300–1541*, 12 vols. (1962–7)
Fasti Angl., 1541–1857	[J. Le Neve], *Fasti ecclesiae Anglicanae, 1541–1857*, ed. J. M. Horn, D. M. Smith, and D. S. Bailey, [9 vols.] (1969–)
Fasti Scot.	H. Scott, *Fasti ecclesiae Scoticanae*, 3 vols. in 6 (1871); new edn, [11 vols.] (1915–)
FO List	Foreign Office List
Fortescue, *Brit. army*	J. W. Fortescue, *A history of the British army*, 13 vols. (1899–1930)
Foss, *Judges*	E. Foss, *The judges of England*, 9 vols. (1848–64); repr. (1966)
Foster, *Alum. Oxon.*	J. Foster, ed., *Alumni Oxonienses: the members of the University of Oxford, 1715–1886*, 4 vols. (1887–8); later edn (1891); also *Alumni Oxonienses … 1500–1714*, 4 vols. (1891–2); 8 vol. repr. (1968) and (2000)
Fuller, *Worthies*	T. Fuller, *The history of the worthies of England*, 4 pts (1662); new edn, 2 vols., ed. J. Nichols (1811); new edn, 3 vols., ed. P. A. Nuttall (1840); repr. (1965)
GEC, *Baronetage*	G. E. Cokayne, *Complete baronetage*, 6 vols. (1900–09); repr. (1983) [microprint]
GEC, *Peerage*	G. E. C. [G. E. Cokayne], *The complete peerage of England, Scotland, Ireland, Great Britain, and the United Kingdom*, 8 vols. (1887–98); new edn, ed. V. Gibbs and others, 14 vols. in 15 (1910–98); microprint repr. (1982) and (1987)
Genest, *Eng. stage*	J. Genest, *Some account of the English stage from the Restoration in 1660 to 1830*, 10 vols. (1832); repr. [New York, 1965]
Gillow, *Lit. biog. hist.*	J. Gillow, *A literary and biographical history or bibliographical dictionary of the English Catholics, from the breach with Rome, in 1534, to the present time*, 5 vols. [1885–1902]; repr. (1961); repr. with preface by C. Gillow (1999)
Gir. Camb. opera	*Giraldi Cambrensis opera*, ed. J. S. Brewer, J. F. Dimock, and G. F. Warner, 8 vols., Rolls Series, 21 (1861–91)
GJ	*Geographical Journal*

Gladstone, *Diaries* — *The Gladstone diaries: with cabinet minutes and prime-ministerial correspondence*, ed. M. R. D. Foot and H. C. G. Matthew, 14 vols. (1968–94)

GM — *Gentleman's Magazine*

Graves, *Artists* — A. Graves, ed., *A dictionary of artists who have exhibited works in the principal London exhibitions of oil paintings from 1760 to 1880* (1884); new edn (1895); 3rd edn (1901); facs. edn (1969); repr. [1970], (1973), and (1984)

Graves, *Brit. Inst.* — A. Graves, *The British Institution, 1806–1867: a complete dictionary of contributors and their work from the foundation of the institution* (1875); facs. edn (1908); repr. (1969)

Graves, *RA exhibitors* — A. Graves, *The Royal Academy of Arts: a complete dictionary of contributors and their work from its foundation in 1769 to 1904*, 8 vols. (1905–6); repr. in 4 vols. (1970) and (1972)

Graves, *Soc. Artists* — A. Graves, *The Society of Artists of Great Britain, 1760–1791, the Free Society of Artists, 1761–1783: a complete dictionary* (1907); facs. edn (1969)

Greaves & Zaller, *BDBR* — R. L. Greaves and R. Zaller, eds., *Biographical dictionary of British radicals in the seventeenth century*, 3 vols. (1982–4)

Grove, *Dict. mus.* — G. Grove, ed., *A dictionary of music and musicians*, 5 vols. (1878–90); 2nd edn, ed. J. A. Fuller Maitland (1904–10); 3rd edn, ed. H. C. Colles (1927); 4th edn with suppl. (1940); 5th edn, ed. E. Blom, 9 vols. (1954); suppl. (1961) [see also *New Grove*]

Hall, *Dramatic ports.* — L. A. Hall, *Catalogue of dramatic portraits in the theatre collection of the Harvard College library*, 4 vols. (1930–34)

Hansard — *Hansard's parliamentary debates*, ser. 1–5 (1803–)

Highfill, Burnim & Langhans, *BDA* — P. H. Highfill, K. A. Burnim, and E. A. Langhans, *A biographical dictionary of actors, actresses, musicians, dancers, managers, and other stage personnel in London, 1660–1800*, 16 vols. (1973–93)

Hist. U. Oxf. — T. H. Aston, ed., *The history of the University of Oxford*, 8 vols. (1984–2000) [1: *The early Oxford schools*, ed. J. I. Catto (1984); 2: *Late medieval Oxford*, ed. J. I. Catto and R. Evans (1992); 3: *The collegiate university*, ed. J. McConica (1986); 4: *Seventeenth-century Oxford*, ed. N. Tyacke (1997); 5: *The eighteenth century*, ed. L. S. Sutherland and L. G. Mitchell (1986); 6–7: *Nineteenth-century Oxford*, ed. M. G. Brock and M. C. Curthoys (1997–2000); 8: *The twentieth century*, ed. B. Harrison (2000)]

HJ — *Historical Journal*

HMC — Historical Manuscripts Commission

Holdsworth, *Eng. law* — W. S. Holdsworth, *A history of English law*, ed. A. L. Goodhart and H. L. Hanbury, 17 vols. (1903–72)

HoP, Commons — *The history of parliament: the House of Commons* [*1386–1421*, ed. J. S. Roskell, L. Clark, and C. Rawcliffe, 4 vols. (1992); *1509–1558*, ed. S. T. Bindoff, 3 vols. (1982); *1558–1603*, ed. P. W. Hasler, 3 vols. (1981); *1660–1690*, ed. B. D. Henning, 3 vols. (1983); *1690–1715*, ed. D. W. Hayton, E. Cruickshanks, and S. Handley, 5 vols. (2002); *1715–1754*, ed. R. Sedgwick, 2 vols. (1970); *1754–1790*, ed. L. Namier and J. Brooke, 3 vols. (1964), repr. (1985); *1790–1820*, ed. R. G. Thorne, 5 vols. (1986); in draft (used with permission): *1422–1504*, *1604–1629*, *1640–1660*, and *1820–1832*]

IGI — *International Genealogical Index*, Church of Jesus Christ of the Latterday Saints

ILN — *Illustrated London News*

IMC — Irish Manuscripts Commission

Irving, *Scots.* — J. Irving, ed., *The book of Scotsmen eminent for achievements in arms and arts, church and state, law, legislation and literature, commerce, science, travel and philanthropy* (1881)

JCS — *Journal of the Chemical Society*

JHC — *Journals of the House of Commons*

JHL — *Journals of the House of Lords*

John of Worcester, *Chron.* — *The chronicle of John of Worcester*, ed. R. R. Darlington and P. McGurk, trans. J. Bray and P. McGurk, 3 vols., OMT (1995–) [vol. 1 forthcoming]

Keeler, *Long Parliament* — M. F. Keeler, *The Long Parliament, 1640–1641: a biographical study of its members* (1954)

Kelly, *Handbk* — *The upper ten thousand: an alphabetical list of all members of noble families*, 3 vols. (1875–7); continued as *Kelly's handbook of the upper ten thousand for 1878* [1879], 2 vols. (1878–9); continued as *Kelly's handbook to the titled, landed and official classes*, 94 vols. (1880–1973)

LondG — *London Gazette*

LP Henry VIII — J. S. Brewer, J. Gairdner, and R. H. Brodie, eds., *Letters and papers, foreign and domestic, of the reign of Henry VIII*, 23 vols. in 38 (1862–1932); repr. (1965)

Mallalieu, *Watercolour artists* — H. L. Mallalieu, *The dictionary of British watercolour artists up to 1820*, 3 vols. (1976–90); vol. 1, 2nd edn (1986)

Memoirs FRS — *Biographical Memoirs of Fellows of the Royal Society*

MGH — Monumenta Germaniae Historica

MT — *Musical Times*

Munk, *Roll* — W. Munk, *The roll of the Royal College of Physicians of London*, 2 vols. (1861); 2nd edn, 3 vols. (1878)

N&Q — *Notes and Queries*

New Grove — S. Sadie, ed., *The new Grove dictionary of music and musicians*, 20 vols. (1980); 2nd edn, 29 vols. (2001) [also online edn; see also Grove, *Dict. mus.*]

Nichols, *Illustrations* — J. Nichols and J. B. Nichols, *Illustrations of the literary history of the eighteenth century*, 8 vols. (1817–58)

Nichols, *Lit. anecdotes* — J. Nichols, *Literary anecdotes of the eighteenth century*, 9 vols. (1812–16); facs. edn (1966)

Obits. FRS — *Obituary Notices of Fellows of the Royal Society*

O'Byrne, *Naval biog. dict.* — W. R. O'Byrne, *A naval biographical dictionary* (1849); repr. (1990); [2nd edn], 2 vols. (1861)

OHS — Oxford Historical Society

Old Westminsters — *The record of Old Westminsters*, 1–2, ed. G. F. R. Barker and A. H. Stenning (1928); suppl. 1, ed. J. B. Whitmore and G. R. Y. Radcliffe [1938]; 3, ed. J. B. Whitmore, G. R. Y. Radcliffe, and D. C. Simpson (1963); suppl. 2, ed. F. E. Pagan (1978); 4, ed. F. E. Pagan and H. E. Pagan (1992)

OMT — Oxford Medieval Texts

Ordericus Vitalis, *Eccl. hist.* — *The ecclesiastical history of Orderic Vitalis*, ed. and trans. M. Chibnall, 6 vols., OMT (1969–80); repr. (1990)

Paris, *Chron.* — *Matthaei Parisiensis, monachi sancti Albani, chronica majora*, ed. H. R. Luard, Rolls Series, 7 vols. (1872–83)

Parl. papers — *Parliamentary papers* (1801–)

PBA — *Proceedings of the British Academy*

Pepys, *Diary*   *The diary of Samuel Pepys*, ed. R. Latham and W. Matthews, 11 vols. (1970–83); repr. (1995) and (2000)

Pevsner   N. Pevsner and others, Buildings of England series

PICE   *Proceedings of the Institution of Civil Engineers*

Pipe rolls   *The great roll of the pipe for . . .*, PRSoc. (1884–)

PRO   Public Record Office

PRS   *Proceedings of the Royal Society of London*

PRSoc.   Pipe Roll Society

PTRS   *Philosophical Transactions of the Royal Society*

QR   *Quarterly Review*

RC   Record Commissions

Redgrave, *Artists*   S. Redgrave, *A dictionary of artists of the English school* (1874); rev. edn (1878); repr. (1970)

Reg. Oxf.   C. W. Boase and A. Clark, eds., *Register of the University of Oxford*, 5 vols., OHS, 1, 10–12, 14 (1885–9)

Reg. PCS   J. H. Burton and others, eds., *The register of the privy council of Scotland*, 1st ser., 14 vols. (1877–98); 2nd ser., 8 vols. (1899–1908); 3rd ser., [16 vols.] (1908–70)

Reg. RAN   H. W. C. Davis and others, eds., *Regesta regum Anglo-Normannorum, 1066–1154*, 4 vols. (1913–69)

RIBA Journal   *Journal of the Royal Institute of British Architects* [later *RIBA Journal*]

RotP   J. Strachey, ed., *Rotuli parliamentorum ut et petitiones, et placita in parliamento*, 6 vols. (1767–77)

RotS   D. Macpherson, J. Caley, and W. Illingworth, eds., *Rotuli Scotiae in Turri Londinensi et in domo capitulari Westmonasteriensi asservati*, 2 vols., RC, 14 (1814–19)

RS   Record(s) Society

Rymer, *Foedera*   T. Rymer and R. Sanderson, eds., *Foedera, conventiones, literae et cuiuscunque generis acta publica inter reges Angliae et alios quosvis imperatores, reges, pontifices, principes, vel communitates*, 20 vols. (1704–35); 2nd edn, 20 vols. (1726–35); 3rd edn, 10 vols. (1739–45); facs. edn (1967); new edn, ed. A. Clarke, J. Caley, and F. Holbrooke, 4 vols., RC, 50 (1816–30)

Sainty, *Judges*   J. Sainty, ed., *The judges of England, 1272–1990*, SeldS, suppl. ser., 10 (1993)

Sainty, *King's counsel*   J. Sainty, ed., *A list of English law officers and king's counsel*, SeldS, suppl. ser., 7 (1987)

SCH   Studies in Church History

Scots peerage   J. B. Paul, ed. *The Scots peerage, founded on Wood's edition of Sir Robert Douglas's Peerage of Scotland, containing an historical and genealogical account of the nobility of that kingdom*, 9 vols. (1904–14)

SeldS   Selden Society

SHR   *Scottish Historical Review*

State trials   T. B. Howell and T. J. Howell, eds., *Cobbett's Complete collection of state trials*, 34 vols. (1809–28)

STC, 1475–1640   A. W. Pollard, G. R. Redgrave, and others, eds., *A short-title catalogue of . . . English books . . . 1475–1640* (1926); 2nd edn, ed. W. A. Jackson, F. S. Ferguson, and K. F. Pantzer, 3 vols. (1976–91) [see also Wing, *STC*]

STS   Scottish Text Society

SurtS   Surtees Society

Symeon of Durham, *Opera*   *Symeonis monachi opera omnia*, ed. T. Arnold, 2 vols., Rolls Series, 75 (1882–5); repr. (1965)

Tanner, *Bibl. Brit.-Hib.*   T. Tanner, *Bibliotheca Britannica-Hibernica*, ed. D. Wilkins (1748); repr. (1963)

Thieme & Becker, *Allgemeines Lexikon*   U. Thieme, F. Becker, and H. Vollmer, eds., *Allgemeines Lexikon der bildenden Künstler von der Antike bis zur Gegenwart*, 37 vols. (Leipzig, 1907–50); repr. (1961–5), (1983), and (1992)

Thurloe, *State papers*   *A collection of the state papers of John Thurloe*, ed. T. Birch, 7 vols. (1742)

TLS   *Times Literary Supplement*

Tout, *Admin. hist.*   T. F. Tout, *Chapters in the administrative history of mediaeval England: the wardrobe, the chamber, and the small seals*, 6 vols. (1920–33); repr. (1967)

TRHS   *Transactions of the Royal Historical Society*

VCH   H. A. Doubleday and others, eds., *The Victoria history of the counties of England*, [88 vols.] (1900–)

Venn, *Alum. Cant.*   J. Venn and J. A. Venn, *Alumni Cantabrigienses: a biographical list of all known students, graduates, and holders of office at the University of Cambridge, from the earliest times to 1900*, 10 vols. (1922–54); repr. in 2 vols. (1974–8)

Vertue, *Note books*   [G. Vertue], *Note books*, ed. K. Esdaile, earl of Ilchester, and H. M. Hake, 6 vols., Walpole Society, 18, 20, 22, 24, 26, 30 (1930–55)

VF   *Vanity Fair*

Walford, *County families*   E. Walford, *The county families of the United Kingdom, or, Royal manual of the titled and untitled aristocracy of Great Britain and Ireland* (1860)

Walker rev.   A. G. Matthews, *Walker revised: being a revision of John Walker's Sufferings of the clergy during the grand rebellion, 1642–60* (1948); repr. (1988)

Walpole, *Corr.*   *The Yale edition of Horace Walpole's correspondence*, ed. W. S. Lewis, 48 vols. (1937–83)

Ward, *Men of the reign*   T. H. Ward, ed., *Men of the reign: a biographical dictionary of eminent persons of British and colonial birth who have died during the reign of Queen Victoria* (1885); repr. (Graz, 1968)

Waterhouse, *18c painters*   E. Waterhouse, *The dictionary of 18th century painters in oils and crayons* (1981); repr. as *British 18th century painters in oils and crayons* (1991), vol. 2 of *Dictionary of British art*

Watt, *Bibl. Brit.*   R. Watt, *Bibliotheca Britannica, or, A general index to British and foreign literature*, 4 vols. (1824) [many reprs.]

Wellesley index   W. E. Houghton, ed., *The Wellesley index to Victorian periodicals, 1824–1900*, 5 vols. (1966–89); new edn (1999) [CD-ROM]

Wing, *STC*   D. Wing, ed., *Short-title catalogue of . . . English books . . . 1641–1700*, 3 vols. (1945–51); 2nd edn (1972–88); rev. and enl. edn, ed. J. J. Morrison, C. W. Nelson, and M. Seccombe, 4 vols. (1994–8) [see also *STC, 1475–1640*]

Wisden   *John Wisden's Cricketer's Almanack*

Wood, *Ath. Oxon.*   A. Wood, *Athenae Oxonienses . . . to which are added the Fasti*, 2 vols. (1691–2); 2nd edn (1721); new edn, 4 vols., ed. P. Bliss (1813–20); repr. (1967) and (1969)

Wood, *Vic. painters*   C. Wood, *Dictionary of Victorian painters* (1971); 2nd edn (1978); 3rd edn as *Victorian painters*, 2 vols. (1995), vol. 4 of *Dictionary of British art*

WW   *Who's who* (1849–)

WWBMP   M. Stenton and S. Lees, eds., *Who's who of British members of parliament*, 4 vols. (1976–81)

WWW   *Who was who* (1929–)

Macquarie, Lachlan (1761–1824), army officer and colonial governor, was born on 31 January 1761 on the Hebridean islet of Ulva, one of six children of Scottish-born parents, Lachlan Macquarie, a carpenter and tenant farmer, and his wife, Margaret, *née* Maclaine. His father was a cousin of the sixteenth laird of the Macquarie clan; his mother was sister to Murdoch, eighteenth chieftain of the Lochbuies. Young Lachlan spent his boyhood on the Isle of Mull before being sent as a boarder to a private schoolmaster in Edinburgh. He enlisted in the Royal Highland Emigrants in 1776, was commissioned ensign on 29 April 1777, and performed garrison duties with the 2nd battalion in Nova Scotia. On 18 January 1781 he was promoted lieutenant and transferred to the 71st Highland regiment, with which he was stationed in New York, Charles Town, and Jamaica. Three years later, when his regiment was disbanded, he was placed on half pay.

As a lieutenant in the 77th regiment, Macquarie left England in 1788 for India, where he won promotion—to captain (1789), major (1801), and finally lieutenant-colonel (1805)—and was military secretary (1800–03, 1805–7) to the governor of Bombay. He served in the sieges of Cananore (1790) and Cochin (1795), was present at the capture of Colombo (1796), witnessed the fall of Seringapatam (1799), and took part in the Egyptian campaign (1801). In a private ceremony at Bombay on 8 September 1793 he married Jane Jarvis (1772–1796), the twentieth of the twenty-one children of a former chief justice of Antigua; within three years she died of consumption at the age of twenty-three. Her death left Macquarie inconsolable for fifty months. On home leave from 1803 to 1805, he officiated as assistant adjutant-general for the London district, visited Jarvisfield (his recently acquired estate on Mull), and courted Elizabeth Henrietta (1778–1835), the daughter of John Campbell of Airds. After further service in India he returned to London on 17 October 1807, having travelled through Persia and Russia, and via the Baltic Sea, carrying dispatches. On 3 November he married Elizabeth in the parish church of St Peter and St Paul, Holsworthy, Devon. She was to fortify her husband's resolve and steel him against his detractors.

Macquarie's military career thus far had included a paymastership and supervision of road building, transport, and supplies. He gained his own promotions—and commissions for certain relations—by ingratiating himself with his superiors and by dissimulation. Facets of instability in his nature had exposed themselves: he drank heavily, showed signs of dissipation, and may have suffered from a form of venereal disease. He owned slaves, opposed democratic sentiments, and preferred order to freedom. Extravagant and snobbish, this self-made soldier of fortune hobnobbed with leisured gentlemen and lesser aristocrats, contrived to talk with Canning and Castlereagh, and by 1809 had even been introduced to George III. Macquarie's earnest deference, his urge to please, his longing to be admired, and his prickliness to criticism revealed his insecurity. Able, ambitious, and benefiting

from a leaven of common sense, on the whole he was sincere in manner and correct in conduct; he retained something of the impatience of youth, but was inclined to think ardour indiscreet and anger rash. His experiences brought him a mine of compassion, a mixture of tolerance, and a measure of understanding, all of which he was prepared to subordinate to his sense of duty, even when it challenged his principles. Resolution and indecision dwelt in him, a dichotomy that was to intensify. He was torn between what he felt he wanted to do and what he thought he should, between his instinctive impulses and his acquired ethics, between concern for himself and generosity to others.

Late in 1808 Macquarie heard that he had been ordered to sail for Botany Bay in command of the 73rd regiment; on 27 April 1809 he learned that he was to be appointed governor-in-chief of New South Wales and Van Diemen's Land. He held office from 1 January 1810 to 30 November 1821, during which he was gazetted colonel (1810), brigadier-general (1811), and major-general (1813). Hard work typified his regime, as did a paternalism that verged on autocracy. The notion of regularity ruled his outlook, stamped his plans, and endorsed his deeds. He brought system and efficiency to the government and brooked no opposition, whether from clergyman or judge. Capable of doing things on a grand scale to implement his dreams, he appreciated that symmetry could be achieved only by orderly, pragmatic, and daily attention to detail. The antipodean outposts progressed materially under his governorship. The population grew from 11,590 to 38,778; sheep multiplied from 26,000 to 290,000, cattle from 12,500 to 103,000; the land under tillage increased from 7500 to 32,000 acres; roads, bridges, towns, churches, schools, hospitals, parks, and gardens were developed; improvements were effected in trade and manufacturing, in banking and currency, and in public morals; and attempts were made to befriend the Aborigines. Macquarie ruled New South Wales during a time of transition: he found a gaol, he left a burgeoning colony. To some extent he recognized local influences that pushed the settlements in a new direction, but he had no sense of the impetus for expansion and reform that was let loose with victory at Waterloo.

Of all the features of his administration, Macquarie regarded his emancipist policy as most worthy of praise. Unlike the 'exclusives' among the minority of the population who had come to New South Wales and Van Diemen's Land as free immigrants, Macquarie insisted that, on the expiry or remission of their sentences, the convict majority—provided they were well behaved—should be treated as if they had never transgressed the law and ought to enjoy the rights of free men. Whether this policy sprang from Christian principle or from mundane pragmatism, it led to divisions in society, and united his opponents in the antipodes as well as in London. Once his resignation was eventually accepted, Macquarie embarked from Sydney on 15 February 1822 in the *Surrey*, which anchored in the Thames on 4 July. He then battled to secure a pension and to salvage his reputation in the face of the reports of John

Thomas Bigge, the royal commissioner who recommended that year that the cost of the penal settlements be reduced and that transported felons be punished with greater severity. Exhausted and sick at heart, Macquarie travelled in Europe in 1822–3 with Elizabeth and their son (*b*. 1814) and then returned to Mull. He died of a bowel disease and strangury on 1 July 1824 in rented rooms at 49 Duke Street, St James's, London. His body was buried on his estate, Gruline, on Mull, on 29 July.

Macquarie's character abounded in paradoxes and contradictions. He could be impetuous and equivocating. Visionary and realist, he was always money-conscious, though seldom greedy. While he was usually energetic and industrious, his strength came in spasms and he lacked robust health. If he had inconsistencies, he also had dedication; if he were loquacious, he listened well. Although he trusted his intimates, he was rarely willing to delegate full responsibility to them. With those he disliked, he preferred enmity to appeasement. Polite and earnest, he found it difficult to unbend in public. He was a practising Episcopalian, a devoted husband, and a doting father. Sound if not clever, shrewd if not clear-headed, he had a mind that was literal rather than contemplative, and his reactions tended to stem more from his emotions than his reason. With sandy hair, brown eyes, an aquiline nose, a brick-red complexion, and broad shoulders, in his prime he stood 5 feet 10 inches tall and weighed 13½ stone. He enjoyed romantic landscapes and historic places, liked the theatre and games of whist, and loved horse-racing, but did not himself ride well. He appreciated cameo portraits, thrilled to the pipes, spoke Gaelic and a smattering of French, and treasured the works of Scott and Boswell. His letters and diaries—which reveal a quiet sense of humour—were written in a large, plain hand, with frequent underlining, capital letters, and exclamation marks. This low-born Scottish exile, distanced from metropolitan Georgian society, was given the chance in 1810 to behave largely as he wished: with self-effacing humanity and a common touch, he chose to use his vast authority to attempt nothing less than the regeneration of the fallen men and women under his sway.

JOHN RITCHIE

Sources M. H. Ellis, *Lachlan Macquarie* (1947) · J. Ritchie, *Lachlan Macquarie* (1986) · Lachlan Macquarie MSS, Mitchell L., NSW · Lochbuie MSS, NA Scot. · Colonial office records, PRO · 'Commission of inquiry into … the colony of New South Wales', *Parl. papers* (1822), 20.539, no. 448 · 'Commission of inquiry on the judicial establishments of New South Wales', *Parl. papers* (1823), 10.515, no. 33 · 'Commission of inquiry on the state of agriculture and trade in … New South Wales', *Parl. papers* (1823), 10.607, no. 136 · [F. Watson], ed., *Historical records of Australia*, 1st ser., 7–10 (1916–17) · [F. Watson], ed., *Historical records of Australia*, 1st ser., 11 (1917) · [F. Watson], ed., *Historical records of Australia*, 3rd ser., 1–3 (1921) · [F. Watson], ed., *Historical records of Australia*, 4th ser., 1 (1922) · F. M. Bladen, ed., *Historical records of New South Wales*, 7 (1901) · *AusDB* · Mitchell L., NSW, Fitzgerald MSS
Archives Mitchell L., NSW, letter-books, journals, and papers · NA Scot., accounts and corresp. · NL Scot., letters to his brother | BL, Bathurst MSS · Derbys. RO, Catton MSS · Lincs. Arch., Jarvis MSS · Mitchell L., NSW, Fitzgerald MSS · National War Museum of Scotland, Edinburgh, corresp. with Sir David Baird
Likenesses J. Opie, oils, 1805, Mitchell L., NSW · R. Read senior, watercolour, 1824, Mitchell L., NSW
Wealth at death left widow £300 p.a.; also assets valued at £4962; landed estate on Isle of Mull, Scotland: will, NA Scot., SC 51/32/2, fols. 67–80

MacQueen, Daniel (*bap.* 1714, *d.* 1777), Church of Scotland minister, was baptized Daniel McQueen on 4 April 1714, the son of Daniel MacQueen or McQueen, an Edinburgh merchant, and Helen Craig or Greig. He was licensed by the presbytery of Edinburgh on 29 June 1735, ordained to the parish of Dalziel in Lanarkshire on 29 October 1736, and translated to the West Church, Stirling, on 31 December 1740. While in Dalziel he married, on 26 December 1738, Elizabeth, daughter of Archibald Nisbet of Carfin, who died giving birth to their fourth child on 9 May 1748. In 1748 MacQueen published anonymously in Edinburgh *Observations on Daniel's prophecy of the seventy weeks*, a book that refuted another anonymous work of 1744–5, *Daniel's prophecy of the seventy weeks explained from the sacred writings, and applied to the history of the Jews*, by arguing that the prophecy concerned Christian rather than Jewish history. It was reissued in London in 1751.

MacQueen was said to be exceptionally learned, though a strict Calvinist and a leading member of the popular or orthodox party in the Church of Scotland. He took offence at some passages on the protestant Reformation in the first volume of David Hume's *History of Great Britain*, which appeared in November 1754, and early in 1756 published anonymously at Edinburgh a lengthy critique entitled *Letters on Mr Hume's History of Great Britain*. The footnotes demonstrate his command of Greek language and philosophy, while the text itself pursues Hume relentlessly for his alleged infidelity, concluding with a tract on the nature of 'true piety' that states: 'How dreadful a thing for anyone to go about, by opposing the essential truths of religion, to weaken the foundations of human happiness and hope; nay of society itself, and of all truth, justice, and probity among men' (MacQueen, 306–7). The book was favourably reviewed by William Rose in the *Monthly Review* and by Tobias Smollett in the *Critical Review*. Hume never acknowledged it, but MacQueen's *Letters* may have caused him to expunge the two most offensive passages from later editions of his *History*. The effect of Hume's revision was to render MacQueen's book obsolete, as Sir Henry Moncreiff Wellwood later observed. Sir Henry claimed that the attack on Hume brought MacQueen (whose identity as the author was soon known) 'so much reputation when it was first published' that an Anglican dignitary offered him 'high preferment' if he would come over to the Church of England (Wellwood, 232–4). Instead, MacQueen accepted a call to Edinburgh dated 13 August 1756, although his admission to the Old Kirk, where he joined his 'intimate friend' Patrick Cuming, was delayed until 15 June 1758. MacQueen enjoyed the patronage of the powerful Lord Milton, who was concerned in his translation to Edinburgh and his assignment to the Old Kirk (NL Scot., Saltoun MS 16719, fol. 167, and MS 16703, fol. 39).

MacQueen received an honorary DD degree from the

University of Edinburgh on 12 April 1759. When its principal died on 19 February 1762 the professor of natural philosophy, George Stuart, immediately wrote to Gilbert Elliot to secure the position for MacQueen, who was, he said, not only connected with Milton but a cousin of the influential magistrate Bailie James Stuart and 'related to Bute through his wife', as well as someone with 'more academic knowledge than any man I ever knew of his profession' (NL Scot., Minto MS 11016, fol. 13). But MacQueen lost the principalship to the earl of Bute's choice, William Robertson, and thereafter he received no other preferments. On 10 September 1762 he married his second wife, Warburton Dunbar, who died in 1766, the year that their third child was born.

MacQueen's only other publication was a sermon on the epistle to the Colossians, 1:23, preached before the Society in Scotland for Propagating Christian Knowledge on 1 January 1759, which attacked scepticism, deism, and the corruption of religious principles by the intellect. In 1773 the mischievous Gilbert Stuart, son of MacQueen's friend George Stuart, deliberately rankled Hume by altering the phrase 'the *celebrated* William Robertson' to read 'the *celebrated* Daniel MacQueen' in the proofs of a book review (ultimately suppressed) that Hume had written for the *Edinburgh Magazine and Review*, but Stuart was also critical of MacQueen's *Letters* in the pages of that periodical. MacQueen died on 22 October 1777.   RICHARD B. SHER

Sources E. C. Mossner, *The life of David Hume*, 2nd edn (1980) • J. V. Price, introduction, in D. MacQueen, *Letters on Hume's History of Great Britain*, repr. (1990), v–x • *Fasti Scot.*, new edn, 1.72 • R. B. Sher, *Church and university in the Scottish Enlightenment: the moderate literati of Edinburgh* (1985) • H. M. Wellwood, *Account of the life and writings of John Erskine* (1818) • W. Zachs, *Without regard to good manners: a biography of Gilbert Stuart, 1743–1786* (1992)
Archives NL Scot., Minto MSS (Sir Gilbert Elliot) • NL Scot., Saltoun MSS (Lord Milton)

MacQueen, James (1778–1870), geographer, was born at Crawford, Lanarkshire. In 1796 he was manager of a sugar plantation in Grenada, West Indies, and subsequently made repeated voyages through all the West Indian colonies. He became interested in African geography, a subject on which he became a leading authority, when he read Mungo Park's *Travels* (1799). He collected much information concerning the features of the country on the upper Niger from the Mandingo slaves under his charge, and the merchants and slave agents with whom he had dealings. He was one of the first to assert, in a treatise of 1816, that the Niger entered the ocean in the bights of Benin and Biafra, before this question was settled by the Landers in 1830.

By 1821 MacQueen had settled at Glasgow, where he became editor and part-proprietor of the *Glasgow Herald*. In that journal, then published three times a week, he ably defended what he regarded as the rights of the 'West India interest'. As a writer he was trenchant and vigorous, and could present statistics attractively. He projected and organized the Colonial Bank and the Royal Mail Steam Packet Company. Eventually he settled in London, and wrote extensively on politics, geography, economics, and

general literature in the newspapers and magazines. He was a fellow of the Royal Geographical Society and contributed several interesting memoirs to its *Journal* and *Proceedings*. In the 1840s he projected a scheme for a chartered company to cultivate cotton at the Niger–Benue confluence. It received little attention at the time, and although he persuaded the Royal Geographical Society to take it up during the American Civil War, when cotton supplies were jeopardized, it again came to nothing. His letters in the *Morning Advertiser* on Speke's claim to have discovered the source of the Nile were deemed by Burton to be so 'valuable and original' that he incorporated them in his *The Nile Basin* (1864).

MacQueen died on 14 May 1870 at 10 Hornton Street, Kensington, London. Among his numerous works, the best are *A geographical and commercial view of northern central Africa: containing a[n] … account of the … termination of the … Niger in the Atlantic Ocean* (1821); *A Geographical Survey of Africa* (1840), with a map by John Arrowsmith; and *Journals of the Missionaries Isenberg and Krapf* (1843), to which he prefixed a geographical memoir of Abyssinia and southeastern Africa.

Although well known in his day as an authority on Africa, it seems that MacQueen had never visited the continent, and made often pointed attacks on the claims of eminent travellers, including Livingstone, Speke, and Grant, based on his knowledge of Ptolemy, the early Arab travellers, and the Portuguese colonists. Such criticism commands some interest, but he is mostly remembered as a staunch defender of imperial commercial interests and their extension, particularly into west Africa, not least as he was one of the first to advocate the extension of legitimate commerce as the way to overcome the slave trade in Africa.   GORDON GOODWIN, *rev.* ELIZABETH BAIGENT

Sources H. R. Mill, *The record of the Royal Geographical Society, 1830–1930* (1930) • R. A. Stafford, *Scientist of empire: Sir Roderick Murchison, scientific exploration and Victorian imperialism* (1989) • C. R. Markham, *The fifty years' work of the Royal Geographical Society* (1881) • A. Adu Boahen, *Britain, the Sahara and the western Sudan, 1788–1861* (1964) • *Proceedings* [Royal Geographical Society], 14 (1869–70), 301–2 • Boase, *Mod. Eng. biog.* • *Morning Advertiser* (17 May 1870), 5 • d. cert.

Macqueen, John Fraser, of Revan (1803–1881), barrister and law reporter, was the eighth, but eldest surviving, son of Donald Macqueen of Corrybrough, Inverness-shire, and his wife, Elizabeth, daughter of Hugh Fraser of Brightmony in the same county. He eventually succeeded his father as chief of clan Revan, the tribal designation adopted by the Macqueens. At first he practised as a writer to the signet at Edinburgh, but subsequently he became a member of Lincoln's Inn. He was called to the bar on 8 June 1838, and commenced practice in the court of chancery. In 1840 he married Georgiana, daughter of George Dealtry, rector of Outwell, Norfolk. He was at one time frequently engaged in Scottish appeals, and in proceedings for divorce both before and, briefly, after the passing of the Divorce Act in 1857.

In 1860 Macqueen was appointed by Lord Campbell official reporter of Scottish and divorce appeals in the House of Lords, and he compiled four volumes of appellate reports (1861–5). He continued his reports for several years after the formation of the Incorporated Council of Law Reporting in 1866, but failing health obliged him to nominate a deputy, and in 1879 he resigned the post. He took silk in 1861, and during the same year was made bencher of Lincoln's Inn. Macqueen, who was deputy lieutenant and JP for Inverness-shire, where he had a seat at Aird, died at 4 Upper Westbourne Terrace, Hyde Park, London, on 6 December 1881.

Macqueen was a man of genial and kindly disposition, and of considerable literary achievements. Among his legal works were several texts concerning the divorce laws, which underwent a great deal of change in the course of his career, and *Chief Points in the Laws of War and Neutrality, Search and Blockade* (1862). He wrote also some legal pamphlets, including an interesting *Lecture on the Early History and Academic Discipline of the Inns of Court and Chancery* (1851).

GORDON GOODWIN, rev. ERIC METCALFE

Sources The Times (8 Dec 1881), 9f · Law Times (10 Dec 1881), 106 · Solicitors' Journal, 26 (1881–2), 129 · Law Magazine, 4th ser., 7 (1881–2), 215–16 · Law List · W. P. Baildon, ed., The records of the Honorable Society of Lincoln's Inn [incl. Admissions, 2 vols. (1896), and Black books, 6 vols. (1897–2001)]
Wealth at death £8491 19s. 7d.: probate, 14 Jan 1882, CGPLA Eng. & Wales

McQueen, Sir John Withers (1836–1909), army officer, was born in Calcutta on 24 August 1836, the eldest son of the Revd John McQueen, chaplain of the Kidderpore Orphan Asylum in Calcutta. He was educated at Trinity College, Glenalmond, Perthshire, and in 1853 received an East India Company military cadetship. In India he was appointed ensign in the 27th Bengal native infantry with effect from 4 April 1854. On the outbreak of the mutiny in May 1857 the 27th native infantry, at Peshawar, was disarmed, and McQueen was posted to the 4th Punjab infantry of the Punjab irregular force. The regiment reached Delhi after a march of 1000 miles on 6 September, just in time to take part in the assault on the city, which began on the 14th. McQueen quickly acquired a reputation for bravery, and on 19 September he made a daring reconnaissance of the royal palace which enabled it to be taken without serious loss the next day. He took part in the second relief of Lucknow, being seriously wounded and recommended (unsuccessfully) for the Victoria Cross during the capture of the *sikandarabagh* on 17 November 1857. He was mentioned in dispatches.

In May 1858 the regiment moved back to the frontier, where McQueen was appointed adjutant and took part in the expedition against the Kabul Khel Wazirs in 1859 and against the Mahsuds in 1860. In April 1860 he became second in command of the regiment although only a substantive lieutenant, not being promoted captain until 1866. In 1870 he was appointed to command the 5th Punjab infantry, a command he held until 1883. In 1872 he married Charlotte Helen Pollard, daughter of Major-General Charles Pollard, Royal Engineers; they had two sons and two daughters. His elder son, Malcolm Stewart, was killed in the Second South African War in 1900.

In the Jowaki expedition of 1877–8 McQueen was repeatedly mentioned in dispatches, adding to his reputation in mountain warfare. When the Second Anglo-Afghan War broke out in November 1878 McQueen and his regiment were valued components of the force under Major-General Roberts which invaded Afghanistan via the Kurram valley. His long frontier experience, his knowledge of the local peoples and their languages, and his skill in mountain warfare made him particularly valuable to Roberts, whose own frontier experience was limited; moreover, they had known each other since Delhi in 1857. In the second phase of the war, which followed the massacre of Sir Louis Cavagnari and his mission at Kabul in September 1879, McQueen and his regiment formed part of the force with which Roberts advanced and occupied Kabul. He was again prominent in the fighting around Kabul in December 1879 and in the siege of Sherpur, but his regiment was not included in the force with which Roberts marched from Kabul to Kandahar, and McQueen returned to India with Sir Donald Stewart's force. He received the CB and a brevet lieutenant-colonelcy.

McQueen commanded the 5th during the expedition against the Mahsud Wazirs in 1881, and later that year was appointed aide-de-camp to the queen and promoted colonel. In 1883 he was appointed military secretary to the Punjab government. In 1885 he commanded the Hyderabad contingent, with the rank of brigadier-general, but in October 1886 was transferred to the prestigious appointment of commandant of the Punjab frontier force. In 1888 he commanded the Black Mountain expedition, with the temporary rank of major-general. Although he received official thanks and was created KCB, he had incurred the strong private displeasure of Roberts, the commander-in-chief, who considered that the expedition's military objectives had not been achieved because McQueen had deferred excessively to the advice of the Punjab political officers, contrary to his warnings and advice. Despite his long friendship with McQueen and the latter's record Roberts concluded that he was not suitable for higher command, and when McQueen finished his command of the Punjab frontier force in 1891 Roberts made it brutally clear that there would be no further appointment.

McQueen was promoted substantive major-general in 1891 and retired in the same year to Bath. He was promoted lieutenant-general on the retired list in 1895 and made GCB in 1907. He died at Richmond, Surrey, on 15 August 1909, and was buried at Wimbledon. His wife survived him. He was a keen student of his profession and left among his papers a two-volume manuscript, illustrated with original miniatures, entitled 'The kingdom of the Punjaub, its rulers and chiefs', written about 1860.

C. B. NORMAN, rev. BRIAN ROBSON

Sources NAM, J. W. McQueen MSS, 6806–6827, 6012–6287 · NAM, Roberts MSS, 7101–7123 · Bengal Army Lists · C. M. MacGregor, ed., The Second Afghan War, 1878–80, official account, 6 vols. (1908) · S. N. Sen, Eighteen fifty-seven (1957) · W. H. Paget, A record of the expeditions against the north-west frontier tribes, since the annexation of the Punjab, rev. A. H. Mason (1884) · Lord Roberts [F. S. Roberts], Forty-one years in India, 30th edn (1898) · H. B. Hanna, The Second Afghan War, 3 vols.

(1899–1910) • J. L. Vaughan, *My service in the Indian army—and after* (1904) • *The Times* (16 Aug 1909)
Archives NAM | NAM, Roberts MSS

Macqueen, Robert, Lord Braxfield (1722–1799), judge, was born on 4 May 1722, the oldest of seven children of John Macqueen (*c*.1687–1771) of Braxfield, Lanarkshire, Scotland, law agent at Lanark, and his wife, Helen, daughter of John Hamilton of Gilkerscleugh. The Macqueens had been servants to the earls of Selkirk, who patronized their social advancement, and the mother came of minor landowners. Macqueen was educated at the grammar school in Lanark. In April 1737 he matriculated at the University of Edinburgh. There is no record of his graduation. In 1740 he was apprenticed to Thomas Goldie, writer to the signet, probably intending to follow his father's branch of the legal profession. But after Goldie's death in 1741 Macqueen turned to the bar. He was admitted to the Faculty of Advocates on 11 February 1744. On 1 March 1745 he became sheriff-substitute in Lanarkshire, holding office jointly with his father for three years. By then he was building up his own practice in Edinburgh, notably as counsel for the crown in intricate cases of feudalism proceeding from forfeitures after the last Jacobite rising.

In June 1753 Macqueen married Mary (1725–1791), daughter of James Agnew, military officer and son of Sir James Agnew of Lochnaw. They had four children: Mary (*b.* before 1760), who in 1777 married William Honyman, later Lord Armadale (1756–1825), of Graemsay, Orkney, advocate; Robert Dundas (*c*.1760–1816), advocate; Katherine (*b.* 1762), who in 1784 married John MacDonald, chief of Clanranald (1765–1794), from whom she was divorced in 1790 on grounds of adultery with Captain William Payne; and John (*c*.1769–1837), military officer. The family lived at 13 George Square, Edinburgh, and at two houses in Lanarkshire, Hardington, and (after John Macqueen's death) Braxfield. Henry Cockburn described Robert Macqueen thus: 'Strong built and dark, with rough eyebrows, powerful eyes, threatening lips, and a low, growling voice, he was like a formidable blacksmith. His accent and his dialect were exaggerated Scotch, his language, like his thoughts, short, strong and conclusive' (*Memorials … by Henry Cockburn*, 113). He was a famous drinker and a ruthless card-player, but also had more refined tastes. Like other old-fashioned members of the Scottish bar he scorned modern literature and stuck strictly to the classics, but let himself go in enjoyment of Scottish music and was a pillar of the Edinburgh Musical Society.

From 1754 Macqueen served as advocate-depute under the lord advocate, Robert Dundas of Arniston. In 1760 he returned to private practice, where he was soon earning £1900 per annum, double the basic judicial salary. So it was at some financial sacrifice that on 13 September 1776 he accepted appointment as judge in the court of session, with the title Lord Braxfield. On 26 February 1780 he was promoted to the high court of justiciary. The award to him of a double gown provoked the jealous James Boswell to publish an anonymous open letter enjoining him to judicial solemnity and religious orthodoxy. On 15 January 1788

Robert Macqueen, Lord Braxfield (1722–1799), by Sir Henry Raeburn

Braxfield became lord justice clerk, head of the criminal judiciary. Cockburn painted his conduct on the bench as outrageous, bullying counsel and sending prisoners to the gallows with a jest. Yet the first Scottish criminal proceedings fully recorded in shorthand, when he presided over the trial of Deacon Brodie in August 1788, do not bear out such criticism. Rather, from the bench he tolerated to excess the provocative rudeness of counsel for the defence, John Clerk of Eldin. After sentencing Brodie to death for a long series of robberies, his concluding admonition ran:

> I hope you will improve the short time which you now have to live by reflecting upon your past conduct, and endeavouring to procure, by a sincere repentance, forgiveness for your many crimes. God always listens to those who seek Him with sincerity.   (Roughead, *Trial of Deacon Brodie*, 209)

Braxfield handed Cockburn the ammunition for his strictures during the trials for sedition arising from disturbances in Scotland prompted by the French Revolution. The first big one was that of Thomas Muir, young advocate turned radical agitator, in September and October 1793. Braxfield presided over the empanelling of a jury drawn from known supporters of the government. Muir and witnesses appearing for him protested his attachment to peaceful change under the king and existing constitution, but the lord advocate, Robert Dundas the younger, put the worst possible construction on his conduct. From the bench Braxfield concurred, in a eulogy of the constitution including the view that 'a government in every country should be just like a corporation; and, in this country, it is made up of the landed interest, who alone have the right to be represented'. Muir was convicted and sentenced to fourteen years' transportation. Soon afterwards, on circuit at Perth, the Revd Thomas Fyshe Palmer got seven years' transportation for sedition. In London, leading whigs such as Lord Lauderdale, Charles Grey, and Richard Sheridan represented to the home secretary, Henry Dundas, that these sentences were far too severe and anyway probably illegal, transportation being a doubtfully valid form of the traditional penalty at common law in Scotland of banishment from the realm. Dundas wrote to Edinburgh asking if there was any doubt about legality on such grounds, and Braxfield replied on behalf of the whole bench that there was none, adding for good measure that neither convicted man should be recommended to the king's mercy.

Braxfield's persecution of radicals went on. In January 1794 he answered doubts of his impartiality raised in open court by giving Maurice Margarot fourteen years' transportation. In March 1794 Joseph Gerrald, on trial for sedition, chose to make his own summing-up speech, in which he recalled that Jesus Christ had been a reformer: 'Muckle he made o'that; he was hanget', Braxfield muttered from the bench. By recording this and others of his *obiter dicta*, Cockburn left no stone unturned to prove Braxfield was 'the Jeffreys of Scotland' (*Memorials … by Henry Cockburn*, 116). Yet he hanged just one radical, the slippery double agent Robert Watt in September 1794. It may have been from this trial that J. G. Lockhart gleaned the comment of Braxfield's, whence a more quizzical intelligence shines through: 'Ye're a verra clever chiel, man, but ye wad be nane the waur o' a hanging' (Lockhart, 425).

Braxfield's first wife died in 1791 and his final years were enlivened by his marriage, in 1792, to Elizabeth (*d*. 1820), daughter of Robert Ord, chief baron of exchequer. He wooed her in inimitable fashion: 'Lizzy, I am looking out for a wife, and I thought you just the person that would suit me. Let me have your answer, off or on, the morn, and nae mair aboot it' (Gray, 120). In her he seems to have met his match. When his butler resigned on the grounds that he could no longer stand her continual scolding, Braxfield retorted: 'Lord! ye've little to complain o'; ye may be thankfu' ye're no married to her' (*Memorials … by Henry Cockburn*, 120). They had no children.

Braxfield died at his home, 13 George Square, Edinburgh, on 30 May 1799, according to Dundas of 'a fistula, a rupture and a violent purgery' (Roughead, *Glengarry's Way*, 306). He was buried on 5 June in his family's lair in the old kirkyard of St Kentigern, Lanark. Conservative in his politics, stern in his judgments, and severe in his sentences, he still does not in the ensemble of his behaviour quite bear out the charges of casual brutality, and the claims that he was illiterate or irreligious are plainly false. Cockburn's always partisan and often unfair slurs on tories are especially suspect when arising from events he had not witnessed himself. His younger generation of whigs, once they took power in Scotland after 1832, were genteel Anglicizers, affecting horror at the blunt ways of their Scottish elders. Braxfield's reputation, committed to paper in vitriol, fell victim to this.   MICHAEL FRY

Sources B. D. Osborne, *Braxfield* (1997) · *Memorials of his time, by Henry Cockburn* (1856) · W. Roughead, *The trial of Deacon Brodie*, 3rd edn (1931) · W. Roughead, *Glengarry's way* (1922) · J. G. Lockhart, *Memoirs of the life of Sir Walter Scott*, 7 vols. (1837–8) · W. F. Gray, *Some old Scots judges* (1914) · A. Young, memoir of Robert Macqueen of Braxfield, U. Edin. L., Laing MSS

Archives NA Scot., Home Office corresp., RH2/4/73 · NA Scot., Melville MSS

Likenesses J. Kay, caricature, etching, 1793, BM · J. Kay, caricature, etching, pubd 1842, NPG · J. Kay, caricature, engraving, repro. in J. Kay, *A series of original portraits and caricature etchings … with biographical sketches and illustrative anecdotes*, ed. [H. Paton and others], 2 vols. (1837–8) · W. & D. Lizars, line engraving (after H. Raeburn), BM, NPG; repro. in J. G. Lockhart, *Peter's letters to his kinsfolk* (1819) · H. Raeburn, oils, Scot. NPG [*see illus.*] · H. Raeburn, oils, Parliament House, Edinburgh

M'Quhae, William (1737–1823), Church of Scotland minister and friend of James Boswell, was born on 1 May 1737, the eldest child of David M'Quhae, Wigtown magistrate, and Margaret Laurie. After graduating MA in 1756 at the University of Glasgow, where he was a favourite pupil of Adam Smith, he was licensed to preach the gospel by the presbytery of Wigtown in March 1762. He was hired by Alexander Boswell, Lord Auchinleck, as domestic tutor to his younger sons, David and John, and resided for a time with the Revd George Reid, minister of Ochiltree, as tutor to his son James, who died in 1762 at the age of eight. M'Quhae impressed James Boswell, three years his junior, who wrote in his diary for 26 February 1763: 'He has excellent parts, and has had a most accurate education. He has a good heart, fine dispositions, and an agreeable vivacity of manners' (*Boswell's London Journal*, 204). It was for M'Quhae and John Johnston of Grange that Boswell wrote his lively 'Journal of my jaunt, harvest 1762', undertaken as a preparatory exercise for the journal he was planning to keep in London, which would become the famous *London Journal* of 1762–3. M'Quhae praised the harvest journal warmly and encouraged its continuation, while regretting the vexation that Boswell's escapades and remarks caused Lord Auchinleck. In one of his affectionate letters to Boswell from this period (26 April 1763, Yale MS C1883), containing news of Ayrshire and Auchinleck family matters, he favours a moderate presbyterianism, speaks with approval of religious toleration in Europe, and praises David Hume as a historian, defending the *History of England* against charges of offensiveness made by some Scottish churchmen.

In August 1763 M'Quhae became assistant minister of St Quivox in Ayrshire, and the following March was ordained as sole minister of the parish. He married first, on 11 November 1765, Elizabeth Park (*d*. 1780) of Barkip, with whom he had seven children, and then, on 3 June 1782, Mary Lawrie (*d*. 1824), with whom he had eight, including Stair Park M'Quhae (1795–1872) who would succeed his father as the minister of St Quivox in 1820. Robert Burns complimented M'Quhae in his poem 'The Holy Tulzie' (1784 or 1785), where he appears as an object of 'Auld Licht' Calvinist anger and is credited with 'a pathetic manly sense'. He has been described elsewhere as a 'learned and able man of business' with a 'cheerful and happy temper' and a 'rich fund of anecdote and flow of wit', which made him an 'agreeable and pleasant companion'. M'Quhae published *The Difficulties which Attend the Practice of Religion No Just Argument Against it* (1775) and the account of St Quivox in Sir John Sinclair's *Statistical Account of Scotland* (1791–9). He was awarded the degree of DD by the University of St Andrews in 1794 and was proposed as moderator of the general assembly of the church in 1806, but declined. At the time of his death at St Quivox on 1 March 1823, at the age of eighty-five, he was father of the synod of Glasgow and Ayr.   GORDON TURNBULL

Sources *Boswell's London journal, 1762–63*, ed. F. A. Pottle (1951), vol. 1 of *The Yale editions of the private papers of James Boswell*, trade edn (1950–89) • F. A. Pottle, *James Boswell: the earlier years, 1740–1769* (1966) • *The general correspondence of James Boswell, 1766–1769*, ed. R. C. Cole and others, 2 vols. (1993–7), vols. 5, 7 of *The Yale editions of the private papers of James Boswell*, research edn • Yale U., Beinecke L., MSS C1881, C1882, C1883, C1884, L915, L916 • *IGI* • W. I. Addison, ed., *The matriculation albums of the University of Glasgow from 1728 to 1858* (1913) • *Fasti Scot.*, new edn
Archives Yale U., Beinecke L., Boswell MSS

Macquin, Ange-Denis (1756–1823), antiquary and writer, of Scottish extraction, was born at Meaux, Seine-et-Marne, France, on 16 October 1756, son of Jean-Charles Macquin, master baker, and Marie-Angélique Chauffé, his wife. He was educated at the college in Meaux, and after his ordination to the priesthood on 23 September 1783 was appointed to its teaching staff, becoming professor of rhetoric and *belles-lettres*. From 1781 he was involved in historical and antiquarian research in editing the *Almanach de Meaux*. In 1783 he published an anonymous pamphlet, *Je ne sais quoi, par je ne sais qui, se vend je ne sais où*, and in 1789 some verses on memory. Openly hostile to the French Revolution, he contributed an article to a Meaux journal which welcomed the Prussian invaders as deliverers.

Exiled to England in 1792, Macquin settled at Hastings, where he began learning English and supported himself by sketching local landscapes. In 1793, following an introduction to Edmund Lodge, he was appointed heraldic draughtsman to the College of Arms, and on 22 May 1794 he was elected honorary fellow of the Society of Antiquaries of London. He designed Nelson's funeral car and a new throne for the old House of Lords. Devoting his leisure to literature and art, he wrote on heraldry and other subjects in the *Encyclopaedia Londinensis*, besides articles for the *Sporting Magazine* on the history of pugilism. He edited W. A. Bellenger's *Dictionary of French and English Idioms*, and published a humorous Latin poem, *Tabella cibaria*, a history of 300 animals, dedicated to the delights of the table (1812), and a *Description of West's Picture of Christ Rejected by the Jews* (1814).

On the fall of Napoleon Macquin revisited France and recovered part of his property, but returned to England. It was on this French visit, in Paris, that he first met William Beckford. Macquin became Beckford's librarian, secretary, and heraldic adviser at Fonthill Abbey, and appears in Beckford's correspondence as a scholar, eccentric, and gourmand:

Never have I seen such eating and drinking. He swallows everything, he tastes everything, he mixes everything up inside himself: milk, then a collation, then lonchon, then dinner, then supper accompanied by a vast deal of rum. If he does not die, if he does not become a fountain of maladies, he must have the special favour not of the Supreme Pontiff but of the Eternal Father Himself.   (Alexander, 236)

Macquin was latterly engaged on a work entitled *Etymological Gleanings*, some of which appeared in W. Jerdan's *Literary Gazette*. He died in Bermondsey Street, Southwark, London, on 17 July 1823, and was buried at Horselydown, Bermondsey, in St John's parish churchyard.

DOMINIC AIDAN BELLENGER

Sources *Almanach du Département de Seine-et-Marne* (1864), 131–6 • B. Alexander, *Life at Fonthill, 1807–1822, from the correspondence of William Beckford* (1957) • D. A. Bellenger, *The French exiled clergy in the British Isles after 1789* (1986) • J. W. Oliver, *The life of William Beckford* (1932) • *GM*, 1st ser., 93/2 (1823), 180
Archives Bodl. Oxf., corresp. with William Beckford

Macquoid [*née* Thomas], **Katharine Sarah** [*pseud.* Gilbert Percy] (1824–1917), novelist and travel writer, was born on 26 January 1824 at Kentish Town, London, the third daughter of Thomas Thomas, a London merchant of Welsh extraction, and his wife, Phoebe Gadsden. She was educated principally at home, but a period of residence in France from the age of seventeen or eighteen gave rise to a lifelong fascination with French society and scenery. At this time she seems to have been known as Katharine Gadsden, but on 28 January 1851 she married Thomas Robert Macquoid (1820–1912), an artist and illustrator. She gave birth to two sons, Percy Macquoid (1852–1925) and Gilbert Samuel Macquoid (1854–1940). The former followed his father in working as an artist, illustrator, and theatre designer, while the latter became a solicitor and occasional author. Both sons attended Marlborough College, and it seems to have been partly the need to pay for their education that stimulated their mother to begin to write professionally.

Macquoid's first efforts to be published were stories and verses for children appearing under the signature Gilbert Percy in John Maxwell's weekly the *Welcome Guest* from 1859, many illustrated by her husband, a regular contributor to the magazine. These were collected in a volume entitled *Piccalilli: a Mixture* (1862). In the same year she produced the first of about fifty novels, most charting the affairs of the heart of their young heroines and aimed mainly at female readers. Perhaps following the advice of G. H. Lewes, Macquoid was to set many of them on the continent. Among the most popular were her first, the fashionably naughty *A Bad Beginning: a Story of a French Marriage* (1862); *Patty* (1871), the story of a more conventionally virtuous and charming heroine, the first to attract attention in the United States; and *At the Red Glove* (1885), a romantic comedy set in a *pension* in Bern. There the heroine is the handsome widowed landlady who competes brazenly, but in the end unsuccessfully, for the hand of her strapping lodger against the timid and pretty assistant at the local glove shop celebrated in the title. *The Spectator* described it as the 'most perfect and enjoyable of Mrs Macquoid's works' (16 Jan 1886), comparing the characterization to that of William Dean Howells 'in his best light comedy vein' (ibid.). From the later 1860s she also contributed tales regularly to monthly magazines, notably the fashionable *Temple Bar* and *Belgravia*, but also the more staid *St Paul's* and *Macmillan's*, which carried *Patty* as a serial. At the same time she wrote uplifting tales for the evangelical *Good Words for the Young*, and in the 1880s produced a series of tract novels for the Society for the Promotion of Christian Knowledge.

The Macquoid family seems to have resided permanently in London, but there were frequent continental holidays which were also turned to literary account. By the end of the century, Macquoid had also published more than half a dozen volumes of travel sketches, most devoted to northern France, like the first, *Through Normandy* (1874). All were collaborative efforts with other family members. Several were jointly authored with either her husband or her younger son, and the former always furnished the illustrations.

At the age of seventy Macquoid was awarded a civil-list pension of £50, later increased to £120, though she was also forced to apply for financial assistance to the Royal Literary Fund on several occasions. After the turn of the century, however, she was still contributing stories occasionally to, among others, the *Illustrated London News* and Tillotson's Fiction Bureau, while her last novel, *Molly Montague's Love Story*, appeared as late as 1911. She died at her home, The Edge, 8 Lucien Road, Tooting Common, London, on 24 June 1917, and was buried on 28 June in Streatham cemetery.   GRAHAM LAW

Sources BL, archives of the Royal Literary Fund, file 2432 (1894–1915) · *The Times* (26 June 1917) · *Streatham News* (29 June 1917) · Allibone, *Dict.*, suppl. · Boase, *Mod. Eng. biog.* · *WWW*, 1897–1915; 1916–28; 1929–40 · F. Hays, *Women of the day: a biographical dictionary of notable contemporaries* (1885) · *BL cat.* · *Wellesley index* · P. D. Edwards, I. G. Sibley, and M. Versteeg, eds., *Indexes to fiction in Belgravia (1867–1899)* [1989] · J. Sutherland, *The Longman companion to Victorian fiction* (1988) · BL, Macmillan archive, Add. MS 54966; corresp., 1870–1913 · BL, Bentley MSS, Add. MS 46618, fols. 242, 301; Add. MS 46621, fol. 265; agreements 1871–84 · m. cert.
Archives BL, Bentley MSS, Add. MS 46618, fols. 242, 301; Add. MS 46621, fol. 265 · BL, corresp. with Macmillans, Add. MS 54966 · BL, archives of the Royal Literary Fund, file 2432
Likenesses Barraud, photograph, repro. in *Men and Women of the Day*, 4 (1891); copy, NPG · drawing (after photograph by Fradelle), repro. in *Harper's Magazine* (June 1888) · drawings, repro. in *Yorkshire Weekly Post* (17 Nov 1888)
Wealth at death £619 17s. 11d.: probate, 14 Aug 1917, *CGPLA Eng. & Wales*

MacRae, Donald Gunn

MacRae, Donald Gunn (1921–1997), sociologist, was born on 20 April 1921 at 22 Westfield Street, Cathcart, Glasgow, the only child of Donald MacRae (1884–1964), an engineer at a flour mill, and his wife, Elizabeth Maud, *née* Gunn (1888–1971), a teacher. He spent much of his childhood at the homes of his grandparents. His paternal grandfather farmed in Kintail, an ancient territory of the MacRaes in remotest Wester Ross, while his mother's father, John Douglass Gunn, was a schoolteacher in Skye, with a library which played a significant part in MacRae's early education. After matriculating from Glasgow high school in 1938, he entered Glasgow University to read history, and

graduated MA in 1942. After taking a further year's economics he proceeded, like many other Glaswegians before him, to Balliol College, Oxford, where he wrote poetry, some of it published in *Poetry Scotland* (1944–6), and in 1945 graduated with a first-class degree in philosophy, politics, and economics. Almost at once he was appointed lecturer in sociology at the London School of Economics (LSE). He spent 1949 back in Oxford with the support of G. D. H. Cole, who wanted to see sociology established there; but he found it a disappointing time, and the hoped-for college fellowship did not open up. Thereafter the LSE was his base for the rest of his working life. He became reader in 1954 and professor in 1961 (going on to take the Martin White chair in sociology in 1978). On 11 September 1948 he married Helen Grace Simpson McHardy (1922–1996), daughter of William McHardy, schoolteacher. She was also a Glasgow graduate (in psychology), and was a secondary schoolteacher and lecturer in psychology. They had two daughters, Mairi (*b.* 1951) and Helen (*b.* 1953).

As a student MacRae held strongly socialist convictions: his first prose publication, a short article on organized labour in the *Fabian Quarterly* of January 1945, showed evidence of the spirit of the 'red Clyde'. Later his politics moved towards the centre, though he retained many contacts in the labour movement. During 1968–9, as a governor of the LSE, he was robust in opposing the student occupations. He was a man of extraordinary erudition, and drew on it brilliantly in lectures, conversation, and the supervision of his research students. As the founding editor of the *British Journal of Sociology* (1950–64), he played a major role in the developing the subject, encouraging work across the whole spectrum from social anthropology to social policy, and drawing together the British tradition of empirical research and the systematic theory building that had emerged in the United States. Up to the mid-1960s he published many articles on sociology, politics, and contemporary issues in culture and education, not only in academic journals but in those addressed to a wider educated public, such as *Twentieth Century*, the *Rationalist Annual*, or *New Society*. Some of the best of these—notably his classic essay 'The Bolshevik ideology'—were collected in *Ideology and Society* (1962).

MacRae held visiting professorships at the University College of the Gold Coast (1956), at the University of California, Berkeley (1959), and at the University of the Witwatersrand (1975). In the 1960s and 1970s he served on several public bodies: a commission on advertising set up by the Labour Party under Lord Reith's chairmanship, the archbishops' commission on divorce, the Council for National Academic Awards, and the International Council on the Future of the University. From about the time that he held a fellowship at the Center for Advanced Study in the Behavioral Sciences at Palo Alto, California (1967), he was understood to be working towards a major study on the history of social thought. To this several shorter works seemed to point the way: the introduction to a reissue of Spencer's *The Man vs. the State* (1969), his Auguste Comte lecture of 1971 (published as *Ages and Stages*, 1973), and a short book, *Max Weber* (1974). Why this work was never completed is unclear; but MacRae published little thereafter. There were shadows over his personal life, and in 1987 his marriage was dissolved. On 14 August in the same year he married Jean Ridyard (*b.* 1935), secretary, and daughter of William Harold Whitley, clerk with the National Coal Board. MacRae had always liked the Kent coast, and in 1995 he and his wife, Jean, settled at Norfolk House, 44 High Street, Sandwich. He died on 23 December 1997 at the Kent and Canterbury Hospital, Canterbury, of renal failure, and was buried on 2 January 1998 in Sandwich cemetery. He was survived by his second wife and by the two daughters of his first marriage.   J. D. Y. PEEL

Sources *The Times* (2 Jan 1998) · *The Scotsman* (6 Jan 1998) · *Daily Telegraph* (15 Jan 1998) · *The Independent* (26 Jan 1998) · *Donald Gunn MacRae (1921–97)* (privately printed) [pamphlet, incl. tributes by S. J. Gould, D. A. Martin, T. P. Morris] · *WW* (1998) · college register, Balliol Oxf. · personal knowledge (2004) · private information (2004) [Jean MacRae; D. Primrose, E. M. Eppel, J. Gould, and D. Martin—colleagues at the London School of Economics] · b. cert. · m. certs. · d. cert.
Likenesses photograph, Scot. NPG · photograph, repro. in *The Times* · photograph, repro. in *Daily Telegraph* · photograph, repro. in *The Independent*

MacRae, Douglas Gordon (1861–1901), printer and newspaper editor, was born on 6 April 1861 in Upper Hill Street, Richmond, Surrey, the son of John Gordon MacRae of Fyvie, Aberdeenshire, then a coal merchant, and his wife, Harriette Elizabeth Tolley.

Little is known of MacRae's early years. One obituary mentions that his father was a director of the Richmond Gas Company (*Financial News*); another that MacRae attended Shoreham grammar school, Sussex, before taking up an apprenticeship in the printing trade (*City Press*). While serving his apprenticeship MacRae also took his first steps in journalism, writing notes on cricket and subsequently supplying weekly items to the *Eastern Province Herald* and other South African newspapers.

Once qualified, MacRae set up business in Catherine Street, off the Strand, London, where he printed a number of papers owned by Horatio Bottomley's Catherine Street Publishing Association. In 1887, seeking capital to expand the business, Bottomley and MacRae approached H. Osborne O'Hagan, the City financier, who arranged a merger between the Catherine Street Association, MacRae & Co., and Curtice & Co., newspaper publishers and advertising agents. O'Hagan was 'much impressed' by MacRae's plan for utilizing the spare capacity of his printing works. The new company quickly justified MacRae's prediction that it would generate a 10 per cent return on O'Hagan's capital (O'Hagan, 1.265–6).

Bottomley's tendency to overreach ensured that his relationship with MacRae was short-lived. It ended in 1888, when Bottomley formed a new company, the Hansard Union, with a view to taking over MacRae's business and various other printing and publishing firms. MacRae severed his connection with the rogue financier, taking with him the *Financial Times* and the *Draper's Record*. 'He was a printer and I was a journalist', Bottomley later recalled, 'but he took the papers and left me the printing

works' (Hyman, 30). It proved a wise decision. Bottomley's over-capitalized enterprise crashed within two years, by which time MacRae was ensconced as editor of the *Financial Times* and managing director of Financial Times Ltd.

The *Financial Times* had first appeared on 9 January 1888 as the *London Financial Guide*, challenging the position established by the *Financial News*, founded four years earlier. Bottomley had taken it over when the original owners could not pay their printing bills. MacRae joined the board in June 1888 and quickly secured control. The *Financial Times* soon matched the *Financial News* in coverage of City affairs but its approach was 'cooler and more pragmatic' (Kynaston, 30). MacRae's most significant editorial decision was to widen its scope by supplying a digest of general news likely to interest 'the intelligent business man' (*Financial Times*, 2 Jan 1893). Despite this initiative the paper struggled to break even; for a number of years MacRae relied heavily on weekly subsidies from O'Hagan. It was rescued by the boom in South African mining companies after 1895 and the abundance of prospectus advertising which followed.

There is ample evidence of MacRae's drive and energy, not least in the intensity of his rivalry with the *Financial News* in the late 1880s. O'Hagan recalled a vindictive side, but the persistence with which MacRae exposed fraudulent enterprises suggests that this could be usefully directed. 'Our chief', noted his paper in its obituary:

> was a man in a thousand—a man of the finest business faculties, of the most intense energy, of the most indomitable pluck and the most unswerving loyalty towards those who worked with him or who enjoyed the privilege of his friendship. (*Financial Times*)

Tributes in rival newspapers were equally heartfelt.

MacRae lived life to the full, working more hours than were good for him and seeking recreation in hunting, yachting, and billiards. On 11 July 1885 he married Caroline Cecilia Colbourne, the daughter of George Colbourne. They had several children. In the late 1890s his health began to fail on account of a renal disorder. MacRae died while on holiday at Kreuzlingen, near Lake Constance in Switzerland, on 2 April 1901. O'Hagan was glad to sell MacRae's interest in the *Financial Times* 'for a very large sum for the benefit of his wife and children' (O'Hagan, 1.109). He was buried at Norbiton, Surrey, on 10 April 1901. MacRae was survived by his second wife, Florence Lucy Frederica MacRae.   DILWYN PORTER

Sources D. Kynaston, *The Financial Times: a centenary history* (1988) · H. O. O'Hagan, *Leaves from my life*, 2 vols. (1929) · A. Hyman, *The rise and fall of Horatio Bottomley: the biography of a swindler* (1972) · *Financial Times* (4 April 1901) · *Financial News* (4 April 1901) · *City Press* (6 April 1901) · *Rialto* (10 April 1901) · *Newspaper Owner and Modern Printer* (10 April 1901) · *Newspaper Owner and Modern Printer* (17 April 1901) · *CGPLA Eng. & Wales* (1901) · b. cert. · m. cert. [C.C. Colbourne] · d. cert.
Likenesses photograph, repro. in *Rialto*
Wealth at death £13,025 4s. 7d.: probate, 24 May 1901, *CGPLA Eng. & Wales*

Macrae, (John) Duncan Graham (1905–1967), actor, was born on 20 August 1905 at 118 Kirkland Street, Maryhill,

(John) **Duncan Graham Macrae** (1905–1967), by William Crosbie, *c.*1938

Glasgow, the fourth of the six children of James Macrae (1871–1945), a sergeant in the Glasgow police force, and his wife, Catherine Graham (1869–1938). He grew up in a strict Presbyterian background, rooted in the highland traditions of his grandparents, but in his later years religion only figured peripherally. Educated at Allan Glen's School, he matriculated in the engineering faculty at Glasgow University in 1923–4, but did not graduate. He trained as a teacher at Jordanhill College of Education from 1925 to 1927, and taught until 1943.

During the 1930s Macrae moved freely in Glasgow's left-wing intellectual and artistic circles. He became involved with its flourishing amateur theatre movement, where the influence of K. S. Stanislavsky's dramatic theories encouraged productions of Maksim Gorky, Henrik Ibsen, and Anton Chekhov. He headed the Project Company in 1934, then directed with the Glasgow Arts Theatre Group. He created the title role in Robert McLellan's *Jamie the Saxt* for the Curtain company in 1937, and was the club's leading actor until the outbreak of the Second World War in 1939. As a conscientious objector, he was granted exemption from military service. He joined Molly Urquhart's company MSU in 1942–3, and played leading roles in plays by J. M. Barrie, J. Bridie, and J. B. Priestley. He married Margaret (Peggy) Scott (1907–1971), a teacher, in Glasgow in 1943. They had two daughters, Ann, born in 1945, and Christine, in 1948.

Encouraged by James Bridie and Alastair Sim, Macrae turned professional in 1943. An original member of the newly founded Glasgow Citizens' Theatre Company, he gradually rose to prominence as a leading player. In a repertory which encompassed Shakespeare, Ibsen, Shaw, and Bridie, his most notable roles were Donald MacAlpine in Bridie's *The Forrigan Reel* (1944), Inspector Goole in Priestley's *An Inspector Calls* (1947), Quince in *A Midsummer Night's Dream*, Flatterie/Pardoner in Robert Kemp's *The Three Estates* (an adaptation of David Lindsay's sixteenth-century morality play) at the Edinburgh Festival (1948), Harry Magog in Bridie's *Gog and Magog*, the dame in *The Tintock Cup* (1949; also by Bridie, under the pseudonym A. P. Kellock), and the title role in Molière's *Tartuffe* (1951). The shift to pantomime at the Glasgow Alhambra in 1950–51 marked the beginning of a run of eight pantomimes, Christmas revues, and many other variety engagements, including 'white heather' tours to America (1960), Canada (1961), and Australia and New Zealand (1962), and *1045 and a' that*, at the Edinburgh Festival (1966). He transferred effortlessly from legitimate stage to variety and back.

Between 1952 and 1955, financially secure as a result of pantomime, Macrae formed the company Scottishshows in partnership with the playwright Tim Watson. Macrae as actor–manager toured Scotland with a different Scottish play each year. In 1956 he headed one of two repertory companies—the second was led by Stanley Baxter—formed by Henry Sherek to alternate between the King's, Glasgow, and the Lyceum, Edinburgh. Between 1957 and 1959 he appeared for the Citizens', Perth Theatre Company, Edinburgh Gateway, Dundee Repertory, and Jimmy Logan's Metropole in a varied selection of plays, including *The Flouers o' Edinburgh* by R. M. McLellan, and *Dr Angelus* and *Let Wives Tak Tent* (both by Bridie). His London appearances included roles in Bridie's *The Forrigan Reel* at Sadler's Wells (1945), *Let Wives Tak Tent* at the Embassy (1949), Bridie's *Mr Bolfry* at the Aldwych (1956), Ionesco's *Rhinoceros* at the Royal Court and the Strand (1960), and Molière's *L'avare* at the Mermaid (1966). He toured in Joe Orton's *Loot* (1965). His last stage performance was in Aristophanes' *The Burdies* at the Edinburgh Festival in 1966.

In 1946 Macrae took the leading role in his first film, *The Brothers*. He went on to appear in a further fifteen films, mainly in supporting roles, including *Whisky Galore* (1948), *Greyfriars Bobby* (1960), and *Tunes of Glory* (1960). His major success was as the grandfather in *The Kidnappers* (1953). In the earlier part of his career Macrae broadcast regularly in radio drama productions, panel games, and variety shows. From 1958, adding to impressive critical and popular acclaim in both legitimate theatre and variety, he worked increasingly in television. In 1959 he created the title role in the *Para Handy* series. The recitation *The Wee Cock Sparra*, on the BBC Hogmanay party in the same year, confirmed his celebrity. He became familiar in *The Avengers*, *The Prisoner*, *Dr Finlay's Casebook*, revues and chat shows such as *Better Late*, and in one particularly popular porridge advert. Songs, poems, and play extracts were commercially recorded by Scottish Records and released by EMI.

Duncan Macrae figured significantly in the history of Scottish theatre, championing the national drama cause, improving the profession's working conditions, and fearlessly challenging the establishment. He was appointed first chairman of Scottish Equity in 1953, a position he held until his death. He wrote many articles and was in constant demand as a speaker. His pamphlet *Be Not Too Tame Neither*, on the state of the arts in Scotland, was published in November 1965 by the Federation of Theatre Unions. Most of his recommendations were adopted. Despite some notoriety over allegedly selfish practices on stage, and although lacking in technical training, his instinctive acting, coupled with an acknowledged genius for comedy, produced a provocative but mesmeric style that influenced a generation of actors.

Macrae's strikingly tall, lean figure, angular face, and voice bearing traces of his Gaelic ancestry matched a singular if eccentric personality. He was devoted to his family, healthy exercise, Scotland, and the theatre. He died from a brain tumour on 23 March 1967 at the Victoria Infirmary, Glasgow. He was cremated at Linn crematorium, Glasgow, on 30 March. Two weeks later, the ashes were buried at Kippen, Stirlingshire.   P. S. BARLOW

Sources private information (2004) · P. Barlow, *Wise enough to play the fool: a biography of Duncan Macrae* (1995) · D. Hutchison, *The modern Scottish theatre* (1977) · W. Findlay, ed., *A history of Scottish theatre* (1998)
Archives NL Scot., corresp. and papers | U. Glas., scripts, programmes, press cuttings, photographs
Likenesses D. Halliday, oils, *c*.1937, Glasgow Museums and Art Galleries · W. Crosbie, oils, *c*.1938, Scot. NPG [*see illus.*] · B. Schotz, bronze statuette, *c*.1951, Art Gallery and Museum, Glasgow
Wealth at death £5500: will, 16 May 1967, registered at Edinburgh, no. 5279

Macrae, James (*c*.1677–1744), administrator in India, was born in Ayrshire of very poor parents. His father died during his infancy, and his mother gained her living as a washerwoman. He owed what little schooling he received to the kindness of Hew M'Quyre, 'violer', or musician, in Ayr. About 1692 he went to sea, and forty years elapsed before he was again heard of in Scotland.

Macrae's career as a captain of ships carrying the trade between England and the East, especially his efforts against pirates in 1720 and a successful salvage operation in 1722, greatly impressed the East India Company's directors with his fidelity, fortitude, and authority. In 1723 the company employed him to investigate and end the corruption and embezzlement endemic to the English settlement on the west coast of Sumatra, and then to go to Madras to be deputy governor at Fort St David. Despite the depth and extent of the abuses Macrae identified in Sumatra, his suggested reforms were not acted upon, and the company's affairs in Sumatra continued to languish in costly obscurity. On 15 January 1725 Macrae succeeded Nathaniel Elwick as governor of the Madras presidency. In June 1725 Macrae's wife died at Blackheath, Kent. She was a sister of David and John Hunter, both captains of local vessels trading between English settlements in India and the East. Mrs Macrae's funeral was attended by prominent members of the East India Company and the Ulster banking families in London.

Macrae was a very successful commercial governor,

effecting reforms on all sides of the fiscal administration. He greatly reduced expenditure, and carried out a thorough revision of the abuses at the mint and in connection with the rate of exchange and the export of silver. In 1727 he instituted a general revenue survey of the town and suburbs, executed a review of the capacities and behaviour of the company's officers, a number of whom were dismissed, and implemented the new charter from George I (24 September 1726), received in Madras in July 1727. Having completed the usual five years' term of office, he was succeeded, on 14 May 1730, by George Morton Pitt.

Macrae was generous to his friends, scrupulous about his obligations, strongly committed to the proprieties in commercial transactions, and forthright in exercising his belief in discipline and the authority of his position. On his retirement complaints were made against both Macrae and his *dubash* (broker), Guda Ankanna, for corruption and oppression. The relationships between all the proponents were extremely complicated, involving as they did relationships between Britons acting on their own and on the company's behalf, Britons transacting with Indian merchants on both accounts, and Indian merchants dealing among themselves. There is no doubt that vindictiveness as a result of Macrae's exercise of authority over British as well as Indian personnel and merchants informed most of the complaints. The company's investigations were exhaustive, resulting in the decision, in August 1732, that the company had no legal case against its ex-governor. On 21 January 1731 Macrae set sail for Britain, taking his fortune, estimated at over £100,000 in specie and diamonds, 'as his best investment'.

On his return to his native country Macrae purchased several estates in the west of Scotland, fixing his own residence at Orangefield in Monkton, Ayrshire. He was admitted a burgess of Ayr on 1 August 1733, when he was described as 'James MacCrae, late governor of Madras'. In 1735 he presented Glasgow with a bronze statue of William III. He died at Orangefield on 21 July 1744, and was buried in Monkton churchyard, where he was commemorated by a monument erected by John Swan in 1750.

On Macrae's arrival home after so many years' absence, he had found none of his own relatives living, but diligently sought out the family of his old benefactor, Hew M'Quyre or Macguire, whose five grandchildren he generously adopted. James, the eldest, was left the barony of Houston, on condition that he assumed the name of Macrae. Macguire's granddaughters were similarly educated and amply dowered by Macrae. The eldest, Elizabeth, to whom the former governor gave the valuable barony of Ochiltree as tocher (or dowry), married in 1744 William Cunningham, thirteenth earl of Glencairn. In December 1745 Macrae's adoptive son-in-law Lord Glencairn lent the borough of Glasgow £1500, at 4½ per cent, to make up the sum levied by Prince Charles Edward—an act which has erroneously been attributed to Macrae himself. The second granddaughter, Margaret, married James

Erskine, Lord Alva, and the third, Macrae, became the wife of Charles Dalrymple, sheriff clerk of Ayr, who succeeded to Orangefield upon Macrae's death.

THOMAS SECCOMBE, *rev.* I. B. WATSON

Sources Sumatra letter-books, 1724–5; Home misc.; Fort St George MSS, 1723–1750, BL OIOC, MS Eur. B 162 • H. D. Love, *Vestiges of old Madras, 1640–1800*, 4 vols. (1913) • J. T. Wheeler, *Madras in the olden time*, 3 vols. (1861–2) • C. C. Prinsep, *Record of services of the Honourable East India Company's civil servants in the Madras presidency from 1741 to 1858* (1885) • J. Paterson, *History of the county of Ayr: with a genealogical account of the families of Ayrshire*, 2 vols. (1847–52) • W. Robertson, *Historic Ayrshire* (1891) • *Scots Magazine*, 6 (1744), 346, 394 • J. Cleland, *Annals of Glasgow*, 2 vols. (1816) • A. Cochrane, *The Cochrane correspondence regarding the affairs of Glasgow* (1836) • *DNB* • letters, PRO NIre., Sir Robert Cowan MSS, D 654/B1/1C [various in 1723 and May 1726]

Wealth at death wealthy; left valuable property: *DNB*

Macray, William Dunn (1826–1916), librarian, historian, and Church of England clergyman, was born on 7 July 1826 in St Pancras, London, the third son of John Macray (1796–1878) and his wife, Ann Downs. He was educated at Magdalen College School, Oxford, and matriculated at Magdalen College, Oxford, in 1844, graduating in 1848.

John Macray was employed by Treuttel and Würz in London and then J. H. Parker in Oxford. He was first librarian of the Taylor Institution in Oxford (1848–71), and compiled and translated a number of volumes of European poetry. His son William Macray's association with the Bodleian Library began when he was only fourteen, on his appointment as a supernumerary under-assistant in July 1840. Five years later he joined the regular staff as an assistant and was in 1850 assigned to the manuscript collections, where he remained until his retirement in 1905, except for a period of eight years' work on the new general catalogue of printed books in the 1860s.

The work for which Macray is best known, his *Annals of the Bodleian Library*, was published early in his career, in 1868. Using the library's official records, the seventeenth- and eighteenth-century correspondence in its manuscript collections, and the diaries of Thomas Hearne, Macray covered the Bodleian's history to 1845. He escaped from the strait-jacket of a year-by-year chronicle by developing themes under the year they first occurred and then using cross-references from later years. He wrote an institutional history, enlivened by firsthand knowledge, which quickly achieved and has retained the status of indispensable manual. He produced a much enlarged second edition in 1890, taking the story to 1880. Macray's account of the forty years that he was on the staff is largely concerned with the growth of the library's collections. He rarely indulges in reminiscence and wisely stops short of E. W. B. Nicholson's troubled librarianship. His own annotated copy of the *Annals*, illustrated with photographs of many of his contemporaries, gives a more personal view of the Bodleian in the nineteenth century. Even there, little evidence survives of Macray's own involvement in the contests for the sub-librarianship in 1861 and 1865 and the librarianship in 1881–2. His failure on each occasion must have been a severe disappointment.

Macray's long career in the Bodleian was distinguished

William Dunn Macray (1826–1916), by Henry Scott Tuke, in or before 1910

by a succession of published catalogues and editions of manuscripts. His catalogues of the Rawlinson and Digby manuscripts, index to the Ashmole manuscripts, and calendar of the Clarendon State Papers remained in daily use over a century after their compilation, monuments to his industry, thoroughness, wide-ranging scholarship, and exemplary accuracy. In addition he edited over a dozen texts, ranging from monastic chronicles to Clarendon's *History of the Rebellion*. His expertise was used by the Royal Commission on Historical Manuscripts, for whom he produced a series of reports between 1888 and 1911, by the Public Record Office, on whose behalf he surveyed archives in Sweden and Denmark, and by Magdalen College, where he spent fourteen years calendaring the muniments. He was elected to a research fellowship at Magdalen in 1891 and thereafter published eight volumes to complete the college register. He contributed sixteen articles to the *Dictionary of National Biography*, including that on Sir Thomas Bodley.

Macray married Adelaide Ottilia Alberta Schmidt before 1858. They had five sons and two daughters; three of his children, like his wife, predeceased him. Macray was ordained in 1851, held various college chaplaincies, and was curate of St Mary Magdalen parish to 1867. In 1870 Magdalen College presented him to the rectory of Ducklington, 10 miles west of Oxford, where he took up residence, thereafter working half-time in the Bodleian. He served there, an exemplary parish priest, for forty-two years. The parish magazine, which he launched, included reports on church restorations, the school reading room and library, choir, bell-ringers, cricket club, penny bank, clothing club, and regular fund-raising and social events, in all of which Macray, loyally supported by his family, took an energetic, leading role. Macray died at his home, Greenlands, Bloxham, on 5 December 1916 and was buried at Ducklington. The surviving records reveal a genial and charitable man, held in affectionate regard by all who knew him.   MARY CLAPINSON

Sources H. H. E. Craster, *History of the Bodleian Library, 1845–1945* (1952); repr. (1981) · W. D. Macray, *A register of the members of St Mary Magdalen College, Oxford*, 8 vols. (1894–1915), vol. 7, pp. 53–9 · W. D. Macray, *Annals of the Bodleian Library, Oxford*, 2nd edn (1890) · *Cogges, Ducklington and Hardwick Parish Magazine* (1892–1903) · *Witney Deanery Magazine* (1880–91) · *Witney Deanery Magazine* (1904–12) · *Oxford Times* (9 Dec 1916) · G. E. Barnes, *Oxfordshire Archaeological Society Report* (1916), 12–14 · Library records, Bodl. Oxf. · IGI · CGPLA Eng. & Wales (1917)
Archives Bodl. Oxf., collections for a history of Ducklington, Hardwick, and Cokethorpe · Bodl. Oxf., notebook · Magd. Oxf., antiquarian papers · Magd. Oxf., muniments, MS 799, fols. i–v · PRO, corresp. as Historical Manuscripts Commission inspector, HMC 1 | U. Edin. L., letters to James Halliwell-Phillipps; letters to David Laing
Likenesses Hill & Saunders, photograph, 1890, Bodl. Oxf. · H. S. Tuke, portrait, in or before 1910, Bodl. Oxf. [*see illus.*]
Wealth at death £2347 0s. 5d.: probate, 8 Feb 1917, CGPLA Eng. & Wales

Macready, Sir (Cecil Frederick) Nevil, first baronet (1862–1946), army officer, was born on 7 May 1862 at 6 Wellington Square, Cheltenham, youngest son of the actor William Charles *Macready (1793–1873) and his second wife, Cecile Louise Frederica Spencer (*d*. 1908), a granddaughter of Sir William Beechey the painter. Nevil, as he was always known, was Cecile's only child, and only one son and one daughter from his father's first marriage survived infancy.

Macready was brought up in artistic and literary circles. In his memoirs he adjudged himself 'far too lazy' to follow a career in painting or drawing (Macready, 1.14), and his father resolutely opposed his going on the stage. After a series of schools he went to the Royal Military College, Sandhurst; and in October 1881 he was commissioned into the Gordon Highlanders. He took part in the Egyptian campaign of 1882, including the battle of Tell al-Kebir. In the summer of 1884 he was appointed staff lieutenant of military police and garrison adjutant at Alexandria, thus establishing a career pattern which he was to follow for most of his professional life: adjutancy, staff duties, and police work. 'It was not a bad thing', recalled Macready 'to have Staff experience when young … The great thing is always to have a ready answer on one's tongue. Even if it is not absolutely correct, there are many generals who will be none the wiser' (Macready, 1.69–70). In 1886 he married Sophia Geraldine Atkin (*d*. 1931) from a co. Cork family. They had two daughters and one son.

After some five years as a military policeman Macready rejoined his regiment early in 1890 and served in Ceylon and India for two years. In 1892, as a captain, he was transferred to Dublin and in 1894 he became adjutant of a volunteer battalion of the regiment based in Aberdeenshire.

In 1899 he returned to the 2nd battalion in India, which in September was sent to South Africa.

Macready, promoted major in 1899, saw active service during the Second South African War, including the defence of Ladysmith, where he was one of the besieged garrison from October 1899 to February 1900. Having been promoted lieutenant-colonel, he was in June 1901 selected to head a commission investigating cattle-raiding in Zululand. Following this he served in a series of staff jobs, including assistant provost-marshal at Port Elizabeth and assistant adjutant-general and chief staff officer of Cape Colony. For his work in South Africa he was twice mentioned in dispatches. He was promoted colonel in 1903.

In 1907 Macready became assistant adjutant-general at the War Office, in the directorate of personal services which was, among other matters, responsible for discipline and the use of troops in aid of the civil power. For a year from May 1909 he commanded the 2nd infantry brigade at Aldershot, but he returned to the War Office in 1910 as director of personal services. The same year he was promoted major-general. His position made him a crucial figure in the deployment of troops during a series of serious labour disputes in Great Britain and anticipated civil disturbance in Ireland. He earned the confidence of the government as a 'safe pair of hands' in circumstances where passions ran high and over-hasty action could have disastrous consequences. He certainly had liberal political sympathies. Writing in 1930 his close colleague Wyndham Childs recalled that they both 'held views which nowadays I suppose would be called sane, though at that time they were thought ultra-democratic' (Childs, 83). In particular, Macready conceded the right to strike and (unlike many fellow officers) favoured Irish home rule.

In November 1910 Macready was sent to command troops in support of police dealing with possible disorders arising from a miners' strike. Although some rioting occurred, especially in the Tonypandy valley, his insistence that the military forces remained subordinate to the police and, perhaps more importantly (though of questionable legality), that they served under the direct authority of the Home Office, rather than taking direction from sometimes alarmist local magistrates, ensured that the use of soldiers, both then and during the 1912 national coal strike, did not inflame the situation.

A potentially much more serious military commitment arose in Ireland in 1912–14, where unionist and nationalist paramilitary formations raised fears of a civil conflict over the issue of home rule. In the aftermath of the Curragh incident of March 1914, Macready was nominated 'military governor' in Belfast in the event of serious disorder, but the outbreak of war in August 1914 temporarily lifted the threat of civil war in Ireland as both unionists and nationalists united against a perceived common foreign enemy.

Macready went to France as adjutant-general of the British expeditionary force. Among the matters under his charge were the burial of the dead and the recording of graves, and he was responsible for appointing Fabian Ware to head a new graves registration and inquiries organization, which provided the basis for the Imperial (later Commonwealth) War Graves Commission. In February 1916 Macready was recalled to the War Office as adjutant-general to the forces, and for most of the rest of the war he tackled the ever-increasing difficulty of keeping up the strength of the armies in the field. He was a powerful proponent of the 'scientific' deployment of the nation's manpower resources and encouraged the use of female labour to replace male wherever possible.

In August 1918 Macready, who was promoted full general the same year, reluctantly accepted the post of commissioner of the Metropolitan Police, after the police had gone on strike over pay and the recognition of a trade union. He brought the men back to work by granting a pay rise and promising machinery for collective representation. When a minority of police went on strike again in August 1919 Macready summarily dismissed the strikers and restored discipline to the force.

In spring 1920, despite averring privately that he loathed Ireland and its people 'with a depth deeper than the sea and more violent than that which I feel against the Boche', Macready accepted the command of the army in Ireland (Townshend, 20). It was, he recorded in his memoirs, only a sense of loyalty to his old chief Lord French (now lord lieutenant in Ireland) that persuaded him to take the job. The move from London, however, was sweetened by £5000 'disturbance allowance'. He was in many respects the ideal candidate for a position which required high administrative powers, experience of military aid to the civil power, and a degree of political finesse. He immediately injected a note of morale-boosting dynamism into the Irish command and reassessed security policy generally, which up to this point had limped along with no very clear direction. He secured additional troops and much needed technical support, including motor transport and armoured cars. But the possibility of his succeeding in defeating the growing Irish challenge was fatally compromised by his refusal to accept charge of the Irish police alongside his military command. While declining this responsibility may personally have been a wise political move, in security terms it made no sense at all. Macready also acquiesced in the reinforcement of the Royal Irish Constabulary with a militarized auxiliary division whose draconian (and not always legal) methods did much finally to alienate Irish nationalist opinion from the British administration in Ireland.

Macready's advice to Lloyd George in the early summer of 1921 that the army in Ireland scarcely had the resources for a sustained campaign against the IRA contributed to the truce of July 1921 and the subsequent treaty which led to the withdrawal of the British administration from what became known as the Irish Free State. He saw to it that the evacuation of troops was conducted without untoward incident. In June 1922, following the assassination of his old friend Sir Henry Wilson, he deliberately delayed implementing orders from London to reduce the republican-occupied Four Courts in Dublin, an action which would undoubtedly have plunged Ireland into a grave crisis. Thus his cool good sense was sustained to the end.

Known as Make-Ready—a nickname echoing the correct pronunciation of his surname—Macready was, in the words of H. A. L. Fisher, 'a man of cool head, good judgement, and, with a dry manner, tact and humour' (Fisher to Lloyd George, 6 July 1916, Lloyd George papers, E/2/23/2). He was a very able military staff officer who expertly fielded some of the most politically sensitive military duties of the time. His reputation, however, is chiefly sustained by his own memoirs, *Annals of an Active Life*, after the publication of which in 1924 he destroyed his diary and other personal papers.

Macready was knighted (KCB) in 1912, appointed KCMG in 1915, promoted GCMG in 1918, and created a baronet on his retirement in 1923. He was sworn of the privy council of Ireland in 1920. His only son, Gordon Nevil (1891–1956), had a distinguished military career and succeeded his father as second baronet when Sir Nevil died in London on 9 June 1946. KEITH JEFFERY

Sources N. Macready, *Annals of an active life*, 2 vols. [1924] · *DNB* · W. Childs, *Episodes and reflections* (1930) · C. Townshend, *The British campaign in Ireland, 1919–1921* (1975) · K. Jeffery, *The British army and the crisis of empire, 1918–22* (1984) · HLRO, Lloyd George papers · Burke, *Peerage* (1999)

Archives NAM, papers [mostly photocopies] | Bodl. Oxf., corresp. with H. H. Asquith · Commonwealth War Graves Commission, Maidenhead, corresp. relating to work for Commonwealth War Graves Commission · HLRO, corresp. with David Lloyd George and others · IWM, corresp. with Sir Henry Wilson · Lpool RO, corresp. with seventeenth earl of Derby

Likenesses W. Stoneman, two photographs, c.1915, NPG · F. Dodd, charcoal and watercolour drawing, 1917, IWM · P. Anderson, oils, Royal Collection · photographs, repro. in Macready, *Annals of an active life*

Macready [M'cready], **William** (1755–1829), actor and theatre manager, was born in Dublin, where his father was highly esteemed both in his trade as an upholsterer and as a civic leader. Although he served an apprenticeship with his father, William Macready embarked on a stage career, with engagements in Kilkenny (1776) and Edinburgh (1776–7). He played at the Smock Alley Theatre in Dublin during 1783–4 and 1784–5, appearing as Egerton alongside Charles Macklin (as Sir Pertinax McSycophant) in that elderly actor's own play *The Man of the World*. The two men, who shared an irascible temperament, struck up a rapport, and Macklin helped Macready to secure engagements in Liverpool and Manchester. In Manchester, Macready met Christina Ann Birch (1765–1803), from a genteel family of clergymen, surgeons, and schoolmasters; they acted together—Bob Acres and Julia in Sheridan's *The Rivals* was a typical pairing—and on 17 June 1786 they were married at the collegiate church.

On 18 September 1786 Macready began his metropolitan career at Covent Garden, where he remained for ten years. While he never progressed beyond the role of supporting player, he had some success as an adapter of old plays. Christina did not act: she gave birth to eight children, three of whom died in infancy. Following his brief management (1797) at the Royalty Theatre in the East End of

London, Macready took the New Theatre, Birmingham, where he had managed a successful summer season in 1796, and finally severed his link with Covent Garden. In the next few years his activities radiated to Leicester, Stafford, Sheffield, and beyond. He was an exacting manager, setting exceptionally high standards for lighting and scenery, attaching great importance to rehearsals (backed up by an elaborate system of fines, strictly enforced), and engaging the most celebrated actors of the day (Mrs Siddons, Thomas King, and Master Betty). By March 1803 he was sufficiently prosperous to send his sons, William Charles *Macready (1793–1873) and Edward, to Rugby School, where William Birch (a cousin of Christina's) was a master. Christina Macready died on 3 December 1803.

In 1807, with economic depression setting in, Macready took the disastrous decision to abandon Birmingham, where the landlord had doubled the rent, for a newly built theatre in Manchester. His affairs were so parlous in December 1808 that his elder son, William, left Rugby to save money and help his father. Macready managed to extricate himself from Manchester, but within a year he was imprisoned—albeit for only a few weeks—in Lancaster Castle, and the sixteen-year-old William set off to rescue his father's companies in Leicester, Chester, and Newcastle upon Tyne. Back in Birmingham, the young William made his stage début, as Romeo, on 7 June 1810, and for the next four years the fortunes of father and son were contiguous, until their similar temperaments and the latter's burgeoning talents hastened a separation of their ways.

The senior Macready settled first in Carlisle, where he had a theatre built, and thereafter in Berwick, Dumfries, and Newcastle upon Tyne, before descending on Bristol, where with William's help he took the Theatre Royal in 1819. His years in Bristol—with less successful forays to Bath—brought him the respectability and relative prosperity which, Micawber-like, he had always expected to 'turn up'. On 26 November 1821, at Whitehaven, he married Kathleen (known as Sarah) Desmond (1789/90–1853), who was certainly his professional partner of several years' standing and, assuming, as most did, that George Macready (b. 8 July 1814) was not the nephew he was claimed to be but the couple's son, already his wife in all but name. A handsome woman, with a commanding stage presence, Sarah Macready was an attraction in her own right, in particular as Meg Merrilies, Lady Macbeth, and Hermione. Macready maintained a strong musical side and a creditable standard of scenery, costumes, and effects; he supplemented his regular company with visiting stars (Maria Foote, John Liston, and Madame Vestris, as well as his increasingly eminent son William, who was always a popular draw), but was not above introducing animal acts.

Irascible, improvident, exacting, and exasperating, William Macready died in Bristol on 11 April 1829, a respected freemason, and was buried in Bristol Cathedral on 18 April. In his will he left all his property and rights in his theatres to his widow, Sarah, their daughter, Mazarina Emily (1824/5–1878), and 'the boy known by the name of

George William Macready'. His son William, with Richard Brunton, actually held the lease of the Theatre Royal, Bristol, until 1833, when Sarah took it over in her own right. Following her death on 8 March 1853, it passed, in accordance with her wishes, to her son-in-law James Chute, the husband of her daughter Mazarina (Maggie), who formed a minor (at least) theatrical dynasty.

RICHARD FOULKES

Sources *Macready's reminiscences, and selections from his diaries and letters*, ed. F. Pollock, 2 vols. (1875) · A. S. Downer, *The eminent tragedian William Charles Macready* (1966) · J. C. Trewin, *Mr Macready* (1955) · W. Archer, *William Charles Macready* (1890) · J. E. Cunningham, *Theatre Royal: the history of the Theatre Royal, Birmingham* (1950) · K. Barker, *The Theatre Royal, Bristol, 1766–1966* (1974) · K. Barker, *Bristol at play* (1976) · K. Barker, *The Theatre Royal, Bristol: the first seventy years*, 2nd edn (1963) · K. Barker and J. MacLeod, 'The McCready prompt books at Bristol', *Theatre Notebook*, 4 (1949–50), 76–81 · Highfill, Burnim & Langhans, *BDA*
Archives Boston PL, prompt book · Folger, MSS · NYPL, MSS
Likenesses W. Ridley, stipple engraving, pubd 1794 (after miniature by Halpin), BM; repro. in Barker, *The Theatre Royal, Bristol*, pl. 9

Macready, William Charles (1793–1873), actor and theatre manager, was born on 3 March 1793 at 3 Mary Street (now 45 Stanhope Street), Euston Road, London, the fifth of the eight children of William *Macready or M'cready (1755–1829) and his first wife, the actress Christina Ann, née Birch (1765–1803). He was baptized at St Pancras parish church on 21 January 1796, when his date of birth was erroneously given as 1792. William Macready senior was the son of a prosperous Dublin upholsterer, with whom he served an apprenticeship before taking to the stage. Following provincial engagements in Ireland, he joined the Smock Alley Theatre in Dublin in 1785 to take over the part of Egerton to the Sir Pertinax McSycophant of the irascible and elderly (at least eighty-two) Charles Macklin in *The Man of the World*. Macklin used his influence to help Macready secure engagements in Liverpool and in Manchester, where on 18 June 1786 Macready married Christina Ann Birch at the collegiate church. Miss Birch came from genteel stock. Her grandfather, Jonathan Birch, was vicar of Bakewell in Derbyshire; two of her paternal uncles were clergymen; and her father, who died—badly off—when she was three, was a surgeon. On her mother's side she was descended from William Frye (d. 17 May 1736), president of the council of Montserrat.

On 18 September 1786 the elder Macready—again through Macklin's good offices—appeared at Covent Garden as Flutter in Hannah Cowley's *The Belle's Stratagem*; he remained in the company for ten years, never progressing from the ranks of supporting player, though he did enjoy some success as an adapter of old plays. Mrs Macready did not appear on the London stage. The couple's first three children died in infancy; their fourth child, Joanna, survived only until her seventh year, though she lived on in the memory of her younger brother William, whose birth in 1793 was followed by that of Laetitia in 1794 and Edward in 1798. While still a member of the Covent Garden company the elder Macready ventured into management, first at the Royalty Theatre, Wellclose Square, London, and

William Charles Macready (1793–1873), by John Jackson, 1821 [in the title role in 2 *Henry IV*]

next—in June 1795—at the newly opened theatre in New Street, Birmingham. Following a quarrel over his salary Macready left Covent Garden in 1797 and, after a further unsuccessful attempt at the Royalty, devoted himself to provincial management in Birmingham and beyond (Leicester, Sheffield, and Manchester), in support of which his wife resumed her stage career.

Early life and education William Charles Macready was, in his own words, 'got out of the way' (*Macready's Reminiscences*, 2) and sent to school at an early age. When he was six he transferred from a preparatory school in Kensington to an establishment in St Paul's Square, Birmingham, where he distinguished himself by memorizing and reciting long extracts from Shakespeare, Milton, and Pope, marred only by his abuse of the letter 'h'. In the school holidays his favourite recreations were performing some of his own compositions with his siblings and witnessing such luminaries as Thomas King, Sarah Siddons, and Elizabeth Billington performing in his father's theatre. On 3 March 1803 he entered Rugby School, where his mother's cousin William Birch was a master.

At the beginning of the Christmas holidays Macready was devastated by the news of his mother's death, which had occurred on 3 December 1803. His parents' motives in sending Macready to Rugby had been to educate him for a more respectable profession than the stage, which Macready told his headmaster, Dr Inglis, he very much disliked. Nevertheless, with his cousin Tom Birch, he absented himself from school to see the Infant Roscius, Master Betty, as Richard III in Leicester; Macready also assisted with (by borrowing books and costumes from his

father) and performed in plays; and, under Inglis's successor, John Wooll, he won prizes for recitation and on speech day 1808 played the title role in the closet scene from *Hamlet*. That year Birch wrote to Macready's father of his son's 'wonderful talent for acting and speaking', which 'may be turned to good account in the Church or at the Bar; it is valuable everywhere' (Trewin, 22–3).

These hopes were dashed by the decline in the elder Macready's fortunes, as a result of which he withdrew his son from Rugby School at the end of 1808, Birch discharging the debt of over £100 for school fees. Though cut short, Macready's time at Rugby was immensely important to him throughout his life. It gave him the educational background—'he knew enough Greek to astonish a dinner party with a quotation from Homer' (Archer, 11)—to mix in cultivated society, and it fired him with a determination to elevate the stage to a status comparable to that of the other professions to which he had aspired.

Early career Aged fifteen, Macready had to bide his time before making his professional acting début. He learned some juvenile roles in readiness and spent a short time in London, observing leading actors perform and taking fencing lessons, though this was a skill of which he never became master. Late in 1809 he was confronted with the task of salvaging the fortunes of his father's Chester company, which had not been paid for three weeks. Macready emerged—successfully—from the experience with the precepts about the hazards of theatrical management and the importance of financial probity which were to inform the rest of his career. By the summer of 1810 the elder Macready, who had spent a short time in prison for debt, was able to resume his Birmingham management, and it was there, on 7 June 1810, that William Charles Macready made his first appearance on any stage, as Romeo.

Macready's image as Romeo was captured in a portrait by Samuel De Wilde: a chubby-faced boy, in a costume including a broad flowered sash, almost under his armpits, an upstanding ruff, white kid gloves, white silk stockings and dancing pumps, and a large black hat with white plumes. After a faltering, mechanical start, Macready, encouraged by sympathetic applause from the audience, got the measure of his role and achieved what the audience, the critics, and the young actor himself recognized as a remarkable début. During the next four years as the juvenile lead in his father's company he played more than seventy different roles. In Newcastle upon Tyne early in 1811 he performed Hamlet, observing that 'a total failure in Hamlet is a rare occurrence' (*Macready's Reminiscences*, 37), and though, with a self-criticism which characterized him throughout life, he described his début in the role as 'my crude essay', it was pronounced a success. Also in Newcastle the young actor underwent the daunting experience of appearing opposite Mrs Siddons, as Beverley to her Mrs Beverley in Edward Moore's *The Gamester* and as Young Norval to her Lady Randolf in John Home's *Douglas*. Understanding and encouraging on stage and off, Mrs Siddons gave Macready some parting words of advice: 'You are in the right way, but remember what I say: study,

study and do not marry till you are thirty!' (Archer, 21)—both of which injunctions he heeded.

Macready also performed with John Philip Kemble, Dorothy Jordan, and Charles Mayne Young; he adapted Scott's *Marmion* for his own benefit. Relations between father and son, who were both quick-tempered, became strained, and on 29 December 1814 Macready began an engagement in Bath, where his roles included Romeo, Hamlet, Hotspur, Richard II, and Orestes (in Ambrose Philips's *The Distressed Mother*). In the spring of 1815 Macready was in Glasgow and there he met—and scolded for not knowing her lines—a pretty nine-year-old girl, Catherine Frances Atkins (1803/4–1852), who was to become his first wife. In Dublin—in April 1815 and again in February 1816—Macready commanded a salary of £50 a week and was attracting the attention of London managers. Having declined an earlier offer from Covent Garden, he took an engagement there for five years at a weekly salary rising from £16 to £18, making his début as Orestes in *The Distressed Mother* on 16 September 1816.

Tragedian Macready made a nervous start, a top-heavy auburn wig emphasizing his chubbiness. Leigh Hunt described him as 'one of the plainest and most awkwardly made men that ever trod the stage. His voice is even coarser than his personage' (Trewin, 44). Certainly the young Macready was not handsomely endowed physically, but other critics commended the power, harmony, and moderation of his voice, the expressiveness of his eyes, and the sharp intelligence of his characterization. Edmund Kean, conspicuous in a private box, joined in the warm applause, and the play was 'given out' for repetition the following Monday and Friday. Montevole in Robert Jephson's *Julia, or, The Italian Lover* on 30 September augmented his reputation, after which Macready was put to a sterner test, alternating Othello and Iago with Charles Mayne Young. His Othello (10 October) was creditable, but, in what was for him a new role, as Iago (15 October) he was judged to be tame—in Hazlitt's description 'a mischievous boy' whipping the 'great humming-top' which was Young's Othello. The quality of roles assigned to Macready by the Covent Garden manager, Henry Harris, who dubbed him the 'Cock Grumbler', was variable. He was deemed to be unsuited in appearance to romantic and heroic roles and was often cast as the villain in melodramas and more ambitious pieces. Macready confided his dissatisfaction to his diary, wondering whether to quit the stage and make a trial of his talents in some other profession. But, even in roles which he despised, he enhanced his reputation. On 15 April 1817, as Valentino, a traitor, in Dimond's *Conquest of Taranto*, he outshone Junius Brutus Booth, whose engagement at Covent Garden had deprived Macready of roles he might otherwise have expected to play. As Pescara in Sheil's *The Apostate* (3 May 1817), he won the praise of the German scholar Ludwig Tieck; he also met the great French actor Talma at the conclusion of John Philip Kemble's farewell season. Gradually better roles came his way—Romeo to Eliza O'Neill's Juliet, and Richard III (25 October 1819), in which he inevitably invited comparison with Edmund Kean. Colley Cibber's version was still preferred to Shakespeare and, as so often happened on big occasions, the first few scenes eluded Macready. He gained in confidence, and by Richard's death the actor's victory was complete.

Macready's success as Richard III restored the fortunes of Covent Garden, but when, following the death of George III, *King Lear* was restored to the repertory, Macready refused Harris's offer of the title role—in competition with Edmund Kean at Drury Lane—playing Edmund instead (13 April 1820), with Booth taking Lear. Macready's opportunity came with Sheridan Knowles's new play, *Virginius*. He took charge of rehearsals, the intensity of which was resented by senior actors unused to taking orders from anyone, let alone from the youngest member of the company. His careful preparation, as both actor and stage-manager, paid dividends: *Virginius* (17 May 1820) was a triumph and remained in his repertory to the end of his life. For his benefit (9 June 1820) Macready made his début as Macbeth, which was to become his favourite and most successful role. On tour in Scotland that summer he was supported by the fourteen-year-old Catherine Atkins, whom he induced his father to engage for the Bristol company of which he was then manager.

Back at Covent Garden for the 1820–21 season, Macready failed as Iachimo in *Cymbeline* (18 October 1820). In *Richard III* (12 March 1821) he partially reinstated Shakespeare's text, but in *The Tempest* (15 May 1821) he countenanced further maltreatment by Reynolds of the Davenant–Dryden perversion. In his London début as Hamlet he presented a lachrymose, self-pitying, inky cloaked Dane (8 June 1821), but scored a success as the King in *2 Henry IV*, staged as a coronation attraction, a performance captured in John Jackson's portrait (now in the National Portrait Gallery). Having fulfilled his original five-year contract at Covent Garden, Macready renewed his engagement for a further five years, beginning in the autumn of 1821. The 1821–2 season was idle and inglorious for him, the only noteworthy event being a successful revival of *Julius Caesar*, in which he played Cassius. In spring 1822 Charles Kemble, by his brother John Philip's gift, became co-proprietor of Covent Garden. The already uneasy relationship between Macready and Charles Kemble deteriorated when Macready returned from a European vacation and found the Covent Garden regime much reduced by ill-advised economies. Many senior members of the company defected to Drury Lane, where R. W. Elliston trebled their salaries. Macready remained at Covent Garden, performing the title role in Mary Russell Mitford's *Julian* (15 March 1823) and adding Cardinal Wolsey and King John to his Shakespearian repertory. Increasingly dissatisfied, after a heated exchange of letters and pamphlets with the Covent Garden management, he terminated his contract and joined the other refugees at Drury Lane, at a salary of £20 a night.

Macready made his Drury Lane début in *Virginius* on 13 October 1823, followed by his London début as Leontes (3 November 1823) and another—inferior—piece by Sheridan Knowles, *Caius Gracchus* (18 November 1823). His only other new part was the Duke in *Measure for Measure* (1 May

1824). In the autumn of 1823, following her father's death by drowning, Catherine Atkins had become Macready's betrothed. Although Macready had attained thirty years of age, he postponed his marriage, at his sister Laetitia's suggestion, if not insistence, so that his bride-to-be could benefit from a period of study and improvement under her future sister-in-law's supervision. The wedding ceremony took place at St Pancras Church on 24 June 1824. Laetitia lived with the Macreadys throughout their married life, surviving her sister-in-law by six years.

Macready appeared at Drury Lane intermittently for thirteen years, during which he did not add materially to his reputation. His success as Remont in Sheil's expurgated adaptation of Massinger's *The Fatal Dowry* (5 January 1825) was interrupted by serious illness (inflammation of the diaphragm) which caused concern for his life. He recovered to play the title role in Knowles's *William Tell* (11 May 1825), which, though turgid and long-winded, provided him with some effectively overwrought scenes suited to his style. Following some provincial engagements, a period of rest in a country retreat near Denbigh, and a short season at Drury Lane (10 April to 19 May 1826) in which he undertook no new roles, Macready, with his wife and sister, sailed from Liverpool on 2 September 1826 for New York. He made his American début, under the management of Stephen Price, at the Park Theatre, New York, on 2 October 1826, as Virginius, and was warmly received by the public and the press. While in New York he attended a performance of *Julius Caesar* in which Mark Antony was played by a vigorous 21-year-old called Edwin Forrest, whom he met socially. By the time he took his farewell benefit in New York on 4 June 1827, playing Macbeth and Delaval, Macready had appeared in Boston, Baltimore, Philadelphia, Albany, and other American cities, in all of which he had been enthusiastically received.

Back at Drury Lane—under Price's management—Macready appeared as Macbeth (12 November 1827), a performance which impressed the German visitor Prince Pückler-Muskau for its striking excellence in the murder scene, the banquet scene, and the last act. He could salvage little from either Reynolds's historical patchwork play *Edward the Black Prince* (28 January 1828) or Lord Porchester's *Don Pedro* (10 March 1828). On 7 April 1828 Macready appeared in Paris as Macbeth, partnered by Harriet Smithson, whose previous performances in that city had been greatly admired (particularly by Hugo, Dumas, and Berlioz), but her Lady Macbeth was exposed as tame, and feeble beside Macready's fiery and energetic Thane. Macready returned to Paris in June and July, adding to his laurels—he was judged the equal of Talma—as Virginius, Tell, Hamlet, and Othello.

After returning home, Macready devoted himself principally to starring engagements in the provinces. His father died on 11 April 1829 and for two years Macready, with Richard Brunton, held the lease of the Theatre Royal, Bristol, until his stepmother, Sarah Macready, took it over in her own right in 1833. Macready's first child, Christina Laetitia, was born on 26 December 1830; he was now in a financial position to support a family, his income in 1828 amounting to £2361 and in 1829 to £2265. On 18 October 1830 he appeared at Drury Lane for the first time in two years, and on 15 December he triumphed over the unpromising raw material of Lord Byron's play *Werner* to achieve a major success as the gloomy, conscience-stricken title character. In 1831–2 Macready's appearances amounted to only fifty-two, compared with ninety-nine in the previous season. The highlight of the 1832–3 season was *Othello* (26 November 1832), with Edmund Kean in the title role infuriating Macready (Iago) by resorting to the old trick of upstaging—standing a few paces further upstage than his interlocutor, who was consequently forced to appear in profile to the audience. Strained though their professional relationship had been, Macready was a pallbearer at Kean's funeral on 25 May 1833.

Even though Macready's recent achievements had not been outstanding, retirements and deaths combined to place him, at the age of forty, at the forefront of his profession. Unfortunately, the control of the two patent theatres (Covent Garden and Drury Lane), which had enjoyed a monopoly over legitimate drama in London since the restoration of Charles II, was now in the hands of one man, Alfred Bunn, whose character and habits were altogether antipathetic to Macready. Macready naturally resisted Bunn's attempt to reduce the large salaries which he considered to be the ruin of the stage. Furthermore, Bunn was determined not to let his principal tragedian rust in idleness, and exacted fifteen appearances from Macready between 5 and 30 October 1833. On 21 November Macready, struggling against illness, insufficient rehearsal, and deplorable mounting, played Antony in *Antony and Cleopatra*. Shortly afterwards he offered to pay Bunn a premium in exchange for release from his contract, but the manager declined. However, he did enjoy some remission in the number of his performances leading up to Bunn's much-heralded production of Byron's *Sardanapalus* on 10 April 1834. For his benefit on 23 April Macready made his metropolitan début as King Lear, having played the role in Swansea the previous year. Though purged of Tate's absurdities, this was still an incomplete text (without the Fool), but Macready had begun his assault on one of the peaks of the Shakespearian repertory, which, eventually, he was to conquer.

On 21 September 1835 Macready signed a contract with Bunn for Drury Lane (Covent Garden having passed out of Bunn's control). Although Macready had a veto over roles which he deemed to be of a melodramatic character, he was still subject to Bunn's will in the classical repertory. He could find no spark in Jaques (3 October), but off-stage, at the end of act III of *Richard III* on 29 April 1836, his anger was ignited by the sight of Bunn attending to his managerial duties. Macready denounced the manager as a 'damned scoundrel' and struck him in the face. Although he had been caught unaware, Bunn seemed to be getting the upper hand in the ensuing struggle before the two men were separated. Macready unburdened both his anger and his shame in his diary: 'this most indiscreet most imprudent, most blameable action' (*Macready's Reminiscences*, 380). The incident reverberated through the press. Bunn sued Macready for assault. The barrister and playwright Thomas Noon Talfourd appeared for Macready, and, though his attempt to present his client as the victim was unconvincing, the actor got off relatively lightly with damages of £150. The warm reception which greeted Macready when he appeared as Macbeth at Covent Garden on 11 May 1836 was indicative of public sympathy. Nevertheless, at the end of his performance he publicly expressed his self-reproach and regret for his intemperate and imprudent act.

Regrettable though the incident with Bunn undoubtedly was, it proved to be the turning of the tide in Macready's affairs which, taken at the flood, led on to fortune, for at Covent Garden he laid the foundations of what were to be the major achievements of his career. In Benjamin Thompson's *The Stranger* on 18 May 1836 he appeared for the first time with Helen Faucit, his future leading lady. On 26 May, after the first performance of *Ion*, by his erstwhile defending counsel Talfourd, he conversed at a celebratory supper with Wordsworth, Walter Savage Landor, Mary Russell Mitford, Clarkson Stanfield, John Forster, and Robert Browning, to whom he said: 'Will you write me a tragedy, and save me going to America?' (Archer, 99). The result, Browning's *Strafford*, was performed on 1 May 1837, before which, on 4 January, Macready and Helen Faucit had appeared in *The Duchess de la Vallière*, by another recruit to the theatre from the ranks of literature— Edward Bulwer (later Bulwer-Lytton). From the Shakespeare canon *King John* (6 October 1836), with Macready as the King and Helen Faucit as Constance, had emerged as a play worthy of further attention.

Early days as theatre manager Macready now nerved himself to take the decisive step of entering into management, with the hazards of which he had been familiar since childhood. He did so at a peculiarly difficult time, for, though the recommendation of the 1832 select committee on the dramatic literature to abolish the patent theatres' monopoly had been defeated in parliament, its eventual implementation was not in doubt. In assuming the management of Covent Garden Macready was asserting not only his professional leadership, but also the status of the patent houses as national theatres devoted to higher ideals than commercial advantage. Charles Kean declined Macready's invitation to join the company, but Samuel Phelps, James Anderson, George Bennett, Mary Amelia Warner, Priscilla Horton (later Reed), and Helen Faucit accepted. The opening production was *The Winter's Tale* (30 September 1837), in which Macready made a slow start as Leontes, but he and his carefully rehearsed company brought the evening to a commanding conclusion. He gave reprises of his established roles—Hamlet, Virginius, and Macbeth—but his *Henry V* (14 November) had no gleam of the famous revival to come. Since he regarded a strong musical side as an integral part of a patent theatre's repertory, Macready staged John Pyke Hullah's new comic opera *The Barbers of Bassora* (11 November) and T. B. Rooke's new dramatic opera *Amilie, or, The Love Test* (2 December). No royalist, he eschewed the practice of raising seat prices for a royal command performance, and as a consequence the house for Queen Victoria's visit to *Werner* on 17 November was uncomfortably overcrowded. This, alas, was exceptional and as Christmas approached Macready was said to have lost £3000. The coffers were replenished by the pantomime *Harlequin and Peeping Tom of Coventry*, of which Clarkson Stanfield's diorama was the centrepiece, but Macready had not entered management to stage spectacle, pantomime, and opera, and on 25 January 1838 he staked his reputation on a revival of *King Lear*. Rehearsals had begun on 4 January; every aspect of the production received Macready's painstaking attention, none more so than the Fool, to whose overdue restoration he was committed. Initially he cast Drinkwater Meadows, but he seized on George Bartley's suggestion that a woman should play the part, and allotted it to Priscilla Horton. John Forster, who described the Fool as 'interwoven with Lear', hailed Macready's performance as 'the only perfect picture we have had of Lear since the age of Betterton' (*The Examiner*, 4 Feb 1838).

Introducing new plays The encouragement of new dramatists was as central to Macready's enterprise as the restoration of the classical repertory. Since mid-November 1837 he had been discussing a new play with Edward Bulwer, and their surviving correspondence reveals the extent of the actor's contribution to the work. *The Lady of Lyons* opened on 15 February 1838, but the author's identity was not revealed until 24 February, by which time, after an uncertain start, the play's success was assured. Bulwer's refusal of royalties reflected the commitment of Macready's circle to his enterprise: Stanfield had accepted only half (£150) of the payment due to him for the pantomime diorama. The success of *The Lady of Lyons* (thirty-three performances) afforded Macready time and money to mount a large-scale production of *Coriolanus* (12 March 1838), in which the scenery and crowd effects eclipsed his own lacklustre performance as Caius Marcius. For his benefit on 7 April he staged Byron's *The Two Foscari* and on 23 May he introduced Sheridan Knowles's new play, *Woman's Wit, or, Love's Disguises*, which was enthusiastically received. During his first season as a manager Macready had devoted fifty-five of the 211 acting nights to performances of eleven Shakespeare plays. Had he not been opposed to the long-run system, he could have exploited the success of *King Lear* and *Coriolanus* further.

Shakespeare at Covent Garden Macready maintained substantially the same company for his second Covent Garden season, which began on 24 September 1838 with *Coriolanus*, in which he ceded the title role to John Vandenhoff. The first great effort was *The Tempest* (13 October), but, although Macready banished Dryden and Davenant, he also dispensed with the dialogue of the first scene in favour of a spectacular shipwreck. Macready's partnership with Bulwer was resumed with *Richelieu*, on which the two men collaborated for several months prior to its successful première on 7 March 1839. Following a rapturous first night, at which Bulwer no longer hedged his bets under the cloak of anonymity, *Richelieu* ran for thirty-seven performances with Macready as Richelieu, Helen Faucit as his ward, Julie de Mortemar, and Samuel Phelps as Father Joseph. For Miss Faucit's benefit on 18 April *As You Like It* was staged, but Macready's major Shakespearian work of the season was *Henry V* (10 June). His own performance as Henry was merely conventional, but Clarkson Stanfield's pictorial illustrations of Chorus's speeches significantly advanced the art of scenic design to critical and popular acclaim, though Macready restricted performances to four a week. The excessive caution of his proposition to the Covent Garden proprietors for a third season suggests that he did not desire or intend it to be accepted. At a public dinner at the Freemasons' Tavern on 20 July 1839, with the duke of Sussex in the chair and Dickens, Bulwer, and Richard Monckton Milnes present, Macready proclaimed that his poverty, not his will, had obliged him to desist from management. His achievements were considerable: the restoration of Shakespeare's plays and their staging on a hitherto unexampled scale; the encouragement of new drama, Bulwer in particular; and, while ensuring that his own pre-eminence was not challenged, a high standard of ensemble acting—all of this within a policy dedicated to maintaining a repertory commensurate with a national theatre and opposed to the exploitation of long runs. At this time Macready sought the post of reader of plays in the lord chamberlain's office. His autocratic and irascible temperament made him ill-suited for such a function, but perhaps he thought it would afford him the opportunity to shape the nation's drama without incurring the financial risks of management. In the event, Charles Kemble was succeeded by his son John Mitchell Kemble.

Return to acting For the next two and a half years Macready worked as an actor, principally at the Haymarket Theatre under Benjamin Webster. He appeared in two further works by Bulwer—*The Sea Captain, or, The Birthright* (31 October 1839) and *Money* (8 December 1840)—with the writing and staging of which he was closely involved. Bulwer's contemporary comedy of manners, *Money*, had been postponed because of the death of Macready's daughter Joan on 25 November 1840. Other personal matters intruded: it was during this period at the Haymarket that Macready was the subject of backstage gossip—by Ellen Tree, Mary Warner, and Harriette Lacy—concerning his relationship with Helen Faucit. The young actress's nightly visits to Macready's room after the performance were avowedly for help with her studies, but even Macready could not entirely discount his protégée's feelings for him or suppress completely his own susceptibility to what he described, in a poem inscribed in her album, as Miss Faucit's 'holier charm' (Trewin, 168).

Managing Drury Lane The days of the patent theatres' monopoly were now clearly numbered, and Macready, who in his evidence to the 1832 select committee had advocated reform rather than abolition, was tempted to seize one last opportunity to manage one of the great metropolitan houses. On 4 October 1841, encouraged by

Dickens, Forster, and the rest of his loyal coterie, Macready took Drury Lane, but the refurbishments required were such that the season did not open until 27 December. He regrouped many of his Covent Garden company with the additions of Miss Fortescue, Marston, Compton, Hudson, and the Keeleys. Following a careful revival of *The Merchant of Venice* (27 December 1841), albeit without either Morocco or Arragon, Macready retrieved *The Two Gentlemen of Verona* (29 December 1841), but it was with *Acis and Galatea* (5 February 1842), arranged and adapted from Handel with sets by Clarkson Stanfield, that he achieved his first great success. Other features of the season were Douglas Jerrold's new play *The Prisoner of War* (8 February)—no role for Macready, but the Keeleys in fine form—and Gerald Griffin's *Gisippus*, which sustained twenty performances with Macready in the title role and Helen Faucit as Sophronia.

Macready's second Drury Lane season opened on 1 October 1842, when his sombre Jaques took his place in an elaborately mounted (the Forest of Arden by courtesy of Clarkson Stanfield) and strongly cast *As You Like It*. This was followed on 24 October by a lavish production of *King John* with Macready at his best as the subtly sinister John, Helen Faucit a high-souled Constance, and Phelps exuding manly pathos as Hubert. William Telbin's scenery set the standard for Victorian pictorial revivals of Shakespeare's histories, and was complemented by historically accurate costumes, attributed by Charles Shattuck to Colonel Charles Hamilton Smith. The importance of the two revivals was both immediate and far-reaching, as Charles Shattuck indicates:

> But taken as a whole—the arrangement of the text, the ensemble playing, the stage decoration, the stage management, and the overall conception—*King John* was, together with *As You Like It* which had opened the season three weeks earlier, the finest work that Macready had ever put together. (Shattuck, *Macready's King John*, 2)

Macready fared less well with new plays. Westland Marston's *The Patrician's Daughter* (10 December 1842), in which he played Mordaunt, proved a barren success, as did Browning's *A Blot in the 'Scutcheon* (11 February 1843), in which he did not appear. For his benefit on 24 February 1843 Macready, whose forte was not comedy, made the surprising choice of *Much Ado about Nothing*; his Benedick was described by James Anderson (Claudio) as being as melancholy as a mourning coach in a snowstorm. Unsparingly, the evening was concluded with *Comus*. By 6 May it was apparent that Macready could not come to satisfactory terms with the Drury Lane committee for the continuation of his management. He made his valedictory appearance on 4 June 1843 as Macbeth. At a dinner at Willis's Rooms on 19 June, the duke of Cambridge presented Macready with a testimonial in the form of a massive and elaborate piece of silver in which Shakespeare and the tragedian both featured prominently. In response Macready proclaimed, 'I aimed at elevating everything represented on the stage', and accepted 'this crowning gift' as an assurance that 'whatever may have been the pecuniary results of my attempts to redeem the Drama, I have secured some portion of public confidence' (*Macready's Reminiscences*, 527). At Drury Lane, Macready had abided by the same guiding principles—restoring Shakespeare, encouraging new plays, improving standards of acting, scenery, and soon—as he had at Covent Garden, and in doing so he had secured a greatly increased portion of public confidence, not only for himself, but also for the profession which he had so reluctantly joined and of which he was now the undisputed leader. But Macready had made little, if any, money as a manager, and it was to the accumulation of sufficient funds to ensure a dignified and comfortable retirement that he devoted the remaining years of his career.

At home and abroad　On 5 September 1843 Macready sailed from Liverpool for America. Samuel Phelps, who under Macready's management had smarted from having his talents held in check, declined to accompany him, recognizing his own opportunity at home during Macready's absence. John Ryder went instead, to play seconds and help with the tour arrangements. In New York the English actors were visited by Edwin Forrest, whose marriage to Catherine Sinclair at St Paul's, Covent Garden, Macready had attended in June 1837. Macready opened at the Park Theatre with *Macbeth* on 25 September 1843 and proceeded to Philadelphia (where he met Charlotte Cushman), Boston, Baltimore, St Louis, New Orleans, and Montreal. He played an extensive repertory, his heavy Shakespearian parts being particularly well received. He was befriended by Emerson, Longfellow, and other men of eminence and returned home after a year's absence some £5500 the wealthier.

In December 1844, accompanied by his wife, Macready went to Paris to carry out engagements with Helen Faucit. Their performances in *Hamlet*, *Othello*, *Macbeth*, and *Virginius* were warmly received; Théophile Gautier, George Sand, Eugène Delacroix, Hugo, and Dumas all expressed their admiration. After returning to England early in 1845, Macready devoted the next three years principally to provincial engagements. In London he undertook a series of short engagements (usually for a stated number of weeks at three nights a week) at the Princess's Theatre in Oxford Street, under the management of J. M. Maddox. His repertory was predominantly Shakespearian, but on 20 May 1846 he created the role of James V of Scotland in *The King of the Commons* by the Revd James White of Bonchurch. On 22 November 1847 he appeared in his own botched arrangement of Sir Henry Taylor's *Philip Van Artevelde*. On 7 December 1847 Macready returned to Covent Garden to play the death scene of King Henry IV in a programme entitled 'Shakespeare Night' to raise funds for the purchase of Shakespeare's birthplace. Back at the Princess's in spring 1848 there was little rapport with his leading lady, Fanny Kemble. From 24 April to 8 May 1848 he appeared for Mary Warner at the Marylebone Theatre, and on 10 July he took a farewell benefit at Drury Lane, commanded by the queen, in which Charlotte Cushman played Queen Katharine to his Wolsey. Receipts totalled over £1100, the house being so crowded that some disturbance marred the occasion.

Disastrous farewell tour of America, 1848–1849　This disturbance presaged Macready's ill-fated farewell visit to America, on which he set forth from Liverpool on 9 September 1848, again accompanied by John Ryder. There were rumours of hostility towards Macready, but his first performance on 4 October (in New York as Macbeth) was warmly received. Unwisely, Macready made a curtain speech thanking his audience for having refuted his detractors. The speech was seized upon as a challenge by James Oakes, a friend of Edwin Forrest, who was generally perceived as the source of anti-Macready feeling. Oakes published a lengthy piece in the *Boston Mail* (30 October) setting out Forrest's grievances, foremost that Macready had treated the American actor with indignity during his 1845 visit to London and that Macready or John Forster had packed the Princess's Theatre with a hostile claque. During Macready's engagement (20 November to 2 December 1848) at the Arch Theatre in Philadelphia, Forrest appeared at the Walnut Theatre, duplicating Macready's role wherever possible. The two actors published rival accounts of what had taken place in 1845 and Macready began an action against Forrest. While awaiting documents from England, Macready continued his tour, visiting Baltimore, Washington, Richmond, New Orleans, and St Charles, without incident until, in Cincinnati, half a raw carcass of sheep was propelled onto the stage by a ruffian in the gallery. Even this was only a drunken gesture, and the audience rallied indignantly round the actor.

During the performance of *Macbeth* at the Astor Place Theatre, New York, on 7 May, the stage was rained with copper cents, eggs, apples, potatoes, and a bottle of horribly pungent asafoetida, which splashed Macready's costume. By the third act chairs were being thrown from the gallery and, though Macready stood his ground apparently unmoved, the performance was abandoned. Meanwhile, at the Broadway Theatre, Edwin Forrest had completed his performance—as Macbeth—uninterrupted. Macready's next appearance was announced for 10 May, when posses of police were stationed in the auditorium. Trouble-makers—fewer in number—who had infiltrated the auditorium were ejected by the police, but this further incited the mob outside, who bombarded the theatre with loose paving stones. Troops retaliated in self-preservation, and between seventeen and twenty rioters were killed and many others injured. Macready finished his performance, thanked his supporters, and then, having changed clothes with another actor, made his escape, accompanied only by Robert Emmett, initially by carriage to New Rochelle, then to Boston, and ten days later home to England. Macready had shown considerable courage, but he had also been characteristically tactless and self-assertive. He was, furthermore, the victim of a nationalist undercurrent sweeping America to which the unfavourable accounts of the country by Frances Trollope and Dickens had contributed. The Astor Place riot and the circumstances surrounding it were to be the subject of Richard Nelson's play *Two Shakespearian Actors* (1990).

Final appearances and last days Following his return to England, Macready undertook farewell performances in the provinces and in London. In two seasons at the Haymarket Theatre (8 October to 8 December 1849 and 28 October to 3 February 1851) he gave reprises of his Shakespearian repertory and his contemporary successes Richelieu and Virginius. On 1 February 1850 he performed at Windsor Castle in *Julius Caesar*, playing Brutus to the Antony of Charles Kean, whose appointment as director of the Windsor Theatricals he had deeply resented. The definitive farewell performance took place at Drury Lane on 26 February 1851, with Mary Warner (Lady Macbeth) and Phelps (Macduff) supporting Macready's valediction as Macbeth. The occasion reverberated with excitement and enthusiasm, but Macready remained dignified and in his curtain speech steadfastly avoided any show of simulated sorrow. The inevitable public dinner followed on 1 March, with Bulwer in the chair, speeches by Dickens, Thackeray, and Bunsen, and the recitation by Forster of Tennyson's sonnet 'To W. C. Macready':

> Farewell, Macready, since this night we part,
> Go, take thine honours home ...
> Thine is it that our drama did not die,
> Nor flicker down to brainless pantomime,
> And those gilt gauds men-children swarm to see.
> Farewell, Macready, moral, grave, sublime ...

Macready retired to a substantial house in Sherborne, Dorset. On 18 September 1852 his wife died unexpectedly while the couple were visiting Plymouth; many of their children went prematurely to the grave. In Sherborne, Macready busied himself with the abbey church, of which he became a church warden; the Sherborne Literary Institute, of which he was a board member; and an evening school, of which James Fraser, later bishop of Manchester, wrote as a member of the 1858 royal commission on popular education:

> the only really efficient one [night school] that I witnessed at work, the only one full of life and progress and tone of the best kind, was the one at Sherborne which owes its origin and its prosperity to the philanthropic zeal and large sacrifices of money, time, and personal comfort of Mr Macready. (*Report of the Assistant Commissioners Appointed to Inquire into the State of Popular Education in England*, 1861, 2.52)

On 3 April 1860, at the age of sixty-seven, Macready married Cecile Louise Frederica Spencer (d. 1908), many years his junior, at Clifton parish church. Shortly afterwards the Macreadys moved to Wellington Square, Cheltenham. A son, Cecil Frederick Nevil *Macready, was born on 7 May 1862; he pursued a military career, becoming a general and a baronet. For the last two years of his life Macready was an invalid—his hands were paralysed and his speech was blurred, though his mind remained active—and he died at 6 Wellington Square, Cheltenham, on 27 April 1873. He was buried in Kensal Green cemetery on 4 May. In 1914 Nevil Macready destroyed what would have been his father's richest legacy, his copious and uninhibited diaries, lest they might be injudiciously used. Sir Frederick Pollock's edition (2 vols., 1875; 1 vol., 1876) was highly selective, and though William Toynbee (1912) was more inclusive he omitted some important passages from the

Pollock text. J. C. Trewin's abridged collection (1967) includes extracts from sixty-four manuscript pages discovered in 1960 and subsequently deposited in the Mander and Mitchenson Theatre Collection. Despite its incompleteness, Macready's diary constitutes a major resource, not only for the author's life and career, but also for the theatrical and cultural world of his day.

Assessment Macready was a complex individual. He had his father's quick temper, of which he was fully aware, although he was not always able to curb it in his professional dealings. His education at Rugby School encouraged his aspirations to the status of a gentleman, and while he resented being obliged to abandon his hopes of the church or the bar as a career, he equally resented any supposed slur upon his personal status or that of his enforced calling, the theatre. He cultivated his own learning and way of life in concert with his friendships with leading intellectual, literary, and artistic figures of his day (Carlyle, Tennyson, Dickens, Thackeray, Forster, Browning, and Bulwer), but, though this benefited the theatre, it also set Macready apart from the rest of his profession. His two periods of management were informed by high principles: he conducted his enterprises as national theatres, eschewing crude commercialism. He materially advanced the art of the theatre in all its facets: his rehearsals were unprecedented in their length and rigour; his attention to *mise-en-scène* set standards for generations to come; his acting versions marked a significant advance in the restoration of Shakespeare's texts; his encouragement of Browning, Bulwer, and Knowles resulted in plays of serious literary intent; and his engagement of actors of the calibre of Phelps, Ryder, and Helen Faucit produced a generally high standard of ensemble acting, even if Macready was sometimes swayed by jealousy of potential rivals. As an actor, although he was not endowed with great physical advantages, Macready had a good figure, a strong stage presence, an expressive face (especially his eyes), and a commanding voice, which, though not naturally musical, was capable of varied modulation. He avoided the excesses of the Kemble school of stately declamation, striving to introduce naturalistic familiarity, often through over-abrupt transitions from the declamatory to the conversational. He was also prone to insert the letter 'a' indiscriminately—thus Burnam Wood was seen 'a-coming'. His greatest quality was his intellectual ability to penetrate and to express the psychological nature of his characters; thus Macbeth's moral decline was charted from the erect martial figure of act I to the self-abased murderer, with crouching form and stealthy felon-like step, at the end. Macready was ill-suited to comedy, but as a tragedian he scaled the Shakespearian peaks of Hamlet, Othello, Macbeth, and King Lear. In contemporary drama he succeeded in investing the works of Knowles, Bulwer, and others with a vitality and stageworthiness which compensated for, and even disguised, their deficiencies. For nigh on twenty years Macready dominated the English stage. Although he was a reluctant member of the acting profession, in it Macready achieved an eminence comparable to the leaders of the other professions to which he had aspired, and it was in large measure thanks to him that, by the end of the nineteenth century, the theatre enjoyed the status and esteem which had been denied it at the beginning.   RICHARD FOULKES

Sources *Macready's reminiscences, and selections from his diaries and letters*, ed. F. Pollock, new edn (1876) · W. Archer, *William Charles Macready* (1890) · J. Pollock, *Macready as I knew him* (1884) · *The diaries of William Charles Macready, 1833–1851*, ed. W. Toynbee, 2 vols. (1912) · N. Macready, *Annals of an active life*, 2 vols. [1924] · G. H. Lewes, *An actor and the art of acting* (1875) · J. W. Marston, *Our recent actors*, new edn (1890) · C. H. Shattuck, ed., *Bulwer and Macready: a chronicle of the early Victorian theatre* (1958) · C. H. Shattuck, ed., *William Charles Macready's King John* (1962) · A. S. Downer, *The eminent tragedian William Charles Macready* (1966) · T. Martin, *Helen Faucit* (1900) · T. Martin, *Essays on the drama* (1889) · J. C. Trewin, *Mr Macready* (1955) · *The journals of William Charles Macready*, ed. J. C. Trewin (1967) · G. Scharf, jun., *Recollections of the scenic effects of the Covent Garden Theatre* (1838) · W. H. D. Rouse, *A history of Rugby School* (1898) · *The Era* · 'Reports of the assistant commissioners appointed to inquire into … education', *Parl. papers* (1861), vol. 21/2, no. 2794-II; repr. in *Education general*, 4 (1969) · 'Select committee on theatrical licences and regulations', *Parl. papers* (1866), 16.1, no. 373; 16.351, no. 373-I; repr. in *Stage and Theatre*, 2 (1968) · *DNB* · d. cert. · C. H. Shattuck, *The Shakespeare prompt books* (1965) · *Oxberry's Dramatic Biography*, 5/67 (1826)
Archives BL, corresp. · Harvard U., prompt books · Hunt. L., letters · Mander and Mitchenson theatre collection, London · Princeton University Library, New Jersey, corresp. and papers | Gwent RO, corresp. with J. E. W. Rolls · Herts. ALS, letters to Lord Lytton
Likenesses G. Clint, oils, 1821, V&A · J. Jackson, oils, 1821, NPG [*see illus.*] · H. Inman, oils, *c*.1827, Metropolitan Museum of Art, New York · W. Behnes, marble bust, 1843–4, NPG · H. P. Briggs, oils, 1844, Garr. Club · G. Wightwick, drawing, 1869, NPG · watercolour, *c*.1870 (after photograph), NPG · J. Boaden, oils (as Orestes), Garr. Club · P. Hollins, plaster bust, Royal Shakespeare Theatre · D. Maclise, oils (after, 1849–50), V&A · D. Maclise, oils, Drury Lane Theatre, London · D. Maclise, portrait (as Werner), Theatre Museum, London · attrib. D. Maclise, watercolour, NPG · Mason, photograph, NPG · Woodman, engraving (as Romeo; after S. De Wilde), Harvard TC · illustrations (as Macbeth), repro. in Downer, *The eminent tragedian* · portraits, repro. in Scharf, *Recollections* · print (as King Lear; with Helen Faucit as Cordelia), repro. in Trewin, *Mr Macready* · prints, BM, NPG
Wealth at death under £18,000: resworn probate, Dec 1873, *CGPLA Eng. & Wales*

Macro, Cox (*bap.* 1683, *d.* 1767), antiquary and Church of England clergyman, was born in Bury St Edmunds, Suffolk, where he was baptized on 20 March 1683, the son of Thomas Macro (1649?–1737), grocer, alderman, and chief magistrate of Bury St Edmunds, and his wife, Susan (1660–1743), only daughter of the Revd John Cox, rector of Risby, near Bury St Edmunds, and great-granddaughter of Dr Richard Cox, bishop of Ely. His unusual forename preserves his mother's surname. He was educated at Bury St Edmunds grammar school and in 1699 went up to Jesus College, Cambridge, where he remained until January 1702. He then transferred to Christ's College apparently for reasons of health, and to benefit from the teaching of two distinguished doctors of medicine then resident. From here he moved to Leiden in 1703 to continue his studies at the university under the famous professor of medicine Hermann Boerhaave. By 1710, however, he had returned to Cambridge and proceeded LLB. In 1716 he was ordained deacon and priest, in 1717 took the degree of DD,

and was, at the time of his death, the senior doctor in divinity of the university. It is often mistakenly claimed that he was appointed chaplain to George II, but in fact he appears never to have held any ecclesiastical preferment.

By 1719 Macro had moved to Little Haugh Hall, a property purchased by his father near Norton in Suffolk. Here he devoted himself to a broad range of studies and to the collection of 'antiquities': coins, medals, paintings, books, and manuscripts. His collection of manuscripts was exceptionally fine and included the great register of Bury Abbey during the abbacy of William Curteys; a ledger book of Glastonbury Abbey; a cartulary of the religious house at Blackborough in Norfolk; a vellum manuscript of the works of Gower; and the original manuscript of Spenser's 'View of the state of Ireland'. He also obtained a large collection of manuscripts relating to Cambridge University which had been amassed by John Covel, master of Christ's College from 1688 to 1722, and a considerable body of charters relating to the immediately surrounding area.

In 1714, before moving to Norton, Macro had married Mary (1689?–1753), the daughter of Edward Godfrey, privy purse to Queen Anne, and about 1717 their first child, a daughter, Mary, was born. According to an account book kept by Macro, another child was born after this but died, and a third and last child was born in 1719 on 24 August. This was a son, whom they named Edward. The number and variety of entries in the account book during the 1730s and 1740s indicate that the running of the family estate took considerable time and attention. But Macro was also much involved in improving his house and in commissioning works of art to decorate it. Chief among the artists he commissioned was Pieter Tillemans (1684–1734) of Antwerp who had been a close friend of the family since about 1715. Tillemans was popular in England as a painter of landscapes, country seats, and horses, and since his first visit in 1708 had executed a number of paintings for various patrons including Lord Byron of Newstead, the earl of Derby, the dukes of Devonshire, Kent, and Kingston, and the earl of Radnor. Macro, however, was one of his most faithful patrons and Tillemans was staying with the Macro family when he died in 1734. Not long before this he had completed an overmantel prospect view of Little Haugh Hall, commissioned some time after the refacing of the front of the house. He had also completed three 'Doorpiece[s]' (Raines, 'Peter Tillemans') and other decorative work in the house as well as some twenty paintings, twelve of them original compositions and the remainder copies or works painted in the manner of other artists. The original works included a painting of the artist's studio (*c*.1716) with 'Mr Macro' standing by the artist, and a portrait of 'Mr Edw. Macro & his Sister' dated *c*.1733. Almost immediately after his death Cox Macro commissioned a terracotta bust of Tillemans from Michael Rysbrack, together with another of the sculptor himself. The former was designed to stand in a specially constructed niche at the top of the stairs, with below it the inscription 'Tillemansio suo Rysbrachius'.

Further work on Little Haugh Hall was undertaken subsequently with Macro employing Francis Hayman to paint the interior of the cupola and the local sculptor and painter, Thomas Ross of Bury, to provide further paintings and some rich wood carvings. In addition to work commissioned from contemporary artists, Macro made a substantial collection of earlier pictures about half of which were Netherlandish works. His own manuscript catalogue lists paintings by or attributed to Bol, Dou, Droochsloot, Griffier, Holbein, Hondius, Hondecoeter, Cornelius Johnson, Lely, Rembrandt, Riley, Rubens, Ruisdael, Stella, Streeter, and Trevisani.

Macro retained links with Cambridge University and formed a strong friendship with Richard Hurd whose acquaintance he made when his son, Edward, was admitted in 1739 to Emmanuel College where Hurd had just taken his BA degree. He was instrumental in finding Hurd his first living and influenced his early taste and interests, including encouraging and helping him to learn Italian. Hurd considered Macro 'a very learned and amiable man, the most complete scholar and gentleman united that almost ever I saw' (*Early Letters*, 93). He remained a close friend of the family for many years corresponding not only with Cox, but also with his wife, Mary, and with Edward. The latter left Cambridge without a degree and during the 1740s and early 1750s spent long periods in London where he enjoyed a reputation as a connoisseur of the arts, whose taste was esteemed and advice sought after. He frequented the sale rooms and the studios of such artists as Benjamin Wilson and the sculptor Michael Rysbrack. In 1753 he took over the management of farmland belonging to his father. However, unlike Cox, who appeared to have inherited much of his father's business acumen and could strike a hard bargain, Edward had little aptitude for and success in the management of these estates. He fell deeply into debt during the 1750s and early 1760s, quarrelled with his father, and was 'turnd out of doors' (ibid., 365). There is no evidence that they were reconciled and Edward died in April 1766, apparently in 'rather mysterious circumstances' (Venn, *Alum. Cant.*).

Cox Macro survived his son by less than a year and died at Little Haugh Hall on 2 February 1767. He was buried on 9 February in Norton churchyard 'in an inclosure between the side of the Vestry and one of the buttresses which supports the Church-wall' (Nichols, *Lit. anecdotes*, 9.365). His daughter Mary inherited his property and, having been prohibited from doing so during her father's lifetime, finally married William Staniforth of Sheffield in May 1767. Although Macro had instructed Mary 'not to sell the Library, or not to Dispose of any of the Manuscripts, but let them continue where they are' (Raines, 'An art collector of many parts', 1692), the collection was dispersed. Mary died without any surviving children on 16 August 1775.

SARAH BREWER

Sources S. Tymms, 'Little Haugh Hall, Norton', *Proceedings of the Suffolk Institute of Archaeology, Statistics, and Natural History*, 2 (1854–8), 279–87 • R. Raines, 'An art collector of many parts', *Country Life*, 159 (1976), 1692–4 • S. Tymms, 'Cupola House, Bury St Edmunds', *Proceedings of the Suffolk Institute of Archaeology, Statistics, and Natural History*, 3 (1860–63), 375–85 • N. Scarf, 'Little Haugh Hall, Suffolk', *Country Life*, 123 (1958), 1238–41 • *The early letters of Bishop Richard Hurd, 1739-1762*, ed. S. Brewer (1995) • R. Raines, 'Peter Tillemans, life and work: with a list of representative paintings', *Walpole Society*, 47 (1978–80), 21–59 • Nichols, *Lit. anecdotes*, vol. 9 • F. Kilvert, *Memoirs of the life and writings of the Right Rev. Richard Hurd* (1860) • J. Hunter, *Hallamshire: the history and topography of the parish of Sheffield in the county of York*, new edn, ed. A. Gatty (1869) • Venn, *Alum. Cant.*, 1/3.124 • J. Peile, *Biographical register of Christ's College, 1505-1905, and of the earlier foundation, God's House, 1448-1505*, ed. [J. A. Venn], 2 vols. (1910–13) • A. Moore, *Dutch and Flemish painting in Norfolk: a history of taste and influence, fashion and collecting* (1988) [exhibition catalogue, William and Mary tercentenary exhibition, Norfolk] • C. Macro, personal account book, 1717–53, Bodl. Oxf., MS Eng. misc. e. 346 • PRO, LC 3/64 • *DNB* • *IGI*

Archives BL, corresp., Add. MSS 32556–32557 • BL, papers, Add. MSS 25103, 25473, 25726 • Bodl. Oxf., commonplace book • Bodl. Oxf., personal account book, MS. Eng. misc. e. 346 • CUL, commonplace books • Suffolk RO, Ipswich, papers, HD695 | Bodl. Oxf., annotated copy of Wood's *Athenae Oxonienses* • priv. coll., letterbook • Suffolk RO, Ipswich, letter-book [microfilm]

Likenesses F. van Mieris, oil on copper, *c.*1703, Norwich Castle Museum; repro. in Moore, *Dutch and Flemish Painting in Norfolk* • P. Tillemans, group portrait, oil on canvas, *c.*1716 (*The artist's studio*), Norwich Castle Museum; repro. in Moore, *Dutch and Flemish Painting in Norfolk* • P. Tillemans, oil on canvas, Norwich Castle Museum; repro. in Moore, *Dutch and Flemish painting in Norfolk*

Macrone, John (1809–1837), publisher, was 'either a Scot, an Irishman, an Italian ("Macrone"), or, most probably, a Manxman' (Sutherland, 244). He arrived in London aged about twenty-one, having presumably cobbled together some schooling in the country. By January 1833 he had become the junior partner of James Cochrane, a former member of the publisher Henry Colburn's staff who had set up on his own at 11 Waterloo Place, Pall Mall, London. In September 1834 Macrone left Cochrane and started his own firm nearby at 3 St James's Square. 'Handsome and intelligent' (*Life and Adventures of George Augustus Sala*, 1.144) but also ambitious and impatient, Macrone used £500 borrowed from an older woman whom he was then cultivating, Sophia, aunt of the journalist George Augustus Sala, in order to purchase copyrights and stock. He never repaid the loan; instead he invested in new projects. And he never married Sophia, who died a spinster in 1837. Instead, in January 1835 he married an American, Eliza Adeline Bordwine (*b.* 1800). They had three children; the first, Frederick Joseph Bordwine Macrone, born on 20 October 1835, died less than a month later, on 16 November. A second son, William John Bordwine Macrone, was born on 30 September 1836. The name of the third child is unknown.

As a publisher Macrone began by emulating Henry Colburn and Richard Bentley, extravagantly advertising republications of standard works and new or reissued three-volume novels. His initial list (January 1835) included a six-volume edition of John Milton, embellished with vignettes by J. M. W. Turner; in April 1836 Macrone inscribed a copy as a wedding present to Catherine Dickens (Stonehouse, *Catalogue*). He was originally asked to serve as best man at Dickens's marriage on 2 April 1836, but his wife insisted that Dickens be attended by a bachelor. During summer 1835 Macrone bought from Bentley a novel by William Harrison Ainsworth, *Rookwood*, which he promptly reissued in a third three-volume edition. He then commissioned original steel etchings for a revised, one-volume fourth edition from the leading illustrator of the day, George Cruikshank; this, appearing in May 1836, was a huge success. During autumn 1835 Macrone, encouraged by the prospects of the *Rookwood* venture, committed to republishing the magazine sketches of Charles Dickens, whom he met through Ainsworth, pairing them with new etchings by Cruikshank. The resulting miscellany, *Sketches by Boz*, appeared in two volumes on 8 February 1836 and was supplemented by a second series, in one volume, published on 17 December.

Until November the Macrones, Ainsworths, and Dickenses were most intimate friends. Offering £200 for the manuscript, Macrone commissioned a three-volume novel, *Gabriel Vardon* (renamed *Barnaby Rudge*) from Dickens in May, their wives exchanged notes and visits, Dickens placed his 'very quick and steady' younger brother Frederick William Dickens in Macrone's counting house in July (*Letters of Charles Dickens*, 1.150, 157), and Ainsworth advised on all sorts of literary and legal matters. *Sketches* sold even better than *Rookwood*. But when in June 1837 Macrone planned to republish the work in monthly parts in imitation of Dickens's successful serial *Pickwick Papers*, Dickens and his publishers Chapman and Hall objected strongly; on 17 June they agreed to pay Macrone in instalments over twelve months £2250 for text and plates—the 'biggest single coup of his publishing career' (Sutherland, 250). But Macrone's relationship with his two star writers deteriorated thereafter.

Between 1835 and 1837 Macrone gathered a substantial stable of authors, including Benjamin Disraeli, W. H. Maxwell, and Leitch Ritchie. He issued enough three-deckers to catapult him into the first rank of fiction publishers. But each success tempted him to greater ambitions. Encouraged by Ainsworth, who wanted Macrone to become 'a publisher of taste and discrimination' (Ellis, 1.290), he bid for copyrights by Robert Browning, Victor Hugo, Paul de Kock, and Thomas Moore. (He was already collecting sculpted busts of literary figures.) Macrone overstretched himself time and again, notably in sharing the exorbitant costs of the *Westminster Review*, merged in 1836 with the *London Review*. Despite the size of his list Macrone did not sell particularly well to circulating libraries because many of his authors were second-raters, some a bit passé, and many recycling titles previously published. When in November 1836 Dickens backed out of writing *Vardon*, Macrone quarrelled with him over republication of *Sketches*, and then Ainsworth dried up, unable to produce promised texts. Macrone's situation grew desperate. He sold off the last items of value, Ainsworth's *Crichton*, to Bentley for £1000 and the merged *London and Westminster Review* to Henry Hooper. He also persisted in advertising titles as 'preparing for immediate publication' when they were not yet written, an expedient that cost him respectability, friendship, and authors. Unable to cope, Macrone succumbed to influenza on 9 September 1837, leaving his family 'in a state of utter destitution' (*Letters of Charles Dickens*, 1.372). Dickens edited, and Ainsworth, Cruikshank, and Hablot Knight Browne (Phiz) contributed to, a three-volume collection, *Pic-Nic Papers*, that came out on 9 August 1841, providing £450 for Macrone's family. Hugh Cunningham, who had joined Macrone's firm shortly before the proprietor's death, continued in business under Macrone's name as the publisher of William Makepeace Thackeray's early work *Paris Sketch Book* (1840), and then with a partner, Mortimer, issued one of the more successful of those Ainsworth–Cruikshank collaborations Macrone had initiated, *The Miser's Daughter* (1842).

ROBERT L. PATTEN

Sources *The letters of Charles Dickens*, ed. M. House, G. Storey, and others, 1–2 (1965–9) • J. Sutherland, 'John Macrone: Victorian publisher', *Dickens Studies Annual*, 13 (1984), 243–59; condensed as 'John Macrone', *British literary publishing houses, 1820–1880*, ed. P. J. Anderson and J. Rose, DLitB, 106 (1991), 196–9 • R. L. Patten, *George Cruikshank's life, times, and art*, 2 (1996) • S. M. Ellis, *William Harrison Ainsworth and his friends*, 2 vols. (1911) • R. L. Patten, *Charles Dickens and his publishers* (1978) • *The life and adventures of George Augustus Sala*, 2 vols. (1895) • *The letters and private papers of William Makepeace Thackeray*, ed. G. N. Ray, 4 vols. (1945–6) • J. H. Stonehouse, ed., *Catalogue of the library of Charles Dickens* (1935)
Archives Dickens House, London, papers

Macrorie, William Kenneth (1831–1905), bishop of Maritzburg, was born at Liverpool on 8 February 1831, the eldest son of David Macrorie, a Liverpool physician, and his wife, Sarah, daughter of John Barber. He was educated at Winchester College from 1844, and at Brasenose College, Oxford, from 2 February 1849; he graduated BA in 1852 and proceeded MA in 1855. In 1855 he also became a 'fellow', or assistant schoolmaster, at St Peter's College, Radley, and was ordained a deacon. After his ordination as a priest in 1857 he successively held the curacies of Deane (1858–60), and of Wingates, Lancashire (1860–61). In 1861 the bishop of London, A. C. Tait, made him rector of Wapping. In 1863 he married Agnes, youngest daughter of William Watson of South Hill, Liverpool, and in 1865 he was nominated to the perpetual curacy of Accrington.

In January 1868 Macrorie was offered the bishopric of Natal by the bishop of Cape Town, Robert Gray. Macrorie hesitated before accepting this contentious post, since J. W. Colenso was still in Natal and the affair concerning him had not yet died down, Colenso refusing to recognize the canonical deposition which had been pronounced in 1863. Since that date Bishop Gray had made unsuccessful efforts to establish a new rival episcopate in the colony. When Macrorie finally accepted the post he became the first colonial bishop not to be appointed by the crown. Since Colenso still had a legal right to the title of bishop of Natal, Macrorie was designated bishop of Maritzburg. Lord Derby's ministry disapproved of the appointment, and refused to grant the queen's mandate for Macrorie's consecration in any place where the Act of Uniformity was in force. Archbishop Longley vetoed the ceremony in the province of Canterbury, and the Scottish bishops declined to take any part in the rite. Eventually Bishop Gray consecrated Macrorie personally at Cape Town on 25

January 1869, disregarding a protest signed by 129 of Colenso's supporters.

Macrorie's uncompromising high-churchmanship helped to prolong the schism in the church in Natal. Macrorie was zealous and energetic and was backed by both the Society for the Propagation of the Gospel and by the Society for Promoting Christian Knowledge, who gave him the financial support which had been taken away from Colenso. But his lack of tact alienated moderate opinion, and his fierce denunciations of Colenso's supporters only increased the gulf between the two parties which Archbishop Benson sought in vain to bridge. When Colenso died in June 1883, Benson suggested to Macrorie that he should either resign or else accept the post of bishop of Bloemfontein. But Macrorie refused to entertain the 'cowardly thought'. Macrorie's difficulties diminished when the archbishop refused to consecrate either George William Cox or William Ayerst, whom the Colenso party, on their leader's death, had elected to the bishopric of Natal.

Macrorie eventually resigned his see in 1891. In the following year he was appointed to a canonry in Ely Cathedral, where he served the diocese as assistant bishop. In 1876 he was created honorary DD of Oxford and DCL of the University of South Africa. He died at the college, Ely, on 24 September 1905, and was buried in the cathedral close. G. S. WOODS, *rev.* LYNN MILNE

Sources *The Times* (25 Sept 1905) · *The Times* (29 Sept 1905) · H. Paul, *History of modern England* (1905), 3.185 · G. W. Cox, *Life of J. W. Colenso*, 2 (1888) · A. T. Wirgman, *History of the English church and people in South Africa* (1895) · [H. L. Farrer], *Life of Robert Gray, bishop of Cape Town and metropolitan of Africa*, ed. C. Gray, 2 vols. (1876) · *Classified digest of the records of the Society for the Propagation of the Gospel in Foreign Parts, 1701-1892* (1893) · E. Stock, *The history of the Church Missionary Society: its environment, its men and its work*, 2 (1899), 362 · *DSAB*

Archives LPL, corresp. with E. W. Benson · LPL, corresp. with A. C. Tait

Likenesses photograph, NPG

Wealth at death £1703 14s. 5d.: probate, 13 Oct 1905, *CGPLA Eng. & Wales*

MacRory, Joseph (*bap.* 1861, *d.* 1945), cardinal, was born in Ballygawley, co. Tyrone, where he was baptized on 10 March 1861, one of ten children of Francis MacRory (*d.* 1867?), a small farmer, and Rose Montague. Little is known of his parents apart from the fact that his father died when MacRory was six years old. He attended the local primary school and went on to St Patrick's Seminary, Armagh, and St Patrick's College, Maynooth. After his ordination in 1885 MacRory became first president of Dungannon Academy. From 1887 to 1889 he was professor of moral theology and sacred scripture at Olton College, Birmingham, returning to Maynooth in 1889 as professor of sacred scripture and oriental languages. In 1905 he was appointed to the chair of hermeneutics and New Testament exegesis and in 1912 became vice-president of the college. His writings include *The Gospel of St John* (1897), *The Epistles of St Paul to the Corinthians* (1915), and *The New Testament and Divorce* (1934). He contributed many essays to the *Irish Theological Quarterly*, of which he was a founder, and

also wrote for the *Irish Ecclesiastical Record* and the *Catholic Bulletin of America*.

MacRory was consecrated bishop of Down and Connor in 1915, a position he held until 1928 when he became archbishop of Armagh and primate of all Ireland. A year later he became cardinal. He represented the pope as papal legate for the laying of the foundation stone of Liverpool Metropolitan Cathedral in 1933 and for the National Eucharistic Congress in Melbourne in 1934. After the death of Pope Pius XI in 1939 he attended the conclave of cardinals for the election of a new pope. MacRory was an outspoken champion of separate Catholic education. In 1919 he condemned plans to involve local authorities in the provision of schools in Belfast. He opposed the transfer of control of primary schools from priests to management committees, but in his latter years considered modifying his position in return for greater financial assistance from public funds. MacRory's forthright views antagonized his opponents. In 1931 he caused outrage by stating that the Church of Ireland was not part of the church of Christ. A year later he engaged in a press debate on theological points with the Church of Ireland archbishop of Dublin, John A. F. Gregg. Private correspondence between the two in later years when Gregg had become Church of Ireland primate indicates that the theological debate continued at a more cordial level.

MacRory was a vocal and eloquent commentator on political affairs. In 1916 he opposed proposals for the exclusion of Ulster or any part of it from home rule. One of four Roman Catholic bishops who attended the Irish Convention of 1917–18, his references to earlier conflicts caused unease. A Sinn Féin sympathizer, he mediated in prison disputes in Belfast in 1918 and 1920. MacRory came under particular pressure during the intense violence of the period 1920–22. Fearing for his personal safety, he moved from the episcopal residence in Andersonstown to St Malachy's College. He highlighted the expulsion of Belfast Catholics from their employment in the summer of 1920, assisting them through appeals for aid and subscriptions of his own to relief funds. Before the election to the first Northern Ireland parliament in 1921 he urged the Catholics to vote in order to register their opposition to partition. During the Irish War of Independence he attributed violence to the British government's denial of Irish rights, and during preparations for the Anglo-Irish negotiations in 1921 he was among those consulted by Sinn Féin on the likely effects of partition. He attended a number of cabinet meetings of the provisional government in Dublin in 1922, advised Michael Collins on matters relating to northern Catholics, and became involved in talks on the implementation of the Craig–Collins pact of March 1922.

A patron of the Gaelic Athletic Association, MacRory's parting gift to the people of Belfast was his purchase of Shaun's Park, renamed MacRory Park. He is commemorated by the MacRory cup, awarded for a college football championship. His support for the Catholic Boy Scouts likewise indicated interest in young people. He maintained an uneasy relationship with the Northern Ireland establishment. Like his episcopal colleagues he supported the formation of a new nationalist party, the National League of the North, in 1928. He was awarded an honorary degree of LLD by Queen's University, Belfast, in 1929, but declined an invitation to attend the awards ceremony.

During the Second World War MacRory approved of de Valera's policy of neutrality, stating that Éire deserved credit in the circumstances for not having allied herself with the axis nations (*Derry Journal*, 15 Oct 1945). He resented the presence of allied troops in Northern Ireland and vehemently opposed proposals for conscription there. At the dedication of Cavan Cathedral in 1942 he said partition was 'not only a grave injustice to Ireland, one of the oldest nations of Europe, but it was a flagrant and intolerable injustice against Catholics doomed to live under the narrow and unjust domination of the Belfast Parliament and Executive' (*Irish News*, 15 Oct 1945).

Cardinal MacRory died of a heart attack at his residence, Ara Coeli, in Armagh on 13 October 1945. His funeral ceremony, which was broadcast by Radio Éireann, was attended by government representatives from both the Irish Free State and Northern Ireland. He was buried in the primate's plot in the grounds of St Patrick's cemetery, Armagh, on 17 October.   MARY N. HARRIS

Sources M. Harris, *The Catholic church and the foundation of the Northern Irish state* (1993) · S. Farren, *The politics of Irish education, 1920–1965* (1995) · *WWW, 1941–50* · *Tyrone Courier and Dungannon News* (18 Oct 1945) · *Irish News and Belfast Morning News* (15 Oct 1945) · *Irish Times* (15 Oct 1945) · *Irish Times* (18 Oct 1945) · *Derry Journal* (15 Oct 1945) · G. F. Seaver, *John Allen Fitzgerald Gregg, archbishop* (1963) · *Irish Catholic Directory* (1929) · *Irish Catholic Directory* (1946) · T. O'Hanlon, 'The new bishop of Down and Connor', *Catholic Bulletin* (Dec 1915), 896–8
Archives Archdiocesan Archives, Armagh · Down and Connor Diocesan Archives, Belfast, pastoral letters [printed] | Irish College, Rome, O'Riordan and Hagan MSS, corresp. | FILM BFI NFTVA, news footage
Likenesses J. Lavery, portrait, 1926–9 · Vannucci and Favilla, bust, 1929, repro. in *Irish Times* (15 Oct 1945) · Keogh, photograph, repro. in O'Hanlon, 'The new bishop of Down and Connor'
Wealth at death £8284 17s. 4d.: probate, 29 March 1946, CGPLA NIre.

MacRuairi, Ranald, of Garmoran (d. 1346), chief of clan Ruairi, was the illegitimate son of Ruairi MacRuairi (styled Ruairi of the Isles in contemporary documents) and a woman whose identity is unknown. Ranald's father was probably the MacRuairi rí Innse Gall (king of the Isles) who was noted in the annals of Ulster as dying alongside Edward Bruce, Robert I's brother, at the battle of Dundalk on 14 October 1318. Ranald's accession to the lordship of Garmoran, which embraced Moidart, Arisaig, Morar, and Knoydart on the mainland, along with the islands of Rum, Eigg, Barra, the Uists, and St Kilda, may have been contested after his father's death in 1318. Ruairi had received formal title to the lands which made up the lordship of Garmoran only after the resignation of the heir to these estates, his legitimate half-sister, Christina, some time in the reign of Robert I (r. 1306–29). After Ruairi's death Christina made a further resignation of her rights in Garmoran, this time in favour of one Arthur Campbell. Despite Christina's grant and his own canonical illegitimacy, Ranald was undoubtedly accepted as the chief of clan Ruairi and the dominant lord in Garmoran after his father's death.

Ranald MacRuairi's earliest appearance in record sources dates from 1337, when, as Ranald, son of Ruairi of the Isles (Latinized as Reginald, son of Roderick of the Isles), he was noted as supporting attempts to obtain a papal dispensation for his sister Amy to marry John MacDonald, first lord of the Isles. At this point Ranald and his new brother-in-law were probably backing the claims of Edward Balliol to the Scottish throne against those of David II, the son and heir of Robert I. However, both men had been reconciled to David II by 12 June 1343, on which date Ranald received a general confirmation of his Garmoran lands from the king. Shortly before the royal grant, in July 1342, William, earl of Ross, gave over the west coast lands of Kintail to Ranald. The political and military expansion of the clan Ruairi into Kintail can probably be dated to the period after the death of William's father, Earl Hugh, at the battle of Halidon Hill in 1333, when William was either a minor or, as some sources suggest, in exile outside the kingdom. In either case the 1342 grant in Ranald's favour seems to have been forced from a reluctant Earl William. That the relationship between the two men was far from cordial is confirmed by Ranald's assassination in Elcho Priory by adherents of Earl William during a muster of the Scottish host at Perth in October 1346.

Ranald MacRuairi seems to have had at least one brother, Hugh, who had a grant of the thanage of Glen Tilt in the period 1342–6. After Ranald's death control of Garmoran passed to his sister's husband, John MacDonald, lord of the Isles. MacDonald continued to exercise lordship over Garmoran despite the end of his marriage to Amy MacRuairi, either through her death or through a divorce which in 1350 allowed John to marry Margaret Stewart, daughter of Robert the Steward (the future Robert II). On 9 March 1372 MacDonald received a grant of Garmoran from Robert II. In January 1373 the king confirmed John's grant of the Garmoran lands to Ranald, the eldest son of his marriage to Amy MacRuairi and the nephew of Ranald MacRuairi (after whom he was named).

From the sons of Amy and John descended the Clanranald and the Glengarry MacDonalds, who continued to dominate the island and mainland territories associated with the lordship of Garmoran. Fifteenth-century Gaelic genealogies suggest that Ranald MacRuairi had at least one illegitimate son; his descendants acted as the leaders of a kindred reduced to political and military dependence on the new MacDonald lords of Garmoran. That the MacRuairis remained a significant force within Garmoran is suggested by the appearance of an Alexander MacRuairi of Garmoran, who was arrested and executed on the orders of James I in 1428 and who was described by the chronicler Walter Bower as the chief of 1000 men.

S. I. BOARDMAN

Sources K. A. Steer, J. W. M. Bannerman, and G. H. Collins, *Late medieval monumental sculpture in the west highlands* (1977), appx 2 · J. Munro and R. W. Munro, eds., *Acts of the lords of the Isles, 1336–1493*, Scottish History Society, 4th ser., 22 (1986) · G. W. S. Barrow and others, eds., *Regesta regum Scottorum*, 6, ed. B. Webster (1982) · J. M.

Thomson and others, eds., *Registrum magni sigilli regum Scotorum / The register of the great seal of Scotland*, 11 vols. (1882–1914), vol. 2, appx 1, nos. 9, 412, 520 • *The 'Original chronicle' of Andrew of Wyntoun*, ed. F. J. Amours, 6 vols., STS, 1st ser., 50, 53–4, 56–7, 63 (1903–14) • W. M. Hennessy and B. MacCarthy, eds., *Annals of Ulster, otherwise, annals of Senat*, 4 vols. (1887–1901) • charter, penes Faculty of Procurators, Glasgow

McShane, Kathleen (1897–1964). *See under* Lucan, Arthur (1885–1954).

Macsparran, James (1693–1757), Church of England clergyman in America, was born on 10 September 1693, probably in Dugive, co. Londonderry. Although his parents are unknown, he was the nephew of Archibald Macsparran, a Presbyterian minister and well-to-do landowner. Macsparran entered Glasgow University in 1708 and left about six years later. Although the subject of his studies is uncertain, he arrived in Boston, Massachusetts, in 1718 and was shortly invited to become the Congregational minister in Bristol, Rhode Island. Doubts about the authenticity of his qualifications provoked an official inquiry, but he was cleared in 1719. The following year he laid the rumour to rest when he travelled to England, where he traded Congregationalism for the Church of England, in which he was ordained deacon in August and priest in September. In 1721 he returned to the American colonies as a minister for the Church of England's missionary arm, the Society for the Propagation of the Gospel. He was soon made the rector of St Paul's Church in Narragansett county, Rhode Island, where his efforts doubled the size of his church and won the favour of that colony's élite. He married one of its daughters, Hannah Gardiner (1704–1755), on 22 May 1722.

Any success Macsparran enjoyed as a clergyman was marred by controversy. He founded several churches and toured the colony giving sermons, and although he had a number of American Indian and black slaves, he actively spread the gospel outside the white community. In 1737 his labours were recognized by Oxford University, which made him an honorary DD. He was a strict conformist, however, and sparked hostility in the denominational diversity that characterized early British America. He went so far as to bring a lawsuit to block a Congregational minister from receiving a substantial tract of land, on the grounds that it had been intended for an 'orthodox' minister, which Macsparran interpreted as Church of England. He lost the case in 1752, but that same year he continued his conformist push by publishing *The Sacred Dignity of the Christian Priesthood Vindicated*, which explicitly attacked irregularities among the Church of England clergy in America and implicitly condemned dissenters. The following year he published *America Dissected* which disparaged colonial Americans as a whole for embracing pluralism and the liberty of conscience. In 1754 he left for England, hoping to receive an American bishopric. His hopes were soon dashed, and disappointment turned to misery when during the trip his wife died in 1755 from smallpox. He returned to Rhode Island the following year and died on 5 December 1757 at South Kingston; he was buried at St Paul's, Kingston, Narragansett. Macsparran had no children and so left his house and farm to the Church of England for the use of an American bishop.

TROY O. BICKHAM

Sources J. F. Woolverton, 'Macsparran, James', *ANB* • *DNB* • W. Updike, *A history of the Episcopal church in Narragansett, Rhode Island*, ed. D. Goodwin, 3 vols. (1907) • *Macsparran's diary*, ed. D. Goodwin (1899) • S. V. James, *Colonial Rhode Island: a history* (1975) • S. P. Dorsey, *Early churches in America, 1607–1807* (1952) • C. Tiffany, *A history of the Protestant Episcopal church in the USA* (New York, 1895)
Archives University of Rhode Island, Kingston, records of the Episcopal church in Rhode Island, MSS group no. 41
Likenesses J. Smibert, oils, 1735, Bowdoin College Museum of Art, Maine • J. Smith, portrait, Bowdoin College, Maine
Wealth at death house and farm for use of any American episcopal bishop: Woolverton, 'Macsparran, James'

MacSwiney, Mary Margaret (1872–1942), Irish republican, was born at 13 Clements Road, Bermondsey, London, on 27 March 1872, the eldest of seven surviving children of John MacSwiney (*c*.1835–*c*.1895), and his wife, Mary Wilkinson (*c*.1840–1904). Both her parents were schoolteachers. The family returned to Cork city where John MacSwiney began a tobacco factory with his brother-in-law. The enterprise was a failure and plunged the two families into bankruptcy. In 1885 the father emigrated to Australia. The mother opened a corner shop to help support the family.

MacSwiney was educated at the Ursuline convent school in Cork city. When she was twenty she took up a teaching post in a private school in England. With a loan received from the Students' Aid Society in Ireland MacSwiney took a teaching diploma from Cambridge University. After receiving her diploma she taught at a convent boarding-school in Farnborough, England. While working here she seriously considered entering the religious life. She began a one-year noviciate with the Oblates of St Benedict but at the end of the period decided not to proceed. Instead she became a member of a lay organization, the third order of St Benedict, whose members made a public promise to lead a charitable and spiritual life. MacSwiney returned to Cork in 1904 after the death of her mother and took a teaching post at St Angela's, an Ursuline convent school.

MacSwiney's first venture into politics occurred with her interest in the suffrage campaign. She was present at the first meeting of the Munster Women's Franchise League and became a member of its committee. She viewed suffrage as an end in itself and was not concerned with the wider feminist aims of the suffrage campaign. She constantly expressed her nationalist views at local suffrage meetings, often to the irritation of other members. She opposed militancy within the suffrage movement, particularly the tactics of English suffragettes in Ireland, believing that violent tactics were 'unsuitable for Ireland and unjust since Ireland was not responsible for women's voteless condition'. The blame lay instead with the 'Parliament and people of England' (memoirs).

By 1914 MacSwiney's nationalism had taken precedence over her suffrage beliefs. She formally resigned from the

Munster Women's Franchise League in November of that year. She also set about establishing a branch of Cumann na mBan, the women's auxiliary to the Irish Volunteers, in Cork. Many suffragists saw Cumann na mBan as a servile organization, and between May and July of 1914 Mac-Swiney engaged in a public debate with suffragists about the precedence of nationalism over suffragism, in the pages of the suffrage paper the *Irish Citizen*.

MacSwiney's politics caused considerable concern to her employers, the Ursuline nuns. In consequence she was sacked from her teaching post in 1917. In order to support herself she opened a private school in her home in Cork city. The school was called St Ita's and was modelled on Patrick Pearse's St Enda's in Dublin.

MacSwiney was particularly attached to her younger brother, Terence *MacSwiney. She campaigned for him when he was elected to the first Dáil Éireann in 1918, and publicized his stance during his fatal hunger strike in 1920. In December 1920 she travelled to the United States, with her sister and her brother's widow, to give evidence to the American commission on conditions in Ireland. She remained in the United States for nine months, giving interviews and raising money for the Irish cause. Her tour was considered to be very successful and she was to tour the United States again in 1925.

MacSwiney returned to Ireland in August 1921 to take her Dáil seat as a member of Sinn Féin. She was also at this time president of Cumann na mBan. Along with five other women TDs she vehemently opposed the Anglo-Irish treaty, which had been negotiated in December 1921 to end the War of Independence. She was elected in June 1922 to the third Dáil, which did not sit because of the outbreak of the civil war. She retained her Dáil seat in the 1923 general election but, as with other republicans, refused to take the oath of allegiance necessary and did not take up her seat. She was committed to the ideal of a republic and remained an inflexible opponent of the Irish Free State, as she later stated in a letter to Eamon de Valera (24 April 1925):

> The people of a nation may not voluntarily surrender their independence; they may not vote it away in the ballot box even under duress and if some, even a majority be found, who through force or cupidity, would vote for such a surrender, the vote is invalid legally and morally and a minority is justified in upholding the independence of their country. (Fallon, 86)

She was arrested on a number of occasions under the Free State and on imprisonment always went on hunger strike, which often brought about her release.

MacSwiney was defeated in the 1927 election, by which time she was vice-president of Sinn Féin and Cumann na mBan. In 1933 she resigned from Cumann na mBan over a dispute about acknowledging allegiance to the republic rather than the second Dáil. In consequence, with a number of other women, she formed Mná na Poblachta (Women of the Republic). By 1934 she had also left Sinn Féin because it allowed its members to accept IRA war pensions. Her health deteriorated from 1938. She died at her home, 4 Belgrave Place, Cork, on 8 March 1942, and was buried in St Joseph's cemetery in the city three days later.   MARIA LUDDY

Sources C. H. Fallon, *Soul of fire: a biography of Mary MacSwiney* (1986) • F. J. Costello, *Enduring the most: the life and death of Terence MacSwiney* (1995) • 'The incomplete memoirs of Mary MacSwiney', typescript, University College, Dublin, P48a/300 (2) • R. M. Fox, *Rebel Irishwomen* (1935), 55–71 • M. Ward, *Unmanageable revolutionaries: women and Irish nationalism*, pbk edn (1983) • b. cert.
Archives Cork Public Museum • University College, Dublin, papers, P48a
Likenesses photographs, University College, Dublin • photographs, Cork Public Museum

MacSwiney, Muriel Frances (1892–1982). *See under* Mac-Swiney, Terence James (1879–1920).

MacSwiney, Terence James (1879–1920), politician and author, was born on 28 March 1879 at 23 North Main Street, Cork city, co. Cork, Ireland, the fifth among the nine children, two of whom died in infancy, of John Mac-Swiney (c.1835–c.1895), schoolteacher and tobacco manufacturer, and his wife, Mary, *née* Wilkinson (c.1840–1904). His Cork-born father had volunteered in 1868 to fight as a papal guard against Garibaldi, such was the strength of his Catholic faith, after which he had worked as a schoolteacher in London, where he had married his English-born wife. The couple had then moved to Cork to establish a tobacco factory which failed, reducing them to bankruptcy. Terence was therefore brought up in a large, well educated, and deeply Catholic family amid some financial hardship, made worse when his father emigrated to Australia in 1885, never to return.

MacSwiney was educated at the North Monastery Christian Brothers' School in Cork, where he was a brilliant pupil. His education was Catholic but also emphasized an Irish patriotism which was reflected in his own success in the study of the Irish language. Patriotism was also an influence on his family, and especially on his father, who claimed to be a descendant of a Donegal clan of MacSwineys driven out by Saxon invaders. MacSwiney left school in 1894 at fifteen, and began work at a Cork warehousing firm. His financial contribution to the family household was vital, and he became a well-respected employee. In his spare time he continued his studies, eventually gaining admission on a part-time basis to Queen's College, Cork, graduating from the Royal (later National) University of Ireland with a degree in mental and moral science in 1907. He subsequently gained part-time employment as a lecturer in business studies at Cork Municipal School of Commerce, and at the end of 1911 he took up the full-time post of commercial instructor for the Joint Technical Instruction Committee for co. Cork.

MacSwiney was one of a generation who became caught up in the cultural and political movements that coalesced into republicanism and the struggle for Irish independence. In 1899 he helped to form a Young Ireland Society in Cork, and in 1901 he became a founder member of the Cork Celtic Literary Society. He contributed numerous poems and articles to the society's journal, most of them under the name of MacEireann ('Son of Erin'), many of

KEATING

Terence James MacSwiney (1879–1920), by Seán Keating

which were published in a collection entitled *The Music of Freedom* (1907). Soon afterwards he became involved in the Cork Dramatic Society, for which he wrote a number of plays, all in verse form, and most concerned with Irish nationality. Over the same period MacSwiney became strongly committed to the importance of the Irish language, and through Gaelic League classes and regular visits to Gaelic-speaking areas he became a proficient speaker.

In 1902 the Cork Literary Society protested against Edward VII's visit to the city. Members of the society unfurled a black banner as the monarch processed through the main street, and as a result MacSwiney was arrested for the first time. From 1911 his activities became even more explicitly political, first manifested in the articles that he began to contribute to the republican journal *Irish Freedom*, which were posthumously collected together in 1921 under the title of *Principles of Freedom* (repr. 1936, 1970). He was a founder and a leader of the Cork brigade of the Irish Volunteers in 1913, and became the publisher of and principal contributor to the weekly republican paper *Fianna Fáil* ('Soldiers of Destiny') before its suppression in December 1914. He was arrested in January 1916 on charges of sedition, and after a month in custody, during which his detention was discussed in parliament, he was acquitted on all but one charge and fined 1s.,

a moral victory which strengthened his reputation with republicans.

MacSwiney's role in the Easter rising of April 1916 was contentious, however. There were conflicting messages about whether the Cork brigade should mobilize in support of their colleagues beleaguered in the Dublin post office, and the British intercepted a ship intended to bring German arms to supply their forces in the south. By the time news of the rising reached Cork crown forces had secured the city militarily, and MacSwiney and Tomás MacCurtain, to whom he acted as second in command, decided that insurrection would be futile. They ordered the volunteers to hand over their arms to the civil authorities, and travelled on British army permits to instruct the Tralee and Limerick brigades to do the same. There was much bitterness over their conduct, although an investigation by the Irish volunteer executive in 1918 absolved them of any blame. There is no doubt that despite this MacSwiney felt uneasy about his part in the Easter rising, as revealed by statements he and others made later.

Within days MacSwiney was arrested and detained until June 1917, with only two months of freedom at the beginning of that year. On 9 June 1917, while still being held at Bromyard, Herefordshire he married Muriel Frances Murphy [*see below*]. They had a daughter, Máire (*b.* 1918). In November 1917 he was arrested again and was sentenced to six months' imprisonment. He instigated a hunger strike in protest, and was released within four days. Further arrest followed in March 1918, and MacSwiney was then detained for almost twelve months. By the time of his release in March 1919 the war for Irish independence had begun. MacSwiney had also been elected as a Sinn Féin candidate in the elections of December 1918 for Mid-Cork, and, along with the others who did not take their seats at Westminster, had become a founding member of the Irish parliament, the Dáil Éireann. He was prominent in helping to establish the Dáil's legitimacy by helping to organize a loan to underpin its operations, and by fostering republican courts in the Cork district. The campaign of assassination and counter-assassination between the Royal Irish Constabulary (RIC), the Black and Tans, and the auxiliary division of the RIC on the one side and the IRA on the other was especially fierce in the Cork district, and reached its apogee when MacSwiney's colleague Tomás MacCurtain was shot dead in his home in March 1920, almost certainly at the hands of crown forces. MacSwiney succeeded MacCurtain as lord mayor of Cork and as commandant of the Cork brigade of the IRA.

On 12 August 1920 MacSwiney was arrested during a raid on city hall. He was charged with possessing a police cipher code and with sedition on three other counts, and was sentenced by a court martial to two years' imprisonment. He began a hunger strike as soon as he was arrested, and told the court: 'I will put a limit to any term of imprisonment you may impose … I have taken no food since Thursday … I shall be free, alive or dead, within a month' (O'Hegarty, 90). He was taken to Brixton prison in London, where he endured the last agonizing days of his life. Mac-Swiney's decision to go on hunger strike was personal, and was not required by his political or military leaders. Among his motives was a desire to atone for failing in 1916 to lead the rising in Cork, and strengthening his resolve was his semi-mystical brand of Catholicism. His own release after he had gone on hunger strike earlier in November 1917, and the freeing of twenty-seven IRA hunger strikers from Wormwood Scrubs in May 1920, may have encouraged him to believe initially that he would be set free. The British government, though, was determined not to give in in this case, nor in that of the eleven republicans in Cork gaol who had begun hunger strikes not long before MacSwiney's arrest.

MacSwiney survived seventy-four days, resisting attempts by the authorities to force-feed him, before he died on 25 October 1920, his death certificate putting his cause of death as 'heart failure … from prolonged refusal to take food'. While he suffered, his plight became an international *cause célèbre*, doing much to increase support for the Irish cause and to undermine British resolve to hold on to Ireland. The British government's intransigence brought increasing criticism, heightened when one of the Cork hunger strikers died a week before MacSwiney, followed by another on the same day as his own death. His body lay in state at St George's Roman Catholic Cathedral, Southwark, where there is a memorial to him, before being returned to Ireland. After a requiem mass in Cork Cathedral he was buried on 31 October in St Finn Barr's cemetery. Huge crowds attended MacSwiney's funeral procession, and in subsequent months and years he became an iconic figure of Irish nationalism.

Muriel Frances MacSwiney [*née* Murphy] (1892–1982) was born on 8 June 1892 in Carrigmore, Cork, the daughter of Nicholas Murphy and his wife, Mary Gertrude, *née* Purcell. The Murphys were one of the richest Catholic families in Cork, the owners of the chief liquor firm in the city. The MacSwineys had settled at an address in Douglas Road, Cork, in September 1917, but from November of that year had spent little time together owing to MacSwiney's frequent arrests. After his death Muriel participated in nationalist activities, especially in the United States, where she was the first woman granted the freedom of New York city. After partition and the creation of the Irish Free State in 1922 she took the side of the defeated anti-treatyites in the civil war, and later joined the Communist Party. She left Ireland with her daughter, Máire, in December 1923, and spent the rest of her life in a peripatetic existence, mostly in Germany, France, and England. In 1932 Terence MacSwiney's elder sister Mary [see MacSwiney, Mary Margaret], a prominent figure within the nationalist movement before and after his death, removed Máire, her niece, to Ireland. The two sisters-in-law did not get on well together, and Muriel claimed that her daughter had been kidnapped. Legal attempts to regain her failed, however, and the daughter herself later repudiated her mother's claims. Muriel MacSwiney's later activities are obscure. She was granted a pension by the Irish government in 1950, and she surfaced briefly on the fringes of left-wing politics in London in the late 1960s and early 1970s. From a relationship with a French intellectual she had a daughter, Alix (b. 1926), with whom she was living in Tonbridge in Kent towards the end of her life. She died in Oakwood Hospital, Maidstone, on 26 October 1982.   SAM DAVIES

Sources F. J. Costello, *Enduring the most: the life and death of Terence MacSwiney* (1995) · P. S. O'Hegarty, *A short memoir of Terence MacSwiney* (1922) · M. Chavasse, *Terence MacSwiney* (1962) · T. MacSwiney, *Principles of freedom* (1921) · A. Clifford, *Muriel MacSwiney: letters to Angela Clifford* (1996) · C. H. Fallon, *Soul of fire: a biography of Mary McSwiney* (1986) · M. Laffan, *The resurrection of Ireland: the Sinn Féin party, 1916–1923* (1998) · 'Irish statute book, 1922–1998', 193.120.124.98/front.html · b. cert. · b. cert. [Muriel Frances Murphy] · m. cert. · d. cert. [Muriel Frances MacSwiney]
Archives Cork Municipal Museum, MSS · NL Ire., MSS · University College, Dublin, archives department, MSS
Likenesses S. Keating, drawing, NG Ire. [*see illus.*] · portrait, repro. in Costello, *Enduring the most*

McSwiny, Owen. *See* Swiny, Owen (1676–1754).

Mactaggart, John (1791–1830), engineer and poet, was born on 26 June 1791 near Plunton Castle, Borgue, Kirkcudbrightshire, one of the eleven children of a Galloway farmer. He attended Kirkcudbright Academy and showed marked mathematical ability. But he left school aged thirteen and worked on the farm, where he developed an interest in rural antiquities and social life and began the observations later used in his publications. In 1817 he entered Edinburgh University, where he specialized in mathematics and physics, but he soon withdrew, feeling that he was learning nothing. He picked up some engineering skills and worked for John Rennie on the Plymouth breakwater. He made his way to London in the 1820s, earned an income tutoring, and, with Thomas Campbell and Henry Brougham, launched an unsuccessful weekly, the *London Scotsman*. In 1824 Mactaggart published *The Scottish Gallovidian Encyclopedia*, which contains his observations and poems, and his notes on folklore and folksongs. However, comments on a local beauty, the 'Star of Dungyle', caused protests and the book was quickly withdrawn; it was reprinted after Mactaggart's death, in 1876 and 1981.

In 1826, on the recommendation of John Rennie's son, Mactaggart went to Canada as clerk of works in the building of the Rideau Canal, working under Lieutenant-Colonel John By. He stayed in Canada, taking on other engineering tasks, travelling, and making notes. After a bout of swamp fever he was dismissed for drunkenness and returned to Britain, where he published *Three Years in Canada* (2 vols., 1829), an important work of social observations. Mactaggart died, unmarried, on 8 January 1830 and was buried in Sandwich churchyard, Galloway. He left plans for an account of the Canadian *voyageurs*, and an unfinished poem, 'The Engineer'. Mactaggart's independent and piquant curiosity gives his works an enduring interest.   H. C. G. MATTHEW

Sources G. S. Emmerson, 'Mactaggart, John', *DCB*, vol. 6 · M. M. Harper, ed., *The bards of Galloway* (1889) · A. Trotter, *East Galloway sketches, or, Biographical, historical and descriptive notices of Kirkcudbrightshire, chiefly in the nineteenth century* (1901) · J. Mactaggart, *The Scottish Gallovidian encyclopedia* (1824); new edn, ed. L. L. Andern (1981)

Archives Stewartry Museum, Kirkcudbright

Mactaggart, Sir John Auld, first baronet (1867–1956), builder, was born on 30 September 1867 in Anderton, Glasgow, the eldest son and second in the family of two sons and two daughters of Neil Mactaggart (1835–1904), coppersmith, and his wife, Anne Auld (d. 1906). Mactaggart was educated in Glasgow and was intended for the civil service, but instead joined Robert Mickel & Co., timber merchants and sawmill owners, where he was trained as a mercantile clerk, and became chief accountant at the firm's Glasgow office. In 1897 he married Margaret Lockhart, daughter of Robert Curtis, a master blacksmith, of Ramelton, co. Donegal, Ireland. They had one son and one daughter. Margaret Mactaggart died in 1927, and in 1928 Mactaggart married Elizabeth Ann (Lena; d. 1958), eldest daughter of the Revd David Orr of Govan, Glasgow. In 1898 he left Mickels to set up his own business, and until 1901 he was in partnership with the builder Robert Pollock, making concrete steps and later building tenements.

In 1901 Mactaggart started his own firm, J. A. Mactaggart & Co. He began by manufacturing concrete pipes, steps, and lintels, but soon started to build large tenement buildings, mainly for middle-class tenants, in west and south Glasgow. Most of the houses had bathrooms: Mactaggart later claimed to be 'the man who had made Glasgow bathroom conscious' (Morgan, 2.154). He kept some of the properties to let himself, and by 1911 eighty-three tenements provided him with an annual rental of £14,000, and also security to raise loans to buy land and finance building operations. In addition to these, Mactaggart built forty-four cottages for the English workers at the new Yarrow shipyards which opened at Scotstoun in 1908.

When the royal commission on housing was set up in 1913 to tackle the housing problem in Scotland, Mactaggart gave evidence, urging the reduction of local property taxes in order to encourage people to move into larger houses, thus helping to solve the problem of overcrowding. He also argued for rent control, and this led to the passing of the rent restriction acts.

During the First World War Mactaggart was occupied with government work, including an Admiralty contract at Gourack. In 1919 he converted the firm into a limited company. The largest shareholders were members of his family, and he became managing director. Mactaggart benefited from the 1919 Addison Act, which tried to fulfil the government's wartime promise to provide 'homes fit for heroes to live in' by obliging local authorities to undertake housing schemes, and providing large subsidies to enable them to do so. His most important single contract was the Mosspark housing scheme for 1502 houses for Glasgow corporation, worth £1.8 million, which Mactaggart completed despite shortage of building materials and disputes with the trade unions. At the same time, through a consortium made up of his wife and other members of his family, Mactaggart was buying land in Glasgow with a view to future property development, including land at King's Park, to the south of the city, and 114 acres of the Kelvinside estate, at its west end.

In 1924 J. A. Mactaggart Ltd went into voluntary liquidation, and Mactaggart's son Jack, and his partner, Andrew Mickel (nephew of Mactaggart's former employer, Robert Mickel), formed Mactaggart and Mickel Ltd, with John Mactaggart as the largest shareholder, to concentrate on building houses for private owner-occupiers, while John Mactaggart took over the Western Heritable Investment Company Ltd in 1925. He applied for permission to build blocks of cottage flats at King's Park, subsidized under the terms of the 1924 Housing Act which promised subsidies to build houses for rent. Mactaggart had encouraged the MP John Wheatley to include these clauses in the bill. By 1930 he had completed 1356 houses, not only subsidized under the 1924 act, but also financed by Glasgow corporation through loans of 75 per cent of the value of the completed houses. In 1931 agreement was reached for a subsidy and loans for a further 1512 houses at King's Park. Following this he built subsidized houses at Kelvinside, and on corporation land at Cardonald. Altogether the company built 6038 houses for rent with subsidies offered by the 1924 act.

Mactaggart turned his attention to the London property market in the 1930s. He formed a new company, the London Heritable Investment Company Ltd, which developed luxury flats on a site in Park Lane, next to the Dorchester Hotel, between 1935 and 1938. After the Second World War he formed a new company, Grove End Gardens Ltd, which built and managed luxury flats in St John's Wood. He visited the United States in 1936 to study housing conditions, and was asked by President Roosevelt to prepare a memorandum. Increasingly consulted by the government as an authority on housing, Mactaggart was created a baronet in 1938.

Although at one time a socialist, and a member of the Independent Labour Party from 1889 to 1902, Mactaggart joined the Liberal Party in 1902 and became secretary of the Glasgow branch, although he refused to stand for election either to Glasgow corporation or to parliament. In 1930 he gave the house and grounds of the Aitkenhead estate, next to the King's Park development, to Glasgow corporation, to be preserved as a public park. He financed the Peace Pavilion at the 1938 Glasgow Empire Exhibition, and, always interested in the film industry, he gave £5000 towards the building of the cinema at the exhibition. Mactaggart was a member of the Royal Philosophical Society of Glasgow, to which he read a paper on housing and planning in 1943. He was also a JP for Glasgow. His interests spread beyond Scotland: he founded the American and British Commonwealth Association in 1941 (it was merged with the English-Speaking Union in 1947), served as president of the Economic Research Council, and was elected president of the National Federation of Property Owners for 1950–52.

Mactaggart died at his Glasgow home, Kelmscott, 110 Springkell Avenue, Pollokshields, on 24 November 1956.

ANNE PIMLOTT BAKER

Sources N. J. Morgan, 'Mactaggart, Sir John', *DSBB* · *The Times* (26 Nov 1956) · *The Builder*, 191 (1956), 927 · Burke, *Peerage* · *WWW*

McTaggart, John McTaggart Ellis (1866–1925), philosopher, was born John McTaggart Ellis at 28 Norfolk Square, London, on 3 September 1866, the second and eldest surviving son of Francis Ellis (d. 1870), county court judge, and his wife, Caroline Ellis. Thomas Flower *Ellis, the author of law reports, was his grandfather. He was named in honour of John McTaggart, an uncle of his father, and soon afterwards acquired McTaggart as a surname also, when Francis Ellis adopted it as a condition of inheriting that uncle's wealth. After attending a preparatory school in Weybridge (from which he was allegedly removed for announcing that he did not believe in God), McTaggart went to a school in Caterham until 1880 and, following a period under a private tutor, to Clifton College, Bristol, from 1882 to 1885. He went to Trinity College, Cambridge, in October 1885, where he studied moral sciences under Henry Sidgwick and James Ward, and was placed alone in the first class of the moral sciences tripos in 1888. He was an active member of the Union Society, of which he was elected president in 1890. In 1891 he was elected to a prize fellowship at Trinity, and in 1897 he was appointed college lecturer in the moral sciences. From 1892 to 1893 McTaggart stayed with his mother, who was by then living in Taranaki, near New Plymouth, in New Zealand. He returned there in 1898 and, on 5 August 1899 at St Mary's Church, New Plymouth, he married Margaret Elizabeth Bird, daughter of Joseph Bird, supervisor of a large district in the colony. They had no children.

McTaggart's writings fall into three groups. His earlier work was devoted to expounding and defending the method, and some of the results, of Hegel's *Logic*. The dissertation by which McTaggart gained his fellowship dealt with the dialectical method, and his first book, *Studies in the Hegelian Dialectic* (1896), was an expanded form of this dissertation. This was followed in 1901 by *Studies in Hegelian Cosmology*. In this book he discusses and criticizes certain applications which Hegel and others made of Hegelianism to ethics, politics, and religion. He also attempts to determine by Hegelian methods, more definitely than Hegel himself did, the nature and structure of the absolute. In 1910 he published his *Commentary on Hegel's 'Logic'*. In this he takes the detailed argument of Hegel's *Greater Logic* category by category from pure being to the absolute idea. He tries to expound in intelligible English the characteristic content of each category, and to explain and criticize the transitions from one category to another. McTaggart considered that the dialectical method, within the *Logic*, could be defended, both as to its validity and its fruitfulness, if it were regarded as a means of gradually making explicit what was implicit in every rational mind. He also held that Hegel's transition from logic, through nature, to spirit could be defended on similar lines. He was convinced that the absolute idea, the highest category of the logic, as interpreted by himself, expressed the complete nature of reality, so far as this could be determined

John McTaggart Ellis McTaggart (1866–1925), by Roger Fry, 1911

by purely *a priori* reasoning. But he rejected many of Hegel's particular steps: he thought that Hegel often deceived himself and his readers by giving to his categories names taken from concrete empirical facts, and he rejected almost all the applications which have been made of Hegelianism to ethics, politics, and religion.

In his exposition of Hegel, McTaggart, along with other British neo-Hegelians of the period, has commonly been regarded as unwarrantedly attributing to Hegel a florid metaphysics which later interpreters of Hegel have disdained. An alternative view of McTaggart's account has been advanced by Robert Stern ('British Hegelianism: a non-metaphysical view?' in *European Journal of Philosophy*, 2, 1994, 293–321), who suggests that in many respects he may be regarded as an important precursor of the non-metaphysical interpretations of Hegel (for example J. N. Findlay's) which prevailed in the last years of the twentieth century.

The second group of McTaggart's writings contains only one book—*Some Dogmas of Religion*, published in 1906. This is the only popular philosophical work which he wrote. He was at once an atheist and a convinced believer in human immortality. He held, on philosophical grounds which he developed in his *Hegelian Cosmology* and his *Nature of Existence* (1921 and 1927), that the absolute is a perfect society of spirits, each of whom loves one or more of the others. He also held that each of these spirits is eternal, and that each human mind, as it really is, is one of these spirits. He thought it most probable that the eternal and timeless existence of these spirits would appear, under the partly delusive form of time, as a series of successive lives of finite duration. In *Some Dogmas of Religion* he takes the doctrine of pre-existence, rebirth, and post-existence as a hypothesis, and defends it with great ingenuity against the more obvious objections. In this book he also discusses free will and determinism, arriving at a completely deterministic conclusion, and the omnipotence of God. On the latter subject he concludes that the existence of a non-omnipotent and non-creative God is the utmost that can be granted to be philosophically possible. In *The Nature of Existence* his conclusions are even more definitely atheistic.

The later years of McTaggart's life were spent in elaborating his own system of constructive metaphysics. This is contained in *The Nature of Existence*, the first volume of which appeared in 1921, the second and concluding volume being published posthumously in 1927. This is a complete system of deductive philosophy of extreme acuteness and ingenuity. It arrives at much the same conclusions as the writings of the Hegelian period by an entirely different method. In volume one he argues that any acceptable metaphysics must satisfy three ontological principles, namely those of the identity of indiscernibles, the infinite divisibility of substances, and the determinacy of the properties possessed by a substance. In volume two he goes on to argue that these principles are satisfied only by his conception of ultimate reality as being composed of the loving perceptions of one another by a community of selves. The work is remarkable for the strenuous attempt which the author makes to deal satisfactorily with the existence of error and illusion, particularly the illusion of time and change, in a world of eternal beings perfectly related to each other. His thesis of the unreality of time continued to attract debate in the decades after his death and is perhaps the most enduring part of his philosophy. A clear but highly condensed account of the arguments advanced in *The Nature of Existence* is in his contribution to *Contemporary British Philosophy* (edited by J. H. Muirhead, vol. 1, 1924).

McTaggart retired from his lecturership at Trinity College in 1923, after completing twenty-five years' service. He continued to give some of his courses of lectures until his death, which took place, after a short illness, on 18 January 1925 in a nursing home at 2 Bentinck Street, London. He was survived by his wife.

McTaggart was a man of great wit and great administrative ability. He felt a passionate affection for his friends, for his school and college, and for his country. His 'extremely virulent' patriotism (Dickinson, 108) was expressed during the First World War when, as well as working in a munitions factory and as a special constable, he took a leading part in the expulsion of the pacifist Bertrand Russell from Trinity. McTaggart was for many years an active member of the governing body of Clifton College, and he gave great help to Trinity College in drawing up the new statutes imposed upon it by the statutory commission. In his youth McTaggart's political opinions were radical but, influenced partly by his reading of Hegel and partly by the great loyalty he developed towards long-standing institutions such as those of Cambridge, he became increasingly conservative, even to the extent that, although an atheist, he was a keen supporter of the Church of England. In national politics he was a free-trade unionist. Traces of his

earlier radicalism persisted. He was a supporter of women's suffrage and in university politics, too, he was a strong feminist and an advocate of wide-ranging reforms. He had an extraordinary knowledge of English novels, both past and contemporary, and of eighteenth-century memoirs. The honorary degree of LLD was conferred on him by the University of St Andrews in 1911 and he was elected a fellow of the British Academy in 1906.

C. D. BROAD, rev. C. A. CREFFIELD

Sources G. Lowes Dickinson, *John McTaggart Ellis McTaggart* (1931) · T. Baldwin, 'McTaggart, John McTaggart Ellis (1866–1925)', *Routledge encyclopaedia of philosophy*, ed. E. Craig (1998), 24–8 · R. Mason, *Dictionary of twentieth century philosophers*, ed. S. Brown, D. Collinson, and R. Wilkinson (1996), 495–7 · R. Stern, 'British Hegelianism: a non-metaphysical view?', *European Journal of Philosophy*, 2 (1994), 293–321 · C. D. Broad, 'J. M. E. McTaggart, 1866–1925', *PBA*, 13 (1927), 307–34 · Venn, *Alum. Cant.* · CGPLA Eng. & Wales (1925)
Archives Bodl. Oxf., letters to G. G. A. Murray; letters to Hastings Rashdall · CAC Cam., letters to Oscar Browning · CAC Cam., letters to Roger Fry · CUL, letters to G. E. Moore · CUL, notes on his lectures taken by G. E. Moore · CUL, letters to Nathaniel Wedd · CUL, letters to Hilton Young · McMaster University, Hamilton, Ontario, letters to Bertrand Russell
Likenesses photographs, 1874–1907, repro. in Dickinson, *John McTaggart Ellis McTaggart* · R. Fry, watercolour caricature, 1911, Trinity Cam. [see illus.] · W. Rothenstein, pencil drawing, 1916, Trinity Cam. · W. Stoneman, photograph, 1917, NPG · R. Fry, oils, 1937, Trinity Cam.
Wealth at death £19,137 8s. 2d.: probate, 25 Feb 1925, *CGPLA Eng. & Wales*

McTaggart, William (1835–1910), painter, was born on 25 October 1835 at Aros in Kintyre, the third of the eight children of Dugald McTaggart (1797–1861) and Barbara Brolochan (also known as Brodie; 1804–1884). He was baptized on 28 October at Campbeltown. In the artist's earliest years his father was a crofter working difficult land. By 1841 the family had moved to School Lane, Campbeltown, where his father made a living digging and carting peats for sale to a whisky distillery. His parents spoke both Gaelic and English, and so too did William.

Education and early career McTaggart was educated at the school of the SPCK in Kirk Street, Campbeltown, leaving at the age of twelve to be apprenticed in the drug dispensary of Dr John Buchanan. Buchanan was a key figure in the transition of McTaggart from crofter's son to the pioneer of modern art in Scotland; McTaggart's biographer Sir James Caw described Buchanan as 'a wise counsellor and a kind friend' (*DNB*). Buchanan was an elder of the Free Church, an institution which had attracted a number of intellectuals and artists at its formation in 1843, for example the physicist Sir David Brewster and the painter and photographer David Octavius Hill. It is in this context that Buchanan's encouragement of McTaggart's early artistic efforts can be seen. In 1852, aged sixteen, he left for Glasgow, against parental advice but armed with an introduction from Buchanan to the portrait painter Daniel Macnee.

Macnee recognized McTaggart's potential, and on 19

William McTaggart (1835–1910), self-portrait, 1892 [*A Study of Oak Leaves in Autumn (Self-Portrait)*]

April of the same year he was admitted, on the older painter's recommendation, to the Trustees' Academy in Edinburgh, the city that was to become his home. The academy provided tuition without fee, thus making it possible for a student of limited means to consider becoming an artist. It was McTaggart's good fortune that in 1852 Robert Scott Lauder had been appointed director of the antique school at the academy. Lauder was a teacher inspired by international vision and experience. McTaggart was one of a remarkable group of Lauder's students that included the painters W. Q. Orchardson, Robert Herdman, John Pettie, Hugh Cameron, George Paul Chalmers, Tom Graham, Peter Graham, John MacWhirter, J. B. Macdonald, W. F. Vallance, John Burr, and Alexander Burr, and the sculptors John Hutchison and George Lawson. McTaggart was a prize-winning student, and he made a number of lifelong friendships with his fellows.

During this period McTaggart supported himself by sketching portraits not only in Edinburgh but, during the summer vacations from 1853 to 1856, in Dublin; indeed his first professionally shown work was a portrait group exhibited at the Royal Hibernian Academy in 1854. Although it was not to be the focus of his career, he retained a penetrating ability as a portrait painter. He first exhibited at the Royal Scottish Academy in 1855, and became an associate in 1859, at the early age of twenty-four. His links to Kintyre remained strong, and on 9 June 1863 he married Mary Brolochan Holmes (1837–1884), the daughter of a Campbeltown builder. Their first child, Annie, was born the next year; she later married the above-mentioned Sir James *Caw, who was distinguished both as a historian of Scottish art and as director of the National Gallery of Scotland in Edinburgh. A second

daughter, Barbara, born in 1865, died at the age of a little over one year, an event that gave rise to a moving portrait from memory.

Early landscapes and seascapes By this time McTaggart had already shown a strong interest in the depiction of children, both individually and in landscape and coastal settings, which remained with him throughout his life. This interest is clear in his most important early oil painting, *Spring*, dated 1864 (National Gallery of Scotland). Caw described this work as 'epoch-marking' on the grounds that it 'marks emergence from the conventional brown tone, so long in favour with Scottish artists' (Caw, *McTaggart*, 39). Modest in scale, it shows two children musing and making daisy-chains on the banks of a burn, with hills in the background. In its fresh colouring and consciousness of the notion of truth to nature it shows a clear awareness of Pre-Raphaelite painting. In 1857, with his friend Chalmers, McTaggart had visited the Manchester Art Treasures Exhibition, where he had been impressed by the paintings of William Holman Hunt and J. E. Millais. The latter's *Autumn Leaves*, with its wistful air of childhood passing and its setting on the edge of the highlands, was in due course also shown in Edinburgh, and is likely to have made a particular impression. At this time McTaggart was contributing illustrations of scenes from the novels of Sir Walter Scott to portfolios of engravings commissioned by the Royal Association for the Promotion for the Fine Arts in Scotland. Another influence on *Spring* can be found in two paintings by George Harvey, illustrations to Robert Burns's 'Auld Lang Syne', which had been engraved for a cognate portfolio published in 1859. However experimentally 'impressionistic' McTaggart's landscapes became in due course, at the heart of his work was a commitment to narrative.

An important influence from the late 1860s onwards was the depiction of everyday life in a coastal environment by the artists of the Hague school. Indeed, one of McTaggart's few visits outside Scotland, along with his friend and patron, the machinery designer James Guthrie Orchar, was a short tour of Europe which included a meeting with Josef Israels at The Hague in 1882. Further trips abroad were limited to a visit to Paris in 1860, along with Pettie and Tom Graham, and a few weeks' holiday on the Riviera in 1876. This lack of travel, unusual for a Scottish artist of his standing, serves to emphasize the fact that McTaggart's art, whatever it may have shared with that of his French impressionist contemporaries in its commitment to observation of light and colour in the open air, developed independently. However, a major debt was to the work of the English painter John Constable; indeed Leslie's *Life of Constable* was one of McTaggart's most valued books.

In 1870 McTaggart was elected academician of the Royal Scottish Academy; he exhibited there frequently until 1895. His diploma work was *Dora* (1869), a subject from Tennyson, yet by this time the illustrative aspect of his work was drawing to a close. From that date onwards his work became increasingly concerned with how to convey the relationship between figures and land or seascape. He did not fully solve the problem until the 1890s, and something of his struggle is reflected in his comment late in life that he found it as difficult to paint after fifty years as when he was a boy. In 1878 the Royal Scottish Water Colour Society was founded and McTaggart became vice-president, his election reflecting his contribution to the development of that medium. He was also a strong supporter of the more radical alternative to the Royal Scottish Academy, the Society of Scottish Artists, and he became their vice-president in 1899.

From c.1870 McTaggart spent several summers at Tarbert on Loch Fyne, and from this date the sea, always of importance from the early *Wreck of the Hesperus* (1861; priv. coll.) onwards, came to dominate his work. In due course he worked on seascapes at locations near his birthplace in Kintyre and on the east coast at Carnoustie and in Fife. He developed a fluidity and directness of technique that enabled him to paint remarkable seascapes in which the subject is the immediacy of the sea, pure and simple, for example *Machrihanish Bay* (1878; National Gallery of Scotland) and *The Wave* (1881; Kircaldy Museum and Art Gallery). At the same time the desire to integrate figures, often children, was always strong, as in *Fisher Children* (1876; priv. coll.) and *Bait Gatherers* (1879; National Gallery of Scotland). McTaggart's knowledge of the realities of fishing at sea from an open boat up against the elements comes out strongly in works such as *Through Wind and Rain* (1875; Dundee Art Galleries and Museums). While such maritime subjects were popular at the time, there were few artists able to match McTaggart's understanding of his subject. Although stylistically very different, he shares much with his contemporary Winslow Homer in this regard. J. D. Fergusson wrote that he found it 'very difficult to believe that anyone has painted the sea better than McTaggart' (Fergusson, 31), and it is easy to concur.

It was during this period of the maturing of his art that McTaggart suffered the loss of his first wife, who died on 15 December 1884. He married again on 6 April 1886, his second wife being Marjory Henderson (1856–1925?), the daughter of the artist Joseph Henderson. From his first marriage McTaggart was survived by two sons and two daughters and from his second marriage by two sons and four daughters.

Later work In 1889 McTaggart moved from Edinburgh to the nearby village of Broomieknowe. From the point of view of the modern impact of the artist's work it is in the following decade that his key contribution was made. By this time he would often paint even large canvases out of doors. A number of paintings exploring highland communities and histories stand out from this late phase. They include *The Storm* (1890), *The Coming of St Columba* (1895), and *The Sailing of the Emigrant Ship* (1895), all now in the collection of the National Gallery of Scotland. In such works he encapsulates the history of the highland Gael from the establishment of Christianity in the sixth century to emigration in the wake of the clearances of the nineteenth century. Along with a remarkable set of landscapes painted at Broomieknowe, for example *Consider the Lilies* (1898; Kircaldy Museum and Art Gallery), in which the lessons of

painting the sea are transposed inland to wonderful effect, these works played a key part in setting the agenda for art in twentieth-century Scotland. If there is one image that enables us to grasp McTaggart's personality as a painter and the physicality of his practice it is not his meditative self-portrait *A Study of Oak Leaves in Autumn* (1892; National Gallery of Scotland), but rather a photograph which shows him braced against the wind while painting on the beach at Machrihanish in 1898. The picture was taken by one of his sons, while another son steadies the large canvas (already anchored with guy-ropes) to stop it blowing away. Such directness of encounter with nature is at the heart of McTaggart's art. McTaggart died at his home, Dean Park, Broomieknowe, on 2 April 1910, and was buried at Newington cemetery, Edinburgh, three days later. The value of his work has never been in serious dispute. It was reaffirmed in 1989 in a major exhibition at the Royal Scottish Academy in Edinburgh.

MURDO MACDONALD

Sources J. L. Caw, *William McTaggart: a biography and an appreciation* (1917) · *DNB* · L. Errington, *William McTaggart, 1835–1910* (1989) [exhibition catalogue, Royal Scot. Acad., 11 Aug – 29 Oct 1989] · L. Errington, *Master class: Robert Scott Lauder and his pupils* (1983) [exhibition catalogue, NG Scot., 15 July – 2 Oct 1983, and Aberdeen Art Gallery, 15 Oct – 12 Nov 1983] · J. D. Fergusson, *Modern Scottish painting* (1943) · P. Bate, *The English Pre-Raphaelite painters*, 2nd edn (1901) · NL Scot., McTaggart MSS · D. Macmillan, *Scottish art in the 20th century* (1994) · D. Macmillan, *Scottish art, 1460–1990* (1990) · D. Irwin and F. Irwin, *Scottish painters at home and abroad, 1700–1900* (1975) · W. Hardie, *Scottish painting, 1837 to the present* (1990) · J. L. Caw, *Scottish painting past and present, 1620–1908* (1908)

Archives Midlothian Council Archives, Loanhead · NL Scot., corresp. and son's corresp. relating to executry · NL Scot., personal and family corresp. and papers · U. Edin. | NG Scot., Caw archives

Likenesses W. Hodgson, pencil and black wash, 1892, NPG · W. McTaggart, self-portrait, oils, 1892, NG Scot. [*see illus.*] · H. McTaggart, photograph, 1898, NG Scot. · G. P. Chalmers, oils, Scot. NPG · O. Edis, photograph, NPG · Nesbitt & Lothian, carte-de-visite, NPG · G. Reid, oils, Aberdeen Art Gallery, MacDonald collection

Wealth at death £17,512 16s. 4d.: confirmation, 18 Aug 1910, *CCI*

MacTaggart, Sir William (1903–1981), painter, was born on 15 May 1903 at Loanhead, Midlothian, the elder son and third of four children of Hugh Holmes MacTaggart, mechanical engineer, and his wife, Bertha, daughter of Robert Little, businessman, of Edinburgh. His father was the eldest son of the Scottish landscape painter William *McTaggart. Although he always revered his grandfather's memory MacTaggart established his artistic personality from the beginning and even his earliest pictures owe nothing to his illustrious namesake. As a child MacTaggart suffered from ill health and was educated privately. From an early age he determined to become a painter. In this he received every encouragement from his father whose collection of pictures not only contained an excellent representation of the elder McTaggart but also pictures by (Louis-)Eugène Boudin and Henri Le Sidaner. Between 1918 and 1921 he attended the Edinburgh College of Art as a part-time student. It was at this time he met the painters W. G. Gillies, Anne Redpath, and John Maxwell who were to remain lifelong friends. An unfinished portrait of Mac-Taggart by W. G. Gillies (*c.*1935) in the Scottish National Portrait Gallery, Edinburgh, is a good likeness. The person who had the greatest influence on MacTaggart at this period, however, was the artist William Crozier (1893–1930). He had studied in Paris with André Lhôte, had travelled extensively, and brought an intellectual approach to painting which was important to MacTaggart.

Between 1922 and 1929 MacTaggart went regularly to the south of France for the sake of his health, sometimes in the company of Crozier: to Cannes, Le Cannet, Cassis, Bormes, and Grimaud. He took advantage of these visits to paint, and a six-week period at Cannes in 1923 was particularly important. The pictures from this period are bright and strong in colour and show an affinity with those of the Scottish colourists, particularly S. J. Peploe. It was appropriate therefore that in 1927 MacTaggart joined the Society of Eight, of which Peploe and F. J. Cadell were also members. MacTaggart held an exhibition of his work at St Andrew's church hall, Cannes, in 1924. His first one-man show in Edinburgh took place at Aitken Dott & Son in 1929.

The inclusion of twelve pictures by Edvard Munch in the annual exhibition of the Society of Scottish Artists in 1931–2 was the occasion for MacTaggart's meeting the person who was largely responsible for bringing them to Edinburgh: Fanny Margarethe Basilier (*d.* 1981), daughter of General Ivar Aavatsmark, of Oslo. She was perhaps the most important influence in his life. She gave him confidence in his work and broadened his outlook. Together they visited Matisse in the summer of 1936 and after their marriage in July 1937 they paid regular visits to Norway. MacTaggart was president of the Society of Scottish Artists between 1933 and 1936, during which period paintings by Paul Klee and Georges Braque were shown at their annual exhibitions in Edinburgh. In 1933 he began his teaching career at the College of Art, Edinburgh, an association that lasted until 1956. In 1937 he was elected as associate of the Royal Scottish Academy. (He became a full member in 1948 and was president between 1959 and 1969.) A bronze bust of MacTaggart by Benno Schotz RSA, which belongs to the Royal Scottish Academy who commissioned it in 1970, is a good likeness.

Between 1939 and 1945 MacTaggart again turned his attention to the landscape of East Lothian which remained an important source of inspiration for the remainder of his life. Visits to Scandinavia resumed after the war and between 1947 and 1952/3 the MacTaggarts stayed regularly at Orry-la-Ville, just north of Paris. The Rouault exhibition at the Musée d'Art Moderne in 1952 had a profound effect on MacTaggart's technical approach to painting. The palette becomes more sombre and the paint surface more richly worked. In the landscapes and still lifes of this period, especially those of flowers seen through an open window against a night sky, colours take on an inner glow. The most important example of the 'window' theme which he often repeated throughout the 1960s is the *Starry Night, the New Town* (1955; priv. coll., Norway). MacTaggart gave up painting directly from

nature in the mid-1950s and increasingly worked from sketches boldly executed on the spot in black chalk.

The MacTaggarts were a focal point of social life in Edinburgh and entertained constantly at 4 Drummond Place, which was their home from 1938. In the later 1960s and 1970s the routine of work, parties, and official functions was broken by the annual visit to the spa town of Skodsborg in Denmark. MacTaggart was a man of great personal charm with a gift for friendship. Position and honours were important to him, if only to prove that he had been able to conquer adversity and ill health. He had an honorary LLD degree from Edinburgh University (1961), was knighted in 1962, and became a chevalier of the Légion d'honneur (1968). He was elected an associate of the Royal Academy in 1968 and Royal Academician in 1973.

MacTaggart's range as an artist was limited and he was no innovator. But he spoke with a distinctive voice and the East Lothian landscapes of the 1960s in which harvest fields and ploughed land glow under an incandescent sun belong to the visual imagery of the Scottish scene and make a small but distinctive contribution to a larger Nordic tradition in painting. He was very popular in his lifetime and his pictures always sold well. MacTaggart stopped painting about 1976. He died in Edinburgh on 9 January 1981, and his wife died nine days later. They had no children.　　　　HUGH MACANDREW, *rev.*

Sources Royal Library of Scotland, MacTaggart MSS, Acc. 8636, 8416, 8755 · [D. Hall], *Sir William MacTaggart* (1968) [exhibition catalogue, NG Scot., 1–30 June 1968] · H. H. Wood, *William MacTaggart* (1974) · studio sale catalogue (1981), 45–74 [Christies and Edmisons, Edinburgh, 2 July 1981] · personal knowledge (1990) · I. Gale, *Sir William MacTaggart, 1903–1981* (1998) [exhibition catalogue, NG Scot.] · L. Errington, *William McTaggart, 1835–1910* (1989) [exhibition catalogue, Royal Scot. Acad., 11 Aug – 29 Oct 1989]
Archives NL Scot., corresp. and family papers
Likenesses W. G. Gillies, oils, *c.*1935, Scot. NPG · B. Schotz, bronze bust, *c.*1970, Royal Scot. Acad.

Mactavish, John McKenzie (1871–1938), shipwright and educationist, was born in the Scottish fishing village of Tarbert, Loch Fyne, on 18 July 1871, the son of Alexander Mactavish, a carpenter, and his wife, Euphemia McKenzie. He had no formal schooling beyond the elementary level but he did much to educate himself, and even in his early years in Tarbert he was an articulate atheist. Having finished his apprenticeship as a shipwright in 1892, he worked on the Clyde, the Tyne, the Mersey, the Thames, in South Africa, and at Gosport. Probably in Liverpool he met and married Emma Cartwright, and in 1906 they moved to Portsmouth, where he worked in the dockyards.

Mactavish was already active in the Independent Labour Party and the Shipwrights' Society, and he soon became an important figure on the local trades council. In 1908 he was elected the first Labour member of Portsmouth city council, on which he served until 1914, when his opposition to the First World War cost him his seat. As a councillor he spoke out on unemployment, municipal housing, council workers' wages, sewers, and public works—but, revealingly, he said little about education.

On 10 August 1907 Mactavish attended an important conference of the Workers' Educational Association

(WEA) at Oxford, where representatives of the university and the working classes met to forge a co-operative plan for continuing education. The two sides failed to come together until Mactavish delivered an electrifying speech: 'I claim for my class all the best that Oxford has to give' (Mooney, 14). According to Albert Mansbridge, first general secretary of the WEA, that declaration moved the conference to create a joint university–WEA committee that included Mactavish. The committee's report, *Oxford and Working-Class Education* (1908), proposed the creation of what became the WEA's distinctive pedagogical vehicle: tutorial classes where university-based tutors brought higher education to working-class communities.

Mactavish's performance at the conference in 1907 helps to explain why he was chosen to succeed Mansbridge in 1916. WEA leaders felt that in building bridges between the workers and the universities they had leaned too far toward the latter, and they hoped that Mactavish would use his personal contacts to strengthen their ties with organized labour. In fact he helped to create, in 1919, the Workers' Educational Trade Union Committee (WETUC), through which the WEA provided educational services to the labour movement, and he eventually secured the affiliation of several important unions.

But Mactavish also faced blistering attacks from a rival organization, the National Council of Labour Colleges (NCLC), which unapologetically promoted Marxist indoctrination. The NCLC denounced the less partisan liberal education offered by the WEA and the WETUC, and competed vigorously for trade union support. Ironically Mactavish, rare among labour leaders of his generation, was both informed and balanced on the subject of Marxism, which he felt deserved a place (along with other perspectives) in WEA curricula. As he put it, he wanted 'to save the memory of Marx from those who make of him a God, and those who make of him a Devil or a trivial fellow, by giving him a niche in the gallery of great thinkers to which he is entitled' (Mooney, 1).

As chief of the WEA Mactavish had shortcomings that should have been foreseen at the time of his appointment. He had no real administrative experience, not much interest in educational issues, and limited prior involvement in WEA activities. Nor was he a diplomat; he alienated H. A. L. Fisher by first promising to support his Education Bill of 1918 and then attacking it as inadequate. For H. D. Hughes, a later WEA leader, Mactavish 'exemplifies the "Peter Principle"—a man of undoubted ability promoted beyond his capacity' (Mooney, vi). The continuing battle with the NCLC wore him down. He began drinking too much, and in 1927 he was compelled to retire. In 1936 he returned to live in his native village of Tarbert, where he died of a stroke on 11 July 1938, and where he was buried. His wife survived him.   JONATHAN ROSE

Sources T. Mooney, *J. M. Mactavish* (1979) · B. Jennings, *Knowledge is power: a short history of the WEA, 1903–78* (1979) · L. Goldman, *Dons and workers: Oxford and adult education since 1850* (1995) · A. J. Corfield, *Epoch in workers' education: a history of the Workers' Educational Trade Union Committee* (1969) · M. Stocks, *The Workers' Educational Association: the first fifty years* (1953) · CCI (1938) · *The Labour who's who* (1927)

Archives Portsmouth city council, minutes
Likenesses portraits, repro. in Corfield, *Epoch*, facing p. 39
Wealth at death £6 3s. 2d.: confirmation, 23 Aug 1938, CCI

McTavish, Simon (1750–1804), fur trader and merchant, was born in Stratherrick, the son of John McTavish (d. 1774) of Garthbeg, a lieutenant in the 78th foot, a Highland regiment. McTavish's rise from humble beginnings to control of a mercantile empire stretching from the Labrador coast to the Canadian Rockies and the Arctic circle with trading contacts in Britain, New York, and Canton (Guangzhou) provides historians with a case study of the dynamism of diaspora Scots in the British Atlantic world. That he came from a poor family background no doubt motivated him to leave Scotland for New York about 1764.

Early career Penniless and in need of work, McTavish obtained employment in New York's thriving merchant community. The popularity of upper New York for Scottish emigrants and its commercial potential explains why McTavish petitioned unsuccessfully the governor of New York for a grant of 2000 acres on behalf of his father, who had served in the campaign against Louisbourg during the Seven Years' War. Drawn to the Great Lakes frontier and its opportunities for mercantile activities, McTavish had by 1772 established himself in Detroit, where he became connected with William Edgar, an important American merchant in that region.

McTavish arrived in the Great Lakes country at a time when it was being buffeted by the imperial government's attempts to develop a coherent strategy for administering the trans-Appalachian country. The New York fur trade had initially benefited from imperial regulations that reduced Quebec's ability to compete against the American traders by restricting trade to stipulated posts. But the restoration of the French system of trading directly with the Indians and colonial boycotts of British goods were only the beginning of a series of events that gradually drove the American traders north to Quebec. The restitution of Quebec's boundaries to their pre-conquest limits as part of the Quebec Act of 1774 and the Quebec Revenue Act were for many merchants the final blows that left them with no choice but to refocus their activities in the former French colony. McTavish echoed the sentiments of his fellow New York traders when he judged the Quebec legislation 'will be of infinite hurt to [the American fur] Trade'. By December 1774 McTavish had written to Detroit informing his partner and fellow Scot, James Bannerman, that they must 'break off [their] connection' with the fur trade centre of Schenectady, New York, and obtain their goods through Montreal (Wallace, *Documents*, 47).

Once in Montreal McTavish began to appreciate the potential of the St Lawrence watershed as a highway for commerce into the rich fur country of the Canadian north-west. McTavish and Bannerman thus became part of a small but active group that saw the enormous potential of a fur trade focused on tapping into the vast territory that was the sole preserve of the Hudson's Bay Company.

Simon McTavish (1750–1804), by unknown artist, c.1800

The American War of Independence and events surrounding the invasion of Quebec in 1775–6 convinced McTavish to break completely from the more limited American trade and re-establish himself permanently in Montreal, where he would continue to have access to British goods and markets and the rich fur country of Rupert's Land.

Move to Montreal McTavish relocated himself in Montreal at a particularly fortuitous moment. American firms with extensive London connections were moving their operations from the New York fur trade centres of Albany and Schenectady to avoid disruptions caused by political upheaval and war. Among the London firms relocated in Montreal was the well-connected firm Phyn, Ellice & Co.; McTavish's previous business association with that metropolitan company allowed him to build his Montreal interests to the point where he could claim status as an important trader with significant transatlantic connections. By 1778 McTavish and his partner, Bannerman, had at least eight canoes in the north-west. That same year colonial officials and Canadian merchants recognized that ventures west of Lake Superior had become 'an object of considerable note' (BL, Add. MS 21759, fol. 1). It was at this time that McTavish also met Benjamin and Joseph Frobisher; the Frobishers were among the first British merchants to realize the enormous potential of the north-west and had already acquired a wealth of experience trading in the area.

The Frobishers and McTavish understood that to carry on a profitable trade it was necessary to reduce damaging competition among the traders and to concentrate on maintaining logistical support for operations extending west to the far west. The solution to the challenges raised

by the long-distance trade was in the formation of alliances that would allow the 'Pedlars from Quebec' to establish trading systems capable of challenging the Hudson's Bay Company. Bannerman's retirement from the trade left McTavish free to be one of nine signatories to the agreement of 1779 which represented an attempt by the Montreal traders to eliminate destructive competition by pooling goods and contributing to the costs of the venture; under this arrangement profits would be shared in proportion to their respective contribution to the undertaking. By pooling their resources the Montreal merchants could maintain a system where they could reduce supply costs through agreements with suppliers in Detroit and Michilimackinac to supply Indian corn, peas, and flour to fur brigades passing to the north-west.

The winter of 1783–4 was particularly important for McTavish. The end of the American War of Independence, with Britain ceding the territories to the south of the Great Lakes, divided the North West Company into those who wished to continue trading south of the Great Lakes and those who believed that the north-west provided the only realistic option for British subjects. The revised company agreement of 1784 saw some partners leaving the earlier accord to concentrate on the south-west Mississippi trade while the Frobishers, McTavish, and their partners focused solely on the north-west. The new arrangement created sixteen shares, of which Benjamin and Joseph Frobisher and McTavish each held three shares. The Frobishers and McTavish set out to dominate the Quebec fur trade through the renewed company agreement; in part this was achieved by their respective houses controlling a total of six shares in the reconstituted concern. But beyond that their respective trading houses acquired the exclusive right to act as supply agents obtaining trade goods and credit in London, hiring labourers, and transporting all manner of supplies to the North West Company's forward base at Grand Portage, on the head of Lake Superior. In exchange for these services the houses of Frobisher and McTavish received a percentage fee for these services provided as well as their respective proportion of all the company's profits. Anxious to implement the agreement McTavish set out with the spring brigades to meet and subsequently secure the approval of the wintering partners at Grand Portage.

Post-war dominance The agreement of 1784 solidified the position of McTavish and the Frobishers as dominant players in the trade. But they believed that the boundary provisions of the peace treaty, which placed the critical carrying place at Grand Portage in American hands, left the trade susceptible to interference by American traders. To counter this threat, Benjamin Frobisher and McTavish vigorously lobbied colonial and metropolitan officials to grant the North West Company exclusive trading rights to the north-west for a ten-year period as recompense for the cost of developing an all British route. The Montreal traders argued that their request did not constitute a monopoly as 'they are the only persons who have any Interest or Connection in that Country' (BL, Add. MS 21877, fol. 396). McTavish and Benjamin Frobisher sought to utilize their London contacts with firms, such as Strettle, Dyer, Allan & Co., to press their case to obtain special protection of the Montreal company's interests in the far west (BL, Add. MS 21736, fols. 6–7). Despite a certain amount of sympathy on the part of imperial officials for the company's arguments, they could never win acceptance for measures that would have established time-limited monopoly rights. In any case the Montreal company pressed ahead with developing an all British route to the west by rediscovering old French trade routes via Kaministiquia. They also sought to reduce transportation costs by obtaining permission to acquire and operate three ships on the Great Lakes.

During this time fate and ambition catapulted McTavish to the forefront of the Canadian fur trade. In April 1787 Benjamin Frobisher, who was the most experienced merchant of the two brothers, died unexpectedly. McTavish immediately wrote to Joseph Frobisher proposing that they amalgamate their two firms, which together controlled about half of the North West Company. Having obtained the surviving brother's acceptance of the new arrangement, McTavish hurried to Grand Portage to defuse a tense situation arising out of the murder of John Ross, a prominent trader in the rival firm of Gregory, Macleod. McTavish responded to the crisis by reorganizing the company to absorb their rivals while maintaining control over the St Lawrence fur trade. Under the terms of the revised 1787 agreement McTavish and Frobisher continued to be solely responsible for financing, importing trade goods, hiring men, and handling the sales of pelts. McTavish moved to strengthen his London contacts by renewing agreements with Strettle, Dyer, Allan & Co. and Brickwood, Pattle & Co. to supply goods and credit to finance the company's activities. While Brickwood and Pattle declined the invitation the firm of Phyn, Ellice, Inglis & Co. agreed to supply the other half of McTavish and Frobisher's needs. The growing complexity of the North West Company's business and McTavish's desire to protect McTavish and Frobisher's control over the lucrative London–Montreal supply business stirred McTavish to use a visit to Britain as an opportunity to found his own London house, McTavish, Fraser & Co. The new entity was managed by his cousin, John Fraser, who had experience in the Canada export trade and numerous contacts in the metropolis, would obtain trade goods, and would dispose of North West Company pelts on the London market. Thus through the establishment of McTavish and Fraser in concert with his interests in McTavish and Frobisher and the North West Company the Scottish merchant had risen from relative obscurity to effectively control a vast commercial empire in little more than a decade.

In the 1790s threats to British shipping and European markets during the Napoleonic wars forced McTavish to develop new markets for North West Company furs. James Cook's voyages in the north Pacific had made British merchants alive to the rich fur resources of the Pacific north-west and the demand for high-value pelts in Chinese markets. McTavish, Fraser & Co. undertook to ship furs to China, but the difficulties of getting their china, porcelain, and other trade returns back to London in East India Company ships, combined with onerous duties, meant that they incurred a loss of £40,000 between 1792 and 1795. In January 1798 McTavish sent the celebrated Alexander Mackenzie, explorer and new partner in McTavish, Fraser & Co., to New York to negotiate with American merchants to act as marketing agents for the company's furs in Canton. McTavish found this option particularly attractive as it would allow McTavish and Fraser discreetly to circumvent the East India Company's monopoly on the China trade by smuggling furs from Canada to New York for shipment to the Far East. However, Mackenzie was able to convince McTavish that it would be more effective if they acquired their own ships, the *Nancy* and the *Northern Liberties*, to enable them to conduct the China trade more independently. The China trade became more important as war in Europe intensified but it also caused problems as the proportion of fine-grade pelts going to China meant that prime furs for the London market were in short supply. This drove John Fraser to complain to McTavish that a balance must be struck or the North West Company would lose its pre-eminent place in London markets.

Challenges to trade and further expansion The Napoleonic wars were not the only challenge to McTavish's hold on critical markets. Throughout the 1790s he was constantly struggling to maintain the North West Company's position in the face of new combinations. Often disgruntled traders were in the forefront of those willing to try and loosen the company's hold on the trade. Jay's treaty of 1794 forced many traders to abandon their traditional territory to the south-west of the Great Lakes in favour of the country long occupied by the Nor' Westers. In 1792 McTavish had been able to defuse rising discontent among many of the south-west traders by yet again expanding the company's share base to accommodate them. But feeling slighted by McTavish's offer of a very minor share in the new entity the Montreal firm of Forsyth, Richardson & Co., a subsidiary of the influential London house Phyn, Ellice, Inglis & Co., spent 1797 and 1798 organizing a partnership with Leith, Jamieson & Co. and a group of disgruntled winterers to challenge the company's hold on the fur trade. The New North West Company, or the X. Y. Company as it was popularly known, dealt a serious blow to McTavish's concern when in 1800 Alexander Mackenzie was convinced to join its ranks. Mackenzie's popularity with the North West Company's clerks and winterers as well as his influence in London allowed the upstart company to pose serious competition for the Nor' Westers.

McTavish took the establishing of the X. Y. Company to be a personal affront to his authority. Reflecting the bitterness of this competition one commentator observed that the rivalry between McTavish and Mackenzie was 'stimulated by revenge and interest to ruin each other' ('Some account', 61). McTavish's first response to the rival company's challenge was to address the winterers' and clerks' frustration that their opportunities for advancement were limited by, once again, bringing in more partners. He asserted his authority by ensuring that McTavish and Frobisher maintained an even stronger role as the exclusive supplier of trade goods and seller of company furs. While mounting a vigorous campaign against the X. Y. Company McTavish also launched an attack on the sleepy monopoly held by the Hudson's Bay Company. In 1802 he was part of a group that obtained a lease for the king's posts that not only allowed them the exclusive right to the trade and fisheries on the Labrador coast but let his company directly challenge the Hudson's Bay Company's hold on the James Bay fur trade by occupying a post on the headwaters of the Rupert River. In 1803 the Montreal company sent a ship into Hudson Bay to set up a post on Charlton Island and a smaller post on Moose River to compete in the London company's backyard.

The rapid growth of North West Company interests and vicious competition between the three fur trade concerns made McTavish devote much of his energy to organizing an efficient trading network. Furthermore, European wars not only caused havoc in global markets but also led to higher labour costs and shortfalls. Scarcity of grain had led to shortages that made prices attractive for habitants who previously looked to the fur trade economy to supplement subsistence farming activities. As the North West Company pushed ever westward in search of new sources of pelts there was greater need to man supply lines at a time when competition was most acute and labour was in short supply.

The development of McTavish's commercial activities on a global scale also meant that his companies had to maintain offices in New York and London as well as Montreal. McTavish drew on family and clan connections to meet his need for loyal and competent merchants. Particularly after 1798, when Joseph Frobisher retired, McTavish had a free hand to promote those he favoured to the upper ranks of his various concerns. William and Duncan McGillivray, nephews from a poor family, had their education paid for by McTavish and were brought into the concern. William was eventually McTavish's successor and Duncan served as an explorer and winterer. John Fraser, his cousin and partner in the London supply house McTavish and Fraser, was joined by McTavish's youngest nephew, Simon McGillivray. Roderick Mackenzie, his cousin, was taken out by McTavish and after an apprenticeship became a partner in the North West Company. James Hallowell and his son William, two of McTavish's countrymen, served the company well. John McDonald of Garth owed his apprenticeship to McTavish's friendship with General Small, his great-uncle. The promotion of family and friends within the company often provoked ill feeling on the part of those who saw their prospects dashed by those connected with McTavish. Indeed the defection of Alexander Mackenzie to the X. Y. Company was partly due to a clash of egos, 'as there could not be two Caesars in Rome', and Mackenzie's perception that McTavish favoured his nephew William McGillivray as his successor (*Askin Papers*, 2.275). Despite McTavish's preference for promoting family members and clansmen, the company's interests were paramount. McTavish might

have extended a paternalistic hand of patronage to many but he still demanded that they serve an apprenticeship to demonstrate their competence before they were raised within the ranks.

Social life and final years With McTavish's interests in capable hands he could devote more energy to other aspects of his life. Considering his almost complete dedication to the fur trade it is not surprising that when he did marry, in October 1793, aged forty-three, his young bride of eighteen was Marie-Marguerite Chaboillez, the daughter of Jean-Baptiste, a Canadian fur trader. The Nor' Wester's marriage was typical of many between Quebec's Scottish merchant élite and a family closely tied to the old French colonial regime; it is telling that although the marriage was held in the Scottish Presbyterian church McTavish still maintained a pew in the Catholic church for his new wife. The theme of the new maintaining contact with the old was echoed throughout all aspects of McTavish's life. As has been noted, McTavish's preference for employing family and members of the clan Tavish was but one example of his continued connections with the land of his birth. In 1794 while visiting Britain with Marie-Marguerite, McTavish visited Lachlin McTavish, the head of the clan Tavish, whom he found in serious financial difficulties. McTavish readily assisted the chief, obtaining a grant of his armorial bearings, and later undertook to pay for the education of the chief's second son, John George McTavish, and to bring him into the trade, as well as to purchase the McTavish ancestral home, Dunardary.

In Montreal McTavish was known for his hospitality as well as a driving ambition to dominate the fur trade. His ambition to control the trade and to develop a powerful transatlantic trading house earned him the epithets the Premier and the Marquis among disgruntled wintering partners (Masson, 1, appx, 44). But the negative image of the hard-driving merchant accepted by many historians belies a much more complex individual. What little correspondence of the Scottish merchant has survived indicates that he was a bon vivant who requested that his correspondents supply him with the latest gossip, and that he professed his love of 'good cheer viz good Wine, good Oysters, and pretty Girls' (Wallace, *Documents*, 48). In 1786 he was a founder member of the Beaver Club, in which members were restricted to gentlemen who had wintered in the north-west but who entertained guests as illustrious as the duke of Kent with prodigious quantities of food and drink. McTavish's generosity and loyalty extended beyond family members. In 1802 McTavish pledged to his friend Commodore Alexander Grant of Detroit that he would 'take care of his [son's] education and prospects in life' if he would send him down to Montreal for that purpose (*Askin Papers*, 2.357). Despite McTavish's sudden death in 1804 a promise made in life was recognized in death—the Nor' Wester's will bequeathed a £1000 legacy to ensure that his undertaking was provided for.

The final years of McTavish's life were extremely active ones. Besides administering a vast fur trade empire the

Marquis showed an interest in developing new commercial interests. In 1796 he purchased the seigneury of Terrebonne, near Montreal, where he operated a store, a bakery, and two flour mills. He also purchased a large parcel of land in Chester county. When McTavish married he had purchased the Montreal house he had long rented but, as befitted the richest man in the colony, he set about building a mansion that was all but finished when he died, at his home, as the result of complications arising from a cold, on 6 July 1804. He was buried on 9 July. In many ways McTavish's last will and testament gives more insight into his priorities than the few surviving letters written in his hand. McTavish's generosity, loyalty to his friends, and his extensive network of family and clansmen with whom he maintained contact are revealed in a will in which, in addition to leaving bequests to relatives, friends, and servants, he even left £1000 for 'assisting such of my poor relatives in Scotland as I may have neglected to provide for'. McTavish's wealth, which amounted to more than £125,000, left his widow and four children well provided for. But his attachment to his Scottish roots is apparent in the proviso that if neither of his sons lived to the age of majority the residual of his estate, valued at £60,000, would be transferred to his nearest male relative, while Dunardary, seat of the McTavishes, would be inherited only if he assumed the name McTavish. Like his family name and its association with his Scottish roots, McTavish sought to ensure the perpetuation of the vast commercial empire that he had fought so hard to build—no legacies over 100 guineas were to be paid out of his estate until seven years after his death and then only if there was 'sufficient money for that purpose … without loss … to the concerns in which I am now a partner' (Wallace, *Documents*, 140).   K. DAVID MILOBAR

Sources L. R. Masson, ed., *Les bourgeois de la Compagnie du Nord-Ouest: récits de voyages, lettres et rapports inédits relatifs au Nord-Ouest canadien*, 2 vols. (Quebec, 1889–90) • letter-book of McTavish, Frobisher & Co., NA Canada, MG 19:5 • W. S. Wallace, ed., *Documents relating to the North West Company* (1934) • *The journals and letters of Sir Alexander Mackenzie*, ed. W. Kaye Lamb, Hakluyt Society, extra ser., 41 (1970) • *John Askin papers*, ed. M. M. Quaife, 2 vols. (1928–31) • BL, MSS of Fredrick Haldimand, Add. MSS 21661–21892 • PRO, colonial office MSS, CO 42 • 'Some account of the trade carried on by the North West Company', 1809, *Report of the public archives of Canada for 1928* (1929) • W. S. Wallace, *The pedlars from Quebec and other papers on the Nor' Westers* (1954) • R. H. Fleming, 'McTavish, Frobisher and Company of Montreal', *Canadian Historical Review*, 10 (1929), 136–52 • H. A. Innis, *The fur trade in Canada* (1984) • R. H. Fleming, 'Phyn, Ellice and Company of Schenectady', *Contributions to Canadian Economics* (1932), 7–41 • *Quebec Gazette* (12 July 1804)
Archives NA Canada, letter-book of McTavish, Frobisher & Co.
Likenesses portrait, *c.*1800, NA Canada [*see illus.*] • J. Hoppner, portrait, NA Canada
Wealth at death £125,000: Wallace, ed., *Documents*

McTier [*née* Drennan], **Martha** (1742–1837), letter writer and political commentator, was the eldest of three surviving children of Thomas *Drennan (1696–1768) [*see under* Drennan, William], a non-subscribing Presbyterian minister, and his wife, Ann Lennox (*c.*1719–1806). Nothing is known of her education, but she probably received some lessons from her father, a leading figure in Belfast intellectual circles and a liberal in politics and religion.

Following her father's death, the family member to whom Martha was closest was her brother William *Drennan (1754–1820), physician and political reformer. In 1769 William went to Scotland to study medicine, and in 1776 he and Martha began a forty-year correspondence that embraced discussion of political and literary affairs as well as family news and details of domestic and social life. Following William's return to Ireland in 1778 he became involved in the Volunteer movement, whose objective of political and parliamentary reform he championed in his writings. Martha's views were similarly radical: in 1792, writing approvingly of the French Revolution, she expressed the hope that Irish reformers would 'keep arms in their hands, think and act with liberality, speak out boldly, and watch each happy moment thrown in their way by others, and they cannot fail of an easy conquest over their oppressors' (*Drennan–McTier Letters*, 1.418).

In 1773 Martha married Samuel McTier (*c.*1738–1795), a Belfast merchant. The marriage was happy, marred only by periodic financial problems and by Martha's ill health. During the 1780s she developed a number of complaints diagnosed as largely nervous in origin, and in 1789 suffered a breakdown from which she did not fully recover until 1792. By that year she was reporting 'a renewal of her wonted spirits' (*Drennan–McTier Letters*, 1.417). Her recovery coincided with a heightening of political tensions in Ireland. The Society of United Irishmen, inspired by French revolutionary ideals, was founded in 1791, with William as its leading propagandist. Sam McTier was a prominent member of the Belfast society, and the McTier home became a centre of United Irish activity. Martha's known radicalism and her correspondence with William made her a target of government surveillance, and in 1797 she was forced to deny rumours that she had written articles for the United Irish newspaper, the *Northern Star*. However, she certainly acted as a conduit for information, and may have collaborated with William on some of his political writings.

Neither William nor Martha was directly involved in the 1798 United Irish rising. However, Martha, while repeatedly denying any knowledge of subversive activities, retained a strong sympathy for the radical cause—she was described by an acquaintance at this time as 'a violent republican' (*Drennan–McTier Letters*, 2.421). In the aftermath of the rising she lamented the 'most awful prospect' of 'this ill-fated country', and the 'detested, presumptuous, impolitic punishment' meted out by the authorities to former insurgents (ibid., 2.507). She strongly opposed the Act of Union (1800), describing its advocates as 'the meanest, most wicked and detestable set of tame, interested, cold-hearted cowards ever infested a country' (ibid., 2.547). Like her brother, however, she opposed Robert Emmet's rising of 1803, favouring the reversal of the Union by constitutional rather than violent means.

Sam McTier died in 1795, leaving Martha in financial difficulties and dependent on the generosity of relatives, but she found a new focus of affection in William's son Tom, who lived with her from 1803 until 1807 when William and the rest of his family settled in Belfast. The move brought the regular correspondence between brother and sister to an end. However, they continued to write to each other during William's occasional absences from Belfast, and it is clear that both retained a lively interest in politics and a caustic awareness of the prejudices and peculiarities of their fellows into old age. Martha McTier died in Belfast in 1837, aged ninety-five.

ROSEMARY RAUGHTER

Sources *The Drennan–McTier letters*, ed. J. Agnew, 3 vols. (1998–9) • *The Drennan letters*, ed. D. A. Chart (1931) • D. Keogh and N. Furlong, eds., *The women of 1798* (1998) • N. J. Curtin, 'Women and 18th century Irish Republicanism', *Women in early modern Ireland*, ed. M. MacCurtain and M. O'Dowd (Dublin, 1991), 133–46
Archives PRO NIre., corresp. with William Drennan, Duffin (Drennan) papers
Likenesses R. Home?, oils, c.1787, priv. coll. • portrait (as a child), priv. coll. • silhouette, priv. coll.

McVail, John Christie (1849–1926), physician and public health administrator, was born in Kilmarnock on 22 October 1849, the second son of James McVail and his wife, Jean Christie. After an early education in Kilmarnock he studied medicine at Glasgow and St Andrews, where he graduated MB, CM, with high honours in 1873. Two years later he graduated MD and entered private practice in Kilmarnock, encouraged by John Borland, the town's leading medical figure.

McVail developed an early interest in vital statistics and public health. In 1885 he took the Cambridge diploma in public health and succeeded Borland as medical officer of health for Kilmarnock and as physician to the Kilmarnock Infirmary. McVail combined these offices with private practice until 1891, when he left Kilmarnock to become the first full-time medical officer of health for the joint counties of Stirling and Dumbarton, formed under the Local Government Act (Scotland) 1889. This post gave him a basis for his pioneering work in Scottish public health.

A large man with large ideas which he vigorously expressed in speech and writings, McVail had already published work on smallpox and vaccination. He appeared before the royal commission on vaccination (1892–3) as an expert on the disease and in 1907 the BMA awarded him the Jenner medal. From 1887 to 1889, and again in 1905, he was president of the Sanitary Association of Scotland. In 1909 he produced a special report on the housing of miners for the Scottish Local Government Board. He also became the expert witness in the sometimes fraught boundary disputes dealt with by the Scottish burgh and county health administration. In 1907 he was appointed medical examiner for the royal commission on poor laws, and, unusually, he reported on the poor-law system covering England and Wales. McVail had a firm commitment to the voluntary principle in general and to workers' insurance schemes in particular: he acted as medical adviser to the Kilmarnock Foresters friendly society.

When the National Health Insurance scheme came into operation in 1912, McVail was appointed deputy chairman of the National Health Insurance Commission for Scotland. In 1919 the board of health for Scotland replaced the insurance commission and the Local Government Board, and McVail and his long-term colleague Leslie Mackenzie became the new board's medical members. Both men were members of the Dewar committee of 1912, whose recommendations formed the basis of the Highlands and Islands Medical Service, instituted in 1913, and both served on its board. During the First World War, McVail gave great service on the emergency committee.

Early in his career McVail was a frequent contributor to the *British Medical Journal*. He was an active member of the British Medical Association, becoming president of the Glasgow and west of Scotland branch in 1905. He was a member of the constitution committee which drafted the association's new constitution in 1901, and later he wrote a historical sketch in the *British Medical Journal* of the steps leading to the changed constitution. McVail presided over the state medicine and medical sociology sections of various BMA congresses. In 1922 he received the Alexander Patrick Stewart prize for research into the origin, spread, and prevention of epidemic disease, at the association's Glasgow meeting. Although involved in the practical application of public health administration, McVail also kept in touch with the academic teaching of his subject. For many years he was external examiner in public health and forensic medicine for all four Scottish universities. In 1908 the University of Glasgow conferred on him the honorary degree of LLD. In 1912 he was appointed crown nominee for Scotland on the General Medical Council, succeeding his elder brother, Sir David McVail, in the post.

McVail married Jessie Schoolbred, daughter of John Rowat, on 17 June 1877. They had two sons and two daughters, of whom a son and a daughter followed their father into the medical profession. McVail was a friend of John Glaister, professor of public health and forensic medicine at Glasgow, and their families were united when McVail's eldest son, Dr John Borland McVail, married one of Glaister's daughters. McVail was a staunch Liberal and a member of the Evangelical Union Congregational church.

Ill health forced McVail to retire from public service in 1922. He lived in Golders Green, Middlesex, for some time afterwards, but later moved to Netherway, Falkland Road, Torquay, where he died on 29 July 1926. He was an acknowledged giant in Scottish public health, and many expressed surprise at the lack of recognition of his services.

BRENDA M. WHITE

Sources *BMJ* (7 Aug 1926) • *The Lancet* (7 Aug 1926) • *Kilmarnock Standard* (31 July 1926) • Kilmarnock parish registers, The Dick Institute, Kilmarnock • M. A. Crowther and B. White, *On soul and conscience: the medical expert and crime* (1988) • T. Ferguson, *Scottish social welfare, 1864–1914* (1958) • D. Hamilton, *The healers* (1981) • D. Hamilton, 'The highlands and islands medical services', *Improving the commonweal: aspects of Scottish health services, 1900–1984*, ed. G. McLachlan (1987) • *Medical Directory* (1902) • private information (1998) • d. cert. • CGPLA Eng. & Wales (1926)
Likenesses photograph, repro. in *BMJ*

Macvicar, John (c.1795–1858/9), textile merchant and civic leader, is a figure about whom nothing is known before his marriage to Isabella Burn (b. 1799), in January 1821 at

South Leith, Midlothian. He remains strangely elusive to the historian, though an important figure in Britain's early nineteenth-century trade with China. For more than anyone, Macvicar promoted and inspired the export of cotton products to exploit the demise of the East India Company's monopoly of the China trade in 1833. He constituted a vital nexus in the trade's supporting infrastructure, providing a personal link and a measure of co-ordination between the disparate worlds of the Canton (Guangzhou) merchant, the Lancashire manufacturer, and the political lobby.

At first dependent on the agency services provided by the older houses in the Far East, Macvicar gradually took all stages of the trade into his own hands. Between 1823 and 1829 John Macvicar & Co., 'agents general and commercial', were located at 4 Barges Yard, Bucklersbury, London, with interests as far afield as Havana. An exploratory visit to the East about 1830 revealed a potential demand for British cotton piece-goods in spite of increasing American competition from the looms of Lowell, Massachusetts. In addition to a partnership with his brother-in-law, David Burn, in Bombay, agency agreements were sealed with Purvis & Co. in Singapore, Anderson and Wardrop in Penang, and Jardines in Canton.

Frustration with Jardines and their apparent sluggishness caused ill-feeling on both sides in the mid-1830s. Hardly their pawn, as once suggested, Macvicar had his own objectives to secure and by 1838 Macvicar & Co. itself was established in Canton, acting as agent for the Bombay Commercial Insurance Society. Surviving the First Opium War (1839–42) Macvicars was still in business at the 'new English factory' in Canton in 1848, having participated in the foundation of Hong Kong by purchasing lots in the first land sale of 1841.

Macvicar's interests lay decidedly with the home manufacturer, and from the early 1830s he was resident in Manchester at 48 Mosley Street. As a partner in the Manchester calico-printing firm of Butterworth and Brooks, and with his links through John Brooks to the Blackburn bankers Cunliffe Brooks & Co., he was well-connected in Lancastrian industrial circles; this attribute was invaluable in Macvicar's successful promotion of the Union Bank of Manchester, of which he had been a founder director in 1836. Cotton was Manchester's lifeblood, and, as continental European and American manufacturing gathered pace, British producers anxiously eyed new outlets to replace those disappearing. However, Macvicar and his associate Samuel Gregson probably over-promoted the potential of China and fostered exaggerated expectations among manufacturers who included Horrocks of Preston, producers of a celebrated cambric much in vogue in Canton.

Macvicar's position as a director and vice-president of the Manchester chamber of commerce, together with his business link with Gregson, later a chairman of the East India and China Association, established him as the leading advocate of the local China interest. As the prime mover behind the chamber of commerce's memorial of February 1836 on the 'unprotected state of trade with China', he can be credited with being the first to throw the weight of British manufacturing behind the lobby to encourage the British government to adopt a coercive or 'forward policy' towards China. Macvicar's credibility as a spokesman was accepted at the highest levels and in October 1839, accompanied by a Mr Garnett of Clitheroe, he briefed Palmerston on the concerns of the manufacturers as war with China loomed.

As both Jardines and Gregson discovered to their cost, Macvicar was a difficult man to handle. Yet he was not totally self-interested. He took his civic responsibilities seriously at a time when the town of Manchester was witnessing both administrative change and social stress. His record as borough reeve (or chief officer) in 1835–6 was sufficiently impressive to warrant further service, following the introduction of a borough council, as alderman for the Oxford ward between 1838 and 1841 (when he was an exact contemporary of Richard Cobden), and as a justice of the borough up to 1852. Together with his support of the Royal Manchester Institution as an annual governor, this at least provides a glimmer of altruism. It is not known whether Macvicar had children. His death is recorded in the minutes of the annual general meeting of 27 July 1859 of the Union Bank of Manchester.

PHILIP K. LAW

Sources W. E. Cheong, *Mandarins and merchants: Jardine Matheson & Co., a China agency of the early nineteenth century* (1979) · M. Greenberg, *British trade and the opening of China, 1800–42* (1951) · *Canton Press* (1838–44) · *Chinese Repository*, 7–17 (1838–48) · trade directories, London, 1820–29 · trade directories, Manchester (1830–60) · letter, 20 June 1828, ING Barings, London, Barings archives, house correspondence, HC 3.7 · Man. CL, Borough reeves' and constables' MSS, M6/1/49/3, p. 24 · A. Redford, *The history of local government in Manchester*, 3 vols. (1939–40) · L. H. Grindon, *Manchester banks and bankers: historical, biographical, and anecdotal* (1877) · IGI

Macvicar, John Gibson (1800–1884), Church of Scotland minister and writer, was born on 16 March 1800 at Dundee, the second son of Patrick Macvicar, minister of St Paul's, Dundee, and his first wife Agnes, daughter of John Gibson, minister of Mains, Forfarshire. From Dundee grammar school Macvicar entered St Andrews University in 1814 where he won a prize for mathematics and a medal for natural philosophy. He then went to Edinburgh University where he studied chemistry, anatomy, and natural history alongside rhetoric, Hebrew, and church history. His first papers, on the germination of ferns and on the air pump, were given at this time.

Macvicar was licensed to preach by the presbytery of Dundee but before receiving a call he was appointed in 1827 to a new lectureship in natural history at St Andrews, and received an honorary MA from there in 1828; the lectureship was advanced to a chair in 1830. Also in 1828 he was appointed editor of the *Quarterly Journal of Agriculture*, started under the auspices of the Highland and Agricultural Society of Scotland. He began the formation of a museum at St Andrews, and lectured there and at the Watt Institution, Dundee, which he had helped to promote. During this time he published *Elements of the Economy of Nature, or, The Principles of Physics, Chemistry and Physiology* (1830, second edition 1856), and *Inquiries Concerning the*

Medium of Light and the Form of its Molecules (1833). In both books he sought to explain the recent advances in molecular science and to resolve these with religious teaching, a subject to which he returned in later years.

On 25 December 1839 Macvicar was ordained chaplain to a new branch of the Scottish church in Ceylon. He married on 2 January 1840 Jessie Robertson MacDonald (*d.* 1900), daughter of Lieutenant-Colonel David Robertson MacDonald; all but the last two of their four sons and five daughters were born in Ceylon where Macvicar was minister of St Andrew's Church, Colombo. His overseas service ended in 1852 and in July 1853 he was inducted into the parish of Moffat, Dumfriesshire, where he remained for the rest of his life. In 1856 he applied for the chair of logic and metaphysics in the University of Edinburgh, vacated on the death of Sir William Hamilton, on the basis of his published works and testimonies commending his theology and his ability to preach with style and clarity, but he did not secure the appointment. His obituarist in *The Scotsman* described his theology as 'broad, living and thorough'. He published several more books on science, philosophy, and religion, much of his earlier material being recycled in these texts. He was ill during the last ten years of his life, and died at the manse, Moffat, on 12 February 1884.   ANITA MCCONNELL

Sources *Fasti Scot.* · *The Scotsman* (13 Feb 1884) · *The Athenaeum* (16 Feb 1884), 220 · *Testimonials in favour of John Gibson Macvicar* (1856) · m. cert. · d. cert.
Archives U. Edin., New Coll. L., letters to Thomas Chalmers · U. Newcastle, Robinson L., letters to Sir Walter Trevelyan · UCL, letters to G. C. Robertson
Wealth at death £2685 5s. 3d.: confirmation, 15 May 1884, *CCI*

McVitie, Robert (1809–1883), baker and confectioner, was born at Nunholm, Dumfries, the son of William McVitie, farmer, and his wife, Jean Green. His father was a failed poet and a friend of Sir Walter Scott, who used his name in *Rob Roy*. After an apprenticeship to a Dumfries baker, Robert McVitie joined his father in Edinburgh, where he helped to run a provision shop in a tenement house in Rose Street that had been inherited from an uncle. When his father returned to Dumfries, McVitie continued to keep the shop. He moved to Charlotte Place and on 30 January 1844 married Catherine, daughter of William Gairns. They had two sons and two daughters.

By 1856 McVitie was advertising himself as a baker and confectioner, the baking being carried out in the shop basement. His two sons were apprenticed as bakers in the firm, and as the business grew McVitie was able to open other retail outlets and to send his sons to the continent, to learn French and German and to study European baking methods. On their return, the firm introduced Vienna bread to Edinburgh and described itself as 'Boulangerie Française et Viennoise'. McVitie retired in 1880, and died from cancer on 21 November 1883 at 6 Mansfield Place, Edinburgh. His wife had predeceased him.

The business was continued by their younger son **Robert McVitie** (1854–1910). Born in Edinburgh he spent his whole working life in the family business, from apprenticeship onwards. His experience, gained on the continent

and elsewhere, convinced him that there was a considerable untapped market for fancy biscuits and similar snack items. As his elder brother had already left the business to become a journalist, he took charge of the firm on his father's retirement. He occupied larger premises in Merchant Street, where he made shortbread and oatcakes as well as biscuits. These won a gold medal and a certificate of excellence at the Calcutta Exhibition of 1883–4. He made a wedding cake for the future George V and Queen Mary, in 1893, and later christening cakes for their children.

Leaving the production side to his manager, Alexander Ross, McVitie opened up distribution centres in England. In 1887 he engaged Alexander Grant, who was soon made foreman. That year he visited plants in the United States to learn about the latest biscuit-making technology, and he made a further visit twelve years later. Then in 1888 Charles Edward Price (*d.* 1934), a former traveller for Cadburys, became a partner of what was renamed McVitie and Price; he concentrated on the marketing side, but retired in 1901 and served as Liberal MP for Central Edinburgh from 1906 to 1918.

The bread and catering activities were now carried out by a separate firm, which in 1898 was named McVities Guest & Co., the other partner being Edward Graham Guest, McVitie's brother-in-law. In 1902 they opened a modern, air-conditioned building in Princes Street.

When Price left the biscuit firm Grant was appointed general manager, and he and McVitie worked hard for much of the decade on starting up a branch factory in London. With the dependable Grant in charge of the Edinburgh activities, McVitie came to spend most of his time in London, and he also built a residence at Northchurch, near Berkhamsted, Hertfordshire, where he lived with his wife, Louisa Elizabeth, daughter of William Thompson; they had no children. For a time he represented the chamber of commerce on the board of management of the Royal Infirmary in Edinburgh, and he was a member of the Merchant Company there.

McVitie had unsuccessfully contested an Edinburgh ward for the town council as a Unionist, and in London he maintained his political links by becoming president of the Harlesden Conservative Association. He was also patron of several charitable institutions. His outside directorships included that of the Employers' Mutual Insurance Association of Scotland Ltd. A quiet, industrious, and conscientious man, he chose able managers to assist him in making the firm one of the leading biscuit manufacturers in Britain. However, his exertions clearly shortened his life; he died, aged only fifty-six, on 15 July 1910, at his home, Woodcock Hill, Northchurch, near Berkhamsted, and was buried on 19 July at Dean cemetery, Edinburgh.

T. A. B. CORLEY

Sources J. S. Adam, *A fell fine baker: the story of United Biscuits* (1974) · *The Times* (18 July 1910) [Robert McVitie, son] · *The Scotsman* (18 July 1910) [Robert McVitie, son] · *Edinburgh Evening News* (16 July 1910) [Robert McVitie, son] · W. McVitie, *The affecting history of Lady Bertha, a poem* (1805) · 'McVitties, Guest & Co. Ltd', *Edinburgh Tatler*, 3/23 (1963), 24–5 · m. cert. · d. cert. · *CGPLA Eng. & Wales* (1910) [Robert McVitie, son]

Archives NA Scot., GD 381 (United Biscuits) 3/1–35 McVitie and Price
Likenesses Moffatt, photograph, repro. in *The Scotsman*
Wealth at death £1505 3*s*. 8*d*.: confirmation, 12 Feb 1884, *CCI* · £154 10*s*. 0*d*.: additional inventory, 8 Nov 1884, *CCI* · £227,454— Robert McVitie, son: Scottish probate sealed in London, 9 Dec 1910, *CCI*

McVitie, Robert (1854–1910). *See under* McVitie, Robert (1809–1883).

McVittie, George Cunliffe (1904–1988), astronomer and cryptanalyst, was born on 5 June 1904 in Smyrna, Turkey, the eldest of three children (two sons and a daughter) of Francis Skinner McVittie (1872–1950), businessman, and his wife, Emily Caroline (1877–1942), daughter of George Weber from Alsace. McVittie was educated privately by tutors, notably the Revd Lucius Fry, under whose gifted teaching he covered most of a normal secondary education in two years. The family were on holiday in England when the Turks sacked Smyrna in 1922. The McVitties lost everything and never returned to Turkey. Help from a group of largely anonymous businessmen enabled McVittie, after a year's delay, to read mathematics and natural philosophy (physics) at Edinburgh University, where he studied under Sir Edmund Whittaker and Sir Charles Galton Darwin. After obtaining an MA with first-class honours in 1927, he moved to Cambridge to research unified field theories of gravitation and electromagnetism under Sir Arthur Eddington, whose remoteness he found a sharp contrast to the warmth of Whittaker and Darwin. His PhD dissertation solved the Maxwell–Einstein equations of general relativity for a specific case, and found corresponding solutions for three unified field theories (one being Einstein's), but with unfavourable results for them. On 3 September 1934 he married Mildred Bond (*b.* 1906), daughter of John Strong, professor of education at Leeds University. They had no children. After spells as a lecturer at Leeds and Liverpool universities, McVittie was appointed reader in mathematics at King's College, London, in 1936. His first book, *Cosmological Theory*, appeared in 1937.

In November 1939, following a short self-organized course in meteorology, McVittie joined the Government Code and Cypher School at Bletchley Park. After training briefly under Colonel J. H. Tiltman and J. E. S. Cooper he formed a meteorological subsection, as part of the air section in Hut 10, to attack the weather codes of Germany and her allies. The subsection also broke Soviet meteorological codes even after the Soviet Union entered the war in June 1941, so as to keep Winston Churchill informed about developments on the Eastern Front, and to help in solving German weather codes.

Although initially understaffed, McVittie's group comprised sixty people at its height in November 1943. McVittie was an excellent organizer, who also solved countless ciphers himself. Under his inspired leadership the group produced invaluable results. Solved keys were sent to a Meteorological Office group, IDA, at Dunstable, to decipher messages intercepted there. By February 1944 about 15,000 enciphered weather reports were being intercepted daily. IDA transmitted the deciphered texts to various allied commands to provide weather forecasts for operations, especially against German-held territory, and for intelligence generally.

The group's solution of a *Kriegsmarine* meteorological cipher, combined with a codebook captured from *U 559* in late October 1942, enabled Hugh Alexander and his team in Hut 8 to end a ten-month blackout on Shark, the Atlantic U-boats' four-rotor Enigma cipher, in mid-December 1942, despite only having three-rotor bombes (high-speed key finding aids). The blackout had almost blinded naval intelligence in the Atlantic; the solution helped to provide the indispensable cribs (probable plain text) required by the bombes. Bletchley's head, Edward Travis, later told Cooper that reading Shark had cut shipping losses in the Atlantic in December 1942 and January 1943 from an expected 1.2 million tons to about 450,000 tons.

McVittie returned to King's College in 1945, mentally and physically exhausted by the constant strain of code-breaking for almost five years: he did not recover until late in 1947. He was appointed professor of mathematics at Queen Mary College, London, in 1948, but the post did not offer him enough scope. He therefore accepted the chair of astronomy at the University of Illinois in 1952, although the department had no staff, students, or modern instruments. He transformed it into a major centre which, when he left, had world-class radio and optical telescopes, and a considerable research reputation. McVittie believed that an extensive catalogue of cosmic radio sources would help to distinguish between different cosmological theories. From 1958 to 1969 his department's new 400 foot radio telescope mapped major portions of the Milky Way, found many new sources and catalogued about a thousand sources. He retired to Canterbury in 1972, where, as honorary professor of theoretical astronomy in the University of Kent, he taught astronomy and mathematics. A gifted lecturer, he was still teaching in 1987. He also continued his research, publishing an impressive paper on perfect fluid configurations when he was eighty.

McVittie's contributions to astronomy lie principally in theoretical astrophysics. Although his papers were mathematically based he described himself as an 'uncompromising empiricist'; they therefore also stressed the importance of observation. As a cosmologist he was celebrated for his penetrating comparisons of observational data with model universes. His *General Relativity and Cosmology* (1956, 1964) is a superb example of such an approach, while his *Fact and Theory in Cosmology* (1961) made cosmology understandable by a wider readership.

A major part of his research concerned spherically symmetric solutions of the equations of general relativity (corresponding to spherical distributions of fluid). His wartime meteorological work led him to research hydrodynamics and gas dynamics in the light of relativity. He was elected a fellow of the Royal Astronomical Society in 1931, of the Royal Society of Edinburgh in 1943, and was appointed OBE in 1946 for his outstanding wartime service. In 1984 the International Astronomical Union recognized his many achievements by naming minor planet 2417 'McVittie'. McVittie died in the Chaucer Hospital, Canterbury, on 8 March 1988. RALPH ERSKINE

Sources R. Chisholm, 'George McVittie: honorary professor, University of Kent', *Vistas in Astronomy*, 33 (1990), 79–81 · *Daily Telegraph* (18 March 1988) · W. Davidson, 'George McVittie's work in relativity', *Vistas in Astronomy*, 33 (1990), 65–9 · R. Erskine, 'Kriegsmarine short signal systems—and how Bletchley Park exploited them', *Cryptologia*, 23/1 (1999), 65–92 · R. Erskine, 'Naval Enigma: the breaking of Heimisch and Triton', *Intelligence and National Security*, 3/1 (1988), 162–83 · private information (2004) [J. Pulokas, A. McVittie] · M. A. H. MacCullum, *Quarterly Journal of the Royal Astronomical Society*, 30 (1989), 119–24 · W. McCrea, 'George Cunliffe McVittie (1904–88) OBE, FRSE, pupil of Whittaker and Eddington: pioneer of modern cosmology', *Vistas in Astronomy*, 33 (1990), 43–58 · G. C. McVittie, 'Autobiographical sketch', CAC Cam. [prepared for Royal Society of Edinburgh] · A. H. Schrieffer, K.-S. Yang, and G. W. Swenson, 'The Illinois 120-foot radio telescope', *Sky and Telescope*, 41 (1971), 132–8 · G. W. Swenson jun., 'Building a department of astronomy', *Vistas in Astronomy*, 33 (1990), 71–3 · G. W. Swenson jun., 'Reminiscence: the Illinois 400-foot radio telescope', *IEEE Antennas and Propagation Society Newsletter*, 28/6 (1986), 13–16 · G. W. Swenson jun., 'Reminiscence: at the dawn of the space age', *IEEE Antennas and Propagation Society Magazine*, 36/2 (1994), 32–5 · *WWW*, 1981–90 · b. cert. · m. cert. · d. cert. · PRO, Government Code and Cypher School, directorate, Second World War policy papers, HW 14 files

Wealth at death £472,608: probate, 6 June 1988, *CGPLA Eng. & Wales*

McWard [Macward], **Robert** (c.1625–1681), Presbyterian minister in the Netherlands, was born in Glenluce, Galloway. He graduated MA at Glasgow and probably also studied at the University of St Andrews, where he was a favourite of Samuel Rutherford and held office as regent. He accompanied Rutherford to the Westminster assembly and was a protester in the religious dispute against the moderate resolutioners in the 1650s. In 1654 he was appointed regent at Glasgow and was ordained to the Outer High Church in that city in September 1656. Robert Baillie objected to both appointments and his opposition may have been responsible for McWard's failure to become vice-chancellor of the university in 1659.

In February 1661 McWard preached a sermon in which he was reported to have offered his 'Dissent to all Acts which are or shall be passed against the Covenants, and Work of Reformation in Scotland' (Wodrow, 1.78). He was imprisoned in Edinburgh Tolbooth and, having been indicted by the king's advocate for treasonable teaching, defended himself before parliament on 6 June. McWard was banished and travelled to the United Provinces, where he became one of the first and most influential members of the Scottish exile community.

McWard enrolled at Leiden University in December 1661 and for the rest of his life retained close links with several prominent Dutch theologians, including Gisbertus Voetius. He spent most of his exile in Rotterdam, preaching for three months in 1662 and being appointed one of the incumbents of the Scots kirk on 23 January 1676. He cared passionately about the congregation, which he called 'the only remaining Model of that once beautiful Fabrick of the Church of Scotland' (R. McWard, *Earnest Contendings*, 1723, 171). He introduced a compulsory levy on Scottish shipping to benefit the poor and helped establish a school linked to the congregation. He married Marion Cullen, the widow of another exile, John Graham (formerly provost of Glasgow) some time between 1665 and 1676 and took on responsibility for raising his stepson, John.

McWard was not known for his compromising attitude and his stay in the United Provinces was full of incident. In February 1667 the Utrecht congregation complained about his refusal to use the Lord's prayer and his upsetting remarks about England, then at war with the Dutch. McWard refused to compromise and gave up his position as locum, so that Sunday sermons had instead to be read by the church's reader. There was further consternation when it was discovered that McWard was preaching two rival Sunday sermons at the house of another exile, Mrs Simson.

McWard was also involved in political correspondence: as a supporter of the Dutch in the war against the English he penned an anonymous tract, *The English Ballance*, in 1672. He was in contact with the spy William Carstares while the latter was in a London prison in November 1674 and was apparently in regular communication with the Dutch court, at least towards the end of his life. His final letter to the high-ranking official Gaspar Fagel asked the official to care for his family after his death and also revealed that he had received money from the states general. While McWard's political machinations were fairly insignificant he—along with his fellow exile John Brown—remained a threat to the Scottish government with continuous attacks on Erastianism and the policy of indulgence from the mid-1660s onwards. From their relative safety the two ministers played a key role in presbyterian debates, stiffening the resistance of those who might otherwise have conformed.

McWard's writings at this time included *The Poor Man's Cup of Cold Water* (1678), intended to support the 'sufferers for Christ' in Scotland, *The Banders Disbanded* (1681), and *Epagōniemoi, or, Earnest Contendings for the Faith* (published 1723), which attacked the indulgences and indulged ministers. Other works included *The True Non-Conformist* (1671), *A Collection of Tracts* (published 1805), and notes and prefaces to the works of his fellow exiles John Livingstone and John Brown. He also assisted with editions of Samuel Rutherford's letters and works, *Joshua Redivivus, or, Mr Rutherfoord's Letter* (1664) and *Examen Arminianismi* (1668).

McWard and Brown also upset several of their brethren by agreeing to ordain the extremist Richard Cameron in Rotterdam in 1679, the event at which McWard is famously said to have predicted the young man's death. Their insistent refusal to compromise with the indulged ministers in Scotland also led to conflict in the exile community as they opposed the more conciliatory attitude of McWard's successor at Rotterdam, Robert Fleming (*Earnest Contendings* was written as a response to Fleming's *The Church Wounded and Rent*).

It is hardly surprising that Charles II made three

attempts to have McWard banished from the United Provinces. In July 1670 he and two other exiles were accused of trying to stir up sedition and treason against the king and of writing defamatory documents. All three were ordered to leave in September but banishment was not enforced. The king's most concerted attempt came in 1676 when he urged the Dutch states general to banish McWard—this time along with Brown and their comrade James Wallace of Auchens. The Dutch authorities were not unsympathetic to the Scots' plight but the exiles realized that the authorities would not risk damaging diplomatic relations with England. In February 1677 the states general passed a resolution to banish the three Scots but again this was not enforced. McWard had to give up his incumbency and seems to have retired to Utrecht, though he was safely back in Rotterdam by 1678. The ambassador, Sir William Temple, noted in his memoirs that negotiations had been particularly difficult because of the high esteem in which McWard was held. In 1680 there were hints that the king intended to act once more against him, but nothing came of it.

McWard died in Rotterdam in May or June 1681 (he was buried in Rotterdam in June at the cost of 367 guilders). Like many of his friends he entrusted the execution of his will to the merchant Andrew Russell. McWard's library of books was auctioned for the benefit of his wife, who remained part of the exile community and was still alive in 1687. McWard was a respected member of the exile community and contributed much to the presbyterian debates during the reign of Charles II. Wodrow referred to him as 'a person of great knowledge, zeal, learning, and remarkable ministerial abilities' (Wodrow, 1.207). He is still remembered with pride by the Scots church in Rotterdam: one of the elders presented a portrait of him to the congregation in 1737, a copy of which was still on display in the church at the beginning of the twenty-first century.   GINNY GARDNER

Sources *Fasti Scot.*, new edn, 3.462–3 · R. Wodrow, *The history of the sufferings of the Church of Scotland from the Restauration to the revolution*, 2 vols. (1721–2) · G. Gardner, 'The Scottish exile community in the United Provinces, 1660–1690', DPhil diss., U. Oxf., 1998 · *DSCHT* · W. Steven, *The history of the Scottish church, Rotterdam* (1832, 1833) · *Album scholasticum academiae Lugduno-Batavae, mdlxxv–mcmxl* (Leiden, 1941) · *Scots Church Rotterdam* [n.d.] [commemoration of 350th anniversary] · *DNB* · NA Scot., Andrew Russell MSS
Archives NL Scot., corresp. | NA Scot., Andrew Russell MSS · Nationaal Archief, The Hague, Raadpensionaris archive
Likenesses portrait, *c*.1737, repro. in *Scots Church Rotterdam*
Wealth at death books auctioned for 697 guilders in 1682: NA Scot., Andrew Russell MSS

MacWhirter [McWhirter], **John** (1837–1911), landscape painter, was born at Inglis Green, Edinburgh, on 27 March 1837, the son of George McWhirter (1786–1850), a paper manufacturer at Colinton, near Edinburgh, and his second wife, Agnes (1789–1873). He was the sixth child and third son in a family of five sons and three daughters; his elder sister Agnes Eliza McWhirter (1833–1882) became an accomplished still-life artist. In 1851, after his schooling in Peebles grammar school, he enrolled at the Trustees' Academy, Edinburgh, where he studied under Robert

John MacWhirter (1837–1911), by Ralph W. Robinson, 1889

Scott Lauder, director of the antique department. His fellow students included W. Q. Orchardson, Peter Graham, John Pettie, William McTaggart, and George Paul Chalmers. They became lifelong friends. Chalmers was best man at his wedding on 17 May 1872 to Katharine Cowan (Katy) Menzies (1843–1929), daughter of Professor Allan Menzies of Edinburgh University and granddaughter of Alexander Cowan, paper manufacturer, of Penicuik, Midlothian. They had two sons and two daughters; the elder daughter, Agnes Helen, married the painter Charles Sims (1873–1928) in 1897. At the age of seventeen McWhirter exhibited his first picture at the Royal Scottish Academy: *Old Cottage at Braid*. By the age of twenty-one a further sixteen works had been exhibited and he had also made the first of his study visits to the continent. He became an associate of the Royal Scottish Academy in 1867, an honorary member in 1882, and a Royal Academician in 1893.

Many of McWhirter's early landscapes reflect the influence of the Pre-Raphaelites. In later years, his more broadbrush technique satisfied the increasing demands of commissions, exhibitions, and illustrating, and his work embraced more fully the teachings of Robert Scott Lauder on the role of colour in painting. His move to London in 1869 (at about which time he began to spell his surname as MacWhirter) followed the success of *Loch Coruisk: Isle of Skye* (exh. RA, 1869; priv. coll.) which, in only his third Royal Academy exhibition, was described in the *Art Journal* of 1869 as 'one of the grandest landscapes of the year' (31.163). He and his wife visited locations abroad annually, including Austria, Italy, Switzerland, and Turkey; they also ventured to New York, Salt Lake City in Utah, and San Francisco. MacWhirter frequently combined family visits to Scotland with outdoor sketching, preferring subjects from his native landscapes and those of Italy to all others since, as he said, 'if Italy is the land of light, Scotland is certainly the land of colour' (J. MacWhirter, *Landscape Painting in Water-Colour*, 1900, 56).

MacWhirter's oil paintings, watercolours, and engravings were prolific and popular: among the works he illustrated were William Nimmo's *Caledonia Described by Scott, Burns and Ramsay* (1878) and David Hannay's *Glimpses of the Land of Scott* (1888). He was most noted for his paintings of trees, especially silver birches, but his works ranged widely from dramatic oil paintings of Scottish and alpine mountains to delicate Turneresque watercolours of Genoa, Venice, and Naples. His *œuvre*, typically devoid of human subjects, is exemplified by such works as *The Lady of the Woods* (exh. RA, 1876; Manchester City Galleries), which featured a solitary silver birch; *The Fisherman's Haven, St Monans, Fife* (exh. Berlin International, 1896; Art Gallery, Rochdale); *A Fallen Giant* (exh. RA, 1901; Tatham Gallery, Natal, South Africa), showing a fallen Scots pine; *A Valley by the Sea* (exh. RA, 1879; Musée des Beaux-Arts, Montreal); and *Spindrift* (exh. RA, 1876; Royal Holloway and Bedford New College, University of London, Egham, Surrey). His attention to natural detail, especially in painting wild flowers, excels in *June in the Austrian Tyrol* (exh. RA, 1892; Chantrey bequest, Tate collection) and in *Harebells and Primroses* (Ashmolean Museum, Oxford), the latter of which was used as an exemplar by John Ruskin in his lectures on landscape painting at Oxford.

MacWhirter was a committed family man whose intellect, genial personality, and broad experience of life won him many friends and the respect of younger artists seeking his help and advice. He died on 28 January 1911 of lymphatic leukaemia and cardiac failure at his home, 1 Abbey Road, St John's Wood. After a private funeral service there, he was cremated at Golders Green crematorium. He was survived by his wife. His works, which remain popular at major auction sales, are in national and provincial galleries throughout Britain, in Australia, Canada, South Africa, and New Zealand, and in private and corporate collections. He published *Landscape Painting in Water-Colour* in 1900 and *The MacWhirter Sketch Book* in 1906. In 1913 *Sketches from Nature* was published posthumously.

JOHN MCWHIRTER

Sources W. McD. Sinclair, 'John MacWhirter', *Christmas Art Annual* (1903) [whole issue] · *Glasgow Herald* (30 Jan 1911) · *The Scotsman* (30 Jan 1911) · *The Times* (30 Jan 1911) · J. Dafforne, 'The works of John MacWhirter', *Art Journal*, 41 (1879), 9–11 · J. Halsby and P. Harris, *The dictionary of Scottish painters, 1600–1960* (1990), 116, 143 · L. Errington, *Master class: Robert Scott Lauder and his pupils* (1983) [exhibition catalogue, NG Scot., 15 July – 2 Oct 1983, and Aberdeen Art Gallery, 15 Oct – 12 Nov 1983] · bap. reg. Scot. · m. cert. · NA Scot., Trustees' Academy nominal roll, NG/2/1/4–NG 2/1/7 · C. B. de Laperriere, ed., *The Royal Scottish Academy exhibitors, 1826–1990*, 4 vols. (1991) · J. McFarlan, *Letters and journals* (privately printed, Edinburgh, 1892) · H. McFarlan, *Letters and journals of Ruthwell manse life, 1871–1899* (privately printed, Edinburgh, 1914) · W. D. McKay and F. Rinder, *The Royal Scottish Academy, 1826–1916* (1917);

repr. (1975), 266–8 · private information (2004) · R. W. Robinson, *Members and associates of the Royal Academy of Arts, 1891* (1892)
Archives BL, Add. MSS 41567, 60634 · National Galleries of Scotland, letters by daughter gifting wild flower studies collection · NL Scot., corresp., MSS 2255, 3217, 5573, 9813, 9828, 9994, 10994, 19609 · Royal Scot. Acad., corresp. and photograph | Hospitalfield House, Arbroath, letters to Patrick Allan Fraser; photograph
Likenesses J. Pettie, oils, 1882, Aberdeen Art Gallery, MacDonald Collection · R. W. Robinson, photograph, 1889, NPG [*see illus.*] · H. von Herkomer, watercolour drawing, 1892, Scot. NPG; repro. in J. MacWhirter, *Sketches from nature* (1913), frontispiece · J. Archer, oils, Scot. NPG · R. Burton, photograph (aged sixteen), Scot. NPG; repro. in *The Strand Magazine* (1887), 476 · Fradelle, photograph (aged forty), Scot. NPG; repro. in *Strand Magazine* (1887), 476 · Hill, sketch (*Mr. John MacWhirter ARA painting in his studio*), repro. in *Art Journal* (1891), 194 · London Stereoscopic Co., photograph, NPG · R. Lynde, photograph (aged fifty), Scot. NPG; repro. in *Strand Magazine* (1887), 476 · J. Mayall, photogravure photograph, NPG · J. Mayall, woodburytype, NPG; repro. in *Men of mark* (1883) · photograph (aged thirty-two; after oil painting by J. Pettie), Scot. NPG; repro. in *Strand Magazine* (1887), 476 · wood-engraving, NPG; repro. in *ILN* (3 May 1879)
Wealth at death £29,983 11s.: probate, 19 April 1911, CGPLA Eng. & Wales

McWhirter, Robert (1904–1994), medical radiologist, was born on 8 November 1904 in the schoolhouse at Ballantrae, Ayrshire, Scotland, the younger son of Robert McWhirter, the village schoolmaster, and his wife Janet Ramsay, *née* Gairdner. His elder brother John was also a medical radiologist. He was educated at Girvan Academy and read medicine at the University of Glasgow, graduating with high commendation in 1927. He spent the next four years as an assistant in general practice in Prestwick, Ayrshire, where he was responsible for the installation of an X-ray unit in the local nursing home. In 1931 he embarked on postgraduate work at the University of Edinburgh, and was elected a fellow of the Royal College of Surgeons of Edinburgh in 1932. Moving to Cambridge later that year, he studied for the diploma of medical radiology and electrology with A. E. Barclay, and attended lectures on the nature of radioactivity given by Lord Rutherford, director of the Cavendish Laboratory. After clinical studies in the radiology department of St Bartholomew's Hospital in London, he moved to the Mayo Clinic in Rochester, Minnesota, USA, to study diagnostic radiology, returning to Britain at the invitation of the radiotherapist Ralston Paterson to take up a clinical research fellowship at the Christie Hospital and Holt Radium Institute in Manchester. He returned to St Bartholomew's Hospital as chief assistant in the X-ray department, where he came into contact with the surgeon Geoffrey Keynes, who was doing pioneering work on the implantation of radium needles in the treatment of breast cancer.

When Barclay was offered the post of head of the X-ray department of the Royal Infirmary in Edinburgh, he accepted on condition that he could bring McWhirter as his assistant, but shortly after his arrival Barclay decided to return to his research in Cambridge, and in late 1935 McWhirter was asked to stay on as director of radiotherapy. He soon began to modernize the department, installing new X-ray equipment for the treatment of cancer. On

26 June 1937, at Kelvinside church, Botanic Gardens, Glasgow, he married Susan Muir MacMurray (b. 1900/01), a doctor, daughter of William MacMurray, a civil engineer. They had one son, William (Bill), a paediatric oncologist who became head of the department of child health at the University of Queensland, Australia.

McWhirter's most important work was in the treatment of cancer through radiotherapy rather than relying on radical surgery, but unlike Keynes he believed that the use of X-rays would be more effective in destroying the malignant cells than radium needle implants. After studying all the cases of breast cancer coming into the Royal Infirmary between 1941 and 1945, he found that in the majority surgery was unlikely to be successful unless supplemented by radiotherapy. His research, published in the *British Journal of Radiology* and the *Proceedings of the Royal Society of Medicine* in 1948, showed that during the period studied the five-year survival rate was 43.7 per cent when simple mastectomy (the removal of the breast) was combined with radiotherapy, whereas when radical mastectomy (the removal of the breast and the surrounding lymph nodes) was the only treatment, the survival rate was 25 per cent. His approach met with considerable opposition, but within a few years it became standard practice in the treatment of breast cancer.

In 1946 McWhirter was appointed to the newly founded Forbes chair of medical radiology at the University of Edinburgh, a post he held, while remaining director of radiotherapy at the Royal Infirmary, until his retirement in 1970. He was responsible for building the Radiotherapy Institute (later the department of clinical oncology) at the Western General Hospital in Edinburgh, which opened in 1953. As the international reputation of the department grew, he attracted large numbers of postgraduate students, many of whom went on to head departments of radiotherapy and oncology in Britain, the United States, and the Commonwealth.

McWhirter was elected a fellow of the Faculty (later the Royal College) of Radiologists in 1944, and was warden of the fellowship, in charge of the education of radiologists, from 1961 to 1966, and president from 1966 to 1969. He was an honorary member of the radiological societies of the United States, France, Italy, Japan, and Australia, and was president of the Medical and Dental Defence Union of Scotland from 1959 to 1990. Appointed CBE in 1963, he received the gold medal of the National Society for Cancer Relief in 1985. A keen golfer, ornithologist, and cine-photographer, he died on 24 October 1994 in the Western General Hospital, Edinburgh. He was survived by his wife.   ANNE PIMLOTT BAKER

Sources *The Scotsman* (7 Nov 1994) · *The Independent* (7 Dec 1994) · *The Times* (14 Nov 1994) · *WW* · b. cert. · m. cert. · d. cert.
Likenesses photograph, repro. in *The Scotsman* · photograph, repro. in *The Times* · photograph, repro. in *The Independent*
Wealth at death £275,811.17—Scotland: confirmation, 23 Dec 1994, *CCI* (1994)

McWhirter, (Alan) Ross (1925–1975), book editor and litigant, was born in Winchmore Hill, north London, on 12 August 1925, the third and youngest son and the younger twin son (there were no daughters) of William Allan McWhirter (1888–1955), national newspaper editor, and his wife, Margaret (Bunty) Moffat Williamson (1900–1972). Ross was educated with his brothers at Marlborough College, which he attended from 1939 to 1943. Having volunteered for the Royal Navy at seventeen he became a midshipman in the Royal Naval Volunteer Reserve in 1944 and served two arduous years in minesweeping. In January 1947 he returned to Trinity College, Oxford (he had spent six months there in 1943–4 in the Oxford University naval division), with his twin, Norris, to resume reading jurisprudence. He graduated in 1948 with a third class in jurisprudence (shortened course), having represented the university in athletics abroad and against Cambridge. In the same year he ran in the Achilles Club team that won the Amateur Athletic Association relay championship.

In 1951 Ross and Norris McWhirter established an agency in London to provide facts, figures, and features to the press, publishers, and advertisers. The business immediately prospered and Ross McWhirter was appointed the lawn tennis and rugby football correspondent of the London evening *Star*. The twins, who always worked as a team, published in 1951 their first book, *Get to your Marks*, on the history of athletics. It was later quoted as being 'distinguished by a degree of precision and thoroughly which no athletics historian had achieved before' (McWhirter, 95).

The first of Ross McWhirter's many law cases was in 1954 against the National Union of Journalism, of which he was an involuntary closed shop member. A union officer had defamed his twin brother and, when the editor of the *Star* declined to give evidence against the union, McWhirter insisted on a subpoena and the case went against the union, along with damages and costs. In the same year the brothers became the only company directors in the country to insist on their names' being placed on the local government electoral register after the county court accepted that the words 'does not entitle' have a different meaning from 'disentitle'.

In 1957 McWhirter married Rosemary Joy Hamilton, daughter of Leslie Charles Hamilton Grice, who worked for Nestlé; they had two sons. In the general election of 1964 he stood, unsuccessfully, as Conservative candidate for Edmonton. In his next legal foray, in 1967, he brought four High Court actions in forty-three days to challenge the conversion of Enfield grammar and secondary modern schools into an entirely comprehensive scheme. After partial success by the defending parents, represented by Geoffrey Howe QC, McWhirter personally intervened to win injunctions against the Enfield council and the secretary of state, who was forced to go back to parliament for new powers. The *Daily Mirror* carried a leader which rejoiced: 'Liberty still has its vigilant defenders'.

In November 1968 McWhirter fought the Home Office single-handed to challenge the miscounting of votes in the Enfield local government elections the previous May. Having lost in the crown court he appeared in person before the High Court and defeated the Home Office to win an order signed by the lord chief justice requiring a unique recount of votes, which confirmed his suspicions of massive mathematical discrepancies between the ballot papers issued and the votes declared. In 1969 he took James Callaghan, the home secretary, to court for not giving effect to the recommendations of the boundary commissions to redistribute parliamentary seats. Since the statutory time limit of fifteen years had been exceeded he moved the court for an order of mandamus. The attorney-general compromised the action by assuring the court that the boundary commissions' orders would be laid forthwith. The home secretary circumvented his undertaking by forcing through the Commons an affirmative motion ending with the words 'be not approved', although the act spoke only of 'a motion to approve'. No appeal was possible because proceedings in parliament are non-justiciable. The press, however, denounced this manoeuvre, which McWhirter always referred to as the 'boundary fiddle'.

McWhirter's attention now turned to the Independent Broadcasting Authority (IBA). A High Court judge refused, on grounds of *locus standi*, to give him a declaration that the IBA had acted unlawfully in transmitting messages by subliminal flashes (expressly forbidden by statute) during a Labour Party political broadcast on 8 May 1970. In the appeal court Lord Denning accepted McWhirter's plea that having a television licence gave him the maximum possible *locus*, and the IBA took the unusual step of giving him a written undertaking that no further subliminal messages would be transmitted. The IBA were again defendants in the Andy Warhol case in 1973, when McWhirter succeeded uniquely, without the fiat of the attorney-general, in getting the transmission of a television programme stopped by court injunction until members of the authority had discharged their statutory duty 'to satisfy themselves' that the programme was not 'offensive to public feeling'.

Between the two IBA cases Ross McWhirter was again before Lord Denning, questioning the legality of the prime minister's action in signing the treaty of accession to the EEC. He contended that this use of the prerogative power by Edward Heath, the prime minister, put the monarch in breach of her coronation oath to govern her peoples 'according to their laws and customs'. The judges exercised their discretion not to make a declaration but accepted McWhirter's view against Treasury counsel that the scope of the exercise of prerogative power is justiciable.

The last case McWhirter personally fought was against Eagle Ferry and the National Union of Seamen, which had impounded the cars of some forty passengers at Southampton as a bargaining lever in a dispute over redundancy notices. McWhirter revived the tort of detinue and got a rare *ex parte* mandatory injunction in nine minutes.

His most important case was concluded almost six years after his death, when the European Court of Human Rights concurred with his view that article 2 of the convention on freedom of association protected citizens against the coercion of compulsory unionism. At a cost above £100,000, and after ten governmental delays, the British Rail closed shop case of *Young, James, and Webster* v. *United Kingdom* was successfully sustained by Viscount De l'Isle VC and by McWhirter's twin through the agency of the Freedom Association, whose charter had been drafted by Ross McWhirter. The judgment was delivered on 13 August 1981 in Strasbourg and resulted six months later in a new employment bill which included a clause to compensate retrospectively some 400 victims who had been dismissed without remedy under the 1974 act.

Ross McWhirter was for twenty-one years co-editor with Norris McWhirter of the *Guinness Book of Records*, which they had started in 1954. Before his death it had already set its own record for any copyright book by selling more than 25 million copies in thirteen languages. He was also the author of the *Centenary History of Oxford University Rugby Football Club* (1969) and the *Centenary History of the Rugby Football Union* (1971). He served for twenty years as the honorary press officer for the Victoria Cross and George Cross Association.

On 27 November 1975 McWhirter was shot by two IRA terrorists at the front door of his home, 50 Village Road, Enfield, and died shortly afterwards in Chase Farm Hospital, Enfield. In the previous weeks he had campaigned to raise £50,000 bounties for people who gave information leading to conviction for the IRA terrorist campaign in London that had killed fifty-four people. On the initiative of his friends the Ross McWhirter Foundation was established with £100,000 subscribed by admirers. It sought to advance Ross McWhirter's qualities of 'good citizenship … personal initiative and leadership, and personal courage as an example to others'. He was buried at Southgate cemetery, London; he was survived by his wife.

HARRIS OF HIGH CROSS, *rev.*

Sources *The Times* (28 Nov 1975) · *The Times* (29 Nov 1975) · N. McWhirter, *Ross: the story of a shared life* (1976) · N. Allen, *The Times* (29 Nov 1975), 16 · *WWW* · personal knowledge (1986, 2004) · D. Griffiths, ed., *The encyclopedia of the British press, 1422–1992* (1992) · *CGPLA Eng. & Wales* (1976)
Likenesses photographs, repro. in McWhirter, *Ross*
Wealth at death £137,082: probate, 20 Feb 1976, *CGPLA Eng. & Wales*

Macwilliam family (*per. c.*1130–*c.*1230), claimants to the Scottish throne, descended from *Duncan II (*r.* 1094), that is, from the first marriage of Malcolm III (*d.* 1093) and so from the ancient line of Scottish kings. But the family took its name from the king's son, *William fitz Duncan (*d.* 1151x4), described in an English source as earl of Moray. The origin of William's claim on Moray is not clear. Alexander II's foundation at Elgin Cathedral in 1235 of a chaplaincy in memory of King Duncan might suggest that the latter had had a right in the area which could have passed to his son. Alternatively, it has been proposed that William's claim came from a first wife related to Angus, earl of Moray, who was killed in battle in 1130 when in revolt against David I. Angus had claimed the crown, and on his death without direct heirs any right he had to that would thus have passed to William fitz Duncan.

William fitz Duncan was strenuously loyal to David I, especially in the campaign of 1138 in the north of England against King Stephen, and no claims to Moray or to the crown were pressed by his heirs soon after his death. No Macwilliam is known to have taken part between 1154 and 1164 in the revolts of Somerled, lord of Argyll, or of a group of Scottish earls against Malcolm IV (1160). Nor were similar claims put forward at any time by the heirs of William's presumed second marriage to Alice de Rumilly (a son, William of Egremont, who died c.1165, and three daughters). But by the 1170s things had changed.

The death of Somerled of Argyll in 1164 and the division of his lordship brought instability to the western seaboard. No earl of Moray was appointed following William fitz Duncan's death, and after 1165 King William the Lion tightened his grip there. He named no successor as earl of Ross after the death of Malcolm Macheth in 1168. Royal government was extending its arm and some local lords, faced with this, preferred to support another line. In 1179 the king and his brother, Earl David, led an army into Ross. Two castles (mottes) were built at Redcastle and Dunskeath and measures were agreed to strengthen the defences of Inverness. The likely reason for the trouble is activity by the *Macheth family, claimants to the earldom of Ross. Possibly the Macwilliams too were involved; they are reliably said to have been restive before 1181, when **Donald Ban Macwilliam** (d. 1187), a son of William fitz Duncan and an unknown mother, and by then the male heir of all the family's claims, took advantage of the absence of the king and his brother in France and led a full-scale revolt in Moray and Ross.

This uprising was a serious blow to the king, who was also at that time trying to restore order in Galloway. A later assertion that Donald Macwilliam controlled the earldoms of Ross and Moray for some considerable time seems to be well founded. The king is not known to have issued charters in Moray between probably 1179 and 1187, and there was no bishop of Moray for nearly two and a half years, from 17 September 1184 to 1 March 1187. A royal servant surrendered the castle of Auldearn and went over to the rebels. That a band led by Aed, son of Donald Macheth, was able to strike as far south as Coupar Angus in 1186 suggests how weak the king's position in the north was. In 1187, however, a major effort by the royal forces brought the rebels to battle on 31 July at 'Mam Garvia' (unidentified, but perhaps north or north-west of the Beauly Firth). Donald Macwilliam and, it is said, 500 of his men were killed, and Donald's head was sent to the king.

After this defeat the Macwilliams, unlike the Macheths, are not known to have taken part in the unrest caused by Harald, earl of Orkney and Caithness, and his wife, Hvarflod (a Macheth), between 1196 and 1203. But a probable result of the expedition of King John of England to Ireland in 1210 was the expulsion of **Guthred Macwilliam** (d. 1212), son of Donald Ban, who, invited by the lords of Ross, arrived there with Irish forces in January 1211. Redcastle and Dunskeath were refortified; a foray by King William's army in 1211 accomplished nothing, and after its withdrawal one of the castles was surrendered and burnt. At a meeting of the Scottish and English courts at Durham

in February 1212 the dispatch of mercenaries was probably agreed. Whether they were effective is unlikely; a little later in the same year Guthred was betrayed, captured, presented to the king's son, the future Alexander II, at Kincardine, and decapitated; the corpse was then left hanging by the feet.

In 1212 and 1214 Alan of Galloway and his brother Earl Thomas of Atholl attacked probable centres of help for the Macwilliams in Ulster. These measures and the death of Guthred were no deterrent. In 1215 there was an invasion (said to be of Moray, but Ross is more likely) by another **Donald Ban Macwilliam** (d. 1215); his exact relationship to Guthred is unknown. He was accompanied by Kenneth Macheth and the son of an Irish king. But the attacks on Ulster had had an effect; the 1215 invasion was probably weaker than earlier ones and the rebels were defeated in May or June by Farquhar Mactaggart (lord of Applecross in Wester Ross and later earl of Ross) without royal intervention; their heads were presented to the king on 15 June 1215.

The family's last fling was in the 1220s, possibly as early as 1223 but certainly by September 1228, when a certain **Gillescop Macwilliam** (d. 1229) and his sons (again the exact relationship to other Macwilliams is unknown) fired a wooden castle in Moray, burnt part of Inverness, and about 8 September plundered some royal lands. William Comyn, earl of Buchan, was made responsible for law and order in the area; in 1229 Gillescop and his sons were captured and killed, and their heads were brought to the king. Then, or possibly in 1230, the last known member of the family, an infant daughter, was publicly put to death in Forfar, when her head was dashed against the market cross.   W. W. SCOTT

Sources APS, 1124–1423 · A. O. Anderson, ed. and trans., *Early sources of Scottish history, AD 500 to 1286*, 2 vols. (1922); repr. with corrections (1990) · A. O. Anderson, ed., *Scottish annals from English chroniclers, AD 500 to 1286* (1908); repr. (1991) · G. W. S. Barrow, *Kingship and unity: Scotland, 1000–1306* (1981) · C. Innes, ed., *Registrum episcopatus Moraviensis*, Bannatyne Club, 58 (1837) · G. W. S. Barrow, ed., *Regesta regum Scottorum*, 1–2 (1960–71) · W. Bower, *Scotichronicon*, ed. D. E. R. Watt and others, new edn, 9 vols. (1987–98) · A. C. Lawrie, ed., *Annals of the reigns of Malcolm and William, kings of Scotland* (1910)

Macwilliam, Donald Ban (d. 1187). *See under* Macwilliam family (*per. c.*1130–*c.*1230).

Macwilliam, Donald Ban (d. 1215). *See under* Macwilliam family (*per. c.*1130–*c.*1230).

McWilliam, Frederick Edward (1909–1992), sculptor, was born on 30 April 1909 in Newry Street, Banbridge, co. Down, the son of William Nicholson McWilliam, medical practitioner, and his wife, Elizabeth Esther, *née* Rounds. An exile for most of his life, McWilliam cherished memories of his childhood in a small country town where craftsmen still pursued their traditional skills—his own work was splendidly imbued with craftsman-like qualities— but he also carried darker memories of Ireland in the 1920s, as it moved towards partition in an atmosphere of bigotry and intolerance. He was educated at Campbell College, Belfast, and at Belfast College of Art (1926–8). He continued his studies, at first intending to become a painter, at the Slade School of Fine Art, London (1928–31). Influenced by a member of the teaching staff, A. H. Gerrard (later Slade professor of sculpture), and by Henry Moore, whom he met for the first time in his second year—both of these men became his lasting friends—McWilliam emerged from the Slade committed to sculpture. After being awarded the Robert Ross leaving scholarship, he went straight to Paris to work: 'It was the mecca … holy ground, full of the memory of Cézanne, and the presence of Picasso', he said later (Flanagan and Marle, 22). His visit coincided with the slump, his money soon dwindled, and he returned to London.

On 31 March 1932 at St John's Presbyterian Church, Kensington, McWilliam married the painter Elizabeth Marion (Beth) Crowther (1909/10–1988), whom he had met at the Slade. She was the daughter of Ramsden Crowther, a mill owner from Golcar, near Huddersfield. They had two daughters. Their first home—at Chartridge, Buckinghamshire—was a rented cottage which they shared with Henry Moore. There McWilliam began in earnest to carve, using cherrywood from the orchards which surrounded the house. His early pieces were semi-abstract, but a visit to the International Surrealist Exhibition at the New Burlington Galleries, London, in 1936 induced a change of direction. In the following year he joined the British surrealist group, and exhibited with them. He had his first one-man exhibition, of sculpture and drawings, at the London Gallery, Cork Street, London, in March 1939.

The outbreak of the Second World War interrupted this steady progress. For six years, while serving in the RAF (in England and then, from 1944 to 1946, in India), McWilliam produced very little. As soon as conditions allowed, he returned to his work in wood, stone, clay, bronze, and concrete. In addition, he was invited in 1947 by A. H. Gerrard to teach sculpture at the Slade, a post which he occupied until 1968.

McWilliam tended to work in series, exploring a theme in a succession of variations, rather as a composer might do. Characteristic of his sculpture produced just before and soon after the war was his exploration of 'the complete fragment', the part standing for the whole, in works which are aptly described by their titles: *Mandible* (1938), *Eye, Nose and Cheek* (1939; Tate collection), *Profile* (1939–40), and the extraordinary *Head in Extended Order* (1948), in which the components of a face—lips, eyeballs, nose, and ear—are laid in a row like excavated fragments of classical antiquity. His later *Legs* series (1977–81) was a more playful excursion into the same territory. Another surreal device much favoured by McWilliam might be called 'the missing torso'. In *Man and Wife* (1948), *Father and Daughter* (1949), and *The Matriarch* (1952), to name but a few pieces, limbs tenderly and convincingly, in defiance of common sense, surround an empty space. Henry Moore's riven sculptures of the same period became more famous but McWilliam's work had a lightness and grace which were all his own.

In 1949 McWilliam was elected to the London group (he resigned in 1963); and in the following year he and his wife, Beth, made what proved to be their final move, to a house and studio in Holland Park, London. The house had a large, tree-lined garden, lovingly tended by Beth, where they entertained their many friends and where, according to the artist and collector Roland Penrose, 'his sculptures, placed appropriately on mounds among trees, seem to join the conversation' (*Women of Belfast*, introductory note).

In 1951 McWilliam was commissioned to create a large figurative work, *The Four Seasons*, for the country pavilion at the Festival of Britain; many public commissions followed throughout the 1950s and 1960s. Probably the most important was his monumental *Princess Macha* (1957) for the Altnagelvin Hospital in Derry, a tall elegant figure which marked the beginning of his re-engagement with his Irish past. He also undertook a number of 'straightforward' portrait commissions, including a fine bronze of his friend and fellow Ulsterman the painter William Scott (1956).

The Irish present—or one brutal aspect of it—announced itself with the commencement of the troubles in 1969. On 4 March 1972 a bomb exploded without warning among the diners at the Abercorn Tea-rooms in Belfast. Two women were killed, two more lost both legs, and a total of 130 people were injured. McWilliam, who never before had used his sculpture for direct comment, was moved by this dire event to create a series of small bronzes, known collectively as *Women of Belfast* (1972–3; Arts Council of Northern Ireland Collection, no. 5). These suffering figures, whirled about, tumbled, and harried by the bomb blast, their faces contorted, their clothing agitated, have undeniable power. Though connected to the Northern Ireland conflict, they had a wider significance: they were emblems of innocence violated in a violent century.

McWilliam received an honorary DLitt from Queen's University, Belfast, in 1964. He was appointed CBE in 1966, and in 1971 he won a gold medal for sculpture at the Oireachtas Exhibition in Dublin. He was briefly an associate of the Royal Academy: he was elected in 1959, but resigned in 1963 in protest at the hanging committee's rejection of a painting by William Gear. A comprehensive photographic survey of his work, by Roland Penrose, was published in 1964. A large retrospective in 1981—held first at the Ulster Museum, Belfast, before travelling to Dublin and Cork—showed how various and inventive his contribution had been. He continued to carve with verve until almost the end of his life; and a second retrospective, at the Tate in 1989, included examples from his latest series, the fantastic *Mulberry Figures*, carved from a gnarled mulberry tree growing in his garden, which the great storm of 1987 had uprooted. He died of cancer at 12 Pembroke Square, Kensington, London, on 13 May 1992. He was survived by his two daughters, his wife having predeceased him.

MARK SORRELL

Sources T. P. Flanagan and J. Marle, *F. E. McWilliam* (1981) · M. Gooding, *F. E. McWilliam: sculpture 1932–1989* (1989) · R. Penrose,

McWilliam, sculptor (1964) · *Women of Belfast: new bronzes by F. E. McWilliam, 1972–73* (1973) [exhibition catalogue, McClelland Galleries International, Belfast, 12–24 November 1973] · *The Independent* (14–15 May 1992) · *The Times* (15 May 1992) · b. cert. · m. cert. · d. cert.
Likenesses C. Rainey, pencil drawing, 1976, Ulster Museum, Belfast · F. E. McWilliam, self-portrait, bronze bust, 1986, University of Limerick, National Self-Portrait Collection of Ireland · photograph, repro. in *The Times* · photograph, repro. in *The Independent*
Wealth at death £1,432,394: probate, 21 July 1993, *CGPLA Eng. & Wales*

Macwilliam, Gillescop (*d.* 1229). *See under* Macwilliam family (*per. c.*1130–*c.*1230).

Macwilliam, Guthred (*d.* 1212). *See under* Macwilliam family (*per. c.*1130–*c.*1230).

McWilliam, James Ormiston (1808–1862), epidemiologist, was born in Dalkeith, Midlothian. He became a licentiate of the Edinburgh College of Surgeons in 1827, and entered the Royal Navy in 1829 as assistant surgeon. After serving abroad from 1829 to 1836 he was appointed surgeon to the *Scout* on the west coast of Africa. Esteemed by all on board, he was awarded the Blare gold medal for his journal of practice (with an appendix on the health of the ship's company).

McWilliam returned to Britain in November 1839, where he improved his professional knowledge at the London schools and hospitals. He became MD of Edinburgh in 1840. In September 1840 he was appointed senior surgeon on board the *Albert*, which joined the government expedition sent to the Niger for geographical and commercial purposes, and to oppose the slave trade.

Although the expedition was well supplied and the crew carefully selected for the voyage (most were familiar with the tropics) it was said in 1862 that 'had the prophylactic influence of quinine been then as well understood as it is now the result might have been far less disastrous'. The *Albert* and two other vessels set sail on 12 May 1841 and entered the Niger on 13 August. For about three weeks all went well, but on 4 September the crew of the *Albert* came down with fever, probably malarial, and, almost simultaneously, the crews of the other two vessels were also affected. These two vessels, filled with the sick and dying, were sent back to the sea, leaving the *Albert* to continue the voyage alone. However by 4 October the *Albert* also turned back, and since the rest of the officers and crew were incapacitated, the ship was managed for some days by McWilliam and by Dr Stanger, the geologist of the expedition. In ten days they reached the open sea, and the crew recovered. A few days later McWilliam himself was taken ill; he firmly believed that it was only the knowledge that the survival of ship and crew depended upon him which had prevented him from becoming ill sooner. Of the 145 Europeans on the expedition, 130 fell ill with the fever, of whom 40 died; but among the 158 Africans there were only 11 cases of fever and 1 death.

McWilliam reached England on 19 November 1841, but the Admiralty did not recognize his services. In 1843 he brought out his *Medical History of the Niger Expedition*, which was well received. It was plain in style, and gave a history of the fever, its description, morbid anatomy, sequences, causes, treatment, and case studies, as well as an account of the state of medicine among the Africans and of vaccination. It also included a description of the ventilation of the ships—which had been based on the plan adopted by David Boswell Reid for the houses of parliament—an abstract of meteorological observations, and a brief account of the geology of the Niger, condensed from the notes of Dr Stanger.

After again serving two years afloat, McWilliam was sent on a special mission to the Cape Verde Islands to investigate the outbreak of yellow fever among the inhabitants of Boa Vista soon after the arrival of the *Eclair*. On his return to England his detailed report, proving that the fever had been carried by the *Eclair*, was published by order of parliament in 1847. He contributed to medical and other learned journals, and published several reports on the yellow fever epidemic.

McWilliam was again overlooked by the Admiralty, but in 1847 he was appointed medical officer to the custom house, a post which he kept until his death. In 1848 he was elected FRS, in 1858 he became CB, and in 1859 FRCP, London. He was an active member of the Epidemiological Society, and was its secretary from 1850 until his death. He was also a secretary to the medical section of the International Statistical Congress held in London in 1860. He promoted naval medical reform and in 1858 the medical officers of the Royal Navy presented him with a service of plate.

McWilliam died on 4 May 1862, after falling downstairs at his home, 14 Trinity Square, Tower Hill, London. He left a widow, Margaret Galloway (*b.* 1819), and several children in straitened circumstances, having left less than £450 at his death.   W. A. GREENHILL, *rev.* LYNN MILNE

Sources *British and Foreign Medical Review*, 16 (1843) · *Medico-chirurgical Review*, 39 (1843) · review, *Edinburgh Medical and Surgical Journal*, 63 (1845), 415–54 · W. Cooke, 'Report on the accident and decease of the late J. O. McWilliam', *Medical Times and Gazette* (17 May 1862), 504–5 [see also review, (15 March 1862); account of death, (10 May 1862); obit., (17 May 1862)] · *BMJ* (1862), 497 · *British and Foreign Medico-chirurgical Review*, 30 (1862), 556 · J. O. McWilliam, *Remarks on Dr Gilbert King's report* (1848) · [J. O. McWilliam], *An exposition of the case of the assistant surgeons of the Royal Navy*, 3rd edn (1850) · J. O. McWilliam, *Further observations on quarantine* (1852) · J. O. McWilliam, *On the health of merchant seamen* (1862) · d. cert. · private information (2004)
Archives Wellcome L., corresp.
Likenesses T. Butler, plaster medallion, 1864, RCP Lond. · oils, Wellcome L.
Wealth at death under £450: administration, 21 July 1862, *CGPLA Eng. & Wales*

Maczek, Stanisław Władysław (1892–1994), officer in the Polish army, was born on 31 March 1892 in the small town of Szczerzec in Galicia, south-eastern Poland, then part of the Austro-Hungarian empire, one of the twin sons of Władysław (Witold) Maczek (*d. c.*1928), advocate and retired judge, of Croatian origin and his wife, Anna Mueller, *née* Czerny (1852–1932), both Roman Catholics. Maczek's twin brother, Franciszek, was killed in the First

World War in 1915, one younger brother was killed in action in 1914, and another in the Polish–Soviet War in 1920: none reached the age of twenty-five. Maczek attended secondary school in the nearby town of Droho-bycz, where one of his best friends was Bruno Schultz, the Jewish writer and artist shot by the Gestapo in 1942. In 1910 he entered the Jan Kazimierz University at Lemberg (Lwów), the nearest city, to read philosophy and Polish philology. He was a member of the Riflemen's Associ-ation, the Polish paramilitary organization headed by Jozef Pilsudski. In 1914, a few months before graduation, he was conscripted at the outbreak of war into the Austro-Hungarian army. He served as an officer in the crack 2nd Kaiser Jaeger regiment, mountain infantry, on the Italian front almost until the end of the war. In the winter of 1917–18 he had three months' leave to recuperate from wounds and completed his university diploma. He wrote his thesis on the psychology of emotions in literature. A good soldier, he reached *Oberleutnant* and, among other decorations, received the bronze medal for valour.

After the First World War Maczek returned home and joined the new Polish army, which fought six border wars in three years. He served in the Polish–Ukrainian War (1918–19), as commander of the volunteer Krosno com-pany marching to relieve Lwów, besieged by Ukrainians, and in victories in other parts of eastern Galicia, and was promoted captain. Promoted major in June 1919, he fought in the Polish–Soviet War (1919–21), serving in the offensive of 1920 which captured Kiev, then the ensuing retreat under the Bolshevik counter-offensive. In summer 1920 he organized and led the *Lotna* mobile assault battal-ion of the first cavalry, which fought the *Konarmiya* Red Cavalry in the Lwów area. He effectively utilized the *taczanka* (cart-mounted heavy machine gun).

Maczek had never intended to pursue an army career, and in autumn 1920 he considered resuming his univer-sity studies. Superior officers persuaded him to devote himself to a military career, though he was unusual among the hierarchy in being a former Austro-Hungarian officer and not coming from Pilsudski's legions. In 1924 he graduated among the top students of the General Staff College, Warsaw, and for three years he commanded the intelligence station at Lwów. On 28 June 1928 he married Zofia Kurys (1910–1995), daughter of Sebastian Kurys, inland revenue civil servant; they had one son and two daughters, the second born in Scotland after the Second World War. He was highly regarded by Pilsudski. From 1929 to 1935 (as colonel from 1931) he commanded the 81st infantry regiment at Grodno, and from 1935 he was dep-uty commander of the 7th infantry division at Czesto-chowa. He was awarded various decorations. Having been an advocate of mobile armoured warfare since 1918, he was appointed commander of the 10th motorized cavalry brigade, Poland's first armoured tactical formation, in October 1938.

Against the German invasion of Poland in September 1939 Maczek's brigade, nicknamed the Black Brigade because of the company's black leather coats, was part of the 'Krakow' army defending Silesia and the southern bor-der area, and fought hard, with some success, to delay the 22nd Panzer corps. The brigade counter-attacked Ferdi-nand Schörner's mountain division outside Lwów and recaptured previously lost ground. Yet such isolated suc-cesses could not prevent German victory. On 19 Septem-ber 1939, following the Soviet invasion of Poland two days earlier, Maczek complied with orders from the Polish general staff to prevent encirclement by Soviet forces and withdrew his brigade, fully armed and with regimental colours, into Hungary where it was interned. He ordered his men to go to France. He arrived there in October, and General Władysław Sikorski, GOC Polish forces, pro-moted him major-general and, for his role in the Septem-ber campaign, awarded him the gold cross of the Virtuti Militari, the highest Polish military decoration. He com-manded Polish units at Coetquidan camp in Brittany and re-formed his 10th armoured cavalry brigade. Under-equipped, it fought with some success against the 1940 German invasion, defeating a German armoured brigade on the day the armistice was signed (22 June). Maczek then ordered his troops to disperse and go to England.

Following the fall of France about one-third of the Polish forces there managed to escape to Britain. Maczek left from Marseilles in disguise on a ship repatriating Algerian soldiers. At Casablanca, amazingly, he was reunited with his wife and two young children. They were flown to England, landing at Bristol on 21 September 1940, then moved to Scotland where many Polish troops were stationed. The Poles, while owing allegiance to the Polish government in exile in London, were under British opera-tional command. Maczek aimed to reconstruct his armoured formation, but meanwhile his troops guarded the Scottish coast between Carnoustie and Montrose. In February 1942 Sikorski appointed Maczek to command the newly formed first Polish armoured division, which trained in Scotland and gained a high reputation for dis-cipline, smartness, and *esprit de corps*.

Following the D-day landings (6 June 1944) Maczek's 13,000-strong division, part of the second Canadian corps and under Montgomery's command, landed on the Arro-manches beaches on 1 August 1944 and entered the offen-sive south of Caen. In British battledress, with American Shermans and jeeps, but with 'Poland' shoulder flashes and traditional Polish insignia, the Poles fought with a very Polish panache and courage. Maczek was rugged, stocky, and short-necked, intensely patriotic, brave, opti-mistic, decisive, intelligent if not intellectual, crafty, and with clear vision. A strict disciplinarian, vehement against plunder, he was adored by his troops, who nick-named him 'Baca' ('Chief Shepherd'). He rarely stayed in his armoured command vehicle but usually went forward in his command tank, directing the battle from the for-ward line. At night, like his men, he slept under his tank. He once ordered his three headquarters tanks, out of ammunition, to circle a hill like a stage army to give the Germans the impression of a large force. His relations with Montgomery were cool; when Montgomery had inspected the division in March 1944 he asked Maczek,

'What language do the Poles use among themselves, German or Russian?' (Stachura, *Poland*, 4).

In France, Maczek's division was involved in heavy fighting. On 21 August, following delay by Omar Bradley's US forces, the Poles closed the Argentan–Falaise gap at Chambois, a turning-point in the Normandy campaign. Fighting notorious SS divisions the Poles suffered heavy casualties, but took many prisoners. On the summit of the 'Mace', the dominating long ridge held by Colonel Koszutski's force, Canadian sappers erected a board with the words 'A Polish Battlefield'. Later Montgomery told Maczek, 'The battle of Chambois was ... of decisive significance. Your division was like a cork of a bottle in which the Germans were trapped' (*The Times*). The division advanced against strong opposition across northern France, and into Belgium and the Netherlands where towns they liberated included Ypres, Passchendaele, and Breda. The people of Breda were especially grateful for Maczek's manoeuvre, which spared their historic Old Town from destruction. Early in 1945 the division advanced into Germany, augmented by Poles freed from the Germans. In May it occupied Wilhelmshaven. It had been exceptionally successful and Maczek, who had never lost a battle since 1939, was among the most successful allied commanders. In May 1945 he was appointed commanding officer of the first Polish corps, with headquarters in Scotland, and promoted lieutenant-general. From December 1945 he was also GOC of Polish forces in the UK, his main responsibility the demobilization of Polish troops through the British-sponsored Polish resettlement corps. He was awarded Polish and allied decorations including the CB, DSO, Croix de Guerre, and Légion d'honneur.

Maczek was demobilized on 9 September 1948. The post-war Soviet-dominated regime in Poland was a bitter disappointment to him and his troops, and it deprived him of Polish citizenship. He never returned to Poland and, despite approaches to him, never recognized or compromised with the communist regime. To exiled Poles he was a 'living legend' (Stachura, *Themes*, 13) and 'came to personify ... the indomitable courage and patriotic spirit of the Free Poland' (Stachura, *Poland*, 83–4). He settled into exile in Edinburgh, did various jobs including bartending at the Learmouth Hotel owned by one of his former soldiers, and retired in 1965. The British government did not grant pensions to Polish officers, but the grateful Dutch granted him a generous pension. He kept apart from émigré politics and, with his wife's support, devoted himself to wounded and disabled Polish ex-servicemen in Edinburgh. Honoured by his men at home and overseas, Maczek emerged as the natural if unofficial leader of the Polish community in Scotland. His recreations included hill-walking and fishing. In 1961 he published his memoirs, *Od Podwody do Czolga*, modest on his own achievement but praising his 'Boys', 'the Old Guard of the Republic' (ibid., 91).

In 1989 the communist regime in Poland collapsed, and in 1990 the new government promoted him full general.

In 1992 he celebrated his 100th birthday, and in his birthday message to his soldiers he declared their 'overwhelming joy that ... we can see a Poland free once more' (Stachura, *Themes*, 4). In February 1994 he was awarded a rare Polish honour, membership of the order of the White Eagle (knight companion). He died of cardiovascular and renal degeneration on 11 December 1994 at the house where he had lived since 1948—16 Arden Street, Edinburgh—and, following a service on 21 December at St Mary's Roman Catholic Cathedral, Edinburgh, was buried on 23 December in the Polish military cemetery at Breda in the Netherlands. His wife and their three children survived him. In 1997 he was commemorated by a plaque on his Edinburgh home. He was 'the quintessential Polish hero' (Stachura, *Poland*, 93). ROGER T. STEARN

Sources P. D. Stachura, *Poland in the twentieth century* (1999) • P. D. Stachura, ed., *Themes of modern Polish history: proceedings of a symposium on 28 March 1992 in honour of the centenary of General Stanislaw Maczek* (1992) • *The Times* (13 Dec 1994) • *The Independent* (13 Dec 1994) • *The Independent* (16 Dec 1994) • d. cert. • K. Sword, N. Davies, and Jan Ciechanowski, *The formation of the Polish community in Great Britain, 1939–1950* (1989) • J. Keegan, *Six armies in Normandy: from D-day to the liberation of Paris* (1992) • N. Davies, *God's playground: a history of Poland*, 2 (1981) • N. Davies, *Heart of Europe: a short history of Poland* (1984) • *The Scotsman* (27 May 1995) • private information (2004) [Dr Andrzej Maczek, son]
Likenesses photograph, repro. in *The Times*
Wealth at death £48,656: confirmation, 28 July 1995, CCI

Madan, Falconer (1851–1935), librarian and bibliographer, was born on 15 April 1851 at Cam vicarage, Gloucestershire, the fifth and youngest son of George Madan (1807–1891), vicar of Cam, and his wife, Harriet (1813–1904), daughter of William Gresley. He was educated at Crewkerne grammar school (1861–4) and Marlborough College (1864–70), and won a scholarship to Brasenose College, Oxford in 1870. There he gained first-class honours in honour moderations, and second-class honours in *literae humaniores* in 1874. He was elected a fellow of Brasenose in 1876, and entered the Bodleian Library as a sub-librarian in June 1880. His college fellowship lapsed at this point, but was renewed in 1889 (when he was also appointed, until 1913, university lecturer in palaeography), and he was made an honorary fellow in 1912. On 29 December 1885 he married Frances Jane (*b.* 1861) daughter of Harrison Hayter. They had three sons and two daughters.

Madan's grasp of minute scholarly detail, already demonstrated in collections for the revision of Liddell and Scott's *Greek-English Lexicon*, found immediate expression at the Bodleian, where he was at first engaged in the cataloguing of accessions and arrears of manuscripts. His classical training also involved him in the cataloguing of printed books in Latin and Greek (including early books). An awakened interest in printing and the book trade in Oxford rapidly assumed importance in his library work, and he was thus able both to fill gaps in the Bodleian's holdings and to amass a major collection of his own.

Bodleian manuscript holdings had hitherto been published (in Latin and in great detail) in a series of volumes known as Quarto Catalogues. In 1890 the curators agreed, upon the suggestion of Andrew Clark, a junior proctor office, and it remained so, and was much valued by his former colleagues, until his death.

Although Madan was somewhat critical of the founding constitution of the Bibliographical Society, he became a member in 1892, and contributed substantially to its first *Transactions* (1893), with a discussion of bibliographical method, illustrated by a specimen of his forthcoming *Oxford Books*. One of the society's earliest preoccupations was with the establishment of a standard for bibliographical description, and Madan contributed forcefully to the debate, in which A. W. Pollard and W. W. Greg also participated. In 1909 he followed this by elaborating his 'degressive principle', by which different levels of detail in description were provided for books, according to their perceived importance. He was the society's president from 1919 to 1922.

It was in his work on the press in Oxford, together with his abilities as a manuscript cataloguer, that Madan's greatest achievement lay. The first volume of *Oxford Books* appeared in 1895, the second in 1912, and the third in 1931. The completion brought him the Bibliographical Society's gold medal in 1932. Madan was a founding member of the Oxford Bibliographical Society in 1921, and its president from 1924 to 1926. He died on 22 May 1935 at his home, 94 Banbury Road, Oxford, and was buried at Wolvercote. Even at the time of his death, he was seen as one of the last scholar-librarians; he was certainly the last to be equally at home in the worlds of both manuscripts and printed books.   R. JULIAN ROBERTS

Sources H. H. E. Craster, *History of the Bodleian Library, 1845–1945* (1952) · *WWW* · F. Madan, *The Madan family and Maddens in Ireland and England* (1933) · F. Madan, *The Gresleys of Drakelowe* (1899) · K. A. Manley, 'E. W. B. Nicholson (1849–1912) and his importance to librarianship', DPhil diss., U. Oxf., 1977 · Library records, 1882, Bodl. Oxf. · *The Times* (23 May 1935), 18c · H. H. E. Craster, *Oxford Magazine* (30 May 1935), 668 · *Bodleian Quarterly Record*, 8 (1935–7), 73–4 · *CGPLA Eng. & Wales* (1935)
Archives BL, letters relating to localization and dating of MSS, Add. MS 37815 · Bodl. Oxf., corresp., notes, papers and collections; draft catalogue of the Clarendon Press MSS | BL, letters to W. C. Hazlitt, Add. MSS 38903–38912 · BL, letters to G. F. Warner and J. P. Gilson, Add. MSS 47686–47687 · Bodl. Oxf., corresp. relating to Lewis Carroll and the London cemetery exhibition; corresp. with members of the Gresley family; corresp., notes and papers relating to the Oxford Millenary Exhibition · Brasenose College, Oxford, notes on Brasenose College business, memoranda of Brasenose men · Lincs. Arch., letters to R. W. Golding
Likenesses P. Bigland, oils, 1920, Bodl. Oxf. [*see illus.*]
Wealth at death £6125 0s. 11d.: probate, 19 July 1935, *CGPLA Eng. & Wales*

Falconer Madan (1851–1935), by Percy Bigland, 1920

and fellow of Lincoln College, who was advised by Madan, that both existing collections and future accessions should be recorded in a briefer form and with an English apparatus. Madan was the principal architect of the *Summary Catalogue*, and worked on it until 1912; three volumes and part of a fourth appeared under his name, from 1895 to 1906, and his work was also acknowledged on the title-pages of subsequent volumes. The accuracy and content of his work are still seen as exemplary.

Madan's relations with E. W. B. Nicholson, Bodley's librarian from 1882, were at first friendly, but deteriorated to a point when librarian and sub-librarian only communicated in writing. Madan not only compiled a series of detailed notes in criticism of the librarian, but from time to time supplied this criticism to curators, to other members of the university, and, anonymously, to the press.

Upon Nicholson's enforced retirement in 1912, Madan succeeded him as librarian, at the age of sixty-one. On the outbreak of war in 1914, he was granted an extension for five years, and retired in 1919. As librarian, he continued his predecessor's policies, although bringing to the office greater caution and stability, a characteristically close attention to administrative detail, and the financial prudence which a time of war demanded. In particular, the library's financial deficit was eliminated. The *Bodleian Library Quarterly* was established by Madan in 1914. He was president of the Library Association from 1914 to 1915.

Upon retirement, Madan devoted himself to his bibliographical interests. The nature of these necessitated a presence in the library as regular as that of a librarian in

Madan [*née* Cowper], **Judith** (1702–1781), gentlewoman and poet, was born on 26 August 1702, probably at the family estate, Hertingfordbury Park, Hertfordshire, the only daughter of Spencer *Cowper (1670–1728), lawyer, judge, and MP, and his wife, Pennington, *née* Goodere (*bap.* 1665, *d.* 1727).

From her mid-teens Judith Cowper composed verse, mainly in heroic couplets, characteristically in imitation and celebration of the poets she was reading. She probably met Pope while sitting to his friend Charles Jervas for her portrait. He compared her favourably with Lady Mary Wortley Montagu:

Tho sprightly Sappho force our Love & Praise,
A softer Wonder my pleasd soul surveys,
The mild Erinna, blushing in her Bays.
(*Correspondence of Alexander Pope*, 2.138–9)

The poem concludes with a version of the comparison of sunset to moonrise, to the latter's advantage, which was later to be applied to Martha Blount at the close of *Characters of Women*. In 1723 he sent Judith 'To a Lady on her Birthday', which she seems to have assumed to have been addressed to her, whereas the 'lady' was actually Martha (ibid., 2.180, 3.18–19). Pope suggested poetic projects as diversions to counter the depression to which Judith was subject, and in 1723 proposed that she should write 'something in the descriptive way on any Subject you please, mixd with Vision & Moral': if she wrote the descriptions, he offered, 'I would undertake to find a Tale that shoud bring em all together' (ibid., 2.202–3).

In 1723 an outburst of rapturously lyrical poems proclaimed Judith's love for Lysander, alias Colonel Martin Madan (1700–1756), whom she married on 7 December. They had nine children, including Martin *Madan (1725–1790) and Spencer *Madan (1729–1813). After her marriage her writing of poetry came to a virtual standstill. Money was short and her husband often abroad, and she suffered recurrent depression. She was confirmed about 1749 and joined the Methodist circle of John Wesley and Selina Hastings, countess of Huntingdon, corresponding with her like-minded nephew the poet William Cowper. Her daughter Maria also published religious verse. Madan was praised as 'Cornalia' in John Duncombe's *Feminiad* (1754), and a few of her poems appeared in the miscellanies of Matthew Concaren (1731), George Colman and Bonnell Thornton (1755), and Robert Dodsley (1755); 'Abelard to Eloisa', written in 1720 in response to Pope's poem, appeared in William Pattison's *Poetical Works* (1728) as his own. However, much of Madan's most interesting work remains unpublished.

Madan died on 7 December 1781 at her home in Stafford Row (now part of Buckingham Gate), London, and was buried in the churchyard of Grosvenor Chapel, Mount Street, Grosvenor Square.   VALERIE RUMBOLD

Sources letters and poems, Bodl. Oxf., MSS Eng. lett. c. 284–5 · poems in Ashley Cowper's commonplace book, BL, Add. MS 28101 · F. Madan, *The Madan family and Maddens in Ireland and England: a historical account* (1933) · *The correspondence of Alexander Pope*, ed. G. Sherburn, 5 vols. (1956) · *The Twickenham edition of the poems of Alexander Pope*, ed. J. Butt and others, 11 vols. in 12 (1939–69) · V. Rumbold, *Women's place in Pope's world* (1989) · V. Rumbold, 'The poetic career of Judith Cowper', *Pope, Swift, and women writers*, ed. D. C. Mell (1996) · R. Lonsdale, ed., *Eighteenth-century women poets: an Oxford anthology* (1989); pbk edn (1990) · *Letters of the late Alexander Pope, esq. to a lady. Never before published* (1769)
Archives Bodl. Oxf., MSS Eng. lett. c. 284–5, d. 286–9; misc. c. 502, d. 636–8, 679–81, e. 588, 642–7; poet c. 62, d. 196 · Surrey HC, family papers | BL, Ashley Cowper's commonplace book, Add. MS 28101 · Bodl. Oxf., letters to her daughter, Maria Cowper · Bodl. Oxf., corresp. with Martin Madan

Likenesses C. Jervas, crayon drawing · J. Vanderbanck, portrait; Sothebys, 23 May 1930 · W. S. Wright, portrait (after lost oil painting), Cowper Museum, Olney
Wealth at death principally house in Bond Street and remainder of lease on house in Stafford Row: will, Madan, *The Madan family*, 90–91

Madan, Martin (1725–1790), Church of England clergyman and advocate of polygamy, was born on 5 October 1725 at his paternal grandfather's house in Bond Street, London, the elder son of Colonel Martin Madan (1700–1756), MP for Hertingfordbury, Hertfordshire, and his wife, Judith *Madan (1702–1781), poet, the only daughter of Judge Spencer Cowper. His younger brother, Spencer *Madan, became bishop of Peterborough, and through their mother's family they were cousins of the poet and hymn writer, William Cowper. Madan was educated at a school in Chelsea under Mr Rothesy and from 1736 at Westminster School, whence he proceeded to Christ Church, Oxford; he matriculated on 9 February 1743 and graduated BA on 9 November 1746. He was called to the bar from the Inner Temple in 1748, but his career took a dramatic turn when he was challenged by his fellow members of a fashionable and lively club, frequented by young men of the town, to accompany some of them to hear John Wesley and then to entertain them with a caricature of his preaching. As they entered the text was being announced: 'Prepare to meet thy God'. Madan was deeply struck and on returning to the club and being asked 'to take the old Methodist off', he stunned his colleagues with the reply: 'No, gentlemen, he has taken me off' (BL, Add. MS 5832, fol. 84). He forsook the bar, his former mode of living, and his erstwhile associates.

Nurtured in his new direction by David Jones (1735–1810) and even more strongly by William Romaine, who at that time at his church, St Dunstan-in-the-West, was the most influential evangelical in London, Madan sought holy orders, not, be it said, without difficulty because of these perceived Methodist connections. Through the efforts, however, of the countess of Huntingdon he was successful and the 'lawyer turned divine' was appointed to All Hallows, Lombard Street, in 1750. He is said to have remarked on one occasion: 'I have long been accustomed to plead at the bar the cause of man; I stand here to plead the cause of God and to beseech sinners to be reconciled to Him' (Binns, 242). He was apparently an impressive preacher, tall of stature with an imposing presence, whose legal training assisted in the ordering and cogency of his sermons. 'He preached without notes; his voice was musical, well undulated, full and powerful; his language plain, nervous, pleasing and memorable, and his arguments strong, bold, rational and conclusive' (Seymour, 1.167).

Madan became chaplain of the Lock Hospital at Hyde Park Corner, an institution for penitent prostitutes. His preaching there, where members of the public were free to attend, became so popular that a new chapel was built in 1762. His association with the Lady Huntingdon meant, however, that his talents were given wider scope for exploitation. He preached at the opening of her first chapel in Brighton in 1761 and again at its enlargement in 1767, as well as at such other fashionable watering places as Cheltenham, Bath, and Tunbridge Wells. Before that he is recorded as being present at her prayer meetings where both Wesley and Whitefield attended at different times. He also joined other clergy who were part of her circle in itinerating. Thus he was with Whitefield and the young Henry Venn in Gloucestershire in 1757 and later in the same year with Romaine in Hertfordshire, Bedfordshire, and Buckinghamshire. In 1759 he was with Romaine again, this time looking at the revivalist activities at Everton, Bedfordshire, where Berridge was the incumbent, and for whom Madan also acted as locum when the latter was itinerating. Madan continued his links with Lady Huntingdon, severing them only when she herself severed those of her Connexion with the Church of England. His affinities with other clergy in these years place him distinctly within the Calvinistic wing of the evangelical movement. His correspondence with Wesley over a period from 1756, together with his *Scriptural Account of the Doctrine of Perfection* (1763), bring out their differences on that subject.

Besides his other talents Madan also possessed high musical gifts, and, in addition to his preaching, another attraction of the Lock chapel was the annual oratorio, where in 1764 and 1765 respectively Wesley attended performances of *Judith* and *Ruth*. Of more lasting significance was the *Collection of Psalms and Hymns* which Madan assembled and published in 1760, the popularity of which was such that it ran to thirteen editions by 1794. It consisted originally of 170 pieces with a further 24 added as an appendix to the second edition in 1763. John Julian remarks of it that

> nearly the whole of its contents, together with its extensively altered texts, were reprinted in numerous hymn-books for nearly one-hundred years. At the present time many of the great hymns of the [nineteenth] century are in use as altered by him in 1760 and 1763. (Julian, 710)

A more recent writer has called it

> a robust, no-nonsense collection ... He aimed for plainness and simplicity ... To assist the reader in decoding the text, therefore, Madan provided biblical references as footnotes to every page. His preface was an uncompromising document, denouncing any deviation from what he saw as orthodox belief. (Watson, 266)

Madan did not hesitate to alter the texts of hymns and many of his emendations became standard. One such example is his extensive alteration of the passiontide hymn by Isaac Watts, 'He dies, the Heavenly Lover dies', where even the first line became 'He dies, the Friend of sinners dies' (Julian, 500), while 'Lo, He comes with clouds descending' is Madan's mixture of the original by John Cennick and a subsequent version by Charles Wesley (ibid., 681–2). He also followed the same practice with tunes, including that for 'Lo, He comes', originally written by Thomas Olivers and named after him, but altered in Madan's *Collection of Hymn and Psalm Tunes* (1769) to the version now known as 'Helmsley'. Apart from this, little of Madan's hymnody has survived, though his 'Wandsworth' was the setting given to 'Father of mercies' in the

1904 edition of *Hymns Ancient and Modern*. In later life he also published *Six Sonatas for a German Flute and Violin* (*c*.1780) and *A Sonata for the Harpsichord or Pianoforte* (*c*.1785).

In 1767 Madan was involved in an ecclesiastical *cause célèbre*, in which a principal player was one of his former assistant chaplains at the Lock, who was another member of Lady Huntingdon's coterie. This was Thomas Haweis, who had been preferred on Madan's recommendation to the rectory of Aldwincle, Northamptonshire, in February 1764 after the patron, one Kimpton, had failed to negotiate the sale of the advowson. Three years later, however, an offer of 1000 guineas for the advowson was made, and Kimpton, not surprisingly given that he was in prison for debt and his family was said to be starving, tried to secure Haweis's resignation on the grounds that the preferment had been made with reservations. Madan, the erstwhile barrister, consulted the lord chancellor, Lord Apsley, and other legal luminaries and advised Haweis to refuse. In the subsequent acrimonious public outcry accusations were made of simony, Methodism, and misrepresentation. Only after the mediation of the wealthy evangelical London merchant, John Thornton, and the satisfaction of Kimpton's creditors by Lady Huntingdon's purchase of the advowson was Haweis able to remain in possession. Some of Madan's friends, Lady Huntingdon among them, suggested the appropriateness of at least a qualified apology for what appeared to have been a narrowly legalistic insistence on his part. Madan was supported in resisting this by others of his friends including Lord Apsley, who shortly thereafter appointed him as his domestic chaplain. The controversy was the occasion of several pamphlets both by and against Madan.

This incident did not sever Madan's friendships, but a later event did, and it is by this that he is chiefly remembered. This was the publication in 1780 of his book, *Thelyphthora*, dealing with a topic which he no doubt thought it proper to entitle in the decent obscurity of a learned language, even though he elaborated the subtitle 'A Treatise of Female Ruin' under the heads of 'marriage, whoredom and fornication, adultery, polygamy, divorce'. Arising from his acquaintance with the plight of the unfortunate inmates of the Lock Hospital, Madan argued at length for the social benefits of polygamy. He realized the daring of what he was doing, calling himself in the preface to the first edition 'a Free-thinker, not in the usual sense of that word' (M. Madan, *Thelyphthora*, 2nd edn., 1.xv) and recognizing that some might think his subject better 'left under the clouds of obscurity ... hidden from vulgar observation' (ibid., 1.xi). He disclaimed any advocacy of polygamy in terms of satisfying sexual appetite, but asserted that it was 'expedient in some cases, necessary in others' to prevent greater damage, citing in support the Mosaic injunctions of Exodus 22: 16 and Deuteronomy 22: 28–9. In doing so he alleged that while society still chose to recognize part of what he called 'God's law' in condemning fornication, adultery, and marriage within the bounds of consanguinity, it nevertheless saw fit to ignore the requirements of these verses. Realizing, however, that in the Christian dispensation he needed New Testament support, he also argued from such texts as 1 Corinthians 6: 15. His idiosyncrasies were not lacking in boldness, such that he could describe marriage as an outward 'human invention' (ibid., 1.24) and contrast divine ordinance and civil contract (ibid., 2.64). The crux of his case was expressed in a single sentence: 'Every man who has seduced a woman, whether with or without a promise of marriage, should be obliged to wed her publicly' (ibid., 2.67).

The genuineness of Madan's intentions was transparent and it is said that his views were shared by others, among them his great-uncle, Lord Chancellor Cowper, but public opinion and especially the religious world thought differently. Lady Huntingdon held a petition with 6000 signatures against the book's appearance, while a fellow evangelical, Henry Venn, wrote, on 9 August 1780, 'I am glad to see that Mr. Madan's book is held in abhorrence. The fruits it will produce are dreadful' (Venn, *Annals*, 107). There were many articles in magazines, especially those by Samuel Badcock in the *Monthly Review* (vols. 63–5), a spate of pamphlets including three by fellow evangelicals, Richard Hill, Haweis, and Thomas Wills, this last writing at the request of Lady Huntingdon, and a number of satires including William Cowper's *Anti-Thelyphthora*. Madan's only responses were *Letters on Thelyphthora* (1782) and *Five Letters Addressed to Abraham Rees, Editor of Chambers's Encyclopaedia* (1783). As a result of the outcry against him Madan resigned his chaplaincy at the Lock Hospital. He had been in possession of considerable private means since the death of his father in 1756. Five years before, on 17 December 1751, he had married Jane, daughter of Sir Bernard Hale. They had two sons, Martin (d. 1809), of Bushey, Hertfordshire, and William (d. 1769), and three daughters, Sarah, Anna, and Maria. Unembittered by the controversy, Madan withdrew into retirement at Epsom, in 1781, and spent his last years preparing his *New and Literal Translation of Juvenal and Persius* (2 vols., 1789). He died there on 2 May 1790 and was buried at Kensington. His wife survived him by four years, and died at Epsom on 15 June 1794.

ARTHUR POLLARD

Sources [A. C. H. Seymour], *The life and times of Selina, countess of Huntingdon*, 2 vols. (1839) · *DNB* · L. E. Elliott-Binns, *The early evangelicals: a religious and social study* (1953) · J. Julian, ed., *A dictionary of hymnology*, rev. edn (1907) · J. R. Watson, *The English hymn: a critical and historical study* (1997) · M. Frost, ed., *Historical companion to 'Hymns ancient and modern'* (1962) · *GM*, 1st ser., 60 (1790), 478 · J. Venn, *Annals of a clerical family* (1904) · *The journal of the Rev. John Wesley*, ed. N. Curnock and others, 8 vols. (1909–16) · R. S. Lea, 'Madan, Martin', HoP, *Commons*, 1715–54 · F. Madan, *The Madan family, and Maddens in Ireland and England* (1933)

Archives Bodl. Oxf., family corresp. and papers · Harvard U., law school, legal notebook · Surrey HC, family corresp. and papers

Likenesses J. Watson, mezzotint, pubd 1774 (with C. E. de Coetlogan; after G. James), BM, NPG · line engraving, 1784, NPG · R. Houston, mezzotint (after Jenkin), BM · R. Manwaring, mezzotint, BM · engraving, repro. in *Gospel Magazine* (1774)

Wealth at death presumed wealthy

Madan, Spencer (1729–1813), bishop of Peterborough, was the second of eight sons of Colonel Martin Madan MP (1700–1756) and his wife, Judith Cowper (1702–1781) [*see* Madan, Judith]. He was the brother of Martin *Madan

Spencer Madan (1729–1813), attrib. Mather Brown, 1797

(1725–1790). His mother's uncle was Lord Chancellor Cowper. He was sent to Westminster School in 1742, whence in 1746 he passed to Trinity College, Cambridge, as a scholar. In 1749 he graduated BA as third wrangler, and he proceeded MA in 1753, and DD in 1766. He was at first intended for the bar, like his elder brother, and had been admitted to the Inner Temple in 1747, but he took holy orders, and was ordained deacon on Christmas eve 1752. In 1753 he was elected to a fellowship at his college, but after a short residence he became vicar of Haxley with the rectory of West Halton, both in Lincolnshire, and vicar of Bossall, Yorkshire. In 1761 he was appointed chaplain in ordinary to the king, a position which he held until 1787, and he was also from 1770 to 1794 prebendary of Peterborough, and at the same time rector of Castor in Northamptonshire. His advancement was in part due to his personal qualities. He was described by Richard Cumberland as 'a young man of elegant accomplishments … [and] no small portion of hereditary taste and talent … [who] reads in chapel to the admiration of everyone' (Cumberland, 105). In 1776 he was appointed to the sinecure rectory of Ashley in Berkshire, and in 1792 was promoted to the see of Bristol, where he was consecrated bishop on 3 June. Early in 1794, on the death of John Hinchliffe, he was translated to Peterborough, where he remained until his death.

Madan married twice, first Lady Charlotte (1725/6–1794), second daughter of Charles Cornwallis, first Earl Cornwallis. The couple had a daughter, Charlotte, and two sons. The elder son was Spencer *Madan (1758–1836), Church of England clergyman and a noted translator of H. Grotius. His brother, William Charles, became a colonel in the army. In 1796 the bishop married, secondly, Mary Vyse, daughter of William Vyse of Lichfield and sister of William Vyse (1741–1816), archdeacon of Coventry. Madan and his second wife had no children.

Madan developed, from his Cambridge days to the end of his life, simple and even austere habits. It was his custom to rise early and light his own fire, in order to pursue the study of the scriptures in the original Hebrew and Greek, before the general work of the day began. It is recorded by those who knew him personally that he was a man of unobtrusive piety, passionately fond of music, and widely read in Hebrew. When starting on his last round of confirmations and visitation in 1813, at the age of eighty-four, he said that he preferred to die in the discharge of his duty rather than to live a little longer by neglect of it. It was this sense of duty that brought a later writer to claim 'his example in the episcopal station, like the precepts which he taught, uniformly displayed in a most engaging light, the genuine character of true religion' (Hill, 251).

Madan published a number of his sermons, as well as *Observations on the question between the present lessee of the prebendal estate of Sawley and the curate of that place* (1810). He died at his palace in Peterborough on 8 November 1813. He was buried in Peterborough Cathedral, and his tomb bears the well-known lines:

In sacred sleep the pious Bishop lies:
Say not, in death—a good man never dies.

He was survived by his second wife.

FALCONER MADAN, *rev.* WILLIAM GIBSON

Sources R. Cumberland, *Memoirs of Richard Cumberland written by himself* (1806) · *GM*, 1st ser., 83/2 (1813), 508–9, 703 · J. R. Tanner, ed., *Historical register of the University of Cambridge … to the year 1910* (1917) · Venn, *Alum. Cant.* · G. Carnell, *The bishops of Peterborough, 1541–1991* (1993) · J. H. Hill, *The bishopric of Peterborough and its prelates* (1870) · J. Wade, ed., *The extraordinary black book*, new edn (1832) · *Old Westminsters*, vols. 1–2 · J. Nichols, *The history and antiquities of the county of Leicester*, 4 vols. (1795–1815) · J. Ingamells, *The English episcopal portrait, 1559–1835: a catalogue* (privately printed, London, 1981) · *IGI* · Foster, *Alum. Oxon.*

Likenesses T. Chapman, engraving, 1794 · T. Cheesman, stipple, pubd 1794 (after J. Barry), BM, NPG · attrib. M. Brown, portrait, 1797, bishop's palace, Peterborough [*see illus.*]

Madan, Spencer (1758–1836), Church of England clergyman, born on 25 August 1758 at Fulford, near York, was the eldest son of Spencer *Madan (1729–1813), bishop of Peterborough, and his first wife, Lady Charlotte Cornwallis (1725/6–1794), daughter of Charles Cornwallis, first Earl Cornwallis. He was educated at Westminster School from 1771, and Trinity College, Cambridge, from 1776. He received an honorary degree of MA on 11 December 1778 and in 1782 won the Seatonian prize for his poem, *The Call of the Gentiles*. During his lifetime, he was best known in academic circles for his English translation of Grotius's *De veritate*, published as *Hugo Grotius on the Truth of Christianity* at Cambridge in 1782 and reprinted in 1797 and 1814.

Madan's aristocratic and clerical connections ensured his rapid preferment, but he was only a minor pluralist. Not only was his father a bishop, his mother was the niece of Frederick Cornwallis, archbishop of Canterbury, and sister of James Cornwallis, bishop of Lichfield (1781–1824). The dean of Peterborough appointed him his curate at Wrotham, Kent (1782–3), at a time when his father was a prebendary of Peterborough. He became rector of Bradley Magna, Suffolk, in 1783, but resigned this living in 1786 when his uncle, the bishop of Lichfield, presented him to the prebend and vicarage of Tachbrook, Warwickshire. Within the year he exchanged the prebend for the rectory of Ibstock, Leicestershire, which he held until his death fifty years later. In 1787 he resigned the vicarage of Tachbrook on being appointed rector of St Philip's, Birmingham.

As a city rector in Birmingham from 1787 to 1809 Madan played a prominent role in the debate on the French Revolution and the suppression of radical thinking in Britain. In 1790 he engaged in controversy with Joseph Priestley, the Birmingham dissenter, over the proposed repeal of the Test and Corporation Acts. His sermon of 14 February 1790, published as *The Principal Claims of the Dissenters Considered*, gave rise to Joseph Priestley's *Familiar Letters Addressed to the Inhabitants of Birmingham* (1790), to which Madan responded in April 1790. In the crisis of authority in the winter of 1792–3 Madan contributed *A Plain Caution to every Honest Englishman Against Certain False Arguments* (1793), an anonymous, fifteen-page propaganda tract, which was sold for 2*d*., urging the lower orders to remain loyal and obedient. He contributed £500 towards the building of a free church 'for the use of the lower classes' (*GM*, 7.206) in Birmingham; and he founded, largely at his own expense, three free schools for poor children in his Leicestershire parish of Ibstock. He published a number of sermons between 1792 and 1805, including a charity sermon for Leicester Infirmary and Lunatic Asylum in 1798.

Madan served as chaplain in ordinary to the king from 1788 to 1832. His Cornwallis connections secured him a canon residentiary of Lichfield (1790–1817); his father appointed him chancellor to the diocese of Peterborough in 1794 and a prebendary of Peterborough Cathedral in 1800. On 5 January 1791 he married Henrietta Inge (*d.* 1816), daughter of William Inge of Thorpe Constantine; they had eleven children before her death, aged forty-six, in 1816. In 1809 Cambridge University made him an honorary DD. In the same year he resigned his Birmingham rectory and was appointed by his brother-in-law, William Phillips Inge, to the family living of Thorpe Constantine, Staffordshire, which he held until 1824. In October 1833 he was attacked by paralysis from which he made only a partial recovery. He died at the rectory, Ibstock, on 9 October 1836, aged seventy-eight, and was buried in a family vault at Thorpe Constantine. His children erected a tablet to his memory in Lichfield Cathedral.

ROBERT HOLE

Sources *Memoir of the rev. Spencer Madan* (1842?) [printed from a MS in Lichfield Cathedral and prefixed to a Bodleian copy of S. Madan, *An Eng. trans. of the six books of Hugo Grotius, on the truth of Christianity*, 1814] · J. Taylor, *A sermon on the occasion of the death of the rev. Spencer Madan* (1836) · *GM*, 2nd ser., 7 (1837), 205–7 · *GM*, 1st ser., 61 (1791), 87 · *GM*, 1st ser., 86/1 (1816), 574 · *DNB* · Venn, *Alum. Cant.*

Madariaga, Salvador de (1886–1978), writer and diplomatist, was born on 23 July 1886 at Corunna, Spain, the second child of José de Madariaga, colonel in the Spanish army, and his wife, Maria de la Ascensión Rojo. After graduating from the Instituto del Cardenal Cisneros, Madrid, he travelled to Paris in 1900 to study at the Collège Chaptal. Although naturally inclined towards literature, at the instigation of his father he embarked on a scientific and technical career, entering the École Polytechnique in 1906, and the École Nationale Supérieure des Mines two years later. After graduation in 1911 he returned to Spain and joined the Compañía del Ferrocarril del Norte as a mining engineer. In 1912 Madariaga married in Glasgow Constance Helen (d. 1970), eldest daughter of Edmund Archibald, a meteorologist, and granddaughter of Sir Thomas Archibald (1817–1876); they had two daughters, Nieves and Isabel.

While conscientiously following his chosen career, Madariaga began writing for Madrid newspapers on French and English topics, and established contacts with literary and political circles in the capital. In 1916 he finally decided to abandon his technical career to devote himself to writing. He moved to London, where he worked for *The Times* and reported on the First World War for the Spanish press. His *Times* articles were collected and translated as *La guerra desde Londres* (1917). In 1920 he published his first book of essays in English, *Shelley and Calderón* (1920). *Guía del Lector del "Quijote": ensayo psicológico* followed in 1926 (Eng. trans., *Don Quixote: an Introductory Essay in Psychology*, 1934). He left London for Geneva in 1921 to become a member of the press section of the League of Nations secretariat, and in the following year he was appointed director of the disarmament section. He held this post until the end of 1927, when he left the League of Nations to occupy the newly created chair of Spanish at Oxford (1928–31). During this time he published, among other books and articles, *Disarmament* (1929); his first historical work, *Spain* (1930); and novels such as the futuristic satire *The Sacred Giraffe* (1925), thus initiating a prolific literary career which was uninterrupted until his death at the age of ninety-two.

Madariaga's academic career ended abruptly during a lecture tour in Mexico and Cuba in 1931, when the new Spanish republican government appointed him ambassador in Washington, a post which he held only briefly, for in January 1932 he was transferred to the embassy in Paris. He was also nominated permanent Spanish delegate at the League of Nations, where he played an active and influential part, particularly in the Manchurian and Abyssinian debates, during which he presided over the committees of five and thirteen which were set up to negotiate a solution.

When in July 1936 the Spanish Civil War broke out, Madariaga took up residence in London and devoted himself to historical research. On the outbreak of the Second World War he moved to Oxford, and continued his work on the New World biographical trilogy, *Christopher Columbus* (1939), *Hernán Cortes* (1941), and the controversial *Bolívar* (1952), as well as on *The Rise and Fall of the Spanish American Empire* (2 vols., 1947), and the essay *On Hamlet* (1948). His researches informed a series of historical novels, of which the most successful was *The Heart of Jade* (1944). He concurrently produced all these works in Spanish, and they were later translated into many languages. Madariaga's eclectic literary output extended to poetry, plays, and innumerable articles for the world press.

During the Second World War and for a period of nine years he broadcast weekly from the BBC to Spanish America. His radio plays were also broadcast to Europe in French, Spanish, English, and German. After the war he became prominent in European affairs and continued to publish works of political argument and analysis which fervently defended the cause of European unity. He was founder and president (1949–64) of the College of Europe, Bruges; a founder member, president, and honorary president of Liberal International, as well as president of its cultural commission; and honorary president of the Congress for the Liberty of Culture (Paris, 1950). Numerous international honours were bestowed on him, including gold medals of the universities of Yale and Bern; honorary doctorates of the universities of Arequipa, Liège, Lille, Lima, Oxford, Poitiers, and Princeton; honorary fellowship of Exeter College, Oxford; the grand cross of the orders of the Spanish Republic, the Légion d'honneur (France), Jade in Gold (China), Aztec Eagle (Mexico), White Lion (Czechoslovakia), and Alfonso el Sabio (Spain).

On 18 November 1970, soon after the death of his first wife, Madariaga married Mrs Emilia Rauman, daughter of Dr Lajos Szekely, a barrister, and head of the Hungarian bar for many years. Emilia Rauman had been his constant collaborator since 1938, and was responsible for translating his books and lectures into German, Italian, and Hungarian. Soon afterwards, and mainly for reasons of health, he left Oxford to take up residence in Locarno. In April 1976 he visited Spain after a voluntary exile of forty years, and delivered his inaugural address—delayed because of the civil war and Franco—to the Real Academia Española, to which he had been elected in 1936.

Madariaga, who considered himself a citizen of the world, inspired international respect for his literary achievements and liberal politics. Always a scintillating conversationalist and lecturer (in three languages), he had a polymathic intellect of rare brilliance. He died in Locarno, Switzerland, on 14 December 1978.

J. L. GILI, *rev.* P. J. CONNELL

Sources S. de Madariaga, *Morning without noon: memoirs* (1974) · personal knowledge (1986) · private information (1986) · *The Times* (15 Dec 1978) · P. Ward, ed., *The Oxford companion to Spanish literature* (1978) · G. Bleiberg, M. Ihrie, and J. Pérez, eds., *Dictionary of the literature of the Iberian peninsula*, 2 vols. (1993)
Archives NL Wales, corresp. with Thomas Jones
Likenesses photograph, 1934, repro. in Madariaga, *Morning without noon* · two photographs, 1948–9, Hult. Arch.

Madden, Cecil Charles (1902–1987), radio and television producer, was born on 29 November 1902 at the British consulate in Mogador, Morocco, the eldest of three sons (there were no daughters) of Archibald Maclean Madden CMG, diplomatist, and his wife, Cecilia Catherine, daughter of Allen Page Moor, canon of Truro. He was educated at French schools in Morocco, schools in Spain, and in England at Aldeburgh Lodge preparatory school and Dover

College. He acquired fluent French and Spanish. While working in a secretarial post with the Rio Tinto Company in Spain, he wrote revues in Spanish and played Freddy Eynsford Hill in a translation of George Bernard Shaw's *Pygmalion*. Four times a year his professional duties took him to New York, where he saw Broadway productions in his free time.

Between 1926 and 1932 every holiday was spent in Paris working in theatre management. Although Madden encountered famous stars such as Fernandel, Maurice Chevalier, Mistinguett, and Miss Bluebell, he was very proud of the fact that he improved backstage conditions for the chorus girls. As well as writing revues in French and Spanish, he wrote several plays in English.

In June 1932 Madden married Muriel Emily, daughter of Brigadier-General James Kilvington Cochrane; they had a son and daughter. In 1933 he joined the BBC talks department, where he produced a series entitled *Anywhere for a News Story* and subsequently produced the outside broadcasting spot on a popular Saturday evening programme, *In Town Tonight*.

Madden subsequently worked as a senior producer in the new empire (later overseas) service of the BBC, and in 1936 joined Gerald Cock, the recently appointed first head of the BBC's television service. In August 1936 they were told to prepare programmes to open the first high definition service in the world on 2 November. Plans changed and Madden was told to produce a show to be transmitted to Radiolympia in ten days' time. *Here's looking at you* was seen by visitors to the exhibition and the few television set owners then living around London. Madden then created *Picture Page*, a magazine programme transmitted from Alexandra Palace on the official opening of the television service. From 2 November 1936, until television shut down on 1 September 1939, Madden organized and produced live programmes of variety, ballets, and drama, as well as Disney cartoons. 'A play a day' was his motto. He created the series *100% Broadway*, *Cabaret Cartoons*, and *Starlight*.

On the outbreak of the Second World War, Madden returned to radio, and in 1940 was made head of the overseas entertainment unit in the Criterion Theatre, broadcasting all radio programmes to British Commonwealth forces serving abroad. He presented the *American Eagle in Britain* programme from 17 November 1940 to 9 September 1945, earning the title of the 'GI's friend'. General Dwight D. Eisenhower visited the studio on 2 March 1944; on 7 June (D-day plus one) his brainchild, the Allied Expeditionary Forces programme (AEF) of the BBC, began with Madden in charge of the integrated production. This programme informed and entertained its listeners until 25 July 1945. Artists included Gertrude Lawrence, Marlene Dietrich, George Raft, Bing Crosby, and Bob Hope. Major Glenn Miller conducted the American band of AEF until he disappeared in December 1944, Madden being the last civilian to see him alive. He was also the man responsible for discovering Petula Clark in 1942 and the Beverley Sisters in 1944.

When television reopened on 7 June 1946, Madden returned to his former post of programmes organizer. In 1950 he was made acting head of children's programmes until April 1951. He then became assistant to the controller of television programmes and created *Picture Parade*, a magazine programme dealing with the film industry. He was also involved with a series of excerpts from West End plays, including *Look Back in Anger*.

Madden retired from the BBC in 1964, but he continued other activities, as a governor of Dulwich College preparatory school, and president of both the Glenn Miller Society and the British Puppet and Model Theatre Guild. His interest in young entrants to the profession was reflected in his work for the Royal Academy of Dramatic Art (RADA), as vice-chairman of the RADA Associates. He was involved with the British Academy of Film and Television Arts (BAFTA) and took part in the National Film School. His personal scrapbooks, containing records of television since 1936, aided research for the 'fifty years of television' celebrations in November 1986, when he was videoed from the studio at Alexandra Palace on 2 November. In the Museum of Film, Photography, and Television at Bradford he is commemorated in a life-sized model, seated in the gallery at Alexandra Palace. He was a BAFTA award winner (1961) and a fellow of the Royal Society of Arts (1950). In 1952 he was appointed MBE. Madden laid the foundation of British television, always with taste and high standards. His popularity with those who worked with him was not always shared by the BBC administration. With his sound knowledge of theatre he was a discoverer of talent as well as an innovator.

Madden was tall, slim, and always immaculately dressed. He was charming, courteous, dignified, and had a great sense of fun, which prevented him from being pompous. Madden died in Westminster Hospital, London, on 27 May 1987.   JUNE AVERILL, *rev.*

Sources BBC WAC · P. Noble, ed., *British film and television yearbook, 1957–8* (1958) · C. Andrews, ed., *Radio and television who's who*, 2nd edn (1950) · *Who's who in the theatre* · A. Briggs, *The history of broadcasting in the United Kingdom*, rev. edn, 5 vols. (1995) · *CGPLA Eng. & Wales* (1987)
Wealth at death £185,433: probate, 12 Oct 1987, *CGPLA Eng. & Wales*

Madden, Sir Charles Edward (1862–1935), naval officer, was born at Brompton, Gillingham, Kent, on 5 September 1862, the second son of Captain John William Madden of the 4th (King's Own) regiment and his wife, Emily, second daughter of John Busby, of Kingstown; he was descended from a long line of Anglo-Irish families. He entered the *Britannia* as a naval cadet in 1875 and on promotion to midshipman in 1877 was sent to the *Alexandra*, the flagship of Geoffrey Hornby in the Mediterranean. In 1880 he went to the *Ruby*, a corvette in the East Indies squadron, for two and a half years, being promoted sub-lieutenant in her in 1881.

Soon after promotion to lieutenant in 1884 Madden decided to specialize in torpedoes and spent two years in the torpedo school *Vernon* with an additional six months as staff officer of that establishment. In 1892 he was

Sir Charles Edward Madden (1862–1935), by Walter Stoneman, 1924

appointed torpedo lieutenant of the *Royal Sovereign*, flagship of the channel squadron, and in 1893 resumed his post as staff officer of the *Vernon* until promoted commander in 1896. After three years at sea as commander of the cruiser *Terrible* and the battleship *Caesar* he returned to the *Vernon* in 1899 for a further two years, being promoted captain in June 1901. A year later he became, for two years, flag captain in the *Good Hope* (cruiser squadron) to Admiral Wilmot Hawksworth Fawkes, who had been his captain in the *Terrible* and had since been naval private secretary to the first lord. During this service he took Joseph Chamberlain on his memorable visit to South Africa at the end of 1902. He married on 28 June 1905 Constance Winifred (d. 1964), third and youngest daughter of Sir Charles Cayzer, first baronet, and sister of Countess Jellicoe; and they had two sons and four daughters.

In February 1905 Captain H. B. Jackson was brought by Lord Selborne from the command of the *Vernon* to the Admiralty as third sea lord and controller. Jackson was the greatest scientific naval officer of his generation, and asked for Madden, now a leading torpedo specialist, to be his naval assistant. It was the time of the great reforms of Sir John Fisher in fleet redistribution, dockyard administration, and shipbuilding policy, and Madden soon became one of his most trusted instruments in carrying them out. Fisher had already, in the previous October, named Madden to Lord Selborne as one of the 'five best brains in the navy below the rank of admiral' and in December 1904 secured his appointment as a member of

the epoch-making ships design committee which produced the *Dreadnought* and *Invincible* designs for battleships and armoured cruisers (later styled battle cruisers). A year later he made Madden his own naval assistant, a post which he held until August 1907. During those stormy years Madden's sound judgement and cool common sense were of the utmost value to his great chief. He was then glad to get to sea again, this time as captain of the *Dreadnought* herself, and as chief of staff to Sir Francis Bridgeman, commander-in-chief of the Home Fleet. In December 1908 he was brought back to Whitehall, first as naval private secretary to Reginald McKenna until January 1910 and then as fourth sea lord until December 1911.

Madden had reached flag rank in April 1911 with unusually short sea service as a post captain, and only fourteen months' fleet experience, but he was now to be at sea continuously for over eleven years as a flag officer in the main British fleet, including the whole period of the First World War. He commanded the first division, Home Fleet (flag in the *St Vincent*) during 1912, the 3rd cruiser squadron (flag in the *Antrim*) during 1913, and then the 2nd cruiser squadron (flag in the *Shannon*) until the eve of the outbreak of war. When Admiral Sir J. R. Jellicoe was appointed to take over the command of the Grand Fleet he asked for his wife's brother-in-law, Madden, who had been designated to rejoin the Board of Admiralty as third sea lord and controller, to accompany him as chief of staff. Madden was accordingly sent to the *Iron Duke*, Jellicoe's flagship, on 4 August 1914 and remained in her until Jellicoe became first sea lord in November 1916, having been promoted acting vice-admiral in June 1915 and confirmed in that rank immediately after the battle of Jutland. In Jellicoe's Jutland dispatch of 18 June 1916 Madden's brilliant work as his chief of staff was recorded thus:

> Throughout a period of twenty-one months of war his services have been of inestimable value. His good judgment, his long experience in fleets, special gift for organization, and his capacity for unlimited work, have all been of the greatest assistance to me, and have relieved me of much of the anxiety inseparable from the conduct of the fleet during the war. In the stages leading up to the fleet action and during and after the action he was always at hand to assist, and his judgment never at fault. I owe him more than I can say. (*Jellicoe Papers*, 1.307)

On the change of chief command in 1916 Madden was appointed to the command of the 1st battle squadron, as second in command of the fleet, with the acting rank of admiral (flag in the *Marlborough* and later in the *Revenge*), and retained it until April 1919, having been confirmed as admiral in February of that year. When Sir David Beatty hauled down his flag as commander-in-chief of the Grand Fleet and the war organization of the navy was broken up, Madden was appointed to the command of the newly constituted Atlantic Fleet (flag in the *Queen Elizabeth*) which he held from 1919 to 1922.

In the autumn of 1919 Madden was created a baronet and granted £10,000 by a vote of parliament, and on finally coming ashore in August 1922 he received a letter of appreciation from the Board of Admiralty for 'the manner in which he exercised command of the Atlantic Fleet and for his services to the Royal Navy and to the Empire'. He was at once appointed first and principal naval aide-de-camp to the king and was promoted admiral of the fleet in July 1924. He served in 1923–4 as chairman of the committee on the functions and training of Royal Marines, and in 1925, under the chairmanship of Lord Chelmsford, on that for the list of executive officers of the navy. He then retired to Broadstone, Forest Row, Sussex, until July 1927, when, on the recommendation of W. C. Bridgeman he was selected to succeed Lord Beatty as first sea lord. Two years later he would have been placed on the retired list, but, in order to retain him in office, Bridgeman procured a special order in council to secure his remaining admiral of the fleet on the active list supernumerary to establishment, so long as he held appointment as first sea lord.

Madden's career had been closely linked with that of Jellicoe since the time of their work together on the ships design committee, and his marriage to Jellicoe's sister-in-law, but it was also believed, at least by Sir Roger Keyes, that Madden could be relied on to be loyal to Beatty and so bring an end to 'the Jellicoe vs. Beatty "talk"' (*Keyes Papers*, 2.267–8). Years later, however, when Madden had frustrated Keyes's ambitions, the latter asserted to Dudley Pound that he had been persuaded to support Madden's appointment against his better judgement, and that Beatty had had 'grave misgivings, but acted on the advice you had given and bitterly regretted it for the rest of his life' (ibid., 3.34). Keyes is a bad witness, but Vice-Admiral W. H. Kelly had concern at the time of Madden's appointment that he 'was too little human, as far as the Service is concerned, and I don't think he would carry any guns at all vis-à-vis with the Politicians' (ibid., 2.183–4), and Ethel Beatty thought he 'had brain but no …' (*Beatty Papers*, 1.376).

Service politics at the time were notoriously bitchy, but it is true that Madden, lacking Beatty's standing with the British public and aristocracy, was unable to sustain Beatty's valiant defence of the naval estimates at a time of tremendous financial difficulty when Winston Churchill, as chancellor, reopened the question of naval procurement as part of his defence of the gold standard.

Even more important than the financial crisis was the need to address the diplomatic one developing between Britain and the United States over naval arms, and over the rights of belligerents to employ naval blockade in the event of war. Having failed at the Paris peace conference to persuade the British government to abandon its definition of maritime rights, it was a major American preoccupation to ensure that Britain could not employ naval force to restrict the growth of American trade. When Madden came to the Admiralty the abortive 1927 Geneva disarmament conference was in session, and he was still in office when Ramsay MacDonald's Labour administration invited the naval powers to meet in London in 1930 to extend the principles of naval arms limitations to cruisers. Limitation in cruiser numbers, besides affecting British trade defence, was also seen as a means of limiting Britain's capacity to blockade neutral commerce.

Austin Chamberlain, the Conservative foreign secretary, and Winston Churchill agreed that it would be an empty, and possibly dangerous, gesture to defend British claims to belligerent rights against American objection. The prime minister, Stanley Baldwin, would only appoint Madden to the committee of imperial defence subcommittee on belligerent rights as an 'expert assessor'. Madden was more effective than anticipated in defending the navy's position, however, and when in October 1927 the report was presented he refused to agree with either the majority or minority reports. Colonel Maurice Hankey, secretary to the committee of imperial defence and to the cabinet, and a stout defender of British naval strategy, recorded Madden's objection in any circumstances to submitting belligerent rights to compulsory arbitration.

These stalling tactics left it to the Labour administration to resolve the crisis in Anglo-American affairs, and it did so by agreeing at the London naval conference to cuts in British cruiser programmes, from the seventy cruisers wanted by the Admiralty to fifty, with an 8 inch calibre and 10,000 ton limit which suited American interests in the Pacific. This surrender was largely hypothetical as Beatty's cruiser programme, abandoned under pressure by Churchill, had no chance of being revived by Ramsay MacDonald. Madden finally retired from the board and the active list in July 1930.

Madden was awarded numerous honours and decorations. He was mentioned in dispatches for service at Suez in 1883, and was appointed CVO in 1907, KCB in January 1916, and KCMG for his services at Jutland. He received the rank of commander of the Légion d'honneur. The Russian order of St Anne, the military order of Savoy, and the Japanese grand cordon of the Rising Sun were conferred upon him in 1917. He was admitted to the rank of grand officer of the Légion d'honneur in 1918, and at the end of the war he was appointed GCB and given the Belgian order of Leopold, the French Croix de Guerre (bronze palms), and the Chinese order of the Striped Tiger. He was appointed GCVO in 1920 and a member of the Order of Merit in 1931. The honorary degree of LLD was conferred upon him by Cambridge University in 1919, and that of DCL by Oxford University in 1928.

Madden acquired during his long career an intimate knowledge of every detail of his profession and was universally esteemed as a man upon whom complete reliance could be placed in any task which he was set. His manner was modest and unassuming; he was popular and an excellent host: he had no enemies, but did not easily make friends. The parts which fell to him during the First World War he played to perfection. As chief of staff to Jellicoe he was responsible for much of the organization of the fleet, and by the care and tact with which he carried out his chief's instructions he contributed largely to its efficiency. While in the closest confidential intimacy with Jellicoe, he was more an interpreter of his views than a contributor to their formation. As second in command to Beatty, while kept fully informed of all developments and consulted on major problems, he was not a man to put forward or insist on strong views of his own, and difficulties which might have arisen had he been of less loyal personality or more ambitious character were non-existent, although he was over eight years older than Beatty.

With hindsight, Madden's insensitivity in early 1919 to the desire of hostilities-only ratings to return to their civilian lives, and as first sea lord his resistance to the Labour administration's attempts to democratize the officer-cadet intake, may be judged more harshly than his limited success in defending the navy's budget and strategic role. Beatty had learned before the war when he was naval secretary to Churchill, the first lord, that 'You have to have a bloody awful row with Winston once a month and then you are all right' (S. Roskill, *Admiral of the Fleet Earl Beatty*, 1980, 58), but Madden was more of an accommodating personality, and did not feel justified on constitutional grounds in going to the length of resignation as a protest at budget cuts. If he had, it might not have had much political impact. Strategically, reconciliation of differences with the United States was worth almost any cost.

In his private life Madden was a devout churchman and a thorough sportsman, and was devoted to his family. During his retirement he was greatly interested in local affairs and gave much time to support of the British Legion. He died at 29 Wimpole Street, St Marylebone, London, on 5 June 1935, and was succeeded as second baronet by his elder son, Charles Edward (*b.* 1906).

V. W. BADDELEY, rev. NICHOLAS TRACY

Sources N. Tracy, 'Admiral Sir Charles E. Madden (1927–1930) and Admiral Sir Frederick L. Field (1930–1933)', *The first sea lords*, ed. M. H. Murfett (1995), 141–56 · *The Keyes papers*, ed. P. G. Halpern, 2, Navy RS, 121 (1980) · *The Jellicoe papers*, ed. A. T. Patterson, 2, Navy RS, 111 (1968) · *The Beatty papers: selections from the private and official correspondence of Admiral of the Fleet Earl Beatty*, ed. B. Ranft, 1, Navy RS, 128 (1989) · S. W. Roskill, *Naval policy between the wars*, 2 vols. (1968–76) · *CGPLA Eng. & Wales* (1935) · Burke, *Peerage* (1980) · private information (1949)
Archives NMM, diaries | BL, letters to Lord Jellicoe, Add. MS 49009 · BL, corresp. with Lord Keyes · NMM, letters to David Beatty · Shrops. RRC, letters to first Viscount Bridgeman | FILM IWM FVA, actuality footage · IWM FVA, documentary footage
Likenesses A. S. Cope, group portrait, oils, 1921 (*Naval officers of World War 1, 1914–18*), NPG · R. G. Eves, oils, 1922, IWM · W. Stoneman, photograph, 1924, NPG [*see illus.*] · F. Dodd, charcoal and watercolour drawing, IWM
Wealth at death £10,590 17s. 2d.: probate, 23 Sept 1935, *CGPLA Eng. & Wales*

Madden, Dodgson Hamilton (1840–1928), judge and legal writer, was born on 28 March 1840, the only son of the Revd Hugh Hamilton Madden, rector of Templemore, co. Tipperary and chancellor of Cashel, and his wife, Isabella Mason. He was educated at Trinity College, Dublin, where he became a scholar in 1860 and graduated with a senior moderatorship in ethics and logic in 1861. He entered the King's Inns, Dublin, in 1860 and the Middle Temple, London, in 1862, and was called to the Irish bar in 1864. He was married twice: first, in 1866, to Minnie, daughter of Lewis Moore of Cremorgan, Queen's county, who died in 1895, and second, in 1896, to Jessie Isabelle,

third daughter of Richard Warburton of Grangehinch, Queen's county.

Madden's practice at the bar was chiefly in Chancery matters. He became queen's counsel in 1880 and third serjeant in 1887. In 1888 he was appointed solicitor-general, in 1889 attorney-general, and in 1892 a justice of the Queen's Bench Division of the High Court. In 1887 he had been elected one of the members of parliament for the University of Dublin. He had a long association with the university, and was later (between 1895 and 1919) to be its vice-chancellor. He took a leading role in the tercentenary celebrations of the granting of the charter of Trinity College in 1892 and received an honorary LLD degree from the university in 1908.

In 1868 Madden published a treatise on the registration of deeds in Ireland, and in 1870 he produced a further work on the landed estates court. A second edition of *A Practical Treatise on the Registration of Deeds, Conveyances, and Judgment-Mortgages* was published in 1901, and *Madden on the Registration of Deeds* became the authoritative work on the subject. While attorney-general he was responsible for the drafting and enactment of the Local Registration of Title Act 1891: this established the Land Registry in a form that facilitated the enormous volume of transactions arising from the Land Acts, which implemented the policy of transfer of estates in Ireland to tenants. In the same year he introduced a bill for the purpose of consolidating and amending the law on the registration of deeds, but this attracted opposition from what Madden described as 'certain advocates of the system of registration of title, who desired the abolition and not the reformation of the existing system of registration' (Madden, vi), and it was withdrawn.

Madden was known outside legal circles for his Shakespearian scholarship, the best-known of his works being *The Diary of Master William Silence; a Study of Shakespeare and of Elizabethan Sport*, written in 1897. He became a member of the Royal Irish Academy in 1901. He retired from the bench in 1919 and then moved to England. Madden died at his home, The Orchard, East Sheen, Surrey, on 6 March 1928. He was survived by his wife. DAIRE HOGAN

Sources *Irish Law Times and Solicitors' Journal* (10 March 1928) · *Irish Law Times and Solicitors' Journal* (17 March 1928) · D. H. Madden, *A practical treatise on the registration of deeds, conveyances, and judgment-mortgages*, 2nd edn (1901) · F. E. Ball, *The judges in Ireland, 1221–1921*, 2 vols. (1926) · *CGPLA Eng. & Wales* (1928)
Likenesses A. A. Wolmark, oils, 1907, TCD
Wealth at death £22,970 8s. 7d.: probate, 16 April 1928, *CGPLA Eng. & Wales*

Madden, Sir Frederic (1801–1873), palaeographer and librarian, was born at 31 St Thomas's Street, Portsmouth, on 16 February 1801, the eleventh of the thirteen children of Captain William John Madden (1757–1833), Royal Marines, and Sarah Carter Madden (1759–1833), daughter of the Revd Arnold Carter, a minor canon of Rochester Cathedral. General Sir G. A. Madden was his uncle. He was educated at local day schools and the Revd Charles Walters's boarding-school at Bishop's Waltham. He contemplated taking orders and matriculated at Magdalen Hall, Oxford,

Sir Frederic
Madden (1801–
1873), by Richard
Cockle Lucas, 1849

in July 1825, but his need to earn his living prevented him from keeping regular terms and proceeding to a degree. He showed a precocious taste for antiquarian and literary pursuits, compiled formidable reading lists, took private lessons in Hebrew, taught himself Syriac, and mastered classical and European languages, including the then little studied Norman French and Anglo-Saxon. In February 1824 he was engaged as a copyist by Sir Henry Petrie, keeper of the Tower records. In 1825 he was invited to help William Roscoe catalogue the manuscripts of Thomas William Coke at Holkham Hall, Leicester, a task beyond Roscoe's abilities. In 1828 Madden completed the catalogue (for which he was paid £350) to the highest standards, but its projected publication was abandoned as too expensive. His annoyance was tempered by Coke's invaluable support for his application for an established post at the British Museum, where, after an unsuccessful application for an assistant librarianship in June 1826, he had been employed as a temporary cataloguer to work on the classed catalogue of printed books. He was appointed assistant keeper in the department of manuscripts in February 1828, and promoted to keeper on 18 July 1837.

Madden's qualities as an administrator have been questioned, but there is no doubt that his energy and industry abruptly ended his department's amiably torpid eighteenth-century ways and advanced it to a standing in the world of scholarship which it has maintained ever since. He instituted the systematic registration and cataloguing of the collections, which doubled in size during his keepership. He was the first keeper to seek out and acquire manuscripts on a large scale through dealers and agents, and he took full advantage of the great buyers' market in manuscripts that followed the Napoleonic wars, acquiring important foreign manuscripts on a scale since unmatched. Serious attention was given to binding and conservation for the first time. He identified and arranged the myriad burnt fragments of the Cotton manuscripts damaged by fire in 1731 and recovered numerous valuable texts, the achievement he himself valued most. No labour was too great for him to undertake

for the public service: he personally cut up a copy of Samuel Ayscough's scarcely usable classified *Catalogue of the Manuscripts Preserved in the British Museum* (1782), and rearranged and mounted the many thousands of individual cuttings in the numerical order of the manuscripts to which they referred, for the first time making it possible to establish the contents of a manuscript from the catalogue. Conservative in some respects—he disapproved of exhibiting manuscripts to the public, for example—he was innovative in others: he perceived at once the value of photography for the copying of manuscripts, and in 1856 he installed Roger Fenton in a studio at the museum to photograph the unique text of the Clementine epistles in the Codex Alexandrinus and make the plates for the first published manuscript facsimile.

Madden's zeal for his department's interests, however, brought him into conflict with his trustees, most of whom he held in the greatest contempt. He was aggrieved that they refused to pay him the stipend of £227 due to him as Egerton librarian, a violation of the terms of the Bridgwater bequest for which they were censured by the royal commission on the British Museum, which reported in 1850. Sir Henry Ellis, the principal librarian, he described as 'always an *ass*; always a *bully*; always a *time-serving, lick-spittle booby and blockhead*' (Madden, journal, 10 Nov 1852), and the 'slave' of his arch-enemy Sir Anthony *Panizzi, the keeper of printed books, who united in himself, according to Madden, 'all the villainy, cunning, fraud and diabolical qualities of both Richelieu and Mazarin' (ibid., 1 Aug 1856). His quarrels with Panizzi poisoned his life at the museum. On first acquaintance they were on civil, even friendly terms. Upon their respective promotions to keeper in 1837, however, Archbishop Howley, the principal trustee, intentionally or not, had dated Madden's appointment three days after Panizzi's, thus nullifying Madden's five years' seniority of service and making Panizzi his senior. From Howley's inexplicable act grew Madden's conviction that Panizzi was perpetually conspiring against him and his department. In their notorious disputes over the custody of the King's and Grenville manuscripts Madden had the better argument, but over the latter he was outmanoeuvred. The royal commission by implication criticized him for obstructing Panizzi, a censure not really justified by the facts. Madden's hatred of Panizzi—shared by many of his colleagues—was fuelled by chauvinism and dislike of his whig politics. Panizzi's appointment as principal librarian in 1856 in preference to himself compounded his hatred; he resented his dictatorial rule and what he described as the 'Russian police system' (ibid., 28 May 1856) Panizzi imposed on the museum. He resisted Panizzi's attempts at reconciliation, and not even the appointment of his son Frederic William *Madden as assistant in the coin department in 1859—effectively Panizzi's doing—could appease him. Panizzi retired in July 1866 and Madden was again passed over for promotion to principal librarian. He resigned in disgust on 29 September 1866. The trustees refused his request to retire with his full salary of £800, a privilege they had granted Panizzi, and he was pensioned at £600 p.a.

These unedifying disputes have overshadowed Madden's deserved reputation as a giant of Victorian scholarship. As a palaeographer he had no equal in the nineteenth century; his readings, datings, and identifications have rarely been faulted. He pioneered the systematic study of the early English language and edited a magnificent series of texts to unprecedented standards of accuracy. *Havelok the Dane* (1828), *William and the Werwolf* (1832), and the Old English *Gesta Romanorum* (1838), were followed by the greatest of medieval English romances and his own discovery (in Cotton MS Nero A X), *Sir Gawayne and the Grene Knight* (1839). For *Layamon's Brut* (1847) he translated 32,000 lines of verse in four years without benefit of dictionaries or competent models, a labour that taxed even his stamina: he came to refer to it as his 'vomit'. His greatest achievement was the definitive edition of the Wycliffe Bible, begun in 1829 in collaboration with Josiah Forshall (though it was largely Madden's work) and finally published in 1850 after prodigious labour, including the collation of 170 manuscripts. He worked at extraordinary speed. His edition of *The Privy Purse Expenses of the Princess Mary* (1831) was begun in October 1828 and ready for the press in March 1829. Edited with absolute fidelity to the manuscript and comprehensively indexed, it included a long introduction remarkable for its unfashionably charitable view of 'Bloody Mary'. Madden was as much at home with medieval history as philology. His last major work was the Rolls series edition (1866–9) of the *Historia Anglorum* of Matthew Paris. Richard Vaughan, Matthew's biographer, has written:

> This edition was an important landmark in medieval studies, for it is one of the finest of all those published in the Rolls Series, and it set a standard of careful accuracy and profound scholarship which has scarcely been equalled since. (*Matthew Paris*, 1958, 155)

A constant flow of lesser publications accompanied these great works: his bibliography totals over 150 items.

Madden was nevertheless no bookish recluse. His enormous and boundlessly entertaining unpublished journal in the Bodleian Library records his daily life from 1819 to his death in 1873. As a young man, his life was an endless round of parties, dinners, dances, and assemblies, at one of which he met Mary Hayton, daughter of Robert and Ann Hayton *née* Whitfield, of Sunderland, co. Durham. He courted her for ten years against the opposition of her family, before finally marrying her on 18 March 1829. Her death on 26 February 1830, followed shortly by the death of his new-born son, Frederic Hayton, on 3 March, almost destroyed his reason, and was thereafter the subject of an agonized annual commemoration. He sought distraction in liaisons with prostitutes and *demi-mondaines*, candidly described in his journal. Of rather less than middle height, slightly built, dark, handsome, and luxuriantly whiskered, Madden was attractive to women. At Holkham, in 1827, he had had a brief affair with the entrancing *femme fatale* Jane Digby, Lady Ellenborough (Madden, journal, 24 March 1827). He abandoned these entanglements on his second marriage, on 14 September 1837, to Emily Sarah Robinson, daughter of William Robinson, of Tottenham, Middlesex. They had six children, of whom two died in infancy, and he found a measure of domestic happiness. He was an indulgent father, never too busy to entertain his children with London's amusements. Insatiably curious, he sought out all the novelties and diversions the town had to offer; his descriptions of great public events such as Queen Victoria's coronation, the Great Exhibition, and the funeral of the duke of Wellington are among the best on record. Money worries are a recurring theme in his journal. An acute sense of his own gentility and a wish to cut a fashionable figure led him into extravagances of dress and expensive misadventures with horseflesh. Pride in his Irish ancestry manifested itself in a sentimental partiality for Irish Railway shares: in 1854 the Newry and Inniskillen line lost him the equivalent of a year's salary. These and other domestic misfortunes and the sense that he was ill-used by the museum reinforced a natural melancholy and pessimism. He was sensitive to any slights, real or imagined: he abruptly ended his long friendship with Sir Thomas Phillipps when the latter tactlessly offered him a post as his paid librarian on his retirement in 1866. He has been described as arrogant and ill-tempered, largely because of his quarrels with Panizzi and the savage invective of his journal. There seems, however, to be no direct evidence that his behaviour mirrored his paper ferocity, and he was on sociable terms with his fellow keepers, apart from Panizzi and Ellis. Francis Espinasse describes him as 'amiable and courteous' (*Literary Recollections*, 1893, 18). He was not an unkindly man: though highly critical of his assistant John Holmes, whom he regarded as Panizzi's creature, he welcomed the appointment of his son Richard as a junior assistant in his department when Holmes died suddenly, calling it 'a proper and gracious act on the part of the Trustees, in consideration of the late Mr. H.'s period of service' (Madden, journal, 5 April 1854). He was conservative in politics, though never a party man, and indifferent to religion. After the death in 1865 of his third son, George, at the age of twenty-four, he dabbled in spiritualism until Panizzi declined to fulfil a planchette prediction that he would die in 1872.

Madden was made KH in 1832 and KB in 1833. He was elected FSA in 1828, FRS in 1830, and was one of the first hundred members selected for the Athenaeum in the same year. He was a gentleman of the privy chamber to William IV and (until she dispensed with them) to Queen Victoria. He died at home at 25 St Stephen's Square, Bayswater, London, on 8 March 1873, just three weeks after the death of Lady Madden. They were buried at Kensal Green.

MICHAEL BORRIE

Sources R. W. Ackerman, *Sir Frederic Madden* (1979) · A. Esdaile, *The British Museum Library: a short history and survey* (1946) · E. Miller, *That noble cabinet: a history of the British Museum* (1973) · M. A. F. Borrie, 'Panizzi and Madden', *British Library Journal*, 5 (1979), 18–36 · F. Madden, journal, Bodl. Oxf. · A. Bell, 'The journal of Sir Frederick Madden, 1852', *The Library*, 5th ser., 29 (1974), 405–21 · [J. Webb], *Sir Frederick Madden and Portsmouth* (1987)

Archives BL, corresp., historical notes, and papers, Egerton MSS 2257, 2337, 2837–2848, 3778 · BL, historical and professional corresp., diaries, notes and papers, Add. MSS 20758, 33278–33285, 38791, 43500–43502, 46138, 50204, 57341–57342, 58080, 62001–62078, 70850, 71174, 71512 · BL, printed works with annotations and marginalia · Bodl. Oxf., historical and literary notes and papers, incl. Hampshire collections · Bodl. Oxf., journals and papers · Chetham's Library, Manchester, transcripts of historical MSS and notes · CUL, notes on Cambridge college MSS · Harvard U., Houghton L., corresp. and papers · Hunt. L., letters · JRL, historical notes and papers · Portsmouth City RO, papers; published works relating to Hampshire and Portsmouth grangerized by subject · S. Antiquaries, Lond., antiquarian notes and drawings · U. Edin. L., notes from ancient MSS · University of Toronto, papers | BL, letters to Philip Bliss, Add. MSS 34569–34582 · BL, papers relating to restoration of Cotton Library, Add. MSS 62572–62578 · BL, corresp. with J. B. Nichols, Add. MS 63652 · BL, letters to J. G. Nichols, Add. MS 51020 · Bodl. Oxf., letters to Francis Douce · Bodl. Oxf., corresp. with Sir Thomas Phillipps and papers · Derbys. RO, annotations and corrections to Frecheville and Mustard family pedigree · Portsmouth City RO, corresp. with R. H. C. Ubsdell · U. Edin. L., letters to James Halliwell-Phillipps; letters to David Laing
Likenesses R. Dighton, watercolour, 1833, priv. coll. · W. Drummond, oils, 1837, BL · lithograph, pubd 1837, BM, NPG · R. C. Lucas, wax medallion, 1849, NPG [*see illus.*] · photograph, 1863, Portsmouth City RO
Wealth at death under £12,000: probate, 12 March 1873, *CGPLA Eng. & Wales*

Madden, Frederic William (1839–1904), numismatist and librarian, was born on 9 April 1839 at the British Museum, the eldest of the six children of Sir Frederic *Madden (1801–1873), antiquary and palaeographer, and his second wife, Emily Sarah (1813–1873), daughter of Dr William *Robinson (1777–1848), a magistrate and deputy lieutenant for the county of Middlesex, and his wife, Mary, *née* Ridge. He was educated at Merchant Taylors' School, London (1846), and St Paul's (1848–51), before eventually becoming a foundation scholar (gownboy) of Charterhouse (1851–6) on the prince consort's nomination. Not wishing to go up to university, in 1858 Madden passed the civil service examination and on 7 August was appointed a second-class assistant in the British Museum's department of antiquities. In 1861, when the department was divided, Madden was allocated to the new department of coins and medals. On 12 September 1860 he married Elizabeth Sarah Rannie (*b.* in or after 1839), daughter of John Rannie, an engineer, which led to an estrangement from his father, who thought that his son had married beneath him. However, Madden's increasing ability as a numismatist led to some rapprochement. On 7 August 1864 Madden was promoted to the lower class of first-class assistants and to the upper class on 9 February 1867.

In 1868 Madden's promising career as a museum numismatist came to an abrupt end. In October 1864 the collector Edward Wigan had donated an important collection of 293 Roman gold coins. After these were incorporated some duplicates were left over. Wigan wrote asking Madden to hold these for him at Madden's home. Madden declared that, having later been told by Wigan that he might dispose of the duplicates as he saw fit, he sold some for approximately £300, which he kept. In 1868 the

museum authorities were informed. Wigan denied the gift but regarded the transaction as a private 'misunderstanding'. Madden was judged to have behaved irresponsibly but was allowed to resign.

From 1871 to 1874 Madden worked for HM commissioners for the Great Exhibition of 1851 as assistant secretary to the executive for the annual international exhibitions, editing special catalogues and *The Key* newspaper, a daily guide. He then moved to Brighton, initially as secretary and bursar of Brighton College (1874–88), becoming involved in the running of the college library. In 1888 he became chief librarian of Brighton Public Library, but resigned in 1902 owing to ill health. He died at his home, Holt Lodge, 86 London Road, Brighton, on 21 June 1904.

The ending of Madden's museum career represented a real loss to numismatics, although he continued to write and study. He had published a useful *Handbook of Roman Numismatics* (1861) but his main contribution was his *Coins of the Jews* (1881), the second volume of the *International Numismata orientalia*, an enlargement of his earlier *A History of Jewish Coinage* (1864), an excellent treatment of an extremely difficult subject which remained the standard work until the middle of the twentieth century. He contributed nearly forty papers to the *Numismatic Chronicle* and wrote for other publications. Madden was elected to the Numismatic Society in 1858, became an honorary member in 1898 and a silver medallist in 1896. He was secretary to the society and joint editor of the *Numismatic Chronicle* (1860–68). A member of the Royal Asiatic Society from 1877, he also belonged to several American numismatic and antiquarian societies. He had two sons and two daughters.

M. L. CAYGILL

Sources *Numismatic Chronicle*, 4th ser., 5 (1905), 27–8 · BM · F. Madden, diaries, Bodl. Oxf., MSS Eng. hist. c. 140–182 · private information (2004) · *WWW* · *The Times* (25 June 1904) · *Testimonials in favour of Frederic W. Madden … candidate for the office of librarian of the Brighton Free Library* [n.d.] · b. cert. · m. cert. · d. cert.
Archives CUL, letters to the Royal Society of Literature · Royal Society of Literature, London, letters | BL, account of his sister E. M. Holley, Add. MS 57342 · Bodl. Oxf., corresp. with Sir Thomas Phillipps
Likenesses photograph, Brighton Public Library; copy, BM
Wealth at death £316 11s. 6d.: probate, 18 July 1904, *CGPLA Eng. & Wales*

Madden, Sir George Allan (1771–1828), army officer in the British and Portuguese services, was born on 3 January 1771 in London, the eighth son and youngest child of James Madden of Cole Hill House, Fulham, Middlesex. He was baptized at St Martin-in-the-Fields, London. After attending private schools, he worked briefly in a merchant's office before his father, in February 1788, obtained for him a commission in the army. On 14 March 1789 he was appointed cornet in the 14th light dragoons in Ireland. On 30 June 1791 he purchased (from Arthur Wellesley, later the duke of Wellington, then promoted in the 58th foot) a lieutenant's commission in the 12th (Prince of Wales's Royal) light dragoons, in which he became captain on 29 June 1793 and major on 25 December 1800.

After serving several years in Ireland, Madden embarked with his regiment at Cork in September 1793 for Ostend. Contrary winds drove them back, and the regiment was counter-ordered to Toulon, then just relieved by Admiral Samuel Hood. Adverse winds and defective supplies caused delays, and Toulon had been evacuated before the regiment arrived. Madden was with the mounted portion of the regiment, which was refused permission to land at Leghorn (Livorno). They landed instead at Portoferraio, on Elba, but were unable to find forage. At length, at the invitation of Pope Pius VI, the regiment was put ashore at Civitavecchia on 6 March 1794, the surviving horses, it is said, having then been nine months aboard ship. During the troops' stay at Civitavecchia the pope presented gold medals to the officers. It appears from the exergue that the medals were originally struck to commemorate the restoration of the port, but a subsequent order of the commanding general directed them to be worn at all times by the recipients out of respect for the memory of the ill-fated pontiff. After the regiment left Civitavecchia in May, it took part in the operations in Corsica which ended with the fall of Calvi in August, and was ordered home in November. Madden's troop was shipwrecked on the coast of Spain, but the men and horses were saved. The Spanish government assigned them quarters in one of the Puntales forts near Cadiz, where they remained until a ship was sent out from England to take them home in August 1795.

Madden's conduct was approved by the British authorities at Gibraltar. In January 1797 he went with his regiment to Portugal, and was stationed three years at Lisbon. In 1801 the regiment accompanied Sir Ralph Abercromby to Egypt and took part in the battle before Alexandria and the advance on Cairo. During the latter, Lord Hutchinson sent Madden, the youngest field officer of cavalry present with the army, with detachments of the 12th and the 26th (later 23rd) light dragoons, on special service towards Rosetta, an indication that he valued Madden's services.

A serious dispute arose between Madden and the officer in temporary command of the regiment, Colonel Browne. An angry altercation over duty matters had taken place between them, and in August 1801 Madden charged Browne with having committed perjury in a recent court martial of a captain of the 12th light dragoons. Madden was arraigned before a general court martial on a charge of unofficer-like conduct and disrespect to his commanding officer. The court martial, of which Major-General John Moore was president, and colonels John Stuart (of Maida) and Alan Cameron of Lochiel and other famous officers were members, was held in the camp before Alexandria on 31 August 1801. The court found Madden guilty of the charge, and adjudged him to be dismissed from the service. However, Lord Hutchinson refused to confirm the proceedings. Although Madden received written testimonials of character and service from Hutchinson, Sir John Cradock, Sir John Doyle, and all of the officers of the 12th light dragoons at the rank of captain and below, he was sent home and permitted to retire by the sale of his commissions, all of which he had purchased. When the 12th light dragoons arrived in England three years later, a duel took place between Madden and Blunden, a major of the regiment, who had taken a part against Madden in the quarrel. Madden, after receiving Blunden's shot, fired in the air, and the matter ended.

Madden was a close friend of the margrave and margravine of Ansbach and lived with the family at Benham, Berkshire, and Brandenburgh House, Hammersmith, Middlesex, during most of 1804 and 1805. On 4 July 1805, on the recommendation of the margrave, the duke of York appointed Madden inspecting field officer of yeomanry cavalry and volunteers in the midland district, with the temporary rank of lieutenant-colonel. On 17 May 1807 his appointment was renewed in the Severn district. He held the post until June 1809, when he was appointed a brigadier-general in the Portuguese army, with pay and allowances as in the British service.

On 10 September 1809 Marshal William Carr Beresford appointed Madden commander of a Portuguese cavalry brigade. Five months later Lord Wellington inspected the brigade and commended Madden for achieving discipline and good order despite operating under great handicaps. In August 1810 Madden's brigade was sent to Spain, to be attached to the Spanish army of Estremadura, commanded by the marqués de La Romana. Wellington, who thought highly of Madden, recommended him to Romana as 'un officer Anglais de beaucoup de talent' (*Dispatches of the Duke of Wellington*, 5.220). Madden's brigade remained with the Spaniards, under Romana and his successor, Mendizabel, throughout the French siege of Badajoz until its surrender to the French in March 1811.

On 15 September 1810, at Fuente de Cantos, Madden led his untested brigade against a French force which had virtually routed the Spanish forces at Carréra. The Portuguese fought well and saved the Spanish from destruction, an achievement Wellington praised in his dispatches. At Gebora on 19 February 1811 Madden's men fled after they observed a nearby Spanish force crumple and flee before an energetic French charge. Madden was unable to rally his men, despite repeated efforts. His brigade was with Beresford's army before Badajoz, but a small portion only was engaged at Albuera, the rest being on detached duty with Madden, who was unaware of the likelihood of a battle. Subsequently the brigade was with the allied cavalry under General William Lumley, and with Wellington's army until the latter raised the second siege of Badajoz and retired behind the River Caía. During the latter part of these operations Madden's command was augmented by two more regiments, raising the Portuguese cavalry under him to the strength of a division. When Wellington's army went into cantonments for the winter, the Portuguese cavalry was sent to Oporto, where it remained during the rest of the year. Early in 1812 it was ordered to Golegão, near Lisbon. The difficulty of procuring remounts caused Beresford to reduce the number of regiments and to give up the idea of employing the Portuguese cavalry in brigades for a time. Madden thus found that his services were no longer needed, and he returned home in the early summer of 1812. In the meantime he had been reinstated in his rank in the British service, 'at the special request of the Prince Regent and the government of Portugal, in recompense for his services in the army of that country' (*LondG*, 3 March 1812). In the annual *Army List* of 1813 his name reappears as lieutenant-colonel, late 12th dragoons, with seniority from 4 July 1805.

Madden returned to Portugal in August 1812 and was appointed to command the 7th brigade of Portuguese infantry, which spent the winter of 1812–13 in villages in the area of the Estrela Mountains and by arduous forced marches joined Wellington at Vitoria on the morning after the battle of 21 June 1813. Madden commanded the brigade, which was attached to the 6th British division, in the operations in the Pyrenees during the blockade of Pamplona, including the actions at San Esteban and Sauroren. He attained the rank of marechal de campo (major-general) in the Portuguese service on 4 June 1813, but to avoid difficulties as to precedence, the promotion appears not to have been announced until after the arrival from Britain of the 4 June birthday issue of *The Naval and Military Gazette*, by which he was promoted colonel in the British army.

Wellington may have cooled to Madden during this time. On the one hand, he believed that Madden denigrated rather than maximized his resources. On the other, he believed that he had engaged in a rash attack at Urdax in August 1813. Notwithstanding the high character of his services with the Portuguese army—he had been third in seniority among the English officers and had commanded a cavalry division—the precedence given by his Portuguese rank was regarded as unfair to the English colonels of equal standing, and he was directed to resign his brigade to the next senior officer, Sir John Douglas. After witnessing the assault on San Sebastian as a spectator, he returned to Lisbon to await orders, and remained unemployed until the peace, when he returned home. He became a major-general in the British army on 12 August 1819.

Madden was made a CB on 4 June 1815, a knight commander of the Tower and Sword in Portugal on 19 December 1815, and a knight bachelor 5 July 1816. He also received the Turkish order of the Crescent, the general officers' gold medal for the Pyrenees, and the Portuguese Guerra Peninsular cross. He died, unmarried, on 8 December 1828, at the age of fifty-seven, in Portsmouth, Hampshire, at the home of his brother, Captain William John Madden, half pay Royal Marines, who was the father of Sir Frederic Madden. He was buried with military honours in Portsmouth royal garrison church, where a tablet was erected to his memory. Madden's second name is misspelt in all army lists, and the date of his death is wrongly given in the *Army List* and in obituary notices.

H. M. CHICHESTER, rev. GORDON L. TEFFETELLER

Sources *GM*, 1st ser., 99/1 (1829) • Fortescue, *Brit. army* • C. W. C. Oman, *A history of the Peninsular War*, 7 vols. (1902–30) • G. L. Teffeteller, *The surpriser: the life of Rowland, Lord Hill* (1983) • *Army List* • *The dispatches of … the duke of Wellington … from 1799 to 1818*, ed. J. Gurwood, 13 vols. in 12 (1834–9) • *Supplementary despatches (correspondence) and memoranda of Field Marshal Arthur, duke of Wellington*, ed. A. R. Wellesley, second duke of Wellington, 15 vols. (1858–72) • W. F. P. Napier, *History of the war in the Peninsula and in the south of*

France, rev. edn, 6 vols. (1876) • J. Philippart, ed., *The royal military calendar*, 3rd edn, 5 vols. (1820) • private information (1893)

Madden, John (*bap.* 1649, *d.* 1703/4), physician and manuscript collector, was born at Enfield, Middlesex, and baptized at St Andrew, Enfield, on 29 March 1649, a younger son of John Madden (1598–1661) and his wife, Elizabeth (*d.* 1671), daughter of Charles Waterhouse. His grandfather, from a family long established at Bloxham Beauchamp, Oxfordshire, although possibly with Irish origins, had moved to Ireland and acquired estates at Maddenton, co. Kildare, and Manor Waterhouse, co. Fermanagh. During the 1641 rebellion these were abandoned as the family fled, but they returned to Ireland in the 1660s. John Madden was educated in Dublin and his elder brother, Thomas, in Enniskillen, near the estate at Manor Waterhouse. Their sister Anne, widow of Josias Stewart, Baron Castlestewart, attempted in the late 1660s to obtain for them jointly the position of transcriptor and foreign opposer in the court of exchequer in Ireland, but without success. While Thomas went on to study law, John entered Trinity College, Dublin, in 1670 to study medicine, graduating MB in 1674. Following Thomas's death in 1677 he inherited the family estates. In 1680 he married Mary Molyneux (*d.* 1695); they had three sons, Samuel Molyneux *Madden (1686–1765), John, and Thomas. He briefly fled to England in 1689, and was attainted by the Irish patriot parliament.

Meanwhile Madden continued with his studies, becoming MD in 1682. Two years later he was elected a fellow of the College of Physicians in Dublin, and served as president of the King and Queen's College of Physicians in Ireland (as it became in 1692) in 1694, 1697, and 1700. Dublin intellectual life at this period revolved around Madden's brothers-in-law, William and Sir Thomas Molyneux. Madden joined the Dublin Philosophical Society, an attempt at an Irish version of the Royal Society, a year after its foundation by William in 1683 (any papers he may have read have not survived). The only extant membership list of the society survives in Madden's manuscript collection, and it was the latter rather than the new learning which was the focus of his interests. In its time one of the three or four largest manuscript collections in Ireland (including institutional ones), it was purchased by John Stearne, dean of St Patrick's, after Madden's death. The fact that it passed as part of Stearne's library to Trinity College, Dublin, in 1741 may account for the lack of recognition Madden has subsequently received for his achievements as a collector and preserver of manuscripts.

A printed catalogue of the manuscripts was included in E. Bernard's *Catalogi librorum manuscriptorum Angliae et Hiberniae* (1697) and at this time Madden's collection extended to 22 folio, 13 quarto, and 3 octavo volumes (a manuscript catalogue of 1700 is also extant). Material relating to genealogy and ecclesiastical history is prominent. Among the highlights are material inherited from Daniel Molyneux, the Ulster king of arms, and grandfather of Mary Madden, records of the court of wards and liveries, proceedings of the court of castle chamber, inquisitions into dissolved houses, the fifteenth-century cartulary of All Hallows' Monastery, Dublin, and the Book of the de Burgos. These and other sources provided the materials for both Madden's manuscript 'Monasticon', often mistakenly credited to Walter Harris, and the well-known and very extensive genealogical notebooks (again not generally credited to Madden). Contemporary or near contemporary manuscripts of political importance are also contained in the collection, most important of which are the notorious 1641 depositions (bought from Matthew Barry, clerk to the Irish privy council). Devotional works include a Hebrew psalter, a copy of a Middle English psalter, a Middle English Thomas à Kempis, and a book of hours from Bective Abbey, probably acquired through his second wife, Frances Bolton, whom he married in 1696, and whose family had lived at the abbey. Madden also compiled a herbarium, the earliest Irish one to survive. An Irish–Latin dictionary is extant in his hand at the back of the Book of the de Burgos and suggests some attempt to make a study of the language.

In addition to manuscript collecting Madden laid the foundations of the art collection from which his son Samuel allowed Trinity College, Dublin, to select twenty of their choice. Its rich contents suggest that Madden travelled extensively in Europe. The foundation of all his collecting and his medical studies was, of course, his estates. Given Samuel's subsequent fame as a pioneer in agricultural management it is unfortunate that almost nothing is known of Madden's management of his estates beyond the fact that he laid out formal gardens and avenues of trees at Manor Waterhouse.

Madden is frequently referred to as 'Sir John', but no evidence surrounding the conferring of a title survives. Madden died on 19 October, probably in 1703, although 1704 has also been suggested. His sons John and Thomas continued the family connection with Trinity College, becoming respectively a fellow and professor of anatomy there. He also left a son, Nicholas, from his second marriage.

MIHAIL DAFYDD EVANS

Sources M. D. Evans, 'The manuscript collection of Dr Sir John Madden: an annotated catalogue' (unpubd typescript), 1995, TCD · W. O'Sullivan, 'John Madden's manuscripts', *Essays on the history of the library, Trinity College, Dublin* (Dublin, 2000), 104–15 · F. Madan, *The Madden family* (1933) · National Library reports on private collections, 'No 9: Madden papers', unpublished typescript, NL Ire., department of manuscripts · A. Crookshank and D. Webb, *Paintings and sculptures in Trinity College, Dublin* (1990) · E. C. Nelson, 'A late seventeenth century Irish herbarium', *Irish Naturalists Journal*, 20 (1981), 334–5 · Burke, *Gen. Ire.* (1976) · IGI
Archives TCD

Madden, Richard Robert (1798–1886), author and colonial administrator, the youngest son of Edward Madden (1739–1830), a silk manufacturer of Dublin, and his second wife, Elizabeth, the youngest daughter of Thaddeus Forde of Corry, co. Leitrim, was born at Wormwood Gate, Dublin, on 22 August 1798. He was educated at a private school in Dublin, and studied medicine in Paris, Naples, and St George's Hospital, London. While in Italy he became acquainted with Lady Blessington and her circle, and

acted as correspondent of the *Morning Herald*. Between 1824 and 1827 he travelled in the Levant, visiting Smyrna, Constantinople, Crete, Egypt, and Syria; he published an account of his travels in 1829. He returned in 1828 to England, where he married Harriet (d. 1888), the daughter of John Elmslie of Jamaica; they had three sons, including Thomas More *Madden.

Madden was elected a member of the Royal College of Surgeons in 1828, and was made an FRCS in 1855. He practised as a surgeon in Curzon Street, Mayfair, until, in 1833, he went to Jamaica as one of the special magistrates appointed to resolve disputes between black apprentices and their white masters in the transitional system which, in 1834, replaced slavery with apprenticeship as a preliminary to full freedom. His energetic support for the apprentices brought him into conflict with the plantation owners, and he resigned in November 1834. He published a two-volume account of his experiences, *A twelve-month's residence in the West Indies during the transition from slavery to apprenticeship* (1835).

In 1836 Madden was appointed superintendent of the liberated Africans and judge arbitrator in the mixed court of commission in Havana. During his four years in Cuba he published a number of works on slavery, including an *Address on Slavery in Cuba, Presented to the General Anti-Slavery Convention* (1840). He left Cuba in 1840 to accompany Sir Moses Montefiore on his mission to Egypt to plead for a group of Jews from Damascus accused of ritual murder. Again he wrote an account of his experiences. The following year he was sent to west Africa as a commissioner of inquiry into the administration of British coastal settlements, where he exposed the 'pawn system', which was a disguised form of slavery. From November 1843 until August 1846 he acted as the special correspondent at Lisbon of the *Morning Chronicle*. In 1847 he was appointed colonial secretary of Western Australia, where he strove to protect the few remaining rights of the Aborigines. After returning to Ireland on leave in 1848, he took up the cause of the famine-stricken peasantry, and in 1850 resigned his Australian office in favour of that of secretary to the Loan Fund board at Dublin Castle, which he held until 1880.

Madden's interest in his homeland provided the source of his most enduring work, *The United Irishmen, their Lives and Times* (7 vols., 1843–6), which was issued in a second edition in 1858; *A History of Irish Periodical Literature from the End of the Seventeenth to the Middle of the Nineteenth Century* (2 vols., 1867); and *Literary Remains of the United Irishmen of 1798* (1887), a collection of ballads, songs, and other united Irish literary works. His other work of importance was the three-volume *The Literary Life and Correspondence of the Countess of Blessington* (1855). Madden had been an intimate of the Gore House circle since his meeting with the Blessingtons in Naples in 1821; despite this advantage, and despite his access to the papers, it has been remarked that 'no one who attempts to use his book can help but deplore the chaotic arrangement, the faults of copying, the digressions and the frequent errors in plain statement of fact which disfigure it' (Sadleir, 388).

Madden was a member of the Royal Irish Academy, and a corresponding member of the Society of Medical Science. He died at his residence, 3 Vernon Terrace, Booterstown, co. Dublin, on 5 February 1886 and was buried in Donnybrook graveyard there.

J. M. RIGG, rev. LYNN MILNE

Sources Memoirs of Richard Robert Madden, ed. T. M. Madden (1891) • The Times (8 Feb 1886) • M. Sadleir, Blessington–D'Orsay: a masquerade (1933) • Boase, Mod. Eng. biog. • G. J. Heuman, Between black and white: race, politics and the free coloreds in Jamaica, 1792–1865 (1981) • N. J. Curtin, The United Irishmen: popular politics in Ulster and Dublin, 1791–1798 (1994) • CGPLA Ire. (1886)
Archives Bodl. RH, corresp. and papers • Royal Irish Acad., corresp. and papers • TCD, corresp. and papers relating to United Irishmen • Wellcome L. | BL, corresp. with John Miley, Add. MS 43684 • BL, letters to Joseph Soul and others
Likenesses Count D'Orsay, pencil and chalk drawing, 1828, NPG • R. J. Hamerton, lithograph, NPG • J. P. Haverty, oils, NG Ire. • B. R. Haydon, group portrait, oils (The Anti-Slavery Society Convention, 1840), NPG • T. W. Huffam, mezzotint (after daguerreotype by Claudet), NPG • T. W. Huffam, mezzotint (after daguerreotype by Claudet), NG Ire. • T. W. Huffam, mezzotint and line engraving (after drawing), NG Ire. • silhouette, NG Ire.
Wealth at death £2659 4s.: probate, 15 March 1886, CGPLA Ire.

Madden, Samuel Molyneux [called Premium Madden] (**1686–1765**), writer and benefactor, was born on 23 December 1686 in Dublin, the eldest of the five sons and one daughter of John *Madden (bap. 1649, d. 1703/4), one of the original members of the Irish College of Physicians and a keen antiquarian whose manuscripts on English and Irish history are now housed in Trinity College, Dublin. His mother was Mary (d. 1695), daughter of Samuel Molyneux and sister of the renowned Irish political writer William Molyneux and of Sir Thomas Molyneux, professor of physic at Trinity College, Dublin. On 28 February 1700 Madden entered Trinity College, Dublin, from which institution he received a BA in 1705 and DD on 23 January 1723. While still an undergraduate student he inherited the family home and estate of Manor Waterhouse near Newtownbutler, co. Fermanagh, on his father's death in 1703.

After his ordination in the Church of Ireland, Madden acquired the living of Galloon, co. Fermanagh, which included the village of Newtownbutler, and later in 1727 he also took charge of the neighbouring parish of Drummally, worth £400 p.a., which lay in the gift of his family. Concurrent to this, Madden was also a colonel of militia in Dublin, a justice of the peace of co. Fermanagh and co. Monaghan, and high sheriff of Fermanagh in 1710. To aid him with his clerical duties Madden employed Philip Skelton as a curate and tutor to his children, who numbered five sons and five daughters. On 22 August 1709 Madden had married Jane (d. 1765), daughter of Hugh Magill of Kirkstown, co. Armagh. According to Skelton, Jane Madden was proud, parsimonious, ruled her husband with supreme authority, and took charge of the Madden estate.

These helpmates enabled Madden to pursue his literary and philanthropic career. In 1729 Madden published Themistocles, the Lover of his Country: a Tragedy in Five Acts and in

Verse, which was performed at the Theatre Royal in Lincoln's Inn Fields. This was followed in 1730 by A Letter from the Rev Mr M[a]d[de]n to the Hon Lady M[oly]n[eu]x, on the Occasion of the Death of the Rt. Hon. S[amue]l M[oly]n[eu]x. In 1733 Madden published anonymously Memoirs of the Twentieth Century; being Original Letters of State under George the Sixth Received and Revealed in the Year 1728, whose 'author', the comte de Gablis, a Jacobite, was assured that his descendants would profit under the Hanoverian regime until one would become prime minister at the end of the twentieth century. The volume is a cumbersome 527 pages long, but caused enough of a stir to be suppressed on its first day of publication. Within a fortnight 900 of the original 1000 copies were returned to Madden in order to be destroyed. This makes the book one of the rarest eighteenth-century publications in English. None of the other five promised volumes ever appeared. In 1738 Madden penned Reflections and Resolutions Proper for the Gentlemen of Ireland, as to their Conduct for the Service of their Country. In this epistle Madden ascribed the low condition of the country to the extravagant and idle disposition of its people, but recommended resident landlords and the encouragement of tillage, linen manufacture, granaries, and credit facilities for Ireland, while stressing that the furtherance of the Irish economy should never harm England's interests. Many of his ideas were not original but came from the works of Thomas Prior, Arthur Dobbs, and George Berkeley. This book was reprinted in 1816 under the patronage of the Dublin benefactor Thomas Pleasants. Other literary works included A Letter Concerning the Necessity of Learning for the Priesthood and Boulter's Monument, a Panegyric Poem, Sacred to the Memory of Dr Hugh Boulter (1745). The finished work contained 2034 lines which, for a payment of 10 guineas, was edited by Samuel Johnson, who included a section in his dictionary under 'sport'. In 1746 Madden composed a tragedy which was later bequeathed to Thomas Sheridan; as a benefactor of the Physico-Historical Society founded in 1744 he commenced an abortive attempt of a 'History of the county of Fermanagh', and in 1748 he published an anonymous poem dedicated to Lord Chesterfield. Finally in 1761 he produced a metrical epistle of around 200 lines as an introduction to Thomas Leland's History of Philip of Macedonia. Despite his whig leanings Madden was a close friend of Jonathan Swift, and he was the means by which Johnston authenticated much of the information for his Life of Swift, including the marriage of Swift and Esther Johnson (Stella).

It was, however, as a philanthropist that Madden obtained the sobriquet of Premium Madden. In 1731 he proposed instituting a system of prizes for students in the quarterly examinations at Trinity College, Dublin. The Madden prizes commenced in 1798 following a bequest from Madden's son Samuel. Madden is usually designated as the founder of the Royal Dublin Society, although in fact he was never a member, but it was he who introduced the premium system to the institution. The idea of premiums was first suggested in his letter to the Dublin Society of 1739, which recommended awards for agriculture, art, and manufactures. Later he settled £150 p.a. during his life for this purpose, but often donated double that amount as well as obtaining a further subscription of £500 p.a. from the nobility and gentry of Ireland. This drew attention to the society and won it the patronage of parliament. It is also believed that he contributed many of the articles to the society's *Weekly Observations* (1739) and *Essays and Observations* (1740). It is therefore of some surprise that on Madden's death, at the age of seventy-nine, on 31 December 1765 at Manor Waterhouse, no official notice was taken by the society. However Dr Johnson declared that 'his was a name which Ireland ought to honour'.

ROSEMARY RICHEY

Sources DNB · *Irish Quarterly Review*, 3 (1853), 693–734 · T. de Vere White, *The Royal Dublin Society* (1955) · S. Burdy, *The life of the late Rev Philip Skelton* (1792) · Nichols, *Lit. anecdotes*, 2.699 · S. Madden, *A proposal for the general encouragement of learning in Dublin College* (1731) · Boswell, *Life* · *Weekly observations*, Royal Dublin Society (1739) · *Essays and observations*, Royal Dublin Society (1740) · Nichols, *Illustrations* · Burke, *Gen. Ire.* (1976)

Likenesses J. van Nost, marble bust, *c.*1751, Royal Dublin Society · J. Brooks, mezzotint, BM, NPG · S. Harding, stipple (after R. Hunter), BM, NPG; repro. in *European Magazine and London Review*, 41 (1802), facing p. 243 · T. Hickey, oils, NG Ire. · R. Purcell, mezzotint (after R. Hunter), BM

Wealth at death £400 p.a. from curacy of Drummally: Burdy, *Life* · income from estates

Madden, Thomas More (1844–1902), gynaecologist, one of the three sons of Richard Robert *Madden (1798–1886) and his wife, Harriet (*d.* 1888), daughter of John Elmslie, a West Indies planter, was born in Havana, Cuba, where his father, who was a doctor, historian, and anti-slavery campaigner, was the British representative at the International Congress for the Abolition of the Slave Trade. The atmosphere of his early life, and the prevailing language of freedom, appears to have made a lasting impression on Madden, who retained a lively independence in his views on medicine and politics, though he never became politically active. When his father returned to his practice in Dublin, Thomas was apprenticed to James William Cusack, a well-known surgeon in the city. He obtained his first medical qualifications in 1859 as LFPS (Glasgow) and LM of the King and Queen's College of Physicians in Ireland, but his deteriorating health and the threat of consumption led to a long sojourn abroad. He combined the completion of his medical education with his search for health during the next three years at Malaga and Montpellier. In 1862 he qualified as MRCS (London). In 1865 he married Mary Josephine, the daughter of Thomas McDonnell Caffrey; they had three sons and two daughters. Madden travelled extensively in Spain, north Africa, and Australia before returning to Dublin in 1868 to set up in practice.

Madden specialized in midwifery and gynaecology, and in 1868 became assistant master of the Rotunda Lying-in Hospital, a post he held until 1871. He was subsequently appointed master of the National Lying-in Hospital, and obstetric physician to the Mater Misericordiae Hospital in 1871, a post which he held until his death. In 1871 Madden organized an Irish ambulance corps to aid the French Republic during the Franco-Prussian War, and in 1872 he was awarded the *croix de bronze* for his service to France. He was soon recognized in the United Kingdom and elsewhere as a leading gynaecologist. Madden also developed a strong interest in the diseases and development of children, and served as consulting physician at the Temple Street Hospital for Sick Children. He was vice-president of the British Gynaecological Society and of the Dublin Obstetrical Society; he became FRCS (Edinburgh) in 1882, president of the obstetrical section of the Royal Academy of Medicine of Ireland in 1886, president of the obstetric section of the British Medical Association in Glasgow in 1888, and honorary president of the first International Congress of Obstetrics and Gynaecology at Brussels in 1892. He was fellow of the Obstetrical Society of Edinburgh and corresponding member of the Gynaecological Society of Boston and of the Associazione dei Benemerite Italiani. His work was recognized by many learned bodies and medical societies, including the Texas Medical College, which awarded him the honorary degree of MD in 1890, and the Queen's University of Ireland conferred on him the degree of MAO in 1896 in recognition of his services as examiner to the Royal College of Surgeons and Apothecaries' Hall, Ireland.

Madden was a voluminous writer, chiefly on medical topics. Besides contributing regularly to the *Dublin Medical Journal*, the *Provincial Medical Journal*, the *British Medical Journal*, and other medical journals, and writing several contributions to Richard Quain's *Dictionary of Medicine*, he published a number of books, some of which ran through several editions, including works on climate and chronic disease, health resorts, the history of spas, rinderpest and contagious cattle distempers, childhood, insanity, hysteria, and nervous disorders. He wrote extensively on gynaecology and obstetrics: puerperal insanity, uterine disorders, dysmenorrhoea, sterility, premature deliveries, and the history of the forceps, including *Contributional Treatment of Chronic Uterine Disorders* (1878), *Mental and Nervous Disorders Peculiar to Women* (1883), *On Uterine Tumours* (1887), and *Clinical Gynaecology: being a Handbook of Diseases Peculiar to Women* (1893). He also edited the *Dublin Practice of Midwifery* and in 1893 he produced a revised and enlarged edition of Fleetwood Churchill's *Manual for Midwives* (5th edn) as *A Handbook of Obstetric and Gynaecological Nursing*.

Madden inherited the literary tastes of his father, was a member of the Royal Irish Academy, and contributed articles on the history of medicine in Ireland to a number of lay journals. He produced a new edition of his father's work, *The Lives of the United Irishmen*, wrote on the castles and abbeys of Ireland, and published accounts of his father and family history in *Memorials of R. R. Madden* (1886), *The Memoirs (Chiefly Autobiographical) of R. R. Madden* (1891), and *Genealogical, Historical, and Family Records of the O'Maddens of Galway and their Descendants* (1894).

Madden's obituaries maintain that he was never interested in the pursuit of money through his medical work. He had a warm Irish temperament, and, while he was cultured and courteous, this stimulated both lasting friendships and enmities. Madden was considered to be one of the most prominent members of the Irish medical profession, and was said to be extremely popular with his students. He took a deep interest in a number of Dublin charities, was a major landowner, JP to the counties of Kildare and Carlow, and an active participant in the medical societies of Dublin. Madden abandoned his practice and his professional residence at Merrion Square, Dublin, in 1901, following a yachting accident, when he received a severe blow to the head. After months of illness he died at his country house at Tinode, co. Wicklow, on 14 April 1902.

HILARY MARLAND

Sources *The Lancet* (26 April 1902), 1218–19 · *BMJ* (3 May 1902), 1127 · *DNB*
Wealth at death £21,223 13s. 1d.: probate, 21 June 1902, *CGPLA Ire.*

Maddison [*née* Tindal], **(Katherine Mary) Adela** (1862/3?–1929), composer, was probably born on 15 December 1862 or 1863 (the year 1866 is given in several sources but her age is given as eighteen in the census of 1881), the youngest child of Vice-Admiral Louis Symonds Tindal (1811–1876) and his wife, Henrietta Maria O'Donnell Whyte (*b.* 1836/7). She grew up in London and was presumably given the private education, including music tuition, deemed suitable for a girl of her class. In 1882 her earliest surviving compositions, a song and a piano piece, were published by Metzler, and on 14 April of the following year she married one of the firm's directors, the barrister Frederick Brunning Maddison (1850–1906). Her two children, Diana and Noel, were born in 1886 and 1888.

In the 1880s and 1890s Maddison played an important part in the musical life of London upper-class society, together with friends such as the patrons Mabel Batten and Frank Schuster. Maddison and her husband were enthusiastic supporters of the French composer Gabriel Urbain Fauré and were responsible for introducing many of his works to a British audience. Fauré, who had a high opinion of her talents, gave Maddison some composition lessons. Her songs from this period, published by Metzler and heard at a variety of London concerts, reveal an increasingly individual musical voice. They include several to poetry by Algernon Swinburne, including a striking setting of his erotic lyric 'Stage Love'.

In the later 1890s Maddison's instrumental pieces and songs to French texts began to be issued by French publishers. It has been suggested that she had embarked on an affair with Fauré and that this relationship was the main reason for her moving to Paris in 1898. However, there is little concrete evidence to support this claim, and it seems more likely that Maddison moved to Paris primarily to further her musical career, always the driving force in her life. She appears to have supported herself financially at this time by taking lodgers. She also continued to arrange concerts of her own and other composers' music, moving in French musical circles which included Frederick Delius, the princess de Polignac, and Maurice Ravel, as well as Fauré.

About 1905 Maddison moved to Berlin, where she looked after her husband (who was unwell), organized concerts of music by her French friends, and began to compose a four-act opera *Der Talisman* to her own libretto after the play by Ludwig Fulda. After her husband's death in 1906 she remained in Germany despite finding that Berlin, unlike Paris, was a city where people had 'contempt for anything done by a woman in the composition line' (undated letter to F. Delius, Delius Trust archive). *Der Talisman* was premièred in Leipzig in 1910, to enthusiastic reviews in the British press. Shortly after this, at the instigation of Polignac, Maddison was made an 'officer of the academy' by the French government for her work in promoting French music.

When the First World War broke out Maddison returned to London, together with Marta Mundt, the woman who became her companion and probably lover for the rest of her life. The two women initially found it difficult to find anywhere to live or a way of making a living. Maddison published several songs in Britain during the war, but her progressive musical language did not make these works easily marketable to the British public. Her Longfellow setting 'Sail on O Ship of State' was dedicated, by permission, to the king and may represent an attempt to find favour in court circles. This uncharacteristically grandiose song was first performed in 1915 at a London concert organized by Maddison which also included performances of eleven others of her own songs, Ravel's *Valses nobles et sentimentales*, and violin sonatas by César Franck and Delius.

By 1917 Maddison was involved with Rutland Boughton's radical Glastonbury festivals. She moved to Glastonbury, where she provided incidental music for Miles Malleson's play *Paddly Pools* and wrote a ballet, *The Children of Lir*, that was performed in Glastonbury and London in 1920. Mundt had eventually returned to Germany, although the two women were reunited at some point after the war. In the 1920s Maddison appears to have divided her time between Glastonbury, Geneva, and London.

Songwriting remained an important part of Maddison's work as a composer. She continued to produce finely judged and atmospheric songs, using texts ranging from Lady Gregory's translations from the Irish, through the poetry of Rabindranath Tagore, to the work of the sixth-century Chinese poet Wang-Sen-Ju. She also produced several larger works, such as the three undated ballets *Foambride*, *Lueurs marines*, and *Pierrot chez Poireau*. Her piano quintet was premièred in 1920 and well received by the press, who found it an interesting example of modern, French-influenced composition. In 1926 the first performance of her opera *Ippolita in the Hills*, to a libretto by Maurice Hewlett, was given, to somewhat mixed reviews, in Chelsea. During the 1920s Maddison continued to organize concerts of new music, such as a chamber concert at the Hyde Park Hotel in London on 11 May 1924 which included Arnold Bax's oboe quintet as well as a selection of her own songs and a suite arranged from her incidental music to the play *The Song of Triumphant Love*, after Turgenev. She was also the music librarian for the Queen's Dolls' House project.

Maddison was a self-confident and highly talented composer whose career stood almost entirely outside the institutions of the British musical establishment and whose music was better known and more highly regarded in continental Europe than in Britain. She died on 12 June 1929 in a nursing home at 53 Castlebar Road, Ealing, after a long illness. Later in that year the Guild of Singers and Players organized a memorial concert in order to initiate an Adela Maddison memorial fund. SOPHIE FULLER

Sources S. Fuller, *The Pandora guide to women composers: Britain and the United States, 1629–present* (1994) · S. Cline, *Radclyffe Hall: a woman called John* (1997) · R. Orledge, *Gabriel Fauré* (1979) · M. Baker, *Our three selves: a life of Radclyffe Hall* (1985) · D. Greer, *A numerous and fashionable audience: the story of Elsie Swinton* (1997) · m. cert. · d. cert. · census returns, 1881
Archives priv. coll., papers | Delius Trust, London, archive, letters to Frederick Delius and Jelka Rosen
Likenesses photograph, repro. in *The Sketch* (16 Nov 1910), 160
Wealth at death £218 18s. 1d.: probate, 10 Sept 1929, *CGPLA Eng. & Wales*

Maddison, Fred (1856–1937), trade unionist and politician, was born on 17 August 1856 at Boston, Lincolnshire, the son of Richard Maddinson, a hotel worker, and his wife, Mary, *née* Yates. When precisely the spelling of his surname changed is unknown. After a period of education at the Adelaide Street Wesleyan school in Hull, he served an apprenticeship as a compositor, and developed into a quintessential late Victorian radical craftsman. In 1879 he married Jane Ann Weatherill of Bewholme in Yorkshire; they had three daughters.

When the Trades Union Congress met in Hull in 1886 Maddison acted as its president, a consequence of his position as president of the Hull Trades Council. He was a committed Liberal, a supporter of the eight-hour day and the payment of MPs. From 1887 he was president of the Hull branch of the Labour Electoral Association, with an agenda of securing the election to parliament and local authorities of working men under Liberal Party auspices.

Maddison's most significant trade union activity began in 1889 when he became editor of the *Railway Review*, the organ of the Amalgamated Society of Railway Servants. He was an effective editor, and had a close association with the railway servants' general secretary, Edward Harford (1837–1898). Both were Liberals and became increasingly the target of criticism from those union activists who espoused independent labour or socialist politics. In 1897 Harford was dismissed; his successor, Richard Bell (1859–1930), although essentially a Liberal, was supportive of the union policy of a more assertive 'all grades' campaign for improved conditions. Maddison felt that a limited union membership made successful industrial action unlikely and argued thus in an editorial. Following criticism from Bell and the union's executive Maddison resigned, admitting his purpose had been 'to avert a general strike' (*Railway Review*, 10 Dec 1897). This rift was a consequence of differences over union strategy, a desire by a full-time official and a union executive to control the behaviour of an employee, and a significant political difference between Maddison and several members of the society's executive.

During the 1890s Maddison emerged as a vigorous anti-socialist and a defender of labour movement links with the Liberal Party. In 1892 and in 1895 he stood unsuccessfully as 'Lib–Lab' candidate for Central Hull. A violent dock strike in 1893 found Maddison attempting to conciliate between Liberal shipowners and trade unionists. One Independent Labour Party member characterized him as 'a paltry mean miserable party hack' (J. Northern to James Keir Hardie, quoted in Howell, 119).

Eventually in August 1897 Maddison was returned to the Commons in a by-election for the working-class constituency of Sheffield Brightside. His Commons career was brief. He opposed the Second South African War as a campaign waged for the benefit of international financiers. His radical sentiments (flavoured with antisemitism) failed to gain endorsement from the Brightside electorate, many of whom were involved in armaments manufacture. Sheffield Liberalism was divided over the war and in the 1900 election Maddison was defeated.

Maddison's response to the formation of the Labour Representation Committee in February 1900 was hostile and dismissive—'the shortest and surest path to Labour representation is by way of Liberalism' (*The Speaker*, 593). In 1906 Maddison successfully contested Burnley in a three-cornered contest, but was run close not just by the Conservatives but by H. M. Hyndman of the Social Democratic Federation (SDF). In a town with a significant SDF presence, the contest saw a sharp juxtaposition of Lib–Lab and socialist rhetoric. His second period as an MP saw Maddison clearly at odds not just with Labour sentiment as articulated by the Parliamentary Labour Party, but also with Liberals prepared to consider some state intervention. In the Commons Maddison, unlike many Liberals, vehemently opposed the Labour Party's 'right to work' bill as 'the first fruit of the Socialist agitation' (*Hansard 4*, 186, 1908, col. 32).

The January 1910 election saw Maddison's defeat at Burnley by ninety-five votes; in December 1910 he unsuccessfully contested Darlington. After the war he stood unsuccessfully as a Liberal at Holderness (1918), South Dorset (1922), and Reading (1923). He continued with two enthusiasms characteristic of his radicalism—industrial co-partnership and international arbitration. From 1897 he had been an organizer for what became the Labour Co-partnership Association and from 1908 was secretary of the International Arbitration League. Much of his later life was spent at Ealing and then at Hounslow. He died at the Grove Nursing Home, 18 The Grove, Heston, Isleworth, on 12 March 1937. His wife survived him.

Maddison was a Victorian radical, strongly influenced by Giuseppe Mazzini. He responded vigorously to the socialist challenge in the 1890s; his ideas changed little and by the 1906 parliament he seemed somewhat outdated. His most productive years were perhaps as editor of the *Railway Review* and his resignation from it arguably marked a critical deterioration in his relationship with the labour movement. DAVID HOWELL

Sources F. Maddison, 'The Labour Representation Committee', *The Spectator* (March 1900), 592–3 · F. Maddison, 'Why some British workmen condemn the war', *North American Review* (April 1900), 518–27 • W. T. Stead, 'The labour party and the books that helped to make it', *Review of Reviews*, 33 (1906), 568–82 • P. S. Bagwell, *The railwaymen: the history of the National Union of Railwaymen*, [1] (1963) • R. Brown, *Waterfront organisation in Hull, 1870–1900* (1972) • R. Brown, 'Maddison, Fred', *DLB*, vol. 4 • D. Howell, *British workers and the independent labour party, 1888–1906* (1983) • R. Price, *An imperial war and the British working class: working-class attitudes and reactions to the Boer War, 1899–1902* (1972) • H. A. Clegg, A. Fox, and A. F. Thompson, *A history of British trade unions since 1889*, 1 (1964) • *Railway Review* (10 Dec 1897) • 'The Labour Representation Committee', *The Speaker* (3 March 1900) • *Hansard 4* (1908), 186.32 • d. cert.

Archives Sheff. Arch., corresp. relating to election campaign
Wealth at death £1578 18s. 4d.: probate, 26 April 1937, *CGPLA Eng. & Wales*

Maddison, Sir Ralph (1574?–1656), writer on economics, was the eldest of the three sons of Edward Maddison (1555–1619), escheator, of Fonaby, Lincolnshire, and his wife, Katherine (d. 1591), daughter of Ralph Bosville of Bradbourne, Kent. He married in 1592 Mary (d. after 1630), daughter of Robert Williamson of Walkeringham, Nottinghamshire. Six sons were born, Edward (1594–1672), Francis, Humphrey (1601–1671), Thomas, Theodore, and John, who appear to have died early and childless, and two daughters, Bridget (d. 1657) and Faith. Like his brothers, Ralph was caught up in foreign wars and served on the side of Henri IV of France. He was knighted by James I at Whitehall on 23 July 1603.

While enjoying the life of a country gentleman on the modest estate inherited from his father, Maddison accumulated an extensive holding acquired by litigation and by purchase from impoverished royalists. Some of the suits in which he was embroiled appear to have arisen from his acting without lawful authority; in 1602 he was accused of breaking into the family house at Fonaby when it was occupied by a tenant in order to remove certain goods. In 1626 complaints were laid against Sir Ralph and his cousin Sir Edward Ayscough for having ploughed and sown two great common fields at Caistor, preventing the people from holding their customary market ouvert for livestock on the land. A family scandal arose when Sir Ralph accused Clement Benson of providing false details in 1614 to obtain a licence to marry his daughter Bridget. The allegation was not made until 1628, when Sir Ralph was in dispute with Richard Benson over a debt incurred at the time of his son's marriage to Bridget.

An improving landlord and investor in coalmines, Maddison made his mark in the public arena in the 1620s by contributing to a series of controversies over the national decline of trade. In these disputes he echoed the theories of Gerard de Malynes, who argued that the nation's economic ills were the result of the activities of foreign exchangers and unscrupulous merchants who undervalued English currency for private gain in the international money market. In spring 1622 he was given his first public platform, when appointed to the committee to examine allegations of abuses in the exchange of English currency. The committee duly castigated the money dealers, but subsequent reviews questioned this thesis, seeing the balance of trade as a more influential force on the par of the exchange. In April and July 1623 he submitted further advice on the exchange issue, acknowledging the importance of the balance of trade, but still stressing the superior importance of regulating the money markets. He failed to find immediate favour under Charles I, even though he protested that the recent improvement of trade had been caused by state intervention resulting from his arguments. Undeterred, in June 1628 he submitted a historical account of the fluctuation of the exchange, but to little apparent effect.

The crisis preceding the civil war provided Maddison with another opportunity to air his views, this time in a published format. *England's Looking in and out; Presented to the High Court of Parliament now Assembled* (1640, reprinted 1641) duly rehearsed his economic theories, his principal demand centring on the provision of an accurate account of the balance of trade. He appears to have played little part in the war, though he did advance money to parliament, and was ready to purchase land from the victorious republican regime. Official recognition came in August 1649, when the council of state appointed a committee to confer with him and other experts on monetary matters, and the following year he was chosen as a member of the Rump's council of trade. Its instructions reflected his economic thinking, for it was charged with perfecting an account of the balance of trade, and with regulating the par of the exchange. His views on monetary matters were received by authority in the winter of 1650–51, and he was a trusted ally of republicans such as the regicide John Jones, who in January 1651 asked Maddison to contact Rumpers on his behalf. These connections probably worked to Sir Ralph's disadvantage after the fall of the Rump, for he appears to have had little public impact thereafter. In 1655 he published an updated version of his 1640 tract entitled *Great Britain's remembrancer, looking in and out; tending to the increase of the monies of the Commonwealth. Presented to his highness the lord protector and to the high court of parliament now assembled* (1655). His recent experience of office can account for new calls for a bank, a council for the mint, and free ports, but his general economic views remained unchanged. The tract did not resuscitate his career, and he died in London the following year, his body being laid to rest in the chancel of St Mary Aldermary on 24 October 1656. By this time three of his sons and a daughter had predeceased him unmarried; another son, Francis, was also dead but left heirs, while a daughter, Bridget, had married Clement Benson. The main portions of Maddison's estate passed to his eldest son, Edward, but in his will Sir Ralph made generous provision for his son Humphrey and for Humphrey's son Ralph, whom he held in affection.   PERRY GAUCI and ANITA McCONNELL

Sources A. R. Maddison, ed., *Lincolnshire pedigrees*, 2, Harleian Society, 51 (1903) • A. R. Maddison, *History of the Maddison family* [n.d.] • B. Supple, *Commercial crisis and change in England, 1600–42* (1959), 186, 205, 220–1 • J. Thirsk and J. P. Cooper, eds., *Seventeenth-century economic documents* (1972), 25 • C. H. Firth and R. S. Rait, eds., *Acts and ordinances of the interregnum, 1642–1660*, 2 (1911), 403 • C. Holmes, *Seventeenth-century Lincolnshire*, History of Lincolnshire, 7 (1980), 69 • BL, Add. MSS 33374, fols. 50–51; 34324, fols. 173, 179 • *Report on the Pepys manuscripts*, HMC, 70 (1911), 306 • *CSP dom.*, 1619–

23, 417; 1625–6, 204; 1640, 538–9; 1625–49, addenda, 283–4; 1649–50, 284 • PRO, PROB 11/267, sig. 319

Maddock, Henry (d. **1824**), legal writer, was the eldest son of Henry Maddock of Lincoln's Inn, barrister. He resided for a time as a fellow commoner at St John's College, Cambridge, but did not graduate. On 25 April 1796 he entered Lincoln's Inn; he was called to the bar on 16 November 1801, and afterwards practised as an equity draftsman. In 1815 he published *A Treatise on the Principles and Practice of the High Court of Chancery*, which reached a third edition in 1837. It was the first general treatise on the principles and practice of modern equity and also the first to sum up the work of the lord chancellors of the eighteenth century. Maddock also produced five volumes of case reports (1817–22), an unfinished biography of Lord Chancellor Somers (1812), and two political tracts—on the Act of Union with Ireland (1799) and in reply to Sir Francis Burdett's reform proposals (1810). Maddock, who was married and had several children, died at St Lucia, in the West Indies, in August 1824.   J. M. RIGG, *rev.* JONATHAN HARRIS

Sources W. P. Baildon, ed., *The records of the Honorable Society of Lincoln's Inn: admissions*, 1 (1896), 557 • W. P. Baildon, ed., *The records of the Honorable Society of Lincoln's Inn: the black books*, 4 (1902), 243 • R. F. Scott, ed., *Admissions to the College of St John the Evangelist in the University of Cambridge*, 4: *July 1767 – July 1802* (1931), 370 • *Clarke's New Law List* (1803) • *Clarke's New Law List* (1824) • Venn, *Alum. Cant.* • Holdsworth, *Eng. law*, 13.577–8

Maddock, James (**1718–1786**), nurseryman and florist, was born on 10 August 1718, at Eaton, Cheshire, the son of Mordecai and Sarah Maddock, active members of the Religious Society of Friends. Maddock made his reputation as a nurseryman first in Lancashire, at Warrington, but after a period working in East Anglia, near North Walsham, during which he probably visited growers in the Netherlands, he established himself in London, at Walworth, south of the Thames. His nursery, which flourished from at least the mid-1770s to the turn of the century, was situated on the south side of Walworth Road and extended to 18 acres. It became noted not only for florist's flowers, about which Maddock was to write the authoritative treatise which was published posthumously, but also for its annual catalogues which, together with other choice items, advertised 320 different kinds of gooseberry, supplied from Lancashire and bearing names as evocative as 'Pendleton's bullock's heart', 'Jerrot's Achilles', and 'Worthington's golden fleece'; varieties were designated as one of six colours—amber, black, green, red, yellow, and white—and ranged in price from 6*d.* each to 10*s.* 6*d.* About 1779 he and his wife, Mary, were joined at Walworth by their son, James Maddock [*see below*]. The elder Maddock devoted himself increasingly to writing; he died at Walworth Road on 24 September 1786 and his wife later moved to Alton, Hampshire, where she died on 27 January 1801.

James Maddock (1764–1825), chemist and druggist, was born at Yarmouth on 22 January 1764. Before working at Walworth, he lived in east Yorkshire, where he was a member of the North Cave monthly meeting of Quakers.

Soon after his father's death he married, on 14 February 1788 at Alton, Mary Curtis (1768–1832), daughter of James Curtis, a surgeon. In 1792 he saw through the press his father's *The Florist's Directory, or, A Treatise on the Culture of Flowers* (1792). This volume, the first book devoted exclusively to florist's flowers, treats the hyacinth, tulip, ranunculus, anemone, auricula, carnation, pink, and polyanthus, and gives detailed instructions for their culture, together with an essay on soils and manures. It was translated into German (1798), and was later revised and extended by Samuel Curtis (1779–1860), Maddock's brother-in-law, and published in new editions in 1810 and 1822.

Within a few years, however, Maddock determined to quit the nursery business. In 1798 he sold the Walworth property to Richard Wright of Goring and Wright, 'successors to Maddock & Son, florists' (*Catalogue*; Hants. RO, Q22/1/2/144–147), for the annual sum of £200 for each of twenty years. Maddock then moved with his wife and young family, Sarah Maria (*b.* 1789) and William (*b.* 1791), to Alton, where he pursued trade as a chemist and druggist for over twenty years and died on 2 April 1825; he was buried in the Quaker burial-ground at Alton on 6 April.

PAUL FOSTER

Sources R. Weston, *Flora Anglicana* (1775) [with suppl., 1780] • J. H. Harvey, 'The nurseries on Milne's land-use map', *Transactions of the London and Middlesex Archaeological Society*, 24 (1973), 191 • Horsleydown Monthly Meeting, list of members, 1782, and other records, RS Friends, Lond. • papers concerning tax enquiries, Hants. RO, Q22/1/2/144–147 [James Maddock jun.] • Hants. RO, 24M54/39, 24M54/54, 24M54/64, 1825/AD25 • *Catalogue of flowers, plants … sold by Goring and Wright* (1798) • B. Henrey, *British botanical and horticultural literature before 1800*, 3 vols. (1975) • *Pigot's Hampshire* (1823–4)

Maddock, James (**1764–1825**). *See under* Maddock, James (1718–1786).

Maddocks [*née* Thomas], **Ann** [*called* y Ferch o Gefn Ydfa] (*bap.* **1704**, *d.* **1727**), tragic heroine, is believed by many to have been the subject of one of the great star-crossed romances of modern Wales. She was probably born at her father's house, Cefn Ydfa, near Llangynwyd, Glamorgan, and was baptized on 8 May 1704. Her parents were the lawyer William Thomas (*d.* 1706) and his wife, Catherine, of Tyn-ton, Llangeinor, Glamorgan, who was the sister of Rees Price, the father of the philosopher Richard Price.

According to popular tradition centred on Llangynwyd and the surrounding region, William Thomas, who died in December 1706, had placed his heir, Ann, in the wardship of Anthony Maddocks, a lawyer of Cwm Rhisga, who eventually compelled her, against her wish, to marry his own son Anthony (*d.* 1764). Although there is no reference to this wardship in William Thomas's will, Ann and Anthony junior, who was also a lawyer by profession, did marry on 4 May 1725 and their detailed marriage contract is extant. There is some evidence to suggest that the marriage was not an entirely happy one. Ann died in Llangynwyd in 1727 and was buried in the church there on 16 June, barely two years after her marriage. Her daughter,

Catherine, the only child of that marriage, died some three weeks previously and was buried on 28 May 1727.

Around these facts a poignant romantic story has been woven. It is claimed that Ann was deeply in love with Wil Hopcyn (1700–1741), a poet from Llangynwyd to whom various Welsh verses are attributed by popular tradition, including 'Bugeilio'r gwenith gwyn' ('Watching the White Wheat'), which, it is believed, he had composed for her.

The story of the Maid of Cefn Ydfa, embroidered with a plethora of sentimental details and associated in particular with the song 'Bugeilio'r gwenith gwyn', became very popular in Wales during the second half of the nineteenth century. It was discussed in detail by G. J. Williams, who cogently argued that, after it had been stripped of the accumulation of details that were manifestly the product of romantic fantasy and conjecture, its central core consisted of a few facts that Taliesin Williams (Taliesin ab Iolo; 1787–1847) claimed in April 1845 to have heard from the parish clerk of Llangynwyd thirty-two years previously, and that it was Taliesin who had initiated the process of conjectural elaboration others later ingeniously continued. Williams believed that it was Edward Williams (Iolo Morganwg; 1747–1826) who first maintained that Wil Hopcyn was the author of the verses and that it was his son, Taliesin, who, after finding the poem in his father's manuscripts, began connecting it with the traditional story. Although it may contain a core that is genuinely old, it seems likely that Iolo himself was the author of the poem in its final form. Taliesin passed the words to Maria Jane Williams (1795–1873), who published them in her *Ancient National Airs of Gwent and Morganwg* (1844). Later, Mrs Mary Pendrill Llewelyn (1811–1874), wife of the vicar of Llangynwyd, began to collect the Welsh verses associated by popular tradition with that area and to claim that some had been written by Wil Hopcyn and were connected with the Cefn Ydfa episode.

The story became the theme of various literary works in the second half of the nineteenth century and some mawkish elements, similar to those frequently found in such romantic tales, were soon added to it—the heartless mother who forcibly confined her love-smitten daughter to her room; messages being carried to the maiden's lover by a servant; love letters, written with Ann's own blood on a sycamore leaf, being concealed in the hollow of a tree; the hapless maiden incessantly languishing and eventually dying of a broken heart. The story was also the theme of an opera composed by Joseph Parry in 1902, with an English libretto by Joseph Bennett.   C. W. LEWIS

Sources Llangynwyd parish registers · Llandaff probate registry · NL Wales, Llanover papers · T. C. Evans, *History of Llangynwyd parish* (1887) · G. J. Williams, 'Wil Hopcyn and the Maid of Cefn Ydfa', *Glamorgan Historian*, 6 (1969), 228–51 · G. J. Williams, *Traddodiad llenyddol Morgannwg* (1948), 251–9 · M. J. Williams, *Ancient national airs of Gwent and Morganwg* (1844), 38–9, 82 · D. Huws, 'Ancient national airs of Gwent and Morganwg', *National Library of Wales Journal*, 15 (1967–8), 31–54 · B. Richards, *Wil Hopcyn a'r Ferch o Gefn Ydfa* (1977) · W. Edwards, ed., *Souvenir of the Wil Hopcyn memorial* (1927) · *The Cambrian* (Oct 1845) · C. W. Lewis, 'The literary history of Glamorgan from 1550 to 1770', *Glamorgan county history*, ed. G. Williams, 4: *Early modern Glamorgan* (1974), 535–639, esp. 619–22 · private information

Maddox, Anthony (*d.* 1758), slack-wire acrobat, was probably the son of James Maddox, a Bristol dancing-master, and his wife, a Miss Hoyle, who both died in 1744. There is no confident knowledge of his activities before the sudden notoriety of his début season at Sadler's Wells in 1751. Maddox was a supreme exponent of slack-wire acrobatics. He would set the wire swinging, then balance his hat on his chin while playing the violin (as a later refinement, he would simultaneously play the trumpet and the violin while swinging), he would lie on the wire or stand on his head as it swung, he would balance several pipes or full wineglasses, and conclude his act with a hornpipe. Contemporary engravings, though, suggest that it was his passing of a straw from foot to face and back again that most caught the popular imagination. It is possible that the Maddox vogue owed something to the iconographic force of a 'balance-master' a decade after the fall of Walpole and with the events of 1745 still vivid in the public memory. Whatever the explanation, Maddox was able speedily to amass sufficient wealth to announce his early retirement in December 1754. Still popular at Thomas Rosoman's 'low' theatre at Sadler's Wells, he had also appeared at John Rich's Covent Garden in a showy revival of Rich's afterpiece *The Fair*, which began a run of twenty-eight nights on 2 November 1752. The last night was commanded by the young prince of Wales, the future George III. Garrick protested when his partner, James Lacy, proposed to 'bring such defilement and abomination into the *house of Shakespeare*' (*Letters*, 1.172), and Lacy had to settle for the Haymarket instead of Drury Lane.

Maddox was as sought after in Dublin as he was in London. He was performing at the Smock Alley playhouse in 1752–3, and he and his wife, Elizabeth, shared a benefit there on 6 June 1753. He was recalled to Dublin in the autumn of 1758, in the company of Theophilus Cibber, who had been one of many to encourage him out of retirement in 1756. Cibber and Maddox set sail in the *Dublin Trader* on 27 October 1758, and were among those drowned when the packet sank in a storm. In his will, dated 3 October 1758, Maddox bequeathed to his wife Elizabeth all his real estate in Bristol, Devon, and elsewhere, and £10 to each of three siblings.

There is no mention of **Michael Maddox** (*b.* 1747), who may have been a nephew rather than a son, and whose extraordinary career as a dancer, equilibrist, and entrepreneur culminated in the award, in 1805, of a pension of 3000 roubles for services to the Russian theatre. While he was known to have performed his slack-wire act in Russia in 1767, Maddox made his first English appearance at the Haymarket on 10 December 1770. He repeated most of Anthony Maddox's tricks, with the additional refinement of simultaneously playing the violin, french horn, and drum while swinging on the wire. From a clipping in the A. M. Broadley Collection at Westminster Public Library, dated 4 January 1772, he is known to have had financially advantageous 'affairs in Sweden', but the nature of those affairs is mysterious. He was probably back in Russia by

1772. There he made and exhibited automata and presented experiments in the physical sciences. He also seems to have invented and installed machinery for the Znamenka Theatre in Moscow, of which he was joint manager with Prince Urasov. PETER THOMSON

Sources Highfill, Burnim & Langhans, *BDA* · D. Arundell, *The story of Sadler's Wells, 1683–1964* (1965) · *The letters of David Garrick*, ed. D. M. Little and G. M. Kahrl, 1 (1963) · M. C. Battestin and R. R. Battestin, *Henry Fielding: a life* (1989)
Likenesses B. Cole, engraving, 1753, BL · R. Houston, engraving (after T. King), BL
Wealth at death real estate in Bristol, Devon, and elsewhere; £10 bequests to three siblings: will, Highfill, Burnim & Langhans, *BDA*

Maddox, Isaac (1697–1759), bishop of Worcester, was born on 27 July 1697 and baptized on 29 July in the parish of St Botolph, Aldersgate, London, the son of Edward Maddox, a stationer, and his wife, Mary. According to Thomas Nowell he 'was from a child bred up at a regular grammar school: but having the misfortune to lose his father, he fell into the hands of friends who were Dissenters' (Nowell, 49). It was intended to apprentice him to a pastry-cook, but, as he proved too bookish for such work, arrangements were made for him to resume his studies.

With the assistance of dissenting patronage Maddox attended the University of Edinburgh and was awarded the degree of MA in 1723. Thereafter Maddox conformed to the Church of England, becoming a protégé of Bishop Edmund Gibson, and was ordained priest in 1723, though his relations with dissenters remained cordial in later life; he was on friendly terms with Philip Doddridge. Entering the Queen's College, Oxford, in June 1724, he was granted his BA degree by decree of convocation in July. He was incorporated in 1728 at Queens' College, Cambridge, was admitted MA, and received his DD in 1731. In the latter year he married Elizabeth Price (d. 1789), daughter of Richard Price of Hayes, Middlesex, and niece of Bishop Waddington of Chichester; they had one son and two daughters, two of the children dying young.

After his ordination to the priesthood Maddox was appointed vicar of Whiteparish, Wiltshire, subscribing in July 1724. He was collated to the prebend of Eartham in 1725, and subsequently to that of Bury, in Chichester Cathedral. In 1730 he was collated to the rectory of St Vedast, Foster Lane, London. In 1729 Maddox was appointed clerk of the closet to Queen Caroline, holding the office until 1736, and thereafter important preferment swiftly followed. In January 1734 he became dean of Wells; on 4 July 1736, he was consecrated bishop of St Asaph; and in 1743 he was translated to Worcester, the see which he held until his death.

Maddox discharged his episcopal duties vigorously and efficiently. Though he did not reside in the diocese he went to St Asaph each year between 1737 and 1742, conducted ordinations and confirmations, and held visitations in 1738 and 1742. At Worcester he undertook his primary visitation in 1745, triennial visitations in 1749, 1753, and 1757, and also peculiar visitations, and confirmed and ordained regularly. In his primary visitation charge he described the importance of the sacraments, preaching

Isaac Maddox (1697–1759), by unknown artist, c.1736–40

'with Diligence, with Plainness, with an affectionate Seriousness' (Maddox, *Charge*, 21), catechizing, and other clerical responsibilities, noting '[i]n many other Cases the private Labours of a Clergyman will be greatly useful; which renders his careful RESIDENCE among his People more desireable and more necessary' (ibid., 25). At both St Asaph and Worcester he showed himself determined to bring the dean and chapter to heel, so that they discharged their duties more effectively. He assigned £200 annually in his lifetime to augment the smaller livings of the Worcester diocese, and was a supporter of the Society for Promoting Christian Knowledge.

Respecting politics, Maddox was a whig supporter though in his later years he sometimes opposed the ministry. He took his parliamentary duties seriously, and his attendance in the House of Lords was good. While bishop of St Asaph he lent his support to John Myddelton, who had recently allied with the government, in the 1741 Denbighshire election; and, when the result was later overturned on petition, he had to make 'disagreeable *Submissions*' before the Commons (Taylor, 141). In September 1745 he wrote to the clergy of the Worcester diocese, denouncing the Jacobite rebellion. On 4 October, when an association and subscription was presented at Worcester's town hall, he made a speech, urging every effort to combat the rising and a possible French invasion—'the last Struggle You may ever have for Your Religion, Your Liberties, Your Lives' (Maddox, *Letter*, 8). His memorial in Worcester Cathedral remarks on his heartfelt patriotism, and he plainly regarded his spiritual and political duties as overlapping if not inseparable.

Maddox was much concerned with the social and physical ills of his age, and was well known as a preacher of charity sermons. Mindful, perhaps, of his own childhood, he preached in 1753 at the chapel of the Foundling Hospital a sermon entitled 'The wisdom and duty of preserving destitute infants', describing these as 'the most pitiable, most helpless, and most innocent Part of the human Species' (Maddox, *Wisdom and Duty*, 4). He promoted inoculation against smallpox, becoming a president of the Smallpox Hospital, London, and also denounced 'the *destructive* and *fatal Use* of *Spirituous Liquors*', which he saw as baneful to society at large as well as to those individuals who spent their days 'in *Idleness, Intemperance,* and *Wickedness,* to the Ruin of their *Health,* and *Substance,* and *Families,*—and … the Ruin of their *immortal* Souls!' (Maddox, *Epistle*, appendix, 30, 31). His most lasting memorial was the Worcester County Infirmary, opened in 1746: he was its prime mover, encouraging subscriptions and undertaking administrative work. Fittingly, his monument in Worcester Cathedral has a relief of the Good Samaritan.

Maddox's most significant work in print was *A vindication of the government, doctrine, and worship, of the Church of England, established in the reign of Queen Elizabeth*, which he published anonymously in 1733. It was a reply to Daniel Neal's *History of the Puritans* (1732) and owed much to material with which Zachary Grey had furnished him. In 1734, siding with Bishop Gibson in the campaign to prevent Thomas Rundle (thought to hold deistical views) being appointed bishop of Gloucester, he published a work attacking Rundle. In addition, he published fifteen of his sermons.

An ambitious man, Maddox was also generous, cheerful, and sometimes humorous. One visitor, writing in the *Gentleman's Magazine* for 1773, recalled his 'affability, ingenuity, and hospitality' (*GM*, 386). At Hartlebury Castle, the bishop of Worcester's country residence, Maddox improved the chapel, the palace, and the grounds. His portrait there, by Joseph Wright, shows a man with an oval face, thoughtful eyes, a long nose, and delicate hands. Maddox died at Hartlebury of 'a consumption' on 27 September 1759, and was buried in the south transept of Worcester Cathedral. His wife survived him.

Maddox's career, like the lives of Edmund Gibson, John Potter, and William Warburton, shows the rise of a man of conspicuous ability but humble origins to the heights of the Hanoverian church. Careful to balance his spiritual duties, his commitments in the Lords, and his various philanthropic concerns, he was an able, if not an outstanding, bishop.   COLIN HAYDON

Sources ordination register, diocese of London, 1675–1809, GL, MS/Microfilm 9535/3 · parish register, London, Aldersgate, St Botolph, GL, MS 3854/2 · *GM*, 1st ser., 43 (1773), 386 · I. Maddox, *The charge of Isaac, lord bishop of Worcester; to the clergy of his diocese, at his primary-visitation, holden at several places in the month of July, 1745* (1745?) · I. Maddox, *An epistle to the right honourable the Lord-Mayor, aldermen and common-council, of the City of London, and governors of the several hospitals; with an appendix, containing the most material extracts from the sermon, &c. concerning the pernicious and excessive use of spirituous liquors*, 3rd edn (1751) [with additions] · I. Maddox, *The lord bishop of Worcester's letter to the clergy of his diocese; and his lordship's speech upon the presenting an association and subscription at the town-hall of the city of Worcester, October 4, 1745* (1745) · I. Maddox, *The wisdom and duty of preserving destitute infants* (1753) · I. Maddox, *A sermon preached before his grace Charles duke of Marlborough, president, the vice-presidents and govenors of the hospital for the small-pox, and for inoculation … on Thursday, March 5, 1752* [1752] · Nichols, *Lit. anecdotes* · T. Nowell, *An answer to a pamphlet, entitled 'Pietas Oxoniensis'* (1768) · T. Stedman, ed., *Letters to and from the Rev. Philip Doddridge, D.D.* (1790) · memorial monument of Isaac Maddox, Worcester Cathedral · J. L. Salter, 'Isaac Maddox and the dioceses of St Asaph and Worcester (1736–1759)', MA diss., U. Birm., 1962 · S. Taylor, 'The bishops at Westminster in the mid-eighteenth century', *A pillar of the constitution: the House of Lords in British politics, 1640–1784*, ed. C. Jones (1989), 137–63 · W. H. McMenemey, *A history of the Worcester Royal Infirmary* (1947) · D. Laing, ed., *A catalogue of the graduates … of the University of Edinburgh*, Bannatyne Club, 106 (1858) · Foster, *Alum. Oxon.* · G. Hennessy, *Novum repertorium ecclesiasticum parochiale Londinense, or, London diocesan clergy succession from the earliest time to the year 1898* (1898) · Venn, *Alum. Cant.*
Archives Bucks. RLSS, Denham estate papers · NL Wales, notebook | BL, corresp. with duke of Newcastle and others · Worcs. RO, Worcester diocesan papers
Likenesses oils, c.1736–1740, Hartlebury Castle, Worcestershire [see illus.]
Wealth at death £1483—purse and apparel £8 5s.; money upon specialty £1459; £16: will, Borth. Inst.

Maddox, Michael (b. 1747). *See under* Maddox, Anthony (d. 1758).

Maddox, Willis [Willes] **(1813–1853)**, painter, was born in Bath. Nothing is known of his parents or training. In his early career he was patronized by William Beckford (1760–1844) of Fonthill, Wiltshire, for whom he painted several religious pictures, such as *The Annunciation, The Temptation,* and *The Agony in the Garden*. He exhibited for the first time at the Royal Academy in 1844, sending a still life of precious objects from Beckford's collection (Beckford Tower Trust, Bath). In the same year he painted Beckford on his deathbed (Brodick Castle, Isle of Arran) and published *Views of Lansdowne Tower, Bath*. In 1847 he exhibited his first important picture, *Naomi, Ruth, and Orpah,* at the academy, and he showed Italian genre and historical subjects in 1845, 1848, and 1850. In 1849 he sent a portrait of Halil Aga Risk Allah, and in 1850 one of the Turkish ambassadors, Mehemet Pasha. Among his British sitters were the duke and duchess of Hamilton, and Thomas James Watson, principal of an asylum for deaf mute people. Owing to his success in painting the portraits of prominent Turks, Maddox was invited to Constantinople to paint the sultan, for whom he executed several portraits. He died of fever at Pera, near Constantinople, on 26 June 1853.   L. H. CUST, rev. KENNETH BENDINER

Sources Bryan, *Painters* (1866) · Redgrave, *Artists* · Graves, *Artists* · Graves, *RA exhibitors* · C. Wainwright, *The romantic interior: the British collector at home, 1750–1850* (1989), 144–5 · *Apollo*, 127 (1988), 36 · *Burlington Magazine*, 118 (1976), 434

Maddy, Watkin (1798–1857), astronomer, a native of Herefordshire, was educated at Hereford grammar school. He graduated as second wrangler in 1820 from St John's College, Cambridge, proceeded MA in 1823, took orders, and in 1830 was awarded a degree of BD. He was elected to a fellowship on 18 March 1823, received the office of moderator, and joined the Astronomical Society. In 1826 he published at Cambridge *The Elements of the Theory of Plane Astronomy*, which was enlarged by John Hymers for a new edition in 1832. About 1837 Maddy resigned his fellowship from conscientious motives, feeling that he should henceforth earn his living, and supported himself by teaching mathematics in St John's Wood, London. He then moved to Sutton Coldfield, near Birmingham, where he died, unmarried, on 13 August 1857.

A. M. CLERKE, *rev.* ANITA MCCONNELL

Sources *Monthly Notices of the Royal Astronomical Society*, 18 (1857–8), 99–100 • *GM*, 3rd ser., 3 (1857), 345 • Venn, *Alum. Cant.* • private information (1893)

Madeleine [Madeleine de Valois] (**1520–1537**), queen of Scots, consort of James V, was the second daughter and fourth child of François I of France (1494–1547) and his first wife, Claude (1499–1524), daughter of Louis XII of France and Anne of Brittany. She was born on 10 August 1520, at St Germain-en-Laye, and joined her elder sister, Charlotte, and brothers, the dauphin François and Prince Henri, in the royal nurseries. Claude had two more children, Charles and Marguerite, but died when Madeleine was four, and little Charlotte died that same year. The princes and princesses had their own household and in 1523 this comprised no fewer than 240 officials and servants, including five chamberlains, nine stewards, and twenty pages. After Queen Claude's death the children's upbringing was supervised by their paternal grandmother, Louise de Savoie. When she died in 1531 the king's mistress, Anne d'Heilly, later duchesse d'Étampes, and his learned sister Marguerite, queen of Navarre, took charge of the girls.

Madeleine's daily companions also came and went. Her brothers the dauphin and Prince Henri were taken away to Spain as hostages and remained there for four years. They came back in 1530 and, three years after that, Henri's young bride, Catherine de' Medici, arrived from Italy. No mention was made, however, of a match for Madeleine. A charming childhood drawing of her shows a plump little girl clutching a rattle, but she seems to have contracted tuberculosis and was judged too sickly for marriage. In October 1536, however, *James V (1512–1542), king of Scots, arrived at Dieppe in search of a French wife. As long before as 1517 the Franco-Scottish treaty of Rouen had promised the then five-year-old James 'a daughter of the French king already living or yet to be born' (Donaldson, 99). He had inherited the throne at the age of one, whereupon his nobility had engaged in bitter power struggles with each other and nothing had been done about the marriage. Now, however, he was ruling for himself, and he had forceful ideas about his country's future. His uncle Henry VIII had broken with Rome and was urging him to do likewise. He refused to listen, instead resolving to strengthen Scotland's traditional alliance with France.

When he asked François for the promised bride, James was offered the duc de Vendôme's daughter Marie. He went to see her for himself, incognito, but made the excuse that she was too ill-shaped. In fact, he seems to

have been determined to have no less than a French princess, and set off for the French court which was then at Lyons. A portrait of Madeleine, probably painted that autumn, shows a rather sallow, serious girl in a jewelled French hood and a dark dress with ermine sleeves. James was handsome, highly-strung, and attractive to women. According to the Scottish chronicler Robert Lindsay of Pitscottie, when Madeleine met him she fell in love with him and persuaded her father, against his better judgement, to agree to the match. Whatever the truth of the matter, negotiations went ahead, in spite of her doctors' warnings that she would never survive the cold Scottish climate.

The marriage contract was finalized in Blois on 26 November 1536. The court then proceeded to Paris, where James spent 1100 crowns on a great table diamond for his bride's spousing ring. The wedding took place at Notre Dame on 1 January 1537, the bridal party standing on a platform which was draped with cloth of gold just outside the cathedral. They then went inside to hear mass, and finished the day with a magnificent banquet. After lengthy celebrations the young couple set out for the coast. They were delayed at Rouen when Madeleine fell ill, but by May she had recovered sufficiently to set out on the long voyage to Scotland. She and James took up residence in the palace of Holyroodhouse while elaborate preparations were made for the ceremonial entry into Edinburgh and coronation of the new queen. Within weeks of her arrival, however, Madeleine fell ill once more, and although she seemed to be recovering in early June, she died in her husband's arms on 7 July 1537.

Thomas Arthur, the royal tailor, laid aside the celebratory garments he had been making and started work on mourning gowns instead. James wrote to tell his father-in-law of the death of 'votre fille, ma tres chere compaigne' (Paris, Bibliothèque Nationale, Fonds Clairambault, MS 48, fol. 5971) and one of his officials began to list the young queen's belongings. There were gowns of cloth of gold, black velvet, and crimson satin, a kirtle of violet satin embroidered with gold, her silver cross and altar plate, and the two little gold cups made for her when she was a child.

Madeleine was buried in Holyrood Abbey, and a few weeks later James sent an emissary to France to ask her father for a replacement bride.

ROSALIND K. MARSHALL

Sources E. Bapst, *Les mariages de Jacques V* (Paris, 1889) • R. K. Marshall, *Mary of Guise* (1977) • D. Mayer and R. K. Marshall, 'Iconography and literature in the service of diplomacy', *Stewart style, 1513–1542: essays on the court of James V*, ed. J. H. Williams (1996), 237–88 • C. Bingham, *James V, king of Scots* (1971) • R. Knecht, *Renaissance warrior and patron: the reign of François I* (1994) • *The works of Sir David Lindsay*, ed. D. Hamer, 1, STS, 3rd ser., 1 (1931), 101–12 • M. Maclagan and J. Louda, *Lines of succession: heraldry of the royal families of Europe* (1981) • G. Donaldson, ed., *Scottish historical documents* (1970), 99
Archives BL, marriage contract of Princess Madeleine of France and James V, Harley MS 1244, fols. 159–163; Add. MS 30666, fols. 204–207
Likenesses J. Clouet, chalk drawing, *c*.1525, Musée Condé, Chantilly • C. de Lyon, oils, 1536, Château and Musée de Blois; [stolen] • colour transparency (after C. de Lyon), Château and Musée de Blois

Maderty. For this title name *see* Drummond, James, first Lord Maderty (1551x61–1623).

Madge, Charles Henry (1912–1996), poet and sociologist, was born in Johannesburg, South Africa, on 10 October 1912, the son of Charles Albert Madge (*d.* 1916), army officer, and his wife, Barbara, *née* Hylton Foster. His father, temporary lieutenant-colonel in the Royal Warwickshire regiment, was killed in action on 10 May 1916, near Bethune. Madge's schooling was clad in the conventional garb of his class of origin and he bore the personal marks of a gentle and superior upbringing—a diffident and self-effacing manner which hid his passionate and impulsively radical nature. He was a clever child, entering Winchester College as a scholar, and going on with a classical scholarship to Magdalene College, Cambridge, where he was determined to read science. He had already begun to write poetry.

The 1930s were times of turbulence for intellectuals. Not only were the economies of the world in disarray but Madge's generation was faced with political and moral upheaval. Dictatorship threatened democracy, and slump brought the menace of social inequality. Madge struggled to combine science and verse in the service of humanity, as did his Cambridge contemporaries J. D. Bernal and Lancelot Hogben. He became an inactive member of the Communist Party. From Paris too he welcomed surrealism (a movement to apply realistically the ideas of psychoanalysis and Marxism in aid of social change). His personal radicalism led to his being 'swept off his feet', as the saying then went, by the glamorous young poet Kathleen Raine—Kathleen Jessie Davies (1908–2003), daughter of George Raine, schoolmaster, and divorced wife of Hugh Sykes Davies—for whom he left Cambridge, his degree incomplete, to seek his fortune in London. They married on 22 December 1937 and had a son and a daughter, but the marriage was dissolved. On 4 March 1942 Madge married the novelist Marie Agnes (Inez) Spender (1913/14–1976), known as Inez Pearn (also known as Elizabeth Lake), only daughter of William Henry Pearn, dock's timekeeper, and divorced wife of Stephen Harold Spender, poet. Madge had a further son and daughter by this second marriage.

Meanwhile Madge had come under the favourable notice of T. S. Eliot, who liked his poetry, if not his politics. Eliot was influential in securing Madge a job as reporter on the *Daily Mirror* (1935–6) and in arranging for Faber to publish his first book of verse, *The Disappearing Castle*, in 1937. His poems were selected by W. B. Yeats for inclusion in the *Oxford Book of Modern Verse* (1938).

At the *Daily Mirror* Madge became increasingly conscious of the gap between what ordinary people thought and what their leaders thought they thought. So deeply impressed was he by this gulf between popular opinion and its representation by the powerful in press, parliament, and party that when Edward VIII abdicated he wrote to the *New Statesman* calling for 'mass observation' to create 'mass science'. He knew both the popular Caribbean calypso 'On the 10th of December 1936 the Duke of

Charles Henry Madge (1912–1996), by Elliott & Fry, 1945

Windsor went to get his kicks …' and the constitutional opinions of the monarchy, Baldwin, and Churchill. He wanted to interpret each to the other and to base democracy on shared scientific fact (*New Statesman*, 20 Jan 1937). By extraordinary chance Tom Harrisson published his first and only poem in the same issue of the *New Statesman* as Madge's letter. Harrisson, recently returned from 'living with cannibals' in the New Hebrides in the Pacific, was setting up a study of the English natives of the north in Bolton (Worktown). He wrote to Madge in Blackheath and within a month the enterprise Mass-Observation was formed. It soon achieved success and national notice: and the Madge–Harrisson partnership produced a Pelican Special, *Britain* (1939), in which their journalistic skills combined to offer a lively picture of contemporary life through the eyes of 'observers' and voluntary diarists from all over the country.

Mass-Observation was, as Madge put it, 'a science of ourselves' (*New Statesman*, 20 Jan 1937). It sprang, according to Tom Jeffery, 'from a realization that ordinary people were being misled by a complacent press and an indifferent government' (Jeffery, 3). Current sociology was dismissed as academic. The urgent need was to amass facts and to circulate them. Madge's day reports after a year confronted him with 2.3 million words, and he needed another year to sort them out. T. H. Marshall and Maria Jahoda both recognized the sincerity of the intention behind the survey of Bolton and the national panel of volunteers' diaries, but denounced the method as unscientific. A total of 1894 respondents replied between 1937 and 1945. They were youngish, left-leaning, and preponderantly middle-class, and therefore not a random sample of the national population. Nevertheless, the archives later deposited at the University of Sussex presented an invaluable source to social historians of the war and immediate pre-war period.

Two such contrasted personalities as Madge and Harrisson could hardly be expected to co-operate permanently, and Madge soon drifted away. Thereafter his career became more conventional. He analysed working-class spending habits for J. M. Keynes at the National Institute for Economic and Social Research from 1940 to 1942, worked on the research staff of Political and Economic Planning in 1943, was director of the Pilot Press in 1944, and became the social development officer at the new town of Stevenage in 1947 before going on to be the first professor of sociology at Birmingham University, from 1950 to 1970. While at Birmingham he published only one book—*Society in the Mind* (1964)—but he was a respected teacher, and was a member of numerous United Nations and UNESCO missions, to Thailand, India, south-east Asia, and Ghana.

From Birmingham, Madge retired with his wife to the south of France, but he returned to England following her death in 1976. On 13 July 1979 he married Evelyn May Brown (1926/7–1984), journalist, and daughter of Robert Edward Brown. In the 1970s and 1980s Madge published a number of books, including (with Barbara Weinberger) *Art Students Observed* (1973) and (with Peter Willmott) *Inner City Poverty in Paris and London* (1981). He also edited, with Mary-Lou Jennings, *Pandaemonium* (1985), a collection of texts compiled by his old Cambridge friend Humphrey Jennings, covering the period 1660–1886, and chronicling contemporary reactions to mechanical invention.

While he never lost his early enthusiasm for social planning on behalf of humanity Madge's later years were dogged by ill health. In old age he was still the same charming and tentatively friendly man, but despite his very considerable talents he became self-critical and seemed somehow defeated. Madge died at his home, 28 Lynmouth Road, Haringey, London, on 17 January 1996, of heart failure.   A. H. HALSEY

Sources A. Calder, 'Mass-Observation, 1937–1949', *Essays on the history of British sociological research*, ed. M. Bulmer (1985), 121–36 · *The Independent* (20 Jan 1996) · *The Times* (25 Jan 1996) · C. Madge and T. Harrison, *Mass-Observation* (1937) · T. Jeffery, *Mass-Observation: a short history* (1978) · M. Green, *Children of the sun: a narrative of 'decadence' in England after 1918* (1977) · A. Calder and D. Sheridan, *Speak for yourself: a Mass-Observation anthology* (1984) · m. certs. · d. cert. · WWW · personal knowledge (2004)
Archives NRA, corresp. and literary papers · U. Sussex, corresp. and papers | BLPES, corresp. relating to his Keynes letters · King's AC Cam., corresp. with John Maynard Keynes · U. Sussex, Tom Harrisson Mass-Observation Archive
Likenesses H. Coster, photograph, c.1937, repro. in Calder and Sheridan, *Speak for yourself* · M. Peake, drawing, 1938, repro. in Calder and Sheridan, *Speak for yourself* · Elliott & Fry, photograph, 1945, NPG [see illus.]
Wealth at death £256,463: probate, *CGPLA Eng. & Wales*

Madge, Thomas (1786–1870), Unitarian minister, was born in 1786 at Plymouth, Devon, and was baptized there on 15 July 1787, the son of John and Betty Madge. Little is known of his parents, except that his father, a miller, died when he was about twelve, and his mother placed him in the care of a relative, Thomas Hugo, a surgeon of Crediton. Following education at the local grammar school (c.1798–1803), he commenced training for the medical profession in his guardian's surgery in 1803.

Brought up in the Church of England, Madge started to attend the Unitarian church in Crediton. The preaching of John Rowe of Lewin's Mead, Bristol, influenced him to enter the Unitarian ministry. While this was not to the taste of his guardian, nothing was done to stop him. Madge entered Timothy Kenrick's theological academy at Exeter in 1804, transferring afterwards to Manchester College at York (1804–9). He married, first, in 1819, Harriet, daughter of Benjamin Travers of Clapton, who died on 22 June 1835; they had two sons and a daughter. On 20 August 1844 he married Ellen (1805–1889), daughter of James Bischoff, a merchant, and his wife, Peggy. Their one daughter died in 1872.

Madge's ministry commenced at Bury St Edmunds early in 1810, and he 'took his place as one of the most eloquent and able of preachers, a place he maintained for more than half a century' (*The Inquirer*, 10 Sept 1870, 593). In 1811 he joined Pendlebury Houghton in the ministry of the Octagon Chapel, Norwich, becoming sole pastor the next year. Being convinced of the truth of Unitarianism as the genuine gospel of Christ, he proclaimed it strongly, thereby causing some secessions, but strengthened the congregation's sense of commitment. He influenced James Martineau, then a young chapel member, who concluded in 1870 that 'in my case, early impressions have something to do with the affectionate veneration with which I regarded him' (Drummond and Upton 1.13). Martineau's sister Harriet, however, saw him as a preacher fitted only for children.

Madge's fame spread, and in 1825 he was appointed assistant to Thomas Belsham at Essex Street Chapel, London. He became minister in 1829, at Belsham's death, of what was then considered the premier pulpit of Unitarianism. He was no administrator or reformer, was seldom seen on platforms, and took no part in politics. The pulpit was his throne: 'In the prayers so devoutly offered, and the hymns and lessons so admirably delivered, he often produced a thrilling effect and an abiding impression' (*The Inquirer*, 29 Oct 1870, 699). For thirty-four years he preached at Essex Street, attracting listeners, including Charles Dickens, from all walks of life, a power which did not diminish with time. He drew so large and select a congregation that the carriages took up nearly all of one side of St Clement's churchyard.

Madge's attraction as a preacher was not intellectual, but lay in a crystal-clear presentation, combined with earnestness and vitality. Madge saw his success arising from his simplicity of style; there had never been any difficulty, he believed, in understanding what he said. He was considered by many as the leading Unitarian preacher of his time, and it was remarked in 1859 that 'his [was a] ministry which for acceptance and popularity had never probably been surpassed in Unitarian congregational history' (James 237–8). Essex Street Chapel never regained its popularity after Madge's retirement. The congregation declined in the 1860s, and moved to Notting Hill Gate in 1887. Madge's published writings consist mostly of sermons and prayers delivered on special occasions, for which he was in much demand until his death. Twice chaplain to sheriffs of London, he also delivered the address from the Presbyterian divines to the queen during the Crimean War and on the occasion of royal marriages.

Madge became widely known: his son Travers (1823–1866), staying at Ambleside in 1843, introduced himself to Wordsworth, and met with the response 'Oh, the son of the clergyman' (Herford, 22). His traditional, Bible-based view of the Unitarian gospel led him to oppose Martineau's theological innovations in the 1860s, but he never joined in the religious rancour that was so common after 1850. Madge died at 20 Highbury Terrace, Highbury, London, on 29 August 1870, and was buried in the grave of his daughter Amelia at Abney Park cemetery, Stoke Newington.   ALAN RUSTON

Sources W. James, *Memoir of Thomas Madge* (1871) · *The Inquirer* (3 Sept 1870), 570, 583 · *The Inquirer* (10 Sept 1870), 593–4 · *The Inquirer* (24 Sept 1870), 623 · *The Inquirer* (22 Oct 1870), 684 · *The Inquirer* (29 Oct 1870), 699–703 · *The Inquirer* (5 Nov 1870), 715–18 · *The Inquirer* (12 Nov 1870), 732 · *The Inquirer* (19 Nov 1870), 751 · *The Inquirer* (10 Dec 1870), 795 · *Christian Life* (27 July 1878), 366 · *Christian Life* (24 Aug 1878), 414 · J. Diprose, *Some account of the parish of Saint Clement Danes*, 2 (1876), 27–8 · *Christian Reformer, or, Unitarian Magazine and Review*, 1 (1835), 511 · *Christian Reformer, or, Unitarian Magazine and Review*, new ser., 1 (1845), 332 · *The Inquirer* (22 April 1845), 271 · *The Inquirer* (3 Feb 1845), 78 · *The Inquirer* (3 Feb 1872), 78 · *The Inquirer* (27 May 1872), 341 · *The Inquirer* (3 June 1872), 345 · *The Inquirer* (22 July 1872), 465 · B. Herford, *Travers Madge, a memoir* (1868) · Boase, *Mod. Eng. biog.* · J. Drummond and C. Upton, *Life of J. Martineau*, 1 (1902), 12–14 · T. Sadler, *London Unitarians fifty years ago* (1900) · W. D. Jeremy, *The Presbyterian Fund and Dr Daniel Williams's Trust* (1885) · J. Carpenter, *J. Martineau* (1905), 9–10 · d. cert. · m. cert. · Plymouth and West Devon Record Office, Plymouth, Charles MS 8
Archives DWL
Likenesses photograph, repro. in James, *Memoir of Thomas Madge*, frontispiece
Wealth at death under £18,000: probate, 26 Sept 1870, CGPLA Eng. & Wales

Madgett [Madget], **Nicholas** (b. c.1738), Irish nationalist, was born in Kinsale, co. Cork. He was educated in France, possibly at the Irish College in Paris, and remained in the country thereafter, securing employment under the *ancien régime* monarchy. During the early 1790s he formed part of a prominent group of pro-revolutionary Irish and British exiles in Paris, based around the radical writer Thomas Paine. After Paine's fall from favour Madgett occupied an increasingly influential role as the most senior spokesman on Irish affairs for the revolutionary government, especially between 1793 and 1795. This was enhanced by his employment, from 1793, at the *bureau de traduction*, attached to the committee of public safety. In 1793 he urged the French government to purge Paris of an alleged English espionage network and suggested that agents should be sent to Ireland to disseminate revolutionary ideals.

Madgett was responsible for the mission of William Jackson to Ireland, as a French agent, in 1794. When Theobald Wolfe Tone arrived in Paris as a United Irish agent in February 1796, he discovered that the Directory had delegated Madgett, then working at the French foreign office, with responsibility for negotiating on behalf of Irish radicals. Madgett provided Tone with an important medium of communication to the French authorities and translated numerous memorials for him. However, Tone quickly became disillusioned with Madgett's protracted negotiations, and effectively bypassed him by approaching Lazare Carnot personally. Tone was also aware of Madgett's self-importance, but realized that he had little real understanding of events in Ireland. During 1796 Madgett recruited among British prisoners of war for an irregular force which he hoped would form a vanguard to a future Irish invasion under the French general Lazare Hoche. The French government subsequently abandoned the idea.

The missions of the United Irishmen, Tone in 1796, and Edward Lewins in 1797, reduced Madgett's importance as an Irish representative. He continued to petition the French authorities, assuring them in 1797 that a successful Irish revolution would lead to the collapse of British naval power. He later urged the Directory to seize British funds held at the Bank of Venice. Despite his less prominent role in negotiations, the informer Samuel Turner explained to Castlereagh that Madgett was 'one of the most active instruments of the French Directory in everything that respects Ireland' (Hayes, 195). He remained prominent within the Paris committee of United Irishmen in 1798. With James Napper Tandy and Thomas Muir he formed an alternative base of Irish radical exiles to the 'official' United Irish missions of Tone and Lewins. In the aftermath of the 1798 rising it appears that Madgett was considered a liability among some Irish exiles for his high profile during the Jacobin period in power. The date of his death is unknown.   LIAM CHAMBERS

Sources M. Elliott, *Partners in revolution: the United Irishmen and France* (1982) · W. T. W. Tone, *Life of Theobald Wolfe Tone*, ed. T. Bartlett (1998) · R. Hayes, *Biographical dictionary of Irishmen in France* (1949) · R. Hayes, 'Madgett's legion, 1796', *Irish Sword*, 1 (1949–53), 142 · P. Weber, *On the road to rebellion: the United Irishmen and Hamburg, 1796–1803* (1998) · DNB · R. R. Madden, *The United Irishmen: their lives and times*, 2nd edn, 4 vols. (1857–60) · R. Hayes, *Ireland and Irishmen in the French Revolution* (1932) · private information (2004) [C. J. Woods and R. B. McDowell]
Archives Archives du Ministère des Affaires Étrangères, Paris, correspondance politique, Angleterre, 587–9

Madison, James (1751–1836), revolutionary politician in America and president of the United States of America, was born on 5 March 1751 in King George county, Virginia, near the Rappahannock River (on the estate of his maternal grandmother, at the site of the future town of Port Conway), the first of a dozen children of James Madison (1723–1801) and Nelly Conway (1732–1829). His father was a vestryman and justice of the peace in Orange county, where he owned 4000 acres and perhaps 100 slaves.

James Madison (1751–1836), by Gilbert Stuart, 1805–7

Early years Madison's father, not himself formally educated, provided his son with more appropriate preparation for a future place among the great Virginia gentry. 'James Madison, jr', as he signed himself until his father's death, attended Donald Robertson's boarding-school in King and Queen county from 1762 to 1767, and was then taught at home for two years by the local rector, the Revd Thomas Martin, who encouraged him to travel north to the College of New Jersey, Princeton. The selection of Princeton possibly arose from the enthusiastic support of Martin and the Madisons for the patriotic party in the growing debate concerning the American colonies' relations with Britain as well as from its progressive and exciting curriculum. Princeton students rejected imported cloth and dressed in homespun, and the college's president, John Witherspoon, an immigrant from Scotland and major figure in the Presbyterian denomination, later signed the Declaration of Independence. Madison passed examinations with the freshman class in September 1769 and graduated two years later instead of taking the usual three. He remained at Princeton during the winter of 1771–2, recovering from debility and reading law, theology, and Hebrew under Witherspoon's direction. On his return to the family plantation, he tutored his younger siblings and pondered a career, two years before the imperial crisis culminated in the Coercive Acts of 1774. As Orange county mobilized, Madison trained with the militia and joined his father on the local committee of safety. As he reflected later, 'he was under very early and strong impressions in favour of liberty both civil and religious' (Adair, 198).

For Madison, civil and religious liberty were closely linked. He did not record his religious views after 1776, but he had been brought up in the Church of England and occasionally attended episcopalian services in later life. Clearer is his commitment to the most advanced Enlightenment position on freedom of religion. His first intervention in Virginian politics, in 1774, had been to oppose the imprisonment of unlicensed preachers in Culpeper county. When his weak health excluded him from active military service, the gratitude of Baptist neighbours perhaps assisted his election to the state convention of 1776, which framed one of the earliest and most widely imitated revolutionary constitutions. When only twenty-five he made his first important contribution to the revolutionary reconstruction: an amendment to replace a commitment to religious 'toleration' with an assertion of an equal, universal right to the free exercise of religion, thus introducing into Virginia's declaration of rights a standard unprecedented in any society's organic law. Madison also supported fully Thomas Jefferson's attempts to liberalize the state's religious statutes.

Madison was defeated at the next election after refusing voters their customary treats, but was selected by the legislature for the executive council and, in December 1779, for congress. There he won a nationwide reputation for his grasp of legislative business. He was active in bringing Virginia to cede its north-west lands—thus facilitating ratification of the articles of confederation and the creation of a national domain—and also supported Robert Morris's attempts to rationalize the department of finance. Madison introduced the compromise leading to the congressional recommendations of 18 April 1783, which asked the states to amend the articles in order to permit congress to levy a 5 per cent duty on foreign imports, to complete their western cessions, and to authorize other measures to meet the interest on the continental debt.

State and federal reform Under the articles of confederation, delegates were chosen annually and limited to three successive terms. Madison retired in November 1783 and promptly stood for the state assembly once more. There he sought approval of the federal reforms proposed in 1783 and also of a variety of state reforms that Jefferson had introduced before replacing him in congress. Madison hoped that peace would facilitate states' satisfaction of their federal requisitions, and that better times and rapid adoption of these limited reforms would enable congress to fulfil its obligations and repair its damaged prestige. He knew, however, that the central legislature's absolute dependence on the states for revenues, as well as for enforcement of its treaties, undermined its effectiveness and could endanger its very existence. Taking an apprehensive, continentalist view, Madison was sure that revolutionary liberty would be doomed by disintegration of the continental union, and with it the republican experiment's protection against foreign intervention and the states' safeguard against the rivalries which condemned Europe to fragmentation, oppressive taxes, enlarged armies, tyranny, and wars. He also urged a grant to congress of a power to retaliate against Great Britain for restrictions on American trade.

In fact the peace was followed by an economic downturn. The states did not approve amendments to the articles of confederation and fell increasingly behind with their federal requisitions, while mutual animosities escalated perilously as several attempted legislative retaliation against commercial restrictions, only to be baffled by their neighbours' conflicting regulations. Without a steady source of independent funds, the continental congress could not manage its domestic debt, and only with increasing difficulty could it secure European loans to meet its foreign obligations. Deadlocked over the negotiation of a commercial treaty with Spain in 1786 and over new proposals for a federal power over commerce, both northerners and southerners talked of imminent separation into smaller, regional confederations.

Madison, who had doubted the usefulness of extra-legal meetings and feared undermining the authority of congress, backed only one motion to consider improved regulation of trade after other motions had failed. He and other delegates assembled in the Annapolis Convention of 1786 in an atmosphere of deep and urgent concern for the union's survival. After seven days it was apparent that attendance would be poor, and reports from congress were increasingly alarming. It was more from desperation than from a real expectation of success that the dozen delegates present recommended the appointment of another general convention to consider all the problems of the union, a course to which Madison was thoroughly committed from September.

By now, moreover, Madison no longer thought that the country's problems could be solved by a revision of the articles. Faced with economic troubles, many of the states passed measures—issuing paper money, suspending private suits for debt, postponing taxation—that he thought interfered with private contracts, threatened security of property, or undermined states' financial ability to satisfy their individual and federal obligations. During the autumn of 1786 Madison's correspondents warned him of increasing disillusionment, leading in Massachusetts to an armed rising by rural inhabitants led by Daniel Shays. Though Virginia was so far immune from insurrection or serious abuses, Madison's motions for major state and federal reform had been often defeated. Madison believed that his single greatest triumph, the statute for religious freedom (19 January 1786), had been successfully enacted only because a bill granting tax support to teachers of religion—in his view, a serious threat to freedom of conscience—had failed owing to rivalry between Virginia's many sects. Disgusted with the multiplicity, the mutability, and the injustices of local laws, Madison feared that such abuses would alienate increasing numbers of people if the revolutionary enterprise appeared unable to advance individual interests or protect fundamental rights. The crisis of confederation government was, he believed, further aggravated by a crisis of republican convictions, neither of which could be overcome by minor alterations to the articles of confederation. An effectual

reform, he told one correspondent, must 'perpetuate the union'; more, it must 'redeem the honour of the republican name' (Madison to Edmund Pendleton, 24 Feb 1787, *Papers*, 9.295).

No one played a more vital part in the subsequent developments. On his return from Annapolis, Madison quickly secured the state assembly's endorsement of the plan for a federal convention and also George Washington's consent to lead the Virginia delegation, encouraging other states also to choose distinguished delegates. Madison was also selected, and—being again eligible—re-elected to the confederation congress. He may already have compiled his notes on ancient and modern confederations; in April 1787 he wrote a formal memorandum entitled 'Vices of the political system of the United States'. Here and in private correspondence he argued that the crisis in both confederation and state government made it necessary to replace the existing federal system with a central government derived directly from the people. He also argued that it should have effective, full, and independent powers over matters of general concern, incorporating so many different economic interests and religious groups that popular majorities could rarely form 'on any other principles than those of justice and the public good'.

The framing and ratification of the constitution Madison, the best-prepared delegate to the convention, made numerous distinctive contributions towards framing the constitution. He had urged other Virginia delegates to arrive in Philadelphia in time to agree some introductory proposals and was the main author of the propositions introduced on 29 May by Edmund Randolph, which served throughout the summer as a basis for the convention's sweeping reconsideration of the federal system. Madison and other supporters of the 'Virginia plan' argued that effective reform must free central government from dependence on the states. He and other delegates from larger states insisted on proportional representation in both houses of congress, popular ratification of the new federal charter, and a careful balance of authority between a democratic house of representatives and branches less immediately responsive to majority demands. Madison also insisted on the need to address not only the confederation's ills but also the vices of republican government apparent in the revolutionary states. He argued that a sound reform had to enable the central government to fulfil its delegated functions but also to respond to majority abuses, limiting states' powers and correcting the frequent structural mistakes of early revolutionary constitutions. In all these respects Madison compelled the great convention to reconsider fundamentally the nature of a sound republic, even as other members compelled him to reconsider his first thoughts on federal reform. In several respects the constitution departed significantly from Madison's original proposals; but his peers and later writers have agreed he was unmistakably its most important framer.

Yet even this does not entirely explain why Madison is often called the father of the constitution. Before he returned to Virginia, where his leadership was vital in securing the approval of a narrowly divided state convention, Madison resumed his seat in the confederation congress, helped provide some central guidance for the ratification contest, and collaborated with Alexander Hamilton in producing the most important exegesis and defence of the finished constitution. Madison's numbers of *The Federalist*, generally regarded as the greatest classic of American political thought, justified the convention's compromises, explained the partly national and partly federal government created by the charter, and served from the outset as an essential guide to the intent of the constitution's framers. Their great theme—the constitution's faithful adherence to the principles of 1776 and its necessity as a democratic remedy for the diseases most destructive to republics—contributed as surely as the convention to the shaping and success of the constitution.

Launching the new republic The newly constituted government assembled in New York in April 1789. Madison immediately assumed the leading role in the first federal congress, which was responsible for filling in the outline of the constitution as well as for the legislation which it had been created to permit. He took the lead in introducing the first federal tariff and in the creation of executive departments, carrying the point that executive officials should be subject to removal only by the president. Most importantly, he took upon himself the preparation of the constitutional amendments that became the Bill of Rights.

Throughout the process of constitutional reform Madison's insistence on a stronger federal government had been accompanied by commitment to a system that could not escape popular control. His numbers of *The Federalist* described the new regime as neither wholly national nor strictly federal in structure, but rather as an unprecedented compound in which state and central governments, each dependent on the people, would each be restricted to the responsibilities each was best equipped to meet while still able to check intrusions by the other. His commitment to a system only partly national in structure, and his recognition that a Bill of Rights would conciliate critics, led him to reverse his opposition to immediate constitutional amendment and persevere against the opposition of others in congress.

These ideas may help explain the 'reversal' of positions often imputed to Madison. Even by the second session of the new congress he was alarmed by the dangers he saw in the proposals of Alexander Hamilton, the secretary of the treasury, including sectional inequities and the broad construction of the constitution involved in their justification. He protested against Hamilton's proposed chartering of a national bank in 1791 as exceeding the powers allowed by the constitution—excessive reliance on implied congressional authority would tend to transmute a limited, republican regime into a unitary system detrimental to the revolution. He and Jefferson encouraged Philip Freneau to found the *National Gazette*, a semi-weekly watchdog over the usurpations of government. Madison

contributed nineteen unsigned essays to this, seeking to alert the people to the danger, while organizing an opposition in the house. Before the end of 1792, he and Jefferson were the acknowledged leaders of a movement that soon became the first political party of the modern sort: the Jeffersonian or democratic republicans, ancestors of the later Democratic Party, but generally referred to in this period as the republicans.

Jefferson resigned as Washington's secretary of state in December 1793; Madison remained in the house of representatives as leader of the opposition party until adjournment of the fourth congress in March 1797, when a number of considerations led him to decline re-election. On 15 September 1794, at Harewood, in the Shenandoah valley, Virginia, after a courtship of four months, the long-time bachelor married the attractive young widow Dolley Payne Todd (1768–1849), daughter of John Payne, a Quaker and former plantation owner from Virginia who had freed his slaves and unsuccessfully set up as a starch manufacturer in Philadelphia, and Mary, *née* Coles. Her first husband, John Todd, a lawyer, had died in the previous year's yellow fever epidemic. The couple were childless, though Dolley had one surviving son from her previous marriage, John Payne Todd. Also in 1794 Madison's brother Ambrose, who had been largely responsible for managing the family plantation, died; with his father ailing and Jefferson newly elected vice-president, Madison decided that his thirty years of steady public service entitled him to retire to Montpelier, as the estate was now called.

This retirement proved brief. In 1795 the Washington administration had avoided a crisis in relations with Britain by concluding a commercial treaty which, to the disgusted Madison and the republicans, sacrificed vital national interests as well as offending Britain's opponent, revolutionary France, which began to prey on US merchant shipping. By the spring of 1798 negotiations with France had failed: the consequent surge of patriotic fury allowed federalists in congress to launch a naval war with France and a bloodless reign of terror against the republican opposition, notably the Alien and Sedition Acts directed against the press.

The quasi-war with France, expansion of the army, and efforts to intimidate domestic opposition seemed to the republicans open signs of a conspiracy to undermine the constitutional republic and to forge a permanent alliance, maybe even reunion, with Great Britain. Jefferson and Madison responded by drafting resolutions condemning the Alien and Sedition Acts as unconstitutional and void, which were respectively passed by the legislatures of Kentucky (16 November 1798) and Virginia (24 December 1798).

No other state was willing to follow Virginia and Kentucky on a path which led, years later, to nullification and secession. This reluctance prompted Madison to stand for re-election to the state assembly in 1799 and to draft his great *Report* (1800), defending the 1798 resolutions, explaining the compact theory of the constitution, and initiating modern, literalist interpretations of the first amendment as proscribing any interference by government with the free development and circulation of opinion. The Kentucky and Virginia resolutions also opened the 1800 election campaign, which ended in victory for the republicans.

The Jeffersonian ascendancy Madison returned to federal office as first lieutenant to his old ally Jefferson—not only secretary of state from 1801 to 1809 but also a principal adviser to the president on the policies arising from the latter's conviction that the federal balance required redress and the central government should be confined within the boundaries set at the ratification of the constitution. The Hamiltonians had relied on rapid economic growth as a path to the emergence of an integrated state with new native manufactures producing exportable goods and a large domestic agricultural market. The Jeffersonians stressed the republic's foundation on independent farmer–owners and the need to revitalize it through continuous overland expansion to the west; they hoped to free its maritime trade and provide new markets for its farmers but to delay urbanization and industrialization. Where Hamilton had seen the national debt as a useful backing for a stable currency supply, the republicans made its reduction a priority, seeing interest payments as a transference of wealth from the productive to the non-productive classes, also connecting dangerously and corruptingly (in the manner of the British system of finance) central government and special interest groups. In foreign policy, the republicans saw themselves as dedicated to a policy of genuine neutrality between Great Britain and the French republic, not the subservience to the former with which they reproached Washington and Adams.

What Jefferson called 'the revolution of 1800' was extraordinarily successful. The interlude in twenty years of European warfare between 1801 and 1803 facilitated his administration's concentration on its domestic programme and consolidation of popular support. The resumption of the war prepared the way in 1803 for the republic's purchase of Louisiana from Napoleon, doubling its size. None the less, Madison's ideas for taking advantage of the renewal of European conflict substantially contributed towards a crisis that damaged his own presidency. By 1805 Napoleon controlled all western Europe while Britain ruled the seas. Neither was willing to allow the other the benefits of trade with neutrals, of which the United States, not itself a military power, was the most significant, and in the next two years they condemned between them some 1500 American ships and passed decrees threatening most of its remaining commerce. Both Jefferson and Madison had believed US trade to be just as effective as war in defending national interests, since (in their view) America exported necessities upon which European countries and their West Indian colonies depended, but imported only 'niceties' or 'luxuries', either dispensable or replaceable domestically. Thus denial of US trade should be able to force to terms a European power, particularly Britain, without resort to war,

with its increased taxation, debt, and armed forces, which would endanger a sound republic.

The complete embargo on American trade with which Jefferson responded in 1807 to French and British depredations led in the next two years to a sharp depression, giving the Federalist Party the opportunity for revival, and the compromising of Jeffersonian concern for civil rights by a ferocious enforcement policy. Congress finally repealed the embargo in favour of non-intercourse with belligerents, a course of which Jefferson and Madison did not approve, but which neither would intervene with his party to oppose.

When Madison succeeded his friend Jefferson in 1809, his administration immediately faced problems it was ill-adapted to resolve. Out of principle a supporter of legislative independence, Madison was diffident in his relations with congress, where his party suffered divisions as the federalists declined. It proved impossible to adjust non-intercourse to hurt the Europeans more than the United States: the policy was therefore abandoned in 1810, with the proviso that it would be reimposed on either belligerent if the other would respect US neutrality. Napoleon gave an ambiguous reply, suggesting possible American exemption; when Britain declined Madison's call to follow suit, he reimposed non-intercourse.

The winter of 1811–12 was thus the fourth year of commercial warfare of some sort, damaging the United States while still producing no British concessions. The federalists capitalized on popular discontent to win state elections; fighting continued with north-western tribes, assisted by British administrators in Canada. Before the twelfth congress met, Madison reluctantly decided that, if he refused submission to British policies, the only alternative was a declaration of war, which was accordingly passed, on a vote that largely followed party lines, on 18 June 1812.

The Anglo-American War of 1812–1814 and Madison's retirement The Anglo-American War of 1812–14 condemned Madison's administration to being assessed by posterity as mediocre. Madison had advocated a high state of readiness for war, but in the event the United States entered war with fourteen warships and fewer than 7000 well-trained troops. Years of economic confrontation had so exacerbated divisions that New England governors would not let their militia, the country's best, leave their states; until the battle of New Orleans, western forces had only limited success. Congress's refusal to preserve the national bank had left the treasury crippled, and Madison sought to limit the war's expense to the republican and federal nature of the country. Thirty months of war imperilled the survival of an intact republic, and the eventual treaty of Ghent (24 December 1814) settled none of the original disputes.

Nevertheless the administration impressed contemporaries, if not historians. John Adams, no admirer, wrote that Madison had won more glory and secured more union than all the preceding presidents combined. His presidency ended in an outburst of national pride and harmony, and with significant readjustments to the fiscal and administrative structure of the country arising from the lessons of the war. The great co-architect of Jeffersonian beliefs finally proposed, in his last annual message (5 December 1815), a federal programme of 'internal improvements' encompassing road and canal construction to improve communication between the states for the purposes of defence and trade, some tariff protection for the nascent industries which had emerged during the war, and the creation of a new national bank—all measures enacted by congress early in 1816 amid federalist collapse. Madison still required, before signing the bill for internal improvements, a constitutional amendment to confirm the federal government's authority to act. His veto of the bill was consistent with his republican principles, but disappointed and puzzled his adherents. Having long feared that such measures would entail civic evils, Madison trusted that these would be checked by education, the capacity for enlargement to the west, and the leadership and integrity of the legitimate defenders of the constitution. He hardly surrendered to federalist ideas, but his partial adoption of them helped heal the division dating back to the adoption of the constitution. James Monroe's essentially unanimous election (1820) to a second term heralded a period of single-party rule by the triumphant Jeffersonian republicans.

Madison retired to Orange county and helped Jefferson create the University of Virginia. He also acted in his last years as an oracle on the creation and interpretation of the constitution, if haunted by his own insistence that the federal charter was a compact between the several states' sovereign peoples and that they alone could definitively decide its meaning. He opposed both the southern use of the Virginia and Kentucky resolutions to elaborate a doctrine of interposition and nullification and the broad constructions imposed by Chief Justice John Marshall that restricted state sovereignty. Respectively he feared that the constitution would be constricted to such narrow limits that the confederation's fatal problems would recur and that it would be stretched beyond endurance. He always aimed above all to preserve the continental union, which could be achieved only by mutual conciliation and restraint—the spirit that had marked the great convention. Madison died at breakfast at Montpelier days before the sixtieth anniversary of independence, on 28 June 1836, and was buried there the following day—the last, as he had once been first, of the framers of the constitution.

LANCE BANNING

Sources *The papers of James Madison*, ed. W. T. Hutchinson and others (1962–) · *The writings of James Madison*, ed. G. Hunt (1900–10) · *Letters and other writings of James Madison* (1865) · A. Hamilton, J. Madison, and J. Jay, ed. J. Cooke, *The Federalist* (1961) · I. Brant, *James Madison*, 6 vols. (1941–61) · R. Ketcham, *James Madison: a biography* (1971) · J. N. Rakove, *James Madison and the creation of the American republic* (1990) · L. Banning, *The sacred fire of liberty: James Madison and the founding of the federal republic* (1995) · D. R. McCoy, *The last of the fathers: James Madison and the republican legacy* (1989) · J. N. Rakove, *Original meanings: politics and ideas in the making of the constitution* (1996) · G. S. Wood, *The creation of the American republic* (1969) · R. A. Rutland, *The presidency of James Madison* (1990) · D. Adair, ed., 'James Madison's autobiography', *William and Mary Quarterly*, 3rd ser., 2 (1945), 191–209 · H. C. Shulman, 'Madison, Dolley', *ANB*
Archives L. Cong. · NYPL · Princeton University, New Jersey · University of Virginia, Charlottesville
Likenesses C. W. Peale, miniature, oils, 1783, L. Cong. · C. W. Peale, oils, *c*.1792, Thomas Gilcrease Institute, Tulsa, Oklahoma · G. Stuart, portrait, 1805–7, Bowdoin College Museum of Art, Brunswick, Maine [*see illus.*] · T. Sully, oils, 1809, Corcoran Gallery of Art, Washington, DC

Madocks, William Alexander (1773–1828), property developer and politician, born in London on 17 June 1773, was the third son of John Madocks of St Andrew's, Holborn, and of Fron Yw in Denbighshire, an eminent chancery barrister, who was MP for the borough of Westbury in Wiltshire (1786–90), and his wife, Frances, daughter of Joseph Whitechurch of Twickenham. Madocks was at Charterhouse from 1784 until 1789, when he appears to have been expelled; he matriculated at Christ Church, Oxford, on 1 March 1790, proceeded BA in 1793, and MA in 1799, and was a fellow of All Souls College, 1794–1818. He first settled at Dolmelynllyn, near Dolgellau, but after his father's death purchased in 1798 the estate of Tan-yr-Allt, adjoining Penmorfa marsh in Caernarvonshire; here he began, about 1800, to bank out the sea, and succeeded in recovering or converting into dry land 1082 acres which previously formed the marsh. In 1807 he obtained a grant from the crown, confirmed by act of parliament, vesting in him and his heirs all the sands known as Traeth Mawr in the estuary close to his residence, which was then washed by the sea, and extending from Pont Aberglaslyn to Gêst Point. He then constructed across Traeth Mawr an embankment nearly a mile in length, which shut out the sea, and was the means of reclaiming nearly 3042 more acres of land. A road was also constructed along the embankment, and formed the line of communication between the counties of Caernarfon and Merioneth. The work was completed in 1811, at an expense of about £60,000. The town of Tremadoc (Tremadog), so called after its founder, with a neat Gothic church and other public buildings laid out in a formal style, was built by Madocks on Penmorfa at his own expense.

Madocks joined the Whig Club in 1796; he was introduced to Boston politics by Major John Cartwright, was elected there in 1802, and sat until 1820, every election being contested. He was an active whig, supported Catholic emancipation, moved (on 11 May 1809) the impeachment of Castlereagh and Spencer Perceval for election bribery, and seconded Burdett's plan for parliamentary reform in June 1809. He was unable to afford to contest Boston in 1820, but was elected for Chippenham and sat until 1826. In 1818, Madocks married Amelia Sophia, daughter of Samuel Hughes, land agent; she was the widow of Roderick Gwynne of Buckland. They had one daughter.

About 1820, Madocks began the development of Portmadoc (Porthmadog), on the other side of the estuary from Tremadock, as a port for the local coal and slate trade; he was also involved in developing the Ffestiniog Railway and in campaigning for a reduction of coal and slate duties. The railway plan was blocked by local objectors

William Alexander Madocks (1773–1828), by Charles Turner, pubd 1812 (after James Ramsay)

and in the speculative year of 1825 Madocks was overstretched. He withdrew to the continent in 1826. He died at 109 faubourg St Honoré, Paris, on 29 September 1828 and was buried in Père Lachaise cemetery (despite rumours of a secret return to Wales). He may have been the model for Squire Headlong in T. L. Peacock's *Headlong Hall* (1816).   D. L. THOMAS, *rev.* H. C. G. MATTHEW

Sources E. Beazley, *Madocks and the wonder of Wales*, 2nd edn (1985) · HoP, *Commons* · R. Williams, *Enwogion Cymru: a biographical dictionary of eminent Welshmen* (1852) · *Y Gestiana: a local history of Portmadoc* (1892) · R. L. Arrowsmith, *A Charterhouse miscellany* (1982) · private information (2004)
Archives Gwynedd Archives, Caernarfon, papers relating to his bankruptcy · NL Wales, family and business corresp. and business records · U. Wales, Bangor, MSS
Likenesses J. Scouler, portrait, 1778, priv. coll. · J. Ramsay, portrait, 1808, priv. coll. · C. Turner, mezzotint, pubd 1812 (after J. Ramsay), BM, NPG [*see illus.*] · drawing, repro. in *Festiniog Railway Magazine*, 62 (1973), 27–9 · mezzotint, All Souls Oxf. · portrait, repro. in *Y Gestiana*

Madog ab Owain Gwynedd (*supp. fl.* 1170), supposed discoverer of America, is not mentioned in *Annales Cambriae*, in *Brut y tywysogyon*, or in any poem of the time, and there is no contemporary evidence of the existence of any son of Owain Gwynedd (*d.* 1170) bearing this name. Two passages in the poetry of Llywarch ap Llywelyn (Prydydd y Moch) have been quoted in support of the theory that Madog made a mysterious voyage to the west and discovered the New World, but neither will bear the significance attached to it. The first, appearing in an ode in praise of Rhodri ab Owain (Jones, William, and Pughe, 202, 'Ker aber congwy') manifestly refers, not to any

expedition over sea, but to the battle of the Conwy estuary, fought by Llywelyn ab Iorwerth at some point in the course of his struggle (1188–95) with his uncles Dafydd and Rhodri. The second (ibid., 205) certainly contains the name Madog, but there is nothing to reveal his identity among many of that name at the time; moreover, the person of whose blood the poet has to prove himself innocent by the ordeal of hot iron clearly was murdered, though by an unknown hand, and cannot have sailed off publicly on an adventurous voyage, as it is assumed Madog did.

The earliest mention of Madog in Welsh literature is in a poem composed by Maredudd ap Rhys, a mid-fifteenth-century poet. Having previously begged (after the bardic manner) a fishing-net of one Ifan ap Tudur and succeeded in his petition, Maredudd thanks him for the gift, and, speaking of his delight in fishing, compares himself to Madog, 'right whelp of Owain Gwynedd', who would have no lands or goods save only the broad sea (*Iolo Manuscripts*, 323–4). The reference to Madog in the third series of triads may very well belong to the same period, though the manuscript is only of the sixteenth century. Madog, it is said, was the third of three who disappeared; he went to sea with ten ships and 300 men, and none knew whither they went. The first two disappearances are obviously mythical, the second being that of Merlin and nine other bards who went to sea in a house of glass; nor is any attempt made to connect that of Madog with discoveries in the west. Thus the triad, taken in conjunction with the allusion of Maredudd ap Rhys, appears to show that already, before the voyage of Columbus, a legend had appeared regarding the mysterious seafaring activities of a son of Owain Gwynedd.

Evidence of Madog appears in some Flemish sources such as the work of Willem the Minstrel in the mid-thirteenth century, but it was in Dr John Dee's 'Title Royal' (1580) that the first reference occurred to his discovery of America, with the intention of proving that England had a stronger claim than Spain to the New World. A reference also appeared in print in Sir George Peckham's *A True Reporte of the Late Discoveries and Possession Taken … by … Sir Humphrey Gilbert …* (1583), again for the same purpose and based on Gilbert's discoveries. The reports of David Ingram, who sailed with Sir John Hawkins in 1568, that he had heard Welsh words spoken by the indigenous people in many parts of the American continent also aroused interest. Both Peckham's and David Powell's versions were published by Richard Hakluyt in *The Principal Navigations, Voyages, Traffiques and Discoveries of the English Nation* (1589). References also appear in the writings of Dr David Powell, who, in the *Historie of Cambria* (1584), gave to the world Humphrey Llwyd's translation and continuation of *Brut y tywysogyon*, with additions of his own. In all probability the passage about Madog was substantially contained in Llwyd's manuscript, and the story may extend as far back as 1559. Powell relates that Madog left Wales to avoid the fratricidal strife that followed the death of Owain Gwynedd in 1170, and that, after leaving Ireland to the north, he came to a strange land, which must, according to Powell, have been Florida or New Spain. He returned after his first voyage, and then with ten vessels made a second expedition, after which he was never heard of more. Reasons are given for believing that he founded a settlement in America, such as the occurrence of certain words of Welsh significance in American languages, the fact that in some parts of the continent the cross was honoured, and the avowedly foreign origin of the ruling class in Mexico.

It has been maintained by the defenders of the Madog theory that Powell's narrative is based upon one by Gutun Owain, who flourished in the age before Columbus. It is only on one point, in fact, that he cites the bard, namely the number of ships that Madog had with him on his second voyage; and tradition, as has already been shown, had fixed upon ten as the number of Madog's fleet before there was any talk of his having discovered America. Powell's real authority was popular tradition—the legend about the mysterious disappearance amplified into a discovery of the New World. He reports that in the popular account there was much exaggeration, so that he only gave what he took to be the basis of fact (Powell, 227–9).

A story so flattering to national pride naturally made great headway. James Howell, the author and historiographer-royal, accepted it, and quoted the four lines from Maredudd ap Rhys that begin *Madoc wif* ('I am Madog'), as having been found on Madog's tomb 'in the West Indies … near upon 600 years since' (Howell, 1.608). It was believed by Theophilus Evans (*Drych y prif oesoedd*, 2nd edn, 1740, 19–21) who also quoted the supposed epitaph upon Madog. Sir Thomas Herbert (1606–1682) told the story in great detail, though his arguments are only those of Powell refurbished. The legend caught the imagination of Welsh radicals in London and elsewhere in the late eighteenth century, especially after the American War of Independence. Among them were the Revd William Richards of King's Lynn, the Revd Morgan John Rhys, and Dr John Williams of Sydenham who, in 1791, published *An enquiry into the truth of the tradition concerning the discovery of America by Prince Madog ab Owen Gwynedd, about the year 1170*.

The principal champions of the theory were Dr W. O. Pughe and his friend Iolo Morganwg [*see* Williams, Edward (1747–1826)]. In 1791 they wrote a series of notes in its defence for the *Gentleman's Magazine*; in the *Cambrian Biography* (1803, ed. W. O. Pughe), it is stated in the most positive form, with the addition that Madog's reputed brother Rhiryd had accompanied him on the second journey; and in the *Cambro-Briton* (ed. J. H. Parry, vol. 1), with which Dr Pughe was closely connected, a Dr John Jones, who had thrown doubt upon it, is very severely treated. It was from Dr Pughe and his circle that Robert Southey heard the story; with the result that in 1805 he published 'Madoc'. So great was the enthusiasm at this period that Iolo Morganwg at one time thought seriously of visiting America on a tour of search for the 'Madogwys', and in 1790 John Evans, a young map maker and adventurer of Waunfawr, Caernarvonshire, actually left Wales with the intention of

preaching the gospel to his imaginary kinsmen. He wandered about the continent a good deal and endured many hardships. Although in September 1796 he reached the district (the Missouri valley) where the Mandan people were at this time living, his evidence to prove their Welsh descent was slight.

During the nineteenth century the adherents of the theory gradually disappeared. George Catlin believed that the Mandans of the upper Missouri were remnants of the Welsh colony (Catlin, 2.259), but his arguments are not convincing. Thomas Stephens expressed himself somewhat doubtfully upon the question in the *Literature of the Kymry* (141–8) but, when a prize was offered in the Llangollen eisteddfod (1858) for 'the best essay on the discovery of America in the twelfth century by Prince Madoc ap Owen Gwynedd', he sent in an elaborate treatise revealing that the discovery could not have taken place. Though the best essay in the competition, it was denied the prize on account of the opinions expressed in it (Stephens, *Madoc*). The Madog story is a myth and will continue to be so. However, it served its purpose in exposing English claims to North America in Elizabethan days. It also stirred minds on both sides of the Atlantic in the 1790s and, in 1805 and 1918, inspired the poets Robert Southey and T. Gwynn Jones respectively to recount, in powerful verse, other aspects of Madog's seafaring skills. It is symbolic as well that, in 1953, a plaque commemorating his landing was erected by the Daughters of the American Revolution in Mobile Bay in the Gulf of Mexico.

J. E. LLOYD, rev. J. GWYNFOR JONES

Sources *The historie of Cambria, now called Wales*, ed. D. Powell, trans. H. Lhoyd [H. Llwyd] (1584) • T. Stephens, *Madoc: an essay on the discovery of America by Madoc ap Owen Gwynedd in the twelfth century*, ed. Ll. O. Reynolds (1893) • J. Williams, *An enquiry into the … discovery of America by Prince Madog ab Owen Gwynedd, about the year 1170* (1791) • R. Deacon, *Madoc and the discovery of America* (1966) • D. Williams, *John Evans and the legend of Madoc, 1770–1799* (1963) • G. A. Williams, *Madoc: the making of a myth* (1979); repr. (1987) • D. Williams, 'John Evans's strange journey', *Transactions of the Honourable Society of Cymmrodorion* (1948) • D. Williams, 'John Evans's strange journey', *American Historical Review*, 54 (1948–9), 277–95, 508–29 • G. A. Williams, 'John Evans's mission to the Madogwys, 1792–1799', *BBCS*, 27 (1976–8), 569–601 • O. Jones, E. Williams, and W. O. Pughe, eds., *The Myvyrian archaiology of Wales, collected out of ancient manuscripts*, 3 vols. (1801–7) • W. O. Pughe, ed., *The Cambrian biography: or, historical notices of celebrated men among the ancient Britons* (1803) • J. H. Parry, ed., *The Cambro-Briton*, 3 vols. (1820) • G. Catlin, *Letters and notes … of the North American Indians*, 2 vols. (1850) • T. Stephens, *Literature of the Kymry* (1849) • T. Williams, ed., *Iolo manuscripts* (1848) • J. Howell, *Epistolae Ho-elianae*, ed. J. Jacobs, 2 vols. (1890–92), bk 4, 1.608

Madog ap Gruffudd (d. 1277). *See under* Madog ap Gruffudd Maelor (d. 1236).

Madog ap Gruffudd Maelor (d. 1236), ruler in Powys, was the son of Gruffudd Maelor (d. 1191), ruler of northern Powys, and his wife Angharad, daughter of *Owain Gwynedd (d. 1170). Following the death of *Madog ap Maredudd and his son and designated heir Llewelyn in 1160 Powys was permanently divided, the south going to Madog ap Maredudd's nephew Owain Cyfeiliog (d. 1197) and the north to his son Gruffudd Maelor. In the south Owain Cyfeiliog was succeeded in turn by his son Gwenwynwyn (d. 1216) and his grandson Gruffudd ap Gwenwynwyn (d. 1286). The south came to be known as Powys Wenwynwyn and the north, after Madog, as Powys Fadog.

Gruffudd Maelor was succeeded by Madog in 1191. According to Gerald of Wales, Madog ap Gruffudd was one of the Welsh rulers who wrote to Innocent III in 1202 or 1203 to protest at the maltreatment of the Welsh church. With most of the other Welsh rulers he joined King John in his campaign against his cousin Llywelyn ab Iorwerth (d. 1240) in 1211. He did not join the Welsh alliance against the king in 1212; the statement in *Brut y tywysogyon* that he did so is incorrect, but by March 1215 he seems to have thrown in his lot with Llywelyn and he was one of those whose support John sought in his struggle with the barons. He did not himself join Llywelyn's campaign in south Wales at the end of that year, but he sent his *teulu*, or household troops, to take part.

Madog was in dispute with Llywelyn some time between 1215 and 1227 over a marriage that had been arranged between his daughter Angharad and the son of Fulk (III) Fitzwarine (d. 1258). Llywelyn objected to the marriage and had Madog's lands placed under an interdict; Hubert de Burgh, the justiciar, was asked to order Llywelyn to stop interfering in the matter, but there is no other information about this episode.

For the rest of his life Madog was Llywelyn's loyal ally. In 1218 he was one of the prince's pledges when he was granted the custody of Carmarthen and Cardigan and in 1223 he and the other leading rulers stood surety that Llywelyn would observe the terms of his submission to Henry III in that year. In 1232 he and Ednyfed Fychan (d. 1246) were named as Llywelyn's representatives at a meeting at Montgomery to remedy breaches of a recent truce.

Madog was the founder of the Cistercian abbey of Valle Crucis near Llangollen. The date of the foundation is usually taken to be 1200 but Madog's grant of the site and of extensive lands in northern Powys probably dates from 1201; a grant of pasture throughout his lands followed in 1202 and a charter of confirmation in 1222. According to most pedigrees he married Gwladus, daughter of Ithel ap Rhys of Gwent; however, one source gives his wife's name as Ysota and in his charter to Valle Crucis of 1222 he states that it was granted with the assent of his wife, the Lady I. They had five sons, Gruffudd (d. 1269) [*see below*], Gruffudd Iâl, Madog Fychan, Maredudd, and Hywel. Three poems to him survive, one by Llywarch ap Llywelyn (Prydydd y Moch) and two, including an elegy, by Einion Wan. Madog died in 1236; the Welsh chronicler described him as 'the man who surpassed all for the renown of his manners and for generosity and piety' (*Brut: Hergest*, 233). He may have spent much of his time in the eastern half of his lands at Overton and in Maelor Saesneg. He was buried at Valle Crucis.

Gruffudd ap Madog [Gruffudd of Bromfield] (d. 1269), ruler in Powys, succeeded his father in northern Powys, although each of his brothers probably had a share of the inheritance under his overlordship. As long as Llywelyn ab Iorwerth lived Gruffudd was loyal to him, but he had no such loyalty to his son and successor Dafydd (d. 1246) and was one of the leading supporters of the claims of Dafydd's elder brother, Gruffudd (d. 1244); his support for Gruffudd is indicated by the fact that he and his brothers Hywel and Maredudd were among the sureties of Gruffudd's wife Senana when she sought her husband's release in 1241. In 1240 he and Hywel and Maredudd had been among the Welsh lords who did homage to Henry III. He was a key figure in Henry's Welsh campaign in 1241 which culminated in the treaty of Gwern Eigron and he was awarded an annuity of £20 as a result. In 1242 Gruffudd and Dafydd ap Llywelyn were invited by the king to contribute troops for his forthcoming campaign in Gascony. With royal lordship becoming increasingly assertive, it was not long before Gruffudd and his fellow rulers began to feel uneasy; in 1244 Henry had to reassure Gruffudd that he had no intention of introducing new laws in his lands and wished to respect their laws and customs and several substantial payments to him are recorded. With Gruffudd ap Gwenwynwyn (d. 1286) and Morgan ap Hywel of Caerleon he stood aside from the coalition of Welsh rulers which Dafydd assembled after the death of his brother in 1244, although the *Brut* claims that Dafydd forced him to submit; his brothers Madog Fychan and Maredudd did join the alliance.

By 1250 Gruffudd ap Madog had made an alliance with Llywelyn ap Gruffudd (d. 1282), the most forceful of the four brothers who were now claiming the rulership of the truncated principality of Gwynedd. The alliance may have been precipitated by the king's plans to divide Gruffudd and Llywelyn's lands with their brothers in accordance with what the king saw, to his advantage, as Welsh custom. But the compact does not appear to have endured; after Llywelyn attained sole power in Gwynedd in 1255 and embarked on the extension of his overlordship to the rest of native Wales he may have driven Gruffudd out of his lands for a time. About Michaelmas 1257 Gruffudd made his peace with Llywelyn and from then on he was one of the greatest men of native-ruled Wales; the alliance was sealed by the marriage of his son Madog [*see below*] to Llywelyn's sister Margaret. He and his brother Madog Fychan were among the parties to the Welsh treaty with the Comyn faction in Scotland in 1258. In September 1262 Llywelyn complained to the king that the justice of Chester and others had raided Gruffudd's lands and threatened retaliation for the raid.

Next to the prince of Gwynedd, Gruffudd ap Madog was the most powerful native ruler in Wales in the 1260s. He had been one of the leaders of the magnate opposition to Dafydd, but with the rise of Llywelyn ap Gruffudd he returned to his father's policy of friendship with Gwynedd; his aim at all times was the preservation of the integrity of Powys Fadog and in this he succeeded. Of his brothers Gruffudd Iâl was killed by Maredudd in 1238 and Maredudd's lands were confiscated by Llywelyn ab Iorwerth, but when Maredudd died he was described in

Annales Cambriae as lord of Iâl. Hywel, who died about 1268, remained loyal to the king, possibly because of territorial claims against his brother; by 1267, however, he was one of Llywelyn's pledges in the treaty of Montgomery.

Gruffudd's main seat was the castle he built at Dinas Brân near Llangollen. He married Emma, daughter of Henry Audley (*d.* 1246), and they had four sons, Madog, Llywelyn, Owain, and Gruffudd Fychan. His grant of dower to Emma was confirmed by his sons soon after his death, with the approval of their overlord Llywelyn ap Gruffudd; Llywelyn may also have supervised the division of the inheritance. Gruffudd died in December 1269, on the same day as his brother Madog Fychan; they were buried at Valle Crucis (*Brut: Hergest*, 259).

Madog ap Gruffudd (*d.* 1277), ruler in Powys, was the eldest son of Gruffudd ap Madog. He and his brothers submitted to the king during the war of 1276–7 and he died soon after, leaving two young sons, Gruffudd and Llywelyn. His death was followed by a series of territorial disputes and extensive litigation over shares of the inheritance and the dower lands of his mother and his widow Margaret. His three brothers fought on the Welsh side in the war of 1282; Llywelyn and Gruffudd Fychan took part in the raid on Oswestry on Palm Sunday 1282 and Llywelyn was later killed in action. Owain may also have been a victim of the war and the young sons of Madog disappear from the historical record; the traditional account of their fate is that they were drowned in the Dee at Holt on the orders of John de Warenne (*d.* 1304) and Roger Mortimer, acting on the instructions of Edward I.

The Edwardian conquest of 1282 was a devastating blow to the dynasty of northern Powys. Most of its members were directly or indirectly implicated in the Welsh revolt and were in effect totally dispossessed by Edward I. Most of their lands were used to create lordships for two of the king's prominent adjutants: the northern lands of Maelor Gymraeg and Iâl became the large lordship of Bromfield and Yale for John de Warenne, earl of Surrey, and his heirs, while the south-eastern commotes became the lordship of Chirkland, granted to Roger Mortimer (*d.* 1326), a cadet member of the Mortimer family, henceforth known as 'of Chirck'. The sole branch of the family able to salvage something from this act of disinheritance was that of **Gruffudd Fychan** (*d.* 1289), son of Gruffudd ap Madog (*d.* 1269) [*see above*]. After some vicissitudes Gruffudd Fychan recovered Glyndyfrdwy in Edeirnion (now formally part of the newly constituted county of Merioneth) and held by Welsh baronial tenure. By 1300 his descendants had also secured Cynllaith Owain, the former patrimony of Owain ap Gruffudd ap Madog. Gruffudd Fychan died in 1289; his great-great-grandson and ultimate heir was Owain *Glyn Dŵr.

A. D. CARR

Sources T. Jones, ed. and trans., *Brut y tywysogyon, or, The chronicle of the princes: Red Book of Hergest* (1955) · J. G. Edwards, *Calendar of ancient correspondence concerning Wales* (1935) · *Littere Wallie*, ed. J. G. Edwards (1940) · J. C. Davies, ed., *The Welsh assize roll, 1277–1284* (1940) · *Chancery records* · J. B. Smith, *Llywelyn ap Gruffudd, tywysog Cymru* (1986) · G. A. Williams, 'The succession to Gwynedd, 1238–

47', *BBCS*, 20 (1962–4), 393–413 · J. E. Lloyd, *A history of Wales from the earliest times to the Edwardian conquest*, 3rd edn, 2 (1939)

Madog ap Llywelyn (*fl.* 1277–1295), rebel, was the son of Llywelyn ap Maredudd (*d.* 1263), who in 1256 had been driven out of his lordship of Meirionydd by Llywelyn ap Gruffudd. Madog failed to regain his inheritance when Llywelyn was defeated by Edward I in 1277. At Michaelmas 1294 revolts against the new order imposed on Wales by Edward I in 1284 broke out simultaneously in Gwynedd, Ceredigion, and the south-eastern marches. The most serious rising, that led by Madog in Gwynedd, gained much initial success. The unfinished castle of Caernarfon was taken, as were the inland castles of Denbigh, Ruthin, and Hawarden, though the coastal castles from Flint round to Aberystwyth held out, provisioned by sea. Edward was taken by surprise and caught off balance, as he was concentrating on sending an urgently needed relief expedition to Gascony; forces mustered for embarkation at Portsmouth had to be redirected to Wales. In November an attempt by the earl of Lincoln to recover his castle and lordship of Denbigh was defeated, and in Meirionydd the castle of Bere fell to the Welsh. From Chester in early December Edward advanced to reduce the rebels in the lordships of Denbigh and Ruthin, while a second force followed the coast. By Christmas 1294 he was in Conwy and in mid-January he led a reconnaissance in force through Bangor and deep into the Llŷn peninsula. The capture of his provision train by the Welsh put his army on short rations when he returned to Conwy. Madog, who had assumed the title of prince, suffered his worst setback not in Gwynedd but in Powys. The earl of Warwick's army, based at Montgomery, was at Oswestry when intelligence was received that Madog was descending into Cedewain. Warwick returned to Montgomery on 4 March 1295, made a night march to meet Madog, and on 5 March, using a combination of cavalry and bowmen, heavily defeated the flower of his forces at Maes Moydog in Castle Caereinion parish. Some miles to the westwards a second English force captured Madog's supply train. Nevertheless, Madog remained in the field and, after Edward had occupied Anglesey and founded Beaumaris Castle in April, three English armies converged in May on Meirionydd, Madog's home ground. Serious resistance was now at an end and the king proceeded on a triumphant circuit of Wales, receiving submissions as he went. It was not until he had returned to England that in late July Madog submitted to John de Havering, justice of north Wales. His life was spared but he was imprisoned in the Tower. The date of his death is unknown.

R. F. WALKER

Sources J. E. Morris, *The Welsh wars of Edward I* (1901) · E. B. Fryde, ed., *Book of prests of the king's wardrobe for 1294–5* (1962), xxvi–xlvi · J. G. Edwards, 'The battle of Maes Madog and the Welsh campaign of 1294–5', *EngHR*, 39 (1924), 1–12 · J. G. Edwards, 'The site of the battle of "Meismeidoc", 1295', *EngHR*, 46 (1931), 262–5 · J. G. Edwards, 'Madog ap Llywelyn, the Welsh leader in 1294–5', *BBCS*, 13 (1948–50), 206–10 · R. F. Walker, 'The Hagnaby Chronicle and the battle of Maes Moydog', *Welsh History Review / Cylchgrawn Hanes Cymru*, 8 (1976–7), 125–38

Madog ap Maredudd (*d.* 1160), king of Powys, was the son of Maredudd ap Bleddyn ap Cynfyn (*d.* 1132) and (according to genealogical sources from the later fifteenth century onwards) Hunydd, daughter of Einudd ap Gwenllian.

Early career Madog succeeded his father as sole ruler of Powys on the latter's death in 1132 and sought to strengthen the kingdom not only by maintaining control over the sons of his elder brother, Gruffudd (*d.* 1128), as well as over his own younger brother, Iorwerth Goch, but also by defending its northern limits from the ambitions of the dynasty of Gwynedd and by expanding it eastwards, especially at the expense of the Normans in Shropshire. Madog married Susanna, daughter of Gruffudd ap Cynan. In 1132, shortly before Madog's accession, Cadwallon ap Gruffudd ap Cynan was killed in the commote of Nanheudwy when he led an attack on Powys. Thereafter no further hostilities from Gwynedd are recorded until 1149, when Madog's brother-in-law, Owain Gwynedd (*d.* 1170), occupied the commote of Iâl and built a castle at Tomen y Rhodwydd. Towards the end of the same year Madog revealed his own capacity for territorial expansion with the capture and refortification of the Norman castle of Oswestry, while he sought to neutralize any threat to his authority from his nephews, *Owain Cyfeiliog (*d.* 1197) and Meurig, sons of his brother Gruffudd ap Maredudd, by granting them the commote of Cyfeiliog (which had formed part of the kingdom of Powys since their father had occupied it in 1116). By 1151 Madog had also established his overlordship in Arwystli in central Wales, for the only surviving charter in his name, issued no later than that year (in which he is styled 'king of the Powysians'), records that he granted land belonging to the region's ruler, Hywel ab Ieuaf, to St Michael's Church at Trefeglwys.

Although a force from Powys had ravaged Maelor Saesneg in 1146 until it was heavily defeated by Robert of Mold, steward of the earldom of Chester, on 3 September of that year, the renewed threat from Gwynedd in 1149 prompted Madog to ally himself with Ranulf (II), earl of Chester, whose lands were likewise the object of Owain Gwynedd's ambitions. However, a joint campaign against Owain by the king of Powys and the earl ended in victory for their adversary at Coleshill in Tegeingl in 1150, allowing the ruler of Gwynedd to maintain his possession of Iâl. This set-back did not halt Madog's plans for territorial consolidation and expansion, for two years later his son, Llywelyn, killed Stephen fitz Baldwin, constable of Montgomery Castle, and the military campaigns in Shropshire and Maelienydd celebrated by the court poets Gwalchmai ap Meilyr and Cynddelw Brydydd Mawr (*fl.* 1155–1195) may also have taken place in the 1150s. In 1156 Madog built a castle near Cymer in the commote of Caereinion: the precise location of this fortification is unknown although it may have been situated at Castle Caereinion, about 4 miles west of Welshpool. The Welsh chronicle *Brut y tywysogyon* also records under the same year that Madog's nephew, Meurig ap Gruffudd, escaped from prison. This event almost certainly inspired the composition of the poem *Hirlas Owain*—ascribed, probably incorrectly, to Meurig's brother, Owain Cyfeiliog—which describes an expedition by Owain's retinue to free his brother from captivity in the district of Maelor. Who was responsible for the imprisonment of Meurig and where precisely he was imprisoned are uncertain, although it has been suggested that he was held at the castle of Wrexham, which belonged to the earldom of Chester by 1160–61. Significantly, Owain's court appears to have been situated at Welshpool by the time of this expedition, suggesting that his authority was not confined to Cyfeiliog, which had shown itself to be vulnerable to external attack when it was ravaged in 1153 by Rhys ap Gruffudd (*d.* 1197) of Deheubarth.

Ascendancy in Powys Madog's territorial expansion owed much to the opportunities created by the weakness of the English crown and marcher lords in Shropshire during the reign of Stephen. However, after Henry II's accession to the English throne in 1154 these opportunities were severely curtailed. The following year William fitz Alan, a marcher magnate who had formerly supported the Empress Matilda, was restored to his Shropshire lands and appointed sheriff of the county, and probably soon recovered Oswestry. The ruler of Powys responded pragmatically to the changed situation by forming an alliance with Henry II in 1157. Madog may have already given support to the Angevins in 1141, for Orderic Vitalis reports that two brothers, 'Mariadoth' and 'Kaladrius', fought on the Angevin side against Stephen at the battle of Lincoln in February of that year: it has been assumed that the names refer to Cadwaladr ap Gruffudd ap Cynan and his brother-in-law Madog ap Maredudd (the former is not known to have had a brother called Maredudd). What is clear is that Madog, together with his brother Iorwerth Goch and Hywel ab Ieuaf, ruler of Arwystli, joined in Henry II's successful campaign against Owain Gwynedd in the summer of 1157; the king's Welsh allies also received payments from the English exchequer in that year.

In the aftermath of Henry's campaign Iorwerth Goch captured and destroyed the castle of Tomen y Rhodwydd, thereby depriving Owain Gwynedd of his authority in Iâl. How far Madog benefited directly from this action is unclear. The medieval Welsh prose tale, 'The dream of Rhonabwy', composed possibly as late as the early fourteenth century, claims that relations between Madog and his brother were strained, since Iorwerth held no lands in Powys during Madog's reign and refused an offer to serve as his brother's *penteulu* ('chief of the military retinue'). If true, this stands in contrast to Madog's treatment of the sons of his elder brother, Gruffudd, to whom he granted the territory of Cyfeiliog and one of whom, Owain, also possessed a court at Welshpool (although whether as a result of a grant by Madog is not known). His lack of lands in Powys could explain Iorwerth's readiness to accept the estate of Sutton near Wenlock and other Shropshire manors in serjeanty from Henry II in 1157 for performing services as Henry's latimer or interpreter. Nevertheless, in that year Iorwerth clearly co-operated with Madog, if only on the basis of common support for Henry II's campaign against Owain Gwynedd, and it is likely that his capture of Tomen y Rhodwydd met with the approval of his brother even if the expedition was undertaken independently of him and, perhaps, resulted in Iorwerth's subsequently holding Iâl under Madog's overlordship.

Death, family, and assessment No further events are recorded of Madog's reign until his death in 1160, which, according to the poet Gwalchmai, took place 'at the beginning of Lent' (Gruffydd, vol. 1, no.7, line 136), and therefore about 9 February. The version of *Brut y tywysogyon* in NL Wales, Peniarth MS 20, states that Madog died at Winchester, but the accuracy of this report has been questioned. All versions of the chronicle agree, however, that Madog was buried at the church of Meifod, Powys, a pre-Norman foundation, 'where his burial-place was' (*Brut: Peniarth MS 20*, 61), a statement which may be compared with Cynddelw's description of Meifod as 'the burial-place of kings' (Gruffydd, vol. 3, no. 3, line 48). Shortly afterwards Madog's son, Llywelyn, was killed. Described in *Brut y tywysogyon* as the one 'in whom lay the hope of all Powys' (*Brut: Peniarth MS 20*, 62), he was quite possibly his father's designated successor to the whole of the kingdom, and his death marked the end of unitary rule in Powys, which was divided between Madog's three remaining sons Elise, Gruffudd Maelor (d. 1191), and Owain Fychan (d. 1187), his brother Iorwerth Goch, and his nephew Owain Cyfeiliog (d. 1197).

Late medieval genealogists claimed that Madog's wife, Susanna, was the mother of two of the king's sons, Elise and Gruffudd Maelor, and she may well also have been the mother of Owain Fychan. Madog also had at least two other sons, Llywelyn (d. 1160) and Owain Brogyntyn [*see below*], as well as two daughters, Gwenllian, who married Rhys ap Gruffudd of Deheubarth, and Marared, wife of Iorwerth Drwyndwn ab Owain and mother of *Llywelyn ab Iorwerth (d. 1240) of Gwynedd. The genealogists, however, name as many as nine sons and four daughters altogether, and identify two extra-marital partners as mothers of three of the former together with a fourth partner, Arianwen, daughter of Moriddig Warwyn.

According to the court poets Gwalchmai and Cynddelw, Madog excelled in his bravery, generosity, and appreciation of fine poetry. Gwalchmai emphasized the king's success in expanding Powys to encompass a territory extending 'from the summit of Plynlimon to the gates of Chester' (Gruffydd vol. 1, no. 7, line 73) and from Bangor Is-coed to the borders of Meirionnydd. Cynddelw was likewise fulsome in his praise of the victorious campaigns led by Madog and his band of warriors and also celebrated the feasts, drink, and warhorses he bestowed on poets at his court. Of the king's relations with the church very little is known: Madog authorized a grant of land to the native monastery of St Michael at Trefeglwys by 1151, and may well have made donations to his burial place of Meifod, at which a new church was consecrated to the Virgin Mary in 1156. There is no evidence, however, that he patronized any of the reformed religious orders of continental origin. The church of Meifod lay near Mathrafal, which was believed by the thirteenth century to be the chief court of

the princes of Powys, and which is mentioned as the site of one of Madog's battles in a poem by Cynddelw; it is therefore possible, but by no means certain, that Mathrafal was the king's principal centre of authority. According to the 'Dream of Rhonabwy', Madog ruled all of Powys 'from Pulford [just south of Chester] to Gwafan in the uppermost part of Arwystli' (*Breudwyt Ronabwy*, 1), and modern scholars are agreed that he was one of the most powerful native rulers of twelfth-century Wales whose greatest achievement was the expansion and consolidation of his ancestral kingdom. However, this achievement barely outlasted his own lifetime and his failure to ensure a unitary succession meant that Madog was also the last Welsh ruler whose authority encompassed the whole of Powys.

Owain Brogyntyn (*fl.* 1160–1215), referred to in contemporary sources as 'Oenus de Porchinton' (or various spellings thereof), was an illegitimate son of Madog ap Maredudd who took his name from Porkington, a village near Oswestry which by the sixteenth century was known in Welsh as Brogyntyn. Later genealogical sources state that Owain's mother was a daughter of the Black Reeve of Rug in Edeirnion. After the death of his father and half-brother, Llywelyn, in 1160 Owain inherited lands and authority in Dinmael, Edeirnion, and Penllyn. From 1160 to 1169 he received regular and substantial payments from the English exchequer, indicating that he maintained the *rapprochement* with Henry II begun by his father and other kinsmen in 1157. Owain was a benefactor of three Cistercian monasteries. From his lordship in Penllyn he granted lands, pasture rights, and Tegid (Bala) Lake to Basingwerk Abbey; in addition, he granted lands to Valle Crucis Abbey in 1207 and made two sales of land to Strata Marcella Abbey. Owain had five sons, Gruffudd, Bleddyn, Iorwerth, Cadwgan, and Hywel, and later genealogical sources also name a daughter, Efa. The identity of their mother is uncertain: the genealogists identify her as either Sioned, daughter of Hywel ap Madog ab Idnerth, or Marared, daughter of Einion ap Seisyll of Mathafarn. Owain probably died between 1215, when he witnessed a charter in favour of Strata Marcella, and 1218, when his son, Bleddyn, submitted to Henry III. The suggestion that the inscribed graveslab at Valle Crucis Abbey bearing the name of Owain ap Madog is that of Owain Brogyntyn cannot be accepted, since the style of the stone dates it to the late thirteenth century. In the later middle ages Owain's descendants continued to exercise rights of lordship in Dinmael and Edeirnion, which they held after the Edwardian conquest by the tenure known as *pennaeth* or Welsh barony.   HUW PRYCE

Sources T. Jones, ed. and trans., *Brut y tywysogyon, or, The chronicle of the princes: Peniarth MS 20* (1952) · T. Jones, ed. and trans., *Brut y tywysogyon, or, The chronicle of the princes: Red Book of Hergest* (1955) · T. Jones, ed. and trans., *Brenhinedd y Saesson, or, The kings of the Saxons* (1971) [another version of *Brut y tywysogyon*] · J. Williams ab Ithel, ed., *Annales Cambriae*, Rolls Series, 20 (1860) · R. G. Gruffydd, ed., *Cyfres beirdd y tywysogion*, 7 vols. (1991–6), vols. 1–3 [the Poets of the Princes series] · *Breudwyt Ronabwy*, ed. M. Richards (1948) · J. E. Lloyd, *A history of Wales from the earliest times to the Edwardian conquest*, 3rd edn, 2 (1939) · K. L. Maund, *Handlist of the acts of native*

Welsh rulers, 1132–1283 (1996) • P. C. Bartrum, ed., Welsh genealogies, AD 300–1400, 8 vols. (1974) • J. Y. W. Lloyd, 'History of the lordship of Maelor Gymraeg [pt 13]', Archaeologia Cambrensis, 4th ser., 7 (1877), 97–116 • A. D. Carr, 'An aristocracy in decline: the native Welsh lords after the Edwardian conquest', Welsh History Review / Cylchgrawn Hanes Cymru, 5 (1970–71), 103–29 • C. A. Gresham, Medieval stone carving in north Wales (1968)

Madog Benfras (fl. 1340), poet, was from Marchwiel near Wrexham; his epithet may be translated as 'Greathead'. He was of age by 1340, when he was plaintiff in a number of court cases. According to a later pedigree, he was the son of Gruffudd ab Iorwerth, a member of one of the noble lineages of north-east Wales. He was a friend and contemporary of *Dafydd ap Gwilym, who playfully introduces him into one of his poems as the priest of a mock marriage with Morfudd. With similar wryness, the two also composed marwnadau (elegies) to each other while they were still alive. Of Madog's other surviving work, most is love poetry, and some shows affinity with continental fabliaux. It is not known when he died.

J. E. LLOYD, rev. MARIOS COSTAMBEYS

Sources R. Bromwich, Aspects of the poetry of Dafydd ap Gwilym (1986) • DWB

Madox, Richard (1546–1583), Church of England clergyman and diarist, was born on 11 November 1546, probably at Uffington, Shropshire, where he lived at some time. His parentage has not been ascertained, but he had two brothers, Thomas being older. He was attending Shrewsbury School by January 1563, and when he was twenty (much older than was usual) entered Oxford University on 25 January 1567. As an undergraduate at All Souls College he has been identified with John Madox, a Bible clerk who in 1581 delivered a sermon 'especially for all mariners' in Weymouth; this was apparently printed. In 1571 he graduated BA and was elected a fellow of All Souls. He proceeded MA in 1575, and was one of the university proctors in 1581. He was ordained priest on 25 November 1580.

On the earl of Leicester's recommendation Madox applied to be the chaplain on the Galleon Leicester for Edward Fenton's trading voyage, ostensibly to the Moluccas. While Tudor diaries are rare, Madox's, for 1 January to 31 December 1582 (now in the British Library), is unusually informative. It chronicles part of Fenton's voyage, as do three other contemporary diaries; but Madox's superior status enabled him, while at sea, to go to other ships. Moreover, his diary shows his earlier movements, noting places he saw and persons he met. On 1 January 1582 he went to Wolverhampton to visit his brother Thomas, who was headmaster of the grammar school, when Thomas's wife, Anne, gave birth to a daughter, Katherine. Following interview by a selection board, including Sir Francis Drake, Madox settled his affairs in Oxford (15 February 1582) and took lodgings in London, at Queenhithe. He dined with William Clowes and John Banister, watched Robert Norman demonstrating his lodestone at Ratcliff, Stepney, and saw 'a scurvy play … by one virgin' at 'the theatre' (An Elizabethan in 1582, 88). He paid Mr Betts of Moorgate (John Bettes the younger) 12s. for making his

'picture'; and, when supping with Mrs Joan Lucar's cultured family in Billingsgate, was given by her some bark—presumably Winter's, from Drimys winteri, a South American evergreen tree—brought back from Drake's voyage of circumnavigation (1577–80).

Madox was one of Captain Fenton's eight 'assistants', and, acting as his secretary, kept an official register of proceedings from 29 April to 21 July 1582. On a lighter note, he remarked that the beer supplied by Mr Duffield (Anthony Duffield of St Katharine's, Middlesex) was 'the very nectar of the gods' (An Elizabethan in 1582, 212). He left Blackwall in the Edward Bonaventure on 2 April for Southampton, where the ships were assembling, although the fleet did not sail from there until 1 May.

The expedition was in the south Atlantic on 19 October 1582, at 21°33′ (probably south-west of Trinidad Island), when, because of the hot climate, Madox had Dr Banister draw 10 ounces of blood from an arm, which was still stiff ten weeks later. On 12 November Luke Ward and he 'set down certain new stars raised to the Southwards' (Hakluyt, 11.180) while sailing to Brazil, but gave no details. Madox's diary finished on 31 December 1582, with a note on the weather.

Sadly, Madox never returned from the voyage. On 27 February 1583, Fenton noted that 'My father Madox died' (Taylor, 137) when in the vicinity of Espirito Santo harbour, near Vitória, Brazil, and was doubtless buried at sea. No will or administration has been found. Madox was unmarried; his brother Thomas, a graduate of Brasenose College, Oxford, died—a yeoman of Astley, Shropshire—in 1605.

JOHN BENNELL

Sources An Elizabethan in 1582: the diary of Richard Madox, fellow of All Souls, ed. E. S. Donno, Hakluyt Society, 2nd ser., 147 (1976) • R. Hakluyt, The principal navigations, voyages, traffiques and discoveries of the English nation, 11, Hakluyt Society, extra ser., 11 (1904), 163, 164, 180 • Foster, Alum. Oxon. • G. Walker, Puritan salt: the story of Richard Madox (1935) • E. G. R. Taylor, ed., The troublesome voyage of Captain Edward Fenton, 1582–1583, Hakluyt Society, 2nd ser., 113 (1959), 137 • E. Calvert, ed., Shrewsbury School regestum scholarium, 1562–1635: admittances and readmittances [1892], 1 • will, PRO, PROB 11/105, sig. 51 [Thomas Madox]

Archives BL, diary, Cotton MS Appendix xlvii, fols. 1–49 • BL, diary, Cotton MS Titus B.viii, fols. 179–221 • BL, documents, Cotton MS Otho E.viii • BL, register, Cotton MS Otho E.viii, fols. 131–43

Madox, Thomas (1666–1727), antiquary and historian, is of unknown origins, although D. C. Douglas suggests that his mother may have been a dissenter. Information is also scarce concerning his early life and education. He appears never to have attended a university, though he later visited Oxford in the course of his researches. He was admitted to the Middle Temple but was never called to the bar. He became a clerk in the lord treasurer's remembrancer office and later joint clerk in the augmentations office. He was acquainted with a number of contemporary scholars and was known to express his views on scholarship, but appears otherwise to have been a retiring individual who had little public life.

Madox was the author of four works of historical scholarship, the first two of which stand among the major achievements of English antiquarianism up to that time.

In the company of like-minded antiquaries such as Thomas Hearne, Humfrey Wanley, and Thomas Rymer, Madox pioneered the accurate diplomatic editing of medieval sources along principles established by the great French scholar Jean Mabillon. His work is significant both for its lasting usefulness to three subsequent centuries of medieval scholarship and for its clear recognition of the primacy of original government records, reproduced with painstaking accuracy.

At the encouragement of Lord Somers, Madox published his first work, the *Formulare Anglicanum*, in 1702. This was a large collection of original charters from the Norman conquest to the death of Henry VIII. Previous scholars as far back as John Selden and Sir Henry Spelman had recognized the importance of charters, but had generally consulted them through later cartularies. Madox examined the originals, principally from the archive of the court of augmentations (erected by Henry VIII to administer the lands of the dissolved monastic houses); he then transcribed them with scrupulous attention to the appearance and precise wording of the text. The *Formulare* was immediately lauded by contemporaries, such as Bishop William Nicolson, who accurately assessed its 'unspeakable service to our students in law and antiquities' (Nicolson, 240). The lengthy 'dissertation' that prefaced its nearly 800 charters can be taken as the first full discussion of the formulas and palaeography of an entire class of English feudal documents. While Madox was persuaded that such labours were a necessary step in the elucidation of medieval records, he also realized that the materials he reproduced were valuable not simply in their own right but as guides to the 'manners and customs' of the middle ages and especially with regard to the mechanics of land transfer. The *Formulare* is thus a seminal document in the development of social and economic history.

Madox's recognition that institutions, and not merely kings and nations, had a history is even more firmly demonstrated in his mammoth *History of the Exchequer*. According to Hearne, he had begun to collect materials for this as early as 1697, having set his sights on a history of one of the most important of medieval departments of state. The records of the exchequer had been consulted for historical purposes as far back as the Elizabethan antiquary Arthur Agarde, and seventeenth-century scholars knew of the early history of the department through the famous *Dialogus de Scaccario*, a twelfth-century text then misattributed to Gervase of Tilbury. Madox correctly ascribed the *Dialogus* to Richard fitz Neal or Nigel, bishop of London, and collated all but one of the surviving manuscripts into an edition that was not superseded until the early twentieth century. It appeared as an appendix to the *History of the Exchequer* in 1711. Madox's greatest work, the *History* was not simply a study of the records of a single institution, but an account of its development over several centuries, and with it much of the legal and financial history of the kingdom. Madox drew here upon documents not only in the exchequer itself but in other archives throughout the kingdom.

In recognition of his scholarship, Madox was elected a fellow of the Society of Antiquaries in 1708. He was appointed to the office of historiographer royal on 12 July 1714, in succession to Rymer. This was an important appointment in that it kept the post in the hands of scholars rather than of literary figures such as James Howell, John Dryden, and Thomas Shadwell who had previously held it, and it is remarkable that Madox's principal rival was no less a scholar than Wanley. For Madox, the position of historiographer royal was no sinecure. During his tenure he prepared two further works, the *Firma burgi*, an essay on the history of medieval boroughs published in early spring of 1726, and a treatise on feudal tenures, *Baronia Anglica*, which appeared posthumously in 1736. In 1756 his widow bequeathed ninety-three volumes of collections, which survive in the British Library (Add. MSS 4479–4572).

Madox drew up his will on 9 March 1726 in the parish of St Andrew's, Holborn, London, and died on 13 January 1727, before he had completed revisions to the *Baronia*. He was buried at Arlesey, Bedfordshire, and was survived by his wife, Catherine (*d.* 1756?), daughter of Vigarus Edwards. The couple had no children. Madox was undoubtedly an important figure in the history of English medieval scholarship between the age of Selden and Spelman three generations earlier, and the great achievements of Maitland, Tout, and Poole in the early twentieth century.

D. R. WOOLF

Sources BL, Madox's historical collections, Add. MSS 4479–4572 · H. A. Cronne, 'The study and use of charters by English scholars in the sixteenth and seventeenth centuries: Sir Henry Spelman and Sir William Dugdale', *English historical scholarship in the sixteenth and seventeenth centuries*, ed. L. Fox (1956) · D. C. Douglas, *English scholars, 1660–1730*, 2nd edn (1951) · *DNB* · W. Nicolson, *The English, Scotch and Irish historical libraries*, 3 pts in 1 vol. (1736) · *Remarks and collections of Thomas Hearne*, ed. C. E. Doble and others, 1, OHS, 2 (1885) · *The diary of Ralph Thoresby*, ed. J. Hunter, 2 vols. (1830) · *Letters of Humfrey Wanley: palaeographer, Anglo-Saxonist, librarian, 1672–1726*, ed. P. L. Heyworth (1989) · *The diary of Humfrey Wanley, 1715–1726*, ed. C. E. Wright and R. C. Wright, 2 vols. (1966)

Archives BL, historical collections, Add. MSS 4479–4572 | Bodl. Oxf., letters to Edward Lhuyd

Wealth at death see will, PRO, PROB 11/614, sig. 68

Máedóc (*fl.* 7th cent.). *See under* Leinster, saints of (*act. c.*550–*c.*800).

Maegraith, Brian Gilmore (1907–1989), university professor, was born on 26 August 1907 in Adelaide, Australia, the fourth son in a family of four sons and one daughter of Alfred Edward Robert Maegraith, accountant, and his wife, Louisa Blanche Gilmore. He was educated at St Peter's, Adelaide, and at the University of Adelaide, from which he graduated MB, BS, first class (1930), and took up a South Australian Rhodes scholarship to Magdalen College, Oxford, in 1931. He graduated BSc in 1933 and DPhil in 1934.

Maegraith was awarded a Beit fellowship in 1933 and the following year was appointed Staines medical fellow and tutor in physiology at Exeter College, Oxford, where he remained until 1940. Also in 1934 he married Lorna, a schoolteacher, daughter of Edgar Langley, schoolmaster (they had one son, Michael, who went into publishing). In 1937 he became lecturer and demonstrator in pathology. One of his proudest boasts was that he came 'from the same town, the same school, the same University in Australia and the same College in Oxford' as Howard Florey, who developed penicillin.

The Second World War proved to be the crucial turning-point in Maegraith's career. Having been in the Territorial Army since 1932, he was recruited in the Royal Army Medical Corps and dispatched to France in 1940. He was evacuated from Dunkirk and sent to Sierra Leone in west Africa. He returned to Oxford to lead, as a lieutenant-colonel, the malaria research unit (1943–5), and he was honorary malariologist to the army from 1967 to 1973. While in Oxford he was also dean of the school of medicine from 1938 to 1944. He became FRCP (London, 1955, and Edinburgh, 1956).

Maegraith first came to prominence in the field of tropical medicine when he was pathologist for the British army in Sierra Leone, where his work on the kidney and malaria attracted a great deal of attention. It soon became clear to him that the pathophysiology of malaria and blackwater fever had been insufficiently studied and was poorly understood. With his background as an Oxford-trained physiologist and pathologist he was ideally suited to study this problem. On being appointed to the Alfred Jones and Warrington Yorke chair of tropical medicine at Liverpool University in 1944, his first task was to make a thorough review of the literature to date and he produced his most erudite publication, *Pathological Processes in Malaria and Blackwater Fever* (1948). The many ideas enunciated in that book were to form the basis of his and the department's research for the next twenty years. Another important achievement of his early days was his work on the anti-malarial drug Paludrine, in collaboration with A. R. D. Adams. In 1946, already at Liverpool, he was also appointed dean of the School of Tropical Medicine there, a post which he retained for nearly thirty years. As dean he was fully convinced that the school's impact had to be in the tropics and he pursued this objective relentlessly for the rest of his life.

The result was an intimate involvement with south-east Asia and the creation of the faculty of tropical medicine in Bangkok, which was later the best in the developing world. Maegraith was also involved in west Africa, especially with the University of Ibadan and the Ghana medical school. He established Ghana's Institute of Health with the support of Kwame Nkrumah, with whom he formed a personal friendship. He was the creator of the Association of European Schools of Tropical Medicine, whose meetings he regularly attended. As vice-president of the interim committee of the international congresses of tropical medicine and malaria he took a prominent part in the organization of a number of the congresses. He retired from his chair in 1972 and as dean in 1975.

A man of strong personality, Maegraith had vision and imagination, and ideas well ahead of his time. He envisaged the escalation of air travel and the increasing importance of imported diseases, with people arriving from tropical areas well within the incubation period of a potential infection, the most important of which was malaria. He wrote a classic paper in *The Lancet* (1963), 'Unde venis?', emphasizing the importance of taking a patient's geographical history.

Maegraith was president of the Royal Society of Tropical Medicine and Hygiene (1969–71) and the recipient of many medals. He was appointed CMG in 1968. He received an honorary DSc from Bangkok University in 1966, of which he was very proud, and was awarded the order of the White Elephant of Thailand in 1982. The Liverpool school presented him with its highest award, the Mary Kingsley medal (1973), and also created the Maegraith wing, where he occupied a room.

For mental relaxation Maegraith taught himself to play the piano, one of his favourite pieces being Beethoven's 'Moonlight' sonata. He was a talented amateur painter and won several prizes in competitions for physicians. He was also a good poet and short-story writer. Although Maegraith spent the whole of his career in Britain, he never lost his Australian approach to life, with its outspokenness, occasional brashness, and healthy disrespect for what he considered outmoded convention. A robust, fair-skinned, good-looking man, he had a striking appearance and strong personality. Maegraith died on 2 April 1989, in Liverpool, where his home was 23 Eaton Road, Cressington Park.   H. M. GILLES, *rev.*

Sources *The Times* (5 April 1989) · *The Independent* (6 April 1989) · *The Lancet* (29 April 1989) · private information (1996) · personal knowledge (1996) · *CGPLA Eng. & Wales* (1989)
Wealth at death under £70,000: probate, 5 July 1989, *CGPLA Eng. & Wales*

Máel Brigte mac Tornáin (d. 927). *See under* Iona, abbots of (*act.* 563–927).

Máel Cétair mac Rónáin (*fl.* 6th–7th cent.?). *See under* Munster, saints of (*act. c.*450–*c.*700).

Máeldub [Maildulf] (*supp. fl.* **mid-7th cent.**), abbot, may have been the eponymous founder and first abbot of the monastery of Malmesbury. He is a shadowy figure whose very existence is questionable. The earliest reference to him is by Bede, who in his *Historia ecclesiastica* states merely that Aldhelm (d. 709/10) was abbot of the monastery *quod Maildubi Urbem nuncupant* ('which they call the *urbs* [that is, monastery] of Máeldub'; Bede, *Hist. eccl.*, 5.18). Máeldub is clearly an Irish name, and Bede might seem to imply that Máeldub was the founder of a monastery there; an implication seemingly supported by place-name forms such as 'Meldubesburg'. An anonymous Irishman, in a letter to Aldhelm, states that Aldhelm had been 'nourished by a certain holy man of our race' (*Aldhelm: Prose Works*, letter 6). Subsequent authors such as William of Malmesbury deduced from such evidence that Aldhelm had been taught at Malmesbury by an Irish scholar named Máeldub, who happened to be the monastery's founder. But Aldhelm nowhere mentions any Máeldub, and other forms of the name, such as that attested in a charter deemed by some scholars to be trustworthy—namely 'Meldunesburg' (*AS chart.*, S 71)—suggest that the eponymous founder was named Máeldún rather than Máeldub. Nothing further is known of Máeldún and his relation to Aldhelm cannot be ascertained. The fact remains, however, that there are various Old Irish words in the Épinal-Erfurt glossaries (*c*.700), which some scholars have associated with Malmesbury. If Máeldub's existence could be proved beyond doubt, the fact of an Irish abbot in a monastery in Wessex in the seventh century would be of the greatest significance.   MICHAEL LAPIDGE

Sources Bede, *Hist. eccl.* · *Willelmi Malmesbiriensis monachi de gestis pontificum Anglorum libri quinque*, ed. N. E. S. A. Hamilton, Rolls Series, 52 (1870) · *Aldhelmi opera*, ed. R. Ehwald, MGH Auctores Antiquissimi, 15 (Berlin, 1919) · *Aldhelm: the prose works*, trans. M. Lapidge and M. Herren (1979) [incl. *Epistolae*] · B. Bischoff and others, *The Épinal, Erfurt, Werden and Corpus glossaries* (1988) · J. D. Pheifer, ed., *Old English glosses in the Épinal-Erfurt glossary* (1974)

Maelgwn ap Rhys (*d.* 1231). *See under* Gruffudd ap Rhys (*d.* 1201).

Maelgwn Fychan (*d.* 1257). *See under* Gruffudd ap Rhys (*d.* 1201).

Maelgwn Gwynedd (*d.* 547/549), king of Gwynedd, was the son of Cadwallon Lawhir ab Einion Yrth of the Gwynedd dynasty of Cunedda Wledig and, according to late genealogies, of Meddyf ferch Maeldaf from Nant Conwy. Maelgwn ruled the kingdom of Gwynedd in north-west Wales in the first half of the sixth century until his death, allegedly of plague, in 547. A certain amount of information about Maelgwn and his reign can be gleaned from the contemporary but brief account by Gildas, who wrote to chastise five kings, of whom Maelgwn was the most notable, for their sinful ways and in order to save Britannia from the Anglo-Saxon threat. This Gildasian account concentrates almost exclusively on the king's sins, which, it relates, were as great as his height—later Welsh tradition knew him as Hir ('the Tall').

There is a problem in dating the beginning of Maelgwn's reign. Robert de Torigni's abstract of the annals of Redon states that a 'Cauallonus, most powerful king of Great Britain' (*Patrologia Latina*, 146, no. 202, col. 1323) died in 534: he has been identified as Maelgwn's father, and this has suggested that Maelgwn himself could not have ruled until after 534. However, the date is probably an error for 634, when the later Cadwallon ap Cadfan is said to have died. It is not clear that Maelgwn's father, Cadwallon, had necessarily ruled as king, for according to Gildas, Maelgwn acquired the kingship having killed his uncle, entitled king, in battle. This uncle may have been Owain Danwyn ab Einion Yrth of Rhos, but alternatively may remain anonymous. The reference to Maelgwn as 'Island Dragon' may imply that he was based on Anglesey, the traditional seat of the kings of Gwynedd. Afterwards, perhaps regretting the murder of his kinsman, Maelgwn is said, following a period of serious deliberation, to have resolved to become a monk. However, this proved only to be a temporary situation and he soon returned to the kingship and his old ways of kin slaying. Gildas claims that Maelgwn slew his wife (whom he had married before his monastic phase) and his brother's son, in the latter case with the collusion of this nephew's own wife. He was thus able to marry this woman and justified the union on the grounds that she was a widow! The later genealogies do indeed name two wives for Maelgwn, called Sanan ferch Cyngen (of the ruling line of Powys) and Gwall(t)wen ferch Afallach (described as his mistress), though their historical authenticity is not beyond doubt. Of course, Maelgwn's nepoticide may have had as much to do with politics as with affairs of the heart, since it is to be assumed that a kinsman must have ruled in his stead during his brief spell as a monk. On rejecting this vocation Maelgwn would have perhaps needed to expel this relative by force. The identity of the nephew (whether king or not) is impossible to determine.

Other notable elements in the Gildasian account of Maelgwn include his alleged preference for the panegyric poems of his bards, particularly those addressed to himself, over the more morally uplifting music of the church. Furthermore, Gildas seems to imply that Maelgwn had been educated in Latin by a secular *rhetor*, probably independently of his monastic training. His ecclesiastical relations were certainly not faultless, but the frequent references to his attacks on monastic sites recorded in lives of the saints probably reflect hagiographical convention and Maelgwn's later reputation rather than genuine historical events. Maelgwn died, according to the Welsh chronicles, in 547 of plague, probably, therefore, the so-called 'Justinian plague'. Some would date his death to 549, because of the mortality mentioned in the Irish annals. Later accounts would add the detail that he died in a church at Rhos attempting to avoid the disease. Maelgwn Gwynedd was certainly regarded as the most important early king of Gwynedd by the ninth century, and the main ruling dynasty claimed descent from him through his son *Rhun. He is also credited with a daughter called Eurgain.
                                                    DAVID E. THORNTON

Sources J. Williams ab Ithel, ed., *Annales Cambriae*, Rolls Series, 20 (1860) · Gildas: *'The ruin of Britain', and other works*, ed. and trans. M. Winterbottom (1978) · P. C. Bartrum, ed., *Early Welsh genealogical tracts* (1966) · R. Bromwich, ed. and trans., *Trioedd ynys Prydein: the Welsh triads*, 2nd edn (1978) · Pope Alexander II, 'Epistolae et diplomata', *Patrologia Latina*, 146 (1853), no. 202, col. 1323 · J. E. Lloyd, *A history of Wales from the earliest times to the Edwardian conquest*, 3rd edn, 2 vols. (1939); repr. (1988) · D. N. Dumville, 'Gildas and Maelgwn: problems of dating', *Gildas: new approaches*, ed. M. Lapidge and D. N. Dumville (1984), 51–60 · M. Miller, 'Dateguessing and pedigrees', *Studia Celtica*, 10–11 (1975–6), 96–109 · M. Lapidge, 'Gildas's education and the Latin culture of sub-Roman Britain', *Gildas: new approaches*, ed. M. Lapidge and D. N. Dumville (1984), 27–50, esp. 50

Máel Muru Othna [Maelmura] (*d.* 887), poet and historian, was evidently connected with the monastery of Fahan (Donegal): his epithet 'Othna' means 'of Fahan' and his name ('devotee of Muru') alludes to that community's founder saint. Accounts of Mael Muru's death describe him as 'royal poet of Ireland' (*Ann. Ulster*), and 'learned poet of the Gaels' (*Chronicum Scotorum*); a eulogistic quatrain in the former praises him in even more elevated terms without, however, adding any further information. The main sources of evidence are three poems bearing attributions to him: 'Flann for Éirinn', 'Can a mbunadus na nGaídel?', and 'Áth Liac Find, cid dia tá?'.

'Flann for Éirinn' (so far unedited) addresses Flann Sinna mac Maíle Sechnaill as king of Tara (high-king of Ireland), and must accordingly have been written between the dates of Flann's accession and Máel Muru's death (that is, between 879 and 887). Flann is exhorted to imitate his legendary ancestor Tuathal Techtmar in gaining mastery of all Ireland; Máel Muru then describes the transmission of the high-kingship from Tuathal to Flann, giving, however, not the standard list of high-kings but rather Flann's own paternal line. In an isolated quatrain preserved in the preface to the martyrology *Félire Óengusso*, he says that it is Flann's descendants 'whom I would choose … henceforth' as kings of Tara. The composition of these poems may have been connected with the events of 880–82, when Flann invaded and took the hostages of Leinster, Munster, and the northern Uí Néill dynasties of Cenél Conaill and Cenél nEógain; it is perhaps on the strength of such propaganda that Máel Muru was accorded the title 'royal poet' (*rígfhili*).

It is difficult, however, to imagine these works being written at Fahan, only 4 miles from the Cenél nEógain stronghold of Ailech; Máel Muru's one-sided insistence on Flann's family's claim to the high-kingship would have been a snub to the local dynasty, which had supplied Flann's predecessor as high-king of Ireland and which was to supply his successor. It accordingly seems likeliest that Máel Muru left the north to attach himself to Flann's household. This hypothesis also makes it easier to accept the attribution to him of 'Áth Liac Find' (edited by E. Gwynn), a poem explaining the name of a ford of the Shannon on the border of the modern counties of Longford and Roscommon.

'Can a mbunadus' (edited by J. Todd and A. Herbert) is composed in the same metre as 'Flann for Éirinn', and the two are almost identical in length. It provides a description of the legendary migrations of the ancestors of the Irish from Scythia to Spain and of their conquest of Ireland; the final third derives the population groups of Máel Muru's own time from various of these fictitious settlers. 'Can a mbunadus' is the earliest surviving extended account of Gaelic origins and was a text of considerable importance in the development of the Irish pseudo-historical tradition: its influence is reflected in the work of Gilla Cóemáin (*fl.* 1072) and in the pseudo-historical treatise *Lebor Gabála*.　　　　　JOHN CAREY

Sources J. Carey, *A new introduction to Lebor gabála Érenn* (1993) · E. O'Reilly, *A chronological account of … four hundred Irish writers … down to … 1750, with a descriptive catalogue of … their works* (1820) · Ann. Ulster · W. M. Hennessy, ed. and trans., *Chronicum Scotorum: a chronicle of Irish affairs*, Rolls Series, 46 (1866) · AFM · T. O'Rahilly and others, *Catalogue of Irish manuscripts in the Royal Irish Academy*, 30 vols. (Dublin, 1926–70) · S. O'Grady, R. Flower, and M. Dillon, eds., *Catalogue of Irish manuscripts in the British Library* (formerly British Museum), 2 vols. (1926–53); repr. (1992) · T. K. Abbott and E. J. Gwynn, eds., *Catalogue of the Irish manuscripts in the library of Trinity College, Dublin* (1921) · E. Gwynn, ed. and trans., *The metrical Dindschenchas*, 1, Royal Irish Academy: Todd Lecture Series, 8 (1903); repr. (1991), 4.36–9, 382 · *Félire Óengusso Céli Dé / The martyrology of Oengus the Culdee*, ed. W. Stokes, HBS, 29 (1905); repr. (1984), 14–15 · J. Todd and A. Herbert, eds., *Leabhar Breathnach* (1848), 220–71

Máel Ruain (d. 792). *See under* Leinster, saints of (*act. c.*550–*c.*800).

Máel Sechnaill mac Domnaill (948–1022), high-king of Ireland, was the son of Domnall mac Donnchada (*d.* 952) and Dúnfhlaith, the daughter of *Muirchertach mac Néill of Cenél nEógain. He was remembered with affection by later writers and the annals of Clonmacnoise have the curious statement that Máel Sechnaill was the last king of Ireland of Irish blood.

Having been king of the southern Uí Néill dynasty of Clann Cholmáin since *c.*976, Máel Sechnaill ascended to the high-kingship on the death of his uncle *Domnall ua Néill in 980. In the same year he won the famous victory over the vikings of Dublin and the Hebrides at the battle of Tara. The vikings were led by a Rögnvaldr, son of Olaf Cuarán (Olaf Sihtricson) of Dublin, and their defeat was so thorough that Máel Sechnaill pursued them back to Dublin and forced them to release their Irish hostages. Máel Sechnaill was hailed as a liberator who broke the power of the vikings in Ireland. He appears to have taken lordship over Dublin, helped by the succession to the kingship of his half-brother Glún Iairn, another son of Olaf Cuarán (with Máel Sechnaill's mother, Dúnfhlaith). The brothers allied to defeat the king of Leinster, Domnall Cláen mac Lorcáin of Uí Dúnchada, and his viking ally Ívarr of Waterford in 983. When Glún Iairn was killed in 989, in a drunken brawl with one of his servants, Máel Sechnaill attacked Dublin and besieged the fortress for twenty days until it capitulated when the fresh water ran out and the inhabitants were reduced to drinking brine.

Early in his tenure of the high-kingship Máel Sechnaill devoted more than a dozen years to pacifying the province of Connacht, leading expeditions there in 985, 992, and 998. In 990 he moved into Munster, and was victorious in the battle of Carn Fordroma. From Munster came his great rival, Brian Bóruma (Brian mac Cennétig). In 988 Brian placed a fleet of 300 boats on Lough Ree to harry Meath, with particular attention given to Uisnech (the ceremonial site of Máel Sechnaill's dynasty). The contest between Máel Sechnaill and Brian for supremacy began in earnest in 999 and, as in previous struggles between the Uí Néill and Munster since the ninth century, the battleground was Leinster. The confrontation began when the king of Leinster, Donnchad mac Domnaill Cláin of Uí Dúnchada, was captured by a rival, Máel Mórda mac Murchada of Uí Fháeláin, and his nephew Sihtric Silkenbeard, the son of Olaf Cuarán. This was a challenge to Máel Sechnaill, as the province's overlord, and he ravaged Leinster. Brian saw an opportunity to intrude into Leinster's affairs, and late in the year he led an army there which defeated the combined forces of Leinster and Dublin at the battle of Glenn Máma (near Newcastle Lyons, co. Dublin); he captured Dublin on new year's day 1000. Adding the men of Dublin and Leinster to his army, Brian invaded the plain of Brega and advanced as far as Ferta Nimhe, Meath, later that year; but the invasion ended badly when an advance party of cavalry, together with the men of Dublin and Leinster, was intercepted by Máel Sechnaill and defeated with heavy losses. A second raid from Munster into Meath in 1001 was also repelled. To face this new threat, Máel Sechnaill turned to military engineering in order to ease the movement of his troops, having a causeway built over the River Shannon at Athlone. The next year Brian led his army there and took the hostages of Connacht and Meath. This was the end of Máel Sechnaill's first possession of the high-kingship. An interesting interpretation of those events is preserved in the tract *Cocad Gáedel re Gallaíb* ('The war of the Irish against the foreigners'), a late eleventh- or early twelfth-century history written in the interests of Brian's descendants, which states that Máel Sechnaill received no support from the northern Uí Néill even though he offered to acknowledge the supremacy of the king of Ailech, Áed ua Néill, rather than allow a high-king from outside the ranks of the Uí Néill.

After his submission to Brian Bóruma, Máel Sechnaill's activities were limited to attendance on Brian's hostings or local warfare. In 1004 Máel Sechnaill nearly died after being thrown from his horse, and he is not mentioned in the annals again for several years, until 1007 when he presided over the fair of Tailtiu. Máel Sechnaill then devoted himself to petty raiding, into Leinster in 1009 and several battles against the rival Uí Néill dynasties of Cenél nEógain and Cenél Conaill in 1012 and 1013. Rebellions against Brian began in the north of Ireland in 1013, and by the autumn Dublin and Leinster had joined the revolt. A battle fought by Máel Sechnaill against the men of Dublin and Leinster at Drinan (in what is now co. Dublin) led to the death of his son Flann. The contest was resumed in April 1014, at the famous battle of Clontarf in which Brian Bóruma fell. Máel Sechnaill was in Brian's army, but his actions are not clear. Several records claim that, on the eve of the battle, he led his forces away and refused to fight. Family ties could have influenced Máel Sechnaill, for his wife Máel Muire was a Dublin princess.

Máel Sechnaill resumed his position as high-king after Clontarf and reasserted his control throughout Ireland. In alliance with Flaithbertach Ua Néill of Cenél nEógain, he raided Leinster in 1015; an expedition from Leinster and Dublin was defeated in 1017 at Odba. Máel Sechnaill harried in Osraige, Ulaid, and southern Leinster in 1016. In 1020 he led an expedition, which included Brian Bóruma's son Donnchad, across the Shannon and took the hostages of Connacht. Thirty days before his death, Máel Sechnaill defeated a raiding party from Dublin at Athboy in Meath. He died on 2 September 1022, at the age of seventy-three, on Cró-inis in Lough Ennell, opposite his fortress of Dún na Sciath (Westmeath); in attendance were the heads of the churches of Armagh, Clonmacnoise, and Kells. He was buried at Clonmacnoise.

Máel Sechnaill was a patron of poets and the church. Poems dedicated to him include verses on the fair of Tailtiu, a poem on the River Boyne, and verses on the hill of Tara. In a poem on Druim Criaich, Máel Sechnaill's defence of his lands is presented in the image of a herdsman guarding his herd. The poem *Maoil Sechloinn sinnser Gaoidhel* ('Máel Sechnaill the elder of the Gaels') is devoted to a recitation of his career. Máel Sechnaill had both ancestral and immediate connections with the church. His brother Flaithbertach was the abbot of Clonmacnoise and of Clonard. Máel Sechnaill is credited with building the great church at Clonmacnoise known as *Tempul na Ríg* ('church of the kings'), although he may have been responsible only for an enlargement or refurbishment of the earlier church built by his great-grandfather Flann Sinna.

Máel Sechnaill was twice married. His first wife was Gormhlaith (*d.* 1030), the daughter of Murchad mac Finn of Uí Fháeláin; she was the mother of his son Conchobar (*d.* 1030). His second wife was Máel Muire (*d.* 1021), daughter of Olaf Cuarán. His other sons included Donnchad (*d.* 1012), Flann (*d.* 1013), Congalach (*d.* 1017), Domnall, who was the abbot of Clonard and died in 1019, Murchad Ruadh (*d.* 1049), and Muirchertach (*d.* 1049).

BENJAMIN T. HUDSON

Sources Ann. Ulster · M. C. Dobbs, ed. and trans., 'The Banshenchus [3 pts]', *Revue Celtique*, 47 (1930), 283–339; 48 (1931), 163–234; 49 (1932), 437–89 · J. H. Todd, ed. and trans., *Cogadh Gaedhel re Gallaibh / The war of the Gaedhil with the Gaill*, Rolls Series, 48 (1867) · B. T. Hudson, *Prophecy of Berchán* (1996) · M. A. O'Brien, ed., *Corpus genealogiarum Hiberniae* (Dublin, 1962) · E. Hogan, *Onomasticon Goedelicum* (1910) · S. Mac Airt, ed. and trans., *The annals of Inisfallen* (1951) · W. M. Hennessy, ed. and trans., *Chronicum Scotorum: a chronicle of Irish affairs*, Rolls Series, 46 (1866) · AFM · F. J. Byrne, *Irish kings and high-kings* (1987) · D. Ó Corráin, *Ireland before the Normans* (1972) · T. W. Moody and others, eds., *A new history of Ireland*, 9: *Maps, genealogies, lists* (1984) · K. Meyer, 'Das Ende von Baile in Scáil', *Zeitschrift für Celtische Philologie*, 12 (1918), 232–8

Máel Sechnaill mac Máele Ruanaid (*d.* 862), high-king of Ireland, was king of Mide before succeeding Niall mac Áeda (Niall Caille) as king of Tara (high-king) after the latter's death in 845. His mother was Aróc, daughter of Cathal mac Fiachrach from a neighbouring Uí Néill dynasty in northern Brega. His father, Máel Ruanaid mac Donnchada (*d.* 843), had been king of Mide (modern Westmeath, with parts of Meath and Offaly) but was one of the least effective rulers to come from the great midland dynasty of Cland Cholmáin. In 841 Máel Sechnaill defeated a coup against his father mounted by his cousin Diarmait mac Conchobair. When Máel Ruanaid died two years later, Máel Sechnaill succeeded, apparently without much opposition.

Threats to Mide The situation for Mide and for its ruling dynasty was exceedingly dangerous. The establishment of the fortified 'ship-ports', *longphuirt*, at Dublin and Lind Duachaill in 841 had shifted the main sphere of viking attacks from the north to the midlands. The vikings had temporary wintering camps, as on Lough Neagh in 839 or Lough Erne in 924–5; but Dublin became the principal permanent base of the vikings in Ireland, comparable with Kiev on the Dnieper, while Lind Duachaill in Louth was occupied until 927. The situation of the two early *longphuirt* of Dublin and Lind Duachaill—astride the low-lying eastern coastlands between the Mourne and Wicklow mountains—posed a direct threat to the kingdom of Máel Sechnaill. In 841, two years before Máel Sechnaill succeeded his father as king of Mide, the vikings of Lind Duachaill marched right across the midlands to Tethbae (approximately the modern co. Longford), immediately to the east of the Shannon. Tethbae, however, was perhaps the most important of the Uí Néill client territories which had to be controlled by Cland Cholmáin, whose own lands lay further east around Lough Ennell. The capacity of the vikings to strike so far west threatened the authority of the king of Mide by revealing his inability to defend his principal clients.

Since 829 Mide had been under severe pressure from the king of Munster, Feidlimid mac Crimthainn. By 831 he had secured overlordship of Leinster, normally a perquisite of the Uí Néill; and, from 832, he began a series of attacks on the border kingdoms of Fir Chell (containing Durrow, Lynally, and other major churches) and Delbnae Bethra (containing Clonmacnoise). His intention was evidently not just to make the kingdoms tributary but to obtain control over major churches normally aligned with Cland Cholmáin. By 840 he appears to have attained this objective, however temporarily. Neither Máel Sechnaill's uncle, Conchobar mac Donnchada (high-king of Ireland; d. 833), nor his father, Máel Ruanaid, were able to repel Feidlimid's attacks. By 843, however, when Máel Sechnaill succeeded his father as king of Mide, the tide of Munster power was on the ebb: Feidlimid was by now an old man and would die in 847. The most immediate threat was, therefore, the vikings, who were now at the high point of their military activity in Ireland and were, moreover, concentrating their attacks on the southern Uí Néill, rulers of the midlands, perhaps precisely because they had been weakened by Feidlimid's attacks.

Military successes Under such severe pressure, the Irish rulers appear to have perceived the necessity of co-ordinating their efforts. In 845 Máel Sechnaill captured a viking leader Turgéis (Turges), who had established himself on the Shannon, and drowned him in Lough Owel (drowning seems to have been the method of execution used for kings who had flouted normal political standards). The year 848 saw a series of viking defeats at the hands not just of Máel Sechnaill but also of the new king of Munster, Ólchobar, of Tigernach, king of southern Brega, and of the Éoganacht of Cashel. These successes were on a scale sufficient to merit notice in the continental annals of St Bertin. In 849 Máel Sechnaill and his ally, Tigernach, were able to sack Dublin itself.

In the years from 849 to 853 neither the Irish nor the vikings maintained any dependable unity. One of the southern Uí Néill rulers, Cináed mac Conaing, king of Ciannacht Breg, 'rebelled against Máel Sechnaill by virtue of the power of the Foreigners' in 850, 'and plundered the Uí Néill from the Shannon to the sea' (*Ann. Ulster*). He took particular care to sack the crannog of the rival Síl nÁeda Sláine king of south Brega at Lagore and to burn the adjacent church of Trevet. If Síl nÁeda Sláine as a whole, namely the Uí Néill of the eastern midland area known as

Brega, had defied the authority of the Cland Cholmáin over-king and had sought an alliance with the Dublin vikings, Máel Sechnaill might have been in severe difficulties, but, as usual, the internal rivalries of the Uí Néill of Brega—shown by the sacking of Lagore and the burning of Trevet—came to his rescue. In the very next year, 851, the power of the Foreigners, in which Cináed mac Conaing had trusted, was not enough to prevent him from being executed by drowning at the command of Máel Sechnaill and Tigernach mac Fócartai, king of Lagore. The inability of the vikings to protect Cináed may have been due to their own divisions. In 849 a fleet of 140 ships 'of the household of the king of the Foreigners' (*Ann. Ulster*) 'came to enforce his power over the Foreigners who were already there and they threw the whole of Ireland into confusion'. Under the year 851 the annals of Ulster record the arrival of 'the dark heathens' in Dublin, where 'they made a great slaughter of the fair foreigners' and plundered the *longphort*. They also attacked Lind Duachaill in the same year, but with less success. The identity of 'the dark heathens' and 'the fair heathens' has been a matter of uncertainty since the eleventh century. What is clear is that the division originated outside Ireland, that it caused some disarray among the vikings for a few years, but that it was soon rendered ineffective by the Scandinavian royal leaders who entered Ireland from 853.

The first of these leaders, Olaf (Amlaíb, Óláfr), is described by the annals of Ulster as 'the son of the king of Laithlind'; and they add that 'the foreigners of Ireland gave hostages to him and tribute was paid by the Irish'. Yet in the next year, 854, Máel Sechnaill led an army into Munster and took the hostages of the Munstermen, a clear demonstration, apparently, that he was not merely still king of Tara, in spite of the hostages given to Olaf, but also that he proposed to make that kingship into an effective monarchy of Ireland by means of military power: he had survived the viking onslaught and could now take revenge on Munster for the humiliations inflicted by Feidlimid mac Crimthainn on his father and uncle. He made another expedition to Munster in 856 in the very year in which the annals of Ulster record 'a major war between the heathens and Máel Sechnaill who was supported by Norse-Irish [Gallgoídil]'. These 'Norse-Irish' appear in the annals for the first time in this year. In 858 he 'came with the men of Ireland to the lands of Munster', and, after defeating the kings of the Munstermen, 'he took their hostages from Bélat Gabráin in the east to the Bull Island in the west, and from the Old Head of Kinsale in the south to Inisheer in the north' (*Ann. Ulster*).

The annalist, almost certainly writing in the territories of the southern Uí Néill, was not disposed to minimize Máel Sechnaill's achievement. Yet it is worth examining carefully what he says. He suggests that the victory was not won over the king of Munster, but over 'their kings', one of whom was left dead on the battlefield. Moreover, even if due allowance is made for rhetorical exuberance, the point of saying that hostages were given from the four quarters of Munster must be that the client kings of Munster, not just their provincial king, had been made to submit personally to the king of Tara. In effect, Máel Sechnaill was bypassing the political authority of the king of Munster, just as Olaf, in taking the hostages of the Irish, had bypassed the authority of the king of Tara.

Assembly at Rahugh In 858 Cenél Fiachach, a client people in Mide, and the Gallgoídil of Leth Cuinn were defeated by Cerball, king of Osraige, himself allied with Ímar, one of the principal viking leaders. Cerball was the brother of Máel Sechnaill's wife, Land (or Fland; d. 890), mother of his heir, *Flann Sinna. Máel Sechnaill responded directly, and in an unprecedented way, to this continued defiance from the king of Osraige. In 859 he held a royal meeting at Rahugh, a church within the kingdom of Cenél Fiachach, at which the king of Munster, Máel Guala, entered into a formal contract, for which he appointed sureties. The terms of this contract were that Osraige was to be permanently alienated to Leth Cuinn (the lands under more direct Uí Néill overlordship) and would thus come under the direct authority of Máel Sechnaill. Cerball himself made his own formal acknowledgement of the authority of Patrick's heir and the community of Armagh.

The royal assembly at Rahugh in 859 was the high point of Máel Sechnaill's reign as king of Tara. He was to die in 862; and, as often in the history of the Uí Néill, an ageing high-king was challenged by his successor. In this instance the challenger was Áed Findliath of Cenél nEogain. The habitual alternation between Cland Cholmáin and Cenél nEogain was maintained, with its usual warlike flurries as one reign ended and another began. What was significant on this occasion, however, was the inability of the vikings to use the growing weakness of Máel Sechnaill to offer their own challenge. There was no question of Olaf or Ímar becoming the next king of Tara. Instead, vikings became part of a distinctively Irish pattern of military and political activity. Moreover, because they became part of that Irish pattern, their military power served the purposes of an Irish king.

Last battles and death In 859, at the great meeting at Rahugh, the ecclesiastical supremacy of Armagh echoed the political supremacy of Máel Sechnaill. Armagh, however, was the traditional ally of Cenél nEogain rather than of Cland Cholmáin. It looks as though Áed Findliath must subsequently have put pressure on Armagh to revert to its customary allegiance. In 860 Máel Sechnaill mounted the last of his great campaigns. He was able to secure contingents from Leinster, Munster, and Connacht as well as from his own southern Uí Néill. With them he marched north towards Armagh. Close to his destination he was attacked during the night by Áed Findliath in alliance with Flann mac Conaing, king of Ciannacht Breg. Máel Sechnaill, however, defeated the attackers. In 861 Áed went further and harried Mide, Máel Sechnaill's own kingdom, in company with vikings. In this instance, later in the year, Máel Sechnaill responded to this intervention on behalf of his rival by defeating 'the Foreigners of Dublin' in a battle fought on the north-western frontier of Leinster. It was his last success: in 862, with Máel Sechnaill only a few months away from his death, Áed Findliath

again invaded Mide with the aid of Flann mac Conaing and of the vikings of Dublin. A new reign had effectively begun; yet when Máel Sechnaill died on 30 November he was described by the annalist as king of all Ireland; and in support of that title more direct military force had been assembled than by any other king of Tara in living memory. T. M. CHARLES-EDWARDS

Sources Ann. Ulster · W. M. Hennessy, ed. and trans., Chronicum Scotorum: a chronicle of Irish affairs, Rolls Series, 46 (1866) · AFM · J. N. Radner, ed., Fragmentary annals of Ireland (1978) · M. A. O'Brien, ed., Corpus genealogiarum Hiberniae (Dublin, 1962) · K. Meyer, ed., 'The Laud genealogies and tribal histories', Zeitschrift für Celtische Philologie, 8 (1910–12), 291–338 · M. C. Dobbs, ed. and trans., 'The Ban-shenchus [3 pts]', Revue Celtique, 47 (1930), 283–339; 48 (1931), 163–234; 49 (1932), 437–89 · F. J. Byrne, Irish kings and high-kings (1973) · D. Ó Corráin, 'High kings, vikings and other kings', Irish Historical Studies, 21 (1978–9), 283–323 · D. Ó Corráin, Ireland before the Normans (1972), 89–95

Maenius Agrippa, Marcus (fl. 122). See under Roman officials (act. AD 43–410).

Maese, Sarah. See Murray, Sarah (1744–1811).

Maffey, John Loader, first Baron Rugby (1877–1969), public servant, was born at 6 High Street, Rugby, on 1 July 1877, the younger son of Thomas Maffey, commercial traveller, and his wife, Mary Penelope, daughter of John Loader, of Thame. He was educated at Rugby School and was a scholar of Christ Church, Oxford, of which he was later an honorary student. He entered the Indian Civil Service in 1899 and transferred to the political department in 1905. On 28 August 1907 he married Dorothy Gladys (1883/4–1973), daughter of Charles Long Huggins of Hadlow Grange, Sussex; they had two sons and a daughter. He served with the Mohmand field force in 1908 and had a distinguished career in the North-West Frontier Province of India. He was political agent, Khyber (1909–12), deputy commissioner, Peshawar (1914–15), and chief political officer with the forces in Afghanistan in 1919. In 1915–16 he was deputy secretary in the foreign and political department of the government of India; and from 1916 to 1920 private secretary to the viceroy, Lord Chelmsford, during a difficult period when, apart from the strains of war, the government of India, the prestige of which had suffered from the handling of the Mesopotamian campaign, was faced with a growing pressure in political circles for constitutional advance. The British responded with the declaration of 20 August 1917 that their goal for India was the realization of responsible government for India within the British empire. During the resulting visit to the subcontinent of E. S. Montagu, the secretary of state for India, which produced in 1918 the Montagu–Chelmsford proposals for constitutional reforms, Maffey's tact, experience, and knowledge played an important part in smoothing relations between the viceroy and the secretary of state. Maffey was chief secretary to the duke of Connaught during his visit in 1920–21 to inaugurate the reformed councils.

As chief commissioner, North-West Frontier Province (1921–4), it fell to Maffey to deal with the rescue of Mollie Ellis, a girl of seventeen who had been carried off by

John Loader Maffey, first Baron Rugby (1877–1969), by Philip
A. de Laszlo, 1923

tribesmen who had killed her mother, into the Tirah, and
was held for a ransom which he refused to give. Realizing
that a military pursuit might be fatal to the girl, he asked
Lilian Agnes Starr of the Peshawar medical mission to go
into the tribal area and intercede, which she did successfully, for the girl's release.

Maffey was an outstanding expert on the north-west
Indian frontier, where frontier policy was a matter of
sharp controversy in the immediate post-war period. The
alternatives were the so-called close border policy of non-
interference, for long successfully applied, save in Waziristan, or a fixed long-term policy of roads, regular troops
well forward, and scouts widely placed in Mahsud country. Maffey, as chief commissioner, with the full support of
the finance member, Sir W. Malcolm (later Lord) Hailey,
was strongly in favour of the close border policy and the
curtailment of expenditure on Waziristan, already very
high at a time of great financial stringency. The governor-
general's council, including the commander-in-chief,
Lord Rawlinson, unanimously agreed, and so recommended to the secretary of state. But, after discussion
with Rawlinson and the committee of imperial defence,
which favoured developing lateral communications, even
at greater cost, the home government decided in favour of
road construction, and the permanent control of Waziristan by military occupation, if no better means could
thereafter be suggested. The viceroy, Lord Reading, and

the commander-in-chief changed their view and accepted
this conclusion. Maffey, however, was not prepared to
compromise. Although the responsible authority for the
north-west frontier, he had not been consulted, and on
the day his pension was due in 1924 he resigned from the
service.

In 1926 he was selected to be governor-general of Sudan,
a vast area with complex problems, which was still
recovering from the troubles following the death of Sir
Lee Stack in 1924. Maffey brought to Sudan the negative
lessons he had learned in India from the rise of nationalism among the educated élite. He determined to reduce
the influence of the educated Sudanese by a policy of
indirect rule which built up the power of the tribal
sheikhs. The policy was retrograde and artificial and had
only limited success. By the time Maffey left Sudan in 1933
indirect rule, in its more dogmatic forms, was losing
favour, and, although Maffey had enjoyed a period of relative quiet, his policies stored up problems for his successors.

In 1933 Maffey was appointed permanent under-
secretary of state for the colonies, a post in which he
served until 1937. His overseas tours, his contacts with
administrative staffs and with non-officials, were of the
greatest value to him at the Colonial Office. After retirement he held directorships in the City (Rio Tinto Company and Imperial Airways) until 1939 when, on the outbreak of war, he was chosen to be the first United Kingdom representative in Éire at a time of great difficulty and
importance. He held this sensitive post with great distinction until 1949. Irish neutrality; the position of Ulster; the
presence in Dublin of representatives of Germany, Japan,
and Italy; the possibility of difficulties over the use of Éire
ports by the allies, were all among the major issues which
he had to face. Maffey earned his reputation by his skill at
mediating between Eamon De Valera's nationalism,
'uncompromising in all that he sensed to touch on his
country's rights', and 'the formidable and aggrieved
imperialist Churchill' (Mansergh, *Unresolved Question* 309),
in the clashes that arose out of Ireland's disputed position
as a neutral dominion. His integrity was accepted and respected by Éire; his kindness and understanding, his discretion, tact, skill, and diplomacy in dealing with individuals, whether in or out of office, in the political field were
outstanding. He maintained throughout cordial relations
with De Valera personally, while retaining at all times the
confidence and esteem of Ulster. When the time came for
him to retire, warm tributes were paid to him in the Irish
press and by Irish political and other spokesmen.

Maffey was appointed CIE (1916), CSI (1920), KCVO (1921),
KCMG (1931), KCB (1934), and GCMG (1935). He was raised
to the peerage in 1947 as Baron Rugby. He died at his
home, Chevington Lodge, 8 Flixton Road, Bungay, Suffolk,
on 20 April 1969, and was succeeded by his elder son, Alan
Loader (*b.* 1913).

GILBERT LAITHWAITE, *rev.* PHILIP WOODS

Sources M. W. Daly, *Empire on the Nile: the Anglo-Egyptian Sudan,
1898–1934* (1986) · E. S. Montagu, *An Indian diary*, ed. V. Montagu
(1930) · *In viceregal India, 1916–1921: the letters of Ralph Verney*, ed.

D. Verney, 2 (1994) • *The Times* (21 April 1969) • R. Fisk, *In the time of war: Ireland, Ulster and the price of neutrality, 1939–1945* (1983) • N. Mansergh, *The unresolved question: the Anglo-Irish settlement and its undoing, 1912–72* (1991) • m. cert. • *CGPLA Eng. & Wales* (1969) • b. cert. • d. cert.

Archives BL OIOC, corresp. and papers relating to Waziristan, MS Eur. F 116 • NRA, papers | PRO, corresp. with foreign office relating to Abyssinia, CO 967/4 • U. Durham L., corresp. with Sir Harold Macmichael | FILM BFI NFTVA, 'Sudan and Mediterranean, 1930–36', 1933

Likenesses P. A. de Laszlo, oils, 1923, NPG [*see illus.*] • W. Stoneman, photograph, 1947, NPG • P. A. de Laszlo, oils, Christ Church Oxf.

Wealth at death £47,998: probate, 11 Sept 1969, *CGPLA Eng. & Wales*

Magan, Francis (1774?–1843), informer, son of Thomas Magan, woollen draper, of High Street, Dublin, was probably born in Dublin and graduated at Trinity College there in 1794. He was one of the first Roman Catholics admitted to the bar by the Relief Act of 1793. In 1795 he left his father's house, and established himself at 20 Usher's Island, in the neighbourhood of the Four Courts. He joined the United Irish Society, but not being successful in his profession, and being in financial difficulties, he was induced by Francis Higgins, the Sham Squire, to become a government informer. During April 1798 he kept a strict watch on Lord Edward Fitzgerald's movements, and it was from information supplied by him through Higgins that Fitzgerald was eventually arrested in Parliament Street. But so cleverly did Magan divert suspicion from himself that on the very night of the arrest he was elected a member of the head committee of the United Irishmen. He continued to pose as a nationalist, and at the meeting of the bar on 9 September 1798 he voted against the union. On 15 December 1802 he received £500 apparently for procuring information against William Todd Jones. But he took an active interest in the Catholic emancipation agitation, subscribed liberally to the association, and possessed the confidence of the leaders of the movement. In 1821 he was appointed a commissioner for enclosing waste lands and commons. He filled a small legal office, afterwards abolished, and until 1834 enjoyed a secret pension from the government of £200 a year. He occasionally went on the home circuit, but never held a brief. He died in Dublin in 1843, was buried in the church of Sts Michael and John in Dublin, and by his will required a perpetual yearly mass to be celebrated by all the priests of the church for the repose of his soul. He never married, but left all his property to his sister, who died possessed of more than £14,000. According to Huband Smith, who as a commissioner for enclosing commons was brought into close relations with him, Magan in later years was 'sufficiently gentlemanlike in appearance; tall, yet rather of plain and even coarse exterior; perhaps a little moody and reserved at times, and something may have been pressing on him of which he said little'.

ROBERT DUNLOP, rev. GERARD MCCOY

Sources W. J. Fitzpatrick, *Secret service under Pitt* (1892) • J. S. Crone, *A concise dictionary of Irish biography*, rev. edn (1937) • Burtchaell & Sadleir, *Alum. Dubl.*

Archives NL Ire., Fortescue MSS

Magauran, Edmund. *See* MacGauran, Edmund (*c*.1548–1593).

Mag Craith, Maol Mhuire. *See* Magrath, Meiler (*c*.1523–1622).

Magee, James (*d.* 1866). *See under* Magee, John (1750?–1809).

Magee, John (1750?–1809), journalist, was born in Belfast, the younger son of James Magee (1707–1797), a Presbyterian printer of books and pamphlets. His brother William founded the *Belfast Evening Post* in 1786. In 1789 John Magee founded *Magee's Weekly Packet, and Hope's Lottery Journal of News, Politics and Literature* in Dublin, and ran a lottery. In 1779 he became proprietor and editor of the *Dublin Evening Post*, a long-running paper, which after a spell in abeyance had been re-founded the previous year. He married a daughter (*d.* 1787) of another Dublin printer, William Gilbert.

The *Dublin Evening Post* soon became one of Ireland's most influential newspapers, with a substantial circulation. This was in part because of the defection of the *Freeman's Journal*, which took subsidies in return for supporting government policies. Under Magee's editorship the *Dublin Evening Post* supported whig policies and Catholic emancipation. In 1783 it argued for legislative independence. Magee's personal experience of the disabilities suffered by those who were not members of the established church made him sympathetic to the rights of Catholics, and he suffered for this and for the support that he gave to the whigs.

Through the articles it published, and through reports of the actions taken by the Dublin Castle party and others against Magee, the newspaper began to expose the nature of the government of Ireland. In November 1784 Magee had printed resolutions from a meeting in Roscommon which called for the impeachment of the attorney-general, John Fitzgibbon. The newspaper was threatened with prosecution, and in January 1785, when Magee published an attack on the government in Dublin Castle, he was arrested. He was charged with contempt of court, was committed to gaol for a month, fined £5, and ordered to give securities to keep the peace.

Following Magee's imprisonment in 1785, the *Dublin Evening Post* went quiet, but in spring 1789 the newspaper began a vendetta against Francis Higgins, the proprietor of the *Freeman's Journal*. It was under the aegis of Higgins, a magistrate and member of Dublin corporation, that the *Journal* had accepted a private subsidy from Dublin Castle, and tailored its once-radical editorial line to the government's advantage. Magee revealed that in the 1760s Higgins, then a poor pot-boy, had married the daughter of a rich Dublin merchant, representing himself as a man with money. Higgins was then tried for fraud, and was dubbed by the judge the 'sham squire'. Later he was convicted of assault and imprisoned for a year, afterwards becoming a government agent. Magee narrated all these details of Higgins's unsavoury past, as well as allegations

John Magee (1750?–1809), by Joseph Wilson, c.1782

of his seduction of a minor and fraud in successive issues of the *Dublin Evening Post*.

As well as inciting one of his employees on the *Freeman's Journal* to assault Magee and destroy his furniture (the man was arrested, but acquitted), Higgins used his friendship with the lord chief justice, John Scott, Baron Earlsfort, to try to silence him. In July 1789 Magee was arrested and charged with libel, and securities were demanded which he was unable to pay. Initially he was confined to a sponging-house, and the case began in his absence. Habeas corpus was at first refused; when it was granted, Magee denied the validity of the court and was returned to gaol. The jury suggested that the trial was unfair, but Earlsfort directed them to find Magee guilty and he was sentenced to another term of imprisonment. While in prison Magee continued to conduct his newspaper, and organized a campaign against Earlsfort by advertising a fair with an 'Olympic pig race', to be held in a field next to Earlsfort's demesne and residence in Dún Laoghaire. A mob came down from Dublin, were plied with drink, dressed dogs as barristers, and set pigs free, causing much damage.

When Magee left prison at the end of October 1789, following the failure of a commission of lunacy against him, he was still subject to fiats which held him to bail. One of these was claimed by Richard Daly, the manager of the Theatre Royal, who alleged that his business had deteriorated because of libellous accusations of dishonesty in the *Dublin Evening Post*. Magee was almost at once returned to prison under a fiat, again issued by Earlsfort, now Lord

Clonmell. In February 1790 Magee was again imprisoned for publishing comments on the king's bench. It was clear that Clonmell intended to keep him in gaol indefinitely, and the *Dublin Evening Post* gave up its campaign. However, Richard Daly continued to press for damages and his case came up in June 1790. Once again the judge was Lord Clonmell. However, in spite of being directed strongly to find Magee guilty, the jury awarded only £200 damages (against the £28,000 claimed) and 6*d*. costs.

By the end of 1790 Magee's finances were in ruins, but he had accomplished what he had intended. Following his allegations concerning Higgins's support of the Dublin gaming houses, in September 1789 the city magistrates took steps to close them down. Higgins was removed from the commission of the peace in 1793 and struck off the roll of electors. Lord Clonmell's reputation was ruined: his successive fiats against Magee, and his directions to juries hearing the cases against Magee, had revealed the partial nature of his court.

Magee's subsequent engagements in politics were more subdued. The *Dublin Evening Post* opposed the Act of Union, but in 1803 it condemned the insurrection led by Robert Emmet. The successive court hearings had broken Magee mentally and he died in an asylum in November 1809, having suffered from mental instability for many years. The judge and author Jonah Barrington subsequently described Magee as 'a little cracked but very acute' (Barrington, 403).

Magee's son **John Magee** (*d.* 1814?) succeeded him as proprietor of the *Dublin Evening Post*. With a change of government, and the appointment of Arthur Wellesley as chief secretary in 1807, the newspaper became the voice of Daniel O'Connell's Catholic Board in its campaign for Catholic emancipation and became an important influence on public opinion. In February 1812 the *Dublin Evening Post* was successfully prosecuted for an article which criticized the performance of the police, after the government had brought an action against the newspaper.

The new chief secretary, Robert Peel, regarded the Dublin press as deeply subversive, describing the *Dublin Evening Post* in September 1812 as the cause of 'most of the dissatisfaction in the country' (Inglis, 139). When the paper published a strong attack on the lord lieutenant of Ireland, Charles Lennox, fourth duke of Richmond, John Magee was summoned to give securities for good behaviour, pending a trial for libel. He was summoned once more in June 1813 this time for an alleged libel on the police magistrates. The Richmond libel trial was held on 26 July 1813 and became a *cause célèbre* in the struggle for Catholic civil rights. O'Connell was John Magee's counsel, and his speech for the defence has been commended as one of his finest performances, though his elegant filleting of the crown's case ultimately did little for his client, who was fined £500, ordered to post securities of £2000, and sentenced to two years' imprisonment. While Magee approved in principle of O'Connell's pugnacious line of defence, he realized that in effect it merely constituted a repetition of the original libels, and that his attack on Saurin, the attorney-general, was particularly likely to worsen Dublin Castle's attitude to the newspaper. When the verdict of the trial was challenged, Magee employed a new counsel, who repudiated O'Connell's defence, much to the latter's annoyance (*Correspondence of Daniel O'Connell*, 1.368 n. 3).

Prior to this Peel had received complaints from the prince regent about a report in the *Evening Post* of a speech by O'Connell; aware that a prosecution instigated at the wish of the regent would stir deep resentment, he took no action. But in August 1813, after the *Evening Post* printed resolutions of the Kilkenny Catholic committee condemning the government action against Magee, he was again prosecuted. It was Peel's intention to shut down the *Evening Post*, whether by prosecuting its proprietor or by withholding the translations of dispatches, on which newspapers were reliant for their foreign news coverage. Magee was convicted in February 1814, and given a further fine of £1000 and six months' imprisonment. It appears that he died in Dublin shortly afterwards (Bigger, 16).

James Magee (*d.* 1866), John's younger brother, who had been a merchant, took over the *Evening Post* after the government withheld newspaper stamps following his brother's libel conviction. A new prosecution was set in train by Peel after the paper printed another speech of Daniel O'Connell, at which F. W. Conway, the new editor of the paper, told the court that he had been instructed by Magee to moderate its tone. Although Magee was found guilty, he undertook to behave in future, and after 1815 the politics of the *Dublin Evening Post* were 'Castle Catholic' and wary of O'Connell. In December 1815 he won a libel case, brought against one O'Gorman, who had induced the paper to publish an incorrect account of a trial which had resulted in Magee paying out yet more damages. James Magee remained as proprietor of the paper until he became a Dublin police magistrate, and died in Bonn, Germany, on 24 September 1866. He was survived by a daughter, Mary-Jane Magee. MARIE-LOUISE LEGG

Sources B. Inglis, *The freedom of the press in Ireland, 1784–1841* (1954) · F. J. Bigger, *The Magees of Belfast and Dublin* (1916) · R. R. Madden, *The history of Irish periodical literature*, 2 (1867) · S. J. Connolly, 'Union government, 1812–23', *A new history of Ireland*, ed. T. W. Moody and others, 5: *Ireland under the Union, 1801–1870* (1989), 48–73 · J. Barrington, *Personal sketches of his own times*, 2 vols. (1827) · M. J. Tulty, 'The *Dublin Evening Post*, 1826', *Dublin Historical Record*, 24/2 (1970–71), 15–24 · *The correspondence of Daniel O'Connell*, ed. M. R. O'Connell, 1, IMC (1972) · *DNB* · F. Griffith, 'Daniel O'Connell's most famous case: the trial of John Magee', *Éire–Ireland*, 9/2 (1974), 90–106 · *The Times* (19 Dec 1815) · *CGPLA Ire.* (1866)
Likenesses J. Wilson, portrait, *c.*1782, Ulster Museum, Belfast [*see illus.*] · portrait, repro. in Bigger, *Magees of Belfast and Dublin* · portrait (John Magee), repro. in Bigger, *Magees of Belfast and Dublin*, 16
Wealth at death under £3000—James Magee: will, *CGPLA Ire.*

Magee, John (*d.* 1814?). *See under* Magee, John (1750?–1809).

Magee [*née* Stewart], **Martha Maria** (*d.* 1846), benefactor, was born, of parents named Stewart, at Lurgan, co. Armagh, where her family had been long settled. She married in 1780 William Magee, who on 12 September of that year had been ordained Presbyterian minister of First Lurgan; she was widowed on 9 July 1800. Left in straitened financial circumstances, with two sons to bring up, she received assistance from the Presbyterian widows' fund. Both her sons entered the army, one as an ensign, the other as army surgeon; they died in early manhood, one from the result of an accident, the other, in India, of rabies.

Mrs Magee's financial circumstances changed dramatically when she inherited a fortune accumulated by her two brothers, both military men—one of them a colonel in the Indian army. She moved from Lurgan to Dublin, where she lived quietly, but contributed generously to various charitable and religious ventures. At first connected with a Presbyterian church in Dublin, she attended for a time the services of the Church of Ireland, before finally settling as a member of Usher's Quay Presbyterian congregation. She died in Dublin on 22 June 1846, leaving no near relative.

It was Mrs Magee's financial legacy, rather than any aspect of her life, which was to ensure her place in Irish Presbyterian history. Various Presbyterian organizations were named as beneficiaries in her will. A large portion of her fortune went to the mission field: the Irish Presbyterian Mission in India received £25,000, the Foreign Mission £5000, and the Home Mission £5000. The Usher's Quay Female Orphan School also received £5000, while the new Presbyterian church on Ormond Quay, to which she had already substantially contributed, received an additional £1350. It was, however, the £20,000 left in trust for the erection and endowment of a college for the education of the Irish Presbyterian ministry which was to prove of lasting significance.

With a history of dispute between the governing body of the Presbyterian Church in Ireland and the Belfast Academical Institution, the general assembly had long desired the establishment of a theological training college over which they could exercise authority and control. While Mrs Magee's legacy brought the realization of that dream closer, it also brought to the surface differences of opinion over the location and design of the project. During a stormy and protracted controversy, which was finally settled by a chancery suit, a majority of the general assembly argued in favour of an exclusively theological college in Belfast, while Mrs Magee's trustees proposed to establish a complete college in Londonderry, with a full curriculum in both arts subjects and theology. In April 1851 chancery ruled that the trustees had full authority over the rules, regulation, discipline, and siting of the college, and that Mrs Magee had indeed intended a college for both literary and theological studies. Magee College was thus established as a college of arts and divinity, the foundation-stone being laid in Londonderry in 1856. Continuing differences between the trustees and the general assembly combined with financial difficulties to delay the opening of the college for a further nine years, but, aided by donations from two of the trustees and a grant from the Irish Society, Magee College was finally opened in October 1865. In 1881 its three theological professors were incorporated by royal charter with the seven professors in the assembly's college in Belfast, as the Presbyterian theological faculty, Ireland, with power to grant degrees in divinity. Magee College became part of the new University of Ulster in 1970.   MYRTLE HILL

Sources R. F. G. Holmes, *Magee, 1865–1965* (1965) · R. F. G. Holmes, *Our Presbyterian heritage* (1985) · J. S. Reid and W. D. Killen, *History of the Presbyterian church in Ireland*, new edn, 3 (1867), 493 · J. McConnell and others, eds., *Fasti of the Irish Presbyterian church, 1613–1840*, rev. S. G. McConnell, 2 vols. in 12 pts (1935–51) · C. H. Irwin, *A history of presbyterianism in Dublin and the south and west of Ireland* (1890), 141 · W. T. Latimer, *A history of the Irish Presbyterians*, 2nd edn (1902), 478 · J. L. Porter, *The life and times of Henry Cooke, D.D.*, [new edn] (1875), 400

Wealth at death £61,350: Holmes, *Magee*

Magee, William (1766–1831), Church of Ireland archbishop of Dublin and theologian, was born on 18 March 1766 near Enniskillen, co. Fermanagh, the third child of John Magee, farmer and linen merchant, and his wife, Jane, *née* Glasgow, a wealthy Presbyterian. Of Scottish origin, the Magee family had been settled in the area since 1640. John Magee had lost a leg while serving as a dragoon which necessitated his giving up farming. He then became a linen merchant, but he was a victim of fraud in his business, and was reduced to poverty. The Conyngham Plunket family were close neighbours and friends of the Magees, and Jane Magee acted on occasion as the wet-nurse of the infant William Conyngham Plunket, who was to become lord chancellor of Ireland and first Baron Plunket; he was to be William Magee's lifelong intimate friend. In spite of his family's reduced circumstances, Magee was educated from the age of five at local schools, firstly (and briefly) at that of a Dr Tew in Enniskillen, and then for a year and a half at the endowed classical school in the same city, where the headmaster was Dr Mark Noble. Further education preparatory to entering Trinity College, Dublin, was provided by his mother's half-brother Dr Daniel Viridet, the learned curate of Ballinrobe.

Magee entered Trinity College as a pensioner in July 1781. His tutor was the notable scholar Richard Stack, who was not on good terms with the provost, John Hely-Hutchinson; the latter did not approve the family's wish that Magee should study law, and in consequence he was directed to study for the church. In the event, this was to prove the beginning of Magee's brilliant career as a theologian, which was to bring him many honours during the thirty-one years he spent at Trinity. He was a scholar in 1784, and a gold medallist when he graduated BA in 1785, with highest distinction. Elected a fellow in 1788, he took his MA the following year. He was appointed Donnellan lecturer in 1795, 1798, and 1800, and in the latter year he was appointed senior fellow and professor of mathematics. Made DD in 1801, he was appointed Archbishop King's lecturer in divinity in 1808, and the following year he became regius professor of Greek. From 1790, when he was ordained deacon in the Church of Ireland in St Peter's, Drogheda (he was ordained priest the next year), Magee was very active in ecclesiastical affairs. That his

William Magee (1766–1831), by Henry Wyatt, exh. RA 1828

theological inclinations were evangelical was revealed in sermons preached between 1792 and 1796 for the Association for Discountenancing Vice and Promoting the Practice of Religion and Virtue.

Magee was very active in college affairs, but sought to avoid identification with either political or religious parties: he opposed the Act of Union, and was ambitious enough to be cautious about publishing his opinions. His first sermon after ordination, delivered in the college chapel on 20 May 1791, was on the subject of the Restoration. In it he strongly criticized Tom Paine and other revolutionary writers of his age, but though the sermon was much appreciated by his audience, it was not published. He did publish two sermons: one in thanksgiving for the deliverance of the nation from invasion (1797), the other a memorial sermon in praise of the life of Lord Clare, the lord chancellor of Ireland (1802). Magee's indifferent health also contributed to the paucity of his publications during his Trinity years. He suffered from a blood circulation disorder which caused him distress if he stooped. He worked standing up, held his head very erect on his small body, and consequently was viewed as a proud man by many, and by his critics as a 'turkey-cock': his lively and playful wit, and other conversational powers ensured that he had his critics. Among the students, however, he was immensely popular when he was junior dean, in spite of his vigorous attempts to discipline them when, for example, they joined in forays of the protestant weavers in the Liberties when they clashed with the Catholic butchers of Ormond Quay. In 1793 he was allowed to keep his fellowship, despite in April marrying Elizabeth Moulson (d. 1825) of Warrington, a member of an old, well-to-do Cheshire family, and niece of the prominent Manchester physician Thomas Perceval. Intelligent, and as ambitious as her husband, Magee's wife was to be a source of great support to him for thirty-six years, during which time she was the mother of sixteen children.

Magee's health problems and his immersion in college affairs ensured that he did not publish his Donnellan lectures on prophecy, but the writings of prominent Socinians, whom he thought presumptuous and ill informed, persuaded him to produce a major theological work in 1801. This was his monumental *Discourse on the Scriptural Doctrines of Atonement and Sacrifice*, based on sermons he had delivered in Trinity College chapel on successive Good Fridays in 1798 and 1799. The work was polemical, immensely erudite, and was directed against what Magee considered were the misguided opinions of Unitarian divines like Joseph Priestley and Thomas Belsham. By the time that the prominent Unitarian theologian Lant Carpenter made a substantial criticism of Magee's work in 1820, it was considered to be a strong defence of orthodoxy. Magee added material to the work, and it went through many editions. In spite of its early popularity, however, Magee's work on the atonement was, by the end of the twentieth century, considered of only antiquarian interest.

This work, which originally appeared in two volumes, brought Magee to scholarly notice in England, as he and W. C. Plunket discovered during a visit to Oxford in 1803. By 1811 the prime minister, Spencer Perceval, was rumoured to be considering appointing this learned Irish theologian to the English see of Oxford when it became vacant. Magee's would have been an unprecedented appointment, complicated further by the opinion of the chief secretary in Ireland, Robert Peel, that the gifted scholar was politically suspect. Magee steadfastly supported his friend Plunket in his campaign to represent Dublin in parliament, though Magee did not support Catholic emancipation, while Plunket was earning a reputation as one of the chief promoters of the measure. By 1812 Magee had concluded that to obtain ecclesiastical preferment he would have to resign his fellowship and move outside the university. In that year he accepted two college livings, the rectories of Cappagh in the diocese of Derry, and Killyleagh in the diocese of Down. His popularity among the students was such that when he left Trinity he received addresses and presentation gifts from the scholars and the college historical society.

Magee's continuing friendship with Plunket still held up preferment, and it was not until 1814 that he became dean of Cork. There he remained for five years in the midst of dissension with the Roman Catholics over local burial customs. His work on the atonement had impressed Princess Charlotte of Wales, however, and in 1819 he was made bishop of Raphoe with royal approval. There he threw himself into the task of improving discipline in a long-neglected diocese. His first visitation charge, which was published in 1821, contained criticism of those clergymen who identified themselves too closely with the

county gentry, and neglected the order of service in the Book of Common Prayer. When he preached before George IV on the second Sunday of the monarch's visit to Dublin in August 1821, the king was so impressed by Magee's sermon entitled 'What must I do to be saved' that he stood up in his pew the better to hear Magee. In 1821 Magee was made dean of the viceregal chapel in Dublin Castle, and when in the following year Lord John George Beresford was translated to Armagh to be primate, Magee succeeded him in Dublin. There he found affairs to be even more chaotic than in Raphoe. Beresford had shown little reforming zeal during his two-year stay in Dublin, and his predecessor, Euseby Cleaver, had been insane for many years.

As a diocesan bishop, Magee was found by some of his clergy to be vain, arrogant, and combative: one of his first actions was to inhibit a clergyman of deist sympathies, Robert Taylor, from preaching at Rathfarnham. Magee's love of controversy was shown clearly by his startling first charge of 1822. He indicated strongly his wish that clergy were to reside in their parishes, and he criticized both clergy and laity who wandered to fashionable churches. He described the Church of Ireland clergy as the true parish priests in the nation, and dismissed the authority of the Roman Catholic prelates who served 'a church without a religion', blindly enslaved to a supposedly infallible ecclesiastical power which ignored the word of God. He also had harsh things to say about the nonconformists, but they were used to Anglican arrogance and largely ignored his polemic. The uproar among the Roman Catholic prelates was immense, however, and furious broadsides against Magee's declaration of religious war were produced by Patrick Curtis, archbishop of Armagh, James Doyle, bishop of Kildare and Leighlin, and Professor John MacHale of Maynooth, among many others. A period of intense sectarian controversy had begun. When Magee gave evidence to a committee of the House of Lords on the state of Ireland in 1825, he proudly described the religious controversies of the time as a representative of a 'second Reformation'.

Daniel O'Connell and others talked of Magee's arrogance, his sacerdotal pride, and his vanity, but in his own eyes Magee was a sober-minded, establishment prelate, intent on defending the spiritual justification of the Church of Ireland. The protestant established church in Ireland was much more than the public utility arguments of William Warburton and William Paley had suggested. Magee took for granted that not only was the protestant religious ascendancy in Ireland inviolable, but that it had the blessing of the Almighty. His 'high' church ideas were presented to his clergy in his triennial charge to the Dublin archdiocese in October 1826, and in the religious controversies which he supported. He strongly opposed Maynooth College, encouraged the distribution of the scriptures, suggested that Bishop James Doyle, who was a Gallican in theology, nevertheless gave his authority to the see of Rome, and at every opportunity Magee helped to increase sectarian animosities in his archdiocese.

Roman Catholic fury was intense when he was accused of forbidding any but Church of Ireland rites from being used in established church graveyards. In 1827 Magee led a deputation of protestant prelates to meet with George IV to express Irish protestant opposition to Catholic emancipation.

Until his wife died on 27 September 1825, Magee was a diligent bishop, noted for the energy with which he tried to put an end to ecclesiastical laxity in the Dublin archdiocese. He had always loved exactness and good order in administration, and he did much to tidy up the ramshackle affairs he had inherited from his episcopal predecessors. His zeal flagged with the death of his wife, however, and by 1829 it was noted that he was being afflicted by small strokes. Despite some contemporary reports, there was no evidence of mental impairment in his later years. He died at the age of sixty-five, on 18 August 1831, at Redesdale House, Stillorgan, near Dublin. His private funeral was attended only by members of his own and the Plunket family, and one clerical friend, and preceded his burial in Rathfarnham old churchyard. One of his grandsons, William Connor *Magee, became archbishop of York in 1891.   DESMOND BOWEN

Sources J. D'Alton, *The memoirs of the archbishops of Dublin* (1838) • A. H. Kenney, *Works of William Magee, archbishop of Dublin, with a memoir of his life*, 2 vols. (1842) • J. Wills, *Lives of illustrious and distinguished Irishmen*, 4/2 (1847), 353–409 • *DNB*
Likenesses H. Wyatt, oils, exh. RA 1828, TCD [*see illus.*] • T. Kirk, marble bust, exh. 1840, TCD • H. D. Hamilton, oils, deanery, Cork • portrait, Archbishopric of Dublin, Dublin
Wealth at death £58,000: J. B. Leslie, *Succession lists of the archbishops of Dublin*, Representative Church Library, Dublin, 45

Magee, William Connor (1821–1891), archbishop of York, was the eldest son of John Magee (*d.* 1837), librarian of the Cork Cathedral Library and curate of the parish, later vicar of Drogheda, prebendary of Raphoe (1825–9), and treasurer of St Patrick's, Dublin (1831–7). His mother, Marianne, daughter of the Revd John Ker, was from a Scottish family. William *Magee, archbishop of Dublin, was his grandfather. He was born in the apartments adjoining the library of Cork Cathedral on 18 December 1821. From childhood he received from his parents religious teaching of a fervent but narrow evangelical type. In 1832 he was sent to the classical school of Kilkenny, and in 1835, when only thirteen, he entered Trinity College, Dublin. He won a classical scholarship there in 1838, and graduated BA in 1842, and MA and BD in 1854. Although he won Archbishop King's divinity prize in 1841, and showed in the examination an exceptional knowledge of theology, he chiefly devoted himself to desultory reading. To his contemporaries he was best known as a ready debater. He successfully agitated for the re-establishment of the Historical Society—an institution analogous to the Oxford Union—in Trinity College, and, becoming the first president, delivered an opening address which gave promise of his future eminence as an orator. At one period he thought of entering the medical profession, and actually walked the wards of a hospital, but decided to join the

William Connor Magee (1821–1891), by James Russell & Sons

ministry. He accordingly took deacon's orders in Advent 1844, and priest's orders in the following year.

After two years' hard work (1844–6) as curate of St Thomas's, a populous Dublin parish, Magee was attacked by a throat ailment, which compelled him to give up work and winter in the south of Spain. He spent two winters (1846–7) at Malaga, and the intervening summer at Ronda. Seville and Granada were visited, and he studied the Spanish language and literature. On his return home in 1848 he accepted the curacy of St Saviour's, Bath, and in 1850 became joint minister, and soon sole incumbent, of the Octagon, a proprietary chapel in Bath. He remained in that capacity for ten years. In August 1851 he married Ann Nisbitt (*d.* 5 May 1901), second daughter of Charles Smith, rector of Arklow. In 1859 he was made an honorary canon of Wells. At Bath his reputation for eloquence and common sense had grown steadily. In May 1860 he was appointed perpetual curate of Quebec Chapel in London. He preached his first sermon there on 7 October. A month later he was instituted to the Trinity College living of Enniskillen. His association with Quebec Chapel ended in March 1861. The large and populous parish of Enniskillen involved Magee in controversies, particularly concerning his support for bringing parochial schools under the national board of education in order to benefit from government grants—at the cost, his critics alleged, of sacrificing the principle of denominational education.

Meanwhile Magee's sermons had attracted general attention in London. In 1860 he preached at Whitehall

Chapel an ordination sermon, which was later published as *The Gospel and the Age* (1884). In 1861 he issued a lecture, *The Voluntary System and the Established Church* (three editions), and was widely acknowledged as a singularly able champion of the establishment; his advocacy of it led to the formation of some church defence societies. In 1860 his university conferred on him the degree of DD, unsolicited and without fees. The earl of Carlisle, while lord lieutenant of Ireland, after two ineffectual attempts to induce the prime minister to give Magee a bishopric in Ireland, promoted him in 1864 to the deanery of Cork, which had been held by his grandfather forty years before. At Cork he took up his residence close to the house in which he had been born, and commenced the building of a new cathedral. In 1865 he was elected Donnellan lecturer at Trinity College. A year later he was also appointed dean of the Chapel Royal, Dublin, and divided his time between the deaneries of Cork and Dublin. The church congress was held in Dublin in 1868, and Magee's opening sermon in St Patrick's Cathedral, on the 'breaking net', rallying the Church of Ireland in the face of the threat of disestablishment, was one of his greatest successes in the pulpit. In the same year he preached before the British Association at Norwich on the Christian theory of the origin of the Christian life, and a few months later he was promoted, on Disraeli's recommendation, to the see of Peterborough. He was consecrated at Whitehall Chapel on 15 November 1868.

On 15 June 1869 Magee made a celebrated speech in the House of Lords in opposition to the second reading of the bill for the disestablishment of the Irish church. He condemned the bill as unjust, impolitic, and against the verdict of the nation. The effort, which was loudly applauded, placed his fame as a parliamentary orator as high as his reputation as a preacher. Lord Salisbury stated publicly that he had heard from the greatest authorities that they considered it the finest speech ever delivered by any living man in either house of parliament (even so, the Lords eventually agreed to pass the bill). Although Magee was an active member of convocation, he intervened only at intervals in parliamentary debates, but always with effect. This was especially the case when he opposed the Licensing Bill of 1872, though the bill was in fact carried. When in 1876 Lord Shaftesbury was appealing for episcopal support for legislation to prohibit the practice of vivisection, Magee, with characteristic readiness, explained his inability to lend his support in an unpremeditated speech of forty minutes' duration, in which he made effective use of his early study of medicine. He completely carried his hearers with him, although he offended the extreme opponents of vivisection. Two measures which he introduced into the House of Lords he was not destined to see become law. One was for the regulation of church patronage, which, after some irritating experiences in his own diocese, he especially wished to see reformed. The other, which he introduced a few months before his death, was for protecting infant life by regulating infant insurance. He also supported the removal of abuses in the church (attacking pew owners in

1886), viewing church reform as an essential element of church defence.

Magee ruled the diocese of Peterborough wisely and vigorously, and although his strong hand occasionally provoked opposition and jealousy, his efficiency was appreciated by both clergy and laity. He still preached with all his former spirit, and from 1880 to 1882 was select preacher in the University of Oxford. He received the honorary degree of DCL at Oxford in 1870, and presided over the church congress at Leicester in 1880. A serious illness in 1883 evoked wide sympathy.

In January 1891 Magee was appointed to succeed Dr William Thomson as archbishop of York. He was enthroned in York Minster on 17 March, and was the first archbishop of York to summon the laity to attend his convocation. He died on 5 May 1891 at a hotel in Suffolk Street, Pall Mall, London, while visiting the capital to attend a committee of the House of Lords on his Infant Insurance Bill. He was buried on 9 May in the burial-ground of Peterborough Cathedral. His wife, with three sons and three daughters, survived him. Two elder children died young.

Magee was one of the greatest orators and most brilliant controversialists of his day. In his oratory, clearness and terseness of expression were accompanied by withering power of sarcasm, much logical reasoning, and humorous illustration. His full-toned voice was capable of sounding every gradation of feeling. In private society he rated in the first rank of conversationalists. Although his religious views were always of an evangelical tone, they broadened considerably in later years. In 1869 he agreed with the protest of some bishops against the consecration of the liberal theologian Frederick Temple as bishop of Exeter. In a sermon of December 1885 Magee accepted evolution. Although he supported the Public Worship Regulation Act of 1874, he later viewed prosecutions of ritualists with disfavour. All fanatical excesses in religion were abhorrent to him. He had little sympathy with the eccentricities of teetotal fanatics and other social reformers, and some remarks in his later speeches that he would rather see England free than sober, and that under certain circumstances betting was not wholly sinful, led to much misconception, but were fully consistent with his hatred of exaggeration and misapplied enthusiasm.

Magee published many sermons and other addresses and speeches. In 1887 he contributed to the series Helps to Belief a volume on the atonement. Selections from his sermons and *Addresses and Speeches* appeared posthumously.

J. C. MACDONNELL, *rev.* IAN MACHIN

Sources J. C. MacDonnell, *The life and correspondence of William Connor Magee*, 2 vols. (1896) · *The Times* (6 May 1891), 5–6 · F. W. Farrar, *Contemporary Review*, 62 (1892), 534–6 · Boase, *Mod. Eng. biog.* · O. Chadwick, *The Victorian church*, 2 (1970) · G. I. T. Machin, *Politics and the churches in Great Britain, 1869 to 1921* (1987) · D. Nicholls, 'Archbishop Magee', *Church Quarterly Review*, 163 (1962), 338–45 · R. P. C. Hanson, 'William Connor Magee', *Hermathena*, 124 (1978), 42–55 · *CGPLA Eng. & Wales* (1891)
Archives CKS, letters to Edward Stanhope · LPL, corresp. with E. W. Benson · LPL, letters to A. C. Tait and related papers · U. Lpool L., letters to William Rathbone

Likenesses J. Watkins, marble bust, 1869, TCD · F. Holl, oils, 1885, Bishop's Palace, Peterborough; copy, 1891, Bishopthorpe Palace, York · C. J. Tomkins, mezzotint, pubd 1886 (after F. Holl), BM, NPG · Lock & Whitfield, woodburytype photograph, NPG; repro. in T. Cooper, *Men of mark: a gallery of contemporary portraits* (1877) · C. Pellegrini, watercolour, NPG; repro. in *VF* (3 July 1869) · J. Robinson, carte-de-visite, NPG · J. Russell & Sons, photograph, NPG [*see illus.*] · J. & C. Watkins, carte-de-visite, NPG · chromolithograph, NPG · photograph, NPG

Wealth at death £21,905 7s. 6d.: probate, 5 Aug 1891, *CGPLA Eng. & Wales*

Magee, William Kirkpatrick [*pseud.* John Eglinton] (1868–1961), writer, was born on 16 January 1868 at 41 Eccles Street in north Dublin, the second of three sons and two daughters of the Revd Hamilton Magee (1824–1902) and his wife, Emily Clare, *née* Kirkpatrick (*d.* 1870). His father, a native of Belfast, after preaching to the famine-stricken peasants in Connaught, was sent by the synod of the Presbyterian church in 1852 to superintend the 'Irish mission' for the conversion of Catholics in Dublin. His wife was the daughter of William Kirkpatrick, the senior Presbyterian minister in the city, so W. K. Magee was descended from protestant clergymen on both sides of the family.

At school in Harcourt Street, Magee sat next to W. B. Yeats, cribbed Euclid from him, and was able to compensate the poet by affording him a glance of his own correct translation of Demosthenes. Yeats introduced his schoolfellows to a book that was to lead Magee and his brothers to a half-way house between their father's evangelical protestantism and outright agnosticism: A. P. Sinnett's *Esoteric Buddhism*: 'I read it, and I believed!' Magee recalled (J. Eglinton, *Irish Literary Portraits*, 1935, 43). Thereafter he became a disciple, if a wayward one, of 'AE' (George Russell) in the Dublin Theosophical Society. In 1887 Magee entered Trinity College, Dublin, where he won the vice-chancellor's prizes for verse in 1889 and 1890, and for prose in 1892 and 1893, prizes judged by Professor Edward Dowden (1843–1913). Magee spent some time picking up German in Göttingen, with his theosophist friend and fellow poet Charles Weekes. After some years of unemployment, and employment as a schoolteacher in Drogheda, Magee was helped to a post at the National Library of Ireland by Dowden, one of its trustees. Magee's early ambition to be a poet soon faltered in the face of Yeats's success. Their friend Charles Weekes set up a press to bring out the first books of AE and John Eglinton, an Anglophile's pen-name taken from the name of the street on which Magee's parents lived in Kingstown. Magee's *Two Essays on the Remnant* (1894) readjusted his father's notions in the light of Wordsworth, Emerson, and Dowden: the 'Chosen People' or remnant, became not Jews or Ulster Presbyterians, but young Magee's 'brethren in unemployment', the last genteel Romantics who would withdraw to the suburban woods rather than accept the professions on offer in the city, with its Darwinian struggle for survival (*Two Essays*, 4).

In autumn 1898 Magee parted company with Yeats and Irish cultural nationalism in a newspaper controversy over the Irish Literary Theatre (republished as *Ideals in Ireland* in 1901). Ancient Irish myths, Irish folklore, or literature in the Irish language could never for Magee be the proper basis for a great literature, but they could turn out to be a dangerous basis for a political separatist movement, one that would extirpate the conditions that gave life to such as him. In *Pebbles from a Brook* (1901), he began to project as the ideal 'the Modern Irishman', by which he meant the university-educated, agnostic-protestant, Anglo-Irish citizen of Europe and a sublimated British empire. Nations he hoped would soon pass away, and leave only individuals behind.

In February 1900 Magee met George Moore, who described him as:

> a thin small man with dark red hair growing stiffly over a small skull … the face somewhat shrivelled and thickly freckled. A gnarled, solitary life, I said, lived out in all the discomforts inherent in a bachelor's lodging, a sort of lonely thorn-tree. (Moore, *Ave*, 124)

(The bachelor lodging was an old coach inn at 5 Cadogan Road where the Tolka flows into Dublin Bay.) At this time, his work at the National Library brought him into contact with the others who would distinguish Irish literature in the period—Oliver St John Gogarty, John M. Synge, and James Joyce. The publication of *Ulysses* (especially chapter nine) twenty years later was sharply to recall to the librarian conversations he had had with the young University College graduate about the Shakespeare–Bacon controversy; Magee was then surprised at 'the half-kindly and painstaking exactness' with which Joyce 'mitigates his cruelty' about 'John sturdy Eglinton' 'ugling Eglinton' 'Steadfast John' and '*Eglintonus Chronololologos*' (Joyce, *Ulysses*, 193–5). In early 1904 Magee had rejected for publication a first draft of *Portrait of the Artist as a Young Man* in *Dana*, a monthly he co-edited with the socialist Fred Ryan from 1904 to 1905.

The stated aim of *Dana* was to open up for discussion ethnic and political issues that had been buried under 'an artificial and sentimental unity' by the cultural nationalists. Moore hoped *Dana* would be simply 'an anti-clerical journal'; 'Fleet Street atheism' was Yeats's dismissal; 'an amusing disguise of the proselytizing spirit', Joyce suspected (*Letters … to Ed. Dujardin*, 49; J. Eglinton, *Irish Literary Portraits*, 1935, 135). Magee published a selection of his own contributions to *Dana* in *Bards and Saints* (1906), including 'The de-Davisation of Irish literature', an argument that the writer should not aim consciously to express, much less exalt, nationality (J. Eglinton, *Bards and Saints*, 1906, 39–43). He also needled the Gaelic League by saying, truly enough, 'The "Irish" language is indeed a title of courtesy: the ancient language of the Celt is no longer the language of Irish nationality. And in fact it never was' (ibid., 13). The real problem with Gaelic literature, he judged (suavely begging the question), was that the Catholic Irish had rejected Bishop Bedell's 1685 translation of the Bible into Gaelic, and thus missed out on that fructifying effect the King James version had had on English literature. Instead, the Irish had to put up with eighteenth-century bards, idlers and bullies for the most part, who wrote only self-serving songs of praise to their hosts.

On his holidays from the National Library, Magee often travelled to Wales and the Lake District, or to Paris, Germany, and Greece (he was fluent in French and German, and well trained in Greek and Latin). In 1913 Magee was considered in place of, or in tandem with W. B. Yeats, for the chair of Edward Dowden at Trinity College; the post went, however, to a more appropriate and ultimately unimportant scholar. Always retentive of his own ideas, Magee became still more costive from 1910 to 1921, although he published *Anglo-Irish Essays* in 1917, to remind 'Irish Ireland' that the protestant descendant of the English settlers 'is still there', though now as a tolerant, melancholy, sceptical 'good European' (J. Eglinton, *Anglo-Irish Essays*, 1917, 3–4). Irish resistance to conscription during the First World War he found 'extraordinary and disconcerting' but, looking over the wreckage of O'Connell Street after the Easter 1916 rising, he was forced to acknowledge that the 'old Catholic population' now held the title deeds to Irish nationality (Eglinton, *An Englishman Talks It Out*, 3–4). From 1919 to 1920, living a tram journey outside wartorn Dublin at 1 Lakelands Park, Terenure, he continued to make a protestant case for inclusive and European conceptions of citizenship in the *Irish Statesman* (edited by George Russell).

In March 1921 Magee began to contribute the 'Dublin letter' to the American *Dial* (T. S. Eliot and Ezra Pound wrote the London and Paris letters). Along with Ernest Boyd's *Ireland's Literary Renaissance* (1916), the *Dial* letters of Magee (1921–9) make up the first serious critical assessment of twentieth-century Irish writers. His commentary on the 'Irish Renascence' insisted on the necessity of biographical and ethnic knowledge to an understanding of literature. Indeed, for Magee in contradistinction to the formalism of Eliot, 'the vitality of a literary work is in proportion to the interest it excites in the author' (*Dial*, August 1926, 91). To gain time to write, and weary of answering inquiries from library patrons, Magee took advantage of the Anglo-Irish treaty (1921) by which the British offered early pensions to those civil servants not wishing to continue employment under the free state. On 31 January 1921 he 'stepped into freedom "with a sigh"' (J. Eglinton, *Confidential, or, Take It or Leave It*, 1951, 6).

Magee's departure from the library may also have had something to do with a great change he had made in his personal life. After her conversion to protestantism, he had married an assistant at the library, Marie Louise O'Leary, on 6 April 1920. The two stayed on into the civil war until 'the ancient archives of Dublin' in the Four Courts were blown up in June 1922—an event he compared with the publication of *Ulysses* as 'conflagrations of pious illusions of provincial and Catholic Ireland' (*Dial*, August 1923, 180; October 1923, 435). The couple moved in late 1923 to a house by the sea in Prestatyn, north Wales, where they had a boy, their only child; and south to Bournemouth in 1929, where Magee remained until his death, brooding over the literary evidence of the turbulence that drove him from Ireland.

In the 1920s, Magee continued an extensive correspondence with George Moore who from 1911 sought advice from Magee on the proofs of all his books. The much admired correctness of Moore's late style owes a good deal to the former Trinity College prizeman. In recompense, Moore found literary projects for Magee: a two-volume edition of Landor, a translation of Homer into the style of Moore's *Brook Kerith*, both unpublished. A few of Moore's proposals, however, did pay off, such as Magee's translation of *George Moore's Letters to Ed. Dujarin* (1929) and the selection of *Dial* essays published as *Irish Literary Portraits* (1935). Magee habitually professed a reluctance to write or, having written, to publish. Moore pictured Magee as the years went by sinking deeper and deeper into his armchair, while he rearranged and dusted his favourite ideas, 'conscious of their familiar presences' but undesirous of writing them out, and out of politeness hiding his contempt for the literary activities of his friends (Moore, *Vale*, 177).

In 1929 Magee shied away from Moore's pleas to become his literary executor, much less his biographer; he also turned down an offer to ghost-write a biography of Synge with Synge's uncle. Magee did, however, accept the commission from Macmillan for *A Memoir of AE: George William Russell* (1937), less a documentary biography than a personal estimate of his old friend, whose poetry, politics, and mystical philosophy, Magee confessed, awoke in him more doubt than admiration. Indeed, the value of Magee as a critic is not just in his vividly etched memories of men he knew, or in the insight he offers into the sectarian energies of Irish literature, but in an intelligence heightened by *ressentiment*. One who confessed himself a failure in the preface to his privately issued booklet of poems (1951) uses world standards to assess the successes of his friends: Yeats did not write out of his 'best self', and was 'more eidolon than man'; the general impression left by Moore's late fiction was 'one of monotony'; Joyce's *Portrait* was 'pompous and self-conscious' in style—'he is a man of one book', *Ulysses*; and the whole work of the 'so-called Irish Literary Renaissance' is 'non-canonical' (that is, it should not be admitted to the British canon) (J. Eglinton, *Irish Literary Portraits*, 46, 97, 142, 149; J. Eglinton, *Dial*, May 1921, 332).

Yet Magee could be profound as well as severe in his appreciation, and he never allowed a badly constructed sentence to leave his desk. Even without a coherent body of convictions, or a talent for invention, Magee wrote periodical essays that count as literature. After 1950 his hand became very shaky as a result of an accident in which he was knocked down by a bicycle, fracturing his wrist. Notwithstanding, up to 1956, the ageing exile continued to send off from Bournemouth his occasional 5-guinea articles to the *Dublin Magazine*, all composed in his 'gaunt, gnarled, masculine prose', and many of them sympathetic second thoughts about the work of friends that he had more strictly judged on earlier occasions (G. Moore, 'An Irish essayist', *The Observer*, 4 Nov 1917, 3). The conscience, in the case of Magee, was a highly developed faculty. In 1952 he was awarded an honorary degree by Trinity

College. He died of cancer on 9 May 1961 at 36 St Catherine's Road, Southbourne, Bournemouth, a writer of the Irish literary revival who lived to tell its story.

ADRIAN FRAZIER

Sources M. Bryson, 'Dublin letters: John Eglinton and *The Dial*', *Éire-Ireland*, 29/4 (1994), 132–47 · H. Magee, *Fifty years in 'The Irish mission'* (1905?) · R. Ellmann, *James Joyce*, rev. edn (1982) · R. F. Foster, *The apprentice mage, 1865–1914* (1997), vol. 1 of *W. B. Yeats: a life* · *The collected letters of W. B. Yeats*, 2, ed. W. Gould, J. Kelly, and D. Toomey (1997) · R. Hogan, ed., *Dictionary of Irish literature*, rev. edn, 2 vols. (1996) · A. Mac Lochlainn, '"Those young men …": the National Library and the cultural revolution', in A. Mac Lochlainn and A. S. Skeffington, *Writers, raconteurs and notable feminists: two monographs* (1993) · *Dublin University Calendar* (1888–94) · G. Moore, letters to W. K. Magee, Ransom HRC · *Letters of George Moore*, ed. J. Eglinton (1942) · *Letters from George Moore to Ed. Dujardin, 1886–1922*, ed. and trans. J. Eglinton (1929) · G. Moore, *Ave* (1937) · G. Moore, *Vale* (1937) · J. Eglinton [W. K. Magee], 'Preface', in A. R. Orage, *An Englishman talks it out with an Irishman* (1918) · E. Boyd, *Ireland's literary renaissance* (1916) · J. Eglinton [W. K. Magee], letters to J. Starkey, TCD, O'Sullivan corr., MSS 4630–4649 · *Report of the Council of Trustees for the National Library of Ireland* (1900) · *Report of the Council of Trustees for the National Library of Ireland* (1916) · *Report of the Council of Trustees for the National Library of Ireland* (1918–23) · E. Boyd, *Appreciations and depreciations* (1917) · D. S. Lenoski, 'Yeats, Eglinton, and aestheticism', *Éire-Ireland*, 14/4 (1979), 91–108 · V. Mercier, 'John Eglinton as Socrates: a study of "Scylla and Charybdis"', *James Joyce: an international perspective* (1982)

Archives Ransom HRC, archives, MSS | TCD, O'Sullivan corresp. · University of British Columbia Library, notebooks | SOUND Radio Telefís Éireann, Dublin

Likenesses J. B. Yeats, pencil drawings, 1901, NG Ire. · J. B. Yeats, pencil drawing, 1905, priv. coll.; repro. in Mac Lochlainn, '"Those young men"'

Wealth at death £18,332 2s. 6d.: probate, 14 Aug 1961, CGPLA Eng. & Wales

Magellan, Jean Hyacinthe de [*formerly* João Jacinto de Magalhães] (**1722–1790**), natural philosopher, was born at Aveiro, Portugal, on 4 November 1722, the son of Clemente de Magalhães Leitão and his wife, Joana Lourença Soares. He was baptized in Aveiro on 22 November as João Jacinto de Magalhães, the name by which he was always known in his native country. The family claimed descent from the navigator Ferdinand de Magellan and were connected to the powerful Castel-Branco family. Throughout his life Magellan drew part of his income from his family property in Aveiro.

In 1733 Magellan entered the Augustinian college of Santa Cruz, the Colégio da Sapiência, at Coimbra. A decade later he joined the Augustinian order as Brother João de Nossa Senhora do Desterro, and later became a canon. The convent had an excellent library that included the works of Newton as well as the classics, and during twenty years there Magellan cultivated a love of science. Eventually he became dissatisfied with convent life, and in 1754 he successfully petitioned Pope Benedict XIV for a letter of secularization. His aim was to improve his acquaintance with the literary, scientific, and industrial progress being made in other countries.

Magellan was in Lisbon during the great earthquake of 1755, and later undertook a 'philosophical tour' of Europe lasting several years. Paris became his first base. There he befriended the famous Portuguese physician António Nunes Ribeiro Sanches, who had been personal physician to the Russian empress Elizabeth. It was probably Sanches who put him in contact with leading French scientists. Sanches subsequently supported Magellan financially for many years, in return for Magellan's having performed a significant service at some risk during a visit to Lisbon.

In Paris, Magellan undertook translating work, including reports of cometary observations by the priest Jean Chevalier, then based in Lisbon, for Sanches' friends the astronomers J. N. de Lisle and Charles Messier, who in mid-1759 were watching for the return of Halley's comet. In 1760 Magellan prepared a version of Luiz de Sousa's life of St Bartholomew, a Dominican classic, and a translation into Portuguese of the Port-Royal Greek grammar. He returned to Lisbon, where his involvement in the religious upheavals led him to publish in 1763 a Portuguese translation of an anti-Jesuit tract. Life in Portugal was not to his liking and, after contemplating living in Italy or America, by late 1763, on Sanches' advice, he settled permanently in England.

In Paris and in Portugal, Magellan, despite his secularization, long continued to be referred to as 'abbé'. He is reported to have been arrested in England for saying mass, which was still a felony. In later life he enjoyed the free-thinking atmosphere of Parisian intellectual life that so scandalized his friend Priestley when they visited Paris together. There are indications that he remained a Roman Catholic even though he was buried in an Anglican churchyard. In 1783, only a few years before his death, he offered to endow a prize at the Lisbon Academy of Sciences using emoluments he had accrued as an abbé that he was still entitled to draw upon. And he was never banished, as happened to another Portuguese who settled in England and became a protestant.

Having arrived in London, Magellan gradually established a place for himself in scientific circles. He attended meetings of the Royal Society with great regularity as guest of one or other of the fellows, and submitted papers that were read there. The most substantial was one read in 1765, in which he described a baro-thermometer that he had invented; but problems arose out of Magellan's prolixity combined with his poor command of English grammar, and the paper was not published. Less ambitious reports, including astronomical observations sent by his friends in Paris and an account of a collection of Roman coins presented to the society's museum on Sanches' behalf, fared better, though most remained unpublished. Magellan helped the society's curator, Emanuel Mendes da Costa, build a collection of Portuguese 'natural productions' for the museum, and was an enthusiastic observer of John Canton's controversial experiments on the compressibility of water, for which Canton received the Copley medal.

Magellan is reported to have added to his income by acting as travelling companion to young gentlemen visiting France and Flanders. He visited both countries regularly, and in 1769 he took to Paris one of Dollond's new achromatic telescopes, which was much admired by the astronomers there. Johann III Bernoulli, who met Magellan in London that year, found him 'well versed in chemistry, experimental physics and practical astronomy', and noted his willingness to take on scientific commissions for continental savants. In 1774 he was elected a fellow of the Royal Society; Franklin, Priestley, Banks, and Solander were among those who signed his nomination certificate.

The commissions to which Bernoulli referred and the associated correspondence became the central feature of Magellan's life. His correspondents were scattered all over Europe and included a number of the leading scientists and most of the leading scientific institutions of the day. His letters carried news abroad of the latest in British science and technology during the early stages of the industrial revolution, when London's scientific instrument makers led the world. Magellan received requests, which he made it his business to satisfy, for books, instruments, and industrial machinery. In the case of the machine invented by James Watt for making wet-press file copies of handwritten documents, Magellan had a formal contract to supply machines to the continental market. In other cases the financial arrangements were more discreet but doubtless saw him rewarded by commissions from suppliers. 'By making himself correspondent of all the savants', wrote the journalist J. P. Brissot, who knew him, 'he achieved a cherished and honourable independence'. At the same time, Magellan satisfied his own genuine commitment to improving the conditions of people's lives by widely disseminating the fruits of scientific advance. His correspondents valued the connection. As early as 1771 he was elected a corresponding member of the Académie Royale des Sciences, Paris. The St Petersburg Academy followed suit in 1778 and later granted him an annual pension of 200 roubles, and he was also elected to the academies in Lisbon, Berlin, and Madrid, and to several other scientific societies in Europe and North America. He was offered, but declined, resident membership of the Imperial Academy of Sciences in Brussels at its foundation in 1773, forgoing the large salary involved because he preferred the freedom of life in England; in 1785 he was elected a non-resident member.

Some of the commissions Magellan took on were very substantial. Volta, who on being appointed to the chair of physics at Pavia was given an almost unlimited budget for new apparatus, ordered a large number of items through him, some of which were extremely expensive. So too did universities such as those of Louvain and Coimbra when reform-minded rulers allocated funds to enhance the teaching of physics. In 1778 Magellan supplied identical sets of expensive astronomical apparatus to the governments of Spain and Portugal, to be used in fixing the disputed boundary between the Spanish and Portuguese territories in South America, and he supplied other English-made instruments to the Spanish naval observatory at Cadiz, including many ordered for the Spanish round the

world expedition under Malaspinas (1789–94). These included instruments by Jesse Ramsden.

Magellan's links with Paris were particularly close. His official correspondent at the Académie Royale des Sciences was Bory, but he also communicated directly with Messier, Macquer, Lavoisier, and Condorcet. Above all, he maintained regular links for many years with Trudaine de Montigny, an honorary member of the academy, who, as France's *intendant des finances*, kept a watchful eye on British industrial innovation. Magellan sent him the latest news and publications; once, despite a British export embargo, he tried to smuggle a new kind of loom across the channel, and was lucky not to be arrested. In the early 1780s he used his contacts to secure exclusive rights in France for the new steam engines being built by Boulton and Watt at their Birmingham works. On at least two occasions he played a crucial role in transmitting news of important British scientific discoveries to France. In several communications in 1771 and early 1772 he drew to the attention of French chemists recent British work on gases, especially that of Priestley, and succeeded thereby in prompting Lavoisier's epoch-making research. His *Essai sur la nouvelle théorie du feu élémentaire*, published in London in 1780, provided the French with their first systematic account of the ideas on specific and latent heat of Black, Irvine, and Crawford—Magellan coined the term 'specific heat'—which inspired Lavoisier and Laplace to undertake their famous experiments on this subject. His new edition of Cronstedt's *Mineralogy* (1788) helped the flow of ideas in the opposite direction because, even though the text retained the old language of the phlogiston theory, in his notes Magellan presented Lavoisier's ideas on combustion and calcination.

In addition to his activities in spreading knowledge, Magellan devised sundry improvements to various mathematical and scientific instruments, including sextants and octants, barometers, thermometers, eudiometers, and pendulum clocks. These he described in articles in Rozier's journal and in a series of tracts that were published in London but written in French, and thus clearly aimed at an international market. Some of Magellan's proposals were incorporated by makers such as Ramsden and Nairne: for example, a sextant made by Ramsden according to Magellan's design was used by Captain Constantine Phipps during his unsuccessful Arctic expedition in 1773. Following the death in 1772 of his friend Gowin Knight, who had entrusted his secret to him, Magellan took over the contract for certifying magnetic compasses made for the Royal Navy by the instrument maker George Adams according to Knight's method.

Magellan was elected a member of the Society of Arts in 1770, and sometimes passed to his correspondents news of inventions described at the society's meetings. He was one of the most active members of the philosophical society that from 1780 met regularly at the Chapter Coffee House under the leadership of Richard Kirwan. He had close links with the Lunar Society in Birmingham, being on particularly friendly terms with Watt, Priestley, and the physician William Withering, and he was elected an honorary member of the Manchester Literary and Philosophical Society. In his last years Magellan's relationship with Watt apparently soured, possibly as a result of controversial evidence he gave in a case brought by François-Pierre Argand, with Watt's support, in defence of his patent over the revolutionary oil burner he had invented.

Magellan prospered: by the early 1780s he seems to have been employing several people on a fairly regular basis. Strongly in sympathy with the American colonists in their struggle for independence, he was elected a member of the American Philosophical Society in 1784 and a year later established a prize with an endowment of £200, the so-called Magellanic premium, for the best work each year in relation to navigation or astronomy. At about the same time he invested a large sum in a money-making scheme devised by the Hungarian adventurer Count Benyovsky, which was irretrievably lost when Benyovsky was killed while attempting to establish a kingdom of his own in Madagascar. Magellan's publication of Benyovsky's memoirs appeared in Paris in 1791.

A tall, heavy-set man, Magellan never married. Mild-mannered and plain of dress, liberal in his politics, he moved easily in the most elevated social circles both in England and abroad. From about 1780 he was subject to recurring bouts of eye pain, headaches, and frequent insomnia, which sometimes prevented him from working for months at a time. In mid-1789 he suffered a complete collapse, perhaps a stroke, from which he never recovered. He died at his home, 12 Nevils Court, Fetter Lane, London, on 7 February 1790, and was buried that month at Islington, London, 'handsomely, but privately', according to his wish, without any tombstone.

R. W. HOME

Sources I. Malaquias, 'A obra de João Jacinto de Magalhães no contexto da ciência do séc. XVIII', PhD diss., University of Aveiro, 1994 · L. Alte da Veiga and others, eds., *João Jacinto de Magalhães (John Hyacinth de Magellan): conference on physical sciences in the XVIII century, 7–10 November 1990* (Coimbra, [n.d.], 1994?]) · A. Birembaut, 'Sur les lettres du physicien Magellan conservées aux Archives Nationales', *Revue d'Histoire des Sciences*, 9 (1956), 150–61 · *GM*, 1st ser., 60 (1790), 184 · J. de Carvalho, 'Correspondência científica dirigida a João Jacinto de Magalhães', *Revista da Faculdade Ciências da Universidade de Coimbra*, 20 (1951), 93–283 · M. F. Thomaz, 'João Jacinto de Magalhães e la ciência europeia do século XVIII', *Colóquio: Ciências*, 3, 78–91 · J. Bernoulli, *Lettres astronomiques* (1771) · J. Brissot, *Mémoires, 1754–1793* (1911), 1. 363 · H. Guerlac, *Lavoisier: the crucial year* (1961) · D. Willemse, 'Suites d'un voyage aux Pays-Bas', *Arquivos do Centro Cultural Português*, 7 (1974), 225–78 · M. Lemos, *Amigos de Ribeiro Sanches* (1912), 43–68 · M. Schrøder, *The Argand burner: its origin and development in France and England, 1780–1800* (1968)
Archives Österreichische Nationalbibliothek, Vienna | Bodl. Oxf., Rigaud MSS · Universitätsbibliothek, Basel, corresp. with Johann III Bernoulli

Magennis, Arthur, third Viscount Magennis of Iveagh (1623/1626–1683), army officer, was the son and heir of Hugh Magennis, later second Viscount Magennis of Iveagh (1599–1639), and his wife, Mary (d. in or after 1641), the daughter of Sir John Bellew of Castletown, co. Louth. He was a minor, aged either thirteen or sixteen, at the time of his father's death in 1639 but, following representations by his kinsman the earl of Antrim, the government did not insist on asserting wardship on the grounds that 'the youth [Arthur Magennis] hath but little time to be in wardship and was soured already' (Ohlmeyer, 54). In other words he was too old to be a likely convert to protestantism. Iveagh's inheritance (some 44,800 acres), like the estates of most surviving native landowners in Ulster, was threatened by indebtedness; it was valued at £1200 per annum but a third of this was tied up in a jointure to his grandmother Viscountess Sara (née O'Neill, daughter of Hugh O'Neill, earl of Tyrone) and the rest was encumbered by a debt of £4500.

Iveagh was in Dublin when the 1641 rising broke out in October of that year. By the following February he had returned to south co. Down where he reportedly participated in the burning of Downpatrick. In April and May 1642 he led an army of some 2500 men in trying to halt the southward advance of Monro's newly arrived Scottish covenanter army. Monro subsequently captured Newry and the town and its hinterland remained in protestant hands throughout the 1640s.

Having been forced to leave Ulster, in November 1643 Iveagh was selected as a member of the supreme council, the standing executive of the confederate Catholic regime. As an inducement for French financial aid, the supreme council in 1644 agreed to permit a regiment of infantry to be raised in Ireland for the French service. In November Iveagh embarked at Galway as colonel of this regiment. He subsequently returned and served as colonel of an infantry regiment in Owen Roe O'Neill's army during the latter's campaign in Connaught in summer 1647. By then the confederate Catholics were beginning to sunder into Ormondist and clericalist factions, divided mainly by the religious guarantees in any proposed peace treaty with the royalists. O'Neill's Ulster army, too, split in May 1649. Those officers who owned land in Ulster before the war, including Iveagh, Alexander Mac Donnell, and Phelim O'Neill, sided with the Ormondist party against Owen O'Neill. Oliver Cromwell's lightning campaign in Ireland (September 1649–May 1650) forced an uneasy rapprochement and in March 1650 Iveagh formally acknowledged to the Catholic primate that he had 'sinned against natural, no less than human law' (O'Ferrall and O'Connell, 4.396). In return the primate lifted the sentence of excommunication laid on him for his adherence to the Ormondist party.

Although Iveagh was away from his regiment when it was attacked by Cromwell in October 1649 as part of the garrison defending Wexford, he remained for the dying days of the Catholic and royalist cause. He was a signatory to last minute reassertions of unity and appeals for foreign aid sent from Inishbofin (off the coast of Galway) in July and August 1652. In March 1653 he signed articles for the surrender of Belturbet (co. Cavan), making this along with nearby Cloughoughter (surrendered in April) the very last Irish strongholds to hold out. The conditions of surrender allowed him to recruit a regiment for service in the Spanish army. Some time after this he transported and, in 1660, was listed as captain-lieutenant (acting company commander) in the duke of Gloucester's regiment of infantry in Spanish Flanders.

Iveagh lost all his estates in the Cromwellian confiscations and after the Restoration these were not restored to him, despite the intervention of Charles II. Iveagh continued in the king's service abroad for a number of years, but about 1662 he was in prison in London, having been obliged to live on credit in England. Some time afterwards the king awarded him an estate of 1860 acres in Ballintober barony, co. Roscommon, and an annual pension of £150, subsequently raised to £500. This was £1600 in arrears and had fallen back to £300 p.a. at the time of his death in Dublin on 30 April 1683. He was buried on 1 May in St Catherine's Church and was survived by his wife, Margaret, daughter of Philip McHugh O'Reilly of co. Cavan, and four daughters, three of whom were married in 1688; his brother Hugh succeeded to the title. The Ballintober estate may have been sold before his death or shortly after; at any rate it is not included in the list of confiscated Jacobite estates dealt with by the Chichester House trustees after the Williamite wars (1689–91). On the other hand the estate may not have been confiscated, because while the eldest son and heir of his brother, Brian, Lord Iveagh, was an active Jacobite, he enlisted in the service of Austria (an ally of William III) rather than France after the war. PÁDRAIG LENIHAN

Sources H. O'Sullivan, 'The Magennis lordship of Iveagh in the early modern period, 1534 to 1691', *Down: history and society*, ed. L. Proudfoot (1997), 159–202 · J. H. Ohlmeyer, *Civil war and Restoration in the three Stuart kingdoms: the career of Randal MacDonnell, marquis of Antrim, 1609–1683* (1993) · B. O'Ferrall and D. O'Connell, *Commentarius Rinuccinianus de sedis apostolicae legatione ad foederatos Hiberniae Catholicos per annos 1645–1649*, ed. J. Kavanagh, 6 vols., IMC (1932–49), vol.3, pp. 161, 171, 177, 605, 678; vol. 4, p.396; vol. 5, pp. 49, 52, 54, 57, 77, 132 · GEC, *Peerage*

Magennis [*formerly* McGinnes], **James Joseph** (1919–1986), submariner, was born on 27 October 1919 at 4 Majorca Street, west Belfast, the second son and third of the five children of William McGinnes and his wife, Mary Jane Murphy. His father was a Scottish-born itinerant musician who soon abandoned his wife and children, leaving Mary to survive on a series of temporary sewing jobs. James attended St Finian's School, Falls Road, Belfast, until 1935, when he enlisted in the Royal Navy, at which point he adopted the surname Magennis. From 1936, as a first-class boy seaman and later ordinary seaman, he served on several warships before being posted to the destroyer HMS *Kandahar* in October 1939. In May 1940 he saw action in the North Sea when the sister-ship HMS *Kelly*, commanded by Lord Louis Mountbatten, was disabled by German torpedoes. He later served in the Mediterranean, and in December 1941, when *Kandahar* struck a mine and sank off Tripoli, he had to swim to safety.

In December 1942 Magennis was drafted into the Submarine Service, and in March 1943 volunteered for special service in X-class 'midget' submarines. He trained as a diver, and in September 1943 took part in the first major use of the X-craft. Two submarines penetrated Kaafjord,

north Norway, and disabled the German battleship *Tirpitz*. For his part Magennis was mentioned in dispatches.

In 1944 Magennis was promoted to leading seaman and began training on a new class of XE submarines designed for use in tropical waters. Early in 1945 his unit was sent out to Australia and trained to cut enemy undersea telegraph cables. In July 1945 they were deployed to attack two Japanese cruisers, *Myoko* and *Takao*, moored in the Johore Strait. Magennis's submarine, XE3, was given the *Takao* as target, and on 31 July Magennis attached limpet mines to the vessel under particularly difficult circumstances. He first had to squeeze through a partly open diving hatch directly below the target and then, handicapped by leaking breathing apparatus, scrape barnacles from the surface of the ship. Having returned exhausted to the submarine he volunteered to go outside again to release a limpet mine carrier that had failed to jettison correctly. For their part in the operation Magennis and the commander of the submarine, Lieutenant Ian Fraser, were each awarded the Victoria Cross.

Magennis's award led to a period of great celebrity just after the war, but the ultimately shabby way in which he, Northern Ireland's only holder of the VC in the Second World War, was treated by his home city formed a painful coda to his story. Although he was given a civic reception in December 1945 and the £3000 proceeds of a public subscription, the Belfast city fathers, perhaps believing that such an honour could not be bestowed on a working-class Catholic from the inner-city slums, refused to grant him the freedom of the city. In 1946 Magennis married Edna Skidmore, with whom he had four sons. He left the navy in 1949 and returned to Belfast, where he found it hard to make a living and at some point sold his Victoria Cross. In 1955 he moved to Yorkshire, where he worked as an electrician. His final years were marred by chronic ill health, and on 11 February 1986 he died of lung cancer in the Royal Halifax Infirmary.

Magennis was commemorated by a memorial in his adopted home of Bradford. In October 1999, following a lengthy local campaign, a 6 foot-high Portland stone and bronze memorial to him was unveiled in the grounds of Belfast city hall. KEITH JEFFERY

Sources G. Fleming, *Magennis VC* (Dublin, 1998) · R. Doherty and D. Truesdale, *Irish winners of the Victoria Cross* (2000) · *The Times* (9 Oct 1999) · b. cert. · d. cert.
Likenesses photographs, repro. in Fleming, *Magennis VC*

Magens, Nicholas (1697?–1764), merchant and author, was born in Germany. Nothing is known about his parents, apart from the fact that they had six children, five sons and a daughter. Gaining early experience as a merchant in Hamburg and Spain, Magens settled in London in the early 1700s. There he became a successful insurance trader and director of the London Assurance Company. His earliest publication in English, *The Universal Merchant* (1753), was allegedly translated from German by William Horsley, although the German edition appeared only in 1762. This book started with a general treatise on trade, which according to Horsley reflected 'many of Mr [William] Woods Sentiments', followed by an enquiry concerning bullion and an exposition of the theory and practice of banking. The work established Magens's reputation as an authority on monetary and commercial matters. The political economist James Steuart, referring to him as Mr Megens, called him 'a very knowing man, and a very judicious author' and quoted among other things his estimate of the amount of coin preserved in the Bank of England (Steuart, 3.212). In the first book of *The Wealth of Nations* (1776) Adam Smith, spelling his name as 'Megens', adopted from *The Universal Merchant* and from *Farther Explanations of Subjects* (1756) the estimates of the precious metals imported into Europe and into Spain respectively.

Magens's second influential study, *An Essay on Insurances* (1755), was a much amended and increased translation of his *Versuch über Assecuranzen* (1753). Additions in the English edition to the general treatise on insurance, with which volume 1 commences, include some interesting mathematical notes on the calculation of insurance premiums. Most of this volume, however, consisted of leading cases. The second volume was a collection of ordinances and laws on insurances from several European states and cities. Magens further demonstrated his detailed knowledge in commercial matters in a memorial and four letters to the duke of Newcastle written in the period 1758 to 1761. Advising on such matters as the best way to finance the provisioning of British troops in Germany, he showed that, as Horsley put it, he was 'an Alien by birth [but] an Englishman by Interest' (N. Magens, *The Universal Merchant*, preface).

That Magens did not neglect his own particular interest either is evinced by the considerable wealth he accumulated, estimated to be about £100,000 at his death (*GM*). In 1763, using some of this wealth, he became lord of the manor by buying Brightlingsea Hall and Moverons, the two manors of Brightlingsea, near Colchester. Not long after, on 18 August 1764, he died. He was buried in All Saints' Church, Brightlingsea, where upon the death of his wife, Elizabeth, in 1779 a sumptuous marble monument was erected to his memory. There is no evidence of any surviving child; his brother William held the manors from 1779.   RICHARD VAN DEN BERG

Sources R. H. I. Palgrave, ed., *Dictionary of political economy*, [3rd edn], ed. H. Higgs, 3 vols. (1923–6), vol. 2, p. 662 · Allibone, *Dict.* · J. Steuart, *An inquiry into the principles of political oeconomy*, ed. A. S. Skinner, N. Kobayashi, and H. Mizuta, 4 vols. (1998) · *GM*, 1st ser., 34 (1764), 398 · will, PRO, PROB 11/901, fols. 149r–154v · private information (2004) [A. L. Wakeling]
Archives BL, Newcastle papers, 32878, fol. 214, 32886, fol. 440, 32904, fol. 266, 32914, fol. 381, 32922, fol. 233
Wealth at death approx. £100,000: *GM*, 398

Mageoghegan [Mag Eochagáin], **Conall** (*fl.* 1596–1644), historian, was the son of Niall Mageoghegan (*d.* 1596), chieftain, of Lismoyny, co. Westmeath, and grandson of Rosa Mageoghegan, a firm supporter of the English, who had been murdered in 1580; his uncle, also Rosa Mageoghegan, became a Dominican friar and was later bishop of

Kildare from 1629 to 1644. Nothing is known of Mageoghegan's date of birth or his early life. He is best known for his translation into English of the so-called annals of Clonmacnoise, a collection of literary, hagiographical, and historical material laid out in annalistic format and purporting to extend from the earliest times to 1408. The original work in Irish is now lost, although there were reports in the middle of the nineteenth century that it was in the possession of Sir Richard Nagle, who was related to the Mageoghegans. Mageoghegan, who undertook the translation for his kinsman Toirdhealbhach Mac Cochláin of Delvin, co. Westmeath, penned the preface to 'Terenc Coghlan' at Lemanaghan, King's county, on 20 April 1627, while the entire work was completed on 30 June. Mageoghegan's own copy of the annals is not extant but there are four seventeenth-century copies, the two earliest dating from 1660 and 1661 respectively, and Sir James Ware made two pages of excerpts in the 1640s. An edition of the work published in 1896, based on a corrupted manuscript, is unsatisfactory, being incomplete and inaccurate.

Soon after completing the annals, Mageoghegan was associated with Míchél Ó Cléirigh who began writing his 'Réim ríoghraidhe na hÉireann accus senchas a naomh' (otherwise 'Seanchas ríogh Éreann accus genealuigh na naomh nÉreannach', later edited by Paul Walsh under the title *Genealogiae regum et sanctorum Hiberniae*, 1918) in Mageoghegan's house at Lismoyny in 1630. On 4 November of that year Mageoghegan appended a note of approbation to Ó Cléirigh's work in which he testifies that he, a gentleman, had seen the source materials from which the book was compiled. On 11 October 1636 he furnished a similar testimonium for Ó Cléirigh's copy of the hagiographical poem 'Naomhsheanchus naomh Innsi Fáil'.

Mageoghegan was also in communication with James Ussher, the scholarly protestant primate. In August 1636 he had the great Connaught manuscript, the Book of Lecan (dating from about 1400), on loan from Ussher and transcribed some portions of it; the manuscript containing those transcripts is now lost but it was copied in September 1644 by Pól Ó Colla in Mageoghegan's house in Lismoyny. It has been suggested that Mageoghegan may have furnished Ussher with translations of Irish texts and that his translation of the annals of Clonmacnoise may well have been prompted by the archbishop. An important fifteenth-century Irish manuscript (BL, Add. MS 30512) was in Mageoghegan's possession for a time and contains colophons penned by him in 1630, 1631, and 1635; one of these recounts a phenomenal shower of hailstones in the counties of Westmeath, King's county, and Meath which occurred on 25 March 1635. The date of Mageoghegan's death is unknown.   NOLLAIG Ó MURAÍLE

Sources T. O'Rahilly and others, *Catalogue of Irish manuscripts in the Royal Irish Academy*, 30 vols. (Dublin, 1926–70), 415–17, 427–8, 1448, 2465 · S. H. O'Grady, ed., *Catalogue of Irish manuscripts in the British Museum*, 1 (1926), 471–3 · K. Grabowski and D. Dumville, *Chronicles and annals of mediaeval Ireland and Wales: the Clonmacnoise-group texts* (1984), esp. 7, 180 · 'Naemsenchus náemh nÉrenn', *Irish texts*, ed. J. Fraser, P. Grosjean, and J. G. O'Keeffe, 5 vols. in 1 (1931), vol. 3, pp. 40–80 · D. Murphy, ed., *The annals of Clonmacnoise*, trans. C. Mageoghagan (1896) · E. O'Curry, *Lectures on the manuscript materials of* ancient Irish history (1861), 130–1, 137–9, 163–4, 548–50 · S. Sanderlin, 'The manuscripts of the Annals of Clonmacnois', *Proceedings of the Royal Irish Academy*, 82C (1982), 111–23 · P. Walsh, *Genealogiae regum et sanctorum Hiberniae, by the four masters* (1918), 9, 145 · P. Walsh, 'Notes on two Mageoghegans', *Irish Book Lover*, 20 (1932), 75–81 · P. Walsh, 'The Mageoghegans', *Irish chiefs and leaders* (1960), 226–69 · R. Welch, ed., *The Oxford companion to Irish literature* (1996), 336, 567 · *DNB*

Archives BL, fifteenth-century Irish MS containing colophons by Mageoghegan, Add. MS 30512

Magheramorne. For this title name *see* Hogg, James Macnaghten McGarel, first Baron Magheramorne (1823–1890).

Maghfeld, Gilbert (*d.* 1397), merchant, was of unknown parentage, and no details of his early years, whether in London or elsewhere, have been traced. He trained as an ironmonger and was elected by his fellow ironmongers in London to represent them in the reforming council assembled in 1376. He seems to have prospered quickly, in particular as a merchant in wholesale and overseas trade. He and his wife, Margery, lived in some style with their cook and other servants and a staff to deal with the business. Their home was on part of a valuable leased property with a wharf in the parish of St Botolph, Billingsgate, and with associates and his brother Geoffrey he extended his holdings and invested in land in nearby counties. He acquired two wardships, one of which brought him control of valuable manors in Kent.

Maghfeld's unique position in the history of late medieval London, however, is due to the survival among the records of the exchequer of one of his ledgers, that kept from 4 July 1390 to 23 June 1395. Maghfeld or his clerk noted, day by day, debts and expenses, cancelling them when settled. Much illuminating detail on aspects of medieval life can be drawn from this volume of forty-seven folios, written chiefly in French, on subjects ranging from the costs of the schooling of two small boys—one of whom, William, may have been Maghfeld's son—to wages for those laying paving tiles in a local church.

The ledger is of the greatest importance for the light it sheds on the business activities of a London merchant. Some of the debts—over eighty debtors are named, some carried over from an earlier ledger—represent straightforward loans. Some of these were sizeable, and were repaid in instalments, sometimes long after the agreed term; others, like the 26s. 8d. borrowed by Geoffrey Chaucer one Sunday in July 1392 and repaid as arranged the following Saturday, involved only relatively small sums. Much of Maghfeld's trade was with south-west Europe, whence his agents dispatched iron, wines, and other products, while cargoes of grain and cloth were shipped to Bayonne. He was well placed at Billingsgate to handle imports of fish and other raw materials such as woad and alum, essential for the cloth industry. While London was his chief market he had contacts as far away as Suffolk and Hampshire. Credit played an essential part in the exchange of goods, although the interest involved is not noted in the ledger.

Maghfeld's financial skills were soon recognized at court. From 1383 he was active on royal business, particularly as collector of customs duties at Boston, Southampton, and London. He was among those to whom Richard II turned for help when he quarrelled with London in 1392. The mayor and leading citizens were summoned to account for disorder, and at councils held in June and July Richard over-rode long-established privileges. He sent the mayor and sheriffs to prison, appointed a warden and sheriffs to rule the city, and imposed a heavy fine. Although Maghfeld, after brief service in 1382, had been elected alderman of the ward of Billingsgate only in the previous March, Richard appointed him on 25 June 1392 one of the two sheriffs, and on 23 July collector of the London wool customs duties. Richard's favour was partly regained by the city by substantial gifts and loans, and when free elections were allowed Londoners found it politic to put forward Maghfeld's name again as sheriff on 21 September 1392. He continued as alderman and customs collector until 1396/7. But his position was not a comfortable one: the city continued to hold its privileges at the royal pleasure.

The impact of his responsibilities on Maghfeld's own finances is clearly shown by the ledger. There was a marked decline in his trading activities, losses for which moneylending could not compensate. Royal favour seems to have harmed his relations with his fellow merchants and therefore his credit. Although he was able to buy a ship and its gear in September 1395, arrears on customs duties for the year 1395/6 led to the seizure of his possessions, including his ledger, on his death in May 1397. He may not then have been worth more than about £500, judging from debts for which the king sought payment. No will is extant.

ELSPETH VEALE

Sources Maghfeld's Ledger, PRO, Exchequer, Accounts Various, E 101/509/19 · E. Rickert, 'Extracts from a fourteenth-century account book', *Modern Philology*, 24 (1926–7), 111–19, 249–56 · M. M. Crow and C. C. Olsen, eds., *Chaucer life-records* (1966) · E. Rickert, ed., *Chaucer's world* (1948) · M. K. James, 'Gilbert Maghfeld, a London merchant of the fourteenth century', *Economic History Review*, 2nd ser., 8 (1955–6), 364–76 · R. R. Sharpe, ed., *Calendar of letter-books preserved in the archives of the corporation of the City of London*, [12 vols.] (1899–1912), vol. H · Court of Husting, Rolls of Deeds and Wills, CLRO · C. M. Barron, 'The quarrel of Richard II with London, 1392–7', *The reign of Richard II: essays in honour of May McKisack*, ed. F. R. H. Du Boulay and C. M. Barron (1971), 173–201 · A. B. Beaven, ed., *The aldermen of the City of London, temp. Henry III–[1912]*, 2 vols. (1908–13)

Wealth at death approx. £500: James, 'Gilbert Maghfield'

Magill, Sir Ivan Whiteside (1888–1986), anaesthetist, was born on 23 July 1888 in Larne, co. Antrim, Ireland, the son of Samuel Magill, draper, and his wife, Sara Whiteside. He was baptized Ivan because his mother, in her second marriage, considered it more romantic than John. After attending Larne grammar school Magill proceeded to Queen's University, Belfast, where rugby football and boxing claimed his attention before he graduated MB BCh BAO in 1913. In 1916 he married a classmate, Edith (*d.* 1973), daughter of Thomas Robinson Banbridge; her MD thesis was accepted by Queen's University whereas his (on blind endotracheal anaesthesia) was rejected, an error assuaged when he received an honorary DSc degree in 1945. There were no children of the marriage.

After qualification, with a certificate to say that he had given one anaesthetic, Magill held resident posts in the Stanley and Walton hospitals, Liverpool. He served throughout the First World War in the Royal Army Medical Corps with the rank of captain and was medical officer to the Irish Guards at Loos in 1915. When demobilization loomed, his commanding officer at Barnet War Hospital encouraged him to enter 'anaesthetic experience' on an official questionnaire. In 1919, when a vacancy for an anaesthetist came up at Queen Mary's Hospital for Facial and Jaw Injuries at Sidcup, Kent, he accepted so as to be near his wife, who was in practice in London. Together with Stanley Rowbotham he worked for the surgeon Harold Gillies.

At that time anaesthesia was provided by insufflating air and ether through an oral tube into the trachea; the method was troublesome because the surgeon and anaesthetist were in each other's way, and the theatre slowly filled with exhaled ether. Late in 1919, however, Magill was faced with a patient who refused ether or chloroform; he knew that insufflation would be useless for nitrous oxide, the only other anaesthetic available. Deciding that the sole solution was to use a wide-bore, angled tube and bag to function as a bellows, he therefore passed the tube through one nostril into the larynx so that the patient could breathe to and fro. Modestly Magill later confessed that the idea came to him as 'a revelation'. Insufflation was abandoned in favour of to-and-fro breathing, after blind nasal intubation with the patient's head held in position to 'scent the morning air' or 'drain a pint of beer', with the result that nitrous oxide was soon in use for long anaesthetics. Later on, bobbin flowmeters were added and bottles were included in the line so that a liquid anaesthetic could bolster the nitrous oxide, and for ease of use Magill incorporated batteries in the handle of his laryngoscope. Working with Arthur Tudor Edwards (1890–1946) at the Brompton Chest Hospital, London, Magill also devised a suction catheter with an inflatable cuff to aspirate bronchial secretions, and developed an endotracheal tube for one-lung anaesthesia in pulmonary surgery.

At Westminster Hospital it was said that to have Magill as one's anaesthetist put the surgeon in a class. Magill railed against unnecessary instrumentation, and recalled that he never intubated any of Terence Millin's prostatectomy patients (Magill, 551). A bibliography of Magill's writings was published in *Anaesthesia* (33, 1978).

Not only did Magill make surgery safer for the patient, he also improved the status of anaesthesia as a medical specialism. He realized that the importance of anaesthetists' service to surgery would not be recognized until their speciality developed a separate existence. When the charter of the Royal Society of Medicine prevented that body from acceding to his request in 1931 for the institution of a diploma in anaesthesia, he turned to the conjoint board of the Royal Colleges in London. The first examination for the diploma of anaesthetics was held in November 1935, thus opening the way for the establishment of the Faculty of Anaesthetists in 1948 and the fellowship in 1954. The detailed reports of the papers and discussions in the *Proceedings of the Royal Society of Medicine* reveal that Magill regularly used the spoken word to put forward his findings, not only on his endotracheal work but also on most new ideas and drugs. He retired from the National Health Service in 1953 and was knighted in 1960.

Magill was an eminently clubbable man who was generous and effortlessly unaffected with juniors. His 'whispered' Rabelaisian asides were relished by those a few feet away. His spare time was devoted to fishing, in which he was adept enough to be made a member of the Houghton Club on the Test in 1932. He remained devoted to Ireland, where he fished and kept a cottage. Magill died on 25 November 1986, at his home, Lake House, Vicarage Road, Leigh Woods, Bristol.   C. S. BREATHNACH

Sources K. B. Thomas, 'Sir Ivan Whiteside Magill, a review of his publications and other references to his life and work', *Anaesthesia*, 33 (1978), 628–34 · A. W. Edridge, 'Sir Ivan Whiteside Magill', *Anaesthesia*, 42 (1987), 231–3 · A. W. Edridge, *The Lancet* (3 Jan 1987), 55 · *BMJ* (3 Jan 1987), 62–3 · I. W. Magill, *BMJ* (1 Dec 1973), 551 [letter] · H. A. Condon, 'Sir Ivan Magill, a supplementary bibliography', *Anaesthesia*, 42 (1987), 1096–7 · d. cert. · WWW

Likenesses photograph, 1984, Wellcome L. · D. Treddinnick, photograph, repro. in A. W. Edridge, 'Sir Ivan Whiteside Magill', *Anaesthesia*, 42 (1987), facing p. 231 · photograph, repro. in A. Bamji, *Queen Mary's, Sidcup, 1974–1994. A commemoration* (1994)

Wealth at death £346,776: probate, 24 April 1987, *CGPLA Eng. & Wales*

Magill, Robert (1788–1839), minister of the Presbyterian General Synod of Ulster and poet, son of George Frederic Magill and Sarah Boyd, was born on 7 September 1788 in the village of Broughshane, near Ballymena, co. Antrim. When he was ten years old the United Irish rising broke out, and his manuscript autobiography contains some vivid pictures of the scenes which he witnessed. After attending local schools, he himself became a teacher, first at Ballyportre, near Loughguile, in his native county, and afterwards in Broughshane. In 1811, having determined to study for the church, he placed himself under the tuition of the Revd John Paul (1777–1848), of Carrickfergus. In 1813 he entered the University of Glasgow, walking, according to the custom of Ulster students of that day, to Donaghadee, a distance of over 30 miles; after a twelve-hour passage to Portpatrick, he spent three days walking to Glasgow. He graduated MA at the university in 1817, and in addition to his proper professional studies attended several of the medical classes. His poetical gifts had already manifested themselves, and two poems which he wrote while at college, 'The Fall of Algiers' and 'Currie's Elegy', were thought worthy to be recited by the public orator. During the long vacations he taught in Broughshane.

On 11 August 1818 Magill was licensed by the presbytery of Ballymena, in connection with the synod of Ulster, and on 20 June 1820, having received a unanimous call after four Sundays on 'trial', was ordained in Antrim as assistant and successor to Alexander Montgomery, minister of

Mill Row Presbyterian Church. He soon acquired the reputation of being a talented preacher. 'He had a vivid imagination, and certain tones of his voice were so exquisitely tender that when touching on particular subjects he could almost at once melt an auditory into tears' (Reid, 3.555). His congregation increased greatly under his care, and a very large new church had to be built. Magill was married, on 11 December 1823, to Ann Jane (b. 1803), daughter of Samuel Skelton. They had a son and a daughter. His wife died on 14 September 1832 and he subsequently married Ellen, daughter of James Liggat, on 11 June 1838.

In the church courts, which were then agitated over the Arian controversy, Magill sided strongly with the orthodox party. At the suggestion of Dr Henry Cooke, the leader of the evangelicals, he wrote *The Thinking Few* (1828), the work by which he is best known. It is a satirical poem of considerable power, directed against the Arians, and had a very large circulation. It was published anonymously. Six years later he published his *Poems on Various Subjects, Chiefly Religious* (1834), some of which are marked by a deep vein of poetic sentiment. He died in Antrim on 19 February 1839, and was interred in the churchyard of Donegore after an initial burial in Templepatrick.

THOMAS HAMILTON, rev. DAVID HUDDLESTON

Sources R. Magill, autobiography, PRO NIre., D 2930/8 · journals, Presbyterian Historical Society of Ireland, Belfast · *Orthodox Presbyterian* (May 1839), 179–80 · W. T. Latimer, *A history of the Irish Presbyterians*, 2nd edn (1902) · J. S. Reid and W. D. Killen, *History of the Presbyterian church in Ireland*, new edn, 3 (1867)
Archives Presbyterian Historical Society of Ireland, Belfast · PRO NIre., diaries and papers

Maginess, (William) Brian (1901–1967), politician and judge, was born at Hillsborough, co. Down, on 10 July 1901, the son of William George Maginess, a well-known Lisburn solicitor, and his wife, Mary Sarah Boyd. His father was secretary of 'Annahilt True Blues' Orange lodge and Maginess would become a member of both the Orange and the masonic orders. A member of the Church of Ireland, he was educated at Downshire School, Hillsborough, at Wallace high school, Lisburn, and at Trinity College, Dublin, where he was a scholar of the house, won a senior moderatorship, and graduated LLD in 1922. He was called to the bar of Northern Ireland in 1923 and became a junior crown prosecutor in co. Fermanagh in 1926.

First elected to the Stormont parliament for the Ulster Unionist Party in 1938 for the co. Down constituency of Iveagh, he continued to represent it until his retirement from politics in 1964. He volunteered in 1939 and was commissioned in the Royal Artillery, but was released at the request of the Northern Ireland prime minister, John Andrews, in 1940 and became parliamentary secretary to the minister of agriculture in January 1941. Three months later he was given the additional responsibility of parliamentary secretary to the minister of public security. He held both posts until he became parliamentary secretary to the minister of commerce and production, Basil Brooke. Maginess, who had become convinced that Andrews was incapable of responding effectively to the demands of wartime mobilization and lacked a strategy

for the post-war period, played a prominent role in the move against the elderly prime minister which forced his resignation in 1943. He earned the respect and gratitude of Brooke, Andrews's successor as prime minister, a factor of some importance later in his career.

Maginess resigned from the government in 1945 and resumed his career at the bar, taking silk in 1946. However he soon returned to the cabinet, first as minister of labour, then briefly as minister of commerce, and in 1949 he took on the politically charged position of minister of home affairs. By this time he was one of the few intellectual heavyweights in the cabinet and its leading liberal. He was convinced that the extension to Northern Ireland of the welfare state and the Butler Education Act had produced a new consciousness in the Roman Catholic middle class of the benefits of the Union and a pride in the achievements of the province as an area of self-government. This was the basis for his pioneering of the idea that the Unionist Party needed to develop a broader and more inclusive conception of the Union which could appeal to at least a section of the minority community.

However, his hope of modernizing unionism was soon challenged by sectarian polarization over the right to march. Maginess had been denounced by the Nationalist Party for the Public Order Act of 1951, which gave the minister of home affairs and the police more power to ban and reroute parades they thought likely to lead to a breach of the peace. Ironically it was Maginess's use of these powers to ban an Orange parade along the Catholic Longstone Road in Down in June 1952 that made him the target of loyalist anger and recrimination for much of his subsequent time in politics. He was opposed by ultra-protestant candidates in the Stormont elections of 1953 and 1958, and so violent and sustained was the opposition that the prime minister had personally to campaign for him. The ban in effect destroyed his chances of eventually succeeding Brooke, who recorded in his diary 'I am distressed to hear from the Whips that Brian is so very unpopular' (Brooke diaries, 5 Oct 1954). He was shifted to the ministry of finance in 1953 but by the time he solicited Brooke's support for a vacant judgeship in 1956 (Brooke diaries, 25 July 1956) it was clear that his future in Unionist politics had been blighted and in that year he moved to a position outside the cabinet as attorney-general. In 1954 he married Miss Margaret Seeton Crawford who was a member of the staff of his private office.

Now less constrained, Maginess made his most memorable intervention in politics in a speech to the Young Unionist Summer School at Portstewart in 1959. It was an eloquent plea for a liberal and inclusive unionism: 'We must look on those who do not agree with us, not as enemies but as fellow members of the community', and attacked words and policies that reflected 'a policy of apartheid' and a 'paleolithic mentality' (*Irish Times*, 3 Nov 1959). The speech and the suggestion made by another participant, Sir Clarence Graham, that Catholics might be eligible for membership of the Unionist Party unleashed a fundamentalist backlash against liberals in the party and further marginalized Maginess. Yet by 1962 he could write optimistically to his friend Jack Sayers, the editor of the *Belfast Telegraph*, that the lack of loyalist opposition to him in the recent election was one indication that 'People are coming round to our point of view' (Gailey, 75–6). In 1963 he was appointed county court judge for Down, and in 1964 he retired from politics at a time when the new prime minister, Terence O'Neill, was setting out in his own patrician way to attempt to realize Maginess's optimistic liberal vision of an inclusive Union. Perhaps his most eloquent epitaph was written by the last Unionist prime minister, Brian Faulkner, who had been a staunch traditionalist in the 1950s:

> I regret now that when Unionists of vision such as Brian Maginess and Sir Clarence Graham tried to stimulate new thinking and broaden the appeal of Unionism in the 1950s and early 1960s I did not come out in support of them. (Faulkner, 283)

Maginess died in the Royal Victoria Hospital, Belfast, on 16 April 1967. He was buried in Hillsborough parish church on 18 April, and was survived by his wife, Margaret, and one son, Dermot.   HENRY PATTERSON

Sources A. Gailey, *Crying in the wilderness: Jack Sayers, a liberal editor in Ulster* (1995) · B. Barton, *Brookeborough: the making of a prime minister* (1988) · B. Faulkner, *Memoirs of a statesman* (1978) · K. Bloomfield, *Stormont in crisis: a memoir* (1994) · 'Letter from Belfast', *Irish Times* (3 Nov 1959) · *Irish Times* (17 April 1967) · *Belfast Telegraph* (17 April 1967) · *Belfast Telegraph* (18 April 1967) · B. Brooke, diaries, PRO NIre., D 3004/D/45 [esp. 5 Oct 1954]; D 3004/D/46 [esp. 25 Jul 1956] · *CGPLA NIre.* (1967)
Archives PRO NIre., diaries of Sir Basil Brooke, D 3004/D/45, D 3004/D/46
Wealth at death £41,425 16s. 0d.: probate, 10 Aug 1967, *CGPLA Éire*

Maginn, Edward (1802–1849), Roman Catholic bishop, the son of Patrick Maginn, a farmer, and Mary, *née* Slevin, was born at Fintona, co. Tyrone, on 16 December 1802; his uncle was a Catholic priest. He was educated at the Irish College in Paris from 1818 and in 1825 returned to Ireland, where he was ordained priest and appointed to the curacy of Moville, co. Donegal. Some time afterwards he took part in a public debate held at Londonderry between protestant and Catholic champions. In 1829 he was appointed to succeed his uncle as parish priest of the united parishes of Fahan and Deysertegny, co. Donegal. During this period he ardently supported Daniel O'Connell and joined in the agitation for the repeal of the union. On 18 August 1845 Maginn was appointed coadjutor to John MacLaughlin, bishop of Derry, and was nominated to the see of Ortosia, in the archbishopric of Tyre, *in partibus infidelium*. The election was confirmed by the pope on 8 September and Maginn was consecrated in the cathedral at Londonderry's Waterside on 18 January 1846.

A politically minded bishop, Maginn promoted all the nationalist and clerical movements of his time. He gave evidence to Lord Devon's commission on the occupation of land in Ireland, wrote a series of letters on tenant right, and published *A Refutation of Lord Stanley's Calumnies Against the Catholic Clergy of Ireland* to defend the loyalty of Catholic subjects against an anti-Catholic polemic of 1847 which had stressed the 'dual allegiance' of Catholics to pope and crown and suggested that the confessional was pernicious, arguing in effect that Roman Catholicism undermined the safe and peaceful governing of Ireland. Maginn died of typhus on 17 January 1849 at St Columb's College, Londonderry, and was buried in Buncrana, co. Donegal, on 22 January. He was eulogized in *A Life of … Maginn … with Selections from his Correspondence* by T. D'Arcy McGee, the only biography, published in New York in 1857.

THOMPSON COOPER, *rev.* DAVID HUDDLESTON

Sources T. D'Arcy McGee, *A life of the Rt. Rev. Edward Maginn, coadjutor bishop of Derry, with selections from his correspondence* (1857) · D. Bowen, *The protestant crusade in Ireland, 1800–70* (1978) · W. M. Brady, *The episcopal succession in England, Scotland, and Ireland, AD 1400 to 1875*, 1 (1876), 322

Maginn, William (1794–1842), writer and poet, was born on 10 July 1794 in Dean Street, Cork, near the cathedral of St Fin-Barre, the first child of the six children of John Maginn (*c*.1750–1819), classics master at the diocesan school, and Anne, *née* Eccles, daughter of William Eccles of Ecclesville, Tyrone. His father quickly discovered a star pupil, and stories circulated in Cork for years about the young William's brilliance. At eleven (1806) he entered Trinity College, Dublin, ranking near the top of examinations in Latin and Greek, and taking the premium in Hebrew. Under the tutelage of Samuel Kyle (later provost of Trinity College, Dublin, and bishop of Cork) and the formidably eccentric John Barrett, he acquired some dozen additional languages, living and dead, though the college reception of his Latin poem *Æneas Eunuchus* left something to be desired. He was awarded an LLD in 1819, reputedly the youngest to be so honoured. His background and education gave him strong unionist and establishment views.

Early years in Cork After Maginn took his BA in 1811, his father opened an academy at 8 Marlboro Street, the family home, and dragooned his teenage son as classics master. The new school rapidly gained a reputation for academic excellence, while the young William raked about town and earned a reputation as a mimic, jokester, and master of lampoons. The closest he came to the church career envisioned for him was through ghost-writing sermons for clerical friends. He moved in both the protestant and Catholic middle classes, and with his fluent Irish mingled freely with the poor. He first published in a local satiric paper, *The Freeholder*, and joined the Cork Literary and Philosophical Society, though a slight stutter kept him from starring as a debater. Using a remarkable variety of pseudonyms, Maginn began sending contributions abroad about 1818, first to London and William Jerdan's *Literary Gazette*, and then in 1819 to Edinburgh and *Blackwood's Magazine* ('Maga'), where his first efforts were a parody of Wordsworth titled 'Don Juan Unread' and a clever rendering of the ballad of 'Chevy Chase' into a rustic Latin (November 1819). (Maginn frequently 'embalmed' folk poetry in classical languages.) Known by Blackwood only as Ralph Tuckett Scott, Maginn was encouraged to expand a squib on Edinburgh University professor John Leslie into

William Maginn (1794–1842), by Daniel Maclise, 1830

'Leslie *versus* Hebrew' (February 1820); the publisher rued his suggestion throughout a lengthy libel case.

On the death of his father in 1819, Maginn became master of the school, while his sisters opened a female academy in a house next door. Leaving all thoughts of the ministry behind, he dutifully supported his family and prepared his brother John for Trinity. Though far away and harassed by pedagogy, he quickly became one of the inner coterie of 'Maga', along with John Wilson, John Gibson Lockhart, and Thomas Hamilton, and during the summer vacation of 1821 he ventured to Edinburgh on a surprise visit to meet the rest of the gang. Turning up in William Blackwood's Princes Street shop, he demanded in his thickest brogue to know the name of the prolific Cork contributor. Blackwood hemmed and hawed until Maginn pulled out Blackwood's own letters and said 'I am that gentleman'. Amused by his youth and learning, his new friends dubbed him the Doctor.

While Lockhart initiated *Blackwood's* most popular feature, the collaborative 'Noctes Ambrosianae', Maginn shortly after enlisted with Wilson and gradually became associated by the public with one of its characters, Sir Morgan Odoherty. Odoherty's speciality was the celebration of drink, cigars, and the convivial life—epitomized in the 'Maxims of Mr Odoherty' in 1824 (reprinted in book form, 1849). Despite attempts to lure him to Scotland, after a scouting trip to London during which he met Jerdan, L. E. L. (the poet Letitia Landon, to whom Maginn may have made a proposal), and Theodore Hook, he determined to move there as soon as possible. When his brother John graduated from Trinity and could replace him at the academy, he made new arrangements, both professional and matrimonial. To the astonishment of his Cork cronies, he married Ellen Ryder Bullen (d. 1859) at Christ's Church, Cork, on 31 January 1824. She was the daughter of a clergyman and her brother had been Maginn's student. Enticed by an offer of employment (£20 a month) with Theodore Hook on an expanded *John Bull* newspaper, Maginn with his new wife and his sister Margaret arrived in London the next month.

Scribbling in London, 1824–1829 In London he renewed his acquaintance with fellow Corkmen and associated with Jerdan, Landon, Thomas Barnes (of *The Times*), publisher John Murray, and the critic John Wilson Croker. The flow of writing to *Blackwood's* continued, regularly remunerated now for the first time, and Blackwood's and Lockhart's visit to London in the spring revealed a man in his element, ensconced in the Salopian Coffee House and surrounded by the gentlemen of the press. In the summer, however, he made a mistake by editing *John Bull Magazine*, a short-lived monthly advertised as written by 'plain People' who 'drink ale with their cheese, and ask twice for their soup if they want it' (*Examiner*, 27 June 1824, 414). It was launched with a forged 'wedding night' episode of Byron's burnt memoirs, and Maginn immediately lost *ton*, being charged with a 'familiar intimacy with all the blackguard publications of the age' (*London Magazine*, June 1826, 208). John Murray, who had toyed with the notion of selecting Maginn to edit Byron's letters, redirected that project to Thomas Moore.

In the autumn the Maginns moved lodgings to Brunswick Square, where their first child, Ellen, was born. By the next year, however, Maginn was in financial difficulties; an attempt to secure a post on a new commission to regularize the state papers was rejected by J. W. Croker, who nevertheless alerted home secretary Robert Peel to Maginn's possible value as tory propagandist. The autumn of 1825 saw him busily attempting to write his way out of debt, when he was rescued by Benjamin Disraeli, then a twenty-year-old with a scheme to use Murray's backing to start a new tory daily (*The Representative*). Maginn accepted the post of Paris correspondent (£500 per annum). After William's trip to Ireland on family business, the Maginns moved to France, where a few days after their arrival in late December Ellen gave birth to Anne, a 'sickly yonker' (Cooke, 627), in their lodgings at Hotel d'Hungerford (31 rue Caumartin). Maginn sent the odd column back to London, but chiefly polished his French (including Parisian thieves' argot) and translated a humorous farrago on food, *Physiologie du goût*. 'The Rip' was badly managed, however, and Murray recalled Maginn in March to salvage things. While his editing produced a more lively and consistent paper, its losses could not be sustained and 'The Rip' was merged with the *New Times* after the summer election. Maginn transferred to this paper, probably as a sub-editor.

In the late 1820s Maginn continued to write sporadically for *Blackwood's*, collaborating with Lockhart on several new 'Noctes'; he also translated Vidocq's memoirs, worked with Crofton Croker on his *Fairy Legends*, contributed a few fine tales to the annuals, and in 1827 published *Whitehall: or, Days of George IV* (a spoof of historical novels). In that year as well his family was completed by the birth of a son, John. He may also have written a true crime version of a famous murder, *The Red Barn* (1828). But his chief livelihood came from the evening *Standard*, a daily launched to support the ultra-tory side after the pro-Catholic emancipation George Canning became premier in 1827. The paper was named after a tag from Livy that also gave Morgan Odoherty the sobriquet the Standard-Bearer, and was edited by Stanley Lees Giffard, a staunch Orangeman whom Maginn knew from Trinity College. After the Catholic Relief Act was passed in 1829, *The Standard* vociferously accused Peel and Wellington of 'ratting'. Maginn served as sub- or co-editor until the late 1830s, drawing an income of more than £400 per annum, and wrote many of the leaders.

Fraser's Magazine, 1830–1842 Late in 1829 Maginn decided that London needed its own 'Maga'. William Blackwood had grown shy of controversy, and Maginn's tendency to 'run-a-muck' in 'personalities' (Gordon, 309) was unwelcome. With a lawyer friend, Hugh Fraser, providing the ready money, Maginn convinced James Fraser (no relation) to make his publishing début with *Fraser's Magazine for Town and Country* (February 1830; nicknamed 'Regina'). The story goes that they were perambulating Regent Street when Maginn spied a bookshop at no. 215 and said, 'Fraser! here is a namesake of yours—let us try him' (Kenealy, 87). While not technically the editor, Maginn was chiefly responsible for its direction and content, and wrote a high percentage of its articles. After a slow start it became an original and powerful organ, combining a rollicking scurrility—not above the occasional hoax or libel—with advanced and intellectually challenging new writing. It was the first to publish, for instance, Thomas Carlyle's *Sartor Resartus*. The most popular feature was a long-running 'Gallery of illustrious literary characters' (collected in book form, 1873) that featured brief and biting prose sketches by Maginn and portraits by Daniel Maclise, a young artist from Cork whom Maginn had befriended. Nine of the first ten writers profiled were Scots or Irish, and the magazine as a whole relied on a Celtic pool of talent. Somewhat later it was enhanced by a young discovery named Thackeray, who later based Captain Shandon in *Pendennis* partly on Maginn.

At the heart of *Fraser's* was a round table in James Fraser's back parlour, where the Fraserians gathered to put together the magazine, write squibs on Lytton Bulwer, or Robert 'Satan' Montgomery, and drink whiskey punch in bacchanalias that were then exaggerated in the magazine. It is no surprise that the chief accusation spread about Maginn by his enemies was that he was constantly inebriated, and this was no doubt true. Odoherty's twenty-fifth maxim was that 'A man saving his wine must be cut savagely' (*Blackwood*, May 1824, 604), and Maginn ran no risk of being cut. He wrote dozens of drinking-songs and once found thirty-seven rhymes for 'a jug of gin-twist'. In defence, it was noted that he did not tipple more than other men; he was just unable to hold it, and this is probably true as well. His 'A Story without a Tail' (*Blackwood*, April 1834) perfectly embodies a life of feckless feasting and reckless drinking.

Maginn was now one of the best-known and most influential literary figures in London, though he deliberately avoided publishing books and preferred anonymity. But despite a substantial income, his liabilities continued to mount and in 1834 he fled to Belgium while Lockhart collected a subscription to settle about £3000 of debt. His reputation was also damaged by rumours that he had not only been writing leaders for *The Age*, but also co-operating with its editor, Charles Molloy Westmacott, a blackmailer. A more personal trouble occurred at about the same time. Maginn was a fond father and husband, though frequently absent from his home at 55 Stanford Street, hiding from duns (often in the Irish-speaking slum of St Giles). In 1834 Landon, who since about 1822 had been the secret mistress of Jerdan, became engaged to John Forster. Rumours flew that she had been or was the lover of Bulwer, Maclise, and Maginn as well. Although the evidence is thin, Ellen Maginn apparently searched her husband's belongings, found letters from Landon that seemed to indicate intimacy, and brought them to Forster's attention, thus breaking off the marriage. Maginn was able to convince his wife that the letters were innocent, but their marriage suffered. Landon was devastated and a few years later made an odd marriage to George Maclean, who took her to his colonial outpost in Africa. When she died there under mysterious circumstances, Maginn was publicly distraught. L. E. L. and Maginn certainly enjoyed a long friendship and close working relationship, though friction occurred when Landon entered the circle of Bulwer and his *New Monthly Magazine*. There is no firm evidence, however, that Maginn was her lover, and much evidence against posthumous allegations that he blackmailed her or sent her anonymous letters.

Oddly enough, Maginn, whom Daniel O'Connell dubbed 'that hoary headed libeller' (Kenealy, 93), caused only two suits against *Fraser's*. The first came when Alaric 'Attila' Watts, dubbed the 'principal fribble among the namby-pambies of the Annuals' (*Fraser's*, July 1831, cover), took umbrage over Maclise's drawing of him sneaking downstairs with pictures under his arms, and Maginn's jibes about his backbiting propensities. Watts won a partial victory (5 December 1835) after Fraser's defence was thrown out on a technicality. The second case was the more serious. Maginn skewered the honourable Grantley Berkeley's egotistical novel, *Berkeley Castle*, in *Fraser's* (August 1836). Grantley, accompanied by his brother Craven, surprised James Fraser alone in his shop, and nearly killed him with a lead-weighted riding crop. They were arraigned at the Marlborough Street station and released on bond—though Fraser later decided to seek damages in civil court, and Berkeley counter-sued him for libel.

Maginn claimed that in Ireland 'for dueling purposes' a

gentleman was a man 'who wore a clean shirt once a week' (*Fraser's*, 'Defence', 14. 368), and he generally found the Code Duello ridiculous. 'Bob Burke's duel with Ensign Brady of the 48th' is one of the great comic takes on duelling (*Blackwood*, 1834). Nevertheless, hearing of the assault he immediately sent his card to Berkeley House. The encounter between the sportsman and crack shot and the tipsy journalist was fought in a field off the Harrow Road on the evening of 5 August. Aim, steady or not, was taken thrice, with both parties missing each time; Maginn's second, Hugh Fraser, then interceded. As they entered Fraser's carriage to return to town, the Berkeley brothers shouted insults after them.

After the duel Maginn wrote a signed 'Defence' for *Fraser's*, and seems to have decided, at long last, to write for posterity. While he contributed to *Fraser's*, his friendship with the publisher understandably cooled, and when Richard Bentley began a new magazine with Charles Dickens at the helm, Maginn was part of the team. After 1836 he wrote much of his best work: the 'Shakespeare papers' in *Bentley's Miscellany* and in *Fraser's* the 'Homeric Ballads', translations from Lucian, and a number of scholarly essays (for example, 'Farmer on the learning of Shakespeare'). Unfortunately, his financial situation sank as fast as works flew from his pen, and he also scribbled for the weekly papers (notably *The Age* and *The Argus*) and briefly edited the *Lancashire Herald* (Liverpool, 1838–9). From debtor's prison itself he contributed to *Fleet Papers*, *The Town*, *The Squib*, and the new *Punch* (their respective editors were briefly fellow inmates).

Sir Robert Peel had brought in a Conservative government in 1841, and despite his lampooning of Peel, Maginn had hoped for some reward for his partisan services. A number of his political essays in *Fraser's* had been popular as pamphlets, and like Peel he urged the development of a post-Reform 'conservative' party. When no government offers surfaced, he believed that Peel held a personal grudge. In fact, Peel had funnelled £100 to Ellen Maginn through Giffard, but she elected not to tell her husband for fear he might turn it down. With money running out after Maginn's death a public subscription was announced (the king of Hanover gave a further £100), and Francis Mahony saw that the Literary Fund Society made a grant. On the form under 'Causes of distress' Mahony entered 'The casualties of a life wholly dependent on literature' (Royal Literary Fund archives, case 1054).

In person Maginn was invariably in good temper, would break into a tune in the middle of conversation, and enjoyed the company of coal-heavers and navvies over that of lords and swells. He was grey-haired by his late twenties, though otherwise youthful in appearance, and when too drunk to walk could get home by breaking into a brisk jog. He was apparently never too drunk to write. Friends commented on his remarkable lack of personal rancour towards the political opponents and literary figures he 'squabashed', and on his extraordinary memory and ability to write accurately and well while carrying on a conversation on a different topic. Even when sick and in the Fleet he impressed Richard Oastler, the Factory Act

campaigner, with his witty conversation, cheerfulness, and radical tory politics. As Thackeray noted, however, for the Victorians he was chiefly 'a famous subject for moralizing' (*Letters*, 2. 140–41).

Maginn's final attempt at fiction was *John Manesty, Liverpool Merchant*, completed by Charles Ollier and published posthumously (1844). He had frequently been urged to collect his best articles in more permanent form. But when he did so, the project was under-capitalized and under-puffed, so a publication in parts called *Magazine Miscellanies* (1841) went mostly unpurchased. With its failure he was sued, and once again lodged in the Fleet prison, where his tuberculosis accelerated. After release on humanitarian grounds, Maginn was reluctantly induced to take advantage of the Insolvent Debtor's Act (18 June 1842). Lacking the funds to travel to the warmer climate his doctors recommended, the Maginns went instead to a little village in Surrey. On 11 August 1842 he wrote to his old Cork friend, Crofton Croker: 'Here I am at Walton-on-Thames, coughing my heart up. The doctors think I am going to die' (Thrall, 205). In the wee hours of Sunday morning, 21 August, the doctors were proved correct, and he died in an upstairs room at Cypress Lodge surrounded by his family. He was buried on 29 August in a pauper's grave in the churchyard of the church of St Mary, Walton-on-Thames; during the service and interment remarkable peals of thunder rang out from a clear blue sky.

Posthumous reputation Maginn remains important to historians of the press, especially for his role in *The Standard*, but he is chiefly remembered for his work in *Blackwood's* and *Fraser's*, where for over twenty years he stirred the pot with learned, witty, and frequently scurrilous essays, reviews, parodies, burlesques, and pasquinades, almost all anonymous or pseudonymous. Politically he supported only the tories; later accusations that he wrote for both whigs and tories are not true, and seem to have arisen from his own satire of such newspapermen in 'The Tobias correspondence' (*Blackwood*, 1840). He brought a unique sensibility to this work: tory, but allergic to any form of aristocratic pretension; proudly Irish, but strongly pro-Union and protestant; anti-bourgeois and a champion of the labourers, because convinced the working classes were naturally conservative; and deeply learned, though rarely pedantic. His debts seem to have accrued through the daily accumulation of not knowing how to say no, and his house was open to any Corkman who found the door. Kenealy, however, believed that the extravagance of Ellen Maginn contributed to his ruin.

Maginn would no doubt be better known if he had spent his critical forces and formidable powers of ridicule on Carlyle, Tennyson, Browning, Dickens, and Thackeray, instead of working with them or praising their work. After all, his friend Lockhart—who wrote a famous epitaph on 'bright, broken Maginn'—is now chiefly remembered for ridiculing Keats and the cockney school. Instead, while the Victorians disowned this brilliant though dissolute Corkman, his unsparing assault on the dominant mediocrities popular in the 1830s helped clear the ground for the greater literature to come.   D. E. LATANÉ, JR.

Sources R. Shelton Mackenzie, 'Memoir', *Miscellaneous writings of the late Dr Maginn*, 5 (1955–7), ix–cx • M. M. H. Thrall, *Rebellious Fraser's: Nol Yorke's magazine in the days of Maginn, Thackeray, and Carlyle* (1934) • E. V. Kenealy, 'William Maginn, LLD', *Dublin University Magazine*, 23 (1844), 72–101 • A. Kersey Cooke, 'Maginn–Blackwood correspondence', PhD diss., Texas Technological College, 1955 • D. Coakley and M. Coakley, *Wit and wine: literary and artistic Cork in the early nineteenth century*, 2nd edn (1985) • Mrs Oliphant, *William Blackwood and his sons* (1897), vols. 1–2 of *Annals of a publishing house* (1897–8) • J. Coleman, 'Biographical sketches of persons remarkable in local history: William Maginn, LLD', *Journal of the Cork Historical and Archaeological Society*, 2 (1893), 125–31 • W. Jerdan, *The autobiography of William Jerdan: with his literary, political, and social reminiscences and correspondence during the last fifty years*, 4 vols. (1852–3) • S. C. Hall, *Retrospect of a long life, from 1815 to 1883*, 2 vols. (1883) • 'Duel between Mr Grantley Berkeley and Dr Maginn', *Morning Chronicle* (8 Aug 1836), 3 • P. Leary, 'Fraser's Magazine and the literary life, 1830–1847', *Victorian Periodicals Review*, 24 (1994), 105–26 • W. Maginn, 'Defence of "Fraser's Magazine" in the Berkeley affair', *Fraser's Magazine*, 15 (1837), 137–43 • Mrs Gordon [M. Wilson], *A memoir of John Wilson* (New York, 1863) • *The letters and private papers of William Makepeace Thackeray*, ed. G. N. Ray, 4 vols. (1945–6) **Archives** Hunt. L., family corresp. and literary MSS | BL, letters to Royal Literary Fund, loan 96 • BL, Peel papers • Cork City Library, letters to Thomas Crofton Croker • NL Ire., letters to Thomas Crofton Croker, Bentley papers • NL Scot., letters to Blackwoods, poems • Yale U., letters to Jerdan, Lockhart, Landon **Likenesses** D. Maclise, pencil and watercolour drawing, 1830, NPG [*see illus.*] • D. Maclise, lithograph, 1831 (after his portrait, 1830), BM, NG Ire., NPG; repro. in *Fraser's Magazine* (Jan 1831) • D. Maclise, group portrait, lithograph, 1835 (*The Fraserians*), BM; repro. in *Fraser's Magazine* (Jan 1835) • J. Kirkwood, etching, pubd 1844 (after S. Skillin), NG Ire. • S. Skillin, drawing, repro. in *Dublin University Magazine* **Wealth at death** close to nil; family left destitute and dependent on charity and public fund: Kenealy papers, Hunt. L. • declared insolvent debtor at Portugal Street Court on 18 June 1842: *Sunday Times* (20 June 1842) • debts at this time were estimated by Lockhart to be £10,000

Maglorius [St Maglorius] (*fl.* late 6th cent.), ascetic, is commemorated on 24 October. There is, however, no contemporary or near-contemporary evidence for his existence. According to his life, he was born in south Wales, to parents named Afrella and Umbrafel and was educated at Illtud's monastery of Llantwit Major. The life also claims that he was the cousin of St Samson; a different tradition makes him cousin of St Malo (Machutus). He was reputed to have been consecrated deacon by Samson, and to have accompanied the latter when he left Britain for Brittany. Maglorius's life asserts that Samson, dying, appointed Maglorius to succeed him as 'archbishop' of Dol but that the saint soon thereafter resigned the office and retreated to a remote monastery, which seems to have been on the island of Sark. He died on Sark and a post-mortem cult subsequently developed there. Maglorius's relics are known to have been translated to Léhon, near Dol, in the middle of the ninth century, and to have been transferred to Paris at the time of the viking invasions of Brittany *c*.920.

Almost everything about Maglorius is problematic. The name itself is the Latinized form of a Brittonic name, the Welsh form being Meilyr and the Breton Maeler, but the saint is not attested as such. His earliest life was written before *c*.1000, probably in Brittany in the late ninth or early tenth century. It has never been fully published; of the various manuscripts in which it survives, none contains the complete text. Its author clearly knew very little indeed about his subject. The claim that Maglorius was 'archbishop' not bishop of Dol reflects the unsuccessful bid to secure metropolitan status for the see of Dol in the 860s, but there are grounds for doubting whether Maglorius was ever bishop of Dol at all, and whether he ever had any contact with Samson, for he is not one of the two immediate successors of Samson mentioned in that saint's early life. There is a good case for arguing that Maglorius was an ascetic on the island of Sark, and that after his remains reached Léhon, his name and cult were appropriated by the clergy at Dol in the later ninth century for their own political purposes.

The author of the life also wrote accounts of some of Maglorius's miracles, and a description of the translation of his remains to Léhon. These are a valuable indication of the literary culture of Carolingian Brittany, for the author shows his familiarity with Christian Latin authors and with Virgil as well as with the Bible. An account of the relics' removal to Paris survives in a twelfth-century form. The life was rewritten in Old French, in both prose and verse, the former in 1315 and the latter in 1319, both in conjunction with the translation of the saint's remains to a new reliquary. John Tynemouth provided an epitome of the Latin life in his *Sanctilogium Angliae, Walliae, Scotiae et Hiberniae*.

The centre for Maglorius's cult was the church in Paris which housed his relics, originally St Barthélemy but renamed St Magloire. From here, liturgical commemoration of his feast day (24 October) spread to a few other churches in the Île-de-France and to places with particular links with St Magloire. His feast is also noted in a handful of late medieval English martyrologies. In Brittany, he is the patron of the churches at Mahalon in Plomodiern (Finistère) and at Châtelaudren (Côtes-d'Armor). It has been suggested on philological grounds that his cult may have become confused with that of the Breton saint Meloir and/or that of the saint attested in Cornwall as Melor and in Brittany as Melar. The truth cannot, however, be established and it remains the case that there is no certain evidence of any church dedication to Maglorius nor onomastic commemoration of him anywhere in the British Isles.

JULIA M. H. SMITH

Sources *Bibliotheca hagiographica latina antiquae et mediae aetatis*, 2 vols. (Brussels, 1898–1901) [suppls., 1911 and 1986] • J.-C. Poulin, 'Sources hagiographiques de la Gaule, II: Les dossiers de S. Magloire et de S. Malo (province de Bretagne)', *Francia*, 17/1 (1990), 159–209 • 'Vita maglorii episcopi', *Acta sanctorum: October*, 10 (Brussels, 1861), 782–91 • A. Denomy and J. Brückmann, 'An Old French poetic version of the life and miracles of S. Magloire [pt 1]', *Mediaeval Studies*, 19 (1957), 251–312 • A. Denomy and J. Brückmann, 'An Old French poetic version of the life and miracles of S. Magloire [pt 2]', *Mediaeval Studies*, 21 (1959), 53–128 • V. Leroquais, *Les sacramentaires et les missels manuscrits des bibliothèques publiques de France*, 3 vols. (1924) • H. Guillotel, 'L'exode du clergé breton devant les invasions scandinaves', *Mémoires de la Société d'Histoire et d'Archéologie de Bretagne*, 59 (1982), 269–315 • S. Baring-Gould and J. Fisher, *The lives of the British saints*, 4 vols., Honourable Society of Cymmrodorion, Cymmrodorion Record Series (1907–13) • G. H.

Doble, *Saint Melor*, Cornish Saints Series, 15 (1927) • J. Loth, *Les noms des saints bretons* (1910) • M. Lapidge and R. Sharpe, *A bibliography of Celtic-Latin literature, 400–1200* (1985), 255

Magniac, Hollingworth (1786–1867), merchant and connoisseur of medieval art, was born in Kensington, London, on 15 April 1786, the fourth son and seventh child in a family of eight sons and three daughters of Colonel Francis Magniac (*d.* 1823) of Kensington and Denton Court, Kent, and his wife, Frances, the daughter of John Attwood. His father was a French Huguenot goldsmith who made clocks and watches for marketing at Canton (Guangzhou) by the firm of Cox and Beale, merchants. In 1801 Hollingworth's elder brother Charles (*d.* 1824) went out to China to oversee the family's interests there, and the firm became Beale and Magniac. About 1805 Hollingworth joined his brother at Canton.

To circumvent the East India Company's monopoly on trade with China, some British merchants undertook to serve as consuls for foreign nations, which was a way to establish themselves at Canton. While Thomas Beale was consul for Prussia, Charles Magniac held the post of vice-consul, and in 1811 Hollingworth Magniac joined the Prussian consulate at Canton as secretary.

By 1817 the firm was designated Magniac & Co., with Charles and Hollingworth as the only partners. Located on the riverfront at Canton, their business was an agency house, providing correspondent merchants in Britain and India with services in marketing, banking, shipping, and insurance. Of the commodities they marketed, Indian opium was the most mercurial, reaching boom prices in 1819, when the Magniac brothers began buying all the opium they could secure. Having seen opium prices increase by 100 per cent between 1819 and 1821, the Magniacs sold all they had, just as Chinese officials were endeavouring to interdict sales of the drug. In the course of this speculation, they had made a fortune. Testifying before a committee of the House of Lords in 1830, Hollingworth stated that, apart from his agency business, his own trade at Canton 'was principally in opium, almost entirely indeed' (Hsin-pao Chang, 238n). He attributed that situation to the inability of the Chinese government to interdict the smuggling which served the needs of those who were addicted.

While Hollingworth Magniac was in Britain, in 1823, Charles fell seriously ill and on advice from his physician he left China in January 1824, but died soon after reaching England. Hollingworth returned to Canton in October 1824, intent on putting his affairs in order and retiring to England. Dr William Jardine, who had conducted the firm in the interim between Charles's departure and Hollingworth's return, was admitted as a full partner in July 1825. By December of the following year, Hollingworth had settled his affairs and prepared to leave Canton after twenty years there. Jardine described Hollingworth as 'honest and liberal beyond what we generally meet with, or even expect to meet with in the general intercourse of business transactions' (*Jardine, Matheson & Company*, 12).

By 1828 the managing partners of the firm were William Jardine and James Matheson, but the firm retained the

Hollingworth Magniac (1786–1867), by unknown artist

name of Magniac until 1832, as time was required for the new partners to buy out the interests of the Magniac family and remit Magniac's capital to England. On 30 June 1832 the name of Magniac & Co. was retired and the firm opened for business the next day as Jardine, Matheson & Co. Magniac came out of his temporary retirement in 1833 to support Jardine Matheson's bills of exchange when a financial crisis brought down their correspondent firm in London. Two years later, when he organized a new agency house to correspond with Jardine Matheson, his partners were John Abel Smith MP, and Oswald Smith, members of a well-established banking family, and the new firm was Magniac, Smith & Co., located at 3 Lombard Street, in the City of London. At Magniac's invitation, William Jardine, after retiring from China, again became his partner, and the firm became Magniac Jardine (1841). In 1848 that firm was reorganized as Matheson & Co., with Hollingworth Magniac remaining as one of the principals.

About 1827 Magniac married Helen, daughter of Peter Sampson of Fitzroy Square, London; they had three sons. Soon after his return from China he leased Colworth House, Sharnbrook, in north Bedfordshire, from John Fiott-Lee, whose principal seat was at Hartwell House in Buckinghamshire. Colworth was an Elizabethan house in origin, altered in the 1760s and again about 1810. It became the principal residence of Magniac, who again extended the house, which he acquired outright in 1854. He played no part in political affairs, although his son Charles later became a local MP and chairman of Bedfordshire county council; he was, however, master of the Oakley hunt, 1847–51. His London house was at 2 Bolton Row (later Curzon Street), Mayfair.

With his ample fortune, Hollingworth Magniac began to form a collection, which was distinguished as one of the finest nineteenth-century collections of medieval art, accumulated in the tradition of William Thomas Beckford. The collection included a series of historical portraits by Jean and François Clouet, Lucas Cranach the elder, and their contemporaries; illuminations and portrait miniatures; ecclesiastical and secular metalwork; Limoges enamels; carvings in ivory and boxwood; maiolica; faience ware of Henri Deux and Bernard Palissy; enamelled German, Venetian, and oriental glass; tazze; reliquaries; dishes; caskets; vases; and armour. Magniac bought many objects at the Strawberry Hill sale of 1842, and was an active buyer from dealers and in the saleroom until the 1850s. The diaries of Joseph Farington state that Magniac 'partly inherited and partly collected the remarkable collection' (*Farington Diary*, ed. Greig, 5.16n.), although no material has come to light to distinguish Hollingworth Magniac's purchases from those of his father or brother.

A considerable part of Magniac's collection was exhibited at the Society of Arts exhibition in 1850, and again in 1862 at the South Kensington loan exhibition. His collection was sold by Christies in an eleven-day sale in July 1892, with 1554 lots realizing £103,040.

Magniac died on 31 March 1867 at his home, 2 Bolton Row, Mayfair, London. His son Charles commissioned the Gothic revival architect William Burges to design a magnificent monument and mausoleum at Sharnbrook.

CHARLES SEBAG-MONTEFIORE, *rev.* RICHARD J. GRACE

Sources M. Keswick, ed., *The thistle and the jade* (1982) · M. Greenberg, *British trade and the opening of China, 1800–42* (1951) · A. R. Williamson, *Eastern traders* (Ipswich, [n.d.]) · W. Jardine, letterbooks, CUL, Jardine, Matheson & Co. MSS · Yrissari letterbook, CUL, Jardine, Matheson & Co. MSS · J. C. Robinson, *Notices of the principal works of art in the collection of Hollingworth Magniac esq of Colworth* (1862) · *The Farington diary*, ed. J. Greig, 8 vols. (1922–8) · J. Mordaunt Crook, *William Burges and the high Victorian dream* (1981) · *Jardine Matheson and Company, an historical sketch. An outline of a China house for a hundred years, 1832–1932* (London, 1934) · Hsin-pao Chang, *Commissioner Lin and the opium war* (1970), 238 note 7
Archives CUL, Jardine Matheson archives, William Jardine letter-books · CUL, Jardine Matheson archives, Matheson corresp. in the Yrissari letter-books
Likenesses oils, unknown collection; copyprint, NPG [*see illus.*]
Wealth at death under £400,000: probate, 16 May 1867, *CGPLA Eng. & Wales*

Magnus, earl of Caithness and earl of Orkney (*c.*1290–1320/21), magnate, is called Magnus 'the fifth' in the fifteenth-century genealogy of the earls, which also tells us that he was the son of the previous earl, John. Very little is known of the line of Angus earls who inherited the northern earldoms in the 1230s, but four of them bore the name Magnus, after their revered ancestor Magnus Erlendsson, martyred about 1115. One of the few certain facts about Magnus is that he had a long minority. Thanks to the efficient government of Edward I there is record that in 1303 the wardship of 'Munes', son and heir of the earl of Caithness, was granted to Weland of Stiklaw. A careerist in the Scottish administration, Weland had left Scotland when Edward invaded in 1296, moving to Norway in the following of Isabel Bruce, who married Erik Magnusson, king of Norway (*r.* 1286–99). He came to

Edward's peace when he was granted the wardship of Magnus for the earldom of Caithness, no doubt because he already controlled Orkney for the Norwegian royal administration. The earldom of Caithness was still in ward in 1309, but Magnus must have come of age before 1312.

Virtually the only evidence surviving about Earl Magnus's career relates to his involvement in high-level diplomatic negotiations. Being an earl in the kingdoms of both Scotland and Norway, his position was not an easy one. There was rivalry between the two in the maritime zones around the north and west of the Scottish mainland. However, the treaty of Perth of 1266 was renewed at Inverness in 1312, when Magnus gave his oath on behalf of the king of Scots as earl of Caithness, but sealed the Norwegian part of the indenture as earl of Caithness and Orkney. In the following spring it was in his Orkney earldom, as earl of Caithness and acting, along with the bishop of Caithness and the chancellor of Moray, on behalf of the king of Scots, that he paid over the 'annual' 100 merks for that year and for the preceding five years to the commissioners of the king of Norway. Seven years later, in 1320, as earl of Caithness and Orkney he was listed seventh of the earls who addressed the declaration of Arbroath to the pope. Only once can we see Magnus acting as earl within his home territory of Orkney on matters concerning his earldom. In a report probably dating from the spring of 1320 and presented to Archbishop Eilif of Nidaros by Kormack, archdeacon of the Sudreys, and Grim, prebendary of Nidaros, it was said that Bishop William of Orkney had promised 'before Lord Magnus, earl of Orkney and Caithness, and Lady Catherine his wife, the chapter and many other worthies' (Lange and Unger, 9, no. 85) to amend the defects of his administration and to assign a certain portion of his rents to each church.

It is thought that Magnus died soon after sealing the declaration of Arbroath in April 1320 since in August 1321 King Robert addressed a letter to the bailies of the king of Norway in Orkney complaining about rebels being received there, which he is unlikely to have done had the earl been alive and active. In 1329 Countess Catherine was making purchases of land in Orkney, and was obviously acting on her own behalf as a widow. It is not clear whether Magnus left any heirs. The genealogy of the earls mentions none, but neither does it say that he left no heirs, as is noted of another earl. His children would certainly have been under age in 1320–21 if he himself came of age only between 1309 and 1312. The absence of other claimants until 1330 suggests that there may have been a minor who did not reach maturity. In that year, however, the two earldoms passed to Malise, earl of Strathearn (*d. c.*1350), whose claim stemmed from his great-great-grandmother. The Scottish element of the joint earldoms was thereafter dominant.

BARBARA E. CRAWFORD

Sources 'Genealogy of the earls', *The Bannatyne miscellany*, ed. D. Laing, 3, Bannatyne Club, 19b (1855), 63–85 · *Diplomatarium Norvegicum*, 2, ed. C. C. A. Lange and C. R. Unger (Christiania, 1852); 5, ed. C. C. A. Lange and C. R. Unger (1860); 9, ed. C. R. Unger and H. J.

Huitfeld-Kaas (1878) • F. Palgrave, ed., *The antient kalendars and inventories of the treasury of his majesty's exchequer*, 3 vols., RC (1836) • *APS*, 1124–1423 • G. Donaldson, ed., *Scottish historical documents* (1970); repr. with corrections (1974) • B. E. Crawford, 'Weland of Stiklaw: a Scottish royal servant at the Norwegian court', *Historisk Tidsskrift*, 52 (1973), 329–39 • B. E. Crawford, 'North Sea kingdoms, North Sea bureaucrat: a royal official who transcended national boundaries', *SHR*, 69 (1990), 175–84

Magnús Erlendsson, earl of Orkney [St Magnus] (1075/6–1116?), patron saint of Orkney, was the son of *Erlend Thorfinnsson, earl of Orkney [*see under* Paul (*d.* 1098/9)], and Thora, daughter of Sumerlidi Ospaksson of Iceland, whose union is the first evidence for close connections between Iceland and the Orkney earldom family. Magnús was thus a relative of the saintly bishop Jon of Holar. He is said to have led a blameless childhood and to have had a good schooling, which enabled him to learn 'holy writings'. While his father, Erlend, and uncle, *Paul, got on well together as joint earls of Orkney, their sons became rivals and enemies. **Hákon Paulsson** [Hákon Pálsson] (*d. c.*1126) eventually went into exile in Sweden leaving Erlend and his sons ruling Orkney. It is said in *Longer Magnus Saga* that Magnús, in his early manhood, kept evil company with viking marauders, participating in their plunder and killings, but his eulogy in *Orkneyinga Saga* says he was 'hard and unsparing towards robbers and vikings. He put to death the many men who plundered the bonder [farmers] and common people' (*Orkneyinga Saga*, chap. 45). It is difficult to get any realistic impression of the character of Orkney's national saint through the standard hagiographical descriptions. He was:

> a man of extraordinary distinction, tall, with a fine intelligent look about him … a man of strict virtue, successful in war, wise, eloquent, generous and magnanimous, open-handed with money and sound with advice, and altogether the most popular of men.
> (*Orkneyinga Saga*, chap. 45)

The events that took place during the first major military expedition to the west of Magnús Barelegs, king of Norway, in 1098 were as portentous for Magnús Erlendsson as for his father and uncle, Paul and Erlend, who were deprived of their power and sent to Norway, where they died. Magnús and his brother Erling, along with their cousin Hákon (who, according to *Orkneyinga Saga*, was responsible for encouraging King Magnús to embark on this conquering expedition) were taken into the king's *hirð* ('war-band')—Magnús being made cup-bearer—and accompanied the raiding expedition through the Hebrides to north Wales. There, at the battle of Menai Strait against Hugh de Montgomery, earl of Shrewsbury, Magnús acted directly against the interest of his overlord and did not participate in the battle. A key tradition in the later cult depicts him refusing to leave the central 'room' in the king's ship, and reading from his psalter he remained there throughout the ensuing battle. He naturally earned the king's displeasure and wisely slipped away from the ship one night, as it was anchored off the Scottish coast. He is said to have spent some years in exile at the court of the Scottish king, with a bishop in Wales (or maybe Cumbria), and with friends in England.

Magnús's absence and the death of his brother Erling left Hákon Paulsson in an advantageous position for claiming his heritage, and he obtained the title of earl and grant of authority over all the earldom from kings Sigurd and Eystein of Norway a year or two after Magnús Barelegs's death on his second expedition west in 1103. Magnús Erlendsson soon after this returned to Orkney and persuaded Hákon to give up half the earldom, which was confirmed to him by a grant from Eystein. The two ruled together for seven years it is said and a poem composed in their honour recorded joint expeditions against troublesome chieftains, one of them in Shetland. Magnús at some point (perhaps when in exile) married a girl 'from the noblest family there in Scotland' (*Orkneyinga Saga*, chap. 45), but according to the later hagiographical interpretation he succeeded in preserving his chastity for ten years. A much later tradition records his wife's name as Ingarth.

Events leading up to Magnús's death are elaborated in the saga accounts with details of a kind suitable for heightening the tension surrounding the doomed earl's progress towards his martyrdom. Basically the circumstances appear to develop from the usual friction between rival earls who could not agree on a harmonious division of power and lands within the islands. The supporters of the earls are mentioned as being the cause of their quarrels, and also as being concerned to enforce agreements, although surprisingly there is no reference to the role of either the bishop or any other churchmen in the events as recorded. Peace meetings were held, one in Lent at the place of assembly in the mainland (probably Tingwall), and the second at Easter on the island of Egilsay (probably because it was one of the bishop's residences). The themes of foreboding and treachery are skilfully interwoven in the saga account, with Hákon arriving prepared for a military encounter, and with a greater number of ships than had been agreed. There was no fighting, however, and Magnús is presented as the innocent victim, who spent some time in the church on the island before being seized. One saga account implies that he had attempted to hide before giving himself up and making an offer to Hákon—either that he would leave Orkney permanently or even that he be mutilated and imprisoned. As recounted—on the cited authority of the Hebridean Holdbodi, who was one of Magnús's companions—Hákon would have agreed to Magnús's imprisonment, but was forced by his followers to execute him as they insisted that one of the two earls should be killed. '"Better kill him then" said Hakon. "I don't want an early death: I much prefer ruling over people and places"' (*Orkneyinga Saga*, chap. 49). The martyrdom was therefore something of a judicial execution, the outcome of a peace meeting that probably went wrong, with a vociferous majority of the local chieftains supporting Hákon as sole ruler.

The description of Magnús's killing, by an axe-blow to his head delivered by Lifolf, Earl Hákon's cook, has been dramatically confirmed by the discovery of skeletal material in St Magnus's Cathedral in Kirkwall. The remains of two individuals were found hidden inside two piers, and the skull of one of them (contained within a small wooden cist which was probably the interior of the saint's shrine) bears the marks of a head wound. Initially the murdered earl was buried at Christchurch, Birsay, in the church built by his grandfather, Earl *Thorfinn (II) Sigurdson—this was permitted by Earl Hákon only after Magnús's mother, Thora, pleaded with him to allow her to bury her son, as described in one of the most moving passages in the whole of *Orkneyinga Saga*. The death-day of the murdered earl was 16 April, probably 1116, and it was not long before a cult developed around his memory. The miracles done in his name are recorded in the 'List of miracles' (*Jarteinabok*) which forms chapter 57 of *Orkneyinga Saga*, while the pilgrimage undertaken by Hákon 'some years later' (*Orkneyinga Saga*, chap. 52), to Rome and the Holy Land was probably carried out as penance for the crime. The convincing of Bishop William (d. 1168) and the furthering of Magnús's cult by his nephew Earl *Rögnvald [*see under* Harald Maddadson] were important stages in the establishment of the sanctity of the murdered earl, and after some twenty-one years his remains were enshrined on 13 December 1137, eventually being housed in the new cathedral built at Kirkwall by Earl Rögnvald.

This process can be regarded as having been deliberately manipulated for the advantage of the rival line of the earldom family. But Earl Hákon himself was not disadvantaged by the murder of his cousin, and the compiler of *Orkneyinga Saga*, or a later reviser, gives a stout defence of Hákon's period of rule, saying that he 'grew to be a fine administrator and brought firm peace to the land, making new laws for Orkney which the farmers found they liked much better than the ones they'd had before' (*Orkneyinga Saga*, chap. 52).

Hákon's sons, **Harald Smooth-Tongue** [Haraldr inn Sléttmáli] (d. 1131) and **Paul the Silent** [Páll inn Ómálgi] (d. c.1137), who were apparently the issue of different marriages, took over the earldom when their father died about 1126. Harald died in 1131, according to *Orkneyinga Saga* by putting on a poisoned shirt which his mother Helga had prepared for Paul. But there was no external threat to Paul's position for some years, and he was remembered as a popular and unwarlike ruler. In 1137, however, Rögnvald, the son of Magnús's sister Gunnhild, came over from Norway to claim Magnús's half of the earldom, and won support through the growing popular belief in the sanctity of his murdered uncle. Paul was captured and deposed, and seems to have died soon afterwards. The establishment of the cult of St Magnus in the islands put the earldom on a level with the Scandinavian kingdoms, each of which had produced a royal saint in the same period, or earlier. The murdered Earl Magnús became venerated throughout Scandinavia, and his fame earned for the earldom's ruling family, and for their cathedral in Kirkwall, the saint's resting-place, much meritorious renown.   BARBARA E. CRAWFORD

Sources H. Pálsson and P. Edwards, eds. and trans., *The Orkneyinga saga: the history of the earls of Orkney* (1978) • 'Longer Magnus saga', 'Shorter Magnus saga', 'Legenda de sancto Magno', *Icelandic sagas and other historical documents*, ed. G. Vigfússon, 1, Rolls Series, 88 (1887), 1 • H. Palsson and P. Edwards, trans., *Magnus' saga: the life of St. Magnus, earl of Orkney, 1075–1116* (1987) • B. Dickens, 'St Magnus and his countess', *Proceedings of the Orkney Antiquarian Society*, 13 (1934–5), 51–2 • J. Mooney, *St Magnus, earl of Orkney* (1935) • GEC, *Peerage*, new edn, 10, appx A

Magnus Maximus (d. 388), Roman emperor in Britain and the western empire, was blackguarded after his death by Pacatus the panegyrist of his conqueror, the emperor Theodosius. The historical tradition is hostile to a failed usurper, as usual, but there are hints that he was respected in his time. St Martin's Gallic biographer says that he was 'a good man in other respects, but corrupted by the advice of bishops' (Sulpicius Severus, *Dialogues*, iii.11.2) and the Spanish writer Orosius comments that he was 'an energetic and honourable man worthy of being Emperor, if he had not broken his oath and become Emperor by usurpation' (Orosius, vii.34.9).

Early career Maximus was born in Spain, at a place unknown; as emperor he created a new province in the north-east, but since he also created one in Gaul, this may not be significant. He was a kinsman and dependant of Theodosius's father, the Roman general Flavius *Theodosius, with whom he campaigned in Britain (367–8) and Mauretania (373–4); in Mauretania he arrested a corrupt Roman official and two disloyal Moorish chieftains. Since the elder Theodosius was executed at the end of 375, Pacatus's reference to Maximus being 'an exile and a fugitive' (Pacatus, 31.1) may mean that he shared his patron's fall; but as this 'exile' is contrasted with the younger Theodosius's army command (presumably in 378), it need only mean that he was posted to Britain. There he was commander of the Roman garrison during Gratian's reign (r. 375–83); it is not known whether he was formally the *dux*, or held the higher rank of *comes*, but the latter is more likely, since it regularly implied command of mobile units.

Gratian made himself unpopular with his army by favouring certain barbarian recruits, and Maximus in Britain is also said to have resented not being more highly promoted. Pacatus guardedly remarks that he 'boasted of his kinship' with the emperor Theodosius and claimed his tacit support (Pacatus, 24.1 and 43.6). Indeed, since Theodosius's father had been executed in the names of Gratian and his infant brother, Valentinian II (although others gave the actual order), and since Theodosius not only recognized Maximus as co-emperor but after his execution protected Maximus's mother and daughter, this suspicion, even if untrue, was not unfounded. Maximus later claimed, like most usurpers, to have been forced into usurpation by the army; the soldiers may have thought he would be a worthier successor of Gratian's father, Valentinian I (r. 364–75), as indeed did Maximus himself, since he struck coins which imitated Valentinian's obverse portrait and reverse types and in his negotiations with Valentinian's younger son, Valentinian II, asserted a father's authority.

Emperor in the west After being proclaimed emperor in Britain in spring or early summer 383, Maximus invaded

Magnus Maximus (*d.* 388), coin

Gaul with an army. Gratian was still at Verona on 16 June 383, but later that summer confronted Maximus near Paris. However, when after skirmishes his soldiers began to desert him for Maximus, and even his commander-in-chief Merobaudes changed sides, Gratian fled with a small escort for Italy. Maximus sent his cavalry commander Andragathius in pursuit, by whom Gratian was captured and perfidiously killed at Lyons on 25 August 383. Maximus, who insisted that he had not ordered Gratian's death, was now *de facto* ruler of Britain, Gaul, and Hispania, and resided at Valentinian I's old capital of Trier. The younger Valentinian (II), aged only twelve, nominally ruled Italy, the Balkan province of Illyricum, and Africa (roughly modern Tunisia) from Milan, and in their first negotiations Maximus insisted to his envoy Ambrose, the sainted bishop of Milan, that Valentinian should come to him 'like a son to his father' (Ambrose, letter 24.7). Ambrose eluded this demand, but after further negotiation the court at Milan grudgingly recognized Maximus's authority beyond the Alps.

The surviving sources are not explicit about the relations between the three emperors, but it can be deduced that Theodosius, who was preoccupied in the east with Goths and Persians, was prepared to recognize Maximus in the west if he left Valentinian alone. There is certainly no evidence that he actually promoted Maximus's rebellion against Gratian. He and Maximus struck a few coins in each other's name, and in 386 Maximus's praetorian prefect Euodius shared the consulship with Theodosius's younger son Honorius; Maximus's portrait was now formally displayed in the eastern empire. In effect, therefore, he was accepted as a member of the imperial college; an inscription from Tripolitania, an African province subject to Valentinian II, honoured all four emperors: Valentinian, Theodosius, his elder son Arcadius, and Maximus (whose name was later deleted). This was only a working arrangement, not a warm collegiality, but it might last

while each emperor was preoccupied by his own problems. Thus Maximus is said by Orosius to have been 'a formidable man, exacting tribute and military service from the most monstrous German tribes by the terror of his name alone' (Orosius, vii.35.4). Orosius is exaggerating Maximus's strength, to prove that it was only by God's will that he fell, but Maximus himself told Ambrose that there were thousands of barbarians in his service who received rations from him (Ambrose, letter 24.4). There is numismatic evidence that he revisited Britain, perhaps to cope with the invasion of Picts and Scots recorded by the Gallic chronicle of 452 (which, however, implies it was in 383). Gildas alleges that Maximus stripped Britain of its army, administrators, and manpower, but his account has no independent value although it accidentally contains this truth: the usurpation was an important step, though it cannot be quantified, in the reduction of the Roman garrison. Maximus, as the last Roman emperor of Britain according to Gildas, was therefore claimed as their first ancestor by medieval Welsh kings, but this is a ninth-century invention. Historical deductions are invalid, for example that Maximus delegated authority in northern Britain to native chieftains; so too should be regretfully dismissed as fiction the medieval Welsh story of 'Macsen Wledig' (King Maxentius), the emperor of Rome who married the princess of Caernarfon.

Religious attitude Maximus like Gratian was an Orthodox (Nicaean) Christian, an embarrassment to some Catholic students of history, as is clear from a comment by Augustine in *The City of God* (5.25); Maximus told Pope Siricius that he had come to the throne 'straight from the baptismal font', and regarded God as his patron and protector (letter 40 in the *Collectio Avellana*). To Valentinian II, whose Arian mother, Justina, was vainly trying to extort a church for Arian worship from Ambrose at Milan, Maximus wrote a disingenuous warning in 386 that it was dangerous to persecute the Orthodox. He asserted his own Orthodoxy by his unrelenting treatment of his fellow-Spaniard, the heretic Priscillian. Certain Spanish bishops had become suspicious of Priscillian's ascetic practices and teaching, which they equated with Manichaeism and sorcery; Maximus ordered that the case be heard by a synod at Bordeaux, but when Priscillian appealed from it to the emperor, Maximus sent him for trial before the praetorian prefect Euodius at Trier. Priscillian was tortured and beheaded, the first heretic to be formally executed, even if it was for sorcery. This intervention by the secular power was resented by leading western bishops like Ambrose and Martin of Tours, and it was in response to such criticism that Maximus told Pope Siricius that by condemning 'Manichees' he was upholding the unity of the church. His downfall, however, was subsequently attributed by Ambrose to quite another action, his edict of 387 or 388 which censured Christians at Rome for burning down a Jewish synagogue; they exclaimed: 'the emperor has become a Jew' (Ambrose, letter 40.23).

Conquest of Italy and death In 387 there were negotiations between Valentinian II and Maximus to improve their accord, in which Maximus deceived Valentinian's envoy and followed after him with an army. His motives for crossing the Alps are unclear: to make Valentinian his puppet, perhaps, or (like Constantine in 312) to strengthen himself against an inevitable civil war. Italy fell without a struggle in summer 387, but Valentinian and his mother escaped by ship to Salonika where they appealed to Theodosius for restoration. The Roman aristocracy acquiesced, however, judging by the decision of the orator Symmachus to deliver a panegyric of Maximus in January 388. Theodosius himself was slow to react. According to the pagan Eunapius's hostile account, he delayed until he was offered the prospect of marrying Valentinian's seductive sister, Galla, but it is more likely that he needed time to mobilize against the formidable western army. In the event, he moved decisively: in summer 388 his army advanced up the Sava valley, defeated Maximus's brother Marcellinus and his other generals at Siscia (Sisak) and Poetovio (Ptuj), and then trapped Maximus himself at Aquileia. Maximus surrendered, perhaps in hope of mercy, but Theodosius's generals immediately executed him, probably on 28 July 388. His son Victor, whom he had left in Gaul as titular emperor (Augustus), was arrested soon after and also executed.   R. S. O. TOMLIN

Sources Pacatus, *Panegyric to the Emperor Theodosius*, ed. and trans. C. E. V. Nixon (1987) · Zosimus, *Historia nova: the decline of Rome*, ed. and trans. J. J. Buchanan and H. T. Davis (1967), iv. 35–46 · *Sulpicii Severi libri qui supersunt*, ed. C. Halm (Vienna, 1866) · Sulpicius Severus, *Vie de Saint Martin*, ed. and trans. J. Fontaine, 3 vols. (1967–9) · Orosius, 'Historiarum libri septem', *Patrologia Latina*, 31 (1846), vii.34–5 · H. Dessau, ed., *Inscriptiones Latinae selectae* (1892–1916) · *L'Année Épigraphique*, no. 58 (1960), 133–5 · Ambrose, *Patrologia Latina*, 16–17 (1845), nos. 24, 40 · T. Mommsen, ed., 'Chronica gallica', *Chronica minora saec. IV. V. VI. VII.*, 1, 615–66, MGH Auctores Antiquissimi, 9 (Berlin, 1892) · Gildas: 'The ruin of Britain', and other works, ed. and trans. M. Winterbottom (1978), chaps. 13, 14 · P. J. Casey, 'Magnus Maximus in Britain', *The end of Roman Britain* [Durham 1978], ed. P. J. Casey (1979), 66–79 · D. N. Dumville, 'Sub-Roman Britain: history and legend', *History*, new ser., 62 (1977), 173–92, esp. 173–82 · Augustine, *City of God*, ed. and trans. H. S. Bettenson (1972), 5.15 · O. Guenther, ed., *Collectio Avellana*, Corpus Scriptorum Ecclesiasticorum Latinorum, 35 (1895–8), nos. 39, 40 · W. Ensslin, 'Maximus', *Paulys Real-Encyclopädie der classischen Altertumswissenchaft*, ed. G. Wissowa and W. Kroll, new edn, 14/2 (Stuttgart, 1930), 2546–55 · A. H. M. Jones, J. R. Martindale, and J. Morris, *The prosopography of the later Roman empire*, 1: AD 260–395 (1971), 588 · J. Matthews, *Western aristocracies and imperial court, AD 364–425* (1975), 165–8, 173–82, 223–5 · H. Chadwick, *Priscillian of Avila* (1976), 42–3, 111–48
Likenesses coin, BM [*see illus.*]

Magnus [*née* Emanuel], **Katie**, **Lady Magnus** (1844–1924), writer and schoolteacher, was born on 2 May 1844 at 101 High Street, Portsmouth, one of six children of Alderman Emanuel Emanuel (*c*.1801–1888), a goldsmith and the first Jewish mayor of Portsmouth, and his wife, Julia Moss of Plymouth. Katie's paternal grandfather, Moses Emanuel, together with his brother Joel, had come to England from Steinhardt in Bavaria, was naturalized in 1801, and lived in Hanway Street, off Oxford Street in the West End of London. His two sons, Ezekiel and Emanuel, moved to Portsmouth where they set up as goldsmiths at 101 High Street. The Emanuel family exhibited a strong creative streak.

Katie Magnus, Lady Magnus (1844–1924), by L. Franklin

Katie's 'favourite' older brother, Barrow *Emanuel (1842–1904) [*see under* Davis, Henry David], became a partner in the successful architectural practice of Davis and Emanuel. Cousins included the artists Charles and Frank Emanuel and Walter Emanuel, who was a contributor to *Punch*.

Brought up in a comfortable, provincial middle-class Victorian Jewish family, Katie Emanuel married into what Chaim Bermant (*The Cousinhood*, 1971) termed 'The Annex' of the Anglo-Jewish 'cousinhood'. Her husband, Sir Philip *Magnus (1842–1933), whom she married on 29 March 1870 in the garden of her parents' home, Grove House, Southsea, was related to all the big families that dominated British Jewry in the nineteenth century: Rothschilds, Montefiores, Goldsmids, and Mocattas. Indeed Katie and Philip were themselves second cousins. Philip was minister of the prestigious West London Synagogue, the 'cathedral' of Reform Judaism, between 1866 and 1880, and served as Conservative MP for London University from 1906 until 1922. The main family home was Tangley Hill, Chilworth, in Surrey, designed by Barrow Emanuel. Of their three surviving children, Laurie (1872–1933) was the best-known, as a writer and journalist, and was himself the father of the biographer Sir Philip *Magnus (1906–1988).

Nevertheless, Katie Magnus was an independent spirit and established a name for herself in her own right as an accomplished author and pioneer of youth clubs for girls. Like many women of her social standing, she had been educated at home and was virtually self-taught in Hebrew. Her obituarist in the *Jewish Chronicle* judged her to have been 'deeply religious, though of course not orthodox in observance'. Katie began her teaching career in the Portsmouth 'sabbath school and synagogue' at the age of seventeen, and continued it at West London and the Bayswater Jewish schools. Her literary output was largely educational in intent. She published her first books for children between 1865 and 1869 under the *nom de plume* H. N., and wrote a number of school textbooks on both Jewish and English historical themes. *About the Jews in Bible Times* appeared in 1881; her best-known work, *Outlines of Jewish History*, was published in 1886, and *Jewish Portraits* in 1888.

She also wrote articles for journals such as the *National Review*, the *Westminster Gazette*, and the *Jewish Chronicle*.

Her privileged position notwithstanding, Katie had a well-developed social conscience. She was involved with several philanthropic causes within the Jewish community, including the ladies' committee of the Jews' Deaf and Dumb Home and the Jewish Home for Incurables, and was active in the Jewish Association for the Protection of Girls and Women, which aimed to combat the white slave traffic during the period of mass Jewish migration from eastern Europe in the late nineteenth century. However, Katie's greatest efforts were directed towards expanding the opportunities available to girls from poor Jewish families in London. When still only twenty-two she founded the Jewish Girls' Club (1886) in Leman Street in the East End—the first institution of its kind in the Jewish community for either of the sexes. Later, she assisted Lily Montagu at the West Central Girls' Club (1893). Lady Magnus died of influenza at her London home, 16 Gloucester Terrace, Hyde Park, on 2 March 1924. Two days later she was buried in the Reform section of the Golders Green Jewish cemetery.

SHARMAN KADISH

Sources *Jewish World* (6 March 1924) · *Jewish Chronicle* (7 March 1924) · *The Times* (22 Feb 1924) · *The Times* (4 March 1924) · F. Foden, *Philip Magnus: Victorian educational pioneer* (1970) · H. Furniss, *Some Victorian women: good, bad and indifferent* (1923) · R. Sebag-Montefiore, *A family patchwork: five generations of an Anglo-Jewish family* (1987) · R. Sebag-Montefiore, 'A quest for a grandfather: Sir Philip Magnus, 1st Bt., Victorian educationalist', *Jewish Historical Studies*, 34 (1994–6), 141–59 · b. cert. · *CGPLA Eng. & Wales* (1924)
Likenesses H. Gibbs, pencil wash, *c*.1860, repro. in Sebag-Montefiore, *Family patchwork*; priv. coll. · photograph, *c*.1912, repro. in Sebag-Montefiore, 'A quest for a grandfather', 154 · photograph, *c*.1920, repro. in Sebag-Montefiore, *Family patchwork*; priv. coll. · L. Franklin, watercolour, 1923, repro. in Sebag-Montefiore, *Family patchwork*; priv. coll. · L. Franklin, miniature, Jewish Museum, London [*see illus.*] · portraits, repro. in Sebag-Montefiore, *Family patchwork*
Wealth at death £1696 19*s*. 7*d*.: administration, 12 April 1924, *CGPLA Eng. & Wales*

Magnus, Sir Philip, first baronet (1842–1933), educationist and politician, was born on 7 October 1842 at 160 High Holborn, London, the second of the five children of Jacob Magnus (1805–1888), a tailor and later a wine merchant, and his wife, Caroline Barnett (1808/9–1894). Jacob Magnus had moved from Chatham to London, where his business enabled him to leave an estate valued at £6800 at his death in 1888. The marriage, though it produced five children, was not a happy one and ended in separation. Laurie, the eldest son, born in 1840, died of meningitis in 1863; Edward, the youngest child, emigrated to Sydney, Australia, where he died in 1922. The two daughters, Sarah and Josephine, did not marry.

Laurie and Philip Magnus began their education at Poland Street Academy (preparatory school, 1850–54), from which they progressed to University College School, London (1854–8). This school had been established in 1829 to provide an efficient middle-class education for Jewish and nonconformist boys at moderate cost. The curriculum emphasized modern studies—mathematics, languages, and science—which at the time were not taught in more

Sir Philip Magnus, first baronet (1842–1933), by Lafayette, 1927

traditionally organized schools for the middle classes. A further aim of the school was to prepare boys for entry to its parent, University College, which Magnus entered in autumn 1858. He graduated in 1863 with a first-class degree in arts and the following year with similar distinction in science.

Magnus was a regular attender at the West London Reform Synagogue and, having determined to dedicate his life to the service of God, spent the next three years at Berlin University, the centre of Jewish Reform, the movement which gave rise to the West London Synagogue. In 1866 he was appointed assistant minister at the Reform synagogue, Margaret Street, Portland Place, London, at a salary of £150 p.a. He served as rabbi in the synagogue for fourteen years, first in Margaret Street and later in its new premises in Upper Berkeley Street. His duties were to preach, teach, and to organize, and he became involved in the affairs of the synagogue and other Jewish causes and enterprises. To supplement his income he began to tutor private students in mathematics, mechanics, and physics. As his reputation grew so his involvement with educational institutions and associations widened. He lectured at University College, its school, and hospital, was appointed visiting lecturer in the theory and practice of education at Stockwell Training College, and was an examiner for the College of Preceptors. As a member of convocation he was drawn into the recurring discussions there for the reform of the University of London. In 1875 he published his first textbook, *Lessons in Elementary Mechanics*, which became a best-seller and the first of a series of elementary science textbooks published by Longmans.

Any tensions between Magnus's duties at the synagogue and his extensive educational commitments were resolved in 1880 when he was appointed director and organizing secretary of the newly created City and Guilds of London Institute for the Advancement of Technical Education. The institute had been set up two years previously by a few of the leading livery companies of the City of London in response to pressure from critics of the unreformed corporation and the privileged companies. Many of these critics were associated with the Liberal Party. They argued that the companies should spend some of their wealth on technical education on account of their historical association with apprenticeship. These Liberal attacks on the companies, including threats of a royal commission to reveal their wealth, stimulated a few companies to take steps to establish the institute of which Magnus was the principal administrator for thirty-five years. Led by the Clothworkers' Company, the companies formed a defence committee which produced in 1878 a 'Report on technical education' containing a detailed plan for action on three fronts: a central institution for the training of technologists; two 'model' trade or technical schools; and a national scheme of technical examinations driven by the principle of 'payment by results'.

Under Magnus's leadership these plans were put into effect. The examinations in trade and technical subjects of the Society of Arts were taken over in 1879; the Finsbury Technical College and the School of Art in Kennington were opened in the 1880s; and the Central Institute or City and Guilds Engineering College was established at South Kensington. As the activities of the institute matured—notably with the increase in entries for its widening prospectus of trade and technical certificates—it came to be seen as a private ministry of technical education with Magnus as its nationally known chief spokesman and representative. At times this gave rise to jealousy on the part of liverymen who resented large expenditure on the Central Institute located outside the City of London. Also, when in 1899 a central authority for all sectors of public education was finally established, officers of the new Board of Education were affronted by the influence over the technical sector of education of what was in effect a private agency.

Now a national figure in technical education, Magnus was a member of the royal commission on technical instruction appointed by the Liberal government in 1881. Chaired by Bernhard Samuelson, the commissioners surveyed technical education at home and abroad and made recommendations for reforms. Magnus reported on the systems in France, Germany, Italy, Austria, and Switzerland and for his work was awarded a knighthood (1886), an early instance of that honour being conferred for services to education. Thereafter he was involved in every important movement for technical education up to 1914. He was a member of the executive committee of the National Association for the Promotion of Technical and Secondary Education, one key source of pressure for educational reform at the time. From 1893 he served on the London school board, where his 'three planks' were the abolition of fees for elementary education, the ending of payment by results, and the broadening of the curriculum by the introduction of instruction in practical arts and skills. He served too on the committee which reported in favour of the creation of the Imperial College of Science and Technology through the combination of the Royal School of Mines, the Royal College of Science, and the City and Guilds College.

In 1910 Magnus published *Educational Aims and Efforts, 1880–1910*, which summarized his many activities promoting 'technical education', at a time when the term referred to modern studies and curricula in general as well as to trade and technical subjects. He retired from the City and Guilds Institute in 1915 after thirty-five years' service which saw the institute established as a body of national and international importance. In this he was acknowledged by colleagues in the technical education movement to have played a major part. His position as the greatest living authority on the subject led to him being asked to contribute the entry on technical education in the famous eleventh edition of the *Encyclopaedia Britannica*. This survey, occupying twenty-three columns, is a rich source for students of the formative period of English technical education.

From 1906 to 1922 Magnus represented London University as a Unionist MP, the first Jew to serve as a representative for one of the university seats. This was a fitting position for Magnus, who had maintained his commitment to the development of the university, notably as a member of convocation active in unsuccessful attempts to reform its structure. In 1917 he accepted a baronetcy.

On 29 March 1870, in the same year that he joined the institute, Magnus married Katie (1844–1924) [*see* Magnus, Katie], daughter of the goldsmith Emanuel Emanuel of Southsea; they lived first in London, then in 1893 moved to Tangley Hill, Chilworth, Surrey. There were five children of the marriage of whom three survived. As the children grew, Katie Magnus became active in Jewish educational and social causes, especially in the East End of London. She was a regular contributor to journals and is remembered for her *Outlines of Jewish History* (1886; rev. edns, 1924 and 1958).

Magnus, too, was proud of his Jewishness but was not a Zionist. He served the community as chairman of the Jewish war memorial council, and as a vice-president of the Jewish board of deputies, of the Anglo-Jewish association, and of Jews' College. He died at his home, Tangley Hill, on 29 August 1933 and was buried on 31 August at Golders Green cemetery. His two sons predeceased him; the eldest, Laurie Magnus (1872–1933), was a publisher and chairman of the Girls' Public Day School Trust. Philip Magnus was succeeded as second baronet by his grandson, the historian Sir Philip Montefiore *Magnus (1906–1988).

BILL BAILEY

Sources F. E. Foden, *Philip Magnus: Victorian educational pioneer* (1970) · R. Sebag-Montefiore, 'A quest for a grandfather: Sir Philip

Magnus, 1st Bt., Victorian educationalist', *Jewish Historical Studies*, 34 (1994–6), 141–59 • b. cert. • m. cert. • d. cert.

Archives King's AC Cam., letters to Oscar Browning • U. Southampton L., corresp. of members of his family with J. H. Hertz

Likenesses Spy [L. Ward], cartoon, 1891, priv. coll. • Lafayette, photograph, 1927, NPG [*see illus.*] • portraits, priv. coll.

Wealth at death £41,955 17s. 11d.: probate, 28 Oct 1933, *CGPLA Eng. & Wales*

Magnus [*later* Magnus-Allcroft], **Sir Philip Montefiore, second baronet** (1906–1988), historian, was born at 8 Craven Hill Gardens, London, on 8 February 1906. He was the eldest child of the two sons and three daughters of Laurie Magnus (1872–1933), publisher and a director of Routledge, and his wife, Dora Marian Spielman (1882?–1972), eldest daughter of Sir Isidore Spielman and granddaughter of Sir Joseph Sebag-Montefiore. His grandfather was Sir Philip *Magnus, first baronet (1842–1933), the educationist. The family was prominent in public and Jewish life in London. Magnus was educated at Westminster School and Wadham College, Oxford, graduating BA in 1928 with a second class in modern history. At Oxford, he was 'a popular figure, almost a dandy, given to wearing top hats' (*The Times*, 22 Dec 1988). In 1928 he entered the civil service as an assistant principal in the office of works and then the Board of Education, but the death of first his father and then his grandfather meant that in 1933 he inherited the title from the latter. He resigned from the civil service and began literary work, in 1939 publishing a life of Edmund Burke. During the Second World War he served in the Royal Artillery and the intelligence corps, ending with the rank of major. On 14 July 1943 in Onibury parish church in an Anglican service he married Jewell Allcroft (b. 1907) of Stokesay Court, Onibury, Craven Arms, Shropshire, daughter of the late Herbert John Allcroft, gentleman, and his wife, Margaret Jane Russell (later Mrs John Rotton). They had no children. His wife's home became his own for the rest of his life. In 1951 by deed poll he added the name of Allcroft to his own and his domestic habits became those of an Anglican squire.

After the war, Magnus returned to the civil service as a principal in the Ministry of Town and Country Planning, but again retired from it in 1951, in which year he published a life of Sir Walter Raleigh (rev. edns 1956, 1968). Magnus's success as a biographer began with his *Gladstone* (1954). This was based on the huge collection of Gladstone papers at Hawarden, which he was the first to use extensively, as well as the collection in the British Museum. Magnus was the first to give details of Gladstone's 'rescue work' with prostitutes, which he charitably described as innocent. The biography was an important work in the rehabilitation of interest in the Victorians, and was written in a markedly different tone from that of Lytton Strachey's *Eminent Victorians* (1918). Magnus took Gladstone seriously, but not very seriously, and his book was an effective combination of research and readability. Magnus did not have access to Gladstone's diaries and their ancillary papers, but he seemed to some a natural choice to be invited to edit them. However, Archbishop Fisher, who owned the diaries, was swayed by objections from

A. Tilney Bassett, the Gladstones' archivist, who felt that Magnus's biography had been too flippant.

On the strength of his *Gladstone*, which over the years sold almost 50,000 copies, and his biography of Kitchener (1958, selling 12,000 copies, revised edn 1968), Magnus was invited to give the prestigious Ford lectures at Oxford. He accepted, but, alarmed by A. L. Rowse, who warned him that he would be 'torn to pieces by third-rate dons', withdrew early in 1961 just as the titles of the lectures were due to be published. Instead, he published a life, *Edward VII* (1964), a fine work of research in the Royal Archives and one of the best of royal lives. It set a new standard with a new tone—scholarly and amusing but not republican—for such works and sold well: over 20,000 copies. He was asked, but declined, to write a life of Wellington, the task then falling to Elizabeth Longford. Poor eyesight made the reading of Victorian handwriting difficult, and in his later years Magnus could hardly read or write at all. With Elizabeth Longford and Janet Adam Smith, Magnus was the best of those who write in the tricky area of the well-researched biography which bridges the popular and the academic.

Magnus was an active Salopian, serving as a JP, county councillor, and alderman, and chairman of the planning committee, 1962–74, and of the records committee; he was chairman of the governors of Attingham College and was governor of Ludlow grammar school, 1952–77. Nationally, he was a trustee of the National Portrait Gallery, 1970–77, and was, his fellow trustee Elizabeth Longford recalled, 'a natural public servant' (*The Guardian*, 23 Dec 1988). Magnus died from myocardial infarction at Stokesay Court on 21 December 1988, his wife surviving him. His body was cremated. The title passed to his nephew, Laurence Henry Philip Magnus (b. 1955).

H. C. G. MATTHEW

Sources *The Times* (22 Dec 1988) • *The Guardian* (23 Dec 1988) • *WW* • Burke, *Peerage* (1999) • Burke, *Gen. GB* (1937) [Allcroft of Stokesay Court] • Oxf. UA, UR6/EH/1, files 3–4 • R. Sebag-Montefiore, *A family patchwork* (1987) • personal knowledge (2004) • private information (2004)

Archives SOUND BL NSA, performance recording

Wealth at death £480,313: probate, 13 March 1989, *CGPLA Eng. & Wales*

Magnus, Thomas (1463/4–1550), administrator and diplomat, was born in Newark-on-Trent, Nottinghamshire, the son of John Magnus and his wife, Alice. His early education is obscure, but he rose in consequence of the patronage of Thomas Savage, archbishop of York, beginning royal service as chaplain to Henry VII and establishing himself as an important figure in northern diplomacy and administration. He had achieved sufficient favour to receive the archdeaconry of the East Riding of Yorkshire from 1504, and he worked as a treasurer with the northern armies, sending diplomatic reports back to the council from Scotland and the north of England. He established a close personal relationship with Henry VIII's sister, Margaret Tudor, queen of Scotland, who describes him as counsellor and chaplain in letters to her brother, and he served on a number of diplomatic missions to Scotland, including commissions to negotiate Anglo-Scottish truces. He was incorporated at Oxford in 1520, having already obtained a doctorate abroad, and was with the king that year at the Field of Cloth of Gold, serving also as a member of the council. Magnus was a notable example of the civil service pluralist who was instrumental, through assiduous royal service, in consolidating the Henrician Reformation.

Rewards heaped on Magnus for loyal service included a canonry at Windsor from 1520 to 1547, and the prebend of North Kelsey in the diocese of Lincoln from 1521 to 1522 and of Corringham from 1522 to 1549. In 1524 Wolsey, fearing the influence of the pro-French lobby in Scotland, entrusted Magnus with the task of reconciling Margaret with her second husband, Archibald Douglas, fifth earl of Angus. The mission proved unsuccessful owing to Margaret's unrelenting antipathy towards Angus. Four years later Magnus was instructed to attempt a reconciliation between James V, following his assumption of royal authority in 1528, and his former chancellor the pro-English Angus. When, early in 1529, James gave Magnus his version of the events of 1528, the latter took the opportunity to deliver a warning to the young king about the dangers of using 'yong consaill', citing as an example the fate of James III in a lecture impertinently threatening to a crowned monarch and inaccurate in its content. Impetus was lent to Magnus's efforts by the fear that James would contract a foreign marriage alliance. In the face of this threat Wolsey was adamant that Angus should be reinstated in order to act as Henry's agent in Scotland. To strengthen the earl's position Magnus was instructed to deny rumours that Angus had ever intended to kidnap James at the instruction of the English king. However, the complexities of Scottish border and national politics rendered it virtually impossible for the earl to regain his influence with James.

In 1525 Henry sent his illegitimate son Henry Fitzroy, duke of Richmond, to head the council of the north. Magnus served as the council's surveyor and receiver-general, devoting great effort to the reorganization of its poorly ordered accounts and records. As a royal agent, he also pressured the northern clergy to pay a large fine to the king to avoid charges under the Statute of Praemunire, and in 1533 he assisted Rowland Lee, bishop of Coventry and Lichfield, to induce the northern convocation to accept the unpopular royal divorce. Henry's gratitude meant that by the mid-1530s Magnus held the masterships of St Leonard's Hospital at York, the college of St Sepulchre, near York Minster, and Sibthorpe College, Nottinghamshire, in addition to being vicar of Kendal, Westmorland, and rector of Bedale, Kirkby in Cleveland and Sessay, all in the North Riding of Yorkshire. It is a measure of his importance that his eight benefices in the diocese of York alone yielded £814 per annum.

On 21 April 1533 Magnus wrote to Thomas Cromwell, the king's secretary, stating that he had sent to Nottinghamshire for his horses to go north to the convocation at York although he had been sick, his 'old body now so oft clogged with infirmity and unwieldiness' (*LP Henry VIII*, 6.361). Nevertheless, he lived for another seventeen years, serving on royal commissions, as JP for all three ridings of Yorkshire from 1538 to 1550, and on the council of the north. He was present in 1535 when Lee preached a sermon supporting Henry's break with Rome and, in a report dated 1 July 1535 concerning the conformity found in the charter house and parish church of Hull, Magnus states that there 'is not a more quiet jurisdiction than my archdeaconry' (*LP Henry VIII*, 8.968).

In 1536 Thomas Darcy, Baron Darcy, wrote to the king mentioning the assistance given to him by Magnus concerning the insurrection in Lincolnshire and the East Riding, and the archdeacon was also involved in the suppression of the monasteries. In a plea to the king from Thomas Howard, third duke of Norfolk, on 16 June 1537 to strengthen the council of the north, he referred to Magnus as a good old man, although less able every day. Indeed, infirmity in the form of a bad leg prevented Magnus from going to see the king in December 1537. He continued to take part in the council, his signature appearing in its records over the next few years, but on 1 December 1539 he surrendered the mastership of St Leonard's Hospital and all his possessions in York in exchange for a pension, a dwelling house, the grange of Beningborough in Yorkshire, and other grants. He was cultivated by the new regime of Edward VI. Edward Seymour, duke of Somerset and lord protector, paid him an annuity of £15 11s. 2d. in 1547-8 out of his own purse.

In 1529 Magnus founded a grammar school and chantry to pray for the souls of his father, mother, and sisters, but his intention was rendered void by the dissolution of chantries in the late 1540s. He died aged eighty-six at Sessay on 28 August 1550 and was buried beneath a portrait brass in the chancel of the parish church there, notwithstanding his wish, expressed in his will, to be buried in York Minster beside his erstwhile patron, Savage.

C. A. MCGLADDERY

Sources A. G. Dickens, ed., *Clifford letters of the sixteenth century*, SurtS, 172 (1962) • J. Cameron, *James V: the personal rule, 1528–1542*, ed. N. Macdougall (1998) • A. G. Dickens, *The English Reformation*, 2nd edn (1989) • *LP Henry VIII* • R. G. Eaves, *Henry VIII's Scottish diplomacy, 1513–1524* (New York, 1971)
Archives BL, Cotton MSS, corresp.
Likenesses brass, parish church of Sessay, Yorkshire

Magnússon, Eiríkur (1833–1913), librarian and Icelandic scholar, was born in the parsonage of Berufjörður in east Iceland on 1 February 1833, the second son and third child of the Revd Magnús Bergsson (1799–1892), then curate of Berufjörður, and his wife, Vilborg Eiríksdóttir (1804–1862). When his elder brother became ill, he was given the chance of advanced education and, after elementary Latin tuition by his father, entered Reykjavík Latin school in 1849 and received his dimissory certificate in 1856. He then attended Reykjavík Theological College and received the degree of *candidatus theologiae* (BD) in 1858 with first-class honours. In 1857 he married Sigríður Einarsdóttir

Eiríkur Magnússon (1833–1913), by Hay, 1867

(1831–1915) of Reykjavík; they had no living children, but they fostered two children of his brother and sister.

Magnússon's initial intention was to offer himself as a curate to his father in his better-endowed living of Kirkjubær í Hróarstungu, but events took a different turn. Among the many British travellers who visited Iceland in the mid-nineteenth century was the Quaker Isaac Sharp, who had been sent by the British and Foreign Bible Society to make arrangements for a new Icelandic version of the Bible, to be made in Iceland and published by the society. An Icelandic proof-reader well-versed in English was needed in London for this project. Magnússon was already noted in Reykjavík as an exceptionally skilful linguist, especially in English, and was chosen by the Icelandic church authorities. He left for London (via Copenhagen and Berlin) in 1862–3; he was to remain in Britain for the rest of his life.

On his journey Magnússon met A. C. Swinburne's friend George E. J. Powell, with whom he struck up a friendship which was to be extremely profitable for him. Not only was Powell to prove a financial crutch in the next eight lean years, but he also helped Magnússon to produce his first English publication, a translation of a large portion of Jón Árnason's classic collection of Icelandic folk-tales (2 vols., 1864–6), and introduced him to William Morris. Morris became Magnússon's faithful friend and collaborator for over thirty years, during which the two men

laboured hard at making medieval Icelandic literature known to a larger public; their efforts culminated in the six-volume *Saga Library* (1891–1905). In order to keep himself and his wife, Magnússon also worked on a miscellaneous collection of linguistic and literary projects, such as an edition and translation of the devotional poem *Lilja* (1870), and he gradually acquired a circle of influential friends who were to support his election to an underlibrarianship at Cambridge University Library, to which he was appointed in 1871, and which he held until his retirement in 1909.

At Cambridge, Magnússon proved an enthusiastic member of the small band, led by Henry Bradshaw, who strove to modernize the workings of the university library. His ingenuity in library matters may be seen in the reports of the library syndicate in the 1870s and 1880s, and the numerous papers which he published on various aspects of librarianship show his endless goodwill and remarkable practical sense in his profession.

Not content with library work, Magnússon also helped W. W. Skeat to build an Old Icelandic component, which he taught from the early 1880s, into the Anglo-Saxon tripos. He was given the title of lecturer in Icelandic in 1893, and retained it until H. M. Chadwick took it over. He proved an excellent, if pedantic teacher, as Sir Israel Gollancz and Dame Bertha Philpotts were to testify. He also published solid contributions to Scandinavian studies, the most notable (after his work with Morris) being his Rolls Series edition of *Thómas saga erkibiskups* (1876–83), a series of papers on runology, work on the Elder Edda, and on the history of the first Commonwealth. At the very end of his life he produced a remarkable verse translation of J. L. Runeberg's epic poem *King Fialar* (1912). Most of this work has been superseded by the efforts of later scholars, but much of it, especially the papers on calendar runes which Magnússon published in the 1870s and 1880s in the *Transactions of the Cambridge Philological Society*, was pioneering work. He also built up a valuable collection of facsimiles of Scandinavian 'clog calendars', which is now held in the Cambridge University Library.

Magnússon's fierce patriotism led him to support every move to set Iceland free from its dependence on Denmark, and here he was to prove an unyielding and furious opponent of anyone who was, in his opinion, acting against Iceland's best interests. He did not confine himself to patriotism on paper: twice (in 1875–6 and 1882–3) he promoted collections to buy food and led expeditions to save people in north and east Iceland from starvation, undergoing considerable personal discomfort when chartering cargo vessels, which he himself led to the harbours of the most affected districts. These works of charity were not always popular with other Icelanders, however, as the country had not been universally affected by these natural disasters: in his later effort he was savagely attacked by his main enemy in England, Guðbrandur Vigfússon, with whom he had already clashed over the 1866 Bible translation. However, for over forty years Magnússon's home in Cambridge was renowned among Icelanders for the warmth of his and his wife's hospitality.

Magnússon died at 7 The Terrace, Camden Square, London, on 24 January 1913 of heart failure after a long urinary illness. His papers and correspondence, both immense, are (other than official papers at Cambridge) in the National University of Iceland Library in Reykjavík.

B. S. BENEDIKZ

Sources S. Einarsson, *Saga Eiríks Magnússonar* (Reykjavík, 1933) · S. Einarsson, 'Eiríkur Magnússon', *Studia centennialia … Benedikt S. Þórarinsson* (1961), 33–50 · H. Pétursson, *Steingrímur Thorsteinsson* (1964) · B. S. Benedikz, 'Guðbrandur Vigfússon', *Andvari* (1989), 166–88 · private information (2004) · d. cert.
Archives National University of Iceland Library | CUL, Steingrímur Thorsteinsson MSS · National University of Iceland Library, Benedikt S. Þórarinsson MSS
Likenesses Hay, photograph, 1867, National Museum of Iceland [*see illus.*] · photographs, repro. in Einarsson, *Saga Eiríks Magnússonar*

Magraidhin, Aughuistín [Augustin Macgradoigh, Augustine MacGrane] (*c.*1349–1405), chronicler, was a canon regular of St Augustine at the priory of All Saints, on Saints' Island, Lough Ree, on the River Shannon in Ireland. Nothing is known of his background. He is described by a colleague as 'undisputed master of sacred and secular wisdom, including Latin learning, history, and many other sciences, … compiler of this book and many other books, including Lives of Saints and histories' (ÓhInnse, 176–7). The book in question survives as a fragmentary set of contemporary Irish annals, contained in Bodleian MS Rawlinson B.488, and often wrongly described as a continuation of the annals of Tigernach. The first section is in Magraidhin's own hand and the entries are noteworthy as the fullest Irish account of Richard II's first expedition to that country in 1394–5, quite distinct from a set of earlier annals from the same location, the 'Book of Saints' Island', used by the four masters for their own work. A translation of a life of St John the Evangelist from Latin to Irish is attributed to Magraidhin in the fifteenth-century manuscript, *Liber flavus Fergusiorum*; but the further attribution by J. Colgan of the anthology of Latin lives of Irish saints in Bodleian MS Rawlinson B.505 to Magraidhin has been disputed by modern scholars. Magraidhin died at the priory of All Saints on Wednesday 28 October 1405.

KATHARINE SIMMS

Sources S. Ó hInnse, ed. and trans., *Miscellaneous Irish annals, AD 1114–1437* (1947), xiv–xix, 176–7 · R. Sharpe, *Medieval Irish saints' lives: an introduction to Vitae sanctorum Hiberniae* (1991), 247–65 · A. Gwynn and R. N. Hadcock, *Medieval religious houses: Ireland* (1970), 194 · S. H. O'Grady, R. Flower, and M. Dillon, *Catalogue of Irish manuscripts in the British Museum*, 3 vols. (1926–53), 1 · E. MacLysaght, *The surnames of Ireland* (1973), 134 · J. Colgan, *Acta sanctorum veteris et majoris Scotiae seu Hiberniae*, 1 (1645)
Archives Bodl. Oxf., MS Rawlinson B.488

Magrath, John Macrory. *See* Mac Craith, Seaán mac Ruaidhrí (*fl.* mid-14th cent.).

Magrath, John Richard (1839–1930), college head, was born at St Peter Port in Guernsey on 29 January 1839, the third son of Nicholas Magrath, surgeon in the Royal Navy, and his wife, Sarah Mauger Monk. He was educated at

John Richard Magrath (1839–1930), by unknown engraver (after John Collier, 1898)

Elizabeth College, Guernsey, before winning a classical scholarship at Oriel College, Oxford, at the age of seventeen. He obtained a first class in *literae humaniores* and a fourth class in mathematics in 1860. The same year he won the Stanhope essay prize with an essay entitled *The Fall of the Republic of Florence*, and was elected a fellow of Queen's College, one of the first to be elected by open competition under the ordinances of 1858. In 1861 he began to read theology, and won the Johnson theological scholarship, finding time also to be president of the Oxford Union. He was ordained deacon in 1863 and priest in 1864. His tastes lay mainly in the direction of *literae humaniores*, especially Aristotelian philosophy, and for some years he was well known as a Greats tutor, numbering among his pupils Edward Talbot, afterwards warden of Keble College and bishop of Winchester, and W. G. F. Phillimore. These, and many more, looked back with gratitude to Magrath's long-vacation reading parties at Beddgelert.

In 1864 Magrath succeeded to a tutorship at Queen's College, where the provost, William Jackson, left the running of the college largely in his hands. From 1864 until 1877 he held the office of dean, and drastically, but with tact and patience, reformed the discipline of the college. He was also chaplain of the college from 1867 to 1878, and in 1874 he assumed the office of bursar, retaining to the end of his life a close knowledge of the college estates. In 1876 he became senior proctor, responsible for undergraduate discipline in the university.

In 1877 Jackson appointed Magrath to assist him as pro-

provost, and a year later Magrath succeeded him as provost. On 27 October 1887 he married Jackson's third daughter, Georgiana Isabella (d. 1899); they had no children. Magrath was elected a member of the hebdomadal council in 1878, and served on it for twenty-one years. He was curator of the university chest from 1885 to 1908, and was for many years also a curator of the Sheldonian Theatre, and a delegate of the Common University Fund and of the University Museum (1903–12). He did particularly valuable work as a delegate of Oxford University Press from 1894 to 1920. It was during his chairmanship of this body that he made himself responsible for the authorization of the proposal made by Henry Frowde in 1896 for the foundation of a branch of the press in New York, a courageous measure from which the press reaped substantial benefits. In 1894 Magrath became vice-chancellor of the university, and for four years he carried out the duties and maintained the traditions of this office with dignity and ability. He was then at the height of his powers, and made a picturesque figure, with his flowing beard, his keen but kindly eyes, and his courtly bearing.

Throughout his life Magrath took a keen interest in municipal affairs, and was, in fact, the first Oxford don to accept civic office, first as a member of the Oxford local board, of which he was chairman from 1882 to 1887, and then, on its dissolution and the reconstitution of the city council, as alderman from 1889 to 1895. He was a JP for Oxfordshire from 1883. In Magrath's earlier days, when Oxford was still a country town, the city was decidedly dominated by the university, and resented its subservience. There was often friction between 'town and gown' and Magrath did significant work in mediating between the two.

In politics Magrath was a Liberal, a supporter and personal friend of Lord Rosebery, and a devoted admirer of Gladstone. In education, also, he was progressive up to a point. He was wholeheartedly in favour of the movement for the higher education of women. He supported Miss Beale in her pioneer work at Cheltenham Ladies' College, and was chairman of the council of St Hilda's Hall (later College), which Miss Beale had founded in Oxford. During his vice-chancellorship he supported the campaign for degrees to be opened to women. In his own college he gradually raised the status of the holders of the exhibitions founded by Lady Elizabeth Hastings for the benefit of scholars from a number of schools in Yorkshire, Cumberland, and Westmorland. His services to St Bees School, Cumberland, were considerable; he was chairman of the governors for many years and was largely responsible for the school's policy of expansion.

At Oxford, Magrath generally identified himself with the modest reforms of the statutory commission appointed in 1877, and was largely responsible for negotiating with the commissioners the new statutes for his own college. In 1882 the commissioners made a statute for the absorption of St Edmund Hall into Queen's College, to take effect at the next vacancy of the principalship. When therefore Dr Edward Moore was nominated to a canonry in Canterbury Cathedral in 1903, Magrath sought to put the statute into operation. He ran into sharp opposition both from St Edmund Hall and within his own college, and a short but sharp contention took place between old friends. He suffered a humiliating defeat when his proposal to take over the hall was rejected by the university congregation in February 1903. He resisted counter-proposals by the hall to secure its independence until, amid considerable internal recrimination, Queen's gave way in 1911. This affair marked the end of Magrath's effective provostship; in that year a pro-provost, Edward Armstrong, was appointed to carry out his duties. In 1922 E. M. Walker became pro-provost.

Although a supporter of some modern developments in Oxford, such as the school of medicine, there was much in the trend of contemporary education which Magrath viewed with apprehension. Particularly he feared that the classics were being gradually ousted by other subjects from their position at Oxford as the chief instrument of education, and he was strongly opposed to the abolition of Greek as a compulsory subject for admission to the university. He believed, in fact, that without such a support, Greek would not survive in the northern grammar schools for more than a generation. Moreover, he dreaded lest the 'Huxley ladder', by which scholarship boys might proceed from elementary school to university, should be made too easy. He also deplored what seemed to him the excessive interference of local education authorities with the independence of schools and schoolmasters and their governing bodies. These views he expressed with no uncertain voice from time to time in his annual progress round the northern schools.

Magrath worked for many years on his history of The Queen's College (2 vols., 1921), assisted by Charles Stainer. He also edited The Flemings in Oxford (vol. 1, 1904; vol. 2, 1913; vol. 3, 1924) for the Oxford Historical Society. Magrath was a keen sportsman, but his innate conservatism limited his activities to rowing and to the kindred sport of swimming. He had a distant respect for cricketers, but none for spectators of games, and for this reason he took little interest in football, until his college gained prestige on the football field as well as on the cricket field and on the river. He himself as a fellow both rowed for the college and was captain of the boats, and for many years he was a conspicuous figure in the 'Ancient Mariners' crew, stroked by W. L. Courtney, and comprising among its members A. L. Smith, L. R. Farnell, and W. E. Sherwood. Magrath was a familiar sight, too, at the all-male dons' bathing place, Parsons' Pleasure, diving from a tree rather taller than himself, and instructing Magdalen schoolboys to do the same. He was one of the earliest and keenest supporters of the volunteer movement, and for seventeen years held the rank of sergeant in the university corps.

On his wife's death Magrath's niece, Miss Eva Lefroy, kept house for him in the provost's lodgings where he lived until his death, at the Boars Hill Hotel, Boars Hill, Berkshire, on 1 August 1930, having been provost for over fifty-one years.　　　　H. A. P. SAWYER, rev. M. C. CURTHOYS

Sources personal knowledge (1937) · J. Foster, Oxford men and their colleges (1893) · Men and women of the time (1899) · R. H. Hodgkin, Six centuries of an Oxford college: a history of the Queen's College, 1340–1940 (1949) · J. N. D. Kelly, St Edmund Hall: almost seven hundred years (1989) · M. E. Rayner, The centenary history of St Hilda's College, Oxford (1993) · A. T. C. Pratt, ed., People of the period: being a collection of the biographies of upwards of six thousand living celebrities, 2 vols. (1897) · CGPLA Eng. & Wales (1930)

Likenesses W. Carter, oils, exh. RA 1894, Queen's College, Oxford · J. Collier, oils, 1898, Queen's College, Oxford · photogravure, pubd 1899 (after J. Collier, 1898), NPG [see illus.] · Werner & Son, photograph, repro. in Foster, Oxford men and their colleges, facing p. 172

Wealth at death £10,949 8s. 6d.: probate, 21 Oct 1930, CGPLA Eng. & Wales

Magrath, Meiler [Maol Mhuire Mag Craith] (c.1523–1622), archbishop of Cashel, was born the eldest son of Donough 'Gillegrowmoe' Magrath (d. in or after 1589), chieftain, on the borders of counties Donegal and Fermanagh. For generations the Magrath sept or clan had been erenaghs, or hereditary wardens, of Termon Magrath, an ancient ecclesiastical district in the parish of Templecarn in co. Donegal. Donough Magrath came into possession of Termon Magrath and other nearby ecclesiastical lands upon acceding to the Magrath chieftaincy some time in the mid-sixteenth century.

Little is known of Meiler Magrath's early years, but he became a Franciscan friar about 1540, was ordained priest in 1549, and travelled the continent for many years before arriving in Rome. On 12 October 1565 he was appointed bishop of Down and Connor by papal provision and shortly thereafter returned to Ireland. However, the see to which he was appointed had come under the control of Shane O'Neill, who was then in open rebellion against Elizabeth I. Through the Roman Catholic archbishop of Armagh, Richard Creagh, whose acquaintance he may have made in Rome, Magrath dined with Shane in August 1566 and appeared ready to support the powerful chief in his struggle against the queen. Following Shane's defeat, however, Magrath surrendered himself at Drogheda, co. Louth, to the lord deputy, Sir Henry Sidney, and expressed a willingness to renounce the pope, Pius V, and hold his bishopric of the queen.

The government, hoping to exploit a native bishop willing to conform, summoned Magrath to England in spring 1570 and (in the hope that his example would be followed by other Gaelic clerics) appointed him bishop of Clogher on 18 September. On 3 February 1571 he was made archbishop of Cashel and bishop of Emly, though he remained the nominal bishop of Clogher until 1605. His relocation to the more prominent see of Cashel coincided with James Fitzmaurice's rebellion. By summer 1571 Magrath had incurred the rebels' enmity following his imprisonment of several Cashel-based friars, who had allegedly preached against the queen. Undaunted, Magrath furnished the government throughout Fitzmaurice's rebellion with valuable information on rebel activity in Munster. He continued to monitor the activities of rebels during the 1570s. His unfounded accusations levelled against Gerald Fitzgerald, eleventh earl of Kildare, and Thomas Butler, eleventh earl of Ormond, in 1572, however, led Sir William Fitzwilliam, the lord deputy, to deem Magrath's writings

to be 'but fancy rather than truth' (PRO, SP 63/37/3). However, despite Fitzwilliam's distrust, Magrath remained one of the few visible successes of a religious reform movement that had made little real progress among Gaelic clerics. His high-profile position was an embarrassment for Rome and on 14 March 1580 the pope, Gregory XIII, finally deprived him of Down and Connor, 'ob crimen haeresis et alia multa scelera' ('for the crime of heresy and many other offences'), which he had held concurrently with the archbishopric of Cashel for nine years (Brady, 1.265).

With letters of recommendation from the Irish privy council, Magrath travelled to England in October 1582, where he complained of the impoverished state of his archbishopric; he also delivered a letter to Elizabeth urging her to require any judge, jury, or witness in Ireland to swear an oath of allegiance to her before passing judgment on known protestants. He was well received and in November was awarded, in commendam, the revenue of the temporalities and spiritualities of the bishoprics of Lismore and Waterford to help offset his financial difficulties. In July 1584 Magrath petitioned to have his ancestral lands in Ulster granted to his ageing father, with remainder to his legitimate male heirs, to hold of the queen. By this time Magrath had married Anne, or Áine, O'Meara (d. in or after 1622), of Lisany, co. Tipperary, with whom he had at least four sons and several daughters. For the rest of the decade Magrath, who had received a grant of English liberty in May 1578, devoted himself to the spread of protestantism and the extension of English law. In 1584 he arrested Maurice O'Brien, Roman Catholic bishop of Emly, and in March 1589 he wrote strongly in favour of the Kerry planter, Sir William Herbert: 'truly I think it were better for Her Majesty to have six like him in this realm to win the people's heart and good will, and to bring them into true and loyal subjection than 6,000 soldiers' (PRO, SP 63/142/17). Yet his religious devotion and loyalty were continually under suspicion. Rumours of his complicity in the rebellion of Gerald fitz James Fitzgerald, fourteenth earl of Desmond (between 1579 and 1583), and his alleged religious ambivalence—fuelled, perhaps, by the continued adherence to Catholicism of his wife and children, and his cousin Dermod Magrath's position as Roman Catholic bishop of Cork—were not easily dismissed. His accumulation of wealth, moreover, led Fitzwilliam to declare that he 'mislikes his greedie mynde to heape together large possessions and contentious nature always bent to quarell with such as were his neighbours' (PRO, SP 63/158/53). However, Thomas Weatherhead's nomination as bishop of Waterford and Lismore on 21 March 1589 deprived Magrath of a lucrative source of income and in 1591 he travelled to England, without licence, to seek remuneration.

During his absence, the rumours surrounding Magrath developed into accusations of treasons, felonies, simony, and extortion. Fitzwilliam, who had emerged as Magrath's most vocal opponent, played no small part in the opposition. Opposition, however, was not limited to English officials: Magrath's religious conversion and his acquiescence in the Tudor state had left him alienated from the Gaelic world. A poem vilifying Magrath and several other clerics who had adopted the new religion was composed by Eoghan Ó Dubhtaigh: 'An chliar—sa anois tig anall, cliar dhall ar a ndeachaidh ceo, ní mó leo Muire ná dog; dar by God, ní rachaidh leo' ('These clergymen who have come by the other side—blind clergy enveloped in fog, respect a dog more than Mary and, by heaven, they should not get away with it'; Mhág Craith, 133). This clever usage of English terminology to satirize Magrath and his colleagues reflects the degree to which the Gaelic learned classes associated acceptance of the new religion with acceptance of English culture. However, Magrath remained popular at court and was restored to Waterford and Lismore following Weatherhead's death in 1592. In May of that year the queen commanded that he produce a tract concerning the state of Ireland with a plan for its reformation. Employing his intimate knowledge of Gaelic Ireland, Magrath wrote and delivered a book to Elizabeth, declaring the state of Ireland, with the means to increase the revenues, amend the government, and withstand Spanish practices. In a letter to Sir Robert Cecil dated June 1593, he responded to the allegations levelled against him. He claimed his enemies: 'have joyned hartes and handes togeather to overthrow and destroy my poore selfe well knowne to be (of that cuntrey birth) theire onlie ey sore and chiefest preventer and detecter of all their mischievous practizes and thirsted for invacon' (PRO, SP 63/170/4). Ultimately it was Fitzwilliam's recall in August 1594 that caused much of the opposition to subside.

Magrath was briefly taken prisoner by Conn, son of Hugh O'Neill, second earl of Tyrone, early in 1599. Tyrone, eager to broaden his confederation beyond Ulster and believing Magrath's loyalty to be firmly rooted in the region, ordered his immediate release. Tyrone's rebellion, however, had upset Magrath's financial interests and in late 1599 he travelled to England to offer his advice on how best to suppress the rebellion. Magrath, who boasted 'although they [the rebels] mislike much of mee in matters of religion, yet they love mee naturally', believed that he could play an integral part in negotiating an end to the rebellion (PRO, SP 63/206/24). Cecil, finding him 'a most turbulent spirit', declined to employ his services against Tyrone, but granted him a pension in 1600. Magrath, approaching eighty, continued to perform his ecclesiastical duties into James I's reign, although he came under criticism in February 1604 when Sir John Davies noted that he was 'an example of pluralities', holding 'in his hands four bishoprics … and three score and ten spiritual livings' (CSP Ire., 1603–6, 143). Magrath, in his own time, had become synonymous with ecclesiastical corruption and greed; in 1607 he was forced to relinquish his right to the revenue of Waterford and Lismore and was granted *in commendam* (though he did not come fully into their possession until 1611) the remote, and poor, bishoprics of Killala and Achonry in Connaught instead.

The political reorganization and plantation of Ulster that followed Tyrone's defeat in 1603 brought Magrath, who spent the preponderance of his later years on his Ulster lands, into conflict with the growing number of English-born planters arriving in Ireland. In 1609 George Montgomery, bishop of Derry, Clogher, and Raphoe, claimed patrimony of Termon Magrath, but Magrath refused to recognize the claim and successfully saw the lands granted to his son the following year. In 1611 differences arose between Magrath and Davies, who claimed possession of certain lands adjacent to Termon Magrath. Though Magrath ceased to wield any political influence in London or Dublin and stood increasingly as an obstacle to both ecclesiastical and political reform, the government found it difficult to curtail his powers. Some attempt was made to limit his influence in Cashel when in 1610 William Knight was appointed coadjutor of the bishopric. However, Knight's stay was a disaster; it became apparent that he shared Magrath's fondness for whiskey and, after appearing pixilated in public, departed in disgrace. In February 1612 the lord deputy, Sir Arthur Chichester, while condemning Magrath's abuses, warned Cecil (now first earl of Salisbury) 'not to discontent that heady Archbishop … for he is a powerful man amongst the Irish of Ulster, and able to do much hurt by underhand practices, in which he is well experienced' (CSP Ire., 1611–14, 241). Magrath sat in the House of Lords in the 1613 parliament and remained in possession of his bishoprics until his death on 14 November 1622, aged nearly one hundred. He was buried in his cathedral at Cashel and left a sizeable inheritance (amassed from years of widespread alienation of ecclesiastical lands) to his four living sons and four daughters. The Catholic tradition holds that Magrath was not buried at Cashel, but was reconciled to Rome and buried, in full Roman vestments, elsewhere. His cryptic epitaph lends some credibility to this belief: 'Hic ubi sum positus non sum, sum, non ubi non sum; sum nec in ambobus, sum sed utroque loco' ('Here, where I am placed, I am not, and thus the case is, I am not in both, yet am in both the places'; Lowry-Corry, 107). In early 1612 the Franciscans expected his conversion and appointed a priest to receive Magrath into the church, but whether in the end he re-embraced Catholicism is of purely personal significance, as he did not disavow his marriage or relinquish the bishoprics which he held of the king.

For the Tudor government, Magrath's Gaelic background, coupled with his exceptional intelligence and ability to communicate fluently in English, Gaelic, and Latin, made him the perfect candidate to advance religious reform in Ireland; and, initially, he eagerly promoted the new religion and the state which he believed would eventually come to dominate Ireland. However, he underestimated the size of the task before him and his campaign against the old religion faltered. Magrath had fallen between the two worlds that he was meant to bridge, and this, together with his avarice, simony, and various other abuses, greatly damaged the protestant cause in Ireland and earned him an infamous reputation among English and Irish alike.

CHRISTOPHER MAGINN

Sources State papers, Ireland, Elizabeth, PRO, SP 63 · J. S. Brewer and W. Bullen, eds., *Calendar of the Carew manuscripts*, 1: 1515–1574,

PRO (1867) • J. Morrin, ed., *Calendar of the patent and close rolls of chancery in Ireland for the reigns of Henry VIII, Edward VI, Mary, and Elizabeth*, 2 vols. (1861–2) • C. Mhág Craith, ed., *Dán na mBráthar Mionúr* (Baile Átha Cliath, 1967) • *Calendar of the manuscripts of the most hon. the marquis of Salisbury*, 24 vols., HMC, 9 (1883–1976) • *The antiquities and history of Ireland, by … Sir James Ware*, 1 vol. in 5 (1705) • B. O'Sullevan, *Historiae Catholicae Ibernniae compendium*, ed. M. Kelly (1850) • W. M. Brady, *The episcopal succession in England, Scotland, and Ireland, AD 1400 to 1875*, 3 vols. (1876–7) • S. R. Lowry-Corry, earl of Belmore, 'The castle and territory of Termon Magrath', *Ulster Journal of Archaeology*, 9 (1903), 48–54, 96–111, 185–90 • J. R. Garstin, *The McCragh tomb in Lismore Cathedral, co. Waterford: with notices of Miler Magrath, archbishop of Cashel* (1905) • R. W. Jackson, *Archbishop Magrath: the scoundrel of Cashel* (Dublin, 1979) • H. Cotton, *Fasti ecclesiae Hibernicae*, 6 vols. (1845–78) • L. Marron, ed., 'Documents from state papers concerning Miler McGrath', *Archivium Hibernicum*, 21 (1958), 75–189

Archives Biblioteca Apostolica Vaticana, Vatican City, Miler Magrath deprived of Down and Connor, March 1580, Barberini Lat. MSS 2873–2874 • NL Ire., abstracts of deeds and draft pedigree of Magrath, GO MS 813(10) • Royal Irish Acad., pedigree of Meiler Magrath, 23D, 17 p. 210

Likenesses portrait, 1570, Clogher Diocesan Collection; repro. in Lowry-Corry, 'Castle and territory', 48

Maguire, Cathal Macmaghnusa. *See* Mac Maghnusa, Cathal Óg (1439–1498).

Maguire, Connor [Cornelius], **second baron of Enniskillen** (*c.*1612–1645), conspirator, was born in co. Fermanagh, Ireland, the eldest of four sons (there were also four daughters) of Brian Roe Maguire, first baron of Enniskillen (*c.*1589–1633), and Rose ny Neale, daughter of Art Mac Avernan O Neile, of co. Armagh. This branch of the Maguires supported the English during the Nine Years' War and was granted the Magherastephana barony in co. Fermanagh, which Maguire still owned in 1641, making him one of the most substantial surviving Gaelic landowners in Ulster. In his youth Maguire attended school with John Clotworthy, and he reputedly spent some time at Magdalen College, Oxford. He was certainly fluent in both Irish and English. Upon the death of his father in 1633 he inherited the title baron of Enniskillen. Related to many of the leading Ulster Irish families, by 1633 Maguire was married to Mary, daughter of Thomas Fleming, of Castle Fleming, co. Cavan; they had several sons.

Maguire attended the Dublin parliaments of 1634 and 1640–41. About February 1641, while in Dublin, Roger Moore initiated him into a plot of the Irish gentry to redress Irish Catholic grievances, playing on the baron's huge debts and valuing his influential kinship ties both in Ulster and (through his wife) in the pale; the activation of such ties seems to have been Maguire's chief role in the plot. With his brother Rory (subsequently Irish leader in co. Fermanagh) Maguire was one of the Irish notables who in May 1641 sent an emissary to his uncle Owen Roe O'Neill in Flanders, asking him to support their plan. In August, Maguire first learned of the plan to take Dublin Castle. At his later examination he alleged that his intention in the plot was to exert pressure in favour of remedying grievances of Roman Catholics, including gaining toleration of their religion. In Ulster and in his native co. Fermanagh, Maguire solicited the support of the Irish gentry for the plot. However, his cousin Brian Maguire was clearly reluctant to become involved: the baron wrote to him, noting his partiality towards the English, and making threatening remarks about those who would not support the Irish action. About 21 October 1641 Fergus O'Howen, follower of Brian Maguire, came to John Carmick in Enniskillen Castle to warn him about the plot to take Dublin and Enniskillen; Carmick told Sir William Cole, who sent word to the lords justices. This report was confirmed by Flartagh McHugh, who was sent by Brian Mac Conaght Maguire to Enniskillen Castle to warn Sir William Cole.

Meanwhile, a day or two earlier Maguire, together with Hugh Mac Mahon and a number of gentlemen from co. Fermanagh and co. Monaghan, had set out for Dublin. The conspirators were to meet in the lodging of Mac Mahon. On the night of 22 October Owen Connolly, servant of Sir John Clotworthy, informed Lord Justice Parsons of the plan to take Dublin Castle; later that evening, Mac Mahon was captured, and a watch was set on the house in Castle Street where Maguire, with about twelve followers, was lodging. A number of weapons was found and linked to Maguire's group. The following morning Maguire was apprehended in Cooke Street, behind the locked door of a cockloft. As an indication of the peer's standing in the conspiracy, and in contrast to the opinion of Sir Henry Bruce, who in the following month referred to the baron as 'but a drunken fellow of no importance' (Ches. & Chester ALSS, MS DCC 47/9), it was alleged that after the Irish took Charlemont Castle, co. Armagh (22 October), they desired to exchange Toby Caulfeild for Maguire; this did not happen, however, and Caulfeild was subsequently killed.

On 26 March 1642 Maguire was examined by order of the lords justices and made a voluntary statement. On 12 June 1642, along with Mac Mahon and Lieutenant-Colonel John Reade, he was transferred to Westminster and lodged in the Tower of London. In February 1643 the prisoners were removed to Newgate prison, where there were complaints about their poor treatment. On 18 August 1644, using saws procured by a Scotswoman, Maguire and Mac Mahon escaped from the Tower; by 13 September they, together with two accessories to the escape, were traced to the Spanish ambassador's house; the escapees were recaptured on 18 September having taken refuge in the house of Mrs Leviston (or Levinsteyn), a Flemish Catholic, where the French envoy resided. The Spanish ambassador, Don Alonso de Cardenas, denied any involvement in the escape bid, while admitting that the accomplices, two priests (one Irish, one English), had been part of his household.

In November 1644 Maguire and Mac Mahon were arraigned before Justice Bacon at the court of the king's bench, and charged with high treason. Mac Mahon was tried first, found guilty, and executed. However, Maguire pleaded that his Irish peerage entitled him to a trial by his peers in Ireland. This was the subject of legal wrangling which entailed that the trial was deferred until February 1645. William Prynne was the leading prosecutor, who argued that trial in England for treason committed elsewhere was valid, citing the precedents of the O'Rourke case (1591), and the trial of Sir John Perrott (1592). Judge Bacon ruled against Maguire's plea, holding that a baron of Ireland was triable by a jury in England. Thereafter the English parliament endorsed Bacon's judgment. Maguire was found guilty, thereby forfeiting his title and lands; he petitioned the Commons to avoid being hanged, drawn, and quartered, citing his dignity as a peer, but the petition was rejected. In court Sir John Clotworthy spoke for the condemned, referring to their schooldays together, and recalling letters of Maguire in which, allegedly, he expressed remorse.

In his will, composed shortly before his execution, Maguire left £50 to be divided among the Franciscan friaries of south Ulster, and entrusted his will to Lisgoole friary. On 20 February 1645 Maguire was drawn by sledge from the Tower to Tyburn. Denied the services of a Franciscan friar, he faced persistent questioning from Sheriff Gibbs and Dr Sibbald, a puritan divine, asking if he were sorry for the deaths of the Irish protestants. Before the crowd Maguire forgave his enemies, and affirmed his adherence to Roman Catholicism and his trust in Jesus Christ. While he was hanging, an officer cut the rope, letting Maguire drop alive, and commanded the executioner to open him. A struggle between condemned and executioner ensued, and, to spare him, the executioner cut the peer's throat.

BRIAN MAC CUARTA

Sources J. T. Gilbert, ed., *A contemporary history of affairs in Ireland from 1641 to 1652*, 1 (1879), 605–49 · 'The relation of the Lord Maguire … to the lords in parliament', *Ireland in the seventeenth century, or, The Irish massacres of 1641–2*, ed. M. Hickson, 2 (1884), 341–54 [chap. dated 1642] · funeral entry of Sir Bryan McGwyer, baron of Enniskillen (d.1633), Genealogical Office, Dublin, MS 69, 16 · M. Perceval-Maxwell, *The outbreak of the Irish rebellion of 1641* (1994), 204–11 · D. A. Orr, 'Sovereignty, state, and the law of treason in England, 1641–1649', PhD diss., U. Cam., 1997, 156–88 · T. Carte, *An history of the life of James, duke of Ormonde*, 3 vols. (1735–6); new edn, pubd as *The life of James, duke of Ormond*, 6 vols. (1851), vol. 5, pp. 254–5 · lords justice to lord lieutenant, 25 Oct 1641, PRO, SP63/260/138r–140v · Irish Genealogical Office · *Report on Franciscan manuscripts preserved at the convent, Merchants' Quay, Dublin*, HMC, 65 (1906), 55, 245 · *CSP Venice, 1643–7*, 139–43 · *JHC*, 3 (1642–4), 628, 633–5 · J. Rushworth, *Historical collections*, 3/2 (1691), 784 · J. Ohlmeyer and E. O Ciardha, eds., *The Irish statute staple books, 1596–1687* (Dublin, 1998), 256 · GEC, *Peerage* · books of survey and distribution, Fermanagh, Royal Irish Acad. · extract of Maguire's will, M. Archdall, *Monasticon Hibernicum*, ed. P. F. Moran, 2 (Dublin, 1876), 167 · Ches. & Chester ALSS, MS DCC 47/9 · D. A. Orr, 'England, Ireland, Magna Carta, and the common law: the case of Connor Lord Maguire, second baron of Enniskillen', *Journal of British Studies*, 39 (2000), 389–421

Maguire, Sir Hugh [Aodh Mág Uidhir], **lord of Fermanagh** (*d.* **1600**), chieftain and rebel, was the eldest son of Cú Chonnacht Maguire, lord of Fermanagh (*d.* 1589), Irish chieftain, and his wife, Nuala, or Fionnghuala, daughter of Manus *O'Donnell, lord of Tyrconnell. Although Hugh Maguire was recognized by his father as his heir, his succession to the position of Maguire was challenged on Cú Chonnacht's death in 1589. Rival branches of the Maguire kin group nominated Connor Roe Maguire as lord 'according [to] all the customs and ceremonies in the country'

(PRO, SP 63/170/11). Maguire's claim prevailed, however, because he received support from the O'Donnells and from the Irish privy council, which had courted Cú Chonnacht and hoped to maintain friendly contact with his son. Government recognition of Maguire was confirmed in 1591 when he was knighted in a ceremony in Christ Church in Dublin.

Maguire's inauguration as chief coincided with a period of considerable instability in the north-west. From 1585 Sir Richard Bingham, president of Connaught, steadily extended his control in the region, establishing crown garrisons and appointing English-style local government officials. The beaching of ships from the Spanish Armada on the northern coast in 1588 led to an intensification of his military rule as rumours circulated that Gaelic lords, including Maguire and Brian O'Rourke, were liaising with the Spaniards and petitioning them to return with a second armada. In 1589 Bingham's brother George Bingham launched an attack on O'Rourke's country of Leitrim which bordered Maguire's territory to the west. O'Rourke fled Ireland but Maguire offered protection to his son Brian Óg O'Rourke, who subsequently married Maguire's sister. Maguire also expressed his support for the MacMahons, whose lordship of Monaghan lay to the east of Fermanagh, and also witnessed increased government interference in 1589 when the ruling MacMahon was executed and plans were initiated by Sir William Fitzwilliam, the lord deputy, to subdivide the entire lordship. While the Monaghan land settlement was being finalized, Bingham entered Fermanagh and, according to Maguire, killed men, women, and children and took away large preys of cattle and horses.

The ruthlessness of the Bingham regime in the north-west was a major factor in the subsequent conflict in Ulster and Maguire's pivotal role in it. Maguire later claimed that he supported the Nine Years' War not 'in respect of any combinations with any foreign enemy or of any malice towards Her Majesty but through the occasion of his hard usage' from English officials and, in particular, from the Binghams (PRO, SP 63/186/96). In 1592 Maguire signalled his opposition to government policy when he welcomed Hugh Roe O'Donnell to Fermanagh following the latter's escape from Dublin Castle. One of O'Donnell's first actions on his return home was to expel the English sheriff, Captain Humphrey Willis, from his territory.

The growing hostility to government policy in north Connaught and Ulster was compounded by the actions of members of the hierarchy of the Catholic church. Maguire was a patron of Edmund MacGauran, titular archbishop of Armagh from 1587 to 1593. At an episcopal meeting in O'Donnell's country in the winter of 1592, MacGauran reported on his recent visit to Spain and the plans of Philip II to send a second armada to England and Ireland. His report was followed by letters from Maguire, O'Donnell, and others to the Spanish king requesting military aid. The spring of 1593 was a crucial time for Maguire and for the developing crisis in Ulster. Much to Maguire's anger, Willis was appointed sheriff of Fermanagh following his expulsion from Tyrconnell. He asserted in vain that he had given Fitzwilliam 300 cows as a bribe to keep English officials out of his lordship. Willis entered Fermanagh in the early months of 1593 with 100 soldiers and as many women and boys, all of whom lived on the spoil of the country. Maguire claimed that Willis's men 'having killed one of the best gents in the country named the son of Edmund Mac Hugh Maguire whose head they cut off they hurled it from place to place as a football' (LPL, Carew MS 617, fol. 286). Maguire confronted Willis and his followers, forcing them to take refuge in a church from which they only escaped with their lives when Hugh O'Neill, second earl of Tyrone, intervened to secure them a safe conduct out of Fermanagh.

It was also in late spring 1593 that Maguire was reported to have married one of Tyrone's daughters, whose name is unknown, the marriage forming part of the labyrinthine network of family connections which the earl created in Ulster. This alliance coincided with an escalation of Maguire's resistance to the Bingham regime. In May 1593 Maguire's troops, led by his brother Shane Maguire, raided George Bingham's headquarters at Ballymote Castle, co. Sligo. The attack was followed up in June by the burning of the territory around Tulsk, co. Roscommon, where Sir Richard Bingham was encamped. Brian Óg O'Rourke and the O'Hagans, Tyrone's foster brothers, accompanied Maguire's soldiers in their expeditions into Connaught, as did MacGauran, who was killed in the raid on Tulsk. Maguire's military network convinced Bingham that he was not acting alone but had the support of O'Donnell and Tyrone.

In summer 1593 the Irish privy council still believed, however, that its best hope of restoring stability in Ulster lay with Tyrone. He was appointed commissioner to conclude a peace settlement with Maguire. The negotiations appear to have stalled on Maguire's demand for reassurance that the Binghams would have no jurisdiction in Fermanagh. Tyrone's failure to reach an agreement with Maguire resulted in the latter being proclaimed a traitor in September and in a military campaign into Fermanagh commanded by Sir Nicholas Bagenal, marshal of the army, aided by Sir Richard Bingham. Tyrone assisted this campaign, which had its most noticeable success in February 1594, when Enniskillen Castle was seized by government troops.

The capture of Enniskillen was followed by a siege of the castle by Maguire, in the company of O'Donnell and Cormac Mac Baron O'Neill, Tyrone's brother. The besiegers won a significant victory in the summer when they attacked a relief force near the River Arney, south of Enniskillen, called thereafter Béal Atha Na mBriosgadh ('the ford of the biscuits') because of the large quantities of biscuit supplies left behind by the fleeing troops. Through the subsequent year Maguire and O'Donnell maintained their military resistance, raiding Longford in April and retaking Enniskillen Castle in May. Although Maguire's actions between early 1593 and May 1595 were crucial in initiating the conflict in Ulster, he never held a dominant position among the rebels. The suspicion of Bingham and other English officials that he was used as a 'forerunner' for Tyrone was probably correct (*CSP Ire.*, 1592–6, 485). When Tyrone assumed the leadership of the rebellion in June 1595 Maguire's subsidiary role became clear: he was assigned the position of cavalry commander under the earl's overall direction. Maguire was included in the negotiations between Tyrone and O'Donnell and crown officials in 1595–6 and 1597 but he was always a junior partner. His requests focused on limiting government involvement in his lordship and, in particular, on keeping Fermanagh free from English troops.

Maguire's subordinate status was also emphasized in the early months of 1598 when the new president of Connaught, Sir Conyers Clifford, received the submission of Brian Óg O'Rourke. Tyrone, concerned that Maguire might be tempted to join with Brian Oge, apprehended him for a short period. By August, however, Maguire was firmly back in Tyrone's camp as he led the cavalry troops at the battle of the Yellow Ford, the rebels' most significant military victory of the war. He also fought in the midlands in 1599 and was among those who accompanied Tyrone when he met with Robert Devereux, second earl of Essex, in September.

In 1600 Maguire travelled with Tyrone to Munster and it was during this expedition that he was killed. He led a troop of cavalry to scour the countryside for prey and on his return made a surprise attack on Sir Warham St Leger of Mollingborne, governor of Leix (Laois), on 18 February, near the town of Cork. In the ensuing skirmish 'Sir Warham St Leger discharged his pistol, and shot the traitor [Maguire]; and he was striken with the other horseman's staff in the head, of which wounds either of them died; but none else on either side was slain' (Carew, 1.14). Giolla Brighde Ó hEodhasa (O'Hussey) composed a poem in honour of Maguire's journey to Munster in 1600. This was later translated by James Clarence Mangan. Maguire was succeeded by his brother Cú Chonnacht (d. 1608), who accompanied Tyrone and Rory O'Donnell, first earl of Tyrconnell, to the continent in 1607.   MARY O'DOWD

Sources AFM · *CSP Ire.*, 1588–1600 · LPL, Carew MS 617, fol. 286 · H. Morgan, *Tyrone's rebellion: the outbreak of the Nine Years' War in Tudor Ireland*, Royal Historical Society Studies in History, 67 (1993) · R. Bagwell, *Ireland under the Tudors*, 3 (1890); repr. (1963) · F. Moryson, *An itinerary containing his ten yeeres travell through the twelve dominions*, 4 vols. (1907–8) · G. Carew, *Pacata Hibernica, or, A history of the wars in Ireland during the reign of Queen Elizabeth especially within the province of Munster under the government of Sir George Carew*, ed. S. O'Grady, 2 vols. (1896) · S. Deane, ed., *The Field Day anthology of Irish writing*, 3 vols. (Derry, 1991), vol. 1, pp. 278–9; vol. 2, pp. 28–9 · D. Greene, *Duanaire Mhéig Uidhir: the poembook of Cú Chonnacht Mág Uidhir, lord of Fermanagh, 1566–1589* (Dublin, 1972) · P. Walsh, *The will and family of Hugh O'Neill, earl of Tyrone* (1930) · L. Ó Cléirigh, *The life of Aodh Ruadh Ó Domhnaill*, ed. P. Walsh and C. Ó Lochlainn, 2 vols., ITS, 42, 45 (1948–57) · P. Livingstone, *The Fermanagh story: a documented history of the county Fermanagh from the earliest times to the present day* (Enniskillen, 1969) · state papers Ireland, PRO, SP 63/168/59; SP 63/170/3; SP 63/170/11; SP 63/171/136; SP 63/183/20; SP 63/186/96; SP 63/187/4 · DNB

Archives LPL, Carew MSS · PRO, state papers Ireland

Maguire, James Rochfort (1855–1925), company director and imperialist, was born at Kilkeedy, co. Limerick, on 4

James Rochfort Maguire (1855–1925), by unknown engraver, pubd 1895 (after Walery)

October 1855, the second son of John Mulock Maguire, rector of Kilkeedy, and his wife, Anne Jane, née Humphries. He was educated at Cheltenham College and at Merton College, Oxford, where he obtained first classes in mathematical moderations in 1875, in mathematical finals in 1877, and in jurisprudence in 1879. He was elected to a fellowship at All Souls, entered the Inner Temple in 1878, and was called to the bar in 1883, but he never practised.

At Oxford, Maguire became a close friend of Cecil Rhodes, who was also a member of the fashionable Bullingdon Club. The friendship lasted until Rhodes's death and had a marked influence on Maguire's career, though he never entered the inner circle of allies and trustees who managed Rhodes's financial legacies. More immediately, Maguire was useful in his capacity as private secretary to Graham Bower, deputy to Sir Hercules Robinson, governor of Cape Colony and high commissioner, who was sympathetic to Rhodes's expansive imperial plans from the mid-1880s. This association and his good connections in English society may account for his selection by Rhodes in August 1888 to accompany Charles Rudd and Frank Thompson to obtain land and mineral rights in Matabeleland from Lobengula. Charming, cultured, and slightly effete, Maguire stood out as a gentleman among the concession hunters, though he does not seem to have used his legal expertise to draft the concession treaty (the 'Rudd concession') to which he was one of the witnesses at Bulawayo on 30 October 1888. Left at Bulawayo with Thompson for some months to hold Lobengula to the agreement, Maguire threatened the use of force to see off rival concessionaires (the Austral African Exploration Company) and received the consignment of rifles which arrived with L. S. Jameson to confirm the transaction.

For these services Maguire was allocated a modest £8000 of the share capital of Central Search Association, formed to manage the concession; he subsequently took 49,000 shares in the United Concessions Company, successor to the title, when the charter for the British South Africa Company was secure. Having returned to England, Maguire helped to limit the damage caused by Lobengula's repudiation of the concession, and he subscribed £18,000

to the company when the charter was formally granted on 29 October 1889. He acted until 1902 as Rhodes's first alternate director to the board of the British South Africa Company, and in 1898 was entrusted with a confidential mission to Antwerp to gather information on diamond resale prices which Rhodes used to negotiate better terms for De Beers with the London diamond syndicate. Thereafter Maguire was based in London to become vice-president of the chartered company in 1906 and president in 1923, as well as chairman of the boards of associated railway companies and a director of Consolidated Goldfields of South Africa Ltd (1900–25).

From his position at the heart of Rhodes's imperial interests, Maguire also shared his patron's admiration for Charles Stewart Parnell and benefited from Rhodes's financial contribution to the Irish nationalist party by an unopposed election to the House of Commons as Parnellite member for North Donegal (1890) and for West Clare (1892–5). He may also have been one of the planners of the Jameson raid at the Burlington Hotel, London, in late 1895 (and sent a 'hurry up' telegram to Cape Town on 20 December); but he disapproved of the armed incursion and its consequences, which were dangerous for the chartered company. On 24 April 1895 Maguire married Julia Beatrice Peel, eldest daughter of Arthur Wellesley Peel, first Viscount Peel, former speaker of the House of Commons. Both Maguire and his wife survived the siege of Kimberley (October 1899 to February 1900) during the Second South African War (of which Julia Maguire left a short unpublished account). The Maguires remained close to Rhodes in his last visits to England and were with him at Rannoch Lodge in the summer of 1901 among other intimates and business partners.

Maguire's principal contribution to Rhodes's projects for development in Africa lay in his planning and supervision of the financial and transport system which made up the infrastructure of the British South Africa Company's rule in Southern Rhodesia. The company acted as banker by issue of debenture shares for its railway subsidiaries and the Rhodesian Railway Trust. Interest obligations to major shareholders kept railway freight rates high and antagonized Rhodesian settlers. Throughout the rest of his career Maguire worked to maintain this monopoly, as railway traffic expanded into Northern Rhodesia and Katanga. Accordingly, he opposed and defeated the plan of the Belgian magnate, Libert Oury, to develop the Beira Railway Junction Company and its port in Mozambique as a rival to Rhodesia Railways Ltd, and he laboured to extract compensation from the British government for administrative costs and loss of land rights following a decision of the privy council in 1918 to vest unalienated lands in Southern Rhodesia in the crown. Unwilling to pay for territorial administration, Maguire and the majority of his board sought to transfer the burden to settlers anxious to exercise power, while safeguarding the railway monopoly from local government control. Maguire played an important part in the long negotiations leading to a financial and constitutional settlement in 1921–3, though he was out of step with the majority of his directors by his opposition to amalgamation of the Rhodesian railway system with the state system of the Union of South Africa. As power passed from the chartered company to the government of Southern Rhodesia, Maguire's death, which occurred at his home, 3 Cleveland Square, St James's, London, on 18 April 1925, removed an obstacle to subsequent company investment in Beira port development, but his policy of rejecting state ownership of railways was confirmed in 1926 in the legal compromise aimed at curbing the transport monopoly of the company through control of profits and railway rates. He was survived by his wife.

COLIN NEWBURY

Sources The Times (20 April 1925) · Rhodesia Herald (24 April 1925) · Bodl. RH, Rhodes MSS, MSS Afr.s.134, Afr.t.5, Afr.t.14 · J. S. Galbraith, Crown and charter: the early years of the British South Africa Company (1974) · R. I. Rotberg, The founder: Cecil Rhodes and the pursuit of power (1988) · J. Lunn, 'Capital and labour on the Rhodesian railway system, 1890–1939', DPhil diss., U. Oxf., 1987 · L. Weinthal, ed., The story of the Cape to Cairo railway and river route, from 1887 to 1922, 1 (1923) · H. M. Hole, The making of Rhodesia (1926) · The gold fields, 1887–1937 (1937) · E. B. d'Erlanger, The history of the construction and finance of the Rhodesian transport system (privately printed, 1938) · J. E. Butler, The liberal party and the Jameson raid (1968) · CGPLA Eng. & Wales (1925) · DNB
Archives Bodl. RH, Rhodes, British South African Company MSS · Derbys. RO, papers relating to British South Africa Co · National Archives of Zimbabwe · PRO, CO 417, 806 | All Souls Oxf., letters to Sir William Anson · National Archives of Zimbabwe, corresp. with Francis Chaplin
Likenesses Spy [L. Ward], chromolithograph caricature, NPG; repro. in VF (1 March 1894) · engraving (after Walery), NPG; repro. in ILN, 106 (1895), 501 [see illus.] · photographs, University of Cape Town, Sibbett collection; repro. in Rotberg, The founder · photographs, repro. in Hole, Making of Rhodesia
Wealth at death £42,423 13s. 11d.: probate, 14 July 1925, CGPLA Eng. & Wales

Maguire, John Francis (1815–1872), Irish newspaper proprietor and politician, was the eldest son of John Maguire, a merchant of Cork, where he was born. He was called to the Irish bar in 1843, and the same year he married Margaret, the daughter of Robert Bailey of Cork. They had seven children and Margaret outlived him. He had already established the *Cork Examiner* in 1841, as an organ of O'Connellite nationalism. He unsuccessfully contested the small borough of Dungarvan as a repealer in 1847 and 1851 before winning it for the new Independent Irish Party built upon the Tenant League of 1850. He held the seat until 1865, after which he represented his native city until his death. Following the demise of his party, he sat as a Liberal from 1859. In its last years he did more than anyone to keep the Independent Irish Party in being, using its dwindling strength to bargain with the transient governments of the 1850s. These tactics elicited abortive land bills falling far short of the league's original demands, and minor concessions in the Catholic interest. Maguire embodied the strong Catholic element in O'Connellite nationalism, and was a prominent defender of the contemporary papacy and its threatened temporal power. Pope Pius IX, to whom he was known, rewarded him with the order of St Gregory for his book *Rome and its Ruler* (1856).

As a Liberal, Maguire continued to press for land reforms, and voiced the growing self-confidence of Irish Catholicism in its uneasy relationship with the protestant state. He joined other Irish Liberal MPs with an O'Connellite background in the National Association of Ireland, set up in 1864 and nicknamed 'Cullen's Association' because of its domination by Paul Cullen (1803–1878), the archbishop of Dublin. This initiative was designed to offer a moderate alternative to the attractions of Fenianism, which repudiated O'Connell's constitutional methods, and to exploit the changing attitude of British Liberals to the Irish problem in the 1860s. Maguire obtained in 1865 a select committee of inquiry into Irish land law for which he had first asked two years earlier. As its chairman, he was unable to secure agreement on even a modest diminution of landlord rights (*Parl. papers*, 1865, 11.343) but the question was back on a Liberal government's agenda. His book *Ireland in America* (1868), the fruit of six months in the United States and Canada, influenced W. E. Gladstone by its argument that industry and order were the characteristics of an Irish population liberated from the accumulated injustices of centuries. Although Maguire gave priority to the land question, he played a full part in agitating for disestablishment of the Anglican church in Ireland. His Commons motion on the state of Ireland in March 1868 provided the occasion for Gladstone's declaration against the church. While his newspaper carried less weight than the Dublin *Freeman's Journal* of another old O'Connellite, Sir John Gray (1816–1875), Maguire was closer than Gray to Gladstone (Lord Derby, *A Selection from the Diaries … 1869–1878*, ed. J. R. Vincent, 1994, 81–2), who listed him as one of the three Irish Catholic Liberals he trusted to convey the reactions of their countrymen to his reforms.

In his correspondence with Gladstone, Maguire depicted himself as a spokesman not for 'Fenians … [but for] honest and logical nationalists', as he said when insisting that only 'irremovability', the real meaning of tenant-right, would still endemic agrarian unrest and demonstrate that 'national improvement and redemption' were possible under the union (Maguire to Gladstone, 7 Oct 1869, BL, Add. MS 44422). Gladstone could not go so far in his Land Bill of 1870, and Maguire's nationalist logic pointed to home rule. He enrolled in the Home Government Association of Isaac Butt in August 1871, and canvassed for the home-rule candidate at the Mallow by-election a year later, shortly before his death. Those actions signalled the end of the attempt to reconcile O'Connellite nationalism with British Liberalism. For most of his career, Maguire's well-defined loyalties had never been exclusive. One of Lord Palmerston's cabinet ministers observed that an article in the *Cork Examiner*, arguing against rebellion in support of a rumoured French invasion, was worth any number of prosecutions for sedition (Lewis to Palmerston, 6 Oct 1860; U. Southampton L., Broadlands MS GC/LE/135). The queen and other political opponents contributed to the national subscription for Maguire's wife and children, left in straitened circumstances.

Maguire was prominent in the civic life of Cork: serving

as mayor in 1853 and again in 1862–4, he used his parliamentary influence to promote the construction of a naval harbour in the port and tried to introduce the linen industry into the south of Ireland. The setback to the post-famine recovery of the Irish economy from a run of poor seasons in the early 1860s led him to solicit some special help for his country from government, with limited success. He was, however, instrumental in securing a mitigation of the Irish poor law that cut to six months the qualifying period of settlement required of applicants for relief. Amid all this activity he found time to make a name for himself as a man of letters. In addition to the two important books previously mentioned, of which *Rome and its Ruler* went to a third and enlarged edition (1870), he wrote: *The Industrial Movement in Ireland* (1852); a biography of the 'apostle for temperance' entitled *Father Mathew: a Biography* (1863); a three-volume novel, *The Next Generation* (1871); and the posthumously published *Young Prince Marigold and Other Fairy Stories* (1873). It was the varied output of a professional writer with, perhaps, more industry than talent.

Contemporaries remembered Maguire as the founder of the *Cork Examiner*, the leading nationalist paper outside Dublin; as an effective publicist for his church; and, not always gratefully, as the archetype of those who endeavoured to be true to O'Connell's memory in Irish politics through the discouraging period that followed the famine and the collapse of repeal and Young Ireland. In the later twentieth century, historians reassessed the Independent Irish Party and the National Association of Ireland and, at least implicitly, conceded their legitimacy in the context of the continuing national struggle: Maguire's reputation benefited as a result. He died in Dublin on 1 November 1872 and was buried in St Joseph's cemetery, Cork.

DAVID STEELE

Sources *Cork Examiner* (4 Nov 1872) • A. D. Macintyre, *The Liberator: Daniel O'Connell and the Irish party, 1830–1847* (1965) • T. W. Moody and others, eds., *A new history of Ireland*, 5: *Ireland under the Union, 1801–1870* (1989), chaps. 21–3 • J. H. Whyte, *The independent Irish party, 1850–9* (1958) • E. Larkin, *The making of the Roman Catholic church in Ireland, 1850–1860* (1980) • E. Larkin, *The consolidation of the Roman Catholic church in Ireland, 1860–1870* (1987) • E. R. Norman, *The Catholic church and Ireland in the age of rebellion, 1859–1873* (1965) • E. D. Steele, *Irish land and British politics: tenant-right and nationality, 1865–1870* (1974) • E. D. Steele, 'Cardinal Cullen and Irish nationality', *Irish Historical Studies*, 19 (1974–5), 239–60 • D. Thornley, *Isaac Butt and home rule* (1964) • Dublin Diocesan Archives, Cullen MSS • BL, Gladstone MSS • *CGPLA Eng. & Wales* (1873)
Archives BL, corresp. with W. E. Gladstone, Add. MSS 44405–44435 • Dublin Diocesan Archives, Cullen MSS
Likenesses cartoon, repro. in *VF* (23 March 1872)
Wealth at death under £5000: administration, 1 April 1873, *CGPLA Ire.*

Maguire, Nicholas (1458/9–1512), bishop of Leighlin, was born at Tulmogima, co. Carlow, and was the natural son of a priest. He 'studied in Oxford, although it was but 2 yrs and 3 months, yet he profited so much in logik, philosophie, the seven liberall sciences and divinitie that in his latter days he seemed to excel' (*Annals of Ireland*, ed. Butler, 32). He was prebendary of Ullard, co. Carlow, from about 1487 and in consequence also a canon of the cathedral;

and from about 1489 he was perpetual vicar of Kiltennel. At Ullard he is said to have 'preached and delivered great learninge' (ibid.). He was elected bishop of Leighlin by the dean and chapter some time before 21 April 1490, aged only thirty-one. Dowling's assertion that 'the King and nobilitie of Leinster' took part in the election points to the dispute that attended his appointment. The election was initially nullified, the pope having reserved the see of Leighlin; but Maguire was later provided by the pope, in deference to local wishes. At the time of his elevation it was discovered he had not received all the dispensations from his illegitimacy necessary to hold his previous cures. He was, however, rehabilitated and allowed to hold them during such time as he was bishop.

According to Sir James Ware, 'he began many Works, but Death prevented him from putting the finishing Hand to any; except his Chronicle' (*Whole Works*, 3.91–2). This chronicle, which can no longer be located, was stated by the Very Revd Richard Butler in 1849 to be copied in the Book of Leighlin. It was used by Thady Dowling, chancellor of Leighlin, in compiling his annals of Ireland. The latter writer says Maguire was commended 'for his hospitalitie and the number of cowes that he grased without losse (so well was he beloved) upon the woodes & mountaines of Knockbrannen' (*Annals of Ireland*, ed. Butler, 32). Harris, in his edition of Ware, says that Maguire also wrote a life of Milo Roche, his predecessor as bishop of Leighlin in 1512 and was buried in the cathedral there. Maguire died at Leighlin in 1512 and was buried in the cathedral there. His life is said to have been written by Thomas Browne, his chaplain, 'about the Year 1513'.

MIHAIL DAFYDD EVANS

Sources *The whole works of Sir James Ware concerning Ireland*, ed. and trans. W. Harris, 1 (1739) • *The whole works of Sir James Ware concerning Ireland*, ed. and trans. W. Harris, 2/2 (1746) • *The annals of Ireland by Friar John Clyn and Thady Dowling: together with the annals of Ross*, ed. R. Butler, Irish Archaeological Society (1849) • Wood, *Ath. Oxon.* • Emden, *Oxf.* • J. B. Leslie, *Biographical succession list of the clergy of Leighlin diocese*, typescript, 1939, Representative Church Body Library, Dublin [revisions to 1947] • *CEPR letters*, vols. 15–16 • W. M. Brady, *The episcopal succession in England, Scotland, and Ireland, AD 1400 to 1875*, 3 vols. (1876–7); facs. edn with introduction by A. F. Allison (1971)

Maguire, Robert (1826–1890), religious controversialist, was born in Dublin on 3 March 1826, the son of William Maguire of Dublin, inspector of taxes there. He was educated at Trinity College, Dublin, where he graduated BA in 1847, MA in 1855, and BD and DD in 1877. In 1849 he was ordained to the curacy of St Nicholas's parish, Cork. In 1852, in the wake of the controversy over the Ecclesiastical Titles Act, he moved to London and became clerical secretary to the Islington Protestant Institute, which had for its object 'the awakening of Protestant Christians to the progress of Popery'. Maguire's efforts increased the number of members from 600 to 1400. In a controversy with Frederick Oakeley, Roman Catholic priest of Islington, and his schoolmaster, William Weale, Maguire published *The Early Irish Church Independent of Rome till A.D. 1172* (1853), which had a large sale.

In July 1856 Maguire was elected Sunday afternoon lecturer at St Luke's, Old Street, and in the following October perpetual curate of St James's, Clerkenwell, one of the few livings in which the parishioners themselves had the right of presentation. His election led to legal proceedings, and he was not inducted until 3 May 1857. While at Clerkenwell he soon became popular as a preacher and lecturer. His extensive writings in the 1850s were highly controversial, disputing the claims of Roman Catholics and Tractarians alike, but he also distinguished himself in 1859 during a debate at Exeter Hall with J. B. Langley of the National Sunday League. In 1864 he was appointed morning lecturer at St Swithin's, Cannon Street. After the Fenian explosion at Clerkenwell (13 December 1867) Maguire was appointed chairman of the relief committee, raising more than £10,000 for the victims. In 1875, on Disraeli's recommendation, he was presented to the rectory of St Olave, Southwark. His later writings were more expository and devotional. His editions of Bunyan's *Pilgrim's Progress* (1859) and *The Holy War* (1863) were very popular, the former being translated into German. His first wife, Effie, died on 13 June 1864, and he married on 5 August 1869 Margaret Mary, daughter of Edward Erastus Deacon, barrister. Maguire died at 6 Lesmore Road, Eastbourne, Sussex, on 3 September 1890, and was survived by his wife.   G. C. BOASE, *rev.* TIMOTHY C. F. STUNT

Sources C. M. Davies, *Orthodox London*, 2nd edn (1874), 108–22 · *The Times* (6 Sept 1890), 7 · *Men of the time* (1879), 673–4 · J. Wolffe, *The protestant crusade in Great Britain, 1829–1860* (1991) · *CGPLA Eng. & Wales* (1890) · S. Silley, 'Maguire, Robert', *The Blackwell dictionary of evangelical biography, 1730–1860*, ed. D. M. Lewis (1995)
Likenesses portrait, repro. in D. J. Pound, ed., *The drawing room portrait gallery of eminent personages* (1859), 14
Wealth at death £2586 15s. 3d.: probate, 6 Oct 1890, *CGPLA Eng. & Wales*

Maguire, Thomas (1792–1847), Roman Catholic priest, polemicist, and Irish patriot, was born in the parish of Kinawley, co. Fermanagh, near Swanlinbar, the son of Thomas Maguire, farmer, and his wife, Judith, *née* Maguire. His maternal uncle was Patrick Maguire, coadjutor-bishop of Kilmore. He attended a classical school in Ballyconnell, but was at least twenty when nominated to St Patrick's College, Maynooth, in 1813 by the bishop of Kilmore, Dr Fergal O'Reilly. He was ordained priest in September 1816 in the church at Kildoagh, co. Cavan, which his uncle had built as parish priest. He remained his uncle's curate until July 1818, when he was appointed parish priest at Drumreilly in co. Leitrim. In early 1825 he became parish priest of nearby Inishmagrath, where he ministered to a poor and largely Irish-speaking population. He moved to Oughteragh, Ballinamore, co. Leitrim, in August 1835, where he became dean of Kilmore.

Maguire rose to national prominence through his support for Daniel O'Connell's campaign for Catholic emancipation and his linked opposition to the 'Protestant crusade' against Irish Catholicism launched in 1822 by the archbishop of Dublin, William Magee. Maguire's remarks at a political meeting at Carrick-on-Shannon on 22 April 1826 led to a debate with the Revd Richard T. P. Pope at the Dublin Institute in Sackville Street held between 11 a.m. and 3 p.m. over six days (19–25 April 1827), Daniel

O'Connell serving as one of the Catholic chairmen, and Admiral Oliver and John Dillon for the protestants. Maguire's easy and passionate eloquence, with its 'flavour of the Leitrim bogs' (*The Devil is a Jackass*, 158), and the help of 'his father', the publisher Richard Coyne, in anticipating his opponent ensured that Maguire got the better of the argument: Coyne had discovered that Pope was cribbing from a work by Charles Leslie of 1713, and supplied Maguire with the Catholic Robert Manning's reply to it of 1716 (this reply was republished by Coyne in 1827, with a dedication to Maguire as 'the Bossuet of the British Churches').

O'Connell was said to have given Maguire a victory present of plate worth £1000 (Bowen, 107), but Maguire had to pay £50 in damages to Power le Poer Trench, the protestant archbishop of Tuam, when in 1827 the Dublin press reported Maguire as claiming that the archbishop had offered him £1000 and a living worth £800 a year to turn protestant. Later in 1827 he was defended by O'Connell when charged by a protestant innkeeper from Drumkeerin, co. Leitrim, Bartholomew McGarahan, with fathering his daughter's stillborn child, and Maguire had to pay 6d. in costs.

Maguire was now embarked on a career as one of the most popular orators of his age, and from 1829 until 1843 he addressed huge crowds and packed congregations in churches and at venues throughout England and Ireland. In 1829 he preached a series of Lenten sermons in St Teresa's Church in Dublin where, in 1835, his charity sermon helped pay for the three churches he built in his parish. His sermon at Waterford on 5 June 1842 attracted a collection of £550. Between 29 May and 7 June 1838 he had another celebrated polemical exchange with the Revd Tresham (by nickname Thrash'em or Trashy) Dames Gregg, chaplain at the Swift's Alley church, Dublin, a learned eccentric who was at war with his own archbishop, Richard Whately, and ended up claiming to be immortal. Gregg afterwards published his own version of his exchange with Maguire to replace their agreed text of the controversy. Bishop Ullathorne recalled 'the wonderful amount of freshness and vigour which Father Tom, as [Maguire] was familiarly called, gave to old and familiar texts', and his habit when, after a lecture, soaked in perspiration, he would drink a glass of whisky hissing from a red hot poker, and then engage with his friends in 'a flow of wit and learning such as I never witnessed before or since' (*The Devil is a Jackass*, 158). Ullathorne was less admiring of Maguire's habit of pocketing half the entrance money.

Much of this speaking was political. At the County Clare election of 1828, which returned O'Connell:

Fitzgerald's own (Catholic) tenants seemed to hang in the balance until … Maguire's stentorian appeal: 'You have heard the tones of the tempter and charmer, whose confederates have through all ages joined the descendants of the Dane, the Norman, and the Saxon, in burning your churches, in levelling your altars, in slaughtering your clergy, in stamping out your religion. Let every renegade to his God and his country follow Vesey FitzGerald, and every true Catholic Irishman follow me'. (O. MacDonagh, *The Hereditary Bondsman*, 1988, 254)

On 15 August 1833 Maguire convened a great meeting for the repeal of the union on Sheena Hill near Drumkeerin. At a meeting in Castlebar in 1843, in the presence of O'Connell and Archbishop MacHale, Maguire explained repeal as 'the consideration next in importance to eternity itself for the Irish people' (McGovern, 281).

Maguire suddenly dropped from public view in 1843, devoting himself to a legendary hospitality and to other country matters as, by his own boast, 'the best shot, the best courser, the best quoit-player, the best breeder of greyhounds, pointers, and spaniels, and the best brewer of "scaltheen" in the whole county of Leitrim', as his obituary in the *Gentleman's Magazine* recalled. His translation of Moore's 'Nora Creina' into Latin for the Dublin *University Magazine* won him free copies of the journal for life. He died on 2 December 1847 at Munroe Lodge, Ardrum, Ballinamore, allegedly of gout. His oration was preached by Dr James Browne, bishop of Kilmore, to 'the most numerously and respectably attended funeral ever witnessed in that part' (McGovern, 285), and parishioners dragged the funeral carriage 6 miles to Kilnavart cemetery in Templeport, where he was buried on 6 December. The sudden deaths of Maguire's brother- and sister-in-law, Terence and Anna, who had lived with him led to the exhumation of his body on 14 January 1848, and the discovery that, like his in-laws, he had been poisoned by arsenic. An inquest brought a charge of murder against his housekeeper Mary Reynolds and an accomplice, Hugh Quinn, but they were acquitted at the Leitrim assizes in 1848. Reynolds and John and Pete Reilly were tried for Terence's murder, and Reynolds was again acquitted, but the Reilly brothers were sentenced to hanging.

Ullathorne described Maguire as 'a tall man with a high, tapering forehead, broad jaws, florid features and a small mouth with tall teeth and, for his proportions, narrow shoulders' (*The Devil is a Jackass*, 158). His career as polemicist and politician embodies one aspect of the nineteenth-century Irish clergy, as a tribune for their people, but as a 'cheery, joyous, independent and … *rollicking* sort of priest' ('Irish poetry', 66). SHERIDAN GILLEY

Sources R. McGovern, 'Father Tom Maguire: polemicist, popular preacher and patriot, 1792–1847', *Breifne*, 4/14 (1971), 277–88 · D. Bowen, *The protestant crusade in Ireland, 1800–70* (1978), 98, 106–9, 115, 127 · P. Brady, 'Father Tom Maguire and the Clare election', *Breifne*, 1/1 (1958), 56–9 · P. M. Lynch, 'Greggism', *Catholic Bulletin and Book Review*, 22/7 (July 1932), 569–71 · P. M. Lynch, 'Greggism', *Catholic Bulletin and Book Review*, 22/8 (Aug 1932), 646–9 · *Irish Catholic Directory* (1849), 251 · 'Irish poetry: rogueries of Father Prout—Father Tom Maguire,—and others unknown', *Kerry Magazine*, 2/16 (1 April 1855), 64–7 · *The devil is a jackass: being the dying words of the autobiographer William Bernard Ullathorne, 1806–1889*, ed. L. Madigan (1995), 157–60 · *GM*, 2nd ser., 29 (1848), 334

Maguire, Thomas (1831–1889), classical scholar and philosopher, was born in Dublin on 24 January 1831, the son of Thomas Maguire, a Roman Catholic merchant, subsequently stipendiary magistrate in Mauritius. After attending a school in Dublin, at the age of fifteen Maguire went with his family to the colony, but returned to enter Trinity College, Dublin, in 1851. He obtained a sizarship, but being a Roman Catholic he could not hold a scholarship or fellowship. He gained high honours in classics and metaphysics, including the Wray prize in the latter (1853), and the Berkeley medal in Greek literature and composition (1857). In 1855 he graduated BA as senior moderator in classics and in philosophy. In the same year the board of Trinity College endowed non-foundation scholarships for the relief of those labouring under religious disabilities. Maguire competed, and was elected. In 1861 he obtained the law studentship at Lincoln's Inn, and in 1862 was called to the English bar. Although highly commended by Lord Westbury, he soon ceased to practise, and, returning to Dublin about 1866, set up as a private teacher in Trinity College. In 1868 he was presented by the college with the degree of LLD, the payment of the usual fees being remitted as a mark of favour. In 1869 the chair of Latin in Queen's College, Galway, became vacant, and Maguire was appointed to it. In 1873 Fawcett's Act for the removal of religious disabilities in Trinity College and the University of Dublin was passed, and Maguire at once prepared to compete for a fellowship.

Maguire was elected the first Roman Catholic fellow of Trinity College, Dublin, on Trinity Monday, 24 May 1880, being then forty-nine years and four months old. His accession to the fellowship was hailed with universal rejoicing. He was personally known to all the fellows and to most of the students who had passed through the college since 1851. He was held in high esteem for the courtesy of his manners, and was socially a charming companion. A special chair of classical composition was immediately created for him, and in 1882 he vacated this to take the professorship of moral philosophy. Although no active politician, Maguire took some part in the transfer to *The Times* of the Pigott letters, which were published by *The Times* in a series of articles called 'Parnellism and crime' in 1887 [*see* Pigott, Richard], and he went to London early in 1889 to give evidence before the commission appointed by parliament to inquire into the truth of the statements made in those articles. He was fully convinced of the authenticity of the Pigott letters, but died, apparently unmarried, at Eaton Place, London, on 26 February 1889 before his examination in court took place. He was buried on 2 March in Dean's Grange, Dublin.

Maguire was a thorough idealist in philosophy, Plato and Berkeley being his chosen masters. He published sets of essays on Plato in 1866 and 1870, an edition of Plato's *Parmenides* in 1882, and a set of philosophical lectures in 1885. He contributed largely to *Hermathena* and *Kottabos*, and many of his translations in the latter appeared in the volume of *Dublin Translations* edited by Professor R. Y. Tyrrell. E. S. ROBERTSON, *rev.* RICHARD SMAIL

Sources Boase, *Mod. Eng. biog.* · R. B. McDowell and D. A. Webb, *Trinity College, Dublin, 1592–1952: an academic history* (1982) · *The Times* (27 Feb 1889) · *The Times* (4 March 1889)
Archives Glos. RO, letters to Sir Michael Hicks Beach
Wealth at death £490 10s. 1d.: administration, 11 April 1889, *CGPLA Ire.*

Mahaffy, Sir John Pentland (1839–1919), college head and classical scholar, was born at Chapponnaire, near Vevey, Switzerland, on 26 February 1839, the seventh and youngest child of the Revd Nathaniel B. Mahaffy, a small landowner in co. Donegal, and his wife, Elizabeth Pentland, who also came of a landowning family with estates in counties Monaghan and Meath. He was thus of Irish descent on both sides. His parents moved from Vevey to Lucerne, and then in 1843 to Kissingen in Bavaria, where his father became first British chaplain and Mahaffy was brought up until the age of nine. His parents then returned to Ireland and settled down on their property in Monaghan. 'An ugly serious looking boy with a broad head, but no other external sign of ability' as he described himself, Mahaffy was educated at home before entering Trinity College, Dublin, in 1855. His career at the university was highly successful; he won a foundation scholarship in classics, and graduated in 1859 with a senior moderatorship in classics and logics, but coming second in both subjects. He was elected to a fellowship in 1864, having earlier in the year become a Church of Ireland clergyman (although 'not in any offensive sense of the term', he is reputed to have said). From his earliest youth he developed, and continued to demonstrate throughout his life, a keen interest and ability in music, and in sport—particularly cricket, which he played several times for All Ireland against All England. He also enjoyed shooting, in which he also won a place on the Irish team, and fishing. In 1865 he married Frances Letitia, daughter of William MacDougall, of Howth, co. Dublin, and led a blissfully happy married life until his wife's death in 1908. They had a family of four children, two sons and two daughters. From his election to a fellowship down to his death he continued to serve the college in one capacity or another as tutor, professor, senior fellow, vice-provost, and provost, for a period of fifty-five years.

Mahaffy's interests were originally philosophical, and the first scholarly work which he published was a translation of Kuno Fischer's *History of Modern Philosophy* dealing with Kant's *Critique of Pure Reason*. He also planned a three-volume commentary on Kant's *Analytic* and *Dialectic*, but only produced two volumes (vol. 1, 1872; vol. 3, 1874). He continued to show interest in philosophy as late as 1880, when he produced a book on Descartes. His election in 1871, however, as the first professor of ancient history in the university gave a new direction to his studies. For the next forty years Greek history and Greek literature were to form the main subjects of his labours. In 1871 he published his *Prolegomena to Ancient History*, which although rendered obsolete in great measure by subsequent investigation was declared by his friend A. H. Sayce to be the best book that he ever wrote (Sayce, 126). Most others would award this honour to his *Social Life in Greece from Homer to Menander* (1874). His first visit to Greece in 1875, for which he absented himself during Trinity term and was severely reprimanded by the board of the college, led to his charming and popular *Rambles and Studies in Greece* (1876). His *History of Classical Greek Literature* (1880) in four volumes ranks

Sir John Pentland Mahaffy (1839–1919), by Fradelle & Young

as one of his major endeavours, and was followed by other important works, such as *Greek Life and Thought from the Death of Alexander to the Roman Conquest* (1887), *The Greek World under Roman Sway* (1890), and *Problems in Greek History* (1892). The year 1890 marked the beginning of a new epoch in his literary activities. Shortly before, a quantity of mummy cartonnage was discovered by W. M. Flinders Petrie in the Fayyum, and handed over to Sayce, of Queen's College, Oxford, for decipherment and publication. Sayce asked Mahaffy to collaborate with him. For the next ten years Mahaffy's interests were centred on the Egypt of the Ptolemies, and to this period belong the first two volumes of *The Flinders Petrie Papyri* (1891–3), followed by a third volume (1905), produced in collaboration with J. G. Smyly, and *The Empire of the Ptolemies* (1895). For the rest of his life Mahaffy's interests were chiefly directed to the history of his university and of Ireland in general. *An epoch in Irish history—Trinity College, Dublin, its foundation and early fortunes, 1591–1660* (1903), *The Particular Book of Trinity College* (1904), and a monograph entitled *The Plate in Trinity College Dublin. A History and a Catalogue* (1918), were among the fruits of his researches in the field of Irish history. He was elected president of the Georgian Society, of which he was the founder, and from 1911 to 1916 he held the office of president of the Royal Irish Academy.

Mahaffy succeeded to a senior fellowship in 1899, and it was the general belief outside Trinity College itself that in view of his eminence in the world of letters and of his long service to his own college, he was certain of the succession to the provostship. When, however, the office became vacant by the death of Dr George Salmon in 1904, he was passed over by the crown in favour of Dr Anthony Traill. Mahaffy had good reason to anticipate that he would be appointed provost, although his was not the only name that might with propriety have been submitted to the king, and it is not too much to say that Traill's appointment came as a shock to many people. Mahaffy had to wait another ten years for the fulfilment of his hopes, and when, on Traill's death, he succeeded to the headship of his college in November 1914 ('ten years too late', he replied to offers of congratulations), he had reached the age of seventy-five. Two years later in 1916 came the Easter rising, during which he directed the organization of Trinity College with coolness and resource. When the Irish convention was summoned in 1917, he was one of the fifteen members appointed by the government, and although then seventy-eight years old, he proved a lively contributor to the proceedings. He was created GBE in 1918. He died in Dublin on 30 April 1919, from the effects of a stroke.

It is by his contributions to the study of the literature, the life, and the history of the ancient Greeks that Mahaffy as a writer must be judged. Few authors, however, have been more versatile, and his range extended far beyond Hellenism to include titles such as *The Decay of Modern Preaching* (1882) and *The Art of Conversation* (1889), and cover subjects as diverse as the architecture and furniture of the great houses of Ireland and the introduction to Ireland of the domestic ass (in a lecture given to the Royal Irish Academy, remembered affectionately as 'Mahaffy on the ass in Ireland'). On all these things he wrote well, and in his treatment of some of them he made valuable, if small, contributions to Irish history. His earliest effort, the translation of Fischer's work on Kant, provoked a generous letter from Mill, then at the height of his influence; his *Sketch of the Life and Teaching of Descartes* (1880) was a good introduction to its subject, although concentrating characteristically on the man himself more than his philosophy. But it is not on these multifarious writings that his reputation rests. Indeed, it is probable that the estimate of him as a student of things Greek has suffered from the variety of his interests; he was assumed to be superficial, because people thought that knowledge so extended must be shallow. 'The Provost's talents, though brilliant, were versatile rather than profound', was the verdict in one of his obituary notices. This was an astute judgement, but in that age of greater scholarly versatility, such skills were highly regarded, as is shown by the innumerable honours bestowed on him. He was elected an honorary member of the academies of Berlin, Munich, Vienna, Athens, and Utrecht, and the Lincei of Rome, and received honorary degrees from the universities of Athens, Louvain, Oxford, St Andrews, and Dublin, and an honorary fellowship from Queen's College, Oxford. In 1877 the king of Greece conferred on him the gold cross of the order of the Redeemer, later raising him two grades.

Although, as Mahaffy himself says in one of his prefaces, his object was to set down results rather than processes of investigation, an essay such as 'On the authenticity of the Olympian register' (*Journal of Hellenic Studies*, 2, 1881, 164–78) indicates that he could, when he so chose, exhibit the processes of investigation equally well with the results. Sometimes cavalier in his approach, he nevertheless had in him much of the stuff of which historians are made: industry and imagination, a superb memory, and a curiosity that was insatiable. One of his greatest gifts was his power of seeing things in the concrete; of so visualizing the past as to make it as real to us as the life we live and see around us. So it is that the books which bear the most distinctive impress of his individuality and ability are the three volumes which treat of the social life and civilization of the Greeks from the age of Homer to the age of Hadrian. His work in this area was, and remains, a remarkable achievement. Concentration on social life was virtually unknown at the time in the world of classical scholarship, and the Hellenistic age was ignored by English-speaking scholars. *Social Life in Greece from Homer to Menander* was, therefore, a pioneering contribution, marked by a typical liveliness and independence of judgement (it opposed, for instance, the prevailing view that Thucydides was a better historian than Herodotus). It also contained the first frank (and balanced) discussion of Greek homosexuality, although this was omitted after the first edition. Whether Mahaffy's open-mindedness on the subject had any effect on his most famous pupil, Oscar Wilde, is difficult to say. From a twentieth-century perspective, his four-volume *History of Classical Greek Literature* is less exciting. At the time it was generally regarded as a solid and useful book, many of the judgements expressed being acute, fresh, and original. It remained a standard work for many years.

As a scholar Mahaffy had limitations and defects. He was interested in persons, rather than in the play of forces or the operation of laws; his strength certainly did not lie in the grasp of historical principles and he lacked any sense of feeling for the nuances of literary style. It was perhaps inevitable that one to whom the past became as real as the present should often allow the present to intrude into the past. He rarely missed an opportunity of introducing modern parallels, many of them fanciful, far-fetched, and irrelevant. He was also notoriously prone to inaccuracies, and aggressively partisan. This latter characteristic led him into a bitter scholarly quarrel with the Cambridge classicist Richard Jebb, and a less bitter 'civil war' with his Trinity colleague Robert Tyrrell. But these faults should not be allowed to obscure his undoubted strengths, and particularly his sense of vision: he was a man ahead of his times in his pursuit of social and Hellenistic history; he was one of the few scholars in the world who appreciated at the outset the revolutionary character of the discoveries of Heinrich Schliemann; and he was one of the first to grasp the importance of papyrology.

When it is remembered that Mahaffy came to the study of papyri with no previous palaeographical training, we may well be surprised at the measure of success which he achieved. He was at his best in the guessing of the sense of obscure passages, the suggestion of supplements, and the lucid summarizing of results; for the task of accurate decipherment and transcription he lacked the patience and the attention to detail which are indispensable to the study of papyrology. None the less, his edition of the *Flinders Petrie Papyri* (the third volume was largely the work of his colleague J. G. Smyly, a much better papyrologist) constituted a work of serious scholarship and secured for Mahaffy a reputation as a real scholar. In fact his book *The Empire of the Ptolemies* shows his skills to better effect—a lively historian prepared to use the exciting new evidence being provided by papyri. It remained for many years by far the best account in English of that period.

Mahaffy's reputation was not merely that of a man of letters or university professor. For nearly half a century he was one of the best-known figures in the social life of his generation. He was an inveterate diner-out, and a constant attendant at congresses and other gatherings of the learned. Thanks in part to a boyhood spent on the continent, he could speak German like a native and French fluently. But it was as a wit and raconteur, as one of the most brilliant talkers of his time, with a fund of apposite anecdote, that he was so widely known and so generally welcome in society. 'Ireland is a place where the inevitable never happens and the unexpected always occurs', is a fair specimen of his epigrammatic power. His caustic wit sometimes made him unpopular, especially in his own university. This is hardly surprising given some of his *bons mots*. When told, for instance, that Provost Traill was ill, he replied, 'Nothing trivial I hope'. And at a *viva voce* examination he asked a student why Dr Barlow had been made a fellow. 'I don't know', replied the student. 'Correct', said Mahaffy. 'You get a mark for that. Nobody knows.' But if he was unpopular in certain circles, he had many attached friends, for he was generous and warm-hearted, and his judgements of men were never tainted by jealousy or bitterness.

Mahaffy played hardly any part in politics until the meeting of the convention in 1917, although in 1914 he did prevent a meeting of the college Gaelic Society from taking place in the college, at which W. B. Yeats and Patrick Pearse were to be speakers. He was both by temperament and conviction an aristocrat, and the Ireland for which he cared and to which he belonged was the nation of Burke and Goldsmith, of Grattan and Charles Lever. He never tired of decrying the cultural pretensions of Celtic Ireland, and he was contemptuous of the provincial note of Irish nationalism. In the convention he recommended a federal scheme on the Swiss model with provincial autonomy for Ulster.   E. M. WALKER, rev. B. C. McGING

Sources W. B. Stanford and R. B. McDowell, *Mahaffy. A biography of an Anglo-Irishman* (1971) • A. H. Sayce, *Reminiscences* (1923) • R. B. McDowell and D. A. Webb, *Trinity College, Dublin, 1592–1952: an academic history* (1982) • F. W. Starkie, 'John Pentland Mahaffy', *Of one company: biographical studies of famous Trinity men*, ed. D. A. Webb (1951), 89–100 • J. Dillon, 'The classics in Trinity', *Trinity College Dublin and the idea of a university*, ed. C. H. Holland (1991), 239–54 • J. V. Luce, *Trinity College Dublin: the first 400 years* (1992) • The letters of Oscar Wilde, ed. R. Hart-Davis (1962) • T. West, *The bold collegians. The development of sport in Trinity College Dublin* (1991) • *Hermathena*, 42 (1920), v–viii • O. St J. Gogarty, *It isn't this time of year at all* (1952) • O. St J. Gogarty, *Tumbling in the hay* (1939) • D. J. Hickey and J. E. Doherty, *A dictionary of Irish history* (1980)
Archives TCD, corresp. and papers • TCD, corresp. | BL, Balfour MSS • BL, Macmillan MSS • BL, corresp. with Macmillans, Add. MS 55118 • King's AC Cam., letters to Oscar Browning • NL Ire., Bryce MSS • NL Ire., Redmond MSS • Plunkett House, London, Plunkett MSS • TCD, Leslie MSS • TCD, Salmon MSS • Trinity Cam., Sidgwick MSS • University College, Dublin, letters to D. J. O'Donoghue
Likenesses W. Osborne, portrait, 1900, TCD • K. Shaw, bronze bust, 1901, TCD • W. Orpen, oils, 1907, Hugh Lane Gallery of Modern Art, Dublin • S. C. Hamilton, portrait, 1916, TCD • Carre, bas-relief, TCD • Fradelle & Young, cabinet photograph, NPG [*see illus.*] • attrib. S. C. Harrison, oils, NG Ire. • W. Osborne, drawing, study (probably for his portrait), TCD • J. Wilcox, bust, TCD, Provost's House • J. Wilcox, oils, TCD • photographs, TCD

Mahatma Gandhi. *See* Gandhi, Mohandas Karamchand (1869–1948).

Mahdi, the. *See* Muhammad Ahmad ibn ʿAbdullahi (1844–1885).

Mahler, Kurt (1903–1988), mathematician, was born on 26 July 1903 in Krefeld in the Prussian Rhineland, with his twin sister, Hilde (*d.* 1934), the youngest of the eight children of Hermann Mahler (1855–1941) and his wife, Henriette, *née* Stern (1860–1942). Both parents were from the Jewish community; his father, a printer, owned a small business. The four oldest children died before Kurt was born. His brother Joseph, who inherited the printing business, died in a concentration camp, probably in 1945. The remaining child, Lydia (*d.* 1984), married and lived in the Netherlands.

Mahler was a sickly child and at five he developed tuberculosis of the right knee. Until the age of fourteen he had only four years of formal schooling. He then studied for two years in elementary technical schools and began an apprenticeship in a machine factory at Krefeld. During this time he became fascinated by mathematics and, entirely self-taught, was eventually reading books at university level. His work was brought to the attention of Felix Klein and his assistant Carl Siegel, and on their recommendation Mahler left the factory and was coached for university entrance while continuing his own mathematical studies.

In 1923 Mahler entered the University of Frankfurt am Main, where Siegel was then professor. Siegel went overseas in 1925 and Mahler migrated to the University of Göttingen; he received his doctorate in 1927 from Frankfurt, and remained at Göttingen for further research, supported by his parents and the Jewish community of Krefeld. At Göttingen he developed new methods in transcendence theory, including his celebrated classification of transcendental numbers, and his work on *p*-adic numbers contributed to their acceptance into general mathematical culture.

When Hitler came to power in 1933 Mahler had just been appointed assistant in the University of Königsberg, but had not yet taken up the post. Realizing that as a Jew

Kurt Mahler (1903–1988), by Walter Stoneman, 1948

he had no future in Germany, he left immediately for the Netherlands, proceeded to Manchester for the academic year 1933/4, supported by the modest Bishop Harvey Godwin fellowship, then, on a stipend raised by a Dutch Jewish group, spent two years at Groningen, where he developed an interest in the geometry of numbers. The cap of his tubercular knee was removed: over the next few years the infection disappeared, but he was left with a permanent limp. In 1937 he returned to Manchester, supported by small fellowships or temporary posts. While he was interned for three months at the outbreak of war, Manchester University awarded him the degree of ScD, and in 1941 an assistant lectureship, his first regular post. He lived from 1938 to 1958 in Donner House, Didsbury, a hostel for single university staff, and when it closed, bought himself a small suburban house.

In the following years Mahler developed his work on convex sets and quadratic forms into a geometry of numbers of general sets in n-dimensional space, including his influential compactness theorem. With his future now assured, Mahler moved steadily up the academic ladder. He took British nationality in 1946 and was elected to the Royal Society in 1948. The London Mathematical Society awarded him its senior Berwick prize in 1950, and its De Morgan medal in 1981; he was also a member of the Dutch and Australian mathematical societies. Manchester University created its first personal chair for him in 1952. Ten

years later he went to Australia as professor at the Institute for Advanced Study in Canberra. This research post gave him freedom to travel and pursue his own studies, which he did with energy and enthusiasm. He also offered courses in number theory in the Australian National University. He was elected to the Australian Academy of Science in 1965 and received its Lyell medal in 1977. In 1968 he reached the statutory age of retirement, whereupon he took up a chair at Ohio State University, returning to Canberra in 1972 as emeritus professor. Mahler did not marry; an attraction of Canberra was that he could live in communal comfort at University House. Mahler was an excellent photographer, and kept up his knowledge of Chinese, begun in 1939 when he had considered taking up a post in China. He remained mathematically active until the end of his life. He died in Canberra at University House on 25 February 1988, leaving the bulk of his estate to the Australian Mathematical Society, which established a lectureship in his memory.   J. W. S. CASSELS

Sources personal record, RS · K. Mahler, 'How I became a mathematician', *American Mathematical Monthly*, 81 (1974), 981–3 · K. Mahler, 'Fifty years as a mathematician', *Journal of Number Theory*, 14 (1982), 121–55 · J. H. Coates and A. J. van der Poorten, *Memoirs FRS*, 39 (1994), 263–79 · J. W. S. Cassels, 'Obituary of Kurt Mahler', *Acta Arithmetica*, 58 (1991), 215–28 [with list of publications, pp. 229–37] · J. W. S. Cassels, *Bulletin of the London Mathematical Society*, 24 (1992), 381–97
Archives Bodl. Oxf., Society for Protection of Science and Learning file · RS · Trinity Cam., corresp. with Harold Davenport, letters
Likenesses W. Stoneman, photograph, 1948, NPG [*see illus.*] · photographs, RS · portrait, repro. in Cassels, *Acta Arithmetica* · portrait, repro. in J. W. S. Cassels, *Bulletin of the London Mathematical Society*

Mahomed, Deen [*formerly* Deen Mahomet] (1759–1851), shampooing surgeon and restaurateur, was born Deen Mahomet in May 1759, in Patna, Bihar, India, the younger son of an Indian officer in the East India Company's Bengal army. Both parents were Shi'i Muslims claiming descent from Afshar Turk and Arab immigrants to India from Persia in the seventeenth century.

After a traditional Islamic education in Patna, and his father's death fighting recalcitrant landholders in 1769, Mahomet left his mother to attach himself as camp follower to Ensign Godfrey Evan Baker of the Bengal army's 3rd European regiment. Together they marched widely across north India, subduing Indian villagers and regional rulers and blocking anticipated French invasions. Under Baker's patronage in 1781 Mahomet rose to the posts of market master and then jemadar (ensign) of the élite grenadier company of the 2nd battalion, 30th sepoy regiment, 2nd brigade. Mahomet fought skirmishes at Kalpi (April 1781) against Marathas and stormed Patita Fort (13 September 1781), rescuing Governor-General Warren Hastings from Raja Chayt Singh of Benares. Promoted subedar (lieutenant) in this regiment, Mahomet helped crush peasant resistance to British control in the Benares region.

Baker, after his recall in July 1782 for alleged extortion

Deen Mahomed (1759–1851), by Thomas Mann Baynes

established a charitable steam bath in his 12 Portman Square mansion, with Mahomet providing 'shampooing' (Indian therapeutic whole body massage). Other London bath house keepers soon imitated his shampooing method.

In 1810 Mahomet started the Hindostanee Coffee House, 34–5 George Street, Portman Square, proffering Indian cuisine and ambience, including hookahs (tobacco water pipes), bamboo furniture, and curries. He also adopted the honorific 'sake' (sheikh, 'venerable one') and altered his name from Mahomet to Mahomed. His restaurant attracted epicures but proved undercapitalized. Mahomed petitioned for bankruptcy on 18 March 1812 and distributed his property among his creditors at London's Guildhall on 27 July 1813. He then sought service as butler or valet but subsequently moved to the burgeoning seaside resort of Brighton, where the reconstruction of the prince regent's Royal Marine Pavilion had made oriental exotica fashionable. Finding employment in a bath house attached to the New Steyne Hotel, 11 Devonshire Place, in 1814, Mahomed sold Indian cosmetics and medicines, including Indian tooth powder, hair dye, steam bath with Indian oils, and shampooing. The last two, bolstered by his hyperbolic advertisements, proved most popular. By December 1815 Mahomed had opened his own Battery House Baths, at the foot of the Steyne. Here his daughter Rosanna (1815–1818) died.

Enhancing his reputation in 1820 Mahomed published a book of testimonials: *Cases cured by Sake Deen Mahomed, shampooing surgeon, and inventor of the Indian medicated vapour and sea-water bath*. Mahomed claimed to be able to cure a range of ills including rheumatism, asthma, and gout. He also identified supporters as well as rivals among orthodox medical practitioners. During 1820–21 he and his silent partner, Thomas Brown, built the magnificent Mahomed's Baths on King's Road, overlooking the sea (later the site of Queen's Hotel); while it was under construction he briefly established a bath house on West Cliff. He also expanded his 1820 book into a medical casebook, *Shampooing, or, Benefits Resulting from the Use of the Indian Medicated Vapour Bath* (1822, 1826, and 1838). In *Shampooing*, he revised his medical credentials to claim ten years' training in Calcutta Hospital and—to accommodate those years—adjusted his reported birth date to 1749. His professional and social prominence received recognition through appointment by royal warrant as shampooing surgeon to George IV and William IV. His popularity and patronage by aristocracy and gentry led jealous competitors to appropriate his method. Mahomed opened a London branch of his bath house at 11 St James's Place (1830–36) and then at 7 Little Ryder Street (1838–58); these were managed by his sons Deen (c.1812–c.1836) then Horatio (1816–1873). Another son, Frederick (1818–1888), taught dance, fencing, and gymnastics in Brighton. He was the father of the physician Frederick Henry Horatio Akbar *Mahomed (1849–1884).

In 1841, after the death of his partner, Brown, Mahomed's Baths went to public auction. Mahomed himself

from villagers, resigned his captain's commission. Following Baker, Mahomet also resigned from the Bengal army and emigrated to Ireland. They sailed from Calcutta on the Danish vessel *Christiansborg* in January 1784, visiting Madras, St Helena, and Dartmouth (November 1784) en route to Cork, Baker's home town. Under Baker's patronage Mahomet studied to perfect his English. In 1786 he eloped with an Anglo-Irish gentlewoman, Jane Daly (*b. c.*1772). They had an Anglican marriage in Cork and Ross diocese, Mahomet having converted to this denomination. In 1794 he published his two-volume *Travels of Dean Mahomet, a native of Patna in Bengal, through several parts of India, while in the service of the Honourable the East India Company written by himself, in a series of letters to a friend*, the first book ever written and published in English by an Indian. This epistolary travel narrative recounted the Bengal army's conquest of India, Indian customs and cities, and Mahomet's autobiography. He elaborated his text with Latin quotations (from Seneca and Martial), citations from Goldsmith and Milton, a portrait of himself in European dress, and illustrations of an Indian sepoy and officer and the panoply of an Indian ruler. He secured the patronage of 320 élite British subscribers, testament to his standing as a man of letters.

By 1807 Mahomet had moved to London, accompanied by at least one son, William (*c.*1797–1833). Slight evidence suggests that his first wife, Jane Daly, may have died and that he married about this time another woman named Jane. Mahomet baptized two children at St Marylebone parish church: Amelia (1808–1894) and Henry Edwin (1810–1823). Mahomet worked for the Hon. Basil Cochrane, recently returned from India and made wealthy as a Madras civil servant and Royal Navy contractor. Cochrane lacked the capital to buy, but he offered to work as manager for the highest bidder. The first auction failed to meet the reserve price but, with no reserve, an 1843 auction succeeded. Since the new owner, William Furner, did not wish to employ Mahomed, he moved to a small rented house at 2 Black Lion Street, where he lived and attempted to compete with his old establishment. While he continued to advertise his services until 1845, his youngest son, Arthur Ackber (1819–1872), carried on the business under straitened circumstances. Jane Mahomed died on 26 December 1850 of uterine cancer; Mahomed died of 'natural decay' on 24 February 1851 at their son Frederick's home, 32 Grand Parade, Brighton. They were both buried together in St Nicholas's parish church, Brighton. From the 1860s his proprietary Indian medicated bath became the Turkish bath and his shampooing mere hair wash.

MICHAEL H. FISHER

Sources Travels of Dean Mahomet: an eighteenth-century journey through India, ed. M. H. Fisher (1997) • M. H. Fisher, The first Indian author in English (1996) • Abu Taleb Khan, Travels of Mirza Abu Taleb Khan in Asia, Africa, and Europe during the years 1799, 1800, 1801, 1802, and 1803: written by himself, in the Persian language, trans. C. Stewart, 3 (1814) • Memoirs of the life of the Right Hon. Warren Hastings, first governor-general of Bengal, ed. G. R. Gleig, 3 vols. (1841), vol. 2 • R. Visram, Ayahs, lascars and princes: Indians in Britain, 1700–1947 (1986) • H. Mahomed, The bath: a concise history of bathing, as practiced by the nations of the ancient and modern world (1843) • B. Cochrane, An improvement on the mode of administering the vapour bath (1809) • The Times (27 March 1811) • The Times (25 March 1812) • The Times (4 April 1812) • The Times (20 April 1813) • The epicure's almanack, or, Calendar of good living (1815) • Visitor's books of Mahomed's baths, Brighton Public Reference Library • LondG (21–4 March 1812) • LondG (2–6 June 1812) • LondG (3–7 July 1813) • Willis's Current Notes (1851) • d. cert. • marriage records of the Cork and Ross Diocese • memorial, St Nicholas's parish church, Brighton • Brighton Guardian (26 Feb 1851)
Archives Brighton Public Reference Library
Likenesses J. Finlay, engraving, 1794 (after Ghaywanimdy?), repro. in M. H. Fisher, ed., Travels of Dean Mahomet • W. Maddocks, portrait, 1822 • W. Maddocks, portrait, 1826 • T. M. Baynes, portrait, c.1830, Brighton Pavilion • S. Drummond, portrait, c.1840, Brighton • T. M. Baynes, lithograph, Wellcome L. [see illus.]

Mahomed, Frederick Henry Horatio Akbar (1849–1884), physician, was born at 2 Black Lion Street, Brighton, on 11 April 1849, the son of Frederick Mahomed (1818–1888), the keeper of a turkish bath, professor of gymnastics, and fencing master, and his wife, Sarah (née Hodgkinson). He was the grandson of Sake Deen *Mahomed (1759–1851). He began medical studies at an early age at the Sussex County Hospital, and from there went to Guy's Hospital, London, where he won several prizes. He became a member of the Royal College of Surgeons in 1872, and soon after became resident medical officer at the London Fever Hospital. He married Ellen Chalk (b. 1847/8), daughter of Charles Chalk, solicitor, in Brighton on 14 June 1873. In 1875 he gained the degree of MD at Brussels and was elected medical tutor at St Mary's Hospital, before returning to Guy's as medical registrar in 1877. Realizing that further progress in the medical profession would not be achieved without a degree from an English university, he matriculated at Gonville and Caius College, Cambridge in 1877 and travelled to Cambridge every evening by the last

train in order to perform the pernoctation essential for keeping a term, returning to London by an early morning train. In 1881 he graduated MB at Cambridge, taking no other degree, and in the same year he was elected assistant physician to Guy's Hospital. In 1880 he was elected a fellow of the Royal College of Physicians.

Employed by the British Association, Mahomed became involved in organizing a system for the registration of diseases, and worked laboriously at this collective investigation. He made many contributions to the *Transactions of the Pathological Society* (vols. 26, 28, 32, 34, 35, 36, 37, 38), the most important being the sphygmographic evidence of arterio-capillary fibrosis; and he wrote a long series of papers on the results of the use of the sphygmograph in the investigation of disease in the *British Medical Journal*. To the *Transactions of the Medico-Chirurgical Society* he contributed a valuable paper on the early stages of scarlatinal nephritis (vol. 57, 1874), and also published many observations in the *Guy's Hospital Reports*.

Mahomed was a tall, muscular man, of dark complexion, and possessed an enormous enthusiasm for his work, which sometimes led him to act impulsively. He died of typhoid on 22 November 1884 at his house, 24 Manchester Square, London.

NORMAN MOORE, rev. RACHEL E. DAVIES

Sources BMJ (29 Nov 1884), 1099 • Journal of the Royal College of Physicians of London, 29 (1995) • Munk, Roll • b. cert. • m. cert. • CGPLA Eng. & Wales (1885) • personal knowledge (1893) • Venn, Alum. Cant.
Wealth at death £1957 1s. 6d.: probate, 24 Jan 1885, CGPLA Eng. & Wales

Mahon, Sir Bryan Thomas (1862–1930), army officer, was born on 2 April 1862 at Belleville, co. Galway, the eldest son of Henry Blake Mahon, a landowner of Belleville, and his wife, Matilda, second daughter of Colonel Thomas Seymour, Ballymore Castle, co. Galway. After attending Dr Wall's school at Portarlington he followed a route into the army common among his Anglo-Irish contemporaries, and was thus commissioned into the militia (4th Connaught Rangers) before being gazetted lieutenant in the 21st hussars in January 1883. He transferred to the 8th King's Royal Irish Hussars three weeks later, and served with them for the next ten years. He was promoted captain in 1888, and was adjutant from 1890 to 1893.

In 1893 he transferred to the Egyptian army in search of adventure and better pay, and this led to his spending the next eleven years in Africa. It was the making of his career. He saw extensive action against the dervishes in the 1896 Dongola expedition as staff officer to a mounted brigade, winning the DSO; in operations in the Nile valley in 1897, during which he was promoted major; and in Kitchener's drive on Khartoum in 1898, as second in command of the Egyptian cavalry. He fought in the battles of the Atbara (8 April 1898) and Omdurman (2 September), being mistakenly reported killed at the latter, and was intelligence officer of the column which finally defeated the Khalifa in Kordofan in November 1899. He was awarded the brevet ranks of lieutenant-colonel in 1898 and colonel in 1899.

Having demonstrated an aptitude for mounted operations, Mahon went to South Africa in January 1900, and led a mounted force during the relief of Kimberley, before in May being given command of the Mafeking relief column, the appointment which established his reputation. Mafeking had been besieged since October 1899, its garrison under Baden-Powell's energetic leadership successfully tying down significant numbers of Boers. But in late April, with rations running low and increasing anxiety at home over the town's fate, Lord Roberts ordered a further attempt to lift the siege, to coincide with his advance on Pretoria.

Mahon's force comprised some 1200 men, including 900 colonial horse, 100 infantry, 4 field guns, and 52 wagons. Covered by General Hunter's advance across the Vaal, Mahon left Barkly West on 4 May. In 11 days he covered 230 miles of enemy-held territory, successfully evading contact with the alerted Boers (other than a skirmish on 13 May). Early on 15 May he reached Massibi, 25 miles west of Mafeking, where he linked up with a force of Rhodesian levies under Colonel Plumer. Reorganizing his force into two brigades, he advanced on the town at dawn on 16 May. Despite stiff resistance, the Boers having reinforced the threatened sector, the column had broken through by late afternoon; Mahon's first patrol reached the town just before 6 p.m., with the main force arriving early the following morning.

News of Mafeking's relief was greeted with hysterical enthusiasm by a British public desperate for success, and Mahon became briefly a household name; but even allowing for the hyperbole, his was a genuine achievement, his drive and dash comparing favourably with the conduct of other British mounted operations during the war. He subsequently took part in further operations in Transvaal, and later that year returned to England to be created CB.

Early in 1901 Mahon was back in Egypt as governor of Kordofan, and in 1904 he moved to India to command a district. After being promoted major-general in 1906 he commanded the Lucknow division from 1909 to 1913, and on returning to England he was made lieutenant-general and created KCVO.

At the outbreak of the First World War in 1914 he held no active command but was soon appointed commander of the 10th (Irish) division, part of Kitchener's New Armies. Although senior for the post, it was hoped his prestige would assist recruitment. This aim was only partly realized—Mahon's protestant, imperialist, and unionist background (he was a close friend of Sir Edward Carson) had only limited appeal for nationalists—but his division's infantry was nevertheless predominantly Irish when it sailed for the Dardanelles in July 1915.

Gallipoli undermined Mahon's reputation, like that of many others. Sir Ian Hamilton, the British commander, was no great admirer of his and refused to accept him as corps commander; Kitchener therefore felt obliged to appoint the elderly Stopford, one of the few available generals senior to Mahon, with unhappy results. The 10th division formed part of Stopford's corps during the Suvla landings on 6–7 August. The operation's failure stemmed largely from the errors and inertia of the commanders on the spot and the troops' inexperience, exacerbated by

Hamilton's own lack of grip. Mahon, who had warned that the plan was over-complicated, also displayed excessive caution, though in fairness the disarray and confusion of the initial landings were for him compounded by the detachment of two of his brigades elsewhere (to the 11th division at Suvla and to Anzac Cove) while his artillery had remained in Egypt, leaving him with just a third of his force. On 15 August, after several days' inconclusive fighting against mounting opposition, Mahon directed two of his brigades in an assault on the Kirech Tepe Ridge in an attempt to expand the bridgehead. The attack failed, despite the troops' bravery, with heavy loss; and in the midst of it Mahon resigned his post in a distinctly inglorious episode. Learning that Stopford was to be replaced by Beauvoir de Lisle, to whom he was senior and whom he detested, Mahon refused to serve under him and retired to Mudros for nine days before relenting. Hamilton was furious, and probably only the likelihood of an adverse reaction in Ireland prevented Mahon's dismissal.

In late September the 10th division was withdrawn to Mudros, having suffered severe casualties. But the decision of the French and British governments to send a division each to Macedonia to assist the beleaguered Serbs offered Mahon a fresh opportunity. The 10th division disembarked at Salonika early in October, Mahon himself arriving on 8 October as overall British commander. The situation he faced was complex: his position was unlike that of the French, because British political and military support for the venture was extremely unenthusiastic; and the neutral Greeks, on whose territory the allied force was based, were obstructive and suspicious. Mahon found himself subject to strict—though frequently changing—political constraints, commanding a force with low priority for equipment and supplies, while having to co-operate with a French commander, Sarrail, determined on an aggressive strategy for both policy and personal reasons. Not until the end of October was Mahon permitted to cross the Serbo-Greek border in support of the French advance northwards. In early December the Bulgarians counter-attacked, and both the French and 10th division—exhausted after Gallipoli and worn down by atrocious weather—were sharply defeated; by the end of the year the allies were back in Salonika. There Mahon received four more divisions, and worked energetically with a makeshift headquarters to create a secure base for future operations. In January 1916 he was placed for political reasons under the command of Sarrail, whose secrecy and high-handedness were causing increasing problems. In May, Mahon was replaced by Lieutenant-General Milne largely because the latter was rightly judged better able to stand up to the French, though the change represented scant reward for Mahon's success in establishing the Salonika base.

Mahon was appointed to a command in Egypt, but within days he was invalided home with sunstroke. In November 1916 he became commander-in-chief in Ireland in an attempt to conciliate opinion there in the wake of the Easter rising. Despite his having achieved some slight success in softening the military's image, in May 1918 the new viceroy, Lord French, replaced him with his own man, Sir Frederick Shaw. From October 1918 to March 1919 Mahon was military commander of Lille. He retired in 1921 and was created KCB in 1922. From 1910 to 1930 he was colonel of the 8th hussars.

In 1920 Mahon had married Amelia Madeline Louisa (1876–1927), daughter of the Hon. Charles Crichton and widow of Sir John Milbanke VC. They had no children. He returned to Ireland, where he devoted himself largely to horse-racing, as owner and administrator. From 1922 to 1930 he served in the Irish Free State senate; in February 1923 anti-treaty republicans burned his home (which was subsequently rebuilt) at Mullaboden, co. Kildare.

For many Mahon epitomized the dashing cavalry officer—a fine horseman who was capable of great charm, though occasionally somewhat volatile. But he was also generally rather a silent and not especially forceful man who grew more cautious with age. That he is remembered as much for the Mafeking relief as for his subsequent senior appointments reflects his relative lack of later success, and by 1914 he was perhaps past his best. But while not the only distinguished colonial soldier to make an uncertain transition to total war, he was not without achievements. He did better than several other commanders in the mishandled Suvla operation, as Hamilton later acknowledged; and at Salonika he helped lay the foundations, in difficult circumstances, for subsequent successes. His appointment to the Irish senate reflected the regard in which he was held in Ireland.

Mahon, who converted to Roman Catholicism in 1927, died at 9 Earlsfort Mansions, Dublin, on 24 September 1930 and was buried at Mullaboden, co. Kildare, on September 26.   NICHOLAS PERRY

Sources *The Times* (25 Sept 1930) · *Irish Times* (25 Sept 1930) · *The Cross-Belts* [eighth king's royal Irish hussars] (Jan 1931) · J. F. Maurice and M. H. Grant, eds., *History of the war in South Africa, 1899–1902*, 4 vols. (1906–10) · T. Pakenham, *The Boer War* (1979) · Marquess of Anglesey [G. C. H. V. Paget], *A history of the British cavalry, 1816 to 1919*, 3 (1982) · C. F. Aspinall-Oglander, ed., *Military operations: Gallipoli*, 2, History of the Great War (1932) · C. Falls, ed., *Military operations, Macedonia*, 1, History of the Great War (1933) · B. Cooper, *History of the 10th (Irish) division in Gallipoli* (1917) · R. R. James, *Gallipoli* (1965) · A. Palmer, *The gardeners of Salonika* (1965) · T. Denman, 'The 10th (Irish) division, 1914–1915: a study in military and political interaction', *Irish Sword*, 17 (1987–9), 16–24 · R. H. Murray, *The history of the VIII king's royal Irish hussars (1693–1927)*, 2 (1928) · Burke, *Peerage* (1939) · WWW · CGPLA Eng. & Wales (1931)

Archives PRO, Kitchener MSS, 30/57 · WO 159 · U. Durham L., corresp. with Sir Reginald Wingate | FILM BFI NFTVA, news footage · IWM FVA, actuality footage

Likenesses photograph, repro. in Murray, *History of the VIII king's royal Irish hussars*, frontispiece · photographs

Wealth at death £6593 3s. 2d.: resworn probate, 31 Jan 1931, CGPLA Eng. & Wales

Mahon, Charles James Patrick [*known as* the O'Gorman Mahon] (**1800–1891**), politician and financial speculator, was born into a prominent Catholic family at Ennis, co. Clare, on about 17 March 1800, the eldest of four children. His father, Patrick Mahon of New Park (*d.* 1821), who took part in the rising of 1798, inherited an estate in co. Clare. His mother, Barbara, a considerable heiress, was the only daughter of James O'Gorman of Ennis. Mahon was one of the earliest pupils at Clongowes Wood College, where he was a contemporary of Maurice, eldest son of Daniel O'Connell. After school he entered Trinity College, Dublin, where he took his BA in 1822 and proceeded MA in law in 1832. Until his father's death in 1821, he was sent an annual allowance of £500; afterwards, he inherited half the family property, becoming also a magistrate for co. Clare. A tall, striking man, he cut an impressive figure at Trinity and then in the Dublin social scene. He adopted at this time the style the O'Gorman Mahon, a conjunction of his parental surnames. He became acquainted with Tom Steele and through him joined the Catholic Association. He was called to the Irish bar in 1834, but never practised. Mahon was instrumental in convincing O'Connell to contest the by-election for County Clare against William Vesey Fitzgerald in 1828, and played a conspicuous part in the ensuing electoral campaign that contributed directly to the Wellington ministry's concession of Catholic emancipation in the following year. As his obituary in the *Freeman's Journal* (17 June 1891) observed, his

> political career could not have opened more brilliantly or with such promise of success in Ireland, where courage and daring, youth and comeliness, physical strength, a noble Irish name, and eloquence—qualities and gifts possessed by The O'Gorman Mahon—are so much admired.

In 1830 Mahon married Christina, daughter of John O'Brien of Dublin. She was an heiress and had property valued at £60,000 in her own right, which gave Mahon the resources to seek parliamentary honours. The couple spent little time together, and she died apart from him, in Paris in 1877. They had one son, St John, who died on 22 September 1883. Mahon was returned for County Clare at the general election of 1830 but was unseated on petition on a charge of bribery. During the election he quarrelled with O'Connell, causing a rift which never healed. At the next general election in 1831, he was easily outdistanced by Major M'Namara and Maurice O'Connell in the race for the representation of County Clare, a struggle that further estranged him from O'Connell senior. Between 1831 and 1835 he resided chiefly at Mahonburgh, becoming a deputy lieutenant of his county, and a captain in the West Clare militia. His most fruitful political period was at an end.

In 1835 Mahon began the travels which gave him a quixotic aura. First he went to Paris, where he made the acquaintance of Talleyrand and became a favourite at the court of Louis-Philippe. From Paris he proceeded to several European capitals, travelled in Africa and the East, and was for a short time in South America before returning to Ireland in 1846. He was returned unopposed for Ennis in the general election of 1847. His political leanings were unclear; he made no mention of repeal of the Act of Union in his election address, terming himself a whig and pledging to follow Lord John Russell. He lost favour in Ireland by supporting Russell's measures against the Young Irelanders, for whom he had no sympathy, in 1848 and because of his subsequent abstention on the Ecclesiastical Titles bill of 1851. However, in Dod's *Peerage, Baronetage* and *Knightage of Great Britain and Ireland* (1850) he affirmed his support for repeal. During this period he made a wide circle of acquaintances in London, including the author William Thackeray. His spendthrift habits depleted his financial resources and in 1851 he was forced to sell most of his co. Clare estates. At the next general election, in July 1852, his attempt to be re-elected for Ennis ended in failure.

On leaving parliament, Mahon was soon off on his foreign travels once more. As earlier, the details are only partially verifiable, and depend upon his own recollections. Reportedly, he returned to Paris, where he was involved in financial, literary, and journalistic projects; proceeded to St Petersburg, where the tsar appointed him a lieutenant in his international bodyguard; subsequently, he hunted bear in Finland with the tsarevich, fought against the Tartars, travelled in China and India, and served under the Turkish and Austrian flags. He went to South America in late 1858 and returned to Europe in late summer 1861. Meanwhile his financial situation worsened. During the next years he moved about extensively, allegedly serving as a general in the government forces during the civil war in Uruguay, commanding a Chilean fleet in the war with Spain, serving as a colonel under the emperor of Brazil, and fighting for the Union in the American Civil War. On returning once more to Paris, in 1866, Louis Napoleon made him a colonel in a regiment of chasseurs. He then, in 1867, went to Berlin, where he established close relations with Bismarck and the crown prince as well as mixing widely in society. During this time he was again plagued by debts and sought to repair his finances through speculative ventures.

Mahon reappeared in Ireland in 1871 and by the next year business liabilities brought him to the verge of bankruptcy. As a consequence of his dealings, he ended up before the central criminal court in London but was acquitted. He then took part in the national conference in November 1873 which established the Irish Home Rule League. His ambition to re-enter parliament was rekindled. At the general election of 1874 he unsuccessfully contested Ennis as a home-ruler and he was defeated in the County Clare by-election on 13 August 1877, when he again stood as a supporter of Irish self-government. Persistence was rewarded when Mahon captured the County Clare seat at a by-election on 15 May 1879, then came at the head of the poll in the same constituency at the general election of 1880. He was a popular figure even with those who differed with his politics. He nominated Charles Stewart Parnell for the chairmanship of the Home Rule Party in 1880 and remained on cordial terms with the Irish leader. He introduced Captain O'Shea to Parnell and acted as an informal channel of communication with the government in 1882, when the Irish leader was in Kilmainham prison. Despite being a nationalist, Mahon sometimes refused to follow party directives and voted with the Liberal government. His independence of mind and whiggish politics made him unacceptable as a nationalist parliamentary candidate in 1885, but Parnell restored him to the House of Commons when the seat at Carlow fell

vacant in August 1887. Even then, he insisted upon standing as a Liberal home-ruler and was not obliged to take the party pledge. He retained this seat until his death at his home, 12 Sydney Street, South Kensington, London, on 15 June 1891. Almost his last act was to repudiate Parnell's leadership during the divorce crisis.

Mahon's dashing reputation was enhanced by his fame with the duelling pistol. Precise details are elusive but he may have participated in between thirteen to eighteen affairs of honour. It is known that he once sent Parnell his card though the difference of opinion was patched up and the Irish chief bore him no grudge, either then or after being abandoned by Mahon over the divorce crisis. Indeed, Parnell attended Mahon's funeral and burial at Glasnevin cemetery, within the O'Connell circle, on 21 June 1891.   F. W. WHYTE, *rev.* ALAN O'DAY

Sources D. Gwynn, *The O'Gorman Mahon* (1934) · *Freeman's Journal* [Dublin] (17 June 1891) · *Pall Mall Gazette* (17 June 1891) · H. Boylan, *A dictionary of Irish biography*, 2nd edn (1988) · *WWBMP*, vol. 1 · B. M. Walker, ed., *Parliamentary election results in Ireland, 1801–1922* (1978) · *Dod's Parliamentary Companion* · C. C. O'Brien, *Parnell and his party, 1880–90* (1957) · A. O'Day, *The English face of Irish nationalism* (1977) · F. S. L. Lyons, *Charles Stewart Parnell* (1977) · D. Thornley, *Isaac Butt and home rule* (1964) · W. L. Arnstein, *The Bradlaugh case: a study in late Victorian opinion and politics* (1965) · T. P. O'Connor, *The Parnell movement* (1886) · *CGPLA Eng. & Wales* (1891)

Archives University of Chicago Library, corresp. and papers

Likenesses lithograph, pubd 1828, NG Ire. · J. P. Havarty, lithograph, pubd 1829 (after his oil painting), NG Ire. · J. Adams-Acton, terracotta bust, 1877, NG Ire. · attrib. T. Bridgford, watercolour drawing, NPG · D. Maclise, black chalk and ink drawing, NG Ire. · Spy [L. Ward], cartoon, NPG; repro. in *VF* (17 Jan 1885)

Wealth at death £702 4s. 7d.: administration, 28 Aug 1891, *CGPLA Eng. & Wales*

Mahon [*née* Tilson], **Gertrude** (*b.* 1752, *d.* in or after 1808), courtesan and actress, was born in Dublin on 15 April 1752, the daughter of James Tilson (*c.*1715–1764), diplomat, and his wife, Gertrude, dowager countess of Kerry (*c.*1720–1775), daughter of Richard Lambart, fourth earl of Cavan, and widow of William Fitzmaurice, second earl of Kerry. Her older half-siblings were Francis Thomas Fitzmaurice, third earl of Kerry; Lady Anna Maria Fitzgerald, *née* Fitzmaurice; and, by an earlier marriage of her father, Elizabeth Anne Tilson. She was brought up in the established church. Little is known about her education but at sixteen she attended the home of Charles Burney, in Poland Street, Westminster, for music lessons. Until she was eleven Gertrude lived at Bolesworth Castle, Malpas, Cheshire, the family home; then her father became consul at Cadiz in Spain. Gertrude and her mother moved to London, where they lived at Wigmore Street. In 1764 Gertrude's father died and she received £3000 in his will.

Gertrude's appearance was striking. 'A mass of raven hair clustered round her pink cheeks, lustrous black eyes lit up her sweet features' (*Morning Herald*, 18 April 1777). She was wilful and spoiled by her ineffectual mother and became an outrageous flirt. Frances Burney described Gertrude's behaviour as 'An amorosa so forward in Cupid's cause!' (*Diary and Letters*, 1.25) after Gertrude wrote lovenotes to Frances's cousin Charles. At seventeen Gertrude fell in love with a disreputable Irish gambler, Gilbreath

Mahon (*fl.* 1740–1795). Knowing of her inheritance, Mahon proposed but Gertrude's mother would not consent. The pair eloped to France and married in 1769. Gertrude became pregnant in 1770. Her mother then insisted they marry in England and the ceremony took place at St George's, Hanover Square, Westminster, on 14 December 1770, their son, Robert Tilson Mahon, being born on 18 January 1771. Gertrude's mother refused to support Mahon and in 1774 he deserted Gertrude, who returned to her mother's home. Gertrude's mother died on 24 October 1775 leaving Gertrude the interest on her large estate, the capital being held for Robert.

Gertrude could have lived a quiet comfortable life but instead began to cavort with notorious courtesans including Grace Eliot, *née* Dalrymple, Dally the Tall, mistress of the prince of Wales (afterwards George IV) and George Cholmondeley, fourth earl of Cholmondeley, and Kitty Frederick, mistress of William Douglas, fourth duke of Queensberry. In her will Gertrude's mother had stated 'I hope that my relations will treat her with kindness and compassion' (PRO, PROB 11/1029, fols. 169–71), but so scandalized were her family that they refused to have anything more to do with her. From 1776 Gertrude appeared at tawdry venues throughout London. Her name was constantly in the press, which referred to her as the Bird of Paradise because of her love of bright immodest colours and large, many-plumed hats. Scandalous stories of her love affairs with wealthy men abounded. 'The Bird of Paradise has taken up residence in the South of France, with Sir J—n L—e, to wash in the pool of Montpelier, famous in the ailment of her trade!' (*The Rambler*, 1784, 359). Gertrude's 'companions' included Queensberry, Cholmondeley, and Thomas Lyttelton, second Baron Lyttelton, who had tired of their previous mistresses, and numerous officers with private fortunes. In 1780 she met the actress Margaret Cuyler and appeared on stage on 12 December at Covent Garden in John Dryden's *The Spanish Fryar*. The play sold out but Gertrude was not a success. After two further plays critics described her acting as 'Intolerable' (*Morning Herald*, 15 Feb 1781). Diminishing public interest cut short her career. Through acting she met the prince of Wales, but his attentions proved short-lived. In 1784 she was left the interest on £3000 by her half-sister Elizabeth and took a house in Great Portland Street. Her son, Robert, left England in 1785 to join the Indian army. Gertrude then appeared on stage in Dublin but was heralded only for her hats. In 1790 Robert died in Madras aged nineteen and the unhappy Gertrude's popularity waned as her beauty diminished. In 1808, aged fifty-six, Gertrude Mahon 'retired' to the Isle of Man and press and public lost interest. There is no obituary or evidence of the date or whereabouts of her death.   SUSAN GARDNER

Sources H. Bleackley, *Ladies fair and frail: sketches of the demi-monde during the eighteenth century* (1909) • *Memoirs of William Hickey*, ed. A. Spencer, 1 (1913), 318–19 • *The Rambler*, 2 (1784), 278, 359 • *European Magazine and London Review*, 1 (1782), 404–6 • *Morning Herald and Daily Advertiser* (18 April 1777) • *Morning Herald and Daily Advertiser* (15 Feb 1781) • *GM*, 1st ser., 41 (1771), 46 • *GM*, 1st ser., 22 (1752), 191 • *GM*, 1st ser., 34 (1764), 303 • Burke, *Peerage* (1999) • will of Gertrude, dowager countess of Kerry, PRO, PROB 11/1029/119, fols. 169–171 • *The early diary of Frances Burney, 1768–1778*, ed. A. R. Ellis, 1 (1889), 25–6 • Dodwell [E. Dodwell] and Miles [J. S. Miles], eds., *Alphabetical list of the officers of the Indian army: with the dates of their respective promotion, retirement, resignation, or death … from the year 1760 to the year … 1837* (1838), 112–13
Likenesses miniature, repro. in Bleackley, *Ladies fair and frail* • print, BM; repro. in Bleackley, *Ladies fair and frail*

Mahony, Francis Sylvester [*pseud.* Father Prout] (1804–1866), satiric poet and journalist, was born at Cork on 31 December 1804, the second son of Mary Reynolds and Martin Mahony (1763/4–1834), a woollen manufacturer who owned and operated a mill near the town. Francis Mahony claimed descent from an old Irish family, the O'Mahonies of Dromore Castle, co. Kerry. With his brother Nicholas, he attended the Jesuits' college at Clongowes Wood, co. Kildare from 1815 to 1819, when they entered the Jesuits' college of St Acheul at Amiens. Determining to become a Jesuit, in spite of his father's desire that he should study law, Francis was soon transferred to the seminary in the rue de Sèvres in Paris, and having spent two years of his noviciate there, he proceeded to the Jesuits' college at Rome to study philosophy (1823–5). A gift for written and spoken Latin attracted the notice of his teachers, but an impatience with discipline made others question his vocation. The Abbé Martial Marest de la Roché-Arnaud, who seems to have met Mahony at Rome, credited him, on the other hand, in his work *Les Jésuites modernes* (1826), with all 'the fanaticism, the dissimulation, the intrigue, and the chicanery' deemed by him to be Jesuitical characteristics.

In August 1830 Mahony was appointed prefect of studies at the Jesuits' college at Clongowes Wood, and in October he was promoted to be master of rhetoric. His pupils included John Sheehan, a popular journalist who wrote under the pseudonym of the Irish Whisky-Drinker, and Francis Stack (afterwards Serjeant) Murphy. In November Mahony went on a trip to Maynooth with his seminarians. They stopped at Sheehan's family home at Celbridge, and Mahony offended the parish priest, Daniel Callinan, with criticism of Daniel O'Connell (whom Mahony was later to pillory in an essay as 'Dandeleon'). A night of drinking with his students led to Mahony's resignation as prefect. After a short stay at the Jesuits' college at Freiburg he went to Florence where he was informed by the provincial of the Jesuits that his association with the order was at an end. Although deeply affected, Mahony showed no animosity against his former colleagues, whom he subsequently defended from conventional accusations in an essay called 'Literature and the Jesuits' (Prout, *Reliques*).

No longer a Jesuit, Mahony sought to become a secular priest. For two years he attended theological lectures at Rome, and was ordained at Lucca in 1832. In that year he joined the Cork mission, and displayed courage and devotion as chaplain to a hospital in Cork during the cholera epidemic. Anxious to see the construction of a new church, to be administered by himself, he argued with his bishop over funding and other matters, and left Cork and went to London, soon after this abandoning the active exercise of his profession. On a few occasions he preached

Francis Sylvester Mahony (1804–1866), by Daniel Maclise, c.1835

and conducted mass in the Spanish ambassador's chapel, but his tone of thought and conversation was unclerical. His interests were mainly literary, and, befriended by William Maginn, he readily adopted the bohemian mode of life, including frequent nights of drinking, which then characterized London literary society.

In April 1834 Mahony sent to *Fraser's Magazine* an article entitled 'Father Prout's Apology for Lent, his Death Obsequies, and an Elegy'. A real Father Prout, parish priest at Watergrasshill, co. Cork, called by Mahony's brother Nicholas 'a man of quiet, simple manners' (Jerrold, 91) was well known to Mahony in his boyhood, and had died in 1830. But Mahony's Father Prout, although also located at Watergrasshill, was a creation of Mahony's imagination, suggested to some extent by Goldsmith's 'Vicar', and described by Mahony as the child of Jonathan Swift and Stella. For two years (1834–6) Mahony regularly contributed his 'Reliques of Father Prout', accounts of fictitious episodes in Prout's career, with his views on life and literature. In entertaining comments on current literature, Mahony, following the example of Christopher North (the pseudonym of John Wilson) of *Blackwood's*, introduced Sir Walter Scott in conversation with Father Prout and his friends, defended Harriet Martineau from her critics, and explained his contempt for Bulwer-Lytton. He also freely interspersed the papers with his original poems and playful translations into Latin, Greek, French, and English verse. In a paper called *The Rogueries of Tom Moore* Mahony rendered some of Moore's best-known verses into Latin or French, and then wittily charged Moore with plagiarism.

His serious translations into English verse, from Horace, Béranger, and Victor Hugo, for instance, are less pleasing. Here he often degenerates into a wordy jingle, which does injustice to his originals, and in his own lyrics, of which 'The Shandon Bells' is the best-known example, the same defect is apparent. The brilliance of the papers, however, secured a wide reputation for their author; Mahony even signed his name for strangers 'Prout Mahony'. He regularly attended the meetings, at taverns or clubs, of the 'Fraserians', the contributors to the magazine, and he came to know many distinguished men of letters of the day. In 1836 he collected the *Reliques*, under the name of a fictitious editor, Oliver Yorke, with illustrations by Maclise.

In 1837 Mahony switched from *Fraser's* to the new *Bentley's Miscellany*, with Charles Dickens as editor, and on the first page of the first number Mahony's poem 'The Bottle of St Januarius' appeared. To the same number he contributed a French rendering of Wolfe's 'Burial of Sir John Moore', which he entitled 'Les funérailles de Beaumanoir', and pretended to regard as the original of Wolfe's poem. Mahony's English parody of Chatterton, with translations into both Pindaric and Horatian verse, also appeared in this issue. Some seventeen or eighteen poems followed in succeeding numbers. Although Mahony enjoyed the convivial society which he found in the literary clubs of London, at Lady Blessington's house at Kensington, and especially with his friend Thackeray, he was always of restless and uncertain temper. Towards the close of 1837 he abandoned London. In January 1838 'A Poetical Epistle from Father Prout to "Boz"' appeared in *Bentley's*, sent from Genoa. After that date he made a long tour through Hungary, Greece, and Asia Minor, and only reached the south of France on his return journey in 1841. From Bordeaux he sent further verse to *Bentley's Miscellany*, and in 1842 he took the publisher's part in the dispute between Bentley and Harrison Ainsworth. Despite his previous friendly relations with Ainsworth, Mahony now attacked him in a mock-heroic poem entitled 'The Cruel Murder of Old Father Prout by a Barber's Apprentice: a Legend of Modern Latherature, by Mr Duller of Pewternose' (*Bentley's Miscellany*, 1842, 11.144). This attack earned scorn for Mahony when he printed in his notes excerpts from private letters by Ainsworth asking Mahony to 'puff' his fiction.

After a short sojourn in London and a visit to Malta, in 1846 Mahony set out for Rome to act as correspondent for the *Daily News*. His contributions ceased at the end of 1847, and he published them in a volume entitled *Facts and Figures from Italy*, under the pseudonym of Don Jeremy Savonarola, Benedictine monk, and addressed to Dickens as an 'appendix' to his *Pictures from Italy*, as Dickens had originally commissioned Mahony to write for the paper, in his brief period as editor. The conservatism which had characterized his papers in *Fraser's Magazine* was here exchanged for liberalism, and he declared himself in full sympathy with the Italian patriots, and with new movements in the church and the papacy. Mahony was well known to English visitors in Rome, and frequently attended Mrs Jameson's Sunday evening parties; he also became friendly with the Brownings, and visited them in Florence.

About 1848 Mahony returned to London from Rome, and spent time there and in Paris, where he settled in the early 1850s. Except for rare visits to England, he remained in Paris until his death, living in an *entresol* in a hotel in the rue des Moulins. He was long a familiar figure in Galignani's reading-room in Paris, where many travelling English literati recorded his increasingly eccentric manners. William Allingham was taken by Thackeray to visit him in his room, where they found him 'loosely arrayed, reclining in front of a book and a bottle of Burgundy' (*William Allingham*, 77). Mahony's moods apparently varied; while there are reports of rudeness and unsociability, others found an amusing and unique cicerone to the sights of Paris. He is described in his best days as a brilliant, witty talker. Mahony owned some shares in *The Globe* newspaper, and in 1858 he became Paris correspondent to the journal, continuing his daily contributions until within a fortnight of his death. He contributed an inaugural ode to the first number of *Cornhill Magazine*, in January 1860, and he was also an occasional writer in the *Athenaeum*.

Mahony became somewhat more religious later in life, and in 1863 he drew up, in scholarly Latin, a petition to Rome asking permission 'to resort thenceforth to lay communion'. The petition was granted, together with a dispensation enabling him, in consideration of failing eyesight and advancing age, to substitute the rosary or the penitential psalms for his daily office in the breviary. He died in Paris in the rue des Moulins of bronchitis and diabetes on 18 May 1866, after receiving extreme unction from his friend Monsignor Rogerson. His sister, Mrs Woodlock, was present during his last illness, and he was buried in the vaults of Shandon church in Cork on 27 May.

Mahony's conversation and works were characterized by a satiric bite. His friend James Hannay described Mahony as 'full of all sorts of anecdotes' who retailed gossip 'flavoured with droll sarcasm' (Hannay, 52–3). It was probably from Mahony, for instance, that Browning picked up the inside information about Cardinal Wiseman which found its way into 'Bishop Blougram's Apology'. Some of his works, such as the Prout paper on *Dean Swift's Madness*, show that he was capable of exploring pathos in an eloquent manner. He himself claimed to be 'a rare combination of the Teïan lyre and the Irish bagpipe; of the Ionian dialect, blending harmoniously with the Cork brogue; an Irish potato seasoned with Attic salt' (Hannay, 53). The particular mixture of polylingual learning and multicultural topical reference, combined with a sense of fun which in both his prose and verse brought him to the verge of nonsense, bewildered many Victorian readers. The same factors make Mahony's works largely unread now except by a few scholars.

SIDNEY LEE, rev. D. E. LATANÉ, JR.

Sources E. Mannin, *Two studies in integrity: Gerald Green and the Rev. Francis Mahony ('Father Prout')* [1954] • B. Jerrold, ed., *The final reliques of Father Prout* (1876) • W. Bates, *The Maclise portrait gallery of illustrious literary characters*, new edn (1898) • C. Kent, 'Memoir', *The works of Father Prout (the Rev. Francis Mahony)* (1881) • M. M. H. Thrall, *Rebellious Fraser's: Nol Yorke's magazine in the days of Maginn, Thackeray, and Carlyle* (1934) • J. Hannay, 'National types of humour', *North British Review*, 45 (1866), 39–55 • private information (1893) • M. Monahan, *Nova Hibernia: Irish poets and dramatists of today and yesterday* (1914) • G. Macpherson, *Memoirs of the life of Anna Jameson*, ed. M. O. W. Oliphant (1878) • *William Allingham: a diary*, ed. H. Allingham and D. Radford (1907); repr. with introduction by J. J. Norwich (1985) • *Pall Mall Gazette* (23 May 1866) • *Cork Examiner* (23 May 1866) • *The Athenaeum* (26 May 1866) • C. Ó Mathúna, 'Rise and decline of Mahony's woollen mills, 1750–1981', *O Mahony Journal*, 11 (1981), 58–65 • T. Eagleton, 'Cork and the carnivalesque', *Crazy John and the bishop: and other essays on Irish culture* (1998), 158–211

Archives Hunt. L., letters • NL Ire., letters | BL, business transactions with Richard Bentley, Add. MSS 46615, 46649–46650 • Bodl. Oxf., letters to Harriet Pigott • Herts. ALS, letters to Henry Drummond Wolff and Lord Lytton

Likenesses D. Maclise, pencil drawing, c.1835, V&A [*see illus.*] • J. Hogan, marble bust, repro. in Mannin, *Two studies in integrity*; priv. coll. in 1954 • D. Maclise, group portrait, lithograph (*The Fraserians*), BM; repro. in *Fraser's Magazine*, 11 (1835), facing p. 1 • M. Weyler, photograph, repro. in Jerrold, ed., *Final reliques* • lithograph (after photograph by Lesage), NPG • wood-engraving, NPG; repro. in *ILN* (11 Aug 1866)

Maidment, James (*bap.* 1793, *d.* 1879), antiquary, was born in London and baptized in St Swithin's parish on 26 October 1793, the son of James Maidment, a solicitor, of Chase Side, Middlesex, and his wife, Jean or Jane Ann Woolley. His father was descended from a Northumberland family, and an ancestor of his mother was the Dutch patriot John van Olden Barneveldt.

Following attendance at arts and law classes at Edinburgh University between 1810 and 1816, Maidment was called to the Scottish bar on 17 June 1817. He soon took a high position as an advocate in cases involving genealogical inquiry, and was much engaged in disputed peerage cases. On general legal cases he was also much consulted, and his written pleadings in the court of session were models of their type. His written style was held to be far superior to his verbal performances. He married Isabella Jane Stewart or Stuart (1820–1862) and with her had two children, a son, James John Barneveldt (*d.* 1884), and a daughter, Blanche Wilhelmina Grace (*d.* 1875). The death of his daughter at the age of fifteen affected him greatly: it is said that he never left his house after this event.

Maidment early showed a taste for antiquarian and historical research, and it was mainly this that led to his friendship with Sir Walter Scott, Charles Kirkpatrick Sharpe, and other men of letters. His publications, mainly of editions of Scottish historical, literary, genealogical, and antiquarian material, were very numerous. Many were anonymous, and as most were privately printed in small editions, some at least for their bawdy or erotic content, they soon became rarities. A more or less comprehensive annotated list of seventy-nine items was issued with memoirs reprinted from contemporary newspaper obituaries in 1883, by Thomas George Stevenson, who, with his father John before him, had in fact published most of them. The most substantial of Maidment's works was one of the last, *Dramatists of the Restoration* (14 vols., 1872–9), in the editorship of which he was assisted by William Hugh Logan. Titles of some others demonstrate the main areas of his productions: *Reliquiae Scoticae: Scotish Remains in Prose and Verse* (1828); *Fragmenta Scoto-dramatica, 1715–1758* (1835); *Analecta Scotica* (2 vols., 1834–7); *Court of Session Garland* (1839); *A Book of Scotish Pasquils, 1568–1715* (1868); *A Packet of Pestilent Pasquils* (1868). He also edited works for the Spottiswoode Society and for the Maitland, Abbotsford, Hunterian, and Bannatyne clubs. At his death, he was the only remaining founder member of the last named club. To support these literary activities, Maidment built up a library of over 5000 titles, plus a fine collection of prints. He is believed to have sold part of his library anonymously in 1869 at a London sale. He died at his home, 25 Royal Circus, Edinburgh, on 24 October 1879, and was buried in the Dean cemetery on 31 October. The auction, in 5059 lots, of what books he possessed at the time of his death, was undertaken by Thomas Chapman & Son in Edinburgh, in April and May 1880. The sale occupied fifteen sessions and raised about £4500. The 1883 Stevenson bibliography reprints a detailed account of these sales, taken from *The Scotsman* newspaper. Lord Crawford purchased Maidment's peerage collections privately in July 1880, and some at least of these are held by the National Library of Scotland. Other goods were sold later in the year.

J. C. HADDEN, *rev.* MURRAY C. T. SIMPSON

Sources T. G. Stevenson, *The bibliography of James Maidment esq., advocate, Edinburgh: from the year MDCCCXVII to MDCCCLXXVIII* (1883) [incl. biographical memoir, contemporary obits. (extracts), details on the sale of his library] · *Catalogue of the extensive, curious and valuable library of the late James Maidment … which will be sold by auction by Messrs. T. Chapman & Son* (1880) [sale catalogue, 27 April 1880] · Irving, *Scots.* · d. cert. · *The Scotsman* (1 Nov 1879) · *IGI* · matriculation registers, University of Edinburgh
Archives Chetham's Library, Manchester, collection of letters incl. Scottish nobility · NL Scot., corresp. and papers relating to genealogical research | Bodl. Oxf., corresp. with Sir Thomas Phillipps · U. Edin. L., letters to David Laing
Likenesses W. Greenlees, watercolour, 1850, Scot. NPG · photograph, repro. in Stevenson, *The bibliography of James Maidment*
Wealth at death £978 8*s.*: confirmation, 24 Jan 1880, *CCI* · £3763 15*s.* 3*d.*: additional inventory, 28 Sept 1880, *CCI*

Maid of Ipswich, the. *See* Wentworth, Jane (*c.*1503–1572?).

Maidstone [Maydestone], **Clement** (*c.*1389–1456), Bridgettine monk and liturgical writer, was the son of Thomas Maidstone, esquire, of Isleworth, Middlesex, and his wife, Elizabeth. His father was a former yeoman-purveyor of Edward III's household, who sat as an MP for Middlesex on several occasions during the 1390s. Clement Maidstone entered Winchester College in 1403 and graduated *ad religionem*, entering the small house of Trinitarian friars at Hounslow. He was ordained subdeacon there on 20 September 1410, and deacon on 10 December of the same year. While still at Hounslow he came in contact with monks from the Swedish mother house of the Bridgettine order at Vadstena and, at some point between 1428 and 1432, transferred to the Bridgettine double house of Syon, founded by Henry V in partial expiation of his father's part in the execution of Archbishop Richard Scrope of

York in 1405. He became one of the deacons, or theological instructors, of the community there, where he died and was buried on 9 September 1456.

Maidstone's reputation was as a liturgical expert. He saw the celebration of the divine office as the defining priestly task, and set himself to remove any grounds for criticism or scandal by an exact exposition of the form such celebration should take. His chief concern was to popularize and explain the intricacies of the Sarum use, and, in particular, to remove the discordances between the actual practice of the cathedral church of Salisbury—'which used to be the bright candle of the whole of England' (Wordsworth, *Tracts of Clement Maydeston*, 10)—and of other churches adhering to the Sarum use. His *Directorium sacerdotum* was a revision of the existing Sarum ordinal which corrected errors and paid particular attention to the liturgical anomalies surrounding the feast of Corpus Christi. A later work, the *Defensorium directorii*, justified at greater length the practice set out in this treatise, and Maidstone also contributed to a composite commentary on the rubrics of the Sarum use known, in its printed editions, as the *Crede mihi*. In addition, Maidstone compiled an account of Archbishop Scrope's death, a topic of natural interest to the Syon community, known as the *Martyrium Ricardi archiepiscopi*, for which he drew heavily on the recollection of the Oxford theologian, Thomas Gascoigne. A composite volume of liturgical and devotional material, including Walter Hilton's *Scala perfectionis*, was copied by Maidstone himself and sent as a gift to Vadstena (now Uppsala University Library, MS C 159).

Although his account of Scrope's martyrdom was notably hostile to Henry IV, Maidstone's writings in general fit easily within the project of ecclesiastical regeneration associated with the Lancastrian episcopate. This laid emphasis both upon the reformation and standardization of the liturgy, encouraging the adoption of the Sarum use throughout the province of Canterbury, and upon the importance of such acts of communal public worship as the feast of Corpus Christi in the defence of orthodoxy. The Henrician foundations at Syon and Sheen were to become forcing-houses of liturgical and devotional change during the fifteenth century. Clement Maidstone played an important part in establishing the intellectual traditions of the Syon community.   SIMON WALKER

Sources C. Wordsworth, ed., *The tracts of Clement Maydeston, with the remains of Caxton's Ordinale*, HBS, 7 (1894) · *Ordinale Sarum, sive, Directorium sacerdotum*, ed. C. Wordsworth, 1, HBS, 20 (1901) · [H. Wharton], ed., *Anglia sacra*, 2 (1691), 169–72 · *HoP, Commons, 1386–1421*, 3.668–9 · M. B. Tait, 'The Brigittine monastery of Syon (Middlesex) with special reference to its monastic usages', DPhil diss., U. Oxf., 1975 · register of Syon, BL, Add. MS 22285 · GL, MS 9531/4 · M. Hedlund and others, eds., *Die Handschriften der Universitätsbibliothek Uppsala*, 2 vols. (1977)
Archives Uppsala University Library, Sweden, MS C 159

Maidstone, Ralph of (*d.* 1245), bishop of Hereford, is of unknown origins. His date of birth is unknown, but is unlikely to have been later than *c.*1195. Since he is referred to, from his earliest occurrences, with the title of *magister,* he probably received a higher education in the first or second decade of the thirteenth century. Where he was educated is uncertain, but either Oxford or Paris is a possibility in view of his later links with both. He made his early career in the diocese of Coventry and Lichfield, perhaps through the patronage of Bishop William of Cornhill (*d.* 1223). He occurs as treasurer of Lichfield Cathedral on 21 September 1219 and between 1215 and 1223, his predecessor in this office last occurring in 1204. Between 1220 and 1221 he is recorded as archdeacon of Shropshire (in the diocese of Coventry), but very soon after this, in or by 1222, he was made archdeacon of Chester. Occurrences of his name in witness lists suggest that he was quite active in this office in the first half of the 1220s; thereafter he seems to have absented himself from the diocese, perhaps to go to Paris to teach, since Matthew Paris names him as one of several English scholars who left Paris for Oxford in 1229 when the university was dispersed following riots. It may have been while he was there that he composed the commentary on the *Sentences*, which he is said to have written while still archdeacon of Chester (extract in London, Gray's Inn, MS 14, fols. 28–32).

By 22 June 1231 Maidstone was chancellor of the University of Oxford, but soon after this he was made dean of Hereford in succession to Master Thomas of Bosbury, who died on 29 September 1231; Ralph first occurs as dean on 28 July 1232. He may have been recommended to Bishop Hugh Foliot of Hereford by the latter's friend and protégé Robert Grosseteste (*d.* 1253), whom Ralph would have known at Oxford. Shortly after Hugh Foliot's death (7 August 1234) he was elected bishop of Hereford; on 30 September 1234 he received the temporalities, and he was consecrated on 12 November of that year by Archbishop Edmund at Canterbury. Already as dean he had received signs of royal favour, being twice granted the right to take stags in the Forest of Dean; as bishop, in November 1235 he baptized Henry, son of Richard of Cornwall, at Hailes, and shortly afterwards was sent to Provence to escort Eleanor, the intended bride of Henry III, to England; in 1235, 1236, and 1237 he was involved with negotiations with Llywelyn ab Iorwerth.

During May 1237 Maidstone seems to have been making plans to resign from his bishopric, since it is at this point that he confirmed, and promised to renew, his predecessor's arrangements for leaving the episcopal manors stocked and provided with money for seed in a vacancy, and furthermore he established posts for four vicarschoral in the cathedral. He made other benefactions to Hereford Cathedral, including houses in London, service books, vestments, and relics. He had apparently made a vow while still archdeacon of Chester to enter the Franciscan order. The Dunstable annals attribute his wish to become a Franciscan to the injuries he received from a fall in 1238, which left him unable to celebrate mass for a time, but this probably was a contributory factor rather than the original cause. On 17 December 1239 at Oxford he was received into the Franciscan order, having resigned his bishopric, and became a member of the Franciscan community at Oxford, where he helped to build the

church. A glossed New Testament which is inscribed as having been given by him, as a former bishop of Hereford, to the Franciscans of Canterbury, survives as BL, Royal MS 3 C.xi. Later he moved to the Franciscan convent at Gloucester, where he died and was buried in the choir. His date of death can be ascertained from the Hereford Cathedral obit book, which says that the time he spent as a mendicant was equal to the length of time he had been bishop, as 27 January 1245.   JULIA BARROW

Sources H. E. Savage, ed., *The great register of Lichfield Cathedral known as Magnum registrum album*, William Salt Archaeological Society, 3rd ser. (1924, [1926]), nos. 31–2, 259, 306, 357–8, 424, 445, 718 · U. Rees, ed., *The cartulary of Shrewsbury Abbey*, 2 vols. (1975), nos. 326, 339 · W. A. Hulton, ed., *The coucher book, or chartulary, of Whalley Abbey*, 4 vols., Chetham Society, 10–11, 16, 20 (1847–9), vol. 1, pp. 43–4, 140 · Hereford Cathedral obit book, Bodl. Oxf., MS Rawl. B.328, fol. 3*v* · Hereford Cathedral, dean and chapter muniments, nos. 795, 1401, 2127 · W. W. Capes, ed., *Charters and records of Hereford Cathedral*, Cantilupe Society (1908), 73–6 · *Ann. mon.*, 1.80, 94, 98, 103, 111, 113; 2.316, 320; 3.141, 144, 148, 156; 4.80, 82, 430 · Paris, *Chron.*, 3.168, 305, 335, 385 · *Chancery records* · A. G. Little, *The Grey friars in Oxford*, OHS, 20 (1892), 3, 182 · Emden, *Oxf.*, 2.1203–4 · J. S. Brewer, ed., *Monumenta Franciscana*, 1, Rolls Series, 4 (1858), 58, 542 **Archives** BL, Royal MS 3 C.xi · Gray's Inn, London, MS 14, fols. 28–32 · Hereford Cathedral, dean and chapter muniments, nos. 795, 1401, 2127

Maidstone [Maydestone], **Richard** (*d.* 1396), Carmelite friar, theologian, and poet, joined the order in Aylesford, Kent. He undertook his early studies in the order's London house, where he was ordained priest on 20 December 1376. He continued to study theology at Oxford, and was a BTh of the university during the late 1380s, when he composed his most popular work, a paraphrase in English verse of the penitential psalms. On 24 March 1390 he was licensed to preach and hear confessions in his home diocese of Rochester. He was promoted DTh, probably soon after. During his time at Oxford, Maidstone was engaged in arguing against Lollard or Wycliffite beliefs and he wrote two sets of *determinationes*, one against heretics and another on the role of the priest. However, it was after some provocative sermons by John Ashwardby, the vicar of St Mary's, Oxford, attacking the ideal of poverty as practised by the mendicant friars, that Maidstone was moved to write his major theological work, *Protectorium pauperis* ('In defence of poverty'). Ashwardby and Maidstone evidently engaged in a series of sermons against each other, but only one later sermon by Maidstone survives, preached in St Mary's Church, Oxford. The details of this controversy are only known through Maidstone's *Protectorium pauperis* and his surviving sermon, neither of which contains any reference as to when it took place. However, as Ashwardby is addressed in both as doctor, and as it is likely that Maidstone would have been a doctor too, the date of the exchange was probably about 1390–92. In 1393 Maidstone wrote a long Latin poem celebrating the reconciliation of Richard II and the city of London. The detailed description of the festivities and the banquet held to celebrate the event, which took place in August 1392, suggest that Maidstone was in London and witnessed them firsthand. Maidstone died on 1 June 1396, and was buried in the cloister of the Carmelite house at Aylesford.

Maidstone was confessor to John of Gaunt, duke of Lancaster, probably during the 1390s, and hence would have been a member of his entourage at the festivities in 1393. Giovanni Grossi, the Carmelite prior-general who visited England in 1413, included a short entry on Maidstone in his catalogue of Carmelite writers, noting that he was Gaunt's confessor and a celebrated preacher, both at Oxford and in court circles. Sadly, apart from the isolated example preached against Ashwardby, none of Maidstone's sermons survives, although John Bale preserves the incipit of a collection of sermons preached at Oxford, which he saw in Queen's College Library, another of sermons for saints' days and the seasons, and a third of eleven preached to the clergy. One other work of Maidstone's survives (BL, Royal MS 12 E.xviii), a commentary written in 1394 on the *Annulus philosophicus*, a perpetual church almanac, of the Carmelite John Avon (John Northampton). Bale saw two more compositions, notably a 'little work' on the *Sentences* of Peter Lombard and a collection of extracts from St Augustine's *City of God*.

Maidstone's *Protectorium pauperis* and his sermon give evidence of his ability to argue concisely and effectively as a theologian. He was clearly, like many of his Carmelite brethren, an able defender of the mendicant ideals, and his sermon shows that he could make some telling points. He accuses Ashwardby of preaching his controversial opinions to the laity in English, whereas he himself had responded in Latin, to an academic audience: Maidstone clearly believed that the forum for discussion of disputed theological points was in the university before those who had studied theology. As for his poetry, Maidstone's Latin ode on Richard II is competent, laudatory, Latin verse, marked more by good intentions and length rather than by any poetical skills. His ability shows better in his paraphrase on the penitential psalms, where he expresses his deep religious feelings in simple, direct English verse. The work clearly spoke to his contemporaries, for twenty-seven manuscripts survive, and excerpts from it were a popular addition to prayer books compiled for both clergy and laity. RICHARD COPSEY

Sources 'Protectorium pauperis, a defence of the begging friars by Richard of Maidstone', ed. A. Williams, *Carmelus*, 5 (1958), 132–80 · V. Edden, 'The debate between Richard Maidstone and the Lollard Ashwardby', *Carmelus*, 34 (1987), 113–34 · *Richard Maidstone's 'Penitential psalms'*, ed. V. Edden, Middle English Texts, 22 (1990) · C. R. Smith, 'Concordia facta inter regem Riccardum II et civitatem Londonis', PhD diss., Princeton University, 1972 · 'Johannis Grossi: Tractatus de scriptoribus ordinis Carmelitarum', *De scriptoribus scholasticis saeculi XIV ex ordine Carmelitarum*, ed. B. M. Xiberta (Louvain, 1931), 42–53, esp. 48–9 · J. Bale, Bodl. Oxf., MS Bodley 73 (SC 27635), fols. 39v, 40v, 51v, 71v, 113, 196v, 197v · Bale, *Cat.*, 1.498–9 · Emden, *Oxf.*, 2.1204 · A. Hudson, *The premature reformation: Wycliffite texts and Lollard history* (1988), 95–7 · Bale, *Index*, 355 · J. Bale, Bodl. Oxf., MS Selden supra 41, fol. 174

Archives BL, Royal MS 12 E.xviii · BL, Harley MS 1819, fols. 183–91 · BL, Add MS 10036, fols. 96v–100v · BL, Add. MS 11306, fols. 1–40 · BL, Add. MS 36523, fols. 71v–87v · BL, Add. MS 39574, fols. 15v–45 · BL, Harley MS 3810, part I, fols. 17–34 · BL, Royal MS 17 C.xvii, fols. 83–90 · Bodl. Oxf., MS e Mus. 86, fols. 160–175v; 94, fols. 121–125 · Bodl. Oxf., MS e Mus. 94, fols. 125–128 [new folio numbering: fols. 5–8v] · Bodl. Oxf., MS Bodley 68 (S.C. 2142), fols. 1–12 · Bodl. Oxf., MS Digby 98, fols. 41–48 · Bodl. Oxf., MS e Mus. 94, fols. 8v–11v (old fols. 128–131) · Bodl. Oxf., MS Ashmole 61 (S.C. 6922), fols. 108–119v · Bodl. Oxf., MS Digby 18 (S.C. 1619), fols. 38–64v · Bodl. Oxf., MS Digby 102 (S.C. 1703), fols. 128–136 · Bodl. Oxf., MS Douce 141 (S.C. 21715), fols. 145v–148 · Bodl. Oxf., MS Douce 232 (S.C. 21806), fols. 1–28 · Bodl. Oxf., MS Eng. poet. e. 17 (S.C. 32690), fols. 9–12v · Bodl. Oxf., MS Eng. poet. a. 1 Vernon manuscript (S. C. 3938), fols. 114, 407–544 · Bodl. Oxf., MS Laud misc. 174 (S.C. 668), fols. 1–24v · Bodl. Oxf., MS Rawl. A.389 (S.C. 11272), fols. 13–20 · Bodl. Oxf., MS Rawl. C.891 (S.C. 12725), fols. 127v, 385–424 · CUL, MS Dd.12.39, final flyleaf · CUL, MS Dd.1.1, fols. 226–228 · Hunt. L., MS HM 142, fols. 22v–41v · JRL, English MS 5, fols. 117–134v · Longleat House, Wiltshire, marquess of Bath MS 30, fols. 26–45v · Morgan L., MS 99, fols. 92–132 · NL Scot., Advocates MS 19.3.1, fols. 97, 87–88 · NL Wales, Porkington MS 20, fols. 96–106v · St George's Chapel, Windsor, MS E.I.I., fols. 32v–52v · TCD, MS 156, fols. 136–141v · University of Pennsylvania, Philadelphia, MS English 1

Maihew, Edward (1568/9–1625), Benedictine monk, was born at Dinton, near Salisbury, Wiltshire, into a firmly Catholic family. As a boy he was sent, in 1583, to the English College, then at Rheims, from where he proceeded in 1590 to Rome, being admitted to the English College there on 23 October. Ordained about 1595 he spent twelve years on the English mission. Talented and well read, he became attracted to the Benedictine order and was professed as a member of the Cassinese congregation by Anselm Beech. Thomas Preston, leader of the first English monks to come from the Italian monasteries of the Cassinese congregation, gave him the monastic habit and took him, with another priest, Robert Vincent Sadler, to meet Sigebert Buckley, last survivor of the Marian community of Westminster Abbey. The meeting probably took place in Buckley's lodgings, somewhere in London and not, as sometimes alleged, in the Gatehouse prison. In a famous scene, on 21 November 1607, Buckley aggregated them to himself not only as the sole member of Westminster Abbey but also of what Augustine Baker considered 'the whole old Congregation of the Order in England' (Connolly, 'Buckley affair', 62). Baker thought that this was planned while the monks were still in Italy.

When the Westminster monks were given an equal share in the property of St Laurence's at Dieulouard, near Metz, in Lorraine, Maihew withdrew from the mission and soon afterwards, in 1614, became prior (superior) of the monastery. His Cassinese background placed him among the supporters of strict observance who went to Dieulouard, and his enthusiasm for old ways may have irritated those of other opinions. He played a considerable part in the negotiations for the uniting of the various groups of English monks into a 'restored and if need be renewed' (*Ex incumbenti*, 1619) English Benedictine congregation, acting as one of the nine definitors elected in 1617 to this end.

As a young man in the English College in Rome (1590–94) Maihew wrote some saints' lives, borrowing text from the Jesuit William Good, the recently deceased college confessor, who as a boy had served mass at pre-dissolution Glastonbury. These he later used when he wrote his *Congregationis Anglicanae ordinis sanctissimi Benedicti trophaea* (4 vols., 1619–25), a paean of praise for what he regarded as the old English congregation from the time of St Augustine. This was subjected to a fierce counter-attack by the brilliant and wayward John Barnes, a Benedictine of the Spanish party, teaching in anti-Spanish France. His *Examen trophaeorum congregationis praetensae Anglicanae* claimed that historically English monasteries had always been under the congregation of Cluny, to which he was now attached. His work in turn promoted the principal manifesto of the renewed Benedictine mission to England, the *Apostolatus Benedictinorum in Anglia* (1626) by Baker and Leander Jones and edited by Clement Reyner.

Maihew had strong views on strict observance of monastic tradition and the rule, and Dieulouard under his leadership gained an impressive reputation. In 1623 he was appointed to be vicar to the nuns at the new English Benedictine convent at Cambrai, near Lille. He died there on 14 September 1625 aged fifty-six, and was buried in the church of St Vedast. He had edited *Sacra institutio baptizandi* (1604), the administration of the sacraments according to the Sarum usage published with his notes, and wrote *A Treatise of the Grounds of the Old and New Religion* (1608), *A Paradise of Prayers and Meditations* (1613), and possibly other works.   ANSELM CRAMER

Sources A. Baker, *Apostolatus Benedictinorum in Anglia, sive, Disceptatio historica*, ed. C. Reyner, trans. Leander [J. Jones] (1626) · A. Allanson, *Biography of the English Benedictines* (1999) · R. H. Connolly, 'The Buckley affair', *Downside Review*, 49 (1931), 49–74 · R. H. Connolly, 'Father Edward Maihew and Glastonbury', *Downside Review*, 50 (1932), 502–4 · J. McCann and H. Connolly, eds., *Memorials of Father Augustine Baker and other documents relating to the English Benedictines*, Catholic RS, 33 (1933) · D. Lunn, *The English Benedictines, 1540–1688* (1980) · Gillow, *Lit. biog. hist.*
Archives English College, Rome, MS

Maildulf. See Máeldub (*supp. fl.* mid-7th cent.).

Maillard [*married name* Briel], **Marie** (1680–1731), beneficiary of miraculous healing, was born in Cognac, St Ouge, France, on 25 September 1680. A Huguenot, in 1689 she escaped from persecution in France with her parents, John Maillard, a sword-cutler, and Charlotte du Dognon, and settled within the Huguenot community of London. Marie Maillard came to prominence when she claimed to have been miraculously and instantly healed from a debilitating lameness that she had suffered since childhood. At the time of her cure, which occurred while she was reading the Bible on Sunday 26 November 1693, Maillard was living with Mademoiselle Renée de Laulan, another Huguenot refugee, as her companion. News of her cure spread quickly in London and attracted attention from prominent figures: she was summoned to appear before the lord mayor of London (Sir William Ashurst); the bishops of Worcester, Salisbury, and London; and four surgeons sent by Queen Mary, who examined her healed body. Several publications about her quickly followed. In 1693 a ballad, 'The happy damsel, or, A miracle of God's mercy', and a narrative of the miraculous events, *A Plain and True Relation of a Very Extraordinary Cure of Marianne Maillard*, were published. In 1694 a sermon on miracles, with particular reference to her case, *Light in Darkness*, and

a further account of the cure, *A True Relation of the Wonderful Cure of Marie Maillard*, appeared. Attached to the latter were affidavits in which people testified to her previous lameness and their observation of her physical cure, and a discourse on miracles by James Wellwood, a fellow of the Royal College of Physicians in London. This account was translated into French and published in Amsterdam in the same year. It was republished in 1730, this time with Maillard's permission, as *An Exact Relation of the Wonderful Cure of Mary Maillard*, with the addition of Maillard's own narrative of events. This text of 1730 was published at least once more, in 1787, indicating the enduring interest of the case throughout the eighteenth century.

Maillard's cure occurred at a significant moment in the history of science in England and just as a philosophical debate on miracles was about to be launched. Some commentators expressed scepticism about the cure or wished to assess the evidence with extreme care. Wellwood, in his published letter, argued that there was something about the cure that was 'above the road of nature', yet tried to steer a middle course between 'enthusiasts', who might too readily believe in a miracle, and 'atheists' (or sceptics), who might too quickly dismiss the possibility of divine healing. Others, such as the anonymous author of the sermon *Light in Darkness*, saw Maillard's cure as a sign in a supposedly atheistical age. Elias Keach, the Baptist minister, in a letter to a fellow minister, John Watts, gave a millennial spin to his comments, seeing the cure of the 'French girl' as part of the 'miraculous effusion' that would usher in the new age, the coming of the kingdom of Jesus Christ.

Maillard's case sparked a number of 'copycat' cases in London, in which women read the Bible and claimed to be miraculously healed of long-standing and apparently incurable ailments. On 22 December 1693 Elizabeth Savage claimed to be healed from the palsy while reading the gospel of Matthew, and on 27 December 1693, Susannah Arch, a Baptist, testified that she had been miraculously cured from leprosy (probably meaning a skin disorder of some sort) after many months of reading the Bible and praying for a cure. On 17 November 1694 Lydia Hills, also a Baptist, claimed that she was cured of a lameness, again while reading the Bible and praying for healing. Each of these cures resulted in a publication.

Marie Maillard married a Huguenot minister, Henry Briel, on 27 April 1700 and they lived in Rose Alley, Bishopsgate, London, probably for the whole of their married life. Briel was pastor of the church at Swanfields, Slaughter Street, from 1721 to 1734. Marie Maillard died on 23 November 1731 and was buried in St Botolph without Bishopsgate, London.   JANE SHAW

Sources *A plain and true relation of a very extraordinary cure of Marianne Maillard* (1693) · *A true relation of the wonderful cure of Marie Maillard* (1694) · *An exact relation of the wonderful cure of Mary Maillard* (1730) [repr. 1787] · *Light in darkness, or, A modest enquiry into, & humble improvement of miracles, in general, upon occasion of this late miraculous cure of Mariane Maillard* (1694) · 'The happy damsel' (1693); H. E. Rollins, ed., *The pack of Autolycus … as told in broadside ballads of the* *years 1624–1693* (Cambridge, Massachusetts, 1927) • *Relation veritable de la guérison miraculeuse de Marie Maillard. Tr. de l'Anglois* (Amsterdam, 1694) • *A relation of the miraculous cure of Susannah Arch, of a leprosy and physick* (1695) • *A relation of the miraculous cure of Mrs Lydia Hills of a lameness* (1694) • *A narrative of the late extraordinary cure wrought in an instant upon Mrs Elizabeth Savage* (1694) • M. Edwards, *Materials towards a history of the American Baptists*, 1: *Materials towards a history of the Baptists in Pennsylvania* (1770) • *Register of the [Huguenot] church of Le Carre and Berwick Street, 1690–1788*, Publications of the Huguenot Society of London, 25 (1921) • *The register of St Botolph, Bishopsgate, London*, 2 (1893)

Main, Robert (1808–1878), astronomer, the son of Thomas and Elizabeth Main and the brother of Thomas John *Main, was born at Upnor in Kent on 12 July 1808. He was educated at Portsea grammar school, became assistant master in the grammar school at Bishop's Waltham, Hampshire, and saved out of his stipend funds for a university career. Having obtained a foundation scholarship at Queens' College, Cambridge, he graduated as sixth wrangler in 1834, was elected to a fellowship, took holy orders, and proceeded MA in 1837. He married in 1838 Mary (*b.* 1809), daughter of Revd Philip Kelland, curate of Dunster, Somerset; they had three sons.

In August 1835 Main was appointed chief assistant at the Royal Greenwich Observatory under Sir George Airy, whom he served with loyalty and efficiency for twenty-five years. At Main's appointment, Airy compared the work to that of 'a head clerk in a bank', and demanded 'punctuality and regularity in a routine of very dull business'. For this service Main received a salary of £300 per annum (plus a tent allowance of £50), which by 1860 rose to £500 (plus £70). He found time, however, to apply the results obtained from the Greenwich observations to the elucidation of several points of scientific interest and to the correction of the fundamental constants of astronomy. On 9 June 1837 he presented to the Royal Astronomical Society the first of a series of papers on the 'Elements of the planet Venus', and on 8 May 1840 he contributed a critical and historical essay 'On the present state of our knowledge of the parallax of the fixed stars'. He established in 1849, from his own micrometrical measures, the elliptical symmetry of Saturn's figure and in 1855 the unvarying dimensions of its rings. In 1850 and 1858 he deduced the proper motions of 1440 stars common to F. W. Bessel's *Fundamenta astronomiae* (1818) and the Greenwich catalogues; in 1855 and 1860 he investigated the constants of aberration and nutation and the annual parallax of γ Draconis; he tested the accuracy of Bessel's table of refractions, and in 1856 communicated the results of twelve years' determinations of the planetary diameters with Airy's double-image micrometer. For these important works he was rewarded in February 1858 with the gold medal of the Royal Astronomical Society. Main's membership of the society dated from 1836; he served for thirty-nine years on the council and acted successively as its secretary and president. He was elected a fellow of the Royal Society in 1860.

Main succeeded Johnson as Radcliffe observer on 19 June 1860, and resided at Oxford from 1 October 1860. Correspondence preserved in the Greenwich observatory archives suggests, however, that the Radcliffe trustees had taken a long time in settling for Main, for he was first considered for the post on 1 April 1859. Perhaps his twenty-five years as Airy's assistant had led some to suspect that he had been too long under Airy's shadow to be an independently creative observatory director in his own right. But the efficiency and prestige of the Oxford establishment was fully maintained by him. He edited in December 1860 the first Radcliffe catalogue, compiled the second Radcliffe catalogue of 2386 stars (1870) from observations made in the years 1854 to 1861, and began a new series of observations, intended for a third catalogue, which, however, he did not live to complete. He issued a total of sixteen volumes of *Radcliffe Observations*, including a valuable series of double-star measurements of position (to check proper motions and parallaxes) made with the heliometer. He also sent to the Royal Astronomical Society for publication his observations of Jupiter's satellites, of the great comet of 1861, of the dimensions of the disc of Mars during the opposition of 1862—made with the same heliometer, by Repsold of Hamburg, which Johnson had obtained for the Radcliffe Observatory in 1848—and of the meteoric shower of 13 November 1866. He also wrote and translated various astronomical and religious works, contributed to Weale's *London in 1851* a chapter on observatories, and re-edited in 1859 Herschel's *Manual of Scientific Enquiry*. Besides being a fair classical scholar, he read fluently nine modern languages. He died at the Radcliffe Observatory, after a short illness, on 9 May 1878.

A. M. CLERKE, *rev.* ALLAN CHAPMAN

Sources CUL, RGO6/1, fols. 321–322 • CUL, RGO6/4, fols. 252–253 • CUL, RGO6/4, fols. 308–309 • *Monthly Notices of the Royal Astronomical Society*, 39 (1878–9), 227–35 • E. Dunkin, *Obituary notices of astronomers: fellows and associates of the Royal Astronomical Society* (1879) • *The Observatory*, 2 (1879), 55 • *Nature*, 18 (1878), 72–3 • R. Grant, *History of physical astronomy, from the earliest ages to the middle of the nineteenth century* (1852) • C. L. F. André, G. A. P. Rayet, and A. Angot, *L'astronomie pratique et les observatoires en Europe et en Amérique*, 5 vols. (Paris, 1874–8) • *National Church*, 7, 123 • *The Times* (13 May 1878) • *The Athenaeum* (18 May 1878), 636–7
Archives Bodl. Oxf., draft articles • MHS Oxf. | RAS, letters to Royal Astronomical Society • RS, corresp. with Sir John Herschel
Likenesses photograph, MHS Oxf.
Wealth at death under £6000: administration with will, 11 July 1878, *CGPLA Eng. & Wales*

Main, Thomas Forrest (1911–1990), psychiatrist and psychoanalyst, was born on 25 February 1911 in Johannesburg, Transvaal, to James Robert Main (1872–1946), shipwright and later mine manager, and Jessie Miller Dundas (1876–1965). Main was one of three children; a fourth died in adolescence. His father joined the South African army in 1914, and the rest of the family returned home to Teesside in some poverty. His disabled father returned after the war.

An intelligent child, Main won a scholarship to the Royal Grammar School, Newcastle upon Tyne, in 1922, and at sixteen obtained a medical scholarship to Durham

University. He was an excellent scholar and an outstanding rugby player. He began writing poetry at school and continued this throughout life, making gifts of poems to children, grandchildren, and godchildren. In 1933 he graduated MBBS with honours and obtained his MD (Durham) in 1937. At Newcastle there was an outstanding medical school where the paediatrician Sir James Spence, who highlighted the emotional components of children's illness, greatly influenced Main. Thereafter his aims turned to psychiatry: he obtained the diploma in psychological medicine (DPM) at Dublin in 1936 and at an early age he became consultant psychiatrist at Gateshead Mental Hospital, Stannington, Northumberland. At medical school he had met his future wife, Agnes Mary (Molly; *b.* 1911), daughter of James McHaffie, a medical practitioner; he married her on 27 February 1937. They both became psychoanalysts after the war. Of their four children two followed his path into psychiatry and psychoanalysis.

Main's adventurous character was well suited to the new role for psychiatrists in the Second World War. To understand the anxieties of parachutists he made several jumps himself, and went to the front line in France to experience battle terror at first hand. Asked to study the causes of the Salerno mutiny, he attributed it to the forced regrouping of soldiers whose loyalty to their own regiments had been disregarded. He also studied the effects of battle training that had attempted artificially to stimulate hatred of the enemy but which had often led to depression. The practice was discontinued following his report. He took part in the outstanding achievements of military psychiatry—officer selection, the handling of delinquents and misfits, and the maintenance of morale. Appointed psychiatrist to the Eighth Army, Main had a disagreement with General Montgomery and became psychiatric adviser to the Twenty-First Army group. As lieutenant-colonel he became a senior member of the team at Northfield Military Hospital, the foundation experience of the therapeutic community movement of which he was a leader in the years after the war. A good wordsmith, he coined the phrase 'therapeutic community', meaning that a hospital as an institution should study its own processes to enhance its therapeutic powers and to recognize its anti-therapeutic aspects. He was mentioned in dispatches.

Main had the opportunity to develop a therapeutic community at the Cassel Hospital for Functional Nervous Disorders, Ham Common, Surrey, of which he became director in 1946. The Cassel Hospital had been a private foundation of the Cassel family but became part of the National Health Service in 1948. The family (in the person of Lady Louis Mountbatten) retained close involvement for many years. Main undertook psychoanalytic training under Michael Balint, and was supervised by both grand ladies of British psychoanalysis, Anna Freud and Melanie Klein. At the Cassel Hospital he developed psychodynamic training for nurses and encouraged doctors to train as psychoanalysts. He involved the whole community—lay staff and patients—in consultation. However, he fought to maintain his position as medical superintendent, insisting that the organization needed a central authority. This suited him as he enjoyed his power and authority and his ability to bring about changes. The Cassel Hospital pioneered the psychotherapeutic treatment of mothers who had become depressed after childbirth, bringing their infants into hospital with them so as not to inflict separation on the nursing pair. Later, whole families were admitted and a nursery school was started. Gleefully he indented for double beds under the NHS. Later, Main joined Michael Balint in a short-term psychotherapy workshop that made a significant contribution to a new area of psychoanalytic work. His final achievement was to create the Institute for Psychosexual Medicine of which he was the principal leader and first president. Main fought orthodox psychiatry for its blindness to the findings of Freud and believed that psychoanalysis would take over biological psychiatry.

Main had charisma: handsome, elegant, silver-haired, and silver-tongued, always with a rose in his buttonhole, he was a stimulating teacher to generations of psychiatrists. Under his direction the hospital constantly evolved. A fine writer, his carefully crafted papers, edited by his psychoanalyst daughter, Jennifer, reached international readership. He became a vice-president of the Royal College of Psychiatrists and would have been an innovative president both of the college and of the Psychoanalytic Society—which ensured that he was not. Main was a sociable man who gave good parties, played the piano enthusiastically, and wrote fluent poems. A fanatical fly fisherman, he invented his own fly. He was an atheist in later life and was left wing in his politics. Main died of carcinoma of the colon at his home, 6 Sherwood Close, Barnes, London, on 29 May 1990 and was cremated on 7 June at Putney Vale crematorium. He was survived by his wife.

MALCOLM PINES

Sources *International Journal of Psycho-Analysis*, 72 (1991), 719 · m. cert. · d. certs. [parents] · private information (2004) · personal knowledge (2004)

Main, Thomas John (1818–1885), mathematician, was the son of Thomas and Elizabeth Main and a younger brother of the Revd Robert *Main. He entered St John's College, Cambridge, on 14 February 1834, graduating in 1838 as senior wrangler and first Smith's prizeman. Elected a fellow of his college that year, he proceeded MA in 1841. He joined the Royal Astronomical Society on 10 January 1840. He took orders and was appointed as a chaplain in the Royal Navy in 1842, serving on HMS *Excellent*, a ship moored permanently in Portsmouth harbour, which was used as a school for instruction in gunnery for officers and men. He was placed on the retired list in 1869. He also served as professor of mathematics for thirty-four years at the Royal Naval College, Portsmouth. He wrote, with Thomas Brown RN, *The Indicator and Dynamometer* (1847; 3rd edn, 1857), *The Marine Steam Engine* (1849; 5th edn, 1865), which was translated into German in 1868, and *Questions on Subjects Connected with the Marine Steam Engine* (1857 and 1863). He married, on 30 June 1842, Emma Louisa

Berry, the daughter of Sir John Theophilus Lee of Mount Radford. He died at his home, 15 Elsworthy Road, Hampstead, on 28 December 1885, aged sixty-seven. At least two sons survived him.   A. M. CLERKE, *rev.* ADRIAN RICE

Sources Venn, *Alum. Cant.* · *The Times* (31 Dec 1885), 1a · *Nature*, 33 (1885–6), 233 · *GM*, 2nd ser., 18 (1842), 200 · *CGPLA Eng. & Wales* (1886)
Wealth at death £35,299 3s. 10d.: probate, 25 Jan 1886, *CGPLA Eng. & Wales*

Mainauduc, John Boniot de [John Boniot Demainauduc] (*c.*1750–1797), surgeon and animal magnetizer, was born in Cork, the son of Elias Mainauduc (*c.*1710–1790), 'one of the greatest mathematicians in Europe', according to the *Gentleman's Magazine* (60, 1790, 575), but, more probably, a linen draper, of French protestant descent. After a classical education, probably in Cork, de Mainauduc studied anatomy under William Hunter. In 1769 he became a pupil and dresser at St George's Hospital, and in 1770 he studied midwifery at Westminster Lying-in Hospital. After a further period of medical training, he opened an apothecary's shop in 1775. In 1777 he became a member of the Company of Surgeons, and resigned his share of his apothecary business to practise surgery and midwifery. On 17 March 1778 on the recommendation of John Leake and George Fordyce, who had taught him, he was awarded the degree of MD from King's College at Aberdeen. He started teaching anatomy and midwifery, but although he continued studying medicine, he was denied entry to the College of Physicians as a surgeon.

In 1782 de Mainauduc went to Paris to seek employment as a royal physician, and in 1784 gained a necessary French qualification at Rheims. But after a dispute over his intended position, he approached Franz Mesmer, who reportedly refused to teach him, notwithstanding the offer of a fee of 200 guineas. Instead he studied animal magnetism under Mesmer's former colleague turned rival, Charles Deslon. By 1785 de Mainauduc was installed in prestigious Bloomsbury Square, London, where he soon became Britain's leading animal magnetizer. He briefly promoted the Hygiaean Society, which stressed the benefits of helping the poor, and published a proposal for its establishment in 1785. But he achieved far greater success by advertising his lectures and therapeutic treatments for wealthy patients. He reputedly earned a fortune, charging between 10 and 50 guineas for his courses on animal magnetism, whose details he obliged his students to swear not to reveal. He taught in Bristol in 1788 and 1789, and probably supplemented his income by tours to other provincial centres.

De Mainauduc attracted several hundred patients and pupils to Bloomsbury Square, including members of the aristocracy (such as the duchess of Devonshire, the prince of Wales, and the duke of Gloucester), the newly wealthy wives of Quaker industrialists, rival medical men, and occult enthusiasts (including the artists Philip de Loutherbourg and Richard Cosway, and the governor of Gibraltar, Charles Rainsford). De Mainauduc's basic technique

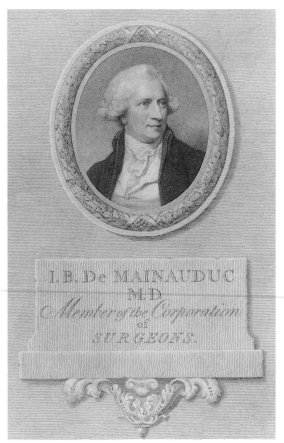

John Boniot de Mainauduc (*c.*1750–1797), by Pierre Condé, pubd 1798 (after Richard Cosway)

resembled hypnotism. Placing himself opposite his patient—usually a woman—he stared intently into her eyes, and moved his hands round her body without touching her. Many women experienced a 'crisis'—manifested as convulsions, hysteria, or sleep—followed by a calm warmth; some of them also claimed that chronic physical ailments were alleviated.

De Mainauduc died suddenly on 22 March 1797 in Bloomsbury Square. The following year his lectures were published, probably by his assistant, Ann Prescott (who may have been his wife). This book describes a comprehensive scheme of health based, like those of many medical contemporaries, on maintaining the body's equilibrium and the free circulation of atomic particles. With a vitalist insistence that life depends on an immaterial principle, de Mainauduc explained how, with God's acquiescence, the mind could control the body. A magnetic therapist supposedly used his own 'volition' to divert diseased atoms emanating from a sick person's body and restore natural harmony.

Marginalized at the time as a quack, de Mainauduc has most often been portrayed as a Mesmeric charlatan. However, he was medically well qualified: his career and his teaching resembled those of some eminent medical contemporaries, who were similarly competing for a wealthy clientele. In contrast with Mesmer, he never used magnetic equipment for treating his patients, and there is no evidence linking him with radical activism. Particularly after the French Revolution, hostile pamphlets ridiculed de Mainauduc and other animal magnetizers. *Animal Magnetism*, the title of a popular pirated farce by Elizabeth Inchbald, became a versatile term of abuse for mocking physicians and natural philosophers, as well as religious and political factions. Robert Southey and other defenders of the British establishment converted de Mainauduc into a symbol of subversive French practices.

PATRICIA FARA

Sources *The lectures of J. B. de Mainauduc* (1798), iii–xii · P. Fara, 'An attractive therapy: animal magnetism in eighteenth-century England', *History of Science*, 33 (1995), 127–77 · newspaper advertisements, BL, Lyson's collectanea, 2 vols., 1881.b.6, 1, fols. 155–63 · G. Winter, *Animal magnetism history of: its origin, progress, and present state; its principles and secrets displayed, as delivered by the late Dr. Demainauduc* (1801), 13–42 · J. De Mainauduc, *Veritas: or a treatise, containing observations on, and a supplement to the two reports of the commissioners, appointed by the king of France to examine into animal magnetism* (1785) · R. Southey, *Letters from England*, ed. J. Simmons (1951), 304–19
Archives RCS Eng., MS 42.e.1
Likenesses P. Condé, engraving (after R. Cosway), NPG; repro. in *Lectures*, frontispiece [*see illus.*]

Mainchín mac Setnai (*fl.* late 6th cent.). *See under* Munster, saints of (*act. c.*450–*c.*700).

Maine, Sir Henry James Sumner (1822–1888), jurist, the son of James Maine MD, of Kelso, and his wife, Eliza, daughter of David Fell of Caversham Grove, Reading, was born at Hockliffe, Bedfordshire, on 15 August 1822.

Education and early legal interests Maine's early years were passed at first on Jersey and then at Henley-on-Thames. When he was still a child his father left home and Maine was cared for exclusively by his mother. He attended the school of a local teacher in Henley, Mrs Lamb, until in 1829 his godfather, John Bird Sumner, then bishop of Chester and afterwards archbishop of Canterbury, nominated him for a place at Christ's Hospital school. A delicate child, Maine suffered throughout life from weak health. He was unhappy at school but was promising as a pupil, and in 1840 he won an exhibition to Pembroke College, Cambridge. He proved to be the best classical scholar of his year, winning the Browne medal in 1842 and 1843, and the chancellor's medal in 1842, and he was senior classic in 1844 as well as a senior optime in the mathematical tripos. His health was always uncertain and he devoted his energies to intellectual matters; he was a member of the Apostles club and formed lifelong friendships with contemporaries such as James Fitzjames Stephen.

In 1845 Maine accepted a junior tutorship, without a fellowship, at Trinity Hall, Cambridge, and in 1847 at the age of twenty-five he was appointed regius professor of civil law. On 20 December of the same year he married Jane Main (1827–1920), his first cousin. He was called to the bar at Lincoln's Inn in June 1850. It was during these early years that Henry Maine linked his classical interests to the

Sir Henry James Sumner Maine (1822–1888), by Lowes Cato Dickinson, 1888

historical study of law and also became committed to improvements in legal education. There is little clear evidence about the development of Maine's legal ideas at this time, but it is likely that he was reading historical studies such as those by Sir William Jones and J. M. Kemble which sought to explain law by reference to its past and placed a particular emphasis on the analysis of language. Whatever the nature of his early speculative reading, by the 1850s Maine had begun to lose interest in the teaching of law at Cambridge: in July 1852 he was appointed the first reader in Roman law and jurisprudence at the Council of Legal Education which had been established in that year by the inns of court in London; consequently in 1854 he resigned his chair at Cambridge.

Following his move to London, Maine developed a strong interest in writing for the press. In 1851 he had contributed to the Peelite *Morning Chronicle*, edited by John Douglas Cook. With Cook he became, in November 1855, a founding editor of the newly established *Saturday Review*. This was to acquire a distinguished reputation for literary and political articles, of which Maine was a frequent contributor until 1861. At the same time he began to practise at the bar, concentrating at first on the common law courts and then turning to chancery. He rapidly came to dislike both types of work and became increasingly critical of his profession and its ideas. His interest in legal thought became stronger, and he started to establish a reputation for the high quality of his lectures on jurisprudence which he now delivered at the inns of court for prospective barristers. No record remains of what he said in his lectures: this omission is perhaps the most unfortunate of all in respect of the information that has been lost on nineteenth-century legal thought in England. However, there is evidence in his published syllabus, in his article 'Roman law and legal education' in *Cambridge Essays* (1856), and in later incidental observations on the part of those who attended his lectures, which suggests that he was developing themes that were to appear in his first and most famous book, *Ancient Law* (1861).

Maine and *Ancient Law* Those who neither attended Maine's lectures nor read his book sometimes assumed that he was an authority on Roman law. In fact *Ancient Law* reveals that he was not greatly interested in Roman law for its own sake; he sought rather to integrate his analysis of the subject into general historical explanations of legal change in societies around the world. He produced these generalizations about law in the course of considering numerous sources of information. Any particular chapter could contain observations on modern politics mixed with comments on statute law, poetry, philosophy, literature, Greek thought, the caste system in India, Roman agriculture, the duties of nineteenth-century bank managers, the nature of scientific theories, American social values, the political influence of women, and many other topics.

For the most part Maine used his sources to explain the history of laws in Indo-European societies. In his view, the first laws of these societies were imposed by individuals who justified their power by reference to divine authority. Their laws were followed by customs (for Maine, custom followed law rather than preceded it), which gradually came to be controlled by minorities such as aristocracies. In the course of time the minorities were deprived of power through revolt, and the authorities which replaced them sought to assert their rule through the creation and development of codes. In some rare cases it was possible for societies to progress further through using fictions, equity, and legislation as successive agencies of legal change. The substance of these later progressive legal phases was described by Maine in his famous phrase as involving a movement from 'status to contract'. For example, the slave had his or her status determined at birth, whereas the citizen of the modern state should be able, under the law, to negotiate with employers and others in such a way as to shape his or her life through the exercise of independent judgement. Early law might concentrate in particular upon the family, and the status of men, women, and children within it; but later law was focused on individuals and the exercise of their rights in accordance with what they saw to be their own interests.

To mention these ideas in this brief manner is to do no justice to Maine's persuasive power. He spoke with clarity and wit and he wrote excellent prose. Maine was all the more attractive to his Victorian audience because of his capacity to integrate popular themes into his arguments. *Ancient Law* was published too soon after the appearance of Darwin's *Origin of Species* for the latter to account for Maine's book; but Maine was sensitive to the ideas produced by geological theorists in the 1840s and 1850s who stressed the possibility of evolutionary change over immense periods of time. To Maine the link with jurisprudence was plain:

> If by any means we can determine the early forms of jural conceptions, they will be invaluable to us. These rudimentary ideas are to the jurist what the primary crusts of the earth are to the geologist. They contain, potentially, all the forms in which law has subsequently exhibited itself. The haste or the prejudice which has generally refused them all but the most superficial examination, must bear the blame of the unsatisfactory condition in which we find the science of jurisprudence.   (H. Maine, *Ancient Law*, 1861, 1–2)

Within the framework of such generalizations Maine persistently asked the question: does law change society or society law? In his view other English jurists, such as Bentham and Austin, had failed to address this question. In considering it he came to believe that lawyers deluded themselves if they saw law as an effective instrument of social change. On the contrary, social developments usually determined both the content and the form of the law, and if law was to be understood it had to be seen in social terms. When he discussed society Maine was candid in stating many of his assumptions. He argued that 'social necessities and social opinion are always more or less in advance of law' (H. Maine, *Ancient Law*, 1861, 24). Fortified by assumptions such as these Maine was prepared to pronounce on the comparative achievements of different groups. For example, he believed that there were inescapable limits to what the ancient Greeks could achieve in legal thought:

> The Greek intellect, with all its mobility and elasticity, was quite unable to confine itself within the straight waistcoat of a legal formula … it confounded law and fact … questions of pure law were constantly argued on every consideration which could possibly influence the mind of the judges. No durable system of jurisprudence could be produced in this way.   (ibid., 75–6)

But Maine's confidence in arguing why some societies had failed properly to develop law was not linked to any assured explanation of progress. Progress could be found in the movement from status to contract but why this movement occurred in certain societies and not others was inexplicable. 'The difference between the stationary and progressive societies is … one of the great secrets which inquiry has yet to penetrate' (ibid., 23).

Lessons of history Despite this Maine was certain that he could reveal many of the 'lessons' of history for Victorian politicians and administrators. In respect of the impact of British law on Indian customs and the caste system he used his historical arguments to suggest that there was no question of British law being able to preserve old ways. Even a British law which declared that ancient customs should be recognized would inevitably ensure that the social role of these customs was changed because, by reason of the new law, they would lose their capacity to adapt over time to new social conditions. Legal recognition fixed them at one moment in time. It followed that informed historical judgement and considerable caution were desirable attributes for a colonial administrator. History was just as useful as a guide to an understanding of rights in modern Western societies. Arguments in favour of the law of nature, or of rights arising out of some supposed ancient social contract, were often treated with hostility and even contempt by Maine. They could not be justified in historical terms.

Maine was more sustained, more subtle, but ultimately no less dismissive, in his analysis of the chief traditions of English legal thought. For him so much of what English lawyers believed was founded on historical misapprehensions. For example, it was nonsense to describe the modern common law as being in some sense unwritten. Such historical errors were of the first importance because they could seriously impede desirable reforms. Undue veneration for the common law obscured the merits of statutory codification. In going beyond the common law and considering the system of equity, Maine argued that:

> it is easily seen by English lawyers that English equity is a system founded on moral rules; but it is forgotten that these rules are the morality of past centuries—not of the present—that they have received nearly as much application as they are capable of, and that though of course they do not differ largely from the ethical creed of our own day, they are not necessarily on a level with it … (H. Maine, *Ancient Law*, 1861, 69–70)

Again and again Maine questioned the historical assumptions of English lawyers. He was as critical of theorists as of practitioners. He respected the clarity of analysis to be found in the works of Jeremy Bentham and John Austin, but he also believed that through their ignorance of the historical relationship between law and society these major utilitarian jurists had arrived at incorrect conclusions about the nature of law. He criticized any attempt to account for law through the use of concepts dear to the utilitarians: he was distrustful of the use of terms such as 'sovereignty' and 'command' without regard to their precise historical and social context. For Maine, Bentham and Austin failed to see that the concepts they were using could not explain changes in the ancient laws of India where such notions had little or no place. A twentieth-century jurist, Sir Carleton Allen, suggested that it was in his lectures of the 1850s that Maine first made the distinction between analytical and historical schools of English jurisprudence (C. Allen, *Legal Duties and other Essays in Jurisprudence*, 1931, 14). The former concentrated on conceptual analysis and sought brief definitions of law. The latter recognized law as a social product and explained it as the creation of contrasting societies evolving over long periods of time. Maine's ideas were a reaction against what he believed was a narrow vision of law reflecting merely modern English experience.

Maine's explanation of law was distinctive. He was not following the views of professional lawyers who believed in what they took to be the immemorial virtues of the common law. Nor was he following the recognized jurists of the day with their emphasis on the demands of utility and the capacity for using law as an instrument of social reform. Instead he was using history to explain law as the product of time and place and, having done this to his own satisfaction, he was always seeking to commend one course of action rather than another. The result was a series of arguments which did little to flatter lawyers. Maine stated that it was the task of a good lawyer to respond constructively to social change rather than produce it. In substance, he asserted that the task of both the practising lawyer and the legal theorist was to clarify the law and to ascertain whether or not it met current social need; if it did not do so, the lawyer should suggest appropriate reform. For Maine it was as if the focal point of legal analysis ceased to be the professional world, or the conceptual work of utilitarian jurists; instead the lawyer was the reflective observer of social change. In a loose sense, he saw the law as a facet of cultural evolution, always and everywhere its improvement requiring historical understanding on the part of the reformer.

Ancient Law was probably the best-selling English law book of the nineteenth century: it sold around the world, sometimes in translation. The mixture of analysis and exhortation was attractive: it seemed to many that Maine was offering the prospect of ordered change at a time when old certainties were being questioned. Evolutionary ideas which many found disturbing in other contexts were being put to use in arguments which justified reflection, comparative analysis, and cautious change, in favour of an enhanced role for individual decision-making. What was more, the informed citizen could contribute to legal debate confident in the knowledge that legal minds had only an instrumental rather than a definitive role in the production of reform.

India and recognition The publication of *Ancient Law* was the central event of Maine's life. The book established his reputation as a jurist and attracted more attention than anything else he wrote. Soon after it appeared, in March 1862 he accepted Sir Charles Wood's offer of the position of legal member of the governor-general's council in India. Assisted there by his friend M. E. Grant Duff, he was involved in giving advice and drafting bills. Between 1863 and 1869 he was also vice-chancellor of the University of Calcutta, and in this capacity he combined a liking for comparative observations on Eastern and Western thought, with some alarm about the possible political roles of the increasing number of Indian law graduates. On his return to England in 1869 he became corpus professor of jurisprudence at Oxford until, in December 1877, he was elected master of Trinity Hall in Cambridge. In these later years he did little to advance the cause of legal education; for example, he did not try to support joint degrees in law and history which were being discontinued at Oxford at this time. Instead he advised successive governments on colonial issues, engaged in political journalism, and published further books which were mostly collected essays, including *Dissertations on Early Law and Custom* (1883).

Maine's reputation as a scholar with an interest in public life achieved wide recognition. In 1871 Maine became Sir Henry when he was gazetted KCSI, and in the same year he was appointed to a seat on the Indian council in London. In 1866 he had been made a member of the

American Academy. He became a member of the Dutch Institute about 1876, of the Accademia dei Lincei in 1877, of the Madrid Academy in 1878, of the Royal Irish Academy in 1882, of the Washington Anthropological Society in 1883, and of the Juridical Society of Moscow in 1884. He became corresponding member of the Académie des Sciences Morales et Politiques in 1881, and foreign member, in place of Emerson, in 1883. He was a fellow of the Royal Society, and was elected an honorary fellow of Pembroke College, Cambridge, in 1887. In that year he had succeeded Sir William Harcourt as Whewell professor of international law at Cambridge. His lectures were edited after his death by Frederic Harrison and Sir Frederick Pollock. At various times in his life he declined other offers: the chief justiceship of Bengal, the permanent under-secretaryships of both the Home Office and the Foreign Office, and the principal clerkship of the House of Commons.

Popular Government and other publications Neither in India nor, later, in England did Maine take the opportunity of further detailed study of ancient systems of law and their social contexts in village and urban life. He never learned Sanskrit and he carried out only minor forms of empirical work. Large parts of his later books constituted general responses to the work of other scholars such as Max Müller, William Stubbs, J. F. McLennan, and Andrew Lang. In the course of considering the ideas of other people he would comment on topics as diverse as the sociological ideas of Herbert Spencer, the ancient Brehon laws of Ireland, French medieval history, ancestor-worship around the world, the dangers of democracy, advances in comparative philology, social change in India, and, as always, the failings of English lawyers. The reader of works such as *Village Communities* (1871), *Lectures on the Early History of Institutions* (1875), and *Popular Government* (1885) could enjoy a lively and very well written excursion through ideas of current concern to educated Victorians. Classical observations were nicely combined with current preoccupations:

> Except the blind forces of Nature, nothing moves in this world which is not Greek in its origin. A ferment spreading from that source has vitalised all the great progressive races of mankind, penetrating from one to another, and producing results accordant with its hidden and latent genius, and results of course often far greater than any exhibited in Greece itself. It is this principle of progress which we Englishmen are communicating to India. We did not create it. We deserve no special credit for it. It came to us filtered through many different media. But we have received it, so we pass it on. There is no reason why, if it has time to work, it should not develop in India effects as wonderful as in any other of the societies of mankind. (H. Maine, *Village Communities*, 4th edn, 1885, 238)

Popular Government, four essays which had previously appeared in the *Quarterly Review*, in particular sold well, was much discussed, and attracted criticisms by John Morley and E. L. Godkin. But it did little to sustain Maine's standing as a scholar. He warned of the dangers of democratic politics, and compared the actions of Gladstone's government to the excesses of the French revolution. He claimed that democracy would become rule by the mob, and that technological progress would be threatened because innovation was opposed by most people, not least by women, who were always suspicious of change. One possible remedy, he believed, might be a written constitution similar to that of the United States of America; this would allow excesses of popular activity to be focused on merely political change, while it would leave individuals free to pursue their own interests in everyday economic life and guarantee the preservation of private property. Maine avoided endorsement of any political party but, in anonymous articles for the *St James's Gazette*, he expressed support for disillusioned Liberals who were alarmed at extensions of the franchise and novel plans for imperial reform such as those furthered by Viscount Ripon in India. His pessimism blended with late Victorian worries as to the nature of democracy.

Criticisms of Maine Maine's grand generalizations were popular but they exposed him to numerous criticisms by scholars which, often unanswered, accumulated as the years went by. Even *Ancient Law* came to be criticized with increasing force: for many authorities there was no convincing evidence to justify Maine's analysis of the phases of legal change, or of the nature of early ownership, or of the role of codes, or of many other topics. His friends, such as James Bryce, privately expressed concern about Maine's preparedness to write about topics on which he was not fully informed. Leslie Stephen observed that 'his inability for drudgery shows itself by one weakness of his books, the almost complete absence of any reference to authorities' (*DNB*). Maine's most earnest defender was his only rival as a historical jurist, Sir Paul Vinogradoff. Speaking of those who questioned Maine's achievements he stated that 'Those who indulge in such cheap criticisms should rather try to realise what accounts for his having been a force in European thought, a potentate in a realm where parochial patronage and a mere aptitude for vulgarisation are not recognised as titles to eminence' (*Law Quarterly Review*, 20, 1904, 119–20). There was substance in this bitter response, for the general ideas in *Ancient Law* (such as those on status and contract) had acquired a strong reputation in Europe and had attracted the attention of major theorists such as Ferdinand Tönnies and Émile Durkheim.

For the greater part of the twentieth century the British response to Maine's work remained unfavourable. Anthropologists and authorities on Roman law were particularly critical of his ideas, and teachers of law gave his works little attention. Stanley Baldwin recalled that he had been taught about Maine's ideas at Cambridge, but the extent of the latter's influence was apparent in Baldwin's observation: 'From Status to Contract—or was it the other way around?' Legal historians looked to Maitland for inspiration, not Maine. Jurists gave little attention to historical issues. In Herbert Hart's major work, *The Concept of Law* (1961), there is no mention of any of Maine's works.

Only the quality of Maine's prose and his succinct generalizations ensured that he was occasionally remembered.

A reviving reputation In the last quarter of the twentieth century Maine's reputation began to revive. In part this arose indirectly out of increasing British interest in the ideas of the continental theorists who had respected Maine. In the 1990s this indirect influence was supplemented by scholars in eastern Europe who pointed out that in the middle of the twentieth century Maine's works had been a precious reminder of the possibility of non-Marxist explanations of legal history: sometimes intellectuals in St Petersburg, Cracow, Budapest, or Sofia instructed their British counterparts in Maine's ideas. But chiefly his enhanced standing arose out of the revival of interest in explaining law by reference to its social context. With this change in perspective Maine ceased to be seen as an inadequate theoretician and became instead the perceptive source of ways of looking at the social reality of legal change. There was praise for his suggestive work in areas including linguistics, sociology, political science, legal history, and jurisprudence. Increasingly he came to be recognized not as a failed 'system-builder' but as a creative innovator who encouraged new forms of enquiry.

Death of Maine Maine died on 3 February 1888 at Montfleury Hotel, Cannes, France, leaving a widow and two sons, the eldest of whom, Charles Sumner Maine, clerk of assize on the south Wales circuit, died soon after his father. Maine was commemorated in Westminster Abbey, but his burial at Cannes was more appropriate as a guide to the standing of his thought. The least parochial of English jurists, after the publication of *Ancient Law*, his ideas became a part of continental thought.   R. C. J. COCKS

Sources G. Feaver, *From status to contract: a biography of Sir Henry Maine, 1822–1888* (1969) • R. C. J. Cocks, *Sir Henry Maine: a study in Victorian jurisprudence* (1988) • J. W. Burrow, *Evolution and society: a study in Victorian social theory* (1966) • S. Collini, D. Winch, and J. Burrow, *That noble science of politics: a study in nineteenth-century intellectual history* (1983) • P. Stein, *Legal evolution: the story of an idea* (1980) • P. Vinogradoff, *The teaching of Sir Henry Maine, an inaugural lecture* (1904) • 'Sir Henry Maine and his work', F. Pollock, *Oxford lectures and other discourses* (1890), 147–68 • [F. Pollock], 'Sir Henry Maine as a jurist', *EdinR*, 178 (1893), 100–21 • M. E. G. Duff, *Sir Henry Maine: a brief memoir of his life* (1892) • [J. F. Stephen], 'Sir Henry Maine', *Saturday Review*, 65 (1888), 150–51 • *DNB* • A. Lyall, 'Sir Henry Maine', *Law Quarterly Review*, 4 (1888), 129–35 • W. A. Robson, 'Sir Henry Maine today', *Modern theories of law*, ed. A. L. Goodhart and others (1933) • A. Diamond, ed., *The Victorian achievement of Sir Henry Maine: a centennial reappraisal* (1991)

Archives BL OIOC, corresp. and papers, MS Eur. C 179 • BLPES, lectures, notebooks, and papers • BLPES, letters to Ilbert • BLPES, letters to Lyall • BLPES, letters to Lytton • BLPES, letters to Merivale | BL, Avebury MSS • BL, Cross MSS • BL, Gladstone MSS • BL, Ripon MSS • BL, lecture on Glanville, Add. MS 46195 • BL OIOC, letters to Lord Elgin, MS Eur. F 83 • BL OIOC, corresp. with Sir Alfred Lyall, MS Eur. F 132 • BLPES, Harrison MSS • Bodl. Oxf., corresp. with Lord Kimberley • CAC Cam., corresp. with Lord Randolph Churchill • CUL, letters to Lord Acton • CUL, Atkinson MSS • CUL, corresp. with Lord Mayo • CUL, Stephen MSS • JRL, letters to E. A. Freeman • King's AC Cam., letters to Oscar Browning • NRA, priv. coll., letters to duke of Argyll

Likenesses photographs, 1863, priv. coll. • photographs, 1865, priv. coll. • photographs, 1871, priv. coll. • T. B. Wigram, drawing, *c*.1878, Foreign Office • photographs, *c*.1884, priv. coll. • L. C. Dickinson, oils, 1888, Trinity Hall, Cambridge [*see illus.*] • J. E. Boehm, marble medallion, 1889, Westminster Abbey; related plaster plaque, FM Cam. • L. C. Dickinson, oils, version, Pembroke Cam. • R. T., wood-engraving, NPG; repro. in *ILN* (11 Feb 1888)

Wealth at death £46,715 6*s*. 7*d*.: probate, 1 May 1888, *CGPLA Eng. & Wales*

Mainwaring. *See also* Maynwaring.

Mainwaring, Arthur. *See* Maynwaring, Arthur (1668–1712).

Mainwaring, Edmund (*b.* 1579, *d.* in or after 1643), civil lawyer, was born in 1579, the second son of Sir Randall (or Randle) Mainwaring (*d.* 1612), of Over Peover, Cheshire, and his first wife, Margaret Fitton. His parents both came from leading Cheshire families, and his maternal grandfather was treasurer of Ireland. In addition to Edmund's elder brother, Randall, the family included Thomas, who entered the church, and Philip *Mainwaring (1589–1661), who achieved distinction as the secretary to Thomas Wentworth. There were also four sisters, and three brothers who died in infancy.

In 1594 Mainwaring entered Brasenose College, Oxford, matriculating on 29 November of that year. Brasenose had strong connections with the north-west of England and gave preference to students and candidates for fellowships who came from Lancashire and Cheshire. He subsequently transferred to All Souls College, where fellowships in civil law were readily available, and whose fellows included the distinguished civil lawyer Arthur Duck, an exact contemporary of Mainwaring. Mainwaring graduated MA on 8 July 1602, and received the degree of BCL on 14 December 1605. He was nominated as dean of All Souls in 1606, and remained as a fellow of the college until 1610, in which year he supplicated for the degree of DCL, although this was not conferred until 1629, the year in which he joined the council of the north.

Having achieved the academic qualifications necessary for practice as a civil lawyer Mainwaring embarked on a career in the ecclesiastical courts of the northern province. Through the influence of George Lloyd, bishop of Chester, within whose diocese the archdeaconry of Richmond then lay, he obtained in 1612 the post of commissary of the Richmond consistory court. The duties of this position, however, he usually carried out through substitutes. He also began to practise as an advocate in the York consistory court from about the same date. In addition, from 1612 until 1620 or later, he was a member of the bench of the York high commission court, which was the most wide-ranging in its powers of the courts controlling ecclesiastical affairs in the northern province. In 1613 he was appointed official of the archdeacon of York, and in this capacity was responsible for visitations of churches in the largest of the three archdeaconries in the diocese.

In 1624 a patent was issued to Mainwaring as chancellor of the diocese of York, jointly with Sir Arthur Duck. This appointment was not confirmed, although Mainwaring did obtain some advancement in the same year, being appointed commissary of the dean and chapter of York. It was not until 1627 that he eventually attained the office of chancellor, which he then held jointly with William Easdall, one of several younger men who at that time were becoming active in enforcing the anti-puritan policies of Bishop Laud within the diocese of York. Mainwaring himself took little part in the work of chancellor, except in the visitation of 1630. A possible reason for this is that he was preoccupied with other duties, since he was one of several new members added to the council of the north in June 1629, following the appointment of his brother's patron, Thomas Wentworth, as lord president. His role was as the civil lawyer who assisted the four common lawyers with the judicial side of the council's work. Mainwaring is sometimes described as having been deputy secretary of the council in 1629 and secretary in 1630. From 1612 the holder of the post of secretary was Sir Arthur Ingram, who appears to have retained the position until 1633. However, as Ingram neglected his responsibilities and failed, at this period, to provide a satisfactory deputy, Mainwaring may have carried out the secretary's duties on a semi-official basis. Mainwaring continued as a member until the council's dissolution in 1641.

After holding the appointment of commissary of the Richmond consistory court for over twenty years Mainwaring gave up the post in 1634 and became chancellor of the diocese of Chester. However, he usually carried out the duties of this office through substitutes. He continued to serve as an advocate in the church courts of York until at least late 1635, when he was appointed one of the prosecutors in the notable case against John Birchall, rector of St Martin's, Micklegate, York, who was accused of holding illicit conventicles. Mainwaring was appointed a justice of the peace in Yorkshire in 1632, and in Cheshire in 1635. By the late 1630s his working life was drawing to a close. He relinquished the posts of commissary of the dean and chapter of York and chancellor of the diocese of York in 1637 and that of official of the archdeacon of York in 1638. He continued to hold the office of chancellor of the diocese of Chester until at least 1643.

Little is known of Mainwaring's family life. His wife, Jane, came from York, and it is likely that they married during the early years of Mainwaring's residence in the city. Three children, Jane, William, and Edmund, were baptized at St Martin's, Coney Street, York, in 1614, 1615, and 1617. William eventually became a royalist lieutenant-colonel who served with distinction at the siege of Chester in 1643. Mainwaring's own estate in Chester was sequestered for his delinquency during the civil war. The date of his death is not recorded.

Mainwaring's personality remains shadowy. In his role as a member of the council of the north he was associated with the administrative rigour of Wentworth's policy of 'thorough'. Nevertheless it seems likely that in ecclesiastical affairs he was a less enthusiastic proponent of Archbishop Neile's enforcement of Laudianism than younger and more active administrators in the diocese of York, such as William Easdall, Henry Wickham, archdeacon of

York, and Edward Mottershead, who was appointed official of the archdeaconry of the East Riding in 1632. His career exemplifies the role that an able civil lawyer could play in ecclesiastical and public administration in the first half of the seventeenth century.   SHEILA DOYLE

Sources B. P. Levack, *The civil lawyers in England, 1603–1641* (1973) • R. A. Marchant, *The church under the law: justice, administration and discipline in the diocese of York, 1560–1640* (1969) • R. Marchant, *The puritans and the church courts in the diocese of York, 1560–1642* (1960) • R. R. Reid, *The king's council in the north* (1921) • A. F. Upton, *Sir Arthur Ingram, c.1565–1642: a study in the origins of an English landed family* (1961), 161–71 • Foster, *Alum. Oxon.*

Mainwaring, Sir Henry (1586/7–1653), pirate and naval officer, was the second son of Sir George Mainwaring (*d.* 1628) MP, of Ightfield, Shropshire, and Anne (*d.* 1624), daughter of Sir William *More MP, and his second wife, Margaret. The Mainwarings were well established in Shropshire and Cheshire. Mainwaring matriculated aged twelve at Brasenose College, Oxford, on 27 April 1599, graduated BA on 15 July 1602, and was admitted to the Inner Temple in November 1604. He was granted (but did not take up) the reversion of the captaincy of St Andrew's Castle on 10 June 1611, was appointed to suppress piracy in the Bristol Channel in 1612, and was chosen to accompany Sir Thomas Sherley to Persia, though Spain, fearing that the real objective was the West Indies, blocked the mission.

The rebuff incited Mainwaring to embark on a campaign of piracy, directed principally against Spain. He soon reigned supreme on the Barbary coast. Spain tried unsuccessfully to buy him off, and then took advantage of his absence on a voyage to Newfoundland in 1614 to seize his base at Marmora. Mainwaring transferred to Villefranca and defeated a Spanish fleet in 1615. Complaints from France and Spain reached such a pitch that James I gave him the choice of a pardon or of facing an expedition. Mainwaring would not fight his countrymen, accepted a pardon on 9 June 1616, and subsequently wrote his *Discourse on Piracy*, which is full of sound common sense.

Although he hated pirates the king was attracted to Mainwaring, knighting him on 20 March 1618 and appointing him a gentleman of the bedchamber. Despite this post and the gains from piracy, however, Mainwaring had financial problems and he needed employment. In 1618–19 plans for him to enter the service of Venice fell through, but Lord Zouche, the lord warden of the Cinque Ports, although allegedly warned not to do so, appointed him lieutenant of Dover Castle early in 1620. He also joined the Virginia Company. Mainwaring undertook his duties as lieutenant seriously, which the corporation of Dover recognized in 1621 by electing him to parliament, where he spoke on issues which affected the Cinque Ports. At Dover he wrote his *Seaman's Dictionary*, the first authoritative treatise on seamanship, published eventually in 1644. But he made enemies in the Cinque Ports and, worse, alienated Zouche, who demanded his resignation on 17 March 1623. Prince Charles intervened on his behalf, but when Zouche surrendered his post to the duke of

Buckingham, it was on condition that Mainwaring should not be given any post in the Cinque Ports.

In 1623 Mainwaring was flag captain of the *Prince Royal*, which brought home Prince Charles and Buckingham from their escapade to Spain in pursuit of a bride for the prince. He failed to secure re-election as MP in 1624 but did, however, secure Buckingham as patron and became one of the group of seamen around Buckingham. He was involved in preparing the abortive naval expeditions of the later 1620s, proposed the development of Portsmouth Dockyard, served on a commission of inquiry into the navy in 1626–7, and was an elder brother of Trinity House by 1627. The assassination of Buckingham on 23 August 1628 deprived Mainwaring of his patron and ended a period of intense English naval activity. His father also died in 1628, leaving him nothing.

Mainwaring was among the suitors in 1629 for the hand of Elizabeth Bennett, widow of a wealthy City merchant, but he failed to find favour. The grant of an island off Brazil was also unproductive. About 1630 he married Fortune Gardiner (*bap.* 1607, *d.* 1633), but without the consent of her father, Sir Thomas Gardiner, who refused to allow him access to her portion until he settled £100 per annum in land on her. They had a daughter, Christian (1633–1639); Fortune died in December 1633 and Mainwaring's brother, Sir Arthur, became guardian of Christian until her death at the age of six.

After performing tasks ashore for the navy in the early 1630s Mainwaring served as a senior captain in the ship money fleets in 1637–40, and was vice-admiral in 1639 in the *Henrietta Maria*. He remained impecunious and is said to have been outlawed for debt in December 1635. Although he failed to become surveyor of the navy in 1638, he was elected master of Trinity House in 1642. Parliament, however, distrusted him, and removed him from all offices in the corporation in November 1642.

Mainwaring went to the king's headquarters at Oxford and received the honorary degree of doctor of physic on 31 January 1643. Age and inexperience in land warfare must have kept him inactive in 1643–4, but early in 1645 he was appointed captain of a ship which lay at Pendennis, ready to transport Prince Charles to the Isles of Scilly if he had to leave England, though the prince eventually travelled in another ship. In dire financial straits, Mainwaring settled first in Scilly, then in Jersey in 1646–8, where he became a friend of Jean Chevalier, the chronicler of Jersey. He may have aroused there the interest of Prince Charles in ships and the sea. After the revolt of part of the parliamentary fleet to the king in the summer of 1648 Mainwaring was appointed captain of the *Antelope*, one of the rebel ships, but played no part in the subsequent operations under Rupert. He eventually made his peace with parliament in November 1651, when he was worth only £8, and returned to England. Mainwaring was buried on 15 May 1653 in St Giles, Camberwell, where his wife was already interred. G. G. HARRIS

Sources G. E. Manwaring and W. G. Perrin, eds., *The life and works of Sir Henry Mainwaring*, 2 vols., Navy RS, 54, 56 (1920–22) • *CSP dom., 1611–35* • Foster, *Alum. Oxon., 1500–1714* [Sir Henry Mainwaringe] • *CSP Venice, 1610–13; 1617–21* • HoP, *Commons, 1558–1603*, 3.2–3, 86 • 'Mainwaring, Sir Arthur', 'Mainwaring, Sir Henry', HoP, *Commons, 1604–29* [drafts] • Chancery proceedings, PRO, C2 Charles I/M74/44; G12/64; M9/64 • A. Thrush, 'The navy under Charles I, 1625–40', PhD diss., U. Lond., 1991 • M. A. E. Green, ed., *Calendar of the proceedings of the committee for compounding … 1643–1660*, 4, PRO (1892), 2894 • parish register, St Giles, Camberwell, LMA, 15 May 1653 [burial] • L. B. Larking, ed., *Proceedings principally in the county of Kent in connection with the parliaments called in 1640, and especially with the committee of religion appointed in that year*, CS, old ser., 80 (1862), xxvi • *The autobiography of Phineas Pett*, ed. W. G. Perrin, Navy RS, 51 (1918), 96, 116–17 • W. H. Cooke, ed., *Students admitted to the Inner Temple, 1547–1660* [1878], 166 • W. A. Shaw, *The knights of England*, 2 (1906), 167

Archives PRO, state papers James I and Charles I, corresp.

Wealth at death very little; total possessions worth only £8 in 1651: Green, ed., *Calendar of committee for compounding*, p. 2894

Mainwaring, Matthew (1561–1652), author, was born on 26 February 1561, the second son of Thomas Mainwaring (*d.* 1573) of Nantwich, Cheshire, and Margaret, daughter of Randall Crewe of the same place. On 10 December 1594 he married Margaret Mynshull (1573–1652), half-sister of Richard Mynshull, to whom he dedicated *Vienna, where in is storied the valorous atchievements, famous triumphs, constant love, greate miseries, and finall happines, of the well-deserving, truly noble and most valiant knight, Sir Paris of Vienna, and the most admired amiable princess the faire Vienna*, a translation, or rather adaptation, of a romance of Catalonian origin. It was licensed on 25 May 1628 and was published that year, with a second edition possibly published in 1632, and another in 1650.

W. C. Hazlitt describes a copy of an early edition which contained a dedication of the book by 'T. M.' to Lucy, countess of Bedford. *Vienna*, published under the initials M. M., has been assigned to Richard Mynshull, but it contains two anagrams and a reference to the arms (those of Mainwaring) in the engraved title, which leave no doubt as to the real author. There are commendatory verses by the playwright Thomas Heywood, various members of the Mainwaring family, and Thomas Croket, from which last it appears that Matthew Mainwaring was already an old man when he wrote *Vienna*. Geffray Mynshull, his nephew, dedicated to him in 1618 his *Essayes and Characters of a Prison and Prisoners*. Mainwaring died in January 1652, having nearly completed his ninety-first year. He was buried on 19 January at Nantwich church.

GEORGE THORN-DRURY, rev. P. J. FINKELPEARL

Sources J. Hall, *A history of the town and parish of Nantwich, or Wich-Malbank, in the county palatine of Cheshire* (1883), 175, 456–8 • E. Brydges, *Censura literaria: containing titles, abstracts, and opinions of old English books*, 6 (1808), 118–21 • *Palatine Note-Book*, 3 (1883), 156–9 • Arber, *Regs. Stationers*, 4.164 • ESTC

Mainwaring, Sir Philip (1589–1661), government official, was born in 1589, probably in Cheshire, the fourth and youngest son of Sir Randall (or Randle) Mainwaring (*d.* 1612), of Over Peover, Cheshire, and his wife, Margaret, daughter of Sir Edward Fitton, president of Connaught. In 1609 he was a student of Gray's Inn and on 29 August 1610 he matriculated from Brasenose College, Oxford. He may have been the Philip Mainwaring who graduated BA on 8

February 1613. His upbringing and career suggest that his protestant beliefs were mainstream.

Mainwaring appears to have served as a useful contact at court for provincial gentry, being described in 1610 as 'my Lord Chancellor's man' (V. Larminie, *Wealth, Kinship and Culture*, 1995, 131). In the second half of the 1610s he worked in the Netherlands as an agent for Thomas Howard, earl of Arundel, some of his correspondence with whom on political affairs has been printed. The possibility that he brought the earl Sebastiano del Piombo's painting *Ferry Carondolet and Attendants*, purchased in 1617, has been noted, as also that Mainwaring's knowledge of this work might have influenced the style of the Van Dyck portrait of himself and Thomas Wentworth, earl of Strafford, painted in 1639 or 1640 (Howarth, 69). It is possible that his work for Arundel brought him into contact with Wentworth, who was on good terms with the earl during the 1620s and early 1630s, and who brought Philip's brother Edmund *Mainwaring (*b.* 1579, *d.* in or after 1643) on to the council of the north and the northern recusancy commission.

By 1629 Mainwaring had begun to report court news and foreign affairs to Wentworth and to keep him abreast of developments that might concern Wentworth's interests, but a bid in July 1632 to serve under Wentworth in a northern office—apparently an ambitious attempt to gain the vice-presidency of the council of the north—was unsuccessful. Mainwaring spent part of 1633 travelling in France. Wentworth's decision in 1634 to appoint him to the post of Irish secretary as a replacement for the elderly Sir Dudley Norton was very much against the advice of one of his allies, Francis, Lord Cottington. Although willing to approach the king with Wentworth's request, Cottington reminded Wentworth that he had himself been critical of Mainwaring in the past. Wentworth's key ally, Archbishop Laud, was less hostile, but was sufficiently concerned to inform Wentworth of Cottington's words on this matter. Mainwaring's appointment on 16 June 1634 brought him membership of the Irish privy council and a knighthood a few weeks later, on 13 July: he evidently served Wentworth well—their portrait is testimony to a good relationship.

Mainwaring was not returned as MP for Steyning, Sussex, in 1621 and 1624, despite Arundel's best efforts, but he sat for Boroughbridge, Yorkshire, in the parliaments of 1624, 1625, and 1626, possibly due to duchy of Lancaster influence, and for Derby in 1628. In 1625 he was a member of a Commons committee handling a bill for the sale and settlement of the late earl of Dorset's estate. He was returned as MP for Clonakilty, co. Cork, in the Irish parliament of 1634 and for Carysfort, co. Wicklow, in 1640. He sat for Morpeth, Northumberland, in the Short Parliament of 1640, and spoke on 23 April, urging the Commons to follow the Irish parliament in its generosity towards the king. He remained in office following Strafford's execution and was resident in Dublin until at least August 1641.

Mainwaring spent the first half of 1642 in London embroiled in a contest with Viscount Mountnorris over the office of secretary and in a dispute with Viscount Loftus regarding land entrusted to Mainwaring, among others, in 1638. He left London in June 1642 and settled in Oxford, where he served Charles I as a receiver of revenue. He claimed to have had no military involvement in the civil war. His entire estate was lost during the rebellion and war in Ireland, but he continued to be pursued by Loftus's heirs until the Restoration. He spent part of 1650 and 1651 in prison following his return to London. In 1660 Mainwaring petitioned Charles II for the mastership of the Charterhouse, but was only awarded the reversion on the death of Sir Ralph Sydenham, the successful candidate. In 1661 he was returned as MP for Newton borough, Lancashire, while living with relatives at Baddiley, Cheshire, but he died in London on 2 August of that year. He never married, although rumour briefly linked him with the widowed countess of Berkshire (Gruenfelder, 83).

FIONA POGSON

Sources *DNB* · Strafford papers, Sheff. Arch., Wentworth Woodhouse muniments, 6, 12–14, 19 · *CSP dom.*, 1623–5; 1631–3; 1641–3; 1649–51; 1659–60; 1666–7 · *Report on manuscripts in various collections*, 8 vols., HMC, 55 (1901–14), vol. 3 · D. Howarth, *Lord Arundel and his circle* (1985) · J. K. Gruenfelder, *Influence in early Stuart elections, 1604–1640* (1981) · J. Nichols, *The progresses, processions, and magnificent festivities of King James I, his royal consort, family and court*, 3 (1828) · M. F. S. Hervey, *The life, correspondence and collections of Thomas Howard, earl of Arundel* (1921) · *Fifth report*, HMC, 4 (1876) · *Ninth report*, 3 vols., HMC, 8 (1883–4) · H. Kearney, *Strafford in Ireland, 1633–41: a study in absolutism*, 2nd edn (1989) · M. Jansson and W. B. Bidwell, eds., *Proceedings in parliament, 1625* (1987) · E. S. Cope and W. H. Coates, eds., *Proceedings of the Short Parliament of 1640*, CS, 4th ser., 19 (1977) · G. Ormerod, *The history of the county palatine and city of Chester*, 2nd edn, ed. T. Helsby, 1 (1882) · Foster, *Alum. Oxon.* · PRO, PROB 6/37, fol. 83v

Archives JRL, papers | Arundel Castle, West Sussex, letters to earl of Arundel

Likenesses oils, *c.*1636 (after A. Van Dyck), Weston Park, Shropshire · Van Dyck, portrait, 1639–40

Mainwaring, Randall (1588–1652), parliamentarian activist, was born at Whitmore, in Staffordshire, the second son of Edward Mainwaring of Whitmore, an esquire from an ancient gentry family, and his wife, Jane, daughter of Matthew Cradock of Stafford, merchant of the staple and a prominent colonial trader. From his marriage on 30 June 1618 at St John's, Hackney, to Elizabeth Hawes, daughter of Humfrey Hawes of London, he was to have four sons and four daughters.

Mainwaring was free of the Grocers' Company and subsequently became a City mercer engaged in colonial trade in partnership with his brothers-in-law and leading transatlantic traders, Joseph and Nathaniel Hawes. A settled resident by 1620 of the affluent Cheapside parish of St Mary Colechurch, he progressed upwards to senior parish and precinct offices over the next two decades. Mainwaring and a number of fellow parishioners were to earn for the parish a reputation for radicalism in the early 1640s. From 1630 to 1644 he sat on common council and, as a citizen with seniority and experience, served on several important City committees from 1640. In addition, he was treasurer of the Honourable Artillery Company from 1631 to 1635 and by 1640 had become a captain in the Red regiment of the London trained bands; promotion was to follow rapidly in 1642–3 to the ranks of sergeant-major, lieutenant-colonel, and colonel.

The early 1640s saw Mainwaring at the forefront of radical politics in the capital. In the summer of 1641, he was one of the six representatives chosen by the citizens to support the claim of common hall to elect both London sheriffs. He was equally prominent in the citizens' petitioning of parliament in 1641–2, protesting at Thomas Lunsford's appointment to the lieutenancy of the Tower of London, calling for urgent assistance for Irish protestants, and complaining about the conduct of Mayor Gurney. In January 1642 he was chosen along with other radical citizens to sit on the London militia committee, and in the following August he was appointed deputy to Gurney's replacement as lord mayor, Isaac Penington.

During the early months of the civil war, Mainwaring gained a well-deserved reputation as a ruthless supporter of the war effort. He raised a new regiment, his 'redcoats', for the earl of Warwick's proposed reserve army in October 1642 which, instead of joining up with the earl of Essex after Warwick's resignation, remained in London throughout the winter of 1642–3. This force was regularly called upon to help police the capital when Mainwaring took over from Philip Skippon the position of sergeant-major-general of the City. Mainwaring also sent a troop of horse to take action against peace petitioners gathered at the Guildhall in December 1642, and later assisted in distraining the goods of those Londoners who failed to pay their assessments for the war. His zeal in executing the latter earned him the sobriquet of 'the crazed mercer' (*Honest Letter*). By January 1643 Mainwaring, along with Penington, John Fowke, and John Venn, had been singled out from their fellow parliamentarian citizens to be accused by the king of treason. His militant credentials were further confirmed in the following March when he was one of the promoters of a radical remonstrance declaring supreme power to reside in the people, who constituted parliaments to manage that power on their behalf. He also saw service on the battlefield in September 1643 when he commanded the Red regiment of auxiliaries at the first battle of Newbury. In November 1645 he joined fellow parliamentarian activists on a Goldsmiths' Hall committee set up to keep on eye on former royalists entering the capital.

During the political upheavals of 1647 in London, Mainwaring was closely associated with the political independents. He was purged from the City's militia committee in May, during the presbyterians' attempted counter-revolution, but was restored to it in July, after the army's intervention. However, he was not nominated to the independent-dominated militia committee of the following September. In January 1649 he was appointed to the high court of justice for the king's trial. He was rewarded for his faithful service of parliament by a grant of land and appointment as comptroller for the sale of royalist lands during the last year of his life. He is not to be confused (as he sometimes is) with Robert *Mainwaring (*bap.* 1607,

d. 1652), a former officer of the London Customs House, and also a parliamentarian activist.

Randall Mainwaring died in October or November 1652 and was succeeded by his son, also named Randall Mainwaring (*d.* 1663). Neither the place of death nor burial of Randall senior are known.   KEITH LINDLEY

Sources vestry minutes of St Mary Colechurch, Guildhall Library, MS 64, fols. 10, etc. · *The visitation of London, anno Domini 1633, 1634, and 1635, made by Sir Henry St George*, 2, ed. J. J. Howard, Harleian Society, 17 (1883), 79 · K. Lindley, *Popular politics and religion in civil war London* (1997) · C. H. Firth and R. S. Rait, eds., *Acts and ordinances of the interregnum, 1642–1660*, 1 (1911), 5–6, 802, 990–91, 1254 · M. A. E. Green, ed., *Calendar of the proceedings of the committee for advance of money, 1642–1656*, 1, PRO (1888), 13, 14, 32 · R. Brenner, *Merchants and revolution: commercial change, political conflict, and London's overseas traders, 1550–1653* (1993) · L. C. Nagel, 'The militia of London, 1641–49', PhD diss., U. Lond., 1982, 85–7 · *Two speeeches spoken by the earl of Manchester and John Pym*, 1643, BL, E 85/7, 6 · *An honest letter to a doubtful friend* (1643) · G. E. Aylmer, *The state's servants: the civil service of the English republic, 1649–1660* (1973), 364, 377 · BL, Harleian MS 986, fol. 4 · H. A. Dillon, ed., 'On a MS list of officers of the London trained bands in 1643', *Archaeologia*, 52 (1890), 129–44, esp. 134 · IGI

Wealth at death £200 p.a. in land to be settled on him and children for service of parliament: Green, ed., *Calendar of the committee for advance of money*, vol. 3, pp. 1251–2

Mainwaring, Robert (*bap.* 1607, *d.* 1652), militia officer and local politician, was baptized in London on 21 June 1607 at St Dionis Backchurch, the son of William Mainwaring, citizen of London and merchant tailor, and his wife, Mary. As a young Londoner, Mainwaring did not immediately follow the customary route into a livery company but became an officer of the London Customs House. Still resident in the parish of St Dionis Backchurch at the time of the 1638 tithe assessment, Mainwaring's rating indicated that he had become a man of substance. He married Martha, the daughter of Francis Hurdman, a London merchant, with whom he had a daughter, Martha. By 1643 Mainwaring had moved into his father-in-law's parish of St Mary Aldermanbury and had become closely associated with him in the collection of duties on the import of sweet wines. He was to be a main beneficiary under Hurdman's 1649 will.

Mainwaring was one of those Londoners who emerged from relative obscurity to make their mark on City politics in the 1640s as supporters of parliament. In March 1642 he was admitted into the Honourable Artillery Company and by April he was a captain in the Green regiment of the City trained bands; he was to reach the rank of major by 1645 and colonel by 1647. He became free by redemption on 17 October 1642 in the Fishmongers' Company, whom he presented with a silver flagon pot in gratitude, and was admitted to the livery on the following 3 November, yet he seems to have played no further part in company affairs. Preparations for war saw Mainwaring acting in the ward of Cripplegate Without as a collector for money and plate in August 1642 and an assessor of parliamentary levies at the end of the year. In February 1643 he was named as one of the militia officers empowered to assist in levying distraints on assessment defaulters in the City. One of

Mainwaring's fellow officers in this task was Colonel Randall Mainwaring, a parliamentarian militant and future political independent, with whom he is sometimes confused. Both men also served in their respective militia companies at the first battle of Newbury in September 1643.

Robert Mainwaring had moved to a substantial dwelling-house with a garden on Grub Street, in the parish of St Giles Cripplegate, by 1645, when he became a common councillor for Cripplegate Without. He served on the assembly for three consecutive years, during which he became one of London's leading political presbyterians. In October 1645 he was appointed one of the lay triers for the eldership for his home parish of St Giles Cripplegate in the sixth classis of the London province, and he also subscribed the citizens' petition of November 1645 calling for an exclusive covenant-based presbyterianism. During the attempted 'counter-revolution' in London Mainwaring was appointed to the presbyterian-dominated city militia committee of May 1647, but he was soon purged from the committee after the army's advance on London. However, in 1646 he had been appointed registrar-accountant for all land sales, with an annual fee of £200, and held the post until his death. By September 1647 he had also become ward deputy for Cripplegate Without and in April 1648 was named a commissioner for the collection of arrears within his ward. He died in his Grub Street home on 19 September 1652 and was buried in the parish church of St Giles Cripplegate. The chief beneficiaries under his will, made on 18 September 1652, were his wife, who was to receive £100 a year, and his daughter, Martha, and son-in-law, Edward Greene, a London goldsmith. KEITH LINDLEY

Sources will, PRO, PROB 11/223/156 · will, PRO, PROB 11/207/57 [Francis Hurdman] · records of Fishmongers' Company, GL, MS 5570/3, fols. 634, 643–4; MS 5576/1, fol. 184; MS 5578A/2, n. p. · journals, CLRO, court of common council, vol. 40, fols. 128, 153, 215 · repertories of the court of aldermen, CLRO, 58, fol. 174 · BL, Harley MS 986, fol. 22 · C. H. Firth and R. S. Rait, eds., *Acts and ordinances of the interregnum, 1642–1660*, 1 (1911), 795, 898, 928, 1129; 2 (1911), 93 · *The obituary of Richard Smyth ... being a catalogue of all such persons as he knew in their life*, ed. H. Ellis, CS, 44 (1849), 32 · committee for the advance of money: orders, Dec 1642–Feb 1643, PRO, SP 19/1/39, 94–5 · parish register, St Dionis Backchurch, GL, MS 17602, 21 June 1607 [baptism] · T. C. Dale, ed., *The inhabitants of London in 1638*, 2 vols. (1931), 48 · CSP dom., 1625–49, 650, 675 · G. A. Raikes, *The ancient vellum book of the Honourable Artillery Company ... from 1611 to 1682* (1890), 63 · 'Boyd's Inhabitants of London', Society of Genealogists, London, no. 24272
Wealth at death £100 annuity for wife; leases in St Martin le Grand and Grub Street; jewels, plate, etc.; interest in a ship: will, PRO, PROB 11/223/156

Mainwaring, Rowland (1783–1862), naval officer, born on 31 December 1783, possibly at Whitmore Hall, Whitmore, near Newcastle under Lyme, Staffordshire, was the second of seven children of Rowland Mainwaring (1745–1817), an army officer, of Four Oaks Park, near Sutton Coldfield, Warwickshire, and his second wife, Jane Latham (d. 1809), daughter of Captain Thomas Latham RN. He probably was educated by a private tutor, and in June 1795 he entered the navy as a first-class volunteer on the *Jupiter*. He served

later as a midshipman in the *Majestic* at the battle of Abu Qir Bay and in the *Defence* at the battle of Copenhagen before being promoted lieutenant of the *Harpy* in 1801. On 31 December 1810 he married Sophia Henrietta Duff (1788?–1824), the stepdaughter of Captain George Tobin RN; they had nine children. By December 1810 he had served continuously throughout the decade, including four years as first lieutenant of the *Narcissus*. In his privately published autobiography, *The First Five Years of my Married Life* (1853), he wrote an interesting account of his subsequent service in the *Menelaus* and as a commander of the *Kite* and the *Paulina* seeing out the war, under the aegis of Sir Edward Pellew, chasing and blockading privateers in the Mediterranean. He moved to Bath when the war ended, and though he did not see active service again, he was promoted captain on 22 July 1830 and was placed on the list of retired rear-admirals on 27 September 1855.

Mainwaring's first wife died in October 1824, and he married, on 15 November 1826, Mary Ann Clark (1786?–1835); they had one child, a daughter. He became very active in the community affairs of Bath, being appointed the honorary secretary of a number of charitable societies. A supporter of the Liberals in later life, on 13 October 1831 he chaired a large open-air meeting of supporters of the Reform Bill in Bath. An energetic man, who once set out to walk from Gosport to Bath (reaching Frome on the third day), he was also a competent artist and a friend of the marine painters Thomas Luny and George Tobin. He published an anthology of writings on painting and several accounts of the affairs of Bath. After the death of his second wife, in January 1835, he decided to settle in Mannheim, Germany. Within a short while he married, on 11 November 1836, Laura Maria Julia Walbugha Chevillard (d. 1891), the only child of one of Napoleon's colonels killed at Leipzig, and the adopted daughter of the baroness de Heygendorf. They had seven children.

In 1837 Mainwaring succeeded his first cousin, Miss Sarah Mainwaring, in the estates of Whitmore Hall, near Newcastle under Lyme, and Biddulph, Staffordshire. His daily diary, kept from 1819 until his death, records the life of an active country gentleman, justice of the peace, and deputy lieutenant of Staffordshire. He died on 11 April 1862 at Whitmore Hall from the effects of a heart attack and was buried on the 21st in the family vault in the parish church of St Mary and All Saints in Whitmore. A memorial tablet was erected in the church.

GORDON GOODWIN, rev. DAVID SMALL

Sources J. G. Cavenagh-Mainwaring, 'The Mainwarings of Whitmore and Biddulph in the county of Stafford', Collections for a history of Staffordshire, William Salt Archaeological Society, 3rd ser. (1933), 92–119 · O'Byrne, *Naval biog. dict.* · J. Marshall, *Royal naval biography*, 3/2 (1832), 126–30 · R. Mainwaring, *The first five years of my married life* (privately printed, Newcastle under Lyme, 1853) · R. Mainwaring, *Lost manuscripts of a bluejacket* (privately printed, 1850) · R. Mainwaring, diaries, 1819–62, priv. coll. · Burke, *Gen. GB* · survey, PRO, ADM 9/4 (1817), 1184 · R. Mainwaring, *Instructive gleanings, moral and scientific, from the best writers, on painting and drawing* (1832) · Captain's log of HMS Kite, 1811–14, PRO, ADM 51 2479 · Captain's log of HMS Paulina, 1813–15, PRO, ADM 51 2677 · GM, 3rd ser.,

12 (1862), 657 · *IGI* · parish register (burial), 1862, Whitmore, St Mary and All Saints **Archives** NMM · priv. coll. **Likenesses** J. Phillip, oils, May 1841, priv. coll. · L. C. Dickinson, oils, *c.*1860, priv. coll. **Wealth at death** under £20,000: resworn probate, Oct 1863, *CGPLA Eng. & Wales* (1862)

Mainwaring, Sir Thomas, first baronet (1623–1689), antiquary and local politician, was born in Cheshire on 7 April 1623, the third, and oldest surviving, son of Philip Mainwaring (1589?–1647) of Baddiley and Over Peover and his wife, Ellen (*d.* 1656), daughter of Edward Minishull of Nantwich, and the great-nephew of Philip Mainwaring (1589–1661), the future secretary to the earl of Strafford. He matriculated on 28 April 1637 from Brasenose College, Oxford, a college favoured by north-western families, and entered Gray's Inn on 15 February 1638 with his elder brother Randle and a Walley cousin. As is evident from his strangely dispassionate diary, begun in 1648, he relied throughout his life on just such an extended circle of kin and friends. From his father, an active county gentleman, who as sheriff in 1639 had to implement unpopular royal policies, and from his contemporaries at the inns, Mainwaring early developed antipathy to Charles I. On 26 May 1642 he married, in Wybunbury, Mary (*d.* 1671), daughter of Sir Henry Delves of Doddington and a distant cousin; they had five sons and six daughters.

During the civil war Mainwaring's father was a captain of horse in the parliamentary forces, and Mainwaring himself took the covenant while still at Gray's Inn. In 1647, he inherited the family estates, and thereafter divided his time between Baddiley and Over Peover. He was assiduous in local committee work, becoming a JP in 1649, sitting as a commissioner for assessment, the militia, and the regulation of ministers, and serving as sheriff in 1657–8, but kept well clear of the wider political scene. He had lifelong leanings towards Independency, but, while patently mistrusting the Stuarts, as a political and social conservative, he came to dislike even more the godly regime which replaced them. Here he echoed his kinsman George Booth, who seems to have been a mentor as well as a friend, and whose career his own paralleled, if on a lesser scale. He was almost certainly involved in Booth's rising in 1659. Like Booth he sat (for Cheshire) in the Convention Parliament, although he proved an inactive member. After the Restoration he was reappointed to his local offices, nominated to the order of the Royal Oak, and, on 22 November 1660, created baronet.

Like his father, Mainwaring loved books and cultivated learning. Between 1673 and 1679 he and his kinsman Sir Peter Leycester exchanged insults and arguments in print over the illegitimacy of their remote common ancestress, Amicia, daughter of Hugh of Cyfeilog, earl of Chester, alleged in Leycester's *Historical Antiquities* (1673) and denied by Mainwaring. Eventually their arguments ranged over much of the social and political life of the twelfth century, and in so doing represented a milestone in historiography. These antagonists—both possessed of legal training, antiquarian zeal, and significant personal muniments—were able to urge each other, and occasionally themselves, to interpret twelfth-century material from the viewpoint of a twelfth-century nobleman, and not as a quaint aberration.

Between 1675 and 1681 Mainwaring served as a deputy lieutenant for Cheshire, but when Charles II moved to purge local government of puritan sympathizers in 1680 Sir Thomas was removed from the commission of the peace. Representations as to his effectiveness and impartiality led to a temporary restoration to the bench, but he was soon deprived again. He and his son John (1656–1702) associated publicly with the duke of Monmouth during the latter's progress through Cheshire in 1682, and after the Rye House plot he was disarmed and bound over at the assizes. Having actively supported John's unsuccessful candidature for a county seat in the 1685 election, Mainwaring was listed as in opposition to James II. On 29 November 1688 he accompanied George Booth's son Henry, Lord Delamere, when he went with a large party to seize arms at Newcastle under Lyme 'in Defence of the protestant Religion' (BL, Add. MS 41805, fol. 234). Within weeks Mainwaring was restored to his deputy lieutenancy.

Mainwaring died at Over Peover in 1689 and was buried there on 28 June in the family vault. Having greatly enhanced the estate bequeathed to him by his father, he left about £25,000. John, his fourth but oldest surviving son, succeeded to the baronetcy and sat as a whig in six parliaments between 1689 and 1701, but was no more an active member than his father. He died in debtors' prison on 4 November 1702. HANS NORTON

Sources M. W. Helms and G. Hampson, 'Mainwaring, Thomas', HoP, *Commons, 1660–90* · J. P. Ferris, 'Mainwaring, John', HoP, *Commons, 1660–90* · G. Ormerod, *The history of the county palatine and city of Chester*, 2nd edn, ed. T. Helsby, 3 vols. (1882) · Foster, *Alum. Oxon.* · J. Foster, *The register of admissions to Gray's Inn, 1521–1889, together with the register of marriages in Gray's Inn chapel, 1695–1754* (privately printed, London, 1889) · P. Leycester and T. Mainwaring, *Tracts written in the controversy respecting the legitimacy of Amicia*, ed. W. Beaumont, 3 vols., Chetham Society, 78–80 (1869) · T. Wooton, *The English baronets*, 4 vols. (1741) · T. Mainwaring, diaries, Ches. & Chester ALSS, DDX 384/1, 2 · 'Over Peover church and its monuments', *c.*1901, Ches. & Chester ALSS, DDX 4487/1–4 · probate of wills, Ches. & Chester ALSS [T. Mainwaring, 1689; P. Mainwaring, 1647/1648] · J. S. Morrill, *Cheshire, 1630–1660: county government and society during the English revolution* (1974) **Archives** Ches. & Chester ALSS, diaries, DDX 384/1, 2 · Folger, corresp. · JRL, diaries and papers **Likenesses** engraving (after 'original picture at Peover'), repro. in Beaumont, ed., *Tracts* **Wealth at death** approx. £25,000: probated wills of Philip Mainwaring (1647/1648) and Sir Thomas Mainwaring (1689), Ches. & Chester ALSS

Mainwaring, William Henry (1884–1971), trade unionist, was born on 14 January 1884 at Fforest-fach, Penderry, Swansea, the third of the ten children of William Mainwaring, a miner, and his wife, Mary Thomas. His first language was Welsh, and he knew no English until he attended St Peter's church school, Cockett (1889–96). At twelve he became a general helper to his grandfather at a small mine, before working as a collier at the Broadoak colliery. In 1903 Mainwaring moved to the Rhondda valleys, where he found work at D. A. Thomas's Cambrian colliery in Clydach Vale.

Mainwaring's political consciousness was stimulated by his reading the American Edward Bellamy's utopian socialist novel *Looking Backward* (1888). He was a member of the Social Democratic Federation and of its Marxian club at Blaenclydach, before joining the Independent Labour Party and the Plebs' League. His political beliefs led to a crisis in his relations with his Baptist church, and he was expelled from the church for refusing to believe that Lot's wife had been turned into a pillar of salt. Thereafter he remained a non-Christian rationalist.

Active in the South Wales Miners' Federation (SWMF) lodge at the Cambrian colliery, Mainwaring served on the Cambrian Combine committee and was prominent in the Cambrian Combine dispute of 1910–11. He helped to establish the Unofficial Reform Committee, a Rhondda-based grouping of union militants that was increasingly drawn towards the principles of industrial unionism, and he acted as the committee's secretary from 1910 until 1913. He participated in the discussion and writing of the committee's influential semi-syndicalist pamphlet *The Miners' Next Step* (1912), which called for the reform of the SWMF along 'fighting lines' and embodied a fierce critique of the existing union leadership. He also contributed regularly to the radical weeklies the *Rhondda Socialist Newspaper* and the *South Wales Worker*. At the same time he led the call for the establishment of a formal Labour Party organization in the Rhondda valleys.

From 1913 to 1915 Mainwaring, with a scholarship from the Rhondda no. 1 district of the SWMF, studied at the Central Labour College in Earls Court. On 19 December 1914 he married Jessie Emily Lizette Hazell (b. 1881/2) of Bristol, daughter of Thomas John Hazell, railway signalman. They had a daughter, Joyce. On returning to the Rhondda valleys he went back to mining, but also began to teach evening classes and developed a reputation as 'the learned Marxian' with a 'caustic tongue' (Pankhurst, 412). During the First World War he was active in the No Conscription Fellowship, the Rhondda Anti-Conscription Committee, the Rhondda Socialist Society, and the South Wales Socialist Society.

By 1918 Mainwaring was secretary of the Rhondda West divisional Labour Party and chairman of the Cambrian lodge. After an unsuccessful challenge in 1919 for the presidency of the SWMF, he became vice-principal of the Central Labour College, where he remained until June 1924. He was not universally popular as a lecturer, being one target of the student strike of 1922–3. During this time he was a member of the Communist Party of Great Britain, but left in disappointment in 1924 after failing to win the backing of the Miners' Minority Movement for the south Wales ballot to nominate a candidate for the post of secretary of the Mineworkers' Federation of Great Britain. Standing anyway in south Wales, Mainwaring was narrowly beaten by the non-communist and eventual victor in the national ballot, Arthur James Cook, whom the Minority Movement had preferred, allegedly for his more

effective militancy and out of a suspicion of careerism on Mainwaring's part. Nevertheless Mainwaring remained, intellectually, a professed Marxist, and was frequently dismissive of what he termed the 'boy-scout' Marxism of prominent members of the Communist Party.

From 1924 until 1933 Mainwaring was miners' agent for the Rhondda no. 1 district of the SWMF and a member of the SWMF executive council. This was a difficult time for the union, with widespread victimization of union activists after the 1926 defeat and bitter strife between Communist and Labour Party members within the union. The target of marked personal hostility from his left-wing critics, Mainwaring was prominent in bringing about the expulsion from the SWMF of the communist-dominated Mardy lodge in 1930.

When sitting Labour MP David Watts Morgan died in 1933, Mainwaring was selected as Labour candidate for the Rhondda East constituency and won the by-election, beating the Communist Arthur Horner and a Liberal candidate. He faced Communist candidates in all subsequent general elections, defeating the Communist Party secretary, Harry Pollitt, in 1935, 1945 (by 972 votes), and 1950. With a power base at the Pen-y-graig Labour and Progressive Club he rebuilt the local Labour Party organization and restored the party's reputation after a corruption scandal in 1934–5. He edited the Labour Party's newspaper the *Rhondda Clarion* (1935–6) and was active in supporting the campaign to resurrect the SWMF in the face of the threat of the 'non-political' South Wales Miners' Industrial Union, and in campaigning against the implementation of part 2 of the Unemployment Insurance Act of 1934 (commonly known as the Means Test).

During and after the Second World War, Mainwaring supported the cause of industrial reconstruction in the south Wales coalfield, and prioritized economic issues over Welsh devolution, opposing the Parliament for Wales Bill in the 1950s. Having been part of a commission inquiring into closer co-operation between Southern Rhodesia, Northern Rhodesia, and Nyasaland in 1938, he maintained a keen interest in imperial and Commonwealth issues, and toured India and Pakistan, independently, in 1956. An advocate of national service, he supported the intervention of the United Nations in the Korean War. With these exceptions, the second half of his parliamentary career (which terminated with his retirement in 1959) was unremarkable. He died at his daughter's home, 38 Harbord Road, Oxford, on 18 May 1971.

Mainwaring was a man who inspired respect among his political colleagues rather than affection. Many thought him egotistical and conceited, with a predilection for bombastic denunciation. In an age when his Communist rivals were often seen as leaders of mercurial brilliance, Mainwaring was deemed to lack charisma and imagination.   CHRIS WILLIAMS

Sources NL Wales, W.H. Mainwaring papers · NL Scot., National Council of Labour Colleges MSS · *The Times* (20 May 1971) · C. Williams, *Democratic Rhondda: politics and society, 1885–1951* (1996) · C. Williams, interview with Idris Cox, Talywaun, 21 June 1987 ·

C. Williams, interview with George Thomas (Viscount Tony-pandy), Cardiff, 17 Aug 1987 · C. Williams, interview with Rev. Cyril E. Gwyther, Pembroke Dock, 28 July 1987 · C. Williams, interview with Cliff Prothero, Penarth, 19 Aug 1987 · E. S. Pankhurst, *The home front: a mirror to life in England during the world war* (1932) · M. G. Woodhouse, 'Rank and file movements among the miners of south Wales', DPhil diss., U. Oxf., 1969 · R. Lewis, *Leaders and teachers: adult education and the challenge of labour in south Wales, 1906–1940* (1993) · b. cert. · m. cert.

Archives NL Wales, corresp. and papers | NL Scot., National Council of Labour Colleges papers · U. Hull, Brynmor Jones L., corresp. with Robin Page Arnot, DAR/1/37 · U. Wales, Swansea, South Wales Miners' Library, corresp. with Rev. Cyril E. Gwyther | FILM BFI NFTVA, party political footage

Wealth at death £14,427: probate, 27 July 1971, *CGPLA Eng. & Wales*

Mainzer, Joseph (1801–1851), music teacher, was born in Trier on 21 October 1801. He was educated as a chorister at Trier Cathedral, and learned to play several instruments. He was employed for a time as an apprentice in the Saarbrücken coal mines with a view to becoming an engineer, but was ordained a priest in 1826 and was subsequently made an abbé. He continued his musical studies and was appointed singing-master at the seminary at Trier, for which he wrote his *Singschule* (1831). Forced to leave Germany on account of his political opinions, which originated in his experience of the poor conditions in the mines, Mainzer renounced the priesthood and fled in 1833 to Brussels where he wrote an opera, taught, and acted as musical editor of *L'Artiste*. Late the following year he moved to Paris. He gave free singing classes in 1835 and contributed musical articles to various journals. Mainzer's classes attracted hundreds of adult labourers and brought his methods to the attention of a much wider audience, including an English one. In fact, similar classes were set up in London in May 1841 following his arrival there in 1839, the authorities in Paris having banned his classes. A textbook, *Singing for the Million* (1841), appeared in numerous editions (the title was apparently taken by Hood as the subject of a humorous poem) and presented his system, which was based on continental 'fixed' sol-fa. The classes, in competition with Hullah's, which had themselves been inspired by Mainzer's work in Paris, were also successful. He established the paper *Mainzer's Musical Times* soon after he arrived in London, and this became the *Musical Times* when taken over by Novello in 1844. In November 1841 Mainzer competed unsuccessfully against Henry Bishop for the chair of music at Edinburgh University. Having settled in Edinburgh, he established classes and published *The Musical Athenaeum* (1842) and *Music and Education* (1848). About 1848 he moved to Manchester.

Mainzer's compositions, including operas, some church music, songs, and choruses, are insignificant, but his system of teaching singing in classes, although superseded after his death, was highly influential and widespread and greatly assisted the development of music among amateurs. Exhausted by overwork, he died in Manchester on 10 November 1851. J. C. HADDEN, *rev.* DAVID J. GOLBY

Sources B. Rainbow, 'Mainzer, Joseph', *New Grove* · H. F. Chorley, 'Foreign correspondence', *The Athenaeum* (12 Dec 1837), 881 ·

A. Guilbert, *A sketch of the life and labours of Joseph Mainzer* (1844) · B. Rainbow, *The land without music: musical education in England, 1800–1860* (1967)

Archives NL Scot., corresp. with George Combe

Likenesses W. Essex, lithograph, 1843, NPG · pencil drawing, BM, Add. MS 35027, fol. 61

Mair [Major], **John** (c.1467–1550), historian, philosopher, and theologian, was born into a farming family in the village of Gleghornie near Haddington, south-east of Edinburgh. He attended the grammar school at Haddington and went on, though not perhaps immediately, to university. Although it has been supposed that Mair was a student at St Andrews University, a passage in his commentary on the *Sentences* of Peter Lombard (*In primum sententiarum*, fol. 34r) makes it clear that as late as 1510 he had not been in that city. So far as is known his first university, exceptionally for a Scot, was Cambridge, where he spent a year, about 1491–2, at Godshouse, a college in the parish of St Andrew—perhaps the reason, a sentimental one, why he chose it.

Mair next moved to Paris, to the Collège de Sainte-Barbe. He received his master's degree in 1494 and the following year incepted as regent in arts, at the same time beginning his studies in theology under Jan Standonck at the Collège de Montaigu. With his colleague Noel Beda he took charge of the college in 1499, on Standonck's banishment from Paris, though about that time Mair also became attached to the Collège de Navarre.

In 1506, while still at Navarre, Mair took his doctorate in theology; he then began to teach theology at the Collège de Sorbonne, the pre-eminent college for theology in Paris and one of the great centres in Europe in that field. The membership, which consisted solely of doctors of theology of Paris, was a highly conservative body: as late as August 1523, after discussing the translations of sacred texts, it passed judgment that such translations from Greek into Latin, or from Latin into French, should be entirely suppressed and not tolerated. Throughout his life Mair remained a conservative on doctrinal matters, despite his periodic severe criticism of the behaviour of the church and of churchmen.

Mair was not wholly opposed to the encroachment of Renaissance humanism. When, against a background of official criticism, the Italian scholar Girolamo Aleandro introduced the teaching of Greek to Paris, Mair was one of his pupils. Aleandro wrote: 'There are many Scottish scholars to be found in France who are earnest students in various of the sciences and some were my most faithful hearers—John Mair, the Scot, doctor of theology and David Cranston, my illustrious friends' (Renaudet, 614 n.).

Few writers of his day were more prolific than Mair. He began in 1499 with a work on exponible terms such as *only*, *except*, and *in so far as*, expressions which contribute in interesting logical ways to the validity or otherwise of syllogisms. Thereafter he contributed to a wide range of fields: ethics, metaphysics, theology, biblical commentary, history, and above all logic, at which he was pre-eminent. As regards ethics, for instance, Mair was the first writer to see the need to place discussions of the appropriate treatment of the American Indians within a moral theological framework, and he went on to provide such a framework in his own *In secundum sententiarum* (1510). His great intellectual drive is demonstrated by the fact that, despite recurrent bouts of illness, he had within twenty years of the start of the series already completed at least forty-six books.

Mair left Paris in 1518 at the height of his reputation—a reputation based on three things. The first was the quality of his writings, many of which ran to several editions and became textbooks for a large number of students in Paris and across Europe. The second reason was the quality of his teaching. There are numerous indications of the respect which his teaching inspired. Juan Gomez, writing to Jerome de Canbanyelle, the Spanish king's envoy in France, said:

> I am following the theology course of John Mair with great interest as he is a deeply knowledgeable man whose virtue is as great as his faith ... May the eternal king deign to grant him long life that he may for long years be useful to our alma mater, the University of Paris.   (Lax, dedication)

The third reason for his reputation was his high-profile leadership of a team of scholars, in most cases former pupils of his, the majority from Scotland or Spain, including, among the Scots, David Cranston (*d.* 1512), George Lokert (*c.*1485–1547), Robert Galbraith (*c.*1483–1544), William Manderston (*c.*1485–1552), and Gilbert Crab (*c.*1482–1522); and, among the Spaniards, Juan de Celaya (*c.*1490–1558), Antonio Coronel (*d. c.*1521), Fernando de Enzinas (*d.* 1523), and Gaspar Lax (1487–1560).

Mair returned to Scotland to become principal of the University of Glasgow, a post he occupied for five years. He was also appointed vicar of Dunlop, in Ayrshire, and a canon of the Chapel Royal in Stirling. During this period he wrote not only his *History*, but also a set of questions on metaphysics, and about this time he also began work on his commentary on the *Nicomachean Ethics* of Aristotle. His commentary on the four gospels must also have been in incubation at that time.

Mair is perhaps best-known today for his *History of Greater Britain, England and Scotland* (*Historia majoris Britanniae tam Angliae quam Scotiae*—which may also be translated *A History of Mair's Britain*), published in 1521. It is possible that he wrote the book with the intention (among others) of promoting the idea of a union of the two countries; and the dedicatee, James V, son of James IV and grandson of Henry VII, was an appropriate symbol of the close relations between the two countries. But the reason Mair gave for writing the book was that 'you may learn not only the thing that was done but also how it ought to have been done'. He adds that the first law of the historian is to tell the truth and that it is 'of more moment to understand aright, and clearly to lay down the truth on any matter, than to use elegant and highly coloured language' (Mair, *History*, cxxxiii). Having told the truth, he had a good deal to say about what ought to have been done or ought not. For example, he criticized David I of Scotland for endowing religious foundations with great wealth in the early twelfth century, arguing that such endowments eventually caused great damage to the church. Similarly, in a discussion of the excommunication in 1217 of the Scottish king Alexander II, Mair writes:

> If it [an excommunication] is unjust to the degree of being null, it is in no way to be dreaded ... unjust excommunication is no more excommunication than a corpse is a man ... Whence it comes that we reckon a vast number of excommunicated persons who are in a state of grace.   (Mair, *History*, 172–3)

In June 1523 Mair left Glasgow for the University of St Andrews, where he was incorporated on the same day as Patrick Hamilton, who had studied under Mair's colleague Manderston at Paris, and who was, five years later, burned before the bishop's palace in St Andrews, so becoming the first martyr of the Scottish Reformation. Mair made it clear that he was utterly opposed to Hamilton's heretical views. His attitude emerges in the dedicatory epistle of his commentary on the gospel of St Matthew, published in 1529 shortly after Hamilton's martyrdom. The dedication is to Mair's friend Archbishop James Beaton of St Andrews, and congratulates Beaton for 'removing, not without the ill-will of many, a noble but unhappy follower of the Lutheran heresy'.

Apart from Hamilton, a strong reminder for Mair of his Paris days was the presence in St Andrews of his own former pupil George Lokert who a year earlier had been elected rector of St Andrews University. During the years 1523–5 Mair was assessor to the dean of the arts faculty and in this capacity served on a committee, on which Lokert also sat, which revised extensively, and along Parisian lines, the St Andrews forms of examination. As well as carrying out administrative duties during this period, Mair also gave courses of lectures in both arts and theology.

By 1526 Mair had returned to Paris, where he resumed his teaching career. During this period students working in his field, who may therefore be assumed to have heard him lecture, included John Calvin, Ignatius of Loyola, François Rabelais, and George Buchanan. Mair continued to write, and in 1529 published his commentary on the four gospels, *In quatuor evangelia expositiones*, in which, as in his *History*, he is frequently judgemental about matters of current concern. For instance, he attacks plural holdings, commendations, absenteeism, the extensive neglect of ordinary pastoral duties, and the personal laxness of many clergymen. In reference to such cases of ecclesiastical corruption, he says: 'Those deceive themselves who think that the approval of even the supreme pontiff can reconcile such things to the dictates of conscience' (Mair, *Commentary on Matthew*, fol. 80). But this criticism, as also his criticism of 'the grasping abbots who make things hard for the husbandmen' (*Commentary on Matthew*, fol. 74*v*), went hand in hand with Mair's unwavering support on doctrinal matters.

After the commentary on the gospels Mair produced one more book, his commentary on Aristotle's *Nicomachean Ethics* (1530). It was dedicated to another friend, Cardinal Thomas Wolsey. Mair gives three reasons for the dedication. The first, harking back to a theme of his *History*, was a shared love of 'our common country', for Scotland and England are 'enclosed in one Britain'. The second reason was their common religion and field of study, and the third was his desire to express his gratitude for the frequent hospitality he had enjoyed in England. It is in this dedicatory note that we learn of the year Mair spent at Godshouse in Cambridge, and we also learn here of Wolsey's offer to Mair of a teaching post in Christ Church, Oxford, the college that Wolsey had just founded. Indication of the genuineness of Mair's feelings for Wolsey is found in the fact that the dedication was written after Wolsey had fallen from grace and had been stripped of his honours.

A year after the publication of the commentary on the *Ethics*, Mair returned to Scotland, to St Andrews, where he remained until his death. A major source of information, the lengthy, chatty, often gossipy, introductory letters to his books dry up following that last publication, and his motives for returning to Scotland are unknown. Perhaps he was simply homesick. Years earlier in the dedication in his commentary on the fourth book of the *Sentences* he had written: 'Our native soil attracts us with a secret and inexpressible sweetness and does not permit us to forget it'.

Mair held two major appointments after his return to St Andrews. From 1534 he was provost of St Salvator's College, and he was also dean of the faculty of theology. Among the friends with whom he was reunited on his return was William Manderston, who had been elected rector of the university in 1530. During this lengthy final period of his life he tutored John Knox, who probably matriculated in St Andrews in 1529. In a famous phrase Knox refers to Mair as a man 'whose word was then held as an oracle on matters of religion' (*History of the Reformation*, 1.15). Knox was a leading instigator of the new order, whereas his teacher Mair was to the end a schoolman of the middle ages. Mair's scholasticism is nowhere revealed more clearly than in his summation of Aristotle at the start of his commentary on the *Ethics*: 'In almost all opinions he agrees with the catholic and truest Christian faith in all its integrity … in so great and manifold a work [the *Ethics*] if it be read as we explain it, you meet scarcely a single opinion unworthy of a Christian gentleman'. By the time Mair died, in 1550, just ten years before the Reformation in Scotland, he must have known that the world to which he had dedicated his life was gone for ever.

ALEXANDER BROADIE

Sources A. Broadie, *The circle of John Mair* (1985) • A. Broadie, *The shadow of Scotus* (1995) • J. K. Farge, *Biographical register of Paris doctors of theology, 1500–1536* (1980) • A. Renaudet, *Préréforme et humanisme à Paris pendant les premières guerres d'Italie, 1494–1517*, 2nd edn (Paris, 1953) • J. Durkan, 'The school of John Major: bibliography', *Innes Review*, 1 (1950), 140–57 • J. Mair, *Ethica Aristotelis peripateticorum principis cum Johannis Maioris theologi Parisiensis commentariis* (1530) • J. Mair, *In primum sententiarum* (1510) • I. Major [J. Mair], *Quartus sententiarum* (Paris, 1509) • *A history of greater Britain … by John Major*, ed. and trans. A. Constable, Scottish History Society, 10 (1892) • J. Mair, *In quatuor evangelia expositiones* (1529) • G. Lax, *De oppositionibus* (1512) • *John Knox's History of the Reformation in Scotland*, ed. W. C. Dickinson, 1 (1949), 15 • J. Mair, *In secundum sententiarum* (1510) • Durkan and Kirk, *The University of Glasgow, 1451–1577*, 155

Mair, Lucy Philip (1901–1986), social anthropologist, was born on 28 January 1901 at Banstead, Surrey, the eldest of four children of David Beveridge Mair (1868–1942) and his wife, Jessy (later Janet) Thomson Philip (1876–1959). Her father was a former mathematics fellow at Christ's College, Cambridge, who had moved on marriage to the civil service commission. Her mother was the daughter of a successful and educated Dundee builder. Lucy Mair referred in later life to her 'awful' family (La Fontaine, interview, 1983): her father was taciturn, her mother dominating and fond of society. From 1906 William Beveridge was a constant visitor to his cousin's house, and lived as a neighbour when in 1913 the Mairs moved to Campden Hill Gardens, Kensington. In 1914 David Mair became an Admiralty cryptographer and was responsible for breaking the coded messages that led to the arrest of Sir Roger Casement. Jessy joined William Beveridge in the Ministry of Munitions, moving with him to the Ministry of Food (where she rose to become director of bacon) and, after the war, to the London School of Economics where she became secretary and Beveridge became director. In 1933 David Mair retired from the civil service commission and thereafter hardly ever lived at home except for occasional visits. He died on 21 July 1942; six months later Jessy and William married.

William Beveridge had befriended Lucy and her sister Marjory: he took them rock-climbing, and went on a walking tour with Lucy. When Lucy was introduced to music by Gustav Holst, then teaching at St Paul's Girls' School, William gave her a silver flute. (A. A. Uthwatt, also a family friend, had given her a wooden one shortly before.) People gossiped about the Mairs' domestic arrangements, and about William's intimacy within the family, but relations were not conventionally immoral. William was clearly taken aback by the suggestion of one of the daughters on the day of David's funeral that he should marry Jessy; and it is unlikely that Beveridge had a physical relationship with Lucy's mother even after their marriage.

Lucy Mair was educated at St Paul's Girls' School in London, and then at Newnham College, Cambridge, where she read the classical tripos, graduating in 1922. She was employed for five years by Gilbert Murray as his secretary-assistant in League of Nations affairs. In 1927 she joined her mother and future stepfather at the London School of Economics, holding a lecturership in international relations. The school has no record of any discussion about the propriety of that appointment. Audrey Richards introduced Mair to B. Malinowski's seminar in anthropology because her work (on mandated territories) involved Africa, and Richards thought that no one could understand Africa unless they understood anthropology. Mair impressed the ebullient Malinowski, but she probably never succumbed to his undoubted charm. She remained a sceptical admirer, with deep reservations about his ideas, throughout her life. He nevertheless arranged for her to go to Buganda to do fieldwork, with a Rockefeller grant. Mair later thought that he had wished to protect her from the influence of A. R. Radcliffe-Brown who was to teach at the school while Malinowski was on leave. She

Lucy Philip Mair (1901–1986), by Lotte Meitner-Graf

spent nine months in Buganda, fieldwork that resulted in her first anthropological work, *An African People in the Twentieth Century* (1934). Returning to the London School of Economics in the early 1930s, she was a member of the group that included E. E. Evans-Pritchard, R. Firth, M. Fortes, M. Gluckman, A. Richards, and I. Schapera, as well as S. F. Nadel and, later, Edmund Leach. It was a stimulating though not always harmonious group, some of the members later dominating British social anthropology, and profoundly influential in America.

Mair continued to teach, taking responsibility for the courses intended to train colonial administrators; the students, at first mostly former members of the British army, later included talented young local nationals from the colonies themselves. Funding was eventually removed: the local students were to go to residential universities where they were thought to be less exposed to radical ideas. Mair also had a reputation, not justified, for believing that Africans were always right, and for being fierce, which may be: until the end of her life she was formidable in conversation, her vehement cleverness sometimes amplified by social awkwardness.

During the Second World War, Mair served in the Royal Institute for International Affairs and at the Foreign Office. On her return to the London School of Economics she was seconded to Canberra to teach members of the Australian military administration of Papua New Guinea. She had two spells there, and wrote *Australia in New Guinea* (1948), with an updated version a few years later. In 1947 she was promoted reader in colonial administration, changing the title to applied anthropology in 1955. She influenced a wide range of pupils at the school, from the young men in the colonial administrators' course to her

BA and PhD students in social anthropology from the 1950s. She became professor in 1963, and taught at the universities of Durham and Kent after her retirement in 1968.

Mair's early publications (many collected in *Studies in Applied Anthropology*, published in 1957, and *Anthropology and Social Change* which appeared in 1969) were concerned with the technical problems of colonial administration and with explaining the aims and achievements of anthropologists to an audience of administrators. *New Nations* (1963), *The New Africa* (1967), and *Anthropology and Development* (1984) summarized and consolidated that work, making it accessible to students and administrators. In the post-war years she began a series of short volumes based on her lectures: *Primitive Government* (1962), *Witchcraft* (1969), and *Marriage* (1971). In 1972 she published her *Introduction to Social Anthropology* which was still in print twenty-five years later. She was scornful of colleagues who would only write specialist work for an audience of their own kind, and these last four books, concise and expository accounts of the state of knowledge, brought her a much wider readership. They were often innovatory—*Primitive Government*, for instance, in its treatment of patronage—but she did not trumpet her resolution of theoretical issues. Her analysis of social organization was centred on individuals who made choices constrained by structures of opportunities and of rules of conduct: she argued, for example, that rural Africans who migrated to cities had more 'room for manoeuvre' (L. Mair, *Studies in Applied Anthropology*, 1957) to arrange their lives. She asked the British how they themselves would choose between good government and self-government, and then why they thought Africans should choose differently. She said she had ceased in the 1920s to imagine that socialism could make the world pleasant for everyone. In teaching the anthropology of economic and social development she said that development was not a separate discipline that could take the findings of anthropology and apply them: it was essential to know the social organization of developing peoples, to be able to assess the likely consequences of intervention.

In the 1960s and 1970s Mair was confronted by socialist and *marxisant* anthropologists who disparaged colleagues who had worked in colonies. She refused to admit that everything colonial administrators had done was completely wrong, and she insisted that they had thought they were doing good. Hers was an ironical anthropology—she compared people's intentions and choices with the outcome of their actions, and deployed as much compassion as the circumstances might allow. This proceeded from her conviction that fairness, social justice, had to be achieved and maintained first by careful scholarship and then by hard work. And this in turn derived from her early life. On her arrival at Newnham College in 1919 she had found women under intense pressure to prove themselves as good as men: the pursuit of anything other than excellence was a betrayal. But when she looked beyond her immediate family she found a world devastated of men, by men. Indeed, like many formidably clever women of her age, she never married; and her chapter in *Marriage* entitled 'What are husbands for?' suggests that she was still preoccupied with the contradictions, not to say absurdities, of women's assumption that men were superior beings, to be emulated.

Mair died in hospital at Blackheath, London, on 1 April 1986, of emphysema. She bequeathed her books to libraries at the London School of Economics, and made various other bequests. The bulk of her estate went to her sister Marjory's children, John and Lucy.   JOHN DAVIS

Sources P. B. Mair, *Shared enthusiasm: the story of Lord and Lady Beveridge* (1982) · R. Dahrendorf, *LSE: a history of the London School of Economics and Political Science, 1895–1995* (1995) · J. S. La Fontaine, A. MacFarlane, and others, interview with Lucy Mair (videotape), 1983, U. Cam., department of social anthropology · J. Davis, ed., *Choice and change: essays in honour of Lucy Mair* (1974) · personal knowledge (2004) · WWW
Archives FILM U. Cam., department of social anthropology, interview footage
Likenesses group photograph, 1918 (with her family), repro. in Mair, *Shared enthusiasm*, facing p. 31 · photograph, 1960?, U. Oxf., Institute of Social and Cultural Anthropology · L. Meitner-Graf, photograph, London School of Economics [*see illus.*]
Wealth at death £396,141: probate, 1986, CGPLA Eng. & Wales

Mair, Dame Sarah Elizabeth Siddons (1846–1941), promoter of women's education and campaigner for women's rights, was born on 23 September 1846 at 29 Abercromby Place, Edinburgh, the youngest of four daughters of Arthur Mair, soldier, and Harriot Murray Siddons, granddaughter of the famous actress Sarah *Siddons. She grew up in a spacious home in Edinburgh's elegant Georgian New Town, where she was taught by private tutors. For most of her life she had no financial worries, but briefly in her childhood the family wealth was drained by losses in railway shares. For a while her mother supplemented the family income by giving readings from English literature in their drawing room. 'We were', Sarah recalled, 'literally fed and clothed on Shakespeare' (Rae, 14).

In 1865 Sarah Mair founded the Edinburgh Essay Society, soon renamed the Ladies' Edinburgh Debating Society. From the age of nineteen to her ninetieth year she was its president. The debating society met, with the encouragement of her parents, each month in the Mair family dining room. It provided the first opportunity for Edinburgh women to discuss public affairs in a formal setting without inhibitions, and gave many of them a training in public speaking. In 1866 they boldly discussed female suffrage, and less boldly voted against it. The society's magazine, *The Attempt*, which became the *Ladies' Edinburgh Magazine* in 1876, attracted such influential writers as Charlotte Yonge and brought the society to the attention of a wide readership in Edinburgh and beyond.

It was around the debating society's large mahogany dining table, moved with the Mair family from Abercromby Place to 5 Chester Street in 1871, that all the organizations and committees associated with Sarah Mair were conceived. The society was at the centre of a web of influence and intrigue, visionary plans, and plodding spade work, from which grew the movement for women's

Dame Sarah Elizabeth Siddons Mair (1846–1941), by unknown photographer, *c.*1876

emancipation in the Scottish capital. Its early members included Louisa Lumsden, founder of St Leonards School; Miss Carmichael (later Mrs Stopes, mother of Marie); Flora Stevenson, who was elected to the first Edinburgh school board; Louisa Stevenson, first woman member of the parochial board; and the group which founded St George's correspondence classes, training college, and school, of which Miss Mair was the leader. Their fathers were bankers, lawyers, landowners, doctors, clergymen, and professors, who had the means to provide their daughters with the leisure and connections essential to their success.

Sarah Mair attended the meeting in October 1867 which led to the formation of the Edinburgh Ladies' Educational Association (from 1877 the Edinburgh Association for the University Education of Women). Their demand was for admission to the arts faculty of Edinburgh University on equal terms with men. She worked closely with Sophia Jex-Blake who campaigned for women's admission to the medical school. Miss Jex-Blake failed and had to turn to England. Sarah Mair, however, accepted a series of compromises which she saw as steps towards her destination. The Edinburgh Association persuaded Professor Masson and others to give a course of lectures for women leading to a diploma which would be of a similar standard to the university's MA degree. Over the next decade the classes attracted hundreds of successful candidates, including Miss Mair herself, but the university refused to offer more than a separate but equal certificate.

Mair's group recognized that equality in higher education was dependent upon equality in the earlier stages of education. In 1876 they placed an advertisement in *The Scotsman* offering a class for women wishing to pass the university local examinations, which were accepted as the entrance qualification for male undergraduates. The response was beyond their expectations. The St George's Hall classes in Randolph Place quickly expanded to offer correspondence courses for women all over Scotland and overseas. The advanced courses led to the LLA (lady literate in arts) certificate of St Andrews University. Sarah Mair was honorary secretary of the classes and the driving force behind them.

In 1886 the group opened St George's Training College. This was the first in Scotland to offer training for women teachers of secondary school subjects. St George's High School for Girls followed in 1888, the first academic girls' day school in Scotland to provide a curriculum which took girls to university entrance standard. Sarah Mair persuaded her close friend Mary Walker to be the principal of the college and school. St George's took the lead over the next thirty years in the education of girls and women in Scotland. Miss Mair remained an active member of its governing council until her death. In 1892 the Scottish universities finally admitted women, and St George's students were among the first graduates. Her skills in committee work were now much in demand. She helped, as treasurer, to promote a scheme for a women's hall of residence in Edinburgh University, Masson Hall, which opened in 1897. She chaired the committees of the Hospital for Women and Children and the Elsie Inglis Maternity Hospital.

Sarah Mair was, from the late 1860s, a strong proponent of women's suffrage. In a review published in *The Attempt* (under the pseudonym des Eaux) she commented favourably on the suffrage essay in Josephine Butler's *Women's Work and Women's Culture* (1869). In 1906 she became president of the Edinburgh National Society for Women's Suffrage and was later president of the Scottish Federation of Women's Suffrage Societies. She chaired debates between constitutionalists and those who favoured more militant tactics to obtain the suffrage, and was an important mediating influence at a period when tensions arose between the different women's societies in Edinburgh. After the partial grant of the franchise to women in 1918 she helped to transform the suffrage society into the Society for Equal Citizenship. Her aim on all her committees was to achieve practical results, 'without', as she put it, 'an inch of red tape about me'. She set out to demonstrate women's equality in her two chief leisure interests, archery and chess. A member of the Ladies' Chess Club, she always maintained that chess both formed and indicated the character of the player.

In 1920 Edinburgh University awarded Sarah Mair the honorary degree of LLD for her work for women's education. At the ceremony she was described as 'a lady whose single aim has been to give her sisters the key of knowledge and power and train them to use it with a due sense of responsibility' (Rae, 16). She was made a DBE in June 1931. Dame Sarah Mair died at the home of her niece, Winton, Hale Road, Wendover, Buckinghamshire, on 13 February 1941. Her funeral service was held in St Mary's Cathedral, Edinburgh.   NIGEL SHEPLEY

Sources St George's School for Girls, Archive, Edinburgh · L. M. Rae, *Ladies in debate, being a history of the Ladies' Edinburgh Debating Society, 1865–1935* (1936) · N. Shepley, *Women of independent mind: St George's School, Edinburgh, and the campaign for women's education, 1888–1988* (1988) · B. W. Welsh, *After the dawn: a record of the pioneer work in Edinburgh for the higher education of women* (1939) · L. Leneman, *A guid cause: the women's suffrage movement in Scotland* (1995) · d. cert.
Archives St George's School for Girls Archive, Edinburgh, corresp. and articles | U. Edin., MSS on founding of Masson Hall
Likenesses photograph, c.1876, St George's School for Girls, Edinburgh [*see illus.*] · J. H. Lorimer, oils, 1928, St George's School for Girls, Edinburgh · photographs, St George's School for Girls, Edinburgh · photographs (aged eighteen, thirty and eighty), repro. in Rae, *Ladies in debate*, facing pp. 16, 36
Wealth at death £5183 11s. 1d.: confirmation, 3 April 1941, CCI

Mair, William (1830–1920), Church of Scotland minister, was born at Savoch, Aberdeenshire, on 1 April 1830, the eldest son and fifth among the twelve children of James Mair, the parochial schoolmaster, and his wife, Christian Johnston (d. 1846), a member of a local farming family. His father was a licentiate of the Church of Scotland and from his earliest days Mair aspired to the ministry. From the local parish school he went on to Aberdeen grammar school and to King's College and Marischal College, Aberdeen, graduating MA in 1849, with special distinction in mathematics. He was licensed in July 1853, becoming assistant to Dr Joseph Paterson in Montrose, but his health quickly broke down. This was to be the most long-lasting bout of ill health in a life largely governed by physical frailty. In his autobiography Mair recorded 'five times I have been taken out of the jaws of death' (Mair, 159), and his longevity was the result of his taking great care in health matters. He had, however, recovered sufficiently by October 1861 that he could be ordained to the mission church in the mining community of Lochgelly, Fife. In April 1865 he was translated to the parish of Ardoch in Perthshire and from there, in 1869, to Earlston in Berwickshire, where he was to remain until his retirement. On 21 August 1866 he married Isabella, daughter of David Edward of Balruddery, Dundee.

It was while he was in Perthshire that Mair's interest in church law was first aroused over a case which came before the general assembly of 1867, involving the introduction of a church organ in Crieff. This interest was deepened by the workings of the Church Patronage Act, which came into force in 1875. Eventually Mair was to distil his knowledge in a *Digest of Church Laws* (1887), which went to four editions and became a standard text. He was honoured with the degree of DD by Aberdeen University in 1885. He was prominent in other church matters, and when the threat of disestablishment loomed he published

The Truth about the Church of Scotland (1891). He was instrumental in enlarging the Assembly Hall in 1893–4 and was appointed moderator of the general assembly in 1897. After his retirement to Edinburgh in 1903 he worked for reunion between the established church and the United Free Church, publishing a series of articles on the subject in *Blackwood's Magazine*. His was a passionately held conviction, and it clearly irritated him that the cause of reunion had not been pursued with more urgency.

Mair's personality emerges positively from the pages of *My Life* (1911) as generous and straightforward, and he enjoyed a reputation for spirituality. He died in his sleep on 26 January 1920. LIONEL ALEXANDER RITCHIE

Sources W. Mair, *My life* (1911) · W. S. Crockett, *Dr Mair of Earlston* (1920) · *Fasti Scot.* · *The Times* (28 Jan 1920) · *The Scotsman* (27 Jan 1920) · *DNB* · *WWW* · *CCI* (1920)
Likenesses G. Reid, oils, 1896, Church of Scotland assembly hall, Edinburgh · photograph (in old age), repro. in Mair, *My life*, frontispiece
Wealth at death £7202 14s. 7d.: confirmation, 4 Sept 1920, *CCI*

Maire, Christopher (1697–1767), Jesuit, son of Christopher Maire of Hartbushes, co. Durham, and Frances Ingleby of Lawkland, Yorkshire, was born on 6 March 1697, and entered the English College at St Omer about 1714. He was admitted to the Society of Jesus on 7 September 1715 at the novitiate at Watten. In 1718 he moved to the college at Liège to study philosophy. After a course of teaching at St Omer he returned to Liège for his theology studies and was ordained priest about 1727. He lectured in mathematics and logic there, returning to St Omer in 1733 as prefect of studies for a year. Back at Liège he taught Hebrew and theology until in 1739 he was appointed to the English College in Rome, becoming rector in 1744. He held that office until 1750. He returned to St Omer in March 1757, and died at the English Jesuit house in Ghent on 22 February 1767.

Alban Butler calls Maire 'an able mathematician'. At Liège, Maire had begun a study of astronomy and to make observations, and while in Rome was able to devote himself to this study. Pope Benedict XIV entrusted to him and Father Boscovich the task of making several precise meridian measurements together with a detailed map of the Papal States, their report being published in Rome in 1755, which concerned the shape and size of the earth as well as the geographical map of the Papal States, *De litteraria expeditione per pontificiam ditionem ad dimetiendos duos meridiani gradus et corrigendam mappam geographicam, jussu et auspiciis Benedicti XIV pont. max.* Between 1744 and leaving Rome in 1750 Maire published a number of other astronomical works as well as a tract on the blessed Trinity in manuscript written in 1737.

THOMPSON COOPER, rev. G. BRADLEY

Sources G. Holt, *The English Jesuits, 1650–1829: a biographical dictionary*, Catholic RS, 70 (1984), 156 · G. Holt, *St Omers and Bruges colleges, 1593–1773: a biographical dictionary*, Catholic RS, 69 (1979), 169 · Gillow, *Lit. biog. hist.*, 4.393 · J. Kirk, *Biographies of English Catholics in the eighteenth century*, ed. J. H. Pollen and E. Burton (1909), 154 · A. M. C. Forster, 'The Maire family of county Durham', *Recusant History*, 10 (1969–70), 332–46 · D. A. Bellenger, ed., *English and Welsh priests, 1558–1800* (1984), 84 · M. E. Williams, *The Venerable English College, Rome* (1979) · G. Holt, '"An able mathematician": Christopher Maire', *Recusant History*, 21 (1992–3), 497–502

Maire, William (1704–1769), Roman Catholic priest, was born on 3 January 1704, the fifth son of Thomas Maire (1672–1752) of Hardwick, co. Durham, and Lartington Hall, North Riding of Yorkshire, and his wife, Mary Fermor of Tusmore, Oxfordshire. He entered the English College, Douai, on 16 August 1719, was ordained priest at Tournai on 23 December 1730, and became professor at Douai, first of rhetoric and afterwards of philosophy. He was chaplain at Lartington 1735–41, and served briefly at Gilesgate, in the city of Durham, before moving to the adjacent mission in Old Elvet in 1742. He was appointed vicar-general to Bishop Francis Petre in 1759 and was nominated as Petre's coadjutor in the northern district in 1767. He was consecrated bishop of Cinna *in partibus* on 29 May 1768. He was in ill health by this time and in November he retired to Lartington Hall, where he died on 25 July 1769. He was buried in the family vault in the parish church of Romaldkirk, and a memorial plaque was later installed in the mausoleum in the grounds at Lartington Hall. He published a translation of Charles Gobinet's *Instruction de la jeunesse en la piété chrétienne* (1687) in London in 1758 under the title *A Treatise of the Holy Youth of our Lord and Saviour Jesus Christ*. THOMPSON COOPER, rev. LEO GOOCH

Sources G. Anstruther, *The seminary priests*, 4 (1977), 184 · A. M. C. Forster, 'The Maire family of county Durham', *Recusant History*, 10 (1969–70), 332–46 · Gillow, *Lit. biog. hist.* · L. Gooch, *Paid at sundry times: Yorkshire clergy finances in the eighteenth century* (1997), no. 61
Archives Ushaw College, Durham, register of visitations

Mairet [*née* Partridge; *other married name* Coomaraswamy], **Ethel Mary** (1872–1952), hand-weaving revivalist and author, was born on 17 February 1872 at High Street, Barnstaple, north Devon, the first of three children of James Partridge (*d.* 1914), dispensing chemist of Barnstaple, and his wife, Mary Ann, *née* Hunt (*d.* 1927). She was brought up in Barnstaple and educated in north London, then briefly at the Municipal Science and Arts Schools, Barnstaple. In 1899 she was awarded the teachers' diploma in pianoforte (LRAM) from the Royal Academy of Music, London; she then found employment as a governess in London and Bonn. Returning to Devon in 1902 she met the young Ananda Kentish *Coomaraswamy (1877–1947), a brilliant, rich, Anglo-Ceylonese geologist, who later became an art historian. They married on 19 June the same year and from 1903 to 1906 travelled in Ceylon, where Coomaraswamy carried out an official mineralogical survey, and Ethel attempted to revive native embroidery; the pair simultaneously studied and collected the indigenous arts and crafts. Their resulting definitive book, containing reports, drawings, and numerous photographs (mostly taken by Ethel Coomaraswamy), was published on their return to England in 1907.

In 1907 and 1910 the Coomaraswamys visited India together, adding to their art and textile collections. Their home and workplace in these years was, however, Norman Chapel near Chipping Campden in the Cotswolds, where C. R. Ashbee, architect and designer, had established his Guild of Handicraft. (Fred Partridge, Ethel

Mary's brother, was a jeweller at the guild.) Ashbee restored and converted the imposing chapel, which rapidly became the centre for an artistic circle, leading Janet Ashbee to recall the striking, dark-haired Ethel Coomaraswamy 'by night coming out like a brilliant moth in eastern plum, cherry and orange colours'. At this time Ethel made her first experiments in hand-weaving.

By 1912 the marriage had broken down and, aged forty, Ethel Coomaraswamy built an isolated bungalow, Broadlys, on the coast near Barnstaple. It contained rooms for weaving and dyeing, where she worked alone; a Samoyed dog and occasional visitors her only company. She secured a divorce and on 28 May 1913 married Philippe (later Philip) Auguste Mairet (1886–1975), a former draughtsman of Ashbee's and secretary of Coomaraswamy's, and fifteen years her junior. They set up workshop and home at the Thatched House, Shottery, near Stratford upon Avon; here Mairet wrote her influential treatise *A Book on Vegetable Dyes* (1916), published by Hilary Pepler, and participated in London craft exhibitions such as the 'Englishwoman'.

A visit to Hilary Pepler and Eric Gill in 1916, who were at the centre of the community of artists forming the Guild of Sts Joseph and Dominic on Ditchling Common, precipitated Mairet's move to the Sussex village. Here she built Gospels, in Beacon Road, the home with weaving workshop and dye house she occupied for thirty-two years, and in which she trained over 130 people: work girls, apprentices, and, in the 1940s, student teachers.

In the 1920s, cloth produced at Gospels was at its simplest: plain weaves in strong, vegetable-dyed colours contrasted with undyed, natural colours using hand-spun British wools and imported cotton and silk yarns. Yardage was made into garments or furnishings, rugs and blankets were woven, and accessories such as stoles, scarves, and ties were sold. Mairet exhibited throughout the country, and orders were regular.

In 1931 Ethel and Philip Mairet separated, following the collapse of their venture running the New Handworkers' Gallery, in London. This changed Ethel Mairet's previously sociable and gentle character, making her austere.

During the mid-1930s an influx of European assistants brought more textured weave patterns to the cloth, through greater technical ability and an interest in combining high quality, hand-spun fibres with industrially produced yarns. These themes persisted until wartime shortages confined Mairet to undyed cotton or chemically dyed Welsh woollen yarns. The war curtailed her travelling which, in the 1930s, had embraced many European countries, especially Denmark, while researching her book *Handweaving Today, Traditions and Changes* (1939). That year she was created an RDI (royal designer for industry), the first woman so honoured by the Royal Society of Arts.

In the 1940s, reduced staff, advancing age, and an interest in craft education caused Mairet to create and hire out 'textile portfolios', with informative booklets, to schools and colleges. They drew on her own weavings as well as her extensive collection of world textiles which, hanging in the barn-like weaving-room, had so impressed visitors

to Gospels. Ethel Mairet died in her sleep at Gospels on 18 November 1952 and was buried at Dyke Road cemetery, Brighton; she was an inspiration to the crafts movement; one who was called, by the Japanese master potter Shoji Hamada, 'the mother of English hand-weaving'.

MARGOT COATTS

Sources M. Coatts, *A weaver's life: Ethel Mairet* (1983) · M. Coatts, *A weaver's life: Ethel Mairet—a selection of source material* (1995) · R. Lipsey, *Coomaraswamy, 3: His life and work* (1977) · A. K. Coomaraswamy, *Mediaeval Sinhalese art* (1908) · A. Crawford, *C. R. Ashbee: architect, designer and romantic socialist* (1985) · C. H. Sisson, ed., *Philip Mairet: autobiographical and other papers* (1981) · b. cert. · m. certs. · d. cert.
Archives Holburne Museum of Art, Bath, corresp., journals and papers | King's AC Cam., Ashbee journals · Museum of Fine Arts, Boston, William Morris Hunt Memorial Library, A. K. Coomaraswamy's photograph albums
Likenesses photographs, c.1903–1945, Holburne Museum of Art, Bath
Wealth at death £6139 10s. 3d.: probate, 8 July 1953, CGPLA Eng. & Wales

Màiri nighean Alasdair Ruaidh [Mary MacLeod] (c.1615–c.1707), Scottish Gaelic poet, was born in Rodel, Isle of Harris, the daughter of Alasdair Ruadh (Red Alexander, or Alexander MacLeod). Through him she was closely related to the family that produced the chiefs of the MacLeods of Harris and Dunvegan, and on her mother's side she was related to the MacDonalds of Clanranald.

Màiri seems to have spent many years serving as a nurse to MacLeod of Dunvegan's family, but to have enjoyed family privileges because of her relationship to the chief's family. The earliest datable poem attributed to her was an elegy for the Mackenzie laird of Applecross, presumably composed in 1646. Her elegy for the MacLeod laird of Raasay can be dated to 1671. Most of her surviving songs are connected with the MacLeods of Dunvegan, some looking back to her early years there, some dating from the end of the seventeenth century and the early years of the eighteenth century. In one of these songs she recalls her teenage years at Dunvegan:

> dancing merrily on a wide floor,
> the fiddle-playing as I went to sleep,
> the pipe-playing wakening me in the morning.
> (*Gaelic Songs*, 34–5)

This song has a reference to Ruairidh Mòr, the Dunvegan chief who died in 1626, and may well have memories of his regime. Her latest datable poem is an elegy for Sir Norman MacLeod of Bernera Harris, who died in 1705. At one point she fell out with the Dunvegan chief, apparently because she composed what he regarded as inappropriate songs, and she was exiled to Mull and its neighbouring islands, but she won her way back to Dunvegan by composing more conventional praise poetry.

Apparently unlettered, Màiri inherited some of the traditional praise-skills of the professional poets, who used classical Gaelic and strict metrics, but she used vernacular language and metrics. These new styles came into prominence in the seventeenth century, but have much older roots. Her verse has great fluidity, and a musical quality often enhanced by the airs of the songs. This body of verse helps to illustrate the transition that was taking place in the seventeenth century from the more formal court-life of the Gaelic chiefs to the less traditional role they were to adopt, embracing non-Gaelic lifestyles. Despite these movements, Màiri's songs are securely anchored in Gaelic tradition. Women poets and songmakers in Gaelic have a long and productive tradition extending from the sixteenth to the eighteenth century in particular, but Màiri is the earliest of the women poets to have a sizeable body of poems firmly ascribed to her. These poems by women are strongly anchored in the community. Màiri's verse does not always appear to have been welcomed by her male contemporaries. Her entire career was punctuated by enforced exiles of one sort or another, and while some of these may be accounted for without reference to her poetry or gender, one does not get the impression that this early Gaelic woman poet had an easy time of it. She died about 1707, and was buried face down, apparently at her own direction, at Rodel.

Màiri's verse appears in collections from 1776 (the Eigg collection), the McLagan manuscripts (second half of the eighteenth century), and a number of nineteenth-century sources. The first detailed edition of her work was edited by James Carmichael Watson in 1934 and republished by the Scottish Gaelic Texts Society in 1965. Various additions and emendations were supplied by William Matheson in his paper 'Notes on Mary MacLeod: (1) her family connections; (2) her forgotten songs' (*Transactions of the Gaelic Society of Inverness*, 41, 1953).   DERICK S. THOMSON

Sources *Gaelic songs of Mary MacLeod*, ed. J. C. Watson, Scottish Gaelic Texts, 9 (1965) · W. Matheson, 'Notes on Mary MacLeod', *Transactions of the Gaelic Society of Inverness*, 41 (1953), 11–25 · D. S. Thomson, *An introduction to Gaelic poetry*, 2nd edn (1990), 132–5 · J. Mackenzie, *The beauties of Gaelic poetry* (1841)
Archives U. Glas., McLagan MSS

Mais, Alan Raymond, Baron Mais (1911–1993), engineer and businessman, was born on 7 July 1911 at Rathmore, Winn Road, Southampton, the only child of Captain Ernest Mais, a master mariner, and his wife, Violet Geraldine, *née* Thomas. He was educated at Banister Court School, Hampshire, and later at the College of Estate Management, a part of London University, where he trained as a surveyor. Upon leaving he entered the construction industry, first with Richard Costain in 1931 and later, in 1936, with Parker Construction. After two years with Parker he established his own consulting practice, A. R. Mais & Partners. On 12 September 1936 Mais married Lorna Aline, the daughter of Stanley Aspinall Boardman, a wool merchant of Addiscombe in Surrey, with whom he had two sons and a daughter.

As a young man Mais became interested in military affairs, and in 1929 he joined the Territorial Army, being commissioned in the Royal West Kent regiment. Two years later he transferred to the Royal Engineers (RE), and he remained a member of the RE throughout the Second World War and afterwards, again as a Territorial, until his retirement in 1958. The occasion of his transfer from the Royal West Kents merits comment. While leading a detachment of that regiment on a march, Mais was overtaken by a mounted column of sappers. The RE commanding officer suggested, perhaps not entirely seriously, that Mais would be better off in a mounted unit. This advice, Mais later admitted, tempted him, and the transfer duly followed.

When war started Mais, by then a major, went first to France and then to Iraq and Iran with special forces. He was twice mentioned in dispatches and awarded the Russian order of Patriotic War for his efforts in keeping supply routes to Russia open. After returning to Britain late in 1943, he became involved in the Mulberry harbour project leading to what was perhaps the most daunting period in his military career. Two artificial harbours were to be constructed on the Normandy coast: a British one at Arromanches and an American one a few miles to the west. When construction began immediately after D-day (6 June 1944) Mais, by now a lieutenant-colonel, was in charge of constructing the pierheads and floating roadways at the British harbour under Colonel S. K. Gilbert of the Royal Engineers, who commanded the port construction force.

Progress, though hectic, went well at first, but disaster struck in the form of a gale which raged from 19 to 23 June and was reckoned to be the worst storm in the channel for eighty years. Because of the determination and courage of those on site, with Mais playing a leading role, the British harbour, though badly damaged, was saved. Unfortunately the nearby American harbour had to be abandoned. For his services in Normandy, Mais was again mentioned in dispatches and appointed OBE (military division).

Mais's beach task force had been part of the First Canadian Army, and he remained with the Canadians in the advance to the Rhine. Promoted full colonel, Mais became deputy chief engineer in Antwerp, and as hostilities came to an end he took charge of ports, waterways, and engineering in the Twenty-First Army group.

Once the war was over Mais returned to his consultancy firm. In 1948 he joined the board of the contractors Trollope and Colls, becoming joint managing director and chairman in 1963 and retiring in 1968 when the firm was taken over by Trafalgar House. During this period he held numerous other directorships, mainly, but not entirely, in construction concerns.

In the mid-1970s the affairs of the Peachey Property Corporation, then under the control of Sir Eric Miller, were found to be in some disorder and Mais, who had become a non-executive board member four years earlier, played a significant part in exposing Miller's mismanagement. The Department of Trade inquired into the company's activities but placed no blame on Mais, who, its inspectors reported, 'was largely instrumental in reforming the company'. After Miller's suicide in 1977, Mais became company chairman and, for a short time, its chief executive. He relinquished the latter role when a new managing director was appointed but remained chairman.

As well as being an astute businessman, Mais was strongly inclined towards public service, and this marked the last thirty or so years of his life. From the 1960s onwards he served on numerous committees, mainly connected with the construction industry; these included the National Contractors' Group, the industry's 'Little Neddy', and governmental committees on the placing and management of contracts and works and on buildings emergency organization. He was also on the British National Export Council's committee for Canada and for two years was a member of the land commission.

Although on the surface Mais did not appear to be a party-political enthusiast, he had a considerable political pedigree, especially in local government. At the general election in 1945 he contested the Orpington constituency for Labour but was unsuccessful. After that somewhat quixotic venture, it was perhaps less surprising than many thought that a Labour prime minister, Harold Wilson, should appoint him to a life peerage in 1967, in recognition of his services to the construction industry. He played an active, but not unduly prominent, part in the Lords until his death, sitting successively on the Labour, Liberal, and finally Liberal Democrat benches.

In local affairs, especially in the City of London, Mais was more conspicuous, becoming master of the Cutlers' Company and a freeman of the City and of the Paviors' Company. He was an alderman in the Walbrook ward from 1963, a sheriff in 1969–70, and lord mayor in 1972, the first peer to be elected to that office since records began in 1192. He was a lieutenant of the City, a justice of the peace and, further afield, from 1976 deputy lieutenant of the county of Kent.

Beside his contribution to politics and public service, Mais was committed to education, and during his term as lord mayor he served, as is customary, as chancellor of City University, which had been founded as the Northampton Institute, a pre-eminent engineering school. He had been a member of the university's governing council since 1965. The chancellor's duties were largely ceremonial, and at the end of his year in office Mais was appointed pro-chancellor, in effect chairman of the governors, a post he held until 1984.

Apart from firm guidance as chairman, Mais's major contribution to the university was the setting up of a fund in his name which raised a substantial sum to establish a new banking and finance unit in the university's business school. The fund was generously supported by the Bank of England and by many leading British and foreign banks and other City institutions. This contribution is recognized by the annual Mais lectures, which are held at the university. Almost as an aside, Mais encouraged the foundation of the university symphony orchestra.

In the course of a long and active life Mais earned many honours and distinctions. In addition to those already mentioned, he held the territorial decoration the ERD, the order of the Aztec Eagle and the order of merit of Mexico, as well as honorary degrees from several universities. In addition, he was a member of several learned societies,

including the institutions of civil and structural engineers, and he was a fellow of the Royal Academy of Engineering. He died on 28 November 1993 at the Sloane Hospital, 125 Albermarle Road, Beckenham, Kent, survived by his wife and children.   WILLIAM HOWIE

Sources private information (2004) [Lady Mais] · *The Times* (30 Nov 1933) · *Royal Engineers Journal* (April 1994) · institution records, Inst. CE · university records, London City University · G. Hartcup, *Code name Mulberry* (1977) · *New Civil Engineer* (19 June 1980) · *New Civil Engineer*, supplement (June 1944) · *Debrett's Peerage* · m. cert. · d. cert.
Archives Institution of Mechanical Engineers, London, corresp. with Lord Hinton
Wealth at death £366,374: probate, 24 Feb 1994, *CGPLA Eng. & Wales*

Mais, Stuart Petre Brodie (1885–1975), writer and radio broadcaster, was born on 4 July 1885 at St Mary Street, Ladywood, Birmingham, the only child of John Brodie Stuart Mais (1860/61–1941), rector of Tansley, Derbyshire, and his wife, Hannah Horden, *née* Tamlin (*d.* 1939).

'S. P. B.', as Mais was known, was educated at Heath grammar school, Halifax, and Denstone College, Staffordshire. He worked as a teacher for two years and then attended Christ Church, Oxford, in 1905. He won a blue for cross-country running and graduated with third-class honours in mathematics and English literature in 1909. From 1909 to 1920 he was a schoolmaster, mainly in English, at Rossall School from 1909 to 1913, where he fought hard to 'bring about an educational reform that most of my colleagues regarded as unnecessary and dangerous' (Mais, *All the Days*, 55). He married on 6 August 1913 and had two daughters with his first wife; Mais does not name his wife in his autobiographies and refers to her as a 'comparative stranger' (ibid., 59). He became an assistant master at Sherborne School in September. He became an officer in the Officers' Training Corps in 1913 and remained as such, much against his will, when the First World War broke out. In July 1914 during an operation to remove his appendix Mais 'died' but was resuscitated.

While teaching, Mais edited Shakespeare for schools and published *An English Course for Army Candidates* (1915) and a series of articles in *A Public School in War Time* (1916). He wrote his first novel, *April's Lonely Soldier* (1916), in epistolary form, followed by a second, *Interlude* (1917), which so closely detailed life at Sherborne that he was forced to resign in 1917. From Sherborne he went to Tonbridge School, where he was elected examiner in English by London University. Immediately after the war he was made professor of English at the new cadet college at Cranwell, but was forced to resign yet again over what were considered to be his 'experimental' teaching methods. His textbook *An English Course for Schools* (1918) sold 20,000 copies.

From 1918 to 1931 Mais was successively literary critic on the *Evening News* (1918) and *Daily Express* (1921–3), and literary editor of the *Daily Graphic* (1923–6). From 1926 to 1931 he was leader writer and book reviewer on the *Daily Telegraph*. This was Mais's last regular employment. About 1922 he had married his second wife, Jill (*b.* 1905?), and in 1927 they rented a large eighteenth-century house in

Southwick, Sussex. A keen cricketer, he became president of the cricket club and when the local council tried to stop cricket on the village green he led the opposition. Truculent by nature, he enjoyed his role of a 'latter day Hampden' and was undeterred by threats of legal action (Mais, *All the Days*, 14). But he overreached himself by refusing to pay his rates, and prosecution led to his eviction. A newly elected council restored the villagers' ancient right and today a plaque on the house commemorates his spirited fight.

In 1932 the BBC commissioned Mais to travel through England, Scotland, and Wales and describe his experience in seventeen talks. They were published later in that year under the title *This Unknown Island*. The book was reprinted three times in as many months. The need to compress his material into 20-minute talks curbed his habit of slack and gossipy writing and produced one of his best books.

This book, together with the earlier *See England First* (1927) and *England's Pleasance* (1935), undoubtedly helped to awaken townspeople to the recreational uses of the English countryside and the need to protect it from the expanding suburbs. In pursuit of this aim Mais worked closely with the railways to produce book-length guides to several counties, footpath guides, and ramblers' booklets. One of his most adventurous ideas was to run night trains from London so that jaded office workers could be shepherded to the top of the south downs by Mais to watch the sunrise. On the first occasion forty walkers were expected; 1440 turned up.

Throughout the 1930s Mais gave radio talks in the United States and Britain. During the Second World War Mais's voice became familiar in most households through his almost daily radio talks entitled *Kitchen Front*. The war restricted his travelling, but as soon as it ended he found publishers, tourist agencies, and foreign governments eager to fund his holidays abroad in return for the holiday guides which he wrote *en route*. These were leisurely cruise holidays on which Mais would take his wife, Jill, and two daughters. Books on Norway, Madeira, Austria, Italy, Spain, Majorca, South America, the Caribbean, South Africa, and many others, flowed throughout the fifties and sixties, culminating in the *Round the World Cruise Holiday* (1965). In *Who's Who* he gave his recreation as 'travel of any sort anywhere'. Mais also wrote two rambling, evasive, and anecdotal autobiographies: *All the Days of my Life* (1937) and *Buffets and Rewards* (1952), several further lightweight novels, and some books of literary appreciation. The latter, such as *From Shakespeare to O. Henry* (1917), lacked any pretension to academic literary criticism but were likeable and enthusiastic studies.

Publishers' records show that few of Mais's books sold more than 3000 copies and none of the 200 or so is now in print. When asked, 'How many books have you written?' he replied, 'Too many'. Yet he continued writing until he was in his late eighties. He died of heart failure on 21 April 1975 at Compton House Nursing Home, Compton Road, Lindfield, Sussex.   BERNARD SMITH

Sources S. P. B. Mais, *All the days of my life* (1937) • S. P. B. Mais, *Buffets and rewards* (1952) • S. P. B. Mais, 'My village, yesterday and today', *Daily Telegraph* (3 July 1965) • *The Times* (24 April 1975) • L. Stapleton, 'S. P. B. Mais: the man who loved Sussex', *Sussex Life* (Sept 1975) • *WWW, 1971–80* • S. J. Kunitz and H. Haycraft, eds., *Twentieth century authors: a biographical dictionary of modern literature* (1942) • b. cert. • d. cert.

Archives U. Reading L., corresp. | U. Reading L., letters to George Bell & Sons • U. Warwick Mod. RC, corresp. with Victor Gollancz

Likenesses Schmidt, photograph, repro. in Mais, *All the days of my life*, frontispiece • photograph, repro. in Mais, *Buffets and rewards*, frontispiece

Maistre, LeRoy Leveson Laurent Joseph de [*known as* Roy de Maistre] (1894–1968), painter, was born LeRoi Leviston de Mestre on 27 March 1894 at Maryvale, Bowral, New South Wales, Australia, the ninth of the ten children of Etienne Livingstone de Mestre (1832–1916), grazier and horse trainer, and his wife, Clara Eliza (1852–1934), daughter of George Taylor Rowe and his wife, Phoebe Melville. The de Mestre and Rowe families settled in Australia in 1818 and 1822 respectively. Etienne de Mestre achieved fame as one of Australia's most successful horse trainers, but by the time of his son's birth he had lost money through land speculation. During LeRoi de Mestre's youth the family lived an impoverished though genteel lifestyle in a succession of rented properties around Bowral, running a dairy and a fashionable guest house. De Mestre was educated at home by his elder sisters and at the local state school, and he took art and music lessons at a local Dominican convent.

In 1913 de Mestre moved to Sydney, where he studied the viola at the state music institution (later the Sydney Conservatorium of Music). He also attended Julian Ashton's Art School and the Royal Art Society; at the latter he was taught by Antonio Dattilo Rubbo, who encouraged his students to experiment with modernist techniques and styles. He first exhibited in 1916, using the name Roi de Mestre. That year he also served briefly in the Australian Imperial Force and then as a medical orderly in the Australian Army Medical Corps. About that time he met Charles Gordon Moffitt, senior medical officer at Kenmore Hospital, Goulburn, New South Wales, and with him devised a colour treatment—consisting of painting hospital walls and furniture in a variety of colours—for shell-shocked soldiers.

De Mestre's background in art and music, together with his interest in modern art, the information available on experiments by overseas artists, the activities of a local colour/music musician, A. B. Hector, the active branch of the theosophical society in Sydney (C. W. Leadbeater made his headquarters in the city from 1914 to 1920), and a lively regional cosmopolitan culture, provided the milieu for him and a colleague, Roland Wakelin, to embark on a series of unique works which were to secure his place in Australian art history. He devised a system in which he allied the seven notes of the octave with the seven colours of the spectrum. Using series of charts, keyboards, and colour wheels based on the system, in 1919 he and Wakelin held an exhibition, 'Colour in art', in which they showed five room designs and eleven small landscape works, simplified in form, flattened in perspective, and painted in highly toned, non-representational colour. The works were the precursors of the first abstract paintings done in Australia. The only documented extant abstract work from the period, however, is de Mestre's *Rhythmic Composition in Yellow Green Minor* (1919, Art Gallery of New South Wales, Sydney). Post-war conservatism inhibited further experimentation.

In 1923 de Mestre won the Society of Artists travelling scholarship and travelled and worked in Europe until 1925. On his return his work, such as *Boat Harbour (St Jean de Luz)* (1925, New England Regional Art Museum, Armidale, New South Wales) showed a strong influence of English post-impressionism. After two major exhibitions in 1926 and 1928 at the Macquarie Galleries in Sydney, teaching, lecturing on modern art, and doing decorative work de Mestre left Australia in 1930, never to return. He settled in London and changed his working name to Roy de Maistre. He later added the names Laurent and Joseph and changed the spelling of Leviston to Leveson. He made an auspicious entry into the European art world: a solo exhibition at the Beaux Arts Gallery, London (July 1930); a joint exhibition of paintings and furniture with Francis Bacon in Bacon's studio at 7 Queensberry Mews (August 1930); an association with the mystic Dimitrije Mitrinovic which resulted in several large surrealist works such as *New Atlantis* (c.1933, priv. coll.); a solo exhibition at the Mayor Gallery (1934); the opening of an art school with Martin Bloch (1934); the devising, with Robert Wellington, of a scheme to provide financial support for artists (1935); and a return to his colour/music experiments, in the form of abstract paintings such as *Arrested Phrase from a Haydn Trio in Orange-Red Minor* (1935, National Gallery of Australia, Canberra) and a plan for a colour/music ballet and film (1934-7).

In the 1940s de Maistre's work matured to a decorative-cubist style usually executed by progressive abstractions of a more realistic version of the subject: for example, the four versions of *The Carol Singers* (1942, 1943; Art Gallery of New South Wales, Sydney, and priv. coll.). Many works were based on the interior of his home and studio at 13 Eccleston Street, Belgravia, London, where he settled in 1937. After a formal conversion to the Roman Catholic faith in 1949, he became known largely as a modernist religious painter: his best-known work in this genre is the series of the stations of the cross (1956) in the Great Corridor of Westminster Cathedral, London. Larger versions of most of the stations, such as the *Pietà* (the thirteenth station of the cross; 1953, Tate collection) and *Christ Falls under the Cross* (the ninth station of the cross; c.1956, Ashmolean Museum, Oxford), are held in private and public collections.

In spite of solo exhibitions at the Calmann Gallery, London (1938), the Leeds City Art Gallery (1943), the City of Birmingham Museum and Art Gallery (1946), the Adams Gallery, London (1950), and the Hanover Gallery, London (1953), and a large retrospective exhibition at the Whitechapel Art Gallery in London (1960), de Maistre remained impoverished all his life, depending on patrons such as Rab Butler and his wife, Sydney Courtauld, who financed his Eccleston Street studio, and the writer Patrick White who purchased a large number of works. Herbert Read and John Rothenstein provided substantial professional support. Roy de Maistre was appointed CBE in 1962. He died, unmarried, of a stroke at his home in Eccleston Street on 1 March 1968, aged seventy-three. After his funeral service at the Brompton Oratory, London, on 5 March, and a requiem mass in the same church on the 8th, his ashes were scattered privately.

HEATHER JOHNSON

Sources H. Johnson, *Roy de Maistre: the English years, 1930–1968* (1995) · H. Johnson, *Roy de Maistre: the Australian years, 1894–1930* (1988) · J. Rothenstein, *Modern English painters, 2: Lewis to Moore* (1956) · *Roy de Maistre: a retrospective exhibition of paintings and drawings from 1917–1960* (1960) [exhibition catalogue, Whitechapel Art Gallery, London, May–June 1960] · R. de Mestre, 'Modern art and the Australian outlook', *Art in Australia*, 3/4 (1925) · Tate collection, John Rothenstein MS 8726 · Art Gallery of New South Wales, Sydney, Roy de Maistre MSS · Australian National Gallery, Canberra, Roy de Maistre MSS · Whitechapel Art Gallery, London, Roy de Maistre MSS · R. Morrow and K. Dundas, 'Roy de Maistre', *Art and Australia*, 2/1 (1964), 38–42 · D. Thomas, 'de Maistre, Leroy Leveson Laurent Joseph, 1894–1968', *AusDB*, vol. 8 · E. Gertsakis, 'Roy de Maistre and colour music, 1916–1920c.', diss., Fine Arts IV, Melbourne University, 1975 · M. Eagle, *Australian modern painting between the wars, 1914–1939* (1990)
Archives AM Oxf. · Art Gallery of New South Wales, Sydney · Art Gallery of South Australia, Adelaide · Art Gallery of Western Australia, Perth · Carrick Hill, South Australia · Contempory Art Society, London · Leeds City Art Gallery · Man. City Gall. · Mayor Gallery, London, sales books · Museums, Art Galleries and Records Service, Leicester · National Gallery of Australia · National Gallery of Victoria, Melbourne · priv. coll. · priv. coll., diaries · Queensland Art Gallery, Brisbane · Tate collection · Thos Agnes and Sons Ltd, London, day book, stock book, picture file · Whitechapel Art Gallery, London | HLRO, Beaverbrook MSS · Royal Arch., MSS Ra Duke of York · Trinity Cam., Butler MSS
Likenesses photograph, c.1930–1939, repro. in Johnson, *Roy de Maistre: the English years*, frontispiece · photographs, repro. in Johnson, *Roy de Maistre: the English years*, pp. 12, 21, 29, 30, 59, 97, 187, 205, 211 passim · photographs, repro. in Johnson, *Roy de Maistre: the Australian years*, frontispiece, pp. 43, 55, 98
Wealth at death £13,713: probate, 1968, *CGPLA Eng. & Wales*

Maitland, Agnes Catherine (1849–1906), college head, was born on 12 April 1849 at 12 Gloucester Terrace, Paddington, Middlesex, the second daughter of David John Maitland, a merchant, formerly of Chipperkyle, Galloway, and his wife, Matilda Leathes Mortlock. When Agnes was five years old the family moved to Liverpool. She received her education at home, though in 1867 she attended the first course of lectures organized by the North of England Council for Promoting the Higher Education of Women. The family was Presbyterian and Agnes grew up to be active in Liberal politics, accomplished as a public speaker. She was involved in the domestic science training school founded in Liverpool by Fanny L. Calder in 1876, and in 1877 became an examiner to the Northern Union Schools of Cookery. From 1881, under the auspices of the Liverpool school, she was a visiting examiner to elementary schools. She produced cookery books which became standard for a generation, and frequently lectured on hygiene and housekeeping. She also wrote

Agnes Catherine Maitland (1849–1906), by William Strang, 1906

improving novels for girls and young women; one of these, *Rhoda* (1886), was reissued in 1920. For a time she was secretary to the Egypt Exploration Fund.

When in 1889 Miss Maitland was appointed warden of Somerville Hall, Oxford, Lord Aberdare described her as 'a thorough lady' (Adams, 45), possibly defensively, if some had contrasted Miss Maitland with her predecessor, Miss Shaw-Lefevre. Somerville now had a principal for whom it was a home and a livelihood. Her ambitions for the hall were unlimited. In 1893 electricity replaced oil lamps, and the building of a gatehouse and lodge (demolished in 1932 when the Darbishire Quadrangle was built) gave Somerville a presence on the Woodstock Road. In 1894 the hall became a college.

Miss Maitland knew that to achieve this status Somerville must have its own tutors. Her initiative was at first considered a betrayal (especially of the Society of Home Students) by the Association for Promoting the Education of Women (AEW), which had arranged teaching for women students under the redoubtable leadership of Mrs Bertha Johnson. Peace was secured by the payment of fees to the AEW. She strongly supported the proposal in 1896 to admit women to Oxford degrees; on its defeat she criticized the suggestion of John Percival, bishop of Hereford, that a separate Queen Victoria University for Women should be established. Where her sympathies were

engaged, Margery Fry wrote, 'Miss Maitland was eager, and sometimes even vehement' (S. M. F., 24). In 1899 Miss Maitland called back Margery Fry, then languishing at home with her parents and unmarried sisters: she was given the title of librarian. Five years later the impressive library building, designed by Champneys, was opened. Munificent gifts followed, including the library of John Stuart Mill and that of Amelia B. Edwards.

Miss Maitland was a tall woman of powerful presence. The tutors, Phoebe Sheavyn said, all liked her but they sometimes had to stand up to her. Her physical and mental energy pervaded the small community. A gymnasium was equipped: dons and students played hockey together. Miss Maitland was forty when she came to Somerville. No one else was over thirty-five. She had a sense of ceremony: there was an arm-in-arm procession into dinner, still served in two separate buildings. She established traditions but did not impose petty rules and restrictions. Though by nature something of an autocrat she had been early trained in democratic procedure. Former students were to be involved in the college council, as electors and members. It was said of her that though she was a brilliant administrator she had a tendency to economize in small matters. This frugality perhaps left its mark on the college. Many of its members, in a later consumerist age, carried this tradition with pride.

Miss Maitland respected the devotion to pure scholarship shown by her tutors, but her own educational interests were in practical affairs. She was a member of the educational section of the National Union of Women Workers and of the committee of the University Association of Women Teachers. In 1904 she was one of a deputation to Lord Londonderry, president of the Board of Education, urging the need for more women as inspectors of elementary schools where the majority of the teachers were women. She was particularly concerned for the teaching and practice of hygiene in state schools. The British Association appointed her to a committee on school hygiene. She was recognized as an eloquent exponent of the history and development of state education.

Agnes Maitland died, after a long illness, at 12 Norham Road, Oxford, on 19 August 1906, and was buried three days later in Holywell cemetery. In 1910, when Miss Penrose was principal, a new residential block was called Maitland. Between this and the original old house rose her memorial, the college hall. There, every evening until the latter half of the twentieth century, when increasing numbers made this impossible, the whole college dined formally, as Miss Maitland would have wished.

ENID HUWS JONES

Sources S. M. F. [M. Fry], 'Agnes Catherine Maitland', *Oxford Magazine* (24 Oct 1906), 23–4 • *Englishwoman's Review*, 38 (1906), 282–3 • *Men and women of the time* (1899) • *Somerville College register, 1879–1971* [1972] • P. Adams, *Somerville for women: an Oxford college, 1879–1993* (1996) • V. Farnell, *A Somervillian looks back* (1948) • Somerville College Archives, Oxford • private information • E. H. Jones, *Margery Fry: the essential amateur* (1966) • *DNB* • *The Times* (22 Aug 1906) • b. cert. • *CGPLA Eng. & Wales* (1906)
Archives Bodl. Oxf., letters to Edith Marvin

Likenesses W. Strang, crayon drawing, 1906, Girton Cam. [*see illus.*] · J. Gunn, oils, 1931 (after photograph), Somerville College, Oxford · W. Strang, chalk drawing, Somerville College, Oxford
Wealth at death no value given: sealed in London, 7 Nov 1906, *CGPLA Eng. & Wales*

Maitland, Anthony, tenth earl of Lauderdale (1785–1863). *See under* Maitland, James, eighth earl of Lauderdale (1759–1839).

Maitland, Sir Arthur Herbert Drummond Ramsay-Steel- [*known as* Sir Arthur Steel-Maitland], **first baronet** (1876–1935), politician, was born in India on 5 July 1876, the second son of Colonel Edward Harris Steel of the Bengal staff corps and his wife, Emmeline Drummond. His parents were from Scottish gentry backgrounds. Arthur Steel, as he was known until 1901, was educated at Rugby School and gained a scholarship to Balliol College, Oxford, where he obtained first classes in *literae humaniores* (1899) and jurisprudence (1900), and was in 1899 the university's Eldon law scholar and president of the Oxford Union Society. In 1900 he was elected a fellow of All Souls. He left Oxford for London in 1900, intending to read for the bar, but did not complete his bar studies. He did, however, continue with his academic studies at the newly founded London School of Economics. On 10 July 1901 he married Mary Ramsay-Gibson-Maitland (1871–1944), with whom he had four children—two sons and two daughters. His wife was the daughter of a Scottish baronet, Sir James Ramsay-Gibson-Maitland, and was heir to the estates of Bainton in Midlothian and the historic domains of Bannockburn and Sauchie in Stirlingshire. The Sauchie estate was to be the principal family home, but they also acquired a London residence at 72 Cadogan Square.

On his marriage Steel changed his name by royal licence to Ramsay-Steel-Maitland, and thereafter was generally known simply as Steel-Maitland. A devout member of the Church of Scotland, he was elected an elder of the church in 1902 at St Ninian's, Stirling. In 1906 he became a member of the church's general assembly, and from 1910 to 1924 he was an elder of St Columba's in Pont Street, London. In 1902 he began his career in public life as unpaid secretary to the chancellor of the exchequer, C. T. Ritchie. When, in the 1903 budget, Ritchie repealed a 1 shilling duty on corn which Joseph Chamberlain had wished to use for purposes of imperial preference, Steel-Maitland resigned his position. Six years later he had occasion to discuss this action, and noted with pride that 'as a Tariff Reformer I left Mr. Ritchie when he took off the corn duty' and that 'mine was the first formal resignation on account of the tariff reform policy' (Steel-Maitland to Sir Charles Follett, 11 Nov 1909, Steel-Maitland MSS, GD 193/144/100). He took up the position again when Austen Chamberlain became chancellor following Ritchie's resignation in the autumn. At the general election of January 1906 Steel-Maitland stood as the unsuccessful Conservative candidate for the Rugby division of Warwickshire. Like many of the younger generation of Conservatives, he was an admirer of Joseph Chamberlain, and a devotee of the cause of tariff reform. Indeed, he became a member of the

secret 'extreme' tariff reform group known as the 'confederacy'. However, he had other political interests and in particular social policy. Between 1906 and 1910 he organized seminars on social questions for Conservative politicians and writers at All Souls. In 1907 he was appointed an assistant commissioner of the poor-law commission, and jointly with Rose Squire undertook an examination of the casual-labour problem, unemployment, and housing conditions. He also undertook a nationwide survey of 'boy labour' problems with Norman Chamberlain, and contributed an essay on labour issues to the collection of Conservative essays, *The New Order* (1908). In 1908 he journeyed to Canada as secretary to Lord Milner, an experience which entrenched Steel-Maitland's interest in imperial problems and forged a bond between the two men.

Thus by the time Steel-Maitland was elected Conservative MP for East Birmingham in January 1910 (a seat he defended successfully in December that year) he had established a reputation as an expert on imperial and social/economic policy questions and was widely regarded as a coming man in the Conservative ranks. His status in the party was confirmed in September 1911, when he became the first person to hold the newly created post of Conservative Party chairman. As chairman, Steel-Maitland presided over important changes in the party's organizational structure. Conservative central office was expanded in terms of both its staffing levels and office accommodation. A press bureau was established to provide Conservative newspapers with advance copy of major speeches by members of the party leadership, and the Conservative publicity machine was further strengthened when the activities of many previously autonomous Conservative pressure groups, such as the Anti-Socialist Union, were co-ordinated by the new central office regime. He also ensured that it became established practice to have parliamentary candidates actively in place well before an election. During his period as party chairman, the post was established as pivotal to the party's operation: his reforms of the party machinery were to be of great benefit to the party in the inter-war years and were to remain in place until the Maxwell-Fyfe reforms in the late 1940s. As chairman, Steel-Maitland was also keenly interested in policy making, and one of his first actions was to oversee the establishment of the Unionist Social Reform Committee.

In May 1915 Steel-Maitland was made under-secretary for the colonies in Asquith's coalition government. He found his post frustrating, and he complained that it provided him with little scope to exercise his talents (Steel-Maitland to Hugh Clifford, 11 Sept 1917, Steel-Maitland MSS). In September 1917 he moved to the more satisfactory position of joint parliamentary under-secretary at the Foreign Office and parliamentary secretary to the Board of Trade—the latter post was *ex officio* in his capacity as the first head of the department of overseas trade at the Foreign Office—and he devoted much effort to improving the consular service.

On 13 July 1917 Steel-Maitland was created a baronet, and a high-flying political career seemed to beckon. At the general election of 1918 he was returned for the constituency of Erdington in Birmingham. In July 1919 he resigned from the Lloyd George government coalition, ostensibly on the grounds that he found it impossible to bridge the demands of the Foreign Office and the Board of Trade, though there had also been a falling-out with the then newly appointed president of the Board of Trade, Auckland Geddes, over administrative responsibility for overseas trade. In addition Steel-Maitland was angry that what he had regarded as a promise of a place in the cabinet had not been kept. After leaving office he devoted much of his time to his business interests. He had been a director of the United Dominions Trust bank since 1911, but soon after his resignation his old friend and mentor Lord Milner invited him to become managing director of Rio Tinto Zinc, and he held this position until 1924. As an active back-bench MP, he represented New Zealand in 1922 as a delegate to the League of Nations, and worked with the league on the care of Greek refugees during the Chanak crisis of that year. He was also president of the joint parliamentary advisory council on industrial and social problems, and played an important role in framing the Criminal Law Amendment Act of 1922 in relation to industrial disputes. In February 1922 he jointly authored, with Lord Robert Cecil, a memorandum critical of the Lloyd George government, which was circulated to back-bench Conservative MPs, and he seemed well placed to benefit from the downfall of the coalition in October 1922. But in September he had been taken ill and, although he retained his seat at the November general election, he was *hors de combat* when Andrew Bonar Law formed his Conservative administration.

By 1924 Steel-Maitland was fit enough to resume an active political role, and when Stanley Baldwin led the Conservatives to triumph at the general election of 1924 Steel-Maitland accepted a place in the cabinet as minister of labour. He was not, however, Baldwin's first choice for the post, and was offered the position at Neville Chamberlain's suggestion only after Sir Robert Horne had declined it. During the mining dispute and the subsequent general strike in 1925 and 1926, he was not one of the cabinet 'hawks'. Although he felt that the miners' position was unreasonable, and criticized the Samuel commission for being too sympathetic to their case, he was also irked by the intransigence of the coal owners. He felt that the solution to the problems of the mining industry, and indeed to many other British industries, was wholesale reorganization, and he was thus critical of those in cabinet, such as Winston Churchill, who he felt were pursuing political rather than industrial ends. By nature and conviction a conciliator, Steel-Maitland wished to see the government act as an 'honest broker' on the industrial front. In 1926 he presided at an international convention on working hours and was disappointed when the convention's proposals for standardized, shorter hours were not ratified by the British government. He was equally disappointed by the failure of the Mond–Turner talks of 1928–9, which he had seen as a sign that employers and employees could achieve a constructive relationship beneficial to industry

as a whole. He was much exercised by the problem of unemployment, and sought cures as well as palliatives. His main legislative achievement as a minister of labour, the 1927 Unemployment Insurance Act, extended the scope of insurance coverage but at the same time sought to discourage 'idlers'. He was also the chief architect of the Industrial Transference Board, established in January 1928, which aimed to facilitate the movement of unemployed workers from depressed to more prosperous areas. Intriguingly, he was one of the first members of the Conservative hierarchy to examine in detail John Maynard Keynes's proposals for extensive public works as a solution for unemployment, and, although he was sceptical about Keynes's ideas, and remained committed to 'sound finance', his interest in and grasp of economic theory led him to adopt a more flexible position than most Conservatives and indeed other politicians of the time. His sceptical but sophisticated approach to proposals to tackle the unemployment problem was expressed in *The Trade Crisis and the Way out* (1931), a reprint of articles which he had contributed to *The Observer* in November and December 1930.

Steel-Maitland lost his seat at the general election of 1929, when he was narrowly defeated by his Labour opponent, but he rapidly re-entered parliament as MP for Tamworth in December 1929, and retained the seat until his death. During the Conservatives' two years in opposition, from 1929 to 1931, he did not take part in the intrigues against Baldwin: 'I cannot play false', he wrote (Steel-Maitland to T. G. Scott, 17 Oct 1930, Steel-Maitland MSS). His political honesty was not, however, rewarded by the offer of a cabinet post in Ramsay MacDonald's Conservative-dominated National Government, and insult was added to injury when his former parliamentary secretary, Sir Henry Betterton, was appointed minister of labour. Steel-Maitland became a largely inactive, almost detached, government back-bencher, who rarely intervened in Commons' debates. In the summer of 1933 he was invited by the Rockefeller Foundation to undertake a four-month tour of the United States, and his observations there led to a broadly sympathetic account of Roosevelt's New Deal experiments, *The New America* (1934).

On 30 March 1935 Steel-Maitland went to Rye in Sussex to play golf with his friends N. R. Swann, Sir Assheton Pownall, and E. R. Peacock, and, having played a near-perfect drive, he collapsed and died of a heart attack. His funeral service was held at St Columba's on 2 April 1935, and he was buried the next day at St Ninian's Church, Stirling. A memorial service was held at St Margaret's, Westminster, on 4 April. His wife survived him and his son Arthur James Drummond (1902–1960) inherited his title and estates. Described as 'a disappointed man' (*Sunday Dispatch*), Steel-Maitland seemed to have had all the attributes for reaching the highest level in politics: 'tall and well looking' (*Brighton Post*, 1 April 1935), he was an excellent athlete and sociable, even clubbable, with a reputation for integrity. He possessed an acute intellect and was well versed in a variety of subjects, especially economics. Yet he never rose politically above the middle ranks and was effectively dispensed with at fifty-five. His exclusion from the National Government may stem from his having advised Baldwin against joining such an administration in July 1931, but he was not the only leading Conservative to take up that stance. More personal factors were at work in thwarting his ambitions. Leo Amery, an old ally from the days of the tariff reform campaign, noted that 'I do not think he would have achieved much more in life. He was too non-committal, and there was something in his manner that never quite did justice to his natural kindness' (Barnes and Nicholson, 393). His weakness as a speaker in the House of Commons was well known. J. C. C. Davidson recorded in September 1926 that a speech by Steel-Maitland on the situation in the coalfields was generally thought to be 'deplorable', and that another of his statements had been 'unconvincing and rambling' (James, 258). Even a generally sympathetic figure, Leo Amery, described a speech by him on tariffs in January 1930 as 'incoherent' (Barnes and Nicholson, 60). He also gained a reputation for being ineffective as a minister, although this may have been a coded reference to his unwillingness to take the offensive against the trade union movement. His cleverness, especially in the realm of economics, may not have been an asset in a party which in his time was suspicious of intellectuals. Nevertheless, Steel-Maitland was an important and intriguing figure. As a Conservative intellectual, his ideas on economic and social questions and on industrial relations are important benchmarks for any serious study of Conservative ideas on these subjects, and they were the subject of a positive appreciation by William Beveridge (*The Listener*). The *Daily Telegraph* described Steel-Maitland as 'too human' (*Daily Telegraph*), and certainly he must be the only cabinet minister who disguised himself as a down-and-out in order to investigate the operation of labour exchanges, which he did when minister of labour.   E. H. H. GREEN

Sources NA Scot., Steel-Maitland MSS · DNB · *Sunday Dispatch* (31 March 1935) · *Daily Telegraph* (1 April 1935) · *The Listener* (10 April 1935) · E. H. H. Green, *The crisis of conservatism: the politics, economics, and ideology of the conservative party, 1880–1914* (1995) · J. Ramsden, *The age of Balfour and Baldwin, 1902–1940* (1978) · P. Williamson, *National crisis and national government: British politics, the economy and empire, 1926–1932* (1992) · Burke, *Peerage* (1939) · *The empire at bay: the Leo Amery diaries, 1929–1945*, ed. J. Barnes and D. Nicholson (1988) · *Memoirs of a Conservative: J. C. C. Davidson's memoirs and papers, 1910–37*, ed. R. R. James (1969) · CCI (1935)
Archives NA Scot., corresp. and papers | Balliol Oxf., corresp. with A. L. Smith · BL, corresp. with Lord Cecil, Add. MS 51071 · BLPES, corresp. with Lord Beveridge · BLPES, corresp. with tariff commission · Bodl. Oxf., Milner MSS · Bodl. Oxf., Round Table corresp. · Bodl. Oxf., corresp. with Lord Selborne · HLRO, corresp. with Lord Beaverbrook · HLRO, corresp. with Andrew Bonar Law · HLRO, corresp. with Herbert Samuel · Lpool RO, corresp. with seventeenth earl of Derby · NA Scot., corresp. with A. J. Balfour · Trinity Cam., Baldwin MSS · U. Birm., A. Chamberlain MSS · University of Sheffield, corresp. with W. A. S. Hewins · Wilts. & Swindon RO, corresp. with Viscount Long
Likenesses W. Stoneman, photograph, 1918, NPG · T. Cottrell, cigarette card, BM, NPG
Wealth at death £109,139 15s. 10d.: confirmation, 1935, CCI

Maitland, Charles, third earl of Lauderdale (c.1620–1691), politician and judge, was the third son of John Maitland, second Lord Maitland of Thirlestane (d. 1645), created earl of Lauderdale in 1624, and his wife, Lady Isabel (1594–1638), daughter of Alexander *Seton, first earl of Dunfermline; John *Maitland, later duke of Lauderdale (1616–1682), was his elder brother. Little is known of his early life. On 18 November 1652 he married Elizabeth, younger daughter and heir of Richard Lauder, thereby acquiring the sizeable estate of Hatton in Edinburghshire. Shortly after Charles II's restoration Maitland was made master and general of the Scottish mint, and on 15 June 1661 was sworn a privy councillor. Despite having no previous legal training or judicial experience, he was admitted an ordinary lord of session on 8 June 1669, assuming the title Lord Hatton, and that year was also elected a parliamentary commissioner for the shire of Edinburgh and chosen as one of the lords of the articles. As he entered the highest levels of Scottish politics, his elder brother had acknowledged his reservations to the earl of Tweeddale the previous November, but relied upon his 'hope [that] he will mend his faults' ('Letters', ed. Paton, 169), since 'he promises me to be a very good bairn' (NL Scot., MS 7023, fol. 299).

In February 1671 Hatton was appointed treasurer-depute and on 12 May 1672 created a baronet. After Lauderdale quarrelled with Tweeddale in 1674 Hatton assumed an increasingly prominent position, taking sole responsibility for the administration of Scottish affairs during his brother's absences in London. Widely unpopular, he became the focus of intense criticism and Tweeddale himself later commented that during the 1670s Hatton's power was so immense that 'the liberties, lives and fortuns of the wholl kingdom depended mor upon him & wer mor at his disposal then ever they have upon any Commissioner or favourite, yea almost any of our Kings' (NL Scot., MS 3134, fol. 119). In 1675 a Scottish informant provided the earl of Shaftesbury with an account of Hatton's controversial attempts to influence town council elections in Edinburgh, but acknowledged that he could also have 'wearied yow with a thousand passages of the Impertinent, passionat Carriage of the Lord Hatton … in whom there is as much folly, Insolency and bossines as ever met in one breast'. Hence the informant wondered why Lauderdale 'will needs mak a Statesman of him', even 'tho God and nature had made him a mad foole' (PRO, PRO 30/24/5/291). The following year William Douglas, third earl of Queensberry, wrote to the duke of Hamilton believing that since 'all complain off him and ar censible of his baisnes', the Scottish political establishment should not delay in 'pitching upon him as the sacrefeis', confident that all political grievances would be removed by that 'single act of justeice to the nation off destroying him' (*Hamilton MSS*).

During the duke of York's temporary Scottish residence in the late 1670s and early 1680s Hatton lived in Canongate House (now Queensberry House), Edinburgh, and aimed to extend his family's political influence by having the property extensively redesigned to incorporate a prominent belvedere tower oriented towards the palace of Holyroodhouse. Following the decline of his brother's political influence, his fortunes began to change, however, and he was found guilty of perjury by the Scottish parliament in 1681, relating to a previous miscarriage of justice in the case of the covenanter James Mitchell in 1678, and further allegations insinuated his likely involvement in bribing witnesses in other covenanting trials. In June 1682 Hatton was also deprived of his office of general of the mint when he was convicted of embezzlement and adulteration of the coinage, having not only circulated a defective silver coinage and issued a light copper coinage, but also having purchased the nation's superior coinage at a vastly reduced rate to use as bullion, culminating in the decision to close the mint itself until 1687.

On his brother's death on 20 or 24 August 1682 Hatton succeeded as third earl of Lauderdale, but did not acquire the additional titles of duke of Lauderdale and marquess of March, which then became extinct. With Sir John Falconer he was found guilty of malversation the following year, but their original fine of £72,000 was reduced to £20,000 by Charles II and on 11 March 1686 Lauderdale was readmitted as a privy councillor. During the revolution of 1688–9 he was sent to Edinburgh Castle 'upon information and refusing to swear allegiance' (Melville, 180), but no further action was taken and he was probably released soon afterwards. He and his wife had two daughters and six sons, of whom the eldest, Richard *Maitland (1653–1695), became fourth earl of Lauderdale when his father died on 6 June 1691. Their second son, John *Maitland, became the fifth earl. CLARE JACKSON

Sources W. C. Mackenzie, *The life and times of John Maitland, duke of Lauderdale* (1616–82) · R. W. Lennox, 'Lauderdale and Scotland: a study in politics and administration, 1660–1682', PhD diss., Columbia University, 1977 · J. C. L. Jackson, 'Royalist politics, religion and ideas in Restoration Scotland, 1660–1689', PhD diss., U. Cam., 1998 · A. J. Patrick, 'The political opposition to Lauderdale in Scotland, 1660–1679', MA diss., U. Birm., 1957 · *The manuscripts of the duke of Hamilton*, HMC, 21 (1887) · 'Letters from John, second earl of Lauderdale, to John, second earl of Tweeddale', ed. H. M. Paton, *Miscellany … VI*, Scottish History Society, 3rd ser., 33 (1939), 111–240 · A. Dalzel, *Short genealogy of the family of Maitland, earl of Lauderdale* (1875) · J. Lowrey, 'Archives and archaeology: the prehistory of Queensbury House, Edinburgh', *Scottish Archives*, 5 (1999), 29–40 · *Ham House*, National Trust, revised edn (1999) · Earl Tweeddale, memorial, NL Scot., Yester MS 3134, fol. 119 · T. Wilson, 'Narrative of the state of affairs in Scotland', PRO, PRO 30/24/5/291 · W. H. L. Melville, ed., *Leven and Melville papers: letters and state papers chiefly addressed to George, earl of Melville … 1689–1691*, Bannatyne Club, 77 (1843) · *DNB*

Archives NL Scot., papers | BL, letters to his brother, duke of Lauderdale, to Charles II, Add. MSS 23113–23249 · Buckminster Park, Grantham, Lincolnshire, Tollemache MSS, corresp. and MSS · NL Scot., Yester MSS · NRA Scotland, priv. coll., volumes of copy letters to Sir Archibald Primrose

Likenesses G. van Honthorst, portrait, Ham House, Richmond-upon-Thames, London

Maitland, Charles (1815–1866), author, was born at Woolwich in Kent, on 6 January 1815, the eldest son of Charles David Maitland (1785–1865) and his wife, Elizabeth Adye Miller, and nephew of General Sir Peregrine *Maitland.

His father was at one time a captain in the Royal Artillery, and served with some distinction at the end of the Napoleonic Wars. After graduating BA in 1824 from St Catharine's College, Cambridge, however, he was ordained and for the last forty years of his life was minister of St James's Chapel at Brighton. Like many others in the early nineteenth century, he took up the study of biblical prophecy, writing two works on the subject, probably while still in the army, and pursuing his interest in it when he became a minister. This interest was obviously passed on to his son, Charles, who was educated first at a large private school at Brighton, and afterwards, when he chose medicine for his profession, in the house of a general practitioner in London. He studied in Edinburgh for three years, and graduated MD in 1838, the title of his inaugural essay being 'Continued fever'. After visiting Malta, Italy, Greece, and Egypt in company with a patient, he returned to England and was admitted an extra-licentiate of the London College of Physicians in July 1842. On 5 November 1842 he married Julia Charlotte [see Maitland, Julia Charlotte (1808–1864)], writer and traveller, widow of James Thomas (d. 1840), an Indian judge in the Madras presidency. Her maiden name was Barrett, and her mother was a niece of Fanny Burney, Madame D'Arblay.

Maitland practised for a few years at Windsor, but his interests drew him more towards theology. He matriculated at Magdalen Hall, Oxford in 1848, graduated BA (with a second class in classics) in 1852, and was ordained deacon in the same year, and priest the following year. He was at first curate at All Saints, Southampton, then at Lyndhurst, Hampshire, and afterwards in the Forest of Dean, Gloucestershire. But his mind gave way, and after being for some years separated from his family, he died at his home, 81 Upper Stamford Street, London, on 26 July 1866, and was buried in the Brompton cemetery.

While at Rome, Maitland was attracted to the catacombs, and, being a good amateur artist, made numerous drawings. In 1846 he published *The church in the catacombs: a description of the primitive church of Rome, illustrated by its sepulchral remains*; a second revised edition followed in 1847. This was apparently the first popular book on the subject, and reflected Maitland's opinion that the Roman church of his day bore little resemblance to that of the Apostolic era. In 1849, while at Oxford, he published *The Apostles' School of Prophetic Interpretation: with its History Down to the Present Time*. This work was clearly premillennial in outlook, although Maitland was somewhat critical of the futurists of that time for what he perceived to be their relative lack of interest in early church figures such as Barnabas and Irenaeus. In this emphasis he appears to have differed somewhat from his father, whom he none the less cited in his study with considerable approval.

W. A. GREENHILL, rev. D. ANDREW PENNY

Sources personal knowledge (1893) · private information (1893) · Boase, *Mod. Eng. biog.* · Venn, *Alum. Cant.* · Bishop's transcripts, St Mary, Woolwich, Kent, 1815, PRO, vol. DW, T 1772 · d. cert. · *CGPLA Eng. & Wales* (1866) · m. cert. · d. cert. [Julia Charlotte Maitland]

Wealth at death under £300: probate, 17 Oct 1866, *CGPLA Eng. & Wales*

Maitland, Edward (1824–1897), author and spiritualist, was born on 27 October 1824 at Ipswich, the second son of Charles David Maitland (1785–1865) and his wife, Elizabeth Adye Miller. His father had been a captain, Royal Artillery, serving in battle at the end of the Napoleonic War, a Cambridge graduate, and from 1828 until his death a perpetual curate at St James's Chapel, Brighton. Maitland was the younger brother of Charles *Maitland (1815–1866) and Brownlow (1816–1902) and nephew of General Sir Peregrine *Maitland (1777–1854), a distinguished soldier and colonial governor. His family were evangelicals and his adverse reaction to their strict principles of belief appears to have coloured his thinking later in life. Maitland was educated first at Morris's large private school in Brighton (1839–43) and at Gonville and Caius College, Cambridge, from 1843 to 1847 (BA 1847). Although intended by his father for the church, he was beset by doubt and emigrated to America in 1849, where he settled for a time in California among the goldminers ('forty-niners'), and eventually to Australia where he became a commissioner of crown lands. There he married Esther, but within a year was widowed and left with an infant son. The son eventually became a surgeon-major in the Bombay medical service, but Maitland apparently took no part in his upbringing.

Maitland returned to England in 1857, intending to devote himself to literary work and searching for a perfect system of thought by which to rule his life. The ensuing ten years are undocumented, but by the late 1860s he emerged to become a contributor to several journals, including *The Spectator*, *The Examiner*, *The Athenaeum*, the *Edinburgh Review*, the *Fortnightly Review*, and the *Westminster Review*. In 1868 he published *The Pilgrim and the Shrine, or, Passages from the Life and Correspondence of Herbert Ainslie, B. A., Cantab.*, a largely autobiographical novel which was well received. This resulted in his moving into society where he was favourably regarded by his contemporaries Richard Monckton Milnes, first Baron Houghton, and Sir Francis Hastings Doyle. *The Higher Law* followed in 1869, a religious romance, and *By and By: an Historical Romance of the Future* (1873) which emphasized mystical material and was set in an African utopia.

By and By attracted the attention of Anna *Kingsford (1846–1888), a 37-year-old woman with advanced views on vegetarianism, anti-vivisection, and women's rights, but also possessed of strong poetical tendencies; she invited him to visit her and her clergyman husband at his rectory at Atcham in Shropshire. In 1874, Anna Kingsford successfully sought permission to study medicine at the University of Paris, and after escorting her there her husband invited Maitland, her step-uncle by marriage, to be her protector in France. Maitland was a large man with a high domed head and Florence Fenwick Miller recorded in her autobiography that he was, at the time of his Paris sojourn, 'old (55 or so), plain, heavy, and dull of conversation' (Miller, 303). During the next six years Maitland began to explore the mystical side of his nature. In 1876 he first saw the apparition of his father, then he experienced other visitations from the dead, which convinced him he was a mystic and had a special spiritual sensitivity. This led him to believe that he had had many past lives, that he had lived in trees and animals, and that in previous incarnations he had been the emperor Marcus Aurelius, St John the Evangelist, and the prophet Daniel. As evidence for these phenomena he relied on a strange medley of so-called inspirations, revelations in dreams, passive writing, and harking to spiritual voices. In 1880, at the conclusion of Anna Kingsford's medical studies, the two returned to London, where she successfully practised medicine for a time, but continued, under Maitland's influence, to explore the supernatural. They published together *The Perfect Way: on the Finding of Christ* (1882), based on a course of Maitland's lectures. She and Maitland joined the London Theosophical Society, of which Kingsford soon became president, but after a philosophical altercation with Madame Blavatsky, the founder of nineteenth-century theosophy, they broke away and founded the London lodge of the Theosophical Society. In 1885 they founded the Hermetic Society, relying on mystic revelations, as opposed to the occult of Blavatsky, and specifically refuting her concept of Mahatmas. In the same year Maitland published *The Hermetic Works*, a translation of the works of Hermes Trismegistus.

After Anna Kingsford's death in February 1888, Maitland lived alone in studios at 1 Thurloe Square, London, where he claimed to receive continual 'illumination' from her, and devoted himself to founding the Esoteric Christian Union, and writing *Clothed in the Sun, being the Book of the Illuminations of Anna (Bonus) Kingsford* (1889); *The New Gospel of Interpretation* (1892); and *Anna Kingsford: her life, letters, diary, and work, by her collaborator … with a supplement of post-mortem communications* (2 vols., 1896). The latter was not well received. Florence Fenwick Miller, who knew them both well, wrote in the *Woman's Signal* (14 October 1897) that the book was more about Maitland and his spiritual revelations than about its subject, and that 'the Anna Kingsford that I knew, the clever, intelligent woman … was absolutely non-existent in the book'.

After the biography Maitland experienced a physical and mental breakdown; in 1896 he went to stay with Colonel Currie at The Warders, Tonbridge, Kent, where he suffered the loss of speech, and died on 2 October 1897. In her obituary notice Fenwick Miller quoted from, and agreed with, *The Athenaeum's* assessment that 'He was a man of fine feeling and much intellectual power, but he lacked balance and drifted into various crazes' (*Woman's Signal*, 14 Oct 1897). Maitland was buried in Tonbridge cemetery on 5 October 1897.   ROSEMARY T. VAN ARSDEL

Sources DNB · J. Sutherland, *The Stanford companion to Victorian fiction* (1989) · *The Academy* (16 Oct 1897), 301–2 · *The Athenaeum* (9 Oct 1897), 492 · *Woman's Signal* (14 Oct 1897) · F. F. Miller, 'An uncommon girlhood', unpubd autobiography, Wellcome L. · BL cat. · Wellesley index · M. Meade, *Madame Blavatsky: the woman behind the myth* (1980) · Boase, *Mod. Eng. biog.* · Venn, *Alum. Cant.* · E. Maitland, *Anna Kingsford: her life, letters, diary, and work*, 2nd edn, 2 vols. (1896)
Likenesses portrait, repro. in Maitland, *Anna Kingsford*

Maitland, Edward Francis, Lord Barcaple (1808–1870), lawyer, was born on 16 April 1808 in Edinburgh, the fifth son of Adam Maitland (*d.* 1843), landed proprietor, of Dundrennan, Kirkcudbrightshire, and his wife, Stewart McWhann. He was educated at the high school and then the University of Edinburgh and was called to the Scottish bar in March 1831. His eldest brother, Thomas *Maitland (1792–1851), also entered the legal profession, rising, as Lord Dundrennan, to be a court of session judge.

Initially Edward was not very successful as an advocate and considered giving up the profession. He had the advantage of family connections, but was apparently gruff and unwilling to flatter or hide contempt. Although never entirely briefless, he had spare time which he spent on literature. He was one of the originators of the Free Church periodical the *North British Review*, contributed several articles to it, and was its editor for a time in 1845 and 1846.

On 21 July 1840 Maitland married Anne Roberts (1813–1854), daughter of William Roberts, a banker in Glasgow. Together they had a family of four sons and two daughters.

A change in the tempo of Maitland's legal career began with his appointment as an advocate-depute in 1847. Maitland came from a whig background, his brother Thomas was MP for Kirkcudbrightshire from 1845 until 1850, and this and his later appointments were made by whig administrations. He was appointed sheriff of Argyllshire in July 1851 and was solicitor-general for Scotland between 1855 and 1858 and again from 1859 until 1862. Especially as holder of the latter office, he was able to build a reputation for conscientiousness and as an earnest and persuasive pleader, though his oratory was not of the kind to attract popular attention. Most notable in bringing Maitland to public attention was probably his conduct, together with the lord advocate James Moncreiff, of the prosecution at the famous trial of Madeleine Smith for murder in 1857. His humour was reportedly subtle and his intellect had a tendency to over-refinement and rigidity. These flaws, however, did not prevent him eventually enjoying a large income at the bar.

Maitland was not attracted by a political career. It was said he would have objected to exercising patronage according to the needs of party rather than in line with his conscience. This aversion did not extend, however, to university politics. After holding office as curator and assessor at Edinburgh University and being awarded an LLD in 1860, Maitland was elected in the same year as the first rector of Aberdeen University, newly created as a result of the union of King's and Marischal colleges. Maitland was put up as the 'peace candidate' in a bitterly contested election overshadowed by the quarrel between supporters and opponents of the union.

In November 1862 Maitland accepted a position as one of the judges of the outer house of the court of session. He took the title Lord Barcaple from a property he had recently purchased from a brother near Dundrennan, the family estate in Kirkcudbrightshire. Reportedly, he soon regretted this step. On the bench his income was significantly reduced and the conscientious thoroughness which had seen him overworked as solicitor-general was

to have fatal consequences when he was a judge. The rule in Scottish courts that a litigant could choose the lord ordinary before whom a case was to be heard meant that a popular judge attracted a lot of business. Maitland's occasional tendency to miss the plain view of a case, the result of characteristic over-refinement, did not help and his roll became longer than he could manage. In addition, he was appointed a commissioner on the courts of law in 1868, and the government failed to fill a vacant chair on the court of session. This workload led to a breakdown in his health at the end of 1869, from which he did not recover. Barcaple died at his Edinburgh residence, 3 Ainslie Place, on 23 February 1870 and was buried on 28 February in the Dean cemetery, Edinburgh.   GORDON F. MILLAR

Sources *The Scotsman* (24 Feb 1870) · *The Times* (24 Feb 1870) · *North British Daily Mail* (24 Feb 1870) · *Glasgow Herald* (24 Feb 1870) · *Proceedings of the Royal Society of Edinburgh*, 7 (1869–72), 242–5 · *Law Magazine*, new ser., 29 (1870), 273–4 · *Journal of Jurisprudence*, 14 (1870), 268–70 · *Solicitors' Journal*, 14 (1869–70), 365 · *Law Times* (19 March 1870), 405 · *The Scotsman* (25 Feb 1870) · *The Scotsman* (1 March 1870) · *ILN* (12 March 1870), 283 · Irving, *Scots.* · *Wellesley index*, 1.664, 998 · F. J. Grant, ed., *The Faculty of Advocates in Scotland, 1532–1943*, Scottish RS, 145 (1944), 143 · S. P. Walker, *The Faculty of Advocates, 1800–1986* (1987), 120 · *DNB* · *IGI* · G. W. T. Omond, *The lord advocates of Scotland, second series, 1834–1880* (1914), 265 · *The Scotsman* (21 Aug 1891) [obit. of John Inglis, Lord Glencorse]
Likenesses W. Brodie, marble bust, Parliament Hall, Edinburgh, Faculty of Advocates
Wealth at death £21,875 11s. 5d.: confirmation, 6 April 1870, NA Scot., SC 70/1/147/910–921

Maitland, Edward Maitland (1880–1921), air force officer and developer of airships and parachutes, was born at 156 Westbourne Terrace, London, on 21 February 1880, the elder son of Arthur Gee (*d.* 1903), a farmer and later barrister and JP, of Shudy Camps Park, Cambridgeshire, and his wife, Margaretha Marianne Maitland. Arthur Gee and his family assumed the surname Maitland in 1903. Educated at Haileybury and Trinity College, Cambridge, Edward Maitland volunteered for service in the Second South African War while he was still an undergraduate. He was commissioned in the Essex regiment and served in South Africa during 1901–2, receiving the Queen's medal with four clasps. Without resuming residence in Cambridge he took a BA (ordinary) in 1906 and obtained a third class.

Remaining in the army, in 1907 Maitland took up ballooning. The following year, with two companions, he made a record 1171-mile voyage to Russia. He also made his first descent from a balloon by parachute. After service at the Balloon School in Farnborough, he commanded the airship company in the short-lived air battalion of the Royal Engineers (1911–12), and then, on the formation of the Royal Flying Corps, was given command of 1 squadron (airships). In 1913, when all British airships came under naval control, he transferred to the Royal Naval Air Service (RNAS). In the same year he made his first parachute jump from an airship.

In October 1914 Maitland was sent to Belgium in charge of an RNAS balloon detachment for artillery spotting. He became impressed with the superiority of the French and Belgian kite balloons over his own spherical type, reported accordingly to the Admiralty, and was promptly recalled to initiate kite-balloon training at Roehampton in March 1915. From this he moved on to command the airship station at Wormwood Scrubs, and then went to the Admiralty to help in airship design and allocation. During this period he made a parachute descent from a balloon at 10,500 feet to investigate 'swinging'. In 1916, as a wing captain, he was appointed to command the airship station in Pulham, Norfolk, where Zeppelin imitations—rigid airships of a greatly improved type—were later to be based.

In June 1917 Maitland was appointed to the DSO for 'extremely valuable and gallant work in connection with airships and parachutes'. Shortly afterwards he returned to the Admiralty as captain-superintendent, lighter-than-air, to take charge of the airships headquarters staff. In this post he helped to build up the airship service into a major weapon in the war at sea. RNAS non-rigid airships, able to stay aloft for many hours and send down reports by wireless, did important work on patrol and convoy escort, many times directing British destroyers into contact with the enemy's U-boats. Further recognition followed for Maitland with appointment as CMG (1919) and the award of the AFC (1919) and the American DSM (1917).

July 1919 saw what was probably his greatest moment, when the naval rigid airship R34, with Maitland as chief observer, crossed the Atlantic successfully in both directions. The following month he received a permanent commission in the Royal Air Force, soon afterwards being promoted air commodore. With the transfer in October of all rigid airships from the Royal Navy to the RAF, Maitland continued at the Air Ministry his work on airship development and operations, but with civil uses now in view.

In 1921 Maitland's previously brilliant career ended in misfortune and tragedy. He was in command of the airship station in Howden, Yorkshire, when on 21 January the R34 struck some high ground, was buffeted in strong winds off the Yorkshire coast, and later broke up. In May the Air Ministry decided to disband the RAF's airship arm. The newly constructed R38, the largest airship yet built, had been sold to the USA in 1919, but was still based in Howden for training and trials. When on 24 August 1921 she broke up over the Humber on a final exercise in sharp turns, Maitland, on board but not in command, died with forty-two others. He was unmarried.

DENIS RICHARDS, *rev.*

Sources ministry of defence, air historical branch · E. M. Maitland, *The log of HMA R34* (1920) · *The Times* (25 Aug 1921) · W. Raleigh and H. A. Jones, *The war in the air*, 6 vols. (1922–37), vol. 1 · R. D. S. Higham, *The British rigid airship, 1908–1931: a study in weapons policy* (1961) · D. H. Robinson, *Giants in the sky* (1973) · b. cert.
Archives NL Scot., journal of flights in airship R 34 · Royal Aeronautical Society, London, papers | FILM IWM FVA, actuality footage | SOUND IWM SA, oral history interview
Wealth at death £1209 9s. 3d.: probate, 22 Nov 1921, *CGPLA Eng. & Wales*

Maitland [*née* Rees], **Emma Knox** (1844–1923), suffragist and educationist, was born on 17 May 1844 at 7 Croft Terrace, Tenby, Pembrokeshire, the only child of John Rees JP, gentleman, and his wife, Emma Brown. Her father died when she was young; her mother was a strong Liberal and she shared her political convictions. Little else is known of her early life other than that she was educated by governesses until she was twelve and then went to a boarding-school.

Having married early in life, to Frederick Maitland, Emma Maitland moved to Kensington and went on to have six children. She had little time for public work until her children were grown up, by which time her eldest daughter ran the family home at 18 Primrose Hill, Hampstead, during her absence. None the less, she did attend one of the first drawing-room meetings to discuss the issue of women's suffrage, held by Mrs Riley Taylor in 1866. A firm believer that the vote should be extended to married women, she refused to join the Women's Suffrage Society (which had sanctioned a partial measure of franchise on the grounds of political expediency). Interviewed by the feminist *Women's Penny Paper* in 1890, she referred to her strong belief that women should work with men, another reason for her refusal to join a women's suffrage society. Three years later she joined the executive of the Women's Local Government Society, a non-party feminist group established to promote the eligibility of women to serve on all local government bodies, serving from 1893 to 1904 and again from 1910 to 1914. She also served as convenor and chair of the organization committee for a three-year period from 1910. A hardworking Liberal Party worker, Emma was president of the women's branch of the Hampstead Liberal and Radical Association and went on to represent that body on the National Liberal Federation and the London Liberal and Radical Union. Finally, by 1890 she was vice-president of the Women's Liberal Federation, formed at the home of Sophia Fry in 1886.

Mrs Maitland always took a keen interest in education, canvassing for Elizabeth Garrett at Marylebone in 1870 during the first triennial election for the London school board. She was also a school manager in the early years of the board and took a practical interest in the administration of a college for working women. Asked to stand as a candidate for Marylebone in 1888, she consented to do so, and was returned in third place (behind Edward Barnes and Lyulph Stanley) with 17,790 votes. Her chief demands were for free education, a more generous curriculum, and simplification of the needlework requirements for girls in order to leave more time for Slojd hand and eye training and Swedish exercises to aid the children's physical development. Unlike her colleagues Margaret Eve (represented Finsbury, 1891–1904) and Rosamond Davenport Hill (longest serving female member, represented the City between 1879 and 1897), who gave special interest to girls' subjects, Emma Maitland spread her work over a larger sphere so that she might offer a female perspective on all aspects of the board's work.

Displaced by the moderate faction, headed by the Revd Joseph Diggle, in 1891, during the furore over the purchase of pianos for board schools, in 1894 Mrs Maitland was returned head of the poll in Chelsea and held the seat until her retirement in January 1903. By 1896 she was responsible for nine schools in Kilburn and Shepherd's Bush and took a keen interest in the education of blind and deaf children, which had been placed under the control of the school board rather than the poor-law guardians in 1893. Like Ruth Homan (represented Tower Hamlets, 1891–1904), Emma Maitland acted on the principle of finding blind children foster homes near their school centres, widening their curriculum, and sending the most able on to training colleges. Mrs Maitland usually spent three days a week at the board's headquarters on the Embankment, as well as alternate Wednesdays, while the rest of the week was devoted to constituency work. Further, she even took advantage of visits to the continent to investigate German and Austrian methods of caring for deaf and deaf mute children.

Elected by her peers to represent the London board on the Association of School Boards (alongside Dr T. J. Macnamara, Mr Thompson, and Graham Wallas), in February 1901 Mrs Maitland attended a special meeting called to discuss the developing crisis over secondary education, after Lord Justice Cockerton ruled that much of the school board's work in this area was unsanctioned and illegal. By the turn of the century education reform was moving up the political agenda and both Mrs Maitland and the Women's Local Government Society played a key role in the campaign to protect the position of women, likely to be disqualified by sex for election to the new local education authorities. As a token of their esteem, her colleagues presented Mrs Maitland with a pair of silver candlesticks on the occasion of her retirement from the board. The chairman, Lord Reay, hoped they 'would help to spread the light around them upon her dining table, as she had spread the light around her' (*School Board Chronicle*, 31 Jan 1901, 86). Although the feminists won a concession enabling women to be co-opted as specialists onto the new institutions, female exclusion from elected office ended with the Qualification of Women (County and Borough Councils) Act, 1907. Emma Knox Maitland, who was widowed, died at her home 43 Howitt Road, Hampstead, on 13 June 1923.   JANE MARTIN

Sources F. Dolman, 'Lady members of the London school board', *Young Woman*, 4 (1895–6), 129–32 · interview, *Women's Penny Paper* (23 Aug 1890) · reports of the Women's Local Government Society, 1896–1923, LMA · *School Board Chronicle* (1888–1904) · b. cert. · d. cert.
Archives LMA, Women's Local Government Society MSS
Likenesses photograph, 1890, repro. in *Women's Penny Paper* · Russell & Sons, photograph, Jan 1896, repro. in Dolman, 'Lady members of the London school board'
Wealth at death £3824 12s. 3d.: probate, 26 July 1923, *CGPLA Eng. & Wales*

Maitland, Frederick (1763–1848), army officer, born on 3 September 1763, was the youngest son of General Sir Alexander Maitland, first baronet (1728–1820), colonel 49th foot, and his wife, Penelope (*d.* 22 December 1805), daughter of Colonel Martin Madan MP and sister of Martin Madan, bishop of Peterborough. Charles Maitland, sixth earl of Lauderdale, was his paternal grandfather. On 1 September 1779 Frederick was appointed ensign in the 14th foot. He served with a company of his regiment doing duty as marines on the *Union* (90 guns, Captain J. Dalrymple) in

the channel in 1779–80, became lieutenant on 19 September 1782, and was on board Admiral Darby's fleet at the relief of Gibraltar in October 1782. He afterwards served for fifteen months in Jamaica.

In 1784 Maitland was transferred to the 30th foot, and placed on half pay; he devoted his leisure time to study. After returning to the West Indies in 1787 he was for a time assistant quartermaster-general in Jamaica. He married at Barbados, in November 1790, Catherine, daughter of John Prettijohn of that island. They had nine children. He had obtained his company in the 60th Royal Americans in 1789, and brought the dispatches announcing the capture of Tobago in April 1793. The sloop *Fairy* (18 guns, Captain John Laforey), in which he came home, was engaged during the voyage with a French 32-gun frigate, which escaped. Maitland was brevet major and aide-de-camp to Sir Charles Grey [*see* Grey, Charles, first Earl Grey] at the relief of Nieuport and Ostend in 1794, and deputy adjutant-general, with the brevet of lieutenant-colonel, at the capture of Martinique, Guadeloupe, and St Lucia in the same year. He was promoted major, 9th foot, in 1794, and lieutenant-colonel in 1795, when he was transferred to the 27th Inniskillings. He went back to the West Indies in 1795, as military secretary to Sir Ralph Abercromby, with whom he served at St Lucia, St Vincent, Puerto Rico, and elsewhere, in 1795–7. While returning home in the *Arethusa* (38 guns, Captain T. Woolley), he was present and commanded the cabin guns of the frigate at the capture of the French corvette, *La Gaieté*, south-east of Bermuda, on 20 August 1797. He afterwards served on Abercromby's staff in Scotland, and in the expedition to the Netherlands in 1799.

As a brevet colonel Maitland returned once more to the West Indies in 1800, and was quartermaster-general there for six years. He commanded a brigade at the capture of the Danish, Swedish, and Dutch West India islands in 1800–01. He was transferred as lieutenant-colonel from the Inniskillings to the 29th, was appointed brigadier-general in 1804, and commanded a brigade at the capture of Surinam. He became a major-general in 1805, and in 1807 was second in command, under General Bowyer, at the recapture of the Dutch and Danish islands, which had been restored at the peace of Amiens. At St Thomas's he received the sword of the governor, Van Schogen, at the spot on which he had received it six years before. He commanded a brigade at the capture of Martinique in 1809 and the subsequent operations at Les Saintes.

Maitland had been appointed lieutenant-governor of Grenada in 1805, and except when absent on active service, as in the West Indies, administered the civil government of the island. This he did until 1810. He was an upright and painstaking administrator. Although his legal knowledge was self-acquired, his decisions as vice-chancellor were never reversed save in a solitary instance on a technical point of law. Privately he was opposed to the abolition of slavery. He became a lieutenant-general in 1811, and on 1 January 1812 was appointed second in command in the Mediterranean under Lord William Bentinck [*see* Bentinck, Lord William Henry Cavendish- (1774–

1839)]. In that capacity he commanded the Anglo-Sicilian army sent from Sicily to the east coast of Spain to make a diversion on Suchet's left flank. The situation in Sicily prevented Bentinck from detaching a force of the strength expected by Wellington, and the motley corps of 9000 British German Legion, Swiss, Sicilians, and Neapolitans, with which Maitland arrived off Palamos on 31 July 1812, was too ill-provided with commissariat and field-train to justify a landing there. Maitland proceeded to Alicante, landed his troops, and opened communication with the Spanish generals in Murcia. After some desultory movements he began to entrench his camp at Alicante at the end of August 1812. But his health was broken, and at the beginning of November, having done nothing, he resigned the command to General Mackenzie, and returned home. He received the lieutenant-governorship of Dominica on 30 June 1813 in recognition of his past services.

Maitland, a full general in 1825, had been appointed in 1810 colonel in succession of the 1st Ceylon regiment and in 1833 he became colonel in succession of the 58th foot. A memoir by him on the defences of Mount's Bay, Cornwall, is extant (*Dispatches of ... the Duke of Wellington*, 7.149–51). He died at Tunbridge Wells on 27 January 1848, aged eighty-four. His wife, and three of their children, survived him; his eldest brother, Sir Alexander Maitland-Gibson (or Gibson-Maitland), second baronet, deputy governor of the Bank of Scotland, survived him by only a few days.

H. M. CHICHESTER, *rev.* ROGER T. STEARN

Sources J. Foster, *The peerage, baronetage, and knightage of the British empire for 1880*, [pt 2] [1880] [Lauderdale, Maitland] · J. Philippart, ed., *The royal military calendar*, 3rd edn, 2 (1820) · *GM*, 2nd ser., 29 (1848) · W. F. P. Napier, *History of the war in the Peninsula and in the south of France*, new edn, 4 (1886) · A. J. Guy, ed., *The road to Waterloo: the British army and the struggle against revolutionary and Napoleonic France, 1793–1815* (1990) · T. C. W. Blanning, *The French revolutionary wars, 1787–1802* (1996) · R. Muir, *Britain and the defeat of Napoleon, 1807–1815* (1996) · Burke, *Peerage* (1959) · *The dispatches of ... the duke of Wellington ... from 1799 to 1818*, ed. J. Gurwood, 7: *Peninsula, 1790–1813* (1837), 149–71

Archives NAM, diaries, corresp., and papers | NA Scot., letters to Lord Seaforth · U. Nott. L., Hallward Library, corresp. with Lord William Bentinck · U. Southampton L., letters to duke of Wellington

Maitland, Frederick Lewis (1730–1786). *See under* Maitland, Sir Frederick Lewis (1777–1839).

Maitland, Sir Frederick Lewis (1777–1839), naval officer, born at Rankeilour in Fife on 7 September 1777, was the third son of Captain **Frederick Lewis Maitland** (1730–1786), sixth son of Charles, sixth earl of Lauderdale. Maitland's father, the godson of Frederick Louis, prince of Wales, commanded with distinction the *Lively* in 1760, the *Elizabeth* in 1778, and served under Rodney in 1782. Between 1763 and 1775 he commanded the royal yacht. He was promoted rear-admiral in 1786, but died before the news reached him. Maitland's mother was Margaret Dick (*d.* 1825), heir in tail general to James *Crichton, Viscount Frendraught, who was heir of the family of Makgill of Rankeilour. Maitland's elder brother Charles (*d.* 1820) inherited the estates of his mother's family and assumed the surname Makgill; he and his wife, Mary Johnston, had a son David Maitland-Makgill-Crichton (1801–1851), who assumed the name Crichton in 1837 as heir to his ancestor James Crichton. He was called to the Scottish bar in 1822, and took a prominent part in the formation of the Free Church of Scotland.

Maitland joined the navy, and, after serving some time in the sloop *Martin* with Captain George Duff and with Robert Forbes in the frigate *Southampton*, in which he was present at the battle of 1 June 1794, he was promoted lieutenant of the *Andromeda* on 3 April 1795. He was shortly afterwards moved into the *Venerable*, flagship of Admiral Duncan in the North Sea, and in April 1797 went out to the Mediterranean to join Lord St Vincent, by whom he was appointed to the sloop *Kingfisher*. In her he assisted at the capture of several privateers with such courage that the ship's company subscribed £50 to present him with a sword. In December 1798 the *Kingfisher* was wrecked as she was leaving the Tagus. Maitland, who was in temporary command, was court-martialled and honourably acquitted. Immediately afterwards he was appointed flag lieutenant to Lord St Vincent, then residing at Gibraltar.

On 7 July 1799, as the combined fleets of France and Spain were retiring from the Mediterranean, Maitland was sent by St Vincent to order the hired cutter *Penelope* 'to go, count and dodge them'. As the lieutenant of the cutter was sick, Maitland took the command, but the next day, owing, it was said, to the cowardice and disobedience of the men, the *Penelope* was captured by the Spaniards and taken into Cadiz. The Spanish admiral Mazaredo, having learned that her commander was the flag lieutenant of Lord St Vincent, to whom he was under some obligation of courtesy, sent Maitland back to Gibraltar free, without exchange. Maitland was promoted by St Vincent to be commander of the sloop *Cameleon*, the promotion backdated to 14 June; he went out to join his new ship, then on the coast of Egypt, under Sir Sidney Smith, and after the signing of the convention of al-'Arish (24 January 1800) was sent home overland with dispatches. He returned almost immediately, and continued in the *Cameleon* to the end of the year. On 10 December 1800 he was appointed by Keith to be acting captain of the store ship *Wassenaar*. As she was then at Malta unfit for service, Maitland obtained permission to accompany the expedition to Egypt. His good service in command of the boats appointed to cover the landing of the army, and to support the right flank in the actions of 13 and 21 March 1801, was specially acknowledged by the commanders-in-chief, on the report of Sir Sidney Smith, and won for him his promotion to post rank, dated 21 March. Maitland was then appointed temporarily to the *Dragon* (74 guns), but in August was moved into the *Carrère*, a recent prize from the French, which he took to England and paid off in October 1802.

St Vincent, then first lord of the Admiralty, immediately appointed Maitland to the *Loire*, a large 46 gun frigate, which, on the renewal of the war, was employed on the west coast of France and the north coast of Spain. In April 1804 he married Catherine (*d.* 1865), second daughter of

Daniel Connor of Ballybricken, co. Cork; their only child died in infancy.

During the three years after his appointment to the *Loire*, Maitland captured or destroyed many large privateers and coastal batteries, especially on 4 June 1805 in Muros Bay, south of Cape Finisterre, where his courage and success won him the thanks of the City of London, the freedom of Cork, and a sword from the Patriotic Fund. He also assisted in the capture of the French frigate *Libre* on 24 December 1805. In November 1806 he was moved into the frigate *Emerald* (36 guns), on the same service as the *Loire*, and with similar success. In April 1809 she was with the fleet outside Basque Roads, under Lord Gambier, and on the 12th was one of the few ships so tardily sent in to support the *Impérieuse*.

In 1813 and 1814 Maitland commanded the *Goliath* (58 guns) on the Halifax and West Indian stations, and in November 1814 was appointed to the *Boyne* (98 guns) under orders for North America. At the beginning of 1815 he was collecting a fleet of transports and merchant ships in Cork harbour, but a succession of strong westerly winds prevented his sailing, until, on the news of Bonaparte's return from Elba, his orders were countermanded, and he was appointed to the *Bellerophon* (74 guns), in which he sailed from Plymouth on 24 May under the immediate orders of Sir Henry Hotham. Maitland, as well as Hotham, had a long experience of the Bay of Biscay, and the *Bellerophon* was stationed off Rochefort to keep watch on the ships of war there. On 28 June the news of Waterloo reached Maitland, and on the 30th a letter from Bordeaux warned him that Bonaparte would attempt to escape from there to America. Maitland, however, considered he would more probably make for Rochefort; and though he sent two small craft, one to Bordeaux and the other to Arcachon, he himself, in the *Bellerophon*, remained off Rochefort. Hotham, in the *Superb*, was in Quiberon Bay, and frigates, corvettes, and brigs kept watch along the whole extent of the coast. Hotham ordered Maitland that if he intercepted Bonaparte he should take him to England.

On 10 July negotiations with Maitland were opened on behalf of Bonaparte, who had then reached Rochefort. Maitland rejected the proposal that he should be allowed to sail to the United States, but offered to take him to England. After four anxious days, Bonaparte, with his staff and servants, embarked on the *Bellerophon* on 15 July. On 24 July the ship reached Torbay; thence she was ordered round to Plymouth to await the decision of the government. She put to sea again on 4 August, and on the 7th, off Berry Head, Bonaparte was removed to the *Northumberland*. To counteract misrepresentation, Maitland wrote for his friends a detailed *Narrative* of Bonaparte's time on the *Bellerophon*, which he subsequently published in 1826.

In October 1818 Maitland was appointed to the *Vengeur* (74 guns), in which in 1819 he went out to South America. In 1820 he carried Lord Beresford from Rio de Janeiro to Lisbon, and went on to the Mediterranean, where he was sent to Naples to take the king of the Two Sicilies to Leghorn. On landing on 20 December, after a rough passage of seven days, the king invested Maitland with the insignia of a knight commander of the order of St Ferdinand and Merit, and presented him with his portrait, set with diamonds, in a gold box. The *Vengeur* returned to England in the following spring, and Maitland was appointed to the *Genoa* (74 guns), guardship at Portsmouth, which he left in October on the completion of his three years' continuous service. From 1827 to 1830 he commanded the *Wellesley* (74 guns) in the Mediterranean. He attained his flag on 22 July 1830. He had been made a CB in 1815; on 17 November 1830 he was advanced to KCB. From 1832 to 1837 he was admiral superintendent of the dockyard at Portsmouth; in July 1837 he was appointed commander-in-chief in the East Indies and China, with his flag in his old ship the *Wellesley*. In February 1839, when co-operating with the army on its advance from Bombay towards Afghanistan, he captured the town and fort of Karachi, and covered the landing of the troops and stores. Afterwards, on the news of some disturbances at Bushehr, he went there and, under the protection of the marines of the squadron, brought away the resident and his staff without punishing the rioters, conduct which the Anglo-Indian press criticized as injudiciously lenient.

Maitland died at sea, on board the *Wellesley*, off Bombay, on 30 November 1839. He was buried at Bombay, where, in the cathedral, a monument to his memory was erected by subscription. Lady Maitland died in 1865 at Lindores, Fife.

J. K. LAUGHTON, rev. ROGER MORRISS

Sources J. Marshall, *Royal naval biography*, 2/1 (1824), 381–400 · W. James, *The naval history of Great Britain, from the declaration of war by France in 1793, to the accession of George IV*, [4th edn], 6 vols. (1847) · J. S. Tucker, *Memoirs of Admiral the Rt Hon. the earl of St Vincent*, 2 vols. (1844) · F. L. Maitland, *Narrative of the surrender of Buonaparte and of his residence on board HMS Bellerophon* (1826) · C. R. Low, *History of the Indian navy, 1613–1863*, 2 (1877) · O'Byrne, *Naval biog. dict.* · *GM*, 2nd ser., 14 (1840)
Archives NL Scot., navals, journals, and papers | NA Scot., corresp. with Lord Melville
Likenesses engraving (after portrait) · monument, Bombay Cathedral, India · watercolour on ivory, Scot. NPG

Maitland, Frederic William

Maitland, Frederic William (1850–1906), legal historian, was born on 28 May 1850 at 53 Guilford Street, London, the only son of John Gorham *Maitland (1818–1863), civil servant, and Emma, daughter of John Frederic *Daniell FRS (1790–1845). He had two sisters: the birth of the younger in 1851 was followed by the death of their mother. Her sister Louisa Daniell maintained a home in various London houses for nearly thirty years. The girls were educated at home, and Maitland valued the German their governesses taught him more than what he learned at his preparatory school in Brighton or, from 1863, at Eton College.

Maitland's father died just before the change of school. Three years later his grandfather Samuel Roffey Maitland also died, and whatever wealth Maitland was to have came to him as a schoolboy. There was some capital from his father, but his grandfather's personalty was probably exhausted by provision for Maitland's sisters. What did come to him from Samuel Roffey was land in Gloucestershire, which brought Maitland much pleasure and, until the agricultural depression of the 1880s, a comfortable

Frederic William Maitland (1850–1906), by Beatrice Lock, 1906

income. It is not clear how well off Maitland was thereafter.

Undergraduate and barrister Maitland left Eton hating Greek, liking strenuous exercise, and devoted to music. In 1869 he went to Trinity College, Cambridge, where he rowed for the college and ran for the university but made a poor academic start. As he disliked classics, Maitland initially read mathematics, but with no success. Then, inspired by Henry Sidgwick, he abandoned the conventional subjects and turned to the moral sciences tripos, in which in 1872 he excelled. His peers also accorded him their own honours, publicly as secretary and later president of the Cambridge Union, and privately as one of the handful (at any one time) of members of the long-lived Conversazione Society, known as the Apostles.

A period of uncertainty followed. Neither joining Lincoln's Inn as a student in 1872 nor winning the Whewell scholarship for international law in 1873 shows commitment to a legal career; and if Maitland was reading law books, he was interrupted when in 1875 Trinity reopened a chance lost when he had turned to moral sciences. A fellowship in philosophy was to be awarded by competition. Maitland did not win, and the 'Historical sketch of liberty and equality' which he submitted lacks the quality of his later writings.

Then Maitland turned seriously to the bar. He was called in 1876, and so impressed the master with whom he read in chambers that when the latter became ill three years later he had his substantial practice managed by Maitland. The loss of this additional business perhaps left an empty feeling when Maitland returned to his own chambers in 1883; and he was soon to change course. He had already started to write. Seemingly encouraged by Sidgwick, he

began an account of property law, but explanation was overwhelmed by anger at the mischievous distinction between real and personal property, and in particular the anachronistic survival of the heir: the landed wealth of one dying intestate passed intact to the eldest male, whereas other property was divided between the children equally. So Maitland stopped explaining and let the anger splendidly loose in an anonymous article of 1879 in the *Westminster Review*. History had played a part in this, if only as villain; and that or chance readings of Stubbs's *Constitutional History* and the work of F. C. von Savigny and H. Brunner may have turned his mind to legal history. Between 1881 and 1883 he published three papers in the *Law Magazine and Review*, suggesting gentlemanly interest rather than dedication, but still a beginning.

Some part in that beginning was played by Frederick Pollock, who had preceded Maitland through Eton and Trinity, was an Apostle, and had been called by Lincoln's Inn. In 1880 Pollock introduced Maitland to Leslie Stephen and his walking club, the Sunday Tramps. Either directly or through the Tramps, Pollock also introduced Maitland to Paul Vinogradoff, then working in England on the feudal structure. After meeting him early in 1884 Maitland, seemingly chagrined that a Russian should know so much and he so little about the early English legal materials, made his first visit to the Public Record Office, and soon he was editing an early Gloucestershire eyre roll. It was published in the same year at his own expense, with a dedication to Vinogradoff and an introduction which ends by acknowledging encouragement and 'ready help out of many difficulties' from Pollock.

Reader in law at Cambridge Maitland's London home was disrupted by the death of his aunt Louisa in 1880 and by the marriage of his elder sister in 1883; and his thoughts may have been turned to the academic life by Pollock's election in March 1883 to the Corpus chair of jurisprudence in Oxford. In the same year Maitland applied unsuccessfully for a readership in Oxford, and Cambridge resolved to establish readerships when money could be found. Sidgwick promptly gave money for a readership in law; and Maitland was elected to it late in 1884, shortly before publication of his Gloucestershire volume. The thrust of his new life was determined by other events in 1884. As editor of the new *Law Quarterly Review*, the ubiquitous Pollock had arranged for the first volume to include papers by both Vinogradoff (on the text of *Bracton*) and Maitland. Maitland's article took him to *Bracton* manuscripts; and he sent Vinogradoff a note of his findings. In July, before returning to Moscow, Vinogradoff published in *The Athenaeum* his suggestion that a manuscript containing transcripts of thirteenth-century plea roll entries was a note book used by Bracton. In admiration, Maitland sent Vinogradoff his copy of the 1569 edition of *Bracton* (*Letters*, 1, no. 12A) and began editing the collection of cases. *Bracton's Note Book* was published in three volumes, again at Maitland's expense, in 1887.

The prefatory matter of the *Note Book* records some bearings of Maitland's life. It is dedicated to Sidgwick as founder of his readership; but 'reverently' (Maitland,

Bracton's Note Book) acknowledges another debt, specified when Sidgwick died: 'to whom I owe whatever there is of good in me' (*Letters*, 1, no. 272). Vinogradoff's part is explained. Acknowledgements to the American scholars M. M. Bigelow and J. B. Thayer draw attention to work in progress on the history of the common law in the neighbourhood of the other Cambridge; and Maitland was soon to correspond with J. B. Ames of Harvard. There is also an acknowledgement to 'my friend Mr Frederick Pollock … from whom I first learnt to find an interest in the history of law' (Maitland, *Bracton's Note Book*, 1.viii).

Work on the *Note Book* was interrupted for a volume in a citizenship series when the chosen author fell out; and the rather slight *Justice and Police* appeared in 1885. But serious historical articles appeared in the *Law Quarterly Review* for each of the three following years. There were also now the duties of his readership: lecture subjects included tort, remote from Chancery chambers and one of the reasons for corresponding with Bigelow. Another obligation was to reside in Cambridge; Maitland lodged first in King's Parade, then for the academic year 1885–6 in rooms in Trinity (though not as a fellow), then in a house in Brookside.

Marriage The last of these moves followed his marriage on 20 July 1886 to Florence Henrietta Fisher (1864–1920), whom he had met through Leslie Stephen. She was the daughter of Herbert Fisher and Mary Jackson, whose sister Julia was Stephen's second wife; one of her brothers was H. A. L. Fisher and a sister was to marry Ralph Vaughan *Williams. The Maitlands had two daughters, the elder born soon after the publication of *Bracton's Note Book* and given a name from it, Ermengard. She was to survive by more than sixty years the father who died on her nineteenth birthday; and her memories of him were to be printed by the Selden Society of which he was the effective founder.

The Selden Society and the Downing chair The Selden Society was formed in 1887 to publish materials for the history of English law. Maitland would have chosen another name, and had no formal role until 1895, when he became first literary director. But the pioneer publishing at his own expense was a prime mover. He was solely responsible for the first two of the society's annual volumes and solely or partly responsible for a third of those published in his lifetime; and he probably supervised all volumes from the beginning. This charge upon his time coincided, perhaps exactly, with knowledge that his time would be limited. He undertook the society's first volume, *Select Pleas of the Crown*, in the summer of 1887, when 'invalided' to Devon (*Letters*, 1, no. 32); probably as a result of the diabetic condition diagnosed then or soon after. In his letters the malady is named only once, to a newly diagnosed friend in 1899: 'Slowly it is doing for me; but quite slowly, and it may cheer you to know that I have had ten happy and busy years under the ban' (ibid., no. 251). At the latest he must have known by March 1889, when he confided a doubt whether he would live another year (*Letters*, 1, no.

62); and the knowledge (and the determination of the former undergraduate runner) helps explain the speed with which his work was driven.

That first Selden volume appeared in time to be available to the electors, together with the *Note Book*, when the Downing chair fell vacant. Maitland's election in the summer of 1888 brought an official residence in the pleasant West Lodge in Downing College. The younger daughter, Fredegond—'After that, don't I belong to the Germanistic school?' (*Letters*, 1, no. 62)—was born there soon after they moved in: and it was the setting for a happy family life, though academic eyebrows were raised at Mrs Maitland's frequent musical gatherings, mostly of young men, and her exotic pets which at one time or another included a capuchin monkey (Fifoot, *Life*, 168–9), a South African meerkat, and 'a stolid English badger' (*Letters*, 1, no. 166).

The illness moved in with them. Maitland was recovering from a bout at the time of his inaugural lecture, 'Why the history of English law is not written' (1888). His answer long seemed unexceptionable, even obvious: a legal historian must be a lawyer and successful lawyers will not turn to history. But when history became a more exclusive discipline, exception was taken by historians who were not lawyers; and T. F. T. Plucknett went so far as to ascribe Maitland's proposition to impaired judgement, caused by his illness (Plucknett, 13).

Maitland's style Maitland was to write other lectures for publication: his Ford lectures in 1897 were published as *Township and Borough*, and his Rede lecture in 1901 as *English Law and the Renaissance*. But there was little difference in style between such works and others written for publication alone. Even when writing directly for print he spoke his words aloud or heard them in his mind (E. Maitland, *F. W. Maitland*, 8); and some other publications took shape in lectures. The strength of Maitland's writing is beyond analysis, but one source must be this directness: he spoke to his readers, and readers hear him still. Another is the directness with which Maitland heard the people he was writing about: they are often imaginary, but Maitland hears them articulate their side of an argument; and this generates a powerful imagery which will be mentioned below. The resulting style is unique. 'The hand of Esau', observed J. H. Round, 'was less distinctive than the pen of the Downing Professor' (Bell, 62).

The inseparability for Maitland of writing from speech had another result. 'I *can* not improvise' (*Letters*, 1, no. 222). Even duty lectures for undergraduates were meticulously written out. One such course was 'horrible bondage' (ibid., 1, no. 33) and firmly not for publication. But after his death it was published; and the *Constitutional History of England* (1908) was long the most widely read of all his writings. Two other posthumous works were similarly undergraduate lectures not meant for publication. Some teachers of the subject still think his *Equity* the best starting point for students; and a revised edition appeared in 1936. At the same time *The Forms of Action at Common Law*, which had first appeared between the same covers in 1909, became a separate book. In seven breathless lectures and eighty pages a coherent development of common law remedies is traced from the beginning to the nineteenth century. Maitland's strength was in imagining people in dispute: but here he had no time for people and conjured up an almost Darwinian evolution of legal entities. In this case alone has the lecturer's simplification probably done more harm than good in the unsought authority of print.

Academic life and duties Beside his lecture courses, many on modern legal subjects, Maitland took a full share of academic duties. He examined in law, moral sciences, and history, and served on the law and history boards and on central bodies of the university; and as fellow of Downing he worried about often worrying college business. Nor was it just time that he gave. He fought for causes both in and out of the senate: for law books in the university library to go to the new faculty library; for Greek not to be required for entrance; and for women to get degrees.

On the last of these Maitland helped reach a compromise and was its principal advocate when the subject was debated in March 1897. The speech was memorable, and decades later his colleague William Warwick Buckland remembered the slight and graceful figure of the speaker, the fine lines of his ever moving face, and eyes which took over the listener's consciousness. His imagery (he envisaged the dignitaries of a proposed women's university waiting to confer degrees in the waiting-room at Bletchley Junction, the women waiting on the platform for trains to Oxford and Cambridge) is like that in his early attack on the law of real property, when he created the sorry figure of the heir consigned to the Society of Antiquaries or, if they would not have him, to rival schools of German scholarship 'who shall write monographs upon him until the end of time'. But the heir lasted until 1925, and women got no Cambridge degrees until 1948; until 1923 they did not receive even those titles of degrees for which Maitland had argued. After the debate feeling was aroused among non-resident MAs and undergraduates, who assembled to cast contrary votes and eggs respectively. An egg is said to have hit Maitland.

Other publications and the History of English Law Nothing slowed the flow of Maitland's publication. In 1889, as well as finishing a Selden volume of *Select Pleas in Manorial Courts*, he also undertook to edit for the Rolls Series a volume of parliamentary petitions from the reign of Edward I. This project was frustrated by difficulties in dating, partly owing to archival disturbance; and before the year was out it had been abandoned in favour of an edition of the parliament roll of 1305 together with the associated petitions and writs. The resulting *Memoranda de Parliamento* marks a stage in the history of parliament, though Maitland might have hesitated over a later inference that the judicial handling of petitions was the essence of the early institution. The work went slowly by comparison with his other editions, and did not appear until 1893. Probably it was never close to his heart.

A much larger and more significant project also conceived in 1889 was to be completed with astonishing speed: 'Pollock and I have mapped out a big work, too big I

fear for the residue of our joint lives and the life of the survivor. Vol. I is to bring things down to the end of Henry III' (*Letters*, 1, no. 78). Though there was no earlier scientific work to serve as a basis, the *History of English Law* went to press in two large volumes only five years later. It still stopped at the death of Henry III; and it was not what had been planned. 'I quite see', Maitland wrote to Pollock in October 1890, 'that a brief history of English law is much wanted and might be written, but I also see that I can not write it' (ibid., no. 87). In the end Pollock contributed just one section, that on the Anglo-Saxon period. Maitland did not like it, not because he disagreed but because he could not now treat the subject in his own way and at his own length. His vision of any scholarly project became too clear to tolerate collaboration; and the Selden volume for 1890, *The Court Baron*, also bears the name of a second editor, for whose work Maitland left no room. He forestalled more from Pollock by hastening to finish the *History* himself, though Pollock's name on the title-page helped sales and allowed the not infrequent first person to appear more comfortably in the plural. It was published in 1895; and the only important changes in a second edition of 1898 concerned corporations, a continuing interest of Maitland's. It must be the only work of history to have had its centenary celebrated (in a British Academy symposium, *The History of English Law: Centenary Essays on 'Pollock and Maitland'*, PBA, 89, 1996) not as a dead classic but as a living authority.

Some of the vitality comes from Maitland's imagery: individuals fight their corner. Instead of reading abstract statements about pasture rights, to take an extreme example, the reader hears an imaginary commoner harangue his lord and fellow tenants in ten lines of emotional speech (*History*, 1898, 1.623). But the imagery is not just an expository device. The groups waiting at Bletchley and the heir consigned to the Antiquaries sprang from Maitland's own feelings about women's degrees and about the unequal distribution of property on death; and the true target of the commoner's tirade was not some thirteenth-century lord but nineteenth-century theories of communalism. Taking sides was a less obvious and more dangerous source for the vitality of Maitland's writing, whether between contemporary scholarly theories or between English and Roman law in the times he was discussing.

Roman law played its part in the *History* at more than one level. Most obviously there are suggestions of Roman influence on specific English results. An example which has come to seem particularly strained is a Roman model for the analysis of the leaseholder's interest: 'English law for six centuries and more will rue this youthful flirtation with Romanism' (Maitland, *History*, 2nd edn, 1898, 2.115). But the germ of that particular idea came from *Bracton*; and the extent of the Roman influence on *Bracton* was probed further by Maitland in his *Bracton and Azo*, the Selden volume for 1894. It was, however, not English law itself that was infected by Roman ideas through the medium of *Bracton*: most scholars now agree that *Bracton* had little effect on English law. The important effect was on Maitland's vision of English legal history. The *De legibus* had permeated his mind while he worked on the *Note Book*, and it may bias the *History* in two ways: the elementary ideas and the meanings of words found in *Bracton* are carried into earlier times, so that what may now seem to be deep changes within the period of the *History* are represented as superficial and mechanical; and the English law of the *History* is assumed to have been of the same nature as the developed Roman law. This, combined with the ideas crystallized in *The Forms of Action*, contributed to Maitland's essentially static vision of common-law development.

Hindsight can see the terminal date of the *History* as contributing to both misconceptions (if such they are). Had Maitland addressed the legislation of Edward I, he might have suspected that many of the separate mischiefs derived from a single underlying change in society. And when later he put his mind to the year-books, he saw a 'stage in the history of jurisprudence' so early that the 'parallel stage in the history of Roman law is represented, and can only be represented, by ingenious guesswork' (*Year Books of 1 & 2 Edward II*, Selden Society, 17.xvii). But this insight came too late for the *History*. Once it reaches beyond its period to quote a year-book case about a bailment: Maitland emphasizes the absence of conceptual analysis, but does not confront this with the conceptualized and Roman account in *Bracton*.

Other work appeared while the *History* was being written, including an edition for the Pipe Roll Society of plea rolls of Richard I (1891). And some of what appeared later arose from the *History* itself. Much of *Domesday Book and Beyond*, published in 1897, was written for the *History* but held over because forestalled by Pollock. The sources were not of the kind with which Maitland felt at home and did not lend themselves to Bractonian modes of thought; and this considerable achievement is proving less durable than the *History*.

Roman Canon Law in the Church of England, published as a book in 1898, reproducing, among others, three major papers from the two preceding years, also dealt with questions which had arisen out of the *History*. Against the finding of a royal commission and in particular its historical amplification by Stubbs, Maitland concluded that the medieval English church was fully bound by the canon law of Rome. He had the better of the argument: but legal questions do not arise in such absolute terms, and modifications have been suggested, mostly arising from studies of church court records. The work elicited personal statements. In his preface, fearing that any writer on this subject would be taken to argue for the English or the Roman church, Maitland declared himself 'a dissenter from both, and from other churches' (p. vi). And much later, he recalled that 'I got more fun out of that than out of any other job I ever did' (*Letters*, 1. no. 418). The sense of enjoyment shows in much of his work and, with his awareness of his own mortality, explains its speed.

This involvement with the medieval church led Maitland into the sixteenth century ('I like most centuries better' (*Letters*, 1, no. 233)) and into the unfamiliar art of narrative history. In 1896 Lord Acton asked him to contribute to the *Cambridge Modern History*, and after some hesitation he agreed to write on 'The Anglican settlement and the Scottish Reformation'. If this seems an unlikely task for Maitland, Maitland equally seems an unlikely choice for Acton: perhaps a notoriously uncommitted outsider seemed safer than entrenched specialists. The chapter was finished in 1899, but Acton's death delayed publication until 1903. As literature it achieves Maitland's customary success; and though the substance of his picture has been questioned it has largely survived.

'Gleanings' from this field appeared in article form in the *English Historical Review* (1900 and 1903) before the chapter itself. And his other sixteenth-century venture, the Rede lecture on *English Law and the Renaissance*, was given early in June 1901 and published with copious notes before the end of the year. At the end of April he had wondered (to R. L. Poole) 'what on earth to say' (*Letters*, 1, no. 283): and he developed a thought that had come to him earlier when discussing the records of Lincoln's Inn. He saw the common law as in decline, and saved from a wholesale reception of Roman law only by the toughness imparted to law by teaching. It was among his most brilliant pieces, and in the end the one most generally agreed to be wrong. He had, as it were, enlisted for his country in a contest that did not happen. There was no Roman threat; and, far from being in decline, English law was staging its own home-made renaissance.

Honours Cambridge's Rede lecture and Oxford's Ford lectures rank among the honours that came to Maitland. Cambridge had made him honorary doctor in 1891; and although not all its honorary degrees were then of their later grandeur, this was remarkable for a man of forty-one in the service of the university whose published books were all editions. Glasgow followed in 1896 and Oxford in 1899; and when he died Oxford was to do him the extraordinary honour of a formal address of condolence to Cambridge. In 1902 he was one of the founding fellows of the British Academy, and became honorary fellow of Trinity (a special pleasure) and honorary bencher of Lincoln's Inn— 'one of the vacant bishoprics would have been less of a surprise' (*Letters*, 1, nos. 344, 352). It was also in that year that the prime minister, A. J. Balfour, offered him the regius chair of modern history in Cambridge, vacant by Acton's death. Maitland declined by return of post, explaining to friends that he was happy with 'such colleagues as it has happened to few to have' and 'We are a peaceful lot at the Law Board': compare, some years earlier, 'I never came upon any Board that had so little cohesion as this History Board has' (*Letters*, 1, nos. 343, 348, 323, 175).

Illness and writing in the Canary Islands Nor was it just that Maitland's lawyer colleagues were congenial: they accommodated his illness. Pleurisy in the summer of 1898 had him sent to winter sunshine; and every winter thereafter had to be spent in the Canary Islands or (once) Madeira. The breakdown was progressive. In 1901 'lumbago has been adding itself to some other ills' (*Letters*, 1, no. 293), and in the last year of his life prolonged intestinal disorder prompted mention of 'the neuralgic fiend' and of recent heart trouble: 'I am always stopping leaks in a crazy ship' (Letters, 2, no. 333). In the islands he worked and took strenuous exercise when he could, and in Cambridge he did all that he could as professor: but lectures in the long vacation must have satisfied honour more than faculty needs, and his debt to his colleagues was as real as their affection for him.

Though nothing would stop Maitland's scholarly work, it had to be redirected. With no libraries in the Canaries and no library time in England he turned to manuscripts which could be reproduced photographically. He had long had in mind the year-books, reports of actual court discussions becoming prominent under Edward I, and may have seen their rise as a turning point which justified the terminal date of the History. There had been various projects for modern editions, including those actually produced by the Rolls Series; Selden Society plans were delayed until the extent of that commitment (and that of its editor) became clear in 1898.

During the winter of 1899–1900 Maitland worked in the Canaries on year-book manuscripts, and early in 1901 wrote: 'I am making up my mind to give what is left of me to starting the Selden Society's edition of the Year Books' (Letters, 1, no. 281). Four volumes appeared under his name from 1903 onward. G. J. Turner is named as joint editor of the last, which he completed after Maitland's death; and he had helped with all, especially in identifying cases in the plea rolls. Maitland is also named among the editors of two of the three volumes of the Eyre of Kent, the first of which appeared in 1910: a manuscript with these reports had been among the first he studied, and a transcription finished in 1901 was found after his death with an instruction to send it to the society.

His work on the year-books must rank next after the History among Maitland's achievements, not just for his ideas about their genesis or his investigation of their language, but for his perception of their place in the intellectual history of all law as well as in the particular development of the common law. But his intention to give them 'what is left of me' was deflected. In May 1895 Leslie Stephen's second wife had died, and in an unusually emotional letter Maitland shows affection and a sense of obligation over his own marriage, in which the Stephens had been instrumental (Letters, 1, no. 157). A little later Stephen asked Maitland to deal with work unfinished at his death and to write any biographical notice that might be called for: not a full life which would be impossible—'the materials do not exist' (Fifoot, Life, 268))—but the kind of notice appropriate to the Dictionary of National Biography. Maitland doubted which would be the survivor—'I know that I shall not be here very long' (Letters, 2, no. 63)—whether he would deal well with any biography, and whether for Stephen he would judge the boundaries of reticence aright. But he promised.

Life of Leslie Stephen, and death of F. W. Maitland Stephen died in February 1904; and modesty carried Maitland beyond his brief. Only one with the powers of Stephen himself, he explained, could catch his essence in the short account Stephen had envisaged. 'If I am to write of him at all, I must use other words and other eyes than mine, more especially his own' (Maitland, Life and Letters of Leslie Stephen, 2). So he brought together many letters written by and about Stephen and worked them into a 500-page book. It is a fine portrait; and perhaps only one who regrets the diversion from the year-books can wonder whether Maitland's own words and eyes, which Stephen wanted, might not have yielded a more compelling miniature. The Life and Letters was finished in the spring of 1906 and Maitland awaited 'the dreadful moment of publication' (Letters, 1, no. 472). For the first time he feared reviews, and feared that he had not done right by Stephen. The book was published in November and he knew that it had been well received; but his wife saw lingering anxiety as he turned its pages just hours before he died (Fifoot, Life, 279).

On 6 December Maitland left Cambridge for the Canaries, and influenza which developed on the voyage became double pneumonia. He died in a hotel in Las Palmas early in the morning of 20 December; and next day his wife and Ermengard, who had preceded him to get a house ready for their usual stay, saw him buried in the English cemetery there.

Reflections on Maitland In his fifty-six years Maitland had lived two disparate lives. The driven scholar who accomplished so much in little more than two decades had emerged in his middle thirties from a more leisurely figure. This is the point of a memoir by his sister (written in 1907 and eventually published in the Cambridge Law Journal, 11, 1951–3, 67), and perhaps she gives a key to that earlier life: in Gloucestershire he was always 'Squire Maitland'. He sought occupation but not, except briefly as an undergraduate, achievement. The family household in London sustained what became a rather aimless life with musical outings and occasional European travels for walking, climbing, or more music.

After Vinogradoff and Pollock and Sidgwick had drawn him into his second life and after illness had taken hold, Maitland never again travelled for pleasure. 'I am compelled to spend the summer in Cambridge in order that I may spend the winter in the Canaries' (Letters, 1, no. 291). He would have liked to visit the United States—'If only Massachusetts were warm in winter' (ibid., no. 472)—but not as a tourist. Declining a visit to Harvard, he wrote: 'I feel as if I lived in the 12th century and was rejecting a "call" to Bologna' (ibid., no. 222). But he corresponded with scholars in the United States as well as in Great Britain and Europe; and since his letters have the spoken immediacy of all his writings, these contacts were close and personal.

Maitland's judgements could be severe. Twiss's edition of Bracton was 'six volumes of rubbish' (Letters, 1, no. 14); and though he thought less badly of the same editor's Glanvill, about which he was consulted only after it had been printed, his opinion still led to its suppression by the Rolls Series (ibid., no. 186). But such judgements were passed in private. He had the lawyer's distaste for personalizing professional differences, and kept out of the perennial battles between historians. Disrespect was reserved for abstractions such as communalism and feudalism; and it was innate respect for people, not just acquired good manners, that underlay his unwavering courtesy. This was in contrast with J. H. Round, who always felt himself entitled to wound; and when his ill-mannered treatment of others provoked Maitland into criticism, Round took lasting umbrage. Even in the offending review (in *The Athenaeum*, October 1899), Maitland expressed his high opinion of Round, but Round was silent until some years after Maitland's death. Then the tribute, though short and paid in passing, was handsome (Round, *Peerage and Pedigree*, 1910, 1.145-7).

There is another contrast. Round's mastery was of detail: Maitland created a subject. But even founding fathers usually die. Maitland's friend and undergraduate rival William Cunningham, who pioneered economic history, is all but forgotten. Maitland's *History of English Law* (together with his *Forms of Action*, which has been taken as an outline continuation of the *History*) is not just remembered: it has been the basis of most of what has been done since. Part of the explanation lies in the volume of scholarly traffic: there have been many economic and few legal historians. And the few have mostly built on Maitland's work, assuming rather than examining his own assumptions. His compelling style and his gift for making difficult things seem obvious still convince; and the work of one who thought orthodox history a contradiction in terms is itself treated as an orthodoxy.　　S. F. C. MILSOM

Sources C. H. S. Fifoot, *Frederic William Maitland: a life* (1971) · *The letters of Frederic William Maitland*, ed. C. H. S. Fifoot, SeldS, suppl. ser., 1 (1965) · *The letters of Frederic William Maitland*, ed. P. N. R. Zutshi, 2 (1995) · H. A. L. Fisher, *Frederick William Maitland* (1910) · W. W. Buckland, 'F. W. Maitland', *Cambridge Law Journal*, 1 (1921-3), 279 · E. Maitland, *F. W. Maitland: a child's-eye view* (1957) [pamphlet format of Selden Society lectures] · S. C. Reynell, 'Frederic William Maitland: a memoir by the late Mrs Reynell', *Cambridge Law Journal*, 11 (1951-3), 67 · B. F. Lock, 'Preface', *Year books of Edward II*, 4: *3 and 4 Edward II*, ed. F. W. Maitland and G. J. Turner, SeldS, 22 (1907), vii-xii · *DNB* · H. A. Hollond, *Frederic William Maitland* (1953) [Selden Society lecture] · *Cambridge University Reporter* (1869-1906), *passim* · T. F. T. Plucknett, 'Maitland's view of law and history', *Early English legal literature* (1958), chap. 1 [first printed in the *Law Quarterly Review* for 1951] · transcript of a radio talk by T. F. T. Plucknett, *The Listener* (12 April 1951) · H. M. Cam, 'Introduction', in *Selected historical essays of F. W. Maitland* (1957) · H. E. Bell, *Maitland: a critical examination and assessment* (1965) · G. R. Elton, *F. W. Maitland* (1985) · M. Philpott, 'Bibliography of the writings of F. W. Maitland', *PBA*, 89 (1996), 261-78

Archives CUL, corresp., papers, mainly relating to research and writings on legal history · Downing College, Cambridge, letters | Bodl. Oxf., letters to J. E. A. Fenwick and T. F. Fenwick · Bodl. Oxf., letters to H. A. L. Fisher and papers relating to biography of him · Bodl. Oxf., letters to Sir Sidney Lee · Bodl. Oxf., letters to Hastings Rashdall · Boston University, letters to Melville Bigelow · CUL, letters to Lord Acton · Duke U., Perkins L., letters to George Neilson · Harvard U., Harvard law school, letters to J. B. Thayer · King's AC Cam., letters to Oscar Browning · LUL, Institute of Historical Research collection, letters to J. H. Round · W. Yorks. AS, Bradford, letters to W. P. Baildon

Likenesses B. Lock, oils, 1906, NPG [*see illus.*] · S. N. Babb, bronze bust, 1908, Squire Law Library, Cambridge · S. N. Babb, marble bust, Lincoln's Inn, London · Cameron Studio, print, NPG · Hills & Saunders, photograph (as president of Cambridge Union), Cambridge Central Library, Cambridgeshire collection; repro. in *Letters*, 2, ed. Zutshi, frontispiece · B. Lock, oils, second version, Downing College, Cambridge

Wealth at death £4657 19s. 5d.: probate, 6 May 1907, *CGPLA Eng. & Wales*

Maitland, James, eighth earl of Lauderdale (1759-1839), politician and political economist, was born on 26 January 1759 at Hatton House, Ratho, Edinburghshire. He was the eldest surviving son of the six sons and six daughters of James Maitland, seventh earl of Lauderdale (1718-1789), landowner and army officer, and his wife, Mary Turner (1733/4-1789), only child of Sir Thomas *Lombe (1685-1739), a silk manufacturer and London alderman.

Education and entry into politics Styled Viscount Maitland from birth, he was educated at Edinburgh high school and at Edinburgh University. His tutor Andrew Dalzel took him to Paris in 1774, and in 1775 he spent a term at Trinity College, Oxford. In 1777 he proceeded to Glasgow University, where he studied under John Millar, and entered Lincoln's Inn. He became an advocate in Edinburgh in July 1780 and had scarcely practised when in September 1780 he was returned to parliament for Newport, Cornwall, on the duke of Northumberland's interest. On 15 August 1782 he married an heiress, Eleanor (1761/2-1856), only surviving daughter of Anthony *Todd, secretary to the Post Office, and Ann Robinson. Described by the writer Elizabeth Grant as 'a nice little painted doll, a cipher as to intellect' (E. Grant, *Memoirs of a Highland Lady*, ed. J. M. Strachey, 1898, 293), Eleanor brought Maitland a dowry of £50,000 and her father's pledge of £10,000 on the birth of each of their children, of which they had four sons and five daughters.

On entering the Commons, Maitland attached himself to Charles James Fox, then in opposition, who valued him. He gave his maiden speech, on 26 February 1781, in favour of Edmund Burke's reforms to the civil list and deplored the extravagance of the war with the American colonies. He praised Fox's East India bill and defended the outgoing coalition ministry in December 1783 against the royal preference for William Pitt. From 1784 he sat for Marlborough on the Wilkins interest and supported the opposition, except when in May 1787 it accused his father-in-law of abuses in administering the Post Office. In the same month he mooted a bill enabling the eldest sons of Scottish peers to sit for Scottish burghs. He was one of the managers of Warren Hastings's impeachment and opposed the exclusion of the prince of Wales from the regency council. He upheld the rights of slave owners in opposing abolition of slavery on 21 May 1789; he reiterated these views in the Lords in 1794 and changed over to the abolitionists only in 1806. His succession to the earldom in August 1789 terminated his Commons career.

Opposition peer In 1790 Lauderdale was elected a Scottish representative peer, and he first spoke in the Lords on 11 April 1791 against the war in India. In the debate on the proclamation against seditious writings on 31 May 1791 he mocked Pitt, the duke of Richmond, and Benedict Arnold

James Maitland, eighth earl of Lauderdale (1759–1839), by Thomas Phillips, 1806

for their desertion of parliamentary reform. Richmond replied heatedly and Lauderdale challenged him to a duel, which was averted. A duel did take place between Lauderdale and Arnold on 1 July, in which neither was injured. In August 1792 he travelled to Paris with Dr John Moore, leaving for Calais during the September massacres and returning in December. A founder member of the Society of the Friends of the People at home, he styled himself Citizen, affected Jacobin costume, and befriended the revolutionary Brissot. Back in the Lords, he twice intemperately attacked the Aliens Bill and on 1 February 1793 attributed French hostilities and atrocities to counter-revolutionary pressure. He subsequently opposed the war with France and the British government's repression of civil liberties. He championed the Scottish reformers Thomas Muir and Thomas Palmer, imprisoned for seditious libel, and visited them aboard the hulks, but was undermined in debate by Lord Mansfield on 15 April 1794.

Having opposed voluntary subscriptions to the war effort, Lauderdale was alleged by government sources to be handling French propaganda funds; he was examined at the Home Office about dealings with William Stone, a supposed French agent. On 30 April he condemned allied endeavours to overthrow the French regime and subsequently supported the duke of Bedford's motions for peace. He led opposition to the suspension of habeas corpus by the British government and in November opposed the bills against treasonable practices and seditious meetings, accompanying Fox to a protest meeting in Westminster. He claimed credit for thwarting government plans to apply the law of treason to utterances and for mitigating the penalties for second offences. In March 1796 he joined Bedford in attacking Edmund Burke's pension, suggesting that the pension fund should be diverted to public works. Burke responded with *A Letter to a Noble Lord*, which targeted Bedford and virtually ignored Lauderdale. On 13 May he and Lord Lansdowne produced fifteen resolutions subverting government versions of public accounts. These, like most of his motions, failed without a division.

Political economist Lauderdale's politics, illustrated in his *Letters to the Peers of Scotland* (1794), written when he was the only Scottish peer left in opposition, prevented his re-election to the Lords from 1796 onwards. Frustrated, he encouraged Fox's secession from the Commons and considered abdicating his peerage. Out of parliament he became a freeman of London and concentrated on writing on finance and the economy. His anonymously published pamphlet *Thoughts on Finance* was followed in 1798 by *A Letter on the Present Measures of Finance*, which was critical of Pitt's budgetary expedients. His *Plan for Altering the Manner of Collecting a Large Part of the Public Revenue* (1799) proposed substituting inheritance tax for income tax and reducing indirect duties. In 1804, the year when Glasgow University made him an LLD, he published *An inquiry into the nature and origin of public wealth, and into the means and causes of its increase*, a thesis which was enlarged in 1819. He questioned Adam Smith's theory of the relationship between labour and value, maintaining that wealth was a compound of labour, land, and capital, and value was a compound of utility and scarcity. He argued that capital was capable of harnessing productive labour to make profits by meeting market demand, and that such profits resulted only when there were no legislative restraints on commerce and no burdens, such as Pitt's sinking fund to redeem the national debt. His thesis was critically reviewed by Henry Brougham in the *Edinburgh Review* (July 1804). His retaliatory *Observations* provoked further *Thoughts* from Brougham in 1805. Lauderdale published two more pamphlets that addressed problems of the Irish currency and the effects of absentee Irish landlords' remission of income.

Return to the Lords The duke of Bedford's death in 1802 raised the possibility of Lauderdale succeeding as opposition leader in the Lords if he obtained a British peerage, but Lauderdale only returned to Westminster four years later when Fox and Lord Grenville formed a coalition ministry. He was created first Baron Lauderdale of Thirlestane in the British peerage on 22 February 1806 but was denied a cabinet seat by Grenville. Fox encouraged his ambition to govern India but Lauderdale was deterred by the hostility of the court of directors and instead became lord keeper of the great seal of Scotland, with an income of £4000 a year. He wished to purge Scotland of Lord Melville's influence but his tenure of the post was short-lived. On 2 August he was sent to Paris to join Lord Yarmouth in peace negotiations with Napoleon Bonaparte; he had been sworn of the privy council on 21 July. After reporting Yarmouth's improper speculations Lauderdale replaced him as chief negotiator, though his mission proved impossible. He left France on 8 October and justified his conduct in the Lords on 2 January 1807. In March he defended the Scottish Judicature Bill and continued to do so from the opposition benches after the change of ministry in April, which deprived him of office. In opposition he joined with Grey, Grenville, and Holland in defending other uncompleted measures of their ministry. He moved resolutions against orders in council regulating licensed trade on 22 March 1808 and remained critical of the conduct of the war.

A deist in religion, Lauderdale questioned the validity of increasing stipends of Scottish clergy, in a speech, later published, of 20 May 1808, and in June opposed the curates' residence bill. Among his other regular targets in debate were the East India Company, which he criticized in print in 1809, and the judicial system. He gave warm support to the reduction of criminal penalties championed by Sir Samuel Romilly and later welcomed the introduction of trial by jury in Scotland in February 1815. Ambitious to return to ministerial office, Lauderdale had long cultivated the prince of Wales and his brother, the duke of York, and wished for the abdication of the incapacitated George III. He sought to reverse the duke's public disgrace over the army contracts affair and in December 1810 took the prince's part in opposing restrictions on his regency. When the prince objected to Grenville's and Grey's principled refusal to take office in his first regency ministry, Lauderdale rebuked him at Carlton House on 22 February 1812 but he failed to overcome the regent's dislike of Grey.

Lauderdale thus remained in opposition and continued to voice his opinions on financial and economic issues. In March 1811 he had deplored excessive issue of paper currency, which had caused coin to disappear and paper money to depreciate. He opposed the gold coin and bank note bill introduced in July by Lord Stanhope in an attempt to stabilize paper currency, arguing that only a resumption of cash payments by the Bank of England could reverse the trend. In February 1812 he spoke out against the Framework Bill, provoked by the actions of distressed Luddites, and advocated retrenchment of public finances. However, his attempt to probe East India Company assets and Bank of England profits failed, as did his motion of 1 May for a committee on the circulating currency; he countered by opposing the Local Tokens Bill. His pamphlets, *The Depreciation of the Paper-Currency of Great Britain Proved* (1812) and *Further Considerations* (1813) provided the basis of his speeches in the 1812 parliament. On 18 May 1813 he again deplored the sinking fund scheme and on 21 June he opposed renewal of the East India Company charter. His motion against over-issue of paper currency failed on 9 July but he persisted by objecting to the renewed restriction of cash repayments on 26 April 1814. He took a protectionist line in his *Letter on the Corn Laws* (1814) which he reiterated in his protests against repeal of corn export bounties and against massive imports of foreign corn. Retrenchment was his main

theme in March 1816 and he tried to hasten the resumption of cash payments by the bank in May. His own preference for a silver standard was overruled by Lord Liverpool in June in favour of the gold standard.

The social policies of Liverpool's administration also kept Lauderdale in active opposition. He opposed the suspension of habeas corpus in March 1817 and appealed for universities to be excluded from the penalties under the Seditious Meetings Bill. In debates in June he characterized a bill to combat unemployment as a chimerical attempt to provide general parochial relief, and attacked the game laws. Soon afterwards, in opposing the Aliens Bill, he attempted to preserve the non-alien status of the Bank of Scotland foreign shareholders. He was critical of the cotton factory regulation bill, particularly its measures regarding child labour, and advocated its extension to factories in other industries, yet he ridiculed a bid to ban boy chimney sweeps. Royal affairs continued to attract his interest and he objected to the duke of Cumberland's exclusion from the Royal Marriages Bill in May 1818, having mediated in Cumberland's quarrel with his mother the queen over his marriage. He also questioned the queen's control over the Windsor establishment.

Throughout Lauderdale kept up pressure for a resumption of cash payments. When the parliamentary committee examining the issue, chaired by Robert Peel, published its report in favour of resumption, he agreed with it that an abrupt recourse to a depreciated metallic currency would cripple commerce. On 15 June 1819 he sought judicial views on the legality of the flawed coinage. He believed that lower taxation would best relieve economic problems, as stated in debates on 21 June, and on 17 December he blamed economic distress on excessive public expenditure. In May 1820 he insisted that the peacetime depression had hit agriculture as well as commerce and manufacture.

Courtier On 19 July 1820 Lauderdale defended the conduct of his brother Thomas as a colonial governor, but his exertions were far greater on behalf of George IV, whose queen faced a trial for adultery. A member of the Lords' secret committee investigating the charges, he delivered a keynote speech on 2 November stating the case against Caroline, which, when it was published, became the talk of the town. The king rewarded him by appointing him a knight of the Thistle, on 17 July 1821. By now a courtier, he had abandoned most of his whig credentials and objected to the disfranchisement of rotten boroughs unless all voters were corrupt. In 1824 and 1825 he attempted to restrain the proliferation of joint-stock companies that lacked sound finances. In 1826 he clashed with Liverpool over the bank charter agreement, contrasting the confidence placed by the Scottish public in their banks with English distrust of theirs. That year, as in 1822, he advocated protection against imports of foreign grain, and on 8 March 1827 he secured a select committee on the sliding scale of duties on imported grain. This remained his favourite subject until 1828 when he supported Wellington's ministry and was reported to have influence over its counsels. On 17 June 1828 he approved a bill enabling

Scottish peers to sit in the Commons. He remained critical of parliamentary reform and in 1829 published *Three Letters to the Duke of Wellington*, which set out the false economies of adopting a sinking fund.

Lauderdale's final speech was made against the Scottish Court of Session Bill on 12 July 1830. He took his seat in the Lords the following year but absented himself for health reasons, though a suspected underlying reason was his embarrassment at opposing Lord Grey's administration. The passage of the Reform Bill, which he opposed by proxy while engineering the election of twelve anti-reformers as representative peers, induced him to retire to his Scottish estate. He died at Thirlestane Castle, near Lauder, Berwickshire, on 15 September 1839 and was buried in the family vault at Haddington Abbey on 20 September. Long dismissed as eccentric, his contribution to economic theory has more recently been acknowledged.

Lauderdale's second son, **Anthony Maitland**, tenth earl of Lauderdale (1785–1863), naval officer, was born on 10 June 1785 at Walthamstow, Essex, and entered the navy, aged ten, as admiral's servant on the *Victory*. A midshipman under Admiral St Vincent in 1798, he was wounded in Nelson's attack on the Boulogne flotilla in 1801. He next served in the Mediterranean and East Indies and from 1811 captained the *Pique* in other stations, seizing an American privateer. As captain of the *Glasgow* he took part in the bombardment of Algiers in 1816, for which he was made CB. He had been elected to parliament on the family interest for Haddington burghs on 16 July 1813 and in the intervals of service voted with the opposition. He gave up his seat in 1818 and resumed service in the Mediterranean until retiring on half pay in 1821. He had been made KCMG on 26 February 1820 and re-entered parliament, for Berwickshire, in 1826, where he gave a general support to government. On 24 March 1831 he defended an anti-reform petition from Berwickshire. In August 1830 he had become naval aide-de-camp to William IV and he was made KMG on 6 April 1832. That year he lost his parliamentary election. He retained his aideship under Queen Victoria until 1841 when he obtained flag rank. He became an admiral in 1857 and on 22 August 1860 succeeded his brother James as tenth earl of Lauderdale and third baron. He became GCB on 10 November 1862 and died unmarried at Thirlestane Castle on 22 March 1863, thereby extinguishing the barony. He was succeeded in the earldom by Thomas *Maitland (1803–1878).   ROLAND THORNE

Sources R. Sturges, ed., *Economists' papers, 1750–1950* (1975), 66–7 · J. Williams, ed., *Guide to the printed materials for English social and economic history, 1750–1850* (1926) · Cobbett, *Parl. hist.* · Hansard 1 · Hansard 2 · Hansard 3 · *DNB* · M. Paglin, *Malthus and Lauderdale: the anti-Ricardian tradition* (1961) · H. R. Vassall, Lord Holland, *Memoirs of the whig party during my time*, ed. H. E. Vassall, Lord Holland, 2 vols. (1852–4) · H. R. V. Fox, third Lord Holland, *Further memoirs of the whig party, 1807–1821*, ed. Lord Stavordale (1905) · *The journal of Elizabeth, Lady Holland, 1791–1811*, ed. earl of Ilchester [G. S. Holland Fox-Strangways], 2 vols. (1908), vol. 1, p. 270; vol. 2, pp. 167–79, 218 · *The correspondence of George, prince of Wales, 1770–1812*, ed. A. Aspinall, 8 vols. (1963–71) · *The letters of King George IV, 1812–1830*, ed. A. Aspinall, 3 vols. (1938) · *The manuscripts of J. B. Fortescue*, 10 vols., HMC, 30 (1892–1927), vol. 2, p. 538; vol. 4, p. 70; vol. 8; vol. 10, pp. 105, 228, 337, 366 · *The Horner papers*, ed. K. Bourne and W. B. Taylor (1994) ·

F. G. Stephens and M. D. George, eds., *Catalogue of prints and drawings in the British Museum, division 1: political and personal satires*, 11 vols. in 12 (1870–1954), vols. 7–11 · *The Creevey papers*, ed. H. Maxwell, 2nd edn, 2 vols. (1904) · Farington, *Diary*, 2.405, 569; 3.838; 6.2359; 7.2760, 2788; 11.4089 · J. A. Cannon, 'Maitland, James', HoP, *Commons, 1754–90*

Archives NA Scot., drafts and papers · NL Scot., corresp. · NL Scot., MSS · NRA, priv. coll., corresp. and papers · priv. coll., corresp. · PRO · Thirlestane Castle, Berwickshire, MSS | Althorp, Northamptonshire, Spencer MSS · Beds. & Luton ARS, Whitbread MSS · BL, Add. MSS · BL, letters to Sir W. A'Court, Add. MS 41536, fols. 20, 34, 40 [Anthony Maitland] · BL, corresp. with John Allen, Add. MS 52180 · BL, corresp. with Charles James Fox, Add. MSS 47564, 51458 · BL, corresp. with Lord Grenville, Add. MSS 58941–58943 · BL, corresp. with Lord Holland and Lady Holland, Add. MSS 51691–51704 · BL, letters to W. Huskisson, Add. MSS 37840–37845 · BL, letters to Lord Liverpool, Add. MSS 38254–38410 · BL, corresp. with Sir Robert Peel, Add. MSS 40347–40402, *passim* · Blair Adam, Fife, Blair Adam MSS, corresp. with William Adam · Heriot Watt University, letters to Sir James Gibson-Craig · NA Scot., letters to Lady Anne Durham · NL Scot., letters relating to Lord Deerhurst · PRO, Chatham MSS · U. Aberdeen, Hamilton papers · U. Durham L., corresp. with Earl Grey · UCL, Brougham MSS

Likenesses Nollekens, bust, 1803 · J. Henning, paste medallion, 1806, Scot. NPG · J. Henning, pencil drawing, 1806, Scot. NPG · T. Phillips, oils, 1806, Scot. NPG [*see illus.*] · C. Smith, portrait, exh. 1868 · G. Hayter, group portrait (*The trial of Queen Caroline*), NPG · J. Sayer, engraving (as Brissot, the French revolutionary), BM, NPG

Maitland, James (1914–1996), Church of Scotland minister, was born on 10 May 1914 at The Gardens, Auchendarroch, Argyll, Scotland, the second of the four children of John Maitland (1878–1953), head gardener, and his wife, Barbara McLeod (1883–1975). He was educated at Oban high school (1926–32), Edinburgh University for arts (1933–7; MA, 1937) and divinity (1937–40), and was ordained as *locum tenens* to Glenorchy and Inishail (1940–42). He served subsequently at Pathhead West, Kirkcaldy (1942–8) and St Bride's, Edinburgh (1948–54). He joined the Iona community, then under the direction of George MacLeod and Ralph Morton and was warden of (Iona) Community House, Glasgow (1954–8). He resumed parish work subsequently at Airdrie West (1958–66). During the Kirkcaldy ministry, on 27 July 1943, he married Elizabeth Mary Simpson (*b.* 1916), a graduate of Edinburgh with teaching and social work qualifications. Maitland finally went to West Lothian and formed part of a remarkable team ministry (1966–83), known as the Livingston Ecumenical Experiment. While in Edinburgh he developed great expertise as a religious broadcaster with the BBC.

Certain features characterized Maitland's ministry, and justify the judgement that he was one of the most visionary and accomplished of the Church of Scotland ministers of the second half of the twentieth century. For example, his preaching was unique, combining as it did profound evangelical fervour and logical persuasiveness, the latter acquired when studying under Professor A. E. Taylor, the former caught from the passion of the Very Revd Dr James Black of St George's West, Edinburgh, where he worshipped as a student. He had, too, gifts of apposite literary reference and quotation as well as of theological exposition, which made him an excellent communicator, not least to the young. The 1950s and 1960s were the years of 'mission weeks' and 'missionary campaigns', and he was much sought after as a speaker. Running through all of his preaching, speaking, and thinking was a deep concern for the underprivileged, whether in Korea, Africa, or Glasgow, depressed by what he once called 'soulless industrialism'.

All of these strands of interest and ability were woven together and strengthened in something which was implicit in Maitland's acceptance of membership of the Livingston Ecumenical Experiment, namely, his commitment to church unity. He tells the story in *New Beginnings: Breaking through to Unity* (1998). From its beginning (1966) with the Revd Brian Hardy of the Scottish Episcopal church and himself, the experiment branched out to include Roman Catholic, Methodist, and Congregationalist representatives, and it developed step by step with the growth of the new town, for which it provided a much needed sense of community and a living soul. Though he would have been the first to deny it, the success of the experiment has to be attributed in the main to his leadership and inspiration, and particularly to his pastoral touch and caring for people, seen in the churches setting up The Forum, a parish group which without statutory authority became a power for the improvement of housing conditions, reallocation of houses, and local educational arrangements. Sadly the success of the experiment has proved to be unique, in that it has not been followed on any similar scale in Scotland.

James Maitland's achievements in church and new town were honoured publicly in two ways—first, in 1969 by the University of Edinburgh with the degree of doctor of divinity, *honoris causa*; and second, in 1990, by the Lothian regional council with the Lothian award for services to the community. Maitland died on 20 August 1996 at his home, 38 Leving Place, Livingston, and was survived by his wife and three daughters. His remains were interred at Adambrae cemetery, Livingston, on 11 May 1998.   JOHN MCINTYRE

Sources private information (2004) [Elizabeth Maitland] · J. McIntyre, *The Scotsman* (2 Sept 1996) · T. Dalyell, *The Independent* (3 Sept 1996) · d. cert.
Archives priv. coll., MSS of sermons, and other addresses
Wealth at death £27,496.45: confirmation, 1997, NA Scot., SC/CO 981/83

Maitland, John, first Lord Maitland of Thirlestane (1543–1595), lord chancellor of Scotland, was the second son of Sir Richard *Maitland of Lethington (1496–1586) and Mary or Mariota Cranstoun (d. 1586); his older brother was William *Maitland of Lethington (1525x30–1573), one of the most powerful politicians in Scotland while he held the office of secretary between 1558 and 1571. Mary *Maitland was his sister. Like his father and brother, Maitland was trained in the law. He probably attended Haddington grammar school; he is listed on the rolls of St Salvator's College of the University of St Andrews for the year 1555. Thereafter he completed his education in France; it is not known when he went or for how long he stayed. In 1563 Queen Mary made him joint factor, with his father, of the lands of the Cistercian nunnery of Haddington. In 1567 he

John Maitland, first Lord Maitland of Thirlestane (1543–1595), by unknown artist, c.1590

became, quite suddenly, a person of importance. In February of that year he became commendator of the priory of Coldingham through a collusive arrangement by which Francis Stewart, the nephew of Mary's all-powerful favourite, James Hepburn, fourth earl of Bothwell, became commendator of the much richer abbey of Kelso. Two months later he became lord privy seal when his father resigned that office in his favour.

His brother's man The keeper of the privy seal was not a powerful official, nor was there much to do: Sir Richard Maitland had held the office for almost five years although he was blind. Secretary Maitland undoubtedly arranged the transfer: he needed an active political supporter, and John Maitland was exactly that, following his brother loyally until the end came for William in 1573. Like William, John Maitland joined the ranks of the queen's opponents in 1567, and was confirmed in his office by the Regent Moray on 26 August, four days after Moray's assumption of the regency. A year later, in June 1568, he became a member of the court of session. Like William, John broke with Moray over Mary's request for a divorce from Bothwell; they were among the few who voted for the divorce at the convention of estates of August 1569. When the fighting between the supporters of the queen and those of the young James VI began in 1570, an English army seized Coldingham. In May 1571 the Regent Lennox's parliament forfeited the Maitland brothers; the privy seal was bestowed on the king's tutor, the famous humanist George Buchanan. The brothers took refuge in Edinburgh Castle, which surrendered to a combined Anglo-Scottish force on 28 May 1573. Sir William Drury, the English commander, took charge of the important prisoners, including the Maitlands. William died within two weeks, possibly a suicide. John was turned over to the Regent Morton, who kept him for a time in his grim fortress at Tantallon. Fortunately for John, Morton did not regard him as worth hanging. In February 1574 the regent permitted him to live with his cousin Lord Somerville at Cowthally, at the western end of the Pentland Hills, under what amounted to house arrest. He did not regain his liberty until 15 September 1578, several months after a *coup d'état* put an end to Morton's regency.

John Maitland's policies and behaviour during his years of power indicate that he had absorbed the lessons of his brother's spectacular and tragic career. Like William he was a *politique*, but he came to understand that William had seriously underestimated the extent to which religious passion determined people's political conduct and, in consequence, the political influence of the spokesmen of the kirk. Making good the Stewart claim to the English succession became William's primary political purpose from the time of Queen Mary's return to Scotland in 1561. He failed to see that in a religious age Anglo-Scottish union could come about only on the basis of a common religion, and so he backed Mary to the end in spite of her Catholicism, which made her unacceptable to the English establishment and, as time went on, to more and more Scots as well. The succession question did not obsess John Maitland, though of course he supported the claims of his master, King James, whom it did obsess. Good relations with England were very important to him, but for domestic political reasons, rather than on account of the succession. Finally, Maitland did not share his brother's, and their father's, view that the upper aristocracy was the only class that counted for anything in Scotland. For him the upper aristocracy was part of the political problem, not the indispensable element in the solution.

Rise to power   John Maitland's rise to power began with the arrival in Scotland of Esmé Stuart in September 1579. Esmé quickly became a favourite of his cousin the king, who made him first duke of Lennox. In 1580 Lennox brought Maitland and other supporters of the fallen queen to court. James always valued such men for their loyalty to his mother, provided they transferred their loyalty to himself, and he came to like and trust Maitland, who, like James, was a poet of modest talents. On 17 February 1581 Maitland was formally rehabilitated; in April he resumed his seat on the court of session. He survived the fall of Lennox in 1582, though the ultra-protestant Ruthven raiders drove him from the king's presence. In January 1583, at the age of thirty-nine, he married Jane Fleming (1554–1609), daughter of James, fourth Lord Fleming, and the niece of his brother William's wife. Jane Fleming's mother was a sister of Lord John Hamilton, the effective head of that great family, an important political connection for Maitland. Two children were born of the

marriage: John, born in 1594, who ultimately became first earl of Lauderdale, and Anne, born in 1590, whose husband, Robert Seton, second earl of Winton, whom she married at thirteen, went mad on their wedding night. Anne died six years later, still a virgin.

With the fall of the Ruthven raiders and the rise to power of James Stewart, fourth earl of Arran, in the summer of 1583, Maitland returned to court. He became a privy councillor in August, and a regular attendant at the council's meetings. Arran had his suspicions about Maitland, who supported a proposal to allow Lord John Hamilton to return from exile: Arran held the Hamilton earldom. But shortly after the suppression of an attempted coup in April 1584 Maitland was knighted and provided with the opportunity to exercise real power, in the future if not now, by being made secretary. Parliament confirmed the grant in May, and at the same time annulled Maitland's forfeiture and restored him to all his honours and estates, save Coldingham. At this parliament Maitland helped to draft the Erastian church legislation known as the Black Acts, which explicitly approved episcopacy and the crown's jurisdiction over all persons and all cases; to deny that jurisdiction, as some ministers had done, was declared to be treasonable. Several ministers refused to accept the acts of 1584. Maitland helped to devise a formula that split the clerical opposition: the clergy would obey the laws in so far as they agreed with the word of God. Maitland also became a member of a commission to adjust ministers' stipends: the carrot for the clerical donkey. The clerical extremists bitterly denounced him in a libel 'wherein Justice is brought in lamenting, that one of Cameleon's clan, one of the disciples of Matchiavell, had so great place in the commonwealth, to the ruin of justice' (Calderwood, 4.349). Another commission on which Maitland served was charged with reforming the court of session, in other words, with replacing politically unreliable members. Maitland thereupon began the process of placing his political allies on the court, which was a matter of great importance for the future.

Maitland also began to try to undermine the seemingly all-powerful Arran, whose violence and greed had never appealed to him. He was not sufficiently well connected and influential to accomplish this by himself, so he became a supporter of Patrick, master of Gray, an ambitious and attractive young man in whom King James was showing a marked interest. James sent Gray to London in the autumn of 1584 to discuss, among other things, a possible Anglo-Scottish league; while he was there Gray persuaded Elizabeth's officials, who disliked Arran, to provide underhand support for his schemes against the favourite. The ensuing intrigue was enormously complicated, one of the complications being the negotiations for the league, in which Maitland as secretary was deeply involved. In the end Gray achieved complete success. He undermined James's confidence in Arran, and leached away the latter's support among the people who counted, so that when the conspirators struck in November 1585 Arran could offer no resistance. He lost his title, his offices, and the property he had accumulated during his two years of power and faded into obscurity.

The overthrow of Arran marked the beginning of the personal rule of James VI, now aged nineteen. It also marked the beginning of Maitland's years of power. His office gave him constant access to the king; he was diligent and capable; English officialdom thought well of him—the English ambassador Sir Edward Wotton, with whom Maitland was negotiating over the proposed league, called him 'the wisest man in Scotland' (*CSP Scot.*, 1584–5, 681–2). The grant of the keepership of the great seal for life, with the title of vice-chancellor, on 31 May 1586 was an indication of his growing influence and importance. He also received a pension of £1000 Scots. His one dangerous political rival, Gray, was ruined by his involvement in the negotiations preceding the execution of Queen Mary in 1587. From 1587 to 1592 Maitland was the king's chief minister and political tutor, the most powerful man in Scotland after the king.

Strengthening the monarchy That Maitland had an agenda quickly became evident. As early as April 1586 Archibald Douglas, one of his enemies, wrote to Walsingham that the Scottish secretary's 'greatness with the king did consist in this, that he had set down certain platts unto the king, how he might preserve his state in obedience' (*CSP Scot.*, 1585–6, 346–7). At first Maitland moved a little uncertainly. He realized, however, that a further clarification of relations between crown and kirk was necessary, and helped to work out an acceptable compromise which acknowledged the pre-eminence of the general assembly and the legality of the recently established system of presbyteries. In return the kirk accepted the existence of the office of bishop and the crown's view that the kirk's jurisdictional authority was limited to matters of doctrine, discipline, and religious offences such as blasphemy and sexual misbehaviour; it did not embrace politics. But it was clear throughout the negotiations, which lasted until May 1586, that Maitland was still very uneasy about the kirk's power and influence. The same uneasiness and uncertainty influenced his attitude during the negotiations for the league with England, which concluded in July 1586. Maitland supported the alliance in principle, but he believed that the English offer was inadequate, and saw no reason to hurry the negotiations to a conclusion. The young king overruled him, however, and agreed to the English terms, after Elizabeth wrote a letter agreeing to do nothing in derogation of James's claim to the succession without just cause. Maitland became even more acutely aware that the succession was uppermost in the king's mind from his reaction to the disclosure of the Babington plot in August 1586, followed, six months later, by the execution of his mother. Maitland prudently avoided involvement in this business. At one point, in November 1586, he did persuade James to threaten to break the league if Mary's life were taken. Elizabeth exploded with rage, and James reverted to his acquiescent stance, which Elizabeth helped him to maintain by ostentatiously denying responsibility for Mary's death and making Secretary William Davison her scapegoat.

The execution of their former queen outraged large numbers of Scots, who put pressure on the king to retaliate in some way. The leadership of the kirk, which did not in the least regret Mary's death, was very helpful in enabling James to resist this pressure and preserve the English alliance. By the middle of 1587 Maitland saw how existing circumstances could be turned to the crown's advantage. The league had turned the English government into a supporter of royal authority instead of a threat to it. The large moderate party in the kirk was supportive also, provided that the king withdrew his favour from the detested Archbishop Patrick Adamson of St Andrews, which James was prepared to do. There remained the upper aristocracy. Although the nobles constituted a group that would follow a decisive royal leader who shared their outlook, Maitland believed that the authority of the crown should not depend upon the uncertain goodwill of this class. So he set out to lessen its power by creating a central government independent of these men, responsible to, and responsive to, the king and only the king. The institution through which Maitland worked was the privy council, which gradually filled with his administrative and judicial colleagues, upon whom he could usually rely for political support.

Reforming legislation The legislation of the parliament of 1587 embodied Maitland's and James's vision in a series of important enactments. The act of James I (1428) authorizing the lairds to elect representatives to parliament, hitherto a dead letter, was revived: Maitland, himself a laird, counted on this class for support. The annexation of the temporalities of benefices to the crown put a great deal of land at the crown's disposal. James used it to reward both the men who comprised the new class of government servants—lairds, lawyers, cadets of aristocratic families, whom Maitland recruited—and those members of the upper aristocracy who were prepared to support Maitland's regime. The revival of justice ayres and the appointment of local gentry to hold quarter sessions on the English model to handle minor crimes, though not very successful, and the expansion of the government's right to prosecute criminal cases, were efforts to eat into the near monopoly of criminal justice enjoyed by the lords of regality. The revival of the general band made landlords responsible for the production in court of any accused resident of their lands; their property was subject to seizure if they failed to meet their obligations. An effort was made, with some success, to meet some of the complaints of the burghs. All these measures were designed to strengthen the crown by creating a *noblesse de robe* and chipping away at the independent power of the magnates—in the phrase of the English ambassador William Ashby in October 1588, to 'bridle the earls' with the support of the lairds and burghs (*CSP Scot.*, 1586–9, 623–4)—and of the kirk. At the end of the parliament, on 29 July, James raised Maitland to the chancellorship.

These measures met with varying degrees of success. The electoral machinery of the act reintroducing the lairds to parliament, which specified an annual election of representatives whether or not parliament met, was too complicated and did not function well. Its main purpose, however, was not to revivify parliament, which did not meet during the years of Maitland's greatest power, but rather to bring the lairds into contact with government and alliance with it. In this respect it resembled the acts reorganizing criminal justice, which also worked less than perfectly. The annexation of church lands, however, accomplished what Maitland had intended. The kirk, although it complained that it gained little financially, saw the act as a death knell for episcopacy as a system of church government, and became Maitland's ally—'he kept true and honest till the day of his death', wrote James Melville, one of King James's severest critics (*Autobiography and Diary*, 271). James later denounced the act because it limited his ability to restore the authority of bishops, but during Maitland's years of power he used it effectively to reward political supporters and build a *noblesse de robe*. Maitland himself received the lordship of Musselburgh, which belonged to the abbey of Dunfermline. The policy of the general band also worked effectively, especially on the borders, where it was combined with crackdowns on recalcitrant landlords like Lord Maxwell and co-operation with English officials to bring border reivers to justice.

Backlash The thrust of James's and Maitland's policy was clear enough to the upper aristocracy, and Maitland was held responsible for it. 'All matters whatsoever, both domestic and foreign, rests [sic] only upon the chancellor's shoulders', wrote one observer in September 1587 (*Salisbury MSS*, 1583–9, 282–3). Inevitably Maitland and his policy provoked resentment. Many aristocrats bitterly hated him, not only for what he planned to do but also for who he was, an upstart and a parvenu—'a puddock-stool of a night', in the phrase of his greatest enemy, Francis Stewart, earl of Bothwell (*Calderwood*, 5.156). His appointment as lord chancellor offended the most aristocratic of his administrative colleagues, Treasurer Thomas Lyon, the master of Glamis, whose brother had been chancellor and who wanted the office for himself—Maitland was the first chancellor who was neither an aristocrat nor a bishop since the reign of James II. The Catholic earls, led by George Gordon, sixth earl of Huntly, one of James's favourites, also disliked Maitland because of his alliance with the kirk. In the autumn of 1588 they planned to assassinate him, or so Maitland was told. In 1589, following the revelation of Huntly's correspondence with Spain, Maitland, by threatening to resign, persuaded James to remove Huntly as captain of the guard. Huntly, together with the other Catholic earls and Bothwell, now planned to seize the king and compel him to dismiss Maitland, who, said Bothwell in a flamboyant speech, was in English pay and was arranging for an English army to enter Scotland, overthrow the nobility, and reduce Scotland to slavery.

The coup misfired and led to a rebellion on Huntly's part which James easily put down. The king, who believed in showing a certain amount of favour to the Catholics so as to forestall Catholic opposition to his succession to the English throne, punished no one very severely. He was about to get married, and was determined that no domestic broils mar his bride's arrival. When he decided in October 1589 to go to Denmark to fetch Anne home himself, he took Maitland with him, partly to ensure Maitland's safety. He left behind a remarkable proclamation denying the truth of the general assumption that Maitland was 'leading me, by the nose as it were, to all his appetites, as if I were an unreasonable creature, or a bairn that could do nothing of myself' (*Reg. PCS*, 4.428–9).

The royal party landed in Norway in October, James was married in November, and went on to Denmark in December, where he remained until spring, enjoying his holiday, meeting with Tycho Brahe, to whom Maitland wrote two Latin epigrams, and holding political discussions with Maitland. Rumours abounded concerning these discussions: Maitland would have the nobility barred from the privy council and not permitted to come to court except on summons. These were canards; what was genuine was a quarrel between the Earl Marischal, James's ambassador to Denmark, and Maitland, which James settled in Maitland's favour. Furthermore, Maitland was unwilling to pay Marischal's (and others') expenses out of Queen Anne's dowry, though he accepted part of a cupboard of plate to cover his own. When the royal party returned to Scotland, and Anne was crowned on 19 May 1590, James raised him to the peerage as Lord Maitland of Thirlestane, the only person so honoured. His colleague the lord treasurer received no more than a knighthood, which further irritated him. Maitland was becoming dangerously isolated, and dangerously unpopular.

As long as Maitland enjoyed James's wholehearted support, however, he was secure enough. He was now at the peak of his influence with the king. He used his position to create a special committee to enforce the policy of the general band in both the highlands and the borders, and to improve the procedure for filling vacancies on the court of session by requiring that the judges examine the qualifications of any nominee before the king formally made the appointment. He also undertook some financial retrenchment. His measures, which included husbanding the queen's dowry, raised a host of new enemies for Maitland among the courtiers. Queen Anne herself turned hostile: James had given her the temporalities of the abbey of Dunfermline, and she wanted them all, including Maitland's lordship of Musselburgh, which was not part of the gift. The allegation in April 1591 that Bothwell had been consorting with witches turned James permanently against the earl, who blamed Maitland, quite unjustly, for the king's implacability. Bothwell was imprisoned, escaped, evaded capture, and on 27 December 1591, with the aid of some disgruntled courtiers, entered Holyroodhouse itself in order to seize the king and kill Maitland. He failed, narrowly. Two months later Huntly, toward whom Maitland had been making friendly gestures, murdered James Stewart, second earl of Moray, who was his rival for local influence in north-eastern Scotland. Maitland was blamed for this by all those who wanted Huntly punished, notably the Stewart family, the kirk, and the English government. Huntly's enemies attributed James's inaction to

Maitland rather than to its real cause, James's obsessive hatred of Bothwell, who was, in the king's view, a far more dangerous offender than Huntly. The political pressure became so great that on 30 March 1592 James ordered Maitland to leave the court. His great days were over.

Last years The last three and a half years of Maitland's life were anticlimactic. He was able to persuade the king to use the parliament of May 1592 to give legal recognition to the existing presbyterian structure of the kirk and repeal the act of 1584 that gave administrative jurisdiction to bishops. This legislation followed logically from Maitland's previous policy toward the kirk. Presbyterian commentators, while giving him credit, declared that his purpose was 'to win the hearts of the ministers and people, alienated from him for his hounding out of Huntly against the earl of Moray' (Calderwood, 5.162), which does Maitland less than justice. It was, in fact, his last act of constructive statesmanship.

During his final years Maitland spent much time at Lethington, and then at his new house, Thirlestane Castle, in Lauder, which was finished in the year of his death. The king often rode out to consult him, and he returned frequently to court, where he manoeuvred among the various factions in order to recover his political footing. In September 1592 James appointed him ambassador to France, partly for his own safety: he was in real danger from Bothwell. He never went; he decided that, if he left, he was likely to lose his offices and property. As it was, he surrendered Musselburgh to the queen in July 1593 to recover her favour. The most significant development of these years was that the administrative machine Maitland and James had built withstood the attacks made on Maitland by Bothwell and the Catholic earls, whose dealings with Spain came to light with the discovery of the so-called Spanish blanks in December 1592. By 1595, after many vicissitudes, Huntly, Erroll, and Bothwell were all driven into exile; Bothwell would never return. This was a milestone: never again would a handful of disgruntled aristocrats threaten royal authority. And the crown had won through without outside aid, apart from a little English money. Thanks to Maitland's work Scotland now had an administration as distinct from a congeries of aristocratic office-holders.

Maitland died on 3 October 1595 at Thirlestane Castle. 'He granted at his death', wrote Calderwood, 'that he had greatly offended that man of God, Mr. Knox; wished often that he had builded a hospital when he builded his castle at Lauder, and cried often for mercy.' Nevertheless he was 'in a very good estate, as appeared, for a life to come' (Calderwood, 5.382). King James wrote a stiff and conventional sonnet of regret; when asked about a successor, he 'said he will well ken who [sic] he chooses for that place, adding that he can have none but in short time they will presume to be equal with himself' (CSP Scot., 1595–7, 39–41). James in fact had no more such equals; Maitland had not only created an administration but also trained his own successor, in the person of the king himself. The

chancellor's portrait, of unknown date, hangs in Thirlestane Castle. His splendid tomb, with a recumbent effigy, is in St Mary's Church, Haddington.

MAURICE LEE JUN.

Sources M. Lee jun., *John Maitland of Thirlestane* (Princeton, 1959) • G. Donaldson, *Scotland: James V to James VII* (1965), vol. 3 of *The Edinburgh history of Scotland* (1965–75) • J. Wormald, *Court, kirk, and community: Scotland, 1470–1625* (1981) • *CSP Scot.*, 1547–1603 • *Reg. PCS*, 1st ser. • *Reg. PCS*, 2nd ser., vol. 1 • *Calendar of the manuscripts of the most hon. the marquis of Salisbury*, 24 vols., HMC, 9 (1883–1976) • *APS*, 1424–1625 • D. Calderwood, *The history of the Kirk of Scotland*, ed. T. Thomson and D. Laing, 8 vols., Wodrow Society, 7 (1842–9) • J. Spottiswood, *The history of the Church of Scotland*, ed. M. Napier and M. Russell, 3 vols., Bannatyne Club, 93 (1850) • *The autobiography and diary of Mr James Melvill*, ed. R. Pitcairn, Wodrow Society (1842) • J. Bain, ed., *The border papers: calendar of letters and papers relating to the affairs of the borders of England and Scotland*, 2 vols. (1894–6) • T. Thomson, ed., *Acts and proceedings of the general assemblies of the Kirk of Scotland*, 3 pts, Bannatyne Club, 81 (1839–45) • *Scots peerage*, 5.298–301 • GEC, *Peerage*, new edn, 12/1.699–701
Likenesses miniature, c.1590, NPG [*see illus.*] • portrait, Thirlestane Castle, Lauder

Maitland, John, duke of Lauderdale (1616–1682), politician, was born at the family seat of Lethington Hall, Haddingtonshire, on 24 May 1616, the eldest surviving son of John Maitland, second Lord Maitland of Thirlestane (*d.* 1645), created earl of Lauderdale in 1624, and his wife, Lady Isabel (1594–1638), second daughter of the prominent Jacobean statesman Alexander *Seton, first earl of Dunfermline. His mother bore fifteen children, of whom four survived her: Sophia, John, Robert, and Charles *Maitland, later third earl of Lauderdale (*c.*1620–1691). Robert died in 1658, and it is the other two sons who feature in public life.

Precocious politician, 1616–1644 The future duke was endowed with the barony of Haddington on 30 March 1622, matriculated at the University of St Andrews in 1631, and married Lady Anne Home (*d.* 1671) in August or September 1632. She was the second daughter of a neighbouring magnate, Alexander Home, first earl of Home, and his second wife, Mary, daughter of Edward Sutton, ninth Baron Dudley. The union produced a daughter, Mary. This is all that is known of his early life, until the young Viscount Maitland (as he was styled) suddenly appears in national view in September 1641, accompanying the commissioners appointed by the Scottish covenanters to negotiate peace with the government of Charles I, first at Ripon and then at London, after their resounding military defeat of the king. From this it must be surmised that he had been a keen supporter of the covenant, but it seems unclear whether he went with the delegation in an official or a private capacity.

Having returned to Scotland with the delegation in 1641, Maitland continued to push himself forward. He was refused leave to attend the parliament of that year in his capacity as a peer's heir, but did sit in the general assembly of the kirk in July, and was chosen to carry its request for uniformity of ecclesiastical government between England and Scotland to the king and the English parliament. This suggests that he had now established a reputation for intelligence and eloquence, and on 8

John Maitland, duke of Lauderdale (1616–1682), by Sir Peter Lely, c.1665

August 1643 he was made one of the commissioners to negotiate the solemn league and covenant, and on 17 August ordered to carry it to Westminster. He was also named to sit in the Westminster assembly of divines as a lay elder, and so by November 1643 had taken up residence in the English capital. In February 1644 he was made one of the Scottish members of the committee for both kingdoms which met there, and on 20 November he was appointed one of the Scottish contingent of the delegation instructed to carry an offer of peace terms to the king at Oxford. By the time of his father's death on 18 January 1645, therefore, the young noble had established himself as one of the main figures in the covenanter alliance with the English parliamentarians, and his fellow commissioners regularly praised him for the energy, dedication, and persuasive skill which he displayed in their work.

Covenanter diplomat, 1645–1648 The first duty of the new earl was to represent Scotland in the fruitless peace talks between the allies and the English royalists at Uxbridge, in February 1645. An invaluable insight into his attitudes at this time is provided by a remark which he made to the French ambassador Sabran, before setting out for Uxbridge. According to the Frenchman, Lauderdale admitted that the religious argument against episcopacy was actually unproven, and stated that the Scottish demand for its abolition in England was a sound practical move, to bring the two nations into harmony with each other. In his pragmatic and opportunist approach to the matter, devoid of any ideological commitment, he already differed from many of his fellow covenanters, and was

establishing a pattern which was to remain consistent throughout his career. None the less, he worked as hard as any of his colleagues to persuade the royalists to concede the removal of bishops from the English church, and only after the talks collapsed did he return to Scotland, in May, to settle his inheritance.

Lauderdale was deeply missed by his fellow commissioners in London, and was back there by February 1646, informing the city's common council of the determination of the Scots to uphold the alliance with parliament and its conditions. In the latter half of the year he was hard at work with his fellows negotiating the terms for the withdrawal of the Scottish forces from England after the defeat of the royalists, and arguing against a proposed resolution of parliament to dispose of the king's person without reference to the views of the Scots. He left England again at the conclusion of the treaty of Newcastle in December, only to return in April 1647 with a deputation briefed to urge parliament to come to terms with Charles on the basis of the terms agreed with the Scots in 1646.

The occasion of Lauderdale's return was the growing crisis in England, as the New Model Army turned upon the dominant presbyterian party in parliament. As it deepened in May, Lauderdale and his fellow commissioners held secret talks with the presbyterians, who were their natural allies, concerning the return of a Scottish army to England to confront the New Model. After the latter seized the king, the earl was sent by the conspirators to obtain Charles's formal consent to this measure, visiting him at Newmarket on 19 June and at Latimer's Cross on 22 July. A third meeting, at Woburn, was prevented by English soldiers suspicious of the existence of such a plan, who burst into the earl's lodgings and expelled him from the town. He had done his utmost both to obtain Charles's consent to the invasion and to urge the Scottish kirk to support it; after his ejection from Woburn he made a formal protest to parliament and then behaved circumspectly for a time, seeing the king only at the formal presentation of parliament's propositions to him on 7 September.

Access to the king's person was restored on 22 October, when Lauderdale visited him at Hampton Court with the earls of Lanark and Loudoun. They renewed the offer of Scottish aid if he would only make concessions regarding the English church. Further discussions with him followed, and the three Scottish nobles met the greatest Irish royalist, the marquess of Ormond, in a wood near Henley and agreed to raise armies in their respective nations to attack the New Model. All that was now lacking was the consent of Charles himself, which was obtained on 26 December, after the king's flight to the Isle of Wight, in the famous document called the engagement, by which Lauderdale and his fellows bound the Scots to assist Charles in return for a trial period of presbyterianism in England. The year 1648 was devoted to the consequences of this agreement. On 17 January, Lauderdale and the other commissioners protested against parliament's vote of no addresses, and so abrogated the alliance. On 24 January he departed for Scotland to advocate the engagement and devoted the next six months to writing and speaking of the danger posed to the Scots by the dominant Independent party in England and the acceptable nature of the deal with the king. On this last point he found himself unable to satisfy the majority of the kirk, which left him out of the commissioners appointed to discuss uniformity of worship with the English. It also estranged him from the more rigid covenanters and pushed him into co-operation with former opponents of the covenants such as the Hamilton faction, a natural consequence of that flexibility of principle which he had revealed to Sabran.

Lauderdale's response to this situation was to seek further concessions from the king concerning the English church while making closer links with English royalists. He corresponded regularly with the latter between April and June, and on 1 May was a signatory of a formal invitation to the prince of Wales to command in Scotland. The prince's reply was that he would come only if no further terms were imposed on him than those in the engagement, whereupon Lauderdale volunteered to visit him in person and coax him into making the concessions that his father would not. The earl took ship at Elie, Fife, in July, and eventually located the younger Charles on board a royalist fleet in the Downs on 10 August. The meeting established a rapport between the two which was to endure through thirty years, and won Lauderdale his three main objectives. The prince agreed to join the Scottish army in England as its titular leader, to leave behind him royalists of whom the covenanters especially disapproved, and to adopt the Scottish form of worship while on campaign. This triumph marked the climax, and apogee, of the earl's career as an envoy for the cause of the covenants.

Exile and prison, 1648–1660 Within a fortnight of the agreement, Lauderdale's whole political position began to collapse like a house of cards. First, news arrived that the Scottish invasion of England had been totally defeated, whereupon the prince withdrew his undertaking to join the Scots. Then the supporters of the engagement were overthrown in Scotland itself, by more extreme covenanters who had always opposed it and who now came to terms with the English parliament and army. Lauderdale found himself stranded in the Netherlands with the prince and his court, out of favour and employment with the new regime. Gilbert Burnet, who later recorded a number of doubtful tales about the earl's activities in the 1640s, asserted that Lauderdale crept back into Scotland at the end of January 1649, but departed again when he found himself in danger of arrest (G. Burnet, *Memories of … James and William, Dukes of Hamilton*, 1677, 377). This story may be correct.

Lauderdale now established himself at The Hague, and set to work to restore his fortunes by persuading the younger Charles, whom regicide had now made king in exile, to come to terms with the hard-line covenanter government in Scotland. In March 1649 his efforts proved unavailing, but a year later he found both sides more willing to agree, and played a prominent part among those advisers who brought Charles II to sign the treaty of Breda

with the covenanters in April 1650. This service secured his return to Scotland with the royal party in June, and the right to live there without molestation, but the Edinburgh regime ensured he was immediately separated from the king's presence and forbidden to engage in public life. Only the crushing defeat of the covenanters by Cromwell at Dunbar rescued him from this enforced retirement, as the government needed a broader basis of support to rebuild its war effort. On 26 December he was allowed to make a public repentance for his part in the engagement at Largo kirk, Fife, and by February 1651 he had rejoined Charles. He remained with and assisted the king in the campaign of that year, and took the risk of accompanying him in its last desperate act of the invasion of England which led to the destruction of the royal army at Worcester on 3 September. He was among those taken prisoner after the battle, in Cheshire after an attempt to flee homeward.

Lauderdale was never brought to trial, but nor was he released. Instead his estates were confiscated, with the payment of an annuity of £600 to his wife, while he was kept in the Tower. He was excepted from the indemnity ordinance issued by the newly established protectorate on 5 May 1654, and the only difference made to his circumstances by Cromwell's rule was that he was moved to other prisons, in the castles of Windsor and Portland. His role in the attempts to destroy the New Model Army in 1647–8 was not deemed forgivable. He seems to have devoted his enforced idleness to study, for which he had a natural aptitude. In later life he was noted as reading Latin, Greek, and Hebrew with ease, having a special enthusiasm for theology and history, and possessing an extraordinary memory. His opinion that no form of church government was prescribed in scripture was clearly based on personal research.

Lauderdale's freedom was automatically restored after the English republicans finally lost power in February 1660. By 23 March he was at liberty in London and immediately concerting plans with the presbyterians once more. He also wrote to the former engagers in Scotland and to Charles in the Netherlands, receiving a reply from the latter on 12 April subscribed 'your most affectionate friend' (Airy, 1.13). Having been sent money by his old acquaintance John Leslie, earl of Rothes, he was able to join the king in person at The Hague, renew their old intimacy, and apply himself to royal favourites such as Hyde 'with a marvellous importunity' (*Life of … Clarendon*, 428). He therefore returned to England in the royal train as a gentleman of the bedchamber, poised to take full advantage of the restoration of monarchy.

Vulnerable courtier, 1660–1663 Lauderdale's windfall of rewards, slowly accumulated in the succeeding years, was immense. In the summer of 1660 he obtained the key office of secretary of state for Scotland, which carried with it the powerful position of constant attendance upon the king's person. He regained his family properties, with a grant of the lordships of Musselburgh, Cranschawis, and Thirlestane, with other land, on 15 May 1661, to which a valuable plot in Leith was added in May 1662 and the Forest of Lauder on 13 October 1664, acquisitions which cemented his status as one of the magnates of south-eastern Scotland. There was, however, a price to be paid for success. His appointment to the post of secretary was opposed by the set of Scots who had been Charles's companions in exile and fought for him in the 1650s, led by John, earl of Middleton, and allied with English royalists such as Hyde. It was the king's own rapport with Lauderdale which had brought him the job. The earl was left caught between Middleton and his friends, who dominated the new government of Scotland, and English ministers such as Hyde (now earl of Clarendon), who wanted their nation to retain a controlling interest in Scottish affairs. The very strength of his position, as the Scotsman with readiest access to the monarch, drew upon him the hostility of both groups.

Lauderdale emerged as the chief champion of the moderate covenanter position once represented by the engagers. In August 1660 he got Charles to sign a letter promising to maintain the 'settled' kirk of Scotland, and in December he ensured that Middleton was instructed to obtain the restoration of former royal powers in the land, but not the restoration of episcopacy. He also persuaded the king, against Clarendon's advice, to withdraw the English garrisons. In early 1661 Middleton outflanked him by obtaining the repeal of the laws against episcopacy in a Scottish parliament. At a meeting of Scottish and English privy councillors in late July, Charles became persuaded that Middleton understood current feeling among Scots better than Lauderdale, and ordered the restoration of bishops on 14 August. Lauderdale struggled to protect himself by attending Anglican communion at the Chapel Royal to please the king while telling friends in Scotland to spread word there of his devotion to the covenanter cause.

Middleton's hatred for his rival now intensified. He was said to have declared that Lauderdale would pimp for any prince in Europe, and in September 1662 he used the Scottish parliament in an attempt to destroy him. On 5 September he obtained an act which enjoined all office-holders to denounce the covenants. This got rid of Lauderdale's last friend in the government, the earl of Crawford-Lindsay, but the secretary himself made the declaration with the alleged sneer that he would take a cartload of others if needed. On 9 September the parliament passed an act of indemnity, with a clause disabling twelve men from office. Middleton's clique ensured both that the twelve would be named by secret ballot and that Lauderdale would be included. The device backfired, for the secretary's agent in Edinburgh sent his master the news at top speed, enabling Lauderdale to be the first to break it to the king, representing it as a means of controlling Charles's power to appoint or dismiss servants. This played directly on the monarch's personal fear of being misled or coerced, and enabled Lauderdale to draw his attention to other recent acts of Middleton which he held to usurp royal authority. The result was that Charles rejected the result of the ballot.

In February 1663 the two earls confronted each other at Whitehall, and Lauderdale finally shattered his rival's reputation by convincing the king that Middleton had countermanded a royal order to suspend the collection of the fines due under the Act of Indemnity. He implicated Clarendon in the action, and so at one blow destroyed one rival and damaged another. In May, Charles formally announced that Middleton would be replaced as his commissioner to the Scottish parliament by the young earl of Rothes, whose timely loan in 1660 had enabled Lauderdale to refound his career. Rothes was instructed to investigate Middleton's activities in power, and Lauderdale was allowed to visit Scotland to assist him. During the course of the summer the two men prepared a devastating report to prove that Middleton had played off monarch and parliament to his own advantage, which prevented any chance of his return to office. They then flattered and delighted Charles by persuading the parliament to increase royal power over legislation, and to provide for an armed force to be used wherever the king desired in Britain.

Finding episcopacy now firmly established, Lauderdale accommodated himself openly to the new order by praising it in parliament while presenting a bill to fine people who worshipped outside the kirk and punish ministers who preached outside it. With this, he finally severed himself from the defeated cause of the covenants and established himself as one of the leaders of Restoration Scotland. For three years he had been penned in a political corner, under attack. Using every strategic advantage of that position, he had now broken out of it, and seized the initiative in his own affairs and that of his country.

First triumvirate, 1664–1667 By 1664 Scotland was dominated by three men. The management of the kirk was left to its primate, James Sharp, who had as yet little influence on politics, dominated by the partnership between Rothes and Lauderdale, the former residing mostly in Scotland and the latter once more at court. Lauderdale tended to keep a low profile in Scottish affairs while quietly building up influence in the land. He attracted a clientage of lairds in his own south-eastern region, and gradually gained them posts, especially in the strategically important legal offices. He also courted popularity, by obtaining royal action against abuses in the collection of tax arrears. At the same time he sought to represent the new regime to the king as one which functioned solely as an agent of Charles's own will: in September 1663 he had informed his monarch that after Middleton's fall 'you govern this poor kingdom yourself' (Airy, 1.184).

The Second Anglo-Dutch War, which broke out in 1665, created a new set of problems, highlighting the existence of religious and political dissent in Scotland, precipitating new taxes and the creation of a new army, and increasing the influence both of Sharp and his bishops and of military men in political life. The process brought Sharp and Rothes closer together, and further from Lauderdale, who began to feel himself tied to an increasingly unpopular administration while losing influence in it. The king was persuaded into supporting a policy of religious repression by visits from Alexander Burnet, archbishop of Glasgow, which threatened the secretary's own influence over Charles. The Pentland rising of November 1666 provoked a crisis, for Lauderdale feared that it would be used to vindicate that policy and that Rothes's repression of the rebellion would raise his stock still higher with the king. Instead he brilliantly turned the tables by using his proximity to Charles to convince him that Rothes had provoked the rising with the same policy, and that Sharp had once collaborated with Cromwell. In January 1667 the archbishop was confined to his see and between April and September, Rothes was gently stripped of his offices. Lauderdale had thus become the arbiter of Scottish affairs, and it was now for him to steer them into new courses.

Second triumvirate, 1667–1672 The earl had his new team of managers ready. Rothes was replaced as the leading man resident in Scotland by a neighbour of Lauderdale's in Haddingtonshire, John Hay, earl of Tweeddale. By 1666 the friendship between them was strong enough for Lauderdale to marry his only child, Mary, to Tweeddale's heir. Both men had been enemies of Middleton, who had reluctantly accepted episcopacy. They were linked by Sir Robert Moray, who carried messages between them, reinforced Tweeddale in Scotland at moments of critical negotiation and intrigue there, and replaced Lauderdale at the side of Charles when the secretary needed to go to his native land in person. These two were Lauderdale's chief allies in obtaining the fall of Rothes, and in devising and promulgating a new religious policy between 1667 and 1669, intended to neutralize religious dissent by dividing it.

At first this consisted of conciliation, as the standing army was disbanded, an indemnity issued to rebels, and moderate presbyterian ministers were appointed to vacant livings in the kirk. When Archbishop Burnet organized a protest against the latter initiative, Moray convinced Charles that this represented disobedience, and Burnet was forced to resign. At that moment (in 1669) Lauderdale was in Scotland, at last equipped with the supreme office of royal commissioner to parliament and steering through an act which recognized the king's supreme power over the kirk; in this manner the whole policy could be sold to Charles as a demonstration of his control of the realm. After its passage, Lauderdale told him that 'Never was king so absolute as you in poor old Scotland' (Airy, 2.164). The second part of that policy was to crush obdurate dissenters, and in 1669–70 parliament and privy council passed a package of measures to harry and punish religious meetings outside the kirk, including the notorious act making death the penalty for field conventicles.

Lauderdale has also customarily been treated by English historians as one of the five royal advisers who made up the body nicknamed 'the Cabal' and who dominated politics between 1668 and 1673. It is certainly true that he sat in the committee for foreign affairs, the inner policy-making ring of England's privy council. Even there, however, he remained primarily an adviser on Scottish dimensions to initiatives, and his influence was further limited by the fact that he was most closely associated with the least important members of the group, Ashley and Buckingham, who had shared with him an old hostility to Clarendon. As such he was screened off with them from the crucial secret diplomacy of the period, although he did play a part in persuading the king to issue the declaration of indulgence of March 1672, as a parallel to his efforts to conciliate and divide dissent in Scotland. These continued in September with the placement of eighty more presbyterian ministers in vacant livings.

Although functioning as a semi-detached member of the Cabal, Lauderdale still received his full share of the round of honours which Charles bestowed upon most of the group to reward and encourage them at the outbreak of his war with the Dutch in the summer of 1672. On 26 May his favourite Scotsman became marquess of March and duke of Lauderdale, and on 3 June the new duke was also made a knight of the Garter. He had reached the highest point of his career.

Master of Scotland, 1672–1679 The year 1672 represented a watershed as well as an apogee for Lauderdale. On 17 February he married his second wife at Petersham parish church, Surrey. She was Elizabeth *Murray (*bap.* 1626, *d.* 1698), eldest daughter of William *Murray, earl of Dysart, whose title she had been allowed to retain as countess in her own right. Her first husband had been Sir Lionel Tollemache, who had died in 1669, and from that moment she had become intimate with Lauderdale. The obvious closeness of the couple had ruined the earl's relations with his first wife, Anne, which had hitherto appeared happy. She abandoned him to live in Paris, where she died on 6 November 1671, clearing the way for the new marriage. It was easy for people to understand Lauderdale's infatuation with Elizabeth, for she was beautiful, charming, and learned. She was also about forty-six years of age at the time of their union, which meant that by marrying her he was effectively giving up his chances of having more children. Abandoning the home at Highgate, just north of London, where he had lived in the 1660s, he moved across the capital to the splendid mansion of Ham House in Surrey.

In public as well as in domestic life Lauderdale was drawing a line underneath old habits, and the two were probably connected. During 1671 he turned upon his partners Tweeddale and Moray, and treated them so badly that they withdrew from the government's affairs. They themselves were bewildered by his change, and historians can supply no certain reason for it, but it is difficult to ignore the contemporary whispers that Elizabeth had disliked them and poisoned her lover's mind against them. She was certainly a proud and greedy woman, who loved to intervene in politics, and may have encouraged Lauderdale's unmistakable tendency to growing arrogance and ruthlessness at this time. His new favourite agents were Alexander Bruce, earl of Kincardine, and his own brother Charles, both lesser men than their predecessors and also much more clearly his servants rather than partners. The change reflected one in the Scottish privy council. Throughout the 1660s it had been a fairly heterogenous body representing different factions and friendships. Between 1669 and 1674 several deaths and enforced retirements enabled Lauderdale to turn it into something like a closed body of his own supporters. In his contributions to the debates of the English committee for foreign affairs, also, he now revealed a brutality and contempt for moral convention which had hitherto not been apparent in his nature.

This trend towards ministerial despotism would probably in itself have produced a new coherence and determination of opposition, but the strains of the Third Anglo-Dutch War caused the latter to develop very swiftly. In 1673–4 Lauderdale faced opposition in parliament, and in 1674–5 in the Faculty of Advocates and the convention of royal burghs. The parliamentary attacks were led by Tweeddale and another noble with whom Lauderdale had now quarrelled, the duke of Hamilton. At the same time he lost his allies in England, Ashley (now earl of Shaftesbury) and Buckingham, by remaining loyal to the government even after they were dismissed during the winter of 1673–4. Shaftesbury in particular could not forgive him for supporting the royal duke of York after the latter's public conversion to Catholicism, and thereafter abetted the growing English suspicions of Lauderdale as an instrument of royal ambitions for more powerful and arbitrary monarchy.

Lauderdale's response to all these pressures was to give up trying to work with the Scottish parliament at the opening of 1674 and to rely on his control of the flow of information to the king. He convinced both Charles and the grateful York that the attacks were motivated solely by jealousy and malice. The king ostentatiously favoured him on his return from Scotland in 1674, raising him to the English peerage on 25 June as Baron Petersham and earl of Guilford, and appointing him to the English privy council. These measures also strengthened his legal position against any attacks which his new enemies might foment against him in the English House of Commons. He made an immediate alliance with the new leading minister in England, the earl of Danby, and henceforth the two worked together. In April 1675 the English Commons indeed addressed the king for Lauderdale's removal, but Charles stood firm, driving around Hyde Park with Lauderdale in his coach and having the duke carry the sword before him at the prorogation of the parliament.

There was a price to be paid for this support. In tying himself to Danby, Lauderdale was also tying himself to the English bishops who were allied with Danby and urging a drive against nonconformists in both kingdoms. It may be that the persistence of large-scale dissent in the wake of the policy of restoration of selected ministers to the kirk would have turned Lauderdale against conciliation in any case, but political circumstance now made this certain. In late 1674 he obtained a string of royal orders to the Scottish privy council to wipe out conventicles, and cultivated the support of the bishops, restoring Sharp to the king's favour and Burnet to his see. A new field army was raised, led by Lauderdale's clients, and

quartered in areas especially noted for dissent. At the same time he changed his chief secular allies and agents, dropping Kincardine when the latter baulked all the new military measures, and with him Charles Maitland. In their place he elevated the earls of Atholl and Argyll.

To Lauderdale's critics, this policy seemed to be part of a general inclination on the duke's part to crush opposition of any sort, and it caught him in a vicious circle of ever greater repression as the presbyterians of the south-west intensified their resistance. He tried to break out of it in 1677 by putting further plans for conciliation before the moderate presbyterians and English bishops alike. The latter, however, allied with both Danby and the Scottish bishops to force the abandonment of the plans and the adoption of yet more savage measures of persecution. Lauderdale had become the virtual dictator of Scotland, on behalf of an absent king. At the same time he had lost the initiative in the making of policy, and been forced into ever more desperate and counter-productive courses.

The crisis which was to end Lauderdale's supremacy was precipitated by another of those measures, a decision to use highland levies to police and terrorize the most disaffected areas in early 1678. Local nobles who did not co-operate were to be declared traitors, a tactic which had the unexpected effect of making two of them desperate enough to bolt to England and appeal to the king. They were joined by old enemies of the duke, and by Atholl who had turned against him in disgust at these events. Lauderdale had to send a new set of agents to represent himself to Charles. The complainants found allies at court and in the House of Commons, where all Danby's efforts were needed to have a new address for the duke's removal defeated by a single vote on 9 May. In June, Charles compromised, declaring his approval of the Scottish government's measures, but ordering Lauderdale to treat the people and nobility of the south-west better. It was the first qualification of royal support for the duke, and the latter regarded it as the beginning of the end of his career.

Lauderdale's position eroded further with the fall of Danby in December, and the new House of Commons of 1679 voted an address for his removal from office on 8 May. Once more this attack was co-ordinated with further complaints made at court by his Scottish enemies, led by Hamilton. Once again, too, the king ostensibly stood firm; the address evaporated with the sudden prorogation of the English parliament on 27 May, and in July Charles signed a succession of documents which upheld Lauderdale against his critics. At the same time it was plain that while the duke remained in power, his period of dominance was over. He had completely lost control of access to the king, so that his enemies could attend court, and the royal person, as they pleased. The Scottish army was put under one of his opponents. The Bothwell Bridge rising of June precipitated a formal condemnation by the king of the policies of repression, and a legalization of conventicles in private houses, made without consulting the Scottish government. It is possible that secret communications between the king and Lauderdale lay behind both initiatives, but by August 1679 it was no longer clear to commentators who, if anybody, was actually steering Scottish affairs. What all agreed was that the duke's replacement was only a matter of time.

Blighted grandee, 1680–1682 It was in September 1679 that Lauderdale himself proposed a way out of his predicament: that his old ally the duke of York be sent to govern Scotland, thereby giving the latter a bolt-hole from an England in the throes of the exclusion crisis while providing a powerful protector for himself. The king adopted this idea in October. Lauderdale was thus freed to return to Whitehall in the winter and bolster his royal master against the demands of the English whigs. Behind his back, however, York created a mixed Scottish government of his friends and enemies, and so effectively brought an end to his regime. It may be that this betrayal landed a final blow upon a constitution long undermined by hard work and political strain, for in March 1680 Lauderdale suffered a stroke which left him a semi-paralysed invalid with a failing memory, vainly seeking cures from the spa waters of Bath and Tunbridge Wells. He was now clearly but one royal adviser on Scottish affairs among many, and in September he finally resigned his post as secretary of state.

Henceforth Lauderdale was a valetudinarian, living mostly at the health resort of Tunbridge Wells. He made what may have been the mistake of attending the English House of Lords in November 1680 for the trial of the Catholic Viscount Stafford. The king, for tactical reasons, was prepared to sacrifice Stafford by allowing him to be condemned and executed, while York was determined to save him. Caught between the two, and perhaps swayed by his old distaste for Catholics, Lauderdale chose to vote for guilt and so allegedly lost York's good opinion. It was also whispered that the royal duke had been scandalized by his discovery of how much money Lauderdale's duchess had been making out of corrupt exploitation of her husband's administration. Whatever the truth, the disabled old man himself was allowed to die in peace, which he did suddenly at Tunbridge Wells on either 20 or 24 August 1682, after taking a purge. He was buried with great ceremony and a huge attendance in the family vault at Haddington kirk on 5 April 1683, although York was ostentatiously absent. His Scottish estates and earldom passed to his brother Charles, but as the latter had never won the king's regard, he was not allowed to inherit the dukedom or English titles. Lauderdale's widow survived until 5 June 1698.

Reputation and legacy Lauderdale suffered two of the worst misfortunes which can attend the posthumous reputation of a statesman: that his enemies left popular and much-admired memoirs while his friends did not, and that the policies with which he was associated were subsequently totally defeated and discredited. He had personally offended the most influential whig and the most influential tory historian of his age, Gilbert Burnet and Clarendon respectively, and their portraits of him are the

more influential for being remarkably similar—of a ruthless, selfish, and unprincipled politician whose sole aim was his own promotion and survival. This was enhanced by the fact that he moved from being one of the foremost representatives of the covenanters to one of their foremost persecutors. As their cause triumphed in 1690, and the kirk of Scotland was finally remade in their image, with Robert Wodrow providing its heroic history and martyrology, it was inevitable that Lauderdale should be implanted in national folk memory as a debauched tyrant, serving an unworthy and absentee monarch. That image was reinforced, like so much else in that folk memory, by Sir Walter Scott.

There is a certain amount of truth in this hostile tradition. The contrast between Lauderdale's brilliant and erudite mind and his physical grossness, upon which Burnet made play, is amply borne out by the Lely portrait in the National Portrait Gallery, London. It shows a man with bushy, ruddy hair (which gave him his nickname of John Red), fat jowls, pursed lips, and cold, heavy-lidded eyes. His growing lack of scruple and aptitude for brutality have been remarked upon here and his supreme talent for political manoeuvre and manipulation should be equally obvious. It has hardly helped his reputation that the only one of his contemporary admirers to have left memoirs, Sir George Mackenzie, played up to the full Lauderdale's ability both to outwit his opponents and to vault over problems which vexed men of more tender conscience. The greatest cameo portraitist of the period, Pepys, has enhanced the impression of coarseness in the man, in his report that Lauderdale declared that 'he had rather hear a cat mew than the best music in the world' (Pepys, 7.225).

On the other hand, Burnet himself paid tribute to the statesman's intellectual interests and prowess, and twentieth-century historiography has been kinder. Lauderdale's biographer W. C. Mackenzie, writing in 1923, pointed out the undoubted truth that he abandoned the cause of the covenants reluctantly, and only after it was apparently wholly lost. The persecution of those who adhered to it was well under way by the time that he acceded to power, and his repeated attempts to alter it failed largely because he was caught between the obduracy of the presbyterians and that of the bishops, ultimately abetted by the king himself. This picture, of a naturally tolerant and flexible politician gradually pushed into more and more savage measures, was endorsed by Julia Buckroyd in her study of Restoration Scotland published in 1980. It must be noted that Lauderdale's immediate successors were no more able to escape the impasse, until the revolution of 1688 made a different policy possible. Furthermore, the pattern which the duke established, of the government of Scotland by a viceroy ruling on behalf of a monarch resident in England, was to be repeated at various times during the following century as one solution to the problem of absentee royalty. The particular odium which Lauderdale incurred in this regard was due partly to the fact that he was the first fully to represent this pattern, partly to the historiographical factors noted earlier, and partly to the sheer size and flamboyance of his personality.

When all this is said, the suspicion still lingers that the odium was in part earned. It is perfectly possible, and proper, for a more secular age than Lauderdale's own to contrast approvingly his doctrinal flexibility and pragmatism—itself based on sound scholarship—with the more rigid presbyterianism and intolerant episcopalianism of many of his contemporaries. Beside figures like Middleton, Sharp, Archbishop Burnet, and many of the nobles who served as his allies or tools, the duke unmistakably appears the greater man, more cunning, adroit, imaginative, open-minded, adaptable, and audacious. None of this, however, alters the simple fact that his sole abiding principle was to take power for himself and to retain it, and beside that all other considerations of honour, loyalty, and belief occupied an ever diminishing supportive role. Even in the rogues' gallery of Restoration politicians, he appears especially devious, ruthless, and brutal. His personal fidelity to Charles II was itself coupled with a willingness to manipulate and misinform the king to his own advantage, while his Scottish patriotism must be questioned by his later clear preference for English residences. When every extenuation is made, his career remains a classic illustration of the corrupting effects of power. RONALD HUTTON

Sources The Lauderdale papers, ed. O. Airy, 3 vols., CS, new ser., 34, 36, 38 (1884–5) • NL Scot., MSS 7006–7025 • NL Scot., MS 3136 • NA Scot., CH 1/1/11 • NL Scot., MSS 2512, 597 • [J. Hamilton, duke of Hamilton], The Hamilton papers: being selections from original letters … relating to … 1638–1650, ed. S. R. Gardiner, CS, new ser., 27 (1880) • R. A. Lee, 'Government and politics in Scotland, 1661–1681', PhD diss., U. Glas., 1995 • W. C. Mackenzie, Life and times of John Maitland duke of Lauderdale (1923) • Bishop Burnet's History • The life of Edward, earl of Clarendon … written by himself, new edn, 3 vols. (1827) • G. Mackenzie, Memoirs of the affairs of Scotland (1821) • The letters and journals of Robert Baillie, ed. D. Laing, 3 vols. (1841–2) • J. Kirkton, The secret and true history of the Church of Scotland, ed. C. K. Sharpe (1817) • R. Wodrow, The history of the sufferings of the Church of Scotland from the Restoration to the revolution, ed. R. Burns, 2 vols. (1836–8) • Reg. PCS, 3rd ser. • Pepys, Diary • R. Law, Memorialls, or, The memorable things that fell out within this island of Brittain from 1638 to 1684, ed. C. K. Sharpe (1818), 234 • GEC, Peerage

Archives BL, corresp. and papers, Add. MSS 23108–23138, 23240–23251, 25125, 32094–32095 • Buckminster Park, Graham, corresp. and papers • NA Scot., papers • NL Scot., corresp. and papers • NL Scot., corresp. • NL Scot., papers • NRA, priv. coll., corresp. and papers | NA Scot., corresp. with Sir William Bruce • NL Scot., corresp. with first and second marquesses of Tweeddale

Likenesses C. Johnson, oils, 1649, Lennoxlove, East Lothian; version, Ham House, Richmond-upon-Thames, London • S. Cooper, watercolour miniature, 1664, NPG • P. Lely, oils, c.1665, Scot. NPG [see illus.] • J. Huysmans, oils, c.1665–1670, NPG • P. Lely, oils, c.1672, NPG • P. Lely, oils, c.1672, Ham House, Richmond-upon-Thames, London • J. Roettier, silver medal, 1672, BM, NPG, Scot. NPG • P. Lely, chalk drawing, c.1672–1673, BM • E. Ashfield, pastel drawing, 1674–5, Ham House, Richmond-upon-Thames, London • J. Riley, oils, c.1680, Syon House, Brentford, Middlesex • A. Simon, silver medal, BM • G. Valck, line engraving (after B. Gennari), BM, NPG

Maitland, John, fifth earl of Lauderdale (c.1655–1710), politician, was the second son of Charles *Maitland, third earl of Lauderdale (c.1620–1691), and Elizabeth, younger daughter of Richard Lauder of Hatton. He graduated MA from Edinburgh on 12 August 1678 and was admitted as advocate on 30 July 1680. He was created a baronet on 18 November 1680. About this time he married Lady Margaret (c.1662–1742), only child of Alexander Cunningham, ninth earl of Glencairn. They had three sons and one daughter.

In March 1685, as Sir John Maitland of Ravelrig, he was elected to parliament as a commissioner of the shires for Edinburgh, and he represented the same constituency in the 1686 parliament. On 4 June 1686 he was appointed a justice of the peace.

Unlike his father and his elder brother Richard *Maitland (1653–1695), Maitland played an active role in the revolution of 1688 in Scotland and supported the Williamite cause. He sat in the 1689 convention of estates as a shire representative for Edinburgh and on 16 March he subscribed the act declaring the meeting of the estates to be free and lawful. On 19 March he was appointed colonel of the foot militia for the shire of Edinburgh and his loyalty to the Williamite cause was further demonstrated on 23 March when he subscribed the letter of the estates thanking him for the administration of public affairs and promoting the cause of union between England and Scotland. Maitland's important political profile in the 1689 convention is further demonstrated by his membership of the convention's delegation appointed on 5 April to oversee the election of new magistrates in Edinburgh as well as his appointment (among others) as a commissioner to treat for a union between England and Scotland. He continued to represent the shire of Edinburgh in the parliamentary sessions of 1689–90. On 9 May 1690 he was one of the members of the parliamentary committee for granting supply to their majesties, and on 7 June he was appointed a commissioner of supply for Edinburgh.

Meanwhile, in May 1689, Maitland had been appointed to the privy council. He was also appointed a lord of session on 28 October, with the title of Lord Ravelrig. On 7 June he was given the important task of distributing collections for Irish and French protestant refugees in parts of Scotland, alongside David Williamson, minister of the West Kirk in Edinburgh. On 15 June he was ordered by the privy council to secure cannon, arms, and ammunition being held by his father at their family home and at Hatton, and to secure them for the Williamite cause; they were subsequently taken to Edinburgh Castle. When Lauderdale agreed to live peacefully, Maitland was appointed one of his cautioners, a role ended by the earl's death in June 1691. In July 1691 Maitland received a charter of the barony of Hatton and took the name of Lauder. He sat for the shire of Edinburgh in the parliamentary sessions of 1693 and 1695 as Sir John Lauder of Hatton, but following the death of his elder brother Richard, succeeded in the latter year as fifth earl of Lauderdale. In remaining sessions of the Williamite parliament he was a member of the committee for trade (1696) and the committee for the security of the kingdom (1700 and 1702). He signed the Association on 10 September 1696 and he was appointed as a commissioner of supply for Haddingtonshire and

Argyll in the 1698 parliament. On 16 January 1701 he voted for a parliamentary address, as opposed to an act, to King William concerning the Darien crisis. He was appointed a commissioner to the 1702 union negotiations between Scotland and England, but recorded sederunts of the meetings indicate his absence at all of the diets.

During the union parliament (1703–7) Lauderdale was affiliated to the court, but he voted in half or fewer of the divisions in the union debate. On 19 October he was excused by parliament for his absence and he failed to turn up for the crucial vote on article 1 of the treaty. However, he did register support for ratification of the treaty on 16 January 1707. He died at Hatton on 13 August 1710. John Macky described him as a 'Gentleman that means well to his Country, but comes far short of his Predecessors, who, for three or four Generations, were Chancellors, and Secretaries of State for that Kingdom' (*Memoirs of the Secret Services*, 230–31). His wife, who survived him, died on 12 May 1742. Their elder son James having died in 1709, their younger son Charles (c.1688–1744) succeeded as sixth earl.   JOHN R. YOUNG

Sources *Scots peerage* · M. D. Young, ed., *The parliaments of Scotland: burgh and shire commissioners*, 2 (1993) · *APS*, 1670–1707 · *Reg. PCS*, 3rd ser., vols. 13–16 · *Memoirs of the secret services of John Macky*, ed. A. R. (1733) · P. W. J. Riley, *The union of England and Scotland* (1978) · GEC, *Peerage*

Maitland, John Alexander Fuller (1856–1936), music critic, was born on 7 April 1856 at 90 Gloucester Place, Portman Square, London, the only child of John Fuller Maitland and his wife Marianne, daughter of George Noble of Dyffryn, Glamorgan. His grandfather was Ebenezer Fuller Maitland, a prominent member of the evangelical and anti-slave-trade philanthropists known as the Clapham Sect.

Fuller Maitland's early education was disrupted by poor health. He was educated privately, with the exception of three terms' attendance at Westminster School. Serious musical instruction began in 1872, when he took piano lessons from Ernst Pauer. Moreover, from his home at Phillimore Gardens in South Kensington (which he later inherited from his father) he soon came into contact with all the major musical events in London. In 1875 he entered Trinity College, Cambridge, where he met Stanford and Barclay Squire (whose elder sister, Charlotte Elizabeth, he married in 1885). With both these men he engaged thoroughly in the blossoming musical activities of the Cambridge University Musical Society and, under their influence, took an interest in music criticism. Piano lessons continued after graduation, first with Dannreuther and afterwards with W. S. Rockstro. But it was in the field of journalism and scholarship that he found his calling, a fact underlined by a request from George Grove to write articles for his *Dictionary of Music and Musicians* and his appointment, through Grove's recommendation, as critic for the *Pall Mall Gazette* in 1882. Between 1884 and 1889 he wrote for *The Guardian*, after which he succeeded Hueffer as critic of *The Times*, a job he retained until 1911.

As well as being one of Britain's most prominent music journalists, Fuller Maitland devoted much of his time to scholarship and editorial work. Having undertaken the appendix to the first edition of *Grove's Dictionary* (published in 1889), he was appointed editor of the second edition (1904–10). His fascination for Renaissance and baroque music manifested itself in numerous ways. With A. J. Hipkins he was an important pioneer in the revival of the harpsichord. From 1879 he worked on a catalogue of the substantial collection of music manuscripts at the Fitzwilliam Museum in Cambridge (published 1893), a task which led to an edition of the *Fitzwilliam Virginal Book* (1894–9) with Barclay Squire. He served as a member of the editorial committee of the Purcell Society, editing several volumes of Purcell's works, among which was the *Ode on St Cecilia's Day*, published in 1895 for the bicentenary of the composer's death. As an energetic participant in the Bach revival—he joined the Bach Choir soon after leaving Cambridge—he and Clara Bell (Mrs Courtenay Bell, mother of C. F. Moberly Bell) translated Spitta's biography of Bach (published 1899), and he was also asked by Oxford University Press to write the fourth volume (*The Age of Bach and Handel*) of the Oxford History of Music (1902). However, his interests were not restricted to early music, as is evident from his monographs on Schumann (1844), Joachim (1905), Brahms (1911), and, at the end of his life, on the music of Parry and Stanford (1934). His autobiography, *A Door-Keeper of Music* (1929), provides a stimulating account of the social and artistic environment of the 'intellectual aristocracy'.

In recognition of his work Fuller Maitland received an honorary DLitt from Durham University (1928), was made a fellow of the Society of Antiquaries, and was an associate of the Belgian Académie Royale des Beaux-Arts. He retired from journalism in 1911 and moved to Borwick Hall near Carnforth, Lancashire, where he died on 30 March 1936.   JEREMY DIBBLE

Sources J. A. Fuller-Maitland, *A door-keeper of music* (1929) · H. C. Colles, *MT*, 77 (1936), 419–21 · F. Howes, 'Fuller Maitland, J(ohn) A(lexander)', *New Grove* · C. V. Stanford, *Pages from an unwritten diary* (1914) · C. L. Graves, *The life and letters of Sir George Grove* (1903) · P. M. Young, *George Grove, 1820–1900: a biography* (1980) · d. cert.
Archives Lancaster District Library, MSS, musical scores, etc. | BL, letters to F. G. Edwards · BL, corresp. with Macmillans, Add. MS 55236 · Elgar Birthplace Museum, Broadheath, corresp. with Edward Elgar
Likenesses W. Strang, chalk drawing, 1905, Royal College of Music, London · S. P. Cockerell, pencil sketch · Elliott & Fry, photograph · portraits, repro. in Fuller-Maitland, *Door-keeper of music*, frontispiece, p. 272
Wealth at death £38,677 11s. 7d.: probate, 12 June 1936, *CGPLA Eng. & Wales*

Maitland, John Gorham (1818–1863), civil servant, was born on 27 October 1818 at Taunton, Somerset, the son of Samuel Roffey *Maitland (1792–1866), historian and religious controversialist, and his wife, Selina Stephenson. He was educated privately before being admitted to Trinity College, Cambridge, in 1835, where he was elected a fellow after gaining the third place in the classical and the seventh in the mathematical tripos of 1839. In 1840 he was admitted at Lincoln's Inn and was called to the bar in 1843, but was not a successful practitioner. He was elected FRS in 1847. He was the author of two pamphlets, *Church Leases* (1849) and *Property and Income Tax* (1853), a critique of Disraeli's 1852 budget. On 12 August 1847 he married Emma (*d.* 1851), second daughter of the physicist John Frederic *Daniell. He was secretary to the civil service commission in succession to his friend, and fellow member of the Cambridge Apostles, James Spedding from 1855 until his death at his London home, 51 Rutland Gate, Knightsbridge, on 27 April 1863. He was survived by his only son, Frederic William *Maitland, and two daughters.

M. C. CURTHOYS

Sources GM, 3rd ser., 14 (1863), 806 • Venn, *Alum. Cant.* • Boase, *Mod. Eng. biog.* • C. H. S. Fifoot, *Frederic William Maitland: a life* (1971) • *DNB* • GM, 2nd ser., 28 (1847), 534
Archives Herts. ALS, Bulwer-Lytton MSS
Wealth at death under £2000: probate, 8 June 1863, *CGPLA Eng. & Wales*

Maitland [*née* Barrett; *other married name* Thomas], **Julia Charlotte** (1808–1864), writer and traveller, was born on 21 October 1808, probably in Richmond, Surrey, the eldest of five children of Henry Barrett (1756–1843) and his wife, Charlotte, *née* Francis (1786–1870), a niece of the novelist Frances Burney (Madame D'Arblay) and the first editor of her journals and letters. Julia Barrett was a favourite of her great-aunt D'Arblay, who thought 'lovely Julia' had 'very good sense, & a truly blyth juvenile love of humour'. She noted that Julia had inherited her 'mother's sweetness, activity to serve, & delight in obliging', though she did not believe that she 'equally inherits that mother's extraordinary talents' (*Journals and Letters*, 11.429). With her mother and her sister Hetty, Julia travelled through France and Italy in search of a cure for her sister's tuberculosis (she was very ill herself in 1827, and Hetty died in 1833). By twenty-two she had taken control of the household, and she was soon befriended by Lady Caroline Morrison, with whom she travelled to Naples, Leghorn, Vesuvius, and Pompeii. She was severely ill on her return in 1833, but by 1834 was fully recovered.

Julia had a 'striking Italianate beauty', and her great-aunt Sarah Harriet thought that she 'ought to marry the Duke of Devonshire' (*Journals and Letters*, 12.622–3). Frances Burney's son Alex was 'deeply smitten' by Julia, but she married James Thomas (*d.* 1840), an Indian judge in the Madras presidency, and a widower with at least two children, on 2 August 1836 at Brighton, Sussex. The marriage disappointed Julia's family, particularly her mother who thought she was 'throwing herself away on a very poor sly fellow' (ibid., 12.895). The couple sailed to India shortly afterwards. They had two children of their own. Julia Thomas spent her first year in India in Madras, and when her husband received a new posting at Rajahmundry they journeyed there together via Calcutta in 1837. Julia Thomas mainly resided in the hills of Rajahmundry (where her son James Cambridge was born on 3 February 1839), but also lived briefly at Samuldavee, Chittoor, and Bangalore.

Julia Thomas and her husband established a school in Rajahmundry that had at its maximum forty-five boys in attendance. The school accepted students of different castes by application and placed a particular emphasis on Christian teaching. Lessons were taught in both English and Gentoo. In addition, Maitland set up a native reading-room in the bazaar that carried Gentoo, Hindi, Tamil, and English books and newspapers. The reading-room at Rajahmundry proved to be popular, and led to her circulating more reading materials in nearby villages. She also helped to establish schools in nearby places, such as Samuldavee. Her book *Letters from Madras* concludes with an impassioned 'Treatise on native education', in which she pleads for the founding of more European schools and for the implementation of a system of national education in India. Thomas believed that education was the route to reform: 'if every civilian up the country were to have a poor little school like ours, it would do something in time' (Maitland, *Letters from Madras*, 254).

Julia Thomas's commitment to education was, however, inseparable from an evangelistic fervour that remained undiluted by contact with native culture during her stay in India. She believed that European education must necessarily conflict with Indian religion, and was critical of instances in which the government proclaimed, 'all respect be paid to native religions' (Maitland, *Letters*, 182). Thomas was well aware of the controversy attached to a Christian education in India, recounting an incident in which two young Parsi boys who had recently converted were attacked as they left a Christian church in Bombay: 'there were great apprehensions of a serious uproar, but the two poor young Christians were rescued. The Government have taken measures to protect them and keep the peace, and all is quiet again' (ibid., 269). In spite of the dangers to which native converts were exposed, Thomas's convictions were such that she did not hesitate to promote missionary endeavours. Despising the liberal objection that the Bible is 'a dangerous interference with native feelings', Thomas wrote that the unwillingness of Indians in the south to receive 'our books' was itself a form of 'bigotry … greatly encouraged by timid or ungodly Europeans, who really put objections into their heads' (ibid., 274–5). She frequently lamented the lack of missionary presence in her district and made every effort to circulate Christian books among her students and in her reading-rooms.

Julia Thomas's attempt to learn local languages made her unusual among many other memsahibs in India in the early nineteenth century. Her letters record her learning Tamil verbs, and enlisting the help of a servant to learn Gentoo. In spite of some typical prejudicial attitudes expressed in her letters towards 'the lazy, inert race' of Hindus, Thomas rebuked English incivility towards the Indian population, particularly towards the upper classes, whom she found 'exceedingly well bred … many of them are the descendents of native princes, and ought not to be treated like dirt' (Maitland, *Letters*, 45, 158). She was also heavily critical of the lack of English intervention in the widow-burning of Ranjit Singh's four wives and seven slave girls, calling it 'another disgraceful story of English ungodliness' (ibid., 279). Thomas was perhaps most horrified by her discovery of the East Indian slave trade, which she called 'just as wicked as its predecessor, the African Slave Trade ... Numbers are *kidnapped*, and *all* are entrapped and persuaded under false pretences.' Characteristically, however, her compassion for Indian slaves was inseparable from her deep and abiding prejudices. 'Some slave-agent tells them they are to go', she wrote, 'and they go: they know nothing about it. A Hindoo does not know how to *make a choice*;—it is an effort of mind quite beyond any but the very highest and most educated among them' (ibid., 214).

Throughout her stay in India, Thomas was fully engaged in her husband's attempts to alleviate the famine in Rajahmundry, in various road building projects, and in educational reform. She also attended Indian festivals and music performances, remained an active and engaged member of Anglo-Indian society, and above all despised the dullness and inertia of English civil ladies. In December 1839 she was forced to return to England owing to the ill health of her daughter, Etta.

After her first husband's death in 1840 Julia Thomas married Charles *Maitland (1815–1866), an author and curate of Lyndhurst, on 5 November 1842. They had one child. Her *Letters from Madras: During the Years 1836–1839* was first published anonymously in London in 1843. It was reprinted in Murray's Home and Colonial Library in 1846. She later wrote three novels for children which went through several editions: *Historical Acting Charades* (1847), *The Doll and her Friends, or, Memoirs of the Lady Seraphina* (1852), and *Cat and Dog, or, Memoirs of Puss and the Captain* (1854). Her children's stories were often humorously narrated from the point of view of an inanimate object or animal, and they sought primarily to promote values of politeness, generosity, and benevolence among children. Her novel *Cat and Dog*, for example, narrated by a dog named Captain, tells the tale of an unusual friendship that develops after a long period of enmity between Captain and a cat called Puss. The epilogue concludes, 'It may seem absurd to suppose that a human being can profit by the history of a dog; but I believe that no creature is too insignificant ... I would propose Puss and Captain as an example of a new and better method of "Living Like Cat and Dog"' (Maitland, *Cat and Dog*, 98–9).

Julia Maitland died from phthisis on 29 January 1864 at Stower Provost, near Shaftesbury, Dorset, where her son-in-law, the Revd David Wauchope, was curate.

JOY WANG

Sources J. Maitland, *Letters from Madras: during the years 1836–1839* (1843) • J. Maitland, *Historical acting charades* (1847) • J. Maitland, *The doll and her friends, or, Memoirs of the Lady Seraphina* (1852) • J. Maitland, *Cat and dog, or, Memoirs of Puss and the Captain* (1854) • I. Ghose, *Memsahibs abroad: writings by women travellers in nineteenth century India* (1998) • J. Robinson, *Wayward women: a guide to women travellers* (2001) • M. Macmillan, *Women of the raj* (1998) • *The journals and letters of Fanny Burney (Madame D'Arblay)*, ed. J. Hemlow and others, 12 vols. (1972–84), vols. 11–12 • *The early journals of Fanny Burney*, vol. 3, ed. L. E. Troide and S. J. Cooke (1994) • d. cert.

Maitland, Mary (d. **1596**), writer, was the daughter of Sir Richard *Maitland of Lethington (1496–1586), poet and keeper of the privy seal, and Mary or Mariota Cranstoun (d. 1586). John *Maitland and William *Maitland were her brothers. She is conventionally understood as the copyist of the Maitland quarto (CUL, Pepys 1408), a collection of religious, moral, political, and amatory poems dating from the mid-sixteenth century (including a copy of a poem by James VI and I) and associated with the Maitland family and circle. In comparison with the Maitland folio, its 'companion' manuscript, it can in part be regarded as a commonplace book, a celebration or commemoration of the Maitland family, closing with a series of laudatory epitaphs and funerary poems on the death of Maitland's wife. Mary Maitland was considered to have acted as 'secretary' to her father, a significant moral and political poet whose work substantially occupies both folio and quarto, and former keeper of the privy seal. On 9 August 1586 she married Alexander Lauder (d. 1622x5), son and heir to Sir William Lauder of Hatton. They had a son, George *Lauder, who became a political and military poet (he was the author of *The Scottish Souldier*, 1629). She died in 1596, and Alexander Lauder remarried.

The inscription 'Mary Maitland 1586', which appears twice on the manuscript's first folio, suggests the date of its completion (appropriately, the year of her parents' death and of her marriage; there is no reference to the latter). The extent of her role as transcriber is undetermined. On the assumption that the italic hand was traditionally taught to women, it is probable that Mary Maitland was responsible for transcribing the manuscript's poetry in italic as opposed to the other secretary hand in evidence. Maitland's importance as transcriber is substantiated by what appears to be several dedicatory poems which pun on the name 'Marie Maitland', and contain a suggestive symbolism of virginity and female creativity. One lyric, inscribed 'To Your Self', alludes to the promise of fame—the poetic crown of immortality—after the labour of the book's compilation is complete, and implies that Mary Maitland is a poet manqué: 'a pleasant poet perfyte sall ye be'. The lyric constructs a literary triumvirate of female poets to whom Mary Maitland is implied as a successor. The lyricist's comparison of 'Marie' to 'sapho saige' seems to endorse the implication of Maitland's own creativity and, in turn, makes more persuasive the case for her actual authorship of several anonymous poems in the quarto, notably one lyric of female homoeroticism, a rare Renaissance poetic example of such desire. A substantial number of secular love poems in the quarto, combined with those written in the female voice, also might suggest Maitland's creative as well as scribal presence. The Maitland quarto is rich in implications regarding women's creative role in manuscript compilation in Renaissance Scotland, and the scope and extent of that expression as dictated by social, moral, and literary orthodoxy.

S. M. DUNNIGAN

Sources CUL, Pepys 1408 (quarto), 2553 (folio) • W. A. Craigie, ed., *The Maitland quarto manuscript*, STS, new ser., 9 (1920) • W. A. Craigie, ed., *The Maitland folio manuscript*, 2 vols., STS, new ser., 7, 20 (1919–27) • S. M. Dunnigan, 'Scottish women writers, c.1560–c.1650', *A history of Scottish women's writing*, ed. D. Gifford and D. McMillan (1997), 15–43 • J. Farnsworth, 'Voicing female desire in "Poem XLIX"', *Studies in English Literature, 1500–1900*, 36/1 (1996), 57–

72 · *Scots peerage* · D. Irving, *The lives of the Scotish poets*, 2 vols. (1804)

Maitland, Sir Peregrine

Maitland, Sir Peregrine (1777–1854), army officer and colonial governor, was born at Longparish House, Hampshire, on 6 July 1777, the son of Thomas Maitland of Shrubs Hall, New Forest, and his wife, Jane, the daughter of General Edward Mathew of Felix Hall, Essex, and the granddaughter of Peregrine Bertie, second duke of Ancaster and Kesteven.

On 25 June 1792 Maitland was appointed ensign in the 1st foot-guards (Grenadier Guards). In this élite regiment he served throughout the revolutionary and Napoleonic wars—in Flanders in 1794, at Ostend in 1798, at Vigo and Corunna in 1809 (medal), at Walcheren, and at Cadiz. In 1803 he married for the first time. His bride, the Hon. Harriet Louisa Crofton, died in 1805. Maitland was second-in-command of the Grenadier Guards at Seville. After becoming their brevet colonel in 1812, he commanded them at the passage of the Bidassoa, at Nivelle, at the Nive in December 1813, and at Bayonne, Bidart, and the passage of the Adour. He was made a major-general in 1813. For his command of the 1st brigade of guards in 1815 at Quatre Bras and Waterloo and in the occupation of Paris he was created KCB. He crowned these achievements by his second marriage, at the duke of Wellington's headquarters in Paris, to Lady Sarah Lennox (*d.* 1873), the second daughter of the fourth duke of Richmond. His life by birth, marriage, and army experience had thus set in a groove of European military convention, tory piety, and an aristocratic detachment and superiority which would ill suit the rough-edged colonial societies and irregular warfare he would henceforth encounter as governor and army general in various parts of the empire.

When his father-in-law, Richmond, was appointed governor-in-chief of British North America, Maitland became lieutenant-governor of Upper Canada, on 3 June 1818. In appearance 'a tall, grave officer, always in military undress, his countenance ever wearing a mingled expression of sadness and benevolence' (Brode, 52), Maitland was content to retire frequently from the capital, York, to his beloved country residence of Stamford Park and leave much of the work of government to trusted subordinates such as the forceful attorney-general, J. B. Robinson. The latter headed a group of old loyalists who disapproved of the ultra-democratic tendencies represented by the 'reformer' opposition of William Mackenzie, John Rolph, and others. Somewhat inaccurately labelled the 'family compact', Robinson's following fairly mirrored Maitland's own views on such controversial matters as alien naturalization and exclusive Anglican clergy reserves. Consequently, his decade of government in Upper Canada (1818–28), while conservatively aligned, has been somewhat harshly seen as laying foundations for the subsequent uprising of 1837.

Nevertheless, Maitland was happier to take over the oligarchic system of Nova Scotia in October 1828. He moved on from there in 1834, and commanded the Madras army after October 1836 until his piety caused him to resign in late 1838, because the East India Company would not enforce the exemptions from compulsory native religious festivals granted to Christian Sepoys.

On 18 March 1844 Maitland became governor of the Cape of Good Hope. Here he made grave errors in severely modifying the treaty systems with frontier peoples and chiefdoms to the north-east and east of the colony. Both beyond the Orange and Great Fish rivers costly entanglements and hostilities followed. In particular, his new and arrogant version of Sir Andries Stockenström's original eastern frontier treaties with the Ngqika Xhosa chiefs was biased towards imperial and colonial interests in that it imposed the main onus of maintaining the treaties on the paramount chief Sandile, his co-chiefs, and their hard-pressed people, but allowed intrusions of colonial patrols and posts into previously declared neutral territory. Over-reacting to minor violations, Maitland was soon involved in transfrontier hostilities. In the Cape Frontier War of 1846–7 the Xhosa enemy provided a major challenge in irregular bush-fighting, particularly in the form of attacks on wagon trains. On the whole this proved beyond the conventional military skills of the ageing governor—who since 1846 had been a full general. Soon his critic, and the able architect of the original treaty system, Stockenström, could point derisively to Maitland's 'ruined cavalry, crippled infantry, and disgusted border force' (Milton, 166). Although by attrition Maitland did eventually achieve stalemate on the frontier by the beginning of 1847, his recall and replacement by more ruthless and energetic men such as Sir Henry Pottinger and Sir Harry Smith were inevitable. Maitland had therefore helped to provoke a major frontier conflagration and had then failed to extinguish it adequately. From this débâcle his political and military reputation did not recover. On his retirement and return to England he did, however, become GCB in 1852. He died at his residence, Eaton Place West, London, on 30 May 1854. Lady Sarah Maitland died on 8 September 1873, and was survived by their three sons and three daughters.

JOHN BENYON

Sources *Narrative of transactions connected with the Kafir War of 1840 and 1847: embracing correspondence between Sir P. Maitland, Lieut.-Col. Johnstone, Sir A. Stockenstrom, and others* (1848) · J. B. Peires, *The house of Phalo* (1981) · B. le Cordeur and C. Saunders, eds., *The war of the axe, 1847* (1981) · P. Brode, *Sir John Beverley Robinson: bone and sinew of the compact* (1984) · G. M. Craig, *Upper Canada: the formative years, 1784–1841* (1963) · J. S. Galbraith, *Reluctant empire: British policy on the South African frontier, 1834–1854* (1963) · W. M. MacMillan, *Bantu, Boer and Briton: the making of the South African native problem*, rev. edn (1963) · G. E. Cory, *The rise of South Africa*, 4 (1926) · DNB · J. Milton, *The edges of war* (1983)

Archives Bodl. RH, letter-book · NA Canada, corresp. and papers | Derbys. RO, letters to Sir R. J. Wilmot-Horton · NA Scot., corresp. with Lord Dalhousie · PRO, Colonial Office files [esp. C.O. 48] · W. Sussex RO, letters to duke of Richmond

Likenesses W. Newton, portrait, repro. in Cory, *Rise of South Africa* · W. Salter, group portrait, oils (*The Waterloo banquet at Apsley House*), Wellington Museum, Apsley House, London · W. Salter, oils (study for *The Waterloo banquet at Apsley House*), NPG · W. Theed, bust, Royal Military Academy, Sandhurst · portrait, South African Library, Cape Town, Elliot Prints · portrait (after W. Newton), State President's residence, Cape Town

Maitland, Sir Richard, of Lethington (1496–1586), courtier and writer, was probably born at Lethington Castle, the son and heir of Sir William Maitland of Lethington (*d.* 1513) and Margaret Seton. The family was descended from Thomas de Matalan, who acquired lands in the eastern lowlands of Scotland in the time of William the Lion (1165–1214). The house and lands of Thirlestane remained the property of the dukes of Lauderdale to present times. Lethington or Ledington (Sir Richard himself used both spellings), from which Sir Richard and his more famous son William *Maitland took their title, and by which they were often known, was a fortified house just south of Haddington (now subsumed into the house of Lennoxlove) which the family acquired by royal charter in 1345. Maitland's mother was a daughter of George, Lord Seton: he was thus connected directly with two of the most important lowland landowning and political families at the court of James IV and his successors. Sir William Maitland of Lethington was killed at the battle of Flodden in 1513, and Sir Richard was served heir to his father on 5 October 1513. He was educated at St Andrews (*c.*1510), and studied law at Paris (*c.*1514).

Probably in 1521, Maitland married Mary or Mariota, daughter of Sir Thomas Cranstoun of Corsbie, who was to outlive him by only a day or two, dying, it was said, on the day of her husband's funeral (Maitland quarto MS, Magd. Cam., fol. 132a). According to an anonymous poem in the Maitland manuscripts they had seven sons, of whom three survived, and four daughters: William (1528?–1573), John *Maitland (1543–1595), his father's heir, and Thomas [*see below*], Helen, Margaret, Mary *Maitland, and Isobel. He became one of the courtiers of James V, but it is not known in what capacity. In 1537 he was given the lands of Blyth near Thirlestane, the estate whose harrying by the English in 1570 he made the subject of a rueful poem ('The Blind Baronis Comfort'). His most celebrated intervention in history is as alleged by John Knox, that he was bribed, along with his relative by marriage Lord Seton, to allow Cardinal Beaton to escape from Seton's custody in 1543. Maitland's instincts for reconciliation, practical tolerance, and moderation would not have endeared him to Knox, and there is no evidence to support Knox's assertion.

In 1552 Maitland was one of the Regent Moray's councillors, and one of the commissioners appointed to settle the disputes in the English and Scottish borders; he was knighted shortly after the successful conclusion of his commission. When in 1559 he was commissioner to the queen of England in the same matter, his opposite number Sir Ralph Sadler described 'the old Lord of Lethington' (he was by then a venerable sixty-three years old) as 'the wisest man among them' (*State Papers and Letters*, 1.448). He had trained as a lawyer, and was appointed an extraordinary lord of session (that is, in Scotland, a high court judge) in 1554, and an ordinary lord in 1561. In that year he became entirely blind, but, remarkably, he continued his judicial duties until 1584. In December 1562 Queen Mary made him her keeper of the great seal for life, and also

appointed him, with his son John, as factor and chamberlain of the royal abbey of Haddington (in the town nearest to Lethington Castle, and the burial place of the Maitland family). In 1567, a year wholly catastrophic for the queen and for her supporters, he resigned the great seal to his son John, and appears to have retired from court and political life, his judicial duties excepted. As early as 1560, as his blindness increased, he recorded his disinclination to meddle with things of importance (preface to his *Tabill or Cathalog of the Kings of Scotland*), and turned to history, genealogy, and literature.

Despite Maitland's age and retirement, the involvement of his son William ('Mr Secretary Lethington') as a strong supporter of the queen in the turbulent conflicts of the queen's and regent's parties meant the seizure of Lethington Castle and its confiscation. His youngest son, Thomas, also working on the queen's behalf, died in Italy early in 1572. After the disgrace and death of William, following the surrender of Edinburgh Castle by the queen's party in 1573, Sir Richard appealed to Queen Elizabeth via Lord Burleigh to intercede for the return of his house and lands, but without result. Not until after the fall and death of the Regent Morton were the Maitland lands restored, in February 1584, when Sir Richard's surviving son, John, was released from prison and made a lord of session. Sir Richard then resigned from the bench, on 1 July 1584, and as a mark of favour to his infirmity and extreme age was allowed to keep the fees of the post. He died on 20 March 1586, and is presumed to have been buried at Haddington one or two days later.

The Maitland Club, founded in 1828 to edit and preserve by publication early Scottish literary and historical texts, took its name from Sir Richard because he was, as the introduction to the club's edition of his poems says, both 'an amiable and accomplished poet, as well as the tasteful and industrious collector and pious preserver of Ancient Scottish Poetry' (*Poems*, [xi]). While this suggests an activity more systematic than it was, nevertheless the Maitland manuscripts are one of the three most important collections of early Scottish poetry in existence (the other two being the Asloan manuscript of 1515 and the Bannatyne manuscript of 1568). Now in the library of Magdalene College, Cambridge, following their gift to Samuel Pepys by Sir Richard's great-grandson, John, first duke of Lauderdale, the Maitland folio manuscript and the Maitland quarto manuscript were edited by W. A. Craigie for the Scottish Text Society (1919–20). The folio contains 182 poems, of which 41 are by Sir Richard and 2 by John; the quarto, largely transcribed from the folio, contains the 41 and 3 more, and 51 other poems, of which only 10 also appear in the folio. The name of Sir Richard's daughter Mary, dated 1586, appears on the quarto, and she is said to have been her father's amanuensis. Prior to 1919 a selection of Sir Richard's poems had been printed by John Pinkerton (*Ancient Scottish Poems*, 1786), by James Sibbald (*Chronicle of Scottish Poetry*, 1807), and by J. Bain for the Maitland Club, already referred to, from a separate manuscript in the Drummond collection of Edinburgh University. The Maitland Club text includes four Scots poems by John

Maitland with a number of Latin epigrams, and two Latin poems by his brother Thomas, which are a panegyric on Lethington House and a poem to the eldest brother, William, 'On Undertaking a Turkish War'. The Latin poems were taken from an anthology by Sir John Scot of Scotstarvet, *Delitiae poetarum Scotorum* (1637).

Sir Richard also wrote a *Historie and Cronicle of the Hous and Surename of Seytoun* (1559), published along with his *Tabill or Cathalog of the Kings of Scotland*, edited by John Fullarton for the Maitland Club jointly with the Bannatyne Club (1829). A revised and more complete version, finished after 1561, remains in manuscript (NL Scot., Adv. MS 34.7.74). The National Library of Scotland manuscript used by the Maitland Club (NL Scot., Adv. MS 31.2.2(1)) also contains what appears to be Sir Richard's legal casebook, compiled between 1550 and 1565, 'Practiques of new [laws of Scotland] wharoff the caisses hes not been frequent'.

Sir Richard's son **Thomas Maitland** (*c*.1548–1572), already referred to, seems to have been at least as brilliant as his brothers; he matriculated at St Mary's College, St Andrews, in 1559 (and was probably therefore born about 1548) and later studied at Paris. George Buchanan made him the prolocutor in his *De jure regni apud Scotos* of 1579, and he was credited by his contemporaries with the authorship of an anonymous pasquinade satirizing the Regent Moray and his advisers after Moray's assassination (1570). He acted as a courier for the queen's party, and died in north Italy early in 1572 while on his way to Rome with the Jesuit Thomas Smeaton. An account of his life has been written by W. S. McKechnie.

MICHAEL R. G. SPILLER

Sources *The poems of Sir Richard Maitland of Lethington, knight*, ed. J. Bain (1830) · *Scots peerage* · J. M. Thomson and others, eds., *Registrum magni sigilli regum Scotorum / The register of the great seal of Scotland*, 11 vols. (1882–1914) · *Reg. PCS*, 1st ser. · R. Maitland, *History of the house ... of Seytoun*, ed. J. Fullarton (1829) · *The state papers and letters of Sir Ralph Sadler*, ed. A. Clifford, 2 vols. (1809) · *CSP for.*, 1572–4 · J. Knox, *History of the Reformation in Scotland* (1895), vol. 1 of *The works of John Knox*, ed. D. Laing (1895); repr. (New York, 1966) · D. Calderwood, *The history of the Kirk of Scotland*, ed. T. Thomson and D. Laing, 8 vols., Wodrow Society, 7 (1842–9) · W. S. McKechnie, 'Thomas Maitland', *SHR*, 4 (1906–7), 274–93 · T. M'Crie, *The life of Andrew Melville*, new edn (1899) · C. Craig, ed., *The history of Scottish literature*, 1: *Origins to 1660*, ed. R. D. S. Jack (1988) · J. Scot of Scotstarvet, ed., *Delitiae poetarum Scotorum*, 2 vols. (1637) · Magd. Cam., Maitland quarto MS

Archives Magd. Cam., MSS | NL Scot., Advocates MSS 31.2.2(1) · NL Scot., Advocates MSS 34.7.4; 34.3.16 · U. Edin., Drummond MSS

Maitland, Richard, **fourth earl of Lauderdale** (1653–1695), Jacobite nobleman, was born on 20 June 1653, the son of Charles *Maitland, third earl of Lauderdale (*c*.1620–1691), and Elizabeth, younger daughter and heir of Richard Lauder of Hatton. He was known by the designation Maitland of Grogar until his father succeeded to the Lauderdale earldom in 1682, after which he assumed the title Viscount Maitland. On 1 July 1678 he married Lady Anne (*b.* 1657/8, *d.* 1734), daughter of Archibald *Campbell, ninth earl of Argyll. They had one son, baptized on 3 May 1679, who died in infancy. On 23 September 1678, he was appointed general of the mint, an office he held jointly

with his father. In October of that year he was named as a privy councillor, and on 8 April 1680 attained further office when he was appointed lord justice clerk. He was, however, not to hold this position for any length of time. In February 1684 he was dismissed from office and replaced by Sir James Foulis of Colinton, on being suspected of complicity in the schemes of his exiled father-in-law, Argyll. It would appear Maitland was implicated by a ciphered letter from the countess of Argyll to her husband, intercepted on its way to the Netherlands. In August he was deprived of his position as one of the commissioners of the exchequer, further evidence of his fall from grace.

Nevertheless, it seems that Maitland had little interest in the machinations of Argyll, and by April 1687 was evidently back in favour with James VII and II. On the 9th of that month he was appointed treasurer-depute, with a pension of £300 sterling, and in May was named in the new commission of the privy council. At the revolution he adhered to King James, and in July 1689 was ordered before the council charged with 'carieing on horid and unjust designes against the present government ... befor his returne from the Viscount of Dundie and his being in armes with him'. Consequently a warrant was issued for his arrest at his 'dwalling hous in Edinburgh, at Hatton and Lauder', and in August he was denounced as a rebel and put to the horn (*Reg. PCS*, 3rd ser., 13.541). Therefore, it was hardly surprising that he chose to join his king in France rather than accept the Williamite settlement. Subsequently, he was said to have joined James's expedition to Ireland, where he was present at the battle of the Boyne.

Although a Catholic and stalwart Jacobite, Maitland disapproved of James's more extreme Catholic policies, and consequently lost favour at the court of St Germain. His wife shared the strong presbyterian sympathies of her father, Argyll, and was apparently ordered to return to Britain, while her husband was forbidden to appear at the Stuart court, and had his pension reduced to 100 pistoles a year. On 9 June 1691 Maitland succeeded his father as fourth earl of Lauderdale, but was outlawed by the court of justiciary on 23 July 1694. He produced a 'mémoriall' on the state of Scotland dating from approximately 1690, and published with Nathaniel Hooke's correspondence in 1870–71, and a two-volume translation of the works of Virgil, perhaps first published in 1707.

Lauderdale died in exile at Paris in 1695 and his wife, who survived her husband and subsequently married Charles Stewart, sixth earl of Moray, died on 18 September 1734, aged seventy-six years. He was succeeded as fifth earl by his younger brother Sir John *Maitland (*c*.1655–1710) of Ravelrig, first baronet.

DEREK JOHN PATRICK

Sources *Scots peerage* · M. D. Young, ed., *The parliaments of Scotland: burgh and shire commissioners*, 2 (1993) · *Reg. PCS*, 3rd ser., vols. 6–9, 13–14 · *APS*, 1670–86 · *DNB* · *GEC, Peerage*

Archives Buckminster Park, Grantham, corresp. and papers | BL, letters to duke of Lauderdale and Charles II, Add. MSS 23242–23249

Likenesses J. Vanderbank, line engraving (aged thirty-one; after G. Kneller), BM, NPG

Maitland, Richard (*c.*1714–1763), army officer, is of unknown origin and parentage. He enlisted with the Royal Artillery as a matross on 1 November 1732, 'when about 18' (Kane, 250). In 1742 he was commissioned a lieutenant-fireworker. His subsequent commissions show the possibility of rapid promotion by merit in the more technical positions during time of war (in this case the War of the Austrian Succession): he was made second lieutenant on 1 May 1743; first lieutenant on 1 April 1744; and captain-lieutenant on 1 August 1747. He fought at Fontenoy in 1745 and probably at some of the less successful battles of the two following years. Following the peace Maitland's promotion was less rapid, but he was made full captain on 1 March 1755.

Maitland was given command of one of the four companies of Royal Artillery formed for service in India in February 1755. One was lost on the way out; the other three arrived safely at Bombay in November 1755, where they joined the garrison. In February 1756 all three companies were engaged in the expedition against the pirates based at Gheria under the command of Lieutenant-Colonel Robert Clive. After returning to Bombay the Royal Artillery companies remained with the garrison and did not take part in the expedition to Bengal in 1757 for the recapture of Calcutta.

On 9 February 1759 all three companies sailed from Bombay with the object of capturing Surat, a prosperous seaport on the River Tapti, 155 miles north of Bombay. The town was defended by a castle, a considerable fortress, which had been taken over by Sidi Masud, admiral to the Mughal emperor, who had installed his own forces and was interfering in the commercial affairs of the town, including trading posts of the Dutch and British East India companies.

As the senior king's officer present Maitland was placed in command of the land force. In addition to the three Royal Artillery companies the expedition included 800 troops from the Bombay European regiment and 1500 sepoys, a total of 2718. Maitland thus has the distinction of being the first Royal Artillery officer to command an overseas expedition comprising a mixed force. The troops took with them six months' supplies and were to receive 200,000 rupees from the merchants of Surat as compensation for not looting the city. Maitland's force landed at Damas (later known as Dentiloury) on 18 February 1759, 9 miles from Surat, where the first camp was formed. On 20 February a new camp was established at Umra, a village on the river bank, close to the city. Maitland assembled his forces to besiege the castle; work began on the breaching of the town's defensive walls on 24 February but on 26 February, Maitland lost about twenty of his men when they drove Sidi Masud's men from Surat's French gardens. However, this action allowed him to bring a battery into close action and bombardment continued for several days, resulting in a small breach in the outer wall. When the frontal assault was repulsed Maitland, fearing heavy casualties, decided on a new plan: to make the main attack from the river, between the outer and inner walls,

under covering fire from the accompanying naval force. After a heavy bombardment during the night of 1 March, Maitland sent an assault party comprising 200 European troops and 800 sepoys, which threw the defenders back and took command of the main gate of the outer wall. On 3 March heavy mortars were landed on the river bank to assist the reduction of the inner wall. In the meantime the East India Company agent had been negotiating with the governor of the castle and terms for capitulation were finally agreed at 10 p.m. on 4 March, when British troops marched into Surat. The losses to the besiegers amounted to some 130 killed and 74 wounded. Maitland had proved the capability of the Royal Artillery as well as his own leadership. His skilful deployment of the artillery had been crucial in the defeat of Sidi Masud's forces, who were worn down by the well-judged bombardment.

Maitland spent the next month putting the castle in good order for the remaining garrison, before moving his troops down the river—the last of which arrived back in Bombay on 21 April 1759. Upon his arrival Maitland received a 13-gun salute as well as the thanks of the East India Company, to whom the acquisition of Surat brought an additional revenue of £50,000 a year.

On 3 April 1760 a payment of 120,000 rupees was distributed among the troops as gratuity money for taking the castle of Surat. Maitland's share as officer commanding was 3560 rupees in addition to 1004 rupees as captain of one of the Royal Artillery companies. On 4 May 1760 Maitland led all three Royal Artillery companies into the campaign against the French forts of the Pondicherry coast, which culminated in the capture of Pondicherry after a long siege on 15 January 1761. Maitland's company returned to Bombay shortly after. He remained in India and in November 1762 learned of his promotion to the rank of major, with effect from the previous March—recognition for having commanded the Royal Artillery in India since 1759.

Maitland died in Bombay on 21 February 1763. The whole council of the Bombay presidency attended his burial, later the same day, and the castle battery fired 60 half-minute guns. JONATHAN SPAIN

Sources J. Kane, *List of officers of the royal regiment of artillery from the year 1716 to the year 1899*, rev. W. H. Askwith, 4th edn (1900) · F. Duncan, ed., *History of the royal regiment of artillery*, 2 vols. (1872–3) · 'The field of Mars, being an alphabetical digestion of principal military and naval engagements in Europe … from the ninth century to the present' (1781) · M. E. S. Laws, 'The royal artillery at Surat 1759', *Journal of the Royal Artillery*, 78 (1951), 38–49 · R. O. Cambridge, *An account of the war in India between the English and the French* (1761), 216–33 [Surat campaign] · *Gunner at large: the diary of James Wood, R.A., 1746–1765*, ed. R. Whitworth (1988)

Maitland, Samuel Roffey (1792–1866), Church of England clergyman and religious controversialist, was born on 7 January 1792 at King's Road, Bedford Row, London, the son of Alexander Maitland, a merchant, and his wife, Caroline Busby, who was descended from the seventeenth-century headmaster of Westminster School, Dr Richard Busby. She provided her husband, Alexander, a nonconformist of Scottish descent, with a Gloucestershire estate.

Education and early career Maitland was brought up early as a nonconformist, and received his early education in a number of private institutions, where he studied Latin and Greek, and also acquired some rudimentary knowledge of French and chemistry. He later remarked on his deficiency in the field of history when he left school in 1807; fortunately, he was subsequently tutored by the Revd Launcelot Sharpe, a master at the Merchant Taylors' School, whose zest for learning seems to have rubbed off on his pupil: Maitland developed a voracious appetite for reading. He was admitted to St John's College, Cambridge, on 7 October 1809, and at about the same time to the Inner Temple. He seems to have done little to distinguish himself at St John's, and switched over the following year to Trinity College, where he could be in closer proximity to his friend W. H. Mill, who instilled in him an interest in Arabic and Hebrew literature.

In 1811 Maitland left Cambridge altogether, finding that he could not, in good conscience, sign the Thirty-Nine Articles, a requisite for obtaining a degree. He later explained that his problem lay not with the articles themselves, but in his own continuing fellowship within the dissenting tradition, which hardly qualified him as a fully committed Anglican. Shortly after, he accepted the task of cataloguing the library holdings of the late Dr Maxwell Garthshorne, on the understanding that he would retain any duplicate volumes for himself. Around 1815 he found his hopes for being called to the bar stymied by his university deficiencies. This situation he endeavoured to rectify by returning to St John's on 10 October 1815, for an additional three terms. During the Easter term of 1816, his application to study paid dividends in a call to the bar. And then, on 19 November of this very busy year, he was married to Selina Stephenson, whose father, Christopher, was vicar at Olney; they had only one child, John Gorham *Maitland.

Meanwhile, Maitland's commitment to law was evidently not strong enough to keep him fully occupied; in fact, his penchant for studying and writing on various subjects seems eventually to have absorbed him almost completely. His first publication, *A Dissertation on the Primary Objects of Idolatrous Worship*, which came out in 1817, was brief and obscure. The publisher was Josiah Conder, and although no one in their right mind could have expected it to become a best-seller, it did serve to introduce Maitland's rather eccentric interests and style to those members of the learned circles who took the trouble to examine his work. By the time his next publication came out, almost a decade later, Maitland's world had been altered considerably.

Ordination and early controversies In addition to a move from London to Taunton, Maitland's spiritual perspectives seem to have undergone a gradual change; accordingly, on 27 June 1821 at Norwich, Maitland was ordained deacon by Bishop Bathurst, becoming curate of St Edmund's there. His stay in Norwich was brief, however,

and before long Bishop Ryder of Gloucester ordained him as a priest. Apparently Maitland's father had just moved to Gloucester himself, and so father and son became next-door neighbours.

The next stage in Maitland's career was an appointment on 22 May 1823 as perpetual curate of Christ Church, Gloucester. The church was relatively new, but it could not hold Maitland's attention for long either. After less than five years in his parish he decided to embark on an extended continental trip. His primary motivation appears to have been his keen interest in the status of the Jews, and his desire to observe their culture for himself in Poland and Germany.

After reaching France in April 1828, Maitland travelled on throughout Germany and Prussia as far as Warsaw. A collection of letters written during this time, together with numerous delightful sketches and illustrations, may still be seen at Lambeth Palace Library (MSS 1943–1945). His facility with languages served him well on his expedition, which lasted until the autumn of 1828. While abroad, Maitland published *A letter to the Rev. Charles Simeon … on the propriety of adopting some means beside those which are now used for promoting Christianity among the Jews* (1828). Here he advocated institutional support for Jews who had converted to Christianity and had thereby been cut off from the means of earning their living. Maitland's suggestions appear to have been well received in Britain, and measures were taken to make his vision a reality; no doubt his decision personally to bear the costs associated with the project for the space of two years was a welcome incentive to many concerned supporters.

Since interest in the fate of the Jews and biblical prophecy had long been linked in the history of the Christian church, it is unsurprising that Maitland had now become deeply engrossed in eschatological issues. As early as 1826 he had published his second work, *An enquiry into the grounds on which the prophetic period of Daniel and St. John, has been supposed to consist of 1260 years*. This piece turned out to be a significant contribution to the discussion regarding the interpretation of Daniel's Seventy Weeks, and especially, the so-called 'Year-day Theory', which had attracted many adherents. Maitland aimed to demonstrate the folly of equating the crucial 1260 days in prophecy with calendar years, so that speculation abounded in many prophetic circles as to when the period in question would end and usher in the consummation. In an era of almost unparalleled fascination with apocalyptic questions of this sort, Maitland's work won much attention. Further interest was fuelled by the appearance of the Catholic Apostolic church and the Plymouth Brethren, movements which foreshadowed the increasing popularity of the 'futurist' method of prophetic interpretation, as opposed to what would be termed the 'historicist' at that time. Clearly, Maitland's stance lent further credibility to the futurist hermeneutic, which would eventually become very popular, especially among evangelicals, though he was careful not to align himself with any particular faction.

Maitland threw himself wholeheartedly into a number

of controversies during his lifetime, and any party or individual so unfortunate as to incur his wrath rarely forgot it. His next target was Joseph Milner, who, with assistance from his brother Isaac, had written *The History of the Church of Christ* (1794–1809), which cast an approving eye upon such controversial sects as the Waldensians and Albigensians. Irked by the favourable review given to these movements, Maitland published the lengthy *Facts and documents illustrative of the history, doctrine, and rites, of the ancient Albigenses & Waldenses* (1832). His views were also aired in his regular contributions to the *British Magazine*, then edited by its founder, Hugh James Rose. In Rose, Maitland appeared to have found a soul-mate, as both men flitted for a time on the outskirts of the Oxford Movement, without ever actually throwing in their lot with, or being completely trusted by, its leaders. A number of Maitland's articles were reprinted in 1844 under the title *The Dark Ages*, while a second collection, *Essays on Subjects Connected with the Reformation in England*, was forthcoming in 1849.

Librarian at Lambeth Rose's untimely death in 1838 led to Maitland's assuming control of the *British Magazine*. Previously, he had served briefly (in fact, for one issue only) as editor of the *British Critic* under the watchful eye of John Henry Newman and his associates. In 1839 Maitland was elected a fellow of the Royal Society, but a greater honour had been bestowed upon him during the previous year. Acting upon the recommendation of Rose, Archbishop Howley had requested his services as Lambeth librarian and manuscript keeper. At the time when the invitation was issued, Maitland was still residing in Gloucester. It is obvious that he accepted the post for reasons other than financial ones: it carried with it an annual salary of only £40, yet Maitland left Gloucester and rented a house in London for £200 per annum. In addition, he brought his books with him, and even hired a clerk to assist him, at his own expense. Later, Maitland's friend William J. Thoms went to great lengths in *Notes and Queries* to establish that 'Dr. Maitland was *not* stall-fed' (Thoms, 50). Moreover, he never enjoyed 'one bit of Church preferment' (ibid.), although he was the recipient of a DD degree from the hands of Howley on 1 February 1848.

The *Acts and Monuments* controversy Maitland is undoubtedly best remembered as the fiercest critic of a new edition of Foxe's *Acts and Monuments*, published in stages, beginning with the second, third, and fourth volumes in 1837. There had not been a complete edition of the *Acts and Monuments* since the late seventeenth century, although numerous edited forms of Foxe, often under the title of the *Book of Martyrs*, had been published. Maitland's attack appears to have been two-pronged: while condemning Foxe for producing an extremely unreliable and slanted work devised to advance the fortunes of the 'puritan' faction, and particularly the Marian exiles whom Maitland so abhorred, he also criticized the Seeley and Burnside project itself, which had been announced in rather extravagant terms by the publisher and a group of prominent clergymen. In the pages of the *British Magazine* Maitland took exception to the editorial 'labours' (for which read

'blunders') of Stephen Reed Cattley, and the introductory material contributed by Canon George Townsend. When Townsend attempted to justify his role in the project, more grist was added to the mill: Maitland dealt with many of the issues involved in the dispute in his *Notes on the contributions of the Rev. George Townsend … to the new edition of Fox's martyrology* (3 parts, 1841–2).

Undoubtedly, Maitland's harsh criticisms embarrassed those involved with the Foxe project, although they did not deter additional editions of Foxe (there were three more issued by 1877). Eventually, Maitland seemed to have tired of the issue and moved on to other publications, which reflect both his eclecticism and his eccentricities, including his *Illustrations and Enquiries Relating to Mesmerism: Part 1* (1849) and his *Superstition and Science: an Essay* (1855). Another unusual book written much earlier, *Eruvin, or, Miscellaneous essays on subjects connected with the nature, history, and destiny of man* (1831), contained essays ranging from such subjects as 'The consequences of the fall' (Essay V) to 'The millennium' (Essay VII).

Later life and death Maitland's fortunes suffered a considerable reversal about 1848, when the new archbishop of Canterbury, John Bird Sumner, appointed his son-in-law, the Revd John Thomas, in Maitland's place as librarian; in addition in the year following, the *British Magazine* ceased publication.

Maitland's expulsion from Lambeth was largely undeserved: despite his acrid pen, it appears that he had gone well out of his way to help those engaged in research while at Lambeth. And, despite inferences to the contrary, he never entered fully into the spirit of the Oxford Movement, but like Rose, represented the old high church rather than the newer, more controversial phenomenon. S. C. Orchard pointed to his progressive disenchantment with evangelicalism fairly early in his career. Perhaps Newman's increasing distance from the old high-church position, which became a source of concern for Hugh James Rose (Nockles, 117), was of equal alarm to Maitland.

Following his experience at Lambeth, this one-time 'Evangelical of the Evangelicals' (Orchard, 165) returned to Gloucester, and though living in retirement, continued to publish on a variety of subjects. He also supported W. J. Thoms at the launching of *Notes and Queries*. At some point in his life Maitland began to write an autobiography, but he did not succeed in getting his manuscript past 1817. While Cambridge University Library possesses numerous printed works including a copy of Strype with notations by Maitland, together with two manuscript essays, the autobiography does not appear to be among the resources held there.

Though obviously a man of letters, Maitland evidently acquired some degree of expertise in a wide range of pursuits, such as music (he played several instruments), draughtsmanship, printing, and bookbinding. Having survived both his wife, Selina, and his son, he died on 19 January 1866 at his home, Spa Road, South Hamlet, Gloucester.   D. ANDREW PENNY

Sources *DNB* • W. J. Thoms, 'Lambeth Library and its librarians', *N&Q*, 4th ser., 1 (1868), 50–51 • S. C. Orchard, 'English evangelical eschatology, 1790–1850', PhD diss., U. Cam., 1969 • D. A. Penny, 'John Foxe's Victorian reception', *HJ*, 40 (1997), 111–42 • D. A. Penny, 'John Foxe, the *Acts and monuments* and the development of prophetic interpretation', *John Foxe and the English Reformation*, ed. D. Loades (1997), 252–77 • P. B. Nockles, *The Oxford Movement in context: Anglican high churchmanship, 1760–1857* (1994) • *The acts and monuments of John Foxe*, ed. S. R. Cattley, 8 vols. (1837–41), vol. 1 • G. R. Elton, *F. W. Maitland* (1985) • D. W. Bebbington, *Evangelicalism in modern Britain: a history from the 1730s to the 1980s* (1989) • J. F. Mozley, *John Foxe and his book* (1940); repr. (1970) • V. N. Olsen, *John Foxe and the Elizabethan church* (1973) • S. R. Maitland, letters and sketches, LPL, MSS 1943–1945 • d. cert. • Boase, *Mod. Eng. biog.*

Archives CUL, notes on John Strype's works • Glos. RO, notes on bishops of Gloucester • LPL, corresp. and papers

Wealth at death under £3000: probate, 13 March 1866, *CGPLA Eng. & Wales*

Maitland, Thomas (*c.*1548–1572). *See under* Maitland, Sir Richard, of Lethington (1496–1586).

Maitland, Sir Thomas (1760–1824), army officer and colonial official, was born on 10 March 1760, probably at the family seat, Hatton House, Ratho, Edinburghshire, the second surviving son of James Maitland, seventh earl of Lauderdale (1718–1789), and his wife, Mary Turner (1733/4–1789), daughter and coheir of Alderman Sir Thomas *Lombe (1685–1739) of Old Jewry, London. He was the brother of James *Maitland, the eighth earl. He was educated at Lincoln's Inn (1774) and Edinburgh (1775–7). He retained his Scottish accent all his life. Shortly after his birth, he was appointed lieutenant in the old Scots 17th light dragoons or Edinburgh light horse, and after it was disbanded in 1763, drew half pay of his rank until 1778.

Army and India, 1778–1790 In 1778 Maitland took up his commission (captain, 14 January 1778) and raised a company for the Seaforth regiment or 78th (from 1786 72nd) Highlanders. With the regiment, in which his younger brother William also held a commission, Maitland served some years in India, ashore against Haidar Ali and Tipu Sultan of Mysore, and afloat under Admiral Sir Edward Hughes against the French under Pierre André de Suffren. In June 1783 he was wounded in Hughes's action with Suffren off Cuddalore on the Coromandel coast. He distinguished himself at the capture of the Mysorean fortress of Palicatchery in November 1784. Later he was brigade major of the king's troops at Calcutta, and was transferred by Lord Cornwallis to a similar post at Madras, at his own request, when war was imminent in 1790.

Member of parliament, 1790–1813 Maitland's brother, the eighth earl, a relatively radical whig with strong electoral interest in the Haddington burghs, decided to return Maitland for them. Following a contested election in 1790 with blatant corruption by both sides, Maitland was elected. He was MP from July 1790 to 1796, from March 1802 to February 1805, and from October 1812 to July 1813. An opposition whig, he supported Charles Grey. In his maiden speech (28 February 1791) he criticized the war with Tipu Sultan, and in April he supported Grey's motion against the Russian armament. His late Victorian biographer, Walter Frewen Lord, wrote that he was 'what we now call a

Sir Thomas Maitland (1760–1824), by John Hoppner

Little Englander' (Lord, 9). In May 1791 he was admitted to the Whig Club and in June to Brooks's. In February and March 1792 he brought in motions against the war with Tipu. One of the Society of the Friends of the People, in 1792 he supported parliamentary reform. On 21 February 1793 he seconded Grey's motion against war with revolutionary France. In 1794 and 1795 he criticized the government's conduct of the war, opposed barrack-building as conducive to military despotism, opposed commissions to French émigrés—Lord wrote of his xenophobic 'ravings'—and criticized the Toulon expedition and the occupation of Corsica. He continued to vote against the government until June 1795, after which he was sent to St Domingue.

After the Belle Île expedition of 1800 Maitland, disappointed at failing to gain further military employment, resumed his seat, vacated for him by the sitting member Robert Baird, in March 1802. W. F. Lord wrote that he 'never appeared again as an obstructionist, or a Little Englander … he rarely spoke, and always as an imperialist' (Lord, 18). He supported the Addington ministry and its defence policy against critics including Pitt. Pitt's return to power in May 1804 left Maitland in the political wilderness, but apparently there were ministerialist hopes of detaching him from the opposition. That winter he accepted the governorship of Ceylon and persuaded his brother to agree to his seat being occupied by a friend of the ministry. Following the 1812 general election he resumed his seat. He advocated suppression of sedition in Yorkshire, and in May 1813 voted for Roman Catholic relief. Soon after, disillusioned with politics and 'not liking to quarrel with Lauderdale and yet neither liking his friends Grey or Grenville' (HoP, *Commons, 1790–1820*, 529), he accepted the governorship of Malta.

St Domingue, 1795–1798 In the 1780s St Domingue (later Haiti), exporting sugar and over half the world's coffee, was the most lucrative French colony, producing more than the entire British West Indies and with more trade than the United States. In 1791 slaves revolted, and some of the colonists requested British intervention. Following the outbreak of war between Britain and revolutionary France (February 1793), Pitt and Dundas's strategy was to destroy France's naval and commercial power by capturing its West Indian colonies. In September 1793 Sir Charles Grey's expeditionary force landed at St Domingue, in co-operation with royalist colonists. They captured Mole St Nicholas, 'the Gibraltar of the West Indies' (Fortescue, *Brit. army*, 330), a key naval base, and the capital, Port au Prince, and occupied about a third of the colony. Opposing them were French republican, ex-slave, and mulatto forces, commanded by Toussaint l'Ouverture and others. Although reinforced by the 1796 'great expedition', the British, weakened by disease, were unable to decisively defeat their enemies and capture the interior and north. They suffered catastrophic losses from yellow fever, malaria, dysentery, and other diseases, exacerbated by lead-contaminated rum. The majority, at least three-fifths, of British troops there died: it was 'among the greatest disasters in British military history' (Geggus, 'British government', 285).

Maitland was appointed major in the 62nd foot in 1790, and promoted lieutenant-colonel in the army in March 1794 and in the regiment in August 1794. From 1795 he commanded a half-battalion of it in St Domingue. A well-connected Scottish aristocrat, he was able to communicate his views to Dundas. Pessimistic and critical of the British intervention and doubting it could succeed, he wrote in July 1796 emphasizing British mortality, alleging that 'St. Domingo will end in being a Brigand Republick' (Geggus, *Slavery, War, and Revolution*, 205), and arguing that if the occupation had to be continued it should be minimal and defensive. He served under General John Graves Simcoe (1752–1806) but reported separately to Whitehall, continuing pessimistic and critical of the French colonists. Appointed brigadier-general at St Domingue (18 April), in August 1797 he returned to England.

The British government, lacking resources, in January 1798 ordered the new commander for St Domingue, Major-General Nesbitt, to implement a partial evacuation, but he died at Madeira. Maitland, appointed brigadier-general in the West Indies (1 January 1798), designated Nesbitt's chief of staff, and informed of the government's intentions, had travelled ahead, leaving England in January and arriving in St Domingue in March. The senior officer there, Major-General John Whyte, 'tacitly abdicated' (Fortescue, *Brit. army*, 555) to Maitland and eventually returned home. Maitland, whose still effective troops and naval blockade enabled him to bargain, negotiated with Toussaint l'Ouverture—whom he considered cunning but not very able or determined—the British surrender of the western province, including the capital, and in

May implemented a successful evacuation of it. Reporting to Dundas he emphasized British mortality—'the British force may now be truly said to be in a galloping consumption' (Lord, 43)—and advocated total evacuation. After the government's instructions to Nesbitt arrived in late July, permitting total evacuation, Maitland seized his opportunity. Despite opposition from Major-General Alexander Lindsay, sixth earl of Balcarres (1752–1825), the governor of Jamaica, and Vice-Admiral Sir Hyde Parker (1739–1807), the naval commander, who both favoured retention of the Mole to defend Jamaica, Maitland, though ill probably with dysentery—he wrote 'I shall never recover the shock to my health' (Lord, 47)—in August negotiated separately with Toussaint and André Rigaud. He secured an agreement with Toussaint for an unmolested evacuation, a guarantee for French colonists remaining, and future non-aggression and trade. He wrote, 'Thank God I have at length got Great Britain rid of the whole of the incumbrance in this Island' (Duffy, 309). Hostilities ceased on 20 August 1798 and he carried out a successful evacuation, taking artillery, stores, and almost everything of military value. He sailed on 31 August, and the evacuation of the Mole was completed by Colonel Spencer on 3 October. Meanwhile in London the government had changed policy, deciding to hold the last strongpoints on St Domingue to defend Jamaica: but, with seaborne communications, they were too late. On his own initiative Maitland had extricated Britain from the St Domingue imbroglio. Later historians criticized Sir John Fortescue's scathing account in his *History of the British Army* of the British involvement in St Domingue. Nevertheless his praise of Maitland arguably remains valid: 'by the supreme strength and courage of a single subordinate officer, England was plucked from the awful morass of confusion, extravagance, death and disaster' (Fortescue, *Brit. army*, 565).

Varied employment, 1799–1805 In 1799 Maitland went on an unsuccessful mission to the United States, arriving in April to negotiate an agreement on trade with St Domingue. In August he returned to England. He went to Cheltenham, then Berkeley Square, London. He was subsequently employed in supporting French royalist military attempts, and in September 1799 was promoted major-general (local rank). He was appointed to command an expedition to capture Belle Île, off the coast of Brittany. As Maitland wished, the naval command was given to Sir Edward Pellew (1757–1833), later Viscount Exmouth. Great difficulty was experienced in finding the required 4000 troops. The expedition, inadequately prepared and equipped—W. F. Lord called it 'this burlesque army' (Lord, 63)—sailed from Cork in May 1800, and destroyed the forts on the south end of Quiberon on 4 June, and on 6 June captured some vessels and prisoners. Maitland's royalist force camped on Ile Houat. Reports of the strength of the garrison of Belle Île, reinforced apparently because of British lack of pre-operational secrecy, caused Maitland to delay his attack until his entire force had arrived. On 21 June he received orders from Dundas to send his troops to Minorca as reinforcements for the Mediterranean. On 4 July Dundas ordered him home. Fortescue later condemned the expedition as 'eminently foolish … a wanton and wicked waste' (Fortescue, *Brit. army*, 779–80).

In 1803 Maitland was appointed colonel of a battalion of the army of reserve. From November 1803, resigning his parliamentary seat, to May 1804, he was a member (at a salary of £1500 p.a.) of the Board of Control for India, under Addington's ministry, and was sworn of the privy council in November 1803. He was promoted major-general in August 1804, appointed colonel in the third garrison battalion in February 1805, and for a short time had a brigade command in Sussex.

Ceylon, 1805–1811 In 1805 Maitland was appointed governor and officer commanding the troops in the crown colony of Ceylon, his exceptional dual appointment presumably resulting from the Colonial Office perception of the problems there. Ceylon government had been troubled under the previous and first British governor, Frederick North (1766–1827), from 1817 fifth earl of Guilford, a well-meaning reformer 'of the most pestilent type' (Lord, 73), under whose lax control finances were disordered and abuses flourished. The previous commander, Major-General David Wemyss, formerly Douglas (1760–1839), was incompetent and extravagant and quarrelled with North and the judges of the supreme court. Moreover, from 1803 a disastrous and expensive war was fought against the inland kingdom of Kandy.

On 18 July 1805 Maitland arrived at Colombo and assumed office. A hard-working, shrewd, and capable administrator, he was a masterful, overbearing, bad-tempered, sometimes unscrupulous autocrat who decided policy, dominated his council, and was disliked by subordinates. In his first six months he investigated the situation, writing a long report. He criticized North's administration as 'in many points totally inefficient' (de Silva, 240), and especially attacked the laxity of his control over the civil service and his tenurial changes. He condemned Wemyss's conduct as 'utterly reprehensible' (de Silva, 239) and his military expenditure as extravagant and often unnecessary, and alleged that the army had 'grown far too independent' (Mills, 47). Realizing the government then lacked the resources to defeat Kandy, and wanting to reduce expenditure, he attempted to make peace. He ended the North–Wemyss policy of economic blockade and military reprisals, remained on the defensive, offered peace terms, and tried to secure them by bribery. The Kandyans refused terms, demanding cession of a sea port, but by tacit agreement hostilities ceased from 1805 to 1815, and Maitland acted largely as if the two states were at peace. He vigorously subordinated the military to the civil authority, suppressed the military board, and reduced military expenditure. He advocated the adequate fortification of Trincomalee, which he claimed was the 'real key' to the 'naval superiority of India' (Lord, 96). Following the July 1806 Vellore Sepoy mutiny in Madras, in

August he sent troops thither, and subsequently wrote to Gilbert Elliot, Baron Minto (1751–1814), the new governor-general of India, scathingly criticizing the Madras government. Following the 1809 Seringapatam mutiny of company European officers he again sent troops, and he proposed a scheme for the reorganization of the East India Company's army.

Maitland declared, 'the sole object of Government is … to ensure the prosperity of the island solely through the medium of generally increasing the prosperity and happiness of the natives' (Mills, 57). He paid off debt, introduced rigorous control of expenditure, stopping large leakages, and attempted to balance the budget. He reorganized the civil service and purged it of corruption, increased salaries, and in 1805 forbade civil servants to trade. He offered rewards for proficiency in Sinhalese. He reorganized the central administration—in 1806 abolishing the board of revenue and commerce and substituting a commissioner of revenue under direct orders of the governor—and the provincial administration, replacing the agents of revenue and commerce by collectors under control of the commissioner of revenue. He retained and tightened the profitable government salt monopoly and introduced stamped paper duties. He tried to prevent native officials oppressing the people, and improved policing. He increased the number and powers of magistrates' courts, extended supreme court jurisdiction, and appointed minor courts of appeal. He also instigated juries in criminal cases, introduced by the 1810 charter. The chief justice, Edmund Henry Lushington, interfered with courts martial and executive decisions and quarrelled with Maitland. In 1808 Maitland suspended him from the council, and early in 1809 threatened to suspend him from judicial office. Lushington resigned in February 1809.

Maitland encouraged agriculture, ending North's restrictions on cinnamon production, and increased the area under cultivation. Hoping to increase coffee production, he persuaded the secretary of state in 1810 to permit Europeans to acquire land anywhere in Ceylon. In 1806 he removed the Dutch-imposed disabilities of Roman Catholics, and he conciliated the Buddhists. He did not favour missionaries. His critics in England called him a pagan, and in 1808 Wilberforce criticized his education policy. In the autumn of 1810 Maitland suffered an attack of fever and his health, seriously affected by the climate, suddenly deteriorated. He returned to England in March 1811. His governorship favourably impressed the British government, and according to the Ceylon historian Colvin de Silva was 'an outstanding success … five years of sound and efficient government' (de Silva, 254).

Maitland was promoted lieutenant-general in June 1811 and appointed colonel of the 10th foot in July. He recuperated in England, taking the waters at Cheltenham. On his recall he was 'perhaps worth £25,000 clear' (HoP, *Commons, 1790–1820*, 529) but lost by the discount on Ceylon paper currency when paying his debts. He wanted employment on the staff, according to the duke of York's secretary, James Willoughby Gordon (1773–1851), who described him as 'a very clever man, but he inclines to be prosy' (ibid.). In 1813 he was proposed as governor of Java.

Malta and the Ionian Islands, 1813–1824 In July 1813 Maitland was appointed the first governor of Malta, and landed at Valletta on 3 October. Reportedly when offered the post it was proposed that a council be established, but he declared, 'Aweel, ye'll just send somebody else, for I'll na be bottle holder for ony mon' (Hedderwick, 80). He insisted on the 'free and unfettered power of the Governor' (Dixon, 137). A benevolent despot, nicknamed 'King Tom', he imposed reforms, including practices he had tried in Ceylon. On arrival he acted rigorously and apparently effectively against the plague, imposing isolation, quarantine, and disinfection of buildings. He centralized finances under his control, reformed local administration, and reduced corruption. He abolished the Universita, an ancient guild which controlled imports of some foodstuffs and, he wrote, 'the most troublesome dunghill of corruption I ever met with' (Lord, 155). He arranged grain purchase from the Black Sea region, and in 1818 established commissioners of the board of supply, directly responsible to the governor. He found 'pure judicial tyranny' (Dixon, 146) and reformed the judicial system. He introduced trial by jury and forbade judges to interfere with the executive or legislation. He tactfully limited the powers of the Roman Catholic church and, concerned for Maltese susceptibilities, prevented the Board of Ordnance moving Maltese armour from Valletta to England.

From 1815 until 1864 when ceded to Greece, the Ionian islands were a British protectorate. In December 1815 Maitland was appointed, in addition to his Malta post, lord high commissioner of the Ionian islands and commander-in-chief in the Mediterranean, excluding Gibraltar. Also in 1815 British consulates on the Barbary coast, excluding Morocco, were placed under him, and he was made a GCB (2 January). The British then dominated the Mediterranean, and W. F. Lord wrote of Maitland, 'He bestrode the Mediterranean like a Colossus' (Lord, 241). He was paid £5000 as governor of Malta, £3500 as commander-in-chief in the Mediterranean, £1000 as high commissioner, and £1000 as former governor of Ceylon. He went to Ionia in February 1816, and thenceforth spent much more time there than at Malta, for which he was criticized.

Maitland was no philhellene, criticizing their 'classic imaginings' (Lord, 217), and dismissing 'fools looking for old stones' (Young, 106). He formed a low opinion of the Ionians, and wrote of their 'duplicity, chicanery and want of principle' (Dixon, 181). He believed that a representative assembly would fail, as it had in Sicily. He wrote that 'if we gave such a people a real constitution, they would simply violate it' (Lord, 186) and that 'a free Government is incompatible with the existence of a strong one' (Dixon, 185). Required by the British government to establish a constitution, he consulted Ionians and drafted a bicameral one, introduced in 1817, which reserved extensive powers to the high commissioner. According to W. F. Lord its only function was 'to throw a decent veil over the despotism of Thomas Maitland' (Lord, 193). Sir Charles James

Napier (1782–1853), who served under Maitland at Cephalonia, described him as 'a rough old despot' (Lord, 114). He ruled despotically and vigorously, preventing liberty of the press, and imposing reforms. He disarmed the islanders, improved administration, increased official salaries, attempted to end bribery and corruption, abolished tax-farming, systematized customs duties, and improved the judicial system and the treatment of Jews. He forbade usurious landlord advances to tenants, and established government banks. He built roads and lighthouses. He resisted expansion of papal prerogatives. However, himself reportedly minimally educated, he took little interest in education and resisted the philhellene project of a university. Made a GCH in 1817, he established in 1818 the Order of St Michael and St George for services in Malta and Ionia. In April 1818 he was appointed its first grand master and GCMG, and he accepted the cross in diamonds. However, he wrote privately of the order with a Swiftian cynicism which later shocked his biographer, and used it to gain influence 'as a mere means of corruption' (Lord, 230). He built the neo-classical palace of St Michael and St George in Corfu town, as headquarters for the order and a residence for the high commissioner.

Despite reforms and prosperity, many Ionians were discontented, and Maitland had to counter the intrigues of local nobles and others, including the Russophile Corfiot Count Ioannis Kapodistrias (later first president of Greece, assassinated 1831). Maitland was required by earlier treaty to cede the formerly Venetian Greek town of Parga, on the Albanian coast, to the Ottoman empire. Privately he opposed cession, and he negotiated relatively favourable terms with the Turks. The cession in March 1819 caused much criticism of him in Britain and elsewhere. During the Greek war of independence he privately sympathized with the Porte as standing for established government, whereas he saw little prospect of the Greeks achieving a successful state. His policy of enforcing the British government's policy of Ionian neutrality and preventing Ionian support for the Greek war was most unpopular. Controversial, he had political enemies also in Britain. Joseph Hume (1777–1855) repeatedly attacked him in the House of Commons. In 1821 he denounced him as a tyrant, and his rule as 'a disgrace to England … a system of misrule' (Lord, 263), and alleged jobbery and financial abuses. The government defended Maitland.

Maitland was capable and hard-working, but also arrogant, imperious, querulous, bad-tempered, and ill-mannered. Napier wrote of him, 'Narrow-minded, he saw many things under false lights, was constantly drunk, and surrounded by sycophants' (Napier, 285). His coarse behaviour and slovenly appearance offended officers and others. According to Napier he was 'insufferably rude' and 'particularly dirty in his person' (Young, 157). Thomas Collings wrote of his 'contempt of all propriety in regard to dress … he looked nothing better than a well to do shopkeeper, and even then not of the superior class' (Hedderwick, 80). He once received the senate in his night attire and told them to 'go to hell!' (Bruce, 83). When visiting a papal official his clothes were shabby, his shirt and waist-coat stained with snuff, and his cap greasy. Though economical in public finance, in private he lived lavishly. W. F. Lord wrote that 'his diversion, his solace, was gross indulgence' (Lord, xiv). He enjoyed 'the pleasures of the table', reportedly 'indulging to excess' (Hedderwick, 80). He indulged in drinking bouts, 'being frequently invisible for several days altogether' (ibid.). Apparently his health was poor, presumably from his tropical service, exacerbated by his lifestyle. He frequently visited the baths at Lucca, Tuscany, for his health, and his enemies scoffed at his valetudinarianism. He never married.

A sick man, Maitland late in 1823 returned to Malta. On 17 January 1824 he visited the forces chaplain's house at Floriana, suffered an apoplectic stroke at half past one, and had died by half past ten that evening. He was buried on 21 January in the Upper Barracca, Valletta, and a simple monument marked his grave. Commemorative services were held in Ionian churches and at one the eulogy by Count Spiridian Bulgaris praised him as like 'a guardian angel', just, humane, and generous, causing 'the progressive improvement of all useful institutions' and entitled to 'the lasting veneration of the Ionian people' (GM, 371–2). He was commemorated by a small Ionic rotunda at the Esplanade, Corfu town. The biography by Walter Frewen Lord, *Sir Thomas Maitland: the Mastery of the Mediterranean*, was published in 1897. Lord wrote that although some considered Maitland a 'gross bully' and 'brutal tyrant', 'his labours were Herculean … his life was illuminated and dignified by his unbending devotion to duty' (Lord, 87, xiv–xv).   H. M. CHICHESTER, rev. ROGER T. STEARN

Sources W. F. Lord, *Sir Thomas Maitland: the mastery of the Mediterranean* (1897) · C. W. Dixon, *The colonial administrations of Sir Thomas Maitland* (1939) · HoP, *Commons, 1790–1820* · GEC, *Peerage*, new edn, vol. 7 · Burke, *Peerage* (1999), vol. 2 · GM, 1st ser., 94/1 (1824), 370–72 · *Army List* (1823) · W. Napier, *The life and opinions of General Sir Charles James Napier, G.C.B.*, vol. 1 (1857) · D. P. Geggus, *Slavery, war and revolution: the British occupation of Saint Domingue, 1793–1798* (1982) · W. N. Bruce, *Life of General Sir Charles Napier G.C.B.* (1885) · L. A. Mills, *Ceylon under British rule, 1795–1932* (1933) · C. R. De Silva, *Ceylon under the British occupation, 1795–1833*, 1 (1941) · M. Duffy, *Soldiers, sugar and seapower: the British expeditions to the West Indies and the war against revolutionary France* (1987) · Fortescue, *Brit. army*, vol. 4 · J. B. Hedderwick, *The captain's clerk* (1957) · R. Cannon, ed., *Historical record of the seventy-second regiment, or the duke of Albany's own highlanders* (1848) · D. Geggus, 'The British government and the Saint Domingue slave revolt, 1791–1793', *EngHR*, 96 (1981), 285–305 · *Oxford history of the British empire*, 2 (1998) · H. Smith, *Britain in Malta*, 1: *Constitutional development of Malta in the nineteenth century* (1953) · H. Luke, *Malta: an account and an appreciation* (1960) · N. C. E. Kenrick, *The story of the Wiltshire regiment (duke of Edinburgh's): the 62nd and 99th foot* (1963) · M. Young, *Corfu and the other Ionian islands* (1977)
Archives NA Scot., letter-books, corresp., and papers | BL, corresp. with William A'Court, Add. MSS 41529–41530 · BL, corresp. with Earl Bathurst, loan 57 · BL, corresp. with William Huskisson, Add. MSS 38735–38739 · BL, letters to William Windham, Add. MSS 37879–37886 · Derbys. RO, Matlock, letters to R. J. Wilmot-Horton · National Archives of Malta, Rabat, corresp. as governor of Malta · NL Scot., corresp. with Lord Minto · U. Nott. L., letters to Lord William Bentinck
Likenesses B. Thorvaldsen, plaster bust, 1818, Thorvaldsen Museum, Copenhagen · J. Hoppner, portrait, Thirlestane Castle,

Berwickshire [*see illus.*] · T. Lupton, mezzotint (after J. Hoppner), NPG; repro. in Lord, *Sir Thomas Maitland*, frontispiece
Wealth at death under £40,000: resworn probate, 1826, Lord, *Sir Thomas Maitland*, 6

Maitland, Thomas, Lord Dundrennan (1792–1851), judge, eldest son of Adam Maitland (d. 1843) and his wife, Stewart McWhann, was born at Dundrennan Abbey, Kirkcudbrightshire, on 9 October 1792. Edward Francis *Maitland, later Lord Barcaple, was his younger brother. Maitland studied at Edinburgh University, and was called to the Scottish bar in 1813. On 3 July 1815 he married Isabella Graham, fourth daughter of James McDowall of Garthland, Renfrewshire. They had four sons and two daughters. The author and judge Henry, Lord Cockburn, was married to a sister of his wife.

After practising successfully for a quarter of a century Maitland was on 9 May 1840 appointed solicitor-general in Lord Melbourne's administration. He vacated the office in September 1841 on the accession to power of the tories under Peel. On the death of his father in July 1843 he succeeded to the family estates, and sat in parliament for Kirkcudbrightshire from 1845 to 1850. Lord John Russell reappointed him solicitor-general in 1846, and he remained in office until 1850. Maitland was a sound lawyer; he became, on 6 February 1850, a judge of the court of session, and took the title of Lord Dundrennan.

Dundrennan was devoted to antiquarian literature, and possessed a magnificent library—'a monument' according to Lord Cockburn, 'honourable to his taste and judgment'. The collection was dispersed by sale over nine days in November 1851. He also edited a collection of his friend Francis Jeffrey's contributions to the *Edinburgh Review*, published in November 1843, and superintended the reissue of works by Marlowe and the poets Thomas Carew, Robert Herrick, and William Drummond, among others. Maitland died on 10 June 1851 at 31 Melville Street, Edinburgh, the home of his brother Edward. He was survived by his wife.   G. C. BOASE, rev. ROBERT SHIELS

Sources F. J. Grant, ed., *The Faculty of Advocates in Scotland, 1532–1943*, Scottish RS, 145 (1944) · Boase, *Mod. Eng. biog.* · B. W. Crombie and W. S. Douglas, *Modern Athenians: a series of original portraits of memorable citizens of Edinburgh* (1882) · *Journal of Henry Cockburn: being a continuation of the 'Memorials of his time', 1831–1854*, 2 vols. (1874) · H. Cockburn, *Life of Francis Jeffrey* (1872) · GM, 2nd ser., 36 (1851), 196–7 · ILN (21 June 1851), 588 · *The Times* (13 June 1851) · private information (1893) [A. C. Maitland, T. G. Stevenson]
Archives BL, letters to Macvey Napier, Add. MSS 34621–34626 · NL Scot., letters to Andrew Rutherfurd
Likenesses B. W. Crombie, coloured etching, 1847, NPG; repro. in Crombie and Douglas, *Modern Athenians*, 111–12

Maitland, Thomas, eleventh earl of Lauderdale (1803–1878), naval officer, born on 3 February 1803 at Frankfort, co. Cork, was the only son of the Hon. William Mordaunt Maitland (d. 1841), general in the army, third son of James, seventh earl of Lauderdale, and his first wife, Mary, widow of John Travers of Fir Grove, co. Cork, and daughter of the Revd Richard Orpen, of Killowen, co. Kerry. He entered the navy in 1816, and was promoted lieutenant of the *Euryalus* on 16 May 1823. In December 1825 he was appointed to the *Superb*, guardship at Portsmouth, and in March

1826 to the *Ganges*, flagship of Sir Robert Waller Otway, on the South American station. On 30 April 1827 he was promoted commander. He married, on 7 February 1828 at Rio de Janeiro, Amelia (*d.* 18 February 1890), daughter of William Young of Rio de Janeiro; they had at least one child. In 1832–3 he commanded the *Sparrowhawk* (18 guns), on the West Indian station, and brought home a treasure freight of 589,405 Mexican dollars and forty-two bales of cochineal. In 1835–7 he commanded the *Tweed* (20 guns), on the north coast of Spain during the civil war, and received the cross of Charles III, which he was permitted to wear. He was advanced to post rank on 10 January 1837, and in June was appointed to command the *Wellesley* (72 guns), flagship, on the East India station, of Sir Frederick Lewis Maitland, and after Sir Frederick's death of Sir J. J. Gordon Bremer. He thus had an active share in the operations in the Persian Gulf in 1839, and during the First Opium War in 1840–41, including commanding the 1st naval battalion at the storming of the heights near Canton (Guangzhou). He was made a CB on 29 June 1841, knighted in 1843, and promoted rear-admiral on 18 June 1857.

In 1859 Maitland was questioned by the royal commission on the defences of the United Kingdom, when he spoke strongly against the proposed fortifications at an expenditure which 'might be more profitably laid out in building ships; because', he said, 'if you can ensure being masters of the Channel, I do not see any absolute necessity, as far as security goes, for fortifying Spithead' (*Parl. papers*, 1860, 23.520). From 1860 to 1863 Maitland was commander-in-chief in the Pacific.

On 22 March 1863, on the death of his cousin, the tenth earl of Lauderdale, Maitland succeeded to the title, and to the hereditary offices of standard-bearer of Scotland and marshal of the royal household. On 30 November 1863 he was promoted vice-admiral. He was made a KCB, on 28 March 1865, and GCB on 24 May 1873. He was a Scottish representative peer (Conservative) from 1867 to 1878. He became an admiral on 8 April 1868, and, by special promotion, admiral of the fleet on the retired list on 27 December 1877. He died at his seat, Thirlestane Castle, Lauder, Berwickshire, on 1 September 1878; as he left no male issue, the title passed to a distant cousin. Mary Jane Maitland [*see* Brabazon, Mary Jane, *under* Brabazon, Reginald, twelfth earl of Meath], his only surviving daughter, married Reginald Brabazon, twelfth earl of Meath.

J. K. LAUGHTON, *rev.* ROGER MORRISS

Sources O'Byrne, *Naval biog. dict.* · *Navy List* · *The Times* (2 Sept 1878) · Foster, *Alum. Oxon.* · G. S. Graham, *The China station: war and diplomacy, 1830–1860* (1978) · E. Holt, *The opium wars in China* (1964) · C. Hibbert, *The dragon wakes: China and the West, 1793–1911* (1970) · E. Holt, *The Carlist wars in Spain* (1967) · GEC, *Peerage* · Burke, *Peerage* (1959) · *CCI* (1879)
Likenesses F. Chantrey, marble bust, Wellington Museum, Apsley House, London
Wealth at death see confirmation, 1879, *CCI*

Maitland, William, of Lethington (1525×30–1573), courtier and diplomat, was the eldest son of Sir Richard *Maitland of Lethington (1496–1586), courtier, judge, and writer, and Mary or Mariota Cranstoun (*d.* 1586), daughter

William Maitland of Lethington (1525×30–1573), by unknown artist

of Sir Thomas Cranstoun of Corsbie. His younger brothers were John *Maitland, later chancellor and first Lord Maitland of Thirlestane (1543–1595), and Thomas *Maitland (*c.*1548–1572) [*see under* Maitland, Sir Richard, of Lethington]; his sister Mary *Maitland (*d.* 1596) was also involved with the worlds of letters and the court. Much has been made of the notion of Maitland as representative of the rise of the 'middling sort' in Scottish society, and the lairds and the legal profession in particular, and there is certainly much in this, but he was not low born. The Maitlands enjoyed a place in Gavin Douglas's *The Palice of Honour*, and numerous marriages into noble families. Maitland's father proudly described himself as a daughter's son of the house of Seton. It is true though that in the mid-sixteenth century the Maitland family were a rising force and were yet to achieve their greatest days.

Education and theological background Maitland was probably educated at Haddington grammar school before entering St Leonard's College at St Andrews University in 1540. He moved on to the University of Paris in 1542. Over fifty Scots entered the university along with Maitland on 16 December 1542, including Quintin Kennedy, the Catholic apologist, William Kirkcaldy of Grange's younger brother Thomas, Maitland's cousin George Seton, the future fifth Lord Seton, Robert Pitcairn, and William Roberton, the future Edinburgh schoolmaster who would cause the reformers so much trouble. Maitland was no doubt helped by the fact that his kinsman William Cranstoun, a staunch Catholic and future principal of St Salvator's College, was elected Scotus rector of Paris in 1542. Given the acknowledged strength of the 'auld Parisiane kyndnes' (A. Ross, 'Reformation and repression', *Essays on the Scottish Reformation, 1513–1625*, ed. D. McRoberts, 1962, 409) between the students which later often transcended sectarian differences, the importance of Maitland's years in Paris from a personal as well as an academic point of view should not be underestimated. Maitland may very well have drunk from the protestant well of St Leonard's along with so many others but his protestantism was of a very different brew from that of John Knox. Maitland had absorbed an Erasmian view of human nature at St Andrews and Paris, and seems to have shared his father's tolerant approach to religion. He may not have been present in his father's house in 1546 when George Wishart preached but he certainly shared his father's civility towards those of different religious views. Knox apparently persuaded Maitland of the sinfulness of the mass at a meeting of the Edinburgh privy kirk in 1555, but that was not an accurate portent for the future of their relationship, which would witness some very acrimonious confrontations.

For a layman, Maitland was remarkably well equipped theologically. Not many were brave enough to threaten Knox with the discipline of his own kirk session for the latter's denunciation of Maitland as an atheist and the allegation that he had dismissed heaven and hell as 'thingis devised to fray bairnis' (Bannatyne, 281–2). Maitland traded scriptural chapter and verse with Knox and was conversant with the teachings of Calvin, Luther, Bucer, Musculus, and Melanchthon. Philosophically, he rejected the 'untractable discipline of the stoickes', preferring instead to be 'a student in that schole where it is taught that wyse men myndes must be ledde by probable reasons which the disciples of Plato and Aristotle have embraced' (PRO, SP 52/19/5). The same preference for flexible reasoning was evident in Maitland's regard for the practicality of the Roman jurisconsults and their awareness that 'the causes, tymes, places, persons, occasions and other circymstances wolde vary the whole decision' (ibid.). As well as being well acquainted with the classics, Maitland was comfortable with the new learning, as his friendship with the Italian protestant and humanist Pietro Bizzarri shows. Regrettably no record of Maitland's library survives.

Early official career Maitland's movements during 1542–50 are unknown. Before 10 November 1553 he married Janet (*d.* before 1560), daughter of William Menteith of Kerse; they had at least one daughter, Marion. The crucial development in his career was his appointment in 1554 as assistant secretary to David Panter. Maitland certainly had powerful friends at court for he was apparently sponsored by Gilbert Kennedy, third earl of Cassillis, and, more significantly as far as Maitland's future career was concerned, Lord James Stewart. This was the first example of the two men working together in close harmony and provides the origin of the partnership that was to be such a feature of the next decade in Scotland's history.

Maitland did not waste his opportunity to establish himself in credit with the queen dowager, Mary of Guise, regent for her daughter Queen Mary, whom he impressed as a partner at cards as well as in his secretarial role. He gained much valuable experience of the royal administration and international diplomacy. In 1557 he was involved with Mary of Guise's attempt to support the French war against Spain through an abortive siege of Wark Castle in Northumberland. Equally illustrative of his high profile in the regent's administration at this time was his proposed embassy to England and France in February 1558 to mediate a peace. While the anger of Mary I of England at the recent loss of Calais ensured that the mission got no further than London, Maitland no doubt made many useful contacts at this time which he was able to exploit to the full after the death of the English queen that November transformed the political landscape completely. He did not attend the marriage of Queen Mary and the dauphin, François, in April 1558, but was probably grateful to keep the most conspicuous absentee from the wedding, the mother of the bride, company, particularly in view of the fact that four of the commissioners failed to return alive.

It can have been no major surprise when Maitland was appointed Panter's successor as royal secretary on 4 December 1558, but he was conspicuous as the only Scottish member of an executive increasingly dominated by the French. By virtue of his access to the highest political circles of the Scottish, English, and French courts, Maitland was in the perfect position to act as a double agent at the expense of Mary of Guise and to the benefit of the newly formed congregation.

The congregation Maitland did not openly defect to the congregation until October 1559, almost two years after the first bond of the congregation, but he had begun to serve their interests as well as those of Mary of Guise long before. In March 1559 he was sent as envoy to London and Paris on behalf of Mary of Guise. He completed his ostensible mission successfully, and returned to Scotland in May with the ratifications of the concluded peace between François and Mary and Elizabeth and his reputation with the regent enhanced. However, his covert agenda was far more significant, as this mission laid the basis for eventual English intervention in Scotland. He played the role of double agent superbly, even winning praise from George Buchanan for managing to deceive the cardinal of Lorraine, 'then esteemed the first diplomatist in Europe' (*Vernacular Writings*, 44). Philip II of Spain was similarly duped, receiving news that Maitland ruled Mary of Guise 'body and soul' (*CSP Spain, 1558–67*, 38). In England, Maitland built on the relationship developed at the border conference of January 1559 between James Hamilton, duke of Châtelherault, and Sir Henry Percy, and established a working relationship with the two most influential people in England, Sir William Cecil and the new queen, Elizabeth. His relationship with Cecil developed in such a way that he described it in filial terms, and the diplomatic community came to regard him 'as a sort of Scotch Cecil' (*CSP Spain, 1558–67*, 492). Maitland's presence at the signing of the treaty of Cateau Cambrésis between France and the Habsburgs in April 1559 enhanced his European perspective of the Scottish crisis, aware that their struggle mirrored that between the French crown and its Huguenot inclined provinces. He could also pose as being in possession of the darkest French secrets and intent towards England.

Maitland defected to the congregation when their fortunes were at an all time low, but he was immediately used to good effect. From December 1559 to February 1560 he led an embassy to London which led directly to the treaty of Berwick. Knox was for once guilty of understatement when he referred to Maitland as his replacement as manager of the civil affairs of the congregation as 'a man of better judgement and greater experience' (*CSP for.*, 1558–9, 69). The congregation were certainly in need of an improved public profile in England, having already been judged 'cold, slow and negligent' (*CSP Scot.*, 1.226–8) while the unfortunate timing of Knox's *First Blast of the Trumpet* rendered his name 'of all others most odious here' (*CSP for.*, 1558–9, 73). During this embassy Maitland provided Cecil with the cogent arguments needed to convince an uncertain English privy council and a parsimonious Elizabeth of the necessity of intervention in Scotland. He countered the perception of the congregation as rebels, and appealed to English self-interest by reminding them of the danger they faced from France. He played on the desirability of a godly and political union between the two realms and also dangled the interesting carrot of the congregation's help in Ireland through the good offices of Archibald Campbell, fourth earl of Argyll, an offer that was actually written into the eventual treaty in February 1560.

The treaty of Berwick, despite securing English military intervention, did not guarantee victory for the congregation and indeed the months between it and the treaty of Edinburgh in July 1560 were among the most precarious in Maitland's career. England's military intervention was disastrously incompetent, as the farcical siege of Leith demonstrated all too embarrassingly, and the congregation achieved victory largely through a series of fortuitous events beyond their or England's control. Most significant of these was the death of Mary of Guise and the all-consuming French domestic strife triggered by the tumult of Amboise. Even the successful treaty of Edinburgh which secured the withdrawal of French and English troops from Scotland would not have been signed if Elizabeth's letter to Cecil ordering him to break off negotiations had arrived sooner. Nevertheless the victory of the congregation was a triumph for Maitland and his ally Lord James Stewart, and won him great credit in England, 'for sustaining the whole burden of foresight' (*CSP Scot.*, 1.364). Not only had he been instrumental in securing English aid but he had also, in the panic-stricken four months between Berwick and Edinburgh, kept a broadly based coalition together, attracting to it the Catholic leader of the north-east, George Gordon, fourth earl of Huntly, and the staunchly protestant but recently politically neutral James Douglas, fourth earl of Morton.

Maitland was chosen as harangue maker, or speaker, at the Reformation parliament of August 1560, a role he was to perform in parliament on three other occasions. He was probably responsible for the disappointment of Knox by preventing what would later emerge as the first Book of Discipline being discussed by the parliament, apparently later dismissing it as a 'devout imagination' (*Works of John Knox*, 2.26–7). The Scottish confession of faith was adopted but it was not, as Knox lamented, a 'perfect reformation' (*Works of John Knox*, 1.338), an accurate portent for the difficult infancy endured by the new kirk. As well as abolishing papal authority and the mass, the parliament supported the proposal of cementing the English alliance by the marriage of Châtelherault's son James Hamilton, third earl of Arran, to Elizabeth. This had the twin benefits of securing the alignment with England and preserving the fragile coalition of the congregation. It was Maitland's misfortune to have to handle the proposal which, while he was in sympathy with it, he knew was unlikely to succeed. Predictably, the reception from Elizabeth was negative, but the international situation was once again transformed by the death of François II of France in December, which Maitland and the other envoys heard about while in England.

Secretary to Mary From January 1561 Maitland and Stewart were preparing the ground for Mary's return to Scotland. They rejected out of hand the solution to the crisis favoured by Elizabeth, the Hamiltons, and Knox of Mary's marriage to the recently rejected Arran, and put forward their own strategy. Maitland admitted that the prospect of Mary's return created a very difficult personal dilemma for him: 'always in France I am taken for a better Englishman than most' (*CSP Scot.*, 1.506–7), which, given his recent record, was understandable. After Stewart's successful embassy to France, Mary admonished Maitland sharply and re-employed him on her own terms. It was a measure of Mary's political acumen that Maitland and Stewart (earl of Moray from 1562) were at the helm of her new regime when Mary began her personal rule in August 1561. Maitland and Stewart had promised Mary that they would win for her recognition of her claim to succeed Elizabeth on the English throne, in return for the maintenance of the religious *status quo* in Scotland. It was a policy which fitted in perfectly with Maitland's ambition for a union of the Scottish and English crowns.

Maitland played a key role in the successful early years of Mary's personal reign. Certainly from 1561 to 1565 he was at the centre not only of her government but of her court too. Apart from his necessary absence on high profile embassies to England and France, he was always present in the privy council and was a constant companion on her progresses throughout the realm. He was indefatigable in restraining the demands of the kirk, and an earnest advocate of Mary's right to hear mass and of the controversial thirds of benefices financial settlement. Astutely, he ensured that substance was not given to protestant discontent by ensuring that Mary rejected the invitation to send Scottish representatives to the Council of Trent in 1562. He played a military as well as his more customary political role in the defeat of the earl of Huntly at Corrichie that year, and was very much to the fore in the glittering atmosphere of the court, whether employing his intellectual gifts, displaying his skill at hawking, hunting, and running at the ring, or participating in court masques. 'Maitland serves me right well', Mary reported to the duke of Guise in January 1562, and he and his family's fortunes rose accordingly (*Letter from Mary*, 28). In 1561 Maitland was appointed an extraordinary lord of session, and in 1562 his father was appointed keeper of the privy Seal.

Most significant were Maitland's diplomatic endeavours on behalf of Mary's claim to the English succession. Within two weeks of Mary's arrival in Scotland he was dispatched to England in pursuit of this objective in exchange for the ratification of a modified treaty of Edinburgh. It was this embassy that saw the first mooting of the proposed interview between the two queens which was to provide the basis for Maitland's next embassy to England in May 1562—his sixth embassy to the Elizabethan court in just three years. An indication of the level of the mutual confidence felt by the queen and the secretary at this point was seen in Maitland's four-month embassy to France and London in 1563. In England he once again demanded parliamentary recognition of Mary's claims to the English throne, but more significant at this time were his intensive negotiations in the highest international political circles for Mary's marriage. The prospect of Don Carlos of Spain, the Archduke Charles of Austria, Charles IX of France, Lord Robert Dudley, and intriguingly her kinsman Henry Stewart, Lord Darnley, were all raised.

This mission arguably represents the peak of Maitland's credit with Mary. She rewarded him with the abbey of Haddington, making him, according to Thomas Randolph, worth '3000 marks sterling in Lothian only' (*CSP Scot.*, 2.28). Maitland applied pressure on the English by displaying his easy access to the French court and his excellent relationship with the Spanish ambassador, La Quadra. Worryingly for the English, he was also seen as a man who could deliver, securing the release from French prison of Sir Henry Killigrew which English diplomatic efforts had failed to achieve. Despite the collapse of meaningful attempts to obtain a Catholic prince as Mary's husband, by mid-1563 Maitland was able to convince the English that it was still an option, encouraging Elizabeth to propose first Lord Robert Dudley as an English spouse for Mary, and then request that Mary rescind the exile of Matthew Stewart, fourth earl of Lennox, whose son Henry Stewart, Lord Darnley, was another strong candidate for Mary's hand, possessing the next best claim to the English throne. The option kept the goal of a union of the crowns alive. Despite Maitland's performance as speaker in the parliament of 1564 and his boastful introduction of the Lennox restitution: 'Justlie it may be affirmed, Scotland in na manis age that presentlie levis wes in greater tranquilitie' (Cameron, 1.41–4), Mary's subsequent marriage to Darnley and the rupture it caused in the amity was a disaster for Maitland and the policy he had advocated since Mary's return. Unlike Moray, Maitland had remained cool-headed after the collapse of the Dudley marriage project in March 1565. He happily accepted his mission to Elizabeth that same month to seek her consent

for Mary's marriage to Darnley and to continue the prosecution of her claim to the succession. His belief that Mary was still only applying pressure on Elizabeth is shown by his reaction, on 8 May, when, *en route* for Scotland, he received a new commission. Maitland was instructed to return to London and announce Mary's decision to marry Darnley, regardless of Elizabeth's objections, and then to pass into France and announce the news there. Maitland was completely dumbfounded by Mary's new tactics and could not conceal his anger. He ignored his instructions and returned to court.

Mary's marriage and fall Despite his defiance of Mary's commands, wisely, Maitland distanced himself from the chaseabout rebellion of Moray and Châtelherault in August and September 1565, but certainly sympathized with their anger. According to Randolph, Maitland and other ostensible supporters of the queen 'did only espy thayr moment and mayke fair wether untyll it come to the pinch' (*CSP Scot.*, 2.162). Mary's brilliant handling of the rebellion ensured that Maitland sided with his queen, but his credit with her would never be the same again. An accurate measure of this was his temporary realignment with Knox and the desperate general assembly of winter 1565 which sent mournful letters to their European brethren lamenting the parlous state of the realm. It was this alienation and despair that led to Maitland's involvement in the murder of David Riccio in March 1566. Maitland's advice to Cecil, just weeks before the murder, of the need to 'chop at the veray root' (*CSP Scot.*, 2.255) has unsurprisingly been interpreted as suggesting that he was prominent in the conspiracy. Maitland had lost much personal prestige by Riccio's rise to favour. His involvement in the murder signalled his willingness to rebel against Mary and her increasingly pro-Roman Catholic policy, of which Maitland and his fellow conspirators had lost control.

Maitland was not officially dismissed from his position as secretary for his part in the Riccio murder, but he was heavily forfeited, losing Haddington Abbey back to James Hepburn, fourth earl of Bothwell. In the most obscure period of his career he was absent from court for the next six months. He was given permission to travel into Flanders but not France or England, but he remained in Scotland. He was warded in Caithness, received the hospitality of John Stewart, fourth earl of Atholl, in Dunkeld and Callendar, and resided in Colin Campbell of Glenorchy's stronghold of the Balloch before his eventual rehabilitation.

The conciliatory policies Mary followed after the Riccio murder facilitated the return of the chaseabout rebels and these were continued after the safe delivery of her son in June 1566. Moray, Argyll, and Atholl lobbied against Bothwell and Darnley for Maitland's return to court and in September 1566 Mary gave way. Her personal reconciliation of Bothwell and Maitland was sealed by Maitland's restoration to the abbey of Haddington. The clear policy of reconciliation was also apparent in what was feared to be Mary's death-bed speech at Jedburgh in October 1566 which Maitland reported. Maitland was also a main figure at the so-called Craigmillar conference, where the Darnley problem was discussed and Darnley's murder allegedly plotted, and which certainly paved the way for the royal baptism. He was present at the spectacular baptismal celebrations of Mary's son Charles James in December 1566 at the Chapel Royal, Stirling. His own return to the inner sanctum of Mary's court was confirmed by his marriage at the same venue just days later, on 6 January 1567, to Mary *Fleming (1542–c.1600) [see under Queen's Maries], daughter of Malcolm Fleming, third Lord Fleming (c.1494–1547), and Janet Stewart (c.1510–1560x63), illegitimate daughter of James IV; her brother John *Fleming, fifth Lord Fleming, was one of Mary's most loyal courtiers. Mary Fleming, raised a Catholic in France, was memorably described by Kirkcaldy of Grange to be as fit a wife for Maitland as Kirkcaldy himself was to be pope. None the less, the marriage was based on affection, and they had a son, James, and daughter, Margaret, who married Robert *Ker, later first earl of Roxburghe, in 1587.

It is hugely unlikely that Maitland was unaware of the plot to murder Darnley. He penned within hours of the deed, on 10 February 1567, the official explanation of the murder sent to Catherine de' Medici, signed by the privy council, including Bothwell, Huntly, Argyll, and Archbishop Hamilton. Even by his own chameleon-like standards, 1567 proved the most tortuous year of Maitland's life. The sheer complexity of his allegiance is revealed by the fact that he fulfils Gordon Donaldson's criteria (as set forth in All the Queen's Men) for committed membership of both the king's and queen's parties in the civil war. He was present at the court of session on 12 May where Mary declared that in marrying Bothwell she was a free agent, was a witness to the marriage contract of 14 May, and was one of the privy councillors present from 17 to 22 May. His king's party credentials are equally impressive; he witnessed the coronation of James VI in Stirling and supported Moray on 22 August when Moray accepted the regency. Only Maitland appears on all these lists.

Establishing the Moray regency Maitland's hand was seen very much at work in the creation of the Moray regency. In August 1567, when Mary was imprisoned but before Moray had accepted the regency, Vincenzo Laureo, papal nuncio to Scotland in 1566, argued that what had helped Moray most was 'the crafty counsel of the Secretary Lethington, a man believed to be so astute and unprincipled that in all the late treasons he is thought to have thrown the stone without seeming to move his hand' (Pollen, 402). Such an interpretation is certainly tenable. After he had assumed leadership of the queen's party in 1570, Maitland issued an apology for his role in Mary's downfall. He even boasted that the king's party could not have done it without him: 'ye and farther without me they had nather the knowledge, wisdome, nor moyen to performe the same' (Calderwood, 3.85–6).

Maitland's customary performance on Moray's behalf as speaker of the parliament in December 1567 was not an accurate portent for the future of the Moray–Maitland relationship, which was soon to collapse, nor of his relations with the kirk. In an ironic tribute to the tolerance of Mary's regime Maitland offered the parliament a timely history lesson, once again stressing the wider European dimension in which Scotland's affairs were cast. Maitland argued that the bloodless triumph of protestantism within the space of eight or nine years was:

> a peculiar benefit only to the realm of Scotland that the true religion has obtained a free course universally through the whole realm and yet not a Scotchman's blood shed. With what nation had God dealt so mercifully? … Germany, France, Flanders, Denmark, you will find the lives of thousands spent before they could purchase the least part of that liberty whereunto we have attained, as it were sleeping upon down coddes.   (PRO, SP 52/14/51)

This was doubly ironic because it paved the way for the radical, Calvinist flavoured legislation Maitland had done much to resist in 1560 and heralded the high point of the kirk's relationship with the state.

Maitland's continued affection for Mary had been suspected during her captivity in Lochleven. A source not well disposed to Maitland strengthens this view. It was alleged that Mary received from Maitland at this time a gold token enamelled with Aesop's fable of the lion enclosed in a net being freed by a mouse, with the Italian legend engraved upon it: 'A chi basta l'animo non mancan le forze' ('he who has spirit enough will not want force'; Nau, 58–9). Mary's escape from Lochleven in May 1568 caught Maitland unawares and the mistaken strategy of the Hamiltons prevented a proper realignment of the queen's party. Mary apparently tried to contact Maitland but failed, and Maitland was found in Moray's camp before Langside. However, even Maitland at this point was struggling to hide his true colours and immediately after the battle of Langside (13 May 1568) was openly referred to by Moray as the 'necessary evil' (ibid., 100). It was on these grounds that he was included by Moray in the party that travelled to York, Westminster, and finally Hampton Court for the Anglo-Scottish conference that became the shambles of a trial of Mary. Moray believed that Maitland would cause less trouble under the watchful eye of the English than he would unattended in Scotland. The trouble he was to cause in England showed the suspicions of the regent to be well founded. The months in England exposed the divergent policies of Maitland and Moray and this was most clearly revealed by the proposal that Mary marry Thomas Howard, fourth duke of Norfolk. If Maitland was not the project's actual architect, then he was a principal supporter. It fulfilled all his conditions for Mary's restitution and the ultimate union of the realms, Maitland's long-term goal.

The inconclusive trial, and Moray's return to Scotland, buoyed by a £5000 English subsidy, brought the rift between Maitland and Moray completely out in the open. Maitland's continued support of the Norfolk marriage project was shown in July 1569 at a convention in Perth. He defied the regent and voted in favour of the motion allowing Mary to divorce Bothwell. This was lost by forty votes to nine, conclusive proof of the changed agenda from Carberry when the professed intention of the confederates was the separation of Mary from Bothwell. Maitland facetiously congratulated the assembly on their concern for Mary's domestic happiness.

Maitland the queen's man Maitland could now be numbered among the ranks of the queen's men and was arrested by Moray on 2 September on the charge of Darnley's murder. Maitland's future looked bleak given the intense enmity he faced from Moray and his allies at this time, but he foiled his enemies in spectacular style, escaping from custody through the good offices of Kirkcaldy of Grange to the sanctuary of Edinburgh Castle. Maitland wrote to his 'friends, actual and potential' (Lee, 269) urging them to attend his trial. Such was the extent of the support he was able to mobilize in Edinburgh that Moray was angrily forced to prorogue Maitland's day of law on 21 November 1569. Moray had been publicly undermined by a popular show of support for Maitland and his pro-Marian policies and matters were to decline further for the beleaguered regent. Moray's arrest of Thomas Percy, seventh earl of Northumberland, following the failed northern rebellion in England fuelled popular discontent which Maitland could exploit. Moray's assassination on 23 January 1570 represented the nadir for the fortunes of the king's party in the civil war against the growing momentum of the queen's party with Maitland increasingly at the helm: 'The son's party daily decays, the mother's daily increases' (*CSP Scot.*, 3.126).

Maitland took the day of Moray's funeral to complete in perfectly stage-managed style his political rehabilitation, insisting on a fully public trial on the charge of the Darnley murder. Public trial and acquittal was followed by a successful return to the privy council. It was from this point that the king's party depicted Maitland as their chief enemy and directed most of their propaganda against him. He was despised as 'the saule and without whom they can do no more than the wheliis can do without the extrie' (Bannatyne, 15). While the propaganda efforts of both sides differed little in the conservative emphasis on the commonweal and the defence of the realm which had been such a feature of Reformation crisis propaganda, it contrasted sharply in its intensity, volume, and bitterness. One piece of civil war propaganda that is of especial significance to Maitland is Buchanan's *Chameleon*. This has had a great impact on Maitland's historical reputation, with its central accusation that Maitland was capable of any type of conduct apart from bravery and loyalty. These virtues are symbolized by red and white, the only colours the chameleon is incapable of disguising itself in. The other is the less well known, anonymously written 'Dialog of the twa wyfies' (PRO, SP 52/17/77) which was received by Sir William Cecil in April 1570. This depicted Maitland as an atheist who dismissed religion as 'bot ane bogill to bairnis' (ibid.) and also gives the earliest known and most detailed contemporary exposition of the popular Scottish interpretation of the political principles of Machiavelli. Maitland was depicted as the Machiavellian 'scole master' imbuing the 'glaikit cumpane' of the queen's party 'as they herd every day and convene as bairns to the scole up

in ye secreataris house' with the principles of Machiavelli (ibid.).

Maitland's pre-eminent position at the helm of the queen's party is usually attributed to his political and diplomatic abilities. He was certainly able, as his rivals feared, 'to lay a plaster over the wound of variance' that lay at the heart of the queen's party (Bannatyne, 38). Those same contemporary rivals were also more aware than subsequent historians have been of Maitland's vast personal influence over so many influential figures over the civil war. Maitland had built up an extensive network of support based upon a combination of kindred and personal ties during his career and from which many of the leading figures of the queen's party were drawn. His marriage to Mary Fleming had added Atholl and Fleming to his list of influential brothers-in-law, and opened up an important Hamilton connection to add to the useful connections his own Maitland family could claim. He was described as 'Athol's head of wit' (PRO, SP 52/17/77) and was decisive in winning Atholl over to the queen's side and in helping to mend the complex Atholl–Argyll feud through his friendship with Colin Campbell of Glenorchy. This helped to create a united Campbell–Stewart front. Maitland's brothers John and Thomas were active in support of the queen, while George, fifth Lord Seton, was his cousin. His friendship with Kirkcaldy of Grange dated back to the congregation and, with his two brothers, to Paris in 1542. To this can be added the loyal Melvilles. Alexander, fifth Lord Home, was described by Maitland as 'one of the dearest friends I have' (PRO, SP 52/18/59), while George Hackett, conservator of the staple at Veere, a fellow student of Maitland's at St Andrews in 1540, provided a vital focus for efforts to obtain Spanish help.

However bullish Maitland was about the prospects of success for the queen's party, he was always aware that success was ultimately dependent on outside aid, be it from Elizabeth or France or Spain. Despite strenuous efforts, he was unable to convince Elizabeth of the righteousness of Mary's plight and endured the enmity of England during the successive regencies of the earls of Lennox, Mar, and Morton. Nor was he able to secure the substantial foreign aid necessary to offset Elizabeth's preference and ultimately crucial military and financial support for the king's party.

While the civil war was never a sectarian conflict, as the allegiance of the participants shows, the queen's party's continuous but unsuccessful attempts to gain overseas aid—necessarily from Catholic powers—were to reap a most destructive harvest. Following the Ridolfi plot in 1571, English parliamentarians called for Mary's head in 1572. Her restoration was from that point more unlikely than ever. Similarly, the fall-out from the St Bartholomew's day massacre in Paris in August 1572 did the cause of the queen's party no good at all. Yet the reason the queen's party and Maitland's fate was not resolved sooner was Elizabeth's irresolution. The magnificent show of strength the queen's party boasted in April 1570 was swept aside by England's decisive and devastating military intervention in the same month under Thomas

Radcliffe, third earl of Sussex. After scattering the Marian triumvirate of Huntly, Argyll, and Châtelherault, despite their territorial strength across northern, central, and western Scotland and the support of 'xxxii erles and lordes in parlement' (*CSP Scot.*, 3.216), and the expulsion of the queen's party from Edinburgh in May 1570, Sussex could not believe Elizabeth's refusal to let him finish the job. There is no doubt Elizabeth's hesitancy kept the queen's party alive at this time.

In August 1571 Maitland described Sussex's military intervention as the turning point in the retrogressive fortunes of the queen's party, lamenting 'in what terms we then stood, since which time for no labours could be made that number could never be assembled again' (Duncan, 56–67). During his year-long absence from the capital Maitland lobbied hard on Mary's behalf to no avail. Despite, on his return to the capital in May 1571, being able to inflict the indignity of the creeping parliament on to the king's party, it was an empty triumph as Maitland knew. He and his brothers felt the pain of the heavy forfeitures of the rival parliament more keenly despite the latter's ceremonial indignity. Hope, however, remained while Elizabeth prevaricated. The last chance the queen's party had to seize the domestic initiative was the botched raid on Stirling in September 1571. Instead of resulting in the capture of the leading lights of the king's party, this led only to the death of Lennox, which, as Maitland laconically admitted, aided the king's party as much as the queen's. Worse was to follow with the subsequent English reaction to the discovery of the Ridolfi plot. Maitland tried to bolster Mary's spirits by reminding her of the advantage their hold of Edinburgh Castle was, being 'aye able to cast the balance' (*CSP Scot.*, 4.376) but Maitland, in declining health, was clutching at straws. The ruthlessness of Morton, following the undynamic Mar regency, coupled with the arrival of English military force, sealed the fate of Maitland and his supporters in the castle. Following the pacification of Perth in February 1573, Maitland and the castle stood alone in support of Mary. The bombardment began on 21 May 1573 and on 29 May, Maitland and Kirkcaldy surrendered.

Maitland, crippled by ill health, died in mysterious circumstances in prison in Leith on 9 June 1573. It was alleged that he 'imitated the auld Romanes' (Melville, 256) and committed suicide to avoid the humiliation of the gallows alongside Kirkcaldy. What is certain is that the realistic hopes of Mary's restitution died with him. Morton's vindictiveness towards Maitland continued after his death, ignoring pleas for a decent burial from Maitland's family so 'that the vermin from it came creeping out under the door of the house' (Calderwood, 3.285).

Assessment There is an irony in the fact that the name Maitland, in its earlier twelfth-century form Maltalent, translates as evil genius, because many of Maitland's contemporaries vituperatively held him to be just that. He was Bannatyne's Michael Wylie, Buchanan's Chameleon, and Knox's atheist. Yet the amount of time his enemies

spent defaming his character is testament to his impressive contemporary reputation. He was regarded by Elizabeth I as 'the flower of the wits of Scotland' (PRO, SP 52/19/8). Even his enemies testified to his academic brilliance, and Robert Sempill, who denounced him as a 'scurvy scholar of Machiavelli's lair', grudgingly respected his ability to:

> both quhissill and cloik,
> And his mouth full of meil.
> (*Satirical Poems of the … Reformation*, 1.131)

John Spottiswoode refers to him as 'a man of deep wit, great experience and one whose counsels were held at that time for oracles' (Spottiswoode, 2.193).

Maitland cuts a brilliant, colourful, controversial and even romantic figure. In the midst of his romance with Mary Fleming he declared love to be the 'most singular remedy for all diseases in all persons' (PRO, SP 52/10/21). He was certainly Machiavellian in the sense that, to him, the end justified the means, and he consistently manipulated religion for political ends, but despite the charges of Buchanan he was capable of both bravery and loyalty. During his doomed defence of Edinburgh Castle he rejected generous offers to abandon Mary and secure his own safety. While it is going too far to agree with the view that he alone in Scotland thought in terms that were neither religious nor personal, it is undeniable that he stayed true to his vision of the ultimate union of the realms.

MARK LOUGHLIN

Sources CSP for., 1558–74 · CSP Spain, 1558–1603 · CSP Scot., 1547–1603 · M. Loughlin, 'The career of Maitland of Lethington, c.1526–1573', PhD diss., U. Edin., 1991 · G. W. S. Barrow, The Anglo-Norman era in Scottish history (1980) · R. Maitland of Lethington, The history of the house of Seytoun to the year MDLIX, ed. J. Fullarton, Maitland Club, 1 (1829) · The poems of Sir Richard Maitland of Lethingtoun, knight, ed. J. Bain, Maitland Club, 4 (1830) · J. M. Anderson, ed., Early records of the University of St Andrews, Scottish History Society, 3rd ser., 8 (1926) · R. Bannatyne, Memoriales of transactions in Scotland, 1569–1573, ed. [R. Pitcairn], Bannatyne Club, 51 (1836) · J. Maitland, The apology for William Maitland of Lethington, 1610, ed. A. Long (1904) · Vernacular writings of George Buchanan, ed. P. H. Brown, STS, 26 (1892) · W. Robertson, The history of Scotland, 3 vols. (1802) · M. Lee, James Stewart, earl of Moray (1953) · E. Russell, Maitland of Lethington, the minister of Mary Stuart: a study of his life and times (1912) · A letter from Mary, queen of Scots to the duke of Guise, ed. J. H. Pollen, Scottish History Society, 43 (1904) · M. Lynch, Scotland: a new history (1991) · M. Lynch, 'Queen Mary's triumph: the baptismal celebrations at Stirling in December 1566', SHR, 69 (1990), 1–21 · D. McRoberts, ed., Essays on the Scottish Reformation, 1513–1625 (1962) · R. Keith, J. P. Lawson, and C. J. Lyon, History of the affairs of church and state in Scotland from the beginning of the Reformation to the year 1568, 3 vols., Spottiswoode Society (1844–50) · D. Calderwood, The history of the Kirk of Scotland, ed. T. Thomson and D. Laing, 8 vols., Wodrow Society, 7 (1842–9) · A. I. Cameron, ed., The Warrender papers, 2 vols., Scottish History Society, 3rd ser., 18–19 (1931–2) · G. Donaldson, All the queen's men: power and politics in Mary Stewart's Scotland (1983) · J. H. Pollen, ed., Papal negotiations with Mary queen of Scots during her reign in Scotland, 1561–1567, Scottish History Society, 37 (1901) · C. Nau, Memorials of Mary Stuart, ed. J. Stevenson (1833) · T. Thomson, ed., A diurnal of remarkable occurrents that have passed within the country of Scotland, Bannatyne Club, 43 (1833) · M. Lynch, Edinburgh and the Reformation (1981) · J. Melville of Halhill, Memoirs of his own life, ed. T. Thomson (1827) · John Knox's History of the Reformation in Scotland, ed. W. C. Dickinson, 2 vols. (1949) · The works of John Knox, ed. D. Laing, 6 vols., Wodrow Society, 12 (1846–64) · Scots peerage, vol. 5 · J. Maitland, *Narrative of the principal acts of the regency during the minority and other papers relating to the history of Mary queen of Scots*, ed. W. S. Fitch (1833) · G. Douglas, *Poetical works of Gavin Douglas* (1874) · W. A. McNeill, 'Scottish entries in the *Acta rectoria universitatis Parisiensis*, 1519 to *c.*1633', *SHR*, 43 (1964), 66–86 · M. Lynch, ed., *Mary Stewart, queen in three kingdoms* (1988) · G. Donaldson, 'The Cistercian nunnery of St Mary, Haddington', *East Lothian Transactions*, 5 (1952), 12–24 · M. Livingstone, D. Hay Fleming, and others, eds., *Registrum secreti sigilli regum Scotorum / The register of the privy seal of Scotland*, 5–8 (1957–82) · state papers, Scotland, Elizabeth, PRO · NL Scot., Advocates MS 34.6.24, fol. 280 · *Reg. PCS*, 1st ser. · J. Spottiswoode, *History of the Church of Scotland*, ed. M. Napier and M. Russell, 2, Spottiswoode Society, 6 (1851) · W. Duncan, ed., *Miscellaneous papers, principally illustrative of events in the reigns of queen Mary and James VI* (1834) · *Satirical poems of the time of the Reformation*, vol. 1, Scottish Text Society, 20 (1891)

Archives NL Scot., corresp. | BL, Cotton MSS, corresp. · NA Scot., letters, mainly to Lady Glenorchy · NL Scot., Lauderdale papers, Advocates MS · NL Scot., Advocates MS · PRO, state papers, Scotland, Elizabeth, SP 52 · PRO, state papers, foreign, Elizabeth, SP 70

Likenesses Flemish school, portrait, 16th cent., Lennoxlove, East Lothian · C. Picart, stipple (after portrait at Thirlestane), BM, NPG; repro. in Lodge, *Portraits of illustrious persons of Great Britain* (1818) · portrait, Thirlestane Castle, Berwickshire [*see illus.*]

Maitland, William (*c.*1693–1757), historian and topographer, was born at Brechin, Forfarshire. Nothing is known of his parentage or of his education. He is known first as a hair merchant, an occupation that took him to Sweden, Denmark, and Germany, and which seems to have enabled him to devote himself to historical study. By 1733 he was in London, working on a history of the city; writing to Richard Richardson on 7 August 1733, Sir Hans Sloane refers to the work in progress. He was elected fellow of the Royal Society on 12 April 1733 and on 13 March 1735 he became a member of the Society of Antiquaries. In April 1737 he appears to have started publishing his history of London in shilling numbers, but only one was announced. About 1738 he contributed to the *Philosophical Transactions* a response to an essay by W. Kersseboom about the population of London. In 1739 he published by subscription his *History of London, from its Foundation by the Romans to the Present Time*, in a folio edition printed by Samuel Richardson. A strongly whiggish history, it was dedicated to the king; the prince of Wales's copy is in the British Library. The work, which owed much to predecessors such as John Stow and John Strype, was not universally well received. In a letter to Joseph Ames dated 1 July 1740 Maitland responds cantankerously to the suggestion that the work was 'not worth keeping', and abuses Ames for his failure to win subscribers. He goes on to declare that since the work has 'met with the approbation of the most judicious and best judges, I despise what others say of it, considering it is not in their power to do me an injury in the sale thereof, seeing I have not one copy left' (Nichols, *Lit. anecdotes*, 5.383).

In the same year Maitland resigned from the Society of Antiquaries and returned to Scotland, where he remained, apart from a six-week stay at Bath for the recovery of his health in the autumn of 1750. He began studying the history of Scotland and proposed to write a general topographical description of it. To this end he prepared a 'large set of queries, with a general letter, and transmitted both to every clergyman in Scotland', but 'the return fell so very far short of his expectation, that he laid aside his design in disgust' (Nichols, *Lit. anecdotes*, 5.383). Some returns from this anticipation of Sir John Sinclair's *Statistical Account* are mentioned in Gough's *British Topography*. Meanwhile Maitland prepared a folio *History of Edinburgh, from its Foundation to the Present Time* (1753), dedicated to the prince of Wales, and based on a fairly thorough examination of the city's archives. This was a work of 'very great labour' which contained much valuable information, though 'the style is mean, and the whole tone of the work is that of a plain, dull old man' (Chambers, *Scots.*, 3.563). A second edition of the *History of London*, extended into two folio volumes, with help from others and by the addition of many more plates, followed in 1756. (Further editions appeared in 1760, 1769, 1772, and 1775, the last continued and expanded by the Revd John Entick.) Maitland resumed his work on Scottish topography by making a tour of the country himself. The results appeared in volume 1 of his *History and Antiquities of Scotland*, published in two folio volumes after his death at Montrose on 16 July 1757. This last work, though it 'did credit to his industry, seems to have been judged deficient in the erudition and critical sagacity requisite for such a design' (Aikin, 6.489). Later it was said to be 'absolutely destitute of reputation' (Chambers, *Scots.*, 3.563). His general reputation within a few years of his death was low. Richard Gough says he was 'self-conceited, credulous, knew little, and wrote worse' (Gough, 2.572). According to Aikin, 'this author has no pretensions to rank among literary characters of the superior class, either in point of style or depth of reflection' (Aikin, 6.489). The *History of London* is, however, still referred to by historians. Early newspaper accounts indicate that he died 'at advanced age' but sixty-four seems to be a reliable consensus (Chalmers, 21.169). He did not marry, and was said to have died worth £10,000.   PAUL BAINES

Sources Nichols, *Lit. anecdotes*, 5.382–3 · A. Chalmers, ed., *The general biographical dictionary*, new edn, 21 (1815), 168–9 · J. Aikin and others, *General biography, or, Lives, critical and historical of the most eminent persons*, 10 vols. (1799–1815), vol. 6, p. 489 · Chambers, *Scots.*, rev. T. Thomson (1875), 3.563 · Nichols, *Illustrations*, 1.287 · R. G. [R. Gough], *British topography*, [new edn], 2 (1780), 572 · *GM*, 1st ser., 7 (1737), 256 · *The philosophical transactions (1732–44) abridged*, ed. J. Martyn, 9 (1747), 329–33 · W. A. Speck, 'Politicians, peers and publication by subscription', *Books and their readers in 18th century England*, ed. I. Rivers (1982)

Archives BL, letter to Thomas Birch

Wealth at death £10,000: Chalmers, ed., *General biographical dictionary*

Maitland, William Fuller (1813–1876), art collector, was born on 10 March 1813, the second, but eldest surviving, son and heir of Ebenezer Fuller Maitland of Stansted, Essex, and Park Place, Henley-on-Thames. He was educated by private tutors until he went to Trinity College, Cambridge, where he graduated BA in 1835, and MA in 1839. Although he never trained as an artist, Maitland quickly developed a remarkable love for, and insight into, paintings. During several journeys to Italy he became acquainted with the works of the early Italian masters—

yet to acquire their later popularity—and was one of their earliest admirers and collectors. His taste for the Netherlandish and German schools of the fifteenth century was unusual in England, and his collection also included many remarkable works of English landscape. Unlike other collectors of the period, his interest was focused mainly on paintings to the exclusion of *objets d'art*.

Maitland's first marriage, to Lydia, only daughter of Lieutenant-Colonel Serjentson Prescott, took place in Florence in 1842; they had four children. A widower, he married again, in London, on 1 June 1852; his second wife was Charlotte Elizabeth Dick, daughter of James Munro Macnabb; they had one daughter. Maitland lived at Stansted in Essex. His interests were by no means confined to art and connoisseurship, but included literature and a love of sport, dogs, and everything connected with the outdoor life.

For many years Maitland lent paintings to the Royal Academy old masters exhibitions, and most unusually, soon after his death, the Royal Academy passed a vote of condolence to his widow and acknowledged his substantial contribution to the loan exhibitions' success. He died suddenly at Stansted House on 15 February 1876, and was buried at Stansted on 19 February. After Maitland's death the bulk of his collection was exhibited at the South Kensington Museum, and subsequently nine of the most important pictures were sold to the National Gallery, including Fraucicbigro's *Portrait of a Knight of Rhodes*, an *Agony in the Garden* ascribed to Le Spaque, and a tondo entitled *Virgin and Child with Saint John* from the studio of Botticelli. Other works are in York, Berlin, and New York.

J. A. F. MAITLAND, *rev.* HELEN DAVIES

Sources G. H. Rogers-Harrison, *A genealogical and historical account of the Maitland family* (privately printed, 1869) · *Graduati Cantabrigienses* · E. T. Cook, *Handbook to the National Gallery* (1912) · personal knowledge (1893) · private information (1893, 2004) · [W. F. Maitland], *Catalogue of the Stansted Hall collection* (1872) · *The Times* (12 May 1879) · m. cert. · d. cert.
Archives National Gallery, London, letters
Wealth at death under £35,000: resworn probate, April 1877, *CGPLA Eng. & Wales*

Maittaire, Michael (1668–1747), classical scholar and typographer, was born in Rouen on 29 November 1668, the son of French protestant parents of whom nothing further is known. He took refuge in England a few years before the revocation of the edict of Nantes in October 1685, and was educated at Westminster School, 'where Dr. Busby well grounded him in the Greek and Latin languages, keeping him some years longer than usual' (Nichols, *Lit. anecdotes*, 4.556). He was a king's scholar there in 1682 and matriculated from Oxford University on 16 October 1688, aged nearly twenty; having been made a canoneer student of Christ Church in 1693 he graduated BA in 1694, MA on 23 March 1697, and was incorporated at Cambridge University in 1708. From 1695 to 1699 he was under-master of Westminster School, but left to keep a private boarding-school at Mile End. According to Thomas Hearne 'he was turned out of the Schools purely out of Malice, to make way for Mr. Rob. Friend, now D. Div. &

Head Master' (*Remarks*, 5.232), although others represent his leaving Westminster as a voluntary retirement 'consecrated to Learning' (Nichols, *Lit. anecdotes*, 4.557). Certainly from the early 1700s he devoted himself to scholarship and began to publish extensively, nearly seventy individual works being attributed to him, mostly in the fields of classics and typography. He lived for much of his life at various residences in London—in the late 1720s in Orange Street, Holborn, and at the time of his death at King Street, near Bloomsbury Square.

Contemporary opinion, both of Maittaire the man and of his scholarly achievement, was somewhat divided. On the one hand he was respected for his probity and strength of conscience, particularly in religious matters. He was a nonjuror and, according to Hearne, a man whom George Hickes had tried unsuccessfully to persuade to take orders. He was also recognized as modest and unassuming, yet convivial, generous, and 'fond of friendly intercourse' (Nichols, *Lit. anecdotes*, 4.564–5). He had a good many friends and acquaintances among the aristocracy, and a number of his extant letters reveal him as a man expert in gaining the favour of patrons both for himself and for others. The earl of Oxford held him in sufficiently high regard to pursue the suppression of several lines in Alexander Pope's *Dunciad* representing Maittaire as an inhabitant of the kingdom of Dullness. The duke of Rutland and Sir Richard Ellis are named in his will as two of his three best friends, to whom he directed his widow for advice and support, and Nichols reports that they each owned a portrait of him. By the standards of the time he was considered a very capable scholar of Latin and more particularly Greek, although his published works were not always highly regarded; while some were considered slapdash others were rated pedestrian and pedantic. Yet his *Graecae linguae dialecti* (1706) was still being reissued in 1742 and an abridged version appeared in 1831, while a number of his editions of classical authors were being reprinted in the late eighteenth century, and in a few cases into the nineteenth. Dr Johnson's opinion of Maittaire's work, as reported by James Boswell, was the harshest eighteenth-century view: 'he seems to have been a puzzle-headed man, with a large share of scholarship, but with little geometry or logick in his head, without method, and possessed of little genius' (Boswell, 4.2).

Among his many publications Maittaire's principal contributions to scholarship were in the fields of classical studies and typography. Between 1713 and 1719 he produced several volumes of Latin classics in a series published by Jacob Tonson and John Watts, and various other editions of Greek and Latin authors, in addition to his work on Greek dialects already mentioned. *Annales typographici* (5 vols., 1719–41), his history of typography from its beginnings until the year 1664, is a major work of great industry. The first three volumes were published at The Hague, the fourth and fifth at Amsterdam and London respectively. Two supplementary volumes by Michael Denis were added in 1789 and a modern reprint was published at Graz in 1965–7. Maittaire wrote a useful grammar of the English language (1712; repr., 1967), edited the

Greek New Testament (1714), and published a new edition of the *Marmora Oxoniensia* in 1732, a work that Thomas Hearne, who had wanted to do it himself, considered beyond Maittaire's capabilities: 'A Grammarian he may be, but he is far from being an Antiquary, and hath not (I fear) those qualifications that are necessary for an Editor of Greek & Roman Inscriptions' (*Remarks*, 10.13). Other publications included his *Stephanorum historia* (1709) and (with others) a catalogue of the Harleian library (1743–5), several religious essays, and some Latin poetry. His final publication was his *Senilia* (1742), a collection of verses on various topics and persons in which, Dr Johnson opined (according to Boswell), 'he shows so little learning or taste in his writing, as to make Carteret a dactyl' (Boswell, 4.2).

In keeping with his classical, bibliographical, and typographical interests Maittaire was a great collector of books. Over about fifty years he had built up a very large library, which included rare early editions of classical authors printed by the major early printing houses of Europe. After his death, on 7 September 1747, his library was sold at auction by Cock and Langford, the sale beginning on 21 November 1748 and lasting forty-four evenings. The sale catalogue was printed from Maittaire's own manuscript catalogue, and a copy with the prices inscribed is in the British Library. He was survived by his wife, Mary.

MARGARET CLUNIES ROSS and AMANDA J. COLLINS

Sources Nichols, *Lit. anecdotes*, 1.338; 4.556–66 · *Remarks and collections of Thomas Hearne*, ed. C. E. Doble and others, 11 vols., OHS, 2, 7, 13, 34, 42–3, 48, 50, 65, 67, 72 (1885–1921), vols. 5, 10–11 · *Old Westminsters*, 2.615 · Foster, *Alum. Oxon.* · J. Boswell, *The life of Samuel Johnson*, new edn, 4 vols. (1826), vol. 4, p. 2 · will, PRO, PROB 11/756, sig. 235 · *A catalogue of the library of Michael Maittaire*, 2 pts (1748) [MS copy with prices, BL, 269. i. 20, 21] · *DNB*

Archives Bodl. Oxf., *Annales Typographici* annotated with additions and inserted papers by him, MSS Rawl. 39, 41–44 (SC 16059–16063) · Bodl. Oxf., note, MS Eng. misc. d. 459 (SC 42302), fol. 24*v* · Bodl. Oxf., notes on chronology, Greek dialects, etc., one set of papers dated 1692, MSS Rawl. G. 148–149 (SC 14872–14873) | BL, letters to P. Desmaizeaux, Add. MS 4285, fols. 208–9, 210 · BL, corresp. with Edward Lye, Add. MS 32325 · BL, letters to Dr C. Middleton, Add. MS 32457, fols 9*r*–10*v*, 56*r*–57*v*, 58*r*–59*v* · BL, letters and verse to Sir Hans Sloane, Sloane MS 4048, fols. 229*r*–230*v*; Sloane MS 4051, fols. 280*r*–281*v*, 282*r*–283*v*; Sloane MS 4059, fol. 307 · BL, letters to Humphrey Wanley, Harley MS 3780 · BL, letters to J. C. Wetstein, Add. MS 32415, vol. 2., fols. 198*r*–201*v* · Bodl. Oxf., receipt signed by him and letter to Edward Lye, MS Autogr. d. 21 (SC 37823), fols. 149–50 · Bodl. Oxf., letters to Rawlinson, MS Rawl. letters 29 (SC 14917) · Bodl. Oxf., sermon on the death of the duke of Rutland, 1711, with a letter from him, 7 May 1743, MS Rawl. E. 1771 (SC 14405) · Bodl. Oxf., letters to William Stukeley, MS Eng. misc. c. 114 (SC 42304), fols. 35–43

Likenesses mezzotint, pubd 1809 (after B. Dandridge), NPG · J. Faber junior, mezzotint (after B. Dandridge), BM, NPG · line engraving, BM, NPG

Wealth at death an estate and valuable library

Majendie, Henry William (1754–1830), bishop of Bangor, was born in London on 7 October 1754, the elder son of John James Majendie (1709–1782) and his wife, Elizabeth Prevost (*c*.1738–1818). Majendie's grandfather André left France in 1688 and settled in England in 1700. He ministered to the French congregation in Exeter and married Susanna Mauzy, the daughter of the French pastor at Barnstaple, Devon. John James Majendie, after serving as pastor of the French church of the Savoy, was ordained in the Church of England. Soon after her arrival in England in 1761, he became preceptor to Queen Charlotte, living at court until 1769. He taught her English and she remained a patron and friend. Appointed a canon of Windsor in 1774, he became the queen's domestic chaplain and a tutor to her two sons, the prince of Wales and the duke of York.

Majendie was educated at Charterhouse School, under Dr Samuel Berdmore, and from 1771 at Christ's College, Cambridge. He secured a scholarship there in 1772, and graduated BA in 1776, proceeding MA in 1785 and DD in 1791. In 1776 he was elected to the fellowship at Christ's just vacated by William Paley. He was ordained priest in 1783 at Worcester, and served as vicar of Bromsgrove, Worcestershire, from 1783 to 1785. In January 1780 he was appointed preceptor to Prince William (the future William IV) at a salary of £200 a year, but had acted as one of his instructors since June 1776. In a letter to the king of 1 November 1782 Prince William noted that Majendie 'has been between 7 and 8 years with me' (*Later Correspondence of George III*, 5.694, no. 4294). As the king told Pitt in a letter of 13 September 1797, Majendie 'attended him with unremitting attention for four years on board the Fleet' (ibid., 2.622, no. 1617) during the American War of Independence. On the *Prince George* they travelled much of the world, including a visit to New York in November 1782. It was as a direct reward for this service that Majendie was appointed a canon of Windsor in 1785 and he deferred marriage until he received that appointment. On 11 April 1785 he married Anne Routledge (*d*. 1836) of Stapleton, Cumberland; they had thirteen children. He was vicar of Nether Stowey in Somerset, where he earned the friendship of Thomas Poole (the correspondent of Coleridge), from 1790 to 1793, and vicar of Hungerford from 1793 to 1798. In that year he resigned his Windsor canonry for a residential prebend at St Paul's, and the vicarage of Hungerford for that of New Windsor. He retained both prebend and living when he became bishop of Chester in 1800, but resigned both in 1809 when he was translated to the bishopric of Bangor. He remained in this see for twenty-one years, until his death on 9 July 1830 at the house of his son the Revd Stuart Majendie, at Longdon, near Lichfield.

A strong supporter of the established order at the time of the French Revolution, Majendie regarded Pitt the younger as 'the ablest Man who ever guided the Councils of this Nation' (H. W. Majendie, *A Charge Delivered to the Clergy of the Diocese of Bangor … 1814*, 15). He understood the need to educate the poor as a means of achieving social control and founded a Sunday school at Nether Stowey. Later he was a vigorous supporter of the National Society, advocating the establishment of parochial and daily schools. He strongly supported legislation relating to the residence of clergy and the appointment of stipendiary curates. He was aware of the growth of industrial occupations in the diocese of Chester, appreciated the problems of clergy 'in populous and commercial districts', stressed the need for them to co-operate with the schoolmaster and the civil magistrate, and encouraged them to serve as magistrates themselves (H. W. Majendie, *A Charge Delivered … Chester*, 19). As well as appearing regularly in the House of Lords, he took his pastoral responsibilities seriously and gave his clergy practical advice. He showed a pragmatic awareness of the necessary attitude of clergy to rich and poor; in 1804 he warned his clergy not to attempt 'private religious discourse in an obtrusive, laboured, or authoritative manner [with] the higher orders of society, whose fastidious refinement' might make it counterproductive, but to save it for 'the poor and unlearned [who] will more readily listen to instruction from their Minister, because they think it very natural and becoming his office whether in the church, the house or the field' (ibid., 30). As a bishop he used his influence to appoint his sons and other relations to lucrative livings, and contemporaries commented on 'the corpulence of the bishop's person and the imperturbable gravity of his countenance' (*Cheshire Sheaf*, 86).   ROBERT HOLE

Sources L. A. Majendie, *An account of the de Majendie family, both French and English, from 1365 to the present century* (1878) · *GM*, 1st ser., 100/2 (1830), 273–4 · Venn, *Alum. Cant.*, 2/4.295–6 · *The later correspondence of George III*, ed. A. Aspinall, 5 vols. (1962–70) · *The correspondence of George, prince of Wales, 1770–1812*, ed. A. Aspinall, 8 vols. (1963–71) · *Cheshire Sheaf*, 2nd ser., 1 (1891) · M. E. Sandford, *Thomas Poole and his friends*, 2 vols. (1888) · *DNB* · H. W. Majendie, *A charge delivered to the clergy of the diocese of Chester at the primary visitation* (1804) · H. W. Majendie, *A charge delivered to the clergy of the diocese of Bangor … 1814* (1814) · H. W Majendie, *A charge delivered to the clergy of the diocese of Bangor … 1817* (1817)
Archives Wilts. & Swindon RO, letters as vicar of Hungerford
Likenesses C. Turner, mezzotint, pubd 1823 (after W. Beechey), BM, NPG · A. Edouart, silhouette, Christ's College, Cambridge · G. Hayter, drawing (study for *The trial of Queen Caroline, 1820*), NPG · G. Hayter, group portrait, oils (*The trial of Queen Caroline, 1820*), NPG

Major, Edith Helen (1867–1951), headmistress and college head, was born on 15 February 1867 at Lisburn, co. Antrim, elder daughter of Henry Major, wine merchant, and Margaret, *née* McCall, daughter of a notable Ulster journalist and local historian. Edith was educated at the Methodist college, Belfast, and was said to have been one of the earliest women students at the Queen's University, Belfast, before entering Girton College, Cambridge, in 1885 and gaining a second class in the history tripos in 1888. She graduated MA from Trinity College, Dublin, in 1907.

Miss Major's first post was that of assistant mistress at Blackheath high school, then a training ground of headmistresses under Florence Gadesden, an example of the networks which expedited the transformation of girls' education. Edith Major appears in a photograph of Miss Gadesden surrounded by sixteen of her staff who had become heads of independent, endowed, and county schools. In 1900 she became headmistress of the thirty-fifth Girls' Public Day School Company school, founded in Putney in 1893. Here her 'outstanding qualities were her wit and scholarship. With the first she enlivened the school and endeared herself to staff and pupils; the second inspired the intellectual effort and enthusiasm which brought academic successes to Putney's university entrants' (Sondheimer and Bodington, 79). Miss Major was one of those who tell good stories and about whom good stories are told.

In 1910 Miss Major was appointed to one of the most important of the schools where endowments were shared with girls under the Endowed Schools Act (1869), the King Edward VI High School for Girls, Birmingham. Its first headmistress, Miss Creak, had become an opponent of women's suffrage and emphasized the domestic education of girls. It was not until 1909 that women governors were appointed. On Miss Major's arrival in 1911 she had to set about modernizing ethos, curriculum, teaching methods, and organization. She did this with speed, but with charm and skill.

A commanding and elegant figure, Miss Major was not a typical headmistress. Once asked whether she was embarrassed by the inevitable adulatory speeches, she replied, 'I never listen on such occasions, I always repeat *The Lay of the Last Minstrel* to myself instead' (Kamm, 73). She 'dispensed with all the attributes of awe and majesty' and 'governed her schools by an understanding that amounted to genius' (*The Times*, 19 March 1951), yet this informality did not imply that she was uncertain as to how things should be done, or was uninterested in whether they were done properly. At Birmingham she introduced a house system, uniforms, and school societies, and insisted on the provision of playing fields. There was already a strong staff, and she increased specialist teaching and encouraged lively and critical methods. In her own history teaching she made clear that children should be 'protected' from such arid matters as the details of the campaigns of the Wars of the Roses. The resources of the city, its libraries, museums, galleries, and sites, were to be exploited. Her gaiety and curiosity, generosity and friendliness delighted her staff and pupils, as did the high reputation she helped them to gain for the school. 'Easily pleased, she was in fundamental things not easy to satisfy' (*Girton Review*). Under her the King Edward VI High School gave Birmingham an outstanding example of the civic education of girls. The school community both profited from and contributed much to civic life. She was appointed OBE for work in helping Belgian refugees, and the school helped to provide a centre for dietary information in the attempt to keep the nation fed during the First World War. In 1919 she became president of the Association of Head Mistresses.

In 1925 Miss Major yielded to strong pressures to become mistress of Girton, in spite of her own misgivings that her scholarship was inadequate to university office. Her appointment was a fortunate one for the college. She came to it at a crucial point in the development of relations between the women's colleges and the university. The work of her predecessor, Bertha Phillpots, the scholar of Scandinavian culture, on the recent statutory commission on Oxford and Cambridge had won many objectives for the college. Although in 1921 membership of the university was refused to women, a new charter placed the government of Girton mainly in the hands of the mistress and resident fellows, and women became eligible for all university teaching offices and for membership of all boards of faculties and courses of research. But the university was distrustful of changes achieved and nervous of further advances. Miss Major's particular achievement was to reassure those in the university who were suspicious of the new developments while consolidating the position of women at Cambridge. Her freedom from teaching and research, and her mastery of administration, gave her genius for friendship time for full play. She soon saw how best she could serve the college. She took Cambridge society, especially that dread of Girton's founder, the 'Cambridge ladies', by storm. Her weekly 'at homes' were crowded with those (of both sexes) who thereafter became friends of the mistress and her college. She even tactfully ensured that the undergraduates did not undo her good work—they were urged to put on hat and gloves when they reached Storeys Way, as the Cambridge ladies were waiting to find fault with them. Her personal qualities and high standards were exactly suited to a period of consolidation and tactful preparation for further advance. At the same time it was necessary to launch an appeal (1929) for new buildings, especially a library, and to create an appointments board for women.

Miss Major's services to education—honoured in 1931 by the CBE—were even wider. She was a member of the council of Birmingham University, and on the governing bodies of the Perse School for Girls, Mary Datchelor School, and Badminton School. In 1932 an honorary LLD was conferred on her by the Queen's University, Belfast. She was a member of the council of the League of Nations' Union. In 1931 she retired from Girton and returned to Ireland. Edith Major died at the Holywell Hospital, Antrim, on 17 March 1951.   MARGARET BRYANT

Sources K. T. Butler and H. I. McMorran, eds., *Girton College register, 1869–1946* (1948) · *Girton Review*, Easter term (1951) · *WWW* · *The Times* (19 March 1951) · *The Times* (30 March 1951) · 'Girton's new mistress', *Daily Telegraph* (6 June 1925) · J. Sondheimer and P. R. Bodington, eds., *The Girls' Public Day School Trust, 1872–1972: a centenary review* (1972) · J. Kamm, *Indicative past: one hundred years of the Girls' Public Day School Trust* (1971) · R. Waterhouse, *Six King Edward schools* [forthcoming] · B. Stephen, *Girton College, 1869–1932* (1933)
Archives Girton Cam.
Likenesses W. Orpen, oils, King Edward VI High School for Girls, Birmingham · Sleator, oils (after W. Orpen), Girton Cam. · photograph, repro. in *Girton Review* · photographs, repro. in Waterhouse, *Six King Edward schools*
Wealth at death £12,429 13s. 5d.: probate, 22 Aug 1951, CGPLA Eng. & Wales

Major, Elizabeth (*fl.* 1656), religious writer, was the author of a single volume, entitled *Honey on the rod, or, A comfortable contemplation for one in affliction; with sundry poems on several subjects* (1656).

Major's identity is unknown, and there is little to be done but quote from her preface to the second part of *Honey on the Rod*:

> I was, till the fifteenth or sixteenth year of my age, brought up by a godly and careful Father (my Mother being taken from me in my infancy) from whom I went to a great and honorable Family, where no vice I think was tolerated; and under a wise and vertuous Governness I lived nere ten years, til God was pleased to visit me with Lameness … Then I was forc't to repair home to my Father again, where I was persued with an inordinate desire of recovery; and having some money in my own hands, I endeavored the

accomplishing of that desire, without an humble and obedient submission to the will of God …
> … upon serious consideration I saw my folly, and found that I had lost much time, in which I had offended God, and deprived my self of that little health I enjoyed, spent my money, and onely gaining a sight and knowledge of those things, I humbly desire my soul may ever abhor; therefore I had no rest in me, till I had shewed my indignation against what so much offended me.   (Major, unpaginated prefatory page)

Honey on the Rod was published under the imprimatur of Joseph Caryl, the leading nonconformist divine and rector of St Magnus, London, during the civil wars and interregnum. Caryl's three-page prefatory recommendation of the volume has led to speculation that Major was a parishioner and protégée of Caryl. Caryl's role as licenser for printing books of divinity from 14 June 1643, however, is enough to explain his involvement in the publication, and there is no evidence that he knew Major personally. Major is likely to have dwelt in London, and it is possible that she was, as some have speculated, the daughter of John Major and Mary Allton of Blackfriars, in which case she was born about 1628.

Major's volume consists of meditations in prose, largely constructed as dialogues between Consolation and the Soul; verses which explore the sins of pride, drunkenness, covetousness, prodigality, and of profaning the sabbath and the name of God; and several acrostics based on her name. Major styles her volume as a child sent forth into the world, and she writes 'onely this may cause some trouble in me, I think it will finde none of so low a birth as it self' (Major, unpaginated prefatory page).

                                                                          SARAH ROSS

Sources E. Major, *Honey on the rod, or, A comfortable contemplation for one in affliction: with sundry poems on several subjects* (1656) · *Calamy rev.* · *The visitation of London, anno Domini 1633, 1634, and 1635, made by Sir Henry St George*, 2, ed. J. J. Howard, Harleian Society, 17 (1883) · *IGI* · G. Greer and others, eds., *Kissing the rod: an anthology of seventeenth-century women's verse* (1988) · Blain, Clements & Grundy, *Feminist comp.* · M. Bell, G. A. E. Parfitt, and S. Shepherd, eds., *A biographical dictionary of English women writers, 1580–1720* (1990) · E. Hobby, *Virtue of necessity* (1988)

Major, Ernest (1841–1908), newspaper proprietor in China, was born on 15 February 1841 at Prospect Place, Clapham, Surrey, the third of the five children of Ebenezer Langley Major (1802–1891), civil servant, and his wife, Emma Jones (*fl.* 1838–1892). The eldest son, Alfred (1839–1907), had a long and successful career at the War Office and was awarded a knighthood on retirement. The second and third sons were twins, Frederick and Ernest, Ernest being the younger by forty-five minutes. About 1861 they travelled together to Hong Kong, where Ernest joined a firm of shipping agents, Fletcher & Co.; in 1865 he moved to the port of Ningbo as commission agent for his own firm, Ernest Major & Co.; five years later he moved to Shanghai, having by this time learned to read and write the Chinese language.

So far Major's career had matched those of many young men who traded with China after the Third Anglo-Chinese War, when some of her ports were opened to foreigners for the first time. He made a special name for himself in

Shanghai, however, by founding an independent Chinese newspaper, something which did not as yet exist. The only news sheet regularly circulated was the *Peking Gazette*, but this was a government publication which confined itself to giving news of the court and official government edicts, while being written in a style understandable only to scholars.

Major called his paper *Shenbao*, or *Shanghai Gazette*, stating on the first day of issue, 30 April 1872, that it was to be a paper for ordinary people to read, written in a language they could understand. He himself retained the financial management of the paper and was also foreign editor, one editor among many. He explained that he regarded the paper as 'essentially a Chinese journal, all the articles in it emanating from Chinese writers, excepting on rare occasions when some special subject is suggested by the foreign Editor' (*North China Herald*, 7 Feb 1882).

Major made the paper cheap to buy, and the advertising rates were low; it was read by all classes and soon became widely distributed and discussed. It did not hesitate to criticize the government and frequently mocked the local officials; at first there were calls from them to ban it, but in a short time the officials came to enjoy it themselves and the *Shenbao* was recognized as an indispensable part of the Shanghai scene.

Among other commercial activities Major introduced lithographic printing with machinery he imported from England; he also reprinted China's great seventeenth-century encyclopaedia, a huge repository of knowledge in 6000 volumes, and by using a smaller type he reduced the size to a more convenient 1620 volumes. When this three-year project was completed he retired from the newspaper and returned to England in 1889. The *Shenbao* continued publication for forty years until 1912, and Major's death in 1908 was announced on the front page with a eulogy for the 'great man' who had, so the paper claimed, introduced new ways and vigorously promoted the newspaper industry. A Chinese history of the *Shenbao* newspaper published in 1988 speaks as warmly as ever of the founder and of his foresight and hard work in establishing the paper, and there is no doubt that he will be remembered in China for as long as the *Shenbao* retains its fame as the first newspaper written by and for the Chinese people.

On 15 July 1885 Ernest Major married Anna Margaret (1856–1937), daughter of Joseph Nadin, the vicar of Crewe; they had two daughters. When he returned to England he and his brothers Alfred and Frederick built themselves houses on a spectacular site at Cookham Dean in Berkshire, overlooking the River Thames. It was there at his home, Waterdale, that he died of pneumonia on 13 February 1908; he was buried in Cookham Dean churchyard five days later.   ANN GOLD

Sources Xu Zaiping and Xu Ruifang, *Qingmo sishinian Shenbao shiliao* (1988) ['Historical material from the late-Qing 40-year *Shenbao*'] · CUL, Jardine, Matheson & Co. MSS, microfilms 141, 574, 577, 578 · *North China Herald* (1870–90) [SOAS library, U. Lond.] · *Maidenhead Advertiser* (1886–1908) [Maidenhead Public Library] · *The Times* · *Celestial Empire* (1870–90) · The *Shenbao*, 1872–3, SOAS · b. cert. · m. cert. · d. cert. · b. cert. [Ebenezer Major] · d. cert. [Ebenezer Major]
Likenesses photograph, 1885, priv. coll.
Wealth at death £12,820 6s. 6d.: probate, 4 April 1908, *CGPLA Eng. & Wales*

Major, Henry Dewsbury Alves (1871–1961), theologian, was born on 28 July 1871 at 10 Boon's Place, Plymouth, Devon, the eldest child of Henry Daniel Major (1844–1902), an Admiralty clerk, and his wife, Mary Ursula, daughter of W. Alves, Admiralty commissioner at Haulbowline, Ireland. In 1878 the family emigrated in the *Lady Jocelyn* to Kati Kati settlement, founded by G. V. Stewart, in the Bay of Plenty, New Zealand, where the climate was congenial for the father's asthma. By then Major had two brothers and a sister. His mother, an admirer of John Keble, exercised a strong religious influence. After tuition from his father, he was influenced by the Revd William Katterns, the local vicar, well known for his ostrich farm, a traditional high-churchman, who encouraged Major in 1890 to enter St John's Theological College, Auckland, where his outlook was broadened by the warden, William Beatty, an admirer of S. T. Coleridge and F. D. Maurice.

As his father opposed his ordination, Major had to support himself in the vacations. In 1895 he gained a pass BA degree from University College, Auckland. Bishop W. G. Cowie of Auckland ordained him deacon in 1895 and priest in 1896. He served a curacy at St Mark's, Remuera, from 1895 to 1899, where Beatty was then vicar, and also gained his MA degree (1896), with first-class honours in natural sciences, having specialized in geology. On 1 November 1899 he married Mary Eliza (d. 1965), daughter of Charles Cookman McMillan, JP, of Remuera and Waingaro, New Zealand. They had two sons, one of whom was killed in action in 1941, and one daughter. Shortly before he was married Major moved into the diocese of Wellington as acting vicar of Waitotara, where he began to have the ear trouble which gradually rendered him deaf. He was later also to have great trouble with his eyesight. In 1900 he became vicar of St Peter's, Hamilton, but left in 1902 because he wished to study biblical criticism in England. He returned to New Zealand once only, in 1929, a visit which inspired his *Thirty Years after: a New Zealander's Religion* (1929).

In 1903 Major entered Exeter College, Oxford, where he graduated with first-class honours in theology in 1905. He had among his teachers William Sanday, S. R. Driver, and W. C. Allen. Here he encountered the modernist theology of which he later became a leading exponent. Allen suggested his name for the vacant chaplaincy at Ripon Clergy College to its principal, John Battersby Harford, an evangelical. The college had been founded in 1897 by William Boyd Carpenter, bishop of Ripon, an eloquent evangelical who had developed broad-church leanings. Major later wrote *The Life and Letters of W. B. Carpenter* (1925). He went to Ripon in January 1906, proved an immense success, and was appointed vice-principal in the same year. Later in the year he brought his family to live at Beech Grove, South Crescent. The bishop, the dean, W. H. Fremantle, an Erastian broad churchman and a disciple of Benjamin Jowett, and A. C. Tait influenced him, but even greater was the impression made by Hastings Rashdall, one of the governors.

Major's first overt link with theological liberalism came with his contribution 'St Paul's presentation of Christ' in *Lux hominum*, edited by F. W. Orde Ward (1907). After a visit to the Holy Land, and a severe illness, Major decided to throw in his lot completely with Anglican liberal churchmen. He joined the Churchmen's Union for the Advancement of Liberal Religious Thought (later the Modern Churchmen's Union) and from 1910 became a fanatical advocate of modernism. He started the *Modern Churchman* in 1911, as a successor to the *Liberal Churchman*, to which he had contributed articles, some of which he republished in *The Gospel of Freedom* (1912). His editing of the *Modern Churchman*, from which he did not retire until 1956, was brilliant and often vitriolic, despite the fact that he was gentle when met in person. He also commenced the series of conferences of modern churchmen, the first of which was held at the Spa Hotel, Ripon, in 1914. He was, in addition, responsible for the *Modern Churchman's Creed* and the *Modern Churchman's Library*.

Major, who had acted as curate of North Stainley from 1908 to 1911, then became rector of Copgrove, where he remained until the end of the war, helping neighbouring parishes and writing *Memorials of Copgrove* (1922). After a series of problems with the management of Ripon College during the war years, Major was instrumental in its being reopened as Ripon Hall, in Parks Road, Oxford, in 1919, with himself as principal. Many notable liberal churchmen subsequently emerged from the college. In 1921, after Major had taken part in the renowned modern churchmen's Girton conference, at which Rashdall and J. F. Bethune-Baker had expounded their new Christology, there was an attempt to arraign him for heresy by the Revd C. E. Douglas, an expert in convocation law and founder of the Faith Press. This caused Major to write *A Resurrection of Relics* (1922), and gain among Anglo-Catholics the title of Anti-Christ of Oxford. In 1925 Major went to the United States to deliver the William Belden Noble lectures at Harvard. These were published in 1927 as *English Modernism: its Origin, Methods, Aims* and gained a reputation as 'the best introduction to the aims and methods of modernism in this period' (*DNZB*, 325). In term-time he lived among his pupils at Ripon Hall, while his family occupied Copgrove Cottage, Bagley Wood, and later a house at Eastleach Turville. In 1929 Major moved near Bicester when he was appointed vicar of Merton by Exeter College, Oxford.

The years 1930–48 saw Major, though getting older, deafer, and white-haired, running Ripon Hall, editing the *Modern Churchman*, and organizing the conferences. He remained the leading apostle of modernism much abused by the *Church Times*. In 1933, at the suggestion of R. W. Macan, he moved the college to Foxcombe Rise, Boars Hill, 3 miles from Oxford, which had recently been the home and laboratory of the earl of Berkeley. In 1937 Major wrote, with T. W. Manson and C. J. Wright, *The Mission and Message of Jesus*, showing he retained the belief that Mark's gospel was the eyewitness testimony of Peter. He had first expounded this idea in *Reminiscences of Jesus by an Eye-Witness* (1925) which had gained him his Oxford DD degree (1924). In 1938 he rejoiced at the publication of the report *Doctrine in the Church of England*, which he regarded as giving modernists the right to worship and serve in the Church of England.

In the Second World War the main buildings of the college became a hospital, and Major moved into Tutor's Lodge, keeping the college going with a handful of students. It reopened fully after the war, but in 1975 it amalgamated with Cuddesdon College. In 1964 the college chapel was refurnished in memory of Major and a Latin inscription described him as 'Praeceptor impiger, et eruditus, veri sine metu studiosus, pastor diligens, hospes liberalis' ('A committed and learned teacher, fearlessly zealous for truth, a diligent pastor, and a generous friend'). By then Major's modernism had been rendered old-fashioned by the new theology of John A. T. Robinson and Paul Van Buren.

Major was a firm believer in the Godhead, but uncertain of traditional Trinitarianism. He was devoted to the person of Jesus Christ, but sceptical of the virgin birth, the physical resurrection, and other miracles. His faith in afterlife was firm. He favoured reunion with nonconformists, considering episcopacy as a non-essential advantage of the church. Although he had affection for the Book of Common Prayer, he advocated its revision and himself attempted it in an article entitled 'Towards prayer book revision' (in G. L. H. Harvey, ed., *The Church and the Twentieth Century*, 1936). His attitude to the Church of Rome is seen in *The Roman Church and the Modern Man* (1934). His special delight was the study of the New Testament in Greek. When at Oxford he had won the Canon Hall Greek testament prize. In 1941 E. W. Barnes appointed Major an examining chaplain and an honorary canon of Birmingham. Much vilified by his opponents, Major tempered his determination with humour and humility and was described as a 'model controversialist' (Fallows, 153). He died at Merton vicarage, Bicester, on 26 January 1961, and was buried in Merton churchyard on 31 January.

A. M. G. STEPHENSON, rev. MARC BRODIE

Sources *DNZB*, vol. 3 · A. M. G. Stephenson, *The rise and decline of English modernism* (1984) · *The Times* (28 Jan 1961) · K. W. Clements, *Lovers of discord* (1988) · W. G. Fallows, *Modern Churchman*, new ser., 4 (1960–61), 153–4 · *WWW* · *CGPLA Eng. & Wales* (1961)
Archives Bodl. Oxf., corresp., sermons, and MSS | St John Cam., corresp., mainly letters to J. S. Bezzant
Wealth at death £15,490 15s. 11d.: probate, 2 June 1961, *CGPLA Eng. & Wales*

Major, John. *See* Mair, John (c.1467–1550).

Major, John (1782–1849), bookseller and publisher, was probably born at Duke Street, West Smithfield, London, the son of Samuel Major. His first business was a shop located in the gateway of St Bartholomew's Hospital, but he moved successively to Skinner Street, Great Russell Street, and Fleet Street. In 1813 he privately printed his own verse, *Rational Madness, a Song for the Lovers of Curious and Rare Books*, which was adapted to the tune of 'Liberty

Hall'. Having an extensive knowledge of bibliography, Major was heavily involved with the famous bibliophile and author Thomas Frognall Dibdin. When Dibdin in 1815 threatened to burn the remaining copies of the fourth volume of the *Bibliotheca Spenceriana* because it was selling badly, Major took them on generous terms.

Major's contemporary the publisher Charles Knight noted that he was also a reprinter of 'beautiful and cheap' standard works (Knight, 1.277). His most famous publication, which he edited himself, was an illustrated edition of Izaak Walton's and Charles Cotton's *Complete Angler* in 1823; there were new editions in 1824, 1835, 1844, and 1847, with many reprints. His other publications included Walton's *Lives* (1825), Walpole's *Anecdotes of Painting* (1826), Bunyan's *Pilgrim's Progress*, and Defoe's *Robinson Crusoe* (1830). Between 1825 and 1836 Major, a minor poet, frequently contributed rhyming commentaries on the politics of the day to the weekly newspaper *John Bull*. He published his own *A Poetical Description of Bartholomew Fair*, by 'One under a Hood', in 1837.

Major continued to support Dibdin's publications, subscribing for fifty copies of Dibdin's edition of Thomas à Kempis (1828), and publishing his *Reminiscences* (1836). However, according to Thomas Rees, in the mid-1830s Major began to accept bills for Dibdin's speculations which Dibdin failed to honour. This eventually caused his financial ruin and a period of mental illness. He struggled on for a few years, first at 29 St Martin's Court, Leicester Square (1838), and then at 6 Museum Street, Bloomsbury (1839). His own rhymed version of Dean Swift's *Advice to Servants* was published in 1843, and in conjunction with his son John Stenson Major, a composer and music teacher, he issued *The Pastoral Week*, in the style of Walton. On the recommendation of the Rt Hon. Thomas Grenville, Major obtained an asylum in the Charterhouse, where he prepared the last and finest edition of *The Complete Angler* (1847), and died on 9 January 1849.

GORDON GOODWIN, rev. JOHN ISSITT

Sources BL cat. [John Major, Thomas Frognall Dibdin, Izaak Walton] · T. Rees, *Reminiscences of literary London from 1779 to 1853*, repr. (1974), 93–5 · A. Lister, 'George John, 2nd Earl Spencer and his "librarian", Thomas Frognall Dibdin', *Bibliophily*, ed. R. Myers and M. Morris (1986), 90–100 · C. Knight, *Passages of a working life*, 3 vols. (1864), vol. 1, p. 277 · *GM*, 2nd ser., 31 (1849), 322–3 · I. Walton, *The complete angler*, ed. G. C. Davies, Chandos Classics Series (1888)

Major, John Henniker-, second Baron Henniker (1752–1821), politician and antiquary, was born on 19 April 1752, the eldest son of Sir John Henniker (1724–1803), who had continued his father's business in the Russian trade and built up landholdings in co. Wicklow and in Essex, and Anne (d. 1792), eldest daughter and coheir of Sir John Major, bt, of Worlingworth Hall, Suffolk. He was educated at Eton College and St John's College, Cambridge (MA by royal mandate 1772, LLD 1811), and was called to the bar in 1777 as a member of Lincoln's Inn. He was elected a fellow of the Society of Antiquaries on 9 June 1785 and a fellow of the Royal Society on 15 December 1785.

Following his father's departure from parliament in 1784, Henniker was elected member for New Romney in 1785, where he generally supported the Pitt ministry. He failed to find a seat in 1790. Following his mother's death, on 10 August 1792 he took the additional surname and arms of Major by royal licence. He returned to parliament as MP for Steyning in February 1794; his continued support for Pitt won his father—a sometime Foxite—an Irish peerage on 30 July 1800. He succeeded his father as second Baron Henniker on 13 April 1803. Henniker-Major was again in search of a seat following the 1802 election, but in January 1805, as a trustee of the young marquess of Exeter, he was returned as MP for Rutland. He withdrew from Rutland in 1812 rather than face a contest, and from then until his retirement in 1818 was MP for Stamford, Lincolnshire, also in the Cecil family interest.

Henniker-Major was renowned as a kind master and good landlord and a generous supporter of numerous charities. On 21 April 1794 he married Emily (1754/5–1819), daughter of Robert Jones of Dyffryn, Glamorgan, who died on 18 December 1819; they had no children.

Henniker-Major's only publications were on the subject of antiquities; these included an essay in *Archaeologia* (1793) on Bicknacre Priory, Essex, two articles on Norman tiles with armorial bearings, and 'Some account of the families Major and Henniker' (1803). Henniker-Major's findings were largely derivative, although he did introduce an element of personal observation, and were mainly focused upon issues of heraldry, genealogy, and Anglo-Norman antiquities. He died on 4 December 1821 at Stratford House, Essex, and was succeeded in his title and estate by his nephew, John Minet Henniker, who resumed the additional surname of Major by royal licence on 27 May 1822.

GORDON GOODWIN, rev. R. H. SWEET

Sources DNB · GM, 1st ser., 91/2 (1821), 562 · GEC, *Peerage*, new edn, 6.438 · L. B. Namier, 'Henniker, John (1724–1803)', 'Henniker, John (1752–1821)', HoP, *Commons, 1754–90* · M. H. Port and R. G. Thorne, 'Henniker (afterwards Henniker major)', HoP, *Commons, 1790–1820*
Archives Suffolk RO, Ipswich, household ledger | BL, letters to Warren Hastings and others, Add. MSS 29179–29182, 29185–29186, 35648, 35729, 38244
Likenesses H. Hudson, mezzotint (after G. Romney), BM, NPG

Major, Joshua (1786–1866), landscape gardener and designer, was born on 28 August 1786 at the estate village of Owston, near Doncaster, Yorkshire, the third of the three children of Richard Major (1736–1809), a general estate labourer, and his wife, Mary, *née* Bramma (1742–1830). It is probable that Major attended the village school founded by Frances Davies-Cooke, the estate owner's wife. In 1793 the landscape gardener Humphry Repton prepared a red book for Owston, laying out proposed physical developments for the estate. It is possible that Joshua's father was involved in their implementation and that the work inspired his boyhood interest in landscape design.

It is not known when Major married his wife, Isabella. They had a son, Henry, who became a partner in the nursery garden Major founded at Knowsthorpe, Leeds, about 1810. Initially the firm practised commercial horticulture, and the gardening magazines of the day recorded their successes at flower shows. Later it became involved in landscape design, and in 1845 Major was awarded the first premium for the design of the first public parks in Manchester. The initial concept was unique: the development of a number of neighbourhood parks within easy walking distance for the majority of the city's population. Financial restraints plus the lack of suitable sites resulted in only Peel, Philips, and Queens parks being made of the four initially planned. Among other landscape works were Hanover Square, Leeds (1824); Derwent Hall, Derbyshire (1833); Oakes Park, Sheffield (1834); Wells House, Ilkley, Yorkshire; and the People's Pleasure Ground, Meltham, Yorkshire (c.1860). All these works showed Major to be pragmatic in his approach to landscape design, creating areas for walking and recreation, including open spaces where cricket or football could be played. But, inevitably, his designs became more picturesque. Joseph Paxton's Birkenhead Park (1843) was similar to Major's Manchester parks, but Major never succumbed to the formal Italianate style of gardening as did Paxton in the People's Park, Halifax, and at Sydenham, London.

Major wrote a number of books: *A Treatise on the Insects most Prevalent on Fruit Trees and Garden Produce* (1829), *The Theory and Practice of Landscape Gardening* (1852), and *The Ladies' Assistant in the Formation of their Flower Gardens* (1861), in which he was assisted by his son. He was a frequent contributor to the *Gardeners' Magazine* and corresponded with the editor, J. C. Loudon, especially on the matter of the 'ideal' garden for the Victorian villa, and a scheme for such a garden (of 100 acres) by Major was extensively illustrated in Loudon's *Encyclopaedia of Gardening* (1871 edn, 1185–91).

In addition to his business interests, Major assisted in the formation of the first Sunday school in Leeds, of which he was the superintendent for many years, and he took an active interest in other religious and charitable institutions of the town. When he died, in Leeds on 26 January 1866, at the age of seventy-nine, his son continued the business, but as a horticultural nursery.

DAVID BALDWIN

Sources D. Baldwin, 'Joshua Major', *Journal of Garden History*, 7/2 (1987), 131–50 · D. Baldwin, 'The establishment of public parks in Manchester', MA diss., University of Manchester, 1981 · T. Wyborn, *Parks for the people: the development in public parks in Manchester, c.1830–1860*, University of Manchester Working Papers, Economic and Social History, 29 (1994)

Major, Richard (1603/4–1660), landowner, was the son of John Major (d. 1630), alderman of Southampton, and his wife, Ann. His grandfather John Major, a brewer, was mayor of Southampton in 1601, while his father, steward of Southampton in 1610–11 and mayor in 1615–16, put his financial skills to acquiring landed property, buying the manors of Candover in 1617 and Allington in 1622. He represented Southampton in parliament in 1628 and at his death two years later left £200 to the corporation which was not paid until they sued his great-grandson in 1671; it established St John's Hospital. The primary fault seems to have been Richard Major's.

Richard Major attended Queen's College, Oxford, from 1621 to 1624, and married Ann (1605/6–1662), daughter of John Kingsmill of Marwell, Isle of Wight, at Carisbrooke in 1625. His father set him up as a prosperous landowner at Sylton in Dorset; he sold Candover on inheriting it and in 1638/9 purchased the manor of Merdon, based on Hursley Park, near Winchester. He was meticulous in keeping records, and his zeal in enforcing his rights led to a later portrait of him by a tenant as witty, and thrifty to the point of miserliness, cancelling tenants' established privileges. Inclined towards puritanism, he served as sheriff of Hampshire in 1640 and supported parliament, becoming a commissioner for sequestration in March 1643 and joining the committee to defend the county. On all assessment committees from 1643 until 1657, he also served on the Southampton town committee aiding Governor Murford. In 1645 he opposed those who sought to prevent a group meeting for spiritual exercises at Newport. He and his colleagues seized control of Southampton's Thursday divinity lecture for Governor Murford's chaplain Nathaniel Robinson, allegedly a Brownist, in 1647.

It was presumably Robinson, intruded into All Saints' parish, who recommended Major to his friend Cromwell and proposed that Major's elder daughter and heir, Dorothy, marry Richard Cromwell. Cromwell cited Major's godliness rather than his money as decisive. On 27 March 1648 Cromwell met him to discuss the proposal, and wrote that he found him 'very wise and honest, and indeed much to be valued', though 'some things of common fame did a little stick' (*Letters and Speeches*, 1.298), on whose side is uncertain. Major insisted that Cromwell settle £400 p.a. of inherited land on Richard and Dorothy, rather than parliamentary grants, which could be rescinded. By March 1649 talks were deadlocked and Cromwell complained that Major was 'very high on all points' (*Letters and Speeches*, 1.424–7) and attempting to levy unreasonable charges on the estate, but the marriage was performed on 1 May at Hursley and the young couple moved in with Major. Cromwell wrote to him from campaign addressing him as his 'beloved brother'.

In 1653 Major lent his support to a Hampshire petition to the Rump Parliament which praised the puritan parochial ministry and sought to defend it against the criticisms of more radical puritans. His family links led to his representing Southampton in the Nominated Parliament in 1653, and on 14 July he was added to the council of state. His only significant contribution was his promotion of a scheme concerning a coalmine in the New Forest. He and Cromwell also seem to have attempted to purchase a property, possibly Fawley Park, for Richard. On 16 December he was nominated to Cromwell's protectoral council of state, subsequently becoming a trier for Hampshire. He was mainly concerned with religion, but his most important role was on the committee determining which petitions should be put to the council and which rejected. Elected MP for Hampshire in the parliament of 1654, he regularly attended council until October, when his lameness inhibited travel. He made several brief appearances in 1655, particularly on Southampton business, and in 1657 was still referred to as a councillor. He is sometimes considered to have been called to the upper house in

December 1657, but had no influence over his son-in-law as protector.

When Richard Cromwell was deposed he and Dorothy eventually retreated to Hursley. Major died at Hursley Park, Merdon, on 25 April 1660 aged fifty-six, the timing leading to rumours of suicide due to his fear of prosecution at the Restoration. He was buried in the chancel of Hursley church on 30 April. His widow died in 1662; Dorothy and her children remained at Hursley during and after Cromwell's stay abroad, and on Dorothy's death in 1676 her son Oliver succeeded. The tenants launched a lawsuit in chancery to regain their rights, which was settled soon after Oliver's death in 1705. Major, despite poor health, was a zealous but grasping estate manager ambitious for his family and dogged in pursuit of money, who acquired prominence by links with Cromwell.

TIMOTHY VENNING

Sources BL, Add. MS 24861 · M. Noble, Memoirs of the protectoral-house of Cromwell, 2 vols. (1787) · The letters and speeches of Oliver Cromwell, ed. T. Carlyle and S. C. Lomas, 3 vols. (1904) · CSP dom., 1653–5 · council of state order book, 1653–4, PRO, SP 25/75 · committee book, 1653–4, PRO, SP 25/121 · VCH Hampshire and the Isle of Wight, vols. 2–3 · R. C. Anderson, ed., The book of examinations and depositions, 1622–1644, 4 vols., Southampton RS, 29, 31, 34, 36 (1929–36) · J. W. Horrocks, ed., The assembly books of Southampton, 1–4, Southampton RS, 19, 21, 24–5 (1917–25) · B. B. Woodward, T. C. Wilks, and C. Lockhart, A general history of Hampshire, 3 vols. [1861–9] · A. J. Willis, ed., Hampshire marriage licences, 2 vols. (1960–63) · J. S. Davies, A history of Southampton (1883) · G. N. Godwin, The civil war in Hampshire, 1642–45, and the story of Basing House, new edn (1904) · J. Speed, The history and antiquity of Southampton, ed. E. R. Aubrey (1909) · C. H. Firth and R. S. Rait, eds., Acts and ordinances of the interregnum, 1642–1660, 3 vols. (1911) · Foster, Alum. Oxon. · A. M. Coleby, Central government and the localities: Hampshire, 1649–1689 (1987) · J. Marsh, Memoranda of the parishes of Hursley and North Baddersley (1808)
Archives BL, corresp. and papers, Add. MSS 24860–24861
Wealth at death estate of Merdon Manor (Hursley Park), Hampshire

Major, Richard Henry (1818–1891), geographer, was born on 3 October 1818 at 38 Old Street (Road), Shoreditch, London, son of Richard Henry Major, surgeon, of an old Jersey family, and Elizabeth Edge, who married in 1816. After her husband's death on 7 January 1822 Elizabeth remarried, leaving Richard and his elder brother to the care of their paternal grandfather. After attending Merchant Taylors' School, London, from 1832 to 1836, Richard was destined for the church, but instead spent the next six years as clerk to a German and then a Spanish merchant's firm in London. He did not regret his decision not to enter the church, although he forwent a considerable legacy thereby and remained interested in religion throughout his life. He became supernumerary assistant at the British Museum in 1844 under the patronage of Sir Henry Ellis. He was also introduced by Ellis to the recently formed Hakluyt Society, where he was honorary secretary, officially between 1849 and 1858 and unofficially for considerable periods after this. His linguistic and historical skills led to his editing eight volumes of travellers' accounts for the society and he also materially helped editors of other volumes.

On 3 June 1847 Major married Sarah Elizabeth Thorn (c.1814–1890), artist, and for twelve years lived with her at 4 Albion Place, Canonbury Square, Islington, London, the house of her parents, Henry (hosier and merino manufacturer) and Elizabeth Thorn. They had two daughters. Sarah—who worked professionally as both Thorn and Major—skilfully illustrated some of her husband's publications. Major continued to work at the British Museum, although, with money inherited from his grandfather and father-in-law, he had a comfortable private income. In 1854 he was elected fellow of the Society of Antiquaries and was active in it for the next twenty years. Elected fellow of the Royal Geographical Society in 1845, he was honorary secretary from 1866 to 1881 and vice-president between 1881 and 1884. In 1861 he was made knight of the Tower and the Sword by Pedro V of Portugal for his claim that the Portuguese discovered Australia in the sixteenth century. Luiz I made him officer of the same order after the publication of The Life of Prince Henry of Portugal, Surnamed the Navigator (1868) and later made him knight commander of the order of Santiago. In 1873 Dom Pedro II of Brazil made him knight commander of the Rose of Brazil. In 1874 Victor Emmanuel II made him knight commander of the Crown of Italy for his Voyages of the Venetian Brothers N. and A. Zeno (1873). He was appointed keeper of the newly created department of maps and charts in the British Museum in 1867. Respiratory illness forced him to retire from the museum in 1880 and from active involvement in professional societies shortly afterwards. He died on 25 June 1891 at his home, 51 Holland Road, Kensington, London, and was buried two days later in Highgate cemetery.

Major was the leading figure of his day in Britain in the history of cartography and discoveries, particularly of America and Australia, and, although subsequent scholarship has forced revision of many of his opinions, he is still recognized as having been a pioneer in his field, with his unique access to the British Museum collections and a considerable say in influential publications.

ELIZABETH BAIGENT

Sources J. H., Biography of R. H. Major, FSA … From materials supplied by himself at the request of the author J. H. (1886) · T. Campbell, 'R. H. Major and the British Museum', Compassing the vaste globe of the earth: studies in the history of the Hakluyt Society, 1846–1996, ed. R. C. Bridges and P. E. H. Hair, Hakluyt Society, 183 (1996), 81–141 · The Times (29 June 1891)
Likenesses R. C. Lucas, wax, 1850, BL · photograph, c.1860–1869, RGS archive · photograph, c.1860–1869, BL, Printed Book Collection · photograph, c.1880–1889, RGS Archive
Wealth at death £3536 15s. 5d.: probate, 20 July 1891, CGPLA Eng. & Wales

Major, Thomas (1720–1799), engraver, may have been the infant baptized on 30 May 1720 at Preston Bisset, Buckinghamshire, the son of Samuel and Elizabeth Major, as Thomas later had property interests in that county. Claims that he was descended from Richard Major of Hursley, Hampshire, father-in-law of Richard Cromwell, are unsubstantiated. Major was taught to draw and etch by Hubert Gravelot, and his first prints are dated 1744. In October 1745 he accompanied the renowned landscape engraver Jacques-Philippe le Bas to Paris, assisted him there, and was befriended by the English-born engraver André Laurent. He published several prints in Paris from his apartment in the rue St Jacques. In October 1746 Major was arrested and spent three months incarcerated in the Bastille as a reprisal for the temporary imprisonment of the Frenchmen of Fitz-James's horse and the Irish regiments after the battle of Culloden. He was freed after strenuous intercession with the marquis d'Argenson by le Bas, Gravelot, and the English banker Selwin. Major dedicated three prints to d'Argenson in grateful recognition of his help. When Laurent died in 1747 Major accompanied his body to its grave in Paris, but he had returned to England by December 1748 when he sold the dealer Arthur Pond a number of prints he had brought back to London. He continued to import prints, acting as an agent for le Bas, and in 1750 auctioned a collection of paintings that he had bought in Paris. Despite his activity as a dealer he published a number of prints in quick succession, including two after Teniers from the collection of the prince of Wales, which earned him an appointment as engraver to the prince. At about this time he married his wife, Dorothy; their first child, Elizabeth, was born in January 1752. In that year the family moved from the Golden Head in West Street to more spacious accommodation in Chandos Street, off lower St Martin's Lane, where a further fifteen children were born between 1752 and 1771.

Major was energetic in providing for his growing family. The patronage of the duke of Cumberland made it possible in 1753 to import André Laurent's plates that Major had bought in Paris. Major completed and in 1753 published Laurent's unfinished *Death of the Stag*, after Wouverman. He engraved the views for two important architectural collections, the *Ruins of Palmyra* (1753) and the *Ruins of Baalbec* (1757). He issued a first broadsheet catalogue of his works in 1754, and in 1756 engraved a title-page for collections of his prints, claiming with some justification that they were 'A collection of prints engraved from the finest paintings of the greatest masters chosen out of the most celebrated collections in England and France'. By then he was able to add to his other qualifications the title of engraver to the king, having been appointed chief seal engraver to the king with an annual income of £50. He was ejected in 1760 but reinstated in 1768 after appealing on behalf of his many children, then reduced by infant mortality to eight. From 1756 until 1797 he was also engraver to the stamp office. His second printed catalogue of his publications listed sixty-four plates, supplemented in that year by *The Ruins of Paestum*, of which he was probably author as well as engraver and publisher. The text was translated into French in 1769 and into German in 1781.

Major joined the Society for the Encouragement of Arts, Manufactures, and Commerce in 1760, but showed prints with them only once, in 1762. He had nothing to do with the Society of Artists but was induced to become an original associate engraver of the Royal Academy in 1770. His most eminent colleagues had declined this honour as a slight to the profession (since they were denied full membership), and according to Robert Strange, Major was blackmailed with the loss of his pension. He exhibited there only once, in 1776, when he showed what may have been his last print, the *Good Shepherd*, after Murillo.

He did not altogether relinquish his craft, however. When in 1784 thieves stole the great seal from the house of Edward Thurlow, the lord chancellor, Major provided within twenty hours a perfect substitute, and afterwards one executed in silver, which was used until the union with Ireland. Specializing in the interpretation of Flemish paintings, Major was the first great English landscape engraver. He was overshadowed by younger rivals after the 1760s, but by then he had already compiled the basis of a comfortable fortune. He died at his house, 5 Tavistock Row, Westminster, on 30 December 1799 and was buried on 6 January 1800 at St Giles's, Camberwell, Surrey. He left his wife an estate valued at nearly £5000, which included properties in Buckinghamshire.

TIMOTHY CLAYTON and ANITA McCONNELL

Sources D. Alexander, 'Major, Thomas', *The dictionary of art*, ed. J. Turner (1996) • T. Major, Memoir of Andrew Lawrence, 1785, BM, 1870/5/14/2357 • Dodd, manuscript history of engravers, BL, Add. MS 33403, fols. 8–13 • Vertue, *Note books*, 3.156; 6.203 • Farington, *Diary*, 3/952, 973; 4/1282; 14/4809 • *GM*, 1st ser., 54 (1784), 230, 378 • will, PRO, PROB 11/1335, sig. 43 • M. Huber and C. G. Martini, *Manuel des curieux et des amateurs de l'art*, 9 (Zürich, 1808), 170–72 • sale catalogue (1800) [Sothebys, 21 April 1800] • H. Dagnell, *Creating a good impression: the history of the stamp office* (1994), 92 • H. A. Hammelmann, 'First engraver at the Royal Academy', *Country Life*, 142 (1967), 616–18 • W. T. Whitley, *Artists and their friends in England, 1700–1799*, 1 (1928), 95–7 • T. Clayton, *The English print, 1688–1802* (1997) • E. Harris and N. Savage, *British architectural books and writers, 1556–1785* (1990) • 'Account of Thomas Major's confinement in the castle of the Bastille in the year 1746 edited by T. Wilson and accompanied by a letter to Thomas Hollis', *Monthly Magazine*, 27 (1809), 429–35; 28 (1809), 540–52

Likenesses T. Major, line engraving, 1759, BM • self-portrait, repro. in Hammelmann, 'First engraver at the Royal Academy', 616

Wealth at death estate valued at nearly £5000: will, PRO, PROB 11/1335, sig. 43

Makarios III [*real name* Michael Mouskos] (1913–1977), Greek Orthodox archbishop and president of Cyprus, was born on 13 August 1913 at Ano Panayia, near Paphos, Cyprus, the eldest child of Christodoulos Mouskos, a peasant farmer, and his wife, Eleni. He was educated at the village school, the monastery of Kykko, and the Pan-Cypriot High School in Nicosia. After ordination as a deacon on 7 August 1938, taking the name of Makarios, he went to Athens to study theology and law at the university. On 13 January 1946 he was ordained priest. In the same year he won a scholarship to study at Massachusetts University. While there, he learned unexpectedly in 1948 that he had been elected bishop of Kition.

Upon installation Makarios became a member of the Cypriot ethnarchy (national leadership) and began to promote the campaign for *enosis* (union with Greece). In January 1950 he organized a plebiscite among Greek Cypriots, who voted overwhelmingly for *enosis*. While the results were being carried to the United Nations, he succeeded as archbishop on 18 October 1950. He was a devout churchman, but he also used his sermons to preach *enosis*. In 1951

Makarios III (1913–1977), by Chris Ware, 1955

he urged the Greek government to raise the issue at the UN. The following year he met Colonel George Grivas to discuss more active measures. Since the British government refused to discuss *enosis*, the Greek government agreed in 1954 to appeal to the UN. Early in 1955 Makarios sanctioned a campaign of sabotage (excluding bloodshed) by Grivas's National Organization of Cypriot Fighters (EOKA). The first explosions took place on 1 April 1955. In the same month Makarios attended the first conference of non-aligned nations at Bandung.

During the next four years Makarios lost control of the violence. EOKA fought the Turkish Cypriots as well as the British. Although negotiations were opened, Makarios spurned every British offer of self-government as insufficient. The British lost patience and deported him on 9 March 1956 to the Seychelles. During his exile things went from bad to worse. In March 1957 Makarios was released, but not being allowed to return to Cyprus he settled in Athens. When the British government decided in 1958 to impose a new constitution, giving the Turks a formal status in Cyprus and hinting at partition, Makarios decided to accept independence in place of *enosis*.

Early in 1959 the crisis was resolved by the Zürich and London agreements, establishing an independent republic. Both *enosis* and partition were excluded, and Britain retained two sovereign bases. Having reluctantly acquiesced, Makarios was elected president on 13 December 1959, with a Turkish vice-president. The republic was inaugurated on 16 August 1960, and joined the Commonwealth in 1961. Makarios still hoped to achieve *enosis* eventually but he made a visit of reconciliation to Turkey in November 1962.

The complex constitution soon broke down. When Makarios proposed to amend it in December 1963, communal fighting began again. The UN intervened with a peace-keeping force in March 1964. Makarios allowed his national guard, commanded by Grivas, to be reinforced illegally from Greece. He rebuffed proposals by UN mediators, appealed to the Soviet Union for help, and toured the developing world seeking support. In April 1967 the threat to his position was aggravated by a military coup in Athens. The Greek junta and Grivas between them almost provoked war with Turkey over Cyprus in November. Grivas and most of the Greek forces were then forced to withdraw. Mutual attempts at assassination followed: an attack on the Greek dictator, Colonel Papadopoulos, instigated from Cyprus in August 1968; an attack on Makarios on 8 March 1970 and on other occasions.

Makarios was now under pressure from many quarters: the communists, the ultra-nationalists, the Greek junta, Grivas (who returned clandestinely in August 1971), and dissident bishops (who criticized his combination of political and ecclesiastical offices). But his popularity was confirmed by re-election to the presidency in 1968 and 1973. He faced a supreme crisis in 1974, when the Greek junta plotted to destroy him, using Greek officers in the national guard and a revived terrorist organization (EOKA-B). Makarios exposed the plot in a letter to the new Greek president on 2 July. On 15 July an attack was made on his residence, but he escaped first to Paphos, then to a British base and to London. The belief that he was politically finished was dispelled when he arrived in New York and addressed the UN on 19 July. Next day the Turks invaded Cyprus, ostensibly exercising their treaty right to restore the *status quo*. On 23 July the Greek dictatorship fell.

Makarios returned to Cyprus in triumph on 7 December 1974, but the *status quo* could not be restored. The Turks occupied two-fifths of the island, which they proclaimed a 'Turkish federated state' in 1975. Discussions at the UN and between the parties concerned failed to produce any improvement during Makarios's remaining years. He died in Nicosia on 3 August 1977, and was buried near the monastery of Kykko, within sight of his native village. He had failed to achieve his life's ambition, but he had established himself as a national hero to the Greeks—too large-scale a hero for his small island to accommodate.

C. M. WOODHOUSE, *rev.*

Sources *The Times* (4 Aug 1977) · S. Mayes, *Makarios: a biography* (1981)
Archives FILM BFI NFTVA, current affairs footage | SOUND BL NSA, documentary recording
Likenesses C. Ware, photograph, 1955, Hult. Arch. [*see illus.*]

Makculloch, Magnus (*fl.* 1477–1484). *See under* Bower, Walter (1385–1449).

Makemie, Francis (*c.*1658–1708), Presbyterian minister, was born near Ramelton, co. Donegal, Ireland. His parents, of Scottish ancestry, are unknown; he had at least two brothers and one sister. Described as blue-eyed and brown-haired, with a fair complexion, he was educated by a local schoolmaster and in February 1676 enrolled in the University of Glasgow. He appeared before Ulster's Presbytery of Laggan on 28 January 1680, was licensed to preach in late 1681 or early 1682, and was ordained in 1682. Restrictions on Presbyterians in Ulster, and an appeal from Maryland's council to his presbytery for ministers, attracted him to the Chesapeake region.

Makemie itinerated along the coasts of Maryland, Virginia, and North Carolina and in Barbados. For a time he ministered in Virginia and by 1687 had a residence there in Accomack county where he began to acquire land and engage in trade. About 1689 he travelled to London, largely to recruit additional ministerial manpower. In Virginia, in 1692, he was visited by George Keith, a Quaker apologist eager to dispute a catechism for children that Makemie had published (no copy of which is known to have survived). Makemie published a verbose theological riposte, *An Answer to George Keith's Libel* (1694). In 1692 he visited Pennsylvania and preached one of the first Presbyterian sermons heard in Philadelphia. By this time he had established trading interests in Barbados and divided his time between the island and Virginia. As early as 1690 he had received from the governor of Barbados a dissenter's licence to preach and by 1693 or 1694 was living there. From Barbados he wrote *Truths in a True Light* (1699), an attempt to build ecumenical bridges to Anglicans on the island and in the Chesapeake. This pamphlet called for protestants to sink their differences in the face of Roman Catholic activity.

Makemie was probably financed during these years by William Anderson, a wealthy Virginia merchant and Accomack county landowner, and some time between 1687 and 1698 he married Anderson's daughter Naomi, about ten years his junior. They had two children, Elizabeth and Anne. Upon Anderson's death in 1698 Makemie and his wife inherited the bulk of his wealth and returned to Virginia from Barbados. The following year Makemie was granted a dissenter's licence on the basis of the one received in Barbados, and registered his home for preaching.

Makemie proved adept at managing both plantation and commercial affairs and added to his inherited wealth by purchase and trade; over the next eight years Virginia records regarding his activities almost exclusively reflected such interests. By 1704 he had become the second largest landholder in Accomack county. In that year he visited England, where the Presbyterian Fund of London promised financial support for two further ministers. Makemie was reacting against the increasing Anglican activity in the American colonies nurtured by the Society for the Propagation of the Gospel. He was also deeply concerned about the lack of civic growth in Virginia and Maryland. Wishing to warn fellow colonists of the pitfalls of scattered settlements, while in London he published *A plain and friendly perswasive to the inhabitants of Virginia and Maryland, for promoting towns and cohabitation* (1705). By uniting in important towns the Chesapeake inhabitants could encourage economic and cultural development, thereby causing self-interest to 'truckle to the Common Good' (Schlenther, *Life*, 139).

Upon his 1705 return to the Chesapeake with two ministerial recruits Makemie experienced the new Anglican aggressiveness, initiated by the Society for the Propagation of the Gospel, first-hand. He quickly moved to organize the first American presbytery, which met in Philadelphia in the spring of 1706, comprising the seven Presbyterian ministers then labouring in Virginia, Maryland, Delaware, and Pennsylvania. Its formation marked the formal foundation of the Presbyterian Church in America, and Makemie was elected its first moderator. Early in 1707 he and another minister visited New York to attempt to broaden the presbytery's scope. There they were confronted by the royal governor, Edward Hyde, Lord Cornbury, who had been actively undermining the rights of the colony's non-Anglicans. Makemie preached in a private home, for which Cornbury ordered his arrest. If various contemporary reports of Cornbury's regular practice of parading in women's clothes were true, Makemie's distaste for the governor was probably flavoured by considerations more than ecclesiastical.

In June Makemie appeared in court. Ever relishing the taste of debate, he participated extensively in his own defence, at first basing it on his two licences to preach—thereby claiming protection under parliament's 1689 Act of Toleration. However, he shifted his stance to denying the need for toleration in colonies where the Church of England had not been legally established. Such was the case, he claimed, in New York. The union of the English and Scottish parliaments just a month before the trial facilitated this alteration in his argument: Presbyterians, he said, 'have now since the Union, a National Establishment in Great Britain, as nighly related and annexed unto the Crown of England, as the Church of England themselves' (Schlenther, *Life*, 225). The presiding judge noted that this was the first such trial in the American colonies, and the jury found Makemie innocent. However, the court affixed upon him the trial's entire costs, which so roused popular opinion that the following year the colony's assembly made such a procedure illegal. A beleaguered Cornbury called Makemie a 'Jack of all Trades he is a Preacher, a Doctor of Physick, a Merchant, an Attorney … and, which is worse of all, a Disturber of Governments' (Schlenther, *Life*, 259).

In Boston following his trial, Makemie arranged for the publication of what is probably the earliest extant American Presbyterian sermon, *A Good Conversation* (1707)—the preaching of which had led to his imprisonment—and of his anonymous *A Narrative of a New and Unusual American Imprisonment of Two Presbyterian Ministers* (1707). This last and most important of his publications brought to public view the trial that served as a milestone in religious toleration in the American colonies. Cotton Mather wrote:

> That brave man, Mr. Makemie, has after a famous Trial at
> N. York … triumphed over the Act of Uniformity, and the
> other Poenal Lawes for the Ch. of England. Without
> permitting the Matter to come so far as to Pleading the Act of

Toleration, he has compelled an Acknowledgement that those Lawes aforesd … have nothing to do with the Plantations.   (Schlenther, *Life*, 17)

Makemie died at some time between 10 June and 4 August 1708, probably at his Accomack home, and it is likely that he was buried on the bank of Holden's Creek. His estate comprised over 5000 acres of land, thirty-three slaves, and a library of 1000 volumes. Called the father of American Presbyterianism, he was its chief early exponent, its leading literary apologist, the main defender of its liberties, the foremost overseer of its congregations, and the moving force in its formal organization. Perhaps of necessity a polemical man, his theology was strictly orthodox, in the style of seventeenth-century Calvinism.

BOYD STANLEY SCHLENTHER

Sources B. S. Schlenther, ed., *The life and writings of Francis Makemie, father of American Presbyterianism (c.1658–1708)* (1999) · J. H. Smylie, 'Francis Makemie: tradition and challenge', *Journal of Presbyterian History*, 61 (1983), 197–209 · C. Miller, 'Francis Makemie: social development of the colonial Chesapeake', *American Presbyterians*, 63 (1985), 333–40 · B. S. Schlenther, 'Religious faith and commercial empire', *The Oxford history of the British empire*, ed. P. J. Marshall, 2: *The eighteenth century* (1998), 128–50 · C. A. Briggs, *American Presbyterianism* (1885) · S. Nottingham, ed., *Wills and administrations of Accomack County, Virginia, 1663–1800* (1973) · H. C. McCook, ed., 'Records of Accomack County, Virginia, relating to Francis Makemie', *Journal of the Presbyterian Historical Society*, 4 (1907), 15–24, 72–90, 109–30, 165–97 · N. C. Landsman, 'Nation, migration, and the province in the first British empire: Scotland and the Americas, 1600–1800', *American Historical Review*, 104 (1999), 463–75 · L. P. Bowen, *The days of Makemie* (1885) · I. M. Page, *The life story of Rev. Francis Makemie* (1938) · C. Torrence, *Old Somerset on the eastern shore of Maryland* (1973) · G. Brydon, *Virginia's mother church* (1947) · L. des Cognets, ed., *English duplicates of lost Virginia records* (1958)

Wealth at death over 5000 acres of land; 33 slaves; at least two houses and one water and grist mill in Accomack County, Virginia: will, Schlenther, ed., *Life and writings*, 260–63; will of William Anderson, Nottingham, ed., *Wills and administrations*, 23; des Cognets, ed., *English duplicates*, 124

Makin [née Reginald], **Bathsua** (*b.* 1600, *d.* in or after **1675**), scholar and teacher, was the elder of two daughters of Henry Reginald (*d.* 1635), a schoolmaster, and his wife, whose name is unknown; her younger sister Ithamaria was baptized at St Dunstan and All Saints, Stepney, in 1601. In 1752, George Ballard apologized for having 'been able to learn very little' about 'Mrs. Makin (who corresponded in the learned languages with Mrs. Anna Maria à Schurman)', not realizing that he had misidentified her as John Pell's sister, rather than sister-in-law. That error confused accounts of her life until the 1960s when Vivian Salmon explained the mistake.

Bathsua Reginald's early years were spent at her father's school in St Mary Axe Street, London. Here she soon acquired a reputation for learning, having, according to Sir Simonds D'Ewes, a fellow pupil, 'exact knowledge in the Greek, Latin, and French tongues, with some insight also into the Hebrew and Syriack'. Indeed, claimed D'Ewes,

much more learning she had doubtless than her father, who was a mere pretender to it; and by the fame of her abilities,

Forma nihil, si Pulchra perit; sed rectoris alma
Divini species, non moritura viget
W.M. *sculpsit*

Bathsua Makin (*b.* 1600, *d.* in or after 1675), by William Marshall

which she had acquired from others, he got many scholars, which else would neither have repaired to him, nor have long staid with him.   (*Autobiography*, 63)

Bathsua was still only sixteen years old when father and daughter collaborated on two publications. In the first, *Ad Annam … reginam* (1616?), Bathsua demonstrated an original shorthand system, radiography, used in recording sermons, in illustrative plates; the surviving sheet from this pamphlet shows her name and the Lord's prayer written out in radiography. A second and far more ambitious project was Henry Reginald's publication of *Musa virginea* (1616), a collection of Bathsua's poems and epigraphs praising King James and members of his family in six languages (Latin, Greek, Hebrew, Spanish, French, and German). This evidently elicited an ungenerous joke: 'When a learned maid was presented to King James for an English rarity, because she could speake and rite pure Latine, Greeke, and Hebrew, the King ask'd "But can she spin?"' (J. Collett, 'Commonplace book', *Anecdotes and Traditions*, ed. W. Thoms, 1839, 129).

While the king showed little regard for the girl's learning, his physician George Eglisham published in 1619 *Duellum poeticum*, a Latin poem that praised 'Bathsua

Reginalda' as 'eruditiones eximiae virgini' ('an exceptionally learned maiden'). Eglisham may have initiated Bathsua's interest in medicine. Certainly she did practise healing: Samuel Hartlib noted in his *Ephemerides* (1650) that the London physician Aaron Gourdain had told him that she 'cured Mr Holsworth [probably Richard Holsworth, one of Charles I's chaplains] of the Palpitation of the heart' (Hartlib, 27/1/48B). According to Hartlib's notes, she was 'very well acquainted' with Carew Ralegh, son of Sir Walter, and had obtained from his mother 'all Sir W. Ralegh's receipts'—knowledge that Bathsua would have used in her work as a healer.

On 5 March 1622 Bathsua married Richard Makin (1599–1659), who was in the king's service, at St Andrew Undershaft, London. One of the guests was D'Ewes, who described being at 'my ould schoolemasters daughters wedding, being the greatest scholler, I thinke, of a woman in England … [T]here was much companye, whence arose that which is the life of a scholler, good discourse' (*Diary*, 68–9). During the late 1620s and the 1630s, Makin cared for her rapidly growing family. She gave birth to eight children: Anna (1623, *d.* 1627), Richard (1626, died in infancy), Anna (1628), Bathsua (1629), Mary (1629), Richard (1630), John (1633), and Henry (1642). Before the birth of her last child, however, she returned to the teaching profession that she had learned from her father.

In the autumn of 1640 the continental scholar Anna Maria van Schurman wrote two letters in Greek to Makin, and a letter in English to D'Ewes that mentions 'the most Learned Matron, Madam Bathsua Mekins' (Schurman, 126–7) as their mutual friend. In her letters to Makin, van Schurman discusses Makin's appointment as tutor to Charles I's daughter the Princess Elizabeth, whom she instructed in Greek, Latin, Hebrew, French, Italian, Spanish, and mathematics. It is not clear when her duties as royal tutor ended, although it must have been after 1644 when the princess was nine years old, since Makin subsequently wrote about the Princess Elizabeth's skills at that age. Makin would later ask the council of state 'for payment of the arrears of 40 £ a year granted her for life, for her attendance on the late King's children', but her petition was dismissed on 16 August 1655 (*CSP dom.*).

As an educator Makin was a firm advocate of the methods espoused by Johan Amos Comenius, whom she probably met in 1641 or 1642, when John Pell (who had married her sister Ithamaria in 1632), Samuel Hartlib, and other English intellectuals brought him to London. In addition to the Princess Elizabeth, she also taught Lucy Davies, later Lucy Hastings, countess of Huntingdon, and her children, including Lady Elizabeth Hastings (later Lady Elizabeth Langham) and (for instance, in 1662) Theophilus Hastings, seventh earl of Huntingdon, and later wrote elegies on Lady Elizabeth, who died in 1664, and on Lord Henry Hastings, who died in 1649. Her other pupils may have included the daughters of Nicholas Love, and the Hebraist Elizabeth Fisher (later Elizabeth Bland).

Beyond her tutorial activities, little is known about Bathsua Makin's life during the 1650s and 1660s. In 1652 she wrote a friendly letter to John Pell asking for information about a comet. Two years later he advised her about renting a house while Richard Makin was away. By 1655, however, John Pell complained that his wife Ithamaria was spending too much time with her sister Bathsua, 'a woman of great acquaintance and no small impatience. She will not sticke to raile at me and you, where ever she comes' (BL, Add. MS 4280.238). None the less, Pell's letters a year later make it clear that Ithamaria and Bathsua continued to see one another. In 1659 Richard Makin was buried in St Andrew's, Holborn, while Ithamaria Pell died two years later.

By the 1670s Makin had embarked on two new projects. She joined Mark Lewis, author of a number of textbooks, who ran a private school for boys in Tottenham. With his help, she opened 'a school for gentlewomen at Tottenham, High Cross, within four miles of London in the road to Ware', described in *An Essay to Revive the Antient Education of Gentlewomen* (1673). Designed to recruit students and set down her philosophy of education, this essay comprises a lively and amusing defence of women, a catalogue of learned women throughout history, an acerbic attack on the traditional humanist text Lily's *Grammar*, and an enthusiastic endorsement of texts by Comenius. It is likely to have influenced Mary Astell and is certainly the first essay by an Englishwoman defending women and their abilities in the classroom.

The last extant letter that Makin wrote was to the physician Baldwin Hamey in November 1675, thanking him for some unspecified favour. The letter shows that her intellect was unimpaired, for she expresses herself in English, Latin, Greek, and a bit of Hebrew. At this date she was living in Long Acre, London; there is no known record of her subsequent life, death, or burial.   FRANCES TEAGUE

Sources F. Teague, *Bathsua Makin, woman of learning* (1998) · J. Brink, 'Bathsua Reginald Makin: "most learned matron"', *Huntington Library Quarterly*, 54 (1991), 313–27 · V. Salmon, 'The family of Ithamaria Reynolds Pell', *Pelliana*, new ser., 1 (1965), 1–24 · V. Salmon, 'Bathsua Makin: a pioneer linguist and feminist in seventeenth-century England', *Neuere Forschungen zur Wortbildung und Historiographie der Linguistik: Festgabe für Herbert E. Brekle zum 50. Geburtstag*, ed. B. Asbach-Schnitker and J. Rogenhofer (1987), 303–18 · *CSP dom.*, 1649–61 · *The autobiography and correspondence of Sir Simonds D'Ewes*, ed. J. O. Halliwell, 2 vols. (1845) · *The diary of Sir Simonds D'Ewes, 1622–1624: journal d'un étudiant Londonien*, ed. E. Bourcier (Paris, 1974) · S. Hartlib, *Ephemerides* (1650) · correspondence of John Pell, BL, Add. MSS 4223, 4278–4281, 4365, 4384, 4397, 4403, 4418–4431 · A. M. van Schurman, *Nobiliss. virginis Annae Mariae a Schurman opuscula Hebraea, Graeca, Latina, Gallica, prosaica & metrica* (1749) · B. Makin, *An essay to revive the antient education of gentlewomen* (1673); facs. edn with introduction by P. L. Barbour (1980) · G. Ballard, *Memoirs of several ladies of Great Britain* (1752) · M. Hobbs, 'Drayton's "most dearely-loved friend Henery Reynolds Esq"', *Review of English Studies*, new ser., 25 (1973), 414–28

Archives Hunt. L., letters and poems to Lucy, countess of Huntingdon, MSS HA 8799, M716; HA 8800; HA literature box 1.1; HAF 18.32

Likenesses J. Brand, pen-and-ink drawing, 1791, NPG · W. Marshall, line engraving, BM, NPG [*see illus.*]

Makins, Roger Mellor, first Baron Sherfield (1904–1996), diplomatist and public servant, was born on 3 February 1904 at 15 Orsett Terrace, London, the oldest of three sons

Roger Mellor Makins, first Baron Sherfield (1904–1996), by Walter Bird, 1962

of Brigadier-General Sir Ernest Makins (1869–1959), army officer and Conservative MP for Knutsford from 1922 to 1945, and his wife, Maria Florence (d. 1972), third of four daughters of Sir James Robert Mellor (1839–1926) of Eastgate, Tenterden, Kent, master of the crown office and registrar of the court of criminal appeal. His mother was an accomplished violinist from a dynasty of Liverpudlian lawyers. The elder of his two brothers, Guy Henry (b. 1906), died following an accident in 1923; the younger, Geoffrey Ernest (b. 1915), was killed in action in Normandy in 1944.

Education and early life After being farmed out to a series of governesses and sergeant-majors by his itinerant parents—his father was at this time a regular officer in the Royal Dragoons—Makins enjoyed a short reign at West Downs, Winchester (1914–17), and then a slightly less glorious one at Winchester College itself (1917–22). From there, as expected, he went up to Oxford—not the way of the true Wykehamist, to New College, but to clubbable Christ Church, to read modern history, which he did, fiercely, during the vacations, there being too many distractions of the hunting, shooting, and socializing variety during the terms. The system worked: he was awarded a congratulatory first (1925). His entire career, one might say, was a congratulatory first. That same year he was elected a prize fellow of All Souls, together with his tutorial partner, A. L. Rowse, historian and amateur of cats and cattiness. At twenty-one, Makins said that he had never known such perfect satisfaction. A lifetime later it was

reprised. At eighty-two, he was elected a fellow of the Royal Society (1986), a signal honour for a non-scientist.

Between elections Makins had a reputation to make. His fellowship prescribed two years in college. He devoted the time to reading for the bar. No sooner was he called than he decided it was not the career for him, and reverted to his original idea of trying for the Foreign Office, his contact with the law and the legal profession 'as brief as it was briefless' (unpublished memoirs). He sat the examinations in 1928. Inevitably, perhaps, he passed first, notwithstanding a certain lack of fluency in French. (Behind him was John Cairncross, later 'the fifth man' among the Cambridge spies.) As top of the list, he had the choice of joining the office without further language study, or taking up a really difficult one like Russian or Chinese. Without hesitation he chose the first option. He was assigned to the American department as a probationary third secretary, in October 1928, and in time-honoured fashion was told to look after Latin America.

Anglo-American relations So began a career of leaps and bounds in the service of his country. Soon Makins was posted across the Atlantic. There he found his second home. He served in Washington as third secretary from April 1931 to May 1934 (being promoted second secretary in October 1933), as minister from January 1945 to February 1947, and finally as ambassador from December 1952 to October 1956. He was also in Oslo, from May to September 1934; at the Foreign Office, being promoted first secretary in September 1939 and counsellor in August 1940; on the staff of the minister resident in west Africa, from July to December 1942; as assistant to the minister resident at allied forces headquarters, Mediterranean command, from January 1943 to September 1944; and again at the Foreign Office, as assistant and then from April 1948 deputy under-secretary of state. His recurrence in Washington sealed his influence and oriented his ambition; for it was there that he met and, on 30 April 1934, married his partner in life, Alice Brooks Davis (1908–1985), eldest of the three daughters of the Hon. Dwight Filey Davis, governor-general of the Federal Reserve Bank and of the Philippines, secretary for war in President Coolidge's administration, and donor of the Davis cup. It was a fortunate partnership. They were well matched, in temperament as in tennis (in golf she had the better of him). Thirty years later, in 1964, Makins (having been made CMG in 1944, KCMG in 1949, KCB in 1953, GCMG in 1955, and GCB in 1960) was made a hereditary peer. The question of a title arose. His account is characteristic, and quietly eloquent of this particular special relationship:

> For some reason which I could not well explain—perhaps euphony—I did not like the sound of Lord Makins, and rationalized it by pointing out that there were too many Lady Makins … It would avoid confusion if I were to take a territorial title. Sherfield was a good old English place name to which I had a better claim than anyone else. For some reason equally difficult to explain, Alice was against a change of name. She said she had changed her name twice and did not want to do it again. But I think it was an expression of her American origins and she had an unconscious prejudice against titles and indeed the idea of an hereditary

aristocracy. She was always critical of pretensions of any kind, and one of the things I am most grateful for is that as I climbed the ladder she never let me get above myself. Anyway, we had quite a sharp argument about it … Alice often returned to this grievance. She claimed that I would be confused with Lord Sheffield, which was true up to a point … She also claimed that nobody would know who Lord Sherfield was—I replied that all the people who mattered to us would know, and that I intended to establish the identity of Lord Sherfield as clearly as that of Sir Roger Makins. (We both had a point there.) (unpublished note)

They made up by choosing the supporters for his coat of arms: a British lion differenced with an atomic symbol on one side, and—to Alice's delight—an American bald eagle differenced with a tennis racket on the other.

There was a history to the atomic symbol, and a sobriquet Makins did not care for: Mr Atom. As minister in the Washington embassy, given free rein by the enervative Ambassador Inverchapel, it fell to Makins to represent British interests in the precarious Anglo-American atomic diplomacy of the post-Hiroshima period. His task was to secure Britain's position, if not by fully-fledged collaboration on the wartime model, then by mutual consultation and appropriate allocation of the vital ingredient, uranium: a tall order. By 1947 the situation was difficult verging on desperate. In 1943 Churchill and Roosevelt had signed an agreement not to use the bomb against third parties without each other's consent (ostensibly an absolute veto), and in 1944 an *aide-mémoire* on full collaboration for both military and commercial purposes after the war. But the fairytale promise of these arrangements never materialized. The perfunctory way in which British consent was requested for the dropping of the bomb in 1945 spoke of the letter rather than the spirit of the original agreement. The passage through the US congress of the notorious McMahon Act in 1946 formally severed the main arteries of atomic information exchange, the vital source of any genuine consultation. After Hiroshima, the constitutional authority of the president and commander-in-chief would not be compromised by written commitments to allies, however special the relationship. Furthermore, the British were clearly (and rightly) worried about the 'coupling' of this issue to the delicate matter of economic assistance from the Americans, and indeed to Anglo-American relations as a whole.

On the other hand Britain was not entirely without cards to play. Apart from her own geostrategic position—Orwell's Airstrip One—there was the submerged issue of access to resources of various kinds, animal and mineral. A much-increased supply of uranium was indispensable to the expansionary US atomic weapons project. Both London and Washington fancied that the key to this supply was held by the British. Certain British scientists were held to be almost irreplaceable in the United States. At the first US post-war bomb test at Bikini in the Pacific, Ernest Titterton, instrumentation group leader at Los Alamos as late as 1947, gave the countdown and detonation order; and William Penney, whose presence had been specially requested for the purpose, played a leading part in the blast measurement and subsequent analysis. Penney

remained *persona gratissima* in Washington throughout the period, as did the unassuming Nobel laureate James Chadwick. It was not all jam and kippers, as Chadwick once remarked, but it was not negligible.

None the less, in 1948, after much transatlantic tergiversation, the so-called *modus vivendi* summarily removed the requirement for consent, made no offer to consult, and restored only limited technical atomic information exchange in return. These were the American terms. The free flow of information would take another ten years: a long sentence, and long-deferred gratification for Mr Atom. The *modus vivendi*, however, was a difficult child. Makins's handling of the negotiations has been variously assessed. No one doubts their exacting nature; but a number of authorities, including the magisterial Margaret Gowing, have suggested that Britain could have done better. Makins himself thought otherwise, resolutely maintaining to his dying day that it was 'the best agreement that could have been secured at the time' (unpublished memoirs)—a defensive construction, and in the final analysis perhaps an insufficiently searching one.

Mandarin At the time, there was no thought of reproof or reproach. Makins had returned to London in an almost impregnable position at the heart of the machine, as assistant and soon deputy under-secretary at the Foreign Office, roaming freely through the jungle of economic and atomic policy making—the critical and the sub-critical, as one might say. This was a daunting brief. It did not daunt Makins. 'He radiated humour, energy and good sense. Bounding from one meeting to the other, he seemed to us in the Office to be plural rather than singular' (A. M. Browne, quoted in Carrington, memorial service address). Cast as the poor relation with ideas above her station—'chief mendicant', in R. W. B. Clarke's biting phrase (Kelly, 114)—Britain had frustratingly little room for manoeuvre. Steering the policy of the poor relation was the redoubtable Ernest Bevin. Whispering loudly in his ear was Roger Makins. In every sense, the whisper carried. Makins was one of the select few: a well-honed and for the most part well-heeled band of brothers who caballed behind the throne in the national interest. Another was the Treasury official Robert Hall. An extract from his diary of 1949 reveals, as Makins himself justly noted, 'the extent and confidence with which we officials were able in this period to influence and indeed manage appointments and policy':

OSF [Franks], RM [Makins], EP [Edwin Plowden] and I had some chat about bodies and whether to move Hall-Patch from Paris. I should be sorry if this had to be done, but it is very bad that he does not get on with Harriman. We have decided that the next steps at home are to cut expenditure and wake up people on the Board of Trade doing the dollar export work. Everyone on the UK talks in Washington agreed that Holmes was a disaster and ought to be shifted, and also everyone except the Ministers that Harold Wilson is no good, ought if possible to be shifted from the Board of Trade, and certainly ought not to succeed Stafford Cripps [as chancellor of the exchequer]. If any young one is to do it it should be Gaitskell!! (unpublished memoirs)

Roger Makins was at the centre of that web of influence.

There can be little doubt that he did much to keep the ship of state afloat during those years of economic reconstruction and diplomatic prestidigitation. Bevin was a heroic figure—not least to his own officials—but as illness and exhaustion took hold he, like Macmillan, became increasingly reliant on the rigorous Roger Makins, whose prudent counsel seemed so difficult to ignore. 'Dominant, but not domineering', in Jeremy Morse's felicitous apposition (memorial service address), Makins was a hard man to gainsay.

This prudence manifested itself in Makins's assessment of personalities and eventualities alike. On the making of Macmillan during the war: 'On his record to date, nobody suspected that [he] had the remarkable diplomatic talents, the political vision and judgement, the powers of persuasion, and the courage to disregard instructions, which he displayed in north Africa, in Italy and in Greece' (unpublished memoirs). On John Foster Dulles as secretary of state:

> My main problem was that he travelled a great deal and I never quite knew what had passed in his dealings with Anthony Eden, Selwyn Lloyd and others … Reports were sent, of course, but it is only if one is actually on the spot that it is possible to know what nods or winks have been exchanged.   (ibid.)

Less happily, on diplomatic golf:

> I played from time to time with the Vice-President, Richard Nixon … I had always been a very bad golfer (indeed, I had given up the game, as I thought, for good). Dick Nixon was equally bad. We formed a bond of misery, and a friendship developed which endured until he was driven from the White House.   (ibid.)

'Driven' may give pause to those brought up on dirty tricks and deleted expletives. Makins lived very much in the here and now, but he was in certain respects an official of the old school. Good order matched good work. Security outbid futurity. The purposive crowded the imaginative. 'He was above all a solver of problems' (Carrington, memorial service address). Expatiating on the difference between a 'realistic' and a 'romantic' view of the world— the prospects for a European Community, for example— there was no mistaking his own affiliation. The realism of the realists was another matter. In 1950 Makins adamantly opposed British participation in the Schuman plan for the first European Community, a coal and steel pool, arguing that 'it let the Americans off the hook'—the hook of continuing engagement in Europe. 'We are not ready', he informed Etienne Hirsch, 'and you will not succeed' (Charlton, 93, 122, 151): the historic misjudgement of a generation of British policy makers.

Suez and after   Deceived by his own masters over Suez in 1956—ambassadors were neither consulted nor informed—on his return to London Makins was astonished to learn at the eleventh hour of the Anglo-French collusion. 'It had never occurred to me the British government would consider taking such action without full American support. I realised immediately that there would be a disaster and I began mentally to prepare

myself for it' (unpublished memoirs). It was a characteristic response. The operation was impracticable. The collusion was deplorable, no doubt, but that was a secondary issue. What mattered was to anticipate the consequences. Remediation, not resignation, was uppermost in his mind. When Anthony Nutting and Edward Boyle resigned, at a moment of high anxiety for the government, Makins said to Boyle, 'privately, I do not blame you; you realise what has happened', and returned to the planning of emergency measures by the Treasury. Privately, also, he gave himself partial credit for the belated 'unblinkering' of the hawkish Harold Macmillan (unpublished memoirs). As Jeremy Morse acutely observed, 'his mind and style were marked by consistency and immediacy' (memorial address). And potency.

After a rather frustrating interlude as joint permanent secretary of the Treasury from 1956 to 1959, alongside Sir Norman Brook—appointed by Macmillan but abandoned to the vagaries of Selwyn Lloyd and the hostilities of the mandarinate—Makins concluded his official service as chairman of the UK Atomic Energy Authority (1960–64), in which post his diplomatic skills were frequently (and successfully) called upon to resolve clashes of personality and of interest within the nuclear industry. He was unready for retirement. In afterlife, as he said, he revelled in a variety of activities in the City, chairing everything from Hill, Samuel (1966–70) to Wells Fargo (1972–84), and in the service of what might be called the public awareness of science and technology, culminating in a notable stint as chairman of the House of Lords select committee on science and technology (1984–7)—a body, and an idea, whose very existence owed much to his inspiration. Makins was the very model of the inquisitive octogenarian.

Character and assessment   Like his contemporary Oliver Franks, with whom he was, as he remarked, 'very much on the same wavelength' (unpublished memoirs), Makins cast a long and impressive shadow in the committees of influence off the corridors of power. If the public pinnacle of his career was as ambassador in Washington, in truth he was a prime mover in the inner circles of the Anglo-Saxons throughout the momentous middle decades of the twentieth century. But it was not only the length and breadth of his career: the pace of his life was breathtaking. Makins was congenitally formidable. The *New York Times* described him as looking like an affable hawk. Colleagues in the Foreign Office plumped for an amiable vulture. More prejudicial accounts move from the avian to the simian. Six feet four inches tall, with a frame and a voice and a zest to match, Makins was an imposing presence. His attack left the lesser primates awestruck and overwhelmed. In wartime Algiers, Harold Macmillan wondered whether he could live up to the standards set by his architectonic assistant:

> It is naturally a great loss—even a great grief—to lose Roger. He has been a most loyal supporter in all my difficulties and a most agreeable companion and friend. I think it is tribute to both of us that we have lived together for nearly two years like subalterns in a company mess without quarrelling (and Roger's temperament is more highly strung than mine). The

inspiring thing about him is his standard of work. He is *never* satisfied with the second best. And this goes through the office and inspires the others.

[His successor] will, I think, be agreeable and efficient. But he has not that rapier-like brain combined with that almost monastic devotion to duty which makes Roger such a unique figure in the public service.   (diary, 29 Sept 1944, in H. Macmillan, *The Blast of War*, 1967, 552–3)

Devotion to duty did not preclude a voracious sociability. ('The Makins of a good party' was an old joke on the diplomatic cocktail circuit. And, in a crowded room, 'Meet you at the British Ambassador.') Makins relished the pleasure of encounter. His charm too was formidable. Unlike Franks, he enjoyed talking, but above all he enjoyed dancing. As a ballroom dancer he was a sensation. In the 1950s he waltzed staid Washington off its feet. Forty years later he was still at it, foxtrotting and quickstepping with the best of them, into the early hours, delighted, at his ninetieth birthday ball. The secret of successful diplomacy, he maintained, was stamina. Stamina was Makins's middle name. Sir Edward Bridges, a paragon public servant, once headed both the Treasury and the civil service. He was asked how he managed it. 'I don't,' Bridges replied. 'I just catch one ball in four' (Hennessy, 144). Makins did better than that. In the arena he was a prodigious all-rounder. In reflection, he might have conceded something to a Monnet or a Spaak or even a Franks. In action, turbo-charged action, he had the measure of them all.

Makins died at the age of ninety-two, at the Hampshire Clinic, Basing Road, Basingstoke, Hampshire, on 9 November 1996, of cancer and heart failure. His wife having predeceased him in 1985, he was survived by the six children of their marriage: twins Mary (Mollie) and Cynthia (*b.* 1935), Virginia (*b.* 1939), Christopher (*b.* 1942), Patricia (*b.* 1946), and Dwight (*b.* 1951). Christopher—like his father a prize fellow of All Souls college—succeeded him as second Baron Sherfield. A memorial service was held at All Souls on 1 March 1997, and another at St Margaret by Westminster Abbey, on 6 March.   ALEX DANCHEV

Sources R. Makins, memoirs, Bodl. Oxf., MSS Sherfield · J. Edwards, 'Roger Makins', *British officials and British foreign policy*, ed. J. Zametica (1990), 8–38 · S. Kelly, '"A very considerable and largely unsung success": Sir Roger Makins' Washington embassy', *Twentieth-century Anglo-American relations*, ed. J. Hollowell (2001), 124–42 · memorial service address by Sir P. Ramsbotham, Sir J. Morse, and Lord Carrington, 1997 · Lord Selborne, *Memoirs FRS*, 44 (1998), 267–78 · Lord Sherfield, 'Britain's nuclear story', *Round Table*, 258 (1975), 193–204 · M. Charlton, *The price of victory* (1983) · private information (2004) [family papers] · M. Gowing and L. Arnold, *Independence and deterrence: Britain and atomic energy, 1945–1952*, 1 (1974) · P. Hennessy, *Whitehall* (1989) · *The Times* (11 Nov 1996) · *The Independent* (11 Nov 1996) · *Daily Telegraph* (11 Nov 1996) · *WWW* [forthcoming] · Burke, *Peerage* · b. cert. · d. cert.

Archives BLPES, interview · Bodl. Oxf., papers · priv. coll., MSS PRO, private office papers, FO 800/614-26 | Bodl. Oxf., Cherwell MSS · Bodl. Oxf., Macmillan MSS · Bodl. Oxf., Sherfield MSS · ICL, corresp. with Lord Jackson · Nuffield Oxf., corresp. with Lord Cherwell · PRO, Foreign Office and Treasury MSS, FO 371, FO 800 · U. Birm. L., Avon MSS

Likenesses W. Bird, photograph, 1962, NPG [*see illus.*] · photograph, repro. in *Memoirs FRS*, 266 · photograph, repro. in *The Times* · photograph, repro. in *Daily Telegraph* · photograph, repro. in *The Independent* · photographs, priv. coll.

Wealth at death £16,036,825: probate, 13 March 1997, *CGPLA Eng. & Wales*

Makkarell, Matthew. *See* Mackarell, Matthew (d. 1537).

Makoni, Mutota (*c.*1835–1896), anti-colonial warrior, is believed to have been born in the Maungwe region, later overlapping with the Makoni district, some 50 miles north-west of Mutare in Mashonaland. Centred on a succession of stone-built villages, whose complex fortifications impressed the British hunter Frederick Courtney Selous, the Makoni dynasty traced its ancestry back to the early 1600s. Mutota Makoni came to the title in 1889, when he succeeded Mukuru Makoni. No detail has survived either about his parents or of any marriage. He is known to have had at least two elder brothers, the elder of whom he poisoned. The other, Ndafunya, plotted against him at every turn, to the extent of siding with the white settlers during the Shona rising of 1896–7. One of Makoni's five acknowledged sons was later enrolled in the Mashonaland native contingent, only to be killed in June 1897 by Shona insurgents.

Regarded as one of the most powerful chiefs in eastern Mashonaland, Makoni was never reconciled to colonial rule. His policies were shaped, however, by the need to bolster his own position against disaffected sections of his followers, his regional rival Mutasa of Manyika, and the sporadic enforcement of 'chata ro', that is, chartered company law and order as understood by Cecil Rhodes's British South Africa Company (BSAC) administration in Fort Salisbury. Towards the end of November 1890 Makoni agreed to fly the Portuguese flag, despite having earlier granted a concession to one of Rhodes's agents, in this way hoping to make good his independence from both, even as he played one against the other. In June 1892 he received the first of several warnings that as neighbouring peoples were now under the BSAC's protection, 'raids and disturbances' would no longer be tolerated. Still more ominous was the threat posed by white farmers taking up land grants in the district. Complaints of trespass and stock theft by Makoni's men multiplied in the course of 1894 and 1895. As far as Makoni was concerned, the fault lay squarely with the white settlers, 'as his land had been given away to strangers up to his very kraal [village]' (Thomson, 106). Attempts by BSAC to impose a hut tax were resisted at every turn. In 1894 an African policeman was killed in Makoni's territory and when the local tax collector seized a number of Makoni's cattle at the beginning of June 1896 they were promptly snatched back.

By this time the Ndebele (Matabele) rising had been under way for several months and on 16 June 1896 the Shona also rose up against the white population. But this was an extremely patchy affair whose uneven spread is best understood as a series of sometimes disconnected local uprisings rather than one co-ordinated rising. Initially Makoni remained aloof. With one eye on Mutasa, he contented himself with expelling native department functionaries, so-called 'messengers', from his district. Some of Makoni's followers were less restrained, however, and murdered three white traders, an act which the authorities in Salisbury immediately attributed to his orders. They also mistakenly blamed him for an attack on a party of settlers at Headlands. Convinced of Makoni's guilt and desperate to reopen communications between Salisbury and Umtali (Mutare), the BSAC singled him out for swift retribution. Following an inconclusive clash in July between his troops and those of Makoni, Colonel E. A. H. Alderson, commander of the imperial Mashonaland field force, instructed Major C. N. Watts and 180 soldiers to invest the cluster of caves near Gwendingwi, north-east Mashonaland, where Makoni and several hundred of his followers, including women and children, were holding out. On 3 September, after four days of fighting, during which dynamite was tossed into the caves to terrible effect, Makoni either surrendered on the promise of a fair trial or was captured, depending on whose testimony is believed.

Watts certainly appeared to be in no doubt that Makoni had been captured. The next day he assembled a field court martial to try him. Makoni was found guilty of armed rebellion and was sentenced to be shot. Unable to spare the men to escort the prisoner to Salisbury, and worried that delay would facilitate a rescue attempt by those of Makoni's followers still at large, Watts took it upon himself to have the sentence carried out immediately. At noon on 4 September 1896 Makoni

> was placed with his back to a corn-bin, on the edge of the precipice on which his kraal stood, and died with a courage and dignity that extorted an unwilling admiration from all who were present … 'Now', he said, 'you shall see how a Makoni can die'. (Thomson, 110)

On hearing what had happened, the high commissioner, Lord Rosmead, had Watts placed under open arrest, but subsequently determined that although the court martial had been illegal, Watts had acted in good faith, 'in the belief that the military situation made his action necessary' (Keppel-Jones, 494). The disreputable circumstances of Makoni's death had entirely predictable consequences. Far from encouraging other 'rebel' Shona rulers to surrender, Makoni's salutary fate stiffened their resolve to fight to the bitter end. IAN PHIMISTER

Sources M. P. Horn, '"Chimurenga", 1896–1897: a revisionist study', MA diss., Rhodes University, 1986 · H. C. Thomson, *Rhodesia and its government* (1898) · D. N. Beach, *War and politics in Zimbabwe, 1840–1900* (1986) · D. N. Beach, *A Zimbabwean past* (1994) · D. N. Beach, *The Shona and Zimbabwe* (Gweru, 1980) · E. A. H. Alderson, *With the mounted infantry and the Mashonaland field force, 1896* (1898) · C. Harding, *Far bugles* (1933) · A. Keppel-Jones, *Rhodes and Rhodesia: the white conquest of Zimbabwe, 1884–1902* (1983) · R. E. Reid, 'The capture of Chief Makoni', *NADA* (1955), no. 32 · D. P. Abraham, 'The principality of Maungwe: its history and traditions', *NADA* (1951), no. 28 · T. O. Ranger, *Revolt in Southern Rhodesia, 1896–1897: a study in African resistance* (1967) · F. C. Selous, *Travel and adventure in south-east Africa* (1893)
Archives National Archives of Zimbabwe, Harare, T. Dhlamini papers, MSS Dh 1/1/1–2
Likenesses caricature, repro. in *Bulawayo Sketch* (12 Sept 1896)

Makonnen, Ras Tomasa [*formerly* George Thomas Griffith] (*c.*1900–1983), political activist, was born George Thomas Griffith in British Guiana. He was educated there, in the United States, where he attended the University of Texas and Cornell University, and in Denmark, where he enrolled at the Royal Copenhagen Agricultural College to study agriculture and the philosophy of the co-operative movement. Extradited from Denmark for alleging that the country's exports were aiding the Italian invasion of Abyssinia (Ethiopia), he settled in Britain. In London, now calling himself Ras Tomasa Makonnen, and claiming Ethiopian ancestry, he began to work with anti-imperialists such as C. L. R. James and George Padmore (Malcolm Nurse). He was a founder member and the secretary of the Pan-African Federation, formed in 1936 to bring together representatives of the whole of Africa and the Caribbean. He was also appointed executive and publicity secretary of the International African Service Bureau (IASB), which worked to achieve 'full economic, political and racial equality and self-determination'. Makonnen organized protest marches and demonstrations, aided delegates from the colonies, corresponded with the Colonial Office and other government departments, and maintained liaison with other black organizations. He and other IASB members addressed meetings around the country and regularly harangued the crowds at Speakers' Corner in London's Hyde Park on Sundays. The bureau published a monthly paper, *Africa and the World*, in 1937; lack of funds led to its demise and also in 1939 to that of its successor, *International African Opinion*, which was banned from most colonies. Nevertheless, the treasurer of the IASB, Robert Broadhurst, managed to raise sufficient funds to continue publishing pamphlets. The IASB office, run by Makonnen, became a haven for anti-imperialists.

About 1938 Makonnen moved to Manchester, where he was active in the Labour Party and the co-operative movement, and worked with the local black organizations. He opened a restaurant, then another, then a bookshop, and used his profits to support the anti-imperialist cause and to aid black organizations. The Pan-African Federation, re-formed in 1944, had its office on his premises. Makonnen was again secretary, and thus played a major role in convening the sixth Pan-African Congress in Manchester in July 1945, which was attended by Africans and West Indians, black Britons, and African Americans. Makonnen spoke on the situation in Ethiopia, and attacked British policies which, he claimed, were to dismember the ancient kingdom.

After the Second World War, Makonnen set up the Panaf Service, 'importers and exporters, publishers, booksellers, printers and manufacturers' representative'. He maintained the Pan-African Federation's political activism, which now included an increasing participation in countering the deterioration of the racial situation in Britain. He also continued his involvement with Ethiopian causes. In 1947 he returned to publishing: he began a monthly journal, *Pan-Africa*, under the editorship of Dinah Stock. His political colleagues Padmore, Jomo Kenyatta, and Kwame Nkrumah were among the associate editors. This journal, too, was soon banned in the colonies, and had to be discontinued in 1948. How long the news releases published alongside the journal survived is not known.

In 1957 Makonnen decided to follow his friend Padmore to independent Ghana. He served Nkrumah as director of the African Affairs Centre in Accra, the training centre for 'freedom fighters', and lectured there. The Bureau of African Affairs under Padmore's leadership published the *Bulletin of African Affairs*, which Makonnen helped to edit. In 1958, when Nkrumah called the All African Peoples' Conference, Makonnen helped to set up its secretariat and was a member of its finance committee. He was also head of the national press set up by Nkrumah, the Guinea Press. Nkrumah appointed him as one of the Ghanaian emissaries to tour African states in preparation for the founding conference of the Organization of African Unity in 1963, which he attended. He also served on the Ghana–British Guiana Committee. However, it seems that the following year Makonnen quarrelled with Nkrumah, perhaps about the pervasive corruption in the administration which he later recorded in his autobiography, *Pan-Africanism from Within* (1973). This, coupled with the hostility to 'outsiders' in leadership positions which was becoming increasingly overt in Ghana, resulted in Makonnen being demoted initially to the post of director of hotels and tourism, and then to the directorship of state bakeries.

After the fall of Nkrumah, Makonnen was imprisoned; an international protest resulted in his release and settlement in Kenya, where Kenyatta was now president. He wrote to Nkrumah, then in exile in Conakry, saying that he would like to join him. Nkrumah's response has not been preserved, but Makonnen remained in Kenya until his death. There his attempts to set up a 'reception and instruction centre … offering a forum of criticism and discussion of the African present' did not materialize, perhaps owing to lack of support from the president. Makonnen's last known political contribution was his attendance at the Pan-African Congress in Dar es Salaam in 1974.

Makonnen was married twice; the second marriage took place in Ghana. He died in Kenya on 16 December 1983, and was survived by children of both marriages.

MARIKA SHERWOOD

Sources R. Makonnen, *Pan-Africanism from within*, ed. K. King (1973) · *West Africa* · H. Adi and M. Sherwood, *The 1945 Pan-African Congress revisited* (1995) · private information (2004) [daughter]
Likenesses photographs, priv. coll.
Wealth at death possibly landholdings in Kenya: private information

Malachy [St Malachy, Máel Máedoc Ua Morgair] (1094/5–1148), archbishop of Armagh, was born into an established ecclesiastical family in either 1094 or 1095, the son of Múgrón (d. 1102), *fer léiginn* (lector) of Armagh.

Early life Malachy (as he is usually known, rather than by his Irish name, Máel Máedoc Ua Morgair) trained as a cleric at Armagh, where he came under the influence of an ascetic teacher, Imar Ua hÁedacháin, who was attached to the *recles*, the church of the monastic community of St Peter and St Paul, Armagh, and who died in Rome in 1134. Notwithstanding the canonical requirements for ordination, he was ordained deacon before the age of twenty-

five and priest before the age of thirty by Cellach (Celsus), archbishop of Armagh. According to Malachy's biographer, Bernard of Clairvaux, Cellach made him his *vices*, or deputy, in which role he showed himself zealous in the cause of reform, instituting the customs of the holy Roman church, especially canonical hours, and the sacraments of confession, confirmation, and marriage at Armagh. So as to ensure that what he taught conformed with the practice of the universal church, Malachy went to Lismore to place himself under the ecclesiastical discipline of Máel Isú (Malchus) Ua hAinmire, bishop of Waterford, who had been trained as a monk at Winchester.

Head of Bangor and bishop of Connor In 1123 Óengus Ua Gormáin, *comarba Comgaill* (that is, head of the church of Bangor) and bishop of Ulaid, died at Lismore. This appears to have occasioned Malachy's recall by those who had sent him there; at the command of Imar, he took ten brethren with him to inaugurate his independent career as a church reformer by reviving conventual life at the secularized monastic site of Bangor, although he faced opposition from locally entrenched interests. Indeed, he failed to gain possession of the landed estates, contenting himself with the monastic site alone, where he erected a new wooden church, subsequently to be rebuilt in stone, despite local opponents voicing the argument *Scoti sumus, non Galli*—'We are Irishmen, not French' (*Sancti Bernardi opera*, 3.365). Bernard of Clairvaux indicates that Malachy had a familial connection with Bangor via his *avunculus*, described as a rich and powerful man, who was prepared to cede Bangor to him. It is not certain whether *avunculus* should be interpreted in the late Latin sense of maternal rather than paternal uncle. Bernard's allusions to events at Bangor are in fact so generalized that it is difficult to reconstruct the circumstances of Malachy's accession. In 1131 the death was recorded of Muirchertach Ua hInnrechtaig, head of the church of Bangor. It is not possible to prove that Muirchertach was related to Malachy; it is equally possible that Malachy was related to Óengus Ua Gormáin. Malachy appears to have taken possession of no more than the old conventual site, and Muirchertach may have remained as lay controller of the Bangor estates until his death.

In addition to his role as head of a reformed monastic community at Bangor, in 1124 Malachy was consecrated by Cellach as bishop for the see of Connor, though he may have remained resident at Bangor. In 1127, according to Bernard of Clairvaux, an attack by an unnamed northern king forced him into exile. The attack may be related to the killings in that year of Áed (Niall) Mac Duinnsléibe and Eochaid Ua Mathgamna, kings of Ulaid, and the subsequent raiding in Ulaid by a son of Mac Lochlainn, king of Cenél nEógain. Malachy sought refuge in Munster, and probably once again at Lismore, where he encountered Cormac Mac Carthaig, temporarily exiled king of Munster, whom he persuaded to return to the kingship, and with whom he was to collaborate in promoting church reform. Cormac's beneficence enabled Malachy to construct within his kingdom the monastery of 'Ibracense' (unidentified).

The archbishopric of Armagh In 1129 Archbishop Cellach, while staying at Ardpatrick, Limerick, and realizing that he was close to death, made what was effectively a testament (*quasi testamentum*) designating Malachy as his successor, enjoining especially on the kings of Munster that his wish be respected. Cellach was buried at Lismore on 4 April 1129; and the very next day Muirchertach Mac Domnaill, like Cellach a member of the hereditary secularized ecclesiastical dynasty of Uí Sínaig which had maintained an almost two-hundred-year monopoly of ecclesiastical offices at Armagh, was installed in the latter city. Three years after Cellach's death, in 1132, on the urgings of Máel Isú, bishop of Waterford, and Gilbert, bishop of Limerick and native papal legate, who had convened the bishops and rulers of the land, Malachy was consecrated for Armagh on the understanding, according to Bernard of Clairvaux, that he would be allowed to resign the see when the Uí Sínaig monopoly had been broken. In 1133 a circuit of Cenél nEógain and collection of tribute by Muirchertach as head of the church of Armagh is recorded, indicating whence Muirchertach derived his main support.

For two years Malachy exercised his episcopal functions without gaining entry to Armagh city, and it was not until 1134, following Muirchertach's death, that he attempted to take possession of the insignia and temporalities of the church of Armagh, which, as Bernard of Clairvaux remarked, was vital to securing recognition as archbishop of Armagh from a 'foolish and unwise people' (*Sancti Bernardi opera*, 3.334). His installation at Armagh was opposed by the Cenél nEógain, but he had the support of Donnchad Ua Cerbaill, king of Airgialla. Another Uí Sínaig candidate, Maíle Niall mac Áeda meic Ísu (*d.* 1139), a brother of Cellach, immediately replaced Muirchertach, attempted to oppose Malachy's installation, and, according to the annals of the four masters, succeeded in temporarily displacing him in 1135. A visitation of Munster by Malachy is recorded in 1134, and he may have been present at the consecration in that year of the Romanesque chapel endowed by Cormac Mac Carthaig on the Rock of Cashel. On 7 July 1135, following the death of Flann Ua Sínaig, its hereditary keeper, Malachy was obliged to pay to gain possession of the *Bachall Ísu*, believed to be the crozier of St Patrick, the principal relic of the church of Armagh.

Bishop of Down In 1136, having asserted the case for canonical consecration and broken the Uí Sínaig monopoly at Armagh, Malachy resigned that see to Gilla Meic Liac (Gelasius), abbot of Derry since 1121, in the interests of conciliation and the expectation that the latter would enjoy the protection of Muirchertach Mac Lochlainn, newly succeeded to the kingship of Cenél nEógain, who had close associations with Derry. Having in the meantime consecrated a bishop of Connor, Malachy now assumed the title bishop of Down, though it is possible that he never actually resided at Down and chose instead

to locate himself at Bangor. In early 1139 he undertook a mission to Pope Innocent II to request formal papal approval and palls for the archbishoprics of Armagh and Cashel, travelling via Scotland and the court of King David, which at this time, when much of northern England had recently come under Scottish rule, was as likely to be at Carlisle as at Roxburgh or Edinburgh. On the way he visited York, where Waldef, the saintly prior of Kirkham, came to meet him, and later Clairvaux, where he formed a warm friendship with his future biographer, Abbot Bernard. He went on to Rome where Pope Innocent II did not accede to his request, but instructed Malachy (whom he commissioned as a native papal legate for Ireland) to return to Ireland and summon a general church council, so that a more formal and demonstrably unanimous request for palls could be made. On his homeward journey, Malachy again visited Clairvaux and left four of his associates to be trained as monks in the Cistercian observance; these were subsequently augmented by others sent from Ireland on his return. He travelled back via northern England and Scotland, and again stopped at the court of King David, who was himself a noted patron of monasticism and of ecclesiastical reform. The first Cistercian monastery in Ireland was to be founded at Mellifont, Louth, in 1142.

In 1139 Malachy had also visited the monastery of Arrouaise near Arras and had its rule and liturgical practices copied, as was recorded in 1179 by its abbot, Gautier. Malachy introduced the austere Arrouaisian observances into Ireland, persuading clergy in cathedral churches in particular to adopt them, the first Arrouasian community in Ireland being established at the cathedral church and priory of St Mary's Abbey, Louth, in 1142. Mellifont and Louth Abbey were situated in the kingdom of Airgialla, the protection and patronage of whose king, Donnchad Ua Cerbaill, enabled Malachy to use Airgialla as a trial ground for his reform strategies. Malachy's brother, Gilla Críst (Christianus), was bishop of Airgialla (or Clogher) between 1135 and 1138; and Malachy also benefited from a close working relationship with Gilla Críst's successor, Áed (Edanus) Ua Cáellaide, whom he chose and consecrated. Bernard of Clairvaux depicts Malachy as travelling extensively in the period 1139–48 in the north of Ireland, in Munster, and in Leinster, preaching reform practices. In Cork he resolved a disputed episcopal election by installing an outsider; in Lismore he confuted a scholar who denied the doctrine of the real presence in the eucharist. His position as papal legate gave him the authority to intervene in such cases, though his legateship may have lapsed temporarily following the death of Innocent II in 1143. In 1148 he consecrated the church of the Augustinian community at Knock, near Louth, which had been built under the auspices of Áed Ua Cáellaide and Donnchad Ua Cerbaill.

Death and sainthood In the same year, availing himself of the circumstance that Pope Eugenius III, a former Cistercian monk of Clairvaux, was visiting France, Malachy undertook a second journey to the continent, for the purpose of making a formal request for palls, having first convened a synod on the island of Inis Pádraig, Dublin. He travelled via Scotland and the court of King David, making arrangements on the way for the foundation of a Cistercian house at what may have been Soulseat in Wigtownshire, and avoided travelling through England because King Stephen denied him passage, possibly because of his status as a papal legate. However, he made a detour to visit the canons of Guisborough, in Yorkshire, near the then Anglo-Scottish border. He arrived at Clairvaux about 13 or 14 October, where he met the English monastic reformer Gilbert of Sempringham, to whom he gave a staff. He fell ill and died, in his fifty-fourth year, in the presence of Abbot Bernard on the night of 1-2 November 1148 and was buried at Clairvaux.

Malachy's aspiration for palls and formal papal approval of the Irish diocesan constitution was to be realized at the Synod of Kells in 1152, presided over by the papal legate, Cardinal Giovanni Paparo. The monks of Clairvaux initiated proceedings for his canonization, which Pope Clement III confirmed on 6 July 1190. His feast day subsequently was celebrated on 3 November, so as to avoid All Souls' day (2 November). Malachy shares with Lorcán Ua Tuathail (Laurence O'Toole), archbishop of Dublin, who also died on the continent, the distinction of having been the only Irish saints to be formally canonized before Oliver Plunket in 1975. The most important sources for Malachy's career are Bernard of Clairvaux's biography, written in 1149, two commemorative sermons preached on the day of his death and on the first anniversary of his death, and a hymn and epitaph, as well as three letters written by Bernard to him during his lifetime. Bernard stated that he wrote his life at the request of Abbot Congan, 'my reverend brother and sweet friend' (*Sancti Bernardi opera*, 3.309), undoubtedly one of the Irish trained at Clairvaux, and that a record of the deeds of Malachy had been provided from Ireland. Malachy (along with his brother, Bishop Gilla Críst) is also mentioned in the *Visio Tnugdali*, written by Marcus, monk of the *Schottenkloster* (Irish monastery) of Regensburg, in 1149, as among the denizens of heaven whom Tnugdal encountered in his vision in the company of St Patrick. He was still remembered late in the following century. About 1272 Robert (V) de Brus, lord of Annandale in south-west Scotland, endowed Clairvaux with land in either Annandale or Cumberland, to pay for lights at Malachy's tomb. His object was to lift the curse which the saint had reputedly laid on a distant ancestor, for hanging a robber after promising Malachy that he would spare him.

Malachy's career has to be set in the context of the church reform movement which sought to bring the Irish church more into conformity with the organizational structures of the contemporary European church. He played a crucial role in securing a canonically consecrated succession at Armagh, in attaining papal recognition for the diocesan constitution of the Irish church as it was first outlined at the Synod of Ráith Bressail in 1111 and later refined at Kells in 1152, and in introducing the Cistercian and Augustinian rules, the latter especially, though not exclusively, according to the Arrouaisian observance. Opposition to his reform policies which he experienced during his lifetime outlived him: Augustinian canons whom he had installed at Saul, Down, were attacked and ejected by local unreformed clerics in 1170.

M. T. FLANAGAN

Sources *Sancti Bernardi opera*, ed. J. Leclercq and others, 3 (Rome, 1963), 295-378, 517-26; 5 (Rome, 1968), 417-23; 6/1 (Rome, 1970), 50-55; 8 (Rome, 1977), 282-3, 300-02, 335-7, 512-13 · M. P. Sheehy, ed., *Pontificia Hibernica: medieval papal chancery documents concerning Ireland, 640-1261*, 1 (1962), no. 23 · W. Stokes, ed., 'The annals of Tigernach [8 pts]', *Revue Celtique*, 16 (1895), 374-419; 17 (1896), 6-33, 119-263, 337-420; 18 (1897), 9-59, 150-97, 267-303, 374-91; pubd sep. (1993) · *AFM* · *Ann. Ulster* · W. M. Hennessy, ed. and trans., *Chronicum Scotorum: a chronicle of Irish affairs*, Rolls Series, 46 (1866), 306, 337, 345, 347 · S. Mac Airt, ed. and trans., *The annals of Inisfallen* (1951) · W. M. Hennessy and B. MacCarthy, eds., *Annals of Ulster, otherwise, annals of Senat*, 4 vols. (1887-1901), vol. 2 · R. Foreville, ed., *The book of St Gilbert*, ed. and trans. G. Keir, OMT (1987), 44-5 · Innocentius III [Pope Innocent III], *Patrologia Latina*, 217 (1855) · Symeon of Durham, *Opera*, 2.321 · *St Bernard of Clairvaux's Life of St Malachy of Armagh*, ed. and trans. H. J. Lawlor (1920) · J. Wilson, 'The passages of St Malachy through Scotland', *SHR*, 18 (1920-21), 69-82 · A. Macquarrie, 'Notes on some charters of the Bruces of Annandale', *Transactions of the Dumfriesshire and Galloway Natural History and Antiquarian Society*, 3rd ser., 58 (1983), 72-9, esp. 76-7 · A. Gwynn, 'St Malachy and the see of Armagh, 1121-37', *The Irish church in the eleventh and twelfth centuries*, ed. G. O'Brien (1992), 193-217

Malachy (*fl.* 1279), Franciscan friar, is first mentioned as a member of the convent of the order of Friars Minor in Limerick in 1279 and as the candidate for the archbishopric of Tuam whom Archbishop Nicholas Mac Maol Tosa of Armagh recommended to Edward I as young, provident, and discreet. Following a disputed election, in which the dean and a minority of the canons favoured Malachy, the case went before the papal court. Malachy was personally present in Rome during part of the hearing but failed to secure papal provision. A *Libellus septem peccatorum venen[orum] eorumque remedia describens, qui dicitur venenum Malachiae* (a treatise on the seven deadly sins and on the pastoral theology of penance), or *Tractatus de veneno*, was printed under his name, and with the title 'doctor theologiae', in Paris in 1518. At least thirty-six manuscripts of the work survive, in fifteen of which the tract is anonymous, whereas eighteen attribute it to Robert Grosseteste, and only three name Malachy as author. However, references to St Francis and especially to Irish affairs, including the papal denunciation of the six wives of the last high-king of Ireland as recorded in the annals of Loch Cé, indicate the authorship of an Irish Franciscan, as does the pastoral intention of the writer: 'for the instruction of simple men who have to teach people' (*Tractatus de veneno*, fol. 25v). It is further notable for the denunciation of the government in Ireland during the author's own lifetime.

There is no contemporary evidence for Luke Wadding's statement that Malachy graduated as a bachelor of theology in Oxford *c.*1310, but the range of sources cited in *De veneno* is commensurate with an academic training in philosophy and theology, and the predominantly English manuscript circulation of the work under the name of Grosseteste further indicates an Oxford connection.

KATHERINE WALSH

Sources H. S. Sweetman and G. F. Handcock, eds., *Calendar of documents relating to Ireland*, 5 vols., PRO (1875–86), vol. 2, no. 1576 · J. H. Sbaraleae, ed., *Bullarium Franciscanum Romanorum pontificum*, 3 (Rome, 1765), 573–5 · *CEPR letters*, 1.487–8 · 'Tractatus de veneno', TCD, MS 115 (formerly A.5.3), MS 281 (formerly C.2.18) · M. Esposito, 'Friar Malachy of Ireland', *EngHR*, 33 (1918), 359–66 · *F. Malachie Hibernici libellus, septem peccatorum mortalium venena eorumque remedia describens* (1518) · M. L. Colker, *Trinity College Library Dublin: descriptive catalogue of the mediaeval and Renaissance Latin manuscripts*, 1 (1991), 239, 241 · H. M. Adams, ed., *Catalogue of books printed on the continent of Europe, 1501–1600, in Cambridge libraries*, 2 vols. (1967), vol. 1, nos. 278, 703; vol. 2, no. 703 · Bale, *Cat.*, 2.242–3 · J. Ware, *De scriptoribus Hiberniae, libri duo* (1639), bk 1, p. 65 · W. M. Hennessy, ed. and trans., *The annals of Loch Cé: a chronicle of Irish affairs from AD 1014 to AD 1590*, 1, Rolls Series, 54 (1871), 313–15 · L. Wadding, *Annales minorum*, ed. J. M. Fonseca and others, 3rd edn, 6 (1931), 176, 198–9 · Emden, *Oxf.* · J. H. Sbaralea, *Supplementum … ad scriptores … S. Francisci*, 3 vols. (Rome, 1908–36), vol. 1, p. 507
Archives BL · Bodl. Oxf. · CUL · TCD, MS 115 (formerly A.5.3); MS 281 (formerly C.2.18)

Malachy MacAedh. *See* Mac Aedh, Malachy (*d.* 1348).

Malan, Adolph Gysbert [*nicknamed* Sailor] (**1910–1963**), air force officer, was born in Wellington, Cape Province, South Africa, on 3 October 1910, one of five sons of William Adolph Malan, a farmer, and his English wife, Evelyn Forde Malan. He was educated at Wellington Public School (1922–4), where he showed an aptitude for competitive sports and became fluent in Dutch. He then chose a career at sea and joined the training ship *General Botha* for two years; he gained his passing out certificate in 1926. The following year Malan became a cadet with the Union Castle Steamship Company, for which he worked until 1935; during this period he gained both second mate's and first mate's certificates. In 1932 he joined the British Royal Naval Volunteer Reserve and became a sub-lieutenant. These maritime associations led to his widely remembered nickname, Sailor.

When the great depression affected shipping, Malan's attention turned to aviation, and early in 1936 he attended the Flying Training School at Bristol. His RAF career (no. 37604) began in March 1936 with a short service commission as acting pilot officer. He was already showing great ability and character, being awarded a special distinction as 'an above average pilot and outstanding officer' (RAF service record, AM form 1406).

In December 1936 Malan joined 74 'Tiger' squadron at Hornchurch, and soon led a flight. On 2 April 1938, at the parish church in Ruislip, Middlesex, he married Lynda Irene Fraser (*b.* 1914/15), a stenographer, the daughter of Alfred Arthur Fraser, a wholesale meat salesman. They later had two children, Jonathan and Valerie. Malan gained wide experience with biplane fighters, especially his squadron's Gauntlets. By the time they converted to Spitfires early in 1939 he was a highly competent pilot and was promoted flight lieutenant.

Malan's introduction to aerial combat came during the French campaign, when the squadron provided air cover over retreating allied forces from 21 to 27 May 1940. He first shot down a Junkers Ju 88 and in six days had a total of three aircraft destroyed, with six others 'shared' or 'probable'. This instant success brought the award of the DFC on 11 June. After returning to England the squadron saw further action when channel convoys were attacked by day, and night bombing began. On the night of 18/19 June Malan shot down two Heinkel He 111s, and by the end of July he had added a Messerschmitt Bf 109, a 'shared', and a 'probable' to his total.

Malan had learned much from the French campaign, where Fighter Command had lost so many experienced pilots. Aged thirty, he was older than most of his fellow airmen and combined calm authority, superb marksmanship, and disciplined aggression in combat. His portraits by Orde and Kennington both show a spirit of determination. These powers of leadership and cool ability brought him command of 74 squadron on 8 August. When the squadron was withdrawn to Kirton in Lindsey, Lincolnshire, Malan wrote his '10 rules of air fighting', an invaluable practical list for airmen in action. The paper was widely distributed throughout Fighter Command.

As the battle of Britain intensified, Malan's airmen played a vital part in the thick of the fighting. He altered formations to meet the new conditions, flying fours in line-astern instead of vic-threes. His tactical awareness of teamwork saved pilots' lives, earning him the reputation of being possibly the daylight battle's outstanding leader and teacher of younger airmen. After further combat success he was awarded a bar to his DFC on 13 August and a DSO on Christmas eve.

Malan was promoted wing commander to lead the Biggin Hill wing in March 1941, as the RAF prepared for an offensive over France. In five days in June he shot down seven Bf 109s, and on 22 July he received a bar to his DSO. At that stage, recognizing his own combat weariness as a danger to his pilots, he was posted first to train airmen at 58 operational training unit, Grangemouth, then, in October 1941, on a lecture tour to the USA.

Following his return to Britain in December 1941, Malan continued training pilots, using his 'Rules'. He became commanding officer of the Central Gunnery School, Sutton Bridge, where he was promoted group captain in October 1942. After a spell as station commander at Biggin Hill from January 1943 he went on to lead fighter wings, and flew an escort sortie on D-day, 6 June 1944. By the end of the war his reputation was unsurpassed, and his score of aircraft confirmed as destroyed stood at thirty-two. He left the RAF as a group captain in April 1946 and returned to South Africa. His foreign awards were the Belgian Croix de Guerre (4 November 1941), the Czech Military Cross (15 March 1946), and the French Croix de Guerre and Légion d'honneur (16 July 1940).

Back in South Africa, Malan entered the mining business as secretary to Harry Oppenheimer MP. After 1948 he opposed the apartheid policy of the government, led by a distant relative, Dr Daniël Malan, launched a campaign involving ex-servicemen, and spoke at demonstrations.

Later he ran his own sheep farm. He developed Parkinson's disease and deteriorated slowly until his untimely death in Kimberley Hospital on 17 September 1963.

In the opinion of Al Deere, a fellow ace, Malan was 'the best fighter tactician and leader produced by the RAF in World War II' (Deere, 229).   JOHN RAY

Sources RAF service record, RAF, Insworth, Gloucestershire, Personnel Management Centre, no. 37604, AM form 1406 · *Daily Telegraph* (18 Sept 1963) · C. Shores and C. Williams, *Aces high* (1994), 421–3 · private information (2004) [J. Young, Battle of Britain Fighter Association] · m. cert. · A. Robinson, *RAF fighter squadrons in the battle of Britain* (1987), 134–64, 215 · M. J. Armitage, ed., *Classic RAF battles* (1995), 36–9 · A. Deere, *Nine lives* (1974), 229 · J. P. Ray, *The Battle of Britain: new perspectives* (1994), 84 · O. Walker, *Sailor Malan* (1953) · N. Franks, *Sky tiger* (1980) · K. G. Wynn, *Men of the battle of Britain: a who was who of the pilots and aircrew* (1989) · R. A. Hough and D. Richards, *The battle of Britain* (1990), 192 · J. Terraine, *The right of the line: the Royal Air Force in the European war, 1939–1945* (1985), 193 · L. Deighton, *Fighter* (1977), 176–8
Archives FILM BFI NFTVA, news footage · IWM FVA, actuality footage · IWM FVA, news footage | SOUND IWM SA, oral history interview
Likenesses E. Kennington, drawing, repro. in E. Kennington, *Drawing the RAF* (1942) · C. Orde, drawing

Malan, Daniël François (1874–1959), prime minister of South Africa, was born on 22 May 1874 in the Cape Colony on the farm Allesverloren, near Riebeek West, the son of Daniël François Malan (1844–1908), a well-to-do farmer, and his wife, Anna Magdalena du Toit (1847–1893). He was the second of six children. Both his parents were descendants of French Huguenots. Malan was raised to have a deep love for the Afrikaner volk.

After schooling in Riebeek West, Malan attended Victoria College, Stellenbosch, where he obtained a BA in 1895. He became a schoolteacher in 1896, but decided to study theology and entered the Victoria College seminary in 1897. Simultaneously, he registered for a philosophy MA, with a thesis on Immanuel Kant. He obtained the degree in 1899. This period strengthened Malan's Afrikaner nationalism. Although the college was predominantly English-speaking, there was a dynamic current of nationalism among Afrikaner students.

Unlike many Cape Afrikaners, Malan did not attempt to join the Boer forces during the Second South African War (1899–1902). In September 1900 he left South Africa to continue his theological studies at the University of Utrecht in the Netherlands. Although in the Netherlands, he was deeply affected by the defeat of the Boer republics, especially after he met the exiled president S. J. P. Kruger in 1901. His meetings with the Boer generals Louis Botha, C. R. de Wet, and J. H. de la Rey in the Netherlands after the war also made a lasting impression. In addition, he developed a firm friendship with President M. T. Steyn, who was then living in Germany. Steyn fundamentally influenced the development of Malan's political views. He subsequently regarded with contempt what he saw as the too submissive and conciliatory attitude of some Afrikaners towards Britain.

On 20 January 1905 Malan became a doctor of divinity when his thesis on the idealism of Berkeley was accepted. On his return to the Cape Colony, he was determined to

Daniël François Malan (1874–1959), by Merlyn Severn, 1948

dedicate himself to the cause of his defeated people. He was formally admitted to the Dutch Reformed church ministry and in July 1905 became a minister in the Transvaal town of Heidelberg. Here he witnessed the devastation of the war and its effect on the Afrikaner. This reinforced the belief he had developed in the Netherlands that the Afrikaner volk could only maintain its separate identity by isolating itself from the British empire.

In February 1906 Malan moved to Montagu in the Cape Colony. It was here that he became a national figure as a puritanical, ecclesiastical, academic, and cultural Afrikaner leader. He played a leading role in the development of Afrikaner education, the recognition of Afrikaans as a written language, and the improvement in social status of poor Afrikaners.

Malan transferred to the Graaff-Reinet congregation in February 1913. This was during the period of estrangement between premier Louis Botha and General J. B. M. Hertzog after Hertzog had rejected the South African Party's policy of conciliation with Britain and English-speaking South Africans. Malan supported Hertzog and opposed South Africa's involvement in the First World War as part of the British empire. He joined the National Party, which was formed in 1914 by Hertzog to articulate and defend purely Afrikaner interests.

A visit to Afrikaner settlers in the Congo and the two Rhodesias in 1912, as well as concern about Graaff-Reinet's large poor white population, also convinced Malan of the need for racial purity. He feared that integration with black people threatened Afrikaner survival. Malan believed that as God's will had established the Afrikaner in South Africa, the volk had to segregate itself from other races. The newspaper *Die Burger* was established in July 1915 to serve as a mouthpiece for the National Party. Malan was appointed editor (a position he retained until 1924). He combined the editorship with his leadership of the National Party in the Cape Province from September 1915. *Die Burger* became the voice of the Afrikaner and played an important part in the dramatic growth of the National Party.

In 1919 Malan was elected to parliament for the Calvinia constituency. He was a formidable parliamentarian who, despite his image of implacability, knew when to compromise. His political skills were bolstered by his natural gift for oratory and magnificent voice. His expressionless face, even under the most bitter personal attacks, also added to his armour as a politician. Malan's strengths as a politician were his patience and the fact that he never doubted that his cause would triumph. He had a cool and sharp mind and his political judgements were never distorted by impatience. This encouraged a view of him as a plodder and led many opponents to underestimate him.

In 1919, encouraged by the statements of allied leaders on the right to self-determination of small nations, the National Party sent a delegation to the peace conference in Paris. Malan was a member of the 'freedom deputation', demanding the restoration of the independence of the two former Boer republics. The deputation, however, was unsuccessful. The right to self-determination as well as the right to secede from the British empire became the major platform of the National Party. Malan strove for independence from Britain, believing that only when independent could South Africa place its own interests first. In 1924, the party after an election agreement with the Labour Party, secured the defeat of Smuts's South African Party government. Malan became minister of internal affairs, education, and public health in Hertzog's cabinet. He was an efficient minister and played a leading role in the government's efforts to protect and encourage Afrikaner interests.

Malan piloted some of the government's most important bills through parliament. He was responsible for the amendment to the constitution which recognized Afrikaans as an official language. He also implemented a policy of bilingualism in the public service. His most controversial legislation between 1925 and 1927 was for a national flag. He saw the British flag as a symbol of defeat and humiliation and wanted a 'clean flag', excluding the union flag. This led to an emotional struggle between nationalists and English-speakers. Eventually Malan had to accept a compromise flag that included the union flag. The flag struggle established Malan as a potential successor to Hertzog.

The worldwide economic depression of the early 1930s forced Hertzog to form a coalition government in 1933 with Smuts's predominately English-speaking South African Party, the political home of big capital. Malan opposed coalition, which he believed would be to the detriment of the Afrikaner. He eventually accepted coalition with reservations, but refused to serve in the new cabinet. However, he rejected the move to fuse the two parties. He feared that without a strong political base Afrikaner culture would be too weak to withstand English cultural and economic influences. When the National and South African parties merged to form the United Party in 1934, he and his supporters founded the 'Purified National Party'. In a parliament of 150 the party had eighteen MPs.

In the 1930s there was a dramatic growth of antisemitism in the Purified National Party. Although not personally an antisemite, Malan did draw political benefit from antisemitism. He also campaigned for stricter racial segregation to maintain white supremacy. The central platform of the Purifieds was secession from the British empire and the creation of a republic. The 1926 Imperial Conference had accepted the Balfour declaration that Britain and her dominions were autonomous within the British empire and equal in status. For Hertzog this had settled the question of South Africa's status as a sovereign independent state, and established that republicanism was no longer a practical policy.

Malan's struggle with Hertzog's United Party was a bitter and emotional contest for the soul of the Afrikaner. The Purifieds, however, remained a rural and predominately Cape-based party and could secure only twenty-seven seats in the parliamentary election of 1938. Malan had to move to the Piketberg constituency to avoid personal defeat. However, the outbreak of the Second World War in September 1939 dramatically altered parliamentary politics. Hertzog's neutrality motion in parliament, supported by Malan, was defeated by Smuts and his followers. For Malan this was final proof that the Afrikaner cause could not be served through co-operation with non-Afrikaners.

Hertzog and his supporters became reconciled with the Purifieds in forming the Herenigde Nasionale Party (Reunited National Party) in January 1940. Malan stood back for Hertzog to be the new leader, but the party was racked by mutual distrust. In November 1940 Hertzog and a number of supporters left it because of conflicting views on the rights of English-speakers. These Hertzogites formed the Afrikaner Party. By 1941 Afrikanerdom had split into opposing factions. In the Herenigde Nasionale Party, Malan had to deal with Oswald Pirow's New Order group which pressed for an authoritarian national socialist state. The biggest threat, however, to the party's leadership of Afrikanerdom was the Ossewa-Brandwag (Oxwagon Sentinel). This was formed in 1938 as a cultural organization, but by 1941 it had become a mass movement under the fascist-influenced leadership of J. F. J. van Rensburg. Its campaign for a national socialist one-party state, and acts of sabotage by more extremist members, alienated Malan. He was a firm supporter of parliamentary democracy (for white citizens only), and adamant that a republic could only be achieved by constitutional means.

The New Order was purged from the Herenigde Nasionale Party, and when it became clear to Malan by

August 1941 that he could not bring the Ossewa-Brandwag under his control he ruthlessly set out to destroy it. This led to a long and traumatic struggle but by the 1943 election, which the United Party won, the Herenigde Nasionale Party was the unchallenged political mouthpiece of Afrikanerdom, with Malan as the volks-leader. After 1943 he shifted the party's focus from opposition to South Africa's involvement in the war to domestic matters: bread-and-butter issues, white insecurity in the face of rising black assertiveness, and the threat of communism. Malan also concluded an election agreement with the Afrikaner Party.

On the eve of the parliamentary election of 1948 the Herenigde Nasionale Party was a highly mobilized mass party. This contributed to its unexpected narrow victory, which Malan termed a miracle of God. He formed a cabinet consisting exclusively of Afrikaners, though it was also the first fully bilingual cabinet. As Malan was determined to entrench Afrikaner supremacy he took steps to weaken the British association. He abolished the right of appeal to the privy council and ended dual British and South African citizenship. It became more difficult for British immigrants to acquire citizenship and the United Party's plan to recruit British immigrants was suspended. The government also passed numerous harsh segregatory measures to bolster white domination. These included eliminating any form of interracial integration. These measures became the cornerstone of the apartheid state. Malan also initiated the process of removing coloured voters from the common voters' roll, a process which led to a subsequent constitutional crisis.

Although Malan's government won the election comfortably in 1953, his premiership was stormy. He was faced with strong parliamentary and extra-parliamentary opposition, as well as growing international pressure. In addition, his own party was racked with internal conflicts over political and personal rivalries. Moreover, firebrands in the National Party also developed doubts about Malan's commitment to secession when after 1948 he accepted that a republic need not leave the Commonwealth. Growing international isolation had persuaded him of the value of the Commonwealth connection. Because of his declining physical powers, he resigned as premier in October 1954 and retired to Stellenbosch, where he died on 7 February 1959. He was buried in Stellenbosch cemetery on 11 February 1959.

Malan was a bald, stout man, with a solemn, pale face behind spectacles with thick lenses. He was aloof and reserved, creating a dour, grim impression. Yet he had a dry sense of humour and could be warm with friends and relatives. He played a crucial role in the renaissance of the Afrikaner after the Second South African War. He strove for Afrikaner self-respect and self-reliance, and secured Afrikaner political supremacy. However, the isolationist, conformist, and oppressive nature of the Afrikaner state he created assured its eventual collapse.

Malan was married twice. On 16 June 1926 he married Martha Margaretha Elizabeth van Tonder, *née* Zandberg (1897–1930), and they had two sons. She died on 26 December 1930 and on 20 December 1937 he married Maria-Anne Sophia Louw (1905–1973). They had no children but they adopted a German orphan girl in 1948.

F. A. MOUTON

Sources B. Booyens, *Die lewe van D. F. Malan: die eerste veertig jaar* (1969) · H. B. Thom, *D. F. Malan* (1980) · H. B. Thom and M. C. E. van Schoor, *Dr D. F. Malan en koalisie* (1988) · H. Saker, *The South African flag controversy, 1925–1928* (1980) · N. M. Stultz, *The nationalists in opposition, 1934–1948* (1974) · A. van Wyk, *Die keeromstraat-kliek: die Burger en die politiek van koalisie en samesmelting, 1932–1934* (1983) · C. F. J. Muller, *Sonop in die suide: geboorte en groei van die nasionale pers, 1915–1948* (1990) · P. J. Furlong, *Between crown and swastika: the impact of the radical right on the Afrikaner nationalist movement in the fascist era* (1991) · L. E. Neame, *Some South African politicians* (1929) · D. F. Malan, *Afrikaner-volkseenheid en my ervarings op die pad daarheen* (1959) · S. W. Pienaar, ed., *Glo in u volk: D. F. Malan as redenaar* (1964) · O. Geyser and A. H. Marais, eds., *Die nasionale party*, 5 vols. (1980–)
Archives University of Stellenbosch, South Africa | FILM BFI NFTVA, current affairs footage · BFI NFTVA, documentary footage · BFI NFTVA, news footage
Likenesses M. Severn, photograph, 1948, Hult. Arch. [*see illus.*] · I. Henkel, bust · I. Henkel, bust, University of Stellenbosch, South Africa · I. Henkel, oils, University of Stellenbosch, South Africa · C. Steynberg, bust, University of Stellenbosch, South Africa · G. Wylde, oils
Wealth at death 57,391 South African pounds: estate 716/59, master of the supreme court, Cape Town

Malan, François Stephanus (1871–1941), politician in South Africa, was born on 12 March 1871 on the farm Bovlei, near Wellington, in the Cape Colony, the second of fourteen children of Daniël Gerhardus Malan (1845–1928) and his wife, Elizabeth Johanna Malan (1848–1926). His parents were both of Huguenot descent.

Malan was raised to be intensely proud of his Afrikaner identity. He was educated at home until 1887, then he attended the Paarl Boys' High School in 1888, proceeding in 1889 to Victoria College, Stellenbosch, where in 1892 he obtained a BA in mathematics and science. He then studied law at Cambridge University, obtaining the LLB degree in 1894. Malan married Johanna Brümmer (c.1871–1926) on 27 September 1897; and they had two sons and two daughters.

In July 1895 Malan was admitted to the Cape bar, but in November 1895 he became the editor of *Ons Land*, a position he retained until 1908. *Ons Land* was the most influential Dutch newspaper in the colony and mouthpiece of the Afrikaner Bond which represented Afrikaner interests. Malan's appointment coincided with the Jameson raid. The raid gave birth to a more exclusive Afrikaner nationalism and Malan's editorship earned him the reputation of an extremist. In 1900 he was elected unopposed as the member of parliament for the Malmesbury constituency.

During the Second South African War Malan was supportive of the Boer republics and he protested against British military tactics. *Ons Land*'s criticism of the British military resulted in Malan's being sentenced to one year's imprisonment for seditious libel in April 1901. His prison experience convinced him of the necessity for reconciliation between Boer and Briton, and for Afrikaners to strive for a united and independent South Africa under the British flag.

In 1904 Malan began a campaign to achieve this goal. This was in tandem with his struggle for Afrikaner rights in the Cape Colony. In 1908 the Afrikaner Bond, which had formed a coalition with independent anti-imperial politicians such as John X. Merriman, under the banner of the South African Party, won the general election. (The South African Party was a party in name alone as it functioned only in parliament and had no local branch structures.) Malan became minister of agriculture in Merriman's cabinet. As the parliamentary leader of the Afrikaner Bond he was the real power in the government. He used this position to campaign vigorously for a unified South Africa.

At the National Convention (1908–9), which framed the South Africa Bill, Malan appealed for a union with a general and non-racial qualified franchise, based on a high qualification test. He believed that total racial segregation was unwise, impractical, and unjust. The convention rejected a general franchise, but Malan did secure the retention of the African and coloured franchise in the Cape.

Malan became a member of the first Union cabinet (1910), remaining so until the defeat of J. C. Smuts's government in 1924. He was appointed to the privy council in 1920. Malan was minister of education (1910–21), of mines and industry (1912–14), and of agriculture and forestry (1920–21) and acting minister for native affairs on numerous occasions, as well as acting prime minister on three occasions between 1917 and 1919. He was a hard-working and efficient minister. The core of Malan's political principles remained reconciliation and an autonomous South Africa within the British empire. He also used his influence in the cabinet to moderate the rigours of racial segregation on black people.

Upon the outbreak of the First World War in August 1914 Malan opposed the South African invasion of South-West Africa. Only his personal loyalty to the premier, Louis Botha, and his commitment to reconciliation, prevented his resignation. This compromise alienated him from Afrikaners who had found a political home in the National Party with its exclusive nationalism. His liberal stance in defence of the rights of black people also alienated many white people. This contributed to his defeat in Malmesbury at the hands of the National Party in the general election of 1924.

This defeat and the death of his wife in 1926 were devastating blows from which Malan never fully recovered. Although a member of the senate from 1927 he gradually withdrew from party politics. In October 1928 he married his wife's sister, Anna Elizabeth Attwell (d. 1967). As a senator Malan saw his main task to be the protection of the interests and rights of the black majority. He played a heroic, albeit unsuccessful, role to prevent the removal of Africans from the common voters' roll in 1936. From January 1940 until his death on 31 December 1941 in Cape Town he was the president of the senate. He was buried at Woltemade cemetery, Cape Town, on 2 January 1942.

Malan was a short and stocky figure with piercing brown eyes. He was an open-minded person of immense moral integrity and courage. He was tireless in his service

to South Africa, always placing this calling above party politics. Outside the political arena he played a prominent role in Afrikaner cultural and religious affairs.

F. A. MOUTON

Sources F. S. Malan, "'n Oud-joernalis kyk terug', *Die Huisgenoot* (7 May–13 Aug 1937) • B. Cloete, *Die lewe van senator F. S. Malan (president van die senaat)* (1946) • J. F. Preller, ed., *Die konvensie-dagboek van sy edelagbare Francois Stephanus Malan, 1908–1909* (1951) • T. R. H. Davenport, *The Afrikaner Bond* (1966) • L. M. Thompson, *The unification of South Africa, 1902–1910* (1960) • P. Kallaway, 'F. S. Malan, the Cape liberal tradition and South African politics', *Journal of African History*, 15 (1974), 113–29 • L. F. Neame, *Some South African politicians* (1929) • J. C. Smuts, *Suiderstem* (2 Jan 1942) • P. Lewson, *John X. Merriman: paradoxical South African statesman* (1982) • P. H. Zietsman, *Die taal is gans die volk* (1992) • O. Geyser and A. H. Marais, eds., *Die nasionale party*, 5 vols. (1980–) • J. F. Preller, 'F. S. Malan', *DSAB* • Venn, *Alum. Cant.* • Dutch Reformed church archive, Cape Town • *Die Huisgenoot* (16 Jan 1942) • death register, Cape Archive, Cape Town, HAWC 1/3/9/5/70 nr 60/1942 • *Die Burger* (2 Jan 1942)

Archives Cape Archive, Cape Town, collection, acc 583

Likenesses H. Naudé, oils, priv. coll. • E. Roworth, charcoal, Africana Museum, Johannesburg • E. Roworth, crayon, University of Cape Town Library, C. J. Sibbeth collection

Wealth at death £17,549: estate 6/9/8506, ref. no. 77112/42, master of the supreme court, Cape Town • estate bequeathed £12,000 to welfare, educational, cultural, and historical organizations, and his church: obituary, *Die Huisgenoot* (16 Jan 1942)

Malan, Solomon Caesar [*formerly* César Jean Salomon] (1812–1894), orientalist and biblical scholar, was born on 22 April 1812 in the rue Verdaine, Geneva, the eldest of the twelve children of César Henri Abraham Malan (1787–1864), a Reformed minister of Huguenot descent, and his wife, Salome Georgette Jeanne, daughter of Salomon Schönberger, a merchant established in Geneva. His early education was given by his father, under whom he not only gained a conversational knowledge of German, Spanish, Italian, and Latin, but also began English, Hebrew, Arabic, and Sanskrit. He was also instructed in natural science, drawing, and various handicrafts.

In 1830 Malan met an Englishwoman, Mary Marsh, only child of John Mortlock, who was visiting Geneva, and the two fell in love. Mortlock initially opposed the match, but eventually consented on condition that Malan passed through an English university. Malan came to Britain in 1831 as tutor to the family of the marquess of Tweeddale (which was when he changed his name to its later form), and in 1833 he matriculated at St Edmund Hall, Oxford. The marriage took place on 1 April 1834. In the same year he gained the Boden Sanskrit scholarship, and in 1837 he won the Pusey and Ellerton Hebrew scholarship, and second-class honours in *literae humaniores*, despite becoming blind in the left eye. After graduating, Malan accepted the post of senior classical professor at Bishop's College, Calcutta, which he reached in May 1838. He took Anglican deacon's orders in the same year. In 1839 he became secretary to the Asiatic Society of Bengal, and gained the friendship of the remarkable scholar Csoma Körösi, from whom he learned Tibetan. Besides learning several Indian vernaculars, he also advanced in Chinese. Leaving India on account of failing health in January 1840, he travelled through the Sudan and Egypt to recuperate, until he learned that his wife, who had returned to England, had died of consumption on 5 April. He returned to England in September to make provision for their three sons, but then resumed his convalescent journeys via Scandinavia and Germany to the Middle East.

After returning to England late in 1842, Malan accepted the curacy of Alverstoke, near Gosport. In 1843 he proceeded MA and moved to Balliol College; he was also ordained priest, and on 24 October that year married his second wife, Caroline Selina, second daughter of Charles Milman Mount, a prebendary of Wells. They had three sons and two daughters; his wife survived him. After a year (1844–5) as perpetual curate of Crowcombe, Somerset, Malan accepted the living of Broadwindsor, Dorset, in September 1845. On 4 November 1845 he was naturalized as a British subject by letters patent. While at Broadwindsor, he served as rural dean and diocesan inspector of schools (1846–53). He held the prebend of Ruscombe-Southbury at Salisbury from 1870 to 1875. He was a frequent traveller, most notably to the Middle East again (1849–50), where he visited the excavation of Nineveh, and to Georgia and the Caucasus (1872).

Malan was regarded as the greatest British orientalist of his day; he was conversant with about eighty languages and published over fifty books. His main concern, however, was not the languages as such but the support of Christianity, for which he was made a DD by Edinburgh University (1880). Most of his orientalist works are accounts of eastern churches or translations of their devotional literatures, notably *History of the Georgian Church* (1866), *The Life and Times of St Gregory the Illuminator* (1868), and *Original Documents of the Coptic Church* (5 vols., 1872–5). Some deal with problems of the mission field, particularly *Who is God in China?* (1855), or with other topical controversies. In 1881 Malan joined in the attack made by John William Burgon on the Revised Version of the New Testament, contributing to his articles, and himself publishing a new version of Matthew 1–4, with an appendix giving the Lord's prayer in seventy-one languages. His *magnum opus* was *Notes on the Proverbs* (3 vols., 1889–93), illustrating the Biblical text with nearly 16,000 passages from some forty eastern languages.

Besides his academic work, and his pastoral duties, which he performed conscientiously, Malan managed to pursue many other interests. He was a keen natural historian, and his collection of birds' eggs, presented to Exeter Museum, was judged one of the finest in the country. He was admired for his skill at calligraphy and drawing, both of which are illustrated in the biography by his son. He drew the portrait of E. B. Pusey in Tract 90 (1841), and the sketches of the excavation of Nineveh in 1850 which illustrate Sir Austen Henry Layard's *Nineveh and Babylon* (1853). His pictures of Palestine were exhibited at Burlington House in 1855 and the Crystal Palace in 1856. His other skills included bookbinding, carpentry, and repairing musical instruments.

Malan's health forced him to retire in May 1855. Before leaving Broadwindsor, he presented forty valuable Tibetan books and manuscripts, given him in India by Csoma Körösi, to the Hungarian Academy of Sciences. His main collection of 4017 volumes became the nucleus of the library of the Indian Institute, Oxford. He spent his retirement at Bournemouth, dying there at West Cliff Hall, Priory Road, on 25 November 1894; he was buried in Bournemouth cemetery.

Despite the remarkable range of his talents, Malan never attained real eminence in any one field. One reason may have been that his energies were too widely dispersed, but another was his strongly conservative temperament and distrust of many developments taken for granted by later generations, including the admission of women to university and transcription of oriental languages into the Roman alphabet. This is shown most clearly in his condemnation of the Revised Version, and of the new Greek text of the New Testament published by Westcott and Hort (both 1881).   R. S. SIMPSON

Sources A. N. Malan, *Solomon Caesar Malan DD: memorials of his life and writings* (1897) · A. Roberts, 'Solomon Caesar Malan and his orientalist library', *SALG Newsletter* [South Asia Library Group], 40 (Jan 1993), 35–9 · A. A. Macdonnell, *Journal of the Royal Asiatic Society of Great Britain and Ireland* (1895), 453–7 · H. V. Malan, *The Malan of Mérindol* (privately printed, London, 1863) · V. Ackland, *Dorset worthies, no. 11: Solomon Caesar Malan* (1969) · *The Times* (28 Nov 1894), 6 · review of *Solomon Caesar Malan*, *The Athenaeum* (12 Feb 1898), 207–8 · Crockford (1886) · d. cert.
Archives BL, sketches and notes relating to journey from Alexandretta to Nineveh and Babylon, Add. MS 45360 · Bodl. Oxf., corresp.
Likenesses charcoal drawing, 1895 (in later life), U. Oxf., Indian Institute Library
Wealth at death £6921 15s. 5d.: probate, 18 Jan 1895, CGPLA Eng. & Wales

Malard, Michael (b. 1676), religious controversialist and tutor in French, was born at Vaurenard, near Mâcon, France, the son of François Malard, a doctor of Vaurenard; his mother later married a M. Patissier de la Fayette of Beaugeu. His parents were Roman Catholics and he was prepared for the priesthood but after serving for some years as pasteur at Belleville, Beaujolais, he came to England about 1700 and was converted to the protestant religion at the French church of the Savoy, London, on 15 April 1705. Shortly after his conversion differences with the French protestants, whom he offended by becoming an episcopalian, drove him abroad.

On his return to England, Malard earned a living by teaching but he also produced a series of bitter attacks on the French committee for the distribution of the £15,000 that, since the beginning of William III's reign, had been annually allocated to the French protestants. His first extraordinary pamphlet, *The Case, and Humble Petition, of Michael Malard* (1717), not only accuses Claude Grostête de la Mothe of stealing Malard's certificates of ordination and references but also of inveigling him into a bigamous marriage. In 1718 Malard published further accusations of malpractice within the French committee in *The French Plot Found out Against the English Church*. Jean Armand Dubourdieu, one of the ministers in the French church of the Savoy, responded with *An Appeal to the English Nation* (1718), in which he accused Malard of repeated adultery and attributed the withdrawal of his allowance to his scandalous life. Malard nevertheless continued his attacks in further publications.

Malard also wrote several manuals on accidence in French grammar, and in *The French and Protestant Companion, or, A Journey into Europe, Asia, and Africa* (1718), which is dedicated to George I, Malard is described as French tutor to the daughters of the prince of Wales, afterwards George II. The *Companion*, a curious mixture of grammar, travel book, and anti-Catholic satire, is offered by Malard to British parents as a safely protestant means of learning the French language. It was reprinted in 1719 and 1722. It is not known when or where Malard died.

THOMAS SECCOMBE, *rev.* EMMA MAJOR

Sources The case, and humble petition, of Michael Malard (1717) · M. Malard, *An appeal to the king* (1720) · M. Malard, *The French and protestant companion* (1718) · D. C. A. Agnew, *Protestant exiles from France in the reign of Louis XIV, or, The Huguenot refugees and their descendants in Great Britain and Ireland*, 2nd edn, 3 vols. (1871–4) · ESTC · Watt, *Bibl. Brit.*
Likenesses print, line engraving, BM, NPG; repro. in M. Malard, *French and protestant companion … with the defence of the Protestant religion* (1719)

Malby, Sir Nicholas (*c.*1530–1584), soldier and president of Connacht, was probably born in the West Riding of Yorkshire. His father died when Nicholas was four years old, and the boy was evidently reared, along with his brother John, in the family of a London merchant named John Malby, probably their father's brother, who had been admitted to fellowship at the Middle Temple in 1516–17. It is not known whether Nicholas or his brother were themselves educated at Middle Temple. Nicholas Malby married Thomasine Lamb, whose father, Robert, was from Leeds and whose mother was a Castell from East Hatley in Cambridgeshire. Thomasine's maternal uncle, Thomas Castell, had studied law at the Middle Temple with the elder John Malby. They had a son, Henry, who matriculated at New College, Oxford, in June 1585, aged thirteen, and a daughter, Ursula. Henry married Elizabeth Jobson, granddaughter of Sir Francis Jobson, lieutenant of the Tower. Ursula married Anthony Brabazon, lieutenant-governor of Connacht. Thomasine Malby survived her first husband and subsequently married George Rawe.

Early career in Ireland It is likely that Nicholas Malby's involvement in Ireland originated in the activities of his relative and guardian, John Malby, who was employed in supplying provisions for the army at Berwick, a point of departure for soldiers bound for Ireland. Nicholas Malby's presence in Ireland is first recorded in 1556, when he was among those Englishmen who were willing to take part in the proposed plantation of Queen's county. Six years later he was back in England when, on 6 August 1562, he and six others were found guilty of coining. The goldsmith involved was executed, but Malby was among those whose death sentence was commuted, probably through the intervention of Sir William Cecil. He was reprieved in September 1562 on condition that he serve under Ambrose Dudley, earl of Warwick, in France. Both Warwick and Cecil were involved in procuring his pardon. By April 1563 he was acting as Warwick's secretary. He served

in the army abroad for some years, being sent to Spain in 1565 where his conduct was commended by the English minister at Madrid.

On his return to England Malby was sent to Ireland to serve as a captain under the lord deputy, Sir Henry Sidney. Having gained extensive military experience abroad he was appointed a sergeant-major of the army in Ireland in 1567. After the death of Shane O'Neill at the hands of the MacDonalds in June 1567, Malby was stationed at Carrickfergus, co. Antrim, sharing the power of martial law with Captain William Piers and charged with keeping in check the Scots who threatened east Ulster. His successful handling of the threat posed by Sorley Boy MacDonald earned him praise from Sir Henry Sidney. In July 1569 he was sent to the assistance of Sir Peter Carew against the Butlers in Leinster. During a skirmish near Carlow he was severely injured in a fall from his horse.

Conscious of his responsibility to provide for his wife and young family, Malby went to London in spring 1571 to pursue his personal suits. He had equipped himself with letters of recommendation from Adam Loftus who considered him 'a right worthy and valiant captain' who could not easily be spared from service in Ireland (PRO, SP 63/31, no. 42), and Sir Edward Fitton who praised his long service and discreet diligence, but judged that Malby would make a 'coarse courtier and a worse suitor' (PRO, SP 63/31, no. 13). On 22 March 1571 he obtained a grant of the office of collector of the customs of the three east Ulster ports of Strangford, Ardglass, and Dundrum. On 5 October 1571 he received a further grant of MacCartan's country, the modern barony of Kinelarty in co. Down, on condition that he planted it with civil and loyal subjects before 22 March 1579. On his way back to Ireland in February 1572 the ship he commanded captured a Spanish ship in the channel.

On 10 April 1572 Malby received a commission to execute martial law in MacCartan's country but his involvement with the proposed plantation of the Ards, led first by Thomas Smith and subsequently by Walter Devereux, earl of Essex, was ultimately unsuccessful. Nevertheless his work in the Ards earned him the respect of the earl of Essex and of Edward Waterhouse, the latter describing him as a man of few words and an ill courtier, but of great reputation among soldiers. A plot by Brian mac Phelim O'Neill to kill Malby while at supper was foiled in November 1574. Malby was sent to London in December of that year to report to the privy council on the state of Ulster. He returned to Ireland on 5 May 1575 with special instructions for the earl of Essex, and with an order for his own admission to the Irish privy council. In the summer of 1575 he took part in Essex's expedition against Sorley Boy MacDonald.

Connacht and its presidency Recognizing that the Ards plantation was not going to succeed, Malby was again in London early in 1576 pursuing his claim to have land to the value of £100 in fee farm in Ireland in exchange for surrendering his patent to MacCartan's country. From this point onward his attention shifted to Connacht and his subsequent land acquisitions were located in counties

Roscommon and Longford. He pursued his interest in establishing an English colony in Roscommon in tandem with his role as provincial governor. In July 1576 Malby was chosen to replace Sir Edward Fitton as chief commissioner and military commander of Connacht. The office was perhaps higher than what someone of Malby's background could reasonably aspire to, but the privy council judged that 'his honesty and discretion will breed better government than would title or dignity' (PRO, SP 63/56, no. 15). His appointment was welcomed by Sir Henry Sidney as 'an apt instrument to frame the rude barbarous people of the province' (*CSP Ire.*, 1574–85, 99). He accompanied the lord deputy, Sir Henry Sidney, to Connacht in September 1576, and was knighted by him on 7 October. During his first winter in the province he succeeded in suppressing the rebellion of John and Ulick Burke, sons of the second earl of Clanricarde.

By the end of 1577, Malby considered that he had concluded his military tasks and was ready to attend to the civil government of Connacht. In particular he sought to implement a plan for taxation that would fund the provincial presidency. The first scheme for a composition of Connacht, devised by Sir Henry Sidney and implemented by Malby in 1577, laid the basis for the success of the English provincial administration in Connacht by making it self-financing. Malby's competence as an administrator and negotiator was clearly demonstrated by his successful implementation of this taxation scheme which did much to ensure the survival of the provincial presidency as an institution and Malby's own continuance in office.

Malby's military endeavours in Connacht were limited in scale. He intervened on behalf of O'Connor Sligo in a dispute with O'Donnell over Bundrowes Castle in October 1577, but was not successful. When his negotiations with Brian O'Rourke proved ineffective Malby used force against him in April 1578. In autumn 1578 he went to England, returning to Ireland in May 1579 with the title of president rather than chief commissioner of Connacht. The province of Connacht being largely peaceful, Malby was free to travel south with 600 troops to assist the lord justice, Sir William Drury, in suppressing James Fitzmaurice's uprising in Munster in the summer and autumn of 1579. After brief military expeditions to Burrishoole in co. Mayo and to O'Rourke's territory in Leitrim early in 1580, Malby was again free to play an active military role outside the province. He travelled to Dublin in summer 1580 to assist Lord Grey in suppressing the Baltinglass rising, and witnessed the defeat of the English forces at Glenmalure. O'Rourke took advantage of his absence from Connacht, and Malby, despite ill health, returned west to deal with the situation. Dissension among the Mayo Burkes threatened to escalate in February 1581 with the arrival of Scots mercenaries, but Malby had advance notice of their coming and prevented them reaching Mayo. He then negotiated a settlement between the rival contenders for the MacWilliam lordship in Mayo. Further unrest was caused in Connacht by the ongoing rivalry over succession to the Clanricarde lordship which was not resolved until after the deaths of the second earl and one of the rival contenders, John Burke, baron of Leitrim, in 1582.

The colonization of Roscommon Malby was rewarded for his early successes in Connacht, receiving a twenty-one-year lease of the castle and lands of Roscommon along with extensive monastic lands in the same county, on 1 November 1577, at an annual rent of £31 5s. 10d. Following Malby's offer to build a walled town at Roscommon and at Athlone, he received a more generous grant from the queen. Athlone was reserved for the official use of the Connacht presidency, but in June 1579 Malby's lease of the lordship of Roscommon and its monastic land was changed to an outright grant of the lands to him and his male heirs. Parts of the castle at Roscommon were remodelled soon afterwards. Malby's son, Henry, was still a minor, and the grant stipulated that where the holder was a minor the chief governor of Connacht would place a guard in the castle of Roscommon at the owner's expense. In July 1579 Malby also received a grant of the annual composition rent of £200 sterling payable by the O'Ferralls in the adjoining county of Longford, and was given power of distraint. He also obtained title to some monastic land in co. Longford. These arrangements allowed him a degree of control over the O'Ferralls, as well as providing an income, but Malby concentrated on his landed interests in co. Roscommon. The lands involved were extensive. He had effectively acquired title to the second largest estate in Connacht after the earl of Clanricarde. The monastic lands in particular were ripe for colonization, and Malby's strong presence in Roscommon attracted English settlers to the area. Some of the soldiers who had previously served with him in Ulster were among those who became his tenants there. His own brother John was also involved. Having learned valuable lessons from the failed Ards colony, Malby calculated that by using monastic lands as a base, and by treating the Irish courteously, an English colony could prosper under the protection of the presidency. Many of Malby's more significant tenants also served as officials of the Connacht presidency. The colony prospered in the 1580s and even after Malby's sudden death at Athlone on 4 March 1584, the English presence in Roscommon continued to expand. His successor as president, Sir Richard Bingham, was forced to pay rent for Roscommon Castle to his son, Henry Malby, when he wished to live there in the mid-1580s. The Malby colony suffered considerable setbacks during the nine years' war, and the death of Sir Nicholas's only son, Henry, in 1602 marked the end of the direct involvement of the Malby family in Roscommon. The descendants of other Elizabethan families who had established themselves in the area under the auspices of Sir Nicholas Malby lived on in the area for many generations.

Character and assessment Malby was a self-made man who rose to prominence in Ireland by virtue of his considerable personal talent as a soldier and administrator. His success aroused jealousies, however, with the influential Thomas Butler, earl of Ormond, numbered among his antagonists. His strength lay in his ability to look after the interests of his soldiers while simultaneously dealing diplomatically with the Irish. He was a shrewd politician and diplomat whose strategic decisions were intelligent and well-informed. In his dealings with O'Rourke and O'Neill he 'had intelligence of all their doings, but dissembled his knowledge', as he explained to the earl of Leicester in 1583 (*Calendar of Carew Manuscripts, 1575–88*, 362–3). Malby understood the political concerns of the Irish and probably understood their language also. His obituary in the annals of the four masters recorded that:

> He was a man learned in the languages and tongues of the islands of the west of Europe, a brave and victorious man in battles fought through Ireland, Scotland, and France, in the service of his sovereign; and this was a lucrative service to him, for he received a suitable remuneration from the Queen, namely the constableship of the town of Athlone, and the governorship of the province of Connacht for seven years before his death, and a grant in perpetuity of the towns of Roscommon and Ballinasloe for himself and his heirs. (AFM, vol. 5, s.a. 1584)

There was more ambivalence in the comment of the Irish obituarists in the annals of Loch Cé who noted of him that:

> there came not to Ireland in his own time, nor often before, a better gentleman of the foreigners than he, and he placed all Connacht under bondage. And it is not possible to count or reckon all that this man destroyed throughout Ireland, and he executed many works, especially on the courts of the towns of Athlone and Roscommon. (*Annals of Loch Cé*, vol. 2, s.a. 1584)

BERNADETTE CUNNINGHAM

Sources CSP Ire., 1509–85 • *The Irish fiants of the Tudor sovereigns*, 4 vols. (1994) • T. Cronin, 'The Elizabethan colony in co. Roscommon', *Irish Midland Studies* [ed. H. Murtagh] (1980), 107–20 • G. W. Lambert, 'Sir Nicholas Malby and his associates', *Journal of Galway Archaeological and Historical Society*, 23 (1948), 1–13 • CSP for., 1562–5 • J. Morrin, ed., *Calendar of the patent and close rolls of chancery in Ireland for the reigns of Henry VIII, Edward VI, Mary, and Elizabeth*, 2 vols. (1861–2), 17, 18, 25, 259 • AFM, 2nd edn, vol. 5, s.a. 1584 • CSP dom., 1547–90 • W. M. Hennessy, ed. and trans., *The annals of Loch Cé: a chronicle of Irish affairs from AD 1014 to AD 1590*, 2 vols., Rolls Series, 54 (1871), vol. 2, s.a. 1584 • B. Cunningham, 'The composition of Connacht in the lordships of Clanricard and Thomond, 1577–1641', *Irish Historical Studies*, 24 (1984–5), 1–14 • J. S. Brewer and W. Bullen, eds., *Calendar of the Carew manuscripts*, 2: 1575–1588, PRO (1868) • PRO, SP63/31, nos. 13, 42 • Foster, *Alum. Oxon.* • W. A. Shaw, *The knights of England*, 2 (1906)
Wealth at death extensive landholding in co. Roscommon and some land in co. Longford

Malchair, John [formerly Johann Baptist Malscher] (bap. 1730, d. 1812), folksong collector, was baptized as Johann Baptist Malscher on 15 January 1730 at Cologne, the son of a watchmaker. He was a chorister at Cologne Cathedral from 1744, moved to Nancy in 1750, and in 1754 came to England, where he was known as John Malchair. In London he played the violin at public-house concerts and taught music to mechanics and others. A gifted artist, he also obtained a post as drawing master at a ladies' school. He lived for some time in Hereford and Bristol, and from 1759 led the second violins at the Three Choirs festival; a peal of bells still rung at Gloucester Cathedral some 250 years later was his composition.

In 1760 Malchair married Elizabeth Jenner, and in the same year won the post of leader of the Oxford Music Room (later the Holywell Music Room) Band over a more prepossessing rival candidate: 'Poor Malchair, tho' a fine figure, was ugly' (Crotch's Malchair, MSS, Bodl. Oxf., MS mus. sch. D. 32), according to a friend, the Christ Church organist William Crotch (1775–1847). Malchair led the band until 1792, when an orange thrown at the orchestra during an undergraduate disturbance broke his Cremona violin. His sight was failing and he never led the band again. When Malchair became blind, Crotch wrote down his violin tunes and provided piano accompaniments for them. Malchair's melodies owe much to the folk tradition; he was a pioneer collector of popular airs, and in Oxford noted several melodies from singers and musicians heard in the streets. These include early notations of the country dance tunes 'Astley's Ride' and 'Davy, Davy Knick-Knack', and of the melody of 'Early one morning', which he obtained in May 1784 from the singing of a poor woman and two children. Malchair's own compositions include several pieces whimsically written for a violin with three strings, after an occasion when he took his violin from its case and discovered one string to be broken.

Both Malchair and Crotch were talented watercolour painters, and through Crotch, Malchair influenced later English landscape painters, including John Constable. Malchair died in Oxford on 12 December 1812.

T. B. HEALEY

Sources *New Grove* • Malchair MSS, English Folk Dance and Song Society • J. H. Mee, *The oldest music room in Europe* (1911) • Crotch's Malchair MSS, Bodl. Oxf., MS Mus. Sch. D. 32 • C. Harrison and others, *John Malchair of Oxford: artist and musician* (1998) [exhibition catalogue, AM Oxf., 22 Sept – 13 Dec 1998]
Archives Bodl. Oxf., topographical sketches • CCC Oxf., sketchbooks • NMG Wales, sketchbook

Malcolm I [Mael Coluim mac Domnaill] (d. 954), king in Scotland, was the son of *Donald II (d. 900) [see under Constantine II], and assumed the kingship of Scotland some time between 940 and 945. The confusion of the sources (if not simply the result of multiple copying errors) may indicate that this was a period of political uncertainty in which he gradually asserted his position against the aged Constantine II (d. 952), who retired (perhaps under duress) and became a monk at St Andrews. Throughout his reign Malcolm was on the offensive to both north and south. In 945 he benefited from Edmund of Wessex's devastation of the kingdom of Strathclyde, which Edmund formally acknowledged to belong to Malcolm's sphere of influence. He attacked the north of England as far as the Tees c.949 (perhaps in support of the attempt of Olaf Cuarán, king of Dublin, to take York) and in the same period or maybe earlier led an army into Moray and killed Cellach, possibly its king. In 952 he formed part of an alliance of Scots, Britons (from Strathclyde), and Saxons which was defeated by a Scandinavian force, probably led by Erik Bloodaxe, former king of Norway (d. 954), who took control of York at this time. Malcolm I was not untroubled by matters at home, however, and in 954 was killed by the men of the Mearns at Fetteresso (Kincardineshire). His body is said to have been taken to Iona for burial. He had two sons, *Dubh (*d*. 966) and *Kenneth II (*d*. 995), both of whom became king in Scotland; he was succeeded by *Indulf, son of Constantine II.   DAUVIT BROUN

Sources A. O. Anderson, ed. and trans., *Early sources of Scottish history, AD 500 to 1286*, 1 (1922), 449–54 · M. O. Anderson, *Kings and kingship in early Scotland*, rev. edn (1980), 249–53, 265–89 · A. O. Anderson, ed., *Scottish annals from English chroniclers, AD 500 to 1286* (1908), 73–4 · A. P. Smyth, *Warlords and holy men: Scotland, AD 80–1000* (1984), 205–7, 222–3

Malcolm II [Mael Coluim mac Cinaeda] (*d*. 1034), king of Scots, was the son of *Kenneth II (*d*. 995); his mother was possibly a daughter of a Uí Dúnlainge king of Leinster. Having challenged his cousin *Kenneth III for the kingship, and killed him at the battle of Monzievaird in Strathearn (now Perthshire) in 1005, he reigned for nearly thirty years and at his death he was described by a contemporary annalist as 'the honour of all the west of Europe' (Anderson, *Early Sources*, 1.572). A fourteenth-century law tract bears the title *Leges Malcolmi MacKenneth*, but has no genuine connection with Malcolm II.

Malcolm was known to medieval chroniclers as 'the most victorious' (Anderson, *Early Sources*, 1.573). His martial record was, however, patchy. He won a famous and decisive victory over Uhtred, earl of Northumbria, at Carham on the Tweed in 1018. As a result Earl Uhtred's brother, and successor as earl, formally recognized Malcolm's possession of all of Northumbria as far as the Tweed, which remained part of the Scottish kingdom's territories thereafter. At the beginning of his reign, however, Malcolm had invaded Northumbria and laid siege unsuccessfully to Durham in 1006. He was repulsed and suffered a crushing defeat at the hands of Earl Uhtred. There are unsubstantiated late accounts of Malcolm defeating Danes in battle, which associate his creation of a bishop's see at Mortlach in what later became Banffshire—from where it was moved by David I to Aberdeen—with one of these victories. An Anglo-Danish invasion which did not culminate in a famous victory for Malcolm was that of Cnut in 1031–2, after which Malcolm II was obliged to submit to Cnut, along with Macbeth, king of Moray, and another unidentified king (possibly of the Isles). By this time Malcolm may have become master of the kingdom of Strathclyde. The last recorded king of the Strathclyde royal dynasty was Owen the Bald, who fought with Malcolm at the battle of Carham and died soon afterwards in 1018. The history of Strathclyde is uncertain thereafter. It has been suggested that *Duncan I was appointed king by his grandfather Malcolm II on Owen's death. This is unlikely, however, because Duncan (who does not appear in the submission to Cnut in 1031–2) was regarded by contemporaries as a young man at his death in 1040. Perhaps Malcolm seized the kingship of Strathclyde for himself while at the zenith of his power following the battle of Carham.

Little is known of Scotland's internal affairs during Malcolm's reign. Although it has been argued that he was responsible for developing a network of thanages throughout his kingdom and even into Moray, these may have been much more ancient in origin, and in any case it

is far from certain that Malcolm was in a position to dominate Moray. Findlaech mac Ruaidrí (*d*. 1020) and Mael Coluim mac Maíl Brígte (*d*. 1029), successive rulers of Moray, are both described in their obits in a (probably) contemporary source as 'king of Scotland', which may suggest that Malcolm's own position in his kingdom was under threat from the north, perhaps after the débâcle of the campaign against Durham in 1006, and again in the 1020s.

Malcolm's successful bid for the throne in 1005 may have ushered in a period of dynastic stability. At the end of his reign, however, strife within the royal kindred was certainly renewed, resulting in Malcolm II having the grandson of Boite mac Cinaeda (probably Malcolm's brother) killed in 1033. Malcolm was doubtless already an old man, and he died at Glamis on 25 November the following year. A late source claims that he was assassinated. It is also alleged that his body was taken to Iona for burial. With his death the male lineage of Kenneth I relinquished the kingship it had held continuously since 889 and had fashioned into the kingdom of 'Scotland', Alba. It is said, on the strength of the killing of the grandson of Boite, that Malcolm II in his final years was paving the way for the succession of his grandson Duncan I. It is possible, however, that in killing Boite's grandson he was simply beating off a challenge to his own position.

It is not known whether Malcolm had any sons, but he may have had as many as three daughters. The only one whose name in known is Bethóc, who married Crínán, abbot of Dunkeld (*d*. 1045). Their son was Duncan I, who succeeded Malcolm as king. Another daughter of Malcolm married *Sigurd (II) Hlödvisson, earl of Orkney (*d*. 1014), whose son was Thorfinn the Mighty, earl of Orkney. The evidence for Malcolm's third daughter is late and uncertain. She is alleged to have married Findlaech mac Ruaidrí king of Moray, whose son *Macbeth (*d*. 1057) succeeded Duncan I as king of Scots in 1040.   DAUVIT BROUN

Sources A. O. Anderson, ed. and trans., *Early sources of Scottish history, AD 500 to 1286*, 1 (1922), 525–75 · A. A. M. Duncan, *Scotland: the making of the kingdom* (1975), vol. 1 of *The Edinburgh history of Scotland*, ed. G. Donaldson (1965–75), 97–100 · M. O. Anderson, *Kings and kingship in early Scotland*, rev. edn (1980), 265–89 · A. O. Anderson, ed., *Scottish annals from English chroniclers, AD 500 to 1286* (1908), 80–83

Malcolm III [Mael Coluim Ceann Mór, Malcolm Canmore] (*d*. 1093), king of Scots, was the eldest son of *Duncan I, king of Scots from 1034 to 1040, and his wife, who is said to have been a cousin of Siward, earl of Northumbria (*d*. 1055). During the reign of *Macbeth (*r*. 1040–57), who had killed Duncan I in order to take the throne, Malcolm was an exile at the court of Edward the Confessor, king of England, and was given a small estate in Northamptonshire. In 1054 Malcolm was present with an army led into Scotland by Siward, probably by command of King Edward, who supplied some of Siward's forces. On 27 July the earl's army defeated Macbeth, traditionally on Dunsinnan Hill in the Sidlaws, with heavy losses on both sides. The victory evidently put Malcolm in possession of Scotland south of the Tay. Three years later (on 15 August 1057) he slew Macbeth at Lumphanan, in what is now Aberdeenshire.

Although Macbeth's stepson, *Lulach [see under Macbeth], was accepted as king by some of the Scots (he can hardly have been made king at Scone, the traditional place for royal inaugurations), Malcolm ambushed and killed him near Rhynie in Strathbogie, in March 1058, and (on 25 April, according to the fourteenth-century historian John Fordoun) succeeded to the throne.

In spite of a peaceful visit to Edward the Confessor in 1059, the first of Malcolm's five raids into English Northumbria took place in 1061, when Holy Island was plundered. Since 1018 at the latest, Scottish Northumbria (that is, Lothian and the merse of Berwickshire) had been part of the northern kingdom. Malcolm seems to have been determined to annex Northumbria between Tweed and Tees, his ambition forming the mirror image of that of the West Saxon kings of England, who regarded the territory from Tees to Forth as part of their lordship. In contrast to the experience of his predecessor Macbeth, Malcolm's relations with the Scandinavian rulers of the northern isles were friendly. About 1060 he married, as his first wife, Ingibjorg (d. c.1067), who was either the widow or the daughter of the earl of Orkney, Thorfinn, son of Sigurd. She is more likely to have been the earl's daughter: Thorfinn's death is usually put at 1064 or 1065, and with his first wife Malcolm had three sons, *Duncan II, Donald, and possibly Malcolm, for whose births there would scarcely have been time between the mid-1060s and the king's second marriage, in either 1069 or 1070.

This second, and famous, marriage, to *Margaret (d. 1093), daughter of *Edward Ætheling (d. 1057) and great-niece of Edward the Confessor, was a consequence, however remote, of the Norman conquest of England. In 1066, following the Confessor's death and Harold Godwineson's assumption of the English throne, Tostig, Harold's brother and until 1065 earl of Northumbria in succession to Siward, plotted with the count of Flanders, Harald Hardrada, king of Norway, and Malcolm, king of Scots, to overthrow Harold Godwineson and, probably, to partition England between them. Although during the summer of 1066 Tostig had been sheltered by King Malcolm, and was said to have been his 'sworn brother', the Scots played no part in the sea-borne invasion of northern England carried out by Tostig and the king of Norway, which ended disastrously for both leaders on 25 September at the battle of Stamford Bridge. Malcolm seems to have viewed the confusion which followed William of Normandy's victory at Hastings as an opportunity to fulfil his ambitions in Northumbria south of Tweed. Although the chronology of events from 1068 to 1071 is hard to establish with precision, it is clear that English resistance to the Normans looked to Scotland for refuge and military support. In the summer of 1068 *Edgar Ætheling, upon whom the aspirations of English nationalists were focused, fled to the Scottish court with his mother and his two sisters, Margaret and Christina. A northern English rising was thwarted by King William's occupation of York and an agreement made with Malcolm which staved off a Scottish invasion. By 1070, however, Malcolm was raiding south of Tweed with a large army. It is not likely that this incursion was intended to support the second Northumbrian rising, which had begun with the killing of Robert Comin (whom William I had appointed earl of Northumbria) in January 1069, for that rising had been effectively suppressed by the Conqueror by Easter 1070. Nevertheless, it was in the period 1069–70 that Malcolm married Edgar Ætheling's sister Margaret. The marriage cannot have been viewed by William I as a friendly act, and must have been meant to give any heirs of the Scottish king's second marriage a claim to English kingship.

Malcolm's aggressive policy led to the Conqueror's only expedition to Scotland. In 1072 William led an army and fleet north as far as the Firth of Tay, and received the homage of the king of Scots at Abernethy. Probably as a result of this submission, Edgar Ætheling made his peace with William, who treated him honourably. The dynasty ruling in Moray still had leaders who could challenge Malcolm's kingship, for in 1078 Lulach's son Mael Snechta was in rebellion, and Malcolm captured his mother and chief adherents. A reconciliation may have followed, as Mael Snechta died peacefully in 1085. In the meantime, the king of Scots carried out his third major raid into Northumberland (1079), sparing the lands and church of Hexham out of reverence for the local saints. The Conqueror's response to this was to send north his eldest son, Robert Curthose, with an army (1080), but he got no further than Falkirk and achieved little beyond building the 'New Castle' on the north bank of the Tyne, near the site of the Roman bridge (pons Aelius). That Malcolm was sensitive in the matter of his authority over Scottish Northumbria is shown by a story told in Symeon of Durham's Historia ecclesiae Dunelmensis. According to this account, Turgot (subsequently Queen Margaret's biographer and bishop of St Andrews), in association with Aldwin, formerly a monk of Winchcombe in Gloucestershire, attempted to revive monastic life at Old Melrose, perhaps in the late 1070s. The Scottish king demanded that the two English monks take an oath of fealty to him, and when this was refused persecuted them in various ways, until at last they were recalled to England by Bishop Walcher of Durham (d. 1080).

For the rest of William I's reign Malcolm's relations with England seem to have been peaceful, and at the accession of William Rufus, Malcolm's eldest son, Duncan, who had been for years a hostage in England, was knighted by the new king and allowed to go to Scotland in freedom. But by 1091 Malcolm was once again raiding Northumbria as far south as Durham. A sea and land expedition mounted by Rufus was severely hampered by bad weather which sank his fleet and played havoc with his cavalry force. Robert Curthose and Edgar Ætheling negotiated a peace which restored English estates to Malcolm which had been given by the Conqueror and, according to some sources, involved Malcolm's homage to Rufus. The latter seems to have been impressed by the fragility of the Scottish border, for in 1092 he went north again and forcibly annexed Carlisle and its district, building a strong castle and settling the area with English peasants. It has been suggested that there had been recent precedent for an English take-over of at least part of Cumbria, inasmuch as Earl Siward is shown exercising authority over a free tenant west of Carlisle, in a writ issued *c*.1050 by an unidentified lord named Cospatric. The authenticity of this writ is uncertain, but even if it is genuine it deals only with a restricted area between Carlisle and Wigton, and can scarcely be regarded as evidence that Siward held territorial lordship even over Cumbria south of the Solway. A statement in the *Historia regum* of Symeon of Durham, that in 1070 Cumberland was under Malcolm's control, 'not possessed by right but subjugated by force' (Symeon of Durham, *Opera*, 2.191), shows both that the region was then being ruled by the Scottish king, and that there were Englishmen who resented this. The status of Cumberland had in fact long been disputed, so that Rufus's seizure of Carlisle and its district hardly needed any precedent, but such an act of aggression nevertheless gave Malcolm a clear grievance.

It was agreed that Malcolm would meet the English king at Gloucester at the end of August 1093. On his journey south he took part in the ceremony of laying the foundation stones for the new (that is, the present) cathedral at Durham. But when the Scottish king reached the English court, William disdainfully refused to see him. An enraged Malcolm (having visited his elder daughter Edith at Wilton) returned to his own land and at once mustered a force with which to inflict maximum damage upon English territory. North of Alnwick he and Edward, the eldest son of his second marriage, were ambushed by the earl of Northumbria, Robert de Mowbray, and were both killed, the king falling victim to Archil Morel of Bamburgh, described as his 'comrade', on 13 November 1093. Malcolm was buried later the same month at Tynemouth Priory and a younger son, *Edgar, carried the news of the death of his father and brother to Edinburgh where his mother, Queen Margaret, lay ill, exhausted by her too severe regime of self-denial. She died of grief on 16 November and was buried in the monastic church she had founded at Dunfermline, where in the reign of her son *Alexander I (*r.* 1107–24) the body of her husband was brought for burial beside her. At the Reformation the remains of both Margaret and Malcolm were transferred by Philip II of Spain to the Escorial at Madrid.

In spite of the brutality involved in his raids into English Northumbria, Malcolm III left a reputation for sagacity, and a story preserved by Ailred of Rievaulx, in which Malcolm placed himself in the power of a conspirator, and then disarmed him with the force of his reproaches, shows that the king was also credited with exceptional moral stature. His byname, Ceann Mór, meaning 'Big Head', from which comes Canmore, is probably to be understood literally. However, the same sobriquet is also recorded in a twelfth-century source as being applied to his great-grandson Malcolm IV, prompting speculation that he suffered from Paget's disease. Malcolm III is not certainly referred to as Canmore before the thirteenth century, though contemporary accounts refer to his florid complexion and long neck. Malcolm was succeeded as king by his brother *Donald III.

Although no significant innovator, Malcolm III, by his vigorous rule and his remarkable second marriage, left Scotland a very different kingdom from what it had been before 1050. It was more clearly defined territorially and more decisively within the orbit of an English kingdom conquered by the Normans, and was appreciably less oriented towards the Scandinavian north. Malcolm and Margaret may be said to have put Scotland on the European map.   G. W. S. BARROW

Sources *ASC* · A. O. Anderson, ed. and trans., *Early sources of Scottish history, AD 500 to 1286*, 2 vols. (1922); repr. with corrections (1990) · R. L. G. Ritchie, *The Normans in Scotland* (1954) · A. O. Anderson, ed., *Scottish annals from English chroniclers, AD 500 to 1286* (1908); repr. (1991) · H. Pálsson and P. Edwards, eds. and trans., *The Orkneyinga saga: the history of the earls of Orkney* (1978); repr. (1981) · Symeon of Durham, *Opera* · A. A. M. Duncan, *The kingdom of the Scots, 842–1292* (2002)

Malcolm IV (1141–1165), king of Scots, was the eldest son of *Henry, earl of Huntingdon and of Northumberland (*c*.1115–1152), and *Ada de Warenne (*c*.1123–1178), and grandson of King *David I. Born between 23 April and 24 May 1141, he became his grandfather's heir when his father died, on 12 or 13 June 1152. In the care of Duncan, earl of Fife (*d.* 1154), he was then taken round Scotland north of the Forth, and thus, by Celtic custom, shown to be heir to the kingdom. When David I died, on 24 May 1153, Malcolm succeeded peaceably. Although he was only twelve years old there was no formal regency. But his early *acta* suggest that real power lay with Walter, son of Alan, the steward (*d.* 1177), Hugh de Morville, the constable (*d.* 1162), and some eight other laymen, with Walter de Bidun, the chancellor, and several bishops.

The long period of internal peace established by David I was broken in November 1154 when Somerled, lord of Argyll, and his nephews, sons of Malcolm MacHeth (claimant to the earldom of Ross, and a dangerous rebel in the previous reign), revolted. Seaborne raids were probably made on the mainland; in 1156 Donald MacHeth was captured at Whithorn and sent to join his father in prison at Roxburgh Castle. In 1157 the king and the MacHeths were reconciled. Deprived of some of his support, Somerled made peace, perhaps in 1159.

Before this pacification the Scots had also faced pressure from England, where King Henry II began to assert himself after his coronation (19 December 1154); in 1157 he was ready to deal with Scotland. Malcolm met him at The Peak in Derbyshire; then, at Chester, in July 1157, he did homage 'in the manner in which his grandfather had been the man of old King Henry' says the Melrose chronicle (Anderson, *Early Sources*, 2.233), tactfully concealing that he was made to give up Cumberland, Westmorland, and Northumberland. Henry subsequently restored the honour of Huntingdon to Malcolm, and gave the lordship of Tynedale to the latter's younger brother *William. The surrenders and regrants were made quickly. The kings met at Carlisle, now an English city, in January 1158 and parted at odds; Henry had publicly snubbed Malcolm's dignity, social expectations, and, in all likelihood, personal wishes by declining to make him a knight. Henry meanwhile recovered castles, revenues, and the silver mines in the northern Pennines. He had weakened Scottish prestige, security, and wealth.

In April or May 1159 a very well-attended court at Roxburgh confirmed the possessions of Kelso Abbey, and probably also considered the need for a new bishop of St Andrews and preparations for a military expedition overseas. Robert, bishop of St Andrews, died early in 1159. A successor had to be found, and a means of denying the archbishop of York's customary claims to a profession of obedience from a new bishop. Malcolm's step-uncle Waldef, abbot of Melrose (d. 1159), was selected but declined. William, bishop of Moray, and Nicholas, the king's chamberlain, were then sent overseas to the pope, probably with proposals to make St Andrews an archbishopric. The bishop returned with powers of a legate and a commendation from Pope Alexander III (r. 1159–81) that he become bishop of St Andrews. This was not acceptable; Arnold, abbot of Kelso, was elected bishop on 13 November 1160 and consecrated by the legate in the king's presence at St Andrews on the 20th. After Arnold's death on 13 September 1162, Richard (d. 1178), a chaplain of the king, was elected as bishop, probably early in 1163. The claims of York were pressed and rebuffed; on 28 October 1164 Ingram (d. 1174), the king's chancellor, was consecrated as bishop of Glasgow by Alexander III at Sens; then, provided with specific papal authority, he and other Scottish bishops consecrated Richard at St Andrews on 28 March 1165 in the presence of the king. In both cases direct links with the papacy had been established, York's claims had been deflected, and the king's candidates had been installed. Long-term effects of these events became clear in the next reign.

The Roxburgh court of 1159 probably also considered Henry II's call-out (March 1159) of his forces from Normandy, England, Aquitaine, and 'other provinces which are subject to him' (Lawrie, 41–2) for an expedition to Toulouse. Malcolm's attendance was no doubt required, and a summons may have been welcome; it gave a chance to be knighted honourably in the field. The king, his brother William, and other Scots crossed the channel on 16 June 1159, and joined Henry's army at Poitiers on the 24th. At Périgueux, about 30 June, Henry knighted Malcolm. Until September the army overran the county of Toulouse; after intervention by King Louis VII of France (r. 1137–80) a siege of the city was abandoned, the army retired, and Malcolm and Henry were at Limoges about the end of September of that year.

Malcolm, possibly after a visit to the earldom of Huntingdon, returned to Scotland early in 1160 to a hostile reception. Ferteth, earl of Strathearn, and five other earls, angered that he had been to Toulouse, besieged him at Perth. Mediation by the clergy ended the immediate dispute. But unrest then appeared in Galloway, and later in the year the king made three military forays there. Fergus, lord of Galloway (d. 1161), submitted and by the end of the year there had been a general reconciliation. Malcolm's Christmas feast at Perth in 1160 was very well attended by prominent laymen (including probably Somerled of

Argyll, earning by his presence the nickname 'Sit-by-the-King') and ecclesiastics. Royal authority had been vindicated and one lesson had been learned; for the rest of the reign and for that of William the Lion (r. 1165–1214) the earls of Scotland were never given cause for armed opposition to the king.

The peace held for three years. The king was now a young adult; an aggressive edge appears in matters where he could use personal influence, such as the bestowal of his sisters Margaret and Ada, married respectively in 1160 to *Conan (IV), duke of Brittany (c.1135–1171), and in 1161 to Florence, count of Holland (d. 1190). The matches linked Scotland with ruling houses then outside the range of Angevin political control. But such gestures had little real effect; Malcolm was again called south in 1163 by Henry II. An illness, perhaps a grave one, at Doncaster on the outward journey did not enable him and his brothers to avoid attendance at Henry's court at Woodstock at the end of June, to find there a group of Welsh rulers; the gathering was evidently meant to demonstrate Henry's lordship within Britain. On 1 July Malcolm again did homage, and handed over as hostages his brother *David (d. 1219), subsequently earl of Huntingdon, and other young noblemen.

In 1163 'King Malcolm transported the men of Moray' (Holyrood Chronicle, 142). This has never been satisfactorily explained; a later tradition of a large-scale removal of population is probably false. Another later view is that it caused the last revolt of Somerled of Argyll in 1164. Supported by a large fleet, and troops from outside Scotland, he attacked Renfrew, the chief residence of Walter the Steward. Rather than a reaction to events in Moray, this might have been a protest against Malcolm's second homage to Henry II, as well as a direct thrust at the steward. In June 1161, at an exceptionally well-attended court at Roxburgh, the king had formally confirmed Walter's extensive lands in Scotland. This sign of trust in an important 'Norman' incomer could scarcely have had a more public demonstration. The invasion failed. Local forces organized by Bishop Herbert of Glasgow (d. 1164) surprised the enemy; Somerled was killed and his head was cut off and presented to the bishop, who attributed the victory to St Kentigern. There was peace for the rest of the reign.

During that time the king completed his major monastic foundation, the Cistercian abbey of Coupar Angus, and secured a refoundation of the Augustinian priory of Scone as an abbey. The first grants for the former had been made in 1161 or 1162; it was fully established by 12 July 1164 when Fulk, the first abbot, was blessed by Bishop Gregory of Dunkeld. Scone had been devastated by a fire, and at Stirling, between May 1163 and May 1164, the king confirmed earlier gifts by kings Alexander I (d. 1124) and David I, added some of his own, and provided an abbot. At various other times he made some gifts to the hospital of Soutra (but probably did not found it), and granted or confirmed gifts to all the major foundations of David I.

After his illness in 1163 Malcolm may not have recovered entirely. He is said to have suffered severe pains in his head and feet, symptoms which, when taken with the contemporary notice of his death in the annals of Ulster, which calls him Cennmor, or 'Big Head', suggest that he was suffering from Paget's disease. An enlargement of the skull is a typical symptom of this affliction; another is pain in the legs. It would thus appear that the original Malcolm Canmore was Malcolm IV, rather than his great-grandfather Malcolm III, who seems to have acquired that nickname only in the thirteenth century. In the last two years of his reign Malcolm was still able to travel within eastern Scotland, but perhaps rarely. He hoped to make a pilgrimage to Santiago de Compostela, no doubt in search of healing, but was unable to do this. He was at Jedburgh in his final illness and died there on Thursday 9 December 1165, aged twenty-four, having reigned for some twelve years and six months. His last bequest was an annual payment of 100 shillings to Dunfermline Abbey, where he was buried, attended at the last by several bishops. On that day Walter the Steward honoured his memory by a gift of land to the abbey.

For an Irish writer Malcolm was 'with regard to charity and hospitality and piety the best Christian of the Gaels to the east of the sea' (Anderson, *Early Sources*, 2.261). Godric of Finchale mentions him in the same breath as Thomas Becket. He was not interested in marriage. His nickname 'Malcolm the Maiden' is not known before the fifteenth century, but well before 1200 his reputation for chastity was fully accepted by several writers. There can be no doubt about his close interest in ecclesiastical matters: the foundation and enhancement of religious houses; appointments to the see of St Andrews; a wish, made too late in life to be fulfilled, to be a pilgrim to Compostela. But Malcolm was no cleric; he ruled as a layman, struggled with internal revolts, and re-established royal authority and peace, which after 1164 was not broken for ten years. After the loss of the northern counties of England, the integrity of the kingdom to which David I had succeeded was maintained; the claims of York over the church in Scotland were consistently and firmly opposed. Although he is also represented on coins and seals, the most striking likeness of Malcolm is that contained in the initial letter of his charter for Kelso Abbey. That he is there shown as a young and beardless figure, seated beside his venerable grandfather David I, may be taken as intended to symbolize dynastic continuity, and within the kingdom David I's innovations were undisturbed or strengthened: for example, more burghs appear, and upper Clydesdale was divided into knights' feus, several of them granted to Flemish settlers. Except, as always, for the loss of Northumberland, his brother William can have had little real cause for complaint when he succeeded.

W. W. SCOTT

Sources A. O. Anderson, ed. and trans., *Early sources of Scottish history, AD 500 to 1286*, 2 (1922) · G. W. S. Barrow, ed., *Regesta regum Scottorum*, 1 (1960) · G. W. S. Barrow, *The kingdom of the Scots: government, church and society from the eleventh to the fourteenth century* (1973) · A. C. Lawrie, ed., *Annals of the reigns of Malcolm and William, kings of Scotland* (1910) · W. Bower, *Scotichronicon*, ed. D. E. R. Watt and others, new edn, 9 vols. (1987–98), vol. 4 · R. Somerville, ed., *Scotia pontificia: papal letters to Scotland before the pontificate of Innocent III* (1982) · G. W. S. Barrow, *The Anglo-Norman era in Scottish history* (1980) · A. A. M. Duncan, *Scotland: the making of the kingdom* (1975), vol. 1 of *The Edinburgh history of Scotland*, ed. G. Donaldson (1965–75) · *The chronicle of Holyrood*, ed. A. O. Anderson and M. O. Anderson (1938) · A. O. Anderson, ed., *Scottish annals from English chroniclers, AD 500 to 1286* (1908) · A. A. M. Duncan, *The kingdom of the Scots, 842–1292* (2002)
Likenesses illuminated initial, c.1159, NL Scot., charter for Kelso Abbey; *see illus. in* David I (c.1085–1153)

Malcolm, Sir Charles (1782–1851), naval officer, tenth son of George Malcolm (1729–1803) of Burnfoot, Dumfriesshire, and his wife, Margaret (d. 1811), daughter of James Pasley of Craig, Dumfreisshire, and sister of Admiral Sir Charles Pasley, bt, was born at Burnfoot in Dumfriesshire on 5 September 1782. Sir Pulteney *Malcolm and Sir John *Malcolm were his brothers. In 1791 his name was put on the books of the *Vengeance*, commanded by his uncle, Commodore Thomas Pasley, and in 1793 of the *Penelope*, of which his brother Pulteney was first lieutenant. He entered the navy in person in 1795 on the *Fox*, then commissioned by his brother, with whom he went out to the East Indies, and whom he followed to the *Suffolk*. He was promoted by the admiral to be lieutenant of that ship, on 12 January 1799, and remained in her until 3 October 1801, when he was appointed acting commander of the sloop *Albatross* (a promotion confirmed by the Admiralty to 28 May 1802). In 1803 he returned home acting captain of the *Eurydice* (24 guns), and on his arrival in England found that he had been previously promoted captain by the Admiralty on 29 December 1802. In 1804 he commanded the *Raisonnable* in the North Sea, and from 1806 to 1809 the frigate *Narcissus* on the coast of France and Portugal; at Oporto in 1807 he was able to save much British property from the French. In the beginning of 1809 he went out to the West Indies, and in April took part in the capture of the Saintes Islands. On his return to England he was moved into the *Rhin* (38 guns), in which during 1812 and 1813 he co-operated with the patriots on the north coast of Spain. In 1813 he went out to the West Indies in convoy; in 1814 he was cruising on the coast of Brazil; and on 18 July 1815, having been joined by the frigates *Menelaus* and *Havannah* and the sloops *Fly* and *Ferret*, he landed a party of seamen and marines at Corrijou on the coast of Brittany, stormed the battery, and brought out of the harbour three small armed vessels and a convoy under their protection. The action was of a type that had become customary, but was the last such during that war.

In September 1817 Malcolm fitted out the *Sibylle* (44 guns), as flag captain to Sir Home Popham in the West Indies, from where he was invalided in February 1819. From 1822 to 1827 he commanded one or other of the yachts *William and Mary* and *Royal Charlotte* in attendance on the Marquess Wellesley, lord lieutenant of Ireland, by whom he was knighted in 1827.

In November 1827 he was appointed superintendent of the Bombay marine, then reorganized and placed under new regulations, which required it to have a captain of the Royal Navy at its head. Malcolm arrived at Bombay in June 1828, where he reformed the navy. On 1 May 1830 its name was officially changed to the Indian Navy, and in addition to the rigorous discharge of its police duties, it became distinguished as a school of surveyors. Malcolm held the post for ten years, and on his being relieved was officially thanked by the governor in council. The introduction and establishment of steam navigation in the Red Sea were also largely due to him. He was promoted rear-admiral on 10 January 1837, and vice-admiral on 28 April 1847, but had no further service.

During his later years Malcolm gave much attention to professional institutions and charities. He also served continuously on the council of the Royal Geographical Society. He was twice married: first, on 4 June 1808, to his cousin Magdalene, daughter of Charles Pasley, his mother's brother; and second, on 11 April 1829, to Elmira Riddell, youngest daughter of Major-General Shaw. With his first wife he had one daughter, and with his second three sons, two of whom became naval officers.

Malcolm died at Brighton on 4 June 1851, and was buried in the catacombs at the Brighton cemetery.

J. K. LAUGHTON, rev. ANDREW LAMBERT

Sources D. Syrett and R. L. DiNardo, *The commissioned sea officers of the Royal Navy, 1660–1815*, rev. edn, Occasional Publications of the Navy RS, 1 (1994) • A. D. Lambert, *The last sailing battlefleet: maintaining naval mastery, 1815–1850* (1991) • J. Sutton, *Lords of the east: the East India Company and its ships* (1981) • H. Popham, *A damned cunning fellow: the eventful life of Rear-Admiral Sir Home Popham* (1991) • O'Byrne, *Naval biog. dict.* • *GM*, 2nd ser., 36 (1851), 431 • C. R. Low, *History of the Indian navy, 1613–1863*, 2 vols. (1877) • *Journal of the Royal Geographical Society*, 22 (1852), lxiv–lxv • Boase, *Mod. Eng. biog.*
Archives NL Scot., letter-books; personal log and notebook • NMM, log and letter-books | BL, letters to Sir Charles Pasley, Add. MSS 41962–41964

Malcolm [Malcolme], **David** (d. 1748), philologist, was licensed as a preacher by the presbytery of Haddington on 11 January 1700 and was ordained on 28 March 1705 to the ministry of Duddingston, at the foot of Arthur's Seat, near Edinburgh. Nothing is known of his life before 1700. He married Susanna Anderson and at least four children of theirs were baptized at Duddingston between 1712 and 1721. Malcolm's celebration of the marriage of George Drummond to Catherine, daughter of Sir James Campbell of Aberuchill, caused him to be summoned before the presbytery on 10 November 1721 and rebuked at the bar for his conduct.

Though not a highlander, Malcolm devoted himself to the study of Gaelic and, according to the Scots antiquary Walter MacFarlan, acquired an amazing knowledge of the etymology of Scottish place names (Gough, 487n.). In 1732 Malcolm proposed to augment, revise, and reprint the Irish–English dictionary from Edward Lhuyd's *Archaeologia Britannica* (1707), adding writings of his own, intended to illustrate Latin, Greek, Hebrew, and Chaldean from Gaelic, and *inter alia* to demonstrate an affinity between Gaelic and the language spoken by natives of the Darien isthmus in Central America. He had the backing of learned societies in Edinburgh and a publication grant of £20 from the general assembly of the Church of Scotland in 1737, but his only traced publication is a hotchpotch of testimonials, correspondence with scholars and possible patrons, and translations and extracts from Lhuyd and

others, under the collective title of *An Essay on the Antiquities of Great Britain and Ireland* (1738). With the addition of more testimonials and correspondence and letter A of the proposed dictionary this collection was reissued under different self-advertising cancel-titles in Edinburgh (1739) and London (1744).

On 12 August 1736 Malcolm was elected FSA, but he evidently spent too much time in London on publication projects because he was deposed from his Duddingston ministry on 24 March 1742 for having deserted his charge for two years without leave. The sentence of deposition was recalled only when he demitted (that is, abdicated) his ministry on 27 April 1743. In the following year he unsuccessfully attempted to ensure that his wife and children could benefit from a newly established ministers' widows' fund. His eldest son, John, an army surgeon and physician in Ayr, was acting for him in financial affairs by 1743, suggesting that he was ill or otherwise incapacitated (Baird, 218). David Malcolm died on 7 February 1748.

JAMES SAMBROOK

Sources D. Malcolm, *An essay on the antiquities of Great Britain and Ireland* (1738) • N. Morren, *Annals of the general assembly of the Church of Scotland* (1838), 1.21, 384 • D. Malcolm, *Letters, essays, and other tracts* (1744) • *Fasti Scot.*, new edn, 1.19 • *Scots Magazine*, 10 (1748), 50 • W. Baird, *Annals of Duddingston and Portobello* (1898), 216–18 • R. G. [R. Gough], *British topography*, [new edn], 2 (1780), 487n. • IGI • D. Duncan, *Thomas Ruddiman* (1965), 36n., 82n.

Malcolm, Sir Dougal Orme (1877–1955), colonial administrator and company director, was born on 6 August 1877 at Walton Manor in Epsom, Surrey, the younger son of William Rolle Malcolm (b. 1840), senior partner of Coutts's Bank, and his first wife, Georgina Wellesley (d. 1880), sister of the fourth duke of Wellington. Malcolm's father was of Scottish descent, and Malcolm cherished his Scottish connections. He was educated at Eton College until 1895, proceeding in that year to New College, Oxford, where he gained a first class in both classical moderations and Greats. In 1899, in a remarkable family double, he followed his father in being elected a fellow of All Souls. Malcolm's liking for masculine collegiality, his lifelong pleasure in classical literature, and his close association, personal, political, and professional, with a number of fellows, including Lionel Curtis and Robert Brand, made the college an important focus of his social and intellectual activity throughout his life.

As was then usual among fellows of All Souls, Malcolm did not linger in academe, but entered the civil service, which then recruited (at graduate level) through a demanding academic examination of the kind at which he excelled. He was appointed to the Colonial Office at the moment when the Second South African War (1899–1902) was the main preoccupation of a department responsible for the political supervision of Cape Colony and Natal and the administration of the conquered Boer republics. Malcolm acted as private secretary to the high commissioner in South Africa, Sir Alfred Milner, during his periodic visits to London. But his real chance came in 1905, when (probably on Milner's recommendation) he went to South

Sir Dougal Orme Malcolm (1877–1955), by Walter Stoneman, 1938

Africa as private secretary to Milner's successor Lord Selborne. This opened Malcolm's lifelong connection with southern Africa. It also brought him into direct contact with the group whose members became his closest friends and associates: the loose fraternity of Milner's aides, the so-called 'Kindergarten', which later constituted the core of the 'Round Table'. They included, as well as Curtis and Brand, Patrick Duncan, Lionel Hichens, Richard Feetham, John Dove, Peter Perry, and Philip Kerr, later marquess of Lothian. The Kindergarten remained after Milner's departure to occupy key posts in the temporary post-war administration. They were also committed to Milner's project to unify South Africa as a British 'dominion' on the Canadian model. They were largely responsible for the 'Selborne memorandum', published in 1907 to promote the idea of federation, to the writing of which Malcolm, as Selborne's closest aide, made an important contribution. On Selborne's retirement in 1910, Malcolm went briefly to Canada as private secretary to Lord Grey, the governor-general. On his return, he moved to the Treasury and acted for a time as secretary to the dominions royal commission, set up in 1911 to inquire into the promotion of intra-empire trade.

Thus far, Malcolm had pursued a conventional enough career for a young man of his class, education, and background. On 20 June 1910 he married Dora Claire Stopford (1883/4–1920), daughter of John Montagu Stopford. In 1913 he made a sharp sideways move. He left the civil service, perhaps out of frustration, perhaps to increase his

income. It seems likely that he lacked the means (as well as the inclination) to seek a parliamentary career. Instead, probably on the recommendation of Lord Grey, himself a former director (1889–1904), Malcolm was appointed to the board of the British South Africa Company, the enterprise which he served for the rest of his career, as a director and as president (or executive chairman) after 1937.

The British South Africa Company was a very unusual company. It was the creation of Cecil Rhodes. In 1889 Rhodes had obtained a royal charter from the government of Lord Salisbury authorizing the company to occupy and administer on behalf of the crown a vast tract of 'Zambezia' (modern Zambia and Zimbabwe), soon renamed Northern Rhodesia and Southern Rhodesia. In this huge domain, the company exercised the functions of a government and exploited the mining concessions Rhodes had extracted from Lobengula, the Ndbele king (the 'Rudd concession'). It was also understood to own all unalienated land. In 1890 the pioneer column had established a rudimentary government in Salisbury (later Harare); Rhodes pressed ahead with building a railway system, and a skeletal presence was established north of the Zambezi.

Since the early days, however, little had gone to plan. Two major rebellions in Southern Rhodesia were a heavy financial drain. The company's reputation was badly damaged by the Jameson raid of 1895, since Sir Leander Jameson was the company's administrator in Mashonaland and his raiders were the company's paramilitary police. Economic development was slow: no second Rand was found. No dividend was paid to the shareholders, nor was to be until 1924. By 1902, with the death of the founder, the board was looking forward to handing over its costly administrative role to the imperial government (Gell to Milner, 4 April 1902, Bodl. Oxf., MS Milner 5). But the Colonial Office declined the poisoned chalice. Nor would it say when such a handover would take place. Instead it quietly encouraged settler discontent with the company's government. In 1913 it referred the settlers' challenge to the company's land rights in Southern Rhodesia to the judicial committee of the privy council, the highest tribunal in the empire.

It was at this critical point in its fortunes that Malcolm had become a director of the company, perhaps commended by his insider knowledge of the Colonial Office, whose ministerial chief was roundly cursed at company headquarters: 'Gott strafe Harcourt' became a regular salutation (Blake, 174). The company had reason to curse. In 1918 the privy council found that unalienated land was owned not by the company but by the crown. It no longer had any prospect of recouping its heavy administrative costs by selling land to new settlers. Indeed, its commercial survival now depended upon shedding the charter and extracting what compensation it could for past expenditure.

Malcolm played a crucial role in the complex negotiations over the future of the Rhodesias between 1919 and 1923–4, together with Philip Gell, a director since 1899 and president from 1920 to 1923. In 1920 he opposed granting self-government to the settlers in Southern Rhodesia: to do so, he told Lord Selborne, would be to repeat 'the Natal blunder in a far worse form' (Malcolm to Selborne, 14 June 1920, Bodl. Oxf., MS Selborne 72). He preferred to see its absorption (with the 'railway belt' in Northern Rhodesia) into an enlarged South Africa under the leadership of J. C. Smuts, now seen as a loyal ally of the imperial system (Wood, 44–5). But the settlers rejected this course. Instead, with the demise of the charter, the Rhodesias were separated: Southern Rhodesia was granted qualified self-government as a settler colony; Northern Rhodesia became a protectorate under the direct control of the Colonial Office. Malcolm's main task became to win the best terms he could for the company and its shareholders from an unsympathetic Treasury. Here he succeeded rather better. The company was paid £2.3 million in compensation for its land rights in Southern Rhodesia, and its war debt of £2 million to the imperial government was waived. More to the point, it was allowed to retain its mineral rights in both Rhodesias: entitling it to a royalty on proceeds, and, in Northern Rhodesia, effective control over prospecting and exploitation. In 1924 the company's first dividend was declared. The best was yet to come.

Between the wars Malcolm's achievement was to capitalize on the company's assets: its mineral rights and ownership of the Rhodesian railway system. In 1933 he agreed to sell the mineral rights in Southern Rhodesia to its settler government for £2 million. Meanwhile—in partnership with the Anglo-American Corporation, the great mineral house formed by Ernest Oppenheimer in 1917, and the American Chester Beatty group—he pressed ahead with developing a huge mineral deposit scarcely known at the time of the charter's surrender: the Northern Rhodesian copperbelt. By 1939, through its royalty and its share of mining profits, the company had become exceptionally profitable, returning an average dividend of 8 per cent between 1924 and 1939 (Malcolm, 54). With the onset of war and the post-war rise in commodity prices, the copper royalty became more valuable than ever, eventually yielding over £100 million before nationalization in 1964. Then in the later 1940s Malcolm became embroiled in the arguments over creating a (white-ruled) federation of the Rhodesias and Nyasaland (later Malawi). He had furiously resisted the demand of the settler politicians in Northern Rhodesia (led by Roy Welensky) for a share of mineral royalties in 1947, and gave way only when the Colonial Office threatened to allow the legislative council to pass a new mining law. Malcolm himself dismissed a central African federation as unworkable, favouring instead amalgamation, with a unitary government under settler control. He died two years after the federation was established but before his prophecy was vindicated.

The company's affairs may have preoccupied Malcolm. But he cultivated a wide range of other interests. He was a director of numerous companies, including the Anglo-American Company, De Beers Consolidated, and the British North Borneo Company. He remained closely attached to the Round Table group, occasionally contributing articles to its eponymous review. He was particularly close to Lionel Curtis. After Lionel Hichens's death in 1940, Curtis later told Malcolm that 'he left a gap in my life which no-one but you could have filled' (Curtis to Malcolm, 18 Dec 1950, Bodl. Oxf., MS Curtis 92). Malcolm remained an ardent supporter of an imperial federation among the white dominions but rejected Curtis's wartime enthusiasm for Atlantic union. He was deeply committed to Anglo-South African partnership. When the question arose in 1934 of transferring the high commission territories (later Botswana, Lesotho, and Swaziland) to Pretoria, Malcolm, like Curtis, was sympathetic. He favoured the promotion of British settlement in South Africa through the '1820 Settler Memorial Association' (but warned against arousing Afrikaner resentment); he chaired its parent body, the South African Settlement Association, from 1947 to 1952.

As a well-connected City figure, Malcolm chaired a government inquiry into education and employment in 1926 and was a member of the British economic mission to Australia in 1928. From 1926 to 1928 he was vice-chairman of the court of governors of the London School of Economics. He was a regular weekender at All Souls, discharging the arcane functions of 'Lord Mallard'. Cosmo Lang, archbishop of Canterbury, and the earl of Halifax (both fellows of All Souls) were intimates. His handsome appearance, conversation, charm, and ease of manner were legendary. A French acquaintance, on being told that Malcolm 'ran Rhodesia', replied 'Who is this Rhodesia; is she very beautiful?' (*Amery Diaries*, 1.445). Malcolm's first wife died in 1920. He married Lady Evelyn Farquhar (1877/8–1962), widow of Colonel Francis Farquhar and daughter of the fifth earl of Donoughmore, on 3 May 1923. There were no children of either marriage. He was appointed KCMG in 1938. Malcolm died at 53 Bedford Gardens, Kensington, London, on 30 August 1955 just after his seventy-eighth birthday. He published two books: *Nuces relictae* (1926) and *The British South Africa Company, 1889–1939* (1939).

J. G. DARWIN

Sources Bodl. Oxf., MSS Lionel Curtis 91–2 · Bodl. Oxf., MS Milner 5 · Bodl. Oxf., MS Selborne 72 · Bodl. RH, Welensky MSS, MS 643/2, 96/7 · P. Slinn, 'Commercial concessions and politics during the colonial period: the role of the British South Africa Company in Northern Rhodesia, 1890–1964', *African Affairs*, 70 (1971), 365–84 · D. O. Malcolm, *The British South Africa Company, 1889–1939* (1939) · J. R. T. Wood, *The Welensky papers: a history of the Federation of Rhodesia and Nyasaland* (1983) · T. E. Gregory, *Ernest Oppenheimer and the economic development of southern Africa* (1962) · A. C. May, 'The Round Table, 1910–1966', DPhil diss., U. Oxf., 1995 · R. Blake, *A history of Rhodesia* (1977) · M. Chanock, *Unconsummated union: Britain, Rhodesia and South Africa, 1900–1945* (1977) · *The Leo Amery diaries*, ed. J. Barnes and D. Nicholson, 1 (1980) · Foster, *Alum. Oxon.* (1885) · m. cert. · d. cert.

Archives Bodl. Oxf., corresp. with L. G. Curtis · Bodl. Oxf., corresp. with Geoffrey Dawson · Bodl. Oxf., Round Table papers · Bodl. Oxf., corresp. with Lord Selborne · Bodl. Oxf., corresp. with Lord Simon · Bodl. RH, corresp. with R. R. Welensky · Derbys. RO, papers relating to British South Africa Company · National Archives of Zimbabwe, Harare, corresp. with Francis Chaplin · Surrey HC, letters to Lord Cranley

Likenesses W. Stoneman, two photographs, 1938–47, NPG [*see illus.*] · J. Gunn, group portrait, oils, c.1954–1959 (*Society of Dilettanti conversation piece*), Brooks's Club, London, Society of Dilettanti; oil study, c.1954–1955, Althorp, Northamptonshire · by or after O. Birley, oils, All Souls Oxf.

Wealth at death £102,446 1s. 1d.: probate, 19 Nov 1955, CGPLA Eng. & Wales

Malcolm, Sir George (1818–1897), army officer, born at Bombay on 10 September 1818, was the only son of David Malcolm (d. 1826), a Bombay merchant (brother of Admiral Sir Pulteney *Malcolm and General Sir John *Malcolm), and his first wife, Maria Hughes (d. 1818). He attended Addiscombe College from 1835 to 1836, and was commissioned ensign in the East India Company's service on 10 June 1836, being posted to the 1st Bombay native infantry (Bombay Grenadiers) on 18 July 1837. He served in the Anglo-Afghan War of 1839 as deputy assistant commissary-general and baggage master with the Bombay division, and was present at the capture of Ghazni and occupation of Kabul. In August 1840, at the head of a detachment of Sind horse, he joined the force sent under Major Clibborn to relieve Kahun in Baluchistan, took part in the attempt to force the Nafusk Pass, and was mentioned in dispatches for his gallantry. He was also engaged in the operations against Nasir Khan and the Brahoes and the capture of their camp near Kanda on 1 December.

Malcolm became lieutenant on 31 August 1840. He served under Colonel John Jacob during the subjugation of Sind, and was at the battle of Shahdadpur and the capture of Shahpur. In the Second Anglo-Sikh War he commanded the 2nd Sind horse, and was present at the siege of Multan and the battle of Gujrat. He was mentioned in dispatches, and on becoming captain in his regiment was given a brevet majority on 22 June 1849. He became lieutenant-colonel on 28 November 1854.

On 19 October 1852 Malcolm married Wilhelmina Charlotte (d. 13 Dec 1911), youngest daughter of the Revd Henry Alright Hughes, and they had four sons. He served in the Anglo-Persian War of 1856–7, and commanded a small field force during the Indian mutiny. On 29 November 1857 he stormed the fortified village of Halgalli, took possession of Shorapur on 9 February 1858, and on 2 June captured the fort of Nargund, the strongest in the south Maratha country. He was mentioned in dispatches and was made CB on 21 March 1859. He became colonel in the army on 30 August 1860 and major-general on 15 December 1867. In the expedition to Abyssinia in 1868 he commanded the 2nd division, which guarded the line of communications. He was made KCB on 14 August 1868. In the same year he printed for private circulation at Karachi a short pamphlet, *Remarks on the Indian Army*, arguing the danger of relying on European troops and of discrediting the native army, as had been the tendency since the mutiny. He was promoted lieutenant-general on 29 May 1875 and general on 1 October 1877, and was placed on the unemployed supernumerary list on 1 July 1881. He received the GCB on 29 May 1886. Malcolm died at his home, Guy's Dale, Leamington, Dorset, on 6 April 1897.

E. M. LLOYD, rev. JAMES FALKNER

Sources Army List · Hart's Army List · Indian Army List · The Times (7 April 1897) · J. W. Kaye and G. B. Malleson, Kaye's and Malleson's History of the Indian mutiny of 1857–8, 6 vols. (1888–9) · LondG (19 April 1849) · Burke, Gen. GB · H. M. Vibart, Addiscombe: its heroes and men of note (1894)

Likenesses photograph, c.1890, priv. coll. · black and white photograph, repro. in The Times · wood-engraving (after photograph by Maull & Fox), NPG; repro. in ILN (17 April 1897)

Wealth at death £8923 19s. 9d.: probate, 22 May 1897, CGPLA Eng. & Wales

Malcolm, George John (1917–1997), musician and choirmaster, was born on 28 February 1917 at 9 Leppoc Road, Clapham, London, the only child of George Hope Malcolm (1870–1950), a chief inspector of insurance, and his wife, Johanna, née Brosnahan (1883–1972). His father was Scottish. Neither parent had a particular interest in the arts, but his mother was a staunch Roman Catholic, so it was the plainsong of the mass in the church of the Sacred Heart in Wimbledon that touched the ear of a very small boy at his devotions; the noble beauty of the singing by the Jesuits affected his whole life, instilled into him his love of music, and revealed his perfect sense of pitch and remarkable memory. At the age of two he reputedly sang 'I'm a poor little robin left out in the cold' with tears streaming down his cheeks, and this prodigious gift was complemented by a powerful intellect and insatiable curiosity; however, the qualities that sustained him during troubled times were his devout Christianity and fearless honesty.

When he was seven years old Malcolm was examined in various musical disciplines by the director of the Royal College of Music, who promptly awarded him a scholarship to its senior department, an extraordinary achievement. After simultaneous studies there and at Wimbledon College, Malcolm went up to Balliol College, Oxford, again with a scholarship. During those brilliant undergraduate years his burgeoning addiction to alcohol inspired him to climb the tower of his college to kidnap its weathervane; for this escapade he was rusticated for a term, but he graduated BMus in 1937. He was made an honorary fellow of Balliol in 1966. On leaving Oxford he was undecided as to what was his true bent. Nevertheless he returned to the Royal College of Music as a Leverhulme scholar in 1938, and in 1939 he won both the Chappell gold medal and a Caird travelling scholarship.

In 1940 Malcolm enlisted in the Royal Air Force Volunteer Reserve and became conductor of the RAF Bomber Command band. This was a time of distress at knowing that so many young men would never return from their nocturnal sorties, but they were also years of experiencing a new interest, in directing the military band repertory with players unaccustomed to a conductor of such charismatic style—a man who knelt at his barrack-room bed to say his prayers, drank with them, and then had to be physically supported during air marshals' inspections.

On demobilization in 1946 Malcolm swiftly embarked upon activities that ultimately brought him dual fame as choirmaster and virtuoso harpsichordist. His reputation had reached Westminster Cathedral, whose ailing music required powerful resuscitation; as an Oxford graduate, and as a master musician steeped in the Catholic liturgy, he was the obvious choice of the cardinal archbishop, and he was appointed master of the cathedral music in 1947. He set about his task without delay and formed a choir that became world famous for the quality of the boys' voices—strong and virile with a dramatic style far removed from the accepted pure angelic sounds of Anglican cathedral choristers, but which produced an electrifying beauty that surely emanated from George Malcolm's own religious devotion.

Malcolm was a regular soloist at the Aldeburgh Festival from its inception in 1948, often helping to train the boys' choirs performing Britten's works. The *Missa brevis* composed in 1959 was dedicated to Malcolm, and he conducted its first performance in Westminster Cathedral on 22 July that year.

Throughout his time at Westminster, Malcolm was in constant demand as a pianist in chamber music with leading artists of the day, and his exploratory interests knew no bounds. On discovering that a fine harpsichord made by Shudi (1702–1773) was to be sold at Sothebys salerooms he felt impelled to buy this interesting example of an instrument he had never played. With his dazzling keyboard skills he soon became its master and a leading exponent renowned for the flair and temperament of his interpretations. Nevertheless, the maintenance of an eighteenth-century harpsichord soon palled; in spite of pleasurable visits to the zoo to see the keeper of the condors 'pluck feathers from the living bird' to provide quills for plectra, it was sold, and Malcolm continued to perform with great success throughout Europe on hired instruments.

After several disagreements with the ecclesiastical authorities Malcolm resigned his cathedral post in 1959. Thenceforth he devoted himself to harpsichord playing and to piano engagements as the partner of distinguished singers and instrumentalists. He also became a much respected conductor of orchestras. Despite his prowess his activities had been overshadowed by his habitual drinking. A fall from an upper window in 1950 had resulted in devastating injuries to his head, and he was aware that friends and admirers remained worried, yet the temptation lingered until a disastrous concert in Oxford indicated that his future was in jeopardy. His absolute integrity and strength, no doubt supported by his Catholic faith, saved him, and for the second forty years of his life he abstained and continued his international career without interruption. He was appointed CBE in 1965 and papal knight of the order of St Gregory the Great in 1970.

Malcolm was wonderfully clever and most amusing. He was often blunt in manner and forceful in his opinions, but he gained the affection and admiration of the many friends who relished his unusual blend of shyness, direct criticism, learning, and kind generosity. His simple truthfulness endeared him to all who knew him well, and fellow musicians regarded him as a latter-day 'eminent master', with all the gifts and imagination of his eighteenth-century predecessors. On his deathbed he telephoned his church to arrange to make his confession, warning them that it would assuredly take rather a long time; later, when the priest came to administer the last rites, he was

asked if he would like the words in Latin or English: 'In Latin please—and do you mind if I smoke?' Slightly taken aback, the smiling priest replied, 'Do—the smoke will be as the incense taking our prayers up to Heaven' (private information).

Malcolm died of cancer on 10 October 1997 at his home, 99 Wimbledon Hill Road, London. His funeral on 21 October, at the church of the Sacred Heart in Wimbledon, was followed on 29 January 1998 by a memorial requiem mass in Westminster Cathedral, at which the principal celebrant was Cardinal Basil Hume, archbishop of Westminster.   GARETH MORRIS

Sources *The Guardian* (14 Oct 1997) · *Daily Telegraph* (14 Oct 1997) · *The Independent* (14 Oct 1997) · *The Times* (15 Oct 1997) · *WWW* · personal knowledge (2004) · private information (2004) · b. cert. · d. cert.
Archives priv. coll., archives
Likenesses photograph, 1971, repro. in *The Independent* · photograph, 1971, repro. in *Daily Telegraph* · G. Turner, photograph, c.1989, repro. in *The Guardian* · photograph, 1989, repro. in *The Times* · J. Bown, photograph, priv. coll.
Wealth at death £967,867: probate, 7 July 1998, *CGPLA Eng. & Wales*

Malcolm, Hugh Gordon (1917–1942), air force officer, was born at Aystree, Broughty Ferry, Dundee, on 2 May 1917, the only son of Kenneth Sinclair Malcolm, a jute merchant (formerly a major in the Royal Field Artillery), and his wife, Marjorie Evelyn Smith. He was educated at Craigflower preparatory school, Dunfermline, and Trinity College, Glenalmond, Perthshire. In January 1936 he entered the Royal Air Force College at Cranwell as a cadet and in December 1937 graduated as a pilot officer. After a short course of instruction in the School of Army Co-operation at Old Sarum, Wiltshire, he joined 26 squadron at Catterick, North Riding of Yorkshire, where he flew the Westland Lysander—a two-seat, high-wing monoplane specially designed for such duty. He was promoted to flying officer, but crash-landed in May 1939 and was severely injured. Helen Catherine Don Swan, the daughter of Andrew Don Swan, a civil engineer, of Forest Dene, Worth, Sussex, helped to nurse him at Halton Hospital, near Morecambe, Lancashire. They married on 24 August 1940 and had a daughter, Carina, in 1941.

Meanwhile, Malcolm returned to 26 squadron in September 1939 and served in a succession of Lysander squadrons (earning promotion to flight lieutenant in September 1940) until December 1941, when he was promoted squadron leader. In April 1942 he joined 18 squadron, equipped with an obsolete light bomber, the twin-engined Bristol Blenheim IV, at Wattisham in Suffolk. The plane was being phased out during that year, and in August the four remaining Blenheim squadrons in England (of which 18 was one) were formed into a wing under the command of Group Captain Laurence Sinclair and re-equipped with Blenheim Vs, known as Bisleys. This was 'a ghastly aircraft', wrote Sinclair:

which had been mucked about with to such an extent it could hardly fly. Its top speed was only 150 mph; it wallowed like a cow and at 10,000 feet it was unstable. It was difficult to

Hugh Gordon Malcolm (1917–1942), by unknown photographer

imagine a more useless aircraft with which to give the Army close bomber support. (Sinclair, 99)

This was the case even though the plane had four nose-mounted machine-guns, two more in a dorsal turret, and an armoured cockpit.

Malcolm was promoted wing commander in September 1942 and given command of 18 squadron, which he took to Blida, near Algiers, that November to help support Operation Torch, the Anglo-American invasion of north-west Africa. On 17 November he led an attack on Bizerte airfield, northern Tunisia. This attack—at low level, in clear daylight, without fighter escort—cost four Bisleys and caused little damage. Malcolm was ordered to return to Bizerte on the 28th, again in daylight and again unescorted. Despite intense ground fire, the Bisleys bombed the airfield and used their machine-guns to attack parked aircraft and other targets.

At 9.15 a.m. on 4 December 1942 Malcolm led six Bisleys from a forward landing-ground at Souk al-Arba (south of Tabarka in Tunisia) to attack a Luftwaffe airfield some 14 miles north of Tebourba, a small town 20 miles west of Tunis. 'On that terrible day', wrote Sinclair, Malcolm 'had known the soldiers had no right to give him an airfield target instead of one in support of their own ground forces' (Sinclair, 105–7), but his long experience as an army co-operation pilot, together with his undoubted courage, persuaded him to accept an order that was unwise as well as improper. The Bisleys, achieving surprise, dropped bombs, machine-gunned ground targets, and escaped unscathed.

Within an hour of landing, however, Malcolm received a request to return to the same area. He took off at 3.15 p.m. with two pilot officers, James Robb (navigator) and James Grant DFC (wireless operator and air-gunner), and led eight Bisleys in tight formation at about 1000 feet towards the airfield. Messerschmitt Bf 109 fighters were waiting for them, and in a few minutes six Bisleys were shot down and the other three crash-landed within allied lines. Malcolm's machine, it seems, was among the last to be destroyed, and all three crew members were killed. Three British soldiers, arriving at the crash site only minutes later, managed to drag Robb's body clear, but fire made it impossible to recover the others. Malcolm was buried at Beja war cemetery, Tunisia. Eighteen of the twenty-seven men who attempted this raid died and of the nine survivors four were injured. On Sinclair's recommendation Malcolm was awarded a posthumous Victoria Cross in April 1943 and DFCs went to three survivors. His was the thirteenth VC won in the air war and the only one awarded to an airman in the three years of the north African campaign.

According to an account of this raid in the squadron's operations record book on 12 March 1943, Malcolm was:

fully alive to the immense danger he was running in not being provided with a close fighter escort ... He also knew that a satellite aerodrome was not a legitimate close-support target and that to attack such an objective needed very accurate timing and close co-ordination with a fighter escort, yet—knowing these things—he never hesitated or queried the necessity for endangering his squadron in this manner; he just led his squadron in his normal cheerfully efficient manner. (PRO, AIR 27/243)

Five weeks later, on 27 April, the *London Gazette* published a blander account in which it was wrongly claimed that the Bisleys 'successfully attacked' their target. Bisleys were never again sent out in daylight, only at night. Although they achieved little, crews survived longer. Two of the four unlucky squadrons were re-equipped in February 1943, but the other two soldiered on with their 'ghastly aircraft' until the end of that year.

On 26 March 1984 Wing Commander Ted Holloway DFC recalled that raid. 'I walked out to our aircraft', he wrote:

with Hughie Malcolm and on the way he asked the Group Captain i/c Fighter Ops ... for an escort and was told that none was available, but a sweep was in progress. Malcolm replied: 'Bullshit' and there was no doubt we were in for a rough time. He knew there were a lot of 109s about. (18 squadron file)

Malcolm was a tall man, darkly handsome and quietly spoken, with a soft Scottish accent. Although friendly and approachable, he had a naturally commanding personality, and crews in all four Bisley squadrons followed him readily.

Thanks to the efforts of Sir Arthur Tedder (head of allied air forces in north Africa) and Mrs Marie Black (who later became Tedder's second wife), a club offering civilized amenities for RAF airmen and named in Malcolm's honour was opened in Algiers in May 1943. Ultimately, more than a hundred Malcolm clubs, formed into a self-financing charity, were opened wherever the RAF served overseas. Helen Malcolm presented a bouquet of Scottish heather to the first Malcolm Club, opened in Normandy in August 1944. VINCENT ORANGE

Sources C. Bowyer, *For valour: the air VCs* (1978) · *The register of the Victoria cross*, 3rd edn (1997) · A. Butterworth, *With courage and faith: the story of no. 18 squadron, Royal Air Force* (1991) · *LondG* (23 April 1943) [2nd suppl.] · 18 squadron file, Air Historical Branch, London · 18 squadron operations record book, PRO, AIR 27/243 · L. Sinclair, *Strike to defend* (privately printed, 1992) · G. F. Howe, *Northwest Africa: seizing the initiative in the west* (1991), 311–20 · W. Green and G. Swanborough, 'Bristol's trim twin', *Air Enthusiast*, 28 (July–Oct 1985), 8–21, 69–73 · private information (2004) [A. Butterworth] · b. cert. · m. cert.
Likenesses photograph, repro. in Bowyer, *For valour: the air VCs* · photograph, repro. in Sinclair, *Strike to defend* · photograph, repro. in Butterworth, *With courage and faith* · photograph, IWM [*see illus.*]
Wealth at death £1119 17s. 7d.: confirmation, 9 July 1943, CCI

Malcolm, Sir Ian Zachary (1868–1944), politician and public servant, was born in Quebec, Canada, on 3 September 1868, the eldest son in the family of six sons and two daughters of Colonel Edward Donald Malcolm (1837–1930), of Poltalloch, Argyll, landowner and officer in the Royal Engineers, and his wife, Isabella Wyld (d. 1927), daughter of John Brown of Ayrshire. He was educated at Eton College (where he was editor of the *Eton College Chronicle* and secretary of the music society) and, briefly, at New College, Oxford. He did not take a degree, and left to prepare for the diplomatic service. He became an honorary attaché at Berlin in November 1891 and at Paris from April to July 1893.

Malcolm entered parliament as Conservative member for Suffolk (North-West) in July 1895. From February to June 1896 he was attached to the embassy at St Petersburg, in attendance on the duke and duchess of Connaught, who represented Queen Victoria at the coronation of Tsar Nicholas II. In August he was appointed assistant private secretary to Lord Salisbury, foreign secretary and prime minister, and he became a lifelong friend of both Arthur Balfour, leader of the House of Commons, and George Curzon, under-secretary at the Foreign Office. In 1897–8 he served as honorary assistant secretary to the Prince of Wales Hospital Fund for London. He resigned his Foreign Office appointment in September 1898. A keen traveller, in 1897 he bicycled with Balfour in Germany; in 1898 he visited New York and Jamaica; in 1899 he visited Spain; and in 1901 he travelled to India and accompanied Curzon, now viceroy, on a tour of Burma. In the same year he became engaged to Jeanne-Marie Langtry (1881–1964), the only child of Lillie *Langtry, Lady De Bathe (1853–1929). They married at St Margaret's, Westminster, on 30 June 1902 and had three sons and a daughter.

Malcolm retained his seat in the general election of 1900 and was appointed parliamentary private secretary to George Wyndham, chief secretary for Ireland, but resigned in 1903. He was a member (and secretary) of a dining club named the Hughligans consisting of younger MPs whose unrealized aim was to rejuvenate a Unionist Party drifting to electoral catastrophe. He did not contest the general election of 1906, and divided his time between

his family, travelling, secretaryship of the Union Defence League (1906–10), which campaigned against home rule for Ireland, and Edwardian social life in the grand style. He visited India and Burma again, in 1906; in 1907 he visited Iceland, Italy, and Spain, and in 1913 Germany. In the first general election of 1910 he unsuccessfully contested North Salford, in the second he was elected for Croydon; he was a popular and active member. In 1913 he sponsored two parliamentary bills placing the Crystal Palace in local authority management. He was elected to the house of laity of the diocesan conference of Canterbury in May 1912.

After the outbreak of the First World War, in August 1914, Malcolm recruited for Kitchener's army. In October he joined the British Red Cross and went to France on an urgent mission to trace British casualties and prisoners of war. This harrowing work was completed in May 1915. He then visited the International Red Cross at Geneva and the Italian Red Cross in Milan. In September he was appointed British Red Cross commissioner in Russia, responsible for the establishment of a joint Anglo-Russian hospital in Petrograd. He was presented to the imperial family and made an honorary colonel in the Russian army. In December 1916 Balfour, now foreign secretary, appointed Malcolm his parliamentary private secretary. In March 1917 he joined an unofficial committee chaired by Sir Alfred Mond that established the National (later Imperial) War Museum, and served until 1919. He contributed valuable ideas to collection policy but his application to become a trustee in 1920 was unsuccessful. In May 1917 Balfour led a special mission to the USA. Malcolm was his private secretary and found himself in demand from the American Red Cross as an expert on Red Cross work in the field.

In the general election of December 1918 Malcolm successfully contested the new seat of South Croydon. In January 1919 Balfour, deputy leader of the British delegation to the peace conference at Paris, appointed him his personal private secretary. In June he was created KCMG. He sought senior diplomatic appointments, and after some disappointments accepted that of British government director of the Suez Canal Company, resident in Paris. He returned to the Foreign Office and became parliamentary private secretary to Lord Curzon (acting foreign secretary) until he ceased to be an MP, on 29 October 1919. Although significant his work at the Suez Canal Company was not full-time, and he kept his home in London. He visited Egypt annually and acquired detailed knowledge of leading Egyptian and French personalities and of the operations of the company. He was British delegate to the International Congress of Navigation at Cairo (1926) and Venice (1931).

Malcolm wrote fifteen books between 1906 and 1939, mainly on politics, travel, poetry, and Scottish folklore. He had a talent for vivid description of events that he had witnessed, as when writing of the First World War in *War Pictures behind the Lines* and *Scraps of Paper* (both 1915) or of pre-revolutionary Russia in *Trodden Ways* (1930). His judgement of friends and parliamentary companions combined affection and shrewd insight, as in his essay on

Lord Curzon in *The Pursuit of Pleasure* (1929) or in his biography of Lord Balfour (1930). He also wrote extensively for newspapers and magazines and was a regular letter writer to *The Times*. He was appointed deputy lieutenant for Surrey in 1924 and was master of the Worshipful Company of Musicians in 1931 and 1935. In 1930 he became seventeenth hereditary chief of the clan MacCallum, on the death of his father, and entertained guests (including King Faisal of Iraq in 1933) in style at Poltalloch House, Argyll. He was a director of the Ritz Hotel, Paris. In 1939 he resigned all public offices and retired to Poltalloch. In 1942 his health began to fail, and in the following year he returned to London, where he took a suite at the Dorchester Hotel. He died there on 28 December 1944, and was buried at St Columba's Church, Kilmartin, Argyll, on 3 January 1945. He was survived by his wife, Jeanne-Marie, and their four children.

Malcolm combined worthy public service with a fashionable social life and travel. His wit and charm attracted a wide circle of friends and acquaintances ranging from most of Edwardian high society to Cecil Rhodes, T. E. Lawrence, John Buchan, General Weygand, and Stanley Baldwin. He was devoted to his family and friends and his party, but cut off those who rejected him. He hoped that his record of service would be rewarded with the revival of the extinct family barony, but this never happened. In their obituaries Scottish newspapers aptly mourned him as 'the last of the Edwardians'.   ROBERT MILLER

Sources Burke, *Gen. GB* (1965–72) • I. Z. Malcolm, *War pictures behind the lines* (1915) • I. Z. Malcolm, *Vacant thrones* (1931) • I. Z. Malcolm, *Trodden ways* (1930) • I. Z. Malcolm, *Lord Balfour* (1930) • M. Egremont, *Balfour* (1980) • L. Mosely, *Curzon: the end of an epoch* (1960) • D. Gilmour, *Curzon* (1994) • *The Times* (23 May 1912); (21 Feb 1917) • R. Miller, *Four Victorians and a museum* (privately printed, 1999) • R. Miller, 'The forgotten founder', *Password* (Dec 2001), 62–6 • I. Z. Zachary, Versailles diary, 1917–19, HLRO • PRO, papers of Sir Ian Malcolm, T206 • *WWW* • private information (2004) [Eton College; Mary Mac Fadyean; Colin Mac Fadyean; Robin Malcolm of Poltalloch] • *The Scotsman* (29 Dec 1944)
Archives BL, corresp., some in French, Add. MS 49458, *passim* • British Red Cross Society, Guildford, Museum and Archives, papers • HLRO, papers, incl. Versailles diary • IWM, archives, papers • IWM, mementoes relating to work in First World War • NL Scot., travel diaries and photograph albums • NRA, papers • NRA, priv. coll., corresp., diaries, and papers • priv. coll., papers and collection of artefacts • PRO, corresp. and papers, T206 | BL, corresp. with Macmillans, Add. MS 55045 • Croydon Local History Studies Library and Archives Service, papers • CUL, letters to Stanley Baldwin • LMA, Prince of Wales Hospital Fund for London, papers • Lpool RO, corresp. with Lord Derby • NA Scot., corresp. with A. J. Balfour • priv. coll., personal papers of the Marquess Curzon of Kedleston
Likenesses C. Cundell, oils, *c.*1876, Duntrune Castle, Argyll and Bute • group portrait, photograph, 1917, IWM • P. A. de Laszlo, oils, 1929, Duntrune Castle, Argyll and Bute • W. Orpen, oils (after First World War); formerly in possession of his second son, Victor • oils (as choir boy), Duntrune Castle, Argyll and Bute • photograph, repro. in C. Hesketh, *Tartans* (1961)

Malcolm, James Peller (1767–1815), antiquary and topographical draughtsman, was born a British subject in August 1767 and baptized at St Peter's Church, Philadelphia, Pennsylvania, the son of the merchant Moses Malcolm (d. 1769) and his wife, Mary, *née* Peller (b. 1742).

His father, whose parents had moved to America from Scotland, died when he was two years old. His mother was the granddaughter of James Peller, who had accompanied William Penn on his journey from Bristol to the banks of the Delaware, where he built a house and eventually settled in 1689. Despite being a member of the Church of England, Malcolm began his education at the Quaker school in Philadelphia; following the horrors of war his family fled to Potts-town, Pennsylvania, where his education continued 'at an enormous expence' (*GM*, 1st ser., 85/1, 1815, 467). After the war ended in 1784 he returned to Philadelphia, where, under the guidance of a Mr Bembridge, he began to concentrate on the study of art and taught himself to engrave. His first published plate was the frontispiece for Colonel John Parke's *Lyric Works of Horace* (1786), after a sketch by Peter Markoe. Towards the end of 1787 he travelled to England to continue his artistic training at the Royal Academy Schools in London. During his three years there he received encouragement from Benjamin West and Joseph Wright of Derby but, realizing that his interests were in history and landscape images, he turned to etching as a more appropriate medium. His potential was recognized at the end of his time at the Royal Academy Schools, when two of his landscape prints were included in their annual exhibition of 1791. Shortly afterwards he began regular work as an illustrator for the *Gentleman's Magazine*, for which he etched numerous, mostly topographical, plates between 1792 and 1814. He was also an active contributor to this periodical, writing numerous letters and articles on antiquarian subjects, including a detailed history of Somers Town, the London suburb where he lived throughout his time in England. It was also in the pages of the *Gentleman's Magazine* that his marriage to 'Miss Chrysogon Vaughan, daughter of the Rev. Richard V[aughan] rector of Leominster Co. Hereford' was announced in January 1797 (*GM*, 1st ser., 67, 1797, 79–80).

In 1850 the antiquary John Britton recalled Malcolm's passion for antiquarianism, recording how he would religiously spend his days making sketches and notes either at his home or at the reading room of the British Museum (Britton, 1.112). Although he was not elected a fellow of the Society of Antiquaries until 27 March 1806, his work from 1797 onwards reflected his enthusiasm for research into English antiquities and topography. Of his eleven illustrated antiquarian publications, the most renowned are *Londinium redivivum* (4 vols., 1802–7), *Excursions in Kent* (1807), and *Anecdotes of the Manners and Customs of London* (3 vols., 1808). In these he compiled an impressive array of unknown parochial and institutional documents and combined these with personal observations and his characteristic and skilful etchings of historical architecture, artefacts, customs, and costume. He also appealed to the more commercial market for antiquarian publications with his series of etchings entitled *Views within Twelve Miles Round London* (1800), where the plates were designed to complement the topographical texts of popular authors such as Thomas Pennant and Daniel Lysons.

Malcolm died on 5 April 1815, after a three-year-long

debilitating illness which is said to have begun with an abscess on his knee. His inability to work during his final months rendered him totally indigent and at his death his wife and ageing mother were left destitute. As a mark of respect for Malcolm's industry and popularity, following his death his loyal friends set up a public subscription to provide for his mother and widow. This appeal was announced in the *Gentleman's Magazine* (May 1815) and was supervised by Malcolm's most regular publishers, Longman & Co., and John Nichols.   LUCY PELTZ

Sources *GM*, 1st ser., 67 (1797), 179–80 · *GM*, 1st ser., 78 (1808), 418–19, 1056 · *GM*, 1st ser., 79 (1809), 692–3 · *GM*, 1st ser., 83/2 (1813), 427–9, 569–70 · *GM*, 1st ser., 85/1 (1815), 467–9 · *DAB* · J. Britton, *The autobiography of John Britton*, 1 (privately printed, London, 1850), 112 · Walpole, *Corr.* · Nichols, *Lit. anecdotes* · Redgrave, *Artists*, 2nd edn, 284 · Graves, *RA exhibitors*, 5.168 · Thieme & Becker, *Allgemeines Lexikon*
Wealth at death destitute: *GM* (1815)

Malcolm, Sir John (1769–1833), diplomatist and administrator in India, was born at Burnfoot, Westerkirk, Dumfriesshire, on 2 May 1769, the fourth son of George Malcolm (1729–1803) of Burnfoot, from younger Malcolms of Lochore, Fife, and of Margaret (*d.* 1811), daughter of James Pasley of Craig, Dumfriesshire. Sir Charles *Malcolm (1782–1851) and Sir Pulteney *Malcolm (1768–1838) were his brothers. Daring and venturesome ('the scapegrace and the scapegoat of the family'; Kaye, 1.5), he left parish school at twelve, was taken to London by his prosperous uncle, and applied for a position with the East India Company. When a director asked 'Why, my little man, what would *you* do if you met Hyder Ali?', he replied that he would 'out with his sword, and cut off his heid!' and was accepted (Kaye, 1.8).

Early career: from soldier to diplomatist Having reached Madras in April 1783, Malcolm was assigned to a regiment at Vellore. He had entered the service of what had become far more than a trading company. On the profits of the cotton textile trade and revenue from its growing territory, particularly Bengal, it was in competition with the many other regional kingdoms which were establishing themselves after the erosion of Mughal power. His first task as an ensign commanding sepoys was to escort to safety English prisoners surrendered by the Tipu Sahib under the treaty of 11 May 1784. Boy Malcolm, as he long continued to be known, became a good horseman and marksman. Later, as adjutant in the 29th battalion of the Madras native infantry at Masulipatam, he paid off his debts and forsook gaming. When his regiment was ordered to Hyderabad in 1790, he determined to become a 'political' (diplomatic) officer. The 'once careless' youth became fluent in Persian. A chance opportunity came in 1792 when the military encampment of Lord Cornwallis at Seringapatam needed a Persian interpreter to serve as liaison between the company's and the nizam of Hyderabad's troops. After the war, in February 1794, he returned to England on medical leave.

Not long after Malcolm landed in England he presented a paper listing grievances of the company's military officers over their scanty pay and slow promotion. This caught the attention of Henry Dundas (later Lord Melville), president of the Board of Control. Dundas persuaded Sir Alured Clarke, the new commander-in-chief of Madras, to add Malcolm to his staff. In May 1795, after visiting his parents and studying at the University of Edinburgh, he returned to India.

Early in 1796, following action against the Dutch on the Cape, Lieutenant Malcolm became private secretary to the commander-in-chief. This service continued under General George, Baron Harris, with extra income as town major of Fort St George. When Lord Mornington landed in April 1798 Malcolm submitted a paper on how to deal with the princes of India. Five months later, after being appointed assistant to the resident at Hyderabad, a crisis erupted. When, under company pressure, the nizam disbanded the 'French corps', sepoys mutinied, seized their French officers, and threatened Malcolm's life. Only action by deserters from Malcolm's old regiment, who were part of the mutinous corps, saved him. Having hastened to the residency and taken command of the company's 'Hyderabad contingent', he overawed the mutineers and persuaded them to lay down their arms. He then made haste to Calcutta, captured colours in hand, and personally laid a report of these events before the governor-general. He was invited to join the expedition then sailing south to deal with Tipu Sultan. After rejoining the Hyderabad contingent (19 January 1799), Malcolm became the key liaison between the governor-general and various military units, especially Colonel Arthur Wellesley and the King's 33rd foot, deploying forces then marching upon Seringapatam during the Mysore campaign. After victory was assured, he was made first secretary of the commission for the settlement of Mysore, and became instrumental in restoring the former Hindu (Woodiyar) maharaja's family to rule over the territories of Mysore.

Envoy to Persia and private secretary to the governor-general Meanwhile, Napoleon's presence in Egypt prompted British efforts to thwart French designs in India. Malcolm was chosen as envoy to Persia, the first person since Elizabeth's reign to undertake such a mission. He travelled overland from Madras, with stops in Hyderabad and Poona, and embarked from Bombay at the end of 1799. At Muscat the imam was induced to accept a company agent, but delays occurred at Bushehr, Shiraz, and Esfahan over stickling slights and protocols of etiquette and ceremonial, and almost a year passed before his audience with the shah took place. Lavish exchanging of presents (*nazrs*) took place before any serious negotiations could begin. Treaties were agreed on 28 January 1801 (but, in the end, never ratified): unrestricted trade, commercial stations, cession of the islands of Kishim, Anjam, and Khargh, and curbs upon French influence and upon actions by the amir of Afghanistan, Zaman Shah, in exchange for military supplies, ships, and troops. Persia adamantly refused to give up its gulf islands. Malcolm returned to India by way of Baghdad, letting its Turkish pasha know that the company was determined to oppose French designs.

As acting private secretary to Marquess Wellesley, as

Lord Mornington had now become, Malcolm soon accompanied the governor-general up the Ganges to settle the affairs of Oudh, another princely state. He then went to Madras to persuade the governor, Lord Clive, not to retire: Wellesley wished to preserve recently enacted revenue and judicial regulations and needed able and experienced officials to remain at their posts. By March 1802 Malcolm was becoming 'Lord Wellesley's factotum and the greatest man in Calcutta' (letter from Col. James Young, Kaye, 1.175). With war clouds again gathering, he went to Hyderabad and Poona to examine relations with their respective princes, the nizam and the peshwa. At Bhore Ghat, anticipating war, a Maratha chief seized and held him for a couple of days. In Bombay the Persian ambassador, Haji Khalil Khan, was killed during hostilities between company sepoys and Persian attendants; Malcolm sent Lieutenant Charles William Pasley, acting resident at Bushehr, with messages and gifts for the shah.

The Second Anglo-Maratha War began when Maharaja Holkar attacked and defeated Maharaja Sindhia and the peshwa, Baji Rao. The peshwa turned to the company for help, and on 31 December 1802 signed the treaty of Bassein. When Malcolm joined General Arthur Wellesley, his role was ambiguous and, hampered by illness, he went on leave. Military actions against Sindhia began in August 1803. Mountstuart Elphinstone took Malcolm's place, and he missed the great battles at Assaye and Argaon. But he then helped to negotiate terms for peace. The settlement made with Sindhia and lesser chiefs, especially his allowing Sindhia to keep his great stronghold at Gwalior, incurred the wrath of Lord Wellesley. This censure, communicated on 22 April 1804, left him so 'perfectly heart-broken' (DNB) that he again retreated to the coast. Early in 1805, others having failed, Wellesley sent Malcolm to deal with Sindhia. From Lord Lake's camp he advocated ways to deal with both Sindhia and Holkar, devising formulas for guaranteeing peace. After the peace treaty, concluded on 7 January 1806, he was assigned to settling hosts of land grants, pensions, and rewards for services rendered to the company during the three campaigns.

Not until April 1807, after half a year in Calcutta, did Malcolm take up his new post as resident of Mysore. He was never thrifty, and often engaged in costly diplomatic missions which, despite extra allowances, left him impoverished, as well as worn out from overwork and exposure to the climate. On 4 July 1807 he married (Isabella) Charlotte (d. 1867), younger daughter of Colonel Alexander *Campbell. They had one son, George, who became a soldier, and four daughters, of whom Margaret eventually married her first cousin, also named Alexander Campbell. But despite marriage, Malcolm stayed restless. He hoped that, as a lieutenant-colonel, he might command a force going to Basrah and combine military with diplomatic functions. The governor-general, Lord Minto, however, was anxious about the impact of the peace of Tilsit upon Indian affairs. Wishing to prevent a French–Russian advance towards India, he decided to send missions to Lahore, Kabul, and Tehran. Malcolm was chosen for Persia, but the court of directors remembered his expensive

and aggressive policies as Wellesley's envoy, and his mission ended ultimately in failure. Sent to the Persian Gulf with a somewhat vague commission, albeit backed by a force of three frigates and 500 sepoys, Malcolm's efforts to overcome French influence failed: his messengers were forbidden to advance beyond Shiraz. He abandoned his efforts, and had hardly returned to Calcutta when yet another expedition was launched. This too was hastily cancelled when Sir Harford Jones arrived in Bombay, determined to carry out his assignment as ambassador to Persia.

In 1809 the Madras ('white') mutiny occurred: a European garrison at Masulipatam had revolted against its commander. Sir George Barlow, Lord Minto's acting successor, sent Malcolm to investigate and make a settlement. When Malcolm arrived, the mutinous regiment was on the point of marching to Hyderabad, where the company's forces were also about to mutiny. Mutineers vaguely talked of a declaration of independence, emulating their erstwhile colonial cousins in America. Faced with this situation, Malcolm negotiated freedom for the commander (Colonel Innes), convened a meeting of company officers, and persuaded mutineers to abandon plans for marching to Hyderabad. While he was successful, and thereby gained time, his conciliatory gestures were not approved. Sir George Barlow wanted nothing less than stern punishment for the mutineers.

Persia, England, and India: ambition frustrated Malcolm returned to diplomatic service, and was again dispatched to Persia. Early in 1810, while at Bushehr, he completed his *Sketch of the Political History of India* (1811), which was later issued in expanded form as *The Political History of India* (1826; repr. 1970). In Tehran he was received with pomp and cordiality while Sir Harford Jones was snubbed. Jones, the crown's ambassador to the shah, was exasperated by lack of success and support from the East India Company, and reacted with fury. Tensions between the two delegations became so acute that a duel nearly took place. Eventually the British government, wishing to keep all diplomatic relations strictly within its own control, took steps to nullify the actions of the governor-general. Sir Gore Ouseley arrived as London's new ambassador to the shah; and Malcolm decided leave Persia. (Perhaps Malcolm's most durable legacy was his introduction to that country of the potato, one local name for which is translated as 'Malcolm's plum'). In vain the shah offered him inducements to remain as a military adviser, even bestowing a newly created order of the Lion and Sun of Persia upon him. On reaching Bombay and before returning to Britain, while awaiting the auditing of his expense accounts (which brought him censure), Malcolm wrote his *History of Persia*. At this time he also wrote his *Observations on the Disturbances in the Madras Army in 1809*, which came out shortly after his arrival in London in 1812. His *Sketch of the Sikhs* was published in the same year.

In England, Malcolm was knighted, allowed to keep the Persian order of the Lion and Sun, and made a KCB (April 1815). His views on the East India Company's army were sought by the Board of Control; and he gave testimony before the Commons on the renewal of the company's charter. He also became acquainted with literary figures, such as Sir Walter Scott; and his *History of Persia*, which appeared in 1815, brought him an honorary doctorate of laws from Oxford. But he was also bereft of funds. The company eventually heeded his pleas and gave him £5000. Yet the destitute Indian officer, debarred from European service, could look only to India and hope for a regimental command as colonel on full pay or for further political service. At forty-six he again embarked for India, leaving his family behind him. While at sea, he wrote a review of William's *History of the Bengal Army* (*Quarterly Review*, 18, January 1818).

Malcolm reached India in 1816, on the eve of the Third Anglo-Maratha War. The governor-general, Lord Moira, gladly welcomed him; and he was soon sent to visit various major princely states. As a brigadier in the Deccan army, he then took part in actions against the Pindaris, and was in the process of pursuing them across the River Narbada at the head of a light field force when formal word about the outbreak of war reached him. Not long after Holkar of Indore joined the Maratha princes of Poona and Nagpur, in November 1817, Malcolm's force engaged Holkar's army in battle. Yet his victory at Mahidipur, following his headlong charge against Maratha cavalry, was more a result of sepoy valour than of good judgement. Holkar sued for peace on 6 January 1818. But it soon became clear that no attempt to 'settle' central India could succeed without a 'voluntary' surrender by the peshwa: Maratha warlords would refuse to lay down their arms and would go on fighting. On 1 June 1818 company forces finally surrounded Baji Rao's encampment. Malcolm offered the peshwa a pension and gave him a twenty-four-hour ultimatum. The peshwa, having little choice, capitulated, and his forces were gradually disbanded. Yet, while the war was over, the governor-general was not pleased. The terms offered by Malcolm had been too generous—costing over £2 million. Nor could full order and peace come to the peshwa's dominions without much more work, and Malcolm spent many months completing this task. Only after suppressing mutinous Arab contingents, building military cantonments, destroying formidable fortresses, and ending the formation of dangerous *bunds* by turbulent warriors did violence gradually subside.

At this point Malcolm's hopes and ambitions were thwarted and his pride offended. Elphinstone was picked to succeed Sir Evan Nepean as governor of Bombay. Malcolm was promoted major-general and GCB, but his wish to become lieutenant-governor of central India was refused by the court of directors; the newly won Poona territories were transferred to Bombay, and his hopes for the Madras governorship were dashed in 1820 when Sir Thomas Munro was chosen to succeed Hugh Elliot. Thus, despite the fact that his pay as brigadier and his stipends as a political officer left him better paid than the governor of Bombay, Malcolm was not mollified. His hopes for other military assignments, possibly expeditions against the amirs of Sind or against Ranjit Singh at Lahore, also

came to nothing. While still popular among notables, officers, and princes in central India, he resigned his position and went to Bombay. While waiting to embark for England, efforts by the marquess of Hastings to dissuade him from leaving having failed, he prepared a vast report on Malwa, which was published in 1820. His homeward journey by way of Suez and the Mediterranean took until late April 1822.

Malcolm spent the next five years in England. Living with his family, initially at Frant, Sussex, near Tonbridge, and then at Hyde Hall, near Sawbridgeworth, Hertfordshire, he cultivated contacts and wrote. His new acquaintances included Madame de Staël, Humboldt, Schlegel, Sedgwick, and Julius Hare. After the appearance of his *A Memoir of Central India* (1823), *Sketches in Persia* (1827), and *Letter to the Duke of Wellington on the State of India*, he sought new assignments. But hopes for another mission to Tehran foundered on his insistence that both crown and company credentials be granted him. His wish to succeed Munro as governor of Madras failed when he was unable to see that Stephen Lushington was already chosen. In contests between the company and the crown that he could never really win, he wore out the patience of friends. Some, like Wellington, wearied of his restless ambition and by now exaggerated sense of self-importance. Finally, the Bombay governorship again became open; and Malcolm accepted it. He hoped for Central India to be added to the Bombay presidency, or that his new post might serve as a stepping stone to the governor-generalship.

Governor of Bombay and final years But what Malcolm encountered, as governor of Bombay, was more trouble than could have been anticipated. No sooner had he assumed office on 1 November 1827 than the *Moru Raghanath v. Pandurang Ramachandra* case came up, and an acrimonious constitutional crisis erupted. The supreme court of Bombay, at that juncture, consisted of one sole judge, its other members having died. That judge, Sir John Grant, issued a writ of habeas corpus against Pandurang Ramachandra, a 'privileged sirdar' who was protected by a company treaty (*sanad*). This action, extending the court's jurisdiction beyond Bombay Island and touching matters 'political', was regarded as going beyond the legitimate limits of judicial authority. On 3 October 1828 the governor-in-council ordered a stay of proceedings in the Raghanath case and in similar writs of habeas corpus. Sir John Grant, piqued, retorted that he was not obliged to heed orders of the company's government. While the matter was being referred to the government of India and the crown, Malcolm forbade officials to discuss such sensitive matters in the press. When the commander-in-chief, Sir Thomas Bradford, coming to Grant's support, threatened to use military force, Malcolm had him arrested and deported. Grant then issued a writ of attachment against Pandurang Ramachandra and, when the governor failed to act on it, closed the court. This prompted Malcolm to issue a proclamation announcing that henceforth, since the court (Grant) was no longer protecting the persons and property of Bombay inhabitants, it was incumbent upon the government to act in its place. Such action was narrowly averted by the arrival of new judges. As they did not share Grant's views, this all but ended the matter—except that a letter from Ellenborough (president of the Board of Control) to Malcolm, referring to Grant as 'like a wild elephant led away between two tame ones' (Kaye, 2.530) found its way into the *Bengal Harkaru*—perhaps by means of a calculated indiscretion on Malcolm's part. This caused considerable embarrassment to the sender when news of the leak reached London.

This all-consuming 'scandal' was the last important event of Malcolm's career. While he tended other duties, such as country tours, visits to Baroda, Kathiawar, and Cutch, retrenchments, public works, road construction, and steam navigation (summarized in his 'Farewell minute' in his *Government of India*, 1833), his administration was not popular. Even though a statue (by Chantrey) was erected after he left Bombay, his day was clearly over. Following his return to England in 1831, his efforts to fulfil further public roles also ended in disappointment. Friends helped to secure his election for Launceston at the general election held that year, but at the election of 1832, held after the passage of the Reform Bill (which he opposed), he was unsuccessful in a contest at Carlisle. Early in 1833 he was still working on his *Government of India* (1833) and *Life of Clive* (posthumously published in 1836) when he came down with flu. He continued to work, collecting documents on the company's charter renewal, and was attending a meeting of the court of proprietors in this connection when he collapsed. After another partial recovery, he died on 31 May 1833, at his lodgings in Princes Street, Hanover Square, Middlesex. He was buried on 7 June at St James's, Westminster. A marble bust by Chantrey, paid for by subscription, was erected in Westminster Abbey, and an obelisk raised on Langholm Hill, Dumfriesshire.

What distinguished Malcolm throughout most of his career was an ability to work with people and to inspire trust. Ambition, sensitivity, and self-confidence, sometimes excessive, accounted for many diplomatic successes. Influence in moulding policies undergirding imperial structures in India marked him out as one of the most able officers ever to have served the East India Company and the rising British empire.

ROBERT ERIC FRYKENBERG

Sources J. W. Kaye, *The life and correspondence of Major-General Sir John Malcolm, GCB, late envoy to Persia and governor of Bombay, from unpublished letters and journals*, 2 vols. (1856) · *Life and letters of Sir Gilbert Elliot, first earl of Minto, from 1751 to 1806, when his public life in Europe was closed by his appointment to the vice-royalty of India*, ed. countess of Minto, 3 vols. (1874) · *The dispatches of … the duke of Wellington … from 1799 to 1818*, ed. J. Gurwood, 13 vols. in 12 (1834–9) · *A selection from the despatches, memoranda, and other papers relating to India of … the duke of Wellington*, ed. S. J. Owen (1880) · *Supplementary despatches (correspondence) and memoranda of Field Marshal Arthur, duke of Wellington*, ed. A. R. Wellesley, second duke of Wellington, 15 vols. (1858–72) · H. Jones Brydges, *An account of the transactions of his majesty's mission to the court of Persia, in the years 1807–11, to which is appended, a brief history of the Wahauby*, 2 vols. in 1 (1834) · F. Rawdon-Hastings, marquess of Hastings [Lord Moira], *Comments excited by the conduct of the chairman at a meeting of the proprietors of the East India Company on the 11th February, 1825* (Malta, 1825) · F. Rawdon-Hastings, *Papers regarding the administration of the marquis of Hastings in India: printed in conformity to the resolution of the court of proprietors of East-India stock of the 3d March 1824*, 8 vols. (1824?) · *Papers respecting the Pindary and Mahratta wars laid before the court of the East India Company to enable the court to judge of the propriety of entertaining the question of further remuneration to the late governor-general*, East India Company (1824), vol. 12, p. 466; vol. 4, p. 135 · *Treaties and engagements with native princes and states in India, concluded for the most part in the years 1817 and 1818*, East India Company (1824), iv, cxxxv · S. Smiles, *A publisher and his friends: memoir and correspondence of the late John Murray*, 2 vols. (1891) · *DNB* · *GM*, 1st ser., 103/2 (1833), 81–4, 559–60 · C. A. Bayly, *Indian society and the making of the British empire* (1988), vol. 2/1 of *The new Cambridge history of India*, ed. G. Johnson · B. Laufer, *The American plant migration* (1938) [Malcolm's plum] · M. E. Yapp, *Strategies of British India: Britain, Iran and Afghanistan, 1798–1850* (1980)

Archives BL, corresp., Add. MSS 13602–13603, 13669, 13746–13748 · BL OIOC, diary, corresp., and papers, MS Eur. F 128, and home misc. series II, pt II, 202–209 · BL OIOC, letters relating to the Anglo-Maratha War, IOR MSS 9899/17 · BL OIOC, minutes on southern Maratha and Gujarat, MS Eur. D 640 [copies] · Bodl. Oxf., collections of history of Persia · JRL, report on judicial administration · NL Wales, letter-book | BL, letters to Sir Charles Pasley, Add. MSS 41963–41964 · BL, letters to Lord Wellesley, Add. MSS 37282–37310, *passim* · BL OIOC, letters to Lord Amherst, MS Eur. F 140 · BL OIOC, letters to Sir Thomas Munro, MS Eur. F 151 · BL OIOC, letters to Henry Wellesley, MSS Eur. E 172–181 · Bodl. Oxf., letters to Sir Graves Haughton · Bodl. Oxf., letters to Richard Heber · Bucks. RLSS, letters to Lord Hobart · Herefs. RO, corresp. with Sir Harford Jones Brydges · NL Scot., corresp. with John Leyden and James Morton · NL Scot., corresp. with Sir Charles Malcolm · NL Scot., letters to Lord Melville · NL Scot., corresp. with first earl of Minto · NL Scot., letters to Sir Walter Scott · RGS, letters to Lord Melville, misc. corresp., and MSS · U. Nott. L., corresp. with Lord William Bentinck · U. Southampton L., corresp. with Arthur Wellesley, first duke of Wellington

Likenesses W. Bewick, chalk drawing, 1824, Scot. NPG · G. Hayter, oils, 1826, Scot. NPG · J. Porter, mezzotint, pubd 1827 (after G. Hayter), BM, NPG · F. Chantrey, statue, 1831, Bombay · F. Chantrey, marble bust, exh. RA 1837, Westminster Abbey · F. Chantrey, bust, AM Oxf. · F. Chantrey, pencil drawing, NPG · S. Lane, oils, Oriental Club, London · S. Lane, oils, Scot. NPG

Malcolm, John, of Poltalloch (1805–1893), art collector and landowner, was the second surviving son of Neill Malcolm (*d.* 1837), twelfth laird of Poltalloch, who owned extensive landed estates in Argyll and sugar plantations in Jamaica, and his wife, Mary Anne (*d.* 1830), daughter and sole heiress of Dr David Orme, the noted physician of London and of the Lamorbey estate, near Sidcup, Kent. He was brought up in the family's London home in Hanover Square and at Lamorbey. Educated at Harrow School (1819/20 to 1823), he matriculated on 6 February 1824 at Christ Church, Oxford, and graduated BA in 1827 and MA in 1830. He studied at Lincoln's Inn in 1829 but was not called to the bar. In 1832 he married Isabella Harriett (*d.* 1858), daughter of the Hon. John Wingfield Stratford, with whom he had three sons, John (*b.* 1833), Edward, and William (*b.* 1840), and a daughter, Isabella. During their early married life they lived at the village of Hunton, near Lamorbey, where Malcolm served as a justice of the peace and deputy lieutenant for Kent; later he served likewise for Argyll.

In 1857 Malcolm succeeded as fourteenth laird of Poltalloch on the death of his elder brother, Neill. He inherited the Poltalloch seat—a vast, uncomfortable mansion near Lochgilphead, Argyll—and also the family's grand London town house at 7 Great Stanhope Street off Park Lane. In the following year Malcolm's wife died. In addition to his inherited estates in Scotland and the profitable sugar and rum plantations in the West Indies, Malcolm ran, as an absentee landlord, a highly successful cattle station named Poltalloch which he had established with his brother Neill in the young colony of South Australia in 1839 and to which he imported the finest breeds of cattle from Scotland. In June 1873 Malcolm sold this and another cattle station, with 4000 head of livestock, for the prodigious sum of £175,000.

It was Malcolm's enormous wealth that enabled him to become one of the leading collectors of his day. In 1860 he purchased *en bloc* the remarkable collection of Renaissance drawings formed by the great connoisseur J. C. Robinson, then superintendent of the art collections of the South Kensington Museum, later the Victoria and Albert Museum. The great strengths of this core collection of some 554 sheets were the works of Italian Renaissance masters, including thirteen drawings attributed to Leonardo da Vinci, twenty-three to Michelangelo, and thirteen to Raphael, many of which had been acquired by Robinson from the London dealers Messrs Woodburn, who had bought the famous collection of Sir Thomas Lawrence. On Robinson's advice Malcolm continued to add to his collection; the large Michelangelo cartoon *Epifania* (BM) was purchased at the Woodburn sale of June 1860 for the ridiculously low sum of £11 0s. 6d., with Robinson acting as his buyer. In March 1866 on Robinson's advice he purchased 135 lots, mostly of seventeenth-century Dutch drawings, at the Leembruggen sale in Amsterdam, and later that year Malcolm bought eighty-three lots, including twenty-four Claude drawings, at the posthumous sale of the Oxford divine Dr Wellesley. By 1866 Malcolm's collection had grown to some 708 old-master drawings. In 1869 Robinson published his *Descriptive catalogue of the drawings by the old masters, forming the collection of John Malcolm of Poltalloch, esq.*, in which he outlined the principles guiding the formation of Malcolm's collection, which by then numbered 870 drawings: to collect genuine specimens of the highest aesthetic quality, by the greatest masters, and with a distinguished provenance. These criteria defined Malcolm as belonging to a new breed of connoisseur whose highly disciplined and selective approach differed from the often indiscriminate accumulations of earlier collectors of drawings.

Malcolm's connoisseurship as a collector was largely formed by his involvement initially with the Fine Arts Club, on his election in 1862, and more importantly its successor, the Burlington Fine Arts Club (BFAC), of which he was a founding member in 1866. His close and lifelong friendship with the collector William Mitchell, dating from the early 1860s, was also significant. Sidney Colvin, keeper of the British Museum's print room, later recalled that Malcolm's 'passion as a collector [was] to a large extent stimulated as well as directed by an inseparable *fidus Achates* in the person of a bachelor friend ... William

Mitchell' (Colvin, *Memories*, 207). The pair were involved with the inner running of the BFAC, lent regularly to its shows, worked together in building up their complementary collections, and were a familiar sight at the salerooms in London and on the continent. By 1870 Malcolm's position as Britain's most important collector of old-master drawings was confirmed by his loan of twenty-three Raphaels and seventeen Michelangelos to an ambitious exhibition of drawings by these two artists at the BFAC, with the Royal Collection as the second largest lender. Malcolm also formed an important collection of old-master prints as well as a very fine group of Venetian Renaissance glass, Limoges enamels, a famous St Porchaire faience *biberon*, and other distinguished *objets d'art*.

On 30 May 1893 Malcolm died at Poltalloch House, and he was buried under the terms of his will (2 May 1888) in the family vault of the Episcopalian chapel at Poltalloch next to his 'dear wife'. The obituary in the *Oban Times* (3 June 1893, 5) described Malcolm as 'a model landlord' noted for 'the consideration shown towards his numerous tenants'. His eldest son, John Wingfield Malcolm, succeeded to the title and his estates; Malcolm bequeathed to him the sum of £100,000 and his collection of old-master drawings and prints.

A few days before he died Malcolm presented the famous Sforza Book of Hours to the British Museum's department of manuscripts (now in the British Library); this is one of the world's finest Italian Renaissance illuminated manuscripts, which J. C. Robinson had purchased in Spain in 1871 and then sold to Malcolm after his initial offer to the British Museum had failed. Less than a month after Malcolm's death his heir donated the Michelangelo cartoon to the British Museum and placed Malcolm's collection of almost 1000 drawings and more than 400 prints on deposit in the print room. Determined that the Malcolm collection should not suffer the same fate as the Thomas Lawrence collection, which had been dispersed following the Treasury's refusal to acquire it for the nation, the keeper Colvin revealed the richness of Malcolm's collection in a loan exhibition at the British Museum in March 1894. With the support of Mitchell, who in January 1895 had presented his unrivalled collection of German woodcuts to the print room, Colvin negotiated to purchase from the heir the Malcolm collection for the nation for the sum of £25,000. In his report to the trustees Colvin argued that the Malcolm collection of drawings 'has long been celebrated ... as the richest that has ever been brought together in England since the dispersal of the Lawrence collections'. Following the trustees' successful application to the Treasury, this single acquisition in September 1895 raised the museum's holding of old-master drawings to a level comparable with the celebrated collections of the Louvre, Paris, and the Albertina, Vienna.

STEPHEN COPPEL

Sources S. Coppel, 'Introduction: John Malcolm of Poltalloch (1805–93)', in M. Royalton-Kisch, H. Chapman, and S. Coppel, *Old master drawings from the Malcolm collection* (1996), 7–20 · S. Coppel, 'William Mitchell (1820–1908) and John Malcolm of Poltalloch (1805–93)', *Landmarks in print collecting: connoisseurs and donors at the*

British Museum since 1753, ed. A. Griffiths (British Museum Press, 1996), 159–88 [exhibition catalogue, Museum of Fine Arts, Houston, TX, 1996, and elsewhere] • S. Colvin, *Memories and notes of persons and places, 1852–1912* (1921), 207 • Foster, *Alum. Oxon.*, *1715–1886*, 3.905 • A. Trollope, *Australia and New Zealand*, 2 (1873), 216 • J. C. Robinson, *Descriptive catalogue of the drawings by the old masters, forming the collection of John Malcolm of Poltalloch, esq.* (privately printed, London, 1869) [reprinted in an expanded edition in 1876 with revised attributions and new preface by Malcolm] • D. Malcolm, 'Neill Malcolm XIII laird [and] John Malcolm XIV laird of Poltalloch', *c.*1992, BM, department of prints and drawings [typescript, privately distributed] • [F. Locker-Lampson], *An autobiography* (privately printed, 1884) [12 copies only; 'Rowfant, August 10, 1883' dated on first page of Bodl. Oxf. copy, Don. d. 161] • *CGPLA Eng. & Wales* (1893) • d. cert. • 'The Sforza book of hours', *The Times* (24 May 1893), 3 • 'The Malcolm collection', *The Times* (17 July 1893), 5 • 'Death of Mr John Malcolm of Poltalloch', *Oban Times* (3 June 1893), 5 • *The Times* (3 June 1893), 14 • N. Gilbert, 'John Malcolm of Poltalloch (1805–1893): a great collector with South Australian connections', 1981, BM, department of prints and drawings [unpubd paper] • S. Colvin, report to the trustees, 6 June 1895, BM

Archives Argyll and Bute archives, Kilmory, Lochgilphead • BM, department of prints and drawings, 'Memorandum of the prices paid at different times for drawings in my collection' • BM, original papers, 'List of drawings, 1866', and book of presents, suppl. vol. 2

Likenesses L. Macdonald, marble bust, 1858, Man. City Gall. • T. L. Atkinson, mezzotint (after portrait by W. W. Ouless, *c.*1860), BM

Wealth at death £413,046: resworn probate, April 1894, *CGPLA Eng. & Wales*

Malcolm [*née* Laing], **Lavinia** (1847/8–1920), local politician, was born in Forres, Moray, where her maternal grandfather, John Kynoch, was provost from 1848 to 1857. Her parents were Alexander Laing (1817–1876), manager of Forres gas works, and his wife, Janet, *née* Kynoch (1820–1884) (not John Laing and Mary Kynoch, as stated on her death certificate). Before her marriage Lavinia Laing was employed as a teacher. On 27 December 1883 she became the second wife of Richard Malcolm (1840–1926), who taught English at Dollar Academy from 1865 to 1910 and subsequently became chairman of the governors of Dollar Academy (1919–23). Richard Malcolm was provost of Dollar from 1896 until 1899.

On 28 August 1907, when Mrs Malcolm was a vice-president of the Clackmannan and Kinross Women's Liberal Association, the Qualification of Women (County and Town Councils) (Scotland) Act was passed, allowing women to be elected as town and county councillors. Although the association had this statute called to its attention by the Scottish executive, the committee 'could think of no woman who would be willing to enter these open doors'. It fell to two male ratepayers to nominate her, and Lavinia Malcolm was elected unopposed to the town and parish councils of Dollar, the only woman in Scotland to be elected at that time (it was two years later before another—Mrs Barlow in Callander—was elected to a Scottish town council).

From 1909 Lavinia Malcolm was also a very active member of the school board. A further connection with children was her responsibility for the many boys attending Dollar Academy who boarded with the Malcolms. As a member of the town council she represented Dollar at the

Lavinia Malcolm (1847/8–1920), by unknown photographer, 1913

Convention of Royal Burghs, one of the first two women to attend the convention. In January 1913 she presented a gold chain to be worn by the provost of Dollar, little thinking that she might soon wear it herself.

Mrs Malcolm was still on the town council in 1913 when a disagreement between the council and some of the ratepayers over the possible acquisition of a town hall led to the refusal of the provost, both bailies, and several councillors to stand in the November election unless an allegation of irregularity was withdrawn. The withdrawal was not made and this left Mrs Malcolm as the senior member of the new council. Councillor McDiarmid proposed that Mrs Malcolm, who was 'wise in counsel, able in administration and wholehearted in the performance of all duties relegated to her', should be appointed provost of Dollar. There being no other nomination she thus became the first woman provost in Scotland, a post which she filled with 'zest and flair' until 1919. An English journal, the *Young Woman*, wrote of her: 'Mrs Malcolm keenly enjoys her work, partly because of her enthusiasm and vivacious personality, and partly owing to her strong sense of humour, which has enlightened many a dull and dreary debate, and enlivened the prosaic details of town lighting and sanitation' (quoted in *Dollar Magazine*, 12, 1914).

It seems to have been the untimely death from pneumonia of her son, Richard (1887–1895), that precipitated Lavinia Malcolm's involvement in the Women's Liberal Association and then local government. She was active in promoting the extension of the parliamentary franchise to women, chairing the Dollar Women's Suffrage Society (a branch of the National Union of Women's Suffrage Societies). When she became provost she said that she considered 'the want of readiness of women to come forward to take part in the privileges of Local Government work as a hindrance to the franchise being given to women' (*Stirling Observer*, 22 Nov 1913). It was only when Lavinia Malcolm retired in 1919 that any other woman stood for election to Dollar town council (and the two who stood that year were defeated in the poll).

In 1920, shortly before her death at Westview, her Dollar home, on 2 November from bronchitis and heart failure, Lavinia Malcolm's valuable services to the community were recognized when she was one of the first women in Scotland to be made a justice of the peace. She was buried in Dollar churchyard.

JANET CAROLAN and LEAH LENEMAN

Sources minutes of Dollar town council, 1907–19, Clackmannanshire Archives, Alloa · *Alloa Advertiser* (1895–1920) · *Dollar Magazine* (1907–14) · Clackmannan and Kinross Women's Liberal Association minutes, 1895–1907, Alloa Museum and Art Gallery, Alloa · census returns for Forres, 1851, 1861; for Dollar, 1871, 1881 · R. Douglas, *Annals of the royal burgh of Forres* (1934) · Cluny graveyard inscriptions, Elgin Library, Elgin · minutes of Dollar parish council, 1907–19, Clackmannanshire Archives, Alloa · minutes of Dollar school board, 1907–9, Clackmannanshire Archives, Alloa · m. cert. · d. cert. · d. cert. [Theodore Laing] · census returns, 1851, 1861, 1871, 1881, 1891

Likenesses photograph, 1913, Dollar Museum, Scotland [*see illus.*] · Whitehead, photograph, 1914, Dollar Museum; repro. in *Dollar Magazine*, 13 (1914) · group portrait, photograph, 1919, Dollar Museum · photograph, repro. in *Alloa Advertiser* (15 Nov 1913)

Wealth at death £434 9s. 4d.: confirmation, 21 Feb 1921, *CCI*

Malcolm, Sir Neill (1869–1953), army officer, was born at 79 Lancaster Gate, Paddington, London, on 8 October 1869, the second son of Colonel Edward Donald Malcolm CB, Royal Engineers, of Poltallach, and his wife, Isabella Wyld Brown. He was educated at St Peter's School, York; Eton College; and the Royal Military College, Sandhurst; and was commissioned second lieutenant in the Argyll and Sutherland Highlanders on 20 February 1889. After promotion to lieutenant on 23 August 1893 he served in India, before travelling to both China and Tibet in 1896. He served in the Tochi valley expedition on the north-west frontier before being posted to Uganda in October 1897. He remained there for the next two years, receiving promotion to captain on 21 December 1898 and winning the DSO for his services during the Uganda mutiny. In November 1899 Malcolm was attached to the headquarters staff in South Africa but he was severely wounded at Paardeburg in February 1900, and was left permanently lame. Malcolm attended the Staff College, Camberley, in 1902 and, in September 1903, was posted to Somaliland. After returning home in June 1904, Malcolm became staff captain in the military operations directorate of the War Office, travelling to Morocco on official business in 1905.

Sir Neill Malcolm (1869–1953), by Walter Stoneman, 1931

He remained at the War Office as deputy assistant quartermaster-general until 1908 and then became secretary of the historical section of the committee of imperial defence (CID). He received a brevet majority in December 1909, being posted as general staff officer, grade 2 (GSO2) on the Staff College directing staff in January 1912. Both at the CID and at the Staff College Malcolm was able to pursue his keen interest in military history, editing the posthumous collection of essays and lectures by G. F. R. Henderson, *The Science of War* (1905), and writing a book on the Austro-Prussian War, *Bohemia, 1866* (1912). In May 1907 he married his cousin Angela (d. 1930), the daughter of the banker William Rolle Malcolm. They had a daughter, Helena, who died in 1934, and two sons.

On the outbreak of war in August 1914 Malcolm was given the temporary rank of lieutenant-colonel and posted GSO2 (operations) on the staff of Sir Douglas Haig's 1st corps; he became GSO1 of 1st corps in November 1914. He was posted chief of staff to the 11th division in January 1915, accompanying it to Gallipoli. In September 1915 he became GSO1 of the Salonika army and, in November 1915, brigadier-general, general staff (BGGS) to the Mediterranean expeditionary force as a temporary brigadier-general. On 14 April 1916 he became BGGS to the new Reserve Army commanded by Sir Hubert Gough. Malcolm was made major-general, general staff (MGGS) of what was now the Fifth Army as temporary major-general on 7 July 1916. He remained Gough's chief of staff until 21 December 1917, being promoted major-general on 1 January 1917. Malcolm's period with the Fifth Army has aroused considerable controversy, Gough's own unpopularity having been attributed to Malcolm's undermining Gough's position by exceeding his own powers. Thus Malcolm's attitude to units within the Fifth Army has been depicted as 'harsh and unsympathetic' (Prior and Wilson, 70) and one of 'unremitting severity' (Farrar-Hockley, 228); Gough in turn is accused of failing to perceive the problem through Malcolm's own loyalty towards himself. Malcolm had known Gough since childhood and had served with Hubert's brother, John Gough, on several occasions. Indeed, John Gough was the godfather of Helena Malcolm and Hubert Gough the godfather of one of Malcolm's sons, Dugald.

In 1936 Hubert Gough suggested in a conversation with Lloyd George and Liddell Hart that Malcolm had not been a good chief of staff. However, in 1931 Gough had written that he should not have taken Malcolm with him on visits to units for it encouraged subordinates to conceal the truth 'which they would not have hidden from him [Malcolm] if he had been alone' (Gough, 134–5). Moreover, while Malcolm has often been blamed for what is perceived to have been poor staff work in the Fifth Army during both the Somme and Passchendaele campaigns, there is contrary evidence that Malcolm was well regarded within the Fifth Army, where he was highly visible in visiting the front, and that there was some surprise when he was removed as chief of staff in December 1917. Certainly Malcolm's determination to overcome his own lameness, which often left him exhausted, gave him a certain disdain for those perceived not to be doing their best. However, the real difficulty was that Gough and Malcolm had a more total concept of command than many others in an army lacking any coherent doctrine. Malcolm's view was evident in his remark that there was 'too much tendency not to command units—that is to say to look upon command as interference' (Malcolm's diary, 6 July 1916, Malcolm MSS).

Malcolm received command of the 66th division on 22 December 1917 but the formation was badly mauled in the German 1918 spring offensive and Malcolm himself was severely wounded in his good leg on 29 March. He returned from convalescence in September 1918 to command the 1st, 39th, and then 30th division before being appointed head of the British military mission in Berlin in April 1919. Malcolm's initial task was to locate Russian prisoners held in Germany but he was then given the task of overseeing the withdrawal of German forces from the Baltic states and ensuring observation of the military restrictions placed on the Germans. In November 1921 he became general officer commanding in Malaya; he retired from the army on 15 February 1924, having been appointed CB in 1919 and KCB in 1922. Malcolm remained associated with the region as president of the British North Borneo Company, and was credited with rationalizing the administration of North Borneo. He was later president of the China Society and helped to found the Oriental Ceramic Society, his own collection of Chinese porcelain being of considerable significance.

Malcolm had shown a level-headed approach to the problem of Germany while in Berlin and remained deeply interested in it, persuading Sir John Wheeler-Bennett, whom he had appointed as his personal assistant, to devote himself to specializing in German affairs. Malcolm and Wheeler-Bennett became founder members of the Royal Institute of International Affairs at Chatham House and Malcolm was its chairman from 1926 to 1933. In the following year he accepted the Geneva-based post of League of Nations high commissioner for German refugees, which he held until 1938. He was also a member of the advisory committee on aliens in Britain as well as pursuing business interests as director and chairman of BKC Alloys Ltd and of Neill Malcolm & Co. Ltd. Malcolm was too old to be recalled for service in the Second World War. He died at his London home, 8 Evelyn Mansions, Carlisle Place, on 21 December 1953.   IAN F. W. BECKETT

Sources priv. coll., Malcolm MSS · A. Farrar-Hockley, *Goughie* (1975) · H. Gough, *The Fifth Army* (1931) · I. Beckett, 'Hubert Gough, Neill Malcolm and command on the western front', *Look to your front*, ed. B. Bond and G. Sheffield (1999) · T. Travers, *The killing ground* (1987) · R. Prior and T. Wilson, *Passchendaele: the untold story* (1996) · D. Williamson, *The British in Germany, 1918–30: the reluctant occupiers* (1991) · I. Beckett, 'The plans and the conduct of the battle', *Passchendaele in perspective*, ed. P. Liddle (1997), 102–16 · A. Wiest, 'Haig, Gough and Passchendaele', *Leadership and command: the Anglo-American military experience since 1861*, ed. G. Sheffield (1997), 77–92 · J. W. Wheeler-Bennett, *Knaves, fools and heroes* (1974) · *Army List* · I. F. W. Beckett, *Johnnie Gough, VC: a biography* (1989) · *CGPLA Eng. & Wales* (1954) · *DNB*
Archives Bodl. RH, diary relating to Uganda mutiny · NRA, priv. coll. · PRO, corresp., CAB 45/136 · PRO, maps and MSS, WO 158/245–254, 333–344, WO 153/505, 584–606 · PRO, report from Berlin, WO 32/5424 · RGS, travel diary in India, Tibet, and China · St Ant. Oxf., papers relating to Rhineland occupation | BL, letters to W. Shaw Sparrow, Add. MS 48204–48205 · IWM, A. J. H. Smith MSS · King's Lond., Liddell Hart MSS · NRA, priv. coll., Hubert Gough MSS
Likenesses W. Stoneman, photograph, 1931, NPG [see illus.] · group portrait (with his family), priv. coll. · photographs, probably IWM · portrait, Chatham House, London
Wealth at death £25,809 2s. 4d.: probate, 27 Feb 1954, *CGPLA Eng. & Wales*

Malcolm, Norman Adrian (1911–1990), philosopher, was born on 11 June 1911 in Selden, Kansas, USA, the youngest of three sons of Charles Malcolm, farmer and pharmacist, and his wife, Adda, *née* Wingrove, schoolteacher. From the age of eight he attended school in Lincoln, Nebraska. On completing his secondary education, he was admitted to the University of Nebraska in 1929. Although he intended to study law, he was attracted to philosophy by Oets Bouwsma, who introduced him to the writings of G. E. Moore. He graduated in 1933 and commenced postgraduate work. In 1936 he went to Harvard for further postgraduate studies. From 1937 until 1939 he was the James Wood fellow. He received his MA in 1938. In the same year he was awarded a Harvard travelling fellowship to go to Cambridge to work with Moore on his doctoral dissertation.

At Cambridge Malcolm met Moore for weekly discussions. Moore's influence was thematic, methodological, and stylistic. Through him Malcolm acquired his early interest in epistemology and his conviction that ordinary language and sound sense are to be respected in philosophy. The greatest influence on Malcolm was Wittgenstein, whose classes he attended in 1939 and again in 1946–7. He later described their friendship in *Ludwig Wittgenstein: a Memoir* (1958), which vividly portrays his great teacher. It is a classic of the genre of biographical sketches. From Wittgenstein he acquired his conception of philosophy and of the roots of philosophical illusion, as well as his later preoccupation with philosophy of mind. He once remarked that Wittgenstein 'made my intellectual life'. While at Cambridge he first met G. H. von Wright, with whom he later established a lifelong friendship. During vacations he cycled extensively on the continent.

In 1940 Malcolm returned to Harvard. C. I. Lewis, knowing that Malcolm was impoverished, generously invited him to stay in his home while he completed his dissertation. He was appointed an instructor in philosophy at Princeton later in 1940. In April 1942 he enlisted in the US navy, serving first on a patrol vessel in the Caribbean, later as executive officer and navigator of a destroyer on north Atlantic escort duty. It was typical of him that his later war reminiscences were not of times of danger and hardship, but of moments of high comedy in naval life. In February 1944 he married Leonida (Lee) Morosova, with whom he had two children, Christopher (b. 1950) and Elizabeth (b. 1957). The marriage was not a happy one and was finally dissolved in 1976, after some years of separation.

On demobilization Malcolm returned to teach at Princeton. He spent 1946–7 in Cambridge on a Guggenheim fellowship, renewing his friendship with Wittgenstein. In 1947 he was appointed assistant professor at Cornell University, where he remained until his retirement in 1978. He was promoted to associate professor in 1950, to full professor in 1955, and to Susan Linn Sage professor of philosophy in 1964. He was chairman of the Cornell philosophy department from 1965 to 1970. Together with Max Black, he transformed the department into one of the finest in the USA, and into the primary centre for the study of Wittgensteinian philosophy.

Malcolm did not believe that philosophy is concerned with problems about a special subject matter, let alone that it is an adjunct or speculative vanguard of scientific theorizing. Rather, it is concerned with special problems about familiar subject matters, namely conceptual problems. Hence his steadfast commitment to careful examination of the uses of words, for to possess a concept is to have mastered the use of a word. His investigations into philosophical problems concerning knowledge, belief, thought, memory, dreaming, consciousness, and so forth exhibited his skill in plotting the contour lines of linguistic usage, the point and purpose of the use of the relevant expressions, and their forms of context dependence. In so doing he demonstrated how the conceptual problems that concern philosophy are typically generated by subtle and little-noticed transgressions of standards of correct use.

Malcolm became renowned as the most influential teacher of philosophy at Cornell. He examined ideas in his

seminars with endless patience and thoroughness. Progress was slow and painstaking, as each problem was investigated from every conceivable angle, with a wealth of examples. 'What's the hurry', he once responded to an expression of impatience, 'we don't have a bus to catch do we?' He was described by Sydney Shoemaker, one of his pupils, as 'tenacious, blunt, and sometimes gruff, but his … single-minded devotion to getting at the truth and exposing confusion, commanded respect. His seriousness was tempered by a sense of the ridiculous, a knack for devising apt and amusing examples, and personal warmth' (Shoemaker, 358). It was primarily through Malcolm that Wittgenstein's ideas were transmitted to the USA.

From July to October 1949 Wittgenstein came to stay with Malcolm in Ithaca. The extensive discussions they enjoyed included examination of Moore's defence of common sense and proof of the external world. These stimulated Wittgenstein into writing his last notes, *On Certainty* (1969), and Malcolm into writing his paper 'Knowledge and belief' (1952).

Malcolm's book *Dreaming* (1959) was a development of an idea in Wittgenstein's work. He argued that dreaming is not a conscious mental state one is in while asleep, and that although one can dream that one thinks, judges, or believes something, one cannot think, judge, or come to believe anything while asleep and dreaming. Hence Cartesian sceptical arguments based on the thought that one is deceived during dreams are mistaken, since deception presupposes false belief. Dream reports on awaking are not descriptions of experiences undergone while asleep. They are descriptions of what one dreamt. And to dream one experienced something is not to experience anything. The book stimulated extensive controversy, and was a lasting contribution to the subject. He spent 1960–61 as a Fulbright research fellow at Helsinki, where he enjoyed extensive conversations with von Wright. These aroused his interest in the subject of memory, and led to his 'Three lectures on memory', delivered at Princeton in 1962 and subsequently published in his first volume of essays, *Knowledge and Certainty* (1963). This, together with *Thought and Knowledge* (1977), exhibits his mastery of the philosophical essay, the clarity of his thought, and the limpid simplicity of his prose. They also display the gradual shift of his interests from epistemology to philosophy of mind. He was a remorseless critic of Cartesian dualism and classical empiricist philosophical psychology, as well as of contemporary materialism, functionalism, nascent cognitive science, and Chomskian linguistic theory.

In 1972 Malcolm was president of the eastern division of the American Philosophical Association. In 1975 he was elected to the American Academy of Arts and Sciences. He spent 1975–6 in London and Oxford, renewing an association with St John's College dating from an earlier visit in 1953–4. It was during this year that he wrote one of his finest works, *Memory and Mind* (1977). With scrupulous fairness he dissected classical empiricist theories of memory, tracing the tangled network of fallacious arguments, and questioned the foundations of current neurophysiologic-ally inspired causal theories of memory.

During his year in England Malcolm met Ruth Riesenberg (*b.* 1929), a Chilean psychoanalyst practising in London. They married in Ithaca in October 1976. On his retirement in 1978 they returned to Britain and settled in Hampstead. His years in London were, according to his friends, the happiest of his life. He took pleasure in the cultural life of London, and enjoyed many continental holidays. He jogged daily on Hampstead Heath. Old American and new and old English friends were welcomed to dinner at home, where he would greet them with an iron handshake and a warm smile that lit up his face. He never lost his slow Nebraskan drawl, which charmed one in the many lighter moments of gaiety in his company, and seemed well suited to the slow but remorseless way in which he gnawed at philosophical confusions, stripping off layer after layer of illusion and humbug.

Malcolm was made visiting professor at King's College, London, in 1978, where he was a key participant in the departmental seminar. He gave graduate classes which were renowned for their lucidity, depth, and intellectual honesty. He set a shining example as a teacher; his high standards of philosophical clarity, his contempt for pretentiousness, and his striving for truth and understanding affected all who worked with him. He was made honorary doctor of humanities by the University of Nebraska in 1979. In 1984 he published 'Consciousness and causality' in an eponymous volume co-authored with D. M. Armstrong, an outstanding work in philosophical psychology, combining exemplary elucidation with ruthless criticism of cognitive scientists, who seemed to him, in von Wright's words, 'a new tribe of philosophical savages' (von Wright, 221). He was elected honorary fellow of Fitzwilliam College, Cambridge, in 1985. In 1986 he published his only full-length study of Wittgenstein, *Nothing is Hidden*, which examines the relations between Wittgenstein's early and later philosophies. He was appointed fellow of King's in 1990.

Malcolm died of leukaemia in London on 5 August 1990, and his ashes were buried at the parish church of St John-at-Hampstead on 10 August. His second wife survived him. He was born into the Methodist faith, but later became an Episcopalian. Shortly before his death he completed a short book, *Wittgenstein: a Religious Point of View*, which was edited and published with a response by Peter Winch in 1993. It was an examination of Wittgenstein's remark 'I am not a religious man but cannot help seeing every problem from a religious point of view'. A volume of his post-1977 essays, *Wittgensteinian Themes*, was edited and published by G. H. von Wright in 1995.

P. M. S. HACKER

Sources G. H. von Wright, 'Norman Malcolm', *Philosophical Investigations*, 15 (1992), 215–22; repr. in N. Malcolm, *Wittgensteinian themes: essays, 1978–1989*, ed. G. H. von Wright (1995) • *The Times* (16 Oct 1990) • S. Shoemaker, 'Norman Malcolm', *ANB* • P. Winch, 'Norman Malcolm', *Philosophical Investigations*, 15 (1992), 223–6 • private information (2004) • personal knowledge (2004)
Archives CUL, letters to G. E. Moore

Likenesses photograph, priv. coll.; repro. in C. Ginet and S. Shoemaker, *Knowledge and mind: philosophical essays* (1983), frontispiece

Malcolm, Sir Pulteney (1768–1838), naval officer, third son of George Malcolm of Burnfoot, Langholm, in Dumfriesshire, and his wife, Margaret, daughter of James Pasley and his wife, Magdalen, *née* Elliot, and sister of Admiral Sir Thomas Pasley, was born at Douglan, near Langholm, on 20 February 1768. Sir John *Malcolm and Sir Charles *Malcolm were his brothers. He entered the navy in 1778 on the books of the *Sybil*, commanded by his uncle, Captain Pasley. With Pasley he afterwards served in the *Jupiter*, in the squadron under Commodore George Johnstone, and was present at the action in Porto Praya and at the capture of the Dutch Indiamen in Saldanha Bay. In 1782 the *Jupiter* carried Admiral Pigot to the West Indies. Malcolm was thus brought to the admiral's notice, was taken by him into the flagship, and some months later, on 3 March 1783, was promoted lieutenant of the *Jupiter*. He continued serving during the peace, and in 1793 was first lieutenant of the frigate *Penelope* on the Jamaica station under the command of Captain Bartholomew Rowley. The *Penelope*'s service was peculiarly active. In company with the *Iphigenia* she captured the French frigate *Inconstante*, off the coast of San Domingo, on 25 November 1793; she captured or cut out many privateers and merchant vessels; and Malcolm, as first lieutenant, commanded her boats in several sharp conflicts. Early in 1794 Commodore Ford took him into his flagship the *Europa*, and on 3 April promoted him to the command of the *Jack Tar*, which he took to England.

On 22 October Malcolm was made a post captain and a few days later appointed to the frigate *Fox* (32 guns). In February 1795 he convoyed a fleet of merchant ships to the Mediterranean; from there he went to Quebec, and afterwards was employed for some time in the North Sea. He was later sent out to the East Indies, and towards the end of 1797 into the China seas under the command of Captain Edward Cooke, in whose company he entered Manila Bay under false colours, on 14 January 1798, and carried off three Spanish gunboats. After some further cruising among the islands the *Fox* returned to India, where, on 18 June, he was appointed by Rear-Admiral Rainier to be his flag captain in the *Suffolk* (74 guns) and afterwards in the *Victorious* (74 guns). He continued to serve in this capacity during the war. On her homeward passage in 1803 the *Victorious* proved very unseaworthy and, meeting with heavy weather in the north Atlantic, was with difficulty kept afloat until she reached the River Tagus, where she was run ashore and broken up. Malcolm, with the officers and crew, returned to England in two vessels which he chartered at Lisbon.

In February 1804 Malcolm went out to the Mediterranean in the *Royal Sovereign* (100 guns) in which, on her arrival, Sir Richard Bickerton hoisted his flag, and he was appointed to the *Kent* (74 guns), then with Horatio Nelson at Toulon. He was, however, almost immediately sent to Naples, where, or in the neighbourhood, he remained during the year. His removal to the *Renown* (74 guns) in July did not change his station. It was not until the beginning

Sir Pulteney Malcolm (1768–1838), by Samuel Lane, exh. RA 1835

of 1805 that he was permitted to rejoin the flagship and to exchange into the *Donegal* (74 guns) in time to take part in the celebrated pursuit of the French fleet to the West Indies. On the return of the fleet to the channel, the *Donegal*, with others, was sent to reinforce Collingwood off Cadiz and was still there when Nelson resumed command on 28 September. On 17 October she was sent to Gibraltar for water and a hurried refit. On the 20th Malcolm learned that the combined fleet was coming out of Cadiz. His ship was then in the Mole, nearly dismantled; but he made a supreme effort and got her out that night, and on the 22nd she sailed from Gibraltar with her foreyard towing alongside. It was blowing a gale from the westward, but she succeeded in getting through the Strait of Gibraltar and on the morning of the 24th rejoined the fleet, too late for the battle of Trafalgar but in time to render valuable assistance to the disabled ships and more disabled prizes. She captured the *Rayo*, which had sallied from Cadiz on the 23rd; and on the night of the 24th, when some of the prisoners on the French ship *Berwick* cut the cable and let her go on shore, on which she almost immediately broke up, the *Donegal*'s boats succeeded in saving a considerable number of her men. She afterwards took charge of the Spanish prize *Bahama* and brought her to Gibraltar. Writing to Sir Thomas Pasley on 16 December Collingwood said:

> Everybody was sorry Malcolm was not there [at Trafalgar], because everybody knows his spirit, and his skill would have acquired him honour. He got out of the Gut when nobody else could, and was of infinite service to us after the action. (Nicolas, 7.242)

The *Donegal* continued off Cadiz until the end of 1805, when she sailed for the West Indies with Sir John

Duckworth and played an important part in the battle of San Domingo on 6 February 1806. Malcolm was afterwards sent home in charge of the prizes, and in a very heavy gale rescued the crew of the *Brave* as she was on the point of foundering. He received the gold medal for San Domingo and was presented by the patriotic fund with a vase valued at 100 guineas. In 1808 he convoyed troops to the Peninsula, and in 1809, still in the *Donegal*, was attached to the Channel Fleet, then commanded by Lord Gambier. In January 1809 he married Clementina, eldest daughter of the Hon. William Fullarton Elphinstone, a director of the East India Company and elder brother of Lord Keith.

The *Donegal* was paid off in 1811, and Malcolm was appointed to the *Royal Oak*, which he commanded off Cherbourg until March 1812, when he accepted the post of captain of the fleet to Lord Keith, his uncle by marriage. He was promoted rear-admiral on 4 December 1813 but remained with Keith until June 1814, when, with his flag in the *Royal Oak*, he convoyed a detachment of the army from Bordeaux to North America and served during the Anglo-American War (1812–14) as third in command under Sir Alexander Cochrane and Rear-Admiral (afterwards Sir George) Cockburn. On 2 January 1815 he was made a KCB and during the 'hundred days' of Napoleon's bid for power commanded a squadron in the North Sea in co-operation with the army under Wellington. In 1816–17 he commanded the St Helena station, specially appointed to enforce a rigid blockade of the island and to keep a close guard on Napoleon, who was imprisoned there. He was promoted vice-admiral on 19 July 1821 and was commander-in-chief in the Mediterranean from 1828 to 1831. In 1832 he commanded on the coast of the Netherlands, with the fleets of France and Spain under his orders; and from May 1833 to April 1834 was again commander-in-chief in the Mediterranean. He was made a GCMG on 21 January 1829 and a GCB on 26 April 1833. He died on 20 July 1838.

J. K. LAUGHTON, *rev.* ROGER MORRISS

Sources J. Marshall, *Royal naval biography*, 1/2 (1823), 582–97 · O'Byrne, *Naval biog. dict.* · *The dispatches and letters of Vice-Admiral Lord Viscount Nelson*, ed. N. H. Nicolas, 7 vols. (1844–6), 7.242 · W. James, *The naval history of Great Britain, from the declaration of war by France in 1793, to the accession of George IV*, [4th edn], 6 vols. (1847) · P. Mackesy, *The war in the Mediterranean, 1803–1810* (1957) · G. S. Graham, *Sea power and North America, 1783–1820* (1941)

Archives NL Scot., family corresp. and papers · NMM, letterbooks and papers · U. Mich., Clements L., logbooks and family letters | BL, corresp. with Sir Hudson Lowe, Add. MSS 20115–20120, 20140, 20147–20148, 20160, 20205 · BL, account of interviews with Napoleon, Add. MS 63107 · BL, letters and papers relating to Napoleon's captivity, microfilm M/570 · BL, notes of interviews with Napoleon, loan 57 · BL, letters to Lord Nelson, Add. MSS 34923–34929 · BL, corresp. with Sir Charles Pasley, Add. MSS 41961–41963 · Cumbria AS, Carlisle, corresp. with Sir James Graham · NA Scot., letters to Lord Melville · NL Scot., letters to Sir Alexander Cochrane · NL Scot., corresp. with Sir Charles Malcolm · NMM, letters to Sir Edward Codrington; letters to Lord Keith · PRO, corresp. with Stratford Canning, FO 352 · U. Durham L., letters to Viscount Ponsonby

Likenesses S. Lane, oils, exh. RA 1835, Scot. NPG [*see illus.*] · W. J. Ward, mezzotint, pubd 1836 (after S. Lane), BM · E. H. Baily, statue, 1842, St Paul's Cathedral, London

Malcolm, Sarah (*c.*1710–1733), murderer, was born in Durham but the family moved to Dublin. On the death of her mother, Malcolm migrated to London, becoming a domestic servant at the Temple. One of her employers was an elderly widow, Lydia Duncomb, who lived with another old woman and their maid. On 5 February 1733 the papers reported a grisly murder of the three women, found in their beds with their throats cut from ear to ear. Four servants were arrested and Sarah Malcolm was later named as the prime suspect. Examined by the magistrate, Sir Richard Brocas, she confessed that 'she, Mary Tracy, together with James and Thomas Alexander, both Brothers, had for some time contrived to rob the Chambers of Mrs Duncomb', saying that they had sneaked into the apartment, accidentally waking the servant and having to murder the women. The evidence produced was 'A Silver Tankard, a bloody Apron and Shift found in a Close-Stool, and Bundles of Cloaths, in her Master's Chambers, where she hid them, and 45 Guineas, concealed in her Hair' (Paulson, *Hogarth*, 2.7).

She was remanded to Newgate and the inquest subsequently brought in a verdict of wilful murder against Malcolm only, refusing to accept her story about the accomplices. She probably expected either to turn king's evidence and get herself off or at worst admit theft while denying murder. Both were capital offences, but the former frequently resulted in transportation rather than the death sentence. At her trial on 23 February she pleaded not guilty and put up a spirited defence, arguing that the blood found on her garments was her own menstrual blood and not that of the murdered women. After her sentence she continued to deny the murder, simultaneously declaring that she was a Roman Catholic and behaving 'very penitent and devout'. Her case was unusual given the scandal of her defence, her alleged Catholicism, and above all her refusal to confess, since confession and penance in the face of death were usual at the time.

As Ronald Paulson suggests, it may well have been the mix of Malcolm's bloody crime and youth, gender, and cool behaviour after the murders that attracted William Hogarth to paint her portrait. Accompanied by his father-in-law, Sir James Thornhill, Hogarth visited her cell and 'took down a very exact Likeness' of Malcolm, which was subsequently published as an engraving. Hogarth is said to have remarked, 'I see by this woman's features that she is capable of any wickedness', but on what grounds he based this conclusion is open to speculation. Her execution two days later on 7 March was almost as melodramatic as her performance in court and prison. She went to the gibbet dressed in a black gown and black gloves, appearing 'very serious and devout, crying and wringing her Hands in an extraordinary manner' (Paulson, *Hogarth*, 2.9–10). Several platforms constructed for the crowds collapsed and a number of spectators were injured. Malcolm's trial and execution reveal the continuing fascination with the idea of women and evil, though it is unlikely that she would have been remembered if Hogarth had not used her as a subject for one of his 'low life' works.   IAN DONNACHIE

Sarah Malcolm (*c.*1710–1733), by William Hogarth, 1733

Sources R. Paulson, *Hogarth*, 2 (1992), 7–10 · R. Paulson, *The art of Hogarth* (1975), 54, 73 · M. A. Doody, 'The law, the page, and the body of woman: murder and murderesses in the age of Johnson', *Age of Johnson*, 1 (1987), 127–60

Likenesses W. Hogarth, engraving, 1733, BM, NG Scot. [*see illus.*]

Malcolme, David. *See* Malcolm, David (*d.* 1748).

Malcom [Malcolm]**, Andrew George** (1782–1823), minister of the Presbyterian General Synod of Ulster and hymn writer, was born at Hill Hall House, co. Down, on 15 September 1782. He was the second son of James Malcolm (*d.* 3 Oct 1805), who was ordained minister of Drumbo, co. Down, on 24 December 1764, in succession to his uncle, Andrew Malcom (*d.* 2 March 1763). His mother was Fanny, third daughter of Andrew Kennedy, Presbyterian minister of Mourne, co. Down. He was educated at Glasgow University, where he graduated MA. On 11 March 1807 he was ordained by Bangor presbytery as minister of Dunmurry, co. Antrim. He was not related to his predecessor at Dunmurry, John Malcome. He resigned from Dunmurry on 11 September 1808, and was installed on 14 March 1809 as minister of the First Newry Presbyterian Congregation in co. Down. Through his mother he was the great-grandson of George Lang (*d.* 25 Jan 1702), the first Presbyterian minister of Newry. Malcom's ministry at Newry was one of marked success, and he was an influential leader of educational and charitable movements in the town. He was one of the founders in 1813 of the *Newry Magazine* and he frequently contributed to it. He married Eleanor Hunter (*d.* 22 March 1854); they had five sons and two daughters. His children reverted to what they believed to be the original spelling of his surname—Malcolm. His eldest son, James

Malcolm (1811–1855), was a Unitarian minister in Ireland and England. His fourth son, Andrew George Malcolm MD (1818–1857), was physician to the Royal Hospital, Belfast.

Although his theology was Arian, Malcom never became involved in controversies with orthodox colleagues. Early in 1820 he received the degree of DD from Glasgow. On 27 June 1820 he was elected moderator of the General Synod of Ulster. On 28 June 1821 the general synod approved an exposition of the principles of Presbyterianism from his pen, and ordered it to be prefixed as an introduction to their forthcoming code of discipline. This order was not carried out, the introduction being set aside in committee as it was considered by the orthodox members of the synod to be somewhat unsound. Malcom died of fever at Newry on 12 January 1823, and was buried in the First Newry Presbyterian graveyard; his wife survived him.

Malcom was best known during the nineteenth century as a hymn writer. He published *A Collection of Psalms, Hymns, and Spiritual Songs* (1811) which contained 405 hymns, twenty-three of them being by Malcom himself, and was for a long time the most considerable collection published in connection with Irish Presbyterianism. Many of Malcom's own hymns are of real merit; six were retained in *Hymns for Christian Worship* (1886), the authorized hymnal of non-subscribing Presbyterians.

ALEXANDER GORDON, *rev.* DAVID HUDDLESTON

Sources W. G. Strahan, *First Newry Presbyterian congregation* (1904) · J. A. Crozier, *Life of Dr H. Montgomery* (1875), 1.36–7 · J. S. Reid and W. D. Killen, *History of the Presbyterian church in Ireland*, new edn, 3 (1867), 441 · J. S. Reid, *History of congregations of the Presbyterian church in Ireland*, ed. W. D. Killen (1886), 140, 206 · minutes of the General Synod of Ulster, 1820, Presbyterian Historical Society, Dublin [privately printed] · minutes of the General Synod of Ulster, 1821, Presbyterian Historical Society, Dublin [privately printed] · minutes of the General Synod of Ulster, 1824, Presbyterian Historical Society, Dublin [privately printed] · *The Disciple*, 3 (1883), 180 · C. H. Irwin, *A history of presbyterianism in Dublin and the south and west of Ireland* (1892), 311 · J. Julian, ed., *A dictionary of hymnology* (1892), 1196

Likenesses silhouette, repro. in Strahan, *First Newry Presbyterian congregation*

Malcome, John (*c.*1656–1729), minister of the Presbyterian General Synod of Ulster, matriculated from Glasgow University in 1672 as 'Joannes Malcolmus, Hybernus' and so was probably born in Ireland; he graduated MA in 1674. In December 1686 the Presbyterian congregation of Killead, co. Antrim, was divided into upper and lower; Malcome was called to Lower Killead in June 1687 and ordained there on 5 December. In 1699 he was transferred to Dunmurry, in the same county, where an old malt kiln was used as a meeting-house.

In 1703 the Presbyterian clergy was divided on the question of the oath of abjuration. Malcome strongly favoured taking the oath and attacked a neighbouring minister, Alexander McCracken (*d.* 1730), who, though a staunch Hanoverian, had preached against the oath as sinful and had retreated to Scotland to avoid it. The affair came before the General Synod of Ulster in June 1704, when Malcome was rebuked and McCracken admonished.

In 1720 the nonsubscription controversy broke out in Belfast in connection with the installation of Samuel Haliday. Malcome was a staunch subscriber and was the first to launch into print with an attack on the nonsubscribers. His *Personal Persuasion No Foundation for Religious Obedience* (1720) was an answer to John Abernethy's published sermon *Religious Obedience* (1720). Although Malcome was not the originator of the phrase he was the first to use in print the term 'new light' about the nonsubscribers. His opposition to them was based on a belief that they were undermining the authority of the church courts rather than on any theological grounds. His argument was that 'a set of men, by preaching and printing, pretend to give new light to the world, by putting personal persuasion in the room of church government and discipline' (Witherow, 218–19).

An anonymous pamphlet, *More Light, being some Remarks on the Late Vindication* (1722), an answer to a work by James Kirkpatrick published in 1721, is often ascribed to Malcome. His final published pamphlet was *The dangerous principles of the sectarians of the last age, revived again by our modern new lights* (1726), which brought forth a response from Abernethy in the same year. Malcome died at Dunmurry on 17 May 1729 and was buried there, in the graveyard of the meeting-house, on 20 May. The location of his grave is now lost.   ALEXANDER GORDON, *rev.* A. D. G. STEERS

Sources *Records of the General Synod of Ulster, from 1691 to 1820*, 3 vols. (1890–98), vol. 1, pp. 82–6; vol. 2, p. 139 · C. Innes, ed., *Munimenta alme Universitatis Glasguensis / Records of the University of Glasgow from its foundation till 1727*, 2/1, Maitland Club, 72 (1854), 40, 125 · J. McConnell and others, eds., *Fasti of the Irish Presbyterian church, 1613–1840*, rev. S. G. McConnell, 2 vols. in 12 pts (1935–51) · J. S. Reid and W. D. Killen, *History of the Presbyterian church in Ireland*, 3 (1853), 163, 252 · T. Witherow, *Historical and literary memorials of presbyterianism in Ireland, 1623–1731* (1879), 217–20 · [A. Gordon], 'Dunmurry. List of Ministers', *The Disciple*, 3 (1883), 179 · A. Gordon and G. K. Smith, *Historic memorials of the First Presbyterian Church of Belfast* (1887), 112 · J. S. Reid, *History of congregations of the Presbyterian church in Ireland*, ed. W. D. Killen (1886), 139, 164–5

Malden, Daniel (*d.* 1736), prison-breaker, was probably born in Canterbury; details of his parents are unknown. He trained as a postilion, and served for a time in the navy. After his discharge he became involved in petty crime in London. He was found guilty and received sentence of death at the Old Bailey on 10 May 1736 for stealing a large parcel of linen at Islington. His wife, Mary, John Holbert, and Holbert's wife, Ann, were also indicted but were acquitted (*Old Bailey Sessions Papers*, May 1736, 103–4). He was ordered for execution on 24 May but on 14 May he escaped from Newgate. This was the first of two escape attempts and there is some confusion about the order of events. According to the *Weekly Miscellany*, acting on a hint from the previous occupant of his cell, he raised one of the floor planks, using the leg of a stool as a lever, and dropped into the cell beneath, which was on the ground floor. He got through the bars into the press-yard and then, by way of the chapel and the ordinary's house, onto the roof of the prison. After traversing the roofs of several adjoining houses he finally gained entry through a garret window to an empty house, 'late a pastrycook's in Newgate Street' (*Weekly Miscellany*, 29 May 1736). Wrapping his irons close to his legs 'with rags and pieces of my jacket, as if I had been gouty or lame', he went 'out at a kitchen window, up one pair of stairs into Phoenix Court, and so through the streets to my home in Nightingale Lane' (*Ordinary's Account*, Nov 1736). According to other sources, however, Malden escaped with six others; they made their way down to the common sewer, from which 'four of them got up a vault in Fleet-lane' (Caulfield, 4.67–9; *GM*, 1736, 230).

Early in June Malden was retaken in Rosemary Lane, London. He was now placed in the 'old condemned hold' in Newgate and doubly loaded with irons (Griffiths, 304). A keeper named Austen left him his rations on the night of Sunday 13 June, when he seemed to be well secured. A few hours later he managed his second escape. Having got hold of a knife, which, according to different sources, had either been secreted about his person, or been given to him by a fellow prisoner, he sawed through the chain that held him, near the staple. He then managed to work a passageway under the seat in the corner of the condemned hold. This led into a funnel which connected with the main sewer. Though still encumbered by chains weighing nearly 100 lb he made his way along the sewer. Newgate runners were at once let into the sewer to look for him and found the bodies of two persons who had been smothered while trying to escape. But Malden, after remaining forty-eight hours in the sewer, eventually got out in a yard 'against the pump in Town Ditch, behind Christ's Hospital' (ibid., 306). He made his way to his wife's room in White's Yard, Rosemary Lane, where he was seen dining. A woman called Elizabeth Shelton, who was later accused of harbouring Malden but acquitted, reported seeing him in a lodging in White's Yard on the night of 14 June with fetters upon his legs 'and the Rivets of a prodigious Bigness, and the great Links of the Chain, and the great Rivets' (*Old Bailey Sessions Papers*, July 1736, 161–3). According to Shelton she approached a smith named Germane to take Malden's irons off but he refused to help.

Malden again lingered about London and on 26 June was reported (apparently in error) to have been taken at Reading (*The Craftsman*, 26 June 1736). He subsequently made for Harwich, by way of Enfield, and journeyed to Flushing in the Netherlands where he was nearly persuaded to take foreign service, but returned to England 'in search of his wife' (Griffiths, 306). He seems to have returned with her to Canterbury, where he may have found employment as a groom or jockey. He was retaken in September by Akerman, a noted constable, and brought to London on 26 September. He reached the capital handcuffed and with his legs chained under the horse's belly yet guarded by thirty or forty horsemen. The roads and streets were lined with spectators anxious to see a criminal so notorious: 'he was as much talked of as the famous Jack Sheppard' (Caulfield, 4.67–9). He was henceforth chained to the floor of his cell in Newgate and constantly and closely watched. Brought into court at the Old Bailey to be sentenced on Friday 15 October, he begged hard that he might be transported, having 'worked honestly at Canterbury, and done no robbery since last June'. But he was hanged at Tyburn with

two other convicts on 2 or 3 November 1736; his body 'was carried to Surgeons' Hall' (*Weekly Miscellany*, 6 Nov 1736; *Old Whig*, 4 Nov 1736). His escapes are the more remarkable because Newgate had been 'strengthened' after the notorious exploits of Jack Sheppard.

HEATHER SHORE

Sources *The proceedings at the sessions of the peace* (1735–6), 103–4, 161–3 [Old Bailey sessions papers, 5–11 May, 21–2 July, 1736] · A. Griffiths, *The chronicles of Newgate*, 1 (1884), 301–8 · J. Caulfield, *Portraits, memoirs and characters of remarkable persons, from the revolution in 1688 to the end of the reign of George II*, 4 (1820), 67–9 · J. Guthrie, *The ordinary of Newgate: his account of the behaviour, confessions, and dying words, of the malefactors, who were executed at Tyburn* (1736) · *Weekly Miscellany* (29 May 1736) · *Weekly Miscellany* (6 Nov 1736) · *GM*, 1st ser., 6 (1736), 230, 354, 550, 617, 681 · *GM*, 1st ser., 1 (1731), 220 · *Old Whig* (4 Nov 1736) · E. Evans, *Catalogue of a collection of engraved portraits*, 2 vols. [1836–53] · H. Bromley, *A catalogue of engraved British portraits* (1793) · *Country Journal, or, The Craftsman* (26 June 1736)
Likenesses J. Clarke, engraving, *c*.1736 · engraving, 1736 · R. Grave, line engraving, 1820, BM, NPG; repro. in Caulfield, *Portraits, memoirs and characters* · portrait, 1822, BM, NPG

Malden, Henry (1800–1876), classical scholar, was the fourth son of Jonas Malden, surgeon, of Putney. He was educated privately, first at the school of the Revd William Carmalt at Putney, and afterwards by the Revd M. Preston at Aspenden Hall, near Buntingford, Hertfordshire, where Macaulay was a fellow pupil. In October 1818 he entered Trinity College, Cambridge. He won the Craven scholarship in 1821, being bracketed with Macaulay and George Long (1800–1879), and was chancellor's classical medallist in 1822. He graduated BA in 1822 and MA in 1825, and was elected fellow of Trinity in 1824. While at Cambridge he wrote for *Knight's Quarterly Magazine* on Longus (no. 2) and on the later Greek philosophy (no. 3). He was also the author of a poem, *Evening*, published in a volume edited by Joanna Baillie. In 1824 he was strongly recommended for the post of rector of the Edinburgh Academy, but failed to obtain it. On 19 March the following year he married Elizabeth Frances (*d*. 23 Nov 1835), eldest daughter of John Taylor MP.

In 1831 Malden succeeded George Long as professor of Greek at University College (then the University of London), and filled this chair until his resignation in 1876. He took an active part 'in promoting the compromise that led to the erection, in 1836, of the University of London as an examining body, and the incorporation of the Gower Street institution as University College'. He published in 1835 an essay entitled 'On the origin of universities and academical degrees', which was written as an introduction to the report of the argument before the privy council in support of the application of the University of London for a charter empowering it to grant degrees.

In 1831, when it faced closure after a difficult first year, Malden was appointed headmaster of University College School jointly with Thomas Hewitt Key, the two men agreeing to take on the school at their own risk. Malden resigned in 1842, though he continued to teach the sixth form Greek until 1868. Malden remarried in 1843; his second wife was Georgina Augusta, daughter of Colonel

Drinkwater Bethune of Thorncroft. He died on 4 July 1876 at his residence, 39 Belsize Square, South Hampstead. A Malden medal and scholarship (of the value of about £20), open to men and women, were established in 1878 by the subscribers to the Malden memorial fund. The medal, by M. Macphail, bears a portrait of Malden.

Malden was a man of a gentle and retiring disposition. His scholarship was 'singularly elaborate and minute'. A tribute by a former pupil, probably R. H. Hutton, recalled his 'fastidious method', deliberately cultivated to counter contemporary critics of the new university in London who alleged that it would dispense superficial instruction (Bellot, 93–4). He was a contributor to the *Philological Museum*, edited by Connop Thirlwall in 1830; to the *Classical Museum*, edited by Dr Leonard Schmitz between 1843 and 1850; and to the *Transactions of the Philological Society*. He reviewed Niebuhr's *Roman History* in the *Edinburgh Review* (56, 1833) and also published for the Society for the Diffusion of Useful Knowledge a *History of Rome to* BC *390* (1830).

W. W. WROTH, *rev.* RICHARD SMAIL

Sources Venn, *Alum. Cant.* • *The Times* (5 July 1876) • *The Athenaeum* (15 July 1876), 81 • *The Spectator* (8 July 1876), 859–60 • H. J. K. Usher and others, *An angel without wings: the history of University College School, 1830–1980* (1981), 15–17 • *Men of the time* (1875) • H. H. Bellot, *University College, London, 1826–1926* (1929) • W. Wroth, *Engraved personal medals in the British Museum* (1887) • *Testimonials in favour of H. Malden* (1824) • *GM*, 1st ser., 95/1 (1825), 364 • *GM*, 2nd ser., 5 (1836), 101 • *GM*, 2nd ser., 20 (1843), 312
Archives UCL, letters to Society for the Diffusion of Useful Knowledge
Likenesses A. B. Joy, bust?, exh. RA 1878, UCL • M. Macphail, medal, 1878 • Lawlor, portrait, UCL
Wealth at death £6000: probate, 28 Aug 1876, *CGPLA Eng. & Wales*

Maldon, Thomas (d. 1404), prior of Maldon, theologian, and preacher, was born in Maldon, Essex, and joined the Carmelite order there. He studied in London, where he was ordained acolyte on 17 February 1353 and priest on 4 March 1357, before moving to Cambridge. He was prior there from 1369 to 1372 and incepted as a doctor of theology shortly after. It is likely that he accompanied the provincial, Thomas Brome (d. 1380), to the general chapter at Le Puy-en-Velay in June 1375, as they were at the papal court in Avignon on 10 October petitioning for a notarized copy of a papal bull. At the following general chapter, held in Verona in 1381, Maldon was appointed procurator-general, but was probably removed from office later in the same year. Some time after his return to England, he was appointed prior of the Carmelite house in Maldon, where in 1394 he received papal permissions to choose his own confessor and possess a portable altar, and in 1397 a further indult to receive plenary absolutions from a confessor of his choice. He died in 1404 and was buried in the chapel there. Bale records an address on the *Sentences*, four sets of *quaestiones*, and works on the Bible, Genesis, the Psalms, and the letters of St James, as well as three books of sermons, made up of twenty-four on the Blessed Virgin, thirty-four on the saints, the seasons, funerals, and dedications, and a collection delivered on academic occasions.

The only surviving work is part of one of his forty-eight lectures on the Psalms given at Cambridge, on Psalm 118 (Oxford, Balliol College, MS 80, fols. 190–232).

RICHARD COPSEY

Sources J. Bale, Bodl. Oxf., MS Bodley 73 (SC 27635), fols. 2v–3, 39, 40r–v, 79, 119 • J. Bale, BL, Harley MS 3838, fol. 87r–v, 198 • J. P. H. Clark, 'Thomas Maldon, O.Carm., a Cambridge theologian of the fourteenth century', *Carmelus*, 29 (1982), 193–235 • Emden, *Cam.*, 385–6 • Bale, *Cat.*, 1.529–30 • E. Boaga, 'Il procuratore generale nell'ordine carmelitano: origine e sviluppo della figura del ruolo', *Carmelus*, 43 (1996), 79 • J. Bale, *Illustrium Maioris Britannie scriptorum … summarium* (1548), 176r–v • C. de S. E. de Villiers, *Bibliotheca Carmelitana*, 2 vols. (Orléans, 1752); facs. edn, ed. P. G. Wessels (Rome, 1927), vol. 2, pp. 822–3 • *Commentarii de scriptoribus Britannicis, auctore Joanne Lelando*, ed. A. Hall, 2 (1709), 409–10 • J. Pits, *Relationum historicarum de rebus Anglicis*, ed. [W. Bishop] (Paris, 1619), 578 • Tanner, *Bibl. Brit.-Hib.*, 503
Archives Balliol Oxf., MS 80, fols. 190–232

Malebisse [Malebysse], **Richard** (c.1155–1209/10), justice, was the eldest son of William of Acaster Malbisse, whom he succeeded in 1176, and Emma, the illegitimate daughter of William de Percy. His only tenancy-in-chief was a single fee of the honour of Eye, but he was nevertheless a considerable landholder in Yorkshire and Lincolnshire, who in 1198 founded the Premonstratensian abbey of Newbo, Lincolnshire, and was a benefactor of other religious houses, notably Fountains Abbey. He acted as a royal justice at Northampton in 1183, and seems to have kept the forest at Galtres in Yorkshire under Henry II. The keepership was confirmed (in return for a large sum) by Richard I. However, indebtedness to the king, arising in part from participation in royal administration and in part from litigiousness, forced him to borrow, and by 1182 at the latest he was heavily indebted to Aaron of Lincoln. Malebisse's leading role in the massacre of the Jews in York in 1190 made him infamous, even in his own lifetime. The chronicler William of Newburgh thought his name 'Mala-Bestia' peculiarly apposite. He makes it clear that the massacre was instigated not by the citizens of York, but by a *conjuratio* of indebted local landholders, who capitalized on popular antisemitic fervour, whipped up by the preaching of the third crusade, as a means of extinguishing their debts. At the climax of the pogrom the *conjurati* marched on York Minster and burned the Jewish bonds—lodged there for safekeeping—in the middle of the church. Thereby they sought to achieve 'liberation for themselves and many others' (William of Newburgh, *Historia rerum Anglicarum*, ed. R. Howlett, Rolls Series, 1884, 321–2).

Malebisse might have liberated himself from debts to the Jewish moneylenders of York, but in doing so he had fettered himself anew. He forfeited his lands for his part in the pogrom, and was allowed to resume them, pending the return of the king, only in return for a fine of 20 marks. He compounded his difficulties by supporting Count John, the king's brother, first against the chancellor, William de Longchamp, for which he was excommunicated in December 1191, and then in open revolt against the king in 1193–4. On Richard I's return to England in 1194 Malebisse had to proffer 300 marks to recover the king's goodwill, and Richard seems to have kept him on a short leash of debt for the rest of his reign. On John's accession Malebisse sought to call in the new king's debt to him: he proffered a substantial fine to recover full seisin of what he had lost through his participation in what the chancery clerk delicately termed 'our service' (*Pipe rolls*, 2 John, 110). He had managed to retain his keepership of the forest during Richard's reign, but he now began to play a fuller part in royal government, as an assessor of tallage, a justice itinerant in several midland shires during the 1201–3 visitation, and a member of John's embassy to William the Lion in 1201. But when he secured permission to fortify his residence at Wheldrake, near York, the citizens of York persuaded the sheriff to intervene with the king and stop the work.

At the same time Malebisse was again finding that fuller participation in royal government could be just as expensive as exclusion. By 1204 he was proffering £100 to recover seisin of lands and chattels taken into the king's hand because of reports that he had kept the forest at Galtres badly. An inquest found that, among other offences, he had taken 250 of the king's oaks to fortify his aborted castle at Wheldrake. He had been caught with his hand in the till, and his administrative career came to another halt. Even his keepership of the forest was not restored to him. By this time he was again in debt to Jewish financiers: so much so that in 1205 the king instructed the sheriff of Yorkshire to grant him respite from his Jewish debts 'for as long as he remains in debt to us' (*Rotuli litterarum clausarum*, 1.58). Ever resourceful, he managed to extract himself from this debt within three years, perhaps by dint of arranging a second marriage for his daughter Emma, widow of Robert de Meisnil, to Robert de Stuteville of Great Ayton, probably a younger son of Robert (IV) de Stuteville (d. 1205), lord of Knaresborough. Stuteville thereby secured Emma's valuable dower, and doubtless made an appropriate expression of his gratitude to Malebisse, who had to pay heavily for royal permission for the marriage. By 1210 Malebisse was dead, for his elder son, John, owed a relief of 300 marks. Little is known of his wife, Helewise, and his second son, Richard.

GEORGE GARNETT

Sources R. B. Dobson, *The Jews of medieval York and the massacre of March 1190*, Borthwick Papers, 45 (1974) • J. C. Holt, *The northerners: a study in the reign of King John*, new edn (1992) • H. M. Thomas, 'Portrait of a medieval anti-Semite: Richard Malebisse', *Haskins Society Journal*, 5 (1993), 1–15 • W. Farrer and others, eds., *Early Yorkshire charters*, 12 vols. (1914–65), vol. 3 • *Pipe rolls* • T. D. Hardy, ed., *Rotuli litterarum clausarum*, 2 vols., RC (1833–4) • T. D. Hardy, ed., *Rotuli de oblatis et finibus*, RC (1835) • T. D. Hardy, ed., *Rotuli chartarum in Turri Londinensi asservati*, RC, 36 (1837) • Chancery Miscellanea, PRO, 11/1/1a, 1b • R. Howlett, ed., *Chronicles of the reigns of Stephen, Henry II, and Richard I*, 1, Rolls Series, 82 (1884) • *Chronica monasterii de Melsa, a fundatione usque ad annum 1396, auctore Thoma de Burton*, ed. E. A. Bond, 3 vols., Rolls Series, 43 (1866–8) • *Chronica magistri Rogeri de Hovedene*, ed. W. Stubbs, 4 vols., Rolls Series, 51 (1868–71)

Malet, Sir Alexander, second baronet (1800–1886). *See under* Malet, Sir Charles Warre, first baronet (1753–1815).

Malet, Arthur (1806–1888). *See under* Malet, Sir Charles Warre, first baronet (1753–1815).

Malet, Sir Charles Warre, first baronet (1753–1815), East India Company servant, was the eldest son of Alexander Malet (1704–1775), rector of Combe Florey, Somerset, and Maiden Newton, Dorset, and his wife, Ann, daughter of the Revd Laurence St Lo of Pulham, Dorset. At an early age he entered the service of the East India Company. He filled various posts, including charge of a mission to the Mughal emperor and of the residency at Cambay from 1774 to 1785, where he formed views in favour of expanding British power in India. Malet also developed an unrivalled knowledge of Gujarat and western India more generally, and was dispatched by the government in Calcutta to persuade the Maratha leader Sindhia to accept the appointment of a company resident to the court of the peshwa at Poona, a post which he took up himself in November 1785.

Malet was by now associated with those, such as David Scott, who argued strongly in favour of consolidating and expanding the East India Company's Bombay presidency. He was keen to use the influence and energy of private traders to bolster the company's position in western India, and in 1780 had noted that 'Surat Broach and Cambay form the shackles of Gujrat' (Malet's letter-book, 1780; Nightingale, 137). For Malet, trade and British power went hand in hand, and he saw clearly the potential value of India's west coast to the China trade. In 1782 he recorded how a forward policy there

> opens a new prospect inviting the exercise of our arms, our policy and that great line of liberal justice by which reducing to order a country plundered by a thousand predatory chieftains is as easy to execute, as worthy of attention of a great and generous people, and the more readily to be adopted when consistent with their interest, their honour and perhaps necessary to the reestablishment of their affairs. (22 Feb 1782; Nightingale, 139)

The company's constant preoccupation with retrenchment meant that Malet's ideas were not immediately accepted. Nevertheless, he has been credited by Pamela Nightingale with 'a new vision … which influenced [Charles] Cornwallis and his successors as Governor General in Calcutta and Henry Dundas and the Court of Directors in London' (Nightingale, 137). His work also helped to lay foundations for Richard Wellesley's forward policy after 1798, Malet's imperialism having a clarity of design and loftiness of vision 'which Wellesley could not add to' (ibid., 174). In 1790 his correspondence with Lord Cornwallis was also influential in persuading Dundas against the proposed abolition of the company's Bombay presidency.

Changing circumstances in western India soon validated Malet's arguments for a more assertive policy. In 1789 Tipu Sultan of Mysore attacked Travancore, a company ally. Cornwallis decided to counter by concluding a triple alliance between the company, the nizam of Hyderabad, and the peshwa. Given the mutual antipathy between these two Indian powers, the alliance was something of a coup. Malet was instrumental in bringing it to fruition in June 1790 after difficult negotiations and despite the counter-efforts of Tipu's *vakils* in Poona. In February 1791 Malet was created a baronet as a reward for achieving the

Sir Charles Warre Malet, first baronet (1753–1815), attrib.
Gilbert Stuart

treaty. The alliance removed the initiative from Tipu in the military campaigns of 1790–92, although Mysore was defeated but not destroyed. Malet had observed to Cornwallis in 1790 that, if Tipu was removed, the company would be drawn into 'an intricate and almost inextricable labyrinth of controversy and altercation' with the nizam and the Marathas over the settlement of Mysore (Forrest, 129–30, 193).

Malet was also concerned to counter French intrigue in western and southern India, especially after the outbreak of the revolutionary war in 1793. By now he had a well-established reputation and style. In 1796 Walter Ewer told Dundas that Malet 'was fit for the highest station in India … and he has a good deal of the Asiatick State about him, is very fond of shew and I should imagine may be easily gained with Titles or gaudy honors' (Nightingale, 137). He remained resident at Poona until 1797, became a member of the council at Bombay, and served for a while as acting governor of the presidency.

Malet retired to Britain in 1798 accompanied by Susanna (d. 1868), daughter of the portrait painter James Wales, whom he had befriended while in India. The couple married on 17 September the following year and had eight sons. Malet retained his interest in India and was instrumental in helping, with the artist Thomas Daniell, in the publication of some of Wales's works, most notably those of the caves at Ellora. In 1801 Malet published an article in *Asiatic Researches* on the architectural and historical features of the same caves. He was created a fellow of the Royal Society and fellow of the Society of Arts, and died at Bath on 24 January 1815, when he was described as living at Wilbury House, Wiltshire (*GM*).

Malet was succeeded in the baronetcy by his eldest son, **Sir Alexander Malet**, second baronet (1800–1886), diplomatist, who was born on 23 July 1800 at Hartham Park, Wiltshire, and educated at Winchester College and Christ Church, Oxford, where he graduated BA in 1822. He entered the British diplomatic service in 1824 as an unpaid attaché and went to St Petersburg. Here he was an eyewitness to the military insurrection that took place on the accession of Tsar Nicholas in 1825. Malet now began his rise through the lower grades of the service, serving next as secretary of legation at Lisbon, under Lord Howden, during the Miguelite War of 1832–4.

On 22 December 1834 Malet married Mary Anne (or Marianne) Dora (1810?–1891), daughter of John Spalding and stepdaughter of Henry, Baron Brougham; the couple had two sons, Henry Charles Eden and Edward Baldwin *Malet. Known as 'Brougham's petticoat' at the Foreign Office, Mary was ambitious for Malet's advancement and immediately plotted to get her husband made précis writer to the foreign secretary, Lord Palmerston. This ploy failed, although Palmerston did make Malet secretary of legation at The Hague, where he remained for almost nine years. He was eventually promoted to secretary of the embassy at Vienna and then British minister at Württemberg. In 1849 he was appointed minister-plenipotentiary to the Germanic confederation at Frankfurt. Here he formed a close friendship with Bismarck during a crucial period in German history which ended with the eclipsing of Austrian influence within the confederation and the emergence of a pre-eminent Prussia. Malet's career failed to progress further and, after the collapse of the confederation, in 1866, he retired and was created KCB. He became a magistrate and deputy lieutenant for Wiltshire, where he lived at Wilbury House. In addition to his diplomatic career, he was author of *Some Account of the System of Fagging at Winchester School* (1828), an English translation of Wace's *Roman de Rou* (1860), and *The Overthrow of the Germanic Confederation by Prussia* (1870). He died on 28 November 1886 at his London house at Queensberry Place, Cromwell Road.

Sir Charles Warre Malet's third son was **William Wyndham Malet** (1803–1885), Church of England clergyman, who held a curacy in Bristol at the time Canon Sydney Smith secured him the living of Ardeley in Hertfordshire. Malet was instituted in 1843 and remained vicar there until his death. A man of firm opinions and acutely conscious of priestly office, he became something of a local character. The Hertfordshire historian J. E. Cussans recorded that 'Malet is one of the best men I ever met, but the manner in which he conducts his services strikes strangers with astonishment. He is an ultra Ritualist … [wearing] … all the vestments of a Roman Catholic priest' (Cussans, 104–5). At other times he wore the costume of a Benedictine monk and, although materially well off, he lived plainly and was generous towards the poor, for whom 'the doors of the vicarage are always open' (ibid.). William Upton's *Survey of Hertfordshire Religions* in 1847–8 described Malet as 'Decidedly Puseyite' (Burg, 6). Not all of his parishioners agreed with his advocacy of increased money for poor relief, of higher agricultural wages, cheap coal for the poor, and the shifting of the burden of rates from the occupiers to the owners of the village's smaller cottages. Few country parish priests petitioned parliament and the monarch to the extent that he did. Such activities provoked friction between him and his vestry, which considered his sermons on poor relief as 'highly dangerous' and a subject for the bishop's attention. Tension also arose over the management of the church buildings and documents, and with the local squires, the Murrays of Ardeley Bury. Malet married Eliza, daughter of E. J. Esdaile, on 9 March 1837; they had four children. No appreciation was recorded on his death on 12 June 1885 after forty-two years' service to the parish. The interesting memorial window in the church was provided by his family and not through any effort of the vestry. Malet was the author of several works, including *An Errand to South in the Summer of 1862* (1863) and *The Olive Leaf: a Pilgrimage to Rome, Jerusalem and Constantinople in 1867* (1868).

George Grenville Malet (1804–1856), army officer, was the fourth son of Sir Charles Warre Malet. He entered the 3rd light cavalry in Bombay in 1822 as a cadet and subsequently rose through the ranks, becoming lieutenant-colonel in 1854. In 1824 he took part in the capture of Godhra, Champaner, and Powanghen in Gujarat; in 1832 he served with Lieutenant-Colonel Jervis in Kathiawar against Sirdar Champoaj, and in 1834 in Gujarat once more against rebels in the Mahi Kantha. In 1839 he became the political superintendent of Mellanee, in Rajputana; he took part in the Anglo-Afghan War in 1842, during which he was wounded, and received a silver medal for his services. The year 1843 saw him serving with Sir Charles Napier at Hyderabad in Sind, and in 1844 he was appointed resident at Khairpur, the court of Mir Ali Murad Khan. In 1845 he accompanied Napier and Meer Ali in an expedition against the Baluchi chiefs. Five years later he became superintendent of the Gwalior contingent of horse.

On 31 March 1851 Malet married Mary Fleming, daughter of Colonel John Taylor; they had one son and three daughters. A keen huntsman (particularly of hogs), Malet narrowly escaped death in 1839 when his head was trapped in a tiger's mouth at the moment the animal was killed by a fellow hunter. Malet wrote a *History of Sind* and translated from the Persian of Muhammad Mᶜa. In 1856 he was in command of the 3rd light cavalry in the war with Persia when he was killed at the capture of Bushehr on 9 December.

Sir Charles Warre Malet's fifth son, **Arthur Malet** (1806–1888), East India Company servant and writer, was educated at Winchester College, Addiscombe College, and the East India College at Haileybury. In 1824 he was appointed to the Bombay civil service and took up his duties in 1826. He began his career as assistant collector and then magistrate at Khandesh. He next became assistant to the resident at Baroda, political agent and resident at Cutch in 1842, and agent in Kathiawar in 1843. In 1846 he was appointed secretary to the Bombay government's political and secret department, and then chief secretary in 1847.

Seven years later he became a member of the Indian legislative council and of the Bombay council, and chief judge of the *sadr diwani adalat* and *sadr faujdari adalat* in 1857. During the Indian mutiny Malet initiated the defensive works for Bombay (which won him high praise from the governor). In 1860, the year he retired, he devised a land reclamation scheme for Bombay harbour.

Malet was twice married: first (on 3 September 1846) to Mary Sophia, daughter of Sir John Pollard Willoughby, and secondly (in December 1854) to Annie Louise, daughter of G. Powney Thompson of the East India Company service. These marriages produced two sons and seven daughters.

Malet published several works, including *A Metrical Version of the Psalms in English* (1863), *The Marriage of Solomon: a Drama* (1876), and *The Books of Job, Ecclesiastes and Revelation in English Verse* (1883). He was also a keen family historian and compiled, in 1885, *Notices of an English Branch of the Malet Family*. He died on 13 September 1888.

DAVID J. HOWLETT

Sources DNB · J. C. G. Duff, *A history of the Mahrattas*, rev. S. M. Edwardes, rev. edn, 2 vols. (1921) · P. Nightingale, *Trade and empire in western India, 1784–1806* (1970) · D. Forrest, *Tiger of Mysore: the life and death of Tipu Sultan* (1970) · M. Archer, *Early views of India: the picturesque journeys of Thomas and William Daniell, 1786–1794* (1980) · GM, 1st ser., 85/1 (1815), 185 · J. Sarker, ed., *English records of Maratha history: Poona residency correspondence*, 2: *Poona affairs, 1786–97*, ed. G. S. Sardisai (1936); 3: *The allies' war with Tipu Sultan, 1790–1793*, ed. N. B. Roy (1937); unnumbered vol.: *Selections from Sir C. W. Malet's letterbook, 1780–1784*, ed. R. Sinh (1940) · Foster, *Alum. Oxon.* · Burke, *Peerage* · J. E. Cussans, *A professional Hertfordshire tramp*, ed. A. Deacon and P. Walne (1987) · J. Burg, *Religion in Hertfordshire, 1847–1851* (1995)

Archives BL OIOC, home misc. series, corresp. relating to India · BL OIOC, diaries, letter-books, and papers as resident in Poona, MS Eur. F 149 · Som. ARS, corresp. and papers, incl. diaries · Wilts. & Swindon RO, letter-books to his family | BL, letters to Lord Grenville, Add. MS 58974 · PRO, corresp. with Lord Cornwallis, PRO 30/11

Likenesses T. Daniell, group portrait, oils, c.1800–1805 (*Sir C. W. Malet, bt resident at the court of Poona in 1790 concluding a treaty in Durbar with the Peshwa*), Metropolitan Museum of Art, New York · C. Turner, acquatint engraving, 1807 (after T. Daniell), BL OIOC · attrib. G. Stuart, oils; Sothebys, 18 Nov 1981, lot 94 [*see illus.*]

Malet, Sir Edward Baldwin, fourth baronet (1837–1908), diplomatist, was born on 10 October 1837 in the British legation at The Hague, the younger of the two sons of Sir Alexander *Malet, second baronet (1800–1886), diplomatist [*see under* Malet, Sir Charles Warre], and his wife, Mary Anne (or Marianne) Dora, *née* Spalding (1810?–1891), stepdaughter of the whig chancellor Lord Brougham. He was educated at Eton College (1850–53) and he matriculated from Corpus Christi College, Oxford, in April 1856. His diplomatic career had already begun in 1854 when, aged just seventeen, he became attaché to his father, then Britain's minister to the Germanic confederation at Frankfurt. Postings to Belgium (1859), Argentina (1860), and Brazil (1861) followed. In 1862, at the height of the American Civil War, he was transferred to Washington. The British

Sir Edward Baldwin Malet, fourth baronet (1837–1908), by
unknown photographer

minister there was Lord Lyons, one of the most able and
highly respected diplomatists of the century. Malet served
under Lyons for nine years, at Washington (until 1865),
Constantinople (1865–7), and Paris (1867–71). In September 1870, during the Franco-Prussian War, he travelled
through the lines to Prussian headquarters with a message from Jules Favre, France's foreign minister, to Count
Bismarck, enquiring whether he would discuss an armistice and peace terms. Bismarck (an old family friend from
Frankfurt days) received Malet warmly, indicated his willingness to speak with the French, and met Favre a few
days later. Malet's next opportunity to shine came during
the popular insurrection known as the commune which
broke out in Paris following the conclusion of peace in
March 1871. Lyons and most of the embassy's staff
decamped to Versailles with the French government and
Malet was left in charge in Paris until the commune's
bloody suppression at the end of May. His courageous service in dangerous circumstances led to his being made CB
in July 1871.

In August 1871 Malet was promoted to be secretary of
legation at Peking (Beijing). He then served at Athens
(1873–5) and at Rome (1875–8) before his promotion to be
secretary of embassy at Constantinople in April 1878. In
spring 1879, with the ambassador, Sir Henry Layard,
absent on sick leave, he took charge of the embassy, as
minister-plenipotentiary, and played an important part in
the delicate negotiations over the implementation of the
treaty of Berlin. In October of that year Malet became
agent and consul-general in Egypt. Partly as an anti-
European reaction, social and political unrest—the Egyptian National Movement—grew apace during his first two
years in Cairo, and was punctuated in February and September 1881 by revolts by the army. With somewhat
unfortunate timing, Malet's knighthood (KCB) was
announced in October 1881 (its award having been
decided some time before). The situation deteriorated further in spring 1882, culminating in June in riots and the
massacre of Europeans at Alexandria. At the height of the
unrest Malet was incapacitated by fever and was obliged
to leave Egypt, not returning to his post until 10 August. By
then British ships had bombarded Alexandria; on 13 September Sir Garnet Wolseley's forces routed the Egyptian
army at Tell al-Kebir and the British occupation had
begun. In November 1882, with Malet still not fully
recovered, Lord Dufferin, Britain's ambassador in Constantinople, was appointed special commissioner to oversee the reorganization of Egypt's administration. The two
worked closely on a scheme of reform until Dufferin's
departure in May 1883. Although Malet was publicly
upheld by the Gladstone administration, his failure fully
to appreciate the complexities of the national movement
undoubtedly contributed to Britain's embroilment in
Egypt, which was to hamstring her freedom of diplomatic
manoeuvre for years to come. He was, perhaps, fortunate
that his career was allowed to continue along its upward
path with his appointment as Britain's envoy at Brussels
in September 1883.

Malet became ambassador at Berlin in September 1884.
The Anglo-German relationship was rarely easy and Malet's arrival coincided with a serious estrangement, caused
largely by colonial rivalries. One of his first duties was to
act as British plenipotentiary during the West African
Conference held in Berlin in late 1884 and early 1885 to settle rival claims in the Congo and Niger regions and to
establish ground rules for future colonial acquisitions by
the powers. Britain's interests were largely safeguarded
during the conference and Malet also contributed materially to the improvement in relations with Germany in
1885. In that year he became a privy councillor and was
made GCMG, becoming GCB the following year. On 19
March 1885 he married Lady Ermyntrude Sackville Russell
(1856–1927), daughter of Francis Charles Hastings *Russell, ninth duke of Bedford [see under Russell, Lord George
William]. The couple were to remain childless. Throughout his eleven years in Berlin, the British government was
well served by Malet's penetrating analyses of German
policy. He established good personal relations with Kaiser
Wilhelm II, and with Bismarck and his successors, and
played a significant part in keeping the Anglo-German
relationship running smoothly.

In October 1895 Malet retired from the diplomatic service and thereafter divided his time principally between
his houses in Sussex (Wrest Wood) and southern France
(Château Malet). He remained a privy councillor, and in

1900 he was appointed to represent Britain on the Permanent Court of Arbitration at The Hague (although his juridical services were never actually called upon). He succeeded to the baronetcy in January 1904, on the death of his elder brother, Henry Charles Eden.

Malet was dark-haired, bearded, and of moderate height. His personal popularity, both in Britain and overseas, greatly contributed to his professional success. Hardworking and ambitious, in public he was the reserved, punctilious career diplomatist *par excellence*, but in private he displayed artistic, even bohemian, tendencies. He wrote a novel, *Nevermore, or, Burnt Butterflies* (c.1869, under the pseudonym John Gaunt), and the libretto of an opera, *Harold, or, The Norman Conquest*, which was performed at the Royal Opera House, Covent Garden, in 1895. He was an enthusiastic amateur poet and playwright and was also a keen golfer and lawn tennis player. He produced two volumes of memoirs, *Shifting Scenes* (1901) and *Egypt, 1879–1883* (1909). His reputation among contemporaries as a man of ability and integrity was well merited. Although not one of the very greatest British diplomatists, he stands out as a man of considerable talent, worthy of a prominent place in the diplomatic history of the nineteenth century.

Sir Edward Malet died at Chorleywood House, Rickmansworth, Hertfordshire, on 29 June 1908. He was cremated at Golders Green on 1 July and his ashes were placed in the Bedford family chapel at Chenies parish church in Buckinghamshire on 2 July.

LYNN WILLIAMS

Sources L. Williams, 'The career of Sir Edward Malet, British diplomat, 1837–1908', PhD diss., U. Wales, 1982 • *The Times* (30 June 1908) • *FO List* (1909), 403 • E. B. Malet, *Shifting scenes, or, Memories of many men in many lands* (1901) • E. B. Malet, *Egypt, 1879–1883* (1909) • *The biographical series: the Right Honourable Sir Edward Baldwin Malet* (1905) • *The Times* (2 July 1908) • *The Times* (3 July 1908) • *The Times* (11 Sept 1908) • A. Schölch, *Egypt for the Egyptians: the socio-political crisis in Egypt, 1878–1882* (1981); trans. of *Ägypten den Ägyptern! Die politische und gesellschaftliche Krise der Jahre 1878–1882 in Ägypten* (1972) • Gladstone, *Diaries* • *The Times* (20 March 1895)
Archives Duke U., Perkins L., corresp. and papers • PRO, corresp., FO 343 • PRO, Foreign Office general corresp. | BL, Dilke MSS • BL, Gladstone MSS • BL, letters to Sir Austen Layard, Add. MSS 39023–39035 • Bodl. Oxf., corresp. with Lord Kimberley • CUL, letters to Lord Hardinge • Hatfield House, Hertfordshire, Salisbury MSS • Lpool RO, Derby MSS • NL Scot., corresp. with Lord Rosebery • priv. coll., Grenville Malet MSS • priv. coll., St Lo Malet MSS • PRO, corresp. with second Earl Granville, PRO 30/29 • Som. ARS, corresp. and papers • W. Sussex RO, Lyons MSS
Likenesses Abdullah Frères, photograph, 1866, Duke U. • Elliott & Fry, photograph, 1883, Duke U.; repro. in Malet, *Egypt* • hand-coloured black and white photograph, c.1886, Duke U. • attrib. circle of H. von Herkomer, oils, c.1895, Dillington House, Ilminster, Somerset; [on loan] • W. Sichelkow, oils, c.1895, Chargot House, Luxborough, near Watchet, Somerset • J. J. Waddington, engraving, c.1905 (after photograph), repro. in *Biographical series*, frontispiece • P. Naumann, wood-engraving (after photograph by J. Russell), BM, NPG; repro. in *ILN* (25 Nov 1893), 669 • R. T., wood-engraving (after photograph by W. & D. Downey), NPG; repro. in *ILN* (5 July 1890) • Spy [L. Ward], chromolithograph caricature, repro. in *VF* (12 Jan 1884) • photograph, Hult. Arch. [*see illus.*] • wood-engraving (after line drawing), NPG; repro. in *ILN* (21 Oct 1882), 416
Wealth at death £47,546 7s. 2d.: resworn probate, 8 Sept 1908, *CGPLA Eng. & Wales*

Malet, George Grenville (1804–1856). *See under* Malet, Sir Charles Warre, first baronet (1753–1815).

Malet, Lucas. *See* Harrison, Mary St Leger (1852–1931).

Malet, Robert (*fl.* 1066–1105), landowner, was the eldest son of the Anglo-Norman landowner William *Malet (d. 1071?) and Esilia, daughter of Gilbert Crispin. He was an adult by 1066 and succeeded his father on the latter's death, probably in 1071. The Malet lands in Normandy lay in the Caennais and the Pays de Caux, where their chief castle was at Graville. In England by 1086 Robert Malet had land in eight counties from Surrey to Yorkshire and was among the dozen richest lay landowners. Four-fifths of his wealth lay in east Suffolk, where his father had made Eye the centre of the estate.

In 1075 Malet took a leading part in suppressing the Bretons who rebelled against William I in East Anglia, and occupied Norwich Castle for the king in the aftermath of the revolt. He was sheriff of Suffolk in 1080. He may have supported Robert Curthose's attempt to win the English crown in 1088 and was certainly out of favour with William II, who took the honour of Eye away from him, no later than 1094, and gave it to Roger the Poitevin. Malet disappears entirely from the historical record during William Rufus's reign: probably he went to Normandy and supported Curthose until the latter went on crusade in 1096. Eventually he attached himself to the king's brother Henry and was with him when he was crowned in England in 1100. Shortly afterwards Malet recovered the honour of Eye. He became Henry I's chamberlain and occupied a central place at court for the next five years, witnessing many royal charters. In later years he was regarded as the first occupant of the new office of master chamberlain. His latest dated appearance on a witness list was in February 1105. Probably between 1100 and 1105 he completed the foundation of a priory at Eye, a project which he had begun before 1087 but which had been interrupted during Roger the Poitevin's ownership of the estate.

Malet's marriages and offspring are uncertain. A much altered copy of a charter names his wife as Maud, but a Robert Malet and his wife, Emmeline, gave land to the abbey of St Taurin at Évreux for the support of their son Hugh, a monk there. Malet may have had other sons called William and Robert, though the William Malet who succeeded him in Normandy has generally been regarded as his brother. Eye and the rest of his English lands passed on his death to Henry I, who in 1113 gave them to Stephen of Blois (later King Stephen).

C. P. LEWIS

Sources V. Brown, ed., *Eye Priory cartulary and charters*, 2 vols., Suffolk RS, Suffolk Charters, 12–13 (1992–4) • C. P. Lewis, 'The king and Eye: a study in Anglo-Norman politics', *EngHR*, 104 (1989), 569–89 • K. S. B. Keats-Rohan, 'Domesday Book and the Malets: patrimony and the private history of public lives', *Nottingham Medieval Studies*, 41 (1997), 13–56 • C. W. Hollister, 'Henry I and Robert Malet', *Viator*, 4 (1973), 115–22 • A. Farley, ed., *Domesday Book*, 2 vols. (1783) • *Reg. RAN*, vols. 1–2 • M. Fauroux, ed., *Recueil des actes des ducs de Normandie de 911 à 1066* (Caen, 1961), no. 220 • Ordericus Vitalis, *Eccl. hist.*, 6.12–13, 18–19

Malet, Sir Thomas (c.1582–1665), judge and politician, was the son and heir of Malachi Malet, of Luxulyan, Cornwall, and his wife, Elizabeth Trevanion. Despite his Norman lineage, and more immediate descent from a solicitor-general to Henry VIII, Malet's immediate family and early life remain obscure. His special admission to the Middle Temple on 29 November 1600 at the request of Chief Baron Sir William Peryam lists his father as 'gent.', a vague and formulaic description. Malet's call to the bar at the summer reading of Sir Henry Montagu in 1606 was confirmed the following November.

In 1614 Malet made his parliamentary début as member for Tregony, Cornwall, being named to five committees and speaking on at least thirteen occasions. Growing professional stature may also be indicated by his appointment in 1616 with two other barristers to organize the Middle Temple's contribution to the tournament staged at Charles's creation as prince of Wales. On 18 March 1620 Malet married Jane, the daughter of Francis Mills, at St Matthew's, Friday Street, London; as their family grew with the birth of successive sons and daughters, eventually eight in all, he leased the Somerset manor of Poyntington in 1624, acquiring the freehold jointly with his uncle Michael Malet in 1630. Malet sat again for Tregony in 1621, where he continued an active speaker and committee man, attacking monopolists, patentees, and judicial corruption. By now, however, Malet was himself beginning to accumulate court preferment, initially via Bishop George Montaigne in his capacities as dean of Westminster and lord almoner, then through his own kinsman Edward Conway, secretary of state, who helped secure not only his return for Newport, Isle of Wight, in 1625 and 1626, but also the office of solicitor-general to Queen Henrietta Maria (September 1626). Hence Malet's lower profile in the first two parliaments of the new reign, and his qualified defence of Conway's patron Buckingham in the 1626 debate on the favourite's impeachment, although the demands of a still expanding practice and his fortnight's Middle Temple reading on 32 Hen. VIII c. 30 (jeofails) in Lent 1626 doubtless also played some part.

Conway's death in 1631 barely checked Malet's advancement; when he was created serjeant in 1636 the patrons who lent their names to the case pleaded at his call were the queen and his old Middle Temple mentor, now the earl of Manchester. As befitted a 'learned man of good report' (Baker, *Serjeants*, 375) he enjoyed a widely based practice in Westminster Hall, served as treasurer of Serjeant's Inn, Chancery Lane, and acquired a Westminster town house. But it may rather have been his connection with a country near-neighbour, John Digby, earl of Bristol, that led to Malet's knighthood and appointment as puisne justice of king's bench on 1 July 1641. Within a year his suspected conniving at the promotion of a royalist petition from the Lent assizes at Maidstone saw Malet imprisoned in the Tower. Released in May 1642, he again rode the home circuit that summer. But when some Kentish MPs were refused permission to read a parliamentary declaration in his court at Maidstone, black rod and a troop of horse brought him back to the Tower. There he remained until October 1644, when he was released in order to negotiate a prisoner exchange at Oxford.

Malet stayed eighteen months with the king, during which time parliament formally disabled him from any future judicial service. After being admitted to compound in December 1646, he retired to Somerset. But on 2 May 1660 the House of Lords summoned 'Serjeant Mallet' (Woods, 128) to attend them, and within the month he was reappointed judge. Disappointed of the chief justiceship, for which he no longer possessed physical or mental capacity, Malet was permitted to retain his judicial place and perquisites, without any requirement to attend court sittings. He died, probably at Poyntington, on 19 December 1665, some two and a half years after being granted a pension of £1000, plus a baronetcy which for unknown reasons he did not take up. He was buried at Poyntington and was survived by his wife.

WILFRID PREST

Sources T. P. S. Woods, *Prelude to civil war, 1642: Mr Justice Malet and the Kentish petition* (1980) · W. R. Prest, *The rise of the barristers: a social history of the English bar, 1590–1640*, 2nd edn (1991) · *The diary of Sir Richard Hutton, 1614–1639*, ed. W. R. Prest, SeldS, suppl. ser., 9 (1991) · Baker, *Serjeants* · C. T. Martin, ed., *Minutes of parliament of the Middle Temple*, 4 vols. (1904–5) · M. Jansson, ed., *Proceedings in parliament, 1614 (House of Commons)* (1988) · A. Malet, *Notices of an English branch of the Malet family* (1885) · HoP, *Commons, 1604–29* [draft] · PRO, PROB 11/319, sig. 28, fol. 221r–v · T. G. Barnes, *Somerset, 1625–1640: a county's government during the personal rule* (1961) · A. M. B. Bannerman, ed., *The register of St Matthew, Friday Street, London, 1538–1812, and the united parishes of St Matthew and St Peter Cheap*, Harleian Society, register section, 63 (1933) · W. Notestein, F. H. Relf, and H. Simpson, eds., *Commons debates, 1621*, 7 vols. (1935) · DNB · C. H. Hopwood, ed., *Middle Temple records* (1904)

Archives BL, notes, Hargrave 402 | CUL, MSS Dd.5.5O (4), fols. 27–40 and Hh.3.7, fols. 59–72

Likenesses woodcut, c.1640, repro. in Woods, *Prelude to civil war, 1642* · portrait, 1661, repro. in Woods, *Prelude to civil war, 1642* · oils (after type, 1661), NPG

Wealth at death substantial; at least eight manors, plus lands in Somerset, Devon, city of Exeter: Woods, *Prelude to civil war*

Malet, William (d. 1071?), landowner, was lord of Graville-St Honorine in the Norman Pays de Caux; his much-debated byname has been explained as meaning 'one who conducts a mail-horse and its baggage'. Of unknown parentage, he was described by Gui of Amiens as part Norman and part English and as *compater Heraldi*, which indicates either spiritual affinity to or close companionship with Harold Godwineson. His father was probably his predecessor as lord of Graville and tenant of the Giffards in numerous other fiefs in the same region. Legends associating his son-in-law Turold the Sheriff with Godgifu (Godiva) of Mercia, mother of Harold's wife, probably indicate a relationship between William's mother and the earls of Mercia or their wives. A strong association of William and his family with Lincolnshire suggests that his English roots lay there.

Between 1060 and c.1066 William Malet occurs with William I in a number of charters relating to the abbeys of Montivilliers and Jumièges. He was associated with the abbey of Préaux in the Lieuvin, of which he was given the fellowship by Abbot Ansfrid in 1060, and with the abbey of Bec, which later mistakenly identified him with his descendant, a monk of the same name. His interests in the region of Lisieux probably originated in his marriage to

Esilia, daughter of Gilbert Crispin, castellan of Tillières in the Vexin. William fought at Hastings and was soon credited with having been ordered to bury Harold's body on the seashore; whether he had anything to do with Harold's burial is uncertain, but it now seems clear that the body was buried at the church Harold founded at Waltham. In 1068 William became castellan of the first castle at York and sheriff of Yorkshire. In September 1069 the city was attacked by Danes. Briefly held captive, William, his wife, and their younger children were among the few to escape alive. He lost the shrievalty of York and the land associated with it soon afterwards, and was thereafter occupied in suppressing the fenland revolt led by Hereward the Wake. Domesday Book makes it clear that he died in the campaign, probably in 1071.

At his death, the bulk of William Malet's wealth lay in the vast lordship (the honour of Eye) granted to him in East Anglia, principally in Suffolk (where he had a castle and a market at Eye), but also in Norfolk, Essex, Surrey, Bedfordshire, and Nottinghamshire. His heir was his eldest son Robert *Malet, who occurs with his father from shortly before 1066. Of William's numerous other children few can be identified. He had another son Gilbert, a daughter Beatrice, wife of Guillaume d'Arques, and a daughter who married Alfred of Lincoln. Another daughter married Turold the Sheriff; their daughter Lucy became the principal heir of the family's Lincolnshire estates. Close examination of Domesday Book strongly indicates that Durand Malet was another of William's sons and not his brother, as is often stated.

K. S. B. KEATS-ROHAN

Sources Ordericus Vitalis, *Eccl. hist.*, 2.178, 222 · Symeon of Durham, *Opera*, 2.188 · *The Carmen de Hastingae proelio of Guy, bishop of Amiens*, ed. C. Morton and H. Muntz, OMT (1972), 38n. · 'Miraculum quo B. Maria subvenit Guillelmo Crispino Seniori', *Patrologia Latina*, 150 (1854), 736–7 · J. H. Round, ed., *Calendar of documents preserved in France, illustrative of the history of Great Britain and Ireland* (1899) · M. Fauroux, ed., *Recueil des actes des ducs de Normandie de 911 à 1066* (Caen, 1961), no. 89 · V. Brown, ed., *Eye Priory cartulary and charters*, 1, Suffolk RS, Suffolk Charters, 12 (1992), no. 1 · C. P. Lewis, 'The king and Eye: a study in Anglo-Norman politics', *EngHR*, 104 (1989), 569–89 · K. S. B. Keats-Rohan, 'Domesday Book and the Malets: patrimony and the private history of public lives', *Nottingham Medieval Studies*, 41 (1997), 13–56

Malet, William (c.1175–1215), baron, lord of Curry Mallet, Somerset, an honour of twenty-two and a half knights, was the descendant of Robert Malet (d. before 1156), first holder of the barony, and the son of Gilbert Malet (d. 1194). He married Alice, the daughter and coheir of Thomas Basset of Headington, Oxfordshire. He accompanied King Richard on crusade and landed at Acre in June 1191. In 1196 he paid a fine and relief of £150 for his inheritance.

Malet was appointed sheriff of Dorset and Somerset at Christmas 1209, after the men of the two shires had offered King John a large fine to have someone resident in the shires other than William Brewer as their sheriff, and he served until Michaelmas 1212. By 1212 he was in financial difficulties with the king, and by 1214 owed 2000 marks, which remained unpaid in 1221, although he had made an agreement in 1214 to serve King John with ten knights and twenty soldiers in Poitou in exchange for cancellation of his debt. In 1215 Malet took a prominent part on the rebel side in the struggle between John and the barons. He joined the confederacy of the barons at Stamford in Easter week, and was one of the twenty-five barons subsequently elected to guarantee the observance of Magna Carta. For the part which he took in the events of that year he was personally excommunicated by the pope, together with thirty others barons.

Malet appears to have died before 20 December 1215, for on that date his estates are known to have been in the possession of his son-in-law, Hugh de Vivonia, his estate having been divided between three daughters: Mabel, who married first Nicholas Avenel and second Hugh de Vivonia (d. 1249) of Chewton, Somerset; Helewise, who married first Hugh de Poyntz (d. 1220), a tenant of the honour of Gloucester (who joined Malet and his own father in the rebellion, and was a prisoner in Bristol Castle in July and August 1216), and second Robert de Mucegros (d. 1253/4), a prominent servant of Henry III; and Bertha, who died unmarried before Easter 1221.   RALPH V. TURNER

Sources I. J. Sanders, *English baronies: a study of their origin and descent, 1086–1327* (1960) · *Pipe rolls* · *Chancery records* · GEC, *Peerage* · L. Landon, *The itinerary of King Richard I*, PRSoc., new ser., 13 (1935)

Malet, William Wyndham (1803–1885). *See under* Malet, Sir Charles Warre, first baronet (1753–1815).

Maley, William [Willie] (1868–1958), football manager and businessman, was born at the barracks, Newry, co. Down, on 25 April 1868, the third of six sons of Thomas Maley, a sergeant instructor with the North British fusiliers, and his wife, Mary, *née* Montgomery. He spent most of his childhood near Cathcart, Renfrewshire, but left school in 1881, aged thirteen, and entered an office in Glasgow with the aim of becoming a chartered accountant.

In 1888 Maley began his long association with Glasgow Celtic Football Club. The club had been formed earlier that year to provide a social focus for the large number of Irish immigrants flocking to the city and to raise money from the proceeds of matches to relieve poverty among the Catholic Irish community in the east end of Glasgow. The club began recruiting players, and Maley's elder brother Tom caught their eye, but Willie happened to be at home when the club's representative called and he was invited to join. A wing-half, he proved good enough to be a club regular for five years, and was selected to represent Scotland against both Ireland and England in 1893, but he played poorly in the latter fixture and was never chosen for his country again. By 1896, when Celtic was in the process of conversion to a limited company, he had decided to confine himself to football administration, and in 1897 he became the club's secretary–manager, a post he was to fill for the next forty-four years.

Maley was arguably the first football manager in the modern understanding of the term, and guided Celtic to become the leading Scottish club in the early twentieth century, winning the league championship in six consecutive seasons from 1905 to 1910. Some of his influence was captured by a newspaper comment: 'He catches the players young and breathes into them the old traditional Celtic fire of which he himself appears to be the very living fountain and source' (*Glasgow Observer*, 14 March 1914). Like his predecessor J. H. McLaughlin, the first Celtic secretary, he was a stout exponent of professionalism. 'Shamateurism', he argued, enabled players to 'debauch themselves without being called to account' whereas open professionalism ensured that clubs could be masters of their players. He also took a wider view of the game's development, encouraging its spread beyond Britain by taking Celtic on exhibition trips to Europe, and especially the Austro-Hungarian empire, where the club played a number of fixtures before 1914.

After the First World War, Celtic lost something of their earlier dominance with the emergence of an ambitious Rangers side under Maley's friend and rival William Struth. Rangers became the dominant league side, but Celtic won the Scottish cup six times in the inter-war years and were popular visitors to the United States. In a period of intense religious sectarianism between the two Glasgow clubs, Maley was always resistant to the notion that Celtic should employ only Catholic players. Apart from his personal repugnance to the policy of sectarianism, he probably realized the disadvantage of confining his recruitment to the smaller community: ecumenism meant that he could sign a protestant and deprive Rangers of a player. At least five of the 1938 Celtic side which won the Scottish cup and league championship were nominal protestants. In that year Maley's fifty years with Celtic were marked by the presentation of a purse containing 200 guineas, and in 1939 he wrote a lively but partisan history of the club, *The Story of Celtic*. In February 1940, however, when the club not unreasonably felt that the time had come for a change in management, Maley took it badly and the parting was bitter. He avoided Celtic Park for a decade, and a reconciliation was effected only shortly before his death.

Maley's overriding characteristic was efficiency, which he combined with a brusqueness of manner which could be, and perhaps was designed to be, upsetting. He also possessed considerable financial acumen: he acquired a sports outfitter's shop at the age of twenty-six, and subsequently owned a thriving restaurant in the centre of Glasgow. He was also the prime mover in attracting the world cycling championships to Scotland and was president of the Scottish Amateur Athletic Association. He was also president of the Scottish Football League from 1921 until 1924, when club managers were debarred from the position. Willie Maley died in Glasgow on 2 April 1958. A requiem mass was said at St Peter's Church, Partick.

ROBERT A. CRAMPSEY

Sources T. Campbell and P. Woods, *The glory and the dream: the history of Celtic F.C., 1887–1986* (1986) · B. Murray, *The old firm* (1984) · R. A. Crampsey, *The Scottish Football League: the first 100 years* (1990) · *CCI* (1958)
Likenesses photograph, repro. in A. Gibson and W. Pickford, *Association Football and the men who made it*, 3 [1906], facing p. 192
Wealth at death £11,404 6s. 10d.: confirmation, 29 May 1958, *CCI*

Malham, John (*bap.* 1747, *d.* 1821), schoolmaster and writer, was baptized on 14 June 1747 at Burnsall, near Skipton in Craven, in the West Riding of Yorkshire, the son of Robert Malham. He had at least one brother, Robert, who was baptized on 7 August 1749, and he was educated at Skipton grammar school. In 1768 he ran a school and corresponded on mathematical subjects in the *Leeds Mercury*. He then took holy orders and served a curacy in Northamptonshire. In 1781 he returned to teaching, and in the following year published the first of many educational works: *The Schoolmaster's Complete Companion and Scholar's Universal Guide to Arithmetic*. By September 1790 he was living in The Square, Plymouth Dock, as a 'teacher of navigation and the classics', as he described himself in his *Navigation Made Easy and Familiar* (1790). In 1792 he vainly petitioned John Pitt, second earl of Chatham, then first lord of the Admiralty, for a naval chaplaincy. His publications at this period included revisions of textbooks by Daniel Fenning, a collection of sermons addressed to seamen, and a naval gazetteer.

About 1798 Malham settled in Salisbury, where he served as chaplain to the county gaol and curate of St Edmund's, and worked as a corrector of the press. He joined in the local controversy about itinerant preaching—between the dissenters and the bishop of Salisbury, John Douglas—that had been sparked off by Douglas's charge to his clergy in summer 1798. After loyally defending his bishop in *A Broom for the Conventicle, or, The Arguments for Village Preaching Examined* (1798) Malham was presented to the vicarage of Hilton, Dorset, on 30 April 1801. Almost immediately he published a pamphlet on clerical non-residence to demonstrate that country clergymen could not afford to reside on their livings, as their current stipends were too low. In an earlier pamphlet he had bemoaned the poverty of curates. His conscience clear, he moved to London, where he found work in the book trade. He continued to write, principally on religious and educational subjects, and grew more ambitious in his projects. He published a life of Christ and a revised edition of Foxe's *Book of Martyrs*, both of which were illustrated, and spent three years on his final work, an impressive folio published in 1816 as *The grand national history of England, civil and ecclesiastical, from the earliest period of genuine record to the year 1816*. He died near London on 19 September 1821.

GORDON GOODWIN, rev. S. J. SKEDD

Sources *GM*, 1st ser., 91/2 (1821), 568 · [J. Watkins and F. Shoberl], *A biographical dictionary of the living authors of Great Britain and Ireland* (1816), 218 · Watt, *Bibl. Brit.* · J. Hutchins, *The history and antiquities of the county of Dorset*, 3rd edn, ed. W. Shipp and J. W. Hodson, 4 (1874), 359 · *IGI*

Malibran, Maria Felicia (1808–1836), singer, was born at 3 rue de Condé, Paris, on 24 March 1808, the second child of the Spanish tenor Manuel García (1775–1832) and his wife, Maria Joaquina Sitchès (1780–1854), a singer and actress. Her elder brother, Manuel Patricio *García (1805–1906), a teacher of singing, founded the English branch of this musical dynasty; her younger sister became the prima donna Pauline Viardot (1821–1910). Owing to her father's profession Maria's childhood was peripatetic, and she

Maria Felicia Malibran (1808–1836), by Henri Decaisne, 1830 [as Desdemona in *Otello* by Rossini]

moved from Naples and Rome, where her father collaborated with Rossini, to Paris, and then to London, where she made a successful début at the King's Theatre on 11 June 1825, in Rossini's *Il barbiere di Siviglia*. She had been trained by her father.

In October 1825 García took his family and a few more singers to New York, where they introduced Italian opera to the New World. Maria was the prima donna, performing operas mainly by Rossini. In 1826 in New York she married a naturalized American merchant, Eugène Malibran (1781–1836), twenty-seven years her senior, probably in order to escape from her tyrannical father. In November 1827 she returned to France, alone.

Maria Malibran arrived in Paris just when the political and artistic ideas which were to culminate in the events of 1830 were gathering momentum. Her success was immediate. Her remarkable voice and musicianship, and her typically Romantic style of acting—passionate, frenetic, highly individual—exactly expressed the mood of the moment. In Paris, where she was prima donna at the Théâtre Italien for the next four years, her influence on the Romantic generation—particularly on writers—was considerable. As Rossini's Desdemona she became a Romantic icon. She also sang frequently in England, where she was acclaimed as an outstanding singer, but did not have the cult status which she soon acquired in France and, later, in Italy.

In 1829 Maria fell in love with the Belgian violinist Charles de Bériot (1802–1870). She succeeded in obtaining a civil annulment of her marriage in 1835, and married Bériot on 29 March 1836. From 1832 until her death she sang in Italy and England. In Italy she became the supreme interpreter of Bellini's music, and her final season at La Scala (1835–6) marked the apogee of her career. She spent the summer of 1836 in London, where she was engaged by Alfred Bunn to sing operas—including *Fidelio*—in English. On 5 July, while riding in Regent's Park with Lord William Lennox, she had a fall, which affected her health.

In September Maria appeared at the Manchester festival. On leaving the stage after a sensational performance on 14 September she became seriously ill; from then on she was attended by three Manchester doctors. But Bériot, losing hope, summoned her homoeopathic doctor, Dr Belluomini, from London. He arrived on 18 September, dismissed the Manchester doctors, and refused to consult them. However, she died in her room at the Mosley Arms Hotel on 23 September. The cause of death was unclear. Immediately after his wife's death Bériot, having given instructions that she should have a simple funeral and that there should be no post-mortem, left Manchester with Dr Belluomini. This created a very unfavourable impression.

The festival committee decided to give La Malibran (as she was known) a grand civic funeral, which took place on 1 October. All the dignitaries of Manchester attended, and thousands of people filed past her grave in the collegiate church (now Manchester Cathedral). However, that afternoon a letter was received from Bériot in Belgium saying that he now wished his wife to be buried there. Public opinion opposed this; and there was criticism from the medical profession, which considered that a post-mortem should have been held. Homoeopathy was fiercely attacked in the national and medical press.

When the diocesan court (Chester) granted a faculty to Bériot to disinter his wife's coffin, a group of Mancunians, the Memorialists, lodged a caveat. It was only when Malibran's mother came to Manchester that the Memorialists relented, and the faculty was granted to her. The coffin was exhumed on 20 December, and reburied at Laeken cemetery, Brussels, on 5 January 1837.

Malibran was dark-haired, slight, attractive rather than beautiful; vivacious and amusing, she nevertheless had an aura of melancholy. She was the most charismatic singer of her epoch, and a charming and intelligent woman. Alfred de Musset's *Stances à la Malibran* (1836) was the finest tribute to her.   APRIL FITZLYON

Sources A. FitzLyon, *Maria Malibran* (1987) [incl. complete bibliography] · H. Bushnell, *Maria Malibran* (1979) · M. Teneo, 'La Malibran d'après des documents inédits', *Sammelbände der Internationalen Musikgesellschaft*, 7 (1906), 437–82 · A. Pougin, *Marie Malibran* (1911) · A. Bunn, *The stage: both before and behind the curtain*, 3 vols. (1840) · W. P. Lennox, *Fifty years' biographical reminiscences*, 2 vols. (1863) · W. P. Lennox, *My recollections from 1806–1873*, 2 vols. (1874) · *The Lancet* (8 Oct 1836) · *The Lancet* (15 Oct 1836) · *The Lancet* (22 Oct 1836) · *The Lancet* (5 Nov 1836) · *The Lancet* (12 Nov 1836) · b. cert.

Archives Bibliothèque de l'Opéra, Paris · Bibliothèque Nationale, Paris · BL · Conservatoire Royale, Brussels · priv. coll.

Likenesses H. Grevédon, lithograph, 1829 · H. Decaisne, oils, 1830, Musée Carnavalet, Paris [*see illus.*] · L. Pedrazzi, oils, 1834,

Museo Teatrale, Teatro alla Scala, Milan · A. Devéria, lithograph, 1836 · C. Baruzzi, bust, Liceo Musicale, Bologna · F. Bouchot, oils, priv. coll., Paris · P. Marchese, bust, Teatro alla Scala, Milan · L. Viardot, lithograph, repro. in *Les Lettres et les Arts*, 14 (1889), 94 · death mask, Conservatoire Royale, Brussels · oils, priv. coll., Paris; repro. in FitzLyon, *Maria Malibran*, 144–5

Wealth at death earned very high fees

Malim, Frederic Blagden (1872–1966), headmaster, was born on 13 June 1872 at Chichester, Sussex, the son of Frederick John Malim, solicitor, of St Wolfram, Blackheath, London, and his wife, Frances Elizabeth Gruggen. He was educated at Blackheath proprietary school, an early nineteenth-century foundation which was prominent in its day. He went there in May 1885, and wrote much later of the strengths of the school in both scholarship and sport. It was, he judged, 'a bustling healthy community with sound ambitions and a good tradition' (Kirby, 135–6). He won an open scholarship at Clare College, Cambridge, but preferred to go the following year to Trinity College, where he matriculated in 1891. He became a scholar in 1892 and won first classes in both parts of the classical tripos (1894 and 1895). He came close to winning a Trinity fellowship with a thesis on Plato's *Phaedo*, and he was president of the union in Michaelmas term 1894.

In 1895 Malim was appointed an assistant master at Marlborough College, and he stayed there until 1907. He was a housemaster, commander of the school cadet corps, and the mainstay of the debating society. Marlborough was, he wrote, 'a good place for a young man to be apprenticed to his craft' (Malim, 26). In 1907 he married Amy Gertrude Hemmerde (d. 1960); they had a family of five sons and three daughters. In the same year he became headmaster of Sedbergh School. This was the first of his three headships (Sedbergh, 1907–11; Haileybury College, 1912–21; and Wellington College, 1921–37). At Sedbergh he had to contend with problems of falling numbers, which he succeeded in arresting. He reorganized the curriculum and the timetable and strengthened the teaching of science. A Board of Education inspection in 1909 commented favourably on the general organization of the school. He was an enthusiast for fell walking, he was strongly interested in the Officers' Training Corps, and he wrote the words of the school song.

Malim's years at Haileybury were dominated by the First World War. It was a period, as he wrote himself, when headmasters were fully stretched to maintain the necessary minimum of efficiency without starting new developments. The school historian, R. L. Ashcroft, commented on the 'briskness, cheerfulness and efficiency' with which he guided Haileybury through those years of trial (Ashcroft, 5). *The Haileyburian* wrote of him:

> whether he was acting as Fifth Form Master in an emergency, touching up the long-suffering time-table (one of his favourite hobbies!), devising a new scheme for an endowment fund, or playing in a servants' cricket match, he never seemed to tire.

The Wellington years (1921–37) were the period when his talents found their fullest expression. His policy during the difficult inter-war years was to keep the numbers high and the fees low while steadily improving the facilities.

The boarding-houses were renovated and new science laboratories built. He was prepared to liberalize the atmosphere of the school, and he dealt sensibly and moderately with the activities of the communist-leaning Romilly brothers, Giles and Esmond, who inserted pacifist leaflets into all the hymnbooks on Remembrance day 1933.

Malim had a remarkable career. Very few men have been head of three major public schools over a period of thirty years, and the writer of his obituary in *The Times* commented: 'he was one of the foremost headmasters of his time and his advice was constantly sought by younger men who became headmasters, as well as by parents'. He was chairman of the Headmasters' Conference in 1930 and 1932, and he made several journeys to schools overseas, the most important being the visit to dominion schools on behalf of the conference (1938–9). He drew upon these experiences in his book *Almae matres: Recollections of some Schools at Home and Abroad* (1948). Of the man and his ideas it is not easy to form a picture because he was a person of strong reserve. One of his Wellington colleagues wrote: 'A certain precision of speech and austerity of public manner, which he seldom discarded, combined with an antipathy towards any expressed emotion, suggested the old Roman virtues' (Talboys, 64). Though he was a fine preacher and public speaker, he was as an individual unpretentious and almost shy. It is interesting that in *Almae matres*, half of which deals with the four schools in which he worked and half with the schools in the dominions which he visited, there are no direct references to himself at all. Yet the book contains a number of revealing pointers. Malim was keenly interested in the British empire and in the opportunities which it offered to Englishmen. He wished to build education in the new nations on the traditions of the English public school, and he laid great stress on the personal influence of individuals. He was keenly concerned for order and discipline, and he was anxious that the headmaster should have freedom and personal control over his school. He was distrustful of state activity and of large-scale educational systems run by officials. In the dominions, he thought, 'a man of vision and courage may meet with remarkable success' (Malim, 143), though he feared the pressures towards standardization which would crush individual achievement. After his retirement in 1937 he lived at Myddylton House, Saffron Walden, Essex. During the Second World War he returned to teach at Haileybury for three years. He died at Myddylton House on 5 June 1966.

JOHN ROACH

Sources F. B. Malim, *Almae matres: recollections of some schools at home and abroad* (1948) · H. L. Clarke and W. N. Weech, *History of Sedbergh School, 1525–1925* (1925) · R. L. Ashcroft, *Haileybury, 1908–1961: the story of Haileybury College from 1908 to 1942, and of Haileybury and Imperial Service College from 1942 to 1961* (1961) · D. Newsome, *A history of Wellington College, 1859–1959* [1959] · R. St C. Talboys, *A Victorian school: being the story of Wellington College* (1943) · J. W. Kirby, *The history of the Blackheath proprietary school* (1933) · *The Times* (7 June 1966) · *The Haileyburian* (20 Oct 1921) · *The Haileyburian and Imperial Service College Chronicle* (19 Oct 1966) · *The Sedberghian* (July 1907) · *The Sedberghian* (Dec 1911) · b. cert.

Likenesses photograph, 1912, repro. in *Wellington College Year Book* (1937) · W. Nicholson, oils, 1920?, Haileybury, Hertfordshire · K. Henderson, oils, 1925, Sedbergh School, Cumbria · F. Dodd, oils, 1945, Wellington College, Berkshire · photograph, repro. in Ashcroft, *Haileybury 1908–1961* · photographs, repro. in *Wellington College Year Book* (1921)

Wealth at death £21,894: probate, 27 July 1966, *CGPLA Eng. & Wales*

Malim, William. *See* Malym, William (1533–1594).

Maling, Christopher Thompson (1824–1901), pottery manufacturer, was probably born in Newcastle upon Tyne, the second son of Robert Maling (1781–1863), pottery manufacturer, and his wife, Eleanor, daughter of William Potts, a Sunderland shipbuilder. The Malings were a family with Huguenot roots. They had secured their wealth by marriage into the Thompson family of Hendon, Sunderland, in the eighteenth century. Maling's great-grandfather had established a pottery at Sunderland in 1762 and his father, Robert, moved the base to Newcastle during the second decade of the nineteenth century. Little evidence remains for Maling's early years except that he worked for his father as a commercial traveller. By the mid-nineteenth century the production of commercial coarseware was firmly established on Tyneside—especially as clay could be conveniently carried as ballast in the returning collier ships. While working for his father Maling became friendly with the renowned 'jam producing' Keiller sisters of Dundee. This relationship was to prove profitable to both families at a later date.

Maling took over the running of the family pottery business in his mid-twenties. Under his control, and in two distinct phases, 'the firm prospered and indeed grew to a size comparable to some of the largest of the Staffordshire potteries' (Atkinson, 50). During the first phase, commencing in 1859, a new and modern pottery was established under the name of the Ford pottery at Ouseburn, Newcastle upon Tyne. As in previous years Maling's main aim was to produce basic containers of various kinds. With eighteen kilns at work, the new Ford pottery was capable of producing three-quarters of a million articles a month—mainly containers for jam, marmalade, potted meat, cream, and ointment. An 1863 report showed the firm producing 90 per cent of jam jars in England and Scotland as well as exports to the empire. During this period the link with the Keillers was cemented. The second phase of Maling's improvements began in 1879 with the building of another pottery on an 18 acre site to the east of the 1859 structure. The older buildings were renamed Ford A and the new ones called Ford B. Ford B was in effect several factories under one roof. In them new ventures were undertaken as Malings moved into the manufacture of decorated toilet and sanitary ware, photographic and chemical apparatus, water filters, electrical ware, and kitchen and dairy equipment. The firm also began to move upmarket with modern decorated tableware bearing the Maling triangular trademark. As a result the London market opened up in the 1880s, as did links with Frank Cooper and Sainsbury's.

Maling was an archetypal entrepreneur, ambitious and keen to keep ahead of rivals. The opening of the first Ford pottery in 1859 enabled him to produce more containers in a week than the previous pottery had in a year. He also had a reputation as a caring employer, although some detractors claimed that his benefaction had mercenary roots. Working conditions at the Maling works were seen as advanced for the time, and safety measures included the adoption of leadless glazes. Ford B had wash-houses, a dining room, and kitchens. There was also a school and chapel on the site. Allotments around the edge of the works were seen as a major benefit to workers, although cynics felt they were constructed as convenient 'safety fences'. Although prominent in terms of his business and enterprise, Maling enjoyed his privacy. He was a church-going man 'but of retiring disposition so far as public service and notoriety were concerned—a man of great but unobtrusive benevolence' (*Newcastle Daily Leader*). The effect of this benevolence may be seen in the number of workers who left the Staffordshire potteries to work for Malings.

Malings continued to be a family affair. Maling married Mary Ford, daughter of an Edinburgh glass manufacturer, at Liberton, Midlothian, on 16 June 1857. The Ford works were named after her. They had a large family—at least nine children, with four boys and four girls still alive at the time of his death. One son, Ernest, left for South Africa, but the other three—John Ford (1858–1924), Christopher Thompson junior (1863–1934), and Frederick Theodore (1866–1937)—were brought into the business. In 1889 it was restyled C. T. Maling & Sons. Ten years later Maling retired.

Maling's later life was not easy. His wife predeceased him by a considerable number of years and ill health forced him to divide his time between the north and the milder south coast. He died at his home, 14 Ellison Place, Newcastle upon Tyne, on 20 July 1901, having been bedridden for six weeks. His body was placed in the family vaults at Jesmond old cemetery, Newcastle, on 23 July. He left Malings as one of the biggest earthenware factories in the world, with a prosperous link with Rington's Tea Company yet to come.   KEITH GREGSON

Sources S. Moore and C. Ross, *Maling: the trademark of excellence* (1989) · R. C. Bell, S. Cottle, and L. Dixon, *Maling: a Tyneside pottery* (1981) · R. C. Bell, *Tyneside pottery* (1971) · E. Cameron, *Encyclopedia of porcelain and pottery in the nineteenth and twentieth centuries* (1986) · J. F. Blacker, *ABC of XIX century English ceramic art* (1911) · R. Hyslop, ed., *Antiquities of Sunderland*, 7, app. 2 (1906) · Sunderland Public Library, Corder MSS · *Newcastle Daily Leader* (22 July 1901) · census returns for Newcastle upon Tyne, 1851 · *Parsons and White directory* (1827); (1838); (1850) · N. McCord, *North-east England: the region's development, 1760–1960* (1979) · F. Atkinson, *Victorian Britain: the north-east* (1989) · IGI

Archives Laing Art Gallery, Newcastle upon Tyne · Newcastle upon Tyne Museum Services · Shipley Art Gallery, Gateshead

Likenesses photograph, repro. in Moore and Ross, *Maling*, 4

Wealth at death £107,785 15s. 8d.: resworn probate, Nov 1901, *CGPLA Eng. & Wales*

Malinowski, Bronisław Kasper (1884–1942), anthropologist, was born on 7 April 1884 in Cracow, Galicia (then part of the Austro-Hungarian empire, now Poland), the only child of Lucjan (Lucian) Feliks Jan Malinowski (1839–1898)

Bronisław Kasper Malinowski (1884–1942), by Samuel Kravitt, c.1939–40

and Józefa Eleonora Zenosia Malinowska, *née* Łącka (1848–1918). Both parents were of noble descent (*szlachta*) and Roman Catholics, though Malinowski was a self-declared agnostic. His father was professor of Slavic philology at the Jagiellonian University in Cracow, with a PhD from Leipzig University. After his father's death Malinowski, a sickly child, was raised by his mother who often took him to warmer, foreign climes in order to improve his health. He was known to family and friends throughout his life by diminutives, the most common of which was Bronio.

The path to anthropology After private tutoring at home in Cracow, Malinowski attended the King Jan Sobieski III Gymnasium and then the faculty of philosophy of the Jagiellonian University (1902–6). A brilliant student, he was awarded a doctorate in philosophy and physics in 1908 with highest imperial honours (*sub auspiciis imperatoris*) for a thesis on the so-called second positivist theories of Ernst Mach (*On the Principle of the Economy of Thought*). Cracow was a centre of intellectual and artistic activity and Malinowski's closest friend was Stanisław Ignacy Witkiewicz, later a noted surrealist author, dramatist, and painter, who depicted Malinowski in some of his works. With other young members of the Polish intelligentsia, budding academics, and artists, Malinowski spent many summers in the Tatra Mountains and around Zakopane pursuing new intellectual ideas and an avant-garde lifestyle.

Between 1909 and 1910 Malinowski studied physical

chemistry at his father's university in Leipzig, and there also attended Wilhelm Wundt's courses in anthropological psychology (*Völkerpsychologie*) and Karl Bücher's in economic history. A romantic attachment resulted in 1910 in a move to London, where he informally attended lectures on ethnology and primitive sociology at the London School of Economics (LSE) before registering as a research student in 1913. In a later construction of his own myth Malinowski identified his reading as a sickly youth of J. G. Frazer's *Golden Bough* as the source of his later interest in anthropology, and he retained a lifelong respect for Frazer. In England he encountered a new generation of science-trained scholars who revolutionized British anthropology, most notably A. C. Haddon, W. H. R. Rivers, and C. G. Seligman. All played an important part in Malinowski's entry into the emergent field of academic anthropology and his integration in English academic life. His first major publication in English, *The Family among the Australian Aborigines* (1913), was based on library research supervised by Seligman and the sociologist Edward Westermarck. Between 1911 and 1915 he also published in Polish works on primitive religion and social organization.

Establishing an ethnographic field Seligman helped Malinowski to gain support for first-hand research among 'primitive peoples', and in 1914 he joined a group of anthropologists journeying to Australia, where meetings of the British Association for the Advancement of Science were held. While he was there the First World War broke out, but Malinowski proceeded to southern Papua where he conducted some rather cursory research among coastal Melanesians. The results were published by the Royal Society of South Australia as *The Natives of Mailu* (1915). This, together with his book on the Australian Aborigines, resulted in his being awarded a doctorate of science by London University in 1916.

Between 1915 and 1918, assisted financially by the Australian commonwealth government and the industrialist Robert Mond, Malinowski spent two ten-month periods in the insular area at the eastern end of Papua known as the Massim, specifically on the island of Kiriwina in the Trobriand group. Seligman had earlier surveyed the area ethnologically, but Malinowski carried out intensive ethnographic research in a single location. Already gifted at languages, Malinowski learned the local language sufficiently well to take notes directly in the vernacular, and accumulated a mass of information which sustained his ethnographic writing for the next twenty years. Between periods in the field Malinowski returned to Australia, where he had established contacts with Australian anthropologists—most importantly W. Baldwin Spencer. A series of muddled love affairs ended with his marriage on 6 March 1919 to Elsie Rosaline (1890–1935), the daughter of Spencer's colleague at Melbourne University David Orme *Masson. An educated woman and an author in her own right, she had three daughters with Malinowski and assisted his career after they returned to Europe in 1920.

To improve Malinowski's health the couple moved to the Canary Islands, where he completed an ethnographic monograph on his Trobriand research. This was *Argonauts of the Western Pacific* (1922), a highly detailed ethnographic account of the *kula* system that linked the Trobrianders with other Massim peoples in a cycle of ceremonial seaborne exchanges. The book was introduced by Frazer, the doyen of British evolutionary anthropology. It began with an appeal for direct research through participant observation, which a future generation of professional anthropologists saw as marking a methodological break with all earlier ethnographic research. The account, in its focused form, style, and attention to detail, also became a model of ethnographic writing. Field research, combined with the resulting interpretation and explanation of a single functioning society, laid the foundation for an ethnographically based anthropology which Malinowski insisted was essential for a new science of human culture. Anthropology thus shifted further from grand evolutionary speculations on humankind and ethnological studies of the historical and geographical interconnection of cultures towards detailed ethnographic accounts of particular cultures.

An English academic career Malinowski declined the offer of a position in a Polish university, accepting instead in 1923 a lectureship in social anthropology at the LSE. He was promoted to reader in 1924 and became foundation professor of social anthropology in 1927. In 1931 he acquired British citizenship. He spent many summers at his villa in Oberbozen in the Italian southern Tyrol. Here, sometimes with graduate students, he would take long walks, his major interest outside his intellectual work, though he also enjoyed dancing, dining, and socializing. His health, however, remained precarious, a situation not assisted by his hypochondria and regular consumption of pills and potions.

During the 1920s Malinowski worked on a number of projects, based mainly on his Trobriand material and intended to throw new light on existing academic concerns with human society and popular intellectual trends of the day. *Argonauts* was concerned in part with economic issues viewed through the activities, pragmatic and ceremonial, of 'South Sea savages'. In *Crime and Custom in Savage Society* (1926) Malinowski addressed the issue of politics and law in a similar way, contrasting the difference between cultural rules and social action. He also sought to test Freud's ideas, at the time a subject of interest and debate in educated society. In various essays and his *Sex and Repression in Savage Society* (1927) he examined claims for the universality of the Oedipus complex against the evidence of his Trobriand research. The Trobrianders trace descent through the female line and the father is not a figure of authority so much as the mother's brother. While Malinowski supported Freud's contention of social-psychological conflict but with a cultural inversion due to matrilineal descent, Freud's supporters would permit no deviation from their master's authority and rejected his argument. Malinowski's *The Sexual Life of Savages* (1929) moved beyond such psychological issues and contained a challenge to established values of sexual prudery through the examination of a society with very different ideas of

courtship, sex, marriage, and domestic relationships. The theme of sex in exotic cultures allowed Malinowski to combine scientific argument with risqué titillation, but the promise of the book's title undoubtedly disappointed many readers.

Malinowski's final two-volume ethnographic monograph based on the Trobriand research, *Coral Gardens and their Magic* (1935), examined magical rites, cultivation, land tenure, and politics. The second volume further developed an 'ethnographic theory of language' in the 'context of situation' which he had first formulated more than a decade earlier with the linguist and Egyptologist A. H. Gardiner, and this influenced J. R. Firth and the London school of linguistics. In shorter essays Malinowski also made important contributions to the study of myth, religion, morality, and social organization.

In teaching, Malinowski's preferred method was the seminar, where he proved 'penetrating, with a quietly relentless Socratic approach broken by a sudden shaft of wit' (Firth, 'Bronislaw Malinowski', 106). His seminars were attended by colonial officials, missionaries, and a number of graduate students with qualifications in a range of disciplines including economics, history, psychology, and classics. His students included almost the entire next generation of British and Commonwealth anthropologists especially Raymond Firth, E. E. Evans-Pritchard, Meyer Fortes, Isaac Schapera, Audrey Richards, Lucy Mair, Ian Hogbin, Phyllis Kaberry, Siegfried Nadel, E. R. Leach, Ralph Piddington, and many others. There were also continental Europeans, Jomo Kenyatta (later the first president of Kenya), Fei Hsiao Tung from China, and figures later influential in American anthropology and sociology: Ashley Montagu, Hortense Powdermaker, and Talcott Parsons.

All Malinowski's students who sought to progress in anthropology were expected to carry out field research. The difficulty of gaining access to the field and research funding was eased by Malinowski's close association with the International African Institute, founded in London in 1929, the award of Rockefeller Foundation funding, and the support of selected colonial governments, particularly in Africa. This emphasis on Africa shifted the ethnographic focus of British anthropology away from ethnological studies of Oceania towards Africa and ethnographic studies of culture contact and change. In numerous essays and addresses Malinowski stressed the practical value of his functional anthropology to formulating African colonial policy. In 1934 he visited southern and eastern Africa to carry out what he referred to as 'survey work', though he left his students to carry out intensive research.

The practical application of anthropological knowledge to everyday problems was undoubtedly grounded in Malinowski's origins in Poland, where the duty of a member of the intelligentsia was to provide support and leadership to society. Malinowski's involvement during the 1930s in promoting progressive views on morality and other social issues reflected similar attitudes. He supported the British Social Hygiene Council on issues of birth control, advised the pioneers of mass observation research, and gave popular talks on BBC radio.

A functional theory of culture: an international figure Malinowski stressed the need for functional studies of culture, and half-jokingly proposed a new 'school of functional anthropology'. His ideas were developed in part as a response to theorizing his ethnographic practice, but also as a counter to competing approaches in anthropology. Emphasizing the value of his ethnographic functionalism in opposition to ethnological reconstructions was not difficult, especially when the latter included the extreme diffusionist Grafton Elliot Smith, who argued that all human culture had emanated from ancient Egypt. But by the 1920s Malinowski's contemporary A. R. Radcliffe-Brown began to promote his view of social anthropology as the comparative study of the structure and function of primitive society in order to establish the natural laws of society. Malinowski developed his functionalism around a theory of cultural universals based on basic human needs and derived cultural imperatives. Culture was ultimately founded in biological needs which in turn created secondary needs and institutional responses. Thus the basic needs of sex and reproduction generated secondary imperatives realized through the institution of the family. These secondary institutions in turn resulted in further cultural imperatives with higher levels of institutional response. Compared with that of Radcliffe-Brown, Malinowski's approach appeared far too instrumental, mechanical, and reductionist, even to many of his own students, most of whom in one way or another favoured Radcliffe-Brown's ideas.

By the 1930s Malinowski had achieved a position of standing in English intellectual society outside the universities. He maintained an active social life even if his often abrasive character and eagerness to challenge conventions—marked by frequent sexual references and 'Rabelaisian adjectives'—shocked sections of polite society (Firth, 'Address', 20). This, combined with his foreignness, probably contributed to his failure to be elected to the Royal Society, an honour which he coveted, though he achieved international recognition, gained membership of foreign learned societies, and delivered public lectures in many European universities.

Malinowski first visited the United States of America in 1926 as the Laura Spelman Rockefeller memorial fellow. The Rockefeller Foundation also provided later financial support for his research in Africa. In 1933 he delivered the Messenger lectures at Cornell University, and in 1936 he attended the Harvard University tercentenary celebrations and was made an honorary doctor of science. Though his public appearances in America were a popular success, many senior American anthropologists viewed Malinowski as 'little better than a pretentious Messiah to the credulous' (Kluckhohn, 208), and his ideas and methods as generally unoriginal.

Malinowski's domestic relationships were complicated by his first wife's long struggle with multiple sclerosis; she died on 18 September 1935. He suffered frequent bouts of illness himself but continued to teach, write, and publish widely. His later works concentrated increasingly on general topics relevant to anthropology and public affairs; for example, his advice to a Church of England committee on the law relating to marriage to a deceased wife's sister. In 1938 he took sabbatical leave in Arizona, but after the outbreak of the Second World War he was advised to remain in the United States. In 1939 he was appointed Bernice P. Bishop Museum visiting professor of anthropology at Yale University. In London he had come to know a divorced artist, Anna Valetta Swann, née Hayman-Joyce (1904–1973), and they were married in Montreal on 6 June 1940. In 1940 and 1941 he carried out new research in collaboration with his wife and Julio de la Fuente into peasant economics and marketing in Oaxaca, Mexico. He resigned his chair in London in 1941 and in the following year he was appointed professor of cultural anthropology at Yale. He found his American students less congenial than his more experienced London graduates, but discovered a community of scholars interested in his anthropological approach. He published articles in social science journals on individualism in relation to society, social change, and war, often with reference to the current world crisis.

Malinowski had long opposed Nazi racist policies and practices. When Germany invaded Poland and most of mainland western Europe he became very active in opposing the Nazis and helped to promote principles of freedom and tolerance. He had long been wary of nationalism in general and had even expressed nostalgia for the old pan-ethnic Austro-Hungarian empire. The Second World War, however, reignited his identification with Poland and he championed the Polish cause in America. It was shortly after delivering the presidential address to the Polish Institute of Arts and Sciences in New York city that he suffered a massive heart attack and died at his home, 154 Everit Street, New Haven, Connecticut, on 16 May 1942. He was buried at the Evergreen cemetery in New Haven two days later.

In obituaries and later biographical sketches Malinowski's students and colleagues speak of his brilliance as a teacher and thinker, his generosity and playfulness, as well as his inconsistency and difficult, highly emotional character. One of his closest students describes him as 'brilliant, witty, sensitive, touchy, egoistic, very dependent on the appreciation of his friends and students and usually quite unfair to his opponents' (Richards, 'Bronislaw Malinowski', 193). Another speaks of his 'cruelty, springing from a mixture of exhaustion and egocentricism', and of his constant demands for loyalty and recognition (Firth, 'Bronislaw Malinowski', 105, 108). Malinowski worked hard for his students: finding research funding, employment and publishing opportunities, and writing forewords to many of their books. At one time or another, however, he fell out with nearly all his male students and some remained hostile to him long after his death. Only his female students appear to have remained basically loyal to him and his memory.

The anthropologist for all seasons Malinowski's reputation declined rapidly in the decade after his death. Academic departments established in British and emerging Commonwealth universities after 1945 were often founded under the rubric of 'social anthropology', a reflection of the triumph of Radcliffe-Brown's vision for the discipline. Malinowski's concept of 'culture' with its behavioural psychological implications was replaced by considerations of social structure as part of a comparative sociology. His ethnographic monographs, however, continued to be recognized as exemplars of method. Some fifteen years after his death his former student, colleague, and successor as professor at the LSE, Raymond Firth, edited *Man and Culture*, a collection of essays by Malinowski's former students on his work and contributions to anthropology. Thus Malinowski's contributions to key anthropological ideas and concepts were rediscovered; his rehabilitation, however, was temporarily delayed by the publication of *A Diary in the Strict Sense of the Term* (1967), his personal, introspective diaries written in Melanesia between 1914 and 1918. By one interpretation, the entries expose Malinowski as a sexist, racist, and self-serving person, ambitious for privilege and power. By another, they reveal a very human person, full of fears and weaknesses, exposed to the confusion and doubt every ethnographer experiences during fieldwork.

Since the 1980s Malinowski's works have taken on a new relevance as anthropologists have increasingly viewed ethnography as a personal interpretative experience rather than a means to objective knowledge. This literary turn has refashioned Malinowski as a pioneer of ethnography as authorship, an identity which has postmodern overtones. In Poland, Malinowski has been rediscovered as a patriot and an outstanding Polish scientist, and this has prompted new research into his formative Polish years. Malinowski's thought has also been examined as a reflection of central European modernist philosophy. However, reassessments of Malinowski in his historical context continue to reveal a complex character and the importance of his contributions to anthropology and to twentieth-century thought.   JAMES URRY

Sources B. K. Malinowski, *A diary in the strict sense of the term* (1967) · *The story of a marriage: the letters of Bronislaw Malinowski and Elsie Masson*, ed. H. Wayne (1995) · A. Richards, 'Bronislaw Kaspar Malinowski', *Man*, 43 (1943), 1–4 · M. F. Ashley Montagu, *Isis*, 34 (1942), 146–50 · G. P. Murdock, 'Bronislaw Malinowski', *American Anthropologist*, 45 (1943), 441–51 · R. Firth, 'Address', in *Professor Bronislaw Malinowski: an account of the memorial meeting held … July 13th 1942*, Association of Polish University Professors and Lecturers in Great Britain (1943), 17–21 · R. Firth, ed., *Man and culture: an evaluation of the work of Bronislaw Malinowski* (1957) · R. F. Ellen and others, eds., *Malinowski between two worlds: the Polish roots of an anthropological tradition* (1988) · G. W. Stocking, *After Tylor: British social anthropology, 1888–1951* (1995) · M. Young, 'Malinowski among the Magi: editor's introduction', *Malinowski among the Magi: the natives of Mailu*, ed. B. K. Malinowski (1988), 1–76 · M. Young, *Malinowski's Kiriwina: fieldwork photography, 1915–1918* (1998) · R. Thornton and P. Skalnik, eds., *The early writings of Bronislaw Malinowski* (1993) · R. Firth, 'Bronislaw Malinowski', *Totems and teachers: perspectives on the history of anthropology*, ed. S. Silverman (1981), 100–37 · A. Richards, 'Bronislaw Malinowski', *The founding fathers of social science*, ed. T. Rice (1969), 188–96 · H. M. Wayne, 'Bronislaw Malinowski: the influence of various women on his life and works', *American Ethnologist*, 12 (1985), 529–41 · A. Kuper, *Anthropology and*

anthropologists: the modern British school, 3rd edn (1996) · M. Young, ed., *The ethnography of Malinowski* (1979) · S. Drucker-Brown, *Malinowski in Mexico* (1982) · C. Kluckhohn, 'Bronislaw Malinowski, 1884–1942', *Journal of American Folklore*, 56 (1943), 208–19 · private information (2004) [M. Young]

Archives BLPES, corresp. and papers; further papers incl. Trobriand diaries and letters to his wife · BM, department of ethnography, notes relating to Trobriand Islands and Robert Mond collection · Bodl. RH, corresp. relating to African affairs · Yale U., Sterling Memorial Library, corresp. and papers | BL, letters, etc., to H. Ellis, Add. MS 70539 · BLPES, letters to P. Kaberry · CUL, corresp. with Meyer Fortes · Jagiellonian University, Cracow, records · National Archives of Australia, 'Dr B. Malinowski, Ethnological Research, Papua', CRS A1, 1914–20, item 21/866

Likenesses photograph, *c*.1906–1908 · S. Witkiewicz, oils, 1910, priv. coll. · portraits, 1910–38, repro. in Stocking, *After Tylor*, 246, 284, 365 · S. I. Witkiewicz, charcoal, 1912, priv. coll. · photograph, *c*.1915–1916 · group portrait, 1930–34 (with his family), priv. coll. · portrait, 1938, priv. coll. · S. Kravitt, photograph, *c*.1939–1940, NPG [*see illus.*] · J. Phillips, photograph, 1942, repro. in *Life magazine* · L. A. White, photograph · S. I. Witkiewicz, portraits, priv. coll. · photograph, repro. in B. Malinowski, *The sexual life of savages in north-western Melanesia*, 3rd edn (1932) · photograph, repro. in Young, *Malinowski's Kiriwina* · photograph, repro. in Richards, 'Bronislaw Kaspar Malinowski' · photographs, priv. coll. · photographs, London School of Economics · photographs, Yale U. archives · photographs, repro. in Ellen and others, eds., *Malinowski between two worlds* · photographs, repro. in Firth, ed., *Man and culture*, frontispiece, following p. 38

Wealth at death £499 5s. 8d.—in England: administration, 7 April 1943, CGPLA Eng. & Wales

Malins, Joseph (1844–1926), temperance activist, was born at 7 Askew Place, Worcester, on 21 October 1844, the third in the family of three sons and one daughter who survived infancy (out of eight children) of John Malins (c.1802–c.1860) of Whittington, near Worcester, and his wife, Jane (1814–1890), daughter of James Allen, cheese factor, of Wellington, Shropshire. John Malins was successively a master builder, carpenter, and cabinet-maker. Soon after Joseph's birth, the family moved to Birmingham, where at the age of eight he entered King Edward VI's School, Bath Row. Two years later his father's drunkenness forced Joseph to file brass-work ten hours a day for 1s. 6d. a week. Later he was apprenticed to a decorative painter. At sixteen Malins took the total abstinence pledge. He was an active Wesleyan most of his life. In 1866 he married Lucy Ellen (c.1842–1922), daughter of Edward Jones, commercial traveller; they had four sons and one daughter. In 1866 he and his wife emigrated to Philadelphia. As a result of his wife's ill health—she was an invalid much of her married life—they returned to Birmingham in 1868.

The crucial moment in Malins's life occurred during his brief residence in the United States. In 1867 he joined the Independent Order of Good Templars, a pseudo-masonic, teetotal, fraternal society founded in central New York State in the early 1850s, which by offering no mutual aid financial scheme made membership relatively inexpensive. Shortly after he returned to England in May 1868, Malins organized its first Good Templar lodge, in Birmingham. The order grew rapidly, but was controversial. Others in the temperance movement regarded it with suspicion and disliked its 'ritual, regalia, titles and degrees' (Shiman, 178), and Quakers initially hesitated to join.

In 1870 Malins instituted the grand lodge of England and was elected grand worthy chief templar. In 1872, less than two years after Malins had to sell his overcoat to pay for handbills, his rapidly growing grand lodge rewarded its leader with a salary of £500, a middle class income presented to a former furniture painter in his twenties. In 1875, after a substantial decline in membership, this salary was reduced to £400. The Good Templars provided predominantly working-class and lower-middle-class members with a quasi-religious sense of community and purpose as temperance militants committed to the prohibition of the sale of alcoholic drink. It also offered individual status and opportunity: one critic alleged Good Templarism was 'a society set on foot to put little men into big places' (Harrison, 170). In 1874 there were over 210,000 adult members in England. A tireless organizer and administrator, Malins reached his office before 6 a.m. and worked there until midnight when not travelling on Good Templar business. At meetings he was an exceptional chairman. By the time he retired in 1914 nearly a million English men, women, and children had held membership, often briefly. Malins also helped build the order in Sweden.

During the 1870s and 1880s conflicts over policy and the extent of Malins's power in the order frequently pitted him against fellow Good Templars. Some of his critics alleged he was a despot who controlled the order through spies. Despite his youth and initial inexperience, he repeatedly triumphed over better known and sometimes wealthy rivals. In the most dramatic of these conflicts Malins led a protest against the racial policies of the Good Templars in the American south, which culminated during 1876–87 in a secessionist Independent Order of Good Templars of the world, dominated by the grand lodges of England and Scotland. His enemies accused Malins of exploiting the racial controversy to consolidate his power in England and to seize control of the international order. The dispute split the English Good Templars, with an acrimonious, expensive, but inconclusive legal action over ownership of the grand lodge's charter. By 1877 perhaps 100,000 of the English Templar membership supported Malins and 13,000 his rival, F. R. Lees, a well-known prohibitionist allied with the North American organization. When the schism ended with a compromise, which accepted *de facto* racial segregation, some of his closest allies in the anti-racist crusade protested. Malins was confirmed as head of the order in England, and it was agreed that his grand lodge should be the only one established there.

Malins's intense commitment to the international character of the order explains his willingness to make concessions to bring about reunion. Eventually he was elected to head the reunited order. In 1899 he undertook a round-the-world mission that symbolized Good Templar internationalism. Malins nearly always opposed compromise in British temperance politics. He took a leading role in forming the National Temperance Federation (1884), of which he became honorary secretary and later chairman.

It functioned as a pressure group that represented militant prohibitionist organizations. The Good Templars were among the most politically extreme of temperance societies and were active both nationally and at constituency level. Malins fought for 'local option' (prohibition by local veto referendums) and against compensation for licence holders. He was prominent among those who rejected any public management of the retail drink trade. For a time he regarded himself as a Liberal Unionist, but as he made policy toward drink the only basis for supporting parliamentary candidates he backed mostly home rule Liberals.

The energetic Malins also served as a Worcestershire county councillor. He was a prolific writer on temperance topics: his works included verse such as *Professor Alcoholico* (1876). The English Order of Good Templars benefited and improved the lives of its members, and especially of Malins, its dominant leader, who made it a lucrative career and was enabled to launch his four sons into middle-class careers: a pharmacist and dentist, a headmaster, a Methodist minister, and a sanitary engineer. He died on 5 January 1926 at his home, 1 Wilton Road, Sparkhill, Birmingham, and was buried on 9 January in Yardley cemetery, Birmingham. DAVID M. FAHEY

Sources J. Malins, *The life of Joseph Malins: patriarch templar, citizen and temperance reformer* (1932) · D. M. Fahey, *Temperance and racism: John Bull, Johnny Reb, and the Good Templars* (1996) · E. H. Welfare, *The world our field: a history of the good templar order* [1954] · J. Malins, 'Random recollections', *Good Templars' Watchword* (1923–5) · L. L. Shiman, *Crusade against drink in Victorian England* (1988) · B. Harrison, *Drink and the Victorians: the temperance question in England, 1815–1872*, 2nd edn (1994) · A. E. Dingle, *The campaign for prohibition in Victorian England: the United Kingdom Alliance, 1872–1895* (1980) · D. W. Gutzke, *Protecting the pub: brewers and publicans against temperance* (1989)
Archives Bodl. Oxf., Harcourt MSS · Castle Howard, Yorkshire, Rosalind Howard, ninth countess of Carlisle MSS · United Kingdom Temperance Alliance, London, United Kingdom Alliance minute books
Likenesses F. S. Ogilvie, oils, repro. in Malins, *Life of Joseph Malins*, 161 · photographs, repro. in Malins, *Life of Joseph Malins*
Wealth at death £1748 0s. 2d.: probate, 1926

Malins, Sir Richard (1805–1882), judge, was born at Evesham, Worcestershire, on 9 March 1805, the third son of William Malins of Ailston, Warwickshire, and his wife, Mary, eldest daughter of Thomas Hunter of Pershore, Worcestershire. He was educated at a private school in Soho, London, before entering Gonville and Caius College, Cambridge, where he matriculated in Michaelmas 1823 and was sixth junior optime. He graduated BA in 1827. He had already joined the Inner Temple in 1825, and was called to the bar on 14 May 1830. On 10 May 1831 Malins married Susanna (*d.* 1881), eldest daughter of the Revd Arthur Farwell, rector of St Martin's, Cornwall.

Malins practised with success as an equity draftsman and conveyancer in Fig Tree Court, Temple, and later in New Square and in Stone Buildings, Lincoln's Inn. He had no family or other connections in the profession, but he was industrious and persevering, and eventually, through his special knowledge of real property law and of the interpretation of wills, he obtained a good court practice in equity. He trained in his chambers numerous pupils, of whom the most eminent, Hugh Cairns, was his responsible assistant for some time. In 1849 he transferred his membership from the Inner Temple to Lincoln's Inn, and was made a bencher, acting as treasurer in 1870. In 1849 also he was appointed a queen's counsel, and soon enjoyed a large leading business in the court of vice-chancellors Parker and Stuart.

Malins was elected as a Conservative MP for Wallingford in July 1852, standing as a supporter of agricultural protection, and held the seat until July 1865, when he was defeated by Sir Charles Wentworth Dilke. He was a frequent parliamentary speaker, and was prominent in the determined opposition which was made to the Divorce Bill of 1857. He carried two bills successfully through parliament, the Infants' Marriage Settlements Act, in 1855, and the Married Women's Reversionary Property Act in 1857, known jointly as 'Malins's acts'.

On 1 December 1866 Malins was appointed a vice-chancellor of the Chancery Division of the High Court in succession to Sir Richard Kindersley. He was knighted in February 1867. He had a considerable gift for marshalling facts, expressed himself with fluency and point, and was esteemed for his amiability and generosity of sentiment; but he was talkative and impulsive, and his judgments did not add much to the law of England. Early in 1879 he was lamed by a fall from his horse. He was seized with paralysis early in 1881, and in March 1881 he retired and was sworn of the privy council. The death of his wife at the end of 1881 hastened his own death, which took place at his London home, 57 Lowndes Square, on 15 January 1882. He was buried on 21 January at Bray, Berkshire. A niece, Henrietta Carey, married the judge Sir Charles James Watkin Williams. He left no family.

J. A. Hamilton, *rev.* M. C. Curthoys

Sources *Law Times* (21 Jan 1882) · *Solicitors' Journal*, 26 (1881–2), 185–6 · *The Times* (17 Jan 1882) · Boase, *Mod. Eng. biog.* · *CGPLA Eng. & Wales* (1882) · *GM*, 1st ser., 101/1 (1831), 463
Likenesses Lock & Whitfield, woodburytype photograph, 1882, NPG · Faustin, chromolithograph, NPG · carte-de-visite, NPG · portrait, repro. in *The Bench and Bar* (1860) · portrait, repro. in *The Graphic*, 30 (1882), 68 · wood-engraving, NPG; repro. in *ILN* (28 Jan 1882)
Wealth at death £93,069 7s. 3d.: resworn probate, Jan 1883, *CGPLA Eng. & Wales* (1882)

Malkin, Benjamin Heath (1769–1842), schoolmaster and antiquary, only son of Thomas Malkin of St Mary-le-Bow and his wife, whose maiden name was Heath, was born on 23 March 1769 in London. He was educated from 1779 to 1787 at Harrow School, where he was head of the school in 1787. He entered Trinity College, Cambridge, as a pensioner on 5 January 1788 and graduated BA in 1792. He was admitted to Lincoln's Inn on 3 February 1791. He married c.1794 Charlotte, the daughter of the Revd Thomas Williams, curate of Cowbridge, Glamorgan, and master of Cowbridge grammar school.

As a young lawyer in London, Malkin made the acquaintance of William Blake, with whom he shared an interest in radical politics, and in 1806 he commissioned

Blake to design and engrave the frontispiece of his book *A Father's Memoir of his Child*, a personal record of his eldest son, Thomas, a gifted child who died in 1802 at the age of six. The published engraving, though designed by Blake, was eventually executed by R. H. Cromek (1770–1812). The introduction to the work, dedicated to Thomas Johnes of Hafod (1748–1816), is valuable as the first and fullest account of Blake's early life and it included a selection of Blake's poems, which it brought to the attention of the general public for the first time. Blake contributed an appreciation of the child's precocious artistic talents. Malkin did much to promote Blake's career and is thought to have been the author of the texts accompanying the latter's plates for Robert Blair's *The Grave* (1808). An illuminated manuscript copy of the *Songs of Innocence*, presented by the author to Malkin and given by him to Johnes, is preserved in the Beinecke Library at Yale University.

From 1809 to 1828 Malkin was headmaster of the grammar school at Bury St Edmunds, where his pupils included Edward Fitzgerald, John Mitchell Kemble, and James Spedding (1808–1881). The last mentioned was later to pay a warm tribute to Malkin as an inspiring and liberal, if idiosyncratic, teacher who encouraged independence of mind and character. The attention he gave in the curriculum to essay-writing and the study of English literature was unusual for the time.

In March 1810 Malkin was awarded the degree of DCL by the University of Oxford, having previously been incorporated of St Mary Hall. In December 1829 he was appointed to be the first professor of history, ancient and modern, at the newly established University of London, and his inaugural lecture was published the following year. His wide interests are reflected in the range of his publications. His tragedy *Almahide and Hamet* (1804), based on Dryden's *Conquest of Granada* (1669), was never acted but was praised for its introductory 'Letter on dramatic composition'. In addition to historical work such as *Classical Disquisitions and Curiosities* (1825) he published in translation *The Adventures of Gil Blas* (4 vols., 1809), illustrated by Robert Smirke, which was frequently reprinted. Malkin's taste for the picturesque is to be seen in his topographical work *The Scenery, Antiquities and Biography of Wales*, published in 1804 and reissued in a two-volume edition in 1807. Written after a tour of south Wales in 1803, it was one of the best travel books of its kind, displaying Malkin's acute observation and considerable knowledge of Welsh history. From about 1830 Malkin lived at the Old Hall, Cowbridge, and took a keen interest in the Glamorgan community. He founded the Society for the Improvement of the Working Population in Glamorgan, for which he edited pamphlets and acted as president and secretary.

Malkin died at Cowbridge on 26 May 1842, and was buried there. A monument was erected to his memory in the church of St James, Bury St Edmunds, with an inscription attesting to the affectionate respect in which he was held by his former pupils. He and his wife had four sons besides Thomas. The eldest, Sir Benjamin Heath Malkin (1797–

1837), a friend of Macaulay, was a fellow of Trinity College, Cambridge, and later a judge of the supreme court at Calcutta. Frederick (1802–1830), also a fellow of Trinity, was the author of a *History of Greece* (1830), while Arthur (1803–1888), a contemporary and friend of Fitzgerald and Spedding, was a pioneer alpinist. Charles Johnes (1808–1825) died young. G. MARTIN MURPHY

Sources G. E. Bentley, *Blake records* (1969) · J. Spedding, 'Remarks on the character of Dr Malkin', in J. W. Donaldson, *A retrospective address read at the tercentenary commemoration of King Edward's School, Bury St Edmunds* (1850), 77–89 · *DWB* · A. K. Terhune, *The life of Edward Fitzgerald* (1947), 13–15 · W. T. J. Gun, ed., *The Harrow School register, 1571–1800* (1934), 102 · Venn, *Alum. Cant.*
Archives BL OIOC
Likenesses F. Chantrey, medallion, St James's Church, Bury St Edmunds, Suffolk · F. Chantrey, pencil drawing, NPG · medallion (after bust by F. Chantrey), St James's Church, Bury St Edmunds, Suffolk

Mallaby, Sir (Howard) George Charles (1902–1978), public servant and headmaster, was born on 17 February 1902 at Worthing, the younger son and the youngest of the three children of William Calthorpe Mallaby, an actor, and his wife, Katharine Mary Frances Miller. He was educated at Radley College and at Merton College, Oxford, where he was an open exhibitioner and obtained a third class in classical honour moderations in 1922. A sound classicist, his tastes in English literature were strongly influenced by H. W. Garrod, who confirmed him in the admiration for Wordsworth he had already acquired.

After a year as assistant master at Clifton College, Mallaby held the same post at St Edward's School, Oxford (1924–6). A temporary breakdown in health led in 1926 to a short recuperative visit to South Africa, where he taught at the Diocesan College, Rondebosch. He returned to St Edward's, where he remained as assistant master and housemaster (1931) from 1927 to 1935. He was an exceptional schoolmaster. His impressive presence gave him complete authority, in which his gentle idiosyncratic wit provided a relaxed atmosphere. He taught literature as well as classics, and had a generous understanding of adolescent writing. He had a sure eye for deficiencies, yet his criticism was always tactful. This talent for inspiring confidence also marked his coaching of rugby football, in which game he was himself a fine player. In personal problems his mature judgement was valued not only by pupils, but by colleagues, some of whom he commemorated appreciatively in his own reminiscences. In later years, as a governor of St Edward's, chairman of the council of Radley College, and vice-chairman of Bedford College, University of London, he drew profitably on his own practical experience as a teacher. From 1935 to 1938 he was headmaster of St Bees School, Cumberland. Outside the educational world, his powers of organization and wise negotiation became recognized. In 1938–9 he was district commissioner for the special area of west Cumberland, where he was successful in attracting industrial concerns needed to alleviate unemployment.

The Second World War gave Mallaby scope to develop these administrative talents. He remained briefly in the north-west as deputy regional transport commissioner for north-western region. After working as a general staff officer in the directorate of military operations at the War Office from December 1940, he was posted to the joint planning staff in mid-1942, and remained there until the end of the war, having been secretary of it from mid-1943. The joint planning staff was a key part of the central machine for the higher direction of the war, and in this capacity he attended the great conferences at Cairo, Quebec, and finally Potsdam. His efficiency and ease, under exacting conditions, were notable. For his work he was appointed OBE in 1945, and was awarded membership of the American Legion of Merit in January 1946. With peace, after a short spell as secretary of the National Trust (1945–6), he became an assistant secretary in the Ministry of Defence (1946–8), and then secretary-general of the Brussels Treaty Defence Organization (1948–50). This was a task for which there was no precedent. Of all his appointments, it provided him with the greatest interest and satisfaction, involving the principles of international co-operation, on which NATO became based. His charm, authority, and persuasive powers were used to weld together an international staff of great complexity, and of interests which often threatened to diverge. Historically, it was his greatest achievement.

As a direct result, Mallaby became from 1950 to 1954 an under-secretary in the Cabinet Office, and a key figure in foreign and defence policy. His appreciation of diverse personalities in government made his contribution, though unobtrusive, far more than merely secretarial. He was known as someone who could always be trusted to resolve an urgent difficulty. In some ways this was a slight disservice to his personal career, since he was apt to be seconded to help in a crisis wherever and whenever it might occur. For instance, he was transferred at short notice in 1954 to undertake some delicate negotiations in Kenya, at the time of the Mau Mau rising, as secretary of the war council and council of ministers; Sir Winston Churchill himself is said to have made noises of protest at this switch. From 1955 to 1957 he found congenial work as deputy secretary of the University Grants Committee, in which his academic interests and administrative flair were happily joined. There followed another overseas appointment as high commissioner for the United Kingdom in New Zealand (1957–9). He had married, on 2 April 1955, Elizabeth Greenwood Locker, daughter of Hubert Edward Brooke, private banker, and widow of J. W. D. Locker. Her high spirits and his quiet sense of fun—perfect foils for one another—made a delightful impact on society there, and aroused goodwill wherever they went. He had one stepson and two stepdaughters.

Appointed in 1959 as first civil service commissioner in charge of recruitment to the civil and diplomatic services, Mallaby exercised fruitfully his gifts of humanity, humour, and judgement. His decisions were the result of high standards, allied with sympathetic encouragement toward the men and women whose claims he examined;

the unseen effect on public life was immeasurable, and later made him sought after as a private recruitment consultant in many organizations. He also did a considerable amount of work for the Overseas Service Resettlement Bureau.

Mallaby retired in 1964 to live in East Anglia. His scholarly interests had been maintained throughout his life, and this was recognized by his election in that year to an extraordinary fellowship at Churchill College, Cambridge; he received a Cambridge MA degree in the year following. His first book had been for Cambridge University Press, when, as early as 1932, he produced a selection of Wordsworth's poems, original in that it included 2000 lines of 'The Prelude'. On the centenary of Wordsworth's death, he wrote in 1950 an admirable short critical life, *Wordsworth: a Tribute*, which forms a lucid and balanced introduction to the poet. In 1970 he selected and edited with an introduction *Poems by William Wordsworth* for the Folio Society. He also published two books of reminiscences, *From my Level* (1965) and *Each in his Office* (1972). These portray, with wit and affection, his many acquaintances, from statesmen to schoolmasters.

Mallaby's activities continued to be varied. In 1967 he was chairman of the committee on the staffing of local government, which culminated in the Mallaby report, and in 1971 he headed the Hong Kong government salaries commission. In 1972–3 he was chairman of the special committee on the structure of the Rugby Football Union. Though not all the committee's recommendations were adopted, a by-product was the important alteration in the rules for kicking to touch, which revivified the game. His final work was a small booklet, *Local Government Councillors: their Motives and Manners* (1976), for which he chose the tongue-in-cheek title, and which contrived to quote Charles Lamb and Samuel Johnson in a far-sighted and inspiring little study. He was appointed CMG in 1953 and KCMG in 1958. He died at his home, Down the Lane, Chevington, Suffolk, on 18 December 1978, having devoted his life to 'human beings, sometimes tenacious, sometimes frail', as he himself understandingly wrote.

ROBERT GITTINGS, rev.

Sources G. Mallaby, *From my level* (1965) · G. Mallaby, *Each in his office* (1972) · personal knowledge (1986) · private information (1986) · Burke, *Peerage* (1959) · *CGPLA Eng. & Wales* (1979)
Wealth at death £46,366: probate, 18 April 1979, *CGPLA Eng. & Wales*

Malleson [née Whitehead], **Elizabeth** (1828–1916), educationist and promoter of rural district nursing, was born on 29 October 1828 in Chelsea, London, the eldest of the eleven children of Henry Whitehead, solicitor, of Chelsea, and his wife, Frances Ann, youngest child of Francis Maguire, British army surgeon. She received a scrappy education at a dame-school near her grandmother's home in Northfleet, from governesses at home, and, for a year at the age of fourteen, at a Unitarian school in Clapton. She had an anxious childhood: her father had lost clients through becoming a Unitarian, the bailiff was a frequent caller, and both parents were often away attending political rallies. At fifteen she accepted responsibility for bringing up her brothers and sisters. Appalled by the poor quality of her own education, she was determined to do better by her siblings, and worked out her own teaching methods from studying everything available on educational theory.

By the age of twenty-four Whitehead was free to seek work outside the home, and she found temporary positions as amanuensis and governess. In 1854 she was appointed teacher at the experimental Portman Hall School endowed by Barbara Leigh Smith (later Barbara Bodichon). She accepted enthusiastically the school's principles of non-sectarianism, co-education up to the age of eleven, mixing middle- and artisan-class children, and making lessons short and pleasurable, and she threw herself wholeheartedly into the teaching until she was forced to resign through ill health.

In May 1857 Whitehead married Frank Rodbard Malleson (d. 1903), son of a Unitarian minister, and partner in a Holborn firm of vintners. They lived in St John's Wood and later in Wimbledon, and had three daughters and a son. After becoming involved with the Working Men's College, established by Frederick Maurice in 1854, Elizabeth Malleson was inspired to found a counterpart for women. Her Working Women's College opened in Queen Square, Bloomsbury, in 1864, offering tuition in a wide range of subjects at very low fees. Malleson personally recruited university-trained teachers, who were prepared not only to provide their services free but also to participate in the social life of the college. Although the enterprise flourished, she remained convinced that adult education ought not to be organized on a single-sex basis, and, after failing to persuade the Men's College to merge, converted the Women's College to co-education in 1874. While still in London she worked for many other causes, campaigning from 1869 for the repeal of the Contagious Diseases Acts and organizing relief for the refugees from Turkish atrocities against the Bulgars in 1876.

After moving to Dixton Manor, near Winchcombe, in 1882, Malleson continued her educational work, helping to set up workers' colleges in Cheltenham and organizing technical education in the Winchcombe district on behalf of Gloucestershire county council. She published *Notes on the Early Training of Children* in 1884 and, with her husband, started reading-rooms and libraries in nearby villages. But she recognized that the most urgent problem in the countryside was the lack of trained district nurses. When her first attempt to sustain a local nursing service failed, she decided that the first essential was a national organization to provide loans, train nurses, and monitor standards. She launched her Rural Nursing Association in August 1889, after securing backing from many doctors and nurses—and overriding opposition from Florence Nightingale. Finding that the recently established Queen Victoria's Jubilee Institute of Nursing concentrated on urban areas, Malleson persuaded its council to accept her association as its rural district branch. She effectively ran this autonomous branch from the position of secretary until 1894, and remained as consultant until it was fully absorbed into the institute in 1897. She also managed a local nursing association from 1889 until 1916. She died on 27 December 1916, from influenza, at home at Dixton Manor. OWEN STINCHCOMBE, rev.

Sources O. Stinchcombe, *Elizabeth Malleson (1828–1916): pioneer of rural district nursing* (1989) • *Elizabeth Malleson, 1828–1916, autobiographical notes and letters, with a memoir by Hope Malleson*, ed. H. Malleson (privately printed, 1926) • *The Times* (6 Jan 1917), 10d
Wealth at death £1537 0s. 9d.: probate, 21 Feb 1917, CGPLA Eng. & Wales

Malleson, George Bruce (1825–1898), army officer and military historian, born in London on 8 May 1825, was the second son of John Malleson of Wimbledon and Lucy (*née* Nesbitt), whose father was colonial secretary in the Bahamas. He was educated at Wimbledon and at Winchester College, where he became a keen cricketer. Through Colonel Oliphant, a director of the East India Company, he was given a direct commission as ensign on 11 June 1842, and was posted to the 65th Bengal native infantry on 26 September. He obtained a lieutenancy in the 33rd Bengal native infantry on 28 September 1847. He was appointed to the commissariat department on 30 November 1852 and served in the Second Anglo-Burmese War. On 28 March 1856 he was appointed an assistant military auditor-general and was engaged in administrative duties at Calcutta during the mutiny. He wrote *The Mutiny of the Bengal Army*, published anonymously in 1857 and known as the 'red pamphlet'. In this he identified Lord Dalhousie's administration, and especially the annexation of Oudh, as mainly responsible for the revolt. In 1856 Malleson married Marian Charlotte, only daughter of George Wynyard Battye of the Bengal civil service, and sister of three distinguished soldiers, Quintin, Wigram, and Frederick Battye, all of the Guides, and all killed in action. She survived her husband.

Malleson was promoted captain on 11 June 1857, major in the Bengal staff corps on 11 June 1862, lieutenant-colonel on 11 June 1868, and colonel in the army on 11 June 1873. He was appointed a sanitary commissioner for Bengal in 1866, and controller of the military finance department in 1868. In 1869 he was chosen by Lord Mayo to be the guardian of the young maharaja of Mysore; he held this post until 1877, when he retired on full pay with the honorary rank of major-general. He had been made CSI on 31 May 1872.

Malleson had been a frequent contributor to the *Calcutta Review* since 1857, and was also a correspondent of *The Times*. After he retired he devoted himself to writing, mainly military history, especially Indian. He had a broad grasp, great industry, and a vigorous and picturesque style, but was apt to be a strong partisan. He did much to draw attention to Russian expansion in central Asia and its potential threat to British rule in India. His many publications included *History of the Indian Mutiny* (3 vols., 1878–80, in continuation of vols. 1 and 2 of J. W. Kaye's *A History of the Sepoy War in India, 1857–1858*, 3 vols., 1864–76), *History of Afghanistan* (1879), *The Decisive Battles of India* (1883), and

The Russo-Afghan question and the Invasion of India (1885). Malleson died at his home, 27 West Cromwell Road, Kensington, London, on 1 March 1898.

E. M. LLOYD, rev. JAMES FALKNER

Sources *Army List* • *Indian Army List* • *Hart's Army List* • *The Times* (2 March 1898) • private information (1901)
Archives BL, corresp. with Florence Nightingale, Add. MS 45782 • CUL, corresp. with Lord Mayo • NL Scot., corresp. with Blackwoods, MSS 4223–4620
Wealth at death £97 2s. 3d.: probate, 4 July 1898, CGPLA Eng. & Wales

Malleson [*née* Billson], **Joan Graeme** (1899–1956), physician, was born at Chitterman Hills, Ulverscroft, Leicestershire, on 4 June 1899, the youngest of four daughters of James Billson, socialist owner of a coal mine and a brickworks, and his wife, Lillian Mary Evans. Along with her sisters, she was educated at Bedales School in Hampshire, which she attended from 1910 to 1918, and was head girl in her final year. In 1918 Joan Billson began to study medicine at University College, London, but in response to the endemic hostility to women students that she found there, moved to Charing Cross Hospital. Before completing her training she married, on 14 June 1923, the actor (William) Miles *Malleson (1888–1969), whose circle included many figures prominent in progressive movements. Among those she came to know were Bertrand and Dora Russell, Clifford Allen, Cyril Joad, A. S. Neill (the Mallesons' first child was educated at Summerhill School), Francis Meynell, Sybil Thorndike, Lewis Casson, and Havelock Ellis.

After qualifying MRCS LRCP in 1925 and MB BS (Lond.) in 1926 Malleson developed a particular interest in the linked areas of fertility, reproduction, and sexuality. This developed in part from her experiences with the patients she encountered in London as medical officer of the comprehensive clinic of the Holborn Borough Council and as clinical assistant at the West End Hospital for Nervous Diseases. It became apparent to Malleson that sexual problems were often the deeper causes of her patients' complaints. Effective treatment, she believed, involved a sympathetic understanding of each individual's case and, in the longer term, the adoption of more enlightened attitudes by both the medical profession and the general public. Malleson was one of the first doctors to provide birth control advice on behalf of a local authority, in Ealing in 1931, following the circular issued by the minister of health, Arthur Greenwood, permitting the opening of clinics for that purpose. In 1935 Victor Gollancz published her short book, *The Principles of Contraception*, which showed her ability to impart practical information in a clear way. For many years she was a member of the executive committee of the National Birth Control Association (from 1938, the Family Planning Association).

More controversially, Malleson was among those who supported the aims of the Abortion Law Reform Association on its formation in 1936. In 1938 her evidence to the inter-departmental committee on abortion, which was chaired by Norman Birkett, influenced Dorothy Thurtle's minority report. She was involved in a notable legal case, the trial in 1938 of Aleck Bourne on a charge of unlawfully procuring a miscarriage, both as a defence witness and as the doctor who had referred to Bourne a girl of fourteen raped and made pregnant by a group of soldiers. Bourne's acquittal helped to safeguard the position of doctors who carried out abortions in comparable circumstances.

Malleson combined hospital consultancies with general practice. She shared a practice with a like-minded doctor, Cecile Booysen, which ended with the latter's death in 1937. For several years Malleson was in charge of a clinic for difficulties of marital adjustment (later more frankly titled the clinic for sexual difficulties) at the North Kensington Women's Welfare Centre. A readiness to question received wisdom in many spheres of life was combined to good effect with the warmth and sincerity of her character. As one of the stage army of the good, she had an infectious belief in the possibility of social improvement. Moreover, her attractive personality was matched by her handsome face and tall figure. Patients as well as fellow professionals appreciated the tact and sympathy she brought to often sensitive matters.

By the end of the Second World War public opinion had moved closer to some of the ideas Malleson espoused. She was invited to give evidence in 1945 to the royal commission on population. As well as supporting groups concerned with birth control and abortion, Malleson was a member of the Eugenics Society and lectured under the auspices of the Socialist Medical Association. Her books, especially *Change of Life in Women* (1948), published under the pen-name Medica, became well known and led to the broadcasting on the BBC's *Woman's Hour* programme of a series of accessible radio talks. Malleson was significant not as a specialist researcher, but as a doctor who encouraged both fellow practitioners and the general public to adopt more progressive ideas and to accept the medical treatments that went with them.

In 1950 Malleson was appointed as the head of the contraceptive clinic at University College Hospital, and published *Any Wife of any Husband: a Book for Couples who have Met Sexual Difficulties and their Doctors*. However, a slipped disc and bouts of depression caused distress during the later years of her life. Partly in the hope of gaining some relief she practised under an exchange scheme in New Zealand for four months in 1956. On the return journey she stopped at Fiji, where, while swimming near Suva on 14 May 1956, she suffered a fatal coronary. She was buried in Fiji, but many of her friends and colleagues celebrated her life at a memorial service held on 25 May at the London church of St Martin-in-the-Fields. Her close friend Kingsley Martin gave the address. Miles and Joan Malleson had divorced in 1940. Their two sons, Nicolas Borel and Andrew Graeme, both qualified as doctors of medicine.

D. E. MARTIN

Sources *The Times* (16 May 1956) · *The Lancet* (26 May 1956) · *BMJ* (26 May 1956), 1242 · *New Statesman and Nation* (26 May 1956) · A. Leathard, *The fight for family planning: the development of family planning services in Britain* (1980) · K. Hindell and M. Simms, *Abortion law reformed* (1971) · D. Russell, *The tamarisk tree*, 3 vols. (1975–85) · J. Croall, *Neill of Summerhill: the permanent rebel* (1983) · private information (2004) · b. cert. · m. cert. · *Medical Directory* · CGPLA Eng. & Wales (1956)

Likenesses portrait, repro. in J. Malleson, *Change of life: facts and fallacies of middle age*, 6th edn (1957)

Wealth at death £21,255 6s. 2d.: probate, 16 June 1956, CGPLA Eng. & Wales

Malleson, John Philip (1796–1869), Unitarian minister and schoolmaster, was born in Battersea, Surrey, on 11 February 1796, the fourth and youngest son of Thomas Malleson (1752?–1820) and his wife, Mary (1759?–1823), third daughter of Frederick Gibson, merchant of Cheapside. Thomas Malleson was a silversmith in Sweeter's Rents, Cornhill, and later a jeweller in Princes Street (later Wardour Street), Leicester Square. The family soon moved to 4 Cheyne Walk, Chelsea, where Mary Malleson opened a boarding and day school for girls to supplement a family income declining with the prosperity of Thomas Malleson's business.

Educated in his mother's school, Malleson was sent in 1810 to Hitchin to board with the Revd John Bailey (1754–1818), who that year became classical tutor at Wymondley House, an Independent academy supported by the Coward Trust, which Malleson entered in 1812; letters to his mother attest to the liberation he felt in his new surroundings. Beginning in June 1817, he supplied the Independent chapel at Wem, Shropshire, but in November, to the disappointment of his congregation, he matriculated at the University of Glasgow, aided by Dr Williams's Trust, taking the BA in 1819.

In 1820, his views on the divinity of Christ having moved to the Arian position, Malleson became minister of a presbyterian congregation in Hanover Street, Long Acre, London; but he resigned two years later on turning Unitarian. He then opened a day school in Leeds and served as chaplain to Mrs Richard Slater Milnes (1760?–1835) at Fryston Hall near Wakefield. When Lant Carpenter (1780–1840) fell ill in 1827 and resigned—temporarily, as it turned out—from Lewin's Mead Chapel in Bristol, Malleson filled in for a time, but proved an unsuccessful candidate; while there he met James Martineau (1805–1900), just out of Manchester College, York, and conducting Carpenter's school.

In 1829 Malleson succeeded the Revd John Morell (1775–1840) as minister of the New Road Chapel, Brighton, and as head of the school at Hove House; he retired from both posts in 1860 and settled in Croydon. He placed far higher value on the role of minister than on the onerous task of teaching, but, while some admired the restrained elegance and sober effect of his preaching, he had no popular gifts in the pulpit, and it is as a schoolmaster that he deserves primarily to be remembered.

On 14 January 1823 Malleson married Anna Sophia (1793–1873), daughter of William Taylor (1755–1843) and his wife, Catherine Courtauld (1760–1826) of London, and granddaughter of the Revd Henry Taylor (1711–1785), rector of Crawley, vicar of Portsmouth, and author of the latitudinarian letters known as *The Apology of Ben Mordecai* (1771–7). The second-generation Taylors were Unitarian, as were the Courtaulds with whom they were associated in the great silk manufacturing firm. The eldest daughter of John Philip and Anna Sophia Malleson died of a fever shortly after the move to Brighton, and within a few weeks their eldest son was killed in a street accident; three other children survived their father, who died of 'softening of the brain' at The Close, Croydon, on 16 March 1869 and was buried in Marylebone cemetery, Finchley.

R. K. WEBB

Sources W. T. Malleson, 'Memoir', in J. Martineau, *The godly man: a sermon in memory of the Rev. John Philip Malleson* (1870) · *The Inquirer* (3 April 1870) · *The Inquirer* (10 April 1870) · P. A. Taylor, ed., *Some account of the Taylor family, originally Tayland* (privately printed, London, 1875) · congregational records, Lewin's Mead Chapel, Bristol, DWL · H. Martineau, letter to J. Martineau, 22 Oct 1827, Harris Man. Oxf. [abstract] · *Memoirs of the life of the Rev. Lant Carpenter, LLD, with selections from his correspondence*, ed. R. L. Carpenter (1842) · d. cert.
Wealth at death under £3000: probate, 7 June 1869, *CGPLA Eng. & Wales*

Malleson, (William) Miles (1888–1969), actor and playwright, was born at Roslyn, Avondale Road, Croydon, Surrey, on 25 May 1888, the son of Edmund Taylor Malleson, manufacturer, and his wife, Myrrha Bithynia Borrell. He was educated at Brighton College, where he was head of the school, captain of cricket, and a good footballer; at Emmanuel College, Cambridge, where he graduated in history in 1911 and passed part one of the MusB examination; and at the Academy of Dramatic Art. A young man variously gifted and of a serious turn of mind, with an interest in sociology and a natural bent for the arts, Miles Malleson was nevertheless best known as one of the subtlest and most resourceful stage clowns of his generation. He very soon found that as an actor his face was his fortune: it was an eccentric collection of strongly contrasted features, in which prominent cheekbones were offset by an almost complete absence of chin. By exaggerating these contrasts with make-up and allowing the intelligence to drain out of his eyes, he could turn himself into a veritable grotesque, which set critics hunting in their descriptive vocabularies for apt comparisons, the happiest of which was perhaps A. V. Cookman's 'an enraged sheep'. In a gentler mood he could tinge his satire with pathos, as he did in his incomparable presentation of Sir Andrew Aguecheek, but it was inconceivable that he could ever have persuaded audiences to accept him in any completely serious part—nature had decreed otherwise and he was wise enough to accept her ruling, becoming the great Shakespearian clown of his generation. At the Court under J. B. Fagan and at the Lyric, Hammersmith, for Nigel Playfair he was able to perfect his particular talent.

Malleson's serious side had, however, its outlets in the theatre. He was an ambitious dramatist and a stage-director of skill. He was a quite prolific writer of 'plays with a purpose' that reflected what one of his friends described as the 'Shelleyan idealism' of his private character. His aim in these plays was always to help on the cause of some social or political reform; but he was apt to allow the urgency of his purpose to show through the pattern of his play, and so lose the attention of playgoers who wished to be entertained rather than instructed. Only once, with

The Fanatics (1927), in which he was pleading for greater freedom for the younger generation and its ideas, did he achieve a long run. Otherwise, as in *Six Men of Dorset* (1938), the play about the Tolpuddle martyrs, which he wrote in collaboration, he had to be content with critical respect.

During the 1930s Malleson made a start in a new direction by writing for films and acting in them also. Among his credits as writer were *Nell Gwyn* (1934), *Victoria the Great* (1937), and *The First of the Few* (1942). In 1937 he became the first chairman of the Screen Writers' Association, and when war broke out in 1939 he continued to collaborate in film work. However, it was always the living stage upon which his heart was set, and in 1943—when London was no longer under intensive air attack and the theatres could once again be run with confidence—he returned to the classic stage as old Foresight in John Gielgud's production of Congreve's *Love for Love*, which ran for a year, after which he stayed on with Gielgud for a repertory season. After that he joined the Old Vic Company, which was making theatrical history at the New Theatre under the leadership of Laurence Olivier and Ralph Richardson, and for another year (1945–6) he played a round of important parts for them and he went with them to New York. Malleson rejoined the Old Vic Company for the 1949–50 season and he played the name part in *The Miser* (his own adaptation from Molière). This version was acclaimed a success; during the last years of his career Malleson devoted his writing talents chiefly to the work of finding an equivalent in English for a whole series of Molière plays. In these, perhaps, consists his chief claim to be remembered as a dramatist.

Malleson was thrice married: his first marriage, on 6 May 1915, to Lady Constance Mary Annesley (1895–1975), daughter of the fifth Earl Annesley, who was on the stage as Colette O'Niel, was dissolved in 1923; he then married, on 14 June 1923, a medical student, Joan Graeme Billson, who as Dr Joan *Malleson (1899–1956) became a pioneer of family planning. They had two sons. The marriage was dissolved in 1940 and on 19 January 1946 Malleson married an actress, Tatiana Lieven, *née* Silbermann (b. 1909/10). Malleson died in London on 15 March 1969.

W. A. DARLINGTON, rev. K. D. REYNOLDS

Sources *The Times* (17 March 1969) · *Daily Telegraph* (17 March 1969) · Burke, *Peerage* (1939) · b. cert. · m. cert. [Tatiana Lieven] · J. Parker, ed., *Who's who in the theatre*, 6th edn (1930) · *Halliwell's filmgoer's companion*, 5th edn (1976)
Archives BL, corresp. with League of Dramatists, Add. MS 63413 · King's Cam., letters to G. H. W. Rylands · McMaster University, Hamilton, Ontario, corresp. with Bertrand Russell
Likenesses C. Klinghoffer, oils, 1946, NPG · H. Schwarz, oils, 1959, NPG · H. Coster, photographs, NPG
Wealth at death £28,362: probate, 17 July 1969, *CGPLA Eng. & Wales*

Mallet [*formerly* Malloch], **David** (1701/2?–1765), poet, was the son of James Malloch (d. 1723) and his wife, Beatrix Clerk, but it is not certain which of two couples of that name were his parents: one James was an innkeeper of Crieff, Perthshire; the other was a well-to-do tenant farmer at nearby Dunruchan. David was educated first at Crieff parish school then at Edinburgh high school, where he was a janitor. In both places his mentor was John Ker, writer of Latin poetry and later professor of humanity at Edinburgh. By 1720 Malloch was tutor to four sons of a Mr Home of Dreghorn, near Edinburgh, and had entered the university, where he made friends with James Thomson (1700–1748) and other budding writers whose earliest published work, including four poems by Malloch, appeared in the *Edinburgh Miscellany* (1720). He was also befriended by the established poet Allan Ramsay (1686–1758).

Malloch spent between three and four years at college but did not at this time proceed to a degree. He was recommended by his professors to James Graham, duke of Montrose (1682–1742), a whig peer in the union parliament, as tutor to the duke's younger sons William and George, aged eleven and eight; so in August 1723 he went south and for the next three and a half years lived in his employer's residences in Hanover Square, London, and at Shawford, near Winchester, enjoying a salary of £30 per annum plus keep.

Early years in London Malloch's first literary success was *William and Margaret*, which is so free an adaptation of the traditional ballad 'Fair Margaret and Sweet William' as to be an original work. First printed with Ramsay's *Jenny and Meggy* (1723), it was reprinted many times in song and ballad collections, including Thomas Percy's *Reliques* (1765), and occasionally as a broadside with music; it first appeared over Mallet's name in Savage's *Miscellany* (1726). Malloch's English imitation of John Ker's *Donaides* (1725), a Latin poem on Aberdeen University, achieved far less notice but earned him an Aberdeen AM degree on 11 January 1726.

William and Margaret made an early appearance in Aaron Hill's *Plain Dealer* (24 July 1724), after which Malloch entered Hill's literary circle and became acquainted with other English poets, including Richard Savage, John Dyer, and Alexander Pope. When Thomson and other Edinburgh friends migrated to London, Malloch, who soon Anglicized his pronunciation and changed his name to Mallet, gave them valuable introductions. Between March and September 1727 Mallet made a short tour of Europe with his pupils the Montrose boys. It was said that when he was in Italy he was challenged by a Tuscan soldier named Flobert over a girl they were both in love with, but there was no duel (Walpole, *Corr.*, 21.377, 386).

After his return Mallet wrote *The Excursion* (1728), a blank verse poem of deistic nature description similar to Thomson's *Summer*, and *A Poem to the Memory of Mr Congreve* (1729), which has been wrongly attributed to Thomson. Pope and Mallet together wrote the prologue to Thomson's tragedy *Sophonisba* (1730), after which Pope interested himself in the writing and staging of Mallet's tragedy *Eurydice*, which opened at Drury Lane on 22 February 1731 and ran for a respectable fourteen performances. (It is about Periander, tyrant of Corinth, not Orpheus or Creon.) Aaron Hill wrote the prologue and epilogue; the printed play was dedicated to the duke of Montrose. The anonymous *Remarks on Eurydice* (1731) is a mock 'Key', absurdly arguing that Mallet's play is a Jacobite allegory about the 1715 rising. Also in 1731 Mallet wrote an epitaph

on his friend William Aikman, the painter, and his son, who died within weeks of one another. Mallet's *Of Verbal Criticism* (April 1733), an epistle in heroic couplets addressed to Pope, satirizes Bentley, Theobald, and other so-called pedants.

Friendship with Pope and opposition to Walpole Pope's friendship for Mallet, 'whom I love and esteem greatly' (*Correspondence*, 3.511), grew in the 1730s. When Mallet left Montrose's service in 1731 it was on Pope's recommendation that he became tutor to James Newsham (1715–1769), stepson of John Knight of Gosfield, Essex. Tutor and pupil were admitted to St Mary Hall, Oxford, as gentlemen commoners and matriculated together on 2 November 1733: Mallet understating his own age as twenty-eight. His congratulatory verses to the prince of Orange on visiting Oxford were published in April 1734, coinciding with his receipt of three degrees: the Oxford BA on 15 March and MA on 6 April, and the Edinburgh MA on 16 April. Mallet and Newsham travelled abroad in 1735–6: their itinerary is unrecorded except for visits to Paris, Geneva, and Hanover.

Mallet married a woman named Susanna (*d.* 1742), probably in 1734, after Oxford. They and their two children, Charles (*b.* 1735) and Dorothea *Celesia (*bap.* 1738, *d.* 1790), lived at Strand on the Green, across the river from Kew, where Thomson lived, and close to Pope in Twickenham. Mallet was often in their company; he associated with Chesterfield, Bolingbroke, and others who opposed Walpole, and readily lent himself to the politico-literary campaign orchestrated by Lyttelton on behalf of the prince of Wales in the later 1730s. Thus it was that Mallet became one of the earliest victims of Walpole's stage Licensing Act when part of his prologue to Thomson's contentious opposition play *Agamemnon* was censored in January 1738. Mallet's own *Mustapha*, which opened at Drury Lane on 13 February 1739 and, like *Eurydice*, ran for fourteen nights, was a typical opposition piece in its parade of high-minded patriotic sentiments and denunciation of evil ministers. Pope and Bolingbroke thought highly of it; Thomson wrote the prologue; the printed play was dedicated to the prince of Wales.

Alfred, a Masque (1740), which glorifies the ideal of a patriot king, implicitly embodied in the prince of Wales, was written jointly with Thomson; the music was by Thomas Augustine Arne. A text revised and enlarged by Mallet, with additional music by Charles Burney and spectacular stage effects, was acted fifteen times at Drury Lane in 1751 and printed over Mallet's sole name; it was the only dramatic work of his to hold the stage after his death. Queen Elizabeth, another idealized patriot, is prominent in Mallet's *Life of Francis Bacon* (1740), which Fielding commended for its judgement and 'nervous manly style' (*Joseph Andrews*, book 3, chap. 6). Gibbon, too, admired the 'vigorous sense' of Mallet as a historian (Gibbon, *Memoirs*, 121). Vivid character sketches and spirited narrative make the *Life* of Bacon the most readable of Mallet's writings and induce regret that he could not or would not complete his life of Marlborough.

Mallet's wife, Susanna, died in January 1742. On 27 May

Mallet was appointed under-secretary to the prince of Wales at £100 per annum. On 2 October he was married by licence at St Andrew's, Holborn, to Lucy Elstob (1715/16–1795), spinster, aged twenty-six. She was the youngest daughter of Lewis Elstob, steward to the earl of Carlisle, and brought a dowry of £10,000, of which £4000 was settled on herself. According to Gibbon, Lucy was a 'talkative, positive, passionate, conceited creature', though 'not destitute of wit and learning' (Gibbon, *Letters*, 2.155; *Memoirs*, 94). On the evidence of several affectionate poems, the most charming of which is 'Cupid and Hymen' (1750), describing how family and friends will celebrate his eighth wedding anniversary, Mallet loved her not only for her money. The children of this marriage were Lucy (*b*. 1743) and Arabella (*b*. July 1745). Mallet's wife took care to see that her husband, a man of diminutive stature, was always very well-dressed, usually in black velvet. These circumstances lend some support to the conjecture that Mallet is the small, black-suited, seated figure on the left in Hogarth's well-known painting of Lord George Graham in his ship's cabin (1745). Graham was Mallet's friend and former pupil. No certain portrait of Mallet has been traced.

In October 1743 Mallet published a collected edition of his poems and plays. In 1744 he was at Pope's deathbed. In the same year Sarah, duchess of Marlborough, died and bequeathed £500 apiece to Richard Glover and Mallet to write a life of her late husband, desiring that 'no part of the said history be in verse' (*GM*, 14, 1744, 590–91). Glover refused; Mallet, who had corresponded with the duchess about Marlborough's papers, accepted the commission, but made little or no progress in the remaining twenty years of his life. In the first half of 1745 he suffered from gout and visited the Netherlands for some unstated purpose, perhaps connected with the life of Marlborough. His *Amyntor and Theodora, or, The Hermit* (April 1747) is a blank verse narrative set on St Kilda and much indebted to Martin Martin's well-known description of that island in 1698. Mallet's poem, which he had originally conceived as a stage play, is dedicated to the earl of Chesterfield and prefaced by an affectionate poem to Mrs Mallet. It was sold to the booksellers for £120 (compared with £25 for *The Excursion*, a poem of comparable length, in 1728).

Bolingbroke's literary executor The prince dismissed Mallet from his under-secretaryship early in 1748 when Lyttelton (Mallet's patron) joined the government, whereupon both Chesterfield and Lyttelton sought a government post for him, but without success. Mallet wrote *A Congratulatory Letter to Selim* (April 1748) to defend Lyttelton against the charge of political apostasy, but continued to associate with Bolingbroke, the unpopular doyen of opposition, who prompted him in 1749 to write an advertisement attacking Pope for having clandestinely printed a garbled edition of Bolingbroke's *Patriot King*. Bolingbroke died in December 1751 and Mallet, as his literary executor, published his works between March 1752 and March 1754. Some had been first published by Richard Francklin and now became the subject of a copyright dispute; arbitrators judged that Mallet owed Francklin £200 but he never

paid; Francklin's consolation was the poor sale of Mallet's expensive edition. More seriously, Mallet included certain hitherto unpublished writings of which Johnson memorably wrote that Bolingbroke was 'a scoundrel for charging a blunderbuss against religion and morality' and 'a coward, because he had not resolution to fire it off himself, but left half a crown to a beggarly Scotchman to draw the trigger after his death' (Boswell, *Life*, 6 March 1754). Mallet was charged with mercenary motives but he had at least the courage of his religiously sceptical convictions.

Since 1748 the Mallets had lived in Putney, where their neighbour and friend was Edward Gibbon, father of the historian. They made a home for the elder Gibbon's niece and ward, Catherine Elliston, and advised on young Edward's tutor. When young Edward became a Roman Catholic in 1753 his father promptly took him to the freethinking Mallets, who plied him with philosophy, by which he was 'rather scandalized than reclaimed' (Gibbon, *Memoirs*, 68), but they remained friends: Gibbon accepted Mallet's advice on his reading and writings, and was a frequent guest in his house. Mallet had a more guarded association with David Hume, who asked him to point out Scotticisms in the manuscript of his *History of England*. Hume lived, as he said, on 'good terms' with Mallet, while conceding that he could be an 'irascible little man', but he cordially disliked Mallet's freethinking and assertive wife, who reportedly spoke of herself and Hume as 'We Deists' (*New Letters of David Hume*, 68; *Letters of David Hume*, 1.307n.).

Working for the government Mallet's patriotic *Britannia, a Masque*, with music by Arne, was performed as an afterpiece at Drury Lane on 9 May 1755 and achieved another dozen performances over the next three years. Its prologue, written and spoken by Garrick in the character of a drunken sailor reading a playbill, was very popular. At this time Mallet was eager to serve the government. In December 1753 he had indignantly rejected an invitation to write an opposition periodical for £400 per annum (BL, Add. MS 32733, fols. 614, 616). Visiting Paris in September 1755 and having highly placed French contacts, he offered to act as a spy (BL, Add. MS 43772, fols. 55–61). He was one of the authors hired to defame Admiral Byng: his pamphlet *Observations on the 12th Article of War*, by 'A Plain Man', was written in October 1756 and vetted by lords Hardwicke and Anson (BL, Add. MS 35594, fols. 103, 236–7, 254); its publication on 27 March 1757 was timed to justify the execution of Byng on 14 March; it earned him £300 from the duke of Newcastle's secret service fund.

In 1758 Mallet moved to fashionable George Street, Hanover Square, and began to grow very corpulent. In 1759 his poems, plays, and *Life* of Bacon were reprinted in a three-volume edition of *Works*; also *Eurydice* was revived at Drury Lane and acted four times. In 1760 appeared his *Verses on the Death of Lady Anson* and *Edwin and Emma*, a ballad of unhappy love similar to but less successful than *William and Margaret*, and in 1761 *Truth in Rhyme*, a compliment to Bute, the new prime minister. These three new works and others were collected in *Poems on Several Occasions* (1763), dedicated to the fourth duke of Marlborough with the promise that Mallet's life of his great ancestor would soon be finished. On 19 January 1763 Mallet's tragedy *Elvira*, based on Houdar de la Motte's *Inèz de Castro*, opened at Drury Lane and ran for fourteen performances; the printed edition carried a politically contentious dedication to Bute. Mallet's recent services to the government were now rewarded with the post of inspector of the exchequer book in the outports of London, worth £300 per annum. George Canning, the statesman's father, wrote 'Davy Malloch the Whig in his old age turn'd *Tory*' ('On the Tragedy of Elvira' in G. Canning, *Poems*, 1767, 89).

Mallet's private letters to Andrew Millar, Thomas Percy, Hume, and others in the 1760s disingenuously claim that his work on the life of Marlborough is nearly complete and would fill two quarto volumes, but no trace of such a work has been found. In 1764 the duchess of Douglas made Mallet one of her commissioners in the famous Douglas cause concerning the legitimacy of her nephew Archibald James Edward Douglas (1748–1827). The cause took Mallet to Paris, the boy's birthplace, in 1764. Leaving his wife in France, he returned to England in poor health early in 1765, died at home on 21 April, and was buried on 27 April in St George's burial-ground, South Audley Street. According to Chesterfield he died 'of a diarrhoea, which he had carried with him to France, and brought back again hither' (*Letters of … Chesterfield*, 22 April 1765); he was said to have been aged sixty-three.

By his will, proved in London on 8 May, Mallet bequeathed all his property to his wife. The contents of their house in Hanover Square, which were sold in July 1765, included a fine-toned French horn with a silver mouthpiece and a chamber organ. Mallet's large library, sold in March 1766, contained as many French books as English. Manuscripts he had inherited directly from Bolingbroke and from Pope via Bolingbroke, including Pope's Homer, were given by his widow to the British Library (Add. MSS 4807–4809 and 4948 A and B). Thereafter Mrs Mallet lived in France. She was imprisoned during the Revolution with her daughter Lucy (Mrs Macgregor), and died in Paris on 17 September 1795, aged seventy-nine. Mrs Macgregor died insane in Paris before her mother. The other daughter, Arabella, who married a Captain Williams RE, and parted from him after two months, was the chief beneficiary of Mrs Mallet's will. The fate of her stepson Charles is not known; his sister Dorothea died in 1790 in Italy, where she had lived since 1759, having married young to escape her stepmother's tyranny (Gibbon, *Journey*, 22 May 1764, 65).

Literary reputation Mallet is best-known in Johnson's hostile *Life*, coloured as it is by an (unexpressed) detestation of freethinking. Johnson charges Mallet rightly with being vain and mercenary, though it is not true that he 'was the only Scot whom Scotchmen did not commend' (Johnson, *Poets*, 3.403), for he had good friends among Scots as well as English. Mallet's poems and plays were reprinted in standard collections into the nineteenth century; French, German, and Italian translations of his *Life of Bacon* were

still appearing after his death; his *William and Margaret* played a significant part in the eighteenth-century ballad revival and has remained a frequent anthology piece; nevertheless these flickers of afterlife do not refute Johnson's judgement that Mallet's works were such as could be kept alive during the author's lifetime by the 'personal influence' of 'a writer, bustling in the world', but which, 'conveying little information and giving no great pleasure, must soon give way' to 'other modes of amusement' (ibid., 410).   JAMES SAMBROOK

Sources F. Dinsdale, 'Memoir', in D. Mallet, *Ballads and songs*, new edn (1857), 3–61 [prefixed] · R. Anderson, *A complete edition of the poets of Great Britain*, 13 vols. (1792–5), vol. 9, pp. 671–8 · *Edinburgh Magazine, or, Literary Miscellany*, new ser., 1 (1793), 3–6, 85–8, 172–4, 413–14 · *Edinburgh Magazine, or, Literary Miscellany*, new ser., 2 (1793), 1–3, 89–90, 169–72, 257–8, 337–42 · *The works of the late Aaron Hill*, 4 vols. (1753), vols. 1–2 · *GM*, 1st ser., 12 (1742), 275 · *GM*, 1st ser., 14 (1744), 590–91 · *GM*, 1st ser., 35 (1765), 199 · *The correspondence of Alexander Pope*, ed. G. Sherburn, 3–4 (1956) · *James Thomson (1700–1748): letters and documents*, ed. A. D. McKillop (1958) · Walpole, *Corr.*, 20.61–2; 21.377, 386; 28.41; 40.151–2 · S. Johnson, *Lives of the English poets*, ed. G. B. Hill, [new edn], 3 (1905), 400–10 · Boswell, *Life* · *The letters of David Hume*, ed. J. Y. T. Greig, 2 vols. (1932) · *New letters of David Hume*, ed. R. Klibansky and E. C. Mossner (1954), 68 · I. Lustig, 'David Malloch's published letters to John Ker redated', *Papers of the Bibliographical Society of America*, 72 (1978) · A. H. Scouten, ed., *The London stage, 1660–1800*, pt 3: *1729–1747* (1961) · G. W. Stone, ed., *The London stage, 1660–1800*, pt 4: *1747–1776* (1962) · *Letters of Edward Gibbon*, ed. J. E. Norton, 3 vols. (1956) · E. Gibbon, *Memoirs of my life*, ed. G. A. Bonnard (1966) · *The letters of Philip Dormer Stanhope, fourth earl of Chesterfield*, ed. B. Dobrée, 6 vols. (1932) · *Boswell's journal of a tour to the Hebrides with Samuel Johnson*, ed. F. A. Pottle and C. H. Bennett (1963), vol. 9 of *The Yale editions of the private papers of James Boswell*, trade edn (1950–89), 140–41 · D. Pope, *At 12 Mr Byng was shot* (1962), 148–9, 194, 199 · E. Gibbon, *Journey from Geneva to Rome: journal 20 April to 2 October 1764*, ed. G. A. Bonnard (1961) · *Scots Magazine*, 27 (1765), 224

Archives Bank of Scotland, Edinburgh, archives department, papers relating to duke of Marlborough · BL, Bolingbroke's manuscripts with subject's annotations and revisions, Add. MSS 4948 A · BL, corresp. with Hardwicke and Anson, Add. MSS 35594, fols. 103, 236–7, 254 · BL, corresp. with 'Thomas Manly', 1753, Add. MS 32733, fols. 614, 616 · BL, letters to duke of Newcastle, Add. MSS 32866–32938 · BL, letters to George Lewis Scott, Add. MS 43772, fols. 56–61, 64

Mallet, Elizabeth (*fl.* 1672–1706), printer and bookseller, was the wife of David Mallet (*d.* 1683), printer, of St Martin Ludgate, London, whom she had married by 1672. Details of her birth and parentage have not been ascertained. On the death, intestate, of her husband on 3 April 1683 she administered his estate and took their son, also named David, as her apprentice on 7 May 1683. At her premises in Black Horse Alley, near Fleet Bridge, she operated two printing presses in 1685. David was made a freeman of the Stationers' Company, by patrimony, on 29 January 1686 but before that date Elizabeth had printed a number of items for him, notably the proceedings of the commissioners of the peace held in the Old Bailey, as well as various items on her own behalf, registering a series of accounts of malefactors and similar popular and lurid items with the Stationers' Company in the period 1683–5. When David set up on his own to embark on a short and undistinguished career in 1686 her activity as a printer slackened.

About 1693, with her son's career ended, Elizabeth Mallet resumed work as a publisher of sensational tracts, possibly succeeding the printer Langley Curtis. She also produced serial publications, including *The New State of Europe*, the first number of which was dated 20 September 1701, but her main claim to fame was that her name appeared in the imprint of issue no. 1 of Britain's first daily newspaper, the *Daily Courant*, on 11 March 1702. The first issue of this two-column newspaper, similar in format to the *London Gazette*, was published from her premises next door to the King's Arms tavern at Fleet Bridge and contained no home news, the content being derived from foreign gazettes. After ten issues publication was taken over by Samuel Buckley, who assured the title's continuing success. There are further imprints recorded for Elizabeth Mallet in 1703 but she probably died not long afterwards, as she granted her estate to Lancelot Head of Stepney on 22 June 1706, in an instrument that was proved in the commissary court of London on 2 August the same year. John Dunton, in his *Life and Errors* (1705), includes her among nine 'honest (*mercurial*) women' (p. 236) who were his contemporaries in the London book trades.

IAN MAXTED

Sources H. R. Plomer and others, *A dictionary of the printers and booksellers who were at work in England, Scotland, and Ireland from 1668 to 1725* (1922), 195 • OPAC, BL • M. Treadwell, working papers, Trent University, Peterborough • D. F. McKenzie, ed., *Stationers' Company apprentices*, [2]: *1641–1700* (1974), nos. 2850–51 • J. Dunton, *The life and errors of John Dunton … written by himself* (1705) • C. Nelson and M. Seccombe, eds., *British newspapers and periodicals, 1641–1700: a short-title catalogue of serials printed in England, Scotland, Ireland, and British America* (1987) • IGI • London commissary court papers, GL, MS 9172, box 99

Mallet, Sir Louis (1823–1890), civil servant and economist, was born on 16 March 1823 in Hampstead, Middlesex, the second son of John Lewis Mallet (*b.* 1775) and his second wife, Frances (*d.* 1851), sister of John Herman Merivale of Barton Place, Exeter. Louis was descended from a Huguenot family which left France because of religious persecution and settled in Geneva. His grandfather Mallet du Pan (*b.* 1749), a celebrated publicist, fled from Paris to Britain in 1798, with John Lewis, to escape the French Revolution. Mallet's father was appointed through Pitt's influence to a clerkship in the Audit Office in 1800 and rose to be secretary to the board of audit.

Mallet was privately educated because of an unspecified constitutional delicacy inherited from his father. In 1839 he was appointed junior clerk in the Audit Office, where monotonous regularity plagued him—as it did throughout his life. He turned to reading poetry and Shakespeare, studying German, playing the guitar, and initiating a lifelong correspondence with 'a brilliantly gifted cousin of about his own age', Louisa Merivale (Mallet, *Sir Louis Mallet*, 12). In 1847 he moved to the more congenial and stimulating atmosphere of the statistical department of the Board of Trade, which expanded vigorously in responsibility and staff during the 1850s. A whig with radical sympathies, he

Sir Louis Mallet (1823–1890), by unknown photographer

studied political economy, embraced free trade before meeting Cobden personally, and rose through the ranks to assistant secretary and head of the commercial department on 2 January 1867. While doing so he became private secretary (1848–52) to the president of the board, Henry Labouchere, and then (1855–8) to Stanley of Alderley as vice-president and president. In 1858 he married Frances Helen, daughter of the Hon. and Revd Edward Pellew. They had four sons, of whom Bernard wrote a biography of his father.

In 1860 Mallet was appointed assistant commissioner, under Richard Cobden, for negotiating the commercial treaty with France. Cobden was impressed by his exceptional competence. This was the turning point in Mallet's career. He became an enthusiastic proponent of Cobden's ideas and was launched into diplomatic work, resulting in some sixty commercial treaties in Europe. Cobden's death in 1865 left him the principal authority on commercial policy, and the chief official representative of free-trade opinion. He was joint plenipotentiary for negotiating treaties of commerce and navigation with Austria in 1866. This established his reputation as chief adviser to the British government in matters of commercial foreign policy. He was accorded the CB in 1866, and was knighted in 1868.

Meanwhile, in 1864, a parliamentary select committee report recommended that the Foreign Office and its consular staff become the clearing house for Board of Trade commercial negotiations and treaties. By 1868 the commercial department withered to an assistant secretary and four under-employed clerks. Mallet pragmatically recommended that the consultative business of the commercial department be transferred to the Foreign Office, and resigned in January 1872.

Largely because of his commercial experience, Mallet was appointed to the Council of India, on which he served from 8 August 1872 until 16 February 1874, when he succeeded his cousin Herman Merivale as permanent under-secretary in the India Office. A stickler for discipline, punctuality, and protocol, he was dismayed by the persistence of the easy-going ways of the East India House, and complained to the newly appointed secretary of state, Salisbury, of the 'laxity' which had been 'allowed to grow up in this office'. Certain heads of department were singled out for criticism of their 'superficial' and 'misguided' opinions, or for being 'literary men' with press connections. In his opinion 'the personality of an official should be vigorously and systematically suppressed'. As for the council, it was 'too young', given to holidays, and rushing off to the train at the end of meetings (Williams, 102–5). He did not discourage Markham, head of the geographical department, from resigning in 1877. Even the young, inexperienced parliamentary under-secretary Hamilton was loaded with work to test his durability (Hamilton, 69).

Mallet's exorcism of the ghost of 'John Company', which included tidying up the secret department, made it easier for his successor, J. A. Godley, to consolidate office reform. Mallet exercised considerable influence on the finance committee. His financial and commercial expertise, underpinned by Salisbury, improved the standing of the office in economic matters. Both were anxious to curb expenditure, especially in public works, which Mallet regarded as 'a bottomless pit of expense and waste', not to be funded by government (Mallet, *Northbrook*, 70; Mallet, *Sir Louis Mallet*, 122).

Mallet's relationship with Salisbury was cordial, with considerable agreement on policy. The viceroy from 1872 to 1876, Northbrook, was a personal friend. Notwithstanding, the 1875 Indian Tariff Act, with its duty on raw cotton, was ill received in the India Office, where Sir Erskine Perry warned Northbrook that Mallet 'as a rigid Member of the Cobden Club would annihilate everything that in the least involves protection …' (Moulton, 197–8). In an unprecedented move, Mallet was sent to India to negotiate suitable amendments. There he fell ill, but he benefited from this valuable, if short-lived, Indian experience. Meanwhile Salisbury disallowed parts of the act. Later Mallet contributed to its repeal, and the reform and reduction of the salt tax. Nevertheless, Indian policy generally was subject to vagaries in the relationship between the home and supreme governments. Ultimately, even Mallet, with his strong aversion to 'feeble and slipshod Government', was convinced that because of this weakness, and lack of knowledge on the part of transient ministers, it was impossible for the India Office to initiate effective measures for reform (Mallet, *Sir Louis Mallet*, 39, 147–9).

Mallet believed in a secure India within the empire, governed according to British ideas, but he disapproved strongly of the title empress of India conferred on Queen Victoria, as encouraging disloyalty among Indians. In 1877, during the Russo-Turkish War, he agreed with Salisbury that restless Muslims did not constitute a threat either in India or to British policy in Europe. He supported the employment of Indians in the lower ranks of the civil service, believing that the material condition of the Indian masses should be improved to equip them for self-government. His strong sense of justice and equity thus laced his view of England's mission abroad, which owed much to Cobden's lifelong aim 'to lay the foundations of her empire in her moral greatness' (Mallet, *Free Exchange*, 71). He opposed the 'forward' policy in India, believing that further expansion of empire generally should not be at the cost of failure to alleviate suffering at home. The surge of imperialism after the Second Anglo-Afghan War (1878) troubled him, since he took no pride in assuming the 'white man's burden'. Increasingly, therefore, he no longer felt at home in government.

Mallet represented the varied interests of India and Britain, as a royal commissioner at the Paris and London exhibitions (1878) and, with Lord Reay, at the international commission on gold and silver in Paris (1881), where he became a convinced bimetallist. In retirement he was a member of the royal commission on the relative value of precious metals (1887–8). Earlier he was a member of the royal commission on the copyright laws (1875).

Mallet, like his father, did not publish extensively, and read widely in French and English literature (including *Treasure Island*) for relaxation. He preferred to live among those who divided their time between 'letters and affairs' (*DNB*). Morley's biography of Cobden owed much to his suggestion and help. His contributions to the publications of the Cobden Club, and various other writings, were collected in *Free Exchange* (1891). Sympathetic to Frederic Bastiat and the French school, and unhappy with Ricardo and Mill, his view of Cobden's ideas identified a carefully conceived political scheme which embraced all aspects of national life, seeking a solution to the social problem. In its international aspect, it was a policy of concord and peace (*DNB*). As he put it:

> If, as an economist and Liberal, I did not believe that the free operation of natural economic laws tended to raise the condition of the masses and to bring about a less unequal distribution of wealth, I should take very little interest in political economy or in public affairs.   (Mallet, *Free Exchange*, frontispiece)

Mallet belonged to an 'inner circle of influential political thinkers' who had personal access to all levels of government (Mallet, *Sir Louis Mallet*, 53). At congenial gatherings in the homes of Grant Duff and Lord Arthur Russell he enjoyed the company of friends who included Indian civilians and soldiers. The Athenaeum also was a meeting-place with, among others, Maine, Cobden, and Matthew Arnold. However, the new spirit in imperial government was at odds with his high principles of peace abroad and retrenchment at home, while living in London had become 'impossible' for health reasons. Accordingly, he resigned on 29 September 1883. A month earlier he had been sworn of the privy council.

Mallet moved to Englefield Green, Surrey, in 1884. As a

young man he delighted in natural beauty and country life, riding his horse to work. But chronic ill health, including a partial failure of eyesight during the 1850s and 1860s, resulted in frequent absences from the office. Persistent infirmity saddened him, but there was no self-pity or shirking of duty. His firm, austere looks denoted a magisterial presence, whose challenging eyes belied unusual sensitivity and compassion. He was essentially a family man, whose wife 'brought him the lifelong devotion and intelligent and cheerful companionship which was precisely what his own deeply affectionate nature needed' (Mallet, *Sir Louis Mallet*, 31). Endowed with many statesman-like attributes, including perspicacity, persuasiveness, and humour, Mallet carried authority graciously and with humility. His unassuming *savoir-vivre* was derived from his forebears, parents, and family connections and friends in Britain and the continent, which he visited regularly from the age of ten. He died of influenza at 13 Royal Crescent, Bath, on 16 February 1890.

There were those who believed that Mallet was too single-minded in his quest for universal free trade as a panacea, failing to appreciate fully the weaknesses of commercial treaties; that he was on the wrong side in the bimetallic controversy, and appeared to have underestimated the capacity of Britain to pay additional taxes. Yet he was admired, especially because he never lost sight of his life's main question: 'Why have I so much and others so little?' For him the solution lay in the teachings of the economists, reflected in his dictum that 'A man may be an economist without being a statesman; he most certainly cannot be a statesman without being an economist' (*Spectator*, 95, 1905, 654).   DONOVAN WILLIAMS

Sources B. Mallet, *Sir Louis Mallet* (1905) · 'A great official', *The Spectator* (28 Oct 1905), 654–5 · T. H. S. Escott, 'Sir Louis Mallet, C.B.', *Pillars of the empire*, ed. T. H. S. Escott (1879), 205–13 · H. Llewellyn Smith, *The board of trade* (1928) · D. Williams, *The India Office, 1858–1869* (1983) · G. Hamilton, *Parliamentary reminiscences and reflections*, 1: *1868–1885* (1916); repr. (1917) · E. C. Moulton, *Lord Northbrook's Indian administration, 1872–1876* (1968) · B. Mallet, *Thomas George, earl of Northbrook* (1908) · G. Cecil, *Life of Robert, marquis of Salisbury*, 4 vols. (1921–32); repr. 2 vols. (New York, 1971) · S. Gopal, *British policy in India, 1858–1905* (1965) · A. P. Kaminsky, *The India Office, 1880–1910* (1986) · L. Mallet, *Free exchange*, ed. B. Mallet (1891) · CGPLA Eng. & Wales (1890) · DNB

Archives Balliol Oxf., corresp. and papers · NRA, priv. coll., corresp. · PRO, Board of Trade MSS | Balliol Oxf., corresp. with Sir Robert Morier · BL, papers relating to Anglo-Austrian Tariff Commission, Add. MSS 38814–38815 · BL, letters to Richard Cobden, Add. MS 43666 · BL, corresp. with Sir Austen Layard, Add. MSS 38922, 39113–39120 · BL, corresp. with Florence Nightingale, Add. MS 45779 · BL OIOC, letters to Arthur Godley, MS Eur. F 102 · BL OIOC, letters to him from Lord Lytton and others, with draft replies, MS Eur. E 218/48 · BL OIOC, corresp. with Sir Philip Wodehouse, MS Eur. D 726 · Bodl. Oxf., letters to Lord Kimberley · Bodl. Oxf., letters to J. E. T. Rogers · CUL, letters to Lord Acton · Hatfield House, Hertfordshire, letters to Lord Salisbury · PRO, letters to Odo Russell, FO 918 · Suffolk RO, Ipswich, letters to Lord Cranbrook · UCL, corresp. with Sir Edwin Chadwick · W. Sussex RO, corresp. with Richard Cobden · W. Sussex RO, letters to duke of Richmond

Likenesses Hill & Saunders, photograph, BL OIOC; repro. in D. Williams, 'Clements Robert Markham and the geographical department of the India Office, 1867–77', *GJ*, 134 (1968), 343–52 ·

photograph, repro. in Mallet, *Sir Louis Mallet* · photograph, BL OIOC [*see illus.*] · portraits, repro. in *Pictorial World* (27 Feb 1890), 260, 283 · wood-engraving (after photograph by Hill & Saunders), NPG; repro. in *ILN* (1 March 1890), 262

Wealth at death £47,254 11s. 5d.: resworn probate, Feb 1891, CGPLA Eng. & Wales (1890)

Mallet [*née* Udny], **Louisa Tempe** (1837–1904), women's activist, was born on 15 April 1837 in Calcutta, the daughter of Bengal civil servant George Udny, of Udny in Aberdeenshire, and Frances Hannay. Little else is known of her private life, other than that on 3 March 1859 she married Charles Mallet (*b.* 1824/5), a civil servant, and in December 1862 she gave birth to a son, Sir Charles Edward Mallet, a Liberal MP and historian.

In the early 1870s Mrs Mallet supported the activities of the sisters Maria Grey and Emily Shirreff to establish a greater number of schools for academically oriented girls, and for a five-year period from 1876 she served on the central committee of the Women's Education Union. The union had two main objectives: firstly, to raise academic standards and to increase provision in the field of secondary education, and secondly, to promote the training and status of women teachers. Mrs Mallet also took a practical interest in the education of the working classes, serving as a manager of the Lisson Grove elementary schools in Marylebone from November 1880. Here the chair of managers was Alice Westlake, an early supporter of Bedford College who was elected on to the London school board in 1876 and, like Louisa Mallet, had connections with the Langham Place circle of feminists and the trade union organizer Emilia Dilke. In 1891 Mrs Mallet stood as a Progressive Party candidate for West Lambeth in the triennial election for the school board, but was narrowly defeated in an election campaign dominated by charges of excessive expenditure from the tory majority. Indeed, her close friend Emma Maitland lost her seat in Marylebone. They shared a concern with the education of girls and women and were active in questions of local government and women's suffrage.

In November 1888 Mrs Mallet helped found the Society for Promoting the Return of Women as County Councillors, with the countess of Aberdeen (president of the executive of the Women's Liberal Federation) as president and Eva McLaren as first honorary treasurer. As joint secretary with Annie Leigh Browne, Louisa supported Jane Cobden in the 1889 election campaign for the London county council and joined the executive of the renamed Women's Local Government Society in 1892. This upper-middle-class, liberal, London-based women's organization was established on a non-party basis for promoting the eligibility of women to elect to and serve on all local governing bodies. Its inner circle included Lady Aberdeen, Annie Leigh Browne, Emma Cons, Emma Maitland, and Eva McLaren. Mrs Mallet defended female involvement in local politics at a number of important meetings in the 1890s, as well as writing articles in the feminist press and producing a campaign leaflet (*Shall Women be Eligible to Serve on County Councils?*) on behalf of the Women's Local Government Society.

By 1893 Mrs Mallet was a well-known figure in London politics, a Liberal Party worker who served on the executive committee of the Women's Liberal Federation, and president of the Guildford, North Kensington, and Mile End women's Liberal associations. Like Annie Leigh Browne, she was also a member of the Albemarle Club. Louisa Mallet remained on the executive committee of the Women's Local Government Society until 1901. She died at the Hotel Burlington, Boscombe, Bournemouth, on 2 July 1904.   JANE MARTIN

Sources 'Women as county councillors: portraits of the vanguard', *Women's Herald* (4 Feb 1893) · *Journal of the Women's Education Union* (1876–81) · *Women's Penny Paper* (29 Dec 1888) · *Women's Penny Paper* (June 1890) · *School Board Chronicle: an Educational Record and Review* (17 Oct 1891) · *School Board Chronicle: an Educational Record and Review* (31 Oct 1891) · *School Board Chronicle: an Educational Record and Review* (21 Nov 1891) · *School Board Chronicle: an Educational Record and Review* (5 Dec 1891) · Women's Local Government Society, minute book one, Nov 1888–15 April 1889, LMA · Women's Local Government Society, reports, 1892–1901, LMA · School Board for London, minutes, 18 Nov 1880, 804 · m. cert. · d. cert. · BL OIOC, N/1/47, fol. 84 · *The Post Office directory* (1880); (1895) · Walford, *County families* (1919) · Burke, *Peerage*
Archives LMA, Women's Local Government Society MSS · Royal Holloway College, Egham, Surrey, Bedford College MSS
Likenesses photograph, 1893, repro. in 'Women as county councillors'
Wealth at death £722 8s. 10d.: probate, 12 Aug 1904, CGPLA Eng. & Wales

Mallet, Robert (1810–1881), civil engineer and scientist, was born at Ryder's Row in Dublin on 3 June 1810, the son of John and Thomasina Mallet. His father came from Devon in 1780 to join his uncle's brass and copper founding business. Mallet received his early education at Bective House in Dublin and entered Trinity College, Dublin, in December 1826, where he studied mathematics and science, graduating BA in 1830.

In 1831 Mallet became a partner in his father's works, the same year marrying Cordelia Watson (d. 1854); the marriage produced three sons and three daughters. He took charge of the Victoria foundry, greatly expanding it and securing large contracts for much of the railway plant, permanent way materials, and ironwork required in the building of the main lines of railway in Ireland. An early undertaking was the raising and strengthening of the 133 ton roof of St George's Church in Dublin, for which he was in 1841 awarded a Walker premium by the Institution of Civil Engineers. In 1836 the firm of J. and R. Mallet erected a number of swivel bridges over the River Shannon. Contracts were also completed for Guinness & Co., the brewers, including boring a deep artesian well, the construction of steam barrel-washing machinery, and large sky coolers. Mallet was elected an associate of the Institution of Civil Engineers in 1839, being transferred to member in 1842. He surveyed the River Dodder in 1841 and devised a scheme to provide a supply of pure water to parts of Dublin city, and to secure a reliable summer water supply to the paper mills along the river. (A similar scheme was eventually built in the 1880s.) Between 1845 and 1848 he supplied and erected the ironwork at many of the railway termini, as well as engine

sheds, workshops, and a 200 ft span timber viaduct over the Nore in co. Kilkenny. His foundry supplied the castings for the first Fastnet Rock lighthouse (1848–9); the structure was replaced in 1904. Mallet invented the buckled plate, which he patented in 1852 (No. 557). Such plates were used widely in structures, particularly for flooring, where they combined maximum strength with minimum depth and weight. In 1854, during the Crimean War, he designed and had built two large siege mortars capable of firing 36 inch shells to distances of over 1 mile, but no opportunity arose to use them before the conclusion of a peace treaty with Russia in 1856.

In 1860, with the completion of the trunk railway lines in Ireland, engineering work became scarce, and Mallet closed the foundry and moved to London, where he had begun to establish himself as a consulting engineer. He lodged with a Mrs Daniel, and in 1861 married her daughter Mary, his first wife having died in 1854. He edited the *Practical Mechanic's Journal*, 1865–9, wrote extensively for *The Engineer*, and gave evidence as a scientific witness in patent cases. In 1863 he reported on the Hibernia and other Ruhr collieries in Germany, and in 1864 was involved in an abortive scheme to connect Dublin's main line railway termini. He investigated the use of the Thames Tunnel by the East London Railway, and the possibility of damage to the Royal Observatory at Greenwich.

Mallet's investigations in physical geology were directed towards four main areas: glacial flowage (1837–45), geological dynamics (1835 onwards), seismology (1845 onwards), and vulcanology (1862 onwards). Between 1850 and 1858, he coined no less than eight terms with the prefix 'seism-', including seismology. His classic paper to the Royal Irish Academy in 1846 on earthquake dynamics is regarded as one of the foundations of modern seismology. He investigated the great Neapolitan earthquake of December 1857 and established the first principles of observational seismology. With his eldest son, John W. Mallet, he compiled a *Catalogue of the World's Earthquakes* (1852–4) and a *Seismographic Map of the World* (1857), both published by the British Association.

Mallet published at least eighty-five papers, on such diverse topics as the corrosion of iron, alloys of copper with tin and zinc, atmospheric railways, the application of water power, fouling of iron ships, earthquakes, and volcanoes. He was elected a fellow of the Royal Society in 1854. He received a Telford medal and premium from the Institution of Civil Engineers in 1859, and the Cunningham medal from the Royal Irish Academy in 1862. In the same year, the University of Dublin bestowed on him an honorary master of engineering degree, followed two years later by an honorary LLD. He was awarded the Wollaston gold medal of the Geological Society in 1877.

Mallet died at Enmore, The Grove, Clapham Road, London, on 5 November 1881. He was buried at Norwood cemetery, London, on 6 November. He was survived by his second wife.   G. C. BOASE, rev. R. C. COX

Sources R. C. Cox, ed., *Robert Mallet, FRS, 1810–1881: papers presented at a centenary seminar* [Dublin 1981] (Dublin, 1982) · *The Engineer*, 52 (1881), 352–3, 371–2, 389–90 · *Irish Builder*, 23/528 (1881), 360 ·

PICE, 68 (1881–2), 297–304 · S. H., *PRS*, 33 (1881–2), xix–xx · private information (1893)
Archives RS, report on Naples earthquake | CUL, letters to Sir George Stokes
Likenesses photograph, *c.*1850, Old Dublin Society · photograph, 1854, RS
Wealth at death £1387 0s. 3d.: 1882, codicil

Mallett, Francis (d. **1570**), dean of Lincoln, was the son of William Mallett of Normanton, Yorkshire. He was a scholar of Queens' College, Cambridge (1519–22), graduating BA (1522), MA (1525), BTh (1534), and DTh (1535), and preached before the university in 1532–3. As a protégé of Thomas Cromwell he became master of Michaelhouse in 1533, retaining this post until the college was subsumed into the larger foundation of Trinity in 1546, when he received a pension of £20. Also in 1533 he acquired the vicarage of Rothwell, Yorkshire (which he resigned in 1543); in 1535 he became rector of Swillington, Yorkshire, retaining it until 1569. In 1536 and 1540 he was elected vice-chancellor of Cambridge. But he was slow to produce the foundation deeds of his own college as required by the royal visitors of 1535. Archbishop Cranmer, whose chaplain he had become by January 1536, asked Cromwell to excuse Mallett's delay because of his preaching duties in the diocese of Canterbury and at Paul's Cross. By April 1539 Mallett was chaplain to Cromwell himself, and employed by him at Cranmer's palace of Ford, Kent, in writing up a liturgical scheme. This was almost certainly a part of the texts (now BL, Royal MS 7 B iv) in which Cranmer first followed Lutheran models in adapting the canonical hours to the twofold office of matins and evensong. Cranmer hoped Mallett's 'diligence and pains in this business' would earn him favour from Cromwell, to whom he commended his 'right judgment in learning, and discreet wisdom' (Cox, 367).

Cromwell's fall in 1540 doubtless impeded Mallett's advancement, but on 13 December 1543 he was granted a canonry of Windsor, in which he was installed on 24 December and which he retained for life. In 1544 he acquired the prebend of Yatton in Wells Cathedral (resigned by 1559). Up to this point he had been a keen reformer—by his own later admission he had been deceived by 'new fangled two-penny books' (*Acts and Monuments*, 8.728). The turning point came when, by 1547, he completed the translation of Erasmus's paraphrase on St John which Princess Mary had begun but then abandoned. As Mary's principal chaplain and almoner in Edward VI's reign (by 1550 at the latest), Mallett (by now a staunch Catholic) was at the centre of the controversy over the princess's mass, which for a time threatened to become a major diplomatic crisis. Mass had been permitted in Mary's houses, but only in her actual presence. In July 1550 Mallett broke this compact by celebrating at Beaulieu in Essex before Mary took up residence there. The sheriff, apparently without waiting for orders from London, indicted Mallett, who fled to the north of England. In December the sheriff, by now backed by the privy council, was still seeking him. Finally in April 1551 the earl of Shrewsbury secured an arrest. Mallett was examined before the privy council at Durham Place and condemned for reoffending after having been forgiven his original fault, and also for persuading others to 'embrase his naughtie oppinions' (*APC*, 3.267). He was committed to the Tower on the 29th. In answer to Mary's complaint the council told her that Mallett had been imprisoned for his original offence, compounded by his flight, and at the king's 'express orders' (*CSP Spain, 1550–52*, 288).

Following Mary's accession in 1553 Mallett's career recovered dramatically. As precentor of St George's, Windsor, he supervised the restoration of Catholic ornament he had previously rejected. On 5 April 1554 he was appointed canon of Westminster, retaining his position until the chapter was dissolved in 1556. On 19 April the queen named him dean of Lincoln; he was installed by proxy on 29 May and in person on 7 September. He was also installed in the prebends of St Martin's (18 December 1556) and Corringham (28 January 1557) in Lincoln Cathedral, but rarely resided there. On 20 July 1554 he was appointed master of the hospital of St Katharine near the Tower of London, and on 23 May 1555 was exempted from first fruits of over £300. To this office he gave his chief attention, refurnishing the church and house, and restoring choral services; but subsequently he could not find adequate singing men for any money, nor 'obedient parishoners' (PRO, SP 12/7, no. 77). In secular affairs he was JP for Middlesex and Berkshire from 1555, and in 1556 helped to interrogate state prisoners. On or before 3 September 1556 he became lord high almoner. In this capacity he gave the queen a gold crucifix as a new year's gift, accompanied by a letter heavy with classical allusion. On 10 April 1558 he was presented to the prebend of Stratton in Salisbury Cathedral.

On 14 October 1558 Mallett received the temporalities of the see of Salisbury as bishop elect, but his advancement was halted by the queen's death on 17 November. In her will he received £200 for masses for her soul. Following Elizabeth's accession Mallett accepted the return to protestantism and so kept his deanery. He resigned the mastership of St Katherine's on 6 November 1561, following a dispute with the executor of the previous master. He had been vicar of Lancaster from 1554 until his nomination to the episcopate. He was also incumbent of Ashbourne and Wirksworth, Derbyshire, in his patronage as dean of Lincoln, and the rectory of South Leverton, Nottinghamshire. As *ex officio* member of the 1563 convocation he assented to the Thirty-Nine Articles by proxy, and defended himself to Archbishop Parker against the accusation that he had preached against the Anglican classification of the sacraments. He died at Normanton, as owner of Malet's Hall there, on 16 December 1570. By his will of 14 December he made bequests to the poor women of Rothwell, Swillington, and Castleford (Yorkshire), to his sister, Jane Burtone, and to other kin. His brother Henry was canon of Lincoln. C. S. KNIGHTON

Sources *Fasti Angl., 1541–1857*, [St Paul's, London], 102 · *Fasti Angl., 1541–1857*, [Salisbury], 1, 75 · *Fasti Angl., 1541–1857*, [Ely], 76 · S. L. Ollard, *Fasti Wyndesorienses: the deans and canons of Windsor* (privately printed, Windsor, 1950), 110 · *CPR, 1554–5*, 117, 224; *1555–7*,

517; 1557–8, 310, 389, 428 · *APC*, 1550–2, 171, 177, 240, 258, 267 · *CSP dom.*, rev. edn, 1553–8, nos. 160, 404, 677 · *CSP Spain, 1550–52*, 150–51, 286–8 · *The chronicle and political papers of King Edward VI*, ed. W. K. Jordan (1966), 60, 67 · C. H. Smyth, *Cranmer and the Reformation under Edward VI* (1926), 74–7 · D. MacCulloch, *Thomas Cranmer: a life* (1996), 225–6 · J. K. McConica, *English humanists and Reformation politics under Henry VIII and Edward VI* (1965), 231, 241–2 · *The acts and monuments of John Foxe*, new edn, ed. G. Townsend, 8 vols. (1843–9), vol. 6, pp. 13–14, 18–21; vol. 8, pp. 579, 727–9 · R. E. G. Cole, ed., *Chapter acts of the cathedral church of St Mary of Lincoln*, 3, Lincoln RS, 15 (1920), 106, 107, 121, 138, 140 · C. S. Knighton, ed., *Acts of the dean and chapter of Westminster*, 1 (1997), 91, 101 · *Miscellaneous writings and letters of Thomas Cranmer*, ed. J. E. Cox, Parker Society, [18] (1846), 318–19, 366–7 · C. Jamison, *The history of the Royal Hospital of St Katharine by the Tower of London* (1952), 64–8 · state papers domestic, Elizabeth, PRO, SP 12/77, no. 77 · PRO, PROB 11/53, fols. 19–19*v* · R. W. Dixon, *History of the Church of England*, 3 (1885), 241–2, 305, 307–8 · R. B. Walker, 'Lincoln Cathedral in the reign of Queen Elizabeth I', *Journal of Ecclesiastical History*, 11 (1960), 186–201 · Cooper, *Ath. Cantab.*, 3.102 · Venn, *Alum. Cant.*

Archives PRO, account of his stewardship as master of St Katherine's by the Tower, SP 12/7, no. 77

Wealth at death owned the family seat; cash bequests totalling £71: will, PRO, PROB 11/53, fols. 19–19*v*

Mallock, William Hurrell (1849–1923), writer, was born on 2 February 1849 at Cheriton Bishop, Devon, the eldest son of the Revd William Mallock, rector of Cheriton Bishop, and his wife, Margaret, daughter of the Ven. Robert Hurrell Froude, archdeacon of Totnes, Devon. His father was a member of an old Devon gentry family, the Mallocks of Cockington Court, and his mother was the sister of Richard Hurrell Froude (1803–1836), William Froude (1810–1879), and James Anthony Froude (1818–1894). He grew up in the traditional world of the local gentry, whose tory and high-church sympaties he was to share fully. He was educated at home and at the school of the Revd W. B. Philpot of Littlehampton, Sussex. In 1869 he went up to Balliol College, Oxford. His academic career was only modestly successful: he took a second in *literae humaniores* in 1874. However, he had spent his time constructively in writing poetry, winning the Newdigate prize in 1871, and in meeting prominent men of letters such as Browning and Swinburne. At Oxford, his interest in religious controversies was awakened by his antipathy to the broad-churchmanship of Benjamin Jowett, the master of Balliol.

At Oxford Mallock had begun work on a satirical novel which portrayed the contemporary state of intellectual and ethical life. After serialization, this was published as *The New Republic* in 1877, winning him immediate acclaim. The novel, set at a country-house party in Devon, took the form of a symposium on issues of religion and morality, Mallock claiming as his models Plato, Petronius, and Peacock. Although the tone was one of ironic humour, he intended it as a serious critique of various *bien-pensants*. It attracted most attention, however, for its skilful parodies of the views of Matthew Arnold, Pater, Huxley, Jowett, and Tyndall in thinly disguised characterizations.

Mallock's later fiction did not really confirm the reputation earned by *The New Republic*. All his novels dealt with the manners and morals of the leisured classes, blending political and religious comment with explorations of

William Hurrell Mallock (1849–1923), by unknown engraver (after Elliott & Fry)

romantic love. The best-known of these were *A Romance of the Nineteenth Century* (1881); *The Old Order Changes* (1886), a 'condition of England' novel; and *A Human Document* (1892), a romance set in Hungary. He also produced more satirical works such as the anti-Bloomsbury novel *The Individualist* (1899), and *The Veil of the Temple* (1904), which returned to the symposium format to defend revealed religion. Although he brought considerable talents of social observation and satiric wit to his fiction, the plots of his novels could be contrived and the characterization superficial. As a result, these works attracted less favourable reviews from the critics.

For most of his life Mallock was best-known as a conservative political and religious polemicist. He was a prolific contributor to the periodical press, sometimes under the pseudonym Wentworth Moore, and was particularly associated with the *National Review*. He had already attacked secular humanism, and Christian compromises with it, in *The New Republic*, but *Is Life Worth Living?* in 1879 established him as a forceful defender of dogmatic Christianity. Mallock berated 'positivists', a term he used for both Comtists and scientific naturalists, for failing to provide a persuasive secular morality to counteract the scepticism unleashed by their 'scientific' criticisms of revealed religion. He argued that the attempt to draw ethical rules from essentially materialist phenomena was doomed, because such phenomena gave equally compelling reasons for cynicism and hedonism. Only supernatural religion could guarantee adherence to moral sanctions.

Mallock believed that political affairs were also being altered by modern materialism. He saw in democratic and socialist thinking the same degree of wishful thinking about the malleability of mankind. Yet the success of Henry George and the land-reformers in the early 1880s convinced him that left-wingers had found attractive arguments, expressed through statistics and sociology, to appeal to a mass audience. Troubled by the intellectual torpor of Conservatives, he proposed a 'scientific' Conservatism to refute egalitarianism, encompassing sociology, psychology, and economics, which was capable of comprehension by both politicians and electorate.

From the publication of his first political work, *Social

Equality, in 1882, and continued in many other works, Mallock was to set out probably the most systematic critique of socialism in pre-1914 Britain. At its heart was a defence of an entrepreneurial élite's contribution to wealth creation. This group possessed a quality of 'ability', which included the qualities necessary to innovate, co-ordinate, and direct industry, and it became progressively more important as capitalism developed. He was disdainful therefore of socialist claims, expressed in labour theories of value, that wealth creation was dependent on the increasing skill and self-organization of the workforce, which was unfairly exploited by passive capitalists. He insisted that on the contrary production was essentially an oligarchic process, while the masses best exercised their influence by stimulating demand. He insisted that great inequalities were inherent in the system because they stimulated entrepreneurs to imagine new possibilities for wealth creation; the leisure class fulfilled a valuable function in encouraging this. His political and economic credo is best summarized in *A Critical Examination of Socialism* (1907).

Mallock's critics, such as Bernard Shaw and J. A. Hobson, cared little for such arguments. They insisted that he had overstated the distinction between manual and mental labour, while disingenuously defending *rentiers*. It was felt that he exaggerated material motivations and ignored possibilities of democratic co-operation. He, in turn, felt gratified by the increasing socialist acceptance of 'rents of ability' as a factor in production, but he maintained that they lacked a sufficient explanation of how entrepreneurial talent could continue to be selected in a socialist society. He was also interested in the practical side of politics, producing numerous statistical leaflets and diagrams for Conservative central office and anti-socialist pressure groups about the ownership and distribution of wealth. However, although he was briefly Conservative candidate for the St Andrews burghs in 1884, he did not feel inclined to enter parliament.

Mallock was a short, portly, dapper figure. He never married, and lived mainly in London and Devon, wintering on the French riviera. He travelled widely and enjoyed visiting old castles and stately homes. At country-house parties he preferred informed conversation to field sports. He earned his living almost entirely from writing, producing over thirty books on a range of subjects, his last book being *Memoirs of Life and Literature*, published in 1920. He was a skilful writer, with gifts for parody and epigram. His political works were always powerfully argued, if repetitive in substance. Philosophically he was a pessimist, whose yearning for religious faith did not entirely succeed in overcoming his intellectual scepticism. He became increasingly sympathetic to Roman Catholicism in later life, but did not convert. Mallock died suddenly on 2 April 1923 at the infirmary, Wincanton, Somerset, and was buried at Wincanton.   J. N. PETERS

Sources W. H. Mallock, *Memoirs of life and literature* (1920) · J. N. Peters, 'Anti-socialism in British politics, *c*.1900–1922', DPhil diss., U. Oxf., 1992 · J. Lucas, 'Tilting at the moderns: W. H. Mallock's criticisms of the positivist spirit', *Renaissance and Modern Studies*, 10 (1966), 88–143 · M. Cowling, *Religion and public doctrine in modern Britain*, 2 (1985), 296–308 · J. M. Patrick, introduction, in W. H. Mallock, *The new republic* (1949) · D. J. Ford, 'W. H. Mallock and socialism in England', *Essays in anti-labour history*, ed. K. D. Brown (1974), 318–42 · A. V. Tucker, 'W. H. Mallock and late Victorian conservatism', *University of Toronto Quarterly*, 31 (1962), 223–41 · A. Adams, *The novels of W. H. Mallock* (1934) · *Wellesley index* · *CGPLA Eng. & Wales* (1923) · register, Cheriton Bishop, 1849, Devon [birth] · *The Times* (5 April 1923) · private information (2004) [family, friends]
Archives NRA, corresp. and literary papers
Likenesses Spy [L. Ward], chromolithograph caricature, NPG; repro. in *VF* (30 Dec 1882) · engraving (after Elliott & Fry), NPG [*see illus.*] · photograph, repro. in Adams, *Novels of W. H. Mallock* · process print (after photograph by Elliott & Fry), NPG
Wealth at death £238 9s. 9d.: administration, 9 June 1923, *CGPLA Eng. & Wales*

Mallon, James Joseph (1874–1961), social reformer, was born on 24 December 1874 at 13 Percival Street, Chorlton upon Medlock, Manchester, of Irish Roman Catholic parents, Felix Mallon (*d.* 1879), a mercantile clerk of co. Tyrone, and his wife, Mary Ann O'Hare, of co. Down. He had two sisters. His father died when he was four. After attending a convent school in Liverpool he was apprenticed to a jeweller and joined the Shop Assistants' Union (he was a member of the union's executive in 1905–6). He also studied at the Victoria University of Manchester, and was drawn at once into what was to prove the main pursuit of his life, social work with the 'under-privileged', at first in the Ancoats settlement, devoted to the poor of Manchester. Mallon was to become known in time as 'the Father O'Flynn of the Labour movement', lively, fluent, charming, and always in demand, a man who, above all else, enjoyed life. His obituary in *The Times* described him as 'the most popular man east of Aldgate Pump'.

Mallon joined the Independent Labour Party and the Fabian Society in 1903. In 1906 he moved from Manchester to Toynbee Hall, the universities' settlement in the East End of London, when he was appointed secretary of the National League to Establish a Minimum Wage. He worked closely with Mary Macarthur of the Women's Trade Union League in the campaign against sweated labour which was followed by the passing of the 1909 Trade Boards Act. Mallon was a member of thirteen of the first trade boards to be set up under the act, and was honorary secretary of the trade boards advisory council. During the anti-sweating agitation he came to know A. G. Gardiner, editor of the *Daily News*, and subsequently (10 August 1921) he married Gardiner's daughter, Stella Katherine (*b.* 1889/90); they had no children.

During the First World War Mallon became a member of the Romney Street Group, a luncheon club of Labour sympathizers founded by the drama critic Joseph Thorp. Another member of the group, Thomas Jones, the deputy secretary to the cabinet, recommended him to Lloyd George, which led to his appointment as a commissioner for industrial unrest, dealing with the grievances of munitions workers. He was also a member of the subcommittee of the government's reconstruction committee, chaired by J. H. Whitley, whose report in 1917 recommended the creation of joint industrial councils (Whitley

James Joseph Mallon (1874–1961), by Sir Jacob Epstein, 1954

councils) of employers and workers as a means of improving industrial relations after the war. He also served on several of the committees set up under the Profiteering Act.

In October 1919 Mallon was appointed warden of Toynbee Hall, a position he was to hold until his retirement in April 1954. There were some misgivings at first since he was not an 'Oxford man', but Jimmy soon became known as a born committee man, conscientious but with a welcome touch of conviviality, even of irreverence. At Toynbee Hall he was the life and soul of an established institution, the place of which in local and in national life was changing considerably during Mallon's long and popular wardenship. Above all, he strengthened its community links and emphasized its educational activities, so that it was sometimes known in his time as 'the poor man's university'. He had been an early member of the executive committee of the Workers' Educational Association, of which he later became honorary treasurer, and was prominent in its counsels. He was a strong advocate of raising the school-leaving age and of expanding further and higher education, including part-time education. He was closely associated, too, with the Workers' Travel Association. In bodies like this he found his ideals realized. During his wardenship three significant pieces of legislation, the Public Order Act (1936), the Education Act (1936), and the Hire Purchase Act (1939), were influenced by initiatives at Toynbee Hall.

Educational and cultural interests mattered more to Mallon than 'straight economics', which he approached in much the same way as R. H. Tawney; and although he served on Ramsay MacDonald's Economic Advisory Council and wrote booklets on the minimum wage and women's work, and articles from time to time on social and economic subjects for *The Observer*, the *Daily News*, and the *Manchester Guardian*, he made no professions to scholarship. The only book he published was *Poverty Yesterday and Today* (1930), with E. C. T. Lascelles. He was happy, however, to receive an honorary doctorate from Liverpool University in 1944: he gave a characteristically stimulating talk in Liverpool in that year on the place of the pub in the community. He was also awarded an honorary MA degree by Manchester in 1921. As secretary to the Labour campaign for public control and ownership of the liquor trade he served in 1929–31 on the royal commission on licensing.

During the Second World War Mallon advised Lord Woolton on the provision of food and refreshment in London's air-raid shelters. By then it was said of him that he knew the East End as an actor knew Charing Cross Road. His friends, who were many, included actors, and he was largely responsible for the foundation of the Toynbee Hall Theatre and later (in 1944) of the Children's Theatre.

It seemed natural that in 1937 Mallon should become a governor of the British Broadcasting Corporation: his tenure, interrupted in 1939, when the number of governors was reduced, continued from 1941 to 1946. One of his broadcasts, a postscript of 1943 following a visit to the United States, was very widely acclaimed. So, too, was his interest in the People's Palace, the Whitechapel Art Gallery, and the London Museum. He also served as a member of the executive committee of the British Empire Exhibition (1924) and the departmental committee on the Cinematographic Films Act.

Mallon hoped at various times to become a Labour member of parliament, and he stood unsuccessfully for Saffron Walden in 1918 and for Watford in 1922 and 1923. His effervescence—and complete lack of *gravitas*—did not help him either with selection committees or with the electorate. 'In this and many other constituencies', he twinklingly told a Burslem audience in 1944, 'I have been rejected by large and enthusiastic majorities.' Although he may have regretted this failure, it was his persistent cheerfulness in dismal times of depression and war which always impressed his contemporaries. He was an energetic chairman of the London Council for Voluntary Occupation during Unemployment during the worst years of the 1930s. He was made a Companion of Honour in 1939 and in 1955 was awarded the Margaret McMillan medal.

In retirement Mallon hoped to write his autobiography to replace an earlier manuscript destroyed during the bombing of London. This was an unrealized ambition, but his work at Toynbee Hall was commemorated in a garden facing Commercial Street known as the Mallon Garden. Mallon died in St Mark's Hospital, London, on 12 April 1961. He was survived by his wife.   ASA BRIGGS, *rev.*

Sources *The Times* (13 April 1961) · *The Times* (14 April 1961) · *The Times* (15 April 1961) · *The Times* (20 April 1961) · A. Briggs and A. Macartney, *Toynbee Hall: the first hundred years* (1984) · b. cert. · m.

cert. • *The Labour who's who* (1927) • *WW* (1932) • *CGPLA Eng. & Wales* (1961)

Archives BL, corresp. with Albert Mansbridge, Add. MSS 65257B, 65261 • BLPES, corresp. with Lord Beveridge • Bodl. Oxf., letters to Sir Alfred Zimmern • JRL, letters to the *Manchester Guardian* • LMA, files of corresp. and MSS as warden • NL Wales, corresp. with Thomas Jones | FILM BFI NFTVA, documentary footage **Likenesses** J. Epstein, bronze bust, 1954, Toynbee Hall, London [*see illus.*] **Wealth at death** £27,623 8s. 6d.: probate, 26 June 1961, *CGPLA Eng. & Wales*

Mallon, John (1839–1915), detective, was born on 10 May 1839 at Meigh, co. Armagh, a small village in the parish of Killeavy. His father, Thomas Mallon, a Catholic tenant farmer, may have belonged to the secret Ribbon Society. Mallon went to the local national school and Newry model school. He was apprenticed to a draper for three years, but in November 1859 went to Dublin, hoping to join the Royal Engineers. He was turned down as insufficiently qualified but a local landlord (Colonel Close) sent him to Sir Henry Lake, chief commissioner of the Dublin Metropolitan Police.

Mallon joined the Dublin Metropolitan Police on 1 December 1859 as a clerk. His intelligence, discretion, and hard work impressed Superintendent Daniel Ryan, head of the G (detective) division. In 1861 Mallon became confidential clerk to Ryan, who delegated much business to him. Mallon's activities against Fenianism gave him extensive knowledge of the separatist movement, and a personal network of spies and informers. In 1869 he became the youngest inspector in the force. In 1874 Mallon succeeded Ryan as head of G division, having been promoted over several senior officers.

Mallon's name became widely known in the early 1880s through his activities against the Land League, its allies and directors in the Irish Parliamentary Party, and the separatist secret societies with which some of its supporters were linked: it was he who arrested Charles Stewart Parnell, leader of the Irish Parliamentary Party, in 1881. After the assassination of Lord Frederick Cavendish and under-secretary Burke in Phoenix Park, Dublin, on 6 May 1882, Mallon was prominent in the 'Star Chamber' headed by Judge John Adye Curran, which gathered evidence against the Invincibles (the group accused of the assassinations) and tricked one of their leaders, James Carey, into turning informer. Lord Spencer, the lord lieutenant, reported in August 1882 that the Dublin detective service depended on Mallon: 'were he to die or be killed we have no one worth a row of beans' (K. R. M. Short, *The Dynamite War*, 1979, 88).

In 1883 Mallon was promoted to chief superintendent, continuing to supervise intelligence operations in Dublin. He claimed his achievement was not fully acknowledged because of his Catholicism, and that some Castle officials suspected his loyalty. This may reflect his necessarily ambiguous relationship with his sources. While Mallon reported regularly on subversive activities, he refused to commit much of his knowledge to paper and kept secrets from his superiors to protect his informants. He gave this reason for refusing to testify at the Parnell commission, though he gathered evidence for *The Times* in its attempt to link the Irish party with political violence. His relations with Patrick Egan, Land League treasurer and Invincible organizer, were particularly shadowy. Some suspected that Egan had given information to Mallon and that Mallon had enabled him to escape to America.

Until his promotion in 1883, when he moved into Dublin Castle, Mallon lived openly on the North Circular Road, Dublin, defying plots against his life. He maintained a tone of affable familiarity with his suspects and claimed that for him preventing crimes by warning conspirators was preferable to making arrests after a crime had been committed. Thus he spread fear and distrust among opponents and promoted a legend of his own omniscience.

Mallon claimed to be a good Catholic and nationalist. He was pious, and perhaps had nationalist sentiments, but used these professions to manipulate potential sources of information and suspects under interrogation. His reports sneer at most of the objects of his surveillance; his recollections exaggerate his own role in the Phoenix Park investigation. This arrogance, encouraged by success in making informers—a £5 note, he said, bought a great deal of patriotism—could be dangerous; some claimed Mallon might have prevented the Phoenix Park murders if he had not despised the Invincibles.

In 1893, with the help of his old adversaries in the Irish Parliamentary Party, Mallon became assistant commissioner of the Dublin Metropolitan Police, the first officer in the force to attain this post from the ranks. He still supervised G division until his retirement (1 January 1902), when he returned to Meigh, bought a small estate, and became a JP for Armagh. He had married, on 8 January 1866, Elizabeth Byrne, daughter of a Dublin greengrocer, John Byrne, and they had three sons and a daughter; his wife predeceased him. Mallon became ill after mass at Meigh on 9 October 1915 and died at the parochial house, Meigh, an hour later. He was buried at Old Killeavy burial-ground.

PATRICK MAUME

Sources F. M. Bussy, *Irish conspiracies: recollections of John Mallon* (1911) • T. Hopkins, *Kilmainham memories* (1896) • Dublin metropolitan police membership register, NA Ire., no. 5838 • *Irish Independent* (11 Oct 1915) • *Belfast News-Letter* (11 Oct 1915) • *Belfast News-Letter* (12 Oct 1915) [funeral report] • L. O Broin, *Revolutionary underground: the story of the I.R.B.* (1976) • L. O Broin, *The prime informer* (1971) • *Reminiscences of John Adye Curran* (1915) • J. Mallon, 'On secret service', *Lloyds Weekly News* (6 June–25 July 1909) • *Irish Times* (11 Oct 1915) • *Dublin Evening Telegraph* (9 Oct 1915) • *Irish News and Belfast Morning News* (11 Oct 1915) • *Northern Whig* (11 Oct 1915) • m. cert. • d. cert.

Archives Garda Siochana Archives, Dublin, administrative records • NA Ire., official papers **Likenesses** portrait, 1882, repro. in Bussy, *Irish conspiracies*, frontispiece • photograph, repro. in Hopkins, *Kilmainham memories*, facing p. 61 • photograph, repro. in *Lloyds Weekly News* (31 May 1909), 5 **Wealth at death** £2900 18s.: probate, 6 March 1916, *CGPLA Ire.*

Mallory family (*per. c.*1100–1300), gentry, of medieval Leicestershire, was first represented by **Richard** [i] **Mallory** (d. *c.*1160), a follower of Robert, earl of Leicester, in the 1130s and 1140s. The Mallory name must have come to

Leicestershire rather earlier, however, for it appears as the name of a family of substantial knights in the county of Meulan, in the French Vexin. It would therefore seem most likely that a Mallory arrived in the county at the time when Robert de Beaumont, count of Meulan, was earl there, that is between 1107 and 1118. The name Mallory is a nickname and could variously be interpreted as 'unlucky' or 'foul-mouthed'. Richard [i] had at least two probable sons, Richard [ii] and Anschetil, who seem to have taken the English and Norman fees of the family respectively on his death about 1160. It is from these two that the many and various branches of the family derive, although only the elder branch, settled at Kirkby Mallory, Leicestershire, will be followed here. However, **Anschetil Mallory** (*d. c.*1190), seneschal of Robert de Breteuil, earl of Leicester, has to be noticed as a prominent character in the reign of Henry II, and a leading rebel of the wars of 1173–4, who defended Leicester Castle against the royalists. Anschetil survived this political mistake and acquired English lands at Tachbrook Mallory, Warwickshire, where his family flourished into the fourteenth century.

Richard [ii] **Mallory** (*d.* before 1175) of Kirkby Mallory, although less important politically than his younger brother and not attached to Earl Robert, had more considerable landed interests. A good marriage to Agnes, coheir of William (II) de Neufmarché, brought Richard estates at Welton and Thrupp, Northamptonshire, held at fee-farm of 40s. from Leicester Abbey, and (from later evidence) land at Broughton Astley, Leicestershire, and the service of Billesley, Warwickshire (see below). Richard died at some time before 1175, and was survived for several years by his wife. He left as his heir William, but left also at least three other sons who obtained subtenancies in the Mallory lands, one of whom, Simon (*d. c.*1208), founded a long-lasting cadet branch of the family at Welton, which survived into the fourteenth century. **William Mallory** (*d. c.*1202) was his father's eldest son, and took responsibility for granting the Welton estate as a subtenancy to his younger brother, Simon. This would seem to have been an internal family arrangement which thus allowed more than one son to succeed while still preserving the integrity of the family's lands. He married a certain Alice, but nothing more of her is known. William had only one known son, **Richard** [iii] **Mallory** (*d.* 1217), who seems to have been active in Leicestershire as early as 1201. He made a rather large number of known grants: the church of Kirkby, first to Philip of Kington and then to Thelsford Priory, Warwickshire; several parcels of land in the same place to the hospitals of St John and the Holy Trinity, Northampton; small estates in Kirkby to his uncle, Luke Mallory, and to one Alexander of Whitby; and the advowson of the chapel of Peckleton to William Motun. He was at one point attached to the retinue of Saer de Quincy, earl of Winchester, in whose service he died at Mountsorrel Castle in 1217. He married Cecilia, sister of Stephen of *Seagrave, the justiciar, and through her obtained three carrucates at Burgh, Leicestershire. Her suits for dower between 1220 and 1222 make it possible to assess Richard [iii]'s interests as being at his death the manors of Kirkby,

Welton, and Thrupp, four and a half virgates subinfeudated at Broughton Astley, and several subinfeudated estates within Kirkby. For this he answered for a half fee to the Montfort half of the earldom of Leicester, a small assessment for such a large estate.

Richard [iii] left four known sons, one of the younger of whom, Anschetil, founded yet another cadet branch of what was by now becoming a widespread family, at Octon in the East Riding of Yorkshire. The eldest son, **Thomas** [i] **Mallory** (*b.* 1201×5, *d.* in or after 1240), succeeded to Kirkby as a minor; he was in wardship to Henry of Seagrave in 1222 and had come of age by 1226, when he presented to the rectory of Kirkby. In 1234 he was involved in a plea concerning the service owed for the old Neufmarché estate of Billesley, Warwickshire, to which he apparently had some claim through his great-grandmother Agnes. Thomas was at that same time associated with the household of Simon de Montfort, but more closely with that of his uncle, Stephen of Seagrave. He was alive in 1240 but thereafter disappears; all that is known is that he was survived by his widow, Christina, and left a son and heir, **Henry Mallory** (*d.* in or before 1277). Little is known of Henry, other than that he instituted a chantry for his father's soul at the hospital chapel of Holy Trinity, Northampton, and that he attested a charter of Earl Simon de Montfort before 1265. Henry was succeeded by one **Sir Thomas** [ii] **Mallory** (*d.* in or after 1299) by 1277, who was probably (but not certainly) his brother. Thomas [ii] was the first of the Kirkby branch of the family known to have been knighted. By contrast, the Mallorys of Tachbrook and Welton were consistently knighted throughout the thirteenth century. Thomas [ii] was a household knight of Edmund, earl of Lancaster, in the early 1290s and is last found in 1299, making purchases of land in Kirkby.

The Mallory family is a singularly well-documented example of the way that a gentry family could multiply and spread in several branches over two centuries, on what was initially a small endowment in land. By 1300 six distinct and related Mallory lineages can be distinguished, settled mostly in the midlands, four of them having produced knights of the county court. The Mallorys of Kirkby, the eldest branch, are an object lesson in how this was achieved on small means: by windfall marriages, magnate patronage, and subinfeudation. It is clear that by 1300 the Mallorys of Kirkby farmed directly comparatively little land, but existed on the services and maintenance owed them. It is also instructive how the Mallorys of several generations varied their magnate allegiance from generation to generation after the mid-twelfth century.

DAVID CROUCH

Sources register of Leicester Abbey, Bodl. Oxf., MS Laud misc. 625, fols. 81v, 128r, 143r · PRO, E40/7070; C144/1901, 1972, 1996, 2036; CP 25(1)/121/7/9–11; CP 25(1)/121/9/59; JUST 1/949 m.2; DL25/2236; DL42/2 fol. 50r · *Curia regis rolls preserved in the Public Record Office* (1922–) · *Inquisitions and assessments relating to feudal aids*, 6 vols., PRO (1899–1921) · *Close rolls of the reign of Henry III*, 2, PRO (1905) · L. C. Loyd, *The origins of some Anglo-Norman families*, ed. C. T. Clay and D. C. Douglas, Harleian Society, 103 (1951), 56

Mallory, Anschetil (*d. c.*1190). *See under* Mallory family (*per. c.*1100–1300).

Mallory, George Herbert Leigh (1886–1924), mountaineer, was born on 18 June 1886 at Mobberley, Cheshire, the eldest son of Herbert Leigh Mallory (1856–1943), rector of Mobberley and later vicar of St John's, Birkenhead, and his wife, Annie Beridge Jebb. He had an elder and a younger sister and a brother, Sir Trafford Leigh Leigh-*Mallory. His father changed his surname to Leigh-Mallory in 1914. Mallory was educated at West Kirby, at Glengorse preparatory school, Eastbourne (1897–1900), and at Winchester College (1900–05). Active as a gymnast, Mallory was taken climbing in the Alps with other students by R.L.G. Irving, a Winchester schoolmaster. In 1905 he entered Magdalene College, Cambridge, where he joined the Fabian Society and the Marlowe Dramatic Club, and captained his college boat. He came under the influence of Arthur Benson, his history tutor, and Charles Sayle, a university librarian who hosted a salon for the bright and beautiful.

Contemporaries admired Mallory more for his beauty than his brain. In 1909 Lytton Strachey wrote:

> Mon dieu!—George Mallory! … He's six foot high, with the body of an athlete by Praxiteles, and a face—oh incredible—the mystery of Botticelli, the refinement and delicacy of a Chinese print, the youth and piquancy of an unimaginable English boy. (Holroyd, 205–6)

After taking a second-class degree in history, Mallory stayed in Cambridge for a year to write an essay which he later published as *Boswell the Biographer* (1912). During 1909–1910 he lived for five months at Roquebrune in the Alpes Maritimes to improve his French in preparation for a teaching career. His circle of Cambridge and Bloomsbury friends fostered many same-sex romances, and there has been some question about his sexual preference in this period. In 1909 he confessed his (unrequited) love to James Strachey (G. Mallory to Strachey, 20 Dec 1909, BL, Add. MS 60679, fol. 18).

Mallory's main passion was mountaineering in the Alps, the Lakes, and north Wales. In their memoirs Geoffrey Winthrop Young, Geoffrey Keynes, and Cottie Sanders (the novelist Ann Bridge) recall climbing with him. Mallory himself wrote little about his climbing. In 'The mountaineer as artist' he compared mountaineering to music as an aesthetic experience (*Climbers' Club Journal*, 1, 1914, 28–40). As a rock-climber he was renowned for his grace and sense of balance, but he also had a reputation for impetuosity, imprudence, and absent-mindedness. He was often argumentative, and his vigorous defence of his ideals earned him the nickname 'Sir Galahad'.

In 1910 Mallory became an assistant master at Charterhouse, Godalming, Surrey, where he taught English, history, and French, and introduced students, including Robert Graves, to mountain climbing. In 1912–13 Duncan Grant painted several nude studies of Mallory. On 29 July 1914 Mallory married (Christiana) Ruth, daughter of Hugh Thackeray Turner, an architect of Godalming. They had two daughters and a son. He was required to remain at

George Herbert Leigh Mallory (1886–1924), by Duncan Grant, 1912

Charterhouse when war came, and wrote a pamphlet, *War Work for Boys and Girls* (1915), to promote international understanding. He was later commissioned in the Royal Garrison Artillery as 2nd lieutenant in December 1915, and assigned to the 40th siege battery, where he participated in the shelling of the Somme.

Transferred to a staff position, he served as a liaison officer with the French and was promoted 1st lieutenant before being invalided home. After the war he became increasingly dissatisfied with schoolteaching and drafted an unpublished public school novel.

Geoffrey Young persuaded Mallory to join the first Everest expedition in 1921 because it would make his name and enhance his career as an educator or writer. In 1921 he explored the Tibetan side of Everest and reached the north col with Guy Henry Bullock (1887–1956) of the diplomatic service, who was a school-friend of Mallory's at Winchester, and several porters. Earlier they had glimpsed a valley on the Nepali side of Everest that Mallory named the Western Cwm. In 1922 he returned to Everest and reached 8200 metres without supplemental oxygen, saving the lives of three companions when they slipped on the descent. After George Finch's party went even higher with oxygen, Mallory led an ill-advised attempt to reach the north col after a heavy snowstorm that resulted in the deaths of seven porters in an avalanche.

Mallory lectured on Everest in Britain in 1922 and in America in 1923. The *New York Times* (18 March 1923) reported that when asked why climb Everest, Mallory replied, 'Because it's there.' This comment has been interpreted as a heroic manifesto, an exasperated evasion, or an editorial invention. Mallory's lecture notes and other news reports suggest that the phrase accurately reflects his ambiguous, sometimes mystical, view of mountaineering (Robertson, 215–20; Holzel and Salkeld, 295–8). In May 1923, he became a lecturer and assistant secretary in the Cambridge University board of extra-mural studies.

In 1924 Mallory was promoted to climbing leader on Everest when Colonel E. F. Norton unexpectedly replaced General C. G. Bruce, who had fallen ill, as overall leader. Despite a prevailing prejudice, which he had shared, against oxygen, Mallory wanted to use it after seeing the benefits in 1922, and as he became increasingly obsessed with conquering the mountain. He developed a plan to give himself the best shot at the top by using oxygen with Andrew Irvine [*see below*]. He told his wife: 'It is almost unthinkable with this plan that *I* shan't get to the top: I can't see myself coming down defeated' (to Ruth Mallory, 24 April 1924, Malory MSS). After two unsuccessful attempts without oxygen, he put his plan into action. Mallory and Irvine left their camp on the north-east ridge on 8 June 1924, and were seen momentarily through a break in the clouds by Noel Odell (1890–1987), who said they were probably on a rock outcrop known as the Second Step, below the final summit pyramid. Their location during this sighting has been the subject of debate. After they failed to return, a memorial cairn was erected at the foot of Everest, and memorial services were held at Magdalene College, Cambridge, at Merton College, Oxford, at St John's, Birkenhead, and on 17 October 1924 at St Paul's Cathedral, London. Mallory was posthumously lionized as a gallant knight and romantic hero in works ranging from schoolboy pulp to W. H. Auden and Christopher Isherwood's *Ascent of F6* (1936).

Mallory's friends wanted to believe that he reached the summit, though this remains unproven, and it is usually assumed that he did not. In 1933 Percy Wyn Harris found an ice axe on bare slabs of rock below the First Step with markings that matched those on Irvine's walking sticks. In 1975 Wang Hung-bao (*d.* 1979), a Chinese climber, found the body of an 'English dead' in old-fashioned clothing on a ledge at about 26,600 feet, also below the First Step. In 1999 an expedition dedicated to searching for Mallory and Irvine found Mallory's frozen body on a snow terrace at 27,000 feet. The body was identified by a name tag sewn into Mallory's clothing. After a brief ceremony, Mallory's body was reburied in the snow on 1 May 1999.

Andrew Comyn Irvine (1902–1924), mountaineer, was born at 56 Park Road South, Birkenhead, Cheshire, on 8 April 1902, the second son and third of six children of William Fergusson Irvine (1869–1962), a merchant trading with Africa and a distinguished Cheshire antiquary, and his wife, Lilian Davies-Colley (*d.* 1950), daughter of

Thomas Charles Davies-Colley, a Manchester solicitor. He had four brothers and a sister. He was educated at Birkenhead preparatory school, Shrewsbury School, and Merton College, Oxford, where he matriculated on 24 January 1922 to study engineering. He was tall and stout, with a muscular physique, and was nicknamed Sandy because of his blonde hair and fair complexion. He was known as a powerful oarsman at Shrewsbury and Oxford, and gained his blue as a freshman in 1922, when he rowed no. 2 against Cambridge. He was taught to ski by Arnold Lunn and he won several slalom races in the Alps. In 1923 he joined a sledging party to Spitsbergen with Noel Odell, who recommended him for Everest in 1924. Despite Irvine's inexperience as a climber, Mallory appears to have chosen him as his partner on Everest because he valued his mechanical ability with the unreliable oxygen apparatus, admired his strength and stamina, and may have seen him as a protégé. A memorial to him, by Eric Gill, was placed in Merton College grove. Irvine's Everest diaries were published in 1979.   PETER H. HANSEN

Sources D. Robertson, *George Mallory* (1969) · T. Holzel and A. Salkeld, *The mystery of Mallory and Irvine*, rev. edn (1996) · Magd. Cam., Mallory MSS · RGS · W. Unsworth, *Everest*, another edn (1991) · D. Pye, *George Leigh Mallory* (1927) · *The Times* (21 June 1924) · *The Nation* (5 July 1924) · *Alpine Journal*, 36 (1924), 381–5 · D. Green, *Mallory of Everest* (1990) · *The Irvine diaries: Andrew Irvine and the enigma of Everest*, 1924, ed. H. Carr (1979) · G. L. Keynes, *The gates of memory* (1981) · R. Graves, *Goodbye to all that* (1929) · M. Holroyd, *Lytton Strachey: a new biography* (1994) · D. Newsome, *On the edge of paradise: A. C. Benson, the diarist* (1980) · Burke, *Gen. GB* (1937) [Leigh-Mallory of Mobberley] · *Winchester College, 1867–1920* (1923) · Oxford University matriculation register, U. Oxf. [Andrew Irvine] · *WWW*, 1961–70 [W. F. Irvine] · b. cert. [Andrew Irvine] · *The Age* [Melbourne] (21 May 1995) · *The Times* (23 May 1995) · *The Australian Way* (Nov 1995), 53–7 · *Daily Telegraph* (4 May 1999) · *CGPLA Eng. & Wales* (1924)
Archives Magd. Cam. · RGS, Everest expedition archives | Alpine Club, London, Geoffrey Winthrop Young MSS · BL, Strachey MSS · CUL, Hugh Wilson MSS · Magd. Cam., A. C. Benson diaries · Merton Oxf., Irvine diary · Ransom HRC, Ann Bridge (1889–1974), Mary Dolling Sanders O'Malley MSS |FILM BFI NFTVA, 'Lost on Everest: the search for Mallory and Irvine', BBC, 21 Oct 1999 · BFI NFTVA, documentary footage · Cary Memorial Library, Lexington, Massachusetts, 'Everest: the mystery of Mallory and Irvine', 1987
Likenesses D. Grant, oil on panel, 1912, NPG [*see illus.*] · S. Bussy, pastel drawing, NPG · photographs, repro. in Robertson, *George Mallory* · photographs, repro. in Holzel and Salkeld, *Mystery of Mallory and Irvine* · photographs, repro. in Green, *Mallory of Everest*
Wealth at death £1706 17s. 6d.: probate, 17 Dec 1924, *CGPLA Eng. & Wales*

Mallory, Henry (*d.* in or before **1277**). *See under* Mallory family (*per. c.*1100–1300).

Mallory, Richard (*d. c.***1160**). *See under* Mallory family (*per. c.*1100–1300).

Mallory, Richard (*d.* before **1175**). *See under* Mallory family (*per. c.*1100–1300).

Mallory, Richard (*d.* **1217**). *See under* Mallory family (*per. c.*1100–1300).

Mallory, Thomas (*b.* 1201x5, *d.* in or after **1240**). *See under* Mallory family (*per. c.*1100–1300).

Mallory, Sir Thomas (*d.* in or after **1299**). *See under* Mallory family (*per. c.*1100–1300).

Mallory, Thomas (**1604/5–1671**), Church of England clergyman, was the son of Thomas Mallory of Davenham, Cheshire (*d.* 1644), dean of Chester, and his wife Elizabeth, daughter of Richard *Vaughan (*c.*1553–1607), bishop of London. He matriculated at New College, Oxford, on 15 October 1624 aged nineteen, graduated BA on 7 May 1628, and proceeded MA on 17 January 1632. In 1635, on the death of William Forster, he was presented by Richard Mallory of Mobberley and William Forster by reason of a grant from the dean (his father) and chapter of Chester, to the church of Northenden, Cheshire. However, doubts about the validity of the presentation seem to have given rise to his re-presentation by the king on 6 August 1635. It was perhaps about this time that Mallory married his first wife. Jane Mallory, however, died very young and was buried at Northenden on 12 February 1639; Thomas must have remarried shortly afterwards, for in 1644 his second wife, Mary, was reported to be looking after six of his children, for whom £6 19s. 9d. was provided by the committee for sequestrations. Mallory later claimed to have been ejected by Sir William Brereton in 1642. A Henry Root was in possession by 18 May 1643.

Mallory was evidently a committed and active royalist. Early in the civil war, as his son John informed John Walker, Mallory was imprisoned for a year at Stafford, but was released in exchange for a notable parliamentarian. From here, reports Walker, he travelled to Oxford, where he often preached before Charles I, and from there he repaired to Lichfield as chaplain to Sir Harvey Bagot, governor of the garrison. When the town fell Mallory returned to Northenden, joining the band of royalists who sought to defend Wythenshaw Hall, and effecting a dramatic escape before besieging troops under the command of Colonel Robert Dukinfeld stormed the building on 25 February 1644. In August the house and glebe at Northenden were sequestered.

Mallory was listed in May 1648 as a delinquent parson, still under sequestration, but in that month it was reported that the estate of his father the dean, who had died in April 1644, had been restored to the use of his mother, Elizabeth. It was at her house at Davenham, Cheshire, in July 1648, that the marriage of the Revd Henry Newcome took place, and Thomas probably officiated. Later Mallory served Norton in Moors, near Stoke upon Trent; his second wife, Mary, was buried at Astbury, just across the Cheshire border, on 26 June 1649. In 1651 Mallory gained a title to the rectory of Eccleston, Lancashire, when the incumbent, Edward Gee, signatory from Eccleston of the *Harmonious Consent* of the Lancashire preachers in 1648, was in prison. It is unclear whether Mallory actually entered this living during the Commonwealth, for Gee was released and in occupation before 27 May 1653. Gee died, however, on 27 May 1660, and Mallory was instituted to the rectory on 6 September on the presentation of the king. The next year he was readmitted to the rectory of Northenden, and on 11 April 1662, a government dispensation was granted to Mallory to hold both rectories, despite the distance of more than 30 miles between them.

Mallory evidently felt that his record warranted the gratitude of the restored house of Stuart. In his petition for the rectory of Houghton, Durham (endorsed on 9 July 1660), he claimed to have 'Served the late King in the war, and his Majesty in the late abortive attempt of the Cheshire gentlemen', that is, that he had been active under Sir George Booth in the summer of 1659 (*CSP dom.*, 1660–61, 112). The bid for Houghton was rejected, and his petition of 13 July for the prebend of Stillington, York, also failed, for on 30 July Henry Bridgeman was presented to that dignity. However, in time Mallory received his reward. On 1 December 1660 he was made a DD by the University of Oxford. On 31 July 1661 he was collated to a canonry of Chester, and on 19 September he was admitted to the prebend of Wolvey, in Lichfield.

Mallory's pastoral efforts did not please everyone. Newcome recalled his 'learned unprofitable sermon to the generality of people' on 9 November 1662, though it might have been worse: 'If the shepherd fed not as desired, yet the watchman smote not as was feared' (*Diary*, 138). Such remarks may reflect the diarist's anxieties in the aftermath of the Bartholomew purge; Newcome later suggested that Mallory had influence with the bishop of Chester. Mallory was still rector when he died in 1671 at nearby Brindle. He was buried at Eccleston on 8 September. STEPHEN WRIGHT

Sources Walker rev. · J. P. Earwaker, *East Cheshire: past and present, or, A history of the hundred of Macclesfield*, 2 vols. (1877–80) · E. Baines and W. R. Whatton, *The history of the county palatine and duchy of Lancaster*, new edn, ed. J. Croston and others, 4 (1891) · Wood, *Ath. Oxon.*, new edn · Venn, *Alum. Cant.* · *Cheshire Sheaf*, 1 (1878) · M. A. E. Green, ed., *Calendar of the proceedings of the committee for compounding … 1643–1660*, 5 vols., PRO (1889–92) · *The diary of the Rev. Henry Newcome, from September 30, 1661, to September 29, 1663*, ed. T. Heywood, Chetham Society, 18 (1849) · *The autobiography of Henry Newcome*, ed. R. Parkinson, 2 vols., Chetham Society, 26–7 (1852) · *Fasti Angl., 1541–1857*, [York] · *Fasti Angl.* (Hardy), vol. 1 · J. S. Morrill, *Cheshire, 1630–1660: county government and society during the English revolution* (1974) · I. M. Green, *The re-establishment of the Church of England, 1660–63* (1978) · *CSP dom.*, 1660–61 · *VCH Lancashire*, vol. 6

Mallory, Thomas (*d.* **1689**), clergyman and ejected minister, was a native of Northamptonshire, although his date of birth and parents are unknown; he is not to be confused with the royalist Cheshire clergyman of the same name. Having matriculated as a sizar from St Catharine's College, Cambridge, at Lent 1630, he graduated BA in 1634 and proceeded MA in 1637. He was ordained priest in the diocese of Peterborough on 9 June 1639.

Little is known of Mallory's wife, other than her likely name, Frances, and the fact that she predeceased her husband, dying in or before January 1669. The couple had, at the least, a son and six daughters, of whom the eldest, Frances, was baptized at St Nicholas, Deptford, on 19 July 1644, not long after her father's nomination on 1 February as vicar of that parish. On 3 August 1645 Bulstrode Whitelocke 'tooke in short hand a Sermon of Mr Mallery att

Deptford & repeated it to his family this Sabbath day' (*Diary of Bulstrode Whitelocke*, 177). Mallory's church politics were not to the taste of John Evelyn, but the diarist recorded in 1653 that though the present incumbent was 'somewhat of the Independent, yet he ordinarily preached sound doctrine, and was a peacable man; which was an extraordinary felicity in this age' (*Diary of John Evelyn*, 2.65). On 6 August 1657, he noted, Mallory 'declaimed against the folly of a sort of enthusiasts and desperate zealots, called the Fifth Monarchy Men, pretending to set up the kingdom of Christ with the sword' (ibid., 2.122). On 29 September 1657 Mallory was named an assistant to the Kent commission into the ministry. Evelyn attended his farewell sermon at Deptford on 17 January 1659. Soon afterwards, Mallory took up a lectureship at St Michael, Crooked Lane, London, where he preached, probably on Sunday afternoons, for a period of two years from 25 March 1659.

In a 1660 list of London congregational ministers Mallory is given as also preaching at St James's, Duke's Place. His sermon, 'How may we have suitable conceptions of God in duty?', was published by Samuel Annesley in *The Morning-Exercise at Cripple-Gate*. Mallory was one of twenty-five signatories of *The renuntiation and declaration of the ministers of congregational churches and public preachers of the same judgment*, a document issued in order to dissociate those churches from the Venner rising in January 1661. Ejected from his lectureship some time later, on 24 March 1662, Mallory accompanied Bulstrode Whitelocke and Dr John Goodwin to the house of the lord chancellor, where it was reported that Clarendon:

> discoursed very freely about liberty of Conscience & professed himselfe a great friend to it, & that he would bring the K[ing] to assure it to them … they thought their desires in this point to be accomplished … [but] after an hours discourse … he dismissed them, & proved afterwards the greatest ennemy that could be to them & their desires. (*Diary of Bulstrode Whitelocke*, 645)

In 1669 Mallory was a signatory of a preface to *Death and Life* by the Amsterdam preacher Samuel Malbon, whose 'name is sweet and precious amongst those saints and people to whom he preaches', together with William Greenhill, Joseph Caryl, and Richard Lawrence, a grouping which testifies to his continuing congregational outlook. He died, probably in London, in January 1689.

STEPHEN WRIGHT

Sources *Calamy rev.* • Venn, *Alum. Cant.* • E. Calamy, *A continuation of the account of the ministers … who were ejected and silenced after the Restoration in 1660*, 2 vols. (1727) • *The diary of Bulstrode Whitelocke, 1605–1675*, ed. R. Spalding, British Academy, Records of Social and Economic History, new ser., 13 (1990) • *The diary of John Evelyn*, ed. A. Dobson, 3 vols. (1906) • R. Tudur Jones, *Congregationalism in England, 1662–1962* (1962) • J. Nichols, ed., *The morning exercises at Cripplegate, St Giles in the Fields and in Southwark*, 5th edn, 1 (1844) • C. H. Fielding, *The records of Rochester* (1910) • will, PRO, PROB 11/329/20

Wealth at death see will, PRO, PROB 11/329/20

Mallory, Sir Trafford Leigh Leigh- (1892–1944), air force officer, was born at Mobberley, near Knutsford, Cheshire, on 11 July 1892, the youngest of the two sons and two daughters of Herbert Leigh Mallory (1856–1943), rector of

Mobberley and later a canon of Chester Cathedral, and his wife, Annie Beridge (b. 1862), the daughter of the Revd John Beridge Jebb, rector of Brampton. His father hyphenated his surname in 1914. Trafford followed his example, but his brother, George Herbert Leigh *Mallory, who died while attempting to climb Mount Everest in June 1924, did not.

Leigh-Mallory was educated at St Leonards, Sussex (1902–6), Haileybury College (1906–11), and Magdalene College, Cambridge (1911–14), where he took history and law. In August 1914 he was commissioned as a second lieutenant in the 4th battalion of the Lancashire Fusiliers, but he remained in England until April 1915, when he went to France with the 3rd battalion of the South Lancashire regiment. He was wounded in June and returned to England. On 18 August he married Doris Jean, the second of the three daughters of Edmund Stratton Sawyer of Upper Norwood, Middlesex, in All Saints' Church, Upper Norwood, his father officiating. They had one son and one daughter.

In January 1916 Leigh-Mallory transferred to the Royal Flying Corps. He qualified as a pilot in June, was promoted lieutenant, joined 7 squadron on the western front in July, and then transferred to 5 squadron in August. He was promoted captain and appointed a flight commander in November. Both were corps squadrons, equipped with the slow but stable BE 2c two-seat biplane and employed close to trench lines to direct artillery fire, take photographs, and drop bombs. Although valuable and dangerous, the work was unglamorous compared with that of faster, better-armed aeroplanes of army squadrons, which provided escorts, carried out long-distance reconnaissances, and, unlike corps machines, could engage in aerial combat with some hope of success.

Leigh-Mallory returned to England in April 1917, was promoted major, and commanded 15 (reserve) squadron until November, when he returned to corps duties on the western front in command of 8 squadron, equipped with a somewhat less vulnerable two-seater, the Armstrong Whitworth FK 8. His squadron was hard worked after March 1918 (when the stalemate of trench war ended) in close support of ground forces until the November armistice. His energy and efficiency earned respect but not admiration: 'a proper little Charlie Chaplin, with turned-out toes and breeches like butterflies' (Dunn, 41) was the verdict of one observer. His brother, George, was little kinder: 'he affects magnificence, rushing about in a splendid Crossley car and giving orders with the curt assurance of an Alexander the Great, or Lord Northcliffe or Rockefeller' (ibid., 45–6). His merits were nevertheless recognized by the award of a DSO on 1 January 1919.

Leigh-Mallory was granted a permanent commission as a squadron leader in August 1919. He found his niche in the School of Army Co-operation at Old Sarum, Wiltshire (1921–3), to which he gladly returned as commanding officer (1927–9), followed by equally congenial service as an instructor at the Army Staff College, Camberley (1930–31). Sadly, he had little opportunity in later years to pursue his undoubted talent for such work. Having been promoted wing commander in January 1925, he attended the RAF Staff College, Andover, in 1925–6. He was promoted group captain in January 1932 and sent to Geneva as air adviser to the disarmament conference in 1932–3. He studied at the Imperial Defence College in 1934 and commanded a flying training school at Digby, Lincolnshire, until December 1935, when he went to Iraq as senior air staff officer at command headquarters; he was promoted air commodore in January 1936. Leigh-Mallory remained in Iraq until December 1937, when he was appointed to command 12 group (responsible for defending the midlands and East Anglia from a headquarters at Watnall, Nottinghamshire) in Fighter Command, even though he had no experience of fighter operations or the organization of an air defence system. He was promoted air vice-marshal in November 1938.

Leigh-Mallory's conduct of pre-war exercises was criticized by Sir Hugh Dowding (head of Fighter Command, at Bentley Priory in Stanmore, Middlesex) and by Keith Park (Dowding's senior air staff officer). In October 1938, for example, Dowding thought he showed 'a misconception of the basic ideas of fighter defence' (Orange, *Park*, 78), and a year later he asked him 'to remember that Fighter Command has to operate as a whole' (ibid., 80).

During the battle of Britain (July–October 1940) Leigh-Mallory and Park (now head of 11 group, responsible for the defence of London and south-east England, at Hillingdon House in Uxbridge, Middlesex) differed sharply over the conduct of operations. Leigh-Mallory resented his place in the rear, behind the front line, and at the end of August he found in the 'big wing' notions of Douglas Bader, one of his squadron leaders, a means of taking a direct part in the battle. However, Park's airfields were left unguarded and his ground controllers were confused by the wing's unexpected arrival in the battle area. Wings took a long time to assemble, using up fuel that was particularly precious to short-range fighters. Once assembled, it proved difficult in cloudy conditions to keep thirty to fifty fighters together *en route* for an interception. Nevertheless, the confident assertions of Leigh-Mallory and his allies, together with extravagant victory claims, enabled them to win the ensuing debate, and in December 1940 Leigh-Mallory replaced Park as head of 11 group. The verdict of most post-war historians and pilots who fought in the battle strongly supports the defensive strategy devised by Dowding and implemented by Park.

An alarming instance of Leigh-Mallory's incompetence was seen on 29 January 1941, when he decided to conduct a paper exercise using the circumstances of an actual attack in September 1940. His intention was to prove correct his opinion on the use of large formations. The exercise was carefully set up and Leigh-Mallory totally mismanaged it. When his several mistakes were pointed out to him, he replied that next time he would do better.

During 1941, instead of intensive combat training—which had been necessarily neglected during the crises of 1940—Sholto Douglas (who had replaced Dowding as head of Fighter Command in November 1940) and Leigh-

Mallory employed their inexperienced pilots on offensive operations across the channel. More pilots were lost—and lost for no tangible advantage—in that year than in the battle of Britain. Before the German assault on the Soviet Union in June, these operations were actually *welcomed* by the Luftwaffe because they offered a chance to join battle in favourable conditions. After June not a single German aircraft was diverted from the Russian front to counter Fighter Command's efforts. Worse still, by accepting victory claims even more inflated than in 1940, Douglas and Leigh-Mallory were encouraged to persist in their offensive and to resist the release of squadrons for service overseas. In the second half of 1941, seventy-five day fighter squadrons were held in England while the Middle East and the Far East had to manage with only thirty-four between them, many of which were equipped with obsolete aircraft.

Leigh-Mallory became head of Fighter Command in November 1942 and was promoted air marshal in December. In November 1943 he was confirmed by the combined chiefs of staff as commander of the proposed allied expeditionary air force (AEAF) to support operation Overlord, the campaign to liberate occupied Europe. Promotion to air chief marshal followed in January 1944.

To paraphrase what his brother, George, said about Mount Everest, Leigh-Mallory was appointed because he was there. Late in 1943, British and American airmen of greater ability, more varied experience, and hard-won mutual respect were still active in the Mediterranean. In January 1944, however, they returned in triumph to England with Eisenhower, appointed supreme allied commander of Overlord. They were reluctant to accept Leigh-Mallory as one of themselves even before they discovered that he was personally uncongenial and professionally unimpressive. Arthur Tedder, Eisenhower's deputy, was overall air commander; Arthur Coningham and Lewis Brereton (later, Hoyt Vandenberg) commanded the tactical air forces, Arthur Harris (the only 'outsider' they recognized) and Carl Spaatz commanded the strategic air forces, Roderic Hill commanded 'the air defence of Great Britain' (a title briefly inflicted upon Fighter Command), and Hugh Saunders was head of 11 group.

Leigh-Mallory's awkward position, as fifth wheel on the coach, and his unpopularity with influential airmen, British and American, explain his eager acceptance in August 1944 of an offer from Lord Louis Mountbatten, supreme allied commander in south-east Asia, that he go to India as air commander. But American objections to a British airman were not withdrawn until mid-September, and he remained in France until 15 October. After a month's leave he left Northolt for India in an Avro York at about 9 a.m. on 14 November 1944. Shortly after midday it struck a mountain ridge some 15 miles east of Grenoble in south-east France and all ten persons aboard (including his wife) were killed. A court of inquiry found that the weather had been very poor on the day of the accident, but that Leigh-Mallory 'was determined to leave and he is known to be a man of forceful personality.' Sir Charles Portal, chief of the air staff, added that Leigh-Mallory had no need for such haste. Tragically, 'the desire to arrive in India on schedule with his "own" aircraft and crew overrode prudence and resulted in this disaster' (PRO, AIR 2/10593).

Leigh-Mallory was a short, burly man with a full head of neatly disciplined dark-brown hair and a trim moustache. He was appointed CB in July 1940 and knighted (KCB) in January 1943.   VINCENT ORANGE

Sources B. N. Dunn, *Big wing: the biography of Air Chief Marshal Sir Trafford Leigh-Mallory* (1992) · V. Orange, *Park* (1984) · V. Orange, *Coningham* (1990); American edn (Washington, DC, 1992) · J. Terraine, *The right of the line: the Royal Air Force in the European war, 1939–1945* (1985) · R. G. Davis, *Carl A. Spaatz and the air war in Europe* (1993) · P. Meilinger, *Hoyt S. Vandenberg* (1989) · J. P. Ray, *The Battle of Britain: new perspectives* (1994) · J. Foreman, *Air war, 1941* (1994) · C. D'Este, *Decision in Normandy* (1984) · R. A. Hough and D. Richards, *The battle of Britain* (1990) · 'The Death of ACM Leigh-Mallory', *After the Battle*, 39 (1983), 1–25 · *After the Battle*, 50 (1985), 4 · *CGPLA Eng. & Wales* (1945) · PRO, AIR 2/10593
Archives Royal Air Force Museum, Hendon, papers | Christ Church Oxf., Portal MSS · L. Cong., Spaatz–Vandenberg MSS
Likenesses E. Kennington, pastel drawing, 1942, IWM · W. Dring, pastel drawing, Fighter Command HQ, Bentley Priory, Stanmore · Y. Jenson, oils, Royal Air Force Museum, Hendon · photograph, Hult. Arch. · photographs, repro. in Dunn, *Big wing*
Wealth at death £2862 1s. 11d.: administration with will, 4 Oct 1945, *CGPLA Eng. & Wales*

Mallory, William (d. c.1202). *See under* Mallory family (*per.* c.1100–1300).

Mallowan, Sir Max Edgar Lucien (1904–1978), archaeologist, was born on 6 May 1904 in London, the eldest of the three sons (there were no daughters) of Frederick Mallowan, a former officer in the Austrian horse artillery and in Britain a quality arbitrator, and his wife, Marguerite Duvivier, of Paris, poet. He records in *Mallowan's Memoirs* (1977) that at little more than four years of age he excavated Victorian china sherds from deep in 'a jet black soil' in Bedford Gardens, Kensington, London. Their photograph he kept all his life. He was educated at Lancing College, where he was a contemporary of Tom Driberg, Roger Fulford, Hugh Molson, Humphrey Trevelyan, and Evelyn Waugh. At New College, Oxford, he obtained a fourth class in classical honour moderations in 1923 and a third in *literae humaniores* in 1925. Thanks to a chance meeting just after his final examinations when he said he feared he might 'be condemned to the Indian Civil Service', he was, with the recommendation of the warden, H. A. L. Fisher, accepted by C. Leonard Woolley as an assistant at Ur of the Chaldees. It was while working for Woolley at Ur that he met Agatha Mary Clarissa *Christie, whom he married in 1930, a marriage of true minds that continued until her death in 1976.

Except for the years 1940–45, when he served in the Royal Air Force Volunteer Reserve as a liaison officer with allied forces and a civilian affairs officer in north Africa, the rest of Mallowan's life was devoted to 'filling in the blank pages of history', to quote his own words—first as an assistant, soon as a leader of expeditions, finally in writing and academic and administrative posts. He came to rank with Woolley and Seton Lloyd as a pioneer whose work formed the frame on which all subsequent Mesopotamian archaeology hung, and was himself very conscious of his place in a long tradition, taking much pleasure for instance in the fact that British School of Archaeology in Iraq, which he was largely responsible for reactivating after the war of 1939–45, could resume at Nimrud 'the work which Austen Layard was obliged to abandon at the outbreak of the Crimean War'.

After five years as assistant to Woolley and a spell with Reginald Campbell Thompson, under whom he made a markedly determined 21 metre-deep shaft to virgin soil through the Quyunjik mound at Nineveh, he became field director in a long series of expeditions jointly sponsored by the British Museum and the British School of Archaeology in Iraq, then recently founded with a legacy from Gertrude Bell. At twenty-eight his discoveries at Arpachiyah, showed the prehistoric villager to have been artistic, ingenious, and energetic, as well as a user of cream-bowls, in Mallowan's words, 'exactly similar to the metal milk cans used in the village of Arpachiyah today'. His writing constantly reflected this interest in the humanity revealed by the artefacts he unearthed.

From Arpachiyah Mallowan moved to north Syria, first to Chagar Bazar, then in 1937 to Tell Brak, selected for excavation after a particularly methodical survey. There he discovered the third-millennium shrines called the Eye Temple and the Palace of Naram-Sin.

In 1947 Mallowan returned to Iraq as director of the British School and soon began his major work at Nimrud, a task that was carried on for twelve years. The accumulated art treasures, inscribed texts, and architectural remains discovered in this period formed a prodigious addition to knowledge of the past and his account, *Nimrud and its Remains* (2 vols., 1966), was hailed as a monumental work 'rivalling the great classics of its nineteenth-century predecessors' (Lloyd).

Nimrud was the crown of his work in the field. In 1962 while writing the book he was elected a fellow of All Souls College, Oxford (he became an emeritus fellow in 1976), and gave up the chair in western Asiatic archaeology at London University which he had accepted in 1947. This latter period of his life was busy in the extreme, and thick with honours. He was fellow of the Society of Antiquaries and became fellow of the British Academy in 1954. He was, among other things, president of the British Institute of Persian Studies (1961), vice-president of the British Academy (1961–2), and member of the Académie Française des Inscriptions et Belles-Lettres (1964). He was appointed CBE in 1960 and knighted in 1968. He was a trustee of the British Museum (1973–8), editor of *Iraq* (1948–71), advisory editor of *Antiquity*, and editor of the Penguin Books Near Eastern and Western Asiatic series (1948–65). He was noted, too, for never failing to answer requests for help from students or colleagues. The busy tenor of those days can be appreciated in Professor Glyn Daniel's recollection of him after a London meeting hailing a taxi and saying simply 'Wallingford'.

In 1977 Mallowan remarried; his second wife was Barbara, daughter of Captain R. F. Parker RN; she had been his assistant in Iraq. He died on 19 August 1978 at the home he had bought with his first wife in 1939, Greenway House, Churston Ferrars, Devon, whose trees and rare garden were an abiding interest.

Sources M. Mallowan, *Mallowan's memoirs* (1977) · M. Mallowan, *Twenty-five years of Mesopotamian discovery, 1932–1956* (1956) · S. Lloyd, *Foundations in the dust: the story of Mesopotamian exploration* (1980) · private information (1986) · D. Oates, 'Max Edgar Lucien Mallowan, 1904–1978', *PBA*, 76 (1990), 499–511 · *CGPLA Eng. & Wales* (1978) · *DNB*
Archives Bodl. Oxf., letters to O. G. S. Crawford · Bodl. Oxf., corresp. with J. L. Myers · U. Glas., corresp. with William Collins and Son
Likenesses W. Stoneman, photograph, 1946, NPG · two photographs, 1974–6, Hult. Arch. · A. Jourdan, photograph, repro. in Oates, 'Max Edgar Lucien Mallowan', facing p. 501
Wealth at death £524,054: probate, 1 Nov 1978, *CGPLA Eng. & Wales*

Malmesbury. For this title name *see* Wharton, Thomas, first marquess of Wharton, first marquess of Malmesbury, and first marquess of Catherlough (1648–1715); Harris, James, first earl of Malmesbury (1746–1820); Harris, James Howard, third earl of Malmesbury (1807–1889).

Malmesbury, William of (*b. c.*1090, *d.* in or after 1142), historian, man of letters, and Benedictine monk, spent his whole life from boyhood as a monk of his order's ancient foundation at Malmesbury.

The monk of Malmesbury Almost all that is known of William of Malmesbury derives from his own writings; even the dates of his birth and death are not easily determined. In his commentary on Lamentations, written soon after 1135, William describes himself as *quadrigenarius*. If this means 'in my forties' rather than 'forty', it would allow him to have been born as early as the late 1080s, to have witnessed and remembered a local 'miracle' which occurred before 1096, and to be of sufficiently mature years when he attracted royal recognition and began to write his major historical works, between 1100 and 1118. He was still alive late in 1142, when his *Historia novella* terminates. Earlier he had said that he intended to chronicle contemporary history as long as life remained to him, and this statement, and the work's abrupt ending, suggest that it was broken off by his death. Although he nowhere says so, he was clearly brought up not far from Malmesbury. 'The blood of two races'—Norman and English—was mingled in William, and that is all he has to say of his parentage and family. His father may have been the Norman partner and was certainly a man of means. William says that his father encouraged his youthful studies, meaning perhaps that he financed private tuition for his son in the first instance.

Whether William studied later on at Malmesbury or another religious house, he does not say. Malmesbury seems unlikely, since William is dismissive of learning there before the abbacy of **Godfrey of Jumièges** (*d. c.*1106). According to William, Godfrey had earlier been a monk of Jumièges, which would suggest that he was Norman. But the matter is complicated. The *Liber Eliensis* describes him as a local monk who became proctor at Ely

following the death of Abbot Theodwin *c.*1075–6. This position he filled with ability for seven or eight years until 1082, obtaining from William I a confirmation of the abbey's liberties. The *Liber* then has him transferred to Malmesbury at the end of this term. But Malmesbury records make it certain that he only became abbot there between 1087 and January 1091. It is therefore possible, either that he came to Ely from Jumièges, perhaps in the company of Theodwin who certainly was a monk of that place, or that he moved from Ely to Jumièges for a few years after 1082, moving on to Malmesbury from there. The former would be the more usual pattern.

At Malmesbury, Godfrey was a vigorous reformer of monastic life and learning: he adorned the church as much as limited resources would permit, and laid the foundations of a library; William describes how the monks, scarcely able to stammer their way through texts in the vernacular, now became competent in Latin. The monastery's reputation grew throughout England, and miracles occurred at its shrine of St Aldhelm. Godfrey died about 1106. William describes him as a man of courteous manners and temperate life, whose abbacy was sullied only by his stripping the treasures of the monastery to pay the tax imposed by William Rufus on the occasion of the mortgage of Normandy by Duke Robert. Tanner supposed Godfrey to have been the author of a chronicle in British Library, Cotton MS Vespasian D.iv (fifteenth century), but this is nothing other than part of the annals of Alfred of Beverley (*fl.* 1143), itself almost entirely based on the *Historia regum Britanniae* of Geoffrey of Monmouth (*d.* 1155). The name Godfridus de Malvesbery in the manuscript is presumably that of an owner, not of the writer.

The scholar and his outlook William was a monk at Malmesbury under Godfrey, and assisted the abbot in building up its library. He gives a valuable outline of his own course of studies:

> I studied many kinds of literature, though in different degrees. To logic, the armourer of speech, I no more than lent an ear. Physic, which cures the sick body, I went deeper into. As for ethics, I explored parts in depth, revering its high status as a subject inherently accessible to the student and able to form good character; in particular I studied history, which adds flavour to moral instruction by imparting a pleasurable knowledge of past events, spurring the reader by the accumulation of examples to follow the good and shun the bad. (Malmesbury, *De gestis regum*, 2, prologue)

This is the programme ascribed to Plato by St Augustine, standard in the West until superseded by the fourfold 'Aristotelian' scheme in the twelfth century. It was therefore rather old-fashioned by William's time. One area within it, logic, had indeed become western Europe's new intellectual obsession, but even that was not one of William's major interests; he was not being overly modest in describing his acquaintance with it as passing.

Like Bede (*d.* 735), his great hero and exemplar, William had no career to speak of. He entered Malmesbury Abbey perhaps as a child, certainly no more than a teenager, and there spent the rest of his life. By the 1120s he was cantor (precentor), in charge of the liturgy as well as effectively librarian. Further promotion he apparently shunned; in

1140 he was offered and refused the abbacy: 'Unless self-love deceives me', he wrote soon after, 'I have proved myself a man of ingenuous mind, in that I gave place to a comrade in the matter of the abbot's office, which I might easily have obtained for myself, more than once' (Leland, *De rebus Britannicis*, 3.272). He represented his abbey at councils held at Winchester in 1139 and 1141, and that is the sum total of his known public activity. As far as is known, only one person outside the abbey wrote about William during his lifetime: Robert of Cricklade (*d.* 1174), canon of Cirencester, who praises him as a writer of devotional works.

The writing of history It is not for his uneventful life, then, that William is remembered, but for his scholarship. Of the genesis of his historical writing he himself says:

> After I had spent a good deal of my own money on getting together a library of foreign historians, I proceeded in my leisure moments to inquire if anything could be discovered concerning England worth the attention of posterity. Not content with ancient works, I began to get the itch to write myself, not to show off my more or less non-existent erudition but in order to bring forcibly into the light things lost in the rubbish-heap of the past. Feeling an aversion to fleeting opinion, I collected chronicles from far and wide—almost, I confess, to no purpose: for when I had gone through them all I remained ignorant, not finding anything to read before I ceased to feel the urge to read it.
> (Malmesbury, *De gestis regum*, 2, prologue)

This suggests that he was self-motivated, but there was more to it than that. Some time before her death in 1118 Queen Matilda visited Malmesbury, and while there asked for a written account of the connection between the English royal family and the abbey's founder St Aldhelm (*d.* 709/10). This was the genesis of what was to be William's most popular and influential work, the *Gesta regum Anglorum*, a full-scale history of England from the death of Bede in 735 until his own day. He says that some of it was written before the queen's death; thereafter he put it aside until the urging of friends caused him to begin again. It was completed *c.*1125–6, but until at least 1134 William continued to revise it spasmodically, mainly to improve it stylistically, with one notable exception. Shortly after the last date he produced a version that incorporated substantial portions from another of his historical works written in the meantime, *De antiquitate Glastonie ecclesie*. This work of local history had been commissioned by the monastic community there, and presumably the version of the *Gesta regum* that included so much of it was specially designed for the same audience. But almost simultaneously William produced what he may have seen as the 'final' version of the *Gesta regum* for a wider audience, with the Glastonbury material pruned back again, and some revisions of judgement in the direction of greater prudence and moderation.

Queen Matilda may have encouraged William to embark on such an ambitious project because he was already active as a historian, engaged on his earliest known work, a remarkable version of the *Liber pontificalis*, the history of the popes, which was finished soon after 1119.

Throughout the decade *c.*1125–35 William was astonishingly prolific as a historian, especially considering how little time was available to a Benedictine monk for such activity. The *Gesta regum* was mainly concerned with secular political history, but as it neared completion William began work on a companion piece of similar scale, the *Gesta pontificum Anglorum*, a church history of England. This too was finished *c.*1125 and revised at intervals over the next decade. As if this were not enough, William visited Glastonbury soon after 1129, and there wrote first the lives of its local saints, Patrick, Dunstan, Indract, and Benignus, and then his famous historical monograph, the *De antiquitate Glastonie ecclesie*. The honesty about the abbey's claims to great antiquity displayed in this work did not satisfy the local monks, and it survives today only in a heavily revised form. Some time between *c.*1125 and 1142 William wrote the life of St Wulfstan for the monks of Worcester.

Travelling and researching All this historical activity must have necessitated some relaxation of the Benedictine rule. There was not merely the time and labour of writing. William had to conduct research, to read and transcribe books and documents at religious houses up and down the country. He was probably at Canterbury (both Christ Church and St Augustine's), Glastonbury, and Worcester more than once; otherwise he records visits to St Frideswide's, Oxford, Thorney, St Ives, Bury St Edmunds, Rochester, Sherborne, Crowland, Hereford, York, Carlisle, Shaftesbury, Bath, Wareham, Corfe, Gloucester, Bangor, Coventry, Winchester, Milton Abbas, and perhaps Tavistock. There is a strong possibility that he crossed the channel into Normandy. William is reticent about his circle of acquaintance, but his travels and historical activity must have brought him friendships, and some can be inferred: Eadmer (*d. c.*1126) and Alexander, monks of Canterbury and disciples of St Anselm (*d.* 1109), John, monk and chronicler at Worcester (*d. c.*1140), and Nicholas, the prior there, Walcher, prior of Malvern (*d.* 1135), interested in astronomy, Faricius, abbot of Abingdon (*d.* 1117), formerly a monk of Malmesbury and biographer of its patron St Aldhelm.

It seems inconceivable that William did not hold conversations with the other great contemporary historian Orderic Vitalis (*d.* 1142), monk of St Evroult, either in Normandy or England; there is too much overlap of content and interest between their historical writings to be coincidental. As to the powers in the land, it has already been observed that Queen Matilda started William on his way as a historian; he eventually sent copies of the *Gesta regum* to her brother David, king of Scots, and to her daughter, the Empress Matilda. But the work itself bore a much more personal dedication to Robert, earl of Gloucester (*d.* 1147), bastard son of Henry I. William had access to Henry's private zoo at Woodstock, which suggests that he knew the king himself, although he does not acknowledge any particular relationship. Two great ecclesiastics, Henry de Blois (*d.* 1171), simultaneously bishop of Winchester and abbot of Glastonbury, and Roger, bishop of

Salisbury and abbot of Malmesbury itself (*d.* 1139), complete what is known of William's circle of acquaintance.

Non-historical writings After this long period of immersion in historical writing William's conscience seems to have troubled him. He says as much in the prologue to his commentary on Lamentations, and about this time he produced a series of works more obviously relevant to the needs and aspirations of a monastic community, his own as well as others. Apart from the commentary itself he wrote a set of miracles of the Virgin and made digests of basic texts to make them more accessible to less gifted monks: the works of St Gregory (*Defloratio Gregorii*) and the liturgical writing of Amalarius of Metz (*Abbreviatio Amalarii*). But he could not stay away from history for long. About 1140 he began the *Historia novella*, a continuation of the *Gesta regum* from 1135. Yet he never adequately covered the decade of English history from *c.*1125 to *c.*1135. In the prologue to the *Historia novella* (Malmesbury, *Historia novella*, 1) he speaks of 'three little books of chronicles', now lost, which perhaps filled the gap.

Already it will be evident that William's original writings shade off into compilations, and these in turn merge into florilegia and 'collected' editions of works by a single author or on a particular theme. It is here that William's astonishing reading and learning are shown, and the mechanics of how he stocked his abbey library revealed. His own hand has been recognized in a handful of books, including the autograph of his *Gesta pontificum*. He seems to have cajoled many of his fellow monks into copying whole books or sections of them, and a few of these survive. Most noteworthy is his knowledge of the Latin classics. Classical and late antique authors account for a quarter of the approximately 400 works by 200 authors which William is known to have read. He compiled a florilegium of such texts, the *Polyhistor*, and all his original writings show how steeped he was in classical literature, especially the poetry of Virgil and Lucan. His love of ancient literature, his scholarship, and the sensitivity that he felt about this preference (as with his historical writing), are all illustrated by the famous preface to his collected edition of Cicero's works:

> This first book of [Cicero's] *Academics* is not to be found in England, nor the second in which Catulus is introduced disputing on behalf of the Academics, as one can tell from much that is written in the two books below ... the third and fourth of the *Academics* ... And Cicero says at the start of his second book *De Divinatione* that he had written a book in which he introduced Hortensius exhorting the study of philosophy; and in the same place he says that he had written six books *De republica*. Now because I have not found these books in England, I William of Malmesbury, according to my usual custom have inserted here whatever of their matter and intention I could find in the works of the blessed Augustine. And I take the opportunity to note that no-one should blame me for reading and copying as many books of the pagans as I do. Certainly whoever reads them because he avoids or despises the holy Scriptures sins gravely and deserves punishment ... But he who reads them so that he may express himself elegantly and eloquently in writings to the glory of God and His saints ... I do not believe that he sins in any way just because he enjoys the pagans' books. (Thomson, 51–2)

Significance and reputation William's importance, then, is twofold: as England's greatest national and local historian since Bede, and as the most learned European of his day. For the period of English history before his own lifetime, it is true that for the most part he had access to written sources still available now. With some notable exceptions, for instance the reign of Æthelstan, he adds only incidentally to this information. Such information and interpretation as is unique to him has to be sifted critically; some of it is legitimate interpretation, some shows the exercise of a lively imagination; some is based upon popular opinion, which itself may or may not be securely based. As he approaches his own time he becomes progressively more independent of other material, and more of a primary source in his own right. But for all periods he sets an example of intelligent and imaginative judgement, of elegant expression and lucid planning, which are the hallmarks of the great historian.

The influence of his writing varies astonishingly from work to work. Most of what he wrote, especially the hagiography, was too sober and sceptical to be widely popular, and survives only in single or few copies. The notable exception is *De miraculis beatae virginis Mariae*, which became the basis for more extensive miracle collections made both in England and on the continent. Of his major works the *Gesta pontificum* enjoyed modest popularity in England over the next century; but it was the *Gesta regum* which was far and away his most influential work over the longest time. Already within his lifetime copies spread throughout southern England, and it was known in Normandy, Flanders, and France. By the end of the century it was being used by chroniclers on both sides of the channel, and continued to be so, increasingly in competition with Geoffrey of Monmouth, until the end of the middle ages. This was partly because he included so much continental history in it, and because of his irresistibly attractive stories of marvels such as 'The Witch of Berkeley' and 'The Two Clerks of Nantes'. William believed that one of the duties of the historian was to entertain by means of such stories, and many of his became detached from the main work and enjoyed a life of their own. But in the end it is as a historian of England that William will be best remembered and his works laid under contribution.

Works William's works were numerous, but some have been lost and others remain unprinted. His importance in the historiography of his age justifies a list: 1 *De gestis regum Anglorum*, ed. W. Stubbs, 2 vols., Rolls Series, 90 (1887–9); new edn with translation and commentary by R. A. B. Mynors, R. M. Thomson, and M. Winterbottom, 2 vols., OMT (1998–9). 2 *De gestis pontificum Anglorum*, ed. N. E. S. A. Hamilton, Rolls Series, 52 (1870). 3 *Historia novella*, ed. and trans. K. Potter, Nelson Medieval Texts (1955); new edn with translation and commentary by E. King, OMT (1998). 4 *De antiquitate Glastonie ecclesie*, ed. and trans. J. Scott as *The Early History of Glastonbury* (1981). 5 *Vita Dunstani*, in *Memorials of St Dunstan*, ed. W. Stubbs, Rolls Series, 63 (1874), 250–324. 6 *Vita Indracti*, previously unprinted and largely lost; see M. Lapidge, 'The cult of St Indract at Glastonbury', *Ireland in Early Mediaeval Europe*, ed.

D. Whitelock, R. McKitterick, and D. Dumville (1982), 194–6; and John of Glastonbury, *The Chronicle of Glastonbury Abbey*, ed. J. P. Carley (1985), pp. xl–xli, 101–5. 7 *Vita Benigni*, previously unprinted and largely lost; see John of Glastonbury, ed. Carley, pp. xxxviii, 69–71, 161–3. 8 *Vita Patricii*, previously unprinted and largely lost; see C. Slover, 'William of Malmesbury's *Life of St Patrick*', *Modern Philology*, 24 (1926–7), 268–83; and John of Glastonbury, ed. Carley, pp. xxxvii, 58–70. 9 *Vita Wulfstani*, ed. R. Darlington, CS, 3rd ser., 11 (1928). 5–9: New editions and translations by M. Winterbottom and R. M. Thomson, in William of Malmesbury, *Saints' Lives: Lives of SS. Wulfstan, Dunstan, Patrick, Benignus and Indract*, OMT (forthcoming). 10 *Liber pontificalis*, as found in CUL, MS Kk.4.6, and BL, Harley MS 633, partly ed. W. Levison, 'Aus englischen Bibliotheken II', *Neues Archiv für Ältere Deutsche Geschichtskunde*, 35 (1910), 333–431. 11 *De miraculis beatae virginis Mariae*, ed. P. N. Carter, 'An edition of William of Malmesbury's treatise on the miracles of the Virgin', 2 vols., DPhil diss., University of Oxford, 1959; *El libro 'De laudibus et miraculis sanctae Mariae'* de Guillermo de Malmesbury*, ed. J. M. Canal (1968). 12 *Abbreviatio Amalarii*, unprinted; see R. Pfaff, 'The *Abbreviatio Amalarii* of William of Malmesbury', *Recherches de Théologie Ancienne et Médiévale*, 48 (1981), 128–71. 13 *Defloratio Gregorii*, unprinted; see D. H. Farmer, 'William of Malmesbury's commentary on Lamentations', *Studia Monastica*, 4 (1962), 283–311. 14 *Commentary on Lamentations*, unprinted; see Farmer, 293–300. 15 *Polyhistor deflorationum*, ed. H. Testroet Ouellette (Binghamton, 1982). 16 *Epistola ad Petrum de Iohanne Scoto*, in *De gestis regum Anglorum*, ed. Stubbs, vol. 1, pp. cxliii–cxlvi. 17 'Three little books of chronicles', mentioned in the prologue to *Historia novella*, lost. 18 *Itinerarium Iohannis abbatis*—a description of the journey of John, abbot of Malmesbury, to Rome in 1140—seen by John Leland at Malmesbury, now lost; see J. Leland, *Commentarii de scriptoribus Britannicis*, ed. A. Hall, 2 vols. (1709), 2.195–6. 19 John Leland also saw at Malmesbury Abbey a copy of a work allegedly by William which he described as 'libri quindecim de serie quattuor euangelistarum uario carminis genere', now lost (ibid.). R. M. Thomson, *William of Malmesbury* (1987), collects together the writer's earlier essays on the subject, and cites earlier literature.

R. M. THOMSON

Sources *Willelmi Malmesbiriensis monachi de gestis regum Anglorum*, ed. W. Stubbs, 2 vols., Rolls Series (1887–9) · *Willelmi Malmesbiriensis monachi de gestis pontificum Anglorum libri quinque*, ed. N. E. S. A. Hamilton, Rolls Series, 52 (1870) · William of Malmesbury, *The Historia novella*, ed. and trans. K. R. Potter (1955) · *The early history of Glastonbury: an edition, translation, and study of William of Malmesbury's De antiquitate Glastonie ecclesie*, ed. J. Scott (1981) · W. Stubbs, ed., *Memorials of St Dunstan, archbishop of Canterbury*, Rolls Series, 63 (1874) · M. Lapidge, 'The cult of St Indract at Glastonbury', *Ireland in early mediaeval Europe*, ed. D. Whitelock, R. McKitterick, and D. Dumville (1982), 194–6 · C. Slover, 'William of Malmesbury's *Life of St Patrick*', *Modern Philology*, 24 (1926–7), 268–83 · *The Chronicle of Glastonbury Abbey: an edition, translation and study of John of Glastonbury's Cronica sive antiquitates Glastoniensis ecclesie*, ed. J. P. Carley, trans. D. Townsend, rev. edn (1985) · *The Vita Wulfstani of William of Malmesbury*, ed. R. R. Darlington, CS, 3rd ser., 40 (1928) · W. Levison, 'Aus englischen Bibliotheken II', *Neues Archiv für Ältere Deutsche*

Geschichtskunde, 35 (1910), 333–431 · P. N. Carter, 'An edition of William of Malmesbury's treatise on the miracles of the Virgin', 2 vols., DPhil diss., U. Oxf., 1959 · J. M. Canal, *El libro 'De laudibus et miraculis sanctae Mariae' de Guillermo de Malmesbury* (1968) · R. Pfaff, 'The *Abbreviatio Amalarii* of William of Malmesbury', *Recherches de Théologie Ancienne et Médiévale*, 48 (1981), 128–71 · D. H. Farmer, 'William of Malmesbury's commentary on Lamentations', *Studia Monastica*, 4 (1962), 283–311 · William of Malmesbury, *Polyhistor deflorationum*, ed. H. Testroet Ouellette (Binghamton, 1982) · *Commentarii de scriptoribus Britannicis, auctore Joanne Lelando*, ed. A. Hall, 2 vols. (1709) · R. M. Thomson, *William of Malmesbury* (1987) · M. R. James, *Two ancient English scholars* (1931) · N. R. Ker, 'William of Malmesbury's handwriting', *EngHR*, 59 (1944), 371–6 · D. H. Farmer, 'William of Malmesbury's life and works', *Journal of Ecclesiastical History*, 13 (1962), 39–54 · A. Gransden, *Historical writing in England*, 1 (1974) · N. Wright, 'William of Malmesbury and Latin poetry: further evidence for a Benedictine's reading', *Revue Bénédictine*, 101 (1991), 122–53 · N. Wright, '*Industriae testimonium*: William of Malmesbury and Latin poetry revisited', *Revue Bénédictine*, 103 (1993), 482–531 · E. Freeman, 'Sailing between Scylla and Charybdis: William of Malmesbury, historiographical innovation and the recreation of the Anglo-Saxon past', *Tjurunga*, 48 (1995), 23–37 · M. Winterbottom, 'The *Gesta regum* of William of Malmesbury', *Journal of Medieval Latin*, 5 (1995), 158–73 · E. O. Blake, ed., *Liber Eliensis*, CS, 3rd ser., 92 (1962) · Tanner, *Bibl. Brit.-Hib.* · chronicle attributed to Godfrey of Jumièges, BL, Cotton MS Vespasian D.iv · J. Smith, ed., *A descriptive catalogue of Friends' books*, 1 (1867) · D. Knowles, C. N. L. Brooke, and V. C. M. London, eds., *The heads of religious houses, England and Wales*, 1: 940–1216 (1972) · *Joannis Lelandi antiquarii de rebus Britannicis collectanea*, ed. T. Hearne, [2nd edn], 6 vols. (1770)

Archives BL, Cotton MS Vespasian D.iv · BL, Harley MS 633 · CUL, MS Kk.4.6

Malone, Anthony (1700–1776), politician, was born in Ireland on 5 December 1700, the eldest son of Richard Malone (1674–1745) of Baronston, co. Westmeath, and his wife, Marcella, the daughter of Redmond Molady, the nephew and coheir of Sir Patrick Molady of Robertstown. His father was the only son of Anthony Malone and his wife, Mary, the daughter of John Reily of Lismore. Edmund *Malone (1704–1774), barrister and politician, was his brother. While a student at the Temple he had attracted the favourable notice of William III through diplomatic work in the Netherlands. He was called to the Irish bar about 1700 and pursued a successful legal career before his death on 6 January 1745.

Anthony Malone was educated at Mr Young's school in Abbey Street, Dublin, before proceeding to Trinity College, Dublin, on 7 November 1717; he was awarded the degree of LLD by Trinity in 1737. On 30 March 1720 he entered the Middle Temple, London; a week later, on 6 April 1720, he matriculated at Christ Church, Oxford. After spending two years at the university he returned to the Middle Temple. He was called to the Irish bar in May 1726, and in the following year he was elected MP for co. Westmeath, being returned at the same time for Blessington, which seat he declined. In July 1733 he married Rose (d. 1773), the daughter of Sir Ralph Gore, bt, speaker of the Irish House of Commons; the couple had no children. At an early date in his career Malone was earning more than £3000 per annum, and by now he had established himself in Dublin as a successful barrister. In the Commons he became noted as an orator and attracted the attention of the Irish administration. In 1737 he voted with the minority against the devaluation of gold, on the grounds that it would harm Irish trade. He became prime serjeant-at-law in 1743, and served as a justice of assize on several occasions between 1744 and 1750, as well as in 1760 and 1763. In parliament he was associated with Gore's successor as speaker, Henry Boyle, who had the greatest influence in the Irish Commons, but he also earned the praise of George Stone, archbishop of Armagh, who described him as 'the most considerable Man here, and the most usefull to the Government; at the same time, He is of all those in the Service of the Government, the most independent and the least importunate for Favours' (Burns, 87).

Relations between Stone and the Boyle party, and as a result between Boyle and the government, later became strained, partly through Stone's failure in 1751 to support the application for the post of solicitor-general of Malone's younger brother Richard (1706–1759), MP from 1741 for Fore. Stone suspected that Malone's Irish and Catholic ancestry made him naturally inclined against the British interest in Ireland. Malone was seen as the leader of anti-government opinion in the early 1750s, and he incurred the displeasure of the duke of Dorset's administration in 1753 for his insistence that the bill allowing the appropriation of surplus revenues should refer to royal recommendation of the measure rather than emphasizing royal consent. He was removed from office by order of the ministry in London. However, he was compensated by Dorset's successor, William Cavendish, marquess of Hartington, in 1756 with a patent of precedence at the bar—one of a series of measures designed to conciliate the Boyle party and leading to accusations that they had surrendered their patriot principles by some colleagues and the mob. He was also offered the post of chancellor of the exchequer, which he at first refused because he feared a loss of income from the bar and was loath to alienate his allies. He was eventually appointed on 10 September 1757, with an additional pension to compensate for the reduction of his law practice, and he was sworn of the privy council on 26 October.

Malone remained an influential member of the Commons, ensuring parliamentary majorities for the administration of John Russell, fourth duke of Bedford. His career was tarnished, though, in 1758, when he became a partner in an unsuccessful bank with Nathaniel Clements, vice-treasurer of Ireland, and Sir Arthur Gore. The collapse of Malone, Clements, and Gore (founded on 3 July 1758, but closed on 1 November 1758) led to the act prohibiting persons holding public funds from engaging in banking, and was considered by Pitt to have contributed to the discontent with Dublin politics manifested in the anti-union riot in December 1759.

Malone was dismissed from the exchequer in 1761, when he resisted the transmission of a money bill to England as a cause for calling a new parliament. Pitt thought the punishment improper, but learned of it too late for his opinion to be counted. Malone and the ministry may have connived at his dismissal, in order for him to retire with honour and return to the bar. In the election of that year

Malone was elected for Castlemartyr on the interest of his old ally Boyle, by then earl of Shannon. The Malones were of Catholic descent, and Malone's mother had been born a Roman Catholic, a heritage reflected in his sympathy for Catholic grievances. He supported Monck Mason's bill for enabling Catholics to invest money in mortgages upon land, and in 1762 he was appointed, with Sir Richard Aston, to try the whiteboys of Munster. The two concurred in ascribing their outrages to local and individual grievances. Malone's political enemies, including William Gerard Hamilton, suspected in 1763 and afterwards that Malone was preparing a return to opposition politics, but their fears were never realized.

At the election of 1768 Malone was returned for both Granard and co. Westmeath; he chose to sit for the county. In his later years he occasionally advised the government. His wife, Rose, died on 22 April 1773, and he himself died on 8 May 1776 at his home in Sackville Street, Dublin. His nephew Edmond *Malone remembered him as a man of large and even robust stature, in later years his abundant grey hair giving him a commanding and venerable appearance. By his will, made in July 1774, Malone left all his estates in the counties of Westmeath, Roscommon, Longford, Cavan, and Dublin to his nephew Richard *Malone [see under Malone, Edmund (1704–1774)], afterwards Lord Sunderlin, the eldest son and heir of his brother Edmund *Malone, 'in the utmost confidence that they will be settled and continue in the male line of the family and branches of it, according to priority of birth and seniority of age'. But Lord Sunderlin, who had no children, did not obey this injunction, and on his death in 1816 the right of succession was disputed.

MATTHEW KILBURN

Sources R. E. Burns, *Irish parliamentary politics in the eighteenth century*, 2 (1990) · 'Malone, Anthony', E. M. Johnston-Liik, *History of the Irish parliament, 1692–1800*, 6 vols. (2002), vol. 5, pp. 183–7 · L. M. Cullen, 'Economic development, 1691–1750', *A new history of Ireland*, ed. T. W. Moody and others, 4: *Eighteenth-century Ireland, 1691–1800* (1986), 123–58 · N. L. York, *Neither kingdom nor nation: the Irish quest for constitutional rights* (1994), 53–4, 66 · S. Murphy, 'The Dublin anti-union riot of 3 December 1759', *Parliament, politics and people: essays in 18th century Irish history*, ed. G. O'Brien (1989), 58 · *Dublin Penny Journal*, 1 (22 Dec 1832), 205–6 · J. Lodge, *The peerage of Ireland*, rev. M. Archdall, rev. edn, 7 (1789), 287–92 · H. Grattan, *Memoirs of the life and times of the Rt Hon. Henry Grattan*, 5 vols. (1839–46) · J. Prior, *Life of Edmond Malone, editor of Shakespeare* (1860) · H. A. C. Sturgess, ed., *Register of admissions to the Honourable Society of the Middle Temple, from the fifteenth century to the year 1944*, 1 (1949), 286 · *DNB*

Likenesses J. Reynolds, oils, 1759, NG Ire. · J. R. Smith, mezzotint, pubd 1779 (after J. Reynolds), BM, NPG · marble bust; at Baronston House, co. Westmeath, in 1893

Malone, Edmond (1741–1812), literary scholar and biographer, was born at Shinglas, co. Westmeath, Ireland, on 4 October 1741, the second son of Edmund *Malone (1704–1774), member of the Irish House of Commons and judge of the court of common pleas, and his wife, Catherine Collier (d. 1765) of Essex. His uncle was Anthony *Malone (1700–1776), distinguished parliamentary orator and chancellor of the exchequer from 1757 to 1761. His elder brother Richard *Malone (1738–1816) [see under Malone,

Edmond Malone (1741–1812), by Sir Joshua Reynolds, 1778, reworked 1786

Edmund] inherited the family's estates at Shinglas and Baronston in co. Westmeath and also sat in the Irish House of Commons; he was raised to the peerage as Baron Sunderlin in 1785. After moving to London to take up a literary career, Edmond was always careful to remain close to his brother and two sisters, Henrietta and Catherine, as well as to a number of Irish connections from his youth.

Education and early years Not much is known of Malone's youth, except that in 1747 he was sent to Dr Ford's Preparatory School in Molesworth Street, Dublin, and in 1757 he entered Trinity College, Dublin, where a year earlier his father had received an honorary LLD. At Trinity he was consistently at the top of his class, earning several 'premiums', books stamped with the college arms. While there he wrote some worthwhile poetry, a translation of *Oedipus*, and a surprisingly erudite history of tragedy. In 1759 he travelled to England for the first time, accompanying his ailing mother to Bath where he left her and then returned home. He took his BA degree in February 1762, one of only three to earn the top mark, *valde bene*. In appearance, he was of less than average height, round-faced, and soft in countenance.

After a year at home in Shinglas reading some law but mainly literature, his great love, in January 1763 Malone followed in the footsteps of his father, uncle, and grandfather by entering the Inner Temple in London on his way to becoming an Irish barrister, notwithstanding a distaste for the profession that he had gleaned from his father. He remained in London for three years, spending much of his time at his favourite haunt, the Grecian Coffee House in Devereux Court, where he picked up literary and social gossip; he also began to interest himself in English and Irish politics, about which he wrote a few fugitive satirical articles. The most important event of this period in London was meeting Samuel Johnson at his rooms in Inner Temple Lane some time in 1764. They met several times over the next two years, meetings which were crucial in turning Malone's mind increasingly toward the muses and away from the law. When he could he visited his mother in Bath. She eventually died there in 1765.

On his return to Ireland after a few months in France, Malone was called to the Irish bar in 1767 and took up his duties as a barrister on the Munster circuit, working hard but taking little pleasure or profit from it. The first years of his practice were darkened by an unfortunate love affair with the enigmatic Susanna Spencer. His family disapproved of her and may have seen to it that she was removed to London, causing him to have a near nervous collapse. He plodded on as a lawyer until his father died in 1774, leaving him and his siblings modest incomes that gave him more time for literary pursuits and some involvement in politics that included friendships with the Irish patriots Henry Grattan and Henry Flood. Among his political writings during this period were contributions to *Baratariana*, a volume of 'Letters' by Flood, Grattan, and others attacking government policy on Ireland; he wrote for the newspapers as well. And in 1774 he also won Trinity College's nomination as its parliamentary candidate for the election in May 1776. He promptly gave up the nomination, however, when his uncle Anthony Malone died leaving him an annuity of about £1000. Without too much reflection, he also gave up the law and decided to dedicate himself to a life of literary scholarship.

First literary pursuits Malone promptly began work toward a new (publishers') edition of Oliver Goldsmith, working on it both in Dublin and (briefly in 1776) in London, where he renewed his literary friendships with Johnson and perhaps others of his circle. He returned briefly to Dublin to settle his affairs and with his independent income moved permanently to London in May 1777, arriving just as *Poems and Plays by Oliver Goldsmith* was published with notes and an eight-page memoir of Goldsmith by him. Impressed, the Shakespearian George Steevens, whom he had met the previous year, invited him to contribute to his second edition of the *Johnson–Steevens Shakespeare*. Malone took up the invitation with alacrity. His first major project was to try to determine the chronology of Shakespeare's plays; he also provided a stream of notes and corrections for Steevens's edition, implying that he did not think highly of Steevens's accuracy and in the process arousing the first signs of Steevens's envy and rivalry. The edition was published in January 1778 and the first volume contained Malone's pioneering *An Attempt to Ascertain the Order in which the Plays Attributed to Shakespeare were Written*. It was an early indication of the emerging literary biographer.

Steevens still encouraged Malone to push on with a supplement to the *Johnson–Steevens* edition, though he irritated Malone by suggesting that the latter need not think he was doing the work for anything but 'mere amuse-ment'. As he worked, Malone received help with notes and commentary from Thomas Percy, Samuel Henley, Edward Capell, Isaac Reed, William Blackstone, and a number of others, but he was firmly in charge. The supplement, containing Shakespeare's apocryphal plays as well as narrative poems and sonnets, appeared in April 1780 in two substantial volumes, generally to very positive reviews heralding Malone as a new Shakespearian prodigy, though a few reviewers cavilled at the particularity of his notes. He was praised especially for his close reading of early texts. In the spring of 1783 he published *A Second Appendix to Mr. Malone's Supplement to the Last Edition of the Plays of Shakespeare*, containing mostly textual emendations to his supplement.

Malone by now had become well known in the luminous Johnsonian circle of literary, social, and political personalities and a close friend of many of them, not least Sir Joshua Reynolds with whom he enjoyed an uninterrupted intimacy until Reynolds's death in 1792. Reynolds painted his portrait in 1778, bringing it up to date a few years later, and Malone acted as his literary executor after his death. It was not until 1782, however, that deeper friendships with the likes of Edmund Burke, Edward Gibbon, Dr Charles Burney, James Boswell, Joseph Banks, William Windham, and Charles James Fox developed from his election to Johnson's famous Literary Club. He soon became the club's first treasurer, holding the office until his death and becoming its greatest promoter and historian. When Johnson died in 1784, Malone's long eulogistic obituary in the *Gentleman's Magazine* was the most detailed and accurate to be published; in homage to Johnson, he and Reynolds also saw to it that a monument to Johnson was set up in St Paul's Cathedral. Later he would do the same for Reynolds. The pattern of his sedentary London-centred, bachelor existence with its endless round of dinners was now well established and continued for the rest of his life. He fell in love two or three times and twice proposed marriage and twice was rejected. Boswell attributed Malone's failure to marry to his 'Irish stare'.

When Malone was not engaged in his scholarship or dining out, he was spending a large portion of his annuity on rare volumes of English literature, mainly Elizabethan poetry and plays, and collecting the 'Heads' (mostly engravings) of English poets which he prized as an important part of the biographer's and literary historian's evidence. He regularly attended book auctions, so that by the end of his life he owned one of the best collections of early English poetry and drama in England, the greatest portion of which was given to the Bodleian Library, Oxford, after his death.

In the early 1780s Malone also became acquainted with Horace Walpole and the actors Sarah Siddons and Philip Kemble in his efforts to revise and get staged a couple of plays by his boyhood friend Robert Jephson. Malone's friendship with Walpole was strengthened when in comprehensively exposing Thomas Chatterton's forgeries of the so-called Rowley poems in his pamphlet *Cursory Observations on the Poems Attributed to Thomas Rowley* (1782) he defended Walpole's treatment of Chatterton's forged poems several years earlier. The pamphlet was well received although it was also ridiculed by Burnaby Greene and others for its alleged pedantry and scholarly arrogance in censuring respected critics. It was not the last time Malone would attack literary forgers or alienate fellow critics. In 1783 he helped Jephson again by editing and seeing through the press the latter's *Roman Portraits*.

Edition of Shakespeare's works In August 1783 Malone asked his friend John Nichols, editor of the *Gentleman's Magazine*, to announce his intended edition of the complete plays and poems of Shakespeare 'with select notes from all the commentators'. He planned two separate editions, the first a 'portable' family edition in duodecimo, the second a complete edition with extensive apparatus. For the latter not only would he provide a history of the English stage and correct and expand the Shakespearian biographical record, drawing on documentary evidence painstakingly (and at great cost to his eyes) unearthed in archives in London, Stratford, and country houses, but he would also consult the early quartos (many of which he borrowed from David Garrick) and folios of the plays more thoroughly than any scholar before him in order to establish an authoritative text, going far beyond the *Johnson–Steevens* edition. His research, especially on Shakespeare's life and the history of the English stage, was encouraged and helped by Johnson, Thomas Warton at Oxford, Richard Farmer at Cambridge, Percy, Reed, Burke, the Irish statesman the earl of Charlemont (with whom he carried on a lengthy correspondence about literature and politics), and a plethora of other scholars, with Steevens excepted, whose envy grew in proportion to Malone's influence. Malone more or less lived at the British Museum; he worked in chancery, at Dulwich College, the stamp office, the Tower of London, the diocese of Worcester, the remembrancer's office in the exchequer, the office of the lord chamberlain, and the Bodleian and Ashmolean libraries; and he spent weeks at Stratford combing through the corporation archives by dim candle-light that seriously damaged his eyesight. He took away with him from Stratford masses of the corporation archives that he kept for years in spite of strident requests to return them, knowing that he could well be using them for the rest of his life.

During these years Malone also struck up correspondence with James Davenport, vicar of Stratford, who lent him the parish registers and did some research for him, and the local poet and amateur historian John Jordan who provided so much romantic legendary chaff about Stratford and Shakespeare that Malone came to distrust almost everything he said on the subject. Malone's correspondence with these two Stratford citizens was published in very limited editions by J. O. Halliwell in 1864. Malone ended up debunking much erroneous tradition about Shakespeare that Nicholas Rowe had perpetuated in his 1709 biography, discovering more about the poet's life than was known before or has been discovered since. Sadly, he never got around to writing a biographical narrative for this edition, delaying that instead (he hoped) for his variorum edition. He also came up with two startling and rich archival discoveries of English stage history in 1789, the office-book of Sir Henry Herbert (master of the revels in the reigns of James I and Charles I) and (at Dulwich) Philip Henslowe's theatre diary and account book.

Malone delayed the 'portable' edition that would have got him into print earlier—it was brought out by Nichols in seven volumes several years later—but in 1786 he published his 'Conjectures concerning the date of ... Macbeth' in the *Hibernian Magazine* and in 1787 his bombshell, *A Dissertation on the Three Parts of Henry VI*, providing exciting new scholarly perspective on Shakespeare's earliest work as a dramatist and new insights into his life.

Not everyone applauded Malone's efforts. Steevens grumbled, but caustic attacks surfaced from other quarters, chiefly from Joseph Ritson, a sound scholar whose bitter jealousies induced him to attack not only Malone, but also Warton, Percy, and other leading scholars within the Johnsonian circle. With Steevens's apparent encouragement, in 1783 Ritson published his *Remarks* angrily and astutely attacking Malone for arrogantly trying to establish the 'genuine' Shakespeare text and setting himself up as the leading Shakespearian. In 1788 Ritson again ridiculed and angered Malone in *The Quip Modest*, attacking his textual preference for the first folio over the second, his notes in the supplement and 1778 *Johnson–Steevens*, and his legion of 'mushroom assistants' in arrogating to himself the crown of Shakespearian studies.

In 1790, after numerous delays caused by new discoveries, Malone published *The Plays and Poems of William Shakespeare* in ten volumes, which included his original and expansive 'Account of the English stage', a revised essay on the order of the plays, and a commentary on Shakespeare's life containing new information exploding many of the legendary stories about the poet. Criticism in the 1980s and 1990s attempted to minimize this monumental achievement in Shakespearian studies by discounting the importance of Malone's unprecedented documentary and textual research, but his work heralded a new age of scholarship in which he helped define the scholar's code for generations to come. Except for some cavilling over the length of the notes, the reviews were enthusiastic. Edmund Burke even praised it as a brilliant scholarly piece of service to the country, repaying Malone's efforts with his own 'brass' offering of 'The reflections on the French Revolution'. Horace Walpole complained that the edition was too heavy with notes but that Malone had been 'indefatigable'. Ritson, however, weighed in again with a caustic attack, *Cursory Criticisms* (1792), accusing Malone of 'profound ignorance' and a total want of 'ear' for poetry. More often than has generally been acknowledged, Ritson made legitimate points. Furious, Malone retaliated against the 'viper' Ritson a few weeks later with his important definition of editorial practice, *A Letter to the Rev. Richard Farmer, D.D.* Steevens, enviously and against his better judgement taking Ritson's side, reissued his own edition in 1793 with frequent criticism of Malone. In recognition of his work on Shakespeare, on 5 July 1793,

Oxford University awarded Malone the degree of DCL (Foster, *Alum. Oxon.*). He was also granted the degree of LLD by Trinity College, Dublin, in 1801.

In a little over a year the edition was almost sold out and Malone announced his intention of producing another in fifteen volumes, a plan he abandoned in 1796 for a new octavo edition in twenty volumes that would become known as the third variorum edition. His scheme was to include as centrepieces of the edition a complete and revolutionary biography of Shakespeare and an expanded history of the English stage. But the prevalent theme of Malone's Shakespearian work for the rest of his life was interruption. He plodded on amassing material and working on the text, but physical and emotional problems conspired to distract him, and in the 1790s especially when he still had the energy and strength, he found it easier and more palatable to turn to other literary projects. He also became the target of considerable ridicule when on a visit to Stratford in 1793 he had Shakespeare's coloured bust in Holy Trinity Church whitewashed, incorrectly assuming that was its original colour. And when in 1792–3 he immersed himself in the John Aubrey manuscripts at the Ashmolean Museum in Oxford, a rich source of biography for Shakespeare, he took the liberty of rearranging the papers with a view to publishing them (which he never did) and high-handedly kept other interested scholars like James Caulfield at bay. Citing Malone's 'big bloated pride', in 1797 Caulfield got his revenge by publishing an extravagant indictment of Malone's scholarly behaviour in his stinging pamphlet, *An enquiry into the conduct of Edmond Malone esq. concerning the manuscript papers of John Aubrey*.

Final years One of Malone's major literary distractions from Shakespeare was James Boswell. They met in 1781 but their famous friendship did not develop until 1785 when Malone, dubbed by Boswell as 'Johnsonianissimus', decided to dedicate himself to encouraging and helping Boswell write and publish his *Tour to the Hebrides with Samuel Johnson, LL.D.* It was one of the greatest literary collaborations in English literature, Malone spending hundreds of hours with Boswell, advising him, revising his manuscript, and helping to bring it to publication later that year. Then after helping Boswell bring out a third edition in 1786, Malone prodded him to proceed immediately with his monumental *Life of Johnson*, over the next five years serving as midwife to the biography, correcting the manuscript as Boswell wrote it, encouraging him against depression with endless advice, and generally keeping him to the task. It is not improbable that without Malone Boswell would never have written the *Life*. The *Life* was published in 1791, after which Malone helped Boswell revise it for a second edition in 1793 and, after Boswell's death in 1795, performed as editor for several more editions, the last (sixth) in 1811. As one of Boswell's executors, he saw to it that after his friend's death in 1795 his manuscripts and collections were organized and sent up to Scotland, where they awaited sensational rediscovery in the first half of the twentieth century.

Other significant interruptions of his work on Shakespeare included a false start on a new edition of Pope to supersede Warburton's, whose scholarship he denigrated; a comprehensive and sensational exposure of the Shakespeare forgeries by William Henry Ireland, *An Inquiry into the Authenticity of Certain Miscellaneous Papers ... Attributed to Shakespeare* (1796); an edition of his dear friend Sir Joshua Reynolds's works, complete with an extensive biography of the artist (1797, 1798); and his edition, *The Critical and Miscellaneous Prose Works of John Dryden* (1800), again with a thoroughly researched biography of the poet on which Sir Walter Scott later would lean heavily for his own edition of Dryden. The latter elicited one of those recurring literary reprisals Malone had to endure on account of his fame for copious scholarship, a hilarious and successful parody by George Hardinge, *The Essence of Malone*, which Hardinge followed up a few months later with *Another Essence of Malone, or, The 'Beauties' of Shakspeare's Editor.*

The upshot was that Malone's work on Shakespeare came virtually to a halt in the late 1790s and, though he fitfully continued with documentary research, he never recovered any momentum with the edition. In spite of encouragement from many friends, ennui set in, he dabbled, and his eyesight worsened. When the Shakespearian Isaac Reid died in 1807, Malone called himself 'the last of the Shakspearians', but by then he had little Shakespeare or any other kind of scholarship left in him. In 1805 he laid out plans and did some research for an essay on Shakespeare's metre that he never completed. After his death it fell to James Boswell jun. to edit it, as well as his incomplete biography of Shakespeare, into something like a coherent work. In 1808 Malone had privately printed his *Account of the incidents, from which the title and part of the story of Shakespeare's Tempest were derived; and its true date ascertained*; and in 1809, *Parliamentary Logick*, an edition of his friend the statesman William Gerard Hamilton's (mostly unpublished) political writings, together with a biographical preface generous with praise. The latter effort won him only ridicule, however, mainly from Francis Jeffrey of the *Edinburgh Review*, for political triviality and extremism. In 1808 Malone also contemplated an expanded edition of Dr Johnson's *Dictionary* that he never published but toward which he systematically annotated the work— almost 3000 annotations in all, an astonishing expenditure (and perhaps misuse) of time and energy. In 1810 he came out with *A Biographical Memoir of the Late Right Honourable William Windham*, another panegyric in memory of the statesman and his dear friend and fellow club member.

After an undetermined illness of several weeks in the spring of 1812 Malone died at Queen Anne Street East, London, on 25 May, survived by his brother Lord Sunderlin and two sisters in Ireland. His body was interred at the family seat of Baronston in co. Westmeath. Lord Sunderlin left most of his brother's library and papers to the Bodleian Library, Oxford, while the rest was dispersed by auction in London in May 1825. Malone left his portrait by Reynolds and his collection of the 'Heads' of English writers to the Revd Thomas Rooper; the collection (now lost) was last seen in the Hove Public Library, Sussex. A few of the papers and Malone's annotated copy of Dr Johnson's *Dictionary* are in the British Library. For most of the time from Malone's death until 1825, Malone's library and papers were at the disposal of James Boswell jun., who in gratitude for Malone's untiring help to his father took his chaotically organized Shakespeare material and spent almost a decade preparing the twenty-one-volume third variorum edition, *The Plays and Poems of William Shakspeare* (1821). Young Boswell also wrote a lengthy memoir of Malone for the *Gentleman's Magazine* in May 1812, describing his mildness and steadiness as a friend, his sincerity and manly independence. More recently, critics and biographers have drawn attention also to Malone's impatience, temper, and indignation where literature and politics were concerned. He is still regarded as the greatest eighteenth-century Shakespearian editor and commentator and one of the earliest scholars to stake all on documentary evidence. PETER MARTIN

Sources P. Martin, *Edmond Malone, Shakespearean scholar: a literary biography* (1995) [incl. bibliography] · S. Schoenbaum, *Shakespeare's lives*, new edn (1991) · J. Prior, *Life of Edmond Malone, editor of Shakespeare* (1860) · M. de Grazia, *Shakespeare verbatim: the preproduction of authenticity and the 1790 apparatus* (1991) · J. K. Walton, 'Edmond Malone: an Irish Shakespeare scholar', *Hermathena*, 99 (1964), 5–26 · *The correspondence of James Boswell with David Garrick, Edmund Burke, and Edmond Malone*, ed. G. M. Kahrl and others (1986), vol. 4 of *The Yale editions of the private papers of James Boswell*, research edn (1966–) · *The correspondence of Thomas Percy and Edmond Malone*, ed. A. Tillotson (1944), vol. 1 of *The Percy letters*, ed. C. Brooks, A. N. Smith, and A. F. Falconer (1944–88) · *The correspondence of Edmond Malone, the editor of Shakespeare, with the Rev. James Davenport, D.D., vicar of Stratford-on-Avon* (1864) · *Boswell: the applause of the jury, 1782–1785*, ed. I. S. Lustig and F. A. Pottle (1981), vol. 12 of *The Yale editions of the private papers of James Boswell*, trade edn (1950–89) · *Boswell: the English experiment, 1785–1789*, ed. I. S. Lustig and F. A. Pottle (1986), vol. 13 of *The Yale editions of the private papers of James Boswell*, trade edn (1950–89) · *Boswell: the great biographer, 1789–1795*, ed. M. K. Danziger and F. Brady (1989), vol. 14 of *The Yale editions of the private papers of James Boswell*, trade edn (1950–89) · F. Brady, *James Boswell: the later years, 1769–1795* (1984) · P. Martin, *A life of James Boswell* (1999) · A. Sherbo, *The birth of Shakespeare studies: commentators from Rowe (1709) to Boswell-Malone (1821)* (1986) · J. M. Osborn, 'Edmond Malone and Baratariana', *N&Q*, 188 (1945), 35 · J. M. Osborn, 'Edmond Malone and Dr. Johnson', *Johnson, Boswell, and their circle*, ed. M. Lascelles (1965), 1–20 · J. M. Osborn, 'Edmond Malone and Oxford', *Eighteenth-century studies in honor of Donald F. Hyde*, ed. W. H. Bond (1970) · J. M. Osborn, 'Edmond Malone: scholar–collector', *Transactions of the Bibliographical Society*, 3rd ser., 19 (1964), 11–37 · A. Brown, 'Edmond Malone and English scholarship' [inaugural lecture at UCL, 21 May 1963] · W. S. Lewis, 'Edmond Malone, Horace Walpole, and Shakespeare', *Evidence in literary scholarship: essays in memory of James M. Osborn*, ed. R. Wellek and A. Ribeiro (1979) · J. Dover Wilson, 'Malone and the upstart crow', *2 Henry VI* (1952) · P. Martin, 'Edmond Malone, Sir Joshua Reynolds, and Dr. Johnson's monument in St. Paul's Cathedral', *Age of Johnson*, 3 (1989), 331–51 · F. A. Pottle, *Pride and negligence: the history of the Boswell papers* (1981) · D. Buchanan, *The treasure at Auchinleck: the story of the Boswell papers* (1974) · [B. Bandinel], *A catalogue of the early English poetry and other miscellaneous works illustrating the British drama, collected by E. Malone ... in the Bodleian Library* (1836) [with memoir of Malone by James Boswell] · J. Caulfield, *An enquiry into the conduct of Edmond Malone Esq. concerning the manuscript papers of John Aubrey, F.R.S. in the Ashmolean Museum, Oxford* (1797) · G. Chalmers, *An apology for the believers in the Shakspeare-papers* (1797) · M. Duff, *Annals of the club, 1764–1914* (1914) · G. Hardinge, *The essence of Malone* (1800) ·

G. Hardinge, *Another essence of Malone* (1801) · Burtchaell & Sadleir, *Alum. Dubl.* [1756] · Farington, *Diary*, 12.4320–21
Archives BL, published works with MS annotations and marginalia · Bodl. Oxf., corresp. and papers · Boston PL, letters and papers · Folger, papers · Shakespeare Birthplace Trust RO, Stratford upon Avon, corresp. · V&A NAL, corresp. · Yale U., Beinecke L., catalogue of his library · Yale U., Beinecke L., corresp. and papers | BL, letters to Charles Burney, M/436 · BL, notes to journal of Reynolds in Netherlands and Belgium in 1781, Egerton MS 2165 · BL, notes on Shakespeare's plays, Add. MS 30943 · BL, corresp. with Thomas Warton, Add. MSS 30375, 42561 · BL, biographical notes on William Windham, Add. MS 37934 · BL, letters to William Windham and others, Add. MS 37854 · Boston PL, letters and papers · NL Scot., corresp. with Sir William Forbes · NRA, priv. coll., letters to Sarah Loveday · Royal Irish Acad., corresp. with Lord Charlemont · Shakespeare Birthplace Trust RO, Stratford upon Avon, corresp. with John Jordan · Sheff. Arch., corresp. with Edmund Burke · Stamford Public Library, Lincolnshire, corresp. with Octavius Gilchrist · V&A, corresp. · Yale U., Beinecke L., corresp. with James Boswell · Yale U., Beinecke L., annotated copy of Peck's *Desiderata curiosa*
Likenesses J. Reynolds, oils, 1778, NPG; reworked 1786 [*see illus.*] · F. Bartolozzi, stipple, pubd 1787 (after J. Reynolds), BM, NPG · O. Humphrey, engraving, 1797 · engraving (after J. Reynolds, 1779), repro. in J. Bell, *The poets of Great Britain*, 109 vols. (1777–83)
Wealth at death valuable collection of books and papers, the bulk of which was given to the Bodleian Library, Oxford; income of approximately £1000 p.a.

Malone, Edmund (1704–1774), barrister and politician, was born in Dublin on 16 April 1704, the second son of Richard Malone (1674–1745), who originally lived in Baronston, co. Westmeath, and his wife, Marcella, daughter of Redmond Molady. Anthony *Malone (1700–1776), politician, was his brother. Educated in Dublin, Edmund Malone arrived in London in 1722 to study law at the Middle Temple. He was called to the English bar on 16 May 1729 and was student of the Inner Temple in 1734. Having established himself as a successful barrister, Malone married Catherine Collier (d. 1765), daughter of Benjamin Collier of Essex, on 26 May 1736. When Malone returned to Dublin in 1740, having been called to the Irish bar, he was already the father of Richard (1738–1816) [*see below*], whose legal and political career followed a course similar to that of his father. In 1741 another son, Edmond (1741–1812) [*see* Malone, Edmond], was born. Edmond entered the law before establishing himself as a noted Shakespearian critic. Malone fathered another four children, two of whom died in infancy. In Dublin, Malone was soon a respected and prosperous barrister, specializing in private litigation. He was sworn in as MP for Askeaton on 26 October 1753 and served until 1760. He was MP for Granard, co. Longford, from 1761 to 1766, but his political career came to an end soon after the death of his wife and he returned to London as a judge in the court of common pleas in 1767. His other appointments included bencher of the Honorable Society of King's Inns (1767–74), commissioner to hear and determine causes in chancery, in the absence of, or on the death of the lord chancellor (1768–74), and commissioner of bankruptcy appointed by the lord chancellor (1772). He was awarded an honorary LLD from Trinity College, Dublin, in 1756 and given the freedom of the city of Cork in 1760.

Malone died on 22 April 1774, probably in London.

Though overshadowed by his second son, Malone epitomizes the successful eighteenth-century professional gentleman.

Malone's first son, **Richard Malone**, Baron Sunderlin (1738–1816), was educated at Dr Ford's school, before entering Trinity College, Dublin, on 18 October 1755. He was student at the Inner Temple, London, in 1757 and graduated BA from Trinity College in 1759 before being incorporated of Christ Church, Oxford, in Michaelmas term that same year. He was called to the Irish bar in 1767. In 1776 he inherited the estates of his uncle Anthony Malone (1700–1776), including Baronston, co. Westmeath, and in 1778 he married Philippa Elizabeth Dorothy, née Rooper (1745–1831), eldest daughter of Godolphin Rooper (1709–1790) of Berkhamsted, Hertfordshire, and his wife, Mary Ann, née Harris (d. 1793), daughter of Timothy Harris. Made sheriff of co. Westmeath in 1780, in 1783 Malone bought a seat in the Irish House of Commons and served as MP for Banagher until 30 June 1785, when he was raised to the Irish peerage as Lord Sunderlin. He was further created Baron Sunderlin of Baronston. In the House of Lords, Malone sought appointment to the privy council without success. Little is known of his life after 1788, but as his brother Edmond's executor he bequeathed many of the Shakespearian scholar's books to the Bodleian Library. Richard Malone died on 14 April 1816, probably at Baronston.   STEPHEN ROBERTS

Sources *DNB* · *IGI* · E. M. Johnston-Liik, *History of the Irish parliament, 1692–1800*, 6 vols. (2002) · Burke, *Peerage*

Malone, Richard, Baron Sunderlin (1738–1816). *See under* Malone, Edmund (1704–1774).

Malone, Sylvester (1822–1906), ecclesiastical historian, born in the parish of Kilmally, co. Clare, was the son of Jeremiah Malone and his wife, Mary Slattery. He was educated for the priesthood and was ordained in 1854. Having served as curate at Cooraclare, Kilkee, and Newmarket-on-Fergus, in 1875 he became parish priest of Sixmilebridge, and in 1889 of Clare Castle. In 1892 he was appointed to Kilrush as vicar-general, and remained there for the rest of his life. He was promoted soon after to the offices of canon and archdeacon.

Malone, an ardent nationalist, was devoted to the study of the Irish language. His *Church history of Ireland from the invasion of the English in 1169 to the beginning of the Reformation in 1532* (1867; 2nd edn, 1880) was a standard work in its time. He was a supporter of the preservation of the Irish language, and a member of the various societies founded for that purpose. He died at Francis Street, Kilrush, on 21 May 1906.

D. J. O'DONOGHUE, *rev.* G. MARTIN MURPHY

Sources *Freeman's Journal* [Dublin] (22 May 1906) · *BL cat.* · private information (1912) · *CGPLA Ire.* (1906)
Wealth at death £1379 13s. 8d.: probate, 8 Aug 1906, *CGPLA Ire.*

Malone, William (1586–1656), Jesuit and religious controversialist, was born in Dublin on 6 December 1586, the son of Simon Malone, merchant, and his wife, Margaret Bexwick of Manchester. He studied at Douai before entering the Society of Jesus at Rome on 24 September 1606. At Antwerp in 1611 he published the first English translation of the autobiography of St Teresa of Avila. He continued his studies at Rome and in Portugal, at Evora (1611–14) and Coimbra (1614–15). He was ordained in Portugal in 1615 before returning to Ireland as part of the Irish Jesuit mission.

Malone is remembered principally for his part in a theological disputation with James Ussher, later archbishop of Armagh, and other protestant controversialists. In 1621 he circulated, possibly in manuscript, a 'Challenge about the judgement of antiquity concerning the Romish religion', a short polemical work questioning the idea that the Church of Rome had deviated from the pure doctrines of Christianity, and challenging what he perceived as protestant disregard for many of the teachings of the fathers of the church on matters like the real presence, confession, and tradition. Ussher replied in manuscript and subsequently in print in *An Answer to a Jesuit* (Dublin, 1624). Three years later Malone's reply to Ussher was printed at Douai under the title *A reply to Mr James Ussher his answere, wherein … the uniform consent of antiquity is declared to stande for the Roman religion: and the answerer is convinced of vanity in challenging the patronage of the doctors of the primitive church for his protestancy.* His reply did not go into circulation in Dublin until 1629 or 1630. George Synge and Roger Puttocke prepared separate rejoinders which were printed in 1632. Christopher Sibthorpe also replied to Malone but his contribution circulated in manuscript only. Joshua Hoyle's rejoinder, the last published text in the Malone controversy, was published in Dublin in 1641.

Malone's published work was not universally well received by Irish Catholic clergy on the continent with reservations expressed about Malone's dedication to Charles I, which to many appeared to award undue influence to the king in the resolution of religious controversy. However, his Catholic critics considered that the least damage would be done if his writings were ignored.

Malone served for a time as superior of the Jesuits in Dublin until in 1635 he became rector of the secular Irish College at Rome, a position he retained until 1647. The college had been founded by Cardinal Ludovisi with the assistance of John Roche, later bishop of Ferns, and the Franciscan Luke Wadding, and following the premature death of the founder in 1632 the Ludovisian college had passed from Franciscan to Jesuit control in controversial circumstances.

In December 1647 Malone was appointed superior of the Jesuit mission in Ireland. Differences with the papal nuncio, Cardinal Rinuccini, in 1648 soon gave rise to requests for his recall. He ceased to be superior in 1650, but was again temporarily in charge in 1653 before being deported from Ireland by the parliamentarians in 1654. In the following year he became rector of the Jesuit college at Seville in Spain; he died in Seville on 18 August 1656.

BERNADETTE CUNNINGHAM

Sources Archives of the Irish Province of the Society of Jesus, Dublin, MacErlean transcripts • D. Gaffney, 'The practice of religious controversy in Dublin, 1600–1641', *The churches, Ireland, and the Irish*, ed. W. J. Sheils and D. Ward, SCH, 25 (1989), 145–58 • F. O'Donoghue, biographical sketches, Archives of the Irish Province of the Society of Jesus, Dublin • B. Jennings, ed., *Wadding papers, 1614–38*, IMC (1953) • F. O'Donoghue, 'The Jesuit mission in Ireland, 1598–1651', PhD diss., Catholic University of America, Washington, DC, 1981 **Archives** Archives of the Irish Province of the Society of Jesus, Dublin, MacErlean transcripts • Archives of the Irish Province of the Society of Jesus, Dublin, MSS A/1–89

Malory, Sir Robert (*d.* 1439/40), prior of the hospital of St John of Jerusalem in England, came from a Warwickshire family: he was the brother or first or second cousin of John Malory of Newbold Revel, father of Sir Thomas *Malory the author.

He may be the Robert Malory, *clericus*, who was rector of Withybrook in Warwickshire in 1407–8, a benefice he would have resigned before going to Rhodes for his noviciate, then of five years. He is first certainly recorded on 11 March 1415, as preceptor of Balsall and Grafton in Warwickshire, and by 18 July 1432 was acting as prior of England, although it was not until 4 May 1433 that the grand master in Rhodes formally appointed him to his priory (Clerkenwell) and its five preceptories, and gave him authority over the hospitaller priory of Ireland and the bailiwick of Scotland.

Malory took his seat in the upper house of the parliament of 1433, by virtue of his position as prior, and afterwards sat on two commissions for Middlesex, one to assess tax rebates, the other to administer an oath not to maintain peace-breakers. He spent 1434 settling into his priory. In addition to routine business, he reorganized its procedures so that the office of the dead should be properly said for deceased members and benefactors of the priory. He also made preparations to lead a contingent, including knights from Scotland, to Rhodes, where an attack from Egypt was expected.

Malory's passport was issued on 25 January 1435, but, although he was supposed to be in Rhodes by March, he was still in England in October. He was in Rhodes by 22 March 1436 and remained there until December 1437, but the danger from Egypt subsided, and his only known duties were more administrative than military. A long-established regulation allowed that once or twice every decade a deserving member of the order residing at headquarters should be granted an extra preceptory, and Malory was given one in Derbyshire, which he then exchanged for one in Yorkshire. He also persuaded the order to grant him his priory for life: it had originally been granted only for ten years. When about to leave he was chosen as one of a commission of three to inform the pope, who was in Florence, of the death of the grand master and the election of a successor. Malory took the opportunity while there to obtain papal confirmation of the life grant of his office.

Malory was back in England by June 1438, and was soon caught up again in the order's business and the king's, carrying out the numerous transactions over the holding of land and ecclesiastical office that went with his position, arranging a safe conduct to get the Scottish members of his party home, acting as trier of petitions for the

Lords in the parliament of 1439–40, and attending the great council. He successfully promoted a private bill in parliament to pursue his priory's interest in property destroyed in the peasants' revolt of 1381. He also saw to his own state and comfort by arranging the duty-free release of a cargo that his party had brought back from Rhodes, including not only armour, but also wine, silk, 'chamlet', and Turkey carpets. His last recorded act was a quittance for rent to one of his tenants, issued on 16 December 1439. He was dead by 10 May 1440, when Henry VI wrote to ask the grand master to confirm the election of Malory's successor.

After Malory's death a number of his kinsmen were working for the priory. That, like the Turkey carpets, suggests that his sense of vocation was not severely ascetic. He looks like a man at ease with himself, able to combine the ecclesiastical and the secular, to work capably with people of every rank, and to give everyone, living or dead, his due. If he ever gave anyone more, there is no record of it. When in Rhodes he sued the king in his own court of chancery by proxy for 8*d*., and won.   P. J. C. FIELD

Sources Royal Malta Library, Valletta, MSS Arch. 340–354 · BL, Cotton MS Nero E.vi · P. J. C. Field, 'Sir Robert Malory, prior of the hospital of St John of Jerusalem in England (1432–1439/40)', *Journal of Ecclesiastical History*, 28 (1977), 249–64 · Essex RO, Chelmsford, MS D/DP T1/1023 · PRO · *Chancery records* · BL, Department of manuscripts · RO, Lichfield · Birmingham RO · GL
Archives Royal Malta Library, Valletta, archives of the Sovereign Military Order of Malta, MSS Arch. 340–354
Wealth at death ex officio, six preceptories (Clerkenwell, Cressing in Essex, Sandford, Oxfordshire, Balsall and Grafton, counting as two, in Warwickshire; Newland in West Riding of Yorkshire; Buckland and Bothmescombe, Devon

Malory, Sir Thomas (1415x18–1471), author, was son and heir of John Malory esquire (*c*.1385–1433/4), and Philippa (*d*. 1441x5), daughter of Sir William Chetwynd of Ingestre in Staffordshire and Grendon in Warwickshire.

Origins and early career John Malory held the manor of Newbold Revel in Warwickshire, that of Winwick in Northamptonshire, and lands nearby in Leicestershire. He was a person of importance in Warwickshire, where he was sheriff, escheator, justice of the peace, and five times MP, and his brother or cousin Sir Robert *Malory was preceptor of the hospitallers of St John of Jerusalem in Warwickshire, and later prior of the hospitallers in England. Philippa Malory was probably a few years older than her husband. They had three daughters, but Thomas was their only known son, and may have been the youngest child.

Thomas Malory must have been born between 25 April 1415 and 22 May 1418, because after John died in 1433 or 1434, it was Philippa who acted as head of the family, proving his will and arranging the marriage of their daughter Isobel. Thomas must have been born by mid-1418, because on 23 May 1439 he witnessed a settlement for his cousin Sir Philip Chetwynd. Prior Robert died a few months later, after which Malory's best hope of serious advancement may have lain with Chetwynd, who was making his mark in the service of the earl of Stafford and elsewhere. His own knighthood, by 8 October 1441, suggests ambition. On 28 December 1441 he acted as a parliamentary elector

for Northamptonshire. He must then have been a Northamptonshire resident: most likely he had married, and Winwick had been settled on him and his wife. She may have been Elizabeth Walsh (*d*. 1479) of Wanlip in Leicestershire, who bore him his son and heir, Robert, in (if his inquisition post mortem can be trusted) 1447 or 1448, who probably bore him one, perhaps two, other sons, and who survived him. There is no evidence of daughters.

For Sir Thomas the routines of provincial life may have been interrupted in 1442 by serving under Philip Chetwynd in the war in Gascony: it is the most likely way for him to have acquired the detailed knowledge of southwest France he shows at the end of the *Morte Darthur*. It was certainly interrupted in 1443 by an accusation of robbery with violence near Winwick, a charge that apparently fell through. Philip Chetwynd died soon afterwards, and in 1445 Malory was elected MP for Warwickshire, and became a commissioner to assess tax exemptions in the county. This would mean both that he had returned, presumably on his mother's death, to live at Newbold Revel, and that he was *persona grata* to the two great Warwickshire magnates, Chetwynd's patron Stafford, now duke of Buckingham, and Henry Beauchamp, duke of Warwick. About this time Warwick was paying him an annuity, and Buckingham may have helped him in 1449 to be returned as MP for his borough of Bedwin in Wiltshire.

Criminal career, trials, and imprisonment With the new decade, however, Malory's life underwent a sudden, startling, and unexplained change. During the first recess of the new parliament, on 4 January 1450, he and twenty-six other armed men allegedly lay in ambush to murder Buckingham in the abbot's woods at Combe near Newbold Revel. This was followed by eighteen months of well-supported allegations of crime, including extortion, theft, rape, cattle rustling, robbery of the local abbey, and deer stealing and enormous damage to property at Caludon Park, a hunting lodge belonging to the duke of Norfolk, but of which Buckingham apparently had the use. Malory's attack was no doubt deliberate provocation of Buckingham, who at the time was hunting him with a large posse, but put him at odds with Norfolk too. His natural protector should have been Warwick, but Duke Henry was dead, and his newly installed successor, Richard Neville, earl of Warwick, was unable or unwilling to help. Malory seems to have turned to the duke of York, who was trying to bring political pressure to bear on the government, and for whose borough of Wareham a Thomas Malory was returned to the parliament that met in September 1450.

It was a bad move. In May 1451 York's efforts collapsed, and in July Buckingham caught up with Malory and committed him to the sheriff, who detained him in his own house at Coleshill. Malory escaped by swimming the moat at night, but was recaptured. He was charged at Nuneaton, the centre of Buckingham's power in Warwickshire, before a court presided over by Buckingham, with a long list of offences including the attempted murder of Buckingham; and when the two juries returned true bills, a writ of *certiorari* transferred the proceedings to the king's bench at Westminster. In January 1452 Malory was in prison in London, awaiting trial. All of this was clearly meant to keep the legal process away from the assize town of Warwick and the influence that Malory's friends might bring to bear there. Someone had also clearly encouraged potential complainants to bring forward every possible charge against him. That does not mean the charges were false.

Malory was to have a long wait for his trial. During his first year in prison he made his peace with Norfolk, and later was bailed to a group of Warwickshire gentlemen. However, a neighbour's complaint that Malory had stolen her oxen probably dates from this period of freedom, and at the end of it he failed to surrender to his bail; Buckingham had to be called out again to recapture him. Bailed a second time, in 1454, to a group of Norfolk's men, he joined an old crony on a horse-stealing expedition across East Anglia that ended in Colchester gaol. From there he escaped again, 'using swords, daggers, and halberds', but was again recaptured and sent back to London. After that he was shifted frequently from prison to prison, and, as far as is known, the penalties imposed on his gaolers for his safe keeping reached a record for medieval England. In 1455, when Henry VI suffered a mental collapse, Malory was granted a pardon by the lord protector, York. However, if his imprisonment had begun as an incautious feud with a powerful and vindictive magnate, it had now become politicized: the Lancastrian chief justice dismissed his pardon. This was the lowest point in his fortunes. He was twice sued for small sums he could not repay, and a young Thomas Malory, presumably his son, died at Newbold Revel. Late in 1457 he was bailed again, this time for two months to Warwick's men, and he seems to have been free again briefly in 1459. When the Yorkists invaded England in 1460, he was moved to a more secure prison, but their victory brought him lasting freedom. He was never tried on any of the charges against him.

In prison again, and death   The new decade looked more promising. A second pardon cleared the legal slate, and in 1462 (after settling an estate on his son Robert), he followed the new king, Edward IV, and his lords north to besiege the castles of Alnwick, Bamburgh, and Dunstanburgh, which had been seized in a Lancastrian coup. When the castles were retaken, he settled down to a more peaceful life. In 1464 he witnessed another family land settlement, and in 1466 or 1467 his grandson Nicholas was born. But soon after that his political sympathies appear to have shifted. The new king was beginning to be at odds with his chief supporters, Warwick's family, and Malory seems to have been drawn into a plot against him that was discovered in June 1468, and arrested and imprisoned without formal charge, probably in the Tower of London. He was certainly imprisoned in relative comfort and with access to one of the best libraries in the country. This is shown by the *Morte Darthur*, which he wrote in prison at this time, and completed by 3 March 1470; but the Yorkists now thought of him as a dangerous enemy, and he was excluded by name from general pardons offered in July 1468 and February 1470.

Outside prison the balance of power shifted uncertainly. In October 1470 a sudden invasion brought the Lancastrians back, and among their first acts in London was the freeing of imprisoned members of their own faction. Six months later, on 14 March 1471, Sir Thomas Malory of Newbold Revel died in London. He was buried under a marble tombstone in St Francis's Chapel, Greyfriars, Newgate, which despite its proximity to one of the gaols in which he had been imprisoned, was one of the most fashionable churches in London. His epitaph called him 'valens miles de parochia de Monkenkyrkby' ('valiant knight, of the parish of Monks Kirby'). On the day of his death the Yorkists landed again in the north, and two months later were back in power. When they held an inquiry into Malory's estate, the jurors testified that he had died owning nothing. In a prudent moment, the rash Sir Thomas had made over all his lands to others.

Malory's *Morte Darthur* and other works   His permanent memorial was to be the *Morte Darthur*. It may not have been his only work. A contemporary Arthurian verse romance called *The Wedding of Sir Gawain and Dame Ragnell* (Bodl. Oxf., MS Rawl. C. 86) bears striking similarities to it in some aspects of treatment of the story and authorial comment. In particular, both end with prayers for the author's deliverance from prison, couched in similar terms. But although *The Wedding* shows some gusto in reworking the old folk-tale theme of 'what women most desire', its 855 lines of near doggerel would not purchase anyone literary immortality.

Le Morte Darthur is a very different matter. It survives in two important texts, the edition printed by William Caxton in 1485 and a manuscript rediscovered at Winchester in 1934 (now BL, Add. MS 59678). The two texts derive independently from a lost common original, and both have suffered from post-authorial tinkering. Modern editions have reversed some of the damage by careful comparison of the two texts with each other and with Malory's known sources, which he sometimes follows very closely.

Malory called what he wrote *The Whole Book of King Arthur and his Noble Knights of the Round Table*. Its usual name, now established too firmly to be altered, was accidentally given by its first printer, William Caxton, who mistook the name of its last section for the name of the whole. As Malory's title implies, he intended to retell in English the entire Arthurian story from authoritative accounts, which for him meant primarily the three major cycles of French Arthurian prose romance, although he knew many other Arthurian stories and drew on them for incidents, allusions, and minor characters that give his story additional solidity.

Malory's book falls into eight tales. The first is based on the end of the second romance in the post-vulgate *Roman du graal*. It relates Arthur's mysterious conception, his achievement of the throne, and the early wars and quests of his knights: it ends with Arthur as undisputed king of Britain. The second adapts a late medieval English alliterative poem, *Morte Arthure*, to tell how Arthur conquers the Roman empire. Malory replaces the poem's tragic ending with a triumphant return to Britain, so making Arthur the greatest monarch in the world, and increases Lancelot's part from a few passing references to that of the rising star of chivalry.

The third tale sets incidents mostly from the third romance of the vulgate cycle in a frame of Malory's devising, to show Lancelot becoming the greatest knight in the world. He is also Guinevere's knight, but Malory's choice of episodes suppresses the adulterous love that is prominent in his source. The fourth tale is almost certainly based on a lost English poem about Gawain's youngest brother, Gareth, in which Malory has transferred much of Gawain's role to Lancelot. It gives Lancelot a follower with followers of his own, who might support him and Lancelot against Arthur.

The long fifth tale is taken from the French prose *Tristan*. Malory cut the extended account of Tristan's ancestry with which his source begins and the grail story with which it ends, leaving as the centrepiece of his book a profusion of adventures without obvious plot and theme. The result, however, is what later authors would imitate or satirize as the characteristic Arthurian world of chivalric quest and adventure.

The sixth tale is based on the fourth romance of the vulgate cycle, and tells the story of the grail, the supreme quest, in which three of Arthur's knights succeed, Lancelot is caught between success and failure, and the rest fail. The seventh tale combines material from the last romance in the vulgate cycle (partly through a derived English poem, *Le Morte Arthur*) with additional material from the third romance and Malory's invention. Its five episodes follow Lancelot's resumption of his affair with Guinevere after the grail quest, through repeated risk of discovery. The eighth tale completes the vulgate cycle story, relating the discovery of the affair, the internecine war that it provokes, and the deaths of nearly all the principal characters.

Malory's influence Malory made his story one of the rise and fall of a great king and his kingdom. The symbolic power provided by this, by the innumerable quests and adventures contained in the book, and by the half-strange, half-familiar world of chivalric romance, reinforced by a transparent colloquial style that made events seem to stand free of any controlling author, quickly made it popular. For sixteenth-century England, despite humanists and puritans, it was the definitive retelling of the Arthurian story. When the round table in Winchester Castle was repainted for Henry VIII, the names of the individual knights on it were mostly taken from the *Morte Darthur*. In the next two centuries different tastes meant that the few readers interested in the 'matter of Britain' mostly looked to Geoffrey of Monmouth; but nineteenth-century medievalism raised the status of Malory's book to previously unimagined heights: Dante Gabriel Rossetti put it second only to the Bible. The twentieth century has seen it less admired but perhaps even more influential, affecting the media of films, cartoons, and computer games as well as established literary genres.

Malory's own reputation followed an even more erratic course. John Bale in 1548 asserted that Malory came from Maelor in Denbighshire, and the *Biographia Britannica* in the mid-eighteenth century misread the closing words of the *Morte Darthur* as implying that its author was a priest. It was only in the 1890s that scholarship jettisoned the imaginary Welsh priest and discovered a trio of real Thomas Malorys, whose various claims to authorship became the subject of vigorous debate. As the only indubitable knight among them, Sir Thomas Malory of Newbold Revel began as favourite, but when the criminal charges against him were discovered, many found them difficult to reconcile with the idealism that was commonly seen in the *Morte Darthur*. Renewed investigation, however, has established that he was the only knight of the right name alive at the right time. If an author's life and writings must echo one another, the criminal charges must be false, or the perceived idealism exaggerated, or the author's personality must have changed in the course of eighteen years, mostly spent in fifteenth-century prisons. It seems most likely that all three notions contain an element of truth.   P. J. C. FIELD

Sources T. Malory, *The works*, ed. E. Vinaver, rev. P. J. C. Field, 3rd edn, 3 vols. (1990) · P. J. C. Field, *The life and times of Sir Thomas Malory* (1993) [incl. copious references to unpubd sources] · PRO, C 140/36/12; E 149/224/18; C 140/75/46 · W. Dugdale, *The antiquities of Warwickshire illustrated*, rev. W. Thomas, 2nd edn, 2 vols. (1730) · J. Nichols, *The history and antiquities of the county of Leicester*, 4 vols. (1795–1815) · G. Wrottesley, 'The Chetwynd chartulary', in G., *Collections for a history of Staffordshire*, William Salt Archaeological Society, 12/1 (1891), 244–336 · 'Brief notes of occurrences under Henry VI and Edward IV from MS Lambeth, 448', *Three fifteenth-century chronicles*, ed. J. Gairdner, CS, new ser., 28 (1880), 148–63 · C. Carpenter, *Locality and polity: a study of Warwickshire landed society, 1401–1499* (1992)

Archives priv. coll., literary MSS | BL, Add. MS 59678 · Bodl. Oxf., MS Rawl. C. 86

Wealth at death widow held lands in Warwickshire, Leicestershire, and Northamptonshire valued at £22: PRO C 140/36/12; E 149/224/18; C 140/75/46; Nichols, *History and antiquities*, 4.362

Malpas, Philip (d. 1469). *See under* Cook, Sir Thomas (c.1410–1478).

Maltby, Edward (1770–1859), bishop of Durham, was born on 6 April 1770 in the Norwich parish of St George Tombland, fourth son of George Maltby (d. 1794), master weaver, and his wife, Mary (d. 1804). He was baptized on 8 April by the Presbyterian Samuel Bourn, minister of the Octagon Chapel where George Maltby was deacon. The family was, however, well-disposed towards the established church: a memorial in the parish church commemorates Maltby's parents and grandparents, while in 1789 George and his brother each contributed 5 guineas to the parish augmentation fund.

Maltby entered Norwich grammar school in January 1778, a year before Samuel Parr became headmaster. Parr, an Anglican priest notorious for whiggery, respected dissenters and was Bourn's close friend. His influence on Maltby was profound. Parr retired in 1785; on his advice Maltby transferred to Winchester College, studying under Joseph Warton from 1785 to 1788. Taylor and Taylor's *History of the Octagon Chapel* states that he also studied under

Edward Maltby (1770–1859), by Sir William Beechey, 1832

William Enfield. In 1784 his cousin Elizabeth Maltby married George Pretyman, later George Pretyman Tomline, confidant to Pitt the younger, who in 1787 became bishop of Lincoln. Pretyman entered Maltby at Pembroke College, Cambridge, in 1789.

At Cambridge Maltby won four medals, was 1791 Craven scholar, and graduated BA as eighth wrangler in 1792, MA in 1794, BD in 1801, and DD in 1806. Unlike his cousin William, he conformed to the Church of England and took his degrees without problem. In 1794 he became Pretyman's domestic chaplain, with a Lincoln prebend and two vicarages: Buckden in Huntingdonshire and Holbeach in Lincolnshire. On 10 July 1794 he married Mary, daughter of Jeremiah Ives Harvey of Catton, Norfolk, with whom he had at least four sons. His *Illustrations of the Truth of the Christian Religion*, published in 1802, enjoyed two further editions in 1803 and helped to establish his reputation as a whig 'bishop-in-waiting'. However, the political upheavals of the new century stalled his career: his intervention in the 1807 Huntingdonshire elections, and an 1809 pamphlet denouncing the Portland administration's nepotism, stranded him at Buckden during the long tory political ascendancy, though, aided by Parr's influence with Canning, he became preacher of Gray's Inn in 1817 and was preacher of Lincoln's Inn from 1824 to 1835. In these years Maltby devoted himself to scholarship, publishing an 1815 *Lexicon Graeco-prosodiacum*, based on Thomas Morell's 1762 *Thesaurus*, which went through two full and three abridged editions, and co-compiling an 1815 hymn collection (revised 1824); a New Testament edition discussed with Parr was never completed. He also tutored

private pupils, including E. B. Pusey. He became a fellow of the Royal Society in 1824 and was a fellow of the Society of Antiquaries by 1834. A committee member of Brougham's Society for the Diffusion of Useful Knowledge (founded in 1827), the Utilitarian counterblast to the Society for Promoting Christian Knowledge, Maltby became a senator of University College, London, and offered the blessing prayer when its foundation stone was laid (1827). His first wife, Mary, died on 2 May 1825 and he remarried on 31 August 1826; his new wife was Margaret, youngest daughter of Major Green.

The Reform Bill crisis of November 1830 put Earl Grey in office, needing Maltby's vote in the House of Lords. Folliott Cornewall, bishop of Worcester, died in September 1831; Grey translated Carr of Chichester to Worcester and appointed Maltby to Chichester, so hastily that the *congé d'élire* for Worcester arrived before Cornewall's funeral and caused a scandal. Maltby was in his place in time to vote for the Reform Bill in the House of Lords on 8 October 1831. The sole active whig among the episcopate—Bathurst of Norwich was eighty-seven and incapacitated—Maltby, branded a 'black swan', met the other bishops' hostility with plainspoken resolve to do his duty 'equally regardless of their smiles or their frowns' (Grant, 401–3). A former schoolfellow at Winchester, Sydney Smith, disappointed to be passed over for the Chichester see, regarded him as an 'excellent man and a great fool' (P. Virgin, *Sydney Smith*, 1994, 27). Scandal certainly dogged his episcopate. He invited a Unitarian minister to a public dinner (1834), and did nothing to quieten the outcry by inviting a Catholic priest to dinner two weeks later.

Translated in March 1836 to be the first bishop of 'reformed' Durham, Maltby had charge of the orb at Queen Victoria's coronation, but presented it at the wrong moment; the queen called him 'remarkably *maladroit*' (*Letters of Queen Victoria*, ed. A. C. Benson and Lord Esher, and G. E. Buckle, 1st ser., 1907, 1.155). In 1838 Maltby again outraged the orthodox when he and Bathurst's successor Stanley subscribed to a volume of sermons by the Unitarian William Turner. Charles Thorp, archdeacon of Durham, denounced Maltby in *The Times*, and an effigy inscribed 'Unitarian Bishop' was burnt in Bishop Auckland market-place. He delivered a series of episcopal charges against Tractarianism from 1840 onwards, and in 1845 also attacked the evangelical party for 'believing that they alone possessed true understanding' (E. Maltby, *Charge*, 1845, 8). His continuing scholarly interests were reflected in calls for the training of ordinands to be based on sound biblical learning. He was a generous benefactor to Durham University (founded 1833) and helped negotiate its royal charter, even persuading the government to honour the agreement with his predecessor Van Mildert that students must subscribe to the Thirty-Nine Articles before graduation. In 1847 criticism arose over his income, which averaged about £12,000 a year and in 1841 exceeded £21,000, whereas the 1836 Established Church Act set it at £8000 (reduced from £19,000). In 1848 he established the Maltby Fund, giving more than £21,000 over ten years for allocation by the ecclesiastical commissioners to parsonage building in Durham diocese.

Considered for archbishop of York in November 1847 by his friend Lord John Russell, Maltby declined; he was growing weary. In 1850 his letter to Russell denouncing the establishment of a Roman Catholic hierarchy in England inspired Russell's 'Durham Letter', which declared the Tractarians a worse threat. In 1855, eighty-five and nearly blind, he offered to retire on a £4500 annuity from the Durham revenues. No bishop since the Reformation had been permitted retirement, and Gladstone denounced the pension request as simony; but after acrimonious debate an 1856 act of parliament granted both Maltby and Blomfield of London pensioned retirement. Maltby died on 3 July 1859 at his London residence, 1 Upper Portland Place; the *Times* obituary took one last swipe at his huge pension. Buried on 11 July at Kensal Green cemetery, London, he shared a family vault with his eldest brother.

E. A. VARLEY

Sources E. A. Harbord, 'Bishop Maltby and his library', 1977, U. Durham L., archives and special collections, Local collection · *The Times* (7 July 1859) · *Durham Chronicle* (8 July 1859) · *DNB* · Venn, *Alum. Cant.* · [J. Grant], *Random recollections of the House of Lords* (1836) · O. Chadwick, *The Victorian church*, 2 vols. (1966–70) · H. C. Fowler, 'Edward Maltby: his episcopal superintendence and views as bishop of Durham', MA diss., U. Durham, 1990 · P. J. Welch, 'The two episcopal resignations of 1856', *Church Quarterly Review*, 165 (1964), 17–27 · G. F. A. Best, *Temporal pillars: Queen Anne's bounty, the ecclesiastical commissioners, and the Church of England* (1964) · J. Taylor and E. Taylor, *History of the Octagon Chapel, Norwich* (1848) · H. P. Liddon, *The life of Edward Bouverie Pusey*, ed. J. O. Johnston, [2nd edn], 1 (1893) · *GM*, 1st ser., 64 (1794), 671 · *GM*, 1st ser., 95/1 (1825), 631 · *GM*, 1st ser., 96/2 (1826), 269 · *The Times* (6 July 1859)
Archives W. Sussex RO, corresp., university notes, and other papers | Balliol Oxf., letters to Henry Jenkyns · BL, corresp. with Bishop Samuel Butler, Add. MSS 34584–34592 · BL, corresp. with third Baron Holland, Add. MS 51597 · BL, corresp. with Sir Robert Peel, Add. MSS 40546–40587 · Durham RO, letters to Lord Londonderry · PRO, corresp. with Lord John Russell, PRO30/22 · U. Durham L., letters to second Earl Grey and Maria, Lady Grey; letters to third Earl Grey · U. Durham L., corresp. with Charles Thorp · UCL, letters to Society for the Diffusion of Useful Knowledge · W. Sussex RO, letters to duke of Richmond · Yale U., Beinecke L., letters to T. J. Pettigrew
Likenesses W. Beechey, oils, 1832, Bishop Auckland Palace, Durham [*see illus.*] · W. Behnes, marble bust, *c.*1844, FM Cam. · H. P. Briggs, oils, University College, Durham · R. Cooper, stipple (after H. Edridge), BM, NPG · H. Edridge, watercolour, BM · G. T. Payne, mezzotint (after H. P. Briggs), BM · D. Turner, etching (after J. S. Cotman), BM · oils, Pembroke Cam.
Wealth at death under £120,000: resworn probate, June 1860, *CGPLA Eng. & Wales* (1859)

Maltby, Sir Paul Copeland (1892–1971), air force officer, was born on 5 August 1892 at Allippey, India, the younger son and fourth in the family of five children of Christopher James Maltby, a tea planter, and his wife, Jessie, the daughter of William Copeland Capper, an eminent Indian civil servant. He was educated at Bedford School and at the Royal Military College, Sandhurst, of which an uncle, Colonel W. B. Capper, was commandant. Commissioned in the Royal Welch Fusiliers, he served from 1911 to 1914 with his regiment in India and France.

Perhaps inspired by the knowledge that another uncle,

Colonel J. E. Capper, had taken part in the first flight over London by a British military airship, Maltby joined the Royal Flying Corps on secondment in 1915. Commanding a squadron from 1916, he ended the war a substantive major and temporary lieutenant-colonel. A daring reconnaissance mission in 1916 earned him the DSO (1917), and on another occasion he was mentioned in dispatches.

In 1919 Maltby accepted a permanent commission in the Royal Air Force, in the belief that he would not be called upon to make a formal renunciation of his commission in the army. He commanded a squadron at Quetta from 1920 to 1924. At Bombay, on 25 November 1921, he married Winifred Russell, the daughter of James Harper Paterson, a businessman of Edinburgh; they had two sons (the elder of whom was killed in action in 1945) and a daughter. Maltby attended courses at the RAF Staff College in 1926–7 and the Imperial Defence College in 1931, and from 1932 to 1934 was commandant of the Central Flying School. At the height of the Abyssinian crisis he commanded the RAF in the Mediterranean and served as a nominated member of the council of Malta. In this post he did much to prepare the island's air defences at a time when precautions against the possibility of war were far from popular. He was promoted wing commander in 1925, group captain in 1932, air commodore in 1936, and air vice-marshal in 1938.

During the next three years Maltby commanded in turn a training group and two army co-operation groups and served briefly as senior air staff officer at general headquarters, home forces. In 1941 he was appointed CB, and in November of that year he was posted to command the RAF in Northern Ireland, but almost immediately was ordered to Singapore for special duties at general headquarters, Far East.

Maltby arrived practically on the eve of the Japanese onslaught there. The commander-in-chief, Air Chief Marshal Sir H. R. M. Brooke-Popham, had been told to rely—in the absence of a strong fleet—on air power, but he had no air strike force apart from a few light bombers and obsolete torpedo-bombers. About half the aircraft in Malaya were lost on the first day, and British North Borneo was almost defenceless. Hong Kong, where Maltby's brother had recently assumed command of the land forces, was not expected to hold out for more than a few weeks. Maltby would always praise highly the determination and fortitude of the aircrews of the RAF, the Royal Australian Air Force, and the Royal Netherlands Air Force in their efforts to defend the region. But, as Sir Maurice Dean has observed, their task was made impossible 'by reason of inadequate numbers and grossly inadequate quality of equipment' (Dean, 249).

When, early in 1942, general headquarters, Far East, was abolished and the Western allies set up a unified command, for the purpose of defending a line from Singapore through the Indonesian archipelago to Darwin, Maltby became deputy to the air commander in Malaya, Air Vice-Marshal C. W. H. Pulford. He took a leading part in the preparation of plans for a staged withdrawal to the Dutch East Indies and the formation of two groups, into which an air force augmented by new arrivals was to be divided. He had difficulty, though, in extracting Pulford from Singapore. The latter had become determined not to leave until the last possible moment and finally departed in a launch which was attacked by Japanese aircraft. With other survivors, he was marooned on a desolate island, where he died.

Maltby arrived in Java in mid-February as air officer commanding, charged by Wavell with the defence of the island and with the evacuation of all surplus units and personnel. He did his best to weld depleted squadrons into a coherent air force, and set up an early-warning and fighter-control system staffed largely by local volunteers. But the fate of Java was sealed when the Dutch Admiral Doorman, with no maritime reconnaissance aircraft to help him, lost the naval battle of the Java Sea. Maltby recognized the inevitable and surrendered his forces in April 1942. Maltby was now responsible for the conditions of his men in captivity; he was aware from an early stage of the extreme hardships to which they would be subjected and 'fought their battles with the Japanese prison camp commanders to the end with exemplary dedication' (Dean, 249).

On his return to England in 1945 Maltby took charge of the compilation of reports on operations in Malaya, but his wartime ordeal as a prisoner of war proved too much, and he retired from the RAF soon after, cutting short a promising career. From 1946 to 1962 he filled the more congenial role of serjeant-at-arms (Black Rod) at the House of Lords. In 1946 he was made KBE, in recognition of his services while a prisoner of war, and in 1962 he became KCVO. He was appointed by Queen Wilhelmina of the Netherlands a grand officer of the order of Orange Nassau, and from 1956 he was a deputy lieutenant for Southampton.

Addicted in youth to pranks which sometimes landed him in trouble, Maltby was better known in later years as an enthusiastic gardener and remaker of gardens. Tall and slim, he both looked and always was at heart a soldier. Fashionable theories of air power did not shake his conviction that air forces ought to help land forces. The courage, energy, and sense of dedication to a cause which were part of the Capper inheritance were tempered in him by a sensibility which might have precluded the ruthlessness sometimes demanded of commanders-in-chief in war. The matter was not put to the test, but what he was given to do he did well. His exertions in the closing stages of the campaign in Malaya saved many lives. That Pulford's was not one of them was a sword in his heart. Maltby died at Rotherwick, near Basingstoke, Hampshire, on 2 July 1971.

BASIL COLLIER, rev. MARK POTTLE

Sources *The Times* (6 July 1971) · Ministry of Defence, Air and Army Historical Branches · Royal Military Academy, Sandhurst · private information (1986) · H. Probert, *The forgotten air force: the RAF in the war against Japan, 1941–1945* (1995) · M. Dean, *The RAF and two world wars* (1979)

Archives NRA, priv. coll., diaries, logbooks, corresp.

Likenesses photograph, repro. in Dean, *RAF and two world wars*

Wealth at death £2828: probate, 29 Oct 1971, *CGPLA Eng. & Wales*

Maltby, William (1763–1854), bibliographer and librarian, is said to have been born in London on 17 January 1763 (*DNB*), though his baptism was not recorded until 13 February 1765 at the Old Jewry Presbyterian Church. He was the youngest of ten children of Brough Maltby (*bap.* 1719), wholesale draper of Mansion House Street, London, and Ann Dyer. The Maltbys came originally from Norwich, where several were elders of the Presbyterian church. Edward Maltby, bishop of Durham, was a first cousin, as was John Dyer Collier (Dyce, 300), father of John Payne Collier, the editor and literary forger. Through the Brough family he was related to Thomas Secker, archbishop of Canterbury. Maltby was educated under the Revd James Pickbourne at Grove Street, Hackney, where he formed a lifelong acquaintance with the poet Samuel Rogers, a fellow pupil; he is frequently mentioned in Archibald Dyce's *Recollections of the Table-Talk of Samuel Rogers* (1856).

Maltby entered Gonville and Caius College, Cambridge, but as a dissenter did not take a degree. Here he was to acquire the classical and literary tastes which lasted throughout his life. He was well versed not just in the classics, but also in the literature of France and Italy. On 23 June 1787 he was called to the bar at Gray's Inn, and practised as a solicitor in partnership with his brother, Rowland Maltby, clerk to the Fishmongers' Company (*Law Lists*). But literature was a greater lure than the law, and Maltby became a familiar figure in the literary circles of his day, particularly in company with Rogers.

Following the death in 1808 of Professor Richard Porson (whom he had known socially for more than twenty years), Maltby was on 1 February 1809 appointed to succeed him as principal librarian of the London Institution. This was a society in the City for subscribers, modelled on the Royal Institution in the West End, and offered lectures, particularly on scientific subjects, and an extensive reference library. Porson was better known for his fondness for the bottle than for books, but Maltby was in his natural element there as a book lover. He assiduously attended the major book auctions and made many large additions to the library. By 1811 the institution (founded only in 1806) already held 12,000 volumes. He had an extraordinary memory and knowledge of books, and was a fount of wisdom on bibliographical matters. Visiting Rome in 1821 Rogers wrote: 'I never pass a bookseller's shop here but I think of M[altby]' (Clayden, 1.329).

Twice Maltby was responsible for the removal and rearrangement of the books. The first occasion was in 1811, when the institution moved from its original home in Old Jewry to King's Arms Yard, Coleman Street. These premises were always too small, and in 1819 the institution removed to a new building in the recently laid out Finsbury Circus. He assisted in the compilation of the original catalogue, printed in 1813, as well as in the first volume (1835) of the new edition. The institution grew slowly and suffered a number of crises in its management, but its heart was always the library, whose development into a major reference library was entirely due to Maltby's labours.

From the beginning the assistant librarian of the London Institution had been William Upcott, the autograph collector. When he was asked to resign in 1834 following unspecified complaints (London Institution minute books), Maltby (then aged seventy-one) expressed his desire to retire at the same time if he could keep his apartments. This was granted, and he was awarded a pension of £100 per annum. He died at the London Institution on 5 January 1854 and was buried at Norwood cemetery, where a memorial was erected by Rogers. He was unmarried. Although Maltby had a reputation for his willingness to communicate his great knowledge of books to others—he was masterly at literary and classical quotations—he never published a single book himself. His sole contribution to literature was his memoir of Porson, published as 'Porsoniana' in Dyce's *Table-Talk*.   K. A. MANLEY

Sources GM, 2nd ser., 41 (1854), 209–10 · *Recollections of the table-talk of Samuel Rogers*, ed. A. Dyce (1856) · R. W. Frazer, *Notes on the history of the London Institution* (1905) · P. W. Clayden, *Rogers and his contemporaries*, 2 vols. (1889) · parish registers · law lists · London Institution, managers' minutes, GL · *DNB*
Archives GL, London Institution archives

Malthus, (Thomas) Robert (1766–1834),

political economist, was born on 13 February 1766 and baptized on 14 February at his parents' home, The Rookery, near Wotton, Surrey. In formal situations he used his full name, but in less formal correspondence referred to himself as T. Robert Malthus or Robert Malthus, and among family and close friends was always called Robert or Bob.

Family and early life Malthus's great-grandfather Daniel Malthus (1651–1717) was apothecary to Queen Anne and George I. His grandfather Sydenham Malthus (d. 1757) was a barrister of Lincoln's Inn. His father, Daniel Malthus (1730–1800), being an only son, appears to have inherited considerable wealth and property, and these independent means enabled him to travel and to cultivate his literary, artistic, theatrical, and scientific interests. He entered Queen's College, Oxford, in 1747 but did not graduate. He was an admirer of Rousseau, who once visited The Rookery when Malthus was an infant. He was said to have published some literary pieces anonymously, but the statement by an obituarist that he had translated works from French and German was firmly contradicted by Malthus. He supported the views of the marquis de Condorcet and William Godwin on the perfectibility of mankind, but also encouraged his son's publication of opposing views. Aspects of his behaviour—for example, the unconventional education he chose for Malthus, and his refusal to allow his wife to wear her wedding ring—were regarded as eccentric, and perhaps show the influence of Rousseau. He married (on 6 May 1752) Henrietta Catherine Graham (1733–1800), his second cousin, the daughter of Daniel Graham (1695–1778), apothecary to George II and George III. She can be seen as a young girl with her brother and two sisters, in Hogarth's painting *The Graham Children* (1742), now in the National Gallery, London. Malthus was the sixth of their seven children (two boys and five girls).

Malthus's elder brother, Sydenham (1754–1821), was the grandfather of Colonel Sydenham Malthus (1831–1916)

(Thomas) Robert Malthus (1766–1834), by John Linnell, 1833

and the great-grandfather of Robert Malthus (1881–1972), whose family papers have provided much valuable information about the life and career of Malthus. Other descendants of Sydenham emigrated to New Zealand, where there are now many Malthus families. Malthus's youngest sister, Mary Anne Catherine (1771–1852), married Edward Bray, of Shere, Surrey. Their daughter Louisa, in her unpublished 'Recollections', provides further insights into the lives of the Malthus and Bray families.

Little is known of Malthus's schooling before the age of twelve. One source (Payne) says that he was educated in private at High Wycombe 'by men well qualified as tutors' (Payne, 101), but no further details are given. It is possible that Malthus's father undertook at least some of his early education at home. Malthus's five sisters were brought up at home without a governess.

For at least three school years, from 1778/9 to 1780/81, Malthus attended a school conducted by Revd Richard Graves at his home, Claverton rectory, near Bath. In letters to Daniel Malthus, Graves commented on the rapid progress made by Malthus in his classical studies and on his precociousness in appreciating the humorous passages. He also reported that the young Malthus loved 'fighting for fighting's sake', but that he and his antagonist were 'the best of friends in the world'—a situation that William Empson later saw as prefiguring Malthus's relationship with Ricardo.

During the academic year 1782/3 (and perhaps earlier) Malthus was sent by his father to the dissenting academy at Warrington, near Liverpool. The dissenting academies of Warrington and elsewhere had been established to provide an education for the sons of dissenters, who at that time, because they refused to subscribe to the Thirty-Nine

Articles of the Church of England, were not admitted to the universities of Oxford and Cambridge and were therefore debarred from professions requiring university degrees. It is not clear why Daniel Malthus chose to send his son to a dissenting academy, rather than to a public school, or why he chose one at such a distance from Surrey. There is no evidence that either Daniel Malthus or Malthus was ever a dissenter. Malthus himself later became a clergyman of the Church of England. It is possible that the concept of a dissenting academy appealed to a radical trait in Daniel's character, or that he was impressed by the scholarly reputation and independence of spirit of the tutors at the academy. According to Gilbert Wakefield, the classical tutor at the Warrington academy from 1779 to 1783, at least one third of the students at that time were members of the 'establishment', who preferred an education at the academy to the 'restrictions and licentiousness' of the universities (Wakefield, 199).

When the academy at Warrington closed down in 1783, Malthus became a private pupil of Gilbert Wakefield for the year 1783/4 at his home in Bramcote, near Nottingham, where he pursued a rigorous and regular programme of study in classics and mathematics, interspersed with walking and shooting in the company of Wakefield, who treated him more as a companion. Wakefield was later to become famous for his radical political views, notably his argument that the poor and labouring classes of England would lose nothing if Napoleon conquered England and imposed on England the egalitarianism of the French Revolution. For these seditious remarks he was imprisoned in Dorchester gaol for two years, 1799–1801.

With the advice and help of Wakefield, Malthus on 8 June 1784 was entered as a pensioner at Jesus College, Cambridge, where Wakefield had been a fellow; he took up residence in October that year. His father supported his desire for a university education, although his mother, it seems, was originally opposed to the idea. Malthus graduated BA and ninth wrangler early in 1788. His studies were mainly in mathematics and classics, although later, after graduation, he was reading books on mineralogy, chemistry, geography, and history. He obtained a prize for a Latin declamation on the ironical topic that knowledge of classical texts would be facilitated if they were studied in translation. He proceeded MA in 1791 and became a fellow of Jesus College on 10 June 1793. He held his fellowship until his marriage in 1804. As an undergraduate he was taught by yet another radical tutor, William Frend (1757–1841), who was later expelled from the university for opposing the policy requiring subscription to the Thirty-Nine Articles.

As early as 1783 Malthus had expressed a desire to enter the church. The only difficulty seems to have been a speech defect resulting from a congenital cleft lip and palate. He was advised that it would prohibit his rising to an eminent position in the church, but, although it proved troublesome to some acquaintances, it did not prevent the successful performance of his preaching and teaching duties. He was ordained deacon by the bishop of Winchester on 7 June 1789 and licensed to the curacy of Oakwood (or Okewood) Chapel in the parish of Wotton, at a stipend of £40 a year. The appointment at Oakwood appears to have been negotiated by his father. He held his stipendiary curacy of Oakwood until about 1805, when he was appointed to the East India College. During this time he probably lived mainly with his parents in the village of Albury, about 9 miles north of Oakwood, where they had moved in 1787, although he also spent time in a 'garret in Town' and resided occasionally at Jesus College. He was ordained priest on 20 March 1791, and on 5 April 1824 he was licensed perpetual curate of Oakwood Chapel. On 21 November 1803 he had been appointed rector of Walesby, in Lincolnshire, a living in the gift of a distant relative, Henry Dalton. He visited Walesby occasionally, but the parish duties were carried out mainly by a succession of curates. William Otter and William Empson attest that Malthus was imbued with the spirit of the gospel and with the doctrines of Christianity; and that in the performance of his clerical duties he was conscientious, devout, and pious. In turn with the other professors, he read prayers and preached regularly in the chapel of the East India College. His sermons, some of which have survived, were said by Otter to have become more earnest and edifying over the years. In his publications Malthus nearly always described himself as Rev. According to Payne, Malthus changed the family motto from *Honor justitiae praemium* to *Honor virtutis praemium* ('Honour is the reward of virtue').

Malthus's first known publication venture occurred in 1796, when he unsuccessfully submitted to the publisher Debrett a paper entitled 'The Crisis', a criticism of the administration of William Pitt. His father urged him to persist in trying to find a publisher, even though it might have jeopardized his clerical career ('might not get you a Deanery'). Extracts were quoted by Otter and Empson, but the paper has not subsequently been found.

The 'principle of population' In 1798 Malthus published (anonymously) his first and most famous book, *An Essay on the Principle of Population*. It arose from discussions with his father on the utopian hopes of Condorcet and Godwin, and argued that they had overlooked the difficulties arising from the tendency of population to increase more rapidly than the food supply. Population, he argued, increases in a 'geometric ratio' (1, 2, 4, 8, 16 …), doubling every twenty-five years, but the food supply can increase at the utmost only in an 'arithmetic ratio' (1, 2, 3, 4, 5, …). Consequently, population is kept in balance with the food supply by various 'checks'. These checks were classified as either 'vice' or 'misery', and included wars, famines, plagues, delayed marriages (later called 'prudential restraint'), prostitution ('vicious customs with respect to women'), and contraception ('unnatural' practices; *Essay on the Principle of Population*, 1798, 100, 154). He also classified the checks as either 'positive' (those that increase the death rate) or 'preventive' (those that reduce the birth rate).

In 1803 Malthus published a greatly expanded second

edition of the *Essay*, incorporating details of the population checks that had been in operation in many different countries and periods. Although nominally a second edition, it was regarded by Malthus as a substantially new work. He did not claim originality for the idea that population tends to outrun the food supply. In the preface to the second edition he stated that in writing the first edition he had deduced the principle of population from the writings of David Hume, Robert Wallace, Adam Smith, and Richard Price, but that in the intervening period he had become aware that much more had been published on the subject. He nevertheless believed that even more remained to be done, especially in describing the means by which populations are checked and in drawing out the practical implications of the principle of population.

In the second edition, he made clear what was only implicit in the first, that prudential restraint should, if humanly possible, be 'moral restraint'—that is, delayed marriage accompanied by strictly moral pre-marital behaviour, although he admitted that moral restraint would not be easy and that there would be occasional failures. Whereas in the first edition he had said that all the checks to population would involve either misery or vice, in the second edition he attempted to lighten this 'melancholy hue' (*Essay on the Principle of Population*, 1st edn, 1798, iv) and 'to soften some of the harshest conclusions of the first essay' (2nd edn, 1803, vii) by arguing that moral restraint, if supported by an education emphasizing the immorality of bringing children into the world without the means of supporting them, would tend to increase rather than diminish individual happiness.

In the concluding two chapters of the first edition of the *Essay* Malthus had argued that the pressure of population on the food supply was providentially ordained by God as a stimulus to human development ('the growth of mind') and was consistent with the notion of divine benevolence. These two chapters, which also contained some radical opinions on other theological questions, were omitted from the second and later editions of the *Essay*, but whether Malthus ever relinquished the views they contain is debatable.

Malthus was despised by some famous contemporaries. Samuel Taylor Coleridge referred to 'the stupid Ignorance of the Man' (MS note in Coleridge's copy of the *Essay*, BL, 6), Robert Southey described him as a 'mischievous booby' (*New Letters of Robert Southey*, ed. Kenneth Curry, 1.357) and a 'precious philosophicide' (ibid., 1.551), and William Cobbett wrote of 'the barbarous and impious Malthus' (*Rural Rides*, ed. G. D. H. Cole and M. Cole, 1930, 1.26). But Charles Darwin acknowledged Malthus's influence in the development of his theory of natural selection (*The Life and Letters of Charles Darwin*, ed. F. Darwin, 1898, 68, 465), and the principle of population became accepted as a central tenet of classical political economy.

Further editions of the *Essay* appeared in 1806, 1807, 1817, and 1826, with important alterations and additions, particularly the appendices added to the third and the fifth editions, in which Malthus replied to some of his many critics. He was accused of advocating wars and immoral practices as ways of controlling population growth, but he insisted that this was a gross misinterpretation and that the only check he advocated was prudential restraint, or preferably moral restraint. Critics also argued that the latter would not be feasible as a general method of controlling population and that in advocating it Malthus was guilty of the very perfectibilism he had condemned in Godwin, but he remained cautiously optimistic about the success of his preferred check. He rejected contraception as a means of population control, partly on moral grounds and partly because he believed that, by providing an easy means of control, it would remove the desirable stimulus to work and self-improvement arising from the need to provide for one's children. He would therefore have been strongly opposed to the later usurpation of his name by organizations such as the Neo-Malthusian League, which advocated contraception. He would also have objected to those who link his name with zero population growth. He insisted that he was not 'an enemy to population' (*Essay*, 3rd edn, 1806, 2.508). He regarded the growth of population as a desirable end in itself, and even as a necessary cause of economic growth, provided that it did not exceed the growth of the food supply. Variorum editions of the *Essay* were published in 1986 and 1989.

For today's readers, living in a post-Malthus era, the world's population problems are well known and serious, but no longer sensational. It is difficult therefore to appreciate the radical and controversial impact made by the *Essay* at the time of publication. It challenged the conventional notion that population growth is an unmixed blessing. It discussed prostitution, contraception, and other sexual matters. And it gave vivid descriptions of the horrendous consequences of overpopulation and of the brutal means by which populations are checked. But perhaps most controversial of all was Malthus's argument against the poor laws, and his denial that the poor have a right to be supported—arguments that were continued through all editions of the *Essay* and in other writings. The arguments were based on a variety of economic, psychological, and political considerations. The poor laws tended to increase the price of food, to undermine the spirit of independence of the people, to encourage early and improvident marriages, and thus to create the poor they sought to maintain—although this last tendency would be offset to some extent by the exercise of prudential restraint. For these and other reasons Malthus hoped for and advocated as a long-term goal the gradual abolition of the poor laws, but in later years, acknowledging that under the current state of public opinion abolition would not be politically practicable, he placed greater emphasis on an amelioration of the existing system through administrative improvements.

In the summer of 1799 Malthus travelled with Otter, E. D. Clarke, and J. M. Cripps to northern Europe. Malthus and Otter travelled through Sweden and Finland to St Petersburg, and returned to Britain at the end of the summer. Clarke and Cripps travelled further north, and then extensively throughout Europe. Malthus kept a diary of his journey, part of which has survived and been published. It shows him busily recording local details of the pressure of population on food supplies, and of the various local customs and institutions by means of which populations were held in check. The other part was lent to Clarke and lost.

The East India Company College In the summer of 1802 Malthus had a five-month holiday with relatives in France and Switzerland. The party included Harriet Eckersall (1776–1864), his first cousin once removed, whom he later married, on 12 April 1804. Her parents were John Eckersall (1748–1837) and Catherine Eckersall (1755–1837), both of whom were first cousins of Malthus, as well as first cousins of one another. Malthus and his wife had three children: Henry (1804–1882), who became vicar of Effingham and of Donnington, and who married Sophia Otter, daughter of William Otter; Emily (1806–1885), who married John Watson Pringle; and Lucy (1807–1825). There were no grandchildren.

In 1805 Malthus was appointed professor of history and political economy at the newly founded East India College, set up by the East India Company to educate young men for service in India. The college was initially situated in Hertford, but new buildings including accommodation for the professors and their families were soon after constructed at Haileybury, about 2 miles south-east of Hertford. Malthus taught and lived at Haileybury for the rest of his life, apart from short holidays to Ireland, Scotland, and Europe, and visits to his relatives and friends.

At times, life at the college was disturbed by the unruly behaviour of the students. Their commotions and riots, resulting in damage to property and on one occasion injury to a college servant, received much adverse publicity, and the college was threatened with closure. Malthus was asked to act as spokesperson for the college, and wrote two pamphlets in its defence: *A Letter to the Rt. Hon. Lord Grenville* (1813), and *Statements Respecting the East India College* (1817). Malthus was apparently well liked by the students. His nickname was Pop, or Old Pop, an abbreviation of Population Malthus, and according to one student he was 'both the favourite and the hero' of the college. Brief records of some lectures he delivered at the college have survived. They include notes written in 1828 by a student, J. D. Inverarity, in an interleaved copy of Adam Smith's *Wealth of Nations*, which Malthus was apparently using as a text. Examination papers on political economy and on history set by Malthus in 1808 have also survived.

Later economic writings The population question was not Malthus's only concern. He became increasingly involved in other aspects of political economy, both theoretical and applied. In 1800 he published *An Investigation of the Cause of the Present High Price of Provisions*, in which he argued that food prices were increasing because of the large amount of money being spent to support the poor. In 1807 he published *A Letter to Samuel Whitbread*, which dealt with Whitbread's proposed amendments to the poor laws. In 1808 and 1809 he published in the *Edinburgh Review* two articles on the problems of Ireland, and a third

on '[William] Spence on commerce', although his authorship of the last has been disputed. In 1811 two further articles in the *Edinburgh Review*, on currency and bullion matters, initiated a friendship with David Ricardo. Their extensive correspondence provides a unique insight into the characters, ideas, and mental processes of the two most important economists of this formative period in the history of political economy in England. Although they differed on some essential points—notably, on the theory of value, the nature of rent, and the role of effective demand—their friendship remained close. Eleven days before his death, Ricardo concluded his last letter to Malthus:

> And now my dear Malthus I have done. Like other disputants after much discussion we each retain our own opinions. These discussions however never influence our friendship; I should not like you more than I do if you agreed in opinion with me. (*Works and Correspondence*, 9.382)

And later Malthus said of Ricardo: 'I never loved any body out of my own family so much' (Empson, 499).

In 1815 Malthus published a pamphlet on rent (he is credited with being one of the discoverers of the classical theory of rent). In 1814 and 1815 he wrote two pamphlets on the corn laws, in the second of which he astonished his whig friends by departing from absolute adherence to Adam Smith's doctrine of free trade, and arguing in favour of some restrictions on the importation of foreign corn. Some commentators have argued that in later life he abandoned his policy of agricultural protection; but whether he did or not, his departure from *laissez-faire* in this instance was clearly reluctant, and motivated by considerations of national security, by a desire to maintain a balance between agriculture and manufacturing, and (particularly in his earlier writings) by a fear of the unwholesome and destabilizing effects of an excessive development of manufacturing.

In 1820 Malthus published his *Principles of Political Economy*. The title was something of a misnomer, as the book was conceived as a series of tracts rather than a comprehensive and systematic treatise. For the rest of his life he assembled copious notes in preparation for a second edition of the *Principles*, but he died before completing it. A second edition was published in 1836 by an anonymous editor, probably John Cazenove, with a considerable number of additions and deletions, and including a 'Memoir of Robert Malthus' by Otter. However, it is not clear to what extent the second edition reflects Malthus's final thoughts. The editor did not incorporate all of Malthus's manuscript revisions, and states that he made other editorial variations, omissions, and additions. Variorum editions of the *Principles* were published in 1986 and 1989.

The *Principles* had only a limited impact at the time, and was severely criticized by J. R. McCulloch and Ricardo; the latter prepared extensive critical notes. But more recently it has received greater recognition, largely as a result of the comments by J. M. Keynes in the 1930s. Keynes argued that Malthus's theory of effective demand provided a scientific explanation of unemployment, and that the hundred-year domination of Ricardo over Malthus had been a disaster for the progress of economics. Keynes believed that if economics had followed Malthus instead of being constrained by Ricardo in an artificial groove, the world would be a much wiser and richer place. When Karl Marx referred to Malthus as 'the contemptible Malthus' (Meek, 121) and as 'a shameless sycophant of the ruling classes' (ibid., 123), he obviously overlooked the passages in the *Principles* dealing with the importance of distribution and effective demand as causes of economic growth.

Between the publication of his *Principles* in 1820 and his death in 1834, Parson Malthus (as he was sometimes referred to) published a further ten works, and appeared as a witness before two select committees of the House of Commons. In 1821, in an *Edinburgh Review* article, he replied to Godwin's *Of Population* (1820). In 1823, in a small work entitled *The Measure of Value Stated and Illustrated*, he thought he had proved that the quantity of labour commanded in exchange is the only, and an invariable, measure of value—an argument that commentators have not found convincing. Also in 1823 he wrote an article for the *Quarterly Review* on Thomas Tooke's *Thoughts and Details*, and another on 'Population' for the *Supplement ... to the Encyclopaedia Britannica*. In 1824 in the *Quarterly Review* he criticized the article by McCulloch on 'Political economy' in the supplement, declaring that Ricardo, McCulloch, and James Mill were representatives of a 'new school of political economy' which had departed from the school represented by Adam Smith and himself. The fact (noted above) that Malthus in 1828 was using Smith's *Wealth of Nations* as a text rather than his own *Principles of Political Economy* indicates his great esteem for Smith. In 1825 he was elected one of the ten royal associates of the Royal Society of Literature and in 1825 and 1827 he presented two papers on the subject of value, neither of which appears to have had any impact on the subsequent development of the theory of value. In 1826 he published the sixth edition of the *Essay*. His *Definitions in Political Economy* (1827) was a valiant attempt to resolve differences of opinion in political economy by codifying its terminology and establishing rules for the definition of terms. It could be regarded as one of the earliest works on the methodology of economics. Finally, in 1830 he published *A Summary View of the Principle of Population*, which was a shorter version, with a few small additions, of his 1823 *Encyclopaedia Britannica* article, motivated by a desire to respond to criticisms being levied at that time by Michael T. Sadler. In addition to these ten post-1820 publications, he gave evidence in 1824 before the select committee on artisans and machinery, and in 1827 before the select committee on emigration. His replies to questions provide an important insight into his views on matters not dealt with explicitly in his published works.

While engaged in these extensive literary activities, Malthus carried out his normal teaching duties at the East India College, often under great pressure to meet examination deadlines, and conducted an extensive correspondence. More than 230 letters to or from more than fifty correspondents are known to have survived, in addition to the Ricardo–Malthus letters. His correspondents included Charles Babbage, Bewick Bridge, Thomas Chalmers, Francis Horner, Robert Wilmot-Horton, John Murray, Macvey Napier, Henry Parnell, Jean-Baptiste Say, Nassau William Senior, William Whewell, Samuel Whitbread, Arthur Young, and his close family.

Malthus became a fellow of the Royal Society in 1818 and, as already noted, a fellow of the Royal Society of Literature in 1825. He was one of the initial members of the Political Economy Club, founded in 1821, and regularly attended the monthly meetings. He proposed questions for discussion and participated in the debates, where with the support of Cazenove he was often opposed to Ricardo and James Mill. In 1834, with Richard Jones, Charles Babbage, and others, he inaugurated the Statistical Society of London (later the Royal Statistical Society).

Personality and death   In appearance Malthus was described as tall, slender, elegantly formed, and handsome, with dark eyes and naturally curled hair. When he was an undergraduate his hair was fair and he let it hang in ringlets on his neck—which was unusual at the time, when the fashion was pigtails and powder—but in later life (as in the 1833 portrait by J. Linnell in Haileybury College) his curled hair was auburn and cut short. In character he was said by Maria Edgeworth to be 'a perfectly unaffected, amiable, gentlemanlike man, who really *converses*; that is, listens, as well as talks' (*Letters from England*, 64), and she declared him to be 'of strict truth, perfect integrity and rational benevolence' (ibid., 331). Her views are corroborated by Otter, who believed that the most remarkable feature of Malthus's mind was his love of truth. Otter and other friends also paid tribute to his steadiness and moderation—characteristics that reflected in his own person the 'doctrine of proportions' (or the concept of the optimum), which played such a key role in his political economy.

Malthus's seriousness of purpose and moderation co-existed with a keen sense of humour and an enjoyment of physical recreation. Especially in his younger days he was said to be habitually cheerful and playful, and a source of amusement to his companions. He once acknowledged that, even as a boy, he had always been of a remarkably mischievous disposition. His recreational activities, encouraged by his father, included skating, boating, cricket, swimming, and shooting, but were interrupted at Cambridge by severe bouts of rheumatism. His correspondence with his father shows that they shared a great interest in the theatre and in botany.

Alongside this mildness and humour there was a combative side to Malthus's character. He insisted that he preferred discussion in private to controversy in public, and he stated that he wished for nothing more than a quiet living in the country, but when the occasion arose he was prepared to debate vigorously in the public arena, and was eager to exert an influence on the course of political events. Empson remarked that Malthus, unlike the storm petrel, did not relish storms, but 'usually turned out in one' (Empson, 496).

Malthus died on 29 December 1834 at Bath while on a family visit to his wife's parents. He died after a few days' illness, the cause being described as a 'disorder of the heart, of which it was believed that he was never conscious' (Otter, xlii). He was buried on 6 January 1835 in Bath Abbey. A memorial tablet, probably written by Otter, reads 'one of the best men and truest philosophers of any age or country ... He lived a serene and happy life devoted to the pursuit and communication of truth' (James, *Travel Diaries*, 302). He bequeathed all his personal property to his wife, and recommended that she in turn divide her property equally between their two surviving children, a request that she duly carried out. In 1949 a great-great-nephew of Malthus, Reginald Arthur Bray, of the Manor House, Shere, presented the Malthus Library (containing items collected by Daniel Malthus, by Malthus, and by other members of the family) to Jesus College, Cambridge, and donated Malthus's working copy of his *Principles of Political Economy*, with extensive manuscript revisions, to the Marshall Library of Economics at Cambridge.   J. M. PULLEN

Sources P. James, *Population Malthus* (1979) · W. Otter, 'Memoir of Robert Malthus', in T. R. Malthus, *Principles of political economy*, 2nd edn (1836) · [W. Empson], *EdinR*, 64 (1836–7), 469–506 · *The travel diaries of T. R. Malthus*, ed. P. James (1966) · L. Bray, 'Recollections of Mary Anne Catherine Bray', 1857, Surrey RO · J. O. Payne, *Collections for the history of the family of Malthus* (1890) · *DNB* · J. Bonar, *Malthus and his work*, 2nd edn (1924) · J. M. Keynes, 'Robert Malthus: the first of the Cambridge economists', *Essays in biography* (1933), 93–148 · J. M. Pullen, 'Some new information on the Rev. T. R. Malthus', *History of Political Economy*, 19 (1987), 127–40 · *The works and correspondence of David Ricardo*, ed. P. Sraffa and M. H. Dobb, 11 vols. (1951–73) · *Maria Edgeworth: letters from England, 1813–1844*, ed. C. Colvin (1971) · R. L. Meek, ed., *Marx and Engels on Malthus* (1953) · G. Wakefield, *Memoirs of the life of Gilbert Wakefield* (1792) · D. Winch, *Malthus* (1987) · D. Winch, *Riches and poverty* (1996), pt 3 · D. Winch, 'Introduction', in T. R. Malthus, *An essay on the principle of population* (1992) · A. Flew, 'Introduction', in T. R. Malthus, *An essay on the principle of population* (1970) · J. M. Pullen, 'Introduction', in T. R. Malthus, *Principles of political economy*, variorum edn, 2 vols. (1989) · W. Petersen, *Malthus* (1979)

Archives CUL, travel journals · Jesus College, Cambridge, Malthus Library · Kanto Gakuen University, Japan, Kanto Gakuen collection of MSS | BL, letters to Macvey Napier · CUL, corresp. with David Ricardo · Derbys. RO, corresp. with Sir R. J. Wilmot-Horton · NRA, letters to John Murray

Likenesses J. Linnell, oils, 1833, Haileybury College, Hertfordshire [*see illus.*]

Malton, James (*d.* 1803). *See under* Malton, Thomas, the elder (1726–1801).

Malton, Thomas, the elder (1726–1801), architectural draughtsman and writer on geometry, began his career as an upholsterer in the Strand, London. He exhibited two drawings of St Martin's Church with the Free Society of Artists in 1761 and others with the Society of Artists in 1766 and 1768; from 1772 to 1785 he showed perspective drawings at the newly established Royal Academy. In 1774 he published *The Royal Road to Geometry, or, An Easy and Familiar Introduction to the Mathematics*, a school book intended as an improvement on Euclid, and in 1775 *A complete treatise on perspective in theory and practice, on the principles of Dr. Brook Taylor*. He also lectured on these subjects, having moved to a house in Poland Street, Soho. On 2 March 1776 a fire in the Savoy destroyed 350 copies of the

book on geometry and 200 of that on perspective; Malton was sued by his printer and paper merchant and from this point his financial troubles seem to have begun. In 1785 he moved with his family to Dublin, a city with which he already had some acquaintance, where he struggled to support himself by teaching perspective, and where he died on 18 February 1801. Examples of his work are to be found in the Victoria and Albert Museum; the Witt collection at the Courtauld Institute holds a very fine, if incomplete, perspective drawing of Temple Bar in the Strand with the houses on either side of the thoroughfare.

His son **James Malton** (*d.* 1803), architectural draughtsman and author, accompanied his father to Dublin, where he found employment in the office of the distinguished architect James Gandon, despite a suspicion that the elder Malton had anonymously published severe criticism of Gandon's designs for the Royal Exchange in Dublin. After three years, however, James Malton 'so frequently betrayed all official confidence, and was guilty of so many irregularities that it became quite necessary to dismiss him from employment' (Gandon, 67). Subsequently Gandon suspected that Malton was responsible for *Letters Addressed to Parliament* (1787), which expressed hostile views on the architect's work, but the authorship was not proved.

In the 1790s James Malton returned to London, where he supported himself as a topographical artist, exhibiting some fifty-one drawings, designs for, and elevations of buildings at the Royal Academy between 1792 and 1803. From 1794 his address was 17 Norton Street (later Bolsover Street), Portland Place. In 1797 he published a handsome volume of illustrations with text, *A Descriptive View of Dublin*. In the following year he published *An Essay on British Cottage Architecture* (which went into a second edition in 1804) and in 1802 *A Collection of Designs for Rural Retreats*, which was attacked by R. Elsam in his *Essay on Rural Architecture* of 1803. These two works of Malton's have aquatint illustrations of an exceptionally high quality and delicacy. Malton's importance as a pioneer of the *cottage orné* has been recognized.

James Malton died at his home in Norton Street on 28 July 1803 from brain fever and was buried in Marylebone churchyard. The brief notice in the *Gentleman's Magazine* describes him as 'an ingenious and distinguished artist' (*GM*, 1st ser., 73/2, 1803, 791). The contents of his studio and his effects were auctioned at Christies on 8 and 9 March 1804. In addition to many original drawings for his various publications, several lots consisted of apparatus and models apparently relating to his father's work on perspective. There are good examples of James Malton's work in the Victoria and Albert Museum and in the British Museum, and two interesting designs in the drawings collection of the Royal Institute of British Architects (RIBA), for a hunting-lodge and a villa 'in the Norman style'.

Thomas Malton the younger (1751/2–1804), architectural draughtsman, son of Thomas Malton the elder, joined his father about 1790 in Dublin, where his portrait was painted handsomely by the American Gilbert Stuart; the original can no longer be traced, but it was engraved by W. W. Barney and copies are to be found in the British Museum and the National Portrait Gallery, London. Before his departure for Ireland, he had, in 1774, won a premium from the Society of Arts and had exhibited at the Society of Artists, the Free Society of Artists, and the Royal Academy, where in 1782 he was awarded a gold medal; between 1773 and 1803 he showed at the Royal Academy no fewer than 128 drawings, paintings, and designs of streets and buildings in London, Oxford, and Cambridge and of various mansions in the home counties, East Anglia, Yorkshire, and Bath. Between 1774 and 1796 he lived at 3 (later 56) Poland Street and thereafter at 103 Long Acre, Covent Garden, where he gave drawing classes; among his pupils were Thomas Girtin and the young J. M. W. Turner. The latter was sent away by Malton, who found his pupil's approach too imaginative for the exact representation required from an architectural draughtsman, but the youth was afterwards readmitted and in later life would say: 'But my real master, you know, was Tom Malton of Long Acre' (Thornbury, 26–7). The Westminster rate books also show him at an address in Conduit Street between 1783 and 1789 and at Great Titchfield Street from 1791 to 1796.

In addition to these activities, Malton painted scenery for the theatre. In 1780–81 he was working for Drury Lane, and from 1790 to 1794 he worked at Covent Garden. Here, among the ambitious sets for James Wild's pantomime *Harlequin and Faustus*, Malton received particular praise for 'a representation of the scaffolding prepared for the building of the new Drury Lane Theatre as it appeared in July [1793] and which changed to a view of that theatre as it would appear when completed' (Highfill, Burnim & Langhans, *BDA*, 19) and in his *London Theatres* (1795) Thomas Bellamy acclaimed his skills:

Judicious Malton! Thy receding scene
Of architectural beauty so deceives
The eye of Admiration, that we ask—
'Is this majestic view *unreal* ALL?
The rising column, and the stately arch
Can ne'er be pictured *thus*! 'tis not in art'
(p. 28)

The younger Thomas Malton felt himself to be well fitted for loftier professional employment. On 10 October 1794 the artist Joseph Farington recorded in his diary that Malton had solicited his vote at the forthcoming Royal Academy elections and had said that there was £350 owing to him from Drury Lane; Farington avoided any commitment. In November of the following year Malton sought election in direct competition with John Soane. Farington recorded: 'Smirke came to us and we conversed on the means to be employed to prevent Malton succeeding'; it was decided that the luckless man should be ruled out as 'only a Draughtsman of Buildings, but no Architect'. A few weeks later, on 17 December 1795, Farington noted 'Hamilton told me Malton proposes to paint views of London in order to qualify himself for the Academy as a painter' (Farington, *Diary*, 1.253, 2.395–7, 399). This stouthearted response to the academicians' rebuff inspired what was to be Malton's most important work—the 100 aquatint plates which make up *A Picturesque Tour through the Cities of London and Westminster* (1792–1801). These catch the expanding metropolis at its most elegant and most self-assured. Among so much good topographical work at this period, Malton's views are particularly valuable because they often show an unexpected angle or record an otherwise neglected building. For example, he shows the north, Threadneedle Street, façade of the second Royal Exchange as well as its better-documented Cornhill, southern, frontage and for good measure he throws in another plate of the now vanished arcade on the northern front as well. The elegant little figures, which lend humanity to the building and which include a street vendor with a trayful of toys and novelties, may well be by Francis Wheatley.

But in spite of the excellence of the work, in spite of a new series begun on Oxford, and in spite of his illustrations of buildings by Sir Robert Taylor, the academicians' ranks remained closed against Malton, and the next reference to him in Farington's diary (24 March 1804) grimly recorded his death at home in Long Acre from a putrid fever on 7 March, leaving seven children (Farington, *Diary*, 6.2274).

The *Gentleman's Magazine* speaks of Malton as an 'ingenious and much-respected artist' and says that he had left 'a wife and six young children' (*GM*, 1st ser., 74/1, 1804, 293). Later that year, on 4 and 5 May, his drawings, 'many of them enriched with Figures by the late W. Hamilton RA', were put up for auction at Christies, along with a 'pianoforte by Beck' and 'the original design for the drop curtain at the opening of the present Theatre, Drury Lane' (Christies catalogues). The drawings and engravings sold well: the piano and a view of the Adelphi went to the Adam brothers, Lord Bessborough bought views of Oxford and Bath, and the collector William Crowle scooped up everything that he could on London. At the time of Malton's death, his eldest son was a cadet in India; the second son, Charles, served a seven-year apprenticeship to John Soane, but the one surviving letter suggests that it was not a happy relationship and the young man does not seem to have practised as an architect.

Works by the younger Thomas Malton are to be found in the Victoria and Albert Museum, the British Museum, and the Ashmolean at Oxford. The Guildhall has some excellent examples of his work, but perhaps the best of all is a large (660 mm x 960 mm) pen and wash drawing of the west front of St Paul's Cathedral, engraved as the last plate of the *Picturesque Tour* (now in the drawings collection at the RIBA); it is for such work that Thomas Malton deserves to be remembered.

ANN SAUNDERS

Sources Graves, *RA exhibitors* · *GM*, 1st ser., 71 (1801), 277 · *GM*, 1st ser., 73 (1803), 791 · *GM*, 1st ser., 74 (1804), 283 · A. Pasquin [J. Williams], *An authentic history of the professors of painting, sculpture, and architecture who have practiced in Ireland ... to which are added, Memoirs of the royal academicians* [1796] · W. G. Strickland, *A dictionary of Irish artists*, 2 vols. (1913) · T. Malton, *An essay concerning the publication of works ... by subscription* (1777) · Farington, *Diary* · J. Gandon and T. J. Mulvany, eds., *The life of James Gandon* (1846); repr. with introduction by M. Craig (1969) · W. Thornbury, *The life of J. M. W. Turner*, new edn (1897) · Highfill, Burnim & Langhans, *BDA* · sale catalogue

(1804) [Christies, 8–9 March 1804] • sale catalogue (1804) [Christies, 4–5 May 1804] • R. T. Lacy, *A biographical dictionary of scenographers, 500 BC to 1900 AD* (1990) • letter, Thomas Malton the younger to Sir John Soane, Sir John Soane's Museum, London • *DNB* • rate books, City Westm. AC • parish register (burial), London, St Marylebone • Colvin, *Archs.*

Archives Sir John Soane's Museum, London, archives

Likenesses G. Stuart, portrait, *c*.1790 (Thomas the younger) • W. W. Barney, mezzotint, pubd 1806 (Thomas the younger; after G. Stuart), BM, NPG

Wealth at death Thomas Malton the younger: left a few hundred pounds; lease of house near Hampstead; drawings (anticipated sale value £500–£600)

Malton, Thomas, the younger (1751/2–1804). *See under* Malton, Thomas, the elder (1726–1801).

Maltravers, Sir John (1266–1341). *See under* Maltravers, John, first Lord Maltravers (*c*.1290–1364).

Maltravers [Mautravers]**, John, first Lord Maltravers** (*c*.1290–1364), baron, was the son of **Sir John Maltravers** (1266–1341) of Lytchett Matravers, Dorset, and Alinore, his first wife. Maltravers the elder spent much time in Ireland as a young adult. He was knighted with the prince of Wales in 1306, was a conservator of the peace in Dorset in 1307, 1308, 1314, and 1329, and took part in the Dunstable tournament of 1308. He served the king in Scotland and Gascony, but does not ever seem to have been summoned to parliament. In 1325, however, he joined the anti-Despenser movement. In July that year he was accused of burglary and theft at the royal manor of Kingsbury in Somerset, and in October he caused a riot at a fair in Dorset. In 1326 his manors were confiscated on the grounds that he was a 'rebel'. Besides his son, he also had a daughter called Matilda, who married, by 1313, John Lenham the younger. His second wife was Joan (*d*. 1348/9), daughter of Sir Walter Foliot, with whom he had three daughters: Alice, Joan, and Elizabeth. After his death, which occurred in 1341, she married Alexander Venables.

John Maltravers the younger, who was also knighted in 1306, probably fought at Bannockburn, and in 1319 he was returned as a knight of the shire for Dorset. In 1320 he accompanied Maurice Berkeley to Gascony on royal service. In the same year he was associated with Thomas Gournay in a case of false arrest, the beginning of a disastrous acquaintanceship. In 1321 Maltravers was pardoned for opposition to the Despensers, but, having sided with Thomas of Lancaster at the battle of Boroughbridge, his estates were confiscated. Throughout 1322 he was involved in attacks on the king's supporters, including one with Roger Mortimer on Despenser holdings in Newport. He probably then fled abroad, but by summer 1326 had joined Mortimer and Isabella to overthrow Edward II. In March 1327 he was granted some Despenser holdings—the manor of Winterborne Houghton and land in Sutton Maudite 'for service to Queen Isabella and the king abroad and at home' (*CPR, 1327–30*, 5.9).

From the end of 1328 Maltravers became a key member of Mortimer's inner circle, and was heavily implicated in the murder of Edward II. In April 1327 he and Thomas Berkeley, his brother-in-law and a relative of Mortimer,

were in attendance on the deposed king at Berkeley Castle, for which accounts still survive. Maltravers is accused by the chroniclers Murimuth and Baker both of treating the deposed king harshly and of ordering his murder on the night of 21 September. At the parliament that followed the coup of 1330 against Mortimer, Berkeley, who was absent on the night, gave a sworn statement that Edward had been murdered by William Ocle and Gournay, but the Bridlington chronicler, the St Paul's chronicler, and Adam Murimuth all write that Maltravers, too, had been responsible.

During the minority of Edward III Maltravers frequently served on commissions of oyer and terminer, and was made keeper of the forest south of the Trent on 5 April 1329. He opposed Henry of Lancaster's rebellion in 1328–9 and then was commissioned to try the rebels, and in 1329 he became a household banneret, accompanying Edward III on his journey to do homage in France that year. By May 1330, still acting for Roger Mortimer, he was steward of the household, and received the forfeited manors of John Giffard of Brimsfield. During 1330 he twice received individual summonses to parliament, being consequently regarded as having become Lord Maltravers. In October 1330 he was made keeper of Clarendon Park. As keeper of Corfe Castle, a post he had occupied since at least September 1329, Maltravers was involved in the conspiracy to convince the earl of Kent early in 1330 that Edward II was still alive, thus leading to the earl's execution for treason. Although the Bridlington chronicler says that Maltravers was arrested in the coup that overthrew Mortimer at Nottingham on 19 October 1330, in fact he was not there. Instead he was indicted in his absence for plotting the murder of Kent, and a reward was placed on his head of 1000 marks. His confiscated lands went to Kent's widow and to William Montagu. In December 1330, along with Ocle, Gournay, and others, he tried to flee the realm, while in July 1331 men from Mousehole, Cornwall, were charged with having helped them to escape to the continent. Murimuth and Walsingham claim he spent many years in Germany, though other evidence suggests he may have been in the Low Countries.

In February 1331 Queen Philippa obtained an income for Maltravers's wife, Agnes (*d*. 1375), from the dowers of John Nerford (*d*. 1329) and John Argentine (*d*. 1318), her former husbands, in order to maintain her family, now destitute following the confiscation of Maltravers's lands. In August 1332 Agnes went abroad, ostensibly on pilgrimage, though this may have been a cover for a visit to her husband. In March 1334 William Montagu was appointed to get in touch with Maltravers, who was said to be 'desirous to reveal to him many things concerning his honour and the estate and well-being of the realm' (*CPR, 1330–34*, 59). Other unofficial contacts appear to have been taking place around this time, as pardons were issued in 1335 to Montagu, Edmund Bereford (Maltravers's brother-in-law), Maurice Berkeley, John Moleyns, and Nicholas Beche for receiving Maltravers on the continent. As a result in 1339 Maltravers was granted a life annuity of £100. A further thawing of relations occurred in 1342 when Agnes was permitted to stay with Maltravers abroad for as long as she wished. Edward III's apparently incongruous attitude towards a condemned traitor is one of the factors regarded as giving weight to fourteenth-century rumours and present-day theories, that Edward II, far from being murdered in 1327, may have survived and fled to the continent in 1330. However, Maltravers's own part in the events surrounding the deposed king's supposed flight is less than clear. According to the letter from Manuel Fieschi to Edward III, composed between 1336 and 1343, the latter's father made his way from Berkeley to Corfe Castle, of which Maltravers was keeper. But although he then stayed at Corfe for eighteen months, he did so without Maltravers's knowledge. Hence it was by pure chance that Maltravers was correct in assuring the earl of Kent that Edward II was still alive, although he was on safer ground in claiming to be innocent of Edward's murder. Maltravers's extended exile from England, from 1330 to 1351, would thus have been intended to prevent the truth about the late king's survival coming to light, and thereby presenting a threat to the position of Edward III.

In 1345 Maltravers was refused permission to return to stand trial for the murder of Edward II, but he was active in Calais during the late 1340s, and appears to have become a self-appointed royal agent in an attempt to win the king's favour. In 1347 he was given permission to return to England to attempt to clear his name, following a meeting with the king at the mouth of the Swyn, which also resulted in his being granted an inn and house in Calais, along with the title of 'Regarder of the land of La Lewe' in France. His restoration to royal favour continued over the next five years. In June 1348 he was sent in a delegation to Ghent, Bruges, and Ypres to negotiate on the king's behalf, and was appointed keeper of the Channel Islands, founding a hospital at Bowes in St Peter Port, Guernsey. Finally, on 20 June 1351, all his confiscated lands and his former position were restored in consideration of his faithfulness 'and of the great place which he afterwards held for [the king] in Flanders and elsewhere with great loss to himself and in spite of large offers from the king's adversaries to draw him from his allegiance' (*CPR, 1330–34*, 110), and he was summoned to parliament in November. His restoration was confirmed by parliament in February 1352. In the final years of his life he settled in England.

Maltravers married twice. With his first wife Ela (also recorded as Milicent), sister of Thomas Berkeley, he had a son, John, who died in 1350. Ela had died before about 1329, and it was probably at about that time that Maltravers married again; his new wife was Agnes, daughter of Sir William Bereford. He died on 16 February 1364 and was buried at Lytchett Matravers. A grandson, Henry, had also predeceased him, and his heirs were his two granddaughters, Joan, wife of Sir John Kaynis, and Eleanor, wife of Sir John Arundel, a son of Richard (II) *Fitzalan, earl of Arundel.   CAROLINE SHENTON

Sources GEC, *Peerage*, new edn, 8.579–86 • *Chancery records* • *CIPM*, 11, 452–5 • *Chronicon Galfridi le Baker de Swynebroke*, ed. E. M. Thompson (1889) • *Adae Murimuth continuatio chronicarum. Robertus de Avesbury de gestis mirabilibus regis Edwardi tertii*, ed. E. M. Thompson, Rolls Series, 93 (1889) • N. Fryde, *The tyranny and fall of Edward II, 1321–1326* (1979) • G. P. Cuttino and T. W. Lyman, 'Where is Edward II?', *Speculum*, 53 (1978), 522–43 • S. A. Moore, ed., 'Documents relating to the death and burial of King Edward II', *Archaeologia*, 50 (1887), 215–26 • *RotP*, vols. 1–2 • 'Pedigree of Mautravers', *Collectanea Topographica et Genealogica*, 6 (1840), 334–61 • C. Shenton, 'The English court and the restoration of royal prestige, 1327–1345', DPhil diss., U. Oxf., 1995 • J. Hutchins, *The history and antiquities of the county of Dorset*, 3rd edn, ed. W. Shipp and J. W. Hodson, 3 (1868); facs. edn (1973), 316–20 • T. F. Tout, 'The captivity and death of Edward of Carnarvon', *The collected papers of Thomas Frederick Tout*, 3 (1934), 145–90 • W. Stubbs, ed., *Chronicles of the reigns of Edward I and Edward II*, 2 vols., Rolls Series, 76 (1882–3) [incl. Bridlington and St Paul's chronicles]

Wealth at death see *CIPM*

Malveisin [Malvoisin], **William** (*d.* 1238), bishop of Glasgow and of St Andrews, may have been a son of his namesake, the Norman nephew of Odo, count of Brittany, or he may have derived from a Malveisin family in the Seine valley nearer Paris; and he may have been born in either France or England. All of this bears inconclusively on the suggestion that he was the Guillaume le Clerc [see William the Clerk] who wrote the *Roman de Fergus*, showing accurate knowledge of Scotland, with expletives 'by St Mungo', and surviving in Picard manuscripts. Since the chronicler Roger Howden (whom he certainly met in 1195) knew details of, for example, Malveisin's consecration in 1199, the latter seems to have been one of his informants at the end of his life. But later Scottish chroniclers have used a lost set of annals for the early thirteenth century, of St Andrews provenance, which fit with Malveisin's career there, and he has been suggested as their author, inspired by the example of Howden.

Malveisin was probably young when he took service as clerk of King William the Lion in the 1180s, receiving the archdeaconry of Lothian as a benefice (1189–93) and becoming the king's chancellor on 8 September 1199, after the death on 10 July of Hugh the Chancellor, who had been first choice to succeed Jocelin as bishop of Glasgow. Only a month later, in October, William was elected to the see of Glasgow and was consecrated at Lyons by its archbishop on 24 September 1200. In his short time at Glasgow he put both the canons and the vicars-choral firmly in their place and his translation to St Andrews in 1202, after the death of Bishop Roger, was a wise decision by the king and (probably) the legate, Giovanni da Salerno. He ceased to be chancellor at about this time.

As bishop for over thirty-five years, Malveisin played a large role in his diocese, in the Scottish church, and at the papal curia, and there is no doubt that, even if he did not attend a law school, he was learned in canon and civil law, for he was involved as litigant and judge in many disputes. He curbed the efforts of the religious of Durham and Arbroath to establish exemption from visitation and procurations, and earned a reputation for suffering no nonsense from other houses; in 1207 he went to Rome to secure support in dealing with the religious, and met there Stephen Langton, archbishop of Canterbury, whose father was given refuge in St Andrews Priory during the quarrel between Langton and John, king of England. Yet Malveisin was an acceptable envoy to John's court.

In 1208 the bishop of Durham built a new and threatening castle at Tweedmouth, calling it Malveisin after the bishop to whose diocese it was a 'bad neighbour'. King William the Lion, who had long been pressing his claim for the earldom of Northumberland, seems to have provoked John, king of England by entertaining overtures from Philip Augustus of France. Bishop William had been in abortive embassies to John after 24 May 1209, and he accompanied his king to meet John at Norham on 7 August 1209, when there was a humiliating Scottish climb-down. The bishop must have played a part, for he witnessed the text, and the terms were kept as secret as possible though they included demolition of the castle of Malveisin. Malveisin was also party to the supplementary agreement between the two kings reached in early February 1212. Later chronicle evidence says that he went to France in that year to visit relatives, but if so the visit was brief, for he was back in 1213, acting as legate with Bishop Walter of Glasgow to preach and collect money for the Albigensian crusade. He helped inaugurate Alexander II at Scone on 6 December 1214 and on 7 July 1215 was sent as envoy to King John, possibly to demand fulfilment of chapter 59 of Magna Carta. But he did not return then, and was overseas during the Anglo-Scottish wars of 1215–17, when the southern part of his diocese was ravaged.

With three other Scottish prelates Malveisin attended the Fourth Lateran Council in November 1215, remaining behind at the curia as Alexander II incurred excommunication, his kingdom interdict. Not until December 1217 did the bishop come home via England, probably attending Alexander II's homage to Henry III at Northampton in that month. His absence from Scotland enabled him to press with Honorius III the Scottish case that the English kings had defaulted on the treaties of Norham, and the matter was remitted in 1218 to the legate Pandulph and inaction. Malveisin was at York to negotiate the marriage of Alexander II to Henry III's sister Joan on 15 June 1220, and for the marriage itself there on 18 June 1221, having presumably attended the three-day council held by the legate James at Perth on 9–11 February 1221.

But the Scottish church remained unable to carry out reforms through a provincial council. Since 1199 several legates had visited, including James seeking a crusading subsidy in 1220. Was the Scottish church to be in need of recurrent legates? Malveisin had helped to establish the cathedral of Moray at Spynie, had claimed unsuccessfully that the bishop of Dunkeld must be consecrated by the bishop of St Andrews, and did consecrate other Scottish bishops without adequate papal authority, all signs of a pretension to metropolitan functions. It was perhaps to halt those ambitions that Honorius III agreed on 19 May 1225 to the bishops of the Scottish kingdom holding *provinciale concilium* by papal authority, a decision, apparently, not for a one-off council, but followed by occasional councils representing all dioceses. Only one such council is known before William's death, held in Brechin diocese in 1230–31, and provincial statutes or diocesan synodalia

for reform (as envisaged at the Lateran Council) are unknown until after the visit of the legate Otto to Britain in 1237–9.

None the less, Malveisin was a busy man in the affairs of his diocese and the Scottish church, after 1218 as before 1215. His problems with his own church of St Andrews are the best attested, for he first sought to resolve the differences between the Augustinian and secular (Culdee) canons of St Andrews. A party of the former brought a case against him at the curia in 1216, and charges flew back and forth over the succeeding years. The bishop certainly seems to have forcibly presented clerics to benefices in the patronage of the priory, but he had a large *familia* to provide for—thirty or more of whom were *magistri*. In 1228 the pope was still protecting the priory from further exactions of pensions in favour of such clerks. None the less, the overwhelming impression left by Bishop William's career is of an able, hard-working ecclesiastical civil servant, learned in the law, who knew how to please his masters, both king and pope, who tried to be fair, but who had little spirituality himself and little feeling for it in others.

In his last ten years Malveisin was probably in declining health, yet about 1232 was commissioned by the pope, with two colleagues, to find a bishop for the vacant see of Dunblane; their nomination of the Dominican Clement (whom he consecrated, not at St Andrews or Dunblane, but at Stow in Lothian, on 4 September 1233) shows appreciation of a new force in the church. He was presumably a very old man when he died on 9 July 1238 at Inchmurdo, near St Andrews. He was buried in the cathedral then slowly rising; he is not known to have raised funds for it with any vigour.   A. A. M. DUNCAN

Sources J. Dowden, *The bishops of Scotland … prior to the Reformation*, ed. J. M. Thomson (1912), 12–13, 300–01 · D. E. R. Watt, *A biographical dictionary of Scottish graduates to AD 1410* (1977), 374–9 · G. W. S. Barrow, ed., *Regesta regum Scottorum*, 2 (1971) · Guillaume le Clerc, *Fergus of Galloway: knight of King Arthur*, trans. D. D. R. Owen (1991), 162–9 · D. E. R. Watt, *Medieval church councils in Scotland* (2000), chaps. 3–5 · A. A. M. Duncan, 'John king of England and the kings of Scots', *King John: new interpretations*, ed. S. D. Church (1999), 247–71 · A. A. M. Duncan, 'Roger of Howden and Scotland', *Church, chronicle and learning in medieval and early Renaissance Scotland*, ed. B. E. Crawford (1999), 135–60 · W. Bower, *Scotichronicon*, ed. D. E. R. Watt and others, new edn, 9 vols. (1987–98), vol. 4, pp. 616–20; vol. 9, pp. 251–9
Likenesses cast, NA Scot., Melrose charters, Laing casts · seal, U. Durham L., Durham dean and chapter archives, Misc. Charters nos. 1301, 1308, 1317

Malvern. For this title name *see* Huggins, Godfrey Martin, first Viscount Malvern (1883–1971).

Malvern, John (d. in or before 1414?). *See under* Higden, Ranulf (d. 1364).

Malvern, John (d. 1422), physician, was probably born in or near the town of Malvern in Worcestershire. His origins remain obscure, but his presence at heresy trials held in the diocese of Hereford, in 1393, and his appointment at some point before 1398 as master of the hospital of St Catherine in Ledbury, Herefordshire, suggest that he came from this area. By 1393, when he took his place among the distinguished commissioners appointed to try the two Lollards, William Swinderby and Walter Bryt, Malvern had already served as a chaplain at Balliol College, Oxford. He had also graduated as a master of arts and doctor of theology, at Oxford University, and may, in addition, have obtained there the doctorate in medicine credited to him later in copies of his short tract, *Contra pestilenciam*.

Malvern owed much of his success to an early connection with Henry Bolingbroke, the future Henry IV, who retained him as one of his domestic physicians in 1395 and may have enlisted his professional services while attempting to restore order in the north ten years later. It is, however, possible that Malvern had actually travelled to York in 1405 to attend the leader of the rebel forces, rather than the king. Malvern was reputedly one of the last bystanders to whom Richard Scrope, archbishop of York, spoke before his execution outside the city walls, on 8 June, and is said to have known him well. If he had, indeed, been treating Scrope as a patient, the latter's parting words appear especially poignant. Not even Malvern's battery of cures, he remarked, could save the life of one who was now beyond earthly medicine; and so he had no further need of physic. Such a potentially embarrassing attachment had no apparent effect upon the upward trajectory of Malvern's career or the support of his royal patron, who continued to regard him with favour. In 1408, for instance, he was promoted to a canon's stall at St George's Chapel, Windsor.

Malvern's other distinguished patients included Richard Mitford, bishop of Salisbury, who employed him at considerable expense during his last illness in 1407. He also had links with Archbishop Thomas Arundel. He acted at the trial of John Badby before the archbishop in 1409, while the Lollard, William Thorpe, in his account of his interview with Arundel at Saltwood Castle in 1407, tells how when the laymen were dismissed, and the archbishop withdrew into a 'privy closet', among the clerics in attendance was 'a phisician that is clepid Maluerne' (Hudson, 29). That his practice was not confined to the narrow, theoretical world of academic medicine is evident from the survival of a vernacular receipt for a prophylactic for 'purging phlegm, choler and melancholy' attributed to him; and, although it was composed in Latin for an educated readership, his plague tract likewise suggests a pragmatic approach to preventative medicine. It provides a succinct précis of the scholarly literature and survives in many copies.

Medieval English physicians were customarily rewarded with lucrative benefices, and Malvern's impressive collection attests his skill as a practitioner. In addition to his mastership of St Catherine's Hospital in Ledbury, which he retained until after 1409, he held a succession of rectories, notably that of St Dunstan-in-the-East, London, which he occupied from 1402 until his death. His appointment as a canon of St Paul's Cathedral followed two years later, and he acquired and exchanged several other livings. Yet London, where the richest and most influential patients were to be found, remained his home. He died there between 12 and 14 March 1422, having requested burial at St Dunstan's, to which he left four of his books. These included a collection of sermons, a 'prophecy of Merlin', a copy of the *Golden Legend*, and works by Seneca and Guillaume d'Auvergne. To Balliol, his old college, went a book of commentaries on Aristotle's *Ethics* and *Politics*. His short, businesslike will contains no mention of any surviving relatives.   CAROLE RAWCLIFFE

Sources C. H. Talbot and E. A. Hammond, *The medical practitioners in medieval England: a biographical register* (1965) · Emden, *Oxf.* · *Chancery records* · will, PRO, PROB 11/2B, sig. 35 · J. H. Wylie, *History of England under Henry the Fourth*, 4 vols. (1884–98) · C. M. Woolgar, ed., *Household accounts from medieval England*, 1, British Academy, Records of Social and Economic History, new ser., 17 (1992) · *CEPR letters*, vol. 5 · A. Hudson, ed., *Two Wycliffite texts*, EETS, 301 (1993)

Malvern, Walcher of (*d.* 1135), prior of Great Malvern and astronomer, was a monk at the Benedictine abbey of Great Malvern near Worcester (founded 1085) and became its second prior; but uncertainty surrounds the period of his priorship, because of the almost complete absence of his name in archival records. As prior he attended the consecration of a new abbot of Tewkesbury in Worcester Cathedral on 23 May 1125, but almost all the remaining information on his life comes from an epitaph discovered buried in the grounds of the abbey in 1711, and now to be seen in St Anne's Chapel in the church:

> Here lies in a cyst, Doctor Walcher, a worthy philosopher, a good astronomer, a Lorrainer, a pious man and humble monk, the prior of this sheepfold, a geometer and abacist. The people mourn, the clergy grieve on all sides. The first day of October brought death to this elderly man [*senior*]. May each believer pray that he may live in heaven.   (Dugdale, *Monasticon*, 3.442)

The date 'mcxxv' follows, but this appears to be a mistake dating from the time of the monument's restoration, since earlier reports record 'mcxxxv' (William Cole's report of 23 June 1746, in BL, Add. MS 5811, fol. 131*r*, is decisive on this point). There is no independent witness for it, but 1135 as the date of Walcher's death is compatible with other evidence.

His epitaph states that Walcher, like his namesake, Walcher, bishop of Durham (1081–90), and several other important churchmen and administrators in the early Norman period, came from Lotharingia, or Lorraine. His continental origins are corroborated by his report to William of Malmesbury of a miraculous event that occurred 'fifteen years earlier' in the abbey of Fulda, which he may have witnessed himself; this report follows an account of the introduction of Marianus Scottus's *Chronicle* into England by another Lorrainer, Robert the Lotharingian, bishop of Hereford (1079–95).

The interest in astronomy attested by his epitaph is confirmed by the survival of two short texts by Walcher. The first is a set of lunar tables, in the Latin tradition, but calculated with the aid of an astrolabe from an eclipse observed on 18 October 1092 (he had failed to have the instrument with him when he witnessed an earlier eclipse of the moon in 'Romona' in Italy on 30 October 1091). This is the first mention in a Latin source of the actual employment of an astrolabe, whose construction and use had been described in texts first translated from

Arabic in the late tenth century. This text is extant in several manuscripts, of which the earliest is Bodleian Library, MS Auct. F.1.9 (written between 1120 and 1140 at Worcester Cathedral priory); it often occurs following Robert the Lotharingian's *Excerptio*—his commentary on Marianus Scottus's *Chronicle*.

The second text is *Sententia Petri Ebrei, cognomento Anphus, de dracone, quam dominus Walcerus prior Malvernensis ecclesie in Latinam transtulit linguam* ('the opinion of Peter the Hebrew, surnamed Anphus, concerning the dragon, which the lord Walcher, prior of the church of Malvern, translated into Latin'), a work reporting the information of Walcher's teacher, Petrus Alfonsi, on the times when the moon's orbit crosses that of the sun (the 'nodes' of the moon, represented in Indian and Arabic astronomy as the head and tail of a dragon). This text immediately follows the first text in the Oxford manuscript, and is also found in Erfurt, Wissenschaftliche Bibliothek der Stadt, Bibliotheca Amploniana, MS Q.351 and British Library, Cotton MS App. vi, fols. 22rb–22va (fragment only). The work was composed after 1 April 1120—a date used in an example—and draws on the astronomical tables of al-Khwarizmi, Adelard of Bath's translation of which immediately follows Walcher's work in the Oxford manuscript.

Walcher was one of the earliest Latin scholars to make use of Arabic astronomical data. He may have acquired his interest in science in Lorraine, but he evidently belonged to a small group of scientists working in the west midlands, which included Robert the Lotharingian, Petrus Alfonsi, and Adelard of Bath. In spite of the silence of the charter records, he appears, too, to have had some prestige as a churchman, for William of Malmesbury warns that 'if anyone does not believe his [Walcher's] words, he insults religion' (*De gestis regum*, 2.346), and Great Malvern's dependence on Westminster Abbey would have given him direct access to England's capital. His position as prior may have led him to look to the new science of the Arabs to obtain more accurate calculations for the church calendar, while his influence may have contributed to the spread of the new astronomical tables of al-Khwarizmi to more central English Benedictine abbeys, such as those of St Albans, Winchester, and St Augustine's, Canterbury.

CHARLES BURNETT

Sources C. H. Haskins, *Studies in the history of mediaeval science* (1924) [extracts of both Walcher's texts ed. pp.114–17] · E. Poulle, 'Walcher de Malvern et son astrolabe, 1092', *Publicações do Centro de Estudos de Cartografia Antiga*, série seperatas, 132 (1980), 47–54 · C. Burnett, 'Mathematics and astronomy in Hereford and its region in the twelfth century', *Medieval art, architecture and archaeology at Hereford*, ed. D. Whitehead, British Archaeological Association Transactions, 15 (1995), 50–59 · D. Knowles, C. N. L. Brooke, and V. C. M. London, eds., *The heads of religious houses, England and Wales*, 1: 940–1216 (1972), 90 · J.-M. Millás Vallicrosa, 'La aportación astronómica de Pedro Alfonso', *Sefarad*, 3 (1943), 65–105 [incl. edn of *Sententia Petri Ebrei … de dracone*, pp. 87–97] · *Willelmi Malmesbiriensis monachi de gestis regum Anglorum*, ed. W. Stubbs, 2 vols., Rolls Series (1887–9), vol. 2, p. 346 · John of Worcester, *Chron.* · Dugdale, *Monasticon*, new edn, 3.442b [transcript of tombstone] · W. Cole, 'Collections', BL, Add. MS 5811, fols. 122v–133v · J. Nott, *Church and monastery of 'Moche Malverne' (Great Malvern)* (1885), 25–34

Archives BL, Cotton MS App. vi, fols. 22rb–22va · Bodl. Oxf., MS Auct. F.1.9 · Wissenschaftliche Bibliothek der Stadt, Erfurt, Bibliotheca Amploniana, MS Q.351

Malvern, William of [*formerly* William Parker] (1485×90–1539), abbot of Gloucester, was born into a Gloucestershire family named Parker, and received his early education at St Peter's Abbey in Gloucester. The monks then sent him to Oxford, where he had received the degree of BCL by April 1507; he subsequently returned to the abbey and became a monk there. Presumably it was then that he took the name of Malvern. Oxford later awarded him three additional degrees: DCL (1508), BTh (1511), and DTh (1515). At St Peter's he soon became supervisor of the works before being elected abbot on 4 May 1514. Like a number of other heads of religious houses of his generation Malvern devoted himself to improving the fabric of the abbey in order to assert its antiquity and wealth. Thus he built a tomb for King Osric, who had founded the abbey about 680, thereby emphasizing St Peter's claim to be one of the oldest religious foundations in the realm, and in 1524 he wrote a history of the founding of the abbey in rhyming verse. He also built an elaborate tomb and chapel for himself, and was probably responsible for adding a gallery range along the inside of the north precinct wall, and for rebuilding the two gates in the south wall. In addition, he carried out other responsibilities incumbent on his office. As a mitred abbot he sat in parliament on several occasions. He also received royal visitors: Princess Mary in 1525 and Henry VIII and Anne Boleyn in 1535.

The abbey was not only the most imposing edifice in the city of Gloucester, it was also the dominant local landlord, holding property worth £155 3s. 5d. in 1539. This, as well as the commoning rights it shared with the city, created animosity that had exploded in conflict just a year before Malvern became abbot. However, his tenure seems to have been relatively peaceful in that respect. He was able to turn his attention primarily to activities and responsibilities that would enhance his own reputation and that of his community. Hence he concelebrated the mass with the archbishop of Canterbury and numerous others when Wolsey received his cardinal's hat on 18 November 1515, and he was one of several abbots chosen to attend upon Wolsey at Dover when Charles V visited England in 1522. He also represented the abbot of Westminster in a reforming visitation of Malmesbury Abbey in 1527.

During the last fifteen years of his life Malvern seems to have dealt with conflicting demands on his position with relative success. In particular, when he had to choose between supporting the king and the pope, he supported the king. He was one of the many signatories to a letter to Pope Clement VII 'praying him to consent to the King's desires' for a divorce (*LP Henry VIII*, 4/3, no. 6513). He also subscribed to the royal supremacy in June 1534 (along with thirty-six members of his house). However, he did not reject traditional theology. In response to questions relating to the Act of Six Articles, he opposed priests' marrying, stated that scripture did not prohibit either auricular confession or private masses, and asserted that administration of the sacrament in both kinds was not necessary. At the time of his death, on or about 9 June 1539, the dissolution of the major monasteries was already in progress, and he undoubtedly realized what lay ahead for his community. Others would surrender St Peter's Abbey, but the chaos surrounding the dissolution may explain why he was not buried in the elaborate tomb he had constructed for himself; his place of burial is unknown. CAROLINE LITZENBERGER

Sources *DNB* · Foster, *Alum. Oxon.* · R. Furney, manuscript history of the city of Gloucester, *c*.1743, Glos. RO, D 327 · corporation records, 1535–80, Glos. RO, Gloucester borough records, GBR B2/1 · *VCH Gloucestershire*, vols. 2, 4, 8 · *The itinerary of John Leland in or about the years 1535–1543*, ed. L. Toulmin Smith, 11 pts in 5 vols. (1906–10) · *LP Henry VIII* · A. Douglas and P. Greenfield, eds., *Records of early English drama: Cumberland, Westmorland, Gloucestershire* (1986) · D. Verey, *Gloucestershire*, 2 vols. (1970) · Emden, *Oxf.*, 4.374 · *Reg. Oxf.*, 1.52, 70
Archives Glos. RO

Malvery [*married name* Mackirdy], **Olive Christian** (1876/7–1914), social observer, was the daughter of Thomas Malvery, a civil engineer working in India. Her mother was Jessie Symonds. No record of her birth has been located, and there is conflicting evidence about its date (the age which she stated at the time of her marriage suggested a birth date of 1881/2). She described herself as coming from an 'old Indian family' (Cox) and referred to India as her native land, though she also celebrated her Scottish ancestry which she derived from her grandmother, a Sinclair. Surviving photographs indicate that she was part Indian.

Malvery's parents separated when she was a child; her father, who was considerably older than her mother, failed to make a success of various business schemes. Olive and her brother were brought up in India by their maternal grandparents and received a good education. Raised an Anglican, she became involved in philanthropic work, raising money for Dr Barnardo's orphanages. She arrived in London from the Punjab about 1900 (though she does not appear in the census of 1901) with the ambition to become a professional singer, and through financial assistance from a friend in India she was enabled to train at the Royal College of Music. Enterprising, hard-working, and a self-publicist, freely exploiting her Anglo-Indian ancestry, she came to prominence in London society by reciting what she called her 'Indian pictures', poems on Indian themes set to music. She gave her first performance at the Westbourne Park Institute while still at college. The press praised her work and 'The Times gave me a splendid notice' (Malvery, *A Year and a Day*, 83).

Malvery became best known for her investigative writing on the condition of working women and child labourers in early twentieth-century London. Driven by religious zeal and a social reforming impulse, evident in her philanthropic endeavours and her lecturing on behalf of the temperance cause in Britain, continental Europe, and North America, she set about a series of descriptions of the poor and destitute using information gathered by undercover participation and observation of their lives. In October 1904 she contributed a series of documentary articles on the London poor to *Pearson's Magazine*. She used her position as an outsider to reveal truths about England that were largely concealed from those born and brought up there.

Malvery claimed to have researched her articles by living in the 'seething parishes' of London's poorest quarters (Malvery, *The Soul Market*, 309). There she mixed, undetected, with thieves, tramps, costermongers, milliners, and match girls. Knowing that in such communities an outsider would be easily spotted, she somehow blended in: 'By maintaining a discreet silence, I managed to get through' (ibid., 134). Her foreign appearance, far from being a disadvantage, actually helped her, and on one occasion she gained the confidence of a coster woman who made direct reference to it:

> 'Is yer foreign?' she asked. 'Not by half,' I said: 'One can't help one's birth, but one can help one's heart.' This sentiment pleased her extremely. Presently she asked me to mind her stall a minute, while she went and had a drink. While she was gone I sold two cabbages. (ibid.)

Phonetic transcription of her dialogues with working poor helped to establish the authenticity of Malvery's account for a predominantly middle-brow, middle-class readership. But they also helped to entertain readers in a commercial publication.

Malvery's articles, published as *The Heart of Things*, were accompanied by photographs depicting her in her various guises—barmaid, costermonger, flower girl—the overall effect falling somewhere between serious social enquiry and play-acting. In 1905 she contributed two further articles to *Pearson's Magazine* on the alien question, by which was understood the settlement of Jewish immigrants from eastern Europe in the East End of London. The articles coincided with the parliamentary debate on a bill to restrict such immigration, and Malvery's unsympathetic depiction of the Jewish poor contrasts markedly with her earlier treatment of the cockney street people.

Malvery married, on 13 May 1905 at the parish church of St Margaret's, Westminster, Archibald Mackirdy (1856/7–1911), the Scottish-born American consul to Muscat, the son of Robert Mackirdy, a banker of Rothesay. Mackirdy reportedly fell in love with his future wife after seeing her photograph in the press, and the newspapers published detailed accounts of her society wedding: one thousand working girls from the East End of London were invited, her attendants were coster girls from Hoxton, and, wearing an Indian dress, she was given away by the bishop of Bombay. Archibald Mackirdy was a supporter of the Salvation Army and shared his wife's concern for the welfare of London's destitute. They had two daughters and a son.

In 1906 Malvery published *The Soul Market*, a revised version of her first series of articles for *Pearson's Magazine*. It was dedicated 'To those who still have faith in humanity and a belief in God', and was written in the hope that it would encourage 'the suppression of some of the more hideous evils which I have in these pages only hinted at' (Malvery, *The Soul Market*, 320). She later claimed that *The Soul Market*, which went through several editions and established her as a social commentator and reformer, was 'the first book that roused the public to shame and sympathy … To-day there are a great many Missions which have been founded by people who were stirred to work by that book' (Malvery, *A Year and a Day*, 18). She took the credit, too, for stimulating the debate on night shelters for destitute women and girls. Profits from her first book, which was a considerable commercial success, and donations from readers established housing for homeless women in London. Her two shelters were later run under the auspices of the Salvation Army and the Church Army. She also ran a girls' club in Hoxton, the Girls' Guild of Good Life. Her response to the appalling working conditions which she witnessed in sweatshop trades was to form a Consumers' League with a white list of firms whose goods were produced under humane conditions.

At one level Malvery's investigative work follows in the tradition of Henry Mayhew, General Booth, and Beatrice Webb, but its theatricality and commercialism set it apart. As a review of *The Soul Market* in the *Daily Telegraph* observed: 'Miss Malvery writes with a running pen … The book should attract the ordinary reader; but there is much within its cover that will be valuable to the specialist investigating modern conditions of city life' (Malvery, *Baby Toilers*, frontispiece). *The Soul Market* was rapidly followed by *Baby Toilers* (1907), in which Malvery and her publishers capitalized on her earlier success. She hoped that her exposé of child labour would persuade parliament to legislate to end this abuse.

Malvery understood the social stratification within the London poor and documented the occupational snobbery that differentiated factory girls, costermongers, and domestic servants. If she perhaps did not have the familiarity that she pretended with her street subjects, she exposed serious social evils to a wide public view. But there was also a harshly practical, eugenicist side to her philanthropic concern for the poor.

> These people are all kept chiefly by the middle classes, and the awful result is while they breed and increase like rabbits, the women who might give wholesome and healthy children to the nation are being disqualified for maternal duties by the heavy burdens which society and philanthropy lay upon them. (Malvery, *The Soul Market*, 314)

Drunken, idle, wife-beating men were her principal target, and she recommended for them a sharp exposure to the rigours of military discipline. Instead of taxing those who worked to subsidize those who did not, she argued, 'it would be better to compel men to work for the support of themselves and their families' (ibid., 317). She blamed the difficulties faced by boroughs such as Poplar on 'extravagant local government' rather than under-investment (ibid.).

Such views became more strident in Malvery's later work. In *A Year and a Day* (1912) she regarded processions of the unemployed as 'simply contemptible; one is not even sorry for the bleary, lazy creatures who make up most of these sad "shows"' (Malvery, *A Year and a Day*, 61). Charitable work, she reflected, had 'so far saved us from dreadful outbreaks of desperate ill-used creatures' (p. 39). She had no sympathy for the organized labour movement or socialism, believing that the latter:

> has nothing to offer women except to propose that they should be made breeding cows, and that their young should be fathered by the State instead of by the animals who bred them … If you meet Socialists and listen to their talk, you will be amazed at the low value they place on women. (p. 35)

She herself belonged to a number of women's organizations, including the Pioneer Club for women and the Women Journalists' Club.

In 1912 Malvery published *The White Slave Market* with William Nicholas Willis, a former member of the Australian parliament and newspaperman of doubtful probity, who provided firsthand knowledge from east Asia. This harrowing book describes the enslavement to prostitution of girls in various countries, laying bare 'the nauseating details of this horrible traffic in white women' (Malvery and Willis, *White Slave Market*, 289). It was a traffic, they pointedly observed, that was carried on in Christian countries, and having put their case before the British public they hoped that parliament would be made to act.

Partly because of the circumstances surrounding the death of her husband, in 1911, Malvery was bitterly prejudiced against the medical profession. She made an exception of women doctors, and was determined to do all that she could to get their work recognized, but her animus against the majority of male doctors knew no bounds. It led her to consider the merits of Christian Science, but she was never fully converted. Instead charitable work, which she pursued with even greater intensity, provided a way out of the personal anguish which she felt after the death of her husband. Her final project was to edit a periodical, *Mackirdy's Weekly*, published from January 1914 to the outbreak of war in August. It was pledged to the causes she espoused—practical Christianity, a living wage for all workers, protection for children, and citizen rights for all those who paid taxes or carried out civic duties, regardless of gender. As a supporter of the constitutional movement for women's suffrage she wrote a series of articles in January and February 1914 attacking suffragette militancy, denouncing the resort to violence as a sign of desperation, and exposing the autocratic way in which Christabel Pankhurst ran the suffragette organization.

Suffering from cancer, Malvery died at her home, Iden, Woodcote Valley Road, Purley, Surrey, on 29 October 1914, aged thirty-seven. At an inquest on 31 October 1914 the cause of death was recorded as 'misadventure, veronal poisoning' (d. cert.), in effect an overdose of sedatives. Her will, drawn up shortly before her death, made provision for the upbringing of her three young children by her devoted secretary, Charlotte Cottrill, at a property owned by Malvery at Reigate, Surrey, named Rahat Munzil, or Underhill. She also requested that the base of the gravestone over her and her husband's grave should bear the inscription, 'Who serves his country and his neighbour earns not wealth but fellowship with God.'

MARK POTTLE

Sources J. Winter, *London's teeming streets, 1830–1914* (1993) · J. R. Walkowitz, 'The Indian woman, the flower girl and the Jew: photojournalism in Edwardian London', *Victorian Studies*, 42/1 (1998–9) · m. cert. · d. cert. · will, 13 Oct 1914 · H. Cox, *Who's who in Kent, Surrey,*

and Sussex (1911) · S. Cohen and C. Fleay, 'Fighters for the poor', History Today, 50/1 (Jan 2000), 36–7 · O. C. Malvery [Mrs Archibald Mackirdy], The soul market: with which is included 'The heart of things' (1906) · O. C. Malvery [Mrs Archibald Mackirdy], Thirteen nights (1908) · O. C. Malvery [Mrs Archibald Mackirdy] and W. N. Willis, The white slave market (1912) · O. C. Malvery [Mrs Archibald Mackirdy], Baby toilers (1907) · O. C. Malvery, 'My life', Mackirdy's Weekly (28 March–23 May 1914) · J. Harris, Private lives, public spirit: a social history of Britain, 1870–1914 (1993) · O. C. Malvery [Mrs Archibald Mackirdy], A year and a day (1912) · Bombay Almanack (1856) · Bombay Almanack (1858) · Bombay Almanack (1861) · The Times (15 May 1905), 6b · The Times (5 Nov 1914), 11d · 'Willis, William Nicholas', AusDB · CGPLA Eng. & Wales (1914) · E. Ross, Love and toil: motherhood in outcast London, 1870–1918 (1993)
Likenesses photograph, repro. in Mackirdy's Weekly (24 Jan 1914) · photographs, repro. in Malvery, The soul market
Wealth at death £8967 19s. 0d.: probate, 24 Dec 1914, CGPLA Eng. & Wales

Malvoisin, William. See Malveisin, William (d. 1238).

Malym [Malim], **William** (1533–1594), headmaster, was the son of Henry Malym of Staplehurst, Kent. He was educated at Eton College from about 1544, was accepted as a scholar of King's College, Cambridge, on 14 August 1548 and graduated BA in 1553. On 11 January 1555 Malym was discommuned from King's for an unknown offence, but was reinstated after two weeks and graduated MA the following year.

In 1561 Malym was appointed headmaster of Eton College. His role in the provocative selection as the college's provost of the Roman Catholic sympathizer Richard Bruarne in 1561 is unclear, but—unlike Bruarne—he remained in office. Malym was the author of a Consuetudinarium, or account of the rules of the college, which bears his name on the fly leaf and which was probably intended as a guide for the commissioners who visited the school in 1561. The work is a vital source for the customs of the Eton calendar and the routines of school life. It reveals that the day began at 5 a.m., and that much of the instruction of younger pupils was in the hands of the senior boys of the seventh or highest form, styled praepositores. It also shows that features of the old religion survived at Eton in 1561. Each of the boys had a confessor, on the basis that 'confession is a wholesome medicine for the sinner', as Malym explained approvingly, though this passage was later crossed through (Lyte, 148). Other features of school life did not change. The day remained extremely long, holidays were meagre, and Latin and Greek dominated the curriculum.

On her visit to Eton in September 1563 Queen Elizabeth was presented with a collection of Latin verses by the scholars, who asked that she look favourably on 'our dearest master, by whose kindness and extreme watchfulness, by day and night, we have attained such proficiency in literature', hoping that he should not 'be ground down by ceaseless labours and studies' (Lyte, 169). It may be doubted whether the students' plea was inspired by spontaneous gratitude for the master's tender care. The tradition of flogging, established under its most celebrated practitioner Nicholas Udall, was continued enthusiastically by Malym, his former pupil. In a meeting at Windsor about this time, William Cecil reported that 'divers

scholars of Eton be run away from that school for fear of beating', news which provoked a debate on the value of the birch, and stimulated Roger Ascham to write The Scholemaster (Ascham, preface, sig. B2r–v).

Most historians of Eton have thought that Malym's headship finished in 1563, but Sterry lists his tenure as lasting until 1571. On his own account Malym travelled to Turkey in 1564, convincing himself of the 'cruelty and beastly behaviour' of the natives, 'having been among them more than 8 months together' (Daye, preface). He toured widely, visiting Antioch, Cyprus, the Aegean Islands, and Venice. There is also a second report of 'his great travayle by sea and land unto Hierusalem. Where he was made knight of the sepulchre as appeareth by his letters patent dated at Jerusaleme the 13th day of September … 1564' (BL, Harleian MS 1116, fol. 69v). Such protracted travels suggest that Malym had left Eton altogether. On 3 April 1569 he was installed in the prebend of Biggleswade in the diocese of Lincoln, an appointment most unusual for one who had not been ordained. When, a few days earlier, Malym had written to thank Cecil for using his influence with the earl of Leicester in his behalf, it was probably in regard to this benefice.

On 19 and 20 January 1573 a meeting of the court of the Mercers' Company was held at St Paul's School, London, which discussed the appointment of a new high master in succession to John Cook. The bishop of London, Edwin Sandys, and the archdeacons of Essex and Middlesex were asked to choose between William Malym and Ralph Waddington. Malym was preferred, and took up his appointment on Lady day 1573. It seems possible that Christopher Holden, the 'surmaster' or usher, was resentful at being thus passed over. Whatever the reason, it is clear that the two men were at loggerheads, and in 1575 it proved necessary to appoint arbitrators to resolve contentions between them. But the trouble, which centred on rights of access to the Mercers' lodgings, continued. In 1576 the Mercers' court resolved the dispute. The school was now accommodating boarders, and it is possible that this had been inaugurated by Malym.

It was on 13 April 1578, while master of St Paul's School, that Malym was married to Mary Strete, at the church of St Thomas the Apostle in London. Mary died before him, for in his will Malym named one Alice as his wife. Malym had two daughters and two sons, of whom one, Dudley, was completely disinherited and disowned by his father as 'undutiful, unthankful and unnatural'. Among Malym's pupils at St Paul's were the soldier Sir Francis Vere, and Sir Thomas Chaloner, later chamberlain to Prince Henry, whose book De republica Anglorum instauranda was edited by Malym in 1579. Malym also translated from the Italian a pamphlet on the siege and capture of Famagusta in Cyprus by the Turks, published by John Daye as The True Report of All the Success of Famagosta, with an epistle dedicated to the earl of Leicester dated 23 March 1572. Malym contributed commendatory letters or verses for Demosthenis Graecorum, by Nicholas Corr (1571), and for Edmund Grant's Spicilegium (1575). In 1578 he delivered an oration in Latin to the Dutch military leader John Casimir on his visit to London.

In February 1580 Malym wrote to Alexander Nowell, dean of St Paul's, asking for release from his duties at the school, but this was not granted. On 29 May 1581 he appeared before the wardens of the Mercers and requested to be discharged, asking them to find a successor within the next twelve months. Malym had constructed a polyglot lexicon for the students, in Latin, Greek, Hebrew, French, Spanish, and high Dutch, for which the college paid 19s. on his departure in autumn 1581. Malym died shortly before 15 August 1594, when he was buried at the church of All Hallows-the-Less, Thames Street, London.

STEPHEN WRIGHT

Sources M. McDonnell, *The annals of St Paul's School* (privately printed, Cambridge, 1959) · H. C. Maxwell Lyte, *A history of Eton College, 1440–1910*, 4th edn (1911) · M. McDonnell, ed., *The registers of St Paul's School, 1509–1748* (privately printed, London, 1977) · Venn, *Alum. Cant.* · Cooper, *Ath. Cantab.* · *Fasti Angl., 1541–1857*, [Lincoln] · W. Sterry, ed., *The Eton College register, 1441–1698* (1943) · J. Daye, *The true report of all the successe of Famagosta*, trans. W. Malym (1572) · BL, Harley MS 1116, fol. 69v · R. Ascham, *The scholemaster* (1570); facs. edn (1968) · Wood, *Ath. Oxon.*, new edn · will, PRO, PROB 11/84, sig. 60

Malynes [Malines, de Malines], **Gerard** [Garrett, Gerald] (*fl.* **1585–1641**), merchant and writer on economics, was the son of a 'mint-master' (Malynes, 281). He claimed that Lancashire was the 'countrey' of his 'ancestors and parents', but he was actually born in Antwerp, close to the town of Malines itself (ibid., 263). His early life remains obscure, but in 1622 he boasted fifty years of 'observation, knowledge and experience' of trade, which suggests that his commercial career started in the early 1570s (ibid., 8). By 1585 he had settled in London as a merchant, and, judging by his £200 loan to the crown three years later, was able to establish himself as a successful European trader. He became a member of the City's Dutch church, and remained a merchant stranger without attempting to secure denizen or naturalized status. His foreign connections were further strengthened by 1590 through his marriage to Marie (*fl.* 1590–1602), the daughter of his business partner Guilliame van Ameyden. This union produced at least three sons and one daughter.

Throughout his career Malynes demonstrated an uncompromising ambition, and the international crises of the age presented him with several opportunities to advance himself. Keen to play the patriotic subject in his adopted country, he acted as an informant for the government, using his international contacts in France and Spain to supply the secretary of state, Sir Francis Walsingham, with news of foreign events. His business dealings were equally full of intrigue, and in the 1590s he became embroiled in a series of legal disputes which threatened to ruin him completely. He was partly to blame for these misfortunes, for he seems to have been ruthless in pursuit of financial gain. He was even charged with having arrested members of a Dutch diplomatic party for a debt, and English observers remarked upon his obstinacy and

suspect motives. His key test came from a dispute with Amsterdam merchant John Honger, who accused Malynes and his father-in-law of conspiring to spirit away some £18,000 which he had entrusted to them as his factors in London. Malynes counter-claimed that Honger owed him significant sums, but his adversary was backed by powerful allies such as the Dutch envoy in London, and it was Malynes who ended up in gaol. It appears that he was imprisoned twice, in 1590–93 and from 1594 to at least 1596, although his enemy Honger suggested that he used the stolen money to live 'in riotous sort' during captivity (*Salisbury MSS*, 6.15–16). Malynes sought to use his government contacts to extricate himself from this mess, reminding Sir Robert Cecil of his services for the crown and his concern for 'the advancement of the true gospel and doctrine' (ibid., 262–3). A bill to settle the affair was unsuccessfully submitted to parliament early in 1598, but his connections served him well, for in June 1600 it was reported that 'for some time' he had been granted royal protection from arrest 'for special considerations' (*APC, 1599–1600*, 365). According to an intelligence report of September 1598, Malynes had dealings with a Spanish agent who had been in England, and thus he might have resumed his espionage duties on gaining his liberty (*CSP dom., 1598–1601*, 91). There is no evidence to suggest that Honger ever regained his money, and this and other civil suits were reported to be still 'undecided' in July 1602. However, Malynes informed Cecil several months later that he was now 'out of danger of all arrest', and hoped that the minister would 'create me *de novo*' (*Salisbury MSS*, 12.245, 528).

Malynes's decision to embark on a career as an economic writer must be linked to these personal misfortunes. Perhaps inspired by his father's profession, Malynes sought to establish himself as an authority on currency and exchange, using his government contacts to resurrect his flagging fortunes. In 1600 he was appointed one of the commissioners to establish the true par of exchange, and although frequently rebuffed in the course of public debate, his concern to free the English coinage from the perceived exploitation of foreign money dealers remained the dominant theme of his life's work. So relentlessly did he explore this field that a leading modern authority sees him as 'something of an exchange crank' (Ashton, 4). His views were first published in two tracts which appeared in 1601–2: *St George for England, Allegorically Described*, and *A Treatise of the Canker of England's Commonwealth*. The latter tract suggested that he had had the opportunity to communicate his ideas to the queen in person, and he boldly claimed that he could save the country £500,000 a year. However, the dedication of the *Treatise* also highlighted his continuing notoriety, since he still feared rivals who would 'endeavour to make me generally odious amongst all men'. He advertised his talents by more direct means, reportedly giving evidence to the Commons concerning a marine insurance bill in November and December 1601, and several months later he offered to settle the exchange between England and war-ravaged Ireland. He subsequently ransacked French history to publicize further his views on exchanges, publishing in 1604 *England's view in the unmasking of two paradoxes, with a replication unto the answer of Maister J. Bodine.*

During the reign of James I, Malynes sought to turn his fiscal expertise to more direct financial benefit, becoming involved in a series of projects associated with the coinage. He first turned his hand to mining, gaining the backing of Lord Eure and several London merchants to extract lead and alum in Yorkshire and silver in Durham. However, this scheme had already come to grief by 1606, despite the recruitment of mining experts from Germany and 'the commodiousness of foreign contracts' of his partners (*Salisbury MSS*, 18.271). He darkly suggested that 'a great personage then in authoritie' had let him down on this occasion in order to pursue 'some other private designs', and also blamed the machinations of other business associates (Malynes, 262). Once again he turned to Cecil (now the earl of Salisbury) for aid, and may well have gained his assistance, for in 1607 Malynes was granted another royal protection against arrest, presumably to save him from his creditors. Two years later he was appointed a commissioner on mint affairs, a position which promoted further commentary on monetary schemes. In 1610 he prepared another tract on his favourite topic, *A Treatise of Tripartite Exchange According to the Three Essential Parts of Trafficque*, stating his patriotic intent to halt the nation's commercial decline. He also proudly recalled his recent summons by the House of Commons to advise on ways to halt the export of bullion. The experience also encouraged him to draft *A Treatise of the Royal Merchant of Great Brittayne* (1610), in which he lectured the sovereign on his duty and interest in attending to the nation's finances and commerce.

In 1612 Malynes prepared another paper attacking foreign money dealers as the cause of the country's export of bullion, and in the following year proposed to coin copper and brass farthings to ensure that small-denomination silver pieces did not leave the country. He was successful in his bid and a patent was duly granted to Lord Harrington to oversee the implementation of the scheme. However, it soon ran into trouble, and after six months only £600 of the tokens had been issued, several counties having refused to take them. Harrington's death further complicated matters, and by 1617 Malynes had to contend with the competition of the countess of Bedford, who had also started to mint the coins. He again sought to use court contacts to salvage his fortune, claiming that his family stood to lose £2500 on account of this project, but compensation was not forthcoming. He also appears to have met further disappointment in 1617 when lobbying to secure part of the income from duties levied on foreigners for fishing in royal waters. Ministerial patience with the truculent courtier was clearly running out, for in the following year the privy council prevented Malynes from using his royal protection of 1607 to avoid paying his arrears for rent. Personal ruin again beckoned, and in February 1619 he was back in debtors' prison, whence he petitioned the king for

aid, his debtors having had the temerity to pay him back with his own tokens.

Demonstrating remarkable resilience, Malynes once again managed to survive this ordeal, and embraced the economic crises of the 1620s as an excellent opportunity to put forward his ideas on the currency. His rant against foreign dealers duly resurfaced in a tract of 1622, *The Maintenance of Free Trade, According to the Three Essentiall Parts of Traffique*; this constituted a direct attack on a recent work by Edward Misselden, who argued that the root of the country's monetary problem was an undervaluing of English coins, rather than the rate of exchange. Malynes took pride in declaring his long experience of advising ministers on such matters, and gave evidence to the standing commission on trade about the state of the coinage. The controversy continued into the following year, when he published *The centre of the circle of commerce, or, A refutation of a treatise intitled the Circle of commerce, lately published by E[dward] M[isselden]*, a work which described exchange as 'the heavenly mystery' (p. 139). However, the essential flaws of Malynes's argument were clear to see, and were most damagingly exposed by Thomas Mun, who argued more successfully that the rate of exchange was only a symptom of a deeper malaise, namely a fundamental imbalance in the nation's trade with other countries.

Although Malynes's reputation was severely bruised by this debate, it was during this controversy that he produced his most influential work, *Consuetudo, vel, Lex mercatoria, or, The ancient law merchant; divided into three parts, according to the essential parts of traffic* (1622). At 500 pages, it is a most impressive testimony to his commercial experience, and became the standard English-language work on the law merchant. A modern study has indeed called it 'the most popular merchants' handbook of its time' (Letwin, 101). Its tripartite format analysing commodities, money, and exchanges had appeared in his earlier works, and he predictably took the opportunity to indulge his views on the abuses of foreign exchanges. However, he ranged much further in his economic remit, and sought to promote several new schemes, most characteristically a regulated system of pawnbrokers to relieve the poor from the tyranny of moneylenders. He claimed to have collected a list of 1500 subscribers to back this scheme to the tune of £2000 p.a., but his hopes once again had been dashed by 'a great personage, who (as it seemeth) was not worthy of the honour thereof' (Malynes, 335–6). The general value of the work as a compendium of mercantile expertise ensured its continuing popularity among seventeenth-century publishers, with further editions in 1629, 1636, and 1686, and several excerpts were also published separately, Samuel Hartlib including a section from this 'great book' in his edition of *The Reformed Commonwealth of Bees* in 1655. Economic historians have also found it a most useful, if not entirely unimpeachable, source.

In the *Lex mercatoria* Malynes confessed to be 'stricken in years' and ready to 'number my days'. His financial difficulties and advanced age can account for the general obscurity of his later years, although he surfaced briefly in 1641 to lobby the House of Commons for controls on exchanges, thereby displaying his unquenchable belief in the propriety of his lifelong campaign. No details concerning his date of death have been found, and, as he himself feared, his continuing money problems helped to ensure that none of his offspring rose to prominence.

PERRY GAUCI

Sources *CSP dom.*, 1591–4, 337–8; 1598–1601, 91; 1603–10, 62; 1611–18, 128, 456; 1619–23, 15; 1641–3, 112–13 · *Calendar of the manuscripts of the most hon. the marquis of Salisbury*, 6, HMC, 9 (1895), 15–16, 262–3, 455; 8 (1899), 157; 12 (1910), 245, 528; 18 (1940), 271 · *Calendar of the manuscripts of Major-General Lord Sackville*, 2 vols., HMC, 80 (1940–66), 255, 350 · *Huguenot Society*, 10/2, 207, 314–15, 383, 389, 412, 414, 466 · *Huguenot Society*, 10/3, 86, 194 · *CSP for.*, 1589, 34; 1589–90, 195–6; 1590–91, 214–15; 1593–4, 189; 1595, 96 · *APC*, 1595–6, 145, 518; 1599–1600, 365, 723; 1616–17, 171–2; 1618–19, 163, 267 · BL, Cotton MSS, Julius C.iii. no. 118; Otho E.x, fols. 328–9; Titus B.v, fols. 419–23; Vespasian C.xiv, fols. 10–12 · BL, Harley MSS 38, fols. 220–21; 513, fols. 1–31; 660, fols. 63–4 · J. O. Appleby, *Economic thought and ideology in seventeenth-century England* (1978), 41–8 · W. Oldys, *The British librarian* (1738), 96–105 · W. B. Bannerman, ed., *The registers of St Helen's, Bishopsgate, London*, Harleian Society, register section, 31 (1904), 9, 276 · W. Letwin, *The origins of scientific economics* (1963), 101 · R. Ashton, *The crown and the money market, 1603–1640* (1960), 4, 195 · G. Malynes, *Consuetudo, vel, Lex mercatoria* (1622)
Archives BL, Harley MSS, copies of various works

Malynne [Malin], **Walter** (*d.* 1556/7), abbot of Glenluce, was perhaps born in Edinburgh, where the family owned a modest property. Having graduated at St Andrews (incorporated in 1512) and become a cleric, he entered the service of John Stewart, fourth duke of Albany, who ruled Scotland as governor during James V's childhood, and in August 1515 was made a canon of Aberdeen Cathedral. From February 1516 he acted as Albany's envoy and, when Albany departed to France in June 1517 and remained there for over four years, Malynne's role assumed greater importance. During 1517 he dealt with Henry VIII and Wolsey over peace between Scotland and England, travelled on to Albany in France, and returned to Scotland in September bearing a two-year extension of the truce.

In March 1519 Malynne brought messages from Albany to the lords of council. Two months later the governor nominated him to Rome for Glenluce, a Cistercian monastery in Wigtownshire. Provided by bulls of 13 June 1519, Malynne was to receive the habit, make his monastic profession, and rule as a regular abbot. He continued, however, to be the governor's secretary; he travelled to Denmark and France, and in December 1521 led a mission to London, clearly enjoying Albany's complete confidence. In 1523 he was involved in a confidential mission in January, was sent by the French king, François I, to Denmark in May, was again in France in the late summer, then returned to Scotland in September and became one of the custodians of the young king.

Malynne now settled at Glenluce. The laird Gordon of Lochinvar, acting with the bishop of Galloway, despoiled Glenluce in July 1525, whereupon Malynne took action and won compensation. In 1530, when attending the Cistercian general chapter, he was appointed to replace Andrew Durie, abbot of Melrose, as visitor for Scotland. At once he set out to reform practices contrary to Cistercian ideals of poverty and common life, which brought him into conflict with Durie, and at the king's request he was replaced as visitor by the French abbot of Chaalis. General chapter then, in 1533, appointed Malynne and another abbot to make the French visitor's enactments effective, modifying them if necessary.

Glenluce in 1545 was embroiled in conflict between two powerful local factions, one headed by the earl of Cassillis, the other by Lochinvar. Both parties in turn invaded Glenluce and Malynne took legal action. He now arranged for the succession to the abbacy. By bulls of 5 December 1547 his resignation was accepted, but he retained all powers and revenues for life. The new abbot was James Gordon, aged about nineteen and brother of John, the young laird of Lochinvar. He was to become a monk and rule as a regular abbot, and meanwhile would be groomed as Malynne's successor.

Malynne continued to act as Cistercian commissary and to influence the restoration of ideals of common life. In February 1556 he confirmed an arrangement for the upkeep of sixteen monks at Melrose, having most probably encouraged the community to obtain this. During the previous two years he had been involved in a dispute at Newbattle, in the diocese of St Andrews, and took decisive disciplinary action, about which the archbishop complained to Rome on 29 March 1556.

Malynne had died by 4 May 1557. He had played a modest part in public affairs, sitting intermittently in parliament and council. The outstanding feature of his career was his zeal and fearlessness in defending the interests of Glenluce and Cistercian observance. Community numbers at Glenluce remained stable, despite factors causing their decline in other monasteries. Although Albany's motive in having him promoted to Glenluce was surely to give his envoy greater status and revenues, Malynne embraced monastic ideals sincerely. He belongs to a class of dedicated men, found apparently only in Scotland, who were not monks before their appointment as abbots.

MARK DILWORTH

Sources M. Dilworth, 'Walter Malin: diplomatic agent and monastic reformer', *Innes Review*, 51 (2000), 147–65 · A. Ross, 'Some notes on the religious orders in pre-Reformation Scotland', *Essays on the Scottish Reformation, 1513–1625*, ed. D. McRoberts (1962), 185–244 · R. C. Reid, ed., *Wigtownshire charters*, Scottish History Society, 3rd ser., 51 (1960) · U. Edin. L., MS La.III.321, fols. 167–8 · *The protocol book of John Foular*, ed. M. Wood, 3, Scottish RS, 75 (1953) · J. M. Anderson, ed., *Early records of the University of St Andrews*, Scottish History Society, 3rd ser., 8 (1926)

Mam Cymru. *See* Katheryn of Berain (*c.*1540–1591).

Mamesfeld, Henry (*c.*1270–1328), ecclesiastic, belonged to a family that may have come from Mansfield in Nottinghamshire. He was ordained deacon and priest during 1296 in Lincoln diocese, the same year that he secured Flintham rectory, Nottinghamshire, in the diocese of York. He received licences of absence from successive archbishops to study for one year in 1297 and 1299 and for three years in 1306. Between 1288 and 1296 he was a fellow of Merton College. An MA of Oxford, he had incepted as a doctor of theology by 1309 when, on 27 October, his election as chancellor of the university was confirmed. In 1311, during his tenure, new statutes were drawn up for the 'scholars of Master William of Durham'—that is, University College. By December of the following year Mamesfeld had vacated the office.

Mamesfeld was one of those who attended the provincial council summoned to York in 1311 by Archbishop William Greenfield (d. 1315) for the examination of the templars in the northern province. A canon of Lincoln, he was collated on 22 May 1311 to the Sanctae Crucis prebend, and in 1316 to that of Asgarby. In 1315 he was elected dean of Lincoln and in January 1320 bishop, but he declined to accept the latter office. He died in the second half of 1328; probate of his will (the details are not extant) followed on 6 December.

The early fourteenth-century painted glass in twelve and possibly all fourteen side windows of the choir of Merton College was given by Mamesfeld. These windows depict saints in central panels beneath elaborate pinnacled canopies. All but two of those on the south-east have the saints flanked by kneeling figures of the donor—also beneath canopies—in gown, hood, and cap with the inscription: 'Magister Henricus de Mamesfeld me fecit'. To Oriel College he gave a copy of Peter Lombard's *Sentences*, but his principal gift was of eight volumes to Merton College, one of which, the *Quodlibeta* of Godfrey de Montibus, is now Balliol College MS 211. The others comprised glossed versions of the gospels, the epistles of St Paul, the book of Exodus, and of the psalter, together with copies of St Thomas Aquinas's *De veritate* and *Contra Gentiles*, and Gregory's *Moralia*. William Wheatley, a master at the schools of Stamford and Lincoln, his contemporary at Oxford, included him in his dedication of a commentary on the *De consolatione philosophiae* of Boethius, which John Pits and Thomas Tanner, following him, attributed to Mamesfeld himself.   ROY MARTIN HAINES

Sources Lincoln Cathedral, chapter acts, probate, A. 2. 23, fol. 11r • *The register of William Greenfield, lord archbishop of York, 1306–1315*, ed. W. Brown and A. H. Thompson, 5 vols., SurtS, 145, 149, 151–3 (1931–40) • H. Bradshaw and C. Wordsworth, eds., *Statutes of Lincoln Cathedral*, 3 vols. (1892–7) • *Snappe's formulary and other records*, ed. H. E. Salter, OHS, 80 (1924) • C. R. L. Fletcher and others, eds., *Collectanea: first series*, OHS, 5 (1885) • M. Burrow, ed., *Collectanea: second series*, OHS, 16 (1890) • G. C. Brodrick, *Memorials of Merton College*, OHS, 4 (1885) • H. Anstey, ed., *Munimenta academica*, 1, Rolls Series, 50 (1868), 1.87–91 • *An inventory of the historical monuments in the city of Oxford*, Royal Commission on Historical Monuments (England) (1939) • H. W. Garrod, *Ancient medieval glass in Merton College* (1931) • F. M. Powicke, *The medieval books of Merton College* (1931) • *Fasti Angl., 1300–1541*, [Lincoln] • *Fasti Angl., 1300–1541*, [Introduction] • Emden, *Oxf.*

Likenesses stained glass (as kneeling figure of donor), Merton Oxf., chapel

Man, Felix Hans (1893–1985), photographer and art collector, was born on 30 November 1893 in Freiburg im Breisgau, Germany, as Hans Felix Sigismund Baumann, one of the five children of Karl Sigismund Ludwig Baumann (1853–1914) and his wife, Johanne Jacobine Helene Hofmann (1863–1915). His father, a banker like his grandfather, had been born in Riga, now in Latvia but then in imperial Russia. His father's usual language was German,

Felix Hans Man (1893–1985), by Roger George Clark, 1983

and when this was banned he moved to southern Germany. In Riga he had been music critic for the *Rigaer Tageblatt* so Felix enjoyed a musical background. Years later this was to show in memorable reportage of performances by Stravinsky in 1929, Furtwängler in 1930, and Toscanini at Bayreuth in 1930.

Baumann always remembered his first experience of photography as a small boy when the flash powder failed to ignite for his school photograph. At the age of eleven he owned a box camera and to economize on pocket money he learned to develop and print his own films. Dissatisfied with his photography and encouraged by his school drawing-masters he started to etch, draw, and paint. Except for a few snapshots taken in the First World War trenches, graphic art was to dominate his artistic life until he took up the camera again in 1927 or 1928. He changed his name about this time to avoid confusion with another photographer also called Hans Baumann.

In 1912 Baumann married Gertrude Jeckeln (1896–1966). After the First World War he restarted his art studies in Munich. His autobiography is silent about the early 1920s, but in an interview he revealed that during the inflation period he had lived on his own smallholding growing vegetables. Dr Nachum Gidal, a photojournalist who had worked alongside him, recalled that Baumann had worked in a printing factory making lithographic plates which explains his complete command of the technical and artistic aspects of lithography, on which he became a world authority.

From 1927 Man was drawing illustrations for Ullstein's daily newspaper, *BZ am Mittag*. As it was published at midday, illustrations had to be prepared overnight. Man returned to photography to ensure speed and accuracy in his drawings, but soon realized that photographs alone earned him more money. He began contributing to more Ullstein papers, including *Tempo* and *Morgenpost*. In 1929 he met Simon Gutmann, the charismatic owner of the photographic agency Dephot (Deutscher PhotoDienst). Gutmann was one of the first to understand the nature of the 'picture story' which was to revolutionize magazines worldwide. Man became Gutmann's chief photographer, a pioneering photojournalist: he, with others from this talented agency, provided hundreds of photo-stories for Ullstein's *Berliner Illustrierte Zeitung* and many other publications during 1929–33. Through Dephot Man formed a long-lasting friendship with Stefan Lorant, a Hungarian Jew like Gutmann, who became editor of the *Münchener Illustrierte Presse*.

In 1933 Man was working in Canada on a story for the *Berliner Illustrierte Zeitung* when the Nazis took over the Jewish-owned Ullstein Press; Lorant, already once imprisoned by the Nazis, left for England. Although not Jewish himself, Man did not relish becoming a compulsory member of the Nazi party and he too emigrated to England. Lorant persuaded the mighty Odhams Press to launch *Weekly Illustrated* and Man to photograph for it. Lorant found it impossible to work with the management and resigned after three months leaving the young assistant editor, Tom Hopkinson, in charge. Man left soon after to join the *Daily Mirror*, becoming one of the photographers producing picture stories under the name Lensman.

The dramatic change in Man's career came in 1938 when Lorant persuaded Hulton Press to start *Picture Post*. Man became a major contributor remaining even after Lorant, apprehensive of a Nazi invasion of Britain, left for America in 1940. Again the assistant editor took over; again he was Tom Hopkinson. Man was interned briefly in the Isle of Man in the early days of the Second World War and became a naturalized British subject in 1948. He estimated that over the years he produced between 150 and 200 picture stories. The exact number for *Weekly Illustrated* and *Picture Post* is difficult to ascertain as for years no photographer credits were ever printed and there is limited access to other sources such as publishers' payment records. An extensive but still only partial list appears in a National Book League and Goethe Institute booklet published in 1977.

Man held very strong views on how his pictures should be used, causing periodic disputes with managements. Between 1945 and 1948 he took few photographs, concentrating on his collection of artists' lithography. He wrote books and articles on lithography as well as editing the *Europaeische Graphik*, Munich, from 1963 to 1975. The climax of his collecting career came in 1971 when the Victoria and Albert Museum staged the exhibition 'Homage to Senefelder' entirely from his collection (it is now in the National Gallery of Australia, Canberra). He married his long-term companion, the German-born Lieselotte Henderson-Begg, late in life, in 1973; there were no children of the marriage. He died on 30 January 1985 in Westminster Hospital, London, and was cremated at Golders Green. He was survived by his wife. Many of his photographs can be found in the Hulton Getty collection, among the *Picture Post* material.   COLIN OSMAN

Sources C. Osman, taped interviews, *c*.1978–1983, University of Cardiff · private information (2004) · F. H. Man, *Man with camera* (1983) · unedited MS copy of autobiography, *c*.1979, priv. coll. · T. Hopkinson, 'Introduction', *Felix H. Man: pioneer of photojournalism* (1977) · C. Osman, introduction, *Felix H. Man: pioneer of photography* (1983) [exhibition catalogue, V&A, 24 May – 24 July 1983] · F. H. Man, *Artist's lithographs: a world of history* (1970) · *Homage to Senefelder: artist's lithographs from the Felix H. Man collection* (1971) [exhibition catalogue, V&A] · d. cert.

Archives priv. coll. | SOUND University of Cardiff, Osman Sound Archive, interviews with him and his contemporaries (*c*.1978–83)

Likenesses F. H. Man, self-portrait, photograph, 1947, NPG · D. Hockney, lithograph, 1969, repro. in Man, *Artist's lithographs*, plate 189 · R. G. Clark, photograph, 1983, NPG [*see illus.*]

Man, Henry (*d.* **1556**), bishop of Sodor and Man, is first recorded in 1528, as a Carthusian monk at Sheen; he became prior of the Witham Charterhouse in Somerset in 1534, but returned to Sheen as prior in the following year, remaining there until the house's dissolution in 1539. During the latter year he became both BTh and DTh at Oxford. In his earlier years he appears to have been a supporter of Elizabeth Barton, the Nun of Kent. Always on the fringes of this circle, he reversed his opinion and early in 1534 disowned her, probably under pressure from Thomas Cromwell. Not long afterwards he held a long conversation with Thomas More about Barton, during which More said little about her supposed revelations, although talking about these seems to have been the purpose of the interview. Man certainly became a servant of Cromwell's with speed and was 'compliant to the point of obsequiousness' on the issue of the royal supremacy in 1535 (Knowles, 237). He seems subsequently to have been instrumental in paving the way for an easy surrender of the house at Sheen in 1539.

Between 1539 and 1546 Man was in receipt of a pension of £133 6*s*. 8*d*. From 1541 to 1546 he was dean of Chester. During this time he was also rector of St Mary's on the Hill, Chester (1543–6) and later of Finningley, Nottinghamshire (1546); he also held the Leicestershire livings of Thurcaston and Sibson. He was made bishop of Sodor and Man on 22 January 1546, a diocese he seems never to have visited.

Man holds the distinction of being the only Carthusian monk to be appointed a bishop in England apart from St Hugh (*d.* 1200), the founder of the order in England. He died in London in 1556, shortly after drawing up his will on 18 October, and was buried at St Andrew Undershaft, London. He showed his religious sympathies by bequeathing his books to the monastery at Sheen, 'if it should be re-edified' (Knowles, 3.413, n. 1).   D. G. NEWCOMBE

Sources Emden, *Oxf.*, 4.375 · *LP Henry VIII*, vols. 6–8, 15, 21 · D. Knowles [M. C. Knowles], *The religious orders in England*, 3 (1959) · A. W. More, *Diocesan histories: Sodor and Man* (1893) · *VCH Somerset*, vol. 2 · *VCH Surrey*, vol. 2

Man, Henry (**1747–1799**), writer, was born in the City of London. His father, a well-known builder in the City, sent him to be educated under the Revd John Lamb at a house school in Croydon. He was a quick learner and soon distinguished himself as a scholar. Family pressure and a nonconformist background meant that progressing to university was impossible, so Man left school at fifteen and became a clerk in a mercantile house in the City.

In 1770 Man published a small work called *The Trifler*. This volume of essays established him as a writer. In 1774 he contributed a series of letters on education to

Woodfall's newspaper the *Morning Chronicle*. In the following year he published a novel, *Bentley, or, The Rural Philosopher*. In 1775 he retired from business and published a dramatic satire entitled *Cloacina*. In the following year Man married. The couple had one daughter, Emma Claudiana. Shortly after his marriage Man obtained a post in the South Sea House, and within a matter of months he was elected deputy secretary there.

It was while Man was deputy secretary that he became acquainted with the writer Charles Lamb, who worked at South Sea House as a teenager between 1791 and 1792. Although they worked together for only a brief time, Man impressed Lamb. Praising Man in *The Essays of Elia* Lamb remarked that in him 'common qualities become uncommon', and that he had a genuine wit and geniality (C. Lamb, *Essays of Elia*, 1902, 10).

Working at South Sea House did not interfere with Man's literary interests. He continued to write letters and essays for the *Morning Gazette* until his death on 5 December 1799. His only daughter died in Sevenoaks, Kent, on 14 August 1858.

Man's works were collected and published in two volumes, with a 'Memoir', in 1802. They consisted of essays, letters, and various other literary fragments. In *The Essays of Elia* Lamb lamented that they had been all but forgotten in so short a space of time, as was his style, 'terse, fresh epigrammatic, as alive'. Lamb owned a set of Man's works and often read them. He was particularly fond of Man's epigram on lords Spencer and Sandwich, credited respectively with making the waistcoat a fashionable item and inventing the sandwich:

> Two noble Earls, whom if I quote,
> Some folks might call me sinner;
> The one invented half a coat;
> The other half a dinner.
> The plan was good, as some will say
> And fitted to console one:
> Because, in this poor starving day,
> Few can afford a whole one.

A. E. J. LEGGE, *rev.* J.-M. ALTER

Sources *Collected works of Henry Man* (1802) • *GM*, 1st ser., 69 (1799), 1092 • *GM*, 3rd ser., 5 (1858), 536 • *The works of Charles and Mary Lamb*, ed. E. V. Lucas, new edn, 6 vols. (1912), vol. 6 • E. V. Lucas, *The life of Charles Lamb*, 2 vols. (1905); repr. (1987)

Man, James (1700?–1761), philologist, was born at Whitewreath, Elgin, Moray, the son of John Man, an impoverished small farmer. He was educated at the parish school of Longbride, Elgin, and King's College, Aberdeen, where he graduated MA on 15 April 1721. He was licensed to preach but, being unable to obtain a church, was never ordained as a minister. He became schoolmaster of Tough (Kirkton-on-Tough), Aberdeenshire, before being appointed master of the poor's hospital in Aberdeen on 11 December 1742.

In 1741 Man advertised his projected *Memoirs of Scotish Affairs from 1624 to 1651*, collected from unpublished manuscripts, to be published in parts at three-halfpence per sheet; but it seems that only the first part was printed, consisting of Man's introduction and four pages of memoirs, mostly extracted from a manuscript 'History of Scots

affairs' by James Gordon (1615?–1686), borrowed from Gordon's grandson. However, two volumes of Man's extracts from seventeenth-century manuscripts survive in the National Library of Scotland.

Other uncompleted projects were an edition of the Latin poems of Arthur Johnston (1587–1641) and a history of the Church of Scotland in which Man was encouraged by the general assembly of the church and for which he was qualified 'by learning and diligence, and above all by his zeal of Presbytery and ardour of Whiggism' (Chalmers, 263–4). He did, however, complete *A censure and examination of Mr Thomas Ruddiman's philological notes on the works of the great Buchanan* (1753), a learned but abusive work, 574 pages long, attacking what Man, like other vocal presbyterian scholars before him, believed was anti-protestant bias and poor Latinity in an edition of George Buchanan's works (1715) by Thomas Ruddiman (1674–1757). Ruddiman responded with only marginally less scurrilous attacks on Man in *Anticrisis* (1754) and *Audi alteram partem* (1756).

Man died in October 1761, bequeathing £60 to his relations and £95 to the hospital of which he was master. His own edition of Buchanan's *Rerum Scoticarum historia* was published in 1762 and proved to be textually inferior to Ruddiman's. It was said that Man 'had from nature a vigorous intellect, and a peevish temper, with a small stature, and a mean look' (Chalmers, 248).   JAMES SAMBROOK

Sources G. Chalmers, *Life of Thomas Ruddiman* (1794), 248–67 • J. Gordon, *History of Scots affairs from 1637–1641*, ed. J. Robertson and G. Grub, 1, Spalding Club, 1 (1841), 27, appx to the preface, xlii • P. J. Anderson, ed., *Officers and graduates of University and King's College, Aberdeen, MVD–MDCCCLX*, New Spalding Club, 11 (1893), 225 • N. Morren, *Annals of the general assembly of the Church of Scotland* (1838), 1.93 • D. Duncan, *Thomas Ruddiman* (1965), 65, 102, 106–7 • A. Walker, *History of the workhouse or poor's hospital of Aberdeen* (1885), 7–10
Archives NL Scot., collection for projected 'Memoirs of Scotish affairs', Adv. MS 35.4.3
Wealth at death £155: Chalmers, *Life*, 263

Man, John (1514/15–1569), diplomat and dean of Gloucester, was a fellow of New College, Oxford, but the presence of two men there of the same name (one from Essex, one from Wiltshire) has caused confusion. It would seem that Anthony Wood, who gives the dean's birth as 1512 at Lacock (alternatively Winterbourne Stoke), was wrong to identify him as the Wiltshire fellow. The latter entered Winchester College in 1523, took his BA in 1530 and his BCL in 1540, was principal of St Alban Hall (later absorbed by Jesus College) from 1548 to 1552, and died in 1565. The future dean, born at Letcombe in Berkshire but later resident at Writtle in Essex, entered Winchester in 1527 aged twelve, became a scholar of New College in 1531, BA and fellow in 1533, and MA in 1538. His knowledge of Italian might suggest that he travelled, but the question is obscure.

Senior proctor of the university in 1540, Man became prebendary of Biggleswade in Lincoln Cathedral in 1542, but was not ordained subdeacon until five years later, when he leased out the prebend for £50 p.a. In 1549 he was made master of St Bartholomew's Hospital, Gloucester, 'although he be not of clerical orders and perhaps married' (*CPR*, 1548–9, 244), later resigning the office to the city for a pension of £38. Though he lived quietly during Mary's reign, suspicions concerning his religion caused him to lose his fellowship in 1553 and his prebend the following year. His retaining his fellowship that long suggests that it was then, rather than 1549, that he married Frances, daughter of Edmund Herenden (*d.* 1563), a London mercer whose will he witnessed in 1560. One of his children was old enough to accompany him to Spain in 1566.

Man had been restored to his Lincoln prebend by September 1560. A chaplain to Archbishop Matthew Parker, Man was nominated by the latter to the wardenship of Merton College, Oxford, on 27 May 1562, after disagreement among the fellows. His entry was opposed by the conservative sub-warden, William Hall, who (according to Wood) boxed Man's ears when the new warden gained entry. This was probably an over-dramatization: in Parker's account it was a servant who received the blow. Hall was expelled; other fellows, such as Roger Giffard, resigned. Man expressed gratitude to Parker by dedicating to him his popular translation of Wolfgang Musculus, *Commonplaces of Christian religion* (1563; repr. 1578). On 12 January 1566 Elizabeth named Man ambassador to Spain; to raise his status he was made dean of Gloucester three weeks later, apparently without any expectation of residence. Elizabeth allegedly punned that as Philip II 'had sent her a goose-man [Guzmán de Silva], so she could not return the compliment better than by sending to him a man-goose' (Wood, 2.151).

Man thus followed the slightly old-fashioned pattern of the decanal diplomat. How he was thought to be qualified is obscure. The Catholic Henry Fitzalan, twelfth earl of Arundel, advertised him to Silva as 'a man of low position and small merits'; Elizabeth, apparently calling him 'Curtene', as 'a worthy person who speaks Italian' (*CSP Spain, 1558–67*, 525, 517). His verbatim quotations of Spanish utterances suggest that he could understand, if not necessarily speak, that language—an ability perhaps uncommon among men Elizabeth could trust. Elizabeth later claimed, ludicrously, to have thought that Man was 'rather an adherent of the old religion than a protestant' or, more reasonably (since he had not been a Marian exile), that he was 'a moderate in religion and had no love for the French' (*CSP Spain, 1568–79*, 30, 33). However, he was associated not only with Archbishop Parker but (as Herenden's son-in-law) with the influential protestant coterie surrounding John Day and John Foxe in the parish of St Anne and St Agnes, Aldersgate, London.

Greater administrative experience has been attributed to Man through identification with the John Man heavily involved in military finance, supply, and fortification from 1545. Some of this might seem rather out of the Oxonian's ambit, and the signature of John Man on the treasurer of the ordnance's accounts in 1547 does not resemble the ambassador's. More probably this John Man was the Lincolnshire gentleman to whom Mary confirmed leases of ex-monastic land on the grounds of service to the crown. Perhaps Robert Hogan, an English retainer of the count of Feria, confused two different men when he gibed that the ambassador had been 'overseer of labourers at Dover' and was 'no gentleman' (*Pepys MSS*, 81).

Man arrived in Bilbao in March 1566; proceeding to Madrid he found the papal nuncio (and future Pope Urban VII) Gianbattista Castagna and others watching for indiscretions, which he was not slow to commit. The hostile Hogan complained Man did 'but dishonour the queen and shame the country' and seemed 'to be meeter to sow sedition than to maintain amity, he is of so simple a judgement and small understanding' (*CSP for., 1566–8*, 417). Philip II came to describe him as not so much '*embajador*' as '*perturbador*' (Gonzales, 84), accusing him of circulating protestant literature. Man himself traced his problems to 'the exceeding hatred of the Conte di Feria' (BL, Cotton MS Galba Cii, fol. 146r), resulting from his intervention in the count's quarrel with Arundel over the financial affairs of his English in-laws. Elizabeth agreed that Man had been the victim of malice.

It seems to have been Man's own idea early in his embassy to request religious freedom like that granted to Spanish ambassadors in England, for his household as well as himself. His petition was refused, albeit without arousing particular outrage among the Spanish, but things were different by January 1568, when Elizabeth officially supported his request for free protestant worship, against a background of religious tension provoked by the situation in the Netherlands. In any case Man finally disabled himself from diplomatic function in Spain by calling the pope 'a canting little monk' (*CSP Spain, 1568–79*, 29). In June Elizabeth yielded to pressure for his recall but only after Philip II, not content with subjecting Man to loud prayers for England's conversion under his window, expelled him from Madrid to the village of Barajas.

Philip explained that he had no choice in questions of 'offence to God Almighty'. 'Nobody had been in fault except the ambassador himself', who 'richly deserved to be burnt at the stake'; Philip hoped for a replacement who would 'avoid similar occurrences' and indeed in 1575 was still suggesting reversion to 'the same order of things as had always existed before the time of John Man' (*CSP Spain, 1568–79*, 30–31, 59, 510). His reaction to Man's indiscretions may have been over-demonstrative, but (as he was still disinclined to offend Elizabeth) it was probably not just 'a ploy' (Bell, 'Man', 88). It was an English decision, not a Spanish requirement, that no replacement for Man as resident was sent. Meanwhile Man was cited as a precedent justifying successive expulsions of Spanish ambassadors from England.

The Spanish and English governments may have used the Man débâcle to test each other, but it had not occurred without personal ineptitude on his part. It is hard to see him as 'conscientious and competent' (Bell, 'Man', 93). Castagna even claimed that he was 'rather touched in the head' (*CSP Rome, 1558–71*, 272). Man apparently returned broken in health (which encouraged later reports of Spanish mistreatment): his journey absorbed the large sum of

£276 2s. 2d., which included provision of a litter from London to Windsor. He seems not to have returned to Merton, where Parker had repeatedly had to enforce order in his absence. He died apparently intestate in the London house of his mother-in-law, Millicent Herenden, on 18 March 1569, and was buried in the chancel of St Anne and St Agnes, Aldersgate. His widow remarried: in 1581, as Frances Stauntonne, she received £20 in her mother's will. Mrs Herenden also left £20 to William Man, presumably Frances's son from her first marriage.

JULIAN LOCK

Sources Emden, Oxf., 4.375–6 · G. M. Bell, 'John Man: the last Elizabethan resident ambassador in Spain', Sixteenth-Century Journal, 7/2 (1976), 75–93 · J. G. Retamal-Favereau, 'Anglo-Spanish relations, 1566–72: the mission of Don Guerau de Spes in London, with a preliminary consideration of that of Mr John Man in Madrid', DPhil diss., U. Oxf., 1972 · J. G. Retamal-Favereau, Diplomacia Anglo-Española durante la Contrareforma (1981) · CSP Spain, 1558–79 · Colección de documentos inéditos para la historia de España (1842–95), vols. 89, 90 · A. Wood, Annals and antiquities of the colleges and halls in the University of Oxford, ed. J. Gutch (1786), 2.149–51 · Registrum Matthei Parker, diocesis Cantuariensis, AD 1559–1575, ed. W. H. Frere and E. M. Thompson, 2, CYS, 36 (1928), 684–717 · CSP for., 1566–8 · Report on the Pepys manuscripts, HMC, 70 (1911), 80–81 · CPR, 1548–9 · BL, Cotton MSS Galba C.i–iii, Vespasian C.vii · CSP Rome, 1558–71 · L. Serrano, Correspondencia diplomatica entre España y la Santa Sede durante el pontificado de S. Pio V, 4 vols. (1914) · T. Gonzales, Apuntamientos para la historia del Rey Felipe Segundo de España por lo tocante á sus relaciones con la Reina Isabel de Inglaterra, 1558–76 (1830) · M. J. C. Douais, ed., Dépêches de M. de Fourquevaux, ambassadeur du roi Charles IX en Espagne, 1565–72 (1896), 1.356–7 · G. M. Bell, 'Elizabethan diplomatic compensation: its nature and variety', Journal of British Studies, 20/2 (1981), 1–25 · H. Ellis, 'Expenses of an ambassador AD 1566', GM, 3rd ser., 1 (1856), 463–5 · J. M. Fletcher, ed., Registrum annalium collegii Mertonenses, 2 vols., OHS, new ser., 23–4 (1974–6) · G. M. Bell, 'Men and their rewards in Elizabethan diplomatic service, 1558–85', PhD diss., U. Cal., Los Angeles, 1974 · G. C. Brodrick, Memorials of Merton College, OHS, 4 (1885) · G. H. Martin and J. R. L. Highfield, History of Merton College, Oxford (1997) · Reg. Oxf., 1.160, 175 · B. Usher, 'Backing protestantism: the London godly, the exchequer and the Foxe circle', John Foxe: an historical perspective, ed. D. M. Loades (1999), 105–34 · S. Haynes, Collection of state papers left by William Cecil, Lord Burghley (1740), 472–3 · E. Lodge, Illustrations of British history, 2nd edn, 3 vols. (1838), 1.437 · G. D. Ramsay, The City of London in international politics at the accession of Elizabeth Tudor (1975), chap. 3 · G. Mattingly, Renaissance diplomacy (1955) · E. R. Adair, The extraterritoriality of ambassadors in the sixteenth and seventeenth centuries (1929), 182–3 · R. E. G. Cole, ed., Chapter acts of the cathedral church of St Mary of Lincoln, 3, Lincoln RS, 15 (1920) · Fasti Angl., 1541–1857, [Lincoln] · W. McMurray, ed., Records of two city parishes: SS Anne and Agnes, Aldersgate, and St John Zachary, London (1925), 445 · H. M. Colvin and others, eds., The history of the king's works, 4 (1982) · accounts of treasurer of the ordnance, 1547, PRO, E 351/44

Archives Merton Oxf., letters to fellows from Spain | BL, Cotton MSS, diplomatic corresp. · CUL, diplomatic corresp., MS Mm.iii.8 · Magd. Cam., Pepys Library, letters to the earl of Leicester · PRO, diplomatic corresp., SP 70

Wealth at death shortage of money implied, though probably reasonable income; £600 p.a. according to Guzmán de Silva: Bell, 'John Man', 78

Man, Judith (fl. 1640), translator, was the daughter of Peter Man, solicitor to Thomas Wentworth, earl of Strafford. By her own account, Man was brought up in Strafford's household where she received some education, including competence in the French language. All evidence regarding her life and interests comes from her own hand,

namely from the prefatory materials to her translation of John Barclay's Argenis, which was originally published in Latin, and had been translated into English by both Kingsmill Long (in 1625) and Robert le Grys (in 1628). Man's translation, Epitome of the History of Faire Argenis and Polyarchus, printed in 1640, was taken from an epitome of Barclay's text written by Nicolas Coëffeteau, bishop of Marseilles, and dedicated to Wentworth's eldest daughter, Anne, apparently as a tribute to the 'Schoole of Vertue' (Man, sig. A2v) where she had been educated. Her translation is very literal, and stresses the virtuous femininity of the heroine, Argenis, rather than the political allegory for which Barclay's work was renowned, although Barclay's commitment to monarchy would have made it a suitable text for Wentworth's royalist household. From the evidence of the dedication it is possible to infer that the translation doubled as an exhortation to Anne Wentworth to marry. One of the more interesting aspects of Man's text is her self-presentation as an author. She sees the text as having a specifically didactic purpose, but views translation as a fitting activity for a woman because it creates diversion and provides self-improvement: 'so … I might make my selfe, so much the more perfect, in the French tongue' (ibid., sig. A6v). Man authorizes her literary undertaking by referring to other romance texts translated by women: 'who have traced me the way, witnesse the translation into French of Sir Philip Sidney's Arcadia, the New Amarantha and Urania' (ibid., sig. A7r). Of Man's later life or writing, nothing is known.

DANIELLE CLARKE

Sources J. Man, trans., Epitome of the history of faire Argenis and Polyarchus (1640) · C.V. Wedgwood, Thomas Wentworth, first earl of Strafford, 1593–1641: a revaluation (1961); repr. (1964) · J. P. Cooper, ed., Wentworth papers, 1597–1628, CS, 4th ser., 12 (1973)

Manasseh ben Israel. See Menasseh ben Israel (1604–1657).

Manby, Aaron (1776–1850), engineer, was born at Albrighton, Shropshire, on 15 November 1776, the second son of Aaron Manby of Kingston, Jamaica. His early years were spent working in a bank on the Isle of Wight. He married Juliana Fewster, with whom he had a son, Charles *Manby. His first wife died in 1806, and in 1807 he married Sarah Ann Haskins (d. 1826), with whom he had one daughter, Sarah Maria (d. 1826), and four sons, three of whom became civil engineers.

By 26 November 1812 Manby was in business at Tipton, south Staffordshire, as a managing partner of the Horseley Coal and Iron Company, a mixed concern operating coal mines, blast furnaces, and engineering workshops, established some forty years earlier. Under Manby, the engineering side of the Horseley business developed greatly, and in 1813 Manby was granted one of his earliest patents, for a means of casting the refuse slag from blast furnaces into bricks and blocks for building. Eight years later, in 1821, he took out a patent for a form of steam engine well suited to marine use, which he called an 'oscillating engine'. He was not the original inventor of this form of engine as it had been proposed by William Murdock in 1785, and patented by R. Witty in 1811, but, with his son Charles, he was the first to build and operate it commercially. The same type of engine was patented by him in France in the same year; he included in the specification a claim for making ships of iron, and an improved feathering paddle wheel. By February 1822 the oscillating engine was in use in at least three wooden steamships owned by the Société des Transports Accélérés par Eau, of 2 rue de Valois, Paris.

Manby's fame rests on the iron steamships he built. The first of these, the *Aaron Manby*, was some 120 feet long and 18 feet in beam. It was made at Horseley, conveyed in pieces by canal to the Surrey Canal dock, Rotherhithe, and assembled. It was completed by 30 April 1822 and tried on the Thames on 9 May. A few days later it left London with a cargo of linseed and iron castings, under the command of Captain Charles *Napier (1786–1860), who with Manby had formed a French company, in early 1820, with the intention of establishing a line of steamers to France. On 18 May it arrived at Boulogne, after a voyage of only fifty-five hours, and went on to reach Paris on 10 June after a brief stop in Rouen. The *Aaron Manby* is widely regarded as the first iron ship ever to go to sea. It continued to ply upon the Seine for many years, and it was still running on the Loire in 1846, but was broken up in France in 1855. Another iron vessel, the *Commerce de Paris*, was also made at Horseley, between 1821 and 1823.

In 1822 Manby set up an engineering works at Charenton, near Paris, entrusting its management to Daniel Wilson, a chemist who was the first to patent the use of ammonia for removing sulphuretted hydrogen from gas. The Charenton establishment was of especial importance, and had great influence over the French iron and engineering industries. In 1825 a gold medal was awarded to the founders by the Société d'Encouragement pour l'Industrie Nationale, at which time upwards of five hundred workmen were employed in the works. The effect of Manby's efforts was to render France largely independent of English engine builders, who, for a time, displayed some resentment against him—as was made clear in evidence given before the 1824 parliamentary select committee on artisans and machinery.

On 12 May 1821 Manby, in conjunction with Wilson and another partner, took out a patent in France for the manufacture and purification of gas, and for what was then called 'portable gas'—that is, compressed gas that was supplied to consumers in strong containers. In May 1822 Manby and Wilson were among the first to obtain a concession to provide gas lighting for several streets in Paris. Their company, known as the Compagnie Anglaise, survived until 1847, despite strong competition from rivals such as the Compagnie Royale. In 1826 Manby purchased the Le Creusot ironworks. These were reorganized and provided with new and improved machinery made at Charenton, and about two years afterwards the two concerns were amalgamated under the title of Société Anonyme des Mines, Forges et Fonderies du Creusot et de Charenton.

Manby returned to England from France at some time about 1840 and went to reside at Fulham, moving afterwards to Ryde and then to Shanklin on the Isle of Wight, where he died on 1 December 1850.

R. B. PROSSER, rev. GILES HUDSON

Sources W. H. Chaloner and W. O. Henderson, 'Aaron Manby, builder of the first iron steamship', *Transactions* [Newcomen Society], 29 (1953–5), 77–91 • H. Davis, *Channel crossing* (1985) • *Patents for inventions: abridgments of specifications relating to the steam engine*, 1: 1618–1859 (1871), vol. 2, p. 194 • 'Select committee on the state of law', *Parl. papers* (1824), 5.109–32, no. 51 [on artisans and machinery] • 'Improvement in naval architecture', *Morning Chronicle* (14 May 1822) • J. Grantham, *Iron as a material for ship building* (1842) • T. Gill, *Technical Repository*, 2 (1822) • M. du Camp, 'L'éclairage à Paris', *Revue des Deux Mondes*, 105 (1873), 766–92 • M. Molard, 'Rapport sur les fonderies et établissements d'industrie de MM. Manby et Wilson, à Charenton près de Paris', *Bulletin de la Société d'Encouragement pour l'Industrie Nationale*, 24 (1825), 123–6 • A. Ferry, 'Sur les fonderies, forges et ateliers de MM. Manby, Wilson et Compagnie à Charenton', *Annales de l'Industrie Nationale et Étrangère*, 23 (1826), 5–16 • *PICE*, 22 (1862–3), 629–30 • *PICE*, 24 (1864–5), 533–4 • *PICE*, 30 (1869–70), 446
Archives Inst. CE, Telford MSS

Manby, Charles (1804–1884), civil engineer, was born on 4 February 1804, at West Cowes, Isle of Wight, the eldest son of Aaron *Manby (1776–1850), engineer, and his wife Juliana, *née* Fewster. He received his early education at a Roman Catholic seminary, from where he was sent in 1814 to the semi-military college of St Servan at Rennes in Brittany. His uncle, Captain Joseph Manby, private secretary and aide-de-camp to the duke of Kent, had already obtained a commission for him, but the end of the Napoleonic Wars caused him to change his plans. He joined his father at the Horseley ironworks, Tipton, in 1815 and assisted in building the first iron steamboat, the *Aaron Manby*. About 1823 Manby went to Paris to take charge of the gasworks established there by his father, and he subsequently superintended his father's foundry at Charenton. After a short stay at the Creusot ironworks, which his father had undertaken to reorganize, he was employed by the tobacco department of the French government, and he also received a commission in the French military engineers. In 1829 he returned to England and took the management of the Beaufort ironworks in south Wales. There he met his first wife, Ellen Jones, whom he married in 1830. After spending a short time at the Ebbw Vale ironworks and the Bristol ironworks, he established himself in London in 1835 as a civil engineer, specializing in the heating and ventilating of buildings. In 1838 he became connected with Sir John Ross's steamer service to India, which was soon absorbed by the Peninsular and Oriental Company.

In 1839 he was appointed secretary to the Institution of Civil Engineers, performing the duties of this office for seventeen years with conspicuous success, his wide range of social contacts being of great help in establishing the status of the institution. Upon his retirement in 1856 he was elected honorary secretary, in which capacity he continued to be heavily involved in institution activities until his death. From 1856 he was the London agent for Robert

Stephenson & Co., travelling widely in Europe to secure work for them.

In 1853 Manby was elected a fellow of the Royal Society, and he received many foreign awards and honours. He was a member of the international commission which met in Paris to consider the feasibility of constructing the Suez Canal. His perfect command of the French language was of considerable service in maintaining a good understanding between the engineers' societies of London and Paris. In 1864 he helped to establish the engineer and railway volunteer staff corps. His interests ranged beyond the engineering world, and for many years he was involved in the management of the Adelphi and Haymarket theatres. His first wife predeceased him and in 1858 he married Harriet, daughter of Major Nicholas Willard of Eastbourne, and widow of W. C. Hood, formerly a partner in the publishing house of Whitaker & Co. There were no children of either marriage, and towards the end of his life he lived with his stepson, Arthur Robert Hood, at The Grays, Eastbourne. He died at his London home, Ranelagh House, 10 Lower Grosvenor Place, on 31 July 1884.

R. B. PROSSER, rev. MIKE CHRIMES

Sources PICE, 81 (1884–5), 327–34 · G. Watson, *The civils: the story of the Institution of Civil Engineers* (1988) · J. S. Allen, 'The history of the Horseley Company to 1865', *Transactions* [Newcomen Society], 58 (1986–7), 113–38 · W. H. Chaloner and W. O. Henderson, 'Aaron Manby, builder of the first iron steamship', *Transactions* [Newcomen Society], 29 (1953–5), 77–91 · W. H. Chaloner and W. O. Henderson, 'The Manbys and the industrial revolution in France, 1819–84', *Transactions* [Newcomen Society], 30 (1955–7), 63–75

Archives Inst. CE, letter-book | BL, letters to Charles Babbage, Add. MSS 37192–37197 · Staffs. RO, Horseley Company MSS

Likenesses Moira & Hargh, photograph, after 1860, Inst. CE · engraving, c.1870, Inst. CE · J. S. Hodges, oils, Inst. CE · engraving, Inst. CE · engraving (after photograph by Messrs Lavis, c.1880), repro. in PICE

Wealth at death £249 13s.: probate, 15 Sept 1884, CGPLA Eng. & Wales

Manby, George William (1765–1854), inventor, was born at Denver, near Downham Market, Norfolk, on 28 November 1765, the son of Matthew Pepper Manby, a captain in the Welch fusiliers. Thomas *Manby (1769–1834) was his younger brother. He attended a school at Downham, kept by Thomas Nooks and William Chatham, a fellow pupil being Horatio Nelson, with whom he formed a close friendship. He then attended school at Bromley, Kent, studying under Reuben Burrow, then teacher of mathematics in the military drawing-room at the Tower. After a short time he entered the Royal Military Academy at Woolwich, but because of a delay in obtaining a commission in the artillery he joined the Cambridgeshire militia, eventually attaining the rank of captain.

Manby married, in 1793, the only daughter of a Dr Preston, and went to live near Denver, but in 1801 domestic problems caused him to leave home and settle at Clifton, near Bristol. Here he devoted himself to literary pursuits and in 1801 he published *The History and Antiquities of St David's*, followed by *Sketches of the History and Natural Beauties of Clifton* (1802) and *A Guide from Clifton to the Counties of Monmouth, Glamorgan …* (1802), all of which were illustrated by engravings from his own drawings. In 1803

George William Manby (1765–1854), by Sir Thomas Lawrence, c.1810

Manby wrote a pamphlet entitled *An Englishman's Reflexions on the Author of the Present Disturbances*, in which he dealt with the threatened invasion of England by Napoleon. This work attracted the notice of Charles Yorke, then secretary of war, and in August of the same year Manby was appointed barrack-master at Great Yarmouth.

Manby's attention was first drawn to the subject of saving life from shipwrecks when he witnessed a naval ship, the *Snipe*, off Great Yarmouth during a storm in February 1807, when sixty-seven persons perished within 60 yards of the shore, and 147 bodies were picked up along the coast. It occurred to him that the first thing, when effecting a means of rescue, was to establish communication with the shore. To this end he borrowed a mortar from the Board of Ordnance, and in August and September 1807 carried out some experiments before members of the Suffolk Humane Society. The apparatus, by which communication was established between land and sea, was used successfully on 12 February 1808 at the wreck of the brig *Elizabeth*. The invention had previously been submitted to the Board of Ordnance, who reported upon it in January 1808. It received rapid acceptance and the Navy Board began to supply it to various stations round the coast. In 1810 the apparatus was investigated by a committee of the House of Commons, and the report was published. Manby embodied the results of his work in a pamphlet published in 1812 entitled *An essay on the preservation of shipwrecked persons, with descriptive account of the apparatus and the manner of using it*, which was reprinted in many different forms. In 1823 the subject again came before the House of Commons on Manby's petition for a further reward (up to that time 229 lives had been saved by his apparatus), and the committee recommended payment to Manby of £2000. The use of the apparatus gradually extended to other countries, and Manby received numerous medals to mark his achievement. After 1878, however, the mortars were superseded by rope-carrying rockets. Manby's claim was disputed by the supporters of Lieutenant Bell, who in 1807 presented a somewhat similar plan to the Society of Arts. Bell's idea was to throw a rope from the ship to the shore; Manby's plan simply reversed this order of procedure.

Manby also interested himself in the improvement of the lifeboat, and about 1811 he submitted his new boat to the Navy Board, who reported on the trial. The boat was tried again at Plymouth in 1826, but does not appear to have come into general use.

About 1813 Manby commenced experiments with a view to the prevention of accidents on ice, and on 19 January 1814 he read a paper before the Royal Humane Society. The paper embodying his experimental results contained numerous illustrations and was subsequently published. He also directed his attention to the extinction of fires, being the first to suggest an apparatus known as the extincteur, consisting of a portable vessel holding a fire extinguishing solution under pressure. This was exhibited before the barrack commissioners in March 1816, and also at Woolwich before a joint committee appointed by the Admiralty and the Board of Ordnance on 30 August 1816. Manby's first wife died in 1814, and in 1818 he married Sophia (d. 1843), daughter of Sir Thomas Gooch of Benacre Hall, Suffolk. In 1832 he published *A description of instruments, apparatus, and means for saving persons from drowning who break through the ice*. Among his other works were his *Reflections and Observations on the Practicability of Recovering Lost Greenland* (1829) and a book entitled *A Brief and Historic Sketch of the Life and Public Services of George William Manby* (1852). He was elected a fellow of the Royal Society in 1831. Manby died at his house at Southtown, Great Yarmouth, on 18 November 1854.

R. B. PROSSER, *rev.* R. C. COX

Sources *GM*, 1st ser., 91/2 (1821), 161–7 · *GM*, 2nd ser., 43 (1855), 208 · G. W. Manby, *Reminiscences* (1839) · *Tables relating to life salvage on the coasts of the United Kingdom during the year ended 30 June 1892* · [G. W. Manby], *General report on the survey of the eastern coast of England: for the purpose of … establishing the system for saving ship-wrecked persons* (1813)
Archives BL, corresp., Add. MS 42712 · BL, autobiographical reminiscences, Add. MS 29893 · Norfolk RO, autobiographical papers incl. MS autobiography; letters to subject · Sci. Mus., papers | Norfolk RO, letters to Robert Cole, papers · PRO, Ordnance MSS
Likenesses T. Lawrence, oils, c.1810, RS [see illus.] · T. Blood, stipple (after S. Lane), BM, NPG; repro. in *European Magazine* (1 Aug 1813) · J. M. Johnson, lithograph (after T. Wageman), BM, NPG · D. Turner, etching (after S. de Koster), BM, NPG · colour transparency (after T. Lawrence), RS

Manby, Peter (d. 1697), dean of Derry and religious controversialist, was of unknown parents and background. He was educated at Trinity College, Dublin, and took orders in the Church of Ireland before 1660, when he became a minor canon at St Patrick's, Dublin. In 1666 he became chancellor of that church. He found favour with Dr Michael Boyle, archbishop of Dublin, who made him his chaplain and promoted him to a canonry at Kildare Cathedral in 1670. Manby became dean of Derry in 1672. Little is known of his personal life at this time beyond that he married a wife, Mary, and started a family. He published some unremarkable sermons and hoped for promotion to a bishopric.

In 1687 Manby became notorious when he published *The Considerations which Obliged Peter Manby, Dean of Derry, to Embrace the Catholique Religion*. His stated reasons for converting included concerns about the lack of authority of the reformers at the English Reformation, a commitment to confession which he saw as a shocking omission in protestantism, and, finally, an insistence that Catholicism was not to be reviled as idolatrous since it was the origin of the Anglican religion. Manby declared that there was much to be admired in Catholic writings and credited the mass as the ultimate inspiration for his conversion. There was nothing original in Manby's arguments, but his timing, his position, and some of his recent activities caused a stir. He fully expected that protestant readers would attack him, and he was not disappointed. William King, then chancellor of St Patrick's, Dublin, his most tenacious and cynical critic, challenged Manby's motives. King accused him of converting because he had not received a promotion and because he was an informer to James II's Catholic court. King's criticisms were justified. In 1686 the dissatisfied Manby had come to the attention of James, who took a personal interest in his case. Manby was to provide a prominent example of the advantages to be had when embracing Catholicism and openly supporting James. The state papers reveal that Manby received James's protection when he turned informer, and that James wished to reward Manby for his services. The king arranged for the proceeds from the deanery of Derry be paid to the exchequer, which would then pay an allowance to Manby, who, 'being a married man', could not be given a living in the Catholic church. By April 1687 this plan had changed, and Manby was given a royal dispensation 'to hold the said deanery with all rights, profits and advantages, any law, statute or custom to the contrary notwithstanding' (*CSP dom.*, 1686–7, 415).

Meanwhile, Manby responded to King's attacks with *A Reformed Catechism in Two Dialogues* (1687), in which he attempted to use the writings of protestant historians of the Reformation to prove the validity of his conversion. King and others were still not convinced of his sincerity. Manby repeated his themes in *Some Queries Humbly Offered to the Lord Archbishop of Canterbury* in 1688. James II continued to favour Manby and made him an alderman of Londonderry as part of a scheme to increase the Catholic presence in the local government of Ireland. When James brought his army to Ireland in 1688 Manby's position in Londonderry became untenable. He was not present at the famous siege of the town in 1688–9, and he fled to France with James's forces after the battle of the Boyne in 1690. Manby died in London in 1697 attended by the prominent Catholic scholar Cornelius Nary. The fate of his immediate family is unknown. Although his writings were heavily criticized and his motives were questioned by his opponents, Manby managed to inspire others to convert. His brother, Robert, left the established church to become a friar, and both Robert's sons joined the Society of Jesus. One of these sons, **Peter Manby** (*b.* 1681), was born in Leinster and educated at the University of Coimbra. He had returned to Ireland by 1724, when he published *Remarks on Dr Loyd's Translation of the Montpelier Catechism* in Dublin, arguing that the catechism contained the condemned propositions of Jansenius and Quesnel. His date of death is unknown.   K. GRUDZIEN BASTON

Sources P. Manby, *The considerations which obliged Peter Manby, dean of Derry, to embrace the Catholique religion* (1687) · W. King, *An answer to the considerations which obliged Peter Manby &c. (as he pretends) to embrace, what he calls, the Catholick religion* (1687) · P. Manby, *A reformed catechism in two dialogues* (1687) · P. M. [P. Manby], *Some queries humbly offered to the lord archbishop of Canterbury* (1688) · W. King, *A vindication of the answer to the considerations that obliged Peter Manby, &c. to embrace, as he pretended, what he calls the Catholic religion* (1688) · *CSP dom.*, 1686–7 · B. Lacy, *Siege city: the story of Derry and Londonderry* (1990) · H. Cotton, *Fasti ecclesiae Hibernicae*, 5 (1860) · J. Cannon, ed., *The Oxford companion to British history* (1997) · *DNB* · J. S. Crone, *A concise dictionary of Irish biography* (1928) · *IGI*

Manby, Peter (*b.* 1681). *See under* Manby, Peter (*d.* 1697).

Manby, Thomas (*bap.* 1611?, *d.* 1679), legal writer, was probably baptized on 18 March 1611 at Langton by Wragby, Lincolnshire, the eldest son of Robert Manby (*d.* 1645) of Wragby and his wife, Joane, daughter and heir of Thomas Manby of Wragby and of Leicester, who was mayor of Leicester from 1613 to 1614. He was admitted to Lincoln's Inn on 16 May 1633, and called to the bar on 18 June 1640. In 1644 he produced a manuscript index to Banks's reports and *Plowden's Quaeries*. Manby appears to have been in practice as a barrister during the interregnum, and in 1651 was appointed by the Rump Parliament to the extraparliamentary law reform committee chaired by Matthew Hale. He drafted a number of the committee's law reform bills—including those on marriage, small debt courts, and probate—and from time to time acted as the committee's chairman. He was a judge of Cromwell's probate court from its beginning until 1658, and in 1656 received a payment of £50 from the exchequer 'in recompense and satisfaction of his labour, pains and expenses in several business concerning his highness' revenue' (BL, Add. MS 196, fol. 116). He became a bencher of Lincoln's Inn on 22 November 1659, and on 10 February 1662 was appointed with two others to manage the office of treasurer of the inn, a position which he held until February 1664.

Manby's *A Collection of the Statutes Made in the Reigns of King Charles the I and King Charles the II* (1667) was based upon Ferdinando Pulton's edition of the statutes. It provided the texts of the Caroline public acts in force, together with an abridgement of the public acts repealed or expired, and the titles of the private acts. Pulton's work was reissued in 1670 with a continuation by Manby covering the reigns of Charles I and Charles II to April 1670, together with a table of the whole work. In 1674 appeared *An exact abridgment of all the statutes as well repealed as in force made in the reigns of King Charles I and King Charles II until the end of the sessions of parliament the 29th of March 1673*, dedicated to Arthur Annesley, earl of Anglesey, lord privy seal. Probably intended for the use of members of parliament as much as for use by lawyers, the work abridged the Caroline statutes under alphabetical heads, and provided a chronological catalogue of the statutes, both public and private, and a list of the members of both houses of parliament. In 1675 appeared *An exact abridgment of all statutes in force and use from the beginning of Magna Carta until 1641* by Edmund Wingate of Gray's Inn, with a continuation to 1675 by Manby, who explained in his dedication to Sir Edward Turner, speaker of the House of Commons, that he had seen Wingate's work in use and had therefore updated it.

Manby was keeper of the black book in Lincoln's Inn in 1669, and in that year was exempted from reading 'upon consideration how the said Mr Manby already hath and may be hereafter further serviceable to the public and this society' (*Records of … Lincoln's Inn*, 2.3, 64), a reference perhaps to his work on the statutes. In 1673 he was required by the inn to show cause why he should not read; though his exemption was continued he perhaps felt his position to be awkward, and on 23 June 1673 was at his own request made an associate of the bench rather than a bencher. A gift of books to the benchers of the inn followed in 1674. The date of his marriage to Mary (1624/5–1691), daughter and coheir of Daniel Caldwell of Horndon on the Hill, Essex, is unknown. Their eldest son, Thomas, who was admitted to Lincoln's Inn on 2 June 1674, and in whose chambers in the inn his father was lodging in 1678, was knighted in 1686 and served as sheriff of Essex in 1688. A justice of the peace in Essex from 1651 until 1660, Manby purchased the manor of Downsell Hall in South Weald, Essex. He died on 2 February 1679 and was buried later in 1679 in the churchyard of St Peter's Church, South Weald.   N. G. JONES

Sources A. R. Maddison, ed., *Lincolnshire pedigrees*, 2, Harleian Society, 51 (1903) · W. P. Baildon, ed., *The records of the Honorable Society of Lincoln's Inn: admissions*, 2 vols. (1896) · D. Veall, *The popular movement for law reform, 1640–1660* (1970) · M. Cotterell, 'Interregnum law reform: the Hale commission of 1652', *EngHR*, 83 (1968), 689–704 · BL, Harg. MS 353 · BL, Add. MS 4196 · *CSP dom.*, 1658–9 · Foss, *Judges* · D. H. Allen, ed., *Essex quarter sessions order book, 1652–1661* (1974) · *An inventory of the historical monuments in Essex*, Royal Commission for Historical Monuments (England), 2 (1921) · Holdsworth, *Eng. law*, vol. 6 · *Records of the borough of Leicester*, 4: 1603–1688, ed. H. Stocks (1923) · *IGI*

Manby, Thomas (*bap.* 1633?, *d.* 1695), landscape painter, was probably baptized on 30 May 1633 at St Martin-in-the-Fields, Westminster, the elder of the two children of Robert Manby and his wife, Susanna. Little is known about his life or career, but he was one of the earliest British artists to work in Italy, and was described by a contemporary as 'a good *English* Landskip-Painter, who had been several times in Italy, and consequently painted much after the *Italian* manner' (Buckeridge, 406). A group of eleven drawings (exh. Sothebys, 10 June 1931, lot 149) constitutes all that is known of his *œuvre*. Italian views in pen and ink with grey wash, they chiefly depict the Roman Campagna. *The Ruins of the Colosseum* is in the Tate collection, and four others are in the British Museum. They show similarities to drawings by Francis Place, both men having been influenced by Dutch-Italianate artists such as Bartholomeus Breenbergh.

Manby was a friend of the portrait painter Mary Beale, and is mentioned several times in her husband's notebooks. On 16 February 1677 Charles Beale recorded that, in return for a landscape which Manby had added to Mary's portrait of the countess of Clare (after Lely), he was rewarding him with some expensive oil-pigments (Beale, 1676/7). This portrait cannot now be identified, nor is it known whether Manby contributed further landscapes to works by Beale or other artists.

Manby acted as a picture dealer, and is recorded as having brought from Italy 'a good Collection of pictures', which were sold at the Banqueting House, Whitehall, c.1680 (Buckeridge, 406). He shared this interest with the sculptor Edward Pierce, and, following their deaths, a large group of their artworks were auctioned on 4 February 1696. The auction, held at the premises of John Cocks, the Golden Triangle, Long Acre, London, included books, drawings, prints, and models of plaster figures. Some lots are thought to have comprised works by Manby and Pierce as distinct from works they acquired in Italy.

Manby died in 1695, and was buried at St Martin-in-the-Fields, London, on 24 November.

L. H. CUST, rev. CHRISTOPHER REEVE

Sources I. Williams, 'Thomas Manby, a 17th century landscape painter', *Apollo*, 23 (1936), 276–7 · K. Sloan, *A noble art: amateur artists and drawing masters, 1600–1800* (2000), no. 7 [exhibition catalogue, BM] · E. Croft-Murray and P. H. Hulton, eds., *Catalogue of British drawings*, 2 vols. (1960), 438–9 · [B. Buckeridge], 'An essay towards an English school of painters', in R. de Piles, *The art of painting, and the lives of the painters* (1706), 398–480 · C. Beale, notebook, 1677, Bodl. Oxf., MS Rawl. 8⁰572 · C. Beale, notebook, 1680–81, NPG, Heinz Archive and Library · H. Walpole, *Anecdotes of painting in England … collected by the late George Vertue, and now digested and published*, 2nd edn, 4 vols. (1765–71) · L. Stainton and C. White, *Drawing in England from Hilliard to Hogarth* (1987), 163–4 [exhibition catalogue, BM] · T. Barber, *Mary Beale: portrait of a seventeenth-century painter, her family and her studio* (1999) [exhibition catalogue, Geffrye Museum, London, 21 Sept 1999 – 30 Jan 2000] · I. O. Williams, *Early English watercolours and some cognate drawings by artists born not later than 1785* (1952), 6 · D. Bull, *Classic ground* (1981), no. 113 [exhibition catalogue, Yale U. CBA] · DNB · IGI · admin, PRO, PROB 6/71, fol. 226r

Wealth at death wealthy: administration, PRO, PROB 6/71, fol. 226r

Manby, Thomas (1769–1834), naval officer, born on 1 January 1769 of a family long settled at Manby in Lincolnshire, was the son of Matthew Pepper Manby (d. 1774) of Hilgay in Norfolk, lieutenant of marines, captain in the Welch fusiliers, and afterwards aide-de-camp to Lord Townshend when lord lieutenant of Ireland (1767–72). George William *Manby was his elder brother. Townshend, when lieutenant-general of the ordnance, gave Thomas Manby a post in the department, but the boy, preferring to go to sea, was entered on the frigate *Hyaena*, on the Irish station, in 1783. In 1785 he was moved into the sloop *Cygnet*, in which he went to the West Indies. He was afterwards in the *Amphion* and, returning in her to England, served briefly in the *Illustrious*. Towards the end of 1790 he joined

the *Discovery*, then fitting out for a voyage to the Pacific and the north-west coast of North America, under the command of Captain George Vancouver. In early 1793, when it was necessary to send some of the officers of the expedition to England and to China, Manby was appointed master of the brig *Chatham*, the *Discovery's* consort, in which he remained for the next two years engaged in the arduous work of the survey. In 1795 he was moved back into the *Discovery* as acting lieutenant, and on his return to England was confirmed in that rank on 27 October 1795. In 1796 he was a lieutenant of the *Juste*, and when Lord Hugh Seymour was preparing for an expedition to the Pacific, Manby, at Seymour's request, was promoted on 5 February 1797 to command the *Charon*, a 44-gun ship that was armed *en flûte* as a store ship. The proposed expedition was afterwards countermanded, and the *Charon* was employed in transporting troops to Ireland during the Irish rising (1798). Reportedly on one occasion she took on board a thousand men at Portsmouth, landed them at Guernsey within twenty-four hours, embarked another thousand, and landed these on the following day at Waterford. She also convoyed the local trade and cruised against privateers. In the two years during which Manby commanded her he is said to have given protection to no fewer than 4753 vessels, not one of which was lost.

Manby was advanced to post rank on 22 January 1799 and towards the end of the year was appointed to the *Bordelais*, a remarkably fine and fast vessel built as a French privateer and captured on her second trip by the *Révolutionnaire*, herself a prize and the work of the same builder. The *Bordelais* was considered to be a most attractive vessel, though dangerous because of the weakness of her frame. During 1800 she cruised off the Azores. Afterwards she was on the blockade of Flushing but proved very unfit for this service, being long, narrow, and low in the water and consequently so wet that her crew became very sickly. She was therefore ordered to Spithead, and thence to the West Indies, sailing at the end of the year with the frigate *Andromache* and a large convoy. The convoy was dispersed in a gale off Cape Finisterre, Spain, and Manby was afterwards sent to look out for the stragglers to the eastward of Barbados. On his way he recaptured two of them, already prizes to a French privateer, and on 28 January 1801 fell in with two large brigs and a schooner, French warships, which had been sent by the governor of Cayenne to prey on the British West India fleet. The brigs had very inferior armament to that of the *Bordelais*, but they carried nearly twice the number of men and apparently thought to carry her by boarding. No sooner, however, did the *Bordelais* open fire on the leading brig, the *Curieuse*, than the others turned and fled. Following a brave fight the *Curieuse* surrendered and sank shortly after. This action helped to save the scattered convoy from danger. During the year Manby was employed in cruising, and when peace came he was moved into the *Juno*, one of the squadron on the coast of San Domingo, and in her returned to England in August 1802.

Manby was shortly afterwards appointed to the *Africaine*, a 48-gun frigate in which, on the renewal of the war, he was stationed off Helvoetsluys with a 24-gun frigate to blockade two large French frigates there with troops on board. This irksome service lasted for nearly two years until, the French frigates having been dismantled and having passed through the canal to Flushing, the *Africaine* joined the squadron off Texel. After serious damage in a heavy gale, she had to go to Sheerness to refit. She was then sent to the West Indies with convoy and arrived at Barbados with a crew of 340 men, all in perfect health. Her orders were to return to England with the homeward-bound trade and to take on some invalids from the hospitals. Within forty-eight hours of her departure from Carlisle Bay virulent yellow fever was raging on board. The surgeon and the assistant surgeon died on the second day. Manby himself carried out their duties and, on the advice of a doctor at St Kitts, dealt out large doses of calomel. However, his anxiety brought on an attack of the fever, which nearly proved fatal. At Tortola in the Virgin Islands a surgeon was procured, and after a terrible passage of six weeks, during which a third of her crew was lost, the *Africaine* arrived at Falmouth. From there she was sent to do quarantine at the Isles of Scilly, after which she was paid out of commission.

About the time of Manby's appointment to the *Africaine* he was presented by Lady Townshend to the princess of Wales, who was friendly towards him. Afterwards several witnesses swore that she conducted herself towards him with undue, if not criminal, familiarity; on 22 September 1806 Manby made affidavit that this testimony was 'a vile and wicked invention, wholly and absolutely false' (*'The Book!'*, 181–2). These allegations continued, however, sometimes making Manby the father of a child of the princess. She herself always maintained that she had humbugged him in this business.

In 1807 Manby, in the *Thalia* in command of a small squadron, was stationed at Jersey, and in 1808 he was sent, in company with the frigate *Medusa* and a brig, to look out for two French frigates supposed to have gone to the Davis Strait to prey on the whalers. After a trying and unsuccessful cruise of twelve weeks, he and his crew stocked up with wood and water at a harbour on the coast of Labrador, which he surveyed and named Port Manvers. They then returned to England by way of Newfoundland, the Azores, and Gibraltar. The Arctic service had severely tried Manby's constitution, which was already impaired by yellow fever. His health was ruined, and he was obliged to give up his command. He purchased an estate at Northwold in Norfolk, where he settled for the rest of his life.

In 1810 Manby married Julia Hamond of Northwold; they had two daughters. On 27 May 1825 he was promoted to the rank of rear-admiral. He died from an overdose of opium at the George Hotel, Southampton, on 13 June 1834.   J. K. LAUGHTON, *rev.* ANDREW LAMBERT

Sources B. Anderson, *George Vancouver* (1960) · G. W. Manby, *Reminiscences* (1839) · *The letters of King George IV, 1812–1830*, ed. A. Aspinall, 3 vols. (1938) · *'The book!', or, The proceedings and correspondence upon the subject of the inquiry into the conduct of H.R.H. the princess of Wales*, 2nd edn (1813) · W. James, *The naval history of Great Britain, from the declaration of war by France in 1793, to the accession of George IV*, [5th edn], 6 vols. (1859–60) · J. Marshall, *Royal naval biography*, 2/1 (1824), 199 · *GM*, 2nd ser., 2 (1834)
Archives NA Canada, journal [copy]

Manchán mac Silláin (*d.* 665). *See under* Meath, saints of (*act. c.*400–*c.*900).

Manchester. For this title name *see* Montagu, Henry, first earl of Manchester (*c.*1564–1642); Montagu, Edward, second earl of Manchester (1602–1671); Montagu, Robert, third earl of Manchester (*bap.* 1634, *d.* 1683) [*see under* Montagu, Edward, second earl of Manchester (1602–1671)]; Montagu, Charles, first duke of Manchester (*c.*1662–1722); Montagu, George, fourth duke of Manchester (1737–1788); Montagu, William, fifth duke of Manchester (1771–1843); Cavendish, Louise Frederica Augusta, duchess of Devonshire [Louise Frederica Augusta Montagu, duchess of Manchester] (1832–1911).

Mancini, Domenico (*b.* before 1434, *d.* 1494×1514), scholar and chronicler, was born in Rome. Little is known about his life. His first recorded appearance was in Paris in 1482, when he described himself as 'old', a term that may indicate that he was at least fifty at the time. In that year he wrote a Latin verse recommendation to a commentary on the *Sentences* of Peter Lombard by the Augustinian hermit Gregorio da Rimini (*d.* 1358). This edition marked a turning point in a philosophical controversy among Paris intellectuals, and Mancini must have been sufficiently well known to be asked to contribute by the printer or editor. His involvement suggests he was an Augustinian hermit himself; elsewhere he described himself as 'dedicated to the faith', and there is evidence that he wore a black habit.

Mancini was a competent Latinist and poet. He wrote occasional verse with elegance and ease and his prose style has been said to have 'the merit of clarity'. Two of his verse works were printed: *Libellus de quatuor virtutibus* (1484), a traditional rehearsal of the four cardinal virtues, and *Tractatus de passione domini* (1480s), a reworking of the Bible texts of Christ's passion. His accomplishments as author and moralist were appreciated by his contemporaries. One of them was the humanist Robert Gaguin, Mancini's neighbour in Paris, a student of classical historians and author of the *Compendium* of the history of France (1495). In the 1480s and 1490s Gaguin was the leader of a circle of literary minded scholars and statesmen that included Angelo Cato, archbishop of Vienne, the French chancellor Guillaume de Rochefort, and Guillaume's brother. Their names can also be linked to those of Erasmus of Rotterdam, the Dutch chronicler Cornelius of Gouda, and Johann Tritheim, a scholar in the service of the emperor. All these men were interested in history and its political and didactic aspects; they visited, corresponded, and dedicated or recommended their writings to each other and used each other's work.

Mancini's reputation in England rests on his eyewitness account of the dramatic events between the death of Edward IV and the coronation of Richard III, from April to July 1483. His only surviving prose composition, *De occupatione regni Anglie per Ricardum tertium libellus* ('A little book about the taking of the realm of England by Richard III', usually translated as 'The usurpation of Richard III') survives in a unique, sixteenth-century copy in the Bibliothèque Municipale at Lille; its contents remained unknown to modern scholars until it was discovered by C. A. J. Armstrong, who edited it.

It is not known why or for how long Mancini was in England, only that he left it shortly before Richard's coronation on 6 July 1483. He finished his account on 1 December 1483, claiming it was put on paper at the request of Angelo Cato, who had heard the story several times, found it interesting, and wished to present it to his patron, Federico, duke of Otranto. The book is carefully laid out, starting with a discussion of the situation at the time of Edward IV's death and the reasons why Richard of Gloucester decided to take the throne. The characters of some of the protagonists are discussed to explain their personal motives, but relatively little is said about Richard himself. In the description of the main events Mancini's account agrees with other sources, showing for example that rumours of the death of the 'princes in the Tower' started very early. The author appears to be free of personal prejudice, setting out to report the truth as he saw it; he wrote in the knowledge that Richard's coup had been successful, but without the animus of later commentators writing after Richard's downfall. Mancini probably knew no English, but there must have been many willing informants among the clergy and merchants of London, fluent in French, Italian, or Latin; the only one mentioned is John Argentine (d. 1508), physician to the young Edward V.

The value of Mancini's factual information is marred by ignorance of English customs and institutions, and a strong tendency to imitate classical authors both in images and language. His report must have been of interest to French readers like Cato and Gaguin, concerned about the minority of their own king, and to men eager to discuss the proper education of princes generally, such as Erasmus and Thomas More, but there is no positive evidence that *De occupatione* became widely known. Mancini's own lack of prejudice left his story open to very different interpretations by modern commentators.

LIVIA VISSER-FUCHS

Sources Bibliothèque Municipale, Lille, France, MS Godefroy 129 · *The usurpation of Richard the third: Dominicus Mancinus ad Angelum Catonem de occupatione regni Anglie per Ricardum tercium libellus*, ed. and trans. C. A. J. Armstrong, 2nd edn (1969) [Lat. orig., 1483, with parallel Eng. trans.] · *Roberti Gaguini epistole et orationes*, ed. L. Thuasne, 2 vols. (Paris, 1903) · A. Renaudet, *Préréforme et humanisme à Paris pendant les premières guerres d'Italie, 1494–1517* (Paris, 1916) · St Thomas More, *The history of King Richard III*, ed. R. S. Sylvester (1963), vol. 2 of *The Yale edition of the complete works of St Thomas More* · A. Hanham, *Richard III and his early historians, 1483–1535* (1975), 65–73 · J. Potter, *Good King Richard?* (1983), 81–6 · R. Horrox, *Richard III, a study of service*, Cambridge Studies in Medieval Life and Thought, 4th ser., 11 (1989), 90–123 · A. Gransden, *Historical writing in England*, 2 (1982), 300–07 · J. Trithemius, *Liber de scriptoribus ecclesiasticis* (Basil, 1494) · Bibliothèque Nationale, Paris, MS fr. 29967, fol. 26

Archives Bibliothèque Municipale, Lille, MS Godefroy 129

Mander, Sir Frederick (1883–1964), headmaster and trade unionist, was born at 172 Wellington Street, Luton, Bedfordshire, on 12 July 1883, the son of Arthur Mander, an iron plate worker, and his wife, Carrie Ellingham. His name was registered at birth as Fred, which was also recorded on his marriage certificate, but in later life he was known as Frederick. He was educated at Luton higher grade school before training to become a teacher at Westminster Training College and obtaining a University of London external BSc degree. He was a schoolmaster when he married, on 2 September 1911, Hilda Irene Sargent (b. 1883/4), the daughter of Thomas William Sargent, gentleman; they had two sons and a daughter.

By 1915 Mander was headmaster of a Luton school, where he remained until 1931. Having become involved in the politics of the National Union of Teachers (NUT) at a local level, he was elected to the NUT executive in 1922. The following year he played a leading role in the well-known Lowestoft strike, when 163 teachers withdrew their labour for eleven months in protest against the local authority's decision to reduce salaries by 10 per cent. The actions of the local education authority (LEA) received widespread censure, especially when the NUT demonstrated that non-union 'blackleg' teachers were substandard. The Lowestoft dispute proved to be a landmark case. In 1926 the Board of Education stipulated that LEAs should pay teachers salaries agreed at a national level by the Burnham committee. Mander, together with Michael Conway, W. G. Cove, and Leah Manning, was seen as a leader of the 'forward movement' within the NUT. In reality, however, it was his conservatism which helped him to advance within the NUT executive. He became vice-president in 1926 and president the following year. In 1931 he resigned his post as a head teacher to become general secretary, a position which he held until his retirement in 1947. He was knighted in 1938.

In Mander's first year as general secretary of the NUT he was a vigorous opponent of demands for teachers' pay to be reduced by up to 30 per cent in response to the economic crisis. The National Government initially sought a reduction of 15 per cent but strong NUT resistance limited the cut to 10 per cent. Having emerged from this difficult period, the second half of the 1930s saw the union renew its campaign for educational expansion, including the raising of the school-leaving age to fifteen and the provision of free secondary education for all. During the Second World War these and other themes were central to government plans for educational reconstruction and Mander was regularly consulted by civil servants and by R. A. Butler, president of the Board of Education from 1941 to 1945. In 1942 Mander was appointed to the inquiry into the supply, recruitment, and training of teachers and youth leaders, chaired by Sir Arnold McNair, which reported in May 1944. He also worked constructively with civil servants and representatives of the LEAs to promote the 1943 white paper *Educational Reconstruction* and the 1944 Education Act.

Mander participated in some delicate negotiations concerning the future of church schools and, when it looked as if the legislation might be wrecked by calls for equal pay for women teachers, he instructed NUT members of parliament to save the bill rather than support an amendment which reflected union policy. When the Burnham committee was reconstituted in 1944 Mander, in his capacity as leader of the teachers' panel, was drawn into a dispute with the LEAs concerning the payment of allowances for additional qualifications and training. A compromise was reached, however, and it can be argued that Mander's good personal relationships with Butler, Sir Maurice Holmes, the board's permanent secretary, and Sir Percival Sharp, secretary of the Association of Education Committees, did much to cultivate the sense of 'partnership' in education policy making which characterized the wartime and immediate post-war period.

Within his own union, however, Mander was never universally popular, particularly among communist members of the executive. Indeed, as the Education Bill progressed through parliament, he found himself having to work with his long-standing opponent G. C. T. Giles, the communist headmaster of Acton School, who was union president during 1944. He retired as NUT general secretary in 1947 but remained active in local politics, chairing Bedfordshire county council between 1952 and 1962, and was a member of the executive of the Association of Education Committees. He died at Luton and Dunstable Hospital, Luton, on 27 February 1964; he was survived by his wife.   DAVID CROOK

Sources *The Times* (28 Feb 1964) · R. Aldrich and P. Gordon, *Dictionary of British educationists* (1989) · L. Manning, *A life for education: an autobiography* (1970) · M. Barber, *Education and the teacher unions* (1992) · R. Gould, *Chalk up the memory: an autobiography* (1976) · D. Crook, 'The reconstruction of teacher education and training, 1941–54, with particular reference to the McNair committee', PhD diss., U. Wales, Swansea, 1997 · b. cert. · m. cert. · d. cert. · *CGPLA Eng. & Wales* (1964)
Likenesses photograph, National Union of Teachers, Hamilton House, London, Mander Hall
Wealth at death £12,471: probate, 9 Sept 1964, *CGPLA Eng. & Wales*

Mander, Raymond Josiah Gale [Ray] (1911–1983), actor and theatre historian, was born at 6B Cato Road, Clapham, London, on 15 July 1911, the only son of Albert Edwin Mander, architect and surveyor, and his wife, Edith Christina, *née* Gale. Albert Mander was related to the film director Miles Mander, but there seems to have been no family connection to inspire Ray Mander's passion for labelling items around the family home, thought at one stage to destine him for a career as a museum curator. Instead, after being educated at Battersea grammar school and perhaps inspired by the bundle of Irving theatre programmes given to him on his seventh birthday, he became an actor when he left school, touring in weekly repertory.

(Francis) Joseph Blackett [Joe] **Mitchenson** (1911–1992), actor and theatre historian, was born at 53 Selborne Road, Southgate, London, on 4 October 1911, the only son of Francis William Mitchenson, general merchant and drama critic, and his wife, Sarah, *née* Roddam.

Mitchenson's father's ancestors had strong theatre connections and his mother (who had Yorkshire family connections) was theatre crazy and an amateur actress. The parents' marriage was not a success and Francis Mitchenson soon disappeared from the scene. Joe Mitchenson was educated privately, and from the age of eight, with financial support from a relative, took dancing classes at the Fay Compton School of Dance. Five years later he decided that his interest was in acting, no doubt influenced by contact with theatricals encountered at a fashionable vegetarian restaurant to which he was frequently taken by his mother after dancing classes. His first experience of the West End came in 1934 when he walked on in *Libel* at the Playhouse (with Alec Guinness similarly engaged).

14 February 1939 saw the first meeting between Mander and Mitchenson, and later in the year they appeared together in *The Merry Wives of Windsor*, Mitchenson playing Fenton and Mander playing Page. They toured the provinces for the rest of the year, with Mander playing Guildenstern among other roles in the Harold V. Neilson company at the Opera House, Manchester, until the Benson tradition ended just before the outbreak of the Second World War. Mander and Mitchenson then followed separate paths during the war. Mander found employment as a pioneer disc jockey for the BBC with thirty-five programmes to his credit, despite the inclusion on one occasion of banned Strauss music. Mitchenson meanwhile joined the Royal Horse Artillery and then transferred to the infantry before being invalided out with a leg injury, which continued to trouble him in later life.

At the end of the war the two friends decided to turn their common interest into something more, and gradually the Mander and Mitchenson Theatre Collection was born, housed in Mitchenson's mother's house in Sydenham, London. Over the years this tall Victorian terraced house at 5 Venner Road overflowed with an amazing treasure trove of playbills and books from seventeenth-century folios onwards, programmes, periodicals, gramophone records, playwrights' prompt scripts, drawings, designs, and china figurines of great actors and actresses in their most famous roles, including a Bloor Derby Garrick. Anything which narrated theatre history was avidly acquired, magpie fashion.

Soon the passion for collecting took over from acting, although Mitchenson continued to make the occasional 'professional' appearance in later life—probably the last was with Coral Browne on television in *Caviar for the General*. Working together, Mander and Mitchenson established themselves as the source for any authoritative theatrical information, willingly dispensing this to actors with whom they had personal connections (Judi Dench was a particular friend and later a patron of the collection's charity) and managements alike. They provided material for journals, television programmes—*This is your Life* was a consistent customer—and innumerable exhibitions—among which was one to Soviet Russia in 1978 of theatre design for the British Council.

It was a natural step for Mander and Mitchenson to use their acquired knowledge as the source for publications, and between 1952 and 1977 seventeen books were written or compiled by them, besides contributions to more than 400 other publications. Their own publications ranged from pictorial histories of British theatre (1957), of opera (1959), of Gilbert and Sullivan (1962), of musical comedy (1969), of revue (1971), and of pantomime (1973), to more narrative accounts—including *Hamlet through the Ages* (1952), *The Gay Twenties* (1958), *The Turbulent Thirties* (1960), and the theatrical companions to Maugham (1955), Coward (1957), and Wagner (1977)—and the authoritative records of London's theatres themselves, *Theatres of London* (1961) and *Lost Theatres of London* (1968).

In the 1960s and 1970s 'Ray and Joe' became a theatrical institution and, dressed in style, invariably held court at first nights, reflecting on previous productions and associated gossip. At Venner Road they dispensed knowledge to those fortunate enough to be invited there—it was a private collection—or to those who could brave a telephone conversation which was always a double act. Noel Coward aptly named them Gog and Magog, quipping 'sort out between yourselves which is which' (private information). Indeed many of their friends secretly found it difficult to distinguish Mander (with the air of a former pugilist and speedy verbal delivery) and Mitchenson (taller, with long silver hair).

Mander and Mitchenson knew from their personal experience of rescuing theatrical records from oblivion (as when they purchased the watercolour poster by Dudley Hardy for Kitty Grey from its use as temporary shop window repair following bomb damage) or when they failed (as with drawings in the Saville Theatre's bar), how easily theatre history might be lost. They first suggested as early as 1944 that their collection might be bequeathed to the nation. Sybil Thorndike aptly summed up their importance with her description of those the profession affectionately knew as 'The Boys' as 'our passport to posterity' (private information).

Initially Mander and Mitchenson hoped that their collection would find a home in the National Theatre on the South Bank, but reasons of space forced rethinking. For a time it seemed that the collection would find a permanent home in the eighteenth-century Beckenham Place Park, with support from Lewisham council (which at one stage had sought to acquire the Venner Road property for road widening). The collection moved there in 1983, but despite support from the Greater London council in its final days the cost of renovating the Beckenham property proved too much for the charitable trust to which Mander and Mitchenson had made over the collection in 1977 (although both retained a hands-on approach to its work, sometimes to the concern of its curators). In 2001, after a brief period in temporary accommodation, it moved to a new home as part of the Jerwood Library of the Performing Arts in the Hawksmoor building at the Trinity College of Music, Old Royal Naval College, in Greenwich. There, while still retaining its independent status and within an academic environment which might have surprised its founders, it was located in a worthy surrounding and atmosphere appropriate for Mander and Mitchenson's life work.

Mander died at Hither Green Hospital, Lewisham, London, on 20 December 1983, of bronchopneumonia and emphysema, when the move to Beckenham Place had only just begun. Mitchenson moved with the collection to Beckenham and lived there until shortly before he died in Orpington Hospital, Bromley, London, on 7 October 1992, of renal failure and prostatic hypertrophy.

RUPERT RHYMES

Sources *The Times* (23 Dec 1983) · *The Times* (9 Oct 1992) · *The Times* (16 Oct 1992) · *The Independent* (3 Nov 1992) · WWW · b. cert. · b. cert. [Francis Joseph Blackett Mitchenson] · d. cert. · d. cert. [Francis Joseph Blackett Mitchenson]
Likenesses double portrait, photograph (with Francis Mitchenson), repro. in *The Times* (9 Oct 1992)
Wealth at death £21,659: probate, 20 March 1985, *CGPLA Eng. & Wales* · £257,996—Francis Joseph Blackett Mitchenson: probate, 6 Jan 1993, *CGPLA Eng. & Wales*

Mander, (Samuel) Theodore (1853–1900), paint manufacturer, was born in St Paul's Terrace, Wolverhampton, on 25 February 1853. Always known as Theodore, he was the eldest of the seven children of Samuel Small Mander (1822–1881), paint and varnish manufacturer, and his wife, Mary, *née* Wilkes (1831–1900). After preparatory schools, Mander attended the Tettenhall proprietary school, Wolverhampton, from 1864 to 1871, and spent his sixteenth year at a small private school in Dijon. His education continued with a year at London University, where he matriculated in 1873; a year at Berlin University studying organic chemistry with Professor Hofmann; and finally at Clare College, Cambridge, where he graduated BA in November 1876. Mander's sincere Christian beliefs (and also his thoughts of an alternative vocation) are evident in the letters to his parents from abroad. He wrote to his mother, 'my desire and I think my duty is to prepare to enter Papa's business and I think I can be quite as useful in that way as in being a minister' (Mander MSS, A89).

On completion of his education, therefore, and with the knowledge of chemistry needed to improve the varnishes, Theodore joined the family paint and varnish business. Founded in 1773 by Benjamin Mander, his great-grandfather, originally as a japanning and tin plate works, the company later became Mander Brothers under the control of his uncle and father. In 1879 Mander, aged twenty-six, and his older cousin Charles were appointed company directors.

On 29 June 1879 Mander married Flora Elvira St Clair Paint (1857–1905), in Flora's home town of Halifax, Nova Scotia. Flora had attended a private school in London with three of Mander's sisters, in 1873, and the following year they were together at finishing school in Wiesbaden, Germany. Mander's choice was much approved of by his sisters, who wrote of Flora as a 'really splendid girl' (Mander MSS, A128). Flora and her younger sister Mary were daughters of Henry Paint, a merchant who later became a member of the Canadian parliament; Mary subsequently married Mander's cousin Charles. After their marriage Theodore and Flora Mander lived at Mornington Place, Tettenhall

Road, Wolverhampton, where the first two of their four children were born. Mander bought land at Wightwick, 3 miles outside Wolverhampton, and the architect Edward Ould, of the Liverpool firm Grayson and Ould, was in 1887 commissioned to build Wightwick Manor, and in 1893 to extend it. Mander's interest in art and design was reflected in the decor of the house, which incorporated many products from the William Morris company and was elegantly decorated with oriental carpets, De Morgan tiles, and Kempe stained-glass windows.

Mander's wide-ranging interests were typical of the wealthy industrialists of his day. Actively involved in education, at the time of his death he was chairman of the school board, and governor of the local grammar school, Tettenhall College, and Birmingham University. A prominent member of the temperance movement, he was a deacon in the Congregationalist church and served as a lay preacher for thirty years. Elected to Wolverhampton council in 1881, he also became an alderman and a magistrate. In July 1900, during his period of office as mayor, the duke and duchess of York (later George V and Queen Mary) visited Wolverhampton orphanage and laid the foundation stone of the New Free Library.

Only seven weeks after the royal visit Mander was taken ill, while on holiday in Llangollen, and he died at Wightwick Manor on 14 September 1900, at the age of forty-seven, of an abscess on the liver. He was given a civic funeral, and after the service at Queen Street Congregational Church, Wolverhampton, he was buried at Pattingham, Staffordshire. Flora Mander survived until 1905. On the death of this respected and kindly man, Mander's family received more than 400 letters of condolence; their constant theme was the high regard in which Mander was held by 'those who worked with him in the many great undertakings of a public nature to which he so generously and with such rare singleness of purpose devoted his life' (Mander MSS, condolence letters).   POLLY HAMILTON

Sources *A very private heritage: the family papers of Samuel Theodore Mander of Wolverhampton, 1853–1900*, ed. P. Pegg (1996) · S. Ponder, *Wightwick Manor* (1993) [National Trust guidebook] · Wightwick Manor, Wightwick Bank, Wolverhampton, Staffordshire, Mander MSS
Archives Wightwick Manor, Wightwick Bank, Wolverhampton, Staffordshire
Likenesses F. Chester, portrait, *c*.1900, Wightwick Manor, Wolverhampton · photograph, *c*.1900 (in mayoral robes), Wightwick Manor, Wolverhampton · family photographs, Wightwick Manor, Wolverhampton
Wealth at death £178,548 4*s*. 2*d*.: probate, 20 Oct 1900, *CGPLA Eng. & Wales*

Manderston [Manderstown], **William** (*c*.1485–1552), philosopher and logician, was born in Haddington, east of Edinburgh, and was educated at the University of Glasgow, where he matriculated in 1503 and graduated BA in 1506. By 1507 he had matriculated at the University of Paris and was attached to the Collège de Montaigu, where he lived with other Scots including John Mair, George Lokert, and David Cranston. He graduated MA in 1510, and eight years later became a bachelor of medicine.

Manderston's name first appears in connection with a publication in 1516, when he was one of the two editors of the index of Lokert's edition of the fourteenth-century writings on physics by Jean Buridan, Judaeus Thimon, and Albert of Saxony. In the following years he published three books. The first, in 1517, was *Tripartitum*, a three-part work on the principles of logic, dedicated to Andrew Forman, archbishop of St Andrews. This was followed a year later by *Bipartitum*, a two-part work on moral philosophy whose first edition likewise was dedicated to Forman. His last book, published in 1522, was on the theologically important topic of future contingent propositions—in particular, propositions about future human acts. Like many medieval theologians Manderston investigated such propositions because he was interested in the question of whether God's certain foreknowledge of our future free acts implied that those acts were bound to be performed and were therefore not, after all, free.

Manderston rose to become a professor at the Collège de Sainte-Barbe in Paris. His servant in the college was George Buchanan, who would in due course be recognized as one of the great Latinists of the age. Buchanan had attended St Andrews University while Mair was working there, and had followed Mair to Paris. During this period Manderston was also the teacher of Patrick Hamilton, who within the decade became the first martyr of the Scottish Reformation.

In 1525 Manderston was elected rector of the University of Paris. His rectorship was a troubled one, for around the time of the election the anti-Lutheran theologian Jérôme de Hangest accused Manderston of plagiarizing him in the *Tripartitum*. Whatever the justice of the claim, and whatever the precise reason for Hangest's animosity towards Manderston, the latter left France and did not return. It has been suggested that Mair's departure from France at about the same time was a by-product of that same accusation. The loss to Paris was a gain for Scotland. Manderston left Paris early in 1528, the year in which his former pupil, Patrick Hamilton, was burned at St Andrews for his Lutheran beliefs. In 1530 Manderston was elected rector of the University of St Andrews. The rectorship was solely an administrative position, but Manderston continued to teach, for in 1536 he is described as lecturer *in actu*, and it was expected that he would be appointed mediciner (lecturer in medicine) at St Mary's College in the university. Two years later he was granted tax exemption in light of his work for the common good of the university. In 1540 he and Mair jointly founded a bursary in theology at St Salvator's College, and in 1546 he founded a bursary in arts.

Manderston died in 1552, some time before 16 May in that year, when arrangements were made for services for his soul in the parish church of Cupar in Fife. He had been one of the leading Scottish intellectuals of his age. His work on logic, and perhaps even more his work on moral philosophy, repay close study. In particular Manderston offers many illuminating insights into the nature of human action and into the determinants of moral goodness, and he pays special attention to the question of whether it is possible to perform a morally good act without God's grace. Like his friend and colleague John Mair,

Manderston dedicated his life to the maintenance of the old order in the church and in the universities; it was his pupil Patrick Hamilton who represented the new.

ALEXANDER BROADIE

Sources A. Broadie, *The circle of John Mair* (1985) • A. Broadie, 'William Manderston and Patrick Hamilton on freewill and grace', *Innes Review*, 37 (1986), 25–35 • J. K. Farge, *Biographical register of Paris doctors of theology, 1500–1536* (1980) • H. Elié, 'Quelques maîtres de l'université de Paris vers l'an 1500', *Archives d'Histoire Doctrinale et Littéraire du Moyen Âge*, 18 (1950–51), 193–243 • J. Durkan, 'The school of John Major: bibliography', *Innes Review*, 1 (1950), 140–57

Mandevile [Mandevil], **Robert** (1578/9–1618), Church of England clergyman, was born in Cumberland of unknown parents. He matriculated from Queen's College, Oxford, on 25 June 1596, aged seventeen, graduated BA on 17 June 1600, and proceeded MA from St Edmund Hall on 6 July 1603. Like many of his fellow students of humble origins under Henry Airay's provostship at Queen's, he was prepared for the ministry in the north-west, and in July 1607 he was elected to the university living of Abbey Holme or Holm Cultram, Cumberland. Here, according to Anthony Wood, he proved 'a zealous puritan', an active 'enemy against popery', and a promoter of sabbath observance (Wood, *Ath. Oxon.*, 2.251).

Although Wood ascribes to Mandevile the authorship of theological discourses, his only known work was *Timothies Taske, or, A Christian Sea-Card* (1619), edited by Thomas Vicars and published in Oxford with a dedication to the vice-chancellor, Thomas Godwin. Consisting of two addresses given to the diocesan synod at Carlisle, it is a scripturally grounded and anti-Catholic exhortation to pastors to live godly lives and faithfully discharge their duties. Mandevile died in 1618. Nothing is known of a wife or family.

BERTHA PORTER, *rev.* VIVIENNE LARMINIE

Sources Wood, *Ath. Oxon.*, new edn, 2.251 • Foster, *Alum. Oxon.* • C. M. Dent, *Protestant reformers in Elizabethan Oxford* (1983), 116–17 • Wood, *Ath. Oxon.: Fasti* (1815), 284 • *STC, 1475–1640*

Mandeville, Bernard (*bap.* 1670, *d.* 1733), physician and political philosopher, was baptized in Rotterdam on 20 November 1670, the second child of Michael de Mandeville (*bap.* 1639, *d.* 1704/5) a leading physician in Rotterdam, and his wife, Judith, daughter of Bernard Verhaar, captain in the Rotterdam admiralty.

Early life and education Notwithstanding the particle (which Bernard dropped when he settled in England), no French ancestry has been traced for the de Mandevilles. They were an established Netherlandish professional family. At least some members of each generation were university-educated back to the sixteenth century. Bernard's great-great-grandfather Johannes de Mandeville can be traced to Leeuwarden in Friesland about 1580. His great-grandfather Michael de Mandeville studied medicine at the University of Franeker; he was appointed city physician and rector of the Latin school in Nijmegen in 1601. His grandfather Immanuel de Mandeville studied law at Leiden, nevertheless succeeding his father as city physician. Bernard's father, Michael, having studied law as well as qualified in medicine at Leiden, was appointed plague doctor in Nijmegen in 1666. After his marriage to

Judith Verhaar in July 1667, the couple moved to Rotterdam. Michael established a (successful) medical practice and held the offices of city physician, regent of the hospital (1679–87), lieutenant of the Rotterdam militia (1673–5, 1686–91), and a minor judicial position in the dependency of Schieland.

The young Mandeville attended the Erasmian School, Rotterdam; he is likely to have heard the two notable French protestant exiles, Pierre Bayle and Pierre Jurieu, appointed professors of the Illustrious School in Rotterdam. In *De medicina oratio scholastica* (1685), he announced his intention of studying medicine. Matriculating in October 1685 at the University of Leiden, he studied philosophy and medicine until 1690. His doctoral thesis in philosophy, *Disputatio philosophica de brutorum operationibus* (1689), adopted the Cartesian view of animals as automata which he later rejected. He returned briefly in 1691 to present his medical thesis, *Disputatio medica inauguralis de chylosi vitiata*, which dealt with the process of digestion and its effects on the brain—hypochondria and hysteria were Mandeville's medical specialism.

In the preface to the revised versions of his *Treatise of the Hypochondriack and Hysterick Diseases* (1730, xiii), Mandeville claimed that he went to London to learn English, found it agreeable, and stayed. But it seems likely that there were other reasons for his decision to emigrate. In 1690 he and his father (who had connections with the anti-Orangist, republican states party) had been involved in the Costerman riot in Rotterdam. The city bailiff, Jacob Van Zuijlen van Nievelt, had prosecuted and executed Costerman, a citizen member of the militia, for killing (with his sword) a tax agent who had discovered a group drinking untaxed wine. On 5 October, verses written by the de Mandevilles, denouncing the bailiff as a hypocritical 'sanctimonious atheist' and petty tyrant, were posted at the merchants' exchange. This ridicule was concerted with an attack upon and partial destruction of the bailiff's house. The city government dismissed Van Zuijlen from his office the following day. But the provincial government and then the stadholder, William of Orange, intervened. Van Zuijlen was restored to office (1692) and took revenge on his enemies. In 1693 Michael de Mandeville was banished; he moved to Amsterdam to set up in practice there. Bernard would have found his prospects adversely affected by having to establish himself in the very competitive medical environment of Amsterdam. By 17 November 1693 he was sufficiently known in London medical circles to have been summoned to appear by the Royal College of Physicians for practising without a licence. Latin verses, 'In authorem de usu interno cantharidum scribentem', contributed to *Tutus cantharidum in medicina usus internus* (1698), by Johannes Groenevelt, a Dutch physician and surgeon prosecuted for malpractice by the college, indicate Mandeville's continued hostility to its authority. (He remained unlicensed.) On 1 February 1699 he married Ruth Elizabeth Laurence (*b.* 1673/4), who was twenty-five years of age, at St Giles-in-the-Fields, Westminster, London. Their first child, Michael, was born on 1 March 1699;

the date of the birth of their daughter, Penelope, is not known.

Early writings Mandeville seems to have wished to establish himself as an author, first attempting to launch a career through verse; *The Pamphleteers* (1703), which defended William III's memory against his (tory) detractors, was followed by translations of La Fontaine's fables (*Some Fables after the Easie and Familiar Method of Monsieur de la Fontaine*, 1703; enlarged to *Aesop Dress'd*, 1704) and a burlesque epic, *Typhon* (1704), after Paul Scarron. *The Grumbling Hive* (1705), a 423-line verse fable deprecating the grumbling of the English (incorporated into *The Fable of the Bees* in 1714) followed. The wealthy, powerful bees of a hive discontentedly grumbled about the prevalent vices—these disgruntled bees being themselves as guilty of the deceits in their own callings as those of which they complained. Granted their prayers, the bees become virtuous. Consequently their wealth and numbers decline. The moral is that vice is beneficial when it is restricted by justice:

> they, that would revive
> A Golden Age, must be as free
> For Acorns, as for Honesty
> (Mandeville, *Fable*, 1.37)

These efforts being (apparently) unsuccessful, Mandeville turned to prose. *The Virgin Unmask'd* (1709) consisted of dialogues between 'an elderly maiden aunt' and her niece. The initial suggestion of a pornographic content quickly disappeared as the discussion turned to the undesirability of marriage and the harmful effects of child bearing on women, two proto-novels, and a discussion of the dangers posed by Louis XIV to Europe's peace and security. Next Mandeville disguised himself as sisters, Lucinda and Artesia, who were members of the 'Society of Ladies' which took over the *Female Tatler* (1709–10), an imitator of Richard Steele's *Tatler*, from its original author, Mrs Crackenthorpe (probably Thomas Baker). Mandeville wrote thirty-two issues from November 1709 to the end of March 1710. These papers foreshadowed his later works in asserting that the main engine of social development had not been those who pursued virtue, learning, and the public interest (as Steele claimed in *The Tatler*), but rather those 'who by the Sollicitous Care they take of their Backs and Bellies, make Money Circulate, and are the real Encouragers of every useful Art and Science' (Mandeville, *Society of Ladies*, 105). Other issues discussed 'honour' and the eligibility of a life devoted to money-making. Perhaps most notable are eight issues, again responding to *The Tatler*, devoted to contending that women are as capable as men of achieving the cardinal virtues, leading armies, and governing states. To support this view Mandeville cited numerous examples, modern as well as classical, biblical, and mythical, many derived (without acknowledgement and often nearly verbatim) from the English translation of Pierre le Moyne's *La gallerie des femmes fortes* (1647) as *The Gallery of Heroick Women* (1652).

Mandeville returned to his professional specialism for his next work, *A Treatise of the Hypochondriack and Hysterick Passions* (1711). In a set of dialogues between a physician and several patients, Mandeville used a classically educated hypochondriacal patient, Misomedon, to describe the history of his ailment and the (failed) attempts to cure it by physicians addicted to various speculative theories. He gave details of and criticized the remedies prescribed by apothecaries as well as by physicians. The medical practitioner, Philopirio, reveals an adherence to 'medical materialism', denigrating theoretical medicine while praising extensive, careful empirical observation, in opposition to the training in the traditional English universities. The book presumably illustrates Mandeville's own practice, with its extensive 'talking cure' of the patient backed by the recommendations of exercise along with moderation in food and drink. Part of the point of the book's publication was to advertise Mandeville's practice—that itself was a rejection of the authority and standards of the Royal College of Physicians. (Of all his publications in England, it was only in this work, and in its 1715 reissue as a 'second edition', that he subscribed himself 'de Mandeville', presumably to enhance his social status.) A variant title-page of the 1711 edition reveals that Mandeville was then living in Manchester Court, Channel Row, Westminster. A letter written by Mandeville to the well-known physician Sir Hans Sloane (after 4 April 1718) suggests that Mandeville achieved a reasonably successful practice. Philopirio's remarks on his own supposed character in *A Treatise of the Hypochondriack and Hysterick Diseases* (the enlarged and retitled 1730 printings, pp. 351–2) may depict Mandeville. If so, he presents himself as too devoted to his enjoyments and diversions to 'slave at an Employment' (ibid.) as well as not being especially acquisitive.

The Fable of the Bees At least one of Mandeville's diversions remained writing and publishing. A small collection of verses in English and Latin appeared as *Wishes to a Godson* (1712). It was followed by his notorious *The Fable of the Bees, or, Private Vices, Publick Benefits* (1714). This first edition of the *Fable* was composed of a short preface, 'The Grumbling Hive' of 1705, a very brief introduction, 'An enquiry into the origin of moral virtue', and twenty 'remarks' which purported to annotate and explain various lines in the verse fable.

The *Fable* anatomizes human nature, alleging that their 'vilest and most hateful Qualities', their passions, render humans sociable animals and make them 'fit for the largest, and according to the World, the happiest and most flourishing Societies' (Mandeville, *Fable*, 1.3–4). Here Mandeville explicitly refers to Montaigne and apparently relies on exponents of the French Augustinian tradition, such as Pascal, La Rochefoucauld, Jacques Esprit, Pierre Nicole, and Pierre Bayle, who emphasized the worldly benefits of the passions. While claiming that almost every profession and calling is marked with its peculiar vices, that the vile ingredients result in a wholesome mixture, and that wealth, power, and politeness are incompatible with innocence and virtue, Mandeville denied (as he was repeatedly to do throughout his works) that he was commending vice. On the contrary, he claimed that he did not recommend vice to individuals, that he exhorted governments to punish crimes and regulate trade, and that he was deprecating the implicit hypocrisy of those who desired a flourishing society but grumbled about its concomitant conditions. Only if London were less flourishing would the streets be cleaner; their dirtiness was a necessary evil. Mandeville admitted that he would prefer to walk in a garden or a grove rather than a 'stinking' London street; and 'true Happiness', he conceded, was more probable in a 'small peaceable Society' than in a great warlike commercial nation. But this was so only if one laid aside considerations of 'the interest or happiness of the city' and all worldly greatness (ibid., 1.6–13).

The 'Enquiry into the origin of moral virtue' reiterates the *Female Tatler*'s rejection of the distinctiveness and dignity of human nature, with its emphasis on rationality, which Mandeville continued to attribute to Richard Steele. Its version of the origin of morality and society transmutes the discussion in the *Female Tatler*. There Mandeville had pitted an Augustinian-Hobbesian view, which emphasized the inherent strife that resulted from conflicting desires, against one that attributed the improving of mankind to public-spirited benefactors. Both were then trumped by the 'Oxford gentleman', who credited civilization to those who invented new luxurious desires as well as seeking to satisfy existing ones. The Augustinian-Hobbesian self-interested element of human nature is retained in the 'Enquiry' which opens the *Fable*. But Mandeville now suggested that 'skilful Politicians' (moralists, lawgivers, and philosophers) had persuaded humans to sacrifice their selfish desires for the praises of others, thus enhancing their good opinions of themselves as virtuous superior beings: 'This was (or at least might have been) how Savage Man was broke' (Mandeville, *Fable*, 1.46). The 'first Rudiments of Morality, broach'd by skilful Politicians' had resulted from distinguishing vice, that is, indulging one's appetites, from virtue: 'every Performance, by which Man, contrary to the impulse of Nature, should endeavour the Benefit of others, or the Conquest of his own Passions out of a Rational Ambition of being good' (ibid., 42–9). Thus 'the Moral Virtues are the Political Offspring which Flattery begot on Pride' (ibid., 51). The procedure can be observed in the training of children into proper behaviour, whether it be Miss Mollie being taught to curtsy or a boy learning the manners of a gentleman; the results can be equally observed in the ambitions of heroes like Caesar and Alexander (ibid., 53–5). Ultimately, in order to judge human conduct, it is necessary to reveal the motives and passions that produce it.

The 'remarks' further illustrate Mandeville's main contentions (remarks are here denoted by the letters in editions from 1723 rather than those of 1714). Pride, the desire to be thought well of, features in several of them. For example, remark R examines honour and in particular courage. Natural courage occurs when the passion of anger overcomes that of fear. Sociable relations, however, require that fear be strengthened in order to inhibit aggression and at the same time that a substitute for natural courage be provided so that society can be defended.

Thus the passions of pride and shame are harnessed to produce 'Artificial Courage'. More generally, Mandeville contrasted 'ancient' and 'modern' honour. Ancient honour was a 'massy' chivalrous compound of courage, honesty, justice, and other virtues. By contrast, modern honour was new-minted on the basis of pride; with the same weight of courage, half the quantity of honesty, and a very little justice, but not a scrap of any other virtue. Modern honour was much more 'portable' than ancient had been. Yet 'such as it is there would be no living without it in a large nation': a man of honour may never go back on his word; he must pay his gambling debts but may put off other creditors; he must protect any woman entrusted to his care but may act as he pleases toward others. He must also fight if insulted; and the resulting practice of duelling, Mandeville pointed out, had effectively curtailed verbal abuse. Honour may be contrary to religion, but it is far easier to achieve than virtue—that requires restraining many passions with little apparent reward; honour requires less restraint and is immediately recompensed by pride (Mandeville, *Fable*, 1.198–223).

Pride is also a passion that promotes luxury. If everything beyond bare subsistence is luxury, then even 'naked Savages', having made some improvement in their way of life, are luxurious—'in one Sense every Thing may be call'd [luxurious], and in another there is no such Thing'. What is thought to be luxurious is relative to a person's position. Far from being a danger to society, luxury is inseparable from a wealthy, flourishing nation. Moreover, whatever the situation of the rich, the 'working slaving People' will be sufficiently hardy for soldiering (remark L, Mandeville, *Fable*, 1.107–23). Continuous refinement in dress, diet, habitation, and ornament is driven by pride, for humans will aspire to emulate their betters, who will in turn adopt new fashions (ibid., remark M, 124–34; see also D, 80–81). The famous frugality of the Dutch, Mandeville argues, actually stems from their paucity of natural resources and the heavy taxes they pay in order to protect themselves from the sea. Moreover, the virtue of frugality is not apparent in their extravagant expenditure on untaxed goods, while the government actually encourages the luxury and extravagance of seamen arriving in port after long voyages (ibid., remark Q, 181–98). The other great example of a virtuous simplicity and hardiness, Sparta, provides a model not desired by the English (ibid., remark X, 246–7).

Remark P explicitly elaborates the suggestion that there has been a gradual evolution of human society from simplicity to opulence, that luxuries formerly available only to the very rich, such as a white linen shirt, have become common even among the poorest. Many distinct operations must be combined to produce such items. Humans have developed such processes as brewing and baking, even without full knowledge of the chemistry involved (Mandeville, *Fable*, 1.169–73). Among those luxuries now enjoyed even by the poor is eating meat, which clearly requires pain and suffering to animals structurally similar to humans (ibid., 172–6). This leads Mandeville to an attack on human pretensions to superiority over animals in a dialogue between a lion and a Roman merchant (ibid., 176–81).

Many of the remarks explain how contraries are mutually dependent. Avarice and prodigality, prostitution and chastity, protestantism and Roman Catholic reform, the Church of England and learning in the sects, all depend on each other. Society itself is like a punch: a mixture balancing individually unpleasant elements (remark K, Mandeville, *Fable*, 1.105–6). Every calling and trade exhibits the human vices of self-interest and pride. Decio, the sugar dealer, vies with Alcander, a West India merchant—each seeking to get the best of the bargain by relying on information not known to the other (ibid., remark B, 61–3). Merchants rely on secret marks, hiding the real cost of goods from their customers (ibid., remark D, 80–1). The apparently lazy porter who refuses to take a letter to Bow for a penny is astonishingly the messenger willingly to rise from his bed on a stormy winter night to run to Hackney and back with a bill of exchange for a crown (ibid., remark V, 240–1). Self-denying virtue is a pretence: the real human pleasures are sensual and worldly ones. John claims he loves pudding, but eats as little as possible while devouring the beef. Mandeville asserted he could outdo the Stoics in contemning riches for a tenth of Seneca's wealth, as well as teaching 'the way to his *Summum bonum* as exactly as I could my way home' (ibid., remark O, 147–68). Mandeville's claim to anatomize human nature and society meant tracing human actions to their motivating passions and showing how luxury and even such evils such as drunkenness, theft, and prostitution contributed to the wealth, power, and worldly happiness of a trading society. Not only moral but also natural evils like the great London fire (1666), it was suggested, produced some good.

The *Fable*'s notoriety The *Fable*, notwithstanding its having two printings in 1714, attracted little immediate attention. Later in the year Mandeville published *The Mischiefs that Ought Justly to be Apprehended from a Whig-Government* (1714), a minor, anonymous pamphlet defending the Hanoverian succession. In 1720 a more substantial work, *Free Thoughts on Religion, the Church, and National Happiness* urged toleration while objecting to priestcraft and exhibiting anti-clerical attitudes: the clergy, and especially those of a state church, had an interest in inciting hostility between religious denominations. In the book Mandeville relied heavily on Pierre Bayle, in fact transcribing substantial passages. *Free Thoughts* maintained a moderate whiggish position. While passive obedience was required to the sovereign authority in all states, in Britain this authority was the triune king, lords, and commons. The book was reissued in 1721 and 1723 with a second edition in 1729; it was also published in French (1722, 1723, 1729, and 1738), in Dutch (1723), and in German (1726).

In 1723 Mandeville published a second edition of the *Fable*, enlarging the remarks, including for example in remark G the contention that even thieves contribute to the public good as well as both a denunciation of gin ('this Liquid Poison') and a demonstration of its benefits by 'a sharp-sighted good humour'd Man' (Mandeville, *Fable*, 1.86–93). He also added 'An essay on charity and charity schools' (hostile to them and their sponsors) and 'A search into the nature of society' (against the third earl of Shaftesbury's moral and aesthetic philosophy and its contention that virtue is natural to humans). His notoriety and his success as an author was guaranteed by the presentation of this edition by a Middlesex grand jury for denigrating virtue and religion as harmful to society and recommending vices as beneficial to it. Middlesex grand juries were selected by London sheriffs, themselves elected by the City's livery companies. The sheriffs involved, elected unopposed in 1722, were both tories. Accordingly the grand jury was predominantly tory and crypto-Jacobite. On 3 July, at the height of a shrieval election hotly contested between tories and opposition whigs, the grand jury had presented the letters of Cato (John Trenchard and Thomas Gordon, 'country' whigs) in the *British Journal*. Trenchard had attacked high-church charity schools as being Jacobite. He was censured for reflecting on the government and the Church of England. Presenting the *Fable* on 8 July along with Cato (for a second time) appears to have been an attempt to reconcile 'country' whigs with tories in attacking the existing Walpole ministry by denouncing a 'court whig'. Mandeville replied with 'A vindication of the book' in the *London Journal* (10 August 1723)—a government-supported newspaper. The 'Vindication' reproduced the grand jury's presentment, along with what Mandeville labelled 'An abusive letter to Lord C' which denigrated the *Fable*, before defending the book by reiterating many of its themes and quoting some of its most offensive passages, while denying that it advocated vice rather than exposed its ubiquity in the world. The 'Vindication' was immediately reissued in a format matching that of the *Fable* and then incorporated in subsequent editions.

Mandeville's immunity from prosecution in 1723 and when the *Fable* was again presented in 1728 may well have been due to his political connections. He is known to have been on good terms with Thomas Parker, earl of Macclesfield (1666–1732); a letter from Mandeville to the former lord chancellor (in 1726) reports details of Mandeville's son's illness and refers familiarly to Macclesfield's family (Mandeville, *Fable*, 1.xxvi–xxvii; letter reproduced facing p. xxvii).

There were further editions of *The Fable of the Bees* during Mandeville's life in 1724, 1725, 1728, 1729, and 1732. *A modest defence of publick stews, or, An essay upon whoring as it is now practis'd in these kingdoms* (1724), which advocates a scheme of public houses of prostitution, is generally attributed to Mandeville, partly on the basis of remark H of the *Fable*, which notes the wisdom of the Amsterdam authorities in tolerating 'Temples of Venus' complete with organ music. Nevertheless the attribution has not been firmly established, especially since the *Modest Defence* was entered in the Stationers' register (13 July 1724) to Lawrence Lefever, who signed 'Law Lafevre' (Goldsmith, *Private Vices*, 149–50). Mandeville also published some short essays in the *St James's Journal* (20 April, 1 May 1723) and the *British Journal*

(27 April–4 May 1725). The latter were collected and published as *An enquiry into the causes of the frequent executions at Tyburn, and, A proposal for some regulations concerning felons in prison, and the good effects to be expected from them* (1725).

Later works *The Fable of the Bees, Part II* (1729) 'by the Author of the First', was in fact an entirely new work. In six dialogues Mandeville has Cleomenes persuade Horatio that the *Fable* is an entirely moral and religious work which has been grossly misrepresented. In addition to explaining and defending the *Fable* and quoting a number of passages from it, the work develops an extensive 'conjectural history' of how human beings developed from savagery to civilization. Now postulating two basic instinctive drives, self-love (the desires aiming at self-preservation) and self-liking (replacing pride and shame), Mandeville explained how society, language, and the arts and sciences gradually developed over a long period of time. Humans came to live together to defend themselves against wild animals; they then developed restrictions on their actions to control the conflicts arising from their striving for superiority over each other; the third step to society was the invention of written language. It turns out that the material arrangements and social institutions at which humans have arrived have been the result of the 'joynt Labour of many Ages' rather than of the literal machinations of 'skilful politicians' (Goldsmith, *Private Vices*, 63–77). Both Cleomenes' account of the development of civilization from savagery and his naturalistic explanation of the origins of religion implicitly undermine the literal truth of the Bible. Horatio challenges Cleomenes, Mandeville's designated spokesman, to explain how there can be savage peoples if all humans originated from a single source (Mandeville, *Fable*, 2.196–9) and accuses him of inconsistency in accepting Moses's divine inspiration and the miracle of Adam and Eve, created as perfect humans with language, while rejecting the equally fabulous pagan myths (ibid., 306–12). There were further editions of *Part II* in 1730 and 1733. After that the *Fable* and *Part II* were published as if they were a single work in two volumes.

Mandeville went on to produce a further set of dialogues between the same interlocutors: *An Enquiry into the Origin of Honour, and, The Usefulness of Christianity in War* (1732). In the book Mandeville repeated his view that the passions of pride and shame are both forms of self-liking. Honour and (worldly) religion are treated as devices that are useful for socializing humans. Honour is discovered to be even less demanding than virtue or the artificial courage discussed in the *Fable of the Bees*. The work again reveals Mandeville's anti-clericalism in his account of how a perverted version of the truly peaceful doctrine of Christianity can be used to motivate soldiers.

Mandeville's last work was a pamphlet entitled *A Letter to Dion, Occasion'd by his Book call'd 'Alciphron', or, 'The Minute Philosopher'* (1732). In the second dialogue in his *Alciphron* (1732), George Berkeley had lampooned Mandeville through Lysicles, a conceited but intellectually shallow, antinomian freethinker and atheist. Not only did the *Letter* contend that Berkeley was mistaken about the views

expressed in the *Fable of the Bees*, which Mandeville reiterated, contending that they were entirely consistent with strict morality and true Christianity, but also it maintained that a person of Berkeley's intelligence and character could only have so mischaracterized the doctrine of the *Fable* because he had accepted common reports of the work rather than actually having read it himself.

Death On 21 January 1733 Mandeville died in Hackney, possibly of influenza. His will, dated 2 April 1729 (reproduced in Mandeville, *Fable*, 1, after p. xx), left 20 shillings to his daughter for a ring, £100 out of £500 of South Sea annuities to his wife, and the remainder of the annuities and the rest of his estate to his son. An annotation on the will indicated that he had been living in the parish of St Stephen's, Coleman Street. He requested that he be buried 'as near by and in as private a manner as shall be consistent with the cheapest Decency'.

There are no known portraits of Mandeville and the only authentic contemporary personal report about him we have is by Benjamin Franklin: Dr Lyons (a surgeon and author of *The Infallibility of Human Judgment*) 'carried me to The Horns pale ale house in — Lane, Cheapside, and introduc'd me to Dr Mandeville, Author of the Fable of the Bees, who had a Club there, of which he was the Soul, being a most facetious entertaining Companion' (*Franklin's Memoirs*, 110; Mandeville, *Fable*, 1.xxix).

Responses to the *Fable* Mandeville's *Fable* evoked a number of responses (see references to Mandeville's works up to 1923 in *Fable*, 2.418–53). Robert Burrow seems to have been the earliest of Mandeville's contemporary critics to publish, preaching against the *Fable* in a sermon before the lord mayor in September 1723, *Civil Society and Government Vindicated* (1723), alluded to in Mandeville's preface. Sermons and essays by William Barnes (preached March 1724, published 1727), William Hendley (1725), Samuel Chandler (1728), and Isaac Watts (1728), specifically defended charity schools, claiming that they promoted loyalty and religion or that they did not educate children beyond their stations. But many replies to the *Fable* also objected more generally to its denigration of rational morality, irreligious tone, or apparent justification of vice. William Law, in *Remarks on a Late Book* (1724), Richard Fiddes, in the preface to his *General Treatise of Morality* (1724), and John Thorold, in *A Short Examination of the Notions Advanc'd in a Late Book* (1726), all attacked the *Fable* in defence of religion and morality. John Dennis, in *Vice and Luxury Publick Mischiefs* (1724), saw the *Fable* as attack on virtue, liberty, and religion. George Bluet's extensive *Enquiry whether a general practice of virtue tends to the wealth or poverty, benefit or disadvantage of a people?* (1725) disputed many of Mandeville's contentions. *The True Meaning of the 'Fable of the Bees'* (1726) did not defend the book but claimed that Bluet had missed the point: the *Fable* really favoured domination by a select few who reaped the benefit of others' vices.

There were other substantial replies in addition to Berkeley's caricature of Mandevilleans in *Alciphron*. Alexander Innes's *Arete-Logia* (1728), a plagiarized version of

Archibald Campbell's *Enquiry into the Original of Moral Virtue* (1733) with his own preface challenging Mandeville to burn his book, as he had promised, should it be shown to be immoral. Innes's advertisements falsely reported that Mandeville had actually done so.

Francis Hutcheson's title-page to his *Inquiry into the Original of our Ideas of Beauty and Virtue* (1725) purported to defend Shaftesbury and oppose the *Fable*, but only a few passages were explicitly concerned with Mandeville. Hutcheson, a Presbyterian and a member of the 'old whig' Molesworth circle, extended his attack on the *Fable* in the following year in the *Dublin Journal*. He identified five distinct meanings of Mandeville's paradox and contended that the social affections and virtues were natural, conducive to happiness, and consistent with prosperity. The criticism was republished in James Arbuckle's edition of *A collection of letters and essays on several subjects, lately publish'd in the 'Dublin Journal'* (1729) and again in *Reflections on Laughter and Remarks on the 'Fable of the Bees'* (1750); the basic view is repeated in Hutcheson's posthumous *A System of Moral Philosophy* (1755).

Mandeville's views were so widely known in the eighteenth century that there is scarcely any intellectual at the time who did not at least mention them. His conjectural history of society and language, emphasis on the role of the passions rather than reason, and claims that progress and commercial civilization were founded on necessary and beneficial vices set the terms for further moral, historical, and economic discussion in the Enlightenment. At the beginning of his *Treatise of Human Nature* David Hume named Mandeville among significant moral philosophers, while denying in the *Enquiry into the Principles of Morals* as well as in the *Treatise* that moral distinctions were entirely the artifice of politicians. His essays 'On refinement in the arts' (originally 'Of luxury') and 'Of the dignity or meanness of human nature' explore Mandevillean themes. Adam Smith devoted a chapter of *The Theory of Moral Sentiments* to rebutting Mandeville's moral theory but adopted some of his descriptions of commercial society in the *Wealth of Nations*. The defence of luxury by Voltaire in *Le mondain* and by Jean François Melon in his *Défense de 'Le mondain'* relied on Mandeville. In the *Discours sur les sciences et les arts* and the *Discours sur l'origine et les fondements de l'inégalité parmi les hommes*, Jean-Jacques Rousseau accepted that material progress coincided with a shift in morality away from primitive simplicity, treating the change as moral decline. Later in the century Mandeville's accounts of human nature and historical development were also used in the work of Immanuel Kant.   M. M. GOLDSMITH

Sources B. Mandeville, *The fable of the bees, or, Private vices, publick benefits*, ed. F. B. Kaye, 2 vols. (1924) [incl. account of life and works] • B. Mandeville, *By a society of ladies: essays in The Female Tatler*, ed. M. M. Goldsmith (1999) • R. Dekker, '"Private vices, public virtues" revisited: the Dutch background of Bernard Mandeville', trans. G. T. Moran, *History of European Ideas*, 14 (1992), 481–98 • M. M. Goldsmith, *Private vices, public benefits: Bernard Mandeville's social and political thought* (1985) • W. A. Speck, 'Bernard Mandeville and the Middlesex grand jury', *Eighteenth-Century Studies*, 11 (1977–8), 362–74 • *Benjamin Franklin's memoirs*, ed. M. Farrand and W. T. Franklin, trans. L. G. Le Veillard (1949) • G. Clark and A. M. Cooke, *A history of the Royal College of Physicians of London*, 1–2 (1964–6) • H. J. Cook, 'Bernard Mandeville and the therapy of "the clever politician"', *Journal of the History of Ideas*, 60 (1999), 101–24 • M. M. Goldsmith, 'Regulating anew the moral and political sentiments of mankind: Bernard Mandeville and the Scottish Enlightenment', *Journal of the History of Ideas*, 49 (1988), 587–606 • E. J. Hundert, *The Enlightenment's fable: Bernard Mandeville and the discovery of society* (1994) • J. M. Stafford, ed., *Private vices, publick benefits? The contemporary reception of Bernard Mandeville* (1997) • I. Primer, ed., *Mandeville studies: new explorations in the art and thought of Dr Bernard Mandeville* (1975) • F. McKee, 'Honeyed words: Bernard Mandeville and medical discourse', *Medicine in the Enlightenment*, ed. R. Porter (1995) • F. McKee, 'Francis Hutcheson and Bernard Mandeville', *Eighteenth-Century Ireland*, 3 (1988), 123–32 • M. M. Goldsmith, '"The treacherous arts of mankind": Bernard Mandeville and female virtue', *History of Political Thought*, 7 (1986), 93–114 • parish register (marriage), Westminster, St Giles-in-the-Fields, 1 Feb 1699

Wealth at death approximately £500 of South Sea annuities and other property: will, 2 April 1729, repr. in B. Mandeville, *Fable of the bees*, ed. Kaye, vol. 1, after p. xx

Mandeville, Geoffrey de, first earl of Essex (*d.* 1144), magnate, was the son and heir of William de Mandeville, constable of the Tower of London, and Margaret, daughter of Eudo de Ryes, royal *dapifer* ('steward') and lord of Colchester. According to a charter of the 1140s in favour of Geoffrey de Mandeville, his paternal grandfather, also Geoffrey, had been constable of the Tower and sheriff of Essex, London and Middlesex, and Hertfordshire. The elder Geoffrey de Mandeville was one of William I's wealthier tenants-in-chief, eleventh (and last) among Corbett's 'Class A' Domesday landholders, with lands worth a total of £740 a year concentrated in Essex, Middlesex, and Hertfordshire, and extending into seven other counties. Unlike the ten other 'Class A' magnates, all of whom came from prominent continental families, Geoffrey and his family were of such minor importance before the conquest that their place of origin in Normandy defies certain identification. It may have been Colmesnil-Manneville (*arrondissement* Dieppe, *canton* Offranville) but it is impossible to be certain: place names such as Manneville, Magna Villa, and Magnevilla occur in France with perplexing frequency.

Loss of the family estates It was during the constableship of William de Mandeville that Henry I's dangerous prisoner, Ranulf Flambard, bishop of Durham, escaped from the Tower of London early in 1101 and fled to Normandy. There Ranulf served as chief organizer of Robert Curthose's invasion of England in summer 1101 that nearly cost Henry his newly won crown. For his carelessness (or worse) William de Mandeville was burdened with an immense fine of more than £2200 and was forced to relinquish his three most valuable demesne manors—Sawbridgeworth, Hertfordshire, and Walden and Great Waltham, Essex—until the debt was paid in full. The Domesday value of these manors (£50, £50, and £60 respectively) amounted to about a third of the value of the entire Mandeville demesne in England (£489), and their confiscation therefore thrust the Mandeville family from the upper ranks of the English aristocracy.

At some time between 1103 and 1105, but probably in

1103, Henry I notified the chief men of Essex and Hertfordshire that, until such time as the debt was repaid, he had granted custody of the three Mandeville manors to his loyal follower and steward Eudo de Ryes, whose daughter Margaret was William de Mandeville's wife. Thus control of the three manors remained in the family but out of William de Mandeville's reach. At his death some time between 1105 and 1116 his son Geoffrey, probably still a minor, stood to inherit only a truncated portion of his ancestral Domesday honour. The pipe roll of 1130 discloses that Geoffrey was burdened with a substantial relief (1300 marks in 1129) for what remained of his inheritance. His chances of having the three lost manors restored to him had been much reduced by the marriage of his widowed mother, Margaret de Ryes, to the royal favourite Othuer fitz Earl, the natural son of Hugh, earl of Chester and vicomte d'Avranches, and the tutor of Henry I's only legitimate son, William Ætheling. Othuer appears to have come into possession of the three forfeited manors well before the death of Eudo de Ryes in February 1120, and he had also acquired William de Mandeville's former constableship of the Tower of London. Besides these Mandeville assets Othuer probably stood to inherit some or all of the cross-channel estates of his father-in-law, Eudo, thus ascending to the heights of the Anglo-Norman aristocracy while Geoffrey de Mandeville floundered. But Othuer's rise was cut short by his death, along with that of his royal pupil, in the wreck of the *White Ship* in November 1120.

As a result of the disaster, which severely damaged Henry I's plans for the peace of north-western Europe, the lands of Eudo de Ryes escheated to the crown and the three Mandeville manors reverted to the king. The constableship of the Tower passed to a certain Aschuill, probably Hasculf de Tanis (south-west of Avranches), who may have been a kinsman of Othuer. The shipwreck also opened prospects for Mandeville. The death of his stepfather meant that he might hope once again to recover the family fortune.

Constableship of the Tower of London   Mandeville's attestations of three royal charters during Henry I's final year in Normandy suggest that he was seeking to rise through service in the king's military *familia* during Henry's campaign against Guillaume Talvas. His hopes remained unrealized at Henry I's death in December 1135 and in the initial years of Stephen's reign, when Hasculf continued to command the Tower and the three confiscated manors remained under royal control.

Mandeville's fortunes suddenly improved in 1139–40, at a time when the spread of rebellion far and wide across the land compelled King Stephen to delegate much of his regional power to a flock of newly created earls. Between 1138 and 1141 he added no less than eighteen earldoms to the eight that had existed at the close of Henry I's reign. One of the new earls was Geoffrey de Mandeville whom Stephen appointed earl of Essex in a charter issued at Westminster probably between December 1139 and December 1140. It was at about this time, and perhaps as a result of the charter, that Mandeville recovered his ancestral right to the constableship of the Tower of London.

According to the late testimony of William of Newburgh, which most historians have accepted at least guardedly, King Stephen, having negotiated the betrothal of Constance, sister of Louis VII of France, to his own son Eustace, suffered humiliation at Mandeville's hands when the latter seized Constance while she and her mother-in-law, the Queen Matilda, were in London *c*.1141. Mandeville, who was then (according to Newburgh) constable of the Tower, kept Constance as his prisoner despite Matilda's urgent protests, until at length he yielded to King Stephen's demand that she be released. Newburgh believed that Stephen, although disguising his anger for the time being, never forgave Mandeville for the affront.

Defection from King Stephen: a disputed chronology   The rise of Mandeville to the height of his power is documented by four charters—two from Stephen, including the aforementioned grant of the earldom of Essex, and two from the Empress Matilda. Round dated these charters in the order of ascending benefits to Mandeville and then reached the fearlessly circular conclusion that Mandeville gained greater benefits from each successive charter:

> To determine from internal evidence the sequence of these charters, we must arrange them in ascending scale. That is to say, each charter should represent an advance on its immediate predecessor … We find each successive change of side on the part of this unscrupulous magnate marked by a distinct advance in his demands and in the price he obtained.   (Round, 43, 98)

Playing one side against the other in the most ruthless and devious fashion, so Round supposed, Mandeville was thus 'the most perfect and typical presentment of the feudal and anarchic spirit that stamps the reign of Stephen' (Round, v). Having obtained from Stephen's first charter (usually designated S1) the earldom of Essex, Mandeville then received from the Empress Matilda (midsummer 1141, Westminster) a recognition of his right to the earldom and to the third penny of the shire, along with a grant in fee and heredity of all the lands of his grandfather Geoffrey de Mandeville, including presumably the three lost manors (the castle of Walden is mentioned explicitly), the hereditary shrievalty and chief justiciarship of Essex, the crown manors of Maldon and Newport in that shire, and other properties (M1). Next on Round's list is King Stephen's second charter (S2), dated Christmas 1141 at Canterbury, after the king's release from imprisonment following his capture at the battle of Lincoln on 2 February 1141. Stephen confirmed in this charter all that Mandeville had received from the empress in M1, along with the Essex manors of Writtle and Hatfield and certain escheated lands, worth collectively £300 a year, an additional fee of sixty knights along with other lands, and the shrievalty and justiciarship of Hertfordshire and of London and Middlesex. Finally, in the empress's second charter, issued at Oxford between mid-1141 and mid-1142 (M2), Mandeville obtained in addition to the aforesaid grants (including once again all the lands held by his grandfather

Geoffrey and his father, William), the lands of his grand-father Eudo de Ryes in both Normandy and England and Eudo's office of royal *dapifer*.

Round's ordering of these four charters was challenged in 1964 by R. H. C. Davis (*EngHR*, 79), who accepted, more or less, Round's dating of S1, M1, and S2, but dated M2 July 1141, thus placing it before S2 and reducing Mandeville's shifts in allegiance from three to two. If Davis is correct, Mandeville defected from Stephen only after the king had been taken captive at Lincoln in February 1141 and had released his adherents from their allegiance to him. Mandeville had then returned to Stephen's cause after the empress had been driven out of London. If this chronology is correct, Mandeville had precisely followed the shifts in allegiance of Stephen's own brother, Henry, bishop of Winchester, who in fact attested M1 for the empress.

Davis's chronology of the four charters—S1, M1, M2, S2—was challenged in 1988 by J. O. Prestwich, who argued cogently for a return to Round's sequence—S1, M1, S2, M2—indicating three changes of allegiance rather than only two. The disagreement turns on the question of whether M2 was issued (at Oxford) in July 1141 (Davis) or between January and June 1142 (Round and Prestwich). The factors to be considered in dating this charter are complex and depend in part on whether the persons listed as 'hostages' were or were not present. Davis's analysis of correspondences between attestors of M2 and persons attesting for the empress at Oxford in July 1141 is very persuasive. But just as persuasive are Prestwich's arguments that Geoffrey de Mandeville, far from epitomizing the 'feudal and anarchic spirit', was a royalist who, in the tradition of his family, sought advancement through service to the king. The freewheeling Ranulf (II), earl of Chester, whom Round regarded as a kindred spirit to Mandeville, was in fact his opposite—Ranulf was a magnate who sought independence from royal authority whereas Mandeville sought royal service and royal offices.

In view of the royal ministries held by Mandeville's father and paternal grandfather, and by his sons, Geoffrey and William de Mandeville, *curiales* of Henry II, Mandeville, as Prestwich sees him, fits into place. He was clearly self-seeking, and Prestwich is convincing in viewing him as striving for the recovery and advancement of his fortunes and those of his family through service to the king. Significantly he married Rohese de Vere, daughter of another ambitious royal servant, Henry I's great *curialis* Aubrey de Vere, master chamberlain of England. Mandeville fought in the royal cause at the siege of Winchester in September 1141. At King Stephen's command he drove a band of rebels from the Isle of Ely early in 1142. The author of the *Gesta Stephani* described him at that time as:

> remarkable for the ability of his shrewd mind and to be admired for the firmness of his unbending courage in adversity and his excellence in the art of war. In the extent of his wealth and the splendour of his position he surpassed all the chief men of the kingdom ... Everywhere in the kingdom he took the king's place and in all transactions was listened to more eagerly than the king and received more obedience when he gave orders.   (*Gesta Stephani*, 161)

His high status aroused the jealousy of other royal councillors, who persuaded the king to arrest him at the royal court at St Albans in September 1143. Stephen, who may not have forgiven him for seizing Constance of France in 1141, was sympathetic to his enemies at court. Mandeville responded to their accusations of treason with mocking contempt, but the king suddenly had him arrested and forced him to relinquish all his castles and lands. He was then released, 'to the ruin of the realm', said the author of the *Gesta Stephani*.

Mandeville would have regarded himself as being betrayed by Stephen, for the customs of the time prohibited a lord from arresting a *fidelis* in attendance at his court. (Stephen had similarly betrayed Roger of Salisbury and his kinsmen four years earlier in precisely the same way, and he arrested Ranulf, earl of Chester, at his court in 1146.) Earl Geoffrey hurled himself away from the royal court 'like a vicious and riderless horse, kicking and biting'. Gathering his knights and other followers around him he took up arms against the king. He 'raged everywhere with fire and sword; he devoted himself with insatiable greed to the plundering of flocks and herds' (*Gesta Stephani*, 165). He sacked Cambridge, looting its churches, and pillaged the Isle of Ely. He sacked Ramsey Abbey and made it his headquarters. With the help of his brother-in-law William de Say, and eventually of Hugh Bigod, earl of Norfolk (d. 1176/7), he dominated the fenland and terrorized East Anglia.

Death and reputation In August 1144 Mandeville was fatally wounded while attacking the royal stronghold of Burwell, and he died on 26 September at Mildenhall in Suffolk. Having been excommunicated for the desecration and plundering of church property, he remained unburied for nearly twenty years until, at the instigation of his son Geoffrey, Pope Alexander III absolved him in 1163 and he was interred at the New Temple in London.

Although he died in rebellion, Geoffrey de Mandeville was by no means the incorrigibly turbulent baron that he was so long thought to be. He was clearly determined to make good his father's losses and advance his family's interests, but almost to the end he sought to do so in the service of the monarchy. His changes in allegiance during the anarchy were prompted in whole or in part by Stephen's capture at the battle of Lincoln, after which he was no more disloyal to the king than Stephen's own brother, Henry of Winchester.

Geoffrey left three known sons. The eldest, Ernulf, was illegitimate. With his wife, Rohese de Vere, he had Geoffrey (d. 1166) and William de *Mandeville (d. 1189), who were successively earls of Essex and important *curiales* of Henry II. In restoring the earldom of Essex to the younger Geoffrey de Mandeville in 1156 Henry II granted him, among other things, perpetual hereditary right to Walden, Sawbridgeworth, and Great Waltham: 'And the lien that my grandfather King Henry had on the aforesaid three manors is quitclaimed forever' (Round, 235–6, 241).

C. WARREN HOLLISTER

Sources C. W. Hollister, *Monarchy, magnates, and institutions in the Anglo-Norman world* (1986), 117–27 · GEC, *Peerage* · J. H. Round, *Geoffrey de Mandeville: a study of the anarchy* (1892) · R. H. C. Davis, *From Alfred the Great to Stephen* (1991) · J. O. Prestwich, 'The treason of Geoffrey de Mandeville', *EngHR*, 103 (1988), 283–312 · R. H. C. Davis, 'The treason of Geoffrey de Mandeville: a comment', *EngHR*, 103 (1988), 313–17 · J. O. Prestwich, 'Geoffrey de Mandeville: a further comment', *EngHR*, 103 (1988), 960–66 · R. H. C. Davis, 'Geoffrey de Mandeville: a final comment', *EngHR*, 103 (1988), 967–8 · *Reg. RAN*, vol. 3 · Ordericus Vitalis, *Eccl. hist.*, 6.444–6 · Dugdale, *Monasticon*, new edn · R. Howlett, ed., *Chronicles of the reigns of Stephen, Henry II, and Richard I*, 1, Rolls Series, 82 (1884) · K. R. Potter and R. H. C. Davis, eds., *Gesta Stephani*, OMT (1976) · K. S. B. Keats-Rohan, 'The prosopography of post-conquest England: four case studies', *Medieval Prosopography*, 14 (1993), 1–52, esp. 8–12 · W. J. Corbett, 'The development of the duchy of Normandy and the Norman conquest of England', *Cambridge medieval history*, 5, ed. J. R. Tanner, C. W. Previté-Orton, and Z. N. Brooke (1926), 481–520 · *The historical works of Gervase of Canterbury*, ed. W. Stubbs, 1: *The chronicle of the reigns of Stephen, Henry II, and Richard I*, Rolls Series, 73 (1879), 128 · R. H. C. Davis, 'Geoffrey de Mandeville reconsidered', *EngHR*, 79 (1964), 299–307

Mandeville, Sir John (*supp. fl. c.*1357), supposed writer, was assumed to have written the *Voyages de Jehan de Mandeville chevalier*, which appeared anonymously in France *c.*1357; the name of the work's author is unknown. The book is a vernacular account of the known world, loosely based upon the alleged travels of its narrator, and was immediately and immensely popular. Alongside the French version and its recensions there were translations (often more than one) into German, English, Italian, Dutch, Spanish, Irish, Danish, and Czech. Altogether over 250 manuscripts survive in twenty-two versions. In England alone there were four Latin and four English translations and a rhymed version. In the book the narrator declares that he is Sir John Mandeville, born and bred in St Albans, who left England in 1322 and travelled the world for many years, serving the sultan of Cairo and visiting the Great Khan, and finally in 1357 in age and illness setting down his account of the world. This account is essentially in two parts, a description of the Holy Land and the routes thither and a description of Asia and other *partes infidelium*. There is no historical corroboration of the author's claims. On the contrary, nine-tenths of the substance of the *Voyages* can be precisely traced to written sources, which range from Pliny to Vincent of Beauvais and include many itineraries of genuine travellers like William of Boldensele and Odoric of Pordenone, and the remaining tenth almost certainly derives from sources yet to be traced. The intention of the author to produce a popular account of the world in French was possibly part of the fashion for such exotica that flourished in and about Paris *c.*1350. Though the framework of the narration by Sir John Mandeville is fictitious, the substance is not. There can be no doubt whatsoever that the author reported in good faith what his authorities recorded and that his book was seriously intended.

The fiction of the author as a genuine English knight–adventurer easily imposed itself on the middle ages. Even the Benedictine Thomas Walsingham lists Mandeville in his *Annales* among the worthies of St Albans; long resident at St Albans Abbey and in the best possible position to investigate the identity of the author, he was as a professional historian content to take the book at its face value. Consequently it is no surprise to find posthumous grafts on the story. At St Albans an effigy of Mandeville in armour was erected and later replaced with a plaque with verses, and various 'relics' of the traveller were on display. At the Benedictine cathedral priory at Canterbury a forged letter from Sir John Mandeville of *c.*1450 appeared to authenticate a piece of *lignum aloes* which the traveller allegedly brought back from a river flowing out of the earthly paradise, and this and other associated 'relics' including an apple miraculously preserved in a crystal orb were shown to the faithful and reported by John Leland. Such inventions helped to sustain the myth of a historical Sir John Mandeville which, despite the disclosure of his sources and his literary context, commands credence in some quarters.

One variation of this myth developed in Liège and ran an extraordinary course. Shortly after the death in 1372 of Jean de Bourgogne, a physician and author of a plague tract, there appeared in Liège a recension of the French version which claimed that Mandeville wrote his book at Liège at the request of Jean de Bourgogne. A Latin translation of this French recension developed this claim *c.*1375, describing a meeting between author and physician in Cairo when both were in the service of the sultan. Behind both claims lies the imagination of Jean d'Outremeuse (*d.* 1400), a Liège chronicler and notary much given to literary fantasies. He extended his fictions even further by writing in his *Myreur des histors* (*c.*1388) that on his deathbed Jean de Bourgogne revealed that he was Sir John Mandeville, 'count of Montfort', who had lived in retirement at Liège since 1343 (thus somewhat curtailing the length of his alleged travels). Even later, in his *Tresorier de philosophie* (*c.*1390), d'Outremeuse cited Mandeville as one of the authorities of his lapidary and claimed that he possessed the gems that were given to Mandeville during his stay in Alexandria. One manuscript of the Liège recension (Musée Condé, Chantilly MS 699) contains four short tracts (a cosmography, a cosmology, a herbal, and a lapidary) allegedly written by Mandeville.

One consequence of these stories was that an epitaph to Sir John Mandeville, with an engraved device resembling the coat of arms of the Montforts, was erected in the Guillelmin church at Liège where Jean de Bourgogne was buried. Another consequence was that a house in Liège which in 1388 had been described as formerly the lodging of Master Jean à la Barbe was in 1459 described as formerly the lodging of Sir John Mandeville. The chronology of the successive accretions of the d'Outremeuse version of the Mandeville myth is plainly obvious, but his fictions still have their champions.

Those who seek a scholarly investigation of authorship must, in the absence of other evidence, search the original French version of the book and its bibliographical context and disregard the embroideries of various redactors, editors, translators, and romancers. Detailed analysis of this primary record reveals that the author had no knowledge of St Albans but was a fluent French-speaker; that he composed his work c.1357 in a large, almost certainly ecclesiastical, library; that he was an ecclesiastic, with a cleric's knowledge of the Bible, and probably a member of a regular order; that he was a fluent reader of Latin but lacked any knowledge of Greek or Arabic; that he was an informed and intelligent reader of books describing the Holy Land and other foreign parts; that he had mastered the theories of Sacrobosco and his commentators, possibly at the University of Paris, on the rotundity of the world and was aware of the possibility of circumnavigation; that he had never travelled to the lands he describes; that he was aware of current French accounts of foreign lands and was in a position to launch his own work into the mainstream of the Parisian book-trade.

This coherent picture of an anonymous religious, perhaps the librarian of his house, is strengthened by certain parallels between his work and one of his major sources, the translations of Haiton, Odoric, William of Boldensele, and others made by Jean le Long (d. 1388), the librarian of the Benedictine abbey church of St Bertin at St Omer, then within the English pale and on the main route between Calais and Paris. Genuine pilgrims and travellers to the Mediterranean and the Near East habitually used this road and stayed at the abbey. Its library contained all the works used by Mandeville in the compilation of the *Voyages*, including the comparatively scarce French translation of the *Directorium ad faciendum passagium transmarinum* made by the hospitaller Jean de Vignay (c.1340). In such a context a Benedictine authorship is entirely possible and the nationality of the author an open question. English monks lived in French houses, especially within the pale, and there are some pointers towards an English presence in the book, though these are probably artful details to support the larger fiction. Whatever his identity, his work is more certainly part of English than of continental literature.   M. C. SEYMOUR

Sources M. C. Seymour, *Sir John Mandeville* (1993), vol. 1 of Authors of the Middle Ages

Mandeville, William de, third earl of Essex (d. 1189), magnate and courtier, was the second son of Geoffrey de *Mandeville, first earl of Essex (d. 1144), and Rohese de Vere. William inherited the earldom of Essex in 1166, after the death of his brother Geoffrey. Little is known of Mandeville's early years and training, but the Walden chronicler relates that he spent most of his youth at the court of the counts of Flanders, and received the belt of knighthood from the hands of Count Philip, Henry II's first cousin. Philip's warm recommendation of Mandeville was partly responsible for Henry's speedy transfer of the earldom to him. The Mandeville lands, from which the earldom had been created in 1141, formed one of the wealthiest honours in England (£740) at the time of Domesday Book, and by 1166 contained 110 knights' fees. The family's hereditary custodianship of the Tower of London and two valuable manors, however, were withheld from Mandeville. If he harboured any grievances

over this reduction of his inheritance, they never came to the surface; and he was more than compensated for their loss by his friendship with the king.

Earl William became a regular member of Henry II's entourage shortly after his investiture. His rise at court was due as much to his own considerable military and diplomatic skills as to the deaths of the king's earlier baronial advisers. And the bond of friendship that existed between the earl and king from the first never diminished. Throughout the 1170s and 1180s the earl was either at Henry's side, or engaged in royal business elsewhere. It is possible to trace his movements back and forth from England and the continent in the pipe rolls. Between 1173 and 1187 no fewer than nineteen channel crossings are recorded, some of them relating to embassies led by Mandeville to the courts of Flanders, France, and Germany. The high respect with which Mandeville was regarded by the Angevin court is illustrated by a passage from the *Histoire de Guillaume le Maréchal* (1.271–5). When in 1188 Philip Augustus of France suggested that he and Henry II should settle their differences through a trial by combat, William Marshal volunteered that the English champions should be himself and William de Mandeville.

There were many rewards for royal service. Over a twenty-two-year period, the minuscule sum of £174 was levied by the English exchequer against Mandeville in the form of scutages, aids, forest pleas, murder fines, and communal taxes. Of this amount, the sum of £3 was all that was ever paid into the exchequer, the remainder being pardoned. In contrast, Mandeville took more than £1600 from the exchequer in *terrae datae*, outright gifts, and the third penny of Essex. An even more valuable reward came to him through his marriage in 1180, arranged by Henry II, to *Hawisa (d. 1213/14), heir to the Anglo-Norman lands and fees of the counts of Aumale. Richard of Devizes characterizes the countess of Aumale as 'a woman who was almost a man, lacking nothing virile except virile organs' (*Chronicon Richardi Divisensis*, 10). Whatever the facts of the matter, the countess was a rich prize, bringing Mandeville the baronies of Holderness and Skipton in England and the county and castle of Aumale in Normandy.

Mandeville's possession of the county of Aumale established him as one of the great border barons along the sensitive eastern Norman frontier, and Henry meant to rely on the earl as the defender of that frontier. This design is revealed in two contemporary sources. The Walden chronicler, after discussing the earl's marriage, goes on to say that he 'was a brave man, mighty in arms and held in esteem by all; and therefore he abode little in England among his own people, but guarded the castles and fortifications in Normandy handed over to him by King Henry, which were stronger than the rest and situated along the frontier' (Dugdale, *Monasticon*, 4.144). A fragment from the Norman pipe roll of 1184 discloses that the castles in question were Gisors, Neaufle, Dangu, Neufchâteau, and Vaudreuil in the region of the Vexin and the Seine River above

Rouen. Henry II's trust was never betrayed and Earl William proved a valued ally in the ageing king's confrontations with his troublesome cousin Philip, count of Flanders.

From 1180 until his death in 1189 Henry II was involved in the tasks of maintaining the integrity of his vast dominions, finding a workable solution to the succession problem brought about by the unfortunate deaths of his elder sons, and preventing a dispute between Philip of Flanders and Philip of France from erupting into a large-scale war which might have upset the tenuous balance of power in western France. In this last endeavour he sought to utilize Earl William's long-standing friendship with the count to help manage the Franco-Flemish conflict. As late as 1177–8 the two boyhood companions had spent a full year in one another's company on crusade in the Holy Land. Indeed, the seals of Earl William and Count Philip from this period exhibit so many similarities that it is likely that the earl's was a close copy of the count's, perhaps even a gift. This friendship, without doubt, is why Henry chose the city of Aumale on at least two occasions for the site of peace talks he arranged between the warring parties, and it also explains why Mandeville was named receiver for Philip's English landed revenues while the count was in disfavour.

Earl William's final meeting with the king he had served so faithfully came a month before Henry's death in July 1189. At this meeting the earl was made to swear with William Fitzralph that if ill befell Henry, they would hand over the castles in their charge to no one except Prince John. John's lack of loyalty to his father in these final weeks released the earl from his oath. As it happened, Richard inherited the Angevin dominion intact, and like his father sought to use the earl's talents in their governance and defence. Mandeville carried the crown at Richard I's coronation on 3 September 1189, and a few days later, at the Council of Pipewell, Northamptonshire, the king named him chief justiciar jointly with Bishop Hugh of Durham. In November 1189 Richard I sent Mandeville on an embassy to the court of Philip of France. The earl never returned to England. Departing from Paris, he fell ill at Gisors and died shortly afterwards at Vaudreuil, five months after the passing of his benefactor and friend, Henry II. Although the earl had once expressed a wish to be buried in the Mandeville family priory of Walden, his men deemed a winter crossing of the channel too dangerous and he was laid to rest at the Cistercian abbey of Mortemer near Aumale—a fitting burial place for one so closely connected with the Angevin royal house, since the abbey had been richly endowed by the Empress Matilda and Henry II, who were responsible for many of its buildings.

William was the last of the Mandevilles. The Countess Hawisa married in succession William de Forz (d. 1195) and Baldwin de Béthune (d. 1212), taking with her on each occasion the Aumale ancestral lands. The descent of the Mandeville honour and Essex earldom was much more complicated. William de Mandeville's aunt, Beatrice de Say, sister of Earl Geoffrey, stood to inherit. But by 1189 Beatrice was too old—almost eighty—to administer the earldom effectively. Her heirs were the daughters of her eldest son, William, who had died in 1177, and her youngest son, Geoffrey de Say. William clearly intended his cousin Geoffrey de Say to succeed him in the event of his dying, as happened, without children. However, the legality of the representative heir inheriting before the younger cadet, a dilemma similar to that faced by the Angevin house itself in the 1190s, eventually prevailed when Beatrice's son-in-law, the practised courtier Geoffrey fitz Peter, manipulated his way into possession of the earldom. Geoffrey, who later became justiciar of England, completed the takeover by having his children adopt the Mandeville surname, thus keeping alive, if only in name, the family's illustrious history of service to the Norman and Angevin rulers.

THOMAS K. KEEFE

Sources R. Howlett, ed., *Chronicles of the reigns of Stephen, Henry II, and Richard I*, 4, Rolls Series, 82 (1889), 3–315 • J. C. Robertson and J. B. Sheppard, eds., *Materials for the history of Thomas Becket, archbishop of Canterbury*, 7 vols., Rolls Series, 67 (1875–85) • W. Stubbs, ed., *Gesta regis Henrici secundi Benedicti abbatis: the chronicle of the reigns of Henry II and Richard I, AD 1169–1192*, 2 vols., Rolls Series, 49 (1867) • Ralph de Diceto, 'Ymagines historiarum', *Radulfi de Diceto … opera historica*, ed. W. Stubbs, 2 vols., Rolls Series, 68 (1876) • *Chronica magistri Rogeri de Hovedene*, ed. W. Stubbs, 4 vols., Rolls Series, 51 (1868–71) • *The historical works of Gervase of Canterbury*, ed. W. Stubbs, 2 vols., Rolls Series, 73 (1879–80) • *Gir. Camb. opera* • *Chronicon Richardi Divisensis / The Chronicle of Richard of Devizes*, ed. J. T. Appleby (1963) • W. Farrer and others, eds., *Early Yorkshire charters*, 12 vols. (1914–65), vol. 7 • P. Meyer, ed., *L'histoire de Guillaume le Maréchal*, 3 vols. (Paris, 1891–1901) • T. Stapleton, ed., *Magni rotuli scaccarii Normanniae sub regibus Angliae*, 2 vols., Society of Antiquaries of London Occasional Papers (1840–44), 1 • 'The foundation book of Walden Abbey', Dugdale, *Monasticon*, new edn, 4.141–4 • H. Hall, ed., *The Red Book of the Exchequer*, 3 vols., Rolls Series, 99 (1896) • A. Charlton, 'A study of the Mandeville family and estates', PhD diss., U. Reading, 1977 • M. Bouquet and others, eds., *Recueil des historiens des Gaules et de la France / Rerum Gallicarum et Francicarum scriptores*, 24 vols. (1738–1904) • *Pipe rolls*, 13 Henry II – 2 Richard I • T. K. Keefe, *Feudal assessments and the political community under King Henry II and his sons* (1983) • T. K. Keefe, 'King Henry II and the earls: the pipe roll evidence', *Albion*, 13 (1981), 191–222 • B. English, *The lords of Holderness, 1086–1260: a study in feudal society* (1979) • J. C. Holt, 'The "Casus Regis": the law and politics of succession in the Plantagenet dominions, 1185–1247', *Law in medieval life and thought*, ed. E. B. King and S. J. Ridyard (1990), 21–42 • R. V. Turner, 'The Mandeville inheritance, 1189–1236: its legal, political and social context', *Haskins Society Journal*, 1 (1989), 147–72 • T. A. Heslop, 'Seals as evidence for metal working in the later twelfth century', *Art and patronage in the English Romanesque*, ed. S. Macready and F. H. Thompson, Society of Antiquaries of London Occasional Papers, new ser., 8 (1986), 50–60, pl. xxva, xxvb • T. A. Heslop, 'Seals', *English romanesque art, 1066–1200*, ed. G. Zarnecki, J. Holt, and T. Holland (1984), 298–319, esp. 319, no. 376 [exhibition catalogue, Hayward Gallery, London, 5 April – 8 July 1984] • H. Collar, ed., 'The book of the foundation of Walden Abbey', trans. C. H. Emson, *Essex Review*, 45 (1936), 73–85, 147–56, 224–36; 46 (1937), 12–16, 88–98, 164–70, 227–34; 47 (1938), 36–41, 94–9, 150–55, 216–20 [BL, Arundel MS 29] • *Radulphi de Coggeshall chronicon Anglicanum*, ed. J. Stevenson, Rolls Series, 66 (1875) • *Feudalism and liberty: articles and addresses of Sidney Painter*, ed. F. A. Cazel (1961) • L. Landon, *The itinerary of King Richard I*, PRSoc., new ser., 13 (1935) • P. Latimer, 'The earls in Henry II's time', PhD diss., University of Sheffield, 1982

Manfield, Sir Moses Philip (1819–1899), shoe manufacturer and politician, was born on 26 July 1819 in Bristol, son of Moses Philip Manfield, a shoemaker. He came from a poor working-class household, and was supported by his mother after his father was paralysed. Unitarian in religion, his mother educated him herself until he was apprenticed at the age of twelve as a boot closer in a shoe manufacturing business, rising to become a manager.

In 1843 Manfield moved to Northampton as a manager but the business failed. With the help of local Unitarians in 1844 he established himself in business, specializing at this stage in the lower end of the market and government contracts. In 1845 he married Elizabeth Cambridge Newman (1819–1852); they had one child who did not survive. Elizabeth died in 1852 and in 1854 he married Margaret Milne (c.1821–1899), with whom he had two sons. In 1856 Manfield opened a large new warehouse to serve his outworkers but more work was gradually done indoors as the mechanization of the industry proceeded. However, even in the early 1890s the 630 indoor workers were outnumbered by outdoor workers employed by the firm. Under Manfield's chairmanship the firm of Manfield & Sons became one of the leading Northampton shoe manufacturing companies and an important influence on the wider development of the town and industry. In 1892 industry attention was attracted when he opened a large purpose-built factory capable of producing some 350,000 pairs of shoes a year. At that point Manfield relinquished day-to-day control of the firm to his sons, who had already established themselves as a key part of the family management team.

The firm remained at the forefront of technical change during Manfield's period of control. He saw both the productivity potential of new technology and its advantage in allowing closer workforce supervision within the factory. He was also a marketing innovator, seeing the value of branded goods and pioneering a chain of shops which numbered thirty at his death. The protracted mechanization of the industry, along with pressure on wages, created periodic labour discontent and as the leading Northampton manufacturer Manfield played a key role in organizing local producers in a Northampton chamber of commerce and then the Boot and Shoe Manufacturers' Association. After some bitter disputes, he encouraged union recognition and arbitration machinery which he later helped to develop elsewhere.

Manfield played an influential political role in a Liberal revival in Northampton and the wider county. He was a member of the Northampton Reform League in the late 1860s. Manfield initially opposed the official Liberal candidature of Charles Bradlaugh in Northampton, but supported him in his fight for his parliamentary seat; he subsequently succeeded Bradlaugh, serving with Henry Labouchere as one of the MPs for the town between 13 February 1891 and 8 July 1895. Manfield made a limited impact on parliament, but saw himself as a representative of a 'working class constituency' and a radical Liberal supporting Gladstone on home rule. He was far more influential in local politics, serving as a councillor from 1866 to 1877 before losing his seat as a result of divisions caused by the radical candidature of Bradlaugh. He served again as a

councillor from 1882 to 1892 and as mayor from 1883 to 1884. He was then involved in a dispute between the town and the government over the latter's refusal to accept a Liberal list for magistrates, but eventually was himself appointed to the bench.

Although Manfield was kindly regarded in his final years as the 'Grand Old Man', his brand of unevenly radical Liberalism was being undercut by the growth of a local socialist movement which was critical of the role of local employers as a class. He was knighted on 18 July 1894 and made a freeman of Northampton shortly before his death. With his wife he patronized many local causes, including the building of a new Unitarian church and school, which they financed shortly before their deaths. He was also involved in the National Educational Association.

Manfield died at his home, Redlands, Cliftonville, Northampton, on 31 July 1899 and was buried on 3 August at Northampton general cemetery. His wife died shortly before him on 12 July 1899.   MICHAEL HAYNES

Sources *Northampton Daily Reporter* (27 July 1899) · *Northampton Daily Reporter* (31 July 1899) · *Northampton Daily Reporter* (1 Aug 1899) · *Northampton Daily Reporter* (13 Aug 1899) · *Northampton Mercury* (4 Aug 1899) · *Northampton Herald* (5 Aug 1899) · *Boot and Shoe Trades Journal* (5 Aug 1899) · *Boot and Shoe Trades Journal* (12 Aug 1899) · K. Brooker, 'Manfield, Sir Moses Philip', *DBB* · W. E. Burnham, 'A century of shoemaking, 1844–1944', c.1944, Northampton Public Library [unpublished typescript] · W. E. Adams, *Our country* (1893) · 'Sir Philip Manfield: a romance in the leather world', *Fortunes made in business* (1905) · *The story of a British industry: Manfield & Sons* (c.1908) · *Hansard 4* (1893), 14.201 · *Where to buy at Northampton: an illustrated local review* (c.1891) · A. V. Eason, 'Saint Crispin's men', a history of Northamptonshire's shoemakers (1994) · d. cert.
Archives Manfield & Sons, Northampton, archives · Northants. RO, papers | Northants. RO, miscellaneous papers
Likenesses A. Hacker, oils, 1899, Northampton Museum · engraving, repro. in Eason, 'Saint Crispin's men'
Wealth at death £68,344 7s. 0d.: probate, 23 Dec 1899, CGPLA Eng. & Wales

Mangan, (James) Clarence (1803–1849), poet, was born James Mangan on 1 May 1803 at 3 Fishamble Street, Dublin, the second son of the grocers James Mangan (1765–1843), a native of Shanagolden, co. Limerick, and his wife, Catherine Smith (1771–1846), of Fishamble Street, daughter of John Smith of Kiltale, Meath. His father had been a hedge-school teacher before taking over the business of his wife's aunt Mary Farrell in Dublin, but after some years he found himself bankrupt through ill-advised speculations in property. There are many myths surrounding Mangan's early life, mostly created by himself in his unfinished *Autobiography* (written in 1848, published in 1960). However, it seems that the family not only endured extreme poverty, but also suffered from James Mangan's ill temper and frustrations. The young James Mangan sought refuge in books and became a loner. He was educated at a Jesuit school in Saul's Court, Dublin, where he learned the rudiments of Latin, Spanish, French, and Italian. He then attended three different schools until the age of fifteen, when he was obliged to obtain employment in order to support his parents, two younger brothers and a sister (the oldest son died in infancy).

For seven years Mangan worked as a scrivener in the Kenrick office at 6 York Street, Dublin. He was skilled at copying documents, but detested the harsh working conditions. At the same time he continued educating himself, reading widely and writing poetry. The poet James Tighe was his friend in the office, and together with Laurence Bligh they wrote riddles and rebus and puzzle poems for William Jones's two Dublin almanacs, *Grants* and the *New Ladies'*, calling themselves the 'diarians'. The first of Mangan's ephemeral poems was published in 1818. In 1826 his first nationalist poem was published in the *New Ladies' Almanac* as an enigma; it was later renamed 'To my Native Land'.

Mangan was not the friendless person he later claimed to have been, but his severe mood swings made him feel constantly alienated from other people. He also suffered from hypochondria and the fear that he would become insane. It is possible that he started to drink heavily and became addicted to alcohol and opium or laudanum early in life.

Nine months after his apprenticeship ended, in winter 1825–6, he found employment in a solicitor's office, Matthew Frank, at 28 Merrion Square North, Dublin, where his fellow clerks ridiculed him because of his eccentric behaviour. He became increasingly unhappy, withdrawing from his old friends and feeling suicidal.

Mangan never married, but he was infatuated or in love with a number of women including Catherine Hayes, whom he taught German. He was also madly in love with an auburn-haired woman called Frances, who did not reciprocate. In winter 1829–30, he suffered again from unrequited love: the object of his desire has never been identified although Yeats speculated erroneously that it was Margaret Stackpole. The affair threw him into a long period of deep depression, and Mangan's early biographers believed that he was so disappointed that he never loved again. But his addictions and isolation seem to be more likely reasons why he never married: he did propose to Margaret Stackpole in 1834 but she declined. They remained friends. Nevertheless he was so ill in 1829–30 that his brother John replaced him in the office. He found employment in the office of a solicitor, Thomas Leland, at 6 Fitzwilliam Square West, where he may have worked from 1830 to 1838. It seems that he was not unhappy there.

Mangan's first political involvement with the Irish nationalist movement dated from a repeal meeting of the law clerks of Dublin in 1830. In 1830–31 he became a member of the Comet Club, an anti-tithe organization, originally composed of twelve liberal protestant and Catholic men of fashion, and from 1832–3 he contributed humorous verse to their journal, *The Comet*, generally over the signature of 'Clarence', which he had previously adopted as his middle name. Mangan's biographers debate whether this name refers to the duke of Clarence in Shakespeare's *Richard III*, to Clarence Harvey in Maria Edgeworth's *Belinda*, or to both. From then on he was always known as (James) Clarence Mangan.

In 1830 Mangan published his first German translations in *The Friend*. He had mastered German in order to read German philosophy, and also worked as a tutor of German. His German was excellent, and he may have visited Germany in 1828–9. If he did, this was the only time in his life when he left Dublin (although he is also rumoured once to have visited Liverpool). In 1834 his first contribution to the *Dublin University Magazine* appeared, and hundreds of poems and prose pieces followed in the same periodical, the majority being translations of German poetry. However, these were often 'transformations' rather than literal translations. Mangan departed radically from the original, changing the poem into what he believed it was meant to be. Some of the 'translations' were far superior to the original, and a considerable number of them were his own poetry and had no German original at all. After 1836 he mainly published in the *Dublin University Magazine*. He also wrote for the *Dublin Monthly Magazine*, the *Dublin Penny Journal* (1832–4), and the *Dublin Satirist* (1833–6); the latter published some of his more serious poetry.

Mangan's poetry is characterized by inventive word play, challenging rhyme, schemes, and an emphasis on the ridiculous and grotesque, and Gothic and Romantic imagery. However, Dublin born and bred, Mangan was at the same time a true urban poet, using hardly any images from nature. One of his favourite figures was the lonely spectre, a lost soul, cursed to wander without hope as a punishment for his sins. He was also interested in masks and dubious identities. Because he experimented with verse techniques, was fascinated by extreme psychological distress, and was able to give frighteningly accurate descriptions of states of anxiety, he has sometimes been compared to his American contemporary Edgar Allan Poe.

In 1836 Mangan became acquainted with Charles Gavan Duffy. When he started editing the *Belfast Vindicator* in 1839 Mangan published some characteristically humorous pieces in it, using the signature of the 'Man in the Cloak'. A year later he began work on Middle Eastern poetry (Turkish, Persian, and Arabic), the *literae orientales*, in the *Dublin University Magazine*. However, he worked from other people's translations, since he was ignorant of those languages. In the same year John O'Donovan employed Mangan to make the printer's copy of the English translation of the *Annals of the Kingdom of Ireland by the Four Masters*. He had become a full-time employee of the Ordnance Survey in the summer of 1838, serving as a copyist under George Petrie, John O'Donovan, and Eugene O'Curry. All three had been involved in copying Irish manuscripts, and this acquaintance encouraged Mangan to investigate Irish documents and translate Irish poetry. However, since his Irish was not fluent enough, he relied on prose translations made for him by O'Curry, O'Donovan, and John O'Daly, which he then put into poetry. His first translation from the Irish appeared in George Petrie's *Irish Penny Journal* in 1840. Mangan worked at the Ordnance Survey until 1841, but his work was interrupted by fits of heavy drinking. At that time he was described as physically worn out and prematurely aged, wearing a huge pair of green spectacles for his weak eyes.

In 1842, on the request of Petrie, Dr James Henthorn Todd, fellow of Trinity College and librarian, employed Mangan as a library clerk for the work on the new library catalogue. He worked there full-time from 1842 to 1844, and then part-time until the end of 1846. John Mitchel remembered the first time he saw Mangan there in 1845:

> an acquaintance pointed out to me a man perched on the top of a ladder, with the whispered information that the figure was Clarence Mangan. It was an unearthly and ghostly figure in a brown garment; the same garment (to all appearance) which lasted till the day of his death. The blanched hair was totally unkempt; the corpse-like features still as marble; a large book was in his arms, and all his soul was in the book. (Mitchel, introduction to *Poems*, xxxv)

When *The Nation* was started in 1842, with Duffy as editor, Mangan wrote the poem 'The Nation's First Number'. Duffy gave him for a time a fixed salary, but already in November 1842, tensions between the two men arose over the authorship of the poem 'Fag an Bealach'. Deeply hurt, Mangan withdrew from the paper, and only after 1845 wrote more regularly for it, contributing patriotic verse and translations from German, Irish, French, and Spanish poetry in a column entitled 'Echoes of Foreign Song'. Mangan adopted various signatures in *The Nation*—'Terrae Filius', 'Vacuus', 'a Yankee', 'Monos', 'Mark Anthony', 'Hi-Hum', 'the Mourne-r', 'Lageniensis', and 'J. C. M.'— making it hard to attribute all his poems to him. He also supplemented his scanty income by working on a translation by his friend Owen Connellan, *Annals of the Kingdom of Ireland by the Four Masters*, for six months in 1844-5. In 1845 Duffy financed Mangan's *Anthologia Germanica*, a collection of previously published translations of German poetry. This was the only collection of his poetry published in his lifetime. From summer 1845-6 Mangan started writing for the staunch unionist *Irish Monthly Magazine*. This stood in contrast to his nationalist views, but he needed money desperately. He was no longer in full employment, and after the death of his father in 1843 he was the sole carer of his ailing mother, and also had to support his unemployed younger brother William.

Mangan is often seen as a rather unpolitical writer. However, he had a deep love for Ireland, and in 1846, disgusted by the famine, he fully committed himself to the nationalist cause, writing forceful patriotic poetry in *The Nation*, such as 'Dark Rosaleen (Roísín Dubh)', 'A Vision of Connaught in the Thirteenth Century', and 'A Warning Voice'. These poems gave him the recognition in Ireland he had not had before. By 1847 he was so poor that his friends collected money for him. His health declined further as his drinking grew worse. He started writing for the publisher James Duffy's *Irish Catholic Magazine* (1847), but the money he made from his poetry was not enough to feed him and his brother. When Duffy turned down his application for membership to the council of the Irish Confederation in February 1847, because he was not respectable enough, he was deeply hurt and again ceased writing for *The Nation* for some months.

When differences arose between Duffy and Mitchel, over Young Ireland policy, and Mitchel left *The Nation*,

Mangan followed him and wrote for his radical revolutionary paper the *United Irishman* in 1848: Mangan's political views were closer to Mitchel's revolutionary Romanticism than Duffy's pragmatism. In a letter to Mitchel in 1848 he stated: 'Insignificant an individual as I am … I thoroughly sympathise with your sentiments, that I identify my views of public affairs with yours, and that I am prepared to go all lengths with you … Yours, in life and death' (Mitchel, introduction to *Poems*, ed. O'Donoghue, xxxvii). Mitchel, unlike Duffy, was very understanding of Mangan's depression and addictions. But he recognized the 'two Mangans': 'one well known to the Muses, the other to the police; one soared through the empyrean and sought the stars—the other lay too often in gutters of Peter Street and Bride Street' (ibid., xxxv). After Mitchel's transportation Mangan wrote for the *Irish Tribune* (1848), edited by Richard Dalton Williams and Kevin Izod O'Doherty, and for *The Irishman* (1849), edited by Joseph Brenan, both radical papers which were quickly prohibited.

In May 1848 poverty and alcoholism led to Mangan's admission to St Vincent's Hospital. After he discharged himself prematurely in June 1848, he fell into the freshly sunk foundation of a house while drunk at night, and was taken to Richmond Surgical Hospital badly injured. Early in 1849 *The Pilot* carried an appeal by 'Honestus', describing Mangan's destitution and asking for donations. By that stage he either lived in shabby lodgings, or was homeless, and wrote his poetry, on a regular basis, in 'low public-houses', where he got pens and ink for free. He caught cholera in the epidemic that raged in Dublin in 1849, and in May spent some time in the cholera sheds of Kilmainham. Again, he discharged himself too early, and when his condition worsened he was taken to Meath Hospital, Long Street, Dublin, where he died on 20 June 1849. It seems that the primary cause of his death was long-term malnutrition. He was buried on 23 June 1849 in the family plot at Glasnevin cemetery, Dublin. Because of the cholera epidemic in Dublin and the imprisonment of many of his friends, only five people attended the funeral. Allegedly, a volume of German poetry, which he had been translating, was found in his pocket, and loose papers were found in his hat. However, it seemed that some of the papers he wrote in hospital were burnt by an overefficient nurse. A portrait of the dead Mangan was executed by F. W. Burton, and is in the National Gallery, Dublin.

James Clarence Mangan played a major part in establishing a distinctively Irish literature in English in the nineteenth century, but his input has often been overlooked for various reasons. A great number of Mangan's writings were published anonymously or under pseudonyms in obscure and short-lived magazines, and were very hard to trace. He also fell victim to his reputation as a poor and pathetic poet, which prevented his poems from being taken seriously. Often the focus was on his well-known patriotic songs, such as 'Dark Rosaleen', and his works were analysed primarily under a nationalist aspect. Furthermore, he has sometimes been seen simply as a translator and not as an original poet.

A collection of Mangan's poems, edited by John Mitchel, was published in 1859 with a biographical preface. A centenary edition of Mangan's poems and prose was issued by D. J. O'Donoghue in 1903–4, anticipating a renewed interest in him. Yeats called him 'our one poet raised to the first rank by intensity' (*Uncollected Prose of W. B. Yeats*, ed. J. P. Frayne, 1, 1970), and for Joyce he was 'the failed standard-bearer of a failed nation', but 'one of the world's most inspired poets' (*James Joyce: the Critical Writings*, ed. E. Mason and R. Ellmann, 1964). But despite Yeats's and Joyce's interest a proper reassessment of Mangan has not taken place. *The Collected Works of James Clarence Mangan* edited by Jacques Chuto, Rudolf Patrick Holzapfel, and Ellen Shannon-Mangan (4 vols., 1997) is the first systematic collection of Mangan's works. BRIGITTE ANTON

Sources E. Shannon-Mangan, *James Clarence Mangan: a biography* (Dublin, 1996) · B. Clifford, *The Dubliner: the lives, times and writings of James Clarence Mangan* (1988) · 'Fragment of an unpublished autobiography by James Clarence Mangan', *Irish Monthly* (1882), 675–89 · J. Mitchel, introduction, in *Poems of James Clarence Mangan*, ed. D. J. O'Donoghue (Dublin, 1922) · J. Kilroy, *James Clarence Mangan* (1970) · J. McCall, *The life of James Clarence Mangan* (1882); facsimile edn (Dublin, 1975) · *Songs, ballads and poems by famous Irishmen: James Clarence Mangan* [n.d.] · R. J. Hayes, *Manuscript sources for the history of Irish civilisation*, 3: *Persons L–O* (1965) · *Manuscript sources for the history of Irish civilisation, first supplement: 1965–1979*, 1: *Persons* (1979) · *DNB* · *The collected works of James Clarence Mangan: poems*, ed. J. Chuto and others, 4 vols. (1996–9) · *The collected works of James Clarence Mangan: prose*, ed. J. Chuto and others, 2 vols. (2002) · J. Chuto, *James Clarence Mangan: a bibliography* (Dublin, 1997)
Archives NL Ire., letters and poems, MS 138 · Royal Irish Acad., fragment of an autobiography, MS 12, p. 18 | NL Ire., collection of autograph letters and other papers, compiled by Revd T. Lee, incl. a translation of *Táin Bó Regomon* by Mangan and some of his letters, MS 4184 · NL Ire., letters to Charles Gavan Duffy, MSS 5756–5757 · Royal Irish Acad., letters to James Hardiman, incl. some of Mangan, MSS 12, N. 20–21 · Royal Irish Acad., letters to W. E. Hudson and others, concerning contributing to *The Nation*; a letter to O'Daly with an MS copy of a contribution to the *Belfast Vindicator*, MS 3, C.6 (1094) · TCD, Seumus O'Sullivan collection, note to Duffy, MS 4629
Likenesses silhouette, 1822, repro. in Chuto and others, ed., *The collected works of James Clarence Mangan: poems* (1997) · F. Burton, chalk drawing, 1849, NG Ire.; repro. in Kilroy, *James Clarence Mangan*; replica NG Ire. · C. Mills, pencil drawing, repro. in O'Donoghue, *Poems of James Clarence Mangan* · drawing, repro. in *Songs, ballads and poems by famous Irishmen*, frontispiece · drawing, repro. in J. McCall, *The life of James Clarence Mangan* (Dublin, 1975) · memorial bust, Stephen's Green, Dublin; repro. in O'Donoghue, *Poems of James Clarence Mangan*
Wealth at death poor, had never possessed anything of value; sheets of poetry allegedly found in pockets and hat after death: Kilroy *James Clarence Mangan*; Shannon-Mangan, *James Clarence Mangan*; O'Donoghue, *Poems*, *DNB* · did not hold onto possessions because wanted to 'travel light': Shannon-Mangan, *James Clarence Mangan*, p. 43

Mangey, Thomas (1683/4–1755), Church of England clergyman and classical scholar, was born in Leeds, Yorkshire, the son of Arthur Mangey, a goldsmith of Leeds. He was educated at the Leeds Free School, then entered St John's College, Cambridge, as a sizar in 1704, graduating BA in 1708 and MA in 1711. In 1715 he was granted a fellowship at St John's, which he resigned in 1718. He proceeded LLD in 1719, and in 1725 he was one of the seven who received a doctorate at the hands of Dr Bentley, when the latter delivered the famous oration subsequently prefixed to his edition of Terence.

Mangey received deacon's orders on 5 March 1710 and was ordained to the priesthood in November 1711. He held the rectory of Stanfield, Norfolk, in 1711–12, and that of St Nicholas's, Guildford, from 1717 to 1720. Subsequently he was presented with the vicarage of Ealing, Middlesex, which he resigned in 1754, and the rectory of St Mildred's, Bread Street, London, which he retained until his death. He became chaplain to the bishop of London, John Robinson, no later than 1719. When Robinson, at the request of Bishop Crew, consecrated Sunderland church, on 4 September 1719, Mangey preached the sermon 'The holiness of Christian churches', for which he may have been rewarded with a promotion to the fifth stall in Durham Cathedral in 1721, whence he moved to the first stall in January 1722. When treasurer of the chapter at Durham, he greatly advanced the fines upon the tenants, and improved the rents of his prebendal lands by nearly £100 a year. He married Dorothy (d. 1780), one of the daughters of John Sharp, archbishop of York, and they had a son, John, who was to enter the church too and be collated to the vicarage of Dunmow, Essex, by Bishop Secker. Thomas Mangey died at Durham on 6 March 1755, and was buried five days later in the east transept of the cathedral, where a monument stands to his memory. His epitaph was composed by John Sharp, his nephew by marriage, then official to the archdeaconry of Northumberland, who was to become a fully-fledged archdeacon, and a prebendary of Durham in his turn.

Mangey was an erudite philologist and a prolific writer. His great work was his bilingual edition, in Latin and Greek, of *Philonis Judaei opera*, with a copious critical footnote apparatus and a long preface in Latin (2 vols., 1742), which Edward Harwood considered as 'magnificent' even though he detected 'a very considerable number of inaccuracies' (Harwood, 76). The voluminous manuscript materials collected by Mangey for this edition, together with his collations of the different readings of scriptural and classical texts and his commonplace book, mostly written in Latin and Greek, bear witness to his meticulous scholarship.

Mangey's other printed works included polemical anti-deistic pamphlets. His *Remarks upon Nazarenus* (1718; 2nd edn, 1719) called forth John Toland's reply in the latter's *Tetradymus* (1720). Similarly, Mangey's anti-Socinian sermon *The Eternal Existence of our Lord Jesus Christ* (1719) was challenged by an opponent writing under the pseudonym of Phileleutherus Cantabrigiensis, who was promptly identified as Thomas Herne. Mangey's other published sermons, many of which were preached to prestigious audiences at Whitehall, before the House of Commons, or at the anniversary meetings of famous charities, either pursued an explicitly apologetic aim or dealt with the commonplace theme of benevolence and philanthropy. FRANÇOISE DECONINCK-BROSSARD

Sources W. Hutchinson, *The history and antiquities of the county palatine of Durham*, 2 (1787), 173–4 · Venn, *Alum. Cant.* · *GM*, 1st ser., 25

(1755), 138 • Nichols, *Lit. anecdotes* • E. Harwood, *A view of the various editions of the Greek and Roman classics*, 4th edn (1790), 76
Archives BL, notes and collections, Add. MSS 6422–6430, 6435–6437, 6440–6441, 6445, 6447, 6449, 6453, 6457, 6459 • BL, Add. MSS 5831, fols. 193–5; 22911, fol. 230; 23204, fol. 41

Mangin, Edward (1772–1852), writer and translator, was born in Dublin on 15 July 1772, the eldest son of Samuel Henry Mangin (d. 1798) of the 5th Royal Irish Dragoons, afterwards lieutenant-colonel of the 14th, and finally of the 12th (Prince of Wales's) light dragoons, and his wife, Susanna Corneille (d. 1824). Both of his parents' families were Huguenot in origin; the Mangins had emigrated to Ireland to escape persecution during the reign of Louis XIV.

Mangin was a contemporary of Southey at Balliol College Oxford, graduating BA in 1793 and MA in 1795. He was then ordained in the Irish church, and on 2 March 1798 was collated to the prebendal stall of Dysart in Killaloe Cathedral, where he served until 15 January 1800. That year he married Emily Holmes (d. 1801), and was collated to the prebend of Rathmichael in St Patrick's, Dublin. A year later his wife died, leaving him with their baby daughter, Emily.

Mangin remained in Dublin until December 1803, when he became prebendary of Rath in Killaloe, a position he held until his death. Shortly after his move, his first translation, from the French, was published as *The Life of C. G. Lamoignon Malesherbes* (1804). It was followed the next year by *The Deserted City*, a poem on Bath in summer which parodied Goldsmith. At yearly intervals thereafter came *Light Reading at Leisure Hours* (1805), *Oddities and Outlines* (1806), and a three-decker novel, *George the Third* (1807). His *Essay on the Sources of the Pleasures Received from Literary Compositions* (1808) was reprinted in 1813.

Between 1810 and 1814 came a number of more significant works. Mangin's translation, *Hector, a Tragedy in Five Acts* was published in 1810; the nineteen-volume *Works of Samuel Richardson, with a Sketch of his Life and Writings* followed in 1811. *Utopia Found: an Apology for Irish Absentees* did not appear until 1813, but was followed by one of Mangin's best-known works, *A View of the Pleasures Arising from a Love of Books* (1814).

Meanwhile, Mangin was navy chaplain on the *Gloucester*, a 74-gun ship, from April to August 1812. He lived in Toulouse for some time, and was in Paris when it was occupied by the allied armies; but for nearly the whole of his working life he lived at 10 Johnstone Street, Bath, 'associating with all the intelligent in that intelligent city' (Forster, *Goldsmith*). On 1 July 1816 at Queen Square Chapel, Bath, he married his second wife, Mary (d. 1845), daughter of Lieutenant-Colonel Nangreave of the East Indian army. They had a daughter, Mary Henrietta, and two sons who later became clergymen, Edward Nangreave Mangin, and Samuel W. Mangin.

Having a substantial income, Mangin was able to study full-time. He continued to publish, though often anonymously, a variety of original and translated works. *An Intercepted Epistle from a Person in Bath to his Friend in London* (1815) went into three editions within the year. His contributions to the *Bath Herald* during this period were later collected as *The Parlour Window, or, Anecdotes, Original Remarks on Books* (1841). He also gave articles to the *Bath and Bristol Magazine*, and issued a short-lived periodical called *The Inspector* (October–November 1825). At the same time, he produced a variety of letters, translations, short stories, and other works. Most renowned among these was *Piozziana, or, Recollections of the Late Mrs Piozzi, by a Friend* (1833), of which, together with his edition of Richardson, the *Gentleman's Magazine* (1853) commented: 'Upon neither of these works did he bestow a very large amount of labour or research'. On the other hand, his contemporary biographers felt that his abilities were not fully realized in his works.

Mangin died in his sleep on the morning of 17 October 1852, at his house in Johnstone Street, Bath, having been for some time experiencing pain and swelling in his throat. He was buried in the old burial-ground of Bathwick.   W. P. COURTNEY, *rev.* JESSICA HININGS

Sources R. E. M. Peach, *Historic houses in Bath and their associations*, 2 vols. (1883–4), vol. 1, pp. 146–7; vol 2, pp. 8, 37–8, 72 • G. Monkland, *The literature and literati of Bath: an essay* (1854), 90 • J. Forster, *The life and times of Oliver Goldsmith*, 5th edn, 2 vols. (1871) • *GM*, 2nd ser., 39 (1853), 97–8 • H. Cotton, *Fasti ecclesiae Hibernicae*, 1 (1845), 426–7; 2 (1848), 173; 5 (1860), 74; 6 (1878), 46 • S. Halkett and J. Laing, *A dictionary of the anonymous and pseudonymous literature of Great Britain*, 4 vols. (1882–8) • Foster, *Alum. Oxon.* • *N&Q*, 3rd ser., 9 (1866), 107 • J. Hunter, *On the connection of Bath with the literature and science of England* (1853), 90 • [J. Watkins and F. Shoberl], *A biographical dictionary of the living authors of Great Britain and Ireland* (1816) • W. B. S. Taylor, *History of the University of Dublin* (1845) • private information (1893) • will, PRO, PROB 11/2163, sig. 942
Archives Bodl. Oxf., Paris journals • NMM, journal | BL, letters to Joseph Hunter, Add. MS 24871 • BL, letters to Royal Literary Fund, Loan 96 • JRL, letters to Hester Piozzi • Princeton University Library, New Jersey, corresp. with Hester Piozzi
Likenesses W. Say, mezzotint (after J. Saxon), BM, NPG

Mangles, James (1786–1867), naval officer and traveller, entered the navy in March 1800, on the frigate *Maidstone* with Captain Ross Donnelly, whom in 1801 he followed to the *Narcissus*. After active service on the coast of France, at the capture of the Cape of Good Hope, and in the Rio de la Plata, he was, on 24 September 1806, promoted lieutenant of the *Penelope* (36 guns), in which, in February 1809, he was at the capture of Martinique. In 1811 he was appointed to the *Boyne* (98 guns) and in 1812 to the *Ville de Paris* (110 guns), flagships in the channel of Sir Harry Burrard Neale. In 1814 he was first lieutenant of the *Duncan*, flagship of Sir John Poo Beresford in his voyage to Rio de Janeiro. He was sent home in acting command of the sloop *Racoon* (rank confirmed, 13 June 1815). This was his last service afloat.

In 1816 Mangles left England, with his old messmate in the *Narcissus*, Captain Charles Leonard Irby, on a tour on the continent, extended to Egypt, Syria, and Asia Minor. Their descriptive letters were privately printed in 1823, and published in Murray's Home and Colonial Library in 1844. Mangles was elected FRS in 1825, and in 1830 was one of the first fellows and members of council of the Royal Geographical Society. He published *The Floral Calendar*

(1839), on window and town gardening; *Synopsis of a complete dictionary … of the illustrated geography and hydrography of England and Wales, Scotland and Ireland* (1848); *Papers and Despatches Relating to the Arctic Searching Expeditions of 1850–1–2* (1852); and *The Thames Estuary: a Guide to the Navigation of the Thames Mouth* (1853). He became a captain on half pay in February 1853. He died at his home, Fairfield, Topsham Road, Exeter, on 18 November 1867, aged eighty-one.

J. K. LAUGHTON, rev. ANDREW LAMBERT

Sources D. Syrett and R. L. DiNardo, *The commissioned sea officers of the Royal Navy, 1660–1815*, rev. edn, Occasional Publications of the Navy RS, 1 (1994) · O'Byrne, *Naval biog. dict.* · *GM*, 4th ser., 4 (1867), 833 · Boase, *Mod. Eng. biog.* · *Journal of the Royal Geographical Society*, 38 (1868), cxliii · *CGPLA Eng. & Wales* (1868)
Archives University of West Australian History, Perth, letter-books relating to botanical matters | Yale U., Beinecke L., letters to T. J. Pettigrew
Wealth at death under £3000: probate, 10 Feb 1868, *CGPLA Eng. & Wales*

Mangles, Ross Donnelly (1801–1877), East India Company servant and politician, son of James Mangles MP (*d.* 1838), of Woodbridge, Guildford, and his wife, Mary, youngest daughter of John Hughes of Guildford, was born on 10 September 1801. He was educated at Eton College and at the East India College, Haileybury. He arrived at Calcutta in 1820 and in 1821 was appointed assistant secretary to the board of revenue in the Ceded and Conquered Provinces. Over the next four years he filled a variety of subordinate revenue posts and in July 1825 briefly officiated as secretary to the board of revenue in the Lower Provinces. In August 1825, during the First Anglo-Burmese War, he became secretary to the commissioner of Pegu and Ava. In April 1826 he was appointed deputy secretary in the judicial and territorial departments.

Mangles took furlough from January 1828 until November 1831. On 16 February 1830 he married Harriet, third daughter of George Newcome of Upper Wimpole Street, London, with whom he had at least two daughters and a son. Upon his return to India he again was engaged primarily in revenue work, and was appointed in March 1835 secretary to the Bengal government in the judicial and revenue departments, a post which he held until his retirement from the service in 1839. In mid-1837 the governor-general, Lord Auckland, embarked on a lengthy tour up-country and Mangles, in Auckland's absence, effectively became the chief administrator of Bengal.

In 1839 Mangles returned to London and launched into politics. A life-long whig, he was returned at the general election of 1841 as the member for Guildford, a borough which his father had represented from 1831 to 1837. He retained this seat until 1858. In parliament he established himself as an authority on Indian matters, and in particular blunted the attacks of John Crawfurd of the British India Society who accused the government of India of causing famine and depopulation through its land revenue system. Mangles was a staunch utilitarian and defended the high assessments, then pressing particularly hard on the North-Western Provinces, in the pure terms of the doctrine of rent as expounded by Malthus, Ricardo and James Mill. His article in the *Edinburgh Review*

of January 1840, 'The revenue system of British India', was explicitly designed to head off a parliamentary assault by tory paternalists on the whig ministry's supposed over-taxation of the Indian peasantry. In July 1840, before the full horror of Auckland's Afghanistan adventure was known, he published a second, more general article in the *Edinburgh Review*, 'Present state and prospects of British India', defending Auckland, whom he admired as both a friend and fellow whig.

Mangles was an evangelical Anglican and regarded education and evangelization as mutually supportive pillars of society's moral regeneration. In India he was a member of both the Church Missionary Society and the general committee of public instruction. He believed that India's moral improvement could be effected only through Christianization, and in 1834, unhappy with the slow progress of evangelization, he proposed the establishment of an élite seminary in Calcutta to train Indian clergymen for the uphill task ahead. In England, too, he campaigned for a more publicly active church and published in 1840 *Christian Reasons of a Member of the Church of England for being a Reformer*. Writing to Macvey Napier, editor of the *Edinburgh Review*, in 1842, he complained that the Anglican laity were denied any meaningful role in the church, an evil compounded in his opinion by the wholesale association of the clergy with the tory party, to the 'necessary disgust and alienation of a very large number of their respective flocks'.

In 1847 Mangles became a director of the East India Company and in 1857 was elected chairman. In 1858 he retired from parliament on his appointment to the new Council of India, a position he held until his retirement in 1866. In this venue too, confronted by the cautious paternalism of the post-1857 administration, Mangles vociferously defended the utilitarian vision of the 1830s which had so coloured his years in India. He died in London at his home, 23 Montagu Street, Montagu Square, on 16 August 1877. His son, Ross, received the Victoria Cross for gallant conduct near Arrah during the uprising of 1857.

KATHERINE PRIOR

Sources *East-India Register and Directory* (1840–60) · *Indian Army and Civil Service List* (1861–7) · H. T. Prinsep and R. Doss, eds., *A general register of the Hon'ble East India Company's civil servants of the Bengal establishment from 1790 to 1842* (1844) · E. Stokes, *The English utilitarians and India* (1959) · BL, Macvey Napier MSS · M. A. Laird, *Missionaries and education in Bengal, 1793–1837* (1972) · *ILN* (9 Oct 1858) · BL OIOC, Haileybury MSS · H. E. C. Stapylton, *The Eton school lists, from 1791 to 1850*, 2nd edn (1864) · *The Times* (21 Aug 1877), 4 · *DNB* · *CGPLA Eng. & Wales* (1878)
Archives BL, letters to Macvey Napier, Add. MSS 34620–34626 · BL OIOC, home miscellaneous series
Likenesses wood-engraving, 1858, NPG; repro. in *ILN* (9 Oct 1858)
Wealth at death under £100: probate, 27 April 1878, *CGPLA Eng. & Wales*

Mangnall, Richmal (1769–1820), schoolmistress, the third daughter of James Mangnall of Hollinhurst, Lancashire, and London, and Richmal, daughter of John Kay of Manchester, was born on 7 March 1769, probably in London. She was the fourth of seven children to survive infancy; of

Richmal Mangnall (1769–1820), by John Downman, 1814

her two brothers, the elder, James, became a London solicitor; the younger, Kay, died in the East Indies in 1801. On the death of her parents about 1781 she was adopted by her uncle, John Kay, solicitor, of Manchester, and was educated at Mrs Wilson's school at Crofton Hall, near Wakefield, Yorkshire. She remained there as a teacher, eventually taking over the school herself and running it successfully until her death there on 1 May 1820. She was able to support two unmarried sisters from her school and publishing earnings, and to provide for them after her death. She was buried in Crofton churchyard.

Crofton Hall was a flourishing school with over seventy pupils. A system of questions and answers allowed teachers or senior pupils to conduct large classes, and Richmal Mangnall's *Historical and Miscellaneous Questions for the Use of Young People* was first published anonymously in 1798 to serve her own school. Longmans bought the copyright for 100 guineas; their 1800 edition, still anonymous, is dedicated to John Kay. Successive editions appeared almost annually, with the author's corrections and additions incorporating recent events, including a new section on astronomy in the edition of 1806, dedicated to the astronomer royal, Nevil Maskelyne. Richmal Mangnall also published *Half an Hour's Lounge, or, Poems* (1805), which she described as 'trifles'; they treated such themes as nature, the sorrow of parting, Laura and Petrarch, Mrs Opie, and, in a poem entitled 'To the Memory of an Officer in the Honorable East-India Company's Service, 1801', the death of her brother. A *Compendium of Geography for the Use of Schools* (1815) had more limited success than her *Questions*.

In 1888 a satirical writer wondered how people had learned before the 'immortal textbook', and placed it

between the *Lyrical Ballads* of 1798 and *Minstrelsy of the Scottish Border* in 1802 as ushering in a new era. Certainly, the catechism-type textbook dominated Victorian school-publishing, and Mangnall's *Questions* continued to appear until late in the century, albeit revised, corrected, updated, and supplemented by such editors as William Pinnock in mid-century and G. N. Wright in 1875. Richmal Mangnall's declared purpose (Preface, 1806) was that the *Questions* should serve to 'awaken a spirit of laudible [*sic*] curiosity', but it is doubtful whether the formulation of the questions (strictly from a teacher's rather than a learner's perspective) and the finality of the answers achieved this purpose. It is to Mangnall, no doubt, that the contemporary *Blair's Universal Preceptor and Questions* refers in contrasting its 'intellectual or thinking system' with 'popular mechanical systems'; despite these criticisms, the predominant textbook format remained interrogative, and the more mechanical or catechetical systems, incorporating Mangnall, were highly valued where the knowledge of the teacher, whether governess or school monitor, was itself limited.   SUSAN DRAIN

Sources T. Coppock, 'Richmal Mangnall', *Journal of Education*, new ser., 11 (1889), 199–200 · C. Smith, 'Mangnall's questions', *Journal of Education*, new ser., 10 (1888), 431–2 · J. W. H., 'Mangnall's questions', *Journal of Education*, new ser., 10 (1888), 329–31 · H. Heginbotham, *Stockport: ancient and modern*, 2 (1892), 361–2 · J. H. Lupton, *Wakefield worthies* (1864), 217–18 · *GM*, 1st ser., 90/1 (1820), 476 · J. H. Burns, 'Clio as governess: lessons in history, 1798', *History Today*, 36/8 (1986), 10–15 · W. G. Briggs, 'Richmal Mangnall and her school at Crofton Old Hall', *Leeds University Institute of Education Researches and Studies*, 15 (1957), 24–32 · PRO, PROB 11/1629/299 · *Wakefield and Halifax Journal* (12 May 1820)

Likenesses J. Downman, watercolour, 1814, NPG [*see illus.*] · engraving (after a portrait), repro. in R. Mangnall, *Historical and miscellaneous questions*, ed. J. Guy, new edn (1875) · silhouette, repro. in Heginbotham, *Stockport: ancient and modern*, vol. 2, p. 362

Wealth at death £1600 in bequests; also two annuities of £50 each: will, PRO, PROB 11/1629/299

Maniar (*fl.* **1781–1782**). *See under* Indian visitors (*act. c.*1720–*c.*1810).

Manigault, Peter (1731–1773), politician in America, was born on 10 October 1731 in Charles Town, South Carolina, the son of Gabriel Manigault (1704–1781), merchant, and his wife, Ann (*d.* 1782), the daughter of John Ashby. After attending a private school in Charles Town, Peter went to London, where he lived with his tutor, Thomas Corbett. In 1752 he enrolled in the Inner Temple and was called to the bar on 8 February 1754. He also sampled the good life, having his portrait painted by a fashionable artist, and travelling on the continent. While his parents apparently worried that he might want to stay abroad, he nevertheless returned to Charles Town in December 1754, and on 8 June 1755, at St Philip's Church, married Elizabeth (*bap.* 1736, *d.* 1773), the daughter of Joseph Wragg, a merchant; they had seven children, four of whom survived to adulthood. On 16 December 1755 Manigault was called to the local bar. Although he practised briefly, other pursuits proved more congenial. His wealthy father gave him considerable sums, and as early as 1758 Manigault was able to advertise in the *South Carolina Gazette* that he had several thousand pounds to lend at interest. He also managed the Carolina affairs of British contacts and absentee planters, as well as several rice and indigo plantations of his own.

More important, Manigault quickly demonstrated an aptitude for politics. Elected to the South Carolina Commons house in 1755, he remained a member for the next seventeen years. Until 1762 his committee assignments placed him among the second rank of leaders; from 1762 until 1765 he was in the top tier during most sessions, and on 29 October 1765 he became speaker. Repeatedly re-elected, he retained the office until 1772. As speaker he presided over the house during the controversy with Great Britain. Parliament precipitated the first major crisis in 1765 by passing the Stamp Act, which imposed a tax on internal American transactions that produced widespread opposition in the colonies. Under Manigault's leadership the Commons house adopted strong resolutions against the act. That the first issue of the *South Carolina Gazette and Country Journal*—printed on unstamped paper in defiance of the law—published these resolutions suggests that Manigault and other members of the house subsidized it 'so that a just Sense of Liberty' and the actions of the representatives would be 'known to their Constituents and transmitted to Posterity' (South Carolina Commons house journals, 29 Nov 1765, 31).

Parliament repealed the Stamp Act in March 1766 but followed it with the similarly formed Townshend duties, which met the same opposition as before in America. When the Massachusetts house of representatives sent a circular letter to other colonial assemblies urging joint resistance, the royal governor of South Carolina urged the South Carolina Commons to treat it with the 'contempt it deserved' (South Carolina Commons house journals, 17 Nov 1768, 6). Manigault referred the letter to his colleagues, who unanimously on 19 November 1768 declared that it was 'replete with duty and Loyalty to His Majesty' (ibid., 19). The governor countered by dissolving the assembly. South Carolinians later joined the colonial non-importation movement that induced parliament to repeal most of the Townshend duties in April 1770.

Meanwhile a newly elected Commons house responded to solicitations from the Society of Gentlemen Supporters of the Bill of Rights, a group formed in Britain to assist John Wilkes, whose clashes with the ministry and eventual imprisonment prompted aggrieved Americans to identify with him. On 8 December 1769 the South Carolina Commons, alone among colonial assemblies, sent his cause a substantial gift of £1500. As speaker, Manigault presided over this action and helped to arrange payment of the sum. These steps offended the British ministry and violated its policy governing the disbursement of public funds in the colonies. Royal officials therefore responded with a new instruction strictly regulating payments from the South Carolina treasury. The South Carolina Commons, however, considered this mandate to be an infringement of its exclusive right to frame money bills. 'I would rather forfeit my whole Estate' than surrender 'the very Essence of true Liberty' (*Papers of Henry Laurens*, 92,

327), the '*Right* of the People to give and grant [funds] voluntarily … free from the Fetters of ministerial Instructions' (ibid., 59), one relatively moderate member observed. The resulting controversy brought other business to a halt, and for the last six years of the colonial period the legislature failed to pass a tax act.

During the latter part of this controversy Manigault was ill, but he continued to support the rights of the house, going so far as to travel in October 1772 from the capital of Charles Town to Beaufort, where Governor Charles Montagu had called the legislature to meet in an attempt to harass it into compliance with the new instruction. The governor's behaviour prompted Manigault to observe that, although he loved to have a weak executive, Montagu convinced him that 'it is not impossible for a Man to be too great a Fool to make a good Governor' (Peter Manigault letterbook, 194). Immediately after his return from Beaufort, Manigault resigned the speakership. His wife died in February 1773, and in May he sailed for England, hoping to recover his health in a more temperate climate.

There, to his surprise, he found himself in an alien land, 'continually making Comparisons … in Favour of my own Country' ('Letters concerning Peter Manigault', 41). He died at the house of Benjamin Stead in London on 12 November 1773; friends placed his body aboard the *Amity*, bound for Charles Town, where he was buried at the Huguenot church on 16 February 1774. The inventory of his estate listed property (exclusive of real estate) worth £32,737, which made him the richest decedent yet discovered among Americans whose estates were inventoried in 1774. His obituary in the *South Carolina Gazette and Country Journal* on 18 January 1774 paid him an appropriate tribute by noting that in ably discharging his duties as speaker, he had demonstrated 'his inviolable and zealous Attachment to the Cause of Liberty, and the true Interest of his COUNTRY'.   ROBERT M. WEIR

Sources South Carolina Commons house journals, South Carolina Archives and History Center, Columbia, · Peter Manigault letterbook, South Carolina Historical Society, Charleston, SC · M. A. Crouse, 'The letterbook of Peter Manigault, 1763–1773', *South Carolina Historical Magazine*, 70 (1969), 79–96, 177–95 · M. L. Webber, ed., 'Letters concerning Peter Manigault, 1773', *South Carolina Historical and Genealogical Magazine*, 21 (1920), 39–49 · *The papers of Henry Laurens*, ed. P. M. Hamer and others, 15 vols. (1968–), vol. 8 · J. M. Clifton, 'Manigault, Peter', *ANB* · W. B. Edgar and N. L. Bailey, eds., *Biographical directory of the South Carolina house of representatives*, 2 (1977) · M. A. Crouse, 'The Manigault family of South Carolina, 1685–1783', PhD diss., Northwestern University, 1964 · J. P. Greene, 'Bridge to revolution: Wilkes fund controversy in South Carolina, 1769–1775', *Journal of Southern History*, 29 (1963), 19–52 · J. P. Greene, *The quest for power: the lower houses of assembly in the southern royal colonies, 1689–1776* (1963) · R. M. Weir, *Colonial South Carolina: a history*, pbk edn (1997) · A. H. Jones, *Wealth of a nation to be: the American colonies on the eve of the Revolution* (1980) · A. S. Salley, ed., *Register of St Philip's parish, Charles Town* (Charleston, SC, 1904); repr. (1971) · W. B. Edgar and N. L. Bailey, eds., *The Commons house of assembly, 1692–1775*, 2 (1977)

Archives South Carolina Historical Society, Charleston, family papers · University of South Carolina, Columbia, South Caroliniana Library, family papers

Likenesses A. Ramsay, portrait, repro. in *Transactions of the Huguenot Society of South Carolina*, 4 (1897), facing p. 64

Wealth at death £32,737 8s.—in personal property located on four unappraised properties: inventory, A. H. Jones, *American colonial wealth: documents and methods* (1977), 3.1543–57

Manina [*married names* Fletcher, Seedo], **Maria** (*fl.* 1712–1736), singer, was probably from Italy, but may well have been living in England for some time when she began her career in the opera company at the Queen's Theatre, Haymarket, London. A soprano, she made her début singing Eucharis, 'Gay, Young, and Fair' (Hughes, 17), in Johann Ernst Galliard's English opera with libretto by John Hughes, *Calypso and Telemachus* (17 May 1712). Signora Manina remained at the Queen's Theatre until June 1714, singing minor roles in Italian operas, including Handel's *Teseo* and *Rinaldo*. As 'Signiora Maria Fletcher, formerly Menene' (*Daily Courant*) she appeared at Lincoln's Inn Fields Theatre on 6 October 1715, and she remained there until summer 1717, singing entr'acte music and taking the title role in a revival of the English version of Giovanni Bononcini's *Camilla* on 2 January 1717. She apparently sang only in concerts in the 1717–18 season, but then returned to Lincoln's Inn Fields for two seasons of English theatre music, including the pasticcio *Thomyris* (9 December 1718) and Galliard's *Circe* (11 April 1719). Apart from her own benefit concert at Hickford's Room in March 1721 there are no recorded appearances until she returned to the theatre in November 1726 for a revival of *Camilla*, which achieved over twenty performances. By 29 September 1727 she had married the German composer Seedo (known in Germany as Sydow or Sidow) (*d.* 1754). Mrs Seedo remained at Lincoln's Inn Fields until summer 1732, appearing frequently in John Rich's pantomime afterpieces, where her roles included Proserpine, Venus, and Helen of Troy. In 1730 she sang the heroes in revivals of Johann Pepusch's masques *Venus and Adonis* and *Myrtillo*. At the Haymarket Theatre in November 1732, Mrs Seedo sang Victory, Concord, and Peace in John Frederick Lampe's opera *Britannia*. Her husband fell into debt, and on 21 May 1733 she appeared at Drury Lane Theatre in a benefit for him, singing Daphne in his masque *Venus, Cupid and Hymen*. Early in 1736 Seedo was offered the position of musical director to Friedrich Wilhelm I of Prussia. The Prussian ambassador, who handled the negotiations and settled Seedo's debts, reported to the king that Mrs Seedo sang well and had a good voice. She arrived in Potsdam with her husband in May 1736, but nothing is known of her life after this.

OLIVE BALDWIN and THELMA WILSON

Sources E. L. Avery, ed., *The London stage, 1660–1800*, pt 2: *1700–1729* (1960) · A. H. Scouten, ed., *The London stage, 1660–1800*, pt 3: *1729–1747* (1961) · *Daily Courant* (6 Oct 1715) · J. Hughes, *Poems on several occasions*, 2 (1735) [commendatory poem on *Calypso and Telemachus* by Topham Foot, pp. 16–17] · W. H. Rubsamen, 'Mr. Seedo, ballad opera, and the Singspiel', *Miscelánea en homenaje a Monseñor Higinio Anglés*, 2 (1958–61), 775–809 · O. E. Deutsch, *Dokumente zu Leben und Schaffen* (1985), vol. 4 of *Händel-Handbuch*, ed. W. Eisel and M. Eisel (1978–85) · J. Milhous and R. D. Hume, eds., *Vice Chamberlain Coke's theatrical papers, 1706–1715* (1982) · J. Milhous and R. D. Hume, eds., *A register of English theatrical documents, 1660–1737*, 1 (1991) · E. V. Roberts, 'Mr. Seedo's London career and his work with Henry

Fielding', *Philological Quarterly*, 45 (1966), 179–90 · K. Sasse, 'Opera register from 1712 to 1734 (Colman-Register)', *Händel Jahr-Buch*, 5 (1959), 199–223

Maning, Frederick Edward (1811/12–1883), writer and judge in New Zealand, was born on 5 July 1811 or 1812 in Dublin, the eldest of the three sons of Frederick Maning of Johnville, co. Dublin, and his wife, Mary Barrett. Both his parents were from Anglo-Irish protestant families of moderate wealth. In 1824 the family emigrated to Van Diemen's Land, where they farmed for several years before moving to Hobart. However, Maning had no liking for town life, and in 1833 he left Van Diemen's Land to seek adventure and profit among the Maori of Hokianga harbour, an area rich in valuable kauri forest on the northwest coast of New Zealand. It was here that he was to spend most of the rest of his life.

At Hokianga Maning fitted easily into the frontier environment of scattered European establishments surrounded by and dependent on the patronage of powerful Maori tribes. He soon learned Maori and adapted readily to Maori ways necessary for economic survival. At first he ran a small trading establishment at Kohukohu, where he lived a rough, simple, often rather riotous life. According to a local missionary baptism register, he fathered a child to a woman called Harakoi while living there. Nothing else is known of the woman or child.

In 1839 Maning bought a block of land called Onoke at the mouth of the Whirinaki River. This was the territory of the Hikutu hapu (sub-tribe) and Maning soon became an important figure in that community, as the local trader, through his marriage in 1839 to Moengaroa and the birth of four children. He gained some notoriety shortly after moving to Onoke, when the new governor, William Hobson, attacked him in print for attempting to dissuade Hokianga Maori from signing the 1840 treaty of Waitangi.

As colonization increased Maning slowly abandoned his bicultural lifestyle. The northern war of 1844–5 against Hone Heke made him feel less secure about his safety in a potentially hostile Maori world, and after Moengaroa's death in 1847 he began to distance himself from his Hikutu kin. In 1848 he expanded his trading activities, and, although these were initially successful, his eventual retirement from business in the early 1860s was accompanied by financial problems, stemming partly from the reluctance of Maori employees to work off debts.

It was the publication of his two books that brought Maning national attention. Both were initially published under the *nom de plume* the Pakeha-Maori (a name then applied to Europeans living with Maori tribes). *A History of the War in the North* (1862) was written from the supposed point of view of a Maori chief fighting against Hone Heke, and drew on Maning's extensive knowledge of the war and its Maori participants. It was well reviewed, and Maning was persuaded to complete quickly the more ambitious *Old New Zealand*. That was published in 1863, to considerable local and British acclaim. Using some of the literary devices of Laurence Sterne, Maning produced a racy, often very funny *tour de force* of autobiography, description, and discussion of Maori history and customs. Both books were published at the height of the New Zealand wars, and have an underlying theme warning fellow colonists that Maori would never willingly accept European domination. In 1865 Maning gained an appointment as one of the judges on the new Maori land court, set up to begin the task of individualizing title to all remaining Maori land. Until his retirement in 1876 most of his time was spent travelling around the Maori centres of the far north, although he was also brought south at times to help adjudicate several large and controversial land cases.

As he grew older Maning's alienation from all things Maori continued to grow. He resented Maori questioning of his court decisions and was contemptuous of the leaders of the new Maori protest movements emerging in the 1870s. In 1880 he had what seems to have been a nervous breakdown. Imagining among other things that his children and their Hikutu relatives were plotting to kill him, he fled Onoke to Auckland, where the comfort of private lodgings and the novelty of town life brought some contentment. In 1882 he sought treatment for cancer in London, and he died there on 25 July 1883. He was later buried in New Zealand, at the Symonds Street cemetery, Auckland.

For almost fifty years Maning was caught up in the turmoil of New Zealand race relations. However, it is on his brief career as an author that his fame now largely rests. *Old New Zealand* in particular has been frequently reprinted or anthologized and has become a classic of New Zealand literature. DAVID COLQUHOUN

Sources D. Colquhoun, '"Pakeha Muosi": the early life and times of Frederick Edward Maning', MA diss., University of Auckland · F. E. Maning, *Old New Zealand: a tale of the good old times* (1863) · [F. E. Maning], *History of the war in the north of New Zealand against the chief Heke, in the year 1845* (1862) · NL NZ, Turnbull L., F. E. Maning MSS · National Archives of New Zealand, Wellington, Old Land Claims Commission records · NL NZ, Turnbull L., Donald McLean MSS · Auckland Public Library, New Zealand, F. E. Maning MSS

Archives Auckland Public Library · NL NZ, Turnbull L. · University of Otago, Dunedin, Hocken Library | Auckland Institute and Museum, Von Sturmer MSS · NL NZ, Turnbull L., McLean MSS

Likenesses photograph, *c*.1833 (after a crayon drawing), Auckland Public Library, Auckland, New Zealand · photograph, Sept 1869, Canterbury Museum, Christchurch, New Zealand, S. D. Barker Collection · photograph, *c*.1880, Auckland Public Library, Auckland, New Zealand

Wealth at death £5370: will and probate, file 1300, National Archives, Auckland

Manini, Antony (*c*.1750–1786), musician, was possibly born in Rome. Manini's early life has been the subject of a great deal of conjecture. Suggestions that he belonged to the Norfolk family of Mann and Italianized his name appear unreliable. It is perhaps more likely, as Sainsbury suggested, that he was related to the Italian composer named Manini who was living in Rome in 1733. This would sit more comfortably with Christopher Hogwood's assertion that he was a pupil of Tartini. It is also possible that the 'Signora Manini, a new and obscure singer' (Burney, 681), who was performing in England in 1712, was connected in some way.

Manini first came to notice in 1770, performing solos by Felice Giardini and Charles Chabran for his own benefit at the New Hall in Great Yarmouth, Norfolk. He led the band in the same year at the opening of Christian's new concert room in Norwich, and also performed nearby in Beccles. He also established himself as a teacher in Great Yarmouth during the early 1770s, instructing ladies on the guitar and gentlemen on the violin.

In 1777 Manini appeared for the first time in Cambridge, as leading violinist at Miss Marshall's concert at St John's College, the programme containing music by Paradies (or Paradisi), Boccherini, and Abel. His *Six Divertimentos for Two Violins*, perhaps his only works to survive, were published in London around this time. One of Manini's violin pupils was Charles Hague. Manini and Hague enjoyed a fruitful musical partnership in later years. In 1779 and the following year Manini played first violin at Scarborough's annual concert at St Ives, Huntingdonshire, and in 1780 he had two benefit concerts at Trinity Hall, Cambridge. A similar concert was given in 1781 in Emmanuel College, close to where he was living at the time. In 1782 he appeared as leading violinist at Peterborough, Huntingdon, and Stamford, and received another benefit at Trinity. In 1783 he was principal violinist at Mrs Pratt's benefit concert in Caius College; in Trinity once again for his own benefit, on which occasion a member of the Cramer family (probably Johann Baptist) performed; and at Peterhouse for the benefit of Joseph Reinagle. In 1784 he held three subscription concerts on three successive days (1–3 July) in the halls of King's and St John's; played first violin at Huntingdon, Hague appearing in the vocal part; and later played there again for Michael Leoni's benefit. He also gave Leoni a benefit concert at King's, with Leoni and Hague singing and Hague and Manini playing the violin. As well as in Cambridge, Manini and Hague appeared all around East Anglia during the period 1783–4. In 1785, the year in which Gertrud Elisabeth Mara caused a stir in London and Oxford by refusing to stand for the 'Hallelujah' chorus when performing Handel's *Messiah*, she also sang for Manini's benefit at Trinity. In November of that year a benefit concert was given at King's for the highly precocious William Crotch, then aged ten and later a violin pupil of Hague. On this occasion, the two future professors of music at Oxford and Cambridge respectively, Crotch and Hague, sang, and Hague and Manini played. Manini also performed at musical entertainments staged by John Montagu, fourth earl of Sandwich, at Hinchingbrooke; he died soon after one of them at Huntingdon on 6 January 1786. He was buried in the parish of St Andrew's the Great in Cambridge. Manini was highly esteemed during his lifetime, both personally and as a musician.

CHARLES SAYLE, *rev.* DAVID J. GOLBY

Sources C. Hogwood, 'Hague, Charles', *New Grove* · [J. S. Sainsbury], ed., *A dictionary of musicians*, 2 vols. (1824) · Venn, *Alum. Cant.* · Burney, *Hist. mus.*, new edn, 2.681 · *Norwich Mercury* (1770–72) · *Cambridge Chronicle and Journal* (1777–86) · John Montagu, fourth earl of Sandwich, MSS, priv. coll.

Manio, Jean Baptiste de [*known as* Jack de Manio] (1914–1988), radio broadcaster, was born on 26 January 1914 in

Hampstead, London, the only child of Jean Baptiste de Manio (*d.* 1913), an Italian aviator, and his Polish wife, Florence Olga. Before he was born his father, the first person to fly across the English Channel in winter, was killed in a flying accident during a race to Lisbon. His mother, an eccentric and fashionable woman, never remarried but had many male admirers. She spoke eight languages but her English was bad, and de Manio later attributed his poor progress in reading and writing to this. He left Aldenham School without any academic qualifications, and got a job as an invoice clerk in a brewery in Spitalfields in the East End of London. For a time he then tried to make a career in the hotel business, first on the kitchen staff at Grosvenor House and as assistant to the wine waiter at the Ritz, and later as a waiter at the Miramar Hotel, Cannes. On 2 March 1935 he married Juliet Graveraet Kaufmann (*b.* 1911/12), daughter of Louis Graveraet Kaufmann, bank president. They had one son. Following his marriage de Manio lived in the United States for a short while, working on his wife's family's farm.

At the outbreak of the Second World War de Manio was called up into the Royal Sussex regiment. In 1939–40 he fought with the 7th battalion in the British expeditionary force in France, and from 1940 to 1944 he was with the 1st battalion, Middle East forces. He was awarded the MC in 1940, and a bar was added to it in north Africa. In 1944 he joined the forces broadcasting unit in Beirut. On leaving the army in 1946 he was able to get a job with the BBC Overseas Service as an announcer. His marriage to his first wife (who remained with their son in the United States throughout the Second World War) ended in divorce in 1946, and on 8 August 1947 he married Loveday Elizabeth Matthews (*b.* 1916/17), a widowed secretary and daughter of Evelyn Robins Abbott (1873–1956), civil servant in India and chief commissioner of Delhi from 1924 to 1928. There were no children of this second marriage.

De Manio was transferred from the BBC's Overseas Service to its Home Service in 1950. He managed to survive the furore over his slip of the tongue when he announced a talk by the governor of Nigeria, Sir John Macpherson, 'The land of the Niger', as 'The land of the nigger', and in 1958 he was invited to join the new BBC programme *Today*. This was a daily breakfast time magazine programme on the Home Service (renamed Radio 4 in 1967) 'bringing you news, views, and interviews'. Despite his inability to give the correct time, de Manio survived as presenter from 1958 until 1971. Although one listener demanded compensation after he had crashed his car in surprise after hearing the wrong time announced on his car radio, most listeners got used to his misreading the studio clock, and his mistakes made him seem more human, a real person. With his relaxed, informal style and his friendly manner he became very popular, regarded by millions of listeners as a personal friend. To the listening public he was the *Today* programme, a national institution. In 1969 he was the first radio broadcaster to interview Prince Charles. He was voted radio personality of the year by the Variety Club of Great Britain in 1964, and by the British Radio Industries Club in 1971. But in 1970 the new editor of morning

current affairs programmes decided to add a co-presenter, and to make *Today* more of a current affairs programme. For a year de Manio was joint presenter with John Timpson. He never felt happy with the new format, feeling that two presenters tended to talk to each other, rather than directly to the listeners.

For the next seven years (1971–8) de Manio presented his own afternoon programme, *Jack de Manio Precisely*. He also presented *With Great Pleasure* (1971–3). His one venture into television, when he was asked to present *Wednesday Magazine*, a women's programme, was not a success. For a short time from 1979 onwards he contributed to *Woman's Hour*, but he did little broadcasting in the 1980s.

De Manio's career and the development of the informal interview marked the end of the old style of impersonal and impartial radio broadcasting. On the air he behaved naturally, and Brian Johnston's advice, when asked how to become a good broadcaster, was 'be like Jack de Manio: be yourself'. As a radio broadcaster it was his voice rather than his face which was well known. The slightly hoarse, gravelly tones became instantly recognizable, and despite his foreign antecedents, he was the epitome of the middle-class, middle-brow Englishman, a *Daily Telegraph* reader. He died at St Stephen's Hospital, Chelsea, London, on 28 October 1988, of cancer of the liver. He was survived by his second wife and the son of his first marriage. A memorial service was held at All Souls, Langham Place, on 18 January 1989.   ANNE PIMLOTT BAKER

Sources J. de Manio, *Life begins too early: a sort of autobiography* (1970) · J. Timpson, *Today and yesterday* (1976) · J. de Manio, *To Auntie with love* (1967) · *The Times* (28 Oct 1988) · *The Times* (19 Jan 1989) · *The Independent* (29 Oct 1988) · *Sunday Times* (30 Oct 1988) · K. Robinson, 'You're all right, Jack', *The Listener* (14 Sept 1978) · BL NSA · private information (2004) [Loveday Elizabeth de Manio] · *WWW, 1981–90* · m. certs. · d. cert. · P. Donovan, *All our Todays*, 2nd edn (1998), 24–5 **Archives** SOUND BL NSA **Likenesses** photograph, repro. in *The Times* (29 Oct 1988), 12 **Wealth at death** under £70,000: probate, 10 April 1989, *CGPLA Eng. & Wales*

Manisty, Sir Henry (1808–1890), judge, was born at Vicarage House, Edlingham, Northumberland, on 13 December 1808, the second son of James Manisty BD, vicar of Edlingham, and his wife, Eleanor, *née* Foster, of whom little is known. He was educated at Durham Cathedral grammar school, and was later articled in the offices of Thorpe and Dickson, attorneys, of Alnwick, Northumberland.

Manisty became a solicitor in 1830, and practised for twelve years as a member of the firm of Meggison, Pringle, and Manisty of 3 King's (afterwards Theobald's) Road, London. In August 1831 he married Constantia Dickson, the fifth daughter of Patrick Dickson, a solicitor from Berwick upon Tweed. She died on 9 August 1836 and he remarried in May 1838. He and his second wife, Mary Anne Stevenson, the third daughter of Robert Stevenson, a surgeon from Berwick, had four sons and three daughters.

On 20 April 1842 Manisty became a student of Gray's Inn, and was called to the bar on 23 April 1845. He was appointed a bencher of Gray's Inn in 1859, and treasurer in 1861. He joined the northern circuit, and soon built up a considerable practice. He was made a queen's counsel on 7

July 1857, and appeared principally in mercantile and circuit cases.

Eventually, in November 1876, when Lord Blackburn quitted the High Court, Manisty was made a judge, and was knighted (28 November 1876). Among his most important decisions were his judgments in *R.* v. *Bishop of Oxford* (1879), *Belt* v. *Lawes* (1884), *Adams* v. *Coleridge* (1884), and *O'Brien* v. *Lord Salisbury* (1889). He had a stroke in court on 24 January 1890 and died on 31 January at his home, 24A Bryanston Square, London. He was buried on 5 February at Kensal Green cemetery.

J. A. HAMILTON, *rev.* SINÉAD AGNEW

Sources *Law Times* (15 Feb 1890), 286 · Boase, *Mod. Eng. biog.* · R. Welford, *Men of mark 'twixt Tyne and Tweed*, 3 (1895), 139–41 · *Law Journal* (8 Aug 1890), 92–3 · *Solicitors' Journal*, 34 (1889–90), 239 · J. Foster, *The register of admissions to Gray's Inn, 1521–1889, together with the register of marriages in Gray's Inn chapel, 1695–1754* (privately printed, London, 1889), ix, x, 464 · *The Times* (1 Feb 1890), 8

Likenesses Lock & Whitfield, woodburytype photograph, 1880, NPG; repro. in T. Cooper, *Men of mark: a gallery of contemporary portraits* (1880), 26 · W. W. Ouless, oils, 1891; replica, Gray's Inn, London · Quiz, chromolithograph, NPG; repro. in *VF* (30 Nov 1889) · Quiz, lithograph, repro. in *VF*, 36 (1886), 4–5 · portrait, repro. in *Green Bag*, 2 (1890), 142 · wood-engraving (after a photograph), NPG; repro. in *ILN* (4 Nov 1876) · wood-engraving (after a photograph), repro. in *ILN*, 96 (1890), 163 · wood-engraving (after a photograph), repro. in *ILN*, 69 (1878), 428

Wealth at death £122,815 4*s.* 9*d.*: probate, 19 March 1890, *CGPLA Eng. & Wales*

Manley, Delarivier

Manley, Delarivier (*c.*1670–1724), writer, was born in Jersey or possibly at sea between Jersey and Guernsey, the third of the six children of Sir Roger *Manley (*d.* 1687), royalist army officer and historian, and his wife from the Spanish Netherlands, probably named Mary Catherine (*d.* 1675). Sir Roger Manley was the second son of Cornelius Manley of Erbistock; one brother, Sir Francis Manley, was also a royalist but another, John *Manley, was a major in the parliamentary army and supporter of the Commonwealth. Manley's father was appointed lieutenant-governor and commander of his majesty's castles, forts, and forces on Jersey in 1667 under Sir Thomas Morgan; Delarivier appears to have been named after the latter's wife, Delariviere Cholmondoley Morgan.

Early years and education In November 1672 Sir Roger left Jersey to serve as a captain of the Royal regiment of foot guards at Windsor. The family, after sojourns at Tower Hamlets, Brussels, and Portsmouth, moved to Landguard Fort in Suffolk where Sir Roger, now widowed, was made governor in February 1680. The principal source for Delarivier's biography is her own account in the 1714 *Adventures of Rivella* (reissued by the publisher Edmund Curll as *Memoirs of the Life of Mrs. Manley* in 1714 and 1717, and as *Mrs. Manley's History of her Own Life and Times* in 1725); a brief account is also provided by Manley in her most successful work of scandal fiction, the *New Atalantis* (1709), in the first-person narrative of Delia given in the second volume. Manley's autobiographical writings are, however, self-justifying and not always reliable as sources of fact about her life. Manley tells us she was educated at home, apart from a short stay with her brother at the French home of a Huguenot minister, where she was sent to

recover from her youthful passion for a young actor and playwright turned soldier named James Carlisle whose regiment visited Landguard Fort in 1685. She claims to have acquired fluent French here, which was to stand her in good stead in her inveterate plundering of French sources for her works. She also claims to have missed the opportunity of a promise to take up a vacancy as maid of honour to the queen with Mary of Modena's precipitate flight from England in December 1687.

Manley's father died in March 1687 and left Delarivier £200, and a share of the residue of his estate. One of her two surviving brothers, Edward, died in 1688, as did William Eyton, Sir Roger's successor at Landguard Fort and one of the two executors of Sir Roger's will (the other, Edward Lloyd, died the year previously). Delarivier's eldest sister, Mary Elizabeth, was recently married to Captain Francis Braithewaite, whom Delarivier disliked. Her brother Francis was at sea, where he died in June 1693. She and Cornelia, on the death of the lady Delarivier Manley describes as 'an old out-of-fashion aunt' (Manley, *New Atalantis*, 223), fell to the sole care of John Manley, son to the puritan uncle John.

John Manley (1654–1713) was a tory lawyer who later became a successful MP. He had married a Cornish orphaned heiress, Anne Grosse, at Westminster Abbey on 19 January 1679, but succeeded in persuading Delarivier (whether she knew the liaison was bigamous or not) to marry him; they had at least one son, John, born on 24 June 1691 and baptized on 13 July 1691 in the parish of St Martin-in-the-Fields, Westminster, as the child of 'John and Dela Manley'. In January 1694, under the protection of Barbara Villiers, duchess of Cleveland and long-term mistress to Charles II, Delarivier either left or was left by her bigamous husband, but only six months later was expelled from the duchess's house in Arlington Street on the grounds of a flirtation with the duchess's son.

Manley appears to have had a winning personality, although she and others admitted that she was not a remarkable beauty. In his *Journal to Stella* on 28 January 1712 Jonathan Swift described her as having 'very generous principles for one of her sort; and a great deal of sense and invention; she is about forty, very homely, and very fat' (Swift, 2.474). Manley herself endorsed this impression, describing herself as 'from her youth … inclined to fat' and complaining that her appearance had been spoilt by smallpox, but 'considering her disadvantage, she has the most easy air that one can have; her hair is of a pale ash-colour, fine, and in a large quantity' and moreover 'none that became acquainted with her, could refrain from loving her' (Manley, *Rivella*, 47).

First publication From 1694 to 1696 Manley travelled around the south-west of England; a series of eight letters composed during these travels to one 'J.H.' (possibly James Hargreaves or John Manley) was published without her permission as *Letters by Mrs Manley* in 1696. It is possible that Manley was travelling with her 'husband', John Manley, who was inspecting Pendennis Castle to determine rents due to its owner in summer 1694; Delarivier's biographer Dolores Diane Clark Duff speculates that a son,

Francis, baptized on 9 August 1694 at the church of St Mary, Truro, as the child of Anne and John Manley, and buried in December 1694, may have been Dela's also, given the fourteen-year gap between this and the birth of his last child by his first wife (Clark Duff, 47).

Manley had the letters withdrawn from publication and they were not reissued until after her death in 1725, when Edmund Curll produced them under the title *A Stagecoach Journey to Exeter*. The letters reveal an early debt to the works of Marie Catherine de la Motte, Baronne d'Aulnoy, the scandalous travel and letter writer, now better known for her fairy tales. Later in her career Manley published another series of letters related to contemporary scandals in two parts as *The lady's pacquet of letters taken from her by a French privateer in her passage to Holland, or, The lady's pacquet broke open* bound with d'Aulnoy's *Memoirs of the Court of England* (January 1707) and *Memoirs of the Earl of Warwick* (November 1707). This collection of letters was republished in 1711 under the title *Court intrigues in a collection of original letters from the island of the new Atalantis &c.*, which Manley disclaimed as a pirated edition in a number of *The Examiner* on 14 June 1711.

Letters by Mrs Manley had been published to coincide with the production of Manley's first play, a comedy called *The Lost Lover, or, The Jealous Husband* (1696). The cast included the young Colley Cibber, but the play was not a success and its author claims in *Rivella* that her reputation was further damaged by unfounded rumours of an affair with the company's ageing part-owner Sir Thomas Skipwith (Manley, *Rivella*, 73–4). However, an oriental tragedy entitled *The Royal Mischief* performed at Lincoln's Inn Fields in April of the same year met with better success, largely thanks to the powerful portrayal of a self-seeking and sexually assertive princess named Homais.

Manley's fame was considerable enough to win her the dubious honour of a satirical representation as Marsilia, a vain female playwright, in an anonymous play of 1696 called *The Female Wits*. Other women writers attacked in the play, Mary Pix and Catherine Trotter, contributed to a small volume of poems by women poets Manley produced to the memory of John Dryden called *The Nine Muses* (1700).

Law, love, and broken loyalties Manley's acquaintance with Catherine Trotter led to a retreat from literary production for some years. In December 1696 Trotter asked her to assist in securing the freedom of John Tilly, governor of the prison at the Fleet, who was under investigation for corruption and taking bribes by a committee of the House of Commons of which Delarivier's 'husband', John Manley, was a member; this introduction resulted in a six-year affair between Manley and Tilly. The couple became involved in another lawsuit, a dispute over the fortune of Christopher Albermarle between the earl of Bath and Ralph, earl of Montagu, in which John Manley was also entangled. In hopes of turning a profit, Delarivier and Tilly undertook the management of one of the claimants to the Albermarle fortune, Christopher Monck, who had been released from debtors' prison at the Fleet into Tilly's custody. Manley gives considerable space in her *Rivella* to

an account of their ultimately fruitless activities. When Tilly's first wife died in December 1702, Delarivier recounts in *Rivella* that she nobly sacrificed her love to allow him to marry a widowed heiress, Margaret Smith (*née* Reresby), and repair his fortunes. Letter 33 of *The lady's pacquet broke open* narrates the same sacrifice.

Over this period Manley made the acquaintance of Richard Steele when he was a young soldier. She assisted him in procuring a midwife for the delivery of his illegitimate daughter and in dabbling in alchemical ventures. Letters 12 to 24 and 34 to 37 of *The lady's pacquet* give their correspondence and volume one of the *New Atalantis* provides a narrative account of their friendship between 1696 and 1702 (Manley, *New Atalantis*, 100–04). The friendship was abruptly severed, however, when Steele refused to assist Manley with money to enable her to travel to the country after Tilly's marriage. Manley and Steele were to be inveterate and public enemies with numerous exchanges in print, particularly in *The Tatler*, *The Examiner*, and *The Guardian* (for a summary of these see Morgan, 115–16). The rift, exacerbated by their political differences, lasted until 1717. The preface to Manley's last performed play, *Lucius, the First Christian King of Britain*, details the reconciliation, sweetened by Steele's payment of £600 for the play's production by his Drury Lane Company.

Despite Steele's refusal, Manley evidently managed to find some means of support since according to letter 33 of *The lady's pacquet* she made two visits to the country to repair her spirits, the second to Bristol where an intrigue with an unidentified man she calls 'Mr Worthy' aided her recovery, but also ended in separation. Manley spent spring 1704 in London before making a visit to her friend the poet Sarah Fyge in Buckingham. Their correspondence is given in letters 5–9 of *The lady's pacquet*. This friendship too ended bitterly when Sarah Fyge gave evidence in the Doctors' Commons in 1705 against Manley, Mrs Mary Thompson, and a forger, Edmund Smith, in their attempt to gain compensation for Thompson from the estate of her common-law husband, a Mr Pheasant of Upwood, Huntingdonshire (Wylie, 392–3; Manley, *Lady's pacquet*, letter 33). Manley had hoped to win £100 a year from her involvement in this lawsuit and here too she attacked a false friend in print presenting Sarah Fyge as a violent wife and poor poet in the first volume of her *New Atalantis*. By 1705 it became necessary for Delarivier Manley to resume her writing career to secure her living and she embarked on her most successful venture as a writer: the production of anti-whig satire veiled as romance.

Mid-career Manley's *Secret History of Queen Zarah and the Zarazians* (1705) drew on French sources for both its preface, a close translation from an essay of 1703 by Abbé de Morvan de Bellegarde (advocating the advantages and pleasures of the short fiction over the romance), and its narrative, derived from a 1680 French satire about Charles II and Barbara Villiers, entitled *Hattigé*. It was, however, also typical of the prose fiction in which she was to become adept, providing an accurate if scandalous account of whig political machination. In all her fiction, but especially in this first work, John and Sarah Churchill are major targets, their dominance over Queen Anne a source of anxiety and rancour for the tory ideals and ambitions of Manley. A second part, exploiting the popularity of the first, appeared in the same year. A second tragedy, *Almyna, or, The Arabian Vow*, was performed in December 1706 at the new Haymarket Theatre—an early example of her tendency to cryptic self-referentiality in the anagrammatical use of her own name for its powerful heroine derived from Scheherezade in the popular *Arabian Nights Entertainment*.

In July 1709 Manley may have turned her hand to the periodical, appearing as Phoebe Crackenthorpe, editor of the *Female Tatler*, although her claim to the title has been disputed. The fact that Mrs Crackenthorpe handed over the editorship to a Society of Ladies in October 1709 at just the moment that Delarivier Manley found herself taken up for seditious libel suggests some support for the conviction of Paul Bunyan Anderson and of Fidelis Morgan that she was (at least one of) its original author(s). Manley was taken into custody nine days after the publication of the second volume of *Secret memoirs and manners of several persons of quality of both sexes, from the new Atalantis, an island in the Mediterranean* on 29 October 1709. She apparently surrendered herself after a secretary of state's warrant had been issued against her, and her publishers John Morphew and John Woodward and printer John Barber had been detained. Four days later the latter were discharged but Manley remained in custody until 5 November when she was released on bail. After several continuations of the case, she was tried and discharged on 13 February 1710. A note in the Public Record Office (State Papers 34, 11, fol. 69) recently uncovered by Ruth Herman recording that a warrant had been issued for the arrest of Morphew and Woodward on 11 November 1709, a full two weeks after Manley was taken into custody, suggests that Manley did not in fact surrender herself for the sake of her colleagues as the only remaining account of the trial, her own in *Rivella*, claims. In this same account, Manley describes her defence of the book on grounds that her information came by 'inspiration' and her rebuke of her judges for bringing 'a woman to her trial for writing a few amorous trifles' (Manley, *Rivella*, 110–11). The two volumes of *Secret memoirs* (the first volume had appeared in May 1709) were *romans-à-clef* with separately printed keys, which offered a succession of narratives of seduction and betrayal by notorious whig grandees told to Astrea, an allegorical figure of justice. The narratives were mainly told by female characters including an allegorical figure of Intelligence and a midwife. In *Rivella* Manley claims that her trial led her to conclude that 'politics is not the business of a woman' (ibid., 112), and that thereafter she turned exclusively to stories of love.

In fact her next work, the two-volume *Memoirs of Europe, towards the close of the eighth century, written by Eginardus, secretary and favourite to Charlemagne*, of May and November 1710 continued the work of propaganda for the tory party and went on to be published as the third and fourth volumes of the *New Atalantis*. These volumes used male narrative voices more extensively. The first volume was addressed to Lord Peterborough and on the strength of this Delarivier Manley sought, with Swift's support, a pension from Peterborough in July 1711 (Swift, 2.306). The second volume was more concerned with stories of love than with politics but the satirical purpose of exposing whig corruption through analogy with sexual depravity remained evident. The author also sought assistance on several occasions from Robert Harley, sending him a copy of the first volume of *Memoirs of Europe* on 12 May 1710. As a result of her patient solicitations she received £50 from Harley, acknowledged in her letter of thanks dated 14 June 1714 (*Portland MSS*, 5.458). This is the only remuneration she is known to have received for her partisan services.

From 1711 to 1713 Manley concentrated on political journalism, editing Jonathan Swift's *Examiner* for number 7 (14 September 1710) and numbers 46 to 52 (14 June to 26 July 1711). These contained a series of direct attacks on whig propaganda, but are without the female narrative frames or striking female protagonists that are her trade mark in prose fiction and drama. She produced a number of pamphlets addressing contemporary controversies and intervening in political debate in this period: *A True Narrative of what Pass'd at the Examination of the Marquis of Guiscard* (1711); *A Learned Comment on Dr. Hare's Sermon* (1711); and *The Honour and Prerogative of the Queen's Majesty Vindicated* (1713).

Final publications Manley's liaison with the Jacobite printer and alderman of the City of London John *Barber (*bap.* 1675, *d.* 1741) may have begun as early as 1705 when he published her *Queen Zarah*. In any case, by spring 1714 she and her sister Cornelia were living at his residence and printing house on the corner of Old Fish Street and Lambeth Hill in London, although Delarivier retained a country residence for the summer months in Oxfordshire (her will cites the house as in Berkley, taken to be Beckley). With Queen Anne's death in 1714 and the decline of tory hopes, Manley seems to have turned away from partisan publication without losing her relish for scandal. Her third-person (auto)biography, *The Adventures of Rivella*, is a tongue-in-cheek riposte to Edmund Curll who had threatened her with the publication of a scandalous account of her life by Charles Gildon. Manley's narrative frame is that of two men discussing Rivella, although she herself is not present. Here, as in other works, Manley complains about the double standard: 'if she had been a man, she had been without fault' (Manley, *Rivella*, 47) but also acknowledges how successfully she had exploited the display of her sex as an author: 'it would have been a *fault in her, not to have been faulty*' (ibid., 114).

Manley's last performed play, *Lucius, the First Christian King of Britain* (Drury Lane, 1717), a work of fervent nationalism, puts centre stage (like her other plays) a powerful woman, Rosalind, Queen of Britain. *The Power of Love in Seven Novels* (1720) reworked five tales from William Painter's 1566 versions of Italian and French novels entitled *The Palace of Pleasure*, and drew on a contemporary scandal for one and, probably, invention for the last. In this underrated work Manley thoroughly transforms her sources to make them relevant to contemporary contexts and debates, delivers racy plotting, and panders to her readers' voyeurism.

According to Edmund Curll, Barber's tyrannous behaviour towards her and his infidelity with the maid he had engaged for her, one Sarah Dovekin or Dufkin, impeded Manley's completion of a second volume of novels, presumably also from Painter, before her death (Curll, *Impartial History*, 47). In a letter to the government, Curll also reported his sighting of a letter from Delarivier Manley stating that 'a fifth volume of the Atalantis had been for some time printed off, and lies ready for publication' (*N&Q*, 2nd ser., 2/49, 6 Dec 1856, 441–3). Delarivier Manley died at Barber's house on 11 July 1724 of a 'cholic' (Curll, *Impartial History*, 44) and was buried as her will requested at the church of St Benet Paul's Wharf, under a white marble stone (later excavated in building work). In her will (dated 6 October 1723) she mentions two plays now lost, a tragedy called the 'Duke of Somerset' and a comedy called the 'Double Mistress', which might turn a profit on publication, but asks for all her other manuscripts to be destroyed so that 'none Ghost-like may walk after my decease' (PRO, PROB 11/599, 194–5); the same instructions held for any correspondence. *The Life and Character of John Barber* (1741) refers to 'a Miscellany, not yet collected, of valuable pieces in verse and prose' (p. 10) which never appeared. She had little else to leave except £352 capital and £352 annuity from £500 worth of South Sea stock bought in 1721, and complex instructions for her executors, Cornelia Markendale (her sister) and Henrietta Essex Manley, a child's coat maker and presumably relation, to endeavour through the offices of Swift, to procure from his executor half of the £50 annual patent owed to her by the bookseller Benjamin Tooke. The remaining half, owed to her by her printer John Barber, was waived in acknowledgement of 'so many favours' already received.

Manley's plays and prose works were highly successful and popular in her own time, though they failed to secure her the financial and political patronage she craved. The remarkably accurate scandalous and political references in her prose works may now be obscure, but her energetic style and plotting made her an important contributor to the development of the modern novel as a vehicle for entertainment. Her clear-sighted exposure of sexual double standards, if leavened with sexual voyeurism and a taste for the scandalous and perverse, reveals her to be an early exponent of Enlightenment feminism.

ROS BALLASTER

Sources R. Herman, 'The business of a woman: the political writings of Delarivier Manley (1667?–1724)', PhD diss., Open University, 2000 • F. Morgan, *A woman of no character: an autobiography of Mrs. Manley* (1986) • P. Köster, 'Delariviere Manley and the DNB: a cautionary tale about following black sheep with a challenge to the cataloguers', *Eighteenth-Century Life*, 3 (1976–7), 106–11 • D. Manley, *The adventures of Rivella*, ed. K. Zelinsky (1999) • D. D. Clark Duff, 'Materials toward a biography of Mary Delariviere Manley', PhD diss., Indiana University, 1965 • P. B. Anderson, 'Mistress Delariviere Manley's biography', *Modern Philology*, 33 (1935–6), 261–78 • D. Manley, *The novels of Mary Delariviere Manley*, ed. P. Köster, 2 vols. (1971) • [D. Manley], *Secret memoirs and manners of several persons of quality of both sexes, from the New Atalantis*, 2 vols. (1991); repr. as *New Atalantis*, ed. R. Ballaster (1991) • E. Curll, *An impartial history of the life, character, amours, travels and transactions of Mr John Barber* (1741) • E. Curll, 'Preface', *Mrs. Manley's history of her own life and times* (1725) • *The manuscripts of his grace the duke of Portland*, 10 vols., HMC, 29 (1891–1931), vol. 4, p. 541; vol. 5, pp. 95–6, 453–4, 458, 491 • J. Sutton, 'The source of Mrs Manley's preface to Queen Zarah', *Modern Philology*, 82 (1984–5), 167–72 • J. Swift, *Journal to Stella*, ed. H. Williams, 2 vols. (1948) • C. Wylie, 'Mrs Manley', *N&Q*, 2nd ser., 3 (1857), 392–3 • G. B. Needham, 'Mary de la Riviere Manley, tory defender', *Huntington Library Quarterly*, 12 (1948–9), 253–88 • N. Luttrell, *A brief historical relation of state affairs from September 1678 to April 1714*, 6 (1857), 505–8, 546 • P. B. Anderson, 'The history and authorship of Mrs. Crackenthorpe's *Female Tatler*', *MP*, 28 (1931), 354–60 • W. Graham, 'Thomas Baker, Mrs Manley and the *Female Tatler*', *MP*, 34 (1936–7), 267–72 • J. H. Smith, 'Thomas Baker and *The Female Tatler*', *MP*, 49 (1951–2), 182–8 • R. Herman, 'Similarities between Delarivier Manley's *Secret history of Queen Zarah* and the English translation of *Hattigé*', *N&Q*, 245 (2000), 193–6 • *Life and character of John Barber, esq.* (1741) • D. Hipwell, 'Mrs. Manley's will', *N&Q*, 7th ser., 8 (1889), 156–7 • will, PRO, PROB 11/599, 194–5

Likenesses engraving, repro. in D. Manley, *The adventures of Rivella* (1714) • engraving, repro. in C. Smart, *The Midwife, or, The Old Woman's Magazine* (1750–52)

Wealth at death £352 capital and £352 annuity from £500 South Sea stock bought 1721; £50 p.a. from Royal Patent profits granted to Benjamin Tooke, bookseller, and John Barber, printer: will, PRO, PROB 11/599, 194–5; repr. in Hipwell, 'Mrs. Manley's will'

Manley [*née* Swithenbank], **Edna** (1900–1987), sculptor, was born on 28 February 1900 at Buxton, Richmond Wood Road, Bournemouth, the fifth child in the family of six daughters and three sons of the Revd Harvey Swithenbank (*d.* 1910), Wesleyan Methodist minister, and his wife, Martha Matilda Elliott (Ellie), daughter of Alexander Shearer, penkeeper. Her father, who had been a missionary in Jamaica, was of English descent; her mother was of part-Jamaican and part-Irish descent. When she was two the family moved to Cornwall, and lived in St Ives, Penryn, Callington, and, after her father's death, Penzance, where she was educated at West Cornwall College. In 1916 she left school to work at the army remount department at Wembley, breaking in Canadian horses. After the war she remained in London, and from 1918 to 1920, with financial support from her paternal uncle Oliver Swithenbank, a Leeds factory owner, attended evening classes at Regent Street Polytechnic. In 1920 she enrolled at St Martin's School of Art but stayed only for the autumn term. Her studies at St Martin's were combined with evening classes at the Royal Academy where she studied anatomy under Arthur Thompson. In 1921 she left the Royal Academy to participate in evening classes at the Sir John Cass Technical Institute. Her early works were dramatic animal sculptures modelled in clay and cast in plaster, for example *The Lion* and *The Eagle*. However, at St Martin's she was encouraged to look for planes and lines in the human figure. On 25 June 1921 she married her first cousin, Norman Washington *Manley (1893–1969), lawyer and politician; they had first met in 1914 when he arrived in England as a Rhodes scholar. They had two sons, Douglas Ralph Manley (*b.* 1922) and Michael Norman *Manley (1924–1997).

Shortly after the birth of their first son, the Manleys moved to Jamaica. In the first year there Edna Manley learned much. She soon realized that the artistic environment that existed in London was non-existent in Jamaica. Plasterina was imported from England to enable her to work. One of the first works she produced in Jamaica was *The Bead Seller*, which was modelled on a black Jamaican woman. She continued to use black people as models for her work at a time when the notion of 'negroes' as subjects antagonized many among the Jamaican élite. She returned to England in 1923 and took the opportunity to see many exhibitions in London as well as visiting friends. She returned to Jamaica early the following year, determined to survive as an artist. *The Bead Seller* was exhibited in London in the summer by the Society of Women Artists.

Boy with Reed (1927) was the first sculpture that Edna Manley made from wood. This was followed by a life-size figure of *Eve* (1928). Both works reflected the current trends in Vorticism and neo-classicism in British sculpture. When she returned to England in 1929 they were shown at the Goupil Gallery and received extensive press coverage, the *Morning Post* describing *Eve* as 'primeval'. In 1930 *Eve* was shown in the Women's International Art Club's exhibition at Suffolk Galleries and the London Group exhibition, and returned to the Goupil Gallery in the summer. Also in 1930 she was elected a member of the London Group, and became friends with the sculptor Koren der Harootian. Her work had a great influence on him, and on the photographer Denis Gich and the sculptor Alvin Marriott; they frequently exhibited together.

Edna Manley's first solo exhibition in Jamaica occurred in 1931. It was a significant event in Jamaican cultural history, since until that point very little locally produced art had been exhibited there. In the same year Kineton Parkes's book *The Art of Carved Sculpture* commented on Manley's original and productive mind. In 1934 Esther Chapman, journalist and art critic, returned to Jamaica; thereafter she wrote frequently about Manley's work. In the late 1930s Manley's work reflected the political and social upheavals in Jamaica. In 1935 she carved *Negro Aroused* (National Gallery of Jamaica, Kingston), which was bought by public subscription for the Institute of Fine Arts in Kingston. It soon became an icon of the Jamaican anti-colonial movement, particularly after the 1938 riots and strikes in Jamaica, which led to the formation of two political parties, one headed by her husband and the other by her cousin, Alexander Bustamante. In 1977 she made a 10-foot bronze replica of *Negro Aroused* which was commissioned by the Jamaican government and installed on Ocean Boulevard, Kingston.

In the 1940s and 1950s Edna Manley continued to produce sculptures and carvings—notable works including *Horse of the Morning* (1943; National Gallery of Jamaica, Kingston) and *Moon* (1943)—but she was increasingly drawn into teaching and other cultural activities. In 1943 she founded *Focus*, the British West Indies' first successful literary and art journal, and in 1950 she founded the Jamaica School of Art (later renamed the Edna Manley School of Art). Her husband's increasing political prominence—he became chief minister of Jamaica in 1955—

required her to scale down her own activities, though she continued to take a great interest in the careers of a younger generation of Jamaican artists, and produced a widely acclaimed sculpture of Paul Bogle (1965), leader of the Morant Bay rebellion, for installation in Morant Bay Square. Following her husband's death in 1969 she resumed her artistic activity with vigour. *Journey* (1973; National Gallery of Jamaica, Kingston) was her last carving, but she continued to work in clay and fibreglass until her final years. She was one of *Ten Jamaican Sculptors* who exhibited at the Commonwealth Institute, London, in 1975, and there were other exhibitions of her work both in Jamaica and in London. She was made an honorary DLitt by the University of the West Indies in 1977 and awarded the order of merit in the national honours in 1980. She died peacefully in her sleep at her home in Jamaica, on the morning of 10 February 1987. After a state funeral she was buried beside her husband in National Heroes' Park, Kingston. She was survived by her sons Douglas, a social scientist, and Michael, prime minister of Jamaica from 1972 to 1980 and again from 1989 to 1992.

PAULINE DE SOUZA

Sources W. Brown, *Edna Manley: the private years, 1900–1938* (1975) · R. Manley, *Edna Manley: the diaries* (1989) · R. Manley, *Drumblair: memories of a Jamaican childhood* (1996) · *The Times* (26 Feb 1987) · *New York Times* (12 Feb 1987) · b. cert. · m. cert.
Likenesses photographs, repro. in Brown, *Edna Manley* · photographs, repro. in Manley, *Edna Manley*, following p. 148

Manley, Gordon (1902–1980), geographer and meteorologist, was born on 3 January 1902 at Douglas on the Isle of Man, the son of Valentine Manley, a chartered accountant. He grew up in Lancashire and was educated at the Queen Elizabeth Grammar School, Blackburn. From the age of twelve he took meteorological readings in the countryside around his home. He went to Manchester University in 1918 to read engineering, graduated in 1921, and proceeded to Gonville and Caius College, Cambridge, to read geography. He gained a double first in 1923. At Cambridge he studied under Frank Debenham, who inspired his interest in high-altitude environments. He obtained employment in the Meteorological Office in 1925 and was stationed at Kew observatory, but in the following year he accepted an assistant lectureship in geography at Birmingham University. In the same year he also accompanied the Cambridge expedition to east Greenland. There he undertook gravitational measurements which formed the basis of his earliest publications.

The foundations of Manley's career were now established. His training at Manchester in an applied science and his keen geographical interest were focused through his experience of scientific instrumentation, which was refined in Greenland and at Kew, where he also first encountered long meteorological records. In 1928 he was appointed to establish geography as a degree subject at Durham University. He remained at Durham until 1939. While there he married, in 1930, Audrey Fairfax Robinson, the daughter of Arthur Robinson, master of Hatfield College. They had no children.

At Durham, Manley began his work on the British climate which became the distinguishing feature of his scholarship. His research developed two related themes. Field observations concentrated on the climate of upland Britain. In 1932 he began to collect data on Cross Fell in the northern Pennines and in 1938 he established a meteorological station close to the summit of Dun Fell. At the same time he began to analyse historic meteorological records. He was curator of the Durham University observatory between 1932 and 1937 and published an account of the observatory's lengthy meteorological records in the *Quarterly Journal of the Royal Meteorological Society* in 1941. In 1939 Manley moved back to Cambridge as a university demonstrator in geography. This involved him almost immediately in teaching responsibilities shaped largely by the war, including service short courses and teaching shared with the geography department of Bedford College, evacuated from London from 1939 until 1944. He remained at Cambridge throughout the war, serving as an officer of the university air squadron and widening his research interests to embrace global climatic change and palaeoclimatology. He gave the Symons memorial lecture to the Royal Meteorological Society in 1944, and his title, 'Some recent contributions to the study of climatic change', gives a clear indication of the focus of his research.

By the end of the war Manley's academic standing was established among both geographers and meteorologists. He was president of the Royal Meteorological Society in 1945–7 and was awarded the Murchison grant of the Royal Geographical Society in 1947. In the immediate post-war years his publications began to indicate his widening interests, beyond the British Isles and into a more distant past affected by the glacial climates of the Pleistocene.

Manley was appointed to a university lectureship at Cambridge in 1947, but in 1948 he accepted the newly established chair of geography at Bedford College in the University of London. Here 'he was welcomed as an entertaining lecturer and for his genial personality and friendly manner with staff and students alike' (Lamb). At this time he was a member of committees of the Royal Society, the Royal Geographical Society, and the Air Ministry, and also of the British national committee for the international geophysical year. His research publications remained prolific and included his important and meticulous work on historic temperature records for central England for the period 1698–1952, which he later extended to cover the period 1659–1973, published in the *Quarterly Journal of the Royal Meteorological Society* in 1953 and 1974 respectively. His memory for the details of this and other meteorological records was prodigious. He also reached a wider public through his book *Climate and the British Scene* (1952) and through his articles in the *Manchester Guardian*. Of the latter, more than fifty appeared between 1954 and 1961, mostly concerned with the unpredictability of Britain's daily and seasonal weather.

In 1964 Manley was invited to found a department of environmental studies at the new University of Lancaster, and this occupied him until his retirement in 1967. In nurturing the departments at both Bedford College and Lancaster he was more concerned with quality than with scale. *Festina lente* was his motto. After retiring to Coton in Cambridgeshire he was a supporter of the village church there, and he remained active in research and writing until the end of his life. Between 1927 and 1981 he published more than 180 papers. He died on 29 January 1980 at Papworth Hospital, Papworth Everard, of heart failure, and was survived by his widow.

Manley was a pioneer in the study of climatic change. He showed how the weather and climates of the past could be reconstructed, sometimes in considerable detail, using data from many different sources. His own main interest was in the historic period with its written and instrumental archives, but he was fully aware of the climatic signal in the geological record and its significance for the more distant past. Seen in its historical context, his work provides part of the insight that has led to the study of such issues as global warming and has enabled palaeoclimatic research to focus on the causes of climatic change.   CHRISTOPHER P. GREEN

Sources *GJ*, 146 (1980), 475–6 · H. H. Lamb, 'The life and work of Professor Gordon Manley', *Weather*, 36 (1981), 220–31 · G. M. Sheail, J. M. Kenworthy, and M. J. Tooley, 'Bibliography of papers by Gordon Manley', *The climatic scene*, ed. M. J. Tooley and G. M. Sheail (1985), 279–85 · J. A. Steers, *Transactions of the Institute of British Geographers*, new ser., 5 (1980), 513–14 · M. J. Tooley and G. M. Sheail, 'The life and work of Gordon Manley', *The climatic scene* (1985) · d. cert. · *CGPLA Eng. & Wales* (1980)

Archives CUL, papers, incl. notes on Hertzell's journal of weather at Exeter · Meteorological Office, Bracknell, Berkshire, National Meteorological Library, unpublished collections of historical weather records

Likenesses photograph, repro. in Tooley and Sheail, eds., *Climatic scene* (1985), frontispiece

Wealth at death £89,691: probate, 27 June 1980, *CGPLA Eng. & Wales*

Manley, John (*c.*1622–1699), parliamentarian army officer and rebel, came from a minor gentry family seated at Brynyffynnon, Wrexham, Denbighshire. He was the third son of Cornelius Manley, who died in 1623 while John was an infant. John's inheritance was a mere £30, and like so many younger sons of gentry he was put into trade, being apprenticed to a London skinner in 1639. Although both his brothers were royalists in the civil war, Manley enlisted in the parliamentarian army and rose to the rank of captain, possibly helped by his radical religious beliefs. As a Baptist Manley rejected infant baptism, but he went further, denying any legitimacy at all to the Anglican clergy and claiming that continuing divine inspiration made him the equal of any of the apostles. He was also interested in millenarianism and corresponded with the Fifth Monarchist preacher and conspirator Walter Thimbleton, who like Manley came from Wrexham.

Manley's career was further assisted by his marriage in 1650 to Margaret Dorislaus (d. 1675), daughter of the distinguished republican apologist and diplomat Isaac *Dorislaus (assassinated by royalists in 1649), with whom he had two sons and two daughters. Parliamentary respect for his dead father-in-law, together with the £500 it had voted to each of Dorislaus's daughters, no doubt helped him to buy the office of postmaster-general in 1653, for the sum of exactly £8259 19s. 11¾d.—'with good securities' (*CSP dom.*, 1652–3, 450). Responsible for the safe delivery of the post both at home and abroad, at fixed rates, Manley was harassed by law suits from previous holders of the office, and claimed that the costs of developing the service gave him little profit in the two years he held the position. Surveillance of the post was of crucial importance to the regime's security, as Manley's instructions to his postmasters in December 1653 made clear. Apart from their collecting and delivering duties they were to watch strangers and travellers closely, be alert for disaffection and plotting, and to open no letters without Manley's express permission. Security considerations explain why Manley had to sell the office to John Thurloe, the powerful secretary to the council of state, in 1655. During this period Manley made two trips abroad, in 1652 and 1655, possibly to the Netherlands in connection with his father-in-law's affairs.

Manley retired to Denbighshire after 1655 but remained loyal to the republican regime, serving as a local commissioner for the assessment in 1657, captain of militia, justice of the peace, and MP for Denbigh in 1659. He helped suppress a royalist insurrection in August 1659 by arresting the Denbighshire high sheriff, and he opposed the Restoration. He kept to his dissenting religious views, too, his house in Wrexham being raided in 1663 and 1665 as an illegal conventicle. On the latter occasion his quick wits enabled many of the 100 persons present to escape, while he argued with the militia officers through an open window over their lack of a search warrant. After the Restoration he returned to London and took up brewing, though he kept his lease of Brynyffynnon. He lost his premises in the fire of London, but in the 1670s was sufficiently prosperous to become a master in his company, the Skinners. His wife, Margaret, died in 1675, and he remarried some time after, having at least one son by his second wife, Mary (*d.* 1701).

Manley may have considered emigrating to America, having acquired 370 acres in Carolina in 1678, but the grant brought him into contact with the earl of Shaftesbury just as the Popish Plot and exclusion crisis commenced, and Manley re-entered radical politics. He helped promote London's 'monster petition' to the king (for the elected parliament to meet) in 1679–80 and became one of Shaftesbury's agents, being sent by the earl in 1681 to organize disaffected seamen at Wapping to take arms if the king should die. Though on the fringe of the confused plotting which led to the Rye House conspiracy, Manley was never sufficiently prominent to be arrested. His business affairs suffered, however, and by the spring of 1684 he was bankrupt. Early in that year he was still associating with John Wildman and other conspirators in London, but by May he had fled to the Netherlands.

Manley joined the duke of Monmouth's ill-fated expedition in 1685, his presence being very welcome as one of the few participants with any military experience. Monmouth promoted him to major, a rank Manley insisted on for the rest of his life. Though over sixty years old Manley was active in the fighting. Shortly after the landing at Lyme Regis he swept militia troops out of nearby Bridport with a much inferior force of a mere dozen horse, contributing to the dominance which the rebels early established over the militias of the south-west. Ten days into the rebellion, while the rebels were at Shepton Mallett, they were joined by Manley's son Isaac bearing a message from John Wildman that there were good prospects of a rising in Cheshire, and asking what could he and the duke's other London friends do. Monmouth had counted on simultaneous risings elsewhere in England to stretch royal forces, and 'young Manley' was sent back with a sharp message for the Londoners to act at once. A week later, just before the battle of Sedgemoor, Manley himself was sent to London to try to stir Wildman and his friends into action. He thus missed the climax of the rebellion, and though an arrest warrant was issued for him he evaded capture and escaped to the Netherlands.

There Manley joined up with other survivors. He was noted as one of the 'godly' faction among them; took an active part in an attempt to establish a woollen factory at Groningen to provide employment for the exiles; threatened to kill an exile suspected of informing for the English government; and was hopeful of another rebellion if James II tried to resume church lands sold at the Reformation. He sought no pardon, and he and his son Isaac were both excepted from James II's general pardons of 1686 and 1688. He was one of three egregious rebel exiles whom William of Orange in December 1685 asked the Amsterdam authorities to arrest, in response to pressure from James II. Manley nevertheless embarked with William in 1688 and did good work, raising support for the prince in the west. He represented Bridport (Dorset) in the Convention Parliament of 1689, where he was very active, sitting on fifty-one committees and participating in the drafting of several important measures, including the oath of allegiance, the Bill of Rights, and the Mutiny Bill. He took part in the discussions concerning religious toleration, and was lobbied by George Fox and the Quakers.

From about 1690, however, Manley fell into oblivion in public matters, being defeated at Bridport in parliamentary elections in 1690 and 1695. He was one of the very few English rebels and exiles whom William III did not quickly favour with some office, however minor. This may have been because his views were too republican for William, or it may simply have been the effect of advancing age and poor circumstances. Described in 1684 as a 'broken brewer' (Greaves & Zaller, *BDBR*, 2.212), he had probably lost more money in the Groningen cloth venture, and in March 1696 he petitioned for a position in the customs, pleading his great loss of estate caused by sufferings in the public service. He obtained no relief, and by 1698 he was sick with the palsy and in prison for debt, with his son Isaac petitioning for an increase in his own salary in order to support his father. This finally produced a pension of £200 per annum, but Manley lived to receive less than a year of it, dying early in 1699, when he was residing at the Old Artillery Ground. He was buried at St Stephen

Walbrook on 31 January 1699. His eldest son, John, married a Cornish heiress, sat as MP for Bossiney and Camelford under William and Anne, and was a strong tory; but his other son, Isaac (a rebel in 1685), remained a whig and was well rewarded, becoming postmaster-general of Ireland and an Irish MP from 1713 to his death in 1737.

ROBIN CLIFTON

Sources Greaves & Zaller, *BDBR*, vol. 2 · D. R. Lacey, *Dissent and parliamentary politics in England, 1661–1689* (1969) · W. M. Wigfield, *The Monmouth rebels, 1685*, Somerset RS, 79 (1985) · R. Clifton, *The last popular rebellion: the western rising of 1685* (1984) · R. L. Greaves, *Secrets of the kingdom: British radicals from the Popish Plot to the revolution of 1688–89* (1992) · J. Ferguson, *Robert Ferguson the plotter: the secret of the Rye-house conspiracy and the story of a strange career* (1887) · M. Ashley, *John Wildman, plotter and postmaster: a study of the English republican movement in the seventeenth century* (1947) · H. Horwitz, *Parliament, policy and politics in the reign of William III* (1977) · P. Earle, *Monmouth's rebels* (1977) · D. J. Milne, 'The Rye House plot with special reference to its place in the exclusion contest and its consequences till 1685', PhD diss., U. Lond., 1949 · *HoP, Commons, 1660–90*, vol. 3 · M. Knights, 'London's "monster" petition of 1680', *HJ*, 36 (1993), 39–67 · *CSP dom., 1650–99* · PRO, PROB 6/75, fol. 35v · PRO, PROB 6/78, fol. 5r
Wealth at death in prison as a debtor; no property: Greaves & Zaller, *BDBR*; *CSP dom.*, 7.74, 9.215

Manley, Michael Norman (1924–1997), prime minister of Jamaica, was born in St Andrew, Kingston, Jamaica, on 10 December 1924, the younger son of Norman Washington *Manley (1893–1969), statesman and lawyer, and his wife, Edna Swithenbank (1900–1987) [see Manley, Edna], artist and sculptor, daughter of the Revd Harvey Swithenbank, Methodist missionary. Both parents were Jamaican. Like his father he was educated at Jamaica College, an Anglican school, until 1 October 1943, when he enlisted in the Royal Canadian Air Force to train as a wireless operator and gunner. After the war he won a serviceman's scholarship to the London School of Economics, which he entered in 1946. There his tutors, Harold Laski and (William) Arthur Lewis, aroused what was to be his lifelong enthusiasm for the Puerto Rican model for industrial development of smaller countries by attracting large injections of foreign capital through guarantees of low wages, disciplined labour unions, and local provision of the infrastructure. As leader of the West Indian students he protested about the condition of the hostel provided by the Colonial Office, and demonstrated against the policy of the Commonwealth Office on Seretse Khama's marriage to an Englishwoman. Bored by formal course work, he left after a year to live with his first wife, Jacqueline Ramellard, *née* Kanellardski, whom he married in 1946, in St Agnes, Cornwall, where he studied Latin. His first daughter, Rachel, was born in 1947, but in 1948 Manley returned to London to finish his degree. He graduated in economics in 1950, and then spent a year in London learning journalism by reporting on cricket matches as a freelance for *The Observer* and the BBC. He was divorced from his first wife in 1951.

In December 1951 Manley returned to Jamaica, and the following year he became associate editor of *Public Opinion*, the newspaper that supported the People's National Party (PNP) founded by his father. He also became an active member of the National Workers' Union affiliated

Michael Norman Manley (1924–1997), by Neil Libbert, 1989

to that party. He was the union's sugar supervisor from 1953 to 1954, and island supervisor and first vice-president from 1955 to 1972. Great antagonism existed between, on the one hand, the PNP and the National Workers' Union and, on the other, the Jamaica Labour Party and the Bustamante Industrial Trade Union, the latter both created by the Manleys' kinsman, Sir (William) Alexander Clarke (known as Alexander Bustamante). In the 1950s Manley organized the workers in the bauxite and sugar industries; he led the strike in the sugar industry in 1959 which led to the Goldenberg commission of inquiry. He supported his father's aim to democratize the trade union movement. Because of his close association with his father, he was known as Young Boy, or Joshua (to his father's Moses). Until 1972 he worked as a trade unionist and journalist, writing on imperialism, racism, and nationalism. He married Thelma Verity in 1955, and they had one child, Joseph (*b*. 1958). The marriage ended in divorce in 1960.

Having overcome his original strong physical aversion to public speaking, Manley emerged as an effective orator and entered Jamaican national politics when the country gained independence from colonial rule in 1962. His father, chief minister since 1955, secured him a seat in the senate. Bustamante, however, won the first free election, in 1962, and remained in power for a decade. Manley was elected to the house of representatives as MP for Central Kingston in 1967. In 1966 he had married, thirdly, Barbara Lewars; their daughter Sara was born in 1967. The death of Barbara, from cancer in 1968, devastated Manley, and nearly ended his political career. Nevertheless he recovered and, shortly before his father's retirement and death in 1969, succeeded him as leader of the opposition. In 1972 he married, fourthly, Beverley Anderson, who led the women's political movement in Jamaica; they had one daughter, Natasha (*b*. 1974), and one son, David (*b*. 1980). Manley and his fourth wife were separated in 1984.

Like his Fabian father, Manley was a strong advocate of social democracy and the economic strength to be derived from West Indian federation, but he was more extreme in his fight against colonialism, capitalism, and authoritarianism. His open criticism of American culture and frank admiration of the social reconstruction of Cuba achieved by his friend Fidél Castro aroused considerable antagonism in the United States. When he became prime minister, following a landslide victory for the PNP in 1972, Manley expelled one particularly hostile American ambassador, while gladly accepting technical assistance and the gift of a school from Cuba. Another friend whom he consulted frequently was Julius Nyerere. Manley was prominent as a supporter of African liberation movements and openly approved Cuba's intervention in Angola. He was awarded a United Nations special award for his contribution to the struggle against apartheid in 1978.

In 1972 Manley undertook the task of revitalizing the Jamaican economy, the decline of which had been ignored for at least seven years. Declaring his four principles of policy for the Jamaican people to be equality, social justice, self-reliance, and self-discipline, he took a pragmatic stance over the economic measures he introduced, such as sugar co-operatives, agricultural loans, and a bauxite levy, while simultaneously facilitating the investment of external venture capital. His economic planning consequently lacked coherence and the economy further declined. In 1974 a policy statement rededicated the PNP to a form of democratic socialism involving a mixed economy and the individual's responsibility to contribute to the welfare and development of the nation. At this time Manley, influenced by his fourth wife, became a supporter of women's liberation. The chief Jamaican newspaper, *The Gleaner*, bitterly and consistently attacked his policies. Violence during the 1976 general election (in which Manley again triumphed), rumoured to be provoked by the CIA, far exceeded the political riots of the 1960s. Three attempts were made to assassinate Manley, the Peruvian ambassador was stabbed to death, and the governor-general declared a state of emergency. Conflict continued between and within the political parties. Manley repeatedly appealed for peace in Jamaica. To help defuse the situation his friend Bob Marley sang at a 'One Love' concert and called Manley and Edward Seaga, leader of the opposition, onto the stage to shake hands and dance a jig.

Eventually Manley was forced to appeal for help from the International Monetary Fund, a course of action he had long resisted because it required a 40 per cent devaluation of the currency. However, this economic solution failed because Jamaica was unable to meet the IMF's requirements. Much of the aid promised did not materialize, real wages continued to fall, there was a 'brain drain' to the American mainland, and a hurricane destroyed 75 per cent of the banana crop. Internal disorder escalated, causing more than 700 deaths during the 1980 election campaign. Manley's party was soundly defeated, and the adulation afforded him earlier vanished in Jamaica, but his offer to resign from the PNP leadership was refused. His reputation overseas survived and was enhanced by his speeches in support of 'third-world' countries at international conventions, and he received several decorations from foreign heads of state. He was prominent in his opposition to American support for the 'Contras' in Nicaragua, and to the invasion of Grenada by the United States in 1983. Through journalism he again attempted to bring about internal peace, to re-educate his party, and to redefine its social and economic policy objectives, thereby gaining precedence for the PNP in local elections.

In February 1989 Manley again led his party to a decisive general election victory, winning forty-five seats to the Jamaica Labour Party's fifteen. In opposition he had written: 'I am grateful that God has given me the kind of mind that does not assume that what I thought I knew yesterday was an eternal guarantee of truth' (*The Times*, 8 March 1997). In office he embarked on a vigorous programme of privatization and deregulation, arguing that the private sector offered the best hope of expanding Jamaica's economic production, and therefore of achieving the social goals to which he was still committed. In 1987 diverticulitis had necessitated a major colonic operation, and in 1991 prostate cancer was diagnosed. In March 1992 Manley announced his resignation as prime minister; he was succeeded by Percival J. Patterson. In the same year he married, fifthly, Glynne Ewart, who survived him. He died at his home, 89 Old Hope Road, Kingston, Jamaica, on 6 March 1997.   PATRICIA M. PUGH

Sources D. E. Levi, *Michael Manley: the making of a leader* (1989) · M. Manley, *A voice at the workplace: reflections on colonialism and the Jamaican worker* (1975) · M. Manley and J. Hearne, *The search for solutions: selections from the speeches and writings of Michael Manley* (1976) · *The Times* (8 March 1997) · *The Independent* (8 March 1997) · *The Scotsman* (8 March 1997) · WWW · WW (1994)

Archives U. Lond., Institute of Commonwealth Studies, corresp. with Richard Hart · U. Lond., Institute of Commonwealth Studies, corresp. with C. L. R. James |SOUND BL NSA, current affairs recording · BL NSA, recorded lecture [Royal Commonwealth Society Collection]

Likenesses photographs, 1962–79, Hult. Arch. · N. Libbert, photograph, 1989, Hult. Arch. [see illus.] · photograph, repro. in *The Times* · photograph, repro. in *The Independent* · photograph, repro. in *The Scotsman*

Manley, Norman Washington (1893–1969), lawyer and chief minister of Jamaica, was born at Roxburgh, Manchester, Jamaica, on 4 July 1893, the eldest son of Thomas Albert Samuel Manley, planter and produce dealer, and his wife, Margaret Ann, daughter of Alexander Shearer, penkeeper. His father was of partly African and partly English descent and his mother of partly Irish descent. He was educated at elementary schools and at Jamaica College where he excelled both as a scholar and as an athlete, setting many inter-scholastic records (his 100 yards record lasted for forty years although equalled by his elder son, Douglas, in 1942). In 1914 he became a Rhodes scholar and entered Jesus College, Oxford, to read law.

In 1915 Manley enlisted as a private in the Royal Field Artillery, became a first-class gunner sergeant, and won the MM. He declined a commission. He returned to Oxford in 1919, where he graduated BA in 1921 and obtained his BCL with second-class honours, and was called to the bar (certificate of honour) by Gray's Inn. On 25 June 1921 in England he married his cousin Edna Swithenbank [see Manley, Edna (1900–1987)], daughter of the Revd Harvey

Swithenbank, an English Methodist missionary who had married Ellie Shearer, sister of Manley's mother; they had two sons. Manley's wife later won considerable renown as a sculptor.

After spending a year as a pupil in chambers in London, in 1922 Manley was admitted to practise in Jamaica, where he showed brilliance immediately and soon became the foremost lawyer of the day. Appointed KC in 1932, by the time he had given up active practice in 1955 he had appeared in every important or sensational case both civil and criminal in Jamaica. He was not only the leader of the Jamaica bar but of that of the British West Indies as well. He added to his reputation by appearances in England, successfully defending a Jamaican charged with murder, and became the first Jamaican counsel to appear before the judicial committee of the privy council in the Karsote trade mark case which he won (*De Cordova and others* v. *Vick Chemical Co.*, 1951).

Yet all this success at the bar was not enough for Manley. By 1936 he was brooding that 'the law was emotionally and intellectually too bankrupting' and that he would have to 'find a way into a wider life'. In 1938 the wider life opened. In May of that year labour disturbances plagued Jamaica as well as others of Britain's colonies in the Caribbean. There was deadlock between employers and labour; Manley offered his services as mediator and succeeded in restoring industrial peace. Later that year he founded Jamaica's first political party, the People's National Party (PNP), with the chief aims of securing universal adult suffrage and self-government for Jamaica. In the first elections, in 1944, having won adult suffrage, both he and his party were defeated. In 1949 the PNP again suffered defeat, but Manley won a seat. It was not until his third try (1955) that the party succeeded and Manley became chief minister of Jamaica.

In the elections of 1959, under the new constitution which gave Jamaica internal self-government, Manley's party won twenty-nine seats against the sixteen which went to the Jamaica Labour Party of Sir Alexander Bustamante. But in 1961 Manley called a referendum to decide whether or not Jamaica should remain in the federation of the West Indies which had been established in 1958. The electorate voted 'No' and Manley, who was a pro-federationist, had to call new elections in 1962 to decide which party should lead the country into full independence. His party lost, and in 1967 lost again. Finally broken in health Manley gave up the leadership of his party, and left parliament in 1969, only a few months before he died in Kingston, Jamaica on 2 September 1969.

It was ironic that Manley who had done more than anybody else to win self-government for Jamaica was denied the honour of leading the country into independence; it was given to his cousin and arch political rival Bustamante to become Jamaica's first prime minister, although for most of his political life Bustamante had opposed self-government.

Manley received an honorary LLD from Howard University in 1946 and from the University of the West Indies (posthumously) in 1970. In 1969, also posthumously, he was made a national hero of Jamaica and in 1971 a public statue was erected to his memory by the government.

Norman Manley was in every sense a big man. Whether in things of the intellect, in the skills of the law, in the arts of life, or in public dedication, his commitment was total and unselfish. The foundations of parliament and the law in Jamaica owe much of their strength to his legal and constitutional skill, and as in the troubles of 1938 when he first assumed a public role he continued at all times to resist the dangers of national turbulence and divisiveness. Manley's younger son, Michael *Manley, succeeded his

Norman Washington Manley (1893–1969), by George Freston, 1962 [centre]

father as leader of the PNP and in 1972 became prime minister of Jamaica; the elder, Douglas, won a seat and became minister of youth and community development.

T. E. SEALY, *rev.*

Sources *Daily Gleaner* (3 Sept 1969) · *The Times* (3 Sept 1969) · R. Nettleford, ed., *Norman Washington Manley and the new Jamaica: selected speeches and writings, 1938–1968* (1971) · personal knowledge (1981) · WWW
Likenesses G. Freston, photograph, 1962, Hult. Arch. [*see illus.*] · photographs, Hult. Arch.

Manley, Sir Roger (*d.* 1687), army officer and historian, was the second of three sons of Cornelius Manley (*d.* 1623) of Erbistock in Denbighshire, and his wife, Mary, daughter of Francis Lloyd of Hardwick in Shropshire. All three sons were minors at their father's death. Roger's brothers took divergent paths in the civil war: the elder, Francis, later chief justice of the Carmarthen circuit, served the royalist party in north Wales, and compounded for delinquency in arms in 1647, while the younger, John, a vigorous nonconformist and son-in-law of Isaac Dorislaus, fought for parliament and held the postal franchise under the Commonwealth. Roger served as a royalist officer in Lord Byron's regiment, and was present at the capture of Powis Castle in October 1644, being taken prisoner but making a daring solitary escape. After Byron's defeat and the capture of Chester in 1646 he left England for the continent.

Manley spent the next fourteen years mostly in the Netherlands, serving in the army of the states general at Maastricht in 1653–4, accompanying an embassy to Sweden in 1655, and commanding a company in the Dutch expedition to Danzig in 1656–7. All this time he sent reports, under various pseudonyms, to his brother-in-law, Isaac Dorislaus the younger, and others in England; these survive among the Thurloe state papers. It seems that by 1659 he had also compiled the account of the war of 1657–8 between Sweden and Denmark that was later published as the first part of his *History of the Late Warrs in Denmark* (1670), because orders issued in March 1659 cite it as an authority for protocol in dealing with the Swedish fleet. With regard to the published version, the close similarities between his account and the one by Sir Philip Meadows printed in 1675 suggest that they derive from the same original (possibly an earlier version of Meadows's text), and that Manley's book cannot be treated as a primary source. Of clearer antecedents is his *True Description of the Mighty Kingdom of Japan and Siam*, translated from the account by François Caron and dedicated to Manley's brother Francis (1663; reprinted 1671).

At the Restoration Manley held an ensign's commission in the regiment of Robert Sidney, second earl of Leicester, an English unit in Dutch service, and was among the officers who refused to swear allegiance to the states general in 1665, which led to their dismissal and recommissioning in English service as the Holland regiment (later to become the Buffs). He also worked as an agent for Sir George Downing, collecting intelligence on Dutch naval preparations for the war that broke out that year. This led to his brief arrest by the pensionary Johan de Witt. Despite these adventures Manley was dissatisfied with the progress of his career and petitioned Arlington, the secretary of state, for better employment, citing his twenty years' experience, particularly in fortification. This experience had doubtless been gained, in part, during earlier service as ensign to a military engineer cousin, John Manley, whose brother Arthur left two houses at Kew, in Surrey, one of which Roger acquired in 1674.

Promoted captain in September 1665 Manley accompanied his regiment to Portsmouth and thence, in December, to Jersey. He was now married, his wife being Maria Catherina, whose parents were Francophone denizens of the Spanish Netherlands; she died on 1 November 1675 aged thirty-two and was buried in Portsmouth. They had at least six children, of whom five survived their father, two sons dying shortly after him, the three daughters (including Delarivier *Manley) living into the next century. He apparently also played some part in the upbringing of his younger brother's son, John, who later seduced and then abandoned Delarivier.

From 1667 Manley acted as lieutenant-governor of Jersey, being sworn in as such in November that year. Details of his duties and his trips home on leave survive in his letters to his cousin Robert Francis, a clerk in Arlington's office, preserved in the state papers (and wrongly calendared as being from Robert Manley). His knowledge of languages, acquired in exile, was occasionally put to use translating letters for Francis. In 1671 he was allowed an allowance of six soldiers' pay to offset expenses incurred in Jersey, chiefly in repairing the island's fortifications.

In or soon after 1673 Manley left Jersey, still a captain but having transferred in 1672 to the 1st regiment of foot guards (later the Grenadiers), and in 1674 his account of the saga of Boris Godunov and the false Dmitry, *The Russian Impostor*, was published. This book drew on material not then available in English and remains very readable. By June 1675 Manley had been appointed deputy governor of Portsmouth, being knighted there by the king on 3 July. From January 1678 he was on the commission for repairing the fortifications of the port, and was commended for his diligence by Sir Bernard de Gomme, engineer-general.

In February 1680 Manley petitioned the crown for the office of receiver-general of the duchy of Cornwall, but was unsuccessful. The same month, however, he was posted to Landguard Fort in Suffolk as governor, his appointment being renewed (like his captaincy in the guards) on the accession of James II in 1685. By now, however, he seems to have been somewhat weary, and in a letter of March 1684 he refers to his 'forty-three years' colonelling' (PRO, SP 29/437/30), presumably a conscious echo of *Hudibras*. His last book, a military history of the civil war, *De rebellione Anglicana* (1686), was well written in reasonably correct Latin, but is no more informative about the theatre in which the author had himself served than about the others described. It was republished after his death in 1691 in English as *The History of the Rebellions of England, Scotland and Ireland*, with a continuation covering Monmouth's rebellion.

On 26 February 1687 Manley, by then living in Westminster, wrote his will. He was dead by 19 March following and on 21 March he was buried in St Margaret's Church there. His successor at Landguard Fort had been appointed two days earlier, although it was not until May 1688 that one of his daughters was admitted heir to the house at Kew, and June 1688 that his will was proved. Described by his daughter Delarivier as 'brave, full of honour and a very fine gentleman' (D. Manley, *Adventures*, 14), he was obviously a man of some charm and ability, not least in telling a good story. This served him well in his literary efforts, though it sometimes seems out of place in his dispatches, and certainly overran the mark on one occasion in 1669 when, journeying home on leave, he had a fellow traveller arrested as a highwayman's decoy, only to recant afterwards and drop all charges. The affair, probably obscure enough at the time, remains a mystery.

C. E. A. CHEESMAN

Sources secretary of state papers, domestic series, 1660–85, PRO, SP 29 · secretary of state papers, domestic entry books, 1669–87, PRO, SP 44 · Thurloe, *State papers*, vols. 5–7 · R. Holme, pedigree of Manley family, 1638–42, priv. coll. [M. R. Manley] · R. Fruin and N. Japiske, *Brieven aan Johan de Witt: eerste deel, 1648–1660* (1919), 244–5 · C. R. B. Knight, *Historical record of the Buffs, east Kent regiment (3rd foot): 1704–1914*, 1: *1704–1814* (1935) · parish register, 21 March 1687, St Margaret's Westminster, Westminster Abbey Muniment room [burial] · will, PRO, PROB 11/391, fol. 291 · inquisition post mortem into the estate of Cornelius Manley, 1636, PRO, E 150/87/46 · herald's visitation of Hampshire, 1686, Coll. Arms, K8 (church notes), fol. 28 · R. Manley, letter, 1644, BL, Add. MS 18981, fol. 281 · A. Stade, 'Manley's history, Meadowes' narrative och Carl X Gustafs första danska krig', *Historisk Tidskrift*, 2nd ser., 23 (1960), 249–301 · [D. Manley], *Secret memoirs and manners of several persons of quality of both sexes, from the New Atalantis*, 2 vols. (1709) · [M. D. Manley], *The adventures of Rivella, or, The history of the author of 'Atalantis'* (1714) · R. Manley, memorial to Sir J. Williamson, 1673?, PRO, SP 47/1/22 · *Actes des états de l'isle de Jersey, 1660–1675*, Société Jersiaise, états 15 (1900), 39 · will, PRO, PROB 11/306, fols. 19–20 [Arthur Manley] · manor of Richmond or West Sheen, court rolls, 1662–88, PRO, LR 3/76, 77 · H. H. Rowen, *John de Witt, grand pensionary of Holland, 1625–1672* (1978) · PRO, SP 18/202/30–31

Archives Bodl. Oxf., Thurloe state papers, MS Rawl. A · PRO, state papers domestic, SP 29, SP 44

Wealth at death £525—monetary bequests; 'considerable sum' to be raised by sale of houses at Wrexham: will, PRO, PROB 11/391, fol. 291

Manley, Thomas (*c*.1628–1676), legal and political writer, was the son of Thomas Manley (*d*. 1656) of Westminster, clerk of the kitchen in the household of Charles I, and his wife, Cassandra Button (*d*. 1633), daughter of Henry Lyde, and can probably be identified with the author of certain juvenilia published about 1650, in which case he was born about 1628. He may have been the Thomas Manley baptized at St Margaret's, Westminster, on 8 November 1627. Thomas Manley senior was at Oxford with the court and may have been responsible for an account of the king's travels called *Iter Carolinum*, published in 1660. He was fined £250 for his delinquency, but paid less than half the sum and placed the rest of his estate in trust for his daughter. Thomas junior, who had displeased his father by marrying without his permission, received only a small

monetary bequest. By 1656 he and his wife, Anne, had a son and a daughter.

Manley was admitted a student of the Middle Temple on 6 February 1655, and on 25 May following was appointed librarian of the society. So unsatisfactory was he in the post, however, that the library doors were padlocked against him and he was eventually dismissed in June 1658. Despite this he was called to the bar at the Middle Temple on 24 January 1673 without having to perform the usual formalities and ceremonies, in accordance with letters from the king dated 18 September 1672. This has been misinterpreted as an appointment as king's counsel (and Manley accordingly appears as such in library catalogues), but there is no evidence that he ever took silk.

Manley's first legal work was *The Sollicitor* (2nd edn, 1663), a handbook stated in the title to be based on the experience of twelve years' practice. In 1670 he brought out an abridgement of Coke's reports, volumes 12 and 13, as a supplement to the work of Edward Trotman who had abridged the earlier volumes. Then in 1672 he produced both an annotated book of forms entitled *The Clerk's Guide*, and a revised and updated edition of John Cowell's well-known law dictionary, the *Interpreter of Words and Terms* of 1607. His additions were not numerous or substantial, largely consisting of a few lines at the end of the longer entries. Cowell's controversial essays on titles such as 'king' and 'royal prerogative' were cut down, while other, more technical entries were criticized by Thomas Blount in *World of Errors* (1673). A second 'corrected' edition appeared after Manley's death in 1684. His name remains, with his preface, in the 1701 revision by White Kennet, but disappears in later editions of Cowell although all continue to include his material. In 1676 Manley produced an appendix to the seventh edition of Thomas Wentworth's *Office and Duty of Executors*; this reappeared with later editions of the same work.

Contemporaneously with these legal works, Manley published several books of a political character. The first was a translation of Grotius's *De rebus Belgicis*, published as *Annals and History of the Low-Country-Warrs* in 1665, with a subtitle claiming that the book illustrates the extent of the Dutch debt to English valour. In two later pamphlets (*Usury at Six per cent*, 1669, directed against Sir Thomas Culpepper, and *A Discourse Shewing that the Export of Wooll is Destructive*, 1676) he aired isolationist views of economics that were clearly political and social in inspiration. Less certainly his is an earlier work, *A Short View of the Lives of … Henry, Duke of Gloucester, and Mary Princess of Orange* (1660); the author is identified only as T. M., esq.

Manley apparently died soon after writing his appendix to Wentworth, for Middle Temple records disclose the payment of £5 to the widow of T. Manley on 24 November 1676. This means that the book usually identified as his last work, *The Present State of Europe Briefly Examined and Found Languishing*, published in 1689, must have been seen through the press by someone other than the author. A note prefaced to this polemical tract, which advocates immediate war against France to save Europe from the despotic designs of Louis XIV, states that it was written in

1671, on the occasion of a parliamentary vote of £800,000 to equip a fleet.

It seems likely, though it cannot be proved, that the legal and political writer described above was the Thomas Manley junior responsible for three rather earlier and rather different works. The first, *Temporis angustiae: Stollen Houres Recreations*, a collection of almost unreadable adolescent *pensées*, is dated 1649, the author being in his twenty-first year at the time of writing. In 1651 there appeared the same author's *Affliction and Deliverance of the Saints*, a verse paraphrase of the book of Job, the preface of which is dated at Westminster. A manuscript of this work survives in Cambridge University Library. The following year saw his translation of Payne Fisher's *Veni, vidi, vici*, a Latin poem in honour of Cromwell, with in addition an elegy by himself on Ireton, the regicide, and verses in Manley's own honour by Samuel Sheppard. By this time Manley's father was attempting to make amends with the Commonwealth authorities, so his son's encomiastic offerings would not be unexpected; certainly no more so than the verses by Sheppard, himself chiefly known for royalist sympathies.   C. E. A. CHEESMAN

Sources C. H. Hopwood, ed., *Middle Temple records*, 3: 1650–1703 (1905), 1076, 1080, 1100, 1121, 1122, 1271, 1294, 1300 · *CSP dom.*, 1645–7, 454, 493 · M. A. E. Green, ed., *Calendar of the proceedings of the committee for compounding … 1643–1660*, 2, PRO (1890), 1582 · state papers, 1646, PRO, SP 23/197/30–35 · will of Thomas Manley the elder of Westminster, dated 25 March 1656, proved (prerogative court of Canterbury), 21 Nov 1656, PRO, PROB 11/256, fols. 406–7 · parish register, St Margaret's Westminster, Westminster Abbey Muniment Room · T. Manley, *Temporis Angustiae* (1649) · C. E. A. B. [C. E. A. Bedwell], *Law Times* (24 June 1911), 173–4
Likenesses T. Cross, line engraving (aged twenty-one), BM; repro. in Manley, *Temporis Angustiae* · T. Cross, line engraving (aged twenty-four), NPG

Manley, William George Nicholas (1831–1901), military surgeon, was born at Dublin, the second son of the Revd William Nicholas Manley. His mother was a daughter of Dr Brown, a surgeon in the army. He was educated at the Blackheath proprietary school, probably followed an apprenticeship in surgery, and was admitted a member of the Royal College of Surgeons (London) in 1852. Manley joined the army medical staff as an assistant surgeon in March 1855 and was then attached to the Royal Artillery, with whom he served in the Crimea from 11 June 1855. Manley was present at the siege of Sevastopol and it was there he was awarded the first of his many decorations for gallantry on the battlefield. He went on to earn both the Prussian Iron Cross and the Victoria Cross.

The peak of Manley's military career came during the New Zealand war of 1863–6, in which he served with the Royal Artillery. At the skirmish of Tauranga Pah his bravery won him the Victoria Cross, and in subsequent actions at Okotukou, Putahi, Otapawa, and Waikohou pahs he was mentioned in dispatches. His conspicuous bravery earned him promotion to staff surgeon. Manley was undoubtedly a courageous man and was also a good swimmer: on more than one occasion he rescued soldiers from drowning. These actions were made public and won Manley a bronze medal from the Royal Humane Society.

In 1869 he married Maria Elizabeth Darton, daughter of Thomas Harwood Darton of Temple Dinsley, Hertfordshire.

Manley's work in 1870 with the Society for Aiding and Ameliorating the Condition of the Sick and Wounded in Time of War was representative of the semi-private involvement of British army surgeons during the Franco-Prussian conflict. His 'Woolwich' ambulance served with the 22nd division of the armies of the Crown Prince Frederick near Orléans. On several occasions he established field hospitals. Manley particularly stressed the importance of feeding the wounded so as to allow them to recover some of their strength. At the end of the siege of Paris, in February 1871, Manley brought fresh supplies to the Parisian hospitals. When the war ended Manley participated in the debate on the evacuation of casualties and on the suitable organization of war ambulances and field hospitals. He produced several reports which favoured the Prussian system with which he was well acquainted. These reports were summarized and translated into French and German. Manley won both the Iron Cross (second class) and the French Red Cross medal for his actions during the Franco-Prussian War.

Manley then resumed his career with the army, serving in Afghanistan in 1878–9 and in Egypt in 1882. During the latter war, Manley was temporarily in charge of the citadel hospital at which he undertook reforms and implemented the latest methods of hygiene. He was promoted to the rank of deputy surgeon-general and retired from the army with the honorary rank of surgeon-general in 1884. He was made CB in 1894 and enjoyed a distinguished service pension from 1896. Manley died on 16 November 1901 at his home, 3 Lansdowne Terrace, Cheltenham, and was buried in Cheltenham. He left five sons, the eldest of whom followed his father into the army, and one daughter.   D'A. POWER, rev. BERTRAND O. TAITHE

Sources *The Lancet* (23 Nov 1901), 1459 · *BMJ* (23 Nov 1901), 1554 · *The Times* (19 Nov 1901) · L. Gluckman, 'Manley VC, surgeon general and other medical medallists of the Second Maori War', *New Zealand Medical Journal* (Dec 1968), 594–9 · *Military History Society Bulletin*, 14/55 (Feb 1964), 64–5 · *Military History Society Bulletin*, 10/44 (May 1961), 84–5 · Wellcome L., RAMC archives, box 157, 801.14
Likenesses photograph, repro. in *Military History Society Bulletin*, 14/55 (Feb 1964), 64–5
Wealth at death £18,021 12s. 10d.: probate, 13 Dec 1901, CGPLA Eng. & Wales

Manlove, Edward (*bap.* 1615, *d.* 1671), lawyer and poet, was baptized on 6 April 1615 at Tettenhall, Staffordshire, the second son of Rowland Manlove, gentleman, of Wanfield in the parish of Kynaston, Staffordshire, and his wife, Magdalen, the daughter of William Wyke of Shifnal, Shropshire. He entered the Middle Temple in May 1635 and was called to the bar in June 1642. He settled at Ashbourne in Derbyshire. A parliamentary supporter during the civil war, Manlove served on a number of local committees during the Commonwealth and was made a JP for Derbyshire in 1648. He proved an energetic magistrate suppressing profaneness and irreligion. He was included in a list of Derbyshire gentlemen and 'how they stand affected', drawn up in the autumn of 1662, when he was described as a Presbyterian (Newton, 8).

Manlove was actively engaged in lead mining, owning a number of rakes (veins), and serving as steward of the barmote court of the wapentake of Wirksworth. In 1653 he published the *Liberties and Customes of the Lead-Mines within the Wapentake of Wirksworth*, which, drawing on exchequer rolls and inquisitions, provided a description of the laws and customs of the court with comprehensive references to the legal evidence in the margin. The work was a remarkable achievement for it provided an accurate digest of the voluminous detail of mining customs cast into 300 lines of verse to assist the illiterate miner in memorizing them. By the eighteenth century the rhyming verses were being cited as evidence of custom. A further edition, though inaccurate, was published at Wirksworth in 1809, and a modern edition with an introduction and glossary by Thomas Tapping in 1851.

Manlove also published a volume of poems, *Divine contentment, or, A medicine for a discontented man: A confession of faith, and other poems* (1667). The poems were on such subjects as effectual calling, justification, saving grace, keeping the sabbath, and 'the Misery of Man, not Reconciled to God in Christ' (p. 45), which although revealing of Manlove's godliness have little poetic value. A final section consists of 'Poems Against Popery', involving a conventional protestant attack on the supposed tenets of Catholicism, and also poetic epitaphs for two local worthies, Anne Cockaine (*d.* 1664) and William Waine, vicar of Ashbourne. It has been suggested that Manlove is the 'Philanthropus' (that is, Man Love), friend of Mark Hildesley, the compiler of a manuscript volume of 'Essayes and contemplations, divine, morall, and miscellaneous, in prose and meter' (Harley MS 4726), but the ascription is dated 1694, twenty years after Manlove's death.

Manlove married first Catherine, daughter of Paul Hull of Ashbourne, and second Timothee, daughter of John Pearce of Lewes, Sussex. Both predeceased him. There were four sons and three daughters from each marriage. Manlove's published writings and activity on the bench indicate that he was a godly gentleman convinced of the existence of an elect and who believed in a national church and a preaching ministry. In his will he committed his soul to God 'trustinge to bee saved by the meritte of Jesus Christ' and gave instructions for his children to be brought up 'in the feare of god' (will). He had divinity as well as law books in his study. There is however no evidence that he supported nonconformity. He is not recorded in the 1669 Conventicle returns as hosting a meeting, but his son Timothy *Manlove was one of the second generation of Presbyterian ministers. Edward Manlove died in late 1671.   DAVID L. WYKES

Sources G. D. Squibb, ed., *The visitation of Derbyshire*, Harleian Society, new ser., 8 (1984), 111–12 · will and probate; inventory 21 Dec 1671, will dated 14 June 1667, Lichfield RO, B/C/11/1671 · G. J. Armytage and W. H. Rylands, eds., *Staffordshire pedigrees*, Harleian Society, 63 (1912), 164 · S. C. Newton, 'The gentry of Derbyshire in the seventeenth century', *Derbyshire Archaeological Journal*, 86 (1966), esp. 8, 24 · J. C. Cox, *Three centuries of Derbyshire annals as illustrated by the records of the quarter sessions of the county of Derby, from Queen Elizabeth to Queen Victoria* (1890), 1.44, 363; 2.80, 84, 86, 255 · H. A. C. Sturgess, ed., *Register of admissions to the Honourable Society of the Middle Temple, from the fifteenth century to the year 1944*, 1 (1949), 131 · H. Kirke, 'Some notes on the minor poets of Derbyshire', *Journal of the Derbyshire Archaeological and Natural History Society*, 44 (1922), 11 · J. Hunter, 'Chorus vatum Anglicanorum: collections concerning the poets and verse writers of the English nation', BL, Add. MS 24,488, fol. 176v · T. Tapping, *The rhymed chronicle of Edward Manlove concerning the liberties and customs of the lead mines within the wapentake of Wirksworth, Derbyshire* (1851) · S. Glover, *The history and gazetteer of the county of Derby*, ed. T. Noble, 1 (1829), 108 · Mrs Meade-Waldo, 'History and customs of lead-mining in the wapentake of Wirksworth', *Journal of the Derbyshire Archaeological and Natural History Society*, 32 (1910), 174–5 · parish register, Tettenhall, Staffordshire, 6 April 1615 [baptism]

Wealth at death £129 9s. 4d.: will and probate inventory, 21 Dec 1671, will 14 June 1667, Lichfield RO, B/C/11/1671

Manlove, Timothy (1663–1699), Presbyterian minister and author, was born on 18 November 1663 at Ashbourne, Derbyshire, the youngest son of Edward *Manlove (*bap.* 1615, *d.* 1671), gentleman and minor poet, and his second wife, Timothee, daughter of John Pearce of Lewes, Sussex. He began a career as a physician, in which 'he had attained to a great skill … and practised it with Ease' (Gilpin), before deciding on the ministry. He was educated at John Woodhouse's academy at Sheriffhales, Shropshire, and received Presbyterian ordination at Attercliffe on 11 September 1688. He then served as a private chaplain to the family of Sir Philip Gell of Hopton Hall, Derbyshire, who regarded him with more than ordinary kindness. His marriage to Sarah Slater (*d.* 1715) on 18 July 1688 was probably the cause of his seeking a congregation.

Shortly after qualifying himself as a nonconformist preacher at the quarter sessions at Bakewell on 7 July 1689 under the recently passed Toleration Act, Manlove became minister at Durham. He was described there in 1690 as 'formerly a preacher in Derbyshire: a young man of great hopes, and usefullness, [with] an encouraging auditory' (Gordon, 36) though he had thereby gained little financial reward. At Durham he engaged in a debate with the dean, Dr Thomas Comber, who tried hard to persuade him on the terms of conformity. It was later said that his 'principals & practices were so large at Durham that he got him respect with the church men & were rather an offence to them of his own communion' (R. Stretton to R. Thoresby, 13 March 1697, Yorkshire Archaeological Society, MS 16). In June 1693 he accepted an invitation from the congregation at Pontefract, Yorkshire, to settle with them, but following the death of Thomas Sharpe, minister of the Presbyterian congregation at Mill Hill, Leeds, in September 1693, he was invited to become their minister. The congregation at Pontefract strongly resisted his leaving, and Manlove at first declined; but, after further application from Leeds and much irresolution on his part, he was finally persuaded in February 1694 by Richard Gilpin, the minister at Newcastle upon Tyne, to accept, on the basis of being more generally serviceable at Leeds. He was admitted an extra licentiate of the Royal College of Physicians in June 1694.

While at Leeds Manlove published *Immortality of the Soul Asserted* (1697), with a commendatory preface by John

Howe and Matthew Sylvester, in answer to Henry Layton's pamphlet published five years earlier. Layton issued a reply in 1703. The following year Manlove published his *Praeparatio evangelica* based on sermons preached at Leeds. Both works were much admired. William Tong believed that 'Mr Baxter will never be quite dead while Dr Manlove, who inherits so much his clear weighty way of writing, lives' (Hunter, ed., *Letters*, 1.356). His ministry, however, though able was not easy. Initially on friendly terms with Ralph Thoresby, the antiquary, who had played an active part in his choice, Manlove quarrelled with Thoresby's wish to continue hearing sermons by the local Anglican clergy. Manlove's censure encouraged Thoresby eventually to leave Mill Hill. Manlove was also in dispute over the size of his stipend. At Leeds his salary was £60 a year and he was said to have earned as much again by practising physic. He was offered £80 a year at Newcastle with less duty, and though strongly urged to stay at Leeds he refused, becoming in 1699 Gilpin's assistant in the place of William Pell who had died.

Manlove's stay at Newcastle was very brief. He caught a fever shortly after his arrival and died on 3 August 1699 at the age of thirty-five. In recording the event, Thoresby remarked, he 'enjoyed his quadruple salary but a little time' (*Diary*, 1.330). Manlove was buried at the parish church of St Nicholas, Newcastle, on 6 August; his funeral sermon was preached and published by Gilpin, with a memoir by John Turnbull. The congregation showed such 'bounty and liberality' to his widow 'as was never shewn upon any such occasion before (at least not in this place)' (J. Cay to Thoresby, 22 Aug 1699, Yorkshire Archaeological Society, MS 7). He was full of promise but often rash in his decisions—Manlove's moves were considered by John Howe 'to have been twice too hasty' (J. Howe to J. Boyse, 3 Jan 1700, BL, Add. MS 4275, fol. 329). He was one of those younger ministers specially commended by Calamy for their learning, of whom neither Oxford nor Cambridge need 'have been asham'd' (Calamy, xxxi–ii).

DAVID L. WYKES

Sources A. Gordon, ed., *Freedom after ejection: a review* (1690–1692) of *presbyterian and congregational nonconformity in England and Wales* (1917), 36, 307 • biographical account, DWL, Walter Wilson MS A 10 [p. 8] • G. D. Squibb, ed., *The visitation of Derbyshire*, Harleian Society, new ser., 8 (1984), 111–12 • [J. Hunter], ed., *Letters of eminent men, addressed to Ralph Thoresby*, 2 vols. (1832) • *The diary of Ralph Thoresby, F.R.S., author of the topography of Leeds, 1677–1724, now first published from the original manuscript*, ed. J. Hunter, 2 vols. (1830) • *The autobiographies and letters of Thomas Comber, sometime precentor of York and dean of Durham*, ed. C. E. Whiting, 2, SurtS, 157 (1947) • E. Calamy, ed., *An abridgement of Mr. Baxter's history of his life and times, with an account of the ministers, &c., who were ejected after the Restauration of King Charles II*, 2nd edn, 2 vols. (1713) • R. Gilpin, *The comforts of divine love. Preach'd upon the occasion of the much lamented death of the Reverend Mr. Timothy Manlove* (1700) • R. Welford, *The church and congregation of the Divine Unity, Newcastle-upon-Tyne* (1904) • J. Hunter, *The rise of the old dissent, exemplified by the life of Oliver Heywood* (1842), 356 • letter, P. Gell to T. Manlove, 29 June 1689, BL, Stowe MS 746, fol. 112r • letter, congregation at Pontefract to T. Manlove, 8 June 1693, BL, Stowe MS 747, fol. 17r • letter, congregation at Mill Hill to T. Manlove, 11 Feb 1694, BL, Stowe MS 747, fol. 29r • letter, R. Gilpin to R. Thoresby, 5 March 1694, W. Yorks. AS, Leeds, Yorkshire Archaeological Society, MS 6 • letter, R. Stretton to R. Thoresby, 13 March 1697, W. Yorks. AS, Leeds, Yorkshire Archaeological Society, MS 16 • letter, J. Cay to R. Thoresby, 22 August 1699, W. Yorks. AS, Leeds, Yorkshire Archaeological Society, MS 7 • letter, J. Howe to J. Boyse, 3 Jan 1700, BL, Add. MS 4275, fol. 329r • letter, R. Gilpin to T. Manlove, 22 March 1699, BL, Add. MS 38856, fol. 115r • T. Manlove, sermons, Leeds City Archives, Mill Hill Chapel records, MH69 • E. Oates, 'History of Mill Hill, Leeds', *c*.1848, W. Yorks. AS, Leeds, MH75, 148–55 • Protestant dissenting preachers, Derbyshire quarter sessions order book, Easter 1682 – Epiphany 1702, 7 July 1689, Derbys. RO, QSM 1, fol. 146r • parish register (marriage), 18 July 1688, Mickleover, Derbyshire • parish register (burial), 1715, Mickleover, Derbyshire

Likenesses M. van der Gucht, engraving, repro. in Gilpin, *Comforts of Divine Love* • M. van der Gucht, line engraving, NPG

Mann, Arthur Henry (1850–1929), organist, was born on 16 May 1850 at 31 Tombland, Norwich, the youngest of the five children of Henry James Mann (1809–1860) and Ann Couzens Jubey (1811–1891). The family forebears had followed the common Norwich trades of weaving and shoemaking, but, although Henry Mann was originally apprenticed as a worsted weaver, between 1841 and his marriage in 1843 he had become a music teacher. Like his eldest brother, Frederick Alexander, Arthur Mann became a chorister at Norwich Cathedral under Zechariah Buck. A probationer from the late 1850s, and a full chorister shortly after his father died in April 1860, he was articled to Buck from June 1865. Buck had promised the dying Henry Mann that he would see Arthur out into the world; he later made an allowance to Ann Mann, and remitted her son's apprentice fees in full when he left.

Buck was a renowned trainer of boys' voices, and Mann acknowledged that from him he gained all his basic musical experience. During his apprenticeship he grew to have a devotion to his master, and he was later to mirror, in the phraseology, emphasis, and style of his handwriting, the same punctiliousness that can be observed in Buck's manuscript. Mann is mentioned in reviews of local concerts acquitting himself well as a boy soloist in the early 1860s. In 1870 he was appointed organist of St Peter's, Wolverhampton. A year later he moved to the nearby village of Tettenhall, with its collegiate church, where he met his future wife, Sarah Ann (1854–1918), the daughter of John Ransford, whom he married on 25 November 1874. He matriculated at New College, Oxford, in 1872, and took the degree of BMus in 1874. He graduated DMus in 1882 with his cantata *Ecce homo*. Following a brief spell, from 1875, at Beverley Minster, Mann applied for the organist's post at King's College, Cambridge. It was the first time that the job was to be filled by open competition, and, from a shortlist of six candidates, Mann was elected on 7 June 1876, beginning what was to be his lifetime's work at King's on 16 July.

The university colleges which had choirs who maintained 'cathedral service', and several of the cathedrals themselves, were at that time in a process of reform. Many of these establishments had been responsible, since their foundation, for the rudimentary education of their choristers, and most now wished to see this put on a proper professional footing. Mann's appointment to King's coincided with that college's desire to start a proper choir school, dispensing with the children of local menials as the choristers, and beginning to attract sons of professional people who might be boarders at the school. From 1881, through the generosity of the Austen Leigh brothers, a fund for choral scholarships was begun, and this allowed a gradual change to take place, with Mann's active co-operation, as retiring lay clerks were replaced by undergraduate choral scholars, thus making the choir an additional educational unit of the college. Mann, however, like most of his contemporaries, was regarded in his post only as a college servant. For his part, he was the professional musician, leading a choir on behalf of a college which did not have any academic musicians among the fellowship. While the college could not criticize his methods in the chapel, there seems to have been some attempt to broaden the very Victorian selection of music proposed by the young organist. His relationship with choristers was strongly personal. A kind man, he was known to the choir and to his friends as Daddy, but he was not to be trifled with.

It was said that, in the notoriously reverberant acoustic of King's College chapel, 'Mann determined to make Echo his friend'. His performance tempi were, inevitably, slow by modern standards, and he required from all his singers a roundness of tone which blended well within the building, yet the music was executed with distinct enunciation. He paid great attention to the performance of the daily psalms, the importance of which he no doubt derived from the strong traditions in that sphere practised in Norwich since the time of J. C. Beckwith at the start of the century. 'Any fool can sing an anthem', Mann used to remark, 'but it takes a choir to sing a service'. At the behest of one of the fellows he experimented with different selections of Anglican chants, eventually drawing up in 1884, with W. H. D. Boyle, a young graduate volunteer singer, a collection which was to remain in use, in large part, until 1968. As an organist he was reputed never to have been heard to play a wrong note, and his improvisations, particularly those which preceded an anthem, weaving together themes from the music, were of great local renown.

Although Mann was no professional academic, he was a great amateur musical antiquary. From 1894 to 1922 he was an assistant master at the Leys School in Cambridge. He did not achieve recognition in Cambridge University until he was appointed university organist in 1897; it was not until 1910, when he was sixty, that the college supplicated for him to be granted an honorary MA, and he was not made a fellow of King's College until 1921. Nevertheless, in his day, Mann must have been one of the most indefatigable gatherers of archival miscellanea concerning Handel, whose music he adored, and musicians and musical events since the eighteenth century in East Anglia. He possessed a mass of remains connected with William Crotch, first principal of the Royal Academy of Music, including a number of his watercolours. His copious loose-leaf notebooks attest to the hours he must have spent in original research, scouring local newspapers and parish documents, and it is to be regretted that he never brought any of this work together in published form. Possibly he felt somewhat cowed, as a mere amateur, in a world of academics. Over the years he amassed a large library of eighteenth- and nineteenth-century musical publications. Between 1889 and 1892 he spent much time and labour rearranging the Handel manuscripts kept at the Fitzwilliam Museum. His own compositions were slight.

While it was held that Mann was hardly ever away from his daily duty in the college chapel, and he seldom delegated a choir practice, he does seem to have been in demand to travel from Cambridge to open organs or to participate in other musical events. Apart from the college choir, he formed a choral society, initially to celebrate Queen Victoria's golden jubilee on 16 June 1887, and from 1889 this became Dr Mann's Festival Choir. Until 1911, through this vehicle for performance, Cambridge was able to hear works as new as *The Apostles* or *The Kingdom* by Elgar or the Requiem by C. V. Stanford, but, as can be imagined, the programmes also featured a steady diet of Handel and Mendelssohn. There was something of the missionary in Mann. In the early years of the century he felt called to start a series—Dr Mann's Symphony Concerts—whereby large-scale works might be heard in Cambridge, performed by London musicians, with a little additional local participation, and usually under the direction of national figures such as Henry Wood, Beecham, or Elgar. Perhaps it was a combination of factors—the changing musical taste and the growth of a Cambridge snobbery that it did not need outside 'help'—which caused these ultimately to fail financially. Mann was choirmaster of the Norwich festival in and after 1902. In 1892 he had become a freeman of the City of Norwich. He was an early member of the Royal College of Organists and a central figure in the Incorporated Society of Musicians.

Mann had four children, of whom two daughters survived and married choral scholars. Two of his grandsons became choristers. He died at the Evelyn Nursing Home, Cambridge, on 19 November 1929, a few days after his last appearance in the chapel. His lasting legacy is the King's College choir, which he established in its modern, recognizable form, and the apposite harmonization of the Christmas hymn 'Once in royal David's city', later heard throughout the world in the regular broadcast from King's College of the festival of nine lessons and carols each Christmas eve.   ANDREW PARKER

Sources King's Cam., archives of the provost and fellows of King's College · Norfolk RO, archives of the dean and chapter of Norwich · Cambridgeshire Collection, Cambridge City Libraries · King's Cam., Rowe Music Library · *Arthur Henry Mann: a memoir* (privately printed, Cambridge, 1930) · *DNB* · *CGPLA Eng. & Wales* (1930)
Archives CUL, music collections · King's Cam., Rowe Music Library · Norfolk RO | King's Cam., letters to Oscar Browning
Likenesses photograph, 1863 (with other Norwich Cathedral choristers), Norfolk RO, DCN 101/1/6 · photograph, 1899, Norfolk RO, MS 11090 · photographs, King's Cam., Rowe Music Library
Wealth at death £1630 11s. 4d.: probate, 4 Feb 1930, *CGPLA Eng. & Wales*

Mann, Arthur Henry (1876–1972), journalist, was born at Warwick on 7 July 1876, the eldest of thirteen children of James Wight Mann, merchant, mayor, and freeman of

Warwick, and his wife, Annie Elizabeth, daughter of William Lake, of Warwick. He was educated at Warwick School and captained the cricket eleven. At seventeen he was apprenticed as a reporter on the *Western Mail* in Cardiff, where he played cricket for Glamorgan.

After three years as a reporter Mann became sub-editor of the company's evening paper, and married, in 1898, Aida (*d.* 1948), daughter of Louis Maggi, ship chandler, of Cardiff. In 1900 he moved to Birmingham, where he spent five years as sub-editor of the *Birmingham Daily Mail* and seven as editor of the *Birmingham Evening Dispatch*. When the ownership of the latter paper changed hands in 1912 Mann went to work for Edward Hulton in London, initially as London editor of the *Manchester Daily Dispatch* and from 1915 onwards as editor of the *Evening Standard* where he started 'Londoner's diary'.

In December 1919 Mann was offered the editorship of the *Yorkshire Post*, a position he held with unusual distinction for twenty years. With his appointment as managing editor in 1928 he was given broad authority also over the editorial policy and staffing of the two other papers in the group. Mann's editorship was associated with a steady growth in the prestige, if not in the circulation, of the *Post*, and will be chiefly remembered for the paper's resolute opposition to Neville Chamberlain's policy of appeasement in 1938–9, as well as for the part it played in precipitating the abdication crisis in 1936, when Mann on his own initiative published a strong leader on the bishop of Bradford's address admonishing the king.

Mann believed that a serious newspaper had a responsibility to inform and educate rather than entertain its readers, and that it needed a directing mind behind it to give it character and to preserve its independence. As editor he insisted on his right to decide what line the *Yorkshire Post* should take on important issues, and on appeasement he made it clear that he would resign if overruled by his board. The fact that the *Post* was a Conservative newspaper did not in his view require it to lend uncritical support to the party, any more than it had in 1922 when it had distanced itself from the Conservative leadership in advocating the breakup of the coalition. The board chairman, Rupert Beckett, constantly urged him to moderate his criticism of Chamberlain, but Mann stuck to his guns, and when an attempt was made at a shareholders' meeting to have the paper's policy changed, Beckett stood by him.

Mann's effectiveness as an editor rested on a flair for news, shrewd judgement of people, great strength and simplicity of character, and deep concern for the national interest as he saw it. A staunch but not a die-hard Conservative, he was twice offered—and twice declined—a knighthood in the 1920s, writing that 'a journalist who receives a title, particularly if that title be regarded as a recognition of political services, may lessen his power to aid the causes he has at heart'.

Mann wrote little himself for publication. He was not an erudite person and spent only a few weeks of his life outside Britain, but he was well informed on foreign affairs and personally acquainted with many of the leading figures in the governments of his day. In his assessment of Hitler's intentions he relied heavily on his chief leader writer, Charles Tower, who knew Germany well and had studied *Mein Kampf*. Any lingering doubts that Mann may have had about Hitler's character were finally dispelled by the 'night of the long knives' on 30 June 1934.

Declining circulation and deteriorating finances in 1936 brought Mann into conflict with the business managers of the *Yorkshire Post*, who wanted to cut editorial costs and seek increased readership by reducing the price of the paper. The issue was temporarily decided in Mann's favour, but it came up again at the beginning of the war when the board decided to merge the *Post* and the *Leeds Mercury* and to sell the combined paper for 1*d*. This led to Mann's resignation in November 1939.

Mann was appointed CH in the 1941 new year honours list. Previously, in 1934, he had received an honorary LLD from Leeds University. He served as a governor of the BBC from 1941 to 1946 and as a trustee of *The Observer* from 1945 to 1956, when he resigned because he disagreed with the paper's criticism of government policy over Suez. He was chairman of the Press Association (1937–8) and became a director of Argus Press in 1946.

Mann was greatly respected by his staff, although some were a little overawed by his imposing figure and seemingly aloof manner. In private he displayed a warm and outgoing personality, had a keen sense of humour, and was a generous host. Always an optimist, he indulged a lifelong passion for racing; golf and bridge were his other favourite diversions. Following the death of his first wife, he was married in 1948 to Alice Mabel (*d.* 1968), daughter of Frank Wright, manufacturer of buttons, town councillor, and magistrate, of Birmingham. His relationship with his second wife, which extended over more than fifty years, was a singularly happy one; they had one son. Active and alert almost to the end, he died at Folkestone, Kent, on 23 July 1972.   E. P. WRIGHT, *rev.*

Sources *The Times* (28 July 1972) · personal knowledge (1986) · private information (1986) · *CGPLA Eng. & Wales* (1972)
Archives Bodl. Oxf., corresp. and papers · U. Birm., corresp. with Lord Avon | FILM BFI NFTVA, 'All those in favour', 1941
Wealth at death £14,427: probate, 10 Aug 1972, *CGPLA Eng. & Wales*

Mann [married name Follett], **Cathleen Sabine** [*other married name* Cathleen Sabine Douglas, marchioness of Queensberry] (1896–1959), painter, was born on 31 December 1896 in Newcastle upon Tyne, the second of the three daughters of Harrington Mann (1864–1937), a Scottish portrait painter, and his first wife, Florence Sabine Pasley, also a portraitist. Although Cathleen Mann's first ambitions were towards the stage, she early showed artistic skill. Having found her vocation, she studied in her father's studio in London, at the Slade School of Fine Art, London, and in Paris. Through her father she came to know Ethel Walker, who gave her private lessons as well as a rare degree of encouragement. Walker's influence is often discernible in Cathleen Mann's best portrait paintings and flower pictures.

Cathleen Mann's artistic development was interrupted

Cathleen Sabine Mann (1896–1959), self-portrait

by the First World War, when she worked in the ambulance service, but as early as 1924 she exhibited two portraits at the Royal Academy. She became a regular exhibitor there after 1930, as also at the Royal Society of Portrait Painters, of which she was a member. On 18 March 1926 she married, as his second wife, Francis Archibald Kelhead Douglas, the eleventh marquess of Queensberry (1896–1954). This had the unfortunate effect of giving her a reputation as a 'painting peeress', which she bitterly resented, not least when financial embarrassment obliged her to exploit it. This unjust reputation did not prevent her from exhibiting with the progressive London Group between 1929 and 1933, though she was never a member. Solo exhibitions of her work were held in London at Arthur Tooth & Sons in 1932, the Leicester Galleries in 1937, and the Reid and Lefevre Gallery in 1938 and 1954. Of her four works in the Victoria and Albert Museum, London, three are signed 'Cathleen Mann'; one is dated 1933 and the other 1934.

In the Second World War, after completing a series of commissions in the United States, Cathleen Mann was appointed an official war artist, working chiefly as a portrait painter; her models included Sir Adrian Carton de Wiart. The post-war years were ones of great distress. Her marriage to Lord Queensberry was dissolved in 1946 and in the same year she married John Robert Follett (1906–1953), a racehorse owner. His death was swiftly followed by that of her first husband, for whom she had never lost her affection.

During this unhappy period Cathleen Mann's painting took on a new intensity through the influence and friendship of Sir Matthew Smith. She did her best work during the last ten years of her life, and this included a portrait of Smith (National Portrait Gallery, London), some remarkable child studies, and Mediterranean landscapes which often drew Smith's warm approbation. She also made a number of interesting drawings of nude models and with her ceaseless love of experiment made some vigorous essays in abstract painting and sculpture. A study of a group of boys by the Serpentine in Hyde Park, completed a few days before her death, has been considered one of the best works she ever did.

Of diminutive stature and infectious vitality, Cathleen Mann appeared to enjoy limitless energy. She worked hard, often starting at dawn and continuing until darkness fell. To this she added a full social life, and she was involved in numerous charitable works about which her friends knew little. In later years a tendency to nervous exhaustion became more frequent. She took her own life by an overdose of sleeping pills in her London studio, 41 Montpelier Walk, on 9 September 1959 and was cremated at Golders Green, where her ashes are interred in the West Chapel. She had a daughter, and one son, David Harrington Angus Douglas, Viscount Drumlanrig, the twelfth marquess of Queensberry, who taught ceramics at the Royal College of Art, London. A memorial exhibition of her work was held at the O'Hana Gallery, London, in 1960. Her work is also represented in the Glasgow Art Gallery and Museum.　　　　C. H. SYKES, *rev.* BEN WHITWORTH

Sources F. C. Roberts, *Obituaries from 'The Times', 1951–1960* (1979) · J. Soden and C. Baile de Laperrière, eds., *The Society of Women Artists exhibitors, 1855–1996*, 4 vols. (1996) · J. Warburton, scrapbook, Tate collection, MS 968.6.4 · B. Stewart and M. Cutten, *The dictionary of portrait painters in Britain up to 1920* (1997) · *WW* (1947) · *WW* (1949) · *WW* (1958) · *WWW, 1981–90* · B. Dolman, ed., *A dictionary of contemporary British artists*, 1929, 2nd edn (1981) · Graves, *RA exhibitors* · Burke, *Peerage* (1959) · *CGPLA Eng. & Wales* (1959) · *The Times* (10 Sept 1959) · personal knowledge (1971)

Likenesses C. S. Mann, self-portrait, oils, 1938, Russell-Cotes Art Gallery, Bournemouth; repro. in 'Self portraits by living artists' [exhibition catalogue, Russell-Cotes Art Gallery, Bournemouth, 27 March – 31 May 1947] · C. S. Mann, self-portrait; Sothebys, 8 Nov 1977, lot 169 [*see illus.*] · H. Mann, portrait (in youth), priv. coll. · M. Smith, portrait, priv. coll.

Wealth at death £27,089 11s. 8d.: probate, 20 Nov 1959, *CGPLA Eng. & Wales*

Mann, Frederick Alexander [Francis] (1907–1991), jurist, was born at Frankenthal, Rhenish palatinate, Germany, on 11 August 1907, the only child of Richard Mann (1873–1953), lawyer, and his wife, Ida, *née* Oppenheim (1877–1936). Both parents were from Jewish families which had been settled near the Rhine in Germany for many generations. Mann was brought up by his father, a successful provincial lawyer, and by his mother's sister. His mother had disappeared from the boy's life at an early age, having suffered a breakdown, and spent the rest of her days in an institution. It was a lonely and austere childhood. But Mann derived from the companionship of his father the personal and professional ethic which sustained him through disappointment and disaster to ultimate honour and success.

Mann's schooling and time at university took place during the turbulent years of the Weimar republic and, above all, of the German inflation, which left a permanent mark on him. He attended the universities of Geneva, Munich, and Berlin. At Berlin in 1930 he became an assistant in the law faculty, a mark of unusual distinction, and in the following year he took a doctoral degree. It was there also that he met his wife, Eleonore (Lore) Ehrlich (1907–1980), a girl from Breslau whose academic record promised as much as his own. They both looked forward to their professional careers, and Mann himself decided to combine academic work with an advocate's practice, as was not unusual in Germany. But his life and prospects were destroyed when Hitler came to power in January 1933. Both he and Eleonore were impatient with those who thought the nightmare would soon pass, and they decided immediately that they must leave. Arrangements were made for him to open an office in London where, in the first instance, he would practise German law. He returned to Berlin in October 1933 to rejoin Eleonore and take his final examinations. They were married on 12 October under the ubiquitous picture of Hitler, and left Berlin at once for London.

Mann was forced to start again from scratch in an alien land. His wife had to defer her own career to his, and it was not until 1966 that she was able to start her pioneering legal practice for poor persons in the Portobello Road. His intention (a reluctant one, driven by the need to earn a living as quickly as possible: he would have preferred to have continued his academic work) was to practise as a solicitor, but he could not do so until he became a British subject by naturalization in 1946. In the meantime he acted as a consultant in German law to the solicitors' firm of Swann Hardman & Co., of 10 Norfolk Street, London. Between 1936 and 1938 he worked on a book on the law of money, the manuscript for which he submitted as a doctoral thesis to the University of London. The book was published by Oxford University Press under the title *The Legal Aspect of Money* (1938) and received highly favourable notices. It was the first systematic study of the law of money in the English language, and a work of monumental erudition. It was also one of the first textbooks to break the convention that the works of living academic writers should not be quoted in court. Uniquely among writers of English legal textbooks, the author was able to draw copiously from his own knowledge of comparative material from other jurisdictions.

In 1946 Mann returned to Berlin with the Allied Control Commission to help remove the imprint of Nazism from German law. He wore the uniform of a lieutenant-colonel. It was bitter for him that he had not been able to wear an army uniform in wartime. But he had become an enemy alien, and it was only because the police turned a blind eye to his case that he was not interned. After the war, he became a partner in the Norfolk Street firm, which changed its name to Hardman, Phillips and Mann. His practice developed rapidly, and in 1958 the firm was merged with the large City practice of Herbert Smith & Co., of which he remained a working member until the day of his death. He became well known as a forceful and tactically ingenious litigating solicitor with an enviable

following. His clients included many international corporations, as well as such diverse characters as Somerset Maugham, Nubar Gulbenkian, and Baron Thyssen. At the same time his writings on international law were increasingly admired not only in England and Germany but elsewhere in Europe, the United States, and more widely. It was a rare combination of academic and practical distinction.

Although he had been educated first in the civil law tradition, Mann came to have a great admiration for the administration of justice in England. But this did not inhibit his legendary criticisms in the learned journals of any judicial decision which fell short of his own exacting standards. Underlying all his work, both practical and academic, was the pursuit of the unifying legal principle. This is perhaps why, of all his admirers among the judges, none gave place to Lord Denning, who described him in his own book, *The Due Process of Law* (1980), as the most learned of all his learned friends.

Mann (who was known in England as Francis, though he published as F. A. Mann) was one of that unique generation of German Jewish refugees who pulled themselves up by their own efforts and enriched and varied the qualities of English life in the 1930s and beyond. He did not practise the Jewish religion but he felt the force and separateness of his cultural inheritance. In his attitude to Israel and Germany he showed the adamantine quality of his integrity. He refused to condone the abduction of Adolf Eichmann from Argentina so that he could stand trial in Jerusalem, because in his view the kidnapping fatally flawed the trial.

Mann was forthright in his opinions. His confidence in his own legal judgement made him reject compromise as weakness, and seem intolerant of other views. But he was in truth a modest man with a genuine horror of the parade of his own attainments. Both inside and outside the law he possessed the life force, a man of energy and enthusiasm. There was a wide European culture in his make-up, with a special and discriminating love of music. It is ironic that his career and achievements were honoured in the country from which he was exiled long before they were fairly recognized in England. In 1977 the president of the Federal Republic of Germany conferred on him the grand cross of the order of merit. As early as 1960 he was appointed visiting professor at the University of Bonn, to give an annual series of lectures and seminars, whereas he never held an established post at an English university. In 1974 he was elected a fellow of the British Academy. He received honorary degrees from the universities of Zürich and Kiel, and, in 1989, from Oxford. In 1980 he was appointed CBE. In the last year of his life he became the first practising solicitor to be appointed an honorary queen's counsel and to be elected an honorary bencher of Gray's Inn.

Apart from *The Legal Aspect of Money*, Mann published two volumes of *Studies in International Law* (1973 and 1990) and a shorter book, *Foreign Affairs in English Courts* (1986), as well as hundreds of writings on international and monetary law. He died of a heart attack on 16 September 1991 at his flat at 56 Manchester Street, London, while he was correcting the proofs of the fifth edition of his book on the law of money. His body was cremated at Hammersmith cemetery on 20 September. He left one son, David (*b.* 1935), and two daughters, Jessica (*b.* 1937) and Nicola (*b.* 1944). His wife predeceased him in 1980.   GEOFFREY LEWIS

Sources F. A. Mann, unpublished memoir, priv. coll. • personal knowledge (2004) • private information (2004) • *The Times* (19 Sept 1991) • *The Independent* (25 Sept 1991) • *Daily Telegraph* (2 Oct 1991) • *WWW*, 1991–5 • L. Collins, 'Francis Mann, 1907–1991', *PBA*, 84 (1994), 393–407 • L. Collins, 'In memoriam: Dr F. A. Mann QC, CBE, FBA', *British Year Book of International Law* (1992) • L. Collins, 'Dr F. A. Mann: his work and influence', *British Year Book of International Law* (1993), 55 • Lord Denning, *The due process of law* (1980)
Archives priv. coll.
Likenesses photograph, repro. in *The Times* • photograph, repro. in *Daily Telegraph*
Wealth at death £2,253,043: probate, 3 Jan 1992, *CGPLA Eng. & Wales*

Mann, Gother (1747–1830), army officer and military engineer, was born on 21 December 1747 at Plumstead, Kent, the second son of Cornelius Mann and his wife, Elizabeth, *née* Gother. His father, a first cousin of Sir Horace Mann (1701–1786), went to the West Indies in 1760 and died at St Kitts on 9 December 1776. Gother was left in the care of his uncle, Mr Wilks of Faversham, Kent, and after passing through the Royal Military Academy, Woolwich, was commissioned practitioner engineer and ensign on 27 February 1763. He was employed on the Sheerness and Medway defences until 1775, and promoted sub-engineer and lieutenant on 1 April 1771. On 1 March 1768, at St Nicholas's, Rochester, Kent, he married Ann, second daughter of Peter Wade of Rushford Manor, Eythorne, Kent, rector of Cooling, vicar of Boughton Monchelsea, and minor canon of Rochester Cathedral. They had five sons and three daughters.

In late 1775 Mann was sent to Dominica, West Indies. He was promoted engineer-extraordinary and captain-lieutenant on 2 March 1777. He commanded a militia detachment when the island was invaded by the French in September 1778. The little garrison resisted but were outnumbered, and surrendered on honourable terms. Mann was a prisoner of war for a few months, and on 19 August 1779 he was appointed to the engineer staff of Great Britain. He then reported on the east coast defences. In 1781 he accompanied Colonel Braham, the chief engineer, on an inspection of the north-east coast of England to assess coastal defences, as seven corporations had petitioned on the subject.

In 1785 Mann went to Quebec as commanding royal engineer in Canada. Promoted captain on 16 September, he was employed throughout the country on civil and military duties, planning against American invasion, erecting fortifications, improving ports, and laying out townships including Toronto and Sorel. In 1788 he reported to the governor, Guy Carleton, first Baron Dorchester, on military posts, harbours, and navigable river routes, showing the posts' faults and decline.

Mann returned to Britain in 1791, and in June 1793 he joined the duke of York's army in the United Provinces. He was present at the sieges of Valenciennes (which capitulated on 28 July) and Dunkirk (from 24 August to 9 September), and at the battle of Hondschoote or Menin (12–15 September). He was promoted lieutenant-colonel on 5 December 1793. On his return to England in April 1794 he was briefly employed under the master-general of the ordnance in London, and then was again commanding royal engineer in Canada until 1804. Described by the colonial secretary, Lord Hobart, as 'an officer of so much merit and experience' (Kendall, 485), Mann reported on the St Lawrence canals and, understanding their commercial and military importance, proposed repairs and alterations. He also reported on the necessity of an adequate permanent defence system at Quebec, advocating more fortifications there, some of which were later constructed. From August 1801 until he left in 1804 he was the second most senior officer in Canada, and successfully requested brigadier's pay because of his additional duties. After his return to England he continued to be concerned with Canadian defence. His services in Canada were rewarded by a grant, on 22 July 1805, of 22,859 acres of land in the township of Acton in Lower Canada. Mann became colonel in the army on 26 January 1797, colonel in the Royal Engineers on 18 August 1797, and major-general on 25 September 1803. From 1805 until 1811 he was employed on particular services in Ireland and on various committees in London. On 13 July 1805 he was made a colonel-commandant of the corps of Royal Engineers; on 25 July 1810 he became lieutenant-general, and on 19 July 1821 general. From 23 July 1811 until his death he was inspector-general of fortifications. In February 1815, on behalf of officers of the Royal Engineers, he protested to the earl of Mulgrave, master-general of the ordnance, at the paucity of honours awarded to them at the end of the war, alleging it cast a stigma on the honour and reputation of the corps. To the inspector-general's responsibilities were added in 1822, at Wellington's instigation, the construction and maintenance of barracks in the United Kingdom. Mann was offered a baronetcy, but declined it as he lacked the financial resources to support it. He was appointed president of the committee to examine cadets for commissions on 19 May 1828. He died on 27 March 1830 at Lewisham, Kent, and was buried in the churchyard at Plumstead, Kent.

Of Mann's sons, Gother served in the artillery, Cornelius in the engineers, John in the 28th regiment, and Frederick William in the marines and later in the staff corps. Cornelius's son William *Mann (1817–1873) was an astronomer. Plans by Gother Mann are in the British Library and Canadian archives.

R. H. VETCH, *rev.* ROGER T. STEARN

Sources *DNB* • J. C. Kendall, 'Mann, Gother', *DCB*, 6.484–5 • W. Porter, *History of the corps of royal engineers*, 1 (1889) • C. M. Watson, *History of the corps of Royal Engineers*, 3 (1954) • *GM*, 100/1 (1830), 477 • J. Holland Rose and others, eds., *Canada and Newfoundland* (1930), vol. 6 of *The Cambridge history of the British empire* (1929–59) • R. Muir, *Britain and the defeat of Napoleon, 1807–1815* (1996)
Likenesses miniature, 1763, repro. in Porter, *History*, vol. 1, p. 215

Mann, Horace (1823–1917), civil servant, was born at Andover, Hampshire, on 4 October 1823, the youngest son of Thomas Mann (d. 1863), a solicitor, and his wife, Elizabeth Stubbings. He was baptized at Andover Independent Chapel on 4 January 1828. When the civil registration of births, marriages, and deaths came into force in 1837 his father was appointed chief clerk of the General Register Office at Somerset House. Mann was educated privately and at Mercers' School, London, before being admitted at Lincoln's Inn (November 1842). He was called to the bar in November 1847, practising on the home circuit. In April 1849 he published a series of letters in the *Morning Chronicle* suggesting improvements to the law governing registration.

While still in his twenties Mann was placed in charge of a government survey, which produced one of the most significant and controversial public documents of the nineteenth century. Probably at the suggestion of Major George Graham (1801–1888), registrar-general, the 1851 census included two additional surveys of public worship and school attendance; Graham's brother, the politician Sir James Graham, had regretted the lack of such statistical data after the defeat of his 1843 Factory Education Bill. Mann, who was appointed assistant commissioner of the census office in October 1850, organized the two voluntary censuses, conducted, in the case of public worship, on Sunday 30 March 1851, and for education over three days, 29–31 March. He seems to have devised the method of the religious census, which recorded attendances at churches on the prescribed day, and drew up the survey questionnaire. It took him and his large team of enumerators more than two years to chase up the unreturned forms—although it was voluntary, they achieved a remarkably high response rate—and to digest the great mass of data.

Mann's report on religious worship in England and Wales was published in January 1854. He prefaced the statistics with an earnest but amateurish history of religion in Britain, from the druids to the revolution of 1688, which Anglican critics of the census were quick to seize upon. But his account of the doctrines and organization of the thirty-five organized religious communities active in England and Wales was welcomed by nonconformists, who were discussed on a basis of complete equality with the established church. The data exposed the extent of non-attendance or 'spiritual destitution', particularly in cities, and Mann speculated, in remarkably modern terminology, about the connection between secularization and urbanization in terms which anticipated later anxieties on the part of the churches. The really sensational result, however, was the finding that in terms of persons attending public worship (as opposed to notional church membership), the total for the Church of England was exceeded by that for other religious bodies. This statistic, which underlay the mid-Victorian political campaigns for religious equality, made the report 'one of the landmarks in the ecclesiastical history of England and Wales' (H. S. Skeats and C. S. Miall, *History of the Free Churches of England,*

1688–1891, 1894, 521). Mann publicly defended the methods of the census and its accuracy in the *Journal of the Statistical Society* (1855), at the Social Science Association Congress of 1859, and in letters to *The Times* (1860). Despite this, the results of the religious census proved so contentious that in Mann's lifetime no government attempted another, though there were calls to do so in every decade up to 1910.

Mann's report on school provision and attendance, dated March 1854, was scarcely less far-reaching in its implications, though it lacked the uniqueness of the religious census (in this context he is to be distinguished from the American educationist Horace Mann (1796–1859), who made an educational tour of Britain in 1843). He arrived at a more optimistic conclusion about the provision of elementary education than other observers, and found that only a very small proportion of children were receiving no schooling. His report speculated at length, and beyond the ordinary remit of a statistician, on the reasons for the existing shortfall and, in particular, why working-class parents were disinclined to educate their children. He subsequently gave statistical evidence on school attendance to the Newcastle commission on elementary education (6 December 1859) and published a paper on the subject in the *Journal of the Statistical Society* (1862).

In June 1855 Mann became registrar of the civil service commission, which was responsible for government appointments. Although he seems to have owed his original position in the census office to his family connection, he was a strong advocate of extending open competitive recruitment to all branches of the civil service, and at an educational conference in 1857 argued that its adoption for even the lowest-grade posts would help to stimulate better teaching in schools. In October 1874 he gave evidence in favour of open competition to a civil service inquiry. He became secretary of the civil service commission in December 1875, retiring on pension in 1887. He received no honours. In retirement he divided his time between the Reform Club in Pall Mall and his home at Hayes Grove Cottage, Hayes Common, Kent.

Mann, who never married, died in comparative obscurity (no obituaries have been found) at the Spa Hotel, Bath, on 24 March 1917. As class replaced religion as the most fundamental perceived division in British society, so interest in Mann's work had declined. His religious census was rediscovered in the 1960s by historians and sociologists of religion, who renewed the discussions of a century earlier as to its meaning, significance, and reliability as a source. A later resurgence of interest in local history led to the publication of many of the original enumerators' returns. A recent appraisal has concluded that Mann's census was conducted with 'commendable rigour and care' and that its 'basic accuracy' can generally be accepted (Snell and Ell, 51). Mann's pioneering official survey was not repeated until 2001 when, in the context of a multi-faith society, the decennial household census included a voluntary question about individual religious profession.

M. C. CURTHOYS

Sources J. Foster, *Men-at-the-bar: a biographical hand-list of the members of the various inns of court*, 2nd edn (1885) · *Men of the time* · IGI · census returns, 1881 · will, London, 2 May 1901 · O. Chadwick, *The Victorian church*, 1 (1966) · D. M. Thompson, 'The religious census of 1851', *The census and social structure*, ed. R. Lawton (1978) · M. J. Cullen, *The statistical movement in early Victorian Britain: the foundations of empirical social research* (1975) · C. D. Field, 'The 1851 census of Great Britain: a biographical guide for local and regional historians', *Local Historian*, 27 (1997), 194–217 · K. D. M. Snell and P. S. Ell, *Rival Jerusalems: the geography of Victorian religion* (2000) · CGPLA Eng. & Wales (1917) · d. cert.

Wealth at death £18,332 10s. 7d.: probate, 2 May 1917, CGPLA Eng. & Wales

Mann, Sir Horatio, first baronet (*bap.* 1706, *d.* 1786), diplomatist, was baptized on 25 August 1706, the second son of Robert Mann (1678–1751), a successful London merchant, and his wife, Eleanor (1680–1752), the daughter and heir of Christopher Guise of Abbot's Court, Gloucestershire. He had an elder brother, Edward Louisa Mann (1702–1775), a younger twin brother, Galfridus (1706–1756), and two younger brothers, James (*d.* 1764) and Robert (1708–1755). He also had four sisters, of whom the eldest, Eleanor (*d.* 1789), married Sir John Torriano; Mary married Benjamin Hatley Foote and Catherine (*d.* 1776) married Foote's brother the Revd Francis Hender Foote.

Mann studied at Eton College in 1718 and about 1720 moved briefly to Clare College, Cambridge. Ill health may have forced him to leave before he took a degree. Although he was never strong, later in life he took solace in hypochondria. His early years were spent in Chelsea, though little is known of his interests. His father purchased an estate in Linton, Kent, where he built a house about 1730 and established himself as 'a fully qualified country squire' (*DNB*). Seeking a climate which would better suit his health, Mann travelled to Italy, and took the extreme precaution of transporting a coffin with him. He is first recorded in March 1732 in Naples, where he stayed for at least a year. There he purchased marble tables, presumably for Linton, and other 'sundry things' (Ingamells, 42). He travelled north with Lady Grisell Baillie and was in Rome by April 1733, in Padua in June, and in Venice a month later. His companion may have taken him to Florence for the first time in April 1733.

In 1737 Mann visited The Hague, but by 3 February the following year he had become 'well known and esteemed by the ministers' in his capacity as assistant to Charles Fane, the British resident in Florence (PRO, SP 98/40, fol. 239). On Fane's return to England in April 1740 Mann took over his duties. He owed his rapid promotion to Sir Robert Walpole, to whom he was distantly related (their great-great-grandmothers had been sisters), and through his influence, and later the support of his son Horace, he steadily gained professional and social advancement. He remained the British representative in Florence until his death, and was appointed envoy on 13 December 1765 and envoy-extraordinary and minister-plenipotentiary on 29 January 1782. He was rewarded with a baronetcy on 3 March 1755 and was invested a knight in the Order of the Bath with much ceremony in 1768.

As Britain had no diplomatic representation in the Papal States, it was Mann's responsibility to report on the whereabouts of the Stuarts. Consequently his official duties were more onerous during the early part of his career. There was a certain amount of rivalry with other British informants, who included Baron Stosch, alias John Walton, Cardinal Alessandro Albani, and Burrington Goldsworthy, the consul at Leghorn. During the War of the Austrian Succession in the early 1740s Mann was asked to advise on the movement of the British fleet in the Mediterranean. Charles Edward Stuart escaped Italy to lead the Jacobite rising in Scotland in 1745, at which time Mann's dispatches became excitable and his concern for detail tiresome. A lack of proportion ultimately prevented him from becoming a diplomat of distinction. Geniality was his real gift and, as Edward Gibbon wrote, his 'most serious business was that of entertaining the English at his hospitable table' (E. Gibbon, *Memoirs of my Life*, ed. G. A. Bonnard, 1966, 134).

Mann kept open house for all British visitors, and they continually report his kindness. As one writer put it, 'his physiognomy speaks his goodness & politeness which is sometimes carried to excess' (Ingamells, 635). He accommodated guests in Casa Ambrogi and, when there was no performance at the theatre on a Saturday night, he held *conversazione* at his residence, the Palazzo Manetti. According to Alexander Drummond:

> all the apartments on the ground-floor … were lighted up, and the garden was a little epitome of Vauxhall. These little conversazione resemble our card-assemblies; and this one was remarkably brilliant, for all the married ladies of fashion in Florence were there.   (Drummond, 40–41)

Mann's kindness was universally acknowledged, perhaps most admiringly by John Boyle, fifth earl of Cork and Orrery, who wrote:

> he does honour to our nation. He lives elegantly and generously. He never fails in any point of civility and kindness to his countrymen. The politeness of his manners, and the prudence of his conduct, are shining examples both to the Britons and Italians. He is the only person I have ever known, whom all Englishmen agree in praising. He has the art of conquering our prejudices, and taming our fierceness. (J. Boyle, *Letters from Italy in the Years 1754 and 1755*, 1773, 107–8)

The importance of Mann for the historian is the letters—almost 1800 of them—to and from Sir Horace Walpole. Walpole met Mann when he first visited Florence in December 1739, and their friendship blossomed, even though, as Mann never left Florence, they never met again after April 1741. Perhaps Walpole's hold over Mann was sexual, and the correspondence was fed by Mann's toadying and Walpole's desire to have a sympathetic, and resilient, ear. The character of the British resident is best presented by William, second Earl Fitzwilliam, who wrote that:

> Sir Horace is the most finical man in the world: if you speak a little loud, he can't bear it, it hurts his nerves, he dies—and he v–m–ts if you eat your petite patee before your soup; take him as he is, without the least notice, he is perfect character for the stage. He has been so long out of England, that he had lost the manliness of an Englishman, and has borrowed the

effeminacy of Italy. But with all his little airs, he is a good kind of man, and is very civil.   (Fitzwilliam MSS)

His close friendships with the homosexual painter Thomas Patch and the effete John, second Earl Tylney, adds weight to this description. None the less, after his death in Florence, on 16 November 1786, the *conversazione* were missed. One visitor, George Baillie, wrote, 'Florence is a dull Town no Society for Eng: since the death of Sir H. Mann' (Ingamells, 636).

To supplement his considerable entertaining expenses Mann dealt to a limited extent in paintings and antiquities, but, unlike some of his contemporaries, he lacked a concerted interest in science or music. In his later years his post was coveted by George, third Earl Cowper, who, with privileged access to the grand duke, had a clear diplomatic advantage over Mann. However, higher authorities ignored Cowper's offer to replace Mann, and after his death the residency was filled by John Augustus Hervey.

Mann was buried on his estate at Linton, Kent, which he had inherited from his elder brother, Edward, in 1755. The baronetcy devolved on his nephew Horatio *Mann (1744–1814), politician, the son of his twin brother, Galfridus, and the title became extinct at his death on 2 April 1814. The property passed to the Right Revd James Cornwallis, bishop of Lichfield and fourth Earl Cornwallis, who had married Mann's youngest niece, Catherine (1742–1811), the daughter of Galfridus Mann and the sister of the younger Horatio Mann.   HUGH BELSEY

Sources J. Ingamells, ed., *A dictionary of British and Irish travellers in Italy, 1701–1800* (1997), 41–2, 635–6, 974–6 • B. Moloney, *Florence and England* (1969), 34–46 • Walpole, *Corr.*, vols. 17–27 • T. C. W. Blanning, '"That horrid electorate" or "Ma patrie germanique"? George III, Hanover, and the *Fürstenbund* of 1785', *HJ*, 20 (1977), 311–44 • Northants. RO, Fitzwilliam MSS • D. B. Horn, ed., *British diplomatic representatives, 1689–1789*, CS, 3rd ser., 46 (1932) • J. Spence, *Letters from the grand tour*, ed. S. Klima (1975) • A. Drummond, *Travels through different cities of Germany, Italy, Greece, and several parts of Asia* (1754) • HoP, *Commons* • B. Burke, *A genealogical history of the dormant, abeyant, forfeited, and extinct peerages of the British empire*, new edn (1883); repr. (1978) • Venn, *Alum. Cant.* • *DNB*
Archives PRO, state papers • Yale U., Farmington, Lewis Walpole Library, letters | Badminton House, Gloucestershire, muniments, letters to duchess of Beaufort • BL, letters to Sir William Hamilton, Egerton MS 2641 • BL, letters to Robert Keith, Sir R. M. Keith, etc., Add. MSS 35468–35622 *passim* • BL, letters to duke of Newcastle, Sir William Hamilton, etc., Add. MSS 32705–33090 *passim* • BL, letters to Richard Phelps, Stowe MSS 257–259 *passim* • BL, letters to Thomas Richardson, Add. MSS 23805–23829 *passim* • East Riding of Yorkshire Archives Service, Beverley, letters to Henry Medley • NRA Scotland, priv. coll., corresp. with Lord Stormont • priv. coll., letters to Thomas Steavens • priv. coll., letters to first Earl Waldegrave • Wilts. & Swindon RO, corresp. with tenth earl of Pembroke • Yale U., Farmington, Lewis Walpole Library, corresp. with Horace Walpole
Likenesses J. Astley, oils, 1751, Lewis Walpole Library, Farmington, Connecticut • T. Patch, *c.*1760 (*Dilettanti around Venus Medici*), Sir Brinsley Ford collection, London • T. Patch, 1761 (*Golden lassess*), Chatsworth, Derbyshire; copy, Lewis Walpole Library, Farmington, Connecticut • T. Patch, *c.*1765 (*Gathering at Casa Manetti*), Lewis Walpole Library, Farmington, Connecticut • A. van Maron, oils, after 1768, Marquess of Cornwallis collection • J. Zoffany, group portrait, oils, 1772–8 (*The tribuna of the Uffizi*), Royal Collection • W. Greatbach, stipple, pubd 1857 (after Astley), BM, NPG • T. Patch, group portrait, caricature in oils, Royal Albert Memorial Museum, Exeter, Devon

Mann, Sir Horatio, second baronet (1744–1814), politician and patron of cricket, was born on 2 February 1744 at Boughton Malherbe, Kent, the only surviving son of Galfridus Mann (*d.* 1756), army clothier, and his wife, Sarah, daughter of John Gregory of London. Horatio (known as Horace) was educated at Charterhouse School and from May 1760 at Peterhouse, Cambridge. On the death of his father, who had supplied uniforms to the British army, he inherited £100,000 and the family estate at Linton Park, near Maidstone. In 1775 his uncle, the diplomat Sir Horatio *Mann, made over to him his own estate of Bishopsbourne near Canterbury in return for an annuity. Mann had married (on 13 April 1765) Lady Lucy Noel, daughter of the fourth earl of Gainsborough; they had three daughters. He was knighted in 1772 and entered parliament as MP for Maidstone two years later.

While critical of Lord North's conduct of the American War of Independence, Mann supported its prosecution, though after Cornwallis's surrender at Yorktown (1781) he voted against its continuance. Sir Horace Walpole, in correspondence with Mann's uncle, commended his speaking abilities. After North's resignation in 1782, Mann was one of the country gentlemen who met in the St Alban's tavern in London and sought (unsuccessfully) to bring about a government of national unity between William Pitt and Charles Fox. He was a regular visitor to Florence, where his uncle was the British envoy in Tuscany, briefly acting as chargé d'affaires there when the elder Mann—whose baronetcy he inherited—died in 1786.

Mann, who had left parliament in 1784, returned as MP for Sandwich (1790–1807). In two speeches, in 1795 and 1797, he bitterly attacked the black designs of France on Britain's commerce and constitution but, in general, took little part in parliamentary proceedings. He was a man 'dedicated to pleasure rather than to business' (Wilson, 363) and it was the patronage of cricket which dominated his life.

The only evidence of Mann's skills as a cricketer lies in some lines of doggerel written in 1773 after he had batted in a match between Surrey and Kent:

> At last Sir Horace took the field,
> A batter of great might,
> Moved like a lion, he a while
> Put Surrey in a fright.
> (Haygarth, 1.10)

Mann's twenty-two runs proved to be his highest known score and only one other innings is recorded. What contemporary fame he had as a player must lie in any achievements in the years preceding 1772 in matches not recorded in Haygarth's *Scores and Biographies*. This 'agreeable, gay and affable' man (ibid., 1.55) found his chief satisfaction in cricket through his ability to organize, his delight in entertaining, and his compulsion to bet.

In 1765 Mann had laid out a ground at Bishopsbourne which became a centre for cricket matches played by teams such as England, *Hambledon Cricket Club, Surrey, Kent, the *White Conduit Cricket Club, and his own

Sir Horatio Mann, second baronet (1744–1814), by Hugh Douglas Hamilton, c.1785

elevens. There were booths selling refreshments and temporary stands for crowds which could reach several thousands:

> From Marsh and Weald their hayforks left,
> To Bourne the rustics hied.
> (quoted in Underdown, 145)

Mann brought many players from the Hambledon club in Hampshire to play for him. After learning that one of them, James Aylward, had made 167 for Hambledon against England in 1777 he subsequently secured his services on a permanent footing for his own sides by giving him employment—though he was 'ill-qualified for the post' (Nyren, 95)—in Kent as his bailiff. It was John Nyren, Hambledon's historian, who recalled Mann's agitation 'cutting down the daisies with a stick' (ibid., 89) as he anxiously awaited a result on which he had placed a heavy bet. As early as 1767 his uncle warned him about his profligacy in betting in hundreds of pounds. His lavish hospitality of suppers and dances, said a Kentish newspaper, ranked 'him with the first characters in the kingdom' (Underdown, 146), though his attempt to keep up with the expenditure of other cricket patrons such as the third duke of Dorset and the ninth earl of Winchilsea contributed to his eventual bankruptcy, in 1805, to which the playing of whist had also contributed. Undaunted, Mann relinquished his tenancy of Bishopsbourne in 1790 and in the following decade promoted a few matches on the Dandelion Fields, near Margate. With a final flourish he entertained there England versus Surrey in two successive matches in August 1796, in which many of the great

names of late eighteenth-century cricket participated. Four years later he staged a match on horseback with specially made bats, a bit of frivolity which perhaps explains why a contemporary, Frederick Reynolds, remembered that Mann 'was too frequently made the object of buffooneries' (quoted in Lord Harris and F. S. Ashley-Cooper, *Lord's and the MCC*, 1920, 25). None the less, patrons such as Mann helped cricket to retain its rural basis in the south-east of England until the realization that the game's immediate future—for both gentry and professionals—lay in the growth and convenience of London. Mann himself was a founder member of Marylebone Cricket Club.

Mann was someone at ease both with his own social class and with the rural peasantry. He agreed to be godfather to the child of his namesake, the Hambledon player Noah Mann. 'Sir Horace, by this simple act, hooked for life the heart of poor Noah' (Nyren, 94). Mann died at Union Crescent, Margate, on 2 April 1814, having spent his last years either there or at Bath, 'a warm promoter of every institution and improvement in these places' (Haygarth, 56).   GERALD M. D. HOWAT

Sources [A. Haygarth], *Frederick Lillywhite's cricket scores and biographies*, 1 (1862) · J. Brooke, 'Mann, Horatio', HoP, *Commons, 1754–90* · J. Nyren, 'The cricketers of my time', *The young cricketer's tutor*, ed. C. C. Clarke (1833); new edn (1893) · *GM*, 1st ser., 84/1 (1814), 420, 526 · D. Underdown, *Start of play: cricket and culture in eighteenth-century England* (2000) · J. Wilson, ed., *A biographical index to the present House of Commons* (1806) · F. S. Ashley-Cooper, *Hambledon cricket chronicle, 1772–1796* (1924) · J. Goulstone, *Hambledon: the men and the myths* (2001)
Likenesses H. D. Hamilton, portrait, *c.*1785, Marylebone Cricket Club, Lord's, London [*see illus.*] · portrait, repro. in G. R. C. Harris and F. S. A. Cooper, *Lord's and the M.C.C.* (1920); priv. coll.

Mann [*married name* Gye], **Dame Ida Caroline** (1893–1983), ophthalmologist, was born on 6 February 1893 at 67 Fordwych Road, West Hampstead, London, the second child and only daughter of Frederick William Mann (1854?–1935), an official in the Post Office, and Ellen Packham (1851?–1936). Her father's family came originally from Norfolk, her mother's from Cuckfield in Sussex, of which rural connection Mann was always proud. As a child she developed a love of reading and especially of writing poetry which lasted throughout her long life. She was educated at Wycombe House School, Hampstead and then, guided by her ultra-cautious father, she began work at sixteen in the safe but stultifying atmosphere of the Post Office Savings Bank. Soon, however, influenced largely by a chance visit to a hospital open day, she developed a strong desire to study medicine, and eventually was able to enter the London School of Medicine for Women in 1914. Her schooling had been interrupted by many childhood illnesses, but from this point her health became robust and thenceforward she showed a daunting capacity for work. With further periods of training at the Royal Free and St Mary's hospitals, she qualified MB BS in 1920. During the period at St Mary's she assisted Professor J. E. S. Frazer in embryological research; her developmental studies were presented as a dissertation for the DSc (London, 1924), and formed the basis of her notable first textbook, *The Development of the Human Eye* (1928), still in print forty years later.

This training in research methods opened up a new world to Mann. She later wrote in *The Chase* (1986), her autobiography, that the greatest joy she ever experienced was when seated alone at her microscope: 'Just the thrill of knowing I had seen something no one else had ever seen before kept me happy for days' (*The Chase*, ed. Golding, 77). No matter what other duties were laid on her (and she was extraordinarily hard-working in her daily clinical activities), Mann was driven to pursue original knowledge in this way. Her exposure during midwifery training as a medical student to the perils of birth and motherhood convinced her that she herself had no desire for marriage or children, and she thereby gained extra time in which to apply her driving curiosity to exploring the complexities of ocular development. Often this involved overturning long-standing but erroneous beliefs. This latter aspect indeed characterized both halves of Mann's professional career: as well as fighting her way into clinical positions hitherto largely closed to women, she revelled also in sweeping away facile and poorly thought out 'conventional wisdom' by finding out the facts and forcing them on the notice of the often reluctant authorities.

After qualifying Mann decided to specialize in ophthalmology, and took her first post under Leslie Paton at St Mary's, becoming FRCS in 1924. She also held several teaching appointments while she progressed up the ladder towards consultant ophthalmologist status, reaching the highest point in 1927 with appointment as senior surgeon on the staff of Moorfields Eye Hospital, London, the first woman ever to do so. At the same time she established a Harley Street practice and consolidated herself as a leading clinical ophthalmologist in London, but still carried on her developmental studies and teaching (including the diploma course in Oxford). In this period up to the Second World War she learned and promoted the then new technique of slit-lamp microscopy of the eye, applying it both to patients and to animals in the London Zoo. She was also instrumental in bringing to London in 1938 Josef Dallos, the Hungarian pioneer of glass contact lenses, just ahead of the Nazi take-over of Hungary, and with him she established the first contact lens centre in the United Kingdom.

With the outbreak of war it became necessary to evacuate Moorfields. At the instigation of Sir Hugh Cairns Mann moved to Oxford in 1941 to undertake the clinical training of medical students diverted from London, and there she was appointed to Margaret Ogilvy's readership in ophthalmology, as well as a personal chair, the first woman ever to hold the title of professor in the University of Oxford, and a professorial fellowship in St Hugh's College. Despite this time-consuming work she still travelled to London to perform surgery, carried out important research on the ocular effects of war gases, and kept up a staggering number of other activities, including the vigorous reorganization of Oxford Eye Hospital. In this period she was the first to use penicillin to treat ocular infection. The Nuffield Laboratory of Ophthalmology was established in Oxford, aided

by a donation from Lord Nuffield, to provide Mann with research facilities and room to treat her private patients separately from her clinical commitments in the neighbouring Oxford Eye Hospital. Here she appointed the biochemist Antoinette Pirie (later her successor as reader) as her research assistant. Together they wrote the influential book, *The Science of Seeing* (1946), in part to refute Aldous Huxley's 'pernicious psychotic book' *The Art of Seeing*.

On 30 December 1944 Mann married the pathologist Professor William Ewart Gye (1884–1952), the son of Charles Bullock, an agricultural worker, and his wife, Ellen Elizabeth Prosser. Gye was the director of the Imperial Cancer Research Fund. Mann retained her maiden name to avoid having two Professor Gyes in the same house. They had no children, but she helped and supported her three stepchildren throughout her life, as well as taking responsibility for her brother's children after his and his wife's early deaths.

At the end of the war Mann returned to London as Oxford still resisted the idea of making ophthalmology an academic discipline. But she was unhappy with the changes in medicine following establishment of the National Health Service in 1948, feeling that the old autonomy and the trust between doctor and patient had been compromised. This, together with her husband's poor health, exacerbated by the post-war restrictions on food and fuel in bitter winter weather, decided them to overwinter in warmer conditions, and they sailed for Australia in 1949. Their intention may have been to return, but they had presciently taken their household goods with them, and once settled in Perth they decided to stay. She resigned her Moorfields appointment in 1950 (and was apparently never forgiven by them for doing so).

Once settled, Mann and her husband used their combined experience to establish pure-bred strains of laboratory animals in Australia for research and pathological purposes. After her husband's death in 1952 Mann felt free to undertake, in addition to a private ophthalmic practice, a long series of journeys throughout Australia and Oceania to study ocular health and the incidence of disease in many lands, races, and cultures; in particular she studied the incidence of trachoma in the Aboriginal communities of Western Australia and Northern Territory. While she described many of her adventures in lighter books, including *The Cockney and the Crocodile* (1962), under the *nom de plume* (although her own name) of Caroline Gye, the serious outcome was the classic *Culture, Race, Climate and Eye Disease* (1966). Sometimes as a representative of the World Health Organization, or the Australian government, and sometimes just to satisfy her own curiosity, she continued these explorations to a considerable age, and at the same time worked tirelessly for the improvement of ocular health throughout Australia, especially through her own ophthalmic practice and by improvements in medical training. In recognition of Mann's many contributions to research, teaching, and clinical practice, she was appointed CBE (1950) and DBE (1980), as well as receiving honorary degrees, prizes, and medals from many countries.

Mann lived at 56 Hobbs Avenue, Nedlands, Perth, where she died on 18 November 1983. She was cremated at Karrakatta cemetery crematorium in Perth. A distinguished ophthalmologist, Mann was equally well known for her pioneering research work on embryology and development of the eye, and on the influences of genetic and social factors on the incidence and severity of eye disease throughout the world.   J. M. TIFFANY

Sources I. C. Mann, 'The chase', Battye Library of Western Australian History, Perth, Western Australia [manuscript of autobiography] · I. C. Mann, *The chase*, ed. R. Golding (1986) · *Australian Journal of Ophthalmology*, 12 (1984), 95–6 · *Archives of Ophthalmology*, 102 (1984), 1713–15 · private information (2004) · *WW* (1983) · C. H. Andrews, *Obits. FRS*, 8 (1952–3), 419–30 [obit. of William Ewart Gye] · I. C. Mann, *Ida and the eye: a woman in British ophthalmology from the autobiography of Ida Mann*, ed. E. I. Buckley and D. U. Potter (1996)

Archives U. Oxf., Nuffield Laboratory of Ophthalmology · University of Western Australia, Perth

Likenesses photograph, *c.*1943, U. Oxf., Nuffield Laboratory of Ophthalmology · photographs, 1963–80, U. Oxf., Nuffield Laboratory of Ophthalmology · photographs, in or before 1980, repro. in Mann, *The chase* · L. Kahan, drawing, repro. in *The Age* (18 July 1964) [Melbourne]

Mann, Sir James Gow (1897–1962), museum director, was born in Norwood, London, on 23 September 1897, the only son of Alexander Mann (1853–1908), Scottish landscape painter, and his wife, Catherine Macfarlane Gow. In 1916 he left Winchester College (where he was educated from 1911) and joined the Oxfordshire yeomanry (Royal Artillery, Territorial Army), in which he served in Flanders and Italy, rising to the rank of major. At the end of the First World War he entered New College, Oxford, in 1919; he remained there after he had taken his BA degree in modern history in 1921 to take a BLitt in 1922, with a thesis on armour.

After obtaining his degree Mann was appointed assistant keeper in the department of western art at the Ashmolean Museum, Oxford, under C. F. Bell, the keeper. There, although he had little contact with arms and armour, he laid the foundation of his wide knowledge of other branches of art. In 1924 he was appointed assistant to the keeper of the Wallace Collection but, although he now worked in a museum containing an important armoury, he was not in charge of it, since it was the principal interest of the keeper, S. J. Camp. At that time Mann wrote the introduction to the English edition of a book by Oswald Graf Trapp, *The Armoury of the Castle of Churburg* (1929), to the compilation of which he had already contributed. At the same time he produced *The Wallace Collection Catalogue of Sculpture* (1931) with admirable dispatch. The wide range of objects described drew on his exceptionally broad knowledge of the applied arts, but he sometimes failed to examine works of art very closely, leading to a number of errors. In 1932 Mann left the Wallace Collection to become deputy director of the newly formed Courtauld Institute of the University of London, a post which included a university readership in history of art, but he returned to the Wallace Collection at the request of the trustees in 1936 as keeper, a position he retained until his death, although from 1946 with the rank of director.

Both his proven organizing ability and his wide knowledge of arms and armour made Mann an ideal choice for the post of master of the armouries at the Tower of London, which fell vacant in 1939 on the death of Charles J. ffoulkes. The outbreak of the Second World War meant that both collections had to be packed away immediately, but from 1945 Mann had the opportunity of rearranging both. The armouries were dated in the methods of display and lacked trained museum staff. Mann began to reorganize the armouries both as a modern exhibition, and as a national museum with fully trained curatorial and conservation staff. His wide influence in the artistic world made it possible for him to attract very substantial grants from the National Art Collections Fund and the Pilgrim Trust for the purchase for the armouries in 1942 and 1952 of pieces of the greatest historical and artistic importance from the Norton Hall collection, originally formed by Beriah Botfield, and the William Randolph Hearst collection. He also purchased a Gothic horse-armour at auction in Switzerland in 1958.

After a generation in which a great part of the nation's heritage of fine English armours had been exported, Mann induced the authorities to reinstate a purchase grant for the armouries. He began a series of important exhibitions at the Tower, including in 1957 the first to cover the armours made in the royal workshop at Greenwich founded by Henry VIII. His most productive period scholastically was from 1929 to 1945, when he produced, among a stream of papers on armour and related subjects, an important series in *Archaeologia* on European medieval and Renaissance armour.

Mann's two papers in the same journal in 1930 and 1938, on the sanctuary of the Madonna della Grazie, near Mantua, resulted from his discovery that the armours decorating this church were not of *carta pesta*, as had been thought, but contained parts of a number of important and rare fifteenth-century armours. He also published the surviving inventories of the Gonzaga armouries in two papers in the *Royal Archaeological Journal* (1939 and 1945). His paper 'The etched decoration of armour' (British Academy, 1940), opened up new ground by linking the history of arms with the early history of etching plates for printed illustrations.

An excellent committee man, who was constantly in demand throughout his life, Mann played an influential part in organizations concerned with art history. He was a member of the committees of the exhibition of British art (1934), of Portuguese art (1955–6), and of British portraits (1956–7), all of which were held at the Royal Academy. In 1937 he visited Spain at the request of the republican government to inspect the measures taken to protect works of art during the civil war. From 1943 to 1946 he was a member and honorary secretary of the British committee for the restitution of works of art in enemy hands. In 1944 he became director of the Society of Antiquaries of London, and from 1949 to 1954 was president, and thereafter honorary vice-president. In 1946 he was appointed surveyor of the royal works of art, a post he held until his death. At different times he was also trustee of the British

Museum and of the College of Arms, a governor of the National Army Museum, chairman of the National Buildings Record, vice-chairman of the Archbishop's Historic Churches Preservation Trust, a member of the Royal Mint advisory committee, of the Royal Commission on Historical Monuments, and of the Historic Buildings Council. He was knighted in 1948 and appointed KCVO in 1957. He was a fellow of the British Academy (1952).

Mann's last major work, *The Catalogue of the European Arms and Armour* in the Wallace Collection, was published only weeks before his death. It was in some ways unsatisfactory, as he reports old authorities inaccurately. The many calls on Mann's time and energy no doubt sometimes prevented him from checking his original sources. However, it was his very wide interests in many artistic fields which made it possible for Mann to reinstate arms and armour as part of the main stream of art-historical studies. Throughout the greater part of his life, he was the unchallenged authority in his field. In his obituary of Mann for the *Proceedings of the British Academy* Francis J. B. Watson noted a 'streak of Scottish austerity in his character which made him increasingly out of sympathy with certain developments in the modern world'; but this puritanism must, however, have been counterbalanced by a cavalier streak, which led him to adopt court dress and sword for a photographic portrait now in the Wallace Collection library. Always ready to help younger enthusiasts in his field, Mann's apparently reserved and even austere manner concealed a warm personality.

In 1926 Mann married Mary (*d.* 1956), daughter of the Revd Dr George Albert Cooke; they had one daughter. In 1958 he married Evelyn Aimée, daughter of Charles Richard Hughes. Mann died at his London home, 23 Chapel Street, Westminster, on 5 December 1962. His second wife survived him. A. V. B. NORMAN, *rev.* PETER HUGHES

Sources *The Times* (7 Dec 1962) · F. J. B. Watson, 'Sir James Mann', *Burlington Magazine*, 105 (April 1963), 162–4 · F. J. B. Watson, 'Sir James Mann, 1897–1962', *PBA*, 49 (1963), 407–11 · A. H., 'Sir James Gow Mann', *Vaabenhistoriske Aarbøger*, 11b (1963), 183–4, 186 · A. N. Kennard, 'Sir James Mann', *Waffen- und Kostümkunde*, 5 (1963), 73–5 · W. Reid, 'Sir James Mann', *Armi Antiche* (1962), 145–53 [with bibliography of Mann's published articles] · personal knowledge (1981) · private information (1981) · *CGPLA Eng. & Wales* (1963)
Archives Courtauld Inst. · Royal Armouries Library, Leeds, corresp., notebooks · S. Antiquaries, Lond. · Tower of London · Wallace Collection, London | TCD, corresp. with Thomas Bodkin · National Buildings Record [Royal Commission on Historical Monuments]
Likenesses Elliott & Fry, photograph, 1953, Wallace Collection library · A. K. Lawrence, chalk drawing, *c.*1955, S. Antiquaries, Lond. · A. Corbett, photograph, repro. in Watson, 'Sir James Mann', pl. xvi · H. Coster, photographs, NPG · G. Mannell, photograph, Wallace Collection library; repro. in Kennard, 'Sir James Mann'
Wealth at death £28,867 4s.: probate, 25 Feb 1963, *CGPLA Eng. & Wales*

Mann [*née* Stewart], **Jean** [Janet] (1889–1964), politician and housing reformer, was born Janet Stewart, at 22 Calder Street, Polmadie, east Renfrewshire, on 2 July 1889. She was the daughter of William Stewart, an iron moulder

Jean Mann (1889–1964), by Bassano, 1946

and active trade unionist, who was an enduring influence on her radical outlook, and his wife, Annie, *née* Morrison. Polmadie was an industrial district dominated by extensive locomotive engineering works, eventually absorbed into Glasgow in 1891. The Stewarts later moved to the Ibrox district of Govan, where she received an education at Kinning Park School and then up to secondary level at the prestigious Bellahouston Academy. She started working life as a cashier with a local firm, but marriage to William Lawrence Mann (*c.*1878–1958), a commercial traveller and a widower, directed her energies towards childrearing. Married on 18 December 1908, the couple had six children, and subsequent appraisals of Jean Mann made much of her ability to combine family commitments with an active public life. It was an image that she assiduously cultivated, to demonstrate that she had a keen understanding of issues pertaining to 'housewives', especially consumer rights and housing.

Rothesay, on the island of Bute, was where Jean Mann first came to prominence in the Independent Labour Party (ILP). The family moved there after the First World War, and her husband, as local branch chairman, persuaded her to take on the task of secretary. She already had a history of social activism in the United Free Church of Scotland in Kinning Park, and her early radical Liberalism gradually developed into Christian socialism. Although latterly she did not emphasize her religious affinities, perhaps because of the pervasive sectarian dimension to west of Scotland politics, they sustained her throughout her life. There was a strong missionary edge to her belief that housing and the environment helped to shape moral character, and were thus fundamental areas for political action.

Although she was an unsuccessful candidate for Rothesay town council in 1923 and 1924, Mann nevertheless built up a reputation as an impressive public speaker, much in demand on the ILP propaganda circuit. In 1927 she and her husband returned to Glasgow, which served as a more effective base to further her political ambitions. She was eventually adopted as Labour candidate for the parliamentary constituency of West Renfrewshire, although she failed to win the seat in 1931 and 1935. In her semi-autobiographical book, *Woman in Parliament* (1962), she wrote about her reaction to ILP disaffiliation from the Labour Party in 1932, describing the Maxton-led decision as 'an honest, but foolish one' (p. 122). She chose to stay within the official party, although the tensions engendered by the split remained with her and coloured her attitude to the bitter internal divisions of the 1950s.

Mann's municipal career took off in 1931 when she topped the poll in a by-election for the Provan ward of Glasgow corporation. This was despite the opposition of the Roman Catholic church, which had been unable to elicit a response from her on the issue of birth control. Mann's stance was less radical than her silence would suggest, as she later made no secret of her concern about the trend towards limiting family size. Glasgow's notorious inter-war housing congestion was by no means representative of Scotland as a whole, and she advocated planned dispersal of the urban population to encourage balanced demographic growth.

As organizing secretary of the Garden Cities and Town Planning Association of Scotland, Mann was also an ardent publicist for the ideas of planning theorists such as Ebenezer Howard and Patrick Abercrombie. This interest made her the obvious choice to serve as Labour's housing convener, after the party won control of Glasgow corporation for the first time in 1933. Her influence was evident in the conscious shift in corporation policy from tenement construction to the low-rise 'cottage' style of dwelling that she believed to be essential for community wellbeing. Inspired by model municipal developments, notably Manchester's Wythenshawe Garden City, Mann attempted to raise standards in the new housing estates being built on peripheral land acquired by the corporation. However, finance ultimately limited her scope for action, and tensions emerged within the Labour group because she implacably opposed more cost-effective multi-storey housing. In 1938 Mann retired abruptly from the corporation, having achieved hitherto unprecedented civic status for a woman in Glasgow as senior magistrate.

After 1935 Mann was adopted as prospective Labour candidate for the Dundee constituency, but asked to be released from the commitment during the Second World War. In the Labour landslide of 1945 she was returned for Coatbridge, covering the Lanarkshire steel-producing community of the Monklands, in succession to James Barr, whose radical sentiments on land reform and sympathies for Scottish home rule she shared. By this time she was well known in Scotland for her forthright views on housing and planning. As a member of the Scottish Housing Advisory Committee, appointed by Thomas Johnston, the wartime secretary of state for Scotland, she strongly criticized recommendations to encourage high-rise building in towns. Mann continued her housing interest in parliament, where she became a noted speaker on a range of issues relating to social welfare. Austerity and food shortages were themes which she pursued relentlessly, taking on the role of housewives' champion in challenging inconsistencies in rationing policy and the notorious activities of black marketeers. In *Woman in Parliament*, she wrote with enthusiasm of her work during the immediate post-war period, although she made pointed reference to the male chauvinism she encountered in the House of Commons and the mutual support this engendered among women MPs.

The reorganization of parliamentary boundaries meant that from 1950 until her retirement in 1959 Mann represented the constituency of Coatbridge and Airdrie. There was a vigorous and well-organized local Unionist (Conservative) Association, which throughout this time persistently pressurized Mann about the stark left–right polarization that had emerged within the Labour Party. Yet Mann was a declared opponent of the Bevanites; a stance which secured the support of the right-wing trade union leader, Arthur Deakin, who helped to promote her to one of the women's seats on Labour's national executive committee (NEC) in 1953. Two years later she was at the centre of an acrimonious NEC argument over whether to expel Aneurin Bevan from the party, after he had voted against a Labour amendment in a Commons defence debate. Mann later claimed that she decided against expulsion in the interests of unity, thus turning the vote in Bevan's favour by the narrowest of margins. Some on the right of the party accused her of a failure of nerve, but there was some consistency in her approach, as throughout her political career Mann had been distinguished by single-mindedness. She also had personal esteem for Bevan, although pointedly not for the Bevanites, whom she regarded as being too tainted by communist influences.

That Mann was not afraid to embrace controversy was demonstrated in 1958, when she resigned from the NEC following an altercation over the appointment of a party organizer for Scotland. As an MP, she devoted much of her time to child-welfare and consumer affairs, and she was closely associated with campaigns to encourage the fostering of children in care and to raise public consciousness on the need for fire safety at home. The latter issue had particular resonance, as years previously one of her own children had died as a result of a fire accident. She did not contest her seat in the 1959 general election, and after leaving parliament she retired to Gourock, in Renfrewshire, where she was active as a town councillor. She died at Larkfield Hospital, Greenock, Renfrewshire, on 21 March 1964 after a long illness and was buried in Gourock cemetery on 23 March. Obituaries paid tribute to her pugnacious qualities and boundless energy.

A small, wiry woman, Mann projected a feisty, down-to-earth approach, which comes across strikingly in her speeches both within parliament and beyond. Although her feminism was ambiguous, given her moral emphasis on motherhood and family values, Mann consistently spoke out on a range of women's issues at a time when such matters were not normally given priority among MPs. She also deserves to be remembered as an important, pioneering woman in Scottish politics.

IRENE MAVER

Sources *Glasgow Herald* (23 March 1964) · *The Times* (23 March 1964) · *The Scotsman* (23 March 1964) · *Daily Record* (23 March 1964) · *Evening Times* [Glasgow] (21 March 1964) · *Airdrie and Coatbridge Advertiser* (27 March 1964) · J. Mann, *Woman in parliament* (1962) · M. 'Espinasse, 'Mann, Jean', *DLB*, vol. 6 [repr. in *Scottish labour leaders, 1918–1939*, ed. W. Knox (1984), 197–9] · *Glasgow Herald* (20 May 1931) · *Forward* (23 May 1931) · m. cert. · 'Busy life of a woman bailie', *Glasgow Herald* (24 April 1938) · 'Know your councillors: Jean Mann, Provan ward', *Evening News* [Glasgow] (9 June 1933) · J. Mann, 'What kind of world? The importance of your vote', *Airdrie and Coatbridge Advertiser* (30 June 1945) · 'Mrs Mann wins in Coatbridge', *Airdrie and Coatbridge Advertiser* (14 July 1945) · 'Your candidates' views on election issues', *Airdrie and Coatbridge Advertiser* (14 Feb 1950) · '"Proud to be MP again": Mrs Jean Mann reviews election campaign', *Airdrie and Coatbridge Advertiser* (4 March 1950) · '"Hat-trick" for Mrs Jean Mann', *Airdrie and Coatbridge Advertiser* (2 Nov 1951) · 'Mrs Jean Mann', *Airdrie and Coatbridge Advertiser* (21 May 1955) [interview] · 'Mrs Mann in again', *Airdrie and Coatbridge Advertiser* (28 May 1955) · *Glasgow Herald* (16 Jan 1958) [W. L. Mann] · M. Horsey, *Tenements and towers: Glasgow working-class housing, 1890–1990* (1990) · *WWBMP*, vol. 4 · *WWW*, 1961–70 · J. Mann, 'Overcrowding in Glasgow: the case for a satellite town', *Glasgow Herald* (24 Feb 1936) · J. Mann, ed., *Replanning Scotland: expert evidence on pre-war conditions in Scotland and post-war speeches, delivered at planning conference, Largs, 1941* (1942) · L. Hunter, *The road to Brighton pier* (1959) · *The diary of Hugh Gaitskell, 1945–1956*, ed. P. M. Williams (1983) · P. Hollis, *Jennie Lee: a life* (1997)
Likenesses photographs, after 1945, repro. in Mann, *Woman in parliament* · Bassano, photograph, 1946, NPG [*see illus.*] · caricature, repro. in 'Know your councillors' · photograph, repro. in *Glasgow Herald* (26 April 1938) · photograph, Hult. Arch.
Wealth at death £2200 5s. 6d.: confirmation, 24 Sept 1964, NA Scot., SC 53/41/76/664–5

Mann, Julia de Lacy (1891–1985), economic historian and college head, was born on 22 August 1891 in London, the daughter of James Saumarez Mann (*b.* 1851), editor and former fellow and tutor of Trinity College, Oxford, and his wife, Amy Gertrude, *née* Bowman. She grew up in Bromley, in a home characterized by 'liberal politics and a strong evangelical atmosphere' (Major, 1), and received a strong grounding in classics at Bromley high school which prepared her to read *literae humaniores* at Somerville College, Oxford (1910–14). Little is known of her childhood or years at Oxford, where a contemporary described her as a tall and imposing young woman, who 'was a fine Hercules' in the first-year play (ibid., 2). Apparently, she developed an interest in social work through her mother, leading her to spend the year 1914–15 living in the Women's University Settlement in Southwark, while reading for the social science certificate at the London School of Economics. At the LSE, however, Mann discovered the emerging field of economic history:

At the beginning of the First World War, I thought I would do social work, and so I went to the L.S.E. and did the Diploma

in Social Science, and that's where I met economic history for the first time, and I thought this is the stuff for me ... I didn't want to teach and teaching and social work were about the only professions you could have in those days if you were a woman. (Berg, 314)

Mann's pursuit of economic history was delayed by the First World War. From 1915 to 1916 she served as a clerk in the Admiralty, and from 1916 to 1919 in the Foreign Office, attending the Paris peace conference as one of the staff.

In 1919 Mann returned to Somerville College, Oxford to do the diploma in economics. Through one of her tutors, J. A. Todd, who was secretary of the empire cotton-growing committee of the Board of Trade during the war, Mann became interested in the cotton industry. After serving for a short time as Todd's secretary, in 1922 Mann returned to the LSE to work for a PhD on the development of the cotton industry prior to the industrial revolution, supervised by Lilian Knowles. The following year Mann left the LSE upon her appointment as vice-principal and tutor in economics at what was then known as St Hilda's Hall, Oxford.

At that time, St Hilda's was the smallest of the Oxford women's colleges: Mann was one of five resident tutors in 1924. Probably because of her habitual shyness, 'as a tutor, Mann was not a great success and old students remember long silences during tutorials' (Rayner, 62). In fact, Mann kept in contact with many of her students long after they left St Hilda's. She proved herself, however, an able administrator when she found herself virtually running the college during the illness of the principal, Winifred Moberly. Julia Mann was elected principal of St Hilda's after Moberly's death in 1928.

Mann served as principal of St Hilda's during the difficult years of the depression, the Second World War, and the post-war period. At her retirement in 1955 she left the college in a strengthened position—free of debt and ready to embark on a major period of expansion in which it would be accepted as a full college of the university. As principal of St Hilda's, Mann needed to balance the college's lack of endowment with the need to expand numbers and to provide more scholarships and research funding. Although the college was limited to 150 members by the university in 1927 (raised to 180 after the Second World War), in practice it could not even expand to this level because of the cost of building additional accommodation for students. Even though Mann disliked appealing for money, she carried through the raising of funds for the building of a new library wing in 1935. Under Mann's leadership after the war, the college launched a major fundraising and building campaign, the first fruit of which, the Sacher Wing, was opened in 1954. During the early 1950s the college also prepared for self-government, leading to the granting of a new charter in 1955.

Possessing little ambition for herself, Julia de Lacy Mann was dedicated to St Hilda's College. During her tenure as principal she performed many routine administrative functions single-handedly, while never accepting her full salary and living in two rooms in the college. After the death of her uncle, a former warden of Merton College, she became a benefactor of St Hilda's. Although Mann's responsibilities at St Hilda's gave her little time to participate in the university, as senior principal of the women's colleges she was a well-respected figure in Oxford, serving on the council of Barnett House, which provided training in the social sciences, and on the appointments board.

Julia Mann's contributions to women's education were matched by her contributions to economic history. During her early years at St Hilda's she continued her research on the cotton industry, publishing *The Cotton Trade and Industrial Lancashire, 1600–1780* with A. P. Wadsworth in 1931. 'Tentative and pathbreaking in the 1930s, it is a book that has remained authoritative and fertile' (Harte and Ponting, xi). During this period, Mann was also active in the Economic History Society, which had been founded in 1926, serving on its council and as assistant editor of its journal, *Economic History Review*, under joint editors R. H. Tawney and Ephraim Lipson, with whom she had studied at Oxford. As principal of St Hilda's, however, Mann limited her research in the subject to publishing bibliographies in *Economic History Review*, supervising postgraduate students, and reviewing books.

Julia Mann's career entered a new phase after her retirement in 1955, when she moved to the town of Melksham in Wiltshire. Mann began to undertake research on the textile history of the region, publishing chapters in the *Victoria County History* of Wiltshire (1959) and *Studies in the Industrial Revolution Presented to T. S. Ashton* (1960) and editing *Documents Illustrative of the Wiltshire Textile Trades in the Eighteenth Century* (1964). She also published a chapter in *A History of Technology* (1958) and articles in *Economic History Review* and the new journal *Textile History*, founded in 1968. Her research culminated in the publication of *The Cloth Industry in the West of England from 1640 to 1880* (1971). Like her earlier study of the cotton trade, this work was noted for its exhaustive research, attention to detail, and clear prose. Mann uncovered many new sources, gaining access to the records of textile firms held in private hands. During her retirement, Mann also gave support and encouragement to a new generation of economic historians, shown by the publication of the festschrift *Textile History and Economic History: Essays in Honour of Miss Julia de Lacy Mann*, edited by N. B. Harte and K. G. Ponting (1973).

Mann was active in her Wiltshire community, serving on the county education committee and the county records committee, and acting as president of the West Wiltshire Historical Society and chair of the Melksham Local History Group. She frequently attended concerts in Bath and enjoyed reading, particularly nineteenth-century memoirs. In the last years of her life she developed a new interest, transcribing the letters of her father's Guernsey ancestors. At her home at Melksham, which she shared at first with three other women, one of whom was her Somerville contemporary Frances Griffiths, she welcomed many friends. Although she did not have close relatives of her own, she took a particular interest in the daughters and grandchildren of a friend. In her last months she was cared for by her devoted housekeeper. Julia de Lacy Mann died at The Cottage, 462 Bowerhill, Melksham, on 23 May 1985 at the age of ninety-three.   FERNANDA HELEN PERRONE

Sources N. Harte and K. Ponting, *Textile history and economic history: essays in honour of Miss Julia de Lacy Mann* (1973) [incl. bibliography] · K. Major, 'Address at Miss Mann's memorial service', 1985, St Hilda's College archives, Oxford · M. E. Rayner, *The centenary history of St Hilda's College, Oxford* (1993) · *The Times* (27 May 1985) · *Textile History*, 17 (1986), 3–6 [incl. bibliography] · V. Brown and M. E. Rayner, eds., *St Hilda's College register* (1993) · [H. Bryant], ed., *Somerville College register, 1879–1959* (1961) · manuscript register, Somerville College archives, Oxford · M. Berg, 'The first women economic historians', *Economic History Review*, 2nd ser., 45 (1992), 308–29 · T. C. Barker, 'The beginnings of the Economic History Society', *Economic History Review*, 2nd ser., 30 (1977), 1–19 · C. W. Boase, ed., *Registrum Collegii Exoniensis*, new edn, OHS, 27 (1894)
Archives Nuffield Oxf., MSS of the Economic History Society · St Hilda's College, Oxford, records of the principal's office | FILM University of Kent, Canterbury, T. C. Barker, 'Interview with Miss J. de L. Mann', video recording
Likenesses P. Greenham, oils, 1949, St Hilda's College, Oxford
Wealth at death £205,000: probate, 31 July 1985, *CGPLA Eng. & Wales*

Mann [*née* Rackham], **Mary Elizabeth** (1848–1929), writer, was born on 14 August 1848 in Norwich, Norfolk, the daughter of William Simon Rackham, a well-to-do merchant who, having prospered in the retail clothing trade, eventually became a distributor of 'Manchester' goods, and his wife, Mary Anne Elizabeth, *née* Smith. Much of Mary's childhood was spent in the imposing family residence of Town Close House, to the west of the city. Recollections of mid-Victorian Norwich inform a number of her later novels, notably *The Memories of Ronald Love* (1907).

On 28 September 1871 the twenty-three-year-old Mary married Fairman Joseph Mann (1836/7–1913), a substantial yeoman farmer whose land lay around the village of Shropham, near Reepham in south-west Norfolk. As the owner or lessee of nearly 800 acres, Mann was a significant local figure: secretary and treasurer of the board of school managers and guardian and overseer of the poor. A substantial part of his wife's early married career, in addition to the care of their four children, was taken up with parochial responsibilities. The family lived at first at Church Farm, later at Shropham Manor, where at least two previous generations of Manns had lived.

Mann seems to have taken up writing some time in the early 1880s. Her confidant and principal source of guidance was Thomas Fairman Ordish, the son of her husband's sister, a literary-minded civil servant and subsequently a notable Shakespearian scholar. Many years later Mann acknowledged the influence of 'my old friend and sympathiser, the champion of my poor powers and defender of all my scribblings' (private information). Encouraged by Ordish, she published her first novel, *The Parish of Hilby*, in 1883.

In a prolific career extending over three and a half decades, Mann produced nearly forty works of fiction. Mostly set in the few square miles around Shropham ('Dulditch'), their point of view is largely that of the yeoman or tenant farmer who functioned both as tenant and *rentier* and, as such, had been badly hit by the agricultural depression of the 1880s (its victims included Fairman Mann himself, whose losses in the first half of 1885 alone amounted to over £800). While unsparing of middle-class pretension, Mann is sympathetic to the plight of the agricultural labouring class: one of her best-known early works, *The Patten Experiment* (1899), covers the efforts of a well-meaning clergyman and his family to live on the 11s. a week that was the standard farmworker's wage in the 1890s. An earlier novel, *Susannah* (1895), covers a similar theme.

In general Mann's novels, among them *Confessions of a Coward and a Coquette* (1886) and *The Parish Nurse* (1903), were well received by contemporary critics. Later admirers included D. H. Lawrence. *The Memories of Ronald Love* is a notably sharp account of an illegitimate boy packed off to a grisly Norwich boarding-school. She also published a mass of short stories in the magazines of the day, many of them subsequently collected. By this time her literary earnings had become a valuable addition to the family income, and she supported two daughters in their efforts to establish professional careers.

Fairman Mann died in 1913. Mary Mann subsequently moved to Sheringham on the Norfolk coast, where she died at Cliff Road aged seventy on 19 May 1929. Like many of her contemporaries Mann wrote too much, doubtless for the best of reasons. But while the novels are perhaps no more than high-grade period pieces, her claim to lasting fame rests on a handful of stories written in the 1890s. At their best, short fictional works such as 'Ben Pitcher's Elly', 'Dora o' the Ringolets', and 'The Lost Housen' are the equal of Hardy, and yet the matter-of-factness of their rural tragedies differs markedly from Hardy's vengeful determinism. Efforts to revive Mann's writing, usually by local publishers anxious to claim her as a 'Norfolk writer', have tended to focus on this aspect of her work. Belated recognition was achieved in 1998, when A. S. Byatt included 'Little Brother' in *The Oxford Book of English Short Stories*. It seems likely that the twenty-first century will bring a renewed interest in her life and work.

D. J. TAYLOR

Sources private information (2004) · M. E. Mann, *Tales of Victorian Norfolk*, ed. J. C. Baxter and E. A. Goodwyn (1991) · J. Sutherland, *The Longman companion to Victorian fiction* (1988) · b. cert. · m. cert. · d. cert. · *CGPLA Eng. & Wales* (1929)

Likenesses photograph, repro. in Mann, *Tales of Victorian Norfolk* · photograph, repro. in members.tripod.co.uk/Adrian_Money, accessed 20 Dec 2002 · photograph, priv. coll.

Wealth at death £4232 16s. 8d.: probate, 5 July 1929, *CGPLA Eng. & Wales*

Mann, Nicholas (*bap.* 1680?, *d.* 1753), theological writer, was born in Tewkesbury and was probably the son of John and Margaret Mann who was baptized in Tewkesbury on 2 January 1680. He was admitted a king's scholar at Eton College in April 1695, aged about fourteen, and proceeded to King's College, Cambridge, where he matriculated in 1700. He was elected fellow, at a very young age, in 1702 and graduated BA in 1704 and MA in 1707. At Cambridge he was a companion of the first marquess of Blandford,

which led Francis, second earl of Godolphin, to appoint him private tutor to his son William Godolphin, Viscount Railton, later marquess of Blandford and heir to the Marlborough estates. He later became an assistant master at Eton and then one of the clerks in the secretary's office under Lord Townshend. He travelled in France and Italy; by 1722 he was in Florence with his former pupil Richard Rawlinson and William Bromley, and he remained abroad for several years. On his return he was appointed king's waiter at the custom house and keeper of the standing wardrobe at Windsor.

Through the influence of Lord Godolphin, Mann was elected master of the Charterhouse, London, on 19 August 1737, against the opposition of Dr Conyers Middleton. At his institution he is said to have shocked the archbishop of Canterbury, Thomas Newton, by professing himself an Arian. This is certainly borne out by the views on Christ's divinity expressed in his *Critical notes on some passages of scripture comparing them with the most ancient versions, and restoring them to their original reading, or true sense*, published anonymously in 1747, in which he criticizes the Athanasian creed in contrast to the apostles' creed. His treatise drew an immediate response in *The Scripture Testimonies of the Divinity of Jesus Christ Compared* (1747), whose author described Mann as one of 'the modern Socinians' and accused him of peddling 'learned mischief'. Mann's other work was *Of the True Years of the Birth and of the Death of Christ: Two Chronological Dissertations* (1733; Latin version, with additions, 1742 and 1752), which he was prompted to write because of the criticisms of Newton's *Chronology*. He was also an antiquary and made copious annotations on his copy of Roger Gale's *Antonini iter*, which found its way into Richard Gough's possession.

Mann, who does not appear to have been greatly liked at the Charterhouse, did not leave his mark on either the hospital or the school beyond his own epitaph, which was affixed over the chapel door—perhaps prudently—several years before his death at Bath on 24 November 1753. He was buried in the piazza at the Charterhouse and, apparently unmarried, left his property to his sisters, Mary and Margaret Mann, both of whom were still living in Tewkesbury. He bequeathed several items, including a portrait of the late earl of Wilmington, a governor of the hospital, to the Charterhouse, and to Eton College he left his manuscripts, except those of his own works, and his printed books.

GORDON GOODWIN, *rev.* S. J. SKEDD

Sources R. A. Austen-Leigh, ed., *The Eton College register, 1698–1752* (1927) · Venn, *Alum. Cant.* · *IGI* · A. Quick, *Charterhouse: a history of the school* (1990) · *The works of … Thomas Newton*, 1 (1782) · will, PRO, PROB 11/805, fols. 273v–275r · [W. Jones], *Observations in a journey to Paris by way of Flanders*, 2 vols. (1777) · J. Ingamells, ed., *A dictionary of British and Irish travellers in Italy, 1701–1800* (1997), 637 · Nichols, *Lit. anecdotes*, 2.165–6, 194 · *GM*, 1st ser., 23 (1753), 541 · F. Harris, *A passion for government: the life of Sarah, duchess of Marlborough* (1991)

Wealth at death £300–£500 annuities and property: will, PRO, PROB 11/805, fols. 273v–275r

Mann, Robert James (1817–1886), medical practitioner and writer on science, was born in Norwich on 5 January 1817, the second of four children and only son of James Mann (*c.*1787–1820/21), watchmaker and jeweller, and his wife, Elizabeth Hilling of Horstead, Norfolk. He was four when his father died, leaving his mother in straitened circumstances. As a result he was brought up by an aunt and uncle in London until about 1830, thereafter in Norfolk. Apart from a little education at a school in London, mostly from the Latin master, the only competent teacher, he was self-taught. He had a craving for books and became especially interested in botany, geology, and the physical sciences. At seventeen Mann was apprenticed to the surgeon of the Norwich Dispensary. Then, in September 1837, he enrolled at University College, London, where he studied anatomy, physiology, medicine, surgery, midwifery, obstetrics, botany, and medical jurisprudence and, for part of 1840, dressed for the professor of clinical surgery, Robert Liston. He became a licentiate of the Society of Apothecaries on 16 April 1840 and a member of the Royal College of Surgeons on 26 June 1840. That same year the first of his many publications appeared, a list of central Norfolk's flowering plants, published in the *Natural History Magazine*.

From 1840 to 1853 Mann made his living in Norfolk as a general practitioner and surgeon, first in Norwich (from the autumn of 1840 for about a year), then in the village of Buxton (until 1849), and finally in Aylsham, where, on 1 October 1850, he married Charlotte Elizabeth (*b*. 1822/3), daughter of the Revd John Neville White of Tivetshall, Norfolk. In the autumn of 1853 he turned to writing as his principal means of livelihood but continued his medical profession on a casual basis. To help alleviate his wife's chest ailments, he chose to spend the next few winters and springs at Ventnor, Isle of Wight, the summers and autumns in Norfolk. He qualified as a physician by gaining, on 27 March 1854, his MD from the University of St Andrews.

At Buxton Mann developed an interest in astronomy. He published *The Planetary and Stellar Universe* (his first book) in 1845 and soon afterwards built his own observatory. His second book, on elementary chemistry, appeared in 1848 and *The Book of Health*, a volume in Gleig's School Series, followed in 1850. While at Aylsham he published further works on astronomy and, in 1851, the first of his many articles for *Chambers's Edinburgh Journal*. At Ventnor he became friendly with the poet laureate, Alfred Tennyson, who sanctioned and approved a sketch he published in 1856, *Tennyson's 'Maud' Vindicated: an Explanatory Essay*. Also at Ventnor he wrote the first of his many articles for the *Edinburgh Review*.

In October 1857, at the invitation of Dr John Colenso, bishop of Natal, Mann became lay head of Colenso's missionary station near Pietermaritzburg and a teacher of medical and scientific subjects. He found the work frustrating and was greatly relieved when, in July 1859, the lieutenant-governor of Natal appointed him the colony's superintendent of education. When he returned to England on secondment in March 1866, he left a system of public education which proved effective and enduring, a legacy of his diligence and zeal and his ability to manage limited means carefully. While in Natal he had taken up photography, pursued his interest in astronomy, served as

a director of the Natal Bank for several years, organized the Natal court at the London Exhibition of 1862, and had written many books and articles, some of them about Natal, others educational. Encouraged by Sir John Herschel he had taken up meteorology. He observed the weather methodically from early 1858 to early 1866, returned his records to the meteorological department of the Board of Trade, and published a number of works on the climate of Natal.

Back in England Mann served as emigration agent for Natal until 1869, when the colony's legislative council closed his office. He thereupon resigned as superintendent of education, remained in London, and devoted the rest of his life to scientific and literary pursuits. He organized scientific exhibitions and published many articles of a popular nature, the majority intended for young people. He belonged to the Photographic Society from 1866 to 1878 and served on its council for several years. He joined the Meteorological Society in 1867 and served it as president from 1873 to 1875. He served the Society of Arts as secretary of its African (later foreign and colonial) section from 1874 to 1886. He was elected a fellow of the Royal Astronomical Society in 1855, the Royal Geographical Society in 1866, and the Royal College of Surgeons in 1878.

Mann's enthusiasm for Natal never waned and he was, indeed, immediately before his death, busy preparing the catalogue of the Natal court for the Colonial and Indian Exhibition held in London in 1886. He suffered a seizure on 2 August 1886 and died two days later at his home, 5 Kingsdown Villas, Bolingbroke Grove, Wandsworth, London, where he had lived since 1870. Thus passed a man who was kindly, honest, unselfish, and modest. He was buried in Kensal Green cemetery on 9 August and his estate passed entirely to his widow, there being no offspring of the marriage.   J. MALCOLM WALKER

Sources Mrs R. J. Mann, *A sketch of the life and work of Robert James Mann* (1888) · *Monthly Notices of the Royal Astronomical Society*, 47 (1886–7), 137–9 · *Quarterly Journal of the Royal Meteorological Society*, 13 (1887), 123–5 · *DNB* · *BMJ* (21 Aug 1886), 400 · *Journal of the Society of Arts*, 34 (1885–6), 961–2 · *List of persons who have obtained certificates of their fitness and qualification to practise as apothecaries from 1 August 1815 to 31 July 1840* (1840) · private information (2004) · National Meteorological Library, Bracknell, Royal Meteorological Society Archive · m. cert. · d. cert. · parish register (baptism), Norwich, Sts Simon and Jude, 2 Feb 1817
Likenesses photograph (after carte-de-visite?), Royal Meteorological Society, Reading, Berkshire
Wealth at death £2473 19s. 10d.: probate, 3 Sept 1886, *CGPLA Eng. & Wales*

Mann, Theodore Augustine [*known as* Abbé Mann] (1735–1809), natural philosopher and historian, was born in Yorkshire on 22 June 1735, the son of a land surveyor. He was educated at a local school and instructed in scientific principles by his father. In 1753 he was sent to London to be educated in the law, but he ran away to Paris in the following year. Since the age of fifteen he had been of deist opinions, but in Paris his reading and re-reading of Bossuet's *Discours sur l'histoire universelle* brought him to the

Roman Catholic faith. He was received into the Catholic church on 4 May 1756 by the archbishop of Paris.

At the outbreak of hostilities with France, Mann travelled to Spain. He joined a regiment in Spanish service and after some months obtained leave to spend a year at the military academy in Barcelona, where he resolved to seek a life more conducive to study. In 1758 he accordingly entered the English Charterhouse in Nieuwpoort, on the Flemish coast, where he was professed on 13 October 1759 and ordained priest on 20 September 1760. Until elected prior in 1764 Mann could dedicate himself to study for thirteen hours each day, and later described these years as the happiest of his life. He made extensive notes on his reading of the Bible and patristic literature, and translated devotional and apologetical works, including St Eucherius's *De contemptu mundi* and Caraccioli's *L'univers énigmatique*. He also wrote an English treatise on phonetics and a French tract explaining Newton's theory of gravitation. After 1764 his responsibilities as prior allowed him less time for study.

Mann was increasingly absent from February 1774, when he was elected to the Imperial and Royal Academy in Brussels, of which his friend John Turberville Needham was director. In July 1775 he submitted a petition for exclaustration so that he could take up more permanent residence in Brussels. In 1776 the British government sought to have him appointed co-adjutor bishop of Quebec, and in Brussels the chancellor of Brabant (M. de Crumpipen), the chief-president of the privy council (count de Nény), and the minister-plenipotentiary (Prince Starhemberg) sought Maria Theresa's influence to expedite his secularization and retain him in the Netherlands. He was released from his monastic vows on 10 May 1777 and settled in Brussels as a secular priest on 5 June. On 28 July he was made a canon of the church of Our Lady in Kortrijk, with dispensation from residence.

Mann was one of the most active members of the academy and contributed numerous treatises on such subjects as meteorology, fire prevention, fluid dynamics, natural history, agriculture and fisheries, population, political economy, antiquities, universal history, and moral philosophy. Many were published individually or in *Mémoires de l'Académie de Bruxelles* (5 vols., 1777–88). At the academy's request he compiled 'Tables des monnaies, poids et mesures anciennes et modernes de diverses nations' (1788).

Three aspects of Mann's academic labours deserve further notice. Firstly he provided the earliest reliable series of meteorological observations from the Austrian Netherlands. Secondly some have seen an early, populationist, formulation of the 'Malthusian law' in Mann's considerations of the best ways to stimulate demographic growth within the constraints of agricultural productivity (Harsin, 155–9). Thirdly his work on fluid dynamics led to practical proposals for drainage and an official survey of the canals of the Austrian Netherlands.

From 1777 to 1783 Mann was heavily involved in government studies on canalization, agriculture, fisheries, and education. For proposed educational reforms he not only drafted reports and recommendations but was also commissioned to write schoolbooks. His textbooks on the natural sciences went through several editions. Preparatory to Joseph II's ecclesiastical reforms, Starhemberg commissioned a revision of Mann's *Réflexions sur la religion* (1778), a statement of the principles of the Cisalpine position. Such involvement in government projects came to an abrupt end with the resignations of Starhemberg and de Nény in 1783. In 1784 Mann embarked on a year-long scientific tour of France, Switzerland, and Germany in the company of the papal nuncio.

Besides writing academic treatises, government reports, and schoolbooks Mann was a contributor to the *Gentleman's Magazine*, the *Journal des Sçavans*, and *L'Esprit des Journaux*, and edited numerous works for the general public, including a children's encyclopaedia, a geographical dictionary, a horticultural dictionary, histories of the reign of Maria Theresa and of the voyages of discovery (with particular emphasis on those of Cook), and a civil, ecclesiastical, and natural history of Brussels. A treatise against theatre-going, *Le pour et contre les spectacles* (1782), has sometimes been attributed to him.

In April 1787 Mann was called to the deathbed of Anthony Joseph Browne, seventh Viscount Montagu, then resident in Brussels, to reconcile him to the Catholic church and 'to make his dying sentiments known to the world'—which he did, in the *Gentleman's Magazine*, leading to a heated correspondence in that journal. In June he became perpetual secretary of the Brussels academy, responsible for its archives and correspondence. In the following years he achieved election to the Royal Society, long his dearest wish, and to the learned societies of Mannheim, Milan, Rotterdam, Middelburg, and Richmond, Virginia, and to the Society of Antiquaries and the board of agriculture.

During the Brabant revolution of 1789–90 Mann remained in the Netherlands, ensuring that the academy survived the change of regime and, with greater difficulty, the first Austrian restoration of 1790. In 1791 he was again brought into projects for educational reform, and was appointed to the Commission for Studies, the board of education of the Austrian Netherlands, as one of two commissioners whose role was more than advisory.

At the French invasion of November 1792 Mann was evacuated by Lord Elgin. Given refuge in Downing Street he composed treatises to provide the ministry with general intelligence on the Austrian Netherlands. He returned to Brussels in April 1793, at the second restoration, and resumed his work for the academy and the Commission for Studies, but was forced to flee a final time in June 1794, at the second French invasion. Moving on in turn from Roermond, Paderborn, Bamberg, Regensburg, and Linz before the advancing revolutionary armies, he reached Prague late in 1797. He sought permission to return to England in the following year but was refused leave to depart from Austrian territory. Being at that time entirely dependent on an imperial pension he was obliged to remain in Prague, where he resumed his literary activities. He wrote a treatise on the agriculture of the Austrian

Netherlands and compiled a *Table chronologique de l'histoire universelle* for the years 1700–1803. His life's work, *Principes métaphysiques des êtres et des connoissances*, was printed at Vienna in 1807. He had sent the English manuscript to the British Museum in 1801, when he feared his death was imminent (BL, Add. MS 5794). He died at Prague on 23 February 1809.

Mann was known and respected in learned circles throughout Europe for his broad erudition, while in the Austrian Netherlands his reputation and influence were out of all proportion to his achievements. The main concerns of his own investigations were moral philosophy, metaphysics, and fluid dynamics. More importantly his writings increased knowledge of Newton's physics, Cook's voyages, and Cisalpine ecclesiology at every level of French-speaking society.   PAUL ARBLASTER

Sources F. A. F. de Reiffenberg, 'Éloge de l'abbé Mann', *Nouveaux mémoires de l'Académie Royale des Sciences et Belles-Lettres de Bruxelles*, 6 (1830), 1–38 · H. Colpaert, 'Th. A. Mann (1735–1809): een bio-, bibliografische studie', diss., Katholieke Universiteit, Leuven, 1981 · H. Colpaert, 'Th. A. Mann (1735–1809): een bio-, bibliografische studie', *Academiae Analecta: Mededelingen van de Koninklijke Academie voor Wetenschappen, Letteren en Schone Kunsten van België. Klasse der Letteren*, 46/3 (1984), 37–119 · P. Harsin, 'Un économiste aux Pays-Bas au XVIIIe siècle: l'abbé Mann', *Annales de la Société Scientifique de Bruxelles, Série D, Sciences économiques*, 53 (1933), 149–227 · H. Ellis, ed., *Original letters of eminent literary men of the sixteenth, seventeenth, and eighteenth centuries*, CS, 23 (1843) · *Lettres de l'abbé Mann sur les sciences et les lettres en Belgique, 1773–1788*, ed. and trans. O. Delepierre (Brussels, 1845) · A.-F. Renard, 'Mann (Théodore-Augustin)', *Biographie nationale*, 13 (Brussels, 1894–5), 343–55 · L. Dufour, 'Mann (Théodore-Augustin)', *Biographie nationale*, 31 (Brussels, 1961), 553–6 · *DNB* · R. Calcoen, 'Th. A. Mann en zijn studie over Nieuwpoort', *Academiae Analecta: Mededelingen van de Koninklijke Academie voor Wetenschappen, Letteren en Schone Kunsten van België*, 46/3 (1984), 123–31 · *Mémoires de l'Académie de Bruxelles*, vols. 1–5 (1777–88) · *Recueil des mémoires académiques de M. l'abbé Mann* (Brussels, 1788)

Archives Royal Academy, Brussels, map 'L'abbé Mann' | BL, letters to Sir Joseph Banks, Add. MSS 8094–8099 · National State Archives, Brussels, reports in various collections · NRA, priv. coll., letters to Lord Lansdowne

Likenesses R. Rogers, stipple (after C. H. Jones), BM

Mann, Thomas [Tom] (1856–1941), trade unionist, socialist, and communist, was born at Bell Green, Foleshill, Coventry, on 15 April 1856, the third surviving child and second son of Thomas Mann, a bookkeeper at the Victoria colliery, and his wife, Mary Anne, née Grant (1821–1858). His mother, a former domestic servant from Forres, Elgin, Scotland, died when he was two years old. His father married her sister, Harriet, in 1863, and they had a further five children.

Early life Mann began work at the age of nine on the Victoria colliery farm, and stayed for a year before going down the pit, where he kept ventilation shafts clear. After fire closed the mine in 1870, he moved with his parents to Birmingham. There he was an apprentice from 1870 to 1877 at the tool making firm of Thomas Chatwin, where his father was timekeeper. Mann developed a thirst for learning, despite having had less than three years' education at Foleshill, first at the Anglican Old Church day school and then at the Congregational Little Heath

Thomas Mann (1856–1941), by unknown photographer, *c*.1880

School. He continued attending an Anglican Sunday school in Birmingham, and at nineteen taught a Sunday school class. He also attended a Society of Friends' Bible class.

With much insight, Mann later wrote of himself that he had 'a temperament easily enthused when favourably impressed' (*Memoirs*, 38), and he was much influenced by strong personalities around him. His early enthusiasms included Shakespeare and violin playing as well as Christianity, vegetarianism, temperance, co-operation, adult education, and various types of socialism. While in Birmingham he heard such influential speakers as John Bright, Joseph Chamberlain, G. J. Holyoake, Joseph Arch, Charles Bradlaugh, and Annie Besant. But it was not until after his move to London in 1877 that he became an advocate of trade unionism and socialism rather than Christianity.

The move to London resulted in a period of unemployment and loneliness. Mann's first London work was as a clerk for the drapery firm Swan and Edgar of Piccadilly; thereafter he became a porter for a tailor in Hampstead Road and then a domestic engineer. On 2 October 1879 Mann married Ellen Edwards (*b*. 1854), from rural Suffolk, who worked in a draper's shop. Their marriage took place in a Swedenborgian church, reflecting Mann's interest in Swedenborgian beliefs, which had begun in Birmingham. They had four daughters, Rosalind, Emmeline, Gertrude, and Effie. This marriage broke up in 1898, quite probably because of the lower priority Mann gave to his family than to his trade union and socialist activities.

From mid-1880 Mann gained a series of jobs as a skilled engineer for a number of engineering and constructional firms in London, and eventually briefly left London for New York, where he worked for four months from May 1883 at Havermeyer and Elder's sugar refinery in Brooklyn. He joined the Marylebone branch of the Amalgamated Society of Engineers (ASE) in 1881.

Labour leader Once Mann became a socialist, he threw himself wholeheartedly into proselytizing for the Social Democratic Federation (SDF). He was quick to join the Battersea branch after it was formed in May 1885 by John Burns. His views were much influenced by such books as Henry George's *Progress and Poverty* (1879), John Ruskin's *Fors clavigera* (1871–84), and Thorold Rogers's *Six Centuries of Work and Wages* (1884). The historic wage data in Rogers's book in particular encouraged Mann to take his own distinctive line of advocating the eight-hour day, a cause he pressed at his branch of the ASE in Hammersmith in February 1885 and later in an influential pamphlet, *What a Compulsory Eight Hour Working Day Means to the Workers* (1886). When he received scant support from within the SDF, Mann organized the Eight Hour League. Mann's Eight Hours campaigns became linked to H. H. Champion's Labour Electoral Association. Under its auspices Mann spoke for Keir Hardie in the 1888 Mid Lanark by-election.

Mann's vigorous campaigning as a member of the SDF on behalf of the unemployed and for socialism resulted in London employers boycotting him. Following a four-month coal dispute in the Newcastle area, he went there in May 1887 as paid organizer for the SDF. After a year he moved on to be SDF organizer in Bolton, this time with a newspaper and tobacconist shop intended to provide part of his income. He did not stay long. This was due to a combination of dissension in the Bolton SDF over a co-operative workshop, his shop's financial weakness, and the fact that he had the opportunity to help H. H. Champion with his national Labour Electoral Association and also the Shop Hours Regulation Committee. Mann returned to London in early 1889 to work as an inspector for the latter body, enforcing the Shop Hours Act of 1888.

In August 1889 Mann became a leader of the great London dock strike. Earlier in the year, with John Burns and Ben *Tillett, he had helped Will Thorne to organize London's gasworkers. Tillett invited Mann and Burns to help the unskilled dockers achieve 6*d*. per hour. Mann was the dynamic organizer of the strike and his activities included being the strike committee's first treasurer. Mann, like Burns, was committed to building up the self-discipline and respect of the dockers, and he expressed himself vigorously on the need for 'the riff-raff' to 'clear off' (*Diary of Beatrice Webb*, 304).

Mann emerged from the London dock strike as one of the foremost figures in the British labour movement. He became president of the Dockers' Union (1889–92) and continued to help unionize such poorly organized workers as waiters. He represented 'new unionism' on the royal commission on labour (1891–4) and was the signatory of a minority report. When the International Federation of Ship, Dock, and River Workers was formed in 1896, Mann became chairman of its central council and travelled to organize on its behalf in Germany, France, and Spain in 1896–8. After the defeat of the Amalgamated Society of Engineers in the 1897 lock-out, Mann took on building a new general union, the Workers' Union, set up on May day 1898. Mann was its unpaid propagandist and vice-president (an honorific post which he held until the 1920s).

A lucid exponent of the new unionism argument that political power would follow effective trade union organization, Mann remained active politically, being secretary of the Independent Labour Party (ILP) from 1894 to 1897, and a keen supporter of the co-operative movement. He worked hard as parliamentary candidate for the Colne Valley from 1893 until the 1895 general election. When taking the candidacy on he had insisted that the proportion of textile workers of the area in trade unions must increase rapidly or he would feel free to withdraw (Clark, 39). Mann failed to win the seat and in 1896 he stood for Aberdeen North in a by-election, with the support of the trades council, ILP, and SDF. In what was then ILP's best by-election result, Mann narrowly lost. In 1897 he stood unsuccessfully for Halifax in another by-election, coming third.

Mann fell out with other leading ILP figures over the issue of fusion with the SDF and over his personal life. He tried unsuccessfully to change the ILP's name to 'Socialist Party' and, to the annoyance of those opposed to fusion, sent out ballot papers to ILP members with no covering circular (85 per cent of those voting supported merger). However, feelings were embittered over allegations that Mann was consorting with women of poor repute and drinking heavily. In fact Mann's marriage had broken down, and his wife would not agree to a divorce. From November 1898 until his death, he lived with Elsie Harker (b. 1868) as man and wife and brought up a family of four. Elsie was also an ILP activist, twelve years younger than Mann, and the eldest daughter of a Congregational minister.

Concern for his new partner and their growing family was probably the major reason for Mann's leaving Britain with them for New Zealand on 5 December 1901. In going to Australasia he was also satisfying his own curiosity, aroused by others, including H. H. Champion; he could also form links with branches of the ASE. After enquiring into labour conditions and supporting his family by lecturing, he went to Australia where—apart from a lecture tour in New Zealand in mid-1908—he remained until early 1910. There he worked from 1902 until January 1905 as organizer of the Political Labor Council of the Trades Hall, Melbourne, the forerunner of the Labor Party, even though he was increasingly openly critical of its failure to adopt a socialist programme. Thereafter he and Elsie put their energy into leading the Victorian Socialist Party, Tom becoming its secretary and editor of its paper, *Socialist*. He spent five weeks in Old Melbourne gaol in November–December 1906 as a result of his campaigning. Mann finally broke with this party when he stayed to organize miners at Broken Hill in a bitter lock-out. He remained involved with this and the associated dispute of smelters at Port Pirie until May 1909.

Industrial unionism The Broken Hill dispute confirmed Mann's developing belief in industrial unionism. There were elements in his intellectual background of scepticism about parliamentary action, going back to his admiration of Prince Peter Kropotkin and other anarchist speakers in London in the late 1880s and early 1890s. In Australia from late 1904 he was increasingly disillusioned with parliamentary means of achieving improvements for working people. The twenty-one-week Broken Hill and Port Pirie disputes convinced him that, even when there were favourable political and judicial conditions, workers would still be thwarted. What was needed was united industrial action. In *The Way to Win*, first published at Broken Hill in May 1909, he argued:

> Experience in all countries shows most conclusively that industrial organisation, intelligently conducted, is of much more moment than political action, *for entirely irrespective as to which school of politicians is in power, capable and courageous industrial activity forces from the politicians proportionate concessions.* (Mann, *Social and Economic Writings*, 145–6)

Mann and his family returned to London on 10 May 1910, after an interlude in South Africa between February and April when he helped to organize Rand diamond miners. Mann next visited Paris with Guy Bowman to investigate the 'syndicalist' policies of the Confédération Générale du Travail (CGT). He campaigned in Britain for syndicalism, publishing the *Industrial Syndicalist* monthly between July 1910 and May 1911 and founding the Industrial Syndicalist Education League (November 1910). He was instrumental in forming the National Transport Workers' Federation in September 1910, a small step in the direction of one big union for this sector. His rejection of parliamentary politics led to his resignation from the Social Democratic Party (successor to the SDF) in May 1911.

Mann was also involved in the pre-1914 wave of industrial unrest. In 1911, when he was an organizer for the Sailors' and Firemen's Union at Southampton, he contributed to the successful thwarting of the Shipping Federation's strike-breaking powers. He went on to be chairman of the strike committee during the Liverpool transport workers' strike. This dispute was marked by severe police brutality to peaceful demonstrators on 'bloody Sunday', 13 August 1911. The strike committee, in assuming wide authority and issuing permits, was a precursor of similar bodies in Belfast and Glasgow in 1919 and more widespread ones in the general strike of 1926. During the Liverpool transport strike the Liverpool chief constable sought Home Office advice as to whether Mann should be charged with sedition for his speeches. He was not charged then with sedition, but was so charged in March 1912, over a leaflet entitled *Don't Shoot* distributed to troops at Aldershot. Mann had neither written *Don't Shoot*, nor distributed the leaflet. He was charged because he was chairman of the committee (the Industrial Syndicalist Education League) which published *The Syndicalist* in which the manifesto had been reprinted before being turned into a leaflet and because he had said at public meetings he agreed with the views expressed in it. The decision to try him was taken at ministerial level. Mann received a six-month prison sentence of which he served seven weeks (in Strangeways, Manchester, as from 1911 to 1918 he lived in Manchester). After his release he was as active as ever, speaking in support of strikers in London and France on tours of Scandinavia (three weeks in August 1912) and the USA (twenty weeks from August 1913) as well as spending March to July 1914 campaigning again among the Rand miners in South Africa.

Leaving South Africa on 1 August 1914, Mann was at sea when war was declared. On his return he regretted 'that the workers of the world are at one another's throats' and reiterated that wars 'are never in the truest interests of the workers' (*Daily Herald*, 27 Aug 1914; Tsuzuki, 178). He came to combine these sentiments with the view that the Kaiser's Germany should be stopped from controlling other countries, and favoured British victory or a negotiated peace. Resuming work as an organizer for the National Sailors' and Firemen's Union, Mann increasingly became alienated from the ultra-patriotism of its leader, Havelock Wilson. He also worked for the National Transport Workers' Federation, being an honorary district secretary in Liverpool. By late 1915 Mann was campaigning for trade union amalgamation, especially in the engineering sector, and was a founder of *Trade Unionist*, a monthly paper dedicated to this cause. In February 1918 the amalgamation committees and the Shop Stewards' and Workers' Committee merged.

Along with other militant trade unionists Mann was encouraged by both 1917 revolutions in Russia. He spoke at the Leeds convention of June 1917 which called for support for the February revolution and for the formation of soviets in Britain. He also rejoined the British Socialist Party and campaigned at large meetings for a negotiated peace. With the end of war Mann considered retiring to Australia. But when the Foreign Office made it clear he would not be granted a passport he bought (with money subscribed by the trade union movement) a poultry farm at Hill View, Biddenden, Kent, where from late January 1919 he lived for six months.

In October 1919 Mann was elected secretary of the ASE for a third time (having narrowly lost in 1892 and come third in 1913), and served until his sixty-fifth birthday in April 1921. He continued to argue for syndicalism, which after the war had the Shop Stewards' and Workers' Committee at its heart, both on the platform and in the union journal. Mann was also prominent in the Hands Off Russia campaign (against British intervention to defeat Soviet Russia) and a signatory of the manifesto calling for a national 'down-tools' policy to enforce non-intervention. Very appropriately it was during his term of office, in July 1920, that the ASE joined with nine smaller unions to form the Amalgamated Engineering Union (AEU).

Communist After retiring from the AEU, in 1921 Mann became first chairman of the British section of the Red International of Labour Unions (RILU). He had joined the

Communist Party of Great Britain (CPGB) at its foundation. He believed in unity on the left and spoke up for the orthodox communist line, writing an article for *Labour Monthly* in October 1922 entitled *From Syndicalism to Communism*. Yet much that he said after 1922 still revealed a distinct syndicalist flavour. He remained a fiery orator. Harry Pollitt, later secretary of the CPGB, commented on how Mann could cover up 'a thin piece of political analysis' with his 'lifetime experience in public speaking and dramatic delivery' and 'an amazing demonstration on how to move on general principles' (White, 198).

Mann's main responsibility in Britain for the RILU was to head the National Minority Movement (NMM), the rank-and-file movement which greatly contributed to the CPGB's strong presence in many British trade unions over the next forty years. He chaired the foundation conference in August 1924 and was elected its president, remaining in post through the vicissitudes of changing CPGB policy until it dissolved in 1932. Mann was in part a symbolic head, epitomizing past heroic labour struggles; but he was also still a dynamic and effective campaigner. In March 1926 he chaired the NMM's special national conference of action, which successfully encouraged the setting up of local councils of action in many places before the general strike.

Mann campaigned for the CPGB in its various endeavours. He stood unsuccessfully for Nottingham East in the 1924 general election, polling 2605 votes. Campaigns to mobilize the unemployed received his support: he greeted south Wales unemployed marchers at Reading in 1929 and addressed a Trafalgar Square farewell rally of marchers from depressed areas in November 1936. In between the two events his support resulted in his being tried again. In December 1932, after the national march, Mann was sentenced to two months in gaol, spent in Brixton prison, for refusing to be bound over to keep the peace (being treasurer of a group calling for a day of action over unemployment). While in gaol he began planning the monthly newspaper *Militant Trade Unionist* which he edited briefly on his release. In July 1934 he and Harry Pollitt were tried for sedition for speeches at a Congress of Action in Bermondsey town hall, but were acquitted. He greeted the British battalion of the International Brigades at Victoria Station on its return from Spain in December 1938. Elected a member of the central committee of the CPGB at its 1937 congress, he chaired its annual conference in July 1938.

Mann kept up his overseas campaigning as well as a heavy schedule within Britain. He went at least eight times to Russia: his first visit was in 1921 to the founding conference of the RILU (before which he spoke with Lenin). He also went in November 1937 for the twentieth anniversary of the Bolshevik revolution, along with Ben Tillett and Tom Bell. A trip to South Africa from October 1922 to February 1923, in which he campaigned among mine workers on behalf of the RILU (appealing to black men as well as white to organize) was also significant. He made a major tour of China as part of an International Workers' delegation between February and June 1927,

addressing large rallies and denouncing British imperialism. In 1932 he was deported from Northern Ireland when he went to join mass protests against the means test. He undertook a further speaking tour in the USA and Canada in October–November 1933 and returned to Canada in April–May 1936. His other overseas speaking engagements took him to Denmark in spring 1935 and July 1938, Paris in early 1937, and Sweden in September 1938. His energetic campaigning was ended only in November 1939, by a blood clot on the brain. He survived until 13 March 1941, when he died at his home, Moorside, Grassington, Yorkshire. He was cremated on 17 March at Lawnswood crematorium, Leeds. He was survived by Elsie.

Significance According to Charles Duncan MP, writing in 1916, 'Tom is about five feet seven in height, and weighs about twelve stones. He is as dark as a Spaniard and as fiery, as lively as a Frenchman and as courteous … He has the energy of a steam engine' (Tsuzuki, 186). Duncan also dubbed him 'the Peter Pan of the Labour movement who resolutely refuses to grow old' (ibid.). In his near hyperactive energy, Tom Mann was the W. E. Gladstone of the left. He was relentless in his restlessness, always on the move. Ben Tillett observed, 'A whirlwind of enthusiasm has sped him along. He has been one of the world's stormy petrels' (Peacock, 4). He combined vitality with an unaffected nature, however famous he became. He was often judged to be one of the most lovable figures in the British labour movement.   CHRIS WRIGLEY

Sources J. Bennett, ed., *Tom Mann: a bibliography* (1993) • T. Mann, *Tom Mann's memoirs* (1923) • C. Tsuzuki, *Tom Mann, 1856–1941: the challenges of labour* (1991) • J. White, *Tom Mann* (1991) • D. Torr, *Tom Mann and his times* (1956) • T. Mann, *Social and economic writings*, ed. J. Laurent (1988) • D. Torr, *Tom Mann* (1936) • W. A. Peacock, ed., *Tom Mann: 80th birthday souvenir* (1936) • R. Hyman, *The Workers' Union* (1971) • R. Martin, *Communism and the British trade unions, 1924–1933* (1969) • B. Holton, *British syndicalism, 1900–1914* (1976) • H. W. Lee and E. Archbold, *Social-democracy in Britain: fifty years of the socialist movement*, ed. H. Tracey (1935) • *The diary of Beatrice Webb*, ed. N. MacKenzie and J. MacKenzie, 4 vols. (1982–5), vol. 1 • D. Clark, *Colne Valley: radicalism to socialism* (1981) • H. A. Clegg, A. Fox, and A. F. Thompson, *A history of British trade unions since 1889*, 1 (1964) • CGPLA *Eng. & Wales* (1941)

Archives Coventry Central Library, papers • JRL, Labour History Archive and Study Centre, corresp., prison letters, and notebook, papers • People's History Museum, Manchester, Tom Mann collection • U. Warwick Mod. RC, corresp. and papers | BL, corresp. with John Burns • BLPES, corresp. with the independent labour party and rough notes of national administrative council meetings • BLPES, Passfield MSS • HLRO, letters to Herbert Samuel • JRL, Labour History Archive and Study Centre, corresp. with R. Palme Dutt • U. Lpool, Glasier MSS • U. Warwick Mod. RC, International Transport Workers' Federation MSS (and guide) • U. Warwick Mod. RC, corresp. with Charles Lindley | FILM BFI NFTVA, actuality footage; documentary footage

Likenesses photograph, *c.*1880, Hult. Arch. [*see illus.*] • A. Brilliant, statue, U. Warwick Mod. RC

Wealth at death £233 4*s.* 2*d.*: probate, 2 Oct 1941, CGPLA *Eng. & Wales*

Mann, William (1817–1873), astronomer, was born on 25 October 1817 at Lewisham, Kent, the third son of Major-General Cornelius Mann RE. He was educated privately and in 1830 went with his family to Gibraltar, where his father had been appointed commander of the Royal Engineers. Regulations prevented him from following an elder brother into the engineers' college, as he had wished, and he obtained the post of second assistant at the Royal Observatory, Cape of Good Hope, under Thomas Maclear, where he arrived, after preliminary training, on 22 October 1839. Maclear intended to remeasure the meridian arc surveyed by the French astronomer Lacaille in 1751–3, as its accuracy was now in doubt; Mann took out some of the apparatus necessary for this task, which required a base-line to be measured with great precision, from where a series of distant points were to be triangulated along a north–south meridian, its ends astronomically surveyed for latitude. Mann was engaged on this task for six years, often working in remote areas without proper provisions or shelter.

In 1846 Mann was promoted to first assistant in place of Charles Piazzi Smyth, who was appointed astronomer at the Royal Observatory, Edinburgh. A few months later he fell from his horse, suffering head injuries which plagued him for the remainder of his life. After a few months' leave in England to recuperate, he returned to take up the duties of an astronomer. In October 1852 he again travelled to London, where he learned the mechanical details of a new transit circle being constructed by Troughton and Simms and supervised its packing for the journey to the Cape. He arrived back in December 1853. The cases containing the new circle reached the Cape early in 1854, and Mann directed its erection and adjustment. Mann's dedication and efficiency had by this time so impressed Maclear that in 1854 he was permitted to marry Caroline, the Maclears' second daughter.

In 1863 Mann declined the post of government astronomer at Sydney, perhaps hoping that the astronomer royal, George Biddell Airy, would support Maclear's wish that Mann should succeed him at the Cape. But Airy was unwilling to concede what he saw as nepotism, and when Maclear finally resigned, in 1870, Mann was considered too old, and perhaps too unwell, to embark on the long-desired major project, a catalogue of southern stars. He had sought relief from a chest infection in Natal in 1866 and in England in 1867. In 1870 an epidemic of scarlet fever struck the observatory families; two of Mann's children succumbed and Mann himself was grievously ill. He was belatedly elected to the Royal Astronomical Society in March 1871. He retired in 1872 and died at Claremont, near Cape Town, on 30 April 1873. A small civil-list pension, which had been granted shortly before his death, was paid to his widow for three years.

Mann was perhaps unfortunate in not having the opportunity for advancement. Maclear's opinion of him had been voiced during his absence in 1846:

His powerful intellect, unflinching integrity, and his industry enable me to trust him with confidence on all occasions and in every department, whether at the observatory or on the triangulation, being certain that whatever is practicable he will accomplish, and that what he does will be sure to be well done. (Warner, 62)

A. M. CLERKE, rev. ANITA MCCONNELL

Sources Monthly Notices of the Royal Astronomical Society, 34 (1873–4), 144–8 · B. Warner, Astronomers at the Royal Observatory, Cape of Good Hope (1979)

Manners. For this title name see Sutton, Thomas Manners-, first Baron Manners of Foston (1756–1842).

Manners, Arthur (1879–1968), brewer, was born on 8 December 1879 at Stapenhill, Burton upon Trent, one of the nine children of William Posnette Manners (1846–1915), brewer, and his wife, Clara Gothard. William Posnette Manners, son of a local draper, had joined the Burton brewers, Worthington & Co., as an office boy at the age of sixteen. He quickly rose to be the firm's cashier and office manager, was appointed a director on the company's incorporation in 1889, and, following the death of William Henry Worthington (1826–1894) five years later, became managing director and deputy chairman. He rapidly gained control of the company (by 1900 he held no less than 73 per cent of its equity) and under his astute leadership Worthingtons acquired a reputation for the quality of its bottled pale ales. By the outbreak of war, the company had regained much of its earlier standing, steadily eroding the market share of its arch rival Bass, Ratcliff, and Gretton. On Manners's death in 1915, control of the company passed to two of his sons, Arthur (who joined the brewery in 1903) and Ernest. Arthur married and had three sons and two daughters.

Arthur inherited all his father's entrepreneurial drive and ambition. Autocratic in style, he consistently refused to sanction trade unions within the firm. As the architect of the merger in 1927 of Worthingtons with Bass—undertaken to resolve problems of over-capacity—he was to prove more than a match for Colonel Sir John (later Lord) Gretton, the chairman and major shareholder of the larger company. Despite Bass's superior capitalization, the terms of the merger (devised by Worthingtons' London advisers) were such that Manners became chairman and joint managing director of Worthingtons, and deputy chairman and joint managing director of Bass; he had obtained a dominant position in both companies and enhanced his own financial status.

The amalgamation, described as 'the biggest non-merger in the history of the brewing industry' (Hawkins, 90), failed to realize its objectives. Apart from greater co-operation in bottled beer production and distribution, there were few economies and the two companies continued to operate as separate entities. Both boards were increasingly dominated by Manners and his family. He received the support of his brother Ernest until the latter's death in 1944 and during the 1930s and 1940s Arthur's three sons, Arthur Geoffrey, William, and Philip, were all appointed directors. After a minor dispute in 1945 which prompted the resignation of Lord Gretton, Manners replaced him as chairman and managing director of Bass.

By the late 1940s the Manners family provided no fewer than four of the company's six directors. However, despite the duplication at board level, the deep-seated rivalry between the firms persisted and there was little attempt to create a coherent entity. James Eadie & Co., acquired in 1933, also maintained considerable autonomy. In the difficult post-war climate, this lack of rationalization was reflected in falling sales. Concern among institutional investors led to the appointment as a director in April 1953 of Sir James Grigg, a distinguished former civil servant and politician. Three months later, Manners retired.

Manners was never deeply involved in public life. He died at his home, Longford Hall, Longford, Derbyshire, on 13 January 1968, leaving an estate worth over £2 million.

CHRISTINE CLARK

Sources C. C. Owen, 'The greatest brewery in the world': a history of Bass, Ratcliff & Gretton, Derbyshire RS, 29 (1992) · Burton Observer and Chronicle (18 Jan 1968) · K. H. Hawkins, A history of Bass Charrington (1978) · Burton Daily Mail (22 Feb 1915) · will of Arthur Manners, Principal Registry of the Family Division, London · b. cert. · d. cert. · CGPLA Eng. & Wales (1968)

Wealth at death £2,248,151: probate, 7 May 1968, CGPLA Eng. & Wales

Manners, Charles, fourth duke of Rutland (1754–1787), politician, was born on 15 March 1754, the second but first surviving son of John *Manners, marquess of Granby (1721–1770), an army officer, and his wife, Lady Frances Seymour (1728–1761), the daughter of Charles *Seymour, sixth duke of Somerset. He was styled Lord Roos from 1760, and marquess of Granby after his father's death, during the lifetime of his grandfather John, the third duke.

Like his father, Manners was educated at Eton College (1762–71) and Trinity College, Cambridge, where he was credited with pamphlets on the mortality of the soul and in defence of modern adultery. He obtained a nobleman's MA in 1774. That year, hastening back from France, and not yet of age, he was returned to parliament unopposed as member for his university. His family had electoral interests in Cambridge, town and county, as well as in Leicestershire, Nottingham, and Scarborough. While maintaining these, Manners began collecting books, furniture, porcelain, and pictures by old masters, including Rubens, Van Dyck, and Dou, as well as Poussin's Sacraments, to embellish Belvoir Castle. In this Sir Joshua Reynolds, from whom he commissioned family portraits, was also one of his agents; others were stationed in Rome and Brussels. Credited with honouring a pledge to redeem his father's substantial debts, he was snagged by his habitual gambling. His extravagance was not tempered by his marriage on 26 December 1775 to a celebrated beauty, Lady Mary Isabella Somerset (1756–1831) [see Manners, Mary Isabella], the daughter of Charles Noel *Somerset, fourth duke of Beaufort [see under Somerset, Henry, second duke of Beaufort], which had been arranged by her mother, Elizabeth Berkeley; it produced four sons and two daughters. Having previously seduced the daughter of one Smith, an Eton shopkeeper, he later indulged, according to Sir Nathaniel Wraxall, in an expensive fling with the singer Mrs Elizabeth *Billington, née Weichsel (1765–1818).

Before he entered parliament, Granby had already committed himself to the opposition to Lord North's ministry, adhering at first to the Rockingham whigs. On 5 April 1775, having acted only as an observer until he came of age, he spoke and voted against legislative restrictions on the trade of the southern American colonies. This maiden speech sparkled with defiance, particularly when Richard Rigby provoked him into arguing that rebellion was acceptable when justice was at stake; his speech praised Lord Chatham, who wrote to thank him. It also earned the admiration of Chatham's son William Pitt, whom he befriended, and who visited him at his then abode at Cheveley, near Newmarket. Horace Walpole maintained that Granby's parliamentary début was 'a great disappointment' to the court. Lord Mansfield, whose wife was sister to the duchess of Somerset, Lord Granby's grandmother, had flattered himself he should govern Lord Granby, and 'had even answered for him to the Court' (Last Journals, 1.455). Granby could not overcome his diffidence when invited by Lord Rockingham to move the amendment to the address in November 1775. His refusal was probably reinforced by a wish not to commit himself exclusively to Rockingham.

Granby nevertheless seconded the amendment on 18 November 1776 and moved it on 18 November 1777 in a speech that echoed Chatham's in the Lords and urged reconciliation with America. His motion was lost by 243 votes to 86. He was subsequently regarded by North and others as a suitable intermediary for ministerial overtures to the concerted opposition, but George III discouraged any such negotiation. Granby and his squad again displayed opposition on the question of Admiral Keppel's conduct on 3 March 1779, but did not follow this through; his brother Lord Robert *Manners (1758–1782), a naval officer, was later killed in action. No further speeches at Westminster are recorded, even after Granby succeeded to the dukedom on 29 May 1779. Having offered to raise a regiment for home defence against the French, he had become colonel of the Leicestershire militia, and on 9 July 1779 he was made lord lieutenant of Leicestershire at North's suggestion. The king thought it best to bestow this on him in person. Failing to procure William Pitt's succession to his university constituency, Rutland at once obtained another seat for him pro tem, promising to return him for one of his own boroughs in future, with complete freedom of action. Meanwhile he attended the Yorkshire reform meeting of 30 December 1779 and supported reform at a Cambridge election meeting in 1780, when he returned six members to parliament. Later that year he guaranteed financial security for Pitt.

The replacement of North's ministry, first by Rockingham's, then by Shelburne's ministry, brightened Rutland's political prospects. He was made a knight of the Garter on 30 October 1782 and was rumoured to be the intended viceroy of Ireland. Instead he became lord steward of the household and was sworn of the privy council on 17 February 1783, Shelburne thereby gratifying his wish for a cabinet seat. This appointment aroused the king's displeasure and was an unprecedented concession to a lord steward. It precipitated the duke of Grafton's resignation from the ministry, which soon collapsed. Rutland's real attachment was by now to Pitt, with whose young friends he consorted. After resigning in April 1783 with Shelburne, whose elevation to a marquessate he was to promote a year later, he opposed the Fox–North coalition ministry. When Pitt became premier in December 1783 he at once appointed Rutland, upon Grafton's refusal, lord privy seal, in the cabinet, which at first met at his town house. Then on 11 February 1784 Pitt made him viceroy of Ireland, an appointment worth a basic £20,000, which had been declined by Lord Cornwallis.

Rutland's acceptance of this post, while still under thirty, was perhaps a *faux pas*, but his admiration for Pitt's superior abilities, no less than Pitt's confidence in him, swamped any scruples. After making his will on 15 February, he took office in Dublin on the 24th. His correspondence with the premier reveals his initial enthusiasm for Pitt's Irish policy, which, he saw, logically entailed Anglo-Irish union within twenty years, but also his growing doubts about its implementation. Soon after his arrival his staff became embroiled in an affray with dissidents in Dublin, which he successfully suppressed, though he was threatened with tarring and feathering, as a contemporary caricature illustrates. He foresaw problems from Irish Foxite whigs with English connections, one of whom, Leinster, the only Irish duke, tended towards opposition, while another, Lord Bristol, bishop of Derry, advocated Catholic enfranchisement. Pitt's reformist views, Rutland feared, would panic the Irish establishment, and the Irish administration would exercise its borough patronage network to retain control of a Dublin parliament which had enjoyed a degree of independence since 1782. When Pitt proposed giving precedence to reform at Westminster, where Rutland had secured two additional nominees in 1784, Rutland was relieved, perhaps more so when reform was checked there in 1785.

As Rutland was recovering from a dangerous fever late in 1784, Pitt was advancing ambitious plans for a commercial entente with Ireland, involving significant concessions to Irish trade in exchange for a guaranteed contribution to the defence of the realm. The leaders of the Irish parliamentary opposition, Henry Grattan and Henry Flood, could not be reconciled to this guarantee unless it was conditional on the amount of the annual Irish revenue surplus from the crown's hereditary Irish funds; with this proviso conceded, the Irish parliament assented in February 1785. In England, however, the commercial opposition to concessions to Irish trade was taken up by the Foxite opposition in parliament, and the proposals were so much amended that Grattan secured their rejection in the Dublin parliament in August. Later Pitt's intentions were better appreciated in Ireland, and Rutland did not face such trying opposition again, or unrest, except for the desultory disturbances of the Whiteboys in Munster, which he countered with a tour of southern Ireland late in 1785. It had, however, demoralized his chief secretary, Thomas Orde, who had to be cajoled into staying put, and whose subsequent ill health was to dash hopes of legislation improving educational provision in Ireland.

Rutland's increasing popularity as viceroy was bought at a price, and not only in terms of the Irish and English patronage requirements which henceforward dominated his correspondence with Pitt, for evidence of his lavish conviviality abounds. Sir Jonah Barrington recalled 'The utmost magnificence signalled the entertainments of the viceregal court, and the duke and duchess were reckoned the handsomest couple in Ireland' (Barrington, *Historic Memoirs of Ireland*, 2 vols., 1833, 2.225). He was to be credited with a record for dining out unequalled by his viceregal successors. His last recorded scruple, of which he informed Pitt regretfully on 10 April 1787, was his inability, because of a pledge made in 1782, to rally his parliamentary henchmen to the ministry's problematic bid to settle the prince of Wales's debts. In the summer of 1787 he embarked on a strenuous tour of the midlands and north of Ireland. He left a brief journal of this, though he was allegedly seldom sober during it: his claret consumption was well established, and he was reported to have consumed six or seven turkey eggs at breakfast every day. These excesses were generally regarded as having hastened his death, of incurable liver disease, after a violent fever, at Phoenix Park Lodge, Dublin, on 24 October 1787. He was embalmed, and buried at Bottesford, Leicestershire, on 25 November. George Crabbe, his domestic chaplain at Belvoir since 1782, and his praise singer in verse, pronounced a funeral oration (also published), and his former Cambridge tutor Bishop Richard Watson eulogized him in the Lords on 27 November 1787. Pitt, to whom he left £3000, was one of his trustees and the guardian of his children. Some of his acquisitions were lost in a fire at Belvoir in 1815.

ROLAND THORNE

Sources GEC, *Peerage* · GM, 1st ser., 57 (1787), 938, 1021–2, 1123 · *The manuscripts of his grace the duke of Rutland*, 4 vols., HMC, 24 (1888–1905), vol. 3; vol. 4, pp. 237–45 · *Correspondence between the Right Honourable William Pitt and Charles, duke of Rutland, … 1781–1787*, ed. Lord Mahon (1890) · L. B. Namier, 'Manners, Charles, mq of Granby', HoP, *Commons, 1754–90* · J. Ehrman, *The younger Pitt*, 1 (1969), 17, 20, 25, 57, 198, 200 · *The correspondence of King George the Third, from 1760 to December 1783*, ed. J. Fortescue, 4 (1928), 71–2, 255, 374, 376–9, 479; 6 (1928), 78, 232, 237–8, 247, 348 · *The later correspondence of George III*, ed. A. Aspinall, 5 vols. (1962–70), vol. 1 · J. Stockdale, ed., *The debates and proceedings of the House of Commons: during the sixteenth parliament of Great Britain*, 19 vols. (1785–90), vol. 1, pp. 423–5; vol. 2, p. 2 · Cobbett, *Parl. hist.*, 18.601–3; 19.414 · *Correspondence of William Pitt, earl of Chatham*, ed. W. S. Taylor and J. H. Pringle, 4 vols. (1838–40), vol. 4, pp. 406, 507 · *The manuscripts of the earl of Carlisle*, HMC, 42 (1897), 544, 552, 558–9, 565, 567, 575, 581, 606, 611, 630, 642–3 · *The last journals of Horace Walpole*, ed. Dr Doran, rev. A. F. Steuart, 1 (1910), 455 · *The journal and correspondence of William, Lord Auckland*, ed. [G. Hogge], 4 vols. (1861–2), vol. 1, p. 2 · *The historical and the posthumous memoirs of Sir Nathaniel William Wraxall, 1772–1784*, ed. H. B. Wheatley, 5 vols. (1884), vol. 3, p. 55; vol. 5, pp. 32–3 · [J. Almon], *Biographical, literary and political anecdotes*, 3 vols. (1797), vol. 1, pp. 43–5 · Walpole, *Corr.*, vols. 1–2, 25, 27, 33 · Venn, *Alum. Cant.*

Archives NRA, priv. coll., papers | BL, letters to second Lord Hardwicke, Add. MSS 35612, 35658, 35682 · BL, corresp. with J. Wilkes, Add. MS 30872, fol. 92 · N. Yorks. CRO, Bolton MSS · NL Ire., corresp. with Thomas Orde · NRA, priv. coll., letters to Lord

Lansdowne · PRO, letters to William Pitt, PRO 30/8 · PRO, Chatham MSS, letters to Lord Sydney, HO 100/14
Likenesses by or after T. Gainsborough, oils, 1773, Belvoir Castle, Leicestershire; version, Eton College · J. Reynolds, oils, 1776, priv. coll. · J. Reynolds, portrait, c.1782 · W. Dickinson, mezzotint, pubd 1791 (after J. Reynolds), BM · H. Hone, miniature, 1805, NG Ire. · R. Cosway, miniature, Belvoir Castle, Leicestershire · R. Cosway, portrait, NPG · W. Dickinson, engraving (after J. Reynolds, c.1782) · W. Lane, stipple (after R. Cosway), NPG · M. W. Peters, oils, Belvoir Castle, Leicestershire · attrib. J. Reynolds, Belvoir Castle, Leicestershire · J. Scott, engraving (after J. Reynolds, c.1782) · caricatures, repro. in M. D. George and F. D. Stephens, eds., *Catalogue of political and personal satires*, 11 vols. (1870–1954), vol. 5, pp. 5309, 5358; vol. 6, p. 6647 [BM, department of prints and drawings]
Wealth at death see will, PRO, PROB 12/161

Manners, Charles Cecil John, sixth duke of Rutland

(1815–1888), politician, born in Lower Grosvenor Street, London, on 16 May 1815, was the third but eldest surviving son of John Henry, fifth duke of Rutland (1778–1857), and his wife, Lady Elizabeth Howard (1780–1825), daughter of the fifth earl of Carlisle. He was styled marquess of Granby from birth until his father's death in 1857. He was educated at Eton College (1829–32) and as a nobleman at Trinity College, Cambridge, matriculating in 1832 and being made MA in 1835. He was elected as a tory as one of the members for Stamford in 1837 (he and his fellow tory candidate received 200 and 201 votes respectively, their Liberal opponent 1) and held the seat unopposed until his last election, in 1847, when he still won comfortably though there was a Liberal revival. In 1852 he moved to North Leicestershire, where he was unopposed.

Granby was a pronounced and voluble protectionist. He lacked the interest and ability of his brother, Lord John *Manners (later seventh duke of Rutland, d. 1906), but moved on the fringe of the Young England group of which his brother was a leader. His present wealth and future dukedom meant that his tory colleagues had to bear with him; 'it is idle to pretend', wrote Robert Blake, that he 'was other than a stick' (Blake, 262). He was a lord of the bedchamber to Prince Albert in 1843–6, his only political office. His opportunity for power came in 1848, when Lord George Bentinck resigned as leader of the protectionists. Granby was elected on 10 February, but gave up on 4 March, 'conscious of his own inadequacy' (Blake, 262), and no successor could be found; for a time the tory party had no leader in the Commons. Granby then formed part of a trio of leadership with Disraeli (then unpopular with his colleagues) and J. C. Herries, an arrangement concocted by Stanley to allow Disraeli, when Granby inherited the dukedom, to become leader. Disraeli had considerable contempt for Granby and the arrangement was always at best uneasy. Granby resigned from the trio early in 1852. Despite the low opinion held of him by many of his colleagues, and his tendency to break down in debate, Granby was included in the various plans for office. However, when Lord Derby (as Stanley had become) formed a minority tory government in February 1852, Granby declined to join it, but became lord lieutenant of Lincolnshire, Charles Greville remarking that the appointment 'will probably have the effect of stopping his

mouth, if it does not remove his discontent' (GEC, *Peerage*, 11.272).

Granby's significance in the leadership of his party rapidly declined from this point. He replaced Lincolnshire with Leicestershire as his lord lieutenancy in 1857, the year in which he succeeded his father as duke of Rutland, and was made KG in 1867. His father had forbidden him to marry Lady Forester, for whom he 'nourished a hopeless passion' (Vincent, 348). He was known as 'a splendid rider to hounds' (*DNB*) and never lost the conviction that protection, and especially agricultural protection, was the answer to all ills. Disabled by gout in his later years, he died, unmarried, at his seat, Belvoir Castle, on 4 March 1888, and was buried in the mausoleum there.

H. C. G. MATTHEW

Sources DNB · *The Times* (5 March 1888) · *The Field* (10 March 1888) · R. Blake, *Disraeli*, another edn (1968) · GEC, *Peerage* · T. L. Crosby, *English farmers and the politics of protection, 1815–1852* (1977) · W. F. Monypenny and G. E. Buckle, *The life of Benjamin Disraeli*, 2–6 (1912–20) · C. Whibley, *Lord John Manners and his friends*, 2 vols. (1925) · *Disraeli, Derby and the conservative party: journals and memoirs of Edward Henry, Lord Stanley, 1849–1869*, ed. J. R. Vincent (1978) · *Benjamin Disraeli letters*, ed. J. A. W. Gunn and others (1982–), vol. 3 · *CGPLA Eng. & Wales* (1888)
Archives Belvoir Castle, Leicestershire · Duke U., Perkins L., letters · NRA, priv. coll., corresp. | Lpool RO, letters to fourteenth earl of Derby · NRA, priv. coll., family corresp., especially with Lady Eliza Drummond, his sister
Likenesses F. Grant, oils, 1846, Belvoir Castle, Leicestershire · C. Silvy, carte-de-visite, 1861, NPG · F. Grant, oils, 1876, Belvoir Castle, Leicestershire · J. Brown, stipple (after photograph by Mayall), NPG; repro. in *Baily's Magazine of Sports and Pastimes*, 6 (1863), 271 · G. R. Ward, mezzotint, BM · chromolithograph caricature, NPG; repro. in VF (16 Sept 1871), pl. 93 · wood-engraving (after photograph by Broadhead), NPG; repro. in ILN, 92 (24 March 1888), 307
Wealth at death £109,951 19s. 5d.: probate, 1 Oct 1888, CGPLA Eng. & Wales

Manners, Edward, third earl of Rutland

(1549–1587), magnate, was born on 12 July 1549, the eldest son of Henry *Manners, second earl of Rutland (1526–1563), and Margaret Neville (d. 1559). His education befitted a nobleman. His father's death from the plague in 1563 made him the queen's ward, and his education was continued by William Cecil, to whom he said he was greatly beholden. In his teenage years he accompanied Queen Elizabeth on her visit to Cambridge in 1564 where he was lodged in St John's College and made an MA. At Oxford in October 1566 he received an honorary degree.

As a nobleman with extensive northern estates, Rutland was sent with his tenants to assist Sussex against the 1569 northern insurgents, and served as lieutenant-general of footmen. He was called 'into council whenever they treat of any matter' and praised for his courage and forwardness. On his return Sadler said to Cecil: 'God has given him good parts and you have instructed him in honesty, it were a pity they should sleep in him for lack of employment' (*CSP dom., addenda, 1566–79*, 163). He travelled in France between January and October 1571, sending Burghley his impressions. On his return he decided to marry Isabel Holcroft (1552–1605). Her mother wrote in January 1572 'she says that you will marry her whether I give anything or no'

(*Rutland MSS*, 1.96). A later rumour spoke of £4000 and 200 marks a year passing with a 'maid of the court'. The marriage took place in mid-1573.

Rutland held no major office in a life shortened by illnesses which included gout. He was a member of the council of the north by 1574 but 'not bound to continued attendance unless required by the president' (*CSP dom.*, addenda, 1566–79, 463). On 17 June 1577 he was appointed to the ecclesiastical commission for the north. The queen apparently thought highly of him, but he rarely went to court unless summoned, despite her expressed hopes of his service—and the possibility that she had designated him as Sir Thomas Bromley's successor as lord chancellor in 1587. Made a knight of the Garter on 23 April 1584, he soon returned home despite letters telling him Elizabeth expected him at court. In 1585 his excuses were rejected and he had to attend the parliament.

Rutland preferred life as a great magnate in his own country, occupied with the local defence of the realm, dividing his time between Belvoir and Newark, and serving as lord lieutenant (of Nottinghamshire by 1574 and of Lincolnshire by 1581) and commissioner for subsidies and musters. In 1571 he was feodary of the duchy of Lancaster for Nottingham and Derby, and he held the traditional family offices of constable of Nottingham Castle and warden of Sherwood Forest. Holles described him as 'That magnificent earl who kept an house like a Prince's Court' (Holles, 215). He kept great state and open hospitality at Belvoir, although his father's remarriage had severely diminished his resources; his stepmother, who lived until 1601, held much of the Rutland inheritance. He had to sell some manors, and was only starting to buy lands again just before his death. Much of his time was absorbed by estate management which included his interest in lead mining and cloth working. Despite his standing, he became embroiled in local feuds with Thomas Markham, John Foster, and the Talbots. He used his patronage for his many clients and 'his' towns and maintained local harmony as far as possible, occasionally arbitrating suits involving other nobles. His uncle, Roger Manners, served as his main link to the court and his brother John managed the northern estates, rebuilding Helmsley Castle and breeding great horses.

Rutland was acutely sensitive to his honour. Contemporaries spoke of him as wise, learned, godly, and honourable. He was also a scholar, interested in legal matters rather than physical sports and pastimes, although in 1580 he acquitted himself well at the Westminster tilts. He was selected in 1586 as the 'man of honor' for the treaty with the Scots at Berwick. He was reluctant to go, and even more reluctant to stay when the Scots started raising difficulties, thinking his honour adversely affected. He stayed until 6 July when the treaty of Berwick was signed and then unwillingly went to court. The Babington plot had just broken, and on 21 September 1586 he was instructed to be at Westminster on the 27th and then to go to Fotheringhay to hear the queen of Scots's case.

By early April 1587 Rutland was ill at Greenwich, and he died on the 14th of that month. James VI was said to be sorely grieved at his death. His funeral, at Bottesford, Leicestershire, on 15 May, was costly, and his death aggravated the family's financial problems. His only daughter, Elizabeth, inherited the barony of Ros, married Sir William Cecil, and died in 1591. Her son William, born in May or June 1590, was confirmed in the barony of Ros in 1616 and died in 1618. Rutland's brother John became fourth earl. The property division was complicated by the legacies which Edward had made to his wife. His executors were John himself, Roger, and Thomas Manners and Sir George Chaworth; but on John's own death on 24 February 1588 the others withdrew as executors, leaving Elizabeth, John's widow, the problems of both wills. In 1590 Garret Johnson was paid £200 for two tombs including four great pictures erected at Bottesford, Leicestershire, for Edward and John.   SYBIL M. JACK

Sources *The manuscripts of his grace the duke of Rutland*, 4 vols., HMC, 24 (1888–1905), vols. 1–2, 4 · *Calendar of the manuscripts of the most hon. the marquis of Salisbury*, 24 vols., HMC, 9 (1883–1976) · *CSP dom.*, 1547–1603 · GEC, *Peerage* · E. Lodge, *Illustrations of British history, biography, and manners*, 3 vols. (1791) · Cooper, *Ath. Cantab.*, 1.13, 542 · R. R. Reid, *The king's council in the north* (1921) · G. Holles, *Memorials of the Holles family, 1493–1656*, ed. A. C. Wood, CS, 3rd ser., 55 (1937) · BL, Titus MS F iii 138 · C. Wriothesley, *A chronicle of England during the reigns of the Tudors from AD 1485 to 1559*, ed. W. D. Hamilton, 2 vols., CS, new ser., 11, 20 (1875–7) · *Guilielmi Camdeni Annales rerum Anglicarum et Hibernicarum regnante Elizabetha*, ed. T. Hearnius [T. Hearne], 3 (1717) · D. Lloyd, *State worthies*, ed. C. Whitworth, 2 vols. (1766) · PRO, C142/303/137, 146; C142/304/19 · L. Stone, *Family and fortune: studies in aristocratic finance in the sixteenth and seventeenth centuries* (1973)
Archives NRA, priv. coll., corresp.
Likenesses G. Johnson, double portrait, alabaster tomb effigy, 1591 (with wife), St Mary's Church, Bottesford, Leicestershire · oils, Belvoir Castle, Leicestershire
Wealth at death land, when unencumbered with dowagers, at least £2000 p.a.

Manners, Francis, sixth earl of Rutland (1578–1632), nobleman, was the second son of John Manners, fourth earl of Rutland (*d.* 1588), and Elizabeth (*d.* 1595), daughter of Francis Charlton of Apley Castle, Shropshire; his elder brother was Roger *Manners, fifth earl of Rutland (1576–1612). He was admitted to Christ's College, Cambridge, in 1595 and later travelled in France, Italy, and the empire before returning in 1600. With his elder brother he took part in the earl of Essex's plot in early 1601 and was imprisoned and fined 1000 marks. Following his release and the cancellation of his fine, he admitted to his uncle, John Manners of Haddon, that he was foolish, 'neither knowing that I went aboute nor the danger when I was in it' (*Rutland MSS*, 1.374). He was admitted to the Inner Temple in November 1601. On 6 May 1602 he married Frances (*d.* 1605), daughter of Henry Knyvet of Charlton, Wiltshire, and widow of Sir William Bevill. She gave birth to their only child, Katherine (1605–1649), in 1605 but later that year, probably in September, died of smallpox; their daughter later became Katherine *MacDonnell. On 6 January 1605 Manners was created a knight of the Bath, in the same ceremony as Prince Charles. On 26 October 1608 he married Cecily (*d.* 1653), daughter of John Tufton of Hothfield, Kent; as she was the wealthy widow of Sir

Edward Hungerford, her nuptial agreement was negotiated by the lord chamberlain and approved by Manners's brother, the fifth earl. Subsequently, possibly under the influence of Cecily, a recusant, Francis Manners, his daughter, Katherine, and his sister, Frances (who married Lord Willoughby of Parham), were all to become Catholics.

When Manners succeeded his brother as sixth earl of Rutland on 26 June 1612 he was already active in masques and tilts at court but he now turned to the improvement of his large inheritance. His lands were in Lincolnshire, where he was lord lieutenant until 23 January 1629, in Nottinghamshire, where he was constable of Nottingham Castle and warden of Sherwood Forest until April 1620, and in Leicestershire, where his favourite seat, Belvoir Castle, was visited by James I on six occasions. There were profitable ironworks on his estate at Rievaulx and other properties produced a surplus that enabled him to buy or lease new lands. He avoided costly new buildings on his estates but improved the facade of Belvoir Castle. When he lost a claim to the barony of Ros in a law suit, he was granted a hereditary title as Lord Ros of Hamlake in July 1616 and was installed as a knight of the Garter on 7 July.

After his appointment as privy councillor on 6 April 1617, Rutland attended the king on his journey to Scotland. His career at court became linked to that of the royal favourite, Buckingham, after his marriage to Rutland's daughter, Katherine; there were initial obstacles, in her Catholicism and in the exorbitant financial settlement that the groom demanded, but when Katherine agreed 'for his sake and his mothers to be converted and to receive the communion this Easter' (*Letters of John Chamberlain*, 2.301), and a less onerous financial arrangement was accepted, they were married on 16 May 1620. At the opening of parliament on 30 January 1621 Rutland bore the cap of maintenance and at his son-in-law's request he was later, in April 1623, appointed admiral of the fleet to carry Prince Charles and the infanta to England. However this 'Spanish match' had failed, much to Rutland's dismay, prior to the fleet's departure in September, so that he brought back an embittered entourage. When the House of Lords was in session in March 1624 he cast the only dissenting vote when the declaration of the Commons annulling the treaties with Spain was put to the question. Later, on 20 May, in the petition of the Commons to the king denouncing the Catholics 'charged with places of trust' in the shires, Rutland and his wife were first on the list as 'suspected popish recusants', for he was lord lieutenant of Lincolnshire, commissioner of peace, and *custos rotulorum* in Northamptonshire (*JHL*, 3, 1767, 394–5).

At Charles's coronation Rutland bore the rod with the dove but he was absent from the parliament of 1625, sending his proxy to Buckingham. At the parliament of 1626 he took the oath of allegiance for the first time and held the proxies of three absent Catholic peers. Again the Commons sent a petition to the king, in which Rutland headed their list as commissioner of peace and of oyer and terminer in Yorkshire—a 'popish recusant' who 'affronted'

the commissioners of the North Riding by licensing convicted recusants as an alehouse keeper and as schoolmaster in his manor of Helmsley (Rushworth, 1.392). At this session the Commons also questioned Buckingham: 'Whether recusants be not borne and increased by reason of the duke's mother and father-in-law being known papists' (*Diary of Walter Yonge*, 91). Early in 1627 Rutland toured Lincolnshire widely, collecting the unpopular forced loan by threats and promises to reach a required amount. At the parliament of 1628 he carried the sword of state and then took the oath of allegiance and received the proxies of two absent Catholic peers. In taking the oath twice he was apparently in the role of a 'church papist', for he was still judged to be a leading recusant in Yorkshire. Sir Thomas Hoby tried to have him convicted in 1631 at the Helmsley quarter sessions, but failed 'since he did not stay over four successive Sundays at Helmsley Castle' by which he could be legally indicted as a resident (Aveling, 284); later the dowager countess was pardoned for recusancy by Charles I. Rutland died on 17 December 1632 at an inn in Bishop's Stortford, Hertfordshire, after giving final advice to his wife and brother John, who was to inherit his title. His personal goods when inventoried were worth £20,206 and his personal debts were paid off by one year's revenue from his estates, with his funeral at 'the phenomenal sum of over £3500' (Stone, 200); he was buried at Bottesford church, Leicestershire, on 20 February 1633. As sixth earl of Rutland he was an astute manager of extensive properties for two decades but his career at Charles's court was not as successful for personal reasons. He was very close to the Spanish ambassador Gondomar, as seen in his opposition to the war that Charles was anxious to begin in 1624, and he was widely considered to be a recusant although he adroitly escaped the penalties. A. J. LOOMIE

Sources L. Stone, *Family and fortune: studies in aristocratic finance in the sixteenth and seventeenth centuries* (1973) · R. Lockyer, *Buckingham: the life and political career of George Villiers, first duke of Buckingham, 1592–1628* (1981) · *The manuscripts of his grace the duke of Rutland*, 4 vols., HMC, 24 (1888–1905), vols. 1–2 · GEC, *Peerage* · *JHL*, 3 (1620–28) · J. Rushworth, *Historical collections*, 5 pts in 8 vols. (1659–1701), vol. 1 · *The letters of John Chamberlain*, ed. N. E. McClure, 2 vols. (1939) · *Diary of Walter Yonge*, ed. G. Roberts, CS, 41 (1848) · R. E. Ruigh, *The parliament of 1624: politics and foreign policy* (1971) · R. P. Cust, *The forced loan and English politics, 1626–1628* (1987) · H. Aveling, *Northern Catholics: the Catholic recusants of the North Riding of Yorkshire, 1558–1790* (1966) · CSP dom., 1639–40
Archives BL, Harley MSS · HMC, Rutland MSS · PRO, state papers, domestic
Likenesses group portrait, alabaster tomb effigy, c.1632 (with two wives), St Mary's Church, Bottesford, Leicestershire · line engraving, pubd 1795, BM, NPG · oils, Belvoir Castle, Leicestershire
Wealth at death £20,200: inventory, *Manuscripts … Rutland*, vol. 2, pp. 348–9 · lands and income: Stone, *Family and fortune*, pp. 194–200

Manners, George (1778–1853), journal editor and diplomatist, was the fourth son of Robert Manners of Kentish Town, London. Of his mother and his early education nothing is known. He entered Lincoln's Inn on 7 March 1793, but evidently discovered activities more congenial to him than study for the bar. In 1806 he published a five-act play in verse, *Edgar, or, Caledonian Feuds*, and in October 1807 he started a paper, *The Satirist, or, Monthly Meteor*, which was, by his own subsequent description, 'devoted to the purposes of exposing and castigating every species of literary and moral turpitude' (G. Manners, *Vindiciae satiricae*, 1809, 5). The journal was strongly tory in its politics, and sought to promulgate this line through satirical articles, stories, and verses: the coloured cartoons that featured in early editions were soon dropped. William Cobbett, Francis Burdett, and Samuel Whitbread were notable targets of its often scurrilous attacks on reformers, while the less prominent William Hallett, the radical candidate for Berkshire at the election of 1812, was the object of a sustained campaign of invective.

The tone, if not the politics, of *The Satirist* was clearly unpalatable to the establishment. On 12 June 1812 Manners was required by the bar, which had declined to hear his final exercise, to explain 'numerous instances of libellous and unjustifiable attacks on private character, evidently inserted [in the paper] with a view to profit'. It was noted that he had been prosecuted and imprisoned for three months for one libel; that his conduct in another case of February 1809 had been 'highly disrespectable', and that a further action was pending. Manners justified his libels on 'public grounds' and cited the plaudits he had received from Sir James Mansfield, the trial judge in the 1809 case. Evidently his persuasive powers were strong, and he was duly, if belatedly, called to the bar (*Black Books*). Very shortly afterwards he sold *The Satirist*, and its premises at 267 Strand, to the journalist William Jerdan, who toned down its content, a move that did not have the desired effect upon its profitability. The paper ceased publication in 1814 (it is not to be confused with the similar title founded in 1831 by Barnard Gregory).

Thereafter Manners appears to have practised law in London: he is listed as a special pleader in 1815 and 1817 at addresses in Gray's Inn and at 22 St James's Place, Westminster. In 1819 he became British consul at Boston, an appointment which he held until 1839. In 1825 he published (in Boston) *The Conflagration: a Poem*, which was written to aid victims of Canadian fires. Jerdan, who had not benefited from his business dealings with Manners, none the less described him as 'a gentleman in every sense, full of fancy and talent, acute and well informed' (Jerdan, 1.108). The sixth Baron Monson remembered him as 'a remarkably tall distinguished looking man', and recalled his appearance at a masquerade breakfast at the height of his journalistic infamy, dressed as an itinerant preacher 'standing inside of a tub, which hid his own legs, [with] short false ones attached before him'. He kept up an ironic tirade against 'luxury and gluttony', in which he occasionally paused 'for the purpose of stretching his hand behind him to the refreshments, and helping himself to wine and dainties' (*N&Q*, 2nd ser., 1, 1856, 361). Manners died at Coburg, Upper Canada, on 18 February 1853.

H. J. SPENCER

Sources *DNB* · J. D. Vann, 'Comic periodicals', *Victorian periodicals and Victorian society*, ed. J. D. Vann and R. T. Van Arsdel (1994) · W. P. Baildon, ed., *The records of the Honorable Society of Lincoln's Inn: the black books*, 4 (1902); repr. (1991), 128 · *N&Q*, 2nd ser., 1 (1856), 314 · *N&Q*, 2nd ser., 1 (1856), 361 · *N&Q*, 2nd ser., 2 (1856), 156 · W. Jerdan, *The autobiography of William Jerdan: with his literary, political, and social reminiscences and correspondence during the last fifty years*, 4 vols. (1852–3).

Manners, Henry, second earl of Rutland (1526–1563), courtier and soldier, was born on 23 September 1526 and baptized after 24 December at Elsinges Manor, Enfield, Middlesex, the eldest son of five sons and six daughters of Thomas *Manners, first earl of Rutland (c.1497–1543), and his second wife, Eleanor (d. 1551), daughter of Sir William *Paston (1479?–1554) and Bridget Heydon. During his father's lifetime he was styled Lord Ros. At a triple wedding on 3 July 1536, when the other bridegrooms were the heirs of the earls of Oxford and Westmorland, he married Lady Margaret Neville (c.1525–1559), daughter of Ralph *Neville, fourth earl of Westmorland (1498–1549), and Lady Catherine Stafford. Given their youth, the couple are unlikely to have lived together for some years. Details of Ros's education are unknown; he does not seem to have attended Oxford or Cambridge universities. By summer 1540 he was in residence at Croxton Abbey, Leicestershire. The elder of his two sons with Margaret, Edward *Manners, was not born until July 1549; the couple also had a daughter.

Following the death of his father on 20 September 1543, he succeeded as second earl of Rutland, and with his uncle Sir Richard Manners, the family leader until he came of age, he was involved in the invasion of France in 1544. He was knighted by Henry VIII at the surrender of Boulogne on 30 September, and in 1546 accompanied the town's governor, John Dudley, Viscount Lisle, and the lord admiral, Sir Thomas Seymour, on an embassy to France. Rutland bore the spurs at the coronation of Edward VI on 20 February 1547. That year he became constable of Nottingham Castle and warden and chief justice in eyre of Sherwood Forest, and began to emerge as the leading magnate in Nottinghamshire. At about this time much of his debt to the crown was forgiven.

After the arrest of the lord admiral in January 1549, Rutland testified that Lord Seymour had actively sought his support in intrigues against his brother the lord protector, Edward Seymour, duke of Somerset. On 1 May Rutland was appointed warden of the east and middle marches on the Scottish borders in succession to Lord Grey of Wilton. In view of his youth and inexperience Sir Thomas Holcroft and others were deputed to advise him, but he 'emerged from his baptism of fire with high credit' (Merriman, 373). Having marched in June to Stichill, near Hume, he drove the French from Jedburgh, recaptured Ferniehirst Tower, and engaged in targeted devastation. In command during the evacuation of Haddington in September, he then accumulated plans of all the key strongholds still in English hands; these survive and constitute important evidence of English activity there from 1547. He went with William Parr, marquess of Northampton, on his mission to France in May 1551. He became joint lord lieutenant of Lincolnshire and Nottinghamshire with Lord Admiral Clinton in

April that year, but sole lord lieutenant of Nottinghamshire only in May 1552.

Rutland associated with extreme reformers. He attended a debate about transubstantiation at Sir Richard Morison's house. In February 1551 he testified against Sir Richard Whalley, who was involved in a bizarre attempt to return Somerset to power. In April Rutland joined a group of thirteen noblemen, each entrusted with a band of men-at-arms. John Dudley, now earl of Warwick, experimented with this virtual standing army financed by the crown and manned by trusted noblemen, who recruited their servants. In December Rutland sat on the commission which tried the earl of Somerset. He strongly supported Dudley, now duke of Northumberland, during the Lady Jane Grey affair. By 29 July 1553 he was in the custody of a knight marshal and on 31 July he was sent to the Fleet prison, apparently still adhering 'to Northumberland with the utmost obstinacy' (R. Wingfield, 'Vita Maria Anglicanae regina', ed. D. MacCulloch, *Camden Miscellany*, 28, CS, 4th ser., 29, 1984, 270).

However, Rutland came to terms with Mary's regime. Released to house arrest on 8 September, he was then pardoned. In 1554 he was one of sixteen members of the élite entrusted with a band of men-at-arms. In 1557 he was appointed captain-general of horsemen, and then lieutenant- and captain-general of the ill-fated army and navy that set out to retain Calais in January 1558. During Mary's reign he finished his father's work of rebuilding the family seat, Belvoir Castle.

Rutland gained immediate favour under Elizabeth. He was commissioned to investigate the affairs of the late Cardinal Reginald Pole and was installed as a knight of the Garter on 3 June 1559. That year he was appointed lord lieutenant in Nottinghamshire and Rutland, where he mustered troops against the threat of a French invasion. On 13 October his wife died at Holywell, Shoreditch, London; she was buried on 21 October at the parish church of St Leonard. Early the following year Rutland married Bridget (1525/6–1601), widow of the diplomat Sir Richard Morison (c.1510–1556) and daughter of John *Hussey, Lord Hussey (1465/6–1537), and Lady Anne Grey. On 20 January 1561 he became president of the council of the north. He travelled north in February and immediately began a refurbishment of the king's manor house at York, which became the council's meeting place. Having been commissioned to inquire into offences against the Acts of Uniformity and Supremacy in the province of York, he noted as early as 25 February in a letter to William Cecil that 'I do not finde the country so forward in religion as I wish it to be' (PRO, SP 59/4, no. 1026). Although he was able to muster troops for the French campaign of 1562–3, the brevity of his tenure of office curtailed his achievements. He died on 17 September 1563 in time of plague (though it is unclear whether he was a direct victim) and was buried in the parish church at Bottesford, Leicestershire, where a fine alabaster monument to him and his first wife was erected. Owing to a dispute over ancestral lands, his will dated 5 July 1560 was never proved. A crown survey lists his per annum income at £2485, though his debts had been accumulating; early death kept him from reaping substantial profits under Elizabeth. He was succeeded as third earl of Rutland by his son Edward. His widow, Countess Bridget, married about June 1566 Francis Russell, second earl of Bedford; she died on 12 January 1601.

M. M. NORRIS

Sources M. M. Norris, 'The first and second earls of Rutland and their part in the central and local politics of mid-Tudor England', PhD diss., U. Edin., 1995 · GEC, *Peerage* · J. Nichols, *The history and antiquities of the county of Leicester*, 2/1 (1795), 44–6 · M. M. Norris, 'The 2nd earl of Rutland's band of men-at-arms, 1551–2', *Historical Research* (Feb 1995), 99–116 · PRO, SP 59/4, no. 1026 · *The manuscripts of his grace the duke of Rutland*, 4 vols., HMC, 24 (1888–1905), vol. 4, pp. 302–3 · Belvoir Castle, Leicestershire, letters, iii, fols. 42–3; calendared in *The manuscripts of his grace the duke of Rutland*, 4 vols., HMC, 24 (1888–1905), vol. 1, p. 69 · wills, Belvoir Castle, Leicestershire, BCW 14 (PRO C142/139, no. 103) · grants, Belvoir Castle, Leicestershire, BC 6 75, 79, 80 · BL, Add. MS 38133, fols. 105–6 · *LP Henry VIII*, vol. 3, no. 6748 · *CPR*, 1548–9, 93 · PRO, SP 10/6, no. 12 · PRO, SC 12/22/36 · C. Wriothesley, *A chronicle of England during the reigns of the Tudors from AD 1485 to 1559*, ed. W. D. Hamilton, 1, CS, new ser., 11 (1875), 50 · H. Miller, *Henry VIII and the English nobility* (1986) · *APC*, 1552–4, 50, 216; 1552–3, 342 · R. R. Reid, *The king's council in the north* (1921); facs. edn (1975) · M. Merriman, *The rough wooings: Mary queen of Scots, 1542–1551* (2000)

Archives Belvoir Castle, Leicestershire, Belvoir Castle MSS · priv. coll., MSS | PRO, C 3 · PRO, close rolls, C 54 · PRO, LC 4 · PRO, PC 2 · PRO, patent rolls · PRO, STAC 5 · PRO, state papers · PRO, WARD

Likenesses Van der Eyden, oils, 16th cent. (as a young man), Belvoir Castle, Leicestershire · alabaster effigy on monument, 1563 (with his wife), St Mary's Church, Bottesford, Leicestershire

Wealth at death £2485 per annum shortly after 1563: PRO, SC 12/22/36

Manners, John, eighth earl of Rutland (1604–1679), politician, born at Aylestone, Leicestershire, on 10 June 1604, was the eldest son of Sir George Manners (d. 1623) of Nether Haddon, Derbyshire, and Grace, daughter of Sir Henry Pierrepoint of Holme Pierrepont, Nottinghamshire. A great-grandson of Thomas *Manners, first earl of Rutland and thirteenth Baron Ros (d. 1543), at the time of his birth there was little apparent likelihood of his succeeding to the earldom. He was admitted a fellow-commoner at Queens' College, Cambridge, in 1618, graduated MA in 1621, and entered the Inner Temple in November of that year. In October 1622 Manners obtained a licence to travel abroad for three years. He succeeded to the Haddon estate on the death of his father in 1623 and in 1628 married Frances (bap. 1613, d. 1671), the daughter of Edward Montagu, Baron Montagu of Boughton, and Frances, daughter of Thomas Cotton of Conington, Huntingdonshire. He represented Derbyshire in the parliament of 1626 and in the Short Parliament of 1640, having also served as sheriff of the county in 1632–3. Manners succeeded to the earldom of Rutland on 29 March 1641 on the death of his cousin George, the seventh earl.

In March 1642 Rutland was made lord lieutenant of Derbyshire by parliamentary ordinance and was among those peers who remained at Westminster when parliament was summoned to Oxford by the king in January 1643. He was a moderate, or more accurately lukewarm, parliamentarian; Sir Griffin Markham wrote in 1644 'I doubt not but Rutland will do anything to keep himself afoot, his nature goeth more that way than the right way' (*CSP dom.*, 1644, 47). He was appointed a commissioner for parliament to Scotland on 13 July 1643 and nominated as a commissioner for the great seal, but excused himself from both charges on the grounds of ill health. Belvoir Castle was taken by the royalists early in 1643 and retaken by parliamentarian forces in 1646. In that year Rutland was again appointed commissioner to Scotland for parliament and the following year chief justice in eyre north of the Trent. He and his growing family had occupied Exeter House on the Strand since 1642 and its chapel became one of the principal centres for the celebration of ceremonial religion until the Restoration. In April 1645 it was reported that the bishop of Durham 'had sprinkled Rutland's child, signing her with the sign of the cross' (Nichols, 53). In 1647 Rutland returned to his Derbyshire estate to find it occupied by local lead miners claiming the historic right of free mining. The Manners family had long opposed the claims of the miners and Rutland responded by leading an armed attack against them. A protracted dispute ensued. The miners, with encouragement from the Levellers, sought to assert their right through the local duchy court; Rutland enlisted the support of the common law and Westminster courts, the parliament, the county gentry, the council of state, and the army in securing his hold over his estate. Not surprisingly he triumphed and a series of legal rulings in 1648–9 declared against the miners' claim.

In May 1649 the council of state, much to Rutland's dismay, ordered that Belvoir Castle should be demolished to prevent any danger of its becoming a royalist base. He subsequently received £1500 compensation. He played little part in the administration of the 1650s, although he retained his position as chief justice in eyre until 1661 when his petition to remain in the office was unsuccessful. The 1660s were dominated by the rebuilding of Belvoir Castle, completed in 1668, and the marital troubles of his son and heir John *Manners, first duke of Rutland (1638–1711). Rutland's political rehabilitation was marked by his appointment as lord lieutenant of Leicestershire in 1667, a position he held for a decade before giving way to his son. His wife, Frances, died in May 1671 and all but one of their four sons died in childhood, but six of their seven daughters lived to adulthood and married. Rutland died at Nether Haddon on 29 September 1679 and was buried on 24 October at Bottesford, Leicestershire, the traditional resting place of the earls of Rutland.   JAN BROADWAY

Sources J. Nichols, *The history and antiquities of the county of Leicester*, 2/1 (1795), 50–59 · GEC, *Peerage* · Clarendon, *Hist. rebellion*, 7.135, 315 · Venn, *Alum. Cant.*, 1/3.134 · Evelyn, *Diary*, 3.95, 124, 203 · will, PRO, PROB 11/361, fols. 304v–305r · A. Wood, *The politics of social conflict: the Peak country, 1520–1770* (1990)
Archives NRA, priv. coll., papers
Likenesses S. Cooper, miniature, 1656, Belvoir Castle, Leicestershire · J. Hoskins junior, miniature, 1656, Belvoir Castle, Leicestershire · G. Gibbons, double portrait, marble tomb effigy, c.1684 (with wife), St Mary's Church, Bottesford, Leicestershire · Van der Eyden, portrait · oils, Belvoir Castle, Leicestershire

Wealth at death apart from a few small bequests whole estate left to son: will, PRO, PROB 11/361, fols. 304v–305r

Manners, John, first duke of Rutland (1638–1711), nobleman, was born on 29 May 1638 at Boughton, Northamptonshire, the third and only surviving son of Sir John *Manners (1604–1679) of Haddon Hall, Derbyshire, and Frances (1613–1671), daughter of Edward, first Baron Montagu of Boughton, and sister of William *Montagu (1618/19–1706). Manners's father became eighth earl of Rutland and inherited Belvoir Castle, Leicestershire, in 1641, following the failure of the senior Manners line. Manners's childhood was disrupted by the civil war. His father was a 'lukewarm Parliamentarian' (Stone, *Family*, 200) but Belvoir was first a royalist then a parliamentary garrison. The old castle was demolished in 1649 and rebuilt 1654–68.

Manners (known as Lord Roos) married three times: first, on 13 July 1658, Lady Anne Pierrepoint (*bap.* 1631, *d.* 1697), daughter and coheir of Henry, first marquess of Dorchester. The total failure of this marriage had legal and potentially dynastic implications. There was at this time no legal divorce, and Manners's quarrel with his first wife initiated a legal process of separation and remarriage for the few who could afford it. Manners was granted judicial separation from bed and board in the ecclesiastical court in 1663 because of Anne's adultery. To protect the succession to his estates, Manners then obtained private acts, that of 8 February 1667 bastardizing Anne's children born since 1659 and that of 11 April 1670 granting him permission to remarry. The ensuing parliamentary debates attracted disproportionate attention because of revelations about Anne's sexual promiscuity, the challenge to beliefs about the indissolubility of marriage, and suggestions that the process could be adopted by Charles II to divorce his barren wife, Catherine of Braganza. Manners married second, on 10 November 1671, Lady Diana Bruce, daughter of Robert, first earl of Ailesbury, and widow of Sir Seymour Shirley; she died in childbirth on 15 July 1672. Manners's third marriage, on 8 January 1674, to Catherine (1657–1733), sixteen-year-old daughter of Baptist Noel, third Viscount Campden, was successful. Two sons and two daughters were born to this marriage.

Manners was a rather inactive MP for Leicestershire from 1661 until 1679, when he entered the House of Lords. He supported the whigs in the exclusion crisis and in the revolution of 1688–9. He never visited London after the coronation of William and Mary in 1689, pleading ill health and leaving his wife and two sons to represent him at court while he indulged his preference for country life and local politics. From 1668 to 1701 he lived at Belvoir or Haddon, and after 1701 solely at Belvoir. Manners replaced his father as lord lieutenant of Leicestershire and recorder of Grantham in 1677, and enjoyed his aristocratic role exercising local social and political power on behalf of the crown. He was generally effective, but suffered a few failures in this local authority. He influenced local elections, maintained order, and sought out illegal arms. He upset the local gentry in 1679 by inviting a second aristocrat to stand with him in the parliamentary election, contrary to the tradition of one aristocratic and one gentry candidate. Manners's election was disallowed by the Commons: he was created Baron Manners of Haddon with a seat in the House of Lords four months before his father died, when he succeeded as ninth earl. He retained the lord lieutenancy in 1681, despite supporting the whigs in the exclusion crisis, but was replaced in 1687 when James II filled offices with his supporters. He was reappointed in 1689 after the revolution, but resigned in 1702 after failing to secure his son's re-election to the Commons, and in protest at government interference in Leicestershire promoting tory interests. He was reappointed lord lieutenant from 1706 to 1711.

Rutland's heir, John, married on 17 August 1693 Katherine, second daughter of William, Lord Russell, the whig magnate beheaded in 1683 for participating in the Rye House plot. On 29 March 1703, partly as a result of Russell influence, the earl was created duke of Rutland and marquess of Granby, in recognition of lifetime support for whig government. Rutland died on 10 January 1711 at Belvoir Castle, and was buried on 23 February at Bottesford church, near Belvoir. JEAN MORRIN

Sources *The manuscripts of his grace the duke of Rutland*, 4 vols., HMC, 24 (1888–1905), vols. 1–2 · O. R. F. Davies, 'The dukes of Devonshire, Newcastle and Rutland, 1688–1714: a study in wealth and political influence', DPhil diss., U. Oxf., 1971 · 'A true and perfect copy of Lord Roos his answer to marquis of Dorchester's letter 25 February 1659', BL, G2032 · L. Stone, *Road to divorce: England, 1530–1987* (1990), 309–13 · CSP dom., 1659–60, 362, 375; 1677–8, 200, 520; 1679–80, 120; 1685, 427 · JHC, 12 (1697–9), 1167–87 · L. Stone, *Family and fortune: studies in aristocratic finance in the sixteenth and seventeenth centuries* (1973), 165–208 · VCH Leicestershire, 2.109–23 · J. Nichols, *History and antiquities of Leicestershire* (1798), vol. 2, pt 1 · JHL, 12 (1666–75), 191 [22 Feb 1668; petition to House of Lords by Dame Anne Roos pleading for financial maintenance from Roos] · J. R. Western, *Monarchy and revolution: the English state in the 1680s* (1972) · GEC, *Peerage*, new edn, 11.263–6 · E. Cruickshanks, 'Manners, John', HoP, *Commons, 1660–90*, 3.14–16 · tombstone, Bottesford church, Leicestershire [John Manners, father, and Frances Montagu, mother]
Archives Belvoir Castle, Leicestershire, MSS · NRA, priv. coll., papers | Leics. RO, letters to Thomas Staveley
Likenesses J. B. Closterman, oils, 1703, Belvoir Castle, Leicestershire · J. B. Closterman, portrait (in coronation robes), Hardwick Hall, Derbyshire · portrait, Belvoir Castle, Leicestershire
Wealth at death rental in 1707 at £15,446 p.a. based on Rutland audit abstracts; Rutland estates valued at nearly £20,000 in rents and profits: Davies, 'The dukes of Devonshire'

Manners, John, marquess of Granby (1721–1770), army officer and politician, was born at Kelham, Nottinghamshire, on 2 January 1721, the eldest son of John Manners, third duke of Rutland (1696–1779), and his wife, Bridget (1699–1734), the younger daughter and heir of Robert *Sutton, second Baron Lexington. He entered Eton College in 1732, and on 2 July 1738 matriculated from Trinity College, Cambridge. Although he did not take a degree, he was awarded an LLD in 1769. From Cambridge he completed the continental grand tour in company with his tutor John Ewer, later bishop of Bangor. While he was still

John Manners, marquess of Granby (1721–1770), by Sir Joshua Reynolds, c.1763–6

abroad his father's political interest saw Granby returned to parliament for the borough of Grantham (June 1741).

The young officer On 4 October 1745, during the Jacobite rising, the duke of Rutland, having raised in support of the Hanoverian dynasty the Leicester blues, one of fifteen 'noble' regiments, inaugurated Granby's military career by making him its colonel. His regiment never saw action, seeing out the rebellion as part of the garrison of Newcastle upon Tyne. Granby could have interpreted his colonelcy as a post taken up out of aristocratic duty at a time of national crisis, but instead he sought to be taken seriously as a soldier. He volunteered to serve on the duke of Cumberland's staff in Scotland, and in March 1746 is reported to have been present during operations at Strathbogie, a prelude to Culloden. Upon the disbandment of his regiment Granby retained his rank and seniority as a colonel in the army and in 1747 campaigned in the Low Countries. At about this time he had a mistress who became the mother of his illegitimate children George (c.1746–1772), MP for Scarborough from 1768 until his death, and Anne, who married her cousin John Manners-Sutton (1752–1826), MP for Newark from 1783 to 1796.

As a young man Granby made his mark not as a soldier or parliamentarian but as an enthusiastic huntsman, a racegoer, and a gambler; on 1 September 1750 Horace Walpole wrote, 'He is in debt £10,000' (Walpole, *Corr.*, 20.183). On 3 September 1750 he married Frances (1728–1761), the eldest daughter of Charles *Seymour, sixth duke of Somerset, and his second wife, Lady Charlotte Finch; among their children were Charles *Manners, later fourth duke of Rutland (1754–1787), and Lord Robert *Manners (1758–

1782). Granby's new bride also had a reputation as a spend-thrift, and Walpole joked that the couple were well matched not only in their lineage but in their lack of ready funds.

In 1752, as a means of securing the support of the Rut-land family's parliamentary interest, the Pelham ministry urged George II to appoint Granby colonel of the Royal Horse Guards (the Blues), one of the army's most presti-gious regiments. The king at first refused, denouncing Granby as 'a sot, a bully, that does nothing but drink and quarrel' (BL, Add. MS 32729, fol. 4). However, Granby's credit with the king gradually increased. He was elected MP for Cambridgeshire in 1754, and although he expressed a genuine loathing of party divisions he allied himself with the government whig Philip Yorke (later sec-ond earl of Hardwicke). Once elected, he defended the duke of Newcastle's administration in speeches in the Commons. In 1755 he was promoted major-general, and in May 1758 he gained the colonelcy requested in 1752.

The Seven Years' War Three months later, Granby was sent to Germany in command of a brigade of cavalry in the British expeditionary force. When the force commander, Charles Spencer, third duke of Marlborough, died in Octo-ber 1758, Granby succeeded Lord George Sackville as sec-ond in command, and in February 1759 he was promoted lieutenant-general. At the battle of Minden in August 1759 Granby led the second line of cavalry and was praised in orders by Prince Ferdinand of Brunswick, overall com-mander of the allied army. Prince Ferdinand did this, how-ever, as a means of indirectly criticizing Granby's super-ior, Sackville, who Ferdinand felt had disobeyed orders by failing to bring forward the cavalry in time to exploit vic-tory. Sackville resigned in protest, and on 14 August Granby became commander-in-chief of the British con-tingent in his place. At Sackville's subsequent court mar-tial Granby, without rancour, stated his belief that the cav-alry had indeed been led forward too slowly. He was uncomfortable at testifying against his former superior officer and endeavoured to suggest that Sackville had not been negligent, but at best could only give the impression that Sackville had been confused rather than disobedient. If Granby had sought to prevent a verdict of guilty, he failed. Sackville later 'always wrote with contempt [of Granby], referring to promises extracted from him "in the midst of riot and dissipation"' (Mackesy, 247).

At the battle of Warburg on 31 July 1760 Granby took the opportunity to show the capability of the cavalry when under his personal command. Three times his impetuos-ity scattered the French troops opposing him; and the loss of his hat when leading the charge gave rise to the expres-sion 'To go at it bald-headed' (Granby, who by his twenties had lost most of his hair, famously disdained to wear a wig). At Vellinghausen on 15–16 July 1761 he showed him-self a general as well as a fighter when, on successive days, his able dispositions repulsed the assaults of the French. He then launched a counter-attack and secured victory. His beaten opponent, the duc de Broglie, so admired Granby that he commissioned a portrait of him by Sir Joshua Reynolds. At the battle of Wilhelmstahl on 25 June

1762 Granby secured another triumph, the troops under his command cutting off the French rearguard and com-pelling the surrender of some of their finest regiments. 'Il a manoeuvré comme un ange … no man ever acted with more courage or more like a commanding officer', com-mented an enraptured Lord Ligonier (Whitworth, 369). Finally, at Brückermühl on 21 September 1762, Granby raised himself from his sickbed to bring two brigades to the relief of the Brunswicker, General Zastrow.

Although a successful battlefield commander, Granby did not possess all the attributes of a general. He was no administrator—a serious failing in someone who was responsible for the welfare of no fewer than 25,000 British troops—and he cheerfully admitted that he hated writing. During the winter campaign of 1760–61, when the com-missariat was under his direct control, payments were late and supplies became scarce. Not only did military operations suffer but costs increased and monthly expenditure by the commissariat rose from a budgeted £150,000 to £340,000. Fraud by contractors was rife. As dis-cipline in a hungry army came under strain, officers schooled under the harsher regime of the duke of Cum-berland became critical of Granby's leniency towards deserters and marauders. Lord Frederick Cavendish, while acknowledging Granby to be 'indefatigable and dili-gent' at the head of an advance guard, believed that his inability to maintain discipline made him an unfit com-mander (Devonshire MSS, Chatsworth, Derbyshire, MS 397.111). Amid such circles the expression 'German disci-pline' took on ironic connotations.

Politics To the wider public, however, this mattered less than Granby's battlefield successes; and at the end of the Seven Years' War his reputation stood at its height. Much of his popularity derived from his well-publicized solici-tude for his men. Edward Penny's painting *The Marquess of Granby Relieving a Sick Soldier*, exhibited in 1765, overturned conventional expectations of the history painting by showing Granby acting heroically in an act of private charity and not on the field of war. The engraving outsold even that of Benjamin West's *Death of General Wolfe*. The large number of public houses called the Marquess of Granby is testimony to the lasting gratitude felt towards him by the disabled non-commissioned officers whom he is believed to have set up as publicans. Horace Walpole might have sneered that he was the 'mob's hero' (Wal-pole, *Corr.*, 21.315), but this simply provided another rea-son why, even before his return home from Germany, Granby was being assiduously courted by politicians. Most importantly, the political world speculated whether he would lead the Rutland parliamentary vote in support of the terms of peace negotiated by the Bute government. That in the end he did vote for the peace of Paris, notwith-standing his personal regard for the duke of Newcastle—who now led the opposition—was a reflection of the fact that he thought the measure right and he knew that the new monarch, George III, wished it. Granby felt an instinctive aversion towards party politics; at most he would work with individuals whom he believed public-spirited. But this was not an easy path to pursue amid the turbulent politics of the 1760s. Initially he gravitated towards George Grenville, whom he trusted even if he disliked his political associates, and on 1 July 1763 he accepted from Grenville's new ministry the master-generalship of the ordnance. He supported the government over Wilkes and general warrants, but on 10 January 1765 he spoke against the dismissal of army officers from their employments on the basis of their votes in parliament. In May 1765, when the London silk weavers rioted, Grenville's colleague George Montagu Dunk, second earl of Halifax, tried to persuade the king to appoint Granby commander-in-chief of the army: 'Lord Granby is a very popular man and might save the lives of these deluded wretches which may be exposed and sacrificed by another commander' (*Correspondence of George III*, 1.105). Although the king, having promised the reversion to the duke of Cumberland, refused, when the Grenville administration fell a month later Granby remained master-general of the ordnance at George III's request. Granby nevertheless declined to act with the new Rockingham ministry and voted against it over the repeal of the Stamp Act.

With the formation of the ministry of William Pitt, earl of Chatham, the following year, Granby was finally appointed commander-in-chief of the army (13 August 1766). He accepted reluctantly, knowing that his predecessor, the octogenarian John, Earl Ligonier, resented being forcibly retired. It was then rumoured that he would leave parliament, but during the general election of April 1768 Granby campaigned more vigorously than ever and increased the Rutland group's parliamentary representation to seven—adding to his debts in the process. By now his personal loyalty was directed towards Chatham. But when ill health prompted Chatham's resignation from office in October 1768, Granby was cut adrift; he remained in a cabinet headed by Augustus Fitzroy, third duke of Grafton, without finding political consistency easy to come by. His biggest test came with the controversy aroused by the return in the general election of John Wilkes to parliament by the electors of Middlesex. Granby had been against moves in government to have him expelled, but his distaste for Wilkes's character and demagoguery eventually overcame his principles, and when, on 3 February 1769, the motion for expulsion was put to the Commons, he voted in favour. Upon Wilkes being returned again by the electors of Middlesex, Granby voted for the seating of Henry Luttrell in his place. The timing of his volte-face was unfortunate. On 21 January 1769 the first letter of the controversialist Junius had appeared in the *Public Advertiser*. Amid an attack on the Grafton administration as a whole, Junius accused Granby of nepotism, brokering the sale of commissions, and servility towards the court. Ordinarily, Granby's continuing popularity would have been proof against the assault, and besides, as Junius later admitted, he had no particular quarrel with him; but when Granby's school contemporary Sir William Draper, the conqueror of Manila, published a defence of his old friend, Junius felt compelled to justify his allegations. His task was made easier by the ineptitude of Draper's reply, which in effect admitted that the convivial

(and famously hard-drinking) Granby was liable to be imposed upon by unscrupulous associates. Junius pounced gleefully: 'It is you, Sir William Draper, who have taken pains to represent your friend in the character of a drunken landlord, who deals out his promises as liberally as his liquor' (*Letters of Junius*, 41). Further ammunition against Granby's reputation was provided by the vote in parliament just four days before on the Middlesex election: 'Does he not at this moment give up all character and dignity as a gentleman in receding from his own repeated declarations in favour of Mr Wilkes?' (ibid., 40). The knife was then given a final twist with a well-informed attack on Granby for the deplorably undermanned condition of the army overseas—in the West Indies, the Mediterranean, and North America—and closer to home in Ireland, lending credence to the argument that Junius was the *nom de plume* of Philip Francis, a senior clerk in the war office.

So counter-productive were Draper's interventions over the following weeks against Junius on Granby's behalf that it was believed he was asked to desist by his friend. Thereafter Junius took notice of Granby only when addressing a public appeal to him (6 May 1769) to cease his continued votes for the seating of Luttrell. That Granby eventually changed his mind on the issue once again had less to do with Junius's strictures, however, than the return to the political arena of Lord Chatham. Strongly opposed to the government, and especially over the Middlesex election, Chatham used John Calcraft, the influential army agent, as his intermediary in persuading Granby to break with the Grafton ministry. As late as November 1769 Granby was reluctant to throw up office, telling Calcraft that it must 'look like skulking to Junius, or that he saw himself as unfit for the command of the army' (*Correspondence of William Pitt*, 3.363). But at the opening of parliament on 9 January 1770 he announced that his opinion on the Middlesex election had changed, and he voted against the government on the address. His resignation as commander-in-chief of the army and as master-general of the ordnance followed eight days later.

Death and assessment Out of office Granby found that his creditors, of whom there were many, became anxious, and he was increasingly dunned for repayment. By resigning as master-general of the ordnance he had given up a salary of £1500 per annum. Moreover, his resignation forfeited him the reversion of the colonelcy of the 1st foot guards, worth £3000 per annum, which on the death of Lord Ligonier went instead to William, duke of Gloucester, brother of George III. In the summer he went to Scarborough to support his candidate, George Cockburne, comptroller of the navy, in a parliamentary by-election. His man was defeated, but Granby remained to recuperate from illness. He died in Scarborough on 18 October 1770 from a seizure brought on by an attack of gout in the stomach. He was buried in Bottesford church, Belvoir, Leicestershire, on 28 October; his remains were reinterred in the mausoleum at Belvoir Castle in 1829.

Granby left debts estimated at £60,000 and assets of just

£23,000. Since he died intestate, his affairs were administered by the army agent John Calcraft, who, as was his wont, had secured Granby's debts to him through life insurance. Horace Walpole for one claimed that Calcraft, with his financial hold on Granby, had been able to wield an excessive influence over him. In his entry on Granby for the History of Parliament, Sir Lewis Namier suspected that Granby was probably indulgent towards Calcraft's contractor friends.

Granby was an instinctive soldier. He achieved rank through his family and political connections without serving an apprenticeship as a regimental officer. Yet on the battlefield his tactical judgement was unerring. When a more considered approach or a measure of application were necessary, whether in military administration or in politics, he was found wanting; but the public could identify with the gifted amateur, especially when he appeared to embody so many of the unsophisticated virtues of the English country gentleman. Even Walpole, one of Granby's severest critics, could on this basis pen a generous obituary:

> His large and open countenance … his robust and commanding person, and a proportion of florid beauty so great, that the baldness of his head, which he carried totally bare, was rather an addition to its comely roundness than a defect … all distinguished him without any extrinsic ornament, and pointed out his rank when he walked without attendance … Intrepidity, sincerity, humanity, and generosity, were not only innate in his breast, but was never corrupted there … His modesty was incapable of ostentation.

But to Walpole's mind, at least, Granby's merits were as often as not vitiated by his lack of understanding:

> Of money he seemed to conceive no use but in giving it away: but that profusion was so indiscriminate, that compassion or solicitation, and consequently imposture, were equally the master of his purse … No man meant to feel more patriotism, or to be more warmly attached to the constitution of the country; yet his unsuspicious nature suffered him to be easily made the tool of its enemies … In a rude age he would probably have been a successful general from his own valour, and the enthusiasm … which his soldiers felt for him; but in times wherein military knowledge is so much improved it was perhaps fortunate for his country that the sole command was never entrusted to him in any capital emergency. (Walpole, *Memoirs*, 2.117–19)

ALASTAIR W. MASSIE

Sources W. E. Manners, *Some account of the military, political, and social life of the right hon. John Manners, marquis of Granby* (1899) • *The manuscripts of his grace the duke of Rutland*, 4 vols., HMC, 24 (1888–1905) • L. B. Namier, 'Manners, John', HoP, *Commons, 1754–90* • H. Walpole, *Memoirs of the reign of King George the Third*, ed. G. F. R. Barker, 4 vols. (1894) • Walpole, *Corr.* • *The correspondence of King George the Third from 1760 to December 1783*, ed. J. Fortescue, 6 vols. (1927–8) • *The letters of Junius*, ed. J. Cannon (1978) • H. M. Little, 'The emergence of a commissariat during the Seven Years' War in Germany', *Journal of the Society for Army Historical Research*, 61 (1983–4), 201–14 • *Correspondence of William Pitt, earl of Chatham*, ed. W. S. Taylor and J. H. Pringle, 4 vols. (1838–40), vol. 3 • *The Grenville papers: being the correspondence of Richard Grenville … and … George Grenville*, ed. W. J. Smith, 2–3 (1852–3) • R. Savory, *His Britannic majesty's army in Germany during the Seven Years' War* (1966) • R. Whitworth, *Field Marshal Lord Ligonier* (1958) • P. Mackesy, *The coward of Minden* (1979) • D. H. Solkin, 'Portraiture in motion: Edward Penny's *Marquis of Granby* and the creation of a public for English art', *Huntington Library Quarterly*, 49 (1986), 1–23 • J. Brooke, *The Chatham administration, 1766–1768* (1956) • R. R. Sedgwick, 'Manners, John', HoP, *Commons, 1715–54* • R. A. Austen-Leigh, ed., *The Eton College register, 1698–1752* (1927)

Archives BL, letter-book and papers, Add. MSS 28553, 28855, 54485 • U. Hull, Brynmor Jones L., corresp. • U. Mich., Clements L., corresp. with Thomas Gage | BL, letters to Lord Grenville, Add. MS 57813 • BL, corresp. with Lord Holdernesse, Egerton MS 3443 • BL, corresp. with duke of Newcastle, Add. MSS 32864–33089 • U. Nott. L., letters to the duke of Newcastle

Likenesses J. E. Liotard, crayon drawing, 1740, Belvoir Castle, Leicestershire • A. Ramsay, oils, 1745, Gov. Art Coll. • D. Morier, group portrait, oils, *c*.1760, Royal Collection • J. Reynolds, oils, *c*.1763–1766, John and Mable Ringling Museum of Art, Sarasota, Florida [*see illus.*] • E. Penny, group portrait, oils, exh. 1765, AM Oxf.; repro. in Solkin, 'Portraiture in motion', 4 • M. F. Quadal, group portrait, oils, 1772 (*George III at a review*), Royal Collection • J. Ceracchi, marble bust, 1778, Belvoir Castle, Leicestershire • J. Nollekens, marble bust, 1814, Royal Collection • S. W. Reynolds, mezzotint, pubd 1834, BM, NPG • C. Spooner, mezzotint, pubd 1834, BM, NPG • R. Houston, mezzotint (after J. Reynolds), NPG • E. Penny, group portrait, oils, NAM • E. Penny, group portrait, oils, Petworth House, West Sussex • J. Reynolds, oils, NAM • J. Reynolds, oils, second version, Royal Collection • chalk drawing (after J. Reynolds, *c*.1759), NPG • mezzotint (after J. Reynolds), NPG

Wealth at death £23,000 assets • debts of £60,000: Manners, *Some account*, 392

Manners, John James Robert, seventh duke of Rutland

(1818–1906), politician, born at Belvoir Castle on 13 December 1818, was the second son in the family of three sons and four daughters of John Henry Manners, fifth duke of Rutland, and Lady Elizabeth, daughter of Frederick *Howard, fifth earl of Carlisle; his elder brother was Charles Cecil John *Manners, sixth duke of Rutland. He was educated at Eton College and at Trinity College, Cambridge, graduating MA in 1839; he became LLD in 1862. At neither place did he show much academic promise, but at Cambridge he began to adopt the outlook which was to lead him into public life.

Young England Manners had a vivid and Romantic historical imagination. He developed a strong attachment to the principles of *noblesse oblige*, chivalry, and patriotism, and venerated the Stuart monarchy and high Anglicanism for their paternalist commitment to an integrated, hierarchical society. He was an active member of the Camden Society at Cambridge; he read the works of Kenelm Digby, Robert Southey, and Sir Walter Scott; and he supported the cause, and visited the camp of Don Carlos, the clericalist claimant to the Spanish throne, in the months after graduating (he wrote about his visit in *Fraser's Magazine* for May and July 1840). In these years of susceptibility he came under the influence of two gifted and intense propagandists, the Romantic tory George Smythe (afterwards seventh Viscount Strangford), and the Oxford fellow Frederick Faber. Faber, in turn, was much taken with the 'delicate holiness' of the young Manners, who was (and remained) a tall, slim, fresh-faced, and vivacious man of openness, integrity, good breeding, and fashion—and thus a fine symbol of noble purity. Both these mentors were poets, and it was to Smythe that Manners dedicated

John James Robert Manners, seventh duke of Rutland (1818–1906), by James Russell & Sons

the first of his two books of poems, *England's Trust* (1841), which pleaded for the restoration of the former power of the church and the reassertion of feudal values. (Unfortunately for Manners, two of its many ardent lines permanently saddled him with the reputation of an impractical and narrow-minded landowner: 'Let wealth and commerce, laws and learning die, but leave us still our old nobility.') Although in the two years after graduating he was a regular member of Lady Blessington's literary salon, wrote poems, lived a gay London and country social life of dancing, dining, and racegoing, and read for the bar, he had a clear sense of the duty of his class to offer political and moral leadership. He had developed skills of public speaking at the Cambridge Union, and, in 1841, in his twenty-third year, anxious to act out his principles, he entered parliament as Conservative MP for Newark, where the Manners family had some influence, W. E. Gladstone being the other MP (Manners was his pallbearer, fifty-seven years later).

Manners's views were not eccentric for a Conservative in the early 1840s. This was because of the threat to the church, traditional aristocratic society, and rural values posed by urbanization, the 1832 Reform Act, and the class tension stemming from severe economic depression. But there was less agreement about the best way of defending these endangered principles. Manners became associated with three other Conservative MPs, Smythe, Alexander Cochrane-Baillie (afterwards first Baron Lamington), and

Benjamin Disraeli, in what became called the Young England group. Young England scorned the practices and views of industrial employers as materialist, and asserted the need for a social politics, led by a regenerated aristocracy, in order to humanize the towns. The group attracted much attention, owing principally to Disraeli's flair for publicity and to its willingness to criticize the prime minister, Sir Robert Peel, for his attachment to political economy and his lack of sympathy with social reform. But its members had different priorities. Manners was particularly concerned about urban conditions; he toured the industrial districts of Lancashire and was distressed to discover the extent and effects of child labour. In 1844, and subsequently, he was an active supporter of Lord Ashley's campaign to secure a ten-hour day in factories; this was achieved in 1847.

But, notwithstanding his genuine sympathy for the urban poor, Manners's priority was to defend the rural order, the gentlemanly political and social code, and the Anglican church establishment. He urged landlords to establish allotments for agricultural labourers, and persuaded his father to do so on the Belvoir estate. In a pamphlet of 1843, *A Plea for National Holy Days*, he advocated the establishment of communal rest days for dancing, archery, and other sports, as in pre-industrial 'merrie England'—hoping that they would brighten working-class lives, bring families together, increase respect for the church, remove 'thoughts of discontent and moroseness', and improve the nation's fitness in case of attack (he figured as Lord Henry Sydney in Disraeli's *Coningsby*, 1844, urging similar reforms). He strongly believed in the role that religion, and religious art and architecture, could play in reassuring the poor and reducing class tensions. After visiting Lancashire in 1841 he wrote that 'nothing but monastic institutions can Christianise Manchester'. He was committed to defending the Church of England, as the national, established church, rooted in the parochial structure and the alliance with land. Unlike some of his friends, he was never tempted by the idea of seceding to the Roman Catholic church. For all his susceptibility to Romantic fashions, Manners remained a straightforward English aristocrat: a patriot, a churchman, and a firm believer in the social order.

Manners criticized Peel for failing to uphold these values sufficiently staunchly, and it was this which led to his separation from his leader in the crisis of 1846 arising from Peel's proposal to repeal the corn laws. Manners was no absolutist supporter of protection. He believed that Peel should have opened the ports to corn imports, in order to mitigate the effects of the Irish famine, and taken the argument for free trade to the constituencies, in which case he would have supported him (though his ideal solution would have involved a moderate fixed duty on grain imported from outside the colonies, thus maintaining imperial preference). But he could not support Peel in his unchivalrous course of forcing repeal through parliament by expecting MPs to flout the principles on which they had been elected in 1841. So, unlike Smythe, he remained with Disraeli and the protectionists after the prime minister's fall in June 1846.

Tory government Young England was now destroyed as a force, having already been damaged in 1845 by division on Peel's proposal to increase the grant to the Roman Catholic seminary at Maynooth. Manners, like Smythe, did not feel that the grant violated the compact between the Church of England and the state. On the contrary, he advocated a generous treatment of the Irish priesthood, and the maintenance of friendly relations with the Vatican. These views, together with Manners's continuing public sympathy for the Spanish Carlists and his friendship with Tractarians—such as Faber, who joined the Roman Catholic church in 1845—displeased some of his Newark constituents. When his lukewarmness on protection became known in 1846, Manners felt obliged to announce that he would look for another seat at the next election, which was held in 1847. However, his choice of Liverpool instead was unpropitious; he fell victim to a No Popery campaign from evangelical protestants, and was unsuccessful. In 1849 he was again defeated—in the City of London by Baron Lionel de Rothschild—and only in 1850 did he return to the Commons as Conservative MP for Colchester. (He sat until 1857, when he was returned instead for North Leicestershire, a seat which he held until becoming MP for East Leicestershire in 1885.) Manners was therefore out of parliament for the three crucial years during which the leadership of the party in the Commons was decided for the next generation. Though probably not a serious contender for this position, owing to his age, dislike of responsibility, and lack of intellectual weight, Manners had by now developed into a self-confident and tenacious debater. His rank was also a great asset, as is suggested by the elevation of his less talented brother, then known as the marquess of Granby, to the joint leadership between 1848 and 1851. By 1851 Disraeli was agreed to be the party's leading MP. Manners was his ally, counsellor on public affairs and political tactics, and unswerving supporter for the next thirty years.

This was Manners's major contribution to Conservative Party history and it ensured him a cabinet place in all the Conservative governments between 1852 and 1892, though he was never given the responsibility of a major department. In the minority Conservative ministries of 1852, 1858–9, and 1866–8 he was first commissioner of works. This was a post to which his artistic and architectural interests made him suited. His most contentious actions during his first tenure included his decision to remove the Crystal Palace to Sydenham after the Great Exhibition, and his appointment of Alfred Stevens to design the monument to the duke of Wellington in St Paul's Cathedral. In 1858, as an admirer of Gilbert Scott and the Gothic style of architecture, he chose Scott to design the new Foreign Office buildings, despite the fact that Scott had not been placed first in the competition arranged by the previous government of Lord Palmerston. His choice was criticized by Palmerston in the Commons in February 1859, and when the latter returned to power

in June 1859 Scott was told to design the offices in an Italianate style instead, which caused Manners in turn to protest, unavailingly, at this flaunting of amateurish taste and slight to the architectural profession.

Manners's tenure of the commissionership reflected his localism; despite his abstract sympathy for working-class living conditions, it was not distinguished by legislative initiatives. His Metropolitan Burials Act of 1852 followed the consensus of the day in giving government power to close insanitary burial-grounds, but vested the power to establish new public cemeteries in parish ratepayers rather than in the Board of Health as the previous Liberal cabinet had proposed. His Metropolis Water Supply Act of the same year did not seriously challenge the vested interests of the water companies. Similarly, he rarely advocated social reform in government after the extension of the borough franchise in 1867. His concern to defend church interests made him unsympathetic to the extension of government responsibility for elementary education. As a firm believer in social order, he was also anxious that government should not appear weak in the face of radical agitation for parliamentary reform. In July 1866, when the government was faced with demands from the Reform League for permission to agitate in Hyde Park for a reform bill, he steadied the nerve of the home secretary, Spencer Walpole, whom he regarded as insufficiently resolute in upholding the law; he also defended Governor Eyre's behaviour in ruthlessly suppressing a black uprising in Jamaica in 1865; and he advocated strong measures in Ireland in the 1870s, especially against the press, in order to secure property rights. However, he was a supporter of Disraeli throughout the discussions on the franchise in 1867. He subsequently spoke at a number of Conservative working-men's meetings, and toyed with the New Social Movement inaugurated by Scott Russell in 1871 in an attempt to build up support for the Conservative Party among the lower classes. Manners claimed to discern support from this quarter for a number of Conservative principles, including defence of the church, property, and the union with Ireland.

But Manners's speeches after 1867, in and outside parliament, were particularly associated with two issues on which he hoped to generate a wide measure of agreement: national defence and import duties. His patriotism led him to call for a strong army—and the determination to go to war if necessary—in order to assert Britain's position in Europe. He repeatedly expressed his belief that Britain needed a standing army of 100,000 men as well as an effective militia, yeomanry, and volunteer movement. He was disturbed by the loss of national face over the Schleswig-Holstein affair and the concession of the Ionian Islands to Greece in 1864, and by the rise of Prussia and the resurgence of Russia in 1870. He was a strong critic of Gladstone's foreign policy and he was particularly hostile to Russia. With David Urquhart he advocated an understanding with the Circassians, the anti-Russian people on the north-eastern shores of the Black Sea; he also argued that the resettlement of many Circassians to the Balkans after the Crimean War fuelled the instability there in

1875–8, and made Gladstone's proposal of regional autonomy impractical. He supported Disraeli in cabinet during 1877–8 in taking a strong line against Russia and risking war, believing that this was the patriotic and popular cause. He remained an advocate of a pro-Ottoman policy until the end of his life, and in February 1899 published an article in *Blackwood's Magazine* criticizing Salisbury's abandonment of it.

Manners was the first leading politician publicly to advocate a return to a system of import duties and imperial preference, capitalizing on the rise of German competition and the slights to national pride apparent in the 1860s. He stressed it in speeches to working men from the late 1860s, citing the dangers of this competition, for example in the Leicester hosiery trade. In the light of the depression of the 1870s, he urged tariff reform in an article in *Blackwood's* for October 1881, arguing that it would benefit commerce and consolidate the empire. He was seen as the representative of agriculture in Salisbury's cabinet of 1886, until the establishment of a special cabinet post for it in 1889. In 1903 he welcomed Joseph Chamberlain's tariff reform initiative.

In the cabinets of the 1870s and 1880s, Manners was postmaster-general (1874–80 and 1885–6) and chancellor of the duchy of Lancaster (1886–92). He presided over the introduction of postal orders (1880) and the reduction of the minimum telegraph charge from 1*s*. to 6*d*. (1885). On leaving office in 1880 he was made GCB and given a pension of £1200 per annum. He had never been a rich man (he wrote extensively in *Blackwood's* between 1881 and 1885 in order to supplement his income), and it was partly on grounds of expense that he declined the prime minister's offers of the lord lieutenancy of Ireland (1866), the governor-generalship of Canada (1868), and the viceroyalty of India (1875)—for which Disraeli proposed him on account of his positive conception of the national destiny. But in 1888 he succeeded his brother as duke of Rutland, and inherited over 70,000 acres, principally in Leicestershire and Derbyshire. In 1892 he sold his Cheveley estate, near Cambridge, claiming that the injurious consequences of free trade necessitated this. He was made KG in 1891, and on 17 June 1896 he was granted the additional title of Baron Roos of Belvoir. After 1892 he spent most of his time at Belvoir, playing the part of the amiable, eager, benevolent landlord to general admiration; his gardens and galleries were freely open to visitors; he was never deeply interested in sport.

Manners married twice: on 10 June 1851 Catherine Louisa Georgina (1831–1854), only daughter of Lieutenant-Colonel George Marlay CB, of Belvedere, co. Westmeath; she died in childbed, of scarlet fever, in 1854, and on 15 May 1862 he married Janetta (1836–1899), eldest daughter of Thomas Hughan of Airds, Galloway. From the first marriage he had one son, Henry John Brinsley, who succeeded him as eighth duke, and who had five children, including the future Lady Diana Cooper. With his second wife Manners had five sons and three daughters. He died at Belvoir on 4 August 1906, and was buried there.

JONATHAN PARRY

Sources C. Whibley, *Lord John Manners and his friends*, 2 vols. (1925) · *Lord John Manners: a political and literary sketch, comprising some account of the Young England Party and the passing of the Factory Acts, by a non-elector* (1872) · I. Toplis, *The foreign office: an architectural history* (1987) · P. Smith, *Disraelian Conservatism and social reform* (1967) · *Benjamin Disraeli letters*, ed. J. A. W. Gunn and others (1982–) · Gladstone, *Diaries* · GEC, *Peerage*

Archives Belvoir Castle, Leicestershire · NRA, priv. coll., corresp. and papers | BL, corresp. with W. E. Gladstone · Bodl. Oxf., corresp. with Benjamin Disraeli · CKS, letters to Edward Stanhope · Lpool RO, letters to fourteenth earl of Derby; corresp. with fifteenth earl of Derby · NL Scot., corresp. with W. Blackwood & Sons Ltd · NRA, priv. coll., letters mainly to Drummond family · NRA, priv. coll., letters to E. De Lisle · U. Nott., letters to C. B. Marlay; letters to E. M. Wrench · Wellcome L., letters to Sir Thomas Barlow

Likenesses F. Grant, oils, 1853, Belvoir Castle; replica, Hughenden Manor, Buckinghamshire · W. Walker, mezzotint, pubd 1853 (after R. Buckner), BM, NPG · F. Grant, oils, *c*.1860, Belvoir Castle · H. T. Wells, chalk drawing, 1872, NPG · E. Lacretelle, etching, pubd 1874, NPG · lithograph, 1877, BM · W. W. Ouless, oils, 1886, NPG · M. Beerbohm, drawing, 1926, Sheffield City Art Gallery · Ape [C. Pellegrini], chromolithograph, NPG; repro. in *VF* (20 Nov 1869) · Bede, portrait, NPG; repro. in *VF* (7 Dec 1905) · T. Chartran, chromolithograph, NPG; repro. in *VF* (5 July 1881) · G. Cook, stipple and line engraving (after photograph by S. A. Walker), NPG · H. Gales, group portrait, oils (*The Derby cabinet of 1867*), NPG · J. R. Herbert, oils (kit-cat portrait), Belvoir · H. von Herkomer, oils, Belvoir · J. Russell & Sons, photograph, NPG [*see illus.*] · cartoon, repro. in *VF* (1881) · photographs, NPG · prints, NPG · statue, Bottesford church, Leicestershire

Wealth at death £99,596: probate, 30 Oct 1906, *CGPLA Eng. & Wales*

Manners [*née* Somerset], **Mary Isabella, duchess of Rutland** (1756–1831), politician and society hostess, was born on 1 August 1756, the fifth and youngest daughter of Charles Noel *Somerset, fourth duke of Beaufort (1709–1756) [*see under* Somerset, Henry, second duke of Beaufort], and his wife, Elizabeth Berkeley (1718/19–1799), sister and heir of Norborne Berkeley, fourth Baron Botetourt. Her mother, who was widowed when her son, Henry Somerset, fifth duke of Beaufort, was still a minor, was politically active and succeeded in maintaining the Beaufort family interest despite the best efforts of a neighbouring political widow, Lady Berkeley. Given this example, it is perhaps not surprising that Lady Mary Somerset (as she was known until her marriage) went on to be an equally, if not more, political wife and widow in her turn. She was not only political; she was also beautiful—and her combination of looks, charm, and impeccably ladylike political conduct won her the approval of such stern critics of political women as Horace Walpole, Charles Pigott, and Nathaniel Wraxall. For Pigott, she was 'a woman modelled as it were by the graces, with a delicacy and cultivation of mind rarely to be found' (Pigott, 30); whereas, for Wraxall, she was simply 'the most beautiful woman in England' (Wraxall, 2.350). Sir Joshua Reynolds painted her four times. Her intelligence and social poise may have been helped by a tour of the continent with her mother and youngest sister from 1769 to 1774.

When Lady Mary Somerset married on 26 December 1775 Charles *Manners (1754–1787), marquess of Granby, fourth duke of Rutland after 1779, she married into one of

Mary Isabella Manners, duchess of Rutland (1756–1831), by Valentine Green, pubd 1780 (after Sir Joshua Reynolds, 1780)

England's great whig families. They made a striking political couple. Rutland was handsome, rich, extravagant, and a *bon viveur*. He was also an ardent politician, using his family interest to support the king and his ministers, and serving first as a whig MP and subsequently in Lord Shelburne's and William Pitt's governments. His close friendship with Pitt would see him appointed lord privy seal and then lord lieutenant of Ireland (1784–7). The duchess was an ideal political wife. As early as 1780, the first general election after her marriage, and despite being in London, eight months pregnant, she campaigned actively, communicating constantly with her husband and canvassing votes in person and by letter.

By the time of the next general election in 1784, the duchess of Rutland and Mary Amelia Cecil, countess of Salisbury, had emerged as the Pittites's leading political hostesses. Although Pitt's niece, the hoydenish Lady Hester Stanhope, would later criticize the duchess's parties as dull in comparison to those of the most exuberant Pittite hostess, Jane, duchess of Gordon, her invitations were eagerly sought after and her more refined tastes earned much her all-round praise. Indeed, during the 1784 Westminster election, when she was one of the leading female aristocratic canvassers for the government candidates, the Pittite press depicted her as the natural rival—and the

superior in terms of 'proper' female canvassing behaviour—to the Foxites' leading political hostess and canvasser, Georgiana Cavendish, duchess of Devonshire. The two women were only a year apart in age, but their differences in character were reflected in their sharply divergent approaches to the electorate. Even years later, when the duchess was a widow seeking to maintain the Rutland family interest for her son, she preferred giving excellent dinners followed by evening entertainments of plays and/ or cards to the better sort of voters to mixing personally with the lower sort at old-fashioned hard-drinking election treats.

In 1784, Rutland was appointed lord lieutenant of Ireland and the duchess accompanied him to Dublin. A glamorous political couple, they were well suited for this most expensive and status-conscious of political societies. They entertained so continuously, however, that her health suffered and she was forced to leave Ireland to recuperate at Tunbridge Wells and Brighton early in 1787. While she soon recovered, Rutland deteriorated rapidly; he died, aged only thirty-three, on 24 October 1787.

Like her mother a generation earlier, the duchess of Rutland was left to safeguard an extensive political interest in the face of a long minority; her eldest son, John Henry Manners, fifth duke of Rutland, was only nine when his father died. She put her years of political experience and her network of connections to good use. Her correspondence, particularly with Pitt, who was a frequent dinner guest, shows her moving confidently into her new role. She supported candidates, secured votes, and managed men and campaigns. In 1789, for instance, with one of the sitting MPs for Cambridgeshire unlikely to live more than a few days, she entered into negotiations with the Yorkes, the county's other leading political family, to secure a public agreement between the families that would settle the representation for the upcoming by-election and she hoped the subsequent general election. As soon as she had determined upon a candidate, she wrote to Pitt to secure his approval—and, knowing Pitt's tendency to be dilatory, she pointedly reminded him that she needed an immediate answer as she intended to propose the candidate the following morning. She was perfectly aware of the need for decisive action; her only frustration came in trying to persuade Yorke of this:

> I wish Mr. Yorke was a little more decided I am afraid He wants a little spunk upon this occasion; He seems afraid of the Dissenters & twenty other things, which I think we should Triumph over with ease if He would but enter into a Junction of Interests. (PRO, PRO 30/8, vol. 174/2, fol. 233, duchess of Rutland to William Pitt, Albemarle Street, 24 Jan 1789)

Like other landowners nurturing political interests, the duchess of Rutland was also continuously involved in seeking patronage for an assortment of clients in order to pay electoral debts or create electoral obligations. She was well aware of Pitt's famous dislike for patronage and targetted many of her applications to emphasize their political importance. For a Mr Mortlock of Cambridge in 1789, she sought Pitt's assurance that all transactions involving government money would still go through his bank: 'It is very material to me to keep Mr. Mortlock in good Humour at present as an Election draws near' (PRO, PRO 30/8, vol. 174/2, fol. 245v, 4 Nov 1789). Similarly, when seeking patronage for a distant Manners relative in 1792, she not only combined forces with her brother to create a two-pronged attack, but reminded Pitt that granting the request would be in his own political interest. Manners was

> very anxious to unite his Interest to ours in Politicks ... I think he will be a great acquisition both to you & to us, as he is extreemly Rich, & by that means has great Interest both in Leicestershire & Lincolnshire.   (ibid., fols. 251v–252, 14 Nov 1792)

The duchess of Rutland's efforts to preserve the family interest for her son were successful. While she no longer needed to be as politically active once he came of age, she, like a number of other politically active aristocratic widows, remained active in social politics and—albeit more selectly than before—in patronage well into her old age. A consummate female politician of the unreformed political world, she died in London on 2 September 1831, not long before the Reform Act of 1832, having outlived her political rival the duchess of Devonshire by a full quarter of a century.   E. H. CHALUS

Sources GEC, *Peerage*, new edn, 2.53–5; 11.266–70 · Badminton muniments, Badminton, Gloucestershire, FmK 1/2/4, 1/2/7, 1/2/15, 4/3/4 · papers of Pitt the younger, PRO, PRO 30/8 · *The manuscripts of his grace the duke of Rutland*, 4 vols., HMC, 24 (1888–1905), vols. 2–3 · C. Pigott, *The female Jockey Club*, 2nd edn (1794) · N. W. Wraxall, *Posthumous memoirs of his own time*, 2nd edn, 3 vols. (1836) · BL, Althorp papers, Coll. MS, fol. 39 · J. Hartley and others, *History of the Westminster election* (1784) · *The manuscripts of the duke of Beaufort ... the earl of Donoughmore*, HMC, 27 (1891) · *The manuscripts of J. B. Fortescue*, 10 vols., HMC, 30 (1892–1927) · Chatsworth House, Derbyshire, Devonshire MSS, 608A · *Lord Granville Leveson Gower: private correspondence, 1781–1821*, ed. Castalia, Countess Granville [C. R. Leveson-Gower], 2nd edn, 1 (1916) · A. Foreman, *Georgiana: duchess of Devonshire* (1998) · Walpole, *Corr.*, vols. 2, 6, 11–12, 23–5, 29, 32–3, 39 · *Collins peerage of England: genealogical, biographical and historical*, ed. E. Brydges, 9 vols. (1812), vol. 1, pp. 240–41
Archives Badminton House, Gloucestershire, muniments | Belvoir Castle, Leicestershire, Rutland papers · PRO, papers of William Pitt the younger, PRO 30/8
Likenesses V. Green, engraving, pubd 1780 (after J. Reynolds, 1780), NPG [*see illus.*] · mezzotint, 1782 (after unknown artist), NPG · J. Reynolds, portraits · J. Scott, mezzotint (after J. Reynolds), NPG
Wealth at death approx. £4000: will (1831), PRO, PROB 11/1791A, sig. 599

Manners, Sir Robert (*d.* 1354), administrator and landowner, was the son of Sir Robert de Manners, whose family had owned Etal in north Northumberland since at least 1232. He was appointed among the commissioners of truce between England and Scotland in January 1328, probably to represent the interest of the bishop of Durham as lord of Norhamshire and Islandshire, outliers of the regalian liberty of Durham. After the renewal of hostilities he was appointed in 1334 as sheriff of Selkirk and keeper of Selkirk Forest, ceded to Edward III by Edward Balliol as king of Scots. In 1335 and again in 1344 he was appointed commissioner of array in the Glendale ward of

north Northumberland. In 1340 he was MP for Northumberland, in which year he aided Thomas Grey of Heaton and others in stopping a raid of the earl of Sutherland. In 1341 he was allowed to crenellate Etal. In the following year he was appointed as a commissioner of truce and peace with Scotland, and when the Scots invaded England, in alliance with the French, in 1346, he took part in the battle of Nevilles Cross. For his services he received lands in Berrington and Buckton in Northumberland, and two parts of Paxton in Berwickshire. He also acquired lands in Goswick and Kyloe. In 1345 he endowed a chantry in Etal chapel. He died on 28 September 1354, and was buried at Ford church, Northumberland. His inquisition *post mortem* (November 1354) notes that he held Etal as a manor for a half knight's fee, and that its assets included a corn mill, a fulling mill, lime kilns, and mines of coal. He married first Ada (*d.* 1344/5), and second Ellen (*d.* 1362). His heir was his son John, born in 1354.

The second **Sir Robert Manners** (1408–1461) was probably the great-nephew of Sir John Manners and great-great-grandson of the earlier Sir Robert. His father was Sir John Manners of Etal and his mother was Margery, widow of Edward Ilderton. He was a justice of the peace for Norhamshire in 1438, when he succeeded to the family property, was sheriff of Northumberland in 1454, and MP for Northumberland in 1459. He died in 1461. His wife, Joan (*d.* 1488), was sister of Robert, first Baron Ogle (*d.* 1469). There were four sons, including Gilbert, John, and Sir Robert Manners, one of the few substantial supporters of the Yorkist cause in Northumberland, who served as sheriff of that county in 1463 and undersheriff to the earl of Northumberland in 1485. He married Eleanor, daughter of Lord Ros, thereby bringing that title into the Manners family. One of Robert and Eleanor's grandsons was Thomas Manners, created earl of Rutland in 1525.

W. A. J. ARCHBOLD, *rev.* C. M. FRASER

Sources W. P. Hedley, *Northumberland families*, 2, Society of Antiquaries of Newcastle upon Tyne, Record Series (1970), 243–7 · *A history of Northumberland*, Northumberland County History Committee, 15 vols. (1893–1940), vol. 11, pp. 442–50 · PRO, Special Collections, ancient correspondence, SC 1/54 [redated lists and indexes 15 to 1347/8, incorrectly], no. 30 · *Chancery records* · *RotS*, 1.271, 389, 621, 638, 644, 649, 678, 713, 717 · *CIPM*, 10, nos. 203, 235 · C. H. H. Blair, 'Members of parliament for Northumberland, 1327–1399', *Archaeologia Aeliana*, 4th ser., 11 (1934), 21–82, esp. 39–40 · *Report of the Deputy Keeper of the Public Records*, 45 (1884), appx 1, p. 235

Manners, Sir Robert (1408–1461). *See under* Manners, Sir Robert (*d.* 1354).

Manners, Lord Robert (1758–1782), naval officer, was born on 6 February 1758, the third son of John *Manners, marquess of Granby (1721–1770), army officer, and Lady Frances Seymour (1728–1761), daughter of the sixth duke of Somerset and his second wife. Robert Manners, whose paternal grandfather was John, third duke of Rutland, was educated at Eton College (1763–71) before entering the navy. An ambitious young man from one of England's most prominent families, he expected his promotion in the navy to be inevitable and swift. This posed problems for the lord of the Admiralty, Lord Sandwich, who was criticized for resisting Manners's promotion to lieutenant until he had served the regulation six years. Manners was finally promoted to this rank on 13 May 1778 in the *Ocean* in which he was present in the action off Ushant on 27 July. On 17 September he was moved to the *Victory*, flagship of Admiral Augustus Keppel, and on 15 July 1779 into the *Alcide*, one of the ships that went out to Gibraltar with Admiral George Rodney and defeated the Spanish squadron off Cape St Vincent.

Soon after his promotion to lieutenant Manners made clear his desire for further advancement. Sandwich again resisted, and was reminded by his colleague Lord Mansfield how 'He [Manners] & the whole family will feel it as a personal injury' if these ambitions were not realized. Sandwich was aware that the issue could bring renewed attacks on him and on Lord North's government. On 8 December 1779 he wrote to Admiral Rodney concerning Manners:

> There is another young man of fashion now in your squadron concerning whom I am tormented to death. I cannot do anything for him at home; therefore, if you could contrive while he remains with you, by some means or other, to give him rank, you will infinitely oblige me. (Mundy, 1.207)

Rodney, who had fewer qualms about promoting Manners, took the first opportunity (17 January 1780) to advance him to captain of the *Resolution*, under Sir Challoner Ogle, whom he constituted a commodore. The *Resolution* returned to England with Rear-Admiral Robert Digby, and was shortly afterwards sent out to North America with Rear-Admiral Thomas Graves. When Rodney returned to the West Indies after his visit to the coast of North America in the summer of 1780 he took the *Resolution* with him, shortly after which Ogle, having been promoted rear-admiral, went home, leaving Manners in command of the ship. In March of that year he had also been elected in his absence MP for Cambridgeshire; he was never to take up the seat.

In 1781 the *Resolution* went north with Sir Samuel Hood, and took part in the action off Cape Henry on 5 September. She was afterwards with Hood at St Kitts in January 1782, and in the battle of the Saints (12 April 1782), was in the centre of the line, the third ship astern of the *Formidable*. In the action Manners received several severe wounds, in addition to having one leg shot off. From the strength of his constitution hopes were entertained of his recovery. He was put on board the frigate *Andromache* for a passage to England, but some days later tetanus set in, from which he died, probably at sea in the Caribbean, on 23 April. Although his early career had been marked by ambition galvanized by social status Manners was by all accounts a brave, talented, and well-respected young officer at his death.

J. K. Laughton, *rev.* Christopher Doorne

Sources J. Brooke, 'Manners, Robert', HoP, *Commons, 1754–90* · R. Beatson, *Naval and military memoirs of Great Britain*, 2nd edn, 5 (1804) · commission and warrant books, Jan 1774–Dec 1782, PRO, ADM 6/21, 22 · G. B. Mundy, *The life and correspondence of the late Admiral Lord Rodney*, 2 vols. (1830) · *Letters written by Sir Samuel Hood*, ed. D. Hannay, Navy RS, 3 (1895) · *The private papers of John, earl of Sandwich*, ed. G. R. Barnes and J. H. Owen, 4 vols., Navy RS, 69, 71, 75, 78 (1932–8) · W. L. Clowes, *The Royal Navy: a history from the earliest times to the present*, 7 vols. (1897–1903); repr. (1996–7) · N. A. M. Rodger, *The insatiable earl: a life of John Montagu, fourth earl of Sandwich* (1993) · GEC, *Peerage* · G. Blane, *Observations on the diseases incident to seamen* (1785)

Archives NRA, priv. coll., corresp.

Likenesses J. Reynolds, oils, *c.*1781, Belvoir Castle, Leicestershire · J. Nollekens, marble bust, *c.*1782–1784, Belvoir Castle, Leicestershire · T. Hudson, oils (as a child), Winton House, Lothian region · P. C., miniature, Winton House, Lothian region · A. N. Sanders, mezzotint (after T. Gainsborough), BM · T. Stothard, oils, Belvoir Castle, Leicestershire · prints, NPG

Manners, Roger (*c.*1536–1607), courtier and landowner, was the third son of Thomas *Manners, first earl of Rutland and thirteenth Baron Ros (*c.*1497–1543), soldier, administrator, and his second wife, Eleanor (*d.* 1551), daughter of Sir William Paston of Paston, Norfolk. He went to Corpus Christi College, Cambridge, in 1550 and was sent to sea in 1554 and 1555, promising to apply himself to learning maritime skills. He served in the army at St Quentin in Aisne in 1557 and Coquet in Brittany. Fighting did not suit him. He later wrote, 'Hunting and hawking is good sport but deling in warlyek causes is trublesom' (*Rutland MSS*, 1.182). His position as esquire of the body to Mary I and Elizabeth I was probably due to his family's long service to the Tudors. He seems to have been a man who made and kept friends as he was little inclined to faction, widely connected, and trusted. Many, including those in strife with his family, endorsed the praise of his brother, Sir Thomas Manners: 'so honest a man … and so wise and kind a man [with] most natural and loyal love to the head of his house' (ibid., 1.214). He stressed to his niece Bridget Manners when she entered Elizabeth's service as a maid of honour in 1589 that the courtier's role was to be 'diligent, secret and faithful and to be no meddler in the cause of others' (HoP, *Commons, 1558–1603*, 3.9).

Although Manners was MP for Grantham in 1563 and constable of Nottingham Castle during the minority of his nephew Edward *Manners, third earl of Rutland, he had no ambitions beyond the court. Perhaps he was, as he constantly said, lazy. When parliament was in session he evidently attended only to keep an eye on Rutland's interests. Although he had good relations with many women, in 1575 was thought to be 'wooing' and in 1582 to be interested in Elizabeth Howard, he never married, assisting instead with the education of various wards who were committed to him and some of his nephews and nieces, as well as his spendthrift brother Thomas Manners. His position enabled him to obtain various crown grants and leases from about 1567 on and by careful management, lending, and borrowing, he amassed a comfortable estate.

Manners was always in high favour with Elizabeth, on good terms with the Cecils and Robert Dudley, earl of Leicester, and the linchpin of the Manners family's relations with the court and central government, the conduit for public and private news and advice. More clandestinely, he was linked to Sir Francis Walsingham, principal secretary, and Sir Thomas Heneage, but how far that made him a part of the spy network is unclear. He was a strongly committed protestant by the 1570s who found sincere comfort in its faith. This did not prevent his being a cynic where court and society were concerned, and increasingly often he wrote of his wish to 'leave the Court to younger folk and learn to keep your plough' (*Rutland MSS*, 1.94). From the mid-1570s he spent several months a year at his country estate at Uffington, Rutland, where he offered unstinting hospitality to family and friends and enjoyed hunting and hawking.

Although in 1583 he was permitted to withdraw from the routine service of an esquire of the body to act as a supernumerary, writing: 'I shall tak my ese and wayt when I list or when her Majestie herself shall command me' (*Rutland MSS*, 1.151), Manners remained in frequent attendance at court until Elizabeth's death, interceding remarkably successfully for family and friends and easing the approach to court of prominent men such as Gilbert Talbot, seventh earl of Shrewsbury, when they were out of favour. He was able to propitiate Elizabeth for friends and family. He defended his friends vocally when he felt they had been wronged but remained aloof from the problems following the deaths of the third earl in 1587 and John Manners, fourth earl of Rutland, in 1588. Manners was critical of Roger *Manners, fifth earl of Rutland, writing: 'They say it is a thankles office to tell youth of their faultes yet is it the office of there best frendes' (ibid., 1.296).

As the political situation became more difficult because of court faction during the 1590s, Manners's letters became cryptic, advising conversation with trusted confidants in his garden, where the servants could not hear. He felt 'it is not good to write of these perylus causes' (*Rutland MSS*, 1.204). He felt relatively secure as long as he remained on good terms with the queen, helped by his access as a courtier, and as long as he continued to be regarded by the government as completely loyal. Rutland's involvement in the rebellion of Robert Devereux, earl of Essex, in 1601 appalled him. Elizabeth sent Sir John Stanhope to comfort him and by using all the credit he had with his friends, including Sir Robert Cecil, principal secretary, he was able to prevent Rutland's execution for treason. Instead, the earl was fined £30,000. In 1603 when Elizabeth was dying Manners would not involve himself in any intrigue regarding the succession, writing 'I will not go about to make kings, nor seek to pull down any; only will obey such as be chosen and crowned' (ibid., 1.387).

Manners lived in retirement in London under James I, becoming steadily more frail, his condition aggravated by jaundice, so that he was unable to ride. He died on 11 December 1607 and was buried with little pomp in Uffington church in a tomb he had had erected for himself and his long-deceased younger brother Oliver Manners. He had given a dowry to at least one niece in his lifetime, and his property was left so that dowries could be provided for the rest and lands for his nephews. He gave generously to the building and upkeep of Corpus Christi College, Cambridge. Perhaps his greatest legacy was the collection of letters he left, which give wonderful insights into the Elizabethan court. SYBIL M. JACK

Sources L. C. John, 'Roger Manners, Elizabethan courtier', *Huntington Library Quarterly*, 12 (1948–9), 57–84 • *The manuscripts of his grace the duke of Rutland*, 4 vols., HMC, 24 (1888–1905), vols. 1–2, 4 • E. Lodge, *Illustrations of British history, biography, and manners*, 2nd edn, 3 vols. (1838) • C. Jamison, G. R. Batho, and E. G. W. Bill, eds., *A calendar of the Shrewsbury and Talbot papers in Lambeth Palace Library and the College of Arms*, 2 vols., HMC, JP 6–7 (1966–71) • J. Nichols, *The history and antiquities of the county of Leicester*, 2/1 (1795), 100–03 • HoP, *Commons, 1558–1603*, 3.8–9 • PRO, Chancery, inquisitions post mortem, series 2, and other inquisitions, Henry VII to Charles I, C142/303/137; C142/304/19; C142/303/146 • *CPR, 1566–9*, no. 425; 1569–72, nos. 82, 3281
Archives priv. coll.
Wealth at death approx. £200: inquisition post mortem

Manners, Roger, fifth earl of Rutland (1576–1612), nobleman, was born on 6 October 1576 at Kirk Deighton, Yorkshire, where he was baptized on 19 November. He was the eldest surviving son of John Manners, fourth earl of Rutland (*d*. 1588), and his wife, Elizabeth (*d*. 1595), fourth daughter of Francis Charleton of Apley Castle, Shropshire, and nephew of Edward *Manners, third earl of Rutland. Roger was one of a large family and his mother was again pregnant at the time of her husband's death on 24 February 1588. Manners was only eleven when he became fifth earl of Rutland. The short time which had elapsed since the death of the third earl meant that his inheritance was encumbered by the conflicting and burdensome demands of two wills and jointures for two dowager countesses. Rutland's wardship was promised to the earl of Leicester, but the latter's sudden death in September 1588 meant that, like his cousin Elizabeth Manners, daughter of the third earl and heir to his barony of Ros, Rutland became a ward of Lord Burghley. The marriage of Lady Ros to Burghley's grandson in 1589 cemented ties between the Manners and Cecil families, but also created long-lasting tensions over property and the Ros barony. Rutland was educated at Cambridge, arriving at Queens' College to study with the vice-president, John Jegon, in late 1587. He followed Jegon to Corpus Christi College in 1590. He was created MA in February 1595, as part of a grand spectacle at Cambridge which was stage-managed by Robert Devereux, second earl of Essex, the queen's favourite and the late Leicester's stepson. Rutland soon became an adherent of Essex.

Although he had received approval from the queen to travel on the continent in December 1594, Rutland's plans were disrupted by the death of his mother in April 1595 and he did not leave until October 1595. Essex summoned his own cousin, Robert Vernon, from Oxford to accompany Rutland on the initial stages of his journey. Essex also wrote Rutland at least three private letters of travel advice, of which only the third (dated 16 October 1595) is known to survive. These provided the inspiration for a quite separate document which was framed as a letter of travel advice from Essex to Rutland but intended for public circulation, and which may have been written by Essex's secretariat or by Francis Bacon. It was designed as political propaganda to demonstrate Essex's statesman-like qualities and proved remarkably successful. Rutland toured through the Low Countries, Germany, and Switzerland. He matriculated at Padua University in 1596, but fell dangerously ill there in July. The writer Robert Dallington was among his servants by this time. Rutland travelled in France during 1597, before rushing back to Plymouth to join Essex's Azores expedition in July. He returned from that unhappy voyage in November, and was admitted to Gray's Inn on 2 February 1598. He married Essex's stepdaughter, Elizabeth Sidney (1585?–1612), the only child of Sir Philip Sidney, in early 1599. Shortly afterwards he went to join Essex's expedition in Ireland, even though the queen had repeatedly denied him permission to go. Rutland served as an infantry officer but received a peremptory summons from Elizabeth to return to England. Before his return he was knighted by Essex at Cahir Castle on 30 May. Claiming ill health and aided by the intercession of friends such as Sir Robert Cecil, he narrowly avoided imprisonment for his defiance of the queen.

In July 1600 Rutland again went abroad in search of military action, spending several months in the Low Countries before returning to London in October. He was soon caught up in the paranoia of Essex and his few remaining followers. Although he was not involved in the planning for an Essexian coup Rutland probably knew more about the plans of the earl and his partisans than he later admitted. On 8 February 1601, allegedly in the belief that Essex was about to be murdered, he joined the earl's disastrous attempt to secure armed support in London. Two of his younger brothers, Francis *Manners (1578–1632) and Sir George Manners, also participated. Rutland was arrested and imprisoned in the Tower. He was spared indictment but fined £30,000, which was reduced to £20,000 on 10 June. Released from the Tower on 8 August, he was subsequently confined to the house of his great-uncle Roger *Manners at Uffington, Lincolnshire, until January 1602. By the time of Elizabeth's death in March 1603, Rutland was on the point of full rehabilitation, but the accession of James I further boosted his fortunes. A highly successful visit by James to the earl's seat, Belvoir Castle, on 22–23 April secured Rutland the new king's favour. His fine (still largely unpaid) was remitted and in June–August 1603 he travelled to Denmark to bestow the Garter upon Christian IV and attend the baptism of the latter's son on James's behalf. Soon after his return he was made lord lieutenant of Lincolnshire and steward of Queen Anne's manor of Grantham. These posts complemented various other local offices (especially in Nottinghamshire) which Rutland had already received from Elizabeth and James and reinforced his status as a magnate in the east midlands.

Although he participated in the entertainments for the visiting Christian IV in 1606 and the creation of Henry as prince of Wales in 1610, Rutland spent an increasing amount of his time on his country estates. His health may have been weak and he may also have been sensitive to comment about his infertility (the result of disease contracted during his continental tour, according to Ben Jonson; Herford and Simpson, 1.138). Rutland's marriage was also increasingly strained. Jonson observed that the countess lived as 'a widow'd wife', stirring an intense but apparently unrequited passion in Sir Thomas Overbury (ibid., 8.224–5; 11.88). In an elegy written upon her death, Francis Beaumont claimed that 'the chief blessing of women, marriage, was to thee nought but a sacrament of misery' (Dyce, 11.508). Rutland failed to attend parliament in 1610 and was so sick by May 1612 that he moved to Cambridge for specialist treatment. After suffering what seems to have been one or more strokes during May and June, he died in Cambridge on 26 June 1612. He was buried beside previous earls of Rutland at Bottesford, Leicestershire, on 22 July. He was succeeded as earl of Rutland by his brother Sir Francis Manners. Rutland's widow died within a fortnight of her husband's funeral, occasioning wild rumours that she had been poisoned by medicine supplied by Sir Walter Ralegh. Pointedly, she chose to be buried privately at St Paul's near her father rather than accept burial with her husband at Bottesford.

PAUL E. J. HAMMER

Sources *The manuscripts of his grace the duke of Rutland*, 4 vols., HMC, 24 (1888–1905) · *Calendar of the manuscripts of the most hon. the marquis of Salisbury*, 24 vols., HMC, 9 (1883–1976) · PRO, state papers domestic, Elizabeth I and James I, SP 12, 14 · LPL, Anthony Bacon papers, MSS 647–662 · LPL, Talbot papers, MSS 3192–3206 · *The letters of John Chamberlain*, ed. N. E. McClure, 2 vols. (1939) · GEC, *Peerage*, new edn · L. Stone, *Family and fortune: studies in aristocratic finance in the sixteenth and seventeenth centuries* (1973) · P. E. J. Hammer, *The polarisation of Elizabethan politics: the political career of Robert Devereux, 2nd earl of Essex, 1585–1597* (1999) · *Report on the manuscripts of the marquis of Downshire*, 6 vols. in 7, HMC, 75 (1924–95), vol. 2 · *Report on the manuscripts of Lord De L'Isle and Dudley*, 6 vols., HMC, 77 (1925–66) · J. Nichols, *The progresses, processions, and magnificent festivities of King James I, his royal consort, family and court*, 4 vols. (1828); facs. edn (New York, 1969) · J. Nichols, *The history and antiquities of the county of Leicester*, 4 vols. (1795–1815) · Venn, *Alum. Cant.* · will, PRO, PROB 11/120, fols. 36r–37r · Ben Jonson, ed. C. H. Herford, P. Simpson, and E. M. Simpson, 11 vols. (1925–52) · T. Mowle, *Elizabethan and Jacobean style* (1993) · R. Tresswell and A. Vincent, *The visitation of Shropshire, taken in the year 1623*, ed. G. Grazebrook and J. P. Rylands, 1, Harleian Society, 28 (1889) · J. Foster, *The register of admissions to Gray's Inn, 1521–1889, together with the register of marriages in Gray's Inn chapel, 1695–1754* (privately printed, London, 1889), vol. 1 · W. A. Shaw, *The knights of England*, 2 (1906) · Wood, *Ath. Oxon.: Fasti* (1815) · J. Woolfson, *Padua and the Tudors* (Toronto, 1998) · W. B. Bannerman, ed., *The registers of St Olave, Hart Street, London, 1563–1700*, Harleian Society, register section, 46 (1916) · *The diary of John Manningham of the Middle Temple, 1602–1603*, ed. R. P. Sorlien (Hanover, NH, 1976) · A. Dyce, ed., *The works of Beaumont and Fletcher*, 11 vols. (1843–6), vol. 11

Archives Belvoir Castle, Leicestershire | Hatfield House, Hertfordshire, Cecil papers · LPL, Talbot papers, MSS 3192–3206 · PRO, state papers, 12 and 14

Likenesses N. Johnson, double portrait, recumbent alabaster effigy on funeral monument, c.1612 (with wife), church of St Mary the Virgin, Bottesford, Leicestershire; repro. in T. Mowle, *Elizabethan and Jacobean style* (1993) · oils, Belvoir Castle, Leicestershire

Wealth at death £4893 p.a.; bequests of £4600; annuities approx. £180 p.a.: will, PRO, PROB 11/120, fols. 36r–37r; Stone, *Family and fortune*, p. 206

Manners, Thomas, first earl of Rutland (c.1497–1543), courtier and soldier, was the eldest son of Sir George Manners (b. in or before 1470, d. 1513) of Belvoir, Leicestershire, and his wife, Anne (1476–1526), daughter of Sir Thomas St Leger and Anne, sister of Edward IV. Sir George inherited the barony of Ros following the deaths of his maternal uncle Edmund Roos, tenth Baron Ros (d. 1508), and his maternal aunt Isabel, Lady Lovell (d. 1508/9) (both children of Thomas Ros, ninth Baron Ros of Helmsley). Owing to Edmund Roos's incapacity, since 1486 the barony's estates had been administered by Isabel's husband, Sir Thomas Lovell (c.1449–1524), and he was still in control in 1513 when Sir George died on 27 October or 4 November, either in France or, more probably, having just arrived back in England. Thomas Manners, who succeeded as twelfth baron, was almost certainly under seventeen years old when his father made his will on 26 October, while the inquisition post mortem of 4 April 1514 put his age at sixteen or more. His wardship, and that of his siblings, was granted to Lovell. He had already married (the settlement was dated 21 February 1513) Lovell's niece Elizabeth, daughter of Sir Robert Lovell.

Like his father, Ros went on the French expedition of 1513. He was summoned to the parliament that first met on 5 February 1515, though on the evidence above he should have been too young. His Plantagenet blood, Ros inheritance, and connection with Lovell, who held among other offices the treasurership of the royal household, advanced his career greatly. From early in Henry VIII's reign he was part of the king's household; a jouster, he formed long-standing friendships with Henry and his intimates, including Charles Brandon, later duke of Suffolk. Between about 1514 and 1518 Ros and his brothers were in attendance at various times on Mary Tudor, the French queen. On 7 July 1519 Lovell and Ros were jointly granted the offices of constable of Nottingham Castle and keeper of Sherwood Forest. Ros was at the Field of Cloth of Gold in June 1520 and at Henry VIII's meeting with Emperor Charles V in July. He was on the panel of peers in four out of six treason trials in the House of Lords, including that of the duke of Buckingham. In December 1521 he was the king's cup-bearer and in May 1522 he was deputed to meet Charles V at Dover. At an unknown date his first wife died; some time in the early 1520s he married Eleanor (d. 1551), daughter of Sir William *Paston (1479?–1554), an occasional attender at court and executor for Lovell following the latter's death on 25 May 1524. On 16 July that year Ros had livery of the rump of the Ros estates which had remained in Lovell's hands.

By this time, although his most significant landed interest lay in Leicestershire, Ros's ancestral properties in Northumberland and Yorkshire had brought him office in the north. In 1522 he was made steward of Pickering in north Yorkshire. Early that year he was given a commission of array and in April was appointed warden of the east and middle marches on the Scottish border, but his lack of personal knowledge of the area proved a handicap, and in October the local gentry's reluctance to participate in the expedition against the Scots led him to seek release from the wardenship. This was granted in October, and did his career no lasting damage. From 1524 to 1526 he was on twelve commissions of the peace, including those for Leicestershire, Nottinghamshire, Rutland, and all three ridings of Yorkshire. After initial election on 24 April, he was installed as a knight of the Garter on 25 June 1525,

having been created a week earlier earl of Rutland; the king acknowledged his Plantagenet descent in the arms granted with the title. By 1528 he had begun rebuilding Belvoir Castle; in the meantime he resided at Elsinges Manor, Enfield, Middlesex, or, when in London, at Holywell, Shoreditch, or at court.

Although he initially appeared hesitant, Rutland supported Henry VIII's religious policies. In 1533 he was verbally attacked by Thomas Boleyn, earl of Wiltshire, for suggesting that the king's marriage to his daughter Anne was a spiritual matter and could not be settled in parliament. However, Rutland was at Anne's coronation as her carver. In 1535 he was involved on behalf of the crown in the notorious trial of the Charterhouse monks. In the rebellions of 1536 he was charged with the defence of Nottingham Castle. Given a joint command with the earls of Huntingdon and Shrewsbury, he marched promptly to Nottingham and then to Newark, Southwell, and Doncaster. His stewardship of many monasteries, and his ancestral claims to the foundation of certain houses, combined with his proven loyalty to work to his advantage in the wake of the dissolution. By a grant of March 1539, in return for selling to the king land including Elsinges, he received at least fourteen manors (mostly in Leicestershire) and several abbeys, including Rievaulx and Beverley, Yorkshire, and Belvoir Priory and Croxton, Leicestershire. Croxton soon became his main provincial residence.

In July 1536 Rutland cemented his ties to other noble families with a triple wedding at Holywell, in which his eldest son Henry *Manners (1526–1563) and daughter Lady Anne (d. in or after 1549) married Lady Margaret Neville and Henry Neville, Lord Neville (1524/5–1564), children of Ralph Neville, fourth earl of Westmorland, and Lady Dorothy Neville married John de Vere, heir of the earl of Oxford. Rutland was lord chamberlain to Jane Seymour, and, though illness kept him from court for a significant period in spring 1537, he was in attendance when she died in October. He was also chamberlain to Anne of Cleves and Katherine Howard. Lady Rutland served in the privy chambers of the first two queens and possibly of the third. Her position and perceived good nature made her a valuable contact at court for those outside it, such as the governor of Calais, Arthur Plantagenet, Viscount Lisle, and his wife, Honor, whose daughters she supervised and assisted. In 1540 Lady Rutland testified against Queen Anne that the royal marriage had not been consummated. In response to the latter's naïve assertion that the king's bedchamber performances were proof of her loss of virginity, the countess responded, 'Madam, there must be more than this, or it will be long or we have a duke of York, which al this realm most desireth' (Strype). Following the subsequent fall of Thomas Cromwell, Rutland acquired his former offices of warden of the forests beyond the Trent and steward of Halifax manor, Yorkshire.

Having refused reappointment to the east and middle marches in 1537, five years later Rutland became constable of Nottingham Castle and then returned to the borders on 9 August 1542 as warden of all three marches. He was soon reassigned to lead the rearguard of an army prepared to invade Scotland in October. Difficulty in finding a replacement led to his reappointment as warden-general on 2 November, but he was quickly recalled owing to illness. He had made his will on 16 August, but lingered well into the following year, dying at Belvoir Castle on 20 September 1543. He was buried in Bottesford church, Leicestershire, where a dignified alabaster tomb was erected. His widow, who died at Holywell in 1551, was buried at St Leonard, Shoreditch. Rutland died a rich man, owning about 100 manors and with an annual income of £2399, according to 1542 receivers' accounts. He brought the Manners family to new heights, ensuring for the dynasty a national presence for centuries to come.

M. M. NORRIS

Sources PRO, SP 1 and SP 3 · M. M. Norris, 'The first and second earls of Rutland and their part in the central and local politics of mid-Tudor England', PhD diss., U. Edin., 1995 · GEC, *Peerage* · J. Strype, *Ecclesiastical memorials*, 3 vols. (1822), 1/2.452–62 · BL, Add. MS 32647 · PRO, E 101/56 (25) m.31 · PRO, PROB 11/17; PROB 11/30 · BL, Lansdowne MS 160, fol. 310 · Bodl. Oxf., MS Ashmole 837, fol. 147 · PRO, DURH 3/3, no. 27; 3/173, nos. 17, 45 · accounts and grants, Belvoir Castle, Leicestershire, BCA 301; BC6, nos. 30, 31, 32, 49, 51 · *LP Henry VIII* · H. Miller, *Henry VIII and the English nobility* (1986) · S. J. Gunn, *Charles Brandon, duke of Suffolk, c.1484–1545* (1988) · M. St C. Byrne, ed., *The Lisle letters*, 6 vols. (1981), esp. vol. 4 · monument, Bottesford church, Leicestershire
Archives Belvoir Castle, Leicestershire, Belvoir Castle MSS | BL, Add. MSS · Coll. Arms, Garter roll muniment, Roll 6/41 · Lincs. Arch., city council minutes · PRO, state papers, grants, letters, etc.
Likenesses oils, 16th cent., Belvoir Castle, Leicestershire · R. Parker, alabaster tomb effigy, c.1543, St Mary's Church, Bottesford, Leicestershire
Wealth at death £2399 p.a. in 1542, excl. £676 arrears: receivers' accounts, Belvoir Castle Accounts, 301, Belvoir Castle, Leicestershire; will, 26 Oct 1513, PRO, PROB 11/17

Manners [*née* Lindsay], (**Marion Margaret**) **Violet**, duchess of Rutland (1856–1937), artist, was born on 7 March 1856, the second daughter of Charles Hugh Lindsay (1816–1889), son of the twenty-fourth earl of Crawford, soldier and courtier, and Emilia Anne Browne (d. 1873), the daughter of the dean of Lismore. Two of her four brothers and both of her sisters died in infancy or childhood. She was educated privately. Her early interest in art was fostered by her family—the aesthete Sir Coutts Lindsay was a distant cousin—and by a lengthy visit to Italy, although she had no formal training. Sir Coutts opened his Grosvenor Gallery in 1877, and Violet Lindsay was among the early exhibitors of both drawings and sculptures. Her many drawings of the men and women of her social circle, in silver-point or pencil, constituted her most successful work, and she exhibited extensively throughout her life at all the major British galleries (including the Fine Art Society, the Royal Academy, and the New Gallery) and in France and the United States. 'Her style', commented a reviewer of an exhibition of her drawings at the Brook Street Art Galleries, London, in 1925, 'is particularly suited to the interpretation of feminine beauty and elegance, but she usually achieves considerable success in her delineations of men' (*The Connoisseur*, 188). A selection of her

portraits was published in 1900 as *Portraits of Men and Women*.

On 25 November 1882 Violet Lindsay married, at St George's, Hanover Square, London, Henry John Brinsley Manners (1852–1925), who in 1888 became marquess of Granby, and in 1906 succeeded his father as eighth duke of Rutland. Manners, who was conventionally handsome, politically Conservative, and aristocratically philistine, had little in common with his radiant, bohemian wife. Having provided her husband with a daughter and two sons to ensure the legitimate succession of the peerage, Violet proceeded to amuse herself without him: her second daughter, Violet (Letty), was apparently fathered by Disraeli's former private secretary, Montague *Corry, Baron Rowton (1838–1903), and the third, Diana, by Harry Cust [*see* Cust, Henry John Cockayne (1861–1917)]. Socially, Lady Granby (as she became in 1888, the year of her liaison with Rowton) moved in very different circles from those of her husband, whose tastes favoured the hunting field and the chorus line at the theatre. She was one of the central figures of the Souls, the group of aristocratic friends which formed around A. J. Balfour and the Tennant sisters in the last decades of the nineteenth century. The Souls prided themselves on their intellectual interests, their avant-garde artistic taste, and their cultural sophistication, and Violet Granby, as the most talented practical artist among them, enjoyed special status. Her beauty, captured in portraits by many hands, including those of G. F. Watts, J. J. Shannon, and her own, was of the type most admired by the Souls. Her auburn hair, pale complexion, hooded eyes, and very slim figure were invariably set off by her Aesthetic-style clothes of faded colours and soft drapings: Mrs Patrick Campbell once described her as 'the most beautiful thing I ever saw' (Lambert, 79).

The death of her eldest son, Lord Haddon, in 1894 at the age of nine, devastated Violet Granby, who poured all her grief into sculpting his tomb. She considered the plaster of his recumbent figure on an elaborate base decorated with relief portraits of her family to be her finest work, and kept it in her London house until a month before her death in 1937 it was accepted by the Tate Gallery. Lady Granby (who became duchess of Rutland in 1906) was entirely serious about her art, considering herself a professional, but her reputation undoubtedly suffered because of her rank. At a time when few women were able to make names for themselves as artists, she laboured under the dual handicap of gender and a title: if women could not aspire to 'genius', how much less so could a woman who, because of her social position, was inevitably viewed as a dilettante.

The duchess of Rutland's other passion was for the theatre. Among her closest friends were the actor–manager Sir Herbert Beerbohm Tree and his wife and three daughters, and she encouraged her own daughters to take walk-on parts in his productions. Entirely at home with actors and in the theatre, Violet Rutland pushed the boundaries of acceptable bohemianism, even among the Souls. Her unconventionality was mirrored by that of her youngest daughter, leader of the younger generation of Souls who styled themselves the Corrupt Coterie; she eventually married to become Lady Diana *Cooper.

The duchess was spared some of the tragedy of the First World War which decimated the ranks of the children of the Souls: her only surviving son was kept away from the fighting front, married into another Souls family, and lived. But her second daughter, Letty, lost her husband, Lord Elcho, in the Egyptian campaign of 1916, while Diana Manners saw most of her friends and suitors killed on the western front. The duchess converted 16 Arlington Street into a hospital for the duration of the war. After the death of her husband in 1925, she sold the Arlington Street house and moved to 34 Chapel Street, Belgrave Square, London, where she had a new studio built and continued to work. She exhibited throughout the 1920s and 1930s, holding her last exhibition in November 1937. She retained the vestiges of her looks, as Chips Channon observed at a ball at Belvoir, Leicestershire, in 1935: 'I thought that old Violet Duchess looked the best, tired, eighty, and in white; she was a romantic, rather triste figure in a castle where she had reigned so long' (Abdy and Gere, 53). Violet Rutland died at her Chapel Street home on 22 December 1937 following an operation, and was buried at Belvoir, Leicestershire.   K. D. REYNOLDS

Sources A. Lambert, *Unquiet Souls: the Indian summer of the British aristocracy, 1880–1918* (1984) · J. Abdy and C. Gere, *The Souls* (1984) · 'The duchess of Rutland's exhibition', *The Connoisseur*, 72 (1925), 188 · *Apollo*, 18 (1933), 40–41 · GEC, *Peerage* · Burke, *Peerage* · d. cert. · Wood, *Vic. painters*, 2nd edn · J. Johnson and A. Greutzner, eds., *The dictionary of British artists, 1880–1940* (1976), vol. 5 of *Dictionary of British art*; repr. (1994)
Likenesses G. F. Watts, oils, c.1879, repro. in Abdy and Gere, *The Souls* · H. S. Mendelssohn, photograph, 1892, NPG [*see illus.*] · M. M. V. Manners, self-portrait, repro. in, *Portraits of men and women* (1900) · J. J. Shannon, oils, Belvoir Castle, Leicestershire? · photographs, repro. in Abdy and Gere, *The Souls*, 48–53 · photographs, repro. in Lambert, *Unquiet souls*, 136ff.
Wealth at death £14,752 16s.: resworn probate, 14 Feb 1938, *CGPLA Eng. & Wales*

Mannheim, Hermann (1889–1974), criminologist, was born in Berlin on 26 October 1889, the only child of Wilhelm Mannheim and his wife, Clara Marcuse. He came from a well-to-do background: his father represented a German firm in the Baltic seaport of Libau, where he was also vice-president of the chamber of commerce. After tuition at home and at a classical *Gymnasium* at Tilsit in East Prussia, Mannheim took up, at the age of eighteen, the study of law and political science at the universities of Munich, Freiburg, Strasbourg, and Königsberg. By 1913 he had obtained the degree of doctor of laws. In the First World War he served in the German artillery in Russia and in France; towards the end he was appointed judge of a court martial. By 1932 he had become a judge of the Kammergericht in Berlin (the highest court for the whole of Prussia) as well as professor extraordinarius of the prestigious law faculty of the University of Berlin. He had to his credit many publications and was held in high esteem in governmental, judicial, and academic circles. He was barely forty-five years old.

The advent of the Nazi regime shattered this honourable and substantial achievement. Mannheim was forced to relinquish his professorship. Aware where all this would end he also retired from the bench, and in January 1934 this proud man moved to London to start life afresh. He became a naturalized British subject in 1940. Inevitably, the process of readjustment could not but be painful and tortuous. Yet, his capacity to face this new challenge

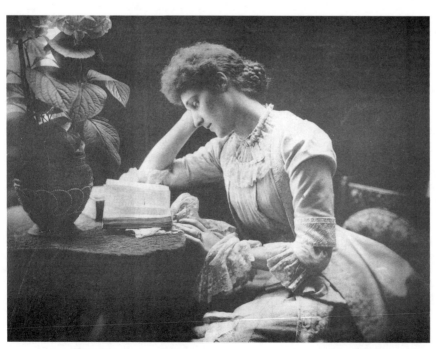

(Marion Margaret) Violet Manners, duchess of Rutland (1856–1937), by Hayman Selig Mendelssohn, 1892

was truly impressive. In this his wife, Mona Mark, whom he married in 1919, proved a gallant companion; they had no children. He switched the focus of his interest from criminal law and procedure to criminology and penal policy, and considerably improved his command of English. The London School of Economics (LSE), with its rich and adventurous tradition in social sciences, was the natural intellectual home for him. In 1935 he was appointed an honorary part-time lecturer in criminology. A year later he received the award of the Leon fellowship. In 1944 he became a permanent full-time lecturer and two years later the reader in criminology—the first post of its kind in Great Britain. He retired in 1955. He was a dedicated and enthusiastic teacher.

Between 1939 and 1965 Mannheim produced eight publications either as the sole author, co-author, or editor. In addition he wrote many articles, notes, and reviews: in the *British Journal of Criminology* alone there were seventy pieces. His most thought-provoking, original, and enduring books are: *The Dilemma of Penal Reform* (1939), in which he traced the implications of Jeremy Bentham's famous principle of 'lesser eligibility' throughout the penological spectrum; *Criminal Justice and Social Reconstruction* (1946; repr. 1949), which is rightly recognized as his most influential and widely read work; and *Prediction Methods in Relation to Borstal Training* (with Leslie T. Wilkins, 1955), the first authoritative study of this kind in England. *Social Aspects of Crime in England between the Wars* (1940) was too ambitious and turned out to be rather uneven but it contained many useful hints for future researches into the environmental contents of crime. *Group Problems in Crime and Punishment* (1955) was largely a collection of his major articles, and still repays rereading. But his three other books (*War and Crime*, 1941; *Young Offenders*, with A. M. Carr-Saunders and E. C. Rhodes, 1942; and *Juvenile Delinquency in an English Middletown*, 1948), though informative at the time of their appearance, were rather mechanical and pedestrian. *Pioneers in Criminology*, which he edited (1st edn, 1960; 2nd edn, 1972), was a splendid pedagogical tool. *Comparative Criminology* (2 vols., 1965) failed to become the *magnum opus*, although it was well received, especially on the continent of Europe. An Italian translation appeared in 1972, a German in 1974. The treatise was confined to the strictly criminological aspect of the subject. It appeared at a time when criminological theory was changing direction and seemed in Britain and the United States already old-fashioned.

Mannheim's intellectual vitality was remarkable: as late as 1975 there appeared (posthumously) his massive comparative study of recidivism 'Rückfall und Prognose' in the new edition of the *Handwörterbuch der Kriminologie* (Berlin, 1975, 38–93). He greatly helped the Institute for the Study and Treatment of Delinquency; he was the founding editor of the *British Journal of Delinquency* (later *British Journal of Criminology*); he helped launch the International Library of Criminology and the British Society of Criminology. For twenty-five years he was closely associated with the Howard League for Penal Reform. He played

a fruitful part in the work of the International Society of Criminology.

It is to the credit of the Federal Republic of Germany that he was appointed in 1952 to the rank of retired president of the division of court of appeal and in 1962 he received the Grosses Verdienstkreuz der Bundesrepublik Deutschland. In the same year he was awarded the Golden Beccaria medal of the German society of criminology. A volume of the German encyclopaedia of criminology (2nd edn, 1975) was dedicated to his memory. He was awarded the Coronation Medal in 1953 and appointed OBE in 1959. He received honorary doctorates from the universities of Utrecht (1957) and Wales (1970) and was made an honorary fellow of the London School of Economics (1965). In 1965 he was presented with a Festschrift edited by three of his former students (*Criminology in Transition*).

Mannheim was short in stature but robust, mild mannered but determined, sensitive but with a bite of his own. He maintained a formality characteristic of a German professor. He was disappointed that after so rich a contribution he was not made a professor by London University. It also grieved him that the first chair and Institute of Criminology found a home not in London but in Cambridge. In tribute to him, a new criminological centre was later established, and named after Mannheim, at the LSE.

Mannheim's reputation as a scholar–criminologist stands high and will remain high. Compelled to leave his country of birth he became a pioneer in the country which received him. He died in London on 20 January 1974.   LEON RADZINOWICZ, rev.

Sources The Times (24 Jan 1974) · T. Grygier, H. Jones, and J. C. Spencer, eds., *Criminology in transition: essays in honour of H. Mannheim* (1965) · personal knowledge (1986) · private information (1986) · WWW · CGPLA Eng. & Wales (1974)
Archives BLPES, papers | Bodl. Oxf., Society for the Protection of Science and Learning and home office files
Wealth at death £20,997: probate, 12 March 1974, CGPLA Eng. & Wales

Mannheim, Karl [Károly] (1893–1947), sociologist, was born on 27 March 1893 at 19 Sas Street in Budapest, Hungary, the eldest child of Gusztáv Mannheim, a textile merchant, and Rosa Eylenburg. His father was Hungarian-Jewish and his mother German-Jewish. After attending a *Gymnasium* Mannheim enrolled as a student of philosophy at the University of Budapest from 1911 to 1915, though for much of the time he studied at German universities. In 1918 he took a doctorate of the University of Budapest *summa cum laude*. He mixed freely in various intellectual circles, but became most closely associated with a group around George Lukács, the Marxist literary critic, who was briefly a commissioner for education in a short-lived Communist–Social Democratic government. Although Mannheim declined to join the Communist Party, Lukács appointed him a lecturer at the college of education of the University of Budapest. After a counter-revolutionary government took over in Budapest Mannheim decided to leave for Vienna in December 1919.

Mannheim soon moved to Germany and many of his

Karl Mannheim (1893–1947), by Elliott & Fry, 1943

most formative intellectual experiences took place in exile in the Weimar Republic. He went initially to Freiburg and Berlin but settled in Heidelberg, where he became a member of the circle that had grown up around Max and Alfred Weber. There, on 22 March 1921, he married Juliska (Julia) Láng (1893–1955), a psychologist, also from Hungary. In 1926 Mannheim received a formal academic appointment in sociology at Heidelberg. In 1930 he became professor of sociology at the Goethe University of Frankfurt am Main. However, in 1933 he was 'retired' from this position by the Nazis and went via Amsterdam to England, where he was given a lectureship in sociology at the London School of Economics. He also lectured on a part-time basis for the University of London Institute of Education between 1941 and 1945. During the war he travelled frequently from his home in Golders Green to Cambridge and Nottingham, to where his two institutions were evacuated. In January 1946 he moved full-time to the chair of education at the institute.

Mannheim was about 5 feet 8 inches tall. His dark hair was receding by the time he was in his twenties and he had a distinguished bald dome well before he came to England. Assessments of his character vary. Some observers regarded him as highly approachable, while others saw him as a somewhat distant figure. Some described him as modest, but others felt he was dominating and opinionated. He seems to have been very popular with students at the LSE but his relations with colleagues, especially Morris Ginsberg, the professor of sociology, became decidedly strained. There, as elsewhere, he often felt denied the status and intellectual recognition he believed he deserved.

Internationally, Mannheim was probably best known as a sociologist of knowledge concerned with the social conditioning of thought and the role of socially unattached intellectuals. This work is particularly relevant to the problem of relativism. Many of his key publications were originally written in Germany in the 1920s, notably *Ideologie und Utopie* (1929). This he revised and expanded in the 1930s, and it was translated into English by Louis Wirth and Edward Shils at the University of Chicago. In his writings of this period, Mannheim took the view that sociology could help make people more aware of the nature of social relationships but should not make judgements.

As the 1930s progressed, however, Mannheim's work became increasingly concerned with the threat to democracy posed on the one hand by totalitarianism and on the other by unbridled individualism and competition. These concerns were reflected in *Man and Society in an Age of Reconstruction*, published in German in 1935 and in English in 1940, and in *Diagnosis of our Time: Wartime Essays of a Sociologist* (1943). Jean Floud, a student at the LSE in the 1930s who subsequently assisted Mannheim with his research, suggested that by the 1940s he had 'turned from the fine points of the diagnosis [of the crisis] to the active political problem of controlling the descent into disaster' (Floud, 'Karl Mannheim', 49). He proposed 'Planning for freedom'—a third way between a *laissez-faire* society and total regimentation. Although Mannheim's obituary in *The Times* claimed that he himself always insisted that he was concerned with diagnosis only, it has been said by another of his former students that his denial of partisanship was 'rather like Mr Roosevelt's claim to be neutral before Pearl Harbour' (Stewart, 21).

Certainly Mannheim became passionately concerned to influence reconstruction after the Second World War. The International Library of Sociology and Social Reconstruction, which he founded, reflected his conviction that sociology could provide the basis for this. Indeed he increasingly saw his own destiny as helping to rebuild Europe on a sound democratic footing. This was one reason why he chose not to follow the well-trodden path of fellow Jewish sociologists to the USA. His *Times* obituary described him as becoming 'more English than the English themselves'; in 1940 he had become a British citizen. His self-appointed role as both friend and critic of the British establishment was reflected in his deep involvement with the wartime Moot. This brought together predominantly Christian lay people and clergy at a series of residential weekends between 1938 and 1947 and came to focus on plans for the post-war social and political reconstruction. It included leading intellectuals such as J. H. Oldham, Adolph Lowe, J. Middleton Murry, Walter Moberly, A. D. Lindsay, and T. S. Eliot. Mannheim quickly became a key member of this group, as did Sir Fred Clarke, director of the Institute of

Education, who helped to tease out the educational implications of Mannheim's general prescriptions about 'Planning for freedom'. As a result some of Mannheim's ideas indirectly influenced the 1944 Education Act.

Although he had shown some interest in education as early as the 1920s, it became the main focus of Mannheim's work only towards the end of his life. He became particularly concerned about social education and the development of the techniques necessary for the creation of the democratic personality (see Kudomi). His 'profound reflections on the problems of human society' had led him to a conviction of the importance of education' (minutes of academic board, Institute of Education, Sir Fred Clarke Archive), so his move to the Institute of Education was not merely an escape from a difficult situation at the LSE. However, Mannheim's actual influence on British education was cut short by his premature death at the age of fifty-three. He had had a heart condition from birth and was generally in poor health throughout his life. In early 1947, during one of London's coldest winters, he contracted pneumonia, ignored medical advice to take total bed rest, and died from a heart attack at his home, 5 The Park, Golders Green, Middlesex, on 9 January 1947. His funeral was held at Golders Green crematorium, where there is a memorial to him and his wife, who had become a practising psychotherapist and outlived him until 1955. The couple had no children.

Much of Mannheim's work, including that on the sociology of education, was published after his death. From the 1960s, however, his contribution to both sociology and education was relatively neglected. Although Kettler and Meja suggested that his project should be 'irresistible to reflective people at the end of the twentieth century' (Kettler and Meja, 1), and there are certainly some fascinating resonances with contemporary sociological concerns in his work, he would probably have had little sympathy with postmodern theorists. His intellectual roots predisposed him towards a 'grand narrative' approach to theory and his solutions to the problems of 'new times' were profoundly modernist ones. However, it is not always easy to understand just what Mannheim was saying. Even though one of his posthumous volumes was entitled *Systematic Sociology* (1957), he was hardly a systematic thinker. Loader charitably termed his work a 'dynamic totality', but even the books compiled during his lifetime under his own supervision are full of inconsistencies and repetitions.

Floud implied that Mannheim would have done better to continue 'to try to understand and diagnose, rather than to plan and legislate' (Floud, 'Karl Mannheim', 62). She also claimed that, within a decade of his death, it was universally recognized that 'Mannheim's "planning for democracy" … was not "democratic planning"; and people were beginning to think in any case that "democratic planning" was a contradiction in terms' (Floud, *Functions, Purposes and Powers in Education*, 8). Yet it is quite possible that, after the experience of deregulation and political hostility to planning in Britain and elsewhere in the 1980s, Mannheim's commentary on the damaging effects of atomization and a *laissez-faire* society will become relevant again. There would certainly be some poetic justice in Mannheim's ideas becoming fashionable in the aftermath of the Thatcherite era, as his views were one of the main targets of his LSE colleague Frederik Hayek's *Road to Serfdom* (1944), which hurt him badly at the time of its publication and later became one of the key texts of the new right revolution of the 1980s.

GEOFF WHITTY

Sources H. E. S. Woldring, *Karl Mannheim: the development of his thought* (1986) · [K. Mannheim], *Mannheim Károly levelezése, 1911–1946*, ed. E. Gábor (Budapest, 1996) · G. W. Remmling, *The sociology of Karl Mannheim* (1975) [incl. bibliographical guide] · C. Loader, *The intellectual development of Karl Mannheim* (1985) · D. Kettler and V. Meja, *Karl Mannheim and the crisis of liberalism* (1995) · Y. Kudomi, 'Karl Mannheim in Britain: an interim research report', *Hitotsubashi Journal of Social Studies*, 28/2 (1996), 43–56 · J. Floud, 'Karl Mannheim', *The function of teaching*, ed. A. V. Judges (1959), 40–66 · J. Floud, *Functions, purposes and powers in education* (1977) · W. A. C. Stewart, *Karl Mannheim on education and social thought* (1967) · W. Taylor, 'Education and the Moot', *In history and in education: essays presented to Peter Gordon*, ed. R. Aldrich (1996), 159–86 · U. Lond., Institute of Education, Fred Clarke MSS · E. Shils, 'Karl Mannheim', *The American Scholar* (1995), 221–35 · *The Times* (11 Jan 1947)
Archives Keele University Library, corresp., papers and lecture notes | BLPES, letters to E. Rosenbaum · Bodl. Oxf., Society for Protection of Science and Learning file · Lukács Archivum, Budapest, Hungary, Magyar Tudományos Akadémia Könyutára · U. Lond., Institute of Education, discussion papers · U. Reading, Routledge and Kegan Paul Archives · U. Reading L., letters to the Isotope Institute · University of Chicago, Louis Wirth MSS
Likenesses Elliott & Fry, photograph, 1943, NPG [*see illus.*] · portraits, repro. in Woldring, *Karl Mannheim*
Wealth at death £4283 15s. 7d.: probate, 31 Oct 1947, CGPLA Eng. & Wales

Mannig [Wulfmær] (*d.* 1066), abbot of Evesham and craftsman, was elected abbot at the general synod held in London in 1044 and consecrated on 10 August. In 1058 incurable paralysis struck him, and he was forced to resign the abbacy and retire from active life; he died between 4 and 6 January 1066, reputedly on the same day as Edward the Confessor. The name Mannig is of Old Danish origin, and may point to Anglo-Scandinavian roots; he was also called Wulfmær.

The Evesham chronicle portrays Mannig as a holy and upright abbot, restoring estates and refusing to accept the profits of criminal justice, but praises him especially as *artificiosissimus*: he was 'richly imbued both with sacred learning and with many other arts, namely singing, writing and painting; he excelled in knowledge of the goldsmith's art, and was considered the greatest master among virtually all others in this land' (*Chronicon abbatiae de Evesham*, 46, 86–8). At his own abbey he rebuilt one of the churches on a larger scale, made a great shrine of gold, silver, and precious stones for St Ecgwine as well as lesser shrines for St Odulf and St Credan, and wrote and illuminated a missal and a great psalter with his own hand. He is also said to have executed works of art at Canterbury, Coventry Abbey, and many other places. The story of a miraculous healing of a goldsmith named Godric, the foreman of 'many artificers' at Evesham, indicates that Mannig supervised a workshop of craftsmen in precious metals based at his abbey. Mannig's career, like that of Spearhafoc, abbot of Abingdon, shows that excellence and versatility in manual skills were esteemed in even the highest-ranking late Anglo-Saxon churchmen. JOHN BLAIR

Sources W. D. Macray, ed., *Chronicon abbatiae de Evesham, ad annum 1418*, Rolls Series, 29 (1863), 44, 46, 86–8, 321–2 · *ASC*, s.a. 1045 [text D] · C. R. Dodwell, *Anglo-Saxon art: a new perspective* (1982), chap. 3 · John of Worcester, *Chron.*, 2.540–41

Mannin [*married names* Porteus, Reynolds], **Ethel Edith** (1900–1984), writer, was born on 11 October 1900 in Clapham, London, the eldest of the three children of Robert Mannin (d. 1949), a postal sorter of Irish ancestry, and Edith Gray, a farmer's daughter. In her first of seven published memoirs, Mannin records that she began writing stories at the age of seven. Her first published pieces appeared on the children's pages of two papers, the *Lady's Companion* in 1910, and *Reynolds Newspaper* in 1913. Mannin attended a boarding-school in Clapham from 1906 to 1914. In 1915 she won a scholarship to attend a commercial school in London and she quickly found employment as a typist for the Charles Higham advertising firm. Soon after, Higham promoted her to the post of copywriter.

From 1915 to 1919 Mannin worked at Highams, writing advertisements and editing two in-house publications. Her skills eventually enabled her to manage *The Pelican*, a theatrical newspaper Higham acquired in 1917; she also wrote drama criticism until the paper ceased publication in 1919. On 28 November of that year, Mannin married fellow writer John Alexander Porteus (1885–1956), who was the general manager at Highams, and she bore her only child, Jean (Faulks) the same year. In 1920, Mannin, who did not believe in mixing housewifery with a professional career, found work as a freelance editor of business and commercial publications and began writing novels in serial form for a guinea per thousand words. When her manuscript *Martha* won a writers' competition for first novels, Mannin published the book in 1923 and launched her second career in the book publishing world. *Martha* was directly followed by *Hunger for the Sea* (1924), *Sounding Brass* (1925), her first critical success based on her years with Highams, and *Pilgrims* (1927), which was inspired by her admiration of Van Gogh. In later years Mannin claimed *Sounding Brass* as the best of her nearly ninety works of fiction.

In 1929 Mannin and Porteus separated and she bought a small house in London, Oak Cottage, Wimbledon, which she had admired as a child. In 1931 she published her first book of short stories, *Green Figs*, and her literary success made her popular with the press, who were eager for her progressive views on sexuality, motherhood and professionalism, and marriage. In the same year, Mannin published *Common Sense and the Child*, which describes the educational theories of A. S. Neill, to whose Summerhill School Jean was sent in 1926. Mannin's novel *Linda Shawn* (1932) is a fictionalized account of a Neill-raised child.

With the publication of *Love's Winnowing* (1932), Mannin more deliberately incorporated her political views into her fiction, as the setting of this novel provides a communist's view of the working class. As early as 1913 Mannin had espoused an admiration for the communist

Ethel Edith Mannin (1900–1984), by Paul Tanqueray, 1930 [background painted by Ida Davis]

system, though she never was a member of the party. She maintained an interest in communism all her life. In 1935 she joined the Independent Labour Party, contributed articles to the *New Leader*, and served as a high-profile spokesperson. In 1936 Mannin went to the Soviet Union—a journey she describes in *South to Samarkand*, a finely written narrative detailing how, as an idealist, she was disillusioned by the reality of communism. In 1938 Mannin divorced Porteus, and married Reginald Reynolds (1904/5–1958) on 23 December 1938. He was a writer with strong ties to the Independent Labour Party.

By 1942 Mannin, after the publication of *Women and the Revolution* (1938) and *Red Rose: a Novel Based on the Life of Emma Goldman* (1941), was described in the press as the most unpopular writer in England. The politics and hard edge she was introducing into her romance fiction was overpowering the love stories in the end. Her awareness of this is indicated in such of her titles as *Bread and Roses: an Utopian Survey and Blueprint* (1944) and *Comrade, O Comrade* (1947), a satirical novel on British Labour and Liberal Party members and sympathizers. Her enthusiasm for travel and travel narrative continued from the 1930s through to the late 1970s. In all, Mannin published fourteen travel books recording her visits to Germany, India, Morocco, Burma, Egypt, Jordan, Italy, and elsewhere. For long-time readers, the humour of *England for a Change* (1968) was not lost.

Mannin kept to her vow, made in the late 1930s, to write two books a year, one fiction and the other non-fiction, until 1974. In 1958 she ventured into children's books with two short-lived series, the Ann and Peter books, whose travelling children go to Sweden, Austria, and Japan, and two later works, *The Saga of Sammy Cat* (1969) and *My Cat Sammy* (1971). Still interested in polemic and philosophy (having studied Bertrand Russell as well as Neill), Mannin published *Loneliness: a Study of the Human Condition* in 1966 and *Practitioners of Love: some Aspects of the Human Phenomenon* in 1969.

Mannin wrote seven autobiographical works beginning with *Confessions and Impressions* in 1930. Her *Connemara Journal* (1948) serves as an early tribute to her Irish heritage, which was more fully explored in her two publications of 1952, *The Wild Swans and other Tales from the Ancient Irish* and *This was a Man: some Memories of Robert Mannin by his Daughter*. The return to the romance-adventure novel is clearly indicated in her works *Curfew at Dawn* (1962), *The Night and its Homing* (1966), *The Lady and the Mystic* (1967), and *Kildoon* (1974). Her popularity returned when she turned from activism to more conventional work.

In 1977 Mannin marked her retirement as a writer of nearly 100 books with the publication of her final memoir, *Sunset over Dartmoor*, and she moved to Shaldon, overlooking the Teign estuary in Devon. For forty years she also maintained a cottage in Connemara, Ireland. In July 1984 Mannin was injured in a fall at home and died of pneumonia and heart failure at Teignmouth Hospital, on 5 December 1984.　　　BEVERLY E. SCHNELLER

Sources *International who's who* (1978) · R. Myers, ed., *A dictionary of literature in the English language from 1940 to 1970* (1978) · S. J. Kunitz, *Authors today and yesterday* (1933) · *The Times* (8 Dec 1984) · A. Croft, 'Ethel Mannin: the red rose of love and the red flower of liberty', *Rediscovering forgotten radicals: British women writers, 1889–1939* (1993), 205–25 · A. Croft, BBC broadcast on Radio 4, 23 Sept 1990 · J. Todd, ed., *British women writers: a critical reference guide* (1989) · R. Welch, ed., *The Oxford companion to Irish literature* (1996) · *CGPLA Eng. & Wales* (1985) · m. certs.
Archives Boston University, corresp. and literary papers
Likenesses P. Tanqueray, photograph, 1930, NPG [*see illus.*]
Wealth at death £78,646: probate, 26 April 1985, *CGPLA Eng. & Wales*

Mannin, James (*d.* 1779), painter and decorative artist, is said to have been a Frenchman but his name is also found in Italy, in Venice and in Genoa. He was engaged on a salary in 1756 by the Dublin Society Schools to teach the art of design, and remained there until shortly before his death. He had earlier been teaching in the schools on the basis of payment for each student he taught, and he had a considerable private practice. Strickland recorded that he was in Dublin during the 1740s (Strickland, 2.100). No painting by him is known, although he exhibited flower pieces, designs for interior decoration, and landscapes at the Society of Artists in Ireland between 1765 and 1777. In 1768 he lived in Dublin at King's Street, Stephen's Green, and following his marriage on 18 October 1769 to Mary Maguire in St Andrew's Church, Dublin, he lived at Lazar's Hill, until 1775 when he moved to King Street. The president's chair at the Royal Dublin Society was designed by Mannin in 1767 and carved by Richard Cranfield, and is in a very Italianate manner. He probably taught landscape painting. His pupils included George Barret, Thomas

Roberts, and J. J. Barralet, who took over his post in the Dublin Society Schools when ill health forced him to retire shortly before his death in Dublin in 1779.
　　　　　　　　　　L. H. CUST, *rev.* ANNE CROOKSHANK

Sources J. Turpin, *A school of art in Dublin since the eighteenth century: a history of the National College of Art and Design* (1995), 43–5 · W. G. Strickland, *A dictionary of Irish artists*, 2 vols. (1913) · A. Crookshank and the Knight of Glin [D. Fitzgerald], *The painters of Ireland, c.1660–1920*, 2nd edn (1979), 70 · G. Breeze, *Society of Artists in Ireland: index of exhibits, 1765–80* (1985)
Archives Royal Dublin Society, minutes of the Dublin Society

Manning, (Elizabeth) Adelaide (1828–1905), social reformer, was the daughter of James *Manning (1781–1866), serjeant-at-law, and his first wife, Clarissa (1796–1847), daughter of William Palmer. Adelaide's grandfather, also James Manning, had been a Unitarian minister in Exeter and Unitarian links were perhaps one factor in her enrolment as one of the earliest students at Bedford College in 1850. Certainly with his friends Matthew Davenport Hill and Benjamin Leigh Smith her father was active in the Law Amendment Society and shared in the society's decision in 1855 to support reform of the law relating to married women's property.

In 1857 Adelaide Manning's father married Charlotte [*see below*], widow of William Speir. The relationship between daughter and stepmother was a close and warm one, and together they became friends with Emily Davies after her move to London in 1862. The Kensington Society, the women's discussion group which ran from 1865 to 1868, met at the Mannings' home.

Besides assisting in the campaign for the suffrage, Adelaide Manning joined the London Association of Schoolmistresses in 1867, taking a particular interest in infant education and the teaching of Froebel. Her cousin Caroline Bishop was appointed by the London school board to advise on the use of kindergarten methods in the board's infant schools, and in 1874 the two were founder members of the London Froebel Society. In 1875 it became a national body, with Adelaide Manning as secretary. In 1874 she had delivered a paper, 'Kindergarten training', to the Social Science Association, subsequently published as a pamphlet, and in 1884 her address to a conference in London in parallel with the International Health Exhibition was likewise published, as *Froebel and Infant Training*. She also engaged with the difficult issue of moral training, reading a paper to the Social Science Association in 1875, which was published as *Moral Teaching in Schools*, and giving a course of lessons on ethics at a private girls' school in the autumn of 1876.

Adelaide Manning's friendship with Emily Davies led to involvement with her infant university college for women, first at Hitchin and then from 1873 at Girton. Emily had enlisted Adelaide's help in persuading her stepmother to become the first mistress. To set an example Adelaide, aged forty-one, took and passed the entrance examination in June 1869 and accompanied Charlotte to Hitchin in the autumn, exceptionally entered on the books as a supernumerary student. Following Charlotte's death in 1871 Adelaide replaced her on the Girton executive committee, remaining a member of the Girton governing body until her own death. She was fully involved, and often acted as both a sounding board and a calming influence. Emily Davies wrote in September 1876,

> It occurs to me to say, as it comes into my head, as it often does, what a comfort you are. I can open a letter from you without fear & about many things one could feel confident & at rest with you. There are not many people who have both judgement and good heart. (Girton College archives, Emily Davies MSS, XVII 13/3)

However, the lion's share of Adelaide Manning's time in the last thirty years of her life was occupied by the affairs of the National Indian Association in Aid of Social Progress in India (NIA). Founded in Bristol in 1870 by Mary Carpenter, a London branch was started from the Mannings' home in 1871, shortly before Charlotte's death. Adelaide continued her involvement from her new home at 35 Blomfield Road in Maida Vale. On Mary Carpenter's death in 1877 the London and Bristol committees were merged and Adelaide replaced her as both general secretary and editor of the monthly *Journal*, renamed the *Indian Magazine* in 1886. She continued in these roles until a month before her own death.

The NIA launched two initiatives in the 1880s, in both of which Adelaide played a major role. The first was the campaign Medical Women for India, launched in 1882, which was designed to train women doctors who would be willing to work in India, with Indian women in particular, for at least part of their professional careers. Adelaide's involvement with the creation of the Royal Free Hospital was of use here. The second initiative was that for the superintendence of Indian students working in England. The NIA produced first notes for guidance and eventually, in 1893, a *Handbook of information relating to university and professional studies etc. for Indian students in the United Kingdom*, prepared by Adelaide Manning. She worked too to reinforce the formal support of the NIA with her own hospitality and friendship. She held open house regularly at Blomfield Road and then at 5 Pembridge Crescent and sought out Indian students wherever they were. Abdul Qadir met her in 1904 when they were both visiting a friend, a medical student who had been taken ill:

> Well-attended as the patient was in the hospital to which he belonged and was well-known, it was a peculiar relief to have somebody else taking an interest in one in this wide and strange world of London. And that was exactly what Miss Manning made every Indian feel in this huge Metropolis. (*Indian Magazine*, Oct 1905, 272)

Within its general commitment to the furtherance of mutual understanding the NIA had a commitment to education and to the education of women in particular. Under Adelaide Manning's editorship the *Journal* and then the *Magazine* gave ample coverage to Indian and British initiatives in this field. The anonymity of many contributions makes it difficult to judge how much she herself wrote, but her accounts of her two visits to India (*Indian Magazine*, May 1889 and May 1899) make the importance of this to her plain, and her first visit was followed by a special appeal for funds, stressing that 'the education of women lies at the root of all social progress in India' (ibid., April 1890, 168). The breadth of her religious sympathies was of help in negotiating ways through the religious and cultural minefields surrounding the issue.

Adelaide Manning's contribution to Anglo-Indian understanding was recognized by the government with the award of the Kaisar-i-Hind medal in 1904. She died of kidney disease at 5 Pembridge Crescent, Kensington, on 10 August 1905. Among the institutions which benefited under her will were the NIA, Girton College, the Royal Free Hospital, the Froebel Society and Institute, and the Theistic Church, Swallow Street, Piccadilly.

Her stepmother, **Charlotte Manning** [née Solly; *other married name* Speir] (1803–1871), Indian scholar and college head, was born on 30 March 1803, the daughter of Isaac Solly of Leyton in Essex. In 1835 she married William Speir MD, who practised medicine in Calcutta, where he died. In 1856, as Charlotte Speir, she published a substantial study, *Ancient India*. It was well received and in 1869, as Charlotte Manning, she published a greatly enlarged second edition in two volumes, *Ancient and Medieval India*.

Following her second marriage, to James Manning on 3 December 1857, Charlotte moved to live in Kensington, at 44 Phillimore Gardens, where she and her stepdaughter became friends with Emily Davies. In 1863 she joined the committee campaigning to secure girls access to university local examinations and in 1865 became president of the Kensington Society. In December 1867 she was one of the four members of the committee formed to plan for a residential college providing higher education for women. After James's death in 1866 Charlotte and Adelaide had moved to 107 Victoria Street, where many of the committee's meetings took place. Emily Davies hoped to persuade Charlotte to preside over the new college at Hitchin for at least a year, setting great store by her unimpeachable social and intellectual standing. Eventually she agreed to serve simply for the first term, Michaelmas 1869, one of the first students recalling that 'her suavity and gentle courtesy complemented perfectly Miss Davies' eager abrupt decisiveness' (Stephen, 222). Charlotte took an active part in the formation of the London branch of the NIA and became its first president shortly before her death at her London home, 107 Victoria Street, Westminster, on 1 April 1871. GILLIAN SUTHERLAND

Sources 'Personal recollectons of Elizabeth Adelaide Manning', *Indian Magazine*, new ser., 94 (1905) · K. T. Butler and H. I. McMorran, eds., *Girton College register, 1869–1946* (1948) · B. Stephen, *Emily Davies and Girton College* (1927) · Girton Cam. · *Journal of the National Indian Association in Aid of Social Progress in India* (1873–85) · *Indian Magazine* (1886–1905) · P. Woodham-Smith, 'History of the Froebel movement in England', *Friedrich Froebel and English education*, ed. E. M. Lawrence (1952); facs. edn (1969), 34–94 · d. cert. · 'Smith, John', *DNB* [Charlotte Manning] · Girton Cam., Davies MSS · *CGPLA Eng. & Wales* (1871) [Charlotte Manning]
Archives Girton Cam.
Likenesses oils (after a photograph by E. MacNaghten), Girton Cam., Stanley Library · two photographs (Charlotte Manning), Girton Cam. · watercolour and body colour (Charlotte Manning), Girton Cam.

Wealth at death £25,458 13s. 6d.: probate, 5 Sept 1905, *CGPLA Eng. & Wales* · under £14,000—Charlotte Manning: probate, 25 April 1871, *CGPLA Eng. & Wales*

Manning, Anne (1807–1879), writer, was born in London on 17 February 1807, the daughter of William Oke Manning (1778–1859), an insurance broker of Lloyd's, London, and his wife, Joan Whatmore, daughter of Frederick Gibson, principal surveyor of the London docks. Manning's family included two notable legal writers: her first cousin Sir William Montague Manning (1811–1895), attorney-general and judge of the supreme court of New South Wales, was co-author of *Reports in Court of Queen's Bench* (1834), and her brother William Oke *Manning (1809–1878) was the author of the 1839 treatise on international law *Commentaries on the Law of Nations*. James *Manning (1781–1866), serjeant-at-law, was her uncle.

Manning spent her first eight years in Brunswick Square until the family moved to Old Chelsea, where they lived in the former home of Scottish author John Galt (1779–1839). Manning was educated by her mother, an accomplished scholar, and her schooling was thorough. She showed interest in the sciences and she was awarded a gold medal from the Royal Academy for a copy of *Flower Girl* originally by Spanish painter Bartolomé Esteban Murillo (1617–1682). She received sound tuition in English literature and knew several languages, including Latin and Old French ([Manning], 'Introduction' to *Thomas More*, xxv).

At the age of nineteen Manning published *A Sister's Gift: Conversations on Sacred Subjects* (1826). That book of essays was succeeded by another, more historically based prose work, *Stories from the History of Italy* (1831). The latter was the only book ever published under her own name. During her lifetime she wrote numerous other essays and articles, a book on the elements of logic (*The Hill Side*, 1854), some verse, and autobiographical sketches. She is best remembered, however, as a prolific writer of historical fiction, mostly set in the sixteenth century.

Of particular note among Manning's many fictional works is *The Maiden and Married Life of Mary Powell, Afterwards Mistress Milton* (1849). The novel purports to be the diary of Mary Powell and, using its own contrived version of sixteenth-century words and spellings, shows a most careful attention to and knowledge of the works of Milton, as well as of the other major poets of that time. This work was extremely popular, went through eight printings in the nineteenth century, and enjoyed French and German translations. After its publication, Manning published as 'the author of *Mary Powell*'. In what was largely an attempt to capitalize on the success of the original *Mary Powell*, the novel was amended in 1859 to include *Deborah's Diary*, the fictional diary of Milton's daughter. Manning's final novel on Milton was *The Masque at Ludlow and other Romanesques* (1866), which she described as an attempt to 'outline [Milton] at an earlier age, full of promises that were to be richly fulfilled' (Manning, viii).

Another significant success for Manning's fiction was *The Household of Sir Thomas More* (1851). Like *Mary Powell*, *Thomas More* combines pseudo-archaic language, considerable familiarity with historical facts, and female observation (this time in the epistolary mode) to create a reverential story that encompasses both public greatness and everyday private domesticity. *The Household of Sir Thomas More* also achieved great popularity, two language translations, and multiple reprintings. Other notable examples of Manning's historical fiction are *Cherry and Violet: a Tale of the Great Plague* (1853) and *A Noble Purpose Nobly Won* (1862), about Jeanne d'Arc.

Manning's bold inventiveness in portraying important historical moments and renowned figures did not go unnoticed or unchallenged. In 1855 a review of her works (including *Mary Powell* and *Thomas More*) lambasted the author for writing books 'which are little else than a tissue of sentimental unrealities and falsehoods' ('Spurious antiques', 106). While her works were never intended to be taken for literal truth, this hostile review highlights the issues that arise in the creation of historically based works of fiction. As a result of such difficulties, some of Manning's later works include disclaimers such as the one which precedes *The Masque at Ludlow*: 'These letters have no pedigree, unless forged by the Cheat'em Society, of which, in an innocent way, I am a member' (Manning, vii). The decidedly 'old-fashioned' tenor of Manning's works (Miller, 109) poses a greater problem for the modern reader, but a novel such as *Mary Powell* can be usefully read today both 'because of and in spite of its sentimentality, its piety, and its didacticism' (Swaim and Culley, 88).

According to her niece, Manning desired that no particulars about herself be published while she lived (Drake, 16). She kept in close retirement, avoided public notice through literary anonymity, and never married. She is remembered by her contemporaries as a 'tall, thin lady with black hair, an aquiline nose, and a bright colour' (Hutton, 'Introduction' to *Mary Powell*, xi). Although an extremely private person, Manning was greatly valued for her willingness to encourage other aspiring authors (Batty, 65). She is also depicted as a 'stout English Churchwoman', restrainedly but sincerely devout (Hutton, 'Introduction' to *Mary Powell*, xii). According to a written memorial, she was 'a chronic invalid' whose final years were racked by increasingly confining discomfort and whose gradual paralysis ended her career as an author in 1876 (Batty, 64, 66). A year before her death, illness forced her removal from Reigate Hill (which had been her home since 1850) to her sisters' home at Tunbridge Wells. She died there on 14 September 1879. She is buried near her parents in Mickleham churchyard, near Dorking.

MARY A. ARMSTRONG

Sources W. H. Hutton, 'Introduction', in A. Manning, *The maiden and married life of Mary Powell, afterwards Mistress Milton* (1898) · K. Swaim and M. Culley, 'Anne Manning on John Milton', *Milton Quarterly*, 10 (1976), 88–9 · [Mrs Batty], 'In memoriam', *Englishwoman's Review*, 11 (1880), 64–6 · DNB · L. Miller, 'Anne Manning's "The masque at Ludlow"', *Milton Quarterly*, 11 (1977), 107–9 · [A. Manning], introduction, in A. Manning, *The household of Sir Thomas More* (1906) · 'Spurious antiques', *Fraser's Magazine*, 52 (1855), 104–14 · W. H. Hutton, introduction, in A. Manning, *The household of Sir Thomas More* (1896) · E. C. Drake, *N&Q*, 8th ser., 8

(1895), 16 · A. Manning, 'Introduction', *The masque at Ludlow and other romanesques* (1868)

Archives NL Scot., letters to Blackwoods

Wealth at death under £200: probate, 9 Oct 1879, *CGPLA Eng. & Wales*

Manning, Bernard Lord (1892–1941), historian of religion, was born at Caistor, Lincolnshire, on 31 December 1892, the only son of George Manning (1863–1935) and his wife, Mary Ann (1863–1934), daughter of William Short Lord, businessman, of Caistor. In 1898 George Manning became a Congregational minister, with the result that his son's home during his schooldays was first at Ravenstonedale, in Westmorland, and then at Lincoln. Bernard Manning was never robust, and a severe illness in boyhood left him a semi-invalid for the rest of his life, with only one effective lung. In 1912, however, he won an open scholarship at Jesus College, Cambridge, from Caistor grammar school. He obtained a double first in the history tripos (1914, 1915), won the Lightfoot scholarship in 1915, a Thirlwall prize in 1917, and from 1916 to 1918 was a bye-fellow of Magdalene College and editor of the *Cambridge Review*.

A short period of national service at the Ministry of Munitions in 1918 was brought to an end by an attack of tuberculosis, but Manning made a rapid recovery and in 1919 was elected a fellow of Jesus College. He was bursar from 1920 to 1933, senior tutor from 1933 until his death, and a university lecturer in medieval history from 1930. He died, unmarried, at Evelyn Nursing Home, Cambridge, on 8 December 1941 and was buried at Ravenstonedale, as were his parents.

Manning was both soundly practical and deeply spiritual. As bursar of his college he proved himself a shrewd businessman and a wise administrator. As tutor he showed a remarkable gift for administering discipline while treating his pupils as friends and equals. He was a staunch Congregationalist but possessed the ecumenical mind to a pre-eminent degree; for he absorbed the spirit of the Christian church throughout the centuries—of the early church and the medieval church no less than the fragmented Christianity of post-Reformation times.

Everything that Manning wrote is conspicuous for scholarship, style, wit, and humour, as he shows in *The People's Faith in the Time of Wyclif* (1919, his Thirlwall prize essay), *The Making of Modern English Religion* (1929), *Essays in Orthodox Dissent* (1939), *The Hymns of Wesley and Watts* (1942), two chapters ('Edward III and Richard II' and 'Wyclif') in vol. 7 of the *Cambridge Medieval History*, and two posthumous volumes of sermons.

F. BRITTAIN, rev. H. C. G. MATTHEW

Sources F. Brittain, *Bernard Lord Manning* (1942) · personal knowledge (1959) · *CGPLA Eng. & Wales* (1942)

Wealth at death £10,115 8s. 11d.: probate, 21 March 1942, CGPLA Eng. & Wales

Manning, Charles Anthony Woodward (1894–1978), scholar of international relations, was born on 18 November 1894 in Cape Town, Cape Colony, the second of the three children of Dumaresq Williamson Manning (1865–1944), successively civil servant and farmer, and his first

wife, Helena Isabella (1860–1908), daughter of Charles Davidson Bell, sometime governor of Cape Colony. Following the death of his wife Dumaresq Manning remarried and had three further children in South Africa. In 1937 he returned to Britain, the country of his birth, where he died.

Charles Manning attended a leading South African public school, Diocesan College, Rondebosch, and went on to South Africa College, Cape Town, and, as a Rhodes scholar, to Brasenose College, Oxford. However, war having been declared, he enlisted, was commissioned in the 7th Oxford and Buckinghamshire light infantry, saw active service in France and at Salonika, was wounded, and was twice mentioned in dispatches. Afterwards, at Oxford, he obtained a distinction in Greats (1920), and firsts in the jurisprudence (1921) and bachelor of civil law (1922) degrees. He was called to the bar by the Middle Temple in 1922. In 1922–3 he worked in Geneva at the International Labour Organization and as personal assistant to the secretary-general of the League of Nations, Sir Eric Drummond.

In 1923 Manning returned to Oxford as a fellow of New College and a law lecturer; there, apart from visiting Harvard in 1925–6, he remained until 1930. He then took the decisive academic step of his life and accepted the Cassel (later Montague Burton) chair of international relations at the London School of Economics (LSE), which he occupied until his retirement in 1962. Throughout this period the very new academic subject of international relations held a highly marginal place in British universities and was often viewed suspiciously by teachers of those subjects with which it had the closest links. Manning tried to remedy this situation but was not best suited for the task, being neither very gregarious nor much given to political intrigue. But he stuck to it. He gave the teaching of international relations a distinctive shape, which later spread, and has endured, throughout Britain and beyond. At the LSE he both consolidated the subject as one in which undergraduate students could specialize and—which he thought of great importance—introduced it as an option for non-specialists. From cognate disciplines he recruited two brilliant colleagues, Martin Wight (from history) and Hedley Bull (from philosophy and politics). He also organized regular 'Bailey conferences' for British university teachers, which included a Saturday session in which interested school teachers were involved. (These conferences were named after a colleague, S. H. Bailey, who, before his early death, had organized the initial such meetings in the 1930s.) Unfortunately for Manning the British higher education sector was broadly static during these years and, except at the LSE, where his department grew, his efforts had little obvious effect. But the subsequent expansion in the teaching of international relations owed much to his dedicated work.

In the earlier phase of that development several of those to whom it was entrusted had been taught by Manning. He was an enthusiastic teacher but an extremely unusual one. His lectures were notably lacking in detailed structure and in no way offered a sustained and detailed analysis of what transpired between states. Rather he sought to throw light on their dealings by 'ceaselessly hunting for some analogy, simile, image, parallel, snatched from anywhere—the everyday world around him, cricket, the theatre or music-hall, that morning's newspaper or radio programme' (Northedge, 3). Not a few found themselves ill at ease with—or even baffled by—this pedagogic style and it was certainly not the route to a well-filled notebook. None the less those who heard Manning often discovered that they had been deeply influenced, a process which was helped by the weekend reading parties that Manning organized for specialist students and colleagues. Largely by osmosis such students came to think that the job of social science was to understand and explain things, not to change them; that the nature of inter-state life was essentially competitive; that, despite the absence of a single government, the world was by no means without order; and—in line with Manning's philosophical leanings—that precision of thought and the drawing of distinctions were supremely important.

Manning's early writings reflected his legal interests. He edited the eighth edition of Salmond's *Jurisprudence* (1930) and his 'Austin today, or, "The province of jurisprudence" re-examined', published in *Modern Theories of Law* (1933), edited by W. I. Jennings, pleased him throughout his life. During the 1930s he focused on the League of Nations (which he viewed sympathetically but realistically), his main publications being *The Policies of the British Dominions in the League of Nations* (1932) and an edited work *Peaceful Change: an International Problem* (1937). But it was after the Second World War (for most of which he was at the Royal Institute of International Affairs, doing work for the Foreign Office) that he made his chief intellectual contribution to the academic discipline that he so largely helped to found. This was twofold. First he vigorously contended that international relations should be a separate university subject, advancing its claim in a succession of articles, notably 'International relations: an academic discipline', published in *The University Teaching of International Relations* (ed. G. L. Goodwin, 1951). He also wrote a report for UNESCO, *The University Teaching of Social Sciences: International Relations* (1954). His second contribution concerned the societal character of the collectivity of sovereign states, on which he published a book, *The Nature of International Society* (1962). This argued that, while the world is politically fragmented, it is a social whole in the sense that inter-state relations rest on certain socially prevalent ideas, which thus constitute the premises of co-existence. For the comprehension of these matters 'sophisticated realism' was required (Manning, *The Nature of International Society*, 35). The book brimmed with insights but was written in Manning's elusive lecturing style (someone called it poetic) and so received relatively little notice. However, it may yet secure a higher profile, for Manning's work is representative of what is now known as constructivism, and it can also be seen as an early instance of what has come to be called the English school's approach to international relations.

Manning was emphatic that social scientists, when acting as such, should strive for detachment and avoid advocacy. While at the LSE he exemplified this belief by keeping very quiet and publishing nothing about the white South African regime's policy of apartheid, notwithstanding—or perhaps because of—the fact that Western criticism of it troubled him deeply (as did South Africa's departure from the Commonwealth in 1961). But after retirement he became publicly active in support of the South African government. He wrote articles and pamphlets and spoke frequently on behalf of the South Africa Society (of which he became chairman in 1964) and at British and American universities. Such was Manning's forensic skill, wit, and speed of thought that he emerged relatively unscathed from these debating encounters. In general (and typifying his marked reluctance to ascribe blame) his approach was that an established and prosperous ethnic group could hardly be expected to hand over power to a quite different one when it was thought that such action would signal the immediate end of its privileges.

Manning's new role offended many of his former colleagues but their hostility did not entail much rupturing of relations for, though Manning was always concerned at another's woes and was a kindly departmental head, he was not the easiest person to get to know. He had a rather distant air, his hugely acute mind had little space for small talk, and he occasionally showed that he did not suffer fools gladly. However, those close to him learnt that beneath his outward calm and modesty lay a very sensitive soul, who could easily feel that he was insufficiently given his due. He was therefore gratified to be included among the eminent scholars who commemorated the establishment of the first chair in his subject in *The Aberystwyth Papers: International Politics, 1919–69* (ed. Brian Porter, 1972) and was particularly pleased, shortly before his death, to be made an honorary president of the South African Institute of International Affairs, in the establishment of which in the mid-1930s he had played, at some personal cost, a possibly crucial role. Very loyal to his school, he was a vice-president of the Old Diocesans' Union from 1964. In 1971 he received an honorary doctorate from the University of Pretoria.

Manning's appearance was striking: he was tall and willowy, carefully dressed, his eyes were often alight with amusement or intellectual excitement, and he had a long, lean face which from early adulthood was crowned by a handsome shock of white hair. His cultivated, slightly strained voice had no hint of a South African accent. His pastimes were those of a loner: he wrote poetry, enjoyed music, and—above all—loved watercolour painting (rarely going far without sketch pad and paintbox). He attended his local Anglican church regularly. On 21 March 1939 he married Marion (Maisie) Somerville Johnston (1898/9–1977), daughter of John Bell Johnston, a farmer; she was a student of Manning, who looked after him solicitously at 34 Newton Road, London. They had no children. She died in 1977; by then Manning had been found to have a serious problem with his larynx (later diagnosed as cancer of the throat). An operation seemed to have been successful but further difficulties emerged. He returned to South Africa after Maisie's death, where, following another operation, he died at his home, Westcliff, Spaanschemat River Road, Constantia, Cape Town, on 10 March 1978, and was buried at Muizenberg cemetery.   ALAN JAMES

Sources F. S. Northedge, 'In memoriam: Charles Manning, 1894–1978', *British Journal of International Studies*, 5 (1979), 1–5 · H. Suganami, 'C. A. W. Manning and the study of international relations', *Review of International Studies* [forthcoming] · *WWW, 1971–80* · m. cert. · personal knowledge (2004) · private information (2004)
Archives JRL, corresp. and papers | CUL, Sir Herbert Butterfield · U. Leeds, Brotherton L., The Liddle collection
Likenesses J. Cast, crayon, 1962, University of Witwatersrand, Johannesburg, South African Institute of International Affairs; repro. in A. James, ed., *The bases of international order: essays in honour of C. A. W. Manning* (1973), frontispiece · black and white copy, 1962 (after portrait by J. Cast, 1962), London School of Economics, department of international relations · Wyld(e?), oils, London School of Economics, department of international relations
Wealth at death approx. 120,000 rand—property and personal possessions: Herold, Gie, and Broadhead, attorneys, Cape Town, letter to the chairman, College Council, Diocesan College, Rondebosch, Cape, South Africa, 2 July 1979

Manning, Charlotte (1803–1871). *See under* Manning, (Elizabeth) Adelaide (1828–1905).

Manning, Edgar [Eddie] (1889/90–1931), criminal, was born in Jamaica and had settled in London by 1916. Employed in a wartime armaments factory and then in the entertainment business, he achieved long-lasting fame from newspaper reports of his criminal career. Metropolitan Police files identified him variously as Alfred Mullin, Edgar Manning, and Edgar Eugene McManning, son of Ben McManning and Cecilia Francaco or Francesco. Newspapers in the 1920s and later histories, memoirs, and biographies stated that Manning was 'an important drug trafficker' (*The Times*, 1 May 1922), a 'drug vice chief' (*News of the World*, 22 July 1922), 'the worst man in London' (*The Times*, 13 Sept 1929), the 'negro dope-king' (Harrison), and 'a notorious drugs dealer' (J. Chilton, *Sidney Bechet*, 1987, 47), 'living on the immoral earnings of a woman' (*The Times*, 20 July 1923); he represented 'the threat of alien savagery' (Kohn, 167). More prosaically, he was the first person convicted under the 1923 amendments to the Dangerous Drugs Act (1920).

Manning was neither charged nor convicted on drug dealing or on immoral earnings charges: he was a victim of misreporting. After reaching London, possibly via America, he worked in the Vickers munitions factory in Dartford from October 1916 to September 1918, valuable war work that ended when he was hospitalized for surgery until late December 1918. He then worked in theatres and as a dance-band drummer, appearing in newspapers and on the police record after he shot three men in central London in mid-1920. He was sent to prison for sixteen months.

On 24 April 1922 *The Times* reported 'Alleged Cocaine Trafficker—Man of Colour Charged'; Manning had been charged with possession of cocaine and morphine. He pleaded guilty but *The Times* headed its report 'important drug trafficker' and the *News of the World* had the headline 'War on Dope Fiends' (30 April 1922). Misreporting by the national press was to continue. After six months' imprisonment Manning was again in custody for possession from April 1923. The Old Bailey heard allegations of his participation in drug trafficking, and of his living on prostitution, and that he was connected to the expulsion of a Greek possessing cocaine and to a death through heroin—although no hard evidence linked him to these events. He was sent to prison for three years (the first conviction under the amended Dangerous Drugs Act, which extended the maximum sentence for possession from six months to ten years). Press reports suggested that Manning had lived off immoral earnings, although there had been no conviction; and detailed his war work as if labouring in an armaments factory was a sinecure. In 1926 Manning permitted a journalistic biographical account to be published; it indicated that he had come from Jamaica in 1912 to study law, and had been led astray.

Manning's public reputation fuelled racist beliefs in a savage alienism, perverting young white women met in London's night-life *demi-monde*. He kept a seedy restaurant–club in Soho. His criminal activities remained petty. In mid-1927 he was found guilty of harbouring prostitutes; late in 1927 he was found not guilty of receiving stolen goods (this time *The Times* did not report his colour or origins), but was fined for obstructing the police. In mid-1929 he was charged with stealing a car and other property. It belonged to the Duff Coopers, a political and high society couple; Manning was sent to prison for three years. The *News of the World* referred to the 'Coloured Man's Amazing Past' and reported that his café harboured 'coloured men' and 'cunning alien thieves and receivers' (15 Sept 1929).

Manning was a failed petty criminal who used drugs and found companionship with dubious characters. His employment in show business resulted from the jazz age fashion which associated new dances and black people with America. Indeed, the police had believed Manning to be an American, and wanted to deport him: he told them he was Jamaican (and so not an alien in Britain), and the island police traced a veteran who recalled an Alfred Mullin born in 1888. Manning died in Parkhurst prison, Isle of Wight, on 8 February 1931, of acute myolitis. He retained until the end of his life the courtesy that had been a distinguishing aspect of his character, and which, had he avoided the drug use which marked his life from 1920, should have been an asset.

Manning's legacy is remarkable: the London press of the 1920s and books by police officers, social historians, and criminologists portray him as the leading drug trafficker of 1920s London. He was not—but the police, the press, and many later commentators assumed that a black male Jamaican would be at the centre of illegal activities. His death certificate stated that he had been a 'journalist'—the final paradox in the life of a small-time criminal whose crimes had been magnified out of proportion by the press.   JEFFREY GREEN

Sources PRO, MEPO 3/424 · M. Kohn, *Dope girls: the birth of the British drug underground* (1992) · R. Harrison, *Whitehall 1212: the story of the police of London* (c.1954) · R. Fabian, *London after dark* (1954) · A. Tietjen, *Soho: London's vicious circle* (1956) · A. Rose, *Scandal at the Savoy: the infamous 1920s murder case* (1981) · D. Streatfeild, *Cocaine: an unauthorised biography* (2001) · contemporary newspaper reports · d. cert.
Likenesses photograph, repro. in Fabian, *London after dark*, facing p. 96 · photograph, repro. in Tietjen, *Soho*, facing p. 60

Manning, Frederic (1882–1935),

writer, was born on 22 July 1882 at 29 Upper William Street South, Sydney, Australia, the sixth of the eight children of Sir William Patrick Manning (1845–1915), accountant and local politician, and his wife, Honora (*née* Torpy). Sir William, whose parents and wife were Irish Roman Catholic immigrants, was a respected and powerful figure in Sydney, knighted in 1894. Frederic was a lifelong asthmatic, and so was educated almost entirely at home. In his early teens he formed a close intellectual friendship with Arthur Galton (1852–1921), a scholarly Englishman who had moved to Sydney as secretary to the governor. Manning accompanied Galton to England in 1898, and returned to Australia in 1900, but settled in England for good in 1903, taking lodgings with Galton, who was by then vicar of Edenham, Lincolnshire.

Sensitive and unassertive, Manning seems to have been dominated by the increasingly ill-tempered, reactionary vicar, who hoped he would write a masterpiece. Manning laboured in vain on a historical novel, and read widely in the classics and philosophy, enjoying the great sceptics and sharing Galton's scorn for Roman Catholicism (although he never quite deserted the faith). He was of slight build, his drawn face and large dark eyes showing the constant strain of asthma, made worse by heavy smoking. Lonely and often unwell, he developed a weakness for alcohol. He probably never had a sexual relationship; Galton and several motherly women were perhaps parent-substitutes. He made several London friends: Max Beerbohm, William Rothenstein, and others, and two young modernists, Ezra Pound and Richard Aldington. Pound said later that 'Fred', whom he always highly esteemed, had been his first literary companion in England.

Manning's first two books, *The Vigil of Brunhild* (1907), a verse monologue, and *Scenes and Portraits* (1909), were well received by a small, discriminating readership. *Scenes and Portraits* is a collection of debates—ironic, elegant, inconclusive—about religion in different periods of society. Manning began to be talked of as an outstanding new talent, although his *Poems* (1910) showed little originality.

It may seem extraordinary that such a man was keen to join the army when war came. Perhaps Manning was driven by Galton's loathing of Germany, or perhaps by the chance of freedom from the vicarage. After various attempts, he was accepted as Private 19022 in the King's Shropshire light infantry in October 1915. He coped well with life in the ranks, observing his fellow soldiers with an Australian's lack of class-consciousness and warmly admiring their spirit. After failing an officer training course, he was sent to France for the second half of 1916,

took part in the Somme fighting, and was promoted lance-corporal. He came home in December for further training, and in May 1917 was posted to Ireland as second lieutenant, Royal Irish regiment. Loathing the ethos of an officers' mess, he was soon in trouble, receiving a severe reprimand in August for excessive drinking; neurasthenia was diagnosed, perhaps generously. His resignation was accepted in February 1918.

Manning had published a collection of verse, *Eidola*, in 1917. The style was still predominantly old-fashioned, but the war poems showed traces of Pound's imagism. Their central theme is the complete self-possession that can be found in battle, where each individual finds secret freedom, fighting for his own dreams.

Needing to supplement the small income he received from his family, Manning accepted a commission to write *The Life of Sir William White* (1923), a meticulous, uninspired biography of the ship designer. He ceased to have a settled home after Galton's death in 1921, except for a brief period when he owned a Surrey farmhouse. He wrote for periodicals, including T. S. Eliot's *Criterion*, but without a mentor he seemed likely to drift, until in 1929 the publisher Peter Davies persuaded him to write a short novel about the western front. The market for war books was suddenly opening up; urged on by Davies, who allowed no opportunity for revisions, Manning worked fast. Unlike most other authors of the time, he wrote about the troops, using their normal language.

The Middle Parts of Fortune appeared anonymously in a small, private edition in 1929 (the standard text since republication in 1977). The expurgated version, *Her Privates We*, by Private 19022, was published by Davies in 1930. Though unobtrusively literary—Manning's friend, T. E. Lawrence, claimed to have seen that it had to be by the same author as *Scenes and Portraits*—the book is a vivid story of archetypal soldiers, their innate strengths brought out by suffering and comradeship. *The Middle Parts of Fortune* is one of the finest accounts of war ever written, as many of its early readers recognized. Manning used his own experiences, and the central character Bourne, a mysterious, detached figure, is his self-portrait. Bourne, however, dies at the end of 1916, and the survivors are left immersed in their own thoughts, 'each man keeping his own secret'.

Manning kept his own secret. Comparatively little is recorded about him. The authorship of his one great book was not widely known, and he was never famous. He died of pneumonia and asthma at a Hampstead nursing home at 12 Merton Road on 22 February 1935, and was buried at Kensal Green cemetery on 26 February.

DOMINIC HIBBERD

Sources V. Coleman, *The last exquisite: a portrait of Frederic Manning* (1990) · J. Marwil, *Frederic Manning: an unfinished life* (1988)
Archives Harvard U., MSS · Mitchell L., NSW, papers · U. Texas, MSS · University of Chicago, MSS · Yale U., MSS | Bibliothèque Nationale, Paris, MSS · NL Aus., James G. Fairfax MSS
Likenesses W. Rothenstein, chalk drawing, 1921, NPG · photograph, repro. in *The Bookman*, 36 (1909) · photographs, priv. coll. · portraits, repro. in Coleman, *Last exquisite* · portraits, repro. in Marwil, *Frederic Manning*

Wealth at death £257 12s. 7d.: administration with will, 30 May 1935, *CGPLA Eng. & Wales*

Manning, Henry Edward (1808–1892), Roman Catholic convert and cardinal-archbishop of Westminster, was born at Copped Hall, Totteridge, Hertfordshire, on 15 July 1808, the eighth and youngest child of William *Manning (1763–1835), West Indies merchant and tory MP, and his second wife, Mary Hunter (1771–1847), who had influential City connections, her brother becoming lord mayor of London in 1811. William Manning had made his fortune from the West Indian sugar trade and his family grew up in circumstances of considerable affluence, as he gained successive offices of prestige within the City, culminating in his appointment as governor of the Bank of England in 1812–14. Henry Edward was baptized by the bishop of Bath and Wells, and one of his godfathers was a former prime minister, Henry Addington, Viscount Sidmouth. In 1815 the family moved to Coombe Bank at Sundridge, near Sevenoaks, where the young Manning soon made friends with Christopher and Charles Wordsworth, the sons of the rector of Sundridge, the brother of William Wordsworth.

Education Until the age of eight, Manning was educated at home; he then proceeded to a private school at Streatham, from which he was speedily removed because his father feared the lingering influence within the school of a boy who had been removed for immoral practices. He returned to Totteridge where the local curate was taking in private pupils. At the age of fourteen he was sent to Harrow School, where he distinguished himself more in games than at study, playing for two successive years (1825–6) in the Harrow cricket eleven. At this stage of his life he exhibited few indications of subsequent eminence. Being somewhat aloof and fastidious, he was nicknamed the General; he was certainly not particularly pious. His mother had instilled in him a not altogether healthy fear of the inevitability of the day of judgment, but the somewhat high-church religious ambience at Sundridge appears to have left him relatively unmoved. It was not until he left Harrow in 1826 that a major transformation occurred, induced by grief at the death in that year of his favourite sister, Harriet, and by the close association he then formed with his brothers-in-law, John Anderdon, his first real mentor. This was less of a religious conversion than a realization that success in life depended upon industry and disciplined will-power. He therefore subjected himself to a rigorous regime of study under the direction of Canon William Fisher at his coaching establishment at Poulshot in Wiltshire. In April 1827 he entered Balliol College, Oxford. For the next three years, although his health was poor—he was a chronic asthmatic all his life—he worked assiduously, owing much to his tutor, Herman Merivale, and forging stronger links of friendship with Charles Wordsworth at Christ Church and his contemporary at the same college, W. E. Gladstone. He also discovered a talent for public speaking as well as an arena in which to display it—the newly founded Oxford Union, where he enjoyed meteoric success, being cast by

Henry Edward Manning (1808–1892), by George Frederic Watts, 1882

his auditors as the rising young statesman of his generation. In December 1830 his industry was rewarded with a first class in Greats.

Ordination and marriage There followed a combination of circumstances which altered the whole direction of Manning's life. His hopes of a distinguished political career were dashed when his father's fortunes collapsed, ominously precipitated by a slump in sugar prices in 1829. In 1831 Manning had the harrowing experience of accompanying his father to the Guildhall to hand in his seals of office, the symbolic last possessions of a bankrupt. For a short period he was grudgingly grateful to obtain a junior clerkship in the Colonial Office, during which unhappy period he came under the influence of the second, if only temporary, mentor of his life—an exceedingly pious evangelical lady, Favell Bevan, the sister of one of his Harrow contemporaries. The extent of Miss Bevan's influence in drawing Manning into a state of evangelical 'seriousness' has been open to some question (O'Gorman), but their association undoubtedly coincided with Manning's decision to abandon his political aspirations for a career in the church. He returned to Oxford and, in April 1832, was elected fellow of Merton, taking deacon's orders in December of that year. In Manning's subsequent quest for a curacy, his friend Henry Wilberforce arranged for him a temporary engagement—until he was ready to take up the post himself—as curate to John *Sargent, the evangelical rector of Lavington and Graffham in Sussex, little realizing what the consequences would be. Manning went to Lavington in January 1833 and fell in love with one of John

Sargent's daughters, Caroline, to whom he became engaged after a courtship of three months. In May of the same year John Sargent died, and Manning was presented to the living by Caroline's grandmother, having taken priest's orders immediately after John Sargent's death. He and Caroline were married in November 1833.

Thus came about the forging of the closest of bonds between Manning and the Wilberforce and Sargent families. Samuel Wilberforce (later bishop of Oxford and of Winchester) had married Caroline's elder sister, Emily, in 1828; his brother Henry, not at all put out by the chain of events, married yet another Sargent daughter (Mary) in July 1834. In the same month, the fourth Sargent daughter, Sophia, married George Dudley Ryder. Tragically, three of the brothers-in-law were to undergo the agonies of early bereavement, through the successive deaths of Caroline Manning (25 July 1837), Emily Wilberforce (1841), and Sophia Ryder (1850).

Manning suffered first, and the loss of Caroline (there were no children) was a lifelong sorrow. He kept all her letters, which were stolen—to his great grief—from a travelling bag when he was *en route* for Rome in 1851; on his deathbed, he entrusted to Herbert Vaughan, his successor at Westminster, a book of Caroline's prayers, from which he had prayed and meditated every day since her death. Thereby he also paid final testimony to his enduring attachment to the Church of England.

Manning and Anglicanism Manning's advance into full sympathy with Newman's stance at Oxford, while never amounting to adulation and always maintaining a measure of independence, progressed in stages: first, an acceptance of the doctrine of baptismal regeneration (at the time of his ordination) and (by 1834) an understanding of the nature of the real presence, gained from a study of Richard Hooker. In 1835, when he preached his first published sermon (*The English Church, its Succession and Witness for Christ*) at a visitation in Chichester Cathedral, he gave eloquent expression to his conviction of the exalted nature of the priestly office; he reverted to this theme in his second visitation sermon, in 1838 (*The Rule of Faith*, published in the same year), by which time he had arrived at the conclusion that the credentials of the Church of England must be seen to lie in its authoritative role as the teacher and interpreter of Christian doctrine (the church as *ecclesia docens*). Although he had shared Samuel Wilberforce's reservations about the severe tone of Newman's first volume of sermons, Manning fully endorsed the concept of the Anglican church as the *via media* between the corruptions of Rome and the heresies of continental protestantism, and he therefore undertook to become a distributor of the Tracts for the Times in his locality. In 1836, in collaboration with Charles Marriott, he contributed a tract himself—Tract 78, a *catena patrum* on the subject of Catholic tradition. In 1837 he pinned his colours to the Tractarian mast by registering his vote at Oxford in protest against the appointment of the allegedly heterodox R. D. Hampden as regius professor of divinity.

Although during these years Manning's strongest bond of affection was with his senior brother-in-law, Samuel

Wilberforce, another close—and probably more formative—friendship had developed with Samuel Francis Wood (younger brother of Charles Wood, later first Viscount Halifax), a brilliant young lawyer, greatly attached to Newman, and himself a keen student of theology. They became firm friends in the course of their joint work on behalf of the National Society for Promoting the Education of the Poor, and recent research has unearthed a highly significant correspondence, as early as the winter of 1835, between Wood (the instigator), Newman, and Manning on the church's role in the development of Christian doctrine, which was later to prove such a decisive issue in Newman's conversion to Rome (Pereiro, 218–53). Manning was himself engaged in patristic studies during these years (offering a contribution to Pusey's Library of the Fathers on Justin Martyr), and his scholarship was clearly demonstrated in his most substantial book, written as an Anglican, *The Unity of the Church* (1842). There is no doubt, however, that he deeply respected Wood's judgement on all theological questions. After Wood's untimely death in 1843, Manning found a second mentor on theological matters in yet another of the Wilberforce family—Robert Wilberforce, archdeacon of the East Riding, brother of Samuel and Henry, and also a future convert to Rome.

Within the diocese of Chichester, and indeed beyond, Manning was making his mark in other ways, as well as by acquiring influential friends. In 1837 he became rural dean of Midhurst, and rapidly established a reputation as the most active and efficient among his diocesan colleagues. He was appointed to the corresponding committee of the National Society and—in the company of S. F. Wood and Thomas Acland—was the leading force in the founding of the theological college at Chichester, securing his friend Charles Marriott as its first principal. The establishment of the ecclesiastical commission on a permanent basis in 1836, with extensive powers to tackle the anomalies and abuses within the Church of England, provoked Manning to follow the lead of Pusey in publishing an intemperate protest against what he conceived to be an unwarranted encroachment by the state upon the independent authority of the church (*Principles of the Ecclesiastical Commission Examined*, 1838), which brought about a renewal of friendship and the beginning of regular correspondence with Gladstone. He was overworking himself, partly as a reaction to the feeling of crushing emptiness after Caroline's death, and William Otter, his bishop, persuaded him to take a complete break abroad. So, in the winter of 1838, Manning decided to join Gladstone who was spending Christmas in Rome. This was to be the first of twenty-two visits that Manning made to the 'eternal city' in the course of his life.

Archdeacon of Chichester Shortly after his return from Rome, Manning received his reward for his industry and influence. In December 1840 he was appointed archdeacon of Chichester in succession to the senile Charles Webber, who had been prevailed upon to retire. It was a preferment hardly to be expected from the new evangelical bishop, William Shuttleworth, who had swallowed his antipathy to Tractarians in response to pressure from Julius Hare, archdeacon of Lewes, and the dean of Chichester, G. Chandler, and also because Webber candidly admitted that Manning had been effectively acting as archdeacon since he became rural dean.

As archdeacon, Manning soon became a national figure. A speech that he delivered in Willis's Rooms in London in April 1841, on the subject of the need for more colonial bishops, was so powerful that Gladstone recalled its eloquence fifty years later, and George Selwyn, who was also in the audience, described it as the turning point of his life. His archidiaconal charges were read nationwide, their main significance today lying in the remarkable similarity between the declared priorities in these charges and those which he was later to define in his pastorals as archbishop of Westminster: urgent attention to the plight of the poor and the outcasts of society; sympathy for the lot of the labouring classes and condemnation of exploitation by greedy landowners and employers; and the crucial need for the education of the poor and for the preservation of its denominational character. A theme of several of his Anglican sermons—the church's obligation to undertake the proper training of ordinands—would reappear in time, once he became archbishop of Westminster, as would his emphasis on the awesome nature of a priest's responsibilities and duties (to be prepared 'to be crucified with Christ', as he put it in an Oxford University sermon in 1843). This would be repeated in his work *The Eternal Priesthood* (1883), a tough challenge for seminarians, since it reads like a counsel of unattainable perfection. A further enduring theme (which would change only in name when he became a Catholic) was the independence of the church from secular interference: the need to combat Erastianism as applied to the Church of England, labouring under unacceptable manifestations of the royal supremacy.

Newman and Roman Catholicism Nevertheless, bold as Manning was in his own championship of the Catholic traditions within the Anglican church, he began studiously to distance himself from the Romeward trend of Newman in 1841 and thereafter. He sincerely believed that Newman's notorious Tract 90 was misconceived; and when called upon to preach the sermon on 5 November at Oxford in 1843—a delicate mission in the circumstances—Manning took the opportunity to inveigh against 'the secular domination of the Roman pontiff' and to declare his own total devotion to 'our highly-favoured Church' (*Sermons Preached before the University of Oxford*, 1844, 81). From the sensitive and sympathetic correspondence that continued between Manning and Newman up to the point of Newman's reception into the Roman Catholic church in October 1845, however, there is no suggestion of personal estrangement on either side.

Difficult years lay ahead for Manning. Samuel Wilberforce became bishop of Oxford in the same month as Newman's reception, and Manning felt less able to share his private anxieties with him. Pressure was being put upon him to apply his own moderating influence and reputation for statesmanship to rally the shaken ranks of those

whom Newman had abandoned. Gladstone begged him, in the winter of 1845, to produce a weighty challenge to the arguments of Newman's *Essay on Development*. Manning was well aware that his friends were looking to the day when he would follow his brother-in-law into the ranks of the episcopate, and a new—rather improbable—friendship with the crusty old doyen of the high-church party, Henry Phillpotts, bishop of Exeter, made such an expectation even surer. Yet, when the obvious opening occurred in December 1845—the offer of the post of subalmoner to the archbishop of York, generally regarded as a springboard to episcopal office—Manning declined it, to the surprise and consternation of his friends.

The truth is that Manning embarked upon the task that Gladstone had set him only to discover that he found Newman's arguments unanswerable. Only to a very few people could he safely communicate his growing fears that he might be ministering within a schismatical church: Henry Wilberforce and Mary, his wife; his own curate, Charles Laprimaudaye, who had become his spiritual director; and Robert Wilberforce, the man whom he hoped would be most able to allay his doubts. In February 1847 he fell seriously ill. He spent ten months of his convalescence abroad, determined to learn for himself as much as he could about continental Catholicism and Catholic theology. Much of the time was spent in Rome, where he had an audience with Pope Pius IX on 11 May 1848. He returned to England still undecided. Three years of spiritual anguish followed, during which—according to the unsympathetic account given by E. S. Purcell, his first major biographer—he spoke with 'a double voice', stoutly defending the Church of England while privately doubting its claims to be a church at all. It should be observed that from this point in Purcell's two-volume biography, published in 1896, indications of strong personal animus appear, amounting to distortion and calumny in the construction that he places on Manning's motives and ruthlessness during the course of his Catholic career. Unfortunately for Manning's reputation in the eyes of posterity, these imputations of unscrupulous personal ambition were to be popularized in 1918 by Lytton Strachey in the first of his essays in *Eminent Victorians*. Purcell's motive and methods have been rightly questioned more recently (see Gilley, 166–98).

A fairer way of representing Manning's dilemma in the years between 1848 and 1851 is to recognize that he could not contemplate injury to the church whose preferments he had accepted, and the sorrow caused to those near to him, until his doubts had become certainties. This eventually came about through an escalating series of considerations and events: his conviction that the Church of England lacked the strength of the penitential system that he had seen at work abroad, as he testified to Henry Wilberforce and T. W. Allies on his return to England in 1848; and the emotional blow of the secession of Henry and Mary Wilberforce in June 1850. On his own admission, however, it was the proof of the inherent Erastianism of the Church of England that forced him to take the decisive step. The church had been impotent in 1847 when Lord John Russell had ignored the howls of protest against his appointment of R. D. Hampden to the bishopric of Hereford. Even more serious, the judicial committee of the privy council (a largely secular tribunal) had presumed to make the final and irrevocable judgment in the Gorham case of 1850, thereby overruling the decision of the court of arches to support the bishop of Exeter's refusal to institute to a living in his diocese a Calvinist who denied the doctrine of baptismal regeneration. Here was proof positive that the Church of England must resign all claims to be an *ecclesia docens*, if the state had the right to dictate on matters of doctrine. Manning's protest, his last publication within the Church of England (*The Appellate Jurisdiction of the Crown in Matters Spiritual*, 1850), went unheeded. When, later that same year, Pius IX proclaimed the restoration of the Roman Catholic hierarchy in England, thereby precipitating outraged protestant accusations of 'papal aggression', Manning was required as archdeacon to convene his clergy to register their repudiation of the papal effrontery. In duty bound he summoned the meeting; but in conscience bound he vacated the chair and announced his intention to resign. On 6 April 1851, in the company of his friend James Hope, he was received into the Roman Catholic communion by Father Brownbill SJ at the Jesuit church in Farm Street.

A Roman Catholic priest 'After this I shall sink to the bottom and disappear', Manning observed to Robert Wilberforce. Did he sincerely believe this, and did it seriously worry him if he did? Loss of friends deeply distressed him; so too did loss of influence in high places. As for personal advancement, when a member of the cabinet told him in 1854 that, if he had remained an Anglican, he would have gained the bishopric of Salisbury (instead of W. K. Hamilton), his reply was, 'What an escape my poor soul did have' (Gray, 153). In fact, he had underestimated the percipience of Nicholas Wiseman, now installed as cardinal-archbishop of Westminster. He was fully aware of the depth of Manning's spirituality and the many gifts and talents that he could bring to the service of the church. Against Manning's own wishes he ordained him priest on 14 June 1851, within ten weeks of his reception. In the autumn of 1851 Manning left for Rome to study at the Accademia Ecclesiastica, where he remained, returning for occasional breaks in England, until the late summer of 1854. Here again he made an immediate impression, both on Pius IX, with whom he was to have frequent audiences, and on his recently appointed papal chamberlain, acting as Wiseman's personal representative in Rome, the Hon. George Talbot, who had been Manning's travelling companion *en route* for Rome. He was awarded a papal doctorate at the conclusion of his studies and the pope tried, unsuccessfully, to persuade him to remain at Rome as a papal chamberlain with prelatial rank.

But Manning's place, at his own wish, was in England. An immediate service which he could offer, on the outbreak of the Crimean War, was to use his influence with former friends in the government (and his diplomatic skills with wary members of the Catholic hierarchy) to supply Florence Nightingale with nuns to act as nurses in the Crimea. A more permanent challenge was to respond to Wiseman's invitation to him to found a community of mission priests to work in the poorest quarters of London. This was the origin of the congregation of the Oblates of St Charles Borromeo, for the headquarters of which Manning secured a partially built church in Bayswater (St Mary of the Angels). Having drawn up a rule, Manning was appointed superior, and the congregation began its active life in 1857. For the next eight years—the happiest years of his life, as he later recalled—Bayswater remained his residence; during that time he converted the area around him into a virtual Catholic stronghold, building three new churches and four convents, and setting up eight schools, a choir school, and a reformatory.

These successes, and the favours lavished upon him, did not endear Manning to many of the old English Catholics. He seemed to be in too much of a hurry, a 'forward piece' as William Hogarth, bishop of Hexham, described him. He was accused of being over-zealous in his determination to gain converts. By 1865 his tally amounted to 346; as some of them came from the ranks of the aristocracy, he was—very unfairly—taunted with the title the 'Apostle of the Genteels'. Wiseman's affection for him did not pass unnoticed. Within a year of his reception Wiseman had invited him, with Newman, to preach one of the two sermons at the first synod of Oscott in July 1852; Pius IX then caused a stir of unrest, amounting almost to a mutiny within the chapter of Westminster, by personally appointing Manning provost of Westminster in 1857.

Understandably, the most resentful were those who had been closest to Wiseman's inner councils before Manning appeared to usurp their place. But the most implacable opponent was Wiseman's own coadjutor, with right of succession to the Westminster see, George Errington, archbishop of Trebizond. Errington was an able canon lawyer who was totally unsympathetic to the religious temper and Italianate usages of the so-called 'new ultramontanism', which coincided with Wiseman's arrival in England and the restoration of the hierarchy. Many of the recent converts rejoiced to see such a day, but it was a wind of change uncongenial to the majority of old English Catholics who responded to it with insular indifference. Errington's many attempts to thwart Manning's influence eventually centred on what he conceived to be a virtual take-over of the seminary at St Edmund's, near Ware, by the Oblates, and the consequent introduction there of Roman usages, both in dress and devotions. The climax of this clash of personalities was fought out in Rome, when Errington's opposition turned into open disloyalty to Wiseman himself. This, then, became Wiseman's battle, and Manning prudently played no direct part in it. But it was to lead to a fateful conclusion. Errington, at the pope's command, was deprived of his coadjutorship and his right of succession to the see.

Already something of a division into parties was becoming discernible among English Catholics, tending to centre on the personalities and priorities of the two most distinguished converts, Newman and Manning. This was almost inevitable, granted their different temperaments and the conflicting interests dearest to their hearts. Newman was anxious to elevate the intellectual standing (and standards) of the Catholic laity; both the tone of his writings and the refreshingly independent spirit displayed within them appealed especially to the Catholic intelligentsia. He became involved, somewhat reluctantly, with Lord Acton and the newly founded organ of liberal Catholicism, *The Rambler*, which was inclined in the subject matter of its articles to trespass on the sacred preserves of the hierarchy and official theologians. Newman's wish to establish a branch of the Oratory in Oxford raised fears that his return to his old stamping ground would encourage the laity to defy the inhibition against Catholics attending the university, imposed for fear of their encountering influences damaging to their faith. Both Wiseman and Manning were uneasy about Newman's influence, Manning going so far (after he became archbishop) as to express his views in a private letter to Mgr Talbot that Newman was attempting to reproduce in the church 'the old Anglican, patristic, literary Oxford tone', unfairly branding such an attitude as 'worldly' or 'diluted' Catholicism (Newsome, *Convert Cardinals*, 257–8). Manning agreed with Newman in putting Catholic education as a top priority, but his main concern was the education of the poor, the founding of Catholic elementary schools, and the provision of seminaries for the training of the secular clergy.

The divergence became a rift, however, over the vexed question of the pope's 'temporal power'. To Newman the retention of papal sovereignty within his traditional patrimony was a thing indifferent. To Manning it was the essential safeguard of the pope's independence from secular control, and he was prepared to fight this issue with almost apocalyptic fervour. It was understandable that he should do so. His visit to Rome in 1847 and 1848 had coincided with the flight of Pius IX to Gaeta and the setting up of the Mazzinian Roman Republic. He saw, more clearly than many of his contemporaries, the hypocrisy that underlay Cavour's facile slogan 'A free church in a free state', which was purely a cover to wrest education out of the hands of the church, to spoliate ecclesiastical endowments, and ultimately to silence its effective voice. Furthermore, Manning had abandoned the Church of England because of its inability to resist Erastianism. On the wider stage of the worldwide Catholic communion, secular pretensions to gain control of the church were what he was wont to describe as 'Caesarism', representing it as the greatest menace of modern times. He had not left the Anglican church in order to see the vicar of Christ become as impotent as the archbishop of Canterbury. For such a fate to overcome Pius IX, to whom Manning felt an intense personal loyalty, was unthinkable. The subject of Caesarism evoked from his pen, for the remainder of his life, some of his most powerful invective, directed against Piedmont, the Paris commune, and, finally, the *Kulturkampf* of Bismarck (for example, in *Caesarism and Ultramontanism*, 1873, repr. in *Miscellanies*, vol. 2).

Archbishop of Westminster and cardinal Wiseman died on 15 February 1865, and Manning delivered his funeral oration in accordance with the cardinal's expressed wish. He had no serious expectations that the mantle of Elijah would fall on his own shoulders. But the Westminster chapter caused great offence to the pope by placing the name of Errington, with the names of two other bishops who declined to stand, in the terna (the three nominations for the succession to the Westminster see). Pius IX therefore took the matter into his own hands, defying the advice of the Congregatio de Propaganda Fide and relying on the guidance of private prayer. So it came about that within fourteen years of his conversion Manning found himself appointed the second archbishop of Westminster. He was consecrated on 8 June 1865 at the pro-cathedral at Moorfields.

The expected opposition to the appointment never came, and for a while there was a closing of the ranks behind the new archbishop. Manning immediately worked for reconciliation. He offered a bishopric *in partibus* to Newman, which he declined. Thereafter, despite his private feelings expressed sometimes intemperately to Mgr Talbot, he offered a series of olive branches to the man who had once been his friend and whose support he was so anxious to obtain. He was not prepared to relent, however, on the inhibition on Catholics attending Oxford and Cambridge. In 1875 Manning persuaded *propaganda fide* not to censure Newman for certain ill-received comments in his *Letter to the Duke of Norfolk*. Putting aside his own personal feelings, Manning agreed to support the petition to Pope Leo XIII in 1879 for the bestowal of a cardinalate on Newman, unfortunately gaining discredit for what was meant to be a kindly act by his misunderstanding of Newman's reply, Manning interpreting certain ambiguous phrases as a courteous refusal of the official offer. Following Newman's death on 11 August 1890, Manning delivered his funeral oration at the Brompton Oratory nine days later, acknowledging his services to the church in a eulogy of great eloquence.

Manning was archbishop of Westminster for nearly twenty-seven years. He was elevated to the cardinalate himself on 29 March 1875 (cardinal-priest attached to the church of St Andrew and St Gregory on the Coelian Hill). On the death of his beloved Pius IX on 7 February 1878, Manning's name was put forward at the ensuing conclave as a possible successor, but he refused to be considered on the grounds that the political situation demanded the election of an Italian. The first years of his archiepiscopate were marked by his determination to set in motion a crisis fund to provide school accommodation for Catholic children, and he insisted that this pressing need must take priority over the building of Westminster Cathedral, as Wiseman's memorial. By the time of his death schooling had been provided for 70,000 children. With a determination reminiscent of his Anglican days, he fought a constant battle to undo the damage to denominational teaching in the Forster Education Act of 1870. He even took the unprecedented step in 1885 of publishing in every Catholic newspaper instructions to Catholic voters on the eve of a general election, in order to thwart the proposals of Joseph Chamberlain (and therefore the Liberal Party) to put an end to voluntary schools. Lord Salisbury duly appointed him in 1886 as a member of the Cross commission on elementary education.

Not all Manning's educational endeavours were successful, however. He appreciated that if he were to have any hope of countering the pressure on Catholics to defy the official inhibition against entry to Oxford and Cambridge, he must at least take the initial steps to establish a Catholic university as an acceptable alternative. In January 1875 the Catholic University College of Kensington began its precarious life. The Jesuits, however, failed to support it; the first rector consistently created more problems than he solved; and within seven years its effective life was over. Another of Manning's grand educational designs—a project to set up a network of diocesan seminaries, on the Tridentine pattern, in order to guarantee a supply of disciplined and professionally trained priests—was also short-lived. The expense proved too great, and the supply of ordinands too few.

Manning's devotion to the interests of the secular priesthood, on which the major burden of the pastoral office lay, led him to resent the independence of the regular clergy from episcopal control (he could not easily forgive the Society of Jesus for their refusal to support his university plans). In 1881 he, with the support of Herbert Vaughan and Bishop Clifford of Clifton, succeeded in obtaining from Leo XIII the bull *Romanos pontifices*, which laid down that in future no religious house, college, or school could be established without the prior consent of the diocesan bishop.

Papal infallibility To Manning, however, this was a minor triumph compared to the issue of the definition of papal infallibility at the Vatican Council of 1869–70, within which he was to play a prominent and a highly controversial role. Against the so-called inopportunists, who feared that a time of political crisis, exacerbated by the designs of Piedmont on the remaining Papal States, was unpropitious for the raising of so sensitive an issue, Manning held precisely the opposite view (again finding himself at odds with Newman). He was determined to secure conciliar confirmation of what was practically universally accepted by Catholics, seeing such a bold assertion of ultramontanism as the most fitting riposte to the revolutionary forces threatening the church on all sides. In three successive pastorals, published as a volume entitled *Petri privilegium* in 1871, he called upon the church to unite against the evil of Caesarism. Once in Rome, where he was in his element (he spoke Italian perfectly), he took upon himself the role of chief whip of the infallibilist party, allowing fervour at times to degenerate into ruthlessness in his contriving to ensure that no member of the opposition should be allowed a place on the committee set up to draft the conciliar decree. He employed all his statesmanship, through the intermediary of Odo Russell (England's unaccredited agent in Rome), to persuade the British government and other hostile European powers not to intervene to close

the proceedings of the council. On 25 May 1870 he delivered at the council one of the most powerful speeches of his life in support of the definition, lasting one hour and fifty minutes, which even his opponents conceded was a masterly performance. The final definition, in the decree *Pastor aeternus*, was actually more moderate than Manning had hoped to achieve, but he had no reservations in his defence of the definition or of the proceedings of the council when he came to respond to Gladstone's published 'expostulations' of 1874–5 against a seeming reversion to medievalism. His answer to Gladstone's attacks came in two books: *The Vatican Decrees and their Bearing on Civil Allegiance* (1875) and *The True Story of the Vatican Council* (1877).

Manning and reform Manning had an enduring affection and respect for Gladstone, harking back to their close friendship in the 1840s. Gladstone, on the other hand, never quite forgave his friend for abandoning the Church of England, and was constantly perplexed by Manning's change of stance from statesmanlike moderation, as an Anglican, to the extremism and inflexibility of his Catholic years. Nevertheless, intermittent and reasonably cordial relations with Gladstone had been resumed after Manning's elevation to Westminster and again, if slightly less cordial, in the years following the council, chiefly because of their common concern over the plight of Ireland. The first necessity was to secure the disestablishment of the Irish church, the established church being an intolerable affront to a largely Catholic nation. In 1868 Manning published his *Letter to Earl Grey* (repr. in *Miscellanies*, vol. 1), forcefully expounding his case, as well as identifying other iniquitous abuses—the grossly inequitable land laws most of all. Gladstone had already come round to the need to tackle the issue of disestablishment without Manning's prompting, but the arguments of Manning's pamphlet were used extensively in the parliamentary debates which eventually saw disestablishment achieved in 1869. The removal of the worst abuses of the land laws, for which Manning tirelessly campaigned, was a slower process, but legislation in 1870 and 1881 gained most of what he sought. Manning felt a genuine sympathy for the Fenian cause, but never condoned the use of violence. He maintained friendly relations with both Parnell and Michael Davitt, doing his utmost to counter pressure upon the Holy See from the British government to issue a papal condemnation of the Irish Land League. Towards the end of his life he came to the reluctant conclusion that some form of home rule was inevitable.

Manning's sympathy for the oppressed and disadvantaged in society, already witnessed in his Anglican days, became more and more marked as he grew older. During his retreat with the Passionists at Highgate on the eve of his consecration, he pledged himself to devote all his energies on behalf of the wretched and the so-called 'worthless' in society. He also recognized the church's obligation to protect honest labouring people against exploitation by employers. His strongest proclamation on this theme came in an address given in Leeds in 1874, published under the title *The Dignity and Rights of Labour* (repr.

in *Miscellanies*, vol. 2). He had already publicly supported Joseph Arch's National Agricultural Labourers' Union, insisting that labour had a right to protect itself against exploitation and to campaign for fair wages and reasonable hours of work. He was later to declare his support for the even more radical union movement in America, the Knights of Labour. In this respect he stood virtually alone within the church in England as a pioneer of social Catholicism, although he had allies among the Catholic hierarchy abroad in men like Cardinal Gibbons, archbishop of Baltimore, and Cardinal Moran in Australia. Manning's concern was not merely Christian compassion; he vehemently believed that the rising labour movement throughout the Western world was waiting for leadership and guidance. If that genuinely sympathetic guidance was not offered by the church, then more dangerous forces, and communism in particular, would not be slow in seizing the initiative.

As early as 1864 Manning had warned his generation that the old order was dying ('The visit of Garibaldi in England' in *Miscellanies*, vol. 1). The church's place was no longer in alliance with princes, but with the common people. The role of the church in modern society was to be 'the Mother, Friend and Protectress of the People. As our Divine Saviour lived among persons of the people, so lives His Church' (Fitzsimon, 142). There is no doubt that Leo XIII's social encyclicals, and notably the great declaration on workers' rights in *Rerum novarum* (1891) owed much to Manning's influence. As early as 1884 his concern for social problems had been recognized at home by his appointment as a member of the royal commission on the housing of the working classes. His greatest triumph in the field of labour relations, however, was his personal intervention in the crippling London Dock strike of 1889, through his friendship with one of the dockers' leaders, Ben Tillett, and his readiness to confront the strike committee to negotiate an acceptable compromise. He was successful in breaking the deadlock, and earned for himself the enduring gratitude of the London dockers and the labour force nationwide.

Many of Manning's co-religionists found his radical sympathies difficult to understand. He faced fierce opposition and ridicule in his campaign to curb the evils of intemperance, believing the demon drink to be the greatest single cause of degradation and misery among the poor. He gave active support to the United Kingdom Alliance, a largely nonconformist pressure group working for legislation to control the drink trade; in 1872 he founded the League of the Cross—an organization unashamedly imitating the successful techniques of the Salvation Army—committed to proselytize on behalf of total abstinence. He would cheerfully share a platform with Bramwell Booth, who—in return—came to reverence him almost as a saint.

It is not surprising that Londoners grew to love Manning. He was always in their midst; and the doors of Archbishop House, an ugly barrack-like building on the corner of Carlisle Place and Francis Street, where the cardinal lived in an atmosphere of bleak austerity, were open to all comers, who rarely went away unsatisfied, because Manning was prodigal in his charity. To the end of his life, he preached two or three times every Sunday, usually choosing churches in the poorest parts of his diocese. He never took a holiday. His occasional relaxations consisted of a visit to the Athenaeum to read the papers or to take part in the rarified discussions of the Metaphysical Society, happy to hold his own against T. H. Huxley demonstrating the spurious credentials of the Christian revelation. Sometimes, during the evening, he would relax in the company of a young Anglican friend, J. E. C. Bodley, to whom he could talk more freely than to members of his own communion.

Wherein lay the secret of the exceptional impact that Manning made on everyone who met him? Great personal charm, certainly, but also a remarkable physical presence. Every artist who met him wanted to sketch his portrait; everyone who encountered him tried to find the words to describe the impression, usually recalling the massive forehead, the piercing look of his eyes, and the hollow cheeks, which gave the cardinal a cadaverous look in his old age. But always, despite the frailty induced by years of austerity and self-denial, the dignity and authority were the lasting impression. As G. W. E. Russell recalled, the sight of Manning as he passed through the anteroom to his throne room to hold an audience was such that 'the most Protestant knee instinctively bent' (Russell, 41).

Death and reputation Manning died at Archbishop House, Carlisle Place, London, on 14 January 1892, following a serious attack of bronchitis. The scenes at his funeral on 21 January and the crowds that thronged the streets for the 4 miles between the Brompton Oratory and Kensal Green cemetery (where he was buried) had no precedent, it was observed, since the death of the first duke of Wellington. Manning's body was later reinterred at Westminster Cathedral.

Forty years earlier, a cardinal seen in the streets of London would have been pelted with mud. The temperature of No Popery agitation within the nation at large had cooled by the closing decades of the century. To what extent this was due to Manning's personal reputation is difficult to quantify, though it was undoubtedly one among other reasons for the easing of the tension. Perhaps his vision of the role of the Catholic church in modern society has been imperfectly appreciated by his immediate posterity. He was neither Liberal nor Conservative, his political stance being most aptly expressed when he described himself as 'a Mosaic Radical': radical in his indignation over the exploitation of the weaker members of society; authoritative and ultramontane in his conviction that the people ask of the church strong guidance and a voice of certainty. One of his greatest services to his church also has an element of paradox in it. Unflinchingly dogmatic and a Roman of the Romans, he also gave his generation the initiative to practical ecumenism by his readiness to recognize the workings of the Holy Spirit in churches other than the 'one true fold'. This was an argument advanced as early as 1864 in his *The Workings of the Holy Spirit in the Church of England*, though Anglicans at the time were affronted by the fact that he allowed the Church of England no higher accreditation than he accorded to dissenting churches. He believed passionately that Christians of different communions could and should learn from one another, and should be prepared to work together in endeavours of 'practical Christianity', as he himself demonstrated in his co-operation with non-conformists and the Salvation Army to save men's bodies as well as their souls. Finally, in the course of his archiepiscopate he taught his fellow Catholics that the time had come for them to emerge from the twilight and to show themselves as a powerful pressure group, whose interests and concerns could not be ignored. If they doubted their ability to do so, they had only to witness the example of his own life.   DAVID NEWSOME

Sources E. S. Purcell, *Life of Cardinal Manning*, 2 vols. (1896) · S. Leslie, *Henry Edward Manning: his life and labours* (1921) · J. E. C. Bodley, *Cardinal Manning, and other essays* (1912) · V. A. McClelland, *Cardinal Manning: his public life and influence, 1865–1892* (1962) · V. A. McClelland, *English Roman Catholics and higher education, 1830–1903* (1973) · R. Gray, *Cardinal Manning: a biography* (1985) · D. Newsome, *The parting of friends: a study of the Wilberforces and Henry Manning* (1966) · D. Newsome, *The convert cardinals: John Henry Newman and Henry Edward Manning* (1993) · J. Fitzsimon, ed., *Manning: Anglican and Catholic* (1951) · W. Ward, *The life and times of Cardinal Wiseman*, 2 vols. (1897) · C. Butler, *The life and times of Bishop Ullathorne, 1806–1889*, 2 vols. (1926) · C. A. O'Gorman, 'A history of Henry Manning's religious opinions, 1808–1832', *Recusant History*, 21 (1992–3), 152–66, esp. 159–61 · J. Pereiro, 'Truth before peace: Manning and infallibility', *Recusant History*, 21 (1992–3), 218–53 · B. H. Harrison, 'Cardinal Manning as temperance reformer', *HJ*, 12 (1969), 485–510 · S. Gilley, 'New light on an old scandal: Purcell's *Life of Cardinal Manning*', *Opening the scrolls: essays in Catholic history in honour of Godfrey Anstruther*, ed. D. A. Bellenger (1987), 166–98 · C. Butler, *The Vatican Council*, 2 vols. (1930) · E. R. Norman, *The Catholic church and Ireland in the age of rebellion, 1859–1873* (1965) · Gladstone, *Diaries* · G. W. E. Russell, *Collections and recollections, by one who has kept a diary* (1898) · H. E. Manning, *Miscellanies*, 3 vols. (1877–88)

Archives BL, letters, mainly to his brother, RP 2824 [photocopies] · Bodl. Oxf., corresp., notebooks, and papers · Catholic University of the West, Angers, France · Emory University, Atlanta, Georgia, Pitts Theology Library, corresp. and papers · St John's Seminary, Camarillo, California, letters · University of Atlanta, letters to Gladstone · Westm. DA, papers | Birmingham Oratory, letters to John Henry Newman and Lady Herbert of Lea · BL, corresp. with Sir Charles Dilke, Add. MS 43896 · BL, corresp. with W. E. Gladstone, Add. MSS 44247–44250 · BL, corresp. with Lord Ripon, Add. MS 43545 · Bodl. Oxf., corresp. with Sir William Harcourt · Bodl. Oxf., letters to Disraeli · CAC Cam., corresp. with W. T. Stead · Exeter Cathedral, archives, letters to Henry Phillpotts · LPL, letters to Charles Wordsworth · LPL, letters to Christopher Wordsworth · NL Ire., corresp. with Lord Emly · NL Scot., corresp. with J. R. Hope-Scott · Northants. RO, letters among the Elwes family papers · PRO, letters to Odo Russell, FO 918 · Southwark Roman Catholic Diocesan Archives, London, letters to Searle and Dannell · St Deiniol's Library, Hawarden, letters from W. E. Gladstone [copies] · Syracuse University, New York, corresp. with Sir John Simeon · U. St Andr. L., letters to Wilfrid Ward and Mrs Ward · Ushaw College, Durham, corresp. relating to Ushaw College · Ushaw College, Durham, letters to Henry Wilberforce · W. Sussex RO, letters to the Otter family · W. Sussex RO, letters to duke of Richmond · W. Sussex RO, personal and family papers incl. letters to Samuel Wilberforce · Westm. DA, corresp. with Edward Thompson, etc. · Westm. DA, letters to Wiseman · Wilts. & Swindon RO, corresp. with Sidney Herbert and Elizabeth Herbert

Likenesses G. Richmond, group portrait, ink, pencil and wash, 1840–45, NPG · F. Holl, stipple, pubd 1851 (after G. Richmond), BM, NPG · J. H. Thomas, bronze bust, 1870–86, Tate collection · G. F. Watts, oils, 1882, NPG [*see illus.*] · J. A. Acton, plaster bust, *c*.1884, NPG · R. Lehmann, chalk drawings, 1890, BM · C. G. Anderson, oils, 1892, Balliol Oxf. · B. Gotto, bronze bust, *c*.1929, Harrow School · A. Legros, bronze medallion, Man. City Gall. · A. Legros, etching, BM · M. Menpes, etching, NPG · Orpen?, Westminster Cathedral, London, archbishop's house · C. Pellegrini, watercolour, NPG; repro. in *VF* (25 Feb 1871) · G. Pilotell, etching, BM · G. Richmond, Westminster Cathedral, London, archbishop's house · J. H. Thomas, marble bust, Westminster Cathedral, London, archbishop's house · A. Wing, portrait, NPG · cartes-de-visite, NPG · death mask, Watts Gallery, Compton, Surrey · photographs, NPG · portrait?, Mannheim collection · prints, NPG · wood-engraving (after photograph by J. & C. Watkins), NPG; repro. in *ILN* (10 June 1865)

Wealth at death £3527 19*s*. 10*d*.: probate, 26 April 1892, *CGPLA Eng. & Wales*

Manning, James (1738–1791), college head and Baptist minister in America, was born on 22 October 1738 in Piscataway, Middlesex county, New Jersey, the son of James Manning, a farmer, and Grace Fitz-Randolph, and great-grandson of Jeffrey Manning, one of the earliest settlers in Piscataway township. Educated early at school at Hopewell, New Jersey, by the Revd Isaac Eaton, he enrolled at the age of twenty in the College of New Jersey and graduated with highest honours in 1762. He entered the Baptist ministry shortly after leaving college and during the remainder of his life was a leading Baptist figure. He married on 23 March 1763 Margaret, daughter of John Stites of Elizabethtown, Pennsylvania, and was ordained to preach the Baptist faith on 19 April. He proceeded to take a tour of the colonies with regard to educating himself about their religious conditions.

In 1763 Manning became active on behalf of a movement led by the Philadelphia Association of Baptist Churches for the establishment of the first Baptist college in the American colonies. After considerable discussions a Latin school was established in Warren, Rhode Island, and Manning was made the pastor of the First Baptist Church in the same town; with the Rhode Island assembly granting a charter in March 1764 for a Rhode Island College. Manning was appointed in September 1765 'President and Professor of languages, and other branches of learning, with full power to act in those capacities, at Warren or elsewhere'. He conducted the Latin school and the new college in Warren until 1770, when they were moved to Providence and the College Edifice (now known as University Hall) was erected.

Manning directed the affairs of Rhode Island College for twenty-five years with great administrative skill and talent. At the same time, he assumed charge of the First Baptist Church, Providence, and until his retirement in 1791 carried on a heavy load also of preaching and pastoral duties. He was a moving force behind the organization in 1767 of the Warren Association, for the 'promotion of harmony' and concerted common activities of New England Baptist churches. He was active in civic and pre-revolutionary affairs, preaching on one occasion in 1774 at the continental congress in Philadelphia on behalf of peace, as well as civil and religious liberty. In 1786 he represented Rhode Island in the congress of the confederation, and later became a strong and active advocate of the adoption of the United States constitution. When the critical Massachusetts ratification convention met, Manning went to Boston to persuade anti-federalist Baptist delegates to vote for the constitution, and just before the final vote Governor John Hancock, the president of the convention, asked Manning to offer a prayer for the convocation. Always a moving force in education, towards the end of his life Manning in the summer of 1791 drew up a report recommending the establishment of free public schools.

But it was as first president of Rhode Island College (Brown University after 1804) that James Manning made his greatest contribution. From the first commencement at Providence, the first Wednesday of September 1770, with a class of seven, until his last days, Manning expanded support among people of liberal learning in the Baptist community for education and sought to raise the funds to achieve academic excellence. During the American War of Independence the college was occupied by American troops from 1776 to 1780, and from 1780 to 1782 was used as a hospital for French soldiers. From the 1770s, as one account stated, for 'a period of twenty years' he carried on 'preaching not only to the satisfaction, but to the delight, of his hearers; while at the same time, he discharged his varied and arduous duties in connection with the College, with the most exemplary fidelity' (Sprague, 94). He died on 29 July 1791 in Providence, and was buried there in the north burial-ground. Manning was the embodiment of the words of the Brown corporation charter, discharging 'the offices of life with usefulness and reputation' and promoting 'institutions for liberal learning' as 'highly beneficial to society'.

MURNEY GERLACH

Sources R. A. Guild, Early history of Brown University, including the life, times, and correspondence of President Manning (1897) · I. Backus, A history of New England with particular reference to the denomination of Christians called Baptists, 3 vols. (1777–96) · Providence Gazette and Country Journal (6 Aug 1791) · J. Maxcy, A funeral sermon occasioned by the death of the Rev. James Manning (1791) · W. G. Goddard, 'Memoir of the Rev. James Manning', American Quarterly Register (May 1839) · W. C. Bronson, The history of Brown University (1914) · W. B. Sprague, Annals of the American pulpit, 6 (1860) · M. Mitchell, Encyclopedia Brunoniana (1993)
Archives Brown University, Providence, Rhode Island, John Hay Library, papers, MS-1C-1 [2 boxes] · Brown University, Providence, Rhode Island, John Hay Library, papers concerning Rhode Island College, MS-1E-1
Likenesses C. Alexander, oils, 1770, Brown University, Providence, Rhode Island, President's Office, University Hall

Manning, James (1781–1866), barrister and serjeant-at-law, was the son of James Manning, Unitarian minister in Exeter, and his wife, Lydia, daughter of John Edge of Bristol. He acquired an early familiarity with history, antiquities, and European languages. He was called to the bar at Lincoln's Inn on 23 June 1817 and went on the western circuit, of which he was for many years the leader. On 7 September 1820 he married Clarissa, daughter of William Palmer of Kimbolton, Herefordshire. Their children included

(Elizabeth) Adelaide *Manning, Froebelian and promoter of Indian education.

Manning's reputation rested mainly upon his learning. He was no orator, and his powers of advocacy were slight, but as a junior he obtained much business. On the basis of his knowledge of copyhold law he secured a perpetual retainer from the lord of the manor of Taunton Dean, Somerset, whose rights were the subject of continual litigation. He enjoyed the friendship of lords Brougham, and Denman, and assisted them in the defence of Queen Caroline. He was appointed recorder of Sudbury in 1835, and recorder of Oxford and Banbury in November 1837, three offices which he held until his death. He was made a serjeant-at-law on 19 February 1840, received a patent of precedence in April 1845, and was made queen's ancient serjeant in 1846. This dignity, revived at his own suggestion after long being dormant, entitled him to a seat in the House of Lords, ex officio, but gave him no right of speaking, unless consulted, or of voting. In March 1847 he became judge of the Whitechapel county court, from which he retired in February 1863 on a pension of £700. His first wife died in 1847, and on 3 December 1857 he married again. His second wife, Charlotte *Manning (1803–1871) [see under Manning, (Elizabeth) Adelaide], widow of William Speir, was sister of the Unitarian social reformer Henry Solly, and the first mistress of the College, Hitchin, later Girton College. Manning died at 44 Phillimore Gardens, Kensington, London, on 29 August 1866. He was survived by his second wife.

Manning's publications included Serviens ad legem: a report of proceedings … in relation to a warrant for the suppression of the antient privileges of the serjeants-at-law (1840); Cases in the Court of Common Pleas (1841, with T. C. Granger), texts on marriage reform and parliamentary reform, and an inquiry concerning possessive augment in English and in cognate dialects. He also published volumes concerned with law reports and court practice.

G. C. BOASE, rev. ERIC METCALFE

Sources Law Magazine, new ser., 22 (1866–7), 174 · Law Times (8 Sept 1866), 767, 808 · CGPLA Eng. & Wales (1866)
Archives UCL, letters to Society for the Diffusion of Useful Knowledge
Wealth at death under £7000: probate, 26 Sept 1866, CGPLA Eng. & Wales

Manning, John Edmondson (1848–1910), Unitarian minister, was born at 5 Derby Street, Liverpool, on 22 March 1848, the son of John Manning, a furniture broker, and his wife, Eliza Edmondson. He was educated at Mount Pleasant School, where he subsequently became a teacher, while preparing for the ministry with his brother-in-law, George Beaumont, Unitarian minister at Gateacre. He studied at Queen's College, Liverpool, in 1866–8, and at Manchester New College, London, in 1868–73, graduating BA from the University of London in 1872 and proceeding MA in 1876. In 1873 he was awarded a Hibbert scholarship and spent a year at the University of Leipzig in 1875–6.

Manning's first settlement was at Swansea in 1876, where he was also visitor and examiner in Hebrew and Greek to the Presbyterian college, Carmarthen. In 1889 he moved to Upper Chapel, Sheffield, where he remained until 1902 and of which he wrote a bicentenary history (1900). He was visitor to the Unitarian Home Missionary College (later Unitarian College), Manchester, in 1892–4, and from 1894 to his death he was tutor in Old Testament studies, Hebrew, and philosophy. He terminated his ministry at Sheffield in 1902 as the college was absorbing much of his time and, facing a choice, he preferred the academic post, where his sound learning gave distinction to his career. He published six *Addresses at the Unitarian Home Missionary College* (1903) on topics pertaining to his chair, and his *Thomas à Kempis and the 'De imitatione Christi'* (1907) is a valuable excursus.

On 15 December 1879 Manning had married Emma (*d.* 1913), youngest daughter of George Browne Brock JP (1805–1886), who had been minister at Swansea in 1837–54; they had three daughters, who survived him. The youngest daughter, Ruth Vernon Manning-*Sanders, was a notable folklorist. He died of the effects of pleurisy, contracted on a holiday in Italy, on 30 April 1910 at his house, Harper Hill, Derbyshire Road, Sale, Cheshire, and was buried in Dan-y-Graig cemetery in Swansea.   R. K. WEBB

Sources *The Inquirer* (7 May 1910) · *Christian Life* (7 May 1910) · b. cert. · m. cert. · d. cert.
Likenesses photograph, Upper Chapel, Sheffield
Wealth at death £9036 18s. 4d.: probate, 19 May 1910, *CGPLA Eng. & Wales*

Manning [*née* Perrett], **Dame (Elizabeth) Leah** (1886–1977), educationist and politician, was born on 14 April 1886 at Burrish Street, Droitwich, the eldest of twelve children of Charles William Perrett and his wife, Harriet Margaret Tappin, both officers in the Salvation Army. Her mother had been a teacher and her father worked for a time in the family timber business. After her parents emigrated to Canada, Leah was brought up in Stamford Hill, London, in her grandfather's family, a household of evangelical Methodism and radical Liberal politics. She attended St John's School, Bridgwater, and then the Misses Thorns' Select Academy for Young Ladies in London, where she met the Revd Stewart Headlam, whose Christian socialism had an important influence on her own beliefs. In 1906 she entered Homerton Teacher Training College, Cambridge. She was introduced to the university Fabian Society by Hugh Dalton, who became a lifelong political friend, and also joined the Independent Labour Party. Her first teaching post was in a slum school in Cambridge, where her indignation at the poverty and malnutrition of the children contributed to the development of her socialism and commitment to progressive education. She set up an after-school play centre and campaigned (through her membership of the Cambridge Trades Council and of the National Council of Women) for the provision of milk for the schoolchildren, almost losing her job when she condemned the policy of the education committee in unequivocal terms.

On 26 July 1913 Leah Perrett married William Henry Manning (*d.* 1952), who worked at the university solar physics laboratory. Their only child, a daughter, was born in 1918, but lived for just three weeks. At the outbreak of

Dame (Elizabeth) Leah Manning (1886–1977), by Bassano

the First World War, the Cambridge education authority relaxed the marriage bar, enabling Leah Manning to continue in her teaching post. As a pacifist and internationalist she abhorred the war and its consequences and made annual visits to Germany from 1918, building links with socialists there.

In 1920 Leah Manning was appointed head of the new Open Air School in Cambridge for undernourished children, a post in which she achieved success and fulfilment. She continued to be deeply involved in Labour Party and trade union activities in Cambridge in the 1920s, supporting the general strike (despite her position as a magistrate), and attempting to unionize women manual workers in the city. She was elected in 1924 to the national executive committee of her own union, the National Union of Teachers (NUT), and was also active in the left-wing Teachers' Labour League and its successor from 1928, the National Association of Labour Teachers.

In 1930 Leah Manning served as president of the NUT, only the fourth woman to be elected to that position. At this time she sought a parliamentary seat, and won East Islington for Labour in a by-election in February 1931, losing it, however, in the general election in October. In the same year she also lost her seat on the national executive committee of the Labour Party, which she had held since 1930. She was appointed assistant education officer to the NUT, and continued in this post until 1942.

Always on the left of the Labour Party, Leah Manning became increasingly involved in opposing the threat of fascism in the 1930s and served as joint secretary of the Co-ordinating Committee against War and Fascism from 1934. She visited Spain at the outbreak of the civil war in 1936, and took a major part in organizing British fundraising for medical supplies and transport. In 1937, at the request of the Basque government, she travelled to the besieged city of Bilbao and successfully arranged the evacuation of 4000 children to Britain. By this time she had modified her anti-war views and accepted the idea of collective military security. During the Second World War, Leah Manning severely criticized the government's handling of evacuation. She was promoted in 1943 to head the organization department of the NUT, and was involved in the preparation of the 1944 Education Bill.

In the 1945 Labour landslide Leah Manning won the marginal seat of Epping and returned to the House of Commons. As in 1931 she made foreign affairs and education her particular interests as a backbencher, as well as the agricultural concerns of her constituency. She supported the idea of a federated Europe and criticized the increasing anti-Soviet policy of the West. She was also known as a forceful advocate of women's rights. Although she described herself as 'never outstandingly feminist', Leah Manning was well aware of male hostility towards powerful women, both in the NUT and the House of Commons, but she did not allow it to cramp her activities. She had worked for equal pay and birth control from the 1920s, and during her post-war parliamentary career pressed the government on equal pay, took up the issue of analgesia in childbirth, and raised a number of other questions concerning women's rights.

Leah Manning lost her seat in 1950 and failed to regain it in the two following elections. After her political career ended she returned to teaching, in a friend's private school in Harlow, until her eventual retirement in 1970. A major post-war commitment was family planning, and in 1964 she started a controversial new clinic in Harlow providing contraception for unmarried couples. She was made a DBE in 1966 for political and public services. Dame Leah Manning died at home at the NUT Home for Retired Teachers at Elstree Manor, Barnet Lane, Elstree, Hertfordshire, on 15 September 1977, aged ninety-one. She and her husband (who predeceased her on 22 January 1952) lived apart in their later years.

Leah Manning was a tall and well-built woman, a hugely energetic campaigner, and a fiery orator. She was a left-wing socialist whose political outlook rested on a warm humanitarian commitment rather than a theoretical position. Her lifelong passion was education and the creation of a more just society for women, men, and children. She bequeathed her body for medical research.

ALISON ORAM

Sources L. Manning, *A life for education: an autobiography* (1970) · *Times Educational Supplement* (19 April 1930), 177 · *Schoolmaster and Woman Teacher's Chronicle* (25 April 1930), 784 · *Schoolmaster and Woman Teacher's Chronicle* (16 Oct 1930), 588 · *Schoolmaster and Woman Teacher's Chronicle* (20 Nov 1930), 795 · *National Union of Teachers Annual Report* (1930) · *Cambridge Daily News* (22 April 1930) · *The Teacher* (23 Sept 1977) · *The Times* (19 Sept 1977) · *Daily Telegraph* (19 Sept 1977) · *Essex Gazette* (11 Nov 1977) · *DLB*, vol. 7 · H. Dalton, *Call back yesterday: memoirs, 1887–1931* (1953) · H. Dalton, *High tide and after: memoirs, 1945–1960* (1962) · *The Vote* (12 April 1918) · L. Manning, *What I saw in Spain* (1935) · b. cert. · *Hansard 5C* (1930–31); (1945–50) · WWW · m. cert.

Archives Labour Party archives, London · Marx Memorial Library, London, corresp. with Emergency Committee in Aid of Democratic Spain · U. Warwick Mod. RC, National Union of Teachers archive

Likenesses Bassano, photograph, NPG [*see illus.*] · photographs, repro. in Manning, *Life for education* · photographs, University of Warwick, National Union of Teachers archive; repro. in *Schoolmaster and Woman Teacher's Chronicle* (1929–30) · photographs, probably Labour Party archive

Wealth at death £21,650: probate, 24 Nov 1977, *CGPLA Eng. & Wales*

Manning [*née* de Roux], **Marie** (1821–1849), murderer, was born in Geneva, Switzerland, and went into domestic service in England. Among her employers were Lady Palk of Haldon House, Devon, and Lady Blantyre at Stafford House, London. When travelling to Boulogne to join her mistress in 1846, Marie met Patrick O'Connor, a well-off, retired gauger in the London docks and moneylender. On 27 May 1847 she married at St James's Church, Piccadilly, a former railway guard named Frederick George (sometimes given as George Frederick) Manning (*d.* 1849), who had left the railway service when suspected of involvement in a bullion robbery and who kept the White Hart inn in Taunton. They shortly moved back to London, where Marie continued her close friendship with O'Connor. On 9 August 1849 O'Connor dined with the Mannings at their house, 3 Miniver Place, Bermondsey, where, in accordance with a premeditated plan, the couple murdered him, she with a pistol and he with a crowbar. They buried the body in quicklime in a grave they had prepared under the flagstones of the kitchen. The next day Marie Manning visited O'Connor's lodgings in Greenwood Street, Mile End Road, and stole the certificates of his railway shares (worth about £4000) and £300 in cash, thus realizing the objects of the murder. The body was discovered on 17 August 1849, and soon afterwards the Mannings were arrested. By then she was in Edinburgh (using the name of Smith), where she had gone to make enquiries with a stockbroker about selling the shares. Manning had gone to Jersey where he was very indiscreet, giving his real name and mentioning a former lodger, Massey, a medical student, from whom he had asked for information about various topics related to the projected murder.

The Mannings were tried for the murder at the Old Bailey on 25 and 26 October 1849, where Manning tried to put all the blame on his wife, saying that she had first shot O'Connor before he used the crowbar to finish him off. She made a plea that as a foreigner she was not subject to the jurisdiction of an English court; this was dismissed because of her marriage to a British subject. They pleaded not guilty, Marie appearing in court in a gaudy shawl, mainly blue, and primrose gloves, with a white lace veil on her head. A great deal of evidence was brought forward, including a medical report of bloodstains on her dress. They were both found guilty and Marie became hysterical about her husband's accusations. The Mannings were, however, reputed to have kissed and made up half an hour before their execution by William Calcraft, which took place on the roof of Horsemonger Lane gaol on 13 November. A vast and unruly mob gathered to witness the scene. Charles Dickens, who based the character of Hortense, Lady Dedlock's waiting woman in *Bleak House*, on Mrs Manning, wrote a letter to *The Times* on the wickedness of permitting such a mob. Mrs Manning wore a black satin dress for the occasion, rendering that material unpopular for many years thereafter.

G. C. BOASE, rev. J. GILLILAND

Sources *The Times* (18 Aug 1849) [*et seq.*] · *The Times* (26 Oct 1849) · *The Times* (27 Oct 1849) · *The Times* (29 Oct 1849) · R. D. Altrick, *Victorian studies in scarlet* (1972) · J. Bland, *The book of executions* (1993) · J. H. H. Gaute, *The new murderer's who's who* (1989) · P. Chapman, *Madame Tussaud's* (1984) · B. Lane, *Encyclopaedia of women killers* (1994) · R. G. Jones, *Mammoth book of women killers* (1993) · D. Nicoll, *Man's revenge* (1890), 71–83 · R. Huish, *The progress of crime, or, The authentic memoirs of Maria Manning* (1849) · *Verbatim report of the trial of G. and M. Manning for the murder of P. O'Connor* (1849) · *The Bermondsey murder* (1849)
Likenesses portrait, in or before 1849, repro. in Huish, *Progress of crime* [not found] · portrait, in or before 1849, repro. in *Verbatim report of the trial* (1849) [not found] · portrait, in or before 1972, repro. in R. D. Altrick, *Victorian studies in scarlet* (1972) · wax sculpture, Tussaud's

Manning, Olivia Mary (1908–1980), novelist, was born on 2 March 1908 at 134 Laburnum Grove, North End, Portsmouth, the elder child and only daughter of Lieutenant-Commander Oliver Manning (*c.*1859–*c.*1950) of the Royal Navy, and his wife, Olivia Mary, daughter of David Morrow from Bangor, Down. It was an unhappy domestic situation: the father, married before, was over forty when he remarried; he had retired early from the navy, and had little money apart from his service pension. A handsome womanizer, he was adored by his two children (the younger, Oliver, was killed in action in 1943). Olivia had a more troubled relationship with her mother, who came of Irish peasant stock with American roots. Her maternal grandfather was a slave owner on the banks of the Missouri River. It was a fraught and mortifying childhood which Olivia Manning used trenchantly in her short stories and early novels. This childhood insecurity and unhappiness shadowed her personality and work: she had, as she said, 'the usual Anglo-Irish sense of belonging nowhere'. Childhood and adolescence described in her books are screams of pain and wounds remembered.

Manning was educated at Portsmouth grammar school, and later studied art at the town's technical college, but her parents could not continue to pay the fees. Her ambition was to be a painter, and, although this was superseded by her writing, it contributed to the intensely visual descriptions of landscape in her work. *Artist among the Missing* testifies to her understanding of the medium she abandoned. Forced by poverty to earn her livelihood in her teens, she worked first in an architect's office in Portsmouth, and wrote in her spare time. Determined to get to London, she left home and worked as a typist in the department store Peter Jones. She was mistaken for someone who had exhibited in Bond Street and was promoted

to painting furniture. She also worked for the Medici Society's book production department and read scripts for Metro-Goldwyn-Meyer. She drew on her experiences as a struggling writer in *The Doves of Venus*. Using the pseudonym Jacob Morrow, she launched herself as a writer, selling the copyright of four 'lurid serials', with titles such as *The Rose and Ruby* and *The Black Scarab*, for £12 each. She was extremely poor, had insufficient money for food, and yet worked far into the night at her writing after a full day's office work. Encouraged by Hamish Miles, an editor at Jonathan Cape, and later her lover, she finished her first literary novel, *The Wind Changes* (1937). It was set in Dublin in June 1921 during the 'troubles', and was about a woman torn between an Irish patriot and an English novelist with pro-republican sympathies.

After this novel Manning did not publish another for twelve years. On 18 August 1939 she married Reginald Donald (Reggie) *Smith (1914–1985), then a lecturer with the British Council and later a BBC drama producer and professor at the new University of Ulster. Her bridesmaid was the writer Stevie Smith, while Reggie's best man was Louis MacNeice. She travelled with Reggie to Romania where she witnessed King Carol's abdication, the rise of fascism, and the tyranny of the totalitarian regime. From Romania they escaped to Greece, then occupied by British troops who retreated at the advance of the German army. In 1942 Olivia Manning was a press officer at the American embassy in Cairo; in 1943–4 she was press assistant at the public information office in Jerusalem, and in 1944–5 held the same position at the British Council in Jerusalem. The couple returned to England after the war; they had no children (Manning had suffered a miscarriage during the war).

During and immediately after the war Manning wrote a few short stories (*Growing Up*, 1948) and a book about the explorer Henry Morton Stanley (*The Remarkable Expedition*, 1947), but the 'emotional upset' resulting from her brother's death had prevented her from writing novels. She drew attention to the fact that such a work gap was also the experience of Katherine Mansfield and Virginia Woolf, thereby firmly placing herself in the literary establishment. The gap in fact provided Manning with a wealth of material for her novels. Her second, *Artist among the Missing* (1949), one of her most underrated works, is richly evocative of life in the Middle East. *School for Love* (1951), her first commercial and critical success, was set in Jerusalem, while *The Doves of Venus* (1955) was her only novel set almost entirely in London. *My Husband Cartwright* (1956) was a collection of sketches about Reggie Smith which she had contributed to *Punch*. There is a more vivid portrait of him as the ebullient, feckless, popular Guy Pringle in her greatest and best-known works, the Balkan trilogy and the Levant trilogy (six interlinked novels), which were also based on her experiences of the war. In the novels the young watchful Harriet Pringle, newly-wed, critical, and sharp-tongued, is a self-portrait. The books are in effect a ruthless and illuminating analysis of Olivia Manning's marriage.

The Great Fortune (1960), *The Spoilt City* (1962), and *Friends and Heroes* (1965) comprise the Balkan trilogy, which relates the progressive story of Harriet and Guy's relationship, while simultaneously (with a reporter's skill) it records the political and social scene and presents English non-combatants abroad during the early war years, viewing the majority of them as corrupt, mean, and self-centred. Olivia Manning's pitiless clarity about human frailty is directed at the greedy, ambitious, and pretentious. Her compassion—which goes deep—is given to the poor, the persecuted, and animals. Her historical touches are unobtrusively inserted into the tapestry of her overall design, authenticated with a sureness of touch and a sense of place. Her understanding of men dealing with other men, politically and socially, is remarkable. Her humour—dark though its implication often is—reaches a peak in her affectionate portrayal of a great comic character, Prince Yakimov, a tarnished yet innocent-at-heart anachronistic time-server.

In between the trilogies Manning wrote *The Play Room* (1969), a disturbing novel supposedly based on Manning's family: the unworldly protagonist develops a crush on a girl who is raped and murdered. It was published in America as *The Camperlea Girls*. *The Rain Forest* (1974) centres on an unhappily married couple on an Indian island who are brought closer by adversity. A selection of her short stories, written over a period of thirty years, was published as *A Romantic Hero* (1967).

But it was with her final series of novels, the Levant trilogy, that Olivia Manning firmly established herself as one of Britain's most outstanding novelists, one who in maturity widened her canvas almost historically, as she juxtaposed her story of Harriet and Guy and important world events. In the Balkan trilogy war is a shadow from which Olivia Manning's protagonists are forever fleeing: in the Levant trilogy a war in the Middle East is the centrepiece of her canvas. Egypt, Jerusalem, and Syria are the landscape of the latter's three parts, *The Danger Tree* (1977), *The Battle Lost and Won* (1978), and *The Sum of Things*, published posthumously in the year of her death (1980). The battle of Alamein is described with a near-Tolstoyan passion for detail, and Olivia Manning's ability to relate to a young man's first experience of battle is particularly noteworthy. Great sympathy is expressed for the fighting soldier, contempt for the establishment civilians and general headquarters, and compassion for the poor and peasants. Death is the all-pervasive element, and love found to be an illusion. Her final coda reflects on 'the pernicious peace' to come, with which the survivors will have to cope. The two trilogies were collectively known as *Fortunes of War*; Anthony Burgess described the series in the *Sunday Times* as 'the finest fictional record of the war produced by a British writer'. The six novels were compressed into a BBC television serial in 1987 by Alan Plater.

In youth Olivia Manning was rather beautiful, in later years 'striking' was the adjective most applied to her physical presence. Slender and seemingly frail, her sharp features were redeemed by the luminosity of her eyes which mostly looked at human beings to mock and at animals kindly. Between books she knew 'black despair', felt that she was not prolific enough, suffered from 'intellectual paralysis', and worried herself with literary reputations. A reputation for malice and gossip was probably the result of her abnormal honesty, in that she would never endorse any opinion she did not hold. She was devoted to the welfare of animals (she published *Extraordinary Cats* in 1967), and was increasingly concerned with environmental matters. She was very anxious about money, although she did fairly well and invested in property. She was loyal to her friends though she sorely tried their patience: she had a particularly volatile friendship with Stevie Smith whom Manning characterized as Nancy Claypole, much to Smith's irritation, in *The Doves of Venus*. At her best she was a delightful companion and full of quirky humour. She had an innate sense of elegance and surrounded herself with beautiful objects, paintings, and books. She and Reggie had several affairs—she with Henry Green, and William Gerhardie, and a married doctor called Jerry Slattery. She also claimed that Anthony Burgess had proposed to her after his first wife's death in 1968, but she and Reggie never contemplated divorce. Physically she was not strong, and frequently suffered from illness, perhaps as a result of the deprivations she had suffered as a young woman. In 1976 she was appointed CBE. On 23 July 1980 Olivia Manning died suddenly of a stroke at the Royal County Hospital, Ryde, in the Isle of Wight, where she had been on holiday. The Isle of Wight was a place where she had been most happy in childhood with her brother. She was cremated at Whippingham crematorium, Isle of Wight. Her ashes are at Billingham Manor on the island. She once said that her aim as a writer was 'to express the inexpressible'. She was happy, she said, only when writing.   KAY DICK, *rev.* CLARE L. TAYLOR

Sources K. Dick, *Friends and friendship* (1974) · I. English, introduction, in O. Manning, *The doves of Venus* (1984) · I. English, introduction, in O. Manning, *The wind changes* (1988) · F. Spalding, *Stevie Smith: a critical biography* (1988) · J. Barbera and W. McBrien, *Stevie: a biography of Stevie Smith* (1985) · P. Parker and F. Kermode, eds., *The reader's companion to twentieth-century writers* (1995) · lion.chadwyck.co.uk [Literature Online (LION)], 10 Sept 2002 · b. cert. · *CGPLA Eng. & Wales* (1980)

Archives BL, notes on *Ladies with escorts*, Add. MS 57727 · Ransom HRC, corresp. and literary papers | BBC WAC, corresp. with members of BBC · CUL, corresp. with W. A. Gerhardie |SOUND BL NSA, recorded interview

Likenesses group photograph, 1949, Hult. Arch. · group photograph, 1972, Hult. Arch. · photograph, repro. in *The Times* (24 July 1980) · photograph, repro. in *The Times* (27 July 1980)

Wealth at death £168,344: probate, 22 Dec 1980, *CGPLA Eng. & Wales*

Manning, Owen (1721–1801), county historian and Old English scholar, was the younger son of Joseph Manning (1688?–1773?) and Mary Manning of Orlingbury, Northamptonshire. He is said to have been born at Orlingbury on 11 August 1721 and was baptized there on 5 September. He was educated at Huntingdon grammar school and at Queens' College, Cambridge, where he was admitted pensioner on 29 March 1737 and graduated BA in 1741; he proceeded MA in 1744 and BD in 1753. While an undergraduate Manning suffered two near-death experiences, the first when he was supposed to have died of smallpox and was laid out for burial, and the second when he fell into the River Cam after suffering an epileptic fit, and was thought to have drowned. From 1742 to 1755 he was a fellow of Queens', but he resigned his fellowship in 1755 to marry Catherine, daughter of Reade Peacock of Huntingdon, 'a reputable and substantial Tradesman … who was bred a Quaker' (Cole MSS, BL, Add. MS 5808, fol. 229v). They had three sons and six daughters.

Manning was ordained deacon at Lincoln on 25 September 1743 and priest at York on 21 September 1746; he held the Queens' living of St Botolph's, Cambridge, from 1749 to 1760. He was prebendary of Lincoln from 1757 to 1801. Dr John Thomas, bishop of Lincoln, to whom he was chaplain, collated him to the prebends of South Scarle (5 August 1757; installed 13 August) and Milton Ecclesia (15 March 1760; installed 5 April). Disappointed in his attempt to be elected president of Queens' in 1760, Manning was appointed that year rector of Chiddingfold in Surrey, which he held until 1768, and in 1763 was presented by Dr Green, dean of Salisbury, to the vicarage of Godalming in Surrey, where he lived until his death. In 1769 he was presented to the rectory of Peper Harow, an adjoining parish, by Viscount Midleton. Like many Queens' men of his time, Manning held strong views in support of civil and religious liberty. This is apparent from his published sermons and pamphlets, including his *Discourses on Election and Justification* (1790) and his *Discretion in Matters Pertaining to Religion* (1788). It is clear from anecdotal evidence that he was most conscientious in the execution of his pastoral duties in Godalming.

However, it was his scholarly contributions in two different but connected fields, Old English studies and county history, that made Owen Manning a significant figure in the history of the study of early English language and history. He is best-known for his *History of Surrey*, completed and published posthumously in three volumes by his collaborator William Bray from 1804 to 1814. It is regarded as one of the best of the older county histories. The first volume in particular, which is largely Manning's work, is distinguished by his careful attention to all available documents, including medieval ones, which he had sought out over nearly forty years, and by its 'terse and workmanlike language' (Simmons, 1.vii). Manning was one of the first historians to make use of the Domesday records for the history of a county and he had prepared a facsimile of them for his *History* as early as 1773.

Manning's earlier work was in Old English studies, and it too is of a high standard. His first achievement was to augment, improve, and publish the Old English and Gothic dictionary of his friend Edward Lye, who died in 1767 with the dictionary unfinished. Manning devoted more than four years to preparing the *Dictionarium Saxonico et Gothico-Latinum* for the press, and, when it was published in 1772, it contained a good deal of original research by Manning himself. A full assessment of the importance of Manning's lexicographical work is yet to be made, but the Manning–Lye dictionary served as the model for the 1838 Old English dictionary of Joseph Bosworth.

Manning was the first to publish the Old English text, with literal and free translations and notes, of the will of King Alfred from the Liber Vitae of the New Minster and Hyde Abbey, Winchester (BL, Stowe MS 944), which had come into the possession of Thomas Astle, who commissioned Manning to prepare an edition of the document. The will was published in 1788, edited by Sir Herbert Croft and with a preface by Astle. On the advice of Richard Gough, Manning also acted as a consultant to Daines Barrington on the text of the Alfredian Orosius which Barrington published in 1773. At various times he worked on material for an edition of the Caedmon manuscript of Old English poetry, as had Lye, although neither of them ever published it. Manning was elected a fellow of the Royal Society on 10 December 1767 and fellow of the Society of Antiquaries in 1770.

In his final years Manning lost his sight, and he died at the vicarage in Godalming on 9 September 1801 after a short attack of pleurisy. He was buried in the churchyard of St Peter and St Paul, Godalming, on 14 September. According to his will, he wanted no memorial but his parishioners held him in such high esteem that 'some of the principal ones amongst them placed a handsome marble tablet to his memory in the Church; and some private friends put an Inscription on a head-stone in the Church yard' (Bray, 1.vii); the memorial is now in the north chapel of Godalming church. He was survived by his wife and all their children, except their eldest son and one daughter.

MARGARET CLUNIES ROSS and AMANDA J. COLLINS

Sources W. Bray, preface, in O. Manning and W. Bray, *The history and antiquities of the county of Surrey*, 1 (1804), v–viii · Nichols, *Lit. anecdotes* · Nichols, *Illustrations* · Venn, *Alum. Cant.* · T. Astle, marked proofs of the preface to 'The will of King Alfred', U. Birm. L., 5/iii/2, 131–7 · W. Cole, 'Anecdote of Mr Manning of Queens' College in Cambridge', BL, Cole MSS, Add. MS 5808, fols. 229v–230r · parish register (baptisms), Orlingbury, Northamptonshire, 1721 · parish register (burials), Godalming, Surrey, 1801 · letters from R. Plumptre, H. Thomas, and J. Green to the duke of Newcastle, BL, Newcastle MSS, Add. MS 32914, fols. 29r–30v, 58r–59v, 94r–95v, 116r–117v · will, 1784, proved 6 Oct 1801, PRO, PROB 11/1364/685–6 · *DNB* · J. Simmons, introduction, in O. Manning and W. Bray, *The history and antiquities of the county of Surrey*, 1 (1974), v–vii · B. Board, 'Surrey', *English county histories: a guide*, ed. C. R. J. Currie and C. P. Lewis (1994), 375–84

Archives S. Antiquaries, Lond., annotated copy of *Caedmonis monarchi paraphrasis poetica* · Surrey HC, accounts of manors of Braboeuf and Pickards · Surrey HC, MS account of Peper Harow, possibly by him · Surrey HC, corresp., pedigrees, historical notes, and papers | BL, letters to Edward Lye, Add. MS 32325 · BL, corresp. with Thomas Percy, Add. MS 32325, fols. 246r–250v; fol. 268v · Bodl. Oxf., corresp. with J. C. Brooke · Bodl. Oxf., corresp. with Richard Gough · Surrey HC, letters to William Bray

Likenesses oils, Godalming Museum, Surrey

Wealth at death everything to wife: will, PRO, PROB 11/1364/685–6 · wife perhaps poor as William Bray states he published *The history and antiquities of the county of Surrey* for her benefit: Simmons, 'Introductory note'; Bray, 'Preface'

Manning, Percy (1870–1917), antiquary and folklorist, was born on 24 January 1870 in Weetwood Road, Headingley, the fourth and last child of John Manning (c.1830–1874), boilermaker, and his wife, Sophia Gotobed (b. 1833?). His father was apparently from Northamptonshire; his mother from Waterhead, Cambridgeshire. Manning's father, a partner in the Leeds engineering firm of Manning, Wardle & Co., died when Manning was only four. The family remained near Leeds until about 1880, then moved with his paternal grandmother to Watford. Manning attended preparatory school in Hove, proceeding to Clifton College in 1884 and New College, Oxford, in 1888. His life thereafter was spent in Oxford.

Manning did not flourish at university, obtaining a third in classical moderations in 1890, failing in *literae humaniores* in 1892, and being removed from the college books at the end of 1893 after repeated warnings, whereupon he enrolled in the private tutorial college Marcon's Hall. In 1896 he finally gained his degrees (BA, proceeding to MA) and was also elected a fellow of the Society of Antiquaries.

Perhaps Manning's extreme aphasia hindered his progress at New College, but he undoubtedly attended more to archaeology and antiquities than to study. During the 1892 examinations he and J. L. Myres were excavating the Roman site at Alchester; he would have lost his place at college then had not Myres won the dean over by persuading him to wield a pick on site himself. In his first year in Oxford, Manning was elected a member of the Oxford Architectural and Historical Society (OAHS) and from 1891 until 1898 was its honorary secretary. He made his first donations to the Ashmolean Museum in 1892 (Roman keys, pottery, and other artefacts), and in 1893 was a founder member of the Oxford University Brass Rubbing Society (later the Oxford University Antiquarian Society). He was its vice-chairman in 1895 and 1899–1912, and president from 1912; in 1899 and 1914 he was also vice-president of the OAHS.

In the 1890s Manning began to collect extensively: by wide reading with meticulously organized notes; by purchase of books and prints; and by fieldwork. He was a substantial contributor to the OAHS's 1894 exhibition of Oxfordshire antiquities, providing 185 items, including many of the Oxford engravings and all 34 engravings of the rest of Oxfordshire. He had the independent means to devote himself to his interests. He was particularly active and innovative in collecting artefacts and details of popular folk customs. When collecting archaeological finds, he marked their locations precisely on a large-scale map of Oxford, taking care to document every aspect of the find. He often relied on intermediaries to alert him to finds, notably on Thomas James Carter, a retired brickmaker and self-taught palaeontologist, whom Manning also used to collect information on local folklore and custom. Carter was able to converse naturally with working people in ways barred to Manning by his class and speech impediment. Carter's notes form a substantial part of Manning's collections; Manning was among the first to use a 'fieldworker' in this way. At the same time Manning did not neglect the traditional antiquarian interests of church and manorial history, assembling one of the finest such collections in the country.

In 1898 Manning took practical steps to revive one local custom, reassembling and equipping the Headington Quarry morris dancers for a performance in the Oxford corn exchange in March 1899. The side continued to perform thereafter, and their encounter with Cecil Sharp that December marked the beginning of the English folk music revival. In 1912 he was assiduous in organizing, as committee chairman, the Oxford Millenary Exhibition.

Of slight build with dark moustache, Manning was self-effacing, making his extensive collections available to others but publishing little himself. For many years the Folklore Society pressed him, unsuccessfully, to provide the Oxfordshire volume in its County Folklore series. Among his few published pieces, written as secretary of the National St Bernard Club, was that breed's entry in the *Kennel Encyclopedia* (1910).

When war began in 1914, Manning formed a rifle club in Yarnton (where he had long had a close friendship with the bookseller C. J. Parker of the Manor House), then joined the Oxford and Bucks national reserve. After a short spell at the Leafield wireless station he was assigned to guard duty at Southampton docks in November 1914, where he rose to the rank of sergeant. He died at Southampton from pneumonia on 27 February 1917; he was buried at St Peter's, Wolvercote, Oxford, on 3 March. His collections, bequeathed to the University of Oxford, were distributed between the Bodleian Library and the Ashmolean Museum in Oxford.   MICHAEL HEANEY

Sources M. Mellor, *Pots and people* (1997) · H. E. Salter, 'In memoriam', *Surveys and tokens*, ed. H. E. Salter, OHS, 75 (1923), 85–6 · *Oxford Times* (10 March 1917) · *Oxford Journal Illustrated* (21 March 1917) · *Oxford Chronicle and Berks and Bucks Gazette* (9 March 1917) · Library records, Bodl. Oxf., C1817 · B. Grant, M. Heaney, and R. Judge, 'Copy of GP morice dancers Mr Manning', *English Dance and Song*, 43/2 (1981), 14–16 · *Whites General and Commercial Directory of Leeds*, 12th edn (1870)

Archives AM Oxf., antiquarian notes arranged by county; papers relating to Berkshire, Buckinghamshire, and Oxfordshire · Bodl. Oxf., notes of antiquities in Oxford

Likenesses H. W. Taunt, photograph, 12 May 1894, Bodl. Oxf., library records, C1817, frontispiece · photographs, 1910, AM Oxf., Manning archive · photograph, *c.*1915, repro. in *Oxford Journal Illustrated*

Wealth at death £7296 15*s.* 3*d.*: probate, 17 July 1917, CGPLA Eng. & Wales

Manning, Robert (1655–1731), Roman Catholic priest, was born in Amsterdam of an English father and Dutch mother, and entered the English College at Douai in 1668, where he was for some time professor of humanities and philosophy. He spent a short time at St Gregory's, Paris, in 1688–9, but returned to Douai and was ordained priest in 1690, and was for two years chaplain to the canonesses of St Augustine at Louvain. He was then sent to the English mission in October 1692. For most of his missionary career he was chaplain to Lord Petre at Ingatestone Hall, Essex, to whose family, as he remarked, he was indebted for all he possessed. In 1719 he spent a year as chaplain to the Poor Clares at Rouen, but soon returned to Ingatestone. Manning composed various controversial treatises, which, says Dodd, were 'much esteemed by the learned on account of their easy flowing style' (Dodd, 3.488), and was with Hawarden and later Challoner one of the leading Catholic polemicists of the age. His *England's Conversion* *and Reformation Compared*, printed secretly in London in 1725, was seized by the authorities as 'seditious and impious'. The proceeds from his *Moral Entertainments*, published after his death in 1742, he generously donated to the London Secular Clergy Fund. Manning died at Ingatestone Hall on 4 March 1731.

THOMPSON COOPER, *rev.* G. BRADLEY

Sources G. Anstruther, *The seminary priests*, 3 (1976), 141 · D. A. Bellenger, ed., *English and Welsh priests, 1558–1800* (1984), 85 · J. Kirk, *Biographies of English Catholics in the eighteenth century*, ed. J. H. Pollen and E. Burton (1909), 157 · Gillow, *Lit. biog. hist.*, 3.453 · C. J. Mitchell, 'Robert Manning and Thomas Howlatt: English Catholic printing in the early eighteenth century', *Recusant History*, 17 (1984–5), 38–47 · F. Blom and others, *English Catholic books, 1701–1800: a bibliography* (1996), 1737–68 · E. Duffy, ed., *Challoner and his church: a Catholic bishop in Georgian England* (1981), 91–2 · C. Dodd [H. Tootell], *The church history of England, from the year 1500, to the year 1688*, 3 vols. (1737–42)

Manning, Rosemary Joy [*pseuds.* Sarah Davys, Mary Voyle] **(1911–1988)**, author and headmistress, was born on 9 December 1911 at Rodwell Lodge, Weymouth, Dorset, the only daughter among four children of Thomas Davys Manning (1868/9–1943), a doctor, and Mary Ann Coles (1869–1960/61), a nurse and social worker before her marriage. Manning describes her childhood in this 'overwhelmingly masculine family' in her autobiography *A Corridor of Mirrors* (1987). She was educated first at a school in Dorchester Road, Weymouth, and then at Camberley, her father having moved the family to Sandhurst in the early 1920s after he had had to resign his practice, following a scandal with an employee. Manning was then sent to a boarding-school in Devon until 1930. At school she wrote and produced several plays and had ambitions to be a writer. The school is fictionalized as Bampfield in her novel *The Chinese Garden* (1962); in her autobiography she recounts a 'very damaging' affair with her housemistress and her first 'ludicrous, hamfisted attempt' to commit suicide, aged seventeen (Manning, 62).

In 1930 Manning read classics at Royal Holloway College, where she was a rebellious student. On graduation with a second class degree in 1933 she got a job as a shop assistant in an Oxford Street department store and was living with her mother, who had recently separated from Manning's father; during this time she studied shorthand and typing, and after two years she left her job to become secretary to a brick salesman in Westminster. She wrote little in her twenties and, with the exception of a 'gloomy sonnet on suicide' that was printed in the *New Statesman*, she did not attempt to get her work published (Manning, 92). During the 1930s her political affiliations were socialist and she became increasingly unhappy in her work. She suffered a nervous breakdown and was unsuccessfully treated at the Maudsley Hospital by a series of doctors who were hostile to her lesbianism. By her own account she was 'rescued' by her former headmistress, who offered her some teaching work. She thus embarked on a thirty-five-year teaching career that she later saw as a 'desperate retreat' which cut her off from her creativity as a writer (Manning, 111–12).

Her interest in left-wing politics led Manning towards the 'progressive' movement in education at a small school in Sussex, where she had an affair with the art teacher. After an unhappy period at a school in Ascot she went into partnership with a friend in buying a small day school in Hertfordshire in 1943. In 1950 they moved to north London to take over a long-established girls' preparatory school. Manning prided herself on giving the arts, especially music, an equal footing with other subjects; she saw herself not as a scholar but as a 'sharer and populariser' (Manning, 132). After two or three years in Hampstead she began to explore both writing and her sexual nature, which she kept hidden throughout her career as a teacher and headmistress. Influenced primarily by Rilke, her writing career began with a clutch of short stories published in the *Cornhill* and the novels *Remaining a Stranger* (1953) and *A Change of Direction* (1955), which were written under the pseudonym Mary Voyle and later disregarded by Manning. She often described her fiction as autobiographical and she certainly used her writing to explore issues emanating from her closeted position as a lesbian. Indeed her work is a strong contribution to the genre of women's confessional writing. *Look, Stranger* (1960) is a moral, if stylized, account of irrational fears towards the outsider, in this case a woman suffering from epilepsy. In the roman à clef *The Chinese Garden* (1962) Manning represents with candour the atmosphere of repressed sexual desire between schoolgirls in an atmosphere of hypocrisy and betrayal.

After a five-year relationship came to an end in April 1962 Manning made a second and nearly successful attempt to kill herself. She used the sleeping pill Luminal, which she had secured through a friend over twenty years previously, 'as a protection in case Hitler was victorious' (Davys, 16). She was saved when a suicide note that she had posted to a friend arrived sooner than she expected. Two months later *The Chinese Garden* was published to rapturous reviews but nothing could console Manning for having failed to kill herself. She embarked upon *A Time and a Time* (1971) shortly afterwards; it is a moving and darkly witty account, first published under the pseudonym Sarah Davys, of her love affairs with women and of her failure to commit suicide, which she ascribed to 'the combined forces of the Post Office, the law and I suppose, fate' (Manning, 139). *A Time and a Time* is perhaps the best summation of Manning's character as self-professed 'clown and melancholic'. Later, in *Man on a Tower* (1965), she explored the destructive nature of introversion and isolation in the artist, while in *Open the Door* (1983) she followed the losses that fracture the lives of a group of archaeologists. She was also an accomplished writer for children of both reference books and fiction, which included *Green Smoke* (1962) and other stories in the Dragon series.

Later in life Manning lectured in evening classes on subjects such as heraldry and symbolism, and in the 1970s she became interested in the Campaign for Nuclear Disarmament and feminism. She came out as a lesbian at the age of nearly seventy, in an ITV programme early in 1980. In her candid autobiography *A Corridor of Mirrors* she explores her development as a writer and as a lesbian with her characteristic wit and tendency towards self-deprecation. *A Time and a Time* was reissued under her own name in 1982 and she hoped that her work would illuminate the lives of many lesbians who were forced to live a similarly veiled existence in the first half of the century. Towards the end of her life she was living in Dorset and London; she died of cancer in 1988 on 15 April at her home, Devey Cottage, Pembury Grange, Tunbridge Wells.   CLARE L. TAYLOR

Sources R. Manning, *A corridor of mirrors* (1987) · S. Davys [R. Manning], *A time and a time: an autobiography* (1971) · P. J. Smith, 'Afterword', in R. Manning, *The Chinese garden* (1962); repr. (2000) · N. Hastie, 'The muted lesbian voice: coming out of camouflage', www.nickihastie.demon.co.uk/muted.htm, 1989, 21 Feb 2003 · b. cert. · d. cert.

Wealth at death under £70,000: probate, 5 May 1988, *CGPLA Eng. & Wales*

Manning, Ruth Vernon. *See* Sanders, Ruth Vernon Manning- (1888–1988).

Manning, Samuel, the elder (1786–1842), sculptor, was born in 1786, and baptized on 28 August at St Leonard, Shoreditch, London, the son of the sculptor Charles Manning (*d.* 1812) and his wife, Sarah Parsons. Charles Manning was the partner of John Bacon the younger (1777–1859) from 1808 until his death. Detailed legal papers relating to this partnership, which came to light in 1954, show that Charles Manning was responsible for the greater part of Bacon's business, mainly in neo-classical memorials (Cox-Johnson). Within six years of his father's death, Samuel Manning the elder took his place in the partnership. No documents relating to his role in the firm have been found so it is not known whether the terms of this partnership were the same as those for his father. Bacon retired soon after, leaving the business under Manning's control. Manning exhibited a number of portrait busts at the Royal Academy between 1806 and 1843 including in 1819, *Colonel Adenbrooke*; in 1820 *Princess Charlotte*; in 1825 *John Wesley*; in 1838 the *Revd Isaac Saunders*; in 1839 *Miss Hunter*; and in 1843 the *Revd Charles Manning*. Monuments signed by Manning or Bacon and Manning are to be found in many English churches. Mostly in the neo-classical style, they are described by Gunnis as 'dull and uninspired' and 'only too prevalent in England' (Gunnis, 252). They include memorials to John Bones (*d.* 1813) at Fen Ditton, Cambridgeshire; Charles Grant in St George's, Bloomsbury (1823); Bishop Charles Warburton (*d.* 1826) and his wife at Cloyne Cathedral, co. Cork; John Wilson (*d.* 1835) at Southborough, Kent, and Lancelot Haslope (*d.* 1838) in the Wesley Chapel, City Road, London. Manning died on 7 December 1842 at his home, 17 Newman Street, London. With his wife, Eliza, Manning had four daughters, Eliza, Ann, Abigal, and Christiana Mary, and a son, **Samuel Manning the younger** (1814/15–1866), who was also a sculptor. He was baptized on 18 July 1819 at St Pancras Old Church, Pancras Road. It seems likely that the younger Manning trained in his father's workshop. He married Honoria, daughter of Captain James Williams, of Stoke Demerel, Devon, at Marylebone on 13 August 1846.

His most successful work, *Prometheus Chained*, won a Society of Arts gold medal in 1834, was shown at the Great Exhibition in 1851, and was engraved for the *Art Union*. Manning exhibited at the Royal Academy between 1831 and 1858, showing mainly portrait busts, including one of John Bacon in 1846. He executed a statue of Wesley (1849) for the Theological Institute at Richmond, Surrey, and various monuments, in much the same style as his father's, such as those to William Lee Warner, at East Deerham, Norfolk (1852), and to the 53rd Shropshire regiment, at St Chad's, Shrewsbury (1860). Manning died on 29 November 1866 at Victoria Road, Surbiton, Kingston, Surrey, when his age was recorded as fifty-one.

EMMA HARDY

Sources R. Gunnis, *Dictionary of British sculptors, 1660–1851* (1953); new edn (1968) · A. Cox-Johnson, 'Gentlemen's agreement', *Burlington Magazine*, 101 (1959), 236–43 · *GM*, 2nd ser., 26 (1846), 528 · M. Whinney, *Sculpture in Britain, 1530 to 1830*, rev. J. Physick (1988) · M. H. Grant, *A dictionary of British sculptors from the XIIIth century to the XXth century* (1953) · Redgrave, *Artists* · artist's file, archive material, Courtauld Inst., Witt Library · m. cert. [Samuel Manning the younger] · *IGI* · d. cert. [Samuel Manning the elder] · d. cert. [Samuel Manning the younger] · will, PROB 11/1973, fols. 361v–362v [Samuel Manning the elder]

Archives Courtauld Inst., photographs of works

Wealth at death bequeathed goods, furniture, and books to his wife; £200 each to his four daughters; tools, materials, business and goodwill therein, and his property, 17 Newman Street, London, to his son: will, PRO, PROB 11/1973, fols. 361v–362v

Manning, Samuel, the younger (1814/15–1866). *See under* Manning, Samuel, the elder (1786–1842).

Manning, Samuel (1821–1881), Particular Baptist minister and journal editor, was born on 26 November 1821 in Leicester. His family were well known there: his father, John Manning, was several times elected mayor, and before his conversion to Baptist principles was a churchwarden at St Martin's, Leicester. Samuel grew up in 'the bracing spiritual atmosphere' (*Baptist Hand-Book*, 308) provided by the ministry of the Revd James Philippo Mursell, a political radical and founder of the Leicester and Leicestershire Political Union. Although little is known of his early education, it seems Manning was destined not for the ministry but for commerce, and aged eighteen he was sent to work for a Liverpool business house. While in Liverpool he worshipped with a Baptist congregation at Pembroke Chapel, and was baptized by the Revd C. M. Birrell on 27 November 1842, the day after his twenty-first birthday. About six months later Manning expressed a desire to enter the ministry, and with the support of Birrell and the church he went to study at Bristol Baptist college in the autumn of 1843. Before completing the course at Bristol, Manning, on his tutors' advice, studied for a time at Glasgow University. At the end of 1847 Samuel Manning was invited to preach (initially on a trial basis) at the church at Sheppard's Barton, Frome, Somerset; he accepted its call and was ordained on 21 April 1848. During his fifteen-year pastorate the chapel was rebuilt and large schoolrooms added.

In 1850 Manning's first serious publication, a collection

of essays defending the historical truth of the New Testament reprinted from *The Church*, appeared as *Infidelity Tested by Fact*. While at Frome, Manning wrote some tracts for the Religious Tract Society and articles for the *Eclectic Review*, the *Christian Spectator*, and *The Freeman*. His literary output earned him the editorship of the *Baptist Magazine*, which he held from 1857 to 1861. His next project, *Selections from the Prose Writings of John Milton*, was published in 1862 for the Bunyan Library series. At Frome he was a popular lecturer on politics (he was a Liberal) as well as on literary and religious subjects. Manning was well liked and was regarded by contemporaries as an entertaining storyteller and a witty conversationalist. He married the daughter of a Mr Hope of Liverpool, and they had three sons and three daughters.

In 1863 the Religious Tract Society appointed Manning its book editor, and he resigned his Sheppard's Barton pastorate. In keeping with the society's goal of producing 'Christian literature' in its widest sense, Manning began what would become a series of travelogues, beginning with *Swiss Pictures: Drawn with Pen and Pencil* (1866). These travel books, attractively produced, proved popular Christmas sellers, and offered not only a physical description of a country (they were lavishly illustrated) but an assessment of the social, moral, and religious life of the people. *Swiss Pictures* was followed by books on Spain (1870), Italy (1872), Egypt and Sinai (*Land of the Pharaohs*, 1875), America (1876), England (1877), and the Holy Land (a compilation of *These Holy Fields*, *Land of the Pharaohs*, and *Pictures from Bible Lands*, 1879); the last two books were produced jointly with his friend Samuel Gosnell Green. He accepted an honorary LLD from the University of Chicago in 1869 and in 1876 was appointed a secretary of the Religious Tract Society, where he supported (along with S. G. Green and Sir Charles Reed) the candidature of G. A. Hutchinson for the editorship of the *Boy's Own Paper*. Manning was a member of the committee of the Baptist Missionary Society and served as a deacon to the church at Cornwall Road, Notting Hill. His health began to fail, but he continued to work at the society's offices in Paternoster Row until about three months before his death. He died at his home, 35 Ladbroke Grove, Notting Hill, London, on 13 September 1881, and on 16 September was buried in Kensal Green cemetery, London.

GORDON GOODWIN, rev. L. E. LAUER

Sources Baptist Hand-Book (1882), 307–10 · S. A. Swaine, *Faithful men, or, Memorials of Bristol Baptist College* (1884), 327–30 · S. G. Green, *The story of the Religious Tract Society for one hundred years* (1899) · J. Cox, *Take a cold tub sir! the story of the Boy's Own Paper* (1982) · church minutes, Pembroke Chapel, Liverpool, 1838–46, Regents Park College, Oxford, Argus Library, fols. 47, 56, 107 · *The Freeman* (16 Sept 1881), 464 · *The Bookseller* (5 Oct 1881), 885 · *The Guardian* (1881), 1309 · J. H. Y. Briggs, *The English Baptists of the 19th century* (1994), 395 · private information (2004)

Likenesses portrait, repro. in Green, *Story of the RTS*, facing p. 71

Wealth at death £4097 4s. 6½d.: probate, 20 Jan 1882, *CGPLA Eng. & Wales*

Manning, Thomas (1772–1840), traveller and writer on China, born at Broome, Norfolk, on 8 November 1772, was the second son of the Revd William Manning, successively

Thomas Manning (1772–1840), attrib. J. M. Davis, *c.*1805

rector of Broome and Diss, who died at Diss on 29 November 1810, aged seventy-seven, and his wife, Elizabeth, the only child of the Revd William Adams, rector of Rollesby, Norfolk, who died at Diss on 28 January 1782, aged thirty-four. Because of ill health, Thomas was educated at home as a boy, and in 1790 matriculated as a scholar at Caius College, Cambridge, where he spent the following five years studying mathematics. However, having adopted the plain dress of the Quakers, and sharing their antipathy to oaths and tests, he did not take a degree. He stayed for some years at Cambridge, studying medicine, teaching mathematics privately, and publishing his *Introduction to Arithmetic and Algebra* (2 vols., 1796–8) and other works on mathematics. He also met Charles Lamb there in 1799. Lamb described Manning as his friend 'M., who with great painstaking got me to think I understood the first proposition in Euclid, but gave me over in despair at the second' ('The old and new schoolmaster', *Elia: Essays*).

While at Cambridge, Manning became interested in the language and people of China, and in 1802 he went to Paris to study Chinese under Dr Hagar at the Bibliothèque Nationale. There he became friendly with several scientists, and especially the elder Carnot, with whom he corresponded regularly on the subject of algebra. When war broke out between France and England in 1803 Carnot and Talleyrand are said to have persuaded Napoleon to allow Manning to return to England, which he did in 1805.

Manning decided to go to Canton (Guangzhou) to perfect his Chinese, and in May 1806 obtained permission from the court of directors of the East India Company to travel there and live in the English factory as a doctor, having spent the previous six months gaining practical medical experience, mainly at Westminster Hospital, to complement his theoretical knowledge of the subject. In May 1806 he left England, and later that year arrived at Parijong. He made several unsuccessful attempts to penetrate the interior of China and, with the exception of a visit to Cochin China in February 1808, stayed at Canton until 1810. Early that year he went to Calcutta, where for a few months, with his flowing beard, eccentric dress and manner, and witty conversation, he was the centre of society. Then, without government permission, with one Chinese servant, he set off to Rangpur heading for Lhasa. He entered Bhutan by the Lakhi Duar in September 1811 and reached Parijong on the frontier of Tibet on 20 October. There he found a Chinese general, some of whose troops he cured of illness, and in their company he travelled as a doctor to Lhasa, where he arrived in December 1811, the first and for many years the only British traveller to reach the holy city. Ignoring the fact that he had been refused permission, he rode up to the *potala* (the Dalai Lama's palace), heavily but ineffectually disguised. Surprisingly he was permitted to stay for five months and was even granted an audience with the Dalai Lama, then a boy of seven. Manning was far from overawed by Lhasa. 'If the palace exceeded my expectations, the town as far fell short of them', he wrote.

> There is nothing striking, nothing pleasing in its appearance. The habitations are begrimed with smut and dirt. The avenues are full of dogs … growling and gnawing bits of hide which lie about in profusion and emit a charnel-house smell. (Hanbury-Tenison, 1995, 49)

Under peremptory orders from Peking, Manning was sent back to India; he left Lhasa on 19 April 1812 and arrived at Calcutta the following summer. His original narrative of the journey was lost, and he refused to give any details to officials at Calcutta, so nothing more was known of this remarkable visit to one of the most politically sensitive and tantalizing areas of the world until his journal was edited by Clements Markham and published in 1879 as *Narrative of the mission of George Bogle to Tibet and of the journey of Thomas Manning to Lhasa*, with an introductory memoir.

Manning returned to Canton to live in the factory. In 1816 he accompanied Lord Amherst's embassy to Peking as junior secretary and interpreter, despite Amherst's initial objection to his flowing beard as 'incongruous' in a British embassy. When the embassy was over, he set off for home in the *Alceste*, but the ship was wrecked near Sunda on 17 February 1817. Continuing homeward in the *Caesar*, in July 1817 he reached St Helena, where he met Napoleon. He returned to England, left again in 1827 to live in Italy until 1829, and thereafter lived in strict retirement, first at Bexley, Kent, and afterwards at a cottage called Orange Grove, near Dartford. The house was never furnished and Manning lived in a library of Chinese books

said to be the most extensive in Europe at the time, and which he later bequeathed to the Royal Asiatic Society. He had a stream of visitors attracted by his scholarship and conversation. In 1838 a stroke disabled his right hand, and to secure better medical attention he moved to Bath, but before leaving his cottage he is said to have plucked out the whole of his beard by the roots, although this and other of his eccentricities may be simply the product of his habitually humorous tone, especially in his letters to Lamb. He died at Bath of apoplexy on 2 May 1840 and was buried in the abbey church there on 8 May.

Manning's scientific and mathematical work is now judged of little importance. For many years he was best remembered for his friendship with Lamb. Manning's were the only letters which Lamb did not destroy, and both they and Lamb's letters to Manning were published. The letters show the two men to have been good friends, but Manning's are remarkably uninformative about the places he visited. His journey to Lhasa has recently been the focus of more interest, although he himself regarded it simply as a necessary stage on his route into China.

ELIZABETH BAIGENT

Sources A. J. Dunkin, *GM*, 2nd ser., 14 (1840), 97–100 · *The letters of Charles and Mary Lamb*, ed. E. W. Marrs, 3 vols. (1975–8) · A. Ainger, ed., *The life and works of Charles Lamb* (1899) · *Letters of Thomas Manning to Charles Lamb*, ed. E. A. Anderson (1925) · R. Hanbury-Tenison, 'A longing for Lhasa', *Geographical Magazine*, 67 (1995), 49 · C. Lamb, *Elia: essays which have appeared under that signature in the London Magazine* (1823) · R. Hanbury-Tenison, *The Oxford book of exploration* (1993) · private information (2004)
Archives NHM, corresp. with Sir Joseph Banks
Likenesses attrib. J. M. Davis, portrait, c.1805, Royal Asiatic Society [*see illus.*] · bust, 1806, repro. in Anderson, ed., *Letters*

Manning, Thomas Henry (1911–1998), Arctic explorer and zoologist, was born at Shrublands, Dallington, Northamptonshire, on 22 December 1911, the only child of Thomas Edgar Manning (1884–1975), brewer and county cricketer, and his wife, Dorothy Frances Randall (1886–1968). Educated at Harrow School from 1925 to 1930, he entered Jesus College, Cambridge. After two years there, Arctic exploration claimed him, and he went down without a degree in 1932.

In the winter of 1932–3 Manning and a schoolfriend journeyed by reindeer sledge through northern Sweden and Finland, and inadvertently into the Soviet Union. They were arrested and imprisoned in Leningrad gaol for three weeks, until released through the intervention of the British consul.

Manning now turned to the Canadian Arctic, thus setting the course for the rest of his life. In 1933–5, during two winters, he sledged alone around the coast of Southampton Island, Hudson Bay, mapping and studying animal life as he went. On his return to England he organized a larger expedition to the same region and north-eastwards to Baffin Island: the British Canadian Arctic expedition of 1936–41. Working sometimes alone and sometimes with Inuit guides, its six members pursued their various projects in archaeology, biology, geology, and survey.

By the end of summer 1938, only Manning remained in

the field, having moved to a camp near Cape Dorset in southern Baffin Island. From here he persuaded his Nova Scotian friend Ella Wallace (Jacky) Jackson (*b.* 1905) to join him by the summer resupply ship. They were married at Cape Dorset on 5 August, and for the next eighteen months they travelled by whaleboat and dog team up the west coast of Baffin Island, mapping the land and studying animal life. They first learned that war had broken out on return to Cape Dorset in January 1940. At this season the only way to reach the south, where their duty lay, was to travel north round Foxe basin, and thence to the railhead at Churchill on the west coast of Hudson Bay. They completed this journey of nearly 2500 miles in January 1941, becoming the first people to have travelled and mapped the entire west coast of Baffin Island.

Manning was commissioned lieutenant in the Royal Canadian Naval Volunteer Reserve in 1941, and spent the next four years mainly on the Labrador coast. Before demobilization, he took part in the Canadian military exercise Muskox in the winter of 1945–6, when tracked vehicles were tested on a journey of nearly 3000 miles north-westward from Churchill and then southward to Edmonton.

Geodetic survey on the Hudson Bay coast then occupied Manning and his wife during two summers. In 1949, as skipper of a Peterhead boat, he led a thorough investigation of Prince Charles Island, newly discovered from the air in Foxe basin, and in 1951, on the Canadian–American Beaufort Sea expedition, he skippered an ice-strengthened ship, carrying out inshore oceanography off Alaska and the Canadian western Arctic, while an American ice-breaker worked offshore. In the summers of 1952 and 1953 he circumnavigated Banks Island by canoe with one companion, surveying its harbours and its birds and mammals. In the summers of 1957 and 1958, again with one companion, he made zoological expeditions to Adelaide peninsula and King William Island, and to Prince of Wales Island.

Manning remained active in the field in most summers until the 1980s, concentrating his interests in later years on James Bay and the southern shores of Hudson Bay. Of independent means, he had always worked on short-term contracts for various Canadian government departments.

Manning was a low-strung, elemental person of iron self-control and iron resolve, who always attained his objectives, appearing to enjoy hardship. In his sturdy frame, 5 feet 9 inches tall, he possessed the endurance of the polar bear, whose movements he had studied. He had worn a beard since his Cambridge days. By nature a man of few words, he was always a good listener to others. His expertise as cabinet-maker and bookbinder was evident in the nineteenth-century farmhouse near Merrickville, Ontario, where he spent the last thirty-five years of his life, latterly with his companion Brenda Helen Carter (*b.* 1943), the Canadian artist, following separation from his wife in 1968.

Manning's important contributions to Arctic zoology were published by the Canadian National Museum and in professional journals. He sought no publicity for his work, but his wife published *Igloo for the Night* (1943) and *A Summer on Hudson Bay* (1949) on their travels. His honours included the patron's medal of the Royal Geographical Society (1948), the Bruce memorial prize of the Royal Society of Edinburgh (1944), the Massey medal of the Royal Canadian Geographical Society (1977), and the order of Canada (1974).

Manning donated to the community of Ikaluit, Baffin Island, his fine Arctic library, and to Cambridge University C$1 million towards the new Shackleton Library at the Scott Polar Research Institute. This was officially opened on 20 November 1998, but Manning had died from Parkinson's disease on 8 November at a hospital in Smith's Falls, Ontario. His ashes were buried four days later on his estate at Merrickville.

Manning will be remembered in the legends of the Canadian Arctic as one of the most undaunted travellers the land has known, as the last of its true explorers, and as a zoologist of distinction.   G. HATTERSLEY-SMITH

Sources E. W. Manning, *Igloo for the night* (1943) • E. W. Manning, *A summer on Hudson Bay* (1949) • T. H. Manning, 'Explorations on the east coast of Hudson Bay', *GJ*, 109 (1947), 58–75 • T. H. Manning, 'The Foxe basin coasts of Baffin Island', *GJ*, 101 (1943), 225–51 • R. J. O. Bray, *Five watersheds, a winter journey to Russian Lapland* (1935) • T. H. Manning and others, 'The voyage of CGMV *Nauja* to Foxe basin, 1949', unpublished report, 1950, Energy, Mines and Resources Canada, Ottawa, Ontario, Canada, Library and Records [Canadian Geographical Branch] • T. H. Manning, 'Narrative of an unsuccessful attempt to circumnavigate Banks Island', *Arctic*, 6 (1953), 171–97 • T. H. Manning, 'Narrative of a second defence research board expedition to Banks Island', *Arctic*, 9 (1956), 3–77 • G. Hattersley-Smith, *Daily Telegraph* (19 Nov 1998) • personal knowledge (2004) • private information (2004) [Brenda Carter, relatives] • *WW* • G. Hattersley-Smith, 'Polar profile: Tom Manning', *Polar Record*, 35 (1999), 149–52 • G. W. Rowley, *Cold comfort: my love affair with the Arctic* (1996)

Archives Canadian Museum of Man, Ottawa • Canadian Museum of Nature, Ottawa • Public Library, Ikaluit, Baffin Island, Canada, collection • RGS, papers and photographs • Scott Polar RI, papers

Likenesses photograph, *c*.1932, repro. in T. H. Harrisson, *Letter to Oxford* (1933) • photograph, *c*.1951, repro. in Hattersley-Smith, 'Polar profile: Tom Manning'

Wealth at death approx. £5,400,000: private information (2004)

Manning, William (1630x33–1711), clergyman and ejected minister, was born at Cockfield, Suffolk, the son of William Manning. He was educated at Stowmarket School before being admitted on 25 October 1649 as a sizar of Christ's College, Cambridge, where the Platonist Henry More was his tutor. (There is a discrepancy as to his date of birth based on his recorded age at admission, sixteen, and that derived from his reported age at death of eighty-one.) Manning graduated BA in 1653 and proceeded MA in 1660. Like his brothers John (*d.* 1694), vicar of Sibton-with-Peasenhall and pastor to Independent congregations at successively Walpole and Sibton, and Samuel, rector of Cookley-with-Walpole, William became a clergyman in Suffolk. In 1652 he married Priscilla (1629/30–1710). In 1654 he was chaplain at Landguard fort. By 1658 he was rector of Middleton, where on 29 December he baptized his son, also William. All three Manning brothers were ejected at the Restoration; William's signature appears for the last time in the Middleton parish register in April 1661, the month in which his daughter Elizabeth was baptized there. Manning settled at Peasenhall, and in 1672 he took out a licence under the declaration of indulgence as 'a congregational teacher in his own house', as did his brother John who continued to live in the same parish after his ejection. In 1674 William was fined £20 for keeping a conventicle.

In 1686 Manning published a small volume of sermons entitled *Catholic Religion … Discovered in some Discourses upon Act X*, in which he exhibited a tolerant and truly Christian spirit. He preached occasionally at Lowestoft, Suffolk, and there became acquainted with Thomas Emlyn, who in 1689 was chaplain at Rose Hall to Sir Robert Rich, a member of the presbyterian congregation at Lowestoft. The two friends read William Sherlock's *Vindication of the Trinity* (1690), but found it too much like a form of tritheism. Both men were led in consequence to doubt the doctrine and Manning became convinced of the Socinian attitude towards Christ, namely a denial of the essential deity and a full acceptance of the humanity of Christ. In letters to Emlyn, who in 1691 moved to Dublin, Manning argued strongly for this position up to the time of his death. Indeed he tried hard to convert others to this view, but not always successfully. His chief opponent was Nathaniel Parkhurst, a vicar of Yoxford, Suffolk. Increasing deafness led Manning to give up preaching (before 1704), but he retained an active mind and took great interest in current developments of theological opinion. Among the ejected he appears to have been the sole example of a Socinian preacher, and Edmund Calamy, while recognizing that Manning was 'a man of great abilities and learning', curtly noted, 'But he fell into the Socinian Principles' (*Calamy rev.*, 337). Manning died on 13 February 1711 and was buried at Peasenhall on 15 February. In his will he left money for the poor of Peasenhall and also 'for the schooling of their children' (ibid.).

ALEXANDER GORDON, rev. H. J. McLACHLAN

Sources *Calamy rev.* • A. Gordon, ed., *Freedom after ejection: a review (1690–1692) of presbyterian and congregational nonconformity in England and Wales* (1917) • M. Watts, *The dissenters: from the Reformation to the French Revolution* (1978) • S. S. Toms, 'Some account of Mr. William Manning, an ejected minister and an unitarian', *Monthly Repository*, 2 (1817), 377–84 • 'Original letters: two letters from Mr. Emlyn to Mr. William Manning', *Monthly Repository*, 2 (1817), 387–8 • 'Original letter of Mr. Emlyn to Mr. Manning, with Mr. Manning's notes', *Monthly Repository*, 21 (1825) • 'Correspondence between Mr. Emlyn and Mr. Manning', *Monthly Repository*, 21 (1826), 33–9, 87–91, 203–6, 333–7 • Venn, *Alum. Cant.* • [T. Emlyn], *The works of Mr T. E. … memoirs of the life and writings of the author*, 3 vols. (1746)

Manning, William (1763–1835), merchant, was born on 1 December 1763, the only surviving son of William Manning, merchant, of the parish of St Mary Axe in the City of London, and his wife, Elizabeth, daughter and heir of John Ryan, a planter in St Kitts and Santa Cruz. The elder William Manning also came from a planter family on St Kitts, and soon after his marriage in 1751 started a merchant house in Bristol, trading to the West Indies, subsequently moving to London. His son joined the firm and took over

on his father's death in 1791; he also inherited two-thirds of the Ryan estates on Santa Cruz from his mother, and purchased the remaining third. His status in the City was marked by his election to a directorship of the Bank of England in 1792. He remained a member of the court until 1831, serving as deputy governor (1810–12) and governor (1812–14). In 1793 he became a commissioner of exchequer bills; he also served as agent for St Vincent between 1792 and 1806, and for Grenada between 1825 and 1831.

In 1786 Manning married Elizabeth, the daughter of Abel Smith, a Nottingham banker, with whom he had two daughters. After her death, he remarried in 1792; his second wife was Mary (1771–1847), daughter of Henry Leroy Hunter, a barrister of Reading, with whom he had four sons (including Henry Edward *Manning, the future cardinal) and four daughters. The connection with the Smith family took Manning into Pitt's circle, and in 1794 he entered the Commons as the member for Plympton Erle, subsequently sitting for Lymington (1796–1806), Evesham (1806–18), Lymington again (1818–20 and 1821–6), and Penryn until 1830. He was a staunch supporter of the government, promoting the loyal declaration of London merchants in 1795, and subscribing to the loyalty loan of 1797. He served as a volunteer in the London and Westminster light horse in 1797, before joining the Bank of England Volunteers in 1798, where he rose to the rank of lieutenant-colonel in 1803. He was also a leading spokesman of the West Indies interest in the Commons, and was particularly active in the campaign for a dock to serve the West Indies trade. A committee of West Indies merchants was formed in 1795, and £800,000 was subscribed to a company to construct the proposed dock. He submitted the petition for the bill in 1796, and was instrumental in the appointment of a select committee against the opposition of the City corporation, which feared a threat to its income from the quays on the Thames. Although the bill failed, it was reintroduced in 1797, and was finally approved at the end of 1799. Manning was also active in urging compensation for slave owners, but he denied that he opposed abolition of slavery.

By the 1790s Manning was a wealthy man at the heart of the City. He had a town house in Spring Gardens and a modest country house, Copped Hall, at Totteridge, on the outskirts of London; in 1813 he purchased the Coombe Bank estate at Sundridge, near Sevenoaks, for £40,000, a property which was more fitting to his status. He was, Cardinal Manning later remarked, 'of the Old Church Established religion; a friend of the bishops, many of whom were his close personal friends', especially Wilberforce and Tomline; and he remembered his father as 'one of the justest, most benevolent, most generous men I ever knew', who had a 'refinement and delicacy of mind' and a modest and sensitive aversion to display (Purcell, 7–8). These memories may say more about the cardinal's filial sentiments in old age than about his father's character, and may reflect the cares which descended on him from the end of the Napoleonic Wars and the depression in the West Indies trade which marked a turning point in his prosperity. He was in difficulties in the 1820s, and in 1831 he became bankrupt. His son Henry, who led him away from his appearance before a commissioner of bankruptcy at the Guildhall, remembered 'his saying to me with much feeling, "I have belonged to men with whom bankruptcy was synonymous with death." It was so to him' (Purcell, 71). He resigned from the Bank of England, sold his estate, and withdrew from business and public life. His friends bought a life interest in his wife's marriage settlement, and subscribed to an income which allowed him to survive in the shabby gentility of Gower Street and a cottage near Petworth. He died at Gower Street on 17 April 1835, probably with his bankruptcy still undischarged, and was buried at Sundridge, Kent. He was survived by his wife.　　　　　　　　MARTIN DAUNTON

Sources P. A. Symonds and R. G. Thorne, 'Manning, William', HoP, Commons, 1790–1820, 4.540–43 · E. S. Purcell, Life of Cardinal Manning, 1 (1896) · W. M. Acres, 'Directors of the Bank of England', N&Q, 179 (1940), 131–4, esp. 133 · D. Newsome, The convert cardinals: John Henry Newman and Henry Edward Manning (1993)
Archives Bodl. Oxf., papers

Manning, William Oke (1809–1878), legal writer, was the son of William Oke Manning, a London merchant, and nephew of James Manning, serjeant-at-law. He was the brother of Anne *Manning, author of historical fiction. He was educated at Bristol under Dr Lant Carpenter, who had been the colleague of his grandfather, James Manning, in the Unitarian ministry at Exeter.

After leaving school Manning entered his father's counting-house. In 1839 he published *Commentaries on the Law of Nations*. He claimed in the preface to be the first English writer to produce a systematic treatise on international law. A closely reasoned work, it was noticeable for its historical method and its appreciation of the combination of the ethical and customary elements in international law. At first it attracted little attention, but it was gradually found useful by teachers, and was cited as an authority in the courts. Manning died, after a long illness, on 15 November 1878, at his home, 8 Gloucester Terrace, Regent's Park. He was survived by his wife, Frances Augusta, and son, Herbert Lane Manning.

G. LE G. NORGATE, rev. CATHERINE PEASE-WATKIN

Sources The Athenaeum (30 Nov 1878) · The Standard (19 Nov 1878) · BL cat. · Holdsworth, Eng. law, vol. 15 · CGPLA Eng. & Wales (1879)
Wealth at death under £35,000: probate, 5 Feb 1879, CGPLA Eng. & Wales

Manningham, John (c.1575–1622), lawyer and diarist, was the son of Robert Manningham (d. 1588) of Fen Drayton, Cambridgeshire, and his wife, Joan, daughter of John Fisher of Bedlow, Buckinghamshire. After his father's death Manningham was formally adopted and made the heir of Richard Manningham, a prosperous, childless London mercer and the younger brother of the diarist's grandfather. John Manningham entered Magdalene College, Cambridge, in 1592 and graduated BA in 1596. On 16 March 1598 he began to study law at the Middle Temple, and on 7 June 1605 he was called to the degree of utter barrister. About one month later, on 16 July 1605, he married Anne (d. c.1656), the sister of his Middle Temple chambermate Edward Curle. They had eight children.

Through inheritance and family connections Manningham led a successful and comfortable life. He practised law and had a position at the court of wards and liveries, probably obtained through his wife's father William Curle, who was auditor in that office. From Richard Manningham, John inherited the manor house of Bradbourne in East Malling, Kent, and throughout his life he kept his chambers at the Middle Temple. There he was apparently on the verge of rising to the office of reader at the time of his death in 1622.

From January 1602, his third year at the Middle Temple, until April 1603 Manningham regularly wrote down material of various sorts in a duodecimo copybook: anecdotes, poems, epitaphs, gossip, Inner Temple customs, jokes and witticisms, recipes, inscriptions, reactions to important public events, legal lore, brief accounts of his family, as well as many summaries (some very long) of sermons. By itself this pot-pourri gives only the cloudiest picture of life at the Middle Temple and London; a social historian requires such documents as Chamberlain's letters, the autobiography of Simonds D'Ewes, and James Whitelocke's recollections to give Manningham's entries sharper focus. But, as such material is pitifully scanty, readers are grateful for his record of wit combats among his fellow students, his account of the professional wisdom he gained from the eminent lawyers with whom he dined and studied at the Temple, and for mention of important historical events. Every Sunday Manningham heard one, often two, sermons at locations all over London, and he devoted at least one-third of the copybook to detailed summaries of them, recording them in an unquestioning, meticulous manner. Manningham rarely expressed his personal views on this, as on most other topics; he was primarily a reporter who apparently found everything interesting.

Unquestionably the most valuable of the entries are those concerning Shakespeare. Manningham records that on 2 February 1602, at the Middle Temple Candlemas day feast, 'wee had a play called "Twelve Night, or what you will"'. Few of Shakespeare's plays can be so precisely placed and dated. What is equally enlightening are Manningham's next words: 'much like the commedy of errores, or Menechmi in Plautus, but most like and neere to that in Italian called Inganni'. Manningham, hardly an aesthete or even a regular theatregoer, instantly recalled an earlier play by Shakespeare, recognized the source in Plautus, and the similarity to a relatively recent Italian play. Moreover he was appreciative of the playwright's 'good practise' (Diary, ed. Sorlien, 48) in concocting the plot against Malvolio. It is apparent from that brief paragraph that Shakespeare could rely on at least a portion of his oft-maligned audience to be appreciative of his best efforts.

Manningham's other mention of Shakespeare is in the fabliau-like story he heard from an older Templar, William Towse. It seems that the actor Richard Burbage, while playing Richard III, was overheard by Shakespeare making an assignation with a lady. Shakespeare usurped his place and was 'at his game' when Burbage announced his arrival with the agreed 'Richard III'. To him Shakespeare sent the triumphant message 'William the Conquerour was before Richard the 3' (*Diary*, ed. Sorlien, 75). At a time when Shakespeare's sexual orientation is much discussed, it is worth noting that the only contemporary gossip on the subject makes him out to be an amiable woman-chaser. Unlike most such allusions this one is precisely contemporary and the source, William Towse, was not a town gossip but a prominent and active bencher deemed responsible enough to be chosen treasurer, the highest office at the Inner Temple, in 1608 and a serjeant-at-law in 1614. (E. K. Chambers, *William Shakespeare*, 2.212, following W. W. Greg, reads the name of Manningham's informant as 'Curle', but R. P. Sorlien argues forcefully that the manuscript reads 'Touse'.)

There are silly and boring passages in Manningham's diaries, but he was also capable of Elizabethan eloquence, as in his description of the death of the queen that he heard from eyewitnesses: 'This morning about 3 at clocke hir Majestie departed this lyfe, mildly like a lambe, easily like a ripe apple from the tree' (*Diary*, ed. Sorlien, 208). Similarly, Manningham captures the relief that was universally felt at the peaceful succession of King James:

> Noe tumult, noe contradiction, noe disorder in the city; every man went about his busines, as readylie, as peaceably, as securely, as though there had bin noe change, nor any newes ever heard of competitors. God be thanked, our king hath his right.   (ibid., 209)

Manningham was no Pepys, but he left invaluable documentation of an ordinary life in the legendary London of Donne, Bacon, and Shakespeare. Manningham died at Bradbourne Manor on 22 November 1622, and was buried at East Malling church.   P. J. FINKELPEARL

Sources The diary of John Manningham of the Middle Temple, 1602–1603, ed. R. P. Sorlien (Hanover, NH, 1976) · Diary of John Manningham, ed. J. Bruce, CS, old ser., 99 (1868) · Venn, Alum. Cant. · A. Ponsonby, English diaries: a review of English diaries from the sixteenth to the twentieth century with an introduction to diary writing, 2nd edn (1923) **Archives** BL, diary, Harley MSS
Wealth at death significant wealth: will, Diary, ed. Sorlien, 289–92

Manningham, Sir Richard (*bap.* 1685, *d.* 1759), man-midwife, second son of Thomas *Manningham (*d.* 1722), later bishop of Chichester, and his wife, Elizabeth (1656/7–1714), was baptized at East Tisted, Hampshire, on 2 March 1685. Like his elder brother he was intended for the church; however, having been admitted as a fellow-commoner to Magdalene College, Cambridge, on 27 September 1717, he proceeded LLB in the same year, before gaining the MD, by mandate, in 1725. Nothing is known of his further education in medicine.

On 10 March 1719 Manningham was elected FRS and on 30 September he became a licentiate of the Royal College of Physicians; on 18 February 1722 he was knighted by George I. He obviously made rapid progress in his career, and was looked on as a leading man-midwife of his day. He was commanded by the king to investigate the case of Mary Toft of Godalming, who claimed to have given birth

to several rabbits. Through contacts at court John Howard, the local Surrey man-midwife, had Mary Toft transferred to Lacy's bagnio in London, there to be exhibited. However, she finally confessed to her fraud, largely because a porter at Lacy's was discovered with a rabbit in his pocket. Manningham, along with others, seems to have been duped by Toft, and attempted to exculpate himself by publishing, in 1726, *An exact diary of what was observ'd during a close attendance upon Mary Toft, the pretended rabbet-breeder of Godalming in Surrey, from Monday, Nov. 28, to Dec. 7, following, together with an account of her confession of the fraud.*

Manningham taught midwifery, for a course fee of 20 guineas, using, as did many of his contemporaries, some kind of model of a pelvis and uterus. His main published work, of 1739 and 1740, was *Artis obstetricariae compendium*, which was translated into English in 1744; the original version was written in inelegant and incorrect Latin. It was expanded, as *Aphorisma medica*, in 1756. Manningham followed the teachings of the Dutchman Hendrik van Deventer (1651–1724) in regard to conservative midwifery and in his descriptions of the shapes of the bony pelvis and the obliquity of the uterus, with their effects on labour. When there was disproportion between the size of the foetal head and the pelvis Manningham advocated internal version, in which, with a hand in the uterus, the foetus is turned so that either the head or the breech is made to present. If the breech then the baby may be born by traction on the feet and legs. Manningham may have favoured turning to the head presentation when others mainly used podalic version. He would not, in difficult labours, resort to the recently introduced obstetric forceps, first depicted by Edmund Chapman in 1735 and afterwards employed by many other man-midwives of the time. Manningham claimed that caesarean section should be performed only after death of the mother, a generally held view at the time. Correctly, he taught that the placenta is usually inserted in the fundus of the uterus. He knew of convulsions in pregnancy (eclampsia) and treated those afflicted with fits by venesection, then a commonplace remedy. He had seen a fallopian tube, at postmortem, closed by infection; this tended to be common after manual removal of the placenta, making it clear, in Manningham's view, how dangerous it was to employ unskilled individuals in midwifery. He thought that children born seven months into the term of a pregnancy rarely survive whereas those born at eight months do, if well nursed. Manningham's major contribution to midwifery was that of establishing, in 1739, for the first time in this country, lying-in beds for mothers; these were in a house next to his own, in Jermyn Street, not in the local parochial infirmary, as was once believed. The idea of lying-in beds was current among some of Manningham's contemporaries in London but he was the first to put it into practice; one of his objectives was to teach midwives. His *Abstract of Midwifery for Use in the Lying-in Infirmary* appeared in 1744; the institution closed a little later. The third edition of his treatise, *The Symptoms, Nature, Causes and Cure of the Febricula or Little Fever*, came out in 1755 but was of little significance; others of his works were on fevers and plague.

Evidence has been adduced that Manningham was politically a whig, with court connections, and that whig man-midwives were conservative in their practices whereas those who used forceps were in the tory tradition. The significance of this is hard to evaluate but suggests that there were separate coteries of man-midwives with differing ideas on the practice of midwifery allied with political affiliations. Thomas Denman, an eminent man-midwife, commented that Manningham was 'successful in practice and very humane in the exercise of his art'.

Manningham lived in Chancery Lane, London, then successively in Haymarket and in Woodstock Street before finally settling in Jermyn Street in 1745, where he remained until his death there on 11 May 1759. His second son, Thomas, graduated MD at St Andrews University on 24 May 1765 and became LRCP on 25 June of the same year. He lived in his father's house in Jermyn Street until 1780, when he went to Bath, where he died on 3 February 1794.

PHILIP RHODES

Sources H. R. Spencer, *The history of British midwifery from 1650 to 1800* (1927), 14–18 · A. Wilson, *The making of man-midwifery: childbirth in England, 1660–1770* (1995) · *DNB* · F. H. Garrison, *An introduction to the history of medicine*, 4th edn (1929) · H. Graham, *Eternal Eve* (1950) · Venn, *Alum. Cant.* · *GM*, 1st ser., 29 (1759), 146 · Munk, *Roll* · *The record of the Royal Society of London*, 4th edn (1940) · *IGI* · Nichols, *Lit. anecdotes*, 1.207–11
Likenesses W. Hogarth, etching, 1726, Wellcome L.

Manningham, Thomas (d. 1722), bishop of Chichester, was born in St George's, Southwark, the son of Richard Manningham (d. 1682), rector of Michelmersh, Hampshire, and Bridget Blackwell. He was admitted a scholar of Winchester College in 1661. He was elected a probationer fellow of New College, Oxford, matriculating on 12 August 1669, graduated BA in 1673, and proceeded MA in 1677; he was a fellow of New College from 1671 to 1681. He received a Lambeth DD on 21 December 1691.

On ordination Manningham became, according to Anthony Wood, 'a high flown preacher' (Wood, *Ath. Oxon.*, 4.555). In 1681 he was presented to the comfortable living of East Tisted in Hampshire, 'Where being settled, he was passionately desirous to collect himself, to be known to few, and to be envied by none' (ibid.). It was there that his two eldest sons were baptized, in 1683 and 1685. Nothing is known of his wife, Elizabeth (1656/7–1714) apart from the high-flown phrases on her monument in Chichester Cathedral: 'Comely in person, meek in her temper, most humble in her behaviour, prudent in all her actions, and pious through her whole life' (Nichols, *Lit. anecdotes*, 1.208).

The king admired Manningham's preaching and in 1684 promised him the prebend at Winchester vacated by the promotion of Thomas Ken to the bishopric of Bath and Wells, but it was found to be in the gift of the lord keeper. Manningham succeeded Gilbert Burnet as preacher at the Rolls Chapel after the latter was dismissed because of his controversial sermon on 5 November 1684, in which he was supposed to have made a disloyal allusion to the lion

and the unicorn. Manningham became a lecturer at the Temple and on 8 September 1691 rector of St Andrew's, Holborn, where, E. G. Rupp says, 'high churchmen and Non-Jurors were thick upon the ground' (Rupp, 69). He retained the living until April 1713, leaving so that Henry Sacheverell, the anti-whig preacher and pamphleteer, might receive a rich reward from Queen Anne after the three-year moratorium imposed upon him after his trial in Westminster Hall. Manningham was an early supporter of the Society for Promoting Christian Knowledge, founded in 1699, further evidence of his high-church sympathies.

Appointed by Sir John Trevor as speaker's chaplain in 1690, four addresses were made by the House of Commons to the king on Manningham's behalf. The second, uniquely, specifically asked that 'the next prebend of Windsor or Westminster that should fall vacant' be conferred on him (*JHC*, 1688–93, 10.736). This came about on 28 January 1693 when he was installed as a canon of Windsor. In 1708 Manningham became rector of Great Haseley, Oxfordshire, and in 1709 dean of Windsor.

Manningham served as a chaplain to William and Mary and had praised the queen's enthusiasm for ensuring the printing of court sermons, believing that the multitude of plain, useful, and practical sermons she caused to be printed were 'her gift to the publick' (Claydon, 97–8). Royal favour continued, Queen Anne valuing his ministrations. On one occasion, when she was confined to her chamber by illness, it was suggested that Manningham should pray in an adjoining room, but he refused saying, 'he did not chuse to whistle the prayers of the Church through a key hole' (Nichols, *Lit. anecdotes*, 1.208). A Hanoverian tory, a high-church supporter of the succession laid down by the Act of Settlement rather than to the Jacobite cause, he became bishop of Chichester on 10 November 1709, an appointment which pleased the queen. At Chichester he found a chapter of whig sympathies and consequently quarrels ensued. He reported to Archbishop Wake his concern about the danger to the church from the strength of dissenters in his diocese and opposed the repeal of the Test Act.

Manningham was one of the bishops who signed a declaration in 1715 deploring the Jacobite rebellion of that year. He died at his house in Greville Street, Holborn, on 25 August 1722, and was buried in St Andrew's, Holborn. Many of his sermons were published in his lifetime. His will mentions ten children, of whom the names of six can be established: four sons (Thomas, Richard, Charles, and Simon) and two daughters (Mary and Dorothea). Thomas Manningham (*bap.* 1683, *d.* 1750) became, like his father, chaplain to the speaker (1718–23); Richard *Manningham, the only one of the sons not to become a clergyman, became a leading man-midwife.

DONALD GRAY

Sources Nichols, *Lit. anecdotes*, 1.207–11 · Wood, *Ath. Oxon.*, new edn, 4.555–6 · *Fasti Angl.* (Hardy), 1.253; 3.376, 405–6 · S. L. Ollard, *Fasti Wyndesorienses: the deans and canons of Windsor* (privately printed, Windsor, 1950), 49 · Foster, *Alum. Oxon., 1500–1714*, 3.966 · N. Luttrell, *A brief historical relation of state affairs from September 1678 to April 1714*, 6 (1857), 380, 403, 409, 474, 478, 554 · Wood, *Ath. Oxon.: Fasti* (1820), 334 · G. Hennessy, *Novum repertorium ecclesiasticum parochiale Londinense, or, London diocesan clergy succession from the earliest time to the year 1898* (1898), 90 • R. Newcourt, *Repertorium ecclesiasticum parochiale Londinense*, 1 (1708), 275 • *Archbishop of Canterbury acts books*, LPL, 4.461; 5.336 • *JHC*, 10 (1688–93), 423, 533, 593, 736 • E. G. Rupp, *Religion in England, 1688–1791*, Oxford History of the Christian Church (1986) • N. Sykes, 'Queen Anne and the episcopate', *EngHR*, 50 (1935), 433–64 • C. Rose, 'The origins and ideals of the SPCK, 1699–1716', *The Church of England, c.1689–c.1833: from toleration to tractarianism*, ed. J. Walsh, C. Hayden, and S. Taylor (1993) • *DNB* • J. S. Chamberlain, *Accommodating high churchmen* (1997) • A. Claydon, *William III and the Godly revolution* (1996) • will, PRO, PROB 11/587, sig. 176 • *Walker rev.*, 187

Mannion, Wilfred James (1918–2000), footballer, was born near Middlesbrough on 16 May 1918, at 31 Lower Napier Street, Eston. He was one of ten children of Irish immigrant parents: Thomas Mannion, a blast furnace labourer, and his wife, Mary Duffy. He grew up around South Bank, which borders the steelworks and shipbuilding sites of the Middlesbrough area. Thousands crammed together in the terraced housing of such districts, and were brought up and educated in the local institutions of the district. Mannion attended St Peter's Roman Catholic school and church, in the heart of South Bank, and played his first football nurtured by local schoolteachers, graduating to play for the local amateur side, South Bank–St Peter's. He signed to play for the professional football club Middlesbrough, in September 1936, and on 2 January 1937 played his début first-team game for the club, against Portsmouth. Becoming a professional player allowed Mannion to leave his job in the local steelworks. The small, chunky South Banker (he stood only 5 feet 5 inches) was one of those precociously skilled footballers bred in the deprived heartlands of England's industrial north. Middlesbrough paid Mannion £3 10s. per week, plus a £2 bonus for a first-team win. With his blond hair and his good looks he became known as Golden Boy.

Military service interrupted Mannion's football. Initially serving in the Auxiliary Fire Service, he was conscripted in 1940 to the 7th battalion of the Green Howards and saw service in France (as a Dunkirk evacuee), Sicily, and the Middle East. His playing career peaked in the years immediately after the Second World War, as if making up for lost time.

Mannion spent the bulk of his career at Middlesbrough, playing 368 games and scoring 110 goals. He also played 26 times for England, scoring three times on his début in a 7–2 victory over Northern Ireland in 1946, and inspiring England to a 4–0 defeat of Italy at Turin in May 1948. Mannion dazzled and fuelled the popular memory on two notable occasions: in May 1947, in a match organized by Sir Stanley Rous and the UK football associations to help the world governing body, FIFA (the Fédération Internationale de Football Associations), re-establish itself financially; and in November of the same year, in a home fixture for Middlesbrough against Blackpool. Great Britain defeated the Rest of Europe 6–1, double-goal scorer Mannion self-effacingly recalling that it was 'the team spirit, and nothing else, which gained that very convincing victory' (Kelly, 160). Of Mannion's qualities of vision, and the Blackpool game in particular, one fan recalls that 'He was magic ...

he 'ad the radar in his fingertips' and that in the Blackpool game "e 'ad the ball on 'is 'ead one moment and ran fifteen, twenty yards with the ball balanced on 'is 'ead ... It was magical' (Tomlinson, 254).

On 9 February 1948 Mannion married a local woman, Bernadette Kathleen Murray (*b.* 1927/8), to whom he had become engaged on the day of the Blackpool game; he attributed his extravagant display in that game to the fact that it was the first game that she had ever watched him play. His career at Middlesbrough was punctuated by some disputes over contracts. In 1948 he spent six months out of the game while Oldham Athletic sought unsuccessfully to raise the funds to buy him from Middlesbrough, where he returned until 1954, when he left for an unrewarding season with lower-division Hull City. His career spiralled downwards thereafter, as in his mid- and late thirties he undertook fruitless spells in playing and management in a number of non-league clubs, and in coaching the game for local authorities. He returned to his native Teesside, working in a series of unskilled jobs on building sites, the railways, and the steelworks, fighting over the years to claim a parsimoniously denied testimonial from his hometown club, selling his football memorabilia, and drawing on support from the Professional Footballers' Association hardship fund. He lived the last few years of his life in Redcar, on the coast.

Wilf Mannion died in Stead Memorial Hospital, Redcar, on 14 April 2000, aged eighty-one, after a prolonged illness. With his wife, Bernadette, who predeceased him, he had one son and two daughters. Where the St Peter's–South Bank football ground once stood visitors are now welcomed to Golden Boy Green, an initiative of Redcar and Cleveland borough council, funded by the European Regeneration Fund, and opened in December 2000. Bordered by the remnants of the old industrial terraces across Normandy Road and the council blocks on the other side, the green is a mix of community facilities, a toddler's play area, half a dozen basketball hoops, a skateboarding park, and a fortified community hall doubling as function room and indoor sportspace. It is a moving memorial to Mannion. There is a pedestrian access through a gate with his name inscribed in the arc at the top. Underneath, sculptured in shiny silver steel, hangs a pair of high-ankled, hard-toecapped football boots, and a thick, heavy-looking, upturned-collared no. 10 football shirt. Complementary sculptures of industrial clothing and plant make this a monument to an industrial culture as well as a sporting legend. But where Mannion learned his skills—on the streets of South Bank, across from Golden Boy Green—signs on gable-ends of houses state 'Ball Games Prohibited'.   ALAN TOMLINSON

Sources A. Tomlinson, 'Flattery and betrayal: observations on qualitative and oral sources', *Ethics, sport and leisure: crises and critiques*, ed. A. Tomlinson and S. Fleming (1997), 245–64 • J. Mapplebeck, Wilf Mannion, 1978, BBC Television North-East [written and produced by J. Mapplebeck] • S. F. Kelly, ed., *A game of two halves* (1993) • I. Ponting, *The Independent* (15 April 2000) • *The Times* (15 April 2000) • *The Scotsman* (15 April 2000) • b. cert. • m. cert. • d. cert.

Likenesses photograph, repro. in *The Independent* · photograph, repro. in *The Scotsman* · photograph, repro. in *The Times*

Mannix, Daniel (1864–1963), Roman Catholic archbishop of Melbourne, was born on 4 March 1864 at the substantial family farm, Deerpark, near Charleville (Rathluirc), co. Cork, Ireland, first child of Timothy Mannix (1826–1910) and his wife, Ellen Cagney (1826–1925). The family was comparatively affluent and of the small farmer middle class. Of eight children, three died in infancy, one at twenty-two. The surviving sons went variously into medicine, law, the family farm, and, in Daniel's case, religion. A daughter was educated in France. Their parents combined intense piety with driving family ambition.

Mannix's early life and schooling were witness to both his mother's strong-willed management and his own abilities. From local schooling with the Sisters of Mercy and Christian Brothers, he was moved, aged twelve, to a more distant classical school for three years of Latin and an education designed for aspirants to the priesthood. He then went to St Colman's College, Fermoy, where he won a scholarship to the élite Irish seminary for priests St Patrick's College, Maynooth. Tall, handsome, bony (at that stage anaemic), and even then forthright and outspoken, Mannix had suppressed a boyhood ambition to be an artist, determining on the priesthood at the age of sixteen. He entered Maynooth in 1882 and demonstrated outstanding intellectual quality and application, but also, presaging the future, a formidable and principled independence. Ordained on 8 June 1890, he spent the next year studying at Maynooth's postgraduate institute, the Dunboyne Establishment. He was quickly appointed to the teaching staff of the college and to a succession of professorships by 1894, and to editorship of the moral theology section of the *Irish Ecclesiastical Record*. In all this he firmly upheld Roman authority against Gallican tendencies, and pursued moral logic with a rigour and austerity which attracted attention as seeming severe.

However, being made secretary of the Maynooth Union in 1896, Mannix took the emphasis of clerical discussion away from theoretical questions toward national, social, and economic issues. His interest then, and for the rest of his life, was to apply religion to the condition of the people—particularly the poor—with respect to housing, the co-operative movement, the sick, and temperance.

Mannix became president of Maynooth in 1903, imposing his strong will and a necessary reforming discipline on that college, and ensuring its incorporation into the Irish university system upon the establishment of the multicollege National University of Ireland in 1908. His sharp imposition of authority, demanding good manners, strict dogma, and student subservience, stood with his patent holiness, compassion, and practical concern for the welfare of college servants, to the confusion of critics. Although Mannix's outlook and disposition were nationalist, his religious priorities and practicality took him into confrontation with the growing tide of Irish nationalism associated with the Gaelic revival. His opposition to compulsory Irish, on the grounds that it was useless to a missionary clergy, led in 1908, after major public conflict, to

Daniel Mannix (1864–1963), by unknown photographer

the dismissal of his own professor of Irish, Michael O'Hickey. Mannix's good manners and acceptance of existing political realities in providing college hospitality to Edward VII in 1903, and George V in 1911, drew attacks from the leaders of Irish nationalism.

Unpopularity, in spite of his acknowledged brilliance, holiness, and remarkable poise, made Mannix's appointment to an Irish bishopric unlikely. Besides, the ageing archbishop of Melbourne, Thomas Carr, aware of Mannix's interest in, and political experience of, education issues, saw him as the right man to revive and spearhead the Australian campaign for state aid to Catholic schools. Mannix arrived in Melbourne as Carr's coadjutor in March 1913. He was forty-nine; fifty-three when he succeeded Carr as archbishop in 1917. After Cardinal Moran's more passive, and unsuccessful, search for community harmony, Mannix embodied a new spirit of Catholic challenge and confrontation, centred on the state aid issue. In this, and wider matters of Catholic social deprivation, Mannix provided electrifying leadership and became the focus for sectarian storms: 'a sort of lightning conductor for all the abuse of the State of Victoria' (*Catholic Press*, 15 March 1917) was the self-description he offered in 1917 at the height of the socially and politically convulsive conscription debate.

Aggressively willing to speak his mind in public, a tall commanding figure, Mannix not only championed religious principles, but attacked a society which he saw as excluding Catholics from wealth, power, and influence: he became a hero to the Catholic underclass. Tensions increased with the outbreak of the First World War. Catholic loyalty was being publicly questioned before the Irish revolution in 1916, but this worsened the situation, particularly as Mannix made clear his criticism of British policy towards Ireland to vast crowds (at times 100,000) assembled to hear him, mainly at religious occasions. His very public opposition to conscription, expressed during the 1916 and 1917 referendum campaigns, earned him the obsessive hatred of the prime minister, W. M. Hughes, though it is doubtful whether Mannix's opposition alone decided the rejection of conscription. These campaigns, Mannix's role, and rampant sectarianism were profoundly divisive, a situation protracted into the early 1920s by Mannix's defiant identification with the cause of Irish independence. He attempted to visit Ireland—via Irish America—in 1920 to visit his aged mother but his ship was intercepted by a British destroyer and Mannix landed in England, to worldwide Irish indignation. Efforts were made to have Mannix recalled to Rome or banned from re-entry to Australia in 1921. Australian Catholics had seen oppression and injustice in Ireland as their own predicament writ large, but the Anglo-Irish treaty of 1921 and the Irish Civil War of 1922–3 saw support disappear for Mannix's intransigence, and the emergence of a distinctively Australian Catholic consciousness.

In this, Mannix's vision of education as the way forward—and socially upward—came into its own in the 1920s and 1930s. His distinctive initiatives were in promoting lay and clerical intellectuality. He fostered the Jesuit order and their initiatives, opened Newman College at the University of Melbourne in 1917, and a major seminary in 1923: other Australian bishops distrusted both universities and lay intellectuality. And unlike other Australian bishops he encouraged lay initiatives in relation to the papal call for Catholic Action in the 1930s. All this fostered the Victorian Catholic conviction—not without basis—that it was the most vital Catholicism in Australia, with Mannix at its head.

In particular Mannix backed the energies of the layman B. A. Santamaria and urged the support of other bishops for The Movement, a Catholic Action organization dedicated to Catholic social policy and the purging of communist influence in the trade unions. This led, in 1954, to a major split in the Australian Labor Party, traditionally supported by most Catholics. In turn this led to a split of opinion in the Catholic hierarchy, which, being referred to Rome, resulted in a win for those who opposed the Mannix position. He continued in support of Santamaria and his organization, and in the view that Catholics in good conscience could not vote Labor. The whole matter was a major and protracted social and political trauma for Catholics, Labor, and Australians generally, with profound and continuing consequences: Mannix remained central to it, as actor and symbol.

Mannix died suddenly on 6 November 1963 at Raheen, Kew, Melbourne (where he had lived), aged ninety-nine, of strangulation of the bowel, and was buried on 8 November in St Patrick's Cathedral, Melbourne. Earlier that year he had communicated to the Second Vatican Council a critique of astonishing pastoral sensitivity and liberality. Despite his commitments prayer occupied four to six hours a day. Yet some of his contentious life invites adverse interpretation—egotism, authoritarianism, impatience with opposition, Irish obsessions. His greatness was such as to contain both contradiction and mystery, his persona and indeed appearance such as to be formidable and magnificent. He died a revered national icon. A man who kept his own counsel, he confided in no one, kept no diary, wrote seldom and formally, and destroyed documentation. His many biographers are without private sources and thus tend to reflect, more than usually, their own standpoints.　　　PATRICK O'FARRELL

Sources B. A. Santamaria, *Daniel Mannix* (1984) · M. Gilchrist, *Daniel Mannix* (1982) · J. Griffin, 'Mannix, Daniel', *AusDB*, vol. 10 · W. Ebsworth, *Archbishop Mannix* (1972) · F. Murphy, *Daniel Mannix* (1972) · C. Kiernan, *Daniel Mannix and Ireland* (1984) · P. J. O'Farrell, *The Catholic church and community: an Australian history*, rev. edn (1992) · N. Brennan, *Dr Mannix* (1964) · J. Murphy, 'The lost (and last) animadversions of Daniel Mannix', *Australasian Catholic Record*, 76 (1999), 54–73 · *Catholic Press* (15 March 1917)
Archives Melbourne Diocesan Historical Commission, Fitzroy, Melbourne, MSS | Society of Jesus Provincial Archives, Hawthorn, Melbourne, Hacket MSS | FILM Australian Broadcasting Corporation, Melbourne · National Film and Sound Archives, Canberra | SOUND Australian Broadcasting Corporation, Melbourne
Likenesses J. Lavery, oils, 1921, Dublin Art Gallery · J. Cato, oils, 1928, St Patrick's Cathedral, Melbourne · H. Newton, photographs, c.1960, Melbourne Diocesan Historical Commission · C. Pugh, oils, 1962, University of Melbourne, Newman College · N. Boonham, statue, 1999, St Patrick's Cathedral, Melbourne · J. Longstaff, oils, Melbourne Diocesan Historical Commission · M. Meldrum, oils, St Patrick's Cathedral, Melbourne · A. Mezaros, medallion on tomb, St Patrick's Cathedral, Melbourne · photograph, NL Ire. [*see illus.*]
Wealth at death virtually nil; small bequests to servants and gold watches worth £150 and £5: Griffin, 'Mannix'

Mannock, Edward [Mick] (**1887–1918**), air force officer, was born in Brighton, Sussex, on 24 May 1887, the third of four children of Corporal Edward Mannock, Royal Scots Greys, and of his wife, Julia O'Sullivan of Ballincollig, co. Cork. The elder Edward Mannock, son of a Fleet Street editor, was at the time serving under his mother's maiden name of Corringhame, though in 1893, after a period of civilian unemployment, he re-enlisted as Trooper Edward Mannock, 5th dragoon guards. His regiment was shortly afterwards posted to India, and there his family joined him in May, at Meerut.

At the outbreak of the Second South African War the 5th dragoon guards were posted to South Africa, and Mannock's family, remaining in India, did not rejoin him until 1901, at Shorncliffe in Kent. Shortly afterwards, in Canterbury, he was discharged at the expiry of his service, and within weeks he deserted the family, taking with him their meagre savings. None of them saw him again.

The desertion of Mannock's father left his family in great poverty, and it was necessary for Edward to earn a

Edward Mannock (1887–1918), by unknown photographer

living, which he did as a greengrocer's (and then a barber's) assistant, before joining his elder brother Patrick in working for the National Telephone Company. Three years' office work were followed, more congenially, in the spring of 1911 by a transfer to a line gang. This entailed a move from Canterbury to Wellingborough, Northamptonshire, where Mannock widened his circle of friends and articulated the social and political opinions that he was to hold until his death—a passionate combination of socialism and patriotism.

His horizons broadened and his ambitions enlarged, in February 1914 Mannock left the National Telephone Company and travelled to Turkey, where in Istanbul he found employment with the Société Ottomane des Téléphones. When Turkey entered the war on the side of the central powers Mannock, like many others, was interned. Several attempts to escape were followed by imprisonment under conditions so harsh that, sick and emaciated, in April 1915 he was repatriated as medically unfit for military service.

Before leaving Canterbury Mannock had joined the home counties (territorial) company of the Royal Army Medical Corps, and on his return, his health restored, he rejoined his company at Ashford, Kent. Promoted sergeant, he chafed at his unit's inactivity and transferred to the Royal Engineers, where he was commissioned as second lieutenant. A chance meeting with an old friend suggested a way out of yet more frustration, and on 1 April 1916 he transferred to the Royal Flying Corps. On gaining his pilot's brevet he was posted for advanced training at Joyce Green, Kent, before, on 6 April 1917, joining 40 squadron at Treizennes, near Aire, in Artois, France.

Mannock was fortunate in that at the beginning of what became known (because of heavy losses) as 'bloody April' he was joining a squadron equipped with what was probably the best fighter in Royal Flying Corps service: the Nieuport 17. Even so, his operational career began inauspiciously. He was lucky to survive a crash landing when a lower wing broke away from the Nieuport that he was flying. He also got offside with many in the officers' mess when, as a fellow officer recalled, he 'offered ideas about everything; how the war was going, how it should be fought, the role of scout pilots, what was wrong or right with our machines' (Smith, 64). But the most serious cloud over Mannock during his first weeks on the squadron was the suspicion that he lacked fighting spirit. Eventually questioned about this he candidly admitted to fear, adding that, having conquered it, he was ready to conquer the enemy. It was to prove no empty boast.

Like many aces Mannock was a slow starter. His first victory, on 7 May 1917, was followed by a second a month later, with the third and fourth coming on successive days, 12 and 13 July. With success (and the award, on 22 July, of the Military Cross) came both growing confidence and acceptance, though a handful of his fellow pilots remained unconvinced that he was an appropriate choice as flight commander, to which he was appointed later that month on promotion to captain. August, however, brought accelerating success, with four victories in six days in mid-month, one of them, on 12 August, taking place almost over Treizennes, and resulting in the capture of the aircraft and its pilot, Joachim von Bertrab, a German ace.

By the end of August 1917 Mannock was credited with nine victories, and September brought six more, earning him on 14 October a bar to his MC. In October 40 squadron converted to the S.E. 5a, one of the finest fighters of the First World War, but the autumn and early winter was a fallow period, both for Mannock and the squadron, and he did not score again until new year's day 1918. The next day he left for home establishment, where he soon became restless at being away from combat. A period of intense frustration, serving with the Wireless Experimental Establishment at Biggin Hill, ended when on 11 February he was posted to 74 training squadron at London Colney, as flight commander.

It was at London Colney, where 74 squadron was working up on the S.E. 5a, that Mannock came fully into his own as a charismatic teacher and leader. His first biographer, Ira (Taffy) Jones, whom he trained, has given a vivid account of Mannock's inculation of the principles of air fighting in a series of lectures that began: 'Gentlemen, always above; seldom on the same level; never underneath' (Jones, 161). 'He had the ability', Jones writes, 'to convince the poorest and most inoffensive pilots that they could knock Hell out of the best Hun' (ibid., 160).

On 30 March 1918 74 squadron flew to France, and by 11 April was settled at its base at Clairmarais, near St Omer. Its first victory, the following day, went to Mannock, and by the end of the month he had raised his total to twenty-one, while B flight, which he led, had proved conspicuously successful. May 1918 proved even more so, with Mannock himself scoring a remarkable twenty victories, including four in one day (21 May). A DSO, awarded on 24 May (with a bar on 30 May), followed. In June he continued to score at a high rate, adding eleven further victories before going on leave on the 18th (and being awarded a third bar to his DSO).

While on leave Mannock was promoted major, as commanding officer of 85 squadron at St Omer. He took up his appointment on 5 July and set about restoring morale in a squadron that under his predecessor, the controversial Canadian ace Major W. A. (Billy) Bishop, had lacked cohesion and a sense of identity. Within days the squadron was transformed, Mannock's tactical skill, combined with his ability to foster team spirit and raise morale, moulding a group of individuals into an efficient fighting unit. He himself continued to score steadily, with seven victories prior to his final sortie, at dawn on 26 July 1918, when he went up with a young pilot who had yet to score a victory. They shot down a German reconnaissance aircraft over the German lines, with Mannock (as he often did to give new pilots confidence) ensuring that his companion completed the 'kill'. Immediately afterwards, however, his aircraft was hit by ground fire, and it crashed in flames near Pacaut Wood. He was buried by the Germans at a point 300 m north-east of La Pierre-au-Beurre, although his grave could not be identified after the war. Dudgeon, however, makes a compelling case (pp. 174–6) that after the war Mannock was exhumed and reinterred as the 'unknown British aviator' in grave 12, row F, plot 3 of the military cemetery at Laventie, some 4 km to the east of the crash site.

Where James McCudden and Albert Ball became legends in their lifetime, Mannock was for some reason little known by the general public until after the war, though intensely admired in the RAF. Agitation for further recognition of his achievements eventually met with success, however, and on 11 July 1919 the award of the Victoria Cross was gazetted. Tall and thin, Mannock had a shock of unruly hair, deep-set, piercing blue eyes, and walked with a stiff, slightly awkward gait. Sensitive and somewhat shy, he was at first handicapped by an awareness of his humble origins and limited education but as he gained confidence he became a charismatic figure, inspiring something approaching devotion in those who served under him. He had a keen sense of fun, often expressed in morale-raising practical jokes, but also a melancholy streak that intensified over the sixteen months of his combat career. On his last leave he was clearly exhausted and under severe emotional strain (Dudgeon, 154–5), though he concealed it well on his return to France. It was perhaps this strain that led him to break his own cardinal rule in flying low over the trenches after shooting down his last victim.

Two frequent claims concerning Mannock need dispelling. One is that he was a fervent 'Hun hater'. That he urged those under his command to extirpate their opponents is clear, as is evidence that he fought for a time with fierce vengefulness after the death of close friends. But it is not entirely clear whether his 'hatred' was a deeply felt personal one or a means of boosting morale and ensuring a single-minded application to the job in hand—winning the war. His diary, covering his first months with 40 squadron, suggests, by implication, the latter. For instance, of his first certain victory, on 7 June 1917, he wrote: 'I saw him go spinning and slipping down from fourteen thousand. Rough luck, but it's war, and they're Huns' (*Personal Diary*, 105). And, after viewing the wreckage of a two-seater he had brought down and seeing the corpse of the pilot, he wrote: 'I felt exactly like a murderer' (ibid., 119). Undoubtedly he became hardened to killing but it may perhaps be fairer to conclude that Mannock was more a hater of 'hunnishness' than of individual Germans.

If the claim that Mannock was a 'Hun hater' cannot be settled either way, the second claim, that Mannock was blind in one eye (McScotch, 139–40), can without doubt be discounted. He certainly suffered a serious eye infection when a child in India, and his sight was for a time impaired, but there is no reliable evidence of permanent damage, and Mannock family sources categorically deny this, while several who flew with him testify to his excellent vision. Neither Mannock's human qualities, which made him loved and admired by those who served under him, nor his standing as perhaps the greatest tactician and teacher of fighting tactics and one of the greatest aces of the First World War (his sixty-one victories, verifiable to a remarkable degree, being second in British service only to the highly questionable and often unverifiable seventy-two of Bishop), needs a fiction of this kind to sustain or enhance it.   DAVID GUNBY

Sources A. Smith, *Mick Mannock, fighter pilot: myth, life, and politics* (2001) · *The personal diary of 'Mick' Mannock*, ed. F. Oughton (1966) · McScotch [W. McLanachan], *Fighter pilot* (1936) [repr. 1985] · J. M. Dudgeon, *'Mick': the story of Major Edward Mannock* (1981) · I. Jones, *King of air fighters* (1934) · D. Gunby, *Sweeping the skies: a history of no. 40 squadron, RFC and RAF, 1916–1956* (1995), 19–42 · C. Shores and others, *Above the trenches: a complete record of the fighter aces and units of the British empire air forces, 1915–1920* (1990), 255–7
Archives Royal Air Force Museum, Hendon, medals and artefacts · Tangmere Military Aviation Museum, Chichester, letters and papers
Likenesses photograph, RAF Museum, Hendon [*see illus.*]
Wealth at death £506 4s. 11d.: administration with will, 3 Oct 1919, *CGPLA Eng. & Wales*

Mannock, John [*name in religion* Anselm] (1681–1764), Benedictine monk and author, was born at Giffords Hall, Suffolk, the third son of Sir William Mannock, third baronet (d. 1714), and his wife, Ursula, daughter of Henry Neville of Holt, Leicestershire. His family were faithful to the Roman Catholic religion and many in the seventeenth and eighteenth centuries joined religious orders on the continent. He was educated at Douai in Flanders by the English Benedictines. While playing with a cannon ball at a first-floor window he accidentally let it slip, and it killed his brother Thomas who was standing below. He was so overwhelmed with distress at this accident that he determined to devote the rest of his life to religion. He joined the community at Douai and made his profession on 7 March 1700. After his ordination to the priesthood he was sent to England, and for fifty years served as chaplain to the Canning family at Foxcote in Warwickshire (1709–59). He was then moved to Kelvedon Hall in Essex, the seat of the Wright family, where he remained until his death.

Mannock held several positions of responsibility in the English Benedictine congregation. He was secretary to the provincial chapter in 1721, and procurator of the province and praepositus of Worcestershire (1725–37). He was elected praedicator generalis in 1733, and definitor of the province in 1755. His final office was as cathedral prior of Worcester and definitor of the regimen from 1757.

Besides his pastoral work Mannock devoted his life to the pursuit of sacred literature, and the surviving manuscripts (more than twenty volumes) preserved in the archives at Downside Abbey bear witness to his studious habits and indefatigable perseverance. Joseph Gillow wrote of him that, 'Among the old controversial writers there are few who have taken higher ground or maintained it more durably than Fr. Mannock'.

Although only two of Mannock's works were published in his lifetime (with a third appearing posthumously), they proved to be popular with monks on the mission in Britain. *The Poor Man's Catechism* (1752) provided helpful practical directions, such as listing the manual works forbidden on a Sunday, as well as the 'impedimenta' involved in marriage cases. 'It served a need precisely at the time when many expanding congregations were moving away from a household chaplaincy and patrons' control' (Scott, 140).

A more complicated work, *The Poor Man's Controversy*, was published posthumously in 1769. Although written in a plain style, 'it tried to reconcile Protestantism to English Catholicism by explaining controversial Catholic doctrines, adopting a minimalist view of the papacy and admitting Catholic excesses' (Scott, 141). The book probably reflected the liberal values of what has been called the Catholic Enlightenment. Both of these works were helped to the press by the secular priest George Bishop of Brailes. Mannock died at Kelvedon Hall, Essex, on 30 November 1764. PHILIP JEBB

Sources A. Allanson, 'Biography of the English Benedictines', 2 vols., 1850–76, Downside Abbey, near Bath, vol. 1, fol. 440 · Gillow, *Lit. biog. hist.* · T. B. Snow, *Obit book of the English Benedictines from 1600 to 1912*, rev. H. N. Birt (privately printed, Edinburgh, 1913), 104 · 'Liber professionum conventus S. Gregorii Duacensis', 1607–1831, Downside Abbey, Bath, fol. 207 · Liber depositi Duaci, 1666–96, Downside Abbey, Bath, fols. 230, 231 · A. Collins, *The English baronetage*, 2 (1741), 57 · *Downside Review*, 4 (1885), 156 · *Downside Review*, 6 (1887), 137 · G. Scott, *Gothic rage undone: English monks in the age of Enlightenment* (1992)
Archives Downside Abbey, near Bath, papers
Wealth at death vowed to poverty

Manns, Sir August Friedrich (1825–1907), conductor, was born at Stolzenburg, near Stettin, Pomerania, on 12 March 1825, the fifth of the ten children of Gottlieb Manns, a foreman in a glass factory. He received his first formal musical instruction when he was twelve and played flute, clarinet, violin, and horn under the musician of the neighbouring village of Torgelow; at the age of fifteen he was apprenticed for three years to Urban, the town music director of Elbing. In his nineteenth year he enlisted in the band of the 5th Prussian infantry regiment stationed at Danzig, and later at Posen, as clarinettist; in 1849 he played first violin in Joseph Gungl's orchestra in Berlin, and from Christmas 1849 until early 1851 was first solo violinist and then conductor of the orchestra of Kroll's Winter Gardens, Berlin. Later in 1851 he was appointed bandmaster to Colonel von Roon's regiment at Königsberg, and later at Cologne. On 1 May 1854 he took up the position of sub-conductor and clarinettist in the band of the newly built Crystal Palace at Sydenham, south London. After unjust dismissal by the conductor, Henry Schallehn, Manns took positions at Leamington Spa, Edinburgh, and, in the spring of 1855, Amsterdam, but returned as full conductor of the Crystal Palace band in October 1855. He retained the position of director of music until his retirement in 1901, undertaking very few outside engagements, notably as conductor of the Sheffield festival in 1896 and 1899 and of orchestral concerts in Glasgow in 1879 and later. He was married three times: his first wife died in 1850 or 1851, his second, Sarah Ann Williams, with whom he had a daughter, died in 1893. His third wife, (Katharine Emily) Wilhelmina Thellusson (*b.* 1865/6), whom he married on 7 January 1897, survived him.

Manns's reputation was built on the establishment of orchestral concerts of the highest quality in the unlikely setting of a garden leisure palace. The original band of the Crystal Palace was comprised entirely of brass and wind instruments, and played twice daily for the patrons. Manns immediately transformed this ensemble into a mixed concert orchestra and obtained additional higher quality strings for special concerts on Saturday afternoons. Over the first ten years the quality of the orchestral playing steadily improved, the numbers were made comparable with those of established symphonic orchestras, and a wide repertory was set in place. After experimentation with performance in different locations, the permanent concert room was erected at the side of the centre transept by summer 1856; its facilities were gradually improved over the next ten years, by which time the 'Saturday Concerts' had achieved international fame. Manns was especially noted in the German classics, then largely unknown in England, and gave innumerable first and early British performances of these and many other standard orchestral works; he was noted particularly in Schubert, Schumann, and Brahms, and introduced new works until the end of his career. He performed many works by British composers, and the palace soon became a focus for the emerging British school—the concerts being regarded as a crucial element in the so-called English musical renaissance. The support of George Grove as first secretary of the Crystal Palace was vital to obtaining the backing of the directors for Manns's ambitious policy, and they worked closely together. The concerts ceased with the disbanding of the daily orchestra, for financial reasons, in 1900.

Manns was noted for his friendly and modest disposition, supportive manner—especially towards young musicians—total commitment to his work, and frank discussion of musical issues. While he was never considered a virtuoso conductor, he was noted as an outstanding orchestral trainer and for his detailed knowledge of, and faithfulness to, the scores he performed. Though he never lost his military bearing on the rostrum, his performances were characterized by nervous intensity, with marked rhythmic energy and fire as well as sensitivity, and a generally excellent ensemble arising from his daily contact with most of the players; he was considered unrivalled in England as an orchestral conductor for a full twenty years until Hans Richter began conducting in London in 1879. He was less successful as a choral conductor (the Crystal Palace Choir rarely received good reviews), and he also took some time to establish his full authority with the triennial Handel festival, held at the Crystal Palace, which he took over at short notice from Sir Michael Costa in 1883, though he steadily improved its standards to 1900. In 1903 he was both knighted for services to British music and awarded an honorary doctorate by Oxford University. He died on 1 March 1907 at his home, White Lodge, Biggin Hill, Norwood, and was buried at Norwood cemetery on 6 March.   MICHAEL MUSGRAVE

Sources H. S. Wyndham, *August Manns and the Saturday concerts: a memoir and a retrospect* (1909) · *MT*, 39 (1898), 153–9 · A. Bonten, *Memoirs, 1858–1930* [1930] · F. G. E., 'Schubert's music in England', *MT*, 38 (1897), 81–4 · *DNB* · *The Times* (4 March 1907) · 'The Handel festival and Mr Manns', *Musical Herald* (July 1900), 204 · 'Manns, Sir August', Grove, *Dict. mus.* (1904–10) · m. cert. · d. cert.
Archives Royal College of Music, London
Likenesses J. Pettie, oils, 1892 · Spy [L. Ward], chromolithograph, NPG; repro. in *VF* (13 June 1895)
Wealth at death £6678 4*s*. 7*d*.: resworn probate, 23 April 1907, *CGPLA Eng. & Wales*

Manny, Walter. *See* Mauny, Sir Walter (*c*.1310–1372).

Mannyng, Robert [Robert Mannyng of Brunne] (*d*. in or after **1338**), poet and historian, was the author of two works, *Handlyng Synne* and *The Story of England* (this is his own title for the latter work, though it is often now referred to as *The Chronicle*), which are translations, adaptations, and expansions of Anglo-Norman moral and historical works respectively, put into English for those who knew no French. *The Medytacyuns of the Soper of Oure Lorde Jhesu*, a translation of Bonaventure sometimes attributed to Mannyng, is probably not by him.

The 'Brunne' (that is, 'brook') of Mannyng's name is usually taken to be modern Bourne, in Lincolnshire, a likelihood strengthened by the manuscript (LPL, MS 131) which names him (albeit in a later hand) as 'Robert de Brunne iuxta Depynge', presumably a reference to Deeping Fen or Market Deeping, only a few miles from Bourne. However, a minority opinion sees him as a Yorkshireman, originally from Nunburnham (recorded as Brunne in 1280), near York. The northern dialect of the Yale manuscript of *Handlyng Synne* is very close to that of the Petyt manuscript of *The Story of England*. The many allusions in his writings to Gilbertine masters and priories suggest that Mannyng himself was most probably a Gilbertine canon, perhaps a master of novices, though no record confirms this connection. References in his two works provide further evidence for his movements, and for the stages of his career.

Thus in *The Story of England* Mannyng says that he attended the 'commencement', or degree feast in Cambridge, in honour of Alexander Bruce, with Alexander's brothers Thomas and Robert (the latter being the future king of Scots) also in attendance; perhaps Mannyng was studying in Cambridge, possibly in the period 1298–1302, although there is no record of his being a student there. Then in his prologue to *Handlyng Synne* Mannyng greets all Christians 'under sun', the good people of Brunne, and especially the Gilbertine community of Sempringham in Lincolnshire. He there records that he began *Handlyng Synne* in 1303, when Dan Felyp (Philip Burton) was master of the Gilbertines, at which time he was himself exactly 6 miles from Sempringham, usually taken to refer to his supposed birthplace, Bourne, in Lincolnshire ('Brunnewake' in the Dulwich manuscript; a minority opinion suggests that the Folger manuscript reading, 'Bringwake', might be a corruption of 'Brig Dike', or Bridge End (Holland Bridge), about 6 miles north-east of Sempringham, where there was a Gilbertine priory, St Saviour's, essentially a cell of Sempringham.) He relates that he was fifteen years (perhaps 1302–1317) with Dan John of Camelton (Hamilton) and Dan John of Clinton (Glinton). Finally, Mannyng places himself at the Gilbertine priory at Sixhills, Lincolnshire, at the time when he finishes *The Story of England*, on 15 May 1338. There are no later references to him or by him.

Handlyng Synne is Mannyng's reaction to the call for yearly confessions for all Christians made by the Fourth Lateran Council of 1215, and has been described as representing 'a development in the whole technique of confession and the parish priest's role therein' (Bennett, 460). The work has a strong homiletic tone to it throughout. Simultaneously a translation, adaptation, and expansion of the Anglo-Norman *Manuel des péchés*, *Handlyng Synne* is Mannyng's masterpiece, characterized by charming retellings of old *exempla* from French and Latin moral treatises, and by its author's often traditional moral commentaries on the theological topics examined, commentaries that are leavened by his own amusing and amused, occasionally pedantic, consideration of the human predicament. The work is a guide to confession, an encouragement to 'shewe' sin (MS H, line 5), but is also, and just as importantly, a guide to help one avoid, or 'eschewe', sin (MS D, line 5), once the individual (a varied audience is frequently addressed directly) understands sin's true nature. Frightening and sobering descriptions, in the stories and in their visions of hell, of the eternal and terrible suffering of those who commit the major sins, must have had their intended effect on at least some of the medieval readers of, or listeners to, this work. Mannyng's collection of tales, with their overriding moral concern, provided a model for such later collections as Chaucer's *Canterbury Tales* and Gower's *Confessio amantis*. It has been suggested that the early audiences of the *Confessio* would have recognized it immediately, from its form as a collection of *exempla* sharing the same verse metre, as a parody of *Handlyng Synne*.

Handlyng Synne, a free verse translation and adaptation from the Anglo-Norman *Manuel*, consists of over 12,630 lines of octosyllabic rhyming couplets, with occasional shorter lines. It contains an additional thirteen tales of Mannyng's own. A short prologue is followed by anecdotes, illustrative *exempla* and social and moral commentary, designed for a popular regional audience, organized according to the ten commandments, the seven deadly sins (about half of the poem), sacrilege, the seven sacraments, the twelve points of shrift, and the twelve graces of shrift; Mannyng omits book 1 of the *Manuel*, containing the articles of the faith, and translates only about half of the 8500 lines in the sections of the *Manuel* that he does include. Like the *Manuel*, he makes particular use of the Bible, Bede, Gregory the Great's *Dialogues*, and the lives of the fathers. His best-known tales include that of the dancers of Colbeck; the witch and her cow-sucking bag (the bag would not work for the bishop because he did not believe in it); and the story of the hermit and his bear, the latter being slain by followers of the hermit Euticius, out of envy of his fellow hermit Florens, who had been enjoying miraculous comfort, companionship, and sheepherding, all provided by the polite and accommodating bear.

There are twelve extant manuscripts of *Handlyng Synne*, none of them complete or entirely satisfactory. Among the most important are the four earlier versions, some of them in later manuscripts: Yale University, Beinecke Library, MS Osborn a.2, once complete but now lacking more than 3000 lines; CUL, MS Ii.4.9, an excerpt of about 2800 lines, containing the ten commandments only; London, Dulwich College, MS XXIV, a fragment of 2894 lines, which has the prologue and most of the ten commandments, stopping with a catchword; and the Vernon manuscript, Bodl. Oxf., MS Eng.poet. a.1, which has only 919 lines, 'Of the sacrament of the altar'. Also very important are the three almost complete manuscripts (two of them base manuscripts of editions) of about 12,638 lines, which represent a later (even though dated earlier in some cases) 'revised' version of the work: Bodl. Oxf., MS Bodley 415; BL, Harley MS 1701; and Washington, Folger Shakespeare Library, MS Folger V.b.236.

Mannyng's only other known work, his metrical *Story of England*, is one of the best-known Middle English chronicles. It has two parts: the first, 16,638 four-stress lines in rhyming couplets, consists of a prologue, the story of Noah's flood, a summary of the Troy legend, and the history of Britain from its founding by Brutus to the death of the last British king, Cadwalader, in 689, followed by the arrival of the Saxons and their conquest of Britain, with substantial Arthurian material. The second part, 8387 lines of six-stress lines of rhyming couplets, with some internal rhyme, continues from 689 to 1307 and the death

of Edward I. It also contains references to Havelok the Dane, and to Gwenllian daughter of Llywelyn, who lived with the Gilbertines for her last fifty-four years. Mannyng's primary sources for *The Story of England*, which, he explains, avoids fancy poetic forms, so that he will be plain and understandable, are the Anglo-Norman *Roman de Brut* of Wace, and the chronicle of Peter Langtoft, but he adds material from other sources. He is writing to delight and instruct 'symple men', so that they can learn which kings were wise and which were foolish. The final product, among the best-known chronicles in Middle English, shows his careful scholarly tendencies and interests, and a willingness to conduct a wide-ranging search for his material. He would gladly copy more of his *Story*, he says at the end, if there were more to copy.

Robert Mannyng of Brunne communicated his moral, religious, and historical concerns to fellow Christians of all conditions through his extraordinarily vigorous, fast-paced, often dramatic narrative skills, even as he avoided the ironies and complexities which are now valued in narrative, so that the moral points of his *exempla* would be clear. These narrative skills, and the energy and intelligence that he brought to his large tasks, provided important new models in English for later fourteenth-century writers who are now more admired and better known—at the moral level, tactful instruction intended to move the reader or hearer to change for the better; at the narrative level, masterful story-telling; and at the structural level, moral instruction and tales within a larger framework, all three levels handled with consummate skill.

RAYMOND G. BIGGAR

Sources B. Golding, *Gilbert of Sempringham and the Gilbertine order, c.1130–c.1300* (1995) · R. R. Raymo, 'Works of religious and philosophical instruction', *A manual of the writings in Middle English, 1050–1500*, ed. A. E. Hartung, 7 (1986), 2255–7, 2467–74 · E. D. Kennedy, *A manual of the writings in Middle English, 1050–1500*, 8: *Chronicles and other historical writings*, ed. A. E. Hartung (1967), 2625–8, 2811–18 · T. Turville-Petre, *England the nation: language, literature, and national identity, 1290–1340* (1996) · A. I. Doyle, 'A survey of the origins and circulation of theological writings in English in the 14th, 15th and early 16th centuries, with special consideration of the part of the clergy therein', PhD diss., U. Cam., 1953, 1.58ff. · R. Crosby, 'Robert Mannyng of Brunne: a new biography', *Proceedings of the Modern Language Association of America*, 57 (1942), 15–28 · Robert Mannyng of Brunne, *Handlyng synne: Robert Mannyng of Brunne*, ed. I. Sullens (1983) · Robert Mannyng of Brunne, *Robert Mannyng of Brunne: the chronicle*, ed. I. Sullens (1996) · M. T. Sullivan, 'The original and subsequent audiences of the *Manuel des péchés* and its Middle English descendants', DPhil diss., U. Oxf., 1990 · J. A. W. Bennett, *Middle English literature*, ed. D. Gray (1986), vol. 1, pt 2 of *The Oxford history of English literature* · D. Pearsall, *Old and Middle English poetry* (1977), vol. 1 of *The Routledge history of English poetry* · P. Boitani, *English medieval narrative in the thirteenth and fourteenth centuries*, trans. J. K. Hall (1982) · *Robert of Brunne's 'Handlyng synne'*, ed. F. J. Furnivall, Roxburghe Club (1862), Introduction · *Robert of Brunne's 'Handlyng synne', AD 1303, with those parts of the Anglo-French treatise on which it was founded, William of Wadington's 'Manuel des pechiez'*, ed. F. J. Furnivall, EETS, original ser., 119, 123 (1901–3) [later printed as one vol.] · F. J. Furnivall, introduction, in *The story of England by Robert Manning of Brunne, AD 1338*, 2 vols., Rolls Series, 87 (1887) · *Monastic Britain: south sheet*, 2nd edn, Ordnance Survey (1954)

Archives BL, Harley MS 1701 · Bodl. Oxf., MS Bodley 415 · Bodl. Oxf., MS Eng. poet. a.1 · CUL, MS Ii.4.9 · Dulwich College, London,

MS XXIV · Folger, MS Folger V.b.236 · LPL, MS 131 · Yale U., Beinecke L., MS Osborn a.2

Man of Ross, the. *See* Kyrle, John (1637–1724).

Mansbridge, Albert (1876–1952), founder of the Workers' Educational Association, was born in Albert Cottages, India House Lane, Gloucester, on 10 January 1876, the youngest of the four sons of Thomas Mansbridge (*d.* 1911) and his wife, Frances Thomas (*d.* 1902). The family, active co-operators and Congregationalists, moved to London in 1880 and settled in Battersea in the following year. Thomas Mansbridge was a carpenter who rose to be a clerk of works. Albert had happy memories of being 'a normal child in a decent working-class home' (Mansbridge, *The Trodden Road*, 14).

Mansbridge attended infant school in Gloucester (1879–80), and from board schools in London (1880–86) he progressed by scholarships to Sir Walter St John's Middle School, Battersea (1886–8), and Battersea grammar school (1888–90), where his academic potential was recognized. With three sons already at work, Thomas Mansbridge could have allowed Albert to stay at school and try for a university scholarship, but at the age of fourteen he became an office boy. He continued his education in the evenings, at university extension lectures, co-operative courses, and other classes.

At about the age of fourteen Mansbridge joined the Church of England, was confirmed, and became active in Sunday school and temperance work. He developed the ambition to go to Oxford or Cambridge and take holy orders. At the age of eighteen he entered for a competitive co-operative scholarship at Oriel College, Oxford, but was beaten by a candidate who was already an undergraduate. Soon afterwards he qualified as a licensed lay reader and met Charles Gore, then a canon of Westminster, who became his friend and mentor.

Mansbridge had worked as a boy clerk in the education department, but his other activities, which included playing cricket frequently in summer, distracted him from qualifying for a permanent clerkship. His twenty-first birthday found him employed in a dead-end job by the Co-operative Wholesale Society, consoled by the outlet for his idealism which he had found in the wider co-operative movement. He spoke at meetings, contributed to co-operative journals, taught a co-operative class in industrial history, and became recognized as a promising young activist.

Mansbridge joined in a 'great debate' about the purposes of co-operative education, including its relations with university extension. The latter movement, pioneered by Cambridge in 1873, had realized its ambition to attract working-class students only in a few places where it had a strong local partner, usually a co-operative society. The costs of courses of six or twelve lectures, each followed by an optional tutorial class and essay work for the keenest students, had to be met locally, and working-class suspicions ruled out middle-class benevolence as a solution. Invited to read a paper to a joint co-operative-

Albert Mansbridge (1876–1952), by John Mansbridge, 1947

university conference in 1899, Mansbridge made a bombastic speech which contained no significant new ideas, but appeared to blame the missionaries of both movements for the difficulties against which they had been struggling. A blast of justified criticism blew him back into private life for a few years. In August 1900 he married fellow Sunday school teacher Frances Jane Pringle, and thereby acquired a loving and cheerful wife, a prudent housekeeper, and a fellow idealist. In the following year he at last found suitable employment, as cashier of the Co-operative Permanent Building Society, and the couple had their only child, John, who became an artist.

The Workers' Educational Association and tutorial classes, 1903–1914 In 1903 Mansbridge turned again to the issue of workers' education, and in a series of three articles in the *University Extension Journal*, supported by one from Robert Halstead, a leading co-operative educationist, proposed the formation of an association to bring together working-class organizations with an educational role and create a new partnership with university extension. He demonstrated for the first time what became a remarkable ability to select the arguments best calculated to sway his readers or hearers. He coupled a warning about the social dangers of ignorance in trade unions and other workers' organizations with a declaration of the infallibility of the truly educated mind which university men found convincing. He showed also the quality which turns ideas into movements. Faced with estimates of substantial sums needed to launch the new body, he and his wife formed the Association to Promote the Higher Education of Working Men in their kitchen, financed by 2s. 6d. from

Frances's purse. A 'provisional committee' (a stage army of Mansbridge's friends) planned the conference at Oxford, in August 1903, at which the association was formally constituted, with the blessing of leading co-operators, university extensionists, and churchmen. Mansbridge became honorary secretary.

By the end of 1905 eight branches of what was now called the Workers' Educational Association (WEA) had been formed, in each case through careful preparation by Mansbridge of inaugural meetings involving leading co-operators, trade unionists, churchmen, academics, and politicians of different persuasions. In the spring of 1906 Mansbridge became the full-time general secretary and the pace of growth quickened. By 1908 there were forty-eight branches and a network of districts was emerging. The branches organized a range of courses and single lectures, but those promoting university extension work found that short courses for large audiences did not meet working-class needs. Mansbridge took up the challenge of devising a system which would permit sustained study to a university level.

Helped by Charles Gore, now bishop of Worcester, Mansbridge formed an alliance with a group of young Oxford academics, including R. H. Tawney, William Temple, and Alfred Zimmern, who wanted to reform their university by simultaneously raising its standards and democratizing its entry. Following a conference at Oxford in August 1907 a committee of fourteen men, half nominated by the university and half by the WEA, was appointed to devise a new strategy for workers' education. Nearly all of the university representatives were supporters of the WEA and three—Sidney Ball, A. L. Smith, and Zimmern—were close allies of Mansbridge. The report of the committee, *Oxford and Working-Class Education*, published in November 1908 and ratified by the university and the WEA, was in terms of university government a revolutionary document. Tutorial classes over a period of three years (seventy-two meetings), with not more than thirty students, were to be provided at a low fee; the programme was to be managed by a permanent joint committee with equal WEA and university representation; and the WEA branch was to have 'a controlling voice' in the selection of tutors for its tutorial classes. Promising worker-students would proceed from the classes to full-time study at Oxford, normally to read for one of the new diplomas to be created in economics and politics.

The new joint tutorial classes committee was effectively independent of the university extension delegacy, with its own officers and funds. The secretary of the delegacy, J. A. R. Marriott, had given much help to Mansbridge and the WEA, but was ruthlessly sidelined. Marriott thought that this was because he was a tory and had doubts about 'workers' control' of syllabuses and tutor selection. Mansbridge's real concern, however, was to keep exclusive control over the grants from the Board of Education and prevent Marriott from using the proposed undergraduate entry scheme for the benefit of students from conventional extension courses.

Mansbridge had secured the grant aid from the Board of Education, without which the tutorial class movement could hardly have made much progress, by winning over the permanent secretary of the board, Sir Robert Morant, who was impressed by his evangelical zeal and respect for academic values. Some months before the 1907 Oxford conference Mansbridge had been invited to join the consultative committee of the Board of Education. One important feature of the grant system was that, with the university and the WEA each responsible for half of the costs, the money from the board was credited to the WEA side of the account.

The tutorial class movement spread rapidly. Several other universities entered the field, in most cases setting up joint committees on the Oxford model. The number of classes grew from 2 in 1907–8 (both taken by R. H. Tawney) to 39 in 1909–10 and 145, with 3234 students, in 1913–14. In 1909 Mansbridge asked the Oxford joint committee to take the lead in forming the central joint advisory committee for tutorial classes. He was appointed honorary secretary of this committee, which became a high-powered body, often attended by vice-chancellors and principals. The university extension officers of Cambridge (D. H. S. Cranage) and London (R. D. Roberts) were unenthusiastic about this development, as they were about the tutorial class movement, being willing to accept the WEA as a junior partner but not as a dynamic new force in adult education. They were, however, no match for Mansbridge, who outmanoeuvred them in negotiation, praised them in public, and berated them in private.

Joint committee summer schools began in 1910 and two years later Mansbridge, with the help of Toynbee Hall, organized a central library for tutorial classes, which later became the nucleus of the National Central Library. By 1914 the WEA had 179 branches with over 2500 affiliated societies, mainly co-operatives, trade unions, and religious societies. Enthusiasts in each region spread the gospel, but Mansbridge took on an immense burden of speaking and writing articles, as well as administration.

In 1907–8 Mansbridge and his allies had been as much concerned to provide full-time university places for worker-students as to develop a network of tutorial classes. A shortage of money severely limited these opportunities, and it was a cause of some relief when the members of tutorial classes began to argue in favour of giving summer school scholarships to the many rather than undergraduate places to the few.

In 1913 Albert and Frances Mansbridge went to Australia. In the course of a four-month tour they helped to establish the WEA and tutorial classes in all six states, although some of the successes were short-lived. Mansbridge, now at the height of his powers, deployed his organizing and diplomatic skills and his ability to appeal simultaneously to the universities and organized labour, in a socio-political environment by no means identical to that of England.

Educational expert after 1914 In June 1914 Mansbridge was stricken with cerebrospinal meningitis, and after being near to death made a slow recovery. He resigned as general secretary of the WEA in September 1915 and soon afterwards gave up his three posts in the tutorial class system. During his long convalescence the pattern of the second half of his working life gradually emerged. As a versatile educational expert with wide connections he was appointed to many committees, including the adult education committee of the Ministry of Reconstruction (1917–19). In co-operation with his Church of England allies, including Gore and Temple, he founded the Church Tutorial Classes Association (1917) and played a leading role in two movements for church reform, life and liberty (1917) and the committee on the church and industrial life (1916–18).

Early in 1918 Mansbridge accepted a temporary appointment at the Board of Education, assisting the parliamentary passage of H. A. L. Fisher's Education Bill. He was later seconded to lecture on residential courses for Australian and British army officers. His experience of this work led him to found the World Association for Adult Education (WAAE, 1919), forming a hand-picked management team out of the empire's army education chiefs and the WEA. The first offshoot of the WAAE was the Seafarers' Education Service (1919), conceived when Mansbridge heard how desperate merchant seamen were for books to read, and launched with the help of Laurence Holt, a fellow member of the prime minister's committee on the teaching of modern languages (1916) whose family owned the Blue Funnel shipping line. In 1921 Mansbridge joined with Lord Haldane to establish the British Institute of Adult Education as a combined learned society and pressure group. In the same year he was appointed to the Board of Education's new adult education committee.

After serving on the royal commission on Oxford and Cambridge (1919–22) Mansbridge was appointed to the statutory commission on Oxford (1923) and fought hard behind the scenes to preserve earmarked funding for adult education work at both universities. In 1922 he made the first of seven lecture tours in North America, choosing for the prestigious Lowell lectures at Boston the subject 'The older universities of England'. In the following year he published a book with the same title to add to his earlier major works *University Tutorial Classes* (1913) and *An Adventure in Working-Class Education* (a history of the WEA, 1920). He had been made an honorary MA by Oxford in 1912, and in the years 1922–38 he was given honorary doctorates by the universities of Manchester, Cambridge, Pittsburgh, and Mount Allison (Canada). In 1931 he was made CH.

Mansbridge's later books included *Margaret McMillan, Prophet and Pioneer* (1932), *Brick upon Brick* (a history of the Co-operative Permanent Building Society, 1934), *Edward Stuart Talbot and Charles Gore* (1935), *The Trodden Road* (autobiography, 1940), *The Kingdom of the Mind: Essays and Addresses* (1944), and *Fellow Men* (1948). He gave away most of the royalties from his books. His income came from a directorship of the Co-operative Permanent Building Society, a small civil-list pension, and trust funds and consultancies created for him by some of his influential friends. His main concerns in the 1920s and 1930s were the development of the National Central Library, of which he was

chairman until 1931, the British Institute of Adult Education, and the Seafarers' Education Service, which was providing libraries for 600 merchant ships by 1939, and had created a correspondence section, the College of the Sea (1937).

In addition to his North American lecture tours, the last of which was undertaken in 1938, Mansbridge gave many hundreds of lectures and sermons in Britain. He retained his power to inspire audiences and attract disciples, his voice and personality breathing life into his simple ideas about life and learning, which had not developed in depth as his role changed from innovator to sage. At times he displayed some frustration at being regarded as the premature 'grand old man' of his first great creations, the WEA and the tutorial classes. He was himself partly to blame, as the essence of his message had shifted from 'education for emancipation' to 'education *is* emancipation'. A member of the Athenaeum, he was in closer touch with bishops and academics than with working-class organizations, and was even on terms of respectful friendship with Queen Mary.

Assessment and death Mansbridge's own accounts of his life and work depict a simple man, enamoured of 'the glory of education', who had many supportive friends of high moral worth and hardly any enemies. This self-portrait has been too readily accepted by writers of different ideological leanings. Selective quotation from Mansbridge's writings and speeches can produce two different men, a Panglossian character barely conscious of the class struggle, and a radical agitating for far-reaching educational reforms. In the period 1906–14 Mansbridge demanded secondary education for all, a school-leaving age of sixteen, maintenance allowances for poorer pupils, university entry for all who could benefit, and even holidays with pay on the grounds that workers wanting to study needed periodic refreshment. He claimed that none of this was controversial, as no one of goodwill could possibly oppose the creation of an educated democracy. This typical piece of Mansbridgean ambiguity was of considerable benefit to the WEA, enabling it to campaign for educational reform while defending its non-party stance.

Mansbridge was not an original thinker, and few of his comments on educational and social issues, taken out of context, merit extensive study. His importance lay in the developments which he initiated or encouraged. This point has not been fully appreciated by some of the historians who have regarded the Labour Party, as well as the WEA, as part of the 'antidote to socialism'. In their view the WEA, because of its alliance with the universities and acceptance of state aid, was a 'top-down' movement, in contrast to the 'bottom-up' labour colleges, which rejected both forms of support. In fact the WEA branch had a high degree of autonomy, a reflection of Mansbridge's faith in the right, and the capacity, of working people to manage their own affairs. He had in any case no appetite for the detailed administrative work required for the centralized control of an organization. When branch autonomy was allied to the 1908 Oxford formula for tutorial classes—joint management at university level and local control over the selection of subjects and tutors—the way was open for the WEA, at least in the industrial areas, to become the educational wing of the labour movement, embracing objectivity and thoroughness of study not as a philosophical ideal, which was Mansbridge's position, but as a guarantee of quality. Whether Mansbridge anticipated this development at the time is doubtful. That he disapproved, in the 1920s, of any departure from the 'ideal' of learning for its own sake is certain.

Historians who do not pay sufficient attention to the 1914 divide are unlikely to reach a proper understanding of Mansbridge. Some of his friends thought that his serious illness damaged his sharpness and subtlety of mind. In any case, by the time he had fully recovered the social situation had changed. Edwardian England saw the last flowering of the alliance between Liberalism, nonconformity, and the co-operative movement. Mansbridge's religious idiom appealed not only to church leaders anxious to do something practical to help the workers, but also to socialists who lambasted capitalism with quotations from the sermon on the mount. The organizations which he founded after 1915 would have guaranteed Mansbridge a place in educational history, but none of them gave him quite the same opportunities to display the remarkable collection of talents, as a superb organizer, a manipulator, and an evangelist with a gift of tongues, which he had employed to such great effect in the years 1903–14. In 1945 he retired to Paignton, Devon; he died at the Mount Stuart Nursing Home, St Luke's Road, Torquay, on 22 August 1952, and was buried in Gloucester Cathedral. His wife survived him.

BERNARD JENNINGS

Sources BL, Add. MS 65231 · private information (2004) [family, colleagues] · A. Mansbridge, *The trodden road* (1940) · U. Oxf., Rewley House MSS · A. Mansbridge, *The kingdom of the mind* (1944) · Workers' Educational Association National Archives, Temple House, London · *Workers' Educational Association annual report, 1905–14* · A. Mansbridge, *An adventure in working-class education: being the story of the Workers' Educational Association, 1903–1915* (1920) · A. Mansbridge, *The making of an educationist* (1929) · A. Mansbridge, *University tutorial classes* (1913) · B. Jennings, *Albert Mansbridge: the life and work of the founder of the WEA* [forthcoming] · B. Jennings, 'Albert Mansbridge', Mansbridge memorial lecture, U. Leeds, 1973 · B. Jennings, 'The Oxford report reconsidered', *Studies in Adult Education*, 7 (1975), 53–65 · B. Jennings, 'Revolting students: the Ruskin College dispute, 1908–1909', *Studies in Adult Education*, 9 (1977), 1–16 · B. Jennings, *Knowledge is power: a short history of the WEA* (1979) · B. Jennings, 'The reception of the report', *The 1919 report: the final and interim reports of the adult education committee*, later edn (1980) · B. Jennings, 'Albert Mansbridge and the World Association of Adult Education', *Convergence* [Toronto, Ont.], 17 (1984) · B. Jennings, 'The making of the Oxford report', *Oxford and working-class education*, ed. S. Harrop, later edn (1987) · B. Jennings, *The university extension movement in Victorian and Edwardian England* (1992) · L. Goldman, *Dons and workers: Oxford and adult education since 1850* (1995) · *CGPLA Eng. & Wales* (1952)
Archives BL, corresp. and papers · National Institute of Adult Continuing Education, Leicester, archives | Bodl. Oxf., corresp. with L. G. Curtis · Bodl. Oxf., letters to Sir Alfred Zimmern · McMaster University, Hamilton, Ontario, letters to Leonard Clark, etc. · NA Scot., corresp. with Philip Kerr · NL Wales, corresp. with Thomas Jones · Temple House, 17 Victoria Park Square, London, Worker's Educational Association national archives · U. Newcastle, Robinson L., letters to Mary Moorman · U. Oxf., Rewley House Papers | SOUND BL NSA, recorded talk
Likenesses H. Coster, photographs, 1930–39, NPG · W. Stoneman, photograph, 1932, NPG · J. Mansbridge, oils, 1947, NPG [*see illus.*] · photographs, repro. in Mansbridge, *The trodden road* · photographs, Workers' Educational Association, London
Wealth at death £10,651 14s. 1d.: probate, 27 Nov 1952, *CGPLA Eng. & Wales*

Mansel, Charles Grenville (1806–1886), administrator in India, was appointed a writer in the East India Company in 1826, following a distinguished career at the East India College, Haileybury. He was made assistant to the secretary of the western board of revenue in Bengal on 19 January 1827. He subsequently held several appointments in Agra, becoming magistrate and collector in 1835. In 1837 he became temporary secretary to Lord Auckland, the governor-general. From December 1838 to April 1841 he acted as *sadr* settlement officer in Agra, and in 1841 published the important *Report on the Settlement of the District of Agra*. In 1841 he became deputy accountant-general in Calcutta and in 1843 one of the civil auditors under Lord Ellenborough. From 1844 to 1849 he was on leave, and on his return to India was appointed a member of the board of administration of the Punjab, under the presidency of Sir Henry Montgomery Lawrence. Because in principle he opposed Lord Dalhousie's annexation policy, in November 1850 he was gazetted as resident at Nagpur, where he remained until 1855, when he retired. He is chiefly remembered for his discomfort as the junior member of the board responsible for the administration and reorganization of the Punjab after its annexation. He was caught between the strong-minded Lawrence brothers, who constantly disagreed over the disposition of the important landowners. He died at his home, 7 Mills Terrace, Hove, Sussex, on 19 November 1886, leaving an unmarried daughter, Fanny Mansel.

G. C. BOASE, rev. PETER PENNER

Sources R. B. Smith, *Life of Lord Lawrence*, 4th edn, 2 vols. (1883) · T. E. Bell, *Retrospect and prospect* (1868) · G. Campbell, *Memoirs of my Indian career*, 2 vols. (1889) · P. Penner, *The patronage bureaucracy in north India* (1986) · G. B. Malleson, *Recreations of an Indian official* (1872) · H. B. Edwardes and H. Merivale, *Life of Sir Henry Lawrence*, 2 vols. (1872) · J. W. Kaye and G. B. Malleson, *Kaye's and Malleson's History of the Indian mutiny of 1857–8*, 6 vols. (1888–9) · R. Temple, *Men and events of my time in India* (1882) · *The Times* (25 Nov 1886), 6
Archives NA Scot., Dalhousie muniments, letters
Wealth at death £90 19s. 11d.: administration, 5 Jan 1887, *CGPLA Eng. & Wales*

Mansel, Henry Longueville (1820–1871), dean of St Paul's and theologian, was born on 6 October 1820 at Cosgrove, Northamptonshire, where his father, also called Henry Longueville (1783–1835), was rector of the parish. His mother, Maria Margaret Longueville, was the daughter of Admiral Sir Robert Moorsom. The Mansel (Maunsell, Mansell) family were for some centuries landowners in Buckinghamshire. Early in the seventeenth century one Samuel Maunsell acquired by marriage the property of Cosgrove, where his descendants thereafter lived. Young Henry's grandfather John was a soldier who attained the

Henry Longueville Mansel (1820–1871), by unknown
photographer

rank of major-general and who fought and fell at the battle of Coteau in Flanders in 1794. The boy's uncle Robert
served in the Royal Navy and became an admiral. The
fourth of eight children, six of whom were girls, Henry
was brought up at Cosgrove, a pleasant village for which
he retained a lifelong affection.

Education After attending a preparatory school at East
Farndon, Mansel entered the Merchant Taylors' School,
London, in autumn 1830. Here he soon displayed the apti-
tudes of a scholar, loving books—on which he readily
spent his pocket money—and despising games. He wrote
regularly for the school magazine and in 1830 published a
little book of verses, *The Demons of the Wind and other Poems*,
with a fairly obvious debt to Coleridge and Shelley but not
without intrinsic merit. On his father's death in 1835 his
mother left Northamptonshire and resided in London for
a few years, but returned to Cosgrove in 1842, where a
house had been bequeathed especially for her use. In 1838
Henry won the school prize for English verse, and also a
medal for Hebrew awarded by Sir Moses Montefiore, distinctions to be followed by further prizes, now in classics,
in 1839, the year in which he matriculated as a scholar of
St John's College, Oxford. Here the promise he showed at
school was borne out by the diligence he applied to his
studies in classics and mathematics. He was likewise
assiduous in his religious observance, attending college
chapel daily. He was no swot, however, and enjoyed the
company of his fellow undergraduates, with whom he
was popular. His tutor in his last two years, Archdeacon

James Augustus Hessey, was impressed both by his refusal
to shirk difficulties and by his keen sense of humour. The
result of his efforts was that he gained a double first in his
finals, although at his *viva voce* examination he risked his
chances by arguing with the examiner about what he
regarded as a false assumption in the first question put to
him, so causing a protracted discussion. Such pertinacity
was to prove not untypical of the mature man. The same
characteristic may even have been present in the child,
coupled, it might seem, with precocity in metaphysics: his
mother used to relate of him that at a still tender age he
would perplex himself with the question: 'My hand: my
foot. But what is *me*?' (Burgon, 2.157).

Career at Oxford University and marriage On graduating
Mansel remained in Oxford, a city which was to be his
home for most of his life. Clearly his work was to teach,
and he began to take in pupils immediately, being very
soon in great demand as a tutor. But ordination to the ministry was his intention; at Christmas 1844 he was made
deacon, and a year later he was ordained priest by the
bishop of Oxford. Mansel continued to apply himself to
his studies, however, learning French and German and
improving his Hebrew. He also started to read ecclesiastical history. His presence in St John's senior common
room was a marked asset to college life by reason of his
conversational gifts, enhanced by wide-ranging knowledge and an often scintillating wit, despite, perhaps, his
fondness for puns. His high-tory politics matched his
high-churchmanship, giving him the air, for all his youth,
of a typical don of the old school. His earliest academic
publications were in the field of logic: *Ars logicae rudimenta*
(1847), a revised version of Henry Aldrich's much-used
textbook, and *Prolegomena logica* (1851), on the philosophy
of science. But his 'fragments of an Aristophanic drama',
Phrontisterion (1850), was a signal demonstration of his talent for satirical verse. In it he depicted the invasion of
Oxford by a host of German philosophers and theologians:

> Theologians we,
> Deep thinkers and free,
> From the land of the new Divinity;
> Where critics hunt for the sense sublime,
> Hidden in texts of the olden time,
> Which none but the sage can see.

A Strauss, a Bauer, a Feuerbach are then each neatly lampooned. So,

> Presbyters, bend,
> Bishops, attend:
> The Bible's a myth from beginning to end.
> (*Phrontisterion*, 2nd edn, 1852, 14–15)

The occasion for this *jeu d'esprit* was the appointment by
Lord John Russell of a commission on university reform.

In 1849 Mansel applied for the university chair of logic,
but unsuccessfully. Five years later he was elected to the
hebdomadal council, heading the poll for members of
convocation regardless, it seems, of his junior standing
and comparative youth. On 16 August 1855 he married

Charlotte Augusta (1824/5–1908), daughter of Daniel Taylor of Clapham Common, London, a union which brought him lifelong happiness; she herself was to outlive him by very many years, dying in 1908 at the age of eighty-three. As a married man he gave up residence in college and took a home of his own in the High Street. On 17 May in the same year he was elected to the Waynflete readership in moral and metaphysical philosophy at Magdalen College, becoming the first Waynflete professor in that subject in 1859, without, however, receiving the full professorial salary until 1862. In April 1864 he was re-elected professor-fellow at St John's, a token of the college's respect, which greatly pleased him.

Mansel's theology Mansel's inaugural lecture on the Waynflete foundation was published in 1855, and another on Kant in 1856, while in 1857 he wrote the article 'Metaphysics' for the eighth edition of the *Encyclopaedia Britannica*. In that year, too, he was selected as Bampton lecturer for 1858. The title he chose for the latter undertaking was 'The limits of religious thought examined', and the delivery and subsequent publication in 1859 of the lectures became the event on which his memory now largely rests. They were certainly arresting—for the Bamptons quite unusually so—and in outcome controversial, particularly for the vigorous attack on their whole argument levelled by Frederick Denison Maurice, one of the best-known theologians of the day.

Mansel derived his thesis from the Scottish philosopher Sir William Hamilton, whose 'philosophy of the conditioned' owed much to Kant. Knowledge, Hamilton contended, is from the very nature of the human mind itself limited to the conditioned: what is unconditioned, free of all determining circumstances, is incognizable and inconceivable, serving only as the negative of the conditioned and relative. When, that is, a fact is said to be known, it is so only as limited or conditioned by other facts known in conjunction with it. But he went on to maintain that what is conditioned necessarily implies the unconditioned as its complement or ground, albeit only as the negative of the conditioned. Hamilton did not himself venture upon the theological terrain, but his remarks that 'a God understood would be no god at all', and that 'to think that God is, as we think him to be, is blasphemy' (W. Hamilton, *Discussions on Philosophy and Literature, Education and University Reform*, 2nd edn, 1853, 15 n.), indicated the way in which his own philosophy, he thought, might provide 'the most useful auxiliary to theology' (ibid., 621). Mansel accordingly pressed the case that the speculative reason has no place in theology, which gains nothing from such spurious metaphysical help. If indeed philosophers had been less ready to assume the possibility of a purely rational knowledge they would have spared themselves the illusions of both idealism and scepticism. And the limits of philosophy in general must be applicable to religious philosophy in particular. In either realm, consciousness of the infinite or the absolute, both of which are contradictory of the finite and relative, whereof alone—such being

the constitution of the human mind—we can have knowledge, is not open to us. Religion speaks of God as personal, but personality, as we understand it, implies limitation. Inevitably the language of religion is anthropomorphic, and is the better for being so:

> It is only by conceiving [God] as a Conscious Being, that we can stand in any religious relation to Him at all, that we can form such a representation of Him as is demanded by our spiritual wants, insufficient though it is to satisfy our intellectual curiosity. (H. L. Mansel, *The Limits of Religious Thought Examined*, 1859, 61)

But for the religious believer this metaphysical incapacity is made good by divine revelation, contained, for the Christian, in the Bible, under forms relating directly to human experience. Its truths are not presentative but regulative only, valid *quoad nos*, in our human and 'fallen' situation. To criticize the revelation is pointless; it must be received as it stands, as a sufficient guide to practice.

> Where the doctrine is beyond the power of human reason to discover, it can be accepted only as resting on the authority of the teacher who proclaimed it; and that authority must be guaranteed by the external evidence of supernatural mission, (ibid., 155)

in the forms of prophecy and miracle. To the implications of biblical criticism, which was then beginning to make some impression, not always adverse, on the minds of churchmen, Mansel was apparently indifferent. His theology remained in the grooves of the orthodox tradition.

This appeal to what amounts to theological agnosticism satisfied some, if a little perversely, as a defensive apologetic in face of rationalism, but it scandalized others, not least Maurice. His indignation overflowed. Mansel, it seemed to him, had substituted theological language for the knowledge of God, and nescience for the assurance of faith. He answered the Oxford divine in *What is Revelation?* (1859), made up of sermons and supposed 'Letters to a student of theology', but expressed with a confused vehemence that did nothing to elucidate the question at issue, as even his friends realized. Mansel promptly retorted, describing Maurice's book as 'a tissue of continuous misrepresentations without a parallel in recent literature' (Burgon, 193), and further exchanges were made, although to no avail in reconciling their antithetical opinions. That there was some personal animosity behind Maurice's strictures was recognized at the time (ibid., 193 n.). Little given to critical analysis, he clearly did not appreciate the extent of the epistemological problem which talk about 'the knowledge of God' raises. But he was not alone in denouncing Mansel's views. J. S. Mill, from a very different standpoint, found them 'loathsome', while F. J. A. Hort wondered 'what a very juiceless and indigestible morsel' Mansel's book 'must be to its orthodox admirers' (A. F. Hort, *The Life and Letters of Fenton John Anthony Hort*, 1896, 1.402). Certainly its publication was no small contribution to the religious controversies with which the following decade was fraught. What is likely to interest the modern reader is the way in which the 1858 Bampton lectures anticipated some twentieth-century developments in religious thinking.

Other scholarly activities But Mansel had other occupations as well. In 1857 he edited the four volumes of Hamilton's lectures on metaphysics and logic in collaboration with John Veitch. From 1860 to 1862 he was university select preacher, a duty to be repeated by him from October 1869 until June 1871, and continued his output of sermons and articles, including a paper entitled 'Modern German philosophy' in the *Quarterly Review* (reprinted in his *Letters, Lectures, and Reviews*, published posthumously in 1873). In 1865, largely for health reasons, he and his wife took a continental holiday, touring Italy for nearly three months, during which his visit to Rome was of special delight to him. On his return he immediately answered Mill's *An Examination of Sir William Hamilton's Philosophy* (1865) in an article in the *Contemporary Review* (January–February 1866; republished in his own *The Philosophy of the Conditioned*, 1866), in which he accused Mill of ignorance of Kant's doctrines. In any case he could not approve Mill's utilitarianism, considering it 'utterly mischievous'.

At the end of 1866 Mansel was appointed to the university professorship of ecclesiastical history, which carried with it a residentiary canonry at Christ Church (he had already, in 1864, been made examining chaplain to the bishop of Peterborough and an honorary canon of Peterborough Cathedral). The ecclesiastical history chair may seem to have been an odd exchange for a noted philosopher, but Mansel had not neglected his theological studies, and in his new capacity he delivered in the Lent term of 1868 a series of lectures, 'The Gnostic heresies', for which his knowledge of ancient philosophy gave him added qualification. Thanks to the editorial work of J. B. Lightfoot, they were published posthumously in 1875.

Dean of St Paul's, death, and reputation In 1868 Mansel was offered the deanery of St Paul's Cathedral and he willingly accepted it. His departure from his beloved Oxford was eased for him by his dissatisfaction with the recent course of events in the university, which appeared to him secularizing, as well as a growing weariness from the pressure of university business that intruded more and more upon his proper vocation as a scholar. He hoped, in fact, that purely ecclesiastical office would afford him more leisure for literary activities, among them the completion of his part in the Speaker's Commentary on the Bible. But in this he was to be disappointed. The administrative duties, which won his full attention, were, he discovered, engrossing. He managed nevertheless to get away to Cosgrove from time to time, staying with his brother-in-law. But on one of these visits, in the summer of 1871, he died suddenly in his sleep on 30 July from the rupture of a blood-vessel in his brain. He was buried, as he would have wished, in Cosgrove churchyard on 6 August. A window in St Paul's erected to his memory was unveiled on St Paul's day in 1879.

As a thinker Mansel was astute and logical, if somewhat narrow in his intellectual sympathies. As a writer he was lucid and incisive, and in controversy could be acerbic. As a man he was, by all accounts, genial and hospitable. He greatly valued friendship, although it was his friends' actual presence he enjoyed: correspondence by letter he disliked, presumably as too impersonal. His biographer J. W. Burgon speaks of his 'profound humility' (Burgon, 274), and, for all his rather dry theologizing, his personal religion was sincere and heartfelt.

BERNARD M. G. REARDON

Sources J. W. Burgon, *Lives of twelve good men*, [new edn], 2 (1889), 148–237 · W. R. Matthews, *The religious philosophy of Dean Mansel* (1956) · K. D. Freeman, *The role of reason in religion: a study of Henry Mansel* (1969) · B. M. G. Reardon, *From Coleridge to Gore: a century of religious thought in Britain* (1971) · V. Sillery, *St John's College biographical register, 1775–1875* (1987)
Archives St John's College, Oxford | BL, corresp. with Lord Carnarvon, Add. MS 60834 · NL Scot., letters to Alexander Campbell Fraser
Likenesses oils, *c*.1850, St John's College, Oxford · C. Pusey, group portrait, pencil, pen and ink, *c*.1856, NPG · E. W. Wyon, marble bust, 1872, St John's College, Oxford · R. Taylor, wood-engraving (after photograph by T. Watkins), NPG; repro. in *ILN* (12 Aug 1871) · photographs, NPG [*see illus.*]
Wealth at death under £7000: probate, 4 Sept 1871, *CGPLA Eng. & Wales*

Mansel, John (d. 1265), administrator and royal councillor, is said by Matthew Paris to have been the son of a country priest. A papal letter of 1259, confirming a dispensation granted to Mansel by Pope Innocent IV, reports that Mansel's father, a man of noble family, married Mansel's mother and lived with her as his wife without revealing the fact that he had previously been ordained a deacon. Repenting of his conduct, Mansel's father later returned to his orders and a divorce was declared between the couple by the local diocesan. The resulting imputation of illegitimacy clung to Mansel and his siblings throughout their lives, and may go some way toward explaining Mansel's own restless pursuit of property and preferment.

Early years in royal service Mansel entered royal service as a young man, but it is not known how or when he did so. He is first recorded as a clerk at the exchequer of receipt, where from July 1234 until October 1236 he kept one set of the receipt rolls. From October 1236 to April 1238 he was chamberlain of the king's wines at Southampton. He continued his associations with the receipt, however, where the bulk of the revenue from the thirtieth of 1237 passed through his hands. In 1238 Mansel went with a detachment of troops supplied by King Henry to support Emperor Frederick II's military campaigns in Lombardy. Mansel may have been sent on this expedition as paymaster, but he also took an active part in the fighting, earning a reputation as a soldier he would further enhance in Gascony.

Mansel's movements from 1239 until 1242 are poorly documented. He was abroad on royal service in October 1239 and in August 1240. Already, however, he had begun to accumulate the vast combination of custodies, lands, and ecclesiastical offices that would make him, by the 1250s, the wealthiest of all King Henry's clerical administrators. In 1235 he was presented to the church at Bawburgh, Norfolk. In 1238 he acquired custody of the lands and heirs of Adam Fitzwilliam. In 1240 and 1241 the king granted him several manors formerly held by the disgraced keeper of the royal seal, Master Simon d'Ételan. In

1241 he received a papal provision to the prebend of Thame, but when Bishop Robert Grosseteste of Lincoln resisted the provision Mansel resigned his claim. King Henry made good the loss, appointing Mansel to the church of Maidstone, Kent, and to two prebends at St Paul's Cathedral. Mansel already held the church at Haughley, Suffolk, and the prebend of Malling South in Kent. In May 1243 the king appointed him chancellor of St Paul's also.

Mansel accompanied the king's expedition of 1242–3 to Gascony, where once again he distinguished himself as a soldier. In July 1242, at the battle of Saintes, Mansel unhorsed and captured Pierre Orige, the count of Boulogne's seneschal. In November 1242 Henry appointed Mansel custodian of Gascony until a seneschal could be found, and in February 1243 made him seneschal. Shortly thereafter, however, his military career came to an end. While participating in the siege of the monastery of Vérines in Bordeaux, he was seriously wounded by a stone hurled by the defenders that crushed his leg. Nursed back to health by Master Pierre de Montibus, physician to Peter of Savoy, Mansel remained in Gascony until the end of September 1243, when he returned with the king to England. Mansel's injury cemented the king's attachment to him. The court poet, Master Henry d'Avranches, addressed a poem to 'John Mansel's Leg', and stories of Mansel's bravery circulated widely.

Royal councillor Mansel's influence with the king continued to grow. In 1244 he became a member of the king's council, a position he would retain until 1263. In 1245 he was much involved in the diplomatic and administrative aspects of the king's campaign in Wales. From 8 November 1246 until 28 August 1247, and again from 17 August 1248 to 8 September 1249, he was keeper of the king's seal, an office he had briefly held in Gascony. Between 1247 and 1248 he carried out an unsuccessful mission to negotiate a marriage between Henry III's eldest son, the Lord Edward, and the daughter of the duke of Brabant. In November 1249 he fell violently ill at Maidstone, probably of food poisoning, but he was sufficiently recovered by March 1250 to take the cross with the king and other members of the royal household. In June 1250 he hosted a famous banquet for the Dominican general chapter meeting at Holborn. In October he went, with Peter Chaceporc, as the king's emissary to instruct the monks of Winchester to elect Henry's half-brother Aymer de Lusignan to the vacant bishopric.

Mansel's influence at court during these years extended well beyond the formal offices or the specific diplomatic duties entrusted to him. Between 1244 and 1258 Matthew Paris described him variously as the king's chief or special councillor and as his *secretarius* (Paris, *Chron.*). The special intimacy such terms imply made Mansel a particularly valuable intercessor for those in need of the king's favour. In 1251 Mansel protected Henry of Bath, a royal justice accused of corruption, from the king's wrath, and then secured a pardon for him. He did the same for Philip Lovel, an exchequer official accused of accepting bribes from Jews in return for favourable tax assessments. Mansel himself had brought Lovel into the king's service. He now paid Lovel's fine, and arranged the petition by Alexander III, king of Scots, that restored Lovel to the king's favour. The following year Mansel engineered Lovel's appointment as royal treasurer. Mansel knew, however, not to press his influence too far. When in 1251 he was an arbiter (with William Button the elder, bishop of Bath and Wells) in a dispute between the abbot and convent of Westminster over the division of goods, although he was a friend of the abbot Mansel settled the affair by a compromise, one approved by Henry III.

The rewards of office Such discretion brought Mansel a continuing series of rewards. In 1244 he acquired properties from the Arundel honour, including Wepeham and Bilsington, Kent, where he established an Augustinian priory. He also received a prebend in Chichester, along with another in a series of dispensations for pluralism. In 1246 Mansel was appointed dean of Wimborne in succession to Ranulf the Breton, and in 1247 became provost of Beverley, Yorkshire. He acquired many other livings also, among them Axminster in Devon; Howden and Hooton in Yorkshire; Wigan in Lancashire; and Ferring in Sussex. In 1251 he became a papal chaplain, and in 1256 the king appointed him treasurer of York, one of the richest benefices in the kingdom. Even before his promotion to York, however, Matthew Paris had declared Mansel the wealthiest cleric in England, estimating his annual income in the early 1250s at 4000 marks. The Melrose chronicler gave an even higher figure, and reported Mansel as having remarked, upon receiving a new benefice worth £20 per year, 'This will provide for my dogs' (*Chronicle of Melrose*, 214).

Mansel also took care to promote the interests of his family. In 1245 his nephew and namesake, Master John Mansel, became parson of the royal church at Lugwardine, Herefordshire, for which he received a series of royal protections. In 1251 he went abroad to study. When he returned, he entered royal service, where he worked closely with his uncle. Master John Mansel was most likely the son of Mansel's brother Reyner, who appears occasionally around the royal court during the 1250s as Brother Reyner, the brother of John Mansel. Sarah of Farlington, described as John Mansel's niece, may have been Master John Mansel's sister; if so, then Amabillia of London, niece and eventual heir of Master John Mansel, would perhaps have been the daughter of Sarah of Farlington.

Mansel seems to have been particularly attached to his two sisters. He arranged their marriages and directed a stream of royal gifts towards them. It was probably for Emma that Mansel was promised a marriage worth £30 or more by the king in 1238. She eventually married Alard the Fleming, a royal tenant-in-chief who served John Mansel as a squire until he was knighted by the king in 1251. Their daughter Joan married Henry Huse, son and heir of Matthew Huse, in a match arranged by Mansel in 1252–3. Like Alard the Fleming, Henry Huse also became a member of Mansel's *familia*, serving Mansel during the early 1260s. Mansel's other sister, Claricia, married Geoffrey of Childwick, a royal marshal and one of the most troublesome of the knightly tenants of St Albans Abbey. Matthew Paris claimed that Mansel sustained Childwick in his quarrels with the abbey, and that Mansel used his influence at court to frustrate the abbey's attempts to get justice against Childwick. Professional pleaders refused to take the abbey's case, and the royal justices declared that John Mansel so dominated the kingdom that they were afraid to give sentence against him. Mansel eventually offered the abbey his good favour, however, and the abbey, realizing they were beaten, settled with Childwick.

Diplomatic activities Mansel had already gained considerable knowledge of Gascony in 1242–3. After the collapse of Simon de Montfort's lieutenancy in Gascony, however, Mansel emerged as the man principally in charge of Henry III's Gascon and Spanish diplomacy. As such, Mansel led the diplomatic mission of 1253–4 to Castile that culminated in the marriage of the Lord Edward to Eleanor of Castile, and that produced, in consequence, King Alfonso's formal cession of Castilian claims to Gascony. Mansel was accompanied on this mission first by the bishop of Bath and later by the bishop of Hereford, but it was upon Mansel and his confidential clerk, Master John Clarel, that the burden of the negotiations rested, and to whom the credit for their success is due. Mansel continued to advise the king on Gascon and Castilian affairs thereafter. He went on several further diplomatic missions himself, and wrote lengthy letters of instruction when other royal officials were sent in his stead.

Less clear is Mansel's role in negotiating the disastrous grant by the papacy of the Sicilian throne to Henry's second son, Edmund. Mansel was absent from court during the last half of 1253 and early 1254. It seems unlikely, therefore, that he could have been one of the principal architects of the Sicilian scheme that came to fruition during these months. He was, however, present with the king in Gascony during March 1254 when Henry accepted the papal offer, and at the king's command he set his own seal on the formal documents accepting the papal terms. There are hints he may have done so reluctantly, but if so, his objections were more likely to the terms of the offer than to the offer itself. He gave steady support to the Sicilian project thereafter, even when other royal councillors, such as Bishop Walter de Cantilupe of Worcester, outspokenly opposed it.

Mansel's direct diplomatic involvements were not limited to Gascony and Castile. He was a key figure in the king's campaign to put Richard, earl of Cornwall, on the throne of Germany. He planned the mission of 1256 by Robert Walerand and the earl of Gloucester to sound out support for Richard among the German princes, and he accompanied Gloucester on a similar mission in 1257. Mansel was also a frequent visitor to the Scottish court during the 1250s, where he was sent several times by King Henry to restore peace between Henry's daughter and her husband, the young king of Scots, and the guardians of the Scottish kingdom.

Relations with the baronial reformers When the baronial reform movement began in 1258, Mansel was one of three royalist representatives appointed to the new royal council of fifteen. He was clearly trusted by the reformist party, despite his long association with the king. His clerk, John Clarel, was sent to Rome to negotiate new terms for 'the Sicilian business', and Mansel himself was put in charge of Aymer de Lusignan's confiscated property at Tickhill. In August Mansel went once again to Scotland, and in September his nephew, Master John Mansel, received the prebend of Fenton, Yorkshire, a gift that quickly embroiled him with the pope, who had provided another claimant. Mansel was a frequent target of complaint in Hugh Bigod's judicial eyre of 1258–9, but he continued as one of the key members of the council throughout the summer and autumn of 1259. He played an active role in negotiating that year's treaty of Paris, including the settlement of Eleanor de Montfort's dower claims, but was reluctant to agree to the alienation of any royal demesne lands to her. Hostility between Mansel and the Montforts grew steadily thereafter.

In November 1259 Mansel went to Paris with the king, and in February 1260 witnessed the letters by which Henry delayed a scheduled meeting of parliament. With Peter of Savoy, Richard of Cornwall, and Robert Walerand, Mansel began now to plan the gradual restoration of the king's authority. The council of fifteen finally collapsed in December 1260; in January 1261 Master John Mansel was sent to Rome to ask Pope Alexander IV to absolve King Henry from his oaths to observe the provisions of Oxford. In February Mansel and the king withdrew into the Tower of London to await events. In May Mansel was appointed constable of the Tower. In June he travelled personally to Winchester to warn Henry of the danger he was in, and to accompany him back to London. Henry and Mansel remained in the Tower continuously from 22 June until 30 July. By the time they emerged, the resistance was over. On 21 November Mansel negotiated the treaty of Kingston, by which the reformers effectively abandoned the provisions of Oxford. The king's coup was completed in May 1262, when Pope Urban IV reissued his predecessor's decree annulling the provisions. The bull was addressed to Archbishop Boniface of Canterbury, Bishop Simon of Norwich, and to John Mansel, treasurer of York.

Last years and death By July 1262 King Henry felt sufficiently secure to return to France. Mansel did not join him until the end of August. By October, however, Mansel was so alarmed by the news from England that he begged the king to abandon his pilgrimage and return to England. Henry would not agree, however, and he and Mansel remained abroad until 20 December 1262. In the spring of 1263 Mansel's lands were a particular target of attack by Montfort's partisans, who blamed him for the papal quashing of the provisions. Once again Henry and Mansel retreated to the Tower, but this time the munitions were inadequate to sustain a siege. Mansel fled down the Thames and across the channel. His properties were immediately confiscated and given to Simon de Montfort the younger.

In September 1263 Mansel appeared at the Boulogne conference between Montfort, King Henry, and King Louis of France, to plead for the return of his lands. In November it seemed briefly that Mansel's pleas would be answered. Henry recovered his authority, revoked the grant to young Simon, and placed Mansel's lands in the hands of royal custodians. Mansel himself, however, remained in exile, his return to England blocked by Henry's failure, in December 1263, to secure control over Dover Castle. In January 1264 Mansel was again at King Louis's court, this time for the mise of Amiens. Louis's arbitration failed, however, and the resulting civil war left King Henry a prisoner in Montfort's hands. During the summer and autumn of 1264 Mansel co-operated with the queen, Archbishop Boniface, Peter of Savoy, William de Valence, and others of the royalist exiles to mount an invasion of England from Flanders. No invasion was ever launched, however, and in early 1265 Mansel died in exile. News of his death had reached England by 7 February 1265, when Montfort appointed his youngest son Amaury to succeed Mansel as treasurer of York.

Mansel's executors were unable to act until after Montfort's defeat and death at the battle of Evesham on 3 August 1265. But in November they were granted free administration of all his property. None of his property, however, seems to have descended to his heirs. His sister Emma outlived him, and was able to have the manors her brother had given her during his lifetime confirmed to her by the crown. Master John Mansel died within the year, leaving his own London houses to his niece Amabillia of Ripon. Nothing of his uncle's property, however, seems to have passed to him. Mansel left Bilsington Priory to King Henry, who in 1272 proposed to give it to the church of St Mary at Boulogne. But the remainder of Mansel's vast estate appears to have been treated as a crown escheat. Perhaps this was appropriate for a man whose labours on behalf of the crown, in so many different spheres, had brought him such rewards. Contemporaries were in no doubt as to Mansel's importance in matters of state. The value which the king placed on his services was noted by Matthew Paris, but most eloquently expressed by Henry III himself, in a message sent to the pope in 1262: 'He was trained under my wing. I have tested his ability, his character and merits since his boyhood. He has always been serviceable and loyal in my affairs and in those of the kingdom' (Powicke, 294).   ROBERT C. STACEY

Sources Chancery records · Rymer, *Foedera*, new edn · Paris, *Chron.* · J. R. Maddicott, *Simon de Montfort* (1994) · N. Denholm-Young, *Richard of Cornwall* (1947) · R. F. Treharne, *The baronial plan of reform, 1258–1263*, [new edn] (1971) · F. M. Powicke, *King Henry III and the Lord Edward: the community of the realm in the thirteenth century*, 2 vols. (1947) · *Gesta abbatum monasterii Sancti Albani, a Thoma Walsingham*, ed. H. T. Riley, 3 vols., pt 4 of *Chronica monasterii S. Albani*, Rolls Series, 28 (1867–9), vol. 1 · W. W. Shirley, ed., *Royal and other historical letters illustrative of the reign of Henry III*, 2 vols., Rolls Series, 27 (1862–6) · A. O. Anderson and M. O. Anderson, eds., *The chronicle of Melrose* (1936) · *CPR, 1258–66*, 502, 508
Archives PRO
Likenesses seal, BL, Harley charter 43 C42
Wealth at death see *CPR*

Mansel, John Clavell. *See* Pleydell, John Clavell Mansel- (1817–1902).

Mansel [Mansell], **Sir Rice** (1487–1559), soldier and administrator, was born in Oxwich in the Gower peninsula, Glamorgan, on 25 January 1487. His father was Jenkin Mansel, known as 'the Valiant' (*fl.* 1450–1510), and his mother was Edith (*fl.* 1450–1510), daughter of Sir George Kene, a knight of Kent. The family estate, in west Gower, had been built up over two centuries by careful management and prudent marriages. It had been forfeited in 1464 when an act of attainder was passed against Philip Mansel (Rice's grandfather) for conspiring with Jasper Tudor against the Yorkist cause. Jenkin (Rice's father) recovered the estate soon after the battle of Bosworth which suggests that he had fought for Henry Tudor at that battle. Jenkin was a client of the powerful Rhys ap Thomas of Dinefwr and may have named his son after him.

In his youth Rice Mansel was placed under the guardianship of his uncle Sir Mathew Cradock, a naval commander and prosperous Swansea merchant, and from 1509 was entrusted with the charge of a number of ships bearing the Cradock family name. Rice received seisin of his estates from his guardian in 1510 and on 17 May in the following year married Eleanor, daughter of James Bassett of Beaupré, the first of his three wives, who died in or just before 1520.

The record of Mansel's career between 1513 and 1526 is virtually a blank, apart from a mention of his service with the earl of Worcester in Flanders in 1517. His knighthood, however, granted in 1526, when he was still comparatively young, points to his having served with distinction as a soldier and administrator in the royal pay. His private life at this period is better documented. In 1520 he married his second wife, Anne Brydges, who bore two daughters. His third marriage, in 1527, to Cecily (*d.* 1558), daughter of John Daubridgecourt of Solihull, forged an intimate link with the court, for Cecily was a lady-in-waiting to Princess Mary (the future queen) and the friendly connection between them continued after Cecily's marriage and Mary's accession.

Mansel played a conspicuous part in suppressing the rebellion of Thomas Fitzgerald, Lord Offaly, in Ireland in 1534–5. The English commander, Sir William Skeffington, wrote that 'Sir Rice Mansel with his band … has done right good exploits and acceptable service' (Maunsell and Statham, 1.299). Mansel was among the first to enter the fortress of Maynooth after a five-day bombardment had breached the walls, probably the first time heavy artillery had been used for such purposes in Ireland. His wife pleaded with Thomas Cromwell to allow him to return, on the grounds that 'most of his living is encumbered with jointures and other charges, so that if God should take him, I and my children are undone' (Maunsell and Statham, 1.302). Mansel's successes in Ireland brought him to the favourable notice of the king and his ministers, for in 1536 he was made chamberlain of Chester. He also became a member of the council of Wales, and was placed on the commission of the peace for a number of counties and pricked as sheriff of Glamorgan.

Mansell, though a religious conservative, was probably not over-concerned with the niceties of theology and had no compunction about profiting from the dissolution of the monasteries. He obtained a lease of the site of the abbey of Margam in 1537, and between 1540 and 1557 he purchased the site of the abbey and much of its estate in four instalments for a total sum of £2482 13s. 1d. His investment tripled the acreage of his estate and secured him a place in the first rank of the landed society of south Wales. Leaving his new residence at Oxwich Castle for his son and heir, Edward, to complete, he set about converting the domestic buildings of the abbey, together with its fine chapter house, into a mansion which became his principal home and survived until its demolition in 1792-3. He dismantled the monks' choir and presbytery, leaving the former lay brothers' nave to function as the parish church.

When war with France and Scotland was resumed in 1542, Mansell as vice-admiral engaged the French rather unsuccessfully in the channel; and in 1544 as knight marshal he led a commando-style raid against Rothesay Castle on the Isle of Bute. His wife's friendship with the Catholic Princess Mary may have prompted Mansell to keep a low profile during the radically protestant reign of Edward VI, but when Mary succeeded to the throne he was rewarded for his services and loyalty with the offices of chamberlain and chancellor of south Wales and the counties of Carmarthenshire and Cardiganshire, as well as the stewardships of many manors and lordships. These offices gave him the power and status of the chief royal representative in south Wales and the influence once enjoyed by the family's patron, Rhys ap Thomas of Dinefwr.

While Mansell's son Edward was defending the family's interests against George Herbert in a celebrated affray at Oxwich Castle in 1557, Rice was raising troops against the French. They were never used. Mary died, peace was restored, and before the new queen, Elizabeth, could reverse the religious changes of the previous reign, Mansell himself died at his town house in Clerkenwell on 10 April 1559. He was given an elaborate Catholic-style funeral and buried at St Bartholomew-the-Great, west Smithfield, a dissolved Augustinian priory, only recently restored as a Dominican priory by Queen Mary. No grave marker now survives, nor does a portrait; but his likeness has been preserved in the effigy on his fine tomb at Margam Abbey church. Three versions of his will are extant and two poems in his praise by the bard Iorwerth Fynglwyd (d. 1527).   F. G. COWLEY

Sources E. P. Statham, History of the family of Maunsell (Mansell, Mansel), compiled chiefly from data collected … by Col. Charles A. Maunsell, 3 vols. (1917-20) • G. Williams, 'Rice Mansell of Oxwich and Margam (1487-1559)', Morgannwg, 6 (1962), 33-51 • G. Williams, 'The Herberts, the Mansells, and Oxwich Castle', Castles in Wales and the marches, ed. J. R. Kenyon and R. Avent (1987), 173-83 • G. Williams, 'The dissolution of the monasteries in Glamorgan', Welsh History Review / Cylchgrawn Hanes Cymru, 3 (1966-7), 23-43 • G. Williams, 'The affray at Oxwich Castle, 1557', Gower, 2 (1949), 2-6 • An inventory of the ancient monuments in Glamorgan, 4/1: Domestic architecture from the Reformation to the industrial revolution, the greater houses, Royal Commission on Ancient and Historical Monuments in Wales and Monmouthshire (1981), 63-76, 382 • P. Moore and D. Moore, 'Two topographical paintings of the old house at Margam, Glamorgan', Archaeologia Cambrensis, 123 (1974), 155-69 • D. M. Williams, Gower: a guide to ancient and historical monuments on the Gower peninsula (1998), 24-7, 30-37 • H. Ll. Jones and E. I. Rowlands, Gwaith Iorwerth Fynglwyd (1975), 58-61 • W. de Gray Birch, ed., A descriptive catalogue of the Penrice and Margam Abbey manuscripts in the possession of Miss Talbot of Margam, 6 vols. (privately printed, London, 1893-1905) • J. Strype, Annals of the Reformation and establishment of religion … during Queen Elizabeth's happy reign, new edn, 1 (1824), 283, 335-6

Likenesses tomb effigy, Margam Abbey church; repro. in Williams, Gower: a guide

Mansel, Thomas, first Baron Mansel (1667-1723), politician, was born on 9 November 1667, at Margam Abbey, Glamorgan, the second but first surviving son of Sir Edward Mansel, fourth baronet (1637-1706), of Margam Abbey, and his wife, Martha, the daughter of Edward Carne of Ewenni, Glamorgan. He was educated privately, by the local presbyterian minister, and then at Exeter College, Oxford; he took his BA from Trinity College in 1686 and his MA, at New Inn Hall, in 1699. On 18 May 1686 Mansel married Martha (d. 1718), the only daughter and heir of a prosperous London merchant, Francis Millington; they had five sons and five daughters.

Reacting violently against his strict upbringing, and in particular the tutelage of an overbearing father, Mansel became in adulthood a man of fashion, a wit, and a rake (he fathered at least three illegitimate children), and was persistently extravagant, in the teeth of parental injunctions to economy. In the same way he abandoned his family's whig politics to become a pillar of the 'church interest', influenced first by his fellow Welshman Francis Gwyn, and later falling under the spell of a fellow refugee from a presbyterian past, Robert Harley, first earl of Oxford. From his earliest experience of parliament, where he sat, as a commoner and then a peer, from 1689 until his death (with one short interval in 1698-9, after which he was MP for Glamorgan until 1712), he 'always made an agreeable figure' without ever establishing a reputation as an orator. A man of considerable charm, but of a facile and shallow intellect, his sparkle was somehow dampened on the public stage.

Not until Queen Anne's reign did Mansel attract much attention, when he took the eye as one of Harley's henchmen in the Commons, and his appointment to office in 1704, as comptroller of the household and a privy councillor, was an integral part of the ministerial reconstruction in which Harley's band of 'moderate' tories came to the fore. The years that followed were in many respects his heyday. Not only was he an important member of the ministry (though without a cabinet place), he was also, from his father's death in 1706, the head of his family and the leader of the tory interest throughout south Wales. Although there are indications that he was increasingly concerned at the drift of the lord treasurer, Sidney Godolphin, to the whigs, he needed the resources of office to settle his debts and pursue his feuds with local Welsh rivals, some of which, notably his quarrel with the industrialist and projector Sir Humphry Mackworth, degenerated into actual physical violence. He promptly resigned, however, with the fall of Harley in February 1708.

After returning to government with his mentor two years later, Mansel was briefly a lord of the Treasury, but in 1711 he became comptroller again and not long after that took a peerage as one of Harley's 'dozen' new lords (created *en bloc* to guarantee the upper house's acceptance of the peace of Utrecht) and retreated to the lucrative but undemanding post of teller of the exchequer. He remained loyal to Harley until the bitter end—though his own influence in the administration was dwindling—lost all offices except a few local honours at the Hanoverian succession, and more or less retired from active politics to follow his mild interest in antiquarian matters and his somewhat keener passion for the refinement and embellishment of his country seat at Margam.

Mansel died at Margam Abbey on 10 December 1723, allegedly of a 'broken heart', following difficulties with his own children, his eldest son having died young and one of his two surviving daughters having contracted what he viewed as a wholly unsuitable marriage. He was buried in Margam with his ancestors.

D. W. Hayton, rev.

Sources *Calendar of the Penrice and Margam manuscripts*, ed. W. de Gray Birch, 2nd ser. (1894) · *Calendar of the Penrice and Margam manuscripts*, ed. W. de Gray Birch, 3rd ser. · W. A. Shaw, ed., *Calendar of treasury books*, 26, PRO (1954); 29 (1957) · GEC, *Peerage* · E. P. Statham, *History of the family of Maunsell (Mansell, Mansel), compiled chiefly from data collected … by Col. Charles A. Maunsell*, 3 vols. (1917–20) · L. Naylor, 'Mansel, Thomas II', HoP, *Commons, 1660–90* · G. Williams, ed., *Glamorgan county history*, 4: *Early modern Glamorgan* (1974) · G. Jenkins, *Foundations of modern Wales* (1993)
Archives NL Wales, corresp.
Wealth at death substantial; Margam Abbey with local Glamorgan manors; Gower estates; lands and mineral rights around Aberafan; collieries at Swansea and Briton Ferry: Penrice and Margam MSS, NL Wales · collieries at Swansea and Briton Ferry brought in £800–£900 p.a. in early 18th cent.: G. Jenkins, *Foundations*

Mansel, William Lort (1753–1820), bishop of Bristol and college head, was born at Pembroke on 2 April 1753, the son of William Wogan Mansel, of Pembroke, and his wife, Anne, daughter of Major Roger Lort, officer in the Royal Welsh Fusiliers. He was educated at Gloucester grammar school, under Mr Sparks, and was admitted pensioner, aged seventeen, at Trinity College, Cambridge, on 2 June 1770. Elected scholar in 1771, he graduated BA in 1774 and proceeded MA in 1777. He was made junior fellow in 1775, full fellow in 1777, and held many college offices, twice serving as junior dean (1783–4 and 1785–6). He was ordained deacon at Peterborough on 18 June 1780 and priest on 28 September 1783, after which he was appointed vicar of Bottisham, Cambridgeshire, by the bishop of Ely. On 6 November 1788 his college presented him to the vicarage of Chesterton, and in the following year, on 20 January, he married Isabella Haggerstone, the daughter of a Cambridge attorney.

In college Mansel was known as a fine wit and mimic,

and delighted in satirizing academic rivalries. His popularity led to his election as public orator in 1788. He often preached before the university and took part in county politics as a strong supporter of William Pitt's government. He was linked to the administration through his position as chaplain to Pitt's master of the rolls, Sir Richard Pepper Arden. His former pupil Spencer Perceval recommended him to Pitt for the mastership of his college; Mansel was duly appointed on 25 May 1798, with instructions 'to maintain the authority of the situation, and (what is much wanted) to improve the discipline of the College' (William Pitt to George III, 12 May 1798, *Later Correspondence of George III*, 3.61). The elements of political and religious radicalism in Trinity—encouraged by two of the fellows, Thomas Jones and James Lambert—certainly dispersed under 'the perfectly orthodox' Mansel (ibid., 3.61), who also served as vice-chancellor in his second year as master. Mansel's loyalty to the political establishment was recognized when Perceval, then chancellor of the exchequer, promoted his candidacy for the bishopric of Bristol, to which he was consecrated on 30 October 1808. He was further rewarded, in 1810, with the wealthy living of Barwick in Elmet, Yorkshire, which was in Perceval's gift as chancellor of the duchy of Lancaster.

Mansel published only three of his sermons. He died at the master's lodge, Trinity College, on 27 June 1820, and was buried in the chapel on 3 July. He had five daughters and at least three sons, the youngest of whom, Spencer Perceval Mansel (1797–1862), was named after his great patron.

W. P. Courtney, rev. S. J. Skedd

Sources Venn, *Alum. Cant.* · *GM*, 1st ser., 59 (1789), 86; 90/1 (1820), 637 · *Fasti Angl.* (Hardy), 1.221; 3.611, 615, 670 · J. Gascoigne, *Cambridge in the age of the Enlightenment* (1989), 219, 234 · *The later correspondence of George III*, ed. A. Aspinall, 5 vols. (1962–70), vol. 3, p. 61; vol. 5, p. 638 · *N&Q*, 2nd ser., 9 (1860), 483; 10 (1860), 41–2, 283–4; 12 (1861), 221; 3rd ser., 12 (1867), 485 · H. Gunning, *Reminiscences of the university, town, and county of Cambridge, from the year 1780*, 2 vols. (1854), vol. 1, pp. 55–6, 194–5, 317; vol. 2, p. 101 · C. Wordsworth, *Annals of my early life, 1806–1846* (1891), 69–70 · will, PRO, PROB 11/1631, fol. 361r
Archives BL, letters to T. J. Mathias and others · Glos. RO, corresp. incl. letters to his son Frederick
Likenesses R. Dighton, caricature, coloured etching, pubd 1810 (*A view from Trinity College, Cambridge*), NPG · W. Say, mezzotint, pubd 1812 (after T. Kirkby), BM, NPG · D. Turner, etching (after sketch by G. H. Harlow, 1815), BM, NPG

Mansell, Bussy (1623–1699), soldier and politician, was born at Briton Ferry, Glamorgan, on 22 November 1623, the second son of Arthur Mansell (d. in or before 1628), himself a second son, and his wife, Jane Price (d. 1638), heir of a Briton Ferry family. The main branch of the Mansell family in south Wales was seated at Margam and was descended from the Somersets, earls of Worcester. Mansell's forename was an acknowledgement of his paternal grandfather's second marriage to the widow of John Bussy of Lincolnshire. Nothing is known of his formative years or education, but it was natural that the Mansell family, within the sphere of influence of the royalist fifth earl of Worcester, should have been mobilized on behalf of the king during the civil war. At the age of twenty-one Mansell was active in the western hundreds of Glamorgan in raising taxes for the royalist war effort and in sequestrating the few parliamentarian activists in the county. When the Glamorgan 'peaceable army' was formed in 1645 as a reaction against the depredations of the royalist commanders he became a prominent member of it, having recently been appointed colonel-general of the king's forces in south Wales. When his disloyalty was discovered he confessed his move had been a misjudgement, and promised on 13 September to prove his allegiance to Charles I. Four days later, however, Mansell was one of those in the peace army to whom the royalists surrendered Cardiff Castle. By 28 October he had espoused the parliamentarian cause at Cardiff, and by 17 November was being recommended for the post of commander-in-chief of parliament's forces in south Wales. The recommendation, by the most committed parliamentarians of Glamorgan, was later accepted by the House of Commons. Mansell was still only twenty-two years old, and although these moves have been taken as evidence of his military prowess and political adroitness, it is also possible to see him at this time as something of a *roi fainéant*, pushed forward in the interests of social respectability by men like Philip Jones, who provided the real steer for winning the political war in south Wales for parliament. On occasions of military crisis in the region—when the royalist gentry rose in February 1646 and June 1647 and when the disaffected Rowland Laugharne turned against his former parliamentary masters in May 1648—Mansell played supporting roles to other commanders.

On 17 April 1646 Mansell married Catherine (d. in or before 1678), widow of Sir Edward Stradling of St Donats, a leading Glamorgan royalist, at a time when the resolve of parliamentarians in the county was hardening. The marriage proved no obstacle to his continuing good standing in the eyes of the king's opponents. Between 1648 and 1653 he was part of the circle of committeemen around Philip Jones, and sat on the commission for the propagation of the gospel in Wales (February 1650) and the high court of justice against royalist insurgents in the principality in 1651. The names of Jones and Mansell were inseparable in south Wales public affairs during the rule of the Rump Parliament, and it was surely Jones's patronage that secured Mansell a place in the nominated assembly of July to December 1653. On this new stage Mansell was able to find some independence from Jones, and it was perhaps as an expression of this freedom that Mansell supported the radical minority in the assembly that sought the abolition of tithes. This was opposed to the pro-Cromwellian line taken by Jones, and Mansell on no other occasion expressed support for the demands of the millenarians. He never again held a parliamentary seat until the Restoration, although he continued to hold local office, proof that his relations with the all-powerful Jones remained amicable.

The Mansell family name and his earlier loyalties made Mansell an attractive target for agents recruiting support for the future Charles II in what had been such a royalist region. On the eclipse of Philip Jones during the revived Rump Parliament he became the leading military figure

in Glamorgan and Monmouthshire; at the same time Edward Hyde considered him an ally. By late September 1659 Hyde had to write off Mansell, who initially stuck to the republican cause before using his local offices to move with George Monck towards the Restoration. He was double returned for Cardiff Boroughs in the Convention of 1660, and had to wait until 27 June to be declared victor. He conformed easily to the restored monarchy, and became a leading figure in Glamorgan local administration, although his sympathies were decidedly whig: he was a patron of dissenting congregations. At some point before May 1678 he married, after the death of his first wife, a woman whose forename alone, Anne, is known. When he returned to parliament to sit for Glamorgan in March 1679 he was sympathetic to the exclusionists, but was not particularly active in that assembly or the succeeding one of October. He did not stand for the county in the 1681 elections, but instead took Cardiff Boroughs. Mansell was imprisoned briefly during Monmouth's rising, and supported the 1688 revolution without reservation. His reputation as a political weathervane persisted: in 1687 he was lampooned as

> Hospitable Bush, who cares not a rush
> What hurries, so himself be secure,
> With his friends and his glass,
> Now and then a private lass,
> Can all these adventures endure.
>
> (J. P. Jenkins, 'Two poems on the Glamorgan gentry in the reign of James II', *National Library of Wales Journal*, 21, 1979–80, 171)

From 1689 Mansell sat once more for Glamorgan and was listed by Robert Harley as a member of the country opposition, but from 1694 he was given leave of absence from the House of Commons, probably on grounds of age and ill health. In 1696, following the attempt on the life of William III, Mansell readily signed the Association for the king's defence. He died at Briton Ferry on 5 May 1699 and was buried there on 25 May. His property passed to his only grandson, his son, Thomas, having predeceased him.   STEPHEN K. ROBERTS

Sources A. M. Johnson, 'Bussy Mansell (1623–99): political survivalist', *Morgannwg*, 20 (1976), 9–36 • M. W. Helms and L. Naylor, 'Mansell, Bussy', HoP, *Commons, 1660–90*, 3.16–17 • 'Mansell, Bussy', HoP, *Commons, 1690–1715* [draft] • G. Williams, ed., *Glamorgan county history*, 4: *Early modern Glamorgan* (1974) • NL Wales, Tredegar MS 105 • *Diary of the marches of the royal army during the great civil war, kept by Richard Symonds*, ed. C. E. Long, CS, old ser., 74 (1859), 217–18 • Bodl. Oxf., MSS Nalson • will, PRO, PROB 11/451, fol. 128 • G. T. Clark, *Limbus patrum Morganiae et Glamorganiae* (1886) • E. P. Statham, *History of the family of Maunsell (Mansell, Mansel)*, compiled chiefly from data collected … by Col. Charles A. Maunsell, 3 vols. (1917–20) • *The manuscripts of his grace the duke of Portland*, 10 vols., HMC, 29 (1891–1931), vols. 5–10 • CSP dom., 1645–7; 1651; 1655; 1659–60 • Thurloe, *State papers*, 3.132–3 • W. de Gray Birch, ed., *A descriptive catalogue of the Penrice and Margam Abbey manuscripts in the possession of Miss Talbot of Margam*, 6 vols. (privately printed, London, 1893–1905), vols. 2 and 3

Wealth at death bequests of £130 to the poor; he was said to be worth £1100 p.a. in 1645: will, PRO, PROB 11/451, fol. 128; Long, ed., *Richard Symonds's diary*

Mansell, Francis (1579–1665), college head, was born at Muddlescombe, Carmarthenshire, and baptized on 23 March 1579, the third son of Sir Francis Mansell and his first wife, Catherine, daughter and heir of Henry Morgan of Muddlescombe. After attending the free school in Hereford, he matriculated from Jesus College, Oxford, on 20 November 1607. He graduated BA on 20 February 1609 and proceeded MA on 5 July 1611. In 1613 he was elected to a fellowship at All Souls as founder's kin.

On the death of Griffith Powell on 28 June 1620, Mansell was elected principal of Jesus College, and was admitted by the vice-chancellor, in spite of opposition from a number of fellows. On 13 July Mansell expelled three of his opponents from their fellowships and proceeded, on the authority of the vice-chancellor, against a fourth. His position does not appear to have been secure, however, and before his year of grace from All Souls expired he resigned from the principalship and retired to his fellowship, proceeding BD and DD on 3 July 1624. When his successor at Jesus, Sir Eubule Thelwall, died on 8 October 1630, Mansell was re-elected, his success on this occasion perhaps a result of the patronage of William Laud, the new chancellor. In the same year he became rector of Easington, Oxfordshire, and in 1631 rector of Elmley Chapel, Kent, prebendary of St David's and treasurer of Llandaff.

During Mansell's second tenure of office Jesus College buildings were altered and enlarged. In 1636–7 the chapel was extended westwards. Thelwall's new library, raised on a colonnade which was insufficiently strong, was pulled down and the north and south sides of the inner quadrangle were completed. Mansell was a tireless fundraiser and gave much of his own money to the college, including £100 towards the second quadrangle.

When war broke out in 1642 Mansell was in Wales settling the details of some benefactions. He returned to Oxford at the end of the year but in 1643 was forced to leave the city to look after the affairs of his brother Anthony, who had been killed at the battle of Newbury. For the next few years he rallied support for the royalists in Wales. He was sequestered from his Kent rectory before 4 March 1646 but on 11 June that year was one of those clergy whom the House of Commons wished to secure in some suitable place. When the parliamentary visitation of the university began in 1647 he returned to Oxford to look after college interests, and although ejected from the principalship in May 1648, took a year to ensure that the college's affairs were in order before handing over to his successor, Michael Roberts.

Mansell then retired to Llantriddyd, Glamorgan, where he encountered some harassment. In 1651 he again returned to Oxford, residing with a Mr Newman, a baker in Holywell Street. He found employment teaching a small group of sons of Welsh gentry at the home of a Mr White, which received the nickname 'little Welsh hall'. Later invited to take rooms in Jesus College, he resumed tutorial duties, teaching among others the young Sackville Crowe. In letters to Crowe's father Mansell advocated a broad curriculum for all commoners, not just those destined for the church or for academe.

Following the Restoration, on 1 August 1660 Mansell was reinstated as principal of Jesus. However, age and bad eyesight induced him to resign the following year, and

having gradually become more infirm, he died on 1 May 1665. He requested burial in the college chapel, where a memorial was placed. By his will dated 3 January 1661, he left small bequests to the poor of parishes in Carmarthenshire and Glamorgan, and the residue of his estate to his friend, executor, and successor at Jesus, Leoline Jenkins, in trust for the benefit of the college and of the church in Wales.   A. F. POLLARD, *rev.* J. H. CURTHOYS

Sources E. G. Hardy, *Jesus College* (1899) • J. N. L. Baker, *Jesus College, Oxford, 1571–1971* (1971) • W. P. Griffith, *Learning, law and religion: higher education and Welsh society, c.1540–1640* (1996) • *Hist. U. Oxf. 4: 17th-cent. Oxf.* • Foster, *Alum. Oxon.* • DWB • Mansell's will, PRO, PROB 11/322, fols. 352–3

Mansell, Sir Robert (1570/71–1652), naval officer and administrator, was the fourth, or possibly the sixth, son of Sir Edward Mansell (1530/31–1585) of Margam, Glamorgan, and Lady Jane Somerset, the youngest daughter of Henry, second earl of Worcester, and his second wife, Elizabeth, daughter of Sir Anthony Browne. A student at Staple Inn in 1585, he attended Brasenose College, Oxford, in 1587, but did not graduate.

Maritime exploits In 1591 Mansell captained a privateer on an expedition to the West Indies led by Thomas, Lord Howard, to whom he was related by marriage through his nephew, Sir Lewis Mansell. Within a few years he had married Elizabeth, daughter of the late lord keeper, Sir Nicholas *Bacon, and widow of Sir Francis Wyndham (*d.* 1592), a Norfolk squire whose property lay at Pentney, about 8 miles from King's Lynn. This union, which proved childless, connected him to the influential Gawdy and Bacon families, and led in 1593 to his appointment to the Norfolk bench. However, he did not settle himself in the county but instead embarked upon a naval career. During the Cadiz expedition of 1596 he rose to the command of a royal warship after the previous captain was killed, and received a knighthood from the earl of Essex (27 June). In the following year he served as Essex's flag captain on the Islands' voyage, and then as vice-admiral in the narrow seas. Between February and October 1599 he was admiral of a small squadron on the Irish station, and saw action against the rebels at Waterford. In 1600 he belatedly attempted to develop his standing in Norfolk, where he was regarded as an outsider. On 24 April he was appointed the county's vice-admiral, and later that year he offered himself as knight of the shire for the parliament which was soon expected to meet. However, his hopes of representing his county were jeopardized by a duel with Sir John Heydon on 9 October 1600, which also cost him the use of his right arm and, briefly, his place on the bench. After helping to round up the accomplices of the rebellious earl of Essex in February 1601, Mansell served as admiral of a squadron in the western channel, capturing six Hanseatic vessels laden with Portuguese merchandise. He failed to overcome the damage done to his reputation by his earlier duel, and in the parliamentary election for Norfolk held on 5 October he was defeated. However, four days later he was chosen as senior burgess at King's Lynn. He made only a modest impact on the 1601 parliament.

During the closing years of Elizabeth's reign Mansell

Sir Robert Mansell (1570/71–1652), by unknown artist

served as admiral of the narrow seas. In September 1602 he performed a notable service when he intercepted six Spanish galleys, driving them into the hands of a waiting Dutch squadron, which destroyed them. On the accession of James I he signalled his desire to give over his employment at sea in favour of 'some place of attendance' (*Salisbury MSS*, 15.43). He achieved his ambition in April 1604 when, aided by his distant relative Lord Admiral Nottingham, and the surveyor of the navy, Sir John Trevor, his associate in a recent privateering venture, he displaced Sir Fulke Greville as treasurer of the navy. About the same time he was also made a gentleman of the privy chamber. As treasurer Mansell proved keen to enrich himself at the government's expense. Corruption was allowed to flourish at every level while he himself regularly exacted exorbitant fees from the navy's suppliers as a condition of payment. In 1605 he hired to the crown the *Resistance*, a new ship of about 140 tons of which he was a part owner, for service as a victualler in the fleet which accompanied Nottingham on the latter's embassy to Spain that year. Although equipped at government expense, the ship's true cargo was 50 tons of lead, which it carried on behalf of a private merchant. Moreover, her hire was paid on the false basis that she was a ship of 300 tons, and none of her rigging, worth £379, was ever returned to the navy's stores. By such underhand means Mansell amassed a fortune, so enabling him to invest in various enterprises such as the Muscovy Company. His fraudulent dealings were exposed in 1608–9 by the commission appointed to investigate corruption in the navy, but although the evidence against him was damning he went unpunished.

Naval administrator During the first Jacobean parliament (1604–10) Mansell acted as a spokesman for the navy. He represented Carmarthenshire, where he apparently leased some property. In 1605, while parliament was prorogued, he accompanied Nottingham to Madrid, and in the following year, during a further prorogation, he commanded the fleet which returned the Danish king, Christian IV, to his native country. By 1610 Mansell had been drawn into the circle of those who advised the young Prince Henry. Improbable though it may seem, Henry hoped to enlist Mansell in a campaign of naval reform, while Mansell supported the prince's bid to discover a north-west passage. It was probably Mansell who suggested that the expedition to find the passage should be commanded by his own nephew, Sir Thomas Button. Henry's sudden death in November 1612 deprived Mansell of his patron. In February 1613 Mansell staged a mock seafight to celebrate the marriage of Princess Elizabeth to the elector palatine, a project over which he took great care. Three months later he was imprisoned in the Marshalsea after he had advised Nottingham to question the legality of a second commission of inquiry into the navy. The immediate cause of his incarceration, however, was his refusal to identify the lawyer whose advice he had solicited. On 12 June he was arraigned before the privy council where he confessed his fault, avoiding the sort of intemperate outburst to which he was prone. Soon after his release he attached himself to the royal favourite, Robert Carr, earl of Somerset, whose agent he was in the parliamentary elections of 1614. He was again returned for Carmarthenshire, and also at Harwich, in recognition of his support for its bid for local admiralty jurisdiction. Mansell plumped for the county seat and again acted as the navy's spokesman.

Mansell was unaffected by the fall of Somerset in 1615. In that year he expanded his commercial interests by obtaining the monopoly on glass production, buying out the other members of a syndicate to which he belonged. To cut production costs he reorganized the works, but his search for a suitable site for a new furnace outside London proved ruinously expensive. Attempts to establish works in Nottinghamshire, Dorset, and Pembrokeshire all ended in failure, and by the time he discovered the ideal location at Newcastle upon Tyne he had expended £28,000, 'almost to the exhausting of all his estate' (BL, Add. MS 12496, fol. 165). The cost of financing the glassworks may have been one of the considerations which induced Mansell in the spring of 1618 to sell the treasurership of the navy to a fellow Muscovy merchant, Sir William Russell. However, his main motive was undoubtedly that he had learned that a further investigation of the navy was now inevitable, allied to which it was clear that the power of his patrons, the Howards, was on the verge of collapse. Before Mansell agreed to sell the treasurership, he sought appointment as lieutenant of the admiralty. This office, which would allow him to retain his links with the navy, was also known as the vice-admiralty of England. Though little more than a sinecure, in status it ranked second only to that of lord admiral. It was duly conferred on Mansell in May 1618 by the young marquess of Buckingham, whom Mansell encouraged to seek appointment as lord admiral in succession to Nottingham. It seems likely that the main reason Buckingham lent his support was that Nottingham made Mansell's appointment a condition of his own resignation.

Over the next few years Mansell was questioned by the newly appointed navy commissioners regarding his accounts as treasurer, many of which he had failed to submit. A clause in his grant of the lieutenancy stipulated that he could not be dismissed for any offences he had previously committed, but he enjoyed no immunity from financial liability for any irregularities which the commissioners might expose. His response to the commissioners' demands was to present them with a bill for travelling expenses amounting to £10,000, which he alleged he had incurred as treasurer. This evidently achieved the desired result, as the commissioners, faced with such an enormous sum, discontinued their investigation, and Mansell's accounts were not finally declared until 1639. Mansell's victory over the commissioners coincided with his appointment in 1620 as admiral of a fleet which was charged by Buckingham, the new lord admiral, to suppress the pirate base at Algiers and free the prisoners held there. The fleet anchored off Algiers on 27 November and after some negotiation forty English captives were released. These, it was maintained, were all that they had, but though Mansell was aware that this was false, his crews were sick and his ships short of supplies. He therefore retired to Spain, returning to Algiers in May 1621. On 24 May he sent five or six fireships into the harbour, though only two of the corsairs' vessels were destroyed. Before Mansell could undertake a fresh assault he was recalled, as it was thought that his ships might be needed in the channel against the Dutch in the dispute triggered by repeated acts of violence against the English in the East Indies.

Parliamentary career During his absence in the Mediterranean Mansell's glass monopoly was condemned by parliament, despite the best efforts of his second wife, whom he had married on 11 March 1617. This was Elizabeth Roper (d. 1658), formerly his mistress and a maid of honour to the late Anne of Denmark. His grant was accordingly revoked in May 1623, but the privy council, noting that Mansell was 'a well deserving servant to his majesty' who had been 'abused in that business' (APC, 1621–3, 406–7), immediately awarded him a fresh patent on terms almost identical to the first. This new grant came under parliamentary attack in 1624, but this time Mansell was himself in the Commons, as knight of the shire for Glamorgan. He obtained an exemption for his patent from the Act of Monopolies, possibly because the Commons valued his views on the feasibility and cost of the forthcoming war with Spain, about which he spoke at length on 11 and 19 March. The government, too, held his long naval service in high regard, and before the parliament was adjourned Mansell was appointed to a newly established council of war. However, he soon grew disenchanted with the council's proceedings and in February 1625 he withdrew from its meetings.

Mansell bore one of the flags at the funeral of King James in May 1625. Returned for Glamorgan to the 1625 parliament, he took little part in its proceedings until 10 August, when, at the invitation of Sir Robert Phelips, he alleged that the council of war had not been properly consulted about strategic matters. Over the next couple of days he bitterly criticized the conduct of Buckingham as lord admiral. Not only had Buckingham ignored Mansell's advice, but he had chosen incompetent commanders for the king's ships and had left the narrow seas without adequate defence. Not surprisingly, his sharp outbursts caused him to be arraigned before the privy council on 14 August. In the event he was treated leniently, presumably because many of the duke's enemies were then present, among them the lord chamberlain, the earl of Pembroke, who by the beginning of the new year had enlisted Mansell in his power struggle with Buckingham. It was Pembroke's agent, William Coryton, who secured Mansell's return to parliament for Lostwithiel in January 1626. During the course of this parliament Mansell was prevented by his colleagues on the council of war from speaking openly regarding the advice that they had given to Buckingham, but he nevertheless renewed his former assault on the duke, whom he lambasted for having lent the French a number of ships the previous year and for failing to guard the narrow seas. Moreover, he supported the house's efforts to impeach Buckingham, and on 9 May he called for the duke to be imprisoned. There was now no possibility that he would escape punishment for his hostility to Buckingham, and on 3 May he was removed from the council of war. On 8 July, following the dissolution, he was also dismissed from the commissions of the peace for Norfolk and Kent.

These punishments, and the *rapprochement* between Pembroke and Buckingham effected after the 1626 parliament was dissolved, may have persuaded Mansell to moderate his criticism of the duke in the 1628 assembly, in which he again represented Glamorgan. Although he remained critical of the conduct of the war, which had been widened to include France, he was careful not to single out Buckingham for blame, and in early July, during the interval between parliamentary sessions, Mansell was reconciled with Buckingham after a two-hour meeting. This accommodation, which led to his restoration to the Kent commission of the peace, encouraged Mansell to hope that he would now be permitted to take a more active role in naval affairs, but this expectation was soon dashed. In the following month Buckingham was assassinated and his place taken by admiralty commissioners, among whom was Mansell's sworn enemy, Sir John Coke. Over the next ten years Mansell's naval duties were largely limited to the naming and launching of new ships, although he was consulted in 1633 over the size of the manning establishment and in 1635 over the proposed dimensions for the *Sovereign of Seas*. By the time the admiralty commissioners were replaced by the earl of Northumberland in April 1638, Mansell was in his late sixties and recovering from a mild stroke, which had left him temporarily paralysed down one side. It was because of his age that in June 1642 the king refused to entrust to him the task of seizing control of the Channel Fleet from the admiral appointed by parliament.

Mansell's Newcastle glassworks were disrupted by the English defeat at Newburn in August 1640, when many of his workmen fled south in fear of the victorious Scots. Later that year Mansell, who presumably feared a renewed assault in parliament on his glass monopoly, canvassed his neighbours in Kent (where he had been living since at least 1626) for a county seat in the Long Parliament, but he was obliged to abandon his candidacy for lack of support. Mansell's patent was subsequently challenged in a petition to the House of Lords in May 1641. While waiting to give evidence to the house, Mansell witnessed members of the Commons fleeing in panic after mistaking the sound of a board breaking for an explosion; though he drew his sword and cried 'stand for shame' (Fletcher, 27) he proved unable to stem the exodus. He was finally forced to surrender his glass patent in June 1642 after a London merchant complained that some of his chests of imported glass had been seized by Mansell, though this did not prevent him from continuing to manufacture glass.

Mansell played no active part in the civil war. The parish register of St Alfege, in East Greenwich, where he lived, indicates that he was buried on 21 August 1652, so it is difficult to explain why licences to export horses were issued in his name in October 1655. He died childless and intestate, letters of administration being granted on 26 June 1656 to his widow, who died in 1658. As a director of the New England Company in 1622 Mansell had sponsored the discovery of Mount Mansell, but his attempt to leave his mark on the map of North America was thwarted by Champlain, who subsequently renamed the mountain Mount Desert.   Andrew Thrush

Sources 'Mansell, Robert', HoP, *Commons, 1604–29* [draft] · N. M. Fuidge, 'Mansell, Sir Robert', HoP, *Commons, 1558–1603*, 3.11–12 · *CSP dom., 1595–1655* · APC, 1613–31 · PRO, HCA 13/30, fol. 187r–v · PRO, HCA 49/106, packet A, no. 65 · Hatfield House, MS 278 · S. Usherwood and E. Usherwood, *The counter-Armada, 1596: the journall of the Mary Rose* (1983), 147 · *The naval tracts of Sir William Monson*, ed. M. Oppenheim, 5 vols., Navy RS, 22–3, 43, 45, 47 (1902–14) · *The letters of John Chamberlain*, ed. N. E. McClure, 2 vols. (1939) · R. F. Dell, ed., *The Glynde Place archives: a catalogue* (1964), 55 · *Calendar of the manuscripts of the most hon. the marquess of Salisbury*, 15, HMC, 9 (1930) · PRO, C54/2374/10 · *The manuscripts of the Earl Cowper*, 3 vols., HMC, 23 (1888–9), vol. 1 · J. Nichols, *The progresses, processions, and magnificent festivities of King James I, his royal consort, family and court*, 4 vols. (1828) · A. P. McGowan, ed., *The Jacobean commissions of enquiry, 1608 and 1618*, Navy RS, 116 (1971) · *The autobiography of Phineas Pett*, ed. W. G. Perrin, Navy RS, 51 (1918) · *The manuscripts of his grace the duke of Portland*, 10 vols., HMC, 29 (1891–1931), vol. 9 · *The life and letters of Sir Henry Wotton*, ed. L. P. Smith, 2 (1907), 27–30 · *GM*, 1st ser., 96/1 (1826), 484 · M. Jansson, ed., *Proceedings in parliament, 1614 (House of Commons)* (1988) · W. Scott, ed., *Secret history of the court of James the First*, 2 vols. (1811), vol. 1 · PRO, E115/279/18 · 16 Oct 1643, PRO, SP 28/157 · D. Crossley, 'Sir William Clavell's glasshouse at Kimmeridge, Dorset', *Archaeological Journal*, 144 (1987), 340–83 · BL, Add. MS 12496, fol. 165 · *Cabala, sive, Scrinia sacra: mysteries of state and government in letters of illustrious persons*, 3rd edn (1691), 297–9 · W. Notestein, F. H. Relf, and H. Simpson, eds., *Commons debates, 1621*, 7 vols. (1935) · M. Jansson and W. B. Bidwell, eds.,

Proceedings in parliament, 1625 (1987) · W. B. Bidwell and M. Jansson, eds., *Proceedings in parliament, 1626*, 2–3: *House of Commons* (1992) · Som. ARS, Phelips MS, DD/PH 219/66 · R. C. Johnson and others, eds., *Proceedings in parliament, 1628*, 6 vols. (1977–83) · J. R. Tanner, ed., *Holland's discourses of the navy*, Navy Records Society, 7 (1896), 392 · G. Radcliffe, *The earl of Strafforde's letters and dispatches, with an essay towards his life*, ed. W. Knowler, 1 (1739), 1.422 · Clarendon, *Hist. rebellion*, 2.219 · A. Fletcher, *The outbreak of the English civil war* (1981), 27 · L. B. Larking, ed., *Proceedings principally in the county of Kent in connection with the parliaments called in 1640, and especially with the committee of religion appointed in that year*, CS, old ser., 80 (1862), 15, 17 · JHC, 1 (1547–1628) · JHC, 2 (1640–42), 527a, 533b, 534a, 600b · parish register, St Alfege, Greenwich, LMA · PRO, PROB 6/32, fol. 132v · J. P. Baxter, ed., *Sir Ferdinando Gorges and his province of Maine*, 1 (1890), 208 · J. W. Kirby, *Royal subsidy of 1641 and the levy of 1644 on the hundred of Blackheath, Kent*, Greenwich and Lewisham Antiquarian Society (1913), 85
Archives BL, corresp. with Sir Walter Aston, Add. MSS 36444–36445
Likenesses oils, Penrice Castle, Glamorgan [*see illus.*]

Mansell, Sir Thomas (1777–1858), naval officer, third son of Thomas Mansell of Guernsey, was born at Guernsey on 9 February 1777. He entered the navy in January 1793, on the frigate *Crescent* with his fellow Guernsey man Captain James Saumarez. He followed Saumarez to the *Orion*, in which he was present in Lord Bridport's action off Lorient, and at the battles of Cape St Vincent and the Nile, after which he was promoted by Nelson acting-lieutenant of the *Aquilon* (confirmed by the Admiralty to 17 April 1799). He subsequently served in the channel and on the French coast, and at the capture of the Cape of Good Hope, whence he was sent home by Sir Home Popham in command of an armed transport. On 1 November 1806 he married Catherine, daughter of John Lukis, a merchant of Guernsey: they had four daughters and four sons.

Mansell was flag-lieutenant to Sir James Saumarez in the *Diomede*, *Hibernia*, and *Victory*, and on 17 September 1808 was promoted to the command of the sloop *Rose*, in which he took part in the capture of Anholt in the Baltic on 18 May 1809, and was at different times engaged with the Danish gunboats. In 1812 the tsar presented him a diamond ring, for piloting a Russian squadron through the Belt; and the king of Sweden awarded him the order of the Sword. In 1813 Mansell commanded the brig *Pelican* (18 guns) on the north coast of Spain, and on 7 June 1814 was promoted captain. Reportedly while commanding the *Rose* and *Pelican* he captured at least 170 vessels, some of them powerful privateers. In 1837 he was nominated a KCH and knighted. On 9 October 1849 he became a rear-admiral on the retired list. After the death of his first wife Mansell married a daughter of John Wood of Guernsey. He died at Guernsey on 22 April 1858. His sons almost all entered the navy or marines. The second, Arthur Lukis, for some years commanded the surveying ship *Firefly* in the Mediterranean, and died, a retired vice-admiral, in 1890.

      J. K. Laughton, *rev.* Andrew Lambert

Sources D. Syrett and R. L. DiNardo, *The commissioned sea officers of the Royal Navy, 1660–1815*, rev. edn, Occasional Publications of the Navy RS, 1 (1994) · *The Saumarez papers: selections from the Baltic correspondence of Vice-Admiral Sir James Saumarez, 1808–1812*, ed. A. N.

Ryan, Navy RS, 110 (1968) · *Memoirs and correspondence of Admiral Lord de Saumarez*, ed. J. Ross, 2 vols. (1838) · O'Byrne, *Naval biog. dict.* · Boase, *Mod. Eng. biog.* · *Dod's Peerage* (1858) · *CGPLA Eng. & Wales* (1858)
Archives States of Guernsey Island Archives Service, St Peter Port, corresp. and papers
Wealth at death under £5000: administration, 1 June 1858, *CGPLA Eng. & Wales*

Mansergh, James (1834–1905), civil engineer, was born on 29 April 1834 at Lancaster, the second son of John Birkett Mansergh, a draper and local politician and philanthropist. After being educated locally and at Preston, he was sent in 1847 to Queenwood College, Hampshire, where John Tyndall and Edward Frankland were among the teachers. Mansergh and his classmate Henry Fawcett edited together the *Queenwood Chronicle*.

In 1849 Mansergh was apprenticed to Hugh Unsworth McKie and John Lawson, engineers, of Lancaster. In 1855–9 he worked in Brazil as engineer to E. Price, the contractor for a short line of railway extending inland from Rio de Janeiro. On his return to England he became a partner of his former master, McKie, then city engineer in Carlisle, where they laid out the first sewage farm in England, and were contractors for a sewage scheme for West Ham. The latter was a financial disaster for Mansergh and the partnership was dissolved. From 1862 to 1865 Mansergh was engaged as contractor's agent for John Watson & Co. on the construction of the Mid-Wales and the Llandeilo and Carmarthen railways. On 7 July 1859 he married Mary (*d.* 1897), daughter of Robert Lawson of Skirton, Lancashire. Together they had two sons, Ernest (*b.* 1866) and Walter Leahy (*b.* 1871), and two daughters.

In 1866 Mansergh entered into partnership with his brother-in-law, John Lawson, who was then associated with Robert Rawlinson. Lawson died in 1873, and thenceforward Mansergh practised alone until he took his two sons into partnership in 1897. Mansergh specialized chiefly in waterworks, and in sewerage and sewage-disposal plants. His greatest work was the Birmingham water supply scheme. He identified mid-Wales as a potential source of supply to the corporation of Birmingham in 1870–71 and repeated his advice in 1890. The corporation obtained powers to construct impounding reservoirs in the valleys of the Elan and Claerwen rivers, and an aqueduct 73½ miles in length to convey the water to Birmingham. The work was commenced in 1894, and the supply was inaugurated by Edward VII and Queen Alexandra on 21 July 1904. The scheme provided 75 million gallons per day for the use of Birmingham and district, and 27 million gallons of compensation water per day to the River Wye. The total cost approached £6 million.

Mansergh also carried out sewerage and sewage-disposal for Southport, Burton upon Trent, Coventry, Derby, and Plymouth, and water supply works for Lancaster, Stockton, Middlesbrough, and many other places, and generally supported municipal ownership of waterworks. His consulting practice and parliamentary work was vast. He appeared more than 600 times before parliamentary

James Mansergh (1834–1905), by William Mainwaring Palin, 1900

committees, acted for 360 municipalities or local authorities, wrote more than 250 reports on sewerage and waterworks alone, and gave evidence at about 300 public inquiries.

Mansergh's practice and reputation were international. In 1884 he visited the United States and reported on Philadelphia's water supply. In 1889 he reported to the government of Victoria on the sewerage of Melbourne; in 1895 on the supply of water for the city of Toronto; and in the same year on the sewerage of Colombo, Ceylon. In 1898 he reported on Budapest's sewerage, and subsequently on water supply and sewerage schemes as far afield as Cape Town, Port Elizabeth, Naples, Antigua, Malta, and Singapore. He prepared two schemes for the sewerage of the lower Thames valley; the first, in 1878, was awarded one of three premiums, while the second (prepared in conjunction with J. C. Melliss) was defeated in parliament. He was a member of the royal commission on metropolitan water supply in 1892–3, and supported the Local Government Board in the London Water Transfer Bill, 1902.

Mansergh had become fond of mid-Wales while working there in the 1860s. He acquired a property, Bryngwy, at Rhayader in Radnorshire, and was high sheriff of the county in 1901–2 and a JP there from December 1902. He was presented with the freedom of his native city of Lancaster in March 1903. He was elected FRS in 1901. He joined the Institution of Civil Engineers in 1859, and was president for 1900–01. His presidential address was a history of waterworks engineering. His lectures on water supply at the School of Military Engineering, Chatham, given in 1882, were published as a book. He was president of the engineering congress held in connection with the Glasgow exhibition of 1901. He was also a member of the Institution of Mechanical Engineers, and served on its council from 1902. He was chairman of the Engineering Standards Committee (the forerunner of the British Standards Institution) from its inception in 1901 until his death. His first wife died in 1897 and in September 1898 he married the widow of Nelson Elvey Irons of Tunbridge Wells.

Mansergh died at his home, 51 Fitzjohn's Avenue, Hampstead, on 15 June 1905, and was buried in Hampstead cemetery. W. F. SPEAR, rev. MIKE CHRIMES

Sources *PICE*, 161 (1904-5), 350-54 · *Engineering* (16 June 1905), 777-9 · *The Engineer* (16 June 1905), 605 · *The Times* (16 June 1905) · *Institution of Mechanical Engineers: Proceedings* (1905), 781-3 · d. cert. · d. cert. [Mary Mansergh] · m. cert. [Mary Lawson]
Archives Inst. CE, membership records
Likenesses W. M. Palin, oils, 1900, Inst. CE [*see illus.*] · T. Kell & Sons, photogravure (after a photograph by T. Fall), repro. in *PICE*, 143 (1901) · W. M. Palin, oils, Lancaster Museum and Art Gallery · photograph, repro. in *The Engineer* (16 June 1905) · photograph, repro. in *Engineering* (16 June 1905)
Wealth at death £103,641 7s. 6d.: probate, 17 July 1905, *CGPLA Eng. & Wales*

Mansergh, (Philip) Nicholas Seton (1910–1991), historian, was born into a middle-ranking Anglo-Irish gentry family on 27 June 1910 at Grenane House, Tipperary, Ireland. He was the second son of Philip St George Mansergh (1863–1928), railway engineer, and his cousin Ethel Marguerite Otway Louise Mansergh (1876–1963). Educated at the Abbey School, Tipperary, and St Columba's College, Dublin (1923–9), he entered Pembroke College, Oxford, in 1929, where he read modern history under R. B. McCallum. Despite a disappointing failure to get a first, he began postgraduate research under W. G. S. Adams, the Gladstone professor of political theory and institutions, who shared his particular interest in Ireland. Mansergh's work for the BLitt (1933) and DPhil (1936) was published in a pair of pioneering 'political science' books: *The Irish Free State: its Government and Politics* (1934) and *The Government of Northern Ireland: a Study in Devolution* (1936). In 1937 he was appointed tutor (but not fellow) in politics at Pembroke, a post which enabled him to produce a major work entitled *Ireland in the Age of Reform and Revolution* (1940, later reissued and expanded as *The Irish Question, 1840–1921*). At the same time he was secretary to the Oxford University politics research group under Sir Arthur Salter, which proved to be a useful experience.

Meanwhile Mansergh was looking for a mixed-doubles partner in tennis, a game at which he excelled. The search resulted in marriage to Diana Mary Keeton (an undergraduate at Lady Margaret Hall, daughter of the headmaster of Reading School) on 12 December 1939. Their long and happy partnership produced five children (three sons and two daughters), while Diana also acted as his devoted research assistant until his death, and beyond.

During the Second World War, Mansergh became the Irish expert and director of the empire division of the Ministry of Information (leading to his appointment as OBE), and then an assistant secretary at the Dominions Office (1946–7). Despite his natural gifts as a civil servant,

(Philip) Nicholas Seton Mansergh (1910–1991), by Elliott & Fry, 1950

he returned to academic life in 1947 as a research professor at the Royal Institute of International Affairs. In 1953 he moved to Cambridge as the first Smuts professor of the history of the British Commonwealth.

Nicholas Mansergh was a striking figure, lean and tall, 6 feet 3 inches and inclined to stoop, until spinal osteoarthritis developed in old age. With a huge head and heavy spectacles, he was the very model of a professorial archetype. He had a prominent mole on his left cheek and outsize fingernails. He had a ready smile, which regularly punctuated even the driest of his lecture material, and which reinforced the general impression of an unfailing good humour and kindliness, a man who enjoyed life. He was slow and deliberate of utterance, curiously adding an 'a' or 'ah' sound after dental consonants in a way which was all too easily (if affectionately) imitated. His speech was not always easy to follow, either, as he tended to talk in hushed tones about anything remotely important, and to drop the ends of his sentences. And what he had to say was invariably cautious and guarded. All the more astonishing, then, that at fellows' lunch in St John's during the Suez crisis of 1956, he should cut short mystified attempts to justify government policy, with the loud, imperious observation, 'I shall never vote conservative again-ah'.

But in general there was a diffidence in discussion, a reticence in answering questions, a reluctance to commit himself in public either to an opinion or a decision, which contrasted sharply with the fluency, confidence, sense of direction, and even stylistic adventurousness which pervaded his prolific written output. Between 1952 and 1983 (essentially to 1974), he published a two-volume *Survey of British Commonwealth Affairs* covering the years 1931 to 1952, three volumes of supporting *Documents and Speeches*, four books on Commonwealth history (including a keenly felt study of British South African policy), three revised new editions of earlier books, two major lecture-booklets, some three dozen articles, and, as editor-in-chief, the twelve magnificent and highly acclaimed volumes of documents, *Transfer of Power in India, 1942–7* (*TOPI*), which appeared from 1970 at the rate of one a year. In many ways the centrepiece of his *œuvre* was *The Commonwealth Experience* (1969; new edn, 1982), covering the years from 1839 to the present; more than one of its chapters were masterly examples of the art of writing history. In retirement he completed *The Unresolved Question: the Anglo-Irish Settlement and its Undoing, 1912–72* (published posthumously, 1991), an unrivalled and humane analysis of contemporary problems in his beloved Ireland, the first major synthesis of Anglo-Irish relations in the wider Commonwealth context, which he understood better than anyone. If in his writing about Commonwealth history, Mansergh retained what was often described as an Olympian detachment, in Irish history this was much harder. As a boy of eight in co. Tipperary he had heard the shots which killed two policemen at Soloheadbeg on 29 January 1919 and which heralded the opening of the War of Independence; for him, the events of Irish history were experienced as 'near realities, not as distant phenomena or as issues in high politics' (*The Unresolved Question*, 3).

As a Cambridge professor (1953–70) Mansergh was notably—and successfully—concerned to raise the profile of the study of both Irish and Commonwealth history; he travelled widely (frequently to Canada and New Delhi, but also to Canberra, Duke, and Cape Town); he cared deeply about his pupils and knew exactly how to help and encourage them. As master of St John's College (1969–79)—to which office he was elected after fourteen years as a fellow—he was well regarded as a patient and courteous 'safe pair of hands'; he was dignified but never pompous, hospitable rather than managerial. At meetings he was perhaps overscrupulous in making sure all views were fully expressed, except his own; it is not the way to guarantee the swift dispatch of business and his chairmanship had its critics. As a contemporary historian his achievements were impressive and influential. The *TOPI* documents should ensure the name of Mansergh an enduring place in learned references. He contributed uniquely to the understanding of what an apparently nebulous Commonwealth actually was, and *The Commonwealth Experience* is widely recognized as the finest book on the subject, exemplifying that 'detachment with sympathetic insight' which he always aimed at. His contributions to modern Irish history place him among its most accomplished and fair-minded practitioners too.

He obtained an Oxford DLitt in 1960 and a fellowship of the British Academy in 1973. He was an honorary fellow of Pembroke College, Oxford (1954), and Trinity College, Dublin (1971). He was presented with a Festschrift in 1980 (*The First British Commonwealth: Essays in Honour of Nicholas Mansergh*, ed. N. Hillmer and P. Wigley).

As he grew older, Mansergh neatly substituted 'lawn mowing' for 'lawn tennis' as his hobby in *Who's Who*. He died at Brookfields Hospital, Cambridge, on 16 January 1991, from pneumonia which set in at the end of a prolonged period of ill health precipitated by a fall on an escalator of the London underground. He was buried on 26 January in the new cemetery, Cashel Road, in his native Tipperary, at a Church of Ireland funeral attended by representatives of all Ireland and many walks of life. The taoiseach, Charles Haughey, read the lesson, a symbolic signal that Mansergh will be remembered as a scholar who tried to bring reconciliation to Ireland.   R. Hyam

Sources D. W. Harkness, 'Philip Nicholas Seton Mansergh, 1910–1991', *PBA*, 82 (1993), 415–30 · F. H. H. [F. H. Hinsley], 'Professor Nicholas Mansergh', *The Eagle* (1991), 35–9 · W. K. Hancock, 'Nicholas Mansergh: some recollections and reflections', *The first British commonwealth: essays in honour of Nicholas Mansergh*, ed. N. Hillmer and P. Wigley (1980), 3–9 · *The Times* (18 Jan 1991) · *The Independent* (18 Jan 1991) · *Irish Times* (25 Jan 1991) · *The Guardian* (31 Jan 1991) · personal knowledge (2004) · private information (2004) [Diana Mansergh]

Likenesses Elliott & Fry, photograph, 1950, NPG [*see illus.*] · W. Narraway, oils, 1973, St John Cam.

Wealth at death £418,058: probate, 24 July 1991, *CGPLA Eng. & Wales*

Mansfield. For this title name *see* Murray, William, first earl of Mansfield (1705–1793); Murray, David, seventh Viscount Stormont and second earl of Mansfield (1727–1796).

Mansfield, Charles Blachford (1819–1855), chemist and traveller, was born on 8 May 1819 at Rowner, near Gosport, Hampshire, the son of John Mansfield, rector at Rowner, and Winifred, eldest daughter of Robert Pope Blachford of Osborne House, Isle of Wight. His younger brother, Robert Blachford *Mansfield (1824–1908) became a sportsman and barrister. Although they lived comfortably, the Mansfields do not seem to have been a happy family. Charles Mansfield was educated first at a private school at Twyford, and afterwards at Winchester College (1831–5), which he detested. At the age of sixteen his health broke down from what seems to have been poliomyelitis, which left him partially deaf and with a stiff arm. In consequence he passed a year with a private tutor in Northamptonshire, where his scientific interests were encouraged by the marquess of Northampton, a council member of the Royal Society. On 23 November 1836 he entered his name at Clare College, Cambridge, but was unable to take up residence until October 1839. Owing to frequent absences due to ill health, and intellectual and social diversions he did not graduate BA until 1846, then MA in 1849. During these years, he read widely and through his charisma rapidly gathered many friends around him. With Charles *Kingsley, who was a contemporary at Cambridge, Mansfield formed a lifelong friendship. Only gradually did such friends learn of Mansfield's secret life, and how to help him during periodic bouts of melancholic depression. Despite earlier illness he had grown into a handsome, athletic young man who easily attracted the opposite sex. On 3 February 1842 he secretly married a widow, Catherine Shafto, daughter of a London merchant, William Warne Higgs, but they separated immediately. He was never able to divorce her and had many love affairs.

A medical career attracted Mansfield for a time, and while still at Cambridge he attended some classes at St George's Hospital in London. However, when he settled in London in 1846 he decided to devote himself to chemistry, while occupying his leisure with a diversity of interests ranging from natural history and mesmerism (he hypnotized Kingsley during the composition of *Yeast*), to abstruse studies in medieval science. Chemistry, he decided, was the central science for a system of quasi-Platonic knowledge that he had already worked out for himself, whose aim would be 'the comprehension of the harmonious plan or order on which the universe is constructed—an order on which rests the belief that the universe is truly a representation to *our* ideas of a Divine Idea, and is in fact a visible symbol of thoughts working in a mind infinitely wise and good' (C. B. Mansfield, *A Theory of Salts*, 1865, ix).

In 1848, after completing the chemistry course at the Royal College of Chemistry, Mansfield undertook, at the request of its director, A. W. Hofmann, a series of experiments which resulted in the fractional distillation of impure benzene, toluene, and xylene from coal tar, and the development of procedures for the large-scale conversion of benzene into nitrobenzene. In premises in Hanover Square, close to the Royal College of Chemistry, he manufactured aniline for Hofmann's researches and helped him prepare scientific papers and reports. The extraction method, which he patented in May 1848 (no. 11,960), effectively laid the foundation of the European coal tar and dyestuffs industries though others were to reap the profits. In 1849 he published a pamphlet, *Benzole, its Nature and its Utility*, to indicate what he foresaw as some of the most important applications of benzene. These included perfuming soaps, urban illumination, surgical plasters, and dry-cleaning.

During the critical cholera years of 1848–9, when Chartism appeared likely to promote political disruption, Mansfield became a Christian socialist, joining J. F. D. Maurice, Kingsley, J. M. Ludlow, Nevil Story Maskelyne, and others in their efforts at social reform among the workmen of London, supporting these efforts financially, and helping to provide pure water for districts like Bermondsey, where every drop was sewage-tainted. He wrote several articles in *Politics for the People*, edited by Maurice and Ludlow, and afterwards in the *Christian Socialist*, and he was strongly supportive of the group's efforts to create a working men's college in 1854. In September 1850 an account of a balloon inflating machine constructed in Paris led him to investigate aeronautics, and in the next few months (following correspondence with Sir George Cayley), he wrote his *Aerial Navigation*, an original and suggestive work that appeared posthumously in 1877. In addition, he published a Utopian fantasy on space travel in *Fraser's Magazine*. In

the winter of 1851–2 he delivered a Royal Institution lecture course on the chemistry of metals, which apart from remarkable generalizations, contained strange triadic speculations concerning chemical classification which were published posthumously as *A Theory of Salts* in 1865, by which time the theory of chemical structure had superseded it.

In the summer of 1852 Mansfield started for Paraguay, partly 'to gratify a whim of wishing to see the country, which I believed to be an unspoiled Arcadia' (C. B. Mansfield, *Paraguay, Brazil and the Plate*, 1856, 8), but also to escape a sexual entanglement with a working-class woman that had shocked his Christian socialist friends. He arrived at Buenos Aires in August, and having obtained permission from Urquiza, the leader of the Argentine confederation, to sail up the River Paraná, he reached Asunción on 24 November, where he remained two and a half months. Paraguay, under José Francia and his successor Carlos Lopez, had been shut off from the world for forty years, and Mansfield was, if not the first English visitor to the capital, certainly the first to go there merely to take notes. His letters, published after his death, contained bright and careful descriptions of Paraguayan society, the scenery, plant and bird life, and a scheme for the colonization of the Gran Chaco, a dream that remained with him for the remainder of his life. A sketch of the history of Paraguay, valuable for the period immediately preceding and following his arrival, formed the conclusion to his letters. Other letters (all originally addressed to Kingsley, Ludlow, and Maskelyne), printed in the same volume, dealt in a similar manner with Brazil. These were translated into Portuguese by Pascual, and published at Rio de Janeiro together with critical essays on Mansfield's narrative, the first volume in 1861, the second in 1862.

Mansfield returned to England in the spring of 1853, resumed his chemical studies, and began a book on the constitution of salts based upon his Royal Institution lectures. He also took up the study of law in emulation of his brother, and became involved in controversy with the manufacturing chemist F. C. Crace Calvert over the validity of Mansfield's 1848 patent. In his private life he became entangled with Mary Ellen Meredith, the unhappy wife of the writer George Meredith. Meanwhile, Hofmann had invited him to prepare specimens of pure benzene for the Paris Exhibition, and on 17 February 1855, while preparing these in a building he had hired for the purposes by the Regent's Canal, a naphtha still overflowed and a benzene/air mixture explosion occurred. Mansfield, in attempting to save the premises by carrying the blazing still into the street, was horribly burned, and died nine days later on 26 February in the Middlesex Hospital, surrounded by friends. He was buried in Weybridge churchyard. His tragic death, with so many of his talents unfulfilled, affected his friends emotionally for several years to come. Even in death his private life continued to embarrass them, for Mansfield left his fortune to a former lover, a Mrs Burrows, *née* Gardiner, even though she had subsequently married another man; she declined the bequest.

Vegetarian, teetotaller, and mesmerist, brilliant conversationalist, and eccentric, Mansfield possessed a personality which dazzled all who fell into his company. His works, published at various intervals after his death by his brother, Kingsley, and Maskelyne, are unfortunately mere fragments to which he had not added the finishing touch, yet each bore the unmistakable impress of a polymathic mind of the highest order. The private testimony of those who knew him well, such as Kingsley, Ludlow, and Maskelyne, confirmed Hofmann's commemoration of Mansfield as 'this highly-gifted young chemist and noble-hearted young man. In him science has lost one of its most ardent and most promising cultivators' (*Report of Juries 1862 Exhibition*, 123).

W. H. BROCK

Sources *Discovery*, 16 (Aug 1955), 322–3 · E. R. Ward, 'Charles Blachford Mansfield, 1819–1855: coal tar chemist and social reformer', *Chemistry and Industry* (25 Oct 1969), 1530–37 · E. R. Ward, 'Eminent Victorian: Charles Mansfield', *Chemistry in Britain*, 15 (1979), 297–304 · E. R. Ward, 'Mansfield and the Merediths: three Victorian intellectuals', *Hampshire Field Club and Archaeological Society: Section Newsletter*, new ser., 7 (1987), 1–3 · E. R. Ward, 'The death of Mansfield', *Ambix*, 31 (1984), 68–9 · T. Christensen, *The origins and history of Christian socialism* (1962) · N. C. Masterman, *John Malcolm Ludlow: the builder of Christian socialism* (1963)
Archives Isle of Wight RO, Newport, papers · U. Southampton L., letters and papers | CUL, corresp. with Ludlow, Add. 7348/9.207–215 · Hants. RO, Blachford MSS
Likenesses L. Dickinson, drawing, repro. in C. B. Mansfield, *Paraguay, Brazil and the Plate: letters written in 1852–1853* (1856) · N. S. Maskelyne, photograph, repro. in V. Morton, *Oxford rebels* (1987), 109
Wealth at death approx. £10,000; left to, but refused by, his former mistress: Ward, 'Mansfield and the Merediths'

Mansfield, Edward Dillon (1845–1924), headmaster, was born on 12 February 1845, at Bathwick, Bath, Somerset, the eldest son of the Revd Joseph Mansfield, rector of Blandford St Mary, Dorset, and his wife, Emily (*née* le Poer Trench). He entered Marlborough College in August 1856, joining C.I. house (the former 'Castle Inn' before the school's development). He left Marlborough in September 1864 and in the following month entered Trinity College, Oxford, where his father had been a member. He obtained a pass BA in 1867 (MA 1877). Mansfield became an assistant master at Clifton College, Bristol, in 1874. Appointed third form master, he became in the same year the inaugural master of the preparatory school, a post he held until 1883 when he left to become headmaster of Lambrook School, Bracknell, a private preparatory school founded by R. J. Burnside in 1860. He married Muriel Edith Campbell-Ross; Sir John Maurice *Mansfield was their son.

Mansfield's success at Lambrook, where he set out to test his ideas of education, established his reputation among his fellow preparatory school headmasters. He was an outstanding leader in the affairs of the Association of Preparatory Schools (APS), the precursor of the Incorporated Association of Preparatory Schools, where he promoted his liberal and progressive ideas in the teaching of young boys. A sturdy champion of the reform of the curriculum and a critic of too early specialization, he played an important role in the negotiations with the public

schools for the institution of the common entrance examination in 1904, being appointed with Herbert Bull to represent the APS on its board of management. It has been said that 'if Frank Ritchie [headmaster of the Beacon school, Sevenoaks] devised the machinery of the examination, Mansfield was the guiding spirit'. With the help of Charles Darnell (of Cargilfield School, Edinburgh) he was also responsible for the setting up, in 1897, of the Oxford diploma course, run by M. W. Keatinge for the training of preparatory-school masters who were without a qualification.

Opinion varies concerning Mansfield's personality: he was said by some to be aloof but by others he was seen to be good with both boys and staff, showing understanding of their problems but showing 'no mercy to the shirker and evil doer'. His teaching was of a high quality, being lucid in explanation, and he was capable of understanding boys' rudimentary problems. He was not in favour of the boys' use of translations and was himself a well-known writer of school books. He co-edited with Evelyn Abbott, a fellow Cliftonian master, a Greek grammar (1877), which went through several editions. He was a keen sportsman and played with, and coached, his boys at both cricket and rugby football, which he regarded as 'the cure for all boyish ailments'. He was also a craftsman, and expert at wood-carving; he ensured that the boys, through the school curriculum, were encouraged to work in wood.

Mansfield retired from Lambrook School in 1904 and threw himself into local politics, becoming an alderman of Berkshire county council and a member of its education committee. He sat on governing bodies of secondary schools and the council of the University of Reading. He died on 10 November 1924 at his home at Pucks Wood, Finchampstead, Berkshire, survived by his wife.

DONALD P. LEINSTER-MACKAY

Sources *Preparatory Schools Review* (June 1925), 142 · [A. H. Wall and D. E. Wall], eds., *Marlborough College register from 1843 to 1933*, 8th edn (1936) · J. A. O. Muirhead, ed., *Clifton College register, 1862–1947* (1948) · D. P. Leinster-Mackay, *The rise of the English prep school* (1984) · W. F. Bushell, *School memories* (1962) · CGPLA Eng. & Wales (1925)
Wealth at death £23,540 11s. 11d.: probate, 16 Jan 1925, CGPLA Eng. & Wales

Mansfield [*formerly* Manfield], **Sir James** (bap. 1734, d. 1821), judge, was baptized at Ringwood, Hampshire, on 30 May 1734, the son of John James Manfield, attorney, of Ringwood, and his wife, Elizabeth. His grandfather was reputedly of foreign descent and was at one time employed in Windsor Castle. Little is known of his personal life, and while most sources state that he never married it is known that he fathered at least five children. He attended Eton College between 1745 and 1750, when he entered King's College, Cambridge, as a scholar. At university he changed his surname from Manfield to Mansfield, and in 1754 was elected a fellow of King's. He graduated BA in 1755 and proceeded MA in 1758.

Like his father Mansfield pursued a career in law. On 11 February 1755 he was admitted at the Middle Temple and on 28 November 1758 he was called to the bar. As a lawyer he acquired prestige and success, and practised at common law as well as in chancery. When John Wilkes returned to England in 1768 Mansfield was appointed one of his counsel and argued in the court of king's bench, albeit unsuccessfully, in favour of Wilkes's application for bail on the grounds that he had been outlawed improperly. He was appointed king's counsel on 24 July 1772 and a bencher of the Middle Temple on 6 November 1772. He was involved in numerous trials, including that of Elizabeth Chudleigh, duchess of Kingston, for bigamy, in 1776, and in the same year that of the four candidates who had stood for parliament at Hindon in 1774, for bribery. He was also defence counsel, in 1777, for James Aitken (John the Painter), the pro-American arsonist who torched naval stores at Portsmouth and warehouses at the port of Bristol, and appeared as crown prosecutor in 1779 against George Stratton and others who took over the administration of Fort St George (Madras) without authorization in 1776.

Mansfield's ability drew interest from political patrons. In 1776 the earl of Carlisle offered to bring him into the Commons for Morpeth but Mansfield declined, as he was hoping for judicial office, which would preclude his sitting in the Commons. In 1778 Lord North, considering the appointment of a new attorney-general and solicitor-general, suggested Mansfield and James Wallace to George III as 'the gentlemen who stand foremost, are sensible men and good lawyers' (Christie), though he doubted the potential of both as parliamentarians. Mansfield was not appointed on this occasion. He eventually stood for the Commons at Cambridge University in 1779, supported by the chancellor (the former prime minister Grafton) against the government candidate, but after his election he voted with North's administration. On 1 September 1780, following Wallace's promotion to attorney-general, he was appointed solicitor-general. In this role he took part in the government's prosecution of Lord George Gordon for high treason in 1781.

Mansfield left office in April 1782, following the resignation of North, and opposed the Rockingham and Shelburne administrations. William Eden observed in September 1782 that he was 'very earnest for the demolition of Lord Shelburne's Government at any rate, and yet he has not fallen in love with Fox' (Christie). In November 1783 he was returned briefly to office in the coalition between North and Charles James Fox, but the ministry was dismissed in December of that year and Mansfield was again forced into opposition. His parliamentary career ended in April 1784, when he was defeated at the general election, and while his oratory achievements in parliament are not distinguished, the *English Chronicle* in 1781 described him as 'a man of keen but not elegant parts—he speaks with point, labour and precision, but without any of those graces which give energy to talents and make eloquence pleasing, as well as instructing' (ibid.).

Mansfield returned to his legal career. In 1782 he had been elected reader at the Middle Temple and in 1785 he was elected treasurer. In 1795 he and John Scott, subsequently lord chancellor and earl of Eldon, represented the fellows of Trinity Hall, Cambridge, in Francis Wrangham's appeal against the fellows' decision not to elect Wrangham to a fellowship. The argument turned upon the proper construction of the words 'idoneus moribus et ingenio' in the college statutes, and Wrangham's counsel cited Terence, Horace, and other Latin authors to prove that 'mores', as applied to an individual, could only mean morals. Mansfield successfully argued that 'mores' referred to manners and character, quoting a line from Ovid describing two mistresses—'Hæc specie melior, moribus illa fuit'—and Wrangham lost his appeal. He was also counsel for the plaintiffs, with Samuel Romilly, in the case of *Thellusson* v. *Woodford*, in 1797, which established that there was no distinction in law between trusts designed to prevent the alienation of property by creating a series of limited interests preventing the vesting of property in an absolute owner in the future, and a trust for accumulation designed to restrict the uses of inherited property by heirs.

Mansfield was appointed chief justice of Chester in July 1799 and chief justice of the common pleas on 24 April 1804, when he was knighted. He also became a serjeant-at-law, taking the motto 'serus in cœlum redeas', alluding to his exclusion from office. As a judge he was known for 'an ungraceful delivery and a husky voice' (*DNB*) and for his unsteady temper, which was easily exploited in court for the amusement of counsel, rather than for the high quality of his judgments. However, a merchant, Joseph Minet, told Joseph Farington that Mansfield 'preserved High Authority in the Court of Common Pleas by his superior knowledge of Law, which was such that in Chancery Lord Eldon was afraid of Him, & was glad to have him appointed to the Chief Justiceship' (Farington, *Diary*, 6.2428). He enjoyed shooting, and on circuit liked to rise at five 'to kill something before breakfast' (*DNB*). In 1806 he was the Grenville ministry's next choice after Edward Law, first Baron Ellenborough, for the lord chancellorship, but like Ellenborough he refused. He opposed the bill in 1807 that prevented the crown granting reversions to office. As chief justice he upheld the earlier rulings by William Murray, earl of Mansfield, that a moral obligation should count as a valuable consideration in contract law, in the cases *Barnes* v. *Hedley* (1809) and *Lee* v. *Muggeridge* (1813). On 15 May 1812 he presided over the trial of John Bellingham for the murder of Spencer Perceval. There he instructed the jury that Bellingham's belief that Perceval was the cause of his mistreatment by the authorities was a '"fancy" and his consequent behaviour "an opportunity to gratify revenge"' (Eigen, 54); unlike the insane, Mansfield argued, Bellingham was able to act rationally and could distinguish right from wrong.

Mansfield resigned on 21 February 1814, on account of ill health. It is clear that he had been a better legal practitioner than a parliamentarian but Sir Nathaniel Wraxall described him as a man 'of acknowledged talents, parliamentary no less than professional' and as one who 'manifested great energies of mind and character' (Christie). He died on 23 May 1821 at his house in Russell Square, London, having instructed, through his will, that all his personal papers be burnt following his death.

MICHAEL T. DAVIS

Sources DNB · I. R. Christie, 'Mansfield, James', HoP, Commons, 1754–90 · J. Barrell, Imagining the King's death: figurative treason, fantasies of regicide 1793–1796 (2000) · Venn, Alum. Cant. · will, PRO, PROB 11/1651, sig. 179 · Holdsworth, Eng. law, 13.532–5; 7.228–31 · J. P. Eigen, Witnessing insanity: madness and mad-doctors in the English court (1995) · S. Romilly, Memoirs of the life of Sir Samuel Romilly, 3 vols. (1840) · Farington, Diary, 6.2428 · Sainty, Judges · Sainty, King's counsel · Foss, Judges, 8.332–5 · IGI
Likenesses C. Turner, mezzotint, pubd 1825 (after H. Edridge), BM, NPG · J. Sayers, aquatint caricature (The master of the inn confers the order of knighthood on Don Quixote), NPG

Mansfield, Sir John Maurice (1893–1949), naval officer, was born on 22 December 1893 in Winkfield Row, Lambrook, Bracknell, Berkshire, the son of Edward Dillon *Mansfield (1845–1924), headmaster, and his wife, Muriel Edith Campbell-Ross. He entered the Royal Navy in 1906 and after passing through the Royal Naval College at Osborne and Dartmouth went to sea in 1911. The outbreak of war in 1914 found him a sub-lieutenant in the cruiser *Warrior* until, in 1915, he joined the Submarine Service where he remained for the next six years, being awarded the DSC in 1917. In 1916 he married Alice Talbot, who survived him, daughter of Commander Gerard Talbot Napier RN. They had one daughter and one son who also entered the navy.

Mansfield served in battleships, as flag lieutenant-commander to the admiral commanding the coast of Scotland, and as executive officer of the cruiser *Cairo*, on the America and West Indies station. Promoted to commander on 30 June 1929, he commanded a destroyer division in the Mediterranean, and in 1931–2 attended the courses at the Royal Naval Staff College at Greenwich and the Royal Air Force Staff College at Andover, after which he was appointed executive officer of the aircraft-carrier *Courageous*. His varied early experience was invaluable in developing his career, and he was promoted to captain on 30 June 1934, at the age of forty.

There followed two years on the directing staff of the Royal Naval War College, Greenwich, until, in October 1937, Mansfield became flag captain and chief staff officer to the commander-in-chief, East Indies, in the cruiser *Norfolk*. The outbreak of war in 1939 found him serving in the same capacity to the flag officer commanding the 1st cruiser squadron, in the *Devonshire*. In this ship he saw lengthy service in the Mediterranean, on the northern patrol, in the Arctic, Norway, equatorial Africa, and the south Atlantic.

In February 1941, when the U-boat war in the Atlantic had become very serious and Sir Percy Noble became commander-in-chief, western approaches, Mansfield became his chief of staff. He contributed a great deal in this role. He played a large part in setting up the new combined sea–air organization. When Canadian–British relations were strained in negotiations over the deployment of the Canadian navy, Mansfield was sent to Ottawa and

'was able to redeem some of the damage done by his masters. Mansfield overcame by his own tact and cheerfulness a great deal of the anger in the RCN' (Terraine, 537). It was such qualities that were most remembered by those who served with him.

Promoted to rear-admiral in 1943, Mansfield commanded a cruiser squadron in the Mediterranean in the *Orion*, with conspicuous service during the landing at Anzio in January 1944; in support of the seaward flank of the United States Fifth Army during the advance towards Rome; and during the landing in southern France in the following August, for which he was appointed DSO in 1945. In October 1944 he very successfully commanded the British naval forces employed in the liberation of Greece. After a short period at the Admiralty in 1945, in which year he was appointed CB, he became flag officer, Ceylon, until in October 1946, as vice-admiral, he became head of his old service as admiral (submarines), where he had the difficult task of demobilization. Forced to relinquish that command in 1948 because of ill health, he was appointed KCB in June of the same year. He died at his home, Magnolia Cottage, Lower Woodford, near Salisbury, Wiltshire, on 4 February 1949.

TAPRELL DORLING, rev. MARC BRODIE

Sources The Times (5 Feb 1949) · The Times (9 Feb 1949) · J. Terraine, Business in great waters: the U-boat wars, 1916–1945 (1989) · Foster, Alum. Oxon. · WWW · CGPLA Eng. & Wales (1949) · personal knowledge (1959) · private information (1959) · b. cert.
Likenesses W. Stoneman, photograph, 1943, NPG
Wealth at death £2436 9s. 8d.: probate, 26 April 1949, CGPLA Eng. & Wales

Mansfield, Katherine. See Murry, Kathleen (1888–1923).

Mansfield [née Fellowes], **Margaret**, **Lady Sandhurst** (bap. 1827, d. 1892), women's suffragist and spiritualist, was the youngest of the seven children of Robert Fellowes (1779–1869) of Shotesham Park, Norfolk, and his second wife, Jane Louisa Sheldon (d. 1871); his father also had a child from his first marriage. She was baptized at Tredington, Worcestershire, on 14 November 1827. On 2 November 1854 she married Lieutenant-Colonel William Rose *Mansfield (1819–1876), who was knighted in 1858 and created Baron Sandhurst in 1871; they spent eleven years in India and had four sons and a daughter.

After her husband's death in 1876 Lady Sandhurst became increasingly involved in both spiritualism and Liberal politics, which interests came together in 1884 when she played host to a private séance for the benefit of the prime minister, W. E. Gladstone. Gladstone commented that she had 'explained to me the spirit & purpose, wholly Christian & biblical, of her proceedings in this matter' (Gladstone, Diaries, 18 April 1884). From 1886 she was active in the Women's Liberal Federation, and in January 1889 she was the first woman elected to the London County Council, as member for Brixton. She was, however, unseated on petition in May, when the objection of her Conservative opponent, Beresford Hope (who maintained that, though empowered to vote in municipal elections, women were ineligible to serve as councillors), was upheld. In the same year she was given the freedom of the city of Dublin, in recognition of her sympathy towards Ireland. She died suddenly in London on 7 January 1892, at her home, 29 Park Road, Regent's Park, and was buried with her husband at Digswell, Hertfordshire.

K. D. REYNOLDS

Sources GEC, *Peerage* · Gladstone, *Diaries* · P. Hollis, *Ladies elect: women in English local government, 1865–1914* (1987) · P. Levine, *Victorian feminism* (1987) · Boase, *Mod. Eng. biog.* · Burke, *Peerage* (1907) · Burke, *Gen. GB* (1914) · CGPLA Eng. & Wales (1892)
Archives BL, letters to W. E. Gladstone, Add. MSS 44466–44513
Likenesses portrait, repro. in *Black and White* (16 Jan 1892), 67 · portrait, repro. in *Daily Graphic* (9 Jan 1892), 9
Wealth at death £4091 5s. 7d.: probate, 10 March 1892, CGPLA Eng. & Wales

Mansfield, Robert Blachford (1824–1908), author and sportsman, born at Rowner, Hampshire, on 1 February 1824, was the second son of John Mansfield, rector of Rowner, and the younger brother of Charles Blachford *Mansfield. His mother was Winifred, eldest daughter of Robert Pope Blachford, of Osborne House, Isle of Wight. He received his early schooling at Romsey and Guildford, after which, in 1835, he was admitted to Winchester College. There he spent five undistinguished years, of which he wrote later a lively account, *School Life at Winchester College* (1866). Prepared by private tutors for Oxford, he entered University College in 1842, graduating BA in 1846. There, in addition to taking up rowing, he hunted with the Heythrop but did little work. He commented, 'I think that I would have passed a better examination when I went up than when I left.' He was admitted to Lincoln's Inn in 1845 and was called to the bar at the Inner Temple in 1849. He joined the western circuit, but never practised seriously. He married on 29 July 1858, at the British embassy, Brussels, Sophie, daughter of Lieutenant-Colonel l'Estrange of Moystown, King's county, Ireland. They had two daughters.

Ample means allowed Mansfield to travel and to indulge his love of sport. He was a good shot and frequently visited Scotland during the season. He also learned to play golf in France in 1857, and became an enthusiastic player, confessing to a missionary zeal for the game. At Oxford he was in the University College eight that went head of the river in 1843. In the same year he rowed briefly as a substitute in the Oxford crew that, with seven men, beat Cambridge in the final of the Grand Challenge Cup at Henley. He broke down in training the next year and never made the university eight.

A pioneer of boating on continental rivers, Mansfield wrote two books about his journeys, first published anonymously: *The Log of the Water-Lily* (1851; 2nd edn, 1854), which described a rowing excursion on the Rhine and other German rivers; and *The Water-Lily on the Danube* (1852). A third trip down the Saône and Rhone in France was less successful. He described his companions on these expeditions in *New and Old Chips from an Old Block* (1896), a small volume of autobiographical gossip. His other publications were as editor of a posthumous work by his brother Charles entitled *Aerial Navigation* (1877), and of *Letters from the Camp before Sebastopol* (1894) by Colonel C. F.

Campbell, a close cousin, whom he had visited in the Crimea at the close of the war.

Among Mansfield's many friends was Charles Kingsley, and he was also acquainted through his brother with J. F. D. Maurice and the members of the Christian socialist movement. Towards the end of his life, he settled in London, at 74 Warwick Square, and was a vestryman of St George's, Hanover Square, and guardian for the poor between 1885 and 1894. He died at Linden House, Headington, near Oxford, on 29 April 1908. His wife survived him.

J. S. COTTON, rev. ERIC HALLADAY

Sources R. B. Mansfield, *New and old chips from an old block* (1896) · *The Times* (19 May 1908) · private information (2004)
Wealth at death £755 10s. 9d.: probate, 28 May 1908, CGPLA Eng. & Wales

Mansfield, William Rose, first Baron Sandhurst (1819–1876), army officer, was born on 26 June 1819 at Ruxley, Kent, the fifth of seven sons of John Edward Mansfield of Diggeswell House, Hertfordshire, and his wife, Mary Buchanan, daughter of General Samuel Smith of Baltimore, USA. He was the grandson of Sir James *Mansfield, and among his brothers were Sir Samuel Mansfield, a senior member of council, Bombay, Colonel Sir Charles Mansfield of the diplomatic service, and John Mansfield, a London police magistrate. He was educated at the Royal Military College, Sandhurst, and passed out in November 1835 at the head of the five most distinguished cadets of his half-year.

Mansfield was commissioned ensign in the 53rd foot on 27 November 1835, and promoted lieutenant in 1838, and captain in 1843. After serving in the Mediterranean and at home, he accompanied his regiment to India, and was present at Badiwal, at Aliwal (28 January 1846), and at Sobraon (10 February 1846), during the First Anglo-Sikh War. During the last-mentioned engagement he acted as aide-de-camp to Lord Gough. On 3 December 1847 he was promoted major, and early in 1848 commanded a small detached force that suppressed civil disturbances in Bihar. Mansfield commanded the 53rd foot during the Second Anglo-Sikh War, and on 21 February 1849 fought at the battle of Gujrat. On 9 May 1851 he became a junior lieutenant-colonel at the age of thirty-two, passing over Henry Havelock, having purchased all his promotions apart from the first. In 1851–2 he was constantly employed in the Peshawar district on the north-west frontier, in operations against the trans-border Pathans, either in command of the 53rd or attached to the staff of Sir Colin Campbell (afterwards Lord Clyde), who commanded the area. During this period Mansfield established a close friendship with Campbell, who formed a high opinion of his abilities.

Mansfield briefly considered an alternative career, either in journalism or in banking, during the 1850s, but finally decided to stay in the army. On 2 November 1854 he married Margaret [see Mansfield, Margaret, Lady Sandhurst (*bap.* 1827, *d.* 1892)], daughter of Robert Fellowes of Shotesham Park, Norfolk; they had four sons and a daughter. He was promoted brevet colonel on 28 November

1854, and in April 1855 exchanged to the unattached list and was appointed deputy adjutant-general in Dublin. In June 1855 he was sent to Constantinople, with the temporary rank of brigadier-general in Turkey, to act as military adviser to the British ambassador, Lord Stratford de Redcliffe. When he arrived in Constantinople a plan for relieving the city of Kars with the Turkish contingent was under active consideration. Mansfield maintained constant communication with the Turkish authorities on the subject, and afterwards accompanied the ambassador to the Crimea where he rendered valuable services. Following the end of the war in 1856 he received the quasi-military appointment of consul-general at Warsaw, with the rank of brigadier-general in Poland. After the outbreak of the Indian mutiny in May 1857 Mansfield was recalled by special request of Sir Colin Campbell, who had been appointed commander-in-chief in India following the death from cholera of Sir George Anson. An entry in Campbell's diary, dated 11 July 1857, reads:

> Before going to the Duke of Cambridge I had settled in my mind that my dear friend Mansfield should have the offer made to him of chief of the staff. His lordship (Panmure) proposed the situation of military secretary, but that I told his lordship was not worth his acceptance, and I pressed for the appointment of chief of the staff being offered to him, with the rank of major-general and the pay and allowances of that office in India.   (Shadwell, 1.405)

On 7 August 1857 Mansfield was appointed chief of the staff in India, with the local rank of major-general. While passing through London, *en route* for India, he was consulted by the government, and submitted a plan of operations based on the same principles as that communicated in confidence by Campbell to the Madras government on his way to Calcutta. Mansfield acted as Campbell's right-hand man and as his strategic mentor throughout the period that followed, and played a key role in planning the reconquest of the area occupied by the mutineers.

In late October 1857 Mansfield left Calcutta with Campbell to take command of the force assembled to relieve the besieged garrison of Lucknow. Mansfield participated in the advance on Lucknow and in the second relief of the city in November 1857 (for which he was made a KCB on 24 March 1858). On 6 December he was present when the Gwalior contingent was routed at the third battle of Cawnpore. During this engagement he was sent by Campbell late in the afternoon to occupy the Subahdar's Tank, blocking the line of retreat of the enemy's centre and right wing. Mansfield halted, however, rather than advancing after dark through a mile of ruined buildings where the rebels were still located, thereby allowing them to escape with all their artillery. He accompanied Campbell in the advance on Fatehgarh and the engagement at Kali Nadi, and at the siege of Lucknow (when he was promoted major-general for distinguished service in the field). He then participated in the summer campaign in Rohilkhand, at the battle of Bareilly and at Shahjahanpur, in the campaign in Oudh during 1858–9, and in the operations in the trans-Gogra. Following the end of the uprising he shouldered the chief burden of reorganizing the shattered fragments of the Bengal army and dealing with the disgruntled European troops of the now defunct East India Company. Although Mansfield was a resolute critic of the company's troops, and played an instrumental role in their eventual transfer to the crown, he did not agree with the official policy towards the company's officers and men which had provoked the 'white mutiny'.

In December 1859 Mansfield was offered the command of the north China expedition, but refused it in the hope he would be appointed commander-in-chief following the end of Lord Clyde's period of command. He was disappointed in this hope, however, and until 23 April 1860 remained chief of the staff in India. He held the command of the Bombay presidency, with the local rank of lieutenant-general, from 18 May 1860 to 14 March 1865. He was appointed colonel 38th foot in 1862 and was made lieutenant-general in December 1864. On 14 March 1865 he was appointed commander-in-chief in India and military member of the executive council, a position he held until 8 April 1870. Throughout this period he was a warm supporter of Lord Lawrence, but his tenure of command in India did not prove a great success. He was unpopular, and on several occasions had painful and discreditable quarrels; he sometimes lacked both good temper and judgement in dealing with subordinates. The incident most damaging to his reputation occurred when he court-martialled a member of his personal staff against whom he had levelled charges of peculation and falsifying accounts, none of which could be substantiated. Mansfield commanded the forces in Ireland between 1 August 1870 and 31 July 1875. He was made a GCB in May 1870, sworn of the Irish privy council in August 1870, and awarded the honorary degree of DCL at Oxford in June 1870. Two years later he was promoted general. Mansfield was also unpopular in Ireland, and several times showed a lamentable lack of judgement. On 28 March 1871, during Gladstone's first administration, Mansfield was created Baron Sandhurst of Sandhurst, Berkshire. A Liberal in politics, he took an active part in debates in the House of Lords, talking on such topics as army organization and the abolition of the purchase system which he believed would result in 'stagnation, tempered by jobbery'. He died on 23 June 1876, aged fifty-seven, of 'congestion of the lungs', at his London residence, 18 Grosvenor Gardens. He was buried at Digswell church, near Welwyn, Hertfordshire. His eldest son, William (1855–1921), succeeded to the peerage, and was governor of Bombay from 1895 to 1900 and lord chamberlain from 1912 to 1921.

Mansfield was tall and wiry, with dark hair. He possessed undoubted intellectual abilities and was a staff officer of considerable aptitude, but his haughty, often contemptuous and arrogant manner made him unpopular with his subordinates and fellow officers throughout his career. He disliked advice, was unable to delegate authority to others, and had many personal enemies. An able and courageous staff officer and administrator, he lacked the necessary leadership ability to prove a successful commander in the field and his personal judgement was frequently questionable.   T. R. MOREMAN

Sources DNB · 'Lord Sandhurst', *The Times* (24 June 1876) · GEC, *Peerage* · *Army List* · L. Shadwell, *The life of Colin Campbell*, 2 vols. (1881) · P. Stanley, *White mutiny: British military culture in transition, 1825–1875* (1998) · C. Hibbert, *The great mutiny, India, 1857* (1978) · J. W. Kaye, *A history of the Sepoy War in India, 1857–1858*, 3 vols. (1864–76) · M. C. Hill, *A guide to the Shropshire records* (1952) · H. L. Nevill, *Campaigns on the north-west frontier* (1912)
Archives BL, letters to H. Bruce, Add. MSS 43992 · BL, corresp. with Lord Ripon, Add. MS 43619 · BL, letters to Lord Strathnairn, Add. MS 42806 · BL OIOC, corresp. with Sir George Russell Clerk, MS Eur. D. 538 · CUL, corresp. with Lord Mayo, Add. MS 7490
Likenesses E. Lundgren, watercolour drawing, 1858, National Museum, Stockholm · double portrait, photograph, 1858 (with Lord Clyde), BL OIOC, 139/2 (1) · Ape [C. Pellegrini], chromolithograph caricature, NPG; repro. in *VF* (30 May 1874) · Becto and Robertson, Day & Son, double portrait, lithograph (with Lord Clyde), repro. in W. H. Russell, *Diary in India*, 1 (1860), frontispiece · W. Roffe, double portrait, stipple and line engraving (with Lord Clyde; after photograph), repro. in Lord Roberts [F. S. Roberts], *Forty-one years in India*, 1 (1897) · T. B. Wirgman, double portrait, pencil drawing (with Lord Clyde), Scot. NPG · group photograph, NPG · group portrait, photograph (with personal staff), BL OIOC, 28/2 (3) · prints, NAM · wood-engraving (after photograph by Hering), NPG; repro. in *ILN* (13 May 1865) · wood-engraving (in uniform; after photograph by T. Cranfield), NPG; repro. in *ILN* (29 April 1871)
Wealth at death under £60,000: probate, 8 July 1876, *CGPLA Eng. & Wales*

Manship, Henry (*c*.1520–1569). *See under* Manship, Henry (*c*.1550–1625).

Manship, Henry (*c*.1550–1625), historian, was almost certainly born in Great Yarmouth, the son of Katherine and **Henry Manship** (*c*.1520–1569), merchant, freeman of the town, and long considered the author of *Greate Yermouthe: a Booke of the Foundacion and Antiquitye of the Saide Towne* (1847) which is now reliably attributed to Thomas Damet. So far as is known, he completed his formal education at the town's free grammar school, though he went on to serve Yarmouth as town clerk from November 1579 to July 1585, as one of four attorneys to the borough court, and in other *ad hoc* capacities on the borough's behalf. By 1613 he had married Joan, daughter of Henry Hill of King's Lynn and his wife, Anne, *née* Gourney.

Manship's perpetual pugnacity and even dishonesty plagued him all his life. An unspecified infelicity cost him a royal appointment to a customs post in 1585; he was temporarily dismissed from his burgess-ship in 1604 for calling Yarmouth's two MPs 'sheep' and 'dunces'; an unauthorized loan in the borough's name placed him under a cloud in 1616; and in 1620 he published a self-serving pamphlet at the borough's expense. The two signal achievements which command attention, Manship's reorganization of the borough's records in 1612 and his completion of *The History of Great Yarmouth* in 1619, seem partly intended to restore his favour with the borough's ruling élite.

On 16 June 1612 Manship received permission from Yarmouth's borough assembly to establish a committee of aldermen and common councillors to set about the methodical retrieval, description, and reorganization of Yarmouth's official documents, which had become widely scattered both within the borough and far beyond. In twenty-three meetings over two months' time, the committee fulfilled its task. A later transcription of Manship's report on this project (BL, Add. MS 23737, fols. 4–31) describes this signal achievement in the annals of local record keeping. It did restore his standing, and gained him several *ad hoc* official assignments on Yarmouth's behalf in the 1610s.

Manship obviously employed his intimate and thorough familiarity with these records in completing his *History* in 1619. It was not published until 1854 when the local freeman and antiquary Charles John Palmer transcribed it from a then-extant manuscript copy. No original copies are now known. Manship's *History* is remarkable for the breadth of its research in authorities both contemporary and ancient, its critical use of source material, and its polemical support for the rule of magistrates and the law. It illuminates the local identity and history of Great Yarmouth, thus encouraging the loyalty and pride of fellow townspeople. Several copies seem to have circulated from an early time and subsequent local historians such as Henry Swinden and Francis Blomefield relied heavily upon it. The failure to publish it in his own time probably had to do with Manship's personal standing and with the expense of so doing. Though rewarded with £50 for completing the *History*, his final disgrace, the offending pamphlet of 1620, seems to have eclipsed his fortunes for the last time. Manship died a relatively poor man in 1625, and was survived by his wife.   ROBERT TITTLER

Sources H. Manship, *The history of Great Yarmouth*, ed. C. J. Palmer (1854) · BL, Add. MS 23737, fols. 4–31 · DNB · W. Rye, ed., *The visitacion of Norffolk … 1563 … 1613*, Harleian Society, 32 (1891) · P. Rutledge, 'Thomas Damet and the historiography of Great Yarmouth [pt 1]', *Norfolk Archaeology*, 33 (1962–5), 119–30 · P. Rutledge, 'Thomas Damet and the historiography of Great Yarmouth [pt 2]', *Norfolk Archaeology*, 34 (1966–9), 332–4 · will, PRO, PROB 11/3, sig. 21 [Thomas Damet]
Archives BL, report of the archives project 1612, Add. MS 23737, fols. 4–31 · Bodl. Oxf., notes on Great Yarmouth hospitals
Wealth at death relative poverty: DNB

Manson, David (1726–1792), schoolmaster, was born in the parish of Cairncastle, co. Antrim, the son of John Manson and Agnes Jamieson. As his parents were poor he worked as a farmer's servant-boy, but was allowed by his employer to attend a school kept by the Revd Robert White in the neighbouring town of Larne. There he made such good progress that he himself opened a school in his native parish—according to tradition, in a cowhouse. He next became tutor to the Shaw family of Ballygally Castle, and then taught at a school in Ballycastle. It was probably at this time that he married Miss Lynn, of Ballycastle; they had no children.

In 1752 Manson moved to Belfast, where he started a brewery, and in 1755 he opened an evening school in his house in Clugston's Entry, where he taught English grammar, reading, and spelling. The school grew, so that in 1760 he moved to larger premises in High Street and employed three assistants. He advertised that his pupils would be taught 'without the Discipline of the Rod by intermixing pleasurable and healthful exercise with Instruction' (Benn, 452), and instead used a complex system of rewards to encourage them in their studies. In 1768 he built a still larger schoolhouse, in Donegall Street, where he was able to accommodate boarders for the first time. He taught both boys and girls; one of his pupils was Mary Anne McCracken. To amuse his pupils he devised various machines, one a primitive kind of velocipede. He wrote and published a number of school books, which enjoyed a long-lasting reputation in the north of Ireland and elsewhere. These were a spelling book, a primer, a pocket English dictionary, and a pronouncing dictionary. *Manson's Spelling Primer* continued to be published in the 1840s, and a new edition of his pronouncing dictionary was printed in Belfast in 1823. He set out his methods of teaching in 'A plan for the improvement of children in virtue and learning', printed in *A New Pocket Dictionary* (1762). He also published a small treatise in which he advised Irish handloom weavers to live in the countryside, where they could supplement their income by cultivating the soil. He invented an improved machine for spinning yarn.

In 1775 Manson was listed among the seatholders in the First Presbyterian Church, Belfast, and in 1779 he was admitted a freeman of the borough. He died on 2 March 1792 at Lillyput, a house which he had built near Belfast, and was buried at night, by torchlight, in the churchyard at the foot of High Street.

THOMAS HAMILTON, *rev.* S. J. SKEDD

Sources E. C. Porter, *Ulster biographical sketches*, 2nd ser. (1884) · *Belfast News-Letter* (1755); (1760); (1768) · G. Benn, *A history of the town of Belfast from the earliest times to the close of the eighteenth century*, 2 vols. (1877); (1880) · J. R. Fisher and J. H. Robb, *Royal Belfast Academical Institution: centenary volume, 1810–1910* (1913)
Likenesses oils, Royal Belfast Academical Institution; repro. in Fisher and Robb, *Royal Belfast Academical Institution*, 25

Manson, George (1850–1876), wood-engraver and landscape and genre painter, was born on 3 December 1850 in Edinburgh, the son of Magnus Manson, a merchant. As a boy he was encouraged to paint by his father, who was an amateur artist. He read the works of John Ruskin and worked his way through all the practical exercises in *The Elements of Drawing* (1857). On leaving school he began an apprenticeship with the publishers William and Robert Chambers, where he worked as a punch cutter, making the steel dies used in the production of printers' type. Rising very early in the morning before work, he would sketch various scenes around his home on the southern outskirts of Edinburgh. He joined the Craigmillar Sketching Association and for their monthly meetings made numerous sketches of the oldest buildings in Edinburgh. This he called his 'religious work' (Gray, 8), since he viewed himself as a conservationist recording the ancient buildings before they were destroyed. This work later led him to have a deep admiration for the haunting Parisian views of Charles Meryon.

Manson worked in pencil, watercolour, and oils but also made wood-engravings from an early age. Inspired by the work of Thomas Bewick, his blocks are simply composed and forthright. In 1870 he competed for a prize offered to apprentices by the Edinburgh Society of Engravers on Wood. Manson's work did not sufficiently meet the exacting stipulations of the award for him to win the main prize, but the quality of his entry—a study of a farm with trees and sheep grazing in a field—was nevertheless noticed by the judge, and he was awarded a special prize in recognition of his 'artistic feeling in landscape'. He first exhibited at the Royal Scottish Academy in 1869 with *Study of a Doorway at Craigmillar Castle*. In 1870 he exhibited *Milking Time* and the following year *Children at a Well*. It was perhaps the encouragement of other artists that prompted him to become a professional painter that year: James Cassie bought the last of these three paintings and became one of many artists who admired and patronized Manson throughout his short career.

Mixing with such artists and studying at the Trustees' Academy in Edinburgh, Manson soon came under the influence of realist European artists, and particularly the Dutch Hague school of painters. In 1873 he visited Europe with W. D. McKay (1844–1924): in Paris they sketched from the paintings in the Louvre and, with a letter of introduction from the art connoisseur John Forbes White, called on the Dutch genre painter Adolphe Artz. In The Hague they visited Josef Israels. Influenced by the work of the Dutch artists with whom he had become acquainted Manson began to concentrate on depicting seascapes and fishing folk: like Israels, he became renowned for his ability to depict the pathos of working-class life.

In 1874 the first signs of consumption pre-empted a visit to Sark, but Manson continued to visit Scotland, touring the highlands and spending prolonged periods of time in Edinburgh and Galashiels. In January 1875 he travelled to France with Patrick W. Adam (1854–1930) and there began to etch, receiving instruction from a M. Cadart. In St Lô he contracted pneumonia, and thereafter his physical decline was rapid. On his return to Britain he settled in Shirley, near Croydon. His last known work was a small study for a scene from Allan Ramsay's *Gentle Shepherd* (1725). He died of consumption at Lympstone in Devon on 27 February 1876 and was buried in Culliford churchyard. Three years later more than 300 subscribers funded the publication of a book on Manson and his art. Compiled by J. M. Gray, it served as a fitting testimonial to Manson's artistic achievements. In 1881 an exhibition of his watercolours was held in London; his expert use of both detailed brushwork and 'wet' watercolour washes attracted great interest and the admiration of critics and artists alike.

JENNIFER MELVILLE

Sources J. M. Gray, *George Manson and his works* (1879) · P. J. M. McEwan, *Dictionary of Scottish art and architecture* (1994) · letters of Sir George Reid, John Forbes White, and others, Aberdeen Art Gallery, Archives · J. L. Caw, *Scottish painting past and present, 1620–1908* (1908), 279–80 · J. Halsby, *Scottish watercolours, 1740–1940* (1986), 70, 126, 241 · W. Hardie, *Scottish painting, 1837–1939* (1976), 66, 78, 79 · *DNB* · C. B. de Laperriere, ed., *The Royal Scottish Academy exhibitors, 1826–1990*, 4 vols. (1991) · d. cert.
Archives Aberdeen Art Gallery, archives of George Reid

Likenesses Elliott & Fry, photograph, 1873, repro. in Gray, *George Manson*, frontispiece · G. P. Chalmers, oil on millboard, Scot. NPG · G. Manson, two self-portraits, watercolour, Scot. NPG

Manson, James Bolivar (1879–1945), painter and art administrator, was born at 65 Appach Road, Brixton, London, on 26 June 1879, the second of six children and eldest of four sons of James Alexander Manson, author and editor, and his wife, Margaret Emily, daughter of Charles Deering. In 1895, on leaving Alleyn's School, Dulwich, Manson worked as office boy and then in a bank, while studying painting in his spare time at Heatherley's School of Art in London. Over the next eight years, with the help of Lilian Beatrice (*b.* 1876/7), a violin teacher, daughter of William Laugher, he saved sufficient money to support full-time studies. On 29 August 1903 he married Lilian, left the bank and went to the Académie Julian in Paris.

The Mansons returned to London in 1904 for the birth of the first of their two daughters. In 1908 they moved to 98 Hampstead Way, their home for the next thirty years. Manson spent the summers of 1905–7 on painting trips in Brittany, where he developed his talent unaffected by the fluctuations of fashion. He was a convinced admirer of the impressionist painters; although in no sense an imitator, his natural outlook was closest to that of Monet and Camille Pissarro. He was thus prepared for his meeting late in 1909 with Lucien Pissarro, son and artistic heir of Camille. In November 1910 he was brought to the Fitzroy Street Group studio to view paintings by Pissarro, on whom he was preparing an article. As their friendship ripened, Pissarro brought Manson more frequently to group gatherings on Saturday afternoons at 19 Fitzroy Street. When the *Camden Town Group was formed in 1911 Manson, with his affable temperament and office experience, was elected secretary. Thus was Manson drawn from the fringes of the London art world into its progressive centre. In 1913 he was a founder member of the London Group and its first secretary, but resigned in March 1914 following its first exhibition. In 1919 he was a founder member and secretary of the Monarro Group, created around Lucien Pissarro to represent those artists who derived inspiration from the leaders of the French impressionist movement, Claude Monet and Camille Pissarro. Advocacy of the work of Lucien Pissarro was a constant theme of his life and work.

Manson supplemented his meagre income from painting by writing articles, catalogue prefaces, and books. His accounts of contemporary art, such as the catalogue introduction to the Camden Town Group section of the exhibition 'Work by English post-impressionists, cubists and others' held at Brighton Art Gallery from December 1913 to January 1914, remain valuable historical records. His short monographs intended for the general reader—on, for example, Rembrandt (1923) and Degas (1927)—are models of their kind.

From 1912, when he took on the post of clerk at the Tate Gallery, Manson's main income came from his successive appointments there. In 1917 he was promoted to assistant keeper and succeeded Charles Aitken as director in 1930.

At that time, additions to the gallery were more dependent on private generosity than on government support. During Manson's directorship the collection was strengthened, particularly its impressionist holdings. His appreciative article, 'Mr Frank Stoop's Modern Pictures' (which appeared in *Apollo* in 1929), refutes the canard that he deplored the acquisition by the Tate in 1933 of paintings by Matisse, Picasso, and Cézanne through the Stoop bequest. However, some opportunities to expand the collection with European art of more contemporary vintage were missed.

Manson found what time he could for painting. His achievement as a painter, especially of landscapes and flower pieces, was recognized during the 1920s with exhibitions at the Leicester Galleries, London (1923), at the Galérie Balzac, Paris (1924), and at the Reid Gallery, Glasgow (1925). He became a member of the New English Art Club in 1927 and exhibited at the Royal Academy from 1939.

In his youth Manson was a tall man with a slim and sensitive face. More thickset in later life, his abundant white hair and bright light-blue eyes gave him a surprisingly youthful aspect. He was 'an amusing companion, spontaneous and without affectation' (*DNB*); often, but not always on wisely chosen occasions, he was extremely funny. It was also Manson's misfortune that he had no head for wine. His liking for pranks and his weak head for liquor led to his downfall. On 4 March 1938, at a solemn moment during an official luncheon in Paris to mark the opening of the British exhibition at the Louvre, he produced his renowned *chants du coq*; later:

> when the guests were dispersing, he lifted the beard of one of the most distinguished Frenchmen present in order to see 'whether he had a tie on underneath'. The French were tolerant, even amused, by these indiscretions but a less lenient view was taken by the British authorities.　(*DNB*)

Manson was forced to resign from the Tate, an event which heralded further upheavals in his financial and domestic circumstances. He ventured his small capital with disastrous results, and he left his wife and house in Hampstead Way.

Manson died of heart failure at his home, 6 Carlyle Studios, 296 King's Road, Chelsea, on 3 July 1945. He had spent the last years of his life with Cicely Constance Hayward (*née* Kettle), estranged wife of the painter Alfred Hayward, who changed her name by deed poll to Elizabeth Manson in 1941. In 1946 a memorial exhibition was held at Wildenstein, London, where he had last exhibited in 1937. His paintings are owned by many public galleries, regional and national; the Tate collection has one of his finest flower pictures, *Michaelmas Daisies* (1923), and a self-portrait of 1912.　　　　WENDY BARON

Sources D. Buckman, *James Bolivar Manson: an English impressionist, 1879–1945* (1973) · W. Baron, *The Camden Town Group* (1979) · J. B. Manson, correspondence with L. Pissarro, AM Oxf., Lucien Pissarro MSS · *DNB* · F. Spalding, *The Tate: a history* (1998) · W. Meadmore, *Lucien Pissarro: un coeur simple* (1962) · m. cert. · *CGPLA Eng. & Wales* (1945)

Archives Tate collection, corresp., writings and photographs | TCD, corresp. with Thomas Bodkin · U. Oxf., Sackler Library, Lucien Pissarro archives

Likenesses S. Halpert, oils, 1903, NPG · J. B. Manson, self-portrait, oils, 1912, Tate collection · H. Coster, photographs, NPG · A. O'Connor, bronze bust, Hugh Lane Municipal Gallery of Modern Art, Dublin

Wealth at death £2270 14s. 7d.: probate, 24 Nov 1945, *CGPLA Eng. & Wales*

Manson, (Thomas) Mortimer Yule (1904–1996), journalist and musician, was born on 9 February 1904 at Lerwick, Shetland, the third son and fourth and youngest child of Thomas Manson (1859–1941), a journalist, printer, and musician, and his wife, Margaret, *née* Cruttwell (1865–1954), a piano teacher and choral singer. Both parents were important influences on Manson, the Benjamin of the family, as he once referred to himself. Their house often swarmed with musical people and other local celebrities. Manson was educated at a small private school in Lerwick and then at the Anderson Educational Institute there. He shone in most subjects, and was devoted to art in particular. He eventually studied English and history at Edinburgh University, and prepared to become a teacher. But his return to Shetland in winter 1929–30 coincided with his eldest brother's departure for South Africa, and Manson took his place in the family printing works in Mounthooly Street, Lerwick. He succeeded his father as editor of the *Shetland News* in 1941, and ran the paper until its demise twenty-three years later. He was conscientious as editor, as in everything else. However, there was an old-fashioned air about the *News*, and its political stance—it had come into existence as Shetland's Conservative organ—did not always commend it to Shetland's largely Liberal population. The Liberal *Shetland Times* gradually ousted it. Manson's subsequent career, as a jobbing printer, was not prosperous either. When he retired, in 1977, he relaxed for the first time for years.

During the 1980s Manson took up an entirely new career. For a few years after his retirement he had reported council meetings for Radio Shetland. In May 1982 he stood for election in the Clickimin ward of Lerwick, knocking personally on each door. He was duly elected. An independent councillor, in every sense, he took the work seriously, especially his position as chairman of the leisure and recreation committee. He liked to be busy: shortly after he left the council, in his eighties, he visited the employment exchange in search of a job.

Manson was also a scholar. In the 1930s he was the founder of *Manson's Guide to Shetland*, a pocket-sized book for discerning tourists. He read up on current archaeological and historical work, and expounded it in his earnest way. An exacting critic, Bruce Dickins, described the *Guide* as an 'excellent piece of work by a good scholar' (*Old-Lore Miscellany*, 10, 1935–46, 290). Manson was also a staunch contributor of historical and political articles to the *New Shetlander* and *Shetland Life* magazines. His essay on Shetland's Spanish Armada shipwreck, written for a Festschrift for his friend Ronald Cant in 1974, was a characteristic piece of work. Ten years later another friend, Barbara Crawford, edited Manson's own Festschrift—this time

called a *heiðursrit*, the equivalent Faroese word—entitled *Essays in Shetland History* (1984).

Dear to Manson's heart was the fostering of contact between Shetland and the Scandinavian countries. In 1933 he accompanied a group of Shetland footballers to Tórshavn in the Faroes, re-creating a link that had long been in abeyance. For the rest of his life he did his best to foster relationships between the two groups of islands. He played a key part in organizing the first Viking Congress, a meeting of Scandinavianists in Lerwick. A measure of his conscientiousness in everything he did is the fact that at one point he sent a telegram concerning an aspect of the congress at four o'clock in the morning. The congress, held in 1950, was a great success, the first of many. A year later Aberdeen University awarded Manson an honorary degree of doctor of laws for his achievement.

Manson's chief love, however, was music. When he was thirteen he joined the Boy Scouts flute band and became besotted with that instrument. Almost self-taught, he was in demand to play it in the local orchestra, since Lerwick lacked flautists at that time. Eventually he taught local scholars and trained and led the Boys' Brigade flute band. When young flautists began to take their place in the orchestra, in the 1970s, Manson took up the violin. He was conductor of the brass band from 1959 to 1964, treasurer of the Lerwick Orchestral Society from 1937, and secretary from 1947 to 1989.

Manson was active in numerous other ways. His campaigns to preserve the old flagstones on Lerwick's Commercial Street, and to restrain industrial depletion of sand at St Ninian's Isle, conducted stubbornly, became legendary. He was a devoted scouter. A tory for most of his life, he left the fold when the party began to look towards Europe, in 1962, and defiantly printed 'A Commonwealth newspaper' on the masthead of the *Shetland News*.

Mortimer Manson was shy, and sometimes a little gruff. Courteous and dutiful, he felt distressed if he thought that he had let someone down. His halting voice and sweet personality made a vivid and lasting impression on people both in Shetland and further afield. He died, unmarried, on 23 January 1996.   BRIAN SMITH

Sources S. Cooper, *Key notes: the history of the Lerwick Orchestra* (1996)

Manson, Sir Patrick (1844–1922), physician and parasitologist, was born on 3 October 1844 at Cromlet Hill, Oldmeldrum, Aberdeenshire, the second son of John Manson, laird of Fingask and manager of the local branch of the British Linen Bank, and his wife, Elizabeth Livingston. Manson was educated at the Gymnasium and later at the West End Academy, both in Aberdeen, where his parents had moved in 1857. He was then apprenticed to an engineering firm in Aberdeen but developed a curvature of the spine and a slight weakness in one arm which forced him to consider another career. During his convalescence he was able to pursue his interest in natural history, and this soon led him to abandon engineering and take up the study of medicine. He entered Aberdeen University in 1860, and in 1865 graduated MB CM; in 1866 he took his

Sir Patrick Manson (1844–1922), by Olive Edis, c.1905

MD degree and was appointed medical officer for a lunatic asylum in Durham.

Through the interest of his elder brother, who by then was in China, in Shanghai, Manson was appointed later in 1866 as medical officer for Formosa (Taiwan) to the Chinese Imperial Maritime Customs. Owing to the political unrest there, Manson left the island in 1871 and went to Amoy (Xiamen). It was there, while in charge of a missionary society hospital and dispensary, and busy with his private practice, that he made observations on patients with elephantiasis. His surgical work in the removal of the massive tumours of this condition, and the prevalence of this and allied illnesses among the Chinese, impressed him with the importance of these diseases. While in England in 1875 he read the work of Vincent Richards and Timothy Richards Lewis (1841–1886). Lewis claimed to have found the filaria embryos and immature worms of microscopic nematodes (microfilariae) in the blood of patients suffering from diseases allied to elephantiasis. Later discoveries, in 1876 by Joseph Bancroft of Brisbane, and in 1877 by Lewis in Calcutta, revealed the adult worms corresponding to the embryonic blood forms.

Manson married in 1875 Henrietta Isabella (b. 1858), second daughter of Captain James Ptolemy Thurburn RN of Norwood, Surrey; they were to have five children. On his return to China early in 1876 Manson made a series of observations which convinced him of the causal relationship of filaria worms to elephantoid diseases. Lewis had published in 1869 an article that speculated on the role of the mosquito as a probable host, and Manson too embarked on a study of mosquitoes. He established that filaria embryos were preserved only in mosquitoes which fed on patients with the embryos in their blood:

> After many months of work … often following up false scents, I ultimately succeeded in tracing the filaria through the stomach wall into the abdominal cavity, and then into the thoracic muscles, of the mosquito. I ascertained that during this passage the little parasite increased enormously in size. It developed a mouth, an alimentary canal and other organs. … Manifestly it was on the road to a new human host. (China customs, *Medical Reports*, September 1877)

In 1879 Manson observed that the embryonic forms of the worm did not appear in the blood until sunset, that they increased in number until midnight, and then decreased, disappearing almost entirely about 6 a.m. He began to speculate on the fate of these embryonic blood filaria—how they left the body. In his autobiography Manson was later to write about his subsequent work on the transmission of filaria: 'A regrettable mistake, the result of a want of books, was my belief that the mosquito died soon after laying her eggs' (Manson-Bahr and Alcock, *Life*, 57). He conjectured that the filarial larvae passed into water at the death of the 'short-lived' mosquito, and then in some unknown way were transmitted back to man. Other researchers including Ronald Ross and G. Low took up the question and demonstrated the stages of development in the abdomen, thorax, and proboscis of the mosquito.

In December 1883 Manson left Amoy and settled in Hong Kong, where he soon built up a large private practice and became a leader in public work. He was one of the founders of the Hong Kong school of medicine, which eventually became the Victoria University and Medical School of Hong Kong. Manson's support of the Hong Kong school helped to foster a faction of the Chinese élite who wanted to seed China with Western values. His support also signalled his interest in medical education. In 1886 he received the honorary LLD degree of Aberdeen University—the first official recognition of his scientific work.

Manson retired from practice in 1889, left China, and went to live in Scotland. A year later, however, he was compelled, through financial losses, to take up practice again in London, where his appointment in 1892 as physician to the Albert Docks branch of the Royal Naval Hospital gave him the opportunity to continue his researches into tropical diseases. Manson was now familiar with certain forms of the malaria parasite which behaved in a peculiar manner when examined under the microscope. In 1894 he published his mosquito-malaria hypothesis in which he drew an analogy between the transmission of microfilaria and the malaria parasite. He argued that mosquitoes or another blood-sucking parasite were the intermediary agents in malaria. Ronald Ross then traced the subsequent steps: 'His brilliant induction', Ross wrote of Manson, 'so accurately indicated the true line of research, that it has been my part merely to follow its direction.'

In 1894 Manson began to give public lectures in London on the subject of tropical diseases, and in 1897 he was appointed as the London medical adviser to the Colonial

Office. He was thereby brought into close association with Joseph Chamberlain, at that time secretary of state for the colonies. Manson suggested reforms of the system of medical reports from the colonies and pressed for the foundation of a school of tropical medicine. During this period at the Colonial Office, there was much discussion over the reorganization of the colonial medical service, with Herbert Read (Chamberlain's private secretary) taking a special interest. In 1899 the establishment of the London School of Tropical Medicine was the outcome of a scheme drawn up by Manson in 1897 for systematic instruction in the diagnosis, treatment, and prevention of tropical disease. Manson had been appalled at the ignorance of, and the lack of training in, the subject with which practitioners had hitherto proceeded to the tropics. His efforts to found the London school resonated with his earlier endeavours in Hong Kong. In both instances he attempted to forge consent among doctors and colonial officials who did not share many common goals. Part of his success lay in his collegiality and a generosity that he extended, especially to junior colleagues. He loyally supported a number of doctors who wished to conduct research in tropical medicine, most famously Ross, but also William John Ritchie Simpson and James Cantlie.

In 1896 Manson delivered the Goulstonian lectures, entitled 'The life history of the malarial germ outside the body'; these were published in the *British Medical Journal* and *The Lancet* in 1896. In 1898 he published *Tropical Diseases: a Manual of the Diseases of Warm Climates*, a work founded on his large experience and numerous original researches in China. Later important contributions to the subject were his *Lectures on Tropical Diseases* (the Lane lectures delivered at San Francisco in 1905) and, in 1908 (with C. W. Daniels), *Diet in the Diseases of Hot Climates*.

Manson, who had been elected a fellow of the Royal Society in 1900, was created KCMG in 1903 and promoted GCMG on his retirement from the Colonial Office in 1912. He was the first president of the Royal Society of Tropical Medicine and Hygiene (1907–9). He received the honorary degree of DSc from the University of Oxford in 1904. At the International Congress of Medicine held in London in 1913 he was described as the 'father of tropical medicine'—a recognition of his achievement which was endorsed by future generations. Manson died in London on 9 April 1922, and was buried on 13 April in Allenvale cemetery, Aberdeen. He was commemorated in the London School of Hygiene and Tropical Medicine by having his name inscribed in the frieze at the front of the Keppel Street building and on a plaque in the entrance hall of the school. Manson also left a bequest to the school, for tropical medicine research.

J. W. W. STEPHENS, *rev.* MARY P. SUTPHEN

Sources P. Manson-Bahr and A. Alcock, *The life and work of Sir Patrick Manson* (1927) • P. Manson-Bahr, *Patrick Manson, the father of tropical medicine* (1962) • D. M. Haynes, 'From the periphery to the center: Patrick Manson and the development of tropical medicine as a specialty in Britain', PhD diss., U. Cal., 1992 • E. Chernin, 'Sir Patrick Manson's studies on the transmission and biology of filariasis', *Reviews of Infectious Diseases*, 5 (1983), 148–66 • 'Pioneer of tropical medicine Sir P. Manson's great work: an empire builder', *The Times* (10 April 1922) • E. Chernin, 'Sir Patrick Manson: physician to the colonial office, 1897–1912', *Medical History*, 36 (1992), 320–31 • W. F. Bynum and C. Overy, eds., *The beast in the mosquito: the correspondence of Ronald Ross and Patrick Manson* (1998) • private information (2004) • IGI

Archives London School of Hygiene and Tropical Medicine • Wellcome L., casebook; casebook while in Hong Kong; papers | London School of Hygiene and Tropical Medicine, Ronald Ross MSS • PRO, Colonial Office archives • Seamen's Hospital, Greenwich, minute books

Likenesses O. Edis, photograph, c.1905, NPG [*see illus.*] • J. Y. Hunter, oils, 1911, Royal Society of Tropical Medicine & Hygiene, Manson House, London • E. Webster, oils, c.1921, London School of Hygiene and Tropical Medicine • J. R. Pinches, bronze medal, 1922, U. Cam., Molteno Institute of Biology and Parasitology • J. R. Pinches, bronze medal, 1922, NPG • bronze bas-relief, 1934, London School of Hygiene and Tropical Medicine • M. L. Gee, watercolour, London School of Hygiene and Tropical Medicine • M. Osborne, mezzotint, Wellcome L. • A. W. Turnbull, etching, Wellcome L. • photographs, Wellcome L.

Wealth at death £57,439 9s. 6d.: probate, 9 June 1922, CGPLA Eng. & Wales

Manson, Thomas Walter (1893–1958), biblical scholar, was born at North Shields, Northumberland, on 22 July 1893, the only son of Thomas Francis Manson, schoolmaster in his own private school, and his wife, Joan, daughter of Walter Johnston, of Cunningsburgh, Shetland. The eldest child, he was followed by eight sisters. He was educated by his father, then at Tynemouth Municipal High School, and Glasgow University where he took his MA with honours in logic and moral philosophy, his course being interrupted by war service in the Royal Field Artillery during which he was wounded in France. In 1919 he was awarded the Clark scholarship by Glasgow University and the Ferguson scholarship in philosophy which was open to all four Scottish universities. At Westminster College, Cambridge, he prepared for the ministry of the Presbyterian Church of England, and also entered Christ's College, Cambridge, gaining a first class in part two of the oriental languages tripos, in Hebrew and Aramaic, in 1923. At Westminster College he was awarded the Crichton–Munro scholarship and the Williams and Elmslie open scholarships; Christ's College made him a research scholar and he won the Tyrwhitt Hebrew scholarship (1924) and the Burney (1923) and Mason (1924) prizes.

After a short period as tutor in Westminster College, Manson was ordained in 1925 at Howard Street Church, North Shields, and served for a year in the Jewish Mission Institute in Bethnal Green. In 1926 Manson married Nora, daughter of James Robert Wilkinson Wallace, master butcher, of North Shields; they had no children. In the same year he took charge of the church at Falstone, Northumberland. There he produced his first book, *The Teaching of Jesus* (1931), for which Glasgow awarded him a DLitt in 1932. His specialized work in Cambridge had been in Hebrew and Semitic studies in which he retained a lifelong interest, but with the publication of this book his eminence as a New Testament scholar was immediately recognized; thereafter, his work lay principally in this field. It was enriched by his expert knowledge of the Old Testament and his access to rabbinical Hebrew and Syriac. Already interested in the Septuagint, he developed an interest in Apocryphal and Pseudepigraphal literature. Later he acquired Coptic, making his linguistic equipment for New Testament work exceptionally strong.

In 1932 Manson was appointed to the Yates chair of New Testament Greek at Mansfield College, Oxford, in succession to C. H. Dodd, and in 1936 he again succeeded Dodd, in the Rylands chair of biblical criticism at Manchester where he remained, despite job offers elsewhere, until his death. For many years he served as dean of the faculty of theology, and for four years as pro-vice-chancellor. He was also a governor of the John Rylands Library and a feoffee of Chetham's Library. In the Second World War he was an operations officer in the civil-defence operations room for the north-west during the heavy bombing. He also took charge of St Aidan's Presbyterian Church, Didsbury.

Manson was awarded many honours, including honorary degrees of DD from Glasgow (1937), Durham (1938), Cambridge (1951), Pine Hill (Halifax, Nova Scotia, 1953), and Trinity College, Dublin (1956), and of DTheol from Strasbourg (1946). He was elected a fellow of the British Academy in 1945 and was awarded the academy's Burkitt medal in 1950. He took a leading part in the formation of the *Studiorum Novi Testamenti Societas* and was its president in 1949–50. He lectured in universities in several foreign countries, was an honorary member of the American Society of Biblical Literature and Exegesis and of the Göttingen Akademie der Wissenschaften. For many years he delivered an annual lecture in the John Rylands Library; these were published in the library's *Bulletin* and a number reissued in a volume edited by Matthew Black, *Studies in the Gospels and Epistles* (1962).

Manson did not write a great number of books, but they were always significant contributions. Among them may be mentioned *The Sayings of Jesus* (part 2 of *The Mission and Message of Jesus*, in collaboration, 1937; published separately, 1949); *The Church's Ministry* (1948); and *The Servant-Messiah* (1953). He was a member of the New Testament and Apocrypha panels for the preparation of the *New English Bible*. He accepted the editorship of the Cambridge Septuagint (he had been Grinfield lecturer at Oxford, 1943–5) and had hoped to devote his retirement to the continuation of this great task.

With all his academic work Manson never lost his interest in his work as a clergyman and preached in many different churches. For ten years he was president of the Manchester, Salford and District Free Church Council, and in 1953 he was moderator of the general assembly of the Presbyterian Church of England. He had great administrative gifts, which Manchester University fully exploited. A gentle man of strong conviction, and a good raconteur, he was a brilliant teacher, commanding the admiration and the affection of his students, over whom he took a great deal of trouble.

Some time before his death, failing health caused Manson to move to Milnthorpe, Westmorland, near waters where he had long delighted to fish. He died at Milnthorpe on 1 May 1958, survived by his wife. His colleagues and friends planned to present him with a Festschrift for his sixty-fifth birthday, but it became a memorial volume, *New Testament Essays* (ed. A. J. B. Higgins, 1959). The wide esteem in which he was held was shown by a memorial service held in Manchester Cathedral at which the bishop of Manchester gave the address.

H. H. ROWLEY, rev. GERALD LAW

Sources M. Black, 'Thomas Walter Manson, 1893–1958', *PBA*, 44 (1958), 325–37 · H. H. Rowley, 'Foreword', *Studies in the gospels and epistles*, ed. M. Black (1962), vii–xvi · *CGPLA Eng. & Wales* (1958)
Archives CUL, papers · JRL, memorabilia, research papers, etc. · NL Scot., corresp. with publishers
Likenesses W. Stoneman, photograph, 1946, NPG
Wealth at death £4822 0s. 5d.: probate, 23 Sept 1958, *CGPLA Eng. & Wales*

Mant, Richard (1776–1848), bishop of Down, Connor, and Dromore, eldest son and fifth child of Richard Mant DD (d. 1817), was born at Southampton on 12 February 1776. His father was the master of King Edward's Grammar School, and afterwards rector of All Saints', Southampton; Mant was educated by his father and at Winchester College. He entered as a commoner at Trinity College, Oxford, in 1793, and in 1794 obtained a scholarship. In 1797 he graduated BA, and in 1798 was elected to a fellowship at Oriel, which he held until his marriage on 22 December 1804 to Elizabeth (d. 1846), daughter of William Wood or Woods of Chidham, Sussex. Mant's essay 'On commerce' obtained the chancellor's prize in 1799. In 1800 he began his long series of poetical publications with verses in memory of his old master at Winchester, Joseph Warton. He graduated MA in 1801, was ordained deacon in 1802, and, after acting as curate to his father, took a travelling tutorship, and was detained in France in 1802–3 during the war.

Having been ordained priest in 1803, Mant became curate in charge (1804) of Buriton, Hampshire. After acting as curate at Crawley, Hampshire (1808), and to his father at Southampton (December 1809), he became vicar of Coggeshall, Essex (1810), where he took pupils. In 1811 he was elected Bampton lecturer, and chose as his topic a vindication of the evangelical character of Anglican preaching against the allegations of Methodists. The lectures attracted notice. Charles Manners-Sutton, archbishop of Canterbury, made him his domestic chaplain in 1813, and on going to reside at Lambeth he resigned Coggeshall. In 1815 he was made rector of St Botolph without Bishopsgate and took a DD at Oxford. He was presented in 1818 to the rectory of East Horsley, Surrey, which he held with St Botolph's.

In February 1820 Mant, though lacking any previous Irish interest or connection, was nominated by Lord Liverpool for an Irish bishopric. He is said to have been first intended for Waterford and Lismore (though this was not vacant), but was ultimately appointed to Killaloe and Kilfenora, and was consecrated at Cashel on 30 April 1820. The Catholic south was not an easy post for a Church of Ireland cleric, and W. B. Mant's memoir of his father reports considerable turmoil during Mant's four years there. He voted against Roman Catholic emancipation in 1821, and again in 1825. On 22 March 1823 he was translated to the more congenial Ulster diocese of Down and Connor, succeeding Nathaniel Alexander who had been

Modern at the end of the twentieth century. The annotated Bible (1814) prepared by George *D'Oyly and Mant, at the instance of Archbishop Manners-Sutton, and at the expense of the Society for Promoting Christian Knowledge, was largely a compilation but was influential in its time, upon the young W. E. Gladstone, among others. It was followed by an edition of the prayer book (1820), on a somewhat similar plan, by Mant alone.

Mant's most enduring work is his *History of the Church of Ireland from the Reformation to the Revolution* (2 vols., 1840). It was undertaken to provide as detailed a narrative of the Church of Ireland as James Seaton Reid provided in the first two volumes of his *History of the Presbyterian Church in Ireland* (1833–7). No one was so well equipped for the task as Charles Richard Elrington, but on his withdrawing owing to ill health, Mant came forward. His style is readable, and his facts are usually well arranged, though his comments and general point of view are those of a committed partisan. The earlier church history of Ireland is ignored, and the period immediately preceding the Reformation is treated somewhat in the manner of a protestant pamphlet; but the real topic of the book, the post-Reformation annals of the Irish establishment to the Union, still stands, more than a hundred and fifty years later, as a useful, if biased, account.

Mant was taken ill on 27 October 1848 while staying at the rectory, Ballymoney, co. Antrim, and died there on 2 November 1848. He was buried on 7 November in the churchyard of St James's, Hillsborough, co. Down. He was survived by a daughter and two sons; the elder son, Walter Bishop *Mant, was his father's biographer.

ALEXANDER GORDON, *rev.* KARL S. BOTTIGHEIMER

Sources W. B. Mant, *Memoirs of the Right Reverend Richard Mant, D.D.* (1857) · D. H. Akenson, *The Church of Ireland: ecclesiastical reform and revolution, 1800–1885* (1971) · Ward, *Men of the reign*
Archives Down and Connor and Dromore Diocesan Library, Belfast, corresp. mainly with Lord J. G. Beresford | BL, corresp. with Sir Robert Peel, Lord Liverpool, Add. MSS 40537, 40550, 40573 · Bodl. Oxf., letters to James Ingram · PRO NIre., corresp. with Primate Beresford
Likenesses E. K., oils, 1831, Oriel College, Oxford · R. Smith, line engraving, pubd 1840, BM, NPG [*see illus.*] · G. R. Ward, mezzotint, pubd 1843, BM

Richard Mant (1776–1848), by Richard Smith, pubd 1840

translated to Meath. There was no official residence connected with his diocese, and Mant made his home at Knocknagoney (Rabbit's Hill), in the parish of Holywood, co. Down, a few miles from Belfast. He had come from a diocese which was largely Roman Catholic to a stronghold of protestantism, mainly Presbyterian, and he succeeded in doing much for the prosperity of the then established church. Mant was on the royal commission of inquiry into ecclesiastical unions (1830); the publication of its report in July 1831 was followed by considerable efforts of church extension in his diocese. He found Belfast with two episcopal churches, and left it with five. He took an active part in connection with the Down and Connor Church Accommodation Society, formed (19 December 1838) at the suggestion of Thomas Drew, which between 1839 and 1843 laid out £32,000 in aid of sixteen new churches. In 1842, on the death of James Saurin, bishop of Dromore, that diocese was united to Down and Connor, in accordance with the provisions of the Church Temporalities Act of 1833. The united diocese was a large one, being 'a sixteenth of all Ireland'. The last bishop who had held the three sees conjointly was the seventeenth-century prelate Jeremy Taylor, to whose memory a marble monument, projected by Mant, and with an inscription from his pen, had been placed in 1827 in the cathedral church at Lisburn, co. Antrim.

Mant was an indefatigable writer; the bibliography of his publications occupied over five pages in the British Library catalogue. His poetry is chiefly notable for its copiousness. Many of his hymns were adapted from the Roman breviary, and four survive in *Hymns Ancient and*

Mant, Walter Bishop (1807–1869), Church of Ireland clergyman, was the eldest son of Richard *Mant (1776–1848), bishop of Down, Connor, and Dromore, and Elizabeth Wood (*d.* 2 April 1846). He was born on 25 June 1807 at Buriton, Hampshire. He matriculated at Oriel College, Oxford, on 6 February 1824, and graduated BA in 1827, proceeding MA in 1830. In 1831 he took holy orders, and was appointed archdeacon of Connor by his father. He married the Hon. Marianne Blackwood, daughter of Hans, third Lord Dufferin and Claneboye, on 15 October 1831. They had two daughters before her death on 22 February 1845. In 1832 he attended Trinity College, Dublin. He became rector of Hillsborough, co. Down, in October 1834, and was appointed archdeacon of Down.

For many years Mant was provincial grand master, and afterwards provincial grand chaplain, of the freemasons of Down and Antrim. On 5 January 1847 he remarried; his new wife was Emily Neville (d. 1865), daughter of Lieutenant-Colonel Marcus Corry, of Hillsborough, co. Down. They had two sons. Mant wrote poetry and was interested in antiquarian subjects, contributing to the *Proceedings* of local societies. His published works include *Horae apostolicae* (1839), *Memoirs of … Richard Mant* (1857), *Christophoros and other Poems* (1861), and *Bible Quartets* (1862). He died on 6 April 1869 at the archdeaconry, Hillsborough, where he was buried in the churchyard on 10 April. A tablet to his memory was erected in the village church there.

ALEXANDER GORDON, rev. DAVID HUDDLESTON

Sources J. B. Leslie and H. B. Swanzy, *Biographical succession lists of the clergy of diocese of Down* (1936), 34 · *Belfast News-Letter* (7 April 1869) · *Belfast News-Letter* (12 April 1869) · H. Cotton, *Fasti ecclesiae Hibernicae*, 3 (1849), 234–58 · H. Cotton, *Fasti ecclesiae Hibernicae*, 6 (1878), 103 · H. B. Swanzy, *Succession lists of the diocese of Dromore*, ed. J. B. Leslie (1933), 21 · Foster, *Alum. Oxon.*
Archives Representative Church Body Library, Dublin
Wealth at death under £800: administration, 24 Sept 1869, *CGPLA Ire.*

Mante, Thomas (*bap.* 1733, *d. c.*1802), army officer and historian, was baptized Thomas Mant on 3 December 1733 at St Faith's parish church, Havant, Hampshire, the eldest of the eight children of Thomas Mant (1702–1768), an estate manager, and his wife, Mary (d. 1781), the daughter of the Revd Joseph Bingham (1668–1723), rector of St Faith's, Havant, a church historian and antiquarian, and his wife, Dorothea Pococke (1672–1755). Nothing is known of his early years until his appointment as senior second lieutenant of the 94th company of marines on 25 June 1756. On 1 November 1759 he transferred to the 56th company of marines as its junior first lieutenant. As a marine officer he participated in the West Indies campaigns of 1759 and 1762, and by 7 June 1762 he was one of seventeen assistant engineers engaged by the earl of Albemarle for the siege of Havana. By 24 June 1762 he was a lieutenant in the 77th regiment of foot, which left for New York late in August 1762 after the capture of Havana from Spanish forces. Following the peace of 1763 newer regiments such as Mant's 77th were disbanded, but Mant's company joined Colonel Henry Bouquet's campaign against Pontiac's coalition of Native American tribes during the summer of 1763. His next post was brigade major in Colonel John Bradstreet's expedition in 1764 to make peace with Pontiac's coalition.

Having been placed on half pay, Mant spent the years 1765–73 primarily in London working on numerous projects. As agent for John Bradstreet, now a general in America, he worked unsuccessfully from 1765 to 1768 with the Board of Trade to set up a colony in Detroit with himself as lieutenant-governor and Bradstreet as governor. He was also unable to earn an adequate income, and his constant borrowing from Bradstreet and Sir Charles Gould, judge advocate-general of the army, alienated these powerful figures who might have advanced his career. Mant was employed during this London period by John Robinson, secretary of the Treasury and head of foreign intelligence, to gather intelligence concerning a possible war with

France. On 29 June 1769 he married Mary Silver at St Peter's parish church, North Hayling, near his ancestral home of Havant.

Mant's first period in London is noteworthy for his literary activity. He prepared four books for the press: his masterpiece, the *History of the Late War in North America* (1772) and three translations of works on military tactics by Colonel Joly de Maizeroy or his school, *A Treatise on the Use of Defensive Arms* (1770), the two-volume *System of Tactics* (written in 1769–71, though not published until 1781), and the *Elementary Principles of Tactics* (1771). The three works on military science provide the theoretical foundation for his *History*, and the four works should be regarded as a tetralogy of 1600 pages offering an epic portrait of men at war. His *History* has been widely praised by historians, and some passages have been quoted repeatedly, such as the description of the horrors of thirst and yellow fever at the siege of Havana in 1762. Mante changed the spelling of his name between 1770, when his *Defensive Arms* was published under the name Thomas Mant, and 1772, when his *History* was published under the name Thomas Mante.

The change in name reflects Mante's permanent move in 1773 to Dieppe, Normandy, where he had lived intermittently since 1769. In 1769 he had been recruited by General Grant de Blairfindy, who regarded him as 'peut être le plus grand génie de l'Europe' (Cole, 102), to spy for the French ministry of war against Britain. Mante was in the employ of the French authorities until 1774, when payments stopped because of suspicions that he was a double agent. However, he was still able to work in France as an excise officer and then, during the years 1775–8, as the owner of an estate near Dieppe for raising British sheep. This project was a failure, and in 1778 Mante's heavy indebtedness threw him into debtors' prison. He was nevertheless able to convert his failure as a farmer into a book, published in 1778 as *Traité des prairies artificielles, des enclos, et de l'education des moutons de race angloise*. The work was officially approved by the keeper of the great seal, and Louis XVI gave his 'Amé le sieur de Mante' (Cole, 120) and his heirs the privilege to publish. From debtors' prison Mante inscribed a copy to Benjamin Franklin, American ambassador to France in 1778, from whom he received several gratuities.

After being released from prison early in 1781, Mante returned to London destitute and in poor health. He was rebuffed by both family and friends as a traitor, but he found a new friend in the London publisher Thomas Hookham, who in 1781–2 published Mante's novels *Lucinda* and *The Siege of Aubigny*, which were paraphrases from French sources. Mante's main effort during this second London period, however, was his monumental *Naval and Military History of the Wars of England* (*c.*1795–1807). While relying heavily on the histories of Hume and Smollett in the early volumes, he trusted his own expertise in volumes 5 and 6 covering the wars of 1714–71. His account of the Seven Years' War in America, in which he had been both participant and chronicler, however, lacks the richness of detail so characteristic of his earlier *History*. Mante wrote only half of volume 7, and an unnamed editor completed volume 7 and wrote volume 8, covering the period 1791–1807. Mante died about 1802 while working on his seventh volume and after publishing under a pseudonym nineteen essays entitled 'Retrospect of the eighteenth century' in the *Gentleman's Magazine* (1800–01).

RICHARD CARGILL COLE

Sources R. C. Cole, *Thomas Mante: writer, soldier, adventurer* (1993) · DNB
Archives NA Canada · NL Wales, Tredegar Park muniments · Yale U., Beinecke L. | American Antiquarian Society, Worcester, Massachusetts, Orderly Books collection, Bradstreet MS, Orderly book · American Philosophical Society, Philadelphia, Benjamin Franklin MSS · U. Mich., Clements L., Gage MSS, vol. 138

Mantell, Gideon Algernon (1790–1852), surgeon and geologist, was born on 3 February 1790 at his family's home in St Mary's Lane, Lewes, Sussex, a middle child among the eight of Thomas Mantell (1750–1807), a shoemaker, and his wife, Sarah Austen (1755–1828), originally from Kent. Precluded from attending grammar school and the universities by his father's well-known political and religious views (radical whig and Methodist, respectively), he was educated by John Button in Lewes and by his uncle George Mantell in Wiltshire. In 1805 he was apprenticed in Lewes to James Moore, a surgeon, with whom (following six months at St Bartholomew's Hospital in London) he entered into partnership. In 1816 Mantell married Mary Ann Woodhouse (1795–1869) of Maida Hill, London, the daughter of one of his first patients, and further established himself in Lewes, eventually buying out his partner, Moore. The four surviving children of his marriage were Ellen Maria (1818–1892?), who married John W. Parker, Walter Baldock Durrant *Mantell (1820–1895), Hannah Matilda (1822–1840), who died unmarried, and Reginald Neville *Mantell (1827–1857).

Although Mantell contributed several medical publications to *The Lancet* and other journals, he is notable primarily for his work in geology and palaeontology, fields that had attracted him in childhood. This work earned him the nickname 'Wizard of the Weald'. His assiduous investigations of the strata and invertebrate fossils of eastern Sussex culminated in *The Fossils of the South Downs* (1822), his first book (of twelve), with lithography by his wife. Having by then explored the rich vertebrate deposits of Tilgate Forest (near Cuckfield), he announced in February 1825 the discovery of *Iguanodon*, one of the various kinds of dinosaurs (not yet so called) with which he was subsequently associated. Although his earliest evidence consisted of teeth only, these were sufficient to establish the, at the time unique, identity of *Iguanodon* as an extinct gigantic herbivorous reptile and to secure for Mantell entry into the Royal Society. He had been admitted to the Geological Society of London as early as 1818 and in 1835 became the second recipient (after William Smith) of its Wollaston medal on the basis of his saurian discoveries.

In 1827 Mantell published *Illustrations of the Geology of Sussex*, which was devoted to the vertebrate fossils of Tilgate Forest and is the earliest book of any to deal primarily

with dinosaur remains. His *Geology of the South-East of England* (1833) then combined text from his books of 1822 and 1827 with a Geological Society paper in which he announced his discovery of a second kind of dinosaur, *Hylaeosaurus*. Heavily armoured, *Hylaeosaurus* confirmed that dinosaurs walked on solid ground and were not amphibian, as had earlier been thought.

Mantell's discoveries, honours, and books, together with a private geological museum he had established, brought him much-sought-after recognition, and even friends among the aristocracy, his lowly social origins notwithstanding. His lifelong hunger for respectability, whetted by a generous grant of £1000 from the very rich third earl of Egremont, led Mantell to abandon Lewes for nearby Brighton, which the king and his retinue visited every winter. Mantell failed to achieve a viable medical practice there but by expanding and eventually institutionalizing his geological museum, he became the local leader of scientific and other learned endeavour. In 1834 his American correspondent Benjamin Silliman of Yale (whom he was not to meet until 1851) secured for Mantell an honorary LLD. On the strength of this blatantly solicited honour, Mantell chose ever after to be known as Dr Mantell, though his distinction was literary rather than medical.

It was also in 1834 that Mantell acquired his most famous specimen, the Maidstone *Iguanodon*, which was bought for him from its discoverer by friends. As one of the two most nearly complete dinosaur fossils then known (his *Hylaeosaurus* being the other), it considerably increased available knowledge and became the chief attraction of his museum. Forced by economic necessity to buy a medical practice (in Clapham Common), and needing money, Mantell sold his fossils to the British Museum in 1838 for £4000. His wife and elder son left him the next year and his favourite daughter, Hannah Matilda, died of tuberculosis in 1840.

After months of despair over his quadruple loss, Mantell recovered his tenacity of spirit and began a decade of remarkable creativity, during much of which he was assisted by his remaining daughter, Ellen Maria, who contributed drawings by herself to several of his books, including the very popular *Wonders of Geology* (1838), *Medals of Creation* (1844, opposing evolution), and *Thoughts on Animalcules* (1846, on microscopy). His last books on geology, *A Pictorial Atlas of Fossil Remains* (1850) and *Petrifactions and their Teachings* (1851), include contributions on rare or recently extinct New Zealand birds by his son Walter.

The word 'dinosaur' was coined only in 1842 by Richard Owen, a brilliant but unscrupulous comparative anatomist whose envy of Mantell's original discoveries spoiled what should have been a congenial relationship between them. It was Mantell, not Owen, who first emphasized (in 1831) what Cuvier had affirmed earlier—that there had been an age of reptiles preceding the age of mammals. Besides *Iguanodon* and *Hylaeosaurus*, Mantell's dinosaur finds included *Megalosaurus*, *Cetiosaurus*, *Regnosaurus*, *Pelorosaurus*, and the later-named *Hypsilophodon*. He also discovered dozens of other prehistoric creatures: new fossil fishes, further vertebrates, and a very large number of invertebrates, together with microspecies and plants.

By the end of his remarkable career (blighted from 1841 on by a painful spinal condition), Mantell had won the gold medal of the Royal Society and numerous domestic and foreign honours. He contributed importantly to stratigraphy, palaeontology, evolutionary biology, ornithology, microscopy, archaeology, and local history; his medical knowledge and astute detective work once saved the life of a local woman, Hannah Russell, who had been falsely accused of poisoning her husband. Though a popular writer and lecturer, most of his publications were specialized, highly technical papers for either the Geological Society or the Royal Society. Mantell died in bed at his final home, 19 Chester Square, London, on 10 November 1852, possibly from an overdose of opium taken to assuage his continual spinal pain. He was buried four days later in Norwood cemetery beside his favourite daughter, Hannah Matilda, the only member of his immediate family who (in his eyes) never rejected him. DENNIS R. DEAN

Sources D. R. Dean, *Gideon Mantell and the discovery of dinosaurs* (1999) · D. R. Dean, *Gideon Algernon Mantell: a bibliography with supplementary essays* (Delmar, NY, 1998) · D. R. Dean, 'A bicentenary retrospective on Gideon Algernon Mantell, 1790–1852', *Journal of Geological Education*, 30 (1990), 434–43 · m. cert. · NL NZ, Turnbull L., Mantell MSS · M. Benton, 'Progressionism in the 1850s', *Archives of Natural History*, 11 (1982–4), 123–36 · P. Taquet, 'Cuvier-Buckland-Mantell et les dinosaures', *Actes du symposium paléontologique Georges Cuvier* [Montbeliard, France 1982], ed. J. M. Mazin and E. Salmon (1983), 475–94 · T. G. Vallance, 'Gideon Mantell, 1790–1852: a focus for study in the history of geology at the Turnbull Library', *Royal Society of New Zealand Bulletin*, 21 (1984), 91–100 · C. Brent, *Georgian Lewes* (1993) · A. J. Woodhouse, letters · R. J. Cleevely and S. D. Chapman, 'The two states of Mantell's *Illustrations of the geology of Sussex*: 1827 and c.1829', *Archives of Natural History*, 27 (2000), 23–50

Archives American Philosophical Society, Philadelphia · CUL · E. Sussex RO, letters; papers · GS Lond., papers relating to Lewes · NHM, catalogue and drawings; corresp. [copies] · NL NZ, Turnbull L., corresp. and papers · RS · Sussex Archaeological Society, Lewes | Castle Ashby, letters to Lord Northampton · GS Lond., letters to Roderick Impey Murchison · NHM, letters to Richard Brickenden · RS, letters to William Buckland · W. Sussex RO, corresp. with John Hawkins · Yale U., Silliman MSS

Likenesses A. Archer, group portrait, oils, 1831, Lewes Town Hall · J. J. Masquerier, oils, 1837, RS · oils, 1840–49, GS Lond. · C. Woolcott or D. Woolcott, oils, 1876?, repro. in S. Spokes, *Gideon Algernon Mantell* (1927) · R. M. Paye, oils, 1879, NL NZ, Turnbull L. · A. Archer, portrait, priv. coll. · W. T. Davey, engraving (after photograph by Myall, 1849), Sussex Archaeological Society; repro. in Dean, *Gideon Mantell*, frontispiece · W. T. Davey, mezzotint, BM, NPG

Wealth at death proceeds from sales of second collection and household goods; over £5000: Dean, *Gideon Algernon Mantell*, 249–50, 263–4

Mantell, Joshua (1795–1865), surgeon and horticulturist, was born on 3 November 1795 at St Mary's Lane, Lewes, the fourth son of Thomas Mantell (1750–1807), shoemaker, and his wife, Sarah Austen (1755–1828). Though hunchbacked and desultory, Mantell displayed an aptitude for science and eventually gave several public lectures on chemical topics to local audiences. In 1821 he managed a stationer's shop in Brighton for John Baxter (1781–1858), a

local printer and publisher. In 1822 he was apprenticed as a surgeon to his older brother Gideon. Joshua moved to London the following year for study at Westminster Hospital and the Fever Institute, returned to Lewes and his brother, and then went back to London (1827–8) for further study at St George's Hospital and other institutions. Now with proper credentials, he established himself as a surgeon in Newick, Sussex, and was both liked and respected by his patients. An avid botanist, Mantell founded the Newick Horticultural Society in 1830 and in 1832 published a short, practical essay on floriculture in the second edition of Baxter's *Library of Agricultural and Horticultural Knowledge*, a volume he may also have edited.

In March 1836 Mantell was thrown by his horse, permanently injuring his brain. His scientific and professional effects were auctioned off that September (by his older brother Thomas) and it was rumoured that Mantell had died. In April 1839 he was admitted as a patient at the respected Ticehurst Asylum; he died there on 28 March 1865 from 'decay of nature' complicated by asthma, and was buried at Newick. He never married.

DENNIS R. DEAN

Sources NL NZ, Turnbull L., Mantell family MSS · Wellcome L., Ticehurst Asylum records · *Sussex Advertiser* (22 Dec 1817) · *Sussex Advertiser* (26 Feb 1827) · *Sussex Advertiser* (19 Sept 1836) · *Diary of the late John Epps*, ed. Mrs Epps [1875]

Archives NL NZ, Turnbull L., family MSS

Mantell, Reginald Neville (1827–1857), civil engineer, was born in Lewes on 11 August 1827, the youngest, somewhat uncontrollable child of the surgeon Gideon Algernon *Mantell (1790–1852) and his wife, Mary Ann Woodhouse (1795–1869). His brother was Walter Baldock Durrant *Mantell (1820–1895). After desultory schooling at Lewes, Hanwell, and Clapham up to 1842, Mantell received valuable practical experience in civil engineering under Henry Carr in 1843. On 27 May 1844 he was formally apprenticed (at a cost to his father of £800) to Isambard Kingdom Brunel. Mantell worked on Hungerford Bridge (over the Thames at London) and, more importantly, on branches of the Great Western Railway. Living successively at Trowbridge and Swindon, he socialized extensively and collected fossils from newly made rail cuts in his spare time. These fossils were at first sent to his father, but Mantell later published on others himself. His finds, mostly interpreted by others, substantially resolved an important controversy regarding belemnites, confirming the identity of *Belemnoteuthis* as an independent genus separate from *Belemnites*.

Brunel was so pleased with the quality of Mantell's work as an engineer that in 1847 he cancelled the last year of Mantell's indentures and paid him a salary instead. Nationwide economic decline prevented Mantell from achieving a permanent position, but in March 1849 he rode aboard several of Brunel's new (and decidedly unsafe) locomotives on a frightful series of test runs to ascertain their consumption of coke and water. Rescued from that dangerous occupation by parental generosity, Mantell toured America later the same year at his father's expense. After some further months in England, he returned to the United States in August 1850 to accept employment as a railway engineer in and around Paris, Kentucky, a frequently violent frontier town that left its imprint on him.

Forced back to England by his father's death on 10 November 1852, Mantell oversaw the disbursement of his estate, returned briefly to Henry Carr, and then accepted a four-year position as district engineer in Allahabad, India. However, he proved unable to get along with the Hindus; he was successfully sued by one for battery and twice had his professional responsibilities curtailed as a result. In India he devoted his spare time to photography, the techniques of which he had learned in England from the well-known American photographer John Mayall.

Caught up in the Sepoy mutiny, Mantell died (unmarried) of cholera on 30 June 1857 in his houseboat on the Jumna River at Allahabad. He was buried in Allahabad the same day, his effects being eventually returned to his brother Walter in England. Gideon Mantell's *Thoughts on a Pebble* (1836; eight editions), a popular introduction to geology, was written for Reginald and dedicated to him.

DENNIS R. DEAN

Sources NL NZ, Turnbull L., Mantell family MSS, MS-Group-0305 · D. R. Dean, *Gideon Mantell and the discovery of dinosaurs* (1999) · D. R. Dean, *Gideon Algernon Mantell: a bibliography with supplementary essays* (Delmar, NY, 1998)
Archives NL NZ, Turnbull L., family MSS | PRO, I. K. Brunel MSS · Yale U., Silliman family MSS
Likenesses photographs (of Mantell?), NL NZ, Turnbull L.
Wealth at death under £5000—in England: probate, 1858

Mantell, Sir Thomas (1751–1831), antiquary, was born on 17 October 1751 at Chilham, Kent, the only son of Thomas Mantell, surgeon, of Chilham, and Catharine, daughter of John Nichols, rector of Fordwich. He belonged to the Kentish branch of the Mantells. The antiquary Samuel Pegge was his godfather. Early in life he settled in Dover as a surgeon but retired on being appointed agent for prisoners of war and transports at Dover. In 1814 he was appointed to the demanding post of agent for packets at Dover. He was for many years a magistrate at Dover, and six times its mayor. He was knighted on 13 May 1820 during his mayoralty. He married on 31 December 1778 at St Mary the Virgin, Dover, Anne, daughter of William Oakley; they had no children.

Mantell was elected fellow of the Society of Antiquaries in 1810. He investigated the tumuli in various parts of Kent, and was a collector of antiquities. In 1811 he published *An Account of Cinque Ports Meetings*; this was republished with additions in 1828. He further published *An Account of Coronation Ceremonies Relative to the Barons of the Cinque Ports* in 1820. He also published two medical papers. Mantell died at his home in Dover on 21 December 1831, aged eighty, and was buried in the family vault at Chilham. He was survived by his wife.

W. W. WROTH, *rev.* J. A. MARCHAND

Sources *GM*, 1st ser., 102/1 (1832), 88, 89, 651 · *IGI* · will, PRO, PROB 11/1798, sig. 238
Wealth at death whole estate bequeathed to wife: will, PRO, PROB 11/1798, fols. 322r–323r

Mantell, Walter Baldock Durrant (1820–1895), naturalist and colonial civil servant, elder son of Gideon Algernon *Mantell (1790–1852), geologist and palaeontologist, and his wife, Mary Ann Woodhouse (1795–1869), was born at Castle Place, Lewes, Sussex, on 11 March 1820. It was intended that he should be a surgeon and naturalist and he was apprenticed to his father in 1835. When this arrangement became unworkable, he served out the remainder of his apprenticeship (1836–9) under Ambrose Dodd (1806–1847) of Chichester.

Mantell refused a partnership with his father and emigrated to New Zealand, having been granted free passage on the *Oriental* in September 1839 as part of the Wakefield colonization scheme. On arrival the following January he took up land at Wainui but soon returned to town and accepted employment with the New Zealand Land Company, helping settlers at Wanganui and Taranaki. Between December 1840 and February 1844 he was variously clerk to the magistrates at Wellington, postmaster, and subcollector of customs. In 1845 he was appointed superintendent of military roads, a position which brought him into contact with the Maori, and enabled him to learn their language. In 1848 he was appointed commissioner for the extinguishment of native titles in Middle (later South) Island. In this capacity he bought from the Ngai Tahu Maori some 30 million acres of land in exchange for cash and such promised improvements as schools, hospitals, and reserves. In 1851 he was appointed commissioner of crown lands for Otago and a justice of the peace.

An active naturalist, Mantell sent large quantities of New Zealand specimens and much information to colleagues in England, including his father, Richard Owen, Charles Lyell, Charles Darwin, and John Gould. The specimens were primarily bones of the moa (*Dinornis maximus*), a large flightless bird only 200 years extinct. He also found, alive, the tahake (*Notornis mantelli*) and the North Island brown kiwi (*Apteryx australis mantelli*), both of which were named for him. The kiwi became a national symbol of New Zealand.

As a condition of his paternal inheritance, Mantell necessarily took a leave of absence and returned to England for three years (1856–9), where he met the distinguished naturalists he had assisted, was elected to the Zoological and Geological societies, and established further friendships with Thomas Carlyle and his literary circle: Jane Carlyle (1801–1866) described Mantell as 'a proud, shy man' (Howe, chap. 8); Geraldine Jewsbury (1812–1880) began a close association with him; others resented his caustic wit. Mantell was infuriated when the British government refused to honour promises he had made to the Ngai Tahu in good faith and resigned his commissioner's position.

On returning to New Zealand in 1859 Mantell entered politics and was elected to the house of representatives for 1861–5. An outspoken friend of the Maori, he was twice appointed native minister and twice resigned. In 1869 he married Mary Sarah Prince (d. 1873), with whom he already had a son (b. 1864). In 1866 he was appointed to the legislative council, serving until his death, at Sydney

Street, Wellington, on 7 September 1895. He was buried in Wellington. Mantell contributed numerous papers to the *Proceedings of the New Zealand Institute*, of which he was a founder and sometime secretary. He was also president of the Wellington Philosophical Society (1870) and occasionally acting director of the Geological Survey and Colonial Museum. Following the death of his first wife he married, on 10 January 1876, Jane Hardwick (*d.* 1906).

DENNIS R. DEAN

Sources NL NZ, Turnbull L., Mantell family MSS · H. Beattie, 'The pioneers explore Otago', *Otago Daily Times* (1947) · A. Ward, *A show of justice: racial 'amalgamation' in nineteenth century New Zealand* (1974) · S. Howe, *Geraldine Jewsbury: her life and errors* (1935) · M. P. K. Sorrenson, 'Mantell, Walter Baldock Durrant', *DNZB*, vol. 1 · A. H. McLintock, ed., *An encyclopaedia of New Zealand*, 3 vols. (1966) · W. B. D. Mantell, diary, NL NZ, Turnbull L.
Archives NL NZ, Turnbull L., family MSS
Likenesses photographs, NL NZ, Turnbull L. · photographs, Museum of New Zealand, Wellington · photographs, Parliament House, Wellington

Manteo (*fl.* 1584–1587). *See under* American Indians in England (*act. c.*1500–1609).

Manton, Irene (1904–1988), plant cytologist, was born on 17 April 1904 in Kensington, London, the youngest of three children and younger daughter of George Sidney Frederick Manton, dental surgeon, and his wife, Milana Angele Terese d'Humy. The eldest child, a son, had died in infancy; the elder daughter, Sidnie Milana *Manton, became a prominent zoologist. The family has been traced to Charles Manton (*b.* 1620), chaplain to Charles II. Her father's hobbies were cabinet-making and gold- and silver-working, and she undoubtedly owed her deftness to early exposure to these manual skills. She was educated at the Froebel Educational Institute and later at St Paul's Girls' School. Oddly enough in view of her later abundant energy, her school found Manton an idle pupil with marked aptitude only in music. Nevertheless in 1923 she won a Clothworkers' scholarship, and an exhibition from the school, which took her to Girton College, Cambridge (of which she became an honorary fellow in 1985). She retained her musical interest and later became an accomplished violinist.

About this time Manton came across E. B. Wilson's book *The Cell in Developmental Inheritance* (1896) and decided to read botany and to spend her life counting chromosomes. She obtained first-class honours in both parts of the natural sciences tripos (1925 and 1926). She then elected to begin her postgraduate work in Sweden in Otto Rosenberg's laboratory. Though without a supervisor, after one year she managed to classify 250 species of the Cruciferae on the basis of chromosome counting, giving her the material for her first important publication, and on the way learned to speak Swedish. Back in Cambridge she completed the mandatory further year's residence with the aid of a Yarrow bursary. She gained her PhD in 1930.

In 1929 Manton became assistant lecturer in botany at Manchester University, where she came under the influence of W. H. Lang, who was working on *Osmunda* and turned her mind to the ferns, an interest which was to last

all her life. By 1946 she had accumulated innumerable data on fern chromosomes, defining genera and species and their phylogenetic relationships, and later she gathered them into a book, *Problems of Cytology and Evolution in the Pteridophyta* (1950), which had enormous influence and established her as an authority.

In 1946 Manton was invited to become professor of botany at Leeds, a post she held until her retirement in 1969. Her medium figure in blouse or cardigan and tweed skirt, with its vigorous stride, strong face, and penetrating voice, became familiar. She had a heavy load of teaching and administration, and in consequence adopted a new lifestyle, working on her researches late into the evening every day, including weekends and holidays. She had no distracting domestic chores since she was, and remained, unmarried and had brought with her from Manchester her kindly, patient, and long-suffering housekeeper, Edith. She acquired an ultraviolet microscope and later took advantage of the extra microscopic resolution afforded by the first electron microscope, obtained in 1950. She dealt first with the flagella of the sperm of ferns and other plant groups, from which it was an easy step to the structure of the organelles inside plant cells. Because of this work, she became as distinguished for her electron microscopy as for her fern cytology. She took up the study of marine flagellates and published extensively on the remarkable structures they revealed. In the course of this work she discovered a number of new species. Her ferns were not neglected either. By her own efforts and that of many students and colleagues she collected from various parts of the world and, with chromosomes as the guide, made the ferns the best-known group in the plant kingdom.

The early years of Manton's retirement were traumatic since her housekeeper also retired, so that she had to fend for herself at home. She began work on the marine flagellates and was freely invited to use the facilities at Nottingham, Lancaster, and Imperial College, London, and occasionally laboratories at Ottawa and at Marburg in Germany. She made frequent arduous journeys in places ranging from the Arctic to South Africa, discovering and recording innumerable new species. She also made a valuable collection of modern paintings, which she bequeathed to Leeds University.

Manton received many honours and medals. She had honorary doctorates from five universities (McGill, Durham, Lancaster, Leeds, and Oslo). Several societies elected her to honorary membership or fellowship. She was president of the Pteridological Society in 1971–2 and of the Linnean Society from 1973 to 1976. In 1961 she was elected FRS. As a final accolade, she and her sister, Sidnie, received posthumously the distinction of having a feature on the planet Venus named the Manton crater. She died on 31 May 1988 in the Chapel Allerton Hospital, Leeds.

R. D. PRESTON, *rev.*

Sources R. D. Preston, *Memoirs FRS*, 35 (1990), 247–61 · personal knowledge (1996) · *CGPLA Eng. & Wales* (1988)
Wealth at death £292,711: probate, 22 July 1988, *CGPLA Eng. & Wales*

Manton, John (1752–1834). *See under* Manton, Joseph (1766–1835).

Manton, Joseph [Joe] (1766–1835), gun maker, was born in April 1766 and baptized on 29 April at St Wulfram's Church, Grantham, Lincolnshire, the youngest of six children of John Manton (1725–1802), farmer, and his wife, Mary, daughter of Henry Gildon, yeoman, and his wife, Ann. He was apprenticed first to William Newton of Grantham and then to his elder brother, John Manton, at 6 Dover Street, London. He married Mary Ann Aitkens on 17 January 1792. They had nine children; of these, Frederick was sent out to India in 1822 where he established a gun making business in Calcutta, and Charles became master furbisher at the Tower of London in 1829. In 1789 Joseph Manton branched out on his own and by 1791 he was established in business at 25 Davies Street, Berkeley Square, London, where he remained until 1818. The possession of one of his guns was an object of ambition to sportsmen, many of whom frequented his shop. Colonel Peter Hawker was a great friend and admirer of Joe Manton, as he was almost universally called, and his *Instructions to Young Sportsmen* abounds with references to Manton's skill.

Manton took out twelve patents between 1792 and 1825 for a variety of ideas. These included an improved hammer and breeching; a spring to prevent the trigger from rattling; cartridges; a perforated hammer to allow air to escape when the charge was being rammed down; the 'elevated rib' connecting the barrels of double guns; the 'gravitating stop' to prevent accidental discharge; and the 'musical sear', by which a musical sound was produced on cocking the piece. Manton applied for a patent in 1790 for a machine for rifling cannon, and for an improved shot with a base of soft wood to take into the grooving. Experiments were carried out at Woolwich and he was offered a sum of £500 for these inventions, which he declined. Finally in 1792 the patent was granted. Had he co-operated more closely with the authorities, Manton would have met with more success but he had already developed those characteristics of doggedness and determination which were to colour his whole life. In his best guns he introduced platinum touch-holes for preventing corrosion, and his barrels were proved by hydraulic pressure. He claimed that none of his guns had ever been known to burst. His famous reputation as the 'king of the gun makers' was founded on the speed of ignition of his flintlocks and the overall excellence of his work. His other inventions comprised a method of enclosing clocks in exhausted cases to make them airless; airtight sliding tubes for telescopes; and a tool for boring holes in horses' feet, so that shoes might be attached by screws instead of by nails. Hawker claimed for Manton the introduction of the copper percussion cap, but this is not borne out by the evidence.

In 1816 Manton started to make guns with percussion ignition, first with a pellet lock and in 1818 with a tube lock. The quality was superb but they were very costly, and whereas in 1815 he had an annual production of 400 arms,

by 1825 the figure was less than 100. Several legal actions for alleged infringements of his patents, one against his own brother John, were also a great expense and in 1825 he was imprisoned for debt. He was declared bankrupt in January 1826. He had recovered by June 1827, but was again imprisoned four times between 1828 and 1831. At the time of his bankruptcy he was carrying on business at 11 Hanover Square and at 315 Oxford Street but the next year he was in the New Road, Marylebone, then in Burwood Place, and in 1834 at 6 Holles Street, in partnership with his son John Augustus. Manton died at 4 Lyon Terrace, Edgware Road, Maida Hill, on 29 June 1835, aged sixty-nine, and was buried in Kensal Green cemetery, his epitaph being from the pen of Colonel Hawker, who printed it in his *Instructions*. Manton's business was carried on by his son at 6 Holles Street until 1838, when it was acquired by Messrs Charles and Henry Egg, also a name of repute in the gun trade. His brother **John Manton** (1752–1834) was also a gun maker, with a reputation little inferior to that of Joseph. He was born on 6 November 1752 at Grantham, the eldest son of John Manton (1725–1802) and his wife, Mary, *née* Gildon. He was apprenticed in 1766 to John Dixon, gun maker, at Leicester, turned over in 1768 to W. Edson at Grantham, and from about 1774 worked for John Twigg of Piccadilly, rising to be his foreman. He and his wife, Catherine, whom he married about 1786, had four children. At Michaelmas 1781 he set up on his own at 6 Dover Street, Piccadilly, where he carried on business until his death. Between 1797 and 1821 he developed a flintlock with a V-shaped flash pan which was very successful, a single trigger action, a vertical sear, and a new breech system, all protected by patents. His business prospered despite a temporary set back in 1823–4 when he continued with flint ignition while other makers were using percussion locks. Eventually he yielded to the increasing knowledge of the times and thereafter his trade recovered.

In 1814 John Manton took his son George Henry into partnership and the firm was known as John Manton & Son. Shortly afterwards annual production was about 250 arms and Colonel Hawker gave this opinion: 'No one can dispute the excellence of Mr John Manton's guns, although he may have left to other members the risk or merit of trying experiments, and bringing out new patents or inventions.' John Manton died at 6 Dover Street on 24 November 1834 and was buried at St George's, Hanover Square, bequeathing the whole of his business to his son George Henry.   D. H. L. BACK

Sources W. K. Neal and D. H. L. Back, *The Mantons: gunmakers* (1967) • W. K. Neal and D. H. L. Back, *A supplement to the Mantons: gunmakers* (1978) • D. H. L. Back, *Great British gunmakers: the Mantons, 1782–1878* (1993) • *The diary of Colonel Peter Hawker, 1802–1853*, ed. R. Payne-Gallwey, 2 vols. (1893) • P. Hawker, *Instructions to young sportsmen* (1814) • D. P. Blaine, *Encyclopaedia of rural sports* (1840) • W. B. Daniel, *Rural sports* (1807) • Thormanby [W. W. Dixon], *Kings of the rod, rifle, and gun*, 2 vols. (1901) • G. T. Teasdale-Buckell, *Experts on guns and shooting* (1900) • J. Davies, *A collection of the most important cases respecting patents of invention* (1816), 333–55 • S. Parkes, *Chemical essays*, 1 (1815) [John Manton] • parish records (baptism), 29 April

1766, St Wulfram, Grantham, Lincolnshire · private information (2004) · 'On a proposed monument', *The Times* (6 April 1836), 3f **Likenesses** H. Adlard, engraving (after Childe), repro. in Paine-Gallwey, ed., *Diary of Colonel Peter Hawker*, vol. 1, facing p. 318 · G. Manton, portrait, Gunmakers' Company, London · portrait, Mitchell L., NSW

Wealth at death £100: administration, 1835 · John Manton: administration with will, 1834

Manton [*married name* Harding], **Sidnie Milana** (1902–1979), zoologist, was born on 4 May 1902 in London, the elder daughter and second of three children (the son died in infancy) of George Sidney Frederick Manton, dental surgeon, of London, and his wife, Milana Angele Terese d'Humy. She was educated at the school of the Froebel Educational Institute, Kensington (1906), and St Paul's Girls' School, Hammersmith (1917–21), from where she obtained a leaving exhibition and proceeded to Girton College, Cambridge. There she won the Montefiore prize and obtained first classes in both parts of the natural sciences tripos (1923 and 1925), topping the list in zoology in the latter examination.

Following a year spent as Alfred Yarrow student at Imperial College, London, in 1927 Manton was appointed university demonstrator in comparative anatomy at Cambridge, and served variously as supervisor in zoology, director of studies (1935–42), a staff fellow (1928–35 and 1942–5), and research fellow (1945–8) of Girton College. She was awarded her PhD in 1928 and her ScD in 1934.

In 1928 she visited Tasmania to study the primitive freshwater syncarid crustaceans *Anaspides* and *Paranaspides*, and then joined the Great Barrier Reef expedition for the last four months of its stay at Low Isles —a never-to-be-forgotten experience.

In 1937 Sidnie Manton married John Philip Harding (1911–1998), son of Philip William Harding, a bank official. Her husband eventually became keeper of zoology at the British Museum (Natural History). They had one daughter and an adopted son.

From 1949 to 1960 Manton was reader in zoology at King's College, London (she had been visiting lecturer there, 1943–6), and subsequently honorary fellow at Queen Mary College, London, and honorary associate of the British Museum (Natural History).

Manton was an all-round zoologist; her particular eminence lay in the fields of arthropod embryology and functional morphology, and in her ability to bring her findings to bear on the problems of evolution. Her embryological work on the crustaceans *Hemimysis lamornae* and *Nebalia bipes* elucidated many of the complex processes that take place during their development and set new standards in this field. Much interested in the enigmatic Onychophora, she discovered how, in *Peripatopsis*, spermatozoa reach the ovary from spermatophores deposited on the surface of the body, and she studied the development of certain viviparous non-placental species of that genus. Later, with Donald T. Anderson, she studied the relationship between the embryo and the oviduct in two viviparous placental species.

Sidnie Manton's work on functional morphology,

Sidnie Milana Manton (1902–1979), by Walter Stoneman

which began with studies on crustacean feeding mechanisms, some of it in collaboration with H. Graham Cannon, extended to a wide-ranging study of arthropod mandibles, and culminated in a long series of investigations on arthropod locomotory mechanisms. The latter embraced a diversity of organisms and, beginning in 1950, the published results, which often broke new ground, appeared at intervals over a period of more than twenty years. She also developed new concepts of arthropod relationships, resulting in the erection of the new phylum Uniramia. Much of her work was summarized in *The Arthropoda: Habits, Functional Morphology and Evolution* (1977), in which she was able to draw out its evolutionary implications.

As well as other contributions to invertebrate zoology, and to meet the needs of students in a different field, Manton produced, with J. T. Saunders, *A Manual of Practical Vertebrate Morphology* (1931), which went through four editions. An interest in the breeding of colourpoint cats, at which, by virtue of her understanding of the genetic principles involved she was very successful, led to a book, *Colourpoint, Himalayan and Longhair Cats* (1971), of which a second edition appeared in 1979.

She was honoured by election as a fellow of the Royal Society in 1948. Her sister, Irene *Manton, professor of botany at Leeds University, later also achieved this distinction, the only case involving two sisters in the history of the society. She was awarded the gold medal for zoology of the Linnean Society (1963) and the Frink medal of the Zoological Society (1977), as well as an honorary doctorate of the University of Lund, Sweden.

Spare of frame and always interested in sport, Sidnie Manton was the Cambridge swimming captain in 1923 and a hockey blue in 1924; she played tennis until well into her sixties. She was forthright in manner, and her criticism of loose thinking could be scathing, but she devoted much time to helping students, and those less gifted than herself, with their work. She died at her home, 88 Ennerdale Road, Richmond, Surrey, on 2 January 1979.

GEOFFREY FRYER, *rev.*

Sources G. Fryer, *Memoirs FRS*, 26 (1980), 327–56 • *The Times* (16 Nov 1979) • W. T. Stearn, *The Natural History Museum at South Kensington: a history of the British Museum (Natural History), 1753–1980* (1981)
Likenesses W. Stoneman, photograph, RS [*see illus.*] • photograph, repro. in Fryer, *Memoirs FRS*, 327
Wealth at death £44,219: probate, 5 March 1979, *CGPLA Eng. & Wales*

Manton, Thomas (*bap.* 1620, *d.* 1677), nonconformist minister, was baptized on 31 March 1620 at Lydeard St Lawrence, Somerset, where his father, Thomas Manton of Whimple in Devon, was probably curate.

Education and early clerical career Manton was educated at the free school in Tiverton, Devon, and on 11 March 1636 matriculated as a plebeian from Wadham College, Oxford. He graduated BA from Hart Hall, Oxford, on 15 June 1639, proceeded BD from Wadham on 20 April 1654 (the degree was incorporated at Cambridge in 1658), and was created DD at Oxford on 19 November 1660. Bishop Joseph Hall ordained Manton to the diaconate in 1640, although his leanings towards presbyterianism prevented him from seeking further ordination. Anthony Wood, the Anglican polemicist of the 1680s, alleged that Bishop Galloway ordained Manton to the priesthood in 1660. The balance of probabilities is against this assertion; Edmund Calamy states, on the basis of Josias Hill's testimony, that it was Manton's 'judgement that he was properly ordained to the ministerial office, and that no powers on earth had any right to divide and parcel that out at their pleasure' (Calamy).

Until September 1643 Manton was lecturer to the parish church of Sowton, near Exeter, where he married Mary Morgan (*d.* 1701) of Sidbury on 15 May 1643. After Exeter fell to royalist forces on 4 September the Mantons were forced to move first to Lyme and then to Colyton. Further royalist advances led Manton to decide to flee the west altogether, and in July 1645 he moved to London, where he was installed by Alexander Popham, the godly MP and parliamentarian colonel, as rector of St Mary's, Stoke Newington.

An impassioned presbyterian During the late 1640s Manton was involved in the campaign to establish presbyterianism in the London region. He established the government at St Mary's, Stoke Newington, in 1646 and was joined by Alexander Popham as the parish's ruling elder. Manton was a committed member of the eighth London classis and was often a delegate to the London provincial

Thomas Manton (*bap.* 1620, *d.* 1677), by Robert White, pubd 1681

assembly, which gave him the task of persuading the ministers of the failed eleventh classis to set up church government.

Manton's ministry at Stoke Newington was a model of rigorous evangelical Calvinism; in particular he preached long expository sermons of the epistles of both James and Jude. In so doing he caught the attention of the House of Commons and, in the troubled years of 1647–8, was twice invited to preach at official parliamentary fasts. He ostensibly chose moderate themes for both of these sermons. On 30 June 1647, at the peak of the crisis between the army and the City of London, Manton preached *Meate out of the Eater, or, Hopes of Unity in and by Divided Times*, a sermon on Zechariah 14: 9. In his epistle to the Commons he stated that the purpose of the sermon was '*to reduce men from their violences & extremities to some better temper and moderation*'. The main thrust of the sermon, however, was that parliament should establish presbyterianism as the official church system in England and allow only a modicum of accommodation for dissenting opinion.

On 28 June 1648, during the second civil war, Manton was again invited to preach before the Commons. His sermon, entitled *England's Spiritual Languishings; with the Causes and Cure*, was on Revelation 2: 3 and had as its doctrine 'That a speciall way to save a Church and people from imminent and speedy ruine is the repairing of decayed godlynesse'. He bemoaned the fact that religion had become the 'stalking horse to every selfe seeking designe' and once again asked parliament to settle presbyterianism as a means to rectify England's sins. Appalled by Pride's Purge and the trial of Charles I, in January 1649 he was a signatory to the London presbyterians' printed protests about both addressed to Lord General Fairfax. Manton also joined the ministers of the London provincial assembly in private fasts convened to seek the guidance of God about the revolutionary events. He preached a sermon for this purpose to the assembly on 6 February 1649.

Commonwealth career During the first three years of the republic the London presbyterians plotted against the regicides' regime for the return of Charles II and the solemn league and covenant. The result of this plotting was the arrest, trial, and condemnation of Christopher Love for treason in the summer of 1651. In August 1652 Manton joined Edmund Calamy and Simeon Ashe in spiritually preparing Love for his execution. Manton intended to preach at Love's public funeral, but when this was forbidden by parliament, who feared rebellion, he was forced to give his oration to a midnight audience at Love's parish of St Lawrence Jewry. Despite the threatening presence of the army a correspondent noted that 'a mighty throng of people' gathered to hear him. He lectured on 1 Corinthians 15: 57 and applied the text in a Calvinist manner against Love's persecutors. Manton used the logic of predestination to interpret the passage, holding that it revealed a 'terror for wicked men' as 'none but a childe of God can have true and solid courage against death'. In condemning those who had executed Love, Manton equated the republic to the Babylonian tyranny of Belshazzar in the book of Daniel.

Although Manton refused to co-operate with the republic's government his star was in the ascendancy during the protectorate of Oliver Cromwell, and on 20 March 1654 he was appointed one of the commissioners for the approbation of public preachers, or 'triers'. The state papers show that he was often called upon to perform this duty. In April 1654 he joined his fellow presbyterians Edmund Calamy, Stephen Marshall, Simeon Ashe, and Richard Vines for talks on accommodation with the congregationalists Joseph Caryl, Philip Nye, Sidrach Simpson, Samuel Slater, and William Carter. He also joined the senior presbyterian and Independent ministers of Oxford, Cambridge, and London in signing a letter recommending John Dury in his mission to create unity among European protestants.

Manton's willingness to seek accommodation with the congregationalist clergy meant that he became the principal presbyterian voice on protectorate committees discussing religious matters. In October 1654 he was chosen for the committee convened to help resolve the rift in the Church of Scotland between the resolutioners and the remonstranters. In November that year a parliamentary subcommittee chose Manton to join ministers such as Thomas Goodwin, John Owen, Henry Jessey, and Richard Baxter to agree on the fundamentals of religion that would be essential for subscription to the protectorate

church. He also sat with the council of state in November 1655 to hear Menasseh ben Israel's proposals for the readmission of the Jews into England.

Manton's connections with the protectorate earned him high appointment. He was chosen to be lecturer at Westminster Abbey on 18 January 1656, and on 21 December following the earl of Bedford called him to be admitted as rector of St Paul's, Covent Garden, whose congregation also included Oliver St John and Sir William Fleetwood. Manton was keen to establish presbyterian discipline at St Paul's, but the policy was resisted by his parishioners, as well as by his assistant Abraham Pinchbecke. Despite his presbyterianism he showed charity to clergymen of other persuasions; in May 1658 the Anglican diarist John Evelyn recalled that Manton arranged a collection for the 'Anglican' clergy sequestered during the civil war. He was also nominated an assistant to the Middlesex commission on 24 October 1657. When Oliver Cromwell was offered the crown by parliament in the same year, Manton was chosen alongside John Owen, Joseph Caryl, Philip Nye, and George Gillespie to pray with the lord protector in order to help him seek God's guidance in making a decision. Although Cromwell finally refused the crown Manton was chosen to deliver the public blessing at the inauguration of the second protectorate parliament in June.

The search for accommodation and ejection Manton welcomed the protectorate of Richard Cromwell and its call for unity among the orthodox godly clergy. On the opening day of Richard's ill-fated parliament Manton wrote to Richard Baxter about the possibility of calling an assembly of divines to seek agreement between presbyterians and Independents, a suggestion Baxter opposed on grounds that agreement was unlikely. When the army deposed Baxter, Manton joined his fellow presbyterians in seeking the restoration of Charles II and was one of the divines who attended Charles at Breda. He was also one of the ministers deputed to give the oath of loyalty to the king on his procession through London in May 1660. Despite these overtures to the king Manton's belief in the need for a godly and disciplined church did not wane. In 1660 he joined his fellow ministers in signing the *Seasonable exhortation … to the people of their respective congregations*, warning of the dangers of popery and heresy. He was also a co-signatory with Edmund Calamy and other London presbyterians in writing a private letter to brethren in Scotland, warning of the threat to the godly cause from the restoration of episcopacy and the Anglican liturgy.

Manton's connection with the king meant that he received some favour in the early days of the Restoration. He was officially instituted at St Paul's, Covent Garden, on 10 January 1661, although some of his parishioners petitioned the bishop of London to make him read the Book of Common Prayer. Despite his opposition to the ceremonies Manton reluctantly complied with the bishop's orders.

With the re-establishment of episcopacy the moderate presbyterian ministers sought to use their favour at court to remodel the national church in the Reformed mould. In

1660 Manton republished the 1641 work of the presbyterian ministers who wrote under the eponym 'Smectymnuus'. This was an extremely provocational act as the work argued that in the New Testament the Greek words for 'bishop' and 'priest' were used synonymously. Smectymnuus claimed that this proved that the hierarchy between bishop and priest was false and thus a sinful human innovation. Manton stated in his epistle, 'if the quarrell of Episcopacy were once cleared, and brought to an issue, we should not be so much in the dark in other parts of discipline.'

The main concern of the presbyterians was to prevent the institution of the revised Anglican liturgy, which they saw as containing the worst abuses of Roman Catholicism. Manton was present at a meeting at Edmund Calamy's Aldermanbury house on 2 April 1660 and attended discussions at Sion College. The purpose of these meetings, also attended by Richard Baxter, was to resolve contents of the presbyterian liturgy. On 22 October, Manton and other senior presbyterian clergy attended the king at Lord Chancellor Manchester's residence to present their proposals. These talks led to the ill-fated conference between the Anglicans and presbyterians at the Savoy on 25 March 1661, the failure of which prompted Clarendon to remark to the thin Baxter that if he 'were but as fat as Dr. Manton, we should all do well' (Keeble and Nuttall, 1.377). Manton was offered the deanery of Rochester if he conformed, but rejected this offer.

The failure of the attempts to reach an accommodation in church matters and the rise of the cavalier party in the House of Commons meant that the puritan clergy were ejected from the Church of England for nonconformity on 24 August 1662. Like other London ministers Manton preached a poignant farewell sermon, choosing Hebrews 12: 1 as his text. He may have been disappointed with Charles II's failure to intervene to stop the great Ejection, for George Wild, the bishop of Derry, noted that Manton seemed to make a slur on the title 'Defender of the Faith' in his prayer for the king. Dr Patrick, later bishop of Ely, replaced Manton at Covent Garden on 23 September 1662. Manton attended his services at Covent Garden, but was accused by Patrick of circulating libels about him among the congregation. In 1669 Manton was referred to the bishop of London's court for not receiving communion.

Restoration nonconformist Manton was at the centre of early nonconformist organization and generally held the chair of dissenters' meetings. This was possibly due to his influence with the king and nobles. In March 1663 Charles II summoned him alongside Edmund Calamy, William Bate, and possibly Richard Baxter to discuss his plans for the comprehension of moderate dissenters in the Church of England. His main influence, however, was with the presbyterian aristocrats and gentry who attended various conventicles at his house in King Street, Covent Garden, at White Hart Yard, near the Strand, and at Lord Wharton's residence at St Giles-in-the-Fields. In January 1664 a government agent noted that Manton preached to the countess of Exeter, Sir William Waller, and Lord Wharton at Arthur Jackson's residence in Whitefriars. In the same

year another agent noted that he regularly met at an unnamed lord's house some 17 miles from London with Edmund Calamy, Richard Baxter, and others to plan nonconformist strategy. Manton's preaching was particularly popular with nonconformist ladies; reports mention ladies Bedford, Manchester, Clare, Clinton, Wortland, Scarsdale, Seymour, and Trevor and the earl of Anglesey's sister as having attended his services. He also seems to have had some influence with Scottish presbyterian peers, especially the earl of Lauderdale.

In September 1668 Manton was asked by Charles II through Sir John Baber to make an address thanking the king for indulgence. In making this request Baber was joined by William Bates and Thomas Jacombe. This prompted hopes for a *rapprochement* between the presbyterians and the established church, and Manton joined Richard Baxter and Bates in discussing comprehension with the king and others at Lord Arlington's residence. Baxter reports, however, that the congregationalist John Owen, who refused to accept anything but full toleration, wrecked the talks.

The breakdown of communication between the king and the nonconformists led to a wave of repression in the form of the revised Clarendon code. In 1670 Arlington received communication that Manton, speaking for the presbyterians, had resolved with the leaders of the congregationalists and the Baptists to resist the Conventicle Act of 1668 as a united body. Manton was also involved in talks with the congregationalist clergy on obtaining a common liberty of conscience. His reward was to be arrested under the Five Mile Act in March 1670 and imprisoned for six months in the Gatehouse. Upon release his peace-making skills were required in the presbyterian camp. In December 1671 he joined William Bates and Thomas Jacombe, the so-called 'dons' (presbyterians who wanted comprehension with the established church), in negotiations with Samuel Annesley, Nathaniel Vincent, and Thomas Watson, called the 'ducklings' because they represented the younger generation of presbyterians who wanted to remain separated from the Church of England.

Reconciliation among the presbyterians came in time for the declaration of indulgence in 1672. Manton was licensed as a presbyterian at his home in Covent Garden on 2 April. He took full advantage of the opportunity created by the indulgence and was elected one of the joint congregational and presbyterian lecturers at Pinners' Hall in Old Broad Street, London. He also preached at the revival of the presbyterian morning exercises. Manton applied Acts 2: 38 to give counsel on baptism at Cripplegate in 1674 and applied 2 Thessalonians 2: 15 in defending the doctrine of the sole sufficiency of scripture in the morning exercises against popery in 1675.

Last years In 1675, with the end of the king's indulgence, Manton's congregation was broken up. He, however, continued to preach to his aristocratic followers at Covent Garden until his death. In April 1675 he joined William Bates, Matthew Poole, and Richard Baxter in more ill-fated accommodation talks with the latitudinarian clergy John

Tillotson, George Morley, Seth Ward, and Edward Stilling-fleet. In the following year he was a co-signatory to Baxter's *The Judgment of Non-Conformists, of the Interest of Reason, in Matters of Religion*.

Manton's health began to fail in late 1675, and he 'languish'd many months but presuming he should be too strong for his infirmity, neglected it, till at last it became insuperable and mortal' (W. Bates, *A Funeral Sermon Preached upon the Death of … Thomas Manton*, 1678, 58). He died on 18 October 1677 and was buried in the chancel of St Mary's, Stoke Newington, on 22 October. Ralph Thoresby noted that the nonconformist ministers were paired with priests of the established church during the funeral procession and that Manton was styled 'the King of Preachers'. William Bates preached Manton's funeral sermon and chose 1 Thessalonians 4: 17 as his text. His former presbyterian colleagues Thomas Case and John Collinges also commemorated his life in sermons.

Manton's wife, Mary, lived until 1701 but few of their children survived them. One daughter, Ann, married John Terry and died on 16 March 1689. A son, Nathaniel, was a bookseller at the Three Pigeons in Poultry. Manton left little money, but a vast library of books was sold at public auction at his house in King's Street on 25 March 1678 for the benefit of his family.

Manton's works were generally well regarded by his contemporaries. Archbishop Ussher described him as a 'voluminous preacher' and William Bates commended his technique of 'represent[ing] the inseperable connection between Christian duties and priviledges' (*DNB*). His Calvinism was, however, too much for Lord Bolingbroke, whose family had been under Manton's ministry at Covent Garden. Bolingbroke told Jonathan Swift that 'Manton taught my youth to yawn, and prepared me to be a high churchman, that I might never hear him read or read him more' (*DNB*). The younger Calamy gave a more favourable judgement, noting that he 'was endowed with extraordinary knowledge of the scriptures, and in his preaching gave a perspicacious account of the order and dependence of divine truths'.   E. C. VERNON

Sources minutes of the London provincial assembly, DWL, MS 201: 12–13 • *CSP dom.*, 1654–80 • *Calendar of the correspondence of Richard Baxter*, ed. N. H. Keeble and G. F. Nuttall, 2 vols. (1991) • R. Wodrow, *The history of the sufferings of the Church of Scotland from the Restauration to the revolution*, 2 vols. (1721–2) • *Calamy rev.* • T. Manton, *Sermons preached by the late reverend and learned divine, Thomas Manton*, ed. [W. Bates] (1678) • *The nonconformist's memorial … originally written by … Edmund Calamy*, ed. S. Palmer, 2 vols. (1775) • Clarendon, *Hist. rebellion* • DWL, MS PP12.50*.4 (21) • D. Neal, *The history of the puritans* (1822) • Evelyn, *Diary* • Foster, *Alum. Oxon.* • *DNB* • will, PRO, PROB 6/53, fol. 91v

Likenesses R. White, line engraving, BM, NPG; repro. in Manton, *Sermons*, ed. [W. Bates] (1678) • R. White, line engraving, BM, NPG; repro. in T. Manton, *One hundred and ninety sermons on the hundred and nineteenth Psalm* (1681) [*see illus.*] • copperplate, repro. in Calamy, *Nonconformist's memorial*

Wealth at death library sold for benefit of his family; will, PRO, PROB 6/53, fol. 91v

Mantovani, Annunzio Paolo (1905–1980), orchestra leader and musical arranger, was born on 15 November

Annunzio Paolo Mantovani (1905–1980), by Harry Hammond, 1950

1905 in Venice, Italy, the son of (Bismark) Benedetto Mantovani and his wife, Iparia Gandino (*d.* 1969). His father, born in Rovigo, was a violinist and leader of the orchestra at La Scala, Milan, and had played under Arturo Toscanini, Hans Richter, Thomas Beecham, Camille Saint-Saëns, and Pietro Mascagni. He was also professor at two Italian conservatories (and held the title cavaliere).

In 1909, when Mantovani was four, his father went to London as leader of the orchestra of the Italian Opera Company at the Royal Opera House, Covent Garden. At the end of one season he decided to stay in England with his family: wife, son, Annunzio, and daughter, Remila (*b.* 1907). A second daughter was born in England. The young Mantovani went to Archbishop Tenison's Grammar School and L'École Notre Dame, London. His father, who wanted him to be an engineer, gave him piano lessons and at an early age he showed great musical aptitude. At fourteen he developed a passion for the violin and his father, now won over, promised that the boy should have his Testori violin, which had been presented to him by a Russian princess, if he could play the Kreutzer violin concerto before he was sixteen. This was accomplished nine months before his birthday. His father now agreed that he should go to the Trinity College of Music, where he studied violin and composition. He became a professional violinist and gave recitals at the Wigmore Hall and played the Saint-Saëns concerto at the Queen's Hall. He played in various hotel restaurant orchestras, including the Midland Hotel in Birmingham in 1923, and by 1927 he was leading a small orchestra at the fashionable Metropole Hotel, London, which had in its ranks such future talents as Reginald Kilbey and George Melachrino, as well as Mantovani's father on violin. He first recorded about 1927 under the name of Leonelli Gandino on the Imperial label, and made many records between 1927 and 1932 with various dance orchestras; he first recorded under his own name on the Regal label from 1928. By 1930 he was leading his Tipica Orchestra, resident at the Monseigneur Restaurant in Piccadilly from 1931 to 1934, where he began to build his national reputation through a series of lunchtime broadcasts. From 1932 to 1935 he recorded for the Homophone group of labels under various names and, with his Tipica Orchestra (title dropped in 1937), for Columbia, in 1935–40. Later he was resident at the Café de Paris, the Mario, and the Hollywood restaurants, and worked at Butlin's holiday camps. He became an experienced theatre conductor, for a time musical director for Noël Coward—with *Sigh No More* (1945), *Pacific 1860* (1946), *Ace of Clubs* (1950), and Noel Gay's *Bob's your Uncle* (1948), among the shows he directed, the last being J. B. Fagan's *And So to Bed* (1951), a musical romp based on the life of Samuel Pepys.

In July 1935 Mantovani became a naturalized British subject, having married Winifred Kathleen Moss (1909–1977), the daughter of a City company director, William James Moss, on 4 August 1934. For most of their marriage they had a house in Bournemouth and kept a flat in St John's Wood, with Winifred his constant support and encouragement during a long and happy marriage. They had a son, Kenneth Paul, and a daughter, Paula Irene.

Monty, as Mantovani was always known, might well have continued as just one of many accomplished and admired orchestra leaders had he not attained great popular fame through his phenomenal success as a recording artist. The fruition of his musical ideas came in a neatly coincidental way with the recording boom prompted by the launching of the hi-fi long-playing record. In the late 1940s the lightly lush Mantovani style had a steady following in the USA as well as in Britain and it was decided to make a fresh appeal to the record market by launching a comparatively large light orchestra of about forty-five players with some thirty-two strings, proportions far beyond the scope of the general palm court sort of ensemble. The talented composer/arranger Ronald Binge (1910–1979), who had played with and arranged for Mantovani since 1935, conceived the idea of a delayed entry device in the string writing which gave a shimmering, cascading effect; it was first successfully employed in the 1951 recording of 'Charmaine', which quickly sold a million copies. The novelty caught on in a big way and the LPs issued by the Decca Record Company, for whom he had started recording in 1940, began to sell in very large numbers. By 1971 his LPs had sold some 35 million copies. Now very popular in the USA, he made the first of many American tours in 1955, also regularly visiting Europe, South Africa, Canada, and the Far East until 1969.

The huge record sales continued into the 1970s, his first twenty-five years with Decca being celebrated in 1965 when Mantovani was presented with a diamond studded baton. By then he had also been rewarded with eighteen gold discs, each celebrating million-selling recordings. He made his last LP in 1975, the year in which ill health forced his retirement. Beyond his skills as a conceptual director and arranger of most of his scores, and the fame that came with the cascading strings, he was also an accomplished composer of orchestral pieces, his works including 'Royal Blue Waltz', 'Toyshop Ballet' (which won a Novello award in 1957), 'Serenata d'amore'—which became his best-known creation—and the song 'Cara mia' which was made a no. 1 hit by the singer David Whitfield.

Mantovani was a strict disciplinarian at work, a trait that was always made acceptable by his innate courtesy and charm. He was appreciated by his players as a thorough technician and a musician of experience and quality. He maintained a quietly dignified manner in his soft-voiced introductions and allowed the music to speak for its flamboyant self; but his quiet and unassuming manner changed when the baton was in his hand. He liked to think that his head was British and his heart Italian—an ancestry that came out in his music-making. He always enjoyed his role as the maestro and would be found seated elegantly at his grand piano, pen in hand, when one visited him at his large flat off Regent's Park. He passed his retirement years in Dorset, and died in the Clarence Nursing Home, 3/4 Clarence Road, Tunbridge Wells, on 30 March 1980. He was cremated at Tunbridge Wells on 8 April and his ashes were interred in Bournemouth, next to his wife's.   PETER GAMMOND

Sources m. cert. · d. cert. · *The Times* (31 March 1980) · private information (2004) [Kenneth Mantovani (son); Peter Cliffe] · *International who's who in music*, 7th edn (1975) · P. Hardy and D. Laing, eds., *Faber companion to 20th century popular music* (1990) · P. Gammond, *The Oxford companion to popular music* (1991) · *CGPLA Eng. & Wales* (1980)
Archives SOUND BL NSA, performance recordings
Likenesses H. Hammond, photograph, 1950, NPG [*see illus.*] · photograph, repro. in *The Times* · photographs, Hult. Arch.
Wealth at death £356,993: probate, 12 Nov 1980, *CGPLA Eng. & Wales*

Manuche, Cosmo (*bap.* 1613, *d.* 1673?), playwright, was baptized on 24 October 1613 at St Andrew's, Holborn, in the liberties of the City of London, the eldest surviving son of James Manuche (*c.*1590–1633), a painter, and Katherine, who lived near the Windmill in Shoe Lane, Holborn. His grandfather Jacomo Manuche (*d.* 1593), first went to England some time before 1573 and worked for many years in England and abroad in Sir Francis Walsingham's intelligence-gathering network. In 1577 he was rewarded by the queen with a £40 annuity for life. James Manuche, a middle child of Jacomo, was a member of the Painters' Stainers' Guild, having been apprenticed to John de Critz the elder about 1610.

In 1626 Cosmo Manuche entered Merchant Taylors' School, London, a few years after John Webster, the future dramatist, whose family were near neighbours of the Manuches in Shoe Lane. He probably would have left school in 1631 or 1632. There is no record that Cosmo Manuche matriculated at either Oxford or Cambridge, the course one might expect, but it must be admitted that university registers for this period are notoriously incomplete. Family difficulties may have prevented him. On 7 March 1633 his father, James Manuche, 'a man a painter', was buried at St Andrew's, Holborn, 'out [of] his house near the Windmill in Shoe Lane' (parish register, St Andrew's, Holborn, Guildhall Library). There is evidence that Cosmo Manuche continued to live in the family home in Shoe Lane in the early 1630s, and on 19 January 1636 he married Anne Cooley (d. 1641) at St Dunstan and All Saints, Stepney. There is no record of any children of the couple being baptized at St Andrew's, Holborn. They almost certainly continued to live there, for when Anne was buried on 11 April 1641 she was buried in this parish. On 27 October 1648 in the parish of St Bartholomew-the-Less, London, Manuche married his second wife, Frances Brewster. There were certainly offspring from this marriage, as Manuche says in the dedication to the earl of Northampton of his play *The Feast* (c.1664) that the manuscript is being carried by his daughters and he hopes Northampton will be able to help them to get on in the world.

When the civil war broke out Manuche joined the forces of the king. Surviving records indicate that he was a serving officer, probably of a company of foot initially, from 1642 until at least 1645, though there is circumstantial evidence that he continued serving until the final collapse of the king's cause. Whatever his initial rank, he eventually rose to the rank of major. On 19 October 1645 Major Cosmo Manuche and Lieutenant Francis Manuche, probably a cousin, and serving under the ultimate command of Sir John Berkeley, governor of Exeter, were taken prisoner by the army of Sir Thomas Fairfax at the siege of Tiverton. However, Cosmo Manuche must have been soon released or exchanged, for on 12 December 1661 Lord John Berkeley of Stratton, Sir Gilbert Talbot, and Sir Lewis Dyves, his commanders in the west during the civil war, testified that he continued to fight in Ireland and the Isles of Scilly for as long as any sort of armed resistance lasted (BL, Egerton MS 2623, fol. 34).

What happened to Manuche after the final defeat of the royalists is not clear, but it seems likely that he had some patronage from the earl of Northampton, although Northampton too was suffering from the deprivations laid on him by parliament. Another play, *Love in Travell* (c.1650), a tragicomedy, was dedicated to Northampton:

> The former favours I have received by your honours free and noble acceptation of my weak endeavours (the productions of a disturbed brain, through want); in point of gratitude and duty (with my soul's affection), could no less than present the first fruits of my last endeavour to your honour. (BL, Add. MS 60275, fol. 3r)

This dedication indicates a previous connection, and all of Manuche's known works, save *The Bastard* (1652), are dedicated to Lord or Lady Northampton, or both together.

There is an implication in the testimony of his former commanders given on 12 December 1661 (previously cited) that Manuche was imprisoned in London several times in the 1650s, but what is certainly known is that he published three plays in 1652: *The Bastard*, *The Loyal Lovers*, and

The Just General, the first a tragedy and the latter two tragicomedies. Various entries in the state papers suggest that Manuche boarded, and perhaps taught, scholars in the country, possibly in Kent, between 1652 and 1656. But Manuche, clearly in need of funds, followed the example of some other royalists and made a sort of peace with the interregnum government. On 4 June 1656 'Capt.' Cosmo Manuche petitioned Cromwell for money for having turned in several seditious persons. He was paid £10 for his 'publique service' (*CSP dom.*, 1655–6).

In 1659 and early 1660 Manuche composed *The Banished Shepherdess*, a political pastoral comedy about the impending restoration of Charles II. In the play the dowager queen, Henrietta Maria, is the banished shepherdess and her son Charles II is Charilaus, but the composition cannot be later than the early spring of 1660 since the restoration is hinted at but clearly has not happened yet. Manuche produced two very careful presentation copies in his own hand, one for Henrietta Maria (Hunt. L., MS EL 8395) and one for the earl of Northampton (BL, Add. MS 60273). When Charles II offered small financial rewards for those officers who had served the crown loyally during the civil war, one who came forward was Cosmo Manuche on 27 June 1661, when he was awarded £20 (*Treasury Books*).

Manuche's sixth and last play, another tragicomedy, is *The Feast* (BL, Add. MS 60274; Worcester College, Oxford). Its date of composition can be no earlier than January 1665 since it contains references to Sir Samuel Tuke's *Adventures of Five Hours*, performed either on 15 or 23 December 1664, and to John Dryden's and Sir Robert Howard's *The Indian Queen* which opened on 25 January 1664. On 7 November 1673 a Major Mullinax was buried in the Dark Cloister of Westminster Abbey, and it is likely that this was Cosmo Manuche, for on 11 January 1676 Mrs Frances Manuche was buried in the cloisters of Westminster Abbey as well (Chester, *Westminster Abbey Registers*). WILLIAM PROCTOR WILLIAMS

Sources W. P. Williams, 'The Castle Ashby manuscripts', *The Library*, 6th ser., 2 (1980), 392–412 • M. Edmond, 'Limners and picturemakers', *Walpole Society*, 47 (1978–80), 60–242 • parish register, Holborn, St Andrew's, GL • *CSP dom.*, 1655–6 • BL, Egerton MS 2623, fol. 34 • W. P. Williams, 'Evidence of performance', *English Language Notes*, 30/1 (1992), 11–16 • W. Van Lennep and others, eds., *The London stage, 1660–1800*, pt 1: 1660–1700 (1965), 59 • *CPR, 1575–8*, 541, no. 3681 • BL, Add. MS 60275

Archives BL, Add. MSS 60273, 60274, 60275 • Hunt. L., MS EL 8395

Manvell, (Arnold) Roger (1909–1987), film critic and historian, was born on 10 October 1909 at St Barnabas vicarage, Leicester, the only child of the Revd Arnold Edward William Manvell, later canon of Peterborough Cathedral, and his wife, Gertrude Theresa Baines. He was educated at King's School in Peterborough. He studied English literature at University College, Leicester, obtaining his PhD on W. B. Yeats at London University. He began work in 1931 as a schoolmaster and adult education lecturer in Leicester, moving to the department of extramural studies at Bristol University in 1937.

In 1940 Manvell joined the films division of the Ministry of Information, screening factual films and lecturing to non-theatrical audiences. Seizing the opportunities offered by current interest in 'film appreciation', he wrote *Film* (1944), which broke new ground as a critical history of the great films of the past. It was an immediate best-seller, introducing a whole generation to an understanding of film as an art form. In the following year he was appointed research officer and lecturer at the British Film Institute and was instrumental in setting up, and at first guiding, the institute's academic series of volumes *The History of the British Film*.

In 1946 Manvell began broadcasting and his name became a household word through the BBC series *The Critics*. Also in 1946 he founded the *Penguin Film Review*, and edited it until 1949, and in 1947 became the first director of the senior film-makers' own organization, the British Film Academy, the forerunner of BAFTA, where he remained until 1959. All the while he busily produced books written or edited by himself alone or in collaboration with experts in various aspects of the cinema. After 1959 he acted as consultant to the British Film Academy, continuing to write, lecture, and sit on numerous committees. He was also prominent in the humanist movement, and was associate editor of *New Humanist* from 1967 to 1975. Books of film criticism, analysis, and history continued thick and fast, interspersed with biographies of Charlie Chaplin (1974) and of several great English actresses. In later years he was involved in film studies at Sussex University, Louisville University (1973), and the London Film School, of which he was a governor (1966–74), and he did useful work for the Society of Authors and other bodies.

Manvell also took up a new interest. Heinrich Fraenkel, a Jewish film journalist and scriptwriter, who had fled Germany in 1933, had founded a Free German movement in Britain and written several slight books to persuade his adopted country that not all Germans were Nazi. Manvell began a fruitful collaboration with him in 1959 with a thoughtful and well-documented biography, *Doctor Goebbels* (1960). Together, during the next dozen years they produced eight solid books on the history of Nazism, including four biographies and an account of the 1944 July plot to kill Hitler. Fraenkel had gone to the Nuremberg trials and interviewed many key people. He had valuable contacts in Germany, as well as access to relevant archives. Manvell's expertise in scholarly presentation, as well as his wide contacts and fluent style, helped make this an important body of work.

By 1975 film studies in Britain and France had developed in directions uncongenial to a man of Manvell's generation and he felt more at home in American universities. He joined Boston University in 1975, was made a professor in 1982, and worked there for the rest of his life, continuing his large and varied output of books, of which two of the most notable were *Films and the Second World War* (1974) and *Elizabeth Inchbald, England's Leading Woman Dramatist* (1987).

In 1970 Manvell was made commander of the order of merit of the Italian Republic, and in 1971 was awarded the order of merit (first class) of the German Federal Republic.

A scholar–teacher of the year award for 1984–5 from Boston University followed, as well as an honorary DFA of New England College (1972), and honorary DLitts from Sussex (1971), Leicester (1974), and Louisville (1979) universities.

These were meagre distinctions for an influential writer who had pioneered the serious study of film in his native land. Brisk and practical, he was a good organizer and a prolific writer, who combined accuracy with a readable middlebrow style. Even his puzzling insistence on the use of his academic title of 'Dr' played its part, perhaps, in the emergence of film as a respectable subject for academic study, belatedly accepted at last by British universities. His assiduous use of contacts, combined with great energy and drive, did much to spread a serious appreciation of the cinema in Britain.

Of medium height, fairly heavily built, and inclined to be pudgy, he always seemed in a hurry to get to the next opportunity that beckoned. As he grew older his hair receded fluffily and his eyes peered shrewdly from behind thick glasses. Ambition and determination almost hid a wry, slightly sardonic humour. In 1936 he married Edith Mary, daughter of John Cook Bulman; they had one son. The marriage was dissolved and in 1946 he married Margaret Hilda, daughter of Percy James Lee, dental surgeon, of Bristol. After a divorce, in 1956 he married Louise, daughter of Charles Luson Cribb, of London. They divorced in 1981 and in the same year he married Françoise Baylis, daughter of René Nautré, company director. There were no children of the final three marriages. Manvell died in Boston on 30 November 1987.   RACHAEL LOW, *rev.*

Sources *The Times* (2 Dec 1987) • *The Independent* (3 Dec 1987) • *Daily Telegraph* (1 Dec 1987) • *Daily Telegraph* (2 Dec 1987) • private information (1996) • personal knowledge (1996) • *CGPLA Eng. & Wales* (1988) • b. cert. • m. certs. [Edith Bulman, Margaret Lee, Françoise Nautré]
Wealth at death £117,369: probate, 13 Sept 1988, *CGPLA Eng. & Wales*

Manvers. For this title name *see* Pierrepont, Charles, first Earl Manvers (1737–1816).

Manwaring, Roger. *See* Maynwaring, Roger (1589/90?–1653).

Manwood, John (*d.* 1610), legal writer, was a relative of Sir Roger Manwood (*d.* 1592), chief baron of the exchequer, with whom he has occasionally been confused. Sir Roger's brother, John Manwood (*d.* 1571), MP for Sandwich in 1571, had a son John who may be the same person. According to the posthumous 1615 edition of the book on forest law for which Manwood is known, he was a member of Lincoln's Inn, though no trace of him can be found in the records of that society and it must be open to doubt whether he was qualified as a barrister. Some, at any rate, of the author's expertise in the forest law was gained by practical experience as gamekeeper of Waltham Forest, and as a justice of the New Forest, which stimulated him to read the law books and records on the subject.

Manwood married Mary (perhaps Crayford); their second son, Jasper, was admitted to Lincoln's Inn in 1624 (as

John) and called to the bar in 1632. The admissions register describes the father as being of Chigwell, Essex, and Manwood also acquired the estate of Priors in Broomfield, near Chelmsford, where his descendants lived until the eighteenth century. According to Manwood's preface of 1598, the forest laws had 'growen cleane out of knowlege in most places', and he had therefore decided to 'hold the candle and begin the first enterprise herein'. Nevertheless, although his book was the only substantial work on the subject ever to reach the press, it was in fact the successor to two detailed and widely circulated inns of court readings by Richard *Hesketh and George *Treherne, which Manwood occasionally cited. Manwood also stated that he had the assistance of 'grave and learned men ... in the perusing of this treatise' and in the provision of legal citations, which tends to confirm his modest admission of a lack of professional expertise on his own part.

Manwood had a first version of his book printed for private circulation, in or about 1592, as *A Brefe Collection of the Lawes of the Forest*. An enlarged edition, with twenty chapters, was published in 1598 as *A Treatise and Discourse of the Lawes of the Forrest*, and dedicated to Charles Howard, earl of Nottingham and chief justice of the forests south of the Trent. Manwood died in 1610; a posthumous edition followed in 1615, which was further enlarged by the insertion of five chapters on forest courts taken from the private edition but omitted in 1598. This version was reprinted in 1665. In 1717 William Nelson of the Middle Temple produced a fourth edition, with the material rearranged under alphabetical headings in modernized English; this was reprinted in 1741. An abridgement was published in Nicholas Cox's *Gentlemen's Recreation* of 1696 and in subsequent editions. Manwood was also the author of a brief 'Project for improving the land revenue by inclosing wasts', submitted to Sir Julius Caesar on 27 April 1609 and first printed as an appendix to John St John's *Observations on the Land Revenue of the Crown* (1787).

J. H. BAKER

Sources HoP, *Commons, 1558–1603*, 3.14 • P. Morant, *The history and antiquities of the county of Essex*, 2 (1768), 77 • T. Wright, *The history and topography of the county of Essex*, 1 (1836), 187 • W. Boys, *Collections for an history of Sandwich in Kent*, 2 (1892, [1792]), 481 • W. P. Baildon, ed., *The records of the Honorable Society of Lincoln's Inn: admissions*, 1 (1896), 196 • W. P. Baildon, ed., *The records of the Honorable Society of Lincoln's Inn: the black books*, 2 (1898) • BL, Add. MS 26047, fols. 161–4 • CSP dom., 1603–10, 418, 645 • STC, 1475–1640, nos. 17290–92 • Wing, STC, 2.515

Manwood, Sir Peter (1571–1625), judge and antiquary, was born at Hackington, Kent, the eldest son of Sir Roger *Manwood (1524/5–1592), a judge, and his first wife, Dorothy (d. 1575), daughter of John Theobald, of Seal. His younger brothers John and Thomas died childless, while his two sisters married into the county's judicial élite: Margaret to John Leveson, of Halling, and Anne to Percival Hart, heir of Sir George Hart. Sir Roger Manwood was a revered judge of great legal learning who was accused of using judicial offices for personal gain. Peter followed his father's intellectual pursuits but not his profession, as he declined being called to the bar. He entered as a student of

the Inner Temple on 20 November 1583, his father having arranged a room for him over benchers' chambers at Serjeants' Inn in 1587. He spent much time at the Inner Temple, where he pursued antiquarian interests throughout his life, and had his own four sons specially admitted to the inn. He married in January 1588 Frances (1573–1638), daughter of Sir George Hart, of Lullingstone.

Manwood inherited his father's Kent, Essex, and London properties in 1592, and leased land from the archbishop of Canterbury. By 1600 he had the manors of Hackington, Ash, Chislet, and Raynhurst, Flint Castle, and houses in Sandwich and St Bartholomew's, London. The Manwoods had six sons and four daughters. Their eldest son, Thomas, graduated BA from Lincoln College, Oxford, in 1611, was a student at the Inner Temple, and drowned in France in 1613; their second, John (d. 1653), became Manwood's heir. The couple were also generous benefactors to local schools, churches, and hospitals. Their legacy was a lease of many lands in trust for charitable uses in 1615.

Manwood was senior MP for Sandwich in 1588–9, 1592–3, 1597, and 1601; for Saltash, Cornwall, in 1603–4; for Kent in 1614; and for New Romney in 1620–21. Though he sat in parliament and was appointed to a few committees concerned with legislation, he did not participate in debates. His political allegiance was anti-Catholic, anti-Spanish, and pro-puritan. A 'moderate Sabbatarian' (Clark, 345), he devoted his public interests to his county as a justice of the peace, where he was a member of the quorum of the court of quarter sessions (1593–1620). He was appointed commander of Dover haven by 1591; a commissioner for grain in 1596, for musters by 1597, and for the oyster fisheries in 1598; deputy lieutenant of the Cinque Ports (1600), and of Kent (1601); sheriff of Kent (1602–3); mayor of Canterbury (1605); and commissioner of sewers for Kent (1619–23). After being knighted at the coronation of James I on 25 July 1603, by the 1620s he was the only one of three Elizabethan governors still prominent in Kent.

As a public official, Manwood was a patron of learned men as well as a scholar in his own right. He collected notes on English affairs from Edward the Confessor to Henry VIII and Cardinal Wolsey in the 1590s, which he exchanged with John Stow, and on Kent topology. He also collected transcripts of state papers between 1564 and 1618, and political tracts on Ireland, France, the Low Countries, north Africa, and Asia Minor. He had a licence to travel beyond the seas 'for his increase in good knowledge and learning' (CSP dom., 1598–1601, 132). Manwood liked to gather scholars at his family seat of St Stephen's, Hackington, near Canterbury, and patronized the translators Edward Grimstone and Richard Knollys. His commonplace books were unique, combining letter-books for the governments of England, Ireland, and the Low Countries and proclamations for kings and sultans. Mentioned with great respect by William Camden in 1607, Manwood became a member of the Society of Antiquaries in 1617. He gave part of the manuscript of Sir Roger Williams's *The Actions of the Lowe Countries* to Sir John Hayward for revision; it was published in 1618 with a dedication to Sir Francis Bacon as 'good history' designed to excite men to take up arms for good causes (Williams, xlv–xlvi). He gave many of his books to the Bodleian Library in 1620.

Manwood's large family, his inattention to his properties, and his lavish style of living brought financial difficulties which caused him to leave the country in August 1621. He had net liabilities of about £3000 in 1593, a total estate valued at only £1500 in 1614, and nothing left in current funds by the early 1620s. After returning to Dover in April 1623, he made arrangements with his creditors that allowed him to remain, and he was steward of the Inner Temple Christmas feast that winter. Lord Zouche, his life-long friend, had written to Secretary Conway begging him to use his influence with the king for his protection. James complied because Manwood was one of those long-suffering county governors who served in numerous local offices at his own expense. He advised his son John to 'keep a good house within the proportion of his living' but his lessons to wife and son in household management were insufficient, and the family fortune was in disarray at the time of his death at Sandwich in 1625. He was buried in St Stephen's Church, Hackington, Kent.

LOUIS A. KNAFLA

Sources Wood, *Ath. Oxon.*, new edn, 1.362–3 · M. R. Pickering, 'Manwood, Peter', HoP, *Commons, 1558–1603* · P. Clark, *English provincial society from the Reformation to the revolution: religion, politics and society in Kent, 1500–1640* (1977) · *CSP dom.*, 1591–1625 · APC, 1595–1625 · F. A. Inderwick and R. A. Roberts, eds., *A calendar of the Inner Temple records*, 1 (1896), 327; 2 (1898), 50, 74, 90, 97, 104, 109, 140 · BL, Add. MS 29759 [family pedigree, estate documents, and correspondence, 1551–1619] · PRO, C142/244/112, C142/451/108 [notes on family and dates] · *Calendar of the manuscripts of the most hon. the marquis of Salisbury*, 7, HMC, 9 (1899); 14 (1923) [addenda]; 15 (1930); 17 (1938); 20 (1968); 24 (1976) · Sandwich year books, 1582–1608, CKS · R. Williams, *The actions of the Lowe Countries. Written by Sr. Roger Williams knight* (1618); ed. D. W. Davies (1964) · S. D'Ewes, *The journals of all the parliaments during the reign of Queen Elizabeth* (1682) · E. Hasted, *The history and topographical survey of the county of Kent*, 2nd edn, 3 (1797); 8–10 (1799–1800) · E. A. Webb, G. W. Miller, and J. Beckwith, eds., *The history of Chislehurst: its church, manors, and parish* (1899), 142–4, 149–51 · *Archaeologia Cantiana*, 16 (1886), 159, 169, 183–8 [Sandwich borough and orphanage account bks] · *Archaeologia Cantiana*, 27 (1905), 53, 293; 45 (1933), 201–2 [household accounts and gifts] · *Archaeologia Cantiana*, 44 (1932), 268

Archives BL, estate documents and personal corresp., Add. MS 29759 · BL, historical collections, Add. MS 38139 · Bodl. Oxf., books and MSS, Bodley MSS 710, 875, 966 | Staffs. RO, letters to J. Leveson

Manwood, Sir Roger (1524/5–1592), judge, was born in Sandwich, Kent, the second son of Thomas Manwood (*d.* 1538), draper, and Katherine (*d.* 1566), daughter of John Galloway of Cley, Norfolk. The offspring of a long-established local merchant family, he was educated at the Thomas Ellis Chantry School, Sandwich.

Legal career Manwood was admitted to the Inner Temple in February 1548 and by July 1553 he was doing legal work for the Cinque Ports. He was called to the bar by 1555, and became counsellor to the ports and recorder of Sandwich. He was one of the borough members for Hastings in the parliament of 1555, and represented Sandwich in 1558 and in every subsequent parliament until his appointment as a judge. He also obtained important clients among local families, including Sir Thomas Cheyney, lord

Sir Roger Manwood (1524/5–1592), by unknown sculptor

warden of the Cinque Ports. By 1557 he had married a twice widowed woman, Dorothy Alleyn (*d.* 1575), daughter of Richard Theobald, who had been married first to Dr John Croke and who brought Manwood her jointure lands and a stepdaughter. In that year he was suing for her jointure in the courts on a difficult technical point. Problems of leasehold were one of his specialities, and he put his knowledge into practice for both himself and his clients. His views on this are known from his readings in 1565 on 21 Hen. VIII c. 3, and his arguments, for example in *Winter's case*, were long accepted as authoritative. His second reading as serjeant-elect in 1567 was on the Statute of Westminster I c. 37.

In 1561 Manwood played the part of chief baron of the exchequer in the Inner Temple entertainment, the *Masque of Desire and Beauty*, which Robert Dudley, the Inner Temple's patron, put on for Queen Elizabeth on St Stephen's day. Sir Christopher Hatton was also involved. Manwood thus had connections to the inner circle at court, and his committed protestantism made him a safe appointment as a JP in Kent and on other commissions. In 1562 he was adjudicating piracy cases. In 1563 he arranged to establish a grammar school in Sandwich. His commitment throughout his life to education for the bright but impoverished is as clear as his desire for a clean water supply. Later he established four scholarships at Oxford and Cambridge. His benefactions to his home parish of Hackington, Kent, included a hospital with six almshouses. He also gave two new bells, augmented the income of the vicarage, and built a conduit and the fourth aisle of the church. His rapid rise in his profession made him increasingly valuable to Sandwich and the Cinque Ports and prominent in Kent. He became steward of the liberties to Archbishop Parker and steward in the chancery and admiralty court of the warden at Dover. In 1566–7 Gresham in a letter to William Cecil begged him to 'Have my friend Mr Manwood in remembrance' (Burgon, 2.175).

Serjeant-at-law Manwood was called to the lucrative order of serjeant-at-law on 24 April 1567. As a serjeant he served as an assize judge, acted as an arbitrator, and gave legal opinions on such matters as the privileges for battery and the use of the calamine stone. In 1570 he surveyed all the grounds previously used for archery near London. On 30 March 1571 he, together with Thomas Leighton, wrote a report on the death of Cardinal Chastillon. With John Jeffreys in 1571 he arbitrated in a matter between Weymouth and Melcombe Regis. As an active adviser to the Cinque Ports he was one of their representatives in the exchequer where he handled issues of their franchises, liberties, privileges, and exemptions from loans and aids. He also remained on close terms with his old inn, and was concerned for the well-being of family and friends, especially his son Peter *Manwood. He was reluctant to become a judge. Gresham wrote on 16 April 1572 that there were others of more ancient standing, and 'because yet his welthe doth not serve to accept anie such office upon him' he should be passed over (Burgon, 2.478). Manwood had prepared for it, however, by settling his already considerable estates, worth approximately £475 a year. On 30 May 1571 he provided for his wife and entailed the property on his only surviving son, and in default to his daughters.

Manwood had resigned as recorder of Sandwich on becoming a serjeant. Becoming a puisne justice of common pleas on 14 October 1572 required him to resign all other lesser offices and to cease to represent clients. In 1572 he aroused comment by appearing twice in *White's case*, first as serjeant and later as judge, even though this might have prejudiced his former client's case. He had long kept records of cases, and there are various references to reports he kept during his tenure of judicial office. He also continued to be involved with Canterbury, Sandwich, and the Cinque Ports in matters of law. Because of his expertise in their abstruse privileges, the crown required him to determine issues involving conflict between the ports and the warden. Sometimes his judgments were unpopular with the ports.

The privy council called on Manwood as a judge to deal with cases elsewhere involving royal rights and local privileges. He was involved in amending the laws of Star Chamber, and gave his opinion on the observation of the penal statutes. He advised on the action to be taken when assizes in Cornwall and Lancaster had charged the wrong man. He assisted Wells with its new charter of incorporation, and was helpful to Southampton, which made him free. Manwood also arbitrated in a festering controversy between Oxford University and the city. In matters of felony he was severe, and routinely charged juries who acquitted against the evidence, but he was also sceptical, so it is not surprising that Reginald Scot dedicated *The Discovery of Witchcraft* (1574) to him. In 1577 Manwood advised that a man persisting in speaking ill of the queen after the pillory and having his ears cut off might either be imprisoned for life or have part of his tongue excised. He was not abrasive to his fellow lawyers—in 1578, when Plowden had given bad advice to a sheriff concerning a writ of extent, Manwood tactfully observed that perhaps Mr Plowden did not know of an entry that indicated that execution had not taken place.

Judge in ecclesiastical matters Manwood's religious commitment explains his role in ecclesiastical affairs. In June 1575 he served on a commission against Anabaptists, and in April 1576 became a member of the high commission. Later he served on commissions for ecclesiastical causes, for reformation of the court of arches and audience, and at a conference concerning the powers of ecclesiastical laws to mulct and otherwise punish offenders. By 1577 he was being considered for the position of chief baron of the exchequer. Francis Walsingham promised to help, knowing 'no man in England so fit for it … but … he hath great enemies and those that have chiefest voice in chapter' (*Finch MSS*, 1.22). Cecil may have been this principal opponent; if so, his opposition may have rested on Manwood's profound commitment to the common law as the subject's protection, and his dislike of the intervention of the privy council at the petition of favoured individuals. Manwood's classical tags, that truth made enemies ('malas causas habentes semper fugiunt ad potentes; ubi non valet veritas, praevalet auctoritas'), were unpopular. However, he was knighted on 15 November and installed as chief baron on 17 November 1578. His one-time client Nicholas Bacon gave the address. In 1582 it was rumoured that Manwood had offered money to be chief justice of common pleas; if so he was unsuccessful. In July 1586 he wrote to Lord Burghley explaining how the people of Kent were grieved by purveyors and suggesting better regulations; and in 1589, when unpaid mercenaries were in distress at Sandwich, he intervened to get them paid.

Manwood's promotion sealed his position in society. His first wife, Dorothy, had died 'of a sore breast' on 14 September 1575; she was buried in the church of St Gregory by Paul, London. His second marriage, c.1580, to Elizabeth (d. 1595), daughter of John Coppinger of All Hallows, Kent, and widow of John Wilkins of Stoke, Kent, was another indication of increased status. He married his daughter Margaret to John Leveson of Harling, and in 1587, by agreeing to a very generous settlement, he arranged with Dame Elizabeth Harte a double marriage by which Percival Harte married Manwood's daughter Anne, and Manwood's heir, Peter, married Percival's sister Frances. He was to pay £200 a year for them to live with Dame Elizabeth.

As lord chief baron, Manwood actively protected the exchequer's jurisdiction in matters relating to the queen's prerogative and rights. In 1585 he sharply forbade Julius Caesar to hear a case in the admiralty. He maintained that cases of controversy over patentees, as well as decisions over the property of Sir Francis Englefield who had 'adhered to the queen's enemies', belonged in the exchequer (Hunt. L., Ellesmere MS 482, fol. 236). He also made legal doctrine. In a case in exchequer chamber concerning variations in the meaning of the term 'corporation' he wrote a letter to Burghley about what was and was not substantial, contradicting Burghley's own views. He required the solicitor-general to answer '*pro bono publico* and to deliver himself in conscience because the matter would be cited for a precedent … to the prejudice of many other suitors' (Hunt. L., Ellesmere MS 2650).

Manwood sat on all the state trials, including the trial of the supporters of the Jesuit Edmund Campion, and argued for heavier punishments. When Cartwright and his puritan fellows refused to take an oath, he claimed this tended to the overthrow of the common justice of the land in all civil and ecclesiastical causes. He was also concerned with the case of Mary, queen of Scots, and sought to show that the queen had dealt honourably with Mary, whereas Mary had dealt dishonourably with the queen. In the Star Chamber case against William Davison he put the crucial argument: 'if the warrant were sealed yet was it not lawful to kill her because the direction was special and not general' (*State trials*, 1.1230). The complaints that Burghley entertained against Manwood for abuse of his office are varied. Some concerned legitimate use of his position in the queen's interest. In others, where undue pressure was alleged, the evidence that he exceeded his legal rights is slender. Those involving mutual recriminations, as in the highway robberies at Gaddeshill where Edward Hoby and Manwood accused one another of maintenance, seem insoluble.

After 1588 Manwood was overtly troubled by royal encroachments on the traditional rights of citizens. His enemy Sir John Smythe reported that Manwood condemned the conscription of soldiers for overseas service. In June 1591 he and most of the other judges formally complained against arbitrary impressment. By 1590 the privy council was entertaining various complaints about his possibly corrupt verdicts, but he produced adequate explanations. He increasingly seems, however, to have come into conflict with Burghley over the use of royal power to override normal process of law. The case over which he was finally humiliated concerned a gold chain, which Manwood had recovered from a goldsmith named Roger Underwood. The law seems to have been on Manwood's side, but the privy council pressured him to admit that justice demanded concessions. His rigid refusal to accept privy council authority in this offended Burghley and the council and he was obliged to submit, confessing his folly first in a letter and publicly two days later on 14 May 1592. Historians believe that he none the less again offered money to be chief justice of queen's bench, although his extant letter to Burghley (in which he gives his age as sixty-seven) refers only to his undoubted seniority as serjeant.

Assessment After this, although his old enemies renewed their complaints, Manwood continued actively in office until his death in St Stephen's parish, Hackington, on 14 December 1592. His will, dated 12 December, left money for annual sermons to be preached at Hackington and St Mary's, Sandwich, in which mention was to be made of

the frailty and vain delights of this world. He recounted all his good deeds—the most recent being a hospital for poor priests in Canterbury and the gaol house of correction there—as *rei publice*, the 'one tenth of his value being the talent in this life to me lent by Almighty God'. Claiming he would 'do as he would be done unto', he gave large sums of money to his extended family. His widow was to receive £550 a year. His heir, Peter, would inherit providing he lived five years beyond Elizabeth's death without committing treason. He was buried in St Stephen's Church, Hackington, under a monument, erected before his death, which depicts him in his robes as a baron, with two wives, five children, and a life-size wooden skeleton. His extensive lands were closely focused in eastern Kent and the Isle of Thanet. He was exceptionally litigious in a litigious age. If his adversaries described him in slanderous terms, he sued. It was said that he brought more cases of *scandalum magnatum* than any other person.

Manwood was a man who aroused strong feeling. His hard dealings in property transactions were legal but not necessarily equitable, as he clawed himself from nothing to own property worth at least £1500 a year. His enemies revived their hatred when they judged him vulnerable. His neighbour at Shorne, Richard Burston, was not assuaged by the provision of free running water to his house, and pursued him for oppression to his death.

Manwood was the centre of many controversies and the subject of myth-making. Christopher Marlowe, perhaps his protégé, perhaps merely grateful that Manwood had released him at the London assizes in 1589, wrote a Latin eulogy, which starts:

Here lies the dour scourge of the profligate
Instrument of the hardened criminals fate
Fearsome to vagrants, Hercules from Jove sent
Celebrate you old lags! If innocent,
Weep with dishevelled hair and mournful breast,
Law's light and glory now has gone to rest.
(Bakeless, 286–7)

Archbishop Parker, thirty years earlier, had praised Manwood's charity, describing him as a living example that not all lawyers were concerned first and last with their own well-being. Richard Mulcaster in his *Elementarie* (1581) wrote of him as one of the 'greate founders to learning both within the universities and in the countries about them'. Sir Edward Coke said he was 'A reverend judge of great and excellent knowledge of the law and accompanied with a ready invention and good elocution' (Coke, pt 3, 26a). Legal historians see him as a sage of the law and a justice of proven reputation. His enemies, however, damned him: 'as proud a man as ever I knew', and 'so given to revenge' that no one dared 'meddle in his causes' (BL, Lansdowne MS 71, no. 1); a cruel man who oppressed his neighbours and used corruption and bribery to further his career. In 1577 Thomas Digges claimed 'he rejoiced that he lived in that estate where Mr Justice Manwood was not the best but that there were Superior Magistrates he doubted not were able to rule and govern him according to equity'. Manwood retorted, 'Rule me. No there is none in England shall rule or govern me'. Digges replied: 'I hope there is one ys able to rule you … The Queen'. 'Tush', quoth Master Manwood. 'She is a woman. I say there is no man in England shall rule me and that I will make you feel' (BL, Lansdowne MS 24, no. 30, fol. 91). Scurrilous stories circulated. When a murder was committed in Canterbury, Manwood allegedly took £240 and obtained the culprit a free pardon. His legal aphorisms, such as 'In the Common Pleas there is all law and no conscience; In the Queens bench both law and conscience, in the chancery all conscience and no law and in the Exchequer neither law nor conscience' (*Diary of John Manningham*, 91), circulated widely and some became legal commonplaces.

SYBIL M. JACK

Sources G. F. L. Bridgman, *All England law reports, reprinted, revised, annotated, 1558–1774* (1968) · W. Boys, *Collections for an history of Sandwich in Kent* (1792, [1892]) · HoP, *Commons, 1509–58* · HoP, *Commons, 1558–1603* · APC, 1558–95 · *State trials*, 1.915, 1162, 1230 · *Correspondence of Matthew Parker*, ed. J. Bruce and T. T. Perowne, Parker Society, 42 (1853) · *Report on the manuscripts of Allan George Finch*, 5 vols., HMC, 71 (1913–2003), vol. 1, p. 22 · *Calendar of the manuscripts of the most hon. the marquis of Salisbury*, 24 vols., HMC, 9 (1883–1976), esp. vols. 2, 13 · *Fifth report*, HMC, 4 (1876) · *The manuscripts of Rye and Hereford corporations*, HMC, 31 (1892) · *CSP dom.*, 1547–80; addenda, 1580–1625 · J. Strype, *Annals of the Reformation and establishment of religion … during Queen Elizabeth's happy reign*, new edn, 4 (1824) · J. Strype, *Historical collections of the life and acts of … John Aylmer*, new edn (1821) · J. Strype, *The history of the life and acts of the most reverend father in God Edmund Grindal*, new edn (1821) · J. Strype, *The life and acts of Matthew Parker*, new edn, 3 vols. (1821) · J. Strype, *The life and acts of John Whitgift*, new edn, 3 vols. (1822) · *Camden's Britannia*, ed. and trans. E. Gibson (1695), 242 · J. C. Davies, ed., *Catalogue of manuscripts in the library of the Honourable Society of the Inner Temple*, 3 vols. (1972), vol. 3 · F. Hull, ed., *A calendar of the white and black books of the Cinque Ports, 1432–1955*, Kent Archaeological Society Records Branch, 19 (1966) · R. Mulcaster, *Elementarie* (1581) · J. W. Burgon, *The life and times of Sir Thomas Gresham*, 2 vols. (1839) · *CPR, 1560–72* · L. W. Abbott, *Law reporting in England, 1485–1585* (1973) · Foss, *Judges*, 5.516–23 · E. K. Chambers, *The Elizabethan stage*, 4 vols. (1923) · BL, Add. MS 16169, fols. 67v, 68v; 48065 [Bacon's speech in 1579] · *The poems of Christopher Marlowe*, ed. M. Marcamer (1968), 263 · W. Urry, *Christopher Marlowe and Canterbury*, ed. A. Butcher (1988) [ed. with introduction by A. Butcher] · J. Bakeless, *Christopher Marlowe* (1938) [for evidence of Marlowe's authorship] · PRO, C142/244/112 · PRO, C2/Eh2 Mm.15, 42 · BL, Lansdowne MSS 24, no. 39; 31, nos. 55, 56; 26, no. 7; 33, no. 41; 50, nos. 24, 31; 62, no. 5; 63, no. 16; 71, nos. 1, 4, 5, 6, 7, 8, 67, 68; 104, no. 32 · BL, Add. MS 33512 · *Diary of John Manningham*, ed. J. Bruce, CS, old ser., 99 (1868), 41, 91 · BL, Harley MSS 6993; 6994; 6995, fol. 49; 5265; 7567 · BL, Add. MS 48019 · Hunt. L., Ellesmere MSS 482, 2650 · G. Wilson, ed., *The reports of Sir Edward Coke* (1793) [Co Rep] · *Inner Temple register* · BL, Add. MS 29759
Archives BL, Add. MS 29759 · Inner Temple, London, records | BL, Lansdowne papers, Harley MSS
Likenesses portrait, 1580, Bunratty Castle, co. Clare · style of G. P. Harding, watercolour drawing, NPG · bust on monument, St Stephen's Church, Hackington, Kent [*see illus.*]
Wealth at death probably c.£1500 in property; arranged to settle £550 p.a. on second wife and 500 marks (300 in possession and 200 in reversion) as his daughter-in-law's jointure in 1587: will

Manzoni, Sir Herbert John Baptista (1899–1972), engineer and surveyor, was born at 14 Jackson Street, Birkenhead, on 21 March 1899, the son of Giovanni Carlo Manzoni, a sculptor, and his wife, Emma Marjorie, *née* Rogers. His father came from Milan but had settled in Birkenhead, where Herbert Manzoni attended the Birkenhead Institute. He served in the later years of the First World War in the 12th lancer regiment and then in the 7th Middlesex regiment. But after the war he returned to Birkenhead and worked there in the borough engineer's office, which he continued to do while studying civil engineering for a year (1920–21) at Liverpool University. On 22 September 1923 he married, at the Primitive Methodist Chapel, Birkenhead, Lillian May Davies (b. 1897/8) of Birkenhead, the daughter of Albert Newton Davies, an insurance superintendent; they had three sons, one of whom died young, predeceasing his father.

Earlier in 1923 Manzoni had moved to Birmingham to work in the city engineer's department. He became chief engineer, sewers and rivers, in the public works department of Birmingham city council in 1927. He rapidly moved up, first to be deputy city surveyor and then in 1935 (at the early age of thirty-six) city engineer and surveyor. He held this post for nearly thirty years until his retirement in 1963. Furthermore he was, in effect, the city architect, for the architectural staff came under him until a city architect was appointed in the 1950s.

Manzoni's period as city engineer saw the great redevelopment of Birmingham. His ideas were developed immediately before the Second World War and were described in his account entitled *The Production of Fifty Thousand Municipal Houses* (1939), but it was in the post-war reconstruction period that they were implemented on a truly massive scale. The post-war redevelopment was made possible by the national Town and Country Planning Acts of 1944 and 1947, which Manzoni had been involved in drafting. This legislation initiated the concept of comprehensive redevelopment in town planning thought and practice in the post-war years; the provisions for wide compulsory acquisition and accelerated vesting at low cost by all-purpose local planning authorities were much more powerful than the former slum-clearance procedures and paved the way for the redevelopment of Birmingham and other cities. His earliest projects involved comprehensive redevelopment plans, which swept away Birmingham's large areas of sub-standard houses and led to the major municipal house-building programme.

Manzoni's most famous achievement lay in major highways. Before the redesign and rebuilding of much of the central area of Birmingham he had planned an inner ring road to speed traffic through the city. Rapid national policy developments made possible linkage of the national motorway system with the city inner ring road with effects that were extraordinary, at that time, on the journey times of peak-hour traffic. Work on the inner ring road commenced in 1957, and the first section opened in 1960, not long before Manzoni's retirement. Its completion in 1971 marked Birmingham's successful regeneration of the post-war years and was the basis for the second successful regeneration of the 1980s and 1990s. In fact, the inner ring road scheme had been developed from a pre-war concept, and the city council was given powers under private act which Manzoni had strongly advocated in pursuance of his great belief in combining planning with execution within the authority for big projects. This scheme was delayed by the post-war stringencies but then was given a favourable start because the local act freed it from a degree of control by central government. Manzoni was also involved in the early work of expanding Birmingham airport.

Manzoni's influence on Birmingham went far beyond what would in later years be the responsibility of any technical or professional chief officer. In part this reflected the circumstances of the time. Reconstruction was accepted and expected immediately after the Second World War. Central government finance was available. And this applied both to the great slum clearances and to the road-building programme—particularly that for the inner ring road—which marked Birmingham out ahead of other cities. But that alone is not an adequate explanation. In his time, long before the extension of political control in local government from the 1970s onwards, a great chief officer could exercise enormous personal power and influence. Manzoni came into this category, as did, for example, Sir Alec Clegg (1909–1986), chief education officer in the Yorkshire West Riding county council. The elected members relied on Manzoni's advice. Power in Birmingham city council came to reside in the public works committee, which nominally was the decision-taking committee for the capital projects which transformed Birmingham in the twenty years after the war, but in reality that committee merely carried through Manzoni's ideas. He, in turn, built up a trusted staff on whom he relied to carry through the series of projects.

In later years there was a reaction against some of Manzoni's work, particularly the dominance of the motor car, which lay behind the redevelopment of the centre of Birmingham, and especially the inner ring road. To that extent he was a man of his time. But his inspirational leadership marked Birmingham as few others have done. He influenced politicians, who usually admired his persuasive and negotiating skills. He had no familiars among his staff, who regarded his far-sighted decisions and controlled judgement with a legendary respect. Most of his thinking was pushed forward in wartime years when Birmingham and many other cities were under active threat and subject to exacting demands for the maintenance of services on all utilities in order to carry on industrial production.

Manzoni's Birmingham career was accompanied by many honours and distinguished appointments. He was made a CBE in 1941 and knighted in 1954. He was a president of the Institute of Municipal Engineers, member of the Town Planning Institute, fellow of the Royal Society of Health, chairman of the Building Research Board of the Department of Scientific and Industrial Research (1954–60), president of the Institution of Civil Engineers (1960–61), president of the British Standards Institution (1956–8), life governor of Birmingham University, national president of the Federation of Master Builders (1964–70), chairman of the Civil Engineering Research Association (1964–7), and trustee of the Civic Trust (1957–64). He was awarded an honorary DSc by Birmingham University in 1961.

Manzoni retired from Birmingham in 1963 and initially went to live in Herefordshire. But he soon moved back to Birmingham, the city he loved and had done so much to reconstruct after the war. He died of cancer at the Queen Elizabeth Hospital, Edgbaston, on 18 November 1972.

TOM CAULCOTT

Sources *Birmingham Post* (20 Nov 1972) · *WWW*, 1971–80 · personal knowledge (2004) [former colleagues] · G. E. Cherry, *Birmingham: a study in geography, history and planning* (1994) · b. cert. · m. cert. · d. cert. · U. Lpool L., special collections and archives · Burke, *Peerage* (1967)
Archives Birm. CA, scrapbooks and papers
Likenesses B. Hardy, double portrait, photograph, 1954 (with A. G. Shephert-Fidler), Hult. Arch.

Map, Walter (*d.* 1209/10), royal clerk, raconteur, and satirist, was probably born in or about the early 1130s. He sprang from a border family, probably living in Herefordshire, and may have been partly Welsh: his surname is a version of the Welsh Vab or Mab or ap, meaning 'son of'. His attitude to his Welsh 'compatriots' (*compatriote*, his own word), as to many people and institutions in his world, was ambivalent: he claimed kinship, but spoke disparagingly of them. His family were probably prosperous Herefordshire landowners of the second rank—prosperous enough to have some access to Henry II. Map may well have been related to the lay lord of Wormsley near Hereford, who was also called Walter Map, as was his son. But the only relative who can be securely identified is a nephew, Master Philip Map, who was also a canon of Hereford Cathedral, and a chaplain of Giles de Briouze, bishop of Hereford (1200–15).

Royal servant Walter may have had early schooling at Gloucester Abbey; by 1154 he was a student in Paris, and was very likely there over a long period in the 1150s and 1160s—hence, doubtless, his title *magister*. Thereafter he followed a very characteristic *cursus honorum* for an aspiring, highly educated secular clerk of the age—in the service of bishop and king, with widely scattered benefices, and dignities in the chapter of Lincoln Cathedral.

Map won patronage from the bishop of Hereford, Gilbert Foliot (1148–63), in whose service he is to be found in the 1160s. Later on, when Foliot was bishop of London (1163–87), Map won a prebend in St Paul's Cathedral, presumably from the bishop, which to this day bears his name—Mapesbury ('Map's *burh*', or 'fortress'), very likely based on one of his jests. Meanwhile, from the early 1170s and certainly by 1173, Map is recorded in royal service: in February 1173 he was in attendance on Henry II at Limoges, and on the king's behalf entertained the saintly Pierre, archbishop of Tarentaise; in 1179 he was one of the king's representatives at the Third Lateran Council in Rome; in 1183 he was at Saumur in Henry's service when Henry, the Young King, Henry II's eldest surviving son, died at Martel. He acted from time to time as a royal itinerant justice.

Work in the see of Lincoln, and death Map seems thus to have spent at least a part of his time in royal service, until the death of Henry II in 1189, and he is the source of a vivid description of the rigour of living in the royal court, which he likened to hell. But some years before 1189 he won patronage in the see of Lincoln, possibly during the long vacancy between 1166 and 1183, during part of which Henry II's illegitimate son, Geoffrey—a particular bugbear of Map—was bishop-elect (1173–82), more probably from his associate in the royal service, Walter de Coutances, who was bishop of Lincoln in 1183–4. In any case Map occurs as canon in the period 1183–5, and as chancellor by 1186. That is to say, he was in charge of the schools of Lincoln at a time when they were about to enjoy an exceptional reputation as a centre of learning, especially in theology—and at the moment when Hugh of Avalon became bishop (1186–1200). In his own writings Map affects the role of a worldly secular clerk, deeply suspicious of the religious orders—though making something of an exception for the Carthusians from whom Hugh sprang. But he must have been acceptable to Hugh, to say the least, for Hugh made him first precentor of the cathedral (c.1189), then archdeacon of Oxford (from 1196 or 1197), an office he appropriately occupied during the period when Oxford was first visibly becoming the home of a university, in the 1190s. In addition he enjoyed the revenues of parish churches as far apart as Westbury-on-Severn in Gloucestershire and Ashwell in Hertfordshire; and he was clearly prosperous. In his *De nugis curialium* (Map, distich 1, cap. 10) he grumbles humorously at the cost of maintaining his nephews and servants, who for ever press him to further expense: 'You are but spending what you have. Trust in the Lord: it's common talk that they'll make you a bishop.' Early in 1199 the cathedral chapter of Hereford, of which Map was or had been a member, petitioned Richard I to ask permission to elect Walter Map their bishop; but Richard died (6 April 1199) before their petition could be answered. King John arranged for Giles de Briouze, son of his favourite William (III) de Briouze, to receive the bishopric. And in 1203, after his friend Gerald of Wales had failed in his attempts to become bishop of St David's, Map was suggested as a possible candidate, but again without result: he died an archdeacon on 1 April 1209 or 1210.

Writings, spurious and authentic Map's was a career clearly illustrating the opportunities open to a talented and able man who enjoyed at least some early patronage; but it was his writings, spurious and authentic, which have given him fame. Two of the poems in the prose cycle of Lancelot of c.1215–30, the *Queste del Saint Graal* and the *Mort Artu*, claim to be French translations of a Latin original preserved at the abbey of Salisbury (which never existed), composed 'by Walter Map at the request of King Henry his lord'. The translation topos appears in many vernacular poems of the twelfth and thirteenth centuries, and is commonly, as in this case, fictitious. No modern scholar believes that Map had a substantial role in the composition of these poems, nor their immediate source; but why they should have been attributed to him remains an intriguing puzzle. Similarly, a large quantity of secular Latin verse—including some of the most sophisticated poetry now attributed to the Archpoet—came, at the end of the middle ages and later, to be attributed to him; but no modern scholar now believes him to be the author of more than a tiny fraction of this goliardic verse.

Map's modern fame depends mainly on the *De nugis curialium* ('Courtiers' trifles'), a work undoubtedly his which survives only in a single late-fourteenth-century copy (Bodl. Oxf., MS Bodley 851 (3041)), which only became at all widely known after the publication of the *editio princeps* by Thomas Wright in 1850. One section of the *De nugis* (Map, distich 4, cap. 3–4) occurs separately in over fifty manuscripts: it is a witty tract against marriage, *Dissuasio Valerii ad Ruffinum philosophum ne uxorem ducat* ('A dissuasion of Valerius to Ruffinus the philosopher, that he should not take a wife'). It was printed among the works of St Jerome in the earliest editions of Jerome's works: though far more entertaining, it clearly owes some inspiration to Jerome's *Aduersus Iouinianum*. Some of the stories in the *De nugis*, with other specimens of Map's wit and prejudices, especially against the Cistercians and the Jews, were reported by Gerald of Wales (clearly a friend of Map, though perhaps not a very close friend), evidently from Map's conversation. The *De nugis* is meant to entertain, and often succeeds; but it is very difficult to define its genre or subject. Therein, indeed, lies its interest; it is a kind of inventory or florilegium of the mental furniture of a learned and witty twelfth-century clerk. At the beginning and end is a heavy satire on the court—with some abuse, too, of his own household. But it soon passes into a jumble of stories—including two very moving accounts of miracles performed by St Pierre of Tarentaise—and descriptions of religious orders. The reader is rapidly transported to 'A Digression of Master Walter Map on Monkery', his celebrated diatribe against the Cistercians. Some of the satire is entirely wild; some—his accusation that Cistercians moved villages and displaced peasants—is now known to have had substance; it is all very readable. 'It is prescribed to them that they are to dwell in desert places, and desert places they do assuredly either find or make' (Map, distich 1, cap. 25, pp. 92–3). For the rest, the book comprises a remarkable gathering of disparate elements: humorous stories, serious stories, ghost stories, satirical stories—some of them exceedingly sophisticated, some crude—and fragments of history. Distich 5 largely comprises a sort of garbled history of England in the eleventh and twelfth centuries; it contains some interesting nuggets of fact amid a great deal that cannot be true; it concludes with a fragment of autobiography:

> This lord king [Henry II] was served by a certain clerk, who has written these matters for you, whose surname was Map. He was dear and acceptable to the king, not for his own merits, but for those of his forebears who had been faithful and useful to the king, both before his accession [in 1154] and after it. (Map, distich 5, cap. 6, pp. 494–5)

As commonly, Map invites the expectation of genuine revelations, but instead breaks into scurrilous tales about Henry's illegitimate son, Geoffrey, who had been Map's predecessor in his London prebend, then (1173–82) bishop-elect of Lincoln, and was later (1191–1212) archbishop of York. The value of his witness is sometimes most difficult to assess when it could be most authentic. The title of the book, *De nugis curialium*, was also the subtitle of John of

Salisbury's *Policraticus*, which is in part a 'mirror of princes'; and it may perhaps be said that Map's book was designed to be a parody of a 'mirror of princes'; yet frivolous and serious elements in it are bafflingly combined. It survived, clearly, as a collection of loose quires, not in any final form—composed originally *c*.1181–2, but added to at a variety of later dates; it never received any final revision.

Style and character of writings Map's Latin style is of its age, heavily charged with biblical echoes, yet revealing too a wide classical learning, especially in Horace, Virgil, Ovid, and Juvenal. It can show extraordinary point and wit; it often illustrates his own peculiar type of humour. Thus in the *Dissuasio* he tells us that:

> Pacuvius, weeping, said to his neighbour Arrius: 'Friend, I have a disastrous tree in my garden: my first wife hung herself on it, so did my second later on, and now my third has done the same.' Said Arrius, 'I wonder that after so many strokes of luck you find it in you to weep.' And again, 'Good gods, what expenses has that tree suspended for you!' And a third time: 'Friend, give me some cuttings of that tree to plant'. (Map, distich 4, cap. 3, pp. 302–3)

The story comes originally from Cicero, the names from Aulus Gellius; Map's version is better than either. But his wide reading does not only show in his use of the Bible and the classics: it is clear, for example, that he had read Geoffrey of Monmouth's *History of the Kings of Britain*, had detected it for the fraud it was, and enjoyed telling stories that parody it. Although many of his stories have morals (or a notable lack of them), very few reveal any interest in theology—a partial exception may perhaps be made for some of his fairy stories, which are classics for the intermediate world between men and angels in which many folk believed, but whose inhabitants were hard to place among God's creatures. Yet Map must have had some knowledge of theology, if his own account that he was officially invited to hold disputation with the future heresiarch Valdès at the Third Lateran Council of 1179 is to be believed (Map, distich 1, cap. 31). Furthermore, he was chancellor of Lincoln Cathedral not long before it became a leading school of theology under Master William de Montibus. But since he was a royal justice it is likely that he had legal learning too. Like John of Salisbury, he was a polymath, a characteristic product of the leading schools in northern Europe in the age of the twelfth-century renaissance, especially Paris.

Gerald of Wales reports a conversation in which Map drew a distinction between Gerald, who wrote, and Walter, who talked—between Gerald's writings (*scripta*) and Walter's sayings (*dicta*); and there is a sense in which much of the *De nugis* reads like a man talking to his friends. Thus he tells the man Geoffrey—not identified—who, he claims, inspired him to write, that he has set his hand to a vast toil, to put down 'the sayings and doings which have not yet been committed to writing … that the reading of it may amuse, and its teaching tend to moral improvement' (Map, distich 1, cap. 12). However this may be, Map in his own day was evidently known for his talk; in the twentieth century he is known for the *De nugis*. A. G. Rigg has established a strong probability that the *De nugis* survived in Oxford, there to be copied in the late fourteenth century for Brother John of Wells, scholar of Oxford and monk of Ramsey: the book (Bodl. Oxf., MS Bodley 851) also contains—besides other matter, some of it added later—a celebrated copy of *Piers Plowman*, called by A. G. Rigg and Charlotte Brewer the Z version. Though Langland seems strange company for Map, it is the eclectic tastes of Brother John that are responsible for the survival of Walter Map's *De nugis*.

C. N. L. BROOKE

Sources W. Map, *De nugis curialium* / *Courtiers' trifles*, ed. and trans. M. R. James, rev. C. N. L. Brooke and R. A. B. Mynors, OMT (1983); repr. with corrections (1994) [incl. bibliography, list of edns, and MS sources] • A. G. Rigg, *Speculum*, 60 (1985), 177–82 [review of W. Map, *De nugis curialium*, OMT (1983)] • *Gir. Camb. opera*, 1.271–89, 306–7, 362, 363 [a poem by Map addressed to Giraldus], 412; 3.92–3, 145, 321, 335–6; 4.140, 219–25; 5.410–11 • M. Manitius, *Geschichte der lateinischen Literatur des Mittelalters*, 3 (1931), 264–74 • Emden, *Oxf.*, 2.1219 • F. J. E. Raby, *A history of secular Latin poetry in the middle ages*, 2nd edn, 2 (1957), 91n. • *Fasti Angl.*, 1066–1300, [St Paul's, London], 59–60 • *Fasti Angl.*, 1066–1300, [Lincoln], 13, 16, 36, 75, 163 • J. Barrow, ed., *Hereford, 1079–1234*, English Episcopal Acta, 7 (1993), esp. xlv, lix–lx, and nos. 135, 179–80, 244–5, 256–7, 282 • R. A. Donkin, 'Settlement and depopulation on Cistercian estates during the 12th and 13th centuries, especially in Yorkshire', *BIHR*, 33 (1960), 141–65 • A. G. Rigg, 'Medieval Latin poetic anthologies (II)', *Mediaeval Studies*, 40 (1978), 387–407 [on Bod. MS Bodley 851]
Archives Bodl. Oxf., MS Bodley 851 (3041)

Maple, Sir John Blundell, baronet (1845–1903), businessman and racehorse owner and breeder, was born on 1 March 1845 at 145 Tottenham Court Road, London, the elder son of John Maple (*d.* 1900) and his wife, Emily Blundell. His father, after some years as an assistant with Messrs Atkinson in Westminster Bridge Road, set up a furnishing and drapery business in 1840 in Tottenham Court Road, under the name Maple and Cook. This became highly successful, and John, who was educated at Crawford College and King's College School, joined his father in 1862. In 1874 he married Emily Harriet, daughter of Moses Merryweather of Clapham, and from 1880 he was practically head of the family business, although his father remained active until shortly before his death. In 1891 the firm was converted into a limited liability company (with a capital of £2 million) of which Maple was chairman.

However, Maple's abundant energies were not wholly absorbed by his business. He contested (unsuccessfully) the parliamentary division of South St Pancras as a Conservative in 1885, and in 1887, at a by-election, he became member for Dulwich. He continued to represent that constituency until his death. For twelve years he was the president of the Voluntary Early Closing Association, and he was also a member of the London county council. Maple was knighted on Lord Salisbury's resignation from office in 1892, and he received a baronetcy at Queen Victoria's diamond jubilee in 1897. Not until 1903, however, was he elected to the Jockey Club.

Maple's major association with the turf began in 1883, when he registered the racing colours of sky blue, black sleeves, gold cap (eventually changed to white and gold stripes, claret cap). For several years he raced under the pseudonym of Mr Childwick, taking the name from that of his country seat, Childwick Bury, near St Albans, where he established an extensive breeding stud. Previously he had run a few horses in hunter races under the *nom de course* of Mr Hodges, the name of one of his friends. During the twenty-one years that he had horses in training—usually between thirty and forty at a time—he won 544 races, valued at £186,169. In each of eight seasons his winnings ran into five figures. His most successful year was 1901, when twenty-four of his horses won fifty-eight races worth a total of £21,364, which placed him at the head of the winning owners.

Although during later years the Childwick Bury Stud was often overstocked, Maple bred many useful racehorses including Siffleuse (1893) and Nun Nicer (1898), each of which won the One Thousand Guineas. In addition to breeding thoroughbreds, he was a bold buyer of bloodstock. He paid 4000 guineas for the yearling filly Priestess, and a then record 6000 guineas for the yearling colt Childwick, with which he won the Cesarewitch in 1894. With the colt Kirkconnel, which he had bought, Maple won the Two Thousand Guineas and gained third place in the Derby in 1895. Maple purchased Common from Lord Alington and Sir Frederic Johnstone for 15,000 guineas the day after that horse won the St Leger in 1891. He is said later to have turned down an offer of 20,000 guineas for the horse from the Austrian government on the grounds that 'the English turf requires Common's services'. Unhappily Common proved to be a disappointment at stud.

Maple died at Childwick Bury on 24 November 1903, and was interred in the churchyard there or at St Albans. His estate was valued for probate at £2,153,000. During his life he had bestowed large sums on charitable institutions and in 1897 he had undertaken the rebuilding of University College Hospital, which immediately adjoined his business premises. The work was nearly completed at the time of his death, and he empowered his executors to carry the scheme through, with the proviso that the total cost was not to exceed £200,000. The new building was opened by the duke of Connaught on 6 November 1906. Maple left no male heir, and the baronetcy became extinct.

EDWARD MOORHOUSE, *rev.* WRAY VAMPLEW

Sources R. Mortimer, R. Onslow, and P. Willett, *Biographical encyclopedia of British flat racing* (1978) · *The Times* (25 Nov 1903) · *The Sportsman* (25 Nov 1903) · J. Porter, *Kingsclere* (1896) · G. Plumptre, *The fast set: the world of Edwardian racing* (1985) · Burke, *Peerage*
Likenesses B. Stone, photographs, 1901, NPG · L. Fildes, portrait; formerly in possession of his widow, 1912 · Spy [L. Ward], chromolithograph, NPG; repro. in *VF* (6 June 1891) · Walery, photograph, NPG · wood-engraving, NPG; repro. in *ILN* (24 Dec 1887)
Wealth at death £2,153,000: *DNB* · £200,000: probate, 5 Dec 1903, *CGPLA Eng. & Wales*

Maples, Chauncy (1852–1895), bishop of Likoma in Nyasaland, was born on 17 February 1852 at Bound's Green, near Edmonton, Middlesex, the third son of a City solicitor, Frederick Maples (*d.* 1899), and his wife, Charlotte Elizabeth, *née* Chauncy (*d.* 1891). He was educated first at Eagle House School in Wimbledon under the Revd Edward Huntingford, and subsequently at Charterhouse School

Chauncy Maples (1852–1895), by Elliott & Fry

from 1865 to 1869. After preparatory study with J. B. Mozley of King's College, London, at his second attempt he entered University College, Oxford, in January 1871. He graduated in June 1875 with a third-class degree in theology, and worked briefly in Liverpool with the Revd John Eyre, before being ordained at Cuddesdon in the autumn and taking up a curacy in Oxford, at St Mary Magdalene (under the Revd Cecil Deedes).

As an undergraduate Maples was one of those aroused by Bishop Steere's visit to Oxford in September 1874 and his appeal for volunteers on behalf of the Universities' Mission to Central Africa (UMCA). He saw Steere frequently in London during December and January 1874–5, and his developing interest in overseas missions prompted him to join the UMCA in the following March. At Kiungani, the mission's settlement in Zanzibar, Maples was ordained priest by Steere on 29 September 1876, together with his Oxford friend W. P. Johnson. Later that year Steere established the new mainland mission station of Masasi, and in July 1877 he sent Maples to take charge there.

Maples possessed to a marked degree the intellectual interests and attractive curiosity characteristic of so many UMCA recruits, including a special appreciation of music and poetry. However, amiable and popular as he seems to have been at college, few contemporaries apparently expected much of him. Suffering a slight deafness (the consequence of a teenage illness), highly strung, and prone to sentimentality, he worked to his own conception of early church practice and experienced difficulties with the organizational problems of the settlement. He found himself at odds with Steere over discipline, and in part, perhaps as a result, the Masasi mission did not flourish.

Maples's talents lay at first in other directions. During spells of leave in England in 1879–80 and 1884–5 he was, like Steere, an effective propagandist for the UMCA. He also lectured to learned societies, to the Philological Society on his linguistic studies, and to geographical societies on his journey during 1881 to the Rovuma River. He continued his wide and critical reading in theology, church history, and other fields, ranging from the works of E. B. Pusey and Jane Austen to those of Karl Pearson, the duke of Argyll, A. C. Sayce (on the science of language), and E. S. Creasy (on the Ottoman Turks). Combining this eclectic selection with his reading of many missionary lives and writings, Maples wrote for the UMCA's own periodical, *Central Africa*, and reflected on the nature of missionary work and the lessons of his own practical experience. As a result he helped to redefine the high-church party's approach to the missionary task.

By the late 1870s missionaries of many denominations were losing sympathy for approaches which linked Christianity, commerce, and western civilization closely together. Maples not only endorsed these criticisms, but also their corollary of a renewed emphasis on the importance of evangelical preaching. In a paper written originally for the Oxford mission to Calcutta in 1882, *On the Method of Evangelizing Uncultured Races*, he emphasized the fundamental importance of achieving a sympathetic understanding of indigenous cultures, arguing that 'the European must become an African to win Africans'. Worried like other contemporaries about the corrupting impact of the West, and beating a retreat from large, Westernized mission stations, Maples spelt out the need to abandon any preconceptions about 'white superiority' or particular methods of evangelism. His message was about the need for an infinite variety of approaches which involved the missionary in serious efforts to understand local conceptions of God, conscience, and moral laws. His linguistic work and preoccupation with the successful expansion of Islam engaged constantly with such questions.

With his ideas clarified, Maples was also able to make a new start. Masasi was abandoned in 1883, after destruction by Ngoni raiders the previous year. After a short time at Newala, Bishop Smythies appointed Maples archdeacon of Nyasa in 1886, based at Likoma. With more maturity and practical experience Maples now came into his own. The goodwill he built up with local chiefs was of inestimable value to a British administrator such as H. H. Johnston, and it also served to exclude the Portuguese. His work provided foundations for what became in 1892 the diocese of Nyasaland, and when the first bishop, Wilfrid Hornby, soon resigned, no one but Maples himself doubted that he was the obvious successor. He returned to England early in 1895 and was persuaded to accept, and was consecrated with the new title of bishop of Likoma on

29 June in St Paul's Cathedral. His anniversary sermon for the UMCA in May indicated just how far the mission had moved since his arrival in 1876, with its declaration that African contact with Christianity would 'bring out and exhibit new sides of Christian life such as our Western and European natures have not in them to develop' (*Journals and Papers*, 223).

Maples, however, was unable to take things further. On his return journey his boat was caught on Lake Nyasa in a storm; on 2 September 1895, weighed down by his cassock, he drowned. Buried at Kota Kota, he was later commemorated by a mission steamer, the SS *Chauncy Maples*. He never married.   ANDREW PORTER

Sources E. Maples and E. G. Maples Cook, *Chauncy Maples, D.D., F.R.G.S., pioneer missionary in east central Africa* (1897) · *Journals and papers of Chauncy Maples, D.D., F.R.G.S., late bishop of Likoma, Lake Nyasa, Africa*, ed. E. Maples (1899) · C. Maples, *The African church and its claims upon the universities* (1879) · A. E. M. Anderson-Morshead, *The history of the Universities' Mission to Central Africa, 1859–1909*, 5th edn (1909) · D. R. J. Neave, 'Aspects of the Universities Mission to Central Africa, 1858–1900', MPhil diss., University of York, 1974 · J. T. Moriyama, 'The evolution of an African ministry—the work of the Universities' Mission to Central Africa in Tanzania, 1864–1909', PhD diss., U. Lond., 1984 · W. P. Johnson, *My African reminiscences, 1875–1895* (1924) · Boase, *Mod. Eng. biog.*
Archives Bodl. RH · United Society for the Propagation of the Gospel, London, archives
Likenesses Elliott & Fry, photograph, NPG [*see illus.*] · photograph, repro. in Anderson-Morshead, *History*, rev. edn (1909), 257 · portrait, University College, Oxford · portrait, repro. in Maples, *Chauncy Maples*
Wealth at death £1487 10s. 2d.: probate, 26 Feb 1896, *CGPLA Eng. & Wales*

Mapleson, James Henry (1830–1901), opera manager, was born in London on 4 May 1830, the son of James Henry Mapleson (1802/3–1869), for forty years violinist and music librarian of Drury Lane Theatre, where the two-week-old infant was brought on for the christening scene in Shakespeare's *Henry VIII*. He spent two years (1844–6) at the Royal Academy of Music, studying the violin and piano, and in 1848–9 he played the violin in the orchestra of the Royal Italian Opera, whose conductor, Michael Balfe, encouraged him to think of a singing career as a tenor. In 1849 he organized an autumn concert tour by eminent musicians. On 7 January 1851 he married, at Shoreditch, Marianne Raper, a butcher's daughter, who six weeks later gave birth to their first child. This marriage, which held for at least some years, did not prevent him from going to Milan, studying singing with Alberto Mazzucato, and performing (as Enrico Mariani) at Lodi and Verona. Back in England in July 1854, he appeared for one disastrous performance at Drury Lane in Auber's *Masaniello* (under his own name) and was never again heard in public.

In 1856 Mapleson opened a concert and dramatic agency, using his Italian contacts and his knowledge of the language to supply artists for Covent Garden and Her Majesty's, and in 1858 was engaged by E. T. Smith, a jack-of-all-trades entrepreneur and lessee of Drury Lane, to manage a season of Italian opera there. Three years later Mapleson took the Lyceum Theatre for a season of his own, and then moved on to Her Majesty's, where he remained until the theatre burnt down on 6 December 1867. These were his most prosperous and significant years as an opera impresario. The Italian works with which he was identified (by Rossini, Donizetti, Bellini, and Verdi) were still dominant; he supplemented them with the fashionable works of Meyerbeer, scored a *coup* with the first London performance of Gounod's *Faust* (1863), and engaged some of the best singers of the day—Marietta Alboni, Antonio Giuglini, Zélia Trebelli, Ilma Di Murska, Christine Nilsson, and especially Therese Tietjens, whose dramatic genius he served with unusual performances of Gluck's *Iphigénie en Tauride* and Cherubini's *Médée*, all of them capably led by the conductor Luigi Arditi. Mapleson also became an honorary officer in the volunteers (lieutenant-colonel in the Tower Hamlets rifle brigade, and captain in the artillery company) and used these unauthorized titles freely. His political sympathies were Conservative and he was a member of the Junior Carlton Club.

After two uneasy seasons in partnership with his former rival, Frederick Gye, at Covent Garden, Mapleson once again launched out on Italian opera, at Drury Lane (1871–6, 1886–7), Covent Garden (1868–71, autumn seasons in 1885, 1887), Her Majesty's (1877–82, 1887), and the New York Academy of Music (1878–86), interspersed with tours of the British Isles and the United States. He also projected a grand national opera house on the Thames Embankment; the first stone was laid in 1875 by Prince Alfred, duke of Edinburgh, but money ran out and the unfinished building was demolished in 1888. In 1877 Mapleson apparently married, possibly in the United States, the French soprano Marie Roze, real name Marie-Hippolyte Ponsin (1846–1926), widow of the American bass Julius Perkins (d. 1875); Mapleson may have been the father of her son, J. H. Raymond Roze (1875–1920), a conductor and composer. The couple separated some time in the late 1880s, and in 1890 Marie Roze returned to France.

In these years Mapleson acquired a reputation for being both financially unreliable (though glibly persuasive) and artistically outdated, until George Bernard Shaw could write in 1888—reviewing Mapleson's entertaining but undependable memoirs—that they covered 'a period of hopeless decay' marked by 'want of life, purpose, sincerity and concerted artistic effort' (Shaw, *London Music*, 39–40). Though he scored another *coup* with the first London performance of Bizet's *Carmen* (1878), he relied on the old Italian repertory, now shopworn. And while he engaged the hugely successful Adelina Patti (especially for his American tours, 1882–5) and other good artists, casting was erratic and productions ramshackle; he could not in the end withstand competition from the new Metropolitan Opera in New York or, from 1888, from Augustus Harris's well-financed management at Covent Garden. He went bankrupt in 1888; his last American tour (1886) and his last London (1889) and New York (1896) seasons all failed disastrously. He died in London of Bright's disease on 14 November 1901, and was buried in Highgate cemetery on 18 November.

HENRY DAVEY, *rev.* JOHN ROSSELLI

Sources *The Mapleson memoirs: the career of an operatic impresario, 1858–1888*, ed. H. Rosenthal (1966) · J. F. Cone, *First rival of the Metropolitan Opera* (1983) · G. B. Shaw, *London music as heard in 1888–89 by Corno di Bassetto* (1937), 39–40, 139–40 · G. B. Shaw, *How to become a musical critic*, ed. D. H. Laurence (1960), 158 · *The Times* (15 Nov 1901) · *The Times* (16 Nov 1901) · J. Bennett, *Forty years of music, 1865–1905* (1908), 188–95 · L. Arditi, *My reminiscences*, ed. Baroness von Zedlitz, 2nd edn (1896) · L. Lehmann, *My path through life* (1914) · H. Rosenthal, *Two centuries of opera at Covent Garden* (1958) · Boase, *Mod. Eng. biog.* [James Henry Mapleson, son] · *New Grove* · m. cert. [Marianne Roper]
Likenesses caricatures, cartoons, repro. in Cone, *First rival of the Metropolitan Opera* · photograph, repro. in Rosenthal, ed., *Mapleson memoirs*, p. 30 · woodburytype photograph, NPG

Maplet, John (d. 1592), writer on natural philosophy, matriculated as a sizar from Queens' College, Cambridge, in December 1560 and graduated BA in 1564. He was a fellow of St Catharine's College in August 1564, and was ordained deacon at Ely on 5 November of that year. He was a fellow of Gonville and Caius College in 1566/7 and proceeded MA in 1567. On 26 November 1568 he was instituted, on the presentation of Sir Thomas Mildmay, to the rectory of Great Leighs, Essex, which he exchanged for the vicarage of Northolt, Middlesex, on 30 April 1576. His marriage to a widow named Ellen Leap (d. 1595) brought five children: Margaret, Ellen, John, Thomas, and Mary, born between 1577 and 1581.

When Maplet was in Cambridge he wrote the first of the two works for which he is known, *A Greene Forest, or, A Naturall Historie*. This was printed in London in 1567 and dedicated to Thomas, earl of Sussex. It is divided into sections on minerals, plants, and animals, each of which consists of alphabetically organized descriptions drawn from classical, Islamic, and humanist sources. A decade and a half later, when installed as vicar in Northolt, Maplet wrote another small book, *The Diall of Destiny*. He finished writing this in December 1581, and it was printed in London, with a dedication to Sir Christopher Hatton, the following year. In this treatise Maplet, again drawing on scholarly sources, argues that the heavens influence earthly events. He discusses the properties, effects, and qualities of each of the known planets in turn (the moon, Mercury, Venus, the sun, Mars, Jupiter, and Saturn), and touches on a range of subjects from elephants to earthquakes. A third work by Maplet, 'Argemonie, or, The prynciple vertues of stone' is reputed to have been printed in London in 1566; although this might have been the first part of *A Greene Forest*, issued separately, no copy of it seems to have survived (C. H. Cooper, 2.135–6). Maplet was buried in the chancel of Northolt church on 7 September 1592. A few weeks later his widow married Matthew Randall, a servant of her husband's glebe; she died at Ealing in 1595.

While Maplet's books number among the few dozen vernacular treatises on natural philosophy printed in sixteenth-century England, they have not figured in histories of these subjects. During Maplet's lifetime John Bossewell included his name alongside Geoffrey Chaucer, Sir Thomas Eliot, and others as sources for information relevant to heraldry, probably referring to *A Greene Forest*.

Maplet's works continued to be read after his death. For instance, about the turn of the century Simon Forman the astrologer physician cited *A Greene Forest* for information about metals and *The Diall of Destiny* on comets; in 1675 William Cooper included *A Greene Forest* in a catalogue of English alchemical books.   LAUREN KASSELL

Sources Venn, *Alum. Cant.* · R. Newcourt, *Repertorium ecclesiasticum parochiale Londinense*, 2 vols. (1708–10) · parish register, Northolt, Middlesex, LMA, 7 Sept 1592 [burial] · Bishop of London, 'Probate act in vice generals' book', 1595 · will, PRO, PROB 11/86, sig. 70 · J. Bossewell, *Workes of armourie* (1572) · Bodl. Oxf., MSS Ashmole 384, 1472, 1491, 1494 · W. Cooper, *A catalogue of chymicall books* (1675) · Cooper, *Ath. Cantab.*, vol. 2

Maplet, John (1611x15–1670), physician, born in the parish of St Martin's-le-Grand, London, was the son of John Maplet, a shoemaker. He was educated at Westminster School, and in 1630 he was elected to Christ Church, Oxford; he claimed to be twenty in 1632, when he matriculated. He graduated BA on 8 July 1634, MA on 17 April 1638, and DM on 24 July 1647. On 9 December 1643 he was elected junior proctor on the death of William Cartwright, and served for the remainder of the year, and in the autumn of 1647 he was nominated principal of Gloucester Hall. He was a delegate of the university appointed to receive the parliamentary visitors, and is said to have submitted to their authority, but he quickly left the university.

About 1648 Maplet became tutor to Lucius Cary, third Viscount Falkland, with whom he travelled in France for two years, staying chiefly at Orléans, Blois, and Saumur. During the tour he made many observations, which he committed to writing, 'in a neat and curious hand, with a particular tract of his travels in an elegant Latin style' (Guidott, 181). He afterwards went with Henry Cary, Lord Falkland, brother of Lucius, to the Low Countries, where an uncle of his seems to have lived. On 5 March 1651 it was certified to the committee for reformation of the universities that he was 'absent upon leave' (Burrows, 329), but while still abroad he appears to have been ejected from his offices at Oxford.

On his return Maplet settled as a physician at Bath, practising there in the summer and at Bristol in the winter 'with great respect and veneration from all people in those parts'. About that time he married Mrs Anne Hull of Bristol. He was acquainted with the leading physicians of his time, and helped Thomas Guidott in his early days. At the Restoration he resumed the principalship of Gloucester Hall, but retired in 1662. He died at Bath on 4 August 1670, said to be aged fifty-five. In the north aisle of Bath Abbey, where they were buried, Guidott erected an elaborate monument, with a black marble tablet bearing a Latin inscription to Maplet's memory. Under it is another small tablet with an inscription to his wife, who died in February 1671, aged thirty-five, and his children, a son John, aged three years, and a daughter Mary, aged three months. Of Maplet, Guidott says: 'He was of a tender, brittle constitution, inclining to feminine, clear skinn'd and of a very fresh complexion' (Guidott, 152). Wood says, 'he

was learned, candid, and ingenious, a good physician, a better Christian, and an excellent Latin poet'.

Maplet left a number of works in manuscript, including the account of his foreign travels. In 1694 Guidott published Maplet's *Epistolarum medicarum specimen de thermarum Bathoniensium effectis*, which was dedicated to the leading contemporary physicians. Guidott also transcribed some Latin verses by Maplet on catarrh in the eyes, and some lines headed 'De catarrhi fuga' and 'In primum canitiem', with a rhymed translation of the latter. He considered Maplet's 'style terse, his words choice, but his periods a little too elaborate' (Guidott, 193).

     G. LE G. NORGATE, *rev.* PATRICK WALLIS

Sources Foster, *Alum. Oxon.* · *Old Westminsters*, vols. 1–2 · A. Chalmers, ed., *The general biographical dictionary*, new edn, 32 vols. (1812–17) · Wood, *Ath. Oxon.* · T. Guidott, *A discourse of Bathe, and the hot waters there* (1676) · M. Burrows, ed., *The register of the visitors of the University of Oxford, from AD 1647 to AD 1658*, CS, new ser., 29 (1881), 329

Maplethorpe, Cyril Wheatley (1898–1983), pharmaceutical manufacturer, was born on 20 April 1898 at 68 Balfour Street, Drypool, Kingston upon Hull, the son of Jack Maplethorpe, a police constable, and his wife, Emeline Annie, *née* Vesiter. He was educated at Hymers College, Hull, where he held a scholarship, before going on to study pharmacy at Chelsea College, London. Towards the end of the First World War, his education was briefly interrupted by service in the Royal Engineers, but after the war he entered the School of Pharmacy, at the Pharmaceutical Society, Bloomsbury Square, London, where he qualified as a pharmaceutical chemist in 1922. On 21 September 1925 he married Margery Bessie Pearce, in Hull. There were no children of the marriage.

After a spell in the research laboratories and museum of the Pharmaceutical Society, in 1924 Maplethorpe joined the staff of Allen and Hanburys Ltd. The modern science-based pharmaceutical industry was then in its infancy, and many British firms were still locked in the Victorian world of the chemist and druggist, with its invalid and baby foods, and various tonics, embrocations, and laxatives. Allen and Hanburys, founded by Quakers in 1715 and famous for its milk foods, cod-liver oil, and surgical instruments, typified the traditional nature of the industry in the 1920s.

Maplethorpe joined Allen and Hanburys as a research chemist, but his organizational talents were soon recognized and in 1932 he was appointed manager at the firm's Ware factory. He was only the second technically qualified pharmacist to have worked there, so he brought with him some much needed technical expertise. In the 1930s he involved himself with research and product development and was responsible for Isogel, a traditional but profitable bulk laxative. But he was also increasingly aware that the days of the old galenicals and food products were numbered, and he slowly began to push the company towards a more scientific future. His appointment to the board as managing director in 1944 increased his influence. In the UK he enlarged the numbers of technical personnel and extended the firm's research interests; abroad he began

Cyril Wheatley Maplethorpe (1898–1983), by Anna Zinkeisen

rationalizing its wide-ranging subsidiaries. By the mid-1950s, Allen and Hanburys began to acquire a more modern look, with products that included antihistamines, antibiotics, and tranquillizers, besides more traditional items such as throat pastilles and Haliborange. In the summer of 1958 the company announced that its production of traditional drugs and galenicals would cease.

Unfortunately, Maplethorpe's reforms took place within a family-owned firm that was still very conservative. Faced by stronger British (and overseas) rivals and with low profitability, Allen and Hanburys was vulnerable. In 1958 it was bought by Glaxo Laboratories for £633,000 and Maplethorpe's dream of running his own science-based pharmaceutical company ended. However, the take-over—which he had helped negotiate—involved no loss of prestige for Maplethorpe, who was elected to the Glaxo board. He and the Glaxo chairman, Sir Harry Jephcott, respected each other, and their views on the future of the industry coincided. Allen and Hanburys, therefore, entered the 1960s with a considerable degree of independence and Maplethorpe was free to pursue his plans for a research division at Ware with considerably more resources. In 1962, largely owing to his initiative, a new research director, David Jack, was appointed at Ware to spearhead a new and greatly expanded research programme.

Meanwhile, Maplethorpe was intent on improving the professional standing of pharmacy, largely through his work at the Pharmaceutical Society. He was a member of its council from 1943 to 1967, chairman of its education committee from 1945 until 1962, and president of the society between 1963 and 1965. For services to pharmaceutical education he was awarded an honorary degree of MSc by Manchester University in 1958 and received the Pharmaceutical Society's charter gold medal in 1968. He was a founder member of the council of the School of Pharmacy and played a part in its transfer to the University of London in 1948. He was also a governor of Chelsea College. For his efforts to introduce a more rigorous pharmaceutical training in universities and elsewhere, Maplethorpe was described by David Jack as 'probably the most influential pharmacist of his generation' (*Pharmaceutical Journal*, 231, 1983, 734).

Maplethorpe retired as the managing director of Allen and Hanburys in 1965 and left the Glaxo board in 1968. The research division at Ware under David Jack and others subsequently achieved spectacular success with science-based drugs, lifting Glaxo to a position among the world leaders in the industry by the late 1980s. Fortunately, Maplethorpe lived to see something of this transformation, in which he had played such a significant part.

Maplethorpe had considerable physical presence—he was well over 6 feet tall—and he could sometimes be intimidating to subordinates. However, he was a humane man, whose early Congregationalist beliefs had been replaced by a firm socialism. Unusually for a leading businessman, he was a supporter of the Labour Party. Much of his personal estate was directed into research fellowships at Chelsea College and the School of Pharmacy and, through the Margery Maplethorpe Trust, he funded old people's homes in Hertford. His estate at death was valued at £765,225.

After a stroke at his home, Stoneyfield, St Mary's Lane, Hertingfordbury, Maplethorpe died in Hertford Hospital on 26 October 1983, and was cremated at Harlow crematorium. He was survived by his wife, who died in 1995, having been a substantial benefactor, in her husband's memory, of St Hugh's College, Oxford.

GEOFFREY TWEEDALE

Sources G. Tweedale, *At the sign of the plough: 275 years of Allen & Hanburys and the British pharmaceutical industry, 1715–1990* (1990) • D. Chapman-Huston and E. C. Cripps, *Through a City archway: the story of Allen and Hanburys, 1715–1954* (1954) • *Pharmaceutical Journal*, 231 (1983), 547–8 • private information (2004) • R. P. T. Davenport-Hines and J. Slinn, *Glaxo: a history to 1962* (1992) • 'Reception for Maplethorpe post-doctoral fellows', *Pharmaceutical Journal*, 243 (1989), 775
Archives GlaxoSmithKline, Greenford, Middlesex, Allen and Hanbury Archive
Likenesses A. Zinkeisen, oils, Royal Pharmaceutical Society of Great Britain, London [*see illus.*] • portrait, repro. in Tweedale, *At the sign of the Plough*
Wealth at death £765,225: probate, 2 March 1984, *CGPLA Eng. & Wales*

Mapletoft, John (1631–1721), physician and Church of England clergyman, was born on 15 June 1631 at Margaretting, Essex, the second of the three children of Joshua Mapletoft (1594–1635), vicar of Margaretting and rector of Wickford, and his wife, Susanna (*d.* 1657), daughter of

John Collett of North Thoresby, Cambridgeshire, and his wife, Susanna. After his father's death his mother married James Chedley and Mapletoft was brought up with his brother and sister at Little Gidding in the well-known, if small, religious community established there by his great-uncle and godfather Nicholas *Ferrar. In 1645 he was sent to Westminster School by his uncle Robert *Mapletoft, later master of Pembroke College, Cambridge, and dean of Ely. He entered Trinity College, Cambridge, as a pensioner on 20 May 1648, and graduated BA in January 1652 and MA in 1655. In May 1652 he was admitted a student of Gray's Inn, but he does not appear to have remained there long, as in October 1653 he was elected a fellow of Trinity College, where he later supported Isaac Barrow's scheme for building a library.

On leaving Cambridge in 1658 Mapletoft became tutor to Joceline, son of the earl of Northumberland. Two years later he travelled abroad to France and Rome, where he lived in the household of Algernon Sidney, in order to study physic. By early 1664 he had rejoined the earl's family at Petworth. He took his MD in 1667 at Cambridge, and incorporated the degree at Oxford in 1669.

Mapletoft established a successful practice as a physician in London, numbering several aristocratic families among his patients. He attended Lord Essex on his embassy to Denmark in 1670, and the dowager countess of Northumberland in France in 1672 and again in 1676. Against stiff competition, he succeeded Jonathan Goddard as Gresham professor of physic in 1675. Mapletoft lived in the college for the next three years until he resigned in order to marry, on 18 November 1679, Rebecca, daughter of Lucy Knightley of Hackney, a Hamburg merchant, with whom, as he told his friend Robert Nelson, he learned the vanity 'of believing myselfe as happy as any man, either single or married' (BL, Add. MS 45511, fol. 1). Together they had two sons, Robert (1684–1716) and John (1687–1763), and a daughter, Elizabeth (d. 1761). Rebecca Mapletoft died in November 1693, on the fourteenth anniversary of their marriage.

Through his distant relation Thomas Firmin, Mapletoft became part of an extensive circle including noted natural philosophers such as Robert Hooke, physicians such as Thomas Sydenham, and clergy, particularly latitudinarians such as John Tillotson. Mapletoft was elected a fellow of the Royal Society in February 1676 and was a member of its council in 1677, 1679, 1690, and 1692, during which time he took part in discussions and experiments. He had been at school with John Locke, and they remained on close terms for many years, corresponding regularly when either of them was abroad and consulting each other over difficult patients. Together they became involved with Sydenham's medical researches, acting as secretaries and examining cases. Mapletoft translated several of Sydenham's works into Latin for publication, most notably much of *Observationes medicae* (1676), which was dedicated to him, and other texts published in 1683. The extent and details of his role are uncertain, although it seems likely that the idiomatic flavour and classical references in *Observationes* reflect his rather florid style.

Mapletoft had always had an inclination towards theology, and following his marriage he gave up physic to prepare himself for ordination. Although he had some scruples about subscribing to the Thirty-Nine Articles, seeking advice from Simon Patrick about the matter (see Patrick's letter of 8 February 1683 in BL, Add. MS 5878, fol. 151), he took deacon's and priest's orders on 3 March 1683. He had already been presented as (non-resident) rector of Braybrooke, Northamptonshire, and in January 1685 became lecturer at Ipswich, and later that year lecturer at St Christopher's, London. In January 1686, with the support of several prominent city figures, he was selected as vicar of the united parishes of St Lawrence Jewry and St Mary Magdalen, Milk Street, London, the parish in which he had been married, where he succeeded the prominent latitudinarian and former provost of King's College, Cambridge, Benjamin Whichcote. He remained vicar there until his death, preaching until he was over eighty years old. In 1690 he graduated DD at Cambridge. Mapletoft was an early member of the Society for Promoting Christian Knowledge, joining in 1699, and of the Society for the Propagation of the Gospel in Foreign Parts. He was also active in Sion College, an institution designed as a guild of the clergy of the City of London and its suburbs, serving as assistant in 1688 and 1689, senior dean in 1694, and president in 1707, and was involved with Greenwich and St Thomas's hospitals. During his time at St Lawrence Jewry he published a number of sermons, minor works on theology, and collections of proverbs and classical extracts, several of which were republished on a number of occasions. His writings were deeply concerned with the everyday faith of his parishioners, and he distributed copies of his *Principles and Duties of the Christian Religion* (1710), a 'True, Plain and Useful' account of religion, to each household in his parish.

For most of the last decade of his life Mapletoft lived in Oxford and Westminster with his daughter, who had married Francis Gastrell, canon of Christ Church, Oxford, and bishop of Chester. Mapletoft died in Westminster on 10 November 1721 and was buried under the communion table of St Lawrence Jewry in the same tomb as Benjamin Calamy on 15 November.   PATRICK WALLIS

Sources Venn, *Alum. Cant.* · Foster, *Alum. Oxon.* · *Old Westminsters* · G. G. Meynell, *Authorship and vocabulary in Thomas Sydenham's Methodus and observationes* (1995) · J. Ward, *The lives of the professors of Gresham College* (1740) [BL copy with MS additions] · *The correspondence of John Locke*, ed. E. S. De Beer, 8 vols. (1976–89) · A. W. Hughes Clarke, ed., *The register of St Lawrence Jewry, London*, 2, Harleian Society, registers, 71 (1941) · A. R. Maddison, ed., *Lincolnshire pedigrees*, 2, Harleian Society, 51 (1903) · K. Dewhurst, *John Locke (1632–1704): physician and philosopher* (1963) · *The diary of Robert Hooke … 1672–1680*, ed. H. W. Robinson and W. Adams (1935) · J. Mapletoft, letter to Robert Nelson, 1679, BL, Add. MS 45511, fol. 1 · *DNB*

Mapletoft, Robert (1609–1677), college head, was born on 25 January 1609, at North Thoresby, Lincolnshire, the son of Hugh Mapletoft, rector of that parish, and his wife, a member of the Stennits family of Wainfleet, Lincolnshire. He was educated at the grammar school at Louth. He was admitted a sizar of Queens' College, Cambridge, on 25 May 1625, graduated BA in 1628, and proceeded MA in

1632. On 8 January 1631 he was elected fellow of Pembroke College and became chaplain to his friend and patron Bishop Matthew Wren. On Wren's recommendation, in 1639, the year he proceeded BD, he was presented to the rectory of Bartlow, Cambridgeshire, by Charles I.

Mapletoft was cousin to Nicholas Ferrar, whom he assisted with his translation of a temperance treatise by Leonard Lessius. He frequently wrote to and visited Ferrar's religious community at Little Gidding, Huntingdonshire. Mapletoft was there when Ferrar died in 1637; he preached the funeral oration and officiated at the funeral. His brother, Joshua, married Susanna Collett, Ferrar's niece, and was father of John Mapletoft (1631–1721), the physician and clergyman.

During the civil war Mapletoft was among the fellows who unsuccessfully attempted to prevent William Dowsing, the iconoclast, from cleansing Pembroke College chapel. Mapletoft was ejected as a malignant from his living at Bartlow in 1643 and at the parliamentary visitation of the university in 1644. The charges against him included refusing the solemn league and covenant and permitting Bishop Wren's son to wear Prince Rupert's colours. He subsequently 'lived as privately and quietly as he could' (Baker MSS, CUL, MS 36, fol. 103) and was sheltered in Sir Robert Shirley's house in Leicestershire, where he met Gilbert Sheldon, afterwards archbishop of Canterbury. During the protectorate Mapletoft provided prayer book services to a private congregation in Lincoln. 'Being discovered, he was like to come into some trouble, but came off safe when it became known that his congregation had made a considerable purse for him, which he would not accept' (ibid.).

Following the Restoration, on 28 July 1660 Mapletoft received the degree of DD by royal mandate. On 23 August he was presented by the crown to the subdeanery of Lincoln Cathedral and the prebendal stall of Clifton, and on 8 December revived the mastership of the Spital Hospital. While subdean he was involved with a dispute with the cathedral's precentor, John Featley, about capitular appointments, and was attacked by him in the manuscript tract 'Speculum Mapletoftianum' (DNB). As master of Spital Hospital he received the practically defunct charity with Dean Michael Honywood. A bill in chancery was exhibited in 1662 against Sir John Wray for the restoration of the estates, and Mapletoft at his own expense rebuilt the demolished chapel and increased its revenues, making the office rather one of expense than profit. He was nominated master of Pembroke College, Cambridge, but Mapletoft's recommended candidate, Mark Frank, served in the office until Mapletoft succeeded him, in 1664. He held the mastership until his death. He was made dean of Ely on 7 August 1667, holding the subdeanery of Lincoln with the deanery until 1671.

When in 1668 Anne Hyde, duchess of York, began to waver in her allegiance to the Church of England, Mapletoft was recommended as her chaplain by his friend Sheldon, as a 'primitive and apostolical divine' (Baker MSS, CUL, MS 36, fol. 103) whose influence might prevent her secession, but feeling himself 'unfit for court life' (Baker

MSS, CUL, MS 38, fol. 191) he was reluctant to undertake the office. Shortly after resigning the subdeanery he moved to Cambridge, serving as vice-chancellor in 1671. He received from the crown the living of Clayworth, Nottinghamshire, which in 1672 he exchanged for the college living of Soham, near Ely, resigning his fellowship; he held the living of Soham until his death.

Mapletoft died, unmarried, on 20 August 1677 in the master's lodge at Pembroke, and, by his desire, was buried the same day in the chapel near Bishop Wren. It is recorded of him that 'wherever he resided he kept a good table, and had the general reputation of a pious and charitable man' (Baker MSS, CUL, MS 38, fol. 192). He was exceedingly thin, 'vir valde macilentus' (ibid.). In his will he made numerous bequests, including his library, the 'small reserves from the late plundering times' (Cambridge University Archives, will, vol. 4, 158), £100 to Ely Cathedral, and the same sum to poor clerical widows in Ely. He also founded catechetical lectures at Queens' and Pembroke colleges, and petty schools at North Thoresby and at Louth.   EDMUND VENABLES, rev. S. L. SADLER

Sources will, CUL, department of manuscripts and university archives, PROB., original will, 1677; will, vol. 4, 158; will inv., 1677/8 · *CSP dom.*, 1660–61, 163 · CUL, Baker MSS, MS 36, fols. 103–4; MS 37, fols. 20–25; MS 38, fols. 191–2; MS 42, fol. 226 · Magd. Cam., Ferrar MSS, box 5, nos. 476, 562, 564; box 8, no. 828 [CUL, Ferrar papers, microfilms] · [J. Barwick], *Querela Cantabrigiensis* (1647), conclusion, appx · J. Walker, *An attempt towards recovering an account of the numbers and sufferings of the clergy of the Church of England*, 2 pts in 1 (1714), 154 · W. Kennet, *A register and chronicle* (1728), 213, 231 · E. Carter, *The history of the University of Cambridge* (1753), 33, 75, 80–81 · E. Carter, *The history of the University of Cambridge* (1753) · E. Venables, 'An historical notice of the hospital of Spittal-on-the-Street, Lincoln', *Associated Architectural Societies' Reports and Papers*, 20/2 (1890), 285–8, 298 · A. Kingston, *East Anglia and the great civil war*, [new edn] (1902), 393 · J. B. Mullinger, *The University of Cambridge*, 3 (1911), 290–91 · Venn, *Alum. Cant.*, 1/3.139 · A. L. Maycock, *Nicholas Ferrar of Little Gidding* (1938), 193, 230–31, 257–8, 272, 299, 300 · *Walker rev.*, 84 · D. Underdown, *Royalist conspiracies* (1960), 182 · J. Twigg, *The University of Cambridge and the English Revolution, 1625–1688* (1990), 249, 291, 294 · *VCH Cambridgeshire and the Isle of Ely*, 3.349, 555 · *The journal of William Dowsing*, ed. T. Cooper (2001)
Archives Bodl. Oxf., MSS Tanner 53, 197 · CUL, Baker MSS 36, fols. 103–4; 38, fol. 191; 42 · Magd. Cam., Ferrar MSS, box 5, nos. 476, 562, 564; box 8, no. 828
Wealth at death £563 13s. 8d.: inventory, 23 Aug 1677, CUL, department of manuscripts and university archives, inv., 1677/1678

Mapondera, Kadungure (1840s–1904), warrior chief in Africa, was born at Nyota, a mountain stronghold of the Negomo dynasty, in what is now northern Mashonaland, Zimbabwe. Mapondera's mother, Mwera, was a *mhondwa*, a slave wife, but there is no agreement as to who his father was. Some accounts favour Gorejena Mororo, others Nyahunzvi Zhenjeni, both of them local rulers. Among the known children of the former who may have been Mapondera's siblings were Rwanga, Mupfunya, Katena, and Chikuwa. Mapondera himself had twenty-five wives, fathering an unknown number of children. The names of two of his wives survive: Mandivanza and Kamvera.

The first mention of Mapondera dates from the early 1860s, when Ndebele (Matabele) raiding parties clashed with the Shona inhabitants of the Mazowe valley and its surrounds. Nyota itself was almost certainly attacked and, according to tradition, it was here that Mapondera fought bravely, 'making a great name for himself' (Beach, *Mapondera*, 16). From this time until the 1880s what little is known about Mapondera turns on incomplete and contradictory oral testimony. Five episodes are recalled, in the main involving dynastic conflict, but also a notable visit to Barwe in Mozambique, where Mapondera acquired the war medicine charm nyembe, whose reputed ability to turn bullets into water rarely failed to attract a following.

By the end of the 1880s foreigners were taking an increasing interest in the region. In July 1889 Mapondera allowed a Goan trader to establish himself at Nyota and fly the Portuguese flag. Two months later, however, Mapondera signed a concession with the hunter Frederick Courtney Selous. In return for conceding mineral rights to a large area over which he had no control whatsoever, he obtained the promise of trade goods worth £100 p.a. and 1.5 per cent of any profits. In doing this, he was in effect declaring himself independent of Negomo.

Over the next four years or so, while Cecil Rhodes's British South Africa Company gradually made its presence felt in the country around Fort Salisbury, Mapondera was left to his own devices, missionary contact notwithstanding. But in July 1894 he and his followers abruptly abandoned Nyota. The previous year he had staged a brutal raid against the Chipadze people, and it seems that his neighbours combined to force him to leave the district: 'Mapondera went away after having murdered people at various places' (Beach, *Mapondera*, 27, 29). Mapondera removed himself to the Dande River, near the escarpment overlooking the Zambezi valley, effectively beyond the reach of either the Rhodesians or the Portuguese. For several years he kept a low profile so far as the colonial authorities were concerned, contenting himself with raids on nearby villages for women and grain. When these activities eventually came to the notice of the administration in Salisbury, Mapondera and his well-armed followers shifted deeper into the Zambezi valley. By October 1900 he was on the lower Ruya River, from where he was reported as exacting tribute from the established population.

Until this point Mapondera had avoided conflict with white people. But convinced that encroaching settler demands for tax and labour threatened his authority, Mapondera and a loose coalition of local allies decided to stand and fight at the battle of Matitima on 3 March 1901. Involving several hundred men on both sides, it was to be the largest single clash of arms on Rhodesian soil in the twentieth century. Although the battle itself ended indecisively, it marked the end of Mapondera's campaign. The Rhodesian government was now determined to settle accounts with him once and for all. In January 1902 Rhodesian forces pushed him over the border into Mozambique, where he eventually gave himself up to the Portuguese authorities. Such evidence as there is indicates that he was subsequently employed by the Portuguese in their campaign against the Makombe dynasty of Barwe. It

appears that he was taken prisoner at some stage by Makombe, but escaped in the general confusion that accompanied the end of the Barwe war in October 1902 (Beach, *Mapondera*, 54). With what remained of his followers starving and desperate to plant crops for the coming season, he returned to Negomo's territory, where in September 1903 he surrendered, much to the surprise of the Rhodesians. In the event, he treated his trial with 'a degree of levity, and danced on hearing his 7 year sentence'. Yet less than two months later, on 20 June 1904, he died in Salisbury prison. His family believed he had committed suicide: 'though I may serve that sentence and go out of gaol, what am I going to do, the chieftainship has gone, the country has gone' (ibid., 55).

Mapondera's reputation was much revised in the late twentieth century. Once hailed as a social bandit who selflessly attacked symbols of colonial oppression such as government posts, tax collectors, and labour recruiters, he came to be seen very much as a product of his times. Far from attacking white people, he spent most of his energy attempting to found a new dynasty. Although he caused early Rhodesian administrators some anxious moments, he was never simply a hero of anti-colonial resistance.

IAN PHIMISTER

Sources D. N. Beach, *Mapondera: heroism and history in northern Zimbabwe, 1840–1904* (1989) · F. C. Selous, *Travel and adventure in southeast Africa* (1893) · T. O. Ranger, 'The rewriting of African history during the scramble: the Matabele dominance in Mashonaland', *African Social Research*, 4 (1967), 271–82 · D. N. Beach, *War and politics in Zimbabwe, 1840–1900* (1986) · P. R. Warhurst, 'A troubled frontier: north eastern Mashonaland, 1898–1906', *African Affairs*, 77 (1978), 214–29 · A. F. Isaacman, *The tradition of resistance in Mozambique: anti-colonial activity in the Zambezi valley, 1850–1921* (1976) · A. F. Isaacman, 'Social banditry in Zimbabwe (Rhodesia) and Mozambique, 1894–1907: an expression of early peasant protest', *Journal of Southern African Studies*, 9 (1977), 1–30

Archives National Archives of Zimbabwe, Harare, oral history, AOH 13–16 | National Archives of Zimbabwe, Harare, corresp., 'Concession from Mapondera and Temaringa, 25 Sept 1889', CT 1/6/7 · National Archives of Zimbabwe, Harare, annual report of Native Commissioner Noah Mazoe, 3 March 1901, 'A short history of the outlaw chief Mapondera' · National Archives of Zimbabwe, Harare, *Rex v. Mapondera*, 17 Feb 1904, D 3/5/10

Likenesses two photographs, 1903, National Archives, Harare, Zimbabwe · G. Armour, portrait (after a photograph by Franceys), repro. in Selous, *Travel and adventure in south-east Africa*, p. 289

Mapother, Edward (1881–1940), psychiatrist, was born on 12 July 1881 at 6 Merrion Square, Dublin, the only son of the seven children of Edward Dillon *Mapother (1835–1908), surgeon to St Vincent's Hospital and president of the Royal College of Surgeons of Ireland (1879–80), and Ellen, daughter of John Tobin MP of Halifax, Nova Scotia. In 1888 the family moved to London when E. D. Mapother went into private practice at 32 Cavendish Square. Edward Mapother was educated at University College school and hospital, from where he graduated MB BS in 1905, winning medals in pathology and medicine. After graduation he served as houseman under Risien Russell at the National Hospital, Queen Square. In 1908 Mapother obtained his MD (London) and was appointed to the new London county council asylum at Long Grove, Epsom. He worked with an exceptionally gifted team of young psychiatrists, including Hubert Bond and Bernard Hart, who were experimenting with the new psychological theories of Janet and Freud. The tension between the neurological work carried out at Queen Square and the psychotherapeutic regime instituted at Long Grove was to inform Mapother's intellectual outlook for the rest of his career.

With the outbreak of war in 1914 Mapother volunteered for the Royal Army Medical Corps. He worked as a surgeon in the military hospitals at Étaples and Millbank and later in Mesopotamia and India. In April 1917 he was invalided back to England with sciatica. He retrained in military psychiatry at Maghull Military Hospital and was appointed neurologist to the 2nd Western General Hospital in Manchester. Mapother demonstrated great energy and organizational ability in his new post, establishing two subsidiary neurological hospitals in Stockport which he administered almost singlehanded until his demobilization in March 1919.

In September 1919, Mapother was appointed medical superintendent to the Ministry of Pensions war neurosis centre in the requisitioned Maudsley Hospital. After the centre's closure in October 1920 Mapother returned to Long Grove, yet he never abandoned his commitment to the Maudsley. He was deeply involved in the protracted discussions concerning its future funding and organization. Mapother was insistent that the institution fulfil its original purpose as a centre for voluntary treatment and psychiatric research. In January 1923 his efforts were rewarded. The Maudsley reopened with Mapother as its medical superintendent. It was a position he was to hold until the end of his career. The post provided the institutional space and intellectual opportunity for Mapother to realize his own vision of psychiatry. At a disciplinary level Mapother strengthened the academic status of the science, forging close links between the Maudsley and the University of London. In 1924 the hospital was recognized as a centre for postgraduate education and in 1936 Mapother was elected to the university's newly created chair in clinical psychiatry.

Intellectually Mapother promoted an eclectic therapeutic. He was suspicious of system-building philosophies which attempted to explain all the symptoms of mental distress through reference to a single cause. In his presidential address to the psychiatric section of the Royal Society of Medicine (*Proceedings of the Royal Society of Medicine*, 1936) and his unpublished Bradshaw lecture before the Royal College of Physicians (1938) Mapother attacked the 'therapeutic chanticleers' of psychoanalysis who mistook diagnostic concepts for clinical entities. Yet within the Maudsley he tolerated the use of all forms of therapy, from hormone treatment to Jungian analysis.

In 1939 Mapother resigned from the Maudsley Hospital due to ill health. In his career he had secured status, funding, and clinical success not simply for the Maudsley but for British psychiatry as a whole. As a teacher, he had trained many of the most influential psychiatrists in postwar Britain, including Aubrey Lewis and William Sargant. As a manager, he had established a programme of research and funding through his close negotiations with the Medical Research Council and the Rockefeller Foundation. He died at Mill Hill Emergency Hospital on 20 March 1940 from asthma and pulmonary fibrosis. His ashes were scattered in the grounds of the Maudsley. Mapother was survived by his wife of twenty-five years, Barbara Mary (*d.* 1945), the daughter of Charles Reynolds. They had no children, but in 1950 their name was commemorated through the Mapother bequest which instituted two research studentships in psychiatry and an eponymous annual lecture at the Maudsley. RHODRI HAYWARD

Sources A. Lewis, 'Edward Mapother and the making of the Maudsley Hospital', *The later papers of Sir Aubrey Lewis* (1979), 135–52 · D'A. Power and W. R. Le Fanu, *Lives of the fellows of the Royal College of Surgeons of England, 1930–1951* (1953), 529–30 · Munk, *Roll* · *BMJ* (30 March 1940), 552 · *The Lancet* (30 March 1940) · *The Lancet* (6 April 1940) · *Journal of Mental Science*, 86 (1940), 747–9 · *The Times* (21 March 1940) · *The Times* (26 March 1940) · *Nature*, 145 (1940), 652–3 · W. Sargant, *The unquiet mind* (1967) · *WWW* · *DNB*
Archives Bethlehem Royal Hospital, Kent, corresp.
Likenesses Elliott & Fry, photograph, repro. in *BMJ*, 552
Wealth at death £16,284 18s. 7d.: probate, 25 June 1940, *CGPLA Eng. & Wales*

Mapother, Edward Dillon (1835–1908), surgeon and dermatologist, was born on 14 October 1835 in Annadale Lodge, Fairview, Dublin, the son of Henry Mapother and Mary Lyons, both of co. Roscommon. His father was a bank official who disappeared from his office mysteriously and without trace.

Mapother was apprenticed to John Hatch Power, professor of surgery at the Royal College of Surgeons in Ireland, and attended the college and a number of other Dublin medical schools, as well as Queen's College, Galway. He obtained the licence of the Royal College of Surgeons in Ireland on 21 April 1854, and in the same year was appointed anatomy demonstrator in the college medical school. In 1857 he graduated MD, with first-class honours and a gold medal, in the Queen's University, and became a fellow of the Royal College of Surgeons in Ireland on 30 August 1862. On 30 May 1864 he was appointed professor of hygiene, or political medicine, in the College of Surgeons, a chair that had been vacant since the resignation of Henry Maunsell eighteen years earlier. On 21 February 1868 he succeeded Arthur Jacob as professor of anatomy and physiology, a position he held for more than twenty years. He was elected vice-president of the Royal College of Surgeons in Ireland in 1878 and president in 1879–80. In 1859 Mapother was appointed surgeon and dermatologist to St Vincent's Hospital, Dublin, which had been established by the Sisters of Charity in St Stephen's Green in 1834. He was also surgeon to the Children's Hospital, and to successive viceregal households from 1880 to 1886. On 7 September 1870 at St Mary's Cathedral, Halifax, Nova Scotia, Mapother married Ellen, youngest daughter of the late John Tobin, MP for Halifax. They had six daughters and a son, Edward *Mapother, who became a psychiatrist.

In 1864, the year when civil registration was introduced in Ireland, Mapother was appointed the first medical officer of health to Dublin corporation, and committed himself to pressing for legislation on sanitary matters. He advocated a properly organized system of sanitary inspection and administration to suppress the causes of preventable diseases and deaths in Dublin, which he attributed to poverty and its consequences. In 1874 an act of parliament constituted the Local Government Board for Ireland the supreme sanitary authority for the country, a development that marked an increasingly professional approach to the pressing problem of public health. On 21 October 1874 Dublin corporation appointed Mapother to the new post of consulting sanitary officer at an annual salary of £300. His professorial colleague at the College of Surgeons, Charles Cameron, replaced him as medical officer of health. Both were extremely able, energetic, and committed public health officials, determined to improve Dublin's notorious sanitary situation. In 1876 Mapother identified twelve of the worst blackspots in the north and south inner city that might be cleared and redeveloped under the 1875 Artizans' Dwellings Act but the high costs involved meant that little remedial action was taken. The Public Health Act of 1878 gave additional powers to the sanitary authorities and resulted in Mapother's promotion to another new post, medical superintendent officer of health. He resigned in the following year and was replaced by Cameron on 21 August 1879.

In 1888 Mapother left Dublin for London, where he established himself as a consultant dermatologist. He had established a reputation as a dermatologist, having practised and lectured on the subject at St Vincent's Hospital. Prior to his departure, he had spent some time studying diseases of the skin, gout, and syphilis at the leading French and German medical schools. He regarded bathing and the taking of spa waters as important elements in treating certain skin conditions and he investigated the waters of various spas in Europe and the United States.

Mapother published widely, on surgery, physiology, public health, dermatology, the curative powers of spa waters, and Irish medical history. His books, most of which ran to several editions, include *A Manual of Physiology* (1862); *Lectures on Public Health* (1864); *The Body and its Health: a Book for Primary Schools* (n.d.); *The Treatment of Chronic Skin Diseases* (1872). In 1868 he was awarded the Carmichael prize of £200 for an essay on the medical profession and medical education, which was subsequently published as *The Medical Profession and its Educational Licensing Bodies* (1868). This distinction was achieved under somewhat questionable circumstances, given that he was a member of the awarding body, the council of the Royal College of Surgeons in Ireland. According to *The Lancet* (9 May 1868, 605) Mapother explained at the prize-giving ceremony that he had submitted under a pseudonym, 'Unite and Prosper', that he had dissociated himself from the adjudication process, and had not influenced it in any way. He offered to publish at his own expense the essay of any unsuccessful candidate who was unhappy with the result, so that 'the highest court of appeal', public opinion, would be the final arbiter of the quality of the submissions. He was 'most proud of the position of Carmichael prizeman', he said, 'for it was not gained by purchase, by

nepotism, or by partisanship, which unfortunately determine too many high places in our ranks'. He concluded his acceptance speech by pledging his assistance 'in reforming those abuses which have caused the medical calling, so honourable, to be so little honoured'.

Mapother was a striking, full-bearded figure, who in his book *The Body and its Health: a Book for Primary Schools* objected to shaving as 'a sore and time-wasting habit', one which 'robs us of a natural ornament, and of a safeguard of our throat from cold and our lungs from dust'. Mapother died at his residence, 16 Welbeck Street, London, on 3 March 1908.   LAURENCE M. GEARY

Sources M. O'Doherty, 'Salus populi—the endeavours of Edward Dillon Mapother (1835–1908)', *Journal of the Irish Colleges of Physicians and Surgeons*, 28 (1999), 169–73 · *BMJ* (14 March 1908), 661–2 · C. A. Cameron, *History of the Royal College of Surgeons in Ireland*, 2nd edn (1916) · J. Prunty, *Dublin slums, 1800–1925: a study in urban geography* (1998) · *The Lancet* (9 May 1868), 605 · E. D. Mapother, 'The lives and writings of O'Ferrall and Bellingham', *Dublin Journal of Medical Science*, 64 (1877), 461–75 · A. Lewis, 'Edward Mapother and the making of the Maudsley Hospital', *British Journal of Psychiatry*, 115 (1969), 1349–66 · *BMJ* (17 Sept 1870)

Likenesses oils, *c.*1879, Royal College of Surgeons in Ireland, Dublin · photograph, repro. in O'Doherty, 'Salus populi'

Wealth at death £3066 8s. 7d.: probate, 21 March 1908, *CGPLA Eng. & Wales*

Mapp [*née* Wallin], **Sarah** (*bap.* 1706, *d.* 1737), bone-setter, was baptized on 26 March 1706 at Hinton, near Chicklade, Wiltshire, the daughter of John Wallin and his wife, Jenny. She had a younger brother, Richard, and a sister who later acted the part of Polly Peachum in *The Beggar's Opera*. John Wallin, also a bone-setter, trained Sarah but instilled in her only the barest knowledge of anatomy. After a family quarrel she 'wander'd up and down the Country in a very miserable Manner' (*London Magazine*, 5.458), and scarcely made a living. Already eccentric in her ways, she dubbed herself Crazy Sally.

About 1735 Sarah found herself in Epsom, Surrey, a watering place with royal connections and a centre of fashionable society; the horse-racing there produced a useful crop of mangled bones. Still a young woman, she was beefy and endowed with unusual strength, which she used to gain an immediate reputation for righting dislocations and for setting fractures, even those of patients who had suffered for decades. Despite her slovenly appearance she was neat in her work, even down to the rolling of bandages. Treating each day a plentiful assortment of the injured, whom with great dispatch she sent on their way rejoicing, she was soon earning nearly 20 guineas a day; the well-to-do also lavished many presents on her. When a rumour spread that her services were to be poached elsewhere, some townspeople clubbed together and offered her 100 guineas to remain for another year.

Having acquired a four-horse chariot, in mid-1736 Sarah began to travel to London once a week. There, at the Grecian Coffee House near the Temple—much frequented by lawyers—she performed some noteworthy feats in the presence of Sir Hans Sloane, the physician. She straightened out the crooked back of Sloane's niece, and of a man from Wardour Street, who for nine years had gone about with his backbone projecting 2 inches out of true. There was even a man who, after an accident, had one leg 6 inches shorter than the other, which she restored to its correct length by manipulating his hip. When some disbelieving doctors tried to hoodwink her with a sound patient who pretended to have a damaged wrist, she angrily dislocated it and bade him go back and have it set by the fools who had sent him.

The *haut ton* of the capital, wild for amazing new cures to surpass those of earlier publicity-seeking quacks, took Sarah Wallin to its collective heart and, metaphorically, put out of joint the nose of the former idol Josiah Ward. Having taken a London residence, in August 1736 at All Hallows, London Wall, Sarah married Hill Mapp (*b.* 1708), from Hopesay, Shropshire, who was a footman to Ebenezer Ibbetson, a mercer of Salisbury Court in London's Fleet Street. Given Sarah's unprepossessing appearance, Mapp was assumed to have married for money; sure enough, within two weeks he had decamped, robbing her of more than 100 guineas. A month later the *Grub-Street Journal*, pursuing its relentless crusade against medical impostors of all kinds, began to ridicule her. It gleefully noted that she had given a plate worth 10 guineas to a race at Epsom, which had been won by a mare named Mrs Mapp, while a still disabled ex-patient indignantly rebuffed claims that he had been cured by her. These reports did not prevent her from being graciously received by Queen Caroline at Kensington.

In October, Sarah Mapp was brazen enough to appear with the itinerant oculist John Taylor (1703–1772) at the Playhouse Theatre, Lincoln's Inn Fields, to see a topical comedy entitled *The Husband's Relief, with the Female Bone-Setter and Worm Doctor*. A packed house cheered an ironic finale, sung from the stage, on her exploits. Sarah Mapp's conduct now became more and more indecorous. In December 1736, when passing through the Old Kent Road in her chariot, she was waylaid by a crowd who mistook her, in her *robe-de-chambre*, for one of George II's detested German mistresses. 'Damn your bloods,' she expostulated, 'don't you know me?' Bawling her name she drove off to loud huzzas.

Although Sarah showed up the poor grasp of bone manipulation among medical men of the day, she was very widely dismissed as a figure of no great consequence, and the general public soon tired of her. It was William Hogarth who gave a push to her downward spiral by featuring her in his print of March 1737, *The Company of Undertakers*. Above a group of twelve physicians were John Taylor, Josiah Ward, and Sarah Mapp. She was depicted as bun-faced, distinctly boss-eyed and double-chinned, and holding a bone. Her mannishness was emphasized by a hat at a rakish angle and being referred to as 'he', her substantial bulk being covered by a harlequin costume. After this savage satire her name disappeared from the press, and she became a heavy drinker, hardly ever sobering up. Sarah Mapp died on 10 December 1737 in her lodgings at Seven Dials, London, 'miserably poor' (*London Magazine*,

6.705), so that she had to be buried at the parish's expense. Too unselfconscious, rumbustious, and disorganized to strive for the highest ranks of charlatanism, she fell victim to the fickleness of those who raised her up to fame and riches and as abruptly dropped her for fresh wonders and sensations.
T. A. B. CORLEY

Sources A. Boyer, *The political state of Great Britain* (1714), 11, 52, 349 · *GM*, 1st ser., 6 (1736), 422, 487, 616–17, 747 · *GM*, 1st ser., 7 (1737), 767 · *London Magazine*, 5 (1736), 457–8, 520 · *London Magazine*, 6 (1737), 705 · J. T. Hillhouse, *The Grub-Street journal* (1928), 264–7, 338–41 · R. Porter, *Health for sale: quackery in England, 1660–1850* (1989), 34–5, 83, 222 · R. Paulson, *Hogarth's graphic works*, 1 (1965), 173–4 · R. Paulson, *Hogarth: his life, art and times*, 1 (1971), 391–4 · *London Journal* (4 Sept 1736), 896 · parish register, Hinton, near Chicklade, Wilts. & Swindon RO, 26 March 1706 [baptism]
Likenesses W. Hogarth, group portrait, etching, 1736 (*Various doctors and quacks*; after W. Hogarth), Wellcome L. · W. Hogarth, print, 1737, repro. in Paulson, *Hogarth: his life, art and times* · G. Cruikshank, coloured etching, 1819 (after W. Hogarth), Wellcome L. · engraving (after W. Hogarth), Wellcome L. · portrait, repro. in R. Porter, *Quacks* (2000)

Mappin, Sir **Frederick Thorpe**, first baronet (1821–1910), industrialist and politician, was born on 16 May 1821 in Sheffield, the eldest of the four sons of Joseph Mappin (1793–1841), cutlery manufacturer, and his wife, Mary, the daughter of Thomas Thorpe of Haynes, Bedfordshire, a land surveyor. He was educated at Mr Wright's school, Sheffield, and at the age of thirteen joined the family firm, taking charge of it on his father's death. On 25 September 1845 he married Mary (*d.* 1908), daughter of John Wilson, a steel manufacturer, of Oak Holme, Sheffield; they had three sons.

Under Mappin's guidance, the firm which became Mappin Bros. rose to the forefront of the Sheffield cutlery trades. It grew from about a hundred workers to five hundred, acquired London's largest cutlery warehouse, and developed an extensive export trade, partly through Mappin's own vigorous salesmanship abroad. In 1855 he became Sheffield's youngest master cutler. His success owed much to his ability to supply high-quality goods to an increasingly affluent Victorian domestic market. Following a partnership dispute, he left the firm in 1859, but it would in 1903 form part of Mappin and Webb, the London business set up by his youngest brother, John Newton Mappin (1836–1913).

After his departure Mappin directed his entrepreneurial energies towards the heavy steel industry, in 1860 purchasing Thomas Turton & Son, a top-quality steel manufacturer but also owners of William Greaves & Co., the pre-eminent file and edge toolmakers in Sheffield. Under Mappin, Turtons now led the mechanization of Sheffield's cutlery trades, but its introduction of the first grinding machine for file-cutting in 1865 precipitated a major strike, at a time when Sheffield's industrial relations were deeply embittered by the challenge to its well-organized handicraft trades. In this particular contest over files, the employers broke union resistance, but the pace of technological change was by no means rapid and Turtons continued to employ much hand labour into the 1890s.

Sir Frederick Thorpe Mappin, first baronet (1821–1910), by Bassano, 1897

Mappin also turned Turtons into the leading manufacturers of railway springs, distributed from its depots in London, Paris, and New York. Appropriately, he became a director of the Midland Railway in 1869, a position he held until 1903. In 1886 Turtons was converted into a private limited company, with Mappin as chairman (until his death), but he now retired from an active managerial role in favour of two of his sons, Frank Mappin (1846–1920) and Wilson Mappin (1848–1925); his other child, Samuel Mappin (1854–1942), became a gentleman farmer in Lincolnshire.

After 1886 Mappin's keenest business interest lay in the Sheffield Gas and Light Company, of which he had become a director in 1863 and was chairman from 1873 until 1908. Under him it became the second-largest provincial gas undertaking, paid the maximum permitted dividends, and produced the cheapest gas in Britain. This, Mappin believed, was a fundamental public benefit for Sheffield, leaving him a confident advocate of enlightened private enterprise against the rising tide of municipal trading.

Mappin's strong belief in the duties of wealth also made him 'benefactor to Sheffield' (*DNB*) in many other ways. Above all, he was the leading advocate of technical education in Sheffield, a vital necessity if its industry was successfully to keep pace with growing German and American competition. He was largely responsible for the creation of the Sheffield Technical School in 1884. He also supported generously Firth and University colleges,

which together became the University of Sheffield in 1905; he was among its charter pro-chancellors and was commemorated in its Mappin Hall in 1911. Mappin served on Sheffield town council (1854–7 and 1876–83), acting as mayor in 1877–8 but retiring disillusioned by the lack of vision of his colleagues, whom he regarded as small-minded men of little experience. He was also a long-serving member of Sheffield's important town trust, playing an instrumental role in its taking over the town's botanic gardens. Besides such civic duties, Mappin was a benevolent practitioner of voluntary action, building a coffee house, supporting churches of several denominations (having abandoned Congregationalism for the Church of England), and, to the lasting cultural benefit of Sheffield, establishing, under the will of his uncle, the brewer J. N. Mappin (1800–1883), the Mappin Art Gallery, to which he gave numerous paintings from his own extensive modern collection. In 1900 his contribution to the welfare of the city of Sheffield was aptly marked by the granting of its freedom. He was also justice of the peace and deputy lieutenant for the West Riding of Yorkshire, a captain in the volunteers, and in 1878 had been awarded the Légion d'honneur as a juror at the Paris Universal Exhibition.

Mappin's local prominence led naturally to an important part in Sheffield politics, as president of both the Sheffield United and Hallamshire Liberal associations. He entered parliament as MP for East Retford in 1880 and sat for the Hallamshire division of the West Riding between 1885 and 1905. An infrequent speaker, he proved a loyal Gladstonian, backing home rule for Ireland and gaining a baronetcy on 27 August 1886. He contributed regularly, if with growing reluctance, to party funds. But he looked with disfavour upon labour representation, purportedly urging at Attercliffe in 1894 that 'we are almost as much giving up the seat if a working man is elected as if a Tory was' (Brown, 56). He also alienated many file-cutters by his failure to support their campaign for the marking of machine-made files, but the miners of south Yorkshire remained his loyal supporters until he retired from parliament in 1905.

Mappin died at his home, Thornbury, Fulwood Road, Sheffield, on 19 March 1910 and was buried on 23 March at Ecclesshall cemetery in Sheffield; his wife had died on 10 April 1908. He was succeeded, as second baronet, by his eldest son, Frank Mappin. Sir Frederick left an estate of almost £1 million, a considerable fortune by the standard of his industrial peers and in the light of his substantial philanthropic and political donations. He may be regarded as typical of a generation of energetic, masterful businessmen, supremely confident in their own abilities, who did so much to shape the economic, political, and cultural identity of late Victorian provincial England.

A. C. HOWE

Sources A. C. Howe, 'Mappin, Sir Frederick Thorpe', *DBB* · *Sheffield Independent* (19 March 1910) · *Sheffield Daily Telegraph* (19 March 1910) · *Sheffield Weekly Independent* (26 March 1910) · *The Times* (21–4 March 1910) · A. W. Chapman, *The story of a modern university: a history of the University of Sheffield* (1955) · W. Odom, *Hallamshire worthies*

(1926) • J. Brown, 'Attercliffe, 1894: how one local liberal party failed to meet the challenge of labour', *Journal of British Studies*, 14/2 (1974-5), 48-77 • *CGPLA Eng. & Wales* (1910) • *DNB*

Archives Sheff. Arch., corresp. with H. J. Wilson • Sheffield Central Library, Sheffield Utd Gas Company records • University of Sheffield, Mundella MSS • University of Sheffield, university archives

Likenesses portrait, *c.*1880, repro. in Chapman, *Story of a modern university* • W. W. Ouless, oils, 1892, Mappin Art Gallery, Sheffield • Bassano, photograph, 1897, NPG [*see illus.*] • W. Eadon, watercolour, 1903, Mappin Art Gallery, Sheffield • E. Moore, oils, Sheffield Town Trustees, Court House • bronze bust, Botanic Gardens, Sheffield • oils, University of Sheffield • portrait, repro. in *Sheffield illustrated: views and portraits* (1885), 98-9 • portrait, repro. in S. O. Addy, *Sheffield and neighbourhood at the opening of the twentieth century: contemporary biographies* (1901), 71

Wealth at death £944,563 9s. 11d.: resworn probate, 13 May 1910, *CGPLA Eng. & Wales*

Mapson, Leslie William (1907-1970), biochemist, was born on 17 November 1907 in Cambridge, the only child of William John Mapson (*d.* 1918/19) and his wife, Elizabeth Chapman. His father was a steward for the Pitt Club in Cambridge and his mother had a position as a housekeeper. Following the death of his father, Mapson's mother was left to arrange her son's education, which she did with help from the Very Revd Geoffrey Hare Clayton, afterwards archbishop of Cape Town, and the Revd C. P. Hankey, dean of Ely. At the age of ten Mapson went to the Cambridge and County high school. After leaving school in 1926 he began in the following year to study for a pharmaceutical career. However, having been recognized as a talented pupil, he was encouraged by his former chemistry teacher to read natural science. He entered Fitzwilliam House (later Fitzwilliam College) at Cambridge in 1928. This led to his taking both parts of the natural sciences tripos—part one, in which he gained a second class (1929), and part two, in 1930, in which he also gained a second class, with biochemistry as the principal subject. In 1932 Mapson undertook research with F. G. Hopkins, in his school of biochemistry in Cambridge. This was an exciting time for the study of nutrition and of enzyme catalysis. Marjory Stephenson had developed her superb microbiological technique for studying the catalytic activities of a bacterium. J. B. S. Haldane was then the reader in biochemistry in Cambridge. The idea which arose from the study of nutrition and the properties of enzymes inspired Mapson to take up scientific research. His early contacts with Hopkins, Haldane, and M. Dixon also encouraged his interest in biochemistry.

Mapson's next research was on a nutritional problem, with B. C. Guha, a well-known authority on the subject. But as the income from teaching in college or in a university department was meagre, Mapson also obtained a position with a commercial venture connected with the whaling industry. This work, which he carried out in the biochemical department, allowed him to be registered as a student for the degree of PhD under the supervision of Haldane and Hopkins. Mapson showed how a concentrated preparation containing a supplementary factor for nutrition could be prepared from the liver of the whale during the normal disposal of the catch. His experiments and critical conclusions from this work formed the basis for his doctoral dissertation.

After Mapson had taken his PhD degree in 1934, there was apparently no satisfactory research appointment available for him, so he left the laboratory and accepted the post of lecturer in biochemistry at Portsmouth College of Technology. However, in 1938 he was appointed as a scientific officer to the Food Investigation Board of the Department of Scientific and Industrial Research. After the outbreak of the Second World War in 1939, he was seconded to the Dunn Nutritional Laboratory of the Medical Research Council in Cambridge. Mapson also became a member of the vitamin C subcommittee of the Accessory Food Factors Committee of the Medical Research Council. (The report of this was published in 1953 as *Vitamin C Requirement of Human Adults*; MRC Special Report, 280.) These activities were followed by enthusiastic study of the biological significance of this vitamin. Mapson was essentially concerned with the relation of the *in vivo* and *in vitro* aspects of a process. He never lacked enthusiasm, and faced with an unsuccessful experiment he quickly decided on a new approach. Throughout his scientific career he collaborated with many different workers and mutual appreciation was always apparent. In 1950 he became principal scientific officer of the Department of Scientific and Industrial Research and in 1956 senior principal scientific officer, a post from which he retired in 1967. He then became head of the plant biochemistry division of the Food Research Institute at Norwich. He published many research papers.

Mapson was twice married, first to Muriel Dodds in 1932 (there was one son who did not survive); second in 1949 to Dorothy Lillian Waldock, daughter of John George Montague Pell, bookseller, of Cambridge. There was one daughter, Elizabeth, of his second marriage.

Mapson lived in the village of Hauxton, Cambridgeshire, where he was an active member of the church community. He was a governor of the Melbourn Village College from its foundation. He was elected fellow of the Royal Society in 1969 and was an honorary professor at the University of East Anglia. He died at his home at Church Hill, Robins Lane, Lolworth, Cambridgeshire, on 3 December 1970. ROBERT HILL, *rev.*

Sources R. Hill, *Memoirs FRS*, 18 (1972), 427-44 • probate, 1971

Likenesses G. Argent, photograph, 1969, repro. in *Memoirs FRS*, 23 (1972)

Wealth at death £8554: administration with will, 9 March 1971, *CGPLA Eng. & Wales*

Mar. For this title name *see* William, fifth earl of Mar (*d.* in or before 1281); Donald, sixth earl of Mar (*d.* in or after 1297); Donald, eighth earl of Mar (1293-1332); Thomas, ninth earl of Mar (*c.*1330-1377) [*see under* Donald, eighth earl of Mar (1293-1332)]; Douglas, William, first earl of Douglas and earl of Mar (*c.*1330-1384); Douglas, James, second earl of Douglas and earl of Mar (*c.*1358-1388); Stewart, Alexander, earl of Mar (*c.*1380-1435); Erskine, John, seventeenth or first earl of Mar (*d.* 1572); Erskine, John, eighteenth or second earl of Mar (*c.*1562-1634); Erskine, John, nineteenth or third earl of Mar (*c.*1585-1653); Erskine, John, styled twenty-second or sixth earl of Mar and Jacobite duke of Mar (*bap.* 1675, *d.* 1732).

Mar, Donald. *See* Donald, sixth earl of Mar (*d.* in or after 1297); Donald, eighth earl of Mar (1293–1332).

Mar, Norman René del (1919–1994), conductor and writer on music, was born on 31 July 1919 at 12 Kidderpore Gardens, London, the youngest of the three sons of Max Levi (1876–1963), a brush manufacturer, and his wife, Vera, *née* del Mar (1891–1964). Max adopted his wife's surname during the First World War; his sons Ronald and Norman were baptized into the Church of England in June 1939, and formally adopted the name del Mar by deed poll in September 1940. Norman was educated at Marlborough College (1932–7) and the Royal College of Music (1937–40), where he studied composition with Vaughan Williams and R. O. Morris, conducting with Constant Lambert, and the horn with Frank Probyn. During the war he served in the RAF central band, a group that included some of the finest young players of the day, among them Dennis Brain. Del Mar played second horn to him then, and later in Sir Thomas Beecham's new Royal Philharmonic Orchestra.

In 1944, with ambitions for a conducting career, del Mar formed the student and amateur Chelsea Symphony Orchestra, with whom his lifelong interest in exploring new or unfamiliar music led him to programme works by Mahler, Dohnányi, Busoni, Poulenc, Hindemith, Britten, and others. Impressed by a performance he attended, Beecham engaged del Mar as his assistant, and in 1947 enabled him to make his professional début conducting Richard Strauss's music in the presence of the composer. Strauss remained a lifelong interest, and del Mar's three-volume study of the composer and his music (1962–72) remains a classic. He was a perceptive and fluent writer. His other books included *Anatomy of the Orchestra* (1981) and a series of practical studies of the problems in various composers' scores that arose from his success as a teacher and which bore witness to his enduring fascination with the craftsmanship of conducting.

On 24 January 1947 del Mar married Pauline Joy Mann (*b.* 1926), an art historian and the sister of the music critic William Mann; they had two sons. During the late 1940s del Mar was frequently called upon to conduct the Royal Ballet, and he was principal conductor of the English Opera Group from 1949 until he occasioned Britten's displeasure in 1956; they were later reconciled. After much freelance work he was appointed conductor in 1960 of the BBC Scottish Orchestra, and did much to improve and stabilize its reputation. He also became chief guest conductor of the Göteborg Symphony Orchestra in 1968, developing a Scandinavian prestige that led to directorship of the Århus Symphony Orchestra. He had meanwhile expanded his English reputation, as a reliable interpreter across a wide repertory but especially of the complex late Romantic scores that lay closest to his heart. Mahler was a composer whose acceptance in England he greatly advanced by the quality of his performances. He also excelled in Delius, and was one of the finest Elgar conductors of his day; in 1963 he gave a studio performance of

Norman René del Mar (1919–1994), by Derek Allen, 1954

Tippett's opera *The Midsummer Marriage* which drew new attention to the work's stature, and which the composer always remembered with gratitude. He continued to be in demand both at home and abroad, where he was an excellent ambassador for British music, and his presence on the rostrum was always a guarantee of carefully prepared, lucid, and skilfully controlled performances.

For all his professionalism, his abundant enthusiasms, and his infinite capacity for hard work, del Mar never achieved the directorship of any of the major British orchestras he often conducted, and it was a particular regret that that of the BBC Symphony eluded him. To some extent this was due to his relationship with his players. Many were fond of him personally and respected his first-hand knowledge of their craft, but, especially in the early days, thought him fulsome in rehearsal when quieter leadership would have been preferable. He also found it difficult to adapt the old-fashioned autocratic relationship between conductor and players to the more democratic style that was emerging during his career. Less at home in classical music than when expounding a large-scale Romantic or modern work, he was himself built on a large scale, and to observe him preparing a work by Strauss or Mahler or some lesser-known Romantic, then animating a huge orchestra in performance, was to be aware of artistic physiques well matched. His tastes and inclinations were formed early and did not greatly develop, which perhaps set a limitation on the growth of his stature as an interpreter. Yet, though not intellectual by temperament, he had as sharp a mind in penetrating the difficulties of a modern score as any conductor of his time, and as great a skill in performing it to best advantage. Iain Hamilton, Hugh Wood, Gordon Crosse, Richard Rodney Bennett, and especially Thea Musgrave were among those whose works were given a sound launch in life through his performances.

Personally del Mar was a man of generous warmth and enthusiasms, with many idiosyncrasies but also a certain innocence, who kindled affection in his friends as well as sometimes amused exasperation. Domestically inept, he lacked most elementary practical skills while being meticulous in such matters as organizing his vast record collection. Although he made a good number of distinguished recordings himself, this consisted almost entirely of old 78 r.p.m. records, which he played through systematically a side at a time in alphabetical order to accompany his morning shave. His recreations included board games, and composition was almost another recreation with which to fill time, though his works (about which he was modest) included symphonies, a string quartet, concertos for Dennis Brain and the flautist Gareth Morris, a cantata on T. S. Eliot's *The Waste Land*, and an opera on James Elroy Flecker's *Hassan*. These reflected his Romantic inclinations and his excellent orchestral craftsmanship. He died at the BUPA Hospital, Bushey Heath, on 6 February 1994, four years after being diagnosed with cancer, and was buried on 14 February in Limpsfield, Surrey, next to Beecham and Delius. JOHN WARRACK

Sources *The Times* (7 Feb 1994) · *The Independent* (7 Feb 1994) · private information (2004) [Pauline del Mar] · personal knowledge (2004) · *New Grove* · *WW*

Archives BL, papers, deposit 9372 · CUL, corresp. · priv. coll., personal MSS |SOUND BL NSA, *Talking about music*, 221, 1LP0202707 S1 BD2 · BL NSA, *Talking about music*, 262, 1LP0204022 S2 BD1 · BL NSA, *Talking about music*, 280, 1LP0204724 S2 BD1 · BL NSA, documentary recording · BL NSA, oral history interviews · BL NSA, performance recording

Likenesses K. Hutton, photograph, 1949, Hult. Arch. · D. Allen, photograph, 1954, NPG [*see illus.*] · E. Auerbach, photograph, 1958, Hult. Arch. · G. Hoffnung, cartoon

Wealth at death £42,469: probate, 27 April 1994, *CGPLA Eng. & Wales*

Mar, William. *See* William, fifth earl of Mar (*d.* in or before 1281).

Mara [*née* Schmeling], **Gertrud Elisabeth** (1749–1833), singer, was born in Kassel, Germany, on 23 February 1749, the daughter of the violinist Johann Schmeling. She received her early musical education from her father, who trained her as a violinist. He subsequently exhibited her as a child prodigy in many countries of Europe, including the Netherlands, Germany, and England. On the advice of some London ladies, she abandoned the instrument, regarding it as unladylike, and took up singing. Her first lessons, while profitable, were fraught with difficulty; she was removed from the so-called care of the London master Pietro Domenico Paradies (formerly Paradisi; 1707–1791), who was said to have been less than discreet in their pupil–teacher relationship, although the details of his aberration are unknown. Her soprano voice was soon noted for its brilliance, rapid execution, and wide range. As a diva, she was unusual in that she sang in tune and

Gertrud Elisabeth Mara (1749–1833), by Joseph Collyer the younger, pubd 1794 (after Philip Jean) [in the title role of *Armida* by Mortellari]

kept accurate time. The brilliance and rapid execution appear to have come from subsequent lessons in Leipzig with Johann Adam Hiller, to whom her accurate timekeeping can also be attributed; his course of instruction included work as a keyboard player, and her study culminated in public performances of harpsichord concertos. There can be no doubt that this conservatory-style training was one of the chief causes of her ability to survive well past the usual age in the less than kind career of a professional singer. However, she was considered to be an extremely poor actress, a factor which was doubtless responsible for the large number of concert and oratorio engagements she undertook, including a close association with the Lenten oratorio season.

Schmeling's personal appearance was the subject of comment by many, and was not prepossessing; Burney, describing her aged twenty-three, thought her 'short and not handsome' (Highfill, Burnim & Langhans, *BDA*) with irregular teeth, but commented on her good humour, which 'rendered her addresses *very* engaging' (ibid.). These physical drawbacks were probably the result of malnutrition; there is evidence that she had rickets in her early childhood, and her father's business as a freelance musician and repairer of instruments suggests if not poverty, at least periods of hardship.

Throughout her career, Schmeling was dogged by controversies both manufactured and otherwise, and her capricious behaviour was destructive both personally and professionally. Perhaps it was the security and wealth she had acquired when she was taken up by Frederick the Great, king of Prussia, in 1771 as a permanent court singer at Berlin and Potsdam on a salary for life (reputed to be in the order of 11,250 francs), or perhaps it was the sudden privileges of being a court *prima donna*, but whatever the reason, she proceeded to live the role of the diva to the full. Against all advice and objections from the king, she married in 1772 Giovanni Battista Mara (1744–*c*.1808), who as a husband proved to be what all those who objected to him thought he would be; an uncouth womanizer, a sub-standard musician, and more attached to alcohol than to his wife. According to Mozart, at a concert in Munich in 1780 Mme Mara, her husband, the orchestra, and the conductor were involved in a public row on the concert platform before the elector of Bavaria. She was restive in Berlin, and antagonized Frederick, who finally released her from her contract. She travelled via a number of cities to Paris, where in 1782 she immediately entered into rivalry with the Portuguese mezzo-soprano Luiza Todi. French musical society divided into the 'Maratistes' and the 'Todistes' in a debate which was conducted with wit and panache.

Mara's London début in 1784 was a triumph. It was witnessed by Mrs Papendiek, who noted that:

> the *tutti* or symphony of the air commenced, and led up in a crescendo to a high note, upon which Mara began. She held it for a few bars, then brought it to a long shake, and from it ran down an octave or more in notes as clear as bells. When she had finished her song the excitement was intense. The people almost screamed.   (Papendiek, 1.215–16)

The performance earned her the recognition of the prince of Wales (afterwards George IV), although he was not, as he later claimed, the first to recognize her talents.

Mara was soon engaged for a short series at the Pantheon, which was a financial failure; Charles Burney blamed the general election. This did not stop the Mara star ascending, and she was in demand to sing opera and oratorio alike, appearing both in the Pantheon concerts and in the concerts of the Academy of Ancient Music. In February 1786 she made her début at the King's Theatre, where she appeared until 1792; her roles included Dircea in *L'usurpatore innocente*, Cleofide in *La generosità d'Alessandro*, and the title role in *Dido, queen of Carthage* by Prince Hoare and Stephen Storace. She also excelled in Handel roles such as Cleopatra in *Giulio Cesare*. As her voice declined, she took on a number of roles in ballad opera, such as Polly in John Gay's *The Beggar's Opera* and Rosetta in *Love in a Village* by Isaac Bickerstaff and Thomas Arne. She also made a number of continental forays to fulfil prestigious singing engagements. During this period her husband, who had accompanied her to London, found work in the London orchestras.

It was not long before a new London rivalry grew up, this time between Mara and the great Elizabeth Billington. The London press loved, fomented, and sometimes created this sort of polarized competition, but as far as the Mara–Billington axis is concerned, their careers naturally followed similar paths—so much so, in fact, that not only was the most famous role for both sopranos—the part of Mandane in Arne's *Artaxerxes*—performed with 'the anticipated and pleasing labour of encores' (Bacon, 219),

but attempts were made to personalize it in a competitive manner by the addition of numerous extra songs; this claim is borne out by the numerous published song sheets of their additional arias.

Mara's English career was blighted by professional incidents. Although she sang successfully at the 1784 Handel commemoration, in 1785 the press were outraged at her 'insolent' behaviour (she laughed during the rehearsals) and at her leaving the abbey before the end of the performance. Her attempts to organize a subscription series which challenged the Professional Concert—referred to by the newspaper *The Register* in November 1785 as the 'Hanover Square phalanx'—met a hostile reaction in the press; she appears to have mishandled some of the administration, laying herself open to charges of deception, of being a dishonest foreigner, of employing only foreigners, and of being a profiteer. By June she was singing in Oxford, where her insistence on leaving the stage after she had sung and her refusal to stand up during the choruses led to her being hissed and booed and ordered to leave the Sheldonian Theatre by the vice-chancellor. She publicly apologized, offering a chronic problem with her leg as an excuse, and carefully placed articles, mostly written by John Taylor, seem to have had some effect. But the following year she was pilloried in a vicious caricature entitled the 'Wapping Concert', an illustration which shows her sitting, and referring to 'Le Genou Inflexible, or (Stiff Knee) which prevents her standing' (Highfill, Burnim & Langhans, *BDA*). By April 1787 she was being attacked again, this time because she was refusing to sing in the Handel commemoration that year in protest at the request by the dean and chapter of Westminster Abbey for £1200 to be deducted before the proceeds were given to charity. Her oratorio performances were cancelled by order of George III in the same year because they clashed with performances by the Academy of Ancient Music, an event which inspired a vicious poem by John Wolcot, which also made use of the stiff knee image.

However, Mara's voice was universally praised, and most contemporary essays and discussions of vocal technique refer to her on at least one occasion, and usually many. They mostly touch on her vocal agility and brilliance, but Bacon reports that she was unusual in being able to dance and sing at the same time. She survived many attacks on both her personal attributes and her integrity, a survival that may well be in part attributable to her 'masculine understanding' (Taylor, 2.103); she preferred male society and 'was animated in company, and uttered humorous and shrewd remarks' (ibid.).

Mara ended her days as flamboyantly as she lived the earlier years of her life. She was financially ruined by imprudent—and well-publicized—love affairs with two obviously unsuitable, much younger, singers. By 1786 she was having an affair with the 26-year-old singer Samuel *Harrison (1760–1812), with whom she visited Margate and Paris, but the relationship ended about 1787.

By summer 1794 she had eloped to Bath with Charles Florio, with whom she remained until the end of his life (she and her husband separated at some point after 1795).

She courted public censure by living openly with him in Brompton, and public disgrace by beating her cook in 1798; although she and Florio were both brought before the magistrate Sir Richard Ford on 11 August, the matter was settled out of court. She left England with Florio in 1801, and after travelling to Paris and to Berlin in 1803, she settled in Moscow in 1807, only to be made destitute by the burning of the city by Napoleon in 1812; she lost two houses and all her worldly goods in the flames. After Florio's death in 1819 (he had starved himself for days and become violent, insisting that Mara was attempting to poison him) she suffered the indignity of attempting a disastrous London comeback on 16 March 1820, unaware that her musical powers had declined. She died in Reval, Russia (now Tallinn, Estonia), on 20 January 1833, not entirely forgotten; Goethe had sent her a birthday poem 'Sangreich war dein Ehrenweg' in 1831.

MICHAEL BURDEN

Sources G. C. Groscheim, *Das Leben der Künstlerin* (Kassel, 1823) · Highfill, Burnim & Langhans, *BDA* · S. McVeigh, *Concert life in London from Mozart to Haydn* (1993) · J. Haslewood, *The secret history of the green room: containing authentic and entertaining memoirs of the actors and actresses in the three theatres royal* (1793) · C. Burney, *An account of the musical performances ... in commemoration of Handel* (1785) · R. M. Bacon, *Elements of vocal science* [1824] [originally pubd as a series of essays in the *Quarterly Musical Magazine and Review*] · J. Taylor, *Records of my life*, 2 vols. (1832) · C. L. H. Papendiek, *Court and private life in the time of Queen Charlotte: being the journals of Mrs Papendiek, assistant keeper of the wardrobe and reader to her majesty*, 2 vols. (1887) · *Jackson's Oxford Journal* (1785)

Likenesses J. Sayers, caricature engraving, 1786 · caricature, 1786, repro. in Highfill, Burnim & Langhans, *BDA* · J. Gillray, caricature engraving, 1787 · Dent, caricature, *c*.1791 · engraving, pubd 1792 (as Mandane in *Artaxerxes*), Harvard TC; repro. in Highfill, Burnim & Langhans, *BDA* · J. Collyer the younger, stipple engraving, pubd 1794 (after P. Jean), NPG, Harvard TC [*see illus.*] · E. Landseer, group portrait, medallion miniature, 1801 (after miniature cameos by H. de Janry; after a plan by de Loutherbourg) · Dal Pian, engraving (after Castelli), Civiza Raccolta delle Stampe Achille Bertarelli, Castello Sforzesco, Milan; repro. in Highfill, Burnim & Langhans, *BDA* · W. Greatbach, engraving (after P. Collyer), repro. in G. Hogarth, *Memoirs of the musical drama* (1838) · A. Hüssner, engraving, Harvard TC; copy, W. Ridley, 1792 · J. Hutchinson, pastel drawing, Garr. Club · W. S. Leney, engraving (after Fouquet), Harvard TC; copy, G. L. Chrétien · J. Nixon, caricature, pen and ink wash, repro. in *New Grove*, 2nd edn, 15.794; priv. coll. · W. Ridley, engraving (after J. L. David), repro. in *Monthly Mirror* (1800) · sketch, repro. in *New Grove*, vol. 7; priv. coll.

Mar and Garioch. For this title name *see* Stewart, John, earl of Mar and Garioch (1457?–1479/80).

Marbeck [Merbecke], **John** (*c*.1505–1585?), composer and writer, was probably born in Beverley, Yorkshire, and may have trained as a chorister of the minster there. The chapter's payment to him during 1531–2 of a gratuity of 4*s*. in return for his donating musical compositions suggests that he had earlier connections with the church, and had made his gift on the occasion of a family visit to the town, where one Robert Marbeck was a substantial tenant of minster property. It is likely that John was taken thence by commission to be a chorister of St George's Chapel, Windsor Castle, and that he received there the rest of his education, since in the preface of his *Concordance* (1550),

addressed to Edward VI, he states that he was 'altogether brought up in your highnes College at Wyndsore, in the study of Musike and plaiyng on Organs'. The earliest mention of his name occurs in an inventory of domestic plate belonging to the vicars-choral and minor canons of St George's dated 1 May 1531; among the items was 'one sylver spone wrytyn theron John Marbeke'. He married about this time, for in 1543 he was reported to have had five or six children; one of them, Roger *Marbeck, later became provost of Oriel College, Oxford, and physician to Elizabeth I. The earliest surviving payment to Marbeck dates from 1541–2, when he received 40*s*. for playing the organ; however, his employment was principally as one of the lay clerks who, with the minor canons, vicars-choral and choristers, sang the liturgy in plainsong and polyphony at eight daily services in St George's.

In September 1540 Marbeck wrote out the will of William Tate, canon of St George's, who bequeathed him £5. However, his activities as a copyist, combined with a thirst for biblical knowledge, nearly brought him to the stake, for in March 1543 he was arrested and charged with heresy along with Henry Filmer, Anthony Peerson, and Robert Testwood, a fellow lay clerk of the Windsor choir. The events surrounding Marbeck's detention are related in the preface to his *Concordance* and in the account that he prepared for the second edition of Foxe's *Acts and Monuments* (1570). During the mid-1530s Marbeck apparently became deeply interested in theology, and when the English 'Matthew' Bible appeared in 1537, he resolved to own a copy. Being unable to afford one, he began writing it out by hand, but later diverted his energies to the more useful enterprise of compiling a concordance to the same publication. However, by the late 1530s a Catholic reaction to reform had set in, and Marbeck and his associates were arrested under the provisions of the Act of Six Articles. On 16 March 1543 Marbeck's house at Windsor was searched, and books and manuscripts, including his nearly finished concordance, were confiscated as evidence. After appearing before the privy council, he was committed to the Marshalsea on charges of expressing contempt for the mass and of writing and possessing heretical documents. His interrogation mainly concerned his work on the concordance, but he was also closely examined on the copy of a John Calvin letter (probably the *De fugiendis impiorum illicitis sacris* of 1537) that had been found in Marbeck's handwriting. His defence was that he had copied it for a priest named Marshall before the six articles became law, and therefore could not be judged guilty. Four months after their arrest, the accused were returned to Windsor where, at their trial on 26 July, all four were found guilty and sentenced to death. Three died in the flames two days later, but Marbeck obtained a royal reprieve and eventually a full pardon. In the first edition of his *Acts* (1563), Foxe reported that Marbeck was martyred with the others, though he corrected this statement in the corrigenda and later editions. On his release, Marbeck returned to his musical duties at Windsor and resumed work *ab initio* on his concordance.

The death of Henry VIII removed one of the main obstacles to protestant reform, and Marbeck greeted the new reign with enthusiasm. On 1 December 1547 his name headed the list of fourteen lay clerks in a petition presented to Edward VI's commissioners. In 1549 he supplicated Oxford University for the degree of BMus, but it is not known if it was granted. A year later Marbeck published his *Concordance* and *The Booke of Common Praier Noted*. Both works broke new ground, the former being the first concordance in English to cover the whole Bible, and the latter the first musical setting of services prescribed by the 1549 prayer book. Initially the *Concordance* could not find a publisher on account of its great length, so Marbeck produced a third, abbreviated version, itself of over 900 folios each divided into three columns. In the preface he expressed regret at having 'consumed vainly the greatest part of my life' as a church musician. *The Booke of Common Praier Noted* was composed for the use of cathedral and collegiate choirs, and represents an attempt to reconcile the austerity of Reformation attitudes to music with the assumption evident in the rubrics of the 1549 prayer book that such choirs would continue to exist. Marbeck provided monodic settings in syllabic style of the preces and responses, matins, evensong, Benedicite, *Quicunque vult*, communion, and burial of the dead, placing utter priority on the audibility of the words. Within two years his book was rendered obsolete by the appearance of the second Edwardian prayer book. Certain later composers, however, used Marbeck's melody for the preces and responses as the basis of their own polyphonic settings.

St George's found itself at the forefront of Edwardian attempts to restrict the scope of music at cathedral and collegiate foundations. The royal injunctions of 8 February 1550 reduced the number of choristers and laid down stringent guidelines for the appointment of future singers, placing more emphasis on virtue than on musical skill. A further set of injunctions issued in October excluded Marbeck and his colleague George Thaxton from duty as organists, though they still received a stipend. In 1552 the Windsor chapter granted Marbeck the reversion of the presentation of the benefice of Tintagel, Cornwall.

After his near-martyrdom in the early 1540s, Marbeck abstained from religious controversy during Queen Mary's reign, which saw the reformed services abolished and the Latin rite restored. The only records concerning him in these years relate to his work as a copyist: in 1553–4 and 1555–6 he received payment for examining and correcting books for the choir, and in 1557–8 he wrote out a collectarium for one of the canons. At the time of Elizabeth I's accession Marbeck was serving as both lay clerk and organist of St George's. In the two terms following Christmas 1558 he was remunerated both as joint organist with Mr Preston and as supervisor of the choristers; however, he had ceased to hold the latter post by 1562–3 when he and Robert Golder are described as 'agitatores organorum'. By 1564 Marbeck was merely a lay clerk and sole organist. He headed the list of lay clerks for the last time in 1571, when Henry Hastings, the puritan earl of Huntingdon, recommended his appointment to the nominal office of chaplain to the Hastings chantry in St George's, a sinecure whose profits doubtless helped to provide financial security in his retirement. He devoted the rest of his life to writing a series of theological works, some of which violently attacked the papacy. They include: *The Lyves of Holy Sainctes* (1574), *The Holie Historie of King David* (1579), *A Booke of Notes and Common Places* (1581), *The Rippinge up of the Popes Fardell* (1581), *Examples Drawen out of Holy Scripture* (1582), and *A Dialogue between Youth and Old Age* (1584). He died presumably in 1585, when John Mundy succeeded to the post of organist.

Marbeck is chiefly remembered for *The Booke of Common Praier Noted* which, since its revival in the mid-nineteenth century, has been widely used and adapted by Anglicans and other denominations. His four surviving polyphonic works include 'A virgin and mother', possibly adapted from a setting of a Latin text, and a five-part mass of about 1530 based on *Per arma justiciae*, the antiphon sung at terce during Lent. His two large-scale votive antiphons, *Domine Jesu Christe* and *Ave Dei patris*, are typical of the genre in falling into triple- and duple-time halves, with passages for reduced voices alternating with those for full choir.

DAVID MATEER

Sources BL, Add. MS 27324 · minor canons, lay-clerks, etc., 1 May 1531, St George's Chapel, Windsor, Archives Department, XI.B.40 · treasurers' rolls, 1541–2, St George's Chapel, Windsor, Archives Department, XV.59.3 · treasurers' rolls, 1562–3, St George's Chapel, Windsor, Archives Department, XV.59.5 · treasurers' rolls, 1563–4, St George's Chapel, Windsor, Archives Department, XV.59.6 · treasurers' rolls, 1566–7, St George's Chapel, Windsor, Archives Department, XV.59.7 · treasurers' rolls, 1568–9, St George's Chapel, Windsor, Archives Department, XV.59.8 · treasurers' rolls, 1568–9, St George's Chapel, Windsor, Archives Department, XV.59.9 · treasurers' rolls, 1571–2, St George's Chapel, Windsor, Archives Department, XV.59.11 · precentors' rolls, 1553–4, St George's Chapel, Windsor, Archives Department, XV.56.39 · precentors' rolls, 1554–5, St George's Chapel, Windsor, Archives Department, XV.56.40 · precentors' rolls, 1555–6, St George's Chapel, Windsor, Archives Department, XV.56.41 · precentors' rolls, 1557–8, St George's Chapel, Windsor, Archives Department, XV.56.43 · precentors' rolls, 1558–9, St George's Chapel, Windsor, Archives Department, XV.56.78 · J. E. Hunt, *Cranmer's first litany, 1544, and Merbecke's 'Book of common prayer noted', 1550* (1939) · H. Aston, J. Marbeck, and O. Parsley, *Tudor church music*, 10 (1929) · R. A. Leaver, *The work of John Marbeck* (1978) · K. W. T. Carleton, 'John Marbeck and *The book of common praier noted*', *The church and the arts*, ed. D. Wood, SCH, 28 (1992), 255–65 · R. Stevenson, 'John Marbeck's "Noted booke" of 1550', *Musical Quarterly*, 37 (1951), 220–33 · P. Le Huray, *Music and the Reformation in England, 1549–1660* (1967); repr. with corrections (1978) · H. W. Shaw, *The succession of organists of the Chapel Royal and the cathedrals of England and Wales from c.1538* (1991) · E. H. Fellowes, *Organists and masters of the choristers of St George's Chapel in Windsor Castle*, 2nd edn (1979) · J. N. Dalton, ed., *The manuscripts of St George's Chapel, Windsor Castle* (1957) · R. A. Leaver, 'Marbeck, John', *New Grove*, 2nd edn · W. H. Frere and W. P. M. Kennedy, eds., *Visitation articles and injunctions of the period of the Reformation*, 3 vols., Alcuin Club, Collections, 14–16 (1910) · H. Baillie, 'Some biographical notes on English church musicians, chiefly working in London (1485–1569)', *Royal Musical Association Research Chronicle*, 2 (1962), 18–57 · H. Benham, *Latin church music in England, c.1460–1575* (1977) · J. D. Bergsagel, 'The date and provenance of the Forrest–Heyther collection of Tudor masses', *Music and Letters*, 44 (1963), 240–48 · H. Byard, 'Farewell to Merbecke?', *MT*, 114 (1973), 300–03 · N. Sandon, 'Merbecke', *MT*, 114 (1973), 597

Marbeck, Roger (1536–1605), college head and physician, was probably born at Windsor, where his father, John *Marbeck (c.1505–1585?), was organist. He is thought to have been educated at Eton College, and in 1552 was elected student of Christ Church, Oxford, where he probably lived for about fifteen years, graduating BA on 26 January 1555, and MA on 28 June 1558.

Although Marbeck was apparently never ordained, he held several clerical positions. On 3 February 1559 he was made prebendary of Withington in Hereford Cathedral. In 1562 he was senior proctor, and again in 1564, and on 18 November of the same year he was appointed first public orator for life, with a yearly pension of 20 nobles (£6 13s. 4d.) from the university chest. Copies of some of his speeches and addresses, which are notable for their elegant Latinity, are among the Rawlinson MSS in the Bodleian Library, Oxford.

Early in 1565 Marbeck was made canon of Christ Church; and after some negotiation with the visitor, Nicholas Bullingham, bishop of Lincoln, he was unanimously elected provost of Oriel College by the whole body of fellows on 9 March 1565. He fulfilled the role enthusiastically, immediately ordering three absentee fellows to return and dismissing the dean, Francis Webber, for refusing to take the oath of allegiance to Queen Elizabeth.

Early in 1566 the queen paid a visit to Oxford, and Marbeck, who was 'deliciae Latinarum literarum', delivered a Latin speech. The queen received him very graciously, and said to him, 'We have heard of you before, but now we know you.' She visited Oxford again in the same year on 6 September, and Marbeck again delivered the customary Latin oration. At this time he seems to have been a particularly popular and distinguished member of the university. However, his marriage to Anne Williams, daughter of Alderman Thomas Williams of Oxford, led to his resigning all his offices, due to her Catholicism, and her 'notorious whoredoms' (Gilpin). His wife died soon after. They do not seem to have had any children.

Marbeck then turned his thoughts to medicine. Where he studied medicine is unknown, but on 1 July 1573 he became bachelor of medicine at Oxford, and the following day, doctor of medicine. Marbeck joined the College of Physicians, London, and was elected fellow about 1578. He was the first registrar of the college, and after filling that office for two years, he was on 3 November 1581 elected for life, with a salary of 40s. a year, plus various fees of 3s. 4d. According to Munk, he was a careful and diligent registrar.

Marbeck filled various other college offices: censor (1585, 1586), elect (1597), and consiliarius (1598, 1600, 1603, 1604). During this time he re-established his acquaintance with the queen, and was appointed chief of the royal physicians. In 1589, at the age of fifty-three, he was admitted to Gray's Inn, an honorary distinction offered to a number of well-known men of the time.

In September 1596 Marbeck accompanied the Lord High Admiral Howard in the expedition against Cadiz. There is in the British Library (Sloane MS 226) a beautiful manuscript, probably written by Marbeck himself (he was a noted calligrapher), entitled 'A breefe and a true discourse of the late honorable voyage unto Spaine, and of the wynning, sacking, and burning of the famous towne of Cadiz there, and of the miraculous ouerthrowe of the Spanishe navie at that tyme, with a reporte of all other accidents thereunto appertayning, by Doctor Marbeck attending upon the person of the right honorable the lorde highe admirall of England all the tyme of the said action'. Another manuscript copy is in the Bodleian Library (MS Rawl. D. 124), and it is printed, without Marbeck's name, in Hakluyt's *Voyages* (1599, 1.607). A pamphlet, entitled *A Defence of Tobacco* (1602), is attributed to Marbeck because his name appears in an acrostic forming the dedication.

Marbeck died at the beginning of July 1605, and was buried in St Giles Cripplegate, London, on 5 July. He left a considerable collection of manuscripts in his own hand, now in the Bodleian Library.

W. A. GREENHILL, rev. SARAH BAKEWELL

Sources A. G. W. Whitfield, 'Roger Marbeck—first registrar', *Journal of the Royal College of Physicians of London*, 15 (1981), 59–60 · Foster, *Alum. Oxon.* · Munk, *Roll* · W. Sterry, ed., *The Eton College register, 1441–1698* (1943), 223 · *Hist. U. Oxf.* 3: *Colleg. univ.*, 113 · J. Gilpin, Christ Church Oxf., MS DPi.a.16 · T. F. T. Baker, 'Williams, Thomas I', HoP, *Commons*
Archives Bodl. Oxf. | BL, Sloane MS 226

Marçay, Étienne de. See Tours, Étienne de (d. 1193).

Marcet, Alexander John Gaspard (1770–1822), physician and chemist, was born in Geneva, Switzerland, the only son of Marc Marcet (b. 1734), a merchant of Huguenot descent, and his wife, Louise-Marguerite, née Nadal. Educated in Geneva, Marcet was apprenticed in commerce but after two years he obtained his father's permission to study science. During the political disturbances in Geneva following the French Revolution he was indicted for serving in the national guard and, after the fall of Robespierre in 1794, he was banished from Switzerland for five years, with his boyhood friend Charles Gaspard De La Rive. Together they studied medicine at Edinburgh, and graduated MD on 24 June 1797. Marcet's thesis, printed at Edinburgh in the same year, was on diabetes. It is a compilation showing no evidence of clinical experience, but it reveals his inclination for chemical experiments.

After moving to London, Marcet became assistant physician to the Public Dispensary, Carey Street. He was admitted a licentiate of the Royal College of Physicians on 25 June 1799 and was appointed physician to the City Dispensary at Finsbury. On 4 December 1799 he married Jane Haldimand (1769–1858) [see Marcet, Jane Haldimand], only daughter of Anthony Francis Haldimand (1740/41–1817), a Swiss merchant living in London, and his wife, Jane, née Pickersgill (d. 1785). They took a house in Russell Square, and later had two daughters, Louisa and Sophie, and one son, François (1803–1883), who became a distinguished physicist. In 1800 Marcet took British citizenship and on 18 April 1804 he was appointed physician to Guy's Hospital, London, on the recommendation of William Saunders. In 1805 Marcet contributed an essay on the Brighton chalybeate spring to a new edition of Saunders's *Treatise on Mineral Waters*. This essay, also published as a separate octavo pamphlet, describes various chemical experiments which show that, unlike the Tonbridge spa, the Brighton mineral water could be taken warm without precipitation of iron. Encouraged by Saunders, Marcet also analysed samples of sea water from various parts of the world.

Marcet attended meetings of the London Medical Society and, discovering dissatisfaction among the members, became a founder member in 1805 of the Medico-Chirurgical Society of London. He was its foreign secretary until his death in 1822. On 2 June 1808 he was elected a fellow of the Royal Society, and in the following year he took charge of a temporary military hospital at Portsmouth for troops suffering from a virulent fever contracted during the expedition to capture Flushing and Walcheren. Marcet himself suffered an attack of this fever.

Between 1807 and 1820, with William Babington and William Allen, Marcet lectured on chemistry at Guy's Hospital medical school. Unusually for that time, the lectures were illustrated by demonstration experiments and the students were also given access to a chemical laboratory. About 1812 Marcet began a friendship with the Swedish chemist J. J. Berzelius, with whom he investigated the properties of carbon disulphide during the latter's visit to London. Marcet also persuaded Berzelius to publish some analyses of animal fluids in the *Medico-Chirurgical Transactions*, thus helping to introduce Berzelius's animal chemistry studies to English chemists. In 1817 Marcet published his most important and original work, *An Essay on the Chemical History and Medical Treatment of Calculous Disorders*, which contained much chemical information and some good drawings of renal and urinary calculi. In chemical tests Marcet used very small quantities, a valuable technique which he derived from the work of William Hyde Wollaston; he also used the blowpipe. He was probably the first to remark that the pain caused by a renal calculus is often due to its passage down a ureter, whereas it may grow in the kidney without causing acute suffering. The book was useful to chemical pathologists, but Marcet regretted that no London hospital then kept any regular record of calculus cases. He identified a new type of urinary calculus, consisting of xanthic oxide, and he later investigated alcaptonuria, the condition in which the urine turns black.

Marcet was punctilious in dress and behaviour. He always sought to improve conditions for his patients, but his enthusiasm for medical practice declined as his interest in chemistry increased. He retired from the staff of Guy's Hospital on 10 March 1819, after inheriting a large fortune from his father-in-law. He had paid a short visit to Geneva in 1815 and he returned in 1821, intending to live

there. He was warmly received and was made both a member of the representative council and an honorary professor of chemistry, sharing lectures with his friend De La Rive. In 1822 he returned to England to settle his affairs prior to moving permanently to Geneva, but while visiting Edinburgh he suffered an attack of 'gout of the stomach' (Munk, *Roll*). He returned to London, and was attended by William Babington and Astley Cooper, but he died at Babington's home in Great Coram Street, London, on 19 October 1822. He was buried at Battersea, and was survived by his wife, who died on 28 June 1858.

N. G. COLEY

Sources A. Garrod, *Guy's Hospital Reports*, 4th ser., 5 (1925), 373–89 · N. G. Coley, 'Alexander Marcet (1770–1822), physician and animal chemist', *Medical History*, 12 (1968), 394–402 · E. Haag and E. Haag, *La France protestante*, 10 vols. (Paris, 1846–59); repr. (1966), vol. 7, pt 13, pp. 217–20 · *Biographie générale* (1863), 33.463 · Munk, *Roll* · *London Medical and Physical Journal*, 49 (1823), 85 · *Quarterly Journal for Medical Surgery*, 5 (1823), 314 · *Medical and Chirurgical Review*, 3 (1822–3), 698 · A. Hirsch and others, eds., *Biographisches Lexikon der hervorragenden Aerzte aller Zeiten und Völker*, 2nd edn, ed. W. Haberling, F. Hübotter, and H. Vierordt, 6 vols. (Berlin and Vienna, 1929–35), vol. 4, pp. 69–70 · C. Bossart, *Schweitzer Arzte als Naturforsche im 19 Jahrhundert* (1979), 111–12 · C. Schaedler, *Biographisch-litterarisches Handwörterbuch der wissenschaftlich bedeutenden Chemiker* (1891), 76 · A. C. P. Callisen, *Medicinisches Schriftsteller-Lexicon*, 33 vols. (Copenhagen, 1830–45), vol. 30, p. 224 · J. C. Poggendorff and others, eds., *Biographisch-literarisches Handwörterbuch zur Geschichte der exacten Wissenschaften*, 2 (Leipzig, 1863), 40 · *American Journal of Science*, 17 (1829–30), 363–4
Archives Duke U., corresp. and papers · LPL, account of public education at Geneva, MS 1309 · NL Scot., corresp., MSS 3649, 3813, 3836 · NRA, corresp. · RCP Lond., corresp.
Likenesses H. Meyer, engraving, Wellcome L. · H. Raeburn, oils, Royal Society of Medicine, London

Marcet, Jane Haldimand (1769–1858), writer on science and political economy, was born in London, one of twelve children and only surviving daughter of the Swiss merchant and banker Anthony Francis Haldimand (1740/41–1817) and his wife, Jane (d. 1785). She was baptized on 23 June 1769. The Haldimands' was a wealthy, comfortable household, which fostered intellectual achievement in its children together with business acumen, a combination typified by the career of Jane's younger brother William *Haldimand, who became a merchant banker, director of the Bank of England, and member of parliament. Jane shared in the excellent home education provided for her brothers. A serious, lively child, highly intelligent but constitutionally literal-minded, Jane read widely and with discrimination in English and French. Her later career indicates that her parents respected her curiosity and encouraged her development as a reader and an intelligent listener, if not as an original thinker in her own right. When Jane was fifteen she took over the running of the family household upon the death of her mother (in October 1785), including the care of her brothers and a sister who appears to have died in childhood. She developed a close, companionable relationship with her father, who was to live with her even after her marriage. Together they travelled to Italy when Jane was seventeen, where she became interested in painting. Through her father she

Jane Haldimand Marcet (1769–1858), by unknown engraver

met and studied with Joshua Reynolds and Thomas Lawrence. Jane served as her father's hostess when he entertained scientists, politicians, and intellectuals.

On 4 December 1799 Jane Haldimand married the amiable and attractive physician Alexander John Gaspard *Marcet (1770–1822); this was a highly successful marriage which was to allow them both to develop as intellectuals. Marcet was born in Geneva, had been imprisoned there for political activities as a young man, was exiled from Geneva after 1794, and studied medicine in Edinburgh. Although Marcet had a successful practice he preferred research and writing in the field of physiological chemistry, to which he made important contributions. For the first twenty years of their marriage he continued to practise medicine, and he and Jane entertained some of the most distinguished scientists and thinkers of their time.

Jane Marcet gave these men her intelligent and undivided attention, sat openly at their feet, remembered every word they uttered, and, if she did not understand a nuance, sought an explanation from her husband. Alexander Marcet appears to have understood the depth of her need both for information and for inclusion in his circle, and to have supported her efforts to become literate in the unfamiliar language of science. During this time their four children were born—their son François Marcet (1803–1883) was to become a well-known physicist—and Jane's friend Maria Edgeworth describes a happy home, their children lively and intelligent, the house full of welcome visitors who were on occasion entertained with elaborate home theatricals, written by Jane and performed by parents and children. Despite their domestic

felicity, Jane began to suffer from depression, the cure for which lay in hard and useful work. Encouraged by her husband, she wrote, but did not publish, a textbook on the basic components of scientific knowledge: physics, mechanics, astronomy, the properties of fluids, air, and optics. Later published as *Conversations on Natural Philosophy* (1819), the book established a format which she was to use successfully in future works. She presented her information in the form of a dialogue among three characters, Caroline, the flippant pupil, Emily, the serious pupil, and Mrs Bryan, their teacher.

Like many fashionable London women, Jane Marcet attended Sir Humphry Davy's lectures at the Royal Institution; unlike many of these, she paid attention to their content rather than to the charms of the speaker, discussed what she had heard with her husband, repeated the experiments at home, and invited Davy and his wife to dine. Inspired by the knowledge she had gained and wishing to impart it to other women, she published her *Conversations on Chemistry, Intended More Especially for the Female Sex* anonymously in 1805. The work had taken her about three years to write and illustrate and was carefully edited, probably with the help of Alexander Marcet and his friend John Yelloly (Crellin, 459–60). It was one of the first elementary science textbooks and became enormously popular. It went through sixteen editions in England, which Marcet updated meticulously, adding new discoveries and deleting those for which she felt she had made overoptimistic claims. It was translated into French and went through twenty-three editions in America, where it was widely plagiarized. Although not intended as a school text, the *Conversations* was adopted in England by students at mechanics' institutes and by medical apprentices, and it became a successful text in the women's seminaries established in America after 1818. There, its insistence on demonstration by experiment and its theoretical rigour appealed to teachers who wished to give girls a sound scientific education, not merely a gloss on more obviously feminine preoccupations such as domestic science or theology. At the same time *Conversations*, though presented in the form of a classroom dialogue, was read with respectful interest by adults of both sexes and all walks of life. Most notably, it was read by the young bookbinder's apprentice Michael Faraday, who credited Marcet with introducing him to electrochemistry and with giving him the courage to propound his early theories. Faraday was to become a friend of the Marcets, and Jane incorporated his work in later editions.

Although Jane Marcet continued to update *Conversations on Chemistry* (lastly at the age of eighty-four), her next publication took another direction, exploring the new science of political economy. As she had done before, Marcet profited from her friendships with a circle including Brougham, Malthus, Jeffrey, Sydney Smith, and, most significantly, Ricardo. Her *Conversations on Political Economy* (1816) utilized principles of Ricardian economics before the publication (1817) of Ricardo's *Principles of Political Economy*. As in all her works Marcet laid no claim to original thought, but she wrote in a lucid, pleasant style, incorporating the latest, often controversial, theories in her popular works. *Conversations on Political Economy* was praised by Macaulay and Say, and was approved by Malthus, McCulloch, and Ricardo. Her confident presentation of complex ideas in the form of appealing dialogue repelled later economists (notably Alfred Marshall) and led others to conclude that hers was economics for schoolgirls (Schumpeter), but the book's popularity with adult readers grateful for a simple introduction to a new and forbidding field of knowledge indicates Marcet's accurate perception of a wide and generally sophisticated readership for an introductory economics text. The book inspired Harriet Martineau to begin writing fiction with economic themes. Martineau became a close friend of Marcet, though an occasionally critical one, for Marcet's secure position at the heart of the whig literary establishment sometimes infuriated the radical outsider Martineau.

Emboldened by the success of her first books, Marcet published her *Conversations on Natural Philosophy* in 1819. It had been written before *Conversations on Chemistry* and was intended as an introduction to it. It, too, proved highly successful and remained in print well after Marcet's death. The Marcets meanwhile inherited a large fortune from Anthony Haldimand, enabling Alexander to resign his position at Guy's Hospital and devote himself to research. They travelled to Geneva in 1820 and intended to settle there, but Alexander died suddenly while on a visit to Britain in 1822. His death threw Jane into a state of nervous prostration, through which she was nursed by her children and by a large circle of friends in Geneva. Her adult children having dispersed in England and Switzerland, she returned to London after a few years in Geneva but retained close ties with her Swiss friends. In London she continued her family tradition of entertaining a wide circle of famous men and women.

Although Jane Marcet continued to write some works on scientific themes (her *Conversations on Vegetable Physiology* was inspired by her friendship with the naturalist Candolle) and finally abandoned her anonymity as the author of her works, it appears that her work took a less challenging direction after the death of her husband. She wrote one important collection of stories with economic themes for working people and many stories for the education and amusement of young children. The former, *John Hopkins's Notions on Political Economy* (1833), was a product of the climate of fear of working-class rebellion that characterized the early 1830s. Possessing none of Martineau's radical sympathies, Marcet believed implicitly in the community of interest between rich and poor; she supported the abolition of the corn laws and was scolded by her friend Malthus for the simplicity of her belief that wages could remain high as the price of corn fell (Malthus to J. Marcet, 22 Jan 1833; Polkinghorn, 'Unpublished letter', 845). Her choice of format made the little book impossible for working people to afford; rather, it was intended to be bought by landowners and distributed to the poor in their neighbourhoods, as Malthus appears to have done.

When the panic of the 1830s subsided, sales of *Hopkins* slumped. It never approached the popularity of her *Conversations* and has not remained readable over time. While she is known for her ability to address young women without patronage, the same can not be said of her tone in speaking to the working man.

Marcet was more successful in her works for children, which made up the bulk of her literary output after 1833. In her widowhood she spent a great deal of time in the company of her grandchildren, and this undoubtedly inspired her interest in writing for the very young. Her works for children were very well received, including *Mary's Grammar* (1835), which became a classic text. They include many stories of the family life of a boy named Willy and his sisters. Willy's curiosity leads him to investigate everything from the building of a new house to the working of a coalmine. In these books working men are polite but not deferential, confident, and proud of their skills; children are boundlessly curious and not overly obedient; parents are kind, tolerant, and endlessly willing to support their children's quest for information. It seems reasonable to suppose that, in her old age, Marcet turned to writing for children in order to recreate in imagination her happy family life, both in her father's house and with her husband.

In the last seven years of her life Jane Marcet increasingly inhabited a world of her own, untouched by events in the outside world. Presumably she suffered a recurrence of the nervous complaint which had always afflicted her in periods of stress; her friend the Swiss physicist and naturalist Auguste de La Rive described it as a 'shadow enveloping an energetic and active spirit' (La Rive, 464). She died peacefully at her daughter's house, 14 Stratton Street, Piccadilly, London, on 28 June 1858, where she had been living, having asked her children not to allow her to be forgotten in Geneva.

Harriet Martineau wrote of Marcet's almost excessive modesty and humility, commenting rather slightingly on the narrowing effects of her conventional way of life upon her thought. Maria Edgeworth wrote that while others talked endlessly of what they knew, Mrs Marcet sat quietly and listened. Her modesty has usually been accepted by critics at its face value, to the detriment of her reputation. After Marshall's denunciation of both Marcet and Martineau as mere popularizers Marcet's work received little attention. More recent writers have tended to view her either as a figure in the history of chemistry (notably as the inspirer of Faraday) or in the history of political science (less exclusively as a popularizer of Ricardo). She may more justly be seen as a figure of great importance in the history of women's education. In her prefaces Marcet addresses the presumed unsuitability of her topics for study by women and dispenses with objections, stating bluntly that public opinion has come to accept these subjects as appropriate for women. For Mrs Marcet writing was the outcome of her restless search for truth, rather than merely a rather canny appreciation of a gap in the market which she could fill. In *Conversations on Political*

Economy Mrs B's flippant pupil, Caroline, says that she would have thought a woman could be excused ignorance of that topic. Mrs B replies tartly, 'When you plead in favour of ignorance, there is a strong presumption that you are in the wrong' (Marcet, 11). By her sheer refusal to accept that scientific subjects lay beyond women's grasp, Jane Marcet used her position as hostess to great thinkers, coupled with great energy, a formidable intelligence, and the ability to express complex ideas clearly, to bring the new developments in science and political economy within the reach of ordinary women.

ELIZABETH J. MORSE

Sources A. de La Rive, 'Madame Marcet', *Bibliothèque Universelle de Genève*, 4th ser., 4 (1859), 445–68 · H. Martineau, *Biographical sketches, 1852–1875*, new edn (1885) · M. S. Lindee, 'The American career of Jane Marcet's *Conversations on chemistry*, 1806–1853', *Isis*, 82 (1991), 8–23 · E. V. Armstrong, 'Jane Marcet and her *Conversations on chemistry*', *Journal of Chemical Education*, 15 (1938), 53–7 · W. Henderson, 'Jane Marcet's *Conversations on political economy*: a new interpretation', *History of Education*, 23 (1994), 423–37 · J. R. Shackleton, 'Jane Marcet and Harriet Martineau: pioneers of economics education', *History of Education*, 19 (1990), 283–97 · B. A. Polkinghorn, 'Jane Marcet and Harriet Martineau: motive, market experience, and reception of their works popularizing classical political economy', *Women of value: feminist essays on the history of women in economics*, ed. M. A. Dimand and others (1995), 71–81 · J. K. Crellin, 'Mrs Marcet's *Conversations on chemistry*', *Journal of Chemical Education*, 56 (1979), 459–60 · B. A. Polkinghorn, 'An unpublished letter from Malthus to Jane Marcet, January 22, 1833', *The American Economic Review*, 76 (1986), 845–7 · N. G. Coley, 'Alexander Marcet (1770–1822), physician and animal chemist', *Medical History*, 12 (1968), 394–402 · *Harriet Martineau's autobiography*, ed. M. W. Chapman, 3rd edn, 1 (1877) · J. Marcet, *Conversations on political economy* (1816) · B. Polkinghorn and D. L. Thomson, *Adam Smith's daughters: eight prominent women economists from the eighteenth century to the present* (1998) · B. Polkinghorn, *Jane Marcet: an uncommon woman* (1993)
Archives Archive Guy de Pourtalès, Etoy, Switzerland · NRA, papers · University of Geneva Library, Switzerland, Salle Senebier | University of Pennsylvania, Edgar Fahs Smith Memorial Collection
Likenesses engraving, University of Pennsylvania Library [*see illus.*] · portrait, Beckman Center for the History of Chemistry, Philadelphia, Pennsylvania, Chemical Heritage Foundation · several likenesses, repro. in Polkinghorn, *Jane Mercet*
Wealth at death under £18,000: probate, 11 Aug 1858, *CGPLA Eng. & Wales*

March. For this title name *see* Dunbar, Patrick, seventh earl of Dunbar or of March (1242–1308) [*see under* Dunbar, Patrick, eighth earl of Dunbar or of March, and earl of Moray (1285–1369)]; Dunbar, Patrick, eighth earl of Dunbar or of March, and earl of Moray (1285–1369); Mortimer, Roger (V), first earl of March (1287–1330); Mortimer, Roger (VI), second earl of March (1328–1360); Dunbar, Agnes, countess of Dunbar or of March (d. 1369) [*see under* Dunbar, Patrick, eighth earl of Dunbar or of March, and earl of Moray (1285–1369)]; Dunbar, George, ninth earl of Dunbar or of March (c.1336–1416x23); Mortimer, Edmund (III), third earl of March and earl of Ulster (1352–1381); Mortimer, Roger (VII), fourth earl of March and sixth earl of Ulster (1374–1398); Mortimer, Edmund (V), fifth earl of March and seventh earl of Ulster (1391–1425); Stewart, Robert, earl of Lennox and earl of March (1522/3–

1586); Douglas, Francis Wemyss-Charteris-, eighth earl of Wemyss and sixth earl of March (1818–1914).

March, John (1611/12?–1657), barrister and legal writer, came from obscure origins and little can be ascertained of his family background. He appears to have been the same John March of St Stephen Walbrook, scrivener, who married Alice Matthews of St Nicholas Olave in spring 1638 at the age of twenty-six. Recent scholarship has challenged the *Dictionary of National Biography*'s contention that March was the second son of Sam March of Finchampstead, Berkshire, on grounds that that John March died unmarried and childless. He was possibly the John March admitted to the degree of BCL at St Edmund Hall, Oxford, on 27 November 1632, and probably the 'John Marche, St. Andrew Holborn London' who entered Barnard's Inn on 15 April 1635 (Brooks, 86) and continued his studies at Gray's Inn, where he was admitted on 18 March 1636 and called to the bar on 11 June 1641 NS.

In 1642 March rose to prominence when he published a defence of the Long Parliament's militia ordinance entitled *An argument or, debate in law: of the great question concerning the militia; as it is now settled by ordinance of both the houses of parliament*. In this tract March argued that, although power to proclaim war and peace and hence control over the militia ordinarily lay with the king, in time of 'imminent danger' to the kingdom and 'extream necessity' the two houses of parliament could lawfully put the militia in a posture of defence without the king's authority (J. March, *Argument*, 1642, 5–7). This tract has sometimes been attributed to John Milton although Thomason's copy is clearly marked 'J. Marsh'. In March 1644 he was in the employ of the committee of both kingdoms at Darby House and in 1647 he published *Actions for slaunder, or, A methodicall collection under certain grounds and heads, of what words are actionable in the law, and what not?* A second, augmented, edition of this work appeared the following year along with a set of printed reports entitled *Reports, or new cases; with divers resolutions and judgements given upon solemn arguments, and with great deliberation*.

At the end of August 1649 the Commonwealth dispatched March to Guernsey as one of four commissioners for the ordering and settling of its affairs there. March also made an important contribution to the debate on law reform during the Commonwealth and protectorate. He represented, along with fellow barristers William Sheppard and Sir Matthew Hale, a branch of the interregnum law reform movement that advocated reform from within the existing structures of the common law. He is best known for his *Amicus republicae, the Commonwealth's friend, or, An exact and speedie course to justice and right, and for preventing and determining of tedious law-suits* (1651; Thomason's copy is dated May). This work, dedicated to the lord president of the council of state, John Bradshaw, was probably an attempt to influence the deliberations of the Hale commission on law reform. March held that although the core of the common law remained pure, over the centuries both procedural and substantive corruptions of it had crept into the administration of justice. He likened the common law to a tree that would grow better 'for the pruning, and cutting off of its exuberant and unnecessary branches' (*Amicus*, preface). In practical terms he advocated an end to benefit of clergy, the abolition of the death penalty for petty theft, the right to legal representation in capital cases, the end of imprisonment for debt, the legitimization of bastards by the subsequent marriage of the parents, and an end to *peine forte et dure*—the practice of 'pressing to death' in instances where the accused refused to enter a plea. He argued more generally that punishments should be proportional to the crime committed. More controversially he called for a fusion of common law and equity on grounds that it would provide uniformity of procedure in all courts and minimize jurisdictional rivalries. Around this time he also published a translation (from law French), *Some new cases of the years and time of King Hen. 8 Edw. 6 and Qu: Mary; written out of the great abridgement, composed by Sir Robert Brook, knight* (1651).

Following the defeat of Scottish and royalist armies in 1652 March travelled to Scotland on the orders of the council of state. There he served until 1653 as one of a commission of four Englishmen and three Scots charged with the administration of justice. About this time he was also one of a commission of nine charged with regulating the church and universities. He appears to have returned to London by 1656, when he served the trustees for the sale of crown lands at Worcester House. He died early in 1657 after 'a long and expensive sickness' in a state so impoverished that his widow, Alice, on 5 February 1657 petitioned Lord Protector Cromwell for assistance in her husband's burial (*CSP dom.*, 1656–7, 264). The council subsequently ordered payment of £20 'For her relief' (ibid., 592). His surviving family also included two small children, one of whom may have been the Elizabeth March of Richmond, Surrey, who married James Howseman of St Margaret's, Westminster, on 20 January 1668, aged about eighteen. Another John Marsh, whose identity remains uncertain, matriculated at Trinity College, Cambridge, during Easter term 1631.   D. A. ORR

Sources DNB · Foster, *Alum. Oxon., 1500–1714*, 3.969 · Venn, *Alum. Cant.*, 1/3.144 · M. del L. Landon, 'March, John', Greaves & Zaller, *BDBR*, 2.213 · C. W. Brooks, ed., *The admissions registers of Barnard's Inn, 1620–1869*, SeldS, suppl. ser., 12 (1995), 86 · Wood, *Ath. Oxon.*, new edn, 3.374–5 · J. Marsh, *An argument or, debate in law: of the great question concerning the militia; as it is now settled by ordinance of both the houses of parliament* (1642) · J. March, *Amicus republicae, the Commonwealth's friend, or, An exact and speedie course to justice and right, and for preventing and determining of tedious law-suits* (1651) · *CSP dom.* · F. D. Dow, *Cromwellian Scotland, 1651–1660* (1979), 55, 176 · S. E. Prall, *The agitation for law reform during the puritan revolution, 1640–1660* (1966) · D. Veall, *The popular movement for law reform, 1640–1660* (1970)

March, John (*bap.* 1640, *d.* 1692), Church of England clergyman and scholar, the son of Richard March, apothecary, was baptized at St Nicholas's Church, Newcastle upon Tyne, on 17 February 1640. His parents, who died while he was a child, were said to have been Anabaptists, and after their death March was entrusted in 'some way' to the care of Ambrose *Barnes, a prominent north-eastern dissenter

(*Ambrose Barnes*, 144). After education at the grammar school in Newcastle under George Ritschel, a kinsman of Barnes, March matriculated as a commoner at Queen's College, Oxford, on 15 June 1657. In December 1658 he followed his tutor, Thomas Tully, to St Edmund Hall, where the latter had been elected principal. March proceeded BA in 1661, MA in 1664, and BD in 1674. From 1664 until 1672 he served as tutor and vice-principal of St Edmund Hall, where one of his pupils was John Kettlewell, later a nonjuror, and where March's son, Humphrey, matriculated in 1695.

March returned to the north-east in June 1672, when he was appointed by Merton College to the vicarage of Embleton in Northumberland. His abilities marked him out for an important part in the ecclesiastical affairs of the region. When Nathaniel, Lord Crewe, was translated to the palatine see of Durham in 1674 March became a chaplain to the new bishop and in 1676 he was appointed afternoon lecturer at St Nicholas's, the principal parish church in Newcastle. In 1679 he became vicar of St Nicholas's at a salary of £60, with an additional £10 as lecturer, and resigned the living of Embleton. In 1682 the corporation of Newcastle increased his salary to £90.

Despite his early upbringing March was a zealous high-churchman, asserting the excellence of the Church of England against dissenters and Roman Catholics alike. An erudite preacher, he was particularly noted for his sermons at annual services held on 30 January and 29 May to mark the respective anniversaries of the martyrdom of Charles I and the restoration of Charles II. Several of these sermons, delivered before the mayor and aldermen of Newcastle, were published at the request of the hearers. One, delivered on 30 January 1677, characteristically apostrophized the dissenters as 'sons of *Belial*' (March, *A Sermon*, 8) and included a notable encomium on Charles I, whose *Eikon basilike* March frequently quoted. Another, *The False Prophet Unmask't, or, The Wolf Stript of his Sheeps-Clothing*, delivered on 30 January 1683, when March's brother-in-law Nicholas Ridley was sheriff of Newcastle, condemned the 'dangerous principle … that all power is originally seated in the people' (p. 16) and employed quotations from Augustine, Chrysostom, Ignatius, and Optatus to show the schismatical condition of the dissenters. However, March was equally prepared to contend against the errors of the Church of Rome, boldly employing arguments from Augustine, Basil, Chrysostom, Irenaeus, Jerome, and Tertullian for this purpose in an undated assize sermon delivered during the reign of James II.

March was not only an able controversialist, he was also a faithful and diligent parish priest. Continuing work begun by the archdeacon of Northumberland, Dr Isaac Basire, he proved remarkably successful in his efforts to restore conformity to the Church of England after the sectarian confusion of the 1650s. Constantly resident, March officiated at daily public prayers and was diligent in catechizing and in visiting the sick, while 'his known abilities in resolving cases of conscience drew after him a great many good people, not only of his own flock, but from remoter distances, who resorted to him as a common Oracle' (March, *Sermons*, preface). He preached effectively, in an eloquent and direct style, exhorting his hearers to holiness of life, warning against the Epicurean tendencies of 'the Infamous Author of the Monstrous *Leviathan*' (ibid., 19) and urging adherence to the Church of England, the nursing mother of Charles I, 'the first Royal Martyr that ever was in the World', of the emperor Constantine, and of '*Lucius*, the first Christian King' (ibid., 123). By 1683 it was reported that 'Newcastle was brought to a very great degree of conformity, by the zeal and diligence of the Vicar' ('Remains of Denis Granville', 167). This achievement earned March the approval of William Sancroft, the archbishop of Canterbury; Leoline Jenkins, the secretary of state; and the bishop of Oxford, Dr John Fell.

During the early 1680s March was a member of a clerical club which met monthly in Durham to promote church principles, 'according to the practice of Dr [Peter] Samways and Dr [Thomas] Comber' (*Remains of Denis Granville*, 171). At least three members of this assembly later became nonjurors (Denis Granville, archdeacon and later dean of Durham; John Cock, vicar of St Oswald's in Durham and later rector of Gateshead; and Thomas Davison, vicar of Norton, whose brother Jonathan Davison, another nonjuror, was appointed lecturer at St Nicholas's, Newcastle, in 1686). Following the revolution of 1688 March remained loyal to James II. He refused to preach at the thanksgiving service ordered by the convention on 31 January 1689 and caused the *Homily Against Rebellion* to be read instead (*Ambrose Barnes*, 435). On the previous day, the anniversary of the martyrdom of King Charles I, in defiance of the order of the House of Lords, which for that year suppressed the official marking of the day, March had preached, as usual, in favour of passive obedience and non-resistance, denouncing the argument from self-defence as 'an old fanatick Principle' and declaring that 'whoever meddled with the King's Forts, Castles, Militia and Revenue, were ... guilty of Damnation' (March, *Vindication*, 3). When criticized by James Welwood, a Scottish doctor practising in Newcastle, March firmly restated his convictions: 'I have always preached this Doctrine on January the 30th ... If the Times be changed, Truth is not, and *English* Ministers of all men ought not to be time-servers' (ibid., 6).

Like many high-churchmen March took the oath of allegiance to William of Orange with deep reluctance and 'with such a declaration or limitation as should still leave him free' to serve James II (*Ambrose Barnes*, 436). Such ambiguous behaviour caused Thomas Hearne to believe that March might have been a nonjuror (*Remarks*, 2.60) and led to a further deterioration in his relationship with the corporation of Newcastle, which had been under strain since a disagreement over the appointment of a preaching curate for All Saints' parish in 1686. On 15 July 1690 March was warned that his salary would be stopped if he continued to refuse to name William and Mary explicitly in the state prayers, and on 3 December 1692, the day after March's death in Newcastle and before he had even been buried, the corporation resolved that his £90 stipend should not be continued to any successor.

March was buried in St Nicholas's Church on 4 December 1692. A collection of twelve of his sermons was published in November 1693, and a second edition, with a brief biographical note of March by his fellow high-churchman John Scot, appeared in 1699.

RICHARD SHARP

Sources J. March, *Sermons preach'd on several occasions*, 2nd edn (1699) · J. March, *The false prophet unmask't, or, The wolf stript of his sheeps-clothing* (1683) · J. March, *A sermon (on Judges xix.30) preached on 30th January 1677* (1677) · [J. March], *A vindication of the present great revolution in England; in five letters passed between James Welwood M.D., and Mr John March* (1689) · *Memoirs of the life of Mr Ambrose Barnes*, ed. [W. H. D. Longstaffe], SurtS, 50 (1867) · 'The remains of Denis Granville, DD, dean and archdeacon of Durham', ed. [G. Ornsby], *Miscellanea*, SurtS, 37 (1861) · *The remains of Denis Granville ... being a further selection from his correspondence, diaries, and other papers*, ed. [G. Ornsby], SurtS, 47 (1865) · E. Mackenzie, *A descriptive and historical account of the town and county of Newcastle upon Tyne*, 2 vols. (1827) · J. Brand, *The history and antiquities of the town and county of the town of Newcastle upon Tyne*, 2 vols. (1789) · H. Bourne, *The history of Newcastle upon Tyne* (1736) · A. R. Laws, *Schola Novocastrensis*, 2 vols. (1925–32) · *Remarks and collections of Thomas Hearne*, ed. C. E. Doble and others, 2, OHS, 7 (1886) · *DNB*

Likenesses oils, 1893; known to be at Blagdon in 1893 · oils, 1893; known to be at Vicarage House, Newcastle, in 1893 · J. Sturt, engraving (after portraits), repro. in March, *Sermons preach'd* · J. Sturt, line engraving, BM, NPG; repro. in J. March, *Sermons preached on several occasions* (1693) · oils; formerly in the possession of Alderman Hornby, 1893

March [de Marchia], **William** (*d.* 1302), administrator and bishop of Bath and Wells, is consistently described in records as 'magister', and is assumed to have been a graduate of Oxford University. First recorded as rector of Thorpe in Nottinghamshire in 1277, he entered the king's service and was employed in the wardrobe, where he was cofferer (1280–84) and controller (15 August 1283 to 1 May 1290), and in the latter capacity had temporary charge of the great seal in February 1290. He was treasurer of the exchequer, in succession to John Kirkby, from 6 April 1290 until his dismissal on 16 August 1295. As treasurer he presided over important reforms in the administration of taxation. Henceforward the exchequer controlled the receipt, auditing, and expenditure of lay subsidies, and the financial independence of the wardrobe was considerably reduced. The king's personal confidence in him was clearly displayed on 13 October 1289, when Edward I appointed him to a prestigious commission of seven trusted men, headed by the bishops of Winchester and Bath and Wells, to hear grievances against the king's ministers over wrongs committed by them during the king's recent absence abroad. Nevertheless March became the only great officer of state who fell permanently from office for political reasons in Edward I's reign. He was dismissed by the king in 1295 in a blaze of unpopularity.

March's involvement in Edward I's financial extortions, particularly the scrutiny of money on 4 July 1294, which gave royal agents access to wealth stored in religious institutions, brought him notoriety among churchmen. *Flores historiorum* claimed that he should be called 'not bishop of Bath but tyrant', and that he was 'not protecting the church but attacking it' (3.274). Edward I was willing to make his treasurer a scapegoat. The scrutiny may have been an important cause of March's dismissal, but another contributory factor was his extraordinary unpopularity in London, arising from his tight grip on civic administration as treasurer while the city was in the king's hand between 1285 and 1298. A roll of two membranes containing unanswered petitions from London citizens to the king and council against March, internally datable to August or September 1295, survives to bear witness to the city's hatred. The Dunstable annals suggest he tried to buy his way out of trouble with a large sum of money. But the Osney annals give a more favourable picture of him at the time of his appointment to the treasury, as a man of foresight, discretion, and circumspection.

March amassed a number of benefices during his career. In 1291 a papal dispensation, at the king's request, to the treasurer March (specifically described therein as subdeacon) listed eight churches in four dioceses, which, in addition to the deanery of St Martin's-le-Grand, he had held without papal dispensation and without being ordained priest within a year of receiving them. He resigned the rectory of Thorpe, and was prepared to resign two more, but sought permission to retain the rest, together with canonries in Salisbury, Chichester, and Wells, and a portion in the chapel of St Clement, Pontefract, and also to accept another or other rectories on resigning one or more of these. On 28 January 1293 he was elected bishop of Bath and Wells, the royal assent was signified on 1 March, temporalities were restored on 19 March, and consecration took place at Canterbury on 17 May, being performed by the bishops of London, Rochester, Ely, and Dublin in the vacancy following the death of Archbishop Pecham.

The precise date of March's death, long cited as 11 June 1302, is now uncertain, but he was buried at Wells on 17 June, and administration of his will was granted on 3 July 1302. A Somerset inquisition recorded ignorance of his heir, but the award of a papal nuncio in a subsequent dispute, in 1313, names two close kin: March left 100 marks to pay his brother, John March, if still living, or his nephew, Robert Urry, to go to the Holy Land for him at the first subsequent crusade. His executors had deposited this money in September 1311 with the dean and chapter of Wells, to be paid at the first expedition; there was no crusade and the money attracted borrowers and claimants for over thirty years.

In June 1324 the dean and chapter of Wells advised their proctors at the papal court of their decision to urge Bishop March's canonization, and began their campaign. The archbishop of Canterbury and eight English bishops wrote to Pope John XXII (r. 1316–34) on 4 December 1325 pressing the case. Edward II and later Edward III lent support to the request, and the diocesan clergy granted a tenth to finance costs. The attribution of healing miracles gives an impression of sanctity beyond the more general claims to moral probity and generous alms-giving, but it is possible that part at least of March's popularity in his own diocese arose from his financial prowess. On 19 January

1295 March had entered a bond to repay on demand £1000 advanced to him and the prior and convent of Bath and dean and chapter of Wells by the bishops of Lincoln and Winchester (agents of the papacy for the crusading tenths granted to Edward I in 1291); the bond stated that the sum had been spent by March on his own and the bishopric's business and indemnified the prior and dean and their chapters. The chapter house at Wells is ascribed to his time as bishop, and is architecturally of the period.

HELEN M. JEWELL

Sources Emden, *Oxf.*, 3.2195 · Tout, *Admin. hist.*, vols. 2, 6 · I. S. Leadam and J. F. Baldwin, eds., *Select cases before the king's council, 1243–1482*, SeldS, 35 (1918), 8–18 · *CEPR letters*, 1.530 · *Calendar of the manuscripts of the dean and chapter of Wells*, 1, HMC, 12 (1907) · W. Hunt, ed., *Two chartularies of the priory of St Peter at Bath*, Somerset RS, 7 (1893) · E. B. Fryde and others, eds., *Handbook of British chronology*, 3rd edn, Royal Historical Society Guides and Handbooks, 2 (1986) · H. R. Luard, ed., *Flores historiarum*, 3 vols., Rolls Series, 95 (1890), vol. 3, p. 274 · *Ann. mon.*, 3.399, 4.324 · W. Stubbs, *Registrum sacrum Anglicanum*, 2nd edn (1897), 68 · *Fasti Angl., 1300–1541*, [Bath and Wells], 1 · *Registrum Roberti Winchelsey Cantuariensis archiepiscopi, AD 1294–1313*, ed. R. Graham, 1, CYS, 51 (1952), 438, 440–41 · J. F. Willard, 'An exchequer reform under Edward I', in L. J. Paetow, *The crusades and other historical essays presented to Dana C. Munro* (1928), 326–40
Likenesses stone effigy (in eucharistic vestments), Wells Cathedral, Somerset; repro. in L. S. Colchester, ed., *Wells Cathedral: a history* (1982), pl. 56
Wealth at death held no lands *in capite* at time of death: *CClR, 1296–1302*, 561

Marchall, Roger (*c.*1417–1477), physician and writer on medicine, embodied three strands of late-medieval English life: Cambridge University and its support through gifts of books; the sphere of London medical practice (including royal service); and the financial world of London merchants which afforded him prosperity. Born at Toddington in Bedfordshire, Marchall was one of at least four siblings in what was probably a landowning family. Still alive in the early 1470s were a brother John, of Toddington, a sister, Alice Awncell, and a brother Nicholas (*d.* 1474), sometime alderman of London and warden of the ironmongers. Whether Thomas Marchall *clericus* (*fl.* 1438–1439), author of a Latin poem on cock-fighting, was another brother is unclear. Roger Marchall married Johan, probably after 1456. By the time Marchall's will was written (14 February 1477) they had a daughter, Anne, who was a minor, and an unborn child. Proved on 6 May 1477, the will specified burial in St Katharine Cree, London (his wife and John Clerk, royal apothecary, were executors). Marchall left to his children lands and tenements in that parish and in Hackney, along with £200 and considerable plate. The will is noteworthy for its minimal religious bequests when compared with those of his brother Nicholas.

The first twenty years of Marchall's recorded life were spent at Cambridge. He was admitted as a fellow of Peterhouse in 1437, presumably having determined as MA. This suggests that he was born about 1417. He lectured as regent master, and afterwards held the position of junior proctor of the university (1443–4). He had been awarded the MD degree by 1453. Some of his manuscripts bear his notes and diagrams from this period. He has also been suggested as the author of *Cum rerum motu*, a 1441 text on invalid and valid horoscopes for Henry VI, which survives in a later manuscript.

London was Marchall's residence from *c*.1456, and during this time he served as physician to Edward IV. References to this service are found in a writ of 1468, recording the examination of a woman for leprosy, and in Bodleian, MS Ashmole 424, where he identifies himself as 'regum medicus'. Peterhouse, MS 95 contains a recipe, 'preservativa Regis Edwardi iiiite', apparently in his hand. Marchall may also have been responsible for royal horoscopes in his codices. In addition to royal service Marchall attended the first wife of John Howard (later duke of Norfolk) in 1465, and in 1471 is recorded as inspecting treacle for the mayor of London. Records surviving from the period of Marchall's London residence also testify to his financial transactions, particularly with members of the Guild of Ironmongers. In 1464 he conveyed money to Peterhouse as an executor of the will of the London ironmonger Thomas Dorchester, and his own will of 1477 records two debts of £100 each, owed him by the ironmongers William Fuller and William Milne.

Marchall's manuscripts are the richest source of information about his interests. In a careful hand he copied out and annotated the text of Petrarch's *De remediis utriusque fortunae*, in what is now Oxford, All Souls College, MS 91. He may have compiled a medical florilegium emphasizing English medical writers in Cambridge, Gonville and Caius College, MS 98/50, and he supplied a number of short texts or notes, as well as diagrams and figures of division, to twelve other manuscripts. Leland also cited him as author of a (mathematical?) text titled *De figuris cata et apodiatis*. Marchall was, however, neither the author nor the scribe of the Middle English surgery treatise in New York, Academy of Medicine, MS 13, which has been attributed to him.

Roger Marchall also assembled manuscripts from booklets, adding tables of contents (for example, BL, Harley MS 531). He appears to have commissioned at least four codices from one London scribe and was particularly interested in Albertus Magnus on the *Parva naturalia*, owning four codices of that group of texts. He left his mark in numerous manuscripts, most of which he owned, by annotating them and supplying contents tables to them: forty-five survive in fourteen libraries; six others may have been his; twelve mentioned in records have not been traced. The overwhelming majority of the more than 400 texts he listed or annotated in his surviving codices are medical or have to do with astronomy, astrology, or natural philosophy.

Wealth from London trade enabled Roger Marchall to acquire scientific and medical manuscripts, which he used and then donated, apparently in the early 1470s, to three Cambridge colleges which supported the study of medicine: Peterhouse, King's, and Gonville Hall. His intellectual tastes and his wealth are revealed in two deluxe manuscripts he donated to Peterhouse; these are now Bodleian MS Ashmole 424, containing Witelo's *De*

perspectiva, and Cambridge, Magdalene College, Pepys Library, Pepys MS 2329, a mathematical compendium. His benefaction of a considerable number of valuable books to fifteenth-century Cambridge colleges is exceptional for one who was neither a member of the aristocracy nor a cleric.

LINDA EHRSAM VOIGTS

Sources L. E. Voigts, 'A doctor and his books: the manuscripts of Roger Marchall, d. 1477', *New science out of old books: studies in manuscripts and early printed books in honour of A. I. Doyle*, ed. R. Beadle and A. J. Piper (1995), 249–314 · will, testamentary records, commissary court of London (London division), GL, Register 6, fols. 241–2; 1478 · M. R. James, 'The old catalogue', in M. R. James and J. W. Clark, *A descriptive catalogue of the manuscripts in the library of Peterhouse* (1899), 1–26 · T. A. Walker, *A biographical register of Peterhouse men*, 1 (1927), 43–5 · will, 1474, PRO, PROB 11/6, sig. 16 [Nicholas Marchall] · *CClR, 1468–76*, 30 · R. R. Sharpe, ed., *Calendar of letter-books preserved in the archives of the corporation of the City of London*, [12 vols.] (1899–1912), vol. L, p.103 · will, 1479, proved, 1483, PRO, PROB 11/7, sig. 8 [John Clerk] · *The household books of John Howard, duke of Norfolk, 1462–1471, 1481–1483* (1992) [with introduction by A. Crawford] · *Joannis Lelandi antiquarii de rebus Britannicis collectanea*, ed. T. Hearne, [2nd edn], 6 vols. (1770), vol. 4, pp. 19–25 · H. M. Carey, *Courting disaster: astrology at the English court and university in the later middle ages* (1992) · J. D. North, *Horoscopes and history* (1986) · Emden, *Cam.* · C. H. Talbot and E. A. Hammond, *The medical practitioners in medieval England: a biographical register* (1965)

Archives Gon. & Caius Cam., MS 98/50 · Peterhouse, Cambridge, MS 95 | All Souls Oxf., MS 91 · BL, Harley MS 531 · Bodl. Oxf., MS Ashmole 424 · Magd. Cam., Pepys MS 2329

Wealth at death very prosperous; lands and tenements in Hackney of unknown value; lands and tenements in parish of St Katherine Cree, London, of unknown value; bequests of £240; extensive bequests of plate; had also given away fifty manuscripts, two of which were deluxe, in the period 1472–4: will, GL, Register 6, fols. 241–2

Marchand, Leslie Alexis (1900–1999), literary scholar, was born on 13 February 1900 near Bridgeport, Washington, United States, the son of Alexis Marchand, a French-speaking homesteader, and Adele Clara, *née* Buckingham.

Marchand graduated BA at the University of Washington in 1922, and in 1923 became the first teacher in the humanities at the Alaska Agricultural College and School of Mines 'Farthest North College', Fairbanks, Alaska, which then consisted of nine faculty members and thirty-five students. In chapters of his unpublished autobiography Marchand described life among the 'sourdoughs' during the long months when the temperature remained far below zero and the only transport was dog-drawn sledges. In the summer of 1926 he explored the glaciers of Mount McKinley, and boated down the Yukon River with some gold prospectors, visiting many Indian villages. He enjoyed the pioneering life, but it all had a purpose. With the money saved, he was able to attend a course on French civilization at the Sorbonne in Paris. He began teaching at Rutgers University, New Jersey, in 1937 and in 1940 he took his doctorate at Columbia University.

Marchand's doctoral dissertation, '*The Athenaeum*: a mirror of Victorian culture' (1941), was a study of the struggle to establish an independent literary review. With the encouragement of his professors at Columbia he decided that as soon as the war was over he would turn his attention to Byron. In July 1947 he sailed for England on board the *Queen Elizabeth*. He was well equipped with the most modern technology, a camera which could take colour pictures. He also knew how to arrange microfilming in London, an innovation in literary research then scarcely known. His luggage included a trunkful of assorted groceries to ease his passage through a Britain deep in postwar austerity plus a supply of woollen underwear. Marchand's Alaskan experience proved invaluable in the unheated British Museum Library.

It was at that time that he met John Grey Murray—of the firm of John Murray, Byron's publisher—with whom he shared his lifelong enthusiasm. Together they explored the boxes of letters into which less dedicated researchers had made only occasional dips. In Wiltshire a member of the Hobhouse family used her precious petrol coupons to enable him to see the diaries of Byron's dearest friend. From England, Marchand followed Byron to Switzerland, to Italy, and then to Greece, where the bitter civil war had not yet ended. It was the first of many research trips to Europe in search of materials relating to Byron in which he was both tireless and outstandingly successful. On 8 July 1950 he married Marion Knill Hendrix (*b.* 1920), an editor.

Marchand was made full professor at Rutgers in 1953 and in 1958–9, under the aegis of a Fulbright fellowship, was Byron professor at the University of Athens. Like Byron he developed a special love for Greece.

Marchand's *Byron: a Biography*, which drew on innumerable primary sources previously unknown, was published in three large volumes in 1956. His edition of the complete *Byron's Letters and Journals*, which appeared in twelve volumes between 1973 and 1982, with a supplementary volume in 1994, made available the results of three decades of searching in libraries and private collections in many countries.

Leslie Marchand enabled the world to appreciate for the first time the extraordinarily rich personality of the poet and the variety and integrity of his life. Along with another American, Newman Ivey White, who performed the same service for Shelley in 1948, Marchand rescued Byron from the semi-fictional romancing of Maurois which dominated inter-war biographical writing on the English Romantic poets. By giving Byron's own unedited words, in his business letters as well as in his intimate confidences to his friends, Marchand not only revealed one of the best letter writers in the English language, but helped readers to understand why Byron was so engaging as well as so influential a figure in his time and later.

Marchand's approach to biography was to transcribe and contextualize the original documents, to reconstruct the historical facts to which they pointed, and to allow Byron to speak for himself. Seldom has a biographer been more modest, keeping well in the background, avoiding making unnecessary or definitive judgements, and offering no overarching psychological or theoretical explanations. But Marchand knew his man. He could tell a forgery at a glance from the style as well as from the handwriting. Most important of all, he was sympathetic to, and he understood, that indefinable mixture of seriousness,

irony, fun, and self awareness which Byron brought to everything he wrote.

Marchand retired in 1966 and was awarded honorary doctorates by the University of Alaska (1976) and Rutgers University (1981). In later years, as a grand old man of scholarship, there were attempts to turn him into a Byronic figure. But he would have none of it. Marchand seemed personally the least Byronic of men, with little of the romantic flamboyance of his subject. He was a fine, slim, athletic figure, conservatively dressed. In appearance he scarcely changed during his long life. At the Byron Bicentenary Conference in 1988, when Marchand was already eighty-eight, he delivered an excellent paper. When the applause died down, he remarked, 'when you get to my age, you only have to sneeze to get a cheer'.

Leslie Marchand died at 570 Foxwood Boulevard, Englewood, Florida, on 11 July 1999, and was cremated there on 12 July; he was survived by his wife.

WILLIAM ST CLAIR

Sources L. A. Marchand, unpublished autobiography, priv. coll. · personal knowledge (2004) · private information (2004) [Marion Marchand] · R. D. Altick, *The scholar adventurers* (1950)
Archives NYPL · priv. coll. · University of Delaware, Newark
Likenesses photograph, repro. in *The Guardian* (20 July 1999)

Marchant, Nathaniel (1738/9–1816), gem-engraver and medallist, came from a family long-established in the village of Mayfield, Sussex. Details of his parentage and birth are obscure, although he was possibly the son of another Nathaniel Marchant (*b.* 1702), at one time an apprentice watchmaker. Marchant was recorded in 1761 as the winner of a premium for gem-engraving offered by the London Society for the Encouragement of Arts, Manufactures, and Commerce, and gained three further premiums in successive years, making him the foremost prize-winner in this field. As prescribed by the society, his winning entries were intaglios reproducing casts from ancient statues in the third duke of Richmond's gallery, where artists were trained in copying from the antique. Until 1765 he was the apprentice of Edward Burch, a fellow prize-winner, whom he joined that year as an exhibitor with the Society of Artists, showing copies of his prize-winning gems. He exhibited his intaglios there until 1768 and remained loyal to the society even after Burch's defection to the Royal Academy, but from 1769 he showed only wax models for future gems and casts from those completed, an indication that the originals were already sold; his *Garrick with the Bust of Shakespeare* became a bestseller in Wedgwood's copy.

The most important of Marchant's early patrons was George Spencer, fourth duke of Marlborough, a passionate gem collector, whose help was probably material in enabling Marchant to travel to Rome to fulfil his ambition to study original works of the ancients *in situ*. He set out in 1772; his last exhibition entry for the society, sent two years later, was pointedly described as 'after the original head of the Antinous in the Villa Albano, near Rome' (exh. Society of Artists, 1774). Henceforth he devoted himself almost entirely to copying Rome's antiquities on his intaglio sealstones. From 1774 to 1786 he lived and worked

Nathaniel Marchant (1738/9–1816), attrib. Hugh Douglas Hamilton, c.1779–88

in via Babuino, in the middle of the artists' and antiquaries' quarter, then until 1788 in strada Felice (later via Sistina) on the healthier heights near Trinità de' Monti. He kept up his connection with the duke conscientiously, informing him about the availability of ancient gems and offering him and other collectors at home his own newly engraved stones; but having attracted the attention of important antiquaries and dealers, he soon found new commissions in Italy itself. His exquisitely engraved gems were sought especially by grand tourists as mementoes of their visits; he also practised very successfully a second popular genre, cutting very accomplished portraits from life, such as that of Emma Hart, later Lady Hamilton (Metropolitan Museum of Art, New York), and came to be considered the only rival to the pre-eminent Giovanni Pichler. From 1781 he began to send gems for exhibition in the Royal Academy.

The Roman diaries and correspondence of Lord Herbert (later eleventh earl of Pembroke) and his circle paint a vivid picture of Marchant's painstaking, thoughtful approach to the lengthy process of engraving and his self-confidence as an artist: 'I have kept the work as light as possible in imitation of the best Greek gems' (*Henry, Elizabeth and George*, 487). As his fame grew he received commissions from European and British royalty and nobility, and was allowed to model the pope from life, but it was among the British visitors that he found not only patrons but influential friends, moving with remarkable ease in high society. He seems to have benefited from good schooling: he wrote fluent letters in a practised hand,

made a point of learned quotations in his published *Catalogue*, and acquired a reputation in Rome for connoisseurship as well as his art. In 1788, after a sojourn of sixteen years, he was at last ready to return home, confidently expecting to build on his fame and his connections.

Settling in Bond Street, Marchant renewed links with artist friends, most now members of the Royal Academy, and was elected an associate in 1791. The following year he exhibited the casts from 100 of his finest gems, a catalogue of which he was preparing for publication; though virtually all after antiquities, he included his masterly essay in modern history, *General Wolfe, Receiving the News of the Victory, as he was Expiring* (Brocklesby Park, Lincolnshire). The catalogue (1792) meticulously documented the ancient models for his stones, together with the names of their prestigious owners: the project attracted 446 subscribers, at their head the prince of Wales and the duke of Gloucester. He received some further important commissions and was elected to membership of the academies of Vienna, Stockholm, and Copenhagen, but to his continuing disappointment, as vividly described in Joseph Farington's diary, the Royal Academy dragged its feet: he had to wait until he was seventy years of age before he was at last elected.

Marchant was, however, appointed to the Royal Mint in 1797 as probationer and later assistant engraver; in 1799 he became senior engraver to the stamp office, which provided him with elegant accommodation in Somerset House. In 1801 he was named his majesty's engraver of seals. Marchant fulfilled his duties conscientiously, although in later years in indifferent health; in 1815 he was superannuated, suffering from a lengthy and debilitating illness. He died a wealthy man, unmarried, on 24 March 1816 at his home, New Somerset House, Somerset Place, and was buried in Stoke church, Buckinghamshire, where he is commemorated by an inscribed memorial by his friend John Flaxman. His contemporary fame as the foremost recorder in miniature of Rome's antiquities is enshrined in the many souvenir collections of its sights, in the form of plaster casts from gemstones, produced for gentlemen's libraries; his reputation as one of the finest glyptic artists of the eighteenth-century revival, equally brilliant in classical subjects and in portraiture, has endured. A representative group of his gems in the British Museum includes the noble portrait *George John, Second Earl Spencer* and an exquisite *Bacchus and a Bacchante*. Plaster impressions are held by the Society of Antiquaries of London; Sir John Soane's Museum, London; Mompesson House, Salisbury, Wiltshire, and Kingston Lacy, Dorset; the Ashmolean Museum, Oxford; and the Fitzwilliam Museum, Cambridge. GERTRUD SEIDMANN

Sources G. Seidmann, 'Nathaniel Marchant, gem-engraver, 1739–1816', *Walpole Society*, 53 (1987), 1–105, 161 · Farington, *Diary* · will, PRO, PROB 11/1580, sig. 270 [duty register will proven 8 May 1816] · epitaph, tomb of Nathaniel Marchant, by John Flaxman, Stoke Poges church, Buckinghamshire · committee minutes (Polite Arts), 1760–65, [now Royal] Society for the Encouragement of Arts, Manufactures, and Commerce, London · exhibition catalogues (1765–74) [Society of Artists of Great Britain] · *The exhibition of the Royal Academy* (1781–1811) [exhibition catalogues] · *Henry,*

Elizabeth and George, 1734–1780: letters and diaries of Henry, tenth earl of Pembroke and his circle, ed. S. Herbert (1939) · F. Haskell and N. Penny, *Taste and the antique* (1981), 97–8 · *DNB* · parish register, Mayfield, E. Sussex RO · J. Ingamells, ed., *A dictionary of British and Irish travellers in Italy, 1701–1800* (1997)
Archives RA, papers | Archivio del Vicariato, Rome, Status Animarum books, 1772–89 · Birm. CA, letters to Boulton family · BL, Blenheim MSS · FM Cam., British artists and general MSS · PRO, Mint MSS · RA, Ozias Humphry MSS · RA, Royal Academy minutes · RA, Society of Artists MSS · RSA, minutes of general meetings and committee of polite arts
Likenesses attrib. H. D. Hamilton, pastel, *c.*1779–1788, Sir John Soane's Museum, London [*see illus.*] · G. Dance, tinted black chalk drawing, 1793, RA · W. Daniell, soft-ground etching (after G. Dance), BM
Wealth at death approx. £24,000, incl. property at Mayfield: will, PRO

Marche, Jean de la (1585–1651), Reformed minister, was born on 6 August 1585, the elder son of Hellier de la Marche (*c.*1558–1643) of St Peter Port, Guernsey, and his wife, Michelle, daughter of Thomas Verin. Thomas Cartwright, minister at Castle Cornet (1595–1601), may have been an early influence. He attended the universities of Cambridge, from 1604 to *c.*1608, and Saumur, from *c.*1608 to 1610, graduating MA on 10 September 1610. He was ordained on 6 August 1613 and became minister in Guernsey of both St Andrew and La Forêt in the following month, of Castle Cornet from 23 May 1623, and of St Peter Port from 15 February 1625.

On 25 January 1616 de la Marche married Esther De Beauvoir, heir to La Ville au Roi, St Peter Port. Of their children, Bertranne and Thomas died in 1622, and Charles (1618–1695), minister of the Castel parish, Guernsey, until 1662, was chaplain to Whitlocke's Swedish embassy in 1653. Jean junior was probably another son, about whom little is known, save his becoming Castle Cornet's gaoler in 1660, suggesting royalist sympathies and familial estrangement.

De la Marche was active in Guernsey's parliament, the *états* or states, in which the clergy sat *ex officio*. In November 1616 James I personally assured him of the continuation of Guernsey's presbyterian regime. From 1626 de la Marche challenged the secular power's claims to certain tithes. Consequently accused of treason and false doctrine, he was imprisoned in Castle Cornet for seven months in 1633. After appealing to the privy council without result he returned in July 1634 and was ejected from the living of St Peter Port, reassuming the rectorship of St Andrew in August.

Following their release from Channel Island prisons, Henry Burton and William Prynne banqueted at de la Marche's home on 19 November 1640. In March 1641 de la Marche was sent to draw parliament's attention to Guernsey church affairs, presumably in support of a national presbyterian settlement. His *Complaint of the False Prophets Mariners* was presented to the Commons on 28 July 1641, at the height of the root and branch debates. Dedicated to Burton, and supposedly based upon Guernsey 'prophesyings' on Revelation, through calendar calculations and allegorical exegesis it looked to episcopacy's fall and the rise of presbyterianism. In April 1642 parliament appointed de la Marche one of two Guernsey ministers in the Westminster assembly of divines.

On 6 February 1642 de la Marche preached at the French church, Threadneedle Street, London, against hierarchy. This provoked a rebuke from its administration, as did a millenarian sermon he delivered a little later. On 6 June 1642 he preached there on the apocalyptic fate of earthly monarchies, a subject to which he was to return, to the point of encouraging regicide. His precocious and ardent opinions did not prevent his appointment to the French church in May 1643, a position made official that September. He presided over the colloquy of the French churches in England in 1644.

De la Marche is not known ever to have returned to Guernsey, although he remained in touch with the island, and in June 1643 there were moves there to dismiss him from St Andrew. Nor did he lack opposition in England. The royalist Louis Hérault, appointed a minister of the French church in 1643, soon returned to France. Between 1645 and 1648 Christopher Cisner complained of de la Marche's radicalism, his dictatorial behaviour, and his own exclusion from the church's ministry. Although this divided the congregation, de la Marche remained in office. His commitment to the presbyterian cause, though radical, was not in doubt. The *Complaint* was reissued in 1645 as *A Revelation of the Time, and Fall of the English Hierarchy of Prelates*, a year before episcopacy was abolished and limited presbyterianism introduced. In a table the book anticipated in 1650 the 'last great period of the … journey, and the end of it' (2–3); de la Marche died in London on 14 October 1651.   D. M. OGIER

Sources 'Jean de la Marche, 1585–1631', ed. W. Rolleston and T. W. M. de Guerin, *Report and Transactions* [Société Guernesiaise], 11 (1930–32), 193–220 · J. De la March, *A complaint of the false prophets mariners upon the drying up of their hieraricall Euphrates* (1641) · J. De la March, *A revelation of the time, and fall of the English hierarchy of prelates* (1645) · F. de Schickler, *Les églises du réfuge en Angleterre*, 3 vols. (Paris, 1892) · *Note-book of Pierre Le Roy, Guernsey*, ed. and trans. G. E. Lee (1893) · H. Burton, *A narration of the life of Mr. Henry Burton* (1643) · Livres de perchage, fief le roi, St Peter Port, 1573, 1603, 1616
Archives Priaulx Library, Guernsey, 'Papier ou livre des colloques des églises de Guernezey', MS, ref. SR · Greffe, Guernsey, Greffe collection, diary, no. 83

Marchi, Giuseppe Filippo Liberati [Joseph] (1735?–1808), painter and engraver, was born in the Trastevere district of Rome of unknown parentage. His date of birth is usually given as 1735, although he told Farington in January 1795 that he was then '73 or 4' (Farington, *Diary*, 2.291). He was probably therefore fifteen, and already showing some talent for painting, when he caught the attention of Sir Joshua Reynolds, whom he accompanied on his leisurely return through the towns of northern Italy and Paris. They arrived in London in 1752. One of Reynolds's first portraits after his return was that of Marchi in a turban, much admired at the time and now in the Royal Academy. In 1764 Reynolds invited Marchi to reside with him for six months and to paint for him, offering to pay him £50. Marchi kept Reynolds's appointment books, set his palette, painted draperies, and became one of Reynolds's most trusted copyists, responsible for many of the replicas of popular pictures that the studio produced. Marchi also took up mezzotint engraving and from 1766 to 1775 exhibited both paintings and mezzotints with the Society of Artists, of which he was a fellow as a painter and a director in 1775. He produced only about a dozen mezzotints but they were of high quality and included fine prints after Reynolds of Oliver Goldsmith (1770) and George Colman (1773). Only one of his mezzotints records a portrait that he himself painted, namely that of Princess Czartoriska (1777).

In 1768 Marchi had made a brief attempt to establish himself as an independent painter in London. In September of that year he also visited Wales with his old friend Thomas Jones the painter. While staying at Pencerrig he painted portraits of Jones himself, his brother Major John Jones, and other family members and friends, before he and Jones returned to London in November. In the following year he returned to Reynolds at a salary of £100. He remained a part of Thomas Jones's lively social set: in 1769, for instance, he was in the party with Jones, Mortimer, Farington, and Lawranson that visited the Indiaman *Duke of Gloucester*. Coming ashore late at night, they beat off the crew of a customs house boat that had taken them for smugglers, an incident in which John Hamilton Mortimer almost lost a hand to a cutlass stroke. Marchi remained with Reynolds until the master's death in 1792. Reynolds made no bequest to him, but the artist's niece arranged that his salary should continue. Subsequently he was much employed on cleaning and restoring paintings by Reynolds, an activity for which he was uniquely qualified since he alone understood Reynolds's idiosyncratic techniques.

Towards the end of his life Marchi, who was unmarried, sought the help of his friend Joseph Farington to write his will; it transpired that at the time of his departure from Rome he had two sisters in a convent at Lodi, another sister in Rome, and a brother, Lorenzo, but he did not know if any was still living. Provision was made for £200 to be divided among any surviving siblings. The rest of his estate, valued at under £1500, was distributed among his friends and colleagues. He died, probably at his Wardour Street home, on 2 April 1808, and was buried at St Anne's, Westminster.

TIMOTHY CLAYTON and ANITA MCCONNELL

Sources W. T. Whitley, *Artists and their friends in England, 1700–1799*, 2 vols. (1928); repr. (1968) · *GM*, 1st ser., 78 (1808), 372 · will, PRO, PROB 11/1478, sig. 321 · Farington, *Diary* · D. Mannings, 'Marchi, Giuseppe (Filippo Liberati)', *The dictionary of art*, ed. J. Turner (1996) · N. Penny, ed., *Reynolds* (1986) [exhibition catalogue, RA, 16 Jan – 31 March 1986] · D. Mannings and M. Postle, *Sir Joshua Reynolds: a complete catalogue of his paintings*, 1 (2000) · J. C. Smith, *British mezzotinto portraits*, 4 vols. in 5 (1878–84), 911–16 · A. P. Oppé, ed., 'Memoirs of Thomas Jones, Penkerrig, Radnorshire', *Walpole Society*, 32 (1946–8) [whole issue], esp. 15, 20
Likenesses J. Reynolds, oils, 1753–4, RA · J. Spilsbury, mezzotint, pubd 1761 (after J. Reynolds), BM, NPG · R. Brookshaw, mezzotint (after J. Reynolds), BM, NPG

Marchmont. For this title name *see* Hume, Patrick, first earl of Marchmont (1641–1724); Campbell, Alexander Hume, second earl of Marchmont (1675–1740); Campbell, Hugh Hume, third earl of Marchmont (1708–1794).

Marckant, John (*d.* in or before **1586**), Church of England clergyman and poet, is of obscure origins. Through the patronage of John, Lord Darcy, he was inducted vicar of Great Clacton, Essex, in August 1559, a living which he retained until his death. He also held the Essex vicarage of Shopland from 1563 until his resignation in 1568. Other biographical details are scant, although he may have been the John Markan who was a scholar of St John's College, Cambridge, and a fellow of Pembroke College, Cambridge, in 1555.

Marckant contributed to the English metrical psalter produced by the court poet Thomas Sternhold and the Suffolk minister John Hopkins, the first complete edition of which appeared in 1562. The singing of metrical psalms had become popular under Edward VI among the continental protestant émigrés sheltering in London, and the tradition continued among the English protestants exiled in Europe during Mary's reign. Although not officially part of the Elizabethan liturgy, congregational psalm singing was allowed under the royal injunctions of 1559, and was swiftly adopted by godly congregations. Marckant translated psalms 118, 131, 132, and 135. These were initialled 'M.' in the earliest editions, but in 1565 his surname was printed in full; it occasionally also appears as 'Market'. The Sternhold and Hopkins psalter reigned unchallenged until the new version by Tate and Brady of 1696, and retained its place in English parish churches well into the nineteenth century. Marckant was also responsible for two additional prayers in the 1562 psalter: the eleven-stanza 'The Lamentation of a Sinner', an urgent entreaty to be admitted at the gate of mercy and not held to strict account, which also became known as a hymn; and a plea for grace, 'The Humble Sute of a Sinner', expressing the plaintiff's real hope of finding a place with the angels and the saints.

Taken together, his devotion to the psalms and his cure of souls in Essex imply that Marckant was influenced by Calvinism. Evidently not one to hide the light of Christ under a bushel, he turned from the metrical psalter to the popular press. In 1571 the Fleet Street printer Wylliam Gryffith produced a broadside ballad by Marckant, *A Notable Instruction for All Men to Beware the Abuses of Dice Wyne and Wemen*. This tells the story of a once affluent man who has frittered away his wealth on wine, gambling, fine apparel, and the base delights of 'Venus Pallace'. The reader is lectured by the anonymous unfortunate, who ruefully reflects upon his lost youth, squandered among women who loved him only for the pounds in his pocket:

> Let this example of my smarte, teache others to be ware
> Of Wemen, Dyce and Wyne also, which have made me thus
> bare.
> For where my Parents gave to me, great summes of golde
> most fyne,

That I consumd at dauncinge schole, on Wemen Dyce and Wyne.

So low has he sunk, admits the wanton, that he has come close to taking his own life at 'Tyborne tree'. But Marckant concludes his vividly imagined portrait of one man's descent into degeneracy with a message of hope: those who hold fast in the love of God 'can not want or quayle'. One further verse ballad can be attributed to Marckant, namely *The Purgacion of the Ryght Honourable Lord Wentworth, Concerning the Crime Layde to his Charge* (1559), for which Owen Rogers was fined for printing without entering. Other of Marckant's compositions are known only from the Stationers' register, including 'With speed retorne to God', and 'Verses to Diverse Good Purposes', the latter licensed to Thomas Purfoote in November 1580. John Marckant was dead by 24 February 1586, when he was succeeded by Hugh Smith as vicar of Clacton.

J. P. D. COOPER

Sources *The whole boke of Psalmes* (1566) · J. Marckant, *A notable instruction for all men to beware the abuses of dice wyne and wemen* (1571) · J. Julian, ed., *A dictionary of hymnology* (1907) · N. Temperley, 'Psalms, metrical: §III, England', *New Grove*, 15.358–71, esp. 358–61 · P. Le Huray, *Music and the Reformation in England, 1549–1660* (1967) · J. Silvester, *An Elizabethan vicar of Great Clacton: John Marckant and his famous hymn* (1922) · *ESTC* · *VCH Essex* · R. Newcourt, *Repertorium ecclesiasticum parochiale Londinense*, 2 (1710) · Arber, *Regs. Stationers*

Marcks, Violet Olivia Cressy- [*née* Violet Olivia Rutley; *other married name* Violet Olivia Fisher] (1895–1970), traveller, was born at the High Street, West Wickham, Kent, on 9 June 1895, the only daughter of Ernest Rutley (*d.* in or after 1931), a butcher, and his wife, Olivia Ada, *née* Leake. Details of her early life are obscure: she was living in Croydon when she married, on 13 October 1917, Maurice Cressy-Marcks (or Marckx; *b.* 1891/2), a captain in the North Lancashire regiment, son of Leopold Eugene Marcks (or Marckx), a cotton merchant. She had one son before divorcing him, and marrying, on 12 December 1931, Francis Edwin Fisher (1874/5–1956) of Duddenhill, Watford, a farmer, whose previous marriage to Mabel Frances Frier had been dissolved; her second marriage produced two further sons.

Elected to the Royal Geographical Society (RGS) in 1922, Cressy-Marcks (as she was generally known) was described by her proposer as of independent means, already having 'travelled extensively' from Alaska to Java and having made private 'explorations in Tibet, Kashmiri etc.' She went on to travel overland from Cairo to the Cape in 1925, and in Albania and the Balkans (1927–8), and spent the winter north of the Arctic circle travelling by sledge from Lapland to Baluchistan (1928–9). Eventually credited with travelling in every country of the world, she was keen to have a scientific grounding to her travels, and was a fellow of the Royal Asiatic and Zoological societies. She was trained in surveying at the RGS and surveyed part of the north-west Amazon basin during her journey through the Amazon and Andes to Peru by canoe and foot (1929–30). Her first major work, *Up the Amazon and over the Andes* (1932), acknowledged the tutelage of Edward Ayearst

Reeves of the RGS. She was also a capable cinematographer and photographer, bringing films and photographs from many of her travels including politically sensitive areas. She studied in Arabia and undertook widespread archaeological studies including Egypt, Syria, Palestine, Persia, Java, China, Ethiopia, Afghanistan, and the Khmer, Inca, Aztec, and Mesopotamian peoples. Although she was regarded primarily as an archaeologist (Robinson, 1990), part of her remit was to collect contemporary ethnological data on ethnic groups little known in the West.

Cressy-Marcks's fourth journey around the world was completed during 1931–2; she revisited Spain in 1933 and travelled through India, Kabul, Tashkent, and Moscow in 1934. In 1935 she took the first motor transport from Addis Ababa to Nairobi (during the Italian invasion) and visited the Ethiopian and Eritrean war fronts taking cine film; in 1937 she travelled from Mandela to Peking (Beijing) over land and in 1938 she travelled from Turkey to Tibet by motor, yak, and mule. The latter included a study of the war conditions and an interview with Mao at the communist headquarters in the cliff town of Yenning, as well as ethnographic studies and reaching Lake Kimono as her end point.

Up the Amazon (1932) was dedicated to Violet's mother, 'the bravest and most noble human I know', who was also credited with both encouraging and financing her journeys. However, her will requesting that a copy of her biography be shown to the chief of MI5 'for his appreciation', as well as entrusting that biography to (the then deceased) Bernard Rickatson-Hatt, who had spent three years in intelligence in Constantinople (as well as editor-in-chief for Reuters), suggests sponsorship from the secret service (a different sort of 'mother') for some of her many travels. These coincided with periods of international political sensitivity on a number of occasions. She often achieved largely unfettered travel, as in the case of Russia where she availed herself of permission to travel wherever she wanted and visited most of the Foreign Office officials (as she reported to Mao). During the Second World War she was an ambulance driver for the British Red Cross abroad, as well as special war correspondent, based in Chungking (Chongqing), for the *Daily Express* from 1943 to 1945. She was also accredited to the War Office as war correspondent at the Nuremberg trials.

In addition to *Up the Amazon* Cressy-Marcks published only one account of her many journeys: *Journey into China* (1940). Both were well received by critics, who realized her serious and determined journeying under often difficult and even life-threatening conditions. Her work on China was valued for its contribution to understanding China in general and the Chinese means of resistance to Japanese invasion. Although writing the Amazon book primarily as a travel account, she included supplementary appendices for those seeking practical and reference information. Dismissing economy travellers as 'not conducive in furthering the prestige of our country' (Cressy-Marcks, *Up the Amazon*, 331), she argued that if a journey was to be of any scientific use then money must be spent on equipment.

Although taking her husband with her as a 'passenger' on her journey in 1938, Cressy-Marcks relished the solitude of travelling without a companion, albeit with porters. Her descriptive writing is at its best in her account of Kokonor Lake. Her style is generally spare, not re-creating experiences as being the more dramatic simply on account of her presence, allowing her observations on culture, war, and politics to speak for themselves. At home she led a society life (giving an 'at home' at the Lyceum Club before travelling to Lapland, for example) and had a taste for hunting and game shooting as well as collecting east European icons and rugs.

After the Second World War, Cressy-Marcks's travels were generally less arduous, though still frequent. They included Indo-China, Katmandu, and Japan (1953–4), and her seventh and eighth journeys around the world, completed in 1955 and 1956. Her husband, Francis, died at Nassau on the journey in 1956. She died at her London home—19 Princes Gate, Westminster—on 10 September 1970 and was buried at Langleybury church, Hertfordshire. Her will included a bequest in her name providing a travelling scholarship for geographical research in the field.

AVRIL M. C. MADDRELL

Sources *The Times* (16 Sept 1970) · WW · WWW · *The Times* (16 Dec 1970) · b. cert. · m. certs. · d. cert. · V. Cressy-Marcks, *Up the Amazon and over the Andes* (1932) · V. Cressy-Marcks, *Journey into China* (1940) · will · J. Robinson, *Wayward women: a guide to women travellers* (1990) · *CGPLA Eng. & Wales* (1970)
Wealth at death £318,259: probate, 7 Dec 1970, *CGPLA Eng. & Wales*

Marconi, Guglielmo (1874–1937), physicist and inventor of wireless transmission, was born on 25 April 1874 in Bologna, Italy, the son of Giuseppe Marconi (1826–1904), a local administrator and landowner, and his second wife, Annie (b. c.1843), daughter of Andrew Jameson of the notable Irish family of whiskey distillers. Owing to his poor health Marconi was educated by private tutors. During his one year at the private Istituto Cavallero in Florence he developed a lifelong friendship with the young Marchese Luigi Solari, later one of his most important collaborators. At Leghorn in 1891 he attended the physics lectures given by Professor Giotto Bizzarini at the technical institute, and concurrently took private instruction in physics from Professor Vincenzo Rosa, and learned the Morse code and techniques of transmission.

Education in physics Marconi's health improved in the maritime climate of Leghorn, and, under his mother's influence, he was more fluent in English than Italian. His understanding of physics improved by reading technical articles about electricity, many of these having been sent from Britain by his relatives, and also by reading the biography of Benjamin Franklin. Contact with Rosa was interrupted when Rosa was transferred to Alessandria, in Piedmont, but resumed during the summer of 1894 when they were on holiday in the same area. This gave them the opportunity to discuss Oliver Lodge's recent publications on Hertz's experiments on electrical waves. Marconi's knowledge in that field had by then been augmented through his attendance at the laboratory of the well-

Guglielmo Marconi (1874–1937), by unknown photographer, 1896

known physicist Professor Augusto Righi of Bologna University. Righi's experiments, like those of Hertz, were concerned with Maxwell's electromagnetic theory of light (1873). Righi confirmed and extended Maxwell's theory, which was not yet accepted by physicists, including William Thomson, formerly Maxwell's adviser and correspondent. In Righi's laboratory Marconi had the opportunity to familiarize himself with Hertz's oscillators and resonators, including those for short waves and microwaves which Righi had improved, and to read Righi's numerous articles on this topic. At this time Hertz and Righi intended only to confirm Maxwell's theory; there is no proof that Righi was interested in signal transmission by means of Hertzian waves. It was Marconi who first had the idea of employing this apparatus to develop a practical and useful system of wireless telegraphy. It is clear that by the end of 1894 he had a thorough grasp of the physical background, and a practical and conceptual understanding of electricity which surpassed that of a student and had matured to that of an expert.

First patent for wireless transmission During the winter of 1894 Marconi devoted himself to improving oscillators (as transmitters) and resonators (as receivers) and every part of a practical system of telegraphy without wires. In the spring of 1895, following experiments over shorter ranges, he arranged to transmit signals from his laboratory to a barn 1.5 km distant and hidden from sight behind a hill. He then sought to interest the Italian government, but received only the advice to apply for a patent. Having decided to leave Italy, and helped by his mother's cousin, the engineer Henry Jameson Davies, he arrived in England on 2 February 1896 with his apparatus. A letter of recommendation from the electrical engineer A. A. Campbell Swinton gained him the confidence and assistance of Sir William Henry Preece, chief engineer of the Post Office, who himself had previously succeeded in transmitting electromagnetic signals by the inductive method. After several demonstrations, including that of 27 July when signals were sent across 300 metres from the roof of the General Post Office at St Martins-le-Grand to a bank in

Queen Victoria Street, Marconi succeeded in the more difficult task of transmitting over 14 km on Salisbury Plain. British army and navy experts were present at these demonstrations, which received good coverage in the newspapers.

Over the same period Marconi worked hard to prepare his patent specification. He withdrew his first application, filed in March 1896, substituting a new specification on 2 June. This, the first British patent for wireless telegraphy, was granted on 2 July 1896 as no. 12,039: 'Improvements in transmitting electrical impulses and signals and in apparatus thereof'. On 13 July an American patent was granted for the same specification. These patents are noteworthy for the drawings of his apparatus, clearly showing his apparatus with aerial antenna and earth, and in particular for the detailed information on his receiver (the coherer). To some extent it resembled those of Calzecchi-Onesti, Branly, and Lodge, but it was smaller and its improvements made it more reliable. Every part of Marconi's apparatus had been thoroughly tested, in the laboratory and out of doors, over longer ranges. In May 1897 signals sent the 15 km across the Bristol Channel were observed by the famous German scientist Professor A. Slaby. The Italian navy then showed interest and in July Marconi organized transmissions from the arsenal at La Spezia to various islands at up to 7 km distant, and then to the battleship *San Martino* 18 km out at sea.

Publicity and further advances After returning to England, Marconi established, on 20 July 1897, the Wireless Signal and Telegraph Company, and in 1900 Marconi's Wireless Telegraph Ltd. During July and August he transmitted messages between Queen Victoria's residence at Osborne House on the Isle of Wight and the royal yacht, *Osborne*, carrying information about her son the prince of Wales. This service was much appreciated by the queen and was of course an invaluable advertisement for Marconi's company. Hoping to extend the transmission distances by the use of long waves and very high antennas, Marconi successfully transmitted from the Needles on the Isle of Wight to a ship 30 km out at sea, and then over the 50 km between Salisbury and Bath. The importance of these transmissions lay in their reception at locations below the horizon. Marconi also made experiments to syntonize the signals (that is, to tune them accurately), perhaps aware that Lodge had filed a patent for syntonic wireless telegraphy the previous year. On 27 March 1899, using aerials about 54 metres high, he transmitted Morse code signals across the English Channel from South Foreland to Wimereux, some 50 km. That same year Marconi followed the America's Cup regatta, sending about 1200 messages from the liner *Ponce* to inform the United States public of the challenges between the American *Columbia II* (the eventual winner) and the English *Shamrock*. It was his great opportunity to spread a wider understanding of the importance of wireless telegraphy for peaceful purposes. During this period, he established an American wireless telegraphy company on the lines of the existing British company.

Some technical aspects remained to be improved: to avoid interference between several transmissions and to preserve the secrecy of messages, Marconi developed, and in 1900 patented in the UK and USA, a syntonic system, which made it possible to send signals simultaneously from several stations without interference, using different wavelengths and appropriate induction coils. The principal was to have the same LC product (where L was the induction and C the capacity) in both primary and secondary circuits. With this system it was possible to have partial privacy and transmission distances up to 300 km out to sea. This experiment was of key importance in achieving confidence in the transatlantic transmission which Marconi intended to organize within a few months. This patent, however, was contested by Lodge and Braun. Their own patents were subsequently acquired by Marconi's company.

First transatlantic transmission When, in 1901, Marconi announced his proposals for a transatlantic transmission some scientists were outraged at the news, believing that electromagnetic waves, like optical waves, must travel along straight paths and that it was impossible to send messages beyond such large visible barriers as the curvature of the earth which would intervene between the two sides of the Atlantic Ocean. They supposed that Marconi did not understand the laws of physics and mathematics. The great French physicist Henri Poincaré declared that electromagnetic waves would fade within 300 km. Marconi, however, relied on his earlier trials, where he had already sent signals to receivers beyond the horizon, and confidently organized a transmission from Poldhu in Cornwall to Signal Hill in Newfoundland, about 3400 km. There were many difficulties to overcome in England and the USA, and in Canada severe storms destroyed his very tall antennas, obliging him to resort to a kite-borne antenna raised to about 180 metres. But on 12 December 1901 Marconi received the signal consisting of three dots of Morse code—the letter S. The transmission had been a success. Overnight Marconi became a household name. He was just twenty-seven years old.

Over the following years, while overcoming the initial deficiencies of his system and developing the technology needed for its practical use, Marconi battled with the telegraph cable companies and struggled against those who claimed priority for inventing wireless telegraphy, meanwhile continuing to develop the technology for its practical use. As the coherer did not function well on a rolling ship, Marconi substituted the magnetic detector as a more reliable receiver, first using rotating magnets, and then fixed magnets. His detector, patented in 1902, was perhaps inspired by Ernest Rutherford's article on this subject, published in 1896. From June to September 1902 Marconi, his friend and collaborator Solari, and their technician undertook experiments on board the Italian navy's royal battle cruiser *Carlo Alberto* during her cruise from Naples to Kronstadt and back through the Kiel Canal via Portsmouth and Gibraltar to La Spezia. During these experiments they discovered the negative effect of solar light on transmission, confirmed that signals could be transmitted beyond the high mountains of continental

Europe without any negative effect on the reception of electromagnetic waves, and tried various prototypes of the magnetic detector.

Marconi was undoubtedly helped by the skilful technicians, engineers, and assistants, all knowledgeable about electricity, whom he recruited to his company. It was his great merit to bring together a scientific team, headed by J. A. Fleming, who had been Maxwell's pupil, was a consultant to Edison, and was professor of electrical technology at University College, London. Fleming was the inventor in 1904 of the thermionic valve (the diode) which, in the following years and with the De Forest triode of 1907, became so important for radio transmission. Marconi organized his team effectively and appreciated their qualities; in turn most of them regarded him with veneration.

The multiple spark generator introduced in 1904 and the rotating disc generator of 1905 resulted from Marconi's efforts to avoid the Rumkorff induction coils and the oscillators of Hertz and Righi with their high resistance which was responsible for wave attenuation. Also in 1905 Marconi developed his horizontal directional aerial, later especially for use with short waves. In the same year he married, in London, Beatrice O'Brien (b. 1882), daughter of Edward Donough O'Brien, fourteenth baron of Inchiquin, whose family had been kings of Ireland until the sixteenth century. There were two daughters and a son from this marriage. In 1909 Marconi shared the Nobel prize for physics with Ferdinand Braun, inventor of the cathode ray oscillator.

When the Italian war against the Turkish empire began in October 1911 Marconi was called in to assist the Italian army and navy, as a civil consultant, to connect the military forces on land and sea. He developed portable radio sets, and organized trench stations and aircraft transmitting systems. In November, with Solari's help, he opened powerful radio transmitting stations at Coltrano, near Pisa, inside the royal estate of San Rossore, to provide a military link to those in Tobruk and Darnah. In 1912 he developed a timed spark system to generate continuous waves, which were then modulated for signal transmission.

In 1912, during these military endeavours, Marconi was seen as a benefactor of humanity following the transmission of an SOS message that led to the rescue of about 700 of the 2300 people on board the stricken SS *Titanic*. Hot on the heels of this praise the Marconi scandal blew up. It began with rumours of certain assistance given to Marconi's company by British government ministers who were shareholders in the company. Journalists publicized the fact that these ministers would benefit financially if Marconi's company secured the passage into law of a bill setting up the British Imperial Wireless Network. Asquith's government was almost brought down, but although Marconi suffered some trouble, in the end his merits were recognized and he received an honorary GCVO in 1914.

Short-wave transmission In 1913–14 Marconi investigated the use of the new thermionic valves as transmitters,

bearing in mind Meissner's existing patent. Developing electronic tubes as transmitters, he created the M-round transmitter. At the start of the First World War he enlisted in the Italian army and was transferred to the navy, during which time he introduced short-wave beam systems for military use in sending secret messages and to economize on the energy needed for long-distance transmissions. He introduced more advanced radio range beacons, ground radio beacons, and radiogoniometers. These researches continued in peacetime and the results transformed and enhanced long-distance wireless communication. This was a bold step: about twenty years later the move to enormous radio stations with high and very costly antennas reversed the line of research, developing short-wave technology to improve reliability of communication. Speaking in Rome in 1928 he admitted having made a mistake in working with long waves, and that henceforth he would work with short waves. As usual, his company and other technicians followed his lead.

In his post-war short-wave experiments Marconi was helped by an outstanding new laboratory that he acquired in February 1919, namely the steam yacht *Rowenska*, previously owned by the archdukes of Austria. Renamed *Elettra*, it became his home, laboratory, and mobile receiving station. The Italian poet Gabriele D'Annunzio lauded it as 'la candida nave che naviga nel miracolo e anima i silenti aerei' ('the miraculous snow-white ship which gives life to the ethereal silence'). In 1919 Marconi attended the Versailles peace conference in Paris as the Italian government's plenipotentiary delegate. From the beginning of 1920, after several trials, broadcast transmissions were begun from *Elettra*, stationed in the Atlantic about 48 km from Lisbon, to Monsanto, near Lisbon, where Solari was listening to a loudspeaker connected to the receiver.

In a speech given on 20 June 1922 at the Institute of Radio Engineers in New York, Marconi described how electromagnetic waves could be reflected by conductive bodies, thereby predicting the possibility of receiving information about other ships or objects along a route although there was no direct line of sight. It was the germ of a radar detection system. In 1923 his wife sought an annulment, which was granted the following year. A few years later, in June 1927, Marconi married Maria Cristina Bezzi-Scali, a young woman of noble birth and member of an ancient and extremely well-connected family. They had one daughter, named Elettra. In the same year, on behalf of the British government, he established a radio telegraph network spanning the empire. Honorary degrees and many other marks of distinction were conferred on him from all over the world. The Italian government bestowed a marquessate on him in 1929 and the same year he became the founder president of the CNR (Italian Research Council), and the following year president of the Italian Academy. Marconi was a great propagandist for his own discoveries, thanks to the fame of his international experiments. He both had and made use of his sense of theatre. He was fond of music, a passion perhaps inherited from a musical mother.

During his last years Marconi was involved in several important experiments concerning microwaves, and is remembered for an official demonstration on 30 July 1934, carried out between S. Margherita Ligure and Sestri Levante, in which he demonstrated a radio-beam microwave (60 cm) technique enabling a ship to be steered blind, without compass or any exterior visibility, relying on an instrument to detect the silent zone produced by the interference of microwaves. Of greater military consequence were his further experiments on reflections from objects. According to A. Landini, one of his technicians, he made experiments near Civitavecchia to see if, with 50 cm microwaves, he could detect the movements of his car—another step along the way to radar detection. A great many fantastic discoveries were attributed to Marconi. Some, like the inevitable 'death rays', were mere journalistic fancy; it was true, however, that Marconi had for many years been exploring the possibility of extracting gold from seawater, of transmitting electrical energy over distance, of improving the yield of harvests, and of eliminating bacteria, all by the use of electromagnetic waves. Marconi died at his home, via Condotti 11, Rome, on 20 July 1937, following a series of heart attacks brought on by a form of angina pectoris which had afflicted him for several years.

Assessment Marconi's character was summed up by Professor Quirino Majorana, professor of physics at Bologna University:

> Guglielmo Marconi was not satisfied with his first success, which would have been sufficient to assure him perpetual celebrity; he always led the way in improving his already outstanding system. Thus it was for the syntonic problem, long-distance transmissions, directional transmissions, radiogoniometry, beam-system signalling and, more recently, the matter of short-waves and microwaves. (Q. Majorana, 1932)

No more appropriate, clear and accurate description of Marconi could have been given. The entire world was his experimental laboratory, and he persevered with confidence in the experimental method, though he often struggled against the 'official' scientific opinion. This capability distinguishes him from the numerous other pretenders to the title of inventor of wireless telegraphy.

GIORGIO DRAGONI

Sources D. E. Ravalico, *Marconi giovane* (1966) · M. C. Marconi, *Mio marito Guglielmo* (1995) · A. Colombini, *La vita di Guglielmo Marconi* (1974) · D. Marconi Paresce, *Marconi mio padre* (1993) · O. E. Dunlap, *Marconi, the man and his wireless* (1937) · W. K. Gesses, *Guglielmo Marconi, 1874–1937* (1974) · W. P. Jolly, 'Marconi: a biography', *Nature*, 140 (1937) · W. J. Baker, *A history of the Marconi Company* (1970) · A. Righi, 'I rapporti fra Marconi e Righi', *Ingeneri, Architetti, Construttori*, 25 (1970), 360–61 · A. Righi, 'Giornale di Fisica', no. 4 (1974) · R. Poli, *L'opera tecnico-scientifico di Guglielmo Marconi* (1985) · G. Tabarroni, R. De Benedetti, and G. Masini, *Marconi: cento anni dalla nascita* (Turin, 1974) · B. Cavalieri Ducati, *Guglielmo Marconi, la vita e l'ultima visita à Bologna nel 1934* (1995) · G. Paoloni, F. Monteleone, and M. G. Ianiello, eds., *Cento anni di radio: da Marconi al futuro delle telecomunicazioni* (Venice, 1995) · G. Pancaldi, ed., *Radio da Marconi alla musica delle stelle: from Marconi to the music of the universe* (1995) · P. Poli, *Conosciamo veramente Guglielmo Marconi?* (1979) · P. Poli, ed., *Radiocommunicazioni a grande e a grandissima distanza: celebrazione nazionale del centenario della nascità di Guglielmo Marconi* (1976) · G. di Benedetto, *Bibliografia Marconiana* (1974) · *CGPLA Eng. & Wales* (1938)

Archives GEC Marconi Archives, Chelmsford · Inst. EE, Preece corresp., SC MSS 22/62–69, 122–176 | FILM BFI NFTVA, actuality footage; documentary footage; news footage

Likenesses photograph, 1896, Hult. Arch. [*see illus.*] · F. S. Baden-Powell, drawing, silhouette, 1900, NPG · H. Furniss, pen-and-ink drawing, NPG · A. P. F. Ritchie, cigarette card, NPG

Wealth at death £48,529 4s. 1d.—in England: administration with will, 16 March 1938, *CGPLA Eng. & Wales*

Marcroft, William (1822–1894), co-operative movement activist and company promoter, was born on 15 July 1822 at Box Cottage, Fog Lane, Middleton, Lancashire, the illegitimate son of Sally Marcroft (1801–1841), a farm servant, and Richard Howarth, a weaver. Shortly after his birth he and his mother moved to Heywood, where she eventually married Jacob Aspinal, a weaver. William Marcroft was put to work at the age of six gathering dung on the local turnpike road. Eighteen months later he became a piecer at a Heywood cotton mill, where he remained until he was twelve. He was then apprenticed to a fustian cutter, but left after three years to work as a piecer again before joining Charles Mills's machine-making works in Heywood, where he became a grinder. Shortly after his marriage on 3 March 1844 to Jane Smith, daughter of David Smith, a local brewer, he moved to Oldham, where he worked in Hibbert and Platt's great machine-making works, eventually being promoted to foreman.

Marcroft appears to have had no formal education and his early attempts to educate himself (he attended John Plant's night school in Heywood about 1837) were frustrated by the need to nurse his mother, whose health had collapsed as a result of constant childbearing and poverty. After her death in 1841 he attended night school at the Heywood Mechanics' Institute, where for a time he was an assistant teacher. On arriving in Oldham, he joined the Oddfellows, Rechabites, and the Machine Grinders' Society (of which he was local secretary), attended Chartist meetings, and became an active supporter of W. J. Fox, the radical MP for Oldham between 1847 and 1863. He later wrote of this period that 'my doings in life were become loose' (Marcroft, *Inner Circle*, 15), but after hearing a temperance lecturer he became an ardent teetotaller for the remainder of his life. His earnings at Hibbert and Platt were about £2 a week, and he was determined to save half of this until he had £1000; he would then retire from an arduous and unhealthy occupation. He refused to lend money to neighbours and discouraged the visits of former friends to his house, which behaviour made him so unpopular that he was forced to move home several times.

The collapse of Chartism in 1848 and the defeat of the Amalgamated Society of Engineers in the 1852 lock-out convinced him that the co-operative movement offered the best hope for the working classes. He was accordingly a promoter of the Oldham Industrial Co-operative Society in 1850, and sat on the board of the Co-operative Wholesale Society in 1865, and 1867–71. Above all, however, he was a vigorous advocate of co-operative production, whereby the workers in an establishment held the share capital and received a bonus on profits. In 1857 he helped to promote the Oldham Building and Manufacturing Company Ltd, and when it appeared on the point of failure suggested that it should build the Sun Mill, which eventually would have 90,000 self-acting mule spindles, an extremely large number for that period. While the mill was being built he served as clerk of works and treasurer, having left Hibbert and Platt in 1861 with his £1000 saved, though for a time he may also have practised as a dentist, a profession he had taught himself to supplement his wages. He served as a director of the company in 1859–61, 1862–4, 1865–71, and 1875–7, and as chairman in 1866–7. More than anybody he was responsible for what, as the Sun Mill Company Ltd, was a brilliant success and a model for the Oldham cotton industry. His years with the company, however, were marked by frequent clashes with the other directors, principal servants, and shareholders. In part this was because they increasingly regarded the company as an ordinary commercial concern (in 1867 only four out of over 1000 shareholders worked there). But it was also a consequence of Marcroft's difficult personality. Blunt of speech and contemptuous of anyone who did not share his ideals, he became obsessed with plots against him. Nevertheless his contribution to the co-operative movement was remarkable for he also helped to promote the Oldham Co-operative Insurance Society (1867), the Oldham House and Mill Company Ltd (1867), the Star Corn Mill (1868), the Central Mill Company Ltd (1871), the Federative Insurance Company Ltd (1875), the Oldham Limited Liability Association (1875), and the Cotton Buying Company Ltd (1881). He also became a prolific author, producing several autobiographical works, a history of the Sun Mill Company, and large numbers of pamphlets and articles on co-operative production.

Marcroft had four sons and two daughters (one of whom died aged four in 1862). His considerable business acumen and thrift allowed him and his family to live in some comfort, despite simple food and home-made clothing, and to travel widely throughout the British Isles, the continent, and the USA. The death of his wife on 18 April 1882, shortly after that of his surviving daughter, Emma, in childbirth, clearly unnerved him. He abandoned plans to establish a co-operative village with a cotton mill, sold off his property and shares, and retired for a time to Southport. He died at his home, 85 Roman Road, Failsworth, Lancashire, on 8 September 1894, and was buried in Oldham on 14 September. By then he was very much an anachronism, not only in his old-fashioned forms of speech, but also in his belief in the principles of co-operative production.

R. E. TYSON

Sources W. Marcroft, *The Marcroft family: a history of strange events* (1886) · W. Marcroft, *The inner circle of family life* (1886) · W. Marcroft, *Sun Mill Company Limited: its commercial and social history from 1858 to 1877* (1877) · R. E. Tyson, 'William Marcroft (1822–94) and the limited liability movement in Oldham', *Transactions of the Lancashire and Cheshire Antiquarian Society*, 80 (1979), 60–80 · University of Manchester, records of the Sun Mill Company Ltd · W. Marcroft, *Ups and downs: life in a machine-making works* (1889) · *Oldham Chronicle* (10 Sept 1894) · *Oldham Standard* (10 Sept 1894) · *Oldham Chronicle* (15 Sept 1894) · d. cert.

Likenesses group portrait, photograph, repro. in *Sun Mill Co. Ltd: the story of a great enterprise, 1858–1958* (privately printed, Sun Mill Co. Ltd), facing p. 62 · photograph, repro. in Tyson, 'William Marcroft (1822–94) and the limited liability movement in Oldham', facing p. 64

Wealth at death £14,753: J. Savile, 'Marcroft, William', *DLB*

Marcuard, Robert Samuel (1756–1788?), engraver, was born in England on 25 December 1756 and entered the Royal Academy Schools as an engraver on 31 May 1777. He was a pupil of Francesco Bartolozzi, whose manner he successfully followed, and it is likely that he remained in Bartolozzi's employ until his own death. He produced a large number of stipples after allegorical and fancy pictures, mainly by Angelica Kauffmann, William Hamilton, and G. B. Cipriani. G. K. Nagler mentions two subjects by Marcuard after his own drawings, and he also produced portraits of both Bartolozzi and Ralph Milbank after Joshua Reynolds. The latest date to appear on one of his prints is 1786, and an advertisement of 1788 for the sale of drawings by Marcuard at Bartolozzi's address suggests that he had probably died shortly before that date.

F. M. O'DONOGHUE, rev. ANNE PUETZ

Sources D. Alexander, 'Marcuard, Robert Samuel', *The dictionary of art*, ed. J. Turner (1996) · G. K. Nagler, ed., *Neues allgemeines Künstler-Lexikon*, 22 vols. (Munich, 1835–52) · Redgrave, *Artists* · Thieme & Becker, *Allgemeines Lexikon* · T. Dodd, 'History of English engravers', BL, Add. MS 33403 · Bryan, *Painters* (1886–9) · Bénézit, *Dict.*, 3rd edn · *Engraved Brit. ports.*, 6.651

Mardall, Cyril Leonard Sjöström (1909–1994), architect, was born Cyril Leonard Sjöström on 21 November 1909 in Helsinki, Finland, the only child of Einar Johannes Sjöström (*d.* 1922/3), architect, and his English wife, Phyllis Eleanor, *née* Mardall (*b.* 1888), opera singer. Educated in Finland, he moved to England in 1927 and was naturalized in 1928. He trained at the school of architecture of the Polytechnic of North London from 1927 to 1931, when he won a scholarship to the Architectural Association School, and was awarded its diploma in 1932. After a year in Finland working for Ole Gripenberg on a design for the stadium for the Olympic games, which won second prize, he returned to London in 1933, and started his own practice in Bedford Square, also teaching part-time at the Architectural Association School until 1939. He was knowledgeable about the use of prefabricated timber houses, which were widely used in Sweden and Finland, and he was asked by Lord Forrester to design terraces to house members of the Subsistence Production Society in Brynmawr, south Wales. He also designed a community centre for Bryn-mawr, and timber farm cottages for Forrester's Gorhambury estate: none of these was built. As part of the government's attempt to deal with the housing shortage in Scotland, he was asked to supervise the erection of 200 timber houses, just before the Second World War. During the war he served as an intelligence officer in the Royal Naval Volunteer Reserve until 1944, when he was seconded to the United Nations Relief and Rehabilitation Administration to head the section dealing with rebuilding in Europe. On 17 January 1947 (by which time he had taken the surname Mardall) he married (Hilary) June

Bosanquet (b. 1920/21), architect, who designed their house in Fitzroy Park, Battersea. She was the former wife of David Francis Rivers Bosanquet, and the daughter of Bertram Charles Percival Park, a photographer. They had one son and one daughter.

In 1944 Mardall joined Francis Reginald Stevens *Yorke (1906–1962), author of *The Modern House* (1934) and a founder member of the Modern Architectural Research Group, and the Czech Eugene Rosenberg (1907–1990) in founding an architectural partnership, originally called by their names including their initials, then just their names, and finally YRM. Dedicated to the modern international style of architecture of the 1930s, to start with it was a loose association of three separate but equal design partnerships, based from 1947 in an office in Hyde Park Place, with regular evening meetings to discuss each other's projects. One of Mardall's first contracts was to build housing at Bryn-mawr in 1950, including a block of flats in timber and brick, and brick terraces. Committed to establishing modern architecture as the architecture of the post-war state, the firm concentrated on work for public authorities, in four main areas: housing, schools and colleges, hospitals, and airports. As the firm grew, the number of partners increased to six, and when they moved to newly built offices in Greystoke Place in 1961, organizational changes were put into place: from then on the partners operated as a single body, while still taking on responsibility for particular projects.

Mardall specialized in housing and schools, and was closely involved in the design of housing for Stevenage and Harlow new towns. As a result of the Education Act (1944) there was a demand for new schools, and the partnership had several local authority clients, especially Hertfordshire county council, which had a strong interest in modern architecture. The first school built by the firm was the Barclay secondary school in Stevenage (1950), famous for its Henry Moore sculpture, *Family Group*. Mardall worked on over forty schools and technical colleges: his designs in the 1950s were strongly influenced by the Scandinavian style, as in Queensmead secondary school in Ruislip, Middlesex (1954), with timber cladding on the upper floor. In the 1960s he developed a brick and concrete design, which was used for many schools in Essex, including Barstable School in Basildon, and Mildmay secondary school, near Thurrock (1964). In addition to his local authority work, he had private clients, and he designed the Finnish Seamen's Mission (1958) in Bermondsey, London. In 1966 he was made a commander of the order of the Lion of Finland. After he retired from YRM in 1975 he entered into private practice with his wife, concentrating mainly on housing projects in Finland and the Caribbean. He died on 1 June 1994 at his home, 5 Boyne Terrace Mews, Kensington, London, survived by his wife and their two children. A funeral service was held at the Finnish church in London on 9 June.

ANNE PIMLOTT BAKER

Sources A. Powers, *In the line of development: FRS Yorke, E Rosenberg, and CS Mardall to YRM, 1930–1992* (1992) · *The architecture of Yorke,* *Rosenberg, Mardall, 1944–1972* (1972), with an introduction by R. Banham · 'The work of Yorke, Rosenberg and Mardall', *Architectural Design*, 36 (June 1966), 276–307 · C. Davies, 'Modern masters', *Building*, 240 (20 March 1981) · *The Times* (15 June 1994) · Grove, *Dictionary of art* · naturalization details, PRO, HO 334/118/B.826 · m. cert. · d. cert.

Archives SOUND BL NSA, oral history interview

Likenesses S. Lambert, group photograph, 1950–54, YRM Ltd, London; *see illus. in* Yorke, Francis Reginald Stevens (1906–1962) · photograph, 1950–54, repro. in *The Times*

Wealth at death £313,465: probate, 22 Sept 1994, CGPLA Eng. & Wales

Mardeley, John (*fl.* 1548–1558), government official and author, wrote a series of polemical protestant poems, including *A shorte resytal of certayne holy doctours whych proveth that the naturall body of Christ is not conteyned in the sacrament of the Lordes supper but fyguratyvely*, partly written in Skeltonic metre (Collier, 1.515–16). It was published by Thomas Raynolde probably in 1548 and, according to W. T. Lowndes, was 'written in answer to John Aungell's *Agreement of the Holy Fathers and Doctors*' (Lowndes, 3.1471).

Mardeley's critique of transubstantiation was continued in a prose treatise, *A Declaration of the Power of Gods Worde Concerning the Holy Supper of the Lord*, published by Raynolde in 1548 and dedicated to Protector Somerset. It attacked those bishops resistant to Edward VI's religious reforms and who sought 'His godly reformacion, utterly to delay' (sig. A1v). Mardeley was committed to the idea of a reformed church, and a further prose treatise, *A Necessary Instruction for All Courteous Men*, published by Raynolde probably in 1548, provided opportunity for a caustic aside on how 'gready al kinde of men' 'be in these dayes, as wel the clergye as the layitie' (sig. A2r).

Under Edward VI, Mardeley was clerk of the mint. Unsurprisingly, considering his strong affiliations to protestantism, he published nothing during the reign of Mary, but greeted the accession of Elizabeth in 1558 with an extended poetic treatise on 'The supper of the Lord' presented to the queen in manuscript form (BL, MS 17 B.xxxvii). In this work Mardeley celebrated England's release from Marian persecutions and urged the new monarch to 'Redresse the abuses of the spiritualitie' (fol. 17v). As a poet, Mardeley tapped into vernacular traditions of Skeltonic metre and the idioms of Wyatt's epistolary satires.

Bale credits Mardeley with various works (now lost) in verse and prose, including a book 'On the ingratitude of the Scots', verse translation of twenty-four psalms, and 'The complaint of the English republic', probably the anonymous *A Ruful Complaynt of the Publyke Weale to Englande*, printed between 1547 and 1553?, owing to which work, according to Bale, Mardeley 'only evaded death with great difficulty' (Bale, *Cat.*, 2.106–7). Some verse translations in the psalter of 1562 signed M and attributed by Haslewood to Mardeley are by John Marckant.

Mardeley may have been the John Mardeley of the parish of St Katharine Cree, London, whose wife, Eleanor, was granted administration of his estate on 25 January 1560.

CATHY SHRANK

Sources W. T. Lowndes, *The bibliographer's manual of English literature*, ed. H. G. Bohn, [new edn], 3 (1864) · T. Warton, *The history of English poetry*, new edn, ed. W. C. Hazlitt, 4 vols. (1871) · W. C. Hazlitt, *Hand-book to the popular, poetical and dramatic literature of Great Britain* (1867) · R. Ruding, *Annals of the coinage of Great Britain and its dependencies*, 3rd edn, 1 (1840) · Bale, *Cat.*, vol. 2 · J. P. Collier, ed., *A bibliographical and critical account of the rarest books in the English language*, 1 (1865) · PRO, PROB 6/1, fol. 3r

Marder, Arthur Jacob (1910–1980), naval historian, was born in Boston, Massachusetts, USA, on 8 March 1910, the son of Maxwell J. Marder, a tailor, and his wife, Ida, *née* Greenstein. He was educated at Harvard University, where he gained his PhD in 1936. On the suggestion of the Harvard diplomatic historian William L. Langer, he had written his senior undergraduate dissertation on the Haldane mission of 1912. Langer thus started Marder's lifetime of work on the Royal Navy.

Marder first taught at the University of Oregon (1936–8), and then returned to Harvard as a research associate (1939–41). His first published work appeared in 1940 in the USA: *British Naval Policy, 1880–1905*. The worsening international situation and Marder's knowledge of German led to his becoming a research analyst in the office of strategic services in Washington, DC, from 1941 to 1942. The rest of his career was as a university teacher, his two main professorial appointments being at the University of Hawaii (1944–64) and finally at Irvine, a new campus of the University of California (1964–77).

Marder's first work to be published in the United Kingdom was *Portrait of an Admiral: the Life and Papers of Sir Herbert Richmond* (1952). Richmond himself was a historian, but Marder first approached him regarding his personal knowledge of Lord Fisher of Kilverstone. During their meeting Marder came across Richmond's diaries, which he used to good effect. Marder subsequently established his reputation among a wider reading public with three volumes (1952–9) based on the correspondence and papers of Fisher entitled *Fear God and Dread Nought*. The great hero of the main corpus of Marder's writing was Fisher.

In Britain doors opened more easily to Marder, an American, than to British-born historians, and his charm allied to persistence gave him a large number of informants, of whom one of the earliest was Nina, duchess of Hamilton, a literary executor of Fisher. A few whom Marder approached, G. M. Trevelyan for one, did not receive him so well, but a burgeoning network of contacts gave him access to materials not readily available to earlier historians of the First World War. His industry and thoroughness combined with a gift for narrative and description produced outstanding historical writing.

Marder's tempo of work was determined by the great distance of his sources and informants from his university teaching posts. Long vacations and sabbaticals were of necessity spent in the United Kingdom. The limited time at his disposal meant a highly structured workday with a furious pace of research. There were no long lunches, though he would enjoy a sherry in the early evening. In contrast to his specialized research in the United Kingdom, Marder's undergraduate teaching in the USA was of the general history variety. He was a dedicated teacher and a reliable colleague but he never taught naval history to American undergraduates and had relatively few graduate students. His narrative history inspired no academic following.

Marder's greatest work came in the years 1961–70 with the publication of his five-volume history of the Royal Navy, *From the Dreadnought to Scapa Flow*; that is, the pre-First World War years through to 1919. The *Battle of Jutland* volume with a second edition in 1978 was particularly distinguished. The continuation and conclusion of this *magnum opus* was delayed by a janitor at the University of Hawaii, who accidentally destroyed most of his materials for the 1915–19 years; but, as Marder readily admitted, his second working on the material only made better the final product.

The years after completion of his greatest work were less felicitous. Marder was no reactionary, but in the late 1960s and the decade of the 1970s the strident non-negotiable demands of radical students and the narcissistic self-indulgence and irresponsibility of junior colleagues were a sore trial. His retirement, short as it turned out, was industrious and exilic rather than golden.

In the last phase of his career, Marder did not rest on his laurels. He moved on to the inter-war period and then to the Second World War. In 1974 came a volume of studies entitled *From the Dardanelles to Oran*. The 1976 *Operation Menace* concentrated on the Admiral Sir Dudley North affair of 1940. Marder accepted the suggestion of Professor Alvin Coox of California State University, San Diego, that he work on the imperial Japanese navy and the Royal Navy in the Second World War. He applied his customary methods in gaining Japanese material, but he could not, partly because of cultural differences, succeed in establishing a similar degree of rapport with former officers of the imperial Japanese navy as he had with those of the Royal Navy. Fatal pancreatic cancer prevented his seeing publication of the first volume of such a study. He was permitted only to start work on the second volume, though he had amassed most of the research material. The first volume of *Old Friends, New Enemies*, published posthumously in 1981, described the relations of the two navies until the sinking of the *Repulse* and the *Prince of Wales* in 1941. The work was received with customary critical acclaim. The second volume, bringing the story to the allied victory in 1945, was completed by two former graduate students of Marder, John Horsfield and Mark Jacobsen, and was published in 1990.

It would be difficult to fault Marder's published work. If he erred, it was in seeing his subjects in too heroic a light. Thus in dealing with the imperial Japanese navy, he might have emphasized to his readers that, despite all the heroism, that navy indulged at times in acts of great cruelty and barbarism. His writing on the Royal Navy amounts to a viewpoint of the élite and the upper deck, reflecting a knowledge of British society very much confined to that of the higher echelons of the public service and academia.

Marder was much honoured. In 1968 he was awarded

the Chesney medal of the Royal United Services Institution. In 1969–70 he was George Eastman professor at Oxford University, and in 1970 he received an Admiralty board citation. In the following year he was particularly honoured as an American with an honorary CBE, while Oxford awarded him an honorary DLitt, the offer of which he accepted with his customary speedy dispatch of business by return of post.

In 1977, on his retirement, Marder and his wife, Jan North (d. 1985), whom he had married in 1955, left Orange county and moved to Montecito, convenient for the University of California at Santa Barbara. He died at his home, 730 Woodland Drive, Santa Barbara, California, USA, on 25 December 1980.   JOHN HORSFIELD

Sources WWW · personal knowledge (2004) · private information (2004) · *The Times* (29 Dec 1980)
Archives U. Cal., Irvine, special collections and archives, corresp. and papers | King's Lond., Liddell Hart C., corresp. with Sir B. H. Liddell Hart | SOUND BL NSA, recorded talk

Mardisley, John (*fl.* 1350–1375), Franciscan friar and theologian, was probably born in the 1320s, and entered the order at its Oxford convent. He studied in Oxford in the 1340s and became doctor of theology soon after 1350. By 1355 he was a member of the York convent; probably in that year he disputed there with the Dominican William Jordan in the chapter house and the chancellor's school on the subject of the conception of the Blessed Virgin Mary. Given these locations, this must have been intended as a formal academic exercise, but Mardisley seems to have attracted bitter criticism for his opinions, from Jordan himself and other observers, and the chapter at York found it necessary to issue letters exonerating him. Mardisley seems to have followed up his verbal defence of this doctrine with a written exposition of his arguments; it was known to Bale but no longer survives.

Scarcely more than a year later he had become involved in further controversy, joining another Franciscan, Roger Conway (d. 1360), in replying to Richard Fitzralph's attacks on the mendicants. Mardisley's growing reputation as an outspoken theologian may explain his appointment in May 1374, together with a Dominican and a Benedictine, to deliberate at a great council in Westminster Hall over the right of the pope to interfere in temporal affairs in England. The meeting of the council, and Mardisley's contribution, is discussed in some detail in a contemporary chronicle, the *Eulogium historiarum*, compiled by a monk of Glastonbury. The Dominican refused to answer, and the Benedictine, Uthred Boldon (d. 1397), resolutely defended papal authority. Mardisley gave a more detailed answer, and somewhat surprisingly, given his status, upheld the claims of the crown that Christ conferred only spiritual rule on Peter, not earthly dominion. His argument can be seen as an attempt by the English Franciscans to improve their political position and to win royal favour. The drama of the scene and the uncompromising nature of the dialogue led earlier historians to assume that the entire episode was fictional, contrived by the chronicler in order to raise some important and controversial issues, but it has since been shown to have taken place.

Mardisley was elected minister provincial of the order in England in 1375. He resigned his office towards the end of the 1370s, and probably died at the York convent within a decade and was buried there. Bale suggests he died in 1376, but his evidence for this is obscure. Several theological works have been attributed to Mardisley, but none is known to survive. A commentary on the *Sentences* of Peter Lombard which survives in Padua, MS Antoniana IX 159, was for some time thought to be the work of Mardisley, but is now believed to be the work of another author.   JAMES G. CLARK

Sources Emden, *Oxf.*, 2.1222 · Bale, *Cat.*, 1.486 · Bale, *Index*, 232 · F. S. Haydon, ed., *Eulogium historiarum sive temporis*, 3 vols., Rolls Series, 9 (1858), vol. 3, pp. 337–8 · M. E. Marcett, *Uthred de Boldon, Friar William Jordan and Piers Plowman* (1938), 52–4 · J. I. Catto, 'An alleged great council of 1374', *EngHR*, 82 (1967), 764–71

Mare, Sir Peter de la (*fl.* c.1365–1387), speaker of the House of Commons, was probably the son of Sir Reynold de la Mare, a Herefordshire knight. His brother Malcolm was also prominent in Herefordshire and in some parliaments. For some years before October 1371 Peter de la Mare had been collector of the tolls from the iron mines of the Forest of Dean. From December 1372 to July 1373 he was sheriff of Herefordshire. In 1373 he was a member of the commission to raise troops in Herefordshire, Worcestershire, and Shropshire to accompany Edmund (III) Mortimer, earl of March (d. 1381), to Ireland, while in November 1374 he was one of the feoffees to whom March was licensed to enfeoff various estates on the Welsh border, which were later leased back to the earl for a nominal rent. The Mortimer link was no doubt the crucial factor behind de la Mare's political importance—he was later said to have been retained for life to serve the earl in peace and war, and to be the earl's steward.

Peter de la Mare came into prominence in the Good Parliament of April to July 1376, which he attended as knight of the shire for Herefordshire and in which he was appointed speaker of the Commons, the first named holder of this position. He probably owed this to his connection with Mortimer, who had become disaffected with the government in the 1370s, and consequently sympathized with the Commons' attack on the court, becoming a member of the council appointed as a result of demands made by the Commons. The Good Parliament was effective because it embodied a remarkable alliance of varied class interests against the corrupt court of the later years of Edward III: commons offended by the waste of taxpayers' money, merchants anxious to reassert the control of the staple over the wool trade, nobles and bishops critical of the crown's foreign policy, which had been managed by the duke of Lancaster rather than the king. De la Mare acted as spokesman for this collection of interests, and the detailed account of the parliament in the Anonimalle chronicle presents dramatically his forthright adoption of the role of spokesman, summing up the Commons' views to be presented to the Lords, as a critical moment in the whole evolution of parliamentary institutions. As speaker he was decidedly not a spokesman for the crown, but was partly responsible for the feast held at the end of the parliament to celebrate the success of the Commons in damaging the position of Alice Perrers (d. 1400/01), Lord Latimer (d. 1381), and others at court.

The political tide, however, turned quickly in favour of the court in the next few weeks. De la Mare was summoned to appear before the council in November 1376, and then imprisoned in Nottingham Castle. During the so-called 'Bad Parliament' early in 1377, when the court was effectively in control, demands by the Commons and by Londoners that he should be released were rejected. His release eventually came immediately after the death of Edward III in June 1377. His return to London under the new king, Richard II, was much celebrated in the city. He was pardoned and later rewarded by the crown, and his expenses in prison compensated. In the parliament of October 1377 de la Mare was again knight of the shire for Herefordshire, and was once again elected speaker, presumably in accordance with the renewed ascendancy of the political wing with which he had been connected in the Good Parliament, and which revived the attack on Alice Perrers, the mistress of Edward III, who apparently regarded de la Mare as an enemy.

In May 1379 de la Mare was appointed to the commission to assess the poll tax in Herefordshire. He was later pardoned for neglect of this duty, on the grounds that he had accompanied the earl of March, appointed lieutenant of Ireland in October 1379. In January 1380, however, he again became knight of the shire for Herefordshire. March crossed to Ireland in May 1380, after appointing de la Mare one of the attorneys for his absence, and also one of his executors. De la Mare was made justice of the peace for Herefordshire in May 1380, and then sat as knight of the shire for the fourth time in the parliament of November and December 1380. When the peasants' revolt broke out in 1381 he was appointed to commissions to resist rebels in Herefordshire. In the same year he appears to have been involved in the administration of the cathedral church of Hereford. After the death of the earl of March in December 1381 de la Mare was one of his executors, and also one of the trustees of the Mortimer estates in many counties; their position as trustees was confirmed by the crown on condition of their paying a rent to the exchequer. He represented Herefordshire in the parliaments of May 1382, October 1382, and February 1383. After the death of Sir Richard Burley in Spain with the duke of Lancaster in 1387 de la Mare was one of his feoffees. That is the last known mention of him. The date of his death is unknown and he may have been unmarried.

GEORGE HOLMES

Sources J. S. Roskell, 'Sir Peter de la Mare, speaker for the Commons in parliament in 1376 and 1377', *Nottingham Mediaeval Studies*, 2 (1958), 24–37 · V. H. Galbraith, ed., *The Anonimalle chronicle, 1333 to 1381* (1927) · [T. Walsingham], *Chronicon Angliae, ab anno Domini 1328 usque ad annum 1388*, ed. E. M. Thompson, Rolls Series, 64 (1874) · *Chancery records* · G. Holmes, *The Good Parliament* (1975)
Archives PRO, E 159

Mare, Petronilla de la (b. 1248, d. in or before 1292). *See under* Dunstanville, de, family (*per. c.*1090–*c.*1292).

Mare, Thomas de la (c.1309–1396), abbot of St Albans, was perhaps born in Northumberland, where he is known to have had family connections. He was related to several noble families: through his father, John de la Mare, and his mother, Joanna (both c.1275–c.1340), daughter of Sir John Harpsfield, he claimed kinship with William Montagu, earl of Salisbury, William, Lord Zouche, and John Grandison, the distinguished bishop of Exeter.

Novice, prior, and abbot Thomas de la Mare was one of five children, and his three brothers and his sister followed him into the religious life, two brothers also becoming monks at St Albans. Nothing is known of his early life, but he probably studied for a time at a local grammar school. He must have entered St Albans in his late teens, because according to the *Gesta abbatum* he made his profession soon after the election of Abbot Richard of Wallingford in 1326. He passed his novitiate year at the abbey's dependent priory at Wymondham, Norfolk, and returned there after his profession to serve as chaplain to the prior. According to the *Gesta*, while at Wymondham, he also devoted himself to the study of the *ars dictaminis* and rhetoric and became so proficient in letter-writing that later, when he became abbot, he composed all his own letters himself, including correspondence with the pope.

De la Mare was recalled to St Albans in 1336 and was made an obedientiary, serving first as kitchener and then in the more substantial office of cellarer. In 1340 he was appointed prior of the abbey's dependent priory at Tynemouth, Northumberland. Located near the Scottish border the community had suffered repeated attacks and had almost fallen into ruin. De la Mare appears to have succeeded in reviving both its material fortunes and religious life. He attracted the support of substantial local patrons, such as the Percys, to whom he became confessor, and implemented a series of wide-ranging internal reforms. In particular, he encouraged the monks to engage in intellectual activities and invited scholars from nearby houses to teach and preach in the community. He forged especially close links with the monks and scholars in the circle of the archbishop of York, John Thoresby, and with the Augustinian friars at the York convent, one of whom, Dr John Waldeby, later dedicated a series of homilies on the apostles' creed to de la Mare. In early 1349, following the death of Michael Mentmore, de la Mare returned to St Albans and was elected abbot. The black death was at its height, fifty monks in addition to Mentmore had died from the pestilence, and although he was not the preferred candidate, de la Mare seems to have emerged as the best prospect after the monks' first choice, Prior Henry Steukly, had himself fallen ill. Following his election de la Mare travelled to Avignon to receive papal benediction. Shortly after arrival he became ill, having drunk infected water. According to the *Gesta* he came near to death, but experienced a miraculous recovery through the agency of St Alban: despite this, news reached the abbey that he had

Thomas de la Mare (*c*.1309–1396), memorial brass

and Alice Perrers, as well as more local figures. His dispute with John Chiltern, a Langley tenant, continued for almost thirty years, between the 1360s and 1390s. He also brought actions against landowners and patrons who threatened the independence of the St Albans cells: his dispute with Henry Despenser, bishop of Norwich, over the latter's appointment of the prior of Binham as collector of a subsidy was only resolved through royal mediation.

In most of these disputes de la Mare emerged victorious, but the cost to the community was considerable and even at his death there remained debts arising from his litigation. De la Mare also continued to negotiate through his proctors in the curia for further confirmation of the abbey's exemptions, and before his death he had succeeded in securing several important new privileges, including certain episcopal rights for the abbot, release from the latter's obligation to receive papal benediction in person, and exemption from the reversion of abbatial resources to the crown during a vacancy. In the first decades of his administration de la Mare also dedicated himself to raising the profile of the shrine of St Albans. He encouraged pilgrimage to the church, inaugurating a lavish procession on the martyr's feast day and building extensive new accommodation for visitors: in 1368 the cortège bearing the body of Blanche, duchess of Lancaster, to London halted for a night's vigil at St Albans. About 1376 he refounded the abbey confraternity, and over the next decades attracted a succession of distinguished figures to become members, including Richard II, his mother, Joan of Kent, Robert de Vere, earl of Oxford, and Sir Lewis Clifford. About 1379 he attempted to establish a similar confraternity for the townsmen in the church of St Peter at St Albans, but their hostility forced him to abandon the project.

De la Mare was above all a determined administrator, but he also did much to encourage education and scholarship among his monks. He introduced a more rigorous curriculum of studies into the cloister and even taught liturgy and song himself. He also encouraged able monks to attend the universities, constructed separate chambers where they might pursue their studies, and made significant benefactions to Gloucester College, the Benedictine studium in Oxford. He bought and commissioned a large number of new books for use in the cloister, and in the 1370s constructed a new scriptorium in which, under the supervision of the chronicler Thomas Walsingham, a wide range of new books was compiled and copied. He also began work on a conventual library above the cloister, which was completed after his death. He was a supportive patron of his own monks' scholarship: he encouraged Walsingham in his historical writing, and between 1377 and 1385 he commissioned Nicholas Radcliffe to compile a series of dialogues on the errors of Wyclif. He also offered his patronage to other scholars and artists, attracting to St Albans such figures as the illuminator Alan Strayler, and the architect Henry Yevele.

died. Before his return de la Mare entered into negotiations with the authorities in the curia to secure confirmation of the abbey's many exemptions and privileges. His efforts were inconclusive, and so costly that no abbot travelled to the papacy again for eighty years.

Reforming abbot of St Albans After his return to St Albans in 1350 de la Mare concentrated his energies on repairing the damage done to community life by the black death. In 1351 he issued a series of reforming constitutions for St Albans and its dependent cells. He also conducted a thorough visitation of all the communities and churches under his jurisdiction, and established an annual chapter at which disciplinary problems were resolved and further reforming constitutions ratified. The rigour of his administration was such that Thomas Walsingham compared his rule to that of Julius Caesar. In addition, he began a substantial programme of rebuilding, renewing the abbot's chambers, the cloister, the dormitory, and the infirmary, and constructing a fortified gatehouse at the main entrance to the abbey. He also sought to increase the community's income, both by improving the administration of his officials and through the acquisition of a wide range of properties in the St Albans area and in London: according to the *Gesta* he even surrendered some of his own income to increase the abbey's resources. De la Mare's efforts to revive the fortunes of St Albans also led him to enter into litigation with a considerable number of local landowners and tenants. He fought protracted and very public battles over rights, rents, and taxation with the king's escheator, John of Gaunt, duke of Lancaster,

Spokesman for the Benedictines In addition to his work for his own community de la Mare also pursued a very public career as a leader and spokesman for the Benedictine order in England. He served as president of the order's general chapter continuously from the 1350s to the end of the 1380s, and played a key role in its efforts to reform English communities. In 1363 he compiled and issued a series of statutes to reinvigorate monastic study at the universities, making substantial changes to the curriculum and requiring each community to support its students with sufficient funds. His reputation led Edward III in the 1360s to appoint him to conduct visitations and introduce reforms at Abingdon, Battle, Chester, Eynsham, and Reading. In the 1370s he was also called upon to settle a rebellion and supervise an abbatial election at Bury St Edmunds. He was, however, also a vigorous and vocal defender of the monasteries' traditional independence. In 1389 he intervened on behalf of Gloucester College in its dispute with William Courtenay, archbishop of Canterbury, over a threatened visitation, and persuaded Courtenay to abandon his plans not only in Oxford but with regard to all exempt houses within his province.

In his defence of his own house and of his order as a whole de la Mare benefited from close relations with the crown—he seems to have been on intimate terms with Edward III almost from the time of his election. Walsingham recalls the 'great love' shown to the abbot by the king, and makes uncorroborated claims that the king appointed de la Mare a member of his privy council. Edward was certainly a frequent visitor to St Albans and a considerable benefactor, but the evidence suggests de la Mare actually enjoyed closer relations with his son Edward, the Black Prince, who intervened on several occasions to defend de la Mare and protect the interests of St Albans. The Black Prince's register records a number of gifts of plate and wine to the abbot.

The exemplary monk In the course of his career de la Mare emerged as a distinguished public figure of no small political importance. But according to the memoir in the *Gesta abbatum* he also continued to adhere to the highest monastic and ascetic ideals in his personal life. He submitted to frequent flagellation and other mortifications of the flesh, and observed frequent vigils, often reciting the psalter alone 'while the other monks slept' (*Gesta abbatum*, 3.403). He was said to have abstained from meat and other rich food, even when entertaining important visitors, and forswore the hawking and hunting enjoyed by many in the community. In the late 1350s he seems to have undergone a spiritual crisis, and encouraged by Jean II, king of France, who was held captive at St Albans, he briefly contemplated retiring from the abbacy to lead a solitary ascetic life. In addition to these mortifications de la Mare also continued to pursue his studies in scripture and other devotional literature. In his theological knowledge, according to Walsingham, he surpassed 'the sum of learned clergy' (*Gesta abbatum*, 3.409).

De la Mare suffered from poor health for much of his life. Although unaffected in 1349, he was struck down in the second wave of pestilence in the 1360s and never fully recovered, his infirmity being compounded by his own punishing regime of abstinence. Even before the end of the 1380s illness had forced him to pass many duties over to his younger officials. From 1390 to his death in 1396 the community was effectively governed by the cellarer, John Moot. De la Mare's long decline undermined much of what he had achieved: his long absences from parliament led to the abbot of Westminster's claim to the title of first among the parliamentary abbots, and St Albans was once more threatened by the king's escheator. But he continued to be regarded as a distinguished elder statesman, and even on his deathbed he was visited by Richard II, John of Gaunt, and the archbishops of Canterbury and York. De la Mare died on 15 September 1396 and was buried in the north aisle of the abbey church beneath an elaborate Flemish brass which he himself had commissioned. He was regarded in later generations as the greatest of all the abbots of St Albans, and his achievements were celebrated in various lives written during the fifteenth century.   JAMES G. CLARK

Sources *Gesta abbatum monasterii Sancti Albani, a Thoma Walsingham*, ed. H. T. Riley, 3 vols., pt 4 of *Chronica monasterii S. Albani*, Rolls Series, 28 (1867–9), vol. 2, pp. 371–449; vol. 3, pp. 1–423 · [T. Walsingham], *Chronicon Angliae, ab anno Domini 1328 usque ad annum 1388*, ed. E. M. Thompson, Rolls Series, 64 (1874) · *Thomae Walsingham, quondam monachi S. Albani, historia Anglicana*, ed. H. T. Riley, 2 vols., pt 1 of *Chronica monasterii S. Albani*, Rolls Series, 28 (1863–4) · *Annales monasterii S. Albani a Johanne Amundesham*, ed. H. T. Riley, 2 vols., pt 5 of *Chronica monasterii S. Albani*, Rolls Series, 28 (1870–71), vol. 1, pp. 418–50; vol. 2, pp. 255–372 · CCC Cam., MS 7, fols. 92r–100r · CUL, MS Ee.4.20 · D. Knowles [M. C. Knowles], *The religious orders in England*, 2 (1955), 38–48 · D. H. Farmer, 'Thomas de la Mare & Uthred of Boldon', *Benedict's disciples*, ed. D. H. Farmer (1979), 212–24 · A. Gwyn, *The English Austin friars* (1940), 119–21 · G. G. Coulton, *Five centuries of religion*, 4 (1950) · H. E. Salter, W. A. Pantin, and H. G. Richardson, eds., *Formularies which bear on the history of Oxford*, 1, OHS, new ser., 4 (1942), 232–3 · *Johannis de Trokelowe et Henrici de Blaneforde … chronica et annales*, ed. H. T. Riley, pt 3 of *Chronica monasterii S. Albani*, Rolls Series, 28 (1866) · BL, Harley MS 3775, fol. 130r

Archives BL, Cotton MS Claudius E.iv · Bodl. Oxf., MS Bodley 292 · CUL, register, MS Ee.4.20

Likenesses memorial brass, St Albans Cathedral [*see illus.*] · portrait, BL, Cotton MS Nero D.vii · portrait, CUL, MS 7

Mare, Walter John de la (1873–1956), poet and writer, was born on 25 April 1873 at 83 Maryon Road, Charlton, near Woolwich, London, the sixth of the seven children of James Edward Delamare (1811–1877), principal of the accountant's bank note office, Bank of England, and his second wife, Lucy Sophia (1838–1920). Her father was Dr Colin Arrott Browning, fiery reformer of conditions on board convict transports and staff surgeon to the naval dockyard, Woolwich. The Delamare forebears were Huguenot silk merchants; the poet restored the French form of their name. The Arrotts and Brownings were Scottish evangelicals with a marked bent for medicine.

De la Mare (known as Jack and later WJ) was a chorister of St Paul's Cathedral choir school, founded its *Choristers' Journal*, and at nearly seventeen joined the statistics department of the Anglo-American Oil Company. He drudged through eighteen ill-paid years (1890–1908), adding, copying, compiling elaborate sales sheets, detesting the company's ruthlessness under Rockefeller. Staying

Walter John de la Mare (1873–1956), by Howard Coster, 1934

late after hours, using office waste paper, he experimented with story and verse, struggling for publication, and pursued an isolated self-education.

On 7 August 1899 de la Mare married (Constance) Elfrida (1862–1943), eldest child of William Alfred Ingpen, clerk to the insolvent debtors' court and clerk of the rules. They had two daughters and two sons; Richard, the elder, became chairman of Faber and Faber and a prolific publisher of his father. De la Mare was passionately paternal.

In youth de la Mare had dark romantic looks, favoured aesthete fashions of the 1890s, and enjoyed amateur acting. Later he grew stocky, his head impressive for its strong, concentrated cast of feature—engaging and mobile in talk. His highly individual conversation consisted mostly of questioning—reflective, humorous, dealing in imaginative ideas rather than personalities, constantly off at a tangent. Though warm and widely sociable, he seemed inwardly essentially private. Besides books (he read omnivorously) he delighted in the English scene (travelling abroad reluctantly and seldom), especially in whatever was minute or odd, romantic or grotesque. Poetry was the ruling passion; this only increased with age.

His own output was prodigious: de la Mare published over a thousand poems and rhymes. The poems are marked by subtle and memorable rhythms, and often minor in key; many are masterly and haunting. His real career began late, when he was nearing thirty, with *Songs of Childhood* (1902), published under the pen-name Walter Ramal (discarded only in 1904). Some of these poems aim

directly at child readers, others recreate the state of childhood itself—to him always life's summit—its pure wonder, intuitions, solitary fantasy, and above all its readiness to see this world as part of another, no less real for being magical and spiritual. Fairy-tale, ballad, incantation, make-believe, and dream provide a symbolism not escapist, but selected for more accurate penetration of this other, elusive, 'Real'.

De la Mare's first prose book, *Henry Brocken* (1904), is tentative; the hero, wandering on horseback, encounters random figures from books—Jane Eyre, Gulliver, the doctor in *Macbeth*. It is critical appreciation in romance form, not by analysis but through a kind of oblique, original illustration. Allied experiments (in verse) on Shakespearian characters brought the eager championship of Henry Newbolt, who succeeded finally in securing for de la Mare a £200 royal bounty grant (1908)—enough to risk quitting oil to rely wholly on fiction, poetry, and reviewing (chiefly for the *Saturday Westminster Gazette* and *Times Literary Supplement*). A civil-list pension followed in 1915.

Once free, de la Mare wrote an arresting novel, *The Return* (1910). The hero, leading a mediocre, suburban life, becomes possessed (almost) by the evil, but much more intelligent, spirit of a long-dead Huguenot suicide. By the time the hero repels him (at the cost of all former security) he has himself changed fundamentally, aware now of a profound, enigmatic spiritual context not guessed at before. De la Mare's sense of death as an opening rather than a shutting door is sharply presented.

'Now and again over one's mind comes the glamour of a kind of visionary world saturating this', de la Mare wrote to Naomi Royde-Smith (8 August 1911). This was for him life's central experience: all he wrote concerned it. Popular recognition came gradually for an outlook so unusual. He became well known only with the poems of *The Listeners* (1912) and, for children, *Peacock Pie* (1913). In these, with *Motley* (1918), his lyric powers reached a climax. This was in part owing to his passionate friendship with Naomi, begun in 1911, when he started reviewing for the *Saturday Westminster Gazette*, of which she was literary editor. Though they were never physically lovers, for four years, until war supervened and the bubble burst, Naomi was his muse. She was far from ethereal—ambitious, combative, much more in the swim of literary society than he. Yet he found in her (or invented, as they sometimes agreed he did) a secret self who lit up his. When this ended, workaday friendship survived for a while. Lyrics she inspired—often obliquely expressed—attain an ardour of longing and regret. Echoes of that infatuation later sound, at reticent remove, in the passion of the heroine of the novel *Memoirs of a Midget* (1921), which also explores his fascination with the uncommon angle and the very small. His knee-high midget is as acute as a Jane Austen gentlewoman, but has links with Emily Brontë's stranger universe.

De la Mare's originality stamped his anthologies, notably *Come Hither* (1923), framed by one of his most beautiful symbolic stories. The anthology juxtaposes official poetry with Tom O'Bedlam and counting-out rhymes, as if to prove that poetry's essence counts for everything, its categories for little. Other very personal studies, part anthology, part discursive meditation, cover most of his main preoccupations: childhood; dream, imagination, and the unconscious; love; time (this last in verse, the long, conversational *Winged Chariot*; 1953). His other sustained poem, *The Traveller* (1946), is a kind of dry-land *Ancient Mariner*: a quest across a huge desert, revealed as the Eye of Earth. The hero, dying, finally stares down into a dark well of truth, the pupil, and 'It seemed to him a presence there gazed back'. Sombre, the end yet suggests that to end in defeat does not ultimately matter, to bless life being the only significant victory.

During the course of his life de la Mare wrote about a hundred short stories for both children and adults: mysterious, often sinister, nearly always poetic in effect. They can be obscure, built up as they are by fine-spun suggestion and the same embroidered, often archaic expressions he used in poetry, indifferent to modern fashion. Danger, enigma, and transience closely dog their most homely or commonplace settings. The accepted is everywhere disturbed by warnings that this universe exists unsafely to bring news of something far more important. De la Mare seems doubtful whether good or evil is the stronger, and his distrust of answers, and hatred of dogma, forbade him any creed; yet he acknowledged a divine creator, was steeped in the King James Bible, and would pray before sleep. He held the fundamental human condition, from earliest childhood on, to be homesickness, exile.

De la Mare's health was not robust, but he had basic stamina, surviving dangerous illness at least four times, and though ailing in his last years wrote constantly, inventive energy flourishing to the end. He moved house often around the south London suburbs, ending as he began, near the Thames. The main homes were 14 Thornsett Road, Anerley, south-east London (1912–25); when prosperity came, Hill House, Taplow, Buckinghamshire (1925–39); and finally, best loved, the top half of South End House, Montpelier Row, Twickenham, Middlesex (1940–56). Here he entertained multitudes of friends and fellow writers, usually to tea parties. He was awarded the OM (1953) and appointed CH (1948), and received honorary degrees from the universities of St Andrews (1924), Bristol (1929), Cambridge (1935), London (1948), and Oxford (1951). Keble College, Oxford, elected him honorary fellow (1944).

De la Mare died at home of his second coronary thrombosis (the first was in 1947) on 22 June 1956. His ashes were buried in the crypt of St Paul's Cathedral.

THERESA WHISTLER

Sources Bodl. Oxf., MSS W. de la Mare · W. de la Mare correspondence, priv. coll. · personal knowledge (2004) · private information (2004) · T. Whistler, *Imagination of the heart: the life of Walter de la Mare* (1993) · L. Clark, ed., *Walter de la Mare: a checklist prepared on the occasion of an exhibition of his books and MSS at the National Book League, April 20–May 1956* (1956) [bibliography] · L. Bonnerot, *L'Œuvre de Walter de la Mare: une aventure spirituelle* (1969), 475–517 [incl. bibliography] · DNB

Archives Bodl. Oxf., corresp. and papers · Hunt. L., letters · NYPL, Henry W. and Albert A. Berg collection of English and American literature · Plymouth and West Devon Area RO, Plymouth, letters to the Plymouth branch of the English Association · Ransom HRC, letters and literary MSS · Syracuse University, New York, corresp. and literary MSS · Temple University, Philadelphia, corresp. and literary MSS · U. Edin. L., special collections division, letters and papers; letters · U. Reading L., letters · University of Bristol Library, special collections, letters to N. L. Bright | BL, corresp. with G. K. Chesterton and F. A. Chesterton, Add. MS 73195, fols. 1–40, *passim* · BL, corresp. with Sir Sydney Cockerell, Add. MS 52712 · BL, letters to Emily Jones, Add. MS 53788 · BL, corresp. with Macmillans, Add. MS 55010 · BL, corresp. with Marie Stopes, Add. MS 58501 · BL, letters to Vera Stacy Wainwright, Add. MS 54329 · BL OIOC, letters to E. F. Younghusband, Eur. MS F 197 · Bodl. Oxf., letters to John Freeman and his wife · Bodl. Oxf., corresp. with E. J. Thompson · CUL, letters to Geoffrey Keynes · Gloucester Public Library, letters to Marion Scott · Harvard U., Houghton L., letters to Sir William Rothenstein · Herts. ALS, letters to Lady Desborough, D/ERV · JRL, letters to Katherine Tynan · JRL, letters to Alison Uttley · King's AC Cam., letters to W. J. H. Sprott · Morgan L., letters to Tom Turner · NL Scot., letters to Marion Lochhead · NL Scot., letters to Alice V. Stuart · NL Scot., corresp. with John Dover Wilson · Northants. RO, corresp. with Elsie Taylor · NRA, priv. coll., letters to Lady Rosalie Mander · NYPL, letters and MSS to Edward Marsh · Somerville College, Oxford, letters to Percy Withers and his family · Temple University, Philadelphia, letters to Edward Meyerstein · U. Aberdeen L., special libraries and archives, letters to J. B. Chapman · U. Birm. L., special collections department, letters to Francis Brett Young · U. Edin. L., special collections division, letters to Gerald Bullett · U. Edin. L., special collections division, letters to J. M. Dent · U. Edin. L., special collections division, letters to Joan Hassall · U. Edin. L., special collections division, letters to J. G. Sime and F. C. Nicholson · U. Edin. L., special collections division, letters to C. V. Wedgwood · U. Reading L., letters to R. L. Mégroz | SOUND BL NSA, performance recordings

Likenesses W. Rothenstein, portrait, 1921, Lockwood Memorial Library, Buffalo, New York · W. Tittle, lithograph, 1922, NPG · H. Coster, two photographs, *c.*1928–1934, NPG [*see illus.*] · W. Rothenstein, chalk drawing, *c.*1929, NPG; repro. in Whistler, *Imagination of the heart* · H. Murchison, photograph, 1930–39, NPG · H. Lambert, photograph, 1937, NPG · W. Stoneman, photograph, 1939, NPG · J. Gay, photograph, 1948, NPG · A. John, chalk drawing, 1950, NPG · M. Gerson, photograph, 1953, NPG · P. George, pencil, 1956, NPG · J. Ward, watercolour, 1956, NPG · death mask, 1956, NPG · D. Low, pencil caricature, NPG · R. S. Sherriffs, ink-and-charcoal caricature, NPG · T. Spicer-Simson, plasticine medallion, NPG · four drawings

Wealth at death £14,872 14s. 7d.: probate, 15 Oct 1956, *CGPLA Eng. & Wales*

Mare, William de la [William de Mara] (*fl.* **1272–1279**), Franciscan friar and theologian, is of unknown origins. Little is known of the events of his life. He studied theology in Paris, where in the early 1270s he commented on the *Sentences* (probably 1272–4) and then was regent master (probably 1274–5). The *Sentences* commentary (books 1 and 2, ed. H. Kraml, 1989, 1995; manuscripts include Florence, Biblioteca Nazionale, Z. MS Conv. soppr. A.2.727, and Toulouse, Bibliothèque Municipale, MS 252, which also contain parts of books 3 and 4) is a largely unoriginal work, closely based on Bonaventure's commentary and also using the commentary by John Pecham, who may have been William's teacher. William also preached sermons in Paris and produced a set of *quaestiones disputatae*.

William de la Mare then returned to England. Recorded as preaching to the Franciscan convent at Lincoln, between 1277 and 1279 he produced a critique of Aquinas, his *Correctorium fratris Thomae*, claiming that many of

Thomas's positions—for instance, that man has no direct intellectual cognition of singulars, that it cannot be demonstrated that the world had a beginning in time, and that the intellective soul is the one substantial form of a man—were heretical. William wrote this *Correctorium* before August 1279. Later he extended and revised it (Vatican City, Biblioteca Apostolica Vaticana, MS Vat. lat. 4413). A much shorter form of the work (*Declarationes magistri Guilelmi de la Mare OFM de variis sententiis S. Thomae Aquinatis*, ed. F. Pelster, 1956, from Assisi, Biblioteca Comunale, MS 174), edited as William's original version, has been shown to be an abbreviation by an unknown writer. The *Correctorium* was very influential. In 1282, at their general chapter at Strasbourg, the Franciscans decided that members of their order should not read Aquinas's *Summa* unless accompanied by the *Correctorium*. For the Dominicans' part, four detailed replies to it had been written before 1284—the authors of these anonymous works were probably Jean de Paris, Robert Orford, Richard Knapwell, and William of Macclesfield. A text of William's *Correctorium* is found within one of these replies, which quotes it so as to respond to it (*Le correctorium corruptorii quare*, ed. P. Glorieux, 1927).

William de la Mare was also one of the most learned and judicious of the thirteenth-century scholars who tried to improve the text of the Vulgate Bible. Using his knowledge of both Greek and Hebrew, he wrote a *Correctorium Bibliae* (Vatican City, Biblioteca Apostolica Vaticana, MS Vat. lat. 4240), in which he sensibly refrains from assuming that the Latin text must be corrected whenever it departs from the Hebrew or Greek. He also used his linguistic knowledge to write *De Hebraeis et Graecis vocabulis glossarum Bibliae* (Toulouse, Bibliothèque Municipale, MS 402; Florence, Biblioteca Laurenziana, MS Plut. xxv sin. cod. 4).　　JOHN MARENBON

Sources Guillelmus de la Mare [W. de la Mare], *Scriptum in primum librum sententiarum*, ed. H. Kraml (Munich, 1989) · Guillelmus de la Mare [W. de la Mare], *Scriptum in secundum librum sententiarum*, ed. H. Kraml (Munich, 1995) · *Declarationes magistri Guilelmi de la Mare OFM de variis sententiis S. Thomae Aquinatis*, ed. F. Pelster (1956) · [R. Knapwell], *Le 'Correctorium corruptorii quare'*, ed. P. Glorieux (Paris, 1927) · Emden, *Oxf.*, 1.562–3 · R. Creytens, 'Autour de la littérature des correctoires', *Archivum Fratrum Praedicatorum*, 12 (1942), 313–30 · F. Pelster, 'Einige ergänzende Angaben zum Leben und zu den Schriften des Wilhelm de la Mare OFM', *Franziskanische Studien*, 37 (1955), 75–80 [cf. L. Bataillon's review of this in *Bulletin Thomiste*, 9 (1954–6), 949–51] · P. H. Denifle, 'Die Handschriften der Bibel-Correctorien des 13. Jahrhunderts', *Archiv für Literatur- und Kirchen-Geschichte des Mittelalters*, 4/3 (1888), 263–311, 471–601, esp. 295–8, 545 · S. Berger, *Quam notitiam linguae Hebraicae habuerint Christiani medii aevi temporibus in Gallia* (Paris, 1893), 32–45 · P. Glorieux, *Répertoire des maîtres en théologie de Paris au XIIIe siècle*, 2 (Paris, 1934), 99–101 · E. Longpré, 'Guillaume de la Mare', *Dictionnaire de théologie catholique*, ed. A. Vacant and others (Paris, 1903–72), vol. 16, pp. xl, 2467–70 · R. Loewe, *Cambridge history of the Bible*, ed. G. W. Lampe, 2 (1969), 149–50 · B. Smalley, *The study of the Bible in the middle ages*, 3rd edn (1983), 335–6, 349 · V. Heynck, 'Zur Datierung des 'Correctorium fratris Thomae' Wilhelmus de La Mare', *Franziskanische Studien*, 49 (1967), 1–21 · F. E. Kelley, 'Introduction', in R. Knapwell, *Quaestio disputata de unitate formae* (1982) · P. Glorieux, 'Non in marginibus positis', *Recherches de Théologie Ancienne et Médiévale*, 15 (1948), 182–4 · D. A. Callus, review of J.-P. Muller, ed., *Le Correctorium corruptorii 'Quaestione'*, *Bulletin Thomiste*, 9 (1954–6), 643–55, esp. 643–50 · D. A. Callus, review of F. Pelster, ed., *Declarationes magistri Guilelmi de la Mare*, *Bulletin Thomiste*, 9 (1954–6), 944–8

Archives Biblioteca Apostolica Vaticana, Vatican City, Vat. lat. MS 4240; Vat. lat. MS 4413 · Biblioteca Comunale, Assisi, MS 174 · Biblioteca Nazionale, Florence, Z. MS Conv. soppr. A.2.727 · Bibliothèque Municipale, Toulouse, MS 402 · Bibliothèque Municipale, Toulouse, MS 252 · Biblioteca Laurenziana, Florence, MS Plut. xxv sin. cod. 4

Maredudd ab Ieuan ap Robert (*c*.1465–1525). *See under* Wynn family (*per. c*.1465–1678).

Maredudd ab Owain (*d*. 999), king of Gwynedd and of Deheubarth, was the son of *Owain ap Hywel Dda of Deheubarth (*d*. 988). Maredudd ruled the kingdom of Gwynedd and other parts of north Wales from 986 and subsequently Deheubarth in the south from 988 until his death in 999. The extent of his power is uncharacteristic of this period, matched only by that of his paternal grandfather, *Hywel Dda ap Cadell, and in records of his death he is called 'the most famous king of the Welsh'. His father, Owain, had inherited Deheubarth and other southern Welsh regions from Hywel Dda in 950, whereas the northern Welsh lands were reclaimed by a different branch of the dynasty. Owain did not die until 988, but Maredudd had been active for at least two years before this. It was perhaps because of his father's longevity that initially he sought power beyond his hereditary kingdom in the south. Indeed, his brother Einion had also acted seemingly independently of Owain until he died in 984, and it is possible that Einion's death enabled Maredudd to assume a more active political role.

Maredudd seems to have exploited the political divisions that fractured Gwynedd on the death of Hywel ab Ieuaf in 985. In that year Hywel's brother Cadwallon is said to have slain one Ionafal ap Meurig (a possible kinsman and rival) and thus to have assumed control of Gwynedd, Anglesey, and Meirionydd. The year 986 witnessed the killings of Maig ab Ieuaf (or Meurig ab Idwal Foel), possibly by Maredudd, and of Cadwallon, most definitely at Maredudd's instigation. Maredudd was thus able to bring this northern kingdom under his power and he subdued it under tribute to him. There is no strong evidence that he lost his dominance in the north until his death. Thus, in 987, when Godred Haraldsson (Gofraid mac Arailt), king of Man, raided Anglesey, capturing 2000 people (or slaying 1000, according to an Irish chronicle), it was Maredudd who took the survivors southwards into Ceredigion and Dyfed. Furthermore, two years later he ransomed what were probably some of those captured in 987 by paying the vikings known as the 'Black Host' a penny per head.

Maredudd no doubt harboured interests in his father's southern kingdom. Thus, if the Llywarch ab Owain blinded in 987 was his brother, this act may indicate a fraternal struggle before Owain's demise. When that king did die, in the next year, it seems likely that Maredudd was in a position to add Deheubarth to his territories. However, he was not free of dynastic rivals: his nephew Edwin ab Einion aspired to this southern part of Maredudd's territories, while Idwal ap Meurig (*d*. 997) and his brothers sought to exercise their hereditary claim to Gwynedd. In 991 Maredudd attacked 'Maeshyfaidd', probably the plain of Radnor, then under Mercian control. This may have antagonized the English, for in 992 Edwin ab Einion, in allegiance with an English leader called Edelisi (possibly Æthelsige), raided Maredudd's southern territories of Ceredigion, Dyfed, Kidwelly, and Gower, taking hostages. One account states that Edwin had taken hostages on at least one previous occasion. Maredudd is also said to have raided the neighbouring kingdom of Morgannwg in 992 with the help of viking mercenaries. His son Cadwallon died in this year. The following year saw trouble in Maredudd's northern territories. On the one hand Anglesey was ravaged by vikings (not necessarily Maredudd's erstwhile allies), and on the other the sons of Meurig ab Idwal Foel raided Gwynedd. Maredudd also fought and was heavily defeated by the sons of Meurig in 994 at Llangwm (in Dinmael), where his nephew Tewdwr ab Einion fell. The political implications of this defeat for Maredudd's position in the north are not apparent. It has been suggested that Idwal had established himself in north Wales before this battle and that it represented an attempt by Maredudd to oust him thence; alternatively, it may have been a further attempt by Idwal and his brothers to regain their rightful kingdom. It is possible that these northern troubles ceased following the death of Idwal ap Meurig in 996 or 997. Maredudd lived for a further two or three years, dying in 999, as far as can be determined of natural causes, despite the aspirations of his dynastic rivals. While none of Maredudd's direct male descendants seems to have succeeded him to the kingship, his daughters Angharad and Lleucu were married into dynasties of later importance.

DAVID E. THORNTON

Sources J. Williams ab Ithel, ed., *Annales Cambriae*, Rolls Series, 20 (1860) · T. Jones, ed. and trans., *Brenhinedd y Saesson, or, The kings of the Saxons* (1971) [another version of *Brut y tywysogyon*] · T. Jones, ed. and trans., *Brut y tywysogyon, or, The chronicle of the princes: Peniarth MS 20* (1952) · T. Jones, ed. and trans., *Brut y tywysogyon, or, The chronicle of the princes: Red Book of Hergest* (1955) · P. C. Bartrum, ed., *Early Welsh genealogical tracts* (1966) · J. E. Lloyd, *A history of Wales from the earliest times to the Edwardian conquest*, 3rd edn, 2 vols. (1939); repr. (1988) · D. E. Thornton, 'Maredudd ab Owain (d.999): the most famous king of the Welsh', *Welsh History Review / Cylchgrawn Hanes Cymru*, 18 (1996–7), 567–91

Maredudd ab Owain (d. 1265). *See under* Gruffudd ap Rhys (d. 1201).

Maredudd ap Bleddyn (d. 1132). *See under* Bleddyn ap Cynfyn (d. 1075).

Maredudd ap Rhys Gryg (d. 1271), prince of Deheubarth, was the son of *Rhys Gryg (d. 1233) [*see under* Gruffudd ap Rhys] and grandson of *Rhys ap Gruffudd, the Lord Rhys (d. 1198). Rhys Gryg was among the contenders for power in Deheubarth after the death of Rhys ap Gruffudd and, by the partition made under the aegis of Llywelyn ab Iorwerth in 1216, he secured the castle of Dinefwr and the greater part of Ystrad Tywi, his share including lands recently won by conquest, further augmented the following year with his acquisition of Gower. Under the terms of

Llywelyn's agreement with Henry III's council in 1218 his adherents were required to cede the lands secured by conquest and return to the king's fealty. Rhys Gryg was reluctant to do so and it was only after armed intervention by Llywelyn in 1220 that he yielded. Subsequent adjustments to the distribution of the patrimonial lands of Deheubarth ensured that he ruled the whole of Ystrad Tywi.

Rhys Gryg left two sons, namely Rhys Mechyll (d. 1244), the elder son, and Maredudd ap Rhys Gryg. Named as 'son and heir' in a document of 1222, but not found acting on his own behalf until several years later, Maredudd may have been the son of Rhys Gryg's marriage, noticed by the Welsh chronicler in 1219, to 'the daughter of the earl of Clare' (*Brut: Peniarth MS 20*, 97), that is the daughter of Richard de Clare, earl of Hertford (d. 1217). The possibility that he was 'heir' by virtue of this marriage, and that Rhys Mechyll was not the son of a marriage, could help to explain Maredudd's forceful territorial ambitions. A Clare connection could also account for the king's inclination to engage Richard de Clare, earl of Gloucester (d. 1262), in negotiations with Maredudd at times of political conflict. Upon Rhys Gryg's death in 1233 Rhys Mechyll secured Dinefwr and much the greater part of Ystrad Tywi, but promptly upon the death of Llywelyn ab Iorwerth in 1240 Maredudd began to assert himself. His efforts were facilitated by his association with Gilbert Marshal, earl of Pembroke (d. 1241), custodian of the king's castles of Carmarthen and Cardigan and his lands in south-west Wales. Maredudd married Gilbert Marshal's niece, Isabel, daughter of William *Marshal, earl of Pembroke (d. 1231), and secured Ystlwyf and Emlyn, lands that Walter Marshal (d. 1245) wrested from Cynan ap Hywel, an earlier adherent of the Marshals. In Ystrad Tywi he established the centre of his authority at the castle of Dryslwyn, probably built by him and first mentioned in 1245 when it was put under siege by the seneschal of Carmarthen during the period when Maredudd joined the Welsh leaders in supporting Dafydd ap Llywelyn of Gwynedd. His barony may have consisted at this time of the commotes of Catheiniog, Mabudrud, and Mabelfyw. The greater part of Deheubarth was still held by Rhys Mechyll, who was succeeded in 1244 by his son, Rhys Fychan.

In 1251 Maredudd ap Rhys Gryg and his nephew, Rhys Fychan ap Rhys Mechyll, joined Owain ap Gruffudd and Llywelyn ap Gruffudd (d. 1282), princes of Gwynedd, in an alliance by which each agreed 'to help and maintain the other against all living men as though we were brothers and neighbours' (*Littere Wallie*, 160–61). By the summer of 1256 the two kinsmen of Ystrad Tywi were in open conflict and, unable to withstand a royal army brought by Stephen Bauzan (d. 1257) in support of Rhys Fychan, Maredudd was forced to withdraw to Gwynedd. He joined Llywelyn ap Gruffudd when the latter advanced into Perfeddwlad in November, and they then embarked swiftly upon a campaign in Ystrad Tywi by which Maredudd secured possession of his lands and those of Rhys Fychan. He enjoyed only a brief supremacy. In May 1257, intervening in the territory for a second time, Bauzan brought a great army to reinstate Rhys Fychan. At a critical moment in the campaign Rhys defected, leaving the invading army to suffer a severe defeat at Cymerau in the Ystrad Tywi in June. Llywelyn endeavoured to reconcile the two kinsmen, but receiving Rhys into his fealty entailed restoring the lands he had previously held. Denied a great part of the reward that his adherence to Llywelyn had brought him, Maredudd was soon in negotiation with the king. Henry III held forth the prospect that Maredudd would receive from him a broad estate the like of which he could no longer hope to secure from Llywelyn. Richard de Clare and Nicholas de Molis were empowered to negotiate his adherence to the king and under their persuasion, and protected from the princes' retaliation by the strong forces they deployed, Maredudd agreed to terms which won him a promise both of his lands and those of Rhys Fychan, along with two commotes from among the lands of Maredudd ab Owain (d. 1265) in Ceredigion. Henry was in no position to give effect to his grant but, by instruments drawn up at Westminster on 18 October 1257, he formally conceded to Maredudd a lordship consisting of the whole of Ystrad Tywi.

When Maredudd and Rhys Fychan had been reconciled the previous summer, Llywelyn had prudently taken Maredudd's son as a hostage for his father's loyalty. In April 1258, despite his understanding with Henry, Maredudd made an agreement with Llywelyn whereby, in return for his homage, he secured the prince's promise that he would never again take his son as a hostage nor seize his castles. But Llywelyn's attempt to retrieve Maredudd's loyalty was to no avail. Maredudd was soon known to be in the king's allegiance once more and the Welsh chronicler observed that his infidelity had disturbed the whole of Wales. During 1258 Llywelyn twice waged war upon him and, eventually captured, he was convicted of infidelity by the prince's council. Maredudd secured his freedom in 1261 only upon very stringent conditions concerning his fidelity, but he appears to have withdrawn from Llywelyn's fealty once more, for his barony was held of Edmund, the king's son, as part of the honour of Carmarthen, in 1265. By the treaty of Montgomery of 1267 Llywelyn ap Gruffudd was granted the homage of all the Welsh lords of Wales with the single exception of Maredudd. If Henry were ever to agree to concede the homage Llywelyn would have to pay 5000 marks for it. An early request went unrewarded but, before his departure for the Holy Land in 1270, Edward persuaded his father to relent. Robert Burnell was sent to Gwynedd with the documents prepared, to be handed to Llywelyn only upon delivery of the sum agreed. It is unlikely that the money was paid and it is not certain with whom, in formal terms, Maredudd's homage rested in his last years.

Maredudd ap Rhys Gryg died on 27 July 1271 at his castle of Dryslwyn and, in a particularly fulsome encomium, the author of the Peniarth 20 manuscript of *Brut y tywysogyon* records that Maredudd ap Rhys Gryg, a brave and powerful man, was taken to the Cistercian abbey of Whitland and was honourably buried in the great church on the steps in front of the altar. Maredudd was succeeded in his barony by his son *Rhys ap Maredudd (d. 1292), who was to make renewed efforts to re-establish the hegemony in Ystrad Tywi that, except for a brief interval in 1257, had eluded his father.   J. B. SMITH

Sources PRO · *Chancery records* · J. E. Lloyd, *A history of Wales from the earliest times to the Edwardian conquest*, 3rd edn, 2 vols. (1939); repr. (1988) · J. B. Smith, *Llywelyn ap Gruffudd, prince of Wales* (1998) · R. R. Davies, *Conquest, coexistence, and change: Wales, 1063–1415*, History of Wales, 2 (1987) · J. B. Smith, 'The *Cronica de Wallia* and the dynasty of Dinefwr', *BBCS*, 20 (1962–4), 261–82 · *Littere Wallie*, ed. J. G. Edwards (1940) · T. Jones, ed. and trans., *Brut y tywysogyon, or, The chronicle of the princes: Peniarth MS 20* (1952)

Maredudd ap Tudur (*fl.* 1388–1404). *See under* Tudor family, forebears of (*per. c.*1215–1404).

Marescoe, Charles (1633?–1670), merchant, was born in Lille (then in the Spanish Netherlands), probably early in 1633, the youngest surviving son of Jacques and Jeanne Marescoe. He was evidently resident in London by 1649 for in 1653 he testified to four years of service as bookkeeper to Jacques Boeve, merchant (Anglicized as James Bovey). By 1654 Marescoe had moved into a partnership with John Buck (1620–1661), which secured a trading agency on behalf of the Baltic dukedom of Courland and also built up trading links with Sweden's major manufacturers of metals, armaments, and naval supplies.

Marescoe acquired naturalization on 26 June 1657 (confirmed by Charles II on 29 December 1660) and was married at the French church, Threadneedle Street, on 7 July 1658 to Leonora (*c.*1637–1715?) [*see under* David, Jacob], a younger daughter of Jan Le Thieullier (1591–1679) and sister of Sir John Lethieullier (1632–1719). The latter drew Marescoe into his extensive trading contacts with Spain and the Mediterranean, where they shared in exports of English tin, lead, and textiles. By 1664 Marescoe's ledgers show him to have been worth over £13,000 net, with large stocks of Swedish products such as iron, copper, pitch, and tar. The Second Anglo-Dutch War (1665–7) ensured him substantial profits from these strategically valuable commodities, and by the close of 1669, when he enrolled his brother-in-law, Peter Joye (1636–1721), as a junior partner, his trading capital stood at nearly £38,000.

Marescoe's marriage had brought him close to the aldermanic aristocracy of London and in November 1662, by lord mayor's prerogative, he was granted the freedom of the City by redemption as liveryman of the Clothworkers' Company. In 1663 he purchased a grant of arms, and by 1665 he was recognized by the privy council as the king of Sweden's official factor. In this role he was engaged in Admiralty court litigation on behalf of much Swedish shipping, seized during the war as Dutch-owned. He also disputed exactions levied on Swedish goods by the Eastland Company and in 1668–9, collaborating with the Swedish resident, Johann Barkman, Lord Leyonbergh FRS (1625–1691), he successfully opposed improper 'water-balliage' levies by the City of London's officials.

Marescoe's acquisition in 1668 of an exclusive contract with the Swedish monopoly Tar Company consolidated his prosperous links with Sweden's greatest industrialists, such as the De Geers, the Momma-Reenstiernas, and the Kock-Cronströms, who began to employ him as their commission agent for sales of iron bars and copper wire. It was in their interests to establish a monopoly in the London commodity market and although they never wholly succeeded there is evidence that Marescoe enjoyed a brief and unpopular pre-eminence in these wares. The reference in Samuel Pepys's diary to 'Morisco's Tarr = Business' on 23 July 1665 is only one indication of the importance which the Navy Board attached to his resources. The East India Company was also a client, as were merchants interested in supplying the African slave trade with specially manufactured bars known as 'voyage-iron'.

Marescoe's activities were diverse: in partnership with John Lethieullier he carried on an active export trade to Spain, Italy, and the Levant. The commodities he dispatched consisted mainly of native English products, such as Colchester bays, Exeter perpetuanas, and Cornish tin, but he also figured largely in England's fast-growing traffic in colonial re-exports, channelling substantial amounts of West Indian sugars and tobacco to the refiners and blenders of Hamburg and Amsterdam. He maintained slender links with Lille, the city of his birth, seized by Louis XIV in 1668, and he also built up a precarious relationship with merchants of Rouen who marketed his sugar. It was on the recommendation of one of these agents that he engaged as a bookkeeper Jacob David of Darnetal near Rouen, who entered the household in 1668 at a salary of £40 per annum.

At this date Marescoe was still inconvenienced by the 1666 fire of London and the destruction of his rented house in Fenchurch Street. For a while he shared a Lethieullier house but in 1669 he purchased plots between Tower Street and Thames Street and began building a mansion house in Bosse Alley, conveniently sited for access to the London wharves. With twenty-seven hearths it was a capacious home for a growing family. Five daughters had been born—Leonora in 1659, Jane in 1661, Elizabeth in 1663, Mary in 1665, and Anne in 1666—and a short-lived son, Charles, arrived in 1668. On 5 September 1670, when he made his will, Marescoe's hopes for a male succession were pinned on another son, James, born earlier that year, but James did not long survive his father, who died at his home on 9 September 1670.

Although Marescoe and his kinsmen had strong ties with St Dunstan-in-the-East and the protestant French church, Threadneedle Street (to whose poor he left £150), his costly funeral was transferred to the parish church at Low Leyton, Essex, where he had rented a country residence since the plague year of 1665. A memorial slab to Marescoe and his children was erected there by his widow, but has not survived. His estate, including real property, was finally valued at about £45,000, of which, by 'the custom of London', he assigned one-third to his widow and two-thirds to the children, but the maladministration of this estate by Leonora and her second husband, Jacob David, was to lead to its dissipation.

H. G. ROSEVEARE

Sources *Markets and merchants of the late seventeenth century: the Marescoe–David letters, 1668–1680*, ed. H. Roseveare, British Academy, Records of Social and Economic History, new ser., 12 (1987); repr. (1991) · PRO, admiralty court depositions, HCA/13 · will, PRO, PROB 11/333, sig. 114 · sentence, PRO, PROB 11/333, sig. 111
Archives PRO, chancery masters exhibits, C 114/63–78 · Riksarkivet, Stockholm, Momma-Reenstierna Sammlung
Wealth at death approximately £40,000—cash, stock in trade, and East India Company shares; £5580—recently purchased London real property: inventory in Common Serjeant's Book 2, fols. 240, 293b, GL

Maret, Philippe [Philip Marett] (*d.* **1637**), legal official in Jersey, was born in the parish of Trinity, Jersey, the second son of Charles Maret and his wife, Marguerite, daughter of Noel Le Cerf. He graduated BA from Merton College, Oxford, in 1598. Although his enemies later claimed that he spent time in Spanish seminaries, there is no evidence for this. Maret served as receiver-general in Jersey from his nomination by the governor, John Peyton, on 21 January 1608 until 1615 and concurrently as solicitor-general from 1607 until 1613. He became attorney-general on 14 October 1613 and held that office until 1616.

Controversy surrounded Maret for most of his life, complaints being frequently made about his tenure of office in the island. The two main issues were his combination of the offices of receiver-general and attorney-general and his appointment to those offices by Peyton. Maret's main opponent was the bailiff Jean Herault, who claimed that the right of presentation lay with the king and not (according to his patent) the governor, with whom Herault was already in dispute. Following the discovery in May 1616 that a paper relating to a court case in progress had been removed by Maret, he was summoned to the royal court of Jersey by the *dénonciateur*. Having initially refused to comply, Maret finally entered the court, with his hat on, while the senior jurat, Philippe De Carteret, seigneur of St Ouen, was giving his opinion, and interrupted him, accusing De Carteret of having sent his men to his house by night to assassinate him. Maret was subsequently ordered to ask pardon publicly of God, the king, and the court for his contempt of court, and he was fined 50 crowns for insulting De Carteret. On his refusal to pay he was suspended from office as attorney-general and ordered to appear within forty days before the privy council. In the meantime De Carteret's brother Elie was sworn in as attorney-general on 13 June. In July, Maret was committed by the council to the Gatehouse prison. When he returned to Jersey, he told the court that his case had not been tried, but the bailiff had a letter from the secretary of the council to the effect that Maret had been ordered back to acknowledge his offence. Since he refused to do this he was imprisoned in Jersey, first in Mont Orgueil and then in Elizabeth Castle. From there he petitioned the king that the case be heard before the commissioners Conway and Bird who were coming to Jersey, and he complained, falsely, that he had been fettered and manacled during his imprisonment in the island. In 1617 he brought before the commissioners charges of tyranny and corruption against Herault and charged his enemies, especially De Carteret, of ousting him from office without reason in order to advance their own candidate as attorney-general. The commissioners declared all his charges to be unfounded. In June 1618 Maret was twice ordered to acknowledge his offence and make public submission, the second time on pain of banishment from Jersey.

Maret was often accused by his opponents of being a papist, but there is no evidence for this charge. He always claimed to support the introduction of Anglicanism to Jersey, and he represented the side favouring it at the inquiry before the privy council in 1614 as to whether the Calvinist form of church government should be continued in the island or the Anglican form adopted. He was involved in a protracted dispute with the Calvinist colloquy of the island, and in 1617 he complained that he had been persecuted for a long time by the elders and consistory of the parish of St Helier and been suspended from the Lord's supper.

In 1628 Maret married Martha Lemprière, the widow of Elie Dumaresq, seigneur des Arbres in the parish of St Brelade. In the same year he bought the Fief des Arbres from his two stepsons and moved to La Haule. He had one child, Philippe. In 1629 he was elected jurat; although the election was disputed, he remained in office until his death. He became deputy lieutenant-governor in 1632, being sworn in by Lieutenant-Governor Francis Raynsford on 28 January. Maret died on 8 January 1637 at La Haule, and was buried two days later in the church of St Brelade.

HELEN M. E. EVANS

Sources G. R. Balleine, *A biographical dictionary of Jersey*, [1] [1948] · J. A. Messervy, 'Liste des receveurs-généraux de l'Île de Jersey', *Annual Bulletin* [Société Jersiaise], 5 (1902–5), 101–14 · J. A. Messervy, 'Liste des jurés-justiciers de la cour royale de Jersey, 1274–1665', *Annual Bulletin* [Société Jersiaise], 4 (1897–1901), 213–36 · J. A. Messervy, 'Liste des gouverneurs, lieut.-gouverneurs et députés gouverneurs de l'Île de Jersey', *Annual Bulletin* [Société Jersiaise], 4 (1897–1901), 373–94 · transcripts of the parish registers of St Brelade, Library of the Jersey Law Society, States Building, Royal Square, St Helier, Jersey [property of Channel Islands Family History Society] · J. A. Messervy, 'Listes des procureurs-généraux, vicomtes et avocats-généraux de l'Île de Jersey', *Annual Bulletin* [Société Jersiaise], 3 (1890–96), 293–306 · *Reg. Oxf.*, vol. 2/3

Likenesses C. J. Ansen?, oils, Jersey Museums Service, St Helier

Marett, Sir Robert Hugh Kirk (1907–1981), author and diplomatist, was born in Oxford on 20 April 1907, the younger son in a family of two sons and two daughters of Robert Ranulph *Marett (1866–1943), anthropologist and rector of Exeter College, Oxford, and his wife, Nora (d. 1954), youngest daughter of Sir John *Kirk (1832–1922), consular official, and his wife, Helen (d. 1914). His father was also seigneur of Franc Fief in St Brelade and owner of the manor of La Haule, in the island of Jersey, possessions which had been in the Marett family since the seventeenth century. As G. R. Balleine stated, 'Though Oxford was his workshop, Jersey was his home' (Balleine, 485).

After attending the Dragon School, Oxford, and Winchester College, Marett embarked on a career in commerce, going to Rio de Janiero in 1926 to work in a coffee exporting business, Norton, Megaw & Co. Ltd, of which his father's friend Guy de Gruchy, seigneur of the neighbouring Jersey manor of Noirmont, was managing director. The world depression hit coffee exports and Marett moved on to posts with the British-owned Mexican Railways (1931–6) and then with the Shell Petroleum Company in Mexico (1937–9). Mexico was the setting for two pivotal events in his life. In 1934 he married Piedad, daughter of Vincente Sanchez-Gavito of Mexico City; they had one daughter. It was also in Mexico that Marett embarked on a literary career, with the publication of two highly successful books, *Archaeological Tours from Mexico City* (1934) and *Eye Witness in Mexico* (1939). From 1932 to 1938 he was Mexican correspondent for *The Times*.

In 1939 Marett joined the Ministry of Information to oversee British propaganda in Mexico. In this capacity he was so influential that an initial advantage to the German side in Latin America was turned around and the German ambassador was expelled from Mexico. Marett's success was recognized by his appointment as OBE in 1942. In December the same year, he was transferred to Washington as press secretary to the British Information Service. There then followed brief appointments in New York and Ottawa, before he was appointed director of the British Information Service in New York in August 1946. Meanwhile, he had been transferred to the foreign service in January 1946, with the rank of first secretary.

Having thus entered the Foreign Office 'through the back door', as he expressed it in his book of that title in 1968, Marett was posted to Lima as consul in October 1948. He returned to the Foreign Office in April 1952 and was secretary of the Drogheda committee, which in 1953 reported on the British Overseas Information Services. In September 1953 he was promoted counsellor and head of the information policy department. He was again posted abroad in December 1955, when he was appointed consul-general in Boston, in which capacity he was called on to justify British policy in the Suez crisis. He travelled widely in the United States of America, lecturing at universities. His lecturing skills were then employed on the world stage, after his return to the Foreign Office in London in December 1958 as assistant under-secretary of state. He was meanwhile appointed CMG in 1955. In August 1963 Marett and his wife were delighted to return to South America upon his appointment as British ambassador to Peru. He was appointed KCMG the following year. He retired from the Foreign Office in March 1967, although in 1970 he served briefly as special ambassador for the inauguration of President Allende of Chile.

Marett's retirement to Jersey was, however, far from an anticlimax as, after resuming the vestigial feudal duties of the seigneur of Franc Fief in St Brelade and settling into Mon Plaisir, the fine house built on manor land by his grandfather, he offered himself for election to the states of Jersey and served with great distinction as a deputy for nine years. In 1978 he was elected president of the policy advisory committee, in which capacity he brought his experience and wisdom to bear on the vexed question of population control in the small island. He also continued to write—publishing guides to Peru in 1969 and Mexico in 1971—and enjoyed chronicling the history of his own family. His book *The Maretts of La Haule, Jersey* was published posthumously in 1982.

Marett's death at Mon Plaisir, La Haule, St Aubin, on 2 November 1981 was widely regretted, and sincere tributes were paid to him in the states assembly and by the local and national press. A memorial service was held on 16 November 1981 at the church of St Aubin on the Hill, St Brelade. He was survived by his wife and his daughter, Suzanne Marett-Crosby, a publisher of books of considerable local interest.

F. L. M. CORBET

Sources R. Marett, *The Maretts of La Haule, Jersey* (1982) · S. Marett-Crosby, 'Marett, Sir Robert', in F. L. M. Corbet and others, *A biographical dictionary of Jersey*, [2] (1998) · G. R. Balleine, *A biographical dictionary of Jersey*, [1] [1948] · *The Times* (5 Nov 1981) · *Daily Telegraph* (5 Nov 1981) · *Jersey Evening Post* (3 Nov 1981) · *Lima Times and El Comercio* (12 Dec 1981) · Burke, *Peerage* · Burke, *Gen. GB* · *WWW* · *FO List* · R. H. Marett, *Through the back door* (1968) · personal knowledge (2004)
Likenesses photograph, repro. in Corbet and others, *A biographical dictionary of Jersey*, [2], following p. 230

Marett, Sir Robert Pipon (1820–1884), politician in Jersey and poet, was born at St Peter, Jersey, on 20 November 1820, the eldest of the eight children of Peter Daniel Marett (*d.* 1838) and his wife, Mary Ann, eldest daughter of Thomas Pipon, lieutenant bailiff of Jersey. Marett belonged to a family established in Jersey for many centuries, and was a descendant of Philip Maret (or Marett). His father had served in the East India Company's Madras infantry with the rank of major, and married his mother on retiring to Jersey.

Marett's early education at McMahon's School, Jersey, revealed great academic potential. A contemporary chronicle records:

> The spiritual activity and love of work, which were already characteristic of him, never deserted him in the course of a career filled not only with legal and professional achievements but also with literary and scientific studies, the gift of great intelligence. (*Almanach de la Chronique de Jersey*, 227)

In 1840 Marett commenced a five-year course of study at the University of Caen. He was called to the Jersey bar in November of the same year. On completing his studies he spent one year in Blois with his family, where his widowed mother had gone for health reasons, and was involved in founding an English church there, building being his lifelong hobby.

Reform was the watchword of the time, and local politics were dominated by two parties, the laurel on the right and the rose on the left. In this contentious atmosphere Marett stood for moderation. He was defeated in the 1852 election for constable of St Helier as an independent candidate, but elected unopposed at the next election, in 1856. As constable (mayor) he used the full weight of his influence to improve the town, widening streets and creating public parks. He took the far-sighted view that as the island had no capital but that which came from outside, everything possible had to be done to make it attractive to outsiders.

The progress of Marett's career was rapid. He was appointed solicitor-general in 1858 and attorney-general in 1866, and sworn in as bailiff in 1880. He was knighted in

May 1881. His opinion on legal reform was valued throughout his career: he gave evidence before a commission of the privy council in 1861, and drafted a law fundamentally changing and simplifying the inheritance of real estate, which was passed in 1879. He edited four volumes of manuscripts encapsulating Jersey law, written by Philip Le Geyt, an earlier lieutenant bailiff, and wrote a learned treatise as preface to the edition published by the states of Jersey in 1882. His standing as a legislator is such that his writings were regularly quoted by counsel in cases before the courts even at the close of the twentieth century.

Marett's other local concerns included designs for a new harbour at St Helier, the founding of the Société Jersiaise, patronage of societies ranging from the orphanage and general dispensary to the Agricultural and Horticultural Society, and being a governor of both Victoria College and the Jersey Ladies' College.

In 1865 Marett married Julia Anne (*b. c.*1830), youngest of the four daughters of Philip Marett, seigneur of La Haule, and a distant cousin, with whom he had one son, Robert Ranulph *Marett, who became a distinguished anthropologist, and three daughters.

Marett's interest both in classical and in English literature was wide, and he built up a valuable library at his home, Blanc Pignon, which was destroyed by fire in 1874, whereupon he and his family moved into La Haule Manor. He was fluent in English, French, Latin, and Jersey Norman French, and is considered a pioneer of Jèrriais as a written language, having published a number of poems in the vernacular in the liberal journal *La Patrie*, of which he was a founder, under the pseudonym Laelius.

Marett's death, on 10 November 1884 at La Haule Manor, plunged the island into mourning, and the local newspapers devoted many columns to the most handsome tributes and to voluminous lists of the multitude of local notables and ordinary citizens who attended his funeral at St Brelade's parish church.

F. L. M. CORBET

Sources *DNB* · G. R. Balleine, *A biographical dictionary of Jersey*, [1] [1948] · R. R. Marett, *A Jerseyman at Oxford* (1941) · R. Marett, *The Maretts of La Haule, Jersey* (1982) · P. Le Geyt, *Recueil des lois*, 3 (1882) · *Almanach de la Chronique de Jersey* (1885) · P. Matthews and S. Nicolle, *The Jersey law of property* (1991) · S. Nicolle, *The origin and development of Jersey law* (1998)
Archives Société Jersiaise, Jersey, collection
Likenesses oils, Royal Court, Jersey

Marett, Robert Ranulph (1866–1943), philosopher and anthropologist, was born on 13 June 1866 at Blanc Pignon on Jersey, the eldest child and only son of the four children of Sir Robert Pipon *Marett (1820–1884), attorney-general and later bailiff, and his wife and cousin, Julia Anne (*b. c.*1830), youngest daughter of Philip Marett of La Haule.

Marett's earliest education was at a local dame-school; from nine to fourteen he attended St Aubin's School and afterwards Victoria College. On his seventeenth birthday he was gazetted to the Jersey militia as lieutenant. In November 1884 he won a senior exhibition at Balliol College, Oxford. He persuaded the college to allow him to come into residence that academic year and he did so in

Robert Ranulph Marett (1866–1943), by Henry Lamb, 1935

Hilary term 1885. In 1886 he sat classical honour moderations, in which he obtained a first class; in 1888, despite spending most of the year convalescing after an attack of meningitis, he obtained a first-class degree in *literae humaniores*. During his undergraduate career he was elected secretary of the Oxford Union and in 1887 he won the chancellor's prize for Latin verse.

After coming down from Oxford, Marett spent two years on the continent: a few weeks in Paris, mountaineering in Switzerland, attendance at the University of Berlin, and then a year in Rome as tutor to Lord Basil Blackwood, son of the British ambassador there.

After returning to England, Marett decided on an academic career, although he had earlier contemplated following his father into the legal profession. He was called to the English bar as a member of the Inner Temple in 1885, and to the Jersey bar in 1891. In 1890 he undertook some tutoring for Balliol and acted as university secretary for Toynbee Hall. In 1891 he was appointed to a fellowship at Exeter College, with which he remained associated for the rest of his life. In 1893 he became sub-rector of the college and tutor in philosophy. That year was also marked by an important event in his intellectual development: he won the Green moral philosophy prize, the subject for which on that occasion was 'The ethics of savage races'.

This marked Marett's arrival on the threshold of the anthropological world, a world he entered fully when invited at short notice by John Linton Myres to address the 1899 meeting of the anthropological section of the British Association in Dover. His paper, 'Preanimistic religion', constituted a critique of Tylor's theory of the origin of religion, which had been the orthodoxy for many years.

Marett's embracing of anthropology required little intellectual realignment, for the distance between classics and anthropology was not then great: many classicists from Frazer to Gilbert Murray and Jane Harrison had turned in some degree to anthropology. Marett also became interested in prehistoric archaeology, and as well as visiting sites in France and Spain he conducted excavations in Jersey until the outbreak of the Second World War.

Marett was much involved with introducing the teaching of anthropology at Oxford, first examined in 1908. In 1907 he became secretary to the committee for anthropology, which had been set up two years before to oversee a diploma in the subject, and he remained active on it thereafter. With others, he founded the Oxford University Anthropological Society in 1909 which survives, although intermittently dormant, nearly a century later. In 1910, on the retirement of Tylor, Marett was appointed reader in social anthropology.

As a bachelor don Marett travelled widely in Greece and north Africa; he was a keen ornithologist and fond of game shooting. He participated in various sports, including tennis, bicycling, and especially golf. During the Second South African War he renewed his military career as a lance corporal in the Oxford University volunteer battalion of the Oxfordshire light infantry.

On 5 July 1898 Marett married Nora (*d*. 1954), daughter of Sir John *Kirk (1832–1922) and Helen Cooke, and had to move out of college. He and his wife set up home in north Oxford, where their four children (two sons and two daughters) were born in the decade succeeding: one of their sons was Sir Robert Hugh Kirk *Marett, the author and diplomatist. In 1914 the family moved from Oxford back to the family home, La Haule, on Jersey, and Marett divided his time between there and Oxford.

Like many of the British intellectual establishment Marett attended the British Association meetings in Australia in 1914 and was caught there by the outbreak of the First World War. He had to cut short his visit, but not before visiting a tribe of Australian Aborigines, his only contact with the people who were the subject of so much of his anthropological writings. Back in Oxford he found he had been selected as part of the skeleton staff to run the university during hostilities, though he joined a battalion of veterans with regular military duties. In the absence of most of his colleagues Marett filled many roles both in the college and university, including, in 1918, that of proctor.

After the war Marett continued as tutor at Exeter until 1928 when he was elected rector of the college. He had obtained a DSc at Oxford in 1913 and to this were added an honorary LLD from the University of St Andrews in 1929 and a DLitt from Oxford in 1937. He was made a fellow of the British Academy in 1931. In 1936 he was due to retire from both his rectorship and readership, but both were extended, the former for five years and in 1941, because of the Second World War, for a further year and made renewable. His obituary in *Exeter College Record, 1939–47* refers to his rectorship as a grand period in the life of the college and to Marett's involvement in every aspect of it and his love of entertaining. The extension of his university post—as acting professor of social anthropology—stemmed from the inability of Radcliffe-Brown, the newly elected professor, to take up his chair until 1937.

Marett's fondness for conversation, especially when he was doing the talking, seems to have been widely recognized. An anonymous contributor in *The Times* (4 March 1943) noted 'the audacity, the effrontery almost, of many of his reminiscences—they were such wonderful stories that, when you heard them, it did not matter whether or not they were completely true'. The *Stapeldon Magazine* (December 1928), welcoming him as the new rector, described his laughter as 'vigorous and almost gargantuan'.

The period of Marett's rectorship was also fruitful as far as publications went, several of his books appearing in that period. Among the best known are his collection of essays *The Threshold of Religion* (1909), which contains his 1899 piece on preanimism; *Anthropology* (1912), an introduction to the subject; *Faith, Hope and Charity in Primitive Religion* (1932); *Sacraments of Simple Folk* (1933); *Head, Heart and Hands in Human Evolution* (1935); and his biography of Tylor (1936). Marett's anthropological works are numerous and a full list of them up to 1936 is to be found in Buxton's *Custom is King*.

Few, however, read Marett's works today. His reputation as an anthropologist has not survived and none of his ideas has had a lasting influence on the subject. This was noticeable even by the mid-1930s; the majority of the contributors to the collection of essays presented to Marett on his seventieth birthday, *Custom is King* (1936), make no reference to his work, and those that do mention it do so merely as a brief, preliminary courtesy. This is equally true today of the annual Marett lecture at Exeter College, which commemorates his name but rarely his ideas.

Marett was unfortunate both in the sort of anthropology with which he became involved and in the timing of his involvement. The debates to which he contributed, such as those on mana and the origin of religion, were those of the nineteenth-century evolutionists, and though there was considerable energy left in them, what was to become mainstream anthropology was already diverging from this course. By 1899 the Cambridge Torres Straits expedition had taken place and marked the beginning of the shift towards a fieldwork-orientated future for the subject. By the 1920s this change had taken place, but had passed Marett by.

Marett's closing years were marred by the loss of his elder son, killed at Narvik aboard HMS *Glorious* in June 1940, and by the German occupation of his beloved Jersey. It was at this time that he wrote his autobiography, *A Jerseyman at Oxford* (1941). He died on 18 February 1943 while still rector of Exeter and still active in university affairs—at the time of his death he was waiting for a meeting of the Indian Institute curators to begin. He was cremated in Oxford, after a service in Exeter College chapel, on 22 February.   PETER RIVIÈRE

Sources R. R. Marett, *A Jerseyman at Oxford* (1941) · G. R. Balleine, *A biographical dictionary of Jersey*, [1] [1948] · J. P. V. D. B. [J. P. V. D. Barber], 'Dr R. R. Marett', *Oxford Magazine*, 61 (11 March 1943), 239–40 · L. H. D. Buxton, *Custom is king* (1936) · *Exeter College Record*, 1939–47 · H. J. Rose, 'Robert Ranulph Marett', *PBA*, 29 (1943), 357–70 · *The Times* (4 March 1943) · *Stapeldon Magazine* (Dec 1928) · *Robert Ranulph Marett: a report of a memorial meeting of the Oxford University Anthropological Society, 4 March 1943* (1943) · *Oxford Mail* (19 Feb 1943) · DNB · m. cert.

Archives U. Oxf., Pitt Rivers Museum, ethnological papers | Bodl. Oxf., corresp. with J. L. Myres

Likenesses W. Stoneman, photograph, 1933, NPG · H. Lamb, oils, 1935, Exeter College, Oxford [*see illus.*] · St H. Lander, portrait · photographs, repro. in Marett, *Jerseyman at Oxford*, 310 · photographs, repro. in *Exeter College Register* (1998), 55

Wealth at death £8285 6s. 8d.: administration with will, 25 Oct 1945, CGPLA Eng. & Wales

Margaret [St Margaret] (d. 1093), queen of Scots, consort of Malcolm III, was the eldest child of *Edward Ætheling (d. 1057) and his wife, Agatha, who was a kinswoman of the emperor Heinrich II (r. 1002–24). Margaret's father was one of the two sons of *Edmund Ironside (d. 1016), briefly king of England in succession to his father, Æthelred. Edward and his brother, Edmund, were exiled by King Cnut, perhaps with the intention that they would be murdered. Instead, they seem to have been sheltered by the king of Sweden and sent to the court of Jaroslav, prince of Kiev. Before 1046 they were persuaded by a fellow exile at Kiev, Andrew, first cousin once removed of Stephen, king of Hungary (d. 1038), to join the successful expedition which secured for Andrew the Hungarian throne. Either while still at Jaroslav's court, or (less probably) after reaching Hungary, Edward was provided with a bride. Although Agatha's parentage cannot be established with certainty, the hypothesis which fits the surviving evidence most convincingly is that she was the daughter of Liudolf (d. 1038), margrave of West Friesland, son of Gisela of Swabia and Bruno, brother of Heinrich II, the Saxon. Through her grandfather, Agatha was the great-niece of Heinrich II, brother-in-law of King Stephen of Hungary, while through her grandmother she was related to Heinrich III, the Salian (r. 1039–56).

In 1057 Edward and his family travelled to England, but Edward died within the year, and his young son *Edgar Ætheling was not seriously considered as a successor of Edward the Confessor, who died childless early in 1066. After the duke of Normandy had secured the English throne for himself by his victory at Hastings, the Ætheling and his family, having briefly come into the Conqueror's peace and protection, became involved in the movement of resistance to the Norman invaders chiefly originating in northern England. In 1068 Edgar, with his mother and sisters, Margaret and Christina, fled to the Scottish court. In either 1069 or 1070 Margaret was married to the Scottish king, *Malcolm III, at Dunfermline. It was said that the marriage was against her inclinations, since she wished to enter the religious life; but in the circumstances she and her brother and mother could hardly defy Malcolm III's will. The marriage lasted for some twenty-three years and produced six sons and two daughters who all survived to adulthood. Three sons, *Edgar (d. 1107), *Alexander (d. 1124), and *David (d. 1153), became kings of Scots, while the elder daughter, *Matilda (d. 1118), otherwise known as Edith or Mold, became queen of England in 1100 on marrying *Henry I.

Margaret converted the church in which she was married, Holy Trinity at Dunfermline, into a Benedictine priory which, under the auspices of Archbishop Lanfranc, drew its first community of monks from the cathedral monastery (Holy Trinity or Christ Church) of Canterbury. In 1128 this priory was raised to the status of an independent abbey at the behest of David I, the first abbot being Geoffrey, prior of Canterbury. Margaret also persuaded her husband to remit the ferry charges at the most popular crossing of the Firth of Forth (later to be known in her honour as Queensferry) for bona fide pilgrims, most of whom would be visiting St Andrews, a shrine which Margaret greatly venerated.

Thus far in establishing Margaret's character and significance the facts are largely incontrovertible. Beyond that, the greater part of the information regarding her is derived from the life written *c*.1100–07, at the request of her daughter Queen Matilda, by Turgot, then prior of Durham but formerly for some years Margaret's chaplain. This work, the fullest version of which relates several miracles attributed to Margaret, may have been designed to put the case for her canonization, the postponement of which for over a century is hard to explain. Evidence more objective than the life shows a woman of outstanding piety and religious devotion, with a zeal which may have stemmed from her childhood in a country only recently and partially converted to Christianity. The life stresses her compassion towards children (especially orphans) and the poor, the severity of her self-denial, including much fasting, her love of formality and etiquette (she was, rather oddly, fond of fine clothes and jewellery), and her anxiety to bring the Scottish church into conformity with what she understood to be the doctrine and practices of western Catholicism. In particular, she urged the clergy and people of her adopted country to receive communion more frequently than once a year at Easter, to abstain from ordinary labour (for example, farm work) on Sunday, to observe the Lent fast from Ash Wednesday instead of the Monday following, to forbid marriage between a man and his stepmother or sister-in-law, and to celebrate the mass by a universally accepted ritual. None of these points touched the fundamentals of Christian doctrine. It may be agreed that Margaret made a deep impression upon the Scottish clergy; that she persuaded many of them to alter their rites and practices must be regarded as doubtful. The life mentions, significantly, Margaret's reverence for the ascetic clergy scattered throughout Scotland, evidently communities of Céli Dé ('Clients of God'), who followed an eremitical regime. This statement is borne out by her recorded benefactions to the Céli Dé of Loch Leven, and lends weight to Orderic Vitalis's report that she tried to restore the church of Iona.

It would have been impossible for Margaret to pursue her reform programme in the Scottish church without the goodwill and co-operation of Malcolm III. The life, indeed, emphasizes the extent to which the king helped his wife, not only in her charitable activity but also in the conduct of conferences with the Scottish clergy. According to Turgot, Margaret's customary language was English (not, as might have been expected, French), and, since her husband was fluent in English as well as in his own Gaelic speech, he acted as interpreter.

Queen Margaret died at Edinburgh Castle on 16 November 1093, three days after Malcolm III had been killed near Alnwick while leading his fifth raid into Northumberland; she was buried before the high altar in Dunfermline Priory church. Grief and shock at hearing of the death of her husband and of her eldest son may have been the immediate cause of Margaret's death, but the life tells that she was greatly exhausted by years of self-denial and undernourishment. She enjoyed a very high reputation in the Anglo-Norman world of the early twelfth century, and was eulogized by William of Malmesbury, John of Worcester, and Orderic Vitalis, the last of whom described her as 'eminent for her high birth, but even more renowned for her virtue and holy life' (Ordericus Vitalis, *Eccl. hist.*, 4.273). The Hexham writers, Prior John and Ailred of Rievaulx, refer to her as 'holy' and 'religious', and in 1199 King William the Lion (*d.* 1214) was dissuaded from invading England by a vision he experienced while spending a night at his great-grandmother's tomb at Dunfermline. But although there developed in Scotland, from soon after her death, a cult of St Margaret which seems to have had a genuinely popular character, it was only in 1249–50, in response to a campaign organized by Scotland's most senior clergy (and doubtless encouraged by the crown as a counterpoise to the cult of Edward the Confessor promoted both by Westminster Abbey and by Henry III), that the papacy authorized her formal canonization. At the Reformation her remains, with those of her husband, were transferred by Philip II of Spain to a chapel in the Escorial at Madrid, and in 1673 Pope Clement X named her patroness of Scotland.   G. W. S. BARROW

Sources Symeon of Durham, 'Vita Sanctae Margaretae Scotorum reginae', *Symeonis Dunelmensis opera et collectanea*, ed. J. H. Hinde, SurtS, 51 (1868) · ASC · A. O. Anderson, ed. and trans., *Early sources of Scottish history, AD 500 to 1286*, 2 vols. (1922); repr. with corrections (1990) · A. J. Wilson, *St Margaret, queen of Scotland* (1993) · R. L. G. Ritchie, *The Normans in Scotland* (1954) · A. H. Dunbar, *Scottish kings*, 2nd edn (1906), 33

Margaret, countess of Kent (1187x95–1259), princess, was the eldest daughter of *William the Lion, king of Scots (*d.* 1214), and *Ermengarde de Beaumont (*d.* 1233). She was born at an unknown date between early 1187 and April or May 1195, when her father's illness caused a succession crisis in Scotland. She was perhaps recognized then as his heir; by another account it was proposed by the English court that she should marry Richard I's nephew Otto, duke of Saxony (*d.* 1218), but the Scottish magnates objected because the king's younger brother, *David, earl of Huntingdon (*d.* 1219), was a suitable heir. But the king recovered, and Margaret's expectations changed again in 1198 when her brother, the future King *Alexander II, was born. Nothing more is known about her until August 1209 when, as a consequence of the treaty of Norham, she was sent south as a possible bride for the future King Henry III of England. But nothing came of these proposals, and clause 59 of Magna Carta suggests that there had subsequently been pressure for her being returned to Scotland. But this, too, had no effect, and on 3 October 1221 she was married at London to Hubert de *Burgh (c.1170–1243), justiciar of England. Henry III gave her away, but the match was a disparagement; de Burgh was of gentry stock and was not ennobled, as earl of Kent, until February 1227. Their only child, Megotta (Margaret), was probably born in the early 1220s. In 1232 de Burgh was reported to be planning to divorce Margaret, but in the same year he fell from royal favour, was stripped of his offices, and was imprisoned; Margaret, deprived of personal treasures and possessions, took sanctuary at Bury St Edmunds until her husband and the king were partly reconciled in 1234, when Henry III made grants for her maintenance. At Bury, Margaret organized the secret marriage of Megotta to Richard de Clare (d. 1262), a boy of about the same age and heir to the wealthy honours of Clare and Gloucester. De Burgh may not have known of this; its discovery in 1236 reopened the breach with the king, and Megotta's death in 1237 made no difference; de Burgh was completely out of public life by 1239 and died in 1243. Margaret succeeded to lands in which they had been jointly seised and held them until her death in the autumn (before 25 November) of 1259; like her husband, she was buried at Blackfriars in London.   W. W. SCOTT

Sources W. Bower, *Scotichronicon*, ed. D. E. R. Watt and others, new edn, 9 vols. (1987–98), vols. 4–5 · A. C. Lawrie, ed., *Annals of the reigns of Malcolm and William, kings of Scotland* (1910) · F. M. Powicke, *King Henry III and the Lord Edward: the community of the realm in the thirteenth century*, 2 (1947) · GEC, *Peerage*, new edn, vol. 7 · *CClR, 1259–61* · A. O. Anderson, ed., *Scottish annals from English chroniclers, AD 500 to 1286* (1908) · J. C. Holt, *Magna Carta* (1965)

Margaret [Margaret of England] (1240–1275), queen of Scots, consort of Alexander III, was the eldest daughter and second child of *Henry III of England (1207–1272) and his queen, *Eleanor of Provence (c.1223–1291). She was born at Windsor in October 1240, about the 5th, although the date of her birth is given erroneously by several chroniclers. The early years of her life were passed there along with her brother *Edward, who was a year older, and the daughter of the earl of Lincoln. Her brother *Edmund was born in 1245. Green's account claims that she was named Margaret after her aunt, Queen Margaret of France, and, quoting Matthew Paris, because her mother in the pangs of childbirth had invoked the aid of St Margaret (of Antioch). On 27 November that year a royal writ ordered the payment of 10 marks to her custodians, Bartholomew Peche and Geoffrey de Caux.

In 1243–4 there was an outburst of hostilities between Henry III and Alexander II, king of Scots, but the treaty of Newcastle on 13 August 1244 restored peace between England and Scotland, and arranged that the marriage of Margaret and Alexander (1241–1286), the infant son of Alexander II, should take place when the children were old enough. In 1249 the death of Alexander II made Margaret's betrothed husband *Alexander III of Scotland. The instability of the Scottish government in the period of

minority made it expedient for both countries to effect the marriage sooner rather than later, and on 26 December 1251 Alexander and Margaret were married at York by Archbishop Walter de Gray of York (d. 1255). There had been elaborate preparations for the wedding, which Paris states was attended by 1000 English and 600 Scottish knights, and so vast a throng of people that the ceremony was performed secretly and in the early morning to avoid the crowd. Enormous sums were lavished on the entertainments and large quantities of food were consumed. Next day Henry III bound himself to pay Alexander 5000 marks as the marriage portion of his daughter. Around the time of the marriage Henry was involved in the replacement of the Scottish government, which had been led since 1249 by the noble faction headed by the Durward family. Their rivals, the Comyns, were installed as the main force in government.

The first years of Margaret's residence in Scotland seem to have been solitary and unhappy. She was put under the charge of Robert le Norrey, Stephen Bauzan (d. 1257), and the widowed Matilda de Cantilupe. Paris, the fullest source for details of Margaret's life, names Robert de Ros (d. c.1270) and John de Balliol as her principal guardians. Geoffrey of Langley (d. 1274) was also sent to Scotland by Henry III, but Paris states that he returned to England because of Scottish objections to him. In 1253 Henry III requested that Margaret should be allowed to visit her (pregnant) mother in England, but the request came to nothing. She was dissatisfied with her treatment in Scotland, and seems to have complained bitterly. Paris uses the issue as an excuse for anti-Scottish venom. He states that in 1255 Queen Eleanor sent a famous physician, Reginald of Bath, to enquire into Margaret's health and condition. Finding the queen pale and agitated, and full of complaints against her guardians, Reginald indiscreetly expressed his indignation in public, and soon afterwards died suddenly, apparently of poison. King Henry sent Richard de Clare, earl of Gloucester (d. 1262), and John Mansel (d. 1265) to act as his agents in assisting another coup in Scotland. Margaret and Alexander III were taken from Edinburgh to Roxburgh, while Henry III and Eleanor were now at Wark. The two royal couples met in both places, and Margaret remained a short time with her mother at Wark. A new settlement of the Scottish government was effected: Ros and Balliol were deprived of their estates and the Durward faction was once again installed as the primary force in the administration.

Early in 1256 Margaret received a visit from her brother Edward. In August of the same year she and Alexander went to England. They attended the festivities of the feast of the Assumption on the 15th at Woodstock and, thence proceeding to London, were sumptuously entertained by John Mansel. Shortly thereafter, however, there was more political upheaval in Scotland, culminating in the couple's capture by the Comyn faction in October 1257. By 1260 Alexander III had gained personal control of the Scottish government, and in that year he and Margaret again visited England. Alexander returned to Scotland before the end of the year, leaving Margaret to celebrate

Christmas at Windsor, where on 28 February 1261 she gave birth to her first child, Margaret. Three years later her eldest son, Alexander, was born on 21 December 1264 at Jedburgh. A second son, named David, was born in 1270.

Margaret and Alexander III met her brother Edward at Roxburgh early in 1267 and in 1268 they again attended Henry III's court. According to the Lanercost chronicle, she was very anxious for Edward's safety during his absence on crusade, and deeply lamented her father's death in 1272. On 19 August 1274 she and her husband attended Edward I's coronation at Westminster. Margaret died at Cupar Castle on 27 February 1275 and was buried at Dunfermline Abbey. The so-called chronicler of Lanercost (really a Franciscan of Carlisle), who claims to have had his information from her confessor, speaks of her in the warmest terms. 'She was a lady', he says, 'of great beauty, chastity, and humility—three qualities which are rarely found together in the same person' (*Chronicon de Lanercost*, 97). She was a good friend of the friars, and on her deathbed received the last sacraments from her confessor, a Franciscan, while she refused to admit into her chamber the great bishops and abbots.

T. F. TOUT, *rev.* NORMAN H. REID

Sources CDS, vols. 1–2 · W. Bower, *Scotichronicon*, ed. D. E. R. Watt and others, new edn, 9 vols. (1987–98), vol. 5, pp. 314–21, 346–7, 354–5, 400–03 · *Johannis de Fordun Chronica gentis Scotorum / John of Fordun's Chronicle of the Scottish nation*, ed. W. F. Skene, trans. F. J. H. Skene, 1 (1871), 297, 299–300, 305 · Paris, *Chron.*, vols. 4–5 · H. R. Luard, ed., *Flores historiarum*, 3 vols., Rolls Series, 95 (1890), vols. 2–3 · *CCIR*, 1251–6 · J. Stevenson, ed., *Chronicon de Lanercost, 1201–1346*, Bannatyne Club, 65 (1839), 81, 95, 97 · Rymer, *Foedera*, 1.257 · J. Stevenson, ed., *Chronica de Mailros*, Bannatyne Club, 50 (1835), 109 · *Calendar of the liberate rolls*, 2, PRO (1930) · D. E. R. Watt, 'The minority of Alexander III of Scotland', *TRHS*, 5th ser., 21 (1971), 1–23 · M. A. E. Green, *Lives of the princesses of England*, 2 (1849), 2.170–224

Margaret [Margaret of France] (**1279?–1318**), queen of England, second consort of Edward I, was the last child of Philippe III of France (d. 1285) and his second wife, Marie de Brabant. The story that Edward initially hoped to marry Margaret's elder sister, Blanche, is unfounded; Philippe IV first suggested his half-sister Margaret as a wife for Edward [*see* Edward I] in 1294, but the project hung fire until negotiations began in 1298 to end Edward's Gascon war against Philippe.

Margaret and Edward married amid rich ceremony at Canterbury on 10 September 1299; according to the *Liber de antiquis legibus*, Margaret was then aged twenty. She wore a crown at her wedding and on great occasions thereafter, but was never anointed queen. Her first son, *Thomas of Brotherton, later earl of Norfolk and earl marshal (d. 1338), was born at Brotherton in Yorkshire on 1 June 1300, apparently prematurely as Cawood had been prepared for her confinement; an early birth would support the story that she named her son for Thomas Becket, whom she invoked during a dangerous labour. The child reputedly languished on a French nurse's milk, but throve when an Englishwoman replaced her. A second son, *Edmund of Woodstock, later earl of Kent (d. 1330), was

born at Woodstock on 1 August 1301; Margaret's daughter, Eleanor, born at Winchester on 6 May 1306, died in 1310.

Margaret was less constantly with Edward than Eleanor of Castile (d. 1290), but contemporary chroniclers remark his great love for her, and his letters reveal him to have been most attentive to her welfare and to that of her children. She was friendly with his daughters by Eleanor and in 1305 helped to reconcile him with his son the prince of Wales; she appeared with her husband on such ceremonial occasions as the Feast of the Swans in 1306 and a commemorative mass for Eleanor in 1307. Her official duties are rarely noted, but in 1301 Edward did designate her to determine whether two of his agents had suitable credentials to conclude a truce with the Scots. Margaret was notably active as an intercessor between Edward and his subjects; perhaps she hoped thereby to allay any lingering distrust of her French connections or of the unpopular treaty that led to her marriage, but a story in the later *Scalacronica*, that she once passed strategic information to Philippe IV, suggests she never entirely escaped suspicion. It is unclear, however, if either Margaret or Edward II knew of Philippe IV's project in 1310 to marry her daughter, Eleanor, to a Sicilian prince.

After Edward I's death Margaret commissioned her chaplain, John London, to write a Latin eulogy of her husband. In 1308 she attended Edward II's wedding to his niece Isabella of France, and in November 1312 witnessed Edward III's birth. Little is heard of her thereafter until her death on 14 February 1318; she was interred in the Franciscans' London church, to the construction of which she had contributed 2000 marks in 1306, and a further 100 marks in her will. Margaret was as richly dowered as Eleanor of Castile, held most of the latter's lands, and enjoyed all the financial perquisites of her office. Her revenues must have been ample, but she was apparently extravagant. By 1302 her debts stood at £4000; to pay them Edward assigned her all receipts from wardships and in 1305 granted her new estates worth £500, while the pope, Clement V, in 1306 allowed her, for her expenses and charities, £4000 from a tenth collected in England for the relief of the Holy Land. She none the less left sizeable debts.

Contemporary English writers hailed Margaret as 'the flower of the French' (Wright, 178), her physical beauty surpassed only by the purity of her morals; Robert Mannyng of Brunne in 1338 called her 'good without lack' (*Peter Langtoft's Chronicle*, 2.306). Her tomb was sold by Sir Martin Bowes about 1550, when the Franciscan priory became a parish church. Two extant pieces of sculpture are often associated with Margaret, though neither is an authentic portrait: a battered queen's head on the tomb of Edward's admiral Gervase Alard in Winchelsea church, and a mid-fourteenth-century statue on the south buttress of Lincoln Cathedral, the features of which may have been recut.

JOHN CARMI PARSONS

Sources *Chancery records* · P. Chaplais, ed., 'Some private letters of Edward I', *EngHR*, 77 (1962), 79–86 · F. Devon, ed. and trans., *Issues of the exchequer: being payments made out of his majesty's revenue, from King Henry III to King Henry VI inclusive*, RC (1837) · M. R. Fawtier, ed., *Registres du Trésor des chartes … inventaire analytique établi par les* archivistes aux Archives nationales, 1: *Règne de Philippe le Bel* (1958) • *Peter Langtoft's chronicle (as illustrated and improv'd by Robert of Brunne) from the death of Cadwalader to the end of K. Edward the First's reign*, ed. T. Hearne, 2 vols. (1725) • M. Prestwich, *Edward I* (1988) • 'Annales Angliae et Scotiae', *Willelmi Rishanger … chronica et annales, regnatibus Henrico tertio et Edwardo primo*, ed. H. T. Riley, pt 2 of *Chronica monasterii S. Albani*, Rolls Series, 28 (1865) • T. Stapleton, ed., *De antiquis legibus liber: cronica majorum et vicecomitum Londoniarum*, CS, 34 (1846) • W. Stubbs, ed., 'Commendatio lamentabilis in transitu magni Regis Edwardi', *Chronicles of the reigns of Edward I and Edward II*, 2, Rolls Series, 76 (1883), 3–21 • T. Wright, ed. and trans., *The political songs of England from the reign of John to that of Edward II*, CS, 6 (1839) • *Scalacronica, by Sir Thomas Gray of Heton, knight: a chronical of England and Scotland from AD MLXVI to AD MCCCLXII*, ed. J. Stevenson, Maitland Club, 40 (1836) **Archives** PRO, exchequer acts, various; chancery miscellany; ancient correspondence **Likenesses** statue, 1330–70, Lincoln Cathedral • head (on tomb of Gervase Alard), Winchelsea church

Margaret [called the Maid of Norway] (1282/3–1290), queen-designate of Scots, was the only daughter of Erik II Magnusson, king of Norway (d. 1299), and his first wife, Margaret, the Maid of Scotland, daughter of *Alexander III, whose marriage took place in August 1281; Queen Margaret died at Tønsberg on 9 April 1283, possibly in childbirth. On the death of the Lord Alexander in January 1284, Margaret was recognized by the Scottish magnates as heir presumptive to her grandfather on 5 February following; but after Alexander III's death on 18 or 19 March 1286 the succession remained in suspense until the following November because his widow was pregnant. Margaret then became heir, despite an unsuccessful Brus rising, and it became a concern of the Scottish community to carry out Alexander III's wish to marry her to a son of Edward I. The first need was to persuade her father to release her, and this was achieved at Salisbury on 6 November 1289, after Erik had been helped financially by Edward; four months later, in March 1290, Edward I sent formal proposals for a marriage between the Maid and Edward (later *Edward II), offering to protect the independence of Scotland and the liberties of its prelates and magnates, but also designating Margaret as queen. The Scots were reluctant to agree because Edward demanded control of their castles, and he confirmed these promises at Northampton on 28 August 1290 because the Maid was about to sail from Norway. The text is ambiguous about her immediate destination: she was to come to Scotland or England in one clause, but in another would go to England and venture to Scotland only if it was peaceable. When she sailed in September 1290 her destination was Orkney.

In and after the treaty Edward I showed his intention to impose his will upon the Scots, through his agent, Antony (I) Bek, bishop of Durham, supposedly acting for Margaret as 'queen', but without waiting for her arrival, marriage, and inauguration. Before this, and after her death, Margaret was 'Lady of Scotland' to the Scots; to see her as queen is misleading, and effectively connives at the manipulative insensitivity of those men, led by the English king, of whose ambition for political power she was the pathetic child victim. She would have become queen only after the traditional ceremonies at Scone. Margaret sailed from Norway in September 1290, accompanied by two Norwegian bishops, fell ill on the voyage, and died about the end of that month 'between the hands of Bishop Narve' in Orkney (Dunbar, 106), while the Scots gathered at Scone, presumably to inaugurate her. Her body was returned to Norway and buried beside her mother's in the choir of Christ's Kirk, Bergen.

In 1301 a woman from Lübeck claiming to be Margaret was tried for treason and burned at Bergen.

A. A. M. DUNCAN

Sources A. H. Dunbar, *Scottish kings*, 2nd edn (1906), 103–9 • G. W. S. Barrow, 'A kingdom in crisis: Scotland and the Maid of Norway', *SHR*, 69 (1990), 120–41 • K. Helle, 'Norwegian foreign policy and the Maid of Norway', *SHR*, 69 (1990), 142–56 • M. Prestwich, 'Edward I and the Maid of Norway', *SHR*, 69 (1990), 157–74 • B. E. Crawford, 'North Sea kingdoms, North Sea bureaucrat: a royal official who transcended national boundaries', *SHR*, 69 (1990), 175–84

Margaret [née Margaret Drummond] (d. in or after 1374), queen of Scots, consort of David II, was the daughter of Sir Malcolm Drummond. She was married at an unknown date to Sir John Logie of that ilk (d. 1363?), almost certainly the grandson of the Sir John Logie executed by Robert I after the Soulis conspiracy in 1320. Her husband was apparently still alive after 1 April 1363, but presumably died soon after. From this marriage Margaret had at least one son, another John Logie [see below].

The first mention of Margaret Logie (as she was then described) in connection with her future husband, *David II (1324–1371), is in a charter to the Friars Preachers of Aberdeen, dated 20 January 1363, making a grant for the souls of David himself and of 'our beloved' Margaret Logie (*dilecte nostre*). This open recognition of their relationship suggests that David already contemplated a second marriage, if Margaret should be free to contract one; his first wife, Joan, the sister of Edward III, had died on 7 September 1362. Since the Drummond family was powerful and involved in a violent feud against kinsmen and allies of Robert the Steward, this relationship may have helped to cause the Steward to join two other prominent nobles, the earls of March and Douglas, in 1363 in a revolt whose origins are complex and obscure. It may have been in part a reaction to the king's seizure of Mar's castle of Kildrummy early in that year (Mar was married to Douglas's sister). And the rebels were probably also concerned that David's failure to pay his ransom might lead to their being sent as hostages to England. Others besides the Steward may have feared the influence of the new mistress's and prospective queen's relations. After the revolt collapsed, and presumably after the death of Sir John Logie, David proceeded to marry Margaret at Inchmurdo in Fife, where the formal submissions of the Steward and the other rebels were performed on 14 May 1363. The date of the marriage remains uncertain: Andrew Wyntoun gives it as early as April 1363. According to the fifteenth-century chronicler Walter Bower, David sought the marriage 'not so much for the excellence of her character … as for the pleasure he took in her desirable appearance' (Bower, 7.333). An even stronger motive was probably his desire for the heir which had been denied his first marriage.

For some years Margaret seems to have been in high favour, while her Drummond relatives made prestigious and profitable marriages; her nephew Sir Malcolm *Drummond (d. 1402?) [see under Drummond family] married the daughter of the earl of Douglas, and her niece *Annabella became the wife of the Steward's son, the future Robert III. By 1368, however, still with no heir in prospect, her position had become less sure. There was an obscure quarrel between David and several members of the Stewart family which Bower attributes to Margaret's influence, though the reasons may have been quite other. David soon after turned on Margaret herself (according to the fifteenth-century *Liber pluscardensis*, because she pretended to be pregnant when she was not) and instituted proceedings for a divorce, on what grounds is unknown. This was duly pronounced, probably early in 1369. But Margaret would not go quietly. She is said to have escaped to England and thence appealed to the pope in Avignon: she received a safe conduct to pass through England in 1372 and there is an acknowledgement of a loan to her made by three London merchants at Avignon in June of the same year. Her proceedings, which were continued after David's death in 1371, were ended only by her death, which occurred on a pilgrimage to Rome, probably in or soon after 1374.

John Logie (*fl. c.*1365–*c.*1395), Margaret's son from her first marriage, had been the beneficiary of special favour from David II, who made several grants of land to him, including the royal lands of Annandale in 1366. In the same year the king granted that the lands of Logie in Strathearn, which had previously been held of the Steward, were in future to be held in barony from the crown; this concession was repeated two years later. Logie continued to be important in the reigns of Robert II and Robert III. A cousin of Annabella Drummond, the wife of John, earl of Carrick, he seems to have attached himself firmly to the Carrick party in the complex politics of the later years of Robert II. Logie was involved in a long-running dispute over Strath Gartney with Carrick's younger brother and rival, Robert, earl of Fife, a dispute which Logie ultimately won after Carrick succeeded to the throne as Robert III in 1390. It was probably he who appeared as chamberlain to the king's eldest son, David, earl of Carrick, in the early 1390s. The date of his death is not known.   BRUCE WEBSTER

Sources *Johannis de Fordun Chronica gentis Scotorum / John of Fordun's Chronicle of the Scottish nation*, ed. W. F. Skene, trans. F. J. H. Skene, 1 (1871), 382 • Andrew of Wyntoun, *The orygynale cronykil of Scotland*, [rev. edn], 2, ed. D. Laing (1872), 506 • W. Bower, *Scotichronicon*, ed. D. E. R. Watt and others, new edn, 9 vols. (1987–98), vol. 7, pp. 332–3, 358–61 • S. I. Boardman, *The early Stewart kings: Robert II and Robert III, 1371–1406* (1996), 15–23, 135–41, 185 • R. Nicholson, *Scotland: the later middle ages* (1974), vol. 2 of *The Edinburgh history of Scotland*, ed. G. Donaldson (1965–75), 169–83 • *CDS*, vol. 4, nos. 22, 28, 197, 401 • G. W. S. Barrow and others, eds., *Regesta regum Scottorum*, 6, ed. B. Webster (1982) • F. J. H. Skene, *Liber pluscardensis*, 2 vols. (1877–80) • W. Robertson, ed., *The parliamentary records of Scotland* (1804) • G. Burnett and others, eds., *The exchequer rolls of Scotland*, 2 (1878), 176

Margaret [Margaret of Scotland] (1424–1445), dauphine of France, was the eldest child of *James I (1394–1437), king of Scots, and Queen *Joan (d. 1445). Her parents were married in February 1424 and her birth can be assigned to the latter part of the same year. In 1428 she and her sisters were given into the care of Michael Ramsay, the keeper of Lochmaben Castle, Dumfriesshire, while the king and queen travelled to Inverness. At the age of three she assumed significance in her father's diplomacy. An embassy arrived from Charles VII of France in July 1428 to renew the alliance with Scotland. It was empowered to ask for Margaret's hand in marriage for the dauphin, Louis (1423–1483), himself born only in July 1423. In return the French wanted an army of 6000 men. The prospect of an alliance with the French royal house raised the status of James and the Stewart dynasty, but the king was not prepared to commit himself to Charles VII for nearly eight years, while Charles too hesitated after his increased success against England from 1429. Meanwhile James used the proposed alliance to negotiate from strength with both England and France, and the possibility of a match between Henry VI and either Margaret or one of her sisters was also mooted. It was not until 1435, after this threat of an Anglo-Scottish alliance had been raised, that the marriage of Margaret to the dauphin was finally agreed. In March 1436 Margaret departed from Dumbarton with an escort of major lords, a 140-strong household in royal livery, and an 'army' of 1200. She sailed in a French fleet, arriving on the Île de Ré, near La Rochelle, on 17 April. From there she made a formal progress to Tours, where she married the dauphin on 25 June in the chapel of the castle.

As dauphine, Margaret was committed to the keeping of Queen Marie of France, wife of Charles VII. After the wedding her Scottish household and following were sent home, the French perhaps remembering the demands and disruption arising from earlier Scottish forces in France. Margaret was allowed just a few Scottish attendants, and may have been provided with her own household only in 1437, when her marriage to the dauphin was consummated. The murder of her father in the same year meant that until her death she was heir presumptive of her young brother, James II. The active role of the dauphine in France was limited. Contemporary accounts of her poor relations with her husband probably have some basis. Comparisons of her beauty with his ugliness may be offset by remarks—admittedly made by English chroniclers—about the dauphin's being unable to stand her 'evil-savoured breath'. One of the dauphin's complaints in his revolt of 1440 against his father was the lack of revenue assigned to his wife, but Margaret seems to have remained on good terms with the king and to have received grants directly from him rather than her husband. She acted as a mediator between King Charles and the city of Metz, and in 1444–5 attended the celebration of the marriage of Margaret of Anjou and Henry VI of England. Her public role in France was restricted to these formal interventions and appearances at court ceremonial. Attempts to place her in court politics overplay the evidence.

However, the dauphine became the subject of criticism, instigated, according to later speculation, by her husband. Suggestions that she deliberately prolonged her childlessness through her diet and clothing, and accusations of immorality with members of her household, were made at the French court, and in July 1445 Margaret's relations with Queen Marie became strained in a dispute over the arrangements for their households. In this atmosphere Margaret became ill on 7 August with what was diagnosed as a brain infection which led to ulceration of the lungs. Her reported comments during her illness suggest that her health had been affected by the criticisms, and she was heard to say that she regretted coming to France. On 16 August 1445, at the age of twenty, Margaret died at Châlons-sur-Marne and she was buried in the cathedral of St Étienne in the city. Her wish to lie at the abbey of Thouars, where she had founded a chapellany, was fulfilled by her husband, now Louis XI, only in 1479.

Much of Margaret's significance derives from her role as a patroness of poets and, reputedly, as a poet herself. One later account ascribed her death to the strain of too many poetic vigils. Although nothing survives which can be proved as her work, as dauphine Margaret was surrounded by a group of poets in her household, including the viscount of Blosseville and one of her ladies, Jehanne Filleul, whose extant works do survive. Margaret's father, James I, certainly shared an interest in literary pursuits, and two of her sisters, Isabella and Eleanor, were similarly patrons and artists within the European princely houses. Margaret's influence is suggested by the existence of three different laments for the dauphine, all composed shortly after her death. One was written by de Blosseville, while another appears in the possession of, and was possibly written by, her sister Isabella. The third account, found in a French manuscript, was incorporated into the *Liber pluscardensis*, a Scottish chronicle, pointing to Franco-Scottish cultural ties.

Margaret's importance apart from literature lay in her position as the crucial link between the Stewarts and continental royalty. Her marriage related her brother and sisters to the house of Valois, and from 1440 the Scots exploited this fact. A whole range of prestigious unions followed. Isabella was married to François, duke of Brittany, in 1442, Mary to the lord of Veere in Zeeland in 1444, and Eleanor, initially proposed as a second wife for the dauphin, married Sigismund, count of Tyrol, in 1447. The Scots relied on the French to make matches for Margaret's sisters, and sent out Eleanor and Joanna for this purpose in 1445. Scotland was able to enter the international marriage market, its efforts culminating in James II's wedding to Mary of Gueldres, niece of Philip the Good, duke of Burgundy, in 1449. If Margaret's marriage produced no half-Scottish kings of France, it raised the prestige of the Stewarts as a dynasty of European consequence.

M. H. BROWN

Sources L. A. Barbé, *Margaret of Scotland and the dauphin Louis* (1917) · P. Bawcutt, 'A medieval Scottish elegy and its French original', *Scottish Literary Journal*, 15/1 (1988), 5–13 · P. Champion, *La dauphine mélancolique* (1927) · F. J. H. Skene, *Liber pluscardensis*, 2 vols.

(1877–80) · M. Brown, *James I* (1994) · C. McGladdery, *James II* (1990) · W. Bower, *Scotichronicon*, ed. D. E. R. Watt and others, new edn, 9 vols. (1987–98), vol. 8
Likenesses illumination (Margaret's arrival in Tours in the 'Chroniques de Charles VII'), repro. in McGladdery, *James II*

Margaret [Margaret of Anjou] (**1430–1482**), queen of England, consort of Henry VI, was born on 23 or 24 March 1430, in France, probably at Pont-à-Mousson or Nancy, in Lorraine. She was the fourth surviving child, and second daughter, of René, duke of Anjou (1409–1480), and Isabelle (*d.* 1453), daughter and heir of Charles II, duke of Lorraine.

Early years and marriage proposals, 1430–1444 Margaret's parental links to a number of important European ruling families destined her from birth to be a pawn in the complexities of European diplomacy. René, second son of Louis II, duke of Anjou and king of Naples, and Yolande, daughter of Juan, king of Aragon, was directly related to the French monarchy by his own parentage and through his sister Marie, wife of Charles VII of France. Although having little by way of patrimony in his own name, in 1419, aged ten, René was adopted by his great-uncle the Cardinal-Duke Louis, ruler of the duchy of Bar, as his heir, and was married to Isabelle, eldest daughter and heir of Charles II, duke of Lorraine. René inherited the duchy of Lorraine on the death of his father-in-law on 25 January 1431 but it was contested by Antoine de Vaudemont, a nephew of the late duke, supported by Philip the Good, duke of Burgundy. On 2 July 1431 René was defeated at Bulgnéville in Lorraine and taken prisoner by Vaudemont, transferred into the custody of the duke of Burgundy, and held prisoner in Dijon until 1437. During his imprisonment René inherited the title to the duchy of Anjou and the county of Provence on the death of his childless brother Louis in 1434. In the following year he also inherited the thrones of Sicily, Naples, and Aragon from Joanna II, queen of Sicily, but his claim was contested by Alfonso V of Aragon, a dispute that was to preoccupy René and his wife intermittently for the next five years, necessitating long periods in Italy.

Her father's fluctuating political fortunes meant that Margaret spent much of her early life either in the care of her mother or, after 1435, her grandmother, Yolande of Aragon (*d.* 1442), living first at Nancy, the capital of the duchy of Lorraine, and then at Saumur and Angers in Anjou. These two strong-minded women played an important part in shaping Margaret's personality during her formative years in a society where, within ruling families, women were able to hold more independent power as regents than in England. She was also exposed to the illustrious court culture of Anjou, both her grandmother and her father being leading patrons of literature and art.

In 1442 René abandoned his fight with Alfonso of Aragon for the crown of Naples and returned to France to devote his time to looking after his more immediate territorial interests, and to ensuring the continued influence

Margaret [of Anjou] (1430–1482), by Pietro da Milano, 1460–64

of his family in European politics by arranging appropriate marriages for his children. Proposed marriage partners for Margaret included a son of the count of St Pol in 1433, the one-year-old Charles, count of Charolais, in 1435, and Charles, count of Nevers, in 1442–3. None came to fruition. The most enduring, and ultimately successful, marriage negotiations with representatives of the English king, *Henry VI (1421–1471), were conducted sporadically from 1439, in the hope of bringing the lengthy and expensive war between England and France to an end. In spring 1444 William de la Pole, earl of Suffolk, led an embassy to Charles VII to negotiate a truce, resulting in a marriage treaty between René of Anjou and the English, agreed on 22 May. The solemn betrothal of Margaret and King Henry was celebrated in the church of St Martin, Tours, on 24 May, Suffolk standing proxy for the king. On 28 May a twenty-month truce between England and France was sealed, though the English claim to full sovereignty over Normandy and Gascony, and refusal to renounce the title to the French throne, remained obstacles to permanent peace. Historians have speculated on the benefits of the marriage alliance for the two countries. While it represented a prestigious match for René of Anjou, it also brought an important source of influence at the English court to Charles VII, who was to use it to good effect. Though Margaret came with a meagre dowry, consisting only of her mother's empty claims to the kingdom of Majorca and 20,000 francs, and renouncing claims to her father's possessions, she brought links with other strategically important areas of France, such as the duchies of Lorraine and Bar. Lecoy de la Marche, René's nineteenth-century biographer, suggests that the English acceptance of so poor a dowry was motivated by nothing more than a desire for friendship with France.

Marriage to Henry VI, 1444–1445 After a delay of six months Suffolk returned to France with a large retinue to escort Margaret back to England. This substantial and expensive

expedition, costing £5573 17s. 5d., left London in November 1444 and returned five months later. The exact sequence of events between November 1444 and April 1445 is confused. Some writers record a second proxy marriage performed at Nancy in early March 1445 by Louis de Heraucourt, bishop of Toul. It was afterwards claimed by the French that the marriage was deliberately delayed by the Angevins until Suffolk had given a firm undertaking to surrender Maine to René of Anjou. There is confusion in the sources between the proxy marriage of Margaret and Suffolk in Tours in May 1444, and that of René's eldest daughter, Yolande, to Frédéric, son and heir of Antoine de Vaudemont, at Nancy in February 1445, attended by Margaret and other members of the French royal family. The latter coincided with the arrival of an English delegation led by the Garter king of arms to finalize the terms for the marriage treaty and convey Margaret on the first stage of her journey from her homeland to Rouen via Paris. When Margaret eventually reached Rouen, accompanied by a small number of Angevin servants, she was not well enough to attend the splendid welcoming pageant, and her place in the procession was taken by the duchess of Suffolk.

On her arrival in England on 9 April Margaret was ill again, and remained at Southampton, where, according to the Milanese ambassador, she was visited by the king in disguise, who was anxious to inspect his young bride in person for the first time. By 22 April she had recovered sufficiently for the king's confessor, William Aiscough, bishop of Salisbury, to conduct the marriage ceremony at Titchfield Abbey. The king presented her with jewels appropriate to a queen, including a gold wedding ring set with a ruby made from a ring previously given him by Cardinal Beaufort at his coronation in Paris. She made her state entry into London on 28 May, and was entertained by pageants and tableaux accompanied by verses written by John Lydgate, expressing the high public expectations of the marriage as a symbol of a permanent peace between England and France. The coronation was performed at Westminster Abbey on 30 May by John Stafford, archbishop of Canterbury. Three days of feasting and tournaments followed.

In July 1445 a French embassy arrived in London to conclude peace negotiations in the wake of the royal marriage. The discussions held now and later were indecisive, and were also bedevilled by Henry VI's readiness to enter into independent diplomatic initiatives and to make commitments which conflicted with the views of his advisers. One of these, a personal letter of 25 December 1445 to Charles VII, promising to surrender Maine by the end of the following April, was ultimately to provide the French king with an excuse for the renewal of war in 1448, with disastrous results for the English. The exact role of the queen in all this, and how much responsibility she should bear for the promise offered by her husband to her uncle, is unclear. A letter of 17 December 1445 to Charles VII, signed by Margaret, indicates that she was under instruction from Guillaume Cousinot and Jean Havart, members of the French king's household, to assist the peace process by encouraging her husband to deliver Maine to the French. In his letter of 22 December to Charles VII, Henry categorically acknowledged the influence of his wife in making the decision to surrender Maine, but it is likely that the peace-loving king would have made this decision of his own free will.

Early married life, 1445–1453 Margaret was assigned the customary dower for fifteenth-century queens of England of 10,000 marks per annum by parliamentary grant on 19 March 1446. Estates worth £2000 per annum were settled on her from the duchy of Lancaster, concentrated on the midland honours of Tutbury, Leicester, and Kenilworth, with additional lands in Essex, Hertfordshire, Middlesex, Surrey, and London, and the 'ancient south parts' of the duchy, comprising lands in Hampshire, Wiltshire, Somerset, Dorset, Devon, Cornwall, Oxfordshire, Herefordshire, and Worcestershire. The midland estates were to become the heartland of her territorial power base in the later 1450s, and close administrative links between the duchy of Lancaster and her household were quickly established. Key duchy officials such as William Cotton, the receiver-general, John Walsh and Nicholas Sharp, auditors, and William Nanseglos, clerk of the receipt, provided her with financial and legal services. She also received a cash annuity from the duchy of £1000, and, after the death of the duke of Gloucester in 1447, a further annuity of 500 marks. Other substantial sources of income included £1000 from the customs of Southampton, £1009 from the duchy of Cornwall, and £1658 directly from the exchequer. She struggled to receive her revenues in full in the early years of her queenship, because she lacked the power to compete successfully with rival claims on exchequer resources, at a time of increasing financial crisis for the Lancastrian monarchy. On 15 June 1446 Margaret was given custody of Anne, the three-year-old daughter and heir of Henry Beauchamp, duke of Warwick, and was assigned £200 per annum from her estates to maintain Anne in her household. She sold the wardship to Suffolk in November 1446, but Anne died three years later. A further annuity of 500 marks was assigned to her from the duchy of Lancaster in 1447. In June 1448 she acquired the castle and lordship of Berkhamsted, and in July 1448 she was granted a licence to ship wool free of customs from any port in the realm to any destination.

The limited evidence for the early years of Margaret's married life indicates that she fulfilled the role expected of a late medieval queen consort, devoting her energies to the support of her husband, but failing for a long time in one important queenly duty, the production of an heir, thereby provoking both speculation and anxiety from contemporary observers. Her letters, household accounts, and jewel accounts reveal both a determined and effective distributor of patronage, and a woman concerned for the welfare of her household servants. Her letters provide clear evidence that she understood the importance of her position as a patron, and show her desire to exploit it to secure loyalty and support. The king's and the queen's household establishments enjoyed a very close relationship, with shared personnel and some intermarriage.

Three of Margaret's French ladies-in-waiting in the escort accompanying her to England in 1445 married members of the king's household. Margaret formed a particularly close relationship with Suffolk and his wife, but there is no contemporary evidence to support the sixteenth-century view, deriving from the chronicler Edward Hall, that the queen and Suffolk were lovers. It is much more likely that, given the age difference (Suffolk was nearly fifty in 1445), Margaret looked upon Suffolk as a surrogate father from the time of the proxy marriage at Tours in 1444. Relations between the queen and the duchess of Suffolk seem to have been close. Alice was the regular recipient of gifts of jewels and other favours from the queen until 1450. A number of the queen's household servants had strong links with Suffolk and rose to positions of prominence through his influence. After his downfall in 1450, their earlier close association was to damage Margaret's reputation and link her with the English defeat in France.

Another strong influence on Margaret in these early years was Andrew Dokett, principal of St Bernard's College, Cambridge, who persuaded her to found what is now Queens' College, Cambridge, in 1448, shortly after Henry's foundation of King's College. There has been considerable speculation as to her motives. In her petition to the king requesting permission for the foundation of a sister college to King's, Margaret refers to her desire to emulate her husband and two earlier founders, Elizabeth de Clare and Mary de St Pol, countess of Pembroke. She does not appear to have taken a close personal interest in the foundation, making no significant grants of property or gifts of money to the college, though some of her closest associates were benefactors, including her chamberlain, Sir John Wenlock, her chief steward, Viscount Beaumont, and Marmaduke Lumley, bishop of Carlisle.

It is difficult to form a clear impression of Margaret's physical appearance or her personality. She was considered good-looking by contemporaries, the French chronicler Thomas Basin describing her in 1445 as 'filiam specie et formam praestantem, quae tunc *maturo viro foret et plenis nubilis annis*' ('a good-looking and well-developed girl, who was then "mature and ripe for marriage"'; Basin, 1.156, quoting Virgil's *Aeneid*, book 7, l. 53). The Milanese ambassador, writing to Bianca Maria Visconti, duchess of Milan, in 1458, reported, with a measure of diplomacy, that she was 'a most handsome woman, though somewhat dark' (*CSP Milan, 1385–1618*, 18–19). Her letters indicate that Margaret enjoyed the conventional aristocratic pursuits of riding and hunting. Sometimes she wrote to her park-keeper in advance of a visit, instructing him to ensure that game stocks were replenished. The Coventry city records indicate that she rode regularly to Coventry from Kenilworth accompanied by her ladies-in-waiting. That it took over eight years for the couple to produce a child has led to speculation that the marriage was not a success, but contemporary evidence indicates that the king and queen spent much of their time together, particularly favouring the royal residences at Windsor, Sheen, Eltham, and Greenwich. In April 1453 Margaret visited the shrine of Our Lady at Walsingham to leave a gift of a pax, a thank-offering for the long-awaited baby that she was expecting later that year. Her joy was short-lived for, within a few months, her husband collapsed with a serious physical and mental illness, and he was totally unaware of the birth of their son on 13 October 1453.

York's challenge, 1453–1456 Margaret's personal circumstances changed dramatically in 1453 with the onset of the king's illness and the birth of her son, *Edward, created prince of Wales on 15 March 1454. She was forced into the centre of the political arena, as control of her husband and son became the focus of competing groups among the nobility. It is hard to detect Margaret's true feelings and response to her enhanced political importance, because of the shortage of personal records, but it is likely that a strong motivating force behind her actions was the desire to see her son inherit the throne sooner rather than later. As long as Edward was a minor, during the incapacity of the king, Margaret had to accept that government was likely to be in the hands of those noblemen most senior in rank, and that she would be excluded from power. Her bid for the regency, advanced in January 1454, failed, being rejected by the Lords in favour of a protectorate established in March 1454, headed by the premier duke, Richard of York.

The queen's relationship with York is crucial to an understanding of power politics in the mid-1450s. Margaret is likely to have regarded York as a serious threat to her son's inheritance, even though the duke swore allegiance to King Henry on many occasions, and claimed that his opposition was directed against his political rival, the duke of Somerset, not against the king. It should not be assumed that the queen had always regarded York as a dynastic threat. He and the duchess are recorded as regular recipients of gifts in the queen's jewel accounts between 1445 and 1453. An undated letter written by Cecily, duchess of York, to Margaret some time during her pregnancy indicates that the duchess saw the queen as a possible mediator between her husband and the king. The birth of her son could be said to have made the queen's position more secure, and to have solved the burning issue of the succession, but the king's incapacity then raised the problem of authority at the centre of government. The choice of York as protector by the Lords could be interpreted as a sign of aristocratic favour towards the dynastic possibilities of his line, the situation being aggravated by the personal rivalry of York and Somerset, another possible claimant to the throne. The queen had long been connected with Somerset, paying him an annuity of 100 marks from the autumn of 1451, and during the power struggle leading to the first battle of St Albans (22 May 1455) she must have regarded him as her natural ally against York.

Somerset's death at St Albans created a power vacuum at the centre of government in opposition to York and increasingly the new focus of interest became the royal household dominated by the queen. Her authority was wholly dependent upon the king's power, which was seriously diminished after St Albans, especially from November 1455 with the establishment of York's second protectorate. Margaret might have feared that her position would be undermined by York's authority, and she may have been particularly concerned about a possible threat to her financial resources. A renewed inquiry into the size and costs of the royal household had been initiated by the Yorkist regime in the summer of 1454, resulting in the issue of ordinances to limit the size of the household on 13 November 1454. This was followed by a resumption petition presented by the Commons in parliament meeting in July 1455 to provide for financial solvency, and to attempt to establish some control over the royal household. A further petition presented in February 1456 provoked a storm of opposition from the Lords and the queen, anxious to secure exemption from its provisions. The strength of opposition was such that York was forced to resign the protectorship on 25 February 1456, thus providing Margaret with the opportunity to set herself up at the head of an anti-Yorkist power base focused on the royal household.

Champion of Lancaster, 1456–1461 In April 1456 Margaret and her son left London to take up residence in the royal castle of Kenilworth and the nearby city of Coventry, being joined in August by the king. The queen spent the summer on a tour of her estates and the prince's patrimony, visiting Tutbury Castle in May and Chester in June. The choice of the midlands as an alternative seat of power was deliberate, for the region lay at the heart of the queen's dower estates and provided ready access to urgently needed sources of revenue and manpower. Two letters from the Paston collection for 1456 indicate that the queen was regarded by contemporaries as an emerging political force. In a letter dated 9 February 1456 John Bocking, writing to Sir John Fastolf, states 'The Quene is a grete and strong labourid woman, for she spareth noo peyne to sue hire thinges to an intent and conclusion to hir power' (*Paston Letters*, 3.75), and in another letter written on 7 June 1456, Bocking observes 'My Lord York is at Sendall stille, and waytith on the Quene and she up on hym' (ibid., 3.92). A number of entries in the Coventry records for 1457 also bear out the impression of the queen as an increasingly powerful figure. Members of the great council meeting in Coventry in 1456–7 were expected to show the queen the same deference as the king. When she departed from Coventry for Coleshill on 16 March 1457 she was accompanied by the mayor and sheriffs with the king's sword carried before her. On the feast of the Exaltation of the Holy Cross later that year (14 September) the queen made a triumphal entry into the city, greeted by a pageant of prophets, patron saints, cardinal virtues, and nine conquerors, whereas the king went silent and unnoticed.

Despite appearances, Margaret had no real basis of independent authority and was forced to work within the established framework of royal power to build up a personal following. She did this partly by controlling appointments to the prince of Wales's council, set up in January

1457, linking her supporters with the wider interests of the Lancastrian monarchy. She used appointments to the prince's council to establish her personal control over the principality of Wales, the duchy of Lancaster, the palatinate of Chester, and the duchy of Cornwall. Many of the key personnel of the council had connections with the queen's household—William Booth, archbishop of York, for example, and his younger brother Laurence Booth, keeper of the privy seal and (from September 1457) bishop of Durham, both of whom were her former chancellors. She formed close links with a number of leading magnates who held estates and local offices in the north-west, most importantly Humphrey Stafford, duke of Buckingham, John Talbot, earl of Shrewsbury, and Thomas, Lord Stanley. The power exercised by the queen is evident from the wording of a number of warrants dating from 1457–9 authorizing appointments and decisions in the name of the prince of Wales, but expressly with the assent of the queen.

The chaotic state of royal finances and uncertainty over payments from the exchequer made the queen heavily reliant on her own resources, especially those derived from her duchy of Lancaster estates, boosted by the revenues assigned to the prince of Wales in his own right from January 1457. Her presence, with the prince of Wales, in the midlands and north-west during this period can only have served to strengthen her control over these important assets. Another method used to bind prominent members of the Lancastrian party was marriage alliances. The queen played a prominent part in the arrangement of a number of key aristocratic marriages between 1456 and 1460, including those of Margaret Beaufort, countess of Richmond, to Henry Stafford, son of the duke of Buckingham, in 1457, and Katherine Stafford, daughter of the duke of Buckingham, to John Talbot, son and heir of the earl of Shrewsbury, in 1458.

On 28 August 1457 there was a French attack on the port of Sandwich, led by Pierre de Brézé, seneschal of Normandy, and confidant of both René of Anjou and Charles VII. The contemporary French chroniclers d'Escouchy and Chastellain believed that Margaret had encouraged the raid, but this view was rejected by Beaucourt and Basin, and it seems most unlikely that she had anything to do with it. This attack added to the increasing pressure on the court to return to the capital, and the king temporarily asserted himself, instigating the return to Westminster in October and attempting a reconciliation between the Yorkist and Lancastrian lords, by means of a 'loveday' procession through the streets of London on 25 March 1458. In the procession the queen walked hand in hand with her enemy, the duke of York, perhaps signifying that the underlying source of conflict lay here, rather than with York and Somerset's heir. The loveday proved to be a sham and served only to demonstrate Henry's tenuous grasp on the complexities of politics. By spring 1459 strained relations between the Lancastrian and Yorkist lords had reached such a pitch that the king and queen again withdrew to Coventry, where, at a meeting of the great council held in late June, in the presence of the queen and her son,

the Yorkist lords were indicted for treason, in their absence. Both sides now prepared for confrontation, the queen touring her Cheshire estates with her son, distributing the prince's livery of the swan and ostrich feathers to the gentlemen of the county.

On 23 September 1459 the Lancastrian army, largely consisting of Cheshiremen, described in Gregory's chronicle as the 'Quenys galentys' (Gairdner, 204), was defeated by the earl of Salisbury at Bloreheath. An unreliable tradition asserts that Margaret observed the fighting from Mucklestone church tower, and, witnessing the defeat of the Lancastrians, took flight, reversing the shoes on her carriage horses in order to evade pursuit. But the Yorkists were in turn routed at Ludlow on 12–13 October, and their leaders were attainted at the parliament which met at Coventry shortly afterwards. Towards the end of the session, on 11 December, the assembled lords swore a solemn oath of loyalty to the king, and promised to preserve the queen and the honour of Prince Edward, whom they undertook to accept as king in due time. The dynasticism implicit in their oath was soon to be drastically repudiated, when on 31 October 1460, following his capture at the battle of Northampton, King Henry himself was induced to accept Richard of York as the heir to the throne, in place of the prince of Wales.

The movements of Margaret and her son after the battle of Northampton are unclear, but it seems that they fled westwards from Coventry to Wales, embarking from Harlech for Scotland at the end of the year. Margaret took refuge at the court of her fellow queen, Mary of Gueldres, regent for the young king of Scotland, James III. Contrary to sixteenth-century accounts as finally embodied in one of the most dramatic scenes in Shakespeare's play *3 Henry VI*, I.iv, Margaret was not present at the battle of Wakefield, fought on 30 December 1460, when both the duke of York and his younger son, Edmund, earl of Rutland, were killed. However, she was quick to take advantage of the Lancastrian victory, and rallied an army of Scottish supporters and northern men bearing the livery of the prince of Wales to march on London. This force clashed with the Yorkists, led by the earl of Warwick, at St Albans on 17 February 1461, winning a resounding victory for the Lancastrians, and enabling the queen to regain control of the king. But she was unable to follow up the victory by gaining entry to the city of London, essential to ensure control of government and to give access to badly needed supplies. Attempts at mediation by the duchesses of Buckingham and Bedford, and Lady Scales, failed to reassure the citizen body of London that the Lancastrian army was under control, and they refused it admission. On the approach of the earl of March, now the Yorkist leader, Margaret was forced to withdraw and retreat northwards, thus losing the initiative. The decisive defeat of the Lancastrians at Towton on 29 March 1461 left the king, queen, and prince vulnerable once again, and they fled to Scotland for safety. The earl of March was crowned king as Edward IV on 28 June.

Campaigns in the north, 1461–1463 From 1461 to 1471 Margaret was involved in increasingly desperate efforts to win foreign support for the recovery of the throne for either her husband or her son. She retained the loyalty of a significant number of noblemen and government officers, including the dukes of Somerset and Exeter and the earl of Pembroke who posed a real threat to Edward IV from across the Scottish borders in the early years of his reign. After 1464, when Lancastrian support was limited to a small group of household servants, effective resistance was severely hampered by shortage of money and of committed political backing. Despite her best efforts to persuade the ruling houses of Scotland and France to provide financial and military aid, neither was prepared to offer anything substantial. The Lancastrian cause was thus caught up in a complex web of European diplomacy.

After the battle of Towton, Margaret took refuge initially at Linlithgow Palace, at the invitation of the bishop of St Andrews, and later in the Dominican convent at Edinburgh. Despite the friendly reception given to Margaret in Scotland, the Scottish court was divided over offering aid to the Lancastrians. Following the death of James II on 3 August 1460, leaving an eight-year-old heir, Scotland was governed by a regency council headed by James's widow, Mary of Gueldres, but split into two factions. Margaret was keen to form a firm alliance with the Scots, offering her son in marriage to the baby sister of James III, but Mary of Gueldres was advised against this by her cousin the duke of Burgundy. Despite this opposition, Margaret offered the fortified strongholds of Berwick and Carlisle to the Scottish council in return for their assistance, handing over Berwick on 25 April 1461. French support for the Lancastrian cause was kept alive by the seneschal of Normandy, Pierre de Brézé, who led a French attack on the Channel Islands in May, setting the south coast of England on the alert. In July Margaret dispatched Somerset, Sir Robert Whittingham, and Lord Hungerford to France to seek out allies at the French court, but the death of Charles VII on 22 July 1461 changed the political climate in France, and the new king, Louis XI, proved unwilling to commit himself to a strong anti-Yorkist stance.

In April 1462 Margaret sailed for France with her son, determined to meet Louis XI in person. She was received cordially by François II, duke of Brittany, who presented her with gifts worth 12,000 gold crowns. She travelled to Angers to visit her father and de Brézé, now out of favour at the French court, and to await a meeting with Louis XI. This she eventually succeeded in obtaining, with the result that a secret agreement was reached at Chinon on 23 June, whereby Margaret agreed to surrender to Louis the English stronghold of Calais in return for a loan of 20,000 francs. More open negotiations were conducted at Tours leading to a treaty of mutual friendship concluded on 28 June, by which Louis agreed to finance an expedition to England led by de Brézé, in return for Calais. When Margaret and de Brézé at last set sail for Scotland in late October it was with only forty-two ships and some 800 men, paid for not by Louis but by de Brézé himself. After taking Henry VI and Somerset on board in Scotland, the force landed on the Northumberland coast at Bamburgh and captured Alnwick for the Lancastrians. But on hearing of the approach of a Yorkist army, Margaret took flight with Henry and de Brézé, leaving behind a small garrison. Their fleet was wrecked by a storm and they took refuge in Berwick Castle. By Christmas the castles of Bamburgh, Alnwick, and Dunstanburgh were back in Yorkist hands, only to be recaptured by a Franco-Scottish force in March 1463. In July the young James III, king of Scots, led a large Scottish army over the border to lay siege to Norham Castle, with Margaret, Henry, and Mary of Gueldres in attendance. The expedition was a fiasco and they were forced back having achieved nothing. Margaret left Scotland for France in August, taking her son with her but leaving her husband behind; they were never to meet again. Accompanying her was a small group of loyal supporters including the duke of Exeter, Sir John Fortescue, Sir Edmund Mountfort, Sir Robert Whittingham, John Morton, bishop of Ely, Ralph Mackerell, and seven women attendants.

Diplomatic endeavours, 1463–1470 Margaret's hopes of enlisting the aid of the French were dashed by the uncompromising attitude of Louis XI, who wanted a settlement with the dukes of Burgundy and Brittany. Edward IV agreed a truce at Hesdin on 8 October 1463, by which Louis specifically renounced all aid to the Lancastrians. Though Margaret was left in a very unfavourable position, she persisted in her efforts to obtain a meeting with her old enemy Philip, duke of Burgundy, eventually succeeding at the beginning of September. She was treated with dignity and respect by the duke, but he was not prepared to commit himself to her cause. He sent her back to St Pol, accompanied by the duchess of Bourbon and her daughter, to whom, according to Chastellain, Margaret recounted her earlier adventures in Scotland, which included an attack by a brigand while she was hiding in woods with her son. Margaret was also received at Bruges by the heir to Burgundy, Charles, count of Charolais, and his brother Antoine, count of La Roche, the Bastard of Burgundy, and was presented with generous gifts. During the winter of 1463–4 she stayed with her father in Nancy, continuing to negotiate with Charolais and Brittany. She kept in touch with her husband, now residing at Bamburgh, via Guillaume Cousinot who reported, in the spring of 1464, that there was still support for Henry VI in England and Wales, and that it would not be difficult to recover the kingdom for the Lancastrians with a little foreign assistance. This was not forthcoming, and a further attempt to recover the country for Henry VI instigated by Somerset in April–May 1464 failed, forcing the remaining prominent Lancastrian supporters to flee overseas.

Margaret was now living at the château of Koeur at St Mihiel in the duchy of Bar assigned to her by her father, with a pension of 6000 crowns. She remained there until 1468, apart from a short pilgrimage to St Nicholas-de-Port at the end of 1464 to offer thanks for the safe recovery of her son from a serious illness, and a visit to her parents at Angers in 1466. The royal household in exile is estimated to have numbered between 50 and 200 people. According to Fortescue, they lived in some poverty, and were very much dependent upon Margaret's father for any extra comforts—he sent his personal physician Pierre Robin to attend Margaret and her son several times. They were also visited regularly by her brother Jean, duke of Calabria, who came to play an increasingly important part in the negotiations with Louis XI. Margaret continued to woo the kings of Portugal and Castile as well as Charles, count of Charolais (all kinsmen of the house of Lancaster). By 1466 it had become clear that the duke of Burgundy and Edward IV intended to seal their alliance with a marriage settlement (between Edward's sister Margaret and the count of Charolais), thus pushing Louis further towards a Lancastrian alliance. An indication of the continued efforts of the Lancastrians to keep the cause of Henry VI alive in England and Wales is given by the arrest of a messenger sent by Margaret to rebels in Harlech Castle in 1467, and in the following year a servant of Sir Robert Whittingham was caught with letters from Lancastrian exiles to friends in England. He was tortured and accused of treasonable intercourse with Queen Margaret. In June 1468 Louis was prepared to lend support to an expedition led by Jasper Tudor, earl of Pembroke, to Wales, but this too failed. In October 1468 a rumour circulated that Margaret and her son were at Harfleur with an army about to invade England, and Edward ordered the English fleet to scour the channel to look for Margaret's ships.

The restoration and defeat of the Lancastrian monarchy, 1470–1471 The marriage of Margaret of York to Charles of Burgundy in June 1468 probably convinced Louis XI of the wisdom of falling in with Margaret of Anjou and her brother, who were pressing for an alliance with Richard Neville, earl of Warwick, as a means of restoring Henry VI to the throne. He was backed by Fortescue, whose memoranda to Louis XI in 1468–70 indicate his persistent attempts to bring the two parties together by arranging the marriage of Prince Edward to Warwick's daughter *Anne, despite the difficulties caused by past allegiances. Louis was reluctant to offer asylum to Warwick and Clarence following their rebellion against Edward IV in 1469–70, but they landed at Honfleur on 1 May 1470, and came to Amboise a month later to arrange a meeting with Margaret. She was eventually persuaded to meet Warwick at Angers, although, according to the tract known as 'The maner and guiding of the earl of Warwick', Margaret was initially 'right dificyle' and said that she could never pardon Warwick 'which had been the greatest cause of the fall of Henry VI, of her and their son' (Ellis, 1.132). After fifteen days of pressure from the king of France and her father's counsellors, Margaret reluctantly agreed to the marriage of her son to Warwick's daughter, but insisted that it should not be 'perfyted' until Warwick had recovered England for Henry VI, and established Prince Edward as regent and governor. The betrothal of Prince Edward and Anne Neville took place in Angers Cathedral on 25 July, and Warwick returned to England in September with a fleet of sixty ships paid for by Louis, under the command of the admiral of France.

Margaret and her advisers were well aware of the delicacy of their position, and of the need to present Prince Edward as a viable alternative to his Yorkist rival, and he does indeed appear to have been an energetic and warlike youth. Margaret must have believed that any future hope lay with her son rather than her husband, despite the fact that Warwick had entered the city of London unopposed on 6 October and immediately released Henry from the Tower, declaring him king once more. On 14 October Louis publicly proclaimed a treaty of alliance with Henry VI and ordered three days of thanksgiving for his restoration. Margaret and her son came to Paris to take part in the celebrations, but she was still not prepared to risk returning to England until convinced that conditions were right for the safety of her son. It was not until after Christmas that she made her way towards the Normandy coast via Rouen. On 7 December, an exchequer warrant authorized the payment of £2000 for a military escort to accompany Margaret and her son across the channel, but there were further delays as Warwick struggled to establish effective control of the country through the aged Henry VI.

French ambassadors arrived in London in January 1471 to remind Warwick of the conditions of Louis's support—an alliance against Burgundy—and Warwick did his best to convince them that it was safe for Margaret to return to England with her son. Warwick had hoped to be able to travel to France to escort them himself, but in February he dispatched the prior of St John's and others to Honfleur to meet the royal party. Bad weather further delayed the expedition which finally set sail on 24 March. Margaret's ship landed at Weymouth on 14 April only to be greeted by the news of the Lancastrian defeat at the battle of Barnet and the death of the earl of Warwick. According to the *Historie of the Arrivall of Edward IV in England*, the news made her 'right hevy and sory' (*Historie of the Arrivall*, 23), but she was encouraged by the duke of Somerset and the earl of Devon to make her way towards Wales in order to join up with the forces of Jasper Tudor, earl of Pembroke. The Lancastrian army camped outside Tewkesbury on 3 May as the Yorkists approached from the east. The following morning Margaret took shelter in a neighbouring religious house (its exact identity is unknown) with her daughter-in-law, Anne Neville, the countess of Devon, and her faithful lady-in-waiting, Lady Katherine Vaux. Here she learned of the death of her son at the hands of the Yorkists, and of the final humiliating defeat of the Lancastrian army. She was found three days later with her fellow widowed companions and handed over to Edward IV. According to the anonymous continuator of the Crowland chronicle, Margaret was borne in a carriage as a prisoner before the king at his triumphal entry into the city of London on 21 May. The death of Henry VI in the Tower that very night meant that Margaret no longer had any political importance as either the wife or mother of a rival king. As a childless widow her status was completely altered, and she became only an embarrassing encumbrance upon the victorious Edward IV.

The final years, 1471–1482 Little is known about the last ten years of Margaret's life. She remained in captivity in England until 1475, being moved from Windsor to Wallingford at the end of 1471, into the custody of Alice de la Pole, dowager duchess of Suffolk. Edward was anxious to see her return to her homeland provided a satisfactory arrangement could be made because, although she no longer posed a political threat, she had to be provided for financially. In his negotiations with Louis XI following his abortive expedition to France in the summer of 1475, Edward ensured that one of the conditions of the treaty of Picquigny, signed on 29 August 1475, was the return of Margaret to France. Edward was to surrender all rights over her, and transfer them to Louis in return for a ransom of 50,000 crowns (£10,000), of which the first instalment of 10,000 crowns should be paid when Margaret was handed over. Margaret had to renounce formally all title to the crown of England, to her dower lands in England, and any other claims she might have against Edward. On 13 November 1475 she was committed to the care of Thomas Thwaytes, who in turn handed her over to Sir Thomas Montgomery for her journey to France. Her formal transfer from English into French hands took place at Rouen on 22 January 1476, where two French commissioners made the first payment of her ransom.

Though technically a free woman, Margaret was still dependent upon others for her livelihood. Her father, now married to his former mistress, Jeanne de Laval, and living in Provence, appeared uninterested in his daughter's fate, and she was left to the mercy of the king of France. Louis forced her to give up all claims to the Angevin inheritance of Anjou, Bar, and Provence from her father, and to Lorraine from her mother, arguing that this was an adequate compensation for the heavy expenses he had repeatedly incurred upon her behalf since 1462. He agreed to provide her with a pension of 6000 crowns and she retired to the château of Reculée near Angers. Following her father's death in 1480, when the Angevin inheritance passed into the hands of the French crown, Margaret went to live at the château of Dampierre, near Saumur, in Anjou. Here she wrote her short will on 2 August 1482, just three weeks before her death on 25 August. She was buried in Angers Cathedral. Margaret had little to leave to either friends or relations, but the witnesses to her will include Lady Katherine Vaux, widow of Sir William Vaux, killed at Tewkesbury in 1471, who no doubt had stayed loyally with her throughout the ten years of shared widowhood, the loneliest of times for a former queen and mother of the heir to the throne.

Historical reputation Of all medieval queens consort, Margaret has received some of the harshest criticism from both contemporary commentators and later historians. Concern about her inability to bear a child was expressed as early as 1447, and from the late 1450s she faced slanders against her good character. In 1456 it was first rumoured that Prince Edward was not her son, and soon after, that she was going to force King Henry to abdicate in favour of his son. These rumours were eagerly picked up by foreign observers, such as the duke of Milan's ambassador, who reported in 1461 that it was believed that she had poisoned her husband. The new Yorkist king Edward IV, keen to establish the legitimacy of his dynasty, sought to blacken the names of his Lancastrian predecessors by any means

he could. Inevitably Margaret's reputation suffered as she was blamed for leading the country into civil war, and she was presented as the domineering queen in contrast to her mild-mannered, passive husband. Thus the prevalent image of Margaret as a hard-headed, ruthless, cruel, vengeful power-seeker was born, an image perpetuated so effectively by Shakespeare, drawing upon earlier sixteenth-century writers such as Vergil, Hall, and Holinshed. Like Isabella of France, wife of Edward II, Margaret has suffered from an almost universally hostile press, as much because of her nationality as on account of the unfavourable political circumstances of her time.

Shakespeare's view of Margaret persisted unchallenged into the twentieth century, influencing biographies of the queen by T. F. Tout and J. J. Bagley. Historians have demonstrated a distinct reluctance to seek out independent contemporary evidence, untainted by either political, xenophobic, or misogynist prejudice. Admittedly such evidence is hard to find, but there are some useful sources such as her letters and household accounts for the period before 1453, which indicate that, at first, Margaret conformed to the conventional role of a queen consort. It could be argued that she was subsequently forced, by political circumstance and the weakness of her husband, to take on a much more active role in politics in order to protect both her own position and that of her son. She never exercised independent power, and was always reliant on others for effective action, ultimately failing to achieve her ends. Another view of Margaret, expressed by many French writers, is that of a tragic heroine, the victim of unfavourable political circumstance. This view is epitomized by her contemporary sympathizer Chastellain, who composed a special treatise for her, entitled *Le temple de Bocace, remonstrances, par manière de consolation a une désolée reyne d'Angleterre*, on the subject of the misfortunes of ruling families related to the house of Anjou, among which Margaret's sufferings occupied 'le première place dans le livre des nobles femmes malheureuses' (Chastellain, 7.vii). DIANA E. S. DUNN

Sources R. A. Griffiths, *The reign of King Henry VI: the exercise of royal authority, 1422–1461* (1981) · B. P. Wolffe, *Henry VI* (1981) · J. Watts, *Henry VI and the politics of kingship* (1996) · C. L. Scofield, *The life and reign of Edward the Fourth*, 2 vols. (1923) · J. J. Bagley, *Margaret of Anjou, queen of England* (1948) · A. Strickland and [E. Strickland], *Lives of the queens of England*, new edn, 1 (1864), 534–640 · *Letters of Queen Margaret of Anjou and Bishop Beckington and others written in the reigns of Henry V and Henry VI*, ed. C. Monro, CS, 86 (1863) · J. Stevenson, ed., *Letters and papers illustrative of the wars of the English in France during the reign of Henry VI, king of England*, 2 vols. in 3 pts, Rolls Series, 22 (1861–4) · A. R. Myers, 'The household of Queen Margaret of Anjou, 1452–3', *Bulletin of the John Rylands University Library*, 40 (1957–8), 79–113, 391–431 · A. R. Myers, 'The jewels of Queen Margaret of Anjou', *Bulletin of the John Rylands University Library*, 42 (1959–60), 113–31 · A. Lecoy de la Marche, *Le Roi René: sa vie, son administration, ses travaux artistiques et littéraires*, 2 vols. (1875) · G. Chastellain, *Œuvres*, ed. K. de Lettenhove, 8 vols. (Brussels, 1863–6), vols. 4–5, 7 · A. Gross, *The dissolution of the Lancastrian kingship: Sir John Fortescue and the crisis of monarchy in fifteenth-century England* (1996) · DNB · M. A. Hookham, *Life and times of Margaret of Anjou*, 2 vols. (1872) · *The Paston letters, AD 1422–1509*, ed. J. Gairdner, new edn, 6 vols. (1904) · J. Gairdner, ed., *The historical collections of a citizen of London in the fifteenth century*, CS, new ser., 17 (1876) · J. S. Davies, ed., *An English* *chronicle of the reigns of Richard II, Henry IV, Henry V, and Henry VI*, CS, 64 (1856) · J. Gairdner, ed., *Three fifteenth-century chronicles*, CS, new ser., 28 (1880) [incl. Gregory's Chronicle] · 'John Benet's chronicle for the years 1400 to 1462', ed. G. L. Harriss, *Camden miscellany, XXIV*, CS, 4th ser., 9 (1972), 151–232 · *CSP Milan* · G. du Fresne de Beaucourt, *Histoire de Charles VII*, 6 vols. (Paris, 1881–91) · *Chronique de Mathieu d'Escouchy*, ed. G. Du Fresne de Beaucourt, new edn, 3 vols. (Paris, 1863–4) · T. Basin, *Histoire des règnes de Charles VII et de Louis XI*, ed. J. Quicherat, 4 vols. (1855–9) · *Recueil des croniques … par Jehan de Waurin*, ed. W. Hardy and E. L. C. P. Hardy, 5 vols., Rolls Series, 39 (1864–91) · D. Dunn, 'Margaret of Anjou, queen consort of Henry VI: a reassessment of her role, 1445–1453', *Crown, government and people in the fifteenth century*, ed. R. E. Archer (1995), 107–43 · B. M. Cron, 'The duke of Suffolk, the Angevin marriage, and the ceding of Maine, 1445', *Journal of Medieval History*, 20 (1994), 77–99 · P. A. Lee, 'Reflections of power: Margaret of Anjou and the dark side of queenship', *Renaissance Quarterly*, 39 (1986), 183–217 · *Hall's chronicle*, ed. H. Ellis (1809) · R. Holinshed and others, eds., *The chronicles of England, Scotland and Ireland*, 2nd edn, ed. J. Hooker, 3 vols. in 2 (1586–7) · H. Ellis, ed., *Original letters illustrative of English history*, 2nd ser., 1 (1827) · *Three books of Polydore Vergil's 'English history'*, ed. H. Ellis, CS, 29 (1844) · J. Bruce, ed., *Historie of the arrivall of Edward IV in England, and the finall recoverye of his kingdoms from Henry VI*, CS, 1 (1838) · P. A. Johnson, *Duke Richard of York, 1411–1460* (1988) **Likenesses** W. Abell?, manuscript illumination, 1430–70 (at prayer from her Prayer Roll), Bodl. Oxf., Jesus College MS 124 · manuscript illumination, 1445 (John Talbot, earl of Shrewsbury, presenting a book to Margaret, seated beside King Henry), BL, Royal MS 15. E.VI, fol. 2*v* · P. da Milano, portrait medal, 1460–64, V&A [*see illus.*] · R. de Gaignières, drawing (after stained-glass window); formerly in the Church of the Cordeliers, Angers · manuscript illumination (at prayer), Skinners' Company, London, Book of the Fraternity of Our Lady's Assumption, fol. 34*v* · manuscript illumination, miniature, Bibliothèque Nationale, Paris, Paris workshop, Book of Hours, MS Lat. 1156a (?) **Wealth at death** goods to be used for burial or payment of debts: will, Lecoy de la Marche, *Le Roi René*, vol. 2, pp. 395–7

Margaret, duchess of Burgundy (1446–1503), Yorkist matriarch and mediator, was the third daughter of *Richard, third duke of York (1411–1460), and *Cecily (1415–1495), daughter of Ralph Neville, first earl of Westmorland. She was born on 3 May 1446, probably at Fotheringhay Castle, Northamptonshire. Little is known of her childhood. She is mentioned by name at Fastolf's house in Southwark with her mother and her brothers, George and Richard, when Richard of York returned from Ireland in September 1460. Following her father's death at Wakefield (30 December 1460) and Edward IV's successful seizure of the crown (March 1461), she usually resided at Baynard's Castle or Greenwich. After Edward married Elizabeth Woodville, whose coronation Margaret attended in May 1465, she frequently accompanied the queen and was well schooled in court etiquette. She practised many of the devotions of her extremely pious mother, and was intelligent and literate. As an unmarried sister of the king she was one of the new dynasty's most valuable diplomatic assets. In 1462 there were rumours of a match with James III of Scotland; a more serious proposal was marriage to Don Pedro of Portugal, claimant to the Aragonese throne, but he died unexpectedly in June 1466. By then a more inviting prospect had already opened up, to consolidate an Anglo-Burgundian alliance—marriage to Charles, count of Charolais. Negotiations had begun almost immediately after the death of Charles's second wife in September 1465, but were delayed by Burgundian reluctance to break with the Lancastrians, and also by Richard Neville, earl of Warwick, who favoured a French match. In 1466–7 Louis XI unavailingly proposed no fewer than four candidates for her hand, but the death of Philip the Good, duke of Burgundy, in June 1467 provided renewed impetus. On 1 October 1467 Margaret declared her willingness to wed Charles, who later that month commissioned his mother, Isabella of Portugal, to draw up terms.

Margaret's dowry of 200,000 écus (£41,666 13*s*. 4*d*.), due within three years, was agreed by February 1468, though only just over a half was ever paid, and arrears remained a bone of contention for the rest of Margaret's life. In May 1468 the necessary papal dispensation was granted and an alliance against France concluded. She ceremoniously left London on 18 June, a temporary reconciliation with Warwick being symbolized by her riding pillion on his horse. Margaret and a large entourage sailed from Margate on 24 June, and arrived at Sluys late on 25 June. Two days later she met Charles for the first time and they were married at Damme at 5 a.m. on 3 July, before making a grand entry into Bruges, where onlookers were impressed by the tall, elegant, fair-haired duchess. For the next ten days widely reported festivities of unsurpassed courtly magnificence were held. Similar events greeted them at Brussels on 23 July, though Margaret fell ill at Aire in September.

Margaret and Charles soon settled into a domestic routine which kept them largely apart; they were together for only 21 days in their first six months of marriage, for 96 days in 1469, and 145 days in 1470, and thereafter, while often residing close to one another, they spent little time in each other's company (a fortnight at most in 1473 and 1474), meeting for the last time in July 1475. Formal relations remained polite, however, and there were many distractions at the splendid Burgundian court, where women had an honoured position. Margaret was on friendly terms with Isabella of Portugal (*d*. 1471), and acted as an elder sister to Marie, the duke's only child and heir, who was only eleven years her junior. The two women often lived together and shared many interests; their portraits appear jointly in several contemporary illuminations and paintings. Margaret commissioned manuscripts, encouraged Caxton, and, especially in her widowhood, indulged a passion for building and charitable works, encouraging education and strict religious movements. Moreover, as Charles's political and military difficulties mounted from 1475, Margaret took a larger administrative role: she led resistance to the French in Artois and negotiated with the Flemish cities. Her skills as a conciliator, displayed in 1471 when Edward IV was an exile in Flanders, mediating between him and Clarence, and again when Edward landed at Calais with an army in 1475 to join Charles, were taxed by the duke's pressing demands for men and money which Margaret presented to the estates general in 1476, before military catastrophe overwhelmed Valois Burgundy.

In the aftermath of Charles's death at Nancy (5 January

1477) and Louis XI's invasion of Burgundian lands, Margaret, ably assisted by the lord of Humbercourt and Chancellor Hugonet, lent invaluable support to the new duchess, Marie, among whose first acts was confirmation of the extensive dower lands which Charles had conferred on Margaret, including Malines which became the dowager's principal place of residence. Margaret also vigorously promoted plans for Marie to marry Maximilian, king of the Romans, despite opposition from the estates, who in defiance executed Humbercourt and Hugonet on 3 April 1477. When Maximilian finally arrived to claim his bride (they were married at Ghent on 18 August), Margaret enthusiastically promised loyalty to him. They seldom disagreed thereafter over policy, with Maximilian solicitous for her personal welfare, while she worked tirelessly in the interests of Habsburg Burgundy. The chief diplomatic purpose of her only visit to England after her marriage (in 1480) was to win back the alliance of Edward IV, in receipt since 1475 of a pension from Louis XI; manuscript illuminations represent her negotiating between her brother and Maximilian.

The accidental death of Marie in March 1482, Maximilian's unpopular regency, which led to civil war in the Low Countries, and the deaths in quick succession between 1483 and 1485 of Edward IV, Louis XI, and Richard III tested Margaret's abilities to the full. Much responsibility devolved on her for the education of the young duke, Philip the Fair, and she refused to recognize Henry VII's accession; her court became a haven for Yorkist exiles and pretenders. Payments for a proposed expedition (*Reyse*) by Margaret to England in 1486–7, and mention at Malines in July 1486 of a 'son of Clarence' (her favourite brother), hint at involvement in the conspiracy of Lambert Simnel whose forces were recruited from Maximilian's mercenaries in the Netherlands and paid by Margaret. After their defeat at Stoke by Newark (16 June 1487) new domestic problems, including the capture of Maximilian by the Flemings in early 1488, required Margaret's urgent attention, but her diplomatic intrigues surface occasionally with mention of her envoys at foreign courts including Scotland.

By February 1492, if not before, Margaret was certainly involved with Perkin Warbeck, a tool of French policy, also subsequently backed by Maximilian, whose coronation as emperor in November 1493 Warbeck attended. In the previous July envoys of Henry VII, led by William Warham (*d.* 1532), future archbishop of Canterbury, had confronted her with knowledge of Warbeck's imposture. But in a letter to Isabella of Castile in August, Margaret maintained he was indeed Richard, duke of York, provided funds for him, and as late as May 1495 wrote to the pope on his behalf. Warbeck's landing in England in that summer was a failure; he eventually found refuge at the Scottish court but Margaret remained in contact. As a result of the Anglo-imperial Intercursus Magnus (27 February 1496) she was obliged to renounce her support for Henry VII's enemies, but it was not until almost a year after the capture and confession of Warbeck (October

1497) that she finally made peace with Henry VII (September 1498).

As a formidable matriarchal figure Margaret's last years were largely devoted to her proxy Habsburg grandchildren and great-grandchildren. In 1500 she stood godmother to the future Emperor Charles V, and in 1501 visited Halle with Margaret of Austria, the daughter of Marie, duchess of Burgundy, who inherited many of the duchess's personal possessions. Margaret died at Malines on 23 November 1503 and was buried there in the house of the Recollects (Observant Franciscans), where her tomb was destroyed in the late sixteenth century. Apart from the many portraits and miniatures of her, and nearly thirty extant manuscripts with which she can be connected, her most poignant surviving memorial is perhaps an exquisite coronet of English make that was part of her trousseau, which she donated during a visit in 1474 to the cathedral of Aachen.   MICHAEL JONES

Sources C. A. J. Armstrong, *England, France and Burgundy in the fifteenth century* (1983) · I. Arthurson, *The Perkin Warbeck conspiracy, 1491–1499* (1994) · M. Ballard and C. S. L. Davies, 'Étienne Fryon: Burgundian agent, English royal secretary and "principal counsellor" to Perkin Warbeck', *Historical Research*, 62 (1989), 245–59 · M. Ballard, 'An expedition of English archers to Liège in 1467, and the Anglo-Burgundian marriage alliance', *Nottingham Medieval Studies*, 34 (1990), 152–74 · M. Bennett, *Lambert Simnel and the battle of Stoke* (1987) · S. B. Chrimes, *Henry VII* (1972) · L. Hommel, *Marguerite d'York, ou, La duchesse Junon* (1959) · W. Blockmans, 'The devotion of a lonely duchess', *Margaret of York, Simon Marmion and the visions of Tondal*, ed. T. Kren (1992), 29–46 · *Marguerite d'York et son temps: British week in Brussels*, Banque de Bruxelles (1967) [exhibition catalogue, 29 Sept – 7 Oct 1967] · A. Morel-Fatio, 'Marguerite d'York et Perkin Warbeck', *Mélanges d'histoire offerts à M. Charles Bémont* (Paris, 1913), 411–16 · O. Pächt, *The master of Mary of Burgundy* (1948) · W. Prevenier and W. Blockmans, *The Burgundian Netherlands* (1986) · C. Ross, *Edward IV* (1974) · C. Ross, *Richard III* (1981) · C. L. Scofield, *The life and reign of Edward the Fourth*, 2 vols. (1923) · R. Vaughan, *Charles the bold* (1973) · C. Weightman, *Margaret of York, duchess of Burgundy, 1446–1503* (1989)
Archives BL · Royal Library of Belgium, Brussels
Likenesses school of S. Marmion, portrait, *c.*1468–1480, Louvre, Paris · H. van der Goes?, portrait, 1500–99; copy, S. Antiquaries, Lond. · illumination, Bodl. Oxf., Douce MS 365, fol. 115 · portrait, Metropolitan Museum, New York, Robert Lehman Collection

Margaret [Margaret of Denmark] (1456/7?–1486), queen of Scots, consort of James III, was the only daughter of Christian I of Denmark–Norway (1448–1481) and Dorothea of Brandenburg. That Maundy alms were given to seventeen people at Easter 1474 probably indicates that Margaret was then aged seventeen and was born in 1456 or 1457. Almost from birth she played a key role in Scoto-Danish diplomatic schemes, which continued intermittently from late 1458 until the treaty of Copenhagen of 8 September 1468. Under this treaty between Scotland and Denmark–Norway, Margaret was to marry *James III, king of Scots. It also brought to an end, as part of Margaret's dowry, Scottish payments of the Norway 'annual', the 100 merks that had been due each year since 1266 for the Western Isles, a sum which the Scots had long neglected to pay. The most significant part of the treaty resulted from King Christian's financial difficulties: as he could not afford the bride's dowry of 60,000 Rhenish florins, he pledged first Orkney (1468) and then Shetland (May 1469) to Scotland for the entire sum owed. Christian had every intention of redeeming his pledge and the islands, but subsequent political events made this impossible.

As soon as Margaret reached the marriageable age of twelve, she was brought to Scotland and married to James III at Holyrood Abbey on 13 July 1469. In the summer of 1470 the queen accompanied her husband on a northern progress, spending a full month in Inverness. Earlier that year the king had granted her the barony of Kilmarnock for life, specifically to pay for her gowns and headgear. In 1478 she was confirmed in the dowry promised her under the treaty of Copenhagen, namely a third of the property and revenues of the crown. This included the lordships of Galloway, Ettrick Forest, Strathearn, Strath Gartney, and Linlithgowshire, the castles of Threave, Stirling, Doune, and Methven, Linlithgow Palace, and much else. She spent a good deal of time at Stirling, though her eldest son, the future *James IV, was born at Holyrood on 17 March 1473. She later gave birth to two more sons: James *Stewart, duke of Ross, early in 1476, and John, earl of Mar, before 12 July 1480.

Margaret played an important, if rather enigmatic, political role. A short biography of the queen, written within a few years of her death by the Bolognese Giovanni Sabadino, credits her with more ability than her husband in governing the realm, claims that she and his brother (clearly Alexander Stewart, duke of Albany, is intended) imprisoned him for the good of the kingdom, and comments that James III was unwilling ever to see her during the last three years of her life. These assertions, though undoubtedly exaggerated in transmission, have some substance. Following the Lauder crisis of 1482, when James III was imprisoned in Edinburgh Castle, Albany visited the queen at Stirling; they discussed the education of the heir to the throne, and Albany later played a part in releasing King James from captivity. Collusion between Albany and Margaret would certainly explain the king's subsequent mistrust of his wife, and there is no firm evidence that the two met again after 1482. Margaret of Denmark died at Stirling Castle on 14 July 1486 and was buried in Cambuskenneth Abbey later that month; rebel propaganda which spread to Denmark in 1488 alleged that she had been murdered, possibly poisoned by the king's familiar John Ramsay. This was clearly untrue; but James III's abortive efforts in 1487 to secure his wife's canonization may have been inspired partly by growing rumours of foul play.

NORMAN MACDOUGALL

Sources G. Burnett and others, eds., *The exchequer rolls of Scotland*, 7–9 (1884–6) · T. Dickson, ed., *Compota thesaurariorum regum Scotorum / Accounts of the lord high treasurer of Scotland*, 1 (1877) · S. B. Chandler, 'An Italian life of Margaret, queen of James III', *SHR*, 32 (1953), 52–7 · B. E. Crawford, 'Scotland's foreign relations: Scandinavia', *Scottish society in the fifteenth century*, ed. J. M. Brown (1977), 85–100 · BM, MS 17 Dxx, fols. 299–308r · *APS*, 1424–1567 · T. Riis, *Should auld acquaintance be forgot … Scottish–Danish relations, c.1450–1707*, 1 (1988), chap. 9 · N. Macdougall, *James III: a political study* (1982) · *CEPR letters*, vol. 14 · TKUA, Skotland, Danske Rigsarkiv, Copenhagen, A1, 1 · N. Macdougall, *James IV* (1989) · J. Norton-Smith, ed., *James I of Scotland: the king's quair* (1971), xxxiii

Likenesses H. van der Goes, altarpiece, before 1483, Royal Collection · S. Armorial, double portrait, 1591 (with James III), NL Scot. · watercolour (after H. van der Goes), Scot. NPG

Margaret [Margaret Tudor] (1489–1541), queen of Scots, consort of James IV, was born at Westminster Palace on 28 November 1489, the eldest daughter and second child of *Henry VII (1457–1509) and *Elizabeth of York (1466–1503), and baptized in St Margaret's, Westminster, later that year. Attended by Alice Bywmble as her special nurse and Anne Maylande and Margaret Troughton as rockers of her cradle, she spent her earliest years at Sheen on the banks of the Thames with her brothers and sisters, until a fire caused the royal nursery to be moved to Eltham Palace. Less studious than her brothers *Arthur and Henry (the future *Henry VIII), Margaret learned to play the lute and clavichord and to dance, became skilled at archery, studied Latin, and learned to speak French. Her tutors included such notable scholars as Thomas Linacre, John Colet, and William Grocyn.

Scottish marriage It was inevitable that thought would soon be given to Margaret's marriage. At first her father considered betrothing her to Prince Christian of Denmark, but his thoughts soon turned to nearer home, and on 5 May 1496 he opened negotiations for marrying his daughter to *James IV, king of Scots (1473–1513). Later that year diplomatic progress was halted by the outbreak of Anglo-Scottish hostilities resulting from James's support for Perkin Warbeck, but resumed after he had deserted the pretender. The need to obtain a papal dispensation also caused delay. But by late 1501 Scottish negotiators were pressing for the marriage. King Henry calmed critics who feared that such a union would lead to a Scottish king succeeding to the English throne by pointing out that the greater unit (England) would none the less draw the lesser one (Scotland) into its orbit. The marriage treaty was concluded on 24 January 1502. Henry pledged a £10,000 dowry, while James promised his bride £1000 Scots per annum together with lands and castles yielding a further yearly income of £6000. Margaret would be accompanied by twenty-four English servants, and would also have an appropriate number of Scottish domestics. Should she be widowed, she was promised £2000 per annum and the continued income of her lands.

The earl of Bothwell represented James IV at his king's proxy marriage to Margaret on 15 January 1503, against a background of church bells, bonfires, jousts and tournaments, dancing, and feasting. Although her mother died just before she travelled north to Scotland, on 8 July 1503, now aged thirteen, Margaret left Richmond Palace for her 33-day journey to Edinburgh, accompanied by a large retinue headed by Thomas Howard, earl of Surrey. Henry went with them on the first stage of the journey north. About 1000 Scots met the English company at Berwick and accompanied their new queen into Scotland early in August, after several days of festivities in which James IV played a prominent part. The formal wedding took place in an elaborate service in the chapel of Holyroodhouse on 8 August. Although James provided Margaret with jewels and rich gowns, he continued to visit Janet Kennedy, his mistress since 1498; moreover, Margaret's dower castle of Stirling contained the nursery for her husband's seven illegitimate children. How the queen responded to this evidence for James's physical exuberance is not recorded.

Early in 1507 Margaret gave birth to a son, James, but the baby prince died at Stirling on 27 February 1508. A daughter, born at Holyrood on 15 July 1508, died the same day. Her brother Arthur had left a significant fortune to Margaret, now in the keeping of Henry VIII, and in spring 1513 Margaret asked the English ambassador, Nicholas West, both for Arthur's bequest and also for the plate and jewels left her by her grandmother Lady Margaret Beaufort. West replied that these would only be handed over if James IV remained at peace with England, instead of joining France. Margaret begged her husband not to go to war against her brother, but in vain, and on 9 September 1513 James was killed at Flodden, along with some 10,000 Scots. Their infant son, born at Linlithgow on 11 April 1512, succeeded his father as *James V.

Remarriage and exile James IV's will provided that Margaret should serve as regent as long as she did not remarry. A council of four nobles was established to help her govern. Henry VIII was now determined to influence Scottish affairs through his sister, a development resented by patriotic Scots, and on 6 August 1514 Margaret played into their hands by taking a second husband, Archibald *Douglas, sixth earl of Angus (c.1489–1557), the greatest Scottish magnate, so forfeiting her right to the regency. Partly because she was distrusted by many Scottish nobles, who also regarded the Douglas family as over-powerful, the council invited a cousin of James IV, John Stewart or Stuart, second duke of Albany, to act as regent until the infant James V came of age. Albany, the son of James III's younger brother Alexander, had grown up in France and was highly regarded as a soldier. The Scots, believing that a man of his eminence was needed to keep order and defend the country against England, persuaded the French to allow the duke to cross to Scotland; he landed at Dumbarton on 18 May 1515 with eight ships bearing supplies and French soldiers.

Many Scots regarded Margaret primarily as the sister of the hated English king, and suspected she favoured England over Scotland. For her part, Margaret bitterly resented Albany's replacing her as regent and urged Henry to restore her authority by force. She also complained frequently to her brother about her inadequate revenues and welcomed his intervention with the pope to secure the see of Dunkeld for Gavin Douglas, her husband's uncle. But although Henry was angry with François I for allowing Albany's passage to Scotland, thereby reducing English influence there, he did little to help his sister. Margaret's circumstances were indeed unhappy, and became more so when her brother's efforts to gain possession of her two sons, James V and Alexander, duke of Ross (born on 30 April 1514), led to the children's being taken from her as a safeguard against English designs. Having lost the regency, her revenues, and control of her own children, the queen fled to England on 30 September 1515, even though she was heavily pregnant. Henry arranged

for her to be welcomed at Harbottle Castle in Northumberland with gifts of fine clothes and money, and by the end of the year she had twenty-two gowns of cloth of gold.

At Henry's behest, Angus and Alexander, third Lord Home, attempted to seize Margaret's sons at Stirling and bring them to England, but the coup failed and they lost sixteen men. Shortly after her arrival at Harbottle, on 7 October 1515, Margaret gave birth to a daughter, Margaret *Douglas, an ordeal which nearly killed her and left her so weak that in late November she had to be conveyed to Morpeth in a litter. Angus, Home, and a few others visited her there, and also promised to promote Henry's interests in Scotland. Margaret was herself determined to visit her brother in London, but Angus returned to Scotland to defend his interests there against Albany. On 18 December, while she lay seriously ill at Morpeth, Margaret's second son, Alexander, died. His mother was not informed immediately for fear the shock might prove fatal. On 3 May 1516 she and her entourage finally arrived in London, to be welcomed with jousts, feasting, and celebrations lasting for a month; there Margaret had her first meeting with Henry for thirteen years. She remained in England for over a year, separated from Angus, while Albany and the Scottish council, hoping to prevent English raids, promised to send the queen's jewels after her and to pay her her rents. But although Margaret received her jewels, her revenues were not restored, and she had to borrow money from Cardinal Wolsey.

Breach with Angus After Henry had launched further raids into Scotland to put pressure on the Scots, and after much diplomacy and many threats, in 1517 François I called Albany back to France. Before he left the duke gave assurances that Margaret could return to Scotland and take possession of her revenues and property. Moreover, she and her company would be 'free from arrest, injury, or impediment', provided they did nothing 'prejudicial to the king, governor, or realm' (Hannay and Hay, 41). The Scottish estates insisted that Albany had treated Margaret 'with fairness and indulgence', despite her plot to place her children in English hands (ibid., 42). Furnished with a safe conduct, the queen began her journey back to Scotland on 18 May 1517, equipped with fine clothes, jewels, money, and horses. Angus met her at Berwick, and on 15 June accompanied her into Scotland, where her return was greeted with relief by a government hoping now to allay tensions with England.

Unfortunately Margaret's marriage to Angus was coming increasingly under strain. While she had been in England her husband had been living with a mistress (and former fiancée), Lady Jane Stewart of Traquair, cohabiting with her on Margaret's money. He had also taken the queen's rents from Methven and Ettrick Forest. Discovering his infidelity (which had also led to the birth of a daughter, Janet), Margaret begged her brother to allow her to return to England. Henry, however, sent neither money nor troops, and instead urged her to return to Angus. Deprived of her revenues, and refused permission to live with her son for fear she would remove him to England, she wrote that she would rather be dead than live among the Scottish lords. Thomas, Lord Dacre, the English march warden, echoed her complaint when he asked that aid be sent to Margaret, who 'lies in Edinburgh like a poor suitor' (*CSP Scot.*, 1509–89, 7).

Following his return to France, Albany played a central role in negotiating the Franco-Scottish treaty of Rouen, concluded on 26 August 1517, which provided for mutual assistance should Henry VIII make war on either signatory. On 2 October 1518, however, François I made an alliance with Henry, whose terms included an undertaking that Albany would be kept in France as long as this second treaty remained in force. The Scots felt slighted by this, and they desperately wanted Albany to return, regarding his links with France as a safeguard against English aggression. Against this background of international diplomacy, Queen Margaret, lacking funds, power, and authority over her son, had become a figure of little account, and in 1519 she again asked to be allowed to return to England. To add to her misery, her estrangement from Angus was now so severe that she contemplated divorce. Seeing no chance of an improvement in the prevailing situation, Margaret reversed her position and began petitioning Albany to return, thinking that the French duke might treat her better than did the Scottish estates. Her brother was furious, however, and at his urging she reluctantly returned to Angus, through whom Henry hoped to exercise leverage in Scotland. But although the estates promised to safeguard her revenues, her position did not improve, and in October 1520 she was again lamenting her desperate need of money and the fact that she was only rarely allowed to see her son. She threatened to give support to anti-English factions if Henry did not relieve her plight.

Relations with Albany Margaret was miserable over her status, the Scots were unhappy that Albany was detained in France, and Henry was angry that Margaret had again separated from Angus and now supported Albany's return. Margaret even persuaded Albany to promote her bid for a divorce, believing he had influence at Rome. Then in 1521 Henry VIII's alliance with Emperor Charles V led to François I's sending Albany back to Scotland. He entered Edinburgh on 3 December and was welcomed by the queen, who continued to hope that he would restore her revenues and help her obtain a divorce. Henry, however, refused to make peace, or even a border truce, while Albany remained in Scotland. The duke did in fact arrange better treatment for Margaret, but this merely fuelled the malicious tales spread by Angus and his followers that Albany supported the queen's divorce so that he could marry her himself, kill James V, and become king. In England there were additional rumours that Margaret had become Albany's mistress, rumours which Henry did not hesitate to convey to his sister in a letter brought to Margaret by Clarenceux herald in February 1522. They reduced her to tears, and prompted an indignant response to Henry's 'sharp and unkind letter' (*LP Henry VIII*, 3/2, no. 2038). Supported by the estates, the duke banished Angus

and his brother George to France, and in September gathered an army with the intention of invading England. But fear of a repetition of Flodden held the Scots back from attacking Carlisle, and Margaret was able to persuade Albany and Dacre to conclude a truce. Disgusted by the reluctance of the Scots to fight, Albany appointed a regency council, from which the queen was excluded, and on 27 October sailed for France.

Albany's departure did not end Anglo-Scottish hostilities. Following devastating English raids in spring 1523, Margaret (who had been ill with smallpox in the previous December, but soon recovered) decided in July to co-operate with Henry, in the hope that the English king would help elevate James V to active rule. Implicit in this volte-face was a willingness to see Albany ousted as regent. The Scottish nobility still trusted the duke, however, and again asked François I to allow him to return to Scotland. François complied, and on 23 September Albany landed at Kirkcudbright with several thousand French troops, planning once more to invade England. Fearing retribution for having urged that his regency be terminated, Margaret yet again petitioned for leave to retire to England, but Henry sent her money and ordered her to stay in Scotland.

On 23 October 1523 a large Scottish army again refused to cross the border, and Albany, his prestige greatly reduced by this failure, decided to return to France. He established a rotating governorship for the young king, whereby groups of four nobles took turns to have custody of James for three months at a time, and with Margaret's support tried to negotiate an Anglo-Scottish truce to which the French would also be party. But when he departed on 20 May 1524 he had failed to secure the terms he sought, while Henry decided to bring Angus back from France. Albany left Scotland intending to return, though in fact he never did so, and before his departure he obtained promises from Margaret that she would do nothing to undermine his authority, would reject any Anglo-Scottish peace which excluded France, and would uphold the treaty of Rouen. He also secured an undertaking from the estates to treat the queen well. But no sooner had Albany gone than Margaret, who had threatened to leave with him should her hated husband return and again withhold her revenues, won the support of the powerful Hamilton family, led by the second earl of Arran, for a coup which formally ended Albany's regency and on 26 July invested James V with full royal authority.

The last years of James's minority James promptly indicated that he would follow Henry's advice, raising the latter's hopes of a rupture in the Franco-Scottish alliance. Meanwhile the English king welcomed Angus in London, causing Margaret, who above all else feared her husband's return, to denounce Henry's plans to exercise influence in Scotland through him. In the hope of keeping Angus away, she and Arran, who with her effectively headed the government, worked for an Anglo-Scottish alliance pleasing to King Henry, who sent large sums to strengthen the position of his sister and her son. There was now a significant additional personal dimension to Margaret's aversion to her husband's return. As the third duke of Norfolk reported to Wolsey on 19 September 1524, 'The Queen is very unpopular for taking so much upon herself, and being ruled only by Arran and Henry Steward; also for her ungodly living, in keeping Angus out of the realm when he is so beloved' (*LP Henry VIII*, 4/1, no. 672). Henry *Stewart (*c*.1495–1553/4) was Margaret's treasurer and eventually became her third husband. In November she was reported to be infatuated with him.

Although the Scottish parliament declared Albany's regency to be over on 26 November 1524, it also resolved to maintain the French alliance; attempts to negotiate peace with England, and even the marriage of King James to Princess Mary, came to grief on this point. Henry provided Angus with 'power, substance and counsaill' in his efforts to prise Scotland and France apart (*State Papers, Henry VIII*, 4.207), and also tried to bully his sister into compliance, threatening to stop paying for her 200-strong bodyguard and affecting outrage over her rejection of Angus and liaison with Stewart. Fearing that her regime would be overthrown by its enemies, Margaret asked Henry to pay for 300 guards instead of 200, and when he refused put on a display of Francophilia, further irritating her brother by suggesting that the English ambassadors should go home.

There was a widespread perception that Margaret lacked good counsel, and that her government was too narrowly based. When parliament met in November 1524 it attempted to remedy this by establishing a council of four to help her rule. But her failure to secure anything more than a two-month truce with England undermined the queen's position, and with the support of Henry VIII, who was tired of his sister's unreliability, her rejection of her husband, and her pleas for money, in February 1525 Angus was able to take a leading position in government. Henry also agreed that Angus should take control of his wife's lands. Presumably it was to strengthen the queen's hand at this difficult moment, and also to prevent James V's marriage to Mary Tudor, that François I offered Margaret the French *comté* of Longy and a pension of 20,000 écus, on condition that her son should in due course marry his own daughter Madeleine. Such personal satisfaction as the French king's intervention may have brought her was followed later in 1525 by political disaster. It became Angus's turn to have custody of James V, but he refused to surrender the king at the end of his three-month turn, instead keeping control of him and of Scottish government until 1528. No longer supported by Henry VIII, and with control of her son lost to the hated Angus, Margaret was reduced to near despair. Moreover, despite the provision made for her in the Anglo-Scottish peace which was ratified on 12 February 1526, Angus still refused to return her lands.

An attempt by the third earl of Lennox to free King James from Angus's custody had been defeated at Linlithgow on 4 September 1526. Lennox was killed, and Angus and the Douglases were left without a rival. Margaret had continued to urge Albany to use his influence at Rome to help her obtain a divorce from Angus, since she was determined never to be reconciled with him but to marry Henry Stewart instead. She had originally attempted to justify the separation on the specious grounds that James IV had not been killed at Flodden, but was still alive when she married Angus; however, when Clement VII finally annulled the marriage, on 11 March 1527, it was by reference to Angus's pre-contract to Lady Jane Stewart. Soon afterwards Margaret secretly married Henry Stewart, openly acknowledging him as her husband about the beginning of April 1528. Angus then had Henry Stewart arrested and confined, claiming that Margaret's remarriage had taken place without royal approval. For the queen, this development meant that she could keep company with her present husband only if her former one was removed from power. In May 1528, however, James V escaped from Angus's clutches, proclaimed himself king in his majority, and mustered enough support to expel the Douglases from government. On 19 June his mother caused James, who had come to loathe his erstwhile stepfather, to order that neither Angus nor any other Douglas should come within 7 miles of him. Henry Stewart was created Lord Methven, and in September parliament sentenced Angus and his associates to death *in absentia*, for treason. No doubt Margaret was delighted. She was less pleased, however, when Angus took refuge in England. She angrily accused her brother of having more regard for the earl than for his own nephew. Angus remained in exile at Henry's expense until 1543.

Disengagement and death After 1528 relations between the young king and his mother were generally good, but they differed over foreign policy, Margaret favouring closer links with England, in contrast to James, who renewed the French alliance soon after assuming personal rule. He sought her advice on the rebuilding or renovation of royal castles, but in matters of government took counsel elsewhere, and it is noticeable that Margaret's name is entirely missing from her son's letters dating from after 1534. When Henry proposed a meeting with James at York late in 1534, Margaret's enthusiasm for the event—partly arising from hopes of arranging the marriage of James to Mary Tudor—seems to have turned the Scottish king against the conference, which never happened. Two years later plans were again made for the two kings to meet. Margaret prepared to visit England and bought expensive clothes in anticipation of the journey, which likewise never took place. Afterwards she asked Henry for money to repay debts incurred at this time, but her brother refused, advising her to stay in Scotland and either return her purchases or put them to other uses. Shortly afterwards her hopes of an Anglo-Scottish marriage alliance were dashed when James married Madeleine of France in Paris on 1 January 1537, but she still had the gall to beg Henry for funds yet again, so that she could appear suitably dressed at the reception of her new daughter-in-law; this time Henry complied.

By the mid-1530s Margaret's personal life had turned sour once more, and she sent a stream of letters to Henry

VIII and his ministers complaining of her husband, Lord Methven: not only had he taken a mistress, with whom he had a son, but he had so wasted her revenues that she was 8000 merks in debt. She had resolved to divorce him, but her efforts were thwarted by her son, after Methven told James that she proposed to go to England and there remarry Angus. Early in October 1537 she tried to escape to Berwick but was intercepted. Later that month, in an outburst of self-pity, she told her brother, 'wyth owt I get remedy, I wol pas to some relygeous place, and byde wyth them, or I be intretyd as I am' (State Papers, Henry VIII, 5.120). Queen Madeleine died on 7 July 1537, and in 1538 James married another Frenchwoman, Mary of Guise. Once more Margaret begged Henry to send her money so that she could appear in attire befitting her rank when her son and his new bride reached Scotland. After their arrival Margaret informed Henry that Mary had 'behaved very honorably toward her' (CSP Scot., 1509–89, 39). But she now had little influence with either her son or her brother, though she was at the Scottish court in 1541, and gave comfort to James and Mary when their infant sons died in May. The husband she now hated controlled her revenues, and she was lonely and unhappy. She wanted to return to England, but Henry would not invite her, and in her last years practically ignored her.

On 18 October 1541, in her fifty-second year, Queen Margaret died after suffering a stroke at Methven Castle. She asked for her son, who was at Falkland Palace, but he did not arrive in time. In her last words she asked her confessors to beseech James 'that He wold be good and gracious unto the Erell of Anguyshe, and dyd extremely lament, and aske God mercy, that She had afendet unto the sayd Erell as She hade' (State Papers, Henry VIII, 5.194). She left just 2500 merks in ready money. Dying intestate, she asked that her valuables should go to Margaret Douglas, but James ignored this request and his mother's goods reverted to the crown. She was buried among the Scottish kings in St John's Abbey, the Carthusian house in Perth.

It is difficult to gain a clear impression of Queen Margaret, in terms either of her personality or of her impact on events. Scottish sources often reflect native suspicions of an English queen, English ones the hopes—usually unfulfilled—of diplomatic advantage. It seems clear that her years in Scotland were generally unhappy. She was only twenty-three when her first husband was killed, her two subsequent marriages both failed utterly, and she had limited contact with both her son in Scotland and her daughter in England. The nature of the sources means that it is usually hard to detach the evidence for her parental feelings from her hopes of material advantage, but she clearly wanted the company of her son during the latter's childhood, and in 1536 she pleaded for Lady Margaret Douglas when she disgraced herself by marrying Lord Thomas Howard. Her choice of husbands was disastrous, however, and her involvement in government usually unsuccessful. Nor was she a skilful manager of her income, and her importunities for money finally exhausted the patience of her brother Henry VIII, who had been remarkably tolerant of her demands. Whether these shortcomings arose from difficult circumstances or from her own lack of judgement, compounded by a greater concern with the trappings than the exercise of power, is again unclear, but her recurrent preoccupation with appearances certainly suggests the latter. But in one respect she was undeniably a successful queen, for it was from her first marriage that there sprang the line that eventually united England and Scotland.

RICHARD GLEN EAVES

Sources LP Henry VIII, vols. 1–16 · CSP Scot. ser., 1509–89 · State papers published under … Henry VIII, 11 vols. (1830–52) · The letters of James V, ed. R. K. Hannay and D. Hay (1954) · M. Perry, The sisters of Henry VIII (1998) · R. G. Eaves, Henry VIII and James V's regency, 1524–1528 (1987) · R. G. Eaves, Henry VIII's Scottish diplomacy, 1513–1524 (1971) · M. L. Harvey, The rose and the thorn: the lives of Mary and Margaret Tudor (1975) · BL, Cotton MSS Caligula · P. H. Buchanan, Margaret Tudor, queen of Scots (1985) · R. Holinshed, The chronicles of England, Scotland and Ireland, 6 vols. (1807–8); facs. edn (New York, 1965) · R. K. Hannay, ed., Acts of the lords of council in public affairs, 1501–1554 (1932) · Hall's chronicle, ed. H. Ellis (1809) · J. B. A. T. Teulet, ed., Papiers d'état, pièces et documents inédits ou peu connus relatifs à l'histoire de l'Écosse au XVIème siècle, 3 vols., Bannatyne Club, 107 (Paris, 1852–60) · J. B. A. T. Teulet, ed., Relations politiques de la France et de l'Espagne avec l'Écosse au XVIème siècle: papiers d'état, pièces et documents inédits, new edn, 5 vols. (Paris, 1862) · M. Wood, ed., Flodden papers: diplomatic correspondence between the courts of France and Scotland, 1507–1517, Scottish History Society, 3rd ser., 20 (1933) · CSP Venice, 1509–54 · The historie and cronicles of Scotland … by Robert Lindesay of Pitscottie, ed. A. J. G. Mackay, 3 vols., STS, 42–3, 60 (1899–1911) · J. Cameron, James V: the personal rule, 1528–1542, ed. N. Macdougall (1998)
Archives BL, Cotton MSS Caligula, letters
Likenesses manuscript, c.1503–1513, Bruges · stained-glass window, c.1518–1528, The Vyne, Hampshire · D. Mytens, oils (after type of, c.1515–1516), Royal Collection · portrait, Scot. NPG

Margaret, Princess [Princess Margaret of Connaught] **(1882–1920)**, crown princess of Sweden, consort of Gustav Adolf, was born Margaret Victoria Augusta Charlotte Norah on 15 January 1882 at Bagshot Park, Surrey, eldest of the three children of Queen Victoria's favourite son, *Arthur, duke of Connaught (1850–1942), and his wife, Princess Louise Margaret of Prussia (1860–1917). Princess Margaret, or Daisy, as she was known, was educated at home and received special training in oil painting from the French impressionist Madeleine Fleury. Her landscapes, now preserved in the Swedish royal collection, are highly regarded by Swedish art historians.

In January 1905 Daisy went to Egypt with her parents, and at Luxor she had a chance meeting with Prince Gustav Adolf (1882–1973), eldest son of the crown prince of Sweden. They became engaged within days and were married in St George's Chapel, Windsor, on 15 June 1905. The Swedish court, which was entirely German in sympathy and rigid in etiquette, was not keen to welcome Daisy, but she struck an immediate chord with ordinary people who responded to her naturalness and charm. She often felt shy, but found that a sense of humour carried her through the most daunting occasions. As she became fluent in Swedish her confidence grew and her days filled with public engagements. She enjoyed active sports and took singing lessons. A keen gardener from childhood, she redesigned the gardens at Sofiero, the summer residence given to her as a wedding present, which had been neglected for years. She wrote and illustrated two books about her gardens in Swedish.

In 1907 Gustav Adolf became crown prince. Their marriage was extremely happy and produced five children. Daisy's delight in them and her close involvement with their upbringing increased her popularity, and informal photographs of the family were used to raise money for her charities. She took special interest in childcare, in blind people, and in teacher training.

The First World War brought new problems. In a country officially neutral and actually pro-German, the crown princess was isolated and unable to express her true sympathies. It was not possible for her to visit her own family in England: not even in 1917, when her mother died after a short illness; she swallowed her feelings and was careful to demonstrate loyalty to Sweden. She created a sewing society to support the Red Cross and organized a candle collection for the poor when paraffin supplies ran low. In November 1917 she started a new scheme training girls to work on the land. But she did find ways of using Sweden's neutrality to help her own family and other families divided by the war. From Sweden she could maintain contact between relatives on the opposing sides and help to trace missing men in prisoner-of-war camps, and she was tireless in her efforts to support prisoners by sending food parcels, organizing bazaars to sell their handiwork, and even by sending garden seeds to supplement their diet. Respect for her in British government circles was high during the war years: later, voices from all parts of the Swedish political spectrum were raised in praise of her conduct and in recognition of the personal cost.

Early in January 1920 the crown princess had a mastoid operation, removing a piece of bone from behind her ear. She appeared to be recovering and was expecting her sixth child, but that spring her health declined, with facial neuralgia and inflammation. She died suddenly at the royal palace in Stockholm on 1 May 1920, and was buried in that city on 13 May. Her husband succeeded as king of Sweden in 1950, having married Lady Louise Mountbatten (formerly Princess Louise of Battenberg) in 1923.

CHARLOTTE ZEEPVAT

Sources general correspondence, Royal Arch. · Royal Arch., Add. A15/8635 [vol. of memorial articles from Swedish newspapers, trans. into English] · J. van der Kiste, *Northern crowns* (1996) · N. Frankland, *Witness of a century* (1993) · [H. Montgomery-Massingberd], ed., *Burke's royal families of the world*, 1 (1977)
Archives Royal Arch., corresp., references, and other MSS | Bodl. Oxf., letters to Lady Edward Cecil · St George's Chapel, Windsor, letters and Christmas cards to J. H. J. Ellison
Likenesses photographs, Royal Arch. · portraits (as a child), repro. in O. Millar, *The Victorian pictures in the collection of Her Majesty the Queen* (1992)

Margaret of England. *See* Margaret (1240–1275).

Margaret of Scotland. *See* Margaret (1424–1445).

Margarot, Maurice (1745–1815), radical, was born of foreign parentage in Devon. His father, normally resident in London, was a merchant dealing principally in wine from France and Portugal. Educated at the University of Geneva, Margarot entered the family business, travelling in the West Indies and Portugal, where he owned some property. It is possible that he had developed some sympathy for radical politics through his father, who is reported to have made his home a centre for radical Wilkites during the 1760s and 1770s. At the beginning of the French Revolution, Margarot was resident in France; when he returned to England early in 1792 he joined the *London Corresponding Society (LCS). Margarot's education and undoubted ability ensured his prominence, and, although he expressed some initial nervousness that too public an involvement with the society might damage his business with London merchants, on 3 May 1792 he was elected chairman of the society's general committee. As chairman he shared the administrative load with Thomas Hardy, the secretary, and while Margarot appears to have been the author of some of the significant addresses, the two signed jointly the more important correspondence, addresses, and proclamations. At a general meeting held in the open air at Chalk Farm on 24 October 1793, Margarot was chosen, together with Joseph Gerrald, to represent the society at the Edinburgh convention. The United Political Societies of Norwich also selected Margarot as their representative and agreed to share his expenses with the LCS.

The radicals in Scotland were reeling from the severe sentences imposed on two of their principal spokesmen, Thomas Muir and the Revd Thomas Fyshe Palmer. The Edinburgh convention had already met, briefly, before Margarot and Gerrald arrived, accompanied by another two delegates from different English societies. It reconvened to discuss proposals for constitutional and parliamentary reform, and the proceedings were dominated by Margarot, Gerrald, and the Scot William Skirving, who acted as secretary. On 6 December 1793 the Edinburgh authorities decided to close the proceedings; Margarot, Gerrald, and Skirving were charged with sedition. Recognizing that there was little chance of acquittal Margarot and Gerrald used their trials, in the following January and March, to express their political ideology. They were duly sentenced to fourteen years' transportation.

Awaiting transportation in Portsmouth, Margarot sought to settle business matters and arrange his wife's passage to New South Wales as a free settler. He also continued to correspond with popular radicals. One particular letter, to the societies in Norwich, speaking of a possible French landing, urged his readers not to relax 'in the Cause of Freedom'. It was subsequently reprinted, with emphasis, in the second report from the House of Commons committee of secrecy investigating treasonable activity later in the year.

The *Surprize*, the transport taking Margarot and the other 'Scottish Martyrs' (Muir, Palmer, Gerrald, and Skirving) to New South Wales, set sail on 2 May 1794. While at sea there was trouble on board; a group of convicts, including Palmer and Skirving, allegedly sought to kill the captain and crew and take over the ship. Palmer's account, *A Narrative of the Sufferings of T. F. Palmer and*

W. Skirving (1797), accused Margarot of exposing the plot to the captain and thus being the cause of the brutal punishment inflicted on Palmer and Skirving. Many contemporaries accepted this version, though Francis Place, investigating the charges after Margarot's death, concluded that the events were not as Palmer described; more recent research, which has highlighted Margarot's continuing radicalism, tends to confirm Place's opinion. He may have been vain and financially lax, but there seems little reason to doubt his genuine passion for reform and social justice.

As a political prisoner in New South Wales, Margarot was allowed considerable liberty. He and his wife took a small cottage with a garden, and from here he commenced a campaign against the profiteering in the colony by military officers and certain privileged individuals, notably Palmer, who had invested in a stock of rum before his transportation. Margarot began a lengthy correspondence with the colonial authorities in London outlining various proposals for reform, but no action was taken. Possibly he was involved in the convict rebellion of 1804. The following year he was moved from Botany Bay to Norfolk Island, thence to Van Diemen's Land, and then in 1806 to Newcastle. He eventually returned to England in mid-1810, protesting that his criticism of the corruption in the colony had led to his period of transportation being extended by two years.

Back in England, and in financial difficulties, Margarot demanded that the Home Office return money bills left in the care of Thomas Hardy which had been impounded when the latter was arrested for treason in 1794. This demand was successful, but his claims for compensation for the additional two years' exile, for the fact that his wife had not been treated as a free settler, and for the seizure of his private papers in Australia were dismissed. In 1812 he gave evidence on corruption to the House of Commons inquiry into the transportation system. At the same time he continued his enthusiasm for reform, urging a restoration of the Saxon constitution, the curtailing of commerce, and a redistribution of land with a plot for every family. He spent the summers of 1813 and 1814 in France endeavouring to re-establish his old business. He died in London on 11 November 1815. Thomas Hardy and other members of the defunct LCS organized a subscription for his widow which grew to nearly £200.   CLIVE EMSLEY

Sources M. Roe, 'Maurice Margarot: a radical in two hemispheres, 1792–1815', *BIHR*, 31 (1958), 68–78 · M. Thale, ed., *Selections from the papers of the London Corresponding Society, 1792–1799* (1983) · A. Goodwin, *The friends of liberty: the English democratic movement in the age of the French Revolution* (1979) · J. A. Hone, *For the cause of truth: radicalism in London, 1796–1821* (1982) · *State trials*, 23.1813–20

Archives BL, Place MSS, Add. MSS 27812, 27816 · PRO, HO 42. 29 · PRO, TS 11. 953. 3497

Margary, Augustus Raymond (1846–1875), traveller and consular official, third son of Henry Joshua Margary (d. 1876), major-general RE, and his wife, Louisa Jane, was born at Belgaum, Bombay Presidency, on 26 May 1846. He was educated in France, at Brighton College, and at University College, London. Having received a nomination from his relative Austen Henry Layard (then under-secretary at the Foreign Office), he three times failed the entrance examination, owing to poor spelling, but was given a fourth chance, on which occasion he was successful. He was appointed a student interpreter in the Chinese consular service on 2 February 1867 and the following month went out to China, where, until 1870, he was attached to the legation in Peking (Beijing).

In 1870 Margary was sent to the island of Formosa (Taiwan), where he took charge of the consulate for twelve months. In 1872 he was awarded the silver medal of the Royal Humane Society for saving lives at sea during a typhoon on 9 August 1871; for this action he also received the Albert medal (first class). He was briefly acting interpreter at Shanghai in 1873, and was interpreter at Chefoo (Yantai) from 24 November 1873 to 9 April 1874.

In August 1874 Margary was instructed to travel from Shanghai, through the south-western provinces of China, to Bhamo in Upper Burma, where he was to meet Colonel Horace Browne and act as his interpreter. Browne's ill-considered mission was to attempt to open up the overland trade route between China and India. Margary successfully completed his outward journey of some 1800 miles through Szechwan (Sichuan), Kweichow (Guizhou), and Yunnan in six months, the first Englishman to make the trip. Having met Browne, he returned with the mission across the frontier. Hearing rumours of danger to the mission, he proceeded alone but for his personal staff into Manyunchieh (Mayunjie), where on 21 February 1875 he and his servants were murdered. His head and those of his servants were then stuck up on the walls of the town; only his cook escaped the same fate.

The 'Margary affair' was exploited by the British to gain concessions from China on a variety of unrelated issues, including the stationing of a British consulate in Chungking (Chongqing) in Szechwan province; an indemnity of £10,000 from the Chinese was held in trust for Margary's recently widowed mother, three brothers, and nine sisters.   G. C. BOASE, rev. K. D. REYNOLDS

Sources P. D. Coates, *The China consuls: British consular officers, 1843–1943* (1988) · *The journal of Augustus Raymond Margary … with a biographical preface* (1876) · DNB · J. Anderson, *Mandalay to Momien: with a narrative of the two expeditions to western China of 1868 and 1875* (1876) · *The Times* (9 April 1875) · *The Times* (22 April 1875) · *The Times* (28 April 1875) · *ILN* (6 March 1875), 233–4 · *The Graphic* (27 March 1875), 296 · Ward, *Men of the reign*

Likenesses C. H. Jeens, stipple, 1876 (after photograph), BM · portrait, repro. in *The Graphic* · wood-engraving (after photograph by Elliott & Fry), NPG; repro. in *ILN* (13 March 1875)

Wealth at death under £200: administration, 13 April 1876, CGPLA Eng. & Wales

Marged ferch Ifan (bap. 1696, d. 1793), harpist and wrestler, was probably born in Beddgelert, Caernarvonshire, and baptized in the parish church on 10 May 1696, one of at least eleven children born to Ifan Powell and his wife, Elizabeth Hughes. She became known far beyond Wales after Thomas Pennant published a lively description of her in his *Tours in Wales* (1778–81), but local oral tradition has also preserved many tales which grew up around her, many of them no less attractive for being impossible to verify. All sources, however, describe her as a large and exceptionally strong woman, a great weightlifter who could wrestle any man to the ground, so that even when she was seventy years old the young men of the district treated her with respect. Her husband, the harpist Richard Morris (d. 1786), was much slighter and no match for her, which suggests that it was she who courted him, for few suitors dared approach her. She is said to have given Richard Morris two severe beatings: after the first he married her, on 8 May 1717 in Beddgelert, and after the second he joined the Methodists.

The couple went to keep an inn called Telyrni between Nantlle and Drws-y-coed, in the parish of Llandwrog. The inn was frequented mainly by the local copper miners, and Marged ferch Ifan played the harp to entertain them. Tradition has it that some of her customers composed extempore two of the surviving *penillion telyn* (popular stanzas for the harp), celebrating her two harps and two bellows.

The decline of the copper mine forced the couple to give up the Telyrni inn, of which no trace now remains. Some time before 1764 they moved to Pen-llyn, a house at the north-western end of Padarn Lake in the parish of Llanddeiniolen. Marged became a boat builder and transported copper ore in a boat from the foot of Snowdon across lakes Peris and Padarn to Cwm-y-glo, where it was loaded onto carts to be transported to the coast. According to one anecdote, she took out in her boat one day the local landowner and industrialist Thomas Assheton Smith of Vaenol (1752–1828), who made sexual advances to her. Quick as a flash she picked him up and dropped him in the lake. When he rose to the surface and begged her to pull him out she refused until he paid her half a guinea.

Marged ferch Ifan, whom Pennant calls 'Queen of the Lake', was out when he called at Pen-llyn in 1786, but he seems to be relying on a local informant when he states that she was a remarkable hunter, keeping a dozen hounds, played traditional Welsh airs on the fiddle as well as the harp, made harps and her own shoes, and shod her own horses. Her strength was legendary, for she is also remembered locally for making the Pont Meibion slate bridge at Nant Peris, she alone lifting one end of the huge slab and several young men the other.

At least three children, a son and two daughters, were born to Marged ferch Ifan. Although some sources claim that she died in 1801 at the age of 105, in fact she died in January 1793 at Pen-llyn and was buried on 24 January in Llanddeiniolen churchyard. W. R. Ambrose quotes English verses which he claims were inscribed on her gravestone, but their authenticity is highly questionable and the stone does not survive.

CERIDWEN LLOYD-MORGAN

Sources Glan Rhyddallt [I. S. Lloyd], 'Brenhines y Llynnoedd. Marged uch Ifan', *Y Llenor*, 23 (1944), 40–43 · T. Pennant, *Tours in Wales*, ed. J. Rhys, 2 (1883), 320 · W. R. Ambrose, *Hynafiaethau, cofiannau a hanes presennol Nant Nanlle* (1872), 59 · G. T. Roberts, 'Arfon', *Transactions of the Caernarvonshire Historical Society*, 1 (1939), 57–60 · M. ap Rheinallt, 'Marged uch Ifan a'i theulu', *Llafar Gwlad*, 30 (1990), 6–7 · D. Whiteside Thomas, 'Brenhines y Llynnoedd', *Llafar Gwlad*, 31 (1991), 14–15 · W. J. Gruffydd, *Hen atgofion* (1936), 88 · M. ap Rheinallt, 'Marged uch Ifan a'i theulu', *Llafar Gwlad*, 36 (1992), 13 · parish register (baptism), 10 May 1696, Beddgelert, Caernarvonshire · parish register (marriage), 8 May 1717, Beddgelert, Caernarvonshire · parish register (burial), 24 Jan 1793, Llanddeiniolen, Caernarvonshire

Margery (*fl.* 1300–1306). *See under* Women medical practitioners in England (*act. c.*1200–*c.*1475).

Margesson, (Henry) David Reginald, first Viscount Margesson (1890–1965), politician, was born in London on 26 July 1890, the third of the five children and the elder son of Sir Mortimer Reginald Margesson (1861–1947), private secretary to the earl of Plymouth, and his wife, Isabel Augusta Hobart-Hampden (d. 1946), daughter of Frederick John Hobart-Hampden, Lord Hobart, and granddaughter of the sixth earl of Buckinghamshire. He was brought up in Worcestershire and was educated at Harrow School (1904–7) and then at Magdalene College, Cambridge, though he left without taking a degree and decided to travel, and seek his fortune, in the USA.

On the outbreak of war in 1914 Margesson volunteered and joined the Worcestershire yeomanry. In November 1914 he was commissioned, and he served with the 11th hussars for the remainder of the war, experiencing trench warfare on the western front. He became adjutant within two years and won the MC for 'helping to pull the line together' (*DNB*). He retired with the rank of captain in 1919.

On 29 April 1916 Margesson married Frances Leggett, the only child and heir of Francis Howard Leggett, a wealthy New York wholesale provision merchant, whose wife was a friend of the Margesson family. They had two daughters and a son. Later they became estranged and lived separate lives before obtaining a divorce in 1940; but after the First World War they lived the life of a squire and his lady in Worcestershire. Yet the round of rural sports and village good works soon palled, and Margesson was recruited by Lord Lee of Fareham as a Conservative candidate in the general election of 1922, winning the Upton division of West Ham. He soon made his maiden speech (which turned out also to be his last from the back benches), seconding the address—a signal honour for a new MP—and was appointed parliamentary private secretary to the minister of labour, Sir Clement Anderson Barlow. It was a propitious start to his parliamentary career, but one cut short by defeat in the general election of 1923.

Government chief whip Yet Margesson's career suffered only a brief hiatus. He had attracted the attention of the Conservative leader, and fellow Old Harrovian, Stanley Baldwin, and of his chief whip, B. M. Eyres-Monsell, both of whom were Worcestershire men. Hence he was found a safe seat, Rugby, and was duly returned to parliament in the election of 1924 which unseated the first Labour government. He remained MP for Rugby until 1942. He entered the whips' office, at first as a junior whip, and was a junior lord of the Treasury from 1926 to 1929. Then, after his apprenticeship under Eyres-Monsell and at the relatively early age of forty-one, he became chief whip in the

National Government, in November 1931, following the general election. He held the position until December 1940. As chief whip he was one of the most powerful political figures in Britain, even if the power was exercised unobtrusively. Baldwin judged him to be 'first rate' (Jones, 228), while Lloyd George considered him the most efficient chief whip he had known (Cato, 92). In 1933 he was sworn of the privy council.

Margesson, who devoted himself to his work in the Commons as his marriage broke down, served as chief whip to four successive prime ministers: MacDonald, with whom relations were distant and whose resignation he was anxious to secure in 1934–5, even going so far as to tell MacDonald that by-election results were so poor because 'the country was tired of its leaders' (Channon, 137); Baldwin, whose confidant he was; Chamberlain, with whose policies he became identified; and Churchill. Over this period he developed a reputation as a formidably strict disciplinarian. A junior whip judged that he could 'put the fear of God into new Members' and that he was 'a real dictator', powers enhanced by his tall, imposing figure and habitual garb of immaculate black morning coat with black and white checked trousers (Harvie-Watt, 31, 133). Critics said he was a man who 'never forgives nor forgets' those who crossed him (Nicolson, 43). His authority was enhanced by his influence over ministerial appointments. Certainly under Chamberlain he was said to share with Sir Horace Wilson 'a commanding influence on political appointments' (Colville, 36–7). Those not in his favour tended to judge that he was swayed too much by the 'old school tie' and the wealth of prospective appointees and that he was unduly brusque (*Headlam Diaries*, 240): indeed he elevated 'obedience over ability', so that the tory front benches by the end of the decade were full of yes-men (Nicolson, 71). It is also said that he clamped down on opposition, thus causing it to become magnified, rather than detailing back-bench concerns to the prime minister.

Yet Margesson's image as a martinet is one-sided. Certainly Harold Macmillan, who as a back-bench critic of the National Government's unemployment strategy fell foul of the chief whip several times, judged that he ruled the party by 'charm' as well as 'military discipline' (H. Macmillan, *Winds of Change*, 1966, 401); and a civil servant found him attractively extrovert—'certainly an unusually agreeable man' (Colville, 71). One going to see him for the first time, aware of his reputation as a strict disciplinarian with the qualities of an admirable school prefect, was pleasantly surprised: 'He bade me sit down, he was friendly, charming, attentive. He completed his inquisition, to which I replied to the best of my ability. He was appreciative … We chatted in easy sympathy' (Mallaby, 89).

Despite large victories for the government in the elections of 1931 and 1935, Margesson needed all his powers of persuasion, coercion, and efficient organization to minimize back-bench revolts and secure government majorities during this decade of crisis and controversy. One source of friction was the premiership of Ramsay MacDonald, the former Labour statesman whose powers were evidently failing from late 1933; another was the gargantuan Government of India Bill, which saw Margesson battling against Churchill's formidable powers of obstruction. In the controversy over the Hoare–Laval plan in 1935 Margesson and Baldwin managed to forestall their critics at the cost of the foreign secretary's resignation, and both emerged successfully from the abdication crisis, Beaverbrook judging, somewhat melodramatically perhaps, that the chief whip had thwarted his efforts to retain Edward VIII as monarch. But it was the issue of appeasement which, more than any other, had tarnished Margesson's image by 1940.

Appeasement and the fall of Chamberlain After the formation of Churchill's government in May 1940 Margesson was seen by many as a 'man of Munich'. He received a whole chapter in Cato's *Guilty Men*, published in July 1940. Yet, unknown to his critics, Margesson had pressed for Churchill's entry to the cabinet in May 1937 and thereafter. In addition, he insisted that he had often warned the government 'to modify its intentions because of feeling in the House' (Colville, 298). But he also had to do his job, and as efficiently as possible—and it was a difficult job because, as he confided to Baldwin, by autumn 1939 Chamberlain 'engendered personal dislike among his opponents to an extent almost unbelievable' (G. R. Searle, *Country before Party*, 1995, 188). That few sensed any difference of opinion between the prime minister and his chief whip is testimony to the skill and determination with which the formidable chief whip performed his tasks.

Margesson was aware, by the beginning of May 1940, that trouble was brewing for the government. Before the debate on the Norwegian campaign he told a sympathetic back-bencher that 'we are on the eve of the greatest political crisis since August 1931' (Channon, 244). This awareness did not stop him deploying all his energies to secure a government majority. Brandishing the carrot and the stick, he intimated that there would soon be changes in government personnel and imposed a three-line whip. When, on 8 May, over thirty Conservatives voted against the government and more than sixty abstained, Margesson gave vent to his pent-up feeling with a string of expletives, for instance describing one young rebel as 'a contemptible little shit' (Jenkins, 583). He now knew that Chamberlain could not survive.

At a fateful meeting on 9 May 1940 with Chamberlain, Halifax, and Churchill, Margesson insisted that unity was essential and that it could not come about under Chamberlain. According to Halifax, he did not 'pronounce very definitely between Winston and myself' (Earl of Birkenhead, *Halifax*, 1965, 454). The choice fell on Churchill. But would he now dispense with the chief whip's services? Many thought he should, but Churchill gave the critics short shrift:

> Even during the bitterest times I have always had very good personal relations with Margesson, and knowing what his duties were I never had any serious occasion to complain … I have long had a very high opinion of Margesson's

administrative and executive abilities. (M. Gilbert, *Finest Hour: Winston S. Churchill, 1939–1941*, 1989, 918)

Churchill offered him a secretaryship of state, but when he declined, retained his services as chief whip. One of Margesson's first duties was to co-operate with Brendan Bracken in filling junior positions in the new government.

War Office and peerage The relative eclipse of the House of Commons during the war, however, meant that Margesson's abilities were not fully utilized as chief whip, even when he was also a member of the palace of Westminster Home Guard. Hence he was able to advise that thought should be devoted to reconstruction so that 'we don't leave it to the Labour people to do all the thinking and planning' (Addison, 361). Churchill appointed him secretary of state for war in December 1940. He made a good start in his first department. He read out his speeches 'with a good voice and delivery' (*Headlam Diaries*, 242) and struck an informed observer as 'keen and energetic' as well as ambitious and interested (*Alanbrooke War Diaries*, 132). He established very good relations with chief of Imperial General Staff Sir John Dill. Yet Leo Amery, calling the War Office 'that home of inertia and circumlocution', judged that Margesson 'always fell back on his officials' (*Amery Diaries*, 778). Certainly he had little impact on grand strategy, and his opposition to the invasion of Greece in March 1941 had no impact whatsoever on Churchill's policy. Hence when a resignation was needed after the fall of Singapore in February 1942, Margesson was told by his replacement as chief whip, James Stuart, that he had to go.

Margesson's resignation, and that of Moore-Brabazon from the Ministry of Aircraft Production, paved the way for Sir Stafford Cripps to enter the government, as indeed Margesson had recommended. Yet his departure was undoubtedly a personal blow which he felt deeply. He is reputed to have given a deliberately unhelpful nomination as his successor at the War Office, the civil servant Sir James Grigg, in an attempt to stave off departure—and to have been astounded when it was accepted. 'This is the last time I recommend anyone for anything', he later lamented (D. Irving, *Churchill's War: Triumph in Adversity*, 2001, 338–9). Few believed that Margesson had merited his dismissal, and according to a partial observer a 'wave of indignation has swept over London at the dropping of David' (Channon, 323), though equally few thought his removal would weaken the government. He was made Viscount Margesson of Rugby in April 1942, an elevation which softened the blow.

Thereafter Margesson's political involvement was minimal. He attended the Lords but did not make a speech. He also turned down Churchill's personal offer of the chairmanship of the Conservative Party in October 1944. He might have accepted office in 1945, and he certainly expected a victory for Churchill: he judged Churchill's 'Gestapo' broadcast of 4 June to be 'a beauty' (M. Gilbert, *Never Despair: Winston S. Churchill, 1945–1965*, 1990) and predicted a Conservative majority of about 100 (Lord Moran, *Winston Churchill: the Struggle for Survival, 1940–1965*, 1968,

285). But Labour's victory seems to have ended his ambitions. Nor did he write his memoirs. His energies were taken up in the City, as a director of the General Electric Company and of Martin's Bank. He was also reputed to be an adept manager 'no longer for prime ministers but for his friends' (*DNB*). He died on 24 December 1965 on an annual visit to Nassau in the Bahamas. He was survived by his three children, his son succeeding him as second viscount.

ROBERT PEARCE

Sources *DNB* · *The Times* (28 Dec 1965) · *The Times* (30 Dec 1965) · *The Times* (5 Jan 1966) · H. Channon, *'Chips': the diaries of Sir Henry Channon*, ed. R. Rhodes James (1993) · G. S. Harvie-Watt, *Most of my life* (1980) · J. Colville, *The fringes of power: Downing Street diaries, 1939–1955* (1985) · G. Mallaby, *From my level: unwritten minutes* (1965) · *Parliament and politics in the age of Churchill and Attlee: the Headlam diaries, 1935–1951*, ed. S. Ball, CS, 5th ser., 14 (1999) · T. Jones, *A diary with letters, 1931–1950* (1954) · *The empire at bay: the Leo Amery diaries, 1929–1945*, ed. J. Barnes and D. Nicholson (1988) · *Field Marshal Lord Alanbrooke: war diaries, 1939–45*, ed. A. Danchev and D. Todman (2001) · R. Jenkins, *Churchill* (2001) · H. Nicolson, *Diaries and letters, 1939–45* (1970) · P. Addison, *Churchill on the home front, 1900–1955* (1992) · Cato, *Guilty men* (1940) · *CGPLA Eng. & Wales* (1966)

Archives CAC Cam., corresp. and papers · PRO, private office papers, WO 259 | CAC Cam., corresp. with E. L. Spears · HLRO, corresp. with Lord Beaverbrook

Likenesses W. Stoneman, photograph, 1930, NPG · two photographs, c.1945, Hult. Arch.

Wealth at death £84,279: probate, 21 March 1966, *CGPLA Eng. & Wales*

Margetson, James (1600–1678), Church of Ireland archbishop of Armagh, was a native of Drighlington, Yorkshire. He matriculated at Peterhouse, Cambridge, in Michaelmas 1619, and graduated BA (1622–3) and MA (1626). Ordained deacon and priest at Peterborough in 1626, he was rector of Thornton Watlass, Yorkshire, from 1626 to 1635. Sir Thomas Wentworth took him as chaplain to Ireland, where he served as dean of Waterford, beginning in 1635, and rector of Arvagh, co. Cavan (1635–7). He became rector of Galloon (Dartry), co. Monaghan, in 1637; dean of Derry in 1638; prebendary of St Fin Barre's, Cork, in 1639; and dean of Christ Church, Dublin, in December 1639. No new dean of Derry was appointed until after the Restoration. Margetson was incorporated doctor of divinity at Trinity College, Dublin, in 1637. He was prolocutor of the lower house of convocation in 1639.

When the rebellion of 1641 broke out, Margetson assisted refugees in Dublin. In August 1646 he signed the document in which eleven bishops and seventy-seven other clergymen congratulated Ormond upon the conclusion of peace, and thanked him for his efforts on their behalf. The parliamentary forces controlling Dublin in June 1647 ordered the protestant clergy to use the directory for worship instead of the Book of Common Prayer. The bishop of Killaloe and eighteen clergymen, of whom Margetson was one, formally protested, unsuccessfully seeking to continue the traditional liturgy.

Ormond left Ireland on 28 August 1647, and Margetson fled to England about the same time. There he conducted services according to the Book of Common Prayer. Imprisoned at Manchester, he was freed in a prisoner exchange. After settling in London, he dispersed alms from wealthier cavaliers to needy loyalists in England and Wales, reportedly including William Chappell, bishop of Cork, Milton's old tutor.

At the Restoration, Margetson was sworn of the Irish privy council in December 1660. On 29 January 1661 he was consecrated archbishop of Dublin and bishop of Glendalough; he also held his old living of Galloon, his Cork prebend, and the treasurership of St Patrick's, Dublin. To augment the revenues of his archbishopric, he and his successors received the lands of those attainted by treason formerly held of the archbishopric and the see of Glendalough, and various properties, rectories, and vicarages in co. Dublin and elsewhere to the value of £1000 p.a. net, but the maximum income was not to exceed £2000 p.a.

Margetson was translated to the archbishopric of Armagh on 20 August 1663, where he succeeded John Bramhall, who reportedly recommended him on his deathbed to Ormond. As an archbishop, Margetson generally followed a moderate course in dealing with protestant nonconformists. The Presbyterian Patrick Adair, who called him 'a man of mild spirit', averred that he was 'not of a persecuting temper, but rather inclinable to engage the country and increase his estate' (Adair, 282, 300). Although as archbishop of Dublin he had prohibited the Presbyterian Edward Bagshaw from preaching, as archbishop of Armagh he later permitted John Howe, ejected from his living but by then Lord Massereene's chaplain, to preach in Antrim's parish church. When Margetson succeeded Bramhall, he implemented a policy of indulgence for six months, infuriating George Wild, bishop of Derry. On his triennial visitation in 1664, Margetson persuaded some dissenters in Derry to conform. Meanwhile, with Michael Boyle, archbishop of Dublin, he endeavoured to protect protestantism in the face of increased Catholic activity in 1664, and six years later he was monitoring the work of Oliver Plunket, Catholic archbishop of Armagh.

By 1669 the growing number of conventicles in Dublin worried Margetson, and as covenanter activity increased in the late 1660s he opposed an indulgent policy, avouching that almost every Ulster parish had a Presbyterian meeting-house, and that presbyteries had been established, ministers salaried, and elders elected. To demonstrate his authority over Roger Boyle, bishop of Down and Connor, Margetson declined in 1670 to prosecute nine Presbyterian ministers, though he left four in prison elsewhere for refusing to subscribe the oath of supremacy.

Margetson acted in numerous ways to uphold the established church, and opposed the practice of holding an ecclesiastical post in Ireland while residing in England. Following Jeremy Taylor's death in August 1667, he insisted that the sees of Dromore, on the one hand, and Down and Connor on the other be separated because they were disorderly and disaffected. He succeeded Jeremy Taylor as vice-chancellor of Dublin University and remained in office until his death. Earlier, in November 1663, he had been appointed the king's almoner, for which he received a stipend of £100 (English). By 1668 his annual income exceeded £3500. Armagh Cathedral had been burnt by Sir Phelim O'Neill in 1642, and Margetson contributed generously to its rebuilding, as he also did to the refurbishing of St Patrick's and Christ Church cathedrals, Dublin. He founded a free school at Drighlington and made the master of Peterhouse its patron. At the king's appointment he was responsible in 1666 for adding special prayers to the Book of Common Prayer for 30 January, 29 May, 23 October, and 5 November, and in 1670 he and other prominent clerics were commissioned to review the profits of all ecclesiastical livings with a view to more accurately assessing first-fruits and twentieths.

In the winter of 1677 Margetson became seriously ill and suffered fainting spells, but nevertheless insisted on communicating publicly the following May. By this point his house had become an oratory for private devotion. He died in Dublin on 28 August 1678, and was buried two days later within the altar rails of Christ Church. His charity and exemplary life had won him such reputation that many came to his deathbed to receive his blessing. At his funeral Dr William Palliser spoke of his conciliatory attitude towards theological opponents. According to Henry Jones, bishop of Meath, who preached his funeral sermon, he left £4000 apiece to two children.

Margetson's son James (BA 1676, MA 1679, Trinity College, Dublin) was ordained at Lincoln in 1699, and served as rector of Little Stukeley, Huntingdonshire (1699–1701), and vicar of Exning, Suffolk (1701–37); he died on 4 March 1737. His son John was killed at the siege of Limerick, being then a major in William's army, leaving a daughter, Sarah, from whom the earls of Bessborough and Mountcashell are descended. The earl of Charlemont is descended from Anne Margetson (d. 1729), the primate's only daughter.   RICHARD L. GREAVES

Sources Bodl. Oxf., MSS Carte 33, 37, 45, 49 · CSP Ire., 1660–70 · P. Adair, A true narrative of the rise and progress of the Presbyterian church in Ireland (1623–1670), ed. W. D. Killen (1866) · Venn, Alum. Cant. · Calendar of the manuscripts of the marquess of Ormonde, new ser., 8 vols., HMC, 36 (1902–20), vol. 4 · H. Jones, A sermon at the funeral of James Margetson (1679) · R. L. Greaves, God's other children: protestant nonconformists and the emergence of denominational churches in Ireland (1997) · R. Lascelles, ed., Liber munerum publicorum Hiberniae ... or, The establishments of Ireland, 2 vols. [1824–30], vol. 2 · E. B. Fryde and others, eds., Handbook of British chronology, 3rd edn, Royal Historical Society Guides and Handbooks, 2 (1986) · J. Lodge, The peerage of Ireland, rev. M. Archdall, rev. edn, 7 vols. (1789) · St J. D. Seymour, The puritans in Ireland, 1647–1661 (1912)
Archives Bodl. Oxf., Carte MSS · PRO, SP 63
Wealth at death left £4000 apiece to two children

Margoliouth, David Samuel (1858–1940), orientalist, born in London on 17 October 1858, was the only son of Ezekiel Margoliouth and Sarah, née Iglitzki. His father had converted from Judaism to Anglicanism, and thereafter worked in Bethnal Green as a missionary to the Jews; he was a close friend and probably a relation of the Anglican convert Moses Margoliouth. The son attended Hackney collegiate school as a day boy, and must have shown promise of academic distinction, because he gained a scholarship to Winchester College in 1872. Winchester has always been somewhat *sui generis* among the 'great public

David Samuel Margoliouth (1858–1940), by Lafayette, 1926

schools', yet even there it is hardly possible that he can have escaped feeling the prejudices almost universal at that period and in that ambience; an academically highly gifted boy of Jewish parentage and coming from an east London day school must have surely—at least intermittently—suffered rough treatment from his schoolfellows. If this was so, it might go some way towards explaining the curious air of withdrawn detachment and introspection that clung to him even in his later years.

Oxford In 1877 Margoliouth went up to New College, Oxford, with a scholarship. In tracing his undergraduate career it is needful to bear in mind that in those days both honour moderations (the first public examination) and the final honour schools were examined twice a year, in Trinity and Michaelmas terms. Margoliouth gained a first class in classical moderations in Trinity term 1878, his third term. This was followed by a first in the final honour school of *literae humaniores* in Michaelmas 1880, his tenth term. It is no surprise that, as a Winchester and New College scholar, he collected most of the classical distinctions available: Hertford and Ireland scholarships (1878) and the Gaisford prize for Greek prose (1879) as an undergraduate, and thereafter the Craven (1881) and Derby (1882) awards; nor that he should with his Jewish background have swept up the Pusey and Ellerton Hebrew scholarship (1879), the

Kennicott Hebrew scholarship (1882), and a senior Kennicott award (1879). But when on top of all this he gained the Houghton Syriac prize (1880) and the Boden Sanskrit scholarship (1881), he begins to seem something of a prodigy.

Within a year after his finals Margoliouth was elected to a New College fellowship. There was nothing out of the ordinary about this, for right up to the outbreak of the Second World War it was normal for college fellowships to be filled by young men who had only just taken their first degrees, provided that their undergraduate careers had shown promise—as Margoliouth's certainly had. In the next few years he did tutorial teaching in classics for New College. But the circumstances of his appointment to the Laudian chair of Arabic at Oxford appear strange by the standards of a century later. Robert Gandell, the previous Laudian professor, died in 1887, but no appointment of a successor was made until two years later, the post being 'suspended' in the interval. In the academic code language of the time, this meant that the electoral board had met promptly on the demise of the previous holder but had been unable to find a suitable successor, and so had asked congregation of the university for leave to adjourn for a couple of years and then try again. Margoliouth was an applicant on both occasions, but the dossier of recommendations that he submitted contained not a single allusion to any knowledge of Arabic, and only two mentioned his qualifications in Hebrew and Syriac. Despite this, after being elected on the second round in 1889, he lost no time in vindicating his claim to the chair. Within five years he had published two works on Arabic each important in a different way. One was a piece of highly recondite scholarship, an edition of the Arabic papyri in the Bodleian Library (1893); the other, *Chrestomathia Baidawiana* (1894), a translation of Baidawi's commentary on sura 3 of the Koran, remained an indispensable standby of students for the next sixty years.

Works Among the impressive array of Margoliouth's other works, only a few can here be mentioned. The edition and translation of the letters of the strange, cynical writer Abu al-ʾAlaʿ al-Maʾarri (1898) was an arduous undertaking, since the letters are stylistically complex (and, in fact, are not nearly so much read as that author's other works). The six volumes of the edition of Yaqut's *Dictionary of Learned Men* (1907–27) was more widely celebrated among his editions. The translation, under the title of *Table Talk of a Mesopotamian Judge* (1933), of a collection of anecdotes made by the Qadi al-Tanukhi, which afford invaluable insights to Abbasid daily life, introduced al-Tanukhi not only to the European world but to Arabs, since though popular in his own time he had been virtually forgotten by literary historians until 'rediscovered' by Margoliouth. His papyrological interests continued with a complete edition of the large collection of Arabic papyri in the John Rylands Library in Manchester (1931). He was moreover the first scholar in Britain to do constructive work on the pre-Islamic inscriptions of the Yemen (not in Arabic but in an allied Semitic language); his edition and interpretation of a couple of important such inscriptions in the *Proceedings of the British Academy* for 1925 (he had been elected to that institution in 1915) remains more plausible than some subsequent rival attempts.

Against all this solid positive achievement must be set some strangely quirky publications, including Margoliouth's alleged detection of anagrams in the opening lines of the *Iliad* and the *Odyssey*, containing the name 'Homer' with details of his birth, life, and so on. Can Margoliouth have seriously believed such nonsense, or was he indulging in a laborious joke at the expense of the learned world? Either supposition must unfortunately flaw his own credit for scholarship. The same sort of ambivalence attaches to his article in the *Journal of the Royal Asiatic Society* for 1925 in which he contended that the corpus of early Arabic poetry, enormously admired in the Arab world and credited to the century preceding Islam, was in fact entirely forged a couple of centuries later; his arguments were ably refuted in 1926 by the German scholar E. Bräunlich. An additional enigma surrounding this is the fact that almost at the same time as Margoliouth's article a similar thesis was advanced by the doyen of Egyptian critics, Taha Husayn (strictly speaking, the latter was slightly later in appearing, but when one allows for the process of press and publication, they must have been drafted practically simultaneously), and one can hardly imagine that the two arrived wholly independently at the same conclusion. Naturally, such a revolutionary idea created far more scandal in the Arab world than in Europe, and a couple of years later Taha Husayn was obliged to modify his views. Margoliouth on the other hand seems never to have reverted to the subject; it is noteworthy that during the next ten years when he lectured to Oxford undergraduates on the poems in question he made no mention whatever of his own article or of any suspicion of their being not authentic. Other more popular and general works on Islam by Margoliouth are period pieces and have been criticized by recent scholars for their polemical and contentious content.

Travel and teaching Both before and after the First World War (during which the War Office sent him on a lecturing tour in India) Margoliouth travelled frequently to the Near East, and is said to have lectured in Cairo and Baghdad with considerable éclat in Arabic—this despite the fact that his enunciation was impaired by a speech defect, namely the inability to pronounce 'r' other than as what the French call the 'Parisian r' or 'r grasséyé' (a sound which in both Arabic and Turkish is a quite different letter from 'r').

From time to time Margoliouth had the help of an Arab lector (as he would now be called) for the teaching of elementary Arabic; but this assistance was intermittent, and there was no other teacher of the language available in Oxford. The professor was hence obliged to shoulder the entire teaching load of all necessary lecturing together with much that would otherwise have been reckoned as the job of a tutor. It must be said, however, that he did not attempt to impart the rudiments of the language; the undergraduate had to acquire those by his own efforts from a grammar book. His lecturing schedule too could be

disconcerting: he reckoned to cover the finals syllabus in two years, and it was just too bad if you found yourself thereby compelled to struggle with the more difficult texts in the year before some of the easier ones. When one adds to this the fact that he did not confine himself to Arabic, but was ready to give instruction in Syriac and Ethiopic whenever asked, it will be seen that he bore a very heavy teaching burden on top of his own research. He did his teaching in a small room allotted to the Laudian professor in the Indian Institute building, where he was to be found every weekday morning in term from ten until one, and always ready to give advice during periods when he was not actually lecturing. It has to be remembered, in assessing this commitment, that there was no first public examination in oriental languages, and the number of undergraduates taking Arabic in the finals was very small, averaging about one and a half a year. As for postgraduates, they were virtually non-existent; the Oxford DPhil was invented only in 1916 and attracted hardly anyone in the years before 1939, and BLitt students were very rare too.

Margoliouth's style of instruction was the exact opposite of that adopted by Cyril Bailey, who in lecturing on Lucretius peppered his audience with a fusillade of tightly compacted pellets of information which they were expected to note down and if possible commit to memory. In contrast, Margoliouth took a text simply as a starting point for wide-ranging ruminations arising out of it, and so great was his dislike of *ex-cathedra* utterances that, if by chance he was betrayed into making a directly informative statement, he often hastily added 'as of course you know', quite irrespective of the likelihood of the item of information being one that an undergraduate could not possibly know. For someone who had encountered this style of teaching already in his sixth form at school, it was immensely stimulating and richly rewarding; for others it could be baffling and frustrating.

A further cause of embarrassment to some hearers was Margoliouth's habit of making occasional remarks of a kind which could be construed as very dry pieces of satirical irony; these were uttered with no change in tone and without the movement of a single muscle of the face, so that many complained privately that they 'didn't know whether they were expected to laugh or not'. The ambiguity was in no way removed by the fact that if the hearer did laugh, this was greeted by Margoliouth with no sign of approval or disapproval, but still the same stony, immovable gravity.

Such remarks were normally quite without any personal application, and completely general in nature. Yet one counter-example can be mentioned, coming from the recollections of Harold W. Bailey, who as a young man at Oxford was an applicant for the Nubar Pasha scholarship 'for the encouragement of Armenian studies'. The awarding body was well aware that this was exceedingly unlikely to attract anyone with a previous knowledge of Armenian, so it was normally given to someone who, on the basis of his other qualifications and of a personal interview, seemed likely to be able to study Armenian successfully. The award to Bailey was certainly justified, since he was to turn out perhaps the greatest linguistic polymath of the twentieth century. But Margoliouth, being chairman of the interviewing committee, said, after announcing the award and just as the candidate was leaving the room, 'By the way, Mr Bailey, do you intend actually to learn Armenian?' Once again, one remains uncertain whether he meant this ironically, or whether it was spoken in all simplicity.

One remark, however, does seem to have come straight from the heart. It was Margoliouth's custom to have the morning's *Times* on his desk every day, and if a student asked to be given a passage for translation into Arabic, he would often be handed *The Times*'s 'fourth leader' of the day. This now vanished journalistic feature was a short essay placed at the foot of the leader columns, and dealt with any subject whatever other than the current issues discussed in the main leaders. On one occasion this included the quotation of an English couplet in verse, and the student took it as his duty (having been so trained at school) to put this into Arabic metrical form. Margoliouth was not pleased; he looked gravely at it for a couple of moments, then said 'I sometimes think that the time in my life I consider most wasted is the time I spent composing Latin verses at Winchester'—and that was all.

Personal life; ordination A scholar through and through, Margoliouth had the good fortune to wed, on 25 April 1896, a like-minded scholar, and the daughter of a scholar, in Jessie Payne Smith (1856–1933) [see Margoliouth, Jessie Payne], daughter of Robert Payne *Smith. The couple had no children, but were deeply attached to each other, and her death in 1933 was a blow from which he never really recovered. They lived for many years at 88 Woodstock Road, Oxford, but moved in 1931 to a house in Foxcombe Lane on Boars Hill, whence he drove himself daily down to Oxford in a large car of rather antiquated design. After his wife's death one of her nieces came to keep house for him until he had to be moved into a London nursing home; he died in the Middlesex Hospital on 22 March 1940. Gilbert Murray, a neighbour on Boars Hill, stated that although his habitual reticence concealed it from most people, he agonized greatly over victims of persecution, particularly in the earlier part of the century the so-called 'Assyrian' Christians of Mesopotamia, and even more, of course, over the plight of the Jews under Hitler.

One unexpected facet of Margoliouth's life has still to be mentioned. In 1899 he was ordained to the Anglican ministry as deacon and priest (both in the same year) in Liverpool Cathedral. Since he never undertook parochial responsibilities it has to be concluded that the 'title' to which he was ordained was that of his New College fellowship, which he retained to the end of his life (it was only in 1925 that Oxford professorial chairs were allotted to specific colleges, and those already holding a chair were not obliged to move to the designated college). For four years after his ordination he served as an examining chaplain to the bishop of Liverpool. Furthermore, in the early years of the twentieth century he occasionally preached in an

Oxford city church, his sermons being characterized by extreme evangelistic tendencies, and these attracted large audiences of undergraduates of a similar leaning. To the end of his life he dressed like a late Victorian low-church clergyman, wearing a narrow white bow tie with its ends (unshaped) tucked under a soft turndown collar.

A drawing of Margoliouth by William Rothenstein appeared in *Oxford Characters* (1896). An oil portrait by Harriet Halhead painted about the same time now hangs in the Oriental Institute in Pusey Lane, Oxford. This shows him with thick raven-black hair, black drooping moustaches, a very high colour in his cheeks, and a fierce eye: very much like what a romantically inclined nineteenth-century young lady might have envisaged a Byronic 'corsair'. Thirty years later he was very changed. He walked stiffly and with a stoop; his hair, though still fairly thick, was snow-white, as was his moustache; all colour had drained from his face, leaving it wrinkled and of the colour of parchment or old ivory; and his eyes were sunken.

A. F. L. BEESTON

Sources G. A. Murray, 'David S. Margoliouth, 1858–1940', *PBA*, 26 (1940), 391–7 · *DNB* · *The Times* (23 March 1940) · A. Bethney, *Muslim World*, 30/3 (July 1940), 295 · J. M. Buaben, *Image of the prophet Muhammad in the West: a study of Muir, Margoliouth and Watt* (1996)
Archives Bodl. Oxf., diaries and papers | Bodl. Oxf., corresp. with Gilbert Murray
Likenesses H. Halhead, oils, exh. 1897, U. Oxf., Griffith Institute · W. Stoneman, photograph, 1917, NPG · Lafayette, photograph, 1926, NPG [see illus.] · W. Rothenstein, drawing, repro. in W. Rothenstein, *Oxford characters* (1896)
Wealth at death £10,058 3s. 6d.: resworn probate, 24 June 1940, CGPLA Eng. & Wales

Margoliouth [*née* Smith], **Jessie Payne** (1856–1933), Syriac scholar, was born on 23 February 1856, at 27 Kensington Square, Kensington, London, the second of four daughters and two sons of Robert Payne *Smith (1818–1895), dean of Canterbury and orientalist, and his wife, Catherine, *née* Freeman (d. 1894). Brought up in Oxford and (from 1871) Canterbury, she was trained in both Syriac and lexicography by her father, and proceeded to assist him in the production of his monumental *Thesaurus Syriacus* (1868–1901), one of the truly great works of British lexicography and one that is unlikely to be superseded. On his death she took over responsibility for the *Thesaurus* and saw it, and its final 293 columns, through to completion in 1901. In this she was assisted by David Samuel *Margoliouth (1858–1940), the Laudian professor of Arabic in Oxford, whom she had married in London on 25 April 1896 (they had no children). Even her marriage can be attributed to her devotion to the *Thesaurus*, for in a letter a friend quotes her as saying:

> She finds Professor Margoliouth of Oxford so very kind and useful in helping her with her Father's book, 'that she is going to marry him so that they can work at it together'—! This is exactly as she puts the fact. (Coakley, 393, n. 303)

In 1927 she completed this great lexical endeavour with her *Supplement to the 'Thesaurus Syriacus'*, an important volume which contains some 345 pages of new entries.

In 1903 Margoliouth published her *Compendious Syriac Dictionary* (which has been frequently reprinted), an abridgement of her father's work with words rearranged in alphabetical order, rather than being listed by their semitic roots, and with English rather than Latin translations. It has been an essential tool for successive generations of Syriac students, and has encouraged many to take up the study of this rich language and literature. Margoliouth's own enthusiasm for Syriac culture, as well as her strong Christian faith and humour, can be detected in the short Syriac imprecations that begin each section of the dictionary, playing as they do with words and roots beginning with the appropriate letters of the alphabet. Her lexical work required her to read an extraordinary range of published and unpublished Syriac texts, leading one eminent contemporary orientalist to comment after visiting her: 'the house is not a *house* but a *store-house* of erudition, where Mrs. Margoliouth, with her extensive Syriac knowledge, supplies the last volume of a living encyclopaedia' (Mingana, 218).

This Syriac expertise led to Margoliouth's involvement, from the 1880s, with the Archbishop of Canterbury's Mission to the Assyrian Christians in Turkey and Persia, which had as its purpose not conversion, which its statutes forbade, but the strengthening of faith and religious practice. At first a consultant, she later became a member of the mission committee, and in 1913 edited a selection of accounts of the mission, *Kurds and Christians*, with the Revd F. N. Heazell. Her own devotion to the Assyrian cause was strengthened by an extended tour of the mission and surrounding regions with her husband in 1901. On the orders of the War Office the couple spent the First World War lecturing in India (he returned in 1917, she in 1918). This was followed by a lengthy stay in Iraq, from which time both were active in their support of the persecuted and massacred Assyrians and Armenians.

In 1931 Margoliouth and her husband moved from 88 Woodstock Road, Oxford, to Romney, Boars Hill, near Oxford, where she died on 18 August 1933. She was buried on 21 August at Hoop Lane cemetery, Golders Green, London.   D. G. K. TAYLOR

Sources 'Payne Smith, Robert', *DNB* · 'Margoliouth, David Samuel', *DNB* · A. Mingana, 'Jessie Payne Margoliouth', *Journal of the Royal Asiatic Society of Great Britain and Ireland* (1934), 217–19 · J. F. Coakley, *The church of the East and the Church of England: a history of the archbishop of Canterbury's Assyrian mission* (1992) · F. N. Heazell and J. P. Margoliouth, *Kurds and Christians* (1913) · 'Preface', R. P. Smith, *Thesaurus Syriacus*, 2 (1901) · J. P. Smith, 'Preface', in J. P. Smith, *A compendious Syriac dictionary* (1903) · b. cert. · m. cert. · d. cert. · *The Times* (Aug 1933)

Wealth at death £9910 15s. 2d.: probate, 3 Nov 1933, *CGPLA Eng. & Wales*

Margoliouth, Moses (1815–1881), Hebrew scholar and convert from Judaism, was born in Suwałki, Poland, son of a prosperous local merchant named Gershon Margoliouth (d. c.1852), apparently originally surnamed Epstein or Epszteyn. In 1834 Moses Margoliouth married Chaja Goldberg (1818–1870), daughter of writer and historian Ber Goldberg (1799–1886) and his wife, Rachel (d. 1874), and a daughter, Miriam, was born in the following year. Margoliouth left Poland alone in 1837, arriving at Liverpool on 28 October. On his very first day in the city he met

Moses Margoliouth (1815–1881), by John William Cook, pubd 1850 [with the marble head of Empress Theodora, discovered among the ruins of Carthage]

a missionary from the Institute for Enquiring Jews, who offered him lodging, employment, and a Hebrew New Testament. Moses Margoliouth was baptized into the Church of England on the following Good Friday, 13 April 1838.

Margoliouth was obviously a young man of learning and potential, and he was soon the protégé of an anonymous benefactor, who from January 1840 paid for his studies at Trinity College, Dublin, which he completed in summer 1843. In that year he published his first book, *The Fundamental Principles of Modern Judaism Investigated*, printed at Chester and dedicated to Dr Alexander M'Caul (1799–1863), the Christian missionary to the Polish Jews and Hebrew professor at King's College, London.

Margoliouth returned to Liverpool, to his old position at the Institute for Enquiring Jews, and he was joined in his house at 5 Juvenal Street by his wife and daughter, newly arrived from Poland. On 30 June 1844 he was ordained into the Church of England and granted the curacy of St Augustine's, Everton, Liverpool. But within a few days a better offer came from Bishop Lindsay of Kildare, who gave him the rectorate of Glasnevin, on the outskirts of Dublin. A son was born just then, named Charles Lindsay, so the position could not have come at a better time. On 23 October 1844 Margoliouth took office, and spent the next three years in an undemanding position that gave him plenty of opportunity to carry on with the scholarly work that led to numerous publications throughout his life. Margoliouth also became a freemason and published a monthly magazine, the *Star of Jacob* (January–June 1847), but it folded after six numbers.

The life of a provincial Anglican clergyman in Ireland was clearly not enough for Margoliouth, so he sent his wife to live with her newly arrived parents, resigned his living, and in July 1847 set sail for the Holy Land, arriving at Constantinople in March 1848 and finally Jerusalem, where he went at once to see the protestant bishop of Jerusalem, Samuel Gobat (1799–1879). He travelled throughout Palestine until May 1848 and returned to Liverpool, becoming early the next year curate in the parish of St Catherine Tranmere on the Wirral. He fell out with the vicar and resigned in the autumn, although his children remained in the care of a family in the parish while he went to London to supervise the publication of his three-volume *History of the Jews in Great Britain* (1851).

In September 1851 Margoliouth was made curate of St Bartholomew's, in Salford. On 4 January 1853 his daughter, Miriam, married William Parker, the son of a local farmer: they and their children emigrated to New Zealand in 1859 and Margoliouth's son Charles followed them a few years later. In May 1853 he resigned his curacy once again, taking a similar post at St Chad's, Wybunbury, Cheshire. This too ended unhappily, and in February 1855 he became curate in Great Coates, near Grimsby, but only for a few months.

Margoliouth spent a year and a half abroad in 1856–7. His wife Chaja, from whom he had separated about 1847, had moved to Paris with her parents in 1852, leaving the children behind. Margoliouth paid a return visit to his native town in Poland, visiting his mother and his brother Hershel, whose son Gershon would himself come to England twenty years later. Upon his return to Britain early in 1857 Margoliouth became curate in Braintree, Essex. But by July 1858 he had gone again, in order to apply himself to another of his unfinished projects, a new edition of the Hebrew Old Testament.

Margoliouth spent the next three years living at 25 Great Russell Street, London, working on his edition and writing a semi-autobiographical novel entitled *The Curates of Riversdale*. In September 1861 he took on another curacy at Wyton, near Huntingdon, and remained for about a year, afterwards taking temporary positions until in 1864 he was given a very satisfying post as assistant minister in the East End parish of St Paul's, Haggerston, where he remained for about ten years. He then moved across London to a curacy at St Paul's, Onslow Square, living at 22 Pelham Crescent in South Kensington. It was while serving in this post that he met a childless widow named Sarah Golding St Osyth Smith (1826–1889), and they were married on 14 October 1874 (his first wife having died in 1870). Two years later Margoliouth was offered a proper living at Little Linford, Buckinghamshire, near Newport Pagnell, and he was inducted as vicar on 30 January 1877 and installed with his wife in a new purpose-built house. The following April he had the pleasure of baptizing there his nephew Gershon (now George), who had recently arrived in England after studying in Germany. Margoliouth died at the Portland Hotel, Great Portland Street, London, on 25 February 1881, attended by his nephew George at the end. He was buried at Little Linford churchyard.

Margoliouth's nephew George Margoliouth (1853–1924) was ordained in 1881 and became keeper of the Hebrew, Syriac, and Ethiopic manuscripts at the British Museum (1891–1914). His son Herschel Maurice Margoliouth (1887–1959) was educated at Rugby School and Oriel College, Oxford, where he became a fellow in 1935 and an expert on early modern English poetry.

Moses Margoliouth was probably related to Ezekiel Margoliouth (1816–1894), also born in Suwałki, the son of the rabbi there, Abraham Margoliouth. The two met in the East End about 1864 and became close friends. Ezekiel was baptized in England in 1848 and worked for the London Society for Promoting Christianity amongst the Jews. His son was David S. Margoliouth (1858–1940), Laudian professor of Arabic at Oxford (1889–1937). 　　DAVID S. KATZ

Sources P. Jones, *Moses: a short account of the life of Reverend Moses Margoliouth* (1999) • M. Margoliouth, *A pilgrimage to the land of my fathers* (1850) • D. S. Katz, *The Jews in the history of England, 1485–1850* (1994) • *CGPLA Eng. & Wales* (1881) • d. cert.
Likenesses J. W. Cook, engraving, repro. in Margoliouth, *A pilgrimage*, vol. 1 [*see illus.*]
Wealth at death under £2000: probate, 26 March 1881, *CGPLA Eng. & Wales*

Margulies, Alexander (1902–1991), businessman and patron of the arts, was born in Skalat, Galicia, on 1 July 1902, the son of Marcus Mordecai Margulies (1862–1921) and his wife, Fanny, *née* Feige (1865–1943). The Margulies were descendants of Rabbi Ephraim Zalman Margulies (1760–1828), who was celebrated for his scholarship and wealth. When the First World War broke out the family took up residence in Germany, and it was from there that Alexander moved to Britain in 1931. In his new country Margulies displayed great business acumen, creating with his brother Benzion Margulies (1890–1955) the firm Time Products, which incorporated clock movements, made overseas, into cases made in Britain. In 1939 the firm was the largest importer of horology, having factories in both China and Hong Kong. It became a public company in 1962, though Margulies continued as president after his retirement. With the coming of the Second World War he set up a factory to make aircraft components; its employees included refugee workers from twenty-five families whom he had helped to escape from Nazi Europe.

Like his wife, Stella, Margulies took a keen interest in art, of which he was an avid collector. He favoured, in particular, contemporary French sculptures and paintings and numbered among his friends the artists Derain, Modigliani, and Soutine. For much of his life, however, he was appalled by what he considered the lack of interest and poor financial support given to the arts by the Anglo-Jewish community. Following his appointment in 1965 as chairman of the Ben Uri Art Gallery in London, founded to support and publicize the work of Jewish artists (in which his brother was also involved), he did much to expand the specializations of the gallery to include not only painting and sculpture, but also orchestral and choral music, drama, and literature. When the gallery was obliged to sell one of its most outstanding paintings, *The Merry-Go-Round* by Mark Gertler, to ensure its survival, Margulies was widely criticized. He defended his action, however—accusing the Jewish community for failing to provide the necessary financial support, and noting that he himself had donated thousands of pounds towards the gallery's maintenance and the purchase of contemporary works of art. He also gave a number of his paintings to the Tate Gallery in London and to the New Art Museum in Tel Aviv.

Throughout his life Margulies was a dedicated supporter of Zionism. At the twenty-third Zionist Congress in 1931 he was elected a member of the actions committee of the World Zionist Organization. He was president of the friends of the Anti-Tuberculosis League of Israel. He served at various times as honorary treasurer, vice-chairman, and president of the Mizrachi Federation and the Bachad Fellowship, and his tireless work on behalf of these organizations was recognized when, in 1983, the Alexander Margulies Youth Centre was opened in Temple Fortune, London. In addition he played a prominent part as one of the vice-presidents in the Joint Israel Appeal and was a powerful driving force in helping establish such centres of Jewish education as Carmel College (the only Jewish public school) and, in 1965, Hillel House, the purpose of which was to provide support for Jewish university students.

Firmly committed to Jewish Orthodoxy all his life, Margulies was a tireless supporter of Jewish culture. During the Second World War—together with his brother Benzion, and with assistance from the distinguished Hebrew scholar Simon Rawidowicz—he established the Ararat Publications Society, with himself as chairman; its purpose was to foster Hebrew literature and to encourage Jewish learning. An outstanding publication to be issued under the auspices of the society was the Hebrew quarterly *Metzudah*, the only European Hebrew magazine, its aim being to provide an outlet for Jewish scholarship on an international basis. Margulies also took a keen interest in the Institute for Jewish Studies, being its treasurer, and gave generous assistance to the *Jewish Quarterly*. A bust of him was made by Jacob Epstein.

Margulies died at his home, 4 Sidmouth Road, London, on 2 May 1991, survived by two sons and a daughter.

G. R. SEAMAN

Sources J. Finkelstone, *The Independent* (10 May 1991) · *Jewish Chronicle* (10 May 1991) · *Jewish Year Book* (1990), 246 · A. Greenbaum, *A history of the Ararat Publishing Society* (Jerusalem, 1998) · H. A. Strauss and W. Röder, eds., *Biographisches Handbuch der deutschsprachigen Emigration nach 1933 / International biographical dictionary of central European émigrés, 1933–1945*, 1 (1980), 476 · d. cert.
Likenesses J. Epstein, bust, 1942
Wealth at death £1,125,624: probate, 4 Dec 1991, *CGPLA Eng. & Wales*

Marham, Ralph (*fl. c.*1380), Augustinian friar and historian, is said by John Bale to have belonged to his order's house at Bishop's Lynn, and to have flourished about 1380. His family presumably came from Marham, a few miles south-east of that town. He studied at Cambridge, where he became DTh, and compiled a history of the world in two volumes, under the title *Manipulus chronicorum*, from the creation to his own times. However, a later claim that he became prior of the Lynn friary arose from confusion with a namesake who became prior of the Benedictine cell at Lynn, and in fact nothing that Bale says about Marham's career can be substantiated, beyond his existence and his authorship of the history attributed to him. The latter survives in two copies, Paris, Bibliothèque Nationale, MS Latin 4928, and Cambridge, Gonville and Caius, MS 26/15, and the incipit of the former contains Marham's name in an acrostic taken from the first letters of its opening words. It is not clear whether Bale is correct in saying that there were two volumes. Both surviving texts end with Christ's ascension, as the author states in his *explicit*, though he also declares his hope of continuing his work at a future date. Passages from a work or works called *Manipulus chronicorum*, relating to Bishop Robert Grosseteste and an episode in the barons' wars respectively, survive among transcripts made by the later antiquaries William Worcester (BL, Cotton MS Julius F.vii, fol. 65) and Brian Twyne (Bodl. Oxf., MS Twyne 21, fol. 133). But in neither case is Marham named as the author, and the problem of the chronological range of his work consequently remains unsolved. It can at least be said that his history suggests that he was a learned man, well-read in the fathers and in other universal histories, with perhaps a working knowledge of Hebrew. HENRY SUMMERSON

Sources F. X. Roth, *The English Austin friars, 1249–1538*, 2 vols. (1961–6) · Bale, *Cat.*, 1.485–6 · Bodl. Oxf., MS Twyne 21, fol. 133 · BL, Cotton MS Julius F.vii, fol. 65 · Emden, *Cam.*, 390 · R. Sharpe, *A handlist of the Latin writers of Great Britain and Ireland before 1540* (1997), 383
Archives Bibliothèque Nationale, Paris, MS Latin 4928 · Gon. & Caius Cam., MS 26/15

Maria, duchess of Gloucester and Edinburgh (*bap.* 1736, *d.* 1807). *See under* William Henry, Prince, first duke of Gloucester and Edinburgh (1743–1805).

Marianus Scottus [Muiredach mac Robartaig] (*d.* 1080×83), scribe, was the founder of the Irish monastic community at Regensburg, Bavaria, from which developed the Irish Benedictine congregation in southern Germany, the Schottenklöster. His name in Irish is given in his own hand as 'Muredach macc Robartaig' in the colophon of his copy of the Pauline epistles now in Vienna. The patronymic (which was probably by this time a surname) shows him as of the family of north Donegal who were traditionally guardians of the early seventh-century psalter codex known as the *Cathach* of St Columba. The case (*cumhdach*) of the *Cathach* was commissioned between 1062 and 1098 by Domnall Mac Robartaig, who was coarb (successor) of Columba at Kells. He and Muiredach seem likely to have been closely related, perhaps brothers, while Domnall's predecessor but one as coarb, Robartach mac Ferdomnaig (*d.* 1057), may conceivably have been their father.

Marianus left Ireland with a group of companions *c.*1068, originally intending to go to Rome. According to the *Vita Mariani Scotti* (composed between 1177 and 1185 by a monk of the Schottenklöster at Regensburg), he resided for about a year at the monastery of Michaelsberg at Bamberg in Bavaria before proceeding to Regensburg in the footsteps of a certain Mercherdach (d. 1075), who had settled there as an incluse attached to the cloister of Obermünster c.1040. At Regensburg, Marianus was received by the nuns of the cloister of Niedermünster, on whose behalf he transcribed many sacred books, and rapidly gained a reputation for sanctity. Later, c.1075, he was granted leave by the abbess of Obermünster to move with his companions to a dependency of her monastery, the small church of Weih St Peter on the outskirts of the city, where anchorite cells were specially constructed. About 1077 Marianus was joined at Weih St Peter by Eóin (Johannes), also a known scribe, who in 1083 completed a manuscript (now at Edinburgh) begun by Marianus three years before. From this it is inferred that Marianus's death occurred in or soon after 1080. 9 February is the date given in the Bollandist edition of his life, based on a note in the source manuscript, but this is not corroborated. He was buried at Weih St Peter (site demolished in 1552).

After Marianus's death the community at Weih St Peter adopted the Benedictine rule and underwent rapid expansion due to an influx of newcomers from Ireland. About 1089 a second Irish foundation was established at St Jakob in Regensburg, and in the course of the twelfth century this became the mother house of a congregation numbering some dozen houses of Irish Benedictines in southern Germany.

Two manuscripts by Marianus Scottus are extant, one written entirely in his hand, and a second partially so. The one in Vienna (Österreichische Nationalbibliothek, Cod. lat. 1247) was written by Marianus in the first half of 1079 and contains a copy of the Pauline epistles with copious commentary and other marginalia, including the signature 'Marianus Scottus' which is entered on the verso of the final leaf and glossed in Irish in the form given above. The other codex, formerly in the Benedictine abbey of Fort Augustus and presently housed in the National Library of Scotland, Edinburgh (Rat. 1), consists of eight ascetical treatises of which the first six are in Marianus's hand and the remainder in the hand of Johannes. According to marginalia in a mixture of Irish and Latin, Marianus was writing during the months of June and July 1080. Marianus's hand has also been identified (by Bernhard Bischoff) in occasional marginalia entered in a ninth-century Bible codex from the library of Niedermünster (Munich, Bayerische Staatsbibliothek, Clm 12741). A further manuscript written by him containing the Psalms and excerpts from the Christian fathers is known only from the text of a colophon cited by fifteenth-century Bavarian sources in which the date of writing is given as 1074, which is specified as the seventh year of Marianus's exile.

PÁDRAIG A. BREATNACH

Sources 'Vita Mariani Scoti', *Acta sanctorum: Februarius*, 2 (Antwerp, 1658), 361–72 · P. A. Breatnach, *Die Regensburger Schottenlegende: Libellus de fundacione ecclesie consecrati Petri* (1977) · P. A. Breatnach, 'The origins of the Irish monastic tradition at Ratisbon (Regensburg)', *Celtica*, 13 (1980), 58–77 · M. Dilworth, 'Marianus Scotus: scribe and monastic founder', *Scottish Gaelic Studies*, 10/2 (1965), 125–48 · A. F. Forbes, 'Account of a manuscript of the eleventh century by Marianus of Ratisbon', *Proceedings of the Society of Antiquaries of Scotland*, 6 (1864–6), 34–40 · P. Mai, 'Das Schottenklöster St Jakob zu Regensburg im Wandel der Zeiten', *100 Jahre Priesterseminar in St Jakob zu Regensburg, 1872–1972* (1972) · J. F. Kenney, *The sources for the early history of Ireland* (1929), 618–19 · B. Bischoff, 'Eine turonische Bibel in München (Clm 12741)', *Mittelalterliche Studien*, 1 (1966), 39

Archives Österreichische Nationalbibliothek, Vienna, Cod. lat. 1247 · Bayerische Staatsbibliothek, Munich, Clm 12741 · NL Scot., Rat. 1

Marianus Scotus [Moelbrigte] (1028–1082), Benedictine monk and chronicler, was a native of Ireland. His true name was Moelbrigte, and he became a monk in 1052 at Moville, Down, during the abbacy of Tigernach Bairrech (d. 1061). Having left Ireland, he entered the Irish monastery of St Martin at Cologne on Thursday 1 August 1056. On 12 April 1058 he left Cologne for Fulda, was ordained priest by Abbot Siegfried of Fulda on 13 March 1059 at Würzburg, and on 14 May following became a recluse at Fulda. There he remained for ten years until on 3 April 1069 he left Fulda by command of Siegfried, now archbishop of Mainz, and on 10 July 1069 settled at Mainz, still as a recluse, where he remained in the monastery of St Alban the Martyr until his death, which is said to have occurred on 22 December 1082.

Marianus composed a universal chronicle, in the tradition of Jerome and Bede, extending from the beginning of mankind to his own lifetime. He thought that the Dionysian date of Christ's nativity was twenty-two years too late, and so dated his annals in two ways, according to his own chronology ('in conformity with the gospel'), and according to that of Dionysius, and appended tables and arguments in support of his theory; but even in his own time, says William of Malmesbury, he had but few supporters.

The chronicle contains some fifty or sixty references to Britain and Ireland. Down to 725 these are largely extracted from Bede; the later ones refer mostly to Marianus himself, to Irish monks, and to the ecclesiastical history of East Francia. In its earlier portion the chronicle is a compilation from various sources, and the part that relates to the writer's own time is very brief. John of Worcester adopted Marianus as the basis of his own chronicle, and through this source the work became familiar to English writers, who, indeed, often cite John under the name of Marianus. In Germany the chronicle of Marianus was not so widely known, though Sigebert of Gembloux made extensive use of it. The chief manuscript of Marianus is Vatican City, Biblioteca Apostolica Vaticana, Pal. lat. 830, a fair copy that was almost certainly written for him by Irish hands, and which he very probably revised himself. There were at least three stages in its compilation, one in 1072–3, a second in 1076, and a third in 1082. The second main witness, BL, Cotton MS Nero C.v, a German twelfth-century manuscript, represents a redaction made in Germany shortly after Marianus's death, and was the version used by John of Worcester. The Vatican manuscript was taken by Waitz for his text of book 3 only in the Monumenta Germaniae Historica, 5.495–562. Books 1 and 3 were printed at

Basel in 1559 from a mutilated manuscript; this is followed in the editions of Pistorius (1601) and of Struvius (1726).   C. L. KINGSFORD, *rev.* P. McGURK

Sources D. G. Waitz, ed., 'Mariani Scotti chronicon', [*Annales et chronica aevi Salici*], ed. G. H. Pertz, MGH Scriptores [folio], 5 (Stuttgart, 1844), 481–568 · Marianus Scotus, 'Chronicon', *Patrologia Latina*, 147 (1853), 623–796 · A.-D. von den Brincken, 'Marianus Scottus als Universalhistoriker iuxta veritatem evangelii', *Die Iren und Europa im früheren Mittelalter*, ed. H. Löwe, 2 (Stuttgart, 1982), 970–1009 · A.-D. von der Brincken, 'Marianus Scottus', *Deutsches Archiv*, 17 (1961), 191–238 · T. Ó Raifeartaigh, *The Royal Irish Academy: a bicentennial history, 1785–1985* (1985) · J. F. Kenney, *The sources for the early history of Ireland* (1929); repr. (1979), 614–16
Archives Biblioteca Apostolica Vaticana, Vatican City, MS Pal. lat. 830 · BL, Cotton MS Nero C.v

Marie [Marie de France] (*fl. c.*1180–*c.*1189), poet, was of French origin, resident in England in the reign of Henry II; she is credited with three works which are signed Marie. In the latest of these, a collection of Aesopic fables translated from the English of a certain Alfred, the author declares 'Marie ai nun, si sui de France', which may indicate that she came specifically from the Île-de-France.

The *Fables* were written for a Count William, who has been variously identified with William (I) Longespée, William (I) Marshal, William de Mandeville (earl of Essex, a friend of Henry II—they both died in 1189), William de Blois (Earl Warenne and earl of Surrey), and William of Gloucester, the choice being connected with possible identifications of Marie herself with a nun at Reading Abbey, the abbess of Shaftesbury (1181–1216), Marie de Meulan (or de Beaumont), wife of Hugh Talbot of Cleuville, or Marie de Boulogne, daughter of Stephen of Blois and Matilda, who was abbess of Romsey, Hampshire. None of these identifications is safe. The *Fables* seems to have been a success, being transmitted in twenty-three manuscripts. In the late twelfth century (probably *c.*1180) the monk Denis Piramus, author of a life of St Edmund, refers to a Dame Marie who wrote verses drawn from *lais* which are 'not at all true' (Piramus, 1.35). These poems must be the twelve assembled in BL, Harley MS 978 (possibly from Reading), where they are preceded by a general prologue containing the name Marie, which also occurs in one of the *lais*, that of *Guigemar*. A few of the Harley *lais* are transmitted separately in four further manuscripts. Baum has emphasized the fragility of the attribution of all the Harley *lais* to a single author, and the identification of that author with Marie de France. The views that Baum criticized none the less persist. Attempts have been made to group the *lais* chronologically, but a dating to the second half of the twelfth century, and specifically to the reign of Henry II (presumed to be the 'noble king' of the general prologue), is all that can be established. A third work attributed to Marie is a notably faithful French translation of a highly successful Latin treatise on St Patrick's Purgatory by the Cistercian monk Henry of Saltrey. The French *Espurgatoire* is dedicated to 'H. abbot of Sartis' (Wardon, Bedfordshire), who is most likely to have been the second Abbot Hugh (1173–85/6). It survives in a single manuscript (Paris, Bibliothèque Nationale, MS fr. 25407) and is followed by no fewer than six Old French verse treatments of

the treatise. It is possible that the Marie who composed the life of Æthelthryth in the early thirteenth century is also to be identified as Marie de France.

Whatever her true identity, Marie de France displays an aristocratic outlook, a knowledge of Latin and English, familiarity with the works of Ovid, acquaintance with Wace's *Brut* and Gaimar's *Estoire des Engleis*, and a variety of Breton lore. As a courtly writer and contemporary of Chrétien de Troyes, Marie surprises by introducing Arthurian material into only one of the *lais* (*Lanval*). All but one of the *lais* were translated into Old Norse in the thirteenth century, while *Le Fresne* and *Lanval* inspired versions in Middle English.   TONY HUNT

Sources R. Baum, *Recherches sur les oeuvres attribuées à Marie de France* (1968) · E. J. Mickel, *Marie de France* (1974) · '*Saint Patrick's Purgatory': a poem by Marie de France*, ed. and trans. M. J. Curley (1993) · D. Piramus, *La vie seint Edmund le rei*, ed. H. Kjellman and A. Erdmann (1935)
Archives Bibliothèque Nationale, Paris, MS fr. 25407 · BL, Harley MS 978

Marie [*née* Marie de Coucy] (*d.* 1284), queen of Scots, second consort of Alexander II, was the elder daughter (there were also three sons) of Enguerrand (III) de Coucy, known as the Great (*d.* 1242), lord of Coucy in Picardy and great-grandson of King Louis VI of France (*r.* 1108–37), and his third wife, Marie de Montmirail. She was admired by Matthew Paris for her beauty and was brought from France to be married at Roxburgh on 15 May 1239 to the forty-year-old Scottish king *Alexander II (1198–1249). Alexander's first wife, Joan of England, had died childless in 1238, and he had urgent dynastic reasons for his remarriage. In terms of European diplomacy, it evoked Alexander's alliance with the French in 1216–17, when he and Marie's powerful father had probably met during the Franco-Scottish invasions of England. Such a reassertion of Scottish independence alarmed King Henry III, and contributed to the tensions that almost precipitated another Anglo-Scottish war in 1244.

Little is known about Marie's influence on the culture of the Scottish court, though her chancellor, Master Richard Vairement, possibly hailed from Vermand, near Coucy, and her nephew Enguerrand de Guines (who ultimately succeeded as lord of Coucy in 1311) became a leading Scottish magnate by wedding Christiana de Lindsay *c.*1280. Politically the most important result of Marie's marriage was undoubtedly the birth of her only child, the future *Alexander III, on 4 September 1241. She played no significant part during her son's troubled minority after Alexander II's death in 1249. According to Matthew Paris, as queen mother she was assigned a third of Scottish royal revenues, and he estimated her share at between 4000 and 7000 merks a year. Marie was at Dunfermline Abbey for the translation of St Margaret's relics on 19 June 1250, and crossed to France in October, but returned with a magnificent retinue for Alexander III's marriage to *Margaret of England at York on 26 December 1251. She then appears to have lived mainly in France until 1268. No doubt the ambitious Comyns had wanted to be rid of her so as to reinforce their dominance over the young Scottish king; but she also had pressing family duties in her homeland, due to the succession of her second brother Enguerrand (IV) de Coucy as a boy in 1250, and his imprisonment by King Louis IX (*r.* 1226–70) in 1256.

Early in 1257, apparently to appease Louis for her brother's indiscretions, Marie married her second husband, Jean de Brienne or d'Acre, butler of France, whose father and namesake had been crowned king of Jerusalem in 1210 and emperor of Constantinople in 1231. They visited Scotland briefly in 1257, and both were appointed to a Scottish regency council in September 1258, though their role in state affairs was purely nominal. When Marie separated from Jean de Brienne in 1268 and returned to Scotland, Alexander III secured an agreement whereby she might remain in Scotland at her pleasure, and Jean (who long outlived Marie, dying only in 1296) would receive from her dower an annual pension of 500 merks. In 1276 she was granted safe conducts by the English government to undertake a pilgrimage to Canterbury and return to Scotland. In 1284 (the precise date is unrecorded) she died overseas, presumably in France.

KEITH STRINGER

Sources Paris, *Chron.*, vols. 3–5 · W. Bower, *Scotichronicon*, ed. D. E. R. Watt and others, new edn, 9 vols. (1987–98), vol. 5 · *CDS*, vols. 1–2 · D. E. R. Watt, 'The minority of Alexander III of Scotland', *TRHS*, 5th ser., 21 (1971), 1–23 · J. Balteau and others, eds., *Dictionnaire de biographie française*, [19 vols.] (Paris, 1933–) · D. E. R. Watt, *A biographical dictionary of Scottish graduates to AD 1410* (1977) · GEC, *Peerage*, new edn, vol. 6

Marie, Princess (1875–1938), queen of Romania, consort of Ferdinand I, was born on 29 October 1875 at Eastwell Park, Kent, the second of the five children of Queen Victoria's second son, *Alfred Ernest Albert, duke of Edinburgh (1844–1900), and his wife, Marie Alexandrovna, grand duchess of Russia (1853–1920). Her full given names were Marie Alexandra Victoria. Educated by tutors, Marie (or Missy as she was known to her family) was raised in the Anglican faith of her father. In 1886 the duke of Edinburgh was named commander of the Mediterranean Fleet and moved his family to Malta, and in 1889 the family moved to Coburg in Germany, in preparation for the duke's future inheritance of his uncle's duchies of Saxe-Coburg and Gotha.

In spite of the wishes of Marie's father, of Queen Victoria, and of the young man himself—all of whom expected Marie to marry her cousin, the future King George V—on 10 January 1893 her Anglophobe mother married off the beautiful, high-spirited seventeen-year-old princess to Ferdinand, prince of Hohenzollern-Sigmaringen (1865–1927), who was the heir designate to his uncle, King Carol I of Romania. Marie gave birth to six children: Carol, subsequently King Carol II of Romania; Elisabetha, later queen consort of King George II of Greece; Marie (Mignon), later queen consort of King Alexander I of Yugoslavia; Nicolas; Ileana; and Mircea, who died at three and was generally believed to be the son of Marie's paramour, Prince Barbu Stirbey. Bored by her timid husband, the humourless king, and the king's arty wife, Queen Elisabeth (Carmen Sylva), Marie escaped

from the uninspiring court on horseback—she was a fearless rider—and in flirtations. During a peasant uprising in 1907 she was sent to a friend's estate for safety, and there she met Prince Stirbey, scion of the ancient ruling family of Wallachia. They fell in love, and Stirbey encouraged the crown princess to become a major political force in her adopted country. During the Balkan wars Marie worked in the cholera camps, gaining a reputation for courage and efficiency.

King Carol tried unsuccessfully to take his country into the war on the side of Germany and Austria, but died shortly before war broke out, leaving his heir, now King Ferdinand I, clinging to neutrality while Queen Marie agitated in favour of joining forces with her native England and her allies. In league with the prime minister, Ion Bratianu, the queen took an active role in contacting various members of her family who sat on the thrones of Europe, and in bargaining for the best terms for her country. When Romania finally entered the war on the allied side in August 1916, Marie, according to the French minister to Bucharest, 'embraced war as another might embrace religion' (Saint-Aulaire, 399). Throwing herself into war work, she established hospitals, visited the wounded constantly, and wrote her first book, *My Country*, to raise funds for the Red Cross. But Romania, situated geographically between its enemies and Russia, then on the eve of revolution, was doomed to defeat. In December 1916 Bucharest fell and the court fled to Jassy, the provincial capital of Moldavia, where Marie increased her inspirational and organization work, making herself famous by visiting her soldiers in the trenches and refusing to wear rubber gloves in the typhus wards of the hospitals. The victory of the Bolsheviks in November 1917 turned Romania, in the words of a British diplomat, into 'an island surrounded on all sides by the enemy, with no hope of assistance from the Allies' (Rattigan, 194–5), though Marie and her family were offered asylum in England by George V. In March 1918 Ferdinand was forced to sign the treaty of Bucharest, which left the royal family intact, but isolated and impotent.

The general victory of the allies eight months later brought other problems, as Bratianu's oriental style of diplomacy lost friends for Romania at the Paris peace conference. In March 1919 Queen Marie, whose English background and connections qualified her to deal with the western European diplomatic establishment, was called to Paris to 'try her philtres' (Saint-Aulaire, 485) on the representatives of the great powers. 'She is magnificent', Colette wrote in *Le Matin* the morning after Marie's arrival, 'The morning was grey, but Queen Marie carried light within her' (*Le Matin*, 6 March 1919). When she left Paris some weeks later, the queen had become a world celebrity, admired for her flamboyant style, her romantic charm, and her ease of communication. With Marie smoothing his way and the spectre of Russian communism looming in the background, Bratianu managed to obtain terms that saw Romania's territory doubled and its population increased by more than 100 per cent.

Marie of Romania spent her remaining eight years on

the throne writing books (mostly fairy tales and a highly successful autobiography, *The Story of my Life*), marrying off her children, and trying to keep her elder son from inappropriate liaisons. This last proved impossible, as in 1925 Carol ran away from his wife with Elena Lupescu, renouncing his place in the succession to his four-year-old son, Michael. As a woman Marie was unable to act as regent for her grandson after the death of King Ferdinand I in 1927, and with the death of Prime Minister Bratianu later the same year, her political influence waned. In 1930 Carol returned to Bucharest, reclaimed the throne from his son, and set out to destroy Marie's enormous popularity with the Romanian people. Excluded from an increasingly dictatorial Romanian court, Queen Marie withdrew to her summer home, with its famous gardens, at Balcic on the Black Sea. She fell ill in the summer of 1937; denied the best medical help, she died at Castle Pelisor, Sinaia, Romania, on 18 July 1938 from a rare form of cirrhosis of the liver (she did not drink, and rumours circulated that she did not die of natural causes). She was buried three days later in the royal family vault at Curtea de Arges in Wallachia; at her own request her heart was placed in a small gold casket in the chapel she had built in the grounds of her summer home at Balcic; it was removed to her castle at Bran shortly before Balcic became part of Bulgaria during the Second World War.

HANNAH PAKULA

Sources H. Pakula, *The last romantic: a biography of Queen Marie of Romania* (1985) · S. D. Spector, *Rumania at the Paris peace conference* (1995) · Marie, queen of Romania, *The story of my life*, 2 vols. (1934) · Marie, queen of Romania, *Ordeal: the story of my life* (1935) · comte de Saint-Aulaire, *Confession d'un vieux diplomate* (Paris, 1953) · F. Rattigan, *Diversions of a diplomat* (1924) · Burke, *Peerage* (1924) · T. Elsberry, *Marie of Romania: the intimate life of a twentieth century queen* (1973) · M. Daggett, *Marie of Roumania: the intimate story of the radiant queen* (1926) · 'Ignat Bednarik (1882–1963)', www.bednarik. non-profit.nl, 18 Oct 2002
Archives Archivele Statului Bucaresti, Romania fond Casa Regaia, Regina Maria Memoires, Regina Maria corresp. · Kent State University, Ohio · Maryhill Museum · priv. coll., letters · priv. coll., letters · priv. coll., letters and papers · priv. coll., letters · Staatsarchiv Sigmaringen · Stanford University, California, Hoover Institution | U. Reading L., Astor collection
Likenesses photographs, priv. coll. · photographs, *Illustrated London News* Picture Library · photographs, Royal Arch. · photographs, Kent State University, Ohio · photographs, George Eastman House, Rochester, New York · portrait, priv. coll.

Marie Louise, Princess (1872–1956), was born at Cumberland Lodge, Windsor, on 12 August 1872, and was given the names Franziska Josepha Louise Augusta Marie Christiana Helena. She was the youngest child of Prince Christian of Schleswig-Holstein (1831–1917) and his wife, Princess *Helena (1846–1923), Queen Victoria's third daughter. Her conventional education at home was relieved by holidays with relatives in Germany, during one of which visits she met Prince Aribert of Anhalt (1864–1933). With the encouragement of her cousin Kaiser Wilhelm II she married him in St George's Chapel, Windsor, on 6 July 1891. He proved an unsatisfactory husband. After nine distressing years the childless marriage was arbitrarily annulled in 1900 by Prince Aribert's father, exercising his medieval

right as a sovereign prince. Princess Marie Louise, a devout churchwoman, believed her wedding vows to be binding and never remarried.

The princess returned to her family in England and devoted more than half a century of her life to furthering charitable causes and social services. Nursing, the care of lepers, youth clubs, the relief of poverty, and organizations for international understanding particularly touched her imagination. She became a familiar figure at balls and bazaars, committees and receptions, commemorative services and picture exhibitions. Standing above average height and with imposing features, she brought to all formal occasions an air of dignity softened by kindliness. Her neat and pointed speeches always refreshed and sometimes surprised her audience. There was charm, too, in her conversation. She was a tireless traveller, and few corners of the world had escaped her curiosity or failed to stimulate her talents for humour and mimicry.

Princess Marie Louise's patronage of the arts enabled her to acquire a wider circle of friends than usually surrounded royal personages. She moved at ease in the society of writers, actors, and musicians, and at one time in her life lived contentedly in a bedsitting-room at a ladies' club. Her happiest years were spent between the wars at Schomberg House, Pall Mall, which she shared with her sister Princess *Helena Victoria. Together they gave memorable parties which became a valued institution among London music lovers. From her mother Princess Marie Louise had inherited a passion for Bach, to which was added a later appreciation of Wagner. She visited Bayreuth more than once, attended Covent Garden regularly, and was the friend of Lauritz Melchior, the tenor.

Among the princess's recreations was the delicate art of enamelling in precious metals. Her work in this medium included the clasp on the cope worn by the prelate of the Order of St Michael and St George. She was also an assiduous collector of Napoleonic relics, though free from the megalomania which often accompanies such a pursuit. A self-imposed task which gave her pleasure was the planning of an elaborate doll's house, now at Windsor Castle, for presentation to Queen Mary. To secure contributions to this record of twentieth-century craftsmanship she wrote 2000 letters in her own masterful but barely legible hand.

Throughout her long life the princess was a voracious reader, particularly of history, biography, and detective fiction. In November 1956 she published a volume of her own reminiscences. *My Memories of Six Reigns*, of which 40,000 copies were sold within a few months, is a penetrating portrait of a vanished age. In a style of confiding intimacy, the princess mingled a playful disrespect for the etiquette of German courts with a loving reverence for her grandmother Queen Victoria. Although in visibly failing health she insisted on attending a luncheon to mark the publication of the book, but was unable personally to deliver her message of greeting.

The princess died a few days later, on 8 December 1956, at her grace-and-favour residence at 10 Fitzmaurice Place, Berkeley Square, London. The funeral was at Windsor on

14 December, that most melancholy of dates in Victorian memory, exactly ninety-five years after the death of her grandfather the prince consort. The congregation in St George's Chapel included three pearly queens and a pearly king who, in the gay colours of their calling, had come from Finsbury to pay a farewell tribute to their friend and patron. Her remains were then buried in the private cemetery at Frogmore.

Princess Marie Louise, the last British princess to bear the style of highness, was also one of the last surviving members of the Royal Order of Victoria and Albert. She was appointed a lady of the Imperial Order of the Crown of India by Queen Victoria (1893), GBE by George V (1919), and GCVO by Elizabeth II (1953).   KENNETH ROSE, *rev.*

Sources Princess Marie Louise, *My memories of six reigns* (1956) · *The Times* (10 Dec 1956) · private information (1971) · personal knowledge (1971)
Likenesses Lenare, group portrait, negative, 1945 (with her family?), NPG · C. Beaton, photograph, NPG · H. Mann, portrait; at the Forum Club, Belgrave Square in 1971 · H. L. Oakley, silhouette, NPG

Marie, Nathaniel (1577–1642), Reformed minister, was born in Beaumont, in Leicestershire, the son of Jean Marie (*d. c.*1589x93), minister of the protestant church at Lion-sur-Mer in Normandy, France, and of the French and Walloon refugee congregation in Norwich, and his wife, Marie le Noble (*d.* 1620). By 1593 the French and Walloon refugee churches in England were raising money to have Nathaniel educated for the ministry and in July 1595 he signed a formal agreement promising his services to the churches. He entered the University of Leiden to study theology in October 1597, and in August 1601 he was inducted as a third pastor of the French church of London, joining Robert le Maçon de la Fontaine and Aaron Cappel. Shortly thereafter, on 10 November 1603, he married Ester or Esther Delaune, daughter of the physician and minister William *Delaune (*c.*1530–1611) (who appointed him a co-executor in his will) and sister of the physicians Gideon *Delaune and Paul *Delaune and of Peter Delaune, minister of the French church at Norwich. Over the succeeding several years they had ten children.

Marie's career does not appear to have been exceptional outside of the normal performance of his pastoral duties. Indeed Isaac Casaubon, for one, does not appear to have thought highly of Marie's theology or preaching ability (Casaubon, 854, 965). However, as a minister of the presbyterian French church in London, he was at the heart of the movement for Calvinist reform in England and of English support for the European Calvinist churches. He maintained constant contact with leading English puritans, Scottish presbyterians, and representatives of the Calvinist churches on the continent. All the events surrounding the stranger churches in England in the early Stuart period directly involved him, and in particular he played a leading role in the churches' defence of their ecclesiastical liberties and separate status in the face of Archbishop Laud's attack on them between 1634 and 1636. He appears also to have written extensively on theology, although without ever publishing his works, for in his will

of 25 May 1639 he bequeaths to his son John 'my seven hand written bookes in folio guilt upon the leafes' and exhorts him 'to show them unto learned men to see if any of them bee worthy of printing' (Guildhall Library, 9171/28, fol. 404*v*); nothing is known of the fate of these manuscripts.

Marie died on 3 or 4 August 1642, and was buried at St Botolph without Bishopsgate, London, on 5 August. He was survived by his second wife, Esther le Fevre, whom he had married on 16 April 1637, and by many of his children.   CHARLES G. D. LITTLETON

Sources F. de Schickler, *Les églises du réfuge en Angleterre*, 3 vols. (Paris, 1892) · French Protestant Church of London, Soho Square, MSS 4–5 [Consistory minutes, 1589–1680] · *The registers of the French church, Threadneedle Street, London*, 1, ed. W. J. C. Moens, Huguenot Society of London, 9 (1896) · A. C. Chamier, ed., *Les actes des colloques des églises françaises et des synodes des églises étrangères refugiées en Angleterre, 1581–1654*, Huguenot Society of London, 2 (1890) · will, commissary court of London, GL, 9171/28, fols. 403–5 · will, commissary court of London, GL, vol. 23, 427*v* [mother's will] · D. C. A. Agnew, *Protestant exiles from France, chiefly in the reign of Louis XIV, or, The Huguenot refugees and their descendants in Great Britain and Ireland*, 3rd edn, 1 (1886), 16, 100 · W. J. C. Moens, *The Walloons and their church at Norwich: their history and registers, 1565–1832*, Huguenot Society of London, 1 (1887–8) · A. W. C. Hallen, ed., *The registers of St Botolph, Bishopsgate, London*, 3 vols. (1889–95) · I. Casaubon, *Ephemerides Isaaci Casauboni*, ed. J. Russell, 2 vols. (1850) · G. du Rieu, ed., *Album studiosorum academiae Lugduno Batavae, MDLXXV–MDCCCLXXV: accedunt nomina curatorum et professorum per eadem secula* (The Hague, 1875), col. 49

Marillac, Charles de (1510x13–1560), diplomat and archbishop of Vienne, was probably born at Aigueperse in the Auvergne; he was the third son of Guillaume de Marillac, a nobleman who had served the duc de Bourbon, and of Marguerite Genest. Nothing is known about his childhood, but he was described as 'much advanced towards letters'. Having studied law, he became a barrister in the *parlement* of Paris by 1534. Two years later he accompanied his cousin, Jean de la Forêt, as secretary on a diplomatic mission to the Ottoman sultan at Constantinople. This resulted in a commercial treaty which Marillac brought back to France for François I's approval. He returned to Constantinople in the summer of 1537 and, following his cousin's death in September, succeeded him as resident. At some point in the middle of 1538 he went back to France and was probably ordained at about this time. He then became resident ambassador at Henry VIII's court, his mission coinciding with a rapprochement between François I and the emperor Charles V which was viewed with apprehension by Henry. The highly informative dispatches which Marillac sent to his government contain a lively account of Henry's first encounter with his new queen, Anne of Cleves, as well as a sympathetic portrait of Mary Tudor, whose hand Marillac sought for the duc d'Orléans. He also witnessed the overthrow of Thomas Cromwell. These dispatches convey a vivid picture of Henry VIII's increasingly tyrannical ways. He describes them as three 'plagues': insatiable covetousness, distrust and fear, and light-headedness and inconstancy.

After Katherine Howard's execution, Marillac tried in vain to reconcile Henry VIII and Anne of Cleves, but when

England had decided to join the emperor in a new war against France, Marillac's embassy ended; he sent his last dispatch from London in September 1542, but was detained as a hostage until 1 April 1543. In reward for his services, he was made a councillor of the *parlement* of Paris. He also received the abbey of Mas, in Gascony (October 1540), and that of St Père de Melun (December 1541). In October 1541 he became a *maître des requêtes de l'hôtel*. Little is known about Marillac's activities in the four years after his return from London, but he apparently managed the household of the dauphin, Henri. Under King Henri II, Marillac became resident ambassador at the imperial court in Brussels, whence he reported on events in England, notably opposition to the rule of Protector Somerset and his fall from power. At the same time, he promoted French interests beyond the Rhine. Meanwhile, in June 1550, he became bishop of Vannes.

Marillac returned home in September 1552, following another breakdown in Franco-imperial relations. In 1553 he was sent to Metz to help pave the way for a French intervention in the next election to the Holy Roman empire and the following year he went to Switzerland to treat with the margrave of Brandenburg. In 1555 he took part in Franco-imperial peace talks held at Marck, near Ardre, under the auspices of Mary Tudor; they led to the truce of Vaucelles in 1556, but this was soon broken. Marillac wrote a pamphlet, blaming Philip II and the duke of Savoy for the breach. In 1557 he was sent to Rome to smooth the way for an invasion of Naples by a French army under the duc de Guise. Meanwhile, he was appointed archbishop of Vienne on 24 March 1557; but his political activities prevented him from residing in his see and he entrusted his pastoral duties to his brother, Bertrand. Early in 1559 Marillac attended the diet of Augsburg: although officially charged with reviving Franco-imperial friendship, he was instructed to seek alliances with various German princes. Henri II's accidental death in July 1559 effectively ended Marillac's political career. At an assembly of notables, held at Fontainebleau in 1560, he pressed for radical reforms but after opposing the policies of François II's Guise ministers, he was banished from court and died soon afterwards, at Melun, on 2 December 1560.

R. J. KNECHT

Sources P. de Vaissière, *Charles de Marillac* (1896) • J. Kaulek, ed., *Correspondance politique de MM. de Castillon et de Marillac, ambassadeurs de France en Angleterre (1537–1542)* (Paris, 1885) • *Catalogue des actes de François 1er*, 10 vols. (Paris, 1887–1908) • *LP Henry VIII* • L. Romier, *Les origines politiques des guerres de religion*, 2 vols. (1913) • A. Tallon, *La France et le concile de Trente (1518–1563)* (Rome, 1997)

Marillier, Henry Currie (1865–1951), writer and expert on tapestries, was born at Grahamstown, Cape Colony, on 2 July 1865, the eldest child and only son of Captain Charles Henry Marillier (*d.* 1875) of the Cape mounted rifles. His mother, Margaret, daughter of Alexander Braithwaite Morgan, surgeon to the 57th regiment of foot, had been brought up in Grahamstown by her uncle Sir Walter Currie who was Marillier's godfather. In 1870 Marillier's father became aide-de-camp to his brother-in-law Major-General John Jarvis Bisset at Gibraltar and died there suddenly in 1875.

Marillier was educated at Christ's Hospital, London, and Peterhouse, Cambridge, where he led an active social and cultural life. He took a second class (division two) in part one of the classical tripos in 1887, and having failed to obtain a Royal Engineers' commission in the Indian army, travelled to Egypt as secretary to F. A. Yeo MP. He then worked at Hinchinbrooke, Huntingdonshire, on the papers of the fourth earl of Sandwich, before entering the turbine works of Charles Parsons at Heaton near Newcastle, as a labourer, rising, over two years, to outside manager. In 1893 he went to London intending to become a consulting engineer, but instead accepted the editorship of *Lighting*, a new electrical weekly. In that year he married Katherine Isabella (*d.* 1901), daughter of John Pattinson of Newcastle upon Tyne, with whom he had two daughters. Having contributed occasional verse and articles to the *Pall Mall Gazette*, Marillier joined the staff as scientific correspondent in 1893.

In 1896 Marillier joined Cameron Swan, his wife's cousin, in the Swan Electric Engraving Company for which he wrote the preface to the *Early Works of Aubrey Beardsley* (1899) and a memoir of D. G. Rossetti (1899) with a chronological list of paintings which remained definitive until 1971. In 1904 he wrote *The Liverpool School of Painters, 1810–67* (1904), which has also remained a standard work. In the meantime Marillier had joined W. A. S. Benson's art metal business as a partner, but the vogue for beaten copper-work was already passing.

In 1897 he purchased Kelmscott House, Hammersmith, William Morris's former home, and in 1905 was invited to join the Morris company as managing director. There again he found a decline, but as the demand for Morris textiles fell, he established a thriving tapestry repair department in 1910. During the First World War, in which Marillier was an anti-aircraft gunner, the Morris Cabinet Works profitably manufactured aeroplane propellers; but the post-war years saw a further loss of business and in 1940 Marillier wound up the company. Many of the original designs were preserved but all the records of the firm were destroyed.

During his last thirty years Marillier's most important work was the compilation of a subject-index and illustrated catalogue of the tapestries of Europe which, when given to the Victoria and Albert Museum, London, in 1945, extended to fifty volumes of script and photographs. Marillier wrote occasional articles on tapestries, including those at Hampton Court (1912) and *The History of Morris's Merton Abbey Tapestry Works* (1927), but only published two sections of his researches, *English Tapestries of the Eighteenth Century* (1930) and a *Handbook to the Teniers Tapestries* (1932).

Marillier left Kelmscott House soon after his second marriage, in 1906, to Winifred Christabel, daughter of the watercolour artist Arthur Hopkins, with whom he had one son. They lived in St John's Wood until 1940, when they joined Sir Ernest Pooley at Westbrook House near Petworth, Sussex. He died on 27 July 1951 at the Royal West

Sussex Hospital, Chichester, and was buried in Brighton cemetery. Marillier was a cultured, sociable, and worldly man.   J. L. NEVINSON, *rev.* DAVID RODGERS

Sources autobiographical notes, priv. coll. · L. Parry, 'Morris and company in the twentieth century', *Journal of the William Morris Society*, 6/4 (1985–6) · *WWW*, 1951–60 · *The letters of Oscar Wilde*, ed. R. Hart-Davis (1962) · *The Times* (28 July 1951) · L. Parry, 'The revival of the Merton Abbey tapestry works', *Journal of the William Morris Society*, 5/3 (1983) · *CGPLA Eng. & Wales* (1951)
Archives V&A, department of textiles and dress, catalogue of European tapestries
Wealth at death £3369 7s. 11d.: probate, 12 Sept 1951, *CGPLA Eng. & Wales*

Marina, Princess [Princess Marina of Greece and of Denmark], **duchess of Kent** (1906–1968), was the youngest of the three daughters of Prince and Princess Nicholas of Greece and of Denmark. Her father (1872–1938) was the third son of George I of Greece and her mother was the Grand Duchess Yelena Vladimirovna (1882–1957), daughter of the Grand Duke Vladimir, uncle of Tsar Nicholas II. Born in Athens on 13 December 1906, she enjoyed a particularly happy early childhood, spent mostly in the Greek capital and at the palace at Tatoi at the foot of Mount Parnes. Her parents, although for their position not wealthy, provided a comfortable home life, which combined discipline with affection and understanding. A childhood visit to her maternal grandmother gave her glimpses of the splendours of the Russian court, but her own upbringing was simple. She had an English governess, Miss Kate Fox.

As well as Greek, Princess Marina early acquired fluency in English, which was habitually spoken within the family, and also in French. She was brought up in the Greek Orthodox church and her affection for the country of her birth survived all its disturbed history, even though this brought two periods of exile. The first was in 1917, when political upheavals forced Prince Nicholas and his family to seek refuge in Switzerland. Some four years later they returned to Greece, but in 1922 were again driven into exile. The family settled in Paris, where Princess Marina went for a time to a finishing school run by Princess Meshchersky, an old friend of the family.

Their financial position and social life were now greatly altered. Prince Nicholas was able to make profitable use of his artistic talents and Princess Nicholas devoted her time and some of her slender wealth to helping less fortunate Russian refugees. Princess Marina aided her mother and also developed her good taste in clothes, many of which she made for herself. So began her lifelong reputation as one of the best-dressed women of her time. After her marriage her elegance greatly influenced the style and appearance not only of other members of the British royal family but also of the British public, while her choice of British fabrics, especially cotton, did much to revive home industries.

In 1923 Princess Marina's eldest sister, Olga, married Prince Paul of Yugoslavia and in 1934 the next sister, Elizabeth, married Count Toerring-Yettenback of Bavaria. In August of that year Princess Marina became engaged to Prince *George Edward Alexander Edmund (1902–1942), fourth son of *George V and Queen *Mary, whom she had met from time to time when she visited London. Princess Marina rapidly won the hearts of the British people. Her attractive beauty and obvious happiness made her wedding in Westminster Abbey on 29 November 1934 a notable event. Prince George had been created duke of Kent shortly before his marriage and the duchess quickly adapted herself to her new role as a member of the British royal family, fulfilling her varied engagements with graceful conscientiousness. Her home life, as in Greece, was unobtrusive and simple. The duke and duchess particularly enjoyed converting into a pleasant home Coppins, near Iver, Buckinghamshire, the Victorian house which was left to the duke by his aunt, Princess Victoria. At their London home in Belgrave Square they extended their hospitality to a widely ranging circle of people: artists, authors, and actors, besides those associated with the charitable organizations in which the duke and duchess were especially interested.

The death of the duke in a flying accident in Scotland while serving with the Royal Air Force, on 25 August 1942, was a cruel blow. Their eldest son, Prince Edward, who succeeded as second duke, had been born on 9 October 1935; their daughter, Princess Alexandra, on Christmas day the following year; and Prince Michael on 4 July 1942. The duchess did not for long allow her loss to interrupt her war work. She had trained for the voluntary aid detachment, but her principal energies were devoted to the Women's Royal Naval Service, of which she had become commandant (later chief commandant) in 1940. She took a detailed and continuing interest in this service, and it was generally accepted that her taste in dress influenced the uniform designed for it. Her other concern was the bringing up of her family in an atmosphere which was well ordered and relaxed.

The duchess's public duties increased with widowhood. She replaced the duke in many of the organizations of which he had been president or patron, and in his work as an unofficial factory inspector. As president of the Royal National Lifeboat Institution she was active in visiting many small harbours; her constant attendance at Wimbledon as president of the All England Lawn Tennis Club was indicative of her genuine interest in the game; and towards the end of her life she took seriously her duties as chancellor of the newly formed University of Kent. Another deep and constant concern was for those suffering from mental illness, manifested in her patronage of the National Association for Mental Health. Nor did she abandon the interest in painting and music which she had so closely shared with her husband.

A number of her duties took the duchess abroad. In 1952 she made an extensive tour of the Far East, beginning and ending at Singapore and including Hong Kong and Sarawak. As colonel-in-chief of the Queen's Own Royal West Kent regiment she saw some of its troops in operation in the Malayan jungle. She represented the queen in 1957 at the independence celebrations of Ghana and in 1966 at those of Botswana and Lesotho. On these and other tours in Australia, Canada, Mexico, and South America her charm and natural friendliness increased the prestige of British royalty overseas. Although basically shy and diffident she never allowed this to stand in the way of her duties, and showed great courage in the adverse events of her life. Her warm-heartedness and generosity made for her strong friendships, and she retained a sense of humour and interest in people which made her an enchanting companion. After her eldest son's marriage in 1961 she was known as Princess Marina, duchess of Kent, and moved to Kensington Palace so that her son might have his independent establishment at Coppins. She had been appointed CI and GBE in 1937 and GCVO in 1948.

Financially the post-war years were far from easy. There was no provision for the duchess in the civil list and the situation was only partially eased through the sale of many of the art treasures which she and the duke had acquired before the war. She died at Kensington Palace after a short illness on 27 August 1968. At the time of his death her husband's body had been placed in the vaults of St George's Chapel, Windsor, but at her wish they were now buried side by side in the private burial-ground at Frogmore, Windsor.

G. K. S. HAMILTON-EDWARDS, rev.

Sources The Times (28 Aug 1968) · The Times (6 Sept 1968) · A. S. G. Lee, The royal house of Greece (1948) · J. Ellis, The duchess of Kent (1952) · J. W. Day, H.R.H. Princess Marina, duchess of Kent, 2nd edn (1969) · S. King, Princess Marina (1969) · private information (1981) **Archives** Royal Arch. | FILM BFI NFTVA, documentary footage · BFI NFTVA, news footage · BL NSA, news recording **Likenesses** J. Cassab, portrait; in family possession in 1981 · W. Dargie, portrait; Clothworkers' Company Hall, 1981 · S. Elwes, two portraits; Queen's Regiment, 1981 · N. Hepple, portrait; Corps of Royal Electrical and Mechanical Engineers, 1981 · P. A. de Laszlo, portrait · P. A. de Laszlo, two portraits; in family possession in 1981 · Sorine, portrait; in family possession in 1981 · photographs, Hult. Arch. **Wealth at death** £76,186: probate, 11 Oct 1968, CGPLA Eng. & Wales

Marindin, Sir Francis Arthur (1838–1900), soldier, railway inspector, and football administrator, was born in Weymouth, Dorset, on 1 May 1838. Of Huguenot descent, he was the second son of the Revd Samuel Marindin (1807–1852), originally from Chesterton in Shropshire, and his wife, Isabella, the daughter of Andrew Wedderburn Colville of Ochiltree, Craigflower, Fife. He was educated at Eton College and at the Royal Military Academy, Woolwich, before being commissioned into the Royal Engineers in 1854. In 1860 he married Kathleen Mary, the daughter of Sir William Stevenson, governor-general of Mauritius, whom Marindin served as aide-de-camp and private secretary between 1860 and 1863. In 1868 he was appointed as adjutant at the Chatham School of Military Engineering, and in 1869 he became brigade major, before retiring from the Royal Engineers as major in 1879. He later became an honorary colonel in the engineer and railway volunteer staff corps.

Marindin joined the Board of Trade in 1877 as inspecting officer of railways, and it was in this field that he received most public recognition, being appointed a CMG in 1887, for services to the Egyptian State Railways, and KCMG in 1897. Marindin's inquiries into railway accidents led to the reform of working practices and the introduction of a number of safety measures designed to protect railway company employees.

Marindin's appointment to Chatham coincided with the early dominance of the Royal Engineers in association football. On the football field Marindin was described as 'clever and shrewd', and as a 'tall, well-built, broad shouldered back' who played up 'the lines' for the 'Sappers' (Ward, 25). This team was described as the 'first to show the advantages of combination over the old style of individualism' (ibid., 24–5), and in 1873 undertook the first football tour, visiting Nottingham, Derby, and Sheffield; it thereby set a pattern of touring which was to be followed by other teams, most famously by the Corinthians. After he ceased playing, Marindin continued to referee matches, a role which he considered as part of his duties as president of the Football Association (FA). Players were said to 'dread his frown'. Professionals referred to him as 'The Majaw', but although aristocratic in upbringing, Marindin was described as 'not dandy or la-de-da' (ibid., 24).

It was as an official that Marindin had most influence in shaping the development of the game. In 1869 he became chairman of the committee of the FA, and in 1874 he succeeded S. H. Bartholomew as FA president, a position he held until 1890. Marindin presided over a period of transition which saw the game of association football transformed from a pleasure pursuit of the few to a pastime and spectacle for the masses. Marindin was part of a powerful coalition of amateur administrators who oversaw the acceptance of open professionalism in the laws of the game. Together with such men as Arthur Kinnaird and Charles Alcock, Marindin recognized that professionalism was a part of the way the game had developed in the north, and that if the FA simply outlawed the professional player the game would split, and would cease to be a national pastime. They argued that professionalism should be accepted, but controlled, and the proposal to legalize it was passed by thirty-five votes to fifteen at a special general meeting of the FA held at Anderton's Hotel, Fleet Street, London, on 20 July 1885.

Marindin resigned as president of the FA five years later, a decision which some contemporaries attributed to his growing disenchantment with the development of the professional game, and his dislike of imported Scottish professionals was well known. He died on 21 April 1900 at his home, 3 Hans Crescent, London, and was buried at Craigflower, Dunfermline. His wife and their only child, a daughter, survived him.

M. A. BRYANT

Sources The Times (24 April 1900) · F. Ward, Fifty years of football (1935), 24–6 · A. Gibson and W. Pickford, Association football and the men who made it, 4 vols. [1905–6] · N. L. Jackson, Sporting days and sporting ways (1932) · Boase, Mod. Eng. biog. · Burke, Gen. GB (1937) **Likenesses** portrait, repro. in ILN (5 May 1900), 601

Mariner, William Charles (1791–1853), traveller, was born on 10 September 1791 at Highbury Place, Highbury, Middlesex, the son of Magnus Mariner (1742/3–1823), who had followed a sea-going career, and his wife, Theodosia. At the age of thirteen, living at Wapping, he joined the privateer and whaler *Port-au-Prince*, about to sail to the Pacific Ocean. After an adventurous voyage the ship arrived at the Tonga (or Friendly) Islands in poor condition, hoping to carry out repairs. The crew met with a hostile reception and many of them were massacred. Mariner, however, was taken under the protection of the principal chief, Finau Ulukalala, who bestowed on him the name of one of his deceased sons, Toki Ukamea, and appointed one of his wives to be Mariner's adopted mother.

Mariner's residence in Tonga, mainly on the island of Vava'u, lasted for four years. During this time he became thoroughly conversant with the language and customs of this Polynesian people and he was on friendly terms with many of the chiefs, especially with Finau's son and successor. Using the guns from the *Port-au-Prince*, and helped by his surviving companions, he took a full and often decisive part in his protector's warlike campaigns against other islands. Eventually times became more peaceful and Toki attained the status of a chief, living on his own cultivated plantations.

When, towards the end of 1810, the brig *Favourite*, under Captain Fisk, from Port Jackson, arrived in Tongan waters Mariner, now nineteen, went aboard and worked his passage to Macao in China. From there he again worked a passage on the ship *Cuffnells*, on charter to the East India Company, and arrived at Gravesend in June 1811. Mariner undertook a further voyage, to the West Indies, of which no details are known, and returned to England the following year.

Mariner's account of the voyage on the *Port-au-Prince*, of his life in Tonga, together with the history, customs, and grammar and vocabulary of the language, was written by Dr John Martin, to whom Mariner had recounted his experiences. It was published in 1817 as *An Account of the Natives of the Tonga Islands*. Other editions followed and there were translations into French and German. The book was well reviewed, particularly by the *Quarterly Review* (April 1817), and remained for many years the principal account of the Tonga Islands.

Mariner spent the remainder of his life in business in the City of London and became a stockbroker. He was involved in the exchequer bill affair of 1836–41 when large sums of money in loans were raised on the security of bills later found to have been forgeries. The investigating commission was not able to decide whether Mariner had realized that the bills passing through his hands were forged. He sought to clear his name in the City by publishing a pamphlet, *Exchequer Bills Forgery: a Statement*, in 1843, which ran to two editions.

In his latter years Mariner lived at Gravesend, the port of departure and of arrival of his early voyages. On 3 May 1818 he had married Margaret Roberts (1796–1871), daughter of Peter Roberts, banker, of Aberystwyth; they had eleven children. Mariner died on 20 October 1853, when he was found drowned in the Grand Surrey Canal at Camberwell. He was buried five days later in Gravesend cemetery.   DENIS J. MCCULLOCH

Sources W. Mariner, *An account of the natives of the Tonga Islands*, ed. J. Martin, 2 vols. (1817) · W. Mariner, *Exchequer bills forgery: a statement by William Mariner*, 2nd edn (1843) · [W. Holden], *Holden's triennial directory for 1805, 1806, 1807, including the year 1808*, 2 vols. (1805–7) · d. cert. · parish register (marriage), St Olave, Southwark, Surrey, 3 May 1818 · parish register (baptism), St Dunstan, Stepney, Middlesex, 1819–33 · parish register (baptism), St Peter-le-Poer, London, 1839 · census returns for Gravesend, Kent, 1851 · *N&Q*, 4th ser., 8 (1871), 305, 407 · cemetery records, Gravesend, Kent, 1853 · cemetery records, Gravesend, Kent, 1871 · parish register (burial), St Dunstan, Stepney, 1823 [Magnus Mariner] · d. cert. [Margaret Mariner]
Archives priv. coll.
Likenesses portrait, 1816, repro. in Mariner, *Account* · watercolour, c.1837, priv. coll.; copy, NPG · Mayall, daguerreotype, 1852, priv. coll.; copy, NPG
Wealth at death £450; excl. leasehold houses, 116–17 Windmill Street, Gravesend, Kent: will, 1854

Mario, Jessie Jane Meriton White (1832–1906), advocate of Italian unity, was born on 9 May 1832, probably at 15 Chapel Row, Forton, Gosport, Hampshire, daughter of Thomas White (c.1800–1863) and his second wife, Jane Teage, *née* Meriton (1805–1834). Her mother, related to a liberal New Orleans family, showed more enthusiasm for the local Pestalozzian school than for the High Street Independent Chapel where Thomas White was a zealous worshipper. She died, however, when Jessie was only two, and was instantly replaced by the schoolteacher, White's third wife, Jane Gain (1813–1866). Jessie White grew up beside Forton inlet among numerous variously mothered siblings.

Thomas White came from a family of shipwrights and wrote a treatise on their profession (1848), but his speciality was designing loading slips and installing them abroad. Despite his narrow righteousness he had a social conscience, and was versed in European democratic movements such as Mazzini's Young Italy. He interested his daughter in these, even though she hated his biblical humbug (noting, for instance, in her diary that Abel was preferred to Cain only because God liked roast lamb better than greens). Her conviction that humanity was the one true basis of belief, gained first from an unconventional local preacher, was strengthened by hearing the reformer George Dawson (1821–1876) during her years at school in Birmingham.

By the age of twenty-one Jessie White was living from private lessons and her writing, which included entries for the *Biographical Magazine* and stories for *Eliza Cook's Journal*. During a period of work and study in Paris, her radical ideas were further encouraged by meetings with Cousin, Martin, and Lamennais. In the autumn of 1854 she accompanied Emma Roberts, a widow who believed herself engaged to Garibaldi, for a stay with the general in Nice and Sardinia. She afterwards described this trip as the realization of a dream, binding her to a cause for which she would live and die. In Florence she became intimate with the Brownings, learning much through them about Italian politics. On returning to England in May 1855, she applied to study medicine but was refused because of her sex; instead she became a sedulous reader at the British Museum, preparing articles on Italy for the *Daily News* and other papers. Through Garibaldi she met Orsini and translated his *Austrian Dungeons in Italy*; through the Ashursts she was introduced to Mazzini, who in 1856 asked her to undertake a lecture tour of British cities.

In 1857 Jessie White went back to Italy and was welcomed like a revolutionary saint, but, following the disastrous Pisacane expedition, she was arrested in Genoa together with Mazzini's associate Alberto Mario (1825–1883). On her release she took Mario home to Portsmouth, where they married on 19 December 1857. During another lecture tour in 1858, witnesses praised the graphic eloquence and truthfulness that emerged from this plump, dowdy figure with her shock of flaming hair and partiality for cigars. In the opinion of a later commentator, she blended 'the staunch tenacity of the Anglo-Saxon race with the poetic enthusiasm of the Latin' (Litta-Visconti-Arese, introduction to *Birth of Modern Italy*, i). In the winter of 1858–9 the Marios rallied support for Mazzini in America, but Jessie's forthright manner and extremist views provoked controversy on both sides of the Atlantic and led to a painful break with the more conservative Brownings. The couple returned to Italy full of hope that France's initiative against Austria would bring freedom, but experienced instead the disillusionment of Villafranca. They were imprisoned again, but released, and wintered in Lugano. By now they were drifting away from Mazzinian idealism. In the summer of 1860 they joined Garibaldi in his Sicilian campaign, Alberto as aide-de-camp and Jessie as nurse; she boldly took charge of hospital activities under conditions of great chaos and corruption. Mario's *The Red Shirt* (1865) portrays this 'Miss Uragano' as tender with the wounded but tough and versatile in the field. She successfully appealed to wealthy Englishwomen for ambulance supplies, but in battle tore up her underclothes to make bandages. She became known as 'Garibaldi's Englishwoman', nursing him after Aspromonte and serving under him in 1866 and again in 1867, in which year they also attended together the Geneva Congress of the League of Peace; she began the anti-Prussian campaign of 1870 as a war reporter, but Garibaldi made her chief of ambulances with the rank of major.

With the unity of Italy complete, the Marios resided there permanently. Jessie still travelled about for purposes of research, but lived chiefly at Florence, where she taught and wrote prolifically for the press, including *The Nation*, for which she was Italian correspondent on and off from 1866 to her death. Among her many books were studies of poverty and the convict system, editions of Mazzini and Bertani, and several works on Garibaldi. Her splendid *Garibaldi et son temps* (1884) was dedicated to the memory of Alberto, who died of cancer on 2 March 1883; she also published a biography of Mario and an edition of his writings. This productivity was achieved with little financial reward and at much cost to herself: she developed writer's cramp and suffered a mild stroke, but struggled on with the help of a typewriter and an amanuensis. Although her grasp on content was seldom perfect, readers were swept along by her commitment and her candid expressiveness, as in her essays on hygiene, abortion, boy-labourers in Sicilian sulphur mines, and a frightful paupers' cemetery with 365 covered pits, one for each day of the year.

Jessie White Mario died at Florence on 5 March 1906 and was cremated after a funeral procession through the city; her ashes were buried beside her husband's at Lendinara. A selection of her posthumous papers was published in 1909 as *The Birth of Modern Italy*—a phenomenon to which she had contributed so much and so courageously.

PATRICK WADDINGTON

Sources E. A. Daniels, *Jessie White Mario: Risorgimento revolutionary* (1972) · *The birth of modern Italy: posthumous papers of Jessie White Mario*, ed. P. Litta-Visconti-Arese (1909) · J. W. Mario, *Supplement* (1889), vol. 3 of G. Garibaldi, *Autobiography of Giuseppe Garibaldi*, trans. A. Werner (1889) · *Mazzini's letters to an English family*, ed. E. F. Richards, 2–3 (1922) · W. P. Garrison, 'Jessie White Mario', *The Nation* [New York] (15 March 1906), 218 · H. W. Rudman, *Italian nationalism and English letters* (1940) · M. C. W. Wicks, *The Italian exiles in London, 1816–1848* (1937) · A. I. Gertsen (Herzen), *Sobraniye sochineniy v tridtsati tomakh* (1954–66), vols. 26, 29 · *Literaturnoye Nasledstvo*, 39–40 (1941) · G. Vinant, *Un esprit cosmopolite au XIXe siècle: Malwida de Meysenbug* (1932) · *The life and adventures of George Augustus Sala*, 2 vols. (1895) · T. A. Trollope, *What I remember* (1887) · J. L. Hammond and B. Hammond, *James Stansfeld: a Victorian champion of sexual equality* (1932)
Archives Museo Centrale del Risorgimento, Rome, Archivio Jessie White Mario · PRO | Cowen Collection, Newcastle upon Tyne · Girton Cam., Bessie Rayner Parkes MSS
Likenesses drawing, c.1850, Museo Centrale del Risorgimento, Rome · photographs, 1857, repro. in Litta-Visconti-Arese, ed., *Birth of modern Italy*, facing, p. 272 · photographs, c.1860, Museo Centrale del Risorgimento, Rome

Marion, Francis (1732–1795), planter and revolutionary army officer in America, was born at Goatfield plantation near the Cooper River, St John's parish, Berkeley county, South Carolina, the sixth of six children of Gabriel Marion (1693–1747), planter, and Esther Cordes (1695–1757). Francis was of French Huguenot ancestry and at birth 'not larger than a New England lobster' (Horry and Weems, 20). The family moved to the Georgetown area about 1738, and Francis may have briefly attended an English school there, but by 1747 he had gone to sea, been shipwrecked, and nearly died; thereafter he devoted himself to landlocked occupations. Francis, brother Gabriel, and their mother returned to St John's in 1755; in 1759 Francis began leasing land on the Santee River and in 1773 he purchased Pond Bluff plantation near Eutaw Springs.

Marion had grown robust, if not tall, in his forty-one years and gained an intimate knowledge of swamp terrain through his pursuit of hunting and fishing. In 1756 he had joined the upper St John's militia, served in Gabriel Marion's company in 1759, and distinguished himself on the 1761 campaign against the Cherokee as a lieutenant in the South Carolina regiment. All the Marions were gaining prestige. When South Carolina chose delegates to its first provincial congress (1775), Gabriel represented St Stephen's and brothers Job and Francis were selected by St John's. The provincial congress began arming the colony and on 11 June elected Francis third-ranking captain in the second regiment of foot.

Marion was a good infantry officer. He was promoted major on 22 February 1776, lieutenant-colonel on 23 November 1776, and became commandant of the second South Carolina continental regiment on 23 September 1777. He commanded the heavy guns against the British fleet at Sullivan's Island on 28 June 1776 and led the regiment in the bloody assault on the Spring Hill Redoubt at Savannah, Georgia, on 9 October 1779.

Had Marion's participation been limited to this stint in the continental army he would be little remembered today, for the second regiment surrendered with the capitulation of Charles Town on 12 May 1780. Two months earlier Marion had broken his ankle escaping from a lock-in drinking party and had been evacuated in April. As the British army tightened its occupation he limped northwards to join Major-General Horatio Gates's new army, but escaped its defeat at Camden on 16 August when he was ordered back to South Carolina to take command of American militiamen of the Williamsburg district and cut off British retreat after Gates's anticipated 'victory'. Marion's first victory was the rescue of American soldiers captured at Camden.

Thus began the guerrilla warfare phase of the career that Parson Mason Weems turned into a romantic legend and morality play in the early days of the American republic. In reality Marion could be ruthless in defence of his men, and he shot down sentinels when the British hanged some militiamen. His tactics were based on swamp skills, American Indian warfare, and experiences as a regular soldier. His mounted men covered great distances, often struck at night, disappeared when pursued, and were the only active resistance in South Carolina immediately after Camden. With a force that came and went, he disrupted British efforts to organize the loyalists (in the final analysis counter-revolution was prerequisite to British victory), blockaded enemy supply and communication routes, created an intelligence network for Major-General Nathanael Greene, and forced the diversion of reinforcements from the main British army. Marion's patrols 'keep the whole country in continual alarm', wrote the British commander, Charles, second Earl Cornwallis, 'and render the assistance of regular troops everywhere necessary' (Scheer, 47). When the British concentrated forces against him he either fought them in detail or retreated to the Great White Marsh in North Carolina.

At the end of December 1780 South Carolina governor John Rutledge appointed Marion brigadier-general of militia with authority over all regiments east of the Santee–Wateree–Catawba River line; as many as 2500 men may have served in his brigade by the war's end. Marion was uncomfortable when his force was subordinated to Nathanael Greene's army but generally co-operated. A notable exception was Marion's failure to halt Lord Rawdon's march on Fort Ninety Six in June 1781. Marion particularly disliked subordination to the senior militia brigadier Thomas Sumter, and suffered his worst losses at Quinby Bridge on 17 July 1781, where Sumter commanded.

He was at his best with an independent command or when associated with Lieutenant-Colonel Henry Lee with whom he captured Fort Watson (23 April 1781) and Fort Motte (12 May 1781), two strongpoints on the British interior defence line. He was successful in an atypical role when he commanded the front line of the assault at Eutaw Springs on 8 September 1781.

As the war wound down Marion was elected to the South Carolina senate where he served five terms (1782–6, 1791–4), but his absence from the brigade to attend the Jacksonboro assembly led to a defeat in February 1782. Having taken time to train his new loyalist troops, he was successful in his final battle at Fairlawn, on 29 August 1782.

With Pond Bluff in ruins, Marion was so poverty-stricken that the state created a sinecure for him as commandant of Fort Johnson, a post he held until 1790. On 26 February 1783 the South Carolina senate voted him a gold medal and its thanks 'for his eminent and conspicuous service to his country' (Rankin, 291). On 30 September the continental congress promoted him full colonel of the continental line. His poverty, however, was ended by his marriage on 20 April 1786 to his first cousin, Mary Esther (1737–1815), daughter of Joseph Henry Videau and Anne Cordes. This union, which produced no children, combined Pond Bluff and a neighbouring plantation. According to the federal census of 1790 Marion had 194 slaves, which suggests substantial wealth.

A mild federalist in politics, Marion attended the state's constitutional convention in 1790. He held command of his brigade until 1794, and died on either 26 or 27 February 1795 at Pond Bluff. He was buried in the family cemetery at Gabriel Marion's Belle Isle plantation in St Stephen's parish, Berkeley county, South Carolina.

CLYDE R. FERGUSON

Sources H. F. Rankin, *Francis Marion: the swamp fox* (1973) · R. D. Bass, *Swamp fox: the life and campaigns of General Francis Marion* (1959) · G. B. Scheer, 'The elusive swamp fox', *American Heritage*, 9 (April 1958), 40–47, 111 · C. Colcock, 'The Marion family', *Transactions of the Huguenot Society of South Carolina*, 22 (1911?), 37–49 · R. L. Meriwether, 'Marion, Francis', *DAB* · W. B. Edgar, N. L. Bailey, and A. Moore, eds., *Biographical directory of the South Carolina house of representatives*, 5 vols. (1974–92), vol. 3 · J. J. Simons, 'Old Berkeley county and Craven county', www.geocities.com/Heartland/Acres/3207/fam00395.htm&00409htm, Aug 1999 · G. W. Kyte, 'Francis Marion as an intelligence officer', *South Carolina Historical Magazine*, 77 (Oct 1976), 215–26 · F. M. Kirk, 'Pond Bluff', www.geocities.com/Heartland/Acres/3207/pondbluff.htm, Aug 1999 · E. A. Duyckinck, *National portrait gallery of eminent Americans from original paintings by Alonzo Chappel*, 1 [1862] · W. G. Simms, *The life of Francis Marion* (1844) · W. E. Hemphill and W. A. Wates, eds., *Extracts from the journals of the provincial congresses of South Carolina, 1775–1776* (1960) · P. Horry and M. L. Weems, *The life of Gen. Francis Marion* (1834) · *Heads of families at the first census of the United States … 1790, South Carolina* (1908)
Archives Hunt. L., orderly books · South Carolina Archives and History Center, Columbia, letter-book | Duke U., Nathanael Greene papers · Duke U., revolutionary collection · New York Historical Society, Horatio Gates papers · U. Mich., Nathanael Greene papers · University of South Carolina, Columbia, South Carolina collection, MSS
Likenesses A. Chappel, engraving, repro. in *National portrait gallery of eminent Americans* · A. Chappel, oils, repro. in *National portrait*

gallery of eminent Americans · H. N. Hyneman, portrait, Mount Vernon, Virginia · J. Sartain, engraving (after J. B. White), Old Print Shop, New York · T. B. Welch, engraving (after T. Stothard), repro. in T. Longacre and Herring, *National portrait gallery of distinguished Americans* (1836) · J. B. White, oils, Capitol, Washington, DC · engraving, repro. in Rankin, *Francis Marion*

Wealth at death tax returns for 1793 list 1527 acres in St John's, 330 acres on Pacolet River, and seventy-three slaves; however 1790 census listed 194 slaves; all property left to wife, and then to an adopted son, but will was not properly executed: Kirk, 'Pond Bluff'; Edgar and others, eds., *Biographical directory*, 3 (1981); *Heads of families at the first census*

Marion, Kitty [*real name* Katherine Marie Schäfer] (1871–1944), suffragette and birth control activist, was born on 12 March 1871 at Riedtberg, Germany, the only child of an engineer. Her mother died when she was two and her stepmother when she was six, both of tuberculosis. Her childhood was spent moving between her father, 'a strict disciplinarian with a fierce, violent, and evidently uncontrollable temper, the full force of which [Kitty] often bore the brunt' (Marion, 'Kitty Marion', 4), and various, more loving, relatives. As early as seven-years-old she dreamt of going on the stage, which merely served to provoke her father's wrath. His favourite taunts for her were 'damned actress' and 'red scoundrel', a reference to her red hair which he inexplicably hated. In 1886, relations with her father having deteriorated, she joined his sister Dora in England.

In 1889, Marion escaped the claustrophobic and overcrowded conditions at her aunt's house near London and found work on the stage as a dancer. Her first job was as a chorus member in *Robinson Crusoe* at the Theatre Royal, Glasgow. Between 1889 and 1903, adopting the name Kitty Marion, she developed a modest but successful career in provincial touring theatre as a singer and dancer in musical comedy and pantomime, graduating from the chorus to minor named roles. At the high point of her stage career, she replaced Emily Soldene as the lead in *La toledad*. Having 'crossed' her principal employer, George Dance, and subsequently finding work in musical theatre difficult to come by, she moved into the music hall where she found circumstances even more precarious. The infamous 'casting couch' tactics of music-hall agents are recounted in her autobiography and were the subject of numerous letters which she wrote to *The Era* and other journals.

The sexual vulnerability of women in the theatre profession was one of the many factors that drove Marion into the Women's Social and Political Union (WSPU) and suffrage militancy in 1908. Her first so-called militant action was in October 1908, when she joined a deputation to the prime minister, Asquith, during which she was badly mauled. Mary Richardson recalls her distinctive hair being pulled out by a member of the mob and pinned to his lapel. Her first arrest came the following year in Newcastle for breaking a window of the General Post Office during a visit by Lloyd George. Sentenced to one month's hard labour, she went on hunger strike and was forcibly fed. As in subsequent imprisonments her protest did not confine itself to hunger striking. She barricaded herself in her cell and set fire to her mattress as a protest at her treatment at the hands of the 'dirty, cringing doormats of the government' (Marion, 'Kitty Marion', 191) as she called the doctors.

Suffragettes admired Marion greatly for her activism and her endurance. Her two most notorious activities were the firing of an empty mansion at St Leonards belonging to the Conservative MP Arthur du Cros (for which she was not charged as there was too little evidence against her and which she does not mention in her autobiography) and the burning of the grandstand at Hurst Park racecourse in 1913, which she carried out with Clara Giveen. This last was not only a protest against the government's obduracy in not giving women the vote, but a commemorative gesture for Emily Wilding Davison's death at Epsom earlier that year. For this offence she was given three years; she served just under four months, and was force-fed 232 times before being released under the 'Cat and Mouse Act'. In total she served seven prison terms.

Following the WSPU's amnesty on the outbreak of war in 1914 Marion returned erratically to the stage under the name of Kathleen Meredith. In 1915, however, persecuted as an 'enemy alien', she had the choice of returning to Germany or trying to set up a new life in America. In America she spent thirteen years fighting with Margaret Sanger in the cause of the birth control movement, protesting, being imprisoned, and earning a living and a reputation by selling the *Birth Control Review* on Broadway.

In the early thirties she wrote her autobiography, one of the few accounts by a 'foot soldier' in the suffrage movement. Other references to Kitty Marion's contribution to the women's movement are few and scattered, but all contain some allusion to her abundant red-gold hair. While the authorities described her as 'a well-known, dangerous suffragette' (PRO, HO 221/874) all the personal tributes after her death speak of her commitment to women's rights and her robust good humour. Even the governor of Holloway prison commended her for 'coming up smiling every time' (Marion, 'Kitty Marion', 262). She herself in one of her public defences claimed to have 'the [spiritual] strength of the British Lion and the German Eagle combined' (PRO, HO 221/874). Following her childhood experiences she resolved never to marry, but she records a number of unwelcome offers of 'keeping' during her stage career.

In the last two years of her life Kitty Marion sent valued materials to what became the Fawcett Library, together with cuttings from American newspapers, and encouraged her friend Mrs Dock to do the same after her death. She died in poverty on 9 October 1944 in the Sanger Nursing Home, 22 West 74th Street, New York, close to Central Park.

VIV GARDNER

Sources K. Marion, 'Kitty Marion', autobiography, Museum of London · PRO, file HO 221/874 'Kitty Marion' · PRO, HO 221/826 'Clara Giveen' · NYPL, Humanities and Social Sciences Library, Schwimmer-Lloyd collection, manuscripts and archives division · NYPL, Humanities and Social Sciences Library, Margaret Sanger microform collection · M. R. Richardson, *Laugh a defiance* (1953) · K. Marion, *Birth Control Review* (Nov 1918) · K. Marion, *Birth Control Review* (Jan 1919) · K. Marion, *Birth Control Review* (Sept 1921) · *The*

Era • *New York Herald Tribune* (11 Nov 1944) • E. Crawford, *The women's suffrage movement: a reference guide, 1866–1928* (1999) • *Annual Report* [London Society for Women's Service], 17 (1943–5)
Archives Museum of London
Likenesses pen drawing, 1902, Museum of London • three photographs, *c*.1912–1914, Museum of London • cartoon, *c*.1920–1928, NYPL • photograph, *c*.1920–1928, Smith College, Northampton, Massachusetts • photographs, repro. in *New York Press* (10 Jan 1916) • photographs, repro. in *Columbus State Journal* (31 Aug 1916) • photographs, repro. in *Brooklyn Eagle* (11 Feb 1930) • photographs, repro. in *New York Herald Tribune* (12 Feb 1930) • photographs, repro. in *New York Herald Tribune* (11 Oct 1944)

Mariotti, Luigi. *See* Gallenga, Antonio Carlo Napoleone (1810–1895).

Marischal. For this title name *see under* Keith family (*per. c*.1300–*c*.1530) [Keith, William, first Earl Marischal (*b.* after 1425, *d.* 1483); Keith, William, second Earl Marischal (*d.* 1526/7)]. *See also* Keith, William, third Earl Marischal (*c*.1510–1581); Keith, George, fourth Earl Marischal (1549/50–1623); Keith, William, fifth Earl Marischal (*c*.1585–1635); Keith, William, sixth Earl Marischal (1614–1671); Keith, William, ninth Earl Marischal (*c*.1664–1712) [*see under* Drummond, Mary, Countess Marischal (1675–1729)]; Drummond, Mary, Countess Marischal (1675–1729); Keith, George, styled tenth Earl Marischal (1692/3?–1778).

Marisco, Adam de. *See* Marsh, Adam (*c*.1200–1259).

Marisco, Geoffrey de (*b.* before **1171**, *d.* **1245**), justiciar of Ireland, was a member of a Somerset family which in that county held one of the manors of Huntspill and the manor of Cloud. He was born shortly before 1171. His mother was a sister of John Cumin (or Comyn), archbishop of Dublin; in 1220 she was said to be on the point of death. Marisco's elder brother, William, was granted Lundy island, which had previously belonged to the knights templar, by Richard I in 1194. William was a naval administrator in King John's service but supported the rebels in the civil war of 1215–17; he is last mentioned in 1229–30. His son Jordan who received land in Ireland through his uncle, Geoffrey, was dead by October 1234.

Geoffrey de Marisco is first mentioned in 1192 in an *inspeximus* (a charter confirming earlier grants) made to him by his uncle, John Cumin, of Holywood, Wicklow, which his brother Walter had previously held. His other lands in Ireland included a manor at Knockainy in Limerick, near which, at Any (now Hospital), he founded a preceptory for knights of St John before 1215. In 1226 he was granted a fair at this manor, and also at Adare on the Maigue, which belonged to him from an early stage. After his outlawry in 1238 both manors escheated to the crown. Knockainy was for some time retained by the king, but Adare soon passed to the Fitzgeralds of Offaly. He also held Killorglin in Kerry.

In 1200 Marisco was with the king at Ledbury, Gloucestershire, and received a grant of 'Katherain' (probably Knockainy) in exchange for other lands in Ireland, together with 20 marks, to fortify a house there for himself. In 1208 he defended William (I) Marshal's position in Leinster against King John's machinations and defeated the justiciar, Meiler fitz Henry, at Thurles, Tipperary. He

was pardoned for this and in 1210 accompanied King John in his campaign in Ireland against Hugh de Lacy. In the same year he led an expedition into Connacht with Thomas fitz Maurice Fitzgerald (*d.* 1213/14) and the English of Munster supported by Ó Briain. In 1212 he joined the other English magnates in Ireland in protesting his loyalty to John in the face of Pope Innocent III's threat to absolve the king's subjects from their allegiance. In 1213 Marisco, who was possibly *custos* (deputy justiciar) at the time, was defeated with the English of Meath at Fircall, Offaly, by Cormac Ó Maoil Sechlainn. In the summer of 1215 he was with the king at Marlborough and on 6 July was appointed justiciar of Ireland, giving two of his sons as pledges for his behaviour. He built a castle at Killaloe, Clare, in 1217 and forced the people to accept an English bishop, Robert Travers, who was also his nephew.

In 1218 Marisco was ordered to raise money to enable the king to pay Louis, the son of the French king, the sum promised to him, and to pay the papal tribute. He was ordered in 1219 to pay the revenues of the crown into the exchequer at Dublin, and to present himself before the king, leaving Ireland in the care of Henry of London, archbishop of Dublin. Having already taken the cross he received a safe conduct to make a pilgrimage to the Holy Land and travelled to England. There in March 1220 he entered into an agreement with the king at Oxford, in the presence of the council, with reference to the discharge of his office, pledging himself to pay the royal revenues into the exchequer, and to appoint faithful constables for the king's castles, and delivering one of his sons to be kept as a hostage by the king. On his return to Ireland he was commanded to resume the demesne lands that he had alienated without warrant. Complaints were made against him to the king by the citizens of Dublin, and in July 1221 the king wrote to the council in Ireland, declaring that he had received no money from that country since he came to the throne and that Marisco, who had while in England made a fine with him to satisfy defaults, had not obeyed his wishes. Henry therefore desired that he should give up his office. Marisco resigned the justiciarship on 4 October, was thanked for his faithful services, quitclaimed of 1080 marks, part of the fine made with the king, and received a letter of protection during the king's minority, and the wardship of the heir of John of Clahull. Marisco had given some crown escheats to his friends and ignored some royal mandates. The cantred of Ossures, Kerry, for instance, was given to his son Robert. These Kerry dealings cost him his job in 1221.

In 1224 Marisco, who had been holding a parley with Áed Ó Conchobhair, joined the justiciar William (II) Marshal and Walter de Lacy in besieging Trim, which was defended by supporters of the rebellious Hugh de Lacy. In November and December of the same year he acted as *custos* in the Marshal's absence and carried on war with Áed Ó Néill in support of Áed Ó Conchobhair, the son of Cathal, who had been ousted from the kingship of Connacht. On 25 June 1226 he was reappointed justiciar and being then in England received on 4 July a grant of £580 a year, to be paid out of the Irish exchequer as salary. English policy towards Connacht had changed with the revival of de Burgh fortunes and Marisco attempted to capture Áed Ó Conchobhair. This action was resented by many of the English lords in Ireland and Marisco wrote to the king to complain in particular of Theobald Walter, his own son-in-law, who, he claimed, had garrisoned Dublin Castle against the king. Áed Ó Conchobhair captured Marisco's son, William, near Athlone and returned him in exchange for his own son and daughter, who were being kept hostage by the English. Áed was killed in the following year in Marisco's house, although whether or not with the justiciar's connivance is not clear. At this time Marisco also built castles at Rindown and Ballyleague, Roscommon, on the Shannon. In his energetic attempts to dispossess the Irish he set the tone for his successors during Henry III's reign. He resigned the justiciarship in February 1228 and with Walter de Lacy and the justiciar Richard de Burgh inflicted a severe defeat on the Irish of Connacht.

Marisco was with Richard Marshal on the Curragh on 1 April 1234 when the latter was fatally wounded by a group of magnates possibly acting on Henry III's behalf. Marisco was suspected of betraying Marshal but this is unlikely. Both he and his son William were gaoled until September 1234 and were each fined £2000. In the spring of the following year, 1235, Henry Clement, a messenger of the Irish justiciar, Maurice Fitzgerald (d. 1257), was murdered in Westminster, almost certainly by a party led by William de Marisco and probably in revenge for the slaying of Marshal. After the murder Geoffrey de Marisco fled to the hospital of St John in Clerkenwell. He was allowed to leave on 9 June 1235 and in November of that year one of those imprisoned after the murder, Walter Comyn, who had lands in Offaly and who was probably a kinsman of Marisco, was delivered to him, having found pledges. Marisco's lands were restored to him on 3 August 1235. In the same year, however, he was excommunicated by Hubert de Burgh, brother of Richard and bishop of Limerick, for keeping Kilmallock from the see. Marisco had enfeoffed his son William of Kilmallock and Hubert de Burgh had unlawfully taken it as an escheat because William had fled to Lundy island after Clement's death and had been outlawed.

In 1238 an attempt was made to assassinate Henry III and suspicion fell on William and Geoffrey de Marisco. Geoffrey was also in trouble because he had not paid the instalments of his fine, and, as he had no lands in England, the Irish justiciar was ordered to distrain his lands there. Some time between then and 1242 he fled to Scotland where he was sheltered by Walter Comyn. In 1244 he was forced to leave Scotland, possibly as part of the agreement reached in that year between Henry III and Alexander II. He died in France in the following year.

Geoffrey de Marisco married three times. The name of his first wife is not known. William de Marisco was a child of this marriage. In 1224 William was taken into king's service as a member of the household. Some time before then he married Matilda, niece of Henry, archbishop of Dublin, whose marriage portion included the castle of

Coonagh. Following the murder of Clement he travelled to Lundy island which was evacuated by William, son of Jordan de Marisco. Jordan was Geoffrey de Marisco's first cousin, and both Jordan and his son William held land in Ireland. This William had been on the Curragh with his great-uncle Geoffrey and recovered his Irish land only in 1237. William son of Geoffrey held out in Lundy island until 1242 and used it as a base for piratical attacks on shipping between England and Ireland, sometimes in collaboration with the Scottish crown. In June 1242 he was captured and was executed at the Tower of London on 25 July 1245. His wife, Matilda, was kept at Gloucester until 1243 and succeeded in 1247 in recovering her marriage portion from the archbishop of Dublin. The other children of Geoffrey de Marisco's first marriage included Walter and Thomas and possibly John, who married Mabel, the daughter of Hamo de Valognes and a granddaughter of Richard de Burgh. One daughter, possibly called Joan, married Theobald Walter, while a second, whose name is not known, married Hugh Tyrel.

Marisco's second wife was Eva, the daughter and heir of Robert of Bermingham, to whom Richard fitz Gilbert, earl of Pembroke (Strongbow), had granted Offaly. She had married first, in 1193, Gerald fitz Maurice *Fitzgerald, who died in 1204. Their son, Maurice *Fitzgerald (d. 1257), came of age in 1215, but did not retrieve Offaly from Marisco until the latter's disgrace in 1234. Eva married second Geoffrey fitz Robert, seneschal of Leinster, who was dead by 1211. She married Marisco between that date and 1217 and died before 1226. Their son Robert, who in 1240 was called the brother of Maurice Fitzgerald, joined his outlaw brother William de Marisco on Lundy island and was dead by 1240. Marisco's third wife was Alice, the widow of Roger Pipard and sister of Walter and Hugh de Lacy. This marriage had taken place by 1232.   B. SMITH

Sources E. St J. Brooks, 'The family of Marisco', *Journal of the Royal Society of Antiquaries of Ireland*, 7th ser., 1–2 (1931–2) • F. M. Powicke, *King Henry III and the Lord Edward: the community of the realm in the thirteenth century*, 2 vols. (1947) • H. S. Sweetman and G. F. Handcock, eds., *Calendar of documents relating to Ireland*, 5 vols., PRO (1875–86), vol. 1 • Paris, *Chron.* • A. J. Otway-Ruthven, *A history of medieval Ireland* (1968) • G. H. Orpen, *Ireland under the Normans*, 4 vols. (1911–20)

Marisco, Richard de. *See* Marsh, Richard (d. 1226).

Marishall, Jean (*fl.* 1765–1788), novelist and playwright, was born in Scotland. She began writing in London, hoping to surpass typical circulating-library novels. Between her first novel and her second, a sister died, her only brother (a lieutenant) left for the East Indies with the Queen's Royal regiment of highlanders, and a stroke disabled her father from business. When Francis Noble gave only 5 guineas for *The History of Miss Clarinda Cathcart and Miss Fanny Renton*, she negotiated an unlimited number of wholesale copies for sale to friends and successfully laboured to win a dedication to the queen; sturdily independent but extremely deferential to her social superiors, she was embarrassed by the royal gift of 10 guineas. Published in October 1765 (2 vols.; new edns 1766, 1767),

Clarinda Cathcart is a sprightly epistolary novel in the Richardson tradition. The *Critical Review* noted some plot inconsistencies but it was favourably reviewed. Despite a cavil at her occasional Scotticisms (*Monthly Review*, July 1767, 76), so was her next novel, *The History of Alicia Montague* (2 vols., 1767), which she published by subscription, a distasteful effort that cleared about 100 guineas. (It was also published, presumably pirated, in Dublin in 1767.) Despite Lord Chesterfield and Lord Lyttleton's polite praise, neither Garrick nor Coleman produced her play, *Sir Harry Gaylove, or, Comedy in Embryo*. Foote at the Edinburgh Theatre offered encouragement but not performance, so she published it with an aggrieved preface (1772): the distinguished list of nearly 800 subscribers shows vigorous Scottish support for a native writer. In London, Marishall also attempted a periodical paper; in Edinburgh she taught and boarded pupils. An epistolary novel addressed to a former pupil, *A series of letters, by the author of Clarinda Cathcart; Alicia Montague; and the comedy of Sir Harry Gaylove* (2 vols., 1789) is also her apologia. Although her name is sometimes Anglicized as Jane Marshall, the writer signs her dedication 'Jean Marishall'. Blending precept with lively anecdote, she boldly defends her choices: her tradition of didactic fiction and its exemplar, Richardson's *Sir Charles Grandison*; the propriety of women writing; women choosing to remain unmarried where financial independence permits. Reproving her pupil's libertinism, she criticizes the morals of Chesterfield's famous letters to his son but denies ingratitude. In letters 31 and 32 Marishall brilliantly describes a determined Scotswoman's struggle to become a writer in London. DAVID OAKLEAF

Sources [J. Marishall], *A series of letters, by the author of Clarinda Cathcart; Alicia Montague; and the comedy of Sir Harry Gaylove* (1789) · [J. Marishall], *Sir Harry Gaylove, or, Comedy in embryo* (1772) · *Critical Review*, 20 (1765), 288–92 · *Critical Review*, 23 (1767), 210–14 · *Monthly Review*, 33 (1765), 405 · *Monthly Review*, 37 (1767), 76

Marjoribankis, Thomas, of Ratho (*d. c.*1561). *See under* College of justice, procurators of the (*act.* 1532).

Marjoribanks, Edward, second Baron Tweedmouth (1849–1909), politician, was born at 4 Upper Grosvenor Street, London, on 8 July 1849; he was the eldest son in the family of four sons and two daughters of Sir Dudley Coutts Marjoribanks, first baronet, and his wife, Isabella, daughter of Sir James Weir *Hogg. His father was an astute businessman and a collector of works of art, who sat in parliament as Liberal member for Berwick upon Tweed from 1853 to 1868 and again from 1874 to 1881; he was created a baronet on 25 July 1866 and raised to the peerage as Baron Tweedmouth (12 October 1881). Educated at Harrow School, 1862–5, Marjoribanks matriculated from Christ Church, Oxford, on 9 March 1868. At the university he devoted himself chiefly to sport—throughout his life he was a renowned sportsman, especially on the hill—and took no degree, being expelled for involvement in the 'great library row' in 1870 (he later apologized to the dean for denying his culpability).

After leaving Oxford Marjoribanks went for a tour round the world, and on his return he studied law, being

Edward Marjoribanks, second Baron Tweedmouth (1849–1909), by H. Walter Barnett

called to the bar at the Inner Temple on 17 November 1874. He worked for a time in the chambers of Sir John Duke Coleridge, afterwards lord chief justice, and was employed by him to collect and arrange material for the Tichborne trial. Coleridge formed a high opinion of his abilities, but he made little further progress at the bar, and left law for politics. His political and family connections were strong in Berwickshire, where his father had purchased considerable estates. An invitation to stand in June 1873 as a Liberal candidate there on the sudden occasion of a vacancy failed to reach him in time. After failing in 1874 in a contest in Mid Kent he became prospective Liberal candidate for North Berwickshire in 1875. He was elected there in 1880 and held the seat until the death of his father in 1894 removed him to the House of Lords.

During his earlier years in parliament Marjoribanks spoke little, but he was a leading supporter of the movement for legalizing marriage with a deceased wife's sister, being destined in due course to conduct the bill to its final victory in the House of Lords in 1907. In 1882 he moved the address in reply to the speech from the throne. He was soon much in demand for political gatherings in many parts of the kingdom but especially in Scotland. When Gladstone formed his home-rule government in 1886 Marjoribanks received his first official appointment as comptroller of Queen Victoria's household and second whip to the party, and was sworn of the privy council. After the rejection of the Home Rule Bill in June 1886 and the downfall of Gladstone's ministry, Marjoribanks, with Arnold

Morley as his chief, served as second whip to the opposition until 1892. On Gladstone's return to office in 1892 Marjoribanks became parliamentary secretary to the Treasury, that is, chief Liberal whip. His engaging manners, assiduity, imperturbable good humour, and devotion to manly sports made him an almost ideal whip, and he successfully saw the second Home Rule Bill through the Commons in 1893, a considerable feat.

On the death of his father on 4 March 1894 Marjoribanks succeeded to the peerage as Lord Tweedmouth, and was invited by Lord Rosebery, who, on Gladstone's resignation, had become prime minister, to join the cabinet as lord privy seal and chancellor of the duchy of Lancaster. Tweedmouth's sure grasp of the internal mechanism and sentiment of the party gave him due weight in the inner counsels of the ministry. When the government of Lord Rosebery fell in 1895 and a general election converted the Liberal Party into a divided, distracted, and enfeebled opposition, Tweedmouth earnestly devoted himself to the uphill task of restoring its fallen fortunes.

Tweedmouth was prominent in society, and entertained on a generous scale both in London at Brook House and at his home in Scotland, Guisachan, at Beauly in Invernessshire. He had married on 9 June 1873 Lady Fanny Octavia Louisa (1853–1904), the third daughter of John Winston Spencer-*Churchill, seventh duke of Marlborough, and his wife, Frances Anne Emily, and sister of Lord Randolph Churchill. Lady Tweedmouth was endowed with a native gift for society, and shared her husband's labour in bringing together Liberal politicians of all shades of opinion. She initiated the Liberal Social Council and did as much as social agencies can to restore courage, confidence, and concord to the party. Her death from cancer on 5 August 1904 dealt her husband a blow from which he never completely recovered. At the same time financial losses, due to a crisis in the affairs of Meux's brewery, which he bore with cheery fortitude, compelled Tweedmouth to part with Brook House and Guisachan (to Sir Ernest Cassell) and to sell many of the art treasures which his father had collected.

When Campbell-Bannerman formed his cabinet in December 1905, he appointed Tweedmouth first lord of the Admiralty. He took office at a critical moment, for the expansion of the German navy was then in full swing and yet there was a section of the Liberal Party which was disposed to insist on a large reduction of naval expenditure. Taking advantage of the superiority of the dreadnoughts, Tweedmouth, in close co-operation with Sir John Fisher, the first sea lord, reduced expenditure on capital ships from almost £8.5 million in 1905–6 to under £6 million in 1908–9, and the number of dreadnoughts to two in 1908–9, thus provoking the tory campaign, 'We want eight and we won't wait.' In March 1908 it became publicly known that the German emperor had written to Tweedmouth on matters connected with naval policy and that in the course of a reply—which came to be known as 'the Tweedmouth letter'—Tweedmouth had communicated to him many details of the forthcoming navy estimates before these had been presented to the House of Commons.

Tweedmouth was on these grounds popularly credited with something like an act of treason. A private and unpublished correspondence with the German emperor had taken place, and the public knowledge of that fact may have been due to a conversational indiscretion on Tweedmouth's part. In other respects the circumstances were misrepresented and Tweedmouth was unjustly censured by public opinion. The first insidious assaults of the cerebral malady which was later to cause his death may account for Tweedmouth's error in talking too unreservedly about the correspondence.

Campbell-Bannerman's resignation followed soon after this misunderstanding (5 April 1908), one of his last official acts being to nominate Tweedmouth for a knighthood of the Thistle. On H. H. Asquith's succession as prime minister and some reconstruction of the government, Tweedmouth relinquished the Admiralty and became lord president of the council. But his ministerial career was practically at an end. Within a few weeks he was stricken down by a cerebral attack from when he never recovered sufficiently to resume any kind of public work. He finally resigned his office in September 1908. During the last few months of his life he resided at the chief secretary's lodge in Phoenix Park at Dublin, which had been lent by his colleague Augustine Birrell in order that he might be under the care of his sister, Lady Aberdeen, the wife of the viceroy. He died there on 15 September 1909. He was interred in the family burial-ground in Chirnside churchyard, Berwickshire, where his wife had been buried. In her memory he had restored and greatly beautified the church there, which was not far from Hutton Castle, a residence which his father had purchased, restored, and enlarged. Tweedmouth was succeeded in the title by his only child, Dudley Churchill.

J. R. Thursfield, rev. H. C. G. Matthew

Sources Edward Marjoribanks, Lord Tweedmouth, ed. [I. M. Gordon] (1909) · The Times (16 Sept 1909) · GEC, Peerage · R. Williams, Defending the empire: the conservative party and British defence policy, 1899–1915 (1991)
Archives NMM, Naval Historical Library | BL, letters to Sir Henry Campbell-Bannerman · BL, corresp. with W. E. Gladstone, Add. MS 44332 · BL, corresp. with Lord Herbert Gladstone, MSS, Add. MS 46022 · BL, Ripon MSS, Add. MSS 43636–43640 · Bodl. Oxf., corresp. with Herbert Asquith · Bodl. Oxf., letters to Sir William Harcourt and Lewis Harcourt · Bodl. Oxf., corresp. with Lord Kimberley · Bodl. Oxf., letters from Kaiser Wilhelm II and related papers · CAC Cam., corresp. with Lord Esher · CUL, letters to Lord Hardinge · Hydrographic Office, Taunton, Admiralty Library, corresp. and papers · NL Scot., Haldane MSS · NL Scot., corresp. mainly with Lord Rosebery
Likenesses M. Beerbohm, drawing, 1907, New Club, Edinburgh · H. W. Barnett, photograph, NPG [see illus.] · E. Gland, portrait, repro. in Gordon, ed., Edward Marjoribanks, Lord Tweedmouth · Spy [L. Ward], chromolithograph, NPG; repro. in VF (12 July 1894)
Wealth at death £204,975 18s. —in UK: administration with will, 22 Nov 1909, CGPLA Eng. & Wales

Markaunt, Thomas (c.1382–1439), benefactor, was the son of John Markaunt and his wife, Cassandria. Markaunt's name, prefixed 'm' (magister), is found in the records of Corpus Christi College, Cambridge, in accounts datable to 1413/14 and sporadically thereafter. From 1437 to 1439 he is regularly listed in an order of seniority placing him immediately below the master. Fellowship at Corpus entailed being in priest's orders, but the degree of BTh (found in later histories) is unsubstantiated.

Markaunt served the university as senior proctor during the year 1417, as is known from his citation in 1418, by name and office, in a petition of complaint made by the mayor and commonalty of Cambridge against the university. A paper of crude verses had been affixed to the mayoral gate by unruly scholars, and Markaunt was involved in the university's defence and counter-complaints arising out of that and other incidents. He subsequently added all the relevant documents to the compendium of texts of university records (mainly statutes and privileges), which he had gathered and indexed for his personal reference during his term of office. The resulting volume, usually known as 'Markaunt's Book', is not unique of its kind, but is of exceptional interest as the earliest relating to the university to have survived, predating existing series of registers. Markaunt was one of four witnesses appearing for the university at the 'Barnwell process' of 14 October 1430, his age at the time given as forty-eight years.

The death of Markaunt 'nuper consortis et confratris Collegii Corporis Christi' (Corpus Christi College, Cambridge, MS 232, fol. 17r) is recorded as 19 November 1439. His will, made on 4 November, is largely quoted in the deed of acceptance of his legacy by the college of 1 August 1440, endorsing the conditions set out by the testator for the future management of the books of his bequest. These were to be kept separately as a lending library for the use of the master and fellows. Detailed rules governed the choice of custodians, the order of the borrowers' selection, and the prayers they then recited. The scheme had similarities to those for contemporary (cash) loan chests, and within the college operated in parallel with one such recent endowment. A full inventory of the seventy-six books by number, title, and identifying incipit, with a valuation list roughly classified by subject, accompany the copy of the deed of agreement prefacing the register of borrowers proper. Markaunt's library seems to have been largely dispersed soon after the borrowing register was discontinued in 1517. Five volumes remain in the college, subsumed into Archbishop Parker's manuscript collection. Another survival, strayed from the college before Parker's time, is 'Markaunt's Book', now after many vicissitudes in the university archives. Although misunderstanding of its purpose subsequently won for its compiler an unfounded reputation as an antiquary, modern scholarship still remains lastingly indebted to Markaunt for his transcripts and the records of his library.

CATHERINE HALL

Sources college accounts, 1376–1485, CCC Cam., Muniments, 31 (104), MS 232 · CUL, department of manuscripts and university archives, collect. admin. 7, fols. 66–73v; Hare II, fols. 40v–70, Roll 108, Hare II, fol. 103 · *Masters' History of the college of Corpus Christi and the Blessed Virgin Mary in the University of Cambridge*, ed. J. Lamb (1831), 42, 307–8 · C. H. Cooper, *Annals of Cambridge*, 1 (1842), 159–63, 182–3 · Emden, *Cam.* · M. B. Hackett, *The original statutes of Cambridge University* (1970), appx 1, 309–31 · D. R. Leader, *A history of the University of Cambridge*, 1: *The university to 1546*, ed. C. N. L. Brooke and others (1988), 220–22 · J. O. Halliwell, *A catalogue of the books given to Corpus Christi College (AD 1439), by T. Markaunt, with their prices*, Cambridge Antiquarian Society, Quarto Series, pt 1, vol. 14 (1847), 15–20 · M. R. James, *The sources of Archbishop Parker's collection of MSS at Corpus Christi College, Cambridge, with a reprint of the catalogue of Thomas Markaunt's Library* (1899), 76–82 · M. R. James, *A descriptive catalogue of the manuscripts in the library of Corpus Christi College, Cambridge*, 2 vols. (1912) [nos. 64, 159, 275, 394, 479] · C. R. Cheney, *A register of MSS borrowed from a college library, 1440–1517: Corpus Christi College, Cambridge, MS 232*, Transactions of Cambridge Bibliographical Society, 9 (1987), 103 · R. Lovatt, 'Two collegiate loan chests in late medieval Cambridge', *Medieval Cambridge: essays on the pre-Reformation university*, ed. P. Zutshi (1993), 129–65

Archives CUL, department of manuscripts and university archives, collect. admin. 7, roll 108

Wealth at death £104 12s. 3d.—value of books: CCC Cam. MS 232

Markby, Sir William (1829–1914), judge and legal writer, was born on 31 May 1829 at Duxford St Peter rectory, Cambridgeshire, the fourth son of the rector, the Revd William Henry Markby (1786–1866), and his wife, Sophia, née Randall (1798–1865). He was educated at King Edward's School, Bury St Edmunds, before matriculating at Merton College, Oxford, in 1846. A mathematics postmaster, he graduated with first-class honours in 1851, having played cricket and rowed for his college. Admitted to the Inner Temple on 9 November 1853, he read in the chambers of Edward Turner, and was called to the bar on 5 June 1856, being made an MA by Oxford and, by incorporation, Cambridge, in the same year.

Markby practised on the Norfolk circuit (1856–66) and was recorder of Buckingham (1865–6), before being appointed a judge of the high court of Bengal (1866–78). On 22 March 1866 he married Lucy (1841–1928), daughter of John Edward Taylor of Weybridge, and niece of the jurist John Austin's widow, Sarah, whom Markby helped prepare Austin's *Lectures on Jurisprudence* for publication (1863).

As a judge Markby was noted for his care and conscientiousness, which were constant features in a life conspicuous for the achievement of excellence and devotion to duty. Politically a Liberal, he was sympathetic to those around him aspiring for Indian self-government. He was vice-chancellor of Calcutta University (1877–8). On retirement from the bench in 1878, he was knighted and returned to England.

Immediately Markby took up the newly created readership in Indian law at Oxford, a post he held until 1900. His duties involved the supervision of probationers selected for the Indian Civil Service studying at the university, as well as lecturing on the Anglo-Indian codes and teaching the elements of Hindu and Islamic law. Active in university committee work, he was a member of hebdomadal council, a curator of the university chest, and a delegate of the Clarendon Press. The university settlement in east London, Toynbee Hall, was one of the liberal causes which he promoted. A fellow of All Souls by virtue of his readership, he also served as its domestic bursar until Balliol recruited him as its bursar and made him an official fellow

Sir William Markby (1829–1914), by unknown photographer

(1883–1900). It was in Markby's rooms at All Souls that he, Thomas Erskine Holland, Frederick Pollock, James Bryce, and William Anson initiated the *Law Quarterly Review*, which became a legal journal of international renown. A county alderman and JP, noted for his business acumen, Markby was appointed KCIE (1889) and served as a commissioner to inquire into administration of justice in Trinidad and Tobago (1892) and as a railway commissioner (1906).

The fruit of Markby's teaching and legal career is to be found in his published works: the eleventh edition (with W. Mills) of H. Roscoe's *Digest of the Law of Evidence in the Trial of Actions at nisi prius* (1866), *Lectures on Indian Law* (1873), *The Indian Evidence Act* (1897), *An Introduction to Hindu and Mohammedan Law* (1906), and, most importantly, his *Elements of Law Considered with Reference to the Principles of General Jurisprudence* (six editions: 1871, 1874, 1885, 1889, 1896, and 1905). Whereas some of his other works were undertaken after deafness had begun to curtail his involvement in committee work, his *Elements* had been written while he was in India teaching Hindu students, and mirrored the interest in legal theory and general jurisprudence which his contact with other legal cultures had

stimulated. The work, once much read, earned him the DCL from Oxford (1879), but belongs to a genre which later became virtually extinct. Undoubtedly, such studies were inspired by the contact with other legal orders afforded by the colonial experience and reached their apogee in the work of scholars such as Henry Maine. The book's importance lies in that it was among the first to present English law in terms of general jurisprudential categories, obtained as a result of comparative analysis. When it was written, there were no textbooks as such dealing with subjects such as tort or crime in English law. Its achievement can be measured by the fact that when such books came to be written, the analytical models they adopted were those pioneered in works such as Markby's *Elements*. Its influence was therefore great, but its fate was to be overtaken and replaced by those later works. Interest in this type of analytical approach waned with the decline of empire and increase in the influence of American theorists together with a return to philosophical rather than comparative and historical perspectives in jurisprudence.

Markby died at his home at Headington Hill, Oxford, on 15 October 1914, and was buried four days later at Headington cemetery. In 1917 his widow published a memoir of his life containing a portrait.   T. G. WATKIN

Sources L. Markby, *Memoirs of Sir William Markby, KCIE, by his wife* (1917) · *The Times* (16 Oct 1914) · *The Times* (28 Dec 1928) [obit. of Lady Lucy Markby] · F. H. Lawson, *The Oxford law school, 1850–1965* (1968), 73–5 · parish register, Duxford St Peter, Cambs. AS, 1 June 1829 [baptism] · *The Times* (20 Oct 1914)

Archives Balliol Oxf., letters · Oxf. UA, committee papers | All Souls Oxf., letters to Sir William Anson · Balliol Oxf., Jowett MSS, letters · LMA, corresp. relating to Toynbee Hall

Likenesses photograph, NPG [*see illus.*] · portrait, repro. in Markby, *Memoirs of Sir William Markby*

Wealth at death £16,924 1s. 10d.: probate, 14 Jan 1915, *CGPLA Eng. & Wales*

Markham, Mrs. *See* Penrose, Elizabeth (*c*.1779–1837).

Markham, Sir Albert Hastings (1841–1918), naval officer and Arctic explorer, was born at Bagnères-de-Bigorre, Hautes Pyrénées, France, on 11 November 1841, the fourth son of Captain John Markham RN (*b*. 1797) and his wife, Marianne, daughter of John Brock Wood. Clements Robert *Markham (1830–1916) was his cousin, whom he much admired, and who apparently became the strongest influence in his life. Educated at home and at Eastman's Royal Naval Academy, Southsea, he entered the navy in 1856 and served eight years on the China station, fighting pirates; in 1862 he was promoted lieutenant. He took part in the advance on Peking (Beijing) in 1860 and the suppression of the Taiping uprising in 1862–4. After serving in the Mediterranean, where he delighted in the ruins of antiquity, he spent several years on the Australian station, where he attempted to suppress the 'blackbirding' quasi-slave trade from the south sea islands to Australia, and punished Nakapa islanders for murdering missionaries. In 1872 he became commander, and in 1873 (after the Admiralty refused his offers of Arctic service) he took advantage of a period of leave to sail as second mate in the whaler *Arctic*

Sir Albert Hastings Markham (1841–1918), by unknown photographer, pubd 1913

to Davis Strait and Baffin's Bay in order to study ice conditions; his account of the voyage was published as *A Whaling Cruise to Baffin's Bay* (1874). In the Arctic expedition of 1875–6, under George Strong Nares, Markham commanded HMS *Alert*. His sledging party, in an attempt to reach the pole from winter quarters in lat. 82°27′ N on the western shore of Robeson Channel, reached lat. 83°20′26″ N, long. 64° W, in May 1876. This was gained without dogs and remained the record for the northernmost point reached by explorers until it was broken by Nansen in 1895. The achievements of the expedition were marred only by an outbreak of scurvy resulting from Markham's forgetting to take lime juice for his party. In recognition of his services Markham was promoted captain, and received a gold watch from the Royal Geographical Society. Markham accompanied Sir Henry Gore-Booth on a cruise to Novaya Zemlya in 1879, described by him in *A Polar Reconnaissance* (1879), and in 1886 surveyed ice conditions in Hudson Strait and Bay, for which he received the thanks of the Canadian government.

From 1879 to 1882 Markham served in the Pacific; from 1883 to 1886 he was captain of HMS *Vernon*, the naval torpedo school at Portsmouth, and from 1886 to 1889 commodore of the training squadron. Promoted rear-admiral in 1891, in 1892 he was appointed second in command of the Mediterranean squadron under Sir George Tryon. During manoeuvres off Tripoli on 22 June 1893 Markham's battleship, *Camperdown*, attempting an evolution signalled by Tryon, rammed the flagship *Victoria*, which sank

with the loss of 358 lives, including Tryon's. The court martial exonerated Markham, since he had obeyed the orders of the commander-in-chief, but some officers, including Fisher, privately criticized his conduct. In 1894 Markham married Theodora, daughter of Francis T. Gervers, of Amat, Ross-shire; they had one daughter. From 1901 to 1904 he was commander-in-chief at the Nore; in 1906 he retired from the navy.

Markham was an aide-de-camp to Queen Victoria, and was made a KCB in 1903. During the First World War he devoted himself to the interests of the mine-sweeping service. In the latter part of his life he also wrote several books on geographical and biographical subjects, and contributed to various magazines.

Brave, with strong religious convictions, puritanical and abstemious—except in the slaughter of birds and animals—Markham neither smoked nor drank, and expressed his disapproval of such indulgence: he told his officers that cigarettes were only for effeminate weaklings. He died at his home, 19 Queen's Gate Place, London, on 28 October 1918.

R. N. RUDMOSE BROWN, *rev.* ROGER T. STEARN

Sources *The Times* (29 Oct 1918) · *GJ*, 53 (1919), 61–3 · M. E. Markham and F. A. Markham, *The life of Sir Albert Hastings Markham* (1927) · R. Hough, *Admirals in collision* (1959) · A. H. Markham, *A whaling cruise to Baffin's Bay* (1874) · A. H. Markham, *The great frozen sea* (1877) · A. H. Markham, *A polar reconnaissance* (1879) · R. Gardiner and A. Lambert, eds., *Steam, steel and shellfire: the steam warship, 1815–1905* (1992) · G. S. Graham, *The China station: war and diplomacy, 1830–1860* (1978) · *WWW* · Kelly, *Handbk* (1917) · Burke, *Gen. GB* (1914) · *CGPLA Eng. & Wales* (1919)

Archives NMM, corresp. and papers · PRO, Admiralty papers · Scott Polar RI, notebooks

Likenesses photograph, pubd 1913, NPG [*see illus.*] · woodengraving (after photograph by Elliott & Fry), NPG; repro. in *ILN* (29 May 1875)

Wealth at death £4747 9s. 10d.: probate, 9 Jan 1919, *CGPLA Eng. & Wales*

Markham [*née* Clutterbuck], **Beryl** (1902–1986), aviator and author, was born on 26 October 1902 at Westfield House, Ashwell, Rutland, the younger child and only daughter of Charles Baldwin Clutterbuck, farmer and formerly a lieutenant in the King's Own Scottish Borderers, from which he was cashiered for absence without leave, and his wife, Clara Agnes, daughter of Josiah William Alexander, of the Indian Civil Service. The Clutterbucks went to British East Africa in 1904 and in the following year bought Ndimu Farm at Njoro, overlooking the Rift Valley, where they built a timber and flour mill. In July 1906 Clara left for England with her son and soon divorced her husband. Left with her father, Beryl did not see her mother again until she was twenty-one. She lived a wild childhood with the farm's African children, particularly Kibii (whose name after initiation was arap Ruta), a Kipsigis boy.

In 1911 Beryl was sent to Nairobi European School, from which she was expelled in her third term. She returned to the farm and possibly a promiscuous early adolescence, not being sent to school again until 1916, when an army officer paid for her to attend Miss Seccombe's school in

Beryl Markham (1902–1986), by Alan Webb, 1936 [in Southampton after her flight across the Atlantic]

Nairobi, providing he could marry her. She was again expelled. On 15 October 1919, at the age of sixteen, she married the officer—Captain Alexander Laidlaw (Jock) Purves, son of Dr William Laidlaw Purves, founder of the Royal St George's Golf Club in Scotland. Purves bought land adjoining Ndimu Farm, but the marriage lasted only six months. Beryl began to train horses, as her father had done, and in 1921 left her husband to live on Soysambu, the farm on the floor of the Rift Valley owned by the third Baron Delamere. She stayed there as a trainer until 1924, when she left for London, where she discovered she was pregnant. She claimed the child's father was Denys Finch-*Hatton, the lover of Karen Blixen, who later wrote *Out of Africa* (1937), but she had been so free with her sexual favours that any of a number of people could have been responsible. She had a late abortion and returned to Kenya, where she met Mansfield Markham, the son of Sir Arthur Basil Markham, first baronet, Liberal MP and owner of collieries in the north of England. He was wealthy and they married in 1927.

In 1928 Edward, prince of Wales, and his brother Henry, duke of Gloucester (1900–1974), visited Kenya. Beryl became mistress to Henry. She agreed to go to London to be with him, and he established her in a suite at the Grosvenor Hotel. On 25 February 1929 she had a son, about whom there was much speculation. However, he cannot have been fathered by Prince Henry, because Beryl must already have been pregnant when she met him. The boy

was given to Markham's mother to bring up. When Markham threatened to cite Henry as co-respondent in a divorce, Queen Mary, in an effort to avoid scandal, made Henry settle on Beryl a capital sum of £15,000, which provided her with an annuity of £500 until her death.

Beryl stayed in England until 1929, and learned to fly. Back in Kenya, she obtained her commercial pilot's licence in 1933. Following a dare, she decided to fly the Atlantic from east to west. On 4 September 1936 she took off from Abingdon, near Oxford, in a Vega Gull, without a radio. After 21 hours 35 minutes she landed in a bog at Baleine Cove, near Louisburg, Nova Scotia, 100 yards from the ocean, having run out of fuel. She was the first woman to fly the Atlantic from east to west, and the first person to make a solo non-stop crossing in that direction.

Fêted in America, she returned there in 1939, and met Raoul Cottereau Schumacher, son of Henri Schumacher, farmer, of Minneapolis. A well-read and articulate man, Schumacher worked as a ghost writer. In 1942 Beryl married him, having divorced Markham in the same year. In June 1942 *West with the Night*, by Beryl Markham, was published in America. A remarkable account of her African childhood, it reached thirteen best-seller lists. The book was lyrically written, with many classical and Shakespearian allusions, and in a style similar in places to that of Antoine de Saint-Exupéry, who had befriended Beryl in Hollywood and who may well have been a help with the manuscript. Beryl later claimed that he encouraged her to write the book. It is thought that Schumacher was also a considerable help in editing the manuscript. Some short stories she wrote were later gathered together by her biographer, Mary Lovell, and published as *The Splendid Outcast* (1987).

In 1950 Beryl returned to Kenya without Schumacher. Schumacher divorced Beryl in 1960 and died in 1962. Her remaining days were spent training horses in Kenya, South Africa, and Rhodesia. She won the Kenya top trainer's award five times and the Kenya Derby six times. In 1971 her son, whom she had seldom seen, died after a car accident in France, leaving two daughters, and Markham died three months later.

In 1979 the Jockey Club of Kenya allocated Beryl a bungalow at its racecourse. *West with the Night* was republished in 1982 and hailed as a lost masterpiece. By 1987, 140,000 copies had been sold and royalties began to pour in. Over a million copies were sold.

Beryl Markham was 5 feet 8 inches tall, of willowy build, with blue eyes, fair hair, slightly wide-spaced teeth, and slim, boyish hips. Her beautiful long oval face had a determined chin. She was exceptionally promiscuous, but retained the loyalty of her male friends. Women found her often ruthless and selfish, although they admitted her stamina, physical prowess, courage, and ability to withstand pain. She died on 3 August 1986 in Nairobi Hospital, from pneumonia, which followed a broken hip. A service of thanksgiving was held in St Clement Danes, London, in September, also marking the fiftieth anniversary of her flight.

C. S. NICHOLLS, *rev.*

Sources B. Markham, *West with the night* (1942) · M. S. Lovell, *Straight on till morning* (1987) · E. Trzebinski, *The lives of Beryl Markham* (1993) · private information (1996) · personal knowledge (1996) · *CGPLA Eng. & Wales* (1987)

Archives priv. coll., Mary S. Lovell MSS · priv. coll., George Bathurst Norman MSS | FILM World without walls, TV documentary, made by a San Francisco company (1987) | SOUND US Sound and Picture Archives, newsreel and sound reports

Likenesses A. Webb, photograph, 1936, Hult. Arch. [*see illus.*] · photograph, 1936, L. Cong. · photographs, repro. in Lovell, *Straight on till morning* · photographs, repro. in Trzebinski, *The lives of Beryl Markham* · photographs, Hult. Arch.

Wealth at death £12,984 in England and Wales: probate, 7 Jan 1987, *CGPLA Eng. & Wales*

Markham, Sir Clements Robert (1830–1916), geographer, was born on 20 July 1830 at the vicarage, Stillingfleet, Yorkshire, the second son of the Revd David Markham, vicar of Stillingfleet and canon of Windsor, and his wife, Catherine, the daughter of Sir William Milner, fourth baronet, of Nun Appleton Hall, Yorkshire. He was a descendent of William *Markham, archbishop of York. After attending private school at Cheam, Surrey, from 1839 to 1842 and Westminster School from 1842 to 1844, he joined the Royal Navy as a cadet. He first sailed on HMS *Collingwood* to South America, where he learned Spanish as well as the normal naval curriculum. He had been interested in Arctic exploration from an early age, and in 1850 succeeded in transferring to the Arctic squadron and sailed on the *Assistance* in search of Franklin (1850–51). The party found evidence of Franklin's expedition, but failed to solve the mystery, although they explored large tracts hitherto unknown.

Markham resolved to leave the navy, finding the life as a whole uncongenial, although he enjoyed its more adventurous side. At his father's request he first sat and passed the lieutenant's examination. He had determined to make a career in exploration and geography. Having written *Franklin's Footsteps* (published 1853) to rebut criticism of the expedition, in 1852 he set off for Peru, with advice from W. H. Prescott as to how he might proceed there. He spent 1852–3 in Peru, exploring Inca sites and reading manuscripts in preparation for his *Cuzco … and Lima* (1856), a work of history, geography, and archaeology. His translation from the Quechua of the Inca drama *Ollanta* appeared in 1871, and a freer translation in his *Incas of Peru* (1910). He retained his interest in Peru and the Incas throughout his life.

After returning to England, Markham was obliged by the death of his father to take a job to support his mother and sister. In his second post, from 1854, at what was to become the India Office, he was commissioned to carry from Peru to India seeds of the cinchona tree, the source of quinine and then found only in Peru; to establish the tree in India and Ceylon; and to make quinine readily available there. The remoteness of the country, the possibility of war between Peru and Bolivia, and the hostility of the Peruvian authorities and entrepreneurs to the scheme, which threatened their hold on the quinine trade, made it hazardous. Markham's *Travels in Peru and India* (1862) and *Peruvian Bark* (1880) recount his adventures in Peru, where he was accompanied by his wife, Minna (the daughter of the Revd James Hamilton John Chichester, rector of Arlington and Loxhore, near Barnstaple, whom he had married in April 1857), and several botanists. He managed to gather plants and seeds, and found time for work on his first Quechua dictionary (1864; the second was published in 1892). Although Markham's own plants did not survive, the party as a whole succeeded in getting seeds and plants out of South America and establishing plantations in India and Ceylon, and making pure quinine available throughout the subcontinent. He was awarded a grant of £3000 for his services.

Back in London, Markham built up around him the geographical department of the India Office, appalled by the

Sir Clements Robert Markham (1830–1916), by Elliott & Fry, 1900s

lack of geographical information to hand, and the failure to use or in some cases even to preserve what there was. His *Memoir on the Indian Surveys* (1871) describes the various Indian surveys whose maps and reports were, under Markham, for the first time properly catalogued and stored. He discovered important accounts of early voyages and edited some of these for publication. He published a life of James Rennell (1895), a pioneer of Indian geography. In 1875–6 he took unauthorized leave to sail to Greenland with the north polar expedition. Since he had already been absent from the office to go to Peru and India, and in 1867–8 to act as geographer and naturalist to the British contingent in the Abyssinian expedition, which he described in *History of the Abyssinian Expedition* (1869), this proved too much for his superiors in the office. He was obliged to resign in 1877, but still received a pension. His *Report on the Geographical Department* (1877) and the second edition of his *Memoir on the Indian Surveys* (1878) summarized his achievements at the India Office and his hopes that his work would be continued.

By the time he left the India Office, Markham was active in both the Royal Geographical Society (RGS) and the Hakluyt Society. His influence in the RGS and his *Threshold of the Unknown Region* (1873) helped muster support for the 1875 north polar expedition (for having joined which, as mentioned above, he was obliged to resign his post). He served as both secretary (1863–88) and president (1893–1905) and helped transform and enliven the society's publications and meetings. He was also secretary (1858–86) and then president (1889–1910) of the Hakluyt Society, for whom he also edited some thirty volumes, many of them translations from the Spanish; in effect he kept the society going.

At the turn of the century Markham again became interested in polar exploration, this time of the Antarctic, and he was largely instrumental in getting under way the *Discovery* expedition (the National Antarctic Expedition) of 1901–4 under Robert Falcon Scott, the naval officer of his choice rather than the scientist others would have preferred. Markham's role was commemorated by Scott in Mount Markham in the Trans-Antarctic Mountains, and it was he who ensured that relief vessels were sent to guarantee the party's safe return.

In the final years of his life Markham continued to support exploration and to write, and after 1905 his rate of publication on a wide range of topics, including Peru, actually increased. A notable work of the period was his *Richard III* (1906), the culmination of his battle with the historian James Gairdner which had been raging in print since the publication of Gairdner's *Life* in 1878. Markham took it on himself to clear the name of Richard, a misunderstood hero, maligned by Tudor propaganda and later scholarship. His was one of the first and most important of the popular defences of Richard which contrasted with the sceptical accounts of professional historians. With his wife, herself an interested linguist and botanist, Markham continued to travel. He was made CB in May 1871, elected FRS in 1873, and created KCB in 1896. On 29 January 1916 at his home in London (21 Eccleston Square), he set fire to his bedclothes while reading by candlelight in bed and, although the flames were speedily extinguished, he fell unconscious, and died on 30 January. He was survived by his wife and their only daughter.

Markham's cousin, close friend, and colleague Albert Hastings Markham wrote his life, which, although very informative, was naturally uncritical. As early as 1952 H. R. Mill, while acknowledging his enthusiasm and hard work for the RGS, pointed to the dictatorial way he had run the society. Several scholars have voiced doubts about his translations for the Hakluyt Society, all done freely with a view to quick publication but unrigorous and even careless. Other publications also bore the marks of haste, perhaps not surprising given that Markham had no regular income after his resignation from the India Office. It is also possible to criticize the nationalism which increasingly tinged his desire to promote scientific exploration. None the less, Markham must be recognized as one of the great geographers of his generation, for his own explorations, for making available, through his edited publications or through his careful cataloguing and storage, the work of other geographers and explorers, for his indefatigable work for the RGS and the Hakluyt Society, and for his service to the geographical department at the India Office, which was the more valuable for being unorthodox. Mill's description of him as 'in all things an enthusiast rather than a scholar' (*DNB*) neatly encapsulated his strength and weakness, and helps to explain his extraordinary influence, probably second only to that of Sir Roderick Murchison, on geography and its institutions in Britain in the nineteenth and early twentieth centuries.

ELIZABETH BAIGENT

Sources A. H. Markham, *The life of Sir Clements R. Markham* (1917) • P. Blanchard, ed., *Markham in Peru* (1991) • A. Savours, 'Clements Markham', *Compassing the vaste globe of the earth: studies in the history of the Hakluyt Society, 1846–1996*, ed. R. C. Bridges and P. E. H. Hair, Hakluyt Society, 183 (1996), 164–88 • D. Williams, 'Clements Robert Markham and the introduction of the cinchona tree into British India, 1861', *GJ*, 128 (1962), 431–42 • D. Williams, 'Clements Robert Markham and the geographical department of the India Office, 1867–77', *GJ*, 134 (1968), 343–52 • G. R. Crone, '"Jewels of antiquitie": the work of the Hakluyt Society', *GJ*, 128 (1962), 321–4 • *DNB* • H. R. Mill, *The record of the Royal Geographical Society, 1830–1930* (1930) • A. Savours, Sir Clements Markham, unpublished MSS, 1996 • C. Ross, *Richard III* (1981)

Archives BL, papers relating to Peru, Add. MSS 46216–46218, 48197–48200 • Bodl. Oxf., genealogical collections • Hants. RO, notebooks • RGS, corresp., journals, notebooks, and papers • Scott Polar RI, corresp. and notebook • U. Mich., Clements L., papers • Wellcome L., corresp. and travel journals | BL OIOC, letters to R. H. Major, MS Eur. A 82 • Hants. RO, letters to William Wickham • JRL, letters to E. A. Freeman • RGS, corresp. with Royal Geographical Society • Scott Polar RI, letters to William Colbeck • Scott Polar RI, letters to K. Scott and Robert Falcon Scott, MS 9, MSS 10, 336 • UCL, letters to Sir Francis Galton

Likenesses chalk drawing, c.1855, Scott Polar RI • photograph, c.1900, repro. in Mill, *Record of the Royal Geographical Society*, pl. 22 • Elliott & Fry, photograph, 1900–09, NPG [*see illus.*] • oils, c.1914, Scott Polar RI • F. W. Pomeroy, bronze bust, 1921, RGS • portrait, repro. in *Royal Academy Illustrated* (1922)

Wealth at death £7740 7s. 8d.: probate, 9 March 1916, CGPLA Eng. & Wales

Markham, Ernest Sowerby (1880–1937), gardener and writer on horticulture, was born on 26 June 1880 at 11 Dalby Villas, Lansdowne Road, London, the son of Henry Markham, a commercial traveller, and his wife, Esther, *née* Sowerby. From his youth he worked in a succession of large gardens: Newbottle Manor, Northamptonshire; Crown Court East, Worcester; The Dell, King's Norton, Birmingham; and Wortley Hall, Sheffield. Having been the leading foreman at King's Walden Bury, Hitchin, he became head gardener to Lady Chichester at Arlington Court, Devon, about 1900. From 1905 to 1910 he worked for Lady Marcus Beresford at Bishopsgate, Surrey.

In 1910 Markham became head gardener to William Robinson (1838–1935) of Gravetye Manor, near East Grinstead, Sussex, living with Miriam, his wife, at The Moat, a cottage on the estate. He loved Gravetye and directed more than a dozen gardeners in the productive and ornamental departments. From 1928 the ageing Robinson conferred upon him sole responsibility for managing and developing the garden, and at Robinson's death Markham was left with the life possession of Moat cottage. He continued to manage the famous Gravetye Garden, refusing many offers of employment elsewhere. In 1933 the Royal Horticultural Society recognized his services to horticulture by making him an associate of honour, and in June 1935 he read a paper on ornamental climbing plants to the society.

Markham contributed regularly to *Gardening Illustrated* and wrote two books, *The Large and Small Flowered Clematis and their Cultivation in the Open Air* (1935) and *Raspberries and Kindred Fruits* (1936). His contributions to the later editions of William Robinson's *English Flower Garden* included sections on lilies and clematis. He kept a large collection of clematis varieties and is commemorated by the hybrid clematis 'Ernest Markham' and *Clematis macropetala* 'Markham's Pink'. He died of a heart attack on 6 December 1937 at the Queen Victoria Cottage Hospital, East Grinstead, survived by his wife; he was buried at West Hoathly, Sussex, on 9 December. Obituaries described him as a modest and diffident man with an encyclopaedic knowledge of plants.   A. A. Sclater

Sources M. Allan, *William Robinson, 1838–1935: father of the English flower garden* (1982) · Desmond, *Botanists* · *Gardeners' Chronicle*, 3rd ser., 102 (1937), 439 · *Gardening Illustrated* (11 Dec 1937) · *Proceedings of the Royal Horticultural Society*, 58 (1933) · *Proceedings of the Royal Horticultural Society*, 60 (1935) · William Robinson's will, 1935 · B. Massingham, 'William Robinson: a portrait', *Garden History*, 6/1 (1978), 61–85 · b. cert. · d. cert. · *CGPLA Eng. & Wales* (1938)

Likenesses photograph, repro. in *Gardening Illustrated*, p. 730 · photograph, repro. in Allan, *William Robinson*, 197

Wealth at death £3850 18s. 10d.: resworn probate, 15 Feb 1938, *CGPLA Eng. & Wales*

Markham, Francis (1565–1627), soldier, was born on 25 July 1565, the second son of Robert Markham, landowner, of Cotham, Nottinghamshire, and Mary, daughter of Sir Francis Leake. He was a page in the service of the earl of Pembroke before spending ten years at Winchester College. He briefly studied under the famous Dutch Calvinist theologian Adrian de Saravia before being sent to Trinity College, Cambridge, in 1582. He quarrelled with a tutor, however, and in 1583 made his first trip to the Netherlands, where he served as a gentleman volunteer in an English regiment. His father did not approve of his abandoning university and cut off his allowance. In 1587 they were reconciled, but Robert Markham allowed his son to return to the Dutch wars in the royal expedition sent to attempt to relieve Sluys. Markham then returned to England and in 1588 entered Staple's Inn, from which he moved in February 1589 to Gray's Inn, where his father had been a member.

In his memoirs Francis claimed that he had to leave his studies because of lack of funds, but it was also the case that only a year after being admitted to Gray's Inn he was one of seventeen gentlemen who were 'put out of the fellowship … for their abuse in outrageous manner' at about two or three o'clock on the morning of 4 February 1590 (Fletcher, 87). His father's patron, the earl of Shrewsbury, obtained for him a place in Sir Robert Sidney's garrison in Flushing. He later moved to Germany, serving a season in the army of Christian of Anhalt, a militant Calvinist, before returning—perhaps initially home, but certainly to the Netherlands, where he stayed with the Dutch Anglophile humanist Carolus Clusius in Leiden in early 1594. This was *en route* for Heidelberg, where—presumably to satisfy his parents—he went to study civil law. But Markham enjoyed law no more in Heidelberg than in London and returned home that summer.

Markham now joined the household of the earl of Shrewsbury, with an annual pension of £20, but in 1599 he went back to the wars, as a captain in the army led to Ireland by the earl of Essex. His association with Essex 'crossed' his career, as he later recalled (Markham, 36). He bought a home, meaning to settle down, yet instead he went back to the Netherlands and served in the Dutch army in 1602–3. The death of the queen induced him to try for a place at court, but the involvement of his cousin Sir Griffin Markham in a Catholic plot against James I disgraced the family. Shortly afterwards he was imprisoned for fifteen weeks for debt, securing release only through the good offices of old military friends such as Sir Francis Vere, Robert, Lord Sidney, and another old Essex man, the earl of Rutland, whose son, Lord Ros, Markham tutored on a trip through France. On 3 January 1609 he married Mary Lovel (*b.* 1594, *d.* in or after 1616). They had at least two children. Markham may have fought in the Jülich–Cleves War of 1610 but finally settled in Nottingham on his appointment in 1612 as muster-master of that city.

Markham was clearly committed to the international protestant cause—he chose carefully whom he fought for, and he had a strong interest in military affairs. As a writer he was a greater stylist, though much less prolific, than his more celebrated sibling, Gervase *Markham (1568?–1637). The main source for his life is the 'Genealogy or petigree of Markham' that he composed some time between 1601 and 1622, which includes a brief autobiographical memoir. In addition, material can be gleaned from his two books *Five Decades of Epistles of Warre* (1622), dedicated to Prince Charles, and *The Booke of Honour, or, Five Decads of Epistles of Honour* (1625), dedicated to him as king.

Both are in the form of five collections, each of ten epistles on subjects relating to war and honour, each epistle being dedicated to a nobleman or bishop. The prose style is lucid and elegant, if a touch florid, though both books are somewhat derivative, revealing (if nothing else) their author's acquaintance with a range of classical and Renaissance literature. However, they are also sprinkled with observations drawn from Markham's personal experience. *Epistles of Warre* contains the greater number of these, and partly as a result, is the more original and interesting work for, as he observed in the epistle dedicatory, 'War hath been ever my Mistrese' (sig. A3r). Markham died intestate in 1627.   D. J. B. TRIM

Sources F. Markham, *Genealogy of the Markhams: 27 July 1601*, ed. C. R. Markham (1872) · Venn, *Alum. Cant.*, 1/3 · 'Markham', two letters to Clusius, University of Leiden, Bibliotheek Dousa, Vulc MS 101/19 · J. Foster, *The register of admissions to Gray's Inn, 1521–1889, together with the register of marriages in Gray's Inn chapel, 1695–1754* (privately printed, London, 1889) · R. J. Fletcher, ed., *The pension book of Gray's Inn*, 1 (1901)
Archives University of Leiden, Bibliotheek Dousa, letters, Vulc MS 101/19

Markham, Frederick (1805–1855), army officer, youngest son of Admiral John *Markham (1761–1827) and his wife, Maria (*née* Rice), and grandson of William *Markham, archbishop of York, was born at his father's house, Ades, in Chailey parish, near Lewes, Sussex, on 16 August 1805. He went to Westminster School, where he was a cricketer and oarsman, and acted Syrus in the *Adelphi*, the Westminster play of 1823. He was expelled for a boating scrape in 1824, and on 13 May of that year obtained an ensigncy by purchase in the 32nd regiment, in which he became lieutenant in 1825, captain in 1829, major in 1839, and lieutenant-colonel in 1842, buying all his steps. When the 32nd was in Dublin in 1830 Markham was second to Captain John Rowland Smyth (*d.* 1873), then of the regiment, in a fatal duel with Standish O'Grady, a barrister, arising out of a fracas in Nassau Street, Dublin, on 17 March. Smyth and Markham were tried for their lives, and each sentenced to a year's imprisonment in Kilmainham gaol. Judge Vandeleur assured them that the sentence implied no reflection on their conduct in the affair.

Markham subsequently served with his regiment in Canada, and received three wounds when in command of the light company covering the advance in the unsuccessful attack on the rebels at St Denis in November 1837, during the insurrection in Lower Canada. He went out in command of the regiment to India, commanding the 2nd infantry brigade at the first and second sieges of Multan during the Punjab campaign of 1848–9 (he was wounded on 10 September 1848). He commanded the division at Suraj Kund, when the enemy's position was stormed and seven guns taken, commanded the Bengal column at the storming of Multan on 2 January 1849, and was present at the surrender of the city on 22 January and the capture of the fort of Chiniot on 2 February. After joining Lord Gough's army with his brigade on 20 February, he was present with it at the victory of Gujrat. He was made CB

and afterwards aide-de-camp to the queen, and attained the rank of colonel in 1850.

Markham, a wiry, active man, was all his life an ardent sportsman. When at Peshawar in April 1852 he made a long shooting expedition in the Himalayas in company with Sir Edward Campbell, bt, an officer of the 60th rifles on the governor-general's staff. They visited Kashmir and Tibet, penetrating as far as Ladakh and bringing back trophies of the skulls and bones of the great *Ovis ammon*, the burrell, gerow, ibex, and musk deer. Markham published a narrative of the journey, *Shooting in the Himalayas: a Journal of Sporting Adventures in Ladak, Tibet, and Cashmere* (1854).

Markham returned to Britain on leave, and in March 1854 was sent back to India as adjutant-general of the queen's troops. In November he was promoted major-general and appointed to the Peshawar division, but when within two days' journey of his command was recalled for a command in the Crimea. On 30 July 1855 he was appointed to the 2nd division of the army before Sevastopol, with the local rank of lieutenant-general. He commanded the division at the attack on the Redan on 8 September 1855. He was just able to witness the fall of Sevastopol before his health, which had suffered much by his hurried journey from India, broke down. He returned home and, apparently unmarried, died in London, at Limmer's Hotel, on 21 December 1855. He was buried in the family vault at Morland, near Penrith.

H. M. CHICHESTER, *rev.* JAMES FALKNER

Sources *Army List* · *GM*, 2nd ser., 45 (1856), 83 · *Hart's Army List*
Archives NL Scot., letters to George Brown, MSS 2845–2851
Wealth at death proceeds from sale of second collection and household goods; over £5000

Markham, Gervase (1557–1637), sheriff, was born at Laneham, Nottinghamshire, the son of Ellis Markham (*d.* 1578), gentleman and former member of parliament for the county, and Rosamund Frecheville. His Nottinghamshire origins and military service have often caused confusion, since they make him difficult to distinguish from his namesake Gervase *Markham (1568?–1637), the author. Between 1573 and 1576 Markham of Laneham studied at St John's College and at Gonville and Caius College, Cambridge, and thereafter seems (like his namesake) to have seen military service in Ireland and the Low Countries. He was reputedly handsome, brave, and a gallant of the countess of Shrewsbury. From at least 1593 he was a bitter enemy of his neighbour Sir John Holles, a feud which culminated in a duel in 1598 in Sherwood Forest in which Holles stabbed him with his rapier 'between the privities and the bottom of the gutts up to the hilt and out behinde' (Holles, 91). However, Markham survived, vowing never to eat supper or take the sacrament until he was revenged. It is claimed that he never did either again.

In 1625 Markham served as sheriff of Nottingham, but he seems to have fallen ill soon afterwards. In 1627, now living at Dunham on the River Trent, he was charged with aiding a recusant, but witnesses attested both to his protestantism and to the fact he was bedridden. In 1636 he disputed his assessment for ship money, but was made to pay anyway. He died on 17 January 1637, and is buried in the church at Laneham, where a tomb commemorates him and his father.   MATTHEW STEGGLE

Sources F. N. L. Poynter, *Bibliography of Gervase Markham, 1568?–1637* (1962) · HoP, *Commons, 1509–58* · G. Holles, *Memorials of the Holles family, 1493–1656*, ed. A. C. Wood, CS, 3rd ser., 55 (1937)
Likenesses tomb effigy, *c.*1636, Laneham church, Nottinghamshire

Markham, Gervase (1568?–1637), author, was probably born at Cotham, Nottinghamshire, one of five sons and three daughters of Robert Markham (1536–1606), member of parliament and former high sheriff, and Mary Leake (*b.* 1538, *d.* in or before 1597). Gervase had two elder brothers, one of whom, Francis *Markham (1565–1627), was the writer of an autobiography. The Markhams were well-connected country gentry: Gervase's father, Robert, had been brought up by the Babington family, who were first cousins, and another first cousin was Sir John Harington.

Gervase's elder brother Francis was educated at Winchester and Cambridge, and it is probable that something similar was true of Gervase. Indeed, he may well be one of the two students simply called Markham who entered King's College, Cambridge, at Easter 1583. But by 1584 a Jarvis Markham is mentioned in a letter as a retainer of the earl of Rutland at Belvoir Castle, 4 miles from the Markhams' seat at Cotham. Markham's movements for the next ten years are unclear, but for part of the time at least he was serving with his brothers in the army in Ireland.

By 1593 Markham seems to have been settled in London, since it was in this year that he registered his first books for publication. One was a poem (now lost) entitled 'Thyrsis and Daphne'; the other was *A Discource of Horsmanshippe*, a prose tract full of practical advice based on Markham's experience of horses. These two publications were a foretaste of Markham's career to come, in which an astonishing variety of literary publications—poetry, drama, and prose—is combined with an equally astonishing variety of non-literary works on topics such as horsemanship, veterinary medicine, husbandry, domestic economy, and even military training.

Throughout the rest of the 1590s Markham wrote a stream of poems strongly identified with the faction of the earl of Essex. Among them are *The Most Honorable Tragedy of Richard Grinvile, Knight* (1595), a poem dedicated to Lord Mountjoy, and including a sonnet dedicated to Southampton. In 1596 Markham's *Poem of Poems*, an adaptation of the Song of Solomon into eclogue form, was dedicated to Elizabeth, daughter of Philip Sidney. *Devoreux, or, Vertue's Tears* (1597), a translation from the French of Madame Genevieve Petau Maulette, has been described as 'almost pure Essex propaganda' (Poynter, 11); it is a lament for the death in battle of Walter Devereux, brother of the earl of Essex, and is dedicated to his sisters Dorothy, countess of Northumberland, and Penelope, Lady Rich. *Tears of the Beloved, or, The Lamentation of St John* (1600) and *Mary Magdalen's Lamentations for the Loss of her Master* (1601) complete the sequence of Markham's early

poetic publications. Markham's closeness to Southampton, with whom he went on the Islands voyage in 1596, has led Robert Gittings and others to speculate he may be the Rival Poet of Shakespeare's *Sonnets*. Several extracts from *Grinvile* and *Devoreux* appeared in *England's Parnassus* (1600), edited by Robert Allott, who had himself written a dedicatory poem for *Devoreux*. One 24-line passage from *Devoreux*, beginning 'I walkt alongst a stream', was misattributed in Allott's collection to Christopher Marlowe, and long had a place in the Marlowe canon. Not until 1947 was Markham given his due credit for these widely admired lines.

Probably also dating from this early phase of creativity, and similarly linked to radical protestantism, is Markham's prose completion of Philip Sidney's *Arcadia*. Volume 1 of this project was published in 1607 and volume 2, *The Second and Last Part of the First Book of the English Arcadia*, followed in 1613. Also during this period, Markham seems to have been writing for the theatre, as evidenced by a 1596 record of a payment by Henslowe to 'marcum'. It has been argued that this is for an early version of *The Dumb Knight*, a play which eventually saw print in 1608 in a version modified by Lewis *Machin. In addition, Markham in 1595 published a new edition of *The Boke of St Albans* by Juliana Barnes, a collection of domestic advice and recipes first printed in 1486 that foreshadows his own later work. *A Health to the Gentlemanly Profession of Servingmen* (1598), yet another product of Markham's indefatigable pen, celebrated the importance of gentleman retainers of great lords. By 1601 Markham had already published eight books of various sorts, not to mention various reprintings; however, in that year his publishing career was interrupted, and he did not print another new work for six years.

Essex's fall was a disaster for all his supporters, and Markham seems to have reacted by leaving London. On 23 February 1601, two days before Essex's execution, Markham married Mary Gelsthorp of Epperstone, Nottinghamshire, at Newark. For some years they seem to have lived quietly in the country. 'Yet did I for nine years follow the plow', commented Markham later, as a tenant farmer on the estate of relatives in Huntingdonshire, and perhaps also on the estate of his cousin Sir John Harington near Bath (Poynter, 18). In 1606 Markham's father died, and the estate passed to his eldest son, Robert, 'a fatal destroyer and unthrift of that eminent family' according to one observer, although the family had been struggling with debts since at least 1595 (ibid., 17). Robert died three years later in 1609, by which time most of the family wealth and property was gone.

By then Gervase Markham had started to resume the two threads of his publishing career. On the literary side, he began with *The Most Famous History of Mervine* (1607), a translation from a medieval French story, and followed this with poems including *Rodomonth's Infernall* (1607), translated from Ariosto, and *The Famous Whore* (1609). On the practical side, he wrote a series of books returning to the subject of horses, starting with *Cavelarice* (1607). Partly through his own productivity, and partly through the sharp practice of publishers repeatedly reissuing his work in different forms, it came to pass that five different books on the subject of horses, all of them by Markham, and some of them repeating one another's material, were on the market simultaneously. On 14 July 1617 Markham was forced to sign an unprecedented agreement with the Stationers' Company: 'I … do promise hereafter never to write any more book or books to be printed of the deseases or Cures of any Cattle, as Horse, Oxe, Cowe, Sheepe, Swine, Goates etc.' (Poynter, 23). Instead, Markham wrote *Hobson's Horse-Load of Epistles* (1617), a book of sample letters ready to be adapted to the sender's own particular circumstances. Next he turned to the subject of wildfowling, producing *Hunger's Prevention* (1621), a practical guide to the art of hunting birds.

In spite of all this, Markham still found time to dust off a tragedy of his entitled *Herod and Antipas*, which had been in existence since at least 1613, but which he now revised with the help of William Sampson. The play was staged at the Red Bull in 1621 and printed the following year.

In 1622, for no obvious reason other than for money, Gervase Markham undertook to travel on foot from London to Berwick without using bridges, 'boats, Shippe, or other Ingin for water more than an ordinarye Leape staffe or staffe to leape with all neither shoulde swyme any water whatsoever'. For a 55-year-old man, and even given that his colleague and rival Ben Jonson had four years earlier walked to Edinburgh and back, this challenge was frankly bizarre, and many of his acquaintance bet sums of 5 shillings or thereabouts that he would be unable to complete it. None the less, Markham duly set out, and returned later that year bearing a certificate from the mayor of Berwick, only to find that thirty-nine people, many of them actors associated with the Red Bull, refused to pay up. Markham took legal action against them, stating that he had 'groune pore' because of his numerous children and needed the money. The papers, which name numerous actors and where they live, are extant; however, for a long time after their rediscovery in 1910 there was uncertainty about whether the Gervase Markham in question was this man, or his namesake Gervase *Markham (1557–1637), or another Gervase Markham entirely. The fact that the list of defaulters includes several actors of Markham's play, and indeed John Trundle, one of his publishers, seems to settle the matter. Less clear, however, is whether Markham succeeded in recovering the money he was owed.

Markham's last years seem to have been spent in poverty in London. He continued his astonishing productivity, writing on the enrichment of the weald of Kent, on garden design, and—in a series of monographs including *The Souldiers Accidence* (1625)—on military tactics. He also wrote *Honour in his Perfection* (1624), a prose treatise celebrating the past and current military exploits of four aristocratic protestant families. Markham was buried in St Giles Cripplegate, London, on 3 February 1637.

Markham's more literary works have never enjoyed a particularly high reputation, although he was noted as a poet as early as 1598 by Francis Meres in his *Palladis tamia*. For the most part, commentators have sided with Jonson who derided him as 'not of the number of the Faithfull … and but a base fellow' (*Ben Jonson*, ed. C. H. Herford, P. Simpson, and E. Simpson, 11 vols., 1925–51, 1.137), while his lengthy poem on Richard Grenville has suffered in comparisons with Tennyson's, which, however, it may have influenced. On the other hand, his factual works include a wealth of detail on many aspects of day-to-day living. For the social historian, or the re-enactor, Gervase Markham's numerous works are indispensable guides to the practicalities of Renaissance life.

MATTHEW STEGGLE

Sources F. N. L. Poynter, *Bibliography of Gervase Markham, 1568?–1637* (1962) · G. E. Bentley, *The Jacobean and Caroline stage*, 7 vols. (1941–68)
Likenesses B. Reading, line engraving (after T. Cross), BM, NPG · line engraving, BM, NPG; repro. in Poynter, *Bibliography* (1962) [for G. Markham, *The perfect horseman* (1656), frontispiece] · line engraving (after unknown artist), BM, NPG
Wealth at death "dyed poore": Aubrey, *Brief lives* (?late C17)

Markham, Sir Griffin (*b. c.*1565, *d.* in or after 1644), army officer and conspirator, was the eldest son of Thomas Markham (1530–1607) of Ollerton, Nottinghamshire, and his wife, Mary Griffin (1540–*c.*1633), only daughter and heir of Ryce Griffin of Braybrooke and Dingley, Northamptonshire. Thomas Markham was prominent in county society and served as standard bearer in the gentlemen pensioners. Griffin, who seems to have become a Roman Catholic early in life at the prompting of his mother, fought as a volunteer in the Low Countries and France. He was one of those knighted before Rouen by the earl of Essex in 1591, and he was present at the siege of Groningen in 1594.

Having been imprisoned briefly in the Gatehouse prison, London, during 1596, for reasons still obscure, Markham participated in Essex's expedition to Ireland in 1599, holding a cavalry command in Connaught. As a soldier he was well regarded—his cousin Sir John Harington acknowledged him versed in both the theoretical and practical aspects of warfare. By 1603, however, Markham was heavily in debt, frustrated in his suit for the reversion of the keeperships of Bestwood and Clipstone parks, held for life by his father, and convinced that he had been opposed at every turn by the Jesuit faction among the English Catholics. He had by this point alienated many influential county neighbours—the earls of Rutland and Shrewsbury among them—and as early as 1601 was complaining to Robert Cecil about his lack of preferment in Ireland. He had high hopes of better days under James I, but despite some fair promises made to Markham during his journey south to London in April 1603, the king granted the reversion of Bestwood to the earl of Rutland on 9 June. Dismayed and angry, Markham sought a means of revenge. Collaborating with the unstable appellant priest William Watson, and with Lord Cobham's ambitious younger brother, George Brooke, he hatched a plot by which sympathetic Catholics would foregather secretly, surprise the court at Greenwich on midsummer night, kidnap the as yet uncrowned King James, and hold him prisoner in the Tower of London. The monarch once in their hands, they would demand a pardon, toleration of their religion guaranteed by hostages and strongholds across England, and the removal of counsellors identified with Elizabethan persecution. Both Markham and Brooke, in their subsequent confessions, recalled detailed and precise military planning, involving an inescapable degree of bloodshed:

> Brooke confesseth that the time of the surprise was by Markhams appointment to be on midsomer night both for the execucion and the concealing of the companies as they came scattred … that Marcam affirmed to him that he had given a plott of Greenewich Howse to Copley.   (Bodl. Oxf., MS Carte 205, fol. 120)

He solicited support from his brothers, the twins Charles and Thomas, but like so many others they were at best noncommittal.

For all the plotters' lengthy discussions about the offices they would hold in their remodelled England, the fantasy was exploded when their hoped-for army failed to materialize. In the new, uncertain politics of Jacobean England, very few Catholics were prepared to commit treason in support of men like Watson or Markham. The plot, known as the Bye in contrast to the Main, a parallel treason involving Cobham and Sir Walter Ralegh, was swiftly betrayed, both to the Jesuits and to the crown.

Markham fled, and a proclamation was issued for his arrest, describing him as a man with a 'large broad face, of a bleake complexion, a bigge nose, one of his hands is maimed by an hurt in his arme received by the shot of a Bullet' (J. F. Larkin and P. L. Hughes, eds., *Stuart Royal Proclamations*, 1973, 1.43). He was soon arrested, and was committed to the Tower of London on 23 July 1603. Although no complete record of his examinations survives it is clear that he was questioned repeatedly, and that, like Watson, he made a full confession. At his trial in Winchester on 15 November he was inevitably (and correctly) found guilty. However, it is possible that his dignified carriage that day—one observer states that Markham made 'many men sory for him, and my Lord Cecill weepe aboundantly' (BL, Egerton MS 2877, fol. 175v)—and perhaps his fellow conspirator William Clarke's assertion that Markham had been 'over scrupulous' in respect of shedding blood (PRO, SP 14/3/29), swayed the king towards mercy. Like lords Grey and Cobham he was brought to the scaffold on 9 December, only to have the death sentence commuted by royal command. On 19 January Markham was moved to the Fleet prison, and he was exiled shortly afterwards. But he was never pardoned. His lands in Nottinghamshire and Essex were granted to Sir John Harington in June 1604.

For the next forty years Markham wandered the continent, seeking employment as a soldier, and attaching himself to the courts of various German princes. Several of his letters survive in English archives, proof of persistent attempts to clear his name. In or before 1595 he had married Anne, daughter of Peter Roos of Laxton. Her husband banished, Anne contracted a bigamous marriage with her manservant, James Sanford. This irregularity was soon common knowledge, and she was forced to perform penance at Paul's Cross in November 1617. Sir Griffin is last

glimpsed in Vienna, in the spring of 1644, expressing regret that old age now prevents him fighting for his king. It has been argued by some that his rapid exile was a considered move by the privy council, keen to infiltrate English Catholic forces engaged in the Low Countries. While this might be a possible interpretation of the far from complete evidence, Markham's efforts to secure information may have been taken on his own initiative, keen as he was to recover ground irredeemably lost.

MARK NICHOLLS

Sources state papers, *domestic*, Elizabeth, PRO, SP 12 · state papers, *domestic*, James I, PRO, SP 14 · state papers, foreign, Holy Roman empire, PRO, SP 80 · exchequer of receipt: miscellaneous rolls, books and MSS, PRO, E407/56 · Hatfield House, Hertfordshire, Salisbury–Cecil MSS · LPL, MSS 3200, 3205 · BL, Egerton MS 2877, fols. 175-6 · *State trials*, 2.61-5 · W. J. Tighe, 'A Nottinghamshire gentleman in court and country: the career of Thomas Markham of Ollerton, 1530–1607', *Transactions of the Thoroton Society*, 90 (1986), 30-45 · M. Nicholls, 'Treason's reward: the punishment of conspirators in the Bye plot of 1603', *HJ*, 38 (1995), 821-42 · W. A. Shaw, *The knights of England*, 2 vols. (1906) · C. Markham, 'Genealogy of the Markhams', *Herald and Genealogist*, 7 (1873), 318-35 · Markham genealogy, *Proceedings of the Society of Antiquaries of London*, 2nd ser., 1 (1859-61), 10-18 · *Report on the manuscripts of the marquis of Downshire*, 6 vols. in 7, HMC, 75 (1924-95), vols. 5-6 · M. Lunn, 'Chaplains to the English regiment in Spanish Flanders, 1605-6', *Recusant History*, 11 (1971-2), 133-55, esp. 138-48 · *DNB*

Markham, John (*d.* 1409), justice, came of a family which traced its origins back to the twelfth century and was established at East Markham, near Retford, Nottinghamshire. His father was Robert Markham, who may have been a serjeant-at-law under Edward III, and his mother a daughter of Sir John Caunton. Markham became a king's serjeant in January 1383. He was made a justice of the common pleas on 7 July 1396, and sat on the bench until February 1408. He was chosen as one of the triers of petitions in the two parliaments of 1397, and in those of Henry IV, from 1401 to 1407. From the early 1380s he served as justice of assize and gaol delivery on the northern circuit and was a justice of the peace in Nottinghamshire and elsewhere. He was retained as counsel by Henry, earl of Derby, 1391-5, and also by the dean and chapter of Lincoln between about 1389 and 1396. He received a pension from Durham Priory, 1395-6. In 1395 he bought the manors of Bothamsall and Upton, both near East Markham.

Markham was a member of the commission whose advice Henry of Lancaster took, in September 1399, as to the manner in which the change of dynasty should be carried out, and who on 29 September received Richard's renunciation of the crown in the Tower of London. His name does not appear on the rolls of parliament among those of the seven commissioners who next day pronounced sentence upon Richard in the name of parliament, but Chief Justice Thirning, in announcing the sentence to Richard on behalf of his fellow commissioners on 10 October, enumerated Markham among them. In Henry IV's reign Markham served as a justice of the peace in the eastern counties, and he retired from the bench in Hilary term 1408.

With his first wife, Elizabeth, daughter of Sir John and sister and coheir of Sir Hugh Cressy (*d.* 1408), of Hodsock,

Markham had a son Robert, ancestor of William Markham, archbishop of York (1777–1807), and a second son John *Markham (d. 1479) who was chief justice of the king's bench, 1461–9. By this marriage he acquired the manors of Risegate and Bratott in Lincolnshire and a moiety of the manor of Melton in Yorkshire. At some time after 1403 he married Millicent (d. 1419), widow of Sir Nicholas Burdon, and daughter and coheir of Sir Thomas Bekeringe. Markham died on 31 December 1409, and was buried in East Markham church, where his monument still remains with the inscription *Orate pro anima Johannis Markham justiciarii*. His widow later married Sir William Mering. JAMES TAIT, *rev.* ANTHONY TUCK

Sources Baker, *Serjeants* · G. O. Sayles, ed., *Select cases in the court of king's bench*, 7 vols., SeldS, 55, 57–8, 74, 76, 82, 88 (1936–71), vols. 6–7 · S. J. Payling, *Political society in Lancastrian England* (1991) · N. L. Ramsay, 'The English legal profession, c.1340–1450', PhD diss., U. Cam., 1985 · C. Given-Wilson, ed. and trans., *Chronicles of the revolution, 1397–1400: the reign of Richard II* (1993) · *RotP* · Chancery records · Duchy of Lancaster, accounts of John Leventhorp, receiver-general of Henry, earl of Derby, 15–18 Richard II, PRO, DL 28/3/4 · *CIPM*, 19, no. 733 · *Nottinghamshire*, Pevsner (1951)
Likenesses memorial, East Markham church, near Retford, Nottinghamshire
Wealth at death estates; offices and marriages brought considerable wealth: Payling, *Political society*, 39–40

Markham, Sir John (b. after **1399**, d. **1479**), justice, was the second son of John *Markham (d. 1409) a justice of the common pleas. His mother was Elizabeth, sister and coheir of Hugh Cressy of Hodsock, Nottinghamshire. He followed his father's profession, and in 1438 was called from Gray's Inn to the coif. Retained by the duchy of Lancaster from 1438 to 1444, he was appointed king's serjeant on 1 July 1443, promoted to king's bench on 6 February 1444, and appointed chief justice of that court on 13 May 1461, after the accession of Edward IV had sent Sir John Fortescue into political exile. At Edward's coronation Markham was created a knight of the Bath (along with his nephew), and his standing was even sufficient to secure William Yelverton a knighthood to compensate for missing promotion. He continued to be closely involved with Edward, particularly in putting down rebellion in Gloucestershire in 1464. From 1459 to 1468 he sat regularly as a royal adviser in the Lords.

John Markham was paid as chief justice of king's bench to Michaelmas 1468, and the warrant appointing Thomas Billing as his successor on 23 January 1469 states that Markham had been discharged 'by his desire and special requeste', on the grounds of 'his grete age and debilite' (Sutton). However, legal and City of London sources agree that Edward IV sacked Markham. The fullest version of what would be the only dismissal of a chief justice in the fifteenth and sixteenth centuries (other than at a change of monarch) is given in the early sixteenth-century great chronicle of London. Markham had presided in the summer of 1468 in a treason trial which could only obtain the conviction of Sir Thomas Cook, a wealthy draper and former lord mayor of London, on the lesser charge of misprision (concealment). With typical anti-Woodville bias the

chronicle says that Edward took revenge on the chief justice because his wife's relations had wanted to pay off a family grudge as well as enjoy the spoils of Cook's ruin. Among lawyers memories were different. Fortescue (who was abroad at the time) implies that the issue was the admissibility of information obtained by torture; Thomas More's *History of King Richard III* states that Markham 'left his office' rather than concur with the condemnation of Thomas Burdet, although that took place in 1477; Chief Justice Thomas Bromley in 1553 identified the case as that of Walter Walker (1460). But confused though they are, the memories do suggest that more than 'age and weakness' was involved. Markham had ten years to live!

A possible explanation can be conjectured if two other sources are brought in—trial records which hint that Cook probably was guilty, but that the evidence was not there, and the report of Chief Justice William Hussey that Markham (whom he knew) had told Edward IV that a king could not in person arrest anyone on suspicion of treason. Together these suggest that Markham had found himself having to inform the king not only that the court could not on the evidence secure a verdict of treason from a London jury, but that neither could Edward act by prerogative. The story Fortescue heard would fit with this, on the supposition that there had been argument over the prosecution evidence, which is known to have been obtained from the torture of alleged accomplices. Markham continued in office after the trial and kept up pressure on Cook until the autumn. Nevertheless he had failed in the essential duty of the chief justice, namely to give the crown the judicial outcome it wanted within the limits of due process. Deprived of the king's confidence he felt he had to go, with a face-saving excuse and a decent interval before a successor was appointed.

The stories of Markham's dismissal made his name a byword for judicial integrity. Sir Nicholas Throgmorton reminded the chief justice presiding at his own treason trial in 1554 of 'the example of your honourable predecessors Justice Markham and others, which did eschew corrupt judgements, judging directly and sincerely after the law and the principles in the same' (*State trials*, 1.894). How deserved this reputation was in other matters it is hard to say. Markham had been a puisne in 1452 when king's bench began to develop legal fictions in order to secure business, and as chief justice did not challenge them, but nothing suggests that he took the initiative in this. Contemporary correspondence shows Markham involved in legal manoeuvres, in one case agitating for a fee, and in another applying pressure in support of colleagues, but equally he appears as capable of a blunt morality and always active in promoting compromise, not litigation. A contemporary private note describes him as *eximi et praeclari* and 'ryghte noble and famous' (Markham, 125–6).

Markham married Margaret, daughter of Simon Leek of Cotham, Nottinghamshire, granddaughter and heir of Sir John Talbot of Donnington. He lived at Sedgebrook in Lincolnshire and built up a substantial estate in the county and in Rutland. Markham died on 20 March 1479 and was survived by three of his five sons. His heir, Thomas, became insane and his principal executor was his nephew, Sir Robert Markham MP, 'a man of great prowess' who fought for Henry VII at Stoke.   E. W. IVES

Sources C. Markham, *Markham memorials* (1913) • E. W. Ives, *The common lawyers of pre-Reformation England* (1983) • Sainty, *Judges* • Sainty, *King's counsel* • Baker, *Serjeants* • A. F. Sutton, 'Sir Thomas Cook and his "troubles": an investigation', *Guildhall Studies in London History*, 3 (1977–9), 85–108 • M. A. Hicks, 'The case of Sir Thomas Cook, 1468', *EngHR*, 93 (1978), 82–96 • P. Holland, 'Cook's case in history and myth', *Historical Research*, 61 (1988), 21–35 • S. E. Thorne and J. H. Baker, eds., *Readings and moots at the inns of court in the fifteenth century*, 1, SeldS, 71 (1954) • N. Davis, ed., *Paston letters and papers of the fifteenth century*, 2 vols. (1971–6) • C. Ross, *Edward IV* (1974) • M. Blatcher, *The court of king's bench, 1450–1550: a study in self-help* (1978) • M. Hastings, *The court of common pleas in fifteenth century England* (1947) • G. O. Sayles, ed., *Select cases in the court of king's bench*, 7, SeldS, 88 (1971) • C. Rawcliffe, *The Staffords, earls of Stafford and dukes of Buckingham, 1394–1521*, Cambridge Studies in Medieval Life and Thought, 3rd ser., 11 (1978) • *The Plumpton letters and papers*, ed. J. Kirby, CS, 5th ser., 8 (1996) • A. H. Thomas and I. D. Thornley, eds., *The great chronicle of London* (1938) • *State trials*, vol. 1 • St Thomas More, *The history of King Richard III*, ed. R. S. Sylvester (1963), vol. 2 of *The Yale edition of the complete works of St Thomas More*

Markham, Sir John (*b.* before **1486**, *d.* **1559**), soldier and member of parliament, was the eldest son of Sir John Markham of Cotham, Nottinghamshire, whose ancestors had been established in Great Markham since the twelfth century, and his wife, Alice, daughter of Sir William Skipwith. He inherited lands in Nottinghamshire and Lincolnshire worth about £450 a year on the death of his father on 28 February 1508. His apprenticeship as a soldier and courtier had been served in the household of Margaret Beaufort, countess of Richmond and Derby. Markham joined Henry VIII's French expedition of 1513 and was knighted at the surrender of Tournai on 25 September 1513.

As a prominent local man Markham served on many commissions in Nottinghamshire, including those for the subsidy (1512, 1523–4) and musters (1513, 1524); he was sheriff in 1518–19 and 1526–7 and JP from 1521 until his death. In 1520 he was named in a papal indulgence obtained by his cousin, Sir John Willoughby, in Rome. Markham probably entered parliament in 1529, serving throughout the 1530s. He attended Henry VIII in Calais in 1532, and was server at the coronation of Anne Boleyn. A friend of Archbishop Cranmer, who praised his devotion to 'God's word' (*Miscellaneous Writings*, 358), Markham was actively involved in the dissolution of the monasteries, and was present at the execution of the prior of Lenton and two monks in 1538. Along with George Talbot, fourth earl of Shrewsbury, he held Newark against the Lincolnshire rebels in 1536, and was a royal commissioner at the subsequent trials. By March 1537 Sir William Parr could report that 'no shire is in better quietness', and he praised Markham as one of those who had 'done good service at their great charges' (*LP Henry VIII*, 12, no. 639). In 1539 John Marshall reported to Cromwell how 'The parts of Notts and Lincolnshire adjoining Newark upon Trent are much ruled by one Sir John Marchaam' (ibid., 14/1, no. 295).

Despite Markham's enthusiastic support for the religious changes rewards in pensions added little to his inheritance. His friendship with Thomas Manners, first earl of Rutland, dates from the 1530s, when they were involved in a long-running battle to break the hold of the bishop of Lincoln, and secure a charter of incorporation for Newark. In 1542, when Rutland was nominated lord warden of the marches, Markham was appointed to his inner council. He served in Scotland in the 1545 expedition of Edward Seymour, first earl of Hertford. The latter, as Protector Somerset, secured Markham's return to the parliament of 1547. The high point of Sir John Markham's career came in 1549 when he was appointed lieutenant of the Tower. By 1551 his prisoners included Somerset and his brother-in-law Sir Michael Stanhope, casualties of the *coup d'état* of October 1549. Markham was dismissed on 31 October 1551 for overgenerous treatment of his prisoners and sympathy towards the recently rearrested former protector. He was present at the funeral of Edward VI, but lived in quiet retirement during Mary I's reign, though in 1557 he led a Nottinghamshire levy of 300 men to Berwick. Rutland secured his return to parliament as one of the knights of the shire for Nottinghamshire at the beginning of Elizabeth's reign. He died probably during summer 1559, for his will was made on 1 April and proved on 28 October 1559.

Sir John Markham was married three times: first to Anne, daughter of Sir George Neville, with whom he had three sons; second to Margery, daughter of Ralph Longford; and third, about 1521 to Anne, *née* Strelley (*d.* 1554), widow of Richard Stanhope of Rampton, with whom he had two further sons and three daughters. His grandson Robert succeeded him in a bare inheritance, owing to provisions made in lands and goods for the children of the third marriage. He was commemorated in a short poem by his son-in-law, the younger John Harington (*d.* 1582).

ALAN CAMERON, *rev.* JONATHAN HUGHES

Sources HoP, *Commons, 1509–58*, 2.568–70 • C. R. Markham, *Markham memorials* (1913) • *CSP dom.*, 1547–80 • *CPR*, 1547–60 • will, PRO, PROB 11/50, Chaynay • *Miscellaneous writings and letters of Thomas Cranmer*, ed. J. E. Cox, Parker Society, [18] (1846) • R. E. Hughey, ed., *The Arundel Harington manuscript of Tudor poetry*, 2 vols. (1960), 1 • *LP Henry VIII*, 12, no. 639; 14/1, no. 295

Markham, John (**1761–1827**), naval officer, second son of William *Markham (*bap.* 1719, *d.* 1807), archbishop of York, and Sarah, daughter of John Goddard, a Rotterdam merchant, was born in Westminster on 13 June 1761. At the age of eight he went to Westminster School where his father was headmaster. In March 1775 he entered the navy on the *Romney*, with Captain George Elphinstone, and in her he made a voyage to Newfoundland; in March 1776 he followed Elphinstone to the *Perseus*, going out to join Lord Howe at New York, from where he sailed for the West Indies in February 1777. During this time he twice acted as prize-master. On a third occasion, in May 1777, during a violent gale, with a sinking ship and a drunken crew, Markham prevented prisoners retaking the prize until her crew were rescued by a passing vessel; some months later in England, Markham found his family in mourning for him, Elphinstone having written that he had been lost with the prize.

In March 1779 Markham was appointed to the *Phoenix*, and in July he was moved into the *Roebuck*, with Sir Andrew Snape Hamond, in which he returned to North America. Hamond appointed him acting lieutenant, and in May 1780 Admiral Marriot Arbuthnot, who had hoisted his flag on the *Roebuck* during the siege of Charles Town, gave Markham a commission as the ship's first lieutenant. In April 1781 he was moved into the *Royal Oak*, and in August Admiral Thomas Graves took him as first lieutenant of the *London*, his flagship. In her Markham was present in the battle off Cape Henry on 5 September, and afterwards he went to Jamaica, where, in March 1782, Sir Peter Parker promoted him to command the fireship *Volcano*. In May Sir George Brydges Rodney moved him to the sloop *Zebra* and sent him out to cruise off Cape Tiburon.

On 22 May Markham fell in with a brig flying a French ensign. He chased her, and she hoisted a union jack at the fore; Markham remained suspicious and fired into her. But it then appeared that she was a cartel, and had meant to display a flag of truce. On the complaint of the French lieutenant in command, Markham was tried by court martial and cashiered, but Rodney, after reviewing the evidence, reinstated him, and the king in council, on the report of the Admiralty, completely restored him on 13 November 1782. Indeed on 3 January 1783 he was promoted post captain.

From 1783 to 1786 Markham commanded the *Sphynx* in the Mediterranean. He was then on half pay for seven years, when he travelled in France, Sweden, Russia, and North America. In June 1793 he was appointed to the *Blonde*, in which, after a few months' service in the channel, he went out to the West Indies with Sir John Jervis (later earl of St Vincent), and took part in the reduction of Martinique. The *Blonde* was then sent home with dispatches, and during the summer of 1794 she was attached to the squadron under Admiral George Montagu, or cruising among the Channel Islands and on the French coast. In August Markham was moved into the *Hannibal*, and in May 1795 he was again sent out to the West Indies, where he was met by the news that a younger brother, David, colonel of the 20th regiment, had been killed at Port-au-Prince on 26 March. From here, in common with many others, Markham was invalided; more than a quarter of his ship's company died, and another quarter was committed to hospital. On his return home in 1796 he married (27 November) the Hon. Maria (*d.* 1810), daughter of the late George *Rice, politician, and his widow, Baroness Dinevor; they had three sons, including Frederick *Markham, army officer, and a daughter.

In March 1797 Markham commissioned the *Centaur* at Woolwich, and during the following months he sat on many courts martial arising from the mutiny at the Nore. He did not get to sea until September, and was then employed during a stormy winter on the south coast of Ireland. In May 1798 he sailed to join Lord St Vincent, off Cadiz, from where he was detached with Commodore

John Thomas Duckworth whom he supported in the capture of Minorca in November. Between May and August 1799 the *Centaur* also took part in the vain chase round the Mediterranean of the French fleet under Admiral Bruix, who eventually returned into Brest. When the bulk of his pursuers retired to the Mediterranean station, the *Centaur* remained in the channel and participated in the blockade of Brest. In 1800 Lord Bridport was relieved of the channel command by Lord St Vincent, with whom Markham shared a political association with Lord Lansdowne. When, in February 1801, St Vincent was appointed first lord of the Admiralty, he selected Markham as one of his colleagues at the board. For the next three years Markham's career was identified with St Vincent's. In November 1801, on the death of Lord Hugh Seymour, he was elected MP for Portsmouth, and became the representative of the Admiralty in the House of Commons. He retired from the Admiralty with St Vincent in May 1804, but returned to it in January 1806 as a colleague of Lord Howick, and afterwards, until March 1807, of Thomas Grenville. He then practically retired from public life, though he continued to sit in parliament for Portsmouth until 1826, with one break from 1818 to 1820.

Markham became a rear-admiral on 23 April 1804, vice-admiral (25 October 1809), and admiral (12 August 1819). In 1826 his failing health compelled him to retire from public life altogether. He was advised to winter in a milder climate and left England in September, travelling by easy stages to reach Naples in January 1827. There he died (13 February) and was buried (27 February).

J. K. LAUGHTON, *rev.* ROGER MORRISS

Sources C. R. Markham, *A naval career during the old war: being a narrative of the life of Admiral John Markham* (1883) · B. Murphy and R. G. Thorne, 'Markham, John', HoP, *Commons, 1790–1820* · GM, 1st ser., 97/1 (1827), 363 · D. Syrett and R. L. DiNardo, *The commissioned sea officers of the Royal Navy, 1660–1815*, rev. edn, Occasional Publications of the Navy RS, 1 (1994)
Archives U. Durham L., letters to Charles, second Earl Grey

Markham, Peter (*fl.* **1757–1758**), physician and writer, exposed with some force the abuses in the manufacture of bread during the great scarcity of 1757. Nothing is known of Markham's biography or medical qualifications, though his writings did much to attract the attention of parliament to the subject and some of his suggestions were adopted in the Act for the Due Making of Bread (31 Geo. II c. 29).

Markham wrote three pamphlets on the adulteration of bread by millers and bakers. His first pamphlet, *Poison Detected, or, Frightful Truths, and Alarming to the British Metropolis* (1757), published anonymously, dealt with the adulteration of bread but also drew attention to the unwholesome methods of colouring tea and preparing wine and beer. This pamphlet was subsequently counter-attacked by Emmanuel Collins's parody, *Lying Detected, or, Some of the Most Frightful Untruths that Ever Alarmed the British Metropolis* (1758). Markham's two other works were published under his own name in the pamphlet war that grew out of the bread controversy. It has been argued that Markham may have had genuine concern for the health of the public but his accounts of the abuses in the food industry were in fact 'biased and distorted' (Drummond and Wilbraham, 225).

W. A. S. HEWINS, *rev.* JEFFREY HERRLE

Sources J. C. Drummond and A. Wilbraham, *The Englishman's food: a history of five centuries of English diet* (1939) · *Monthly Review*, 18 (1758), 493 [bks received] · H. Higgs, *Bibliography of economics, 1751–1775* (1935)

Markham, Violet Rosa (1872–1959), public servant, was born on 3 October 1872 at Brimington Hall near Chesterfield, Derbyshire, the fifth of five children (three sons and two daughters) of Charles Markham (1823–1888), engineer and managing director of a coal and iron company, and his wife, Rosa (*c.*1840–1912), daughter of Sir Joseph *Paxton. Markham's family were staunch Liberals, and Markham was a lifelong, although not always very enthusiastic, Liberal. Initially she was strongly influenced by her mother, but over the years she gradually shed many of her mother's views, such as religious scepticism (she gained inspiration from Herbert Hensley Henson's sermons at St Margaret's, Westminster) and opposition to women's suffrage.

Social reform, empire, and anti-suffragism Markham was educated at home, apart from the period from 1889 to 1890, when she spent eighteen months at West Heath School, Ham Common, Surrey. She sat no public examinations, although it was a growing practice for girls in her position to do so, and she received no further formal education. She was, however, widely read. As a young woman she took up unpaid charitable work, visiting the workhouse, and then in 1897 she was elected to the Chesterfield school board.

Life would have continued along the well-trodden path for an unmarried middle-class woman but for a bequest in 1901 from a friend of her father which enabled Markham to establish her own settlement (where middle-class people lived and worked in order to help the local poor) in Chesterfield. She did not share the Charity Organization Society's view that poverty results largely from individual failing, and she was concerned that such views should not dominate the training of those entering social work. At the end of the First World War, along with social workers such as Elizabeth Macadam, Markham helped to shape the nature of social work training in Britain.

More significantly for Markham, the legacy meant that she was able to take a house in London at 8 Gower Street, and to launch herself on a financially independent metropolitan lifestyle. She built up contacts in London and around the empire with politicians, civil servants, and journalists such as Lord Cromer, Lord Milner, Leo Amery, Mackenzie King, J. A. Spender, John Buchan, and Sir Robert Morant. These contacts later provided her with numerous opportunities to take on government work, by personal recommendation and appointment, never by election or open competition. She used her personal contacts not only to further her own position but also to press her views on government. In the 1930s, for instance, she

Violet Rosa Markham (1872–1959), by unknown photographer, 1938

attempted unsuccessfully to influence cabinet appointments (through Thomas Jones) and policy (through Neville Chamberlain).

Throughout her life foreign travel played an important part in shaping Markham's views. On leaving school she had stayed with a French family in Paris; she enjoyed annual family holidays in Cannes and with her mother in 1895 she visited Egypt, where she first met empire administrators, including Lord Cromer. There she read Arthur Milner's *England in Egypt*, which turned her into a staunch imperialist. Her enthusiasm for the empire took her to South Africa in 1899, which prompted her to write several studies of the country: *South Africa, Past and Present* (1900), *The New Era in South Africa, with an Examination of the Chinese Labour Question* (1904), and *The South African Scene* (1913). Her books on South Africa aimed to promote links between the two countries and to underline Britain's responsibilities and interests in South Africa, to which she returned in 1912 and 1924.

Strongly committed to the British empire, Markham believed in a hierarchy of races, with 'stronger' races 'guiding' 'weaker' ones towards social progress, and wrote in 1900 that it was both the 'mission' and the 'fate' of the British to govern. Her writings and activities supported the imperial cause and led to her fellowship of the

Royal Geographical Society and an increasing number of contacts and friends who would prove useful in her subsequent public career. Under the influence of Mackenzie King whom she met in Canada in 1905, her views on the empire evolved from seeing it as an instrument for spreading British values of justice, integrity, and good government to seeing it as a mutual system of support within a commonwealth of nations. In the 1920s Mackenzie King arranged for Markham to represent Canada at the International Labour Organization, for which Canadians heavily criticized him. So close were they in outlook that when Mackenzie King visited Britain in 1937 for the coronation he asked her to help with his speech writing.

In Edwardian Britain, Markham worked with such women as May Tennant, Lucy Deane Streatfield, Lady Dilke, Gertrude Tuckwell, and Mary MacArthur in a campaign to end the appalling working conditions of women in what were known as the 'sweated trades'. It was as a leader of the anti-suffrage campaign, however, that Markham made a public splash. Her anti-suffrage convictions were based primarily on the belief that parliamentary votes for women would increase the number of inexperienced and ignorant voters; instead, as she argued at a major anti-suffrage rally at the Albert Hall (28 February 1912), women should contribute to local government, so complementing men's role in national politics. She believed that a strong sense of duty, coupled with appropriate education, was essential for good citizenship, but also that citizenship was gendered. There were contradictions in Markham's advocacy of the anti-suffrage cause, given her strong interest in national and even imperial politics. During the First World War, as she later explained, Markham's opposition to votes for women was moderated by a growing knowledge of the disabilities from which women suffered, and from a developing belief that the country could not be divided between the enfranchised and unenfranchised, especially as political rights for women were based on spiritual as well as political principles. Even so, she would have liked everyone to pass a test in citizenship before voting.

Despite this change of mind on the suffrage question, Markham continued to advocate different roles for women and men. While she was keen to see expanded employment opportunities for middle-class women, she never wavered in her belief that women's chief joy in life was procreation. She saw an absence of children in her own life as something for which she needed to seek compensation, and she found it in writing.

Marriage and war work The First World War was significant for Markham's private and public life. On 11 February 1915 she married James Carruthers (1876–1936), a career army officer and racehorse owner, to whom she seems to have been happily married until his death. She kept her maiden name for public work and never allowed marriage to interfere with her public life. There were no children.

Sir Robert Morant recommended that Markham serve on the national relief fund, set up in the early days of the war to relieve poverty resulting from the war, and she seized the opportunity. From this committee she then side-stepped to the central committee on women's employment, which promoted employment for working-class girls and women. It continued after the war as the central committee on women's training and employment, with responsibility for training schemes for unemployed females; it rapidly confined its schemes to domestic service, unpopular with working-class girls, but thought to be of benefit to the middle classes, who complained about the shortage of good domestic servants.

Early in 1917 Markham was appointed deputy director of the women's section of the national service department (NSD), which was charged with co-ordinating military and civilian recruitment. May Tennant was director of the women's section, and Neville Chamberlain overall director. Interdepartmental rivalries with the War Office and Ministry of Labour, and personality clashes, quickly surfaced, which meant that the NSD never fulfilled its initial role. In August 1917 Tennant and Markham resigned, bitter towards Chamberlain, who they believed had not supported them sufficiently in their negotiations with other departments. In 1917 she was appointed a Companion of Honour, one of the first to receive this newly created distinction.

Markham's services remained in demand for government inquiries. Many in authority feared that war heightened passions and lowered morals. Women, not men, were the focus of concern, indicating a reinforcement of double moral standards in wartime, rather than a growing equality between women and men. Allegations about the immorality of WAACs stationed in France reached such a level that the government appointed a committee of inquiry, with Markham as honorary secretary. The committee visited France for eight days and concluded that the allegations had no foundation. She did not escape gossip, however, as her husband went to visit her and was found in her bedroom, leading to rumours about Miss Markham, who had come to investigate other women's morals, entertaining an officer in her bedroom!

Public service after 1918 After standing unsuccessfully, and unenthusiastically, in the 1918 general election in her deceased brother's Mansfield constituency as an Asquithian Liberal, Markham went in March 1919 to live in Germany with her husband, who was serving with the army of occupation. On returning to Britain in 1921 she wrote about her experiences in *A Woman's Watch on the Rhine*.

In the early 1920s Markham resumed her local and national work. She was appointed to the lord chancellor's advisory committee on women justices of the peace (1919–20) and was among the first women to be appointed a JP. She was a member of an industrial court from 1920 and of the Sheffield cutlery trade board; she was a local councillor in Chesterfield and from 1927 to 1928 mayor of Chesterfield. Although heavily involved in government work, she also continued to pursue charitable work, seeing a significant role for voluntary welfare alongside state provision.

In 1934 the Unemployment Assistance Board was created to administer a national system of means-tested relief to the unemployed. Markham was appointed the statutory woman member; her close friends Thomas Jones and Sir Henry Betterton also sat on the board. In 1937 she became deputy chair. She took a special interest in unemployed women in general and older unemployed women in particular. The work of the board continued during the war, but shifted its attention (as risks shifted from unemployment to the blitz) to providing cash payments for food, shelter, and clothes to those bombed out.

During the Second World War Markham—now a well-known figure in governmental circles—sat on the 18B advisory committee which heard appeals against the internment of aliens and fascists. Again, she was involved in a government investigation into the morals of working-class women in the auxiliary services. Ernest Bevin, the minister of labour and national service, feared that rumours of rampant immorality were dampening recruitment. The report of the committee on amenities and welfare conditions in the three women's services, appointed in March 1942 and chaired by Markham, bluntly refuted the allegations in an attempt to reassure public opinion. In both wars the focus of attention was on the morals of working-class women, not men, and on both occasions, following superficial investigations, the committees failed to find any evidence of 'immorality'.

Markham had grown up surrounded by domestic servants with whom she developed close emotional ties, and the domestic service 'problem' was a subject close to her heart. It is one of the few examples of her acknowledging that the organization of life in the private sphere significantly influences women's ability to function in the public one. Her reliance on domestic servants was reflected in much of her public work. Unemployed girls were prepared only for domestic service by the central committee on women's training and employment. When on the Unemployment Assistance Board she took a close interest in domestic service for unemployed women; and during the Second World War she co-wrote, with Florence Hancock, an official *Report on Postwar Organisation of Private Domestic Employment* (1945), which recommended formal qualifications for domestic service and a home-help service for all who might require it. Markham wanted to provide domestic support which would enable middle-class women to contribute to public life.

Markham advocated civic duty underpinned by education, which she herself pursued through her local and national government work, extensive reading, and foreign travel. Education for better citizenship always remained high on Markham's agenda. One of her last public activities was to visit Germany during the allied occupation following the Second World War to talk to German women about education for active citizenship.

As well as her political publications Markham, who was a fellow of the Royal Historical Society, wrote *Romanesque France* (1929), *Paxton and the Bachelor Duke* (1935), *May Tennant: a Portrait* (1949), *Friendship's Harvest* (1956), and *Return Passage: the Autobiography of Violet R. Markham C. H.* (1953). In her autobiography she explains her views on women's suffrage, imperialism, and citizenship. She provides an efficient but not especially illuminating account of her public and private life; she makes brief complimentary comments about her husband's gaiety but does not weave him into the unfolding story of her life—the reader learns more about her dogs than about her husband—emphasizing that he always left her free to pursue her public work. She received a Sheffield University honorary LittD (1936), an Edinburgh LLD (1938), and the freedom of Chesterfield (1952).

Violet Markham influenced national and local politics for over half a century, yet she supported a political party which collapsed under her, she was never an MP or career civil servant, she had less formal education than might be expected, and her husband provided her with no entrées into political circles. Her family and domestic circumstances, her commitment to Liberalism, and her views on the appropriate role for women in society influenced the causes with which she became involved. Her class position, financial independence, and personal contacts provided her with opportunities for manoeuvring herself into positions of potential influence. She possessed attributes, such as being a good public speaker and an effective committee member, which ensured that she was able to exploit her opportunities to participate in running both voluntary and governmental bodies. She died on 2 February 1959 at her home, Moon Green, near Wittersham, Kent.

HELEN JONES

Sources V. R. Markham, *Return passage* (1953) · *Duty and citizenship: the correspondence and political papers of Violet Markham, 1896–1953*, ed. H. Jones (1994) · J. Lewis, *Women and social action in Victorian and Edwardian England* (1991), chap. 5 · M. Bell, '"Citizenship not charity": Violet Markham on nature, society and the state in Britain and South Africa', *Geography and imperialism, 1820–1940*, ed. M. Bell, R. Butler, and M. Heffernan (1995), 189–220 · T. Jones, *A diary with letters, 1931–1950* (1954) · B. Harrison, *Separate spheres: the opposition to women's suffrage in Britain* (1978) · DNB · Burke, *Peerage* (1939)

Archives BLPES, corresp. and papers · NA Canada, corresp. | Balliol Oxf., corresp. with A. L. Smith · BLPES, accounts and notebooks of her mother · Bodl. Oxf., corresp. with L. G. Curtis · Girton Cam., corresp. with Eugenie Strong · Mitchell L., NSW, letters to G. E. Morrison · NL Scot., letters to Lord Haldane · NL Wales, corresp. with Thomas Jones · RGS, letters to Sir David Gill · University of Cape Town Library, letters to Patrick Duncan, BC 294 · University of Cape Town Library, letters to J. Newton Thompson

Likenesses photograph, 1938, repro. in Markham, *Return passage* [see illus.] · photograph (aged two), repro. in Markham, *Return passage* · photographs, London School of Economics

Wealth at death £201,206 14s. 4d.: probate, 1959, CGPLA Eng. & Wales

Markham, William (*bap.* 1719, *d.* 1807), archbishop of York, was baptized at Kinsale, in the county of Cork, on 9 April 1719, the eldest of the four children of Major William Markham (*d.* 1771) and his wife, Elizabeth (1686–1772), a distant cousin and the daughter of George Markham of Worksop Lodge, Nottinghamshire. His father was an army officer of literary tastes who ran a school to supplement his half pay. The family claimed descent from the Markhams of Cotham.

After early education at home from his father Markham was admitted to Westminster School as a home boarder

William Markham (*bap.* 1719, *d.* 1807), by Benjamin West, *c.*1775

on 21 June 1733; there his academic talents were complemented by skills as an oarsman and a boxer. In 1738 he obtained a studentship at Christ Church, Oxford, and matriculated on 6 June 1738. He took the degrees of BA (13 May 1742), MA (28 March 1745), BCL (20 November 1752), and DCL (24 November 1752). He held the college lectureship in rhetoric from 1747 to 1750 and was appointed junior censor the following year. Markham's literary talents and wide-ranging classical scholarship flowered during these years at the house. His 'Judicium paridis', a Latin verse version of Shakespeare's 'Seven Ages of Man', was published in volume 2 of Vincent Bourne's *Musae Anglicanae* in 1741, while other specimens of his Latin verse appeared in the second volume of *Carmina quadragesimalia* (1748).

After ordination and continental travel Markham followed his father's example and took up teaching. In 1753 the headship of Westminster School fell vacant on the retirement of Dr John Nicholl, and Markham's familiarity with the school and his high academic standing secured him the post. There he remained for the next eleven years, taking what the *Public Advertiser* in 1755 called 'the first Seminary of School Learning in Europe' through its two hundredth anniversary in 1760. Markham established a reputation as one of the most formidable headmasters of the eighteenth century, though more for his managerial than for his pedagogical skills. Teaching was never Markham's first priority but he had an undeniable presence in the classroom. One of his pupils, Jeremy Bentham (Westminster, 1755–60, and himself the son of a Christ Church canon), famously described Markham in the form room as

'an object of adoration' (*Works of Jeremy Bentham*, 10.30). Many other members of the later Georgian élite received their schooling at his hands. Without personal wealth or high birth Markham sedulously but never fawningly cultivated the powerful throughout his life. He watched over the interests of former pupils, while many of them tended his.

Markham meanwhile accumulated church preferments, thanks to the friendly interest extended by that old Westminster, the duke of Newcastle. He was appointed chaplain to George II in 1756, and Bishop Richard Trevor nominated him to the second prebendal stall in Durham Cathedral on 22 June 1759 (installed 20 July). There were murmurings that the headmaster was putting personal interests before those of the school, and indeed by 1763 Markham was angling for a crown appointment. He eventually resigned the headmastership (pleading ill health) on 8 March 1764 but only received a fresh post towards the end of the Grenville ministry when the Rochester deanery fell vacant. Markham was instituted as dean on 20 February 1765 and in the same year was presented by the chapter to the vicarage of Boxley, Kent. His stay at Rochester was brief. The death of David Gregory in September 1767 offered an opening for Markham to return to Christ Church, and he exchanged one deanery for another the following month with the blessing of both Newcastle and Archbishop Secker. Thus began a decade in academic office which saw Markham at his most creative as a teacher and administrator. He brought to Christ Church some of his best former pupils at Westminster and strengthened the historic connection between the two institutions. He had ambitious reform plans for the college which he summarized for Charles Jenkinson: 'My great object is to bring the noblemen and gentlemen commoners to the same attendance on College duties, and the same habits of industry with the inferior members' (11 Jan 1768, BL, Add. MS 38457, fol. 11). Such changes added signally to the college's reputation, along with the institution of public lectures, the addition of new authors to the curriculum in Greek studies and ancient history, and the reform of 'collections' to underpin the programme as a whole.

It was not long before the ambitious dean enhanced his status further with a bishopric, thanks to the sponsorship of Lord Mansfield. Markham succeeded Edmund Keene as bishop of Chester and was consecrated on 17 February 1771 at the Chapel Royal, Whitehall; he thereupon resigned Boxley and his Durham prebendal stall but retained the Christ Church deanery *in commendam* until 1777 to supplement the £1000 annual income derived from Chester. Markham became a non-resident prelate with responsibility for a huge diocese despite minimal pastoral experience. He made a visit to Chester every summer and confirmed extensively but otherwise his diocesan duties took their place alongside his other responsibilities.

Markham's friendship with Lord Mansfield and his pedagogic reputation secured him the post of preceptor to the young prince of Wales and his brother Prince Frederick, bishop of Osnaburg, on 12 April 1771 (Walpole, *Memoirs*, 4.311). After five years in that difficult role Markham left office in May 1776 in the 'nursery revolution' precipitated by the resignation of the boys' governor, Lord Holdernesse. Markham took the side of Cyril Jackson, his subpreceptor, in his disagreement with Holdernesse. The prince of Wales had got on well with Markham's family and wanted the bishop to remain in post. George III, however, would not make this concession to the wishes of his son, whom he saw as primarily responsible for the affair. The prince remained on very cordial terms with Markham for the rest of his life.

Compensation from the crown was not long delayed. Markham's appointment to the archbishopric of York was announced on 21 December 1776 (enthroned by proxy 28 January 1777). He was also appointed lord high almoner and sworn of the privy council. Within weeks of having received office Markham, on 21 February 1777, had preached a sermon before the Society for the Propagation of the Gospel in Foreign Parts (in the parish church of St Mary-le-Bow) on the calamities that had overtaken Anglicans in the American colonies, and had argued for deploying the machinery of state to assist the spread of Christianity. The sermon was interpreted by opposition politicians as a bellicose endorsement of the government's coercive policy, and Markham found himself at the centre of a political storm for his alleged high-flown monarchism and veiled threats to dissenters. On 30 May in the House of Lords, Markham replied 'with great warmth' to the attacks made on him by the duke of Grafton and Lord Shelburne for preaching doctrines allegedly subversive of the constitution—'pernicious' doctrines, according to Lord Chatham's subsequent denunciation (Cobbett, *Parl. hist.*, 19.327–8, 344–50, 491). Markham received much private support from close friends like Viscount Stormont, who was delighted that his sermon opposed the 'senseless licentious sophistry' of the day 'with all the Powers of Reason enforced by that irresistible Eloquence that Virtue alone bestows' (letter, 21 May 1777, Mansfield muniments, National Register of Archives for Scotland, 0220). Markham derived only limited comfort from this backing. He was enduringly offended by the insults and was one of the four peers who signed the protest against the third reading of the Chatham annuity bill on 2 June 1778 (Rogers, 2.177–8).

After this incident Markham's conduct in parliament was more circumspect and he rarely spoke in the Lords. He supported Lord North's administration until its fall in 1782, and subsequently that of Pitt the younger, but his defence of Anglican interests was low key and private; he had no wish to draw on himself afresh the public hostility that had undoubtedly damaged his standing. Even so Markham's personal courage was never in doubt. *En route* for the House of Lords on 2 June 1780 he was attacked by the protestant petitioners and, subsequently hearing of Lord Mansfield's danger, he tore down from a committee room to rescue his friend. His town house in Bloomsbury

Square adjoined that of the lord chief justice; in a letter to his son John, Markham offers a graphic description of the attack on Mansfield's property by the Gordon rioters, and of his own narrow escape from the violence of the mob (D. F. Markham, 60–65).

John *Markham, who rose to the rank of admiral of the blue, was the second son of Markham and his wife, Sarah (1738–1814), daughter of John Goddard, a wealthy English merchant of Rotterdam, whom he had married on 16 June 1759 (the settlement was worth £10,000). They had a large family of six boys and seven girls, of whom eleven survived. Markham was known as an affectionate family man and Bishopthorpe had an atmosphere 'of kindness and good-humour' in his time (Warner, 1.295). He put much effort into finding professions or eligible marriage partners for his children. The eldest child, William (*d.* 1 Jan 1815), was appointed private secretary to his father's school contemporary Warren Hastings. This connection inextricably involved the Markham family in the impeachment of the former governor-general before the House of Lords. Markham made no secret of his support for Hastings and once again drew criticism from the whig opposition. On 25 May 1793 he interrupted Burke's cross-examination of defence witnesses to accuse the managers of treating James Peter Auriol, former secretary to the supreme council and a relative of Archbishop Robert Hay Drummond, as no better than a pickpocket. He went on: 'if Robespierre and Marat were in the Managers Box they could not say any thing more inhuman and more against all sentiments of honor and morality' (BL, Add. MS 24243, fol. 56). Markham was highly agitated. His daughter Georgina was dying, and that fact curtailed discussion of his intervention in the House of Commons. The archbishop was undeterred from complaining again about the conduct of the trial; on 24 March 1795 he declared that Hastings had been 'treated not as if he were a gentleman, whose cause is before you, but as if you were trying a horse-stealer' (Bond, 4.lxi). He was one of only three prelates to vote Hastings not guilty on all charges, and his staunch support for Hastings wrecked what little remained of his friendship with Edmund Burke.

Markham's thirty-year tenure of the York archdiocese was one of modest distinction. To York Minster he gave new velvet coverings for the high altar, pulpit, and archbishop's throne, and he also encouraged repairs at Ripon and Southwell minsters. His visitational activities were restricted by comparison with predecessors like Drummond and Thomas Herring (there were none after 1791), a fair reflection of his pastoral limitations. Respected for his integrity and sense of honour rather than loved by his clergy he took some time to overcome the rumpus caused by his early public criticism of those priests who had joined the associating movement for parliamentary and economical reform. He devoted much energy to securing key positions in the see for his sons; George was appointed dean of York in 1802, Robert held the archdeaconry of York, and Osborn was named chancellor of the diocese in 1795. Such nepotism was conventional in the late Georgian church, Markham had a large family to provide for, and his status as senior archbishop in England after 1783 and through the war years with France was unassailable. He held back from a conspicuous metropolitan role but was uncompromising in his assertion of the rights of the established church. Markham was not an inspired spiritual leader. As one obituarist closely observed: 'His religion was a religion of the mind; practised in all the concerns of life, without austerity, and free from ostentation' (*GM*).

Markham died at his house in South Audley Street, London, on 3 November 1807, and was buried on the 11th in the north cloister of Westminster Abbey, where a monument was raised to his memory by his grandchildren (he had no fewer than fifty, and three great-grandchildren). His widow died in Mortimer Street, Cavendish Square, London, on 26 January 1814, aged seventy-five, and was buried beside him on 3 February. Throughout his life Markham retained a headmasterly presence that could, to his political opponents, appear overbearing and pompous; to his friends it recalled his father's martial bearing and was well suited to the dignity of the offices he filled. Beneath the surface was a man of strong emotions which occasionally, as in the trial of Warren Hastings, broke through, often in the form of petulance. The elder Richard Burke told his nephew that Markham's 'manner exceeded the matter. Such furious agitation, and bodily convulsion, not producing death were wonderful' (*Correspondence*, 7.369). In the 1770s, because of his political allegiances, he was the butt of a number of satirical cartoons. Unfortunately for Markham historians have turned first to Horace Walpole's unflattering view of him: 'a pert, arrogant man', as the *Memoirs of the Reign of George III* describes him (4.206), that 'warlike metropolitan archbishop Turpin' (Walpole, *Corr.*, 28.313). A much fairer assessment was offered by Samuel Parr, no political ally of Markham's, who singled out inertia for preventing the prelate from making that mark on British public life, either as a scholar or as an archbishop, to which his native abilities entitled him: his 'powers of mind, reach of thought, memory, learning, scholarship, and taste were of the very first order, but he was indolent, and his composition wanted this powerful aiguillon' (D. F. Markham, 66). Apart from his verse, Markham published only sermons.

NIGEL ASTON

Sources C. Markham, *A memoir of Archbishop Markham, 1719–1807* (1906) • D. F. Markham, *History of the Markham family* (1854) • C. Markham, *Markham memorials* (1913) • *GM*, 1st ser., 77 (1807), 1802–3 • *Annual Register* (1806), 789 • J. Sargeaunt, *Annals of Westminster School* (1898) • J. Field, *The king's nurseries: the story of Westminster School* (1987) • *The works of Jeremy Bentham*, ed. J. Bowring, [new edn], 11 vols. (1843–59), vol. 10, p. 30 • Foster, *Alum. Oxon.* • *Fasti Angl., 1541–1857*, [Bristol], 83 • *Fasti Angl., 1541–1857*, [York], 5 • E. G. W. Bill, *Education at Christ Church, Oxford, 1660–1800* (1988) • H. Hodson, *Cheshire, 1660–1780: Restoration to industrial revolution* (1978), 45–8 • J. Addy, 'Two eighteenth-century bishops of Chester and their diocese, 1771–1787', PhD diss., U. Leeds, 1972 • H. Walpole, *Memoirs of the reign of King George the Third*, ed. G. F. R. Barker, 4 (1894), 206, 311 • *The last journals of Horace Walpole*, ed. Dr Doran, rev. A. F. Steuart, 1 (1910), 49–53 • *The political memoranda of Francis, fifth duke of Leeds*, ed. O. Browning, CS, new ser., 35 (1884), 5–9 • A. Tindal Hart, *Ebor: a history of the archbishops of York* (1986), 152–4 • Walpole, *Corr.* • J. E. T. Rogers, ed., *A complete collection of the protests of the Lords*, 3 vols. (1875) • E. A. Bond, ed., *Speeches of the managers and counsel in the trial of Warren Hastings* (1859–61), 3.v–vi, xxiii–iv; 4.lxi • R. Warner, *Literary recollections*, 2 vols. (1830), vol. 1, pp. 294–6 • *The correspondence of Edmund Burke*, 7, ed. P. J. Marshall and J. A. Woods (1968), 369–70 • Cobbett, *Parl. hist.*, 19.327, 347–8, 491; 30.983–94

Archives Borth. Inst., corresp. and papers; family papers | Birr Castle, Birr, Offaly, corresp. with Henry Flood • BL, Add. MS 24243, fol. 56 • BL, letters to Warren Hastings, Add. MSS 29147, 29152, 29154, 29155, 29158, 29167, 29169 • BL, letters to Charles Jenkinson, Add. MSS 38208, 38233, 38305, 38310, 38311, 38457, 38578 • BL, corresp. with the earl of Liverpool, Add. MSS 38208–38311, 38457 • NRA, priv. coll., letters from earl of Mansfield

Likenesses J. Reynolds, oils, 1759–62, Christ Church Oxf. • B. West, oils, *c.*1775, NPG [*see illus.*] • J. Reynolds, oils, 1777, Christ Church Oxf.; copy, Bishopthorpe Palace • J. S. Copley, group portrait, oils, 1779–80 (*The collapse of the earl of Chatham in the House of Lords, 7 July 1778*), Tate collection • G. Romney, oils, 1790–95 • J. Hoppner, oils, 1798–9, Royal Collection • J. Ward, mezzotint, pubd 1800 (after G. Romney), BM, NPG • J. Bacon, marble bust, 1804, Christ Church Oxf. • A. Salvin, C. Haymond, T. Willement, tomb chest with black marble top, *c.*1840, York Minster • E. Fisher, engraving (after J. Reynolds) • Heath, engraving (after Hoppner); copy, Royal Collection • S. W. Reynolds, engraving (after J. Reynolds) • J. R. Smith, engraving (after J. Reynolds) • bust, Westminster School

Wealth at death approx. £10,000 in property, stocks, and shares; divided equally among sons; house left to widow; distributed £1000 each to forty-seven grandchildren at Christmas 1806: will, probate register, Borth. Inst., vol. 152

Markievicz [*née* Gore-Booth]**, Constance Georgine**, **Countess Markievicz in the Polish nobility** (1868–1927), Irish republican and first woman elected to parliament, was born on 4 February 1868 at 7 Buckingham Gate, Pimlico, London, the eldest of the three daughters and two sons of Sir Henry William Gore-Booth (1843–1900), philanthropist and explorer, of Lissadell, co. Sligo, and Georgina Mary Hill (*d.* 1927), of Tickhill Castle, York. Eva Gore-*Booth, the campaigner for women's suffrage, was her sister. Constance Gore-Booth spent most of her childhood at the family house at Lissadell, and although she lived most of her adult life in Dublin and abroad she retained a strong attachment to the west of Ireland.

Descended from seventeenth-century planters, the Gore-Booths were prominent landowners whose wealth and social standing ensured that their children enjoyed a privileged childhood. The family entertained lavishly, hosting such guests as W. B. Yeats, whose poem 'In Memory of Eva Gore-Booth and Constance Markievicz' (1927) chronicled both his early visits to Lissadell and the subsequent careers of both women. Taking advantage of the family's extensive grounds Constance Gore-Booth enjoyed country pursuits, including hunting, driving, and riding, and became especially well known for her skill with the rifle and in the saddle. With Eva she was educated by governesses at home, her tutelage consisting mainly of instruction in the genteel arts of poetry, music, and art appreciation. In 1886 she made a grand tour of the continent, and in the following year was presented to Queen Victoria.

Constance Gore-Booth hoped to study art, and finally persuaded her disapproving parents to fund her studies in 1893, when she enrolled at the Slade School of Art, in London. Having moved to Paris to further her studies she met fellow art student Count Casimir Dunin-Markievicz, a Polish widower whose family owned land in the Ukraine. They married in London in 1900 and their daughter, Maeve, was born the following year. Constance Markievicz's relationship with her daughter was strained; the couple returned to Paris in 1902, leaving their daughter in the care of Lady Gore-Booth. The child's family was reunited when her parents moved to Dublin, but from about 1908 she lived almost exclusively with her grandparents at Lissadell House.

The Markieviczes' move to Dublin coincided with a period of literary and cultural renaissance, and they soon became involved in the city's liveliest artistic circles, displaying their paintings and producing and acting in plays at the Abbey Theatre. They co-founded the United Arts Club in 1907 but Constance Markievicz's interest in Irish nationalism soon took precedence over her artistic ambitions. She joined Sinn Féin and Inghinidhe na hÉireann (Daughters of Ireland) in 1908 and helped to found—and became a regular contributor to—*Bean na hÉireann* ('Women of Ireland'), Ireland's first women's nationalist journal. She had become interested in women's suffrage as a young woman, presiding in 1896 over a meeting of the Sligo Women's Suffrage Society; she remained committed to this cause but she gave increasing time to overtly nationalist organizations.

Markievicz became something of a celebrity in Dublin's radical circles. A strident and flamboyant orator, her background and penchant for military uniforms and weaponry made her a figure of fun in some circles, while attracting deep suspicion in others. In 1909 she founded Na Fianna Éireann, a youth movement whose aims included establishing an independent Ireland and promoting the Irish language. By 1911 she had become an executive member of both Sinn Féin and Inghinidhe na hÉireann, and was arrested in the same year for protesting against George V's visit to Dublin. She grew increasingly interested in socialism and trade unionism, becoming a strong supporter of the Irish Women Workers' Union and of the political programme advocated by the prominent socialist James Connolly. She assisted striking workers during the lock-out of 1913, organizing soup kitchens in Dublin slums and at Liberty Hall. Strongly opposed to Irish involvement in the allied war effort, she co-founded the Irish Neutrality League in 1914 and became a vocal advocate of the small group of men who split from the nationalist Volunteer movement over the question of Irish participation in the war. She had separated amicably from her husband about 1909; while he worked as a war correspondent in the Balkans she continued to assist in training and mobilizing the Irish Citizen Army and the Fianna.

Markievicz made no secret of her support for armed rebellion against British forces, and joined wholeheartedly in the Irish Citizen Army's involvement in the Easter rising of 1916. She was second in command of a troop of Irish Citizen Army combatants at St Stephen's Green; her battalion was hopelessly outmanoeuvred by British soldiers and was forced to retreat to the College of Surgeons. After a week of intense fighting Markievicz and her fellow rebels surrendered. She was sentenced to death for her part in the rebellion but this was commuted to penal servitude for life on account of her sex. She served fourteen months of her sentence at Aylesbury gaol before being released in the general amnesty of June 1917. She

Constance Georgine Markievicz, Countess Markievicz in the Polish nobility (1868–1927), by Keogh Brothers

claimed to have experienced an epiphany during the Easter rising, took instruction from a priest while in prison, and converted to Catholicism shortly after her release.

In 1918 Markievicz was arrested along with many fellow Sinn Féin members on account of their alleged involvement in a spurious 'German plot'. While in prison she stood successfully in the general election of 1918 as a Sinn Féin candidate for Dublin's St Patrick's division, and became the first woman elected to the British parliament; like all Sinn Féin MPs she refused to take her seat. Released from gaol in March 1919 she was appointed secretary for labour in the first Dáil Éireann, but like her colleagues in the proscribed Dáil she spent much of her time on the run. She was arrested again in June for making a seditious speech, and was sentenced to four months' hard labour—her third prison term in four years. After another arrest a sentence of two years' hard labour in the following year was interrupted by the general amnesty that followed the signing of the Anglo-Irish treaty. A vocal opponent of the treaty, she denounced it in the Dáil and continued to work against it through Cumann na mBan, a republican women's organization of which she was president.

Markievicz's stand against the treaty forced her into another period of exile and abstention from the Dáil. She publicized the anti-treaty position during a speaking tour of America and through several publications in which she continued to extol the republican cause. Markievicz lost her seat in the general Dáil election of 1922 but was elected to the Free State parliament in August 1923. In common with other elected republicans she refused to take the oath of allegiance to the king, thus disqualifying herself from sitting. Her characteristic flamboyance—she insisted, for example, on wearing her Cumann na mBan uniform while addressing the Dáil—and an increasingly hostile general attitude to female politicians ensured that she was viewed with growing suspicion by a number of her fellow republicans. She was arrested for the last time in November 1923 but was released soon after she went on hunger strike in protest. She joined Fianna Fáil on its establishment in 1926 and stood successfully as a candidate for the new party in the general election of 1927. She remained an outspoken republican but her influence waned and her health suffered as a result of hard work and often rough conditions. She died, of peritonitis, in a public ward at Sir Patrick Dun's Hospital in Dublin on 15 July 1927, and was buried in Glasnevin cemetery in the city, following a well-attended public funeral.

S. PAŠETA

Sources *Prison letters of Countess Markievicz (Constance Gore-Booth)* (1934) • B. Farrell, 'Markievicz and the women of the revolution', *Leaders and men of the Easter rising*, ed. F. X. Martin (1967) • A. Marrelo, *Rebel countess: the life and times of Countess Markievicz* (1967) • J. Van Voris, *Constance Markievicz: in the cause of Ireland* (1967) • S. O' Faolain, *Constance Markievicz* (1968) • E. Coxhead, *Daughters of Erin: five women of the Irish renascence* [1969] • E. Ni Éireamhoin, *Two great Irish women: Maud Gonne MacBride and Countess Markievicz* (1971) • M. Ward, *Unmanageable revolutionaries: women and Irish nationalism*, pbk edn (1983) • A. Maverty, *Constance Markievicz: an independent life* (1988) • D. Norman, *Terrible beauty: a life of Constance Markievicz* (1988) • Burke, *Peerage* (1959) • b. cert.
Archives NL Ire. • NRA, priv. coll., corresp., sketch pads, news cuttings • PRO, papers, CO 904 | NL Ire., letters to Eva Gore-Booth
Likenesses Keogh Brothers, photograph, NL Ire. [*see illus.*] • photographs, repro. in www.spartacus.schoolnet.co.uk/Wmarkiewicz, 4 Oct 2002

Markland, Abraham (1645–1728), Church of England clergyman, was born on 25 June 1645 in the parish of St Dionis Backchurch, London, the third surviving son of Michael Markland (*d.* 1663), apothecary, and his second wife, Anne Perry (*d.* 1662). He was educated at Merchant Taylors' School from 1658 and elected to a scholarship at St John's College, Oxford, on 14 July 1662. He graduated BA in 1666, became a fellow of the college, and proceeded MA in 1669. While at Oxford he composed his *Poems on his majesties birth and restoration; his highness Prince Rupert's and his grace the duke of Albemarle's naval victories; the late great pestilence and fire of London* (1667). In 1692 he was admitted to the degrees of bachelor and doctor of divinity at Oxford.

Markland was ordained into the diocese of Winchester on 2 June 1672 and was appointed rector of Brixton on the Isle of Wight in 1674; he was instituted rector of Easton, Hampshire, in 1677, of Houghton (1678), and of Meonstoke (1684). In July 1679 he was installed as a canon of Winchester Cathedral. In October 1682, with the government of the City of London firmly under tory control, Markland preached a fervently loyalist sermon before the court of aldermen in which he compared London, fallen into degeneracy and contempt for its governors and riven by whig and nonconformist factionalism, directly and unfavourably with the Jerusalem that Christ had wept over. He rejoiced that the City had been miraculously delivered from the hands of those who were resolutely impenitent for the death of Charles I, men who were 'no more concern'd on the Thirtieth of January, than the Jews are on Good-Friday' and who would have treated Charles II the same way as they had his father (A. Markland, *A Sermon Preached before the Court of Aldermen … Octob. 29 1682*, 1683, 27). Markland married Catherine Pitt (*c.*1637–1693), daughter of Edward Pitt and Rachel Morton of Stratfield Saye; their son, George, was born on 18 November 1678, and they also had a daughter, Jane. With his second wife, Elizabeth (*d.* 1734), he had a son, Abraham (*d.* 1705), who died in infancy, and two daughters, Elizabeth and Anne.

In August 1694 Markland was appointed a master of the hospital of St Cross in Winchester. During his tenure it was alleged that the hospital records had been destroyed and so a new custumal was drawn up and approved by the bishop in 1696. These statutes made the master the recipient of all hospital revenue but he was to finance the provisions made for the thirteen brethren and for the maintenance of the hospital. The brethren were to take oaths of obedience to the master; they were to bequeath all personal possessions to the master and were to be subject to his discipline. This custumal resulted in a legal challenge in the nineteenth century when it was castigated as 'a willfull breach of trust'; the controversy over St Cross was one of the cases which inspired Anthony Trollope's *The Warden* (1855). Markland died on 29 July 1728 and a memorial to him (as well as his wife and sons George and Abraham) was erected in the choir of St Cross, Winchester. A collection of his sermons preached at Winchester Cathedral was published in 1729.   ANDREW SPICER

Sources J. L. Chester, ed., *The reiester booke of Saynte De'nis Backchurch parishe ... begynnynge ... 1538*, Harleian Society, register section, 3 (1878) · *Fasti Angl., 1541–1857*, [Canterbury] · Foster, *Alum. Oxon.* · Mrs E. P. Hart, ed., *Merchant Taylors' School register, 1561–1934*, 2 vols. (1936) · J. Cook, ed., *The wainscot book: the houses of Winchester Cathedral Close and their interior decoration, 1660–1800*, Hampshire RS, 6 (1984) · B. B. Woodward, T. C. Wilks, and C. Lockhart, *A general history of Hampshire*, 3 vols. [1861–9] · *VCH Hampshire and the Isle of Wight* · will, PRO, PROB 11/624, sig. 269, fols. 223v–224r · IGI

Markland, James Heywood (1788–1864), antiquary, born at Ardwick Green, Manchester, on 7 December 1788, was fourth and youngest son of Robert Markland (*d.* 1828), a check and fustian manufacturer at Manchester, who afterwards succeeded to the estate of Pemberton, near Wigan. His mother was Elizabeth, daughter of Robert Hibbert of Manchester. In his twelfth year he was sent for his education to the house of the headmaster of Chester School, and from the associations of the cathedral buildings he acquired his taste for antiquarian pursuits. He was trained as a solicitor at Manchester, but in 1808 moved to London and practised there. By 1811 he was residing in the Inner Temple, and on 4 April 1814 he was admitted as a student. The same year he was appointed by the West India planters their parliamentary agent. On 24 September 1821 he married at Marylebone church, Charlotte (*d.* 1867), eldest daughter of Sir Francis *Freeling; they had a daughter, Elizabeth Jane, who married the Revd Charles R. Conybeare, vicar of Itchen Stoke, Hampshire, in 1853.

Markland remained in London in practice, being the head partner in the firm of Markland and Wright, until 1839, when he withdrew to Malvern, where he lived until 1841. He then moved to Bath and spent the rest of his days in that city.

Markland is best-known as a writer on antiquarian subjects and literary history, a staunch churchman, and a collector of fine books. Contemporaries regarded him as a man of high literary taste, refined manners, and lively conversation. His earliest publications, written when he was living in Manchester, were short and anonymous: *A Few Plain Reasons for Adhering to the Church* (1807), and a biographical note on the poet William Mason for volume 5 of Brydges' *Censuria literaria* (1807). Shortly after moving to London, in 1809, he was elected fellow of the Society of Antiquaries. He was a member of the select Antiquaries dining club from 1822 to 1834. He contributed several articles to *Archaeologia* (1815–38) and was director, in charge of publications (1827–9). While director he wrote to the president, Lord Aberdeen, recommending that the society establish a museum of antiquities on the Scottish model. His letter was printed in the *Gentleman's Magazine* in 1828, but he was disappointed as the society failed to adopt his proposal. In 1816 he was elected fellow of the Royal Society, though he had little interest in science.

The world of book collecting was more to Markland's taste, and he was elected to the Roxburghe Club at its inaugural dinner in 1812. He edited their publication of the *Chester Mysteries* (1818), and was treasurer from 1838 until 1845, when he resigned. His father-in-law was a member of the club, as was George Hibbert, about whom he wrote, anonymously, *A Sketch of the Life and Character of George Hibbert* (1837). He gradually built up an extensive library of books, especially rich in fine bindings, presentation copies, and privately printed works. Various authors acknowledged his help, including John Nichols in volumes 1, 4, and 8 of his *Literary Anecdotes* (1812–14), Alexander Chalmers for the memoir of Jeremiah Markland in volume 21 of his *Biographical Dictionary* (1815), and George Ormerod in his *Cheshire* (1819).

While resident in Bath, Markland was an active member of both the (Royal) Archaeological Institute and the British Archaeological Association, and contributed to their journals. He gave the opening address at the Somerset Congress of the association in 1856, 'On the history and antiquities of Bath'. He was president of the Literary Club of Bath in 1858 and vice-president of the Somerset Archaeological and Natural History Society from its foundation in 1849 until his death. In the same period *Notes and Queries* published numerous articles from him on literary history. His most popular writings on religious matters were *Remarks on Sepulchral Monuments*, which was enlarged in 1842 as *Remarks on English Churches*, *On the Reverence Due to Holy Places* (1845), and *The Offertory the Best Way of Contributing Money for Christian Purposes* (2nd edn, 1862). In recognition of his services to the Church of England he was awarded the degree of DCL at Oxford University, in 1849.

Markland was a strong and constant supporter of all church societies; he was entrusted by Mrs Ramsden with the foundation of mission sermons at Cambridge and Oxford, and while resident in Bath three ladies, the Misses Mitford of Somerset Place in that city, selected him for the distribution of £14,000 in charitable works in England and the colonies. He died at his house in Lansdown Crescent, Bath, on 28 December 1864, and was buried in the new Walcot cemetery on 3 January 1865; the first window in Bath Abbey west of the transept was filled with glass in his memory. His library was sold at Sothebys on 11 June 1859 and 29 May 1865. His wife died on 9 October 1867.

W. P. COURTNEY, rev. BERNARD NURSE

Sources GM, 1st ser., 91/2 (1821), 278 · GM, 3rd ser., 19 (1865), 649–52 · *Journal of the British Archaeological Association*, 21 (1865), 262–4 · *Proceedings of the Society of Antiquaries of London*, 2nd ser., 3 (1864–7), 111–12 · C. Bigham, *The Roxburghe Club* (1928), 31 · T. F. Dibdin, *Reminiscences of a literary life*, 1 (1836), 376, 381–2 · R. E. M. Peach, *Historic houses of Bath and their associations*, 1 (1883), 108–9
Archives Ches. & Chester ALSS, corresp. and papers | BL, letters to Philip Bliss, Add. MSS 34568–34582 · BL, letters to Sir Frederic Madden, Add. MSS 2837–2847 · BL, letters to T. Sharp, Add. MS 43645 · Cornwall RO, corresp. with John Hawkins · W. Sussex RO, Hawkins MSS
Likenesses J. Hoppner, oils (as a young man), priv. coll.; Christies, 17 June 1966, lot 17
Wealth at death under £30,000: probate, 7 Feb 1865, CGPLA Eng. & Wales

Markland, Jeremiah (1693–1776), classical scholar, was born on 29 October 1693 at Childwell, Lancashire, one of the twelve children of Ralph Markland, vicar of that parish. He was admitted on the foundation of Christ's Hospital, London, in 1704 and in 1710 proceeded to St Peter's College, Cambridge, with an exhibition of £30 p.a. for seven years. He graduated BA in 1714, proceeded MA in 1717, and was elected fellow and tutor of his college in 1718. In 1714 he contributed to the *Cambridge Gratulations* and in 1717 he wrote some verses vindicating Addison against Pope's satire. He probably intended to take holy orders but his 'extreme weakness of the lungs' (Chalmers, 21.319) prevented him from pursuing a clerical career. Instead he remained at St Peter's until 1728, when he left to become private tutor to William Strode of Ponsbourne, Hertfordshire. He remained in this position for several years, accompanying Strode abroad to France, Flanders, and the Netherlands before returning to Cambridge in 1733.

From 1744 to 1752 Markland lived in Uckfield, Sussex, where he supervised the education of the son of his former pupil, William Strode. In 1752 he moved to Milton Court, near Dorking, Surrey, where for the remainder of his life he lived as a semi-recluse, maintaining contact with only a few friends, who included the printer William Bowyer, Strode, and the physician William Heberden. Despite the best efforts of his friends to persuade him he twice declined to compete for the Greek professorship at Cambridge declaring that 'instead of going an hundred miles to take it, I would go two hundred miles the other way to avoid it' (Nichols, *Lit. anecdotes*, 4.278). In 1765 he became involved in a costly court case to defend Martha Rose, the widow with whom he lodged, against the claims on her money and property made by her son. The case was lost, as was Markland's 'whole fortune' that had been 'expended on relieving the distress of the family' (ibid., 290). Although in much straitened circumstances he continued to refuse offers of financial help from his friends until in 1768 Strode persuaded him to accept an annuity of £100.

Markland was an outstanding classical scholar and was described by John Nichols as 'one of the most learned and penetrating critics of the eighteenth century' (Nichols, *Lit. anecdotes*, 4.272). He first distinguished himself in his *Epistola critica* (1723); this was followed by an edition of the *Silvae of Statius*, which restored the integrity of a much corrupted text. More controversially, in his *Remarks on the Epistles of Cicero to Brutus, and on Brutus to Cicero* (1745) he set out to prove that the attribution to Cicero of the four orations was spurious. Not all were convinced by his arguments, which have been subsequently disproved, and he became involved in a long and acrimonious debate with Conyers Middleton and others. In 1761 he published an excellent grammatical tract, *De Graecorum quinta declinatione imparisyllabica, et inde formata Latinorum tertia*. Probably the most esteemed and elaborate of his critical works was his edition of the *Euripedes drama supplices mulieres*, published anonymously in 1763 and reprinted in 1775. His other writings were either fragments that mainly were destroyed by himself in a spirit of dejection or contributions to other authors' works. Markland's contribution and character were summed up by Peter Elmsley:

> he was very laborious, loved retirement, and spent a long life in the study of the Greek and Latin languages. For modesty, candour, literary honesty and courteousness to other scholars, he is justly considered as the model which ought to be proposed for the imitation of every critic. (*QR*, 7, 1812, 442)

In later years Markland suffered increasingly from painful attacks of gout. One such attack, accompanied by a fever, led to his death at Milton Court on 7 July 1776. He was buried in Dorking church, where a brass plaque, with an epitaph composed by his friend William Heberden, was placed on his gravestone. In accordance with his will his books and papers were bequeathed to Martha Rose.

C. W. SUTTON, rev. M. J. MERCER

Sources Nichols, *Lit. anecdotes*, 4.272–362 • Venn, *Alum. Cant.*, 1/3.142 • A. Chalmers, ed., *The general biographical dictionary*, new edn, 21 (1815), 318–29 • Allibone, *Dict.* • J. Aikin and others, *General biography, or, Lives, critical and historical of the most eminent persons*, 10 vols. (1799–1815) • *IGI* • M. L. Clarke, *Greek studies in England, 1700–1880* (1945) • C. O. Brink, *English classical scholarship: historical reflections on Bentley, Porson, and Housman* (1986) • C. Collard, 'Jeremiah Markland', *Proceedings of the Cambridge Philological Society*, 202 (1976), 1–12 • tombstone, Dorking church

Archives Ches. & Chester ALSS, letters • St John Cam., corresp. and papers • V&A NAL, letters

Likenesses J. Caldwell, stipple, BM, NPG; repro. in Nichols, *Lit. anecdotes*

Marks, David Woolf (1811–1909), rabbi and Hebrew scholar, was born in London on 22 November 1811, the eldest son of Woolf Marks, merchant, and his wife, Mary. His early education was at the Jews' Free School in Bell Lane, Spitalfields, and when just thirteen years old he was placed in charge of the management of the school for three months during the absence of the master through illness. He then spent five years as a pupil teacher at Mr. H. N. Solomon's Boarding-School for Jews at Hammersmith. After acting as assistant reader at the Western Synagogue, St Alban's Place, Haymarket, he became in 1833 assistant reader and secretary to the Hebrew congregation at Liverpool. There he taught Hebrew to John Simon, later a serjeant-at-law and an MP, and the two became close friends. Simon, who was an early advocate of reform in Jewish ritual and practices in England, enlisted Marks's aid in the movement, and in 1840 Marks was appointed minister of the newly established Reform west London congregation of British Jews; he retained the post until the end of 1895, first at the synagogue in Burton Street, which was opened on 27 January 1842. In his consecration sermon Marks gave notice of his advanced views on the need for religious instruction for girls. The congregation moved to Margaret Street in 1849, and lastly to the building in Upper Berkeley Street which was opened in 1870. Marks fathered the two central reforms that distinguished the new synagogue from the existing Orthodox synagogues, the abolition of the second days of the festivals and the denial of the oral law. He introduced an element of flexibility and freedom to respond to change and not to be bound by ages-old rabbinical decisions. With his colleague Albert Löwy he prepared the Reform prayer book, and mainly owing to his persistent efforts his synagogue was legalized for marriages. Sir Moses Montefiore, the Orthodox president of the Board of Deputies of British Jews, a body which alone enjoyed the right of registering or certifying places of worship for Jewish marriages, long refused to certify the Reform synagogue. A clause covering Marks's synagogue was removed in 1857 by Montefiore's influence during the committee stage in the House of Commons from a bill for legalizing dissenters' marriages in their own places of worship. Bishop Wilberforce and the second earl of Harrowby, however, at Marks's persuasion, reintroduced the clause in the House of Lords, and it became law.

Marks was Goldsmid professor of Hebrew at University College, London, from 1844 to 1898, and was dean of the college during the sessions 1875–7. He was also for a time professor of Hebrew at Regent's Park Baptist college, and was one of the Hibbert trustees, a trustee of Dr Williams's Library, and for thirty-five years member of the Marylebone vestry. He was a member of the council of the Anglo-Jewish Association, which was formed in 1871. Politically he was a Conservative Party sympathizer. The Hebrew Union College in Cincinnati conferred the honorary degree of DD upon him. Marks published four volumes of sermons (1851–85); a biography of Sir Francis Goldsmid (1879, part 1, part 2 being by his colleague Löwy); and *The Law is Light*, a course of lectures on the Mosaic law (1854). He was a contributor to Smith's *Dictionary of the Bible*.

In 1842 Marks married Cecilia (d. 1882), daughter of Moseley Woolf of Birmingham; with her he had two daughters and four sons, of whom Harry Hananel *Marks JP was MP for the Isle of Thanet and proprietor and editor of the *Financial News*, and Major Claude Laurie Marks DSO (1863–1910) served with distinction in the Second South African War. Marks died at his home, Belmont House, Maidenhead, on 2 May 1909, and was buried at the Ball's Pond cemetery of the West London Synagogue. A tablet in commemoration of his long ministry was placed in the hall of the West London Synagogue, Upper Berkeley Street.   M. EPSTEIN, *rev.* GERRY BLACK

Sources G. Black, *JFS: the history of the Jews' Free School, London, since 1732* (1998) · A. J. Kershen and J. A. Romain, *Tradition and change: a history of Reform Judaism in Britain, 1840–1995* (1995) · J. Picciotto, *Sketches of Anglo-Jewish history* (1875) · G. Alderman, *Modern British Jewry* (1992), 98, 101 · J. Neuberger, *On being Jewish* (1996) · *Jewish Chronicle* (7 May 1909) · private information (1912) · *CGPLA Eng. & Wales* (1909)

Likenesses A. Solomon, crayon drawing, 1853, priv. coll. · J. Goodman, oils, *c.*1877, West London Synagogue · S. Marks, engraving (after a crayon drawing by A. Solomon)

Wealth at death £11,441 3s.: probate, 12 June 1909, *CGPLA Eng. & Wales*

Marks, Derek John (1921–1975), political journalist and newspaper editor, was born on 15 January 1921, at 31 Eastnor Road, Reigate, Surrey, the eldest son of Henry James Marks, bank manager, and his wife, Ellie Burlinson. He was educated at Seaford College, Sussex, and joined the Royal Air Force in 1940. He graduated to flying Mosquitoes alongside many Rhodesians, whom he remembered each armistice day by laying his personal wreath at the Cenotaph—a typical example of his lifelong respect for and love of comradeship.

After leaving the Royal Air Force in 1946 Marks entered journalism as a reporter on the *Huddersfield Examiner*, and entered politics as a prospective Liberal candidate for the Cleveland division of Yorkshire. Thus at an early stage of his career he had established the links between journalism and politics which were to govern his working life. He then briefly served on the *East African Standard* in Nairobi before joining the London office of the *Yorkshire Post* in 1950. Two years later he was a political correspondent on the *Daily Express*, where he was rapidly promoted to political editor. He was the outstanding lobby correspondent of his day, and could frequently record the private proceedings of parliamentary committees for his newspaper within minutes of the close of a meeting. Many tried to trace the 'leaks'; nobody succeeded. He was the first to break the news that Harold Macmillan, and not R. A. Butler, was to succeed Anthony Eden as prime minister.

Marks's working day was a punishing schedule: the editor's morning news conference in the *Express* office; lunch with colleagues, often in El Vino, the Fleet Street wine bar where judges, barristers, and journalists congregated to indulge in gossip and to generate ideas; then to Westminster where, as one friend wrote, 'his bulky figure moved through the Lobby with almost the soft-shoe glide of a Lord Chancellor in daily procession to the Lords' (*UK Press Gazette*, 17 Feb 1975). He knew no limit to his working day.

Throughout all these years of twenty-four-hour activity, Marks was suffering increasingly from diabetes. He was greatly comforted and supported by his wife, Jean Greenhalgh (b. 1922), the servicewoman daughter of Edward and Emily Greenhalgh, of Edgerton, Huddersfield, whom he had married on 9 October 1942. One son and two daughters were born of the marriage. In the family's London home, well within division-bell range of the House of Commons, he found a quiet happiness and relaxation that enabled him to recharge his frequently overworked batteries. These intervals of peace were very necessary to a man of deep convictions who, however exuberant he might be at the office or in the lobby, was essentially a shy and intensely private individual.

In the mid-1960s the *Express* organization was going through turbulent times. Lord Beaverbrook, the proprietor, had died in 1964, leaving a management with a somewhat uncertain touch and no well-established editor. Marks had moved to the *Express*'s sister paper, the *Evening Standard*, as deputy editor, but Sir Max Aitken, Beaverbrook's successor, who greatly admired Marks, brought him back to the *Express* in 1965, as editor and a director of Beaverbrook Newspapers.

Marks was able to provide the leadership which had faltered in the previous year or two, but his diabetes was becoming an increasing handicap. Moreover, his devotion to politics, which for years had added enormous strength to the paper, was now at times limiting his performance as an editor. The *Daily Express*, at that time the supreme modern popular newspaper with a circulation of about 4 million, needed a broadly based appeal that Marks occasionally fell short of providing. Indeed, there were moments—although he had always wanted to be editor—when he would say that he regretted the move; but this was invariably followed by a boisterous declaration of his love of the life and the friendships that journalism had brought him.

Then, in 1967, Marks stepped into the limelight in what became known as the D-notice affair. On 21 February the *Express* published a page one story headlined 'Cable Vetting Sensation' which claimed that thousands of private cables and telegrams were regularly being made available to the security authorities for scrutiny. The authorities took the view that this contravened D-notices—secret government warnings to newspapers alerting them to sensitive matters of defence—and brought considerable pressure upon Marks, Sir Max Aitken, and the author Chapman Pincher to suppress the story. Marks refused and published the story in full, whereupon the prime minister, Harold Wilson, set up a committee of privy councillors—Lord Radcliffe (chairman), Emmanuel Shinwell, and Selwyn Lloyd—to inquire into the D-notice system and the *Express* revelations. The committee reported in June on improvements to the D-notice system but, while criticizing the *Express*, did not recommend any action or penalty. Marks was the journalistic hero of the hour.

In the late 1960s Marks's health deteriorated and he finally decided to retire as editor in 1971. He remained a director of Beaverbrook Newspapers and special adviser to Sir Max Aitken. Later still, he was compelled to go into hospital to have a leg amputated. He worked on, hobbling around the office with a stick and continuing to write regular vigorous political columns in the *Daily Express* and *Sunday Express*. In 1971 an honorary degree of LLD was conferred upon him by the University of New Brunswick, Canada. He died at his home, 14 Westminster Gardens, London, on 8 February 1975 from a coronary thrombosis and diabetes, survived by his wife. His remains were cremated at Putney Vale crematorium.

For much of the 1950s and 1960s Derek Marks bestrode the worlds of Fleet Street and Westminster, and he had the Colossus-like frame to enable him to perform that intricate role with an exuberant authority. His memorial service was held at St Margaret's, Westminster, and was attended by MPs from all parties. Edward Heath, who gave the address, said of Marks: 'He was one of the great political journalists of our time. The information he always had at his command was matched by his intuitive perception of men and events' (*Sunday Express*, 9 Feb 1975).

EDWARD PICKERING

Sources personal knowledge (2004) · private information (2004) · *The Times* (10 Feb 1975) · *WWW*, 1991–5 · *UK Press Gazette* (17 Feb 1975) · *Sunday Express* (9 Feb 1975) · J. McMillan, *Daily Express* (10 Feb 1975) · 'Report of the committee … appointed to inquire into "D" notice matters', *Parl. papers* (1966–7), 48.545, Cmnd 3309 · b. cert. · d. cert. · m. cert. · *CGPLA Eng. & Wales* (1975)
Likenesses thirty-five photographs, *The Express* picture library, London

Wealth at death £35,317: probate, 28 May 1975, *CGPLA Eng. & Wales*

Marks, Geoffrey (1864–1938), actuary and insurance company manager, was born on 15 November 1864 at Beddington, near Mitcham, Surrey, the third of five sons of John George Marks, sherry shipper of Croydon, and his wife, Sarah, *née* Walker. He was educated at Whitgift Grammar School, Croydon, where he was head boy and captain of rugby and cricket. His love of sport continued throughout his life: he became captain and scrum-half of Croydon rugby club, and was an amateur boxer and a golfer with a handicap of one. He kept wicket for Middlesex in 1894–5, which probably accounted for his curiously gnarled hands.

Marks left school in 1882 and joined Scottish Amicable Life. In 1885 he moved to Mutual Life, and he became a fellow of the Institute of Actuaries in 1890. In 1893, aged only twenty-nine, he was appointed by Mutual Life as actuary and manager. In 1896, on the merger of his office with National Life, he was appointed actuary and manager of the new company, the National Mutual Life Assurance Society, a position he held for the next thirty-six years. He was a member of the board of directors between 1925 and 1935, though he retired as general manager in 1932.

Marks stamped his authority on National Mutual Life. He reduced costs, expanded business cautiously, and paid particular attention to fund management so that the company paid higher bonuses than any other life office before the First World War. Between 1918 and 1921 Marks secured the election of a number of economists as directors. These included O. T. Falk, John Maynard Keynes (elected chairman in 1922), and Walter Layton, who were to change radically the face of British life-assurance investments. Following Keynes's emphasis on a positive investment policy, assets were rapidly moved out of traditional fixed interest securities into the volatile but expanding field of industrial equities. Most other assurance offices only belatedly followed suit. As a result National Mutual achieved record profits at a time when life assurance was generally stagnating. Marks supervised this innovative investment strategy, and proved a strong enough personality to exercise some control over the charismatic Keynes.

Marks's talents were much in demand outside the company, so that he became one of the best-known of insurance men. He was chairman of the Life Offices' Association (1914–16), president of the Institute of Actuaries (1918–20), chairman of the British Insurance Association (1926–8), and chairman of the Joint Board on Unemployment Insurance (1921–37). He served on two royal commissions, on decimal coinage (1918–19) and on income tax (1919–20), and held a wide range of other positions, including finance officer to the metropolitan special constabulary (1914–16), member of the Insurance Offices' advisory committee on the mobilization of dollar securities, chairman of Miss Holman's Home and Club for Disabled Officers, council member of the Royal Patriotic Fund Corporation (1918–20), governor of the Prince of Wales General Hospital, Tottenham, and, in his later years, governor of

Whitgift School. For his wartime services, particularly as personal assistant to the controller of the navy and army canteen board (1917–19), he was made a CBE in 1920.

Marks was a rather formidable character—stern, impatient, quick-tempered. He was forceful in debate and valued precision in language. He was generous in friendship and to those in whom he had confidence. He married Alys Mary Bridges, who died in 1930; and, lacking children of his own, he took a keen interest in the careers of his junior staff. An omnivorous reader, and something of an aesthete and epicure, he was a connoisseur of wine and his dinner parties were perfect exercises in gastronomy. He had a satirical sense of humour and was a flamboyant, colourful dresser.

Marks died on 25 August 1938 at his home, Nately Lodge, Newnham Road, Nately Scures, near Basingstoke, of exhaustion, a duodenal ulcer, and cerebral thrombosis. He was cremated on 29 August 1938 at Golders Green crematorium, Middlesex.   ROBIN PEARSON

Sources The Times (30 Aug 1938) • E. E. G. Street, 'Marks, Geoffrey', DBB • R. Finch, The history of the National Mutual Life Assurance Society, 1830–1930 (1930) • R. C. Simmonds, The Institute of Actuaries, 1848–1948 (1948) • W. L. Catchpole and E. Elverston, BIA fifty, 1917–1967 (1967) • d. cert. • CGPLA Eng. & Wales (1938)
Likenesses H. Lamb, oils, 1932, National Mutual Life Assurance Society
Wealth at death £26,570 2s. 2d.: resworn probate, 27 Sept 1938, CGPLA Eng. & Wales

Marks, George Croydon, Baron Marks (1858–1938), engineer, patent agent, and politician, was born in Eltham, Kent, on 9 June 1858, the eldest of eight children (four of whom died in infancy) of William Marks, an artisan at the Royal Arsenal, Woolwich, and his wife, Amelia Adelaide, daughter of Thomas Croydon of Crediton in Devon. George attended a private day-school in Eltham and at the age of thirteen entered the Royal Arsenal School, where he continued his basic education while gaining valuable practical experience. He became one of the first Whitworth scholars in 1875 and completed his education at King's College, University of London. On 30 July 1881 he married Margaret, daughter of Thomas John Maynard, a Bath boat builder. They had no children.

Between 1877 and 1882 Marks gained further experience with several well-known engineering firms. In 1882 he joined Tangye Ltd in Birmingham and soon became head of the lifting-machinery department and an expert in hydraulically operated machinery. In July 1887 Marks put up his plate in Temple Street, Birmingham, as a consulting engineer and patent agent. Following a serious illness in 1889, he formed a partnership with Dugald Clerk, a former colleague at Tangye Ltd and inventor of the two-stroke internal combustion engine. The partners practised as Marks and Clerk and were joined by Marks's younger brother Edward in 1894. Initially Marks concentrated upon the design and construction of 'water balance' cliff railways and steep-incline tramways. While he was with Tangye Ltd he had been responsible for machinery used by the Saltburn, North Riding of Yorkshire, cliff railway. In 1888, in association with George Newnes, a

local benefactor, founder of Tit-Bits and Liberal MP for Newmarket, he designed and built the Lynton and Lynmouth Cliff Railway. This was followed by similar railways at Clifton Spa in Bristol, Bridgnorth in Shropshire, and Constitutional Hill in Aberystwyth. A steep-incline cable-hauled tramway was completed in Matlock, Derbyshire, in 1893. In 1894 Marks was appointed consulting engineer to the duke of Saxe-Coburg and Gotha and he built another cliff railway in Budapest, for which he was rewarded with a knighthood of the ducal order of Ernest.

In 1893 Marks and Clerk moved to London, with premises in Lincoln's Inn Fields from 1909, leaving Edward to run the Birmingham and Manchester offices. Marks opened an office in New York in 1910 and became closely associated with Thomas Edison as patent agent, advocate, and personal confidant.

In 1906 Marks successfully stood as Liberal MP for the Launceston and North Cornwall constituency, which he held until 1924. In 1911 he was knighted. He joined the Ministry of Munitions in 1914 and three years later was appointed CBE for his outstanding work as a commissioner for the dilution of labour. In 1929 Marks left the Liberal Party and offered his support to Ramsay MacDonald. In July that year he was raised to the peerage. In the House of Lords, as in the House of Commons, he was regarded as a leading authority on patent and trademark law. He was a member of the institutions of Civil and Mechanical Engineers and of the Chartered Institute of Patent Agents, council member for the London chamber of commerce, president of the Institute of Fuel, and a member of the royal commission on decimal coinage.

Following the First World War, he played a major role in the gramophone industry as chairman of the Edison Phonograph Company and the Columbia Graphaphone Company. In 1931 he was closely involved in the merger of these companies with the Gramophone Company (HMV) which resulted in the formation of Electrical and Musical Industries Ltd (EMI). He was also chairman of the British Equitable Assurance Company.

He was a lifelong Congregationalist and believed in the gospel of work and strict self-discipline, although his hospitality was renowned and his greatest pleasure was shipboard life on the great Atlantic liners. He was chairman of the Sunday School Union and treasurer of the Girls' Brigade. In later life his philanthropic deeds were legion.

Marks died at his home, Cerne Abbas, The Avenue, Branksome Park, Poole, on 24 September 1938 and was buried in the North Bournemouth cemetery on the 28th. He was survived by his wife. The peerage became extinct.
                                                    MICHAEL R. LANE, rev.

Sources M. R. Lane, Baron Marks of Woolwich (1986) • m. cert. • d. cert. • CGPLA Eng. & Wales (1938)
Archives Bodl. Oxf., notes and papers relating to work as special commissioner for the dilution of labour • NRA, business papers
Likenesses R. A. Wolstenholme, repro. in Lane, Baron Marks of Woolwich, jacket
Wealth at death £136,948 16s. 3d.: probate, 1 Dec 1938, CGPLA Eng. & Wales

Marks, Harry Hananel (1855–1916), journalist, newspaper proprietor, and politician, was born on 9 April 1855 in London, the fifth of six children of David Woolf *Marks (1811–1909), eminent Hebrew scholar and chief rabbi of the West London Synagogue, and his wife, Cecilia (d. 1882), daughter of Moseley Woolf of Birmingham and his wife.

Marks attended University College School, London, from 1864 to 1868, before completing his formal education at the Athenée Royale, Brussels. At the age of sixteen he travelled to New Orleans, where his father had friends, and remained in the United States until 1883. These were truly formative years. To the end of his life he admired American 'know-how'. Marks married Annie Estelle Benjamin of Montreal in 1884; they had a son and a daughter.

After a spell selling sewing machines Marks entered journalism on the strength of 'previous experience'—of which he had none. *Chutzpah* he had in abundance. He learned his trade on various Texas newspapers, 'the roughest and most thorough literary training that America offered' (*Financial News*, 27 Dec 1916). Marks moved to New York, working for the *New York World* from 1873 to 1878, and editing the *Daily Mining News* after 1880. A selection of his articles, published in 1882, included reflections on the 'precarious and Bohemian sort of existence' of the American newspaper reporter. 'My own experience', he wrote, 'is that a gentleman can be a reporter, and still be a gentleman. But it is difficult' (Marks, *Small Change*, 10–11). A master of irony, in 1879 Marks wrote and published himself *Down with the Jews! Meeting of the Society for Suppressing the Jewish Race*. This savaged those American politicians who sought to whip up hostility towards Jews.

While in New York, Marks combined journalism with speculation in mining and oil shares. Rumours of sharp practice followed him back to London in 1883; so too did the malicious accusation that he had defrauded and deserted the widow of a business associate with whom he had been intimate. Later, Marks sought to clear his name by suing George Butterfield, an aggrieved company promoter, who had published particulars of his alleged New York indiscretions. Marks failed to convince an Old Bailey jury, which found against him, though the judge made it clear that he regarded the verdict as perverse (*Financial News*, 18 Dec 1890). Thereafter Marks never quite shook off the suspicion that he was rather shady.

By this time Marks had established himself as the chief proprietor and editor of the *Financial and Mining News*, London's first financial daily. Its début, on 23 January 1884, predated the *Financial Times* (with which it merged in 1945) by four years. The *News* initiated a transformation in the British financial press, which had acquired a reputation for dullness. Marks imported cross-headings, short paragraphs, and a breezy style which irritated competitors but appealed to financial sector professionals and their clerks. The *News* also sold among the wider investing public whose interest it claimed to serve. It quickly developed into a crusading journal with a strong line in investigative company reporting. Exposing a vein of corruption in the Metropolitan Board of Works in 1888 was a major journalistic *coup*.

'Yankee bounce' triumphed over 'eighteen-hundred-and-fast-asleep conservatism of the old school' (*Financial News*, 29 April 1884). The *News* became the flagship of the new financial journalism, accessible as well as authoritative, which characterized the money pages of most London newspapers by 1900. There was, however, a darker side. Corruption was endemic in the largely unregulated financial sector and Marks was sorely tempted. In the late 1880s he appears to have used his newspaper to create a market for shares in the Rae (Transvaal) goldmine, unloading his holding through dummy vendors before the price collapsed. It also seems that Marks could be 'squared' by company promoters anxious to secure a favourable reception for a new issue. Edward Hooley's explanation, in 1898, that he had given Marks £17,000 prior to the flotation of the New Beeston Cycle Company because he was 'a friend' failed to convince sceptics (Porter, 8–10). Such abuses were not uncommon among financial journalists at the time.

Marks entered politics in 1889 as a member of the first London county council. A Conservative with progressive inclinations, Marks was an unsuccessful parliamentary candidate at Bethnal Green in 1892. Three years later he gained a narrow victory at St George-in-the-East, another East End constituency, subsequently reinforcing his position when charges relating to corrupt electoral practices were not upheld in court. Although he stood down in 1900, Marks was later praised for his political work in London by Akers-Douglas, Conservative chief whip, who recalled 'a regular attendant and constant supporter of the Government, and a first-rate speaker' (Akers-Douglas to Cobb, 6 Feb 1904, Chilston MSS). In 1904 he re-entered parliament, winning a by-election at Thanet where he had built his principal residence, Callis Court, near Broadstairs. Opinion about Marks among Thanet Conservatives was divided: some of them believed that he was a 'dishonest rogue' and unfit to sit in parliament, but he was popular among local working men, winning again in 1906 despite the intervention of a second Conservative candidate. He retired undefeated in 1910.

Marks suffered a stroke in 1909 and was thereafter in poor health. He retained, as editor-in-chief, a connection with the *Financial News*, interfering in its affairs to the intense irritation of Ellis Powell, who had succeeded him as editor. Powell's revenge, exacted posthumously, was to allege that Marks had tried to sell the paper to a German agent in 1915 (Kynaston, 78–81). Marks died from complications of diabetes at 119A Mount Street, Mayfair, London, on 21 December 1916. His wife also died in 1916.

DILWYN PORTER

Sources H. H. Marks, *Down with the Jews! Meeting of the Society for Suppressing the Jewish Race* (1879) · H. H. Marks, *Small change, or, Lights and shades of New York* (1882) · H. H. Marks, *The metropolitan board of works: a brief account of the disclosures which have led to the appointment of a royal commission* (1888) · H. H. Marks, 'A retrospect', *Financial News* (23 Jan 1904) · D. Porter, '"Trusted guide of the investing public": Harry Marks and the *Financial News*, 1884–1916', *Business History*, 28 (1986), 1–17; repr. in R. P. T. Davenport-Hines, ed., *Speculators and patriots: essays in business biography* (1986) · D. Kynaston, *The Financial*

Times: a centenary history (1988) • *Financial News* (27 Dec 1916) • *Margate, Ramsgate and Isle of Thanet Gazette* (30 Dec 1916) • *The representation of Thanet* (1905) • *Financial and Mining News* (23 Jan 1884) • *Financial and Mining News* (29 April 1884) • *Financial News* (18 Dec 1890) • 'Marks, David Woolf', *DNB* • *CGPLA Eng. & Wales* (1917) • CKS, Chilston papers, U 564 CLp7 • *WWW* • d. cert. • *Financial News* (1884–1916)

Archives BL, Balfour MSS, Add. MSS 49762, 49771 • CKS, Chilston MSS, U 564 CLp7 • Northumbd RO, Newcastle upon Tyne, corresp. and papers relating to Thanet by-election controversy • Powell-Cotton Museum, Birchington, Kent, Powell–Cotton albums **Likenesses** A. J. M., cartoon, repro. in *VF* (8 June 1889) **Wealth at death** £30,933 17s. 4d.: probate, 2 March 1917, *CGPLA Eng. & Wales*

Marks, Henry Stacy (1829–1898), artist, was born on 13 September 1829 at 92 Great Portland Street, London, and baptized at the church of All Souls, Langham Place, on 9 October 1829, the fourth child and eldest surviving son of John Isaac Marks and his wife, Elizabeth Pally. His father was a former solicitor who had given up that profession before his birth in order to take over the running of the family coach-building business, an unwise decision since under his management the business declined. Although he was baptized into the Church of England, Marks was brought up as a dissenter. Compelled to attend lengthy sermons at Craven Chapel, off Regent Street, during his childhood, he developed a streak of anti-clericalism which later manifested itself in his fondness for preaching bogus sermons.

Marks was educated at small private schools near Regent's Park and later at Eythorne in Kent, where, to enable him to assist in the carriage-making business, his father sent him to learn to paint crests and coats of arms. In 1845 he began work as a ledger clerk at a warehouse owned by a friend of his father and soon afterwards joined his father's business. To improve his skill as a painter Marks began about 1846 to attend evening classes at J. M. Leigh's art school in Newman Street. After an earlier rejection, Marks enrolled at the Royal Academy Schools in December 1851. Early in the following year his father was forced to sell the carriage works; this left him free to attend the day classes at the academy, but instead his friend P. H. Calderon persuaded Marks to accompany him to Paris to study at the atelier of François Edouard Picot. Marks also attended the École des Beaux-Arts, but he returned to England in June 1852, leaving Calderon to continue his studies in Paris.

Marks first exhibited at the Royal Academy in 1853, showing a scene from Shakespeare's *Much Ado about Nothing: Dogberry Examining Conrad and Borachio*. It was hung under the line next to Holman Hunt's *Strayed Sheep* and sold to a fellow student for £15. Marks commented: 'I have never enjoyed the sale of any other [work] so much' (Morris and Milner, 61). The works Marks exhibited at the Royal Academy during the 1850s and 1860s were generally either scenes from Shakespeare's plays, for example, *Bardolph* (exh. RA, 1853) or *Francis Feeble, Woman's Tailor* (1865; reproduced in Morris and Milner, 63), or historical genre paintings of medieval scenes. Of his Shakespearian

scenes, G. C. Williamson remarks that, 'few men were so much at home in Shakespeare as was Marks, and that he knew by heart whole plays' (Bryan, *Painters*, 287). Painting scenes of medieval life allowed Marks to practise a neomedieval style of painting which tended to give his figures a naïve quality, for example, *Toothache in the Middle Ages* (exh. RA, 1856; reproduced in Marks, 1.53).

With the failure of his business, John Marks had emigrated to Australia during his son's stay in Paris, and Marks for a time had to support his mother and three younger brothers. His responsibilities increased when on 4 October 1856 he married Helen Drysdale (1829–1892). To supplement his income from painting he took on commissions for wood-drawings for illustrations in *The Home Circle* books, and was art critic of *The Spectator*. He carried out porcelain decoration for the Minton works, church decoration for the firm of Clayton and Bell, friezes for theatres, furniture painting for the architect William Burges, and even Christmas cards. His painting *A Bit of Blue* (1877; Royal Albert Memorial Museum, Exeter), which depicts a porcelain collector examining an addition to his collection, was probably inspired by his earlier work for Minton. The patronage and friendship of the publisher C. E. Mudie and the sale of one of his humorous medieval genre paintings, *The Franciscan Sculptor and his Model* (exh. RA, 1861), for the handsome sum of 300 guineas, brought Marks greater financial security, although he continued to carry out commissions for decorative work. For example, he designed a frieze for an outside wall of the Albert Hall. Most of his later decorative work, however, was for private houses, including that of the neo-classical painter Sir Lawrence Alma-Tadema. His largest commission for house decoration was from Hugh Lupus Grosvenor, first duke of Westminster; he worked on decorations for Eaton Hall, Cheshire, between 1874 and 1880, painting two canvasses 35 feet long of Chaucer's pilgrims for the saloon, and in 1879 twelve panels of birds for the drawing-room.

Marks became a member of the St John's Wood Clique when in 1862 he moved with his wife to Hill Road, St John's Wood. The clique was an association of young artists who shared an interest in historical genre painting. Marks's friend P. H. Calderon also became a member, and his brother-in-law Frederick Walker (who did not live in St John's Wood) was associated with the group. Members aimed to improve their work by submitting it to the rigorous and constructive criticism of the group. Their motto, as framed by Calderon, was, 'the better each man's picture, the better for all' (Marks, 1.147). The clique also had a recreational function, and at meetings Marks would entertain the company by preaching bogus sermons and singing comic songs he had composed. He is depicted in Walker's cartoon *A Vision of the Clique* (1865; reproduced in Marks, 1.90) holding a fool's bauble. Marks was high-spirited but prone to moods of melancholy and misanthropy. His sympathy with, and generosity to, his fellow artists made him very popular in artistic circles.

Marks had been fond of birds since his childhood, but he did not begin to use them as subjects for painting until the middle of his career. *The Convent Raven* (1870; Bristol City Art Gallery) is an early bird painting in oils. *St Francis Preaching to the Birds* (1870), one of his key works, sold for £1155 seven years after Marks sold it to Agnews for £450. His favourite subjects, however, were long-legged birds, particularly storks, cranes, and herons. He also took great delight in parrots and frequently visited the parrot house at London Zoo in order to sketch them. These visits inspired what is probably Marks's most famous painting, *A Select Committee* (1891; Walker Art Gallery, Liverpool). *Convocation* (exh. RA, 1878), which depicts a group of adjutant storks, secured his election as Royal Academician following his election as associate in 1871. It won high, though not unqualified, praise from the eminent art critic John Ruskin. His diploma work, *Science is Measurement*, was regarded as 'one of his highest achievements' (*DNB*). Most of Marks's pictures of birds were watercolours, which he exhibited either at the Old Watercolour Society, of which he became associate in 1871 and member in 1883, or at the two 'bird exhibitions' at the Fine Art Society, which he held in 1889 and 1890. The Victoria and Albert Museum has three of his finished watercolour studies of birds and eleven watercolour sketches for larger bird paintings. Although he was interested in parallels between human behaviour and bird behaviour, Marks did not anthropomorphize his avian subjects. Mr Bartlett, the superintendent of London Zoo, for whom Marks had great respect, discouraged him from imputing human characteristics to birds. His higher reputation as a bird painter rather than as a genre painter rests on the fact that his birds tend to display considerably more animation than his human figures. In his later years Marks painted land- and seascapes 'of notable serenity and breadth' of scenes around Southwold and Walberswick in Suffolk (*DNB*).

Marks's first wife died in 1892. The following year, on 21 December, he married Mary Harriet Kempe (*b.* 1848), a still-life and genre painter. Marks died on 9 January 1898 at his home, 5 St Edmund's Terrace, Regent's Park, and was buried four days later in Hampstead cemetery.

A. R. PENNIE

Sources DNB · H. S. Marks, *Pen and pencil sketches*, 2 vols. (1894) · Graves, *RA exhibitors* · Bryan, *Painters* (1903–5) · E. Morris and F. Milner, *And when did you last see your father?* (1992) [exhibition catalogue, Walker Art Gallery, Liverpool, 13 Nov 1992 – 10 Jan 1993] · Graves, *Artists* · Mallalieu, *Watercolour artists* · F. Lewis, ed., *A dictionary of British bird painters* (1986) · H. Blättel, *International dictionary miniature painters / Internationales Lexikon Miniatur-Maler* (1992) · Bénézit, *Dict.* · J. Turner, ed., *The dictionary of art*, 34 vols. (1996) · S. Houfe, *The dictionary of 19th century British book illustrators and caricaturists*, rev. edn (1996) · B. Hillier, 'The St John's Wood clique', *Apollo*, 79 (1964), 490–95 · G. Leslie, *Letters to Marco* (1893) · www.emory.edu/ENGLISH/classes, 24 April 2002 · parish register, All Souls, Langham Place, 1829, LMA, DL/T/056/006, 49 [baptism] · parish register, Bloomsbury, St George, July 1856–July 1858, LMA, P82/Geo 1/37, 29 [marriage] · m. cert. · d. cert. · *The Times* (14 Jan 1898) · CGPLA Eng. & Wales (1898)
Likenesses D. W. Wynfield, photograph, c.1862–1864, NPG · W. Ouless, oils, exh. RA 1875, repro. in Marks, *Pen and pencil sketches*, frontispiece · H. S. Marks, self-portrait, oils, 1882, Aberdeen Art Gallery · P. H. Calderon, portrait · R. Cleaver, group portrait, pen and ink (*Hanging Committee, Royal Academy, 1892*), NPG · B. L. A. Damman, etching (after W. Ouless, 1875), NPG · H. von Herkomer, watercolour drawing · G. G. Marton, group portrait, watercolour (*Conversazione at the Royal Academy, 1891*), NPG · R. W. Robinson, photograph, NPG · D. W. Wynfield, photograph (members of the St John's Wood Clique), repro. in Hillier, 'The St John's Wood Clique', 490 · wood-engraving (after photograph by Elliott & Fry), NPG; repro. in ILN (8 May 1875)
Wealth at death £9607 12s. 5d.: probate, 23 March 1898, CGPLA Eng. & Wales

Marks, Michael (1859–1907), retailer and chain store founder, was born in Slonim, Russia, in June 1859, the youngest child of Mordecai Marks, a tailor, and his wife, Rebecca. His mother died in childbirth and he was raised by his elder sister. The family lived in considerable poverty and social oppression, typical of so many Jewish communities in nineteenth-century Russia. In his early twenties Marks fled a rising tide of antisemitism and arrived penniless in the north of England. He made his way to Leeds hoping to find employment with John Barran, a manufacturer of clothing who favoured East European refugees. By chance he came across Isaac Dewhirst, a wholesaler, who offered him help and loaned Marks £5 to buy goods from his warehouse. Marks intended to make a living as an itinerant peddler, but he was physically frail and unsuited to such work. As an alternative he took a stall at Kirkgate open market in Leeds, which operated on Tuesdays and Saturdays, and at Castleford and Wakefield, which had different market days. In a short time he expanded his turnover in Leeds by working a stall in the covered market, which was open all week. All his goods were clearly priced and available for customer inspection, and his practice of offering a wide range of products for 1*d.*, under the slogan 'Don't ask the price, it's a penny', was especially popular. From a business point of view it made for simple accounting, as Marks kept no written records in his early years, though he was obliged to rely on a large turnover to compensate for his small margins. His search for products that could sell for 1*d.* led him to stock an increasing variety of wares, from all types of household goods to toys, haberdashery, and stationery. In 1886 he married Hannah (Fanny), daughter of Moses Cohen, a tailor. They had four daughters, including the feminist Rebecca Dora *Sieff, and a son, Simon *Marks (1888–1964), who followed his father in business.

As the business expanded in Leeds, Marks was forced to recruit assistants who could run the stalls while he concentrated more on buying and distribution. He then expanded his business into the markets of the fast growing cotton towns, opening 'penny bazaars' in Warrington in 1887, Birkenhead in 1890, and most importantly in Wigan market-hall in 1891. Wigan was better placed as a distribution centre and he opened a warehouse there and set up home with his family, in order better to supervise his growing retail empire. In 1892 he established another outlet in Bolton and in 1894 a shop in Manchester. Such expansion was proving too difficult for Marks to manage alone and he began to search for a partner; he first

Michael Marks (1859–1907), by unknown photographer

approached Dewhirst, but when he declined, Marks formed a partnership with Thomas Spencer, Dewhirst's cashier. Spencer brought with him much needed organizational skills together with some useful business contacts. The firm of Marks and Spencer was established in 1894 with each partner making share contributions of £300. Marks remained in charge of all the buying operations and the retail side while Spencer focused on the wholesale side and the distribution of goods from the warehouse. It was at this time that Marks moved to Manchester, living above the shop and also leasing a warehouse in the city which was to become the new focus of operations.

Shortly after the firm became a limited company in 1903, Spencer retired and Marks was faced with an increased burden of work. He was now the director of a fairly large organization that had over sixty retail outlets in 1907, all based on the popular principles of open displays and fixed prices. Marks lacked any formal education and was certainly unaware of any of the theories of retailing, but he did have a unique understanding of the market and what customers wanted. He set out to offer consumers value for their money. This was a reflection of his humanitarian outlook, best seen in his treatment of employees. This benevolent attitude was also strongly apparent outside business: he regularly gave money to charities, including the working men's club in Manchester. He also avoided confrontation, inspiring confidence and affection from employees as well as his many friends. He died on 31 December 1907 at Knoll House, 396 Bury New Road, Higher Broughton, Salford; he was survived by

his wife. He left a thriving retail business in the hands of managers until his son was old enough to take responsibility for it.   GARETH SHAW

Sources G. Rees, *St Michael: a history of Marks and Spencer* (1969) • I. Sieff, *Memoirs* (1970) • C. Shaw, 'Marks, Michael', *DBB* • *CGPLA Eng. & Wales* (1908) • m. cert. • d. cert.
Archives Marks and Spencer plc., London, archive
Likenesses photograph, Marks and Spencer, London, archive [*see illus.*]
Wealth at death £27,256 4s. 2d.: probate, 28 Feb 1908, *CGPLA Eng. & Wales*

Marks, Richard (1778–1847), missionary to seafarers, was born on 31 December 1778 at North Crawley, Buckinghamshire, the son of Thomas and Mary Marks. Enlisting in the wartime navy in 1797, he found a ready outlet for a self-described partiality for water, gunpowder, and 'deeds of dangerous enterprize' (Aliquis, *Retrospect*, 1843 edn, 8). Here he recalls with a candour reminiscent of John Newton how he immediately immersed himself in the opportunities for 'unabated licentiousness' of contemporary shipboard life, 'posting down the broad road of destruction, loud in blasphemy, and ever ready to burlesque … the Holy Scriptures' (ibid., 1821 edn, 15). Two narrow escapes from shipwreck in successive ships seemed only to confirm him in a life he openly describes as deliberate rebellion against God.

Meanwhile, Marks clearly took pride in his profession and was popular with his peers. As master's mate on HMS *Defence*, he fought with such distinction at Trafalgar that he was one of the first to receive promotion from Collingwood at the close of the battle. Yet none of this, he would later confess, could dispel the depth of dissatisfaction and despondency which continued to consume him.

At length, after transferring to HMS *Conqueror*, now as lieutenant, Marks managed to find peace of mind and conscience during shore visits while in the Channel service. Thankful for the transformation he had now experienced through the preaching and counselling of the evangelical rector of Old Stoke church, Marks soon sensed a compelling commitment to share with others, particularly fellow seafarers, the key to that gospel of grace he had himself finally found. Through the rest of his life that commitment was destined to manifest itself in three distinct yet complementary ministries, each of fundamental groundbreaking significance in the evolution of organized mission to seafarers during the early 1800s: lay ministry at sea, the provision of Christian literature from shore, and advocacy of the cause in church and society.

Marks's call to lay ministry at sea was quite categorically conveyed by the *Conqueror*'s commander. Impressed with the young lieutenant's resolute response to anti-scriptural scoffing by fellow officers, he summarily ordered Marks to 'turn parson', whereupon the command to 'rig Church' brought the whole ship's company out on deck, an instant congregation of 'six hundred bare heads and attentive looks' (Aliquis, *Retrospect*, 1821 edn, 78). Thus began the public ministry of a pioneer seafarers' missionary. During Marks's remaining three years on board the *Conqueror*, he introduced a whole series of innovative inspirational and educational group activities. While he made light of snide remarks by some about 'Psalm-singing Methodists' on the ship, others were amazed at dramatic manifestations of change among the most 'abandoned characters' in their midst. Eventually a new commander, hostile to Marks's endeavours, presented an insurmountable impediment.

After returning to England in 1810, following thirteen years of unrelenting sea service, Marks relinquished promising prospects of further advancement in the navy, against the advice of well-meaning friends, in order to follow an inner call which had matured in the meantime to ordained ministry among 'poor and plain people' in the established church ashore. He was admitted as a sizar at Magdalene College, Cambridge, on 12 April 1813. In June 1813, on completing his studies at Cambridge, he was ordained as a priest. He gave up as a matter of principle his naval half pay, and served an initial seven-year curacy in a remote village parish of 750 souls. From 1820, following these 'wilderness years', as he later called them, he ministered for the remaining quarter century of his active life among 'the humble cottagers' of Buckinghamshire, as vicar of Great Missenden.

However, Marks gave early and convincing evidence that his decision to leave the sea was by no means motivated by lack of sympathy for followers of his former profession. The concept of full-time shore-based seafarers' missionary service had, at the close of the Napoleonic war, simply not fully dawned on the Christian church. Meanwhile he had himself experienced the scarcity of Christian literature at sea, while witnessing how pornographic books of 'superlative abomination' were widely available 'to debase and pollute' young minds (Marks, *Christian Guardian*, 1826, 174). Well aware of the way fellow seafarers would dismiss with disgust as 'lubberly' even the best of books by well-meaning landlubbers using nautical imagery in an unprofessional manner, Marks saw the need for authentically contextualized literature, and from 1816 led the way with a series of seven booklets, written in popular, readable style, which he presented to the Religious Tract Society for anonymous publication.

Much to Marks's amazement, the impact of his 'sea tracts' within all ranks was immense. Moreover, this happened at a time when thousands of seafarers were transferring from naval to peacetime merchant service. Many of these had already been influenced by the so-called 'Naval Awakening', which had—as on board the *Conqueror*—manifested itself in lay-led Christian cell-group activity on more than eighty men-of-war by the time peace came. Within a decade, half a million of Marks's tracts had been circulated and a wave of similar publications had begun to build on both sides of the Atlantic. It was no coincidence that precisely this decade also saw the emergence of the first comprehensive seafarers' mission organizations in both Britain and America.

It was likewise no coincidence that many who assumed leadership responsibilities in these organizations, at least on the British side, were—like Marks himself—former naval officers. In 1816 Marks had also managed to publish, under the pseudonym Aliquis, a remarkable collection of personal reminiscences from his naval service entitled *The Retrospect, or, Review of Providential Mercies*. Although it attracted a wide-ranging readership and was destined, during the next three decades, to go through numerous editions on both sides of the Atlantic, it was primarily addressed to fellow officers in the Royal Navy. As such, it proved to be a masterpiece of maritime apologetics, with an impact among those officers comparable to that of Marks's maritime tract series among other ranks.

However, not content to provide literature addressed principally to seafarers (which he still continued to do), Marks also launched the first co-ordinated campaign to motivate the national church as such to organize for mission to seafarers. This determined advocacy initiative took the shape of 'An appeal to the Christian public in behalf of British seamen', published in five strongly worded letters to the *Christian Guardian* from January to May 1826, followed by five further letters entitled 'The seaman's friend' from September 1826 to June 1827. While deploring the indifference of those who could leave thousands of their own seafaring kinsfolk with no more knowledge of the gospel than 'savage Hottentots in the wilds of Africa' (Smith, 1826, 55), he had only high praise for the initiatives of existing non-denominational societies, particularly those of their foremost Baptist-affiliated promoter, the Revd George Charles Smith. Realistically recognizing that many years might yet elapse before his own denomination could overcome the irregular nature of church ministry to the peripatetic seafarer, he warmly encouraged fellow evangelical Anglicans to support non-denominational efforts, while leaving no doubt as to where their loyalty belonged once an episcopal establishment for seamen might emerge.

In addition to his extensive maritime authorship, Marks published several more general works of an inspirational, devotional, and theological nature (the last against Socinian and Tractarian positions). After continuing to serve his flock until 1844, Marks died on 22 May 1847 at Great Missenden, Buckinghamshire. A slab marks his grave in the south aisle of Great Missenden parish church. A mural tablet on the south side of the nave testifies to his 'life of piety, usefulness and honor in this village', a tribute eloquently affirmed in two sermons by his successor, the Revd J. B. Marsden, published the same year.

Richard Marks was not the actual originator of organized Anglican maritime mission. The Missions to Seamen, maritime arm of the Church of England, traces its foundation to 1856, and ascribes it to the Revd Dr John Ashley. However, the one who first and fundamentally prepared the way for that event was incontestably an unassuming former lieutenant in the Royal Navy who turned parson.

ROALD KVERNDAL

Sources Aliquis [R. Marks], *The retrospect, or, Review of providential mercies, with anecdotes of various characters, and an address to naval officers* (1816) • [R. Marks], *Nautical essays, or, A spiritual view of the ocean and maritime affairs: with reflections on the battle of Trafalgar and other events by the author of 'The retrospect'* (1818) • [R. Marks], *The ocean, spiritually reviewed, and compared to passing scenes on the land; with various* *anecdotes and reflection by the author of 'The retrospect', 'Morning medita-tions', 'Village observer' &; c.*, 4th expanded edition of *Nautical essays* (1826) · R. Marks, 'An appeal to the Christian public in behalf of British seamen', *Christian Guardian* (1826), 8–14, 49–52, 89–94, 129–36, 169–76 [letters] · R. Marks, 'The seaman's friend', *Christian Guardian* (1826), 337–40, 410–12, 484–6; (1827), 140–42, 209–15 · G. C. Smith, ed., *Sailor's Magazine* (1820), 156 · G. C. Smith, ed., *Sailor's Magazine* (1821), 415–17 · G. C. Smith, ed., *Sailor's Magazine* (1826) [reproducing Marks's letters 1–5 from *Christian Guardian* (Jan–May 1826) with comments] · J. B. Marsden, *Two sermons on … the Rev. Richard Marks* (1847) · R. H. Mackenzie, *The Trafalgar roll* (1913), 182 · lieutenant's passing certificate, PRO, Adm. 107/30, fol. 32 · baptismal certificate, PRO, Adm. 107/30, fol. 33 · [C. Dunford], *Great Missenden parish church: a short history and guide* [1973] · R. Kverndal, *Seamen's missions: their origin and early growth* (1986), 80, 106–9, 167, 210, 275, 286–7, 307, 316, 332, 336, 342 · mural tablet, Great Missenden church, Buckinghamshire · R. M. [R. Marks], letter, *Evangelical Magazine and Missionary Chronicle*, 25 (1817), 168–72

Marks, Simon, first Baron Marks (1888–1964), retailer and business innovator, was born in Trafalgar Street, Leylands, Leeds, on 9 July 1888, the only son and eldest of the five children of Michael *Marks (1859–1907) and his wife, Hannah Cohen. His father came to England as a poor Jewish immigrant from Russia. Within a few years, in 1884, he set up a stall in the open Kirkgate market in Leeds with the slogan 'Don't ask the price—it's a penny'. In 1894 he went into partnership with Thomas Spencer; in 1903 the firm became a private limited company; and when Michael Marks died in 1907 Marks and Spencer Ltd was a chain of sixty 'penny bazaars'.

Simon Marks left Manchester grammar school in 1905 and spent the next two years in France and Germany studying languages and business methods. He joined his father shortly before his death, first as a manager at the company's head office and then as chief merchandiser. He was appointed director in 1911, and in 1916 assumed control as chairman. He occupied this position for forty-eight years, during which he transformed the company into one of the most progressive retail organizations in the world and a national institution.

Marks maintained that there were three factors of success for a retail business: the customers, the suppliers, and the staff, all of whom must derive benefits and contentment from their association. Marks himself enjoyed a fruitful association with Israel (later Lord) *Sieff, whom he met at school. In 1910 Sieff married Marks's eldest sister, Rebecca [see Sieff, Rebecca Dora]. In 1915 Marks married Sieff's sister, Miriam (1894–1971), and asked him to join the board of Marks and Spencer. The two men were to enjoy an intellectual, social, and business partnership lasting over sixty years, their similar outlook on life and business creating what Marks described as a David and Jonathan relationship.

During the First World War Marks joined the Royal Artillery as a signaller, but following the issuing by the British government of the Balfour Declaration he was seconded to Chaim Weizmann to establish and direct the Zionist headquarters in London. The two had met in 1913 at the University of Manchester, where Weizmann taught biochemistry, and this association provided Marks with his first experience of statesmanship. It also gave him an

Simon Marks, first Baron Marks (1888–1964), by Sir Oswald Birley, 1934

appreciation of the potential of science in modern business which he used to develop the distinctive nature of Marks and Spencer stores and their goods.

By 1916 Marks found himself in full command of his father's business, following a Chancery court's ruling against the executors of the Spencer estate, who wanted to have its control. In 1926 Marks and Spencer was incorporated as a public company. In the same year Sieff left his family textile firm to become its full-time vice-chairman and joint managing director, providing Marks with added support at a critical phase in the company's evolution.

Marks called the twenties the formative years. Troubled by both the rapid growth of the rival Woolworth chain and his own inexperience in retail management, Marks visited America in 1924 and undertook an intensive study of retail practices. This enabled him to lay down the principles which not only revolutionized his own business but were to have an effect on the whole of British retailing and beyond. Essentially, Marks set about meeting the latent demand for quality goods at affordable prices, turning a chain of jumbled bazaars into one of modern stores with an increasing emphasis on clothing and food lines. In order to achieve this Marks transformed key elements of the firm's business strategy, establishing a new pricing policy, revolutionizing the firm's relationship with its suppliers, and initiating a new store development programme.

The First World War put an end to the penny price point, and the simplicity of this original pricing policy was not regained until Marks returned from America. Impressed by the goods offered there within the dollar limit, he established a new 5s. price ceiling, which enabled Marks and Spencer to use economies of co-ordinated large-scale production and distribution to create a range of clothing for the family. As part of this process Marks determined to eliminate the wholesaler from the distribution system. Instead, the firm dealt directly with the manufacturer. This was a revolutionary step for a retailer to take and required the development of an educational programme for its suppliers, advising the manufacturer what the public wanted and assisting with expert advice on technology, production engineering, and so on. To ensure better and more consistent quality, the company established its own technological organization to research and test materials and garments, to set specification standards, and to enforce quality control.

'St Michael', the brand name of Marks and Spencer, was registered in 1928 and gradually all the goods sold in the stores were produced under this name to the company's own specifications. Convinced of the quality of domestic manufacturing and dependent on their complete co-operation, Marks and Spencer turned increasingly to British suppliers, so that by 1939 Marks was able to say that 99 per cent of the goods were British made.

The capital available from the public issue of shares made it possible to implement a policy of progressive enlargement, rebuilding, and modernization of the stores, and of continuous improvement of standards, both for the customers and the staff. The new stores provided Marks with a deep satisfaction and were fundamental to his strategy of transforming the company from a 'working class' firm to an 'all class' firm. This aspiration was symbolized in the opening of the state-of-the-art Pantheon store in Oxford Street, London, in 1938, although it was not fully realized until the 1960s. Very little was spent on advertising. Marks always laid great stress on the importance of direct communications through good human relations and personal contact; he introduced efficient stock control to speed up the flow of goods directly from factories to stores. A firm believer in what he termed 'management by walking about', Marks would visit the Marble Arch store on an almost daily basis to assess its operation and to determine what was selling.

From the beginning, the company initiated an enlightened welfare policy towards its staff, starting with the provision of a good hot midday meal and extending to unrivalled medical, dental, catering, and social services, generous pensions, and comfortable quarters. This humane attitude to his shop employees was further demonstrated by Marks's careful and considerate manner on his frequent visits to the stores. In contrast, however, he could be both autocratic and demanding with senior managerial staff, retaining a tight, 'old fashioned' control of the company and its dealings.

During the Second World War Marks served as deputy chairman of the London and South-East Regional Production Board and as adviser to the petroleum warfare department. A co-founder and benefactor of the Air Defence Cadet Corps before the war, he served as one of the first directors of British Overseas Airways.

Marks's talent as a merchandiser was demonstrated again in the post-war years by his decision to increase the company's commitment to provide affordable yet high-quality and fashionable clothing, particularly for women. This strategy met with considerable success during the 1950s and established the 'St Michael' brand name as one of the most popular in the country. Indeed, its impact was such that the company's historian claimed that it helped to begin what has been described as a democratic revolution in women's clothing. The expansion into foodstuffs followed a similar path, with the emphasis on quality and freshness reflecting Marks's almost fanatical interest in hygiene and cleanliness.

Although conservative by nature Marks was aware of the need to adapt. He was always ready to examine and re-examine both merchandise and systems and to reconsider any approach that had taken root. Visionary and sometimes instinctive in his decision-making, he often said to those he led and guided: 'I am the greatest rebel of you all.' Very impatient with rising costs, in 1956 he started the 'good housekeeping campaign' to simplify his business and eliminate unproductive paperwork. This led to higher efficiency, lower prices, and a greater sense of involvement among the staff. This 'operation simplification' was widely reported and caught the popular imagination.

Marks had a strong sense of social responsibility and was ready to give generous help to those who wanted to learn from his success. He was also personally warmly and lavishly generous. His interests included the Royal College of Surgeons, University College, London, Manchester grammar school, the British Heart Foundation, and always Israel.

Marks was knighted in 1944 and raised to the peerage in 1961; the speeches he made in the House of Lords showed pride in British achievement and a desire to enhance it. Parallel with his love for England was a passionate commitment to Zionism. He was president of the Joint Palestine Appeal and honorary vice-president of the Zionist Federation. Following the establishment of Israel he worked tirelessly to help the fledgeling state overcome its many problems.

Honours conferred on him included the honorary DSc (economics) of London, LLD of Manchester and Leeds, PhD of the Hebrew University of Jerusalem; the honorary fellowship of the Royal College of Surgeons, of the Weizmann Institute of Science at Rehovot, and of University College, London. In 1962 he was the first recipient outside the United States of the Tobé award for the most distinguished retailers.

Marks conveyed an impression of youthful enthusiasm and spontaneous warmth, with his sensitive and mobile features. Of small build, he had appraising eyes under heavy eyebrows and a full head of hair. His spirit was vibrant but his manner and humour were understated. He had a mercurial personality: soft in sympathy but passionately relentless in determination, with an earthy sense of fun, particularly at the expense of pomposity.

Marks had great personal charm and was a good companion, with an extraordinary zest for life and a capacity to surprise. He liked to be surrounded by his family in his Grosvenor Square flat or the Berkshire farm; he had one son and one daughter. Once an ardent tennis player, he enjoyed the theatre and concerts, yachting and the races, collecting French Impressionists or antique furniture, and reading. Most of all, though, he was tied to the business which he had nurtured, and continued to play a fully active role in its activities throughout his final years despite declining health. Marks died of heart failure on 8 December 1964 at the head office of Marks and Spencer at 47 Baker Street, London. He was survived by his wife and two children and was succeeded as company chairman by Israel Sieff and in his title by his son, Michael.

SIEFF, rev. ANDREW ALEXANDER

Sources I. Sieff, *Memoirs* (1970) · G. Rees, *St Michael: a history of Marks and Spencer* (1969) · P. Bookbinder, *Marks & Spencer: the war years, 1939–1945* (1989) · *The Times* (9 Dec 1964) · *The Guardian* (9 Dec 1964) · *Yorkshire Post* (9 Dec 1964) · A. Briggs, *Marks & Spencer, 1884–1984* (1984) · M. Sieff, *Don't ask the price* (1986) · private information (1980)
Archives Central Zionist Archives, Jerusalem, corresp. · Marks & Spencer plc, London, corresp. and papers · Weizmann Archive, Rehovot, Israel, corresp.
Likenesses W. Stoneman, photograph, 1933, NPG · O. Birley, oils, 1934, unknown collection; copyprint, Courtauld Inst. [*see illus.*] · double portrait, photograph, 1959 (with Archibald McIndoe), Hult. Arch. · F. O. Salisbury, oils, Marks & Spencer plc, London; in company boardroom · photograph, Marks & Spencer plc, London
Wealth at death £1,830,935: probate, 21 Dec 1964, *CGPLA Eng. & Wales*

Markus [*née* Scharfstein], **Erika** [Rixi] **(1910–1992)**, bridge player and writer, was born on 27 June 1910 in Gura Humora, then in the Austro-Hungarian empire (but now in Romania), the youngest daughter of Michael and Louise Scharfstein, a prosperous Jewish couple with interests in forests and vineyards. After the First World War the family moved to Vienna, where Rixi (as she became known) was educated in music, literature, and the theatre. She learned from one aunt to play poker, and from an uncle in the Netherlands to play whist at ten and bridge (*plafond*) at thirteen; she had natural card-playing sense. Her parents did not approve, but after attending finishing-school in Dresden (Frau Wallenstein's *Pensionat* for Jewish daughters of good families) she took up bridge in Vienna and was regarded as a prodigy.

Through bridge Rixi met Salomon Markus. Twice her age, and in the shoe business, 'Salo' first admired her ability but soon resented her success, objecting to her playing in coffee houses, surrounded by men. Rixi married him in 1928, partly to remain in Vienna after her parents moved to Berlin, but equally to continue playing. Marriage proved a complete disaster (the only mistake to which Rixi would admit). Pregnant at nineteen (her only daughter was born in 1929), she fell seriously ill. This ruined any chance of an active career and led her to become a professional bridge player in 1934.

Rixi caught the attention of Dr Paul Stern, who invited her to join the Austrian women's team, in defiance of her husband's will. Partnered by Ethel Ernst, she won the first

European women's championship (Brussels, 1935) and the second (Stockholm, 1936), then the world women's championship (Budapest, 1937), her team remaining unbeaten in international play. The Anschluss ruined her plans for Oslo in 1938. She left for England, where her parents had moved in 1936, as Hitler entered Vienna. Her husband followed, but the marriage was dissolved in 1942. An elder sister, living in Poland, died in a concentration camp. Salomon Markus later became a millionaire property developer in Austria, and her daughter Margo led a glamorous life in America but died in 1976 from cancer, aged forty-six. Rixi had many affairs, including a thirteen-year alliance with (Norman) Harold *Lever, Baron Lever (1914–1995), millionaire lawyer, Labour cabinet minister, and a bridge player of international class; but she never remarried.

Bridge offered Rixi an entry into society, through Lady Rhodes, Manning Foster, and other influential figures. During the Second World War she was a fire-watcher and translator for the Red Cross. Naturalized in 1950, she played for Britain, partnering Doris Rhodes in the ladies' team which won the European championship in 1951 (Venice) and 1952 (Ireland), and toured the USA in 1953. Her partnership with Fritzi Gordon [*see below*] began in 1951 when Sidney Lee, trailing Denmark in the final, successfully reshuffled his pairings. Universally known as Frisky and Bitchy for their free-wheeling style and willingness to confide to all that the other was 'a selfish bitch' (*Daily Telegraph*, 6 April 1992), the pair were a formidable partnership which often disintegrated, but both recognized the special chemistry that made them the top women's pairing of all time. Rixi's highlights included winning the European women's championship (1951, 1952, 1959, 1961, 1963, 1966, mostly with Fritzi); the gold cup (1961); the world women's pairs (1962, 1974); the world mixed teams of four (1962, with Nico Gardener); the women's team Olympiad (1964); and the inaugural European bridge cup (1974–5). Rixi had numerous victories in the spring foursomes and masters pairs, and the Whitelaw, Lady Milne, Queen's, and Hubert Phillips cups. With over 100 international and national titles, she was the outstanding woman player of her day; but Fritzi was close behind.

Friederike [Fritzi] **Gordon** [*née* Leist] **(1906–1992)**, bridge player, was born in Vienna on 25 January 1906 (she claimed 1916), of middle-class Jewish parents. She worked as a buyer for a Salzburg store before marrying Paul Gordon and moving to Graz. After the Anschluss she fled to London and supported her family through playing poker. Paul Gordon was an excellent bridge player, and her brother Hans Leist a gold cup winner. Fritzi represented Britain fifteen times in the women's European championship, winning seven gold medals. She shared many of Rixi's triumphs, notably in the world women's pairs (1962, 1974), mixed team Olympiads (1962, with Boris Schapiro), and women's team Olympics (1964—Britain's only Olympiad successes). She twice won the gold cup (1957, 1961), and was the second woman to attain world grandmaster status, Rixi being the first. Their last major tournament together was the Monte Carlo Olympiad (1976). Survived by one daughter, Fritzi died on 9 February 1992 in the Royal Free Hospital, Camden.

Despite their similar backgrounds, the two were not friends, sharing only their bridge skills, a tigerish appetite for success, and a knack for disconcerting opponents. Rixi was regarded as friendly away from the table, but intolerably aggressive at play, preferring to be respected and feared rather than liked. She disliked artificial bidding, advocating a simple system with a strong NT and CAB responses to 2C and relying on flair and technique. Her slogan was 'Bid boldly, play safe', which became the title of her first and best book (1966). Her 'Rixi bids', as Terence Reese christened them, were notorious: intuitive leaps to 'lucky' contracts ('Soaring fancy, wild illogicality and comical resource'), which were, she insisted, the outcome of inexorable logic plus aggression, with the thrill of danger. She had a photographic memory, and an uncanny sixth sense. As a woman respected in a man's world she often scorned the abilities of other women.

Rixi contributed regular columns to *The Guardian* (1955–92) and the *Evening Standard* (1975–80), many syndicated widely. She was a contributing editor to *The Bridge Player's Encyclopedia* (1967). She regularly organized the *Guardian* Easter tournament, the *Evening Standard* charity congress (August), and the *Harpers & Queen* festival (December); and she initiated the annual Lords v. Commons challenge match. The author of a dozen books (the early ones written with the assistance of Derek Senior), she at first offered excellent analysis, then tended to recycle her *Guardian* gossip or simply present hands. Some she translated into German. *Aces and Places* (1972) and *Bridge around the World* (1977) reflect the international circuit, from St Moritz in January to Marrakesh in December, offering insights into the foibles of the rich and famous but too often name-dropping and excessively promoting her own interests. In her memoirs, *A Vulnerable Game* (1988), a minor classic without a single bridge hand, she discusses her life and interests in ballroom dancing, gourmet cooking, music, theatre, and sport.

Rixi Markus received many honours. She won five world titles and four Olympic gold medals, ten European championships, and a gold medal from the European Bridge League as best ladies' player (1959); she was recognized by the World Bridge Federation as best woman player (1972) and first woman grandmaster (1974), and was named 'bridge personality of the year' by the International Press Association (1974) and Charles Goren player of the year (1976); and she was awarded the Common Market medal of honour and, prized above all, the MBE for services to bridge (1975). The Rixi Markus cup (women's individual) was named after her, and she participated in Channel 4's *Master Bridge* series (1983). She died on 4 April 1992, two months after Fritzi Gordon, at 42 Nottingham Place, Westminster, from pneumonia, having written her *Guardian* columns almost to the end.   CHRIS ACKERLEY

Sources R. Markus, *A vulnerable game* (1988) · WWW, 1991–5, p. 366 · *Sunday Times* (5 April 1992) · P. Jourdain, *Sunday Telegraph* (5 April 1992) · *Daily Telegraph* (6 April 1992) · A. Hiran, *The Independent* (6 April 1992) · *The bridge player's encyclopedia* (1967) · www.bridgeguys.com/winners/BritishGoldCupwinners.html, 10 Sept 2001 · *The Times* (12 Feb 1992) · *Daily Telegraph* (11 Feb 1992) [Fritzi Gordon] · d. cert. [Fritzi Gordon]
Likenesses J. Cassab, oils, 1958, NPG
Wealth at death £1,115,759: probate, 1992, CGPLA Eng. & Wales

Markwick [Markwith], **Nathaniel** (1664–1735), Church of England clergyman, son of James Markwick of Croydon, was born in April 1664. He was admitted to Merchant Taylors' School in 1677, and matriculated as a commoner at St John's College, Oxford, on 14 July 1682, aged eighteen. He graduated BA in 1686, and proceeded MA in 1690, and BD (under the name of Markwith) on 1 February 1696. After being ordained a priest he was vicar of Westbury, Buckinghamshire, from 1692 to 1694, and of St Mary Magdalen's, Taunton, from 1696 until 1703. He had, in addition, become a prebendary of Bath and Wells on 4 October 1699. From 1703 until his death, on 20 March 1735, he was vicar of East Brent, Somerset.

Between 1728 and 1734 Markwick published a number of works calculating the date of the apocalyptic destruction of Jerusalem foretold in the Old Testament. The first of these, subsequently extended and supplemented, was *A Calculation of the LXX Weeks of Daniel, Chapter IX Verse 24* (1728) or *Stricturae Lucis*.

    G. LE G. NORGATE, *rev.* ROBERT BROWN

Sources Foster, *Alum. Oxon.* · C. J. Robinson, ed., *A register of the scholars admitted into Merchant Taylors' School, from* AD 1562 *to* 1874, 2 vols. (1882–3) · *Fasti Angl.* (Hardy)

Markyate, Christina of (b. c.1096, d. after 1145), hermit and prioress of Markyate, was born c.1096, the daughter of an Anglo-Saxon nobleman, Auti, whose family had large possessions in Huntingdon, and his wife, Beatrix. Her baptismal name was Theodora, but she later took the name Christina, presumably to underline her position as one vowed to Christ. At an early age she was taken to the abbey of St Albans, where she made a secret vow of virginity and scratched a cross on its walls as a sign. Some years later her aunt, Alveva, who had been the mistress of Ranulf Flambard before he became bishop of Durham, entertained him on his way to London, and after the feast Christina was left with him in his room, where he attempted to seduce her. On the plea that she feared others might intrude, she asked permission to lock the door and promptly did so from the outside. The bishop, enraged at being deluded by a mere girl, determined to have his revenge. About 1115 he persuaded her parents to give her in marriage to a friend of his named Burhred, and by constant threats and ill treatment she was forced to consent. On refusing to consummate the marriage she was brought before the prior of Huntingdon. She defended her case so well that the prior gave judgment in her favour. The parents then appealed to Robert Bloet, bishop of Lincoln, who also declared in her favour. Subsequently he was persuaded by liberal bribes to reverse his judgment. From that time she was kept in close confinement and treated with cruelty. Eventually, she secretly engaged a local hermit to describe her plight to Ralph d'Escures, archbishop of Canterbury, and on hearing that he supported her case, she decided to escape.

Christina arranged with the servant of the hermit to bring horses early one morning while her parents were away, and, dressed in man's garb, she escaped on horseback, riding 30 miles to Flamstead, where she took refuge with Alfwen, a recluse. She stayed hidden at Flamstead for two years, eventually moving to Markyate, another hermitage ruled over by Roger, a former monk of St Albans. She remained there for four years, confined to a cell that would allow her neither to sit nor lie down: it was closed by a large stone that could be moved only by Roger. After four years Roger died and, owing to the enmity of the bishop of Lincoln, she appealed for protection to Thurstan, archbishop of York. Probably about 1120, with Thurstan's help, she obtained the annulment of her marriage.

In 1123 Christina returned to Markyate, where a community which would eventually be formally constituted as a nunnery gathered round her. It may well have been for this community that the celebrated St Albans psalter (now in Hildesheim) was prepared or adapted, with its drawings of episodes in the life of St Alexis (who also made a chaste marriage) and of the appearance of the risen Christ to two disciples as they walked to Emmaus, mirroring events in Christina's own life. By 1130 her reputation had spread far and wide and she was sought after as superior for many communities. Archbishop Thurstan wanted her to rule his foundation of St Clement in York, and suggested her as abbess of Marcigny and Fontevrault in France. By this time she had become friendly with Geoffrey de Gorham, abbot of St Albans, who persuaded her to make her monastic profession before Alexander, bishop of Lincoln. Her life now became peaceful and she gave counsel and encouragement to Abbot Geoffrey when he became involved in the ecclesiastical politics of the early years of Stephen's reign. At this point, apparently around the year 1140, the manuscript containing Christina's biography is cut off, though other sources reveal that a priory was built for her at Markyate in 1145. Gifts of her embroidery were sent to Pope Adrian IV in 1155, but it cannot be safely deduced from this that she was herself still alive at that date and the date of her death is unknown. A contemporary account of her life (which may even have been written before her death) survives in the second volume of BL, Cotton MS Tiberius E.i, which was badly damaged in the fire which devastated the Cottonian Library in 1731, though the fire was not responsible for the loss of the manuscript's concluding folios. Until the mid-twentieth century the story of Christina's life was known only through an abridgement of it made by the recusant writer Nicholas Roscarrock at a date about 1600. However, a careful and prolonged investigation by C. H. Talbot, helped by the resources of modern science, led to the publication in 1959 of as much of the surviving text as remains legible, which is considerably more than might have been expected. As a result, the story of Christina of Markyate

has come to be appreciated as one of the fullest and most vivid accounts of a woman's life to survive from the twelfth century.

C. H. TALBOT, rev. HENRY SUMMERSON

Sources *The life of Christina of Markyate*, ed. C. H. Talbot, 2nd edn (1987) · S. Thompson, *Women religious: the founding of English nunneries after the Norman conquest* (1991) · C. J. Holdsworth, 'Christina of Markyate', *Medieval women*, ed. D. Baker (1978), 185–204 · O. Pächt, C. R. Dodwell, and F. Wormald, *The St Albans psalter* (1960)

Marlborough. For this title name *see* Ley, James, first earl of Marlborough (1550–1629); Ley, James, third earl of Marlborough (1618/19–1665); Churchill, John, first duke of Marlborough (1650–1722); Churchill, Sarah, duchess of Marlborough (1660–1744); Spencer, Charles, third duke of Marlborough (1706–1758); Spencer, George, fourth duke of Marlborough (1739–1817); Churchill, George Spencer-, fifth duke of Marlborough (1766–1840) [*see under* Spencer, George, fourth duke of Marlborough (1739–1817)]; Churchill, George Spencer-, sixth duke of Marlborough (1793–1857); Churchill, John Winston Spencer, seventh duke of Marlborough (1822–1883); Churchill, Gladys Marie Spencer-, duchess of Marlborough (1881–1977).

Marlborough [Marleburgh], **Henry** (*d.* in or after 1421), chronicler, was probably a member of the Marleburgh family which appears in Dublin archiepiscopal records from 1219, and in connection with Swords, Dublin, from 1256. In 1359 the surname is found in the Christ Church deeds in connection with property in the Dublin parish of St John. According to J. T. Gilbert, two Latin deeds (now lost) relating to house property in Dublin were executed by Henry Marlborough at Dublin on 6 June 1418 and attached to them were Marlborough's seal with his initials and also the official seal of the Dublin mayoralty. In 1395 all the lordships, messuages, rents, and services in Bakbystown, that Henry Marlborough, clerk, had conveyed by deed to the king, were granted to the prior of St Wolstan. Three years later Marlborough is named as rector of Kylladown in the diocese of Dublin, in a letter proposing that he should have the more profitable vicarage of St Cumnyra in the same parish. In 1412 he is named as vicar of Balscadden and in 1413 as vicar of Donabate. Marlborough also had some interests in England, as there is record of letters of attorney granted to cover journeys there in 1413 and, perhaps more significantly, on 22 April 1421.

The potential significance of the latter date lies in the fact that Marlborough was the author of seven books of annals of England and Ireland down to 1421, under the title of *Cronica excerpta de medulla diversorum*. This work is said to have been begun in 1406. The final year of the annals, 1421, describes the parliament held at Dublin at Easter, and this is followed by brief notices from May and June in the same year. The final entry, still under the year 1421, refers to 29 September 1435, and may not have been Marlborough's work. His death is recorded in the *Book of Obits and Martyrology* of Holy Trinity priory, Dublin, under 12 May, but no year is given.

Although Marlborough's annals are said at the outset to

be heavily indebted to Ranulf Higden, they have a particular importance for early fifteenth-century Ireland, and not least for its parliaments. Thus it is Marlborough who reports among the events of 1413 a native Irish attack on the English lordship at a time when parliament was in session, 'as their usuall custome was in time of other parliaments' (Ware, 2.25). He also records how in August 1408 the Irish attacked and wounded the king's lieutenant and younger son, Thomas of Lancaster, shortly after the latter's arrival in Ireland, and how in 1420 a subsequent lieutenant, Sir John Talbot, left office amid universal execration, due to his failure to pay for goods he had taken by purveyance. Marlborough also has information for the fourteenth century not found elsewhere. For example, he is aware that Sir Walter Bermingham claimed benefit of clergy in 1332; and under the following year points to an important Irish contribution to Edward III's successful campaign in Scotland.

Parts of Marlborough's annals have been printed in William Camden's *Britannia*, of 1607, and in *Ancient Irish Histories: the Chronicle of Ireland, Collected by Meredith Hanmer, 1571*, which was published in 1633 in an edition by Sir James Ware, reissued in 1809. BERNADETTE A. WILLIAMS

Sources [J. Ware], ed., *The historie of Ireland* (1633), vol. 2 · G. Camdeno [W. Camden], *Britannia, sive, Florentissimorum regnorum, Angliae, Scotiae, Hiberniae*, later edn (1607) · C. McNeill, ed., *Calendar of Archbishop Alen's register, c.1172–1534* (1950) · M. J. McEnery, ed., 'Calendar to Christ Church deeds, 1174–1684', *Report of the Deputy Keeper of the Public Records in Ireland*, 20 (1888); 23 (1891) · *CEPR letters*, vol. 5 · E. Tresham, ed., *Rotulorum patentium et clausorum cancellariae Hiberniae calendarium*, Irish Record Commission (1828) · *CPR, 1399–1401* · J. C. Crosthwaite, ed., *The book of obits and martyrology of the cathedral church … Dublin*, Irish Archaeological Society, 4 (1844) · *DNB* · P. Connolly, 'An attempted escape from Dublin Castle: the trial of William and Walter de Bermingham, 1332', *Irish Historical Studies*, 29 (1994–5), 100–08

Marlborough, Thomas of (d. 1236), historian, lawyer, and abbot of Evesham, presumably came from Marlborough in Wiltshire. He studied at Paris under Stephen Langton (d. 1228), most likely arts, when Richard Poor or Poore (d. 1235) was his fellow student: this was probably in the 1180s. He describes John of Tynemouth, Simon of Sywell, and Master Honorius as his 'masters in the schools', and as the common bond between these three is that they were all canonists active at Oxford, he must have also studied there, presumably canon law. It is clear from the chronicle he wrote that he was well versed in law, and had taught at Oxford, before he was professed at Evesham. His teaching must have been in the growing university because there were no grammar schools of importance at Oxford, such as those attached to cathedrals, but the statement that he taught also at Exeter is likely to be the result of a miscopying or mishearing of the text. He was thus no ordinary young novice when he arrived at Evesham to be professed in 1199/1200. By this date, given his previous training and career, he must have been at least in his thirties. Circumstances then arose that were to thrust him into prominence.

In 1202 the newly appointed Bishop Mauger of Worcester (d. 1212) attempted to visit Evesham. From this point until the settlement of the case, Marlborough's activities were taken up with the convent's determined struggle to prove its exemption from the bishop. For its defiance in refusing entry to the bishop, the convent was excommunicated. The monks sought to bring the abbey's case before the archbishop of Canterbury. But the case was too complex for settlement by any other court than the final one and appeal was made to the pope. The main case over the exemption from the diocesan, and the complementary case of the monastery's jurisdiction over the local area known as the Vale, were both fought out at Rome before the masterly Pope Innocent III and his advisers. Marlborough went to Rome to present the abbey's case and during this time he attended the schools at Bologna. In the struggle against the bishop, the abbot and convent attempted to present a united front, although the infamous Abbot Roger Norreis had never been accepted by the monks. He had mercilessly tyrannized over them, keeping them short of food and clothing, calling them 'dogs', acting more like a layman than a priest, and wasting the convent's lands. He was a drunkard and a lecher, and reputed to be a murderer. He was adept at making friends in influential places, which allowed him to be promoted and to survive for so long without censure. It was agreed that any charges against the abbot would not be raised at Rome, though the abbot's treatment of the convent's proctors at Rome was infamous.

After the triumph in 1205, when the abbey's exemption was declared, and the judgment on jurisdiction over the Vale (1207), the main struggle at Evesham was to control Abbot Roger Norreis and to restore the monastery. In both these matters Marlborough was closely involved, and from 1206 he acted as dean of the Vale. Matters were made more difficult by the interdict on the English church from 1208 to 1214, and, indeed, by the abbey's newly won exemption from any kind of correction by the diocesan. The convent was not finally relieved of the abbot until his deposition in 1213. As dean of the Vale, Marlborough attended the Fourth Lateran Council in Rome with Abbot Randulf, and while they were there the pope approved on 16 February 1216 the constitutions that had been drawn up to specify the properties of the obedientiaries and their rights and privileges—an attempt to restore the position of the convent after Abbot Norreis's depredations of their lands and revenues. In this remarkable document Marlborough doubtless had a hand. In 1217 he was made sacrist, and a year later he was appointed prior.

During his time as prior Marlborough completed what has misleadingly been called his chronicle of the abbey. It is in fact a unique account of the lawsuit fought out at Rome, which he prefaced with an abbreviated edition of Prior Dominic's life of St Ecgwine and *Gesta* of the abbots, written in the early twelfth century, and of the continued *Gesta* up to the time of Abbot Norreis (1191). The whole of the description of the lawsuit is written with a frankness and verve that makes the work remarkable on those counts alone. His vivid description of the journey to Rome, of the way in which the curia operated, of the pope and the cardinals, of the trials and tribulations of the petitioner, are without parallel at this date. He was observant and perceptive, and could tell a good story. There are small and important details: the advice of the pope to go to study at Bologna (which he did for six months), Marlborough's fainting for joy when the exemption was declared, and many other memorable vignettes. The great speech made by Marlborough nearly ten years later before the legate, Nicolò, bishop of Tusculum (mistakenly identified as Pandulf by earlier historians), prefacing the final fall of Roger Norreis, is memorable.

Marlborough's subsequent career was taken up with paying off the debts consequent upon the lawsuit and maintaining every aspect of the abbey's rights (perhaps condoning further forgeries). He did, however, submit the convent to archiepiscopal visitation. The continuation of the 'chronicle' includes lives and acts of the abbots and reveals that it was due to him that the customs and revenues were finally written down and approved at the time of the Lateran Council. The biographer is fond of detailing building works: according to him, Marlborough, as sacrist, repaired much of the damage that had been caused to the windows and tombs in the presbytery by the collapse of the tower. He renewed the shrine of St Wigstan, had a reading-desk made for the choir, put a stove in the church at the base of the clock, and had twelve albs made. All this he did in the year before he was appointed prior and much of it was paid for by his careful financial management as sacrist. As prior he brought with him a considerable number of books, including law books, unfortunately not specified. There were also works on natural science, classical authors, sermons, commentaries, and books on grammar and music. He had several books produced (including what is now Bodl. Oxf., MS Rawl. A. 287, to fol. 181v) and he purchased others. He continued to beautify the church, particularly concentrating on the story of St Ecgwine (Evesham's premier saint) in the stained glass of the presbytery and on his shrine, for which he built a throne.

On the death of Abbot Randulf, Marlborough was elected abbot on 20 December 1229, confirmed by the pope in 1230, and blessed by the bishop of Coventry, and finally, after the king had had granted possession of the abbey, installed by the bishop at Michaelmas. The period during which the king had had possession was costly, as was the election process, so Marlborough began his abbatiate in debt. However, judicious management enabled him to enhance the dignity and appearance of the church, to construct comfortable quarters for the abbot, and to build his own tomb. He died at Evesham on 12 September 1236 and was buried there.   JANE E. SAYERS

Sources W. D. Macray, ed., *Chronicon abbatiae de Evesham, ad annum 1418*, Rolls Series, 29 (1863) [Bod., MS Rawlinson A.287] · J. Sayers and L. Watkiss, eds. and trans., *Chronicon abbatiae de Evesham*, OMT [forthcoming] · BL, Cotton MS Vespasian B.xxiv · BL, Harley MS 3763 · BL, Cotton MS Augustus ii.2 · Emden, *Oxf.*, vol. 2 · J. Sayers, '"Original", cartulary and chronicle: the case of the abbey of Evesham', *Fälschungen im Mittelalter*, MGH Schriften, 33/4 (Hanover, 1988), 371–95 · S. Kuttner and E. Rathbone, 'Anglo-Norman canonists of the twelfth century', *Traditio*, 7 (1949–51), 279–358 · L. E. Boyle, 'Canon law before 1380', *Hist. U. Oxf.* 1: *Early Oxf. schools* ·

R. Sharpe and others, eds., *English Benedictine libraries: the shorter catalogues* (1996) · A. Gransden, *Historical writing in England*, 1 (1974)

Marleberge, Thomas de. *See* Marlborough, Thomas of (*d.* 1236).

Marley. For this title name *see* Aman, Dudley Leigh, first Baron Marley (1884–1952).

Marley, Hilda Gertrude [*name in religion* Marie Hilda] (1876–1951), psychologist and educationist, was born at Gaunless Mill, Bishop Auckland, co. Durham, on 13 October 1876, the youngest of seven children of George Marley, a miller, and his wife, Marie Anne Caroline, *née* Simonds. One of her older sisters, Louise, entered the order of the Sacred Heart and spent most of her life at that order's convent in Aberdeen. In 1879 the four youngest children went with their parents to Wynberg near Cape Town, Cape Colony. There Hilda went to a school run by Dominican nuns. After the family's return to England in 1881, she attended the Notre Dame boarding-school in Sheffield, Yorkshire, before going to the Notre Dame Training College for Teachers at Mount Pleasant, Liverpool, in 1896. She then joined the order of Notre Dame de Namur, an order dedicated 'to teach the poor in the most neglected places', entering the mother house in Belgium on 24 September 1898; she took the name Marie Hilda. After becoming a professed sister in August 1901 she returned to England to teach and pursue her private studies.

In 1904 Sister Marie Hilda became a lecturer at the Notre Dame Training College, Dowanhill, Glasgow, the only Roman Catholic teacher training college in Scotland, and continued her external study at London University, graduating with a BA (honours) in history in 1910. She was appointed principal lecturer in psychology in 1921, and until 1931 was engaged in experimental work and research, testing children, advising parents, devising a textbook, and building a psychological laboratory. From June to September 1924 she undertook psychological studies at Louvain University. In May 1930 her first publication, 'A mental survey of a Scottish suburban school', assessing the suitability of intelligence tests for school children, appeared as a supplement to the *Scottish Educational Journal*.

Sister Marie Hilda's engagement in the psychology of individual differences and the emergence of the notion of maladjustment led her to take up the challenge of Robert Robertson Rusk (1879–1972), lecturer in education at the Jordanhill Training College for Teachers, who suggested in 1930 that she establish a child guidance clinic in Glasgow. The child guidance movement at that time was developing techniques to help the child fulfil its potential and she visited two clinics in London, the Islington Clinic and the London Child Guidance Clinic at Canonbury Place, to study methods and procedures. In April 1931 she helped Lady Margaret Kerr to establish a Catholic child guidance clinic in Edinburgh. With a grant from the trustees of the Commonwealth Fund, a personal legacy of £300, and the sanction of the archbishop of Glasgow, she established a child guidance clinic in Notre Dame College in September 1931. Initially the clinic was housed in one room and a team of three undertook the work. The London Child Guidance Clinic lent a fully trained psychiatric social worker for two years and Sister Marie Hilda became director and psychologist, as well as continuing her college teaching.

Sister Marie Hilda retired from the training college in 1941 and opened the clinic full time, the work expanding from 30 to about 800 cases per year within ten years. In 1945 premises at 20 Athole Gardens were acquired and the staff increased to around thirty. The clinic dealt with problem children; it was non-denominational and free to all children attending. It became a training centre for students, from the UK and overseas. A second Notre Dame Child Guidance Clinic was set up with her help in Liverpool in 1942.

Sister Marie Hilda lectured in almost every large centre in England and Scotland, and in 1947 made a lecture tour of Ireland. At the invitation of the Foreign Office she went to Germany in 1949 to give talks on child guidance. Her work as director of the clinic was recognized by her election as a fellow of the British Psychological Society in 1942. She was vice-president of the Guild of Catholic Social Workers in 1943, vice-president of the British Psychological Society (Scottish Branch) in 1944, a fellow of the Educational Institute of Scotland in 1947, and vice-president for the Catholic International Congress of Psychiatrists and Psychotherapists in 1951. She was appointed a member of the Advisory Council on the Rehabilitation of Juvenile Offenders and served on the executive committee of the Scottish Association for Mental Hygiene. In 1947 she was presented with the papal cross *pro ecclesia et pontifice*. She died at 74 Victoria Crescent Road, Glasgow, on 19 November 1951, after a cerebral haemorrhage fourteen days earlier during Child Health Week, held to celebrate her fifty years in the order of Notre Dame and to increase resources for the clinic. News of her appointment as OBE had just been announced.

Sister Marie Hilda was dedicated to creating a clinic that built up 'integrated personalities capable of taking their place as members of the family, of the Church, and of the State' (Marie Hilda, 16). Like all pioneers she had many difficult situations to face—not least, censure from members of her own denomination for her willingness to work with Freudians. For her, difficulties existed to be overcome. She was deaf, but an expert lip-reader. Small in physical stature, being less than 5 feet tall, she possessed infectious good humour, and was able to inspire those around her.   LESLEY M. RICHMOND

Sources Sister Jude [M. McAleer], *Freedom to grow: Sister Marie Hilda's vision of child guidance* (1981) · *Scottish Catholic Herald* (23 Nov 1951), 3 · Sister Marie Hilda, *Child guidance* (1950) · *Golden Jubilee, 1895–1945: Notre Dame Training College, Dowanhill* (1945) · D. Gillies, *A pioneer of Catholic teacher-training in Scotland: Sister Mary of St Wilfrid* (privately printed, Quidenham, 1978) · J. Worrall, *Jubilee sisters of Notre Dame de Namur celebrate 150 years in Britain* (1995) · T. A. Fitzpatrick, *Catholic secondary education in south-west Scotland before 1972* (1986) · b. cert. · d. cert.

Archives U. Glas., Archives and Business Records Centre, St Andrews College collection
Likenesses photograph, 20th cent., U. Glas., Archives and Business Records Centre, St Andrews College collection; repro. in Sister Jude, *Freedom to grow* · photographs, repro. in Sister Jude, *Freedom to grow*

Marlow, William (1740/41–1813), landscape and view painter, was born probably in London or Southwark. He was apprenticed to the marine painter Samuel Scott, in whose London studio in Covent Garden he trained for five years from 1754 to 1759 and from whom he learned to paint carefully observed London scenes and river views in oil and watercolour which, like his teacher's works, clearly show the influence of Canaletto on English topographical painting at the time. Marlow probably also studied at the St Martin's Lane Academy. In the early 1760s he extended his repertoire to include picturesque landscapes which reflect seventeenth-century Dutch influences. He exhibited regularly at the Society of Artists from 1762, showing London scenes and views of east Wales, Twickenham, Worcester, and York which indicate that he was touring the countryside in search of landscape and topographical subjects. In his early years he also showed a number of 'country house portraits' (among them Ludlow Castle in Shropshire and Burton Agnes Hall near Bridlington) and associated views of local scenery, indicating that he was finding patrons among the landed nobility and gentry as well as in London. At an early date in his career he was employed by the duke of Northumberland, who was also a patron of Canaletto and Samuel Scott. Later Marlow 'went on his travels to France and Italy in 1765 by the advice of the late Duchess of Northumberland' according to an obituary notice which appeared soon after his death in January 1813 (Whitley papers, BM); a group of eight Italian paintings of Tivoli, Arriccia, and scenes in the Bay of Naples by him at Alnwick Castle suggests that the duchess was the principal sponsor for his tour of France and Italy. The earliest note of his departure is found on a drawing of an English river scene inscribed 'William Marlow the Author of this Drawing is now studying in Italy—July 8th 1765' (Sothebys, 1 April 1976, 166); the only other dated record of his absence occurs in Richard Hayward's list of artists in Rome in February 1766. The itinerary he followed through France and Italy is well documented by drawings and paintings, and after his return to London later in 1766 he largely specialized in producing watercolours and paintings of continental subjects which evidently proved popular as grand tour souvenirs. He showed his first such pictures at the Society of Artists in 1767, and the great majority of his 134 paintings and watercolours exhibited with the Society of Artists, the Free Society of Artists, and the Royal Academy from then onwards were of French and Italian subjects together with London views which continued the Canaletto–Scott tradition. He was one of the first English painters to exhibit views of Vesuvius erupting (Society of Artists, 1768) and dramatic alpine mountain scenery (Society of Artists, 1769).

Marlow's early success is evidenced by the painter

Thomas Jones who recorded in his *Memoirs* for 1769 that when he was beginning his own career Marlow was one of the artists 'in full possession of the landscape business' (Oppé, 20), and later the Royal Academician Edward Garvey recalled to Joseph Farington that when he had first arrived in London in the 1760s he found Richard Wilson and William Marlow especially successful, and that 'Marlow's work captivated him so much that ... he thought that as a Young Man he would rather be Marlow than Wilson' (Farington, *Diary*, 14 Feb 1804). In 1782 Marlow was listed among the 'six most eminent landscape painters of our country' by Joseph Pott in his anonymously published *Essay on Landscape Painting*. Marlow continued to enjoy some critical success until the end of the 1780s, and the large number of views he painted between 1767 and 1790 earned him an income large enough to move from his studio premises in Leicester Fields to the manor house at Twickenham in 1775. His patrons in the 1770s and 1780s included the dukes of Devonshire, Grafton, and Rutland, Frederick Howard, eighth earl of Carlisle, Lord Palmerston, and Horace Walpole, but business seems to have declined later and he resorted to selling his pictures at Christies St James's salerooms. Professionally he achieved recognition by his election to the Society of Artists in 1765, and he became one of its directors in 1768. His loyalty to the society led him to decline to seek membership of the Royal Academy when it was founded in the same year. Towards the end of his career, apparently in an attempt to restore his fading fortunes as an artist who had been overtaken by a new, more accomplished and adventurous generation, Marlow ventured into publishing etchings and prints, but without success. Among his last works was a series of six etchings of Italian coastal scenes (Baiae, Civitavecchia, Naples, and Pozzuoli), and two engraved London views reproducing pictures he had painted in 1792; both sets were issued by his pupil John Curtis in 1795. He virtually retired from painting about 1796 (the year he ceased exhibiting, apart from two pictures shown at the Royal Academy in 1807).

Very little is known about Marlow's personal circumstances, other than what was reported intermittently by Joseph Farington. In 1808 he recorded that:

> Marlow resides at Twickenham with a man whose name is Curtis. He was a Butcher when Marlow first became acquainted with his wife, who he met at Vauxhall. He has lived more than 20 years with them, & there are now 6 or 7 children, some of them very like Marlow. A strange instance of infatuation. He still applies to painting, but with very little of his former power.   (Farington, *Diary*, 28 June 1808)

In 1813 he was told by the painter James Northcote that 'Marlow died possessed of property which brought him in £100 per annum' and that 'He was charitable, so as to expend the whole of his income. He had long given up painting for an amusement more agreeable to Him, the making of Telescopes & other Articles' (ibid., 10 Feb 1813). When he died at Twickenham in early January 1813 aged seventy-two Marlow's estate was valued at less than £1000, and probate was granted to a sister, Eleanor

Northorp. His one pupil, the same John Curtis who published his etchings in 1795 and who was part of the artist's Twickenham 'family', painted London views and river scenes on the Thames around Twickenham and Richmond which closely imitated those of his teacher. The Yale Center for British Art, New Haven, Connecticut, and the Victoria and Albert Museum, British Museum, and Tate collection have a number of his works.

M. J. H. LIVERSIDGE

Sources M. J. H. Liversidge, 'Six etchings by William Marlow', *Burlington Magazine*, 122 (1980), 547–53 · M. J. H. Liversidge, '"... a few foreign graces and airs ...": William Marlow's grand tour landscapes', *The impact of Italy: the grand tour and beyond*, ed. C. Hornsby (2000) · M. Liversidge and J. Farrington, eds., *Canaletto and England* (1993) [exhibition catalogue, Birmingham Gas Hall Exhibition Gallery, Birmingham, 14 Oct 1993 – 9 Jan 1994] · J. Ingamells, ed., *A dictionary of British and Irish travellers in Italy, 1701–1800* (1997) · Society of Artists, minutes of directors, 1765–83, RA, SA 10 · W. T. Whitley papers, BM, department of prints and drawings · Farington, *Diary* · A. P. Oppé, ed., 'Memoirs of Thomas Jones, Penkerrig, Radnorshire', *Walpole Society*, 32 (1946–8) [whole issue] · L. Stainton, 'Hayward's list: British visitors to Rome, 1753–1755', *Walpole Society*, 49 (1983), 3–36 · will, PRO, PROB 6/189, fol. 263*v* · PRO, IR 1/20 CAPS 29659

Archives Herts. ALS, letters to his lawyer, etc.

Wealth at death under £1000: will, PRO, PROB 6/189, fol. 263*v*

Marlowe [Marley], **Christopher** (*bap.* 1564, *d.* 1593), playwright and poet, was baptized at St George's, Canterbury, on 26 February 1564, the second of the nine children of John Marlowe (*c*.1536–1605), shoemaker, and his wife, Katherine (*d.* 1605), daughter of William Arthur of Dover (*d.* 1575). His father was a native of Ospringe, near Faversham; he had migrated by the late 1550s to Canterbury, where he was apprenticed to an immigrant shoemaker, Gerard Richardson, and where he married in May 1561. The spelling of the family name was fluid: John Marlowe was often called Marley and sometimes Marle, while Christopher appears as Marlowe, Marlow, or Marlo on his title-pages, Marley in his only extant signature, Marlin or Merling in Cambridge University records, and Morley in the coroner's inquest on his death.

Early years, 1564–1580 Christopher was the eldest son and, after the death of his sister Mary in 1568, the eldest child of the family. A couple of months after his birth, his father became a freeman of the Shoemakers' Company; he progressed through a series of minor offices to become 'searcher' (inspector) of leather in 1581, and warden of the company in 1589. Though never prosperous, the family typified that aspirant artisan class which nurtured so much of the literary talent of the period, not least that of Marlowe's exact contemporary, the glover's son William Shakespeare. Other future writers growing up in Canterbury at this time were John Lyly and Stephen Gosson. Local records contain many instances of John Marlowe's pugnacity and quarrelsomeness, qualities inherited by his son, who was involved in violent 'affrays' and in other more dangerous confrontations with authority. Nothing is specifically known of Marlowe's boyhood, though it is possible that he is named in a Canterbury court case of 1573, in which a serving girl brought a case of sexual assault against one John Roydon, and mentioned in the course of her evidence that he employed 'a boy named Christopher Mowle' as a waiter or pot boy in his 'victualling house' (Canterbury Cathedral, archives, MS DCc X.10.4, fols. 165v–166; Butcher, 1–16). Mowle is conceivably another variant of Marlowe, though the deponent estimates the boy's age as twelve, while Marlowe was then only about nine.

About Christmas 1578 Marlowe was enrolled as a scholar of King's School, Canterbury. Scholarships worth £4 per annum, paid quarterly in arrears, were provided for 'fifty poor boys … endowed with minds apt for learning'; the earliest payment to Christopher 'Marley' was on Lady day 1579 (Canterbury Cathedral, archives, CAC misc. accounts 40), indicating his admission the previous Christmas. He was then about fourteen, unusually late to be entering the school; he may have been a fee-paying pupil before this. If so, he probably received some financial assistance, possibly from the rich Kentish judge Sir Roger Manwood, MP for Canterbury: an element of gratitude might explain the rather uncharacteristic Latin elegy he wrote on the occasion of Manwood's death in 1592. His first headmaster was John Gresshop. An inventory of Gresshop's library, drawn up on his death in 1580 (Urry, appx 2), offers a glimpse of the intellectual world opening up to the cobbler's son. Among its 350 volumes were editions of Ovid, Petrarch, Chaucer, and Boccaccio; Munster's *Cosmographia* and More's *Utopia*; the comedies of Plautus and the Neoplatonic philosophy of Ficino. The inventory hints also at the dangers of these broadened horizons, for on these same shelves was an old theological tract, John Proctour's *Fal of the Late Arrian* (1549); Marlowe was later accused of owning a 'vile hereticall' manuscript which was, in fact, a transcript of part of Proctour's book.

Marlowe's documented period at King's lasted for less than two years, for in late 1580 he went up to Corpus Christi College, Cambridge, on a Parker scholarship. The scholarships had been endowed by Archbishop Matthew Parker, a former master of Corpus; one of them was reserved for a King's scholar native to Canterbury. The recipients, it was stipulated, 'shalbe of the best and aptest schollers, well instructed in the gramer, and if it may be such as can make a verse'; they should also be 'so entred into the skill of song that they shall at the first sight solf and sing plaine song' (Wraight and Stern, 63). These indicate Marlowe's accomplishments by this time; the fact that the scholars were intended for holy orders was perhaps less congenial to him. Marlowe's departure for Cambridge did not quite sever his links with his home town or family—he is recorded in Canterbury at least twice after this—but it was undoubtedly a decisive moment.

University, 1580–1587 The first notice of Marlowe at Cambridge occurs in the Corpus Christi 'buttery books' detailing the students' expenditure on food and drink. They show that he spent 1*d*. during the first week of December 1580. As the accounts were reckoned weekly, and 1*d*. was an average spending in the buttery for one day, he perhaps arrived on the last day of the week, Saturday 10 December. He was chambered with three other Parker scholars in a converted 'stoare-house'. A sketch plan of the college

dated *c*.1576 (Corpus Christi College, archives, Misc. MS 138; Roberts, 23) shows that this room was in the northwestern corner of what is now Old Court. He matriculated on 17 March 1581. On 7 May he was formally elected to his scholarship, though he had already received his first quarterly allowance on Lady day (25 March); the scholarship entitled him to 1*s*. for every week in residence. His academic career proceeded smoothly enough. He graduated BA in March 1584, though with no great distinction: in the *ordo senioritatis* he was 199th out of 231 candidates (J. Venn, *Grace Book Δ, Containing the Records of the University of Cambridge, 1542–89*, 1910, 372–3).

In the following year, the evidence of the buttery books and scholarship payments suggests that a change had taken place in Marlowe's circumstances. From 1585 his attendance became irregular, and his spending at the buttery conspicuously higher. This implies some paid employment which took him away from Cambridge, and a privy council memorandum of 1587 offers some clues to its nature, but the only certain sighting of him away from Cambridge is almost piquantly parochial. From the will of Katherine Benchkin of Canterbury (CKS, PRC 16/36) it is known that on a Sunday in November 1585 Marlowe was present at her house on Stour Street, together with his father, his maternal uncle Thomas Arthur, and his brother-in-law John Moore. There they witnessed Mrs Benchkin's will; Marlowe himself read it out to the company 'plainely and disticnktly'. Discovered in 1939, this document contains Marlowe's only extant signature. The hand is graceful and unpretentious; its similarity to the handwriting of the 'Collier leaf'—a single-page manuscript of a scene from Marlowe's *Massacre at Paris* (Washington, DC, Folger Shakespeare Library)—seems to confirm that this too is holograph.

There were literary stirrings at Cambridge in the 1580s of which Marlowe was doubtless a part. Two writers later associated with him in London, Robert Greene and Thomas Nashe, were both at the university, as was his future antagonist, Dr Gabriel Harvey. Nashe recalled a throwaway remark about Gabriel's brother, the astrologer–parson Richard Harvey: 'Kit Marloe was wont to say that he was an asse, good for nothing but to preach of the Iron Age' (*Have with You to Saffron-Walden*, 1596, sig. N3v).

Although there is no consensus on the chronology and dating of Marlowe's works, some are traditionally associated with his period at Cambridge. An early date for his verse translations of Ovid's *Amores* (or 'Elegies') is certainly plausible, though there is no direct evidence for it. These translations have a curious publishing history. A selection of them first appeared in an undated edition, *Epigrams and Elegies* 'by J. D. and C. M.', the epigrams being by John (later Sir John) Davies. According to the title-page this was printed 'at Middleborough' (that is, Middelburg, Netherlands); this is generally thought to be a false imprint, disguising an unlicensed edition printed in England, but the fact that Marlowe and Davies were both separately in the Netherlands in 1592 raises the possibility that it was genuinely printed there. The book was among the 'unsemely' works banned by the archbishop of Canterbury in 1599 (Arber, *Regs. Stationers*, 3.677). A later edition, *All Ovids Elegies*, datable to 1602 or after, contains the full complement of forty-eight poems, including the much anthologized 'In Summers Heate'. Another translation, from Lucan's *Pharsalia*, is less certainly ascribed to Marlowe's university days; it was published in 1600 by Thomas Thorpe, who wrote a preface in memory of the author, 'that pure elementall wit' (*Complete Works*, 2.279). No trace remains of Marlowe's translation of Coluthus's *Helenae raptus*, described by the eighteenth-century bibliophile Thomas Coxeter as done 'into English rhime' in 1587 (Bodl. Oxf., MS Malone 131; Bakeless, 2.293–4).

Marlowe's choice of Latin models—the risqué Ovid and the rebel Lucan—is suggestive of his mentality at Cambridge. So too, perhaps, is the opening scene of his earliest play, *Dido Queene of Carthage*, a languorous vignette featuring Jupiter and his 'female wanton boy', Ganymede. That Marlowe was homosexual is implied by the informer Baines, who famously quotes him as saying 'all they that love not tobacco and boies were fooles' (BL, Harley MS 6848, fol. 185), and can be inferred from some of his writings, notably *Edward II*: these do not constitute proof, but add up to a convincing probability. *Dido*, also close to its Latin source (Virgil's *Aeneid*), is generally thought to have been written at Cambridge. The mounting of plays and entertainments was part of university life; they were mostly in Latin, but it is possible *Dido* was some kind of spin-off from a college production. It was first published in 1594; Nashe is named as joint author, but it is uncertain whether he collaborated with Marlowe on it, or merely edited it for publication. According to the title-page it was performed by the 'Children of Her Majesties Chapel': they are recorded as having been in East Anglia in May 1587, and may possibly have played *Dido* then (C. Tucker Brooke, *Life of Marlowe*, 1930, 116).

The last payment of Marlowe's scholarship allowance was on 25 March 1587; as the buttery books are not extant for the period immediately after this there is no way of knowing how long he remained at Cambridge. He received his MA degree in July, not without some difficulty, but had probably moved to London before then. In his last weeks at Cambridge he may have met Thomas Fineux of Hougham, near Dover, who entered Corpus in the Easter term. According to a well-informed contemporary, Simon Aldrich (a native of Canterbury, and from *c.*1593 a student at Cambridge), young Fineux fell drastically under Marlowe's spell. Aldrich's comments were recorded by the diarist Henry Oxinden in 1641:

> Mr Ald. said that Mr Fineux of Dover was an atheist, & that he would go out at midnight into a wood, & fall down upon his knees, & pray heartily that the Devil would come … He learned all Marlowe by heart, & divers other books. Marlowe made him an atheist. (Washington, DC, Folger Shakespeare Library, MS 750.1)

The influence was perhaps mainly literary—*Dr Faustus* springs to mind—but may also have been the result of their personal acquaintance at Corpus in 1587; the earliest printed allusion to Marlowe's 'atheism' appears in the following year.

Government service, *c.*1585–1587 It is at this point of transition, in the summer of 1587, that there is the first indication of Marlowe's involvement, during his time at Cambridge, in certain political 'affaires'. On 29 June, meeting at St James's Palace, the privy council considered the case of a Cambridge student named Christopher 'Morley', who had been the subject of defamatory reports, and whose MA degree, 'which he was to take at this next Commencement', was being called into question. There is little doubt that the Morley due to graduate in mid-1587 was Marlowe; he cannot have been the Christopher Morley of Trinity College who had commenced MA without discernible difficulty in the previous year. The testimonial issued in Marlowe's favour has not survived, but a digest of its contents is found in the council minutes:

> Whereas it was reported that Christopher Morley was determined to have gone beyond the seas to Reames [Rheims] and there to remaine, their Lps thought good to certefie that he had no such intent, but that in all his accions he had behaved himself orderlie and discreetlie, wherebie he had done her Majestie good service, & deserved to be rewarded for his faithfull dealinge. Their Lps request was that the rumor thereof should be allaied by all possible meanes, and that he should be furthered in the degree he was to take at this next Commencement, because it was not Her Majesties pleasure that any imployed as he had been in matters touching the benefit of his country should be defamed by those who are ignorant in th'affaires he went about. (PRO, PC register Eliz. 6.381b)

This document seems to offer two contradictory accounts of Marlowe's recent behaviour: on the one hand, there are those reports circulating at Cambridge that he is a militant young Catholic intending to defect to the English seminary at Rheims in northern France; on the other hand, there is the council's assertion that he really had 'no such intent', and had been acting on the queen's service for 'the benefit of his country'. One interpretation is that Marlowe had been moving in Catholic circles as a spy or 'intelligencer' for the government, an activity increasingly common in the 1580s, typically (but not exclusively) under the aegis of Sir Francis Walsingham. The document drawn up by the council on Marlowe's behalf is by no means unique: it is a certificate or 'warranty' of the kind often issued by the government to safeguard its agents— see, for example, the 'certificate of allowance' for the spy John Edge, 9 October 1590 (J. Strype, *Annals of the Reformation*, 1822, 4.30); its wording is very similar to that of the Marlowe memorandum. The latter is vague, no doubt intentionally, as to where, when, and how Marlowe had performed his 'service'. He could have done so at Cambridge itself, where the covert recruitment of graduates to Rheims certainly worried the authorities; but those recorded absences of 1585–7 suggest he also travelled elsewhere on government business, perhaps to France (though probably not, given the council's statement to the contrary, to Rheims itself). Four men later associated with Marlowe—Richard Baines, Robert Poley, Thomas Watson, and Thomas Walsingham—were all involved in intelligence work in France during the 1580s, and Marlowe may have first met them in this context. Nicholas Faunt, a 'secretary' of Walsingham's from c.1578 who was both a native of Canterbury and a former student at Corpus, may have employed him; he was on a diplomatic mission to Paris in 1587, at a period when Marlowe was absent from Cambridge.

Marlowe's status as a government servant or agent is the only possible context for the supposed portrait of him, discovered at Corpus in 1953 during refurbishment of the master's lodge. Its only indisputable link with Marlowe is that the age of the sitter ('Anno Dni 1585 Aetatis sua[e] 21') is correct for him. The circumstances of the discovery suggest that it had been in the college for some time, concealed or forgotten, though it is unlikely to have been there continuously since 1585. The rather dandified figure in the portrait does not look like an impoverished student, but may look like an ambitious young political servant whose 'faithfull dealinge' has brought its rewards. The portrait's motto reads, *Quod me nutrit me destruit* ('That which feeds me destroys me'); the emblem associated with this motto was a torch 'turning downeward' (S. Daniel, *A Worthy Tract of Paulus Jovius*, 1585, sig. Hvii), an image of doomed brilliance which seems apt for Marlowe. The painting now hangs at Corpus; the college correctly describes it as a 'putative' or 'apocryphal' likeness, but it is hard now to remember that this sardonic young man in a slashed velvet doublet may not be Marlowe at all.

There are further hints of political dealing in Marlowe's later career, but two red herrings can be conveniently discarded. Mention of a Mr Morley in a letter written at Utrecht in 1587 (Robert Ardern to Lord Burghley, 2 Oct 1587, PRO, SP 15/30, fol. 85) has led to a mistaken belief that Marlowe was then in the Netherlands on a mission for Burghley. In fact the letter concerns a property dispute in Northumberland, and the man referred to is probably John Morley, who was dealing with properties on Burghley's behalf in 1587 (*Salisbury MSS*, 3.277, 287). Nor is Marlowe the 'Mr Marlin' who couriered dispatches from Dieppe in March 1592; this is now known to be a sea captain, William Marlin or Mallyne (Nicholl, 340).

Fame and controversy, 1587–1590 Marlowe's first theatrical success in London was his thunderous drama of conquest and ambition, *Tamburlaine the Great*, based on the exploits of the fourteenth-century Tartar warlord Timur-i-leng. The exact date is uncertain, but a first run in the summer of 1587 is indicated. According to the title-page of the first edition (1590) it was performed by the Admiral's Men; its eponymous hero certainly suits the declamatory talents of the troupe's lead actor, Edward Alleyn, who would be associated with other Marlowe roles—Dr Faustus, Barabas in *The Jew of Malta*, and the duke of Guise in *Massacre at Paris*. The play's success led to the swift cobbling-up of a sequel, *The Second Part of the Bloody Conquests of Mighty Tamburlaine*. It was probably during a performance of the latter that an accident occurred, as described in a letter dated 16 November 1587: 'My L. Admyrall his men and players

having a devyse in ther playe to tye one of their fellowes to a poste and so to shoote him to death', one of the 'callyvers' (muskets) proved to be loaded; the player 'swerved his peece being charged with bullet, missed the fellowe he aymed at, and killed a chyld and a woman great with chyld forthwith' (*Letters of Philip Gawdy*, ed. I. Jeayes, 1906, 23). A scene in act 5, where the governor of Babylon is executed by firing squad, seems to have been the likely occasion. With success came controversy, and early in 1588 Robert Greene, jealous of his position as chief literary lion, complained:

> I have had it in derision for that I could not make my verses jet upon the stage in tragical buskins, every word filling the mouth like the fa-burden of Bow Bell, daring God out of heaven with that atheist Tamburlan.   (*Perimedes the Blacke-Smith*, in *Complete Works*, ed. A. Grosart, 1881–6, 7.8)

The allusion is to *Tamburlaine the Great*, act 1, scene 2: 'his looks do menace heaven and dare the gods'.

Greene also speaks of Marlowe 'blaspheming with the mad priest of the sun', possibly referring to the controversial occultist Giordano Bruno; and to 'mad and scoffing poets that have propheticall spirits as bred of Merlins race' (a pun on Marlowe or Marlin is certainly intended). It has been observed that these cryptic notes of blasphemy and magic seem less appropriate to *Tamburlaine* than to another play, *Dr Faustus*. The dating of *Faustus* is an enigma and its textual history a maze. The earliest recorded performance on 30 September 1594, over a year after Marlowe's death, was certainly not the first. The earliest known printed edition (1604) may not have been the first either; the copy had been entered at Stationers' Hall three years previously. A different and longer text was published in 1616. The relationship between these two versions (known as the 'A-text' and 'B-text') is controversial. Some of the material unique to 'B' is probably by Samuel Rowley and William Birde, who were paid £4 for 'adicyones in doctor fostes' in 1602 (*Henslowe's Diary*, ed. W. W. Greg, 2 vols., 1904–08, 1.172). 'A', long considered inferior, is now thought closer to Marlowe's original text; some of its structural defects may be the results of censorship (see W. Empson, *Faustus and the Censors*, 1989). Stylistic arguments over the date of composition are unresolved, but the play's monolithic structure and scholarly trappings tend to favour an earlier date, c.1588–9. A sourcebook used by Marlowe was *The Damnable Life of D. Iohn Faustus*, translated from the German by 'P. F., gent', but the date of the lost first edition of this is not known.

In his acerbic preface to Greene's *Menaphon* (1589), Thomas Nashe seems to renew the attack on Marlowe when he speaks of certain 'Alcumists of eloquence' who 'mounted on the stage of arrogance, thinke to out-brave better pennes with the swelling bumbast of bragging blanke verse' (sig. A2), but these rivalries must not be taken too seriously. Nashe was certainly more a friend than an enemy: he later defended the memory of 'poore deceased Kit Marlow' from the slanders of Gabriel Harvey (*Christs Teares*, 2nd edn, 1594, 2*1), and recalled Marlowe as one 'that usde me like a frend' (*Have with You to*

Saffron-Walden, 1596, sig. V2v). Other members of this literary group—the so-called 'university wits'—who were personally associated with Marlowe were Matthew Roydon and Thomas Watson, both of whom also had connections with government service, and George Peele. Shakespeare was not of this set; his relations with Marlowe are unrecorded except in the form of Marlowe's literary influence on him, though their collaboration on the *Henry VI* cycle, or some antecedent version of it, remains a possibility.

In the summer of 1589 Marlowe and Watson were both living, perhaps as room-mates, in Norton Folgate, Shoreditch. On the afternoon of 18 September, in nearby Hog Lane, Marlowe fought William Bradley, son of the landlord of The Bishop inn on Gray's Inn Road, with sword and dagger (PRO, chancery misc. MS 68/12/362; Eccles, *Marlowe in London*, 9–101). It appears that the real quarrel was between Bradley and Watson, and when Watson appeared on the scene, Bradley called: 'Art thou now come? Then I will have a boute with thee'. In the course of this 'boute' Bradley was killed. Marlowe and Watson were detained by the constable of Norton Folgate, Stephen Wyld, brought before a local JP, and committed to Newgate. At the inquest the following day, the Middlesex coroner recorded a verdict of self-defence. Marlowe was now eligible for bail, and on 1 October he was released, bound on a surety of £40 to appear at the next sessions at Newgate. The surety was provided by 'Richard Kytchine of Clifford's Inn, gentleman, & Humfrey Rowland of East Smithfield, horner': Kitchen was a lawyer, and was perhaps already associated with the theatre owner Philip Henslowe, whom he later represented; Rowland was probably a professional surety lender. During the twelve days he spent in Newgate, Marlowe seems to have met John Poole, a Catholic imprisoned there in 1587 'on suspicion of coiginge'. Among the charges later laid against Marlowe by Richard Baines was 'that he was acquainted with one Poole, a prisoner in Newgate, who hath great skill in mixture of metals, and having learned some things of him, he meant … to coin French crownes, pistolets, and English shillings' (BL, Harley MS 6848). On 3 December Marlowe appeared at the sessions; the judge presiding was Sir Roger Manwood, who may already have known him. This marked the end of the case for Marlowe, though Watson remained in Newgate, awaiting the queen's pardon, until the following February.

Patrons and politics, 1590–1592 Between his appearance at the Newgate sessions in December 1589 and his arrest in the Netherlands in January 1592, there is virtually no biographical knowledge of Marlowe's movements. The possibility that he acted as a tutor to Arabella Stuart has been aired, further to a letter from her guardian, Elizabeth, countess of Shrewsbury ('Bess of Hardwick'), who wrote to Burghley on 21 September 1592 concerning 'one Morley', who had 'attended on Arbell, and read to her for the space of three year and a half', but had now been dismissed and was 'much discontented'. The countess wrote that she had 'some cause to be doubtful of his forwardness in religion, though I cannot charge him with papistry' (BL, Lansdowne MS 71.2; E. St John Brooks, *TLS*, 27 Feb 1937).

Without further evidence the identification with Marlowe is doubtful; he could not have been employed continuously since early 1589, as the countess's wording suggests.

Other than this, there is only a glimpse of Marlowe in mid-1591, writing plays in a 'chamber' which he shared with the dramatist Thomas Kyd. In the summer of 1593, in a letter of self-justification concerning his relations with Marlowe, Kyd explained:

> My first acquaintance with this Marlowe rose upon his bearing name to serve my Lo: although his Lp never knew his service but in writing for his plaiers, ffor never could my L endure his name or sight when he had heard of his conditions, nor wold in deed the forme of devyne praiers used duelie in his Lps house have quadred wth such reprobates. (Kyd to Sir John Puckering, BL, Harley MS 6849, fol. 218)

This 'Lord' was almost certainly Ferdinando Stanley, Lord Strange, whose company gave the first recorded performance of *The Jew of Malta* at the Rose Theatre on 26 February 1592. The *Jew* is Marlowe's most cynical play, a tale of greed and betrayal suggestive of that Machiavellian *demimonde* of 'policy' or *realpolitik*, that world of 'climing followers', which was in some measure his own milieu. The 'ghost of Machevil' speaks the prologue, voicing sentiments that would soon be dangerously associated with Marlowe himself:

> I count religion but a childish toy,
> And hold there is no sinne but ignorance.
> (prologue, 14–15)

Whether Marlowe could have been present at the play's opening in February is uncertain, for a month earlier he had been arrested for 'coynage'—coining money—in Flushing, or Vlissingen, in the Netherlands, and deported back to England 'to be tryed'. A letter from Sir Robert Sidney, governor of Flushing, to Lord Burghley, dated 26 January 1592, explains something of the circumstances. Sidney had sent, under the escort of his ensign David Lloyd, two prisoners:

> the one named Christofer Marly, by his profession a scholer, and the other Gifford Gilbert a goldsmith, taken heer for coining, and their mony I have sent over to yowr Lo: … A Dutch shilling was uttred [circulated] and else not any peece … Notwithstanding I thowght it fitt to send them over unto yowr Lo: to take theyr trial as yow shal thinck best. (PRO, SP 84/44, fol. 60; Wernham, 344–5)

The man who had informed on Marlowe and Gilbert was 'one Ri: Baines … their chamber fellow'. This was the spy Richard Baines, who later compiled the notorious 'Note' about Marlowe's blasphemous opinions. Baines also accused Marlowe of 'intent to go to the Ennemy or to Rome'; there was, Sidney noted, 'malice' between them. Coining was accounted treason ('petty' rather than 'high' treason, but none the less punishable by death) and the allegation that Marlowe intended to defect to the Catholic enemy made it doubly so. The fact that he escaped serious punishment—he was certainly at liberty by May—suggests there may have been some political dimension to his presence in the Low Countries, and that he could claim, as he had in 1587, that he was working for 'the benefit of his country'.

Under questioning at Flushing Marlowe named two noble patrons in his favour. As Sidney reported it: 'the scholer sais himself to be very wel known both to the Earle of Northumberland and my Lord Strang'. The latter relationship is confirmed by the theatrical connections mentioned above, and may also have been relevant to Marlowe's presence in Flushing. Lord Strange, of royal blood and Catholic extraction, was a figurehead for English Catholic exiles, chief among them his cousin, Sir William Stanley; the exile group at Brussels, of which Stanley was a leading part, was a target for spies and infiltrators, and possibly Marlowe was one of these. The other patron named was Henry Percy, ninth earl of Northumberland, whose philosophical and scientific pursuits earned him the nickname 'the Wizard Earl'. This places Marlowe with other poets—Peele, Roydon, George Chapman—who expressed their praise of 'deep-searching Northumberland' in the early 1590s. The earl was a close friend of Sir Walter Ralegh, with whom Marlowe's name is traditionally associated. Ralegh's poem 'The Nymph's Reply' is an answer to Marlowe's famous lyric 'The Passionate Shepherd', but neither piece can be securely dated. Also part of this circle were the scientists Thomas Harriot and Walter Warner, whom Kyd named as Marlowe's friends, 'such as he conversed withal' (letter to Sir John Puckering, BL, Harley MS 6849, fol. 218). This grouping is sometimes called the 'Durham House set', after Ralegh's town house on the Strand; and sometimes the 'School of Night', after a supposed allusion in Shakespeare's Love's Labour's Lost.

Two further brushes with the law mark this as a troubled year for Marlowe. On 9 May 1592 Christopher 'Marle' was bound over in the sum of £20 to 'keep the peace' towards Allen Nicholls and Nicholas Helliott, constable and beadle of Holywell Street, Shoreditch (London Guildhall, Middlesex County Records, session roll 309/13). It is not recorded what incident or behaviour occasioned this, but it clearly took place in Shoreditch, where Marlowe had been living in 1589. He was ordered to appear at the next session of the peace, to be held at Finsbury court at the beginning of October, but he does not seem to have done so, probably because he was by then detained on court business in Canterbury following a street fight with a tailor, William Corkine. This took place on 15 September 1592, near the corner of Mercery Lane, in Westgate ward. It may have involved Marlowe's arrest by his father, then acting constable of Westgate; the 'mainprise' of 12d. which kept him out of gaol was certainly paid by his father. In a civil suit filed on 25 September, Corkine alleged that Marlowe had assaulted him 'with staff and dagger', causing 'loss and damage' to the value of £5 (Canterbury Cathedral, archives, BACJ/B/S/392; Urry, appx 4). On the following day Marlowe's attorney, John Smith, made a counter-charge at the quarter sessions, claiming that Corkine was the assailant; this indictment was thrown out, however. The case came to court on 2 October but was adjourned for a week; in the interim the litigants seem to have patched up their differences, and no further

action was taken. In 1612 a composer named William Corkine, probably the tailor's son, published an 'air' to Marlowe's 'Passionate Shepherd'.

Two occasional pieces in Latin belong to late 1592. The dedication signed 'C. M.' prefixed to Thomas Watson's Amintae gaudia is almost certainly by Marlowe. It is addressed to Mary, countess of Pembroke; it seeks her patronage for 'this posthumous Amyntas', and was therefore written after 26 September, the date of Watson's funeral. The copy was licensed at Stationers' Hall on 10 November and was published by the end of the year. Another death, that of Sir Roger Manwood on 14 December 1592, occasioned a twelve-line epitaph in Latin hexameters, celebrating the judge as the 'terror of the night prowler' and 'scourge of the profligate'. A seventeenth-century copy, ascribed to Marlowe, survives in the commonplace book of Henry Oxinden (Washington, DC, Folger Shakespeare Library, MS 750.1); another version was written (probably also by Oxinden) in a copy of the 1629 edition of Hero and Leander, though this has since disappeared.

The Massacre at Paris was apparently performed by Lord Strange's Men in late January 1593; the entry in Henslowe's diary is difficult to interpret in detail. This lurid account of the St Bartholomew's day massacre in 1572 (an atrocity ingrained in the mind of English protestants, and no doubt in the mind of the young Marlowe in Canterbury, a city which received a large share of Huguenot refugees) is the most topical and overtly political of his plays. A truncated version of it survives in an undated octavo edition of some 1200 lines, but the fragmentary nature of the text is in part a deliberate technique, in which the brevity and rapidity of the scenes create a vivid kind of reportage: this has been likened to the cinematic style of 'jump-cutting'.

Edward II, with its sophisticated narrative structure and controlled poetic intensity, is generally considered Marlowe's last play. The first edition (1594) describes it as played by Pembroke's Men, but there is no record of a performance during Marlowe's lifetime. It is the only Marlowe play set in England. Its account of Edward's homosexual infatuation for Piers Gaveston may contain an undertone of comment about James VI of Scotland and the earl of Lennox; the play thus touches obliquely on the question of the succession, and on the pro-Jacobean factions already forming in the early 1590s. Marlowe's interest in the latter is suggested by Thomas Kyd, who wrote: 'he wold pswade wth men of quallitie to goe unto the K of Scots whether I heare Royden is gon and where if he had livd he told me when I sawe him last he meant to be' (BL, Harley MS 6848, fol. 154). There are glimpses again of a hidden stratum of political activity, faintly reflected in his writings, but no corroboration of Kyd's claim has been discovered.

Another late work, perhaps Marlowe's last, is the lushly evocative Hero and Leander, a narrative poem based on the sixth-century Greek poem by Musaeus. The work, consisting of two sestiads totalling 818 lines, is apparently unfinished. It was one of a clutch of Marlowe manuscripts copyrighted by John Wolfe shortly after the author's death, but the first edition (1598) was published by Edward Blount, with a dedication to Sir Thomas Walsingham, recalling how Marlowe had enjoyed 'the gentle aire of your liking', and how 'in his lifetime you bestowed many favours, entertaining the parts of reckoning and woorth which you found in him' (*Complete Works*, 2.430). The wording suggests some warmth of friendship. There is evidence that Marlowe was resident at Walsingham's house at Scadbury, Kent, in the last weeks of his life; he may have written *Hero* there. Another edition of 1598, dedicated to Walsingham's wife, Lady Audrey, contains a continuation of the poem by Marlowe's friend George Chapman. His comment about Marlowe's 'late desires' (*Hero and Leander*, sestiad 3.207–9) has been misinterpreted: the desire that Chapman should 'to light surrender [his] soules darke ofspring' refers to the publishing of Chapman's own poem, *The Shadow of Night* (1594), not to the writing or publishing of his continuation of *Hero*. There is no reason to suppose, therefore, that Chapman began his sequel in Marlowe's lifetime.

'Monstrous Opinions', 1592–1593 The last year of Marlowe's life was clouded by allegations about his controversial religious and political views. The *locus classicus* of these is the infamous 'Baines note', a signed statement itemizing nineteen instances of Marlowe's atheistic and seditious talk. But this was delivered to the authorities just a few days before Marlowe's death, and was the culmination of other, vaguer charges which had been circulating for some time.

Late in September 1592, while Marlowe was in Canterbury, there appeared *Greenes Groatsworth of Witte*, a collection of writings by Robert Greene, edited after his death by the printer and playwright Henry Chettle. In a letter to 'those Gentlemen his Quondam acquaintance' who 'spend their wits in making plaies' (sig. E4v–F2v), Greene addressed Marlowe ('thou famous gracer of Tragedians'). He accused him of having said 'There is no God', and of embracing 'pestilent Machivilian pollicy' and 'diabolicall Atheism'. It seems that Marlowe reacted to this, for later in the year Chettle wrote: 'The letter written to divers playmakers is offensively by one or two of them taken … With neither of them that take offence was I acquainted, and with one of them I care not if I never be' (*Kind-Harts Dreame*, 1592, sig. A3v). The latter was almost certainly Marlowe (the other being Shakespeare, who had been derided as 'an upstart Crow' in the same passage.) Chettle admired Marlowe (his 'learning I reverence') but wished to be dissociated from him: a taste of attitudes to come. He claimed he had actually toned down the attack: '[I] stroke out what then in conscience I thought he [Greene] had in some displeasure writ: or had it beene true, yet to publish it was intollerable'. This suppressed material may have been more about Marlowe's atheism, or a reference to his homosexuality.

About the same time a Catholic broadside was circulating, which spoke of 'Sir Walter Rauleys schoole of Atheisme', and of the 'Conjuror that is M[aster] thereof',

and of Christ and the Bible being 'jested at' ('A. Philopater', *An Advertisement*, 1592, 18). The 'conjuror' was Marlowe's friend Thomas Harriot, and Marlowe himself was doubtless suspected of involvement—a suspicion later made explicit by the spy Richard Cholmeley, who asserted that Marlowe 'hath read the Atheist lecture to Sr Walter Raliegh & others' (BL, Harley MS 6848, fol. 191).

The links, if any, between Marlowe's supposed atheism and the circumstances of his death on 30 May 1593, remain a matter of debate. He was certainly under some kind of government surveillance at the time of his death, having been called before the privy council on 18 May, and ordered to report daily until 'lycensed to the contrary'. Three documents offer some clues to the nature of the council's suspicions about him. The first is the so-called 'Dutch Church Libel', an inflammatory doggerel poem posted on the wall of the Dutch church in Broad Street, London, on the evening of 5 May 1593. It was one of a series of 'placards' advocating violence against immigrant traders, but was deemed by the authorities to 'exceede the rest in lewdness'. The text, which survives in a manuscript copy of *c*.1600, bears the hallmarks of being written by an admirer of Marlowe: it is signed 'Tamburlaine', and it contains overt reference to what was then probably his latest play ('Weele cutt your throtes, in your temples praying,/ Not paris massacre so much blood did spill'). A council directive of 11 May (*APC*, 24.222) ordered the immediate apprehension of suspects, who were to be 'put to the torture in Bridewell' if necessary, and by the following day Marlowe's former room-mate Thomas Kyd was under arrest, 'suspected for that Libell that concerned the State'. In his lodgings was found a three-page transcript from Proctour's *Fal of the Late Arrian*, which he correctly described as 'some fragments of a disputation', but which his interrogators endorsed as 'vile hereticall Conceiptes denying the deity of Jhesus Christ or Savior fownd emongest the paprs of Thos Kidd prisoner, wch he affirmeth that he had ffrom Marlowe' (BL, Harley MS 6848, fols. 187–9). Kyd surmised that this document had been 'shuffled' with his own papers 'by some occasion of our wrytinge in one chamber twoe years synce', and said it contained an 'opinion' (Arian or anti-Trinitarian) which Marlowe was known to hold. A third document, almost certainly in the authorities' hands by this time, is an unsigned report detailing the seditious and blasphemous utterances of Richard Cholmeley, spy and provocateur (ibid., fols. 190–91). Among these is Cholmeley's reported belief 'that one Marlowe is able to showe more sounde reasons for atheisme then any devine in Englande is able to geve to prove devenitie'. This was later corroborated by Baines, who said Cholmeley 'confessed that he was perswaded by Marloe's reasons to become an Atheist' (ibid., fols. 185–6).

The case against Marlowe was probably further strengthened by Kyd. Although his statement of Marlowe's 'monstruous opinions' (BL, Harley MS 6848, fol. 154) was certainly written down after Marlowe's death, it doubtless echoes what Kyd told his interrogators in mid-May: 'It was his custom … to jest at the devine scriptures, gybe at praiers, & stryve in argument to frustrate & confute what hath byn spoke or wrytt by prophets & such holie men'. Among Marlowe's alleged 'jests' was that St John was 'Christs Alexis' and 'that Christ did love him with an extraordinarie love'; this homosexual blasphemy is repeated by Baines, who quotes Marlowe as saying St John was 'bed-fellow to C[hrist] and … used him as the sinners of Sodoma' (BL, Harley MS 6848, fols. 185–6).

These accumulated allegations and innuendoes resulted in the issuing of a warrant, dated 18 May, directing a messenger of the chamber, Henry Maunder

> to repaire to the house of Mr Tho: Walsingham in Kent, or to anie other place where he shall understand Christofer Marlow to be remayning, and by vertue hereof to apprehend and bring him to the court in his companie. And in case of need to require ayd. (*APC*, 24.224)

(The last phrase is conventional and does not indicate special powers.) Maunder found his man (whether at Scadbury or elsewhere), and on 20 May the council clerk noted: 'Christofer Marley of London, gent, being sent for by warrant from their Lps, hath entered his appearance accordinglie for his Indemnitie herein; and is commaunded to give his daily attendaunce on their Lps untill he shalbe lycensed to the contrarie' (ibid., 24.225). He thus remained at liberty, albeit on bail and under watch. Given the treatment meted out to Kyd a week earlier this leniency seems surprising. It suggests, once again, that Marlowe had some kind of protection, or could claim some kind of usefulness if kept at liberty.

A few days later the most damning of the indictments against him was delivered: the charge sheet compiled by Richard Baines, entitled 'A note containing the opinion of one Christopher Marley concerning his damnable judgment of religion and scorn of Gods word'. It succinctly itemizes Marlowe's heretical views—'that the first beginning of Religioun was only to keep men in awe', 'that Christ was a bastard and his mother dishonest', 'that the sacrament … would have bin much better being administred in a tobacco pipe', and so on—and concludes darkly: 'I think all men in Cristianity ought to indevor that the mouth of so dangerous a member may be stopped'. The 'Note' survives in two manuscripts: one (BL, Harley MS 6848, fols. 185–6) is autograph; the other (ibid., 6853, fols. 307–8) is a scribal copy, endorsed 'Copye of Marloes blasphemyes As sent to her H[ighness]'. The copy has some alterations in the hand of Sir John Puckering, lord keeper of the privy seal, who together with another court official, Lord Buckhurst, played an important role in the investigation of Marlowe and his associates. A contradictory annotation states that the 'Note' was delivered three days before Marlowe's death (that is, 27 May) and that it was delivered 'on Whitsun eve last' (2 June).

The proportion of truth and invention in the Baines 'Note' is hard to gauge. It can be interpreted as an accurate report of Marlowe's opinions (and even as a précis of that 'atheist lecture' he was supposed to have given); or it can be seen as the final act of an orchestrated campaign of black propaganda against Marlowe and Ralegh. The involvement of another professional snoop, Thomas

Drury (younger brother of Sir William Drury of Hawstead, Suffolk), is revealed in a letter to Anthony Bacon, dated 1 August 1593, in which he claims a leading role in the production of the Baines 'Note':

> There was a command layed on me latly to stay on[e] Mr Bayns, which did use to resort unto me, which I did pursue … and got the desired secrett at his hand … Ther was by my only means sett doun unto the Lord Keper [and] the lord of Bucurst the notablyst and vyldist artyckeles of Athemisme [*sic*] that I suppose the lyke was never known or red of in any age. (LPL, Bacon MS 649, fol. 246)

Some support of Drury's claim is found in a letter from Buckhurst to Puckering, dated 8 November 1592, in which Drury's fitness to do some unspecified 'service' is discussed (BL, Harley MS 6995, fol. 137). Drury's previous connection with another figure involved in the case, Richard Cholmeley, is also documented (*APC*, 21.119, 291, 354).

Death and aftermath, 1593 On the evening of Wednesday 30 May 1593 Marlowe was stabbed to death at a house in Deptford Strand, near London. He was about twenty-nine. The circumstances are generally described as a 'tavern brawl', but there is no evidence that the house was a tavern, and since the killing occurred in a private room it can hardly be called a 'brawl' either. The events of that day can be partially reconstructed from the inquest, held on 1 June, by the royal coroner, William Danby, and a jury of sixteen local men (PRO, C 260/174, no. 27; Hotson, 28–34). At 10 o'clock in the morning Ingram Frizer, Nicholas Skeres, Robert Poley, and Christopher Marlowe met at a house in Deptford Strand belonging to a widow, Eleanor Bull. Rather than the shabby alehouse keeper of legend, Mrs Bull was of an ancient armorial family, the Whitneys of Herefordshire, and was the cousin of the queen's confidante Blanche Parry; her husband, Richard Bull (d. 1590), had been under-bailiff of nearby Sayes Court.

The four men dined together, and in the afternoon walked in the garden; they were in a 'quiet' mood. At six o'clock in the evening they returned to the house, and had supper in a room there. After supper Marlowe lay down on a bed; his companions were seated at the table. There was an argument over the bill: Frizer and Marlowe 'uttered one to the other divers malicious words' because they 'could not agree about the sum of pence, that is, *le recknynge*'. Marlowe, 'moved with anger', leapt from the bed, snatched Frizer's dagger from its sheath, and struck him twice about the head: the wounds (measured at the inquest) were shallow, and were perhaps inflicted with the hilt of the dagger. A struggle ensued:

> and so it befell, in that affray, that the said Ingram, in defence of his life, with the dagger aforesaid of the value of twelve pence, gave the said Christopher a mortal wound above his right eye, of the depth of two inches and of the width of one inch. (PRO, C 260/174, no. 27; translated in Hotson, 28–34)

From this wound, Marlowe 'then & there instantly died'. The actual cause of death was probably a brain haemorrhage. On the basis of this account the coroner found that Frizer had killed Marlowe in self-defence; on 15 June a writ of *certiorari* brought the case into Chancery, and on 28

June Frizer received a royal pardon (PRO, patent rolls 1401).

The discovery of the inquest by Leslie Hotson in 1925 scotched three centuries of rumour and romance. The earliest independent accounts of the killing proved to have been approximate at best. Thomas Beard (*Theatre of God's Judgement*, 1597, 147–8) described it as a street fight: Marlowe died 'in London streetes, as he purposed to stab one whom he ought a grudge unto with his dagger'. Francis Meres (*Palladis tamia*, 1598, sig. Oo6) had Marlowe 'stabbed to death by a bawdy serving-man, a rival of his in his lewd love'. The most accurate account was William Vaughan's (*The Golden Grove*, 1600, C4v–C5), which correctly named the killer ('one Ingram') and the location ('at Detford'). Vaughan had family connections with Mrs Bull's cousin Blanche Parry, and with the earl of Northumberland, and perhaps had privileged information. His statement that it was Frizer who invited Marlowe to Deptford, for a 'feast', may also be correct; the fact that Frizer was a business associate of Marlowe's patron Thomas Walsingham—the connection is documented from 1593—lends credence to this.

The authenticity of the inquest is not in doubt, but whether it tells the full truth is another matter. The nature of Marlowe's companions raises questions about their reliability as witnesses. Nicholas Skeres was a swindler who, a month previously, had been accused in Star Chamber of 'entrapping young gents' (PRO, STAC 5/S9/8); in another case he 'combined' with Frizer to 'undermine and deceive' a young heir, Drew Woodliff (Hotson, 69–73). Robert Poley was the Walsingham spy who had infiltrated the Babington conspiracy; contemporary accounts of his cunning and 'knavery' abound (Nicholl, 31–3). Frequently employed on missions abroad, he had recently returned from the Netherlands, and was still nominally 'in Her Majesties service' when present at Deptford (chamber accounts, 12 June 1593, PRO, E351/542, fol. 182v). That the inquest's account depended on these two men—the only independent witnesses of the fatal 'affray'—is at the least unsatisfactory. They also brought to the scene certain high-up political connections: Skeres served the earl of Essex, whom he described in Star Chamber as his 'Lord and Master'; Poley reported to Sir Robert Cecil, who correctly described him as 'no fool' (Cecil to Sir Thomas Heneage, 25 May 1592, PRO, SP 12/242, no. 25). That these links betoken some covert intrigue against Marlowe has yet to be proved, but they add to a sense that something more complex is concealed beneath the story of the 'recknynge'. The involvement of the royal coroner has no sinister connotation, however: he automatically dealt with cases that fell 'within the verge' (that is, a 12-mile radius of the queen), as this one did.

Marlowe was buried on 1 June 1593 at St Nicholas's, Deptford; the location of the grave is unknown. The publisher Blount, dedicating *Hero and Leander* to Thomas Walsingham, wrote: 'Wee thinke not our selves discharged of the dutie wee owe to our friend when wee have brought the breathlesse bodie to the earth ... albeit the eye there

taketh his ever-farewell of that beloved object'. This possibly indicates their presence at the funeral. The entry in the Deptford burial register states that Marlowe was 'slaine by ffrancis ffrezer', an error compounded by a nineteenth-century vicar of St Nicholas's, who misread the surname as 'Archer'; in the century before Hotson's recovery of the inquest Marlowe's assassin was called either Francis Frazer or Francis Archer.

The earliest epitaph, calling Marlowe 'Marley the Muses darling', is in Peele's *Honour of the Garter*, dedicated to the earl of Northumberland and datable to mid-June 1593. Nashe's *Unfortunate Traveller*, also completed in June but not published until 1594, has a tribute to the dramatist and reputed atheist Pietro Aretino (sig. F3v–F4v) which has been interpreted as referring to Marlowe (who had been compared to 'Aretine' by Gabriel Harvey):

> His pen was sharpe pointed lyke a poinyard; no leafe he wrote on but was lyke a burning glasse to set on fire all his readers ... He was no timerous servile flatterer of the commonwealth wherein he lived ... His lyfe he contemned in comparison of the libertie of speech.

By contrast, Nashe's comments about 'scripture-scorning' atheists in *Christs Teares*, published in October 1593, suggest his desire to distance himself from the Marlovian taint of irreligion. His 'elegy' on Marlowe, perhaps in Latin, was seen in certain copies of *Dido* in the eighteenth century, but is now lost. In *As You Like It* (*c*.1599) Shakespeare calls Marlowe the 'dead shepherd' (III.v), and seems to refer to the circumstances of his death: 'It strikes a man more dead than a great reckoning in a little room' (III. iii; cf. 'infinite riches in a little room'; Marlowe, *Jew of Malta*, I.i). The most beautiful epitaph is Michael Drayton's:

> neat [unadulterated] Marlow ...
> Had in him those brave translunary things
> That the first poets had; his raptures were
> All ayre and fire.
> (*Of Poets and Poesy*, 1627)

However, the anonymous author of the *Returne from Parnassus* (part 2, *c*.1601) perhaps summed up his reputation more accurately: 'Wit lent from heaven but vices sent from hell'.

During the seventeenth century Marlowe's fiery raptures and 'high astounding termes' (*Tamburlaine the Great*, prologue, 5) fell swiftly out of fashion. Ben Jonson derided 'the Tamerlanes and Tamer-chams of the late age' which offered nothing but 'scenicall strutting and furious vociferation to warrant them then to the ignorant gapers' (*Discoveries*, ed. G. Harrison, 1923, 33), though in his ode to Shakespeare (1623) he coined the famous phrase 'Marlowes mighty line'. The eighteenth century cared little for the line and less for the man. William Hazlitt was among the first to reshape Marlowe in a semi-daemonic Romantic mould: 'There is a lust of power in his writings, a hunger and thirst after unrighteousness, a glow of the imagination, unhallowed by any thing but its own energies' (*Literature of the Age of Elizabeth*, 1820, 43). Alfred Tennyson called him the 'morning star' which heralded Shakespeare's 'dazzling sun', while for Algernon Swinburne he was 'the most daring pioneer in all our literature'. The twentieth century discerned in the plays more 'modern' subtexts of irony and dissidence; T. S. Eliot redefined the dominant mode of his plays as 'serious, even savage' farce, rather than tragedy (*The Sacred Wood*, 1920, 92). Behind the exalted poetry and the lurid reputation Marlowe remains an elusive, troubled character. One senses a personal flair both magnetic and dangerous; he was, said Kyd, 'intemperate & of a cruel heart'. Learned, sardonic, aggressive, and reckless, Marlowe leaves more questions than answers, and the profoundly questioning temper of his plays suggests that this is as he would have wanted it.

CHARLES NICHOLL

Sources J. Bakeless, *The tragicall history of Christopher Marlowe*, 2 vols. (1942) · *The complete works of Christopher Marlowe*, ed. F. Bowers, 2 vols. (1981) · F. S. Boas, *Christopher Marlowe* (1940) · W. Urry, *Christopher Marlowe and Canterbury* (1988) · M. Eccles, *Christopher Marlowe in London* (1934) · L. Hotson, *The death of Christopher Marlowe* (1925) · C. Nicholl, *The reckoning: the murder of Christopher Marlowe* (1992) · A. D. Wraight and V. Stern, *In search of Christopher Marlowe* (1965) · A. Butcher, '"Onelye a boye called Christopher Mowle"', *Christopher Marlowe and English Renaissance culture*, ed. D. Grantley and P. Roberts (1996) · P. Roberts, '"The studious artisan"', *Christopher Marlowe and English Renaissance Culture*, ed. D. Grantley and P. Roberts (1996) · *Calendar of the manuscripts of the most hon. the marquis of Salisbury*, 24 vols., HMC, 9 (1883–1976) · M. Eccles, 'Christopher Marlowe in Kentish tradition', *N&Q*, 169 (13 July 1935); (20 July 1935); (27 July 1935) · R. B. Wernham, 'Christopher Marlowe at Flushing in 1592', *EngHR*, 91 (1976) · Arber, *Regs. Stationers* · parish register, Canterbury, St George's, 26 Feb 1564 [baptism] · parish register, Deptford, St Nicholas's, 1 June 1593 [burial]
Likenesses oils?, 1585, CCC Cam.

Marlowe, Thomas Henry (1868–1935), journalist, born at 39 St James's Street, Portsmouth, on 18 March 1868, was the eldest son of Thomas Henry Marlowe of Auchnacloy, co. Tyrone, and Kate, the daughter of John Conway. He was educated in Dublin, at Queen's College, Galway, and at the London Hospital. He did not complete his medical training, but abandoned medicine for journalism. He did not enjoy his first experience as a reporter in Dublin and Manchester. Then, in 1888, he joined *The Star*, where he soon proved that he possessed the successful reporter's eye for the unusual and the picturesque. In the following year he married Alice Warrender, second daughter of John Morrison *Davidson, the radical journalist. They had four sons and four daughters. Friendship with Kennedy Jones meanwhile brought him into contact with the Harmsworth brothers. In 1894 they engaged Marlowe as a reporter for the *Evening News*. An interview by him of the notorious financier E. T. Hooley so impressed Alfred Harmsworth that he promoted the young reporter to be news editor of the recently launched *Daily Mail*. In October 1899 he was promoted to managing director.

Marlowe was obliged first to demonstrate that he, not his predecessor in the post, S. J. Pryor, was the undisputed editor of the *Mail*. Thereafter he very soon established himself as a significant figure in Fleet Street. He was given most credit for the *Daily Mail*'s burgeoning circulation. But, with a chief proprietor like Alfred Harmsworth (soon to be ennobled as Northcliffe), editors were expected to take second place. Nevertheless, it was important to Northcliffe that his editors should look the part. Some

whispered that Marlowe was no more than a sheep in wolf's clothing, but he exuded a quiet masterfulness and possessed 'all round ability in every aspect of newspaper work ... He was not a great editor. Had he been so he would not have stayed long working for Northcliffe' (Fyfe, 82). Like Northcliffe's other editors, Marlowe danced to the proprietor's tune. On one occasion he morosely observed, 'I have carried on your paper under circumstances of great difficulty ... I have always endeavoured to carry out your wishes when I was informed of them' (Marlowe to Northcliffe, 20 May 1907, correspondence with Lord Northcliffe). A successful suit for libel brought by the Lever Brothers against a campaign that Northcliffe had promoted and maintained in all his newspapers, almost cost Marlowe his job. Thereafter, he had every reason to question his proprietor's news judgement. And there were occasions when he successfully resisted Northcliffe's bullying and insisted upon having his own way—most successfully and significantly, in the opening week of the First World War, when Northcliffe was both frightened and uncertain. But for the most part Marlowe, with more or less good grace, 'accepted his status as a hireling' (Koss, 2.206); during the negotiation of the Anglo-Irish treaty, he was required by Northcliffe to take editorial instructions directly from F. E. Smith (*Lloyd George: a Diary by Frances Stevenson*, ed. A. J. P. Taylor, 1971, 235). Northcliffe never underestimated the massive contribution that his 'faithful, devoted servant' (H. W. Wilson, quoted in Pound and Harmsworth, 305) made to the success of the *Daily Mail*. He hoped to secure a title for his editor, and to enhance his chances made Marlowe, in 1918, chairman of Associated Newspapers, while assuring him that the new appointment would 'not mean any extra work' (Northcliffe to Marlowe, 1 Jan 1918, correspondence with Lord Northcliffe).

After the war Marlowe was closely involved in two historic events. Through his contacts with Reginald Hall, former head of naval intelligence and principal agent of the Conservative Party, Marlowe obtained a copy of the famous 'Zinoviev letter' containing instructions from the Comintern to the British Communist Party to foment insurrection, and was largely responsible for circulating its contents. Whether or not the letter was a forgery, its publication on 25 October 1924, four days before the general election, was intended to undermine the Labour government. Two years later, his actions precipitated the general strike. On the night of 2–3 May 1926, while the tense negotiations between the cabinet and the Trades Union Congress general council over the miners' grievances were in progress, he rejected the demands of the machine men at the *Daily Mail* to alter a provocative leading article, headed 'For King and Country', which denounced the trade union movement as disloyal and unpatriotic. On hearing from Marlowe of the men's refusal to print the newspaper, an action which Baldwin described as a 'gross interference with the freedom of the Press' (H. H. Fyfe, *Behind the Scenes of the Great Strike*, 1926, 24), the cabinet broke off negotiations and the general strike was called.

Marlowe, the longest-serving of the *Daily Mail*'s editors, came close to resigning on a number of occasions. But he admired Northcliffe and, for his genius as a newspaper man, was prepared to suffer his wilfulness. He did not extend the same tolerance to Rothermere when Northcliffe's brother succeeded as the *Mail*'s owner in 1922. He increasingly questioned the proprietor's political judgement, doubts that were confirmed when Rothermere championed Lloyd George, not Baldwin and the Conservatives. Also, he resented Beaverbrook's increasing influence not only with Rothermere but also in affairs at Carmelite House. In 1926 Marlowe, together with the *Mail*'s manager, Sir Andrew Caird, finally resigned. Their departure was 'a bad loss: the *Mail* group lost its journalistic punch' (Bourne, 98). His bitterness at a professional lifetime's subservience to overweening, interfering proprietors, was reflected in a letter to a fellow newspaper editor, H. A. Gwynne: 'Journalism has been killed by newspaper owners' (Marlowe to H. A. Gwynne, 20 May 1932, Gwynne MSS, Bodl. Oxf.).

Marlowe's health had been grievously undermined by his years of struggle. He became extremely deaf. Friends noted with regret how he had grown old beyond his years. He was returning from a visit to South Africa when he died at sea, on 3 December 1935. One of his sons, Anthony Alfred Harmsworth Marlowe (1904–1965), a barrister, sat as a Conservative MP, 1941–65.

HAMILTON FYFE, *rev.* A. J. A. MORRIS

Sources *The Times* (6 Dec 1935) · *WW* · S. E. Koss, *The rise and fall of the political press in Britain*, 2 vols. (1981–4) · R. Pound and G. Harmsworth, *Northcliffe* (1959) · P. Ferris, *The house of Northcliffe* (1971) · R. Bourne, *Lords of Fleet Street: the Harmsworth dynasty* (1980) · H. H. Fyfe, *Sixty years of Fleet Street* (1949) · *Memoirs of a Conservative: J. C. C. Davidson's memoirs and papers, 1910–37*, ed. R. R. James (1969) · Bodl. Oxf., MSS Gwynne · BL, correspondence with Lord Northcliffe, Add. MSS 62198–62200
Archives BL, corresp. with Lord Northcliffe, Add. MSS 62198–62200 · Bodl. Oxf., letters to H. A. Gwynne · Ransom HRC, letters to J. L. Garvin
Likenesses photograph (in middle age), probably Daily Mail Library; repro. in Pound and Harmsworth, *Northcliffe*, facing p. 513
Wealth at death £70,952 0s. 11d.: probate, 24 Feb 1936, *CGPLA Eng. & Wales*

Marmion, Joseph Aloysius [*name in religion* Columba] (1858–1923), abbot of Maredsous and author, was born on 1 April 1858 in Dublin, the son of William Marmion (1820–1878), a corn factor, and his wife, Herminie Cordier (1820–1894), a Frenchwoman and language teacher who had recently gone to Ireland. They lived first at 57 Queen Street, but later moved to 2 Blackhall Place, Dublin. There were nine children in the family.

Marmion received his first formal education at St Laurence O'Toole's school, St John's Lane, Dublin. In January 1869 he began his secondary education at Belvedere College, Dublin, remaining there until December 1873. By then he had passed his matriculation examination and also successfully gained a scholarship which entitled him to a place in Holy Cross College, Clonliffe, the Dublin diocesan seminary. During the next five years he obtained the degree of BA from the Royal University of Ireland, and

studied both philosophy and theology with a view to becoming a priest in the Dublin diocese. In December 1879 he was sent to Rome to complete his theological studies. He lodged at the Irish College, but enrolled as a student at the College of Propaganda, Rome, where in 1881 he completed his studies for the priesthood, being awarded the gold medal as the most outstanding student of the year. He was ordained priest in Rome on 16 June 1881.

In the summer of 1881 Marmion returned to Ireland. His first appointment, in September 1881, as priest in the archdiocese of Dublin, was to a curacy in the parish of Dundrum, co. Dublin. There he built up a considerable reputation for himself as a very caring pastor. His name was still remembered in this parish at the end of the twentieth century in the name of the large day-care centre in Dundrum village, Marmion House, managed by a voluntary group, the Marmion Society, to look after the old and the infirm in the parish. After only a year in Dundrum, Marmion was appointed professor of philosophy at his former alma mater, Holy Cross College, Clonliffe. He held this position from September 1882 to October 1886. At the same time he served as chaplain to the Redemptoristine convent in Drumcondra, Dublin, and to the prisoners in Mountjoy gaol.

Despite his success as pastor and professor Marmion felt himself called to lead a more contemplative life. For some years he had been in touch with the Benedictine monks of the abbey of Maredsous, Belgium, which had been founded in 1872. There were no Benedictine monasteries in Ireland at this time, but in any case Marmion wished to emulate the ancient Irish monks, who went into exile as the supreme sacrifice. He entered Maredsous on 21 November 1886 as a novice. Following the custom of the time Marmion was given a new name, Columba. At the end of his time as a novice, on 10 February 1888, Marmion made his first profession as a monk. Three years later, on 10 February 1891, he made his solemn or final profession. He remained in Maredsous, living the monastic life of study and prayer, until 1899, when he was sent to Louvain, the leading Catholic university town in Belgium, as part of a team to establish a monastery there called Mont César (later called Kaisersberg). He spent the next ten years in Louvain as prior of Mont César with special responsibility for the studies of the young monks. During this time Marmion built up a reputation as a popular retreat giver and spiritual director, and was also in demand as external examiner in theology at the university. Much of his time was also taken up writing letters—some two thousand of which have been preserved—giving spiritual advice to people who sought his counsel.

On 28 September 1909 Marmion was elected the third abbot of Maredsous. He received the abbatial blessing in Maredsous on 3 October 1909. During his long tenure of office (1909–23), he ruled over a community of some 130 monks, which proved a time consuming and tiring business. However, these domestic or monastic commitments did not deter him from numerous external interests and pursuits. From March 1913 to October 1914 he became involved in the Caldey affair. The Anglican Benedictine community on Caldey Island, under their abbot, Aelred Carlyle, decided to join the Roman Catholic church. Marmion was one of those who helped to see this transition successfully carried through.

Soon after the First World War broke out, in August 1914, Marmion was obliged to leave Maredsous, and brought his junior monks to Ireland, where they found asylum at Edermine House, near Enniscorthy. He remained in Ireland until early 1916, when he made his way back, via England and Holland, to the abbey of Maredsous. In the post-war years he found himself caught up in a number of physically exhausting enterprises. First he was asked to send a group of Belgian monks to occupy the Benedictine abbey of Dormition in Jerusalem, replacing temporarily the German monks, who had been expelled by the occupying British authorities. This venture lasted from December 1918 to September 1920, when the German monks were allowed to return. Marmion's second, and perhaps most lasting, undertaking, was the setting up, in 1922, of the Belgian congregation of Benedictine abbeys. This meant a separation from the pre-war Beuronese (German) congregation or confederation, a necessary step, given the anti-German feelings in Belgium at this time.

During his final years as abbot of Maredsous, Marmion produced three books of spirituality in French, which have since become classics, translated into fifteen languages. The English titles are: *Christ, the Life of the Soul* (1917), *Christ, in his Mysteries* (1919), and *Christ, the Ideal of the Monk* (1922). Marmion's last public appearance was at the golden jubilee celebrations of the founding of the abbey of Maredsous, on 15 October 1922. Two months later he had an attack of influenza, being one of the many who succumbed to the epidemic then raging in Belgium. He rallied somewhat and was able to spend a week in Antwerp in early January 1923, when he had his portrait painted by Joseph Janssens. By 26 January he was diagnosed as having bronchial pneumonia, which was complicated by uraemia and a high fever. He died on 30 January 1923 at 10 p.m. in Maredsous. The funeral took place on 3 February. He was laid to rest in the abbots' vault, under the shadow of the abbey church. Marmion was beatified on 3 September 2000. His feast day is 3 October.

D. MARK TIERNEY

Sources Maredsous Abbey, Denée, Belgium, Marmion MSS · 'Annals of Maredsous', Maredsous Abbey, Denée, Belgium · acta capitulorum, Maredsous Abbey, Denée, Belgium · Maredsous Abbey, Denée, Belgium, Edermine MSS · Mont César Abbey, Belgium, archives · R. Thibaut, *Abbot Columba Marmion* (1961) · M. Tierney, *Dom Columba Marmion* (1994) · monks of Glenstal, ed., *Abbot Marmion: an Irish tribute* (1948) · curriculum vitae of Columba Marmion, Vatican Archives, Congregatio de Causis Sanctorum, prof. 948 · parish register, Arran Quay, St Paul's, Dublin, 6 April 1858 [baptism] · 'Memoir of Rosie Marmion', 19 Oct 1927, Maredsous Abbey, Dénée, Belgium [daughter of William Marmion and Herminie Cordier] · messager des oblats, 1923, Maredsous Abbey, Belgium, 21.5–11 · *Holy Cross College, Clonliffe, Dublin, 1859–1959* (1961)
Archives Maredsous Abbey, Denée, Belgium | Downside Abbey, near Bath, Bede Camm MSS · Maredret Abbey, Denée, Belgium, C. de Hemptinne MSS · New Norcia Abbey, Western Australia,

Salvado MSS · Sind Andries Abbey, Zevenkerken, Belgium, Mont-César MSS
Likenesses V. de Melle, oils, 1917, Glenstal Abbey, Murroe, co. Limerick, Ireland · L. de Hepcée, oils, 1922, Maredsous Abbey, Denée, Belgium · V. de Melle, oils, 1922, Glenstal Abbey, Murroe, co. Limerick, Ireland · J. Janssens, oils, 1923, Maredsous Abbey, Denée, Belgium

Marmion, Sir Philip (d. 1291), baron, was the son of Robert Marmion and Juliana, daughter of Philippe de Vassy. He succeeded to his estates about 1241–3. He married Joan, daughter and coheir of Hugh of Kilpeck, and on 7 February 1244 he performed homage for his wife's share of the Kilpeck estates. In July 1249 he was appointed sheriff of Warwickshire and Leicestershire, and on 6 February 1252 was pardoned for trespasses in that office. Partly as a result of this he became heavily indebted to the crown, and an arrangement was made for paying this off by instalments in 1253. In that year he went with the king to Gascony, and was captured on his return journey with the earl of Warwick and others at Pons in Poitou. From 1258 he was summoned on several occasions to expeditions against Llewelyn. In 1260 he replaced James Audley as a justice on special eyres arranged for the redress of grievances in Bedfordshire and Buckinghamshire.

A royalist, Marmion was sheriff of Norfolk and Suffolk during 1261–2, and was appointed warden in the counties of Nottingham and Derby in December 1263. He was among the party who submitted evidence on behalf of the king to Louis IX, resulting in the mise of Amiens in January 1264. After Evesham he was granted the lands of Montfortian rebels in seven counties, and on 26 September 1266 he received the king's demesnes of Tamworth and Wigginton for life. This was to bring him into serious conflict with the tenants of both manors. He bought houses in London and, when leasing them, reserved the right to reside there on visits to the capital. In the fourteenth century it was stated that the Marmion manor of Scrivelsby, Lincolnshire, was held by the grand sergeanty of performing the office of king's champion at the coronation, but whether Marmion actually performed that office for Edward I is unknown. He died on or before 5 December 1291. He had four daughters, three with Joan, namely Joan, Mazera, and Maud, and a fourth, another Joan, with his second wife, Mary. The estates were divided between these children. There was also an illegitimate son, Robert.

PETER COSS

Sources GEC, *Peerage* · C. F. R. Palmer, *History of the baronial family of Marmion* (1875), 68, 71 · *Report on the manuscripts of Lord Middleton*, HMC, 69 (1911), 71–4 · *CIPM*, 3, no. 29 · *Chancery records* (RC) · *Chancery records* · Rymer, *Foedera*, 1st edn, 1.777 · D. Crook, *Records of the general eyre*, Public Record Office Handbooks, 20 (1982), 189

Marmion, Robert (d. 1144), baron and soldier, was the son of Roger Marmion of Lincolnshire. He had succeeded his father by Michaelmas 1129 and the pipe roll of 1130 shows that he owed the sum of £176 13s. 4d. as relief for his father's lands, of which £60 had been paid by that date. He married Milicent, said to be a kinswoman of Queen Adeliza, widow of Henry I. Together Marmion and his wife granted the church of Polesworth and the lordship of

Warton to the nuns of Polesworth and the vill of 'Bute-yate', Lincolnshire, to Bardney Abbey. Marmion took King Stephen's part in the struggle with the Empress Matilda. In 1140 he appears as castellan of Falaise, where he successfully held out against Geoffrey, count of Anjou. His own castle at Fontenoy-le-Marmion was destroyed as a reprisal. In England he was in contention with William de Beauchamp over the castle and honour of Tamworth, where he had received a grant of free warren from Henry I.

Marmion faced a more formidable opponent, however, in Ranulf (II), earl of Chester. Here the struggle centred on the town of Coventry. Marmion was no mean figure himself militarily, being described as a warlike man, almost unequalled in his time for ferocity, adroitness, and daring, renowned for his many successes far and wide. At Coventry he expelled the monks and fortified the priory, using its stone buildings as a fortress from which to launch frequent attacks on the earl's castle. He also covered the field between the two with ditches to impede the enemy's forces. It was an act of desecration from which the chroniclers were soon able to draw a moral. The story is told in outline by Henry of Huntingdon, referred to by John of Salisbury, and given detail by the later twelfth-century chronicler, William of Newburgh. When the earl came with a considerable force to relieve the castle, Marmion's forces went out to engage him. During the action he was thrown from his horse into one of his own ditches. As he lay immobilized, with a broken thigh, he was decapitated, in full view of all, by a common soldier of the opposing army. He was apparently the only man killed in the action, 'crushed under the weight of divine judgement' (William of Newburgh, *Historia rerum Anglicarum*, ed. R. Howlett, Rolls Series, 1884, 1.71). This occurred about 16 September 1144. Marmion was buried at Polesworth, in unconsecrated ground as an excommunicate, and was succeeded by his son Robert. His widow, Milicent, married Richard de Camville.   PETER COSS

Sources GEC, *Peerage* · William of Newburgh, *The history of English affairs*, ed. P. G. Walsh and M. J. Kennedy, bk 1 (1988), 71, 163 · Henry, archdeacon of Huntingdon, *Historia Anglorum*, ed. D. E. Greenway, OMT (1996), 744–5 · *Ann. mon.*, 2.230 · *CPR, 1396–9*, 287; *1446–52*, 200 · *Pipe rolls, 31 Henry I*, 111 · R. Howlett, ed., *Chronicles of the reigns of Stephen, Henry II, and Richard I*, 4, Rolls Series, 82 (1889), 139 · Dugdale, *Monasticon*, 1.633 · B. R. Kemp, ed., *Reading Abbey cartularies*, 1, CS, 4th ser., 31 (1986), 402–3 · H. A. Cronne, *The reign of Stephen, 1135–54* (1970), 173 · C. F. R. Palmer, *History of the baronial family of Marmion* (1875), 35–7

Marmion, Robert (*d.* 1216×18), baron and justice, was the son of Robert Marmion of Tamworth, Staffordshire, and his wife, Elizabeth, the daughter of Hugues, count of Rethel, near Rheims. The death of his father, about October 1181, made the younger Robert a leading baron in the English midlands, with important estates also at Scrivelsby in Lincolnshire and Berwick in Sussex, and at Fontenay-le-Marmion in Normandy (Calvados). Identity of name makes it impossible to tell whether it was father or son who witnessed a number of Henry II's charters in Normandy in the 1170s, but it was probably Robert junior who in January 1178 sat on a judicial assize at Caen. After his

father's death he was active in the king's service in England; he is recorded as a justice in the *curia regis* at Melksham, Wiltshire, on 25 January 1184, while in 1187 he headed a circuit of eyres in the west midlands, during which he also imposed a tallage on the counties visited. Between Easter 1185 and Michaelmas 1189 he was sheriff of Worcestershire.

In common with many sheriffs Marmion lost his shrievalty at the accession of Richard I, and in 1190 had to promise a fine of £1000. This was subsequently commuted to 700 marks, which he paid in Normandy. In 1191 he was in Wales, paying £300 to the garrison of Carmarthen Castle. But in 1194 he joined Richard I in Normandy, and was still there in 1197, when he swore on the king's behalf to observe the treaty between Richard and the count of Flanders, and in July 1198. At some point he vowed to go on pilgrimage to the Holy Land, but about 1200 gave £500 angevins instead to the Norman abbey of Barbéry, of which his father ranked as second founder. Marmion seems to have remained in Normandy during the early years of John's reign; he witnessed one of that king's charters at Caen on 7 August 1203, and on the same day was granted the lands of such of his own men as had joined the French.

When Normandy was lost in 1204, Marmion returned to England, but his eldest son remained in France, and this, combined with Marmion's obvious determination to retain his position in both realms, seems to have prompted John's mistrust. Although Marmion acted as a justice in the king's court when it sat at Worcester in August 1204, and in 1205 was entrusted with the custody of a royal hostage, thereafter he appears in the record of government only as paying scutages and clearing old debts. The latter may have been achieved by borrowing, for at his death Marmion was indebted to two London Jews, owing at least £170. In 1210 three of his knights went on the king's Irish expedition, but Marmion does not appear to have gone himself. Estranged from John, he subsequently joined the baronial rebels. At about the end of 1215 the king ordered that Tamworth Castle be demolished; the order was not carried out, but at least some of Marmion's lands were confiscated. On 25 September 1216 it was ordered that the manor of Quinton, Gloucestershire, be restored to him, and early in November he was offered a safe conduct to enter into negotiations, but there is no evidence that he accepted it. He died, probably at Scrivelsby, some time before 9 May 1218.

Robert Marmion married twice, first to Maud de Beauchamp, and second, before about 1200, to Philippa (*d.* in or after 1221), whose surname is unknown. There were children of both marriages, though, confusingly, the eldest son of each was named Robert. In the provision that he made for his sons Marmion showed himself determined to keep his cross-channel lordship in being. The elder Robert remained in Normandy after 1204. The younger Robert came to England with his brother William, who became a secular clerk. Their father provided for both his younger sons, giving lands by charter to Robert in Lincolnshire,

Gloucestershire, and Sussex, and in Lincolnshire and Sussex to William, whom he also presented to two Warwickshire churches during the civil war. There can be little doubt that these grants were intended to shape arrangements subsequently made for the Marmion inheritance, when on 15 May 1218 the younger Robert (who had also been a rebel against John, and was captured at the battle of Lincoln) promised £500 for Tamworth and his father's lands, to be held until England and Normandy were reunited. If his elder brother Robert came into Henry III's allegiance, the lands were to pass to him, except for those that their father had already granted to the younger Robert and to William. In the event the elder Robert did return to England, and for a while reunited almost all his father's Anglo-Norman lordship.   HENRY SUMMERSON

Sources Chancery records (RC) · Chancery records · Pipe rolls, 32 Henry II – 2 Henry III · D. M. Stenton, ed., Pleas before the king or his justices, 1198–1212, 3, SeldS, 83 (1967) · H. C. M. Lyte and others, eds., Liber feodorum: the book of fees, 3 vols. (1920–31) · Curia regis rolls preserved in the Public Record Office (1922–), vol. 16, nos. 1943, 2128 · T. Stapleton, ed., Magni rotuli scaccarii Normanniae sub regibus Angliae, 2, Society of Antiquaries of London Occasional Papers (1844) · H. E. Salter and A. H. Cooke, eds., The Boarstall cartulary, OHS, 88 (1930) · W. W. Shirley, ed., Royal and other historical letters illustrative of the reign of Henry III, 1, Rolls Series, 27 (1862) · J. H. Round, ed., Calendar of documents preserved in France, illustrative of the history of Great Britain and Ireland (1899) · H. Cole, ed., Documents illustrative of English history in the thirteenth and fourteenth centuries, RC (1844), 305 · T. D. Hardy, ed., Rotuli Normanniae, RC (1835), 101 · The historical works of Gervase of Canterbury, ed. W. Stubbs, 2: The minor works comprising the Gesta regum with its continuation, the Actus pontificum and the Mappa mundi, Rolls Series, 73 (1880), 111 · GEC, Peerage, new edn, 8.508–10 · VCH Staffordshire, 1.226 · L. Landon, The itinerary of King Richard I, PRSoc., new ser., 13 (1935) · C. R. Cheney, Medieval texts and studies (1973) · F. M. Powicke, The loss of Normandy, 1189–1204: studies in the history of the Angevin empire, 2nd edn (1961) · N. Vincent, Peter des Roches: an alien in English politics, 1205–38, Cambridge Studies in Medieval Life and Thought, 4th ser., 31 (1996) · C. F. R. Palmer, History of the baronial family of Marmion (1875)

Wealth at death land worth £800: Pipe rolls, 2 Henry III, 54–5

Marmion, Shackerley (1603–1639), playwright and poet, was born in the village of Aynho in Northamptonshire on 21 January 1603, the eldest of four children of Shackerley Marmion (1575–1642) and his wife, Mary, née Lukyn (d. 1632). The family estate at Aynho had been secured by the playwright's great-grandfather Rowland Shackerley, who died in 1565. Shackerley Marmion senior was the eldest son of Thomas Marmion of Lincoln's Inn, who died in 1583 but who in 1577 had married Mary, the youngest daughter of Rowland Shackerley of Aynho. He married Mary, the daughter of Bartrobe Lukyn, a London gentleman, on 16 June 1600 at the church of St Dunstan-in-the-West (Nichols, Collectanea, 5.518). He evidently encountered financial difficulties and mortgaged part of his estate to Sir Thomas Penyston of Stanton in Buckinghamshire; in 1615 he sold his remaining interest in the estate at Aynho to Richard Cartwright of London. By 22 June 1616 the family had moved to Adderbury in Oxfordshire and thereafter there is no further reference to them there. A reference appears in the parish records of the church of St Bartholomew in Smithfield of the burial in 1632 of Mary Marmion, presumed to be the playwright's mother, and there is a

further record of the burial of a Shackerley Marmion in the register of the church of St Margaret's, Westminster, dated 5 September 1642.

Marmion was educated at Thame School under the tutelage of Richard Butcher and proceeded thereafter to Wadham College, Oxford, as a commoner, in 1618. His caution money was received on 28 April 1618 and he matriculated on 6 February 1621; he obtained his BA on 1 March 1622 and proceeded to his MA on 7 July 1624. There is no record of Marmion's activities between the years 1625 and 1629, although it is thought that following graduation, and as an impoverished member of the gentry, his father sent him into the Netherlands, where he may have become part of a troop commanded by Sir Sigismund Alexander, identified by Marion Jones as Sir Alexander Zinzan.

Marmion was back in England by 11 July 1629 and living in the parish of St Giles-in-the-Fields, in the highway of St Giles, since on that date he is alleged to have attacked a certain Edward Moore, wounding him in the head. He was released on bail of £80, £20 having been put up by his father, a further £20 by one Richard Browne, and a further £40 by Marmion himself, and ordered to appear on the following 1 September. Nothing more is heard of the case but it had evidently been resolved satisfactorily by December 1631, the date when Marmion's first play, Hollands Leaguer, was performed by the newly constituted Prince Charles's Men at the Salisbury Court theatre. Marmion took the title of his play from a celebrated event involving the siege of a brothel run by the notorious Southwark prostitute Elizabeth Holland; the siege had become the subject of popular ballads and an anti-Catholic prose account by Nicholas Goodman. The play was entered in the Stationers' register on 26 January 1632 by John Grove and was printed by John Beale, but only after the master of the revels, Sir Henry Herbert, had demanded certain 'alterations'. In addition to the heavy influence of the writings of Ben Jonson that play reveals an awareness of the conflict between platonic and profane love, which had also been the subject of the court masques Love's Triumph through Callipolis and Chloridia, both of which were performed at court in January and February 1631.

Marmion's second play, A Fine Companion, was performed at the Salisbury Court theatre in 1633 by the Prince's Men and also received a royal performance at Whitehall before Charles I and his queen. The play took its title from a well-known dance (printed by Playford in 1652) and appeared in the same year that Charles I reissued James I's declaration of sports, which had been originally formulated in 1618; its emphasis on festivity indicates a degree of sympathy with Charles's championing of such 'sports'. The play was entered in the Stationers' register on 15 June 1633 by the bookseller Richard Meighen and was printed in quarto shortly afterwards by Augustine Mathewes, with a dedicatory epistle to Sir Ralph Dutton, Marmion's third cousin and a distant relative of Sir Christopher Hatton, Elizabeth I's 'dancing chancellor'. Such was Marmion's burgeoning reputation that Richard Meighen solicited from him a poem dedicated to the actor Joseph

Taylor, who had performed in John Fletcher's *The Faithful Shepherdess* before the king and queen on twelfth night 1633, and which Meighen printed as part of the quarto that he published in 1634.

Although Marmion's third play, *The Antiquary*, was not entered in the Stationers' register until 11 March 1639 and was not printed by Felix Kingston in quarto until 1641 it is almost certain that it was performed some time during 1635–6. All that is known about its performance is that it was acted by Queen Henrietta's Men at the Cockpit theatre. Like Marmion's two previous plays it incorporates an actual historical event, the closure in 1629 of an antiquarian library, presumed to be that of Sir Robert Cotton (K. Sharpe, *Sir Robert Cotton, 1586–1631*, 1979). It is thought to have been revived twice in 1718 to celebrate the revival of the Society of Antiquaries (Dodsley, *A Selection of English Plays*, 1780). In its borrowings from various of Shakespeare's plays and poems, as well as from the works of Petronius and Virgil, and from books of 'characters', such as Overbury's *Characters*, John Earle's *Microcosmographie*, or Wye Saltonstall's *Picturae loquentes*, it is possible that Marmion was burlesquing the earlier texts that his audience could not have failed to recognize. In each of Marmion's plays there is an opposition between romantic and profane love, and this is sometimes aligned with the opposition between youth and age. Characters are driven by Jonsonian 'humours' and in each case idiosyncrasies are corrected through the celebratory power of comedy. Threats to the well-being of society are overcome by ingenuity but in the end all that is potentially harmful is rehabilitated within a social order that is shown to be capable of dynamically recharging itself. Marmion aligns the 'turbulenta prima, tranquilla ultima' ('turbulent beginning, tranquil conclusion') definition of the structure of comedy derived from his friend Thomas Heywood with Ben Jonson's Ciceronian definition: 'Imitatio vitae, speculum consuetudinis, imago veritatis' ('Imitation of life, mirror of manners, image of truth').

In addition to Marmion's three known plays his name was associated with a fourth play, *The Sodder'd Citizen*, the manuscript for which was brought to the British Museum by its owner, Lieutenant-Colonel E. G. Troyte-Bullock, in 1932. The first mention of Marmion's association with the play was in 1653 in an entry in the Stationers' register under the name of the publisher Humphrey Moseley. The play was acted between 1631 and 25 January 1632, the latter being the date when the actor Richard Sharpe, who had delivered both the prologue and the epilogue in performance, died. It is now generally thought that the author of this play was the highwayman–poet John Clavell, whose name, alongside the date, 1633, appears on the manuscript (Clavell).

Marmion also contributed occasional poems to Mathewe Walbancke's *Annalia Dubrensia, or, Celebration of Captain Dover's Cotswold Games* (1636), Thomas Heywood's *The Phoenix of these Late Times, or, The Life of Mr. Henry Welby, Esq.* (1637), *A true description of his majesties royall ship, built in this year 1637 at Wooll-witch in Kent* (1637), and *Pleasant Dialogues and Dramas* (1637), and a memorial poem to a collection commemorating the achievement of the dramatist and poet Ben Jonson, who died in 1637, *Jonsonus virbius* (1638). As well as occasional poetry Marmion published a long allegorical poem, *The Legend of Cupid and Psyche, or, Cupid and his Mistress* (1637), based on Apuleius's *The Golden Ass*. The poem was entered in the Stationers' register on 24 June 1637 by John Okes and the quarto was subsequently printed by Nicholas and John Okes, with prefatory verses by Richard Brome, Francis Tuckyr, Thomas Nabbes, and Thomas Heywood, who had treated this theme in his masque *Love's Mistress, or, The Queen's Masque* (1636); it was dedicated to Charles Lewis, prince elector and count palatine of the Rhine. It is thought that a second edition of the poem may have appeared in 1638 (Maxwell, 278ff.). In January 1639 Marmion joined Sir John Suckling's expedition against the Scots. He contracted a cold at Selby in Yorkshire and returned to London, where he died later that month. He was buried in the church of St Bartholomew in Smithfield.

With the exception of *The Antiquary* (1641) all of Marmion's plays and his poetry were published during his lifetime. Dodsley's *A Selection of Old English Plays* (1780) and Sir Walter Scott's *Ancient British Drama* (1810) both contain editions of *The Antiquary*, while W. H. Logan and J. Maidment produced a complete but poorly edited edition of the plays in 1875. In the twentieth century *A Fine Companion* was edited in 1979 by Richard Sonnenshine, and A. J. Nearing published an edition of *The Legend of Cupid and Psyche* in 1944. There have been three significant research theses on Marmion: Sue Maxwell (Yale University, 1941), Marion Jones (University of Oxford, 1956), and John Drakakis (University of Leeds, 1988), the last of which contains a complete old-spelling edition of the plays and a full textual analysis.   JOHN DRAKAKIS

Sources G. Baker, *The history and antiquities of the county of Northampton*, 1 (1822–30) · J. C. Jeaffreson, ed., *Middlesex county records*, 4 vols. (1886–92), vol. 3 · Wood, *Ath. Oxon.*, 2nd edn, 2.647 · J. Drakakis, 'The plays of Shackerley Marmion (1603–39): a critical old spelling edition', PhD diss., U. Leeds, 1988 · S. Maxwell, 'Shackerley Marmion, poet and dramatist', PhD diss., Yale U., 1941 · M. Jones, 'The life and works of Shackerley Marmion, 1603–39', BLitt diss., U. Oxf., 1956 · *The dramatic works of Shackerley Marmion*, ed. J. Logan and W. H. Maidment (1875) · *Cupid and Psyche by Shackerley Marmion: a critical edition with an account of Marmion's life and works*, ed. A. J. Nearing (1944) · Arber, *Regs. Stationers*, 4.270 · J. Q. Adams, ed., *The dramatic records of Sir Henry Herbert* (1917) · [J. Clavell], *The soddered citizen*, ed. J. H. Pafford and W. W. Greg (1936) · G. E. Bentley, *The Jacobean and Caroline stage*, 7 vols. (1941–68)
Archives Northants. RO, Cartwright muniments

Marney, Henry, first Baron Marney (1456/7–1523), courtier, was the son of Sir John Marney of Layer Marney, Essex (d. 1470/1472), and his wife, Jane (d. 1479), daughter of John Throckmorton. On 1 April 1472 his wardship and marriage were granted to Richard, duke of Gloucester, who sold them on 31 July to Robert Tyrell and Thomas Green. In 1484 he was a commissioner in Essex. He accommodated himself with ease to the Tudor regime, being made a privy councillor in 1485 and 1486–7, and in 1492–3 sheriff of Essex and Hertfordshire. He fought at Stoke in 1487 and at Blackheath in 1497. Appointed JP for Essex in 1490 and subsidy commissioner in 1504, he was an MP for the county in 1491–2, 1497, and 1504, and was knighted in 1494. Henry VIII, who retained much of his father's old council upon his accession, made him a privy councillor in 1509, as well as chancellor of the duchy of Lancaster; Henry also appointed him to a number of other positions—vice-chamberlain and captain of the king's guard, constable of Castle Rising, warden of Rochester Castle, steward of the duchy of Cornwall, and master forester of Dartmoor. As chancellor of the duchy, Marney made his son-in-law receiver-general and provided his own son with several minor offices. In 1509 he was granted the office of the constable of Clare Castle in reversion of John de Vere, thirteenth earl of Oxford, but Oxford outlived him. He was one of the executors of Lady Margaret Beaufort's will, and in April 1510 he was elected knight of the Garter. He served in the French campaign of 1513. Thomas, Lord Darcy, considered him one of the men most in favour early in Henry's reign, and at the time of the Yorkshire uprising Henry himself remembered him as one of the 'scant well born gentlemen' of his first council. Marney was present at the Field of Cloth of Gold and obtained many of the third duke of Buckingham's lands after the latter's fall in 1521. Appointed high steward of Sudbury in 1522 and lord privy seal on 14 February 1523, he was issued letters patent as a baron on 9 April 1523, and died at his house in the parish of St Swithin's, London, on 24 May in the same year.

By the terms of his will, dated 22 May 1523 and proved on 15 June, Marney was to be buried at Layer Marney and to have a tomb of marble with his image in black marble on it, as well as images of both his wives. The tomb still survives, executed in terracotta and showing Italian influence. The panels and shields of the tomb-chest, the lid, and the effigy are in black marble. His first wife, Thomazine, daughter of Sir John Arundell of Lanherne, Cornwall, was the mother of his son John, whose career he promoted by arranging his marriage with an heiress—Christian, daughter of Sir Roger Newburgh of East Lulworth, Dorset. (In his *Itineraries* John Leland confused father and son, stating that it was Henry who married 'the doughter and heyre of Newborow'.) Marney's second wife was Elizabeth, daughter of Sir Nicholas Wyfold and Margaret Chedworth, whose third husband, John Howard, became first duke of Norfolk. John Marney died in 1525 and the barony became extinct. John's tomb, although simpler, is similar to that of his father.

Marney, who had a household of thirty-two servants, began the building of a grand house to commemorate his family's rise in importance. Only the huge gatehouse, which has four towers and makes use of terracotta in Italian forms, was completed. Work must have begun around 1520 and Marney's death presumably put an end to the construction of the house, which was intended to stand to the south of the gatehouse. JAMES P. CARLEY

Sources GEC, *Peerage*, new edn, 8.523 · J. C. Wedgwood and A. D. Holt, *History of parliament*, 1: *Biographies of the members of the Commons house, 1439–1509* (1936), 575–6 · H. Miller, *Henry VIII and the English nobility* (1986) · M. K. Jones and M. G. Underwood, *The king's mother: Lady Margaret Beaufort, countess of Richmond and Derby* (1992) · S. J. Gunn, 'Henry Bourchier, earl of Essex (1472–1540)', *The Tudor nobility*, ed. G. W. Bernard (1992), 134–79

Marnock, Robert (1800–1889), landscape gardener, was born on 12 March 1800, at Kintore, Aberdeenshire. He is first recorded as a gardener at Bretton Hall, Yorkshire, and while there he won the competition to design the Sheffield Botanic Garden, which he laid out in 1834; he was also appointed its first curator. While at Sheffield he was involved in the publication of a number of gardening magazines: from 1836 to 1842 he edited the monthly *Floricultural Magazine*, and for several years, beginning in 1845, he edited the weekly *United Gardeners' and Land Stewards' Journal*. With Richard Deakin, he wrote the first volume of *Florigraphia Britannica, or, Engravings and Descriptions of the Flowering Plants and Ferns of Britain* (1837).

In 1840 Marnock won a second competition to design the garden of the Royal Botanic Society in Regent's Park. The design kept 'the number of walks to a minimum', left 'the central mass of the garden an open lawn' and screened 'the specialist gardens behind shrubberies and an elevated rockwork; the garden was bisected by a straight walk leading to the great conservatory, thus imposing an axis of symmetry' (Elliott, 40). It led to the recognition of Marnock as one of the leading landscape gardeners of the day. During much of his time at Regent's Park he was aided by the Irishman William Robinson, most of whose early work after his arrival in England was carried out under Marnock's aegis. As curator of the garden, Marnock also successfully managed the exhibitions at the Royal Botanic Society's gardens. He relinquished his post there in 1862, after which date he practised as a landscape gardener.

Marnock's style was that usually described as 'natural' or 'picturesque', while his work was sound and severely economical. The maxims of his approach are expressed in extracts from letters compiled by Mungo Temple in 1870. Among the practices Marnock objected to were 'The dotting of trees and shrubs on lawns like sentinels … or placing anything on a lawn at all which in any way interrupted the view or defaced the space', 'formal avenues, where they could easily be dispensed with', and 'roads to the dwelling house, taking long out-of-the-way turns, where they could be concealed and the distance shortened' (Elliott, 168). As a general principle, he sought the easy, unimpeded movement of the eye over the scene ahead. His chief designs are those at Greenlands, Henley-on-Thames, made for the Rt Hon. W. H. Smith; at Hampstead, for Sir Spencer Wells; at Possingworth, Sussex, for Lewis Huth; at Blythwood, near Taplow, for George Hanbury; at Brambletye, near East Grinstead, for Donald Larnach; at Leigh Place, near Tonbridge, for Samuel Morley, and at Weston Park, Sheffield; Park Place, Henley; Taplow Court; Eynsham Hall; Sopley Park; and Montague House, Whitehall. His work for Prince Demidov at San Donato, near Florence, in 1852, added greatly to his reputation, and to the increasing taste for English gardening on the continent. His last public work was the Alexandra Park at Hastings, laid out in 1878. He retired in 1879, leaving his business to Joseph Weston, although he continued to give professional advice on landscape gardening until the spring of 1889, in which year he designed his last private garden, that of Sir Henry Peck at Rousdon, near Lyme Regis.

Marnock spent the last summers of his long life in Aberdeenshire with his two daughters, rambling over the high mountains in search of wild flowers. He died at his home, 1B Oxford and Cambridge Mansions, Marylebone Road, London, on 15 November 1889. In accordance with his wishes his body, after a religious service, was cremated at Woking, and his ashes were deposited in his wife's grave at Kensal Green cemetery on 20 November.

GORDON GOODWIN, rev. AUDREY LE LIÈVRE

Sources 'Robert Marnock', *Gardeners Chronicle* (29 April 1882), 567–8 · *Gardeners' Chronicle* (23 Nov 1889), 558 · *Gardeners Magazine* (23 Nov 1889), 733–44 · private information (2004) [Henry Vivian-Neal] · *The Times* (21 Nov 1889) · B. Elliott, *Victorian gardens* (1986) · d. cert. · *CGPLA Eng. & Wales* (1889)
Archives Essex RO, Chelmsford, MSS relating to laying out of gardens at Hassobury
Likenesses T. B. Wirgman, oils, exh. RA 1879, Royal Horticultural Society, London
Wealth at death £3167 11s. 6d.: probate, 12 Dec 1889, *CGPLA Eng. & Wales*

Marochetti, (Pietro) Carlo Giovanni Battista, Baron Marochetti in the nobility of Sardinia (1805–1867), sculptor, was born on 14 January 1805 in Turin, the son of Vincenzo (Vincent) Marochetti (*b. c.*1768), a former priest who had served as secretary-general to the provisional republican Piedmontese government and was professor of eloquence at Turin University and under-prefect of Chivasso, and his wife, whose maiden surname was Isola. With the waning of Napoleonic influence in the area Vincenzo Marochetti moved with his family to France, where he practised as an advocate in the Paris court of cassation. Carlo Marochetti was educated at the Lycée Napoléon and went on to study sculpture at the École des Beaux-Arts under François-Joseph Bosio. His one attempt at the *prix de Rome* of the École was rewarded only with an honourable mention, but since his mother was resident in Rome, having returned to Italy about 1814, he was enabled, without state assistance, to pass lengthy periods there between 1822 and 1827. In Rome his contacts were with other French students, such as François-Joseph Duret and Antoine Etex. He is also reported to have spent time in the studio of Bertel Thorvaldsen, the celebrated Danish sculptor. For all his neo-classical training, Marochetti increasingly identified, after the July Revolution of 1830, with the Romantic school of sculpture, pursuing on the one hand a colourful historicism, and on the other, sartorial realism in contemporary portraiture, accompanied sometimes by a lively textured treatment of surfaces.

Following his move back to Paris, Marochetti married in 1835 Camille de Maussion (*d.* 1893); they had two sons and a daughter. Two major commissions were given to him by the new constitutional monarchy, a relief of the battle of Jemappes for the Arc de Triomphe de l'Étoile, and a colossal group, *The Elevation of Mary Magdalene*, for the high altar of the church of La Madeleine in Paris. Completion of the

(Pietro) Carlo Giovanni Battista Marochetti, Baron Marochetti in the nobility of Sardinia (1805–1867), by Gabriele Ambrosio, 1888

latter was delayed by work on a monument which would win for Marochetti a contested celebrity as a creator of lively equestrian statues. This was the historical portrait of Emanuele Filiberto of Savoy (1528–1580), fully armed, in the act of sheathing his sword while reining in his charger. Marochetti made a gift of this statue to his birthplace, but before its erection in the piazza San Carlo in Turin it was temporarily exhibited in the courtyard of the Louvre in 1838. The support of Louis-Philippe and his family which this privilege denoted was further demonstrated when Marochetti was asked to execute an equestrian statue of Ferdinand, duke of Orléans, after the duke's accidental death in 1842. One version stood between 1844 and 1848 in the Louvre courtyard. Marochetti was also an early contributor to the wave of commemorative sculpture, which this period witnessed, to great men of the nation in the places of their birth.

Tireless in his search for new arenas for public statuary, Marochetti in 1840 was simultaneously attempting to secure a commission in Glasgow for a monument to the duke of Wellington, and also preparing models for the tomb of Napoleon I for the church of Les Invalides in Paris. He was ultimately successful in his bid for the Glasgow statue, which would be inaugurated in 1844, but the commission of one who was seen as both unqualified and foreign as the sculptor of so national a memorial as Napoleon's tomb inspired a storm of protest in France. Relieved of the tomb memorial, Marochetti was appeased with another related commission for an equestrian statue of the emperor for the esplanade of the Invalides. This statue, though modelled by Marochetti, remained at his country house at Vaux-sur-Seine, outside Paris, until the commission was finally annulled by the government of Napoleon III in 1853.

Following the abdication of Louis-Philippe in 1848, Marochetti remained briefly in France. Having been mayor of Vaux since 1846, he now campaigned for election as its deputy to the new republican national assembly. When this and other projects failed he moved permanently to London late in 1848. He already had influential contacts in Britain. In 1849 he met Queen Victoria and Prince Albert for the first time, impressing the queen, who found him 'very agreeable, gentlemanlike and unassuming' (Queen Victoria, journal, 1 July 1848, Royal Archives, Windsor). Quite soon he established his reputation with the plaster equestrian statue of Richard I, which stood outside the western entrance to the Crystal Palace in 1851. A group of supporters campaigned for the statue's erection in bronze 'on some conspicuous site in the metropolis' (*Proposal for the Erection of the Statue of Richard Coeur de Lion by Baron Marochetti, 23 May 1853*). Prince Albert was responsible for the decision to place it outside the Palace of Westminster, where it has stood since 1860.

Despite the support of the royal couple and John Ruskin, Marochetti met with a chauvinistic reaction to his admittedly far-reaching ambitions. Hoping to circumvent competition for the tomb of the duke of Wellington, in 1859 he exhibited a seated figure of a Winged Victory, part of his proposed monument, in the garden of Apsley House, London, overlooking Rotten Row, and tried to muster royal support for his scheme. In this he failed, as he did also in a project of the early 1860s for a series of statues in St Margaret's churchyard, Westminster, commemorating a triumvirate of great engineers. These statues were later erected in different locations (that of Isambard Kingdom Brunel on the Victoria Embankment, George Stephenson at Euston Station, and Joseph Locke in Locke Park, Barnsley, Yorkshire). A colossal statue of Sir Robert Peel in Parliament Square was also later removed, to be replaced by a smaller figure by Matthew Noble. As a reporter for *The Athenaeum* observed, Marochetti appeared to be aiming at hegemony in the heartlands of Westminster ('Fine art gossip', 29 June 1861, 867). Despite these reverses, his vast studio and foundry in the mews behind his home, 34 Onslow Square, South Kensington, were always full of work in progress. The two forms which dominated his production in these years were equestrian statues (Queen Victoria and Prince Albert for Glasgow, Viscount Combermere for Chester, Sir Mark Cubbon for Bangalore, India) and monumental mourning seraphim, deployed in individual or group commemorations (the monument to the lords Melbourne in St Paul's Cathedral, London; the monument to British soldiers killed in the Crimea, known as the Scutari obelisk, in Haydarpaşa cemetery, Turkey; and the Cawnpore memorial in Cawnpore, India). While living in England, Marochetti produced

important monuments for Italy (those of Carlo Alberto of Savoy for Turin, and Gioacchino Rossini for Pesaro) and for France (the tomb of the comtesse de Lariboisière for the Hôpital Lariboisière in Paris).

Marochetti followed in the footsteps of the sculptor John Gibson in his promotion of sculptural polychromy. His most spectacular excursion in this line was a coloured marble statuette of Queen Victoria as 'Queen of Peace', exhibited in the Bayswater studios of the society photographer Camille Silvy in 1862 (lost; photograph, National Portrait Gallery, London).

On the death of Prince Albert in 1861, Queen Victoria chose Marochetti to execute the private monument to the prince and herself for the Royal Mausoleum at Frogmore, in Windsor Great Park. This tomb, with its four kneeling bronze angels, is one of his finest achievements. He seems to have had less success with the seated figure of the prince, designed as centrepiece for the national memorial for Kensington Gardens in London. His second model had just been completed when he himself died, and the queen deemed the portrait figure unworthy of the monument. A new statue was commissioned from the Irish sculptor John Henry Foley.

Marochetti died suddenly at Passy, near Paris, on 29 December 1867 and was buried in the cemetery of Vaux-sur-Seine. The elder of his two sons, Maurizio (Maurice) Marochetti, entered the Italian diplomatic service but also practised as a sculptor.   P. WARD-JACKSON

Sources M. Calderini, *Carlo Marochetti* (1927) · *DNB* · G. Hubert, *Les sculpteurs italiens en France sous la révolution, l'empire et la restauration, 1790–1830* (1964) · M. Vicaire, 'Les projets de Marochetti pour le tombeau de l'empereur Napoléon', *Bulletin de la Société de l'Histoire de l'Art Français* (1974), 145–51 · M. P. Driskel, *As befits a legend: building a tomb for Napoleon, 1840–1861* (1993) · S. Lami, *Dictionnaire des sculpteurs français au XIXe siècle* (1914–21) · B. Read, *Victorian sculpture* (1982) · C. de Remusat, *Mémoires de ma vie* (1958–67) · PRO · Royal Arch. · Archives Nationales, Paris · Dorset RO, Bankes papers · Departmental Archives, Yvelines, Versailles · Archives of the City of Paris, Paris · CGPLA Eng. & Wales (1868) · R. A. [R. Alby], 'Marochetti, Vincent', *Biographie universelle, ancienne et moderne*, ed. J. F. Michaud and L. G. Michaud, 73 (Paris, 1843) · personal knowledge (2004) · A. Bovero, 'L'opera di Carlo Marochetti in Italia', *Emporium* (May 1942), 185–99

Likenesses attrib. A. C. Sterling, salt print, 1845–9, NPG · C. Silvy, carte-de-visite, 1861, NPG · G. Ambrosio, bronze statuette, 1888, NPG [*see illus.*] · V. Brooks, chromolithograph (after J. Ballantyne), NPG · Caldesi, Blanford & Co., carte-de-visite, priv. coll. · W. Murden, group portrait, wood-engraving (*Associates of the Royal Academy in 1861*), BM, NPG; repro. in *ILN* (23 Feb 1861) · C. Silvy, carte-de-visite, priv. coll. · J. & C. Watkins, carte-de-visite, NPG · oils, Château de Vaux-sur-Seine, Hedengren collection · two photographs, Château de Vaux-sur-Seine, Hedengren collection

Wealth at death under £9000: probate, 5 Feb 1868, *CGPLA Eng. & Wales*

Marot, Daniel (1661–1752), architect, designer, and engraver, was born in Paris in 1661, the son of the protestant Jean Marot (1619–1679), engraver and architect, and his wife, Charlotte, daughter of the Dutch cabinet-maker Abraham Garbrand. Daniel assisted his father on his engravings of contemporary French architecture, published in 1670 as *L'architecture françoise*, known as the Grand Marot. From 1677 Daniel worked independently as

Daniel Marot (1661–1752), by Jacob Gole (after Jacques Parmentier)

an engraver for the designers Jean Le Pautre (1618–1682) and Jean Berain (1637–1711), then *dessinateur du cabinet et de la chambre* to Louis XIV. Marot's prints after Berain included the designs for Lully's opera *Le triomphe de l'amour* (1681) and for the funeral in 1683 of Queen Marie Thérèse, wife of Louis XIV. Marot's reputation was enhanced by the engraving of the celebrations marking the birth of the dauphin, 25 August 1682:

> Faite par un jeune homme qui égale deja les plus habile graveurs, et qui se sera autant connaîtres par luy-mesme, qu'il est connu à Paris par le nom de feu son pere. Il est fils du Sr Marot, architecte et graveur, qui a laissé beaucoup ouvrages au Public.   (*Mercure de France*, Sept 1682)

Daniel Marot left France as a consequence of the persecution of protestants that led to the revocation of the edict of Nantes in October 1685. He went to Holland to join his mother's relatives. There, Jacob Gole, Marot's future brother-in-law, engraved *c.*1700 Marot's portrait by James Parmentier.

Marot at the court of William and Mary in Holland The earliest recorded print by Marot in Holland commemorates the ball held in December 1686 at the huis ten Bosch, near The Hague, given by Mary, princess of Orange, to celebrate her husband's birthday. The festive scene, set in the famous Oranjezaal, is framed with allegorical figures and an ornamental cartouche. This etching is signed by Marot as both draughtsman and printmaker and was sold from his house in The Hague and by Jacob Gole in Amsterdam. It

carries an effusive dedication to the princess demonstrating that Marot was anxious to attract her patronage.

Two years later Marot engraved *The order of the fleet of his serene highness the lord prince of Orange coming to the help of the English protestants on 11 November 1688*, an impression of which is in the Bodleian Library, Oxford. The forty-nine warships are depicted diagrammatically so that individual vessels can be identified. The coat of arms indicates that the print was published after William and Mary had been crowned joint English monarchs in April 1689.

Marot's role as a visual propagandist for William and Mary was not limited to the production of prints of royal or political events. He became active as a designer encouraging a taste for unified interiors and gardens for royal palaces and for the stately homes of courtiers, in Holland and in England. A wide range of furnishings and decorative paintings were executed to Marot's designs by teams of artists and craftsmen. His first such commission in 1686 was for the staircase, Willemszaal, and marble room at Slot Zeist, near Utrecht, built to the designs of Jacob Roman (the town architect of Leiden) for Willem Adriaan, count of Nassau-Odijk (1632–1705), ambassador to France and a cousin of William of Orange. At Zeist, Marot was also responsible for the layout of the gardens. In the same year, Mary of Orange had laid the foundation stone for the hunting lodge at Het Loo near Apeldoorn. Also built to the designs of Jacob Roman, after 1689 it was extended as a royal palace. In 1692 Daniel Marot designed the illusionistic painting for the staircase inspired by the escalier des ambassadeurs at Versailles. This was painted by a team of decorative artists including the French protestant refugees Pierre Berchet and James Parmentier, both of whom had previously worked in England and were to return there.

At Het Loo, Daniel Marot was responsible for most of the interior decoration. The original painted decoration in the audience room has survived intact, with landscapes painted by Glauber and figures by Gerard de Lairesse. Further evidence for Marot's role is provided by the printed versions of these designs which appeared in The Hague in 1703. They include the new dining-room and the king's library—which was originally intended as a porcelain cabinet for Queen Mary, with a mirrored ceiling—it was only adapted for the king after Mary's early death in 1694. These prints were published in Holland by Marot after William III's death in an endeavour to compensate for the loss of royal patronage and to encourage new commissions. A later print of a state bedchamber which appeared in the *Second livre d'appartements* in 1712 may have been based on the original design for the king's bedchamber at Het Loo. It shows the extent to which such a room depended on upholstery for its effect. The walls are draped in fabric which echoes that on the state bed. The set of upholstered chairs is, like the wall hangings, enriched with appliqué motifs.

Marot, patronage, and contemporary furniture In England as in Holland, courtiers were swift to realize Marot's potential and supported his role as a designer of interior furnishings. A rare design drawing signed and dated 1700 by

Marot for a mirror, table, and candlestand for William III at Het Loo is endorsed on the back 'table at miroir dore pour Loo 17 Sept 1701' (Rijksmuseum, Amsterdam). Similar mirrors with applied carving at the corners and middles were supplied for English patrons. Examples were made for Thomas Coningsby's seat at Hampton Court, Herefordshire.

There is no distinction in quality between the furnishings made to Marot's designs for the monarch and those for leading courtiers. A set of upholstered chairs, dating from the 1690s, with a daybed and paned hangings *en suite*, survive at Penshurst, Kent. They may have come from one of the English royal palaces, for they belonged to Henry Sidney, first earl of Romney, who was William III's groom of the stole. Or they may have been commissioned for Leicester House, London, refurbished for Lord Romney's elder brother. A daybed and sofa (Temple Newsam, Leeds) made for Thomas Osborne, first duke of Leeds, after 1694 by Philip Guibert may have been designed by Marot; the same maker produced very similar pieces for William III in 1697.

Marot and garden design As at Zeist, Marot was responsible for designing the garden layout at Het Loo under the supervision of Hans Willem Bentinck, first earl of Portland. The grotto in the corner of the queen's garden consisted of three rooms. The first room was lined with shells and paved with black and white marble; the second room contained a couch or daybed for repose; the third was decorated with porcelain. The king's garden was dominated by a bowling green and the fountain in the centre of the upper garden rose to a height of 45 feet, with thirty-two jets around it.

Marot in England It was Marot's skill as a garden designer which led to his first documented English commission, the design for the parterre at Hampton Court Palace, dated August 1689. The design was apparently sent by Marot from Holland and was not executed until 1698. Marot's presence in England is not documented until 1694, although a payment to 'Mr. Maro' in September 1693 (Petworth) may indicate that he was already in England. He was not paid for work on the Hampton Court parterre until after he had returned to Holland. In March 1698 Caspar Frederick Henning (paymaster of the money for the use and service of his majesty's gardens at Hampton Court and Newmarket) wrote to the council of Nassau demesne suggesting that Mr Marot should be paid £236 11s. 11d. sterling . In London, Marot was employed by the francophile Ralph, first earl of Montagu, at Montagu House, Bloomsbury, rebuilt after a fire in 1686. Marot also worked for Montagu's son-in-law, Charles Seymour, sixth duke of Somerset (1662–1748), at Petworth, Sussex. As master of the king's wardrobe from 1689, Montagu was aware of Marot's work as an interior designer in both the Dutch and English royal palaces. William III's visit to Montagu's London house in May 1689 stimulated the wish to emulate that unity of interior decoration in his own royal palaces.

A set of record drawings of decorative panels at Montagu House, Bloomsbury, is annotated in Marot's hand (V&A). They relate to five painted panels at Boughton, Northamptonshire, that originally lined a closet in the London house. These drawings were not subsequently published by Marot. One is inscribed 'la hauteur de la tapisserie de monsieur Loire est de 7 pied 6 pouce' indicating that the panels were probably based on designs by Alexis Loir (1640–1713), Parisian engraver and goldsmith. Similar drawings in the National Museum, Stockholm, correspond to Loir's *Nouveau desseins d'ornemens de paneaux, lambris, carosse etc.* As Loir is not recorded in England, Montagu may have imported the panels from France. Marot's contribution to the interior decoration at Montagu House was as co-ordinator of design although he may have directed operations from Holland. Decorative painting was bordered by architectural woodwork and matching picture frames. Although the house was demolished in the 1840s, surviving picture frames demonstrate that their design answers to Marot's later published designs for frames. The Montagu House frames may have been made from original drawings by Marot.

As at Montagu House, London, Daniel Marot's work at Petworth for the duke of Somerset is largely undocumented. Similar to the second Montagu House, Bloomsbury, said by Colen Campbell to be the work of 'Pouget', the exterior originally had a pronounced central squared dome (destroyed by fire in 1714). The interior—in particular the marble hall realized during 1692, with its giant doorcases, huge bracketed frieze, and overmantels crowned by segmental pediments—is similar to Daniel Marot's Trèveszaal in the Binnenhof at The Hague, completed in 1698. The west front is similar to Marot's De Voorst, designed from 1697 for William III's favourite Arnold Joost van Keppel, first earl of Albemarle; the busts on fluted tapering plinths over the ground-floor windows of the pavilions are reminiscent of an overmantel there. The central section of the frieze is close to one of Marot's prints in his series *Trois diferentes corniches*. Marot's influence is present in the military trophies on the gates to the forecourt, a form of trophy which reappears in his published designs for triumphal arches.

On 30 September 1693 John Bowen the agent 'received of my Lord Duke twenty Pounds which was paid to Mr. Maro' (sixth duke of Somerset's personal receipt book, W. Sussex RO). Marot is also recorded as borrowing a book from the duke's library.

Royal patronage in England Probably inspired by the interior of Montagu House, William III entrusted the earl of Montagu with the supervision of his palace interiors. At some time in the early 1690s Daniel Marot became involved, indeed Marot later referred to himself as 'Architecte des appartments de sa Majesté Britanique'. Correspondence from Constantijn Huygens dated April 1694 records that Marot had been sent for from Holland by Queen Mary. In October he was back in Amsterdam where he married Catherine Mary, daughter of Adrian Gole, but the registers note that Daniel was resident in London. His brother Isaac witnessed the marriage. Daniel, Catherine, and Isaac returned to London. The records of Queen

Mary's privy purse document annual fees paid to Daniel Marot and specific payments to Daniel's younger brother, Isaac, in 1694 for 'designing and drawing 3 large pieces of silk during 3 weeks at 5s a day. For designing during 6 days some ornaments for a bed and cushions' (BL, Add. MS 5751). Thus the series of eight embroidered panels in Queen Mary's closet, Hampton Court Palace, traditionally believed to have been designed by Daniel Marot for the queen, may have been the work of Isaac Marot—they were probably not completed and therefore not hung until after Mary's death. It was Daniel who probably took overall responsibility for the decoration of Queen Mary's water gallery at Hampton Court, a suite of private apartments on two floors overlooking the River Thames, adjoining the privy garden. The *piano nobile* had a gallery and a great room with four closets at the corners; the lower floor housed a dairy and a bathing room. Celia Fiennes described the closets opening off the great room as 'panelled all with Jappan, another with Looking Glass and two with work under panells of glass' (C. Morris, ed., *The Travels of Celia Fiennes*, 1947, 59–60). Could this 'work under glass' be the hangings embroidered to Marot's designs which have now returned to Hampton Court? The upper floor was decorated in blue, white, and gold; the gallery furnished with four couches upholstered in sky-coloured satin, twenty-five cane chairs, and twelve round stools japanned blue and white. In addition two sets of tables, mirrors, and stands, decorated *en suite*, were supplied for the piers. One of these tables has been identified and carries the inscription 'La Galerie Thames' on the underside of the stretcher (priv. coll.). The dairy was furnished with tiles (examples in the Rijksmuseum, and in the V&A) and Delft milk pans (V&A; Hampton Court Palace) made in Delft to Daniel Marot's designs. There were also urns, vases, and tall pyramids, made up of tiers of box-like units, each with a number of protruding nozzles. Usually referred to as tulip vases, they were probably used to grow hyacinths (see A. Pavord, *The Tulip*, 1999, 182). The delftware bears the 'AK' monogram of Adrianszoon Koex (who ran the Greek A factory at Delft from 1687 to 1701) and the 'PAK' monogram of his son Pieter Adrianszoon who ran the factory until his death in 1703, when it was managed by his widow until 1722. Marot also designed some features of the interiors for William III at Hampton Court—a ceiling design in the collection of the Royal Institute of British Architects incorporating a royal crown is thought to be part of this commission—but in the main palace Marot worked under the supervision of William Talman (1650–1719).

Marot almost certainly designed interiors for Queen Mary at Kensington Palace. There the queen's bed was of seven-colour velvet, lined with gold satin and adorned with green and silver *passementerie*, with an embroidered gold satin counterpane. Her closet was hung with Indian damask and furnished with a blue and gold embroidered couch, with a tented canopy of gold and gauze curtains. These could be raised up and down with pulleys round a framework. The design of the latter may have been inspired by Turkish practice. Recent research has indicated that Daniel Marot was also responsible for the layout of the twelve-acre slope garden to the south of Kensington Palace from 1689 to 1690. A broad gravel walk centred on the south front of the palace was flanked by arrangements of grass and gravel forming 'parterres à l'Angloise' with *plates bandes* and topiary. This formal garden was cleared in 1727.

Daniel Marot was based in London for at least two more years. In June 1695 his eldest son, Daniel, was baptized at the Huguenot church of Leicester Fields and his daughter Marianne was baptized there in June 1696. The family were still in London in December 1696 when Daniel's wife (then named as Catherina Maria van Goolen) witnessed the baptism of Abraham, son of her cousin the cabinet-maker Cornelius Gole, at the same church. By the autumn of the following year, Daniel, Catherine, and their two young children had returned to Holland; their second son was baptized in Amsterdam on 1 September 1697. How was Marot's time in England occupied for the two years that he is definitely recorded in England and in particular from January 1695, after the death of Queen Mary?

Other English commissions Leading courtiers created in their own country palaces suites of apartments worthy of their monarch. They commissioned grand beds in imitation of those made for the royal palaces. Other furnishings also imitated royal decoration. Delftware believed to have been made to Daniel Marot's designs survives at Boughton and Drayton in Northamptonshire, Castle Howard, Yorkshire, Dyrham, Gloucestershire, and Petworth and Uppark in Sussex. One courtier, Thomas Coningsby (1656–1729), appears to have commissioned the king's own designer to achieve the necessary effect. At Hampton Court, Herefordshire, the king's state bedroom was hung with the same crimson damask that was used to upholster the state bed and the accompanying set of seat furniture. The damask was identical to that used in William III's presence chamber at Hampton Court Palace. Woven in Genoa, it was provided by the London-based Huguenot merchant William Portal. The state bed (Het Loo Palace, Apeldoorn, Netherlands) with its flying tester has little cantoon wings at the end corners, a feature also found on the great crimson velvet bed from Melville House, Fife (V&A), made for William III's former secretary of state for Scotland, George, earl of Melville. Melville House was designed from 1697 by the Scottish architect James Smith. Not satisfied with creating a bed for the king's use, Coningsby ordered for himself a four-poster bed upholstered in blue silk damask (Metropolitan Museum of Art, New York).

Both the Melville state bed and those from Hampton Court, Herefordshire, are attributed to the London-based Francis Lapiere, the leading French émigré upholsterer of the late seventeenth and early eighteenth century, although no bills have survived to prove this. The attribution is based on a comparison with the remaining canopy, headboard, and cloth of a crimson damask state bed embellished with silver braid (Hardwick Hall, Derbyshire) originally made for William Cavendish, first duke of

Devonshire's seat at Chatsworth, Derbyshire, for which Lapiere charged £497 in 1697. Another state bed, created about 1704, two years after William III's death, can be seen at Dyrham Park, Gloucestershire, the seat of William Blaythwayt, former secretary of war to that king. Upholstered in crimson and yellow velvet, and lined with a sprigged satin, it was created for the 'Best Bed Chamber above Stairs' where the walls were lined with tapestry and the windows had matching yellow damask silk curtains and red and white striped case curtains. Even the doors had similar curtains and valances. The names Lapiere and Marot are directly associated with the provision of upholstered furnishings for Montagu House, London, and Boughton House, Northamptonshire. In 1705 Lapiere was paid £6 0s. 0d. for 'taking a crimson & gold damask bed all to pieces & new making it up again to go to Boughton' (MS, Boughton House), a reference to the Boughton state bed (V&A). Lapiere also made new beds for Montagu and in 1706 supplied a bed of striped tapestry needlework and charged for 'Mr. Marrot' for 'drawing the Cornishes and for drawing the Cupps' (MS, Boughton House). This rare reference to the designer is unexpected, as by 1697 Daniel Marot had returned to Holland. The most likely explanation is that this refers to Daniel's younger brother, Isaac, the 'dessinateur' whose son Charles was baptized at the Huguenot chapel at the Savoy in September 1707.

Historical significance In England, it was Daniel Marot's skill as a designer which resulted in a unified approach to interior decoration. This was realized under his supervision through a team of other designers, artists, and craftsmen. The importance of Daniel Marot's younger brother, Isaac, as a designer has only recently emerged and as yet no drawings have been firmly attributed to him. But there were other designers working in a similar style. Mr Boujet signed drawings for the overmantel at Dunham Massey, Cheshire (drawings collection, RIBA), and a sculptured relief for a pediment (Metropolitan Museum of Art, New York). A series of elaborately carved walnut hall benches at Dunham Massey are Dutch in inspiration and, if not imported from Holland, may well have been designed by Marot, or another member of his circle. Many of those who worked with Marot in England were foreigners; some were Huguenot refugees from France, others came to England via Holland. Apart from the upholsterer Lapiere, they included the cabinet-makers Gerrit Jensen and Cornelius Gole, the carvers and gilders Jean, Thomas, and Réné Pelletier, and the goldsmith Peter Archambo. Through his published designs, Daniel Marot's influence in England was long-lived, and inspired the work of later designers including the architect William Kent. Marot's published designs were reissued in 1892, and the resulting resurgence of interest produced a spate of articles and Marot revival interiors, of which the blue drawing-room at Stansted, Sussex, designed by Goodhart Rendel in 1926, is most remarkable in its close adherence to Marot's printed designs.

Marot's return to Holland On his return to Holland, Daniel Marot worked for Arnold Joost van Keppel, first earl of

Albemarle (1669–1718), at De Voorst (destr.) near Zutphen. Here Marot supervised the interiors of a building designed by Jacob Roman and designed the garden layout. The drawing for the *trompe-l'œil* staircase decoration (Cooper Hewitt Museum, New York) is signed by the decorative artist Isaac de Moucheron. This demonstrates how closely Daniel Marot worked with his team of artists and craftsmen.

Although Marot continued to receive annual payments from William III until 1701 (PRO t38/193, fol. 98), the king's death in 1702 led Marot to seek patronage from citizens of The Hague and Amsterdam. He lived in The Hague until 1704, then moved to Amsterdam and developed his career as an architect. There his clients included the stadholder of Friesland, John William Friso, for whom he created new state apartments and a staircase at Oranienstein Castle between 1707 and 1709.

From 1687 Marot issued series of printed designs in suites of about six sheets. The first collected edition consisting of 108 plates appeared in 1703; many of the prints proclaim Marot's former appointment as 'architecte de Guillaume III, Roy de Grande Bretagne'. The second edition of 1712 consisted of 126 plates and was published in The Hague as *Œuvres de Sieur D. Marot*. His sets of designs included *Nouveaux livre da partements* (first published in The Hague in 1700–01); *Second livre dappartements* (1702); *Nouveaux livres d'ornements* (before March 1702); *Second livre d'ornaments* (1702–3); *Nouveaux livres de pintures de salles et d'escaliers*; *Nouveaux livre de tableaux de portes, et cheminée utiles aux peintres enfleurs*; *Nouveaux livres de placfond*; *Nouvelles chiminée de la Hollande* (before March 1702); *Nouveaux livre de boîtes de pendulles de coqs et estuys de montres et autres necéssaire au orlogeurs* (1706); and *Nouveaux livre d'orfevrerie* (before March 1702). The latter included designs for silver tables. Some of Marot's printed designs from the library of Ralph, first duke of Montagu (priv. coll.), bear contemporary annotations. They include his *Livres de statues propres a taillière en marbre* and *Vases de la maison royalle de Loo*—some are similar to a set of four lead vases with relief decoration which survive at Boughton which were probably supplied by Thomas Pelletier in 1705. There are designs for gardens, coaches, embroidery, stage sets, and funerary monuments.

With the help of Isaac Marot and the Huguenot booksellers David and Pierre Mortier who maintained shops in both Amsterdam and London, Daniel Marot's designs were successfully marketed in Britain as well as in Denmark, Sweden, Germany, and Austria. In England they were used by artists and craftsmen who had already worked to his drawings. They continued to inspire—a set of seventeen painted panels incorporating the Montagu arms and garter star and ribbon (priv. coll.), which were painted for the second duke of Montagu after 1718, bear witness to their influence fifteen years after they were first published.

In Holland, Marot developed a second career as an architect. At The Hague, his patrons were government officials and members of the cultivated upper class. For François Fagel (1659–1746), secretary of the states general, he rebuilt a house at Noordeinde in 1707. In 1715 for Cornelis van Schuylenburch (1683–1763) Marot converted two town houses into one mansion—here he applied typical Louis XIV interior ornament to exterior architecture. About 1717 Johan Hendrik van Wassenaer-Obdam (d. 1745), a member of the council of state, commissioned a house on the Kneuterdijk. In 1734–6 Marot designed the interiors of a palatial residence for Adriana Margareta Huguetan (d. 1752) on the Lange Voorhout; the façade was the work of Jan Pieter van Baurscheit. One of his last important commissions was to extend the huis ten Bosch for William Charles Henry Friso of Orange Nassau (later Stadholder William IV). He added two wings and a new entrance hall in 1745–7.

Throughout his life Marot continued to draw on late seventeenth-century French design for inspiration and it is surprising how little his style changed and developed. This must reflect conservative taste in Holland and the extended dominance of the Louis XIV style. Daniel Marot's eldest son, also Daniel (1695–1769), assisted his father. His earliest drawing dates from 1716. He continued to paint decorations for garden pavilions after his father's death on 4 June 1752.   TESSA MURDOCH

Sources M. D. Ozinga, *Daniel Marot de Schepper van den Hollandschen lodewijk XIV-stijl* (1938) · P. Jessen, *Daniel Marot: das Ornamentwerk* (1892) · R. Baarsen, G. Jackson-Stops, P. M. Johnston, and E. E. Dee, *Courts and colonies: the William and Mary style in Holland, England and America* (1988) · A. K. Placzek, ed., *Macmillan encyclopedia of architects*, 3 (1982), 108–10 · T. Richardson, 'Hampton Court, Middlesex, the newly restored king's privy garden', *Country Life* (31 Aug 1995), 46–51 · F. Hopper, 'Daniel Marot: a French garden designer in Holland', *Dumbarton Oaks Colloquium on the History of Landscape Architecture*, 12 (1990), 131–58 · W. Harris, *A description of the king's royal palace and gardens at Loo* (1699) · G. Jackson-Stops, 'The palace of Het Loo', *Country Life*, 176 (1984), 1626–31 · G. Jackson-Stops, 'Slot Zeist, Netherlands', *Country Life*, 160 (1976), 594–7 · G. Jackson-Stops, 'Huis Schuylenburch', *Country Life*, 164 (1977), 786–9 · T. V. Murdoch, ed., *Boughton House: the English Versailles* (1992) · M. Hinton and O. Impey, *Kensington Palace and the porcelain of Queen Mary II* (1998) · A. Turpin, 'A table for Queen Mary's water gallery at Hampton Court', *Apollo*, 149 (Jan 1999), 3–14 · R. Smith, 'Five furniture drawings in Siena', *Furniture History*, 3 (1967), 1–15 · A. Lane, 'Daniel Marot: designer of Delft vases and of gardens at Hampton Court', *The Connoisseur*, 123 (1949), 19–24 · J. Ayers, 'The ceramics surviving at Hampton Court', *Apollo*, 140 (Aug 1994), 50–54 · M. Archer, 'Delft at Dyrham', *National Trust Yearbook* (1975–6), 12–18
Archives École des Beaux Arts, Paris, drawings · Cooper Hewitt Museum, New York, prints, drawings · V&A, prints, drawings
Likenesses J. Gole, engraving (after J. Parmentier), NPG, Rijksmuseum, Amsterdam [see illus.]

Marow, Thomas (1460×65–1505), lawyer, was the third son of William Marow of Bishopsgate, alderman of London and grocer, and his wife, Katherine, daughter of Richard Rich, sometime sheriff of London. He was admitted to the Inner Temple in the 1480s. There he seems to have been a protégé of Thomas Frowyk, to whom (according to his brother's will) he was related; he later took over Frowyk's chambers in the Inner Temple, and in the British Library there is a manuscript year-book which belonged successively to Frowyk and Marow.

In 1491 Marow succeeded Frowyk as common serjeant of London, and in 1495 was promoted to under-sheriff, holding that office until he became a serjeant-at-law in 1503. Meanwhile he became a bencher of his inn, delivering a reading in 1497 on part of the Statute of Gloucester, and another in 1503 as junior serjeant-elect. It was for his serjeant's reading that he was long remembered in the legal profession, and is still known to legal historians. It was an elaborate exposition of the jurisdiction of justices of the peace, founded on the first chapter of the Statute of Westminster I (1275), 'that the peace of Holy Church and of the land be well kept', and included the fullest exposition at that time of English criminal law. Though not printed until 1924, it was widely circulated in manuscript and exerted an influence upon later commentators on criminal law.

The year of Marow's first permanent appointment, 1491, was also the year of his marriage. His wife, who predeceased him, was Isabel, daughter and coheir of Nicholas Brome of Baddesley Clinton, Warwickshire, who brought him property in Warwickshire. He doubtless maintained a house in that county, where he became a justice of the peace himself in 1497; there was formerly a window in Knole church with his arms and an exhortation to pray for the soul of Serjeant Marow and his wife. His brother William (d. 1499), who was a member of Thavies Inn but not a lawyer, left him a life interest in Marow's Quay in Billingsgate, which brought him a London income from the fishmonger licensees.

Marow did not long enjoy the benefits of his serjeant's coif. He served as an assize judge on the western circuit in 1504 and 1505, while in December 1504 he entered into an agreement with Sir Thomas Grene to marry the latter's daughter Anne, but died before the marriage could be solemnized, aged little more than forty. The record of the suit by his executors against Grene for the recovery of the marriage-money gives the date of his death as 10 April 1505. He left £5 to Lady Frowyk, and made Chief Justice Frowyk his chief executor. By his will he desired to be buried in St Botolph's Church, Billingsgate (where his father lay), with a memorial plate. His only child, Dorothy, married first Francis Cokayne of Ashbourne, Derbyshire, and second Sir Humphrey Ferrers of Tamworth, Staffordshire. Marow's nephew and ward, Thomas Marow (d. 1538), son of his brother William, succeeded to the London property but settled in Warwickshire; this Thomas's son, another Thomas (d. 1561), represented the county in the 1553 parliament and became lord of the manor of Birmingham.

                                                           J. H. BAKER

Sources *The records of King Edward's School, Birmingham*, 1, ed. W. F. Carter, Dugdale Society, 4 (1924), xxviii–xxxi · B. H. Putnam, *Early treatises on the practice of the justices of the peace in the fifteenth and sixteenth centuries* (1924) · E. W. Ives, *The common lawyers of preReformation England* (1983) · Baker, *Serjeants* · *The notebook of Sir John Port*, ed. J. H. Baker, SeldS, 102 (1986) · S. E. Thorne and J. H. Baker, eds., *Readings and moots at the inns of court in the fifteenth century*, 2, SeldS, 105 (1990) · W. Dugdale, *The antiquities of Warwickshire illustrated*, rev. W. Thomas, 2nd edn, 2 vols. (1730) · BL, Add. MS 37659 · HoP, *Commons, 1509–58* [2.573–4] · will, PRO, PROB 11/14, sig. 28 · *CIPM, Henry VII*, 3, nos. 141, 825 · court of common pleas, plea rolls,

PRO, CP40/975m, 409 · marriage settlement, Shakespeare Birthplace Trust RO, Stratford upon Avon, MSS DR 3/275–276

Marples, (Alfred) Ernest, Baron Marples (1907–1978), politician and businessman, was born at 45 Dorset Road, Levenshulme, Manchester, on 9 December 1907, the only child of Alfred Ernest Marples, an engine fitter and later foreman engineer, and his wife, Mary Hammond. His grandfather had been head gardener at Chatsworth. Ernest Marples was educated at a local council school before winning a scholarship to Stretford grammar school. He gave early indications of the entrepreneurial spirit that characterized his whole career by taking a variety of jobs during his school holidays, including that of gatekeeper at a football ground. Despite obvious intelligence and academic promise he left school early to train as an incorporated accountant. One of his first professional duties was to audit the books of bankrupt firms which, he later claimed, gave him early experience of how not to run companies or government departments.

Marples moved to London in the late 1920s and purchased a house on a mortgage while letting part of it to cover his outgoings. This was the start of a successful career in property development in which he bought up Victorian houses and converted them into flats. Before long he had set up a construction firm which he financed from his savings and a loan offered by the civil servant Jack Huntington, whom he had met on holiday and who became a lifelong friend. Huntington also introduced Marples to cultural and intellectual issues, including the study of political philosophy, which his own limited formal education had not encompassed.

Conservative minister: housing, national insurance, and the Post Office By the coming of the Second World War Marples was a man of some substance. His company Marples, Ridgway & Partners had built a number of power stations. Shortly before the outbreak of hostilities he joined the London Scottish territorials. He rose to the rank of captain, transferred to the Royal Artillery in 1941, and was wounded in 1944. By now he had developed political ambitions, and at the general election of 1945 secured entry to the Commons as Conservative member for Wallasey in Cheshire, a seat that he held until 1974. At a time when the typical tory MP was a well-heeled old Etonian, he soon made a distinctive impression, not least through his liking for blue suits and orange-brown shoes. He became secretary of the party's housing committee and produced a well-received booklet on housing problems. He probably ensured his future ministerial career by responding positively to the commitment given to the party conference in 1950 that the next Conservative government would build 300,000 houses in a year. This was, he told the 1922 committee shortly afterwards, something which could be achieved in five years and at a reasonable cost.

When, therefore, Churchill appointed Harold Macmillan minister of housing in October 1951, Macmillan chose Marples as his parliamentary secretary—thus starting a political partnership which ultimately led to the latter's elevation to the cabinet. 'In Marples', Macmillan later

(Alfred) Ernest Marples, Baron Marples (1907–1978), by Elliott & Fry, 1950

recalled, 'I had a colleague of outstanding loyalty and devotion. He was, moreover, a man of infinite resources, great ingenuity and untiring energy' (Macmillan, 460). It was an unlikely partnership, uniting the Edwardian whose pretensions at least were aristocratic and the entirely self-made and somewhat brash businessman who had once been a bookie's 'dodger'. But, as Anthony Sampson has put it, 'between Macmillan with his languid style and Marples with his boasting efficiency, there existed an alliance of mutual advantage, between the amateur and the professional' (*Macmillan: a Study in Ambiguity*, 1968, 98). It was his spell at housing that catapulted Macmillan into the front rank of Conservative politicians, and he never forgot the debt he owed to his junior minister. 'In fact', he once confessed, 'Marples made me PM' (Horne, 1.337). Among Marples's tangible contributions was to initiate the design of a house which needed almost no timber, then in short supply, using concrete instead. But his greatest value was in terms of his no-nonsense common sense, his limitless energy, and a capacity for self-publicity which was then rare in Conservative politics.

Marples was moved sideways to the Ministry of Pensions and National Insurance in October 1954; here his talents were less well employed than at housing, and he returned to the back benches and his business career in December 1955. But when in January 1957 in the wake of the Suez crisis Macmillan became prime minister, Marples had his reward, becoming postmaster-general. He brought his ministry into the public limelight in a way in which few if any of his predecessors had done. His was the right sort of ingenious mind to bring new technology into the running of a government department which was more susceptible than most to the techniques and practices of the business world. During Marples's tenure subscriber trunk dialling was introduced, a new Atlantic cable transformed communications with the New World, and a series of efficiency studies was carried out to improve the profitability of the Post Office. Macmillan had recently introduced premium bonds, in the face of considerable opposition on moral grounds, and it seemed entirely appropriate that Marples, with his flair for publicity, should inaugurate the 'electronic random number indicating equipment'—known by the acronym 'Ernie'—to select the lucky winners. Overall, the minister enhanced his public standing as someone who could get things done, and it was no surprise when he was promoted to the cabinet as minister of transport following the Conservatives' victory in the general election of 1959.

Minister of transport This was not a post that usually figured prominently among Whitehall departments, but there was by the late 1950s a growing concern about Britain's transport problems, especially about those resulting from the rapid and seemingly inexorable growth in the number of motor vehicles, and Marples approached his brief with an infectious conviction that such problems could be resolved. He concentrated his early efforts on London, where road traffic was already approaching gridlock, and soon achieved considerable success in improving the flow of traffic. Many of his schemes were controversial and aroused motorists' hostility, but later came to be accepted as indispensable features of urban life. It was during his five-year tenure at transport that yellow no-parking lines and parking meters, with fixed fines imposed by traffic wardens without trial unless the offending motorist insisted on a court appearance, became commonplace in Britain's towns and cities. He also laid the groundwork for some of the reforms usually associated with his Labour successor, Barbara Castle, especially the introduction of the breathalyser as a means of tackling the problem of drink-driving.

To his credit Marples recognized that short-term palliatives, however useful, were not enough to deal with the problems of Britain's roads, and he invited Sir Colin Buchanan to produce a comprehensive report on the entire road network. Entitled *Traffic in Towns*, it was published in 1963 and called for the systematic planning of urban development so as to reconcile the needs of road transport with those of social amenity. The minister had already authorized the building of a full-scale network of motorways across the country, expanding the plans initiated by his predecessor Harold Watkinson. Many schemes for new bridges, flyovers, and embankments were also put in place. Overall it amounted to a considerable record of achievement.

Marples's legacy to the railway industry was perhaps less fortunate. The nationalized network was making heavy losses and losing customers to the roads in an apparently irreversible fashion. Marples brought in Dr Richard Beeching, a leading executive from ICI, to join the British Transport Commission, with a view to succeeding the existing chairman, Sir Brian Robertson. Beeching then became the first chairman of the British Railways board with instructions to carry out a searching inquiry. He recommended concentrating resources on long-distance inter-city routes and the provision of special goods-carrying services to industry, conclusions which entailed the closure of about 2000 stations, particularly in rural areas, and 5000 miles of track, on the grounds of underutilization. Marples, who believed that the railways must, in the last resort, compete in the market with road transport, with the customer as final arbiter, gave Beeching's recommendations his full support, despite fierce opposition in the country and from the Labour opposition in parliament. At the time, Marples seemed to have had the courage to do something about the intractable problems of a remorselessly declining industry, but later concerns about the environmental pollution caused by an ever-growing number of motor cars and his refusal to recognize the railways as at least in part a necessary social service render his achievements somewhat less impressive.

Marples also set about reorganizing Britain's ports, providing long-term credits for the shipbuilding industry and seeking to protect the country's shipping interests from the competition of state-protected American shipping lines. Seldom, if ever, had a minister of transport embarked upon as wide-ranging a series of policy initiatives, and Marples enjoyed a recognition among the general public far beyond that indicated by the status of his office. Though many of his measures were unpopular, 'Marples Must Go' car-stickers were soon replaced by others bearing the words 'Come Back Ernie, All is Forgiven' once he had left office.

Marples retained the transport portfolio until the defeat of the Conservative government in the general election of 1964. Macmillan admired his dash and energy, regarding him as a 'sword' man in a cabinet composed largely of 'gown' men. But he was perhaps fortunate to survive the tide of scandal which threatened to engulf the Conservative Party during 1963. The loyalty of the prime minister may have proved his salvation. When Lord Denning, the master of the rolls, was asked to investigate the wider ramifications of the Profumo affair, he reported privately to Macmillan that, although unconnected to the disgraced minister of war, the conduct of one cabinet minister in consorting with prostitutes had the potential to bring discredit on the government as a whole. Though Denning's letter has never been published, it is widely believed that Marples was the minister in question.

Life peer By the time when the Conservatives lost office, Marples's career had probably peaked. He did shadow the new Ministry of Technology, but his relations with Edward Heath, who became leader of the party in July 1965, were never easy; he was dropped from the shadow cabinet, with some bitterness, after the general election of 1966. Heath did, however, make some use of his talents from the back benches. It seemed to make good sense to employ a self-proclaimed technocrat to consider ways of improving party organization. But Marples lacked a specific brief beyond looking at possible money-saving schemes, and he soon resigned, making it known that he had received no clear remit. Later he was put in charge of a public sector research unit, designed to study the application of modern management techniques to the machinery of government. There was, however, no place for him when Heath formed his government in June 1970. Marples left the Commons in February 1974 and became a life peer as Baron Marples, though he was never prominent in the upper chamber.

Marples was a more significant politician than his relatively meagre list of offices might suggest. Some ministerial colleagues were inclined to look down on him as being interested only in technical matters. Macmillan apart, the Conservative hierarchy never fully trusted him, perhaps because of his working-class origins. Reginald Bevins, also a Conservative minister from a humble background, recalled a ministerial weekend at Chequers where 'only Ernest Marples and I were without landed estates' (Bevins, 102). Born a generation later, he might have risen considerably higher in the party's ranks, especially given his belief in the primacy of the market and his commitment to the notion of individual freedom and enterprise. Many found him too self-confident and self-advertising, but his was a fertile mind, brimming with ideas which, as even Edward Heath once conceded, 'might be the grain of sand that produces the pearl' (Ramsden, *Conservative Party Policy*, 195). His boundless energy found many outlets outside politics in such diverse activities as skiing and bee-keeping. In later years he became something of a fitness fanatic as well as a connoisseur of fine wines, and he took great pride in the vineyard which he bought at Fleurie in the Beaujolais country. His first marriage, on 6 July 1937 to Edna Florence (*b.* 1921/2), daughter of Arthur Henry Harwood, was dissolved in 1945. Eleven years later he married his former secretary, Ruth Dobson, the daughter of a Nottingham businessman, who survived him.

Marples died in the Princess Grace Hospital in Monte Carlo on 6 July 1978. He left estate in England and Wales valued at £388,166. D. J. DUTTON

Sources *The Times* (7 July 1978) · *DNB* · K. Robbins, ed., *The Blackwell biographical dictionary of British political life in the twentieth century* (1990) · *The Guardian* (7 July 1978) · R. Lamb, *The Macmillan years* (1995) · H. Macmillan, *Tides of fortune, 1945–1955* (1969) [vol. 3 of autobiography] · J. Ramsden, *The age of Churchill and Eden, 1940–1957* (1995) · A. Seldon, *Churchill's Indian summer* (1981) · J. Ramsden, *The winds of change: Macmillan to Heath, 1957–1975* (1996) · J. Ramsden, *The making of Conservative Party policy* (1980) · R. Bevins, *The greasy pole* (1965) · A. Horne, *Macmillan*, 2 vols. (1988–9) · b. cert. · m. cert. (1937)

Archives JRL, Guardian archives, letters to the *Manchester Guardian*, B/M192/1–10

Likenesses Elliott & Fry, photograph, 1950, NPG [*see illus.*] · Emwood [J. Musgrave-Wood], pen-and-ink cartoon, 1963, NPG · N. Colvin, pen and ink, NPG · Emwood [J. Musgrave-Wood], pen-and-ink cartoon, NPG · S. Franklin, pen-and-ink cartoon, NPG · Papas [W. Papas], four pen-and-ink cartoons, NPG · Vicky [V. Weisz], five pen-and-ink cartoons, NPG · photographs, Hult. Arch.

Wealth at death £388,166—in England and Wales: *The Times* (2 Oct 1978)

Marprelate, Martin (*fl.* 1588–1589), pamphleteer, was the pseudonymous author of satirical treatises that attacked the Elizabethan church, particularly church government by bishops, and advocated an alternative, presbyterian polity. Witty, irreverent, and swashbucklingly self-confident, the Marprelate tracts scandalized contemporaries and sparked a pamphlet war that provided an important point of reference in contemporary debates about church reform, polemical decorum, and the use of print to appeal to a popular audience.

The Marprelate tracts are the culmination of the radical strain in English presbyterianism; at their heart are arguments honed by reformers such as Thomas Cartwright, Walter Travers, and William Fulke. But faced with the apparent determination of John Whitgift, archbishop of Canterbury, to restrict discussion of godly reform and to impose uniformity within the church, Martin sought to broaden awareness of the presbyterian platform through a strategy of serious jesting. Wielding the weapons of mockery, parody, colloquial prose, a persona similar to theatre's Vice figure, fictive techniques such as dialogue and direct address, and *ad hominem* anecdotes about the 'proud, popish, presumptuous, profane, paultrie, pestilent, and pernicious prelates' (*The Epistle*, 6), Martin took ecclesiological battle out of the study and into the street: 'hold my cloake there sombody, that I may go roundly to worke. For ise so bumfeg the Cooper, as he had bin better to have hooped halfe the tubbes in Winchester, then write against my worships pistles' (*Hay any Worke for Cooper*, 6). In this case the figure singled out for ridicule is Bishop Thomas Cooper of Winchester; other targets for abuse and merriment include Archbishop Whitgift, his close friend Andrew Perne, master of Peterhouse, Cambridge, and Bishop John Aylmer of London.

The identity of Martin Marprelate has long tantalized investigators, Elizabethan and modern. Many candidates have been proposed, including John *Udall (present when several of the tracts were printed), John *Field, Giles *Wigginton, George *Carleton, Sir Roger *Williams, and Henry *Barrow. But John *Penry and Job *Throckmorton are the only two for whom there is serious evidence. The argument for Throckmorton as the writer responsible for Martin's distinctive style has been generally accepted, though Penry was certainly a collaborator. More than twenty people were eventually discovered to have been involved in the tracts' production, and behind them was a well-organized network of suppliers, distributors, and sympathizers; all risked charges of treason.

The seven extant tracts were printed on a press owned by Robert *Waldegrave and moved from one household to another. Waldegrave himself printed the first four tracts: *The Epistle* (October 1588), in the house of Mrs Elizabeth *Crane in East Molesey, Surrey; *The Epitome* (November), in Fawsley House, Sir Richard *Knightley's Northamptonshire estate; and the broadsheet *Certaine Minerall, and Metaphysicall Schoolpoints* (late January 1589) and *Hay any Worke for Cooper* (late March), in Whitefriars, Coventry, the house of Knightley's nephew John Hales. Waldegrave then quit the project, partly because the ministers he consulted disapproved of the Martinist approach. The press remained silent until July 1589, when John Hodgkins, assisted by Valentine Simmes and Arthur Thomlyn, printed *Theses Martinianae* (known as *Martin Junior*) and *The Just Censure and Reproofe* (known as *Martin Senior*), pamphlets that deployed the personae of Martin's sons, in Wolston Priory, Coventry, the house of Roger Wigston. Disliking Waldegrave's press, Hodgkins then packed up his own and moved the operation to Manchester. In August 1589 agents employed by the earl of Derby discovered the press, seized and destroyed the sheets of *More Work for the Cooper*, a tract in progress, and sent the captured printers to London where they were put to the rack. In early September the project's 'stitcher' Henry Sharpe was also arrested, and his evidence enabled the authorities to round up almost everyone involved. The final tract, *The Protestatyon*, was defiantly published in late September, probably at Wolston on the press that remained there. Its first pages appear to have been set by amateurs, probably Throckmorton and Penry themselves; the printing quality improves with the second gathering, when Waldegrave returned to lend a needed hand.

Depositions generated by the subsequent investigation suggest print runs for all the tracts of between 700 and 1000 copies. Prices ranged from 6*d*. to 9*d*., though one buyer claimed that copies were available for only 2*d*.; perhaps this was for the broadsheet. Distribution was managed by the cobbler Humfrey Newman, who delivered bundles of the stitched pamphlets to towns and houses across the country as well as to other distributors in London. The pamphlets were sold out of the homes of sympathizers or under the counter in shops; some copies appear to have made their way to the continent. Startled officials complained that Martin's works were available in every county in the realm.

Within weeks of the appearance of the first tract church and state were co-operating at the highest administrative levels to find the press and to counter Martin's influence. The official response included a proclamation, a sermon by Richard Bancroft, and *An Admonition to the People of England* (1589), edited by Thomas Cooper, in which various church officials attempted to clear their names from Martin's 'untruethes, slaunders, reproches, raylings, revilings, scoffings, and other untemperate speeches' (Cooper, 35). But the government also sponsored a pamphlet campaign that sought to combat Martin by turning his own style against him. Richard Bancroft is usually credited with this strategy, which involved commissioning anti-Martinist texts from hired pens, including John Lyly and probably Thomas Nashe; these imitations of Martinist style served primarily to give the Marprelate tracts a role in the development of late Elizabethan comic prose. Supplementing official efforts were pamphlets by the independently outraged, stage burlesques, and eventually commentary by those (including Sir Francis Bacon, Richard Harvey, and Gabriel Harvey) who deplored the tactics of both sides.

Martin Marprelate wrote on behalf of a losing cause: a judicial crackdown on the reform leadership accompanied the trials of those involved with the Martinist press, and within a few years organized presbyterianism had collapsed. Many contemporaries attributed the decline in part to disapproval, even among the reform community, of the Marprelate project. But while Martin's immediate influence was more literary than ecclesiological, the Marprelate persona played a role in pamphlet wars through much of the following century. During the 1640s the tracts provided a polemical model for radicals like Richard Overton, and in the Restoration Martin's name was used as pejorative shorthand for political or religious opposition: John Milton and Andrew Marvell were accused of Martinist tendencies. Not until the late seventeenth century did Martinism and anti-Martinism become subjects of antiquarian interest rather than ways of discussing issues vital to church and state.

JOSEPH BLACK

Sources L. H. Carlson, *Martin Marprelate, gentleman: Master Job Throkmorton laid open in his colors* (1981) • E. Arber, ed., *An introductory sketch to the Martin Marprelate controversy, 1588–1590* (1905) • W. Pierce, *An historical introduction to the Marprelate tracts* (1908) • J. L. Black, 'Pamphlet wars: the Marprelate tracts and "Martinism", 1588–1688', PhD diss., University of Toronto, 1996 • *The Marprelate tracts, 1588, 1589*, facs. edn (1967) • *The Marprelate tracts, 1588–1589*, ed. W. Pierce (1911) • R. A. Anselment, 'Betwixt jest and earnest': Marprelate, Milton, Marvell, Swift and the decorum of religious ridicule (1979), 33–60 • P. Collinson, *The Elizabethan puritan movement* (1967) • T. Cooper, *An admonition to the people of England* (1589)

Marquand, Hilary Adair (1901–1972), economist and politician, was born on 24 December 1901 at 4 Marlborough Road, Cardiff, the elder son of Alfred Marquand, a clerk in a coal-exporting firm, and his wife, Mary Adair. His grandfather, who had come from Guernsey, and an uncle were shipowners in Cardiff. His mother was Scottish. Marquand was educated at Cardiff high school and the University College, Cardiff, where he went with a state scholarship. He graduated with first-class honours in history (1923) and economics (1924) and obtained the Gladstone and Cobden prizes. There followed two years in the United States on a Laura Spelman Rockefeller Foundation fellowship spent mainly at the University of Wisconsin, and from 1926 to 1930 a lectureship in economics at the University of Birmingham. He married on 20 August 1929 Rachel Eluned (*b.* 1903/4), a teacher, and the daughter of David James Rees, owner of the *Llais Llafur* ('Voice of labour'), the first Labour newspaper in Wales, founded by his father and later to become the *South Wales Voice*.

In 1930 Marquand returned to his old university in Cardiff as professor of industrial relations. He was then twenty-nine years old and the youngest university professor in Britain. From that time until the outbreak of the war Marquand continued his academic work of teaching and research, including a year in 1932–3 studying industrial relations in the USA and a further year in 1938–9 as visiting professor at the University of Wisconsin. His period as professor at Cardiff was particularly productive.

Hilary Adair Marquand (1901–1972), by Elliott & Fry, 1947

In 1931 he published his first book, *The Dynamics of Industrial Combination*. This, based in part on American experience, was a major contribution to a subject relatively new in British economic literature. In 1934 he published a study entitled *Industrial Relations in the United States of America* and in 1939 he was editor and co-author of *Organized Labour in Four Continents*. But his main preoccupation during the decade preceding the war was the study of the industrial and economic conditions in south Wales. He made a survey for the Board of Trade, *Industrial Survey of South Wales*, published in 1931, and a second one for the commissioner for special areas in 1937. In the meantime, in 1936, he wrote a book, *South Wales Needs a Plan*, which established him with a wider audience as an important contributor to pressing problems of economic policy. During the war he was a temporary civil servant, first in the Board of Trade, later in the Ministry of Labour and in the Ministry of Production.

Marquand had been a member of the Labour Party since 1920, having broken away from a family tradition which, unlike that of his wife's, was thoroughly Conservative. Believing that post-war problems were not going to be either in the field of economic theory or administration but essentially in the political field, he took the earliest opportunity to stand for parliament. In 1945 he was elected for Cardiff East, of which he remained the member until 1950; then, from 1950 to 1961, he was member for Middlesbrough East, a seat held with big majorities until

he resigned in 1961. The initial momentum of his political career was striking. He achieved office immediately on election, becoming secretary for overseas trade, a post, subsequently held by Harold Wilson, in which he travelled widely. In 1946 he led the British delegation to the Havana conference on trade and employment which set up the General Agreement on Tariffs and Trade. Between 1947 and 1948 Marquand was paymaster-general. He had no specific departmental responsibilities but again travelled widely in Africa on trade promotion missions. From 1948 to 1951 he was minister of pensions (being sworn of the privy council in 1949), and then succeeded Aneurin Bevan as minister of health, a post, however, with reduced scope and no longer in the cabinet.

After the 1951 election, in which Marquand maintained a large majority, he became an active member of the opposition front bench, from 1959 as chief spokesman on Commonwealth affairs. The prospect of more long years in opposition and possibly some disillusion with the new tendencies in his party led him to abandon active politics. In 1961 he resigned his seat to take up the post of director of the newly created Institute of Labour Studies at the International Labour Office in Geneva, a post in which his large circle of international friendships served him well. He returned to England in 1965 and for three years served as deputy chairman of the Prices and Incomes Board. His last years were spent in relative inactivity and this, together with failing health, contributed to a sense of frustration, relieved, however, by a happy family life. He had two sons and a daughter. The eldest, David Ian Marquand, born in 1934, showed the same academic and political inclinations as his father, holding various university teaching posts; he was Labour MP for Ashfield (1966–77), and principal of Mansfield College, Oxford, from 1996.

Hilary Marquand, a gentle and kindly man, was not without ambition, but a strong, at times passionate, concern with the welfare of the underprivileged of society probably militated against his energetically pursuing the highest academic laurels, while a deeply founded respect for the criteria of scholarship made him less than wholly comfortable in the turmoil of politics. In a period in which political economy was increasingly forsaken for the more austere and mathematical forms of economics, his researches into the practical problems of modern industry gained less notice in professional circles than they otherwise might have done. On the other hand, his lack of skill in, indeed distaste for, the small change of trafficking in day-to-day politics probably prevented him from reaching the higher offices of state to which his intellectual equipment and scholarly background entitled him.

In a small circle Marquand could be witty, entertaining, and eloquent; and his consistently high polls in elections, though in a safe Labour seat, were evidence of a somewhat surprising talent for the requirements of the hustings. In the House of Commons, though his style lacked the stirring quality of many of his contemporaries, his quiet, scholarly manner and obvious mastery of intricate subjects always commanded respectful recognition. His life and work were characteristic of a new generation of scholars who emerged in public affairs on the early post-war British political scene. He died at Hellingly Hospital, Sussex, on 6 November 1972.   ERIC ROLL

Sources personal knowledge (2004) · *The Times* (8 Nov 1972) · *WWW* · b. cert. · m. cert. · d. cert.
Archives Bodl. Oxf., papers relating to service with the UN, MS Eng. C.4732 · Bodl. RH, corresp. on colonial issues | NL Wales, letters to Graham F. Thomas | FILM BFI NFTVA, party political footage
Likenesses Elliott & Fry, photograph, 1947, NPG [*see illus.*] · photograph, repro. in *The Times*
Wealth at death £12,604: probate, 8 May 1973, *CGPLA Eng. & Wales*

Marquis, Frederick James, first earl of Woolton (1883–1964),

politician and businessman, was born on 23 August 1883 at 163 West Park Street, Salford, the only child of Thomas Robert Marquis (*d.* 1944), a saddler, and his wife, Margaret (*née* Ormerod). They were determined that their son would rise beyond the lower middle classes into which he was born and focused their support and hopes on him. After Ardwick higher-grade school they sent him to the best school they could afford, Manchester grammar school. However, their straitened circumstances prevented him reading classics at Cambridge; instead he went to the University of Manchester, from where, in 1906, he emerged with a combination science degree (mathematics, chemistry, and physics).

Social concerns While an undergraduate Marquis became involved with the activities of Ancoats Hall, a settlement for the poor connected with the university, and became interested in the application of the social sciences to the understanding and alleviation of the problem of poverty. He would have liked to have gone on to further academic study in this area. However, limited family finances were to frustrate this desire and he had to turn down the offer of the Martin White fellowship in sociology at the University of London. Consequently he accepted the position of senior mathematics master at Burnley grammar school and occasionally lectured in the evenings on mathematics and general science at the local technical school. He continued to study poverty and labour mobility while at Burnley, an industrial town with a substantial urban proletariat, which for him was an ideal locality to examine, and he began publishing scholarly articles. For his work he was appointed research fellow in economics at the University of Manchester in 1910 and was awarded an MA in 1912.

In 1909 Marquis was appointed warden of the David Lewis Hotel and Club Association in Liverpool, a social experiment established by the Liverpool retailing firm of Lewis's in the city's docklands area. Run on a profit-making basis it provided cheap beds for the night, recreation in a 'people's palace', and a large theatre. Marquis was then invited by the vice-chancellor of the University of Liverpool to take on the additional responsibility of the wardenship of the Liverpool University Settlement. He took full advantage of these opportunities to research and give practical help to the poor by establishing a successful free dental care unit and a maternity clinic. At this stage of his life, in 1912, he finally felt financially secure enough to

Frederick James Marquis, first earl of Woolton (1883–1964), by Elliott & Fry

marry his long-time fiancée, Maud (*d.* 1961), daughter of Thomas Smith of Manchester. The couple had a daughter and a son. Marquis's political views, however, were in a state of flux. His social concerns initially inclined him towards Fabian socialism and during this period he began wearing a trade-mark red tie, which was interpreted by many as a visual expression of his commitment to socialism. However, his background and his training as an economist at the University of Manchester made him place a high value on personal initiative and, by extension, private enterprise.

Such views were to be further developed through Marquis's experiences as a civil servant during the First World War. Never robust, he was judged unfit for active military service and, as he was already known in Whitehall for his work in Liverpool, was drafted into the war effort, first as an official in the requisition department of the War Office and then at the Leather Control Board. As civilian boot controller he liaised with manufacturers and distributors, and established a system whereby the industry managed distribution itself, with only a small number of temporary civil servants. His interaction with businessmen in the trade made him appreciate their abilities and confirmed his suspicion of the undesirability of government intervention, although he saw that central direction would be necessary in periods of emergency—like war. Once normalcy returned after the end of the First World

War, he joined the Boot Manufacturers' Federation as secretary. To support a growing family he supplemented his income by freelance journalism, often writing about his favourite topics: public welfare and the role of the socially responsible entrepreneur. During this time he went to the United States to observe American sales and production methods which instilled in him the view that 'the customer knows best'.

Business and government In 1920 Marquis joined Lewis's, with which he had developed a close personal and professional relationship since his wardenship of the David Lewis Club. Henceforward he would become known more as a successful businessman than a social scientist. Nevertheless this did not mean the end of his interest in social welfare; that remained, but he would approach it from the perspective of a businessman. Working for Lewis's was probably supremely appealing to Marquis because it had provided him with an example of how business could work to improve the lives of the under-privileged. He quickly rose up the ranks of the company, the only practising Christian (a devout Unitarian) to do so in a firm dominated by a close Jewish cousinhood, becoming director in 1928 and chairman in 1936.

Through the rest of the 1920s and the 1930s Marquis established for himself a key position at the interface of business and government through participation in various government-appointed committees. Nationally, his appointments included: member of the advisory council of overseas development committee, 1928–31; member of the advisory council of the Board of Trade, 1930–34; member of the advisory council to the General Post Office, 1933–47; member of the Cadman committee on civil aviation in 1937; and member, 1936–9, and then chairman, 1939, of the Council for Art and Industry, which was linked to the Board of Trade. In recognition of these services and his success as a businessman he was knighted in 1935. All the while, he steadfastly refused to be identified with any political party or cause.

After Hitler's annexation of Austria in 1938 Marquis declared in a speech in Leicester that Lewis's would henceforward not trade in German goods and made a plea for other companies to do the same. As a result, he was reprimanded in person by the prime minister, Neville Chamberlain. However, this incident did nothing to prevent his deepening involvement with government. On 9 May 1939 he was appointed as honorary adviser to the secretary of state for war, Leslie Hore-Belisha, to ensure that the armed forces were adequately clothed in the event of conflict with Germany and Marquis completed this task efficiently and quickly. Previously he had, through his committee work, come into contact with two supremely powerful civil servants, Sir Horace Wilson, who advised Stanley Baldwin and then Chamberlain, and Sir Warren Fisher, the permanent secretary to the Treasury and head of the civil service. Marquis was involved from 1937 onwards in various covert war preparation committees and had been brought in through the good offices of Wilson. Either Fisher or Wilson, or both, was responsible for recommending him for a peerage in 1939 to Chamberlain.

This was done to allow Marquis to undertake high-level administrative and governmental work if and when war broke out. He was ennobled in mid-1939 and took the name of Woolton, an affluent Liverpool suburb, for his title. (It had been suggested to him that he become Baron Windermere, as he had property in the Lake District; his wife, on account of Oscar Wilde's play, *Lady Windermere's Fan*, refused to countenance it.) Wilson was subsequently instrumental in recommending to Chamberlain in April 1940 that Woolton be appointed to head the Ministry of Food.

Cabinet minister Woolton was to be a non-party minister, one of a number of businessmen (including Sir Andrew Duncan, Lord Leathers, Oliver Lyttelton, and P. J. Grigg) brought into government to help with the war effort. At that time outside Liverpool and the precincts of Whitehall Woolton was largely unknown. This did not last long, as through regular radio broadcasts he was brought to the nation's attention. In them he reassured his listeners that everything was under control and he celebrated the British housewife's ability to cope. He also bequeathed his name to the Woolton pie, a dish designed to maximize the use of vegetables and leftovers. His biggest triumph was getting people to accept rationing as not only necessary and patriotic but also equitable and efficient. He soon became, next to Churchill, the most popular and identifiable government minister. Woolton took the opportunity to implement positive social reform when he began the provision of milk to schoolchildren and orange juice to expectant mothers.

The fact that Woolton was officially non-party may have worked to his advantage in his subsequent promotion to cabinet. In November 1943 he became minister of reconstruction in a compromise which Churchill made with the Labour Party representatives in the war cabinet. The support of Labour leader Clement Attlee, who had first come across Woolton when he was warden of the David Lewis Club, was probably pivotal in his appointment. As a non-party member of government Woolton could more easily fulfil the role of minister of reconstruction which was, as he was to find out to his distress, to act as mediator between the conflicting claims and aims of the Conservative and Labour members of the reconstruction committee and to find the limited common ground on which both sides could agree. Thus he produced the wartime coalition government's famous white papers on health, education, social security, and employment. He continued to refuse to acknowledge political colours throughout the period of the war and after Germany's defeat when he accepted the post of lord president of the council in Churchill's brief caretaker administration in 1945.

Party chairman Woolton officially joined the Conservative Party when Churchill appointed him chairman of the party organization on 1 July 1946. Woolton had become alarmed by the prospect of permanent and substantial government intervention in the economy after the war, and for him Labour's landslide general election victory in

1945 posed a serious threat to free enterprise and the entrepreneurial spirit.

A 'Woolton revolution' was popularly supposed to have taken place during the years in opposition, 1946–51, which resulted in the entire machinery of the Conservative Party being overhauled and improved under his guidance. Woolton supervised organizational, financial, and structural changes. He succeeded in stimulating constituency associations, at their nadir at the time of the 1945 election, and encouraged the professionalization of party functionaries, both at Conservative central office and in the constituencies. The Maxwell-Fyfe committee's 1948 interim report on party organization endorsed the improvements in the conditions of work and the pension scheme he had devised for party agents.

Woolton's success as party chairman guaranteed him a place in Churchill's cabinet after the 1951 general election win. He was appointed lord president of the council and was also co-ordinating minister for food and agriculture. His combination of responsibilities made him one of the three 'overlords'. Woolton was arguably the most successful of the overlords, but this was probably because the ministries he was to co-ordinate were related, and because he attempted only light control. During the Conservative Party's 1952 annual conference at Scarborough he fell seriously ill and could not resume duties until the following spring. He only returned to full ministerial work in September 1953, by which time the overlords system had effectively ceased to function. He was then made chancellor of the duchy of Lancaster and minister of materials. He remained at the duchy until he retired from the chairmanship of the Conservative Party and from politics in the latter half of 1955.

As a minister Woolton was anxious that the government should honour pledges made during the 1950 and 1951 election campaigns, which committed the Conservatives to the welfare state but with increased emphasis on individual and business freedom. If his health had remained robust and if he had retained his post as lord president, he probably would have been a more effective and a more important minister. Before he fell ill in 1952, he urged all government ministers to take steps to reduce government expenditure and intervention. Also, while lord president, he was one of the few ministers urging fulfilment of the election pledges the party had made concerning denationalization; he suggested the Conservative government should begin with road haulage. Housing, which had been a crucial election issue during both the 1950 and 1951 election campaigns, was one of Woolton's concerns: he supported the extension of the 'property-owning democracy' and a shift away from the emphasis, which the Conservatives had inherited from the Attlee governments, on the provision of council housing, towards subsidizing or providing incentives to the private sector.

Chancellor of duchy of Lancaster As chancellor of the duchy of Lancaster and minister of materials Woolton dropped in cabinet rank and had much less to do. He was charged with the task of winding up the Ministry of Materials and dismantling many of the controls on food and raw materials that had been in place since the war. Although this process had in fact begun before he took over, he was to receive all the public credit for its disbandment—people cheered him when sugar and sweets were finally derationed. He found the post at the duchy an empty one as far as serious departmental administration was concerned, but it gave him great pleasure to manage part of the queen's estates and increase her income. It was a period when he was marking time before retiring from active political life.

While a minister Woolton pushed measures in which he was personally interested. A passionate believer in the virtues of competition, he wanted to see the dismantling of the BBC's monopoly on television broadcasting and knew that this was the general view of Conservative backbenchers. Before the Conservatives won the 1951 election he had arranged to get Selwyn Lloyd, who was like-minded, onto the all-party parliamentary committee which investigated the future of broadcasting and was to be one of Lloyd's staunchest supporters. When Woolton became lord president, he chaired the committee which bound the government to the establishment of independent television, in the face of considerable hostility from Churchill and most other members of the cabinet. When it became evident that Lord De La Warr, the postmaster-general, who was entrusted with the task of establishing the Independent Television Authority, had some reservations about his task, Woolton pre-empted any change of heart by the Conservative government by publishing in August 1953 a pamphlet entitled *There's Free Speech! Why not Free Switch?*. This did not allow the government to retreat from its stated position. He had ensured that the government made an important concession to backbench opinion and demonstrated that the Conservatives were committed to consumer choice and freedom, and also to private investment and profit.

One of the outstanding features of Woolton's chairmanship was his popularity with the rank and file of the party. They thought of him as 'Uncle Fred' and saw him as accessible and avuncular. He was sensitive to what they were thinking and what they wanted. The most obvious example of this was his acceptance at the party's 1950 annual conference of the target to build 300,000 houses if the Conservatives were returned to power after a general election. His broad popularity with the party was also rooted in the fact that he was a successful man who did not come from a patrician or a traditional political background, thus representing a welcome break with the past: he embodied the post-war 'democratization' and modernization of the party. Nevertheless Woolton actually revelled in the traditional social distinctions and enjoyed his titles. He was elevated to viscount in the 1953 coronation honours and finally to earl in the 1955 new year's honours list. He was deeply proud to have been made a privy councillor in 1940 and a Companion of Honour in 1942. He also remained for many decades a governor of Manchester grammar school and chancellor of the University of Manchester.

Final years Marquis's public image of avuncularity shielded a very private man. 'Tall, fastidiously dressed and consciously squaring his shoulders, Woolton was a formidable figure both in private and on the platform' (*DNB*). After his devoted wife died in 1961, as a gesture of friendship in 1962 he married his personal physician, Dr Margaret Eluned Thomas. He was never comfortable with professional politicians, apart from David Maxwell-Fyfe (later earl of Kilmuir) and his wife, Sylvia, both of whom he knew from their mutual Liverpool connections. Certainly he was not an intimate of Churchill or most other Conservative leaders. Nevertheless, he remained interested in the activities of the Conservative Party until his death at the country home he had acquired at Walberton House, Arundel, Sussex, on 14 December 1964. He was survived by his second wife and was succeeded as second earl by his son Roger.   MICHAEL D. KANDIAH

Sources M. D. Kandiah, *The political biography of Lord Woolton* (1998) · Lord Woolton, *The adventure of reconstruction: peace, expansion and reform, selected speeches* (1945) · Lord Woolton, *The memoirs of the Rt Hon. the earl of Woolton* (1959) · Lord Woolton [F. J. Marquis], *The Rt Hon. Maud Marquis, countess of Woolton* (privately printed, 1962) · J. Ramsden, *The age of Churchill and Eden, 1940–1957* (1995) · K. Jeffreys, *The Churchill coalition and wartime politics, 1940–1945* (1991) · S. Brooke, *Labour's war: the labour party during the Second World War* (1992) · A. Calder, *The people's war: Britain, 1939–1945* (1969) · M. Gilbert, *Winston S. Churchill, 8: Never despair, 1945–1965* (1988) · J. D. Hoffman, *The conservative party in opposition, 1945–1951* (1964) · Lord Redcliffe-Maude, *The experiences of an optimist: the memoirs of John Redcliffe-Maude* (1981) · A. Seldon, *Churchill's Indian summer: the conservative government, 1951–55* (1981) · *DNB* · *CGPLA Eng. & Wales* (1965) · b. cert.
Archives Bodl. Oxf., corresp. and papers | BL, letters to Albert Mansbridge, Add. MS 65253 · Bodl. Oxf., conservative party archives · Nuffield Oxf., corresp. with Lord Cherwell · PRO, conservative party archives · PRO, corresp. with Sir William Jowitt, CAB 127/160 · U. Warwick Mod. RC, letters to Sir Leslie Scott | SOUND BL NSA
Likenesses W. Stoneman, three photographs, 1939–52, NPG · A. C. Davidson-Houston, oils, 1945, Salters' Company, London · H. Coster, photographs, NPG · G. Davien, caricature, plaster bust, NPG · Elliott & Fry, photograph, NPG [*see illus.*] · J. Gunn, portrait, University of Manchester, Whitworth Hall · Lady Kennet, bronze bust; in family possession in 1981 · D. Low, pencil caricature, NPG
Wealth at death £407,790: probate, 18 Jan 1965, *CGPLA Eng. & Wales*

Marr, James William Slesser (1902–1965), marine biologist and polar explorer, was born on 9 December 1902 at Cushnie, Auchterless, Aberdeenshire, the second son of John George Marr, a farmer, and his wife, Georgina Sutherland Slesser. He was educated initially at Aberdeen grammar school, and then at Aberdeen University from 1919. He was one of the two Orcadian scout patrol leaders selected to accompany Shackleton (in the *Quest*) to the Antarctic. During 1920, while still a student at Aberdeen University, Scout Marr departed from St Katharine's Dock on the Shackleton–Rowett Antarctic expedition, the primary objective of which was the collection of scientific data and observations in the Antarctic and subantarctic regions. However, the death of Sir Ernest Shackleton, on 5

January 1922, altered the course of the voyage. While the expedition (which lasted a year) failed to achieve its main goal much information was gained, notably on the islands of South Georgia, Elephant, Gough, and Tristan da Cunha.

On returning to Aberdeen Marr resumed his studies in the academic year 1923–4, graduating both BSc and MA in 1925. In the latter year he acted as zoologist to the British Arctic expedition in Iceland with Captain Frank A. Worsley and G. Algarsson. He also provided botanical descriptions of West Spitsbergen, Franz Josef Land, and Northeast Land (in the *Journal of Botany* for 1927), and information on benthic ecology from sample dredging in the area 78°–82° N (in the zoological section of Worsley's 1927 work, *Under Sail in the Frozen North*).

Marr occupied the Carnegie scholarship at the Aberdeen Marine Laboratory (with the Scottish Fishery Board) in 1925–6. In the latter year he was appointed zoologist on the scientific staff of the colonial service *Discovery* investigations, where he was primarily concerned with the biology and migratory habits of whales (with some emphasis placed on the whaling industry). In this service he took part in three expeditions to the Antarctic. An initial whale marking cruise on the RRS *William Scoresby* (1927–9), incorporated oceanographic work around the Falkland Island dependencies, South Georgia, and South Shetland Islands, and some hydrographic charting in the latter location.

In the summer of 1929 Marr, then described as hydrologist and plankton specialist, was seconded to the British, Australian, New Zealand Antarctic research expedition (BANZARE), in the RRS *Discovery*, under Sir Douglas Mawson. During this cruise Marr carried out research into plankton, experimented with new sampling techniques, and attempted to find a practical method for accurate quantitative sampling. The expedition included extensive work in the Crozet, Possession, Kerguelen, and Heard islands and off Enderby Land. In *Mawson's Antarctic Diaries* Marr and his colleague, J. Frank Hurley, were described as 'remarkably capable fellows' who could 'turn their hands to any job at all' (p. 256). After reaching Australia (April 1930) Babe Marr (as he was then nicknamed) was prevented by ill health from embarking on the second leg of the BANZARE expedition.

With the RRS *Discovery II* (1931–3), Marr carried out oceanographic observations round the Antarctic winter ice limits, which enabled an examination of the region between the ice edge and warmer waters. This cruise was also the fourth ever circumnavigation of the Antarctic continent (and the first during winter). During his third cruise, on the RRS *Discovery II* (1935–7), an impromptu mission to rescue Lincoln Ellsworth and H. Hollick Kenyon caused a diversion from the planned voyage tracks. The revised survey included oceanographic observations in the Ross Sea, Indian and Atlantic parts of the Southern Ocean, a more specialized cruise in the region of the Falkland Island dependencies, and an outstanding study of krill (*Euphausia superba*).

On 6 July 1937, at Bramshott, Marr married Dorothea

Helene (*b*. 1914/15), fourth daughter of the late Gottlieb Friedrich Plutte, a director, of Sydenham. At the outbreak of the Second World War, Marr carried out research in the Antarctic into the canning, drying, and freezing of whale meat for human consumption (1939–40). In 1940 he was made a lieutenant in the Royal Naval Volunteer Reserve (RNVR), and served in Iceland, at Scapa Flow, and with the Eastern Fleet. He was also seconded to the South African naval forces during 1942–3. In 1943 he was made lieutenant-commander of the RNVR, and was given the special task of organizing and commanding advance parties of the Falkland Islands dependencies survey in the Grahamland region of Antarctica (1943–5). From 1949 he continued his work as a principal scientific officer in the Royal Naval Scientific Service (National Institute of Oceanography), where he resumed his work on *Euphausia superba*.

Marr was author of a number of works, from papers in scientific journals, to a number of *Discovery* reports, including 'The South Orkney Islands' (*Discovery Reports*, 10, 1935, 283–382), for which he was awarded the W. S. Bruce memorial prize of the Royal Scottish Geographical Society in 1936. He also wrote the 'Natural history and geography of the Antarctic krill, *Euphausia superba* Dana' (*Discovery Reports*, 32, 1962, 33–464), which provided a detailed description of Antarctic biology and marine exploration and science, in particular the behaviour and life history of the euphausiid which fulfils such a vital role in the food chain. This latter work was regarded as a history and textbook of marine exploration and science, and in 1963 he was awarded a DSc by his alma mater primarily in recognition of the latter publication. In this field he made a considerable impact to the understanding of marine and polar biology. His last major work examined the ecology and distribution of Antarctic shelf unstalked crinoids.

In 1919 Marr was awarded the scout silver cross and the bronze medal of the Royal Humane Society for saving bathers from drowning. He was also awarded the polar medal in bronze (1934); the bar to polar medal (1942); the polar medal in silver (1954): and the Back grant of the Royal Geographical Society (1946). Marr died from emphysema and bronchopneumonia on 29 April 1965 at Milford Chest Hospital, Busbridge, Surrey. He was survived by his wife and five (two sons and three daughters) of their six children.   YOLANDA FOOTE

Sources *The Times* obituaries (1965) · *WWW* · *Nature*, 207 (1965), 350–51 · *New Scientist* (1 July 1965), 41–3 · J. W. S. Marr, *Into the frozen south* (1923) · *Scottish biographies* (1938) · private information (2004) [Aberdeen University] · W. C. Smith, ed., *Report on the geological collections … made during the voyage of the 'Quest' on the Shackleton-Rowett expedition to the South Atlantic and Weddell Sea in 1921–1922* (1930) · J. Coleman-Cooke, *Discovery II in the Antarctic: the story of British research in the southern seas* (1963) · *Mawson's Antarctic diaries*, ed. F. Jacka and E. Jacka (1988) · H. Fletcher, *Antarctic days with Mawson* (1984) · *Report on the progress of the Discovery committee's investigations* (1937) · b. cert. · m. cert. · d. cert. · *CGPLA Eng. & Wales* (1965)

Archives Mitchell L., NSW, corresp. and papers · Scott Polar RI, corresp. and papers | NL Scot., corresp. relating to the *Discovery* committee

Likenesses J. F. Hurley, photograph, 1929, repro. in Fletcher, *Antarctic days* · J. F. Hurley, photograph, 1930, repro. in F. Jacka and E. Jacka, eds., *Mawson's Antarctic diaries* (1988)

Wealth at death £9323: probate, 22 June 1965, *CGPLA Eng. & Wales*

Marr, John Edward (1857–1933), geologist, was born at Morecambe Terrace, Poulton, Lancashire, on 14 June 1857, youngest of the nine children of John Marr and his wife, Mary (*née* Simpson). His father, who had retired in 1850, had been a Lancaster merchant trader and partner in a silk mill at Wray. Following his family's removal to Caernarfon in 1863, Marr became interested in geology, especially when a fossil he discovered was named after him. While at the Royal Lancaster Grammar School (1867?–1875?) Marr met R. H. Tiddeman of the geological survey and accompanied him on a number of field excursions. In 1875, Marr went up to St John's College, Cambridge, as an exhibitioner. Receiving tuition from, among others, T. G. Bonney, Marr was awarded a first, with geology as his main subject, in 1878.

After graduating, Marr worked as a university extension lecturer for four years, developing an interest in the relationship between geology and scenery. During this period he also worked briefly at Leeds University, and was elected, in 1881, to a fellowship at St John's. In 1886 he was appointed university lecturer in geology and in 1917 he succeeded McKenny Hughes as professor, a position Marr held until 1930, when he retired due to ill health. In 1893 he married Amy, daughter of John Stubbs of Shap Wells, Westmorland, and through the years, Amy Marr regularly acted as hostess to her husband's students. Their son, Alleyne, who used to assist his father's fieldwork in the Lakes, fought in the First World War and was killed in the Second World War.

Marr's early work was carried out among the rocks near Haverfordwest, in Caernarvonshire, in the Dee valley, and especially in the Lake District. But, before beginning his work in England and Wales, he determined to examine the work of geologists in Bohemia and Scandinavia, to which regions he journeyed in 1879 and 1880 with the assistance of the Cambridge University Worts travelling fund. In Bohemia, Joachim Barrande had proposed the notion of 'precursoral forms' or 'colonies', in cases where certain fossils appeared to be out of order according to the usual stratigraphic sequence. This idea had received some favour with British geologists such as Roderick Murchison, but Marr showed that the seeming colonies were in fact the result of younger rocks having been faulted into older strata. So there was no Bohemian contradiction of the stratigraphic principles of William Smith. (Like criticisms of Barrande's hypothesis had been made by Charles Lapworth in connection with his work on the southern uplands of Scotland.)

In conjunction with Henry Alleyne Nicholson, Marr carried out exemplary studies of the Palaeozoic rocks of the Lake District, working out successions at key sites such as Ash Gill near Coniston, Skelgill near Ambleside, and Stockdale in Longsleddale. Graptolites were used as zone fossils, and the evolutionary history of these organisms was investigated. Attention was also given to the conditions under which the ancient rocks were deposited. In further Westmorland researches, Marr worked with Alfred Harker on the igneous rocks at Shap, source of the famous Shap Granite. Marr was chiefly responsible for the map work and stratigraphy, while Harker concentrated on the petrology.

In his Lakeland work, Marr proposed the notion of 'lag faulting' to account for the structure of the region; and he gave particular attention to the effects of earth movements and glaciation on topography and scenery, considering their roles in the formation of lakes and drainage patterns. In his earlier work, he ascribed much of the topography to erosion along 'shatter belts', but after visiting the Lakes with the American geologist W. M. Davis in 1907 Marr placed greater emphasis on the erosive powers of glaciers. His investigations were eventually linked in a much-admired and used book, *The Geology of the Lake District* (1916). In his later years, Marr turned his attention towards prehistoric archaeology, studying the Pleistocene deposits in the neighbourhood of Cambridge, and examining the claims for the existence of flint implements of Pliocene age.

Marr was elected fellow of the Geological Society in 1879 and served the institution as secretary (1888–98), vice-president (for several periods), and president (1904–6). He served on the council for thirty-four years and was awarded the Lyell medal (1900) and the Wollaston medal (1914). He was president of section C (geology) of the British Association (1896) and was elected FRS in 1891, serving on the society's council from 1904 to 1906. He received the royal medal (1930), was awarded a Cambridge ScD (1904), and an honorary doctorate from Prague (1908). He was considered an exceptionally fine teacher. Marr was afflicted by failing sight in old age; he died of a stroke at his home, 126 Huntingdon Road, Cambridge, on 1 October 1933, and was buried in Cambridge. DAVID OLDROYD

Sources Obits. FRS, 1 (1932–5), 251–7 • 'Eminent living geologists: John Edward Marr', *Geological Magazine*, new ser., 6th decade, 3 (1916), 289–95 • I. S. Double, 'President's address', *Proceedings of the Liverpool Geological Society*, 16 (1934), 117–18 • E. J. Garwood and H. H. Thomas, *Quarterly Journal of the Geological Society of London*, 90 (1934), lx–lxiv • A. H. [A. Harker], 'John Edward Marr', *The Eagle*, 48 (1934–5), 64–5 • CGPLA Eng. & Wales (1933) • b. cert. • D. Oldroyd, 'John Edward Marr (1857–1933): Lakeland geologist', *Proceedings of the Cumberland Geological Society* (2000)
Archives U. Cam., Sedgwick Museum of Earth Sciences, notebooks and papers
Likenesses K. Green, oils, 1925, U. Cam., Sedgwick Museum of Earth Sciences • J. P. Clarke, photograph, repro. in 'Eminent living geologists', facing p. 289 • photograph, GS Lond.; repro. in *Obits. FRS*
Wealth at death £5469 12s. 1d.: administration with will, 18 Nov 1933, CGPLA Eng. & Wales

Marrable, Frederick (*bap.* 1819, *d.* 1872), architect, was baptized on 19 January 1819, the son of Sir Thomas Smith Marrable, secretary of the board of green cloth to George IV and William IV, and his wife, Charlotte. He was articled to the architect Edward Blore, and on the expiration of his time studied abroad. On his return he established a small private practice from an office in Lancaster Place, next to

Waterloo Bridge, London, but his career did not flourish until 1856, when he was appointed superintending architect to the newly established Metropolitan Board of Works. This difficult office involved the settling of compensation claims, especially in connection with the building of new streets, and the writing of innumerable reports, and through it he gained the esteem of his profession. The main improvements carried out under his superintendency were Garrick Street (1857–61), Southwark Street (1857–64), and Burdett Road (1858–62), which served as part of an improved approach to Victoria Park from Limehouse; he also prepared an unexecuted design for Holborn Viaduct, eventually built in 1864–9 by the city corporation, designed and built the offices of the Metropolitan Board of Works in Spring Gardens, near Trafalgar Square (1860; dem.), but resigned his post in 1861 on the grounds that he was grossly underpaid (the board responded by offering to increase his salary by £200 to £1000, but he refused to reconsider). He was succeeded by George Vulliamy, but continued to work privately for the board on compensation cases. In 1864 he married the painter Madeline Cockburn (1833–1916) [*see* Marrable, Madeline Frances Jane]; the couple had two children.

Marrable's most important surviving building is the Garrick Club, Garrick Street (1860), a competent essay in the Italian Renaissance manner, which he also employed in the board's offices and in Archbishop Tenison's School in Leicester Square (1869; dem.). He also designed the church of St Peter, Deptford (1866–70), and that of St Mary Magdalen, St Leonards, Sussex (1852; enlarged 1872). Marrable resided at 28 Avenue Road, Regent's Park, and on 22 June 1872 went to Witley in Surrey to inspect the buildings of the Bethlehem Hospital for Convalescents. While thus engaged he was taken ill, and died almost immediately.
GEOFFREY TYACK

Sources DNB • *The Builder*, 30 (1872), 500–01 • D. Owen and others, *The government of Victorian London, 1855–1889*, ed. R. MacLeod (1982), 43 • P. J. Edwards, *The history of London street improvements, 1855–1897* (1898), 25–32, 43–5 • G. H. Gater and F. R. Hiorns, *The parish of St Martin-in-the-Fields*, 3: *Trafalgar Square and neighbourhood*, Survey of London, 20 (1940), 66–7 • Redgrave, *Artists* • Graves, *RA exhibitors* • d. cert. • IGI
Wealth at death under £1500: probate, 26 July 1872, CGPLA Eng. & Wales

Marrable [*née* Cockburn], **Madeline Frances Jane** (1833–1916), painter, was born in London and baptized on 20 July 1833 at St Botolph without Bishopsgate, the daughter of James Cockburn, army officer, and his Scottish wife, Madeline Susan. Her mother died while she herself was still young, whereupon her father became a merchant. She was the niece of Ralph Cockburn, a member of the Old Watercolour Society (OWS) and first custodian of Dulwich Picture Gallery, who introduced her to Henry Warren, president of the OWS, who became her tutor. Later she was taught landscape painting in oil by Peter Graham and also studied at Queen Square School of Art (later the Female School of Art), Bloomsbury. She began to exhibit with all the major London art societies in 1864, and in that year married the architect Frederick *Marrable (*bap.* 1819, *d.* 1872), who died suddenly, leaving her with two young children. From then onwards she supported her family by the sale of her works.

Madeline Marrable painted primarily landscapes, especially mountains with snow but also figures and portraits, and travelled extensively abroad, particularly in Italy, Switzerland, Austria, Ireland, and France; her *View of Cannes* (*c.*1880) was with Comenos Fine Arts, Boston, in 2001. She was a prolific artist, exhibiting well over 200 works at the Society of Women Artists (SWA) alone, as well as contributing regularly to the other major London exhibitions, including those at the Alpine Club Gallery; the Dudley Gallery; the Grosvenor Gallery; the London Salon; the New Gallery at the Royal Academy; the Royal Society of Painters in Water Colours; and the Society (later Royal Society) of British Artists. Outside London she showed works at the Royal Society of Artists, Birmingham; the Walker Art Gallery, Liverpool; and Manchester City Art Gallery. In 1886 she became the first president of the SWA—initially known as the Society of Female Artists (1855–73) and then the Society of Lady Artists, until 1899— and held the post for the next forty years, until 1912; in 1913 she was made its first and only honorary president. She was also an honorary member of the Belgian Society of Watercolours, and of the Verein der Schriftstellerinnen und Künstlerinnen in Vienna, as well as an associate of the Roman Watercolour Society. Her long and active devotion to the SWA was recognized in 1902 when Queen Alexandra consented to be patron and was joined by the princess of Wales. In 1911 Queen Mary and Queen Alexandra were the society's patrons. Edward VII and other members of the royal family commissioned paintings from her.

Madeline Marrable died in London on 26 April 1916. Her daughter Edith (Mrs A. Ferguson) also became a professional artist in watercolours, specializing in flower paintings and participating in SWA activities, as well as exhibiting elsewhere. CHARLES BAILE DE LAPERRIERE

Sources J. Soden and C. Baile de Laperrière, eds., *The Society of Women Artists exhibitors, 1855–1996*, 4 vols. (1996) • P. Dunford, *A biographical dictionary of women artists in Europe and America since 1850* (1990) • Graves, *Artists* • *IGI* • J. Johnson and A. Greutzner, eds., *The dictionary of British artists, 1880–1940* (1976), vol. 5 of *Dictionary of British art*; repr. (1994) • *CGPLA Eng. & Wales* (1916)
Wealth at death £5058 19s. 7d.: probate, 12 Aug 1916, *CGPLA Eng. & Wales*

Marrant, John (1755–1791), missionary and autobiographer, was born in New York on 15 June 1755. When he was four he moved with his mother to Florida after his father's death. There he learned to read, continuing his education in Georgia until the age of eleven, when they moved to South Carolina. He also learned to play the French horn and violin and was apprenticed to a carpenter. Aged thirteen Marrant reluctantly underwent a Christian conversion experience when he heard the Methodist evangelist George Whitefield preach.

In response to his family's opposition to his new faith Marrant wandered in the wilderness, depending upon God to feed and protect him. He was brought by an Indian hunter to a Cherokee town, where he was condemned to a

John Marrant (1755–1791), by unknown engraver, pubd 1795

painful death, but was saved by the miraculous conversion of the executioner. After living with the Indians for two years Marrant returned to his family, who initially failed to recognize him. He continued his missionary work, teaching religion to slaves, despite the objections of their owners.

During the American War of Independence, Marrant claimed that he was pressed into the Royal Navy as a musician and served at the siege of Charles Town in 1780 and in the battle with Dutch forces off the Dogger Bank in the North Sea (1781). Naval records do not support his claims, however. Other records suggest that he may himself have been a slave owner. After the war he worked for a London clothing merchant.

A letter from his brother, who was among the refugee slaves evacuated to Nova Scotia, from the former American colonies, convinced Marrant that he was needed to minister to the refugees' spiritual needs. He was ordained on 15 May 1785 in Bath as a minister in the Huntingdon Connexion, a Calvinistic offshoot of Methodism led by Whitefield's patron, the countess of Huntingdon. Marrant soon left England for Nova Scotia to preach to the native Mi'kmaqs and doctrinally more moderate black and white Wesleyan Methodists. His success earned him the opposition of several white ministers, who lost parishioners to his all black chapels. In the same year his *Narrative of the Lord's Wonderful Dealings with John Marrant* was published in London. Notwithstanding that Marrant was free-born, as an account of the tribulations and ultimate triumph of a black man the autobiography has been considered a founder of the genre of slave narrative.

Despite Marrant's success in Nova Scotia he did not receive the financial aid he requested from Lady Huntingdon. In a destitute state he moved to Boston in 1787, becoming chaplain to the first lodge of African masons, founded by Prince Hall in 1784. He returned briefly to Nova Scotia to marry the black loyalist Elizabeth Herries on 15 August 1788. He published *A Sermon* (Boston, 1789) before returning to England in 1790, never having heard from the countess. He continued his ministry in Whitechapel, and at the Independent chapel on Church Street in Islington while resident at 2 Black Horse Court, Aldersgate Street. His last publication was *A Journal ... to which are Added, Two Sermons* (1790). Marrant died in Islington on 15 April 1791 and was buried in the graveyard adjoining the chapel in Church Street. VINCENT CARRETTA

Sources J. Marrant, *A narrative of the Lord's wonderful dealings with John Marrant, a black* (1785) · *A journal of the Rev. John Marrant, from August the 18th, 1785 to the 16th of March 1790. To which are added, two sermons* (1790) · S. Whitchurch, *The negro convert: a poem, being the substance of the experience of Mr. John Marrant, a negro, as related by himself* (1785?) · J. W. St G. Walker, *The black loyalists: the search for a promised land in Nova Scotia and Sierra Leone, 1783–1870* (1976) · V. Carretta, ed., *Unchained voices: an anthology of black authors in the English-speaking world of the eighteenth century* (1996) · J. W. St G. Walker, 'Marrant, John', *DCB*, vol. 4
Archives BL, Add. MSS 41262A, 41262B, 41263, 41264 · PRO, 30/55/100, fols. 52–3 · PRO, ADM 36/8377, 36/8378, 36/9165, 36/9985 · Public Archives of Nova Scotia, Halifax, Charles Inglis docs., MG 1, 479, no. 1 [transcripts]
Likenesses mezzotint, pubd 1795, AM Oxf. [*see illus.*]

Marras, Giacinto (1810–1883), singer, was born on 6 July 1810 at Naples, the son of the Cavaliere Giovanni Marras and his wife, Maria Biliotti, a famous Florentine beauty. His father was court painter to the grand duke of Tuscany and the sultan of Turkey, and was himself a son of the Roman poet Angelica Mosca. In 1820 Giacinto entered the preparatory school of the Real Collegio di Musica at Naples. Shortly afterwards, probably on account of his success in the soprano part of Bellini's first opera, *Adelson e Salvini*, performed in the college theatre, for which he was chosen by the composer because of the beauty of his voice, he was elected to a free scholarship at the college, where his masters for composition and singing were Niccolò Zingarelli and Girolamo Crescentini, and Bellini and Michael Costa were sub-professors. While studying in Naples he sang in and wrote music for the city's churches.

On leaving the college Marras made a professional tour through Italy, and in 1835 he was invited by the marquess of Anglesey and the duke of Devonshire to visit England. He was immediately engaged for most of the important concerts, including those of the Philharmonic Society and the Ancient Concerts. In 1842 he made a concert tour of Russia, and he had such success at St Petersburg that Tsar Nicholas offered him the post of director of court music, which he declined. He later sang in Vienna, Naples, and Paris.

In 1846 Marras settled permanently in England, and he was naturalized on 12 January 1850. In 1855 he turned down an offer of the principal professorship of singing at the Royal Academy of Music, and was later elected an honorary fellow. About 1860 he started his Après-midis Musicales at his house at 10 Hyde Park Gate. Between 1870 and 1873 he made a successful tour through India, and in 1879

he went to Cannes and Nice, where he made his last public appearances. In 1883 he left Cannes for Monte Carlo for change of air, after a severe attack of bronchitis, and died at the Hôtel de Londres, Monte Carlo, on 8 May 1883. He was buried at Cannes in the protestant cemetery, close to the memorial to the duke of Albany. He had married his pupil Lilla Stephenson, daughter of a major in the 6th dragoon guards, and they had one daughter, later Madame Schulz, who became a singer.

During his long career Marras made many operatic tours with performers including Fanny Tacchinardi-Persiani, Jeanne Castellan, and Jan Pischek, and he sang the leading tenor parts in most of the Italian operas then in vogue. He was equally at home in oratorio and chamber music. As a teacher of singing he was much in demand, and among his pupils were the duchess of Cambridge, Princess Mary of Cambridge, and the grand duchess of Mecklenburg-Strelitz. He composed more than a hundred songs, mainly in Italian. His *Lezioni di canto* (1849) and *Elementi vocali* (1850) were important contributions to the art of singing, for which the king of Naples sent Marras a gold medal. Marras also composed an opera, *Sardanapalus*. Though never publicly performed, it met with considerable success when given privately at Lord Dudley's house, Witley Court. R. H. LEGGE, *rev.* ANNE PIMLOTT BAKER

Sources Boase, *Mod. Eng. biog.* · *Morning Post* (18 May 1883) · *Morning Post* (21 Dec 1872) · *The Athenaeum* (30 Nov 1872), 707 · *Times of India* (20 Jan 1873) · private information (1893) · CGPLA Eng. & Wales (1883)
Likenesses Costantino, miniature, 1830 · Epaminondas, lithograph, 1842 (as Gualtiero in *Il pirata*), Odessa · Baugniet, lithograph, 1848, London · M. Ciardiello, group portrait, oils, 1865, London · Sturges, crayon drawing, 1882, Nice
Wealth at death £10,756 6s. 2d.: probate, 23 Aug 1883, CGPLA Eng. & Wales

Marrat, William (1772–1852), topographer and teacher of mathematics, was born on 6 April 1772 at Sibsey, Lincolnshire, the son of John and Jane Marrat. Self-taught, he acquired a broad knowledge of literature and science, as well as French and German, and his writing on mechanics demonstrates a familiarity with continental mathematics.

For some years Marrat followed the trade of a printer and publisher at Boston, Lincolnshire. At other times he taught mathematics, both in Lincolnshire, and in New York, where he lived from 1817 to 1821. For most of his adult life he contributed articles to the popular press. His attempts to establish similar journals on his own behalf, however, met with little success; while in America he published the *Scientific Journal*, which ran for only nine issues in 1818; the magazine which he and Pishey Thompson had edited from Boston, Lincolnshire, *The Enquirer, or, Literary, Mathematical, and Philosophical Repository*, was issued only during 1811–12. Marrat also wrote on the topography of his native county. His *History of Lincolnshire*, written during 1814–16, was stopped after three volumes covering Holland and much of Kesteven, Marrat alleged, through Sir Joseph Banks's refusal to allow access to his papers, but his *Historical Description of Stamford* appeared in 1816.

On his return to England Marrat settled at Copperas

Hill, Liverpool, where he published lunar tables, compiled tide tables for the port, and wrote his *Elements of Mechanical Philosophy* (1825). From 1833 to 1836 he taught mathematics in a school at Exeter, but on the death of his wife (whose identity is not known), he returned to Liverpool where his son, Frederick Price Marrat, was a conchologist at the Liverpool Museum. He died at his son's house, 15 White Mill Street, on 26 March 1852, and was buried at the city's necropolis.

C. W. SUTTON, *rev.* ANITA MCCONNELL

Sources T. T. Wilkinson, 'Biographical notices of some Liverpool mathematicians', *Transactions of the Historic Society of Lancashire and Cheshire*, new ser., 2 (1861–2), 29–40, esp. 35–6 · *Liverpool Chronicle* (10 April 1852), 6f · parish register (baptism), 7 April 1772, Sibsey, Lincolnshire · E. Baines, *History, directory and gazetteer of the county palatine of Lancaster*, 1 (1824), 289 · d. cert.
Archives S. Antiquaries, Lond., collections relating to Lincolnshire

Marre, Sir Alan Samuel (1914–1990), civil servant and ombudsman, was born on 25 February 1914 in Bow, London, the fourth child and second son in the family of three sons and three daughters of Joseph Moshinsky, who ran a tobacconist's shop near Aldgate East Station, and his wife, Rebecca. His parents were Russian Jews who had settled in England in 1907. Marre (who, in 1941, like his elder brother, changed his name by deed poll) won a scholarship to St Olave's and St Saviour's Grammar School, Southwark, and an open scholarship to Trinity Hall, Cambridge. There he won the John Stewart of Rannoch scholarship and secured first-class honours in both parts of the classical tripos (1934 and 1935).

Marre entered the Ministry of Health in 1936, as an assistant principal. Though in a reserved occupation, he tried to volunteer for the Royal Air Force when the Second World War began, but he was rejected because of his very short sight. He worked in a variety of departmental posts, and helped to launch the National Health Service. He became a principal in 1941, assistant secretary in 1946, and under-secretary in 1952. Eleven years later he moved to the Ministry of Labour, where he handled policy on industrial relations. He returned to the Ministry of Health as deputy secretary in 1964, spent a further two years in the Department of Employment and Productivity, then went back to his home department in 1968 as second permanent under-secretary. This was a time of adjustment to the creation of the composite Department of Health and Social Security, of which Richard Crossman was the first secretary of state. Crossman's personality was not well adapted to the role of departmental minister, and he was notoriously difficult to work with. It was not an easy or comfortable period for Marre; but he managed to establish and maintain a satisfactory relationship with Crossman, who in his diary referred to him as 'a charming sweet man'.

In 1971 Marre became parliamentary commissioner for administration (parliamentary ombudsman), the second holder of the post. In 1973 he additionally became the first health service commissioner, carrying both responsibilities until his retirement in 1976. He was subsequently requested by the government to carry out two difficult and sensitive inquiries, one into the position of those children disabled because of the drug thalidomide who had not benefited from an earlier overall settlement, the other into a £130 million discrepancy in the report on teachers' pay by the standing commission on pay comparability, chaired by Hugh Clegg (seventh report, 1980). From 1979 to 1985 he was vice-chairman of the advisory committee on distinction awards for NHS consultants, and from 1983 to 1987 chairman of the newly established committee on rural dispensing, when he did much to defuse a bitter and long-standing dispute between the medical and pharmaceutical professions. He also devoted time and energy to a range of voluntary organizations, being chairman of Age Concern England in 1977–80. He was appointed CB in 1955 and KCB in 1970.

Marre, with his horn-rimmed spectacles and bald dome, was friendly and approachable, though cool and restrained. His gifts were not so much originality and imagination as excellent judgement and analytical ability, and he was also a good negotiator. His specific strengths included precision in thought and expression, thoroughness, respect for the facts, detachment, and a sense of justice. In his official work he maintained a scrupulous political neutrality, and the tradition of civil service anonymity was thoroughly congenial to him. There were some (including Crossman) who criticized his appointment as ombudsman, doubting whether, despite the strengths which had served him so well as a departmental civil servant, he had the public relations skills and the radically questioning, even aggressive, attitudes which the post required. In fact, he managed to come to terms with the public aspects of his task and, though unabrasive and disinclined to attack the general ethos of contemporary government, proved himself just, persistent, and firmly independent. He gained public credit for his handling of some of the difficult cases which came his way. His career is of particular interest because in its later years it reflects the transition from a civil service imbued with the traditions of neutrality and anonymity, begun in 1853 as a result of the Northcote-Trevelyan report, to one where senior officials appear in the public arena and are held personally accountable. For Marre, this change was against his personal grain, but he had the adaptability to adjust to it successfully.

Marre had a happy domestic life. In 1943 he married Romola Mary (*b.* 1920), daughter of Aubrey John Gilling, bank manager. She herself had a distinguished career of public service, particularly on the London Voluntary Service Council, being appointed CBE in 1979. They had one son and one daughter. Marre died of cancer on 20 March 1990, at his home, 44 The Vale, Golders Green, London.

PATRICK BENNER, *rev.*

Sources *The Times* (23 March 1990) · *The Independent* (6 April 1990) · personal knowledge (1996) · private information (1996) [Lady Marre] · *CGPLA Eng. & Wales* (1990)
Wealth at death £85,099: probate, 20 June 1990, *CGPLA Eng. & Wales*

Marre [Marrey], **John** (*d.* 1408), prior of Doncaster and theologian, was born in the village of Marr, near Doncaster. He was traditionally thought to have entered the Carmelite order in Doncaster, but as this house was not founded until 1351, he must have joined the order in York and undertaken his early studies there, for he was ordained subdeacon in York on 18 December 1350, deacon on 11 June 1351, and priest on 17 December 1351. He completed his theology at Oxford, incepting as a doctor of theology and lecturing there. On 26 February 1377 he was one of the commissioners appointed by the king to settle a dispute in the university. Later he returned to Doncaster, where he was prior until his death on 18 March 1408. He was buried in the choir with the epitaph: 'Jesus Christ have mercy on br. John Marre; whose body is buried in this tomb' (BL, Harley MS 3838, fol. 88). During his period at Oxford Marre was a noted theologian opposed to Wyclif, against whose beliefs he wrote a set of *determinationes*. In addition to his lectures on the *Sentences*, Bale records a work by Marre on the epigrams of Martial, and a compendium of extracts from other authors with an index, all now lost.

RICHARD COPSEY

Sources J. Bale, Bodl. Oxf., MS Bodley 73 (SC 27635), fol. 112*v* · J. Bale, Bodl. Oxf., MS Selden supra 41, fol. 171*v* · J. Bale, BL, Harley MS 3838 fols. 88–88*v* · Bale, *Cat.*, 1.531–2 · Emden, *Oxf.*, 2.1225 · Borth. Inst., Reg. 10 Zouche, fols. 50, 52, 54 · J. Bale, *Illustrium Maioris Britannie scriptorum … summarium* (1548), 179–179*v* · A. Bostius, 'Speculum historiale', before 1491, Milan Biblioteca, Brera AE, xii.22, p. 569 · J. Trithemius, 'De scriptoribus ecclesiasticis, 1492', *Speculum Carmelitanum*, ed. Daniel a Virgine Maria, 2 vols. (Antwerp, 1680), 901 · J. Pits, *Relationum historicarum de rebus Anglicis*, ed. [W. Bishop] (Paris, 1619), 585 · Tanner, *Bibl. Brit.-Hib.*, 512

Marrian, Guy Frederic (1904–1981), biochemist, was born on 3 March 1904 in London, the only son and youngest of the three children of Frederic York Marrian, civil engineer, of London, and his second wife, Mary Eddington Currie; his father and his first wife, who had died, had two sons and a daughter. He was educated at Tollington School, London, but his subsequent entry into University College, London, was delayed by one year in order to meet county scholarship conditions. This administrative problem proved beneficial as Marrian took a technician's job at the National Institute for Medical Research in London, where he was introduced to the topic that formed the core of his future work—endocrinology. This was the era when what subsequently became known as insulin was being isolated and characterized. Marrian appreciated the importance of that work and utilized to great effect the principles of large-scale isolation and biological testing learned during that period when he eventually set up his own research team.

Marrian graduated BSc in chemistry in 1925 and remained at the college for a further eight years, during which he initiated the work for which he became famous: the identification of two chemicals, pregnanediol and oestriol, involved in female sexual function. His ability was acknowledged by the award of a DSc degree by London University in 1930, when Marrian was only twenty-six; he did not bother with the more conventional PhD. He became FRIC in 1931. On 5 November 1928 he married Phyllis May, a fellow chemist, daughter of Albert Robert Lewis, pharmacist. She provided him with valuable practical and moral support. They had two daughters.

In 1933 Marrian moved to Toronto University in Canada where he further enhanced his scientific reputation with pioneering work on oestrogen assay and metabolism. Marrian considered this to be his most productive period and his research activity was recognized by his election as a fellow of the Royal Society of Canada in 1937. He returned to the United Kingdom in 1939 to occupy the chair of chemistry in relation to medicine at Edinburgh University, and the ensuing war years were spent studying the poison gas arsine. With the experiences of the First World War in mind, the authorities were concerned that the Germans would again use poison gas, and arsine was thought to be the most likely candidate. He was elected a fellow of the Royal Society of Edinburgh in 1940, and of London in 1944.

The post-war years saw Marrian re-establish himself in the forefront of steroid-hormone research, playing an important role in persuading the Medical Research Council to establish the clinical endocrinology research unit, the forerunner of the reproductive biology unit in Edinburgh. However, he moved yet again in 1959, this time to become director of research at the Imperial Cancer Research Fund, where he remained until his retirement in 1968. Although taking a major role in rapidly expanding the activities of that charity, his period there was less than happy, in part due to personality clashes.

There is no doubt that Marrian made a lasting contribution to steroid endocrinology, both through his own work and through the many top-class students he trained. What remains debatable is whether his full potential was truncated by the move from research to the running of a large institute. Perhaps his best environment was the laboratory and not the office. The high international status achieved by the Medical Research Council unit in Edinburgh, and the Imperial Cancer Research Fund in London, remain fitting memorials to Marrian's scientific and medical foresight.

Marrian's personal behaviour would, in every respect, be identified as gentlemanly, with occasional lapses when he thought that scientific principles were being undermined. His characteristic manner of speaking could be used to devastating effect on those rare occasions. At the scientific level he generated strong loyalties in his co-workers and students but this was rarely translated into personal associations. His life was not all science, however: having been no mean athlete in his youth he retained his sporting interests, and he took particular pride in his daughter's international achievements in this sphere.

Marrian became a fellow of University College, London, in 1946, was appointed CBE in 1969, and became an honorary MD of Edinburgh in 1975. He received the Meldola medal of the Royal Institute of Chemistry in 1931, the Francis Amory prize of the American Academy of Arts and

Sciences in 1948, and the Sir Henry Dale medal of the Society of Endocrinology in 1966. Marrian died at his home, School Cottage, Ickham, near Canterbury, Kent, on 24 July 1981. R. J. B. KING, *rev.*

Sources J. K. Grant, *Memoirs FRS*, 28 (1982), 347–78 · personal knowledge (1990) · *CGPLA Eng. & Wales* (1982)
Archives Wellcome L., corresp., notebooks, papers, and records
Likenesses photograph, repro. in Grant, *Memoirs FRS*
Wealth at death under £25,000: probate, 31 Aug 1982, *CGPLA Eng. & Wales*

Marriott, Charles (1811–1858), Church of England clergyman and college teacher, was born at the rectory, Church Lawford, near Rugby, on 24 August 1811, the third of the five children of the rector of the parish, John *Marriott (1780–1825), and his wife, Mary Ann (*d.* 1821), the daughter of Thomas and Ann Harris. His father also held the curacy of Broadclyst in Devon, and, on account of his mother's poor health, the family mainly lived there during Marriott's youth. Charles received his elementary education at the village school. Both his parents died while Marriott was still a boy, and he was privately educated at Rugby by his aunts and a private tutor in Shropshire. He was a day pupil at Rugby School in 1825, but his delicate health led to his rapid removal. In March 1829 Marriott entered at Exeter College, Oxford, and in the autumn won an open scholarship at Balliol. George Moberly, afterwards bishop of Salisbury, was his college tutor, and exercised great influence over him. In his undergraduate years Marriott showed great ability and application, and when in Michaelmas term 1832 he took a first class in classics and a second in mathematics, there was some surprise that he had missed a double first. At Easter 1833 he was elected a fellow of Oriel, was ordained deacon, and was at once appointed mathematical lecturer, and afterwards tutor of the college. He took his MA in 1835.

At Oriel Marriott fell under the influence of John Henry Newman, and became his devoted disciple. In February 1839, after spending the winter in southern Europe, he became principal of the Diocesan Theological College at Chichester, at the invitation of Bishop William Otter, and was ordained priest on 19 May, Whitsunday. Although the numbers of students were small, the college was one of the first residential exercises in priestly formation in the Church of England. After two years' conscientious work ill health obliged Marriott to resign: he returned to Oriel and was appointed subdean and later dean of the college, taking his BD in 1848. On Newman's advice he declined Bishop George Augustus Selwyn's invitation to accompany him to New Zealand (1841), though they were to maintain a warm correspondence; his poor health similarly prevented him from joining Newman's community at Littlemore.

Marriott remained a close friend of Newman during the latter's years of increasing alienation from the Church of England, though his confidence in his own position does not appear to have wavered. On Newman's secession in 1845 Marriott to a great extent took Newman's place in Oxford, and increasingly became one of E. B. Pusey's most valuable allies. He had been prominent in the organization of Pusey's defence when the latter was suspended from preaching in 1843; later Pusey sought Marriott's advice on the controversial developments of the late 1840s, including the building of St Saviour's, Leeds, and Priscilla Lydia Sellon's early attempt to establish an Anglican sisterhood. Marriott also provided Pusey with some of the historical information that formed part of his controversial writings. There was, moreover, no doubt about Marriott's unshaken loyalty to the university. He became the correspondent, confessor, and spiritual adviser of many within it, especially young men, and was influential in keeping a large number of Newman's followers in the Church of England in the late 1840s and early 1850s. In 1850 Marriott was appointed vicar of the university church of St Mary the Virgin, which was in the gift of his college. A convinced celibate, he threw himself with his usual thoroughness into his parochial work. When cholera and smallpox broke out in 1854, he fearlessly visited sufferers and caught the latter disease himself. His sermons were always effective, though he was no orator, and it was in personal contact that he made his most profound mark. Edward King, later bishop of Lincoln, wrote: 'If I have any good in me, I owe it to Charles Marriott' (Burgon, 372).

Marriott had an abiding interest in education. He supported Henry Stevens, rector of Bradfield, Berkshire, and his newly founded Bradfield College, and made unsuccessful efforts to establish a hall for poor students in Oxford. He acquired possession of Newman's buildings at Littlemore 'partly because I did not wish that he should be embarrassed with them, and that any of his new friends should be led to urge him to put a Roman colony there, which would be no good to them and a great annoyance to us' (Charles Marriott to Fitzherbert Marriott, [12 April] 1846, Marriott MSS). The buildings were used to house a printing press for religious works, a scheme that caused Marriott endless worry and expenditure, though he grew into the administrative and commercial side of publishing. He also threw himself into a commercial scheme at Oxford, named the Universal Purveyor, an attempt to regulate the quality and price of daily essentials. It was started for the most benevolent purposes, but was quite out of his experience, and became a fruitful source of anxiety. Marriott was at the same time a member of the hebdomadal council, and 'took a considerable part in working the new constitution of the university' (Church, 91). The variety and pressure of his work damaged his health: on 29 June 1855 he suffered a stroke, which left him partially paralysed and hampered his speech. On 23 August he was moved to Bradfield, where he lived with the curate, his devoted brother John, for three years. He died there on 15 September 1858, and was buried in a vault under the south transept of Bradfield parish church on 20 September.

Marriott's reputation was out of all proportion to the number of works published under his name; but much of his most valuable work appeared without acknowledgement of his authorship. In 1843 he published *Sermons*

Preached before the University and in other Places, in 1849 *Reflections in a Lent Reading of the Epistle to the Romans*, and in 1850 *Sermons Preached in Bradfield Church, Oriel College Chapel, and other Places*. Besides numerous single sermons, lectures, and pamphlets, he also published *Hints to Devotion* (1848). After his death his brother John edited his *Lectures on the Epistle to the Romans* (1859), which had been delivered at St Mary's during the last two years of his incumbency; they were the only results of what was intended to be the great work of his life, a commentary on the epistle to the Romans, which was to be his contribution to a commentary on the Bible projected by Pusey but never completed. From 1841 to the time of his stroke, Marriott edited the Library of the Fathers in conjunction with Pusey and Keble. It was Marriott who undertook most of the work: Pusey, in the advertisement to the thirty-ninth volume, while paying a graceful tribute to his departed friend, frankly admitted that 'upon Charles Marriott's editorial labours "The Library of the Fathers" had, for some years, wholly depended' (p. iii). In 1852 Marriott also edited, as part of a series of the original texts of the fathers, Theodoret's *Interpretatio in omnes B. Pauli epistolas*, and in May 1855 he became the first editor of the *Literary Churchman*, in the first seven numbers of which he wrote at least sixteen articles. He edited, for the use of Chichester students, *Canons of the Apostles* (1841) in Greek, with the English version and notes of John Johnson of Cranbrook; *Analecta Christiana* (1844–8), patristic readings intended for the use of Bishop Selwyn's ministerial candidates; and four of St Augustine's shorter treatises (1848).

J. H. OVERTON, *rev.* K. E. MACNAB

Sources J. Marriott, 'Memoir [of Charles Marriott]', *c*.1859, Pusey Oxf., Marriott papers · Pusey Oxf., Marriott papers · Pusey Oxf., Ollard papers · bound volumes, Pusey Oxf., Liddon papers · J. W. Burgon, 'Charles Marriott: the man of saintly life', *Lives of twelve good men*, [new edn], 1 (1888), 296–373 · R. W. Church, 'Charles Marriott', *The Oxford Movement: twelve years, 1833–1845*, 3rd edn (1892), 79–91
Archives NRA, corresp. · Pusey Oxf., diaries and corresp. | BL, corresp. with W. E. Gladstone, Add. MS 44251 · Pusey Oxf., Liddon bound volumes · Pusey Oxf., Ollard papers · Pusey Oxf., Pusey papers
Likenesses J. Drummond, engraving, 1853, Pusey Oxf.; copy, Oriel College, Oxford · J. Posselwhite, stipple, 1853, BM
Wealth at death under £2000: administration, 25 March 1858, *CGPLA Eng. & Wales*

Marriott, Sir James (1730–1803), judge and politician, was born on 29 October 1730, probably at Twinstead Hall, Essex, the son of Benjamin Marriott, a Hatton Garden attorney, and his wife, Esther (*d.* 1771), daughter of Abraham Chambers of Twinstead. He entered Trinity Hall, Cambridge, on 17 June 1746, was elected a scholar on 27 October 1747, and graduated LLB on 17 June 1751. In November 1755 he altered his intended profession from the church to the law 'for family reasons' (Marriott to the duke of Newcastle, BL, Add. MS 32860, fol. 465). His mother's second husband, Everard Sayer, had been a prominent civilian lawyer. Marriott took his LLD on 25 March 1757 and entered the College of Advocates on 3

November. He published two pamphlets on topical controversies over neutrals' rights but it was neither his legal talents nor the very slender literary accomplishments exemplified by his contributions to the university's verses on several public occasions that secured him advancement.

In 1754 Marriott was employed to arrange the library of the university's chancellor, Thomas Pelham-Holles, first duke of Newcastle, and proclaimed himself his 'most devoted dependant' (15 Feb 1755, BL, Add. MS 32852, fol. 495), zealously furthering his patron's interests in Cambridge, where he became a fellow of his college in 1756, and in Suffolk.

In 1760 Marriott wooed the nineteen-year-old Hester Salusbury (later Mrs Thrale) but found her indifferent and her father hostile. Devoted to his mother, he never married but was more persevering and promiscuous in his political pursuits. Marriott was an indefatigable, insatiable, and indiscriminate suitor for patronage and although he was made receiver of land tax for Suffolk, he was disappointed by Newcastle's tardiness in finding him a seat in the House of Commons and when George III became king he shamelessly sought the favour of the king's new ministers while trying unsuccessfully to avoid alienating the Pelhams. His election as master of Trinity Hall (June 1764) owed more to college politics than ministerial favour but on 9 October he was made king's advocate by John Montagu, fourth earl of Sandwich, secretary of state, albeit only 'because it absolutely now goes a-begging' (*Jenkinson Papers*, 299). He served as vice-chancellor of the university in 1767, but was disappointed in his hopes of augmenting by public subscription a legacy of £500 which Walter Titley had left at the vice-chancellor's disposal, in order to erect an amphitheatre for concerts and lectures to his own designs.

Still avid for preferment, Marriott put himself forward in 1768 for the vacant professorship of modern history but Thomas Gray was preferred and despite his importunities (which drove one prime minister, Augustus Fitzroy, third duke of Grafton, to distraction), he obtained nothing more until October 1778, when he was knighted (9 October) and appointed judge in Admiralty (12 October).

As king's advocate Marriott had shown himself capable of effective legal argument, but as a judge he did not enhance the standing of his court despite the opportunities presented by two wars. Described in his youth as 'gay and volatile' (Coote, 125), he never acquired the discretion needed for judicial office and his courtroom manner was said rather to resemble 'the jocular effusions of the president of a festive meeting' (ibid.) than a judge. He was also prone to intemperate outbursts, notably against the American colonists and eminent jurists. Roscoe's verdict that he did 'not leave a single judgment of historical value' (p. 37) is severe, but there is little reason to regret that the only collected reports of his court are those he himself began publishing in retirement. A more valuable undertaking was his compilation of the forms and practice of the court, *Formulare instrumentarum* (1802); freely drawn on by American writers, it was a major influence on American admiralty law.

In 1781 Marriott finally achieved his ambition of becoming MP for Sudbury in Suffolk, not far from Twinstead. He was initially a supporter of North's ministry and wrote a pamphlet in defence of British conduct towards the Americans, but he proved very maladroit and earned a footnote in history when, to the great merriment of the Commons, he solemnly rebutted the colonists' claim to 'no taxation without representation' by arguing that they were 'represented by the members for Kent, since in the charters of the thirteen provinces they are declared to be "part and parcel of the manor of Greenwich"' (*The Parliamentary History of England from the Earliest Times to 1803*, vol. 22, col. 1184). In keeping with his past record he deserted North on the fall of his administration and attached himself to William Petty, second earl of Shelburne, voting for the peace and Fox's India Bill. He did not seek re-election in 1784 but was returned for Sudbury in 1796 in a rather questionable manner when, having initially supported the sitting member, John Coxe Hippisley, and argued against a contest, he allowed several influential citizens to persuade him to stand himself, Hippisley withdrawing in disgust. A silent supporter of William Pitt the younger, he hoped in 1801 to be able to resign his seat in favour of a relative of his friend Charles Jenkinson, first earl of Liverpool, but in the event retained it until the dissolution in 1802.

After quarrelling with the fellows, Marriott seldom visited his college, though he did present it with a bust of Lord Mansfield, whom he greatly admired. In 1786 he successfully evaded a second term as university vice-chancellor on the plea that judicial office exempted him. He was treasurer of Doctors' Commons in 1780 and in the 1790s he sat on the board of longitude. In 1793 he drafted a bill to remove some anomalies in prize law, but towards the end of the century his inability to cope with the court's heavy wartime workload led to memorials seeking his removal. When he resigned on 26 October 1798 with a pension of £2000 p.a., the king wrote that his replacement by Sir William Scott was 'highly advantageous to the credit of the court of admiralty' (George III, *Later Corr.*, 3.147). Marriott made many alterations to Twinstead Hall, where he died peacefully on 21 March 1803, and rebuilt the church, where he was buried on 29 March.

PATRICK POLDEN

Sources L. B. Namier, 'Marriott, Sir James', HoP, *Commons, 1754–90* • J. A. Cannon, 'Sudbury', HoP, *Commons, 1754–90*, 1.382–3 • *The Jenkinson papers, 1760–1766*, ed. N. S. Jucker (1949) • D. A. Winstanley, *Unreformed Cambridge: a study of certain aspects of the university in the eighteenth century* (1935), 266–98 • [C. Coote], *Sketches of the lives and characters of eminent English civilians, with an historical introduction relative to the College of Advocates* (1804) • F. L. Wiswall, *The development of admiralty jurisdiction and practice since 1800* (1970), 12 • W. Stokes, 'Marriott, Sir James', HoP, *Commons, 1790–1820* • A. Clark, 'Sir James Marriott/Twinstead church and hall', *Essex Review*, 15 (1906), 82–90, 190–98 • E. S. Roscoe, *Studies in the history of the admiralty and prize courts* (1932), 28–37 • *The letters of Thomas Gray*, ed. D. C. Tovey, 3 (1912) • C. Crawley, *Trinity Hall: the history of a Cambridge college, 1350–1975* (1976), 120–21 • T. Wright, *The history and topography of the county of Essex*, 1 (1836), 482 • G. D. Squibb, *Doctors' Commons: a history of the College of Advocates and Doctors of Law* (1977), appx 3 • *GM*, 1st ser., 73 (1803), 294, 379 • letter, J. Marriott to the duke of Newcastle, BL, Add. MS 32860, fol. 465

Archives Bodl. Oxf., letters and poems, MSS 31519–31520, 40688 | BL, Hardwicke MSS, 35636–35640 • BL, letters to Lord Liverpool, Add. MSS 38202–38344, 38458, 38469, 38473 • BL, corresp. with duke of Newcastle, Add. MSS 32852–32991 • BL, corresp. with Sir Joseph Yorke, Add. MSS 17386–17387 • NMM, letters to Lord Sandwich • NRA, priv. coll., letters to Lord Shelburne

Wealth at death under £5000: PRO, death duty registers, IR 26/74, fol. 144

Marriott, John (1780–1825), poet and Church of England clergyman, born at Cotesbach Hall, Cotesbach, near Lutterworth, Leicestershire, and baptized at Cotesbach church on 11 September 1780, was the third and youngest son of Robert Marriott DCL (*d.* 1808), rector of Cotesbach and Gilmorton, and his wife, Elizabeth (*d.* 1819), daughter and only child of George Stow of Walthamstow, Essex. He entered Rugby School at midsummer 1788, and matriculated from Christ Church, Oxford, on 10 October 1798. He was one of two who achieved first-class honours in classics in the first honours school in 1802, and was awarded a BA and a studentship at Christ Church. In 1806 he proceeded MA. He was ordained priest in the Church of England on 22 December 1805. His feelings about Oxford, and a clue to his reason for leaving, are contained in a manuscript 'Sonnet Composed under the Shadow of Joe Pullen, a Tree in Headington Hill' of 1806 (Bodl. Oxf., MS top. Oxon. e. 364, fol. 120).

Marriott went to Dalkeith, Scotland, in 1804 to become tutor to George Henry, Lord Scott, brother of the fifth duke of Buccleuch. By 1805 he was describing himself as 'half a Scotchman' (Sharpe, 236). Robert Southey, meeting him then, was impressed by his ability to 'tell by the track what horse has past (*sic*) and how long ago', 'as in a savage country' (*Southey's Common-place Book*, 530). Marriott's naturalization is testified to by his neighbour Sir Walter Scott, who dedicated the introduction to the second canto of *Marmion* (1808) to his friend, celebrating their enjoyment of hunting and poetry. Intervals 'between each merry chase' were free from dullness:

> For we had fair resource in store,
> In Classic and in Gothic lore;
> We marked each memorable scene,
> And held poetic talk between.

Although Marriott disapproved of the introductory epistles he realized that his name stood 'a fair chance of riding down to posterity on the back of one of them' (Sharpe, 308).

Marriott's other claim to posterity's attention lies in his own writing. Fired by the enthusiasm in Scott's circle for ballads, he contributed three poems to the fourth volume of the *Minstrelsy of the Scottish Border*: 'The Feast of Spurs', 'On a Visit Paid to the Ruins of Melrose Abbey', and 'Archie Armstrong's Aith'. Southey describes in his *Common-Place Book* an evening in 1805 with Scott and Marriott reciting ballads. He did not realize that a 'deplorably bad business upon Purlin Jane' (p. 530) was Marriott's 'Pearlin Jean', in which a jilted girl's ghost takes revenge. This poem and others on Scottish subjects, and several letters by Marriott, are published in *Letters from and to Charles Kirkpatrick Sharpe*.

Marriott's tribute to Scott is his poem 'The Poet Released from the Law', which appeared in the *Edinburgh Annual Register, 1809* (1811), 652–3. Composed in 1806, the poem concludes:

Oh may it be my lot to wander near,
Some strains of his enchanting minstrelsy to hear!

That wish, and his intention to marry Mary Scott, of the Buccleuch family, and set up house with his pupil was foiled early in 1807 by a pulmonary disorder, which forced him to resign his post and retreat to Penzance. On 28 April 1807 he became rector of Church Lawford and Newnham Chapelry in Warwickshire, a benefice in the gift of the Buccleuch family. On 19 April 1808 he married Mary Anne Harris (*d*. 1821), daughter of a Rugby solicitor, Thomas Harris, and his wife, Ann Harrison. Her poor health caused them to move to Devon, where Marriott served as curate of St James, Exeter, St Lawrence, Exeter, and Broadclyst. During this time Marriott wrote several hymns, including 'Thou whose almighty word', 'A saint, O would that I could claim', and 'When Christ our human form did bear'. He also turned to secular verse, and wrote his best known poem, the gently satirical 'Devonshire Lane', which describes the narrowness and bumpiness of marriage. It is printed in several places, including Joanna Baillie's *Collection of Poems* (1823) and William Everitt's *Devonshire Scenery* (1884), which also contains 'A Devonshire Sketch'. The poems' merits are wit, humour, and intelligence, rather than metrical ingenuity or originality. A volume of Marriott's autograph poems is held by Exeter Central Library.

Marriott collected and published his sermons in 1818, and after his death his sons John and Charles edited another volume in 1838. His sympathies were with the low-church party. In the summer of 1824, being diagnosed with 'ossification of the brain' (*GM*, 1825), Marriott moved to London for medical treatment. He died there on 31 March 1825 and was interred in the burial-ground of St Giles-in-the-Fields adjacent to Old St Pancras Church. Marriott had five children: John, Thomas, Charles *Marriott (1811–1858), George, and Mary Ann.

W. P. COURTNEY, *rev.* BONNIE SHANNON MCMULLEN

Sources *Rugby School register*, 1: *From 1675 to 1849 inclusive* (1881) · Foster, *Alum. Oxon.* · *The letters of Sir Walter Scott*, ed. H. J. C. Grierson and others, centenary edn, 12 vols. (1932–79) · *GM*, 1st ser., 95/1 (1825), 571 · *GM*, 1st ser., 91/2 (1821), 477 · [C. K. Sharpe], *Letters from and to Charles Kirkpatrick Sharpe*, ed. A. Allardyce, 2 vols. (1888) · J. Julian, ed., *A dictionary of hymnology*, rev. edn (1907) · *Southey's common-place book*, ed. J. W. Warter, 4 (1851) · J. W. Burgon, 'Charles Marriott: the man of saintly life', *Lives of twelve good men*, [new edn], 1 (1888), 296–373 · R. W. Church, *The Oxford Movement: twelve years, 1833–1845* (1891) · *N&Q*, 7th ser., 8 (1889), 208, 277, 332–3 · *N&Q*, 7th ser., 9 (1890), 112 · Bodl. Oxf., MS Top. Oxon. e. 364, fol. 120

Archives NL Scot., letters, MS 865, fol. 70; MS 866, fol. 98; MSS 3878–3893 | Bodl. Oxf., MS Top. Oxon. e. 364, fol. 120 · Devon RO, corresp. with Sir T. D. Acland · JRL, letters to C. K. Sharpe

Marriott, Sir John Arthur Ransome (1859–1945), educationist and politician, was born at Bowdon, Cheshire, on 17 August 1859, the eldest son of Francis Marriott (1830?–

Sir John Arthur Ransome Marriott (1859–1945), by Howard Coster, 1940

1871), a solicitor in Manchester, and his wife, Elizabeth (1835?–1895), second daughter of Joseph Atkinson Ransome, surgeon to the Manchester Royal Infirmary. The Marriotts were from a line of minor landholders in Derbyshire. John Marriott was educated at Repton School (1872–8) and went up to New College, Oxford, in 1878. As an undergraduate he was active in the Canning Club, and took a second class in modern history in 1882. He was appointed lecturer in modern history at New College in 1883, and to a similar position at Worcester College shortly afterwards; he was elected fellow of Worcester College in 1914. Marriott helped to consolidate the modern history school in Oxford, but his major contribution to education dates from 1886, when he was recruited as an Oxford University extension lecturer by the secretary of the extension delegacy in Oxford, M. E. Sadler. Extension lecturers had been sent out by the university to give academic courses in provincial towns and cities in England since 1878. Marriott was immediately attracted to the work: he was a natural platform orator, able to hold large audiences. A tall man, of imposing bearing, his delivery was notable for characteristic gestures and the full sweep of his gown. His impact on individuals, such as the young Vera Brittain, who wrote about him in her *Testament of Youth* (1933), was often profound. He combined an extensive circuit of lectures outside Oxford with college tutorials.

In 1895 Marriott succeeded Sadler as secretary of the

Oxford extension delegacy, a position he only relinquished in 1920. Despite a slightly pompous exterior, he had a capacity for friendship, and was held in high regard by the lecturers he recruited. Marriott was more comfortable lecturing in county towns than in working-class communities. As a Conservative he was in a minority among the many extension lecturers who held progressive sympathies. This was inconsequential until the coincidence of two developments in the Edwardian period: the growth of a movement specifically for workers' education, and Marriott's growing commitment to politics. The foundation in 1903 of the Workers' Educational Association, and its development, in association with Oxford, of the first university tutorial classes, taught in 1908 by R. H. Tawney, not only undermined Marriott's position in the extension delegacy, but was opposed by him because intrinsically partisan. This led to his isolation, and Oxford's tutorial classes committee was established in independence of the existing extension administration. Marriott contributed to this isolation by presenting his political views in Conservative journals. Although sympathetic to the education of working people, he deprecated trade union activism, the growth of socialism, and measures after 1908 for public welfare. He was regarded by some students as 'an obscurantist and reactionary' (J. Marriott, 139) and his influence diminished. From 1910 he turned towards national affairs, especially maintenance of the union with Ireland.

Marriott had been adopted as a Conservative parliamentary candidate for East St Pancras in 1885, though he subsequently withdrew his candidacy. In the following year he was defeated in the general election as Conservative candidate for Rochdale. In 1914 he was defeated in a contest for the Conservative candidacy for the vacant Oxford University seat in parliament. But in March 1917 he was elected unopposed as Conservative MP for Oxford City, a beneficiary of the party-political truce under the wartime coalition. He was re-elected in the 'coupon' election of 1918, but defeated by the Liberal candidate in the general election of 1922. He returned to the Commons after the general election of 1923 as MP for York. There he was defeated in 1929 by a Labour candidate, and retired from active politics.

Marriott was an effective back-bencher, but his platform style was not well suited to parliamentary debate, and he entered the Commons at fifty-seven, which was too old for ministerial office. He was prominent on the select committee on national expenditure (1917–20), and as chairman of the select committee on estimates (1924–5), where he made the reduction of expenditure his concern. His academic work on British government made him an obvious member of the second chamber conference of 1917–18, which considered reform of the House of Lords: on this matter, at least, Marriott favoured change. He was notable as intermediary in negotiations between the coal owners, miners, and prime minister on 14 April 1921, the day before the triple alliance of unions broke down on 'black Friday'.

Marriott was a prolific historian. He began writing in the early years of the century, and in 1907 published his favourite book, *The Life and Times of Lucius Cary, Viscount Falkland*. Marriott, who saw himself as a political moderate and centrist, identified with Falkland's position between king and parliament in the early stages of the English civil war, and admired Falkland's many personal qualities. Of all his books, this received the greatest critical acclaim and popular approval. Thereafter, Marriott's work fell into four main divisions: books on modern English history, notably *England since Waterloo*, which went through thirteen editions between 1913 and 1946; on modern European history, among which *The Eastern Question: a Study in European Diplomacy* (1917) is accounted a classic; on the history of the empire, including *The Evolution of the British Empire and Commonwealth* (1939); and studies of political institutions, including *The Mechanism of the Modern State* (1927). Although he wrote biographies, Marriott's approach was not bound by the lives of great men: he favoured narrative political histories with attention to the interconnection of events and movements. These books owed much to his extension lectures: they presented complex historical questions for an educated but non-specialist audience.

Marriott married Henrietta Robinson, daughter of the Revd W. Percy Robinson, warden of Trinity College, Glenalmond, on 7 April 1891; they had one daughter, Elizabeth Dorothy Cicely (known as Cicely), who was born in 1892. Marriott was knighted in 1924, and he died at the Montpellier Hotel, Llandrinod Wells, on 6 June 1945.

LAWRENCE GOLDMAN

Sources J. Marriott, *Memories of four score years* (1946) · L. Goldman, *Dons and workers: Oxford and adult education since 1850* (1995) · S. Marriott, 'Marriott, John Arthur Ransome', *International biography of adult education*, ed. J. E. Thomas and B. Elsey (1985), 399–408 · V. Brittain, *Testament of youth* (1933) · G. G. R., *Oxford Magazine* (21 June 1945), 317–18 · *The Times* (8 June 1945) · *Rewley House Papers*, 2/9 (1946), 363–4 · *CGPLA Eng. & Wales* (1945)
Archives Oxon. RO, papers relating to his estate · York City Archives, corresp., literary MSS and papers | BL, corresp. with Albert Mansbridge, Add. MSS 65196, 65257A · Oxf. UA, department for continuing education
Likenesses photographs, c.1870–1938, repro. in Marriott, *Memories of four score years* · H. Coster, photograph, 1940, NPG [*see illus.*] · W. Stoneman, photograph, NPG · group photograph (the Joint Committee of Oxford University and working class representatives), Workers' Educational Association, Temple House, London
Wealth at death £200,694 12s. 7d.: probate, 4 Sept 1945, CGPLA Eng. & Wales

Marriott, Stephen Peter [Steve] (1947–1991), singer and guitarist, was born in East Ham Memorial Hospital, Essex, on 30 January 1947, the son of William James Bernard Marriott, electrical engineer, and his wife, Kathleen Beatrice, née Devo. At thirteen he made his West End stage début as the Artful Dodger in Lionel Bart's *Oliver!*, a part he played for one year. This disrupted his education at Sandringham secondary modern school, Manor Park, East Ham, Essex, from which he was expelled for setting fire to the woodwork room. He enrolled at the Italia Conti Drama School in Islington, London, and within months got his first television role in the BBC serial *Mr Pastry*, starring Richard Hearne. He subsequently appeared in the Sid James vehicle, *Citizen James*, and in *Dixon of Dock Green* with Jack Warner, and in the films *Heaven's Above* (1963), with Eric Sykes and Peter Sellers, and *Live it up* (1963) and *Be my Guest* (1965), both with David Hemmings.

Marriott played in a number of bands, including Steve Marriott and the Moments and Steve Marriott and the Frantic Ones, subsequently known as the Frantics. In 1965 he formed the Small Faces with Ronnie Lane (song-writer and bass), Jimmy Winston (keyboards), and Kenney Jones (drums). All four shared a love of the Kinks and the Beatles (John Lennon was a major influence on Marriott), rhythm and blues, and soul, and, as a sharply dressed East End mod band, were to be hailed as the mid-1960s equivalent of West End band the Who. The mods originated in the East End of London about 1963, and have been interpreted as a subculture responding to the contradictions facing young, upwardly mobile working-class men of that period. Typically engaged in semi-skilled manual work, or basic white-collar jobs, and attracted by the idea of 'swinging London', their short hair, well-cut suits, obsessive neatness, and narcissism have been seen as a parody of the consumer society in which they were situated. In a reaction against the music and style of the 'rockers'— whom they considered both dated and boorish—their stylistic influences included Tamla Motown, Jamaican bluebeat, and, later, American rhythm and blues.

The Small Faces (to be a 'face' was an accolade in mod parlance) initially toured clubs and pubs, playing cover versions of soul classics by artists such as James Brown, Bobby Bland, Otis Redding, and Wilson Pickett, and were spotted in London at the Cavern Club, Leicester Square, by the manager Don Arden. Licensed to the recording company Decca, their début single, 'Watcha Gonna Do About It?' was released in October 1965, and broke into the charts. Over the next three years the band dominated the British charts with hits such as 'Sha la la la Lee', 'Hey Girl', 'All or Nothing' (which was their first number one), and 'My Mind's Eye'. In 1967 they switched to Andrew Loog Oldham's Immediate label, and released 'Here Comes Nice', 'Itchycoo Park', 'Tin Soldier', and 'Lazy Sunday', followed by 'The Universal' in 1968. On 29 May 1968 Marriott married Jennifer Rylance (*b.* 1944/5), a model. The marriage ended in divorce.

Marriott's early experiences as a child actor and his love of soul, blues, and rhythm and blues were matched by a keen eye for observation. His ability to tap into a particularly English mentality and to fuse simple pop melodies with the 'in' sounds of the 1960s led to his recognition as one of the foremost pop composers of the decade. 'Lazy Sunday', for example, combines theatricality with a quirky humour ('Cor blimey, Mrs Jones, how's your Bert's lumbago?'), and provides a perceptive insight into contemporary drug culture (with which the band was heavily involved). 'Itchycoo Park' exemplifies the band's idiosyncratic use of phasing, while 'Tin Soldier', arguably the finest Marriott–Lane song of the period, is notable for its sinuous guitar riff, Hammond organ, and Marriott's powerful soul vocal. All were to influence the Britpop scene of the 1990s.

Marriott was frustrated by the labelling of the Small Faces as a chart singles band; their albums achieved little success until *Ogden's Nut Gone Flake*, which reached the top of the charts in 1968. It had a revolutionary, circular sleeve which became much sought after by collectors. Problems also arose over the band's inability to perform the more musically sophisticated songs live: of a disastrous attempt to play 'Itchycoo Park' at Alexandra Palace in 1969, Marriott recalled: 'It was a horrible mess—a nightmare. One of those gigs you dream about with your pants down. As the frontman I felt the nightmare more than anybody. I put my guitar down and walked off stage. I quit' (*The Independent*, 22 April 1991). Marriott left the Small Faces (who reformed as the Faces with Rod Stewart as their singer) to form Humble Pie with the singer and guitarist Pete Frampton, Jerry Shirley (drums), and Greg Ridley (bass). Their first two albums, *As Safe as Yesterday* and *Town and Country*, were overly influenced by the American group the Band, and their success came initially in the singles market with 'Natural Born Bugie'. *Humble Pie* (1970) moved towards a heavier rock feel and achieved a minor success in the United States, and the follow-up albums, *Rock on* (1971) and *Performance—Rockin' at the Fillmore* received international acclaim. Frampton then left the band, and was replaced by Dave Clempson, and Humble Pie moved towards an even heavier rock identity. The album *Smokin'* (1972) was joined in the charts by *Lost and Found and Eat it* (1973), a double set of part-live, part-studio work. By 1975, after twenty-two tours in the United States, and a non-stop round of parties, drugs, and drink, the band split up. Marriott played concerts with the All-Stars, before regrouping the Small Faces in 1977, without Ronnie Lane. They released two albums, *Playmates* (1977) and *78 in the Shade* (1978), but they had little success, and in 1980 Marriott reformed Humble Pie, releasing two albums, *On to Victory* and *Go for the Throat*. Then, after some years in obscurity, Marriott staged a comeback, with the power-rock trio Packet of Three, which became popular on the pub and club circuit, and fronting bands on the European circuit. Reunited with Peter Frampton, Marriott planned to reform Humble Pie, and had played a gig with Frampton in London before going to Los Angeles in 1991 to work on recording plans. However, he died in a fire at his home, Sextons, at Arkesden, near Saffron Walden, Essex, on 20 April 1991, survived by his second wife, Toni, whom he had married about 1988. Everything was destroyed, except his blond Gibson 335 guitar and his records, which were strangely untouched. The Small Faces hit 'All or Nothing' was played at his requiem, which was held on 4 May at the crematorium in Saffron Walden. SHEILA WHITELEY

Sources P. Hewitt, *Small Faces: the young mods' forgotten story* (1995) · C. Larkin, ed., *The Guinness encyclopedia of popular music*, concise edn (1993), 1620 · C. Welch, 'Steve Marriott', *The Independent* (22 April 1991), Gazette, 11 · C. Jones and A. Martin, 'All or nothing', *Mojo* (Dec 1994), 56–74 · *The Times* (22 April 1991) · D. Hebdige, *Subculture: the meaning of style* (1979) · G. Melly, *Revolt into style* (1972) · b. cert. · m. cert. [Jennifer Rylance]
Archives FILM BFI NFTVA, documentary footage · BFI NFTVA, performance footage | SOUND BL NSA, documentary footage · BL NSA, performance footage

Likenesses group photographs (with the Small Faces), Hult. Arch. • photographs, Hult. Arch.
Wealth at death under £125,000: administration, 17 March 1991, *CGPLA Eng. & Wales*

Marriott, Wharton Booth (1823–1871), schoolmaster, seventh son of George Wharton Marriott (1777/8–1833), barrister and magistrate at the Westminster police court, and his wife, Selina Anne, only child of Revd Fitzherbert Adams of Charwelton, Northamptonshire, and rector of Ulcombe, Kent, was born at 32 Queen Square, Bloomsbury, London, on 7 November 1823. Following the death of his father, friends paid for his education at Eton College, 1838–43. He was a scholar of Trinity College, Oxford, from 1843 to 1846, and an officer of the Union Society after taking a second in classics in 1847. He graduated BCL in 1851, MA in 1856, and BD in 1870. He was elected a Petrean fellow of Exeter College on 30 June 1846, but vacated his fellowship by marrying, on 22 April 1851, at Bletchingley, Surrey, Julia, youngest daughter of his godfather William Soltau of Clapham.

Marriott was ordained in 1849 by Bishop Wilberforce and intended to serve in Little Brickhill, Buckinghamshire, but instead took up an appointment as assistant master at Eton in 1850. He never held any benefice, but was a preacher by licence from the bishop in the diocese of Oxford. In 1853 he became a housemaster. He also found time for ministerial work among the poor, holding mission services on a Thames barge for those who would not go into a church. Marriott was on the board of guardians and worked for the Society for Improving the Dwellings of the Poor.

Marriott was influenced by his cousin, Charles Marriott, a fellow of Oriel and vicar of St Mary's and a leader in the Oxford Movement, but was not himself a party man. In 1865 the ritual controversy led him to the question of ecclesiastical ceremony and vestments. He published his opinions in *Vestiarium Christianum: the origin and gradual development of the dress of holy ministry in the church* (1868) and other works. In 1857–9 he wrote a series of letters on the eucharist in the *Clerical Journal*, and his correspondence with a friend, Revd Thomas Thellusson Carter, rector of Clewer, originating from the declaration issued in Oxford in 1866, was published in two parts, 1868–9.

Marriott enjoyed the study of language and the Bible. He planned and partly prepared a critical concordance to the New Testament in 1863. This was later set aside in favour of his antiquarian researches. He edited selections from Ovid and was a contributor to Smith's *Dictionary of Christian Antiquities*. On 30 May 1857 he was elected a fellow of the Society of Antiquaries, and a member of the council in 1871. After his resignation from Eton in 1860 due to ill health, Marriott became absorbed in his literary work and in preaching in his neighbouring church. He became select preacher in Oxford in 1868 and Grinfield lecturer on the Septuagint in 1871. Marriott delivered only one of these lectures, and, before he was able to take up his appointment as Bampton lecturer, died at Eton College on

16 December 1871. His funeral was conducted on 21 December by the dean of Windsor. His wife died in April of the following year.   ELLIE CLEWLOW

Sources *Memorials of the late Wharton Booth Marriott*, ed. F. J. A. Hort (1873) • Foster, *Alum. Oxon.* • C. W. Boase, ed., *Registrum Collegii Exoniensis*, new edn, OHS, 27 (1894) • *Proceedings of the Society of Antiquaries of London*, 2nd ser., 5 (1870–73), 309 • *Eton portrait gallery* (1876), 195–6
Likenesses J. Saddler, engraving (after a sketch by Severn), repro. in Hort, ed., *Memorials*
Wealth at death under £7000: probate, 15 March 1872, *CGPLA Eng. & Wales*

Marriott, William [John, Ben] (*d.* 1653), reputed gourmand and lawyer, was the son of John Marriott of Ashton, Northamptonshire. He is known variously as John (the name given him in the pamphlets which made him notorious) and Ben (the name under which he appears in the anecdotes retailed in Will Oldys's commonplace book in 1718). But it was as William Marriott, gentleman, that he was admitted to Gray's Inn on 3 August 1605. He was called to the bar there six years later, on 8 November 1611, and at the time of his death in 1653 was its eldest member.

Marriott was thrust into the public limelight in 1652 with the publication of a pamphlet entitled *The great eater of Graye's Inn, or, The life of Mr. Marriot the cormorant, wherein is set forth all the exploits and actions by him performed, with many pleasant stories of his travells into Kent and other places*. The author was listed only as 'G. F., gent.', but is now generally accepted to be George Fidge, writer of many titillating pamphlets. The forty-page work is highly entertaining and wholly libellous. Grotesque accounts of how Marriott devoured a meal for twenty men, voided a worm, and consumed dogs and monkeys baked in pies are all colourfully related. Outlandish recipes, claiming to be Marriott's own, form the latter section of the pamphlet. These recipes were reprinted separately in the same year under the title *The English Mountebank, or, A Physical Dispensatory*. Its purported author was J. Marriott himself. These, and the charge that Marriott knew 'better how to handle a chin of beef than a cause', provoked his friends to rise to his defence. *A letter to Mr. Marriot from a friend of his, wherein his name is redeemed from that detraction G. F., gent., hath endeavoured to fasten upon him by a scandalous and defamatory libel* was published 'for the friends of Mr. Marriott' in 1652. It deplored the 'libel of lies, scandal and defamation' of the previous works, and lauded Marriott as the 'most ancient' member of Gray's Inn whose forty-seven years' experience, abilities, and knowledge of the law were widely reputed.

This rebuttal was not sufficient to save Marriott's name from infamy. Charles Cotton's *Poems on Several Occasions* (1689) include two on Marriott, entitled 'The Greater Eater of Gray's Inn' and 'On Marriott'. Both revile the man and celebrate his death. Recording further Marriott lore, Oldys relates in his commonplace book how the infant Marriott 'sucked his Mother and a half dozen Nurses Dry' and how, at the age of fifteen, he 'could Master a Turkey at a Meal' (BL, Add. MS 4245, fol. 97r). Such tales made Marriott's name synonymous with gluttony, and John Dunton mentioned in his *Life and Errors* (1705) how the brisk New England air made him eat 'like a second Marriott' (Dunton, 90). The motivation for Fidge's original attack on Marriott is lost, though it is possible that he had either pecuniary gain or revenge for some ill deed in mind. There is little to suggest that the tales of Marriott had any foundation in fact. In spite of this, the pamphlet endured and was reprinted in a limited edition in 1871 'for subscribers only'. Marriott's burial in London on 25 November 1653 is recorded in Richard Smyth's *Obituary*. He died unmarried and, according to George Fidge, penniless.

ELEANOR O'KEEFFE

Sources *N&Q*, 2nd ser., 2 (1856), 6, 31–3 · G. F. gent. [G. Fidge], *The great eater of Graye's Inn, or, The life of Mr. Marriot the cormorant* (privately printed, London, 1652) · J. Marriott, *The English mountebank, or, A physical dispensatory* (1652) · *A letter to Mr Marriot from a friend of his* (1652) · C. Cotton, *Poems on several occasions* (1689), 349–417 · J. Granger, *A biographical history of England, from Egbert the Great to the revolution*, 2nd edn, 4 (1775), 242 · *The obituary of Richard Smyth … being a catalogue of all such persons as he knew in their life*, ed. H. Ellis, CS, 44 (1849) · J. Foster, *The register of admissions to Gray's Inn, 1521–1889, together with the register of marriages in Gray's Inn chapel, 1695–1754* (privately printed, London, 1889) · J. Dunton, *The life and errors of John Dunton … written by himself* (1705), 90 · R. J. Fletcher, ed., *The pension book of Gray's Inn*, 1 (1901), 195 · commonplace book of William Oldys, BL, Add. MS 4245, fol. 97r
Archives BL, Add. MS 4245
Wealth at death penniless in 1652: G. F., *The great eater of Graye's Inn*

Marriott, William Mark Noble (1848–1916), meteorologist, was born at 8 Church Terrace, Pancras Road, Camden Town, London, on 9 August 1848, the only child of William Marriott (*b*. 1821/2), dairyman, and his wife, Sarah (*b*. 1824/5), daughter of Mark Cordwell of Greenwich. He was educated at Colfe's Grammar School, Lewisham, and afterwards at University College, London. From 1869 to 1872 he was a supernumerary computer at the Royal Observatory, Greenwich, working under James Glaisher in the magnetical and meteorological department. Thereafter, from 1 May 1872 until he retired forty-three years later, he was employed as assistant secretary of the Meteorological (from 1883 Royal Meteorological) Society. He was elected a fellow of that society on 20 April 1870.

In his application for the post of assistant secretary, Marriott stated that he was well acquainted with meteorological work in all its branches and that he frequently compiled the Royal Observatory's weekly and quarterly meteorological reports. He also stated that he had a knowledge of French and had translated letters and other works for several gentlemen. He said he was not unacquainted with the duties of secretary, having served as secretary of the Greenwich Wesleyan Mutual Improvement Society for the previous three years.

Marriott married Jane Saunders Old, daughter of Peter Old, engineer, on 9 August 1875, coincidentally his twenty-seventh and her twenty-fourth birthday, and their only child, William James Marriott, was born on 1 June 1876. A year or two after his marriage he moved from Stockwell to Norwood, south-east London, where he lived until his death.

As assistant secretary Marriott was methodical, meticulous, efficient, and energetic. His manner was quiet, courteous, and unobtrusive, and the kindness of his heart showed in his unhesitating readiness to help anyone who consulted him. He was personally well known to most members of the society, in particular to those who maintained the society's observing stations and to whom he gave valuable hints and helpful advice as to the methods and instruments they should use. He was officially inspector of these stations from 1878 to 1911. He was also for many years official lecturer of the society, in which capacity he delivered more than a hundred popular lectures to schools and scientific societies in different parts of Britain. Whenever the society's council required a special investigation of a storm, frost, tornado, or, indeed, any other form of abnormal weather, they turned to Marriott to undertake the task. In the period 1876 to 1916, he wrote for the society no fewer than thirty reports on such weather events. He was a faithful and devoted servant, and it was due in no small measure to him that the society progressed and prospered during the time he was assistant secretary.

Marriott was a prolific author, with more than 100 publications to his name, many of them short articles published in the *Quarterly Journal of the Royal Meteorological Society*. Although he wrote on a wide range of meteorological subjects, the majority of his articles were concerned with abnormal weather, meteorological phenomena, instruments and their usage, or observations made at various places in the United Kingdom and overseas. He also wrote a number of obituaries and, in addition, compiled the mass of statistics published in the *Meteorological Record* from 1881 to 1911. The most substantial of his publications were his three books, *Hints to Meteorological Observers* (1881; 8th edn, 1924); *Some Facts about the Weather* (1906; 2nd edn, 1909); and *Our Weather* (1911), which he wrote with J. S. Fowler.

After he retired on 30 September 1915, Marriott continued to attend meetings of the Royal Meteorological Society. His retirement was, however, short, for he suffered a heart attack and died at Gipsy Hill railway station, London, on 28 December 1916.

J. MALCOLM WALKER

Sources *Quarterly Journal of the Royal Meteorological Society*, 43 (1917), 226 · *WWW*, 1916–28 · annual reports of the Meteorological (later Royal Meteorological) Society, *Quarterly Journal of the Royal Meteorological Society*, 1–42 (1872–1916) · letter of application from Marriott, addressed to Dr J. W. Tripe, president of the Meteorological Society, 25 March 1872, RMS archive · *British writers on meteorology prior to 1920*, Royal Meteorological Society (1986) · *CGPLA Eng. & Wales* (1917) · b. cert. · d. cert. · m. cert. · b. cert. [Jane Saunders Old]
Archives Meteorological Office, Bracknell, Berkshire, National Meteorological Library and Archive, letter-books as assistant secretary of Royal Meteorological Society
Likenesses portrait, repro. in *Quarterly Journal of the Royal Meteorological Society* (1917), pl. 21
Wealth at death £1646 13*s*. 4*d*.: probate, 21 April 1917, *CGPLA Eng. & Wales*

Marriott, Sir William Thackeray (1834–1903), lawyer and politician, was the third son of Christopher Marriott of Crumpsall, near Manchester, and his wife, Jane Dorothea, daughter of John Poole of Cornbrook Hall, near Manchester. He was admitted in 1854 to St John's College, Cambridge, where he spoke in undergraduate debates at the Union Society. He graduated BA in 1858, and was immediately ordained deacon, and appointed curate of St George's, Hulme, a mainly working-class parish. In 1859 he started the so-called Hulme Athenaeum, one of the first working-men's clubs established in England, whose members were all working men. In 1860 Marriott issued a pamphlet, *Some Real Wants and some Legitimate Claims of the Working Classes*, advocating parks, gymnasiums, and clubs for working people. A year later, when he was to have been ordained priest, he declined on conscientious grounds, giving his reasons in the preface to his farewell sermon, *What is Christianity?* (1862).

Renouncing clerical orders, Marriott became a student of Lincoln's Inn on 4 May 1861 and began writing for the press. He was called to the bar on 26 January 1864, and the following year published a pamphlet on the law relating to clerical disabilities. On 17 December 1872 he married Charlotte Louisa, the eldest daughter of Captain Tennant of the Royal Navy, whose home was Needwood House, Hampshire. Marriott's considerable rhetorical powers helped him quickly to acquire a lucrative practice in railway and compensation cases. He was made a QC on 13 February 1877, and was elected a bencher of Lincoln's Inn on 26 November 1879.

Like many rising lawyers, Marriott had political ambitions, and was elected Liberal member of parliament for Brighton on 5 April 1880. In his election address he described himself as a follower of Lord Hartington, then the official head of the Liberal Party. When Gladstone became prime minister, however, he became dissatisfied. He strongly opposed the government's proposal to remedy obstruction in the House of Commons by means of the closure, and on 30 March 1882 he moved an amendment to the closure resolution, which was defeated by 39 votes. In 1884 he published a pamphlet entitled *The Liberal Party and Mr Chamberlain*, a violent attack on what he regarded as the revolutionary radicalism of Joseph Chamberlain; there ensued an acrimonious personal controversy, which Marriott afterwards regretted. Meanwhile his alienation from the Liberal Party became complete. Repeated visits to Egypt confirmed his opinion of the disastrous consequences of Gladstone's Egyptian policy, which he denounced in an open letter to Lord Salisbury, entitled *Two Years of British Intervention in Egypt* (1884).

Marriott vacated his seat early in 1884, offered himself for re-election as a Conservative, and was elected (3 March 1884). On the accession of the Conservatives to office Marriott was made a privy councillor (9 July 1885), and was appointed judge-advocate-general in Lord Salisbury's first administration (15 July). He was again gazetted judge-advocate-general on 9 August 1886 in Lord Salisbury's second administration, and retained the office until 1892. He was knighted in 1888.

Marriott supported the Conservative cause with ardour.

He joined the grand council of the Primrose League, and in May 1892 he succeeded Sir Algernon Borthwick, Lord Glenesk, as chancellor of the league. He was also instrumental in organizing the monster petition against the Irish Home Rule Bill of 1893. In the same year he retired from parliament to resume practice at the parliamentary bar. He had been re-elected as a Conservative for Brighton at the general elections of 1885, 1886, and 1892. In 1887 and 1888 he had also acted as counsel for the former khedive Isma'il Pasha in settling claims for the arrears of his civil list against the Egyptian government. He persuaded the former khedive to moderate his demands, with the result that he secured for him compensation of £1.2 million. He was less successful in prosecuting similar claims of Zobehr Pasha, the Sudanese slave trader.

After retiring from parliament Marriott made an unfortunate financial speculation and on 3 May 1899 he obtained a judgment of £5000 and costs against a Mr Hooley. Later he migrated to South Africa where he carried on legal business at Johannesburg and acted as political adviser of the Dale Lacy party in opposition to Lord Milner's policy. He died at Aachen on 27 July 1903.

G. S. WOODS, *rev.* HUGH MOONEY

Sources *The Times* (30 July 1903) · *Morning Post* (30 July 1903) · *The Eagle*, 25 (1904), 73–6 · *Men and women of the time* (1899) · L. Stephen, *Life of Henry Fawcett* (1885), 29 · *Annual Register* (1888), 382

Archives PRO, corresp. with Sir Evelyn Baring concerning Khedival family affairs and Zobeir's case, FO 633

Likenesses T. Chartran, caricature, lithograph, NPG; repro. in *VF* (24 March 1883)

Wealth at death £189 14s. 3d.: probate, 30 June 1904, *CGPLA Eng. & Wales*

Marris, Sir William Sinclair (1873–1945), administrator in India, was born at Cookley, Worcestershire, on 9 October 1873, the eldest son of Charles Marris, chartered accountant, of Birmingham, and his wife, Jessie, daughter of Donald Sinclair MD, of London. When he was eleven years old his father's health made it necessary for the family to leave England and they went to Wanganui in New Zealand. There he was educated under an inspiring headmaster, and afterwards at Canterbury College in Christchurch, New Zealand. Recognizing his exceptional abilities, his family decided that he should return to England with a view to entering the Indian Civil Service, and after a year's preparation in London he took the first place by a very large margin in the examination of 1895. He spent his probationary year at Christ Church, Oxford, where he was awarded a scholarship, and in 1896 went out to the North-Western Provinces and Oudh, later the United Provinces of Agra and Oudh.

Marris soon made his mark, and in 1901 was appointed under-secretary to the government of India, home department, just when the government of India secretariat was at the height of its reputation under Lord Curzon, and in this stimulating atmosphere his unusual powers of thought and exact expression were soon recognized. In 1904 he became deputy secretary in the home department. On 27 April 1905 he married Eleanor Mary Eliza

(1880/81–1906), daughter of James Fergusson FRCSE, of Richmond, Surrey. Her death after only one year, when their son, Denzil, was born, cast a profound shadow over his life.

In 1906 Marris was lent to the government of the Transvaal (1906–8) to help in reorganizing the local civil service. There he came into close association with Milner's 'Kindergarten', particularly Lionel Curtis and Philip Kerr. Marris participated in the formation of the Round Table movement which aimed at imperial federation, and he argued the case for India's full participation in any imperial parliament.

After accompanying Curtis and Kerr to Canada in 1909 Marris returned to India in the following year where he served as collector of Aligarh (1910–14) and for a short period as inspector-general of police in the United Provinces. Towards the end of 1917 Marris went back to the home department of the government of India, this time as joint secretary, to assist with constitutional reform. E. S. Montagu, the secretary of state for India, arrived in India in November 1917 for discussions with a wide range of interested parties, after his famous declaration that year of the goal of responsible government for India within the empire. The Montagu–Chelmsford report was signed at Simla on 22 April 1918. During that period of little more than five months it was necessary to obtain opinion from many interests and different parts of India, to discuss a great variety of proposals, and to take crucial decisions. The drafting of the report had to proceed while inquiries were still being made and ideas were fluid. Marris was soon asked to undertake the task of drafting. This formidable task brought out many of his chief characteristics. His grasp of principle and power of exposition helped to win the report recognition as a great state paper. But he felt his personal responsibility as draftsman acutely. He remained doubtful whether India was really suited to Western political institutions, and feared that the pace of constitutional change was too fast. However, he was eager that the scheme should be the best that was practicable, and that the conditions and facts should be stated with scrupulous fairness. He thus came to exercise a marked influence on the proposals themselves, as well as on the method of their presentation.

Marris returned with Montagu to London for six months, and then after a rest became reforms commissioner with the government of India, having been appointed KCIE in January 1919. In January 1921 he was appointed KCSI and in March he was made governor of Assam. In December 1922 he succeeded Sir Harcourt Butler as governor of the United Provinces, a post which he held for five years. In strong contrast to his predecessor he was one of the least political of the governors under the new constitution. He did not have the experience of having rubbed shoulders with the Indian politicians in the legislatures, and the tone of his mind inclined him to prefer the written to the spoken approach.

Marris operated the system of diarchy in the new constitution much more rigidly than his predecessor had done, and allowed his Indian ministers no say in the 'reserved' half of the administration. At an early stage in his administration the Indian Liberal (moderate nationalist) ministers in his government resigned, and Marris was forced to rely thereafter on ministers drawn from the landlord interest, the most conservative element in the legislature. However, he proved himself quite willing to stand up to the landlords when necessary, as was shown by his perseverance with legislation to give life tenancy to non-occupancy tenants under the Agra Tenancy Act (1926), and his withdrawal of compensating legislation to ease revenue assessments when he felt that the landlords went too far in protecting their position. Marris was fortunate in that his government of the United Provinces coincided with a relatively quiet period, after the years of political turmoil and nationalist non-co-operation of 1920–22.

On completion of his governorship in 1928 Marris returned to England and was appointed a member of the secretary of state's council. A post more of dignity than of responsibility made little appeal to him, and in 1929 he was glad to accept the principalship of Armstrong College, Newcastle upon Tyne, in succession to his friend Sir Theodore Morison. He held this post until 1937 when the two Newcastle colleges were combined, as he had advocated. He was also vice-chancellor of Durham University between 1932 and 1934. On 16 July 1934 he married Elizabeth (Lizzie) Wilford (b. 1877/8), daughter of Dr Robert Charles Earle of Wanganui, New Zealand, and the former wife of Harry Edward Good, also of Wanganui, which marriage brought him great personal happiness.

During an exacting official life Marris found time to make translations of considerable merit from Horace (1912), Catullus (1924), and Homer (*Odyssey*, 1925; *Iliad*, 1934) into English verse. He also contributed to the *Oxford Book of Greek Verse in Translation*. He was a man whose great intellectual powers were always directed by an unswerving integrity. In his administration the intellectual side predominated. He grasped with great speed and certainty the essentials of a problem, but the impetus in matters of detail was of less interest to him. Although outwardly reserved, he was capable of great depth of feeling and could inspire strong friendships. He died at his home, Dollar House, Cirencester, Gloucestershire, on 13 December 1945. His wife survived him.

HARRY HAIG, *rev.* PHILIP WOODS

Sources *The Times* (14 Dec 1945) · *The Times* (11 Jan 1946) · E. S. Montagu, *An Indian diary*, ed. V. Montagu (1930) · P. Robb, 'The bureaucrat as reformer: two Indian civil servants and the constitution of 1919', *Rule, protest, identity: aspects of modern south Asia*, ed. P. G. Robb and D. Taylor (1978), 49–82 · L. Curtis, *Dyarchy* (1920) · P. Reeves, *Landlords and Governments in Uttar Pradesh: a study of their relations until zamindari abolition* (1991) · A. C. May, 'The Round Table, 1910–1966', DPhil diss., U. Oxf., 1995 · m. cert. · d. cert. · *CGPLA Eng. & Wales* (1946)

Archives BL OIOC, Chelmsford MSS · BL OIOC, Meston MSS · BL OIOC, Reading MSS · BL OIOC, letters to Sir Malcolm Seton, MSS Eur. E 267 · Bodl. Oxf., corresp. with L. G. Curtis; Round Table corresp. · NA Scot., corresp. with Lord Lothian

Wealth at death £73,492 13s. 6d.: probate, 22 March 1946, *CGPLA Eng. & Wales*

Marrowe, George (*fl.* **1437**), alchemist and Augustinian canon, is known only from a single tract preserved in two later transcripts, made from an 'anceynte booke written in parchment' which survive among the Ashmole manuscripts at the Bodleian Library. The earlier of these, in Bodleian, MS Ashmole 1423, was made in 1596 by Thomas Mountford, a London doctor and collector of alchemical manuscripts. The second, made in 1600 and found in MS Ashmole 1406 in Bodleian Library, is probably in the hand of another London doctor, Simon Forman (*d.* 1611), who had read and written his name into Mountford's text in 1598. The heading of Marrowe's treatise, which is dated 1437, states that he was a canon of Nostell Priory in Yorkshire. Monastic libraries were the traditional repositories of alchemical learning. Marrowe's tract is a record of alchemical practice, comprising sixty-two recipes, forty-seven in English, eleven in Latin, two in German, and one each in French and Italian, all making frequent use of the symbolic alphabet of the Hermetic vocabulary.

Later in the fifteenth century, probably after 1480, another monk, described only as Brandon, wrote a verse coda to the treatise, claiming that Marrowe had bestowed his receipts on him and setting him on a par with Lully (a mythologized Ramon Lull) and George Ripley. In fact, it is likely that Ripley, a fellow Augustinian from another Yorkshire house, Bridlington Priory, knew Marrowe personally; and it is possible that the title of one of Ripley's most famous works, *Medulla alchemiae* ('The marrow of alchemy'), was a deliberate play on words.

ANTHONY GROSS

Sources Bodl. Oxf., MS Ashmole 1406 art.iv, 2–35 · Bodl. Oxf., MS Ashmole 1423, 1–71 · L. M. Eldredge, *A handlist of manuscripts containing Middle English prose in the Ashmole collection, Bodleian Library, Oxford* (1992) · W. H. Black, *A descriptive, analytical and critical catalogue of the manuscripts bequeathed unto the University of Oxford by Elias Ashmole*, 2 vols. (1845–66)

Archives Bodl. Oxf., MSS Ashmole 1406, 1423

Marryat [*married names* Church, Lean], **Florence** (1837–1899), novelist, was born at Brighton, Sussex, on 9 July 1837, the youngest of eleven children of the novelist and naval officer Captain Frederick *Marryat (1792–1848) and his wife, Catherine (1791?–1882?), daughter of Sir Stephen Shairp of Houston, Linlithgowshire. She was educated at home and developed a love of reading, which she always maintained. Although her parents legally separated when she was an infant and her childhood was divided between them, she remained particularly devoted to her father and to his memory, reverting to his name professionally and naming her oldest son after him. On 13 June 1854, when she was sixteen, she married, at Penang, Malaya, Thomas Ross Church (1831–1926), a career officer in the Madras staff corps of the British army in India; with him she travelled over nearly the whole of India, before returning to England in 1860. Marryat and Church had children (seven of whom survived to adulthood) but divorced in 1879. On 5 June 1879 she married her second husband, Colonel Francis Lean (1832?–1902), an officer in the Royal Marine light infantry. Both Church and Lean survived her, though she mentioned neither in her will.

Marryat wrote her first novel, *Love's Conflict* (1865), to distract her mind while nursing her children with scarlet fever. Between then and the year of her death she published over seventy-five novels, primarily popular romances for women, many of which were translated into German, French, Swedish, Flemish, and Russian. Her books were popular in the United States, though she received few American royalties because the lack of international copyright laws allowed American publishers to pirate her work freely. Because she was a popular contributor to the subscription-based lending libraries, many of her novels were published in the three-volume format prescribed by the libraries. While most of her heroines superficially conform to Victorian feminine paradigms, she advocated that women should be capable of earning their own livings within the context of femininity; her heroines are often strong-minded, independent working women—actresses, writers, teachers, nurses, and, in one instance, even an estate manager.

Between 1872 and 1876 Marryat edited the monthly periodical *London Society*, which featured engravings and light literature aimed at the middle and upper classes. In 1872 she published in two volumes the *Life and Letters of Captain Marryat*; while it does not present a complete portrait of her father, the memoir does give details of their family life. A convert to Roman Catholicism, in her later years, she was attracted to spiritualism, a fascination sanctioned by her spiritual director, Father Dalgairns of the Brompton Oratory in London. *There is No Death* (1891) gives a detailed account of the various mediums with whom she came in contact and of the séances she attended. *The Risen Dead* (1893) and *The Spirit World* (1894), as well as several of her novels, deal with the subject. Other non-fiction works include *Tom Tiddler's Ground* (1886), an account of her travels in the United States, and *Gup* (1868), sketches of garrison life in India.

A woman of varied accomplishments, Marryat added to the roles of author and novelist those of playwright, comedy actress, operatic singer, lecturer, and entertainer; she also managed a school of journalism. At the age of forty-three, on the advice of her doctors following a lengthy illness, she became an actress, performing in a drama that she had written entitled *Her World Against a Lie*, produced in London in 1881. Marryat died at St John's Wood, London, where she lived, on 27 October 1899, leaving her assets to two of her children and to a close male companion. She was buried at Kensal Green cemetery in London.

JEAN G. NEISIUS

Sources DNB · PRO, St Catherine's House, London · Principal Registry of the Family Division, London · military records, PRO · *New York Times* (28 Oct 1899) · letters, U. Texas · letters, BL · *Life and letters of Captain Marryat*, ed. F. Marryat, 2 vols. (1872) · V. D. Dickerson, 'Marryat, Florence (1838–1899)', *Victorian Britain: an encyclopedia*, ed. S. Mitchell (1988), 479–80 · C. J. Hamilton, 'Florence Marryat', *Womanhood*, 3 (1900), 2–4 · Allibone, *Dict.* · F. Hays, 'Marryat, Florence (Mrs. Francis Lean)', *Women of the day: a biographical dictionary of notable contemporaries* (1885), 127 · H. C. Black, *Notable women authors of the day* (1893) · CGPLA Eng. & Wales (1899) · will [proved 25 Nov 1899]

Archives BL, novels, letters · U. Texas, novels, letters

Likenesses A. Weger, stipple, NPG · photograph, NPG
Wealth at death £1479 16s. 8d.: probate, 25 Nov 1899, *CGPLA Eng. & Wales*

Marryat, Frederick (1792–1848), naval officer and novelist, was born at Catherine Court, Tower Hill, London, on 10 July 1792. Of Huguenot descent, he was the second son of Joseph Marryat of Wimbledon, who was MP for Sandwich, chairman of Lloyd's, and colonial agent for the island of Grenada; Frederick's mother, Charlotte, daughter of Frederick Geyer of Boston, Massachusetts, was of German origin. He received his early education at private schools, one of which was at Ponder's End, Middlesex. His boisterous temperament brought him into repeated trouble and several times he ran away, always with the intention of escaping to sea. At last, in September 1806, his father got him entered on board the frigate *Impérieuse*, commanded by Lord Cochrane. The service of the *Impérieuse* was exceptionally active and brilliant, not only in its almost daily episodes of cutting out coasting vessels or privateers, storming batteries, and destroying telegraph stations, but also in the defence of the castle of Trinidad, near Rosas on the east coast of Spain, in November 1808, and in the attack on the French fleet in Basque Roads in April 1809. The daring and judgement of Cochrane were subsequently reproduced in Captain Savage of the *Diomede* in *Peter Simple* and Captain M—— in *The King's Own*. In June the *Impérieuse* sailed with the fleet on the Walcheren expedition, from which, in October, Marryat was invalided with fever. Before leaving the vessel he had formed friendships with William Napier and Houston Stewart which lasted life long. In 1810 he served in the *Centaur*, flagship of Sir Samuel Hood in the Mediterranean, and in 1811 was in the *Aeolus* in the West Indies and on the coast of North America. He was afterwards in the *Spartan* (Captain E. P. Brenton) on the same station, and was sent home in the sloop *Indian* in September 1812.

On 26 December 1812 Marryat was promoted to the rank of lieutenant, and in January 1813 was again sent out to the West Indies in the sloop *Espiègle*. From her he was invalided in April, and though in 1814 he returned to the coast of North America as lieutenant of the frigate *Newcastle*, and assisted in the capture of several enemy merchant ships and privateers, his health gave way, and he went home in the spring of 1815. On 13 June he was made commander.

In January 1819 Marryat married Catherine (1791?–1882?), second daughter of Sir Stephen Shairp of Houston, Linlithgowshire, for many years consul-general in Russia. They had four sons and seven daughters before they separated in 1843. Marryat outlived all of his sons except the youngest, Frank, favourably known as the author of *Borneo and the Indian Archipelago* (1848) and *Mountains and Molehills, or, Recollections of a Burnt Journal* (1855), who died aged twenty-eight in 1855. Three of his daughters—most successfully Florence *Marryat—were novelists.

In June 1820 Marryat was appointed to the sloop *Beaver*, which was employed on the St Helena station until the death of Napoleon, when he came home in the *Rosario* with dispatches. The *Rosario* was afterwards employed in

Frederick Marryat (1792–1848), by John Simpson, in or before 1826

the channel for the prevention of smuggling, and was paid off in February 1822. Marryat's pamphlet published in 1822 attacking impressment injured his career and earned him the hostility of the duke of Clarence (later William IV).

In March 1823 Marryat commissioned the *Larne* for service in the East Indies, where he took an active part in the First Anglo-Burmese War. From May to September 1824 he was senior naval officer at Rangoon, and was officially thanked for his able and gallant co-operation with the troops. He was the first Royal Navy officer to use a steamship in wartime. The very sickly state of his ship obliged him to go to Penang, but by the end of December he was back at Rangoon, and in February 1825 he had the naval command of an expedition up the Bassein River, which occupied Bassein and seized the enemy magazines. In April 1825 he was appointed captain of the *Tees*, in which in early 1826 he returned to England, and on 26 December 1826 he was nominated a CB. In November 1828 he was appointed to the *Ariadne*, which he commanded at the Azores or at Madeira until November 1830, when he hotheadedly resigned on the nominal grounds of 'private affairs'.

Marryat was known hitherto as a distinguished naval officer. He was made a CB because of his conduct in Burma, and in 1818 was awarded the gold medal of the Royal Humane Society for his gallantry in saving life at sea, in addition to which he held certificates of having saved upwards of a dozen people by jumping overboard to help them, often endangering his own life. He was also elected a fellow of the Royal Society in 1819, having been proposed by his schoolfriend Charles Babbage, mainly in recognition of his adaptation of Sir Home Popham's signalling system to a code for the mercantile marine (1817). This earned him a large and regular income and, some years later (19 June 1833), membership of the Légion d'honneur.

In the meantime, while still in the *Ariadne*, Marryat wrote and in 1829 published a three-volume novel, *The Naval Officer, or, Scenes and Adventures in the Life of Frank Mildmay*, for which he received immediate payment of £400. The vivid and lifelike narrative of naval adventure, much of which he had experienced, took the public by storm: the book was a literary and financial success. He had already written *The King's Own* (published in 1830), and, having settled down to his new profession of literature, he rapidly produced *Newton Forster* (1832); *Peter Simple* and *Jacob Faithful* (both 1834); *The Pacha of many Tales* (1835); *Mr. Midshipman Easy, Japhet in Search of a Father, The Pirate and the Three Cutters* (all 1836); *Snarleyyow, or, The Dog Fiend* (1837); *The Phantom Ship* (1839); *Poor Jack* (1840); *Joseph Rushbrook, or, The Poacher* (1841); *Percival Keene* (1842); *The Privateer's Man* (1846); and *Valerie*, published, after his death, in 1849.

But novel-writing was not Marryat's only literary work. From 1832 to 1835 he edited the liberal/radical journal the *Metropolitan Magazine*, and kept up a close connection with it for a year longer. In it most of his best novels first appeared: *Newton Forster, Peter Simple, Jacob Faithful, Midshipman Easy*, and *Japhet*, and, besides these, many miscellaneous articles afterwards published collectively as *Olla Podrida* (1840). In 1836 he lived abroad, principally at Brussels, where he was popular as he spoke French fluently and was full of humorous stories. He spent 1837 and 1838 in Canada and the United States, his impressions of which he published as *A Diary in America, with Remarks on its Institutions* (1839).

After his return from America at the beginning of 1839 Marryat lived mainly in London or Wimbledon until his marriage broke down in 1843; he finally settled at Langham, in Norfolk, on a small farm that had been his for thirteen years but had brought in little rent. Notwithstanding a patrimony in excess of half a million pounds and the large sums he made by his novels, he seems to have been permanently short of money, owing partly to the ruin of his West Indian property, and partly to his own extravagance and carelessness. When in need of ready cash he drew cartoons, which were made into etchings by his friend George Cruikshank. When the readiness with which he had poured out novels of sea life at the rate of as many as three a year began to fail, he found a new source of profit in his popular books for children. He devoted himself chiefly to these during his last eight years. The series opened with *Masterman Ready, or, The Wreck of the Pacific* (1841) and continued with *Narrative of the travels and adventures of Monsieur Violet in California, Sonora, and western Texas* (1843), *The Settlers in Canada* (1844), *The Mission, or, Scenes in Africa* (1845), *The Children of the New Forest* (1847), and *The Little Savage* (1848–9, probably finished by Frank Marryat).

The work told on Marryat's health, which was never very strong. He imagined that a change of occupation and

scene might re-establish it, and in July 1847 applied for service afloat. The Admiralty's refusal to entertain his application so angered him that he broke a blood-vessel of the lungs. For six months he was seriously ill, and was barely recovering when the news of the death of his eldest son, Frederick, lost on the *Avenger* on 20 December 1847, gave him a shock that proved fatal. He died at Langham on 9 August 1848.

As a writer Marryat has been variously judged. He wrote quickly and often carelessly and was complained at by the critics, but his position as a story-teller was assured. He drew the material of his stories from his professional experience and knowledge: the terrible shipwreck, for instance, in *The King's Own* is a coloured version of the loss of the *Droits de l'homme*, while *Frank Mildmay* was avowedly autobiographical. Marryat made his sailors live, and in this and his robust sense of fun and humour lay the secret of his success, for, with the exception perhaps of *The King's Own*, his plots were poor, relying on lost heirs and other artificial narrative devices. His children's stories have held their place and several have been filmed. He also published several caricatures, both political and social.

J. K. LAUGHTON, rev. ANDREW LAMBERT

Sources C. Lloyd, *Captain Marryat and the old navy* (1939) • O. Warner, *Captain Marryat* (1953) • A. D. Lambert, *The last sailing battlefleet: maintaining naval mastery, 1815–1850* (1991)
Archives BL, letters, RP2340 • NMM, corresp. and papers • Norfolk RO, farming and household accounts | BL, letters to Edward Howard, RP1299 [copies] • BL, letters to Royal Literary Fund, loan 96
Likenesses J. Simpson, oils, in or before 1826, NPG [see illus.] • line engraving, pubd 1826, BM • E. Dixon, oils, exh. RA 1839, NMM • Count D'Orsay, portrait, 1841, repro. in Lloyd, *Captain Marryat* • Count D'Orsay, portrait, 1841, repro. in Warner, *Captain Marryat* • H. Cook, stipple (after W. Behnes), BM, NPG • R. J. Lane, lithograph (after Count D'Orsay), NPG • F. Marryat, self-portrait, repro. in Lloyd, *Captain Marryat* • F. Marryat, self-portrait, repro. in Warner, *Captain Marryat*

Marryat, George Selwyn (1840–1896), angler, was born on 20 June 1840 at Chewton Glen, Milton, Hampshire, the second of the eight children of Lieutenant-Colonel George Marryat and Georgiana Charlotte, *née* Selwin, and nephew to the author Frederick *Marryat. By 1854 the family had moved to Mapperton House, Dorset, and George Marryat's passion for fly-fishing first blossomed on the River Frome at Maiden Newton in Dorset. After his education at Winchester College (1854–7) his family bought him a commission in the 6th dragoon guards (the carabiniers). He served in India (1859–61) and after deployment on the subcontinent his regiment returned to England, where Marryat received his promotion to second lieutenant on 28 January 1862. After resigning and selling his commission in 1864 he travelled to Australia, where he became a stock rider in the bush.

Marryat returned to his homeland after a sojourn of about five years. He was living in Edinburgh by about 1872, probably the year in which he married Lucy Dorothea, *née* Clinton (1843–1911), daughter of Colonel Frederick Clinton of Ashley Clinton, in Hampshire. They moved back to Hampshire at the end of 1874, and settled at Shidfield

(Shedfield), Hampshire. Over the next five years they had three daughters.

While at Winchester College Marryat had fished on the River Itchen, at a time when the dry fly was the established way to catch trout. Following his return from Australia he became the most expert and celebrated dry-fly fisherman on the southern chalk streams. A chance meeting in April 1879 between Marryat and Frederic Michael Halford, in the hut by the Sheepbridge shallows on the River Test in Hampshire, formed a fishing partnership that has not been equalled. Halford had admitted to Marryat his many shortcomings with tying artificial flies; Marryat resolved to help in any way he could. The partnership produced two very significant books, *Floating Flies and How to Dress Them* (1886) and *Dry Fly Fishing in Theory and Practice* (1889). Without Marryat's input it is arguable that Halford would not have written them; but Marryat refused Halford's request to become co-author on the ground that 'it would be impracticable to have two writers'. His only known publications were two letters, one in *The Field* of 8 January 1881, entitled 'Quill bodies for flies', and one in the *Fishing Gazette* of 28 June 1884, entitled 'Who invented dry-fly fishing?'. Marryat conducted much of the early fieldwork on the development of the up-eyed 'Snecky Limerick' hook and the new methods of dressing the artificial split-winged dry flies on these new hooks, working closely with Henry Sinclair Hall.

By 1885 Marryat and his family had moved to the cathedral close in Salisbury, Wiltshire. It was here that he did his most important work on the entomology of the fly-fisherman's natural insect and its matching artificial fly. An accomplished fly-dresser, amateur photographer, and microscope-user, he linked the last two enthusiasms in his fascination for karyokinesis (cell division). He had endless patience, setting about all this research and documentation with a will that was typical of the Victorian country gentleman. He was modest by nature, but widely read, knowing his Shakespeare almost by heart. Marryat could be the life and soul of the party when in the right company, but did not suffer fools gladly.

Marryat died on 14 February 1896; he suffered influenza followed by a coma, and finally succumbed to a stroke. He was cremated four days later and his ashes were scattered beneath the cedar trees in the cloisters of Salisbury Cathedral. The dry-fly discipline today would not be as complete without Marryat's mastery. He died leaving behind him the most uncontested reputation in the history of trout fly-fishing.   SIMON J. WARD

Sources F. Francis, 'A Christmas maunder anent grayling, etc.', *The Field* (25 Dec 1880), 928 · R. Spinner, 'George Selwyn Marryat: in memoriam', *The Field* (22 Feb 1896), 280 · Red Spinner of *The Field* [W. Senior], W. G. Turle, H. S. Hall, and R. B. Marston, 'Some reminiscences of George Selwyn Marryat', *Fishing Gazette* (29 Feb 1896), 150–53 · Major Carlisle, 'The late Mr G. S. Marryat', *Fishing Gazette* (7 March 1896), 168 · T. Sanctuary, 'Stray memories of Selwyn Marryat', *The Field* (7 March 1896) · C. F. Walker, *Fly tying as an art* (1957), chap. 3 · private knowledge (2004) · b. cert. · Winchester College, archives · d. cert. · T. Hayter, *F. M. Halford and the dry-fly revolution* (2002)

Archives priv. coll., box of self-dressed dry flies | priv. coll., books inscribed by M. Halford

Likenesses photograph, repro. in F. M. Halford, *An angler's autobiography* (1903) · photograph, repro. in *Fishing Gazette* (29 Feb 1896) · photograph, repro. in Hayter, *F. M. Halford and the dry-fly revolution*

Wealth at death £1474 6s. 0d.: probate, 31 March 1896, *CGPLA Eng. & Wales*

Marryat, Thomas (1730–1792), physician, born in London, was descended from a Huguenot family and was educated for the Presbyterian ministry. He possessed great natural talents, a brilliant memory, and a love for literature. His appearance was, to say the least, plain, but his wit, though frequently coarse, was irresistible. From 1747 until 1749 he belonged to a poetical club which met at the Robin Hood, Butcher Row, the Strand, every Wednesday at five in the afternoon, and seldom parted until five the next morning. Among its members were Dr Richard Brookes, Moses Browne, Stephen Duck, Martin Madan, and Thomas Madox. Each member brought a piece of poetry, which was corrected and, if approved, thrown into the treasury from which the wants of the *Gentleman's Magazine* and other periodicals were supplied. A supper and trials of wit followed; Marryat, whom Brookes nicknamed 'Sal Volatile', frequently kept the table amused, though he was never known to laugh himself.

In 1754 Marryat was ordained a minister at Southwold, Suffolk. He married Sarah, the daughter of John Davy of Southwold; their first son, Joseph, father of the novelist Frederick Marryat, was born there on 8 October 1757. Marryat published his *Medical Aphorisms* in 1756 or 1757. This was followed by his *Therapeutics, a New Practice of Physic*, published in Latin in 1758. It was re-titled *The Art of Healing* for a pocket edition. Marryat gave up the ministry in 1760, but there is no evidence to support the claim that he studied medicine at Edinburgh University. It is said that for a while he sought practice in London, and that in 1762 he made a tour of continental medical schools, and subsequently visited America, obtaining practice where he could.

On his return to the British Isles in 1766 Marryat resided for several years in co. Antrim and the northern parts of Ireland. Here he set aside two hours every day to non-paying patients, allowing him to test his medicines on them; in this he tended to administer enormous doses of drastic medicines regardless of the patient's constitution. For dysentery his favourite prescription was paper boiled in milk. The poor, however, maintained a high regard for his skills as a doctor. In February 1774 Marryat moved to Shrewsbury, but finally settled in Bristol about 1785. Here he delivered a course of lectures on therapeutics which was well attended. He also published a book called *The Philosophy of Masons* (1790), a work that contained views which managed to offend even his best friends. Although his good fortune in restoring to health some patients who had been given up by other doctors gained him a reputation that quickly enabled him to achieve a good lifestyle, his improvident habits eventually reduced him to poverty. When Marryat found his friends deserting him, he fixed a note on the window of The Bush coffee-room,

Thomas Marryat
(1730–1792), by
unknown engraver

enquiring 'if any one remembered that there was such a person as Thomas Marryat' and reminding them that he 'still lived, or rather existed, in Horfield Road' (Marryat, xi). Despite his distress, however, he persistently refused assistance from his relatives. In 1791 he published a new edition of his *Sentimental Fables for the Ladies*. Dedicated to Hannah More they had originally been published in Ireland.

Marryat's manners were disagreeably blunt, and towards the end of his life he became morose; but he is represented as a man of integrity and of genuine kindness, especially to the poor. He died in Bristol on 29 May 1792, and was buried in the ground belonging to the Presbyterian chapel in Lewin's Mead, Brunswick Square, Bristol.   GORDON GOODWIN, rev. MICHAEL BEVAN

Sources T. Marryat, preface, *Therapeutics, or, The art of healing*, 21st edn (1806) · 'Marryat, Joseph', HoP, *Commons* · Watt, *Bibl. Brit.* · *Nomina eorum, qui gradum medicinae doctoris in academia Jacobi sexti Scotorum regis, quae Edinburgi est, adepti sunt, ab anno 1705 ad annum 1845*, University of Edinburgh (1846)

Likenesses Johnson, stipple, 1865, Wellcome L. · engraving, AM Oxf. [*see illus.*]

Marryott, Matthew (*bap.* **1670**, *d.* **1731/2**), workhouse promoter and contractor, was born in Olney, Buckinghamshire, where he was baptized on 18 September 1670, the son of Matthew Marryott. The younger Matthew described himself as a yeoman. He is recorded as the father of two children, Elizabeth (*b.* 1695) and John (*b.* 1699). In November 1700 he married Anne Hinde, who was probably his second wife. Anne actively assisted her husband throughout his involvement in the management of workhouses and working charity schools until her death about 1731.

Marryott first comes to prominence as a participant in the discussions leading to the establishment of what is arguably the first characteristically eighteenth-century parochial workhouse, founded at Olney in 1714. From a base in Olney, Marryott became involved in a range of local institutions. In particular, he was instrumental in the running of the working charity school at Artleborough, near Kettering, Northamptonshire, and was probably involved in a series of workhouses set up between 1718 and 1723 in the east midlands, in the vicinity of Olney. It was as a result of his role in the working school at Artleborough that he first came to the notice of the SPCK.

By 1720 Marryott was running a new workhouse established at Hemel Hempstead, Hertfordshire, and during the next seven years he took over the management and supply of a range of new workhouses established in London, Middlesex, and Hertfordshire. By 1727 he can be identified as running, or having run, workhouses at Greenwich, Luton, Peterborough, Putney, Tring, and Watford, and in the parishes of St George, Hanover Square, St James, St Margaret, and St Martin-in-the-Fields in Westminster, and St Giles-in-the-Fields, St Leonard, Shoreditch, and St Mary, Harrow on the Hill, in Middlesex. His normal procedure was to contract for the care of the poor to be housed and employed in a building supplied by the parish. He then installed an assistant to take care of the day-to-day management, and would also contract for the supply of furniture, clothing, and foodstuffs. By the mid-1720s Marryott was by far and away the most successful and important of the three or four individuals who were actively seeking to contract for workhouse management in this period.

During this same decade Marryott also built up a substantial relationship with the SPCK. The society transferred its attention from charity schools to workhouses in the late 1710s, and made extensive use of Marryott as an adviser on workhouse management. It was through the SPCK that he was regularly put in contact with parishes seeking to establish workhouses or seeking the recommendation of an appropriate workhouse master. It was also through the society's publication of *An Account of Several Work-Houses* (1725) that Marryott's activities were brought to the attention of the reading public.

In many respects Marryott's active entrepreneurial approach to the running of workhouses allowed isolated parishes, normally dependent on the work of unpaid parish officers, to establish sophisticated bureaucratic systems for the control of their poor-relief expenditure. For many communities Marryott was their first regular paid employee, and to this extent his activities represent an important transition in the nature of English local government. But more than this, Marryott was instrumental in the creation of the notion of a 'workhouse test'. From his involvement with the house at Hemel Hempstead onwards, he always insisted that poor relief should be denied to any applicant who refused the offer of a place in the workhouse. And there is some evidence to suggest that it was Marryott's example and practice which contributed to the passage of the Workhouse Test Act of 1723 (9 Geo. I c. 7). A pamphlet published two years after it became law suggested that 'it was, in some measure owing to … [Marryott] that the legislature passed the Act' (*The Case of the Parish of St Giles in the Fields*, 14). It should be noted, however, that the pamphlet from which this quotation is drawn, and one published the following year, *A Representation of some Mis-Managements by Parish-Officers* (1726), are so self-serving as to suggest that Matthew Marryott himself was substantially responsible for their drafting and publication.

By the second half of the 1720s, however, Marryott had substantially overreached himself. In 1726 the SPCK complained about the excessive charges that he was making for training provincial workhouse masters, and from that date the society increasingly distanced itself from his activities. And during 1727 he lost his contracts for the management of the four large workhouses he was then managing in Westminster. The vestry of St Martin-in-the-Fields noted that since Marryott had 'under his care and management other workhouses, that he did not nor could not give such attendance at and take such care of the workhouse of this parish as was and is necessary and requisite' ('St Martins-in-the-Fields, Westminster, Vestry minutes, 1716–1739', Westminster Archive Centre, MS F2006, 289).

The last straw came with the anonymous publication of *The Workhouse Cruelty, Workhouses Turn'd Gaols and Gaolers Executioners* (1731). This pamphlet accused Marryott of mistreating a series of inmates of the workhouse belonging to St Giles-in-the-Fields, and of directly contributing to the death of one, Mary Whistle, by confining her to a 'black hole' for long periods without food or water. An investigation into conditions in the workhouse was undertaken, and Mary Whistle's body was subjected to an exhaustive autopsy, but no evidence of deliberate cruelty and culpability was established. In combination with earlier accusations that Marryott had allowed the bodies of workhouse inmates to be illegally used in the creation of anatomical specimens, this signalled the end of Marryott's involvement with workhouses in London. He died in the parish of St Giles-in-the-Fields between 27 November 1731 and 26 January 1732, and was survived by his daughter, Elizabeth Stanton. He was buried at the parish church in Olney and left a substantial estate, composed primarily of agricultural land in north Buckinghamshire.

TIM HITCHCOCK

Sources T. Hitchcock, 'Paupers and preachers: the SPCK and the parochial workhouse movement', *Stilling the grumbling hive: the response to social and economic problems in England, 1689–1750*, ed. L. Davison, T. Hitchcock, T. Keirn, and R. B. Shoemaker (1992), 145–66 • T. Hitchcock, 'The English workhouse: a study in institutional poor relief in selected counties, 1696–1750', DPhil diss., U. Oxf., 1985 • L. W. Cowie, *Henry Newman: an American in London, 1708–43* (1956) • *A representation of some mis-managements by parish-officers in the method at present followed for maintaining the poor* (1726) • *An account of several work-houses for employing and maintaining the poor* (1725) • *The case of the parish of St Giles in the Fields as to their poor and a work-house designed to be built for employing them* (1725) • M. G. Jones, *The charity school movement: a study in eighteenth century puritanism in action* (1938) • J. Simon, 'From charity school to workhouse in the 1720s: the SPCK and Mr Marriott's solution', *History of Education*, 27 (1998), 113–29 • *IGI* [registers of Olney, Buckinghamshire] • will, PRO, PROB 11/649, fols. 142–4

Wealth at death at least several hundred pounds in land in Buckinghamshire: will, PRO, PROB 11/649, fols. 142–4

Mars, Forrest Edward (1904–1999), confectionery manufacturer, was born in Tacoma, Washington, USA, the only son of Franklin (Frank) C. Mars (1883–1934), a confectionery maker, and his first wife, Ethel (*née* Kissack), whom he

had married in 1902. Following his parents' divorce in 1910, Mars was sent to live with his maternal grandparents in Saskatchewan and knew his father only as 'that miserable failure' with three business defeats under his belt. Frank Mars's reputation as a loser was pressed upon Forrest and he was urged to improve on his father's efforts. At Lethbridge high school in Alberta he proved an industrious pupil, and while the majority of his classmates were being recruited by local mining and timber companies he remained there until graduation in 1922, when he was awarded a partial scholarship to study mining engineering at the University of California at Berkeley.

While at Berkeley Mars discovered his entrepreneurial muscle. By 1923 he was regularly making $100 a week by renegotiating wholesale meat prices for the campus kitchens, and that summer he joined a sales force for Camel Cigarettes, plastering their posters all over Chicago's State Street. His unorthodox sales pitch made the city news but also saw him in gaol. Frank Mars, no longer a failure but president of the Mar-O-Bar Company, learned of his son's scrape and went to bail him out. Although the two men had last been in contact when Forrest was six years old, within a short time Forrest had changed the future course of his father's business by giving him the idea of putting a chocolate malted drink into a chocolate bar. This new confection, the Milky Way, was to blaze a trail for Mars as first-year sales approached $800,000. Although Mars returned to Berkeley after the summer break of 1924, by the following year he had transferred to Yale to study commerce. There he read all he could on corporate wire pulling so that by the time he graduated in 1928 he felt ready to enter the world of business.

After Yale Mars joined his father's Chicago-based company, renamed Mars Inc. Yet by 1932 father and son were at odds over the future direction of the company. Frank Mars found his son's shop-floor tirades and his endless needling to simplify the production process increasingly objectionable and decided to send him packing with $50,000 and the foreign rights to Milky Way. In 1933, following a year learning the chocolate business in Switzerland, Mars set up shop in a one-roomed unheated flat in Slough, Buckinghamshire, with his wife, Audrey (*d.* 1989), and baby son, Forrest jun. By 1934 the Mars Bar, a sweeter version of the Milky Way, had been successfully launched and Forrest Mars was on course to create the foundations of a private empire which eventually would generate an annual global revenue of $20 billion from brands ranging from Mars confectionery to Uncle Ben's Rice and a pet food empire accounting for nearly half of total company sales.

Although 1939 saw Mars Confectionery as the third-ranking confectionery maker in Britain after Cadbury and Rowntree, Mars returned to the USA in protest at being expected to pay the tax levied on resident aliens for the war effort. Frank Mars had died in 1934 and the Chicago operation was being run by Forrest's stepmother and her brother, neither of whom cared for his services. While it would be another twenty-five years of fierce board-room battles before Forrest Mars finally was able to gain complete control of Mars Inc., it was a period that witnessed the introduction of America's favourite candy, M&Ms, named after Bruce Murrie, son of the president of the Hershey Corporation, and Mars. The sugar-shelled candy, immortalized in the 1954 slogan 'the milk chocolate that melts in your mouth, not in your hand', first came off the production line at the M&M plant in Newark, New Jersey, in 1940. However Forrest Mars's interest in the Hershey partnership extended only as far as the supply of the chocolate centres for the new candies. His insufferable demands and razor tongue saw to it that the business could not function with two heads, and within a decade Mars's had severed Hershey's connection. It was the last time the company was to rely on any outsider for its production needs.

In 1964, when Forrest Mars finally acquired the last 20 per cent of the company, he lost no time in flattening out the entire structure of the business. No longer were there company perks and pecking orders. Instead, all employees became 'associates', all offices were open, every desk was the same size. Importantly there were only six pay levels throughout the entire organization, permitting easy movement of personnel. In addition, the company's wages were generally three times higher than those of their rivals, attracting top-rate executives. Yet the corporation was closed to outsiders. Mars refused to speak to the press, join any trade organization, or participate at conferences, and by keeping the company in private hands he ensured that those conditions were maintained. By the time he handed over the business to his three children in 1973 his obsessional control over its products and its workforce, together with the public humiliation of those who failed to act according to the book, had become legendary. After his wife's death in 1989 he lived with his companion, Janet, a former Mars secretary. Forrest Mars died in Miami, Florida, on 1 July 1999.   BARBARA TROMPETER

Sources J. G. Brenner, *The emperors of chocolate: inside the secret world of Hershey and Mars* (1999) • J. R. Hall, 'M&M's', *Encyclopedia of consumer brands*, ed. J. Jorgensen, 1: *Consumable products* (1994), 353–5 • D. M. Maxfield, 'Snickers', *Encyclopedia of consumer brands*, ed. J. Jorgensen, 1: *Consumable products* (1994), 543–5 • *Sunday Telegraph* (4 July 1999) • *The Times* (5 July 1999) • *Daily Telegraph* (6 July 1999) • *The Guardian* (6 July 1999) • *The Independent* (6 July 1999)
Likenesses photograph, 1960?–1969, Mars Company Offices, Slough, England

Marsden, Alexander Edwin (1832–1902), surgeon, was born on 22 September 1832, the son of William *Marsden (1796–1867), surgeon and founder of the Royal Free Hospital, London, and his first wife, Elizabeth Ann (d. 1846). He was educated at Wimbledon School and King's College, London, and was admitted a licentiate of the Society of Apothecaries in 1853 and MRCS in 1854; he graduated MD at St Andrews in 1862 and became FRCS (Edin.) in 1868.

Marsden entered the army in 1854 as staff assistant surgeon, and served in the Crimean War. For three months he was in the general hospital at Scutari. Early in 1855 he was sent to Sevastopol with the 38th regiment; he then acted as a surgeon to the ambulance corps until the end of the war, when he received the Crimean and Turkish medals. On his return to England he was appointed surgeon to the Royal Free Hospital, London, where he was also curator of the museum and general superintendent. At the Brompton cancer hospital (also founded by his father) he was surgeon from 1853 to 1884; consulting surgeon from 1884 until his death; trustee from 1865; member of the house committee from 1870; and chairman of the general committee from 1901. In 1856 he married Catherine, only daughter of David Marsden, banker.

In 1898 Marsden was master of the Worshipful Company of Cordwainers, and on his retirement he presented to the company the service of plate given to his father in 1840 in recognition of his philanthropic work in opening the first free hospitals in London. He published many works on malignant diseases, including *A New and Successful Mode of Treating Certain Forms of Cancer* (1869). Marsden died at 92 Nightingale Lane, Balham, London, on 2 July 1902, and was survived by his wife.

D'A. POWER, rev. B. A. BRYAN

Sources *Men and women of the time* (1899) • *The Lancet* (12 July 1902), 118 • *BMJ* (12 July 1902), 157 • *CGPLA Eng. & Wales* (1902)
Wealth at death £17,817 5s. 1d.: probate, 2 Aug 1902, *CGPLA Eng. & Wales*

Marsden, Betty (1919–1998), actress and comedian, was born on 24 February 1919 at 12 Southall Street, Walton, Liverpool, the daughter of John Marsden, a bombardier in the Royal Garrison Artillery, and his wife, Mary Elizabeth, née Atkinson. Her parents were too poor to raise her and when she was six she left home for Somerset, where a music teacher, Betty Allen, became her guardian and mentor. She saw the child's potential as an entertainer, as did Betty herself who, aged seven, told her sister: 'One day I will be an actress in London with my name in lights and people will know about me' (*The Guardian*). After meeting the upper-crust mother of a schoolfellow in Fortt's teashop in Milsom Street, Bath, she started giving recitations at fêtes and local Conservative clubs; when she was eleven she was the First Fairy in *A Midsummer Night's Dream* at Bath's Pavilion Theatre. She made her London début on 26 December 1931 in a musical fairy tale, *The Windmill Man*, as the Prince. At the age of twelve she won a scholarship to the Italia Conti Stage School, where she studied for six years.

Marsden's first big West End role came in 1935, when she played Pamela in *Closing at Sunrise* at the Royalty, followed by roles in Basil Dean's production of *Autumn* (1937), in Ivor Novello's *Comedienne* (1938), and in a revival of J. B. Priestley's *Johnson over Jordan* (1939). She also appeared at the Malvern festival. She joined the Entertainments National Service Association for the duration of the Second World War, entertaining the troops in productions including *Gaslight* and *In Good King Charles' Golden Days*. During the war she married, in a Nigerian bamboo hut, Dr James Wilson Muggoch (d. 1975), a consultant anaesthetist whom she had met on a troopship. Theirs was a happy marriage, and they had a son and daughter and grandchildren to whom she was devoted.

After the war Marsden won critical praise as an amorous lady in James Bridie's *Doctor Angelus* (1947) with Alistair Sim, and in Sacha Guitry's *Don't Listen, Ladies* (1948). For years colleagues had been greatly amused by her off-stage sense of the ridiculous and gift for mimicry, but it was only when she entered the world of intimate revue that these qualities surfaced professionally. She started at the tiny Irving Club (1950–51) and went to the Edinburgh festival with *After the Show*, but was dropped from the London production. Noël Coward, meeting her at the first night, was indignant. He swore he would go and see her whenever she was in a play, and he did. She was in *Airs on a Shoestring* (1953–5), its successor *From Here and There*, and *On the Brighter Side* with Stanley Baxter. Her versatility and wicked sense of burlesque in these shows led to the radio work for which she became nationally famous.

Marsden continued to work in the theatre through the 1970s to the 1990s, playing Lady Bracknell at the Shaw Theatre and the nymphomaniac wife in Lindsay Anderson's revival of *What the Butler Saw*. At the Oxford festival (1979) she gave two renditions of Wildean dowagers in *An Ideal Husband* and *Lady Windermere's Fan*, parts in which her slow basso profundo delivery and daring pauses produced laughs which might even have surprised Wilde himself. She was also a hilariously stupid, snobbish, yet not wholly unlikeable Mrs Hardcastle in *She Stoops to Conquer* (1983). Towards the end she played some effective National Theatre roles.

Marsden never much enjoyed film work, which included *The Young Lovers* (1954) and *Carry on Camping* (1969)—feeling uneasy before a camera and without an audience. Her television work was rather more distinguished, and included parts in such series as *The Bill*, *Inspector Morse*, and *The Darling Buds of May*, but a restrained Betty Marsden was almost a contradiction in terms.

Although her audience missed seeing her round eyes and cheeks, expressive mouth, and robust figure, Marsden, with her inimitable vocal range, was a consummate broadcaster. The two series *Beyond our Ken* (1958–64) and *Round the Horne* (1965–8) gave superlative entertainment—combining the anarchy of the Goons (better controlled), the wit and satire of *Take it From Here*, and an outrageous line in camp innuendo which was part risqué revue, part sixties permissiveness. The benign, ultra-respectable Kenneth Horne was an inspired anchor man, off whom the hysterical Kenneth Williams, the more slyly camp Hugh Paddick, and the astonishingly versatile Betty Marsden—the show's only female—could play to perfection. Among her characterizations were the reminiscing ex-Gaiety girl, Lady Counterblast (*née* Bea Clissold), with her near-salacious catchphrase 'Many times, many, *many*, times'; Dame Celia Molestrangler, who with ageing juvenile Binkie Huckaback (Paddick) played wonderfully hushed *Brief Encounter* burlesques; Daphne Whitethigh, the husky-voiced domestic adviser; ingénues, vamps, and a hilariously sex-obsessed Australian, Judy Koolibar. As Barry Took, one of the writers, said, 'Nothing was beyond her, nothing escaped her' (*The Independent*). Behind the

caricature there was always a recognizable person—sometimes almost poignantly so.

Marsden had a mischievous, raucous sense of humour and also a profound seriousness about her craft. Playing in the theatre night after night, she never stopped exploring the possibilities of a scene. A mistress of timing, she made superb exits, drawing applause from the thinnest of houses. She was extraordinarily generous in giving advice to fellow players—especially young ones—provided she thought them talented. Ninety per cent of her suggestions were excellent; just occasionally she encouraged people to overplay. She was endearingly aware of this tendency in her own work: 'Tell me darling—am I going too far?', she would say (personal knowledge). At times overbearing, she was generous-hearted, bringing enormous pleasure to friends and public alike. For many years she, her family, and dogs lived on an 80 foot converted coal barge, *Chilham*, moored in Brentford; there she entertained lavishly. She died on 18 July 1998 at Denville Hall, 62 Duck's Hill Road, Northwood, of a heart attack, while enjoying a drink and a laugh with friends. She was survived by her son and daughter. JONATHAN CECIL

Sources A. Foster and S. Furst, *Radio comedy* (1996), 211–17, 259–63 · *The Independent* (22 July 1998) · *The Guardian* (20 July 1998) · *Daily Telegraph* (20 July 1998) · *The Times* (21 July 1998) · personal knowledge (2004) · private information (2004) [Jane Myerson] · b. cert. · d. cert.
Likenesses photograph, 1964, repro. in *The Independent* · photograph, 1964, Hult. Arch. · photograph, repro. in *Daily Telegraph* · photograph, repro. in *The Guardian* · photograph, repro. in *The Times*

Marsden, (Charles) David (1938–1998), neurologist and neuroscientist, was born on 15 April 1938 at 4 Sydenham Road, Croydon, the elder of the two sons of Charles Moustaka Marsden, CBE, a captain in the Royal Army Medical Corps, and his wife, Una Maud, *née* Bristow. He was educated at Cheltenham College, and entered St Thomas's Hospital medical school in 1956. In addition to winning three scholarships, an exhibition, five prizes, and two medals he also represented the hospital at cricket and rugby, and had earlier captained England Schoolboys as scrum half. After preclinical training he obtained a first in his intercalated BSc in 1959, and went on to obtain an MSc in 1960, with a thesis on pigmentation in the substantia nigra that established his abiding interest in diseases of the basal ganglia of the brain, foremost among which is Parkinson's disease. He qualified MB BS in 1963, and obtained his MRCP in 1965.

Within two years of qualifying Marsden became lecturer in medicine at St Thomas's for two years and spent the following two years as a senior resident house physician at the National Hospital for Nervous Diseases, Queen Square. In 1970, only seven years after qualifying, he was appointed senior lecturer in neurology at the Institute of Psychiatry and honorary consultant neurologist to the Maudsley and Bethlem Royal Hospital and King's College Hospital. Two years later, aged thirty-four, he was the first appointee to the newly established chair of neurology at the Institute of Psychiatry and King's College Hospital medical school. He was elected FRCP in 1975, MRCPsych in 1978, FRS in 1983 (and was on the Royal Society council 1991–4), and obtained his DSc from London University in 1984.

After seventeen years south of the River Thames, Marsden moved back to Queen Square in 1987 to succeed Roger Gilliatt, who had been the first incumbent of the chair of clinical neurology at the Institute of Neurology. He held this chair until 1995, when he stepped aside to become dean of the institute. (He was delighted that Professor Anita Harding, with whom he had a close professional relationship, was appointed to succeed him in October 1995, but was greatly affected by her death, aged forty-one, in September 1995, only four months after being diagnosed with cancer.)

Marsden was outstanding as a clinical neurologist and as a neuroscientist, and one of very few people to achieve eminence in both. He established the first specialist clinics in the country for patients with Parkinson's disease and other movement disorders. Among these patients he recognized and delineated new diseases and new syndromes, devised and applied new treatments, and explored the pathophysiology underlying their conditions. In order to accomplish these goals he established a purpose-built unit to accommodate teams investigating the pharmacology and neurochemistry (with Peter Jenner), the physiology (with John Rothwell, Brian Day, Pat Merton, and Bert Morton), the neuropsychology (with Marjan Jahanshahi and Richard Brown), and the neuropathology (with Andrew Lees) of movement disorders. He was on the council of the Royal Society from 1991 to 1993, of the Royal College of Physicians from 1995 to 1998, and of the Medical Research Council from 1988 to 1994 and founded and directed the Medical Research Council human movement and balance unit and the UK Parkinson's Disease Society brain bank as vehicles for these enterprises. Among his many significant scientific contributions were the pioneering of evoked responses, and transcranial electrical and magnetic stimulation as methods of demonstrating conduction in neuronal pathways, and establishing the existence and importance of long latency reflexes in maintaining posture. Clinically, he delineated a number of hitherto poorly recognized neurological conditions, in particular the dystonias, which had often previously been incorrectly claimed to be of psychiatric origin. Together with Professor Stanley Fahn, of the Neurological Institute in New York, he founded the Movement Disorder Society and its scientific journal *Movement Disorders*.

The MRC movement and balance unit and the Parkinson's Disease Society brain bank, and many of their staff, followed Marsden to Queen Square, where their work developed further. However, after his death the former was disbanded but the latter has been reincarnated as the Queen Square Brain Bank for Neurological Disorders.

Marsden was a brilliant teacher and educator who inspired many doctors to specialize in neurology, and to sub-specialize in movement disorders. He received clinical fellows from the UK and very many countries abroad, where many of them became professors of neurology specializing in movement disorders. His lectures were marvels of lucidity and precision, and he was much in demand, having held forty visiting professorships in eighteen countries. He gave thirty-four named lectures, including the Milton Shy, Wartenburg, Geschwind, and Merritt Putnam lectures in the USA, the Charcot lecture in France, and the Aubrey Lewis and Maudsley lectures in the UK. He edited the *Journal of Neurology, Neurosurgery and Psychiatry* for a decade, and was on the editorial boards of a further twenty-one journals. His publication record was prolific, with more than 1100 publications (an average of one every eleven days for thirty-five years), including more than 800 original papers.

As befits a scrum half, Marsden was short in stature, but few people noticed this because of the towering presence of his personality. On 7 October 1961 he married Jill Slaney, a physiotherapist, daughter of William Bullock, a general practitioner. They had three daughters and two sons, one of whom predeceased him. The marriage ended in divorce, and on 26 July 1989 he married Jennifer (Jenny) Mudditt, sales manager, and daughter of Peter Henry Sandom, a businessman, with whom he had three daughters. This marriage also ended in divorce. After stepping down as dean, in September 1998 he started his first ever sabbatical year, as a visiting professor at the National Institutes of Health in Bethesda, Maryland. He died suddenly and unexpectedly, in Washington, DC, aged sixty, on 29 September, only four weeks into his visit.

NIALL QUINN

Sources *The Guardian* (6 Oct 1998) · *The Times* (21 Oct 1998) · *The Independent* (21 Oct 1998) · WWW · b. cert. · m. certs.
Likenesses photograph, repro. in *The Guardian* · photograph, repro. in *The Times* · photograph, repro. in *The Independent*

Marsden, Dora (1882–1960), suffragette and philosopher, was born on 5 March 1882 at The Hey, Marsden, Yorkshire, the fourth of five children of Fred Marsden (1851–1913), woollen waste manufacturer, and his wife, Hannah (1852–1936), daughter of a millwright, William Henry Gartside, and his wife, Elizabeth. Fred Marsden's business was in decline and he emigrated with his eldest son to Philadelphia, USA, in 1890 leaving Hannah to support her children alone by returning to her maiden trade of seamstress.

It was an inauspicious beginning for a woman the writer Rebecca West described as 'one of the most marvellous personalities the nation has ever produced' (*Time and Tide*, 16 July 1926). Yet it partly explains Marsden's subsequent feminism and lifelong commitment to the ideal of economic independence for women. Marsden's escape from dependence was through education. A pupil teacher at thirteen who qualified fully at eighteen, she won a queen's scholarship to become an undergraduate at Owens College, Manchester, in 1900.

In Manchester Marsden's political awareness developed as she came into contact with a range of feminists whose activity was beginning to coalesce around the struggle for women's suffrage. Influential in this group were Isabella Ford, Teresa Billington, Eva Gore-Booth, and Christabel

Pankhurst, a fellow student at Owens College. Marsden graduated in 1903 with an upper second-class degree and embarked on a successful career in teaching which in 1908 culminated in her appointment as a headteacher of a teacher-training centre in nearby Altrincham.

In spite of this remarkable professional success Marsden remained active in the Pankhursts' Women's Social and Political Union (WSPU) which had been formed in Manchester in 1903. Wishing to devote herself full-time to the suffrage movement she resigned her post in March 1909. She became a paid organizer for the WSPU and quickly established a reputation for ingenuity and bravery—a reputation enhanced by her own diminutive size and in West's view 'exquisite beauty' (*Time and Tide*, 16 July 1926). She was arrested and imprisoned several times in 1909–10 and though there is no firm evidence she was forcibly fed, she suffered physically in this period. Following one particularly daring escapade involving the then home secretary, Winston Churchill, she nearly fell to her death from the top of the Empire Hall in Southport where she had perched overnight to evade the alleged impregnable security. She appeared on the front page of the *Daily Mirror* (31 March 1909) looking especially waif-like and bedraggled following a long battle with the police.

Yet in spite of her high profile both nationally and within the WSPU, the 'sweetest, gentlest and bravest of suffragettes' (Emmeline Pethick-Lawrence to Dora Marsden, 6 Oct 1909) became increasingly critical of the union. In common with a growing number of other activists, Marsden was disillusioned with Emmeline and Christabel Pankhurst's leadership and resentful of their autocratic style. Dora Marsden also thought their political strategy, largely devoted to ever increasing acts of militancy, was flawed, and restricted feminist debate and analysis to the single pursuit of the vote. Having served the WSPU so well and bravely, she resigned in January 1910.

Marsden resurfaced in November 1911 to publish and edit *The Freewoman: a Weekly Feminist Review*. Though described by some as 'a disgusting publication … indecent, immoral and filthy' (Edgar Ansell to Dora Marsden, 14 July 1912), in its forthright discussions of sex, marriage, motherhood, and 'women's sphere', it stands out as the most outstanding feminist journal of the early twentieth century. It attracted articles from writers such as Rebecca West and H. G. Wells, and rates as Marsden's finest achievement.

However, Marsden began to retreat from feminism into an individualist philosophy inspired by the German anarchist Max Stirner, and after a short break, the paper became the *New Freewoman: an Individualist Review* in June 1913, and following Stirner's *The Ego and his Own*, *The Egoist* in January 1914.

As Marsden concentrated on her philosophical analysis of egoism, the literary content of the paper grew. Indeed, some commentators claim that in attracting such talents as West, Wells, Ezra Pound, and others to the *New Freewoman* and *The Egoist*, Marsden became a seminal figure in the development of imagism and early modern

British and American literature. Though this is contentious, Marsden was, however, certainly involved in the career of the Irish writer James Joyce. She published in serial form Joyce's *Portrait of the Artist as a Young Man* in 1914 and was later willing to defend his *Ulysses*. One instalment of this then highly controversial work appeared in the January–February 1919 issue.

By 1912 Marsden was living in Southport, eventually setting up a permanent home with her mother, Hannah, and Grace Jardine, an active suffragette and worker on *The Freewoman*. Marsden never married but enjoyed close friendships with a number of women including Jardine, Rona Robinson, and Mary Gawthorpe. Both Rona Robinson, who taught with Marsden in Altrincham, and Mary Gawthorpe, were active in the WSPU and became fervent supporters of *The Freewoman*. Marsden was close to her mother throughout her life and she lived with her from this time until her death in 1936.

From 1913 onwards Marsden did not take part in any formal political activity. During the war she occasionally attacked both jingoism and pacifism from an individualist, Stirnerian viewpoint in *The Egoist* and could not resist the odd scathing attack on the Pankhursts. In isolation, she concentrated on developing her philosophical work. *The Egoist* collapsed in December 1919 and Dora Marsden moved to an aptly named cottage, Seldom Seen, in the Lake District the following year. She continued to work on her *magnum opus* which had become more obscure, including proposed volumes on time, space, and religion. She became increasingly reclusive and delusionary and her mental and physical health began to suffer. However, with the generous help of her long-standing friend and benefactor Harriet Shaw Weaver (who had supported her financially since 1913), two volumes, *The Definition of the Godhead* (1928) and *Mysteries of Christianity* (1930), were published. As a result of their poor reception and her isolation Marsden suffered a nervous breakdown in 1934 and she attempted suicide in 1935. Diagnosed as suffering from psychotic depression, she became a patient at Crichton Royal Hospital, Dumfries, where she remained until her death on 13 December 1960. She was buried in Dumfries high cemetery on 16 December. Again with Weaver's help one further slim extract of her previous work, *The Philosophy of Time*, was published in 1955.

Marsden died a lonely and forgotten figure. It was an ignominious end for a 'brave and beautiful spirit' (Emmeline Pethick-Lawrence to Dora Marsden, 6 Oct 1909) whose prime importance lies in her remarkable contribution to suffragism and early twentieth-century feminism, but whose later life serves as a warning of the perils of political and personal individualism and isolation.

LES GARNER

Sources L. Garner, *A brave and beautiful spirit: Dora Marsden, 1882–1960* (1990) · L. Garner, *Stepping stones to women's liberty: feminist ideas in the women's suffrage movement, 1900–1918* (1984) · J. Lidderdale and M. Nicholson, *Dear Miss Weaver: Harriet Shaw Weaver, 1876–1961* (1970) · b. cert. · JRL · Crichton Royal Hospital records, Dumfries
Archives BL, corresp. and MSS · BL, papers incl. letters from Rebecca West and Ezra Pound, RP 3387 [photocopies] · Princeton

University Library, Dyson collection, corresp. and papers | BL, letters to Harriet Shaw Weaver, Add. MSS 57345–57365 · Huddersfield Public Library, Huddersfield Technical College annual reports · Huddersfield Public Library, Marsden Town School reports · UCL, corresp. with Jane Lidderdale

Likenesses photograph, repro. in *Votes for Women* (10 Dec 1909) · photograph, repro. in *Votes for Women* (22 July 1910) · photograph, repro. in *The Freewoman* (13 June 1912) [photo supplement] · photographs, priv. coll. · three photographs, repro. in *Daily Mirror* (31 March 1909), 9 · two photographs, repro. in *Daily Mirror* (1 April 1909)

Wealth at death poor; financially supported by others for most of life; brother-in-law paid hospital fees, 1935–1960

Marsden, Sir Ernest (1889–1970), physicist and scientific administrator, was born on 19 February 1889 in Rishton, near Blackburn, Lancashire, the second of the five children of Thomas Marsden (1864–1925), successively a weaver, household draper, and hardware merchant, and his wife, Phoebe, the daughter of Fish Holden and Esther Place Holden. The Marsdens and Holdens were long established families in Darwen, Lancashire. Academic success brought Ernest scholarships at Queen Elizabeth's Grammar School, Blackburn, where his interest in science was stimulated, and in 1906 at the University of Manchester, one of the strongest scientific institutions in Britain.

Manchester's physics professor, Arthur Schuster, retired in 1907 to enable Ernest Rutherford to succeed him. An unusual feature of the department was the emphasis on research by honours students in their final year. Since the new laboratory director characteristically endeavoured to involve others in his own research speciality of radioactivity, it is not surprising that Marsden found himself learning about this phenomenon, discovered only a dozen years before. Rutherford had observed evidence that alpha particles emitted from radioactive sources were scattered through small angles when they struck a target. Under the direction of Rutherford's assistant, Hans Geiger, Marsden sought to determine if any alphas suffered a large angular deflection when fired at metal foils. Most alphas were turned less than one degree from their path, but one in several thousand was bent more than ninety degrees. The effect increased with the atomic weight of the metal. While small angle scattering could be explained by the so-called 'plum pudding' model of the atom proposed by J. J. Thomson, the Geiger–Marsden results, published in 1909, could not. This discovery was so surprising because, as Rutherford later embellished his reaction, it seemed comparable to a 15 inch artillery shell being bounced back by a sheet of tissue paper. Two years later Rutherford proposed a different structure of the atom: a tiny but dense nucleus exerting electrostatic forces caused the alpha particle to reverse direction.

Marsden received his bachelor's degree in 1909, taught physics at East London College for a while, and then returned to Manchester in 1911 to hold the John Harling fellowship. His superior experimental skills were again allied with the similar talents of Geiger to verify Rutherford's new nuclear picture of the atom. When Geiger returned to Germany in 1912, Marsden succeeded him as

Sir Ernest Marsden (1889–1970), by Vandyk, 1948

lecturer and research assistant. He continued to investigate radioactivity, most notably certain steps in the decay series and the passage of alpha particles through hydrogen and through air. Inexplicable results were obtained with air, for he detected particles that seemed to be hydrogen, but he could not determine their source. When events caused Marsden to drop this topic Rutherford picked it up and eventually showed that the hydrogen arose from the artificial disintegration of nitrogen. Marsden thus was intimately associated with two contributions by Rutherford of Nobel prize quality, the nuclear atom and induced nuclear transformations.

On 4 August 1913 Marsden married elementary schoolteacher Margaret (Maggie) Sutcliffe (1888/9–1957), the daughter of Hartley Sutcliffe, a retired blacksmith of Colne. They had a daughter, Esther Mary (Mrs R. J. Nankervis), and a son Dr Ernest David Lindsay Marsden. In 1914 Marsden received the DSc degree from Manchester and declined a lectureship at the University of Sheffield, but he accepted the professorship of physics at Victoria University College, Wellington, New Zealand. This was the newest of the four colleges that comprised the University of New Zealand. Taking up his new post early in 1915 he was one of four science professors in the college, with other science faculties of a similar number. The First World War interrupted this career and Marsden served in uniform between 1916 and 1919, including action in France with the Royal Engineers sound ranging section, where he helped to pinpoint the location of enemy artillery; he was mentioned in dispatches twice and awarded the Military Cross (1919). Although he left active duty he retained his commission after the war, retiring from the service as a major in 1928.

In Wellington Marsden fought successfully for a new physics wing to the college building to serve the institution's 700 students. His interests, which had never been limited only to radioactivity, broadened. Indeed, at the time he published on alpha particle deflection he also co-authored papers on the electrical state of the upper atmosphere. In New Zealand it appears that he found it difficult to initiate a programme of basic research, but quite happily became absorbed in scientific problems of an applied nature. Thus, in the few post-war years that he held the physics chair in Wellington (1919–22), he pursued such topics as the interference between power circuits and communication circuits, the efficiency of various fuels for domestic purposes, high-voltage insulators, and tropical heat insulators. A decade before the social relations of science movement in Britain alerted scientists to be more conscious of the public good, Marsden made his own personal career transition in that direction. It corresponded well with his desire frequently to undertake a new task, leaving the execution of past ideas to others.

From 1922 to 1926 Marsden served New Zealand as assistant director of education, showing interest in the new field of intelligence testing. The government then appointed him to assist Sir Frank Heath, the permanent secretary of the UK Department of Scientific and Industrial Research (DSIR), in evaluating the islands' needs to organize science for economic development. Heath's report led to the creation of the NZDSIR, with Marsden as permanent secretary. Thus began a whirlwind of more than two decades' involvement in advancing the technical basis for commerce and in promoting New Zealand's civilian and military scientific interests abroad.

Agriculture was of far greater importance to the nation than manufacturing industries, and the biological sciences were of much greater relevance to these needs than the physical sciences. Marsden had the gift to view unfamiliar sciences and quickly comprehend their techniques and capabilities. Under him the DSIR soon encouraged research in dairy, leather, and wheat production; the goal was to convince the industries of the benefits in establishing their own co-operative research centres. Eventually meat, wool, flax, tobacco, hops, and other products were improved. The government itself established a plant research bureau, where investigations were conducted into fruit production, plant diseases, soil chemistry, and insects. Land use was another subject that interested Marsden. Nor were the physical sciences neglected, as he was involved, either personally or through building agencies, in meteorological research, the efficiency of lighthouses, geophysical prospecting, and physical testing. His buoyant optimism and his obvious enjoyment in dealing with others contributed in no small part to his success as a science administrator. He further

endeared himself to his staff by his focus upon issues rather than bureaucratic procedures.

During the Second World War Marsden was appointed scientific adviser to the New Zealand fighting forces, and was attached to army headquarters in Wellington, with the rank of lieutenant-colonel. He simultaneously held other posts, including director of defence scientific development and chairman of the defence science advisory committee. In such roles he travelled to the UK and USA, and in the south Pacific in support of the American naval forces. He also found time to further geophysical exploration for oil, and research on the uses of forest products, and was involved in New Zealand's development of dehydrated foods and substitutes for unavailable imports, as well as improvements in munitions production and submarine detection. Marsden also visited England to learn about radar; he brought back prototypes that were placed into production for ships, aircraft, and amphibious landings.

In 1935 Marsden had been appointed CBE. After the war a steady stream of awards flowed to him in recognition of his contributions to science and to defence: he was created CMG in 1946, and in the same year became FRS and was given an honorary DSc, Oxford; the US medal of freedom, with bronze palms, followed in 1947. In 1958 he was created knight bachelor and in 1966 he was appointed commander, royal Swedish order of the north star. Additional honorary doctorates were conferred by Manchester (1961) and the Victoria University of Wellington (1965).

In 1947 Marsden visited Australia for official discussions on an Australasian nuclear reactor, long-range weapons, and rainmaking experiments. Immediately thereafter he left home to serve as permanent representative of the NZDSIR in London, having concluded that it was time for the agency to have new leadership in Wellington. He was elected president of the Royal Society of New Zealand, but resigned only a few months later upon his departure for England. In London, as during the war, he wore other hats as well, including those of scientific liaison officer, New Zealand government scientific adviser, and New Zealand representative at the British Commonwealth Scientific Office headquarters. He was appointed a governor of the Imperial College of Science and Technology, London, in 1947, a mark of his stature as a senior statesman of science, and served as New Zealand's representative to international conferences on geodesy and geophysics, radio research, and aeronautics. He led the New Zealand delegation to the UNESCO general conference in Paris in 1952.

In 1954, when Marsden was sixty-five, he retired from government employment, though not from public life. He was appointed to the council of scientific and industrial research (1954–8) and chaired the New Zealand defence science advisory council (1956). He served as his country's representative to Commonwealth meetings on defence science, aeronautical research, agriculture, animal nutrition, and oceanography. Marsden also ventured into the private sector, becoming a director of a geothermal development company and a technical adviser to a petroleum exploration company. His wife of forty-four years died in November 1957, and the following year in July he married Joyce Winifred Chote, the daughter of W. A. Chote of Wellington.

Marsden ended his career as he began it, with research on radioactivity. Now it focused on radioactive fallout from nuclear weapons testing, on natural radioactivity of soils and rocks, and on the medical consequences of radioactivity. As a significant alumnus of Rutherford's laboratory he was called upon often to describe his years at Manchester. In particular he delivered in London a Rutherford memorial lecture, sponsored by the Physical Society (1949), in South Africa a Rutherford memorial lecture sponsored by the Royal Society of London (1954), and he was president of the Rutherford Jubilee International Conference in Manchester (1961), attended also by Sir James Chadwick, Sir Charles Darwin, E. N. da C. Andrade, and Niels Bohr—all Rutherford 'boys' from that pre-First World War period.

Marsden was small in stature, solid, and fit. He spoke with the accent of his Lancashire origins, and remembered his humble roots in dealing with others without affectations. He retained his energy and infectious grin throughout his life, as well as his interest in science. A stroke in 1966 confined him to a wheelchair; he died at Lowry Bay, Wellington, on 15 December 1970. He was unusual among Rutherford's students in leaving the academic life and in having such strong applied science interests. This was of immense value to New Zealand, for he was among the pioneers of scientific administrators and science advisers in a period when governments became more cognizant of the value of science.

LAWRENCE BADASH

Sources C. A. Fleming, *Memoirs FRS*, 17 (1971), 463–96 · P. van Asch, F. R. Callaghan, C. A. Fleming, and W. H. Ward, eds., *Sir Ernest Marsden: 80th birthday book* (1969) [incl. bibliography and chronology] · *DNB* · m. cert. [Maggie Sutcliffe]
Archives NL NZ, Turnbull L., papers | CUL, letters to E. Rutherford · University of Copenhagen, Niels Bohr Institution for Astronomy, Physics, and Geophysics, corresp. with Niels Bohr
Likenesses photographs, 1946–61, repro. in van Asch and others, eds., *Sir Ernest Marsden* · Vandyk, photograph, 1948, NPG [*see illus.*] · O. Laurenson, portrait, 1968, Royal Society of New Zealand, Wellington · J. Fanning, portrait, 1969, priv. coll.

Marsden, Isaac Moses (1809–1884). *See under* Moses, Elias (1783–1868).

Marsden, John Buxton (1803–1870), ecclesiastical historian, was born at Liverpool. He was admitted sizar of St John's College, Cambridge, in April 1823 and he graduated BA in 1827 and MA in 1830. He was ordained in 1827 to the curacy of Burslem, Staffordshire, from where he moved to that of Harrow, Middlesex. There he married, on 10 April 1833, Elizabeth Evans, the daughter of the Revd B. Evans of Harrow. Subsequently, from 1833 to 1844, he held the rectory of Lower Tooting, Surrey, and from 1844 to 1851 he was vicar of Great Missenden, Buckinghamshire. In 1851 he became perpetual curate of St Peter, Dale End, Birmingham, where he remained until his death.

Marsden was a liberal-minded evangelical: in 1847–8 he protested against the treatment of the broad-church Renn Dickson Hampden, who was attacked by Tractarians and evangelicals alike on his appointment to the see of Hereford. Marsden also edited the *Christian Observer* from 1859 to 1869, and wrote three important works of church history, *The history of the early puritans, from the Reformation to the opening of the civil war in 1642* (1850); *The History of the Later Puritans, from the Opening of the Civil War to 1662* (1852); and the *History of Christian Churches and Sects from the Earliest Ages of Christianity* (1856). He also wrote memoirs of several clergymen and published sermons and lectures.

For five years before his death ill health incapacitated Marsden; he died on 16 June 1870 at 37 Highfield Road, Edgbaston, Birmingham. Two of his sons, Charles Bateman Marsden and John Frank Marsden, followed in their father's footsteps, also becoming clergymen.

GORDON GOODWIN, rev. NILANJANA BANERJI

Sources Venn, *Alum. Cant.* · *Birmingham Daily Gazette* (17 June 1870) · *Christian Observer* (Aug 1870) · *Guardian* (22 June 1870) · *CGPLA Eng. & Wales* (1870)
Wealth at death under £1500: probate, 4 Oct 1870, *CGPLA Eng. & Wales*

Marsden, John Howard (1803–1891), antiquary, eldest son of William Marsden, curate of St George's Chapel, Wigan, and afterwards vicar of Eccles, was born at Wigan on 7 May 1803 and was admitted on 6 August 1817 into Manchester grammar school, where he was head scholar in 1822. He was an exhibitioner from the school to St John's College, Cambridge, where he was elected a scholar in 1822 on the Somerset foundation. In 1823 he won the Bell university scholarship. He graduated BA in 1826 and proceeded MA in 1829 and BD in 1836. In 1829 he gained the Seatonian prize, the subject of the prize poem being 'The Finding of Moses' (2nd edn, 1830). He was select preacher to the university in 1834, 1837, and 1847; was Hulsean lecturer on divinity in 1843 and 1844; and was from 1851 to 1865 the first Disney professor of archaeology, with the sole duty of giving one lecture a year. He published his first two lectures in 1852.

In 1840 he married Caroline, elder daughter of William Moore, prebendary of Lincoln, and in the same year he was presented by his college to the rectory of Great Oakley, Essex, which he held until 1889, when he resigned it on account of old age. He also held for some years the rural deanery of Harwich. Having been elected canon residentiary of Manchester in 1858, he became rural dean of the deanery of Eccles, and he was one of the chaplains of James Prince Lee, first bishop of Manchester. Marsden died at his residence, Grey Friars, Colchester, on 24 January 1891, a very wealthy man.

Marsden published various sermons and works on a wider range of other subjects. His first work was *The Sacred Tree: a Tale of Hindostan* (1840). He then published on Sir Thomas More's *Philomorus* (1842) and in 1844 and 1845 published his own Hulsean lectures. He wrote a history of the Gentlemen's Society at Spalding (1849) and *College Life in the Reign of James I* (1851), derived from the autobiography of Sir Symonds D'Ewes. His article on classical works at Felix Hall appeared in *Transactions of the Essex Archaeological*

Society (1863), and he concluded with a memoir of William Martin Leake (1864) and *Fasciculus* (1869), a collection of comic verses.

THOMPSON COOPER, *rev.* H. C. G. MATTHEW

Sources Crockford (1882) · *The Times* (26 Jan 1891) · Venn, *Alum. Cant.* · *CGPLA Eng. & Wales* (1891)
Wealth at death £152,939 18s. 4d.: resworn probate, Jan 1894, *CGPLA Eng. & Wales* (1891)

Marsden, Kate (1859–1931), traveller and nurse, was born on 13 May 1859 at the Parade, Edmonton, Middlesex, youngest of the eight children of Joseph Daniel Marsden, solicitor, and Sophia Matilda Willsted. She was educated at home, except for a brief stay at a boarding-school in Margate. Her father's death on 4 August 1873 plunged the family dramatically from affluence to poverty. In 1876 or 1877 Kate was accepted to train as a nurse at the Tottenham Hospital, Snell's Park, Edmonton, a protestant evangelical institution which gave equal weight to evangelism and nursing in the training of its 'deaconesses'. In 1877 she volunteered to join a party of nurses going to Bulgaria to tend Russian soldiers wounded in the Russo-Turkish War. Here she had her first encounter with leprosy, an event which had a lasting impact on her life. She returned to Britain to take up a nursing position at the Westminster Hospital and in 1878 became sister in charge of the Woolton Convalescent Home in Liverpool. Ill health forced her retirement in 1882.

In November 1884 Kate went with her mother to New Zealand to look after a sister dying of consumption. There is no full record of how she spent her time in New Zealand but the visit cannot have been a happy one. A 'serious accident' terminated her short period as lady superintendent of Wellington Hospital. During her service there, however, she had greatly improved the hospital.

Kate decided to dedicate her life to the care of sufferers from leprosy. When she returned to Britain in 1889 she was presented at court to Queen Victoria and obtained an introduction from the princess of Wales to her sister, the empress of Russia. She set off for Russia, using the presentation of a Red Cross medal for her work in Bulgaria as the occasion to investigate the incidence of leprosy throughout Russia and the Near and Middle East. Finding that the lot of the Siberian leprosy sufferers was particularly bad, on 1 February 1891 she set out for Siberia with a Russian-speaking friend, Ada Field. Travelling by sledge in bitterly cold weather and great discomfort they reached Omsk, where Field gave up and Kate pressed on alone to Irkutsk, via Tomsk and Krasnoyarsk, visiting prisons as she went. She reached Yakutsk by barge and from there, in June, left on horseback for Vilyuysk, a zigzagging ride of 2000 miles. Pestered by mosquitoes and summer storms, she rode through forests and swamps and over land burning below the surface so that there was 'always danger of a horse breaking the crust and sinking into the fire' (Middleton, 142). On this most arduous section of her journey she found the plight of the leprosy sufferers truly piteous. She gave what immediate relief she could and interested civil and church authorities in her mission. After returning exhausted to Moscow, she continued to canvas for support, raising through a London committee some £2400 to build and equip a leprosy hospital which was opened in Vilyuysk in 1897. *On Sledge and Horseback to Outcast Siberian Lepers* (1893) described her remarkable journey.

In 1892 Kate Marsden was elected one of the first female fellows of the Royal Geographical Society. On 16 August 1894, however, a letter to *The Times* from Alexander Francis, pastor of the St Petersburg British–American church and the secretary of a committee of investigation into Kate Marsden's work, destroyed her reputation in Britain, though not in Siberia, and brought to an end her humanitarian work. The powerful British Charity Organization Society wrote an unfavourable report on her fund. Quite

Kate Marsden (1859–1931), by unknown photographer, in or before 1893 [on a sledge, travelling in Siberia]

what it was that led to Kate's fall from grace has never been clear. Hints of financial impropriety and lesbianism cannot explain why Isabel Hapgood, an American translator, worked so remorselessly for her destruction. Kate tried to defend herself in the press but she abandoned her libel action against Francis in 1895, perhaps because of lack of money, perhaps because she wanted to be spared a damaging cross-examination. Some continued to believe in her: in 1906 she was presented for a second time at court and in 1916 she received the rare distinction of honorary life fellowship of the Royal Geographical Society. These, a sympathetic biography of 1895, and her own *My Mission in Siberia: a Vindication* (1921) failed to re-establish her good name, and she died poor, unmarried, and forgotten at Springfield House, Beechcroft Road, Wandsworth, London, on 26 March 1931, having been an invalid for thirty years.

In her prime, however, Kate Marsden must have had a magnetism and urgency which are not conveyed by the stilted phrases of Johnson's *Life of Kate Marsden*, which speaks of her tall stately appearance in her 'nurse's garb'. The real Kate Marsden, who charmed the tsarina and her ladies-in-waiting and blasted her way through the embattled bureaucracy of imperial Russia, must have been a very different and infinitely more impressive figure.

DOROTHY MIDDLETON

Sources D. Middleton, *Victorian lady travellers* (1965) · *The Times* (16 Aug 1894) · *The Times* (15 Aug 1994) · M. Bell and C. McEwan, 'The admission of women fellows to the Royal Geographical Society, 1892–1914: the controversy and the outcome', *GJ*, 162 (1996), 295–312 · *GJ*, 1 (1893), 80 · b. cert. · d. cert. · H. Johnson, *The life of Kate Marsden* (1895)
Likenesses photograph, in or before 1893, RGS [*see illus.*]

Marsden, Richard (1802/3–1858), weaver and Chartist, was born in humble circumstances in or near Manchester in 1802 or 1803. Nothing is known about his early life, but he was a hand-loom weaver by trade. He left Manchester in search of work during the slump of 1829 and settled with his family in the weaving township of Bamber Bridge, near Preston. Marsden became the most prominent representative of the Preston Chartists, and played a significant role in the national movement for democratic reform in the late 1830s and 1840s. He was secretary of the Preston committee which submitted evidence to the royal commission on hand-loom weavers, and was the principal witness before Commissioner Muggeridge during the latter's visit to Preston in May 1838. He chaired the first Chartist demonstration in the town in November of that year, when he introduced Feargus O'Connor to a large and enthusiastic audience. After making a fiery speech supporting the Charter, Marsden was elected to represent north Lancashire at the national convention in London. He was a consistent and unyielding advocate of 'ulterior measures', urging the need to prepare direct action for the day when the Chartist petition would be rejected by parliament. During the spring of 1839 Marsden travelled as an official 'missionary' for the convention in Sussex and the Welsh borders, toured Ireland on his own initiative, and made a speaking tour of north Lancashire, continually asserting the people's right to armed self-defence.

Although he became known nationally as a spokesman for 'physical force' Chartism, Marsden seems to have believed that its use would never be necessary. In August 1839 he returned to Preston for the unsuccessful general strike in support of the Charter, vanishing almost immediately to avoid arrest on a warrant relating to a violent speech he had made in Newcastle earlier in the month. Marsden was in Bradford during the abortive Chartist rising in January 1840 and then moved to Bolton, where he lived under an assumed name and worked at his trade. Arrested there in July, he was soon released, and eventually returned to Preston as a full-time itinerant lecturer for the Chartists. He was again arrested in a confrontation between strikers and the military just outside Preston in August 1842, but this time no charges were laid against him. In the mid-1840s he rarely left Preston, but remained an active Chartist and exerted a wider influence through a series of letters to the *Northern Star*.

Unlike many more prominent national figures, Marsden became less liberal and more vigorously anti-capitalist after 1839, coming increasingly to stress that Chartism was a class movement aiming at the emancipation of working people and opposed to all middle-class involvement. He took an active part in the Ten Hours movement, in the campaign of 1844 against proposed changes to the master and servant laws, and in promoting trade unionism in the cotton mills. At the end of 1845 he was appointed secretary of the newly established Preston Powerloom Weavers' Union, and in 1847 moved to Blackburn to take charge of the weavers' union there. Chosen again to represent north Lancashire at the Chartist national convention of 1848, Marsden was sent out once more as a missionary to the north-east and the midlands. His speeches were now subdued and pessimistic, in keeping with the dismal prospects for the Chartist movement as a whole. With its virtually complete collapse in north Lancashire after April 1848, Marsden's withdrawal from political life was immediate and almost total. There is no further record of his presence at public meetings, and his flow of letters to the local press ceased. Unlike many old Chartists, Marsden played no part in the great Preston strike of 1853–4. He died in obscurity, from chronic bronchitis, at 16 Club Street, Bamber Bridge, on 28 January 1858; he was fifty-five. Nothing is known of his private life; the mark of Jane Moss, who was present at his death, is on his death certificate.

J. E. KING

Sources J. E. King, *Richard Marsden and the Preston chartists, 1837–1848* (1981) · *People's Paper* (27 Feb 1858) · d. cert.

Marsden, Samuel (1765–1838), missionary and farmer, was born on 25 June 1765 at Bagley, near Farsley, Yorkshire, the eldest of the five surviving children of Thomas Marsden, butcher, and his wife, Bathsheba Brown. He went to school at Farsley, and subsequently worked for his uncle John Marsden, a blacksmith at Horsforth. His reputation as a lay preacher drew the attention of the evangelical Elland Society, which sought to train poor men for the

Samuel Marsden (1765–1838), by Richard Read, 1833

ministry of the Church of England. Under the society's sponsorship he attended Hull grammar school, where he was taught by Joseph Milner and came into contact with William Wilberforce. In 1790 the society sent him to Magdalene College, Cambridge, but he cut short his university studies to respond to the call of the evangelical leader Charles Simeon for service in overseas missions. On 1 January 1793 he accepted the appointment of assistant to Richard Johnson, chaplain of New South Wales. On 14 March he wrote to Elizabeth (1772–1835), daughter of Thomas Fristan of Hull, inviting her to 'take up your Cross' (Mitchell Library, A1677, vol. 3, fols. 1–4) and share in his missionary labours. They married at Holy Trinity Church, Hull, on 21 April; a month later, on 26 May, Samuel was ordained at Exeter. In July they sailed for Australia.

The Marsdens arrived to find Johnson, the senior chaplain, deep in conflict with the acting lieutenant-governor of New South Wales, Major Francis Grose, over the priorities urged by the secular and the religious authorities. The secular authorities were predominantly concerned with the maintenance of discipline among the convicts and were heavily influenced by the opportunities for material advancement available in the colony; these imperatives sat uneasily with the chaplains' religious mission to the convicts and settlers. Marsden was soon drawn into the materialism of the colony, making his home at Parramatta, some 14 miles west of Sydney, and acquiring a farm of considerable proportions: he sent the first commercial cargo of wool to England in 1811, and made important contributions in sheep-breeding and the marketing of wool. More importantly, in 1795 Governor Hunter, who had replaced Grose, made the chaplains magistrates. They saw their civil power as a means of 'bringing the inhabitants ... under some proper government and subordination' (Yarwood, 50–51), but in the convict colony their moral and spiritual influence was undermined by their identification with the establishment of judges, gaolers, and floggers. Johnson left for England in 1800, worn out in mind and body, while Marsden acquired a reputation for severity as a magistrate, which he deserved in the light of his frequent recourse to flogging. He had come to doubt the possibility of reclaiming the souls of convicts, and believed that rigorous discipline was the only way to maintain morality in the penal colony.

Marsden's evangelistic instincts were thus frustrated among the convicts and met with no greater success among the Australian Aborigines, and so he turned his energies to the Pacific islanders, and particularly the Maori of New Zealand, through the London Missionary Society (LMS) and the Church Missionary Society (CMS). In 1804 he became the agent for LMS operations in the Pacific. A prolonged visit to England in 1807–9 laid the foundations for a mission to the Maori, while also drawing attention to the state of the church in New South Wales and recruiting additional chaplains. He was encouraged by the CMS to establish a mission at the Bay of Islands in northern New Zealand, and he drew together a group of settlers to prepare the ground for the missionaries. The setting up of the mission was delayed by administrative and financial differences and government prohibition until 1814, when Marsden bought his own ship, the *Active*; in December of that year he made the first of his seven voyages to New Zealand, and he preached his first sermon at Rangihoua on Christmas day 1814. He negotiated secure conditions for the missionaries, and made the first purchase of land for the mission. On subsequent trips he continued to preach, to explore, and to encourage the settlement and economic development of the islands. He also fostered missionary work among the South Sea islanders. On his last visit to New Zealand in 1837 he was greeted with veneration by both Maori and settlers.

In Australia itself Marsden's reputation was less gilded. His material success cast doubt on the sincerity of his missionary ventures; the rift between him and Lachlan Macquarie, governor of New South Wales from 1810 to 1821, over everything from the evangelization of the Aborigines to convict and emancipation policy placed Marsden in the position of a *de facto* leader of the illiberal opposition. Censured by the colonial secretary for his conviction of Ann Rumsby in the face of the evidence, suspended from the bench for refusing to sit with Henry Douglass, a political opponent, and passed over for the position of archdeacon in 1824, Marsden remained unpopular with Macquarie's successor, Brisbane, although under Darling he received some official appointments and encouragement in his missionary work.

Elizabeth Marsden died in 1835, after twenty years of

poor health and bearing ten children (the first on board the ship which brought them to Australia in 1794). Marsden's own health broke down in 1837, and he died on 12 May 1838 at St Matthew's parsonage, Windsor, New South Wales, where he had gone for a rest. He was buried in the churchyard of St John's, Parramatta.   A. T. YARWOOD

Sources A. T. Yarwood, *Samuel Marsden, the great survivor* (1977) · *The letters and journals of Samuel Marsden*, ed. J. R. Elder (1932) · S. M. Johnston, *Samuel Marsden* (1932) · A. T. Yarwood, 'Marsden, Samuel', *AusDB*, vol. 2 · G. S. Parsonson, 'Marsden, Samuel', *DNZB*, vol. 1
Archives Bodl. RH, papers · Mitchell L., NSW · NL NZ, Turnbull L., corresp. and papers · NRA, personal and family corresp. · University of Otago, Dunedin, Hocken Library | NL Aus. · SOAS, Council for World Mission archives · U. Birm. L., Church Missionary Society archives
Likenesses R. Read, watercolour drawing, 1833, NL NZ, Turnbull L. [*see illus.*] · oils, Old Colonists' Museum, Auckland, New Zealand · portrait, priv. coll. · stipple, NPG
Wealth at death £30,000: will, 1838, Australia

Marsden, William (1754–1836), orientalist and numismatist, was born on 16 November 1754 at Verval, co. Wicklow, Ireland, the tenth of the sixteen children of John Marsden (1715–1801), shipping merchant and banker, and his second wife, Eleanor Bagnall (*d.* 1804). John Marsden retired from 'extensive mercantile and shipping concerns' in 1764, and became one of the first directors of the National Bank of Ireland after helping to establish it in 1783. William underwent a conventional classical education at schools in Dublin, with the intention that he should enter Trinity College to read for a career in the church. But in 1770 he followed the recommendation of his eldest brother, John, already a writer in East India Company service at Fort Marlborough in Sumatra, to join him there. Though not yet sixteen, Marsden successfully petitioned the East India Company for a Fort Marlborough writership for himself, and he left Dublin on 9 December 1770 and England on 27 December 1770 *en route* to Sumatra. On his arrival on 30 May 1771 he was appointed to the secretary's office before rising to sub-secretary in November 1773 and assuming the full responsibilities of secretary to the company's government in Sumatra in January 1774, though without formal appointment until October 1776. Marsden enjoyed the company of his brother, particularly in performances in the theatre which John Marsden had built at Fort Marlborough (until it burnt down in January 1774).

From early 1778 Marsden began to reconsider following
> the plan commonly adopted, of remaining in the Company's service until the annual savings from the emoluments of office should accumulate to what is termed a fortune—that is, such a sum as, when invested in English securities, would permit the owner to enjoy the conveniencies of life, without further exertion on his part.

He was attracted instead, through reading accounts published of Captain James Cook's *Endeavour* voyage, to the prospect of joining the milieu of scientific and learned meetings in London. In April 1779 he resigned his East India Company position, and he left Sumatra on 6 July, arriving in England on 24 December with slender resources. Literary pursuits, and attendance at theatre, parliament, and the law courts occupied his time. On 1

William Marsden (1754–1836), by George Dance, 1794

March 1780 Thomas Forrest, navigator of the eastern seas, introduced him to Sir Joseph Banks at Banks's house in Soho Square, where Marsden records meeting Daniel Solander, Nevil Maskelyne, Alexander Dalrymple, James Rennell, Charles Blagden, William Herschel, Joseph Planta, and others. He was invited to dine at the Royal Society Club, and to attend Royal Society meetings that month, and he became a regular participant in Banks's Soho Square breakfasts. In 1782 Marsden fortuitously declined a proposal to serve as secretary to Admiral Sir Hyde Parker, about to sail in the ill-fated *Cato*, wrecked on Madagascar, the Maldives, or the Malabar coast. In the following year he published his *History of Sumatra*, on which, inspired by the company at Soho Square, he had been working for two years while lodging at Caroline Street, Bedford Square. The *History*—drawn from his own records of Fort Marlborough, and especially the Redjang people, and dedicated to the establishment of 'facts, rather than systems … to things as they exist, rather than to display the powers of creative imagination' (Marsden, 373)—established Marsden's reputation as both a talented writer and a scholar of zoology, botany, linguistics, and geography. Marsden 'gradually ceased to look forward to obtaining an official appointment': he withdrew from the East India Company formally in 1783, and two years later set up with his brother John an East India agency which continued until John's death in 1786. Marsden was elected a fellow of the Royal Society on 23 January 1783 and of the Society of Antiquaries in December 1785. He was a founding member of the Royal Irish Academy in 1785, and received an honorary DCL at Oxford in June 1786. Elected a member of the Royal Society Club on 2 August 1787, he became treasurer the following year, a position he held until 1804. He declined a suggestion to stand for parliament, and continued the private study of oriental languages, receiving through Banks's influence the oriental vocabularies compiled and submitted by ships' officers after their voyages.

In February 1795 the cartographer James Rennell brought to Marsden Earl Spencer's offer of the second secretaryship of the Admiralty, which he eventually accepted, as much for the amiable society of Admiralty board members and staff as for the satisfaction of duty done. Unlike first secretary Sir Evan Nepean, Marsden survived the changes of ministry in 1801 and 1804. Pressed by Henry Addington, Marsden deferred retirement in that year to accept the first secretaryship of the Admiralty at a salary of £4000 a year, a position he retained until 1807. He records in his posthumously published autobiography that it fell to him in October 1805 to wake Lord Barham, as first lord of the Admiralty, with the news of victory at Trafalgar and the death of Nelson.

Marsden was elected to the Literary Club in 1799, and to the treasurership of the Royal Society in November 1802, presiding at meetings also of the Royal Society Club in Banks's absence. He developed his considerable collection of oriental coins by the purchase in September 1805 of the Kufic coin collection of Sir Robert Ainslie: this and a common interest in oriental languages and literature brought him increasingly into contact with Sir Charles *Wilkins, later librarian of the East India Company. In 1805 Marsden sought a baronetcy without success, and again, on the change of ministry in March 1807, he sought to retire from the Admiralty on grounds of ill health. Eventually insistent on retirement, he ceased to officiate in the Admiralty on 24 June 1807, and on 22 August the same year married Elizabeth Wilkins (*d.* in or after 1860), daughter of Sir Charles, the latter having for some time assisted him in the arrangement of his coin collection.

At the anniversary meeting in November 1810 Marsden relinquished the treasurership and vice-presidency of the Royal Society. Earlier that year he had bought the country house of Edge Grove, Aldenham, Hertfordshire, and moved his books from Wimpole Street to the country in 1812. His married years were his most productive in terms of writing and publication, as he built on the standing he had achieved with his *History of Sumatra* (2nd edn, 1783; 3rd edn, 1784) and *A Catalogue of Dictionaries, Vocabularies, Grammars and Alphabets*, privately printed in 1796. In 1812 he published *A Dictionary of the Malayan Language*, a project he began in 1786 but for which he had found little time with his subsequent appointments. Though not the first such study, Marsden's dictionary was distinctive for its focus on the Malay–English section—the 'essential part of the work'—at 371 pages, and in his use of 'examples of phrases and sentences … as they have occurred in the writings of the natives' (Jones, 1.xii). In 1818 he produced *The Travels of Marco Polo*, a translation from the Italian, and in 1823 and 1825 the two volumes of *Numismata orientalia illustrata* from his own coin collection. In 1827 he had printed a catalogue of his library, as *Bibliotheca Marsdeniana philologica et orientalis, a catalogue of works and manuscripts collected with a view to the general comparison of languages and to the study of oriental literature*. He added to this *Nakhoda Muda, Memoirs of a Malayan Family*, issued for the Oriental Translation Fund in 1830, and in 1834 a volume of miscellaneous *Works* comprising three tracts, one on the Polynesian languages, one on a conventional roman alphabet for oriental languages, and, in a return to the subject of lexicography, 'Thoughts on the composition of a national English dictionary'. Besides this he contributed papers to academic society journals, most notably 'The era of the Mahometans' for the *Philosophical Transactions of the Royal Society* in 1788, and a piece on the language and Indian origin of gypsies for *Archaeologia*.

After moving to Edge Grove, Marsden leased a house at 50 Queen Anne Street from 1825 in order to have a London residence again. He was present at the founding of the Raleigh Club in 1827, and of the Royal Geographical Society in May 1830. As a gesture to the government he publicly forwent his Admiralty pension of £1500 a year from 1831, on the grounds that he had accumulated enough wealth for the remainder of his life. Marsden presented his collection of over 3400 oriental coins to the British Museum on 12 July 1834 and, on the premiss that the British Museum already possessed duplicates of many of the books he owned, his library of books and manuscripts to King's College, London, on 30 January 1835. Marsden's library is now shared by the libraries of King's College and the School of Oriental and African Studies in the University of London.

Marsden had suffered from apoplexy in 1833, and died of an attack on 6 October 1836. He was buried in Kensal Green cemetery. He was survived by his wife; there were no children of the marriage. Elizabeth subsequently remarried; her second husband was the numismatist Lieutenant-Colonel William Martin Leake. In 1838 she edited and published *A brief memoir of the life and writings of the late William Marsden, D.C.L., F.R.S., &c. &c., written by himself*. Orientalist, numismatist, and antiquary, Marsden had developed the means to be a successful private scholar, as well as an effective public servant. He valued the society of which he found himself a part more for the stimulus and the intellectual quality of the company it afforded him, and he contributed in turn. Self-indulgent in his ambitions, he was conscientious in pursuit of them.

ANDREW S. COOK

Sources *DNB* · E. Marsden, *A brief memoir of the life and writings of the late William Marsden* (1838) · H. B. Carter, *Sir Joseph Banks and the plant collection from Kew sent to the empress Catherine II of Russia* (1974) · J. Bastin, introduction, in W. Marsden, *The history of Sumatra*, new edn (1986) · R. Jones, introduction, in W. Marsden, *A dictionary and grammar of the Malay language*, 2 vols. (1984)
Archives BL OIOC, natural history drawings, NHD 1–2 · King's Lond., corresp. and papers | BL, letters to Lord Bridport, Add. MSS 35198–35201 · BL, letters to Thomas Grenville, Add. MSS 41857–41859 · BL, corresp. with Lord Nelson, Add. MSS 34902–34936, *passim* · BL, letters to Lord Spencer · BL OIOC, letters to Thomas Raffles, MS Eur. D 742
Likenesses G. Dance, pencil and wash drawing, 1794, NPG [*see illus.*] · oils, *c.*1805–1810, Gov. Art Coll. · S. Cousins, portrait, 1820 ·

F. Chantrey, pencil drawing, NPG · D. Turner, etching (after T. Phillips), BM, NPG

Marsden, William (1796–1867), surgeon, the eldest of the eight children of David and Elizabeth Marsden, was born in Sheffield in August 1796 and baptized on 18 September 1796 at the church of St Peter and St Paul, Sheffield. After spending his early years in Sheffield he travelled to London and entered St Bartholomew's Hospital, where he was influenced by John Abernethy. While at St Bartholomew's, Marsden also served an apprenticeship to Mr Dale, a surgeon practising at Holborn Hill. Marsden also studied anatomy under Joshua Brookes. He obtained the membership of the Royal College of Surgeons on 27 April 1827.

Later in that year Marsden's inability to obtain admission to a hospital for an eighteen-year-old girl, whom he found on the steps of St Andrew's churchyard, gravely ill from malnourishment and disease, turned his attention to the question of hospital relief. Treatment was then granted only to those who could obtain a governor's letter or produce other evidence of being known to the subscribers to these institutions—a situation which allowed subscribers to exercise considerable patronage. Marsden sought to rectify this situation by establishing in 1828 a small dispensary in Greville Street, Hatton Garden, to which the poor were admitted without such regulation. This institution at first met with great opposition, but in 1832 its value became widely recognized because, out of all the London hospitals, only Marsden's received cholera patients.

In 1843 the hospital was moved to Gray's Inn Road, to a site which was afterwards purchased through the generosity of wealthy friends; on it was built the Royal Free Hospital, of which Marsden became the senior surgeon. In 1838 he obtained the degree of MD from the University of Erlangen and in 1840 a handsome testimonial was presented to him by the duke of Cambridge on behalf of subscribers, in recognition of his work for the poor.

Marsden married twice and had one surviving child, a son, Alexander Edwin *Marsden, from his first marriage (on 29 January 1820), to Elizabeth Ann (d. 1846). His second wife was Elizabeth, daughter of Francis Abbott, a solicitor. In 1851 Marsden opened a small house in Cannon Row, Westminster, for the reception of cancer patients. Within ten years the institution was moved to Brompton, where it later became the Royal Marsden Hospital. Marsden enjoyed a large practice, and throughout his life was a follower of Abernethy, and used his methods. Considered an acute observer by his contemporaries he employed a broad range of approaches to treatment. A busy clinician, he published only one text, *Symptoms and treatment of malignant diarrhoea, better known by the name of Asiatic or malignant cholera* (1834). He died of bronchitis at the Star and Garter Hotel, Richmond, Surrey, on 16 January 1867, and was buried in Norwood cemetery.

D'A. POWER, *rev.* RICHARD HANKINS

Sources *The Hospital* (14 May 1887) · *The Lancet* (26 Jan 1867) · private information (1893) · *Medical Times and Gazette* (26 Jan 1867), 98–9 · R. Flanagan, 'Dr William Marsden (1796–1867)', *Friends of Norwood Cemetery*, 25 (1996), 7–9 · *IGI* · *CGPLA Eng. & Wales* (1867) ·

William Marsden (1796–1867), by Henry William Pickersgill, exh. RA 1866

F. Sandwith, *The compassionate surgeon: the story of Dr William Marsden* (1960)
Likenesses T. H. Illidge, oils, 1850, Royal Free Hospital, London · H. W. Pickersgill, oils, exh. RA 1866, Royal Marsden Hospital [*see illus.*] · portrait, repro. in Flanagan, 'Dr William Marsden', 7
Wealth at death under £12,000: resworn probate, Oct 1867, *CGPLA Eng. & Wales*

Marsh, Adam [Adam de Marisco] (*c.*1200–1259), Franciscan friar, biblical scholar, and teacher, according to the Dominican annalist Nicholas Trevet (*d.* 1328) was born in the diocese of Bath. Possibly he was related to the important Marsh family of Somerset, which was prominent in the royal service under King John. He was a nephew of Richard *Marsh (*d.* 1226), the royal chancellor who became bishop of Durham. A master of arts of Oxford University by 1226, he was presented by his uncle to the rich rectory of Bishopwearmouth, which he held until 1232, when he followed the example of his pupil, Adam Rufus, and joined the Friars Minor at Worcester. Returning to Oxford as a friar, he studied theology under the secular masters who lectured to the Franciscan school, the first of whom was Robert Grosseteste (*d.* 1253), and incepted as a doctor and lector to his Oxford brethren probably in 1242–3. He was the first Franciscan to incept and teach in the theology faculty of Oxford.

Marsh had known Grosseteste since boyhood, and the

two became devoted friends. At Grosseteste's insistence, Marsh accompanied him to Lyons in 1244–5 to attend the general council there. On the return journey Marsh was delayed at Mantes by the illness of his friar companion, and Grosseteste wrote anxiously to the provincial of the English Franciscans, urging him to send another friar to relieve Marsh, for fear that he would be commandeered to fill the Franciscan chair at Paris vacated by the death in 1245 of the famous Alexander of Hales, and so be lost to the English province. This was striking testimony to Marsh's standing as a theologian. His regency in theology ended in 1250. Although his provincial minister directed him to resume teaching in 1252, the pressure of public duties prevented him from doing so. But he continued to reside at Oxford, and his provincial, William of Nottingham (d. 1254), constantly relied upon his advice on the progress of student friars and the choice of lectors for the English province. On one occasion he was called on to mediate between the university and Grosseteste, who as bishop of Lincoln had been incensed by the masters' presumption in using a corporate seal.

Adam Marsh's reputation as a biblical scholar and as a counsellor made him much sought after by the outside world as well as by the rulers of his order. He was persuaded by the archbishop of Canterbury, Boniface of Savoy (d. 1270), to accompany him on his forceful metropolitan visitations. The queen requested his presence at court. He was sent abroad on the king's diplomatic business in 1247, and in 1257 he was one of the royal delegates sent to France to negotiate a peace treaty with Louis IX. He became the mentor and spiritual director of Simon de Montfort and his wife, Eleanor, and he loyally supported Montfort when he was arraigned by Henry III in 1252 for his conduct as governor of Gascony. In addition to his diplomatic activities, he received a number of papal commissions to act as judge-delegate in politically sensitive cases. He was one of three commissioners appointed by the pope in 1256 to investigate the merits of Richard of Wyche (d. 1253) with a view to his canonization. As growing demands were made upon him from all sides, his letters become increasingly querulous over failing health, overwork, and the interruption of his studies. An attempt was made by the king and the archbishop to secure his election to the see of Ely in 1257, in place of Hugh of Balsham (d. 1286) who had been chosen by the monks. It is unlikely that he would have welcomed such a preferment. In any case, it came to nothing. He was already old and ailing, and he died on 18 November 1259.

Marsh shared with his friend Grosseteste an ideal of a church purged of abuses, with a clergy selflessly devoted to the cure of souls. Like many Franciscan writers, he was a fierce critic of the shortcomings of the secular clergy. The chief targets of his invective were the careerists and benefice hunters, the absentee rectors and pluralists, who neglected the pastoral care of their parishioners. Touched by the millennial speculations of Joachim di Fiore, he believed the friars had been raised by divine providence to succour the elect in the final struggle with the Antichrist as the end of the world approached.

To the thirteenth-century Italian chronicler Salimbene, Adam Marsh was 'one of the greatest clerks of the world' (*Cronica*, 235). Roger Bacon (*d.* 1294) credited him with a knowledge of the biblical languages. He collaborated with Grosseteste in the study, transmission, and translation of Greek texts. The manuscript of Grosseteste's famous *tabula* or subject-index to the fathers and the works of Aristotle names Marsh as a contributor to the index. But, surprisingly in view of his academic reputation, none of his biblical commentaries has been traced. His only literary remains that can be confidently identified are his letters. These, which cover the period of his life from 1241 to 1259, survive in a single manuscript (BL, Cotton MS Vitellius C.viii). Their compilation, probably the work of an Oxford Franciscan, appears to have been abandoned at an advanced stage, and never put into circulation. Nevertheless they are an important source for the ecclesiastical and political history of England in the middle years of the thirteenth century. Marsh's influence on the Franciscan theological tradition seems to have been limited. His lasting monument was the Oxford Franciscan school and the academic organization of the English province of the Friars Minor.   C. H. LAWRENCE

Sources 'Adae de Marisco epistolae', *Monumenta Franciscana*, ed. J. S. Brewer, 1, Rolls Series, 4 (1858), 77–489 · *Fratris Thomae vulgo dicti de Eccleston tractatus de adventu Fratrum Minorum in Angliam*, ed. A. G. Little (1951) · *Roberti Grosseteste episcopi quondam Lincolniensis epistolae*, ed. H. R. Luard, Rolls Series, 25 (1861) · [*Cronica fratris Salimbene de Adam ordinis Minorum*], ed. O. Holder-Egger, MGH Scriptores [folio], 32 (Hanover, 1905–13) · Paris, *Chron.* · *F. Nicholai Triveti, de ordine frat. praedicatorum, annales sex regum Angliae*, ed. T. Hog, EHS, 6 (1845) · Chancery records · The 'Opus maius' of Roger Bacon, ed. J. H. Bridges, 3 vols. (1897–1900) · A. G. Little, 'The Franciscan school at Oxford in the thirteenth century', *Archivum Franciscanum Historicum*, 19 (1926), 803–74 · C. H. Lawrence, 'The letters of Adam Marsh and the Franciscan school at Oxford', *Journal of Ecclesiastical History*, 42 (1991), 218–38 · P. Raedts, *Richard Rufus of Cornwall and the tradition of Oxford theology* (1987) · R. W. Southern, *Robert Grosseteste: the growth of an English mind in medieval Europe* (1986)
Archives BL, Cotton MS Vitellius C.viii

Marsh, Alec (1908–1996), jockey and horse-racing official, was born on 12 August 1908 at Staunton in the Vale, Nottinghamshire, the son of George Ernest Marsh, farmer, and his wife, Lily Gertrude, *née* Bramley. He hunted from an early age, graduated to point-to-point racing, and won his first race under National Hunt rules on Common Ground over hurdles at Warwick in February 1929. He was leading amateur rider for three consecutive seasons from 1934–5 but gave up riding in 1940 after a fall too many. He had ridden in over 1000 races, and had won 163 of them, including 21 on the flat. He won the Cheltenham foxhunters twice, in 1935 on Empire Night and in 1936 on Herod Bridge; the Liverpool foxhunters in 1936, on Don Bradman; and dead-heated for the Grand Sefton that year on the same horse. At one stage the National Hunt committee, anxious to protect the livelihood of paid riders, counselled him to turn professional himself, but he ignored their advice. Under the existing Jockey Club regulations this would have prevented him pursuing a career as a racing official. On 31 March 1937 he married Elizabeth Mary Jessop (*b.* 1910/11), daughter of Major Thomas Jessop of the Lincolnshire yeomanry. There was one son of the marriage.

During the Second World War Marsh served with the RAF in Europe, Singapore, Burma, China, and India. On demobilization he acted as a starter for the Royal Calcutta turf club before returning to Britain to be appointed an official starter by the Jockey Club in 1947. He officiated at his first classic in 1952 and in that year also became the senior starter for the club. A further 100 classic starts were to come before his retirement in 1972, after a career in which he began over 25,000 races. As starter his job was to assist in keeping a race fair to all participants, including the punters, by ensuring that all horses were at the start in the correct draw and ready to go when he gave the signal. In the days before starting stalls this also required keeping the horses in line to prevent one being left or allowing a jockey to steal a flying start. Marsh compared starting to driving a car:

> Just as, with the right timing it is possible to overtake six cars at once, so with keen anticipation, one should eventually catch all the horses facing the right way simultaneously. No use panicking or losing one's temper. It all hinges on timing. (Sharpe, 119)

Initially he did not like the mechanical aspects of starting stalls, first used at Newmarket in 1965, which, of course, much changed his job. However, he later admitted that they benefited the sport.

Marsh always arrived at courses wearing his tweeds and bowler hat and carrying a red flag for use by the recall man stationed down the course in case of a false start. In wet weather he would wear galoshes; in dry, shiny brown brogues. As an ex-rider himself, his authority was generally respected by the jockeys. He made it a point seldom to speak to jockeys 'because it is irrational to speak to them in one breath, and shout at them in the next' (Sharpe, 119). His authority could be mistaken for arrogance: one jockey described him as 'a cold fish with no favourites', but added that he was 'damned good at his job' (*Daily Telegraph*, 22 Nov 1997). On retirement Marsh reflected that 'they have been good years, neither free from criticism nor from strain—but they fulfilled my ambition' (ibid.).

His first marriage having ended in divorce in 1959, Marsh married second, on 22 June 1972, Marjorie Minnie Cole (*b.* 1910/11), widow, of Easthorpe, Bottesford, Nottinghamshire, and daughter of Henry Norris, farmer. He died on 17 November 1996 at Grantham and District Hospital, Grantham, Lincolnshire, of ischaemic heart disease; he was survived by his second wife.   WRAY VAMPLEW

Sources *Daily Telegraph* (22 Nov 1996) · P. Smyly, ed., *Encyclopaedia of steeplechasing* (1979) · R. Mortimer, ed., *The encyclopaedia of flat racing* (1971) · G. Sharpe, *The William Hill book of racing quotations* (1994) · b. cert. · m. certs. · d. cert.
Likenesses photograph, 1955, repro. in *Daily Telegraph*
Wealth at death £909,241: probate, 14 March 1997, *CGPLA Eng. & Wales*

Marsh, Alphonso (*bap.* 1627, *d.* 1681), musician and composer, baptized at St Margaret's, Westminster, on 28 January 1627, was the son of Robert Marsh, one of the royal musicians to Charles I. Alphonso Marsh was married

twice; his first wife, Mary Cheston, whom he married on 8 February 1648, was probably the mother of his two children, Elizabeth and Alphonso [*see below*]. His second wife, Rebecca, outlived him. Following his father into royal service as a musician, Marsh was appointed to the king's musick in the voices and lutes on 20 June 1660 in the place of a deceased singer for £40 per year plus livery costs. Marsh's salary fell in the middle of the salary range for royal musicians. As a member of the Chapel Royal he sometimes accompanied the king on progress, for example joining the royal household in Oxford when it escaped the plague in 1665–6. Samuel Pepys was not impressed with Marsh's voice; after an evening outing on 19 August 1661 Pepys commented that his 'voice is quite lost'. However, the condition of Marsh's voice was probably affected by the alcohol Pepys had been buying during the evening (Pepys, 2.158).

Marsh is a good example of two features of the king's musick: dynasties and problems with payment. The Marshes were not the only family that provided the royal household with several generations of musicians; others included the Laniers, the Bassanos, and the Strongs. Alphonso also experienced the Restoration court's inability to pay its servants in a timely manner. In his will, Marsh left his widow, Rebecca, two-thirds of his court arrears and his son one-third. Three years after her husband's death, Rebecca Marsh was still owed £10 from his arrears.

Marsh experienced some opposition to his status as a royal musician. In November 1668 he obtained a warrant to arrest several local musicians who had assaulted him and defamed the special status royal musicians enjoyed. These privileges included exemption from the subsidy assigned in 1662. Marsh also was a member of the Corporation for Regulating the Art and Science of Music, a guild begun by royal musicians in the early seventeenth century to regulate the performance and teaching of music in the capital. However, the corporation closed in 1679 because it could not force local musicians to adhere to its regulations and was unable to collect dues from members, many of whom suffered from the crown's inability to pay its servants on time.

Marsh wrote music for several theatrical productions: Sir William Davenant's *Law Against Lovers* (1662), John Dryden's *An Evening's Love* (1668), part 1 of Dryden's *The Conquest of Granada* (1673), and Thomas Duffett's *The Spanish Rogue* (1673). He was also a regular contributor to John Playford's musical publications, including his series *Choice Ayres, Songs, & Dialogues* in the 1670s and books such as *The Treasury of Musick* (1669). Some material also survives in manuscript form (BL, Harley MS 1911 and PRO, LC9/195–200). Marsh was buried at St Margaret's, Westminster, on 2 May 1681.

Marsh's son, **Alphonso Marsh** (1648–1692), was also a royal musician and composer and performed alongside his father for many years. A tenor, the younger Marsh, who was married to Cicilia (*d.* 1690/91), was sworn on 25 April 1676 into Charles II's service and had to be readmitted into the royal household after taking the oath of allegiance to William and Mary in July 1689. Father and son performed on stage together in Crowne's masque *Calisto* at Whitehall in 1675, the father receiving £10 and the son, who performed Africa in the prologue, £5, sizeable payments compared with their salaries. Alphonso the younger also contributed songs to John Playford's series *Choice Ayres, Songs, & Dialogues*. Marsh died on 5 April 1692 and was buried in the west cloister of Westminster Abbey. JOANNA T. NEILSON

Sources A. Ashbee, ed., *Records of English court music*, 9 vols. (1986–96) · *New Grove*, 2nd edn · A. Ashbee and J. Harley, eds., *The cheque books of the Chapel Royal*, 2 vols. (2000) · J. Neilson, 'The patronage of pomp: music in the Restoration court', MA thesis, Florida State University, 1998 · A. Ashbee and D. Lasocki, eds., *A biographical dictionary of English court musicians, 1485–1714*, 2 vols. (1998) · *DNB* · Pepys, *Diary* · *IGI* · private information (2004)

Marsh, Alphonso (1648–1692). *See under* Marsh, Alphonso (*bap.* 1627, *d.* 1681).

Marsh [*née* Caldwell; *later* Marsh-Caldwell], **Anne** (*bap.* 1791, *d.* 1874), novelist, was born at her father's estate, Linley Wood, Staffordshire, and baptized at Newcastle under Lyme, Staffordshire, on 9 January 1791, the third daughter and fourth child of James Caldwell (*d.* 1838), lawyer and recorder of Newcastle under Lyme, and deputy lieutenant of Staffordshire, and his wife, Elizabeth, daughter of Thomas Stamford of Derby. On 30 July 1817, at St James's, Audley, Staffordshire, she married Arthur Cuthbert Marsh (*d.* 1849), of Eastbury Lodge, Hertfordshire, son of William Marsh, senior partner in the London bank Marsh & Co. of Berners Street. The bank was ruined in 1824 as a result of the depredations of a junior partner, Henry Fauntleroy, who was subsequently hanged for forgery. Anne and Arthur Marsh had eight children: two sons, both of whom died young, and six daughters. Given that her first book was not published until ten years after the collapse of Marsh & Co., there is probably no foundation for the commonly held belief that she turned to authorship in order to help support her large family and, for the same reason, had to redouble her literary efforts after her husband's death in December 1849. Her mother had been an heiress.

The publication of Marsh's first volume of fiction, *Two Old Men's Tales* ('The Deformed' and 'The Admiral's Daughter', 1834), was arranged by Harriet Martineau, an old friend. Marsh had read 'The Admiral's Daughter' to her one night after dinner, and Martineau had been moved to tears by the penitential miseries and sacrifices of its adulterous heroine. Marsh's husband, fearing that the book might injure their daughters' marriage prospects if it attracted unfavourable criticism, insisted that it be published anonymously. 'The Admiral's Daughter' became perhaps her best-loved story. Her second book, *Tales of the Woods and Fields* (1836), was a sequel to the first, comprising further tales by the 'two old men'; she continued to refer to herself as 'the Old Man' for long afterwards. Eight years elapsed before her first and most popular full-length novels began to appear: *The Triumphs of Time* (1844), *Mount Sorel* (1845), *Father Darcy* (1846), *Emilia Wyndham*, her best-known novel (1846), *Norman's Bridge* (1847), and *Angela* (1848). At least twelve more novels followed, not counting

two—*Adelaide Lindsay* (1850) and *Heathside Farm* (1863)—which were described as having been 'edited' by her but were probably her own work, and one—*The Longwoods of the Grange* (1853)—described as by 'the author of *Adelaide Lindsay*'. She also published a further volume of shorter tales, *Chronicles of Dartmoor* (1866); two translations from the French; a two-volume historical work, *The Protestant Reformation in France* (1847); and probably two stories for children, again described as by 'the author of *Adelaide Lindsay*'. Five anonymously published novels by Julia Stretton were mistakenly attributed to Marsh in both the *Cambridge* and the *New Cambridge Bibliography of English Literature*.

At the peak of her reputation Marsh was hailed by the *London Weekly Chronicle* as 'the best lady novelist of the day' (Allibone, *Dict.*). In 'Modern novelists—great and small', an article in *Blackwood's Edinburgh Magazine* (May 1855), Margaret Oliphant grouped her with Catherine Gore and Frances Trollope as 'the respectable elder sisters of the literary corporation', contrasting 'the goodness that lies in her old-fashioned moral' with the passionate rebelliousness given free rein in the novels of Charlotte Brontë, Elizabeth Gaskell, and other younger writers. After her death *The Athenaeum* (17 October 1874, 513) remarked that 'No writer had greater power than she of compelling tears'. Her explicit didacticism was extreme even by early Victorian standards, and her heroines, of whom Emilia Wyndham was the best-known, were seemingly devoid of sexual desires, living only for self-sacrifice. She protested vehemently at the demeaning view of married women presented in the *Punch* series 'Mrs. Caudle's Curtain Lectures', branding the anonymous author (Douglas Jerrold) a 'vulgar penny-a-liner' and suggesting that *Punch* might, for a change, try teaching husbands to 'correct themselves as well as their wives' (*Emilia Wyndham*, chap. 4, chap. 57).

Little information seems to have survived about Marsh's private life, or about her character and appearance. From their childhood she and her siblings were on intimate terms with the children of other notable Staffordshire families, including the Wedgwoods. Her sister (Margaret) Emma was the first wife of Dr Henry Holland, a relative of the Wedgwoods and cousin of Elizabeth Gaskell. Holland later became Queen Victoria's physician, and he and his family remained part of Marsh's social circle after her sister's death in 1834. In February 1838 Harriet Martineau quoted a mutual friend's report that Marsh was 'sadly excited and restless', with an 'uncontrollable' nervous disorder which Martineau evidently attributed to excessive self-absorption (*Harriet Martineau's Letters*, 11). Many years later, in February 1860, Martineau complained to the same correspondent, Fanny Wedgwood, that Marsh had never learned 'self-knowledge or modesty' (ibid., 186).

By this time Marsh had succeeded to her father's estate, Linley Wood, following the death of her brother James Stamford Caldwell on 17 November 1858, but was involved in litigation to have her three unmarried daughters, Eliza Louisa, Georgina Amelia, and Rosamond Jane, recognized as the reversionary heirs to the estate in preference to the heir-at-law, Henry Thurston Holland, her sister Emma's son (who later became a tory cabinet minister and was created Viscount Knutsford). On 18 May 1860, after the case was decided in her daughters' favour, she changed her surname to Marsh-Caldwell by royal licence. She died at Linley Wood on 5 October 1874.   P. D. EDWARDS

Sources *The Athenaeum* (17 Oct 1874), 512–13 · Boase, *Mod. Eng. biog.*, vol. 2 · *Harriet Martineau's letters to Fanny Wedgwood*, ed. E. Sanders Arbuckle (1983) · 'Marsh and others v. Marsh and others', *The Times* (13–14 Jan 1860); (16 Feb 1860) · [M. Oliphant], 'Modern novelists—great and small', *Blackwood*, 77 (1855), 554–68 · P. Schlueter and J. Schlueter, eds., *An encyclopedia of British women writers* (1988) · J. Sutherland, *The Longman companion to Victorian fiction* (1988) · 'Novels by the author of *Two old men's tales*', *Dublin University Magazine*, 34 (1849), 575–90 · Burke, *Gen. GB* (1882) · IGI · CGPLA Eng. & Wales (1874) · d. cert. · DNB
Likenesses portrait, repro. in S. J. Hale, *Woman's record*, 2nd edn (1855), 735
Wealth at death under £10,000: probate, 21 Nov 1874, *CGPLA Eng. & Wales*

Marsh, Catherine (1818–1912). *See under* Marsh, William (1775–1864).

Marsh, Charles (1735–1812). *See under* Marsh, Charles (c.1774–1835).

Marsh, Charles (c.1774–1835), barrister and politician, was born in Norwich, a younger son of Edward Marsh, manufacturer and merchant, of St Saviour's, Norwich, and his wife, Catherine. He was educated at Norwich grammar school under Dr Forster. On 5 October 1792 he was admitted pensioner of St John's College, Cambridge. He resided for four terms but did not graduate. He became a student of Lincoln's Inn on 26 September 1791 and was called to the bar on 3 July 1797. He married Mary Hale, daughter of Thomas Lewin of Bexley, Kent. They had one son, Hippisley Marsh (1808–1884), who became a colonel in the Bengal army.

In 1804 Marsh obtained an Indian judicial appointment through the intervention of Sir John Coxe Hippisley and went to Madras, where he practised with great success. He returned to England in 1809 and was elected MP for East Retford in 1812. It was said that he tricked his way into parliament, falsely representing himself to the electors as the whig candidate. Once there, he was a consistent supporter of Catholic relief and an opponent of attempts to impose Christianity in India. On 1 July 1813 he spoke in a committee of the house in support of the amendment moved by Sir Thomas Sutton on a clause in the East India Bill providing further facilities for people to go out to India for religious purposes. His speech, which occupies thirty-two columns of Hansard's *Parliamentary Debates* (Hansard 1, 26, 1813, 1018), was described by a contemporary as 'one of the most pointed and vigorous philippics in any language' (*Quarterly Review*, 70.290). During his first session he voted as a Wellesleyite. Subsequently he was a supporter of the government. In parliament and elsewhere he was critical of Sir George Barlow in Madras and of General Gore, the governor of Upper Canada. He contested Sudbury unsuccessfully in 1818 and Petersfield in 1831. He was known to be in great financial difficulties in the 1820s. He died in 1835.

Marsh was a contributor to *The Cabinet: by a Society of Gentlemen* (3 vols., 1795). He also wrote several pamphlets, including *An Appeal to the Public Spirit of Great Britain* (1803). This revised version of an earlier pamphlet supporting the political actions of William Windham was prepared with Windham's help. Marsh's speech on the East India Bill was printed in pamphlet form and also in volume 2 of *The Pamphleteer* in 1813. The famous 'Letters of Vetus' in *The Times* (1812) were wrongly ascribed to him. In fact they were written by Edward Sterling, father of John Sterling (1806–1844). Two lively volumes of gossip, *The Clubs of London*, are thought to be his work. He frequently contributed to the *New Monthly Magazine*.

The lawyer and MP is not to be confused with **Charles Marsh** (1735–1812), the only son of Charles Marsh, a London bookseller. He was admitted to Westminster School in 1748. He was elected to Trinity College, Cambridge, where he matriculated in 1753, and graduated BA in 1757 as senior classical medallist. He became a fellow of his college in 1758, proceeding MA in 1760. He was subsequently a clerk in the war office. On 15 January 1784 he was elected fellow of the Society of Antiquaries, and the following May he gave a Latin dissertation to the society entitled 'On the elegant ornamental cameos of the Barberini vase', which was printed in *Archaeologia* (8.316–20). In 1811 he published a translation of John Milton's *L'allegro*. He possessed a valuable library of old books. After many years' employment in the war office he retired, on a pension of £1000 a year. He lived at Rodnor House, Twickenham, and died, unmarried, either there or in Piccadilly, London, on 21 January 1812. He was buried in Westminster Abbey.

GORDON GOODWIN, *rev.* ERIC METCALFE

Sources HoP, *Commons* · *N&Q*, 3rd ser., 3 (1863), 431, 478 · *N&Q*, 3rd ser., 4 (1863), 363, 529 · H. S. Smith, *Parliaments of England* (1849–50), 1.255 · Venn, *Alum. Cant.* · J. Welch, *The list of the queen's scholars of St Peter's College, Westminster*, ed. [C. B. Phillimore], new edn (1852) [Charles Marsh (1735–1812)] · J. L. Chester, ed., *The marriage, baptismal, and burial registers of the collegiate church or abbey of St Peter, Westminster*, Harleian Society, 10 (1876) [Charles Marsh (1735–1812)]

Marsh, Charlotte Augusta Leopoldine (1887–1961), suffragette and social worker, was born on 3 March 1887 at Alnmouth, Northumberland, the third daughter of Arthur Hardwick Marsh (1842–1909), watercolourist and genre painter, and his wife, Ellen Hall. She was educated at St Margaret's School, Newcastle upon Tyne, and Roseneath, Wrexham, and then spent a year studying in Bordeaux. She was one of the first women to train as a sanitary inspector but, appalled by the insight her work gave her into the lives of many women, gave up a promising career to join the women's suffrage movement in 1908, to give women a voice in public affairs. She became a member of the most militant organization, the Women's Social and Political Union (WSPU).

Charlotte Marsh was a regional organizer for the WSPU, working in many cities and towns, including Nottingham and Portsmouth, and was imprisoned three times for 'the cause', hunger-striking on two occasions and being forcibly fed. On 30 June 1908 she was one of twenty-five women arrested following a demonstration in Parliament Square. Charged with obstructing the police in the execution of their duty she was sentenced to one month in the second division at Holloway. On 17 September 1909, along with fellow suffragette Mary Leigh, Charlotte was arrested in Birmingham after staging a roof-top protest at the Bingley Hall where the prime minister, H. H. Asquith, was addressing a meeting. The police attempted to move the two women by, among other methods, turning a hosepipe on them and throwing stones. However, Charlotte Marsh and Mary Leigh proved to be formidable opponents and were only brought down from the roof when three policeman dragged them down. For her part in this, Charlotte Marsh was sentenced to three months' hard labour at Winson Green gaol. In protest at the refusal of the authorities to treat her as a political prisoner Charlotte adopted the hunger strike and, one of the first suffragettes to be forcibly fed, was tube-fed 139 times. She was imprisoned for the last time in 1912 for her part in the window-smashing raid in London's West End on 1 March. As she had previous convictions she was sentenced to six months' imprisonment, which she served in Aylesbury prison (Holloway was being redecorated). Once again she staged a hunger strike and was forcibly fed and released four and a half months into her sentence.

A beautiful and striking figure with long golden hair and an elegant poise, Charlotte Marsh was often chosen as standard-bearer for WSPU processions. In December 1908 she was the colour-bearer at the procession organized to celebrate the release from Holloway of Christabel and Mrs Pankhurst. On 14 June 1913, a more solemn occasion, carrying a large wooden cross, she led the funeral procession of her comrade Emily Wilding Davison, who had died as a result of the injuries she sustained when she fell under the hooves of the king's horse at the Epsom Derby on 4 June.

Charlotte Marsh continued to work with the Pankhursts until the outbreak of the First World War, when the WSPU declared a cessation of militancy. Ironically, during this political truce, having first worked as a motor mechanic, she became Lloyd George's chauffeur, accepting his suggestion that the relationship would promote the victory of the cause of women's enfranchisement. She later worked as a land girl in Surrey before returning to feminist politics in 1919 when she worked for a brief time on the staff of the Women's International League for Peace and Freedom. Following the granting of the full franchise in 1928, Charlotte devoted her time to social welfare work. She worked first for the Community Chest Organization in San Francisco and then with the Overseas Settlement League, and when this organization closed down in the 1930s she became an officer of the National Assistance Board until her retirement. In later years Charlotte Marsh worked as a technical adviser on a BBC documentary, written and produced by Norman Swallow, to celebrate Mrs Pankhurst's birthday, the story of which was woven around Charlotte's life. She continued to be involved with suffrage commemorations and gave many years' service to the Suffragette Fellowship of which she was the vice-president until her death, unmarried, at 31 Copse Hill, Wimbledon, on 21 April 1961. MICHELLE MYALL

Sources *Memories of Charlotte Marsh* (June 1961) [leaflet published for the Suffragette Fellowship] · A. Raeburn, *The militant suffragettes* (1973) · interview with Lady Jessie Street, March 1960, Museum of London, Suffragette Fellowship MSS, (transcript) [recorded at the White House, Albany Street, London] · *The Times* (24 April 1961) · b. cert. · d. cert.
Archives Museum of London, Suffragette Fellowship MSS
Likenesses photograph, Museum of London, Suffragette Fellowship MSS; repro. in D. Atkinson, *The suffragettes in pictures* (1996) · portrait, repro. in *Votes for Women* (24 Dec 1909)
Wealth at death £4185 13s. 5d.: probate, 29 Nov 1961, *CGPLA Eng. & Wales*

Marsh, Sir Edward Howard (1872–1953), civil servant and patron of the arts, was born in London on 18 November 1872, the second child and only son of Frederick Howard Marsh (1839–1915), and his first wife, Jane, daughter of Spencer Perceval, Irvingite angel to Italy and eldest son of Spencer Perceval, the prime minister who was assassinated in 1812 in the lobby of the House of Commons. Jane Perceval had become a nurse and had founded in Queen Street the Alexandra Hospital for Children with Hip Disease where she had met her husband, a surgeon who later became professor of surgery at Cambridge and (1907–15) master of Downing College. Their elder daughter died in infancy; the younger married Sir Frederick Maurice. Marsh was educated at Westminster School and at Trinity College, Cambridge, where he obtained first classes in both parts of the classical tripos (1893–5), and in the latter year was awarded the senior chancellor's medal. At Cambridge his view of life was influenced by his close friendship with his fellow Apostles G. E. Moore and Bertrand Russell, while through Maurice Baring he was brought to the notice of Edmund Gosse, who admitted him to his literary circle in London. His association with Oswald Sickert, editor of the short-lived *Cambridge Observer*, gave him the opportunity for his first essays in criticism, and through his ardent championship of Ibsen, whose work was then making its first appearance on the English stage, Marsh attracted considerable attention before ever he was launched upon a professional career.

In 1896 Marsh was appointed a junior clerk in the Australian department of the Colonial Office, where he served as assistant private secretary to Joseph Chamberlain and subsequently Alfred Lyttelton. By December 1905 he had become a first-class clerk and was at work in the west African department when Winston Churchill became parliamentary under-secretary for the colonies and invited Marsh to become his private secretary. For the next twenty-three years Marsh was at Churchill's right hand whenever he was in office. He toured British East Africa, Uganda, and Egypt with him in 1907–8, and served with him successively at the Board of Trade (1908–10), the Home Office (1910–11), the Admiralty (1911–15), and, from May to November 1915, the duchy of Lancaster. After Churchill resigned this office and left on active service in the army Marsh became an assistant private secretary to the prime minister, his especial responsibility being the civil-list pensions, in which capacity he was able to be of assistance to James Joyce and others. After Asquith's fall in December 1916 Marsh was virtually unemployed until Churchill was appointed minister of munitions (July 1917) and subsequently (1919–21) secretary of state for war. Marsh went with him in 1921 to the Colonial Office, where he remained until 1924, serving as private secretary to the duke of Devonshire and later J. H. Thomas. He then served for the last time under Churchill, at the Treasury (1924–9). When Labour came into power in 1929 he returned to J. H. Thomas, moving with him to the Dominions Office in 1930. There he remained until his retirement in February 1937, serving from November 1935 as secretary to Malcolm MacDonald.

Although Marsh enjoyed a distinguished career as a civil servant, he never attained the highest eminence and he is to be remembered, in Churchill's words, as 'a deeply instructed champion of the arts' (*The Times*). It was in 1896, after meeting Neville Lytton, then an art student in Paris, that Marsh began to cultivate the eye of an art connoisseur and started collecting pictures. With Lytton's guidance he specialized at first in the English watercolourists, in particular Thomas Girtin, Paul Sandby, John Sell Cotman, and Alexander and John Robert Cozens. In 1904, through the good offices of Robert Ross, he acquired the Horne collection of drawings, so that almost overnight he became one of the most important private collectors in the country. The turning point came in December 1911, when his purchase of a painting by Duncan Grant, contrary to Lytton's advice, led him to launch out on his own as a patron of contemporary British painting, and he gathered around him several of the young men from the Slade School of Fine Art, chief among them John Currie and Mark Gertler. Turning his back on the past, he also took under his wing the brothers John and Paul Nash and Stanley Spencer, and by 1914 had brought together the nucleus of what became one of the most valuable collections of modern work in private hands. It covered every inch of the wall space in his apartments at 5 Raymond Buildings, Gray's Inn, London.

Meanwhile Marsh had been no less active in the field of literature, and his apartments had become the rendezvous of poets as well as painters and, from 1913, a virtual second home for Rupert Brooke. Early in 1912 his critical appreciation of Brooke's poems in the *Poetry Review* brought him the acquaintance of Harold Monro; a casual remark of Brooke's led to the scheme of an anthology of modern verse which Marsh undertook to edit, under the title *Georgian Poetry*, with Monro's Poetry Bookshop as the publishing house. The anthology appeared in December 1912 and eventually developed into a series of five volumes published over a period of ten years. During those years Marsh introduced to the general reader almost three generations of poets. Among the original 'Georgians' were Brooke, J. E. Flecker, Lascelles Abercrombie, Gordon Bottomley, W. H. Davies, Walter de la Mare, and D. H. Lawrence. In 1917 a new group appeared, characterized by the powerful 'realistic' war poetry of Siegfried Sassoon, Robert Nichols, and Robert Graves. The fourth volume (1919)

revealed a certain limitation of theme and a pervading mannerism of style, and although the fifth volume of the series (1922) introduced Edmund Blunden, yet another new poet of high promise, it was clear that the movement had played itself out, yielding place to a less traditional conception of poetry derived from the pre-war work of T. E. Hulme and Ezra Pound.

By instituting a royalty system instead of outright payment Marsh, with characteristic generosity, was able to make the anthologies of considerable benefit to his contributors over the years. And through undertaking to do the accounting himself he not only kept himself in regular touch with his poetical 'family' but was often able to supplement their portion with a small gift wherever there was hardship. For this Marsh used what he called his 'murder money', a source of income which he had inherited on the death of an uncle in 1903, being one-sixth of what remained of the compensation granted to the Perceval family in 1812. This fund, now reserved for the patronage of the arts, was augmented by the royalties from Marsh's memoir of Rupert Brooke, a biographical essay attached as introduction to the *Collected Poems* which he edited and brought out in 1918. Marsh was deeply affected by Brooke's death and from 1915 until 1934 he was indefatigable as literary executor, editing Brooke's posthumous prose and verse, thereby laying the basis of Brooke's reputation. His difficulties in completing this work were greatly increased by the objections raised against it by Brooke's grief-stricken mother.

By the end of the Georgian enterprise a new interest had entered Marsh's life when he began translating the *Fables* of La Fontaine. These came out in two small volumes, followed by a complete edition in two volumes in 1931. Thereafter he published translations from French and Latin, notably the *Odes of Horace* (1941), and in 1939 'an urbane, almost too urbane' book of reminiscences entitled *A Number of People* (*The Times*). In 1952 his translation of the *Fables* was reissued in Everyman's Library. He also corrected proofs for other authors, notably Winston Churchill, a form of scholarly hobby that he undertook with painstaking attention to detail.

On his retirement from the civil service in 1937 Marsh was appointed KCVO. He was also made a trustee of the Tate Gallery and a governor of the Old Vic, having for several years served on the committee of the Contemporary Art Society (of which he was chairman, 1936–52) and the council of the Royal Society of Literature. His taste in contemporary painting advanced with the times with easier adaptability than his appreciation of verse, yet he remained loyal to the principles of representational art as against the various abstract manifestations which won favour in his time. His finely balanced aesthetic sensibility was everywhere evident, except at the theatre where, by his own admission, he enjoyed the play like a child, and showed it. Through his friendship with Ivor Novello he developed an ardent enthusiasm for first nights. But, as Violet Bonham Carter later recalled: 'The one theatre which failed to focus his attention was "World Theatre". The sweep and crash of world events left him unmoved, uninterested and almost unaware' (Hassall and Mathews, 49).

Marsh died on 13 January 1953 in the Knightsbridge flat, 86 Walton Street, London, that had been his post-war home. He was unmarried. He was mourned in a leading article in *The Times* as possibly 'the last individual patron of the arts' and later that year the Contemporary Art Society published a literary tribute, *Sketches for a Composite Literary Portrait*, with contributions from many distinguished figures. Max Beerbohm, who recalled never hearing his friend called Edward Marsh, only ever Eddie, described 'his tufted eyebrows and his monocle, and his sharply chiselled features, and his laconic mode of speech' (Hassall and Mathews, 51). Marsh's somewhat stiff demeanour could indeed be forbidding to a stranger, and if he was always anxious to please in conversation, his favourite pastime, he could nevertheless be ruthlessly uncompromising whenever one of his cherished principles of scholarship was at stake. But his 'great kindness of heart … somehow shone through the rather frigid surface of his social form' (ibid.), while the genuineness of his love of art, and the quality of his judgement, meant that he was respected by generations of poets and painters who otherwise 'might have dismissed him as a back number' (*The Times*).

C. V. HASSALL, *rev.* MARK POTTLE

Sources *The Times* (14 Jan 1953) · C. Hassall, *Edward Marsh: a biography* (1959) · C. Hassall and D. Mathews, eds., *Sketches for a composite literary portrait* (1953) · E. Marsh, *A number of people: a book of reminiscences* (1939) · E. Marsh, memoir, in *The collected poems of Rupert Brooke* (1918); with an intro. by G. Ewart (1992) · *TLS* (25 March 1939) · personal knowledge (1971) · C. Hassall, ed., *Ambrosia and small beer: the record of a correspondence between Edward Marsh and Christopher Hassall* (1964)

Archives BL, corresp. with Macmillans, Add. MS 55045 · Bodl. Oxf., letters to R. W. Chapman · Bodl. Oxf., letters to Sir George Rostrevor Hamilton · CAC Cam., corresp. with Sir Winston Churchill and related papers [copies] · CUL, letters to G. E. Moore · Durham RO, letters to Lord Londonderry · Harvard University, near Florence, Italy, Center for Italian and Renaissance Studies, letters to B. Berenson · King's AC Cam., corresp. and papers relating to trusteeship of Rupert Brooke's estate · King's AC Cam., letters to John Hayward · LUL, corresp. with T. S. Moore · Royal Society of Literature, London, letters to Royal Society of Literature · Tate collection, letters to David Bomberg [copies] · Tate collection, corresp. of Marsh and his executors with Contemporary Arts Society · U. Glas. L., letters to D. S. MacColl · U. Leeds, Brotherton L., letters to Sir E. W. Gosse | SOUND BL NSA, performance recording

Likenesses N. Lewis, oils, *c*.1937, Royal Society of Literature, London · F. Dobson, bronze head, *c*.1938–1939, Doncaster Museum and Art Gallery · O. Birley, oils, 1949, NPG · N. Egon, drawing, 1951, Trinity Cam. · L. Appelbee, portrait · M. Beerbohm, caricature, drawing · W. Churchill, portrait · H. Coster, photographs, NPG · A. Devas, group portrait, priv. coll. · J. Hassall, pencil drawing · N. Lytton, portrait · K. Pollak, photograph, NPG · Violet, duchess of Rutland, pencil drawing, priv. coll.

Wealth at death £11,986 17*s*. 6*d*.: probate, 2 May 1953, *CGPLA Eng. & Wales*

Marsh, Francis (1627–1693), Church of Ireland archbishop of Dublin, the son of Henry Marsh of Edgeworth, Gloucestershire, was born in or near Gloucester on 23 October 1627. He was admitted as a pensioner at Emmanuel College, Cambridge, on 22 April 1642, and graduated BA in 1647 and MA in 1650. On 14 October 1651 he was elected a fellow of Gonville and Caius College, Cambridge, and held the office of *praelector rhetoricus* for 1651–2. Though learned in Greek and known for his studies in Stoic philosophy, his royalist sympathies stood in the way of his further preferment. In February 1653 he obtained four months' leave of absence to travel to Ireland, possibly in order to take orders from one of the Irish bishops then in Dublin (perhaps John Leslie, bishop of Raphoe). On returning to Caius College he was again *praelector rhetoricus* in 1654–7, and remained in residence until April 1660.

Marsh's residence at Cambridge seemed assured by the king's letter of 8 October 1660, requesting the continuance of his fellowship, but he decided to return to Ireland on the advice of his patron, Jeremy Taylor. Shortly after the latter's accession to the sees of Down and Connor (January 1661), Marsh was appointed as dean of Connor (8 February 1661), having been ordained by Taylor on 27 January 1661. By 1 June 1661 he had, however, resigned this deanery, having, through the earl of Clarendon's influence, been moved to Armagh, where he was elected dean on 19 June 1661—holding at the same time the rectorship of Clonfeacle. Three years later, again thanks to Clarendon, he was made archdeacon of Dromore. At the end of 1667 (elected 28 October, consecrated at Clonmel 22 December) he succeeded William Fuller as bishop of Limerick, Ardfert, and Aghadoe. He was translated on 10 January 1673 to Kilmore and Ardagh, and on 14 February 1682 was made archbishop of Dublin, holding *in commendam* the treasurership of St Patrick's and the prebend of Desertmore in St Fin Barre's, Cork.

It was in Marsh's palace that the privy council assembled on 12 February 1687, when Tyrconnell was sworn in as lord deputy. Early in 1689, feeling his position unsafe, owing to his opposition to the administration of Tyrconnell, Marsh returned to England, having attempted to appoint William King, then dean of St Patrick's, to act as his commissary. King declined the commission as not legally executed, and prevailed upon the chapters of Christ Church and St Patrick's to elect Anthony Dopping, then bishop of Meath, as administrator of the spiritualities. Marsh, who favoured the transfer of the crown to William of Orange, was included in the act of attainder passed by James's Dublin parliament in June 1689, his name being placed in the first list for forfeiture of life and estate. He returned to Dublin after the battle of the Boyne, but was not present at the thanksgiving service in St Patrick's on 6 July 1690, excusing his absence on the ground of age and infirmity, though in the same year he published his only work: *An Address Given into the Late King James, by the Titular Archbishop of Dublin* (1690). In his last years he repaired and enlarged the archiepiscopal palace of St Sepulchre's at his own cost. He died there of apoplexy on 16 November 1693, and was buried on 18 November in Christ Church, Dublin, Dopping preaching the funeral sermon. Marsh had married Mary, youngest daughter of Jeremy Taylor, and they had four children: Francis, Jeremiah, Barbara, and Mary, the second son succeeding him as treasurer of St Patrick's and afterwards becoming dean of Down. He was apparently not related to Narcissus Marsh, his successor in the see of Dublin. His will, dated 24 October 1693 and proved on 20 November 1693, left all his property to his wife and children.

ALEXANDER GORDON, rev. ELIZABETHANNE BORAN

Sources The whole works of Sir James Ware concerning Ireland, ed. and trans. W. Harris, 1 (1739), 358, 515 · J. B. Leslie, Armagh clergy and parishes (1911), 16–17 · H. K. Bonney, The life of the Right Reverend Father in God, Jeremy Taylor, D.D. (1815), 367–9 · Clergy of Down and Dromore, pt 2: Before 1930, ed. J. B. Leslie and H. B. Swanzy (1996), 5, 42 · R. Mant, History of the Church of Ireland, 1 (1840), 710–11 · Venn, Alum. Cant., 1/3.144 · H. Cotton, Fasti ecclesiae Hibernicae, 3 (1849), 33, 253, 296 · J. B. Leslie, 'Fasti of Christ Church Cathedral, Dublin', Representative Church Body Library, Dublin, 30 · A. Dopping, A sermon preached … at the funeral of … Francis, lord archbishop of Dublin (1694) · Wing, STC, 2.404 · J. Wills, Lives of illustrious and distinguished Irishmen, 4 (1847), 266 · Burtchaell & Sadleir, Alum. Dubl., 2nd edn, 533 · S. J. Connolly, 'Reformers and high flyers: the post revolution church', As by law established: the Church of Ireland since the Reformation, ed. A. Ford, J. McGuire, and K. Milne (1995), 154 · W. A. Phillips, ed., History of the Church of Ireland, 3 (1933), 149–51 · P. Kilroy, Protestant dissent and controversy in Ireland, 1660–1714 (1994), 75 · C. McNeill, ed., The Tanner letters, IMC (1943), 462, 498, 501

Likenesses photograph of portrait (1682x93), 1913, Representative Church Body Library, Dublin

Wealth at death real estate plus £35 cash: Leslie, Armagh clergy and parishes, 17

Marsh, George (c.1515–1555), clergyman and protestant martyr, was born at Dean, Lancashire, probably the son of George Marsh of Dean. He became a farmer, and married when he was about twenty-five years old. Upon the death of his wife, and having made arrangements for the care of his children, he went to study at Cambridge, where he matriculated at Christ's College in 1551 and petitioned for a degree. He probably converted to protestantism while at Cambridge, and was ordained a deacon by Nicholas Ridley, bishop of London, in 1552. Early in 1553 Marsh became the curate for both of the livings (Church Langton, Leicestershire, and All Hallows, Bread Street, London) held by Laurence Saunders, a clear indication that Marsh's career was being fostered by zealous protestants in the Edwardian church. Marsh appears to have remained at Cambridge for the next few years and from this base he conducted preaching forays into his native Lancashire; he may very well have done so in the company of Saunders, who is known to have preached in the area in 1552 or early 1553.

Marsh's missionary efforts seem to have made an impression: the earl of Derby later claimed that he had heard of Marsh while in London and had resolved to arrest him either in London or Lancashire, while (as letters printed by Foxe reveal) Marsh had become one of the leaders of the tiny minority of protestants in Lancashire. Among his converts were Geoffrey Hurst, a nail maker from Shakerley, Lancashire, who was married to Marsh's sister Alice. (Only Queen Mary's death prevented Hurst from meeting the same grisly end as his brother-in-law.) At the beginning of 1554 Marsh returned to Lancashire. He later claimed that he had returned in order to visit his family and friends before going into exile in Germany or Denmark. In fact his activities were less innocuous than this

would suggest; he was charged with having preached heresy publicly in Dean, Eccles, Bolton, Bury, and other Lancashire parishes in January and February 1554. Marsh did not deny this charge but merely claimed that what he had preached had been orthodox doctrine under Edward VI.

In early March 1554, while staying at his mother's house, Marsh was informed that the servants of a local JP were searching for him. His family advised him to flee, but Marsh was afraid that his flight would discredit his previous preaching and undermine his missionary work. A few days later, after anxious soul-searching and prayer, Marsh surrendered to the authorities and was sent to the earl of Derby. Marsh was interrogated about his religious beliefs but initially declined to answer questions about the sacrament, claiming that his accusers sought his death by asking him such questions. Marsh was held in the earl's custody, and was examined again by Derby on Palm Sunday. On being informed by a cleric who had questioned Marsh that the prisoner could be brought to conform, Derby had Marsh held in less rigorous conditions. But Marsh was conscience-stricken by his lack of 'boldness' and resisted further efforts to persuade him to recant. These efforts were intensive—throughout Marsh's ordeal the authorities sought his submission, not his death. Marsh was asked to endorse articles that Edward Crome, the celebrated evangelical preacher, had subscribed to in one of his recantations; Marsh refused to sign them, even when they were reduced to only four articles covering the sacrament and confession.

After Easter, Derby abandoned his attempts to convert Marsh and had his prisoner taken to Lancaster Castle, where he was brought before the quarter sessions. Marsh was held in Lancaster, in secular custody, for nearly a year (probably because the authorities did not want to put him on trial in a spiritual court until statutes against heresy were enacted by parliament). During this time Marsh had many visitors, both priests trying to convert him and sympathizers offering him money and encouragement. Together with Thomas Warberton, a fellow prisoner who would later join the English protestant exiles at Aarau, Marsh read every day from the prayer book and the Bible to townspeople gathered outside the window of his cell. Bishop George Coates of Chester upbraided the gaoler for the lax conditions of Marsh's imprisonment and ordered that he be more strictly confined. In March 1555 Marsh was transferred to Chester, where he was repeatedly examined by Bishop Coates. During these examinations Marsh remained obdurate in his refusal to renounce his beliefs. At Marsh's condemnation the vicar-general of the diocese twice interrupted Coates, while the bishop was passing sentence on Marsh, in futile efforts to give him a final chance to recant and save his life.

On 24 April 1555 Marsh was taken outside the walls of Chester and, after refusing the offer of a royal pardon if he would recant, he was burnt in the adjacent district of Spital Boughton. According to Foxe's informant the people were impressed by Marsh's stoicism and acclaimed him as a martyr. In response Bishop Coates preached a sermon in Chester Cathedral denouncing Marsh as a heretic who met his deserved end and was eternally damned.

THOMAS S. FREEMAN

Sources J. Foxe, *The first volume of the ecclesiasticall history contayning the actes and monumentes of thynges passed*, new edn (1570), 1731–45 · J. Foxe, *Actes and monuments* (1563), 1118–35 · J. Foxe, *Rerum in ecclesia gestarum … commentarii* (1559) · Venn, *Alum. Cant.* · C. Haigh, *Reformation and resistance in Tudor Lancashire* (1975) · C. H. Garrett, *The Marian exiles: a study in the origins of Elizabethan puritanism* (1938) · Cooper, *Ath. Cantab.*, vol. 1
Likenesses portrait (of his execution), repro. in Foxe, *Actes and monuments*

Marsh, Sir Henry, first baronet (1790–1860), physician, was born at Loughrea, co. Galway, son of Robert Marsh, rector of Killinane, co. Galway, and Sophia, daughter of William Wolseley, rector of Tullycorbet, co. Monaghan. Marsh's mother was a granddaughter of Sir Thomas *Molyneux, physician and patriot. His paternal ancestry consisted of a long line of Anglican divines, the most celebrated being Dr Francis Marsh, originally from Gloucestershire, who was archbishop of Dublin from 1682 to 1693. Marsh was educated locally in Loughrea and then entered the University of Dublin as a pensioner in 1807; he graduated BA in 1812 and went on to study for holy orders. However, he came under the influence of the 'Walkerites', a sect named after the Revd John Walker, a fellow of Trinity College, Dublin, and separated from the Anglican communion.

On 9 March 1813 Marsh was indentured to his relative, Philip Crampton (1777–1858), then one of the surgeons at the Meath Hospital, Dublin. In 1818 Marsh received a dissecting wound, which resulted in the amputation of the forefinger of his right hand and the abandonment of surgery as a career. Later in the same year he graduated in medicine from the University of Dublin and obtained the licence of the King and Queen's College of Physicians in Ireland. He spent the next two years studying on the continent, chiefly in Paris.

In 1820 Marsh was appointed assistant physician to Dr Steevens' Hospital, Dublin. In the following year he was one of the founders of the Pitt Street Hospital for Diseases of Children, and in 1824 he helped to establish the Park Street school of medicine, where he lectured on the principles and practice of medicine. In 1828 he was appointed professor of medicine at the Royal College of Surgeons in Ireland, but he resigned his chair in 1832 because of the demands of his expanding private practice. In 1837 he was appointed physician-in-ordinary to the queen in Ireland, and he was created a baronet on 13 March 1839. He was elected a fellow of the King and Queen's College of Physicians in the following October. He served as president of the college for three sessions: 1841–2, 1845–6, and 1857–8.

Marsh acquired all the trappings of a successful Dublin medical practice—a house in Merrion Square, a seat in the country, and a baronetcy. Contemporaries attributed his success to his determination, energy, and intelligence, rather than to any originality on his part, still less to his

Sir Henry Marsh, first baronet (1790–1860), by John Kirkwood, pubd 1841 (after Sir Frederic William Burton)

contributions to the medical journals of the day. The relative paucity of his publications was a matter of contemporary comment. In 1820 Marsh had married Anne, daughter of Thomas Crowe, Ennis, co. Clare, and widow of William Arthur; their only child, Henry Marsh, was born on 3 April 1821, and she died on 2 November 1846. Marsh was married a second time, on 28 August 1856, to Mary Henrietta, daughter of the Revd Robert Jelly, and widow of Thomas Kemmis, of Shane House, Queen's county (later co. Laois).

Marsh died suddenly at his house in Merrion Square on 1 December 1860 and was buried in Mount Jerome cemetery, Dublin. After his death a memorial fund was launched. It was decided to commission a full-length marble figure by John H. Foley (1818–1874), Ireland's leading nineteenth-century sculptor, and to place it in the main hall of the King and Queen's College of Physicians in Kildare Street, Dublin. The inauguration took place on 9 November 1866. Sir Dominic Corrigan, the chairman of the organizing committee, eulogized Marsh's contribution to medicine and his commitment to the dignity and propriety of the profession. Its members were indebted to

Marsh, he said, for his exemplary tact and courtesy, and his humanity and charity. According to Corrigan these qualities were 'exhibited in the profession in Dublin to a degree not excelled throughout Europe'.

Marsh's personal estate and effects amounted to £18,520 10s. 7d. His son Henry, then a major in the 3rd regiment of dragoon guards, succeeded to the title, to most of the personal estate, and to property in co. Kilkenny, which had a net annual value of £819 9s. 5d. He died unmarried and without issue on 27 May 1868 and the baronetcy became extinct.   LAURENCE M. GEARY

Sources Marsh MSS, NL Ire., PC 12, 429 • 'Our portrait gallery, no. XXV: Sir Henry Marsh', *Dublin University Magazine*, 18 (1841), 688–92 • *Dublin Quarterly Journal of Medical Science*, 33 (1862), 251–2 • *Dublin University Magazine*, 57 (1861), 222–8 • C. A. Cameron, *History of the Royal College of Surgeons in Ireland*, 2nd edn (1916), 616–20 • Memorial statue of Sir Henry Marsh, Bart, M.D., in the hall of the King and Queen's College of Physicians of Ireland, 1867
Archives NL Ire.
Likenesses C. Moore, bust, 1843?, Royal College of Physicians of Ireland, Dublin • J. R. Kirk, profile on monument, 1862, Mount Jerome cemetery, Dublin • J. H. Foley, marble statue, 1866, Royal College of Physicians of Ireland, Dublin • Geary Bros., daguerreotype, repro. in *Dublin Quarterly Journal of Medical Science*, 16 (1853), facing p. 1 • J. R. Kirk, marble bust, Royal College of Surgeons in Ireland, Dublin • J. Kirkwood, etching (after F. W. Burton), NPG; repro. in *Dublin University Magazine*, 18 (1841) [*see illus.*] • G. Sanders, engraving (after F. W. Burton, 1843)
Wealth at death under £20,000: probate, 22 Dec 1860, *CGPLA Ire.*

Herbert Marsh (1757–1839), by John Ponsford, 1834

Marsh, Herbert (1757–1839), bishop of Peterborough and biblical critic, was born at Faversham, Kent, on 10 December 1757 and baptized there on 3 January 1758, the eldest son of Richard Marsh (1727–1778), vicar of Faversham and a minor canon of Canterbury, and his wife, Elizabeth Frend, the daughter of a stonemason. There followed another son, Richard, who became a Fleet Street printer, and a daughter, who married a lawyer.

Family and education Marsh's paternal grandfather, Richard Marsh (1670/71–1732), initiated a clerical family tradition: having been admitted a sizar at St John's College, Cambridge, in 1688, he obtained a fellowship in 1696 and became vicar at St Margaret Atcliffe, Kent, in 1700. As chaplain to Edward Villiers, first earl of Jersey, Richard Marsh was committed to the revolutionary settlement of 1689. Opposed to Newtonian physics, which he regarded as a hubristic alternative to Mosaic cosmology, he advocated that reason and learning should be subordinate to revelation. He believed that only a learned clergy of the established church could maintain the mystery of religion and uphold the need for good works inspired by grace, against the threats posed by religious enthusiasm, deism and Socinianism. Apart from his anti-Newtonianism, Richard Marsh's ideas re-emerged in the mature thought of his grandson.

Herbert Marsh was educated at Faversham grammar school and then, from 1770, at the King's School, Canterbury, in company with his cousin William Frend, whose later unitarian and republican views were at odds with Marsh's own. He was admitted a king's scholar on 4 March

1771. His headmaster, Osmund Beauvoir, was an accomplished modern linguist who had assisted Archbishop William Wake in his negotiations at the Sorbonne over a possible union between the Gallican church and the Church of England. Marsh went up to St John's College, Cambridge, on 19 October 1775 and was admitted a foundress scholar on 7 November. He chose as his tutor a fellow undergraduate, Thomas Jones (1756–1807), of Trinity College. Marsh did not share his tutor's unitarian leanings yet defended freedom of thought. He greatly admired Jones's interest in natural theology, although he later subordinated it to biblical revelation. Besides, Marsh's current interests were mathematics and physics; his theological interests developed later (from 1790). In 1779 he graduated BA as second wrangler and second Smith's prizeman; he proceeded MA in 1782 and BD in July 1792. He was admitted foundress fellow of his college on 23 March 1779 and was ordained deacon by the bishop of Ely on 16 May 1780. For the next five years he fulfilled his college teaching obligations. At the general election in 1784 he canvassed for the new prime minister, William Pitt the younger, for one of the Cambridge University seats; he was an admirer of Pitt throughout his life.

Travel and intellectual development In 1785 Marsh received permission to travel to Egypt and Arabia. After passing through Belgium and the Netherlands, in 1786 he consulted the eminent biblical scholar Johann David Michaelis in Göttingen about learning Arabic. While wintering in Leipzig, where he lodged in the Burgstrasse and read the Koran, his lifelong asthmatic condition worsened. He was confined to bed for the best part of the next three years, but was able to visit Christoph Martin Wieland in Weimar, a writer whom he held in awe. During his illness he became fascinated with Enlightenment authors, although his reading of Hermann Samuel Reimarus's writings shook his faith in biblical inspiration. As a partial antidote Marsh began translating Johann Gottfried Eichhorn's *Einleitung in das alte Testaments*, but his hopes for publication were crushed by Dr Thomas Kipling's advice that Cambridge University Press would not sanction the work. Kipling regarded Eichhorn's comparative criticism of biblical books with other Semitic texts as too controversial. Instead Marsh was commissioned to translate the fourth edition of Michaelis's *Einleitung in die göttlichen Schriften des neuen Bundes*, his introduction to the New Testament. Sensing a change in the intellectual climate in England, he feared the odium of heresy even for translating the less controversial work. He added extensive notes to Michaelis's text that primed his readers in continental biblical criticism.

With improving health, Marsh returned to England in 1793 to take his delayed BD examination. His two qualifying sermons registered a reconstructed orthodoxy: one defended Mosaic authorship of the Pentateuch and the other urged rigorous theological education for ordinands in the Church of England. However, during William Frend's university trial in May 1794 for sedition, Marsh was politically compromised for helping his cousin by refusing to give evidence against him in court. He returned to Leipzig under a cloud. Stung by the criticism, he published a thorough refutation of George Travis's defence against Edward Gibbon of the authenticity of 1 John 5: 7, entitled *Letters to Archdeacon Travis, in Vindication of one of the Translators' Notes to Michaelis's Introduction* (1795). Marsh was not defending the unitarian interpretation of the text suggested by Gibbon but was attacking the slipshod theology current in England and evident in Travis's *Letters to Edward Gibbon*.

Marsh's greatest work, however, arose from his notes on Michaelis. In 1795, dissatisfied with Michaelis's account, he began investigating the sources of the synoptic gospels, publishing in 1801 a sophisticated hypothesis that argued for their historical reliability. His *Dissertation on the Origin and Composition of the Three First Canonical Gospels* rigorously developed Eichhorn's theory that the first three gospels shared a common source (now lost) and was taken up by both Eichhorn and Paulus. In conservative wartime Britain, however, Marsh's hypothesis aroused fear and engendered a counter-hypothesis of 'detached narratives' that maintained the integrity of authorship of each gospel, which was successively developed by John Randolph, George Gleig, Daniel Veysie, and Connop Thirlwall. Although Marsh rejected the argument that Mark was the first of the three gospels to have been written, he anticipated the 'two-document' hypothesis, whereby Mark and the lost document were the sources for Matthew and Luke.

Politics In 1797 changing events shifted Marsh's interests to politics. German Anglophilia was replaced by hostility on account of Pitt's maritime blockade of continental Europe. Together with his expatriate democrat friend James Macdonald, Marsh lamented the new German mood. When in 1797–8 the *Allgemeine Literatur Zeitung* printed essays attacking British politics and culture, Marsh was anxious to reply. In March 1798 he published anonymously articles in the *Allgemeine Literatur Zeitung* and the *Neue Teutsche Merkur*. The disillusioned Anglophile Johann Wilhelm von Archenholtz responded with invective in his journal *Minerva*, arousing Marsh to write openly in the July edition of the *Allgemeine Literatur Zeitung*. He had by now lost interest in theology and entered the lists as a political-historical writer. The result was his *Historische Uebersicht der Politik England und Frankreichs* (1799), in which he argued that France not Britain was the aggressor in the current war. The *Allgemeine Literatur Zeitung* in 1799 reported that Marsh had proved his case, and Friedrich von Gentz's influential *Historische Journal* followed suit. Flushed with success, Marsh translated the *Historische Uebersicht* into French and English. In Britain only the Foxite whig William Belsham wrote a rebuff, to which Marsh replied with conclusive satisfaction.

By May 1799 Marsh was engaged to marry Marianne Emilie Charlotte (1774–1844), the daughter of a Leipzig merchant, John Lecarriere. Soon afterwards he rented rooms near the Neumarkt, Leipzig, in preparation for his bride. Seeking financial independence to free him from his college fellowship so that he could marry, he attempted to enter commerce. He proposed a smoked herring industry based in Stornoway, on the Hebridean Isle of Lewes, and manned by Dutch prisoners of war, which would supply the German market hit by Pitt's maritime blockade. He subsequently offered his services to the board of agriculture as an overseas adviser. But, unable to leave Marianne, he refused both a place on Lord Elgin's expedition to Istanbul and the reportedly strenuous post of director of the Weimar Belvedere Academy. Instead in 1802 he pressed in turn to deputize for the aged regius professor of history at Cambridge, to become royal historiographer for England (though based in Leipzig), and for a consulship at Leipzig. While awaiting news from London, Marsh was elected fellow of the Royal Society on 8 January 1801 and held office as junior bursar of St John's from 21 March 1801 to 20 March 1802.

In 1800, through the influence of Pitt's adviser George Tomline, Marsh had been interviewed by Pitt and offered a £500 pension from the secret-service fund. Hoping for more substantial preferment or a title that might carry weight in the German principalities, Marsh delayed, then accepted. The pension was established under Henry Addington only in 1803 and withdrawn by Lord Liverpool on the accession of George IV in 1820, in view of Marsh's then substantially larger income. In 1806 he began canvassing covertly for election to the Lady Margaret professorship of divinity at Cambridge. In the event he was elected without opposition in 1807 and was awarded a DD by mandate the following year. Finally released from his college fellowship, he married Marianne by special licence at Harwich on 1 July 1807.

Doctrinal disputes Until returning to Britain in 1800 Marsh, despite his trinitarian allegiance, had been unconcerned about matters of Christian doctrine. Furthermore in 1798 he thought that political views alone divided Anglican churchmen from dissenters. Between 1800 and 1805 his alarm at the fragile balance of church and state increasingly focused on the supposedly doubtful loyalty of the evangelicals in the Church of England and their non-denominational co-operation with dissent. In accord with family tradition and a growing high-church mood, Marsh responded to recent evangelical challenges by preaching in 1805 four 'strongly anti-Calvinist' sermons which attacked the doctrine of double predestination, which he believed was conducive to antinomianism. In expounding the Thirty-Nine Articles, he appealed to the authority of 'the Bible alone', not to tradition or to the church fathers. He astutely cultivated politically sympathetic patrons, principally the Hardwicke family in Cambridgeshire, for which his Bene't Street house in Cambridge was targeted by an angry mob in March 1810.

Marsh's attempts to build a political base were eclipsed by the Bible Society controversy that broke out in Cambridge in 1811. His public opposition to the society—an interdenominational and evangelically led society that distributed bibles at home and abroad—had been preceded by a successful campaign to promote Church of England educational provision for the poor. This came in response to the opening by Joseph Lancaster of a non-denominational school in Cambridge in 1808 and the gathering momentum of the Royal Lancastrian Society. Alarmed, Marsh used a charity schools sermon at St Paul's Cathedral, London, on 13 June 1811 to appeal for a parallel society to be founded that would be guided by the principles of the established church. In October he met with the Hackney phalanx to plan the scheme. Marsh's sermon proved the catalyst for the formation that year of the National Society for Promoting the Education of the Poor in the Principles of the Established Church. The society mushroomed with support from Anglican churchmen of all persuasions, and Marsh was delighted at the way in which it united the church. But he misinterpreted this support as opposition to non-denominational enterprises. Thus, when undergraduates proposed forming a Bible Society auxiliary in Cambridge, Marsh industriously opposed them with a personally distributed *Address to the Members of the Senate of the University of Cambridge* (1811). But his strategy was defeated when the Bible Society group won the support of the evangelical William Farish, professor of chemistry, Lord Hardwicke, who agreed to chair the meeting, and the university chancellor, the duke of Gloucester, who agreed to preside over the society. The Bible Society meeting, swept by a prevailing apocalyptic mood, was a massive success, and Marsh conceded defeat.

Marsh's principal objection to the Bible Society lay in his insistence that the Book of Common Prayer should be distributed together with the Bible. In his subsequent *Inquiry into the consequences of neglecting to give the Prayer Book with the Bible … with … other important matter relative to the British and Foreign Bible Society* (1812), he depicted the consequences of such neglect as a possible repetition of the civil war, in which the evangelicals and dissenters were presented as new puritans who fostered undisciplined interpretation of the Bible. He warned that disestablishment and perpetual conflict between warring sects could follow. He still sought to win back the evangelicals in the church, but was not mollified when William Wilberforce instituted an evangelical Prayer Book and Homily Society. He wanted evangelicals to forsake the Bible Society for the Society for Promoting Christian Knowledge (SPCK).

Marsh regarded the overseas distribution of bibles in a different light, however. In countries where there was no established church he supported Bible distribution by Roman Catholics or evangelicals, and he personally subscribed to the work of the Baptist Society in India and the London Missionary Society in Africa. But in his *History of the Translations which have been made of the Scriptures* (1812) he successfully challenged the Bible Society's inflated claims about the extent of its work abroad. Although he failed to win back leading evangelicals such as Isaac Milner, there were positive achievements. He had pressurized many evangelicals into protesting their loyalty to the establishment, helped galvanize the SPCK, and inspired a movement for Anglican education of the poor. He also rebuffed the Roman Catholic congratulations offered by Father Peter Gandolphy in his *Comparative View of the Churches of England and Rome* (1814), which became a standard work of anti-Catholic apologetics. Reprinted in 1816, 1841, and 1852, the book delivered him from any suspicion of popery.

Lady Margaret professor of divinity Marsh began his first series of professorial lectures in 1809 and, hoping to reach a wider audience, he broke with tradition by writing the lectures in English rather than Latin and by lecturing in the church of Great St Mary rather than the divinity schools. He intended to lecture in three-year cycles but, because of the Bible Society dispute, the need to pursue his own research, and episcopal duties from 1816 onwards, he lectured only in 1809–10, 1813, 1816, 1822, and 1823. While he published thirty-six lectures, he delivered lectures on only three of the seven branches of divinity he planned to cover. He privately printed an abstract of the fourth branch for his Peterborough clergy in 1820 and a 46-page 'History of interpretation' in 1828. Thereafter his interest waned, due to his ill health and episcopal duties. Besides, he felt a new sense of beleaguerment by the repeal of the Test Act in 1828 and the achievement of Catholic emancipation in 1829, which was reflected in his *Charge to his Clergy* of 1831.

The lectures as published covered the topics of biblical criticism, interpretation, authenticity, and credibility, and the evidences of Christianity. The content was bibliocentric and expressed characteristic themes from the latitudinarian tradition of the eighteenth century. Marsh was keen to echo the protestant reformers' abandonment of church tradition in favour of reason and learning instructed by scripture. This meant a rigorously grammatical interpretation which, he argued, only the learned clergy of an established church could provide. Public response to his lectures was generally favourable. Some Unitarians were disappointed, as they had hoped that Marsh's earlier refutation of Travis had indicated his rejection of trinitarian dogma. Evangelicals rejoiced that Marsh had abandoned the uncommitted divinity of his Michaelis notes for a clearly apologetic purpose, even if they regretted his intellectualist emphasis. From America, the New England biblical critic John Stevens Buckminster sent students to Marsh on the strength of reading his lectures. In contrast, Bishop John Hobart of New York felt that a few lectures were no substitute for the comprehensive training that could be provided by dedicated theological colleges. Marsh did not seek to restructure the training of ordinands in Cambridge, although he considerably raised current learning standards. He certainly stirred controversy by calling for a revision of the Authorized Version of the Bible. But on the whole, while in his lectures he introduced his audiences to new critical methods, he deliberately shielded them from knowledge of more radical higher criticism, such as that of Eichhorn or Paulus. In opting for a safe and gentle introduction to his subject, he little prepared his audience for the coming onslaughts of higher criticism. Instead he cautiously married a digest of biblical criticism to the 'evidence-writing' of Hanoverian theology. His Michaelis notes in this respect were ahead of his *Lectures* both in discussing new critical methods and in facing awkward challenges.

Llandaff and Peterborough Marsh's learning and his loyalty to the religious and political establishment were rewarded with preferment. On 13 July 1816 he was nominated bishop of Llandaff and on 25 August was consecrated in Lambeth Palace chapel by Archbishop William Howley. As the junior bishop, Marsh was chaplain to the House of Lords and so resided in Delahaye Street, London, until 1819, during which time he incurred debts of £4000. Despite the inadequate stipend that accompanied his appointment, he attended to his diocese with vigour. To expedite improvements in building stock and church fabric, he revived the office of rural dean. Seeking an effective clergy, he made facility in the Welsh language a condition for institution, and formulated eighty-seven doctrinal questions for prospective candidates in his diocese. In February 1817 he was elected a fellow of the Society of Antiquaries.

On 8 April 1819 Marsh was elected bishop of Peterborough. Aware of a phalanx of evangelical clergy in his bishopric, he made clear that he would brook no irregularities, such as hymn singing. Nor would he sanction unnecessary non-residence or neglected glebe houses. He also promoted double rather than single services and revived the office of rural dean in his new diocese, subdividing existing deaneries for greater efficiency. A significant if modest amount of repair work was completed by 1823 and double services increased over the following decade. Setting an example of dedication, Marsh frequently preached charity sermons and conducted confirmations between triennial visitations. He regarded his examination for curates as a legitimate exercise of episcopal

power, a view recently reinforced by the 1817 Consolidation Act. His eighty-seven questions, nicknamed 'Cobwebs to catch Calvinists', were designed to 'exhibit a connected View of God's dealings with Man under the New Covenant' and excluded Calvinist doctrines of election and eternal security. Instead they emphasized baptismal regeneration, a synergistic doctrine of grace, the need for good works following justification, and the error of unitarianism. In 1821 and 1822 frustrated evangelical incumbents, whose curate appointees had been excluded by Marsh's examination, unsuccessfully petitioned the House of Lords in protest. Their petitions did, however, arouse misgivings in the upper house about Marsh's methods. Both he and his opponents went to print. Sidney Smith's satirical attack on 'Persecuting bishops' in the *Edinburgh Review* damaged Marsh's reputation, even though conservative journals defended him. Marsh made some concessions by reducing the number of questions from eighty-seven to thirty-six, by licensing at least five evangelical curates in Peterborough in the early 1820s, and by nurturing others. His intervention on behalf of one evangelical curate, Samuel Paris, however, was defeated in the court of arches and at the king's bench in 1824. Such failures underlined the limits of episcopal power, though Marsh's examination was itself legal. Indeed, some bishops, such as William Magee of Dublin in 1822 and Henry Philpotts in 1841, instituted rigorous examinations despite the odium Marsh suffered.

Final years Marsh's relations with the county were as mixed as those with the diocese, for political interests often shaped relationships. He was a focus for tory loyalty in Northamptonshire, while Lord Fitzwilliam led the whig interest. The relationship between the two men varied from businesslike politeness to outright hostility, with clashes over the leasing of episcopal land, the rights of which Marsh tenaciously defended. Even a joint project to build a national school in Peterborough in 1823 nearly foundered on Fitzwilliam's suspicion. But Marsh learned tact. In a conflict about a Catholic claims petition in 1825, he carefully explained his position. In 1832, when Fitzwilliam tried to engineer the purchase of a glebe farm, Marsh negotiated firmly but with legal correctness. He had learned his lesson. Though his many commitments continually encroached on his private life, he and his wife maintained a solicitous friendship with the poet John Clare from 1819 to 1835.

From 1835 Marsh was senile and bedridden. While he lay on his deathbed in 1839 the diocese was run by his wife, his elder son, and the diocesan registrar, John Gates. The trio clashed with the third Earl Fitzwilliam over property transfers and voting interests. Although Fitzwilliam was forced to apologize for insulting Marianne Marsh, it was an unfortunate end to Marsh's episcopate.

Marsh died on 1 May 1839 in Peterborough and was buried in the eastern chapel of his cathedral on the 8th. He had been patriotic, gregarious, and industrious. Although combative in public, he was uniformly gracious in private, even with opponents. If self-promoting, he was courageous and loyally devoted to the established church. He was survived by his widow, who died in Peterborough in 1844, and by his sons Herbert Charles Marsh (1808–1851), whom he appointed vicar of Barnack in 1832 and who died insane, and George Henry Marsh (1814–1896), who became vicar of Great Snoring.   ROBERT K. FORREST

Sources R. K. Braine, 'The life and writings of Herbert Marsh (1757–1839)', PhD diss., U. Cam., 1989 · T. Baker, *History of the college of St John the Evangelist, Cambridge*, ed. J. E. B. Mayor, 2 vols. (1869) · MSS, Sächsische Landesbibliothek, Dresden, Germany · BL, Egerton and Hardwicke papers · MS, Boston, Athenaeum · St John Cam., H. H. Norris collection · MSS, LPL · papers, Northants. RO · MSS, Bodl. Oxf. · *Northampton Mercury*
Archives Northants. RO, family papers | BL, letters to Lord Spencer
Likenesses J. Ponsford, oils, 1834, St John Cam. [*see illus.*] · S. W. Reynolds, mezzotint, pubd 1835 (after J. Ponsford), BM · J. Cochran, stipple (after J. W. Wright), BM, NPG; repro. in W. Jordan, *National portrait gallery of illustrious and eminent personages* (1831)

Marsh, James (1794–1846), chemist, was born in Woolwich on 1 September 1794. Little is known of his early life and education; in 1815 he married Mary Watkins in Erith. By 1822 he occupied the post of practical chemist at the Royal Arsenal, Woolwich—a very junior position. In 1829 he became, for 15s. per week, assistant for the chemical lectures that Michael Faraday delivered at the Royal Military Academy, Woolwich. The limited surviving evidence suggests that he and Faraday enjoyed a good working relationship. Marsh held both these positions until his death, and also acted as a consulting engineer to the New Gas Works, Woolwich.

In the 1820s Marsh assisted Peter Barlow, who taught mathematics at the academy, with his work on electromagnetism, including the invention of Barlow's wheel. In 1822 Marsh himself improved André-Marie Ampère's electromagnetic rotating cylinder. This innovation led Marsh to devise a portable electromagnetic apparatus for which he received, in 1823, the large silver medal of the Society of Arts together with 30 guineas. He and Barlow continued their work on electromagnetism in 1824 and 1825 when they investigated the induction of magnetism in rotating metals. However, in this research they had been anticipated by Dominique François Jean Arago.

In November 1833 Marsh was asked to analyse some coffee which a George Bodle of Plumstead had drunk just before his death. Marsh found arsenic present—as he testified to the inquest jury, which returned a verdict of wilful murder against Bodle's grandson John Bodle. Though acquitted (on non-forensic grounds) at his trial, Bodle later admitted the crime. The case turned Marsh's attention towards the problem of detecting arsenic. By 1836 he had developed a method of combusting arsenic such that it was unmistakably deposited on cold porcelain. For this extremely sensitive test he received the large gold medal of the Society of Arts that year. He continued improving the test in the ensuing years, and in 1840 it came to widespread public notice during the trial of Marie Lafarge for the murder of her husband. The original forensic examination found no trace of arsenic in his body, but the court asked for a new test. The body was exhumed and

was found, using Marsh's test, to contain arsenic. This evidence convicted Lafarge, who was sentenced to life imprisonment. The case caused a sensation on both sides of the channel and ensured that Marsh's name became a familiar one to the public.

In 1837 Marsh invented a percussion cap for naval guns for which he won the silver medal of the Society of Arts and was rewarded financially by the Admiralty. Marsh died at Beresford Street, Woolwich, on 21 June 1846, leaving two married daughters and a widow unprovided for; in late 1847 the Ordnance office awarded his widow an annual pension of £20.   FRANK A. J. L. JAMES

Sources *GM*, 2nd ser., 26 (1846), 219 · W. T. Vincent, *The records of the Woolwich district*, 2 vols. [1888–90] · *The Lancet* (29 Aug 1846), 255–6 · W. A. Campbell, 'Some landmarks in the history of arsenic testing', *Chemistry in Britain*, 1 (1965), 198–202 · *The correspondence of Michael Faraday*, ed. F. A. J. L. James, [4 vols.] (1991–) · *Catalogue of scientific papers, 1800–1863*, Royal Society, 6 vols. (1867–72) · *Literary Gazette* (27 Nov 1847), 836
Likenesses portrait, repro. in Vincent, *Records of the Woolwich district*, vol. 1, facing p. 340

Marsh, John (1752–1828), musician and writer, was born on 31 May 1752 at Dorking, Surrey, the first of the five children of Henry Marsh (1713–1772), captain in the Royal Navy, and his wife, Mary (Molly; 1715x20–1759), probably the daughter of Edward Tyler, a dissenting tradesman of Dorking. The loss of eleven days after the introduction of the Gregorian calendar in August 1752 resulted in John Marsh's celebrating his birthday on 11 June. In 1757 Marsh's father was posted to one of the royal yachts at Greenwich, where in 1759 young John started his education at Greenwich Academy. Five years later Captain Marsh was sent to Portsmouth, a move that led to Marsh's being sent to complete his education at Bishop's Waltham school. In 1765 he commenced a diary, subsequently transferred to a series of journals, that would prove the foundation of his principal claim to fame. These journals, or 'History of my private life', as Marsh entitled his work, were assiduously maintained until a few weeks before his death. Running to thirty-seven volumes and a total of 6704 pages, the journals are now housed in the Huntington Library, San Marino, California, USA, which purchased them at auction in 1990. The previously known version in the University of Cambridge Library is a much-abridged adaptation by Marsh's youngest son, Edward Garrard Marsh.

Today the journals are of value not only for the details they provide of Marsh's own life, but for the vivid account of life in the cathedral cities of southern England in which he lived and worked. From them we learn that Marsh incurred parental displeasure by resisting attempts to persuade him to follow his father into the Royal Navy. Instead in 1768 he became articled to a solicitor in Romsey, Hampshire, completing his legal training at the Inner Temple in London in 1773–4. While Marsh was in Romsey he developed the early interest in music formerly discouraged by his father, teaching himself to play several instruments, inaugurating a series of subscription concerts, and making his first attempts at composition. Returning from London, where he took every advantage to experience the vibrant musical life of the capital, Marsh set up as a lawyer in Romsey. On 15 November 1774 he married Elizabeth Catherine Brown (1756/7–1819), daughter of a Salisbury apothecary, Henry Brown, and his wife, Dorothea. Their first son, John (*d.* 1832) was born the following year. He was followed by four other sons, and a daughter, of whom only Edward Garrard and Henry reached adulthood.

Feeling restricted by the small-town atmosphere of Romsey, Marsh moved his family to Salisbury in 1776, entering into a legal partnership. He rapidly became fully involved in the thriving musical life of the city, playing in the subscription concerts and annual festival. This fresh stimulus was conclusive in deciding where Marsh's true interests lay. During the next seven years he was more likely to be found composing symphonies or anthems than attending to legal matters. After inheriting a large family estate in Kent and removing his family to Nethersole House near Barham, in 1783, Marsh unsurprisingly gave little time to the legal profession. He was now offered the management of the ailing Canterbury concerts, which immediately benefited from his organizational skill and ability to work with the sometimes uneasy mixture of professional and amateur players who performed in eighteenth-century provincial orchestras. However, Marsh soon found the expense of running a large country house too great. Nethersole was sold and, after a short interregnum in Canterbury, the family moved to a house in North Pallant, Chichester, Sussex, in April 1787. This remained his home for the last forty years of his life. As at Canterbury, Marsh found concert life in Chichester in a poor state following a schism. Here too he was offered management of the subscription concerts, skilfully reconciling the warring parties into a management committee while retaining overall control of repertory and the financial affairs of the orchestra. The orchestra, utilizing the services of the wind and brass players of the local Sussex militia, was expanded in size, enabling Marsh to programme a judicious combination of the ancient (primarily Corelli) and modern styles. Many of his own symphonies and other orchestral works were introduced into the repertory, along with those of J. C. Bach and Haydn. Marsh's success in reviving concert life in Chichester is reflected in a report in the *Sussex Weekly Advertiser* of 14 April 1804, at the end of the 1803/4 season: 'The concert, as usual, was distinguished for the excellence of selection, under the influence of its leader and director, J. Marsh, Esq., an amateur of fortune, whose compositions and skill have long since obtained him the highest estimation'. The Chichester concert continued in a flourishing state until 1813, when after twenty-five years Marsh finally stepped down from the directorship.

While music forms the principal thread running through John Marsh's life, it was by no means the only interest of the lively mind revealed in his writings. A lifelong interest in astronomy was stimulated by a meeting with William Herschel in Bath and led to his publishing two books on the subject. His other literary works included a satirical novel, *A Tour through some of the Southern Counties of England, by Peregrine Project and Timothy Type*

(1804). As a gentleman with a reasonably comfortable income from the Kentish estate retained after he moved to Chichester, Marsh was an inveterate traveller whose reaction to the death of his wife in 1819 was to undertake a tour to Scotland involving a round journey of some 1440 miles. His observations on musical life in London, to which he was a frequent visitor, are among the most valuable of the period. A staunch Anglican who in 1822 became involved with a society concerned with the conversion of the Jews, Marsh's faith did not preclude withering criticism of some of the clerics with whom he came into contact. In his later years Marsh turned increasingly to charitable work, being involved with the first Lancastrian schools to be established in Chichester and the anti-slavery movement. In accord with the times in which he lived, Marsh reveals little of his own emotions in his journals, but the picture that emerges is of a man of great energy, considerable leadership qualities, and an innate kindness which was not to be imposed upon. A natural family man, his consideration for his frequently ailing wife is one of many endearing traits to emerge from his writings.

The catalogue of John Marsh's musical compositions, many of them now lost, is substantial. It includes over fifty symphonies and other orchestral works, nearly thirty chamber works, organ music, a large number of services and anthems, and secular vocal works. He died at his home in North Pallant, Chichester, on 31 October 1828 after a short illness, and was buried at All Saints, West Pallant, on 7 November. BRIAN ROBINS

Sources J. Marsh, 'History of my private life (1797–1828)', Hunt. L., MS 54457 · *The John Marsh journals: the life and times of a gentleman composer*, ed. B. Robins (1998) · J. Brewer, *The pleasures of the imagination: English culture in the eighteenth century* (1997) · IGI **Archives** CUL, journals · Hunt. L., journals

Marsh, John Fitchett (1818–1880), promoter of municipal libraries and antiquary, was the son of a solicitor of Wigan, Lancashire, John Marsh, and his wife, Ann. He was born at Wigan on 24 October 1818, and was educated at Warrington grammar school under the Revd T. Vere Bayne. On the death of his father he came under the care of his uncle John *Fitchett (1776–1838), whom he afterwards succeeded in his business as a solicitor. On the incorporation of Warrington in 1847 he was appointed town clerk, and held that office until 1858.

Marsh was instrumental in establishing the Warrington School of Art and the public museum and library. In 1847 he proposed the amalgamation of the Warrington Town Library (founded in 1760) with the Warrington Natural History Society (1838) and the vesting of both in the corporation. This was accomplished in 1848, and Warrington thereby acquired Britain's first municipally funded library. Marsh wrote several articles of local antiquarian interest for the Historic Society of Lancashire and Cheshire and other learned societies, but it is for his pioneering role in the establishment of the first municipal library that he deserves to be remembered.

Marsh retired in 1873 to Hardwick House, Chepstow, Monmouthshire. There he began collecting materials for a history of the castles of Monmouthshire. He had hardly completed that of the first (Chepstow), when he died, unmarried, at Hardwick House, on 22 June 1880. His *Annals of Chepstow Castle* was edited by Sir John Maclean and printed at Exeter in 1883.

C. W. SUTTON, *rev.* ALAN G. CROSBY

Sources *Warrington Guardian* (26 June 1880) · *Palatine Note-Book*, 1 (1881), 168 · *Manchester Guardian* (30 June 1880) · d. cert. · A. M. Crowe, *Warrington ancient and modern* (1947) · parish register (baptism), Wigan, St Catherine, 21 Jan 1819

Archives Warrington Public Library, Warrington borough records

Wealth at death under £35,000: probate, 23 July 1880, *CGPLA Eng. & Wales*

Marsh, Narcissus (1638–1713), Church of Ireland archbishop of Armagh, was born on 20 December 1638 at Hannington, near Highworth, Wiltshire, the son of William Marsh, who owned an estate worth £60 p.a., and Grace Colburn. He was the youngest of his family, with two brothers and two sisters. He was educated in a series of five local schools and noted in his diary that 'in all of which schools I was never so much as once whipt or beaten'. At sixteen he was entered as a commoner at Magdalen Hall in Oxford. He studied 'Old philosophy, Mathematics and Oriental languages', graduated BA (1658), was elected to a Wiltshire fellowship in Exeter College (1658), and proceeded MA (1660), BD (1667), and DD (1671), being incorporated at Cambridge in 1678. As an undergraduate he reported that he kept 'an entire fast every week, from Thursday, six o'clock at night, until Saturday, eleven at noon, for which God's name be praised', though possibly only during Lent.

Clerical career and writings Marsh was under age when ordained priest by the bishop of Oxford in March 1662 and, troubled, noted 'The Lord forgive us both, but then I knew no better but it might be legally done'. Appointed chaplain to Seth Ward, bishop of Exeter, who offered him the living of Swindon, he discovered he was expected to marry a daughter of a friend of the bishop. He was horrified, as he had no intention of ever marrying. Ward, furious, demanded his resignation as his chaplain. Marsh thanked God 'for delivering me out of the snare which they laid for me' and returned to Oxford. In 1664 he delivered his first sermon, at St Mary's, Oxford, and in 1665 was made proproctor of the university. He learned to play the bass viol and reported that 'after the Fire of London, I constantly kept a weekly consort (of instrumental musick and sometimes vocal) in my chamber on Wednesday in the afternoon, and then on Thursday, as long as I lived in Oxford'. He worked even harder at his studies but felt guilty over his recreation—'Yet O Lord I beseech Thee to forgive me this loss of time and vain conversation.'

In 1665 Marsh was appointed chaplain to Lord Chancellor Hyde who advised him to continue with his studies. At this period 'he had many advantageous offers for marriage', 'one who had £800, to her portion, another £1500, another £2400 and another of meaner fortune than either, but all very desirable (I might rather have said beautiful lovely persons)'. He was not tempted by these

Narcissus Marsh (1638–1713), by unknown artist, *c.*1704

offers and also refused appointment as domestic chaplain to the lord keeper, Orlando Bridgeman, in order to continue his studies. Instead he was interrupted by agreeing to the request of the vice-chancellor, Dr Fell, to revise the notes and supervise the printing of Belsamon's and Zonaras's *Comments on the Canons of the Greek Councils* (1672), a monumental task which took almost a year. He had earlier gained some experience of this type of work when he revised Du Trieu's *Logick* (1662), which he later had published for the benefit of Dublin University students as *Institutio logicae in usum juventutis academicae Dubliniensis* (1679). He also wrote an 'Essay touching the sympathy between lute or viol strings', printed by Robert Plot in his *Natural History of Oxfordshire* (1676). In 1673 Fell and the chancellor, the duke of Ormond, appointed him principal of St Alban Hall. His success in this position, and his administrative and organizational abilities, encouraged Ormond and Fell, now bishop of Oxford, to suggest his appointment as provost of Trinity College, Dublin.

Career in Ireland Marsh was invested as provost on 24 January 1679. He recorded in his diary his

finding this place very troublesome partly by reason of the multitude of business and impertinent visits the Provost is obliged to, and partly by reason of the ill education the

> young Scholars have before they come to College, whereby they are both rude and ignorant; I was quickly weary of 340 young men and boys in this lewd and debauch'd town; and the more so because I had no time to follow my allways dearly beloved studies.

Despite his complaint he oversaw some important changes in the college, including the building of a new hall and chapel. He reorganized the library, improving the classification, shelving, and numbering of books, revising the regulations, and demanding greater accountability from the junior fellow annually appointed as librarian, but he was unable to change the statutes which entitled only the provost and fellows to study there unattended.

Marsh discovered that under the statutes thirty of the seventy scholars chosen each year had to be natives, and that while these scholars could speak Irish they could not read or write it. He employed, at his own expense, a former Catholic priest, Paul Higgins, to teach Irish and to preach in Irish once a month. The lectures and sermons, which he attended, were a great success but were severely criticized for promoting the Irish language, among others by the primate, who drew attention to an act of parliament to abolish the language. Marsh ignored these warnings and continued with his work.

Marsh's next project at Trinity College was the preparation for printing of Bishop William Bedell's Irish translation of the Old Testament. With the help of a number of associates he prepared the transcripts which they then sent to Robert Boyle in London. Marsh gives an interesting description of their work:

> when a quantity of sheets was transcribed, I got Dr Sall, Mr Higgins, Mr Mullen and some gentlemen well skilled in Irish to compare the transcript with the original copy, then to render the Irish into English, whilst I had the Polyglott Bible before me, to observe whether it came up to the original [Hebrew] and where any doubt did arise, after a debate, and their agreement upon a more proper expression, twas written in the margin, and left to Mr Boyle to advise with Mr Reilly thereupon. But I think very few alterations were made in the impression. (*Christian Examiner*)

The Irish translation of the Old Testament was printed in London in 1685. Marsh's interest in the Irish language, which had led him at one time to attempt the publication of an Irish grammar, was mainly with a purpose to propagate the reformed religion through the language of the majority in Ireland.

On 6 May 1683 Marsh was consecrated bishop of Ferns and Leighlin, with the rectory of Killeban *in commendam*. Before he took up his appointment he became a member of the newly formed Dublin Philosophical Society and contributed a paper, 'An introductory essay to the doctrine of sounds, containing some proposals for the improvement of acousticks', published in *Philosophical Transactions* (1684). Although the Oxford Philosophical Society thought the article of 'great consequence', a later assessment notes few original conclusions but points to Marsh's use of new words—'diacoustics' to describe the study of refracted sound and 'catacoustics' for that of reflected sound, and his being the first scientific writer to use the word 'microphone' (Hoppen). Marsh was also interested in comets and scientific instruments, and invented a lamp to enlighten a large hall or church. To William Molyneux, who had invented the Dublin hygroscope for indicating moisture in the air, he suggested substituting a lute string for the more fragile whipcord Molyneux was using. He tried to discover a more reliable and logical method of insect classification, incorporating classification by follicles and aurelias. Some years later he was made a vice-president of the Dublin Philosophical Society.

Marsh did not stay long in his diocese. Following the accession of James II he was subjected to threats by disorderly soldiery and, after briefly staying in Trinity College, fled to England. In 1690 he preached before Queen Mary at Whitehall and before the University of Oxford. Bishop Lloyd of St Asaph appointed him vicar of Gresford, Denbighshire, and he was made a canon of St Asaph. He noted the hospitality and financial assistance he received in England, and in return assisted many of his fellow clergymen. In his diary Marsh recorded:

> my time for many days have been in hard study, especially in knotty Algebra, to divert melancholy thoughts these sad calamitous times wherein I am forced to live from home; and do hear almost every day of the murther of some [or] other Protestant, yet my heart and hope is always steadfastly fixed on the Lord my God and I trust it shall never be moved.

He gives vivid accounts of his dreams, illustrating his fear of the pope and the Catholic church. In August 1690 he returned to Ireland and was promoted archbishop of Cashel in February 1691.

As archbishop Marsh forbade preaching in private houses, warned clergy not to praise the dead overmuch, and laid down that every incumbent should preach every Sunday. He worked extremely hard in his diocese and recorded long, difficult journeys to visit and inspect his clergy and parishes. If he was distressed at the consecration of William Fitzgerald as bishop of Clonfert, glad he did not participate and noting 'may I never be concerned in bringing unworthy men into the Church', he was obviously pleased at the consecration a few weeks later of Nathaniel Foy, who would prove an influential bishop of Waterford and Lismore.

Marsh was translated to Dublin in 1694 and enthroned on 26 May. On six occasions between 1699 and 1711 he served as one of the lords justices—effective governors in the absence of the lord lieutenant. To this involvement in 'worldly business', which he hated, was added his service in the House of Lords, including membership of the committee for religion and grievances, and chairmanship of the committee for temporary acts. He appears to have taken a leading part in the drafting of legislation in 1697 including the Banishment Act, directed against Catholic bishops and regular clergy, the act against intermarriage of protestants and Catholics, and the act confirming the treaty of Limerick. He was unsympathetic towards the Limerick articles, fearing 'the effect of the unhappy conditions that (I know not how or why) have been granted to a rebellious people that were not able to defend themselves'.

In 1703 Thomas Emlyn, removed by his fellow Presbyterians from his ministry for unitarian views, was charged with publishing a blasphemous book; Marsh sat on the bench at the trial. Emlyn was sentenced to a year's imprisonment with the condition he not be released until he had paid a £1000 fine. When, after two years, his friends secured the reduction of the fine to £70, Marsh demanded a shilling in the pound of the original fine as queen's almoner, though he was eventually persuaded to a reduction to £20. He personally instituted a case against a Mr Fleming, Presbyterian minister at Drogheda, but the case was withdrawn due to the then government's sympathetic policy to dissenters. In contrast to his treatment of Catholics and Presbyterians he was sympathetic towards Huguenots, some of whom had been given permission to worship in the lady chapel in St Patrick's Cathedral, on condition they were bound by the discipline and canons of the Church of Ireland. Yet Marsh approved and praised the alternative discipline, with a much more liberal interpretation of conformity, which the French congregation prepared and submitted to him.

Foundation of Marsh's Library and reputation   When at Trinity College, Marsh wrote to his friend Dr Thomas Smith that the booksellers' shops were furnished with nothing but 'new Triffles and Pamphlets and not well with them'. He noted the lack of a library for the public in the capital and that

> twas this and this consideration alone that at first mov'd me to think of building a library in some other Place (than in the College) for publick use, where all might have free access, seeing they cannot have it in the college.   (*Christian Examiner*, 764)

Almost twenty years later he had the opportunity, building his library in the grounds of the palace of St Sepulchre, which he held as archbishop. Designed by the surveyor-general of Ireland, Sir William Robinson, it was influenced by the design of the Bodleian Library and was furnished with dark oak bookcases each with carved and lettered gable topped by a mitre. Four main collections were obtained, the most important being the library of nearly 10,000 books of Edward Stillingfleet, bishop of Worcester, which Marsh bought for his library in 1705 for £2500. He donated his own books, reflecting his special interest in books in Arabic, Syriac, Hebrew, Russian, and oriental languages, but bequeathed his oriental manuscripts to the Bodleian. The first librarian at Marsh's Library, a Huguenot refugee, Dr Elias Bouhéreau, donated his books, mainly relating to France, on his appointment in 1701, and in 1745 John Stearne, bishop of Clogher, bequeathed his collection to Marsh's Library.

In February 1703 Marsh was promoted to the Irish primacy. In Armagh he repaired the cathedral and rebuilt churches at his own expense. He bought in impropriated tithes and restored them to the church, and instituted and largely endowed the almshouses for the widows of clergymen in the Armagh diocese. He also contributed large sums of money to the Society for the Propagation of the Gospel. He died on 2 November 1713 and was buried four days later in the churchyard of St Patrick's Cathedral, Dublin, adjoining his library. The large monument erected to him, the work of Grinling Gibbons, was damaged by the weather, and in 1728 the governors and guardians of the library decided to move it inside the cathedral.

Marsh's contemporaries took a fairly sympathetic view of him. Archbishop William King thought Marsh 'though an excellent person and a scholar is yet too modest and unacquainted with the world' (McCarthy, 21), while the bishop of Oxford described him as a man of 'learning, virtue, gravity and diligence' (*Church of Ireland Gazette*, 9 Dec 1927, 714). The exception was Jonathan Swift, who blamed Marsh for his having to produce his 'penitential letter' for his lack of promotion in the church and, unfairly, for removing him from the management of the petition for first fruits for the church just short of success. Swift, a member of the lower house of convocation, unsuccessfully opposed the act setting up Marsh's Library on the grounds that laymen on the library's governing board might become a majority and have authority over the precentor or treasurer of St Patrick's, to one of which posts that of librarian was to be annexed. About 1710 Swift wrote a spiteful 'Character of Primate Marsh':

> Doing good is his pleasure; and as no man consults another in his pleasures, neither does he in this … without all passions but fear, to which of all others he hath the least temptation, having nothing to get or to lose; no posterity, relation, or friend to be solicitous about; and placed by his station above the reach of fortune or envy. … He is the first of the human race, that with great advantages of learning, piety and station ever escaped being a great man. (McCarthy, 26)

Whatever Marsh's failings he was, in great contrast to many of his contemporaries, an exemplary prelate, pious, and sincere—if not effective—as a reformer. He is remembered for his generosity in building the first public library in Ireland, one of the few eighteenth-century buildings in Dublin still used for its original purpose.

MURIEL MCCARTHY

Sources   Archbishop Marsh's diary, 1690–96, Marsh Library, Dublin · M. McCarthy, *All graduates and gentlemen: Marsh's Library* (1980) · *DNB* · G. T. Stokes, *Some worthies of the Irish church*, ed. H. J. Lawlor (1900), 65–111 · *Christian Examiner and Church of Ireland Magazine*, new ser., 2 (1833), 761–72 [original letter of Archbishop Marsh] · J. H. Bernard, *The registers of baptisms, marriages, and burials in the … church of St Patrick, Dublin, 1677–1800* (1907) · parish register, Hannington church, 23 Dec 1638 [baptism] · K. T. Hoppen, *The common scientist in the seventeenth century: a study of the Dublin Philosophical Society, 1683–1708* (1970) · G. E. C. [G. E. C. Cokayne], 'Some notice of various families of the name of Marsh', *The Genealogist*, new ser., 16 (1900), suppl., pp. 34–42

Archives   BL, letters to earl of Rochester, Add. MS 15895 · Bodl. Oxf., letters to Thomas Smith, etc. · NL Scot., corresp. with Robert Boyle [copies] · TCD, corresp. with William King

Likenesses   oils, 1704, Exeter College, Oxford · portrait, *c*.1704, Exeter College, Oxford [*see illus.*] · attrib. H. Howard, portrait, Marsh's Library, Dublin · oils, TCD · portrait, TCD · portrait, Irish Museum of Modern Art; copy, nineteenth century, Marsh's Library, Dublin

Wealth at death   lands purchased to support library and widow's houses in Drogheda; legacies to friends and relations supposedly totalled £8000–£9000: G. E. C., 'Some notice'; will, Marsh Library, Dublin

Marsh, Dame (Edith) Ngaio (1895–1982), detective novelist and theatre director, was born in Fendalton, Christchurch, New Zealand, on 23 April 1895 (although she persistently stated that she was born in 1899, when her father registered the birth), the only child of Henry Esmond Marsh (1863–1948), an English immigrant to New Zealand, holder of a bank clerkship in the Bank of New Zealand, and his wife, Rose Elizabeth Seager (1864–1932), an amateur actress and a New Zealander of longer standing. Marsh's grandfather, Edward William Seager, was a New Zealand pioneer. Known by the Maori name of Ngaio (popularly pronounced 'Nyo' and denoting, among other things, a sturdy New Zealand coastal tree which Maori legend says also grows on the moon), she was educated at St Margaret's College, where she edited the school magazine, acted (she was usually cast in a male role because of her height and deep voice), and composed and produced her own plays. She went on to become a student of painting at Canterbury College School of Art from 1915, but through amateur acting and playwriting she secured an invitation to join the professional Allan Wilkie Shakespeare Company, touring Australasia in 1919–1920, as an actress.

After a stint with the Rosemary Rees Company, Marsh spent the next few years writing and painting with what came to be known as the Christchurch Group, which comprised Evelyn Polson and Margaret Anderson. Feeling that she was not developing an individual style, she turned to language as her medium and toured with her play 'Little Housebound' with members of the Rosemary Rees Company. On her return she was asked to join the newly founded Wauchop School of Drama and Dancing and to produce a number of plays for local amateur groups. From 1928 to 1929 she was commissioned to write a series of travel articles for New Zealand newspapers, which included pieces about England. She first visited England from 1928 to 1932 in the company of the Rhodes family, who were the models for her fictional Lampreys. In London she worked with theatre groups, as a fashion model, as an interior designer, and she ran a shop called Touch and Go with Nelly Rhodes, which was stocked with their handmade gifts.

More importantly it was in England that Marsh first turned her hand to writing detective novels. In her reticent and evocative autobiography, *Black Beech and Honeydew* (1966, rev. 1981), she told how on a rainy London Sunday, in 1931, having devoured a detective story, the notion entered her head of writing one herself. The novel that resulted, *A Man Lay Dead* (1934), was the first of thirty-one, and introduced Chief Detective-Inspector Roderick Alleyn, CID, named after the founder of her father's old school, Dulwich College. It was in many ways a formulaic crime novel based on the idea of a 'murder game', but Marsh matured into one of the great practitioners of the genre.

From that time on Marsh divided her time between England and detective fiction and New Zealand and the theatre. In London she lived the life of a glamorous celebrity,

Dame (Edith) Ngaio Marsh (1895–1982), by unknown photographer, 1936

impeccably dressed and seen walking her Siamese cat on a lead with a jewelled collar; while in New Zealand she was a less ostentatious public figure who preferred gardening to society. Marsh's second novel, *Enter a Murderer* (1935) and the later *Vintage Murder* (1937), set in New Zealand, made convincing use of her knowledge of the theatre. *The Nursing Home Murder* (1935), written in collaboration with Dr Henry Jellett, was the most popular novel of her career and has outsold all her other titles. In 1937 she travelled around Europe in an old police car and completed *Artists in Crime* (1938) on board ship. *Death in a White Tie* (1938) surprised readers with Alleyn's marriage to Agatha Troy, a painter. Extended periods in England in various country houses gave Marsh the material for *Death of a Peer* (reprinted as *Surfeit of Lampreys*, 1941), one of her most ingeniously crafted novels. *Overture to Death* (1939) is often regarded as Marsh's best book.

During the Second World War Marsh was a driver for a Red Cross transport unit in New Zealand and during this time produced plays, the proceeds of which went towards the war effort. She also wrote a patriotic book, *New Zealand*, in 1942. She returned to crime writing with *Colour Scheme* (1943), which uses Maori myth, and which Marsh considered her best-written novel. In 1943 she was asked by the Canterbury University College Drama Society to work with them. In the early 1940s Shakespeare had not been played in New Zealand since the Allan Wilkie tour of the 1920s. Ngaio Marsh cajoled her untried students into tackling *Hamlet* and, despite fearful prognostications, achieved a sell-out success. Her production of *Othello* attracted the notice of D. D. O'Connor, who offered to act as a professional manager for a nationwide tour. Thenceforth a considerable part of her life was devoted in New Zealand to Shakespeare and other dramatists of repute. Her books *A Play Toward* (1946) and *Play Production* (1948) outline her technique.

Meanwhile detective novels such as *Final Curtain* (1947) and *Opening Night* (1951) pleased her reading public. On another trip to London in 1949 William Collins and Penguin threw a 'Marsh Million' party to celebrate the publication of a million copies of Marsh titles. While in London Marsh founded a British Commonwealth Theatre Company; it later toured New Zealand and Australia, but did not prove viable. Also in London she directed Pirandello's *Six Characters in Search of an Author* at the Embassy Theatre. An actor member of her company described her as 'a perfect coach', a director excelling in inspiring the young. In 1948 she was appointed OBE for services to New Zealand drama and literature (she was advanced to DBE in 1966). In 1949 she was made an honorary lecturer in drama at Canterbury University, New Zealand (honorary DLitt, 1962), and in 1963 the Ngaio Marsh Theatre was founded at that university. Marsh continued to write prodigiously until her death, producing eleven Alleyn novels between 1965 and 1981. She died after a stroke on 18 February 1982 at Marton Cottage, 37 Valley Road, Cashmere Hills, the wooden house her father had built overlooking Christchurch and in which she had lived since a child. Her ashes were interred in the churchyard of the Holy Innocents, Mount Peel, New Zealand, beside her lifelong friend Sylvia Fox. She never married, and her private life remains obscure.

Marsh rose to prominence in the 1930s during the golden age of crime writing when Agatha Christie, Margery Allingham, and Dorothy L. Sayers were expanding the genre. Marsh herself developed the form far beyond the conventions of the 'locked-door' mysteries; she was more interested in character and social manners than plot, and adhered to a 'nervous' and 'taut' structure which she likened to that of metaphysical poetry (Marsh, 'Entertainments'). She also injected distinctive elements of her New Zealand heritage and from her theatrical career into her writing.

Marsh is revered in New Zealand for her work in the theatre; she herself thought this her most 'valuable contribution', and she did not consider detective fiction a serious art form, barely discussing it in her autobiography (McDorman, 2, 14). In spite of this her reputation in other parts of the world, particularly Britain, rests on her fiction. It was the vision of a certain kind of Englishness in her work that was one of the factors accounting for her success. Marsh always had a highly romanticized view of England, and a deep attachment to England's cultural heritage. Roderick Alleyn was a product of this affinity; he was 'a new "type" of detective' (McDorman, x), a cross 'between a grandee and a monk', in his creator's words, free from affectation, and quietly humorous.

For her detective fiction Marsh was awarded the Grand Master award from the Mystery Writers of America in 1977, the first female colonial to achieve such a distinction. She was one of the most popular Commonwealth novelists in the 1930s and 1940s and her novels are continuously in print.

H. R. F. KEATING, *rev.* CLARE L. TAYLOR

Sources M. Lewis, *Ngaio Marsh* (1992) • N. Marsh, *Black beech and honeydew: an autobiography* (1981) • K. S. McDorman, *Ngaio Marsh*, Twayne's English Author Series, 481 (1991) • B. J. Rahn, *Ngaio Marsh: the woman and her work* (1995) • N. Marsh, 'Entertainments', *Pacific Moana Quarterly*, 3 (Jan 1978) • *The Times* (19 Feb 1982) • personal knowledge (1990) • private information (1990) • www.freesearch.org.peelforest/marsh.htm, 14 Nov 2000
Archives Boston University • NL NZ, Turnbull L. • St Margaret's College, Christchurch, New Zealand | SOUND BBC Sound Archives
Likenesses photograph, 1936, NL NZ, Turnbull L. [*see illus.*] • V. Elsom, oils, 1981, Robert McDougall Art Gallery, Christchurch, New Zealand • P. Chandler, photograph, priv. coll. • photograph, University of Canterbury, New Zealand, Macmillan Brown Library • photograph, Harvard TC
Wealth at death £65,360: probate, 10 Dec 1982, *CGPLA Eng. & Wales*

Marsh, Richard [Richard de Marisco] (d. 1226), administrator and bishop of Durham, was of unknown origins. The fact that he was styled *magister* indicates that he attended a university, but it is not known where. He first appears in royal records in 1196/7, when he accounted for the issues of the vacant bishopric of Durham on behalf of the appointed custodians, Gilbert fitz Reinfrey and Richard Brewer. In that same year he also paid into the treasury two large sums on behalf of Archbishop Hubert Walter. It appears, therefore, that he was already developing the expertise in financial administration that would characterize his later career. Under King John, Marsh became first a chamber clerk (by 1207), and then, from 1209, senior chancery clerk, with occasional custody of the great seal. He continued as clerk of the chamber, however, until 29 October 1214, when he was appointed chancellor. Yet even as chancellor Marsh continued to be closely involved with both the chamber and the exchequer until 1217, when he left the court to become bishop of Durham. Although Marsh remained titular chancellor until his death in 1226, from November 1218 it was Ralph de Neville who, as keeper of the new king's seal, performed the day-to-day functions of the chancellor's office.

Like most of John's clerical administrators, Marsh remained at the king's side throughout the interdict, and was rewarded for his loyalty with a series of ecclesiastical positions and promotions. In 1209 he became canon of Exeter and rector of Bampton, Oxfordshire; in 1212 he was appointed to the vicarage at Kempsey, Worcestershire. By November 1211 he was archdeacon of Northumberland, and in February 1213 he became archdeacon of Richmond, offices he held concurrently until his appointment as bishop of Durham in 1217.

There is no doubt of Marsh's influence with King John. Along with William Brewer, Robert of Thornham, and Reginald of Cornhill, he was named specifically as one of the 'evil counsellors' who encouraged John's exactions from the Cistercian order in 1210. He was named again among the king's most influential advisers in 1211. During Michaelmas term 1212, when rumours of incipient rebellion reached the king, it was Marsh whom John sent to supervise the exchequer. During this same year he also served as sheriff of Somerset and Dorset, yet another sign of the trust the king reposed in him. Years later a monk of St Albans reported a dream in which King John appeared before him, lamenting the sins that Richard Marsh had encouraged him to commit against the church during the interdict.

When the interdict was finally lifted, Archbishop Stephen Langton threatened Marsh with suspension from his ecclesiastical benefices. In August 1213 Marsh went personally to Rome to explain himself to the pope, and also to negotiate on the king's behalf the final terms for ending the interdict. He succeeded on both counts. In February 1214 he left Rome with letters of special papal protection for all his ecclesiastical benefices, and with the terms for ending the interdict substantially modified in the king's favour.

Upon his return from Rome Marsh quickly resumed his administrative duties at court. He went first to Poitou, where he assisted in organizing John's military campaign of 1214. During this time, between April and June 1214, John attempted to have him elected bishop of Winchester in succession to Peter des Roches, whom the king hoped to postulate to York. Nothing came of this scheme, however, and by June 1214 Marsh was back in England, advising on the munitioning of castles, and compelling monastic houses to seal blank charters surrendering their claims to compensation for their losses during the interdict. Marsh was also active during these years in pressing the king's candidates upon monastic electors, most famously in the disputed election of Hugh of Northwold to the abbacy of Bury St Edmunds. In October 1214 John appointed Marsh chancellor, official confirmation of the position he had already attained as one of the principal men upon whom the king relied in governing England.

Marsh remained a loyal supporter of King John throughout the Magna Carta rebellion. In August 1215 he was in Poitou, attempting to raise troops for John's service. In September he went on another mission to Rome, where he secured the suspension of Archbishop Langton. After John's death, Marsh continued as chancellor in the new regency government, and in this capacity sealed the November 1217 version of Magna Carta. By this date, however, he had already become bishop of Durham. Appointed in May 1217 by the legate Guala, with the support of Pope Honorius III (r. 1216–27), Marsh was consecrated at Gloucester on 2 July 1217 by Archbishop Walter de Gray of York. From that date on he spent most of his time in his northern diocese. Marsh remained in close touch with the royal government, however, acting as a diplomatic intermediary with the king of Scotland and serving, from December 1218 to April 1219, as justice on eyre in Yorkshire and Northumberland. He remained, at least formally, a member of the royal council, and he continued to insist upon his dignity as chancellor, angrily rejecting

Ralph de Neville's claims to be officially the vice-chancellor.

As bishop of Durham, Marsh was engaged in almost constant conflict, first with Philip of Oldcotes, the wartime custodian of the vacant bishopric, and then with the prior and convent of Durham over the proper division of revenues between priory and bishop. Marsh's methods in pursuing these conflicts were brutal. Oldcotes's estates were attacked, his houses burnt, and his men imprisoned. The monks of Durham accused Marsh before the pope of bloodshed, adultery, simony, robbery, and sacrilege, and complained to the king that he was violating their rights under Magna Carta. The pope ordered the bishops of Salisbury and Ely to investigate the charges against him, but Marsh appealed to Rome, and after great expense to all parties the case was remanded to England for a hearing at London. It was on his journey south to attend this hearing that Marsh died in his sleep, without warning, at Peterborough Abbey on 1 May 1226, leaving behind him a heavy burden of indebtedness upon both priory and bishopric, and a personal reputation for heavy drinking. His heir was his nephew Adam *Marsh, subsequently a notable theologian, to whom he bequeathed his library.

ROBERT C. STACEY

Sources Chancery records · Pipe rolls · Paris, Chron. · W. W. Shirley, ed., Royal and other historical letters illustrative of the reign of Henry III, 1, Rolls Series, 27 (1862) · R. M. Thomson, ed., The chronicle of the election of Hugh, abbot of Bury St Edmunds and later bishop of Ely (1974) · N. Vincent, 'The origins of the chancellorship of the exchequer', EngHR, 108 (1993), 105–21 · N. Vincent, Peter des Roches: an alien in English politics, 1205–38, Cambridge Studies in Medieval Life and Thought, 4th ser., 31 (1996) · D. A. Carpenter, The minority of Henry III (1990) · Selected letters of Pope Innocent III concerning England, 1198–1216, ed. C. R. Cheney and W. H. Semple (1953) · J. C. Holt, The northerners: a study in the reign of King John (1961) · S. Painter, The reign of King John (1949) · Emden, Oxf., 3.2195–6 · T. D. Hardy, ed., Rotuli litterarum clausarum, RC, 2 (1834), 136
Wealth at death see Hardy, ed., Rotuli litterarum clausarum, 2.136

Marsh, Walter (bap. 1560, d. 1595), spy and protestant martyr, was baptized on 17 October 1560 at St Stephen, Coleman Street, London, the third or fourth of the four children of John Marsh (b. before 1516, d. 1579), MP, mercer, and governor of the Merchant Adventurers' Company, and his wife, Alice, daughter of William Gresham of Holt, Norfolk, and cousin of Sir Thomas Gresham. The family held the Northamptonshire manors of Bozeat and Sywell. Walter was educated at Merchant Taylors' School and St John's College, Cambridge (BA, 1582; MA, 1585). He was ordained on 13 March 1586 at Peterborough, becoming in the same year prebendary of Gaia Major in Lichfield Cathedral and rector of Hamstall Ridware, Staffordshire (near Lichfield), and in 1588 archdeacon of Derby. By 1590, however, he had vacated his benefices, including the archdeaconry, which he had lost to another clergyman.

Marsh next appears in a letter of 19 March 1591 written by the noted recusant Sir Thomas Tresham, describing an unexpected visit from one Marshe, a '[privy] Councellers Chaplen; and Archedeacon of Darbie', who had come to declare his intention to 'depart beyond the seas to ye

Semenary'—that is, Douai, the English College for Catholics temporarily located at Rheims. In preparation Marsh had cut off his beard; but even had he left it on, Tresham opined, he would have lacked 'ane hare of ane honest manne' (Northants. RO, SS 234). Scenting a spy, Tresham reported Marsh's plans to the authorities.

Marsh did indeed register at Douai on 5 September 1591. In February 1592, however, he left to visit England, first detouring to Flushing to see Sir Robert Sidney, the resident governor. A letter of 11 March 1592 on his behalf from Sidney to Lord Burghley relates that Marsh had confessed his 'error' and offered to 'discover matters wch do greatly concearn her Ma:' (PRO, SP 84/44, 145). This could not have been a simple letter of introduction. Marsh's father had gathered information for Burghley; both Burghley and Walter Marsh (and Walter's near contemporary, Burghley's son Robert) were St John's men, and Marsh's college verses against idolatry survive in Burghley's papers, endorsed in the minister's hand.

Back in Rheims in July 1592, Marsh departed on 14 January 1593 for the English College at Rome. Admitted on 14 March, he proved, in the words of the Jesuit Robert Persons, 'an unquiett scoller' ('Memoirs', 208). The college's entry for Gualterus Marshaeus, headed *Hereticus* and fiercely scored through, briefly records that Marsh was burnt to death in 1595 for knocking the host from the hands of a priest in the procession of the forty hours before St Agatha in Rome, on 15 June. An Italian *avviso* dated two days later reveals that Marsh had spent the last six months under the supervision of the Inquisition, doing penance for offences against Catholics in England and for having been paid by the queen to spy on Catholics, which he had abjured, vowing to live a retired life to save his soul.

Marsh's fatal act appears to have represented a moment of open revulsion against the eucharist. A letter of 23 June from Cardinal Arnaud d'Ossat observed that Marsh gave the monstrance a great blow, 'criant que c'étoit une idole' (*Lettres*, 80). Retribution was swift: on 20 June Marsh's tongue and hand were cut off, and he was burnt to death in the Campo dei Fiori. Marsh's action should be seen as part of a series of attacks upon the host, most notably for Marsh, perhaps, that of Richard Atkins on the 'foolish Idoll' of the sacrament in St Peter's in 1581, described in Anthony Munday's *English Romayne Lyfe* (1582; repr. 1590) and by John Foxe in the 1583 revision of his *Acts and Monuments*. Marsh himself can be found in the *Continuation* added to the 1641 and 1684 editions of Foxe, where he appears as an unnamed 'English man', in a hagiographical tale which contains no trace of his earlier career as a clergyman or of his later activities as a spy. His name lives on only in the tribute of Richard Sheldon, a fellow student in Rome who at first preached against Marsh's act but later attributed to him his own conversion to the Church of England.   RICHARD S. PETERSON

Sources R. Peterson, 'In from the cold: an Englishman at Rome, 1595', *American Notes and Queries*, new ser., 5 (1992), 115–21 · R. Peterson, 'Laurel crown and ape's tail: new light on Spenser's career from Sir Thomas Tresham', *Spenser Studies*, 12 (1998), 1–35 · Sir Thomas Tresham, letter, 19 March 1591, Northants. RO, SS 234 · Sir Robert Sidney, letter to Lord Burghley, 11 March 1592, PRO, state papers foreign, Holland, SP 84/44, fol. 145 · *Calendar of the manuscripts of the most hon. the marquis of Salisbury*, 13, HMC, 9 (1915), 196 · Hatfield papers, 140/76, 172/7r–v · W. Kelly, ed., *Liber ruber venerabilis collegii Anglorum de urbe*, 1, Catholic RS, 37 (1940), 89–90, no. 65 · avvisi di Roma, 17 and 24 June 1595, Biblioteca Apostolica Vaticana, Vatican City, Urb. MS 1063, fols. 386, 399, 407 [transcript in Rome, archives ser. 2, PRO, 31/10/4, pp. 1082–3, 1086] · *Lettres du Cardinal d'Ossat*, rev. edn (1624), 80 · A. Munday, *The English Romayne lyfe* (1582), chap. 8 · J. Foxe, *Actes and monuments*, 4th edn, 2 (1583), 2151–2; 8th edn, 3 (1641), 84; 9th edn, 3 (1684), p. 951 · PRO, PROB 11/61, sig. 2 [will of John Marsh, proved 28 Jan 1579] · HoP, *Commons, 1558–1603*, 3.20–22 · Venn, *Alum. Cant.*, 1/3.146 · ordination book (13 March 1586), diocesan records of Peterborough · R. Clark, 'Lists of Derbyshire clergymen', *Derbyshire Archaeological Journal*, 104 (1984), 41 · D. M. Nolan, W. J. Watkinson, P. Rider, and M. Walton, eds., *Chesterfield parish register, 1558–1600*, Derbyshire RS, 12 (1986), 134 · APC, 15.350 · bills and answers of the court of the Exchequer, PRO, E 112/9/33 · register of Archbishop Whitgift, 23 Nov 1590, LPL · T. F. Knox and others, eds., *The first and second diaries of the English College, Douay* (1878), 241 · *Calendar of the manuscripts of the most hon. the marquis of Salisbury*, 5, HMC, 9 (1894), 258–9 [on Marsh, unnamed, executed in Rome] · R. Sheldon, *The motives of Richard Sheldon, priest, for his just, voluntary, and free renouncing of communion with the bishop of Rome* (1612) · 'The memoirs of Father Robert Persons', ed. J. H. Pollen, *Miscellanea, II*, Catholic RS, 2 (1906), 12–218, esp. 209

Marsh, William (1775–1864), Church of England clergyman, third son of Colonel Sir Charles Marsh (d. c.1805) of Reading and his wife, Catherine (c.1745–1824), daughter of John Case of Bath, was born on 20 July 1775 in Reading, and until the age of eleven or twelve was educated under Dr Valpy in the grammar school there. His intention was to enter the army, but when he was eighteen the sudden death in his presence of a young man in a ballroom deeply shocked him, and under the influence of the Hon. and Revd William Cadogan he became an evangelical. He matriculated from St Edmund Hall, Oxford, on 10 October 1797, and started his studies the following year, graduating BA in 1801, MA in 1807, and BD and DD in 1839.

At Christmas 1800 Marsh was ordained to the curacy of St Lawrence, Reading, and was soon known as an impressive evangelical preacher. In 1801 Thomas Stonor gave him the chapelry of Nettlebed in Oxfordshire. His father presented him to the united livings of Basildon and Ashampstead in Berkshire in 1802, soon after which he resigned Nettlebed, but retained the curacy of St Lawrence, which he served without pay for many years. On 27 November 1806 he married Maria Chowne (1776–1833), the youngest child and only daughter of John Tilson and his wife, Maria (*née* Lushington), of Watlington Park, Oxfordshire. They had five children. The Revd Charles Simeon paid a first visit to Basildon in 1807, and was from that time a friend and correspondent of Marsh. In 1809, with the consent of his bishop, Marsh was appointed as perpetual curate of St James's Chapel, Brighton, but the vicar of St Nicholas's, Brighton, Dr R. C. Carr, afterwards bishop of Worcester, refused his assent to this arrangement, and after some months Marsh resigned. Simeon presented him to St Peter's, Colchester, in 1814. His attention was early drawn by Simeon to the subject of biblical prophecy and the conversion of the Jews, and in 1818 he went with him to the Netherlands to inquire into the condition of the Dutch Jewish community. His continuing interest in this subject led him to publish several works on eschatological themes in later years. *A Few Plain Thoughts on Prophecy* (1840) was particularly well received. Marsh's evangelical influence extended to the family of his wife's brother James Tilson, and through them for a time to Jane Austen.

Ill health obliged Marsh in early 1829 to leave Colchester, and in October, after some months in Guernsey, where he ministered to the English church, he accepted the rectory of St Thomas's, Birmingham. In spite of the restless and riotous times during which he arrived he soon won the respect of what was initially an undisciplined congregation. The excitement and expectations of these years gave a certain topicality to his frequent sermons on the second coming, from which he came to be known as Millennial Marsh. However, his ministry in Birmingham was overshadowed by the death of his wife on 24 July 1833. Early in 1837 Marsh was appointed principal official and commissary of the royal peculiar of the deanery of Bridgnorth. In 1839, finally leaving Birmingham, he became incumbent of St Mary's, Leamington Spa. On 21 April 1840 he married Lady Louisa, third and youngest daughter of Charles, first Earl Cadogan, and his wife, Mary Churchill. After a year of growing blindness from cataract, he was successfully operated on in November 1840. His second wife died in August 1843, and on 3 March 1848 he married the Hon. Louisa Horatia Powys (*d*. 1871), seventh daughter of Thomas, first Baron Lilford, and his wife, Mary Mann. From 1848 he was an honorary canon of Worcester, and in 1851 went to live with his daughter Matilda, whose husband, Frederick Chalmers, was the rector of Beckenham, Kent. In 1860 he accepted the rectory of Beddington, Surrey, where he was assisted by two younger curates. Few men preached a greater number of sermons, and many of these were later published. His conciliatory manners gained him friends among all denominations. On 24 August 1864 he died in the rectory at Beddington and was buried in Beddington on 2 September.

Catherine Marsh (1818–1912), philanthropist and writer, was the youngest of William Marsh's five children and his fourth daughter. Born on 15 September 1818 at St Peter's vicarage, Colchester, she lived with her father and later wrote his biography. During the 1850s in Beckenham, she became concerned for the spiritual welfare of the labourers working on the re-erection of the Crystal Palace nearby and for the many soldiers setting out for the Crimean War. *Memorials of Captain Hedley Vicars* (1855), her emotive biography of an earnest Christian killed in the war, caught the heroic mood of the day, selling 78,000 copies in its first year of publication. Likewise, the account of her work among the navvies given in *English Hearts and English Hands* (1857) was reassuring in its positive approach to the labouring masses. She also established a convalescence hospital in Brighton during the cholera epidemic in 1866. She died on 12 December 1912 at Feltwell rectory, Norfolk, and was buried at Upshire, Essex, on 17 December.   G. C. BOASE, *rev.* TIMOTHY C. F. STUNT

Sources [C. Marsh], *The life of the Rev. William Marsh* (1867) · L. E. O'Rorke, *The life and friendships of Catherine Marsh* (1917) · W. T. Marsh, *Home light, or, The life and letters of Maria Chowne, wife of the Rev. William Marsh*, 3rd edn (1859) · *Jane Austen's letters*, ed. D. Le Faye, new edn (1997)

Archives BL, corresp. with W. E. Gladstone, Add. MS 44246 [Catherine Marsh]

Likenesses W. L. Colls, portrait, 1842 (Marsh, Catherine), repro. in O'Rorke, *Life and friendships*, frontispiece · T. Rogers, photograph, *c*.1858 (Marsh, Catherine), repro. in O'Rorke, *Life and friendships*, following p. 144 · L. Fawkes, watercolour, 1895 (Marsh, Catherine), repro. in O'Rorke, *Life and friendships*, following p. 344 · Elliott & Fry, photograph (Marsh, Catherine), repro. in O'Rorke, *Life and friendships*, following p. 204 · Elliott & Fry?, photograph (Marsh, Catherine), repro. in O'Rorke, *Life and friendships*, following p. 274 · W. Holl, engraving, repro. in Marsh, *Life*

Wealth at death under £3000: resworn probate, March 1866, *CGPLA Eng. & Wales* · £10,635 11s. 0d.—Catherine Marsh: probate, 15 April 1913, *CGPLA Eng. & Wales*

Marshal, Andrew (1742–1813), physician and anatomist, born at Park Hill, Fife, was the son of John Marshal, a farmer with a numerous family living near Newburgh. He lived for some time with his maternal grandfather who taught him to read before he attended first Mr Taylor's school at Newburgh, in 1750, and then Abernethy School in 1752. At first he intended to become a farmer, but when he was about sixteen he decided to become a minister among the Seceders, a body to which his father belonged, and which had separated from the established kirk in 1732. With a view to accomplishing this Marshal studied Latin and logic. He also published an essay on ambition, and one on composition in the *British Magazine*. Unfortunately for Marshal the latter article offended members of his sect and he was excommunicated. For some time subsequently he led a desultory life, without any stable employment. He was for four years tutor in a family on Islay, 'striving to instruct unmanageable children' (Marshal, vi). He then carried on his studies both at Edinburgh and Glasgow while supporting himself by teaching private pupils, and in 1774 travelled abroad for about a year with Lord Balgonie, the eldest son of the earl of Leven and Melville. He translated from the Latin the first three books of Robert Simson's *Elements of the Conic Sections* (1775), and gave some attention to Greek, Latin, trigonometry, logic, metaphysics, and theology. At last, when thirty-five years old, he decided to concentrate on medicine, and in 1777 went to London to continue his studies, although he was invited to become a candidate for the professorship of logic and rhetoric at the University of St Andrews.

In London, Marshal attended the lectures of William Cruikshank and of John and William Hunter in Windmill Street. In 1778 he was, through the interest of Lord Leven, appointed surgeon to the 83rd or Glasgow regiment, which he accompanied to Jersey. Here he remained until 1783, when the regiment was disbanded. He performed his duties with great zeal and ability, and with a rigid probity that occasionally involved him in disputes with his commanding officers. In 1782 he graduated MD at Edinburgh, with an inaugural dissertation, *De militum salute tuendâ*. In the next year he settled in London, on the suggestion and with the support of David Pitcairn, who was at that time physician to St Bartholomew's Hospital. He at first intended to practise surgery, and was admitted to the Company of Surgeons in January 1784; but he afterwards became a licentiate of the Royal College of Physicians (September 1788).

For the first seventeen or eighteen years of Marshal's life in London he was known almost exclusively as a successful teacher of anatomy. His anatomical school was in Thavies Inn, Holborn, where he settled in 1785, and built a dissecting room. It was at first intended that the lectures should form part of a scheme (suggested by Pitcairn) for establishing a kind of school of physic and surgery for the pupils of St Bartholomew's Hospital, but this plan, to Marshal's disappointment, did not materialize and led to a cooling in his friendship with Pitcairn. Marshal then lectured on his own account. Both his appearance and his voice were against him, but he was knowledgeable of his subject and the content of his lectures was excellent, and 'the whole was given with a constant reference to the infinite wisdom of the contrivance exhibited in the structure, so as to form the finest system of natural theology'. In April 1786 Marshal quarrelled with John Hunter about a paper of Marshal's on hydrophobia. This dispirited Marshal to such an extent that he published nothing more.

In 1800 Marshal gave up his lectures on account of his health, and devoted himself entirely to medical practice, which he had before neglected. He died, after a painful illness, at his home at Bartlett's Buildings, Holborn, on 4 April 1813. He was unmarried. He was always of an unsocial temperament, and in his later years was very much alone. He left behind him numerous papers and memorandum books which were entrusted to the care of Solomon Sawrey, who had been his assistant in preparing his lectures. He had also a valuable anatomical museum, of which a detailed catalogue raisonné was being prepared at the time of his death. The only papers that were found to be fit for publication were edited by Sawrey with the title, *The morbid anatomy of the brain, in mania and hydrophobia; with the pathology of these two diseases* (1815).

W. A. GREENHILL, rev. MICHAEL BEVAN

Sources A. Marshal, *The morbid anatomy of the brain … to which is prefixed a sketch of his life by S. Sawrey* (1815) · *GM*, 1st ser., 83/1 (1813), 483 · Munk, *Roll*
Archives NA Scot., letters to Lord Balgonie, GD 26/9/520
Likenesses line engraved silhouette, 1814, Wellcome L.

Marshal, Anselm (d. 1245). *See under* Marshal, William (II), fifth earl of Pembroke (c.1190–1231).

Marshal, Ebenezer (d. 1813), historian and Church of Scotland minister, was licensed as a preacher by the presbytery of Edinburgh on 30 October 1776, and ordained on 3 April 1782 as chaplain to the Scottish regiment in the Dutch service. On 22 November 1782 he was presented to the living of Cockpen in the presbytery of Dalkeith, Edinburghshire. On 29 December 1784 he married Christian Goodsman (d. 1824); they had two children, Archibald, who later became an accountant in Edinburgh, and Susan Gloag.

In later years Marshal published *The History of the Union of Scotland and England* and *An Abridgment of the Acts of Parliament Relating to the Church of Scotland* (both 1799), followed by *A Treatise on the British Constitution* (1812). He also contributed an account of the parish of Cockpen to the first edition of Sir John Sinclair's *Statistical Account of Scotland* (1791–9). Marshal died at Cockpen on 19 May 1813 and was survived by his wife, who died on 13 August 1824.

GORDON GOODWIN, rev. PHILIP CARTER

Sources *Fasti Scot.*, new edn · *Scots Magazine and Edinburgh Literary Miscellany*, 75 (1813), 479

Marshal, Gilbert, seventh earl of Pembroke (d. 1241). *See under* Marshal, William (II), fifth earl of Pembroke (c.1190–1231).

Marshal, John (d. 1165), marshal, son of Gilbert, marshal of Henry I, first appears in records when, with his father, he successfully defended the family's right to the marshalcy against rivals at some time in Henry I's reign. This plea occurred before 1130, as John was recorded in that year's pipe roll as paying for succession to his father's lands and office. He features by name as master marshal in the *Constitutio domus regis*, drawn up for Stephen in the early part of his reign, and he seems to have joined King Stephen soon after Henry I's death. He appears constantly in the king's charters between 1136 and 1138, and accompanied the king on his Norman tour of 1137. But there is no trace of him in Stephen's charters after the outbreak of rebellion in the west country. The annals of Winchester say that in 1138 he garrisoned the Wiltshire castles of Marlborough and Ludgershall, which he appears to have had at farm or in fee from Stephen. The king certainly came to regard him as a rebel, because John of Worcester notes that Stephen was conducting a siege of Marlborough when disturbed in September 1139 by news that the empress and Robert of Gloucester had landed in Sussex. In March 1140 a rogue mercenary, Robert fitz Hubert, was captured by John Marshal. The *Gesta Stephani* says that John Marshal was at this time a member of Gloucester's party, while John of Worcester believed that he was a supporter of the king. It may well be, then, that it was in his own interest that John was working, beginning to define a sphere of lordship in north Wiltshire and the Kennet valley.

After the capture of Stephen at Lincoln in February 1141, John appears unequivocally in the empress's following, at Oxford in July and at the siege of Winchester in August and September. He seems to have been that John 'supporter of the empress' who, according to the continuator of John of Worcester's chronicle, was detached with a force to prevent the relief of Winchester. He was trapped at Wherwell Abbey which was set on fire around him. The verse biography of his son says that this incident cost him an eye, but is otherwise unreliable on the details. He remained firmly committed to the empress's cause after 1141; his brother, William Giffard, became the empress's chancellor. But his chief preoccupation seems to have been the extension of his power in Berkshire, where the abbey of Abingdon recorded him as one of its chief oppressors, and in Wiltshire, where he came into conflict with Patrick of Salisbury. In 1141 John acted with Patrick's elder brother, William of Salisbury, in the keeping of Wiltshire, but he had fallen out with the Salisbury family by 1145. The *Histoire de Guillaume le Maréchal* preserves a number of stories deriving from this period of private warfare in Wiltshire between two Angevin supporters. However, it cannot disguise John Marshal's ultimate defeat, and the fact that he was forced to come to an agreement with Earl Patrick by which he divorced his first wife, Adelina (who later married an Oxfordshire landowner, Stephen Gay), and married the earl's sister, Sybil. John continued to support the Angevin party, appearing with Henry fitz Empress at Devizes in 1147 or 1149.

In 1152 it was the siege of John's forward post of Newbury in Berkshire that provoked the final crisis of Stephen's reign. Under pretext of negotiation, the Marshal (who was not in the castle) surrendered his son William to the king as hostage, but then abused the truce by running provisions and men into Newbury. When informed by the king's messenger that his son's death would follow from this, he is credited with the remark that he still had the hammers and anvil to make more and better sons. As it happened the humane king refused to execute William, and held him at court until the general peace was made the next year.

John Marshal remained prominent at Henry II's court in the first year or so of the new king's reign and was allowed to keep most of his gains from Stephen's reign, but it seems that he lost Ludgershall Castle. It probably reflects the general decline in his fortunes that he lost Marlborough Castle in 1158. In 1163 John Marshal was in disgrace; he had indiscreetly disclosed his belief that one of the prophecies of Merlin referred to Henry II and that the king would die before he could return to England. In 1164 John was involved in the persecution of Becket. He had been deprived of the manor of South Mundham in 1162, when the archbishop reclaimed all lands held of him at fee farm. When his suit to regain the manor failed in the archiepiscopal court, he appealed to the king, alleging unfair treatment. Henry II heard the case at the Council of Northampton in October 1164, and although John's case failed, grounds were found to turn the plea against Becket. John Marshal died in 1165, some time before Michaelmas. He was succeeded initially by his eldest sons, Gilbert and John, but the former died before Michaelmas 1166, leaving the entire estate and office of marshal to John, who was succeeded in turn (after 1194) by his younger brother William *Marshal, later earl of Pembroke.   DAVID CROUCH

Sources P. Meyer, ed., *L'histoire de Guillaume le Maréchal*, 3 vols. (Paris, 1891–1901) • *Florentii Wigorniensis monachi chronicon ex chronicis*, ed. B. Thorpe, 2 vols., EHS, 10 (1848–9) • K. R. Potter and R. H. C. Davis, eds., *Gesta Stephani*, OMT (1976) • J. Stevenson, ed., *Chronicon monasterii de Abingdon*, 2 vols., Rolls Series, 2 (1858) • J. C. Robertson and J. B. Sheppard, eds., *Materials for the history of Thomas Becket, archbishop of Canterbury*, 7 vols., Rolls Series, 67 (1875–85) • *Ann. mon.* • *Radulfi de Diceto ... opera historica*, ed. W. Stubbs, 2 vols., Rolls Series, 68 (1876) • S. Painter, *William Marshal* (1933) • D. Crouch, *William Marshal* (1990) • M. Cheney, 'The litigation between John Marshal and Archbishop Thomas Becket in 1164', *Law and social change in British history* [Bristol 1981], ed. J. A. Guy and H. G. Beall, Royal Historical Society Studies in History, 40 (1984), 9–26 • *Pipe rolls*

Marshal, Sir John (*d.* 1235), baron and justice, of Hingham (or Hockering), was on the evidence of one of his charters to Walsingham Priory an illegitimate son of John Marshal of Hampstead Marshall (*c.*1145–1194), the elder brother of William *Marshal the elder, earl of Pembroke. His mother was probably Alice de Colleville, wife of a Sussex landowner, William de Colleville. This John is therefore one of the few instances where both parents of a child born of an adulterous aristocratic relationship can be discovered. John Marshal was acknowledged by his father and brought up in his household, and after 1194 in the household of his uncle. He was with his uncle in Flanders in 1197 and in Normandy in 1198. But John's success at court may not have been entirely his uncle's doing. His father had been seneschal of King John while the latter was count of Mortain, and may have died while doing him military service. This would account for the fact that the bastard John Marshal was able to survive untroubled his uncle's fall from grace in 1205 and continue to accumulate grants and favour. As castellan of Falaise in 1203 Marshal fought the French advance into Normandy. He retired to England early in 1204. His uncle sent him to Leinster in April 1204 to act as his seneschal for Ireland; he is to be found active there in 1205 and he may have still been there to greet Earl William on his arrival in February 1207.

John Marshal returned with the earl when summoned by King John in autumn 1207, receiving a royal grant of the marshalcy of Ireland and land there. Seemingly untouched by his uncle's disgrace, he stayed with the royal court, and was a banneret in the king's army that sailed to Ireland in 1210. With suspicious ease he resumed the role of Earl William's lieutenant when his uncle returned to England and royal favour in May 1213. It may be that his independent presence at the royal court had been useful to his uncle for intelligence and partisan purposes. He was one of the royalist barons at Runnymede in June 1215, and in its unhappy aftermath the keeping of several key shires (Somerset, Dorset, and Worcestershire), within the area where his uncle was powerful. In September 1215 he was one of John's ambassadors to Rome, and was back in England before the new year. He then attended the king on his northern campaign, and was at his deathbed at Newark in October 1216. In March 1217 John Marshal's position in the west country was enhanced by a grant of the keeping of Devizes Castle. Here he established himself as a dominant regional castellan, and, in partnership with Earl William (I) Longespée of Salisbury, subjected a wide area of Wiltshire to forced exactions. In May 1217 he was one of his uncle's bannerets at the battle of Lincoln, and acted as his uncle's emissary to summon the Anglo-French besiegers of the castle to surrender. With Philip d'Aubigny, Marshal was a leader in the decisive sea battle off Sandwich.

John Marshal accumulated great rewards from victory. In November 1217 he became chief justice of the forests, a post he held until February 1221. In 1217–18 he had custody of the earldom of Devon and the Isle of Wight. In 1218 he was a justice on eyre in the north midlands. Following his uncle's death in May 1219 he entered into an even closer political partnership with the younger Earl William *Marshal, his cousin. Just after his father's death the new Earl William used Sir John's seal until he could have his own dies cut, and acknowledged him as 'my beloved cousin': when William died, John Marshal was to be his chief executor. The Irish interests of Earl William (II) Marshal kept John Marshal frequently engaged in Ireland as a justice both for the king and his cousin. In 1223–4 he had the keeping of the Lacy lordship of Ulster. Elsewhere, he was an ambassador to France in the summer of 1225, and confronted the papal nuncio Otto on the king's behalf in January 1226. In June 1230 he was commissioner in an assize of arms for Norfolk and Suffolk. After Earl William (II)'s death in 1231 he was appointed as castellan to keep Pembrokeshire until the succession of Richard *Marshal was confirmed; the succession ended his active link with the Marshal affinity, although he acted frequently in his capacity as executor for Earl William (II). He did not support the rebellion of Richard Marshal in 1233–4, and was at the royal court in 1234–5.

John Marshal had died between February and 27 June 1235, when his elder son, John, did homage for the manor of Haselbury, Somerset, which was held in chief. John Marshal made a significant number of donations to monastic houses: to Luffield Priory, near his Northamptonshire seat of Norton, and to Walsingham Priory, near his other estate centres in Norfolk. Like his uncle he was also a patron of the templars. He had married his wife, Aline de Ryes, heir of the East Anglian barony of Hingham or Hockering in 1200. She survived him, holding the Ryes lands until 1267, when she died in her nineties. Their elder son, John Marshal, married Margaret, sister and heir of Thomas, earl of Warwick, who died in June 1242, and was briefly earl of Warwick before his own death in October 1242. He was succeeded by his younger brother, William Marshal of Norton, who participated in the baronial rebellion on the Montfortian side and died in 1265, during the fighting. William was succeeded by his son John Marshal, who succeeded his grandmother in the barony of Hockering two years later, came of age in 1278, and died in 1282. The family became extinct in the male line in 1316, with the death of John's grandson, John, whose father, William Marshal of Norton, had been killed at Bannockburn two years earlier.

DAVID CROUCH

Sources P. Meyer, ed., *L'histoire de Guillaume le Maréchal*, 3 vols. (Paris, 1891–1901) · *Chancery records* (RC) · *Chancery records* · Cartulary of Walsingham, BL, Cotton MSS, MS Nero E.vii · G. R. Elvey, ed., *Luffield Priory charters*, 2 vols., Northamptonshire RS, 22, 26 (1968–81) · A. M. S. Leys, ed., *The Sandford cartulary*, 2 vols., Oxfordshire RS, 19, 22 (1938–41) · GEC, *Peerage*, new edn, 8.525–8; 12/2.366–7 · I. J. Sanders, *English baronies: a study of their origin and descent, 1086–1327* (1960) · D. Crouch, *William Marshal* (1990) · D. A. Carpenter, *The minority of Henry III* (1990) · J. T. Gilbert, ed., *Register of the abbey of St Thomas, Dublin*, Rolls Series, 94 (1889)

Marshal, Richard, sixth earl of Pembroke (d. 1234), magnate and courtier, lord of Leinster, Longueville, and Orbec, was born in the early 1190s, the second son of William (I)

*Marshal, earl of Pembroke and Striguil, regent of England, and Isabel de *Clare, daughter and eventual heir of Richard de *Clare (Strongbow) and his wife, Eva, daughter of Diarmait Mac Murchadha, king of Leinster. First mentioned in 1203, Richard Marshal occasionally appeared in the background of the great events of King John's reign in which his father participated. In 1207, when relations between the king and Earl William were deteriorating and the earl wished to visit his Irish lands, King John, who already held the earl's eldest son, William (II) *Marshal, as a hostage, demanded Richard as a second surety for his father's behaviour. Except for a short interval Richard remained in royal custody until 1212. In 1214 he accompanied King John on the disastrous Poitevin expedition and nearly died from sickness there. He is not known to have participated in the baronial wars of 1215–17; indeed, at his father's death in May 1219 he was at the court of King Philip Augustus of France, where he was probably preparing to inherit the Marshal lands in Normandy.

After the death of Richard's mother, Isabel, in 1220, her eldest son, William (II) Marshal, ceded these Norman lands to his brother Richard. After paying a heavy relief to Philip Augustus, Richard Marshal thus became the lord of the Norman honours of Longueville-sur-Scie and Orbec, and until 1231 he was primarily a French nobleman. In November 1226, for instance, after the sudden death of Louis VIII, the regency council of France wrote to him and ten other leading Norman nobles, appealing to them to aid the accession and coronation of the young Louis IX. One English annalist said that Richard was the marshal of the French royal army, another that he learned the skills of warfare in French battles. Moreover, about 1222 Richard married Gervaise (d. c.1239), daughter and heir of Alain de Dinan (d. 1198), one of the greatest nobles of Brittany; Gervaise was also the widow of Juhel de Mayenne, the greatest nobleman in Maine, and of another great Breton noble, Geoffroi, vicomte de Rohan. Such a match raised Richard to an important position in Brittany, and in May 1225 he was present at a great gathering of the Breton nobles with their duke, Pierre Mauclerc, at Nantes.

Yet at the same time Richard Marshal continued to hold his mother's manor of Long Crendon, Buckinghamshire, and he successfully claimed the manors of Ringwood, Hampshire, and Burton Latimer, Northamptonshire, to which Gervaise de Dinan had long-standing claims. To hold lands in England and France simultaneously was a mark of royal favour to his family, which Richard exploited to secure privileges in England for Norman merchants. However, continuing Anglo-French hostility created political difficulties at times for Richard and embarrassed his elder brother, William (II) Marshal. During the Anglo-French war of 1224–7 Richard's English manors were taken into royal hands for a while. Fresh problems arose when Henry III landed in Brittany in May 1230 and occupied Richard's castle of Dinan. Richard appears to have had some initial involvement in the English expedition, but he earned the hostility of Henry III because he did not renounce his allegiance to the king of France.

When William (II) Marshal died in England at Easter 1231, Richard Marshal was at the Norman exchequer in Rouen, and Henry III at first prevented his succession to the Marshal lands, warning the port bailiffs to refuse him entry into England. In view of Richard's French fealty, this was a natural precaution; but according to Wendover, when he came to England to seek his inheritance, Hubert de Burgh, the justiciar, encouraged King Henry to spurn his offer of homage and to order him to leave England at once. Undaunted, the Marshal roused his family's followers in Ireland and Pembrokeshire into revolt, so forcing the king to accept his succession. This story should be treated with some caution. Certainly the king felt constrained to justify his confiscation of the Marshal lands in a letter to the barons of Ireland; but in the same letter he accepted that Richard Marshal was the rightful heir of William (II) Marshal. The good offices of the priory of Notley and the earl of Chester secured a safe conduct for Richard Marshal to come to the king in late June, and the king invested him as earl of Pembroke and lord of Leinster early in August. From then until his death Richard Marshal was at the heart of English politics.

In November 1232 the Marshal was one of four earls assigned to guard the now disgraced Hubert de Burgh at Devizes Castle. The king also conferred the manor and hundred of Awre, Gloucestershire, upon the Marshal. Yet the harmony between the king and the Marshal was short-lived. Richard put up some resistance to providing sufficient dower for his brother's widow, Eleanor, the king's sister; he eventually agreed to pay her the crippling sum of £400 a year for her dower rights in Ireland and south Wales, but by June 1233 he was defaulting on payments. By then the king had fallen under the influence of the bishop of Winchester, Peter des Roches, and his kinsman Peter de Rivallis. From Christmas 1232 these so-called 'Poitevins' and the new justiciar, Stephen of Seagrave, seemed to be monopolizing the distribution of royal patronage, and among the officials they ousted was William of Rowden, Richard Marshal's deputy marshal at court. Throughout the spring of 1233 tensions were rising between the Poitevins and members of the Marshal's affinity, particularly Gilbert Basset and his brothers and Richard Siward; and the Marshal was drawn, probably against his will, into armed protest and eventually a calamitous revolt. Some English chroniclers chose to portray Richard Marshal, hitherto a French nobleman, as a champion of English liberties against the king's foreign counsellors. Yet the revolt was not a struggle between the 'natural-born' barons and 'alien' favourites of Henry III, nor was it a constitutional dispute, although the king's disregard of the rule of law served to stoke the rebellion. Rather, it was a factional conflict over patronage and access to the king, and the descent into war was a startling indication of the mistrust that had built up at court against the king's advisers.

By mid-June Gilbert Basset was in arms against the king. On 9 July Richard Marshal, Basset, and Richard Siward are said to have retired in anger from the royal court because the king had denied justice to Basset and Siward. There are conflicting accounts of what happened next. Wendover

claimed that before 1 August the Marshal fled to Wales, warned by his sister, the countess of Cornwall, that his enemies were plotting to have him arrested at court; he rebelled and the king ordered the destruction of his property and formally 'defied' him (renounced the ties of lordship). More likely, the Marshal was not yet prepared to lead an open revolt. He attempted to organize an armed gathering at Gilbert Basset's manor of Wycombe, Buckinghamshire, in early August, but most sympathizers recoiled from the brink of revolt, leaving the Marshal isolated outside the Welsh marches. In mid-August, when the king was still so unaware of this simmering discontent that he was preparing to go to Ireland, the Marshal's more ardent followers seized the castles of Hay and Ewyas Lacy, and Basset and Siward renounced their homage to the king. In reply Henry III turned upon the Marshal, confiscating his English manors and besieging his castle at Usk. The Marshal had no choice but to make terms, giving pledges for faithful service on 8 September.

The first phase of the conflict was over, although the Marshal was by now at war with Morgan ap Hywel of Caerleon, his family's traditional enemy. A settlement with the king and court might have been within reach, but the Bassets and Siward remained outlawed, raiding the estates of the bishop of Winchester with particular glee—and possibly with the Marshal's connivance. Meanwhile, no doubt mistrusting the intentions of the king and his counsellors and lacking active support from the English baronage, the Marshal negotiated an alliance with Llywelyn ab Iorwerth, reversing his family's former hostility to the Welsh prince. In early October, perhaps to appease his still outlawed followers and fearful of royal support for Morgan, the Marshal launched a campaign to seize Glamorgan. In response King Henry ordered the confiscation of all the Marshal's English castles and manors on 18 October, and their destruction ten days later. As open war erupted along the marches, the daring rescue of Hubert de Burgh from Devizes on 29 October by Siward and the Bassets served only to deepen King Henry's fury. Henry, who by then had certainly 'defied' the Marshal, gathered an army at Hereford and invaded the Marshal lands in south Wales.

The desperate rebels successfully held the royalists at bay, though they could not hope for victory. On the evening of 11 November the Marshal's Welshmen surprised the royal forces at Grosmont, Herefordshire, and succeeded, it was said, in stealing 500 packhorses, the Marshal refusing to attack the king himself. Although Richard narrowly escaped capture during a bloody skirmish outside Monmouth on 25 November, another ambush against the royal army on 26 December prevented further royal advances. Early in January 1234 the Marshal and Llywelyn devastated Shropshire and even burnt part of Shrewsbury; but the next month some of their allies were repulsed with heavy loss from Carmarthen. From Welsh bases, meanwhile, Siward and the Bassets continued to plunder their enemies' manors in England with impunity until May. King Henry's fury knew no bounds, and he demanded that the Marshal should come to him with a rope round his neck to plead for mercy. But the two sides had in reality reached a stalemate; and the English and Welsh bishops, who had already tried to intervene in the autumn of 1233, now stepped into the breach. In February 1234, led by Edmund of Abingdon, archbishop-elect of Canterbury, the bishops told the king that only the removal of the bishop of Winchester and his allies from his counsels would end the crisis. The king eventually yielded, and a truce with Richard Marshal and Llywelyn was arranged late in March; this heralded the fall from grace of the Poitevins and Seagrave in April.

Meanwhile, however, war had broken out in Ireland between the Marshal's brothers and the partisans of the king, including the justiciar of Ireland, Maurice Fitzgerald, the Lacys, and Richard de Burgh. So Richard Marshal crossed to Ireland in February or March to retrieve the situation. There disaster overtook him. On 1 April 1234 he met his enemies in open battle in the Curragh, a plain near Kildare; he was defeated and captured, and died from his wounds in his castle at Kilkenny on 16 April, while the victors divided his lands. Such are the bare details recorded in the Irish sources; but, owing to the popularity of the Marshal and the cause with which he was associated, the English and Welsh chroniclers retold his death as a heroic epic, and it is impossible to separate the truth of the affair from the literary motifs which immediately became attached to the event. Richard Marshal, it was said, was tricked into attending a parley on the Curragh by Geoffrey Marsh, who was secretly in league with Fitzgerald; but the royalists came not to confer but to fight, while Marsh and all the Marshal's Irish knights deserted their lord. Richard could have escaped, but he preferred to fight and 'die with honour for the sake of justice' (Flores historiarum, 3, 84) than to turn tail upon his enemies. He had a mere 15 faithful marcher knights whereas his enemies numbered 140: he fought on until almost alone, when he was mortally wounded from behind, taken prisoner, and borne stricken to his castle. An inept or treacherous surgeon caused the wound to fester, and he died. He was buried at Kilkenny, either in the Dominican convent founded by his brother or, less probably, the Franciscan convent.

The news of Richard Marshal's death shocked the English court and compounded the disgrace of the Poitevins. Henry III was reported to have bemoaned his passing like David mourning Saul and Jonathan; and the story soon spread that the Poitevins had forged the royal letters that had provoked the Irish war. But the king's true attitude is more clearly revealed in the gratitude he expressed to the Marshal's killers for their resistance to the earl, and in the heavy pledges and ransoms which he took from the Marshal's Irish supporters, including Geoffrey Marsh, who was nothing more than a convenient scapegoat for the chroniclers.

Richard Marshal was held in almost universal esteem by contemporary writers, not only for his courage in arms but also for his refinement and erudition, as his friendship with Robert Grosseteste demonstrates. Matthew Paris called him 'the flower of knighthood in our times'

(Paris, Chron., 3.289). In part the Marshal was singled out for such repeated praise because he seemed to be the 'native-born' champion whom contemporary writers keenly pitted against the hated 'aliens', notwithstanding the Marshal's own French career and connections. Yet his violent death in an essentially factional struggle should not obscure his undoubted abilities, which reminded contemporaries forcefully of his great father; it was Richard Marshal's misfortune that events were simply too much for him. He was also a benefactor of a number of religious houses in Normandy, Brittany, England, and Ireland.

Richard Marshal died childless, but his brother Gilbert *Marshal [see under Marshal, William (II), fifth earl of Pembroke] was permitted to inherit the earldom of Pembroke and the other Marshal lands in England, the Welsh marches, and Ireland. The family never recovered its lands in Normandy, which Louis IX had seized on Richard's death. **D. J. POWER**

Sources Paris, Chron. · Rogeri de Wendover liber qui dicitur flores historiarum, ed. H. G. Hewlett, 3 vols., Rolls Series, [84] (1886–9) · Ann. mon., vols. 2, 3, 4 · M. L. Colker, 'The Margam chronicle in a Dublin manuscript', Haskins Society Journal, 4 (1992), 123–48 · P. Meyer, ed., L'histoire de Guillaume le Maréchal, 3 vols. (Paris, 1891–1901) · 'Annals of Ireland', Chartularies of St Mary's Abbey, Dublin: with the register of its house at Dunbrody and annals of Ireland, ed. J. T. Gilbert, 2, Rolls Series, 80 (1884), 293–401 · Chancery records · H. S. Sweetman and G. F. Handcock, eds., Calendar of documents relating to Ireland, 5 vols., PRO (1875–86), vol. 1 · N. Vincent, Peter des Roches: an alien in English politics, 1205–38, Cambridge Studies in Medieval Life and Thought, 4th ser., 31 (1996) · R. F. Walker, 'The supporters of Richard Marshal, earl of Pembroke, in the rebellion of 1233–1234', Welsh History Review / Cylchgrawn Hanes Cymru, 17 (1994–5), 41–65 · R. C. Stacey, Politics, policy and finance under Henry III, 1216–1245 (1987) · G. H. Orpen, Ireland under the Normans, 4 vols. (1911–20) · B. Wilkinson, 'The council and the crisis of 1233–4', Bulletin of the John Rylands University Library, 27 (1942–3), 384–93 · J. Geslin de Bourgogne and A. de Barthélemy, eds., Anciens évêchés de Bretagne, 4 vols. (1855–64) · P. H. Morice, Mémoires pour servir de preuves à l'histoire ecclésiastique et civile de Bretagne, 3 vols. (Paris, 1742–6) · G. MacNiocaill, ed., The Red Book of the earls of Kildare (1964)

Marshal, Walter, eighth earl of Pembroke (d. 1245). See under Marshal, William (II), fifth earl of Pembroke (c.1190–1231).

Marshal, William (I) [called the Marshal], **fourth earl of Pembroke** (c.1146–1219), soldier and administrator, was the son of John *Marshal (d. 1165) and Sybil (fl. c.1146–c.1156), daughter of Walter of Salisbury. He is one of the few medieval laymen to be the subject of a biography, L'histoire de Guillaume le Maréchal. The biography (here referred to as the History) is in fact an extended poem of over 19,000 lines in rhyming couplets. It was commissioned by William (II) *Marshal, the eldest son of the Marshal, and the old Marshal's executor, John (II) of *Earley. It is believed that it was written by an expatriate Tourangeau layman, called John, probably in the southern march of Wales at some time in the years 1225–6, before August of the latter year. The writer worked from the memoirs of those who had been witnesses of the Marshal's life, from the recollections of those to whom the Marshal had told stories of his early days, and also from documents in the

William (I) Marshal, fourth earl of Pembroke (c.1146–1219), tomb effigy

Marshal family archive. The biography is naturally the principal source for much of what follows here.

Upbringing and education, c.1146–1166 William was born the fourth son of John Marshal, the second son by his second wife, whom John had married c.1145 in order to conciliate Patrick, earl of Salisbury, with whom he was engaged in a local war in Wiltshire. The evidence of the *History* indicates that William was born late in 1146 or early in 1147. In 1152, at the age of five or six, William was offered as hostage by his father, who needed a pledge for a truce with King Stephen, who was blockading John's new castle at Newbury, and who expected the truce to be used to negotiate its surrender. John Marshal, reckless of his son's life, used the truce to provision the castle instead. When challenged that his son would die as a result, he is said to have uttered the notorious response that he did not care about the child, since he still had the anvils and hammers to produce even finer ones. The king made several attempts to convince the indifferent garrison that he would execute the boy, but did not in the end permit it. William seems to have remained at court, more as the king's ward than a captive, until perhaps as late as the settlement of November 1153. He next appears as assenting, with his elder brothers, to his father's grant of the manor of Nettlecombe to Hugh de Ralegh in 1156.

It must have been two or three years after this that William was fostered into the household of William de Tancarville, chamberlain of Normandy, who was his mother's cousin. He remained as a squire in the chamberlain's household in Normandy until 1166. Little is known of his training or adolescence, although it is clear from later evidence that he was not put to learn his letters. The only story surviving of this period in his life is that his nickname at Tancarville was Gaste-viande (the Glutton), it being said that when there was nothing to eat, he slept,

although the chamberlain predicted great things for him none the less.

The household knight, 1166–1182 In 1166, just after his father's death, William was knighted, when he was twenty or thereabouts. His father's testament left him no share of the family lands, which ultimately came to his elder full brother, John Marshal (*d.* 1194). The chronology of the *History* is confused at this point, but it seems that after his knighting he became involved in a brief frontier war between Henry II and the counts of Flanders, Ponthieu, and Boulogne, which led to an invasion of the Pays de Caux. The Tancarville household was in garrison at the castle of Neufchâtel-en-Bray, and William found himself in the rare position for a medieval knight of commencing his career in a pitched battle. Apart from a rebuke from his master for being too forward in action: 'Get back, William, don't be such a hothead, let the knights through!' (*History*, ll. 872–4), he distinguished himself in the skirmish. Unfortunately he lost his horse in the cut and thrust of a street fight in the suburbs of Neufchâtel, and failed to take advantage of the opportunity to seize the ransoms that would have retrieved the situation. This was ironically pointed out to him by the earl of Essex, who, at the victory banquet, asked him loudly for various items of saddlery and harness, which he could not produce—but of which he could have had his pick, had he fought professionally, rather than boyishly, in the manner of a knight of the romance.

William was confronted immediately after the battle by the problem of the obvious reluctance of William de Tancarville to offer him further maintenance in his household, forcing him to sell his clothes in order to buy a horse to ride. The chamberlain gave him a reprieve when he decided to lead his household to a tournament in Maine, and it was at this point that William Marshal (as he was known long before he inherited the office of royal marshal on his brother's death in 1194—for William and his other brothers Marshal was a surname rather than, or as well as, an occupational title) found his true calling. By the account of the *History*, the Marshal distinguished himself by capturing a prominent courtier of the king of Scots among others. With the proceeds of his success and the permission of William de Tancarville he threw himself into the tournament circuit for over a year. Late in 1167 or early in 1168 he amicably severed his connection with Tancarville, crossed to England, and took service with his uncle, Earl Patrick of Salisbury. He accompanied the earl to Poitou, where Patrick was given responsibility for the province jointly with Queen Eleanor. William was present at the earl's assassination by a member of the Lusignan family early in April 1168, and was himself cornered by Lusignan soldiers against a hedge, wounded in the thigh by a slash from behind, and captured. He had to undergo a period of uncomfortable captivity, ill from his wound and half-starved by his uncourtly captors. He was eventually released when Queen Eleanor paid his ransom, following which she took him into her retinue.

In 1170, following the coronation of Henry, the Young King, in June, William Marshal was transferred into the boy's household to act as his tutor in arms. He was rapidly established as a favourite and infected the boy with his own love of the tournament. He was given responsibility for the organization of the Young King's retinue, and would seem indeed to have acted as his marshal (*History* gives a wealth of detail about his life on the tournament circuit in the twelfth century, and is indeed the best source for the early history of the tournament). William Marshal is named by Hoveden as one of those who joined the rebellion of the Young King against his father in April 1173. The *History* asserts that his hero knighted the Young King in the early days of the campaign, but there is some confusion here, for it is known that Henry II himself delivered arms to his son immediately before the boy's coronation in 1170. But the Marshal was certainly with the Young King throughout the period of the rebellion. He was still at his lord's side in October 1174, when he attested the agreement between Henry II and his sons. His attendance on the Young King was constant until 1182.

The result of this relationship, together with the rewards of the tournament circuit, was that the Marshal obtained sufficient wealth to maintain his own household knights, and had the resources to raise his own banner at the great tournament of Lagny-sur-Marne in 1180. However, success bred enemies in the Young King's court, and a cabal of William's colleagues succeeded in opening up a gulf between Henry and the Marshal. The principal accusation against him seems to have been that he showed contempt for the Young King in promoting his own interests on the tourney field. A further accusation against him of adultery with Queen Margaret, the younger Henry's wife, would seem to have had little foundation other than in subsequent unsavoury gossip. The two men parted company late in 1182, and an attempt by the Marshal to get redress against his accuser before the Old King at Caen at Christmas 1182 was dismissed. Following this the Marshal went into exile, first making a pilgrimage to the relics of the 'three holy kings' in Cologne, and later (apparently) taking service with the count of Flanders, from whom he accepted a large money fee in the city of St Omer.

Courtier and magnate, 1183–1189 Increasing difficulties between the Young King and his father in Poitou seem to have persuaded the younger king to take the Marshal back into his service at some time after February 1183, when he began to feel let down by his household. However, the Marshal returned only to witness the last illness and death of his young master (on 11 June near Limoges). The Marshal was at the deathbed and was charged near the end to take the Young King's cloak to Jerusalem to fulfil the vow the king had taken to go to the Holy Land. There were some initial difficulties in accomplishing this. He was seized as security for the payment of their wages by a company of the Young King's mercenaries, and only obtained release with difficulty. After attending the younger Henry's corpse on its troubled journey to burial at Rouen, the Marshal received the permission of Henry II to discharge the obligation laid upon him, and with some financial support from the Old King departed for Jerusalem, after taking leave of his own family in England.

William Marshal was in the kingdom of Jerusalem from early 1184 for nearly two years. On his return to Normandy (probably by March 1186) he was received into the royal household. He began to accumulate some of the rewards that went with office. He had a grant of the wardship of the lordship and heir of William of Lancaster soon after his return, and of the royal estate of Cartmel, before July 1188. The Marshal served with distinction in the campaigns against Philip Augustus of France late in 1188, and played a leading part in the last months of the reign of Henry II, as one of the commanders of the royal household guard. He was nowhere more prominent than in the escape of the Old King from Le Mans on 12 June 1189, and was in command of the party that acted as rearguard in the king's flight to Angers. In the course of the action he encountered Richard, the king's son, who was leading the pursuit. Richard was alone and unsupported, having ridden lightly armed ahead of his troops. He is said to have begged the Marshal to spare him, as to kill him would be dishonourable. The Marshal shouted, 'Indeed I won't, let the Devil kill you, I shall not be the one to do it', and shifted his lance to kill Richard's horse beneath him (*History*, ll. 8837–49). After this escape, and a fortnight in garrison at Alençon, the Marshal was recalled to the king in time to witness the conference at Azay and the king's death at Chinon on 6 July 1189. During 1188–9 he was offered marriage first to the heiress of Châteauroux (Berry) and then to the heiress of the honour of Striguil in return for giving up the wardship of the Lancaster lands. He is represented as remonstrating with the seneschal of Anjou that he should open the treasury to give alms to the poor, and as taking responsibility for properly arraying the dead king and escorting him to burial at Fontevrault, but the role the *History* assigns him may have been retrospectively prominent.

None the less, there is no doubt that the heir to the throne, Count Richard of Poitou, was determined to bring William Marshal forward in public affairs on his accession, despite their encounter on the retreat from Le Mans some weeks earlier. The Marshal was confirmed in his possession of Striguil (Chepstow), the honour of the late earl Richard de *Clare (Strongbow) (*d.* 1176) in England and Wales. He married Clare's daughter, Isabel de *Clare (1171x6–1220), probably in August following his arrival in London late in July 1189, on what appears to have been a confidential mission to Queen Eleanor, Richard's mother, then at Winchester. In addition to Striguil, by right of his wife the Marshal received half of the Giffard honour of Longueville in Normandy and some Giffard manors (including Caversham) in England. He shared the Giffard lands with the earl of Hertford, who also had a claim to the Giffard inheritance. As well as this, the Marshal's wife brought a claim to the lordship of Leinster, conquered by her father in 1170–71. To consolidate his power in the southern march William Marshal was granted the shrievalty of Gloucester and the keeping of the Forest of Dean.

In the service of Richard I, 1189–1199 The Marshal was in constant attendance on the new king from the time of Richard's coronation (in which he carried the sceptre) on

13 September 1189, to his departure on crusade in July 1190. His elder brother, John Marshal, shared in his success, having grants of office and lands. Henry Marshal, a younger brother, was given the deanery of York. So prominent did the Marshal group now appear at court that there is evidence of hostility to it in the actions of Geoffrey Plantagenet, the archbishop of York, and William de Longchamp, the chancellor. The latter acted in the spring of 1190 to remove the shrievalty of York from John (II) Marshal for alleged incompetence, and at the same time moved unsuccessfully to blockade the Marshal's castle of Gloucester, for unknown reasons. William Marshal's star continued to rise, however, for he was made one of the four men appointed by King Richard to monitor William de Longchamp's conduct as justiciar. In October 1191 the Marshal and his fellows co-operated with Count John, the king's brother, in his campaign to remove Longchamp from power, and the Marshal supported the substitution of Walter de Coutances, archbishop of Rouen, as the new justiciar. There was a period of stability when power was balanced between Count John and the justiciars, but that ended in December 1192, when news reached England of King Richard's capture and imprisonment in Germany. The Marshal and his fellows were forced into reluctant confrontation with the count in March 1193. John finally withdrew from England in the summer, and in February 1194, with the king's return imminent, the justiciars acted to confiscate the count's lands in England.

In March 1194 the king returned, and at the same time John Marshal died at Marlborough without a legitimate heir (perhaps resisting the justiciars at Marlborough in John's interests, for he was the count's sometime seneschal). This brought William Marshal the family inheritance and completed his landed power base in the west country and southern march. Without waiting to attend his brother's funeral the Marshal joined the royal household on its way to confront John's loyalists at Nottingham, and he played a part in the successful siege of the castle there. However, relations between the Marshal and King Richard were not entirely even. The Marshal refused to do homage to the king for his lands in Ireland, saying that Count John was still his overlord for Leinster. Although the king accepted his reasons, at least one onlooker (William de Longchamp) was brave enough to voice the conclusion that the Marshal was keeping his bridges open to John, as the heir presumptive, saying: 'Here you are planting vines!' (*History*, ll. 10312–26). The Marshal carried a sword of state at King Richard's solemn crown-wearing at Winchester on 17 April 1194.

Thereafter William Marshal was closely engaged with the royal court until the very end of the reign, spending much of the period between 1194 and 1199 campaigning in Normandy and elsewhere in northern France. However, he had other tasks. In the early summer of 1197 he was entrusted with negotiations for an alliance between King Richard and the counts of Flanders and Boulogne. In August 1197 he returned to Flanders with Count Baldwin (his lord for a fee in St Omer) and apparently played a prominent part in the action outside Arras in which King Philip was trapped and forced to surrender on terms. He remained very much a military man, and the *History* has much to say of his campaigns and achievements at this time. For instance, it recalls the active part he played in the taking of the castle of Milly-sur-Thérain, near Beauvais, in 1198, when he climbed a scaling-ladder and defended a section of wall: at that time he was over fifty years of age, but age was not enough to stop him flattening the constable of Milly as he met him on the wall walk. But he did need to sit down on the man's unconscious body, to catch his breath.

The Marshal and King John, 1199–1203 While King Richard was dying on 6 April 1199 the Marshal was at Vaudreuil, acting as a ducal justice. There he heard the news of the king's danger, receiving a writ directing him to take charge of the tower of Rouen and secure the city. He heard of the king's death three days later while on the point of going to bed. He crossed the city in the night to discuss the succession with Archbishop Hubert Walter. He declared himself a supporter of Count John for the succession, rather than the king's nephew, Arthur of Brittany, 'since the son is indisputably closer in the line of inheritance than the nephew is'. Despite the archbishop's warning, 'that you will never come to regret anything you did as much as what you're doing now' (*History*, ll. 11900–6), the Marshal was sent to England with the archbishop to bring his fellow magnates to support John. He then returned to Normandy and joined John's household as it prepared to make the crossing. Immediately before John's coronation (27 May 1199) the Marshal's loyalty was rewarded by investiture as earl of Pembroke. Along with investiture went a promise of Pembrokeshire itself, which the Marshal's late father-in-law had lost to the king in 1154, and which the king still withheld. He had secured the marcher lordship from which he took his title by 1201. It is clear that the Marshal visited the march himself to claim Pembroke late in 1200 or early in 1201. There is strong evidence that, while in west Wales, the Marshal made the crossing to Ireland to visit Leinster and take the homage of his men there, leaving his knight, Geoffrey fitz Robert, behind him as seneschal. He also received once more the shrievalty of Gloucester (lost in 1194) and the keeping of Gloucester and Bristol castles, thus consolidating his power in the southwest of England. He secured for his bastard nephew, John *Marshal, son of the late John Marshal (d. 1194), the barony of Hockering in Norfolk, and the lordship of Ryes in Normandy.

William Marshal maintained the place at the royal court he had held under Richard in John's first years, and certainly found little cause at this time to regret his choice in 1199, whatever the archbishop is alleged to have warned. He had reached a peak of personal influence and power by 1201, being very close to the new king's counsels. But his career slowly became tainted by the king's failure to maintain his position in northern France. The Marshal had been detailed from 1201 onwards to protect Upper Normandy, but his efforts were increasingly compromised by the king's political misjudgements. At the end of 1203 the

Marshal led an unsuccessful attempt to relieve the garrison of the border castle of Château Gaillard, when his energy was defeated by a failure of river-borne and land forces to link up, and his force was decisively defeated by the French commander, Guillaume des Barres. In December 1203 the Marshal accompanied the king on his departure from Normandy for England, after which the duchy fell rapidly to the French invaders.

Problems of allegiance, 1203–1206 The loss of Normandy was a serious matter for William Marshal. It had been the theatre for many of his greatest achievements over the past thirty years, and he plainly loved the place. King Philip's conquest of the duchy involved William in serious losses of land, which he was not prepared to let go without more of a struggle than the king was making. When King John sent him and the earl of Leicester to negotiate with the French king in May 1204, the Marshal took the opportunity to open private negotiations about his continued possession of his Norman lands. He and the earl of Leicester paid for a year's grace before they met King Philip's condition of homage for the continued enjoyment of their Norman lands. King John seems to have understood the Marshal's predicament, and was willing to be as obliging as he could to his old ally. In the summer of 1204 he allowed the Marshal to get away with some sharp practice over the Dorset lands of the count of Meulan, which he claimed. He also allowed the Marshal to seek compensation in the southern march of Wales. He granted the Marshal the lordship of Castle Goodrich, and licensed, and perhaps even funded, the Marshal's campaign to recover Cilgerran in Ceredigion from the princes of Deheubarth, which he achieved in December 1204.

In spring 1205, however, Normandy was still on the Marshal's mind, and he took advantage of another embassy to do homage to King Philip. From the evidence of the *History*, King John seems to have been sympathetic to the Marshal's wish to do homage, but was less than pleased when he heard that Philip had prevailed on the Marshal to do liege homage for his Norman lands, obliging the Marshal to do military service to him when in France. This led to a public rift between King John and the Marshal on his return to the English court, for the Marshal refused to accompany him to campaign in Poitou. The king accused him of treason and demanded that the magnates present pass judgment on him, but, remarkably, they refused, perhaps impressed by the Marshal's harangue that they 'Be on alert against the king: what he thinks to do with me, he will do to each and every one of you, or even more, if he gets the upper hand over you' (*History*, ll. 13171–4). The king then attempted to get one of his household knights to challenge the Marshal, but (despite the Marshal's being now nearly sixty) they all refused. None the less, despite this narrow escape, the Marshal had misjudged the situation, and King John decided that he had gone as far as he wished to go in helping the earl of Pembroke recover his losses. The king as a consequence demanded the Marshal's eldest son as a hostage for his faith, and the flood of favours to the earl dried to a trickle. The Marshal was still at court and in November was detailed with other earls to escort King William of Scots from the border south to York. He remained at court nearly until John's departure to Poitou in June 1206, but did not return when the king came back to England in September.

In the political wilderness, 1206–1213 From 1206 to 1213 the Marshal spent a biblical seven years in the political wilderness. This would seem to have been (initially) a matter of his own choice, rather than the result of the king's expelling him from court. The king was still well disposed enough towards the Marshal to repay a debt incurred before his departure on campaign. He was even prepared to humour for a while the Marshal's request that he be allowed to cross the sea to his Irish estates, and licences to depart were issued both to him and his principal followers in February 1207. However, he had second thoughts about having a man of the Marshal's prestige trampling about in the lordship of Ireland, which the king seems to have regarded as his own private garden. Messages were sent to the Marshal asking him to hand over his second son, Richard, as hostage for his good behaviour, and also intimating that the king would rather he did not go. But the Marshal was by now determined, and, despite the king's hints, sailed to Ireland with his wife and military household. The king immediately retaliated by relieving the Marshal of his responsibilities in Gloucestershire and the Forest of Dean. The fortress of Cardigan was also taken from him and given to a royal warden.

The Marshal was almost immediately drawn into conflict with King John's justiciar, Meiler Fitz Henry, a veteran of the old days of conquest in the 1170s and a willing tool in the king's hand to reduce marcher influence in Ireland. William had already sent his nephew, John Marshal, ahead of him in 1204 to try to assert his interests in Leinster against Meiler, who had laid claim to the region of Offaly. Now he took up the struggle himself. The Marshal would seem to have been the motivating power behind a party of Meiler's enemies, calling itself 'the barons of Leinster and Meath', who petitioned the king that Offaly be restored to the lord of Leinster. This the king refused, and demonstrated that he had been told by Meiler who was to blame by promptly recalling the Marshal to England. About 29 September 1207 the Marshal returned to meet the king with only a small escort, leaving his interests in Leinster in the hands of his wife and his household knights. He seems to have expected the worst when he left, and was not disappointed. In the meantime a meeting with the king, Meiler, and a number of Irish barons at Woodstock in October 1207 went singularly badly for the Marshal: many of his former supporters promptly defected to the king with little pressure.

Meiler's kinsmen and followers, and a number of the Marshal's own tenants in Leinster, began a military campaign against him in his absence. This was reinforced in January 1208 by Meiler himself, whom the king sent off to Ireland armed with letters of recall to the Marshal's men. Fortunately for the Marshal his military household was up to the challenge, and happy to defy the king. His party negotiated for support with the Lacy family; between them Meiler's men and the rebel knights of Leinster were crushed, and Meiler himself was captured. The countess, William's wife, was more or less left in control of Ireland. Recognizing the inevitable, the king came to terms with the Marshal and restored Leinster to him on new terms, but returned Offaly. Meiler himself was offered as sacrifice to the Marshal, and was in the end disinherited. But the Marshal was certainly no longer required at court, and was allowed (and maybe even encouraged) to leave for Ireland once more. His two elder sons remained hostage in England for his behaviour.

The Marshal lived in Ireland in isolation from his former habitat of the court for several years, and amused himself in a reorganization of his lordship there and in some campaigning against the native Irish. He included in his hostilities the native Irish bishop of Ferns, a Cistercian called Ailbe Ó Máelmuaid, who was a friend and intimate of King John from the days when the latter had been count of Mortain. Bishop Ailbe was doubtless persecuted because he had been an ally of Meiler Fitz Henry. The treatment of the bishop of Ferns brought the Marshal under the church's ban by 1216. The only occasion on which the Marshal came into direct contact with the king in his six years' exile from court was in 1210, when he came under suspicion for sheltering the king's enemy, William (III) de Briouze. Briouze had taken refuge in Ireland after falling into disgrace at court, and was briefly entertained by the Marshal in Leinster, before being passed on to his relatives, the Lacy family. The Marshal protested his innocence, crossing over to Pembroke to appear before the king, who was preparing an expedition against the Lacys. He escaped with only a few harsh words and the loss of the fortress of Dunamase, and was sent back across the Irish Sea.

Pillar of the throne, 1213–1216 In August 1212 a thaw in relations between the Marshal and the king began, when the Marshal made ostentatious demonstrations of loyalty in Ireland while John was under threat of a baronial conspiracy. The king had perhaps originally suspected the Marshal's involvement, for he had placed his fleet on alert against threats coming from the Marshal's lands, but the king was eventually reassured. The Marshal's elder sons were released into the custody of his friends. Eventually, in May 1213, the Marshal was recalled to the court, where his renowned loyalty was suddenly in demand once more. He was restored to his former position of dominance in south Wales: Cardigan was returned, and the lordships of Carmarthen, Gower, and Haverford added to his responsibilities. He was left virtually justiciar of the march.

Following the disaster of Bouvines in 1214 the Marshal was more than ever in demand as mainstay for the royalist cause against the emerging rebel baronial party. The Marshal was chief lay negotiator for the king at London in January and at Oxford in February 1215. When war came despite his efforts, he was sent off to secure the march against the rebels who had allied there with Prince Llywelyn of Gwynedd. Following the king's defeat William Marshal resumed his role of middle man in negotiations with the barons. He may have been assisted—rather than hindered—in this by the defection of his eldest son, William (II) Marshal, to the baronial party at some time in May or June 1215. Far from being a blow to the Marshal, this may have been a deliberate move of father and son (who were devoted to each other) to make sure they had a foot in whichever camp ultimately won; the Worcester annals provide evidence that there was some contemporary suspicion of their motives. This was the sort of game the elder Marshal had already played with his elder brother, John, in 1190–94. For John Marshal had been close to the then Count John, while the Marshal had favoured King Richard.

When the crisis came in July 1215 and open war broke out, the Marshal was once again sent off to secure the march and contain the Welsh. Here he stayed while London and the south-east of England fell to the baronial insurgents and Louis of France, in spring 1216. The king's sudden death in October 1216 somewhat retrieved the situation for the loyalist party, and led to the Marshal's greatest political challenge. The Marshal was appointed by King John's last testament as one of a council of thirteen executors to assist the king's sons in the recovery of their inheritance. The assertion by the *History* that the Marshal was appointed by the king as protector and regent for his son on his deathbed is patently incorrect. However, the Marshal's subsequent actions excuse the mistake. He did indeed start to act the part of regent. He took responsibility for the staging of John's funeral at Worcester Cathedral; convened a council at Gloucester for early November to ratify the arrangements for a protectorship; and took responsibility for the boy king, Henry III, who was brought to Gloucester from Devizes. The only potential rival for the position of loyalist leader was Ranulf (III), earl of Chester, and when Ranulf arrived at Gloucester he made it perfectly clear that he would rather that the Marshal took the lead at that time. The evidence of papal correspondence shows that Earl Ranulf later changed his mind, and was agitating for the Marshal to accept him as coadjutor-regent in the weeks before the battle of Lincoln sanctified the Marshal's rule.

Guardian of England, 1216–1219 The Marshal and his royal charge left for Tewkesbury on 2 or 3 November 1216, and thence to another great council at Bristol. At this point his title was decided as 'guardian [*rector*] of the king and the kingdom', a title he first used on 12 November. All royal acts were carried out in his name, and his own seal affixed to chancery writs. He associated with himself the papal legate, Cardinal Guala Bicchieri, who lent his rule not just moral authority, but some legitimacy, England being a papal fief at this time. The Marshal presided over a political stalemate in England until May 1217, but he had the satisfaction of seeing a growing number of barons returning to their allegiance, including his own son, William (II) Marshal, who rejoined him in February. In May 1217 the Marshal led the loyalist column that took first Mountsorrel Castle, Leicestershire, and then moved on to relieve the siege of Lincoln Castle. On 20 May 1217 the Marshal took the field in person, first haranguing his small force and then leading it to the attack against the rebel force at Lincoln, which was commanded by his own first cousin, the count of Perche. He rode into battle with his son, leading the main royalist column that forced an entry into the city through its north gate, while an outflanking force distracted the Anglo-French force by reinforcing the loyalists in the castle. So keen for battle was he that as he was beginning to move his column a page noticed and reminded him that he had not put his helm on. The Marshal (aged about seventy-two) engaged in personal combat in the streets of Lincoln, still able to use his weight and skill as a horseman to force himself deep into the enemy ranks. In the fighting under the west towers of the cathedral he was able to knock from his horse with a sword-stroke Robert of Ropsley, a rebel, who had himself just unseated the earl of Salisbury. There the Marshal witnessed with regret the killing of the count of Perche by a sword splintering through the eyehole of his helm. He supervised the rounding-up of the defeated rebels, and then concentrated his armies on the south-east.

It now became the Marshal's chief concern to get Louis of France out of the country with as much decency and haste as possible. The naval defeat of the relieving French force off Sandwich in August proved conclusive. Louis was persuaded to leave London and return to France in return for a general amnesty and an indemnity of 10,000 marks. In later days the Marshal was much condemned for these easy terms, when the French invaders were apparently at the mercy of the loyalists. Maybe the personal embarrassment of having his liege lord's son at his mercy played its part in his policy, but equally well he may have calculated that England needed peace at this time more than anything else.

William Marshal held power for nineteen months after the departure of Louis from England. His regime had some successes: the exchequer was re-established and the machinery of the eyre set in motion again. Peace returned to the marches of Wales and an accommodation was reached with Prince Llywelyn of Gwynedd at Worcester in March 1218. The Marshal took full advantage of his opportunities for patronage by furthering his men's interests, most particularly those of his eldest son, who was heavily subsidized out of royal revenues. Mortality caught up with him in January 1219, when he became suddenly ill at Westminster. The symptoms of his last illness suggest a bowel cancer, though this can only be a matter of inference. He was in bed until mid-February, but a remission allowed him to resume the business of government. On 7 March he rode to the Tower of London, but soon fell ill once more. Suspecting his death was upon him, he had himself rowed up the Thames to the former Giffard manor of Caversham in the modern county of Berkshire, opposite Reading, which had become one of his chief residences over the years. He reached his home after three days on the river, and there for a while he carried on in his role of regent; the king was brought to Reading with his tutor, the bishop of Winchester. At a council held in his sick-chamber on 8 and 9 April 1219 he relinquished power to the legate, snubbing the pretensions of Bishop Peter des Roches of Winchester.

The Marshal's biography dwells on the events at his deathbed with great detail. A testament was drawn up the day after the Marshal's resignation of power in his own household council, and although a text no longer exists its provisions can be reconstructed. His eldest son, William (II), received the earldom and the bulk of the lands in England, Wales, and Ireland. Richard, his second son, received the Norman lands and the Giffard manors in England. His third son, Gilbert, was a clerk. Walter, the fourth son, received his father's acquisitions: Goodrich Castle and several other English manors. The fifth son, Anselm, was left a large cash legacy, at his father's council's urging. There were other legacies to abbeys and chapter churches in his advocacy, and he left his body to be buried at the New Temple Church in London. He left as his executors David, abbot of Bristol, and his household bannerets, John of Earley and Henry fitz Gerold. The elder Marshal was over a month dying after that, and before the end he was received by the master of the Temple into his order. None the less he was earl of Pembroke to the end, distributing robes from his wardrobe to his household the day before his death, despite the suggestion of a household clerk that he sell them and distribute the cash in alms to the poor. He died in his crowded death-chamber at about midday on 14 May 1219, his head supported by his eldest son, and in possession of a plenary indulgence for his sins.

The Marshal's body was laid that afternoon in the chapel of Caversham manor, where it was presumably embalmed. The next day it was taken to Reading Abbey, and lay the night in a side chapel he had financed, in neighbourly fashion. On what must have been 16 May it was borne by wagon to Staines to meet an escort of earls and barons, who accompanied it to Westminster Abbey. At every halt a mass was said, and the funeral exequies were performed, probably on 18 or 19 May, at the New Temple, where the body was laid under a military effigy (one of the first of its type) in the nave. The effigy currently identified as the Marshal's (restored in the nineteenth century, and damaged by a German bomb in the Second World War) has been thought to be his since at least 1661, when the Dutch traveller Schellinks viewed and described it. The corpse did not rest entirely peacefully beneath it. Bishop Ailbe of Ferns (a sometime follower of Count John, later persecuted by the Marshal) caused a scandal by refusing to lift his excommunication from the dead Marshal when brought to the tomb by the king. His curse was said to be responsible for the poor state of the corpse when it was exhumed in the mid-thirteenth century to accommodate building alterations. It was also supposed to account for the extinction of the Marshal line in 1245.

The Marshal and the historians The Marshal's immediate posthumous reputation was not as shining as the sponsors of the *History* had perhaps hoped to establish. Matthew Paris in the next political generation repeated views of him as a figure of some ambiguity, too easy on the French and too harsh to the church. The discovery of a text of the *History* by Paul Meyer in the sale of the Savile Library in 1861, and its subsequent edition and publication by him, has projected William Marshal into the foreground of modern interpretation of the medieval noble mentality. Modern interpreters have tended to find what they themselves expected. Meyer himself, and Sidney Painter, fulfilled the expectations of the Marshal's executors and saw him as the chivalric hero of his day: taking up the description of him attributed by the *History* to King Philip of France, 'the best knight in all the world'. But the Marshal was only one of several contemporaries who were regarded in that light: Guillamme des Barres the elder, and Robert de Breteuil, earl of Leicester (*d.* 1204), were quite as prominent as warriors and statesmen. Georges Duby dispelled the mythology of the Marshal as a hero of chivalry, but went too far in stressing his physical, animal nature at the expense of his undoubted gifts as a courtier.

In fact the Marshal was a military captain of some international repute, and a physically accomplished sportsman and warrior. Principally he was a courtier, and trained to be such from boyhood. He cultivated and practised carefully the deferential and affable behaviour necessary for survival in the retinues of greater men. He was in his mid-forties before he was placed into any situation where a broader political judgement was needed. As one of Richard's appointees to oversee William de Longchamp in 1190–94 he demonstrated an eagerness to offend neither the king nor Count John which showed him to be a political trimmer at heart—compelled by early training to avoid offending anyone powerful—and a self-serving trimmer he always remained. Trimming was behaviour that might be mistaken for sagacity, but in his case it was really no more than caution masking incomprehension. The only thing his vision comprehended was the direction of his own interests, and these he could pursue ruthlessly, and sometimes recklessly as can be seen in his complaints of poor reward to Henry II in 1188. It is unlikely that anyone took him seriously as a political figure of any great weight (as opposed to a military captain) until the reign of John, who (ironically in view of the verdict of the *History* on him) vigorously promoted the Marshal's political fortunes. It was consistent misjudgement in pursuing his own interests that brought the Marshal down in 1205, and his tired decision to retreat into self-imposed exile in Ireland in 1207 should have been the end of his active career. But King John's own difficulties, the Marshal's undeserved reputation for political wisdom, and his deserved reputation for military success, pulled him out of retirement. His luck was that he was the ideal man for the moment in 1216, and his greater luck was that the moment was not so prolonged as to reveal his political weaknesses. Perhaps, too, by this time his great age made it easier for him to command obedience and respect.

William Marshal was very successful as an estate owner and regional magnate. He could be as charming and affable to social inferiors who were of use to him, as to his superiors. There is no doubt that, if let be, behind the courtier and opportunist was a well-disposed and kindly man. However, the Marshal followed his father and the spirit of his age in being remorselessly vengeful to lesser men who opposed his local ambitions, as was seen both in Leinster and south Wales. His closeness to the king between 1189 and 1205 made his service very attractive to the politically mobile class of lesser bannerets and county knights. He created one of the first recognizable regional political affinities, basing his power in the south-west of England and southern march of Wales. This affinity in turn enhanced his position at court. King John made great use of the Marshal's local power base in his difficulties with rebels. The Marshal's ecclesiastical patronage was conventional for a magnate of his day. He was a generous patron of the regular orders: he greatly favoured the templars; he founded an Augustinian priory at Cartmel about 1189, and the Cistercian houses of Duiske and Tintern Parva in Leinster in the first decade of the thirteenth century. He was survived by his wife, Isabel, for less than a year: she died at Chepstow in February 1220, and was buried at Tintern Abbey. They left five sons: William (II), Richard *Marshal, Gilbert *Marshal, Walter *Marshal, and Anselm *Marshal [*see under* Marshal, William (II)], successive earls of Pembroke. They also had five daughters: Matilda, who married successively Hugh Bigod, earl of Norfolk, and William (IV) de *Warenne, earl of Surrey, Isabel, who married successively Gilbert de *Clare, earl of Gloucester and Hertford, and *Richard, first earl of Cornwall; Sybil, who married William de Ferrers, earl of Derby; Eve, who married William (V) de Briouze; and Joan, who married Warin de *Munchensi. DAVID CROUCH

Sources P. Meyer, ed., *L'histoire de Guillaume le Maréchal*, 3 vols. (Paris, 1891–1901) • A. Holden, S. Gregory, and D. Crouch, eds., *The history of William Marshal*, 3 vols., Anglo-Norman Texts [forthcoming] • S. Painter, *William Marshal* (1933) • G. Duby, *William Marshal: the flower of chivalry*, trans. R. Howard (1984) • D. Crouch, *William Marshal* (1990) • GEC, *Peerage*, new edn, 10.358–64 • *The journal of William Schellinks' travels in England, 1661–1663*, ed. M. Exwood and H. L. Lehmann, CS, 5th ser., 1 (1993) • *Ann. mon.*, vol. 4 • *Chronica magistri Rogeri de Hovedene*, ed. W. Stubbs, 2, Rolls Series, 51 (1869) • N. Vincent, 'William Marshal, King Henry II and the honour of Châteauroux', *Archives*, 25 (2000), 1–15
Likenesses tomb effigy, Temple Church, London [*see illus.*]

Marshal, William (II), fifth earl of Pembroke (*c.*1190–1231), magnate, was born in Normandy, the eldest son of William (I) *Marshal, earl of Pembroke and regent of England (*c.*1146–1219), and his wife Isabel de *Clare (*d.* 1220). In 1205 King *John, unworthily doubting the elder William's loyalty, demanded his eldest son as a hostage, and a hostage he remained until 1212, by which time the king was in urgent need of the Marshal's support.

In the great crisis of his reign King John enjoyed the unswerving loyalty of the elder William, but his son aligned himself with the baronial opposition, possibly as a family insurance policy, and appeared in arms with the barons at Stamford in February 1215; he was later one of the twenty-five barons appointed to enforce the terms of Magna Carta. These proved unacceptable to both sides, and in the civil war that followed the younger William joined Prince Louis of France and was appointed marshal of his army. Though active in the field on the barons' behalf, he avoided any hostile confrontation with his father. Denied possession of Marlborough, once held by his paternal grandfather, John *Marshal, by Louis he changed sides, capturing Winchester and Southampton for the royalists and Marlborough for himself, and fought in the decisive battle of Lincoln on 20 May 1217.

On his father's death in 1219 Marshal succeeded him as earl of Pembroke and marshal of England, and on his mother's death in 1220 succeeded to the lordships of Leinster and Netherwent. The Clare lands in Normandy passed by agreement to his younger brother Richard *Marshal. A major problem faced by the government during the minority of Henry III was regaining for the crown or their rightful owners castles seized and retained by royalists during the civil war. Among the castles held by the earl were Fotheringhay and Marlborough. The return of Fotheringhay to John the Scot, earl of Huntingdon, was desirable to promote good relations with Scotland. The Marshal ignored orders to surrender Fotheringhay in 1219 and 1220 until events in Wales forced his hand. The peace of Worcester in 1218 had established Llywelyn ab Iorwerth as the king's bailiff, during his minority, of Cardigan and Carmarthen. Llywelyn promised to restore to marcher lords lands they had lost since 1215, but when in 1220 he stripped Rhys Gryg (one of the lords of the Welsh principality of Deheubarth) of two lordships, he disposed of them as he pleased. Then, alleging that the Marshal's tenants, with help from Leinster, had attacked their Welsh neighbours, he launched a savage attack on Pembrokeshire, capturing Narberth and Wiston castles and burning the town of Haverfordwest. To buy peace, the men of Pembroke were forced to promise not to repair the captured castles and to surrender lands to be held by Llywelyn on the king's behalf. William now demanded that the justiciar, Hubert de Burgh, should release his men from their obligations and assure them that Llywelyn had acted without royal authority. The answer was a new demand to surrender Fotheringhay. Eventually receiving the desired letters from the justiciar, the Marshal quietly gave up the castle.

In 1214 the marriage arranged in 1203 between the younger William Marshal and Alice, daughter of Baldwin de Béthune, count of Aumale, finally took place; but Alice soon died, probably in 1216. In 1221 the justiciar and the papal legate, Pandulf, in order to avoid the Marshal's making a foreign match and to attach him to the justiciar's party, proposed that he should marry *Eleanor (1215?–1275), the younger sister of *Henry III. The marriage took place on 23 April 1224 and the Marshal surrendered Marlborough, a small price for a royal bride. Up to 1226 the Marshal remained a close ally of Hubert de Burgh.

In March 1223 Llywelyn suddenly attacked and captured the castles of Kinnerley and Whittington in Shropshire, and was consequently caught on the wrong foot by William Marshal, who attacked him in south-west Wales. A truce between the two was due to end on Easter Sunday (23 April). On 15 April the Marshal landed near St David's with an army from Leinster, and on Easter Monday, with a nice observance of the rules worthy of his father, attacked and took Cardigan. Two days later he took Carmarthen. Llywelyn sent an army south under his son Gruffudd, who burned Kidwelly and awaited attack. The Marshal appears to have had the better of the ensuing battle, before proceeding to strengthen the defences of Carmarthen and starting to build the immensely strong castle of Cilgerran. Attempts to reconcile the Marshal and Llywelyn having failed, the justiciar sent a large force of cavalry to the Marshal's help, enabling him to consolidate his gains, which included the castle and lordship of Kidwelly. Wisely, the Marshal secured two Welsh allies, Rhys Mechyll and Cynan ap Hywel, grandsons of the Lord Rhys of Deheubarth. Southern Ceredigion was overrun and given to Cynan. In September the justiciar with a large army occupied the lordship of Montgomery and established a castle on a new site. Llywelyn made peace in October, surrendering Kinnerley and Whittington, ceding Montgomery to the king, and accepting the *fait accompli* in the south-west. It was conceded that Welsh lords should regain lands they had held lawfully. Cynan ap Hywel ultimately surrendered southern Ceredigion to Maelgwn ap Rhys, and was compensated by the Marshal with the commote of Ystlwyf (Oysterlow) and the eastern commote of Emlyn. The earl retained the western commote as his lordship of Cilgerran, while in November 1223 he was granted the custody of Cardigan and Carmarthen. In south-west Wales the Marshal had effectively restored the *status quo* of 1215, and enabled the lords of Cemais, St Clears, Laugharne, Llansteffan, and Kidwelly to resume possession.

Following his successes in south-west Wales in 1223, William Marshal's attention switched to Ireland in 1224. The immediate occasion lay in the claim of Hugh de Lacy to the lordship of Ulster, of which he had been deprived by King John in 1210. Failing to negotiate its restoration, Lacy returned to Ireland late in 1223 to seize it by force, supported by his half-brother William and by many of the tenants of Mide, though not by his brother Walter, lord of Mide. William Marshal was appointed justiciar of Ireland on 2 May 1224, and crossed to Waterford in June. Basing himself on Dublin he besieged Trim, the principal castle of Mide, and sent a force to relieve Carrickfergus. Hugh de Lacy's alliance with the Ó Neills was countered by alliance with the Irish lords of Connacht, Thomond, and Desmond. Trim fell in August, and Hugh was eventually forced to submit, Walter de Lacy regaining control of Mide. Surprisingly, Hugh was generously treated and was restored in Ulster in 1226.

Another awkward issue for William Marshal in Ireland lay in the de Burgh claim to Connacht. This had originated in the gift of Connacht which Prince John, as lord of Ireland, had made in the 1190s to William de Burgh, the brother of Hubert de Burgh, the future justiciar of England. However, in 1215 John as king made simultaneous grants of Connacht to Cathal Ó Conchobhair and William de Burgh's son Richard. Cathal was succeeded in possession of Connacht by his son Áedh, who aided the Marshal during the Lacy rebellion. A plan to support Richard de Burgh's claim against Áedh was strongly opposed by the Marshal, who was consequently replaced as justiciar by Geoffrey Marsh in June 1226. He had to return to Ireland in 1227 to persuade his tenants of Leinster to surrender royal castles to Marsh. He continued to support Áedh Ó Conchobhair, and lost the custody of Cardigan and Carmarthen as a further mark of the justiciar's displeasure.

In 1228, apparently considering that it was now time to compel Llywelyn to make good his promises of restoring march lands taken in 1215, Hubert de Burgh led a large army into the commote of Ceri. The Marshal was among the earls summoned to the army, but nothing is known of his part in a campaign which was a miserable failure, memorable only for the capture by the Welsh of William (V) de Briouze, and for the nickname, Hubert's Folly, which was given to a new castle started by the justiciar but abandoned within a month. A French campaign based on Brittany, aimed at recovering lost Angevin lands, was planned for 1229, but had to be postponed for a year. With twenty knights the Marshal sailed on the expedition in May 1230. Henry III received little save promises from the fickle lords of Poitou on a march from Nantes to Bordeaux and back. The Marshal, who conducted raids into Normandy and Anjou, was one of the few to come out of the campaign with any credit.

While he was a prisoner of Llywelyn in 1228–9, William de Briouze had started a love affair with Llywelyn's wife Joan. In 1230, while visiting Llywelyn's court, Briouze's adultery was discovered and he was hanged, leaving no male heir to the Briouze marcher lordships. Their custody was entrusted to William Marshal, who, still overseas, deputed the task to his steward of Netherwent. Then in November 1230 Gilbert de Clare, lord of Glamorgan, died in Brittany, leaving his eight-year-old son Richard as his heir. The justiciar undertook the care of the Clare lordships. Finally, William Marshal returned to England for the wedding of his widowed sister, Isabella, to *Richard of Cornwall (1209–1272), but died suddenly on 6 April 1231 in London. He had been the master of a huge accumulation of lordships in southern England and Ireland, as well as in south Wales and the Welsh march. Within a year the three most powerful marcher lords of south Wales had died, giving Llywelyn an opportunity which he promptly seized.

William (II) Marshal was buried on 15 April beside his father in the Temple Church. Undoubtedly a good administrator and soldier (he was a notable builder of castles, responsible for Carlow in Leinster, and for Cilgerran and much of Chepstow on the Welsh march), he did not display the statesmanship of his father. Nevertheless, his successful campaign of 1223 secured for the south-western marches a period of comparative security which lasted until the late 1250s. In Pembrokeshire he granted three charters to Haverfordwest. Leinster, where he continued his father's work, bringing in new settlers, founding boroughs and new castles, and fostering religious houses, enjoyed a period of stability and peace under his rule.

Because there were no children of William (II) Marshal's marriage to Eleanor, his heir was his brother Richard, who was killed in 1234 when in rebellion against Henry III. As part of the subsequent reconciliation between king and rebels, Richard's brother and heir **Gilbert Marshal**, seventh earl of Pembroke (d. 1241), was permitted to succeed to the earldom of Pembroke. Although in the years 1234–5

Gilbert received many marks of royal favour and held important posts in Wales, he was never fully trusted and there was much in his behaviour to antagonize the king. When Llewelyn died in April 1240 Gilbert and his brother **Walter Marshal**, eighth earl of Pembroke (d. 1245), were quick to resume hostilities in south-west Wales. Walter recaptured Cardigan, lost to the Welsh in 1231, but Gilbert's scheme to force Maelgwn Fychan to hold southern Ceredigion as his vassal was soon frustrated by the king. In June 1241 Gilbert was killed in a riding accident at an unlicensed tournament at Dunstable. After some delay Walter was admitted to the earldom. He served in the army which went to Gascony in 1242, but although his Pembrokeshire tenants were active in the Welsh war which broke out in 1244, Walter does not seem to have taken part in person. He had fallen ill by July 1245 at Goodrich and died on 24 November, to be followed about a month later by his younger brother **Anselm Marshal** (d. 1245) who was never admitted to the earldom of Pembroke. All five Marshal brothers died without legitimate children and their massive inheritance was subsequently divided between the representatives of their five sisters and coheiresses. Among the families which benefited, then or later, were those of Bigod, Clare, Ferrers, Mortimer, Bohun, Cantilupe, Valence, and Hastings.

R. F. WALKER

Sources GEC, *Peerage*, new edn, 10.358–77 · D. A. Carpenter, *The minority of Henry III* (1990) · D. Crouch, *William Marshal* (1990) · R. F. Walker, 'Hubert de Burgh and Wales, 1218–32', *EngHR*, 87 (1972), 465–94 · P. Meyer, ed., *L'histoire de Guillaume le Maréchal*, 3 vols. (Paris, 1891–1901) · R. R. Davies, *Conquest, coexistence, and change: Wales, 1063–1415*, History of Wales, 2 (1987) · J. E. Lloyd, *A history of Wales from the earliest times to the Edwardian conquest*, 2 (1911) · J. Lydon, 'The expansion and consolidation of the colony', *A new history of Ireland*, ed. T. W. Moody and others, 2: *Medieval Ireland, 1169–1534* (1987), 165–204 · G. H. Orpen, *Ireland under the Normans*, 4 vols. (1911–20), vol. 2 · *Rogeri de Wendover liber qui dicitur flores historiarum*, ed. H. G. Hewlett, 3 vols., Rolls Series, [84] (1886–9), vol. 2 · T. Jones, ed. and trans., *Brut y tywysogyon, or, The chronicle of the princes: Peniarth MS 20* (1952) · Chancery records

Marshall family (*per.* 1848–1922), agricultural engineers, came to prominence with **William Marshall** (1812–1861), born at Gainsborough, Lincolnshire, the son of John Marshall, who was in business there. His father has been described in different sources as a shipwright, or as a block and tackle manufacturer. William was sent to Manchester to serve an engineering apprenticeship with William Fairbairn (1789–1874), whose business as millwright and machine engineer was one of the most important in that city. After completing his apprenticeship Marshall secured permanent employment with Fairbairn, and soon afterwards, in 1834, he married Eliza Dickenson (d. 1845). The couple lived at Stalybridge, and moved to Ancoats in Manchester in 1840. They had two sons.

In 1840 Marshall was appointed Fairbairn's representative in St Petersburg, responsible for negotiating sales and overseeing the installation of textile machinery and water-wheels for customers in Russia. At the end of 1845, however, Eliza Marshall became ill and died, and this led William to return to Manchester. He married again on 1

April 1847; his second wife was Frances Grandage (*d.* 1859), a widow.

In 1848 Marshall took over a small engineering works in Back Street, Gainsborough, and set up on his own account as millwright and engineer. The works had been established in 1835 by William Garland and consisted of machine-making workshops and a small foundry. The business Marshall took over derived most of its trade from the oil and cake mills of Gainsborough, making and repairing machinery. This continued to be the basis of trade in the early years of Marshall's management, but his ambitions were clearly stated when he exhibited a portable threshing machine at the Royal Agricultural Society's show at Norwich in 1849. He was awarded a prize for this machine, which helped to establish a reputation for his new business. By the mid-1850s business had grown sufficiently for larger premises to be needed. Land was bought on Beaumont Street in the centre of Gainsborough in 1855, and there Marshall's new Britannia ironworks were built. In September 1859 Marshall's second wife died, and he himself died of a heart attack at Gainsborough on 15 June 1861, at the age of forty-nine. His two sons, **James Marshall** (1836–1922) and **Henry Dickenson Marshall** (1840–1906), had played a part in the business from an early age and they continued to manage and develop the business. It was said that the two young sons had persuaded their father to start making portable steam engines as well as threshing machines in the mid-1850s.

James Marshall was born on 17 May 1836 at Manchester, and he served his apprenticeship with his father's firm. Made a partner in 1857, he played an active part in the technical development of his firm's products; and there are several patents in his name for improvements to threshing machines. He also patented a design for a tennis racket, tennis being one of his main leisure interests. Active in local politics as a Conservative and a supporter of tariff reform, he served as justice of the peace on the Gainsborough bench, and he was an alderman of Lindsey county council. He was a devout Christian, and belonged to All Saints' parish church at Gainsborough. He married in 1863 Fanny Manning, and they had four sons and five daughters. His wife died in 1891, and in her memory he built the Fanny Marshall Institute in Gainsborough. William Marshall's younger son, Henry Dickenson Marshall, was born on 5 May 1840. He, too, was apprenticed in his father's firm. In 1861, only a few weeks before William died, he was made a partner.

Following William Marshall's death the firm was restructured as a company with limited liability, registered as Marshall, Sons & Co. Ltd in August 1862. James Marshall was named as chairman and joint managing director in 1864, and Henry as joint managing director and company secretary. Under their direction steam engineering became one of the major parts of the business and it remained so until at least the First World War: portable engines of all sizes, traction engines, stationary engines, and boilers were manufactured and exported to markets around the world. As well as providing power for the firm's threshing machines the steam engines were made for a variety of uses, including tea-drying, electricity generation, pumping, and drainage.

The brothers divided the responsibilities: James dealt with most of the engineering and manufacturing matters, and Henry managed the commercial and administrative affairs. Henry toured widely on behalf of the company to India, Russia, and South America. He was a member of the Institution of Mechanical Engineers from 1885, and served on its council from 1889 to 1905. He was a member of council and served as president of the Agricultural Engineers' Association, and he was a member of the board of the Engineering Employers' Federation. He was a member of the council of the Royal Agricultural Society of England.

Among his other business interests Henry Marshall was a director of Shireoaks colliery, Worksop, a major shareholder in the Gainsborough Toll Bridge Company, and a vice-president of the Gainsborough Trustee Savings Bank. Together with his brother he founded the Gainsborough Building Society in order to help their employees buy houses. He was committed to educational improvement, promoted classes for his employees, and was a member of the local technical education committee. Active in local politics as vice-president of Gainsborough Divisional Conservative and Unionist Association, he was a trustee of the constitutional clubs. A supporter of tariff reform, he represented agricultural machinery interests on Joseph Chamberlain's tariff commission. He was a member of Lindsey county council from its formation in 1889 and became an alderman; he was a county magistrate from 1892. He was also a member of the Trent fishery board. Henry Marshall married Mary Ann Woolvine in September 1862, and they had four sons and six daughters. Illness forced him to retire from work in 1905, and on 8 March 1906 he died at Carr House, Gainsborough. He was survived by his wife. One of his sons, Herman Dickenson Marshall, then became joint managing director of the company with Herbert John, one of James's sons. James Marshall lived on until his death at Cleveland House, Gainsborough, on 27 February 1922.

The business founded by William Marshall in 1848 had, by the end of the nineteenth century, become one of the greatest firms of steam and agricultural engineers in Britain. Marshall's sons, James and Henry, were responsible for its rapid development from a modest concern employing 21 men and 10 boys in 1861, to a workforce of 3500 at the turn of the century. By 1906 the Britannia ironworks at Gainsborough occupied more than 29 acres, and Marshalls was recognized as an engineering firm of international repute.   JONATHAN BROWN

Sources M. R. Lane, *The Britannia iron works* (1993) · 'Henry Dickenson Marshall', *The Engineer* (16 March 1906), 270 · 'Henry Dickenson Marshall', *Implement and Machinery Review*, 31 (1905–6), 1411 · 'James Marshall', *Implement and Machinery Review*, 47 (1921–2), 1660 · business records of Marshall, Sons & Co. Ltd, U. Reading, Rural History Centre · d. certs.
Archives Lincs. Arch., engineer's notebook; foundry order book; minutes, ledgers, accounts, plant books, articles of association, patents, pensions records, catalogues, records of subsidiaries · priv. coll., Marshall, Sons & Co. Ltd, business records · Sheff. Arch.,

corporate records • U. Reading, Rural History Centre, sales ledger, productions and staff records, technical notebook, agency agreement, inventory and valuation books

Likenesses photographs (William Marshall, James Marshall, and Henry Marshall), repro. in Lane, *Britannia iron works*, 5, 17, 18

Wealth at death under £300—William Marshall: resworn administration, Jan 1863, *CGPLA Eng. & Wales* (1861) • £178,485 6*s*. 3*d*.—James Marshall: probate, 26 June 1922, *CGPLA Eng. & Wales* • £443,523 17*s*. 8*d*.—Henry Dickenson Marshall: probate, 25 July 1906, *CGPLA Eng. & Wales*

Marshall [*née* Smith], **Agnes Bertha** (1855–1905), ice-cream maker, was born on 24 August 1855 at Walthamstow, Essex, the daughter of John Smith, a clerk, and his wife, Susan. After her father's early death her mother remarried. Nothing is known about her early education or where she learned to cook, but it was later stated in the *Pall Mall Gazette* that 'Mrs Marshall has made a thorough study of cookery since she was a child, and has practised at Paris and with Vienna's celebrated chefs' (Weir and others, 12). On 17 August 1878 she married Alfred William, son of Thomas Marshall, a builder.

Agnes Marshall became one of the foremost Victorian cookery writers, and was the best-known writer of the day on ice-cream. Her *Book of Ices* appeared in 1885, followed by *Mrs A. B. Marshall's Cookery Book* (1888). Her *Larger Cookery Book of Recipes* was published in 1891. A book entitled *Fancy Ices* appeared in 1894. Agnes Marshall and her husband also established the Marshall School of Cookery—one of only two major London cookery schools—at 31 Mortimer Street, London, in January 1883. From 1886 they began to produce *The Table*, a weekly newspaper devoted to 'Cookery, Gastronomy [and] food amusements', and for the first six months Agnes produced a new recipe for each issue.

Unlike Mrs Beeton, who edited a work that also contained readers' recipes, Mrs Marshall featured dishes which she herself devised. The introduction to her first book assured the reader that 'every recipe in it has been tried out by myself, and that I have written each accordingly, and have not copied from other authors'. Her recipes were models of exact detail, simplicity, and accuracy; and, according to the *Oxford English Dictionary*, that for Cumberland rum butter was the earliest recorded.

Marshall's most lasting contributions were her two classic books on ice-cream: only one earlier book on the subject in English is known. Her innovations included the design of a fast ice-cream machine (patented by her husband). In 1888 she suggested putting ice-cream in an edible cornet or cone—a practice previously thought to have originated in the USA. The use of liquefied gas in the making of ice-cream can also be credited to her. She helped popularize ice-creams and sorbets, at a time when they were still novel, enabled to do so by the importation of inexpensive ice from both Norway and the USA. An adept publicist, Agnes Marshall gave demonstrations all over the country to audiences of anything up to 500 people, and these helped promote not only her cookery school and publications, but also the business that she ran with her husband. This involved the manufacture and retail of cooking equipment, stocked by top department stores like Harrods. The firm also fitted out country house kitchens.

Mrs Marshall's reputation rapidly declined after her death. She never properly recovered after being thrown from a horse in 1904; and she died at The Towers, Pinner, on 29 July 1905. She was cremated at Golders Green crematorium, her ashes being interred at Paines Lane cemetery, Pinner. Her husband got married again within a year, to a secretary she had previously sacked. The rights to her books were sold to Ward Lock, the publishers of Mrs Beeton. The culinary equipment business declined and was also eventually sold.

Recent publications, however, have restored Agnes Marshall to her rightful place in the pantheon of Victorian cookery experts. Elizabeth David refers to the 'famous Mrs Marshall' in her posthumously published *Harvest of the Cold Months: the Social History of Ice and Ices* (1994), and reproduces an illustration of 'A bomba a la Fedora' from *Fancy Ices*. A recent biographical study has the title, *Mrs Marshall: the Greatest Victorian Ice Cream Maker* (1998).

ROBIN WEIR

Sources R. Weir and others, *Mrs Marshall: the greatest Victorian ice cream maker* (1998) • E. David, *Harvest of the cold months: the social history of ice and ices* (1994) • T. Masters, *The ice book: a history of everything connected with ice, with recipes* (1844) • m. cert. • d. cert.
Likenesses G. S. Knowles, portrait, exh. RA 1890, priv. coll.; repro. in Weir and others, *Mrs Marshall*, frontispiece • E. Tofano, engraving, *c*.1891, repro. in Weir and others, *Mrs Marshall*, 27

Marshall, Alfred (1842–1924), economist, was born on 26 July 1842 at 66 Charlotte Road, Bermondsey, London, the second son of William Marshall (1812–1901), clerk at the Bank of England, and his wife, Rebecca Oliver (1817–1878), daughter of Thomas Oliver, butcher. He had two brothers and two sisters.

Family and education The story of Marshall's family background and schooling was properly researched only at the end of the twentieth century. The received version was one that his wife, Mary Paley *Marshall, perhaps herself unaware of the true story, had passed on to John Maynard Keynes. Keynes used this material in 1924, when he wrote the brilliant, if at times imaginative, *Memoir* of his old master that remained the standard work of Marshall biography for sixty years. The work of R. H. Coase and P. D. Groenewegen has revealed the truth of Marshall's parental heritage, which, if it lacks the social distinction felt by the Victorians to be so important, lends added weight to Marshall's achievements. It also helps in our understanding of Marshall the man, and the importance that he attached to the role of parents and individuals in overcoming social disabilities. Marshall's background was not that of clerical intellectuals of several generations, as Keynes suggested. His paternal grandfather's financial enterprises failed and he began to slide down the all-important Victorian social ladder. On his early death, his children were cared for by his dead wife's relatives. The eldest child, Marshall's father, eventually achieved the

Alfred Marshall (1842–1924), by Sir William Rothenstein, 1908

rank of a middle-grade civil servant who through hard work and sacrifice was able to move his family to suburban Clapham from its first home near east London's tanneries.

Marshall was educated at a dame-school, probably in Sydenham, then at a private school in Clapham before gaining a place at Merchant Taylors' School in London in 1852. His father recognized that his second son showed promise and from an early age seems to have kept him hard at his school books. William Marshall secured a nomination for Alfred from a member of the Merchant Taylors' Company, which meant that the boy's schooling was subsidized by the company. This enabled him to attend a school that otherwise would have been far beyond the family's means. None the less, Alfred's schooling involved them in considerable financial sacrifice and it must, therefore, have been all the more difficult for Marshall in his final school year to reject the classics scholarship that he won to St John's College, Oxford, and the automatic right to a life fellowship there, in favour of mathematics at St John's College, Cambridge, on money borrowed from his uncle and, later, college prizes and exhibitions. He graduated in 1865 as second wrangler in the highly competitive and prestigious mathematical tripos.

Legend has it that Marshall proposed to study molecular physics—an unlikely suggestion since there were no laboratories and very limited teaching in physics at Cambridge at that time. It is also suggested that he intended to put himself forward as candidate for priesthood in the Anglican church, the career path followed by most Cambridge graduates at that time. This, however, was a time of doubt regarding Christian dogma and the role of priests and Marshall was never ordained. None the less, as his wife commented, 'he was a great preacher'.

Immediately after his tripos examination results Marshall was engaged as a temporary mathematics master by Clifton College, Bristol, a recently founded public school for middle-class boys. This brief interlude in his life led to several valuable contacts. These included: Canon Percival, the school's headmaster, who took a particular interest in community service for both the masters and boys at his school; Henry Dakyn, a master at the school, who introduced Marshall to a group of radical dons at Cambridge who were members of the Grote Club; and, most probably, Henry Sidgwick. Sidgwick was to be Marshall's guide and mentor in a number of projects at Cambridge intended to bring education to deprived sections of the community and to improve academic standards at Cambridge University.

Early career Marshall returned to Cambridge in the autumn of 1865 following his election to a fellowship at St John's College. He was drawn to study metaphysics, ethics, and then psychology, especially in connection with the possibilities of moral and material progress among the working classes. In this he was encouraged by his reading of John Stuart Mill and association with like-minded, progressive young dons whom he met at the Grote Club, where, on several occasions, he listened to the Christian socialist Frederick Dennison Maurice. The depth of his interest in these subjects was such that in 1868 St John's appointed him lecturer in the moral sciences, a relatively new tripos which involved the study of moral and mental philosophy, political economy, and logic. The tripos attracted a small but growing band of students who believed the study of the moral sciences was pertinent to the social and economic problems that had accompanied Britain's transition from an agrarian to an urban, industrial society.

In 1868 Cambridge established the higher local examinations for women, which were intended to test and attest the competence of young women who planned to become school teachers or governesses. (There were at that time no examinations or qualifications available to women beyond secondary-school age.) One group of subjects in which women could be examined was the moral sciences. Marshall offered his services as an examiner and then lecturer, as he became closely involved in Sidgwick's scheme to provide a hall of residence for women in Cambridge attending lectures on examination topics. For four years (1873–6) Marshall funded a prize for the best essay submitted by a woman moral sciences examinee on a socio-economic topic of his choice. Impressed by the intellectual abilities of two of his women students at Cambridge, including his future wife, Mary Paley, he suggested that they should try the moral sciences tripos and then coached them in political economy. Marshall was also involved on several occasions as examiner in the scheme for university extension teaching in the provinces and new industrial towns, which in part grew out of the initial programme of women's lectures. He shared the goal of the scheme's promoters, which was to bring further education to the lower-middle and working classes.

During these first postgraduate years Marshall displayed what he later called 'a tendency to socialism' (Marshall, *Industry and Trade*, vii), which included taking a 'progressive' view on the contribution to society that women could and should make outside the confines of their families, and the achievements that could be made by the working classes in combination through trade unions and the co-operative movement. In 1875 Marshall spent the long vacation on a visit to the United States to examine economic forces at work in a young country. He returned with somewhat modified views on the value of collective action and with greater faith in the importance of individual achievement. He regarded this trip as one of the most formative experiences of his life.

On 17 August 1877 Marshall married Mary Paley (1850–1944), daughter of the Revd Thomas Paley, rector of Ufford, near Stamford, Northamptonshire, and great-granddaughter of Archdeacon William Paley. His marriage meant the loss of his college fellowship, and he accepted the post of principal and professor of political economy at the recently founded Bristol University College. The selection panel was particularly anxious to employ someone who shared the ideals of the movements for female and worker education. Mary Paley also taught at the college and took over much of the burden of her husband's economic classes when he fell ill in 1879 with kidney trouble and stress, the latter caused by what Marshall felt were the onerous administrative duties of his post as principal and the need to attract financial support to the poorly funded college. Ill health forced him to resign from the college in 1881 and the couple travelled to Sicily, where Marshall recovered his health after several months' rest. He remained, however, convinced that his life would be cut short and retreated into ill health whenever he felt subject to unwelcome stress or controversy.

Professor at Cambridge After briefly taking up his post again at Bristol as professor of political economy in May 1882, he moved to Oxford the following term to fill the vacancy left at Balliol College by the death of Arnold Toynbee. It seemed that he might stay at Oxford and develop the teaching of economics there, when the sudden death of Henry Fawcett in December 1884 left the chair of political economy at Cambridge vacant. Marshall was widely recognized as the only possible candidate for the post and he was duly elected, to the satisfaction of most of the younger moral sciences dons. Marshall's claim to the post is, however, something of a mystery. He had published very little: a simple textbook with his wife, a few newspaper and journal articles, newspaper reports of some of his lectures, and some theoretical diagrams privately printed and circulated. Yet his status as the man who could rescue the 'dismal science' from its reputation as a set of natural laws by which the country and a small group of its inhabitants could remain wealthy only at the expense of the majority who must remain poor, ignorant, and hopeless was widespread among his students and others who had been inspired by his public lectures.

Although Marshall had initially taught both moral philosophy and political economy, he became strongly attracted to the latter, perhaps because of the ease in which some elements of economic theory could be expressed in mathematical terms. Algebraic formulae were generally kept for his own private use but from an early date (between 1872 and 1874) he taught his students to express economic relationships in terms of curves. Marshall believed that economics dealt with regular features of human behaviour that could be measured by the earning, spending, saving, and investment of money. Money could thus be used as a measuring rod for most behaviour. It could measure the strength of motives, and was susceptible to mathematical and logical manipulation. It could be captured in a diagram or a formula and then described in simple English. Marshall was quick to point out that human beings were not motivated solely by a selfish interest to make and spend money, but often had other, more complex motives, such as the care and well-being of their families, the approval of the public or their peers, the pleasure of using a skill, or a sense of duty. By widening and deepening the motives for economic behaviour, Marshall made economics more human or even humane, counteracting its 'dismal science' image inherited from the classical economists. This shift of outlook, combined with the apparent rigour that the use of mathematics gave the subject, led to the new economics being described as 'neo-classical'. While Marshall was not alone, nationally or internationally, in its creation, he has been described as the subject's great synthesizer and prime mover in the establishment of neo-classicism as the central paradigm in British economics from the turn of the nineteenth century onwards. He also held that humans were far from perfect optimizers of their economic well-being, giving him the opportunity to preach both to the working classes for their lack of foresight and self-control, and to members of other classes who wasted their opportunities and shirked their duties. His interpretation of economics stemmed largely from his evangelical upbringing, with its great emphasis on duty, reinforced with ideas culled from English idealism and Herbert Spencer's interpretation of evolution which so successfully encapsulated the Victorian belief in progress. When, after the turn of the century, these value judgements were replaced by others, Marshall's 'preaching' became increasingly irrelevant, while his techniques of analysis were refined by academic economists and far removed from his original intention, that of understanding the causes of poverty which is 'the cause of the degradation of a large part of mankind' (Marshall, *Principles of Economics*, 1.3).

Major writings Initially Marshall planned a book on international trade and protection; several short essays containing his theoretical ideas on the subject were privately published and circulated by Sidgwick in 1879, when he and his friends feared he would not live to publish much else. The simple textbook *The Economics of Industry*, written with his wife, was published the same year and contained an early, elementary exposition of his theoretical position. The first full version of his theories covering consumer demand, the supply of the agents of production—

land, labour, and capital—the relationship between demand and supply and the creation of value, and the distribution of this value between the agents of production, finally became available in 1890 with the publication of the first edition of *The Principles of Economics*. This weighty tome was described for many years by Marshall as 'volume 1' since he planned to follow it with a companion volume covering foreign trade, money, trade fluctuations, taxation, collectivism, and aims for the future. It contained in its final version familiar Marshallian constructs, such as elasticity, consumer surplus, increasing and diminishing returns, short and long terms, and marginal utility, many of which are still part of the traditional economist's toolkit. Yet if these tools were all Marshall wanted to give the world, they could have been elaborated in far fewer than the 750 pages of the first edition of his book (which grew to 870 in the eighth edition, thirty years later).

From the time Marshall first became interested in economics, he was 'hungry for facts'. His reading, vacation observations in England and in Europe, his trip to the USA, his discussions with trade unionists, reformers, captains of industry, leading churchmen, his excursions into economic history, were all designed to provide him with facts to underpin his theoretical work. This 'fact-gathering' worked against him since the facts of economic life were constantly changing and caused lengthy delays in the publication of his books. The plan for a companion volume to the *Principles* was finally scrapped in 1910, much of its proposed material appearing shortly before his death as *Industry and Trade* (1919) and *Money, Credit and Commerce* (1923). More significantly, although Marshall understood the need for 'economic biology', which would take account of economic life as something evolutionary, he was a mathematician unable to create an economic theory that was other than static and mechanistic, relying on assumptions of individual optimization and market equilibrium with given preferences, technology, and institutions. He was also hindered by misunderstanding Darwin, as did so many of his contemporaries, accepting instead Herbert Spencer's interpretation of evolution as meaning 'progress' rather than simply 'change'.

Marshall prepared evidence for several royal commissions and inquiries, including those on the aged poor (1893), the Indian currency (1899), and local taxation (1899). He served on the royal commission on labour (1891–4), which he felt was especially important in examining the problems of poverty in depth. In 1903 he wrote a memorandum on the fiscal policy of international trade for the Treasury, as a contribution to the tariff reform question, Marshall providing an interesting, post-Ricardian defence of free trade; it was published as a white paper in 1908. Many of these *Official Papers* were originally published by John Maynard Keynes in 1926, and supplemented by Groenewegen in 1996. A great deal of other Marshall material, lectures, papers, letters, and critical writings, has been published, most significantly by J. K. Whitaker, as *The Early Writings of Alfred Marshall, 1867–*

1890 (1975) and *The Correspondence of Alfred Marshall, Economist* (1996), and Groenewegen, *Alfred Marshall: Critical Responses* (1998).

As the importance of much of his published work has become outdated, increasing recognition has been given to Marshall's role in developing economics from a branch of general knowledge into an academic subject and profession. In 1890 he was instrumental in the foundation of the British Economic Association (later the Royal Economic Society) and the *Economic Journal*, which remained the central professional journal in Britain for many years. However, it took him many years to convince Cambridge that the subject had the depth and breadth needed for independent status, instead of continuing as one subject among many in the moral sciences and history triposes. It can be questioned whether it was his powers of persuasion or the wish on the part of the existing triposes to be rid of economics and its venerable but troublesome representative that finally converted the university and led to the founding of the independent economic and political science tripos in 1903. Remembering her husband on the hundredth anniversary of his birth, Mary Paley Marshall saw the Cambridge economics tripos as Marshall's greatest achievement.

Marshall claimed he hated controversy, and avoided it or left his lieutenants to fight his battles. However, on his return to Cambridge in 1884, he never failed personally to intervene on the university's political stage to promote the independence of his own subject; he also strongly opposed moves that would give women students a firmer foothold in the university and sometimes went to extreme lengths to keep them out. He engaged publicly in bitter professional battles on behalf of free trade against economists who supported protection, and insisted on the paramount importance of parental influence and the quality of life and work in promoting social progress, against those social scientists and statisticians who emphasized nature over nurture.

Marshall died on 13 July 1924, two weeks before his eighty-second birthday, at Balliol Croft, the home in Cambridge that the couple had built following their return there in 1884. He had been fading physically and mentally for some years. Following a short service in the chapel of St John's College, Marshall was buried in St Giles's cemetery, Cambridge, not far from his home. 'At the time of his death', J. M. Keynes wrote in the *Dictionary of National Biography*, 'he was recognised as the father of economic science as it then existed in England.'

RITA McWILLIAMS TULLBERG

Sources P. D. Groenewegen, *A soaring eagle: Alfred Marshall, 1842–1924* (1995) · J. M. Keynes, 'Alfred Marshall', *The collected writings of John Maynard Keynes*, ed. D. Moggridge and E. Johnson, 12 (1983) · J. K. Whitaker, 'Alfred Marshall', *The new Palgrave dictionary of economics*, 4 vols. (1987) · DNB · A. C. Pigou, ed., *Memorials of Alfred Marshall* (1925) · R. H. Coase, 'Alfred Marshall's father and mother', *History of Political Economy*, 18 (1984), 519–27 · R. H. Coase, 'Alfred Marshall's family and ancestry', *Alfred Marshall in retrospect*, ed. R. M. Tullberg (1990), 9–27 · A. Marshall, *Principles of economics*, ed. C. W. Guillebaud, 9th edn, 2 vols. (1961) · A. Marshall, *Industry and trade* (1919) · J. K. Whitaker, *Centenary essays on Alfred Marshall*

(1990) · R. M. Tullberg, ed., *Alfred Marshall in retrospect* (1990) · *Alfred Marshall's 'Lectures to women'*, ed. T. Raffaelli, E. Biagini, and R. M. Tullberg (1995)
Archives U. Cam., Marshall Library of Economics, corresp. and papers | BL, corresp. with Macmillans, Add. MSS 55174 · BLPES, letters to Sir A. L. Bowley · BLPES, letters to Edwin Cannan · BLPES, corresp. with Francis Edgworth · BLPES, corresp. and papers relating to Royal Economic Society · Col. U., Rare Book and Manuscript Library, letters to Edwin Seligman · King's AC Cam., letters to Oscar Browning · King's AC Cam., Keynes MSS · priv. coll., Foxwell MSS · U. Cam., Marshall Library of Economics, letters to Charles Fay; letters to John Maynard Keynes; letters to John Neville Keynes · University of Sheffield, letters to William Hewins
Likenesses W. Rothenstein, oils, 1908, St John Cam. [*see illus.*] · W. Stoneman, photograph, 1917, NPG · W. Rothenstein, oils, second version, U. Cam., Marshall Library of Economics · photographs, U. Cam., Marshall Library of Economics
Wealth at death £13,001 2s.: probate, 18 Oct 1924, *CGPLA Eng. & Wales*

Marshall, Andrew (1779–1854), United Secession minister and religious controversialist, was born at Westerhill in the parish of Cadder, Lanarkshire, on 22 November 1779. He was educated locally before attending classes at Glasgow University. He also went to the Secession Divinity Hall at Selkirk, making the lengthy journey on foot over two days. In November 1802 he was ordained to the church in Kirkintilloch, Dunbartonshire, where he was to remain for the rest of his life. He married Agnes (1785–1847), the daughter of John Dick, a merchant, and his wife, Henrietta Easton, and they had two daughters and four sons. He served as moderator of the synod of the United Secession church in 1836, and was honoured with the degrees of DD from Jefferson College (1841) and LLD from Washington College (1842) in the United States.

Marshall's disputatious nature involved him in two major controversies. In the first, the 'voluntary' controversy, he articulated the growing conviction among Scottish dissenters that church establishments were unjust and that churches should look to their members alone for support. This view was expressed in a sermon preached by him in Greyfriars Church, Glasgow, in April 1829, later published as *Ecclesiastical Establishments Considered*. A fierce and widespread debate, in which Marshall was prominent, continued throughout the following decade. The second controversy, the atonement controversy, was to prove Marshall's undoing. It began in 1841 with the suspension of James Morison from his duties as a United Secession minister. The principal charge against him related to his view of the universal nature of the atonement, a view which challenged the traditional Calvinist orthodoxy of his church. Marshall thought that Morison's views were, in effect, those of the church's own professors Robert Balmer and John Brown. Marshall restated the conservative view of the atonement in *The Death of Christ the Redemption of his People* (1842), and in *The Catholic Doctrine of Redemption Vindicated* (1844) he attached an appendix which made a specific attack on the professors. However, his extended campaign against them ended in defeat and earned him a humiliating public rebuke from the synod. Marshall broke away from the United Secession church in October 1846, the breach further embittered by attempts

to evict him from his church buildings. In spite of contacts with the Free and Original Secession churches, he formed no new attachment before his death on 26 November 1854 at Kirkintilloch. He was buried at Cadder.

Marshall was a major influence on the presbyterian churches in Scotland, if never quite in the way that he intended. Arguably, he did as much as any other individual to bring the Free Church of Scotland into existence by the debate on church–state relations which he initiated. The thorough rehearsal of arguments in the course of the atonement controversy made it clear that the theology of his colleagues was increasingly liberal, and Marshall's departure helped to clear the way for union with the Relief church, not least because he had been on the union committee. Even by the standards of Secession ministers Marshall was a difficult man, with an obstinate loyalty to principle untempered by any tendency towards conciliation. His isolation at the end of his life would have been complete had it not been for the loyalty of the majority of his congregation and of his son William (*d*. 1860), a United Secession minister in Leith, who seceded at the same time as his father and eventually succeeded him in his Kirkintilloch charge, by then a Free Church congregation.

LIONEL ALEXANDER RITCHIE

Sources J. D. Marshall, *Memoir of Andrew Marshall, DD, LLD* (1889) · W. Mackelvie, *Annals and statistics of the United Presbyterian church*, ed. W. Blair and D. Young (1873), 328–33 · R. Small, *History of the congregations of the United Presbyterian church from 1733 to 1900*, 2 (1904), 151–3 · A. Robertson, *History of the atonement controversy* (1846) · DSCHT
Likenesses Gibson, portrait, repro. in Marshall, *Memoir of Andrew Marshall*, frontispiece
Wealth at death £1440 12s. 10d.: confirmation, 1855, Dumbarton

Marshall, (Charles) Arthur Bertram (1910–1989), humorist and broadcaster, was born on 10 May 1910 in Barnes, Surrey, the younger son of Charles Frederick Bertram Marshall, consulting engineer, and his wife, Dorothy Lee. His father was a loving husband, but although he quite liked the idea of children, to Arthur's disappointment he preferred to be where they were not. In 1920 the family moved to Newbury, Berkshire, and Arthur was sent away to boarding-school. First he went to Edinburgh House, an uncomfortable but enjoyable preparatory school in Lee-on-Solent, Hampshire, and then to Oundle School in Northamptonshire. He was happy at Oundle— he seems to have been happy almost everywhere—and during a debate in his last winter term a great burst of laughter at something he said gave him such a whiff of power and pleasure that he decided to make the raising of laughter the prime consideration of his life. He then went to Christ's College, Cambridge, where he obtained a second class (second division) in part one of the modern and medieval languages tripos (French, 1929, and German, 1930) and a third class in part two (1931).

Marshall acted at every opportunity at Oundle and at Christ's and was determined on a career in the theatre. He mostly played female parts at university, for which he collected some excellent press notices, notably for his playing of Lady Cicely, opposite Michael Redgrave, in G. B.

Shaw's *Captain Brassbound's Conversion*. He became president of Cambridge's Amateur Dramatic Society.

Down from Cambridge, armed with his glowing press cuttings, Marshall had his heart set on going to the Royal Academy of Dramatic Art in London, but his mother pointed out that the acting profession would hardly give an ecstatic welcome to an amateur female impersonator. She persuaded him to go back to Oundle instead and make a career as a schoolmaster. In 1931 Oundle offered him a job as a house tutor and teacher of French and German, which he accepted, quaking in his shoes. To his own surprise he turned out to be a good teacher and, as the terms sped happily by, he spent a good deal of his free time writing and performing to friends what were then called 'turns', three-minute comic monologues in which, inspired by Angela Brazil's girls'-school stories which he found hilarious when read aloud, he impersonated hearty botany mistresses and stern school matrons.

In 1934 a BBC radio producer saw Marshall perform his botany mistress turn at a party and booked him to broadcast it on *Charlot's Hour*. Thus his professional career began by his becoming the world's first drag act on radio. In the same year Raymond Mortimer, literary editor of the *New Statesman*, asked him to review a clutch of schoolgirl stories. His review was much enjoyed and for many years was a popular Christmas feature of the magazine.

During the Second World War Marshall, like many a schoolmaster, was drafted into intelligence; he had a busy time, surviving the evacuation of Dunkirk in the British expeditionary force and working with combined operations headquarters and Supreme Headquarters, Allied Expeditionary Force. In 1945 he was a lieutenant-colonel on General Dwight D. Eisenhower's staff. He was appointed an MBE in 1944. In 1943, while still in uniform, he wrote and starred in a BBC comedy series on the radio, *A Date with Nurse Dugdale*, which was a wartime success.

After the war Marshall returned to Oundle in 1946 as a housemaster, but his fascination with the theatre was still strong and, afraid that he might end up as a rotund Mr Chips before his time, he left Oundle in 1954 at the age of forty-four and became a social secretary to his old friend Victor, third Baron Rothschild. In 1958 he changed jobs again and went to work in London as a script reader for one of the leading figures of Shaftesbury Avenue's commercial theatre, H. G. (Binkie) Beaumont of H. M. Tennent Ltd. Marshall was in his element at last. He was such pleasant company that everybody in the theatre seemed to know and like him, and this charming, funny, and uncompetitive person was invited everywhere. He spent many long weekends at Somerset Maugham's Villa Mauresque at Cap Ferrat on the French riviera and months with Alfred Lunt and Lynn Fontanne in the USA. No doubt part of his attraction as a guest was that when conversation sagged his host would call upon him to entertain the company with a turn, and he was delighted to oblige.

In 1953 Marshall began to publish his humorous prose pieces in book form, beginning with *Nineteen to the Dozen* (1953); many more followed. He also published some gratifyingly successful compilations from the *New Statesman*

competitions and his own book reviews, *Salome Dear, not in the Fridge!* (1968), *Girls will be Girls* (1974), *Whimpering in the Rhododendrons* (1982), and *Giggling in the Shrubbery* (1985). In 1975 he started writing a regular column for the *New Statesman* and another for the *Sunday Telegraph*. He also became a regular broadcaster and chat-show guest and in 1979 was enlisted as a team captain in the BBC television game show *Call my Bluff*, which he graced for ten years.

In the world of broadcast humour in the 1980s it was Arthur Marshall who was the 'alternative comedian'. This was the era dominated by young writers and comics who appealed to young viewers and readers with a stunning display of aggressive, sexual, and politically simplistic routines nurtured on the student union circuit. For those for whom this sort of comedy ceased to appeal much after the first excitement, Marshall's charming, intelligent, witty, and affectionate humour came as a breath of fresh air. He was perhaps the last flowering of the humour which Joseph Addison and Sir Richard Steele pioneered in the early eighteenth century and called 'polite comedy'.

With his unconventional attitudes towards such things as religion and erudition, his distaste for foreigners, and his eyes sparkling and chins a-wobble at some absurdity he had noticed, a line of Rupert Brooke's should be bent to Arthur Marshall, this happiest of humorists, as 'an English unofficial sunbeam'. His last years were spent in Devon where he lived at Pound Cottage, Christow, near Exeter, and during his final illness he was fortunate to have an old friend, Peter Kelland, a retired schoolmaster, to look after him and share his life. He died, unmarried, on 27 January 1989, and a memorial service was held in London on 19 July of that year.   FRANK MUIR, rev.

Sources A. Marshall, *Life's rich pageant* (1984) · *The Independent* (28 Jan 1989) · *The Times* (28 Jan 1989) · *CGPLA Eng. & Wales* (1989) · private information (1996)
Archives King's AC Cam., letters and postcards to G. H. W. Rylands
Wealth at death £472,080: probate, 29 March 1989, *CGPLA Eng. & Wales*

Marshall, Arthur Calder- (1908–1992), writer, was born on 19 August 1908 at El Misti, Woodcote Road, Wallington, Surrey, the second of two sons of Arthur Grotjan Calder-Marshall, a civil engineer, and Alice Poole. After a peripatetic childhood, following his father's career, the family settled at Steyning, Sussex, when Calder-Marshall was fifteen. He depicts his rebellious and questing adolescence there in his partial autobiography, *The Magic of my Youth* (1951). This centres on his friendship with an individual named Vickybird or the Poet (the otherwise unnamed Victor Neuburg) and on the then infamous occultist Aleister Crowley, whom he records as a thoroughly seedy and disillusioning character.

Calder-Marshall attended St Paul's School, London, before going up to Hertford College, Oxford. As secretary of the Oxford University Poetry Society, he invited Crowley to come and speak in 1930. He was fascinated by the idea of anyone so reassuringly evil 'in a world where blacks and whites were breaking up so fast into various shades of grey' (Calder-Marshall, *The Magic of my Youth*,

Arthur Calder-Marshall (1908–1992), by Howard Coster, 1934

177). This became the scandalous 'banned lecture' on Gilles de Rais, which was not allowed to take place and was instead printed as a notoriously boring pamphlet. Like so many of his class and generation, Calder-Marshall did an early stint of schoolmastering, teaching from 1931 to 1933 at Denstone College, a minor public school. His misgivings about the public-school system, and indeed about English bourgeois society and capitalism as a whole, were later expressed in his Hogarth Press pamphlet, *Challenge to Schools* (1935). Calder-Marshall became a full-time writer in 1933, and during the 1930s he was a productive experimental novelist whose strong leftward views were in tune with the era that he looked back on ruefully in his 1941 *New Statesman* article 'The pink decade'.

Calder-Marshall's contribution to the 'Writing in revolt' issue of *Fact* (no. 4, 1937) was something of a manifesto for non-bourgeois writing. In contrast with bourgeois literature's emphasis on the individual, Calder-Marshall believed, the progressive writer should depict society as a whole, for which he advocated some form of 'the composite method' as found in the work of John Dos Passos and others. Calder-Marshall admired Dos Passos for his democratic vitality and formal boldness, such as the incorporation of 'newsreel' sections into *USA*.

In accordance with this, Calder-Marshall's early fiction attempted to find composite forms for a more interpersonal, collective, and socially conscious writing, focusing on relationships and institutions rather than on the subjectivity of the individual character. *About Levy* (1933) consists of forty-odd sketches and vignettes—two washerwomen talking, some men in a pub, a judge addressing a jury, and so on—which add up, with a little work from the reader, to the story of a sympathetic Jewish doctor accused of murder. *Dead Centre* (1935) anatomizes the life of a public school through sixty-odd short chapters, each narrated by different boys and masters. Calder-Marshall's methods are those of an era when both cinematic montage and the Mass-Observation movement of Charles Madge and his associates were very much in the consciousness of writers and intellectuals.

On 6 July 1934 Calder-Marshall married Violet Nancy (*b.*

1912/13), daughter of Benjamin Sales, a director of a manufacturing chemist's. They had two daughters. Calder-Marshall became a Hollywood scriptwriter for Metro-Goldwyn-Mayer in 1937. During the war he was employed by the British Petroleum warfare department and, from 1942 to 1945, by the films division of the Ministry of Information. In 1946 he wrote the screenplay for the award-winning Paul Rotha documentary *The World is Rich*. After the war he branched into writing biographies, including that of the pioneering sexologist Havelock Ellis. One biography in particular, *No Earthly Command* (1957), the life of Vice-Admiral Alexander Riall Wadham Woods DSO, was a turning point in Calder-Marshall's own life. During the battle of Jutland, while he was signals officer to the admiral of the Grand Fleet, Woods allegedly received an 'interposed message' instructing him to serve God, and he ended his life as a poor parson working with down-and-outs in the East End of London.

Having initially been cynical about the commission to write Woods's biography, which came from an American film producer, Calder-Marshall came to believe while researching it that Woods was praying for him from heaven, and the book became the emotive story of Calder-Marshall's own conversion to Christianity. It is possible that Calder-Marshall felt this religious change independently, to some extent, and that he chose to dramatize it in the biography project.

Calder-Marshall continued to write fiction, and *The Scarlet Boy* (1961) is often considered to be his finest novel, exploring the effects on a group of people of a house haunted by two boys who have committed suicide. As in *No Earthly Command*, the narrator finds his own character and beliefs changing as he tries to report events.

Calder-Marshall wrote many documentary film scripts, a play, three books for children, and several fictions under the pseudonym of William Drummond, as well as editing editions of Thomas Paine and Jack London, among others. Notable later non-fiction includes *Wish you Were Here: the Art of Donald McGill* (1966), about the saucy seaside postcard artist, and *Prepare to Shed them now: the Ballads of George R. Sims* (1968), which comprises a substantial introduction to the life of the social reformer and sentimental balladeer who wrote 'Christmas Day in the Workhouse'. Calder-Marshall's *Lewd, blasphemous and obscene: being the trials and tribulations of sundry founding fathers of today's alternative societies* (1972) revives a clutch of Victorian free-speech controversies, framed by the contemporary *Oz* magazine obscenity trial.

Calder-Marshall's move away from thirties leftism towards the Christian faith was underpinned by unchanging ethical concerns. His 1930s work has dated to some extent, but the best of his later fiction has an enduring psychological and moral finesse. However, his most enduring work may well be *The Magic of my Youth*, a minor classic of English autobiography. Shrewdly intelligent, his best non-fiction has an unusual combination of down-to-earth social awareness and steady moral concern, together with a wit and an urbanity of a kind that is not prominent in academic cultural studies. About 5 feet 9 inches tall with a stocky build, Calder-Marshall was, as his daughter Anna recalled, 'a Spencer Tracy type when young. As he grew older, his sandy hair went a lovely grey. He had very blue eyes … and a deep voice. He gave off goodness' (private information).

Arthur Calder-Marshall lived latterly at Twickenham, and died at the William Harvey Hospital at Ashford, Kent, on 17 April 1992.   PHIL BAKER

Sources A. Calder-Marshall, *The magic of my youth* (1951) · A. Calder-Marshall, *No earthly command* (1957) · *The Times* (22 April 1992) · A. Calder-Marshall, 'Fiction', *Fact*, 4 (July 1937) ['Writing in revolt' issue] · A. Calder-Marshall, 'The pink decade', *New Statesman and Nation* (15 Feb 1941) · P. Parker and F. Kermode, eds., *The reader's companion to twentieth-century writers* (1995) · *Contemporary Authors*, new revision series, vol. 72, pp. 185–6 · b. cert. · d. cert. · m. cert.
Archives BBC WAC, corresp. and papers · U. Reading L., corresp. and literary papers · University of Bristol Library, corresp. and statements relating to trial of *Lady Chatterley's lover* | BL, corresp. with Françoise Lafitte-Cyon, Add. MSS 70582–70584
Likenesses H. Coster, photograph, 1934, NPG [*see illus.*]
Wealth at death £139,816: probate, 24 Sept 1992, *CGPLA Eng. & Wales*

Marshall, Arthur Milnes (1852–1893), zoologist, was born on 8 June 1852 at 54 New Hall Street, Birmingham, the second son of William Prime Marshall, secretary of the Institution of Civil Engineers, and his wife, Laura (*née* Stark). He went to school in Birmingham where in 1870 he sat and passed the examinations for the London University (external) BA degree. The following year he entered St John's College, Cambridge, to read for the natural science tripos. As a boy he had shared his father's enthusiasm for natural history; as an undergraduate he pursued this interest through laboratory courses, learning the techniques which were beginning to transform biology into a more experimentally based discipline. He attended the courses of Michael Foster, Trinity College's new praelector of physiology, whose elementary biology classes closely resembled T. H. Huxley's courses in London, introducing students to 'type' specimens, emphasizing the relationships between species and groups of animals. Foster actively encouraged senior students to embark upon experimental research and Marshall took advantage of this by joining a distinguished group of enthusiastic and talented young biologists who were to establish an impressive reputation for Foster's laboratory.

In 1874 Marshall was placed in the senior position of the first-class list of the natural science tripos. Shortly after graduating he secured a place at Cambridge University's research table at the new Stazione Zoologica at Naples, accompanying the brilliant embryologist Francis Balfour (1851–1882), who had graduated the previous year. Balfour had become a protégé of Foster, who had encouraged his interest in embryology and had assisted him to publish research papers while still an undergraduate. Balfour in turn encouraged Marshall. The two continued to work closely together on their return from Naples in the summer of 1875. In the autumn of that year Marshall assisted Balfour in teaching laboratory courses in embryology and

animal morphology. Marshall was elected fellow of St John's College in 1877.

In the 1870s there were still few career opportunities in experimental research, even for those who showed Marshall's promise. Consequently, in 1877, he left Cambridge to train as a medical doctor at St Bartholomew's Hospital, London. However, in 1879, before he had begun to practise as a doctor, he was appointed to the newly created chair of zoology at Owens College, Manchester. Although he completed his medical training by taking the Cambridge MB degree the following year, he was able to devote his whole time in Manchester to teaching and research in zoology.

Owens College had been founded in 1851 under the terms of the will of a wealthy local hatter, John Owen. After a fairly dismal start, the college had been transformed during the 1860s into the nucleus of a science-based university on the German model, largely through the efforts and energy of its charismatic professor of chemistry, Henry Enfield Roscoe. Teaching in zoology had been part of the duties of the professor of natural history, W. C. Williamson, but in 1877 the college council decided to divide Williamson's chair. Williamson was asked to continue to teach botany, a subject for which he had established a distinguished reputation, and Marshall was invited to teach zoology with the assistance of a demonstrator, Marcus Hartog. The college authorities clearly hoped that a zoologist with Marshall's background in experimental research would establish in Manchester a biological research school to complement Roscoe's highly successful chemistry department.

Marshall had begun his research career at Cambridge with investigations on the vertebrate nervous system. He had been educated in the Darwinian tradition of comparative embryology and at Owens College he continued to investigate the development of the nervous system, concentrating particularly on cranial morphology. His published research papers were considered influential and in 1885 he was elected fellow of the Royal Society. His address to the British Association for the Advancement of Science in 1890 as president of the biological section provided an outline of contemporary theories in embryology.

In Manchester most of Marshall's time and energy as professor of zoology were devoted to teaching and administration. He organized lecture and laboratory courses and assisted in the development of the zoology collections of the Manchester Museum. He was highly regarded as a teacher—he was able to communicate enthusiasm for zoology, capturing the attention and imagination of his students. His textbook, *The Frog*, first published in 1882, became a popular introduction to elementary zoology, running into five editions during Marshall's lifetime. He produced two further textbooks, a junior course on practical zoology (1887) and one on vertebrate embryology (1893), both of which proved popular. However, although Marshall conducted a number of original investigations as professor, his laboratory did not become a major centre for zoological research during the 1880s. Most of his students were studying for medical degrees and very few availed themselves of the opportunities it offered for original research.

Marshall was a gifted administrator and played an important role in the development of Owens College into the Victoria University, established by royal charter in 1882 with Owens its sole constituent college. Marshall served first as secretary and later as chairman of its board of studies, establishing regulations for the university's degrees. He was secretary of the extension movement, which encouraged lecturers to give popular courses on their subjects to the general public. He also played a prominent role in Manchester life, as an active member of the Literary and Philosophical Society and as president of the Manchester Microscopical Society for many years.

Marshall's main recreation was mountain climbing. His enthusiasm had been temporarily dimmed by the death of Balfour in a climbing accident in the Swiss Alps in 1882, but while professor in Manchester he spent part of many winter vacations climbing in Wales or the Lake District and most summers included a visit to the Swiss Alps. On 31 December 1893 he was climbing with a party of friends on Scafell in the English Lake District when a rock gave way beneath him and he fell. He died instantly. His death aged only forty-one shocked colleagues, who mourned the loss of such a promising academic. Marshall never married.

STELLA BUTLER

Sources PRS, 57 (1894–5), iii–v · *Nature*, 49 (1893–4), 250–51 · *The Lancet* (6 Jan 1894), 44–5 · *Memoirs of the Literary and Philosophical Society of Manchester*, 4th ser., 8 (1894), 209–13 · b. cert. · d. cert. · CGPLA Eng. & Wales (1893)
Archives JRL, papers · NRA, notebooks | Oxf. U. Mus. NH, letters and postcards to Sir E. B. Poulton
Wealth at death £4576 12s. 10d.: administration, 9 Feb 1894, CGPLA Eng. & Wales

Marshall, Benjamin (1768–1835), painter and racing journalist, was born on 8 November 1768 at Seagrave, Leicestershire, the only surviving son of eight children born to Charles Marshall and his wife, Elizabeth (d. 1772). Benjamin Marshall married Mary Saunders (d. 1827) of Ratby on 12 November 1789 and is recorded as being a schoolmaster in the will of his brother-in-law, dated 1791. However, he must have already shown a talent for portraiture for in the same year, on the recommendation of William Pochin of Barkby Hall, MP for the county, he was apprenticed to the portrait painter Lemuel Francis Abbott.

It is said that Ben Marshall (as he was known) was so impressed by Sawrey Gilpin's life-size painting *Death of a Fox*, exhibited at the Royal Academy in 1793, that he decided to change from portraiture to sporting subjects (*Sporting Magazine*, Aug 1835, 298). By 1795 the Marshalls were living in London at Beaumont Street, Marylebone, their elder son, Charles, having been born the previous year. Soon after their arrival Marshall met William Taplin, the author of *The Gentleman's Stable Directory*, and this was to be a turning point in his career. Taplin not only commissioned a portrait of himself, but also paintings of several of his horses. These were hung in Taplin's newly erected

purpose-built 'equestrian repository' in the Edgware Road, where they would have been seen by the many fashionable and influential subscribers to his equestrian services. Marshall's portrait of Taplin was engraved for the February 1796 issue of the *Sporting Magazine* and in August of the same year his first horse portrait appeared, *A Son of Erasmus*, whose owner is recorded as a Taplin subscriber. Both these works were engraved by John Scott and the working relationship between them developed into a lifelong friendship which, as both admitted, did much to enhance their respective talents. Marshall's connection with the *Sporting Magazine* continued throughout his life. Sixty of his paintings were engraved as illustrations between 1796 and 1833, and from 1821 to 1833 under the name Observator he became their southern racing correspondent. The *Sporting Magazine* also records in 1796 that on the completion of three paintings for George III, Marshall was granted an audience of almost an hour with the king and 'all the princesses' (*Sporting Magazine*, Aug 1796, 255).

Marshall's early works owe much to both George Stubbs and Gilpin, for example *Diamond with Dennis Fitzpatrick up* (1799, exh. at RA, 1800; Yale U. CBA) and *Grey Arab Stallion and Mare* (FM Cam.). However, they already show the individuality that in the first years of the nineteenth century was to develop into his own very personal style. This change is best represented in the series of six paintings of horses commissioned by George, prince of Wales, probably executed between 1801 and 1803. These, unlike the three painted for George III, remain in the Royal Collection.

Joseph Farington recorded in his *Diary* of 28 March 1804 that 'Bourgeois spoke of Marshall a horse painter as having extraordinary ability and that Gilpin had said that in managing his backgrounds he had done that which Stubbs and himself never could venture upon'. This ability to capture the vagaries of the British climate and landscape together with the depth of character in his portraits of all those connected with the sporting world raise Marshall well above the range of the average sporting artist. However, he made no attempt to be elected to the Royal Academy and exhibited there only intermittently between 1800 and 1819. The Marshalls remained at Beaumont Street until 1810, Marshall painting both sporting subjects and portraits including the celebrated boxers John Jackson, John Gully, and James Belcher (Tate collection) and, most strikingly, Marshall's Leicestershire friend Daniel Lambert, the celebrated fat man, who had exhibited himself at a shilling a visit in London during summer 1806 (exh. RA, 1807; Leicester Museums and Art Galleries).

Prompted by Ben's great love of racing, the Marshalls moved to near Newmarket in 1812. There, Marshall 'could study the second animal in creation … in all his grandeur, beauty and variety' (*Sporting Magazine*, Sept 1826, 318), adding the much quoted adage that 'a man would give me fifty guineas for painting his horse who thought ten too much to pay for the best portrait of a wife' (*Sporting Magazine*, Jan 1828, 172). His absence from London did not lessen his success and for the next seven years he produced some of the finest sporting paintings of the first quarter of the nineteenth century and arguably the best studies of jockeys ever painted. In September 1819, while he was travelling to his patron Lord Sondes at Rockingham Castle, the mail coach overturned and both Marshall's legs were broken, his head badly cut, and his back injured. He made a remarkable recovery, and the *Sporting Magazine* reported in October 1820 that he 'had built himself a new painting room at Newmarket and was busily employed' (*Sporting Magazine*, Oct 1820, 42). That his abilities were not impaired is shown by the striking portrait *Thomas Hilton and his Hound Glory* of 1822 (Royal Museum and Art Gallery, Canterbury, Kent).

In 1825, aged fifty-seven, Marshall returned to London, purchasing a house in Hackney Road but keeping on his house in East Anglia. His succinct and descriptive racing journalism was still signed 'Observator, Norfolk'. One of his reasons for returning was to promote his younger son Lambert (born in November 1809 and named after Marshall's old friend Daniel Lambert who had died suddenly in June the same year) as his successor as sporting artist and illustrator for the *Sporting Magazine*. Sadly, Lambert had little more than schoolboy talent: the earlier works are almost entirely by his father and there are few that do not have some assistance. It is not surprising that not a single painting attributed to him dates from after Marshall's death.

Although there appears to have been no fall in demand for Marshall's paintings or writing, the effects of his coaching accident were gradually lessening his mobility and hence output. In 1834, when the dress of the youngest of his three daughters, Elizabeth (*b.* 1812), caught fire, he was unable to move out of his chair to assist her and was forced to watch her burn to death. This tragedy, compounded with the death of his wife in 1827, hastened his own end and he died on 24 July 1835 at his home in London Terrace, Hackney Road, London. He was buried with his wife and daughter at St Matthew's, Bethnal Green. Marshall's effects were valued at only £200. There was no studio sale of his unsold paintings and studies, and although the *Gentleman's Magazine* noted the death of 'the celebrated artist Ben Marshall' (*GM*, 2nd ser., 4, 1835, 531), he was soon forgotten. He left little mark on the next generation of sporting painters, for despite the fact that John Ferneley was apprenticed to him and Abraham Cooper had lessons with him, his broad style of painting and somewhat bucolic approach to his subjects had little appeal to the Victorians and it was not until early in the twentieth century that he began again to be appreciated.

Marshall is not widely represented in British public collections, where his portraits are more numerous than his sporting subjects. For a broader view of his work one has to turn to private collections. Many of his paintings were exported to the USA in the first half of the twentieth century and are now represented in a number of galleries there, most notably at the Yale Center for British Art at New Haven, Connecticut, which holds the best portrait of the artist.   DAVID FULLER

Sources *Sporting Magazine* (1796–1835) • W. H. Scott [J. Lawrence], *The sportsman's repository* (1820) • W. S. Sparrow, *British sporting artists* (1922) • W. S. Sparrow, *George Stubbs and Ben Marshall* (1929) • W. S. Sparrow, *A book of sporting painters* (1931) • L. Lambourne, *Ben Marshall/John Leech* (1967) [exhibition catalogue, Leicester Museums and Art Galleries] • J. Egerton, ed., *British sporting and animal paintings, 1655–1867* (1978) • A. Noakes, *Ben Marshall* (1978) • catalogue [Leicester Museum]

Likenesses attrib. I. R. Cruikshank, pencil drawing, NPG • B. Marshall, self-portrait, oils, Yale U. CBA • L. Marshall, oils, NPG • stipple (after B. Marshall), BM, NPG; repro. in *Sporting Magazine* (1826)

Wealth at death £200: administration, Sparrow, *Stubbs and Marshall*

Marshall, (Claude Cunningham) Bruce (1899–1987), novelist, was born on 24 June 1899 at 8 East Fettes Avenue, Edinburgh, the son of Claude Niven Marshall, a stockbroker, and his wife, Annie Margaret Seton Bruce. After schooling at Edinburgh Academy (1906–9) and at Trinity College, Glenalmond (1909–15), he read classics at the University of St Andrews in 1916–17, but his studies were interrupted by the First World War, in which he served from 1917 with the Royal Irish Fusiliers. Shortly before the armistice he was wounded and taken prisoner, subsequently losing a leg because of poor treatment.

In 1919 Marshall published the first of more than forty books: his only collection of short stories. He did not return to St Andrews, but in 1922 took up his studies again at the University of Edinburgh, graduating MA in 1924, the year in which he published the first of what he himself described as nine very bad religious novels, inspired by his conversion to Roman Catholicism. In 1925 he graduated BCom at Edinburgh and the following year, after qualifying as a chartered accountant, joined the Paris branch of Peat Marwick Mitchell. In Paris, on 31 October 1928, Marshall married Mary Pearson Clark (1908–1987), known as Phyllis, daughter of William Glen Clark, a schoolmaster. Their only child, Sheila Elizabeth Bruce Marshall (later Ferrar), was born on 19 March 1931. In that year he also produced the first of his novels to be widely noticed (although more so in the United States than in Britain), and the first the older writer wished to acknowledge: this was his tenth novel, *Father Malachy's Miracle*, a humorous clerical fantasy set in Edinburgh. Revised in 1947, it was a bestseller in Italy and Germany in 1949 and 1950, and in Britain, as a children's book, survived the author's death.

In the years leading up to and including the Second World War Marshall's stream of novels kept flowing, and he continued his accountancy work until June 1940, when, two days before the Germans entered the French capital, he returned to Britain. He served in the Royal Army Pay Corps before joining intelligence, where he was valued for his perfect French and knowledge of France. From 1945 to 1946 he was in Rome and then Vienna, working with displaced persons; these experiences of international bureaucracy inspired *The Red Danube* (1947), later filmed, and *A Girl from Lübeck* (1962).

After Marshall was demobilized in 1946 he and his wife returned to Paris, then in 1948, when he retired from accountancy to devote himself to writing, moved to the south of France, where he found the climate kinder to his war wound. Here he wrote the book by which he was best-known; ironically, it was not a novel. *The White Rabbit* (1952), the harrowing story of the capture and torture by the Gestapo of the resistance hero Wing Commander F. F. E. Yeo-Thomas, was a book that Marshall, who also served in the Special Operations Executive, of which his hero was an agent, was ideally qualified to write. It was acclaimed for its graphic power, and successfully dramatized on television.

As Marshall's own experiences helped with the biography of Yeo-Thomas, likewise his life invariably fed into his novels. Examples, apart from those already cited, are not hard to find, and too numerous to list exhaustively. His own schooldays informed *George Brown's Schooldays* (1946), trenchant on savagery and homosexuality in public schools. His knowledge of accountancy enabled him to write *The Bank Audit* (1958), perhaps the most technical of financial novels. Memories of St Andrews lent colour to *A Thread of Scarlet* (1959), a novel about priestly ambition that showed that the convert could still criticize the church he loved. That church's attitude towards birth control and celibacy was tackled in *The Bishop* (1970), a novel Marshall thought one of his best, and best-written. However, he suffered by the inevitable comparison with two other novelists who were converts to Roman Catholicism, Evelyn Waugh and—especially—Graham Greene. Marshall's achievement is altogether lighter, and slighter; but it is equally distinctive and wide-ranging, and in his accessible and enjoyable farces he comes across to readers as more warmly humorous than either of his greater contemporaries.

In the south of France the Marshalls lived first at Juan-les-Pins and then went to the Cap d'Antibes; they spent the last thirty-four years of their lives at Clos Riant, 104 boulevard du Cap, shared with up to ten cats. The writer had many good friends, who regarded him with great affection, and many visited him in France and were welcome, though unexpected invasions of his privacy by acquaintances making Antibes a stepping-stone on their holiday journeys could elicit unfavourable comment from the very forthright Scot. He was also notably cheerful, which may be partly why he got on especially well with children, enjoying long conversations with them. He was particularly delighted that his granddaughter followed him in becoming a chartered accountant with his old firm, now called KPMG, in which he accurately predicted she would become a partner, though he did not live to see this. Marshall died in hospital in Biot on 18 June 1987, a month after being operated on for cancer. After his funeral in Biot, his ashes were scattered in the garden of the crematorium at Nice. His widow survived him by only two months.

MICHAEL HERBERT

Sources private information (2004) · *The Times* (23 June 1987) · 'Bruce Marshall, British novelist', *Annual Obituary* (1987), 310–11 [obit. of Bruce Marshall] · D. L. Kirkpatrick, ed., *Contemporary novelists*, 4th edn (1986), 576–8 · b. cert. · m. cert.
Archives Georgetown University, Lauinger Library, corresp. and papers · University of Bristol Library, corresp. and statements relating to *Lady Chatterley's Lover* · Westm. DA, corresp.
Likenesses photographs, priv. coll.

Marshall, Catherine Elizabeth (1880–1961), suffragist and internationalist, was born on 29 April 1880 at Harrow on the Hill, Middlesex, the elder of two children of Francis E. Marshall (1847–1922), mathematics master at Harrow School, and his wife, Caroline, *née* Colbeck (d. 1927), formerly a teacher. Catherine Marshall was first educated privately and then for three years (1896–9) at St Leonard's School, St Andrews, and was stimulated by music, travel, and discussion (which had a politically and ethically liberal bias). But no career seems to have been planned for her.

The suffrage movement transformed Marshall's life. Assisted by her parents, she built up a strong local suffrage society in Keswick (where the family lived after her father's retirement): it was a branch of the non-militant National Union of Women's Suffrage Societies (NUWSS). She developed her remarkable flair for organization and became known for innovative and effective work. The London-based executive and administration of the NUWSS did not well serve the dynamic new societies at the periphery (and especially in the north), so Marshall and kindred spirits in the NUWSS used the organization's fundamentally democratic, but out-of-date, constitution to gain acceptance for a new structure. Based on a balance between the national council and new provincial councils the new constitution was accepted at a tense council meeting in March 1910 against considerable opposition from the old guard. Power was distributed more evenly between London and the provinces, giving an effective voice to a whole new constituency with a wider geographical and class base.

Although the activities of the militant suffragettes are more widely known, the essential work of one-by-one conversion of the public, members of parliament, and ultimately of party leaders, was accomplished largely by the NUWSS. The organization had been developed into a remarkable political tool under the leadership, as honorary parliamentary secretary and honorary secretary respectively, of Catherine Marshall and Kathleen Courtney, who both worked full-time at national headquarters between 1911 and 1914. Tall, well dressed, well informed, and dynamic, Marshall could hold the attention of an outdoor audience of miners, and was also a familiar figure to members of parliament, as she pressed the converted for action, cultivated sympathizers, and shamed backsliders.

When private members' bills on women's suffrage were stalled repeatedly by the Liberal government, Marshall worked towards having suffrage adopted as party policy. First the Labour Party was brought to full official support for the cause by intense lobbying in the trade unions, among working women, and in the party hierarchy, and by help from the NUWSS in elections. By 1913 some leading Liberals and Unionists also recognized the inevitability of adopting franchise reform, but the war, by delaying the expected general election of 1915, prevented the culmination of Marshall's strategy. At the outbreak of war in August 1914, the NUWSS put its political work on hold. Soon divisions, previously papered over, surfaced in a new form. Marshall, with like-minded suffragists in Britain and elsewhere, wanted the suffrage movement to work towards a well-informed and hate-free climate for peacemaking after the war. Millicent Fawcett, president of the NUWSS, saw talk of peace as treacherous, finding approval especially among those who had disliked the Labour Party connection. By the end of the struggle the NUWSS was back in the hands of middle-class Londoners and Marshall and her friends had resigned from office.

The history of the non-militant women's suffrage campaign, written by Marshall's opponents, omitted not only any in-depth account of the débâcle but almost all mention of Marshall's pre-war achievements: even the archives of the NUWSS may have been 'weeded'. Marshall herself, throughout her life, wrote only short articles addressing current causes.

Marshall had thought deeply about the role of force in politics, and rejected the force-based arguments of antisuffragists and militants alike. Her conclusions, that good government rested on the consent of the governed, and that to base governance on physical force was particularly inimical to the rights of women, translated readily to the international sphere. For Marshall, to work for a more peaceful world was to work for the women's cause. She helped to plan the Women's International Congress at The Hague in April 1915, but she was prevented by government action from attending it. She went on to help develop the British section of the International Committee of Women for Permanent Peace, later the Women's International League for Peace and Freedom (WILPF), and from early 1916 she became involved with the No-Conscription Fellowship, where, with Bertrand Russell, she was particularly engaged in the political field, monitoring the experiences of conscientious objectors and keeping the issues in the public and parliamentary eye.

Meanwhile, Catherine Marshall fell in love with (Reginald) Clifford Allen, later Lord Allen of Hurtwood (1889–1939), the charismatic chair of the No-Conscription Fellowship, and suffered deeply when he was imprisoned; he was physically frail, and his health deteriorated rapidly in prison. By mid-1917, Catherine Marshall was compulsively driving herself towards breakdown, and Allen's health was further threatened by his intention of embarking on a hunger and work strike in prison. By the end of the year, Marshall had collapsed and Allen was released seriously ill. When both were convalescent they spent several months together in what seems to have been a 'trial marriage'; Marshall was devastated when the relationship ended. She found solace in theosophy and in spiritual dancing, and, more concretely, in renewed work for peace. She recovered her health just in time to go to the Women's International Congress in Zürich in May 1919, attended by women from defeated as well as victorious nations; the congress was among the first to critique the peace terms and the covenant of the League of Nations.

Throughout the inter-war years, Marshall's career was on a roller-coaster, swinging between time spent caring for ailing parents, bouts of phlebitis and other severe (but unnamed) illness, and periods of intense international peace work. She was present (with the protection of Prince Max of Baden) when the Reichstag in Berlin accepted the humiliating peace terms of 1919; and at the time of the invasion of the Ruhr in 1923–4, she went as WILPF envoy to the heads of state in France and Germany, and also visited workers involved in non-violent resistance in the Ruhr itself.

During the early years of the League of Nations, Marshall was often in Geneva, at the headquarters of the WILPF. Refusing to be sidelined into causes thought suitable for women, she directed her attention to those issues which might serve in the overall objective of an enduring peace, and used her lobbying skills in the cause of treaty revision, increased openness in League of Nations membership and procedure, disarmament, protection of minorities, the principle of self-determination, the just working of the mandate system, and economic reform, as well, always, as the appointment of more women to positions of international power. As in the pre-war suffrage movement, the work was mostly carried on out of the spotlight, attempting to build opinion by influencing individual statesmen behind the scenes. Unlike the suffrage cause, however, successes were small and rare, and no ultimate triumph came. Marshall was increasingly debilitated by ill health, as the peace movement was by the rise of fascism.

In the late 1930s Marshall brought renewed energy to bear on the cause of Czech refugees, working for their reception and settlement in Britain, and making a home for some at the house by Derwentwater inherited by herself and her brother Harold; but her service to them was palliative rather than political. After the Second World War she settled in Golders Green, Middlesex, in a remarkable house at 2 Linnell Drive, built in the 1920s for herself and Harold, who, however, married in 1927 and lived elsewhere. Her lifelong incompetence in managing money caused Harold considerable concern, and once landed her in court for non-payment of taxes, but theirs remained an affectionate relationship. She continued to be active in the local Labour Party branch, and with other social, political, and international concerns. Remembered as a woman of humour and courage, Catherine Marshall died in the New End Hospital, Hampstead, on 22 March 1961 after a fall at her home.

The trajectory of Marshall's life, rising to a brilliant effectiveness in her late thirties and forties, and declining thereafter, is in part attributable to the lack of openings for a gifted woman in public life, and in part to poor health; the two may have been connected. When she died, her achievements were little known, but were to be recovered by the end of the century.   JO VELLACOTT

Sources Cumbria AS, Carlisle, Marshall papers · J. Vellacott, *From liberal to labour with women's suffrage: the story of Catherine Marshall* (1993) · J. Vellacott Newberry, 'Anti-war suffragists', *History*, new ser., 62 (1977), 411–25 · J. Vellacott, 'A place for pacifism and transnationalism in feminist theory: the early work of the WILPF', *Women's History Review*, 2 (1993), 23–56 · University of Colorado, Boulder, Colorado, USA, Women's International League for Peace and Freedom MSS · BLPES, WILPF MSS [Women's International

League for Peace and Freedom] · Women's Library, London, Fawcett Library collections · S. S. Holton, *Feminism and democracy: women's suffrage and reform politics in Britain, 1900–1918* (1986) · G. Bussey and M. Tims, *Women's International League for Peace and Freedom, 1915–1965* (1965) · J. Vellacott, *Bertrand Russell and the pacifists in the First World War* (1980) · Man. CL, Arts Library, Suffrage collection · J. Vellacott, second book of Marshall's biography, incomplete, in progress · W. G. Rimmer, *Marshalls of Leeds, flax-spinners, 1788–1886* (1960) · Labour History Archive and Study Centre, Manchester · d. cert. · *Plough my own furrow: the story of Lord Allen of Hurtwood as told through his writings and correspondence*, ed. M. Gilbert (1965)

Archives BLPES, corresp. and papers · Cumbria AS, Carlisle, corresp. and papers · Women's Library, London | BLPES, WILPF MSS · Man. CL, suffrage collection · McMaster University, Hamilton, Ontario, corresp. with Bertrand Russell · Swarthmore College, Swarthmore, Pennsylvania, Peace collection, WILPF and Jane Addams MSS · University of Colorado, Boulder, Women's International League for Peace and Freedom (International section) MSS · University of South Carolina, Columbia, Allen MSS

Likenesses photographs, Cumbria AS, Marshall collection · photographs, priv. coll.

Wealth at death £44,746 0s. 1d.: probate, 8 June 1961, *CGPLA Eng. & Wales*

Marshall, Charles (1637–1698), Quaker preacher and apothecary, was born at Bristol in June 1637. He noted in his short journal that his 'education and bringing up was after the strictest manner of religion', his parents 'being such as feared the Lord' (Marshall, sig. d1r). He went on to recount how at the age of five or six he started to read the Bible, and that at about eleven or twelve years he accompanied his mother to meetings of Independents and Baptists. As he grew older he wrote of his spiritual state, 'I became like the solitary Desart, and mourned like a Dove without a Mate' (ibid., sig. d2r). About 1654 he joined a group of people who met weekly for fasting and prayer. John Audland and John Camm attended one of these meetings, and Marshall describes how he was convinced by the former's 'powerful Ministry' and became a Quaker (ibid., sig. d4r).

On 6 May 1662 Marshall married Hannah, daughter of Edward Prince, an ironmonger of Bristol. She too became a Quaker, and in 1664 they were convicted under the Act for Banishment for attending Quaker meetings and committed to prison, along with 217 others. In 1668 they settled at Tytherington, Wiltshire. They had a number of children: two sons, Beulah and Charles, and two daughters, Sarah, who became the wife of Richard Scott, and another who married 'Ja: Honour'.

Marshall appears to have been an apothecary and published a number of medical works. In 1670 he wrote *A Plain and Candid Relation of the Nature, Use, and Dose of Several Approved Medicines*, in which he described a number of his preparations such as 'Spiritus Sedativus' and 'Expulsive Cordial' that were to be sold at his house near Castlegate in Bristol (pp. 10, 13). This was published again in 1681, with changes and additions, under a similar title. It contained some general guidelines for the preservation of health, and was written while Marshall was living in London at the Golden Bull, Winchester Street. Letters of recommendation for his medicines, subscribed by Richard

Snead with a few lines from William Penn, were printed as a broadside in 1681.

In 1670, Marshall later wrote, he 'faithfully gave up Liberty, Estate and Relations' and began preaching in Bristol and the surrounding areas (Marshall, sig. e3r). He went on to describe how he 'received' a 'Commission from God' to travel through the nation (ibid., sig. e3r), writing that 'the Word of the Lord was as a Fire in my Bones, to run through the Land' (ibid., sig. f5v). In the space of two years he held 400 meetings in most parts of England, returning home only twice—once through illness, and once owing to the death of a favourite child. Through his work he noted that 'Thousands received the Word of Life, and many were added to the Church in divers places' (ibid., sig. f6v).

Marshall recounted that during his travels he was not persecuted at all and 'no Man was suffered to lay Hands on me, to stop my Way' (Marshall, sig. f6r). However, some years later, in December 1674, while at prayer in a meeting at Claverham, Somerset, he was injured when justices violently dragged him through the gallery rail; he was later fined for non-attendance at church.

On his return to Bristol, Marshall worked hard to counteract the divisions made by the Quaker separatists John Story and John Wilkinson, whom he believed were trying to oppose 'Order and Discipline' by 'endeavouring to lay waste the Quarterly, Monthly, Yearly, and Women's-Meetings, by opposing the settled methods thereof; calling them, *Forms* and *an Idol*' (Marshall, sig. f7v). He took part with George Fox in a large meeting at Bristol in 1677 at the house of William Rogers, another separatist. George Whitehead noted that Marshall 'Zealously often Testified against the Spirit of *Division* and *Separation*, and against *Treacherous Apostates* and *Sowers of Discord*' (ibid., sig. b2v).

Marshall lost much property by distraints for tithes, and in 1682 or 1683 was prosecuted by the vicar of Tytherington and committed to the Fleet prison, where he remained for two years. During his incarceration he wrote *A Tender Visitation in the Love of God* (1684), addressed to his parish neighbours and the inhabitants of Wiltshire, Gloucester, and Bristol. Once released and back in Winchester Street, London, he tended the sick 'and was frequently concerned with some in the Government, on behalf of his suffering People' (Marshall, sig. i3r). He appears to have become a very important leading Friend, as in 1697 he was a chief signatory along with William Penn, Leonard Fell, and others to the postscript to an epistle of John Bellers regarding Bellers's proposals for a college of industry.

A number of testimonies to Marshall's good character exist. George Whitehead called him 'a Loving and Tender hearted Man' who 'was truly Tender and Zealous of the Glory of God' (Marshall, sig. b2r). His wife, Hannah, wrote that 'He was a Lover of the Poor, and a Friend to the Rich, often putting the latter, at their well-furnished Tables, in mind of the former'. She added that he visited the poor, 'supplying the Sick, with Advice and Physick; the Hungry, with Bread; and the Naked with Clothes' (ibid., sig. c6v).

Marshall was the author of many works, chiefly epistles

containing warnings and reproofs, twenty-six of which are included in his posthumous collection of works, *Sion's Travellers Comforted* (1704). This also contains his journal, a preface by William Penn, and testimonies by his wife and other Friends. Works included in it are *The Way of Life Revealed, and the Way of Death Discovered* (1674) and *The Trumpet of the Lord* (1675); the former tract contained a discussion of the fall of man together with the Quaker idea of salvation, via the inner light, which Marshall described as 'a measure of the divine fullness', which was 'communicated to, and placed in all immortal souls' (p. 14). Along with Thomas Camm, Marshall also edited *The Memory of the Righteous Revived* (1689), a collection of writings and testimonies concerning the Quakers John Camm and John Audland.

Marshall's last journey was to Bristol at the beginning of 1698. On his return to London he fell ill and was moved to the house of John Padley, near the riverside at Southwark, where after four months he died of a fever and consumption on 15 November 1698, aged sixty-one. The Quaker digest registers state that he was buried at Chequer Alley, London, two days later. The esteem in which he was held can be seen from a letter from John Tomkins to Sir John Rodes, dated 18 November 1698, concerning his funeral, in which it was noted that 'it's thought to be the greatest appearance of Friends at his burial … as of any yet, exceeding in number either G.F's, S.C. or F.S. [George Fox, Stephen Crisp, Francis Stamper]' ('Large gatherings of Friends', 8). Marshall left a will in which he bequeathed estates in Pennsylvania to his son Beulah, his shares in mines in Cumberland to his other son, Charles, and his property at Tytherington and Bromhill to his wife, who survived him.

CHARLOTTE FELL-SMITH, rev. CAROLINE L. LEACHMAN

Sources C. Marshall, *Sion's travellers comforted* (1704) · J. Gough, *A history of the people called Quakers*, 3 (1789) · J. Smith, ed., *A descriptive catalogue of Friends' books*, 2 (1867) · J. Besse, *A collection of the sufferings of the people called Quakers*, 2 vols. (1753) · Quaker digest registers, RS Friends, Lond. · 'Large gatherings of Friends', *Journal of the Friends' Historical Society*, 8 (1911), 7–8 · W. C. Braithwaite, *The second period of Quakerism*, ed. H. J. Cadbury, 2nd edn (1961); repr. (1979) · will, PRO, PROB 11/450, sig. 45

Archives RS Friends, Lond., letters, portfolio MSS 25/105, 25/39, 23/183, 23/132–133, 23/153

Wealth at death difficult to estimate, but considerable: will, PRO, PROB 11/450, sig. 45

Marshall, Charles (1806–1890), scene-painter, was born on 31 December 1806 at 1 Cumberland Street, St Pancras, London, and baptized in St Pancras on 24 May 1807, the son of Nathan Marshall, butcher (d. 1848), and his wife, Mary, née Randall (d. 1852). He studied oil painting under John Wilson, and at the age of twenty-two received a gold medal from the Society of Arts. He became a pupil of Gaetano Marinari, scene-painter at Drury Lane Theatre, and subsequently became one of the most prominent and successful scene-painters of the day. Marshall was employed by a number of London theatre managers, including Robert William Elliston at Drury Lane and David Osbaldiston at the Surrey Theatre. Under William Macready at Covent Garden and Drury Lane he designed

scenery for many plays including *The Tempest*, *As You Like It*, *Coriolanus*, *Virginius*, and the first productions of Lord Lytton's plays. On the death of William Grieve in 1844, Marshall became scene-painter to the opera at Her Majesty's Theatre, London, and contributed much to Benjamin Lumley's revival of the ballet. That year he married on 15 February Anna Maria (d. 1883), daughter of James Kittermaster MD, of Meriden, Warwickshire.

Marshall is credited with introducing limelight on the stage. He originated and developed transformation scenes. In general his scenery depended more on illusion than on solid pictorial effects as practised by Clarkson Stanfield and others. In common with the other leading theatre scene-painters of the day, including Stanfield, David Roberts, Thomas Grieve, William Grieve, and William Telbin, he energetically involved himself in the production and exhibition of panoramas. At the Surrey Theatre in 1829, for instance, he exhibited a *Grand Moving Panorama* with a view of Constantinople as part of the performance, and at the Victoria Theatre in 1834 a moving panorama of the burning of the houses of parliament, completed and displayed within a week of the event. His *Kineorama*, a moving panorama of a trip from Constantinople to Cairo, which opened in London at 121 Pall Mall in March 1841, maximized the use of dioramic effects. The premises caught fire on 20 July during a performance. His most ambitious panoramas were those performed in exhibition halls rather than in theatres. His *Tour through Europe* was performed at the Linwood Gallery in Leicester Square in 1851; and his *Life and Exploits of Napoleon Bonaparte* at the Regent Gallery, 69 Quadrant, in 1853. Both panoramas toured the provinces. Scene-painters misleadingly called their moving panoramas dioramas. Marshall provided James Wyld at the Great Globe in Leicester Square with a *Grand Moving Diorama of a Tour from Blackwall to Balaclava* in 1856, and a *Diorama of Russia* in 1856–7. In 1842 he designed *A General Representation of the City of Hamburg*, the scenic element in a pyrotechnic display at Vauxhall Gardens; and in 1844 he painted the scenery at the Glaciarium, a skating rink at 8 Grafton Street East, Tottenham Court Road.

Marshall retired in 1858. Since 1828 he had regularly exhibited landscape paintings at the Royal Academy, the British Institution, and the Society (later Royal Society) of British Artists, and landscape painting now became his principal preoccupation. He died at his home, 7 Lewisham Road, Highgate Road, London, on 8 March 1890, and was buried at Highgate cemetery. He left three children; of these two sons, Charles James Kittermaster Marshall and Roberto Angelo Kittermaster Marshall, also became artists.

L. H. CUST, rev. RALPH HYDE

Sources P. Marshall, *Charles Marshall RA (1806–90): his origins, life and career* (2000) · R. Hyde, *Panoramania! the art and entertainment of the 'all embracing' view* (1988–9) [exhibition catalogue, Barbican Art Gallery, 3 Nov 1988 – 15 Jan 1989] · playbills, description booklets, handbills, and contemporary advertisements · *Hampstead and Highgate Express* (22 March 1890) · CGPLA Eng. & Wales (1890)

Likenesses C. Marshall, oils, c.1846, priv. coll.

Wealth at death £88 6s.: administration with will, 9 June 1890, CGPLA Eng. & Wales

Marshall, Charles Ward (1808–1876). *See under* Marshall, William (1806–1875).

Marshall, Edward (1597/8–1675), sculptor and master mason, was apprenticed to John Clerke under the auspices of the Masons' Company of London; he became free of the company in 1627, a liveryman in 1630–31, and served as warden in 1642–3 and 1646–7, and as master in 1649–50. On 26 June 1627 he married Anna (*bap.* 1604, *d.* 1673), almost certainly the daughter of the sculptor Isaac James, at the church of St Martin-in-the-Fields, Westminster, where their son Joshua [*see below*] was baptized the following year; they had a further eight sons and five daughters. By 1629 Marshall had moved to the parish of St Dunstan-in-the-West in the City of London and he remained there for the rest of his life.

Professionally, Marshall first emerges as a maker of church monuments. His signature appears on the finely detailed brass of Sir Edward Filmer (*d.* 1629) and his wife at East Sutton, Kent, and in 1643–4 he was paid by the churchwardens of his own parish of St Dunstan's for 'altering the inscripcons in Brasse upon Div[e]rs grave stones' (churchwardens' accounts, City of London, Guildhall Library, MS 2986/3, fol. 651; J. Page-Phillips, *Palimpsests: the Backs of Monumental Brasses*, 1980, 1.22, 76). Numerous other monumental brasses have been attributed to him; however, he was probably more prolific as a sculptor of memorials in stone and marble for in this field he is known to have signed at least eight works while two others are documented as his and over thirty more can confidently be assigned to him. They come in a variety of shapes and sizes and tend to show strongly the influence of Nicholas Stone the elder who was roughly ten years his senior and whose career followed a similar path to his own. The memorial to Henry Curwen, for example, at Amersham, Buckinghamshire, which bears Marshall's signature and the date 1638, shows the deceased in his shroud, like Stone's famous effigy of John Donne, but he is flanked by two angels holding open doors, a device derived from another of Stone's monuments, that of Anne, Lady Cutt (*d.* 1632), at Swavesey in Cambridgeshire.

From the 1650s onwards a second phase of Marshall's career, as a mason–contractor, is traceable, though he remained active as a sculptor. Under the architect John Webb he built the portico at The Vyne, Hampshire (1654), and carried out work at Northumberland House in the Strand, London (1655–7), and Gunnersbury House, Middlesex (1658). At Aynho Park, Northamptonshire, he appears to have worked to his own designs on the rebuilding campaign that began in the 1660s. He was appointed master mason in the re-established office of works at the Restoration and he retired from the post in 1673. Following the death of his first wife in 1673 he married Margaret, *née* White, the widow of Henry Parker of Barnet. He died at the age of seventy-seven on 10 December 1675 in the parish of St Dunstan-in-the-West, and was buried there four days later. His family monument is in the church.

Joshua Marshall (*bap.* 1628, *d.* 1678), master mason, the eldest and sole surviving child of Edward Marshall and Anna James, was baptized on 24 June 1628. He probably received his training from his father, and like him he held office in the Masons' Company of London of which he was twice warden in the 1660s and twice master in the following decade. In 1667 he followed John Stone as master mason at Windsor Castle and from 1673 he combined the office with that of master mason in the central office of works to which he had succeeded on his father's retirement. In addition to his work for the crown he was active privately as a mason–contractor, being much involved with the rebuilding of the City of London after the great fire. He worked on St Paul's Cathedral and Temple Bar and built the monument and six of the City churches. He also found time to produce memorial sculpture, though in this field he showed no special talent, having a tendency to mass-produce designs which were themselves heavily dependent on his father's work. Joshua Marshall married Catharine (1649/50–1716), daughter of John George of London, with whom he had five children, two of whom survived him. He died on 6 April 1678 and was buried six days later at St Dunstan-in-the-West, Fleet Street. His wife survived him by thirty-eight years. ADAM WHITE

Sources A. White, 'A biographical dictionary of London tomb sculptors, *c*.1560–*c*.1660', *Walpole Society*, 61 (1999), 1–162, esp. 83–106 · Colvin, *Archs.*, 641 · M. Whinney, *Sculpture in Britain, 1530 to 1830*, rev. J. Physick, 2nd edn (1988), 80–84, 135 · H. M. Colvin and others, eds., *The history of the king's works*, 5 (1976) · Marshall family monument, St Dunstan-in-the-West, London · parish register, London, St Dunstan-in-the-West, 14 Dec 1675 [burial] · parish register, London, St Martin-in-the-Fields, 24 June 1628 [Joshua Marshall: baptism]

Wealth at death £14,661 1s. 7d.—£4326 4s. 5d. in tangible assets plus recoverable debts; Joshua Marshall: inventory, PRO, PROB 4/12829

Marshall, Emilie Hawkes. *See* Peacocke, Emilie Hawkes (1882–1964).

Marshall, Emily Esther (1832–1915), advocate of an ordained ministry for women and founder of an Anglican Franciscan third order, was born on 4 December 1832 at Upper Clapton, Hackney, Middlesex, the fourth of seven children, one son and six daughters, of Laurence Jopson Marshall (*d.* 1845), underwriter, and his wife, Jane (1801–1866), daughter of Bernard and Ann Ogden of Sunderland. She was educated at home. After her father's death she settled in Sunderland and lived, unmarried, upon independent means.

In 1889 Emily Marshall sent her pamphlet *A Suggestion for our Times* to J. B. Lightfoot, bishop of Durham, who had stated that he wished to see the female diaconate restored to the Church of England. She suggested that an organization should be formed in his diocese specifically to prepare women for this ministry. According to her account, Lightfoot believed that her proposal 'should be productive of much good' and asked her to give it 'a practical form'. She was always adamant that her 'idea, encouraged in its embryo form by Bishop Lightfoot, suffered from his death' in December 1889 (Marshall, *The Parochial, or Third Order*, 7).

On 27 October 1891 Canon George Body, who was responsible for training women to be 'church workers' in

Durham, admitted Miss Marshall and five other women in Durham to the League of St Cuthbert. She soon learned that Canon Body intended to keep local development of the pastoral, charitable, and liturgical ministries of women firmly under his control. Indeed, in the Durham diocese the organization which Miss Marshall initiated became known as 'Canon Body's Third Order'. She was told not to speak in public or to ask others to speak on her behalf at the church congress. However, Canon Body was not wholly successful in silencing her. She wrote tracts, for example *District Visitors, Deaconesses and a Proposed Adaptation, in Part, of the Third Order* (1891), disguising her identity as an anonymous 'author of *A Suggestion for our Times*', and paid to have them printed and distributed by post. In them she revealed that Bishop Lightfoot had also spoken with her of the Franciscan third order formed in the thirteenth century for men and women, ordained and lay, married and unmarried, who served their local communities without 'cowl or cloister'.

Miss Marshall's interest in the third order was further stimulated by reading Paul Sabatier's *Vie de S. François d'Assise*, which she bought on a visit to Paris in 1894. Captivated by the French Calvinist's controversial portrayal of the saint and his account of the origins of the Franciscan movement, she went to Assisi. There she met Sabatier, who clarified for her his view of the vision and intentions of St Francis and told her that the organization she envisaged for the Anglican communion was 'dans le sens de S. François' (Marshall, *Dawn Breaking*, 7). Her advocacy of a full and equal diaconate, a third order of Apostolic ministry for men and women, was thwarted when B. F. Westcott, Lightfoot's successor as bishop of Durham, commissioned the first deaconess (that is, not a woman deacon, and therefore not in the holy orders of the Church of England) in the diocese. This fell short of her objectives, but, undeterred, she wrote and distributed more pamphlets, the most important being *The dawn breaking, and some thoughts on the third order of St. Francis, with translation from the French* (1896), in which she argued the case for the revival of the Franciscan order in the Anglican communion.

Since the death of Lightfoot Emily Marshall had not been able to claim the authority of a bishop for her pioneering projects. This changed in 1893 when William Proctor Swaby, her brother-in-law, was consecrated bishop of Guiana. She had served a pastoral apprenticeship in his Sunderland parish, and with her assistance he fostered a Franciscan third order in his colonial diocese. In 1900 he was translated to the diocese of Barbados and the order grew rapidly there also. Fortunato Pietro Luigi Josa, an Italian priest, who became Swaby's archdeacon, the third order's priest-chaplain, and Miss Marshall's friend, brought the new Franciscan order into the public arena with the publication in England of *St. Francis of Assisi and the Third Order in the Anglo-Catholic Church* (1898). He paid tribute to the foundress without naming her and quoted extensively from her anonymous tracts. Miss Marshall meanwhile had recruited members in England and

abroad who joined the order with the consent of their parish priests. In 1901 she set up to protect the order an Inter-Provincial Council, which H. C. G. Moule, Westcott's successor at Durham, joined at her request. There are no complete extant lists of members but it seems that by the outbreak of the First World War there were several hundred Franciscan tertiaries (as the members now called themselves) distributed across the Anglican communion.

Miss Marshall died at her home, Whitcliffe Lodge, Ripon, Yorkshire, on 23 June 1915. Although others considered that she 'saw the desire of her heart being fulfilled' in that 'she did start anew' the Franciscan third order, which 'spread far and wide in the British Empire' (*The Guardian*), her own writings reveal her sadness that her *Suggestion for our Times* had not resulted in women being ordained to the diaconate.

ROSEMARY A. SHARPE

Sources [E. E. Marshall], *District visitors, deaconesses and a proposed adaptation, in part, of the third order*, 1st edn (1890) • [E. E. Marshall], *Deacons, deaconesses and a proposed adaptation, in part, of the third order of St. Francis, or, A proposed outer order for men and women living in the world*, 3rd edn (1891) • [E. E. Marshall], *The dawn breaking, and some thoughts on the third order of St. Francis, with translation from the French* (1896) • [E. E. Marshall], *Some thoughts on the third order of St. Francis, ancient and modern: with translations from the French by an Anglican* (1897) • [E. E. Marshall], *The parochial, or third order, (Anglican): thoughts and experiences, the order at work* (1901) • F. P. L. Josa, 'In memoriam Emily Esther Marshall', *Third Order Quarterly Magazine* (Aug 1915), 52–3 • *The Guardian* (8 July 1915) • R. A. Sharpe, 'Emily Marshall of Sunderland: a Victorian campaigner for women's work in Anglican parish life', *Antiquities of Sunderland*, 33 (1992), 1–14 • R. A. Sharpe, 'Franciscan values and social contexts: a sociological study of founders of Anglican Franciscan third orders, 1882–1939', PhD diss., U. Lond., 1993 • d. cert. • GL, MS 4402 • F. P. L. Josa, *St Francis of Assisi and the third order in the Anglo-Catholic church*, 1st edn (1898)

Wealth at death £14,832 15s. 5d.: probate, 4 Sept 1915, CGPLA Eng. & Wales

Marshall [*née* Martin], **Emma** (1828–1899), novelist, was born on 29 September 1828 at Northrepps Hill House, near Cromer, Norfolk, the youngest of the eight children of Simon Martin (1774–1839) and his wife, Hannah Ransome, a Quaker. Although a partner in Gurney & Co., a Quaker family bank based in Norwich, Simon Martin was not a member of the Society of Friends, in which denomination the Martin children were apparently brought up. During her happy (although rather solitary) childhood, Emma Martin was educated by a governess in the family home in Norwich. She later depicted her early youth in *The Dawn of Life* (1867), in which she relived the pain of her father's death when she was ten years old. The family subsequently moved to Thorpe, a village on the outskirts of the city, and Emma Martin was sent to a boarding-school where she received 'a sound education of the old-fashioned kind' (Marshall, 29). A keen musician, she afterwards took organ lessons with Zachariah Buck, the cathedral organist.

About 1849 the Martin household moved to Clifton, near Bristol, where their new friends included John Addington Symonds, a physician, who cultivated Emma's literary, artistic, and musical tastes. She also struck up a correspondence with the American poet Longfellow, which continued until his death. In March 1850 she was baptized into the Church of England by James Marshall (1796–1855): this may have been the prelude to her marriage, on 5 October 1854, to his son Hugh (c.1825–1899), a clerk in the West of England Bank. In 1855, when Marshall was appointed manager of the West of England branch there, the young couple moved to Wells. Seven of their nine children were born in Wells, but Emma Marshall's 'almost passionate maternity' (Marshall, 65–6) did not prevent her from embarking upon a career as a novelist; *Happy Days at Fernbank* (1861) was the first of nearly 200 tales. The story of the moral education of two little girls, it drew on Emma Marshall's own experience of everyday family life, as many of her works were to do. From 1868 she reached a wide audience with contributions to the evangelical periodicals edited by the Revd Charles Bullock (1829–1911), such as *Home Words* and the *Fireside News*.

In 1869 Hugh Marshall got a new post at Exeter and the family moved again. Here Emma Marshall began to visit the penitentiary every week to read to the girls and women there, and with the assistance of Jennetta Temple, sister of the bishop of Exeter, she established lectures for the higher education of women. It was at Temple's house that she met Charles E. Moberly (d. 1893), a master at Rugby School, who later featured as Mr Buchanan, the unusually elderly hero of *Life's Aftermath* (1876). In 1874 the Marshalls moved to Gloucester, following Hugh Marshall's appointment to a post there. Emma Marshall continued to arrange lectures for women (lecturers included T. H. Ward and J. A. Symonds) and enjoyed the triennial music festivals. Family finances had been tight for some time, following some unlucky investments, but upon the failure of the West of England Bank in 1878, Hugh Marshall lost his job and was left with large debts. Friends undertook to fund the education of the Marshall children, and the family moved to lodgings in Weston-super-Mare.

Emma Marshall, determined to clear the debts, now wrote at 'a white heat' (Marshall, 151). In 1880 she published the first of her historical romances, *Memories of Troublous Times*, in which the civil war reminiscences of the imaginary royalist Dame Alicia Chamberlayne were interspersed with the genuine seventeenth-century autobiography of a Quaker ancestor, Mary Penington. This literary experiment was not well received, and Emma Marshall returned to the publication of domestic tales until her leading publisher, Richard Seeley, suggested a romance based on the life of the seventeenth-century Bristol philanthropist Edward Colston. Published in 1884, this established the pattern for a series of historical novels, such as *Under Salisbury Spire* (1890) and *Penshurst Castle* (1894). She regarded her historical romances as the most important of her publications, but the amount of time and effort which they demanded was made possible only by a continued output of her domestic tales. These seem to have remained the more popular of her works with her considerable adolescent following: her works

were read in translation as far away as Russia, and Tauchnitz was to include thirty of her novels in his library.

In the early 1880s, after Hugh Marshall found clerical work, the family moved to Bristol. In this area Emma Marshall lived for the rest of her life. Several of her daughters attended Clifton High School for Girls, and Emma Marshall received boarders from the school. A keen promoter of women's education (her daughter Christabel [see St John, Christopher Marie] read history at Somerville College, Oxford), she was also a supporter of women's suffrage: in 1886 she published a pamphlet entitled *Thoughts on Women's Suffrage*, in which she argued persuasively for 'the true womanly element' which a female voter could bring to bear on party politics. When the central conference of the National Union of Women Workers was held in Bristol in 1892, she chaired a meeting and attended other sessions. Emma Marshall died on 4 May 1899 at Woodside, Leigh Woods, near Clifton, after an attack of influenza; she was buried in Long Ashton parish churchyard, Somerset, on 9 May. Hugh Marshall died later that year and was buried beside her.

For nearly forty years Emma Marshall was the consistently popular writer of tales for a range of juvenile audiences. The family sagas of C. M. Yonge were her strongest literary influence; like Yonge, she found her forte in depicting the moral education of a child or young adult within a family setting. Written in a straightforward and readable style, with plenty of incident, Marshall's tales lack in-depth psychological analysis of character. Her own liberal and optimistic religious faith prevented her from adopting fully the traditions of evangelical children's literature: bad ends, dramatic conversions, and pious deathbeds are few in Marshall's tales. Despite her ability to adapt to changing literary tastes (passages of moralizing grew fewer in her later works) and her keen eye for a topical theme—such as women's education in *Lady Alice* (1878) and the plight of street arabs in *Eastwood Ho!* (1890)—Marshall's central educative message remains much the same: self-knowledge and Christian care of others are portrayed as essential for a useful and happy life.

ROSEMARY MITCHELL

Sources B. Marshall, *Emma Marshall: a biographical sketch* (1900) · V. R. Hughes, 'The works of Mrs Emma Marshall in relationship to her life and the educational concepts of her time', PhD diss., U. Lpool, 1989
Likenesses Elliott & Fry, photograph, repro. in Marshall, *Emma Marshall*
Wealth at death £1379 10s. 11d.: probate, 3 Aug 1899, *CGPLA Eng. & Wales*

Marshall, Florence Ashton (1843–1922). *See under* Marshall, Julian (1836–1903).

Marshall, Francis [Frank] (1845–1906), rugby administrator and schoolmaster, was born on 19 September 1845 at Witton Lane, West Bromwich, Staffordshire, the son of John William Marshall, a schoolmaster, and his wife, Sarah Salt. He was educated at Brewood School, then entered St John's College, Cambridge, in 1864, graduating BA as thirty-eighth wrangler in the mathematical tripos in 1868. He proceeded MA in 1880. He was ordained in 1869 and between 1868 and 1870 was vice-principal of Carmarthen Training College. From 1870 to 1878 he was headmaster of Wednesbury Collegiate School and in 1878 was appointed head of King James's Grammar School in Almondbury, near Huddersfield, in Yorkshire.

Marshall was the embodiment of the late nineteenth-century quest for the purity of amateur ideals in rugby. His influence was such that the centenary history of the Rugby Football Union acclaimed him as 'one of the game's immortals'. He had played rugby as a schoolboy, but it was only when he took up the headmastership at Almondbury that he began to make his mark on the game. He became a well-respected referee, and was noted for occasionally smoking a cigar while refereeing. But it was following his election to the committee of the Yorkshire Rugby Union (YRU) in 1887 that he became most famous. Seeking to exorcize the evil of professionalism from rugby, Marshall helped to conduct more than twenty trials of clubs and players accused of professionalism, including two of the future England captain Dicky Lockwood. In 1890 he was elected president of the YRU.

Although initially supportive, Yorkshire rugby clubs discovered that the suspension of players and clubs caused by Marshall's campaign was incompatible with the business exigencies of running successful teams. Growing support for payments to players to compensate them for time lost from work—'broken time'—alienated Marshall from the leadership of Yorkshire rugby. In 1893 he was instrumental in helping to suspend his own club, Huddersfield, for breaches of rugby's amateur code, an act which estranged him from any remaining sympathizers in Yorkshire rugby union. In 1896 he left Almondbury to become rector of Mileham in Norfolk.

As a muscular Christian, Marshall was a firm believer in the importance of rugby in 'developing the physique, in influencing the character, and in improving the moral as well as the physical well being of the working man player' ('Payment for Broken Time at Rugby Football', *Athletic News Football Annual*, 1893). Unfortunately for Marshall, these values were rarely shared by their intended recipients and he found himself heckled at meetings, stoned by schoolboys, and, on one occasion, jostled at his local railway station.

To posterity Marshall is mainly remembered for his book *Football: the Rugby Union Game* (1892), still regarded as the definitive work on the history and development of rugby in the nineteenth century, combining Marshall's own work with contributions from many of the game's leading players and administrators. Although written to demonstrate the importance of the public schools to a game increasingly dominated by working-class players and spectators, the book is notable for the absence of any mention of William Webb Ellis, ostensibly the founder of rugby football. This apparent anomaly is explained by the fact that the book was published three years before the Old Rugbeian Society, on dubious grounds, ascribed to Ellis his place in history. Marshall was also the author of school textbooks on Shakespeare, Sir Walter Scott, Euclid,

and the Bible. He died at Mileham on 19 April 1906, following an operation. He was buried six days later at Mileham church, leaving a widow, Catharine Ann, the daughter of John E. Taylor of Almondbury.   TONY COLLINS

Sources G. Hinchliffe, *A history of King James's Grammar School in Almondbury* (1963) · *Yorkshire Post* (21 April 1906) · U. A. Titley and R. McWhirter, *Centenary history of the Rugby Football Union* (1970) · b. cert. · d. cert. · Venn, *Alum. Cant.*

Wealth at death £100: probate, 22 Dec 1906, *CGPLA Eng. & Wales*

Marshall, Francis Albert (1840–1889), playwright, was born at 41 Upper Grosvenor Street, London, on 18 November 1840, the fifth son of William Marshall (1796–1872) of Patterdale Hall and Hallstead, Westmorland, and his wife, Georgina Christiana (*d.* 1866), seventh daughter of George Hibbert of Munden, Hertfordshire. His father was MP for Petersfield (1826–30), for Carlisle (1835–47), and for East Cumberland (1847–65). Francis Marshall was educated at Harrow School, and matriculated from Exeter College, Oxford, on 14 June 1859, but did not take a degree. He was for some years a clerk in the Audit Office in Somerset House, but soon began contributing to newspapers and periodicals, and in 1868 resigned his appointment.

By this time, Marshall had already gained some reputation as a playwright, and afterwards became theatre critic for the *London Figaro*. His plays included farces, comic operas, comedies, and dramas, which were produced on the London stage between 1863 and 1887. His comedies *False Shame* (1872) and *Brighton* (1874) were among his best-known works. *Biohn*, a romantic opera in five acts, with music by Lauro Rossi (Queen's Theatre, 17 January 1877) featured his first wife, Imogene Fitzinman Marshall, as Elfrida, but was a failure. His first wife died on 19 February 1885. On 2 May 1885 he married Ada *Cavendish (1839?–1895), a well-known actress.

With William Gorman Wills, Marshall produced *Cora*, a drama in three acts (Globe Theatre, 28 February 1877). For his friend Henry Irving he wrote two pieces: a drama in four acts, founded on the history of Robert Emmet, and a version of *Werner*, adapted for the stage. The latter was produced at the Lyceum Theatre on the occasion of the benefit given to Westland Marston by Henry Irving on 1 June 1887. Marshall's *Robert Emmet* was never produced.

During his last years Marshall edited, with assistance from many scholars, a new edition of the works of Shakespeare, called the Henry Irving Edition, to which Henry Irving contributed an introduction. Marshall died of cirrhosis of the liver and jaundice at his home, 8 Bloomsbury Square, London, on 28 December 1889.

G. C. BOASE, *rev.* MEGAN A. STEPHAN

Sources *ILN* (18 Jan 1890), 70 · *The Times* (30 Dec 1889), 6 · Boase, *Mod. Eng. biog.*, 2.756 · Gillow, *Lit. biog. hist.*, 4.470–72 · Allibone, *Dict.* · *WWBMP*, vol. 1 · *The Tablet* (4 Jan 1890), 24 · b. cert. · m. cert. · d. cert.

Likenesses portrait (after photograph by Lambert, Watson & Son), repro. in *ILN*

Wealth at death £4536 2s.: probate, 5 Aug 1890, *CGPLA Eng. & Wales*

Marshall, George (*fl.* 1554), poet, is known only by one work, *A compendious treatise in metre declaring the firste originall of sacrifice, and of the buylding of aultares and churches,* *and of the firste receavinge of the Christen fayth here in Englande*, published at London by John Cawood, on 18 December 1554. Only the author's initials are on the title-page, but his full name is given by an acrostic in the preface. The work is dedicated to Mr Richarde Whartun esquire, who is described as a soldier and a good Catholic. This is presumably Richard Wharton, esquire, of Suffolk, who served in Mary Tudor's forces during her successful bid for the throne in 1553, and subsequently appeared on the Suffolk commission for the peace. The poem itself (fifty-nine eight-line stanzas rhyming *aabccbdd*) celebrates England's Catholic past and the restoration of Catholicism under Mary (who is likened to Judith and Esther). It excoriates the heresies of Wyclif and Luther, blames them for the recent prevalence of disease in England, and crows over the fate of Thomas Cromwell and John Dudley, who

> are to us example and warning
> To serve our lorde God, and obeye the Kynge.
> (Marshall)

Although the author describes himself as 'empty of learning' (Marshall), he refers to Bede, Josephus, and Eusebius, mentions Luther, Oecolampadius, Melanchthon, Bullinger, and Karlstadt, and alludes to the refutation of John Wyclif by William Woodford. Together with his reference to Henry VII, whose 'noble workes in Cambrydge you may se' (ibid.), this suggests that he may have been an educated man. In that case, while his name is hardly uncommon, it is tempting to identify him with the George Marshall who was allowed to graduate BA at Cambridge in 1532 after twelve terms of study at Oxford and Cambridge, and whose subsequent East Anglian connections are shown by his appointment as rector of Cockley Cley (Norfolk) on 18 July 1554. If he may also be identified with the George Marshall instituted to Long Stanton St Michael in 1555 on the presentation of the local gentleman Thomas Burgoyne (this parish usually went to a Cambridge graduate), then he was dead by 3 December 1558, when the benefice went to Dr William May.   RICHARD REX

Sources G. M. [G. Marshall], *A compendious treatise in metre* (1554) · Emden, *Oxf.* · W. G. Searle, ed., *Grace book Γ* (1908) · Ely diocesan registers, G/1/8 · *DNB*

Marshall, George William (1839–1905), genealogist, was born on 19 April 1839 at Ward End House, Aston juxta Birmingham, Warwickshire, the only surviving child of George Marshall (1794–1855), a Birmingham banker, and only child of his second wife, Eliza Henshaw Comberbach (1799–1883). His paternal antecedents had been settled for several generations at Perlethorpe, Nottinghamshire. Educated initially at Radley College (1850–51), he entered Magdalene College, Cambridge, in 1857 and moved to Peterhouse in 1859. He graduated LLB in 1861, and proceeded LLM in 1864 and LLD in 1874. At Cambridge he became a freemason, an interest he was to continue subsequently. He entered the Middle Temple in 1862, was called to the bar on 9 June 1865, and for some time practised on the Oxford circuit.

On 26 September 1867 Marshall married Alice Ruth Hall (1843–1870), youngest daughter of the Revd Ambrose William Hall with whom he had two sons and one daughter.

He married second on 28 May 1872 his deceased wife's elder sister, Caroline Emily Hall (1842–1891), with whom he had six sons and two daughters.

Genealogy was Marshall's lifelong study from his Cambridge days. Apart from articles in periodicals his earliest publication was *Collections for a Genealogical Account of the Family of Comberbach* (his mother's family) in 1866. This was the first of a number of books on families to which he was related, the most extensive being the two-volume *Miscellanea Marescalliana* (1883–8). He registered his paternal pedigree at the College of Arms in 1868, having in 1867 been granted arms with an extension of limitations to the other descendants of his grandfather William Marshall, a banker in Birmingham.

A member of the council of the Harleian Society from its foundation in 1869, he edited two volumes of the society's publications—volume 4, *The Visitations of Nottinghamshire in 1569 and 1614* (1871), and volume 8, *Le Neve's Pedigrees of Knights* (1873)—and two further visitations: *Northumberland, 1615* (1878), and *Wiltshire, 1623* (1882). In 1872 Marshall was elected a fellow of the Society of Antiquaries. He founded *The Genealogist* in 1877 and edited the first seven volumes of the periodical (1877–83). His chief work was *The Genealogist's Guide* which in his lifetime ran to four editions: 1879, 1885, 1893, and 1903. It contained an alphabetical list by surname of printed pedigrees of British families; he defined a pedigree as any descent of three generations in the male line. The value of it can be adduced from the fact that the original work was updated by the issue of a four-volume supplement edited by J. B. Whitmore (Harleian Society, 1947–52) and a further supplement by G. B. Barrow (1977). Marshall's *Handbook to the Ancient Courts of Probate* (1889; 2nd edn 1895) and his list of printed parish registers (privately printed 1891, with subsequent editions) were his other principal genealogical publications of a general nature. He also edited six Nottinghamshire parish registers between 1887 and 1896 and in 1896 was one of the founders of the Parish Register Society.

On 6 September 1887 Marshall was appointed Rouge Croix pursuivant, bringing the number then of qualified barristers at the College of Arms to three, the others being G. E. Cokayne (1825–1911) and W. A. Lindsay (1846–1926). In 1889 he was a member of a College of Arms committee which recommended stricter rules on the acceptance of evidence for pedigree registration. In the same year he gave his collection of printed parish registers to the College of Arms and was appointed librarian of the printed parish registers. He encouraged the purchase of manuscripts for the College of Arms at sales of the collections of Sir Thomas Phillipps in the 1890s and his suggestion for the construction of a fireproof muniment room in the basement of the College of Arms was approved in 1894. His generosity in support of the college library when he was an officer of arms was second only to that of G. E. Cokayne. He was promoted York herald on 18 August 1904 though serious illness (almost certainly rectal cancer) prevented him from reading out his patent, and he died on 12

September 1905 at Holmbush, his house in Upper Richmond Road, Barnes, Surrey. He was buried at Sarnesfield, near Weobley, Herefordshire, on 16 September 1905. On his death he left to the corporation of the College of Arms any of his manuscripts in his office which the corporation might be pleased to select.

Marshall purchased the Sarnesfield Court estate in 1891 and was high sheriff of Herefordshire in 1902. Outside genealogy his interest lay in the improvement of his property, he was fond of shooting, and his great collection of Chinese armorial porcelain remained at Sarnesfield until dispersed in 1978. A keen and truth-seeking antiquary, with an intuitive power of research, he had a lawyer's love of conciseness and accuracy. J. P. Rylands described him as 'a cheerful and genial host, blessed with a keen sense of humour … his really kindly disposition largely concealed under a quite undemonstrative exterior led him to perform many friendly acts' (*The Genealogist*, new series, 22, 1906).   THOMAS WOODCOCK

Sir Guy Anstruther Knox Marshall (1871–1959), by Walter Stoneman, 1930

Sources *The Genealogist*, new ser., 22 (1905–6), 198–202 · pedigrees, Coll. Arms, 18D14, 22; Surrey 2, 78; Surrey 5, 204; Norfolk 12, 89 · *Miscellanea Genealogica et Heraldica*, 2 (1869–76), 62–9 · W. H. Godfrey, A. Wagner, and H. Stanford London, *The College of Arms, Queen Victoria Street* (1963), 191 · A. Wagner, *Heralds of England: a history of the office and College of Arms* (1967), 533 · A. R. Wagner, *The records and collections of the College of Arms* (1952), 51 · *The Times* (15 Sept 1905) · *The Times* (18 Sept 1905) · P. Reid, *Burke's and Savills guide to country houses*, 2 (1980), 56 · *DNB* · d. cert.

Archives Coll. Arms, corresp. and collections · Herefs. RO, antiquarian and historical notes, family papers, and photographs · Herefs. RO, corresp. and papers · S. Antiquaries, Lond., notes relating to bastardy

Likenesses Levine?, oils, 1884?, Coll. Arms · photograph, *c*.1904 (in tabard), repro. in *The Genealogist*, frontispiece

Wealth at death £216,966 18*s*. 8*d*.: probate, 23 Nov 1905, *CGPLA Eng. & Wales*

Marshall, Sir Guy Anstruther Knox (1871–1959), entomologist, was born on 20 December 1871, in Amritsar, Punjab, the only son of Charles Henry Tilson Marshall, Bengal staff corps, and his wife, Laura Frances, daughter of Sir Jonathan Frederick *Pollock, first baronet. Both his father and his uncle, a major-general in the Royal Engineers, were keen naturalists. Marshall's father was joint author with A. O. Hume of *The Game Birds of India, Burmah and Ceylon* (3 vols., 1879–81), and his uncle wrote *Birds' Nesting in India* (1877), and about the butterflies of India, Burma, and Ceylon.

Marshall was sent at an early age to a preparatory school at Margate, where his interest in natural history was further stimulated by his headmaster. At Charterhouse (on the governing body of which he later served) he transferred his attentions from butterflies to beetles, considered a less eccentric hobby. He failed the Indian Civil Service examinations to his father's disappointment but perhaps not greatly to his own. His father's reaction was to pack him off at the age of nineteen to a sheep farmer in Natal; for the next fifteen years he had a most varied career, leaving the sheep farm to become a cattle man and later to join a firm of mining engineers in Salisbury, Rhodesia. Finally he became co-manager of the Salisbury Building and Estates Company.

Despite these activities Marshall maintained his interest in entomology. By 1896 he was in touch with Edward Poulton, Hope professor of zoology at Oxford, who encouraged him to carry out a series of experiments on mimicry and protective resemblance, the results of which appeared under their joint authorship in the *Transactions of the Entomological Society of London* in 1902. It was presumably through Poulton's influence that Marshall was appointed curator of the Sarawak Museum in 1906, but on his way there he was taken ill in London with a complaint contracted in Africa and had to relinquish the post.

In 1909 Marshall was appointed scientific secretary to the Entomological Research Committee (Tropical Africa) by the secretary of state for the colonies. It was from this committee that there evolved in 1913 the Imperial Bureau (later the Commonwealth Institute) of Entomology of which Marshall was director until he retired in 1942. Soon after the bureau came into being, the First World War broke out and Marshall's energy, foresight, and guidance helped it to survive this critical period. The function of the bureau was to act as a centre of information on all matters relating to insect pests, and so successfully was this carried out that it formed the model on which two new institutes and ten bureaux covering all branches of agricultural science were subsequently based. All these information services were brought together in 1933 under an organization later known as the Commonwealth Agricultural Bureaux.

It was in 1933 that Marshall married Hilda Margaret (*d.* 1964), daughter of David Alexander Maxwell, and widow of James Ffolliott Darling. They had no children.

Marshall advised the Colonial Office on entomological matters between the two world wars and thus influenced the development of economic entomology; he was always ready to welcome and assist entomologists from the colonies. He was well known personally or by repute to entomologists throughout the world. These contacts enabled him to amass an encyclopaedic knowledge of both world entomology and entomologists.

Marshall's career was remarkable in that he received no formal education in science. Moreover, he did not take up entomology as a profession until the age of thirty-eight, but his family background, coupled with his enthusiastic amateur spare-time work, stood him in good stead.

Consequently he was not unduly impressed by academic degrees, despite the fact that the University of Oxford conferred an honorary DSc on him in 1915. He believed that commercial companies and insecticide manufacturers should employ their own entomologists, and his influence did much to raise the standard of insecticide products. In later years he developed an interest in commercial entomology and founded one of the first companies for pest control, which occupied him for some years after his retirement.

After he left Africa in 1906 Marshall's personal research work was almost exclusively taxonomic. He had a wide knowledge of all groups of insects but he came to specialize on the beetles of the family Curculionidae. This particular field was chosen for him by the curious accident that when he returned to England on leave in 1896 the greater part of his beetle collection was lost in transit and only the Curculionidae, packed separately, survived. He was therefore able to study only this weevil material at the British Museum during his leave. Subsequently he published some 200 papers on the Curculionidae, including several major works, and he described some 2300 species new to science. He was an acknowledged authority on this family, on which he continued to work at the Natural History Museum, until a very few weeks before his death at his home, 31 Melton Court, London, on 8 April 1959.

Marshall was an able administrator, who believed in delegating responsibility and seldom interfered unless it became necessary, or his advice was sought; he was most approachable. He was of medium height, compact build, and distinguished appearance; he never sought publicity and was of a retiring disposition. He consistently refused to accept the presidency of the Royal Entomological Society of London. He was elected FRS in 1923 and was an honorary member of many overseas societies. He was appointed CMG in 1920, knighted in 1930, and advanced to KCMG in 1942; and he received the Belgian order of the Crown.

W. J. HALL, *rev.*

Sources W. R. Thompson, *Memoirs FRS*, 6 (1960), 169–81 · *Annals and Magazine of Natural History*, 13th ser., 1 (1958), 753–4 · *Nature*, 183 (1959), 1364 · W. T. Stearn, *The Natural History Museum at South Kensington: a history of the British Museum (Natural History), 1753–1980* (1981) · *CGPLA Eng. & Wales* (1959)

Archives Oxf. U. Mus. NH, letters to Sir E. B. Poulton · Oxf. U. Mus. NH, letters to G. H. Verrall and J. E. Collin · Royal Entomological Society of London, letters to Roland Trimen with related notes; letters to C. J. Wainwright

Likenesses W. Stoneman, photographs, 1930–46, NPG [*see illus.*] · black and white photograph, repro. in Thompson, *Memoirs FRS*, 169

Wealth at death £63,401 10s. 2d.: probate, 28 May 1959, *CGPLA Eng. & Wales*

Marshall, Henry (1775–1851), military surgeon, was born on 23 November 1775 at Kilsyth, Stirlingshire, the son of John Marshall, a farmer. He studied medicine at Glasgow College, and in May 1803 was appointed surgeon's mate in the Royal Navy. In January 1805 he left the navy and became assistant surgeon to the Forfarshire regiment of militia; in April 1806 he moved to the 89th regiment. With the latter he served in Buenos Aires, at the Cape of Good Hope, and in Ceylon.

In 1809 Marshall was gazetted as assistant surgeon to the 2nd Ceylon regiment, and in 1813 he was promoted surgeon of the 1st Ceylon regiment. He served in the Second Kandyan War (1815–18), and in 1817 his botanical observations on Ceylon's main export, cinnamon, were read before the Royal Society by Sir Joseph Banks. This work was characterized by the accurate observation and attention to detail common to his later publications on military matters. In 1821 he published a book on the medical topography of Ceylon, and that same year he returned home and served as staff surgeon in Edinburgh and at Chatham. In 1825 he supervised the medical inspection of recruits at Dublin. He was promoted to the position of deputy inspector-general of hospitals in 1830, shortly before his retirement. In 1832 he married Anne (1801–1890), eldest daughter of James Wingate of Westshiels, Roxburghshire.

Marshall was deeply interested in statistics, and many of his writings were concerned with comparative statistical analyses of disease and mortality among the troops of different military stations. He used statistics to highlight the conditions of service endured by the common soldier. In 1835, with A. M. Tulloch, he made an investigation of the health of the troops in the West Indies, the findings of which laid the foundation for improvements in the sanitary conditions of the troops. Marshall became known as the father of medical statistics. In 1828 he published his *Hints to Young Medical Officers of the Army on the Examination of Recruits*, in which he described forms of malingering and feigning of disease popular among the troops. The *Edinburgh Medical and Surgical Journal* recommended this book to all medical officers in the army. Four years later Marshall wrote another book dealing with the enlistment and pensioning of soldiers. He argued that the conditions of the army actively encouraged malingering. Soldiers were enlisted for life and the only means of discharge was through disability. He thus urged the implementation of a new scheme where soldiers could obtain pensions through good conduct and length of service. This new attitude towards the soldier was reflected in the pension warrant of 1833 and in subsequent warrants. Marshall was elected a fellow of the Royal Society of Edinburgh in 1839.

Marshall was instrumental in improving the conditions of the soldier both in service and in retirement. He campaigned for shorter service, better general and sanitary education of the troops, and the reduction of brutal punishments such as flogging and branding. His work in this area gained widespread attention in 1847, when a soldier died from injuries received as a result of whipping. Marshall was not just a medical reformer, but an army reformer. In 1847 he received an honorary MD degree from the University of the State of New York. He contributed regularly to the *Edinburgh Medical and Surgical Journal* and the *United Service Journal*. He died in Edinburgh after a prolonged illness on 5 May 1851, and was buried in Dean cemetery, Edinburgh.

GEORGE STRONACH, *rev.* CLAIRE E. J. HERRICK

Sources R. L. Blanco, 'Henry Marshall (1775–1851) and the health of the British army', *Medical History*, 14 (1970), 260–76 · T. James, 'The Cape and Sir Henry Marshall', *South African Medical Journal*, 48 (1974), 63–4 · *Edinburgh Medical and Surgical Journal*, 76 (1851), 264, 489–92 · N. Cantlie, *A history of the army medical department*, 1 (1974), 449–51 · N. Cantlie, *A history of the army medical department*, 2 (1974), 392–4 · A. Peterkin and W. Johnston, *Commissioned officers in the medical services of the British army, 1660–1960*, 1 (1968), 173 · Chambers, *Scots.* (1835) · J. Brown, 'Dr Henry Marshall and military hygiene', *Horae subsecivae*, 1 (1858)
Likenesses D. Macnee, oils, Scot. NPG
Wealth at death over £4400; left papers to Dr John Brown, for editing, compilation, or possible publication: Blanco, 'Henry Marshall', 275

Marshall, Henry Dickenson (1840–1906). *See under* Marshall family (*per.* 1848–1922).

Marshall, Herbert Brough Falcon (1890–1966), actor, was born on 23 May 1890 at 36 Fitzroy Road, Primrose Hill, London, the son of Percy Falcon Marshall, comedian, and his wife, Ethel May Turner. He was educated privately and at St Mary's College, Harlow, Essex, after which he was engaged as an articled clerk with a firm of chartered accountants in the City. He became the business manager of impresario Robert Courtneidge before making his acting début at the Opera House, Buxton, as a servant in *The Adventure of Lady Ursula* by Anthony Hope (1911). His London début was at the Prince's Theatre as Tommy in *Brewster's Millions*, the comedy by G. B. McCutcheon, W. Smith, and B. Ongley (1913), after which he toured the United States and Canada with Cyril Maude's company. He served in the British expeditionary force during the First World War but lost a leg. Subsequently, although he had a slightly stiff walk, his career was unaffected. On 14 August 1915 he married Hilda Lloyd Bosley, known as Mollie Maitland; they were later divorced.

After the war Marshall initially joined the company of the Lyric Theatre, Hammersmith, but soon became a popular and busy West End star. Additionally he toured the United States and Canada with Marie Lohr (1921), and appeared in New York in *The Voice from the Minaret* by R. S. Hichens and *Fedora* by H. Merivale (both 1922), and *These*

Charming People (1925). He played Prince Keri in Noël Coward's *The Queen was in the Parlour* in London at the St Martin's (1926) and was in New York again, in *The High Road*, a comedy by Frederick Lonsdale (1928), with Edna Best (1900–1974). She became his second wife in 1928. Marshall and Best became a popular team, both on stage (*Michael and Mary* and F. Molnar's *The Swan*, both 1930, and *There's always Juliet*, 1931–2), and on screen. Marshall's film début was *Mumsie* (1927) but it was his performance as the lover in *The Letter* (1929), made in Hollywood from Somerset Maugham's novel, which attracted attention and led to a contract with Paramount Studios. The Marshalls had film commitments in Britain: he was excellent in Alfred Hitchcock's *Murder* (1930), and together they appeared in *Michael and Mary* and *The Calendar* (both 1931) and *The Faithful Heart* (1932). Back at Paramount he was suddenly starring in big films opposite major actresses—in Josef von Sternberg's *Blonde Venus* with Marlene Dietrich and as the suave jewel thief in Ernst Lubitsch's wonderful *Trouble in Paradise* with Miriam Hopkins and Kay Francis (both 1932).

During the 1930s Marshall starred with many of Hollywood's leading actresses. 'He was urbane, soft-spoken and somewhat distant, but he let the ladies act rings round him—except perhaps in comedy, where his skill added much to the sophistication of some of the screen's best pieces' (Shipman, 369–70). Certainly his polish and assurance enabled him to appear well at ease in any setting of culture and gentility. Among the highlights were *Riptide* with Norma Shearer and *The Painted Veil* with Greta Garbo (both 1934), *If You Could Only Cook* with Jean Arthur, William Wyler's excellent *The Good Fairy* with Margaret Sullavan, and *The Dark Angel* with Merle Oberon (all 1935), *A Woman Rebels* with Katharine Hepburn (1936), *Breakfast for Two* with Barbara Stanwyck (1937), and *Mad about Music* with Deanna Durbin (1938). He also appeared back on the stage, in Santa Barbara, California, alongside Helen Hayes in *Ladies and Gentlemen* (1939). Marshall's second marriage, which had produced a daughter, later the actress Sarah Marshall, broke up in the mid-1930s, leading to divorce in 1940. In the same year he married Elizabeth Russell, known as Lee. They, too, had a daughter.

Marshall then enjoyed a brief purple patch, being in Hitchcock's splendid *Foreign Correspondent* and Wyler's remake of *The Letter*, although this time as the cuckolded husband (both 1940). He also appeared in William Wyler's film *The Little Foxes* from Lillian Hellman's play (1941), and played the narrator in the film adaptation of Somerset Maugham's *The Moon and Sixpence* (1942) but this was virtually his last leading role. Marshall's natural reserve, his mannered style, and his age were forcing him into character roles, although his charm and his cultured voice ensured that he remained busy. He was one of over eighty chiefly British stars of *Forever and a Day* (1943), appeared (for the first time on screen with a walking stick and a limp) in *The Enchanted Cottage* (1945), and also in the underrated *Crack-up* (1946). He was again cast as Somerset Maugham in a film version of that author's philosophical novel *The Razor's Edge*, and was in David O. Selznick's epic production, *Duel in the Sun* (both 1946). In an excellent film adaptation of *The Secret Garden* by Frances Hodgson Burnett he played the unfeeling guardian (1949). *The Underworld Story* was his first 'B' film (1950). He also starred in the radio series *The Man called X* (1944–52), hosted the television series *The Unexpected* (1952), and made a number of other television appearances through the 1950s. After a divorce from Lee Russell, in 1947 he married the actress Patricia Mallory (1913–1958) (known professionally as Boots Mallory), with whom he had a third daughter. Better films in his final decade of film-making were *The Virgin Queen* as Robert Dudley, earl of Leicester, opposite Bette Davis's Elizabeth (1955), *The Fly* and Sidney Lumet's *Stage Struck* (both 1958), *Midnight Lace* (1960), and John Huston's gimmicky *The List of Adrian Messenger* and *The Caretakers* (both 1963). His final film was *The Third Day* (1965). Marshall divorced Mallory (who died in 1958) and married again in 1960; his fifth wife was Dee Anne Kahmann. He died of a heart attack on 22 January 1966 in Beverly Hills, Los Angeles, California. His wife survived him.

ROBERT SHARP

Sources D. Shipman, *The great movie stars: the golden years* (1970) · *The Times* (24 Jan 1966), 12g · WWW · www.uk.imdb.com, 15 Jan 2001 · F. Gaye, ed., *Who's who in the theatre*, 14th edn (1967) · b. cert. · m. cert. [Hilda Lloyd Bosley]

Marshall, Howard Percival (1900–1973), broadcaster and writer on sport, was born on 22 August 1900 at Leicester Villa, Mulgrave Road, Sutton, Surrey, the only son of Percival Marshall, an editor and later a publisher, and his wife, Zoe Beatrice, *née* Bridger. He was educated at Haileybury College and entered Oriel College, Oxford, in January 1920. A keen sportsman with a strong build, Marshall played cricket for the Oxford Authentics club and was in the university tug-of-war team at Olympia in 1921. His principal interest was rugby and he won his blue as a second row in the 1921 varsity match, the first to be played at Twickenham, which was won by Oxford. He later played for the Harlequins club, the Barbarians, and the South, and came close to winning an England cap. On leaving university (without taking a degree) Marshall worked as a special correspondent for a number of newspapers, including the *Daily Telegraph*, *Daily Mail*, and *Westminster Gazette*. He married, on 1 October 1925, Ruth ffolliott Shackle (b. 1902/3), daughter of Edward Neild Shackle, an estate agent; they had two sons. In 1927 he joined the British Broadcasting Corporation, where he became assistant news editor in 1928, and, from 1930, was sports and special events commentator. His forte was radio cricket commentary, where his 'soft, purring voice' was ideal for filling the gaps in play; it was said that 'he could make the listener see the grass growing' (Warner, 55).

During the 1930s Marshall was involved in the national campaign against slum housing. With Alice Trevelyan he wrote *Slum* (1933), an exploration of the problem and possible solutions. Marshall regarded the shortage of decent housing for the poor as 'a national emergency' which could be met only by creating a government-backed 'national housing corporation' to encourage house construction, maintenance, and repair (p. 165). He also sat on the advisory council of a public utility society dedicated to house-building in the Isle of Dogs. It was an area, he observed, 'inhabited by people who are facing unemployment and poverty with amazing pluck and good-humour' (H. Marshall, *Isle of Dogs Housing Society*, 1938).

During the Second World War Marshall was director of public relations at the Ministry of Food (1940–43) and director of war reporting with the BBC (1943–5). As a war correspondent he followed the north Africa campaign, described in his book *Over to Tunis* (1943), and the invasion of Europe. After his first marriage ended in divorce Marshall married, on 10 March 1944, Elizabeth Nerina (b. 1908/9), the daughter of Cameron Shute, and the divorced wife of James Wentworth *Day. He subsequently married again; his third wife's name was Jasmine Lydia.

In his day Marshall was the country's 'most famous radio voice', and his long career included commentary on the coronation of both George VI, in 1937, and Elizabeth II, in 1953 (*The Times*, 29 Oct 1973). On the latter occasion he worked alongside John Snagge. He was also a prolific author and editor of books on exploration and sport, including *With Scott to the Pole* (1936), *Rugger Stories* (1932), *Great Boxing Stories* (1936), *Coronation Day* (1953), and *Men Against Everest* (1954). One of the best was *Rugger* (1927), written with the great England forward W. W. Wakefield ('Wakers', as he was introduced to readers), against whom Marshall had played in the 1921 varsity match. *Rugger* expounds the spirit of the game as it was viewed between the wars: a form of 'friendly and controlled war, if such a conception be possible', breeding 'hardiness, which in these days of cocktails and lounge-lizards is a quality to be encouraged' (p. 106). The section on equipment included a warning about boot studs wearing down and exposing the retaining nails, 'thus becoming a danger to other players, on whom you may trample' (p. 115). The wearing of shin-pads, it was suggested, was not a sign of cowardice. But if such hearty sentiments have a period ring to them, the emphasis on the need for all fifteen players to be 'complete footballers' sounds thoroughly modern and anticipates the ethos of the professional era.

Marshall was also a keen angler and was co-founder of *Angling Times* and *Trout and Salmon*. After the war he developed a career in public relations, and was director of personnel and public relations with Richard Thomas and Baldwins Ltd (1945–64). He died on 27 October 1973 at Newbury District Hospital, Newbury, Berkshire. His third wife survived him.

MARK POTTLE

Sources *The Times* (29 Oct 1973) · A. R. McWhirter and A. Noble, *Centenary history of Oxford University Rugby Football Club* (1969) · WWW · H. Marshall and J. P. Jordan, *Oxford v Cambridge: the story of the university rugby match* (1951) · H. Marshall, *Over to Tunis: the complete story of the north African campaign* (1943) · P. Warner, *The Harlequins: 125 years of rugby football* (1991) · b. cert. · m. certs. [Ruth ffolliott Shackle, Elizabeth Nerina Wentworth Day] · d. cert.

Archives FILM BFI NFTVA, sports footage | SOUND BL NSA, 'Howard Marshall', T6395BWC2 · BL NSA, documentary recording · BL NSA, performance recording

Marshall, James (1796–1855), Church of England clergyman, was born at Rothesay, Bute, on 23 February 1796, the son of Hugh Marshall, a doctor, and his wife, Elizabeth

Wilson. When Dr Marshall died, in 1806, the family removed to Paisley. James was educated at Paisley grammar school and subsequently at the universities of Glasgow and Edinburgh. On 2 September 1818 he was licensed to preach by the presbytery of Glasgow, and after assisting his mother's friend Dr Robert Balfour at the Outer High Church, Glasgow, succeeded to Balfour's charge at his death in 1819. Marshall married in 1822 Catherine Mary, daughter of Legh Richmond, rector of Turvey, Bedfordshire. Sir James *Marshall (1829–1889), convert to Rome and colonial judge, was their son. In 1828 Marshall was appointed by the Edinburgh town council to the Tolbooth Church, Edinburgh. Marshall was an effective preacher, and as a young man he attracted the favourable notice of Thomas Chalmers in that capacity. His calm demeanour in the pulpit strikingly contrasted with the vehemence commonly characteristic of the Scottish clergy.

Although for some years Marshall generally sympathized with the opponents of the establishment in the controversy which led to the Disruption in 1843, he disliked the extremities to which what became the Free Church party seemed to be committing itself. Ultimately he embraced episcopacy, which (encouraged perhaps by his wife's family) he had convinced himself was the only scriptural form of church government, and severed his connection with the Scottish church. He sent his resignation to the presbytery of Edinburgh on 29 September 1841, and, after being confirmed by the bishop of Edinburgh, was ordained on 19 December 1841 by the bishop of Durham as curate to Canon Gilly at Norham. He took priest's orders on 6 February 1842, and was appointed to the rectory of St Mary-le-Port, Bristol. In 1845 Marshall became secretary to the newly founded Lay Readers' Association, which he energetically developed for many years. In May 1847 he was appointed by the Simeon trustees to the living of Christ Church, Clifton, which he held until his death.

Marshall published, besides sermons and addresses, *Inward Revival, or, Motives and Hindrances to Advancement in Holiness* (1840) and *Early Piety Illustrated in the Life and Death of a Young Parishioner* (n.d.), both of which had a large circulation. He also edited *The Letters of the Late Mrs Isabella Graham of New York* (1839), his aunt. After three years' ill health Marshall died on 29 August 1855 at his house in Vyvyan Terrace, Clifton, and was buried on 4 September in the Clifton parish church burial-ground.

G. Le G. Norgate, rev. H. C. G. Matthew

Sources J. Marshall, *A memoir of the Rev. James Marshall* (1857) • *Bristol Mercury* (1 Sept 1855) • *Bristol Mercury* (8 Sept 1855) • *Clifton Chronicle* (5 Sept 1855) • *GM*, 2nd ser., 44 (1855), 551 • *Fasti Scot.* • bap. reg. Scot.
Archives U. Edin., New Coll. L., letters to Thomas Chalmers

Marshall, Sir James (1829–1889), colonial judge, the son of James *Marshall (1796–1855), vicar of Christ Church, Clifton, Bristol, and his wife, Catherine Mary Richmond, was born at Edinburgh on 19 December 1829. The loss of his right arm through a gun accident prevented his joining the army, and, after graduating from Exeter College, Oxford, in 1854 he took holy orders almost immediately, and for two years held a curacy. In November 1857 he joined the Roman Catholic church, and as his physical handicap debarred him from being a priest he became procurator and precentor in the church at Bayswater, London. Later he was for a time a private tutor, and in 1863 he became classical master at Birmingham Oratory School, where he became a friend of Cardinal Newman. In 1866 he was called to the bar at Lincoln's Inn. He joined the northern circuit, and eventually settled in Manchester.

In May 1873 Marshall was appointed chief magistrate of the Gold Coast and assessor to the native chiefs. When the Second Anglo-Asante War broke out in 1873, he negotiated the agreement of the chiefs to the recruiting of their people, and was of great use throughout the campaign in raising levies. He received the special thanks of the secretary of state, and later the Ashanti medal. In 1875 he was stationed at Lagos, and in November 1876 he was promoted to be senior puisne judge of the supreme court of the Gold Coast. In October 1877 he married Alice, the daughter of C. Guillym Young of Corby, Lincolnshire. In 1879 he became chief justice, and on his retirement in 1882 he was knighted. In 1886 he was executive commissioner for the west African colonies at the Indian and Colonial Exhibition and was created CMG. The following year he once more went abroad to Africa for a few months, as chief justice of the territories of the Royal Niger Company. He died at Margate on 9 August 1889.

C. A. Harris, rev. Lynn Milne

Sources *The Times* (14 Aug 1889) • W. R. Brownlow, *Memoir of Sir James Marshall* (1890) • *Colonial Office List* (1882) • private information (1893) • *CGPLA Eng. & Wales* (1889)
Wealth at death £2113 7s. 6d.: probate, 8 Nov 1889, *CGPLA Eng. & Wales*

Marshall, James (1836–1922). *See under* Marshall family (*per.* 1848–1922).

Marshall, Jane. *See* Marshall, Jean (*fl.* 1765–1788).

Marshall, John (1642–1677), Indian scholar, was the third son of Ralph Marshall and of his wife, Abigail, daughter of Robert Rogers of Netherthorpe, Yorkshire. He was baptized at East Theddlethorpe, Lincolnshire, on 1 March 1642, and was educated at Louth, also in Lincolnshire, at the school of a Mr Skelton. He matriculated at Christ's College, Cambridge, in December 1660, taking his BA in 1664. Although a person of scholarly inclination, he left Cambridge in January 1668, being unable to hold a fellowship at Christ's because the college could not appoint two fellows from the same county and already had one from Essex, where Marshall's family now lived. Having 'a great desire to travell', he applied to enter the service of the East India Company (*John Marshall in India*, 39). Through the influence of his elder brother he was appointed a factor in the company's service on the Coromandel coast of southeastern India, where he arrived in September 1668 after a nine-month voyage on one of the company's ships. The following year he moved up the coast to Balasore in Orissa, one of the company's trading posts in what was then called The Bay, that is the region round the Bay of Bengal. He was to live out the rest of his life in the company's Bay settlements, serving mainly at Balasore, at Patna in Bihar, and at Hooghly and the silk-producing centre of Cossimbazar in lower Bengal.

In all his postings Marshall seems generally to have earned the respect of his colleagues for the manner in which he managed the company's commercial business in obtaining cotton cloth, silk, and saltpetre to be shipped to England or dealt on its behalf with local officials, although his 'naturall modesty, calme disposition, and soft (though quick) utterance of speech' (Foster, 306) meant that he was thought to lack the necessary 'audacity' (ibid.) to hold his own in a major Indian court. He was clearly a fine linguist, proficient in Persian, Arabic, and 'Hindostand' (presumably Hindi or Urdu). He was at least aware of Sanskrit and able to give a specimen of its script, which he 'writ from the Bramin Doctor in Pattana' (*John Marshall in India*, 423).

Marshall was not only a conscientious servant of the company, but he was also intensely interested in the surroundings in which he lived, and his linguistic abilities were such that he was able to communicate easily with Indians in order to elicit information from them and obtain texts. The legacy of his interests is a deposit of manuscripts, consisting of translations and of 'notes and observations', apparently intended for his old friends at Cambridge. Nothing of Marshall's, apart from an essay in the form of a letter later published in the *Philosophical Transactions of the Royal Society*, appeared in print before the twentieth century, and thus what was the most significant body of material about India to be brought to Britain before James Fraser's collection was acquired by Oxford in the mid-eighteenth century remained largely unknown to contemporaries.

Marshall was especially interested in religion. Whereas knowledge of other religions shook the faith of some of his contemporaries, Marshall wrote that he had always had 'a profound Veneration for the Dictates of Nature, and the universal Traditions of Nations, for thereby are infinite things to be learned for the establishing of our Glorious Religion against Atheists, and the more easie propagation of the same amongst Infidels and Heathens' ('Letter from the East Indies', 729). He records a number of discussions with Muslims, but his main efforts were to elucidate Hinduism. Here his principal informant seems to have been a Brahman at Cossimbazar called 'Muddoosoodun Raure' (Madhusudhana Radha), who gave him a Persian version of the *Bhagavad purana*, one of the most revered texts of Vaishnavite Hinduism, which Marshall translated in six instalments between 1674 and 1677. Madhusudhana also gave him a version of the Sama Veda or 'Epicomie of the sum of the four Beads [Vedas] or the most materiall things in them' to translate. Also surviving is Marshall's English version of 'A familiar and free Dialogue' with Madhusudhana about Hindu beliefs and such questions as 'How shall I know that before the world was, God was?' (BL, Harleian MS 4253, fol. 3). Marshall concluded from his inquiries that Hindus were monotheists who acknowledge 'the being of a mighty God' and did not deserve condemnation as 'Barbarians, Heathens and Idolaters' ('Letter from the East Indies', 729-32).

Marshall's two manuscript books of 'notes and observations' are extremely diverse. They include more about religious beliefs and much else besides, such as natural history, topography, customs, astrology, and medical practices. He set down without comment 'a great many Secrets in Physick' and 'many Traditions and Stories' that he had learned from his informants. He was, however, unimpressed by Indian 'Learning and Knowledge', which he dismissed as 'but little' and full of 'Absurdities and Cabalistick Complications of Figures' ('Letter from the East Indies', 737). Marshall died at Balasore, where he was in charge of the company's affairs, on 31 August 1677 after a short illness. Evidently he never married and had no children. P. J. MARSHALL

Sources *John Marshall in India: notes and observations in Bengal*, ed. S. A. Khan (1927) · W. Foster, ed., *The English factories in India*, 13 (1927) · C. Fawcett, ed., *The English factories in India*, new ser., 2 (1952) · 'A letter from the East Indies, of Mr John Marshal to Dr Coga', *PTRS*, 22 (1700-01), 729-38 · *Diaries of Streynsham Master*, ed. R. C. Temple, 2 vols. (1911)
Archives BL, diaries and papers relating to India, Harley MSS 4252-4256, 7199 · BL, works by him relating to India, Add. MSS 7037-7040 · BL OIOC, translation of the Samaveda 1676, MS Eur. C 461
Wealth at death insignificant: *John Marshall in India*, ed. Khan, 26-7

Marshall, John (*bap.* 1659, *d.* 1723), maker of optical instruments, was baptized on 10 February 1659, the son of Thomas Marshall, a cordwainer (shoemaker) in Covent Garden, and his wife, Jane. He was apprenticed on 13 November 1673 to John Dunnell of the Turners' Company. Dunnell made the wooden and pasteboard parts of scientific instruments, especially of telescope tubes, at his establishment in Charing Cross; he was employed by Robert Hooke and John Flamsteed. John Aubrey may have lodged with him for a time. Dunnell was probably associated in business with Smethwick, a glass-grinder (not to be confused, according to Hooke, with Francis Smethwick FRS), who made the lenses for Dunnell's instruments. Marshall may well have learned his speciality of lens making from Smethwick.

Marshall became a freeman of the Turners' Company on 2 December 1685. In 1688 his address was the Three Keys in Ivy Lane, and from 1693 until his death, the sign of the Archimedes and Spectacles in Ludgate Street, London, opposite the west end of St Paul's Cathedral. His rival, the highly skilled lens maker John Yarwell (*d.* 1708), lived next door. By the end of the century Marshall had an outstanding reputation as a telescope and microscope maker. The typical Marshall microscope had gold stamps to decorate the tube and a fine focus, but did not have a substage mirror, which was introduced by Edmund Culpeper at about the time of Marshall's death.

Marshall boasted on his trade card that he was 'the inventor of true Spectacle Grinding & the only person that has, or ever has had, the Approbation of the Royal Society'. This testimonial was given by Edmond Halley in a letter written 'by the command of the Royal Society' in 1693:

> I have, by Order of the Royal Society seen and examined the method used by Mr John Marshall, for grinding Glasses, and find that he performs the said Work with greater ease and certainty, than hitherto has been practised, by means of an invention, which I take to be his own, and new, and whereby he is enabled to make a great number of Optick-Glasses, at one time, and all exactly alike, which having been reported to the Royal Society, they were pleased to approve thereof, as an Invention of great Use, and Highly to deserve encouragement. (Bryden and Simms, 3)

The method, whereby several lens blanks were set on a dome, to be polished simultaneously by a concave brass form, was not new, though it was little used in London at that time. Marshall's lenses were superior to those of his competitors, who polished on iron forms. To his chagrin they soon adopted his method, prompting him to add a note to his trade card:'There are several Persons who pretend to have the Approbation of the ROYAL SOCIETY; but none has, or ever had it, but myself; as my letter can testifie' (Bryden and Simms, 24). In 1715 he was appointed spectaclemaker to George I.

Marshall was twice married. His first wife may have been Katherine Underwood, whom he married in 1681 and with whom he had at least one daughter, Catherine (bap. 1689). He married secondly a widow, Esther Johnson, who had a son, Isaac. In 1703 the younger Francis Hauksbee (1689–1763) was apprenticed to him, as, in 1709, was John Smith, who later married Marshall's daughter Catherine. Marshall died on 20 January 1723, and was buried on 25 January at St Gregory by Paul's. He was survived by Esther and two daughters and had settled two houses at Islington on Esther to provide her income. Smith inherited the tools in his shop and continued Marshall's business; Esther's son, Isaac Johnson, inherited Marshall's tools kept at another house (where he had probably worked for Marshall).   W. D. HACKMANN, rev.

Sources D. J. Bryden and D. L. Simms, 'Spectacles improved to perfection and approved by the Royal Society', *Annals of Science*, 50 (1993), 1–32 · G. Clifton, *Directory of British scientific instrument makers, 1550–1851*, ed. G. L'E. Turner (1995), 180 · will, PRO, PROB 11/589, quire 32 · M. A. Crawforth, 'Evidence from trade cards for the scientific instrument industry', *Annals of Science*, 42 (1985), 453–554 · parish register, St Paul's, Covent Garden, 10 Feb 1659, City Westm. AC [baptism] · parish register, London, St Gregory by Paul's, 25 Jan 1723, GL [burial]

Marshall, John (bap. 1762, d. 1825), schoolmaster and poet, was baptized in All Saints' Church, Newcastle upon Tyne, on 11 March 1762, the only child of John Marshall (d. 1780), master mariner, and his wife, Eleanor Pembroke (d. 1777). He was educated at the Newcastle Free School, where he received a classical education under the guidance of the Revd Hugh Moises. His father, who was a member of the Guild of Trinity House, died in January 1780 and was buried next to his wife in St Nicholas's Church, Newcastle. He left his son substantial wealth, for he had owned property in Newcastle as well as ships and shares in ships. This wealth soon dissipated and Marshall lost what he referred

to in his poem 'The Village Pedagogue' as 'his summer friends'. He was admitted into the Guild of the Freemen of Newcastle as master and mariner in 1782, probably through patrimony. He pursued a life at sea for a time but by 1804 he was again searching for work.

In his autobiographical work 'A walk from Newcastle to Keswick', Marshall described how he left Newcastle on a 'fine morning' in August 1804 to walk towards Cumberland. Following a recommendation from his only acquaintance in Cumberland, Mr Crossthwaite, proprietor of the Museum of Natural and Artificial Curiosities in Keswick, who had formerly commanded a ship in the service of the East India Company, Marshall was appointed teacher at the vestry school in Newlands, near Keswick. He commenced teaching on 13 August 1804 at a salary of £10 per year and then in 1805 he became schoolteacher at Loweswater with an increased salary of £15 per year. It is not known how long he remained there, but in November 1807 he was teaching at Murton School, North Shields.

It was in 1810 that Marshall published the first edition of *'The Village Pedagogue', a Poem, and Lesser Works*, his only published work. His poetry demonstrated his erudition and intimate knowledge of classical literature nurtured during his formative years, while his autobiographical prose piece 'A walk from Newcastle to Keswick' showed his love of lakeland scenery and his bonhomie. Of his lesser works, 'On viewing Percy Main colliery, Westoe, and Jarrow from the heights near Howdon on the River Tyne' gives a fascinating glimpse of Tyneside before heavy industrialization. By 1817 Marshall was running a school at Newburn, Newcastle. It was also in this year that the second edition of his works was published with a few amendments from the first edition. By 1819 his teaching career was over and on 23 December 1819 he was appointed to one of the lesser rooms of the Peace and Unity Hospital in Newcastle. This hospital together with the Freemen's Hospital had been established to care for impoverished freemen and their dependants. He went to the Freemen's Hospital on 22 January 1821 and died there, unmarried, from a lingering illness on 19 August 1825. He was buried in All Saints' churchyard, Newcastle, on 21 August. Although he lost his family wealth and suffered hardship and poverty, Marshall was well thought of by his contemporaries. John Sykes, compiler of *Local Records*, collected together some of Marshall's autobiographical notes after his death and published them in the *Newcastle Magazine* as a tribute.   ANN KENT

Sources J. Marshall, *'The village pedagogue', a poem, and other lesser pieces; together with 'A walk from Newcastle to Keswick'*, 2nd edn (1817) · J. Sykes, 'Biographical notice of Mr John Marshall', *Newcastle Magazine* (Oct 1825) · will of John Marshall (d. 1780), U. Durham · common council minutes, Newcastle Corporation · records, Newcastle Guild of Freemen · parish register, Newcastle, All Saints' Church, 11 March 1762 [baptism] · parish register, Newcastle, All Saints' Church, 7 April 1747 [marriage] · parish register, Newcastle, All Saints' Church, 21 Aug 1825 [burial] · parish register, Newcastle, St Nicholas's Church, Nov 1777, Jan 1780 [burials] · *Newcastle Courant* (27 Aug 1825) · M. A. Richardson, ed., *The local historian's table book … historical division*, 5 vols. (1841–6), vol. 3, pp. 315–16 · *DNB*

Wealth at death impoverished: common council minutes, Newcastle Corporation

Marshall, John (1765–1845), flax spinner and politician, was born on 27 July 1765 at 1 Briggate, Leeds, the third, but only surviving, child of Jeremiah Marshall (1731–1787), linen draper, and his wife, Mary (1728–1799), daughter of John Cowper of Yeadon. For health reasons he did not live in Leeds until 1772, when he returned to start learning his father's business. On Jeremiah Marshall's death, John Marshall inherited £9000, £1500 of which was made up of a new-built house and warehouse on Mill Hill, Leeds.

In 1788 Marshall and two partners struck out as pioneers in mechanized flax spinning under a licence from the inventors, Kendrew and Porthouse of Darlington, renting a water-powered corn mill in the wooded gorge at Adel, 5 miles north of Leeds. Their venture was poorly rewarded until the mechanical experiments of a young employee, Matthew Murray, produced improved machines, which were patented in June 1790. A less remote and restricted site was purchased on the Hol Beck at Water Lane, just across the river from Leeds. By September 1791 a four-storey mill was erected, and Marshall withdrew from the drapery business.

In 1793 Marshall broke with his partners, and on the strength of a new patent from Murray persuaded Thomas and Benjamin Benyon of Shrewsbury, two of his customers, to join him in financing an additional larger mill at Water Lane, where eventually there was an industrial complex of nine units, strategically placed next to the Round Foundry (1802) of the engineers Fenton, Murray, and Wood, and culminating in Joseph Bonomi's large one-storey mill of 1840, designed after an Egyptian temple. At Shrewsbury in 1796 the partners had erected the world's first multi-storey building to be defended from fire risk by iron beams and columns.

Marshall bought out the Benyons in 1804, and henceforward chose his partners from able but more subservient employees. Increasing profits enabled him to move house in 1805 to New Grange, Headingley, which stood in a small park on the fringe of Leeds, with space enough for ten servants to minister to the family and visitors, among whom were Dorothy and William Wordsworth, Thomas Carlyle, and the painter John Russell.

In a town with a closed tory council and bench, direct involvement in local politics was denied to a whig and a dissenter but, like many members of the Mill Hill congregation, he was active in secular organizations and in intellectual life. He was a founder and sometime president of the Lancasterian School, the Leeds Philosophical and Literary Society, and the Mechanics' Institution. He was generous in the provision of a school for Holbeck and another for the part-time education of his more promising workers for whom he set out the principles of *The Economy of Social Life* (1825), his only known publication.

His life came to be centred on the Lake District, where, on his marriage to Jane Pollard (1765–1849), he had spent his honeymoon, and where in 1815 he built a house, Hallsteads, on the shore of Ullswater. He became high sheriff of Cumberland in 1821. At the general election of 1826 he

John Marshall (1765–1845), by John Russell, 1805

had the distinction of being a manufacturer nominated by the whig gentry of Yorkshire to an uncontested seat. However, he did not find that the Commons ran with the efficiency of a flax mill, and was glad to retire in 1830.

From 1796 Marshall kept an introspective diary, 'My Life'. He was a self-confessed workaholic; confident that hard work and deliberate risk-taking accounted for his success. His active years were marked by many presidential addresses to Leeds organizations, and by vocal support for Benthamite causes in London (including membership of the council of the university), and in Leeds where, in 1826, in the columns of the *Leeds Mercury* he advocated a university eighty years ahead of the event. He was a founding council member of University College. In retirement he maintained a house in London and continued to support liberal and Benthamite principles.

Marshall died at Hallsteads on 6 June 1845, and was buried at the adjoining church, which he had rebuilt. It would seem that, like many dissenting manufacturers in Leeds, he had attached himself in later life to the Church of England. His fortune at death was variously assessed at £1.5–2.5 million; he reckoned that he had spent £0.5 million on philanthropy, politics, and paintings, and he had made generous gifts to his large family of eleven children. Unfortunately he was not able to bequeath his passion for the detailed supervision of a large enterprise nor that alertness for mechanical ingenuity in employees, which had taken him so far. The Marshalls withdrew from the mills, which were sold in October 1886, and the male line died out by 1939.   MAURICE BERESFORD

Sources W. G. Rimmer, *Marshalls of Leeds, flax-spinners, 1788–1886* (1960) · R. V. Taylor, ed., *The biographia Leodiensis, or, Biographical sketches of the worthies of Leeds* (1865), 411–15 · A. Elton, *The house that*

Jack built (1993) • *Leeds Mercury* (14 June 1845) • *Leeds Intelligencer* (14 June 1845) • *Leeds Times* (14 June 1845) • parish register, 1837, W. Yorks. AS, Leeds [baptism]
Archives U. Leeds, Brotherton L., private ledger, travel journals, and other papers, MS 200
Likenesses J. Russell, oils, 1802, U. Leeds • J. Russell, pastel, 1805, U. Leeds [*see illus.*] • marble bust (*Macdonald of Rome*), Leeds Philosophical and Literary Society
Wealth at death £1,500,000–£2,500,000: Rimmer, *Marshalls of Leeds*

Marshall, John (1782/3–1841), writer on statistics, was for many years a supernumerary at the Home Office. He compiled *An account of the population in each of six thousand of the towns and parishes in England and Wales, as returned to parliament at each of the three periods 1801, 1811, and 1821* (1831) while he was employed on the commission to inspect the boundaries of the cities and boroughs, for purposes of the Reform Bill, and made some disingenuous efforts to secure the enfranchisement of a few very small places. Marshall was subsequently made an inspector of factories. He produced *A digest of all the accounts relating to the population, productions, revenues, financial operations, manufactures, shipping, colonies, commerce of the United Kingdom* (2 vols., 1833). Three thousand copies of this book, on the motion of Joseph Hume, were bought by the government at 2 guineas each and distributed among the members of both houses of parliament, who treated them with the disrespect incidental to parliamentary papers. He also compiled topographical and statistical details of Berkshire (1830), the palatine of Lancashire (1832), and London (1832). He compiled a report, *Mortality of the Metropolis, 1629–1831* (1832), made a study of the returns made to parliament since the start of the nineteenth century (1835), and supervised a 'remodelled edition' of Brookes's *London General Gazetteer* (1831). Marshall died on 11 March 1841 in Stamford Street, Blackfriars.

GORDON GOODWIN, *rev.* ALAN YOSHIOKA

Sources *GM*, 2nd ser., 15 (1841), 548–9

Marshall, John (1784?–1837), naval officer and author, himself recorded that he went to sea at nine years of age, and served throughout the French Revolutionary and Napoleonic wars in vessels of a class to which no schoolmaster was allowed, that is, in sloops, cutters, or other small craft. He was therefore probably born in 1784, and first went to sea in 1793. At the conclusion of the war he was promoted to the rank of lieutenant, on 14 February 1815, but had no further service in the Royal Navy.

In 1823 Marshall began the publication of *Royal Naval biography, or, Memoirs of the services of all the flag-officers … post captains, and commanders whose names appeared on the Admiralty list of sea officers at the commencement of the present year* (1823), *or who have since been promoted*. The work was continued until 1835, extending to twelve octavo volumes. This collection of biographies had no pretensions to literary merit, and the author seldom attempted any critical judgement of the conduct he described. Many of the lives were evidently contributed by the officers themselves; though events were thus sometimes described in

too favourable manner, entries commonly included copies of official or private letters, and other documents, which added value to the work. Marshall died early in 1837 at Haslar Royal Naval Hospital, Gosport, Hampshire.

J. K. LAUGHTON, *rev.* ROGER MORRISS

Sources *Navy List* • J. Marshall, *Royal naval biography*, 4 vols. (1823–35) [with 4 suppls.] • *GM*, 2nd ser., 7 (1837)

Marshall, John, Lord Curriehill (1794–1868), judge, son of John Marshall of Garlieston, Wigtownshire, and his wife, Marion, daughter of Henry Walker, was born in Wigtownshire on 7 January 1794. His family were poor, and he walked from his home to Edinburgh in order to attend the university there. He was in November 1818 called to the Scottish bar, and the proceeds of an extensive practice enabled him in course of time to purchase the estate of Curriehill, near Edinburgh, Midlothian. On 25 July 1826 he married Margaret Todd Bell (*d*. Nov 1866), daughter of Andrew Bell of Kilcunean, minister of Crail, Fife. In March 1852 he was elected dean of the Faculty of Advocates, and on 3 November in the same year he became a judge of the court of session, with the title of Lord Curriehill. He was notably well versed in the laws relating to heritage (inheritance), and employed a literary style in the court room. In October 1868 he retired from office, and died on 27 October at Curriehill. His son, John Marshall, born in Edinburgh on 15 October 1827, was educated at the Edinburgh Academy and the universities of Edinburgh and Glasgow. He was called to the Scottish bar in 1851, became a judge of the court of session, also with the title of Lord Curriehill, in October 1874, and died on 5 November 1881.

G. C. BOASE, *rev.* ROBERT SHIELS

Sources F. J. Grant, ed., *The Faculty of Advocates in Scotland, 1532–1943*, Scottish RS, 145 (1944) • B. W. Crombie and W. S. Douglas, *Modern Athenians: a series of original portraits of memorable citizens of Edinburgh* (1882), 123–4 • *ILN* (7 Nov 1868), 459 • *The Times* (29 Oct 1868), 5, 7 • *The Times* (7 Nov 1881), 9 • Boase, *Mod. Eng. biog.*
Likenesses portrait, repro. in Crombie and Douglas, *Modern Athenians*
Wealth at death £31,484 18s. 9d.: inventory, 9 Dec 1868, NA Scot., SC 70/1/141/420

Marshall, John (1818–1891), surgeon and teacher of anatomy, was born on 11 September 1818 at Ely, Cambridgeshire, the second son and third child of William Marshall (1776–1842) and his second wife, Ann Cropley (*c*.1793–1861), also of Ely. William Marshall was a successful solicitor, whose eldest son, also William (1815–1890), took over the legal practice. The Marshalls were a long-established Ely family, and even after John settled in London, he often brought his family back for extended holiday stays there.

The law being chosen for the elder son's career, medicine became John's option. He received his schooling in Hingham, Norfolk, and was then apprenticed to a Mr Wales, a surgeon and general practitioner in Wisbech. In 1838 he enrolled in University College, London, where he enjoyed a distinguished career as a student, winning a gold medal in physiology under William Sharpey, and becoming a private assistant to the surgeon Robert Liston. He also obtained the post (1842) of curator of the anatomy museum, which was followed in 1845 by a demonstratorship in anatomy. He assisted Richard Quain in producing the 1848 edition of *Elements of Anatomy* ('Quain's Anatomy', the early editions having been written by Jones Quain, Richard Quain's brother).

In 1844 Marshall set up in practice in Mornington Crescent, where he befriended Ford Madox Brown, the first of a number of artists who became his friends and patients. In the same year he became MRCS, and the fellowship in the Royal College of Surgeons followed in 1849. By then he was an assistant surgeon (1847) at University College Hospital. He was subsequently full surgeon and in 1866 he succeeded Eric Erichsen to the chair in surgery, a post for which Joseph Lister also applied. Marshall, who was elected FRS in 1857, retired from University College Hospital and the Brompton Hospital, where he was also surgeon, in 1884. On 12 October 1854 he married Ellen Rogers (1831–1919), daughter of Charles Williams (1792–1865), with whom he had two sons and two daughters. One son died young. Except for a period when they rented a villa in what was then the airy suburb of Kentish Town, so that the children might have more space, the family lived at 10 Savile Row, near Piccadilly. Shortly before Marshall's death, he bought a fine house in Cheyne Walk, Chelsea.

Marshall was a competent but traditional surgeon, much of whose private practice was more of the nature of general practice. He pioneered the surgical excision of varicose veins and was an early advocate of Listerian antisepsis, but he contributed little to the surgical literature. His most successful publications were intended for more general audiences. *A Description of the Human Body* (1860, 4th edn, 1882) summarized anatomy and physiology for schoolteachers and their pupils, especially those intending to study medicine. *Outlines of Physiology: Human and Comparative* (1867) was aimed at medical students, but its morphological approach was soon superseded by the newer experimental physiology. *Anatomy for Artists* (1878, 3rd edn, 1890) grew out of his long-standing interest in artistic anatomy, a subject he taught at the government school, first at Marlborough House, and then at South Kensington. He became professor of anatomy at the Royal Academy in 1873, his candidacy being supported by one of his patients, Dante Gabriel Rossetti. He lectured on artistic anatomy to classes of men and women, and also pioneered the teaching of physiology at University College, London, to mixed classes. Consistent with his liberal principles, he encouraged his daughters to attend classes at University College, London.

Marshall also published a few original papers in anatomy and embryology. He was a keen microscopist who appreciated continental developments in cellular pathology and germ theory. An advocate of the public health movement, Marshall and Henry Whitehead produced in 1854 a report on the Broad Street pump (more famously associated with the work of John Snow). He examined the water microscopically, and he and Whitehead reached similar conclusions to Snow about the role of contaminated water in the spread of cholera. Marshall designed a circular hospital ward, believing that their shape would improve ventilation, cleanliness, and light, as well as improve nurse efficiency. He attended the openings of several circular wards in British hospitals and visited one in Antwerp that had been designed and built independently of Marshall's well-publicized advocacy.

In these and many other ways, Marshall espoused the liberal, progressive values of a scientifically based medical profession. He was an excellent committeeman, serving on the councils of the Royal Society and the Royal College of Surgeons, whose president he became in 1883. He was also an experienced examiner, both for the University of London and the Royal College of Surgeons. He sat for many years on the General Medical Council and was its president at the time of his death. He played an important role in the introduction of the 'Conjoint exam' in 1886, administered jointly by the royal colleges of physicians and surgeons, and aimed at giving general practitioners broadly based medical and surgical qualifications (LRCP and MRCS).

Marshall was nominally an Anglican, but religion was not especially important to either him or his wife. He suffered increasingly from winter bronchitis, and died at his home, Belle Vue House, 92 Cheyne Walk, probably from bronchopneumonia, on new year's day 1891. He was buried in the public cemetery in Ely on 6 January 1891.

W. F. BYNUM

Sources Z. Shonfield, *The precariously privileged* (1987) · J. Taylor, 'Circular hospital wards: Professor John Marshall's concept and its exploration by the architectural profession in the 1880s', *Medical History*, 32 (1988), 426–48 · 'John Marshall, FRS, FRCS, LLD, MD etc.', *The Lancet*, 1 (1891), 117–19 · 'John Marshall, FRCS Eng, FRS, LLD', *BMJ* (10 Jan 1891), 93–5 · H. H. Bellot, *University College, London, 1826–1926* (1929) · W. R. Merrington, *University College Hospital and its medical school: a history* (1976) · CGPLA Eng. & Wales (1891)
Archives University of Exeter Library, corresp.
Likenesses T. Brock, marble bust, 1891, RCS Eng. · H. J. Brooks, group portrait, oils (*Council of the Royal College of Surgeons of England of 1884–5*), RCS Eng. · H. J. Brooks, group portrait, oils (*Court of Examiners, 1894*), RCS Eng. · A. Legros, oils, V&A · photograph, repro. in Shonfield, *Precariously privileged* · wood-engraving, NPG; repro. in *ILN* (28 July 1883)
Wealth at death £21,359 15s. 4d.: probate, April 1891, CGPLA Eng. & Wales

Marshall, Sir John Hubert (1876–1958), archaeologist, was born on 19 March 1876 at Everton House, Curzon Park, Chester, the sixth and youngest son of Frederic Marshall (d. 1910), a barrister who took silk in 1893, and his first wife, Annie (d. 1900), daughter of J. B. Evans, of Wanfield Hall, Staffordshire. He was educated at Dulwich College and King's College, Cambridge, where he was a senior scholar (1894), took first classes in the classical tripos and part two archaeology tripos (1898–1900), was Porson prizeman (1898), Prendergast Greek fellow (1900), and Craven archaeology student (1901). From 1898 to 1901 he was at the British School at Athens and took part in excavations and exploration in Crete, Greece, and southern Turkey. In 1902, on the basis of his academic excellence and other qualities, and in spite of his youth and inexperience, he was appointed to the director-generalship of archaeology in India, a post which, after more than a decade of neglect, had just been revived and greatly enlarged by the viceroy,

Lord Curzon. On the eve of sailing for India he married Florence, daughter of Sir Henry Bell Longhurst, surgeon-dentist. They had one son and one daughter.

The task which awaited Marshall when he took up office in India on 22 February 1902 was immense. Throughout the land age-long indifference had imperilled ancient structures, sculptures, and painting, often of great beauty and importance. Little methodical effort had been made to explore the buried history and prehistory of the sub-continent. There was no antiquities law on a modern pattern. Marshall, improvising as he went along, resurrected the archaeological survey of India on an adequate scale and turned it first to the clearance and conservation of upstanding structures. Previous conservation work by regional surveyors had often been misguided, involving artistically and academically unacceptable reconstructions. Marshall laid down guidelines for appropriate care of monuments in his *Manual of Conservation* (1907, 1923), which is still regarded in India as the basic handbook for conservators.

Alongside this urgent work of salvage he began to survey and dig, and in 1913 inaugurated the systematic exploration of the ancient Taxila, near Rawalpindi, a project which was to occupy some part of his attention for more than twenty years. The results, published in 1951, justified his persistence. For a thousand years (500 BC–AD 500) Taxila had been both a local capital and a trading station on an arterial route into India; with it were associated the names of Alexander the Great, the Buddhist king Asoka, King Gondofares, St Thomas, and Kaniśka. It was also a major centre of classically influenced Buddhist art, of which Marshall made an important study (*The Buddhist Art of Gandhara*, 1960). Taxila's periodical removal from site to site in the same general locality helped incidentally to provide an automatic substitute for archaeological stratification, which Marshall never adequately understood, adhering instead to stratification based on structural levels, an advance on methods previously used in the subcontinent.

Even more important than Taxila in a wider view was Marshall's development, in and after 1922, of discoveries made by members of his staff in the Indus valley of the Punjab and Sind. His announcement in 1924 that he had there found a new civilization of the third millennium marked an epoch in modern discovery; the so-called Indus valley civilization is now recognized as the most extensive civilization of the preclassical world. Parallel with these enterprises he directed a large number of projects which partook rather of conservation than of excavation: notably on the great Buddhist site of Sanchi in central India, where his restorations gave a new meaning and security to a remarkable group of buildings and carvings mostly of the last two centuries BC.

Marshall's methods were often summary, and have been criticized; and it is true that, preoccupied from an early age and largely in isolation with a task of gigantic proportions, he was insufficiently aware of developing standards and modes in the West. But alike at Taxila and in his exploration of the Indus valley civilization at Mohenjo-daro, his wholesale and speedy methods revealed expressive, if synthetic, pictures of great cities in a measure which more scientific and necessarily slower techniques would have failed to approach. His mass excavation of large areas at Mohenjo-daro, for example, published in 1931, showed a great city, dating from before and after 2000 BC, planned and drained on a vast scale and in a regimented fashion, with wide thoroughfares and closely built houses and workshops. Detail, and often important detail, was lost; but, like Schliemann before him, Marshall got to the heart of the matter and gave what was needed first in the current state of knowledge, namely the general shape, the sketch, of a hitherto unknown civilization. He was a pioneer of a high order.

His two major excavations, at Taxila and at Mohenjo-daro, are his outstanding contributions. Nevertheless, they represent but a fraction of his actual achievement. There is scarcely a part of India, or Pakistan, or indeed of Burma, which also came within his province, where his care and zeal, particularly in conservation, are not manifest in one form or another. Behind all this lay the tedious negotiation and persuasion constantly necessitated by a government and people which, apart from Curzon's initial stimulus, were not yet ready to appreciate the value of the country's immense heritage. As an administrator in these circumstances Marshall was personally brilliant; Wheeler, who succeeded him, considered that, if he failed at any point, it was in the training of his colleagues in individual responsibility and in technical practice and that his retirement from the director-generalship to take up special duties in 1928 (from which he finally retired in 1934) was followed by a sharp decline in standards (though this may have been the consequence of budget cuts necessitated by the depression). It has been said of him, with some truth, that he was 'a tree under which nothing grew'; but there are no two opinions about the splendour of the tree.

In the course of his work Marshall prepared a comprehensive antiquities law on the lines of those which had already been tried out by British authorities in western Asia and Europe. In modified form this law has remained in force and is a testimony to its draftsman. In this and in other ways he gradually brought under firm central control the monuments and ancient sites of British India, and, by example and advice, those of the Indian states where his writ did not run. His successful work as conservator of ancient buildings aided this process; he began to create an appreciative if still uninstructed public opinion. He took especial delight in the restoration of the gardens which, particularly in Mughal India, had formed an essential feature of tombs and palaces but which had been allowed to decay or even to revert to jungle. Good taste lies at the core of good conservation and Marshall's taste was nearly impeccable. Thus it was that the consolidation of ancient structures was in general accompanied by the re-creation of their ancient amenities and the recapture of much of their original beauty and significance. His work has remained as an accepted pattern and challenge to his successors, many well trained by him.

Marshall laid heavy emphasis on the rapid publication of the results of survey and excavation. During his active period of office he produced a substantial annual report which is a permanent source and, from 1919, a series of memoirs. Otherwise his principal published works are *Mohenjo-Daro and the Indus Civilization* (3 vols., 1931); *The Monuments of Sanchi* (with A. Foucher, 3 vols., 1940); and *Taxila* (3 vols., 1951).

Marshall was appointed CIE in 1910 and knighted in 1914. He was elected an honorary fellow of King's College, Cambridge, in 1927 and FBA in 1936. He also received many British and overseas honours for his scholarship. He died at his home, Avondale, Sydney Road, Guildford, Surrey, on 17 August 1958.

MORTIMER WHEELER, rev. JANE MCINTOSH

Sources WWW · D. K. Chakrabarti, *A history of Indian archaeology* (1988) · N. Lahiri, 'Sir John Marshall's appointment as director-general of the archaeological survey of India: a survey of papers pertaining to his selection', *South Asian Studies*, 13 (1997), 127–40 · Venn, *Alum. Cant.* · personal knowledge (1971) · private information (1971) · N. Lahiri, 'Coming to grips with the Indian past: John Marshall's early years as Lord Curzon's director-general of archaeology in India', *South Asian Studies*, 14 (1998), 1–23 [pt 1]

Archives AM Oxf., MSS | Bodl. Oxf., corresp. with Sir Aurel Stein

Likenesses W. Stoneman, photograph, 1937, NPG

Wealth at death £8344 18s. 10d.: probate, 17 Oct 1958, *CGPLA Eng. & Wales*

Marshall, Joshua (*bap.* 1628, *d.* 1678). *See under* Marshall, Edward (1597/8–1675).

Marshall, Julian (1836–1903), music and print collector and writer, was born at Headingley, near Leeds, on 24 June 1836, the youngest of the five children of John Marshall jun. (1797–1836), MP for Leeds from 1832 to 1835, and his wife, Mary, daughter of Joseph Ballantyne Dykes of Dovenby Hall, Cockermouth, Cumberland. He was educated at the Revd John Gilderdale's private school at Walthamstow, Essex, and at Harrow School (1852–4), where he was champion racket. His grandfather John *Marshall of Headingley (1765–1845), MP for Yorkshire (1826–30), had established flax-spinning factories at Leeds and Shrewsbury, and on leaving school Marshall took part in the family business, though with no great liking, until 1861, soon after which he moved to London. In Leeds, Marshall, an amateur musician, had sung in the choir of the parish church when, under S. S. Wesley, it was being brought close to cathedral standards, and served on the committee of the first music festival in 1858.

Marshall's collection of prints, begun before he was twenty, included Italian, Dutch, German, and French as well as English items; catalogued by G. W. Reid of the British Museum, its sale at Sothebys in 1864 occupied twelve days and raised well over £8000. Books on the technique of engraving and catalogues of earlier sales of prints featured in a sale of items from Marshall's library at Sothebys in 1870. Although he retained his interest in prints, writing an introduction to the 1895 catalogue of British portraits in the National Art Library at the Victoria and Albert Museum, he subsequently collected principally printed and manuscript music. No catalogue of his

collection as a whole exists, and its extent and nature is apparent only from his disposal of it. He sold part of his Handel collection, comprising early editions of printed music and librettos, to Arthur J. Balfour (later first earl of Balfour) in 1876; these are now in the National Library of Scotland.

Marshall married Florence Ashton [*see below*], daughter of Canon Thomas, vicar of All Hallows Barking by the Tower, on 7 October 1864; they had three daughters. He and his wife were founder members of the Musical Association. At a time when the association wanted more importance given to music in the British Museum Library, Marshall began to sell music manuscripts to the museum. In 1878 and—after protracted negotiations—in 1880–81 the museum acquired well over 400 volumes of music from him (BL, Add. MSS 30930–30934, 31384–31823). The manuscripts range from the thirteenth to the nineteenth centuries. They include substantial groups of English sixteenth-century sources and of Handel scores (all copies), as well as autograph music by Purcell, Haydn (symphony no. 103), Mozart, and Beethoven (the major part of the sketchbook for the 'Pastoral' symphony). Marshall also owned the autographs of Mozart's C minor keyboard sonata and fantasia (now in the Mozarteum, Salzburg), and in 1880 attempted to buy the autograph of *Don Giovanni* from Pauline Viardot. Letters of musicians from Marshall's collection were sold in London in 1884; much of the remainder of his library was sold after his death in a two-day sale at Sothebys in 1904, and there was a further sale in 1922.

The most important of Marshall's writings about games is *The Annals of Tennis* (1878), which had first appeared as a series of articles in *The Field* in 1876–7. He was among the major contributors to *A Dictionary of Music and Musicians*, which appeared under the editorship of Sir George Grove in 1879–89. The longest of his articles was the entry for Handel, and there, as in some of his other contributions, he drew on items in his collection. The majority of his other contributions are for Italian singers of the baroque and classical periods, though he also contributed the article on the Mendelssohn Scholarships Foundation, of which he was secretary from 1871. Marshall died at his home, 13 Belsize Avenue, Hampstead, London, on 21 November 1903.

His wife, **Florence Ashton Marshall** (1843–1922), writer and composer, was born in Rome on 30 March 1843, and studied at the Royal Academy of Music. Like her husband she contributed to Grove's *Dictionary*, though on a lesser scale. Some of her articles survived unchanged into the fifth edition. She was elected an associate of the Philharmonic Society. Her biography of Handel was published in Hueffer's Great Musicians series in 1883, and her two-volume *Life and Letters of Mary Wollstonecraft Shelley* in 1889. She was the composer of two operettas, *The Masked Shepherd* (written by 1879) and the fairy operetta *Prince Sprite* (1897). Her published works include solo songs, part songs, and educational pieces. She conducted the South Hampstead Orchestra, a substantial enough body to perform under her direction in 1908 a Brahms symphony and the violin concerto of Saint-Saëns with Mischa Elman as soloist. She died on 5 March 1922; the last of her husband's collection was sold the same year.   ARTHUR SEARLE

Sources DNB · A. Searle, 'Julian Marshall and the British Museum: music collecting in the later nineteenth century', *British Library Journal*, 11 (1985), 67–87 · Brown & Stratton, *Brit. mus.* · A. H. King, *Some British collectors of music, c.1600–1960* (1963) · R. V. Taylor, ed., *The biographia Leodiensis, or, Biographical sketches of the worthies of Leeds* (1865) · J. A. Sadie and R. Samuel, eds., *The new Grove dictionary of women composers* (1994) · sale catalogue (1922) [incl. items from 'the collection of the late Julian Marshall'; Hodgson, London, 22–3 June 1922] · d. cert. [Florence Ashton Marshall]
Archives BL, music MSS from his collection, Add. MSS 30930–30934, 31384–31823 | U. Texas, letters to Edward Rimbault Dibdin
Wealth at death £8974 12*s*. 1*d*.: probate, 9 Jan 1904, *CGPLA Eng. & Wales*

Marshall, Marian Sutton (1847/8–1901), secretary and trade unionist, was born at Huddersfield in Yorkshire, and went with her mother to New Zealand where, it is said, she married Thomas Sutton Marshall, one of a military family and sometime deputy assistant commissary-general, Ireland, who survived her. The marriage did not last, however, and being obliged to support herself in England again she took the advice of the novelist Charles Reade to follow the new career of 'type-writing' and did her first piece of professional work for him. In 1884 she established the Ladies Type-Writing Office, probably the first of its kind, in Chancery Lane, London, and later moved her business, which was prospering, to 126 Strand. Among her clients was Oscar Wilde, who later wanted her to oversee the copying of his prison letter *De Profundis*, for 'Mrs Marshall can be relied on' (20 July 1897; *Letters of Oscar Wilde*, 624). She was a founder member of the Society (later the National Union) of Typists in June 1889 and wrote for its small membership, which included both employers and employed and had the character of a craft guild. Her own standards of accuracy and speed in secretarial work (including shorthand which she thought should be taught routinely to children) were very high; she looked for intelligence and an excellent level of both general and special education in women workers. Adequate payment at standard rates to prevent undercutting and proper sanitary conditions where women were employed were her chief concerns as a unionist. She was an able speaker and organizer, and photographs indicate a woman of poise. The Society of Arts made her its first examiner in type-writing in 1891 and she held that position until her death, and also examined for the London chamber of commerce. She published a short pamphlet of examples in 1892 entitled *Practical Type-Writing Cards for Use in Offices and Schools*, of which a copy survives in the British Library.

In the same year Mrs Marshall moved to Cambridge: 'I have no fear for the future; good work and punctuality will tell here as much as they did in London' (*London Phonographer*, Aug 1892). She was proud of her competence in deciphering technical matter in what she politely called 'hurried' handwriting and her office was soon patronized by senior members of the university, and thanks to them it was granted the title of the Cambridge University Type-Writing Office in July 1898 by the vice-chancellor. She introduced a Remington typewriter with Greek characters for classical texts and extended her service to library research. She was a steady though not a headline-making member of the Women's Suffrage Society and represented the Liberal women of Cambridge at the International Congress of Women Workers held in London in 1899, when she spoke at length on the personal qualities she looked for in employees and on business training. 'To train for a teachership in a high-class commercial school ought to be looked upon as one of the most favourable openings for highly educated women, and one in which their talents will find a remarkable and gratifying outlet' (countess of Aberdeen, 4.118).

Mrs Marshall's health failed rapidly and she was forced to sell the Cambridge business in the spring of 1900 to her pupil Miss Minnie Pate. She returned to London, where she had arranged to act as private secretary for G. P. Gooch, then a young historian of independent means and sympathetic to female suffrage, whose family were long-standing friends. She also joined the local women's Liberal organization. With her funds almost exhausted, she faced death supported by a firm religious faith and among friends with 'my mind at peace with all the world' (Greenwood, 220). Mrs Marshall died of cancer at 61 Hamlet Gardens Mansions, Ravenscourt Park, London, on 7 April 1901 aged fifty-three and was buried in Hammersmith old cemetery on 10 April. No monument was erected on her grave.   JOHN D. PICKLES

Sources M. Greenwood, 'Mrs Sutton Marshall', *Englishwoman's Review*, 32 (1901), 219–20 · *London Phonographer* (Aug 1892) · countess of Aberdeen, ed., *International Congress of Women of 1899*, 7 vols. (1900), 4.115–18 · *Cambridge Independent Press* (12 April 1901), 5, 6 · M. Pate, scrapbook, CUL, Add. MS 7637 · *Portrait album of who's who at the International Congress of Women* (1899), 32 · *Women's Penny Paper* (8 June 1889) · *The letters of Oscar Wilde*, ed. R. Hart-Davis (1962) · d. cert. · *CGPLA Eng. & Wales* (1901) · will
Archives CUL, scrapbook of Minnie Pate, Add. MS 7637
Likenesses photograph, *c*.1899, repro. in *Portrait album*, 32 · photograph, repro. in *London Phonographer* · photograph, CUL, scrapbook of Minnie Pate, MS 7637
Wealth at death £50: probate, 15 April 1901, *CGPLA Eng. & Wales*

Marshall [*née* Paley], **Mary** (1850–1944), economist, was born on 24 October 1850 in the village of Ufford, near Stamford, the second daughter of the Revd Thomas Paley and his wife, Judith Wormald. She was the great-granddaughter of Archdeacon William Paley. Her sister and a younger brother also survived into adulthood.

Although the subject of a lengthy obituary and autobiographical memoirs published after her death, Mary Paley Marshall remains a shadowy figure, a devoted assistant and appendage to her famous husband, Alfred *Marshall (1842–1924). Shortly before his death, she claimed that 'to have helped, however little, in a life such as his is an enviable and delightful lot' (M. P. Marshall to J. M. Keynes, 27 July 1922, King's Cam., Keynes Collection). Yet this picture of her as a typical Victorian wife overlooks her importance as a pioneer woman student and university teacher, her unusual role as a middle-class working woman, her considerable talents as a painter, and, more controversially, the evidence of her rejection of the second-class status that her husband increasingly held to be the place of women in society.

Educated mainly at home, both by her father and by a German governess, Mary Paley's father encouraged her to enter in 1870 for the Cambridge higher local examinations for women over eighteen. She continued her studies in Cambridge, where she lived with Anne Jemima Clough and was one of the first five students at Newnham Hall (the famous Newnham Five), attending lectures given by progressive Cambridge dons who supported the cause of women's higher education. She passed the moral sciences papers of the higher locals with distinctions in political economy and logic, and Alfred Marshall persuaded her to enter informally for the moral sciences tripos, although women at that time had no right to use Cambridge degree examination papers. In December 1874 she was unofficially classed between a first- and second-class degree.

From October 1875 until her marriage to Alfred Marshall in August 1877, Mary Paley was resident lecturer in economics at Newnham College. After their marriage, which was childless, the Marshalls settled in Bristol, where Alfred became principal and professor of political economy of the new University College. The couple had already begun co-operation on a short text book of elementary economics, *The Economics of Industry* (1879). While he stood for the book's analytical content, she ensured its freshness and simplicity of style. The book proved a success, being reprinted nine times.

Bristol was the first university college to experiment in co-education, and, as 'both Alfred and I were anxious that I should help in the work of the College' (Tullberg, 'Mary Paley Marshall', 157), Mary gave her husband's morning lectures. When he fell ill a year later, she took over more of his work, including advanced classes. Her dedication to students was long remembered and, in 1926, she was awarded the degree of DLitt by Bristol University for her lifelong work as a teacher of economics. After an interlude of four terms in Oxford, 1883–4, during which Mary was a popular lecturer in political economy to women students, the couple returned to Cambridge in 1884 on Alfred's appointment to the Cambridge chair of political economy.

Alfred Marshall's views on the position of women in society and on their academic potential had meanwhile grown conservative, even reactionary. Mary Marshall returned to Newnham as economics lecturer but maintained a low profile. However, her review of Clara Collet's *Educated Working Women* reveals her clear understanding of the need for women to gain economic independence through education and not face the 'destructive humiliation' of being obliged to marry for a living (*Economic Journal*, 12, 1902, 252–7). She retired from teaching in 1916 and devoted the following eight years to the care of her husband, who was becoming increasingly infirm, physically and mentally. She assisted him closely in the production of *Industry and Trade* (1919) and especially his final work,

Money, Credit and Commerce (1923). After his death in 1924, she became honorary librarian of the Marshall Library, and catalogued the many books donated by her husband.

Any assessment of Mary Marshall's own work as an economist is difficult because she published so little. As a teacher, it may be said that while in her early years she inspired many other women to enter and succeed in 'men's examinations', she later failed to respond to developments in the educational standards of women students and to attitudes to research in late nineteenth- and early twentieth-century Cambridge. In an unpublished obituary Claude Guillebaud summarized his aunt's life in Cambridge from 1884: 'Until [Alfred Marshall's] death … she lived only for him, collaborating with him in his writing and tending him with a self-sacrificing devotion that could hardly be exceeded.' After his death 'her individuality blossomed forth in what became for her a real St. Martin's summer. … Age never warped the kindly, tolerant and humorous attitude towards life which made her such a delightful companion' (Tullberg, 'Mary Paley Marshall', 184).

Mary Marshall died in Cambridge at her home, Balliol Croft, 6 Madingley Road, Cambridge, on 19 March 1944, and her ashes were scattered in the grounds of Balliol Croft, where she and her husband had lived since their return to Cambridge. RITA McWILLIAMS TULLBERG

Sources M. P. Marshall, *What I remember* (1947) · J. M. Keynes, 'Mary Paley Marshall', *The collected writings of John Maynard Keynes*, ed. D. Moggridge and E. Johnson, 12 (1983) · R. M. Tullberg, 'Mary Paley Marshall, 1850–1944', *Women of value*, ed. M. A. Dimand, R. Dimand, and E. L. Forget (1995) · P. D. Groenewegen, 'A weird and wonderful partnership: Mary Paley and Alfred Marshall, 1877–1924', *History of Economic Ideas*, 1 (1993), 71–109 · R. M. Tullberg, *Women at Cambridge* (1975) · [A. B. White and others], eds., *Newnham College register, 1871–1971*, 2nd edn, 1 (1979) · R. M. Tullberg, 'Alfred Marshall's attitude towards the *Economics of industry*', *Journal of the History of Economic Thought*, 14 (1992), 257–70 · *CGPLA Eng. & Wales* (1944) · d. cert.
Archives Newnham College, Cambridge | King's AC Cam., Keynes collection · U. Cam., Marshall Library of Economics, Marshall collection
Likenesses R. Fry, oils, 1931, U. Cam., Marshall Library of Economics · photographs, Newnham College, Cambridge
Wealth at death £29,608 9s. 11d.: probate, 9 June 1944, *CGPLA Eng. & Wales*

Marshall, Mary Adamson Anderson (1837–1910). *See under* Edinburgh Seven (*act.* 1869–1873).

Marshall, Nathaniel (*bap.* 1680, *d.* 1730), Church of England clergyman and religious writer, was the son of John Marshall (1660–1730), rector of St George's, Bloomsbury Way, and his wife, Anne, daughter of Dudley Ryder, was born in London and baptized on 20 October 1680 at St Andrew's, Holborn. He was admitted to Emmanuel College, Cambridge, on 8 July 1696 and was awarded the degrees of LLB, in 1702, and DD, by royal mandate, in 1717. On 2 March 1700 he married Margaret Wood at St Pancras parish church, Middlesex. They had eight children, the eldest of whom, John (*d.* 1731), became rector of St John the Evangelist, Bedford Row. Marshall was ordained on 3 June 1705 and his first clerical appointment was in 1706, as vicar of St Pancras, a position he held until 1716, when he became rector of the united parishes of St Vedast, Foster Lane, and St Michael-le-Querne. His other clerical appointments were rector of Finchley (1707–30); lecturer at Aldermanbury church and curate of Kentish Town (1715–30); canon of Windsor (1722–30); and lecturer at St Lawrence Jewry and St Martin Pomeroy, Ironmonger Lane (1727–30). William Whiston's intimation, in his *Life of Samuel Clarke*, that Marshall was inclined to Arianism was not widely subscribed to and appears unfounded.

Marshall was the author of several religious works, the first of which was *The Penitential Discipline of the Primitive Church* (1714), which was republished in 1844 as part of the Library of Anglo-Catholic Theology. In this work, described as an 'excellent and most serious book' (Whiston, 99), Marshall demonstrated an extensive knowledge and keen understanding of the history of the early Christian church, a level of scholarship that he maintained in his annotated translation, in 1717, of the works of St Cyrian, archbishop of Carthage, who died in AD 258. These studies earned him a reputation as an authority on Christian antiquity. A more controversial work was *A defence of our constitution in church and state, or, An answer to the charge of the non-jurors accusing us of heresy and schism, perjury and treason* (1717). This drew replies from some leading latitudinarians and nonjurors, including Arthur Ashley Sykes, Matthew Earbury, and Hikiah Bedford. Marshall was also the author of numerous occasional sermons on such subjects as the union of England and Scotland (1707), the death of Queen Anne (1714), and charity schools in London (1724), as well as funeral sermons for friends and colleagues, including those for the Revd John Rogers (1729) and the surgeon Richard Blundell (1718).

Marshall died on either 4 or 5 February 1730 and was buried at St Pancras. His collection of books and manuscripts was sold by auction in 1732. His widow published a collection of his sermons under the title *Sermons on Several Occasions* (3 vols., 1731), dedicated to Queen Caroline; a fourth volume was published in 1750.

THOMPSON COOPER, *rev.* M. J. MERCER

Sources Venn, *Alum. Cant.*, 1/3.147–8 · Nichols, *Lit. anecdotes*, 1.141, 481–2 · A. Chalmers, ed., *The general biographical dictionary*, new edn, 21 (1815), 349–50 · Allibone, *Dict.*, 2.1228 · W. Whiston, *Historical memoirs of the life and writings of Dr Samuel Clarke*, 3rd edn (1748), 99–101 · IGI
Archives BL, letters to R. Nelson, Add. MS 45511, fol. 110

Marshall, (James) Norman Hamilton (1901–1980), theatre director, was born at Rawalpindi, India, on 16 November 1901, the second son of Lieutenant-Colonel Daniel Grove Marshall of the Indian Medical Service and his wife, Elizabeth (*née* Mackie). He was educated at Edinburgh Academy and at Worcester College, Oxford, where he gained a second in English in 1925. After a false start as a journalist in London and a brief spell as an actor in a touring company, he found his real—and lifelong—niche when appointed 'stage director' ('stage manager' in later terminology) by Terence Gray at the Cambridge Festival Theatre in 1926. After less than a year he was promoted one of the resident directors of the theatre, his first production there being C. K. Munro's *The Rumour* in 1927. In

the next six years the Festival Theatre gave Marshall, in his late twenties, play-producing opportunities that were then unique. A selection of the plays produced there illustrates the kind of theatre that Marshall and the brave, celebrated but short-lived Cambridge Festival Theatre were excited about: *The Insect Play* (Čapek), *Beggar on Horseback* (Kaufman and Connelly), *The Knight of the Burning Pestle* (Beaumont), *The Emperor Jones* (O'Neill), *The Shoemaker's Holiday* (Dekker). They were different, both from each other and—especially when put together in a single programme at one theatre—from the great mass of plays produced at other theatres at the time, and established Marshall as a pioneer of non-commercial theatre.

Marshall's first London production was in June 1928, a single Sunday-evening performance for the Stage Society, the play being Franz Werfel's *Paul among the Jews*. In his book *The Other Theatre* (1947), Marshall himself says:

> The actual performance went off without mishap but as a production it did not make much impression on any of the critics except St. John Ervine, who in *The Observer* advised me to abandon forthwith all hopes I might have of ever becoming a producer [director]. He helpfully suggested the profession of a nonconformist minister as more suitable.

Fortunately, the alternative profession was never needed because from 1932 onwards he was continuously in demand as a director of plays in London, New York, and elsewhere (including Israel and South Africa). Especially notable is his work as the artistic director at the Gate Theatre, London, throughout the 1930s where, among many other things, he introduced London audiences to the plays of Jean-Jacques Bernard (for example, *Martine*, *The Unquiet Spirit*, *The Springtime of Others*).

From 1940 to 1942 Marshall served in the army. In December 1942 he was discharged from the fighting forces and formed his own theatre company, in association with the Council for the Encouragement of Music and the Arts (the forerunner of the Arts Council of Great Britain). The company toured extensively in England for the rest of the war. From 1943 to 1949 he directed no less than fifteen London productions, following these with a production of *Hamlet* which toured the British, French, and American zones of occupied Germany. In 1950 he directed *Twelfth Night* at the Florence festival and in 1952 Jonson's *Volpone* at the Cameri Theatre in Israel. His long string of London productions continued until 1972. Some of these, so far as choice of play is concerned, show a distinct decline of his formerly artistically adventurous spirit; he was, in many cases, content to ride the easy waves of current commercial success.

Norman Marshall wrote two highly regarded books: *The Other Theatre* (1947) and *The Producer and the Play* (1957). He also published an edition of Congreve's plays (1959). He was the head of drama for Associated Rediffusion Ltd from 1955 to 1959, chairman of the British Council's drama committee (1961–8), chairman of the British Theatre Association (1961–4), and joint chairman, with Sir Laurence Olivier, of the National Theatre building committee. He served for a number of years as one of the governors of the

Old Vic and was Shute lecturer on drama at the University of Liverpool, for the academic year 1953–4.

Marshall was enormously sensitive to what he saw as a developing danger in British theatre. Particularly in the latter part of his career he often referred to it both in his lectures and in private conversation, and he included a trenchant reference to it in the 1975 edition of *The Producer and the Play*:

> Seventeen years ago I finished this book by declaring my belief in the Director's Theatre as the healthiest form of theatre. Now I have my doubts. It is all too possible, as John Barbour [Barber] warned in an article in the *Daily Telegraph*, that we may be approaching the days when directors are richer, cleverer, more famous and more in demand than authors—or indeed actors. 'I find it', says Barbour, 'a disturbing thought'. So do I.   (p. 344)

There were no distractions from his continuous, incessant theatre work, and no digressions; scarcely any recreations or 'hobbies'. Over the luncheon table or the dinner table he was silent until the theatre was mentioned. Instantly he would become quietly animated, illustrating his often-challenging views with a wealth of remembered incidents and instances. 'Go to the theatre all the time', he would say: 'Even if some of the plays are awful, still go: it's the only way to learn. Don't just *talk* about it. Go to the theatre.' Although invariably the most knowledgeable person present, he presented that vast range of learning and experience with charm, almost with diffidence. On one occasion he turned to his nearest neighbour at table and said 'Do just remind me—how does *The Man with a Load of Mischief* end?' This was in 1978: the play in question (written by Ashley Dukes) was last played in London in 1924 and the rest of the luncheon party had either long forgotten it or had never even heard of it.

Marshall was appointed CBE in the birthday honours list of 1975. He never married. He died at St Stephen's Hospital, Chelsea, after a brief illness, on 7 November 1980.

ERIC SALMON

Sources M. Banham, ed., *The Cambridge guide to world theatre* (1988) • N. Marshall, *The other theatre* (1947) • N. Marshall, *The producer and the play* (1957) • J. Parker, ed., *Who's who in the theatre* • P. Hartnoll, ed., *The Oxford companion to the theatre*, 2nd edn (1957) • *The Times* (12 Nov 1980) • *WWW* • personal knowledge (2004) • *CGPLA Eng. & Wales* (1981) • d. cert.

Wealth at death £43,352: probate, 8 Jan 1981, *CGPLA Eng. & Wales*

Marshall, Peter (1902–1949), minister of the Presbyterian Church of the United States, was born on 27 May 1902 at 70 Henderson Street, in industrial Coatbridge, the son of Peter Marshall, insurance agent, and his wife, Janet Muir. He was four years old when his father died. Domestic discord followed his mother's remarriage, and Marshall sought enlistment in the Royal Navy, but at fourteen was rejected as under age. He found employment with an engineering firm and studied at evening classes. During his next nine years in the iron and steel industry he became active in churches and was drawn to the Christian ministry, thanks to the influence of missionaries such as Eric Liddell, the Scottish Olympic champion. Hopes of being sent to China by the London Missionary Society failed to materialize as he lacked academic qualifications.

A visiting cousin drew his interest to America, and in 1927 Marshall became an immigrant, arriving alone in New York with no prospects. He dug ditches across New Jersey and took other jobs until a former classmate invited him to Alabama, where he was promised work on a Birmingham newspaper. Marshall travelled south, worked as a galley proof-reader and became active at the city's First Presbyterian church. The pastor, Dr Trevor Mordecai, befriended the young Scot, and he soon became a scoutmaster, ministerial candidate, and teacher of the men's Bible class. He was accepted at Columbia Theological Seminary, Decatur, Georgia, where his schooling in Scotland was accepted as equivalent to the American degree of bachelor of arts. For two years his seminary expenses were paid by the Birmingham Bible class. Graduating *magna cum laude* in 1931, he spent two years as pastor of the Covington Presbyterian Church, Georgia, before accepting a call to the Westminster Presbyterian Church, Atlanta.

Marshall's renown as a dynamic preacher and orator of irreproachable character began spreading through the south. One popular sermon he titled 'Azaleas and agnostics'. On 4 November 1936 he married a member of his church, Catherine Wood, a 22-year-old student at Agnes Scott College. Negotiations had already begun by New York Avenue Presbyterian Church, Washington, DC, enquiring whether the tall, impressive Marshall would consider becoming senior pastor of 'the church of Abraham Lincoln'. In 1937 he accepted and began a magnificent ministry of faith and prayer in the nation's capital, attracting large weekly crowds. A year later he became a naturalized US citizen, and received an honorary doctor of divinity degree from the Presbyterian college, Clinton, South Carolina.

In March 1946, while delivering a sermon, Marshall suffered a heart attack. Upon recovering, he resumed the strenuous pace of his ministry, and in January 1947 was elected by the United States senate to be its chaplain. He quickly established a reputation in the senate chambers for the sharp and pungent quality of his prayers. During a debate on foreign aid in 1947, he opened one session with 'O God our Father, give us the determination to make the right things happen, and the courage to stand for something, lest we fall for anything. Amen' (Marshall, *Prayers*). Senators of both parties began arriving early to hear the prayers offered by their chaplain. Despite the dangerous condition of his heart Marshall continued to accelerate the pace of his ministry, as outside invitations to preach increased. On 25 January 1949 he awoke very early with pains in his chest and arms. He was taken to the George Washington Hospital, Washington, DC, but he died from a severe heart attack. On Thursday 27 January 1949 Dr Clarence W. Cranford, Baptist minister, offered before the senate the last prayer prepared by Peter Marshall: 'Deliver us, our Father, from futile hopes and from clinging to lost causes … We know that we cannot do everything, but help us to do something. For Jesus' sake, Amen' (ibid.). His wife,

Catherine, wrote a best-selling biography of him, entitled *A Man called Peter* (1951); and she also edited a volume of his sermons and prayers, *Mr Jones, Meet the Master* (1951). His life story became the subject of an acclaimed film.

SHERWOOD E. WIRT

Sources P. Marshall, *John Doe, disciple*, ed. C. Marshall (1969) · P. Marshall, *Prayers offered by the chaplain, Rev. Peter Marshall, D.D., at opening of daily sessions of the U.S. Senate, 1947–1949* (1949) · P. Marshall, *Mr Jones, meet the master: sermons and prayers*, ed. C. Marshall (1951) · P. Marshall, *New and inspiring messages* (1969) · A. Rothe, ed., *Current Biography Yearbook* (1948) · *Time Magazine* (7 Feb 1949), 13 [article on Marshall's prayers] · J. D. Douglas, ed., *New international dictionary of the Christian church*, 2nd edn (1978), 635–6 · C. Marshall, *A man called Peter* (1951) · C. Marshall, *Something more* (1974) · b. cert.

Marshall, Rebecca [Beck] (*fl.* **1660–1683**), actress, was accused by Nell Gwyn of being 'a Presbyter's praying daughter' and Samuel Pepys was told that she and her sister Anne Marshall (later Anne *Quin) were the daughters of the famous puritan divine Stephen Marshall (Pepys, 8.502–3). He was misinformed: their father was probably another, much more obscure, clergyman, chaplain to Lord Gerard of Gerard's Bromley, Staffordshire. Their father's first name is unknown; their mother was named Elizabeth. Rebecca Marshall may have been active in the King's Company at Vere Street in their first season of 1660–61, having been sworn a member of that company in 1661 according to lord chamberlain records; however, these lists are difficult to interpret. One 1663 roster of sworn actors lists her.

As with many performers of this period, the biographical evidence that exists about Marshall concerns her stage life. Her first recorded role was Colona in John Ford's *Love's Sacrifice* (no later than August 1664). She was primarily known for her portrayal of tempestuous, passionate women, usually in tragedies. For example, she played the queen of Sicily in John Dryden's *Secret Love* (1667), Lyndaraxa in both parts of Dryden's *The Conquest of Granada* (1670–71), Fulvia in William Joyner's *The Roman Empress* (1670), and Calphurnia in Shakespeare's *Julius Caesar* (c.1672). The roles usually offset those played by another actress of the same company, Elizabeth Bowtell. Numerous rival pairs were written so the company could take advantage of the contrast between Marshall's fiery characters and Bowtell's sweet ones (demonstrating how contemporary playwrights deliberately created roles to match the strengths of individual company players). For example, Marshall played Olivia against Bowtell's Fidelia in William Wycherley's *The Plain Dealer* (1676), and she played Roxana against Bowtell's Statira in Nathaniel Lee's *The Rival Queens* (1677).

The characters Marshall played on stage seem to reflect her own character. In a deposition of February 1667 she stated that she 'taxed' Sir Hugh Middleton 'with some ill language he had cast out against the women actors of that house', and she accused him of 'calling her Jade, and threatning he would kick her and that his footman should kick her'. Middleton waited outside the playhouse, 'which gave her some apprehension that he lay in wait to doe her some mischief or affront', and finally, she complained,

some ruffian she believed to have been hired by Middleton followed her home and approached her in the street, where he 'clapd a Turd upon her face and haire' and ran away (Highfill, Burnim & Langhans, *BDA*, 7.426). This was not the only time Marshall had public problems with men. Some time about spring 1665 she petitioned the king for protection from one Mark Trevor. Actresses were often vulnerable to threats and insults from spectators and others who regarded them as servants of the public.

Later legal papers indicate that Marshall sued Mary Meggs, the King's Company orangewoman, in November 1669 for 'abusing' her, and that Marshall was sued for debt by Richard Uttings, beginning in May and continuing at least into late June 1672 (Milhous and Hume, 1.110). The evidence suggests a woman not much afraid of speaking her mind, nor of confrontation. Some time in the spring of 1677 Marshall left the King's Company and joined the Duke's Company at their Dorset Garden theatre. Her only known role after this move was as Maria in Thomas D'Urfey's *A Fond Husband* (1677). She seems to have left the stage after that date, and no death date has been discovered.

The only two other pieces of information about Beck Marshall that survive from after 1677 concern her personal life. An anonymous manuscript 'Lampoon' (c.1678) at Harvard suggests that she had had a daughter, though no other evidence supports this. This poem also calls her a 'Proud Curtizan' and, although this is not an unusual accusation for an actress of this period, an anonymous 'Satyr on both Whigs and Tories' of 1683 implies that she had been the mistress of the 'famous fop' Sir George Hewitt. This is the last known reference to this colourful and important Restoration actress.

CHERYL WANKO

Sources Highfill, Burnim & Langhans, *BDA*, 7.426–7; 10.106–8 · Pepys, *Diary* · J. Milhous and R. D. Hume, eds., *A register of English theatrical documents, 1660–1737*, 2 vols. (1991) · E. Howe, *The first English actresses* (1992)

Marshall [Martial], **Richard** (*b.* **1517**, *d.* in or after **1575**), dean of Christ Church, Oxford, and Roman Catholic priest, was born in Kent, probably the son of William *Marshall (*d.* 1540?), the anti-Catholic polemicist. He entered Corpus Christi College, Oxford, in 1532, and was a probationary fellow from 1538 to 1540. He was one of a group of younger members of the college (called 'neo-Christiani' by their seniors) who supported Henrician religious policy, and in 1538 he caused offence by striking out the word 'papa' from the library's edition of the works of St Gregory: in 1535 the government had ordered the removal of the word from all service books, and college conservatives complained that the instruction did not apply to 'profane books' (*Miscellaneous Writings*, 382). He was in trouble in 1539 for breaking the prohibition on eating meat in Lent.

Marshall took his BA degree in 1537 and MA in 1540, but was in financial difficulties: in 1539 he asked Thomas Cromwell for assistance, reporting that his father could no longer afford to support him and enclosing his own Latin poem on adversity, 'Sustine et abstine'. Marshall was given an exhibition funded by the new Westminster Cathedral. In 1545 the exhibition was switched to the embryonic Christ Church, and at the foundation of the college in 1546 he was elected a senior 'student' (or fellow). He proceeded BD in 1544 and DD in 1552; he seems to have been a popular tutor, with six pupils in 1550. He was elected vice-chancellor of Oxford in October 1552, and is said to have been a reformer under Edward VI, but at some point he must have shown Catholic sympathies, and his career took off under Mary. He became chaplain to the earl of Arundel, dean of Christ Church, on 14 September 1553, canon of Winchester and then St Paul's, vicar of Pyrton, Oxfordshire, and rector of Westbourne, Sussex (an Arundel living). He served as vice-chancellor in 1554 and 1555: he presided at the Oxford disputation against Thomas Cranmer, Nicholas Ridley, and Hugh Latimer; appeared as a witness at Cranmer's trial; took part in the degradation of Ridley; and, as a commissioner at the burning of Ridley and Latimer on 16 October 1555, silenced Ridley's attempt to respond to the official preacher. Little is known of his rule at Christ Church, the Marian records of the house having been removed by Anthony Wood. He was described by a college contemporary as 'parum sobrius et furiosus' ('a raging drunkard'; Calfhill, sig. A3), and it was said that Marshall 'regnavit tyrannice' ('ruled tyrannically'; Humphrey, 81). Within a year he had provoked disobedience from the senior students of Christ Church. Later, on the orders of Cardinal Pole, he had the body of Peter Martyr's wife removed from her grave in the cathedral, and apparently reburied it in the deanery dung-hill—an event which brought opprobrium later.

The accession of Elizabeth brought an end to Marshall's promising ecclesiastical career: he refused to recognize the authority of the royal visitors, and was deprived or forced to resign as dean by May 1559. Marshall then became an underground Catholic priest in the north of England, and stayed for a time with the earl of Cumberland and with Christopher Metcalf in Wensleydale. At some point he was arrested, and, on the orders of the privy council, sent to confer with Bishop Grindal: he was persuaded to subscribe to the Thirty-Nine Articles, probably on 21 December 1563. Earlier authorities (including the *Dictionary of National Biography*) declare that he died in prison in 1563: he did not. Presumably his subscription secured release, and by 1568 he was again operating as a Catholic priest, in Lancashire. In February 1568 the sheriff of Lancashire was instructed to seek out a number of recusant priests working in the area, including 'Marshall, once dean of Christ Church in Oxford', and from 1568 to 1570 'Marshall alias Bradfield' was listed among the priests. His name disappears from these lists in 1571; he seems to have gone into exile at Louvain, and to have moved to Douai by 1575. He probably died soon after.

Marshall was castigated by Lawrence Humphrey in 1573 as 'homo versipellis' ('a chameleon'), and was later condemned as the turncoat dean who went from Romanist to reformer to Romanist to reformer. In fact, his public sympathies under Edward VI followed naturally from his youthful radicalism and, except for his subscription under pressure, he was a consistent Catholic from 1553. Marshall changed his adult religion only once, less than most of his contemporaries. He might have become an academic elder statesman, an Oxford Andrew Perne: instead, and perhaps surprisingly, he sacrificed his career for a secret pastorate and exile.

CHRISTOPHER HAIGH

Sources Emden, *Oxf.*, vol. 4 · Wood, *Ath. Oxon.: Fasti*, new edn · CSP dom., 1547–80; rev. edn, 1553–8 · *Miscellaneous writings and letters of Thomas Cranmer*, ed. J. E. Cox, Parker Society, [18] (1846) · *The acts and monuments of John Foxe*, ed. S. R. Cattley, 8 vols. (1837–41) · J. Calfhill, *De Katherinae nuper uxoris D. Petri Martyris … effosae exhumatione* (1561) · ecclesiastical commission act book, 1562–72, Ches. & Chester ALSS, EDA 12/2 · H. Aveling, *Northern Catholics: the Catholic recusants of the North Riding of Yorkshire, 1558–1790* (1966) · J. Strype, *Annals of the Reformation and establishment of religion … during Queen Elizabeth's happy reign*, new edn, 4 vols. (1824) · lists and accounts, Christ Church Oxf., MS iii. b. 99; MS iii. c. 4; D. & C. 1 B. 1. · L. Humphrey, *Ioannis Juelli Angli … vita et mors* (1573) · J. G. Milne, *The early history of Corpus Christi College, Oxford* (1946)

Marshall, Sheina Macalister (1896–1977), marine zoologist, was born at Stewart Hall, Rothesay, Isle of Bute, on 20 April 1896. She was the second of three daughters of John Nairn Marshall (*b.* 1860) and his wife, Jean Colville, *née* Binnie (*b.* 1861/2). John Nairn Marshall was a general practitioner in Rothesay and a keen amateur naturalist. He founded the Buteshire Natural History Society and encouraged his daughters' interest in the subject. Sheina Marshall, like her sisters, was educated by governesses up to the age of twelve or thirteen. She then went to Rothesay Academy, and St Margaret's School, Polmont, but her education was interrupted by attacks of rheumatic fever. Confined to bed for long periods, she read the works of Charles Darwin, and her father gave her books on geology and zoology; these determined her to become a zoologist. She entered Glasgow University in 1914, but the First World War led to a year's work (1915–16) for J. S. Macarthur, an uncle by marriage, making luminous clock-faces and instrument dials for the armed forces. Returning to university in 1916 she studied zoology, botany, and physiology and obtained a BSc with distinction in 1919. She held a university Carnegie fellowship from 1920 to 1922, working with John Graham Kerr, professor of zoology. He suggested she should take a job at the marine station at Millport on the Isle of Cumbrae in the Firth of Clyde. The laboratory, belonging to the Scottish Marine Biological Association, had just received a grant from the development fund enabling it to expand. Marshall joined the staff in 1922 and continued to work there for the rest of her life.

Following a suggestion from Kerr that she should investigate marine food chains Marshall began a seasonal study of plankton, looking in particular at the micro-organisms forming the food of *Calanus finmarchicus*, a copepod important in the diet of herring. The biology of copepods was to become her life's work. In this, and in the study of marine productivity, she was joined in an extremely fruitful collaboration (between 1923 and 1962) by the chemist

Andrew Picken Orr. They began by looking at the relationship between physical and chemical changes and plankton distribution throughout the Clyde sea area, but the scale of the undertaking proved too large. Thus in 1926 they monitored seasonal changes in nutrients and phytoplankton in Loch Striven on a weekly basis, obtaining results since considered a 'landmark in the study of marine production' (Russell, 372).

Between 1928 and 1929 Sheina Marshall and Orr were members of the Great Barrier Reef expedition. Back at Millport, Marshall resumed her early interest in copepods as chief consumers of phytoplankton. She and Orr made an exhaustive study of the biology and physiology of *Calanus*, looking at aspects of its seasonal distribution, reproduction, and growth. Their joint book *The Biology of a Marine Copepod* appeared in 1957. Following Orr's death in 1962 Sheina Marshall worked closely with E. D. S. Corner, a biochemist from the Plymouth laboratory.

During the Second World War Marshall took part in the search of British coasts for seaweeds suitable as a source of agar, both on field surveys in the west of Scotland, and in laboratory work with Orr. She worked on methods of harvesting the selected species, *Gigartina*, and supervised collection by volunteers. From 1942 she also took part in a field study on the effect on marine productivity of the addition of artificial fertilizers in Loch Craiglin.

In the late 1960s the Millport laboratory moved to Dunstaffnage, near Oban, and the buildings were taken over by the University Marine Biological Station. Sheina Marshall decided to stay in Millport, and continued to work at the station in retirement. She spent 1970–71 at Scripps Institution of Oceanography in the USA and was a visiting worker at the Villefranche laboratory in 1974. In her final years when her eyesight deteriorated, making microscope work difficult, she began writing a history of the Scottish Marine Biological Association (published in 1987). She remained in vigorous health until an attack of pneumonia in 1975 undermined her constitution. She died at Lady Margaret Hospital, Millport, from a heart attack two years later, on 7 April 1977.

Marshall was elected a fellow of the Royal Society of Edinburgh in 1949 and was awarded its Neill prize. She became a fellow of the Royal Society in 1963, and was made an OBE in 1966. The University of Uppsala awarded her an honorary degree in 1977. She was a dedicated and hardworking scientist but also had many outside interests, including walking and foreign travel. She was a gifted needlewoman and enjoyed poetry and listening to music. She had a delightful personality, unassuming but shrewd, and with a keen but kindly sense of humour. She never married.   MARGARET DEACON

Sources F. S. Russell, *Memoirs FRS*, 24 (1978), 369–89 · M. Deacon, tape-recorded interview of Sheina Marshall, 9 Aug 1970 · S. M. Marshall, *An account of the marine station at Millport* (1987) · E. L. Mills, *Biological oceanography: an early history, 1870–1960* (1989) · b. cert. [J. Marshall] · m. cert. [J. C. Binnie] · d. cert.
Archives University Marine Biological Station, Millport, Isle of Cumbrae, personal and scientific papers | SOUND priv. coll., tape-recorded interview

Likenesses photograph, 1923, University Marine Biological Station, Millport, Isle of Cumbrae, Marshall MSS; repro. in Mills, *Biological oceanography* · G. Outram & Co., Glasgow, photograph, c.1963, RS; repro. in *Memoirs FRS* · photographs, repro. in Marshall, *Account of the marine station* · photographs, University Marine Biological Station, Millport, Isle of Cumbrae, Marshall MSS
Wealth at death £148,004.31: confirmation, 5 July 1977, CCI

Marshall, Stephen (1594/5?–1655), Church of England clergyman, was born in Godmanchester, Huntingdonshire, the son of a poor glover. He was educated at Queen Elizabeth Grammar School in Godmanchester and matriculated as a pensioner in Easter term 1615 from Emmanuel College, Cambridge, which exercised patronage over his school. He graduated BA in 1618.

Early career That year Marshall left university and became chaplain to the Barnardiston family at Clare Priory, Suffolk, probably acting as lecturer at Clare and attending the informal graduate seminary run by the puritan minister Richard Blackerby at nearby Ashen, Essex. In 1619 he succeeded the puritan Richard Rogers as lecturer at Wethersfield, Essex. This seems to have been on the recommendation of his former tutor, John Garnons. He was ordained deacon in London on 19 December 1619, when he was described as aged twenty-four, and priest on 12 March 1620. His preaching was very successful; he lodged with William Wiltshire, whose conversion he had effected, and he was given a library worth £50 in return for a promise he would stay at Wethersfield.

However, when Thomas Pickering, the vicar of Finchingfield, Essex, died, the patron, Sir William Kempe of Spains Hall, hoped for Marshall as Pickering's successor. The cure was offered to Marshall and he took his scruples to a committee of puritan ministers who judged that his promise was not binding and authorized Marshall to accept the offer, noting the attractions of the security of tenure attached to a vicarage. He was instituted as vicar of Finchingfield on 25 October 1625, and there he established his reputation as a puritan minister in several ways. He became renowned for his preaching, delivering moving sermons in a direct fashion with rather more passion than rhetorical decoration. His hostile biographer describes him as 'of middle stature, thick shouldered, swarthy Complexion, his eyes always rowling in his head … His deportment was clownish, like his breeding: his garb slovenly … his Gate [gait] shackling, and the Furniture within not unlike the outside' (*Godly Man's Legacy*, 27). His style proved popular, however, and he was a regular visitor to many pulpits across Essex.

Marshall also met with success in his pastoral duties, in particular in bringing his patron out of his withdrawn, silent state and back into society. In addition, he was very active in remodelling the vestry and town meeting in his parish, providing a campaign to reform the morals of the town, closing down unruly alehouses and conducting attempts to reduce vagrancy and to reduce numbers of illegitimate children. A 'privie watch' was established to keep an eye on those townspeople suspected of being disorderly. On a more positive side, the vestry provided emergency housing, wood and grain, and other relief for the poor and generally improved the local amenities with no clear boundary between civil and ecclesiastical business.

Social connections Marshall's role in the reformation of manners was partly to act as a broker, on the one hand communicating local concerns to the magistracy and enlisting the help of local and country gentry in improving town life, and on the other propagating from the pulpit the ethical basis of vestry actions and informing the community or the particular townspeople of the consequences. In this work his connections with the puritan gentry, the 'noble professors', were crucial. He maintained his relations with the Barnardistons, and in 1633 preached the sermon at the funeral of Katherine, Lady Barnardiston, at St Michael Cornhill in London. In Essex his connections were more diverse. By 1628 he was a favourite in the Barrington household, receiving gifts from Joan, Lady Barrington, in the 1630s. He also won the respect of different branches of the Rich family. He preached at Maldon in 1628 before the parliamentary election in support of Sir Nathaniel Rich and was noted as foremost among 'those ministers who gave their voices for [Robert Rich] my lord of Warwick' and those who 'preached often out of their parishes' before the election for the Short Parliament in the spring of 1640 (Webster, *Marshall*, 17). These connections took Marshall's influence beyond the east of England; for instance, he was consulted by the godly Herefordshire gentleman Sir Robert Harley over a minister whose godly credentials seemed suspect. His connections also assisted in Marshall's career. In 1629, in the process of arranging his BD exercise, in which he preached orthodox anti-Catholicism, questions were raised regarding his MA and it became necessary to acquire a royal mandate to allow him to gain his degree. The mandate was gained at the recommendation of Sir Nathaniel Rich through his kinsman Henry Rich, earl of Holland, who was chancellor of the university. About this time Marshall married a wealthy widow, Elizabeth, daughter of Robert Castell of East Hatley, Cambridgeshire, and Woodham Walter, Essex, and his wife, Elizabeth Alleyn. Her brother was Edmund *Castell (*bap.* 1606, *d.* 1686), another graduate of Emmanuel College, who went on to hold livings in Essex and Cambridgeshire.

Marshall's contacts with, and respect from, the noble professors was matched by a similar place among puritan ministers. In the early years of his ministry Marshall was introduced to this network through Emmanuel College, through Richard Blackerby, and then through the similar spiritual exercises organized by Thomas Hooker, lecturer at Chelmsford, Essex. Marshall was one of forty-nine beneficed and 'conformable' ministers putting their names on 10 November 1629 to a petition in favour of Hooker when he was under threat of discipline for nonconformity. In the same year Marshall was among a number of divines suspected of helping a Cambridge printer to distribute the subversive tracts of William Prynne. He may well have been the force encouraging a donor from Finchingfield for the feoffees for impropriations, an organization promoting puritan preachers.

Ministry in the 1630s As he matured, Marshall's prestige, combined with his organizational skills, placed him in a more central role in godly affairs. Lady Barnardiston had left provision in her will for £200 to be distributed in godly causes at Marshall's advice. £50 was given to Anthony Thomas to support preaching in Welsh in the principality, while £150 was given in support of John Dury's scheme for spiritual union between Lutherans and Calvinists. Marshall had been involved in the latter project, an evangelical effort partly conceived to bolster orthodoxy against the advance of Laudianism, which since at least 1630 had been seen by puritans as theologically suspect. About April 1631 Dury canvassed a meeting in London and left with a testimony subscribed by thirty-eight of the leading puritan ministers committing themselves to the task of compiling the manual of practical divinity which featured in his scheme. Marshall represented Essex alongside John Rogers, the elderly lecturer of Dedham. He helped to organize a nationwide network of ministers, offering his own current work on free grace and also employing his contacts, clerical and lay, to raise funds for the cause. An unintended compliment lies within Archbishop William Laud's visitation report for 1636, in which close observation of Marshall was recommended as 'he governeth the consciences of all the rich Puritans in those partes, and in many places far removed' (Webster, *Marshall*, 17). His interest in Dury's work continued through the 1640s and as late as 1654 Marshall worked with presbyterians and Independents, intending to lend credibility to his plans.

Marshall's standing as a minister rose in the 1630s as many of his puritan colleagues were silenced or fled to the Netherlands and New England. Marshall skilfully walked the difficult line which allowed him to keep his preaching post without compromising to an extent which would lower his godly credit. When Laud, then bishop of London, conducted a visitation in 1631, godly ministers met to discuss 'whether it was best to let such a swine to root up God's plants in Essex, and not to give him some check' (Webster, *Marshall*, 9). Marshall was also present at the resulting demonstration but was one of the less vociferous in his protest. When he was questioned about his conformity he showed a willingness to compromise and escaped with merely a warning. He was closely watched but his circumspection was remarkably successful. In 1632 Robert Aylett, the bishop's commissary in Essex and Hertfordshire, reported that Marshall 'onely preacheth on the holy days and is in all very conformable' (Webster, *Marshall*, 10). In 1637 Sir Nathaniel Brent reported that he was 'held to be a dangerous person but exceeding cunning. Noe man doubteth but he hath an inconformable heart, but externally he observeth all' (ibid.). As Thomas Fuller's less than complimentary observation puts it, he 'was of so supple a soul, that he breake not a joint, yea, sprained not a sinew, in all the alteration of the times' (Fuller, *Worthies*, 52–3). Marshall established his priorities: he was not prepared to place uncompromised nonconformity regarding ceremonies he regarded as *adiaphorous*, or things indifferent, before the prime goal of fervent godly preaching.

Godly reform, 1640–1642 Marshall's survival within the established church allowed him to enhance his prestige as a prominent preacher around the county, to procure ministers for other vacant pulpits, and to maintain the tradition of practical divinity in the region. His reputation helps to explain how he came to the centre of parliamentarian politics in the early 1640s. In 1640 he was nominated as a preacher to the Short Parliament, renowned as a 'painful' (i.e. painstaking) preacher but not notorious for nonconformity and thus unlikely to put a strain on the fragile alliance of conservatives and reformers. Parliament was dissolved before he had a chance to preach at a fast, but he was also nominated when parliament returned later in the year and became one of the preachers before the Commons at a solemn fast at St Margaret's, Westminster, on 17 November 1640. This was the first of many such sermons, many of which were printed. He played a crucial role in exhorting the houses to godly reform and religious conviction in their struggle with royalist forces. Between 1640 and 1653, when he delivered his last sermon to the Barebone's Parliament, sixteen such sermons were printed by order of the houses. His passion was disseminated by more than print. His most famous sermon, 'Meroz Cursed', first delivered to the Commons in February 1642, a characterization of passive moderates as just as guilty as active royalists, was apparently preached over sixty times.

Marshall became a popular preacher across London and occupied many of the most prestigious pulpits in the capital, performing at Westminster Abbey and St Paul's Cathedral as well as Marylebone, Spitalfields, and St Olave's. In early 1642 the Commons sanctioned the wish of the congregation of St Margaret's, Westminster (many of them included), to have him as one of seven ministers preaching daily in rotation at 6 a.m. with a salary of £300 apiece. The Finchingfield parishioners petitioned against the arrangement and, although the petition was rejected, Marshall remained vicar of Finchingfield, with a Mr Letmale taking on most of the parochial duties as an assistant.

Marshall's contribution to the cause of godly reform was by no means limited to the pulpit. From November 1640 a group of godly ministers including Marshall, Cornelius Burges, John White, Matthew Newcomen, Thomas Young, and William Spurstowe had been meeting regularly at the home of Edmund Calamy senior in Aldermanbury. This group played an important role in advancing the cause. Marshall was crucial in the ministers' 'petition' and 'remonstrance', signed by more than 700 clergymen and delivered to the Commons on 23 January 1641. He was named among the ministers accused by Edward Hyde, later earl of Clarendon, of having taken signatures from one document and attaching them to a different one. There was some truth in this, in that the final petition was an amalgamation of several petitions forwarded to the central committee, with specific grievances drawn together into a remonstrance comprising nearly eighty articles. There was, as Hyde later claimed, a complaint from ministers but this was merely that the length of the remonstrance would try the patience of the house.

Out of the same circle emerged some of the most famous pamphlets of the ecclesiological debate. Marshall's initials provided the first two letters of the authorial acronym Smectymnuus, the rest belonging to Calamy, Young, Newcomen, and Spurstowe. *An Answer* (1641) was an engagement with the work of Joseph Hall, then bishop of Exeter, which had defended *jure divino* episcopacy. *An Answer* is similar to the 'petition' and the 'remonstrance' in that it pleads for reform. It is, however, more a vigorous critique of Laudian-style episcopacy, delivered in caustic and lengthy prose, than an alternative model. At this stage Marshall was more of an advocate for a reformed, 'primitive' episcopacy and liturgy than a presbyterian. The 'middle-ground' outline of reduced episcopacy being cautiously circulated by James Ussher, bishop of Armagh, fed into this common area. The hopes for moderation could be seen in Marshall's being summoned by John Williams, bishop of Lincoln, to join a 'committee for innovations' that he was chairing. The committee, appointed by the Lords on 1 March, met six times at Westminster Hall and was quite amicable, despite the presence of Hall and three of the Smectymnuans. On 12 May the committee broke up over the Commons' proposal to abolish deaneries and chapters, a sign of diminishing shared ground.

On 27 May the root and branch bill, for the 'utter abolishing' of the existing episcopacy, was introduced in the Commons. On 10 June Marshall was among those present at a conference where it was decided to push the bill forward. The following day he was at the house, hurrying Simonds D'Ewes (and presumably others) into the house to contribute to the debate. Marshall was becoming more hostile to episcopacy as it stood but was not yet a 'full-blooded' presbyterian. This can also be seen with the second Smectymnuan treatise, *A Vindication*, which appeared at the end of June. Much of the earlier work is reiterated and expanded and there are passages that seem to advocate something akin to presbyterianism but no more than that. He was testing the water very carefully: on 12 July he joined a number of English ministers dispatching a letter to the general assembly in Scotland exploring Scottish responses to Independency. He was more resolute by 22 July, joining with other ministers in writing to the general assembly again, this time expressing a desire for 'the Presbyterian Government, which hath just and evident Foundation, both in the Word of God and religious reason' (*Acts and Proceedings of the General Assemblies*, 1863, 1.328). In November 1641 he was party to an agreement of puritan ministers meeting at Calamy's house to minimize ecclesiological debate within the disparate supporters of parliament in order to present a united front against episcopacy. The agreement held sway for a relatively short period.

As hostilities moved from rhetoric to military action Marshall became chaplain to the regiment of foot of Robert Devereux, third earl of Essex, preaching to the soldiers and on 23 October 1642 riding among the troops at the battle of Edgehill, persuading the forces that God was behind them; he later wrote an account of the event. Clarendon charges him and Calibute Downing with absolving the 150 prisoners taken by the royalists at Brentford on 23 October of their oath, when released, not to bear arms against the king, although Oldmixon, with good cause, questions this story and Marshall denied this and similar allegations in print the following year in *A Copy of a Letter* (1643). He certainly justified the struggle but presented the cause as the legitimacy of parliament contesting the dangerous faction surrounding the king. However, the usual distinction between the party and the person of the monarch, which he employed, was enhanced by the starker emphasis of religion in that 'the question in England is whether Christ or Antichrist shall be Lord' (Marshall, *A Sacred Panegyric*, 1644, 21).

The Westminster assembly and parliamentary politics On 12 July 1643 Marshall was among the first to be summoned to join the Westminster assembly of divines. Shortly afterwards he was dispatched to Scotland with Philip Nye as one of the assembly's commissioners. They landed at Leith on Monday 7 August and on 20 August Marshall preached in the Tron Kirk in Edinburgh to general acclaim. They both took part in the unanimous acceptance of the solemn league and covenant and returned to London in September. Marshall's stature among the puritans is further reflected in his selection as the minister to deliver the funeral sermon for John Pym in December 1643, published as *Threnodia* (1644).

In his work in the assembly over the following years Marshall contributed a reasonable amount of theological knowledge but mainly operated as a careful pragmatist, holding the Erastians at bay while constantly seeking, as far as was possible, accommodation with those in favour of Independent church government. On 16 December 1643 he was appointed chairman of a subcommittee of five who were to meet the Scottish delegates and prepare a directory for public worship. He drafted the section on 'preaching of the word' which was accepted despite some reservations from the Scottish commissioners. He used his political acumen to make the resolutions as accommodating as possible. For instance, he joined with John Lightfoot to remove the prohibition on feasting on the sabbath and with George Gillespie to prevent the catechism from being too prescriptive. He drafted *Certaine Considerations to Diswade Men from Further Gathering of Churches*, a declaration issued by the assembly on 23 December 1643, discouraging the formation of Independent churches but retaining a respect for the rights of particular congregations. By early March 1644, perhaps as a response to fears of the ecclesiological mélange in London, he made a clear statement of *jure divino* presbyterianism. However, he was still willing to respond on 20 September when the parliamentary 'committee of accommodation' chose him to appear on a subcommittee of six clerics to devise a modus vivendi between presbyterians and Independents. Negotiations were suspended when the presbyterians demanded their own legal establishment as a preliminary to the offer of

toleration for others. Marshall worked for a more accommodating system in what Robert Baillie called 'a middle line of his own' (*Letters and Journals of Robert Baillie*, 2.230). An openness to the Independents threatened relations with the stricter presbyterianism of the Scottish delegates.

A certain moderation is also evident in Marshall's sermons. At a conservative estimate he must have preached well over 1000 times between 1640 and 1649. His normal routine, even at the height of his 'political' activism, was to preach three times a week. From February 1644 he was one of the daily speakers to parliament, leading prayers from 7.30 to 8.00 every morning. He used this opportunity to deliver a series of lectures on the sacraments, among the fruits of which were *A Sermon of the Baptising of Infants* (1644) and *A Defence of Infant Baptism* (1646). As is evident, his sermons to parliament are far from being solely the 'blood and thunder' calls to war that might be expected. The strongest themes are pleas for unity and an appetite for religious reform at the personal and national levels. The most renowned call to war contains a more peaceful tone, one which might serve as Marshall's motto: 'The Church is the common storehouse to which all our wealth must be carried. Salus Ecclesiae Suprema Lex …. All our blessednesse stands or falls with the blessednesse of the Church' (Marshall, *Meroz Cursed*, 1641, 18–19).

Parliament appointed Marshall as one of the ministers to wait on William Laud between 4 and 10 January 1645, the time between his sentencing and execution, and Marshall seems to have been present on the scaffold. Between 30 January and 18 February he attended the Uxbridge conference as a chaplain to the parliamentary commissioners and preached to them in the large room of their inn. The *jure divino* presbyterianism espoused by Marshall and his colleague Alexander Henderson left no ground for compromise with the episcopalians. Once he had returned to London, on 7 July he was chosen by the assembly to deliver the draft of church government to the Commons, and he performed the task with considerable aplomb, being careful not to test the patience of the house or to tread on sensitive Erastian toes. On 9 November the 'committee for accommodation' was revived, and held meetings until 9 March 1646. Negotiations broke down, with the presbyterians complaining that the Independents called for a broader liberty of conscience than was appropriate; the Independents themselves could be accepted but the more extreme groups were judged to be beyond the pale.

On 14 March 1646 the Commons approved an ordinance naming lay commissioners in every shire and city charged with establishing presbyterian structures. Six days later Marshall presented the ordinance to a meeting of the assembly. With rare unanimity, they endorsed his view that the proposal was unacceptable and that it subverted their authority. Indeed, most of them agreed with his statement that the divines could not accept the system envisaged by the ordinance, and could not continue in the ministry with a clear conscience if it was implemented. He presented their response in a petition to the Commons on 23 March but after a lengthy debate it was judged to be a breach of privilege. He was the main force behind the petition of 29 May signed by 300 ministers of Suffolk and Essex defending clerical authority against the Erastianism of the ordinance.

Marshall seems never to have lost sight of the fundamental necessity of a solution which could be effected at parish level. If *jure divino* presbyterianism was not the way to achieve national salvation, then it could be sacrificed in good conscience to the greater need of practical reformation. He was not reconciled to Erastianism, although his practical experience at Finchingfield and his early fast sermons showed him to be inclined to allow the secular arm a role in reformation in partnership with the clergy. Not until near the end of his life, in a work published as *The Civil Magistrate* (1657), was he prepared to argue, from Isaiah 49: 23 and 60: 10, that as the Old Testament provided examples of reform led by the magistracy, so the current regime should undertake such a mission. In 1653, as in the 1640s, this was probably little more than an accommodation with the status quo, aided by a moderate confidence in the Cromwellian regime. Once the more Erastian system of presbyterianism was established in Essex by the end of 1647, Marshall and his assistant joined their patron in the tenth or Hinckford classis.

In the next two years Marshall was most visible in various parliamentary duties. He received the thanks of the assembly for his book against the Baptists. He accompanied the commissioners to Newcastle in January 1647 with Joseph Caryl, with whom he went on to act as a chaplain to the king at Holmby House, Northamptonshire, the ministers receiving £500 each. The king refused to attend their sermons, and when Marshall launched into prolonged prayer before dinner expressed his impatience by saying his own grace and beginning to eat. Between February and March 1648 Marshall returned to Scotland as part of an attempt to repair the Scottish alliance, making his last recorded appearance at the assembly on 21 June when he was placed on the committee for selecting the proof texts for *jure divino* presbyterianism. He played an active role in the ecclesiological debates in the Isle of Wight from September to October, taking on the episcopalian clergy on the royalist side.

Marshall's part in the dénouement of the revolution is ambiguous. He preached the sermon to the Commons two days after Pride's Purge, but Hamon L'Estrange's allegation that he was one of the justifiers of the king's execution seems groundless. More reliable is the assertion of Giles Firmin that he was 'so troubled about the king's death' that on Sunday 28 January 1648, he interceded with the heads of the army, 'and had it not been for one whom I will not name, who was very opposite and unmovable, he would have persuaded Cromwell to save the king. This is true'.

Later career Marshall was never so central a figure after 1649 although it cannot be said that he withdrew from politics. Indeed, he preached at least once to the Rump Parliament and in April 1649 he was employed along with Caryl, Nye, and others in an unsuccessful attempt to persuade the members excluded to resume their places in

parliament. In the following year, temporarily at least, his attention turned to lesser duties. He established funds for his earlier haunts in giving a 'messuage and tenement' with 'Boynton meadow, containing three acres' worth £2 a year to pay for wood for the poor of Finchingfield and gave 'Great Wingey, a nominal manor' to fund a lecture at Wethersfield. It is as though he was 'closing his accounts' in Essex, and, for reasons which are not quite clear, he did indeed leave Finchingfield in 1651, becoming town preacher at Ipswich, Suffolk, based in St Mary's at the Quay. On Easter Monday 1652, however, he was again in London, preaching to the lord mayor and aldermen; when the sermon was published he was still described as minister at Finchingfield.

In November 1653 Marshall met with Cromwell and others in an attempt to persuade Blackfriars millenarians to moderate their language. Three days later he preached to the Barebone's Parliament with an ecclesiology well suited to his congregation. Late in 1653 he was one of the commissioners appointed by parliament to draw up the 'fundamentals of religion' as part of the loose-limbed ecumenism of the 1650s. On 20 March 1654 he was appointed as one of the 'triers', men given the task of assessing and accepting or rejecting candidates for ministerial posts. He was working with a fairly broad spectrum of ministers, from reconciled presbyterians like himself to baptists such as Henry Jessey.

Marshall's health was declining—he was beginning to suffer from gout. About the middle of 1655 he lost the use of his hands to the disease and started to suffer from consumption. He died at Ipswich on 19 November 1655 with Giles Firmin at his side. He was given a prestigious funeral and resting place, being buried on 23 November in the south aisle of Westminster Abbey with great solemnity. He rested for only six years in this grave as his remains were taken up on 14 September 1661 and cast into a pit at the back door of the prebendary's lodgings in St Margaret's churchyard.

Marshall's wife, who had predeceased him, had exercised her power of disposal of her estate to their children. Their only son had drowned at Hamburg, and of their six daughters, three died before their father, including Elizabeth (*d.* 1654), who had married John *Nye (*bap.* 1620, *d.* 1686?), nephew of Marshall's colleague Philip *Nye. Their daughters Mary, wife of Thomas Langham, and Susanna proved the will.

Conclusion Many of the surviving accounts and appraisals of Marshall date from immediately after the Restoration, so it comes as no surprise that the vast majority are negative. Writers such as Peter Heylyn, Anthony Wood, Laurence Echard, and Zachery Wood have clear reasons for animosity, while more rigid presbyterians such as Robert Baillie regarded him as a traitor. Clarendon, despite his own, more graceful, invective, gives a rather more careful assessment, particularly in his remark that 'the archbishop of Canterbury had never so great an influence upon the counsels at court as Dr [Cornelius] Burges and Mr Marshall had then upon the Houses' (Clarendon, *Hist. rebellion*, 1.401). In contrast, Samuel Pepys, taking a certain satisfaction that they had fallen so low, reported that two of Marshall's surviving daughters had become actresses at the king's theatre; while the women in question were indeed daughters of a clergyman called Marshall, they were not the daughters of Stephen Marshall. His first biographers emerged in the charged atmosphere of the exclusion crisis, and were heavily influenced by news of history then current. *The Godly Man's Legacy to the Saints* (1680) is written by someone who evidently knew Marshall from his career as a minister in Essex and has some trustworthy biographical details albeit ones with an attached anti-fanatic twist. The response, by Marshall's close friend Giles Firmin, 'Vindication of Stephen Marshall', is rarely guilty of idolization but still has to be read in the political climate of the early 1680s and its debates on the consequences of the civil war. The fact that biographies, hostile and sympathetic alike, should be produced in this context is testament to Marshall's stature. He occupied an important place in the religious politics of the 1640s and remained a useful figure for laudatory accounts of godliness and hostile accounts of fanaticism more than two decades after his death.

TOM WEBSTER

Sources T. Webster, *Stephen Marshall and Finchingfield* (1994) · *Godly man's legacy to the saints upon earth* (1680) · G. Firmin, 'Vindication of Stephen Marshall', *Questions between the conformist and the nonconformist* (1681) · R. S. Paul, *The assembly of the Lord: politics and religion in the Westminster assembly and the 'Grand debate'* (1985) · *The letters and journals of Robert Baillie*, ed. D. Laing, 3 vols. (1841–2) · T. W. Davids, *Annals of evangelical nonconformity in Essex* (1863) · H. Smith, *The ecclesiastical history of Essex* (1932) · G. H. Turnbull, *Hartlib, Dury and Comenius: gleanings from Hartlib's papers* (1947) · W. A. Shaw, *A history of the English church during the civil wars and under the Commonwealth, 1640–1660*, 2 vols. (1900) · T. Webster, *Godly clergy in early Stuart England: the Caroline puritan movement, c.1620–1643* (1997)

Archives BL, notes on sermons, Add. MSS 39940–39942 · BL, Sloane MSS 1465 and 654 · CUL, notes on B. D. exercise; notes from post-Pride's Purge sermon · Essex RO, Finchingfield parish records · University of Sheffield, relating to John Dury, etc.

Marshall, Sir Stirrat Andrew William Johnson- (1912–1981), architect, was born on 19 February 1912 in India, the elder son of Felix William Norman Johnson-Marshall, a civil servant of Scottish descent who administered the salt trade, and his wife, Kate Jane Little. Stirrat's childhood was overshadowed by the fact that his father worked abroad in India and Baghdad: while he and his brother Professor Percy Johnson-Marshall had stirring adventures, there were attendant miseries connected with being at boarding-school in England, and having to spend the holidays with the headmaster and his family. He left the Queen Elizabeth School at Kirkby Lonsdale in 1930 as head boy and captain of cricket and rugby. He then attended the Liverpool University school of architecture, which was in transition from classical architecture to the modern movement promoted in schools such as the Dessau Bauhaus. Walter Gropius, its founder, made a deep impression on Johnson-Marshall during a visit to Liverpool. This may have been the point where the latter's devotion to the ideal of service to the community fused with his love of science and engineering, and his strong aesthetic feelings for a humane and inspiring environment for people to live in.

Johnson-Marshall left Liverpool in 1935 with a first-class honours degree and in 1936 became ARIBA. On 30 March 1937 he married Joan Mary Brighouse (*b.* 1914/15), a fellow architect from the Liverpool school whose father was an architect in Ormskirk and had given Stirrat holiday jobs; the couple had three sons and a daughter. Local authority posts in Willesden and the Isle of Ely confirmed his conviction that public service was the right vehicle for the pursuit of social architecture. During the Second World War he served with the Royal Engineers; in 1942, with the Japanese about to defeat the British, he organized a daring escape from Singapore with two colleagues which involved island-hopping by small boat and running the Japanese gauntlet to Colombo. He rarely spoke about this ordeal but was fascinated by the nature of courage for the rest of his life. The tragic death of his second son brought him back to Britain in time for D-day preparations. He was posted to the camouflage development and training centre at Farnham Castle, where he worked on the design and construction of inflatable tanks and guns, decoys which successfully fooled the Germans into defending non-existent landing sites. This was a seminal experience in the organization of designing and manufacturing skills to make a new product, and it remained fundamental to his dream of a revitalized building industry for the rest of his life.

From 1945 to 1948 Johnson-Marshall was deputy architect of Hertfordshire county council and from 1948 to 1956 chief architect of the architects' and buildings' branch at the Ministry of Education in partnership with his client, a senior civil servant. His principal concern during these years was to promote cycles of cheap, practical, and flexible schools which could be improved year on year in response to user needs and advances in technique. He was particularly interested in prefabricated systems of construction, which he saw as a key to reforming the building industry. The schools built in this period under his leadership gave Britain an international reputation for school-building.

During this time Johnson-Marshall was friendly with Henry Morris, the chief education officer of Cambridgeshire. A proponent of the community college, Morris devoted his life to the cause of architecture and the arts as essential ingredients of education and the good society. Morris's efforts to enrol the architects' and buildings' branch in his plans for a Cambridgeshire Bauhaus came to nothing, but it was no accident that Harry Ree and John West-Taylor—both close friends of Morris—later became respectively the first professor of education and the first registrar of the new University of York, a collegiate foundation in whose planning and design Johnson-Marshall was to become intimately involved.

Johnson-Marshall was generous to his colleagues, and made sure that the younger architects in his team got credit for ideas which may well have originally been his. At the same time his modesty disguised a ruthless determination to get done what he believed it was right to do, which astonished those who mistook his shyness for timidity. He was passionate about the basic elements of interaction between buildings and people, such as colour, light, sound, the control of temperature, and air movement, and the more tactile experiences from the ergonomics of furniture design to the feel of a handrail. These passions united the design teams which he led and heightened their awareness, raising their creativity to high levels. He was fond of quoting the painter Fernand Léger: 'Architecture is not an art. It's a natural function of the social order.' He despised what he called 'hat fashion architecture' and was unhappy about architects who failed to take their clients' needs seriously and saw architecture rather as an opportunity for the monumental expression of their own egos. His ideal was a vernacular architecture created by the community, in which client and architect were almost indistinguishable.

During the 1950s Johnson-Marshall was one of the leaders of the revolt of public architect members of the Royal Institute of British Architects, in a majority for the first time in its history, who aimed to turn the institute into a socially concerned body dedicated to improving the competence and political influence of the profession. His partnership with Robert Matthew, whom he joined in private practice in 1956, was not a happy one in terms of personalities, for the two architects responded differently to the pressures of survival in the market place. The Edinburgh and London offices of the firm went on to work as virtually separate practices for a number of years.

Stirrat's brother Percy pursued a parallel career in planning, first at the London county council when Robert Matthew was chief architect and then subsequently when he joined Matthew at Edinburgh University as professor of planning. He combined his talents as a brilliant teacher with distinguished contributions to research and consultancy worldwide. Although the two brothers respected one another's work, their shop talk was amusingly argumentative, perhaps a reflection of their childhood roles, with Stirrat as surrogate father responsible for an irrepressible younger brother.

The Robert Matthew/Johnson-Marshall partnership flourished, and the two founding partners shared the high ground of strategy while agreeing to differ on tactics. In London, Johnson-Marshall pursued his ideal of a better way of building through prefabrication in, for instance, the University of York, the earlier buildings of which were constructed in a heavily modified version of CLASP, the user-driven building system promoted by a group of local authorities. This project, preceded by the Commonwealth Institute and followed by the Central Lancashire New Town, was typical of his contribution to architecture and planning after he left public service.

Johnson-Marshall retired in 1978. Towards the end of his life he knew that he was swimming against the tide of a more materialistic political environment and this saddened him. However, the record shows that he had his chance in his time to make history and seized it with distinction. He became FRIBA in 1964, was appointed CBE in 1954, and was knighted in 1971. He was awarded an honorary doctorate by the University of York in 1972. He died in his Bristol office on 16 December 1981.

Andrew Derbyshire

Sources A. Saint, *Towards a social architecture: the role of school-building in post-war England* (1987) · S. Johnson-Marshall: *five commemorative speeches given at the Royal Society of Arts, 24 March 1982* (1982) [privately printed] · private information (2004) · personal knowledge (2004) · m. cert. · d. cert. · *WWW* · A. Derbyshire and C. Knevitt, 'RMJM: 40 years on', *Architects' Journal* (12 June 1997), 29–34
Wealth at death £21,914: probate, 4 June 1982, *CGPLA Eng. & Wales*

Marshall [Beche], **Thomas** (d. 1539), abbot of Colchester, is of unknown parentage and place of birth. His family name was probably Beche, but, having become a Benedictine monk, he adopted the name Marshall. He was educated at the University of Oxford, where he spent nine years studying logic, philosophy, and theology before supplicating for the degree of BTh on 24 January 1509; he was admitted to the degree on 10 December 1511. He supplicated for the degree of DTh on 20 April 1515. Marshall was prior of Wallingford Priory in Berkshire between 1518 and 1523, but he may have left the priory before its dissolution by Wolsey: Prior Geoffrey was named as surrendering the house in 1525. Marshall was elected abbot of St Werburgh's Abbey, Chester, in 1527, and held this office until 1529 or 1530, when the former abbot, John Birkenshaw, was restored after Wolsey's fall.

Thomas Marshall was elected abbot of the monastery of St John the Baptist, Colchester, on 10 June 1533, the temporalities being restored early in 1534. He had subscribed the petition to the pope of June 1530, appealing for the annulment of Henry VIII's marriage to Katherine of Aragon, but although he and sixteen monks acknowledged the king's supremacy over the church in 1534, Abbot Marshall was not entered on the list in the Colchester records of those taking the oath of succession. There was clearly some criticism of the king's policies about this time; the sub-prior, John Fraunces, was alleged to have called the king and council heretics. Two years later, on 15 December 1536, conversation at the abbot's dinner table turned to the Pilgrimage of Grace, and the diners were given information about the settlement reached at Doncaster nine days before. The abbot may have had some sympathy with the northern rising, if only for its opposition to the dissolution of the monasteries. Marshall's own opposition to royal policies, and the dangers inherent in his attitude are reflected in the examinations in November 1539 of Thomas Nuthake, physician and mercer, and Robert Rouse, mercer, both of Colchester; Nuthake pointed out that he ceased to be in the abbot's company about Christmas 1536, and Rouse ceased to socialize with him in 1537 because of his opposition to the royal supremacy and to the dissolution.

In his examination Nuthake reported that in Marshall's view the pope (referred to as the bishop of Rome) was the sole supreme head of the church, and Henry VIII only made the break with Rome in order to get his divorce from Katherine of Aragon. Marshall was especially critical of

Archbishop Cranmer, and of Thomas Audley and Thomas Cromwell; it is ironic that Audley in fact opposed the dissolution of St John's Abbey, recommending instead that it should be turned into a college. According to Nuthake, Abbot Thomas described those who had put Fisher and More to death as 'wretched tyrants and bloodsuckers' (*LP Henry VIII*, 14/2 no. 454) and said that they had died as martyrs and saints for upholding the pope. Most of these statements were corroborated by Rouse. Edmund Trowman, the abbot's servant, denied that Marshall opposed the royal supremacy, but made clear his opposition to the dissolution, alleging that the abbot said that he would die sooner than surrender his house. Marshall was also suspected of embezzling money, plate, and jewels, and had allegedly handed over two coffers to Trowman.

Cromwell's order for the dissolution of St John's Abbey was dated 6 November 1538. In a letter from Sir John Seyncler to Cromwell of 21 November, Marshall is reported to have said that the king would only have his house against his will, as the dissolution was contrary to right and law. Seyncler commented that he feared that Marshall had a 'cankered heart' (*LP Henry VIII*, 13/2 no. 887). Clearly Marshall was suspected of treason, principally, but not solely, for his hostility to the government's policy towards the monasteries, and he was put on trial at the end of November 1539. According to the indictment, he was accused of trying to deprive Henry VIII of the title of supreme head of the church and of asserting that all who supported and carried out the king's religious policies were heretics and tyrants. Marshall denied the allegations against him during his imprisonment in the Tower of London and pleaded not guilty at his trial. However, he was found guilty by a jury of Essex gentry and men of Colchester, and was hanged, drawn, and quartered at Colchester on 1 December 1539. JENNIFER C. WARD

Sources LP Henry VIII, vols. 4, 6–7, 11, 13–14 • J. E. Paul, 'The last abbots of Reading and Colchester', *BIHR*, 33 (1960), 115–21 • *Reg. Oxf.* • Emden, *Oxf.*, 4.382 • *VCH Essex*, vol. 2 • *VCH Cheshire*, vol. 3 • W. G. Benham, ed., *The red paper book of Colchester* (1902) • D. Knowles [M. C. Knowles], *The religious orders in England*, 3 (1959) • G. R. Elton, *Policy and police: the enforcement of the Reformation in the age of Thomas Cromwell* (1972), 155–60 • J. Caley and J. Hunter, eds., *Valor ecclesiasticus temp. Henrici VIII*, 6 vols., RC (1810–34)

Wealth at death £523 net income of St John's Abbey, Colchester, 1535: Caley, ed., *Valor ecclesiasticus*

Marshall, Thomas (1621–1685), dean of Gloucester and philologist, the son of Thomas Marshall (d. 1628), an illiterate blacksmith, and Helen James, was born at Barkby, Leicestershire, on 13 January 1621. Educated by Francis Foe, vicar of Barkby and alumnus of Lincoln College, Oxford, Marshall matriculated as a servitor of that same college on 23 October 1640. On 31 July 1641 he was elected to a Robert Trappes scholarship which he held until 1648. An ardent royalist, in 1644 Marshall joined at his own expense the university regiment commanded by Henry, earl of Dover, for which he was excused payment of the normal fees at his graduation as BA in 1645. Before his expulsion for absence by the parliamentary visitors on 14 July 1648 he went to Holland and in 1650 became chaplain to the Company of Merchant Adventurers in Rotterdam.

In 1656 he moved with the company to Dordrecht where he resided until his return to England in 1672.

At Oxford, Marshall developed a taste for theology and philology, undoubtedly inspired by the orientalist Edward Pococke and James Ussher, archbishop of Armagh, whose sermons he attended and whom 'he made the pattern for all religious and learned actions in his life' (Wood, *Ath. Oxon.*, 2nd edn, 1721, 2.782–3). In Holland, Marshall continued to cultivate and expand his knowledge of theology as well as of ancient languages, and met leading scholars such as the Arabist Jacob Golius, the polymath Isaac Vossius, and the philologist Francis Junius. In the late 1650s or early 1660s Junius requested Marshall to edit the Anglo-Saxon gospels, which he intended to publish with the Gothic translation facing. In the following years Marshall produced this edition and two volumes of commentary: *Observationes de versione Gothica* and *Observationes in versionem Anglo-Saxonicam*. The whole was published in 1665 as *Quatuor D.N.J.C. Evangeliorum … versiones*. The *Observationes* were the first manifestation of Marshall's scholarly versatility, combining his knowledge of the Bible with both Germanic and oriental languages. They incorporate the truly humanist combination of theology with philology and grammar that was so characteristic of his work.

Junius, Marshall's teacher of Gothic, stimulated his interest in Germanic languages, and provided him with material. Marshall briefly collected notes for an Old English and a Gothic grammar, both of which he abandoned prematurely, but made serious attempts to produce an edition of King Alfred's Old English translation of Orosius. His annotations to an incunable edition of Old Frisian law reveal his interest in Anglo-Saxon canon law. Marshall also pioneered the study of Icelandic, and possessed seventeen Middle Dutch manuscripts, mostly religious texts. His Germanic studies are characterized by sagacity and precision, and differ from Junius's in their deliberate attention to grammar.

In the course of the 1660s Marshall's contacts with Oxford show his increasing occupation with oriental studies. He corresponded with English orientalists such as Thomas Smith, Robert Sheringham, Edward Bernard, and Samuel Clarke, whom he supported by procuring manuscripts and books, including Apollonius's *Conics*, from the Low Countries. In Holland he bought some of his Coptic manuscripts, as well as several Armenian books. Marshall presumably edited Abudacnus's *Historia Jacobitarum, seu, Coptorum in Egypto* (1675), to which he supplied a preface announcing his forthcoming edition of the Coptic gospels. Collations and transcripts of Coptic, Greek, Arabic, and Ethiopic gospels, as well as his Coptic vocabulary are the preliminaries to a project that never materialized. Together with Thomas Hyde, Marshall supervised the publication of the gospels and Acts in Malay (1677), to which he wrote the preface. Marshall's publications never matched his erudition. His most important contribution to oriental studies consists of his generous assistance to others.

Marshall also contributed to the development of the

Oxford University Press by procuring types on the continent, including Junius's matrices of Old English letters, at the request of Bishop John Fell. He was furthermore involved in the compilation of Richard Parr's life of Ussher, and published anonymously *The Catechism Set Forth in the Book of Common Prayer* (1679).

After the Restoration Marshall took his BD in Oxford *in absentia* by the licence of Archbishop Sheldon. Still in Holland, he was elected fellow of Lincoln College (17 December 1668), and received his DD (28 June 1669). On the resignation of Nathaniel, Lord Crewe, Marshall was elected rector of Lincoln (19 October 1672), after which he returned to Oxford for good. He was made a royal chaplain and held the rectorship at Bladon from May 1680 to February 1682. In 1681 he became dean of Gloucester. Marshall, who never married, died in Lincoln College on 18 April 1685, and was buried in All Saints' Church. He bequeathed 453 books and 159 manuscripts to the Bodleian Library, and 1040 books and 77 volumes of civil war pamphlets to Lincoln College. Marshall's executor John Kettlewell inherited his Socinian books, on condition that they 'not come into the hands of others, that may be corrupted by them'. The remainder of his estate was sold and most of the proceeds were left to Lincoln College to provide financial support for 'poor scholars'. 'Marshall's scholars' were regularly elected from 1688 to 1765, when the scholarships ceased to be distinctively designated.

K. DEKKER

Sources G. J. Toomer, *Eastern wisedome and learning: the study of Arabic in seventeenth-century England* (1996) · V. Green, *The commonwealth of Lincoln College, 1427–1977* (1979) · Wood, *Ath. Oxon.*, 2nd edn, 2.782–3 · F. Madan, H. H. E. Craster, and N. Denholm-Young, *A summary catalogue of Western manuscripts in the Bodleian Library at Oxford*, 2/2 (1937), 992–1008, 1205–11 · *DNB* · J. A. W. Bennett, 'The history of Old English and Old Norse studies in England from the time of Francis Junius till the end of the eighteenth century', DPhil diss., U. Oxf., 1938 · H. Hart, *Notes on a century of typography at the university press* (1900) · A. Hamilton, 'The English interest in the Arabic-speaking Christians', *The 'Arabick' interest of the natural philosophers in seventeenth-century England*, ed. G. A. Russell (1994), 30–53 · W. D. Macray, *Annals of the Bodleian Library, Oxford*, 2nd edn (1890) · M. Burrows, ed., *The register of the visitors of the University of Oxford, from AD 1647 to AD 1658*, CS, new ser., 29 (1881), 165, 507 · A. Hamilton, 'An Egyptian traveller in the republic of letters: Josephus Barbatus or Abudacnus the Copt', *Journal of the Warburg and Courtauld Institutes*, 57 (1994), 123–50 · M. Balen, *Beschrijvinge der Stad Dordrecht* (1667), 194–5 · K. Dekker, 'The old Frisian studies of Jan van Vliet (1622–1666) and Thomas Marshall (1621–1685)', *Approaches to old Frisian philology*, ed. R. H. Bremmer, T. S. B. Johnston, and O. Vries (1998), 113–38 · private information (2004) [S. Postles]
Archives BL, corresp., Add. MSS 4276, 4277, 22905 · Bodl. Oxf., corresp. · Bodl. Oxf., MS collection and papers · Bodl. Oxf., inventory of books · Bodl. Oxf., MSS · Lincoln College, Oxford, papers | Bodl. Oxf., MS Rawl. · Bodl. Oxf., MSS Tanner, corresp. · Bodl. Oxf., MSS Wood
Likenesses engraving, repro. in *Oxford Almanack* (1743) · portrait, Lincoln College, Oxford

Marshall, Thomas Falcon (1818–1878), painter, was born at Liverpool in December 1818. His prolific practice chiefly lay in Manchester, and in Liverpool where he lived until 1847. After 1836 he exhibited regularly at the Liverpool Academy and, after 1839, at the Royal Academy in London. In 1840 he was awarded a silver medal by the Society of Arts for an oil painting of a figure subject. In total he exhibited sixty works at the Royal Academy, forty at the British Institution, and forty-two at the Suffolk Street Gallery in London, remaining well represented at the Liverpool and Manchester exhibitions throughout his life. A versatile artist, he undertook portraits, landscapes, genre, and history paintings. *The Parting Day* and *Sad News from the War* were probably his best-known works. He died on 2 April 1878 at 31 Ducie Street, Chorlton upon Medlock, Lancashire. He was survived by his wife, Amelia Jane, and at least one son.

ALBERT NICHOLSON, rev. EMILY M. WEEKS

Sources Bryan, *Painters* · Wood, *Vic. painters*, 3rd edn · *Art Journal*, 40 (1878), 169 · Graves, *Artists*, 3rd edn · d. cert. · *CGPLA Eng. & Wales* (1878)
Wealth at death under £2000: probate, 3 June 1878, *CGPLA Eng. & Wales*

Marshall, Thomas Humphrey (1893–1981), sociologist, was born in fashionable Bloomsbury, in London, on 19 December 1893. He was the second son and the fourth of six children of a successful architect, William Cecil Marshall, and his wife, Margaret, the daughter of Archdeacon J. F. Lloyd of Waitemata, New Zealand. The family home has been described in the *Memories* (1981) of Tom's younger sister Frances Partridge. His Anglicanism was strongly reinforced at Rugby School, but he subsequently lost his faith at Trinity College, Cambridge, where he gained a first in part one of the history tripos in 1914. That summer, destined for a career in the foreign service, he went to Germany to learn German, only to be interned in a prisoner of war camp at Ruhleben, near Berlin.

The making of a sociologist Ruhleben was an enforced escape for Marshall from the narrow social confines of his background in the English bourgeois intelligentsia. A prison camp, being non-producing, cannot be a class society in the ordinary sense. But the merchant seamen and fishermen, the 'camp proletariat', introduced Marshall to an unfamiliar subculture of class: 'without its seafarers Ruhleben would have been a very different camp, softer, less virile, top-heavy with intellectuals' (Ketchum, 126). In a formal academic sense, it was an unknowing introduction to his future profession. The experience of Ruhleben was morally and intellectually crucial: it generated in Marshall a new dimension of social sensibility reaching well beyond Victorian London and Edwardian Cambridge. Superficially and initially, however, it was not so. Marshall returned to Cambridge to compete successfully for a fellowship at Trinity College on the basis of a dissertation on seventeenth-century guilds, a topic suggested by J. H. Clapham.

But Marshall soon made a diversion, at least temporarily, from the normal path of the don into another encounter with working-class people. He stood as a Labour candidate for Farnham, a safe Conservative constituency in Surrey, at the general election of 1922. He was beaten, and returned to Cambridge knowing that he was not suited to a career as a politician. Campaigning did not fit his temperament. Though politics engaged his deep interest, he

Thomas Humphrey Marshall (1893–1981), by Howard Coster, 1944

methods of survey, the powers and limits of social measurement, and the logic of multivariate analysis. But he remained a sophisticated consumer and did not become a professional practitioner of these statistical techniques; for this he advanced the dubious rationalization, by analogy with his experience as a skilled if amateur violinist, that a sociologist must not only learn to use instruments but also 'learn to grow them on the tips of his fingers' (Marshall, *Sociology at the Crossroads*, 42). This also, some believe, was a mistake by the man and a lost opportunity for his subject.

For better or worse Marshall never acquired the driving puritanical dedication to research and writing which might have been possible in the ethos of Houghton Street. His professionalism was never so narrow. Teaching was at least as important as research. Administration at the LSE, burdensome as he found it, was a compelling duty, especially as professor of social institutions and head of the social work department (1944–9) and later (1954–6) as Martin White professor of sociology. Public service, though never sought, was always felt as a call to be unstintingly answered. He served in the Foreign Office research department from 1939 to 1944, with the Allied Control Commission for Germany (British Element) 1949–50, and as director of the social sciences division of UNESCO from 1956 to 1960. And beyond both professional and public duty there remained the constant pull of a highly civilized private life of music and friendship where he expressed perhaps his greatest gifts of character.

In his extra-academic excursions from 1939, and during his retirement to Cambridge from 1960, Marshall applied his sociology. He did so in the analysis of German war propaganda, in planning the post-war reconstruction of German education, and in directing the UNESCO effort towards applying the social sciences to the problems of development. In his retirement he devoted himself to social policy and administration, writing and revising the standard text on that subject as well as a series of occasional papers which Robert Pinker persuaded him to put together and publish. Again the work is applied sociology, indebted to, yet independent of, the definition of social policy and social administration which was so strongly advanced after 1950 by Richard Titmuss and the productive group of academically passionate advocates of welfare at the LSE. Marshall's definition was wider, and more securely grounded in history, though it lacked the detailed empirical foundation of much of Titmuss's work. It was also less sharply egalitarian, and more an advocacy of the 'Butskellite' welfare state.

Marshall's definitive studies in social policy were not written until after his retirement. In particular, *Social Policy in the Twentieth Century* (1967) and the last collection of essays, *The Right to Welfare* (1981), demonstrate his unique ability to relate the sociological aspects of social institutions to issues of social policy. Marshall believed that the value conflicts generated by the interaction of competitive economic markets, representative democracy, and statutory social services indicate the resilience rather than the weakness of democratic welfare capitalism in

decided at that point that the academic cloister must be his base. He went on with his historical studies, revising G. T. Warner's *Landmarks in Industrial History* (1924) and writing a short life of James Watt (1925), but here too was a limitation of personal character. For he also knew that 'it was not in his nature to spend his working life poring over original documents to the extent demanded by reputable historical research' (Marshall, 'British sociological career', 91). As the end of his fellowship approached he realized that he must get away from Cambridge and, accordingly, he applied for the first post he saw advertised, that of a tutor to students of social work at the London School of Economics (LSE). Beveridge appointed him in 1925. Thus his formal journey into sociology began; it was soon confirmed by his promotion to a readership in 1930.

Sociological appointments: LSE and social policy During the 1930s Marshall came to identify himself wholeheartedly as a professional sociologist. He helped to launch the *British Journal of Sociology* and developed interests in social stratification and social policy, editing major studies such as *Class Conflict and Social Stratification* (1938) and *The Population Problem* (1938). In neither of these fields, however, did he equip himself with the statistical skills which might have been available to him from his colleagues A. L. Bowley or, later, D. V. Glass. Such expertise would have been well within his competence. It is clear from his essays and reviews that he thoroughly understood the

the context of social change. He also challenged the convention that the abolition of poverty requires strictly egalitarian policies, arguing that certain inequalities which facilitate economic growth are a precondition of the elimination of poverty, provided that the state guarantees the right to a basic level of social services.

In Marshall's writing there is elegance and economy: sociological jargon is avoided, and meticulous citation shunned. In his teaching there was a personal style of clear, cool analysis dominating a lightly carried but wide erudition. In his public and administrative work there was the rigorous honesty of a Leonard Woolf combined with no less rigorous standards of professional skill. Courtesy and competence, diffidence and dedication marked all his activities. Marshall's qualities of mind have been described as 'a finely balanced tension of opposites' (Lockwood, 363).

Citizenship How is it possible to explain the transition from the Victorian order of class inequality, evangelical religion, and social deference, to the consensus which produced the welfare state and the Butskellism that Marshall spent his life in analysing? His answer was to emerge as sociology. Yet it was rooted in the intellectual culture of Cambridge. First, it was an extension of Maitland's view of history to take in the development of civil, political, and social rights in the twentieth century. Second, it represented the further development of a corpus of work in the 'moral sciences' in Cambridge from the middle of the nineteenth century—with Henry Sidgwick, Alfred Marshall, and Leslie Stephen as the founding fathers—which aimed to produce a secular substitute for the traditional theological justifications of social morality and explanations of social integration.

T. H. Marshall absorbed these ideas and preferences into his personal life. They also appeared later in his writing and most cogently when he revisited Cambridge in 1949 to deliver the Marshall lectures, published in the following year, *Citizenship and Social Class*. By that time a mature sociologist, he found it natural to expound his theme from Alfred Marshall's equally characteristic phrasing in 1873 of the question 'whether progress may not go on steadily, if slowly, till, by occupation at least, every man is a gentleman' (T. H. Marshall, *Citizenship and Social Class*, 1950, 4). Alfred Marshall had held that it would. T. H. Marshall was to go on to show how, and to what extent, it actually did—through the development of citizenship. His method was that of the detached and civilized observer from the study and the library, rather than the party activist on the hustings. R. H. Tawney (his senior by thirteen years) had gone from Balliol to Toynbee Hall in the East End of London and to the Workers' Educational Association in Rochdale. George Orwell (ten years his junior) went to the slums of Paris, the spike, and Wigan Pier. Marshall never moved far from the Cambridge and Bloomsbury connection. Except that he went to Houghton Street.

Marshall went to LSE stamped with the personal and professional morals and manners of the Cambridge élite.

But he was not merely a representative of that high culture. His assured gentlemanliness was more than convention: it was expressed exquisitely by a shy and handsome man of critical but generous sympathy towards others. His austere blend of irony, diffidence, and duty made him a delightful colleague and a punctilious public servant. His quiet passion for justice took him momentarily to the hustings, made him a co-signatory of the memorial to the master of Trinity College in favour of reinstating Bertrand Russell to a lectureship, and impelled him to a lifetime's study of class inequality and social policy. His awareness of his own limitations tended to draw a modest veil over what can now be seen as a genuinely original sociological mind.

For Marshall civil rights are the bulwark of a free democracy. Legal rights as rights of citizenship are dispersed through many institutions: they are intrinsic to all social relations, not simply to the polity; and they refer to citizens as political actors not merely, as with social rights, to people as consumers. They are more than an institution: they are a culture. The rights to freedom of thought, speech, and assembly, and the right to justice and the rule of law are externalized expressions of principles internalized by upbringing.

> They thus become part of the individual's personality, a pervasive element in his daily life, an intrinsic component of his culture, the foundation of his capacity to act socially and the creator of the environmental conditions which make social action possible in a democratic civilisation. (Marshall, *Right to Welfare*, 141)

Marshall, the inheritor of high civility and the scholar of high sensibility, was here describing his own best self, his ideal for his country, and the ultimate hope of ethical socialists for all societies.

Marriages, honours, and legacy Marshall was twice married. On 28 March 1925, the year of his first appointment at the LSE, he married Marjorie (*b.* 1898/9), daughter of Arthur Tomson, artist. She died in 1931. There were no children. In 1934 he married Nadine, daughter of Mark Hambourg, pianist; their son Mark was born in 1937. Appointed CMG in 1947, Marshall received other honours and awards in his retirement, including the presidency of the International Sociological Association from 1959 to 1962, and honorary fellowship at the LSE and honorary degrees from the universities of Southampton (DSc, 1969), Leicester (DLitt, 1970), York (DUniv, 1971), and Cambridge (LittD, 1978). In effect Marshall never retired, and his last book, *The Right to Welfare*, was published only a few months before his death, which occurred at his home, 6 Drosier Road, Cambridge, on 29 November 1981.

Marshall's contemporary relevance outlived him, and forms the title, *Citizenship Today*, of the edition of the twelve T. H. Marshall lectures delivered since their inauguration at the University of Southampton in 1983. The lecturers, all leading British social scientists, agree that T. H. Marshall was a highly significant figure in sociology after the Second World War. His analysis of citizenship and social class with its historical framework of evolving civil, political, and social rights and its contention that citizenship and social class 'have been at war in the twentieth century' (Marshall, *Sociology at the Crossroads*, 87, 115) are both applauded and attacked. Raymond Aron detects *histoire raisonnée*. Giddens blames Marshall for leaning towards the ethical evolutionism of L. T. Hobhouse and his neglect of Marx. Dennis and Halsey argue that Marshall's was a crucial contribution to the sociology of ethical socialism. For Mann the thesis is too English. For Giddens it omits women. All these aspects of the schema are disputable. What is beyond dispute is that Marshall set the stage on which argument about citizenship will continue for the foreseeable future. A. H. HALSEY

Sources M. Bulmer and A. M. Rees, eds., *Citizenship today: the contemporary relevance of T. H. Marshall* (1996) · N. Dennis and A. H. Halsey, 'The theory of citizenship: T. H. Marshall (1893–1981)', *English ethical socialism* (1988) · D. Lockwood, 'For T. H. Marshall', *Sociology*, 8 (1974), 363–7 · T. H. Marshall, *Sociology at the crossroads* (1963) · T. H. Marshall, *The right to welfare and other essays* (1981) · F. Partridge, *Memories* (1981) · J. D. Ketchum, *Ruhleben: a prison camp society* (1965) · A. Giddens, *Profiles and critiques of social theory* (1982) · T. H. Marshall, 'A British sociological career', *International Social Science Journal*, 25/1–2 (1973) · D. G. MacRae, *LSE*, 64 (Nov 1982) · *DNB* · m. cert. [Marjorie Tomson] · *CGPLA Eng. & Wales* (1982)
Archives BLPES, papers
Likenesses P. Adams, caricature, 1932, repro. in R. Dahrendorf, *LSE: a history of the London School of Economics and Political Science, 1895–1995* (1995) · H. Coster, photograph, 1944, NPG [*see illus.*] · photograph, repro. in Bulmer and Rees, eds., *Citizenship today*
Wealth at death £62,432: probate, 23 March 1982, *CGPLA Eng. & Wales*

Marshall, Thomas William (1818–1877), Roman Catholic controversialist, was the son of John Marshall, government agent for emigration to New South Wales. After attending Archdeacon Burney's school in Greenwich, in October 1835 he was admitted to St John's College, Cambridge; he migrated a year later to Trinity, from which he graduated BA in 1840. After ordination the same year he was appointed curate of Swallowcliffe and Anstey, Wiltshire, and on 8 July 1845 he married Harriet, the daughter of the Revd William Dansey, rector of Donhead St Andrew, Wiltshire.

Marshall and his wife were received into the Roman Catholic church at Wardour in November 1845. Poverty drove them abroad for a time, but in 1848 he was appointed an inspector of schools, with responsibility for Catholic schools in the southern counties of England and Wales. The ill feeling aroused by his pamphlet *Christianity in China* (1858), which subjected protestant missionary methods to ridicule, led to his resignation in 1860. His major work, *Christian Missions*, published in three volumes in 1862, though partisan, was thoroughly researched and widely acclaimed. Subsequently Marshall made several lecture tours in the United States, where his forceful and incisive style was much appreciated. In 1873 he received the honorary degree of LLD from Georgetown University. On his return from America he continued his career as a polemical writer and journalist, attacking the Church of England in abrasive style. He died at Surbiton, Surrey, on

14 December 1877, and was buried at Mortlake. He was survived by his wife, son, and daughter. His brothers Frederick and Arthur were also converts to Roman Catholicism. G. MARTIN MURPHY

Sources Gillow, *Lit. biog. hist.* · Venn, *Alum. Cant.* · *The Tablet* (22–9 Dec 1877), 775, 822 · J. Gondon, *Motifs de conversion de dix ministres Anglicans* (1847), 20–37 · J. Gondon, *Conversion de cent cinquante ministres Anglicans* (1846), 90–102 · *The letters and diaries of John Henry Newman*, ed. C. S. Dessain and others, [31 vols.] (1961–), vol. 11 · m. cert.

Marshall, Walter (1628–1679), clergyman and ejected minister, was born on 15 June 1628 at Bishopwearmouth, co. Durham, the son of Walter Marshall, the curate there from 1619 to 1629. In 1639 at the age of eleven he was elected a scholar of Winchester College. At New College, Oxford, he graduated BA on 28 April 1652; he was a fellow from 1648 to 1657. On 10 May 1654 he was admitted to the rectory of Fawley, Hampshire, and in the same year acted as an assistant to the commissioners into the ministry in the county. On 28 November 1656 he was admitted to the living of Hursley, 4 miles from Winchester, but did not get on well with the patron, Richard Major, Richard Cromwell's father-in-law. On 15 December 1657 he was also elected a fellow of Winchester.

Marshall resigned from Winchester in 1661. In August 1662 he was ejected from Hursley following the Act of Uniformity, but soon after he settled as minister of an Independent congregation at Gosport. He was presented at the assizes in autumn 1662, for taking a service without reading from the Book of Common Prayer. Marshall was still living at Hursley in November 1667, but appears in the episcopal returns of 1669 as preaching at Winchester and Alton. In 1672 he was living under the protection of Richard Norton, patron of the donative cure of Southwick in Hampshire, and obtained a preaching licence there as a congregationalist on 10 August. It is reported that Marshall was continually troubled by an unquiet conscience and even consulted Richard Baxter about it. When he made his will on 24 July 1679, Marshall was living in the parish of Alverstoke. He named his wife, Rebecca, as executor, gave to his son, Walter, most of his books and the reversion of a living granted him by Winchester College, and left £80 to Anne, one of two daughters. By 1 August he was dead. His funeral sermon was preached by Samuel Tomlyns of Andover. It was published with a preface dated 23 August 1680 and dedicated to Lady Anne Constantine, Mrs Mary Fiennes, and the inhabitants of Gosport. Marshall's *The Gospel Mystery of Sanctification* was published posthumously in 1692. James Hervey stated in a preface to the sixth and many subsequent editions that, if banished to a desolate island with only a bible and two other books, he would choose this work as one of them.

CHARLOTTE FELL-SMITH, *rev.* STEPHEN WRIGHT

Sources *Calamy rev.*, 341 · T. F. Kirby, *Winchester scholars: a list of the wardens, fellows, and scholars of … Winchester College* (1888) · Foster, *Alum. Oxon.* · J. T. Cliffe, *The puritan gentry besieged, 1650–1700* (1993) · S. Tomlyns, *Faith of the saints … preached at the funeral of … Walter Marshall* (1680) · will and inventory, Hants. RO, 1679 B 030/2
Archives Cambs. AS, letters to Richard Cromwell and Dorothy Cromwell

Wealth at death see will and inventory, Hants. RO, 1679 B 030/2

Marshall, Walter Charles, Baron Marshall of Goring (1932–1996), physicist and public servant, was born on 5 March 1932 at 15 Tymawr Road, Rumney, Newport, Monmouthshire, the last of three children of Frank Marshall (*d*. 1939), a baker, and his wife, Amy, *née* Pearson. His father died when he was seven years old. There was no record of academic ability in his family; his exceptional mathematical gifts were recognized at his grammar school, St Illtyd's College, Cardiff, and he won a scholarship to study mathematical physics at the University of Birmingham. He also became Welsh junior chess champion. He graduated with first-class honours at Birmingham and was awarded a PhD degree at the early age of twenty-two for his thesis, 'Antiferromagnetism and neutron scattering from ferromagnets'.

Early career in physics Marshall joined the theoretical physics division at the Atomic Energy Research Establishment, Harwell, Berkshire, in 1954. He first investigated the behaviour of shockwaves in magnetically confined plasmas, but soon returned to his interests in solid state physics and magnetism. On 12 April 1955 he married Ann Vivienne Sheppard (*b*. 1933/4), a schoolteacher, and daughter of Ernest Vivian Sheppard, a commercial traveller; they later had a son and a daughter. Marshall then had two periods of study leave in the USA, at Berkeley, California, in 1957–8, and Harvard, in 1958–9, where he made a great impression and formed many lifelong friendships. He remained strongly pro-American in outlook. On his return to Harwell he was promoted to group leader and then, at the age of twenty-eight, to be head of the theoretical physics division, a powerful group of forty outstanding scientists covering a range of subjects. It was a remarkable opportunity for an able, ambitious, and supremely confident young man, and Marshall exploited the situation brilliantly. The Harwell laboratory became known as a centre of excellence in materials physics and attracted a number of researchers from Britain, Europe, and the USA.

Marshall's major personal contributions were to the theory of the solid state related to magnetic properties, but his interests were wide and he developed, with many colleagues, experimental programmes to expand the theoretical understanding of materials. In particular he sought to expand and promote the use of the new technique of neutron diffraction for the study of the structures of solids and liquids, which had become possible with the generation of beams of neutrons from research reactors. He was the author or co-author of more than sixty papers between 1956 and 1969, and his book *The Theory of Thermal Neutron Scattering* (1971), written with Stephen Lovesey, remained the standard text on the subject for many years. In 1964 Marshall delivered the Kelvin lecture to the British Association for the Advancement of Science, entitled 'The study of solids and liquids using thermal neutrons'. In the same year he was awarded the Maxwell medal for outstanding contributions to theoretical physics by the Institute of Physics, and in 1971 he was

Walter Charles Marshall, Baron Marshall of Goring (1932–1996), by Godfrey Argent, 1973

elected to the Royal Society, becoming the youngest fellow at that time. He continued to work on problems in magnetism and superconductivity for mental relaxation, recording the results in a series of handwritten notebooks, but he published no papers on theoretical physics after 1971.

Technical direction: the Harwell years Marshall's demonstrated capacity for scientific leadership and his ability to inspire the work of others led to his appointment as deputy director of the Atomic Energy Research Establishment at Harwell in 1966 and director in 1968. At this time the laboratory was seeking new objectives. Many of the scientific questions that had been vitally important to the early development of nuclear power had been met, and some subjects pioneered at Harwell were being moved to independent organizations. Marshall first attempted to institute at Harwell a high field magnetic laboratory and a research reactor producing high-flux neutron beams, in order to further the scientific leadership he had won in these areas, but the proposals failed to win government support because of lack of funds and because they did not promise the early industrial applications sought by the Ministry of Technology (the responsible department). Marshall accepted that the days of academic freedom at Harwell were over, and that a large, multidisciplinary laboratory like Harwell had to be seen to contribute to the national welfare. He argued for and later implemented a policy of diversification aimed at assisting British industry in specific areas and meeting government objectives outside the nuclear-energy field.

There were formidable difficulties, both internal and external. Legal permission to pursue topics that were not covered by the original nuclear remit of the Atomic Energy Authority (AEA) had to be obtained from the Ministry of Technology, and any government funding through the requirement boards set up by that ministry. In addition, nuclear work for external organizations, mainly the exploitation of irradiation facilities and the provision of radioactive sources, now had to be charged for and the work given a commercial edge. Success depended on gaining funding from an initially uninterested and even hostile industry. The internal problems were also severe. Turning the Harwell of the early 1960s into an organization earning a large fraction of its income from sources outside the AEA involved a cultural revolution. Marshall introduced a project system, cutting across the traditional divisional structure, and gave the main responsibility for making industrial contacts and earning industrial money to the project managers themselves, supported by a contracts and marketing organization. This key decision forced a large number of Harwell staff into close contact with industrial firms and other potential customers, with the result that external hostility fell away as the quality of the scientific support on offer was appreciated.

By 1976 the new 'industrial programmes' accounted for 50 per cent of the total effort at Harwell, and the laboratory had a new lease of life. The staff had been reduced by 25 per cent over the previous ten years, but numbers had stabilized by 1975. Marshall was awarded the Glazebrook medal of the Institute of Physics in 1975 for his outstanding administrative achievement. The pattern of work for external customers established at Harwell was followed by other national laboratories, and paved the way for later reorganizations of the AEA.

Nuclear power advocacy and the Department of Energy Marshall was appointed to the board of the UK Atomic Energy Authority in 1972. He became deputy chairman in 1975 and chairman in 1981, and was knighted for distinguished public service in 1982. Over this period he became known in Britain and other countries as a consistent, strong supporter of nuclear power.

Paradoxically, a task which brought Marshall to wide public notice concerned energy policy but not nuclear power. He was appointed as part-time chief scientist to the Department of Energy in 1974, with a remit to reorient and expand the department's research programme in the light of the 'oil shocks' of the early 1970s. To this end he chaired the Advisory Council on Research and Development for Fuel and Power, and the new Offshore Energy Technology Board. He organized studies of the potential value of new energy technologies against different scenarios of supply projections, and inaugurated the energy technology support unit at Harwell to encourage schemes of energy conservation and to evaluate the potential of renewable sources of energy. He also led a group of academics and members of the electricity supply industry in

a study of the feasibility of introducing into Britain large-scale schemes of combined heat and power linked to district heating. The conclusions were that such schemes would not be viable unless gas prices in Britain increased substantially, though a majority favoured building a lead scheme. At the same time Marshall was vigorously pursuing nuclear interests, and he engaged in several attempts to sell British nuclear services in countries starting nuclear power programmes. A clash between him and Tony Benn, who as secretary of state for energy was increasingly suspicious of the nuclear lobby, was, perhaps, inevitable. In 1977 Marshall was asked abruptly to return to full-time duties at the AEA.

Marshall's work on energy policy and projections of fuel supply only strengthened his enthusiasm for nuclear power. He considered that a growing nuclear-power component backed by an efficient nuclear industry was essential both to the long-term stability of energy supplies in this country and to meeting the energy requirements of an expanding world population. He played an important part in the debate in the 1970s about reactor choice. He became convinced that the UK should follow most of the rest of the world and build pressurized water reactors (PWRs), because of the advantages of increased factory fabrication, international technical support, and possible entry to foreign markets. But there were doubts about the safety of high-pressure systems. The most serious criticism, voiced by the government's chief scientist (Sir Alan Cottrell), was that the steel pressure-vessel surrounding the reactor core might fracture under operational or accident conditions. Marshall saw that this concern could be addressed only by a comprehensive analysis of all relevant features of design, fabrication, fracture analysis, non-destructive testing, and quality assurance. He assembled a group of theoreticians and materials scientists, including many academic members, who reported finally that safety criteria could be met by rigorous attention to detail and, in particular, to non-destructive testing during commissioning and in service that was validated independently. This report marked a significant stage in the overall safety case for PWRs, and the exercise demonstrated again Marshall's intellectual ability and technical leadership. He later chaired a task force from the Central Electricity Generating Board (CEGB) and the nuclear industry, charged with determining how the design of a PWR based on that of an American reactor could be altered to accommodate the requirements of the safety regulators in Britain.

Marshall also took a leading role in the British involvement in the International Fuel Cycle Evaluation Exercise launched by President Jimmy Carter in 1977 to assess and reduce the danger of the proliferation of nuclear weapons arising from civilian nuclear power. President Carter had deferred indefinitely the reprocessing of spent fuel from nuclear power stations to recover uranium and plutonium for future use as fuel; he had also cancelled the development of fast (neutron) reactors in the USA, which were most efficient in using plutonium as fuel. Such a strategy was the core of the AEA's programme at the time, and the British, with others, mounted a vigorous defence. Marshall was thanked officially for the part he played. He remained convinced that the long-term future of nuclear power depended on the development of fast reactors which would enable a large proportion of the world's uranium to be used as nuclear fuel, and he considered that fast reactors could be used in ways that would minimize the threat of the proliferation of nuclear weapons. He summarized these arguments in the fifth Cockcroft lecture, published in *Nuclear Energy* in 1980. Later, as chairman of the CEGB, he agreed that the board would fund 30 per cent of the total AEA expenditure on fast-reactor development. However, he came to accept that fast reactors would not be economic commercially for many decades, and the British programme did not survive the later break-up of the CEGB.

The CEGB and later years Marshall was appointed chairman of the Central Electricity Generating Board, at the time a state-owned monopoly responsible for electricity in England and Wales, in 1982. He and others believed that a major reason for his appointment was the government's wish to increase the contribution made by nuclear power through building a series of PWRs. However, he accepted that coal would remain the most important fuel for electricity generation for the foreseeable future—gas was barely considered in 1983—and that the board faced organizational problems owing to the increase in size (and hence the decrease in number) of individual power stations.

The first crisis that Marshall faced was linked to the dependence on coal as the main fuel—the long miners' strike in 1984–5. The CEGB had made plans to meet such a situation by building up coal stocks and planning to burn oil in both oil- and coal-fired stations. Marshall believed that the CEGB had an overriding responsibility to maintain electricity supply, and thought that the strike might be a long one. He therefore won board support to burn more oil, at greater cost, since the output from the nuclear stations could not be increased quickly. This strategy was successful in that electricity supplies were not interrupted and the extra cost of oil fuel was borne by the government. Marshall was rewarded with a life peerage, as Baron Marshall of Goring, in 1985. He later confessed that he had enjoyed the excitement of the struggle.

Marshall always insisted on basing policy on sound science, as in the position he took in the debate over acid rain. He was opposed at first to spending large sums on reducing emissions of acid gases from coal-fired stations, but he supported a joint research programme with Norway and Sweden into the effects of acid deposition, and later agreed that control was necessary. Similarly he was concerned that the language used in the debate about nuclear power was scientifically accurate and reflected properly the probability of future events; he disliked jargon and hated sound bites. He gave a series of lectures between 1980 and 1986 on those aspects of nuclear power that caused public unease, including the threat of large accidents and of the proliferation of nuclear weapons, and the problem of radioactive waste disposal, and he

inspired and edited a comprehensive set of papers entitled *Nuclear Power Technology*, published in 1983.

All nuclear power plans suffered a serious set-back following the accident to a reactor at Chernobyl in the USSR in April 1986. Marshall led the British delegation to the meeting organized by the International Atomic Energy Agency to examine the reasons for and consequences of the accident. He also led a comparative study of design standards and of operating and regulatory practice. He became convinced that such an accident could not happen to a reactor under the conditions imposed in Western countries by the late 1980s, but he saw the danger to the world's nuclear industry posed by the public reaction to Chernobyl and played a leading role in the formation of a worldwide organization aimed at raising safety standards in all utilities operating nuclear power plants. The World Association of Nuclear Operators (WANO) was based on the Institution of Nuclear Power Operators in the USA. WANO provided a mechanism by which information on safety standards and practices could be exchanged directly between the organizations responsible for operating plants, thus encouraging comparison and emulation. Marshall was elected the executive chairman in 1989, and could report by 1991 that the organization included every nuclear utility in the world.

Privatization of electricity generation in 1989 finally ended Marshall's career in public service. He had argued for retaining a single national organization for the generation and transmission of electricity, but lost the argument. He regretted the demise of a public service company with an obligation to continuous supply in favour of energy companies whose priority would be to gain commercial contracts, but he accepted the government's decision to introduce competition into the industry and agreed to be chairman-designate of National Power, the company originally intended to run nuclear reactors as well as some other stations. However, this scheme foundered in 1989, when the government decided to withdraw nuclear stations from the planned privatization, and Marshall resigned. In a valedictory address to the British Nuclear Energy Society he described the industrial and financial difficulties which had led to the decisions to retain the nuclear stations in the public sector and to cancel the plan to build several PWRs after the Sizewell B reactor; the main reasons cited were the high capital charges and high return on investment expected in the private sector.

Marshall continued to work on nuclear projects in other countries after leaving the CEGB, and he also became a consultant to a syndicate insuring nuclear risks at Lloyds as well as a Lloyds name. He was chairman of WANO until 1993, and undertook a large number of visits to overseas utilities. He remained an ambassador for WANO after 1993 because of the close relations he had built with utilities in eastern European countries. He also became an adviser to the Kansai Electric Power Company of Japan.

Marshall dominated the nuclear power scene for two decades. He could be intimidating and very demanding, but he earned the respect of his close colleagues and of the technical community by his intellectual gifts, total commitment to his causes, and his willingness to lead from the front. He was not so successful in his dealings with politicians, who had different priorities. He collected many national and international honours, including being made a freeman of the City of London in 1984, and an honorary fellow of St Hugh's College, Oxford.

Marshall enjoyed a notably happy marriage with his wife, Ann, who entertained for him at their home, Bridleway House, near Goring, Oxfordshire, accompanied him on all his travels, and finally nursed him during a long terminal illness. He died of cancer at the Royal Marsden Hospital, Sutton, London, on 20 February 1996. He was survived by his wife, son, and daughter. He had become ill during the making of a television programme about his life, but he insisted on completing it and requested that the programme's producer give the address at his funeral. This took place on 1 March 1996 at St Andrew's, South Stoke, Goring, the church where Marshall and his wife had been members for many years, and the address was given again at his memorial service at St Margaret's, Westminster, London. L. E. J. ROBERTS

Sources D. Fishlock and L. E. J. Roberts, *Memoirs FRS*, 44 (1998), 297–312 · *The Times* (23 Feb 1996) · *The Guardian* (23 Feb 1996) · *Daily Telegraph* (23 Feb 1996) · *The Independent* (26 Feb 1996) · *WWW* · b. cert. · m. cert. · d. cert. · private information (2004) [family]
Archives United Kingdom Atomic Energy Authority, Harwell, Oxfordshire, archives
Likenesses G. Argent, photograph, 1973, RS [*see illus.*] · oils, Bridleway House, Goring · photograph, repro. in *The Times* · photograph, repro. in *The Guardian* · photograph, repro. in *Daily Telegraph* · photograph, repro. in *The Independent* · photographs, RS · photographs, UKAEA archives, Harwell

Marshall, William (*d.* 1540?), printer and translator, may have been the William Marshall who in 1527 was a clerk to the chief baron of the exchequer and a protégé of Sir Thomas More. If so, he and his patron soon parted ideological company. By 1533 Marshall had developed an enthusiasm for evangelical religion, and was trying to persuade Thomas Cromwell to put his talents to use in the service of the regime. In that year he completed a translation into English (the first such) of Marsilio of Padua's early fourteenth-century political treatise, *Defensor pacis*. Cromwell promised to lend him £20 towards the publication costs but the money was not forthcoming until 1534, and the edition did not eventually arrive until 1535. If Cromwell had misgivings about the project, they seem to have been justified. Two years later, Marshall was pleading his inability to repay the loan on the grounds that the *Defensor pacis*, although 'the best book in English' against the papacy, had sold poorly (*LP Henry VIII*, vol. 11, no. 1355).

This edition was the centrepiece of an array of continental reformist and antipapal propaganda which Marshall published in 1534–5. He does not seem to have established himself firmly in the book trade: his premises in Wood Street are not recorded on any of his colophons, and he used a wide range of printers. His output was dominated by his own translations (notably of Lorenzo Valla's attack on the donation of Constantine) but also included translations by others, for instance one by William Turner of a

Latin version of the Swiss reformer Joachim Vadianus's treatise *Vom alten und neuen Gott* (1534). He may also have been planning to write against religious conservatism in the University at Oxford, as he asked a correspondent for details of 'unreasonable' statutes and the 'griefs' with which students were encumbered (*LP Henry VIII*, vol. 7, no. 308); both his sons were studying there at the time. His interests extended beyond narrowly religious matters: he produced an edition of the new poor-relief ordinance of Ypres in 1535, and may have been the author of a comprehensive and radical set of proposals for reforming poor relief drawn up for Cromwell at much the same time.

If the *Defensor pacis* failed to spark public interest, Marshall's 1535 translation of a Latin version of Martin Bucer's treatise against images, *Das einigerlei Bild*, faced the opposite problem. The book provoked an immediate reaction, perhaps because of the additions which Marshall made to the text, such as a call for images to be burnt. Cromwell's agent Thomas Broke and Lord Chancellor Audley both warned Cromwell that Marshall had gone too far, claiming that the book was already causing disquiet and urging that it be banned. Cromwell was more sanguine; the book was permitted to remain, and indeed was in such demand that it was reprinted later the same year. The Yorkshire rebels of 1536 paid Marshall the compliment of naming him as one of five English authors whose heresies should be stamped out.

Marshall's most influential publication, however, was a primer, printed in 1534 and 1535. It was not the first time this traditional devotional text had been recast for evangelical use (his text borrowed freely from George Joye and Martin Luther), but it was the first English primer to have official backing. The semi-official doctrinal formulary of 1537 (the so-called Bishops' Book) drew heavily on Marshall's text. More significantly, the litany which Marshall introduced in the 1535 edition was the model for Archbishop Cranmer's English litany of 1544, which passed over almost unchanged into the 1549 and 1552 prayer books.

Marshall's personal commitment to these projects is unmistakable. However, Cromwell at least encouraged him, and other scholars vying for government patronage saw Marshall as one of Cromwell's favoured clients. He may also have been connected with Anne Boleyn, to whom he dedicated one of his translations. After 1535 his publishing career petered out: he produced an anonymous translation of a tract by Luther in 1536, and a third edition of his primer in 1538. Perhaps Anne Boleyn's fall sidelined him, or Cromwell may have come to doubt the propaganda value of such heavyweight translations. Marshall did remain in Cromwell's circle; he continued to send reports to the minister, and in 1536 he was one of those sent to persuade the London Carthusians to accept the royal supremacy. He presented them with twenty-four of his unsold copies of the *Defensor pacis*; they burnt one copy and returned the rest unread.

Thereafter Marshall fell on hard times. By 1539 he could no longer afford to support his son Richard at Oxford. Richard *Marshall was born in 1517, and there was another son, Thomas; nothing is known of the marriage or of any other children. He is likely to be the William Marshall of St Alban's Wood Street whose death and probate administration is recorded for 1540.   ALEC RYRIE

Sources STC, 1475–1640 • LP Henry VIII, vols. 4–14 • GL, MS 9168/9, fols. 49, 51v, 62, 65, 66v, 69 • C. C. Butterworth, *The English primers (1529–1545)* (1953) • D. MacCulloch, *Thomas Cranmer: a life* (1996) • A. Eljenholm Nichols, '"Books-for-laymen", the demise of a commonplace', *Church History*, 56 (1987), 457–73 • G. R. Elton, 'An early Tudor poor law', in G. R. Elton, *Studies in Tudor and Stuart politics and government*, 2 (1974), 137–54 • Emden, *Oxf.*, 4.380–81 • G. R. Elton, *Policy and police: the enforcement of the Reformation in the age of Thomas Cromwell* (1972) • E. Gordon Duff, *A century of the English book trade* (1905)
Wealth at death suffering from 'increasing poverty' shortly before presumed death; unable to support son at Oxford: *LP Henry VIII*, 14/2.758

Marshall, William (*fl.* 1617–1649), engraver, was the most prolific of his profession working in London during the reign of Charles I. Nothing is known about his life apart from what can be deduced from the more than 250 plates he engraved. The catalogue compiled in 1964 by Margery Corbett and Michael Norton shows that the great majority of these were made on commission for members of the London book trade, whether as engraved title-pages or portrait frontispieces. Since many of these books were the first editions of classics of English literature (among them works by John Donne and John Milton), Marshall's fame is assured despite the generally low quality of his work.

Marshall's earliest datable plate is the frontispiece to *A Solemne Joviall Disposition Briefly Shadowing the Law of Drinking* by Richard Brathwaite, published in 1617 with its second part, *The Smoaking Age with the Life and Death of Tobacco*. This, like the vast majority of Marshall's works, is too crude to reveal with any clarity who might have trained him. But it is more closely related to the style of the recent incomers from the Netherlands, Simon de Passe and Francis Delaram, than it is to the native tradition of Renold Elstrack. The quality of Marshall's plates was always dependent on his model, as can be clearly seen in his title-page to Philemon Holland's 1632 translation of Xenophon's *Cyrupaedia*. The portrait of Charles I in it is copied from Willem de Passe and preserves something of the high quality of the original. But the figure of Cyrus, for which no model was available to copy, and which Marshall must have designed himself, is wretched.

Marshall never published any plates himself, and only occasionally was commissioned to make single sheet prints for print publishers (as opposed to plates for the book trade). He seems to have worked for only two print publishers. One was William Riddiard, for whom he made portraits of Charles I and of Thomas Scott. The other was Thomas Jenner, for whom he made three portraits (of Charles II as a baby, Gustavus Adolphus, and the earl of Hamilton) in the 1630s, and two sets of allegorical figures of the four temperaments and the four elements. To these can be added a newly discovered set of emblems which was used for trenchers. A few other plates bear the address of Peter Stent, but most if not all of these were reprints.

Marshall's best-known plate is his frontispiece to the *Eikon basilike: the Pourtraicture of his Sacred Maiestie in his Solitudes and Sufferings*. This book, which purports to be written by Charles I himself, appeared within a few days of his execution in January 1649, and became a best-seller despite the efforts of the puritan government to suppress it. So great was the demand that the book was reprinted in various forms fifty-seven times, and the frontispiece had to be re-engraved seven times by Marshall himself, and once by Robert Vaughan copying Marshall's design. Also well known are his illustrations to Francis Quarles's *Emblemes* of 1635—a book whose fame is largely dependent on its being, with George Wither's *A Collection of Emblemes*, the earliest emblem book published in England. Marshall's last datable plates were produced in 1649, and there is no sign of any later activity; presumably he died late in that year. His prints are not rare, and many are held in the British Museum, London.   ANTONY GRIFFITHS

Sources A. M. Hind, *Engraving in England in the sixteenth and seventeenth centuries*, 3, ed. M. Corbett and M. Norton (1964), 102–92 • F. F. Madan, *A new bibliography of the Eikon basilike of King Charles the First* (1950) • P. Daly and M. Silcox, 'William Marshall's emblems (1650) rediscovered', *English Literary Renaissance*, 19 (1989), 346–74 • M. Bath and M. Jones, 'Emblems and trencher decorations: further examples', *Emblematica*, 10 (1996), 205–10
Likenesses J. W. Cook, group portrait, line engraving (*Early masters*), BM, NPG; repro. in H. Walpole, *Anecdotes of painting in England*, new edn, rev. J. Dallaway, 5 vols. (1828)

Marshall, William [Billy] (1671/2?–1792), Gypsy leader, was born either in the parish of Kirkmichael, Ayrshire, or in Minnigaff, Kirkcudbrightshire. The Gypsy clan to which he belonged was ruled by a chief, or 'king', called Isaac Miller; tradition has it that Marshall stabbed Miller to death and assumed the kingship in his place.

In the 'additional note' to *Guy Mannering*, Sir Walter Scott states that Marshall was 'pressed or enlisted in the army seven times, and deserted as often; besides three times running away from the Naval Service'. Marshall himself claimed to have been present at the battle of the Boyne, as a private soldier in King William's army; later he deserted from the Royal regiment of dragoons (Scots Greys) when serving under the first duke of Marlborough in Flanders. Back in Scotland, in 1712 he attempted to extend his dominions, which stretched from Dumfries to the braes of Glenapp in south-west Ayrshire, into the heart of the latter county; however, his troops were defeated at Newton of Ayr by 'a powerful body of Tinkers from Argyll and Dumbarton'.

This was not Marshall's last military exploit, however. In 1724 a popular insurrection was organized among farmers, crofters, Gypsies, and labourers against the Galloway lairds, who were enclosing with dykes land considered by the people to be held in common. These rebels, who became known as Levellers, appointed him their leader, and he directed successful operations, demolishing by night the dykes constructed during the day. He also organized the insurgent peasants into companies, and instructed them in the use of firearms. The government brought dragoons from Edinburgh to restore law and order, and after a skirmish at Duchrae 200 rebels were taken prisoner. Marshall himself was captured, but escaped with the help of Andrew Gemmil (the original of Scott's Edie Ochiltree).

Basing himself in Minnigaff village, from which, when necessary, he could quickly retreat with his gang into the hill country, Marshall conducted a profitable trade for years with the local smugglers. Mountain redoubts ideal for concealing plunder were the Fell o'Barullion in Wigtownshire—hence Billy's sobriquet the Caird o'Barullion—and a large cave in the high grounds of Cairnsmore, in the Stewartry.

According to Scott, Marshall was seventeen times lawfully married, and after his hundredth year was the avowed father of four illegitimate children. His reputedly herculean virility long remained a byword throughout the district over which he held sway. Furthermore, although he was believed to have committed more than one murder, he enjoyed a surprisingly mild and genial reputation. Andrew McCormick summarizes the general opinion thus:

> probably the very crimes attributed to him were essential to terrorize his gang and bring them to subjection. A strong man physically; a splendid wrestler; a good boxer; famous at the quarter-staff; a master handicraftsman, and member of the Hammerman's Guild; possessed of ingenuity and an ever-ready wit; quick to assert the rights and avenge the wrongs of his gang, he was an ideal leader for such a tribe. (McCormick, 474–5)

Marshall died in Kirkcudbright on either 23 or 28 November 1792, said to be aged 120. An obituary in the *Annual Register* provided him with a veiled compliment by stating that of 'all the thievish wandering geniuses, who … led forth their various gangs to plunder, and alarm the country, he was by far the most honourable of his profession'. His tombstone in the kirkyard was decorated on the back with two tup's horns and two horn spoons.

HAMISH HENDERSON, rev.

Sources W. Scott, *Guy Mannering* (1829) · A. McCormick, *The tinkler-gypsies of Galloway* (1906) · *Annual Register* (1792) · personal knowledge (1993)

Marshall, William (*bap.* 1745, *d.* 1818), agricultural writer and land agent, was baptized on 28 July 1745 at Sinnington, North Riding, Yorkshire. The younger son of a yeoman farmer, according to his own account he could trace his blood through the veins of agriculturists for upwards of four hundred years. At the age of fifteen, however, he was apprenticed in the linen trade in London, and after forsaking this for insurance he spent some years engaged in commercial activities in the West Indies.

In 1771, after returning to London, a sudden and severe illness made Marshall decide to take up farming. He had already been in the habit of spending his leisure hours in studying agriculture, and a legacy of £500 received on the death of his father in 1772 helped him to pursue his new career. In 1774 he undertook the management of a farm of 300 acres at Addiscombe, near Croydon in Surrey. Marshall's first work was written there in 1778 and entitled *Minutes of agriculture made on a farm of three hundred acres of various soils near Croydon … published as a sketch of the actual business of a farm*. Marshall swam against the tide of opinion in

advocating the use of oxen instead of horses, and believed in keeping his farmworkers under strict control.

In 1778 Marshall's partner, who held the lease of the Addiscombe land, became bankrupt, and Marshall was obliged to leave. He published *Experiments and Observations Concerning Agriculture and the Weather* in the following year, and he put forward his long-advocated plan for the establishment of government-supported agricultural colleges. An approach to the Society of Arts for funds to enable him to reside in six or seven different agricultural districts and record their farming practices was rebuffed. This reverse he blamed on Arthur Young (1741–1820), who was becoming the best-known agricultural authority of the day, and whose method of collecting information by visiting leading landowners and farmers on lengthy tours Marshall had attacked.

In 1780 Marshall accepted an appointment as agent to Sir Harbord Harbord of Gunton, Norfolk, a minor figure in the promotion of agricultural improvement, but left this post after only two years following a disagreement with his employer. He returned to Yorkshire before visiting Gloucestershire in 1783. In all his country visits Marshall compiled notes with a view to achieving his aim of publishing a series of volumes on regional farming practices. In 1783 he contributed to Dodsley's *Annual Register* for 1783 a pioneering study of the black canker caterpillar, responsible for destroying turnips in Norfolk.

Then, in 1784, Marshall became agent to Samuel Pipe-Wolferstan, agreeing to manage land at Statfold, near Tamworth, and to act also as adviser on landscaping the estate. But after a series of quarrels with Pipe-Wolferstan, arising in part from Marshall's independent and irascible temperament, he left Statfold in 1786. For some years he then resided in London during the winters and examined farming in a variety of regions during the summers. His stay at Statfold had proved fruitful, however, in providing him with a new career in landscape gardening, and it was there that he had completed his book entitled *Planting and Ornamental Gardening* (1785).

In 1787 Marshall published the first of his major studies of the farming practices of six different regions of England, *The Rural Economy of Norfolk*; this was followed by studies on Yorkshire (1788), Gloucestershire (1789), the midland counties (1790), the west of England (1796), and the southern counties (1798). To a second edition of the last he added in 1799 a *Sketch of the Vale of London*. Many of these works were translated into French and published in Paris in 1803.

In his Rural Economy of the midland counties Marshall proposed the establishment of a board of agriculture, a suggestion which the influential Sir John Sinclair (1754–1835) persuaded Pitt to adopt in 1793. Marshall was greatly angered that his old rival, Arthur Young, was chosen for the post of secretary to the board, rather than himself. However, the board adopted his plan of provisional surveys, though on a county rather than his favoured regional basis, and his own work, *Central Highlands*, appeared under the board's auspices. After this Marshall took no further part in the board's publications, preferring to continue with his own Rural Economy series; in addition he published *On Planting and Rural Ornament* (1796), and *On the Appropriation and Inclosure of Commonable and Intermixed Lands* (1801). Marshall was highly critical of the procedures and consequences of the current modes of enclosure, and advocated a general enclosure act to regulate the matter. The General Enclosure Act of 1801, however, proved a half-measure which did not meet his views. He next wrote an important work on estate management, *On the Landed Property of England*, which appeared in 1804. It was some consolation for his disappointments over the board of agriculture that in 1792 he had been appointed reviewer of agricultural books for the *Monthly Review*; in 1796 he had also become agricultural reporter for the *Monthly Magazine*.

Marshall had been assisted in the preparation of his Rural Economy series by his visits in 1791 to Sussex as a guest of the earl of Egremont, and to Devon and Cornwall as adviser to Sir Francis Drake on the improvement of his estate at Buckland Abbey. In 1792 Marshall visited the Scottish highlands as adviser on estate management and garden landscaping to the earl of Breadalbane at Taymouth in Perthshire, and from this visit resulted his *General View of the Agriculture of the Central Highlands of Scotland* (1794).

Marshall did not marry until 1807, when already in his sixties. His bride was a distant cousin, Elizabeth Hodgson, a woman of considerable property, of Middleton, near Pickering, in the North Riding. Marshall now went to Middleton to live, and he remained there until after his wife's death in 1816. He then moved to Beck Isle House at Pickering, where he had inherited various pieces of land following the death in 1811 of his brother John, a successful local farmer. At Pickering, Marshall built a large schoolroom on to one end of Beck Isle House, a first stage in his plan for founding an agricultural college. Its design was one he had first advocated forty years before, and had also elaborated on in *Proposals for a Rural Institute or College of Agriculture* (1799). But on 18 September 1818, before his college could become a reality, Marshall died at Beck Isle House. His estate was sworn for probate at £6600. His monument in Pickering church stated that 'he was indefatigable in the study of rural economy', and that 'he was an excellent mechanic, and had a considerable knowledge of most branches of science, particularly of philology, botany, and chemistry'. Marshall had been the first to form a collection of words peculiar to the Yorkshire dialect. The vocabulary appended to the *Rural Economy of Yorkshire* contains about eleven hundred words, and his *Yorkshire Words* was reprinted by the English Dialect Society.

In 1808 Marshall had begun his tremendous self-imposed labour of compiling and commenting on abstracts from the board of agriculture's county reports, rearranged on a regional basis, a project which filled his declining years. It gave him much scope for attacking the inadequacies of the board's authors and their views, and he lived to see it completed; the fifth and final volume of *The Review and Abstracts of the County Reports to the Board of Agriculture* appeared in 1817. The whole was republished in 1818, the year of his death. 'The registry of the existing practices of England, at the commencement of the nineteenth century', he wrote—the 'leading object' of his life for forty years—'IS NOW FINISHED' (Horn, 39).

Modern agricultural historians have generally held that Marshall's works on English farming are superior to those of his rival, Arthur Young, as they are more systematically arranged and based on a more thorough knowledge of a district by personal residence there. Unlike Young, Marshall was cautious about experimentation, preferring rather to advocate the best practices approved by experienced farmers. On the other hand, he lacked Young's pithy and more readable style, and acquired fewer close contacts with the leading farming figures of the time. Marshall's career, indeed, suffered in some degree from his native bluntness and acid tongue, his pride, and his sensibility to slights. Nevertheless, from the independence of his views arose his remarkably early support for agricultural education, and his belief in the necessity of studying agriculture on a regional basis, both of which were ideas well before their time. A portrait of him in the National Library of Scotland, Edinburgh, is reproduced in Pamela Horn's work, *William Marshall (1745–1818) and the Georgian Countryside* (1982).　　　　G. E. MINGAY

Sources P. Horn, *William Marshall (1745–1818) and the Georgian countryside* (1982) · G. E. Fussell, 'William Marshall, self-appointed national farm surveyor', *Journal of the Land Agents' Society*, 52 (1953), 485–90 · G. E. Fussell, 'My impressions of William Marshall', *Agricultural History*, 23/1 (1949) · G. E. Mingay, ed., *The agricultural revolution: changes in agriculture, 1650–1880* (1977), 78–84, 101–3, 257–9 · monument, Pickering church, Yorkshire

Archives U. Reading, Rural History Centre, minute book of Board of Agriculture, letters, B. VI

Likenesses monument, Pickering church, Yorkshire · portrait, NL Scot.

Wealth at death £6600: Horn, *William Marshall*

Marshall, William (1748–1833), composer and servant, spent his life near Fochabers, Morayshire, where he was born on 27 December 1748, one of at least three children of Francis Marishal and his wife, Isabel Innes. At the age of twelve, after 'some instruction from his father' and 'six months at a grammar-school' (MacGregor, 1), he gave up the idea of joining the army and went into service with the duke of Gordon at nearby Gordon Castle, where he advanced to head butler and house steward. He married Jean or (Jane) Giles (1740/41–1825), eight years his senior, on 31 May 1773 in Fochabers. Four of their sons received commissions in the army. The deaths of Alexander (1773/4–1807), John (*bap.* 1782, *d.* 1829), and George (*c.*1782/3–1812) occurred during active service, while William (1779–1870) lost his right arm at Waterloo but survived to die aged ninety. Francis (*bap.* 1776, *d.* before 1857) became a jeweller in London, and Jean (Jane; 1778–1873) married locally, had a large family, and died aged ninety-five years and ten months.

'Self-taught in … mechanics and other … natural sciences' (Glen, vii) as well as on the violin, Marshall is best-known as the composer of more than 280 Scottish dance tunes for the fiddle, his two-part *A Collection of Strathspey*

Reels (Edinburgh, 1781) preceding those of Niel Gow and his son Nathaniel. The tunes Marshall wrote were all based on the Scottish dance music tradition, with each one being quite short and many able to be played in less than a minute. He 'did not write music for bunglers' (Alburger, 84) but provided technical challenges of key and position then unusual in Scottish fiddle music. His slow airs and strathspeys ('slow, when not danced' (Marshall, *Scottish Airs*, 3), reflecting a shift among his audience from dancing to listening) are still particularly influential.

'... Above middle size, [Marshall] was compactly built, and considered handsome in his youth. In his old age he was portly and venerable ... [and] particular in his dress' (MacGregor, 7). Marshall was also skilled in fishing, falconry, and shooting, and an excellent athlete. Meticulous in penmanship and speech, he was 'a capital dancer' (ibid., 2) and 'a very accurate performer ... [who] stamped the instrument and semi-tones with correctness' (Grant, 2). Two of his violins and bows are in Edinburgh University's Reid Collection of Historic Musical Instruments, while a long-case clock (Fochabers Museum) and a sundial (Bourtie House, Inverurie, Aberdeenshire) show him to have been proficient in clockmaking and astronomy.

Marshall left Gordon Castle in 1790 after thirty years' service, ostensibly because of poor health but possibly as a punishment after he was robbed of £100 17s. 11d. belonging to the duke while in London in May 1789. Marshall spent two years farming at Burnside before being installed by the duke at his farm at Keithmore. Rehabilitation was completed when in 1794 Gordon appointed Marshall estate factor. In that post he built roads and bridges and served as a justice of the peace; the Gordons also allowed his trips to Edinburgh to work with the printers and publishers of his music. He had retired by 1823 to Newfield, a cottage he had designed and built by Craigellachie, Banffshire, where he was able to devote more time to preparing his collection *Marshall's Scottish Airs, Melodies, Strathspeys, Reels, &c.*, published in Edinburgh in 1822. Marshall included a composition by the duke of Gordon in the work and was supported by other members of the Gordon family: the marchioness of Huntly ordered 700 copies for herself and her husband. *Volume 2nd of a Collection of Scottish Melodies, Reels, Strathspeys, Jigs, Slow Airs &c.* was published in 1845, after Marshall's death, and enhanced his reputation for strong and characterful melodies.

'A man of rare integrity', Marshall died at Newfield on 29 May 1833, 'his mental faculties ... entire to the last' (MacGregor, 6). An informative tombstone marks his burial place in the parish churchyard at Bellie, by Fochabers.

MARY ANNE ALBURGER

Sources J. MacG [J. MacGregor], 'Memoir of William Marshall, composer', in W. Marshall, *Volume 2nd of a collection of Scottish melodies* (1845) • M. Cowie, *The life and times of William Marshall* (1999) • W. Marshall, *Marshall's Scottish airs, melodies, strathspeys, reels, &c.* (1822) • Grant [C. Grant], uncatalogued letter from Charles Grant, schoolmaster, Aberlour, to John Glen, 21 Aug 1891, U. Edin., Collection of Historic Musical Instruments • J. Glen, *The Glen collection of Scottish dance music*, 2 (1895) • D. Johnson, 'Marshall, William', *New Grove*, 2nd edn • M. A. Alburger, *Scottish fiddlers and their music* (1983); repr. (1996) • J. M. Bulloch, *William Marshall: the Scots composer, 1748–1833* (1933) • C. Gore, ed., *The Scottish fiddle music index* (1994) • *DNB* • m. reg. Scot. • bap. reg. Scot.

Archives NL Scot., corresp. and papers • U. Edin., Collection of Historic Musical Instruments | NL Scot., letters to Sir William Forbes

Likenesses C. Turner, mezzotint engraving, pubd 1817 (after J. Moir), BM, Scot. NPG • J. Moir, portrait, Scot. NPG

Marshall, William (1806–1875), organist and composer, was born in Oxford, the son of William Marshall, a local music-seller. He was sent to London at an early age and gained his musical education as chorister of the Chapel Royal under John Stafford Smith and William Hawes. In 1825 he was appointed organist to Christ Church and St John's College, Oxford, and for some time he also officiated as organist at the church of All Saints. He took the degree of MusB on 7 December 1826, and that of MusD on 14 January 1840. His published compositions were *Three Canzonets* (1825) and *Cathedral Services* (1847), and in collaboration with Alfred Bennett he edited *A Collection of Cathedral Chants* (1829). His most important work, however, was *A Collection of Anthems used in the Cathedral and Collegiate Churches of England and Wales* (1840), to which an appendix was added in 1851, and which reached its fourth edition in 1862. He also wrote *The Art of Reading Church Music* (1842).

At the urging of his friend Thomas Legh Claughton, then professor of poetry at Oxford and for a long period vicar of the parish church of Kidderminster, Marshall was persuaded in 1846 to leave Oxford and become organist and choirmaster to St Mary's, Kidderminster. He spent most of the rest of his life in the town and devoted his spare time to giving instruction in music. He was spoken of as a fine organist, and as being specially admirable as a teacher and conductor. On various occasions he conducted the rehearsals of the Philharmonic Society in London with great success. He continued to be involved in music throughout his life, for he was professionally engaged in Liverpool only a month before his death, which took place at Handsworth, Birmingham, on 17 August 1875.

William's younger brother **Charles Ward Marshall** (1808–1876), singer, achieved some success as a tenor on the London stage about 1835, under the assumed name of Manvers. In 1842 he turned his attention to concert and oratorio singing, which brought him greater acclaim, but some six or eight years afterwards he withdrew from public life. He died at Islington on 22 February 1876.

R. F. SHARP, rev. NILANJANA BANERJI

Sources Grove, *Dict. mus.* (1954) • Foster, *Alum. Oxon.* • Brown & Stratton, *Brit. mus.* • J. D. Brown, *Biographical dictionary of musicians: with a bibliography of English writings on music* (1886) • *A catalogue of all graduates ... in the University of Oxford, between ... 1659 and ... 1850* (1851), 438 • *Musical World* (4 Sept 1875), 607

Marshall, William (1807–1880), minister of the United Presbyterian church, was born in the hamlet of Meadowmore, Perthshire, early in 1807. He was educated at the village school at Tullybelton and at a superior school in Perth, where he attended a single session. In 1820 he went on to Glasgow University for two years, spending a further two years at Edinburgh University. He entered the Divinity Hall of the United Secession church in Glasgow in 1824, where he studied under Professor John Dick. In 1829 he was licensed, and in December of the following year was ordained to the church at Coupar Angus in Perthshire, where he was to remain for almost fifty years.

Marshall took a prominent role in the 'voluntary' controversy, a national debate sparked off by a sermon by Andrew Marshall in 1829 which argued the case against ecclesiastical establishments. He edited a monthly magazine, *The Dissenter*, in 1833 and also became secretary of the Voluntary Church Association. He was the public champion of other causes in concert with his colleague, Dr David King, particularly in anti-slavery agitation and opposition to the corn laws. His views were so outspoken that *The Times* called attention to one speech in 1842 on the latter topic, suggesting that the lord advocate might prosecute him for sedition.

Marshall was a keen supporter of the union between the Relief and United Secession churches, which came about in 1847. He was also well-disposed towards the abortive union negotiations between the United Presbyterian and Free churches. In 1865 he was moderator of the United Presbyterian synod and in that same year was honoured with the degree of DD from both the University of New York and the Presbyterian College of Hamilton, Canada. In 1872 he was presented with £1500 collected by his friends. By this time he was ailing, and a colleague was appointed to assist with the church while Marshall devoted more time to writings of a local historical nature. He did, however, consent to preach at Dysart, and it was while he was on this visit that he was taken ill. He died at the United Presbyterian manse there on 23 August 1880, and was buried at Coupar Angus.

Much may be deduced about a man's character on the basis of the charges from which he is defended. In his funeral sermon Dr David Young rejected the view that Marshall had been sour, narrow, bigoted, or tending to contention for contention's sake. He contrasted this view with the enlightened causes, such as anti-slavery, missions, and church union, which Marshall had espoused. However, his praise was highly qualified, and even the denomination's own historian acknowledged that 'for much of the awe he inspired as a debater he owed more to the roughness of the weapon than either to the strength or the skill of the arm that wielded it' (Small, 2.569).

LIONEL ALEXANDER RITCHIE

Sources *United Presbyterian Magazine*, new ser., 24 (1880), 452–8 • R. Small, *History of the congregations of the United Presbyterian church from 1733 to 1900*, 2 (1904), 569 • W. Mackelvie, *Annals and statistics of the United Presbyterian church*, ed. W. Blair and D. Young (1873), 609 • *Dundee Advertiser* (25 Aug 1880) • *DNB*

Marshall, William (1812–1861). *See under* Marshall family (*per.* 1848–1922).

Marshall, William Calder (1813–1894), sculptor, was born on 18 March 1813 in Gilmour Place, Edinburgh, the eldest son of William Marshall, a goldsmith, and his wife, Annie Calder. He was educated at the high school, Edinburgh,

and at Edinburgh University, and attended the Trustees' Academy from 1830. In 1834 he went to London, where he worked in the studios of Francis Chantrey and Edward Hodges Baily; on 21 April 1834, on the recommendation of Chantrey, he entered the Royal Academy Schools, and the following year he gained the academy's silver medal. Like most sculptors of his generation, he was intent on completing his education in Rome, and he went there in 1836, via Paris. He befriended the British sculptors John Gibson and Lawrence Macdonald and designed several 'ideal' works based on his studies of the antique.

Marshall received few commissions while in Rome, and had to rely on his family for financial support; on his return to Britain in 1838 he worked for a short time in Edinburgh, and in 1839 settled permanently in London. He married twice: first to Marianne Lawrie in 1842 (she died in the same year) and second in 1845 to Margaret Calder; he and Margaret had four sons and two daughters. Following the exhibition held in Westminster Hall in 1844, Marshall was selected to execute statues of lords Clarendon (1852) and Somers (1855) for the new houses of parliament. He gained many commissions for public statues in the following years, including those for the poet Thomas Campbell (1848) for Westminster Abbey and the inventor Samuel Crompton (1862) for Bolton, Lancashire. His greatest success in public competition was in 1857, when his model for the proposed monument to the duke of Wellington in St Paul's Cathedral was awarded first prize out of eighty-three entrants. However, the commission, amid much controversy, went to Alfred Stevens, whose design was considered more suitable for the intended setting. Marshall subsequently made three biblical reliefs (1863) for the cathedral.

Marshall did not restrict his production to commemorative monuments; he also designed schemes of architectural sculpture (for example, the pediment figures for Bolton town hall, *c.*1870) and several church monuments. His group symbolizing Agriculture (1864) is included on the Albert memorial in Kensington Gardens, London. He also showed some 120 'ideal' and narrative works at the Royal Academy between 1836 and 1891, probably the largest contribution of any Victorian sculptor. These encompassed the broad range of themes popular with artists of the period, including classical, biblical, and literary subjects, as well as some quite novel areas—mirroring those of contemporary painting—such as ancient history and Pompeian genre. Despite its variety, his work seldom showed any great originality of conception and usually adhered to conventional classicizing types. He adopted a businesslike approach to his art, which brought him considerable wealth: at his death his estate was valued at £48,709.

Marshall was described by the painter George Dunlop Leslie as 'rather quiet, and very Scottish and shrewd' (Leslie, 171); a portrait of the sculptor by Patrick Allan-Fraser is at Hospitalfield House, Arbroath, Forfarshire, and a plaster self-portrait bust showing him as a young man is in the Scottish National Portrait Gallery, Edinburgh. He was elected an associate of the Royal Scottish Academy in 1840 but resigned in 1844 and was made an honorary member in 1861; he became an ARA in 1844 and RA in 1852, and was made a chevalier of the Légion d'honneur in 1878. Marshall died at his home, 115 Ebury Street, Chester Square, London, on 16 June 1894, and was buried in Kensal Green cemetery. MARTIN GREENWOOD

Sources R. Gunnis, *Dictionary of British sculptors, 1660–1851*, new edn (1964), 256–7 · Graves, *RA exhibitors* · B. Read, *Victorian sculpture* (1982) · R. L. Woodward, '19th century Scottish sculpture', PhD diss., U. Edin., 1977, 152–7 · *DNB* · M. Greenwood, 'Marshall, William Calder', *The dictionary of art*, ed. J. Turner (1996) · W. D. McKay and F. Rinder, *The Royal Scottish Academy, 1826–1916* (1917), 268–70 · 'Lives of the sculptors no. 3: W. C. Marshall, RA', *The Sculptors' Journal and Fine Art Magazine*, 1/3 (March 1963), 96–7 · private information (2004) · J. Plupick, *The Wellington monument* (1970) · G. D. Leslie, *The inner life of the Royal Academy* (1914), 171 · *Art Journal*, new ser., 14 (1894), 286 · *Building News* (24 Oct 1890), 594 · CGPLA Eng. & Wales (1894) · records, Trustees' Academy, Edinburgh, NA Scot., NG 2/2/24–25

Archives Henry Moore Institute, Leeds · NL Scot., journals · RA

Likenesses P. Allan-Fraser, oils, exh. Royal Scottish Academy 1856, Hospitalfield House, Arbroath · J. Pettie, oils, 1883, Aberdeen Art Gallery · Done and Ball, cabinet, NPG; repro. in *Building News* (24 Oct 1890), 594 · Elliott & Fry, carte-de-visite, NPG · Lock & Whitfield, woodburytype, NPG; repro. in T. Cooper and others, *Men of mark: a gallery of contemporary portraits* (1876–7) · W. C. Marshall, plaster bust (self-portrait), Scot. NPG · R. W. Robinson, photograph, NPG; repro. in R. W. Robinson, *Members and associates of the Royal Academy of Arts, 1891* (1892) · J. & C. Watkins, carte-de-visite, NPG

Wealth at death £48,709 7s. 4d.: probate, 3 Aug 1894, CGPLA Eng. & Wales

Marshall, Sir William Raine (1865–1939), army officer, was born at Stranton, near Hartlepool, co. Durham, on 29 October 1865, the younger son of William Marshall, solicitor, of Foggy Furs, Stranton, and his wife, Elizabeth Raine. Having been educated at Repton School and at the Royal Military College, Sandhurst, he was commissioned lieutenant in the Sherwood Foresters (Derbyshire regiment) in January 1886. He served for eight years with the 1st battalion, mainly in Ireland, where he made a reputation as a horseman, which he had increased on the polo-ground and the racecourse when in 1893 he was, on promotion to captain, transferred to the 2nd battalion in India. In 1897 he was attached to the 1st battalion, Queen's Own Royal West Kent regiment in the Malakand campaign and was at the action of Landakai (16 August). In October 1897 he returned to the 2nd Sherwood Foresters for the Tirah expedition, in which he led his company with the Gordon Highlanders in the storming of Dargai and was at the capture of the Arhanga and Sampagha passes.

Marshall studied to enter the Staff College, but was with his battalion in Malta in 1899, when the Malta command was ordered to raise mounted infantry companies in the Second South African War, and his fame as a horseman marked him out for these. His company formed part of the 7th mounted infantry battalion, and he led it in the fighting round Bethlehem and the Wittebergen, where he was slightly wounded, in the summer of 1900. In the following November he took a leading part in the actions round Bothaville, in which his commander, Lieutenant-

Sir William Raine Marshall (1865–1939), by unknown photographer, c.1917

Colonel P. W. J. Le Gallais, was killed. General Sir Ian Hamilton, who commanded the mounted infantry division in South Africa, wrote of this action in the introduction to Marshall's memoirs, *Memories of Four Fronts* (1929):

> Marshall was awarded the rare distinction of a double Brevet. A fine reward, but could they have given him less when, by his cool yet desperate valour, he, and he alone, had saved the whole column from destruction? He would no doubt have got the Victoria Cross as well: also, afterwards, another Victoria Cross at the Dardanelles; only, being each time the senior on the spot, there never was anyone to recommend him. (Marshall, vii)

Marshall had married on 12 November 1902 Emma (Emmie) Cundell, daughter of John Hett, of Headlam Hall, co. Durham, and widow of John Stephen-Stephen, of Edinburgh and Elgin. They had no children.

The Second South African War brought Marshall the brevets of major and lieutenant-colonel, and when in 1908 he became a substantive major, promotion to brevet colonel followed automatically. In 1911 he was appointed assistant commandant of the mounted infantry school at Longmoor, and in the February 1912 he was given command of the 1st battalion, Sherwood Foresters in India, at Bombay and Deolali.

In October 1914 Marshall's battalion was ordered home to form part of the 8th division, with which he served on the western front in the winter of 1914–15 in the waterlogged trenches before Neuve-Chapelle, where he was slightly wounded. On one occasion his life was apparently saved by 'a very stout cigarette case' (Marshall, 35) in his breast pocket. In January 1915, by the request of his old friend and former commanding officer, General Fred

Shaw, who commanded the 29th division, he was appointed to command the 87th brigade of the 29th division, then forming for the Gallipoli campaign. He was in command at the landing at X Beach on 25 April and, as at Bothaville, his coolness and quick decisions saved the situation when the Turks counter-attacked. He was again slightly wounded. Twice in the early operations he was in temporary command of the 29th division and, his reputation established, he was promoted major-general in June 1915, commanding successively the 42nd, 29th, and 53rd divisions. The 53rd, reduced to a skeleton by casualties, was sent in the late autumn to Egypt to refit, Marshall remaining to help in the successful evacuation.

From Gallipoli, Marshall went to Salonika to command the 27th division, with which he served from January to September 1916, a period of stagnation on the Macedonian front. He was then given command of the 3rd (Indian) corps in Mesopotamia (soon afterwards Iraq), where in August Sir Stanley Maude had been appointed commander-in-chief of a reorganized army. Marshall led his corps in the operations which culminated in the victory at Kut el Amara (24 February 1917) and the capture of Baghdad (11 March). When Maude died of cholera in November, Marshall was, to his surprise, appointed commander-in-chief of the Mesopotamian expeditionary force. His methods differed from his predecessor's. He wrote in his memoirs:

> When I first took over command I had felt it my duty to try to live up to the example of my distinguished predecessor in the matter of work in the office, but, with my very able Staff to cope with the details … and confining myself to major points on which a decision was required, I very soon began to curtail my office hours. (Marshall, 268)

Marshall spent the time he saved mainly with his troops. His immediate task was to secure Baghdad against a Turco-German counter-attack, and he succeeded. He realized Palestine had become strategically the more important theatre and readily released a division to reinforce Sir Edmund Allenby. Despite this he finished the war in Mesopotamia triumphantly by enforcing the surrender of the Turkish army on the upper Tigris (October 1918). He also quietly countered French intrigue in Mesopotamia.

Having received promotion to lieutenant-general in January 1919, Marshall was appointed commander-in-chief, southern command, India, in August before his arrival in November. Peacetime administration made no appeal to him, and in 1924, the year after his term of command expired, he retired from the army to a life of hunting, shooting, and fishing. In his memoirs Marshall criticized the 'absurd worship of ground' (Marshall, 29) on the western front, praised Ian Hamilton, and claimed the Gallipoli campaign failed because it was given insufficient resources; and he praised Maude as perhaps the greatest British general since Roberts. He was colonel of the Sherwood Foresters from 1930 to 1935.

Marshall made no pretence of being a student of war. He was a natural leader of imperturbable courage, with a quick eye for the essential in a critical situation, and the gift of making the right decision quickly.

Marshall was appointed CB in 1916, KCB in 1917, KCSI in 1918, and GCMG in 1919, and awarded foreign orders. He died of heart failure at Le Grand Hotel, Bagnoles de l'Orne, France, on 29 May 1939, and was survived by his wife.

F. B. MAURICE, rev. ROGER T. STEARN

Sources *The Times* (1 June 1939) · W. R. Marshall, *Memories of four fronts* (1929) · *WWW* · Burke, *Peerage* (1924) · *Hart's Army List* · T. Wilson, *The myriad faces of war: Britain and the Great War, 1914–1918* (1986) · personal knowledge (1949) · *CGPLA Eng. & Wales* (1939)
Archives King's Lond., Liddell Hart C., letters to his brother from the Near East | FILM IWM FVA, actuality footage
Likenesses photograph, *c*.1917, IWM [*see illus.*] · W. Stoneman, photograph, 1919, NPG · F. Whiting, oils, 1919, IWM · J. S. Sargent, group portrait, oils, 1922 (*General officers of World War I*), NPG · photograph, repro. in Marshall, *Memories*, frontispiece
Wealth at death £15,607 18s. 5d.: probate, 16 Aug 1939, *CGPLA Eng. & Wales*

Marsham [*née* Warry], **Dame** (**Muriel**) **Joan** (1888–1972), philanthropist, was born at 19 Montague Street, Marylebone, London, on 4 January 1888, the daughter of William Taylor Warry (1836–1906), barrister and banker, and his wife, Elisa Jane, *née* Gosling. Little is known of her early life before her marriage on 2 February 1911 to Sydney Edward Marsham (1879–1952), a stockbroker, the youngest son of Charles Marsham, fourth earl of Romney. They had one son.

Joan Marsham was a committed Anglican, and the primary arena for her life of public Christian service was the national women's auxiliary of the Young Men's Christian Association (YMCA). The YMCA's desperate need for volunteers for war work during the First World War led it to turn to women to undertake the work formerly done only by men. Marsham founded with Princess Helena Victoria the women's auxiliary, which formally came into existence in 1918. Marsham's war work resulted in her being made an OBE but it was during the succeeding decades that she clearly became 'the driving force and inspiration' (private information) of the auxiliary. In 1931 she was elected its chairperson, a position she did not relinquish until her death in 1972.

During the Second World War, Joan Marsham was responsible for the half-million women throughout the world working for the YMCA by providing canteens in army camps, air stations, and devastated areas. As R. E. Roberts, the general secretary of the national council of the YMCA, said at her funeral, 'her chairmanship was no sinecure for she was personally responsible for the recruitment of hundreds of women who served through the YMCA in every military zone overseas' (private information). She continued in this work after the war as the women's auxiliary staffed canteens for the armed forces throughout the world, most notably during the Berlin airlift.

Marsham's energy and management skills were also deployed in the Girl Guide Association. After serving as the chairperson of its executive committee for ten years from 1938 she continued to apply her financial and organizational acumen to the association. She was one of the founders, in 1948, of the Girl Guide Club in Belgrave Square, and was involved in its administration until her death. She also chaired the Personal Service League and the British War Relief Committee of America. In 1945 she was created DBE.

As Roberts observed, Marsham's public life was her way of living out St Paul's injunction 'that ye present your bodies as a living sacrifice, wholly acceptable to God, which is your reasonable service' (Romans 12: 1). Her devotion to her work arose out of her sensitivity to the suffering and needs of others which in turn was the fruit of her deep commitment to her Christian faith. While seen by her work colleagues as a formidable or forceful character, she was also noted for her personal charm and her kindly humour. She died at the Westminster Hospital, London, on 13 March 1972 after collapsing at the Girl Guide Club, which in her last few years she had made her home. Her life of service was celebrated at her funeral at St Michael and All Angels, Sunninghill, Berkshire, eight days later.

CORDELIA MOYSE

Sources *The Guider* (May 1972), 187 · private information (2004) · YMCA, London, Women's Auxiliary MSS · *The Times* (16 March 1972), 19 · *WWW* · Burke, *Gen. GB* (1914) [Warry of Shapwick House] · Burke, *Peerage* (1959) [Romney] · b. cert. · m. cert. · d. cert.
Archives YMCA, London, Women's Auxiliary MSS
Wealth at death £6422: probate, 5 May 1972, *CGPLA Eng. & Wales*

Marsham, Sir John, first baronet (1602–1685), antiquary, was born on 23 August 1602 in St Bartholomew's Close, west Smithfield, London, the second surviving son of Thomas Marsham (1556–1625), alderman of London, descended from a Norfolk family, and his wife, Magdalen (1567–1618), daughter of Richard Springham, merchant, of London. He attended Westminster School from 1617, and in 1619 matriculated from St John's College, Oxford, graduating BA and MA in 1623 and 1625 respectively.

Marsham travelled widely from 1625 to 1627, first in England and then in France, Italy, and Germany. In 1628 he was admitted a student at the Middle Temple, but in 1629 was again abroad, travelling in the Netherlands and France. He was present at the siege of Bois-le-Duc by the prince of Orange, and in September of that year was in attendance on Sir Thomas Edmondes, sent to Fontainebleau to ratify a peace treaty between France and England.

In 1630 Marsham purchased Whorne's Place in Cuxton, near Rochester in Kent, and on 13 January 1631 married Elizabeth Hammond (*bap.* 1612, *d.* 1689), daughter of Sir William Hammond of St Albans, Nonington, Kent. They had ten children. During the 1630s Marsham purchased other properties in the Rochester area. In February 1638 he was appointed one of the six clerks in chancery, and later the same year was presented with the freedom of the city of Rochester.

The civil war of the 1640s caused a reversal in Marsham's fortunes. He followed the king to Oxford, with the result that he was deprived by the parliamentarians of his chancery post and had his estates sequestrated—losing, according to his son Robert, around £60,000. He was

Sir John Marsham, first baronet (1602–1685), by Robert White, pubd 1672

eventually allowed to compound for his estates for the sum of £356 6s. 2d. and retired to Cuxton, devoting himself to his antiquarian studies.

Marsham was MP for Rochester in the Convention Parliament which restored the monarchy in 1660. He was knighted on 5 July 1660, was able to resume his position in the six clerks' office, and was created a baronet in August 1663.

Years of private study at Cuxton had already borne fruit in Marsham's *Diatriba chronologica*, a treatise on the dating of the Old Testament, published in London in 1649. About 1665 he brought out a much longer work, incorporating most of the *Diatriba*, entitled *Chronicus canon Aegyptiacus, Ebraicus, Graecus et disquisitiones*, dealing with the dating of ancient history. A note in a surviving copy states that 500 copies of this edition were destroyed in September 1666 in the fire of London, in which Sir John's library also suffered. Marsham profited by this setback to enlarge his work. An expanded edition of the *Chronicus canon* came out in 1672. The 1672 version subsequently appeared in two foreign editions, one at Leipzig in 1676 and the other at Franeker, in Friesland, Netherlands, in 1696.

Another early work had been the preface, entitled 'Propulaion', to the first volume of Sir William Dugdale's *Monasticon Anglicanum* of 1655. The seriousness of the seventeenth-century scholar is here underlined by the copious references, of which there are more than three hundred in a mere thirty-two pages. Marsham was admired by many European scholars for his knowledge of history, chronology, and languages: all three of his published works, and several left in manuscript at the time of his death, were written in Latin, with the occasional note or comment in Greek. His 'Pandectae nostri temporis', annals for the years 1600–85, is in the Bodleian Library.

But Sir John's interests were not limited to antiquarian matters. The family archive contains papers bearing on the education of his sons, and towards the end of his life Marsham was concerned in a scheme to provide the towns of Rochester, Strood, and Chatham with fresh water. This required a channel to be cut, partly through his own lands; 2 miles of this had been completed and an act of parliament obtained for the remainder, when the scheme was brought to a sudden end by Marsham's death. This occurred on 25 May 1685 at Bushy Hall in Hertfordshire, the home of his younger son, Robert. Sir John's body was brought back to Cuxton and buried in Cuxton church on 3 June 1685. Of his many children only two sons and a daughter survived him. The elder son, Sir John, the second baronet, inherited Whorne's Place and an interest in history, particularly English history, although he never published. Robert, the younger son, succeeded to his father's position as one of the six clerks in 1680 and was knighted in 1681, becoming in 1696 the fourth baronet and ultimately father of the first Baron Romney.

SHIRLEY BURGOYNE BLACK

Sources R. Marsham-Townshend, *Chart and narrative pedigrees of the Marshams of Kent* (1908) • R. Marsham, 'Account of the life of Sir John Marsham, the writer's father', CKS, MS U1300/Z10 • M. A. E. Green, ed., *Calendar of the proceedings of the committee for compounding … 1643–1660*, 5 vols., PRO (1889–92) • E. Hasted, *The history and topographical survey of the county of Kent*, 1 (1778) • E. Hasted, *The history and topographical survey of the county of Kent*, 2 (1782) • *Collins peerage of England: genealogical, biographical and historical*, ed. E. Brydges, 9 vols. (1812), vol. 5 • Marsham manorial and literary documents, deposited by the earl of Romney, 1965, CKS, U1121 • Birch collection, BL, Add. MS 4223, fol. 9 • Wood, *Ath. Oxon.*, new edn, vol. 4
Archives Bodl. Oxf., annals • CKS, corresp. and papers
Likenesses R. White, line engraving, NPG, BM; repro. in J. Marsham, *Chronicus canon* (1672) [*see illus.*] • pen-and-ink drawing, NPG

Marsham, Thomas (1747/8–1819), entomologist, possibly of China Row, Chelsea, London, received a good education and was later employed at the Exchequer Loan Office, and then engaged as secretary to the West India Dock Company for several years. Marsham began the first authoritative work on British insects based upon the Linnaean system, entitled *Entomologia Britannica*, of which only one volume, *Coleoptera Britannica*, was published in 1802. In this work he described 1307 species native to Britain. Nine papers on various entomological subjects were read by him before the Linnean Society and published in its *Transactions*, and he was also author of 'A system of entomology', in Hall's *Royal Encyclopaedia* (1788).

Marsham was a co-founder of the Linnean Society; he was appointed secretary at the first 'fellows' meeting' on 26 February 1788. The other two primary co-founders,

Samuel Goodenough (1743–1827) and Sir James Edward Smith (1759–1828), became treasurer and president, respectively, and the first general meeting was held on 8 April 1788. By September 1796 Marsham was staying at Upper Berkeley Street, London, from where he wrote to Smith about his worries for the society's future. Marsham was secretary of the Linnean Society until 1798, the year he was elected treasurer.

By 1802 Marsham was married to a Miss Symes of Ufford, Northamptonshire; the couple had two daughters. In that year he joined the volunteer corps as an officer. Several months later, on 14 November, Alexander MacLeay wrote to William Kirby: 'I do not believe that I have seen our friend Marsham four times since the beginning of the war … [and] Mrs Marsham says she is more bored with soldiering than she ever was with insect hunting' (Jarvis, 92).

Marsham was treasurer of the Linnean Society until his resignation in 1816, after it became apparent that the society's funds had been mismanaged. Marsham had incurred heavy losses from the publication of his book and, having used society funds to clear his debts, found himself unable to repay the moneys. He died in stricken circumstances on 26 November 1819, having parted with his collections shortly before. He was survived by his wife. The specimens of British Coleoptera which featured in Marsham's book were acquired by James Francis Stephens (1792–1852).

YOLANDA FOOTE

Sources private information (1893) [J. E. Harting] • *GM*, 1st ser., 89/2 (1819), 569 • A. T. Gage and W. T. Stearn, *A bicentenary history of the Linnean Society of London* (1988) • C. Mackechnie Jarvis, 'A history of the British Coleoptera', *Proceedings and Transactions of the British Entomological and Natural History Society*, 8/4 (1976), 91–112 • DNB
Archives Linn. Soc., letters to Sir James Smith

Marshe, John (c.1516–1579), mercer and merchant, was either the eldest son of Walter Marshe of London and his wife, Eleanor, or of John Marshe his namesake, with whom he is sometimes confused, who died in 1565 or 1566. He was a lawyer by training, and in 1536 he was admitted to Lincoln's Inn. As a young man he may also have been a sewer in the chamber of Henry VIII, a position either he or his namesake held by 1543. In that year he married Alice, the daughter and heir of William Gresham, and a cousin of Thomas Gresham, with whom he had at least three sons and one daughter.

During the 1560s and 1570s Marshe became one of the most prominent and well-connected merchants in London. His main interest in overseas trade was in the export of wool and cloth to Flanders and northern France. He was also a shipowner and occasional moneylender. By 1559 he was a merchant of the staple, and served as one of its constables in 1561–2. He was a founder member of the Russia Company in 1555 and a leading figure in the Company of Merchant Adventurers. He served as governor of the company from 1555 to 1556, and for much of the period from 1559 to 1572. He was a warden in the Mercers' Company from 1558 to 1559 and from 1565 to 1566. Though he did not trade with Spain, he played a leading role in the establishment of the Spanish Company in 1577, claiming to have been the 'first mover' behind its incorporation (*CSP dom.*, *1566–79, addenda*, 505).

As governor of the Merchant Adventurers, Marshe was determined to protect the privileges of the company against the threat of interloping. He was a key figure in the complex international crisis of 1563 and 1564 when trade was severely disrupted by an embargo on English wool and cloth in the Netherlands. His resolute leadership, and his support for government plans to move the Merchant Adventurers' mart from Antwerp to Emden, enabled the company to ride out the crisis. His influence with Sir William Cecil was instrumental in the issue of a new charter in 1564 which regularized the move to Emden, though the company returned to Antwerp in 1565.

In addition to these commercial positions, Marshe held a number of important posts in London. As common sergeant from 1547 to 1563 he was responsible for much of the City's legal business. After retiring from that office in 1563 he became a judge in the sheriff's court. He served as an under-sheriff in Middlesex from 1545 to 1546 and from 1563 to 1566. He was on the commission of the peace for Middlesex from 1547 to 1554, and during 1562 and 1564. His experience enabled him to pursue a long and active parliamentary career; he may have sat as MP for Reading in 1547, though it is possible that this refers to his namesake. He was MP for London in 1553, 1554, 1558, 1559, 1563, 1571, and 1572. In 1555 he sat for Old Sarum. His strong protestant convictions led him to oppose Catholicism in the parliaments of Mary's reign. During the Elizabethan parliaments in which he sat, Marshe used his influence to support mercantile and corporate interests in London. He was put in charge of a variety of bills in 1559 and 1563, and was appointed to serve on a wide range of committees in 1566, 1571, 1572, and 1576, including the committee to examine Peter Wentworth in February 1576. During 1572 he made speeches on subjects including the Commons' right to freedom of speech; Mary Queen of Scots, against whom he spoke on 9 June; the bill dealing with the export of leather; and the bill for dyeing cloth. He wholeheartedly opposed the last measure, particularly as the proposed restriction on the export of undyed cloth struck at the commercial privileges of the Merchant Adventurers.

Marshe was one of a small group of merchants who fostered the connection between the court and the City. He was close to Cecil, whom he provided with valuable diplomatic information when he was overseas on company business in 1559, 1565, 1568, and 1570. It was probably at Cecil's prompting that he organized the abduction of Dr John Story from the Netherlands in 1570, on the grounds that he was treasonably conspiring against the queen. Through Cecil's influence he was appointed to numerous commissions dealing with a wide range of matters. He was also involved in handling the commercial problems arising from the Anglo-Spanish crisis from 1568 to 1573.

Although he was not among the wealthiest élite of merchants in London, Marshe was comfortably off. He owned land in Northamptonshire, including the manors of Bozeat and Sywell. In 1571, 1574, and 1576 he was awarded grants of concealed lands. A capable, trustworthy, and discreet man of business, he was acknowledged by Walsingham as 'a great favourer of the common cause to the utmost of his power' (*CSP for.*, *1577–8*, 609). He died in London in 1579, leaving Bozeat to his eldest son, William, and Sywell to his son-in-law, Anthony Jenkinson, the pioneer of English trade with Persia. John Stow records that a monument to him was placed in the parish church of St Michael in Wood Street, where he was buried, and the advowson of which he had purchased from Sir Thomas Gresham in 1565.   JOHN C. APPLEBY

Sources *CSP dom.*, *1547–80*; *1566–79*; addenda · *CSP for.*, *1558–61*; *1566–71*; *1577–8*; *1583–4* · *CPR*, *1547–78* · *APC*, *1558–70, 1575–77* · A. B. Beaven, ed., *The aldermen of the City of London, temp. Henry III*–[1912], 2 vols. (1908–13) · P. Croft, *The Spanish Company*, London RS, 9 (1973) · G. D. Ramsay, ed., *John Isham, mercer and merchant adventurer: two account books of a London merchant in the reign of Elizabeth I*, Northamptonshire RS, 21 (1962) · *LP Henry VIII* · A. M. Mimardière, 'Marshe, John', HoP, *Commons* · T. E. Hartley, ed., *Proceedings in the parliaments of Elizabeth I*, 1 (1981) · G. D. Ramsay, *The City of London in international politics at the accession of Elizabeth Tudor* (1975) · *VCH Northamptonshire*, vol. 4 · T. S. Willan, *The Muscovy merchants of 1555* (1953) · J. Stow, *A survay of London*, rev. edn (1603); repr. with introduction by C. L. Kingsford as *A survey of London*, 2 vols. (1908); repr. with addns (1971) · will, PRO, PROB 11/61, sig. 2
Archives Guildhall, London, City records, court of aldermen proceedings · Guildhall, London, Mercers' Company records · Hatfield House, Hertfordshire, Cecil MSS · PRO, customs records, London port books · PRO, state papers

Marshman, Hannah (1767–1847). *See under* Marshman, Joshua (1768–1837).

Marshman, John Clark (1794–1877), journalist and historian, eldest son of Joshua *Marshman (1768–1837) and his wife, Hannah *Marshman, *née* Shepherd (1767–1847) [*see under* Marshman, Joshua], Baptist missionaries, was born on 18 August 1794 at Broadmead, Bristol. He accompanied his parents to Serampore, India, in 1799, and from 1811 made increasingly important contributions to the various undertakings of the Serampore missionaries, including their expansion in 1816 of Bengali elementary schools, which he superintended and for which he wrote the textbooks. He helped to found and manage a savings bank. Marshman became in effect the business manager of the Serampore mission, and his own earnings helped to provide for a body of missionaries, catechists, and Indian Christians. But as the dispute developed between Serampore and the Baptist Missionary Society in conjunction with their missionaries in Calcutta, he became a particular object of their suspicion, until in 1837 agreement was reached for the BMS to take responsibility for the Serampore mission. Meanwhile Marshman managed the press and also a paper-mill at Serampore, for many years the only one in India; and he emerged as a significant pioneer of Indian journalism. He founded with his father, and edited, the first newspaper in Bengali, the *Sumachar Durpun*, on 23 May 1818 (continuing until 1841) and he established, also with his father, the first English magazine, the *Friend of India*, as a monthly in 1818, then as a quarterly. In 1835 he re-established it as a weekly, editing it until 1852; subsequently it was incorporated into *The Statesman*, which still continues.

Marshman published a series of law books, one of which, the *Guide to the Civil Law* (1845–6), was widely used and highly profitable. The profits of his undertakings were largely devoted to promoting education, which he regarded as a forerunner of Christianity. He was closely associated with Serampore College for education in arts, science, and theology from its foundation in 1818 until his departure from India in 1855. Through the *Friend of India* he supported Bentinck's policy (1835) of funding English education, but also called for some continued patronage for classical Indian literature, and consistently warned against the neglect of vernacular elementary education. His advice influenced Sir Charles Wood's adoption of a grants-in-aid system in 1854. His concern for education was linked to his advocacy of the appointment of qualified Indians to responsible posts in the administration.

Marshman accepted the post of official Bengali translator to the government and he worked to promote the economic development of India, not least through articles and pamphlets: on the cultivation of cotton and tea and the mining of coal; on communications and public works including roads, the railway system, and the Ganges Canal; and on forest conservation. He became chairman of the Red Sea Telegraph Company. Generally he took the view that government and private enterprise each had complementary roles.

An earnest student of Indian history, Marshman produced the first, and for years the only, history of Bengal (1848), and he was long engaged on his *History of India*, which he finished and published after his return to England (1863–7). He was critical of aspects of British rule especially in its earlier stages, including the permanent settlement of Bengal which, he argued, left the peasants at the mercy of the *zemindars* (landholders). But he commended the reforms of governors-general such as Bentinck and particularly Dalhousie, and believed British rule to be providential for India. Other historical and political works included *The life and times of Carey, Marshman, and Ward, embracing the history of the Serampore mission* (2 vols., 1859); *Memoirs of Major-General Sir H. Havelock* (1860); and the pamphlets *How wars arise in India: observations on Mr. Cobden's pamphlet entitled 'The origin of the Burmese War'* (1853) and *Letter to J. Bright, esq., MP, relative to the recent debates in parliament on the India question* (1853).

Marshman's reading was very wide, and he was a distinguished oriental scholar. He studied Chinese, knew all the great Sanskrit poems, and gave much attention to Persian. He published an English–Bengali dictionary (1828) and various Bengali textbooks; also articles in the *Journal of the Royal Asiatic Society*, the *Calcutta Review*, and other periodicals. In England, however, he was not recognized. He was refused a seat in the Indian council, and although his services to education were, at the instigation of Lord Lawrence, eventually recognized by the grant of the Star of India in 1868, he had to seek occupation as chairman of the committee of audit of the East India Railway. He made

three unsuccessful attempts to obtain a seat in parliament, for Ipswich in 1857, Harwich in 1859, and Marylebone in 1861.

Marshman was married twice: to Margaret Anderson in 1831, and, in 1846, to Alice Sparrowe, who survived him. He died at 2 Redcliffe Square North, Kensington, London, on 8 July 1877. His daughter Florence married Lieutenant-Colonel Frederick Bailey; their son was Lieutenant-Colonel Frederick Marshman Bailey (1882–1967), Indian army, Indian political service 1906–38.

Marshman was respected for the independence of his character, his strong convictions, and his knowledge of Indian affairs. Precocious as a young man, he matured as an unostentatious philanthropist with a remarkable range of interests and achievements.

G. C. BOASE, *rev.* MICHAEL LAIRD

Sources G. Smith, *Twelve Indian statesmen* (1897) · *The Times* (10 July 1877) · *Baptist Magazine*, 69 (1877), 337–41 · *Law Times* (14 July 1877), 201 · J. Marshman, *Statement relative to Serampore* (1828) · E. D. Potts, *British Baptist missionaries in India, 1793–1837* (1967) · M. A. Laird, *Missionaries and education in Bengal, 1793–1837* (1972) · B. Stanley, *The history of the Baptist Missionary Society, 1792–1992* (1992) · *CGPLA Eng. & Wales* (1877)

Archives BL OIOC, corresp. and papers of subject and his family, MSS Eur F 157 · N. Yorks. CRO, corresp. and papers · Regent's Park College, Oxford, Angus Library, corresp. and papers | BL OIOC, Wood MSS

Likenesses photographs, BL OIOC, Bailey MSS · portrait, Serampore College, West Bengal, India

Wealth at death under £16,000: probate, 24 July 1877, *CGPLA Eng. & Wales*

Marshman, Joshua (1768–1837), orientalist and missionary, son of John Marshman, weaver, who was said to be descended from an officer in the parliamentary army, and Mary Couzener, of Huguenot ancestry, was born at Westbury Leigh, Wiltshire, on 20 April 1768. After some scanty education at the village school, he was apprenticed at fifteen to a London bookseller named Cater, a native of Westbury Leigh, but after five months Joshua returned to assist his father at weaving. Both in London and at home he read omnivorously, mastering, it is said, more than five hundred volumes before he was eighteen. He usually had a book before him on the loom. On 8 August 1791 he married Hannah Shepherd [*see below*].

Weary of weaving, Joshua Marshman became in 1794 master of the Baptist school at Broadmead, Bristol, and studied classics, Hebrew, and Syriac at the Bristol Baptist college. The accounts which he read of the labours of William Carey (1761–1834) in India led him to offer himself to the Baptist Missionary Society, and in company with William Ward and two others he sailed from Portsmouth for India on 29 May 1799. He arrived at the Danish colony of Serampore, near Calcutta, where Carey soon joined them, on 13 October. At that time the East India Company did not allow missionaries into their territory, so Marshman and Carey lived there under Danish protection, translating the Bible into various languages. They preached and taught in Serampore and travelled throughout the surrounding country; in a few years they established several stations, and rendered the scriptures, in whole or in part, into Bengali, Oriya, Sanskrit, Telugu, Punjabi, Hindustani, Marathi, Hindi, Sikh, and other languages including Chinese. Marshman took the foremost part in this work, and he also handled many of the often difficult negotiations with the British authorities, notably in obtaining their acquiescence for new recruits to mission work in India. In 1811 he received the degree of DD from Brown University in the USA.

Marshman took the main responsibility for the educational work of the Serampore mission, pioneering an important development in Indian elementary education in the vernacular. In 1816 he published *Hints Relative to Native Schools*; within a year funds had been raised for the establishment of 100 schools conducted according to the then fashionable monitorial system, with a relatively broad curriculum. Textbooks compiled by the missionaries, which included elements of Western learning, were accepted also in pre-existing indigenous elementary schools. To crown this work for education, in 1818 Marshman drew up the prospectus of a missionary college 'for the instruction of Asiatic Christian and other youth in Eastern literature and European science', which was built at Serampore on the banks of the Hooghly, and which, as Serampore College, continues to exist. In 1827 he received a charter for the college from King Frederik VI of Denmark.

In 1818, in conjunction with his son, John Clark *Marshman, and other missionaries, Marshman established the first newspaper ever printed in any Eastern language, the *Sumachar Durpun, or, Mirror of News*, and in the same year he commenced the publication of the *Friend of India*, a monthly magazine. In 1820 Marshman vigorously asserted the divinity and atonement of Christ in a controversy with the Hindu reformer Ram Mohan Roy. In 1827 the connection between the Baptist Missionary Society and the Serampore missionaries was severed, owing to differences about administration, and a painful and protracted controversy took place, Marshman acting as the representative of the missionaries. Like Carey he suffered at times from melancholia. He died at Serampore on 5 December 1837 and was buried in the mission cemetery on the following day.

Marshman was undoubtedly one of the ablest orientalists and most earnest missionaries that worked in India. He published several works on the Chinese language and a Chinese version of the Bible, the first complete edition printed in that language and the first Chinese book printed from moveable metal type, which took him fourteen years. He also assisted Carey in the preparation of his Sanskrit grammar.

His wife **Hannah Marshman** [née Shepherd] (1767–1847), born on 13 May 1767 at Bristol, was the granddaughter of John Clark, pastor of the Baptist church at Crockerton, Wiltshire, and the only daughter of John Shepherd, a farmer, and his wife, Rachel. She was outstanding among the missionaries' wives in India at the time in playing an active part in the work of the mission, particularly in the field of education. In 1800 she opened a fee-paying boarding-school for girls, which flourished and soon

became a vital source of funds for the mission; and from 1822 she was one of the pioneers of elementary schools for Bengali girls, in which teaching was in the vernacular. She became a matriarchal figure in the domestic life and organization of the Serampore community, and died there on 5 March 1847, a few weeks before her eightieth birthday. The Marshmans had twelve children, six of whom died in infancy.

THOMAS HAMILTON, *rev.* MICHAEL LAIRD

Sources J. C. Marshman, *The life and times of Carey, Marshman and Ward*, 2 vols. (1859) · J. Fenwick, *Biographical sketch of Joshua Marshman … of Serampore* (1838) · E. D. Potts, *British Baptist missionaries in India, 1793–1837* (1967) · M. A. Laird, *Missionaries and education in Bengal, 1793–1837* (1972) · B. Stanley, *The history of the Baptist Missionary Society, 1792–1992* (1992) · S. K. Chatterjee, *Hannah Marshman* (1987)
Archives N. Yorks. CRO, corresp. and papers · Regent's Park College, Oxford, Angus Library, Baptist Missionary Society archives, corresp. and papers
Likenesses attrib. G. Chinnery, oils, Serampore College, West Bengal, India · portrait, Regent's Park College, Oxford · portrait (Hannah Marshman), Regent's Park College, Oxford

Marsin [Mersin, Mercin], **M.** (*fl.* **1696–1701**), theologian, is somebody about whose life absolutely nothing is known beyond the very scanty personal information contained in her published works. Internal evidence confirms that she was female, and that during the mid-1690s she travelled some hundred miles to London in order to publish her views. Beyond this, her life is a closed book. She is generally credited with having written a guide to marriage for women in 1683, but it was in the period 1696–1701 that she published the vast majority of her fifteen pamphlets and books, and during which she developed her unique method of biblical exegesis and a powerful critique of male authority in both religion and society as a whole.

Marsin was first encouraged to develop her own analysis of the Bible in 1696 when, in response to what she perceived as sure signs of the second coming of Christ, she was struck by

a fervent longing desire for the coming of the Lord … whereupon I took to the Lord's direction, resolving to search the scriptures with more diligence than ever I had done; the which I no sooner had performed, but I found the certainty of the coming of the Lord, and that it was very nigh at hand; but still I was to seek how, and in what manner; for I could then no ways make the Old and New Testament agree. (*Near Approach of Christ's Kingdom*, Preface)

Her first pamphlet after this conversion experience is dedicated to simply recounting the signs of the second coming as they appeared to her. Earthquakes, comets, and the European wars of the period were all important indicators, and to this extent she conforms to a relatively common form of millenarian thinking at the end of the seventeenth century. But she also points to the 'miraculous cure of four women' in the city of London, and to Christ's 'working of miracles on women' in general, prefiguring the substantive critique of gender and women's role in Christianity which she was to develop over the next five years.

In the second half of the 1690s Marsin published a series

of pamphlets in rapid succession unfolding her method of distinguishing the metaphorical, or 'figurative', elements of the Old and New Testaments from those passages she counts as literal description. Throughout, she sets herself in opposition to a scholastic tradition of biblical scholarship and suggests that the failures of that tradition were essentially the failures of men in general and of patriarchal authority in particular. More than this, she claims that the new insights and growing knowledge of the Bible which her new method allowed was published through her as a woman precisely because of the previous failure of men to understand God's word and, by extension, their failure to fulfil God's design.

Marsin's last two pamphlets, *Good News to the Good Women* and *Two Remarkable Females of Womankind*, both published in 1701, contain her most explicit and consistent critique of Christian patriarchy. In *Good News to the Good Women* she essentially claims that although Eve acted in ignorance when she succumbed to the blandishments of the serpent in the Garden of Eden, God had visited patriarchy and the pain of childbirth on women as a temporary punishment for Eve's actions. She also suggests that men and women had been equal partners in the Garden of Eden, and that they would be so again after the resurrection; that

> then the punishment that sin brought into the world will be excluded from all God's people, so as then the husband will not be above the wife nor the wife above the husband … women will be delivered from that bondage which some has found intolerable. (Marsin, *Good News*, 4)

More than this, in these two pamphlets of 1701 Marsin expresses a firm belief that she has been appointed by God to publish his word, and that her sex is consistent with a broader pattern of revelation in which women would have a greater part than men. These later pamphlets are largely taken up with a rendition of the roles of women in the Old Testament and in the exercise of authority. She makes a great deal of the relationship of the Virgin Mary to the Holy Ghost, and the extent to which men were essentially excluded from the birth and creation of Christ, and were likewise largely responsible for his crucifixion. She also attacks St Paul's interdiction on women as teachers and preachers, and claims that the internal contradictions in St Paul's statements entirely negate his authority in this matter.

By the publication of her final pamphlet, *Two Remarkable Females of Womankind*, Marsin had created an essentially female-centred story of biblical history, in which the Virgin Mary and a latter-day prophetess (presumably M. Marsin) are the key figures in the transitions between the various stages of Christian eschatology.

Simply in terms of her statement of a radical adherence to gender equality, Marsin is a unique figure in the history of late seventeenth-century Britain. She is more directly concerned with issues of gender than are the many Quaker prophetesses of the second half of the century, and develops a more sharply focused and coherent analysis of the role of women in the Bible and in Christianity

than do any of her radical protestant contemporaries. Several of her pamphlets are dedicated to William III and parliament, and she makes positive reference to the prophetic writings of George Wither, but she gives no clear indication of any sectarian allegiance. While she is clearly a protestant, her views do not conform to any of the plethora of theological positions which characterize British and European protestantism at the end of the seventeenth century. She is a unique figure with a unique theological perspective and methodology, and can only be described as the first and only 'Marsinite'.

TIM HITCHCOCK

Sources C. Hill, *The English Bible and the seventeenth-century revolution* (1993) · [M. Marsin], *The women's advocate, or, Fifteen real comforts of matrimony* (1683) · [M. Marsin], *Some of the chief heads of the most miraculous wonders* (1696?) · [M. Marsin], *A treatise proving three worlds* (1696) · [M. Marsin], *A practical treatise shewing when a believer is justified by faith* (1696) · M. M. [M. Marsin], *The near approach of Christ's kingdom clearly proved by scripture* (1696) · [M. Marsin], *A rehearsal of the covenant by Moses* (1697) · [M. Marsin], *A clear and brief explanation upon the chief points of the New Testament* (1697) · M. Marsin, *The figurative speeches* (1697) · [M. Marsin], *Truth vindicated against all heresies* (1698) · M. M. [M. Marsin], *All the chief points contained in the Christian religion* (1699) · M. Marsin, *Two sorts of latter days proved from scripture* (1699) · M. Marsin, *A full and clear account the scripture gives of the deity* (1700) · [M. Marsin], *Good news to the good women, and to the bad women that will grow better* (1701) · [M. Marsin], *Two remarkable females of womankind fore-prophecied of in the scriptures* (1701) · W. E. Burns, '"By Him the Woman will be Delivered from that Bondage, which some has found intolerable": M. Marsin, English millenarian feminist', *Eighteenth-Century Women*, 1 (2001), 19–38

Marson, Charles Latimer (1859–1914), Church of England clergyman and folk-song collector, was born on 16 May 1859 at Goldsworth, Woking, Surrey, the third child and eldest son among the three sons and five daughters of Charles Marson (1822–1895) and his wife, Ann Jane (1827–1888), daughter of Joseph Woolley of St Leonards. His father was vicar of Christchurch, Birmingham, from 1864 to 1871 and vicar of St Andrew's, Clevedon, from 1871. His paternal grandfather is recorded as an ironmonger in Southwark and an ironmaster in Staffordshire; his paternal grandmother was a daughter of Dr Gatti, perfumer, of Bond Street.

While attending University College, Oxford, from 1878 to 1881 (BA 1881, MA 1885) Marson became a close friend of Ronald and Charles Bayne, his future brothers-in-law. He joined the Whitechapel Settlement (later Toynbee Hall) in 1881 when Samuel Barnett was warden. He stayed until 1884, then took up a curacy in Petersham. During this period he was contributing to many journals including the *Christian Socialist*, of which he was editor between 1884 and 1887; his first publication in book form was his reply to the arguments of the atheist E. B. Aveling in the latter's *Christianity and Capitalism* (1884). After several short-lived appointments Marson's poor health caused a transfer to Orlestone, Kent, in 1886.

Most of Marson's later Christian texts were published after 1900, but *The Psalms at Work* (1894) and *The Following of Christ* (1895), with a preface by Canon Scott Holland, were well received. A popular booklet was *Huppim and Muppim:*

a Few Words on the Sore Need for Religious Education (1903), reissued after his death as *Huppim, Muppim and Ard* (1915), both issues with a memoir by Scott Holland. *God's Co-operative Society* (1914) was reissued in 1930 with two biographical memoirs.

Clothilde or Chloe Bayne (1865–1952) was a student in her third year at Newnham College, Cambridge, where she completed the classics tripos in 1888, when she met Marson while working in the poorer districts of London. Born in Germany on 12 December 1865, the daughter of Dr Peter Bayne and Klothilde Dorothy Gerwein, Chloe had begun her education in Germany and continued it in England. In 1889 Marson was due to accompany his brother Frank to Australia but in May he sailed alone on the SS *Austral* to serve as curate of St Peter's, Glenelg, Adelaide. He was soon in trouble for his 'eccentricities', both in church services and in contributions to the local newspapers. He advocated the confessional and defended barmaids, he preached sermons in favour of Aboriginals, and addressed striking maritime workers. He formed the first branch in Australia of the Fabian Society, but was forced out of St Peter's for being 'too socialistic'. In January 1890, 'distracted in mind', Chloe telegraphed Charles 'coming May, Marson, Glenelg, Adelaide', and by early April she was on her way to Naples where she joined the *Orizaba*, and landed in Adelaide on 3 June 1890. Two days later they were married, with the folk-song collector Cecil Sharp giving away the bride. In Adelaide, Chloe tutored and was active in campaigning for women's suffrage. Their only daughter, Mary, was born in 1891; a son, John (1896–1915), was killed at Gallipoli.

After serving briefly at St Oswald, Parkside, Adelaide, Marson returned to England hoping to pursue an academic career. Between 1892 and June 1895, when he was appointed perpetual vicar at St James the Less, Hambridge, Somerset, he occupied various positions where he upset the establishment. At Hambridge he drew attention to the singing of John English and provided the initial stimulus for Sharp's long career as a folk-song collector. Of major and lasting importance to the study of English folk-songs was *Folk-Songs from Somerset*, gathered and edited with Sharp and published in five parts in 1904–9. In the preface to the new edition (with memoir) in 1916 of *Village Silhouettes* (1914) Marson recalled 'people were once kind enough to applaud the writer for his discovery of a great gold mine of beautiful songs in Somerset and he is glad to have discovered this' (preface, v).

On 3 March 1914 the 'much esteemed Vicar of Hambridge' died at his rectory. Marson had appeared bright and cheery earlier, according to an obituary, as 'with a kind word for all, he passed through the village, making many calls among his people, by whom he was always welcomed'; apart from his striking personality, he 'was an eminent scholar, and the author of many well-known works on religious, social, economic and piscatorial subjects'; he was 'an angler of anglers ... a wonderful caster of a fly' and an authority on all aspects of fishing (*Langport and Somerton Herald*, 14 March 1914). Marson's funeral on 14 March, attended by more than 500 people, was led by George Wyndham Kennion, bishop of Bath and Wells, who indicated that he had known Marson longer than most, since he had been Marson's bishop also in Adelaide. Kennion spoke extravagantly about his troublesome priest: 'he had watched all along with admiration the consistency of his character, the devotion of his life and the fearlessness with which he spoke out to people who might disagree with him' but had admitted in 1905 that 'Mr Marson and I are unable to see things from the same point of view'. Marson was buried in the churchyard of St James the Less.

Chloe Marson supported herself by writing and lecturing, and by historical research in the 1930s. She died on 20 December 1952, having lived in Hendon, Middlesex, for several decades.　　　　　　　　　　　HUGH ANDERSON

Sources F. M. Etherington, life of C. L. Marson, Ralph Vaughan Williams Library, Cecil Sharp House, London · *Langport and Somerton Herald* (7 March 1914) · *Langport and Somerton Herald* (14 March 1914) · *Cambridge Letter* [Newnham College Club] (1885–8) · 'Royal commission on ecclesiastical discipline: minutes of evidence', *Parl. papers* (1906), 33.201–11, Cd 3069; 33.229, Cd 3070 · corresp. between C. L. Marson and Cecil Sharp, 1906–8, English Folk Dance and Song Society, Cecil Sharp House, London · J. R. Warner, 'The episcopate of George Wyndham Kennion, 1883–1894', BA diss., University of Adelaide, 1958 · M. B. Reckitt, *For Christ and the people* (1968) [mostly from the unpubd biography] · E. K. Miller, *Reminiscences of 47 years* (Adelaide, 1895) · b. cert. · m. cert. · d. cert. · IGI
Archives NL Aus., journal of Clothilde Bayne
Likenesses photographs, *c.*1905–1912, English Folk Dance and Song Society, Cecil Sharp House, London
Wealth at death £304 4s. 4d.: administration, 1 April 1914, *CGPLA Eng. & Wales*

Marson, Una Maud Victoria (1905–1965), writer and feminist, was born on 6 February 1905 at Sharon Mission House, Sharon village, near Santa Cruz, St Elizabeth, Jamaica, the youngest of the six children of Solomon Isaac Marson (1858–1915), Baptist minister, and his wife, Ada Marson (d. 1930). Solomon Marson was a respected and charismatic preacher. He remained the minister at the Sharon Mission House until his death in 1915, when the family was forced to move to Kingston. Una Marson planned, but never wrote, her autobiography, using the title 'Autobiography of a brown girl', but there is evidence that she was very attached to her father and profoundly affected by his death. There is little information available about her relations with her mother.

From 1915 to 1922, with the help of a Free Foundationers scholarship, Una Marson attended Hampton high school, a fee-paying boarding-school in Malvern, Jamaica, modelled closely on the English public-school system. Of her time at this school, Marson writes nostalgically in a poem, 'To Hampton':

> How oft in dreams I live those days again,
> Chasing a hockey ball with might and main,
> Or sit and list without a thought of fear
> To dearest Mona reading great Shakespeare.
> (Marson, *Tropic Reveries*, 70)

Her biographer, however, has suggested that this idealized view of Hampton is qualified by comments made in Marson's unpublished papers which attest to the snobbery and racism endemic in a colonial school, whose

Una Maud Victoria Marson (1905–1965), by unknown photographer

intake was predominantly white and privileged and where the 'dark-skinned scholarship girl', Una, was snubbed (Jarrett-Macaulay, 19). Marson gained the Oxford and Cambridge Board's lower certificate (letters) in 1921, pursued commercial skills, and left Hampton in 1922 with satisfactory but unexceptional academic qualifications.

Una Marson's first job, with the Salvation Army in Kingston, allowed her to make use of her secretarial skills and to develop her commitment to, and interest in, helping the large numbers of Jamaica's unemployed and socially disadvantaged. After a year with the Salvation Army, Marson took a job with the newly established YMCA, and it was not until 1926, when she was made assistant editor of the socio-political monthly journal *Jamaica Critic*, that Marson was able to develop her writing talent. In 1928 she started the magazine *The Cosmopolitan*, becoming the first Jamaican woman to edit her own publication. Thereafter Marson consolidated her interest in Jamaican culture and her commitment to promoting women's rights in an impressive variety of ways and in diverse contexts.

In June 1932 Marson's play *At What a Price* was staged in Jamaica and with the profits generated from it she travelled to England in July 1932. In London she became involved with the League of Coloured Peoples and in November 1933 *At What a Price* was performed by an all-league cast and was hailed as the first play by 'coloured colonials' to be staged in London. In 1935 she was the first, and only, black representative to take part in the First International Women's Conference, held in Turkey. In 1935 Marson took up a post at the League of Nations headquarters in Geneva where, in 1936, she acted as Haile Selassie's secretary in his negotiations with the League of Nations. On her return to Jamaica in 1936 she founded the

Readers and Writers Club and the Kingston Dramatic Club, and two of her plays, *London Calling* and *Pocomania*, were performed; the latter was extremely successful and was hailed as indicating the future trajectory of a truly Jamaican theatre. In March 1941, appointed as full-time programme assistant on the BBC Empire Service, Marson compèred and co-ordinated a series of programmes, *Calling the West Indies*, which continued until her return to Jamaica in 1945. In 1960 she was briefly (and secretively) married to Peter Staples, a dentist. There were no children, and they separated in 1961.

Marson's commitment as a feminist and nationalist activist in Britain, the West Indies, and further afield has earned her a considerable reputation as a pioneering figure in Jamaican cultural history and, increasingly, in accounts of black British history. Una Marson refused to accept the limits and constraints of her time which relegated her, as a black woman, to the margins of cultural activity. She published four collections of poetry: *Tropic Reveries* (1930), *Heights and Depths* (1931), *The Moth and the Star* (1937), and *Towards the Stars* (1945). Though uneven in quality, these works attest to Marson's defiance, vitality, and restless energy.

While many of Marson's poems reveal her indebtedness to canonical English poets, her work experiments with poetic voices and themes which both challenge and subvert canonical notions of the poetic. In 'Black is Fancy' she asserts her poetic agenda with disarming clarity and panache:

> I used to feel ugly
> I was so ugly
> Because I am black,
> But now I am glad I am black,
> There is something about me
> That has a dash in it
> Especially when I put on
> My bandana.
> (Marson, *Moth and Star*, 75)

Marson wrote many deeply ambivalent poems of love in which she explored the pleasures—and pain—of living as a single woman. She died on 6 May 1965 in Kingston, Jamaica, after suffering a heart attack, and was buried at St Andrew's Church in Kingston on 10 May.

DENISE deCAIRES NARAIN

Sources D. Jarrett-Macaulay, *The life of Una Marson, 1905–1965* · E. Smilowitz, 'Una Marson: woman before her time', *Jamaica Journal*, 16/2 (1983) · L. Brown, *West Indian poetry* (1984) · C. McFarlane, *A literature in the making* (1956) · U. Marson, *The moth and the star* (1937) · U. Marson, *Tropic reveries* (1930)

Likenesses F. Man, photograph, 1943, Hult. Arch. · photograph, BBC Picture Archives, London [*see illus.*]

Marston, Edward (1825–1914), publisher, writer, and angler, was born on 14 February 1825 in Lydbury, Shropshire, the son of Richard Marston (1791–1875), a farmer, and his wife, Elizabeth, *née* Bright (1793–1845). Three years later the family relocated to Montgomeryshire, and two years after that to a farm in Lucton, Herefordshire. Marston attended the Lucton School from 1832 to 1840, and then was apprenticed to a bookseller from 1840 to 1844 in a nearby town. His wife, Mary, *née* Pratt (*d.* 1888), whom he married on 9 August 1851, was from the area.

Marston is a significant figure because, more than most Victorian publishers, he was steeped in the international market for print. His first job was with the Liverpool firm of Willmer and Smith, publishers of the *European Mail* and exporters of newspapers and magazines. In 1846 he went to London to work for Sampson Low, who had a bookshop, circulating library, and reading-room in Lamb's Conduit Street. Low also owned and edited the *Publishers' Circular*, a trade weekly: Marston was assigned to collect titles of newly published books from local publishers and Stationers' Hall, and later he would make the rounds of booksellers throughout the United Kingdom. He would eventually become chairman of Publishers' Circular Ltd.

In 1852 Marston left Sampson Low to set up an Australian import–export business in Fenchurch Street. Shipping books to Sydney, Melbourne, and Adelaide proved to be a profitable sideline which blossomed into a major business. Fifty-two years later he estimated that he had sent at least 20,000 letters to overseas correspondents and dealt with as many as 10,000 authors. Since Sampson Low and his son, Sampson Low jun., had developed a similar trade with the United States, Marston became their partner on 1 January 1856. Samuel Warren Searle joined the partnership in 1872, followed by William John Rivington and, in 1883, Marston's son Robert (*b.* 1853). Sampson Low retired in 1875.

Initially based at 47 Ludgate Hill, the firm of Sampson Low, Son, and Marston became notable for its global reach. It would specialize in books about Africa, Australasia, the American west, Canada, the Arctic, and Asia. In 1875 Marston was elected a fellow of the Royal Geographical Society. Of all his authors he corresponded most with the explorer Henry Morton Stanley: Marston met him in Egypt to bring home part of the manuscript of Stanley's *In Darkest Africa*.

Marston visited the United States twice. A vacation in the Rocky Mountains resulted in the popular travelogue *Frank's Ranche* (1886). His company had a substantial list of American writers, including Harriet Beecher Stowe, Louisa May Alcott, Oliver Wendell Holmes, and Captain Alfred Thayer Mahan. Marston also travelled to Paris in order to secure the rights to Victor Hugo and other French authors. His firm published at least fifty-five works by Jules Verne, starting with *Twenty-Thousand Leagues under the Sea* (1871). Marston also served as secretary of the Relief Fund for Paris Booksellers, a committee of publishers and booksellers which shipped food aid to the besieged city during the Franco-Prussian War. With his worldwide contacts he became an expert on international law governing intellectual property, publishing numerous journalistic articles on the subject as well as a pamphlet, *Copyright, National and International, from the Point of View of a Publisher* (1879; new and enlarged edn, 1887).

Marston also worked with many British authors, among them Charles Reade and G. A. Henty. Thomas Hardy published with him, though he felt that he needed a more adventurous house for *Tess of the d'Urbervilles*. A grateful R. D. Blackmore thanked Marston for his support: 'But for you', he wrote, '*Lorna Doone* might never have seen the light' (Marston, 135). Another of his authors, W. Clark Russell, remembered him with equal fondness: 'I was struck by his good looks, his soft, dark intelligent eyes, his agreeable manner, and a pleasant reserve which as I afterwards came to know, easily thawed when you gained his acquaintanceship or friendship' (ibid., 144).

Marston had been fond of fishing as a boy but gave it up for nearly forty years of urban life. Only in the early 1880s did he return to his old hobby. Then, starting with *An Amateur Angler's Days in Dove Dale* (1884), he acquired some fame as the author of several light volumes on angling, all paying homage to Isaak Walton.

Edward Marston retired from publishing in 1903 and died at Coombeheigh, The Downs, Wimbledon, Surrey, on 6 April 1914. He had been a devout though tolerant member of the Church of England. His memoir *After Work* (1904) and his writings on copyright have some value for historians of the book trade. His *Sketches of Booksellers of other Days* (1901) and *Sketches of some Booksellers of the Time of Dr. Samuel Johnson* (1902) represented early attempts to popularize the history of books. JONATHAN ROSE

Sources E. Marston, *After work* (1904) · *The Times* (7 April 1914) · F. A. Mumby, *Publishing and bookselling: a history from the earliest times to the present day*, 4th edn (1956) · R. Blathwayt, 'A talk with Mr Edward Marston', *Great thoughts* (1902) · m. cert. · d. cert.
Likenesses photograph, repro. in Marston, *After work*, facing p. 268
Wealth at death £11,740 1s. 10d.: probate, 24 Oct 1914, *CGPLA Eng. & Wales*

Marston, John (*bap.* 1576, *d.* 1634), poet and playwright, was baptized on 7 October 1576 at Wardington, Oxfordshire, the son of John Marston (*d.* 1599), lawyer, and Maria (*d.* 1621?), daughter of Andrew Guarsi, possibly a descendant of Katherine of Aragon's Italian physician, Balthasar Guarsi. His parents married at Wardington on 19 September 1575, where his maternal grandmother, Elizabeth Grey, had resided since her marriage to her second husband, John Butler.

The law and early dramatic career Marston's father belonged to the Middle Temple but retained strong midlands connections. He was appointed counsel to the city of Coventry (22 September 1585) and its steward (13 April 1588), and he acted as lawyer to Thomas Greene, Shakespeare's 'cousin' and solicitor to the corporation of Stratford upon Avon. Marston senior's grant of arms (29 November 1587) describes him as 'late of the Middle Temple … now of the city and county of Coventry' although the family retained property in Wardington and Cropredy as well as acquiring a new house in Cross Cheaping, Coventry. By 1592 the Middle Temple records were listing Marston senior as 'of Coventry' and his son, who matriculated at Brasenose College, Oxford, in February 1592, described himself as a gentleman from Warwickshire. Marston junior may in fact have been at Oxford since 1591 and he graduated BA in February 1594. Although he continued at Oxford until 1594 he was also 'specially' admitted to the Middle Temple (on 2 August 1592) by his father during his term as reader. By November 1595 Marston resided at the Temple (he and his father stood surety for Thomas Greene as a new entrant) studying under the tutorship of John Armitage and probably sharing chambers with his father.

As the son of a prosperous and prominent lawyer, Marston was expected to follow his father into the law but in 1598 he published the Ovidian erotic poem and Juvenalian verse satires *Metamorphosis of Pigmalion's Image and Certaine Satyres*, and later in the same year his *The Scourge of Villanie* appeared. His father's will (written 24 October 1599) shows that although he had 'hoped that my son would have profited in the study of law', he feared that his son might even sell his precious law books as he took 'delight in plays and vain studies and fooleries'. These lines, cancelled in the final version, reveal that Marston had theatrical interests some time before 1599; they may also show that the burning of his poems under the bishops' ban on 4 June 1599, often assumed to have caused Marston to adopt a dramatic career, probably occurred after he had begun to write plays. Unfortunately, the opening work of Marston's dramatic career cannot be determined, and although it has been generally accepted that he began with the revision of an older play, *Histriomastix* (published 1610), possibly written for the inns of court for Christmas 1598, the evidence remains far from convincing. *Histriomastix* was never attributed to Marston during his life and, indeed, the attribution (only made by Richard Simpson in 1878), rests on limited internal evidence complicated by the poor state of the text and the likelihood of further revision.

It is possible, then, that Marston's dramatic career began as early as 1598, although the auspices, exact date, and even the title, remain unknown. By September 1599 his literary fame was sufficient for Henslowe to employ him as a jobbing writer for the public stage although most of his earlier work was written for the Paul's Boys, one of the new 'private' children's companies. Marston produced *Jack Drum's Entertainment* (1600), *Antonio and Mellida* (1600), and *Antonio's Revenge* (1601) for this company, combining Italianate settings, romance, and Senecan and revenge elements with witty satire of contemporary literary and social fashions and his particular, extravagantly inventive vocabulary. Throughout his career Marston's work is characterized by an acute awareness of new literary fashions and styles, drawing on Aretino (possibly directly from the Italian), Montaigne through John Florio's translation, and upon the fashionable, intellectual cultures of the inns of court. By 1601 Marston was an established literary figure, praised as a satirist by Francis Meres (*Paladis tamia*, 1598), while for John Weever he 'enharbour[ed] Horace vein', and he merited enough attention to be one of the central targets of the Cambridge satirical play, *The Return from Parnassus, Part Two* (1601–2). Extracts from his plays appear in the commonplace book of Edward Pudsey, a Warwickshire gentleman who recorded the fashionable plays he had seen about 1600–01 (including *Merchant of Venice* and *Every Man in his Humour*), and Marston also contributed to Robert Chester's *Love's Martyr* (1601) along with others of the 'best and chiefest of our modern writers' (as they were described on the title-page).

Marston was notoriously quarrelsome. John Manningham's *Diary* (21 November 1602) records his gratuitous rudeness to Alderman More's wife's daughter (he first commended her beauty and then when she saluted him as a poet, he retorted 'poets feign and lie, and so did I … for you are exceeding foul'), although this rebarbative tone also belongs to Martson's poetic persona. In *Certaine Satyres* he signed himself as 'Kinsayder', a punning name ('kinsing' is the castration of a dog) alluding to the dog-like barking of satire which, though rough and cynical, can equally fawn and flatter. In *The Return from Parnassus, Part Two*, Marston's poetic mask is criticized as merely 'lifting up your [his] leg and pissing against the world' (I.ii, ll. 266–70) while the braggart Furor Poeticus imitates Marston's poetic violence and linguistic experiments. Furor's 'roister doister' 'cuts, thrusts and foins at whomsoever he meets' (I.ii, ll. 272–3), and encapsulates Marston's fractious relations with contemporary satirists, such as Joseph Hall (who may have authored the *Parnassus* plays), who had angered Marston due to his attack on *Pigmalion*.

Marston and Jonson Marston's other famously difficult relationship was with his poetic rival and sometime collaborator, Ben Jonson. Jonson told William Drummond in 1619 that he had beaten Marston and taken his pistol from him (an incident that underlies Jonson's *Epigrams*, 68), although in 'On Playwrights' their relations are characterized by sly admiration for Marston's folly and perseverance. This epigram implies that the two writers continuously compared themselves and debated each other's work. The relationship exploded into public disagreement during the 'War of the theatres' (*c*.1600–02), when Jonson attacked Marston, first in *Every Man out of his Humour* (1600) (through Clove and Orange) and in *Cynthia's Revels* (1600) (as Hedon) and then at greater length in *Poetaster* (1601), where the idiotic, effeminate Crispinus is forced to vomit up his Marstonian fustian. The precise occasion of this public spat remains opaque but Marston may have satirized Jonson in *Histriomastix* (as Chrisoganus, if the attribution is accepted) and possibly again in his farce-like *Jack Drum's Entertainment* (as Brabant Senior). Although many of the motives for the 'war' are unclear, Weever's comparison of both Jonson and Marston as the heirs of Horace, and Thomas Dekker's devastating satire on Jonson as a false Horace in *Satiromastix* (1601), may suggest a genuine debate over the role and method of the satirist, perhaps combined with or fuelled by the commercial rivalries between the boy companies. Marston's unjustly neglected play, *What You Will* (1601), dramatizes the failure of the railing Lampatho Doria to achieve moral reform of the debauched 'duke' of Venice. Indeed, even the play's epicurean philosopher Quadratus fails to appeal to the duke's sensual side sufficiently. The incapacity of both satirist and philosopher presents a bleak view of the inability of writers to reform their society, while the play's depiction of Lampatha Doria as both Jonsonian and Marstonian (he is called a 'Don Kinsayder') suggests the failure of both approaches to social satire.

Despite the antagonism and violence in their relationship, Jonson and Marston had much in common. Certainly Marston admired Jonson, writing a prefatory poem to *Sejanus* (1605) and dedicating *The Malcontent* to his fellow writer and 'amico suo candido et cordato'. This published dedication to a living person, unique in Marston's œuvre, conveys the primacy of Jonson's role in shaping Marston's sense of himself as a writer. In contrast to Jonson, Marston's independent means allowed him to disdain the search for patronage that preoccupied his rival. Instead, Marston offered his works to 'the most honourably renowned Nobody, bounteous Maecenas of Poetry' (*Antonio and Mellida*) or 'to the world's mighty monarch, Good Opinion' (*Certaine Satyres*) and 'To Everlasting Oblivion' (*Scourge of Villanie*).

Some time in 1603–4 Marston exchanged the Paul's Boys, now devoted to developing a more citizen-oriented market, for another 'private' company, the Children of the Blackfriars (also briefly known as the Children of Queen's Revels after 1604), at some point also becoming a shareholder in the company. It was for this company, notorious for a 'railing' style that constantly tested the authorities' patience and the limits of privilege granted by their connection to Anne of Denmark's court, that Marston produced his two most successful and sustained plays, *The Malcontent* (c.1603; revised c.1604 by Webster for the King's Men) and *The Dutch Courtesan* (c.1604–5). In particular, *The Malcontent*, a harsh comedy that debates both the possibility and desirability of revenge and political and social reform, became Marston's trade-mark play. The appeal to a 'reformed muse' may echo the hopes for political reform at the outset of the Jacobean regime, but the restless, darkly cynical humour embodied in its central figure, Malevole, also suggests a stark realization of the unlikelihood of its achievement in a pervasively corrupt world.

In 1605 Marston collaborated with George Chapman and Jonson on *Eastward Ho*, a play that satirized both citizen mores and their literary taste for romance, repentance narratives, and moral dramas, while also not sparing the pretensions to gentility of the impecunious knight, Sir Petronel Flash, and his deluded search for fabulous wealth in Virginia. Although the play appears to have been performed in 1605, during the court's summer progress, it attracted the attention of the authorities. One copy of the play retains a cancel leaf with a vicious satire on colonial enterprises, borrowing from Thomas More's *Utopia* to describe Virginia's fantastical plenty, where the dissolute adventurers may also 'live freely … without sergeants, or courtiers, or lawyers, or intelligencers—only a few industrious Scots' (III.iii, ll. 42–4). The authors were 'delated to the king' by Sir James Murray, brother of John Murray, a member of the king's bedchamber, and Chapman and Jonson were imprisoned for 'writing something against the Scots' ('Conversations with Drummond', ll. 273–7, in *Ben Jonson*, ed. C. H. Herford and P. E. Simpson, 11 vols., 1925–52, vol. 1). Marston appears to have escaped.

The precise cause of the offence (Chapman and Jonson claimed it was 'but two clauses' and shuffled the blame on the actors) and the exact sequence of events remain unclear but the offence seems to have either been mitigated or explained away. In 1606 Marston produced his *Parasitaster, or, The Fawn*, widely held to satirize King James, even though, as the printed text suggests, he may have done this from a safe distance from London. However, *The Dutch Courtesan* was staged during the king of Denmark's visit in July and August 1606 and Marston wrote some Latin verses for the king's ceremonial entry into London on 31 July. The presentation of a holograph copy of these verses to James VI and I (BL, Royal MS 18 A.xxxi) might suggest that Marston either had arrived back in favour or was seeking forgiveness.

Leaving the stage During 1605–6 Marston finally parted company with Jonson as the prefatory epistle to *Sophonisba, or, The Wonder of Woman* (1606) criticizes Jonsonian pedantry by its refusal 'to transcribe authors, quote authorities, and translate Latin prose orations into English blank verse', a pointed critique of Jonson's *Sejanus*. *Sophonisba*, a heroic tragedy set in the Carthaginian wars, prefigures Fletcherian drama and marks an increasingly serious temper in Marston's writing. By 1607 he had left the professional stage, his final work (published 1613, although it may have been begun as early as 1603–4), *The Insatiate Countess*, was left unfinished and was completed by William Barkstead and Lewis Machin (c.1608–13). The only other work which can be certainly attributed to Marston, *The Entertainment at Ashby* (1607), is a country-house masque, written to be performed at the home of the earl and countess of Huntingdon to celebrate the arrival of Alice, dowager countess of Derby (the countess of Huntingdon's mother). The masque circulated in manuscript among the midlands gentry who had commissioned and performed the piece (such as Sir Gervase Clifton of Nottinghamshire, the addressee of Marston's one extant holograph letter) and the manuscript, Huntington Library, MS EL 34 B9, originates from the Egerton (Bridgewater) Library. None of the other later works attributed to Marston, such as *The Mountebank's Masque* (1616) or the satires on the duke of Buckingham (c.1628), can confidently be ascribed to his authorship.

Although Anthony Nixon's *The Black Year* (1606) suggests that Marston was 'sent away westward for carping both at court, city and country', in *The Dutch Courtesan*, and perhaps *Eastward Ho*, there is no evidence that Marston was compelled to leave the stage. It may be that the furore created by *Eastward Ho* or financial exigency impelled him to give up writing for the public stage by late 1606, but a more likely reason was his marriage to Mary (d. 1657), daughter of William Wilkes, one of James VI and I's favourite chaplains. Documentary evidence for the marriage date has not survived but in his will (6 May 1630), Wilkes forgave Marston 'all that is or may be due unto me for lodging and diet, for himself, his wife, his man and maid which he had of me eleven years'. As Marston left the Wilkes household some time in 1616, the 'eleven years' lodging implies a marriage in 1605. Marston also sold his shares in the Blackfriars company to Robert Keysar some time between 1606 and 1608 (probably in 1606 or 1607) and in 1609 when he supplicated to read at the Bodleian Library in Oxford he stated that he had been studying philosophy for the past three years. Although it has been conjectured that he was the John Marston condemned to Newgate in 1608, the extant extracts from the privy council registers omit any offence and do not identify the prisoner precisely. E. K. Chambers and others incorrectly identified and dated the author of a letter to Lord Kimbolton with the playwright rather than with the radical Canterbury cleric of the same name and argued that Marston could have written the infamous 'Scots Mine' play (or plays) that precipitated the closure of the Children of Blackfriars. There is, however, no evidence to suggest that Marston was either in prison or responsible for this dramatic satire.

By 1609–10 Marston had transformed himself into a cleric. He was ordained deacon on 24 September 1609, joined St Mary Hall, Oxford, and became a priest on 24 December. This conversion caused some comment at the time and Thomas Floyde, in a letter to William Trumbull in Brussels, received in February 1610, noted that 'Marston the poet is minister and hath preached at Oxon'. In 1619 Jonson wryly observed that 'Marston wrote his father in law's preachings, and that his father-in-law his comedies' ('Conversations with Drummond', ll. 273–7, in *Ben Jonson*, ed. C. H. Herford and P. E. Simpson, 11 vols., 1925–52, vol. 1), while more contemporary comments convey the surprise at Marston's change of direction. John Davies ascribed the translation to 'malcontentedness' over 'Time mis-spent' (*The Scourge of Folly*, 1610, epigram 217, 'To acute Mr. John Marston') while Francis Beaumont's verse epistle to Jonson (before 1616, possibly *c*.1610–11) comments on Marston's 'wretched' 'state'

ordained to write the grin
After the fawn and fleer.

By 18 June 1610 Marston appears as 'clerk' (priest) at Barford St Martin, Wiltshire, presumably acting as a curate to his father-in-law who held the living, and in October 1616 he was preferred to the living of Christchurch, Hampshire, the first fruits of which were paid in 1617.

After 1616 Marston fades into obscurity. In 1621 he inherited lands from his mother and in 1624 his only son, John, died. In 1631 he resigned his living and returned to London. His only activity connected to his former literary career was to lobby, through William Whalley, to have his name removed from the title-page of the 1633 collected edition of his plays printed by William Sheares. He died in London on 24 June 1634 (his will was dated 17 June) and was buried in Middle Temple Church, where the inscription on his tomb read *Oblivioni sacrum*. His wife died in 1657.   JAMES KNOWLES

Sources will, 6 May 1630, Wilts. & Swindon RO, probate records [William Wilkes] · will, PRO, PROB 11/166/71 · A. R. Braunmuller, ed., *A seventeenth-century letter-book: a facsimile edition of Folger MS V.a.321* (Newark, 1983) · I. Donaldson, ed., *Ben Jonson* (1985) · E. A. J. Honigmann, *John Weever: a biography of a literary associate of Shakespeare and Jonson, together with a photographic facsimile of Weever's* '*Epigrammes*' (1599) (1987) · *The diary of John Manningham*, ed. R. Sorlien (1978) · P. Beal, *Index of English literary manuscripts*, ed. P. J. Croft and others, 1/1 (1980), 329–33 · J. W. Binns and N. Davies, 'Christian IV and *The Dutch courtesan*', *Theatre Notebook*, 44 (1990), 118–23 · R. E. Brettle, 'John Marston, dramatist', 2 vols., DPhil diss., U. Oxf., 1927 · R. E. Brettle, 'John Marston, dramatist: some new facts about his life', *Modern Language Review*, 22 (1927), 7–14 · R. E. Brettle, 'Marston born in Oxfordshire', *Modern Language Review*, 22 (1927), 317–19 · R. E. Brettle, 'John Marston, dramatist at Oxford, 1591(?)–1594, 1609', *Review of English Studies*, 3 (1927), 398–405 · R. E. Brettle, 'Notes on John Marston', *Review of English Studies*, new ser., 13 (1962), 390–93 · R. E. Brettle, 'John Marston and the duke of Buckingham', *N&Q*, 212 (1967), 326–9 · E. K. Chambers, *The Elizabethan stage*, 4 vols. (1923) · M. Eccles, *Shakespeare in Warwickshire* (Madison, Wisconsin, 1961) · M. Eccles, 'Brief lives: Tudor and Stuart authors', *Studies in Philology*, 79/4 (1982), 92–3 · P. Finkelpearl, 'Henry Whalley of the Stationers' Company and John Marston', *Papers of the Bibliographical Society of America*, 56 (1962) · P Finkelpearl, *John Marston of the Middle Temple* (Cambridge, Massachusetts, 1969) · J. George, 'John Marston in the Trumbull correspondence', *N&Q*, 202 (1957), 226 · A. Gurr, *The Shakespearian playing companies* (1996) · R. F. Hardin, 'Marston's Kinsayder: the dog's voice', *N&Q*, 227 (1982), 134–5 · G. Jenkins, 'Manningham, Marston and Alderman More's wife's daughter', *N&Q*, 202 (1957), 243–4 · J. D. Knowles, 'Marston Skipwith and the *Entertainment at Ashby*', *English Manuscript Studies, 1100–1700*, 3 (1992), 137–92 · M. O'Neill, 'The commencement of Marston's career as a dramatist', *Review of English Studies*, new ser., 22 (1971), 442–5 · R. Simpson, *The school of Shakespeare*, 2 vols. (1878) · A. H. Tricomi, 'John Marston's manuscripts', *Huntington Library Quarterly*, 43 (1979–80), 87–102 · F. P. Wilson, 'Marston, Lodge, and Constable', *Modern Language Review*, 9 (1914), 99–100

Marston, John Westland (1819–1890), poet and playwright, was born on 30 January 1819 at Boston, Lincolnshire, the son of Stephen Marston, an Anglican priest who converted to the Baptist church, and ministered to congregations in Boston, and later at Grimsby. After schooling at Grimsby, Marston proceeded to London in 1834, and was articled to his uncle, a solicitor with offices near Gray's Inn. While Stephen Marston had a 'horror of playhouses' and saw actors as 'legitimate children of Satan' (Moulton, 'Five friends', 96), his son was fascinated as early as the age of twelve by plays and the theatre, and once in London soon found his way to Sadler's Wells. With nights spent at the theatre and days spent in the company of mystic writers such as James Pierrepont Greaves and John A. Heraud, to whose periodical *The Sunbeam* he contributed, Marston's law studies suffered, although he may have persevered and been called to the bar around 1838 (Wood, 8). In that year he was appointed secretary of Greaves's Pestalozzian Association, and published a pamphlet entitled *Poetry as an Universal Nature*; in 1839 another lecture, *Poetic Culture*, appeared, and he helped edit a new periodical, *The Psyche*.

Inevitably, it was among the followers of the mystic Greaves, centred in Cheltenham, that Marston met his future wife, Eleanor Jane Potts (d. 1870), eldest daughter of the proprietor of *Saunders's News Letter*; they were married on 18 May 1840, though Marston's feeble prospects were panned by the Potts family, who opposed the match. She was a woman 'of much cultivation,—a good critic, a fine linguist, a loving reader' (Moulton, 'P. B. Marston', 11) and the marriage was a happy one. Marston transformed his own courtship into *The Patrician's Daughter*, a play published in pamphlet form in 1841, and sent in October to William Charles Macready. By the spring the Marstons, settled in London, were acquainted with the Macready circle, and had met Thomas Carlyle, John Forster, Charles Dickens, and Robert Browning at the actor's dinners. Marston's next volume, *Gerald, a Dramatic Poem, and Other Poems* (1842) betrays the influence of another new friend, Philip James Bailey, the author of *Festus* (1839). Thus when *The Patrician's Daughter* appeared at Drury Lane in December of 1842, with Helen Faucit in the title role and with a prologue by Dickens spoken by Macready, the twenty-three-year-old Marston's rise to literary eminence would seem to have been certain. Marston's blank verse play with a contemporary and domestic setting quite naturally put him in the company of his friend Browning, also enamoured of the poetic drama; R. H. Horne's and Elizabeth Barrett's *A New Spirit of the Age* (1844) grouped the two young writers together, and Barrett's *Lady Geraldine's Courtship* betrays the influence of Marston's play. Controversy erupted over the behaviour of the central character of Mordaunt, but *The Patrician's Daughter* was an undoubted success, and might have been a larger one had Marston taken Macready's advice and made the ending a happy one.

In 1846 Marston became a contributor to *The Athenaeum*; he continued for about twenty-five years, and reviewed many important figures, including Tennyson, Thackeray, Browning, and Dickens. His first child, Cecily, was born in 1846, and a second daughter, Eleanor, in 1848. Marston's second play, the prose comedy *Borough Politics*, opened at the Haymarket on 27 June 1846 (claims that it was first published as a pamphlet in 1838 remain unsubstantiated); the manager, Benjamin Harrison, would go on to present two other plays by Marston, *The Heart and the World* (1847) and *Strathmore* (1849). The first, a comedic flop, was withdrawn after a week; however, *Strathmore*, a historical drama about the covenanters with Charles and Ellen Kean in the leading roles, enjoyed a great success. The plot is a more even-handed reworking of Scott's *Old Mortality*, with the complication of misallied love versus duty. Marston thought it his best play, and in the quality of its blank verse as well as its fairly well constructed plot, it is certainly above the average for its time.

In the 1850s Marston was a central fixture of literary London, and in one of the theatre's least memorable epochs the chief author of serious dramatic literature that actually reached the stage. He was an early and enduring friend of Dante Gabriel Rossetti (he was visiting Rossetti when the painter had his final stroke in 1882) and acted in his friend Dickens's amateur theatricals. When his only son, Philip Bourke *Marston (1850–1887), was born, his godparents were the poets Philip Bailey and Dinah Mulock (later Craik, better known as a novelist). A steady stream of plays appeared on the London stage: *Philip of France* and *Marie de Méranie* in 1850, then another domestic drama *Anne Blake* (1852, again starring the Keans), and *A Life's Ransom* (1857), which puts domestic

blank verse into the era of the revolution of 1688. The prose *A Hard Struggle* was praised by Dickens and proved to be a success at the box office. But Marston, still only in his thirties, was spreading his efforts and energies in many directions; in addition to book reviewing, he helped found and was the initial co-editor (with John Saunders) of the *National Magazine* in 1856, which published spasmodic and pre-Raphaelite writers and artists, and he also began writing fiction, although he possessed no gift in that genre. He even found the time to pen the second-best newspaper poem on the charge of the light brigade.

In 1860 Marston moved with his family to a fine house at 7 Northumberland Terrace, Regent's Park, and he and his wife began to hold Sunday evening open houses for literary London, as well as for those with interest in spiritualism. Marston had corresponded with Elizabeth Barrett Browning about spiritualism as early as 1853, and his entire family shared his strong interest in it. Visitors report him as a fluent conversationalist, tending towards the epigrammatic, and as an exceptionally good listener. In 1863 he was made an honorary doctor of laws by Glasgow University, and was henceforth usually addressed as Doctor Marston. One of his most durable plays, *Donna Diana*, was staged at the Princess's Theatre in 1864; a comedy, it was adapted from Moreto's *El Desden con el Desden*, and it was frequently performed in Britain and in the United States for the next thirty years, which was not the case for *Life for Life*, another neo-Elizabethan drama produced in 1869.

In 1870 Marston's wife died, and her death affected him deeply. He gave up the house in Regent's Park, and turned to a collaboration with the melodramatist W. G. Wills, *Broken Spells* (1872). The play is aptly titled, for the spell that allowed audiences to enjoy neo-Elizabethan verse dramas was also gone. Marston's two-volume *Dramatic and Poetical Works* (1876) is a self-conscious capstone to his career, and he seems to have taken delight chiefly in the successes of his son, who had overcome his blindness and become a poet. His daughter Cecely died, however, in 1878, followed in 1879 by Eleanor, who had married the poet Arthur O'Shaunessy in 1873.

Marston's last play was acted at the Vaudeville Theatre on April fool's day 1885. It was titled *Under Fire*, and *The Graphic* laconically reported that 'tokens of disapprobation were unpleasantly numerous' (Wood, 50). A harder blow, however, came with the death of his son on 14 February 1887. Despite a modest civil-list pension, Marston's last years were spent in straitened circumstances; his lodgings were modest, his meals taken in cheaper foreign restaurants. His friends, led by Sir Henry Irving, attempted a rescue with a benefit performance of Byron's *Werner* at the Lyceum (1 June 1887), realizing £928. Marston repaid the acting profession in the next year with the publication of the two-volume *Our Recent Actors*, which is now an indispensable primary source for Victorian theatre history. In his last year he suffered from ill health, and lost much of what had been a portly figure. He died in his lodgings at 191 Euston Road, London, on 5 January 1890, and was buried four days later in Highgate cemetery, Middlesex, alongside his wife and children. A few years later, Bernard Shaw, in a review of 7 November 1896 of what for him was an alarmingly powerful revival of *Donna Diana*, spoke of it as a 'pure-bred drama engendered solely by the passion of the stage-struck, uncrossed by nature, character, poetry, philosophy, social criticism, or any other alien stock'; in the age of Ibsen, Marston's was indeed an 'obsolete play' (*Shaw's Dramatic Criticism*, 188). The artificial theatricality of Marston's best work, as well as its deployment of blank verse, has doomed him to a murky corner of theatre history, though any new accounts of serious mid-Victorian drama should begin with a rediscovery of his work.   D. E. LATANÉ, JR.

Sources L. A. Wood, 'John Westland Marston, L.L.D.: neo-Elizabethan dramatist in the Victorian age', PhD diss., Case Western Reserve University, 1955 · J. W. Marston, *Our recent actors*, 2 vols. (1888) · L. S. Moulton, 'Five friends: the history of an extinct household', *The Cosmopolitan*, 12 (Nov 1891), 95–101 · E. Reynolds, *Early Victorian drama (1830–1870)* (1936) · L. S. Moulton, 'Philip Bourke Marston: a sketch', in P. B. Marston, *Garden verses* (1887) · *The Brownings' correspondence*, ed. P. Kelley, R. Hudson, and S. Lewis, 8–9 (1990–91) · F. C. Thomson, 'A crisis in early Victorian drama: John Westland Marston and the syncretics', *Victorian Studies*, 9 (1965–6), 375 · *Shaw's dramatic criticism: a selection*, ed. J. F. Matthews (1959) · *The diaries of William Charles Macready, 1833–1851*, ed. W. Toynbee, 2 vols. (1912) · A. Nicoll, *Late nineteenth century drama, 1850–1900*, 2nd edn (1959), vol. 5 of *A history of English drama, 1660–1900* (1952–9) · *The Times* (8 Jan 1890), 10 · *The Times* (10 Jan 1890), 10 · *The Times* (5 Feb 1890), 5 · R. H. Horne, *A new spirit of the age*, 2 vols. (1844); repr. in 1 vol. (1907) · *CGPLA Eng. & Wales* (1890) · m. cert.
Archives BL, corresp. · Boston PL, letters and literary MS · NL Scot., corresp. · Notts. Arch., corresp.
Likenesses oils, *c.*1840, priv. coll. · H. Linton, woodcut, 1858 (after E. Morin), BM, NPG · caricature, woodcut, BM
Wealth at death £2654 6s. 9d.: probate, 29 Jan 1890, *CGPLA Eng. & Wales*

Marston, Philip Bourke (1850–1887), poet, was born at 123 Camden Road Villas, Camden Town, London, on 13 August 1850. He was the son of John Westland *Marston (1819–1890), a trained solicitor who abandoned this career for the theatre and poetry, and his wife, Eleanor Jane Potts (d. 1870). The novelist Philip James Bailey and the poet Dinah Mulock Craik were his godparents, and a popular poem by Craik, 'Philip, my King', is addressed to him.

When Marston was only three years old his sight became impaired, a loss attributed variously to an infection following an accidental blow, to the use of belladonna against scarlet fever, and to cataracts. For many years he could still see, in his own words, 'the tree-boughs waving in the wind, the pageant of sunset in the west, and the glimmer of a fire upon the hearth'; but by the time he was twenty he was completely blind. Nevertheless, his contemporary biographers all commented on his large, beautiful, dark brown eyes. As a consequence of his disability, he never learned to read, and his poetry was always dictated.

Some work done when Marston was only fifteen was included in *Song-Tide and Other Poems* (1871). It was dedicated to his mother, who had helped him prepare it for the press, but who had died in 1870. In November 1871 he was devastated by the death of his fiancée, Mary Nesbit, and in 1874 his close friend Oliver Madox Brown also died.

Marston had grown up in a house whose regular visitors included Algernon Charles Swinburne and Dante Gabriel Rossetti, and their reception of his work was very favourable: Rossetti famously declared some of his lyrics worthy of Shakespeare. Their compliments remained a source of pride until the end of his life, and he maintained a wide literary circle. After Mary's death his sister Cicely acted as his eyes, and they lived together in London. They made frequent trips together to France, and one to Italy. In 1875 he published *All in All*, which, though dedicated to his father, consisted mainly of poems to Mary. In that anthology, the single poem dedicated to Cicely begins with the line 'What were I, dear, without thee?' She died of consumption, very suddenly, in 1878. Marston and his father were in France at the time and could not be reached; they returned to find that they had missed even her funeral. Eleanor, the surviving sister, was by then an invalid and she died early the next year, followed by her husband, the poet Arthur O'Shaughnessy (1844–1881). Rossetti, Marston's lifelong mentor, died in 1882.

Deeply grieved by these losses, Marston had also, in 1880, run out of money. His friends, in particular Dinah Mulock Craik, raised enough to support him on that occasion, but his living was always precarious. Although he still lived in London with his father, the main market for his writing was in the United States. Marston's short stories were published in *The Cornhill*, and he was a regular contributor to *Harper's*. He did not particularly enjoy writing these potboilers, though the best of them was, he felt, 'Miss Stotford's Speciality'.

In 1883 *Wind-Voices* appeared—the last of Marston's works to be published within his lifetime—and from then his health began to decline and he became an alcoholic. From that time, too, he established a literary club, 'The Vagabonds', which met monthly at his home at 191 Euston Road. In early 1887, while on a summer tour in Brighton with his father, he was taken ill, and he died at home of apoplexy on 14 February. According to his own wishes, he was buried in unconsecrated ground without a religious service at Highgate cemetery in London on 18 February.

Marston's remembrance was secured largely by his two friends, the American poet Louise Chandler Moulton, and William Sharp. She published two posthumous collections of his poems, *Garden Secrets* (1887) and *A Last Harvest* (1891). She also produced, in 1892, *The Collected Poems of Philip Bourke Marston, with Biographical Sketch and Portrait*. Sharp collected his short stories under the title *For a Song's Sake and other Stories* (1887). Marston's poem 'After' was set to music by Edward Elgar, and Swinburne dedicated a sonnet to his memory. Throughout, Marston's works are characterized by a melancholy which has been attributed to the many tragedies of his life, particularly to the number of bereavements that he experienced. The mournful quality of his writing, however, was ultimately criticized by his contemporaries as repetitive, if beautiful.   JESSICA HININGS

Sources L. C. Moulton, 'Biographical sketch of Philip Bourke Marston', *The collected poems of Philip Bourke Marston, with biographical sketch and portrait* (1892), xxi–xxxviii • C. C. Osborne, *Philip Bourke Marston* (1926) • personal knowledge (1893) [*DNB*] • Allibone, *Dict.* • D. Patrick, ed., *Chambers's cyclopaedia of English literature*, new edn, 3 (1903) • *DNB* • d. cert.
Archives American Antiquarian Society, Worcester, Massachusetts, papers • L. Cong., papers | Bodl. Oxf., letters to Dante Gabriel Rossetti [copies]
Likenesses R. T., wood-engraving, NPG; repro. in *ILN* (26 Feb 1887)
Wealth at death £670 8s. 6d.: probate, 22 March 1887, *CGPLA Eng. & Wales*

Marston, Roger (*d.* 1303?), Franciscan friar and theologian, was a student at Paris under John Pecham from 1269 to 1271 and was there closely associated with the so-called 'neo-Augustinians'. Proponents of Augustinian theology wary of, when they were not opposed to, Aristotelianism, they included Pecham himself, Guillaume de la Mare, Eustache d'Arras, and Bartolommeo da Bologna. Marston was probably among the 160 Franciscans who heard Bonaventure preach his *Sermons on the Hexaëmeron*, attacking Aristotelian philosophy, in 1274. He had followed Pecham back to England by 1276, and lectured on the *Sentences* of Peter Lombard at Cambridge, where he is recorded as the thirteenth Franciscan lector. He later became the sixteenth regent master of the Franciscans at Oxford, probably incepting in 1281. After a number of years as a non-regent master at Oxford, he was in 1292 elected the thirteenth provincial of the English Franciscans and held that office until 1298. A letter which as provincial he wrote to Edward I in 1294 survives. He is said to have died and been buried at Norwich in 1303.

Of Marston's writings only his four *Quodlibeta* and his *Disputed Questions* survive. All are attributable to the years of his regency at Oxford, probably dating from the period between the first month of 1282 and the end of the scholastic year 1283–4. His *Disputed Questions*, namely, *De lapsu naturae humanae* ('On the fall of human nature'), *De emanatione aeterna* ('Concerning the eternal processions in God'), and *De anima* ('On the rational soul') are cited in his various *Quodlibeta*, some in earlier, some in later ones. The principal sources for all these works are Pecham, Thomas Aquinas, and Henri de Gand. Marston's lesser fonts are Guillaume de la Mare, Eustache d'Arras, and Matteo d'Acquasparta. His devotion to Pecham, in particular, has drawn the charge that he is more a compiler than an author—indeed, that he is a plagiarizer. Such a charge is a complicated one, but even those who try to absolve him from it still admit the strong influence of Pecham.

However, if it is considered that Thomas Aquinas is a principal source for Marston, it is in a way completely different from Pecham. In the *De lapsu naturae humanae* of 1282, Marston disagrees with Aquinas, but he does so in a moderate manner. This all changes in 1283–4, after the appearance of Richard Knapwell's *Correctorium quare*, a fervent restatement of controversial Thomist doctrines. Marston launches very explicit attacks on Aquinas. His *Disputed Questions 'De anima'* of 1283–4 incorporate into the *determinatio* itself a very detailed critique of Aquinas, with

long citations from the *Summa theologiae*. He criticizes Aquinas as a 'philosophizing theologian' who attempts to develop a true theology while basing himself on a philosophy that is false and plagued with errors. Marston finds many things worthwhile in Aristotle that could be of use for the Christian theologian, but only provided that they are fitted into a framework provided by the Fathers, and especially by St Augustine. He greatly wishes to reconcile Aristotle and Augustine, but on condition that the former is read according to the light provided by the latter. In the later Marston, the Franciscan order at Oxford has begun its open war against the thought of Aquinas.

S. F. BROWN

Sources *Fr. Rogeri Marston, OFM: Quaestiones disputatae: 'De emanatione aeterna', 'De statu naturae lapsae' et 'De anima'*, ed. Z. van de Woestyne and others, Bibliotheca Franciscana Scholastica Medii Aevi, 7 (1932), vii–lxxx • *Fr Rogeri Marston OFM Quodlibeta quatuor: ad fidem codicum nunc primum edita*, ed. G. F. Etzkorn and I. C. Brady (Florence, 1968); 2nd edn (Grottaferrata, 1994), 5*–83* • D. Douie, *Archbishop Peckham* (1952), 13, 284–5 • R. Schönberger and B. Kible, *Repertorium edierter Texte des Mittelalters* (Berlin, 1994), nn. 17767–72 • F.-X. Putallaz, *Figure Francescane alla fine del XIII secolo* (1996), 26–31, 134–5 • G. Bonafeda, 'Il problema del *lumen* in frate Ruggero di Marston', *Rivista Rosminiana di Filosofia di Cultura*, 33 (1939), 16–30 • G. Cariola, 'L'opposizione a S. Tommaso nelle *Quaestiones disputatae* di Ruggiero Marston', *Scritti* (Turin, 1954), 132–44 • S. Belmond, 'La théorie de la connaissance d'après Roger Marston', *La France Franciscaine*, 17 (1934), 153–87 • E. Gilson, 'Roger Marston, un cas d'augustinisme avicennisant', *Archives d'Histoire Doctrinale et Littéraire du Moyen Âge*, 8 (1933), 37–42 • A. G. Little, 'The Franciscan school at Oxford in the thirteenth century', *Archivum Franciscanum Historicum*, 19 (1926), 803–74, esp. 855–7 • Emden, *Oxf.*, 2.1230–31 • J. I. Catto, 'Theology and theologians, 1220–1320', *Hist. U. Oxf.* 1: *Early Oxf. schools*, 471–517, esp. 499–501

Martel, Sir Giffard Le Quesne (1889–1958), army officer, was born in Millbrook, Southampton, on 10 October 1889, to a family claiming descent from Normandy. He was the only son of Sir Charles Philip Martel (1861–1945), Royal Artillery officer and later chief superintendent of ordnance factories (1912–17), and his wife, Lilian Mary, daughter of W. H. Mackintosh MD.

Education and early military career Martel was educated at 'an excellent preparatory school' (Martel, 1), Stratheden House School, Blackheath, London, under the Revd W. M. Chitty, and in the holidays was coached in boxing by a professional. He then attended Wellington College (1904–7), where he won the Wellesley scholarship awarded annually to the top boy on the modern side, and represented the school in gymnastics. In 1908 he entered the Royal Military Academy, Woolwich. Owing to the perceived possibility of war with Germany the two-year course was shortened, and in July 1909 he was commissioned in the Royal Engineers, then attended the two-year course at the School of Military Engineering, Chatham. The army considered it needed more electrical and mechanical engineers, so Martel was selected for a year's training, from September 1911, at the North Eastern Railway Shops at Darlington where he 'lived almost exactly as a workman … and enjoyed every moment' (Martel, 6). In autumn 1911 he was posted to the 9th field company, Royal Engineers, at

Sir Giffard Le Quesne Martel (1889–1958), by Elliott & Fry, 1942

Woolwich. He acquired his nickname, Q, which continued for the rest of his career, though in the First World War he was also nicknamed Slosher. In 1912 and 1913 he won the welterweight boxing championship not only of the army but of the combined services. Later he won the army championship (1920) and the imperial services championship (1921 and 1922), and continued boxing for pleasure until the loss of one eye in 1944. His sporting prowess was a notable asset to his military career.

The First World War tank corps In August 1914 Martel went to France where he served as a field company officer—largely on demolition and bridging—attaining command of his unit in the second year (captain 1915). In summer 1916 he was sent home temporarily to design a practice battlefield, based on the trench-front in France, in the secret area at Thetford, Norfolk, where the crews for the new tanks were being trained under Colonel E. D. Swinton. This had a far-reaching effect on Martel's career: early in October, three weeks after the tanks had made their September début on the Somme, he was chosen for the key appointment of brigade-major in the small administrative and technical headquarters of the new arm (heavy branch, machine-gun corps, which was to become the Royal Tank Corps in July 1917), at the rather dilapidated château of Bermicourt, near St Pol, under Lieutenant-Colonel Hugh Elles, where he assisted on the technical side Major J. F. C. Fuller, Elles's senior general staff officer, and a keen proponent of tank warfare. Later, in his memoirs, Fuller described Martel as a remarkable officer and

constitutionally fearless. In May 1917, as the result of enlargement, Martel became General Staff Officer, grade 2 (GSO2) and was promoted major.

In November 1916 Martel wrote a remarkably futuristic paper, 'A tank army' (reprinted in *Our Armoured Forces*, 1945), which showed his long-range vision at a time when the tank was generally regarded as only a limited aid to infantry assault, and had limited capability and very low speed. He forecast 'tank armies' and their domination of future great wars. Then and between the wars the term 'tank' was often loosely used, for not only tanks proper but also other tracked vehicles including those which would later be classified as armoured personnel carriers (APCs) and infantry fighting vehicles (IFVs). Influenced by the idea of the tank as a 'landship', he proposed that they should be organized and operate like fleets at sea, with 'destroyer', 'battle', and 'torpedo' tanks, carrying with them in 'supply' tanks their requirements for an extensive operation, and all able to 'swim' rivers. His forecast overlooked some basic differences between the conditions of sea and land warfare, and was only fulfilled in part, but it was of great value in lifting thought out of the rut of trench warfare. The extent to which Martel overshot the mark of potentiality was less than that by which the general run of military thought fell short. His paper influenced J. F. C. Fuller, who drew on it, unacknowledged, for his 1919 Royal United Service Institution gold medal prize essay.

Martel contributed to the tank corps' performance in 1917–18 by his activity and boldness in reconnaissance. He was continually at the front and lived there with unit representatives during the preparatory period before offensives. He was described by Sir Evan Charteris as

> Of a desperate bravery, … He was a small, loose-limbed man, a natural bruiser … with a deep hoarse laugh which … had a most peculiar note of good-humoured ferocity in it. Tales which made the ordinary mortal's flesh creep produced from him regular salvos of this notable laughter … On leave, his idea of recreation was to shut himself up in a mobile workshop of his own and work at a lathe. At the front, his idea of pleasure was to get into a shelled area and dodge about to avoid the bursts.

He was mentioned in dispatches, awarded the MC (1915) and DSO (1916) and promoted brevet major.

Inter-war career After the war Martel returned to duty with the Royal Engineers, and remained with them when the Royal Tank Corps (RTC) was formed on a permanent basis in 1923, a choice for which he was later criticized by some of his comrades in the wartime tank corps and by others who joined it after its creation. But he continued to take a very active interest in the development of tanks and armoured warfare, writing much on the subject as well as conducting experimental work—initially in the problems of tank-bridging. Shortly before the 1918 armistice he had been sent home to command a tank-bridging battalion of the Royal Engineers formed at Christchurch, Hampshire, and which after the war became an experimental establishment. There he developed the Martel box girder bridge, which became the standard army girder bridge—

replacing the more expensive, less adaptable tubular girder bridge—and the Royal Engineers' tank, predecessor of the AVRE (armoured vehicle Royal Engineers).

On 29 July 1922 he married Maud, daughter of Donald Fraser MacKenzie, of Collingwood Grange, Camberley; they had a son, Charles Peter (b. June 1923), and a daughter, Valerie Lois (b. October 1925), the latter killed tragically in December 1941 in a riding accident.

In 1921 Martel went to the Staff College, in a batch selected by war experience, not the usual examinations, and after graduating was appointed in 1923 deputy assistant director, fortifications and works, the War Office, where he remained until summer 1926. The French had used light tanks in the First World War, and, influenced by them, Colonel Henry Karslake advocated light tanks. Martel adapted the concept. At least until 1935 he favoured the use of large numbers of small, inconspicuous, cheap, tracked fighting vehicles with machine guns, to support, and partly replace, infantry by their mobile firepower. In 1925, in his workshop in his garden at Camberley he built—partly from an old car and from wood—a prototype 'one-man tank', which he demonstrated to serving officers and to Captain Basil Liddell Hart (then *Daily Telegraph* military correspondent) who publicized it. From it the War Office, Morris Motors, and others developed experimental 'tankettes'; a few were ordered for the 1927 experimental mechanized force. It became a prototype of the British light tank and machine-gun carrier.

In 1926 Martel himself had been given command of the first field company Royal Engineers to be mechanized, and with it took part in the trials of the experimental force during the next two years. In this period he devised a 'stepping-stone' bridge, of timber crates spaced at short intervals, which a tank pressed down into the bed of the stream as it crossed them—a device which the Russians used during their 1943 advance and later. He also devised a 'mat bridge' of a chain of timber panels, or rafts, which were pushed across the stream and over which vehicles could cross so long as they kept moving—an idea revived for the 1944 Normandy landings.

Between the wars Martel was one of the officer and former officer tank enthusiasts—in his memoirs he called them 'crusaders'—who advocated mechanized and armoured warfare. However, though he had amicable contacts with others of this group, his views sometimes differed from theirs and were less extreme than some, notably those of J. F. C. Fuller. He has been categorized as a reformer rather than a revolutionary or radical. He favoured—against the 'all armoured' concept and independent tank formations—mobile forces which integrated tanks with mechanized artillery and motorized infantry. In the 1930s he was more sympathetic to the infantry tank concept than were the Royal Tank Corps radicals such as Charles Broad and Percy Hobart.

Martel's numerous articles in the military journals during the 1920s made a wide impression, at home and abroad. General Heinz Guderian, creator of the German Panzer forces, referred to Martel in his memoirs as one of the three men—the others were Fuller and Liddell Hart—who 'principally' excited his interest in such forces and described Martel as one of those three 'who became the pioneers of a new type of warfare on the largest scale' (Guderian, 20). Martel was promoted brevet lieutenant-colonel in 1928; in 1929 he went to India where he served briefly with the King George's own Bengal Sappers and Miners at Roorkee. He was an instructor at the Staff College, Quetta (1930–34, lieutenant-colonel July 1933), teaching military engineering, mechanized warfare, and air co-operation. He advocated the use of light tanks in India. In 1931 he designed and had built an experimental four-track light tank, which was not subsequently developed. Studying possible intervention into Afghanistan, he proposed an armoured and mechanized force supplied by air. In 1933 he visited Afghanistan to assess unofficially the feasibility of his scheme. In 1934 he was sent on a reconnaissance of routes for a mechanized force to intervene in Iraq. In 1935 he attended the Imperial Defence College. In 1931 he published *In the Wake of the Tank* (enlarged edition 1935) but on the whole he did not write as much in that decade as in the previous one.

Much of Martel's technical inventive work had been done at his own expense and with little or no official aid. He was not given an opportunity to participate in directing tank development and production until 1936, by which time Britain had lost her former lead. He was, however, promoted colonel in October 1936 (antedated to January 1932), and as assistant director of mechanization, War Office (1936–8), and from January 1938 to 1939 as deputy director (brigadier January 1938), he strove vigorously to make up the lost years. In 1936 Stalin, wanting British and French support against Nazi Germany, despite the USSR's usual obsessive secrecy permitted a small group of British army officers to attend Red Army manoeuvres. Martel, Wavell, and others went in September and were lavishly entertained. At the manoeuvres Martel was much impressed by the number of tanks, and especially by the BT fast–medium tank, based on the American J. Walter Christie's design. He also watched an infantry brigade drop by parachute, at a time when Britain had no airborne troops. Back in England later in 1936 he arranged, through Lord Nuffield, the purchase from its inventor of a Christie tank, and instigated the development from it of the cruiser medium tank.

The Second World War In the autumn of 1937 the new secretary of state for war, Leslie Hore-Belisha, considered making Martel master-general of the ordnance, although he was still only a colonel. Martel's own diffidence about such a promotion over his seniors was one of the factors which led to a different decision. He was promoted major-general in February 1939 (back-dated to May 1938) and early that year left the War Office to command a motorized division—the 50th (Northumbrian), Territorial Army. In January 1940 it moved to France to join the British expeditionary force under Lord Gort.

After the German breakthrough on the Meuse in May 1940 and the Panzer forces' drive to the channel, Martel's division was rushed to the scene. He was put in charge of the improvised counter-attack delivered at Arras on 21

May by two of his battalions and all the serviceable tanks of the First Army tank brigade. This stroke hit the flank of Rommel's Panzer division, causing disorder, and the news so alarmed the German higher command that their drive was nearly suspended; the shock effect was out of all proportion to the small size of the force, but Martel does not seem to have made a favourable impression in this 'forlorn hope' action. His conduct of the operation and its faulty co-ordination led to sharp criticism from the tank officers taking part, who felt his powers as a commander and tactician did not match his gifts as a technician. On 1 and 2 June his division was evacuated from Dunkirk.

After the fall of France there was growing pressure for the appointment of a single chief of the armoured forces in Britain. Churchill supported the proposal and wished the post to be given to Percy Hobart. Although the army council reluctantly agreed to the appointment of a single head of the armoured forces, they were unwilling to meet Hobart's conditions and felt that Martel was likely to be the most amenable of the few armoured experts available: in December 1940 he was appointed commander of the Royal Armoured Corps, under the commander-in-chief home forces.

This soon brought Martel into conflict with Hobart, and the tension between these old friends became severe. It was sharpened when Churchill created what he called a 'tank parliament' where the various armoured division commanders and other experts could meet and express their differing points of view. Martel disliked the arrangement as interfering with his authority and showing a lack of confidence in himself. Moreover, like many champion boxers he was basically a gentle and conciliatory man, anxious to please as well as to avoid trouble, and in his over-tactful efforts to reconcile differing views and interests, particularly of cavalrymen and tankmen, he eventually lost the confidence of both.

Martel was promoted lieutenant-general in 1942, and in September went to India and Burma on a lengthy tour; while he was away his post was abolished. On return he was sent in 1943 to Moscow as head of the military mission, another frustrating post. He was shocked by the Soviet 'slave army' (Martel, 269) of political prisoners. He returned to London in February 1944 and a fortnight later lost an eye in the bombing of the Army and Navy Club. He was placed on retirement pay in 1945, having been appointed CB (1940), KBE (1943), and KCB (1944).

In the 1945 general election Martel stood unsuccessfully as Conservative candidate for the Barnard Castle division of Durham, a strong Labour area in which the Conservatives had almost no local organization. He published *Our Armoured Forces* (1945), which aroused wide interest and considerable criticism. In subsequent years he wrote several more books on his experiences in Russia, all strongly anti-communist; his writings received more attention in the USSR than at home. In 1949 he published his memoirs, *An Outspoken Soldier*. He was a director of Greenwood and Batley Ltd, Leeds, and chairman of the Royal Cancer Hospital (later the Royal Marsden Hospital), London, 1945–1950.

Although his career ended in a series of disappointments Martel deserves recognition for his contribution to the development of modern warfare. He died at his residence, Bulford Lodge, Heatherside, Springfield Road, Camberley, Surrey, on 3 September 1958, shot in the head: the inquest returned an open verdict. He was survived by his wife.   B. H. L. HART, rev. ROGER T. STEARN

Sources G. Martel, *An outspoken soldier: his views and memoirs* (1949) • private information (1970) • personal knowledge (1970) • J. P. Harris, *Men, ideas and tanks: British military thought and amoured forces, 1903–1939* (1995) • *WWW* • Burke, *Peerage* (1959) • *Debrett's Peerage* (1924) • B. H. Liddell Hart, *The memoirs of Captain Liddell Hart*, 2 vols. (1965) • B. Bond, *British military policy between the two world wars* (1980) • B. Bond, *Liddell Hart: a study of his military thought* (1977) • D. Fletcher, *Mechanised force: British tanks between the wars* (1991) • K. Macksey, *Tank warfare: a history of tanks in battle* (1976) • H. Guderian, *Panzer leader* (1952) • M. Allen, ed., *Wellington College register, January 1859–December 1962* (1965) • J. F. C. Fuller, *Memoirs of an unconventional soldier* (1936) • *CGPLA Eng. & Wales* (1958) • d. cert.
Archives IWM, corresp. and papers | King's Lond., Liddell Hart C., corresp. with Sir B. H. Liddell Hart | SOUND IWM SA, oral history interview
Likenesses Elliott & Fry, photograph, 1942, NPG [*see illus.*] • W. Stoneman, photograph, 1945, NPG • oils, Royal Engineers, Chatham, Kent
Wealth at death £37,115 19s. 5d.: probate, 5 Nov 1958, *CGPLA Eng. & Wales*

Martel, Linda (1956–1961), healer, was born on 21 August 1956 at Amherst Maternity Home, St Peter Port, Guernsey, the fifth of the six children of John Royston (Roy) Martel (1916–1979), commercial traveller, and his wife, Eileen Ethel, née Allchin (b. 1926). At birth she was suffering from water on the brain and spina bifida, and her legs were paralysed. The doctor in charge of the case, Dr Webber, was of the opinion that she would not live a year. Her mother remained at the maternity home for ten days after the birth. On the eleventh day she returned home; the baby was transferred to St Peter Port Hospital, and soon after her arrival at this hospital was baptized. Her head grew disproportionately large, and on at least one occasion her imminent death was predicted by the hospital. However, she reached her first birthday, and three months later was taken to the Alder Hey Hospital, Liverpool, where she received from Mr Rickham a new treatment for hydrocephalus.

Linda responded well to the treatment. Back in Guernsey she remained in the St Peter Port Hospital until she was two years and nine months old. She was then considered well enough to live at home. It gradually became apparent to her family that she possessed the power to 'see' the pains and illnesses of other people and the gift to cure these afflictions. Her fame spread; reports appeared in national newspapers such as the *Daily Herald* and people increasingly travelled to visit the infant 'miracle worker'. Her parents in no way tried to exploit her healing powers. They were Christians but not churchgoers. Linda herself hated churches and organized religion, but frequently spoke about Jesus and Our Lady. Some have conjectured that this dated from her prolonged stays in hospital and the nearness of Irish (Catholic) nurses. Roy Martel believed that the real reason for Linda's existence was 'to prove to people that there is such a being as God' (Graves, 124).

On 19 October 1961 Linda told her father: 'My Jesus Christ has been, he put both his hands on my chest' (Graves, 114). She died the next morning at her home, Calgary, Palm Grove estate, rue Sauvage, St Sampson, Guernsey. Her father was determined that the funeral service should not take place inside a church. Consequently the order of burial took place by her grave in the cemetery of St Sampson's Church. After her death scraps of her handkerchiefs and blankets were given to those seeking a cure; many believed that remission was brought in this way. With the passing of the years such fragments became harder to obtain. Many then took soil from her graveyard.

The 'legend of Linda Martel' was investigated by Charles Graves. Under that title he published in 1968 a series of case studies, together with the memories of Roy Martel and the verdicts of five medical practitioners. One of these, Dr Bolt, commented:

> If you study Linda's record you will find that a majority of the patients who benefited from her suffered from acute headaches, migraine, asthma and backache, all of which are classical examples of psychosomatic ailments. In this connection the power of suggestion can produce apparently miraculous results. (Graves, 137)

This became a popular understanding. Nevertheless in 1972 Roy Martel approached James Stevens Cox, proprietor of the Toucan Press, Guernsey, with a manuscript of memories about Linda. Stevens Cox had heard of Linda but had not, hitherto, taken much interest in the subject. He explained to Martel that he would first interview some of the people whose cases were discussed in the manuscript. Having served as a detective with Bristol city criminal investigation department throughout the Second World War, he approached the task with a sceptical attitude. However, when he came to investigate the cases he was impressed by the fact that several people acknowledged the reality of their cure, which they attributed to Linda, while protesting that they had had no faith in her ability to effect a cure. Stevens Cox published Martel's manuscript in 1973. Interest in Linda has since continued unabated. In 1990 Bob Bloomfield wrote a book (*Linda Martel: Little Healer*) with an introduction by Dr M. H. S. Bound. This Cambridge-educated practitioner concluded: 'Linda's life teaches how misfortune can be transcended, by contacting the life in it and living its reality, thus becoming crucified with Christ' (Bloomfield, xi–xii).

GREGORY COX

Sources C. Graves, *The legend of Linda Martel* (1968) · R. Martel, *The mysterious power of Linda Martel* (1973) · R. Bloomfield, *Linda Martel: little healer* (1990) · private information (2004) [family] · d. cert.
Likenesses photograph, repro. in Martel, *Mysterious power*, frontispiece · photographs, repro. in Graves, *Legend of Linda Martel*

Marten [Martin], **Anthony** (c.1542–1597), courtier and author, was the son of David Marten (d. 1556) of Westminster and Twickenham, Middlesex, and his wife, Jane Cooke (d. 1563), of Greenwich, Kent. Apparently he had

five sisters. David Marten had been senior clerk to the surveyor of the king's works since 1531, and in 1535 he became comptroller. Anthony Marten was at Trinity Hall, Cambridge, in August 1564 when Elizabeth I visited; he does not seem to have graduated, but entered the royal household. By 27 April 1570 he had become the queen's 'sewar'; on that night, having been 'at Whitehall ... serving at ... the queen's dinner', he was waylaid by George Varneham of Richmond, Surrey, 'with malice aforethought ... and having a sword and buckler'. Forced to fight somewhat outside the palace, 'near the bridge towards Scotland Gate', Marten, though presumably without a buckler, wounded Varneham mortally (Jeaffreson, 1.65). Marten—and also his servant, which might imply that the fight was less clear-cut than alleged—had to give recognizances to appear at the next gaol delivery, but seems to have avoided further repercussions.

In July 1579 Marten, styled the queen's steward, was granted the bailiffship of Ledbury, Herefordshire, but he surrendered it in March 1586. On 1 August 1587 he was present at Peterborough as sewer for the funeral of Mary Stewart. In August 1588 Elizabeth granted him a lease of a house at Richmond, and made him keeper of the royal library in the palace of Westminster for life at 20 marks per annum. In November 1591, as royal cup-bearer (*dapifer*), he was granted a monopoly for licensing exports of tin, being paid 4*d*. per hundredweight. This apparently survived a competitive tender in 1595 by Edward de Vere, earl of Oxford, who claimed that through the licence to 'one Martin', 'being not diligently looked into, her majesty loseth very near half the custom due for want of entering the just weight' (*Salisbury MSS*, 5.137).

Both professional and religious considerations made it fitting for Marten to dedicate to Charles, Lord Howard of Effingham, the lord chamberlain, his translations of John Bernard's *Tranquillitie of the Minde* (1570) and *The Commonplaces of Peter Martyr* (1583), the first of which he rather mysteriously described as fulfilling 'my promise ... in my former epistle made to your lordship' (*Tranquillitie*, sig. *2r). By the second he felt some need to justify 'to the Christian reader' such an undertaking from one 'living in court, as it were in continuall peregrination, and as a Rechabit among the children of Israel' (*Commonplaces*, sig. Air). Marten recommended the work of Pietro Martire Vermigli (known as Peter Martyr) for 'a particular discoverie of the Romaine Antichristian kingdome'; this provided the focus for his next publication, *An exhortation, to stirre up the mindes of all her majestie's faithfull subjects, to defend their countrey* (1588). His sense of England as an Israel beleaguered by a new Sennacherib was not uncommon that year, but more eccentric was *A second sound, or, Warning of the trumpet unto judgment, wherein is proved that all the tokens of the latter day are not onelie come, but welneere finished* (1589). His prediction that Antichrist's war against the professors of the gospel was now so far advanced as to indicate the end of the world within the next five years allowed him to fulfil a pretension already immanent in his earlier prefaces—to preach theology and morality to bishops. He warned them against self-advancement 'by some corrupt and sinister meanes' and admonished them to eject 'unlearned pastors' and pursue England's moral reformation (*Second Sound*, 27).

The apotheosis of Marten's bishop-lecturing was his intervention in the presbyterian controversy with *A Reconciliation of All the Pastors and Cleargy of the Church of England* (1590). It attracted the ire of Sir Francis Knollys, who accused not only John Whitgift but 'Mr Martyn the sewer, an ordynarye servant to hir majestie' of treason or *praemunire* in denying her authority to be the origin of episcopal power (PRO, SP 12/233/62). Knollys's position as treasurer of the household seems to have provoked an oversensitive reaction to the sewer's essentially adiaphorist view of episcopacy and presbyterianism, the latter as practised in Scotland being 'the harder and more dangerous course'. Marten's professed wish for reconciliation, involving the general abandonment of 'unprofitable wrightings', seems genuine, while his continued obsession with the threat of 'the bloudy beast of Rome' and his 'present expectation of Christ unto judgement' hardly made him a natural ally of Richard Bancroft or Adrian Saravia. In approving the latter's 'Latin labours' published 'when I had wellneere finished all these matters' and in attacking John Udall, Marten betrayed some confusion (*Reconciliation*, sigs. 6v, ar, 3v, 1v, A4r). His 'position would appear to be little different from that of Knollys himself'; 'at heart a theologian *manqué*', his last work was affected by 'personal inability to think clearly' but was notable as 'almost the only Elizabethan defence of episcopacy to be written by a layman' (Thompson, 'Marten', 70, 46, 75).

Apparently unmarried, Marten made his will on 21 August 1597. He died at Richmond, and was buried with his father at Twickenham church on 25 August. Besides the Richmond lease, he left £19 to charities—£17 at Richmond (£10 for the relatively conservative object of a church bell), implying continued residence there, and only a token £2 at Twickenham—and some £162 to individuals, mostly to the families of four of his sisters.

JULIAN LOCK

Sources W. D. J. Cargill Thompson, 'Anthony Marten and the Elizabethan debate on episcopacy', *Essays in modern English church history: in memory of Norman Sykes*, ed. G. V. Bennett and J. D. Walsh (1966), 44–75 · W. D. J. Cargill Thompson, 'Sir Francis Knollys's campaign against the *jure divino* theory of episcopacy', in W. D. J. Cargill Thompson, *Studies in the Reformation: Luther to Hooker*, ed. C. W. Dugmore (1980), 94–130, 123–5 [repr. from *The dissenting tradition*, ed. C. R. Cole and M. Moodie (1976), 39–77] · will, PRO, PROB 11/127/107 · will of Jane Marten, PRO, PROB 11/46/15 · will, GL, MS 9171/14 [David Marten], fol. 20 · PRO, lord chamberlain's accounts, state funerals, LC 2/1, fol. 207r · PRO, state papers domestic, Elizabeth I, SP 12/233/62, 12/243/106, 12/249/7, 12/249/9 · *CPR, 1578–80* · J. C. Jeaffreson, *Middlesex county records*, 1 (1886); repr. (1972), 65–6 · *Calendar of the manuscripts of the most hon. the marquis of Salisbury*, 5, HMC, 9 (1894), 95 · H. M. Colvin and others, eds., *The history of the king's works*, 3 (1975) · Cooper, *Ath. Cantab.*, 2.242 · *DNB* · W. H. Price, *The English patents of monopoly* (1906), 143 · J. Lock, '"How many tercios has the pope?": the Spanish war and the sublimation of Elizabethan anti-popery', *History*, new ser., 81 (1996), 197–214, esp. 200–01 · B. T. Whitehead, *Brags and boasts: propaganda in the year of the Armada* (1994), 99, 142

Wealth at death bequeathed over £181; also Richmond lease (income of £10 p.a.): will, PRO, PROB 11/127/107

Marten, Benjamin (*fl.* **1722**), medical writer, was the author of *A New Theory of Consumptions: More Especially of a Phthisis, or Consumption of the Lungs* (1720). Though the author of a remarkable book, he himself attracted little attention from his colleagues, and it is difficult to establish the facts of his life. All that can be definitely stated is that Marten described himself as MD on the title-page of his book, and that he dated its preface from his house in Theobald's Row, near Red Lion Square, Holborn, London.

It is probable that Marten was born in the second half of the seventeenth century, most likely after 1680, and that he was the 'Benjamin Martin, *anglus*' who purchased an MD degree from the University of Aberdeen in 1717. It is likely that he was the 'Benjamin Martin' who served as a surgical pupil and assistant to Johannes Groenevelt (John Greenfield), a London physician and lithotomist, who had emigrated from Holland. It is also likely that he is the 'Benjamin Marten Doctor of Physick' who is named as a brother in the will of John *Marten, a London surgeon and specialist in venereal disease, who had translated two of Groenevelt's works from Latin into English. John Marten had another brother, James, who became a London apothecary, and a sister, Elizabeth, who married a London tailor named Spooner. One contemporary implied that the Marten brothers were themselves the children of a London tailor.

It is possible that the author was the Benjamin Marten who married Mrs Hannah Fisher on 17 November 1716, and also the Benjamin Martin who wrote a will in May 1751, since the writer of the will was a resident of St James's, Clerkenwell, near Theobald's Row.

Marten's book is remarkable because it contains the first completely worked out theory of the transmission of human contagious diseases by micro-organisms. Marten argued that phthisis (tuberculosis) was a contagious disease and, like other contagious diseases, was caused by 'some certain species of *Animalcula* or wonderfully minute living Creatures … which being drove to the Lungs by the Circulation of the Blood … or … being carried about by the Air, may be immediately convey'd to the Lungs …' (*New Theory of Consumptions*, 1720, 51).

It is equally important that Marten recognized that this theory implied that each contagious disease was specific to its own causative organism: 'How can we better account for the regular Types [of diseases] … than by concluding they are severally caus'd by innumerable *Animalcula* … that variously offend us according as their Species are different …' (*New Theory of Consumptions*, 65). Marten argued that even a severe cough could not become a consumption unless animalcula or their eggs were present in the blood or fluids of the body. When they were present, even a trifling cough or chill could become a 'secondary cause', permitting the animalcula to proliferate. He noted that these animalcula differed in their contagiousness, and that the ones that caused consumption required prolonged close contact with a consumptive person. He noted the hereditary transmission of diseases such as syphilis, and pointed out that this theory could explain the geographical and epidemic patterns of particular diseases, such as smallpox and the plague. He also argued that the life cycle of particular animalcula might determine the sequence of symptoms shown in certain diseases.

Marten's book was successful enough to require a second edition in 1722. In the preface to that edition he claimed that 'many learned Gentlemen' approved of his theory and several had adopted it. However, there is little evidence that physicians at the time read his work. The most extensive contemporary citation, by Cotton Mather, appears in his unpublished manuscript *The Angel of Bethesda*. The book disappeared from notice, and was only rediscovered by the medical historian Charles Singer, who published large extracts in 1911.

Marten's ideas did not develop in a vacuum; his putative teacher, Johannes Groenevelt, was a learned man who had studied with François de la Boë Sylvius in Leiden. Although as a foreigner he lived on the fringes of the London medical world, Groenevelt found friends among the fellows of the Royal Society. Marten himself was well read: among the authors he cited were the Dutch microscopist Antoni van Leeuwenhoek FRS, the Frenchman Nicholas Andry de Boisregard, William Harvey on generation, and Richard Morton on phthisis. However, Marten was the first English author who drew these works together into a coherent theory of living contagion.

Although there is no evidence that Marten's work greatly influenced subsequent authors aside from Cotton Mather, his book must be placed within the intellectual milieu of the Royal Society, which generated several similar works over the next two decades. The specific influence of Marten's own work, like the specific details of his life, will probably always remain imponderable.

MARGARET DeLACY

Sources R. Doetsch, 'Benjamin Marten and his "New theory of consumptions"', *Microbiological Reviews*, 42 (1978), 521–8 · C. Singer, 'Benjamin Marten, a neglected predecessor of Louis Pasteur', *Janus*, 16 (1911), 81–9 · private information (2004) · H. J. Cook, *Trials of an ordinary doctor: Joannes Groenevelt in 17th-century London* (1994), 198, 192–3, 64, 120–31 · C. Wilson, *The invisible world: early modern philosophy and the invention of the microscope* (1995), 164–9 · P. J. Wallis and R. V. Wallis, *Eighteenth century medics*, 2nd edn (1988)

Marten, Sir Henry (*c.*1561–1641), civil lawyer and judge, was the eldest son of Anthony Marten, citizen and grocer of London and gentleman of Berkshire, and his wife, Margaret, daughter of John Yate of Lydford, Berkshire. Henry was reputedly born in the London parish of St Michael Bassishaw, although his baptism is not recorded in its parish registers. He was educated at Winchester College and at New College, Oxford, where he matriculated as the son of a commoner on 24 November 1581, aged nineteen, and was admitted a fellow the following year. He graduated BCL in 1587, proceeded DCL in 1592, and was admitted a member of the college of advocates (Doctors' Commons) on 16 October 1596. With his wife, Elizabeth (1573/4–1618), whom he married in August or September 1597, he had two sons, Henry *Marten (1601/2–1680) and George, and three daughters, Elizabeth, Jane, and Mary.

Marten had a long and distinguished career under the first two Stuarts but like many public officials who served

both he found himself somewhat more comfortable with the former than with the latter. His legal career developed with notable speed and success. He had distinguished himself in the profession sufficiently to be invited to participate in the disputations before King James at Oxford in 1605 and three years later made a presentation against the use of prohibitions before the privy council. Perhaps as a consequence of those performances, he was named king's advocate on 3 March 1609. Appointments to a succession of important offices followed in due course: in 1616 he was named chancellor of the diocese of London; in January 1617 he was knighted at Hampton Court and in October that year he was appointed judge of the high court of admiralty; in 1620 he was named to high commission; and in 1624 he was made judge of the prerogative court of Canterbury and dean of the arches. As a civilian he had by 1625 reached the pinnacle of his profession. As James I once remarked to him, he was now 'a mighty monarch, in his jurisdictions over land and sea, the living and the dead' (*DNB*). Clearly he had also established a personal rapport and a significant level of trust with James I. The king sent him on a mission to the Palatinate in 1613 to help negotiate the marriage of his daughter Elizabeth to the Elector Frederick. Six years later Marten was asked to serve as a commissioner in the trade negotiations between the English and Dutch East India companies, and his success in securing a treaty no doubt led James to call on him again in 1624 when relations between English and Dutch merchants deteriorated disastrously in the so-called Amboyna Affair. The seemingly unprovoked and senseless massacre of English subjects by principals of the Dutch East India Company created a diplomatic nightmare for James on the eve of England's entry into the Thirty Years' War, when the alliance with the Dutch took on singular importance, and Marten's attempts to finesse the crisis were no doubt of considerable help.

Marten's political career began in 1625 when he was elected to parliament as a member for St Germans, Cornwall—an election he owed to fellow Cornish MP Sir John Eliot. He served again in 1626 (St Germans), 1628 (Oxford University), and in the Short Parliament of 1640 (St Ives). He started in parliament rather inauspiciously by criticizing the duke of Buckingham for his failed 'ambassadorship' in Spain the previous year, but his criticism was particular and did not reflect anything like ideological opposition to the crown. Marten can be found days later supporting the king's requests for supply, suggesting, quite logically, that since parliament had pressured the king into the war they were morally obliged to offer him financial support—'let us take heed how we discontent a prince whom we have put into a course of war' (Gardiner, *Commons Debates*, 121–2). In the 1626 parliament Marten again became involved (this time inadvertently) in the parliamentary proceedings against the duke of Buckingham. As judge of the admiralty court he had frequently crossed swords with the duke as lord admiral, and MPs had come to focus on one such incident involving cargo in a French ship called the *St Peter*. The ship had been taken as prize along with a number of others in September 1625, and its cargo, including nearly £10,000 in gold and silver, had been sequestered on orders from Buckingham. King Charles subsequently ordered the gold and silver to be confiscated to the government's use—ostensibly as contraband—and the remaining goods sold at auction, this without investigation, proper due process, or any decree from the court of admiralty, and over the protests of Marten. In the event the sale did not go forward, the goods were restored, and the ship eventually released, only to be suddenly rearrested a week later on orders from Buckingham when relations with France took a sudden turn for the worse. The matter was eventually resolved, but Buckingham's (and the king's) cavalier treatment of the French vessels and their merchants' interests had provoked retaliation against English merchants in France and the episode was seized upon by the duke's enemies as further evidence of his venality and incompetence. Marten was caught in the middle and was forced to stage a vigorous defence of his own part in the matter in the House of Commons. The episode did little to improve relations between Marten and the lord admiral. The following year Buckingham again attempted to interfere with Marten's deliberation's in the court of admiralty on matters of prize and in so doing provoked a bitter quarrel which led to Marten's resignation. The quarrel was resolved very quickly, but Marten returned to his place only after he had been reassured (albeit implicitly) of his future independence as an officer of the court.

This incident seems to have accentuated Marten's growing concerns about Charles I's government. He took an active role in the 1628 parliament, and while he cannot in fairness be described as an 'opposition' MP—he staunchly defended the king's discretionary right to declare martial law—he did play an active and important role in the passage of the petition of right. Together with John Glanvill, a prominent common lawyer, Marten was chosen to draft and present the Commons' objections to the Lords' so-called 'saving clause', a proposed amendment to the petition which reserved to the king the discretionary exercise of his 'sovereign power'. Marten's speech in conference on 23 April pointed out the logical inconsistency of the Lords' amendment, suggesting that it contradicted the language of the petition and hopelessly undermined its intent by robbing its specific provisions of any persuasive power—'Sovereign Power', he claimed, 'is a transcending and a high word' (Levack, 119). His speech certainly contributed to the decision to drop the saving clause and it was later printed for public consumption.

During the years that followed Marten also found himself increasingly at odds with Charles I's religious policies. A confirmed moderate, he often used his position as dean of arches (and, before that, as official of the archdeaconry of Berkshire and as chancellor of the diocese of London) to mitigate the harsh treatment meted out to puritans for religious nonconformity. In 1628 he publicly supported a parliamentary bill which would have prevented prosecution for 'gadding to sermons' and claimed that as dean of arches he had in the past assessed damages against prosecuting ordinaries and 'would ever do it' (Levack, 191). He

also became the focal point of the notorious controversy surrounding the position of the communion table. In 1633 the parishioners of St Gregory's, London (a peculiar of St Paul's), appealed to the court of arches to overturn the decision of the dean and chapter to remove their communion table to the east end of the church and rail it in 'altarwise'. Marten was sympathetic to their position and ordered the table to be returned to the chancel but before he could pronounce sentence the king himself intervened—at the urging of Bishop William Laud—and removed the case for hearing before the privy council. The king eventually declared his support for the ordinaries' decision (and for their authority to determine such matters) and consequently ordered Marten to reverse himself and declare against the parishioners. The incident left Marten embarrassed and clearly out of step with official policy and, perhaps not surprisingly, he was summarily removed as dean of arches later that year when Laud replaced George Abbot as archbishop of Canterbury.

Marten found himself at odds with Laud again in the autumn of 1640 when he appeared before the council to argue against the controversial canons of 1640. His opposition on this occasion had less to do with doctrinal matters than with professional concerns. A number of the new canons were designed to circumscribe the jurisdiction and powers of diocesan chancellors and officials in favour of their bishops. These offices were almost always filled by civilians and Marten, together with Sir John Lambe—ironically his replacement as dean of arches—staged a spirited, if ultimately unsuccessful, defence of their professional class.

Despite these disagreements Marten appears to have remained in good standing with the king. He retained his membership on the high commission until its abolition, and kept his posts in both the prerogative court of Canterbury and in the admiralty until his death in London on 26 September 1641 'in the yeare of his Age 81' (Ashmole, 1.160). He was generally admired for his professionalism and his integrity, though as with other members of Charles I's administration his behaviour came under intense scrutiny during the Long Parliament. Marten was fined £250 by the House of Lords for his part in the high commission prosecution of Sir Robert Howard, and proceedings in at least a half-dozen other cases in the admiralty were being reviewed in the upper house at the time of his death. Marten was reportedly one of the wealthiest men in Doctors' Commons—he lent the king £3000 in 1639—and he left substantial properties in Berkshire to his eldest son, the future regicide Henry Marten. He was buried at Longworth, Berkshire.   JAMES S. HART JR

Sources DNB · R. C. Johnson and others, eds., *Commons debates, 1628*, 6 vols. (1977–83), vol. 2, pp. 315, 542–3, 548–9, 552–3, 555–61; vol. 3, p. 307 · S. R. Gardiner, ed., *Debates in the House of Commons in 1625*, CS, new ser., 6 (1873), 26, 28–9, 30, 55, 121–2 · JHC, 1 (1547–1628), 903, 930 · JHL, 4 (1628–42), 106, 114, 266 · main papers, 19 Jan 1641; 21 Jan 1641; 26 Jan 1641; 26 Aug 1641, HLRO · CSP dom., 1625–41 · APC, 1627, 210, 246, 411 · B. P. Levack, *The civil lawyers in England, 1603–1641* (1973) · S. R. Gardiner, *History of England from the accession of James I to the outbreak of the civil war*, 5–7 (1883–4) · C. S. R. Russell, *Parliament and English politics, 1621–29* (1979) · J. Davies, *The Caroline* *captivity of the church: Charles I and the remoulding of Anglicanism, 1625–1641* (1992) • S. R. Gardiner, *Reports of cases in the courts of star chamber and high commission*, CS, 39 (1886) • Foster, *Alum. Oxon.* • will, PRO, PROB 11/187, sig. 124 • E. Ashmole, *The antiquities of Berkshire*, 3 vols. (1719), vol. 1, pp. 160–62

Archives W. Yorks. AS, Leeds, papers

Likenesses J. J. Van den Berghe, stipple, 1798 (after unknown artist), BM, NPG; repro. in J. Adolphus, *The British cabinet*, 2 vols. (1799–1800) • oils, Trinity Hall, Cambridge

Wealth at death numerous charitable bequests; property left to heirs: will, PRO, PROB 11/187, sig. 124; Levack, *Civil lawyers*, 252

Marten [Martin], **Henry** [Harry] (1601/2–1680), politician and regicide, was the eldest son and heir of Sir Henry *Marten (c.1561–1641), civil lawyer and judge, and his wife, Elizabeth (1573/4–1618). He was born in his father's Oxford house opposite Merton College chapel and had a younger brother, George, and three sisters, Elizabeth, Jane, and Mary.

Early life and career to 1640 After attending school in Oxford, Henry (or Harry as he was known by friends) matriculated, aged fifteen, on 31 October 1617 as a gentleman commoner from University College, graduating BA in 1620. He may have been the Henry Marten admitted to Gray's Inn in August 1618 and was certainly admitted to the Inner Temple in November 1619. In the 1620s he toured Europe and enjoyed much high living accompanied by, among others, Mildmay Fane, later earl of Westmorland. During his time in France he was much impressed with the French stoical philosophers.

Many details of Marten's life, particularly during his early years, remain unclear. He probably married twice. On 25 September 1627 he married a woman named Elizabeth (c.1612–1634), with whom he appears to have had three children: Margaret (*bap.* 1629), Mary (*bap.* 1632), and Elizabeth (*bap.* 1634). His wife died shortly after the birth of her third child and was buried on 28 April 1634 at Hurley in Berkshire. On 5 April 1635 Marten married Margaret Lovelace Staunton (*d.* 1679), widow of William Staunton and daughter of Richard, first Baron Lovelace. The union was the idea of his father and according to John Aubrey, Henry acceded 'something unwillingly' (*Brief Lives*, 193). The couple had three children, two daughters and a son, Henry (*bap.* 1639).

Marten earned a reputation for licentiousness as both a womanizer and a drunkard early in his career. Aubrey describes him as 'a great lover of pretty girles' and he is said to have cost his father £1000 a year for the upkeep of his wild lifestyle (*Brief Lives*, 193). Much of his own money was also rumoured to have been frittered away on women and wine. This reputation allegedly earned him the ire of Charles I. Upon seeing Marten at a race meeting in Hyde Park the king is said to have exclaimed

> Let that ugly Rascall be gonne out of the Parke, that whoremaster, or els I will not see the sport. So Henry went away patiently, *sed manebat alta mente repostum* [but it lay stored up deep within his heart].   (ibid.)

Marten's business affairs are obscure during this period. In the 1630s he was described as merely a 'farmer' of Hinton Waldrist, Berkshire (now Oxfordshire). During the latter part of the decade he and his brother managed their

Henry Marten (1601/2–1680), by Sir Peter Lely, 1650s

father's considerable estate, which stretched along the south bank of the Thames and the River Cole and centred on the village of Shrivenham. The brothers had run up considerable debts by the outbreak of the civil wars.

Political and military career, 1640–1646 In April 1640 Marten was returned to the Short Parliament as a member for Berkshire. The following November he was returned for the same seat to the Long Parliament. Prior to the civil wars he developed a reputation as an assiduous committee member. He was part of the group that drew up the protestation of May 1641 and regularly attended the important committee of safety created in July 1642. In that year he and his brother George used contacts to elicit information about the activities of the court. Marten was subsequently paid £500 towards intelligences and later bequeathed £2000 to the 'service of the Commonwealth' (*JHC*, 2, 1640–42, 408). He offered his merchant vessel, *The Marten*, as part of the naval summer watch and, commanded by George, it was part of the parliamentary fleet whose mutiny secured the appointment of the earl of Warwick as lord admiral. It is reported that when the king issued a commission of array for Berkshire, Marten tore up the document in front of his tenants. On the outbreak of war in August 1642 he subscribed £1200 to the parliamentary cause and was named governor of Reading, but abandoned his post when the royalists marched on Oxford. He then raised a regiment by commandeering horses. During summer 1643 he chaired the committee for the general rising in London and although a plan to raise the whole country was not implemented, it formed part of the pressure against the aristocratic leadership of the parliamentarian army. Throughout his parliamentary career Marten enjoyed good living, but seems to have had little stomach for alcohol and was soon drunk. Yet he was capable of using this reputation as a political tool, pretending to sleep in the Commons chamber until, seizing his opportunity to make a rapier intervention, he would leap up from his feigned slumbering.

As early as 1641 Marten confessed to his friend Sir Edward Hyde that he did not believe that one man was wise enough to rule a whole nation. By 1642 he was identified as a key figure among those Sir Simonds D'Ewes referred to as the 'fiery spirits' who used language disparaging towards the royal dignity. Having proclaimed kingship to be forfeitable he was excluded from pardon for life or estate by Charles I in the same year. In support of the puritan divine John Saltmarsh, the author of a pamphlet proposing the deposition of the king, Marten stated in the Commons on 16 August 1643 that 'it were better one family be destroyed than many' (*Mercurius Aulicus*, 19 Aug 1643). On being challenged to reveal to whom he referred he added without hesitation that he meant the king and his family. He was immediately imprisoned in the Tower of London and barred from the Commons. His imprisonment was to last fourteen days but his parliamentary ban was to span almost three years. Despite his non-attendance in the house he claimed to have signed the solemn league and covenant, although in retrospect he admitted doing so on grounds of political expediency rather than conviction. He commanded a troop in the Berkshire-trained bands and was appointed governor of Aylesbury on 22 May 1644. During the winter of 1645–6 he acted as commander-in-chief, under Colonel Dalbier, of the infantry at the siege of Donnington Castle.

Republican and regicide, 1646–1649 The narrative of Marten's return to the Commons is unclear. On 6 July 1646 the house voted to erase from the *Journals* the sections referring to the Saltmarsh affair. The following business was the disablement for delinquency of the Abingdon MP, Marten's brother-in-law, Sir George Stonehouse. Marten may first have stood for Abingdon and then transferred to the county seat. His close political ally and friend, William Ball of Barking, was then elected as a recruiter MP for Abingdon. Ball wrote pamphlets in a similar vein to Marten, and, when Ball died in 1648, his writings continued to appear in the presses, possibly edited or reissued by Marten. Marten subsequently helped Henry Nevile to the Abingdon seat.

After his return to the Commons, Marten emerged as the chief political ally of Thomas Chaloner. Chaloner questioned the involvement of the Scottish commissioners in the peace negotiations with the king, which were taking place at Newcastle upon Tyne. In October 1646 he made a speech in the house, subsequently dubbed the 'Speech without Doors', which called for peace to be settled without reference to the Scots or their wishes. Marten wrote several pieces in support of Chaloner, some published and others that remained in manuscript. His published pieces were issued anonymously, as befitted their extreme statements of hostility towards Charles Stuart, the barely hidden imputation of which was that

Charles should be executed for murder. The aim of these tracts was to reduce Charles Stuart to the status of an ordinary citizen, and thus make him as liable as any Englishman to the same punishment for any crime he committed. The main pieces to appear in the press were *A Corrector of the Answerer to the Speech out of Doores* (1646) and *An Unhappie Game at Scotch and English* (1646). Marten's hostility towards the Scots continued and in 1648 he published two pieces of invective against the Scottish commissioners, arguing that the peace of England ought to be settled without reference to either the Scots or the king. The first of these was *The Independency of England Endeavoured to be Maintained*. He was instrumental in pushing through a vote of no addresses on 3 January 1648, by which the parliament agreed to cease sending overtures for peace to Charles. He explained this move in *The Parliaments Proceedings Justified in Declining a Personall Treaty*.

Marten developed a close working relationship with the Leveller leaders during the late 1640s. He was closest to John Wildman, who was to marry Lucy Lovelace. Wildman was named with Marten in a cipher outlining sympathetic individuals and regiments, as well as identifying opponents, during the army agitation of summer 1647. Throughout their lives Marten and Wildman retained their cipher letters as pen-names for each other. John Lilburne also trusted and respected Marten. The latter chaired the committee charged with examining Lilburne's imprisonment, a committee that was unable to secure Lilburne's release, and in *Rash Oaths Unwarrantable* the Leveller published an invective against Marten. Marten was hurt by Lilburne's personal attack and drafted a reply, 'Rash censures uncharitable', but did not publish it. The two seem to have mended their relationship and developed a mutual respect. Marten also knew several minor Leveller figures. He took part in negotiations to draw up an *Agreement of the People*, and was praised by Lilburne as the only parliamentarian to actively do so in late 1648. Marten approved of the idea of a fundamental constitution and was later, with Edward Sexby, to assist the frondeurs in drawing up a similar agreement for the French rebels.

In December 1647 King Charles signed the engagement with the Scots and this was to lead eventually to a second outbreak of war. Marten returned to Berkshire, and interpreted the Commons order to defend the counties as an opportunity to raise another regiment. This one was entirely unauthorized and its recruitment and actions were opposed both by the army commanders and by the Commons. He refused to answer for his conduct and moved his regiment around the midlands. It was called a regiment of Levellers and a combination of radical political views and a reputation for womanizing made the slur useful in denigrating both Marten's public and his private life. An ejected minister, William Turvil, sent news to London that appeared in a newsletter, *Bloody Newes from the North*. This was a sensationalist but exaggerated account imagining the regiment's extreme actions in Leicestershire. The frontispiece depicted Marten and his soldiers committing atrocities, which helped to foster a reputation as a violent incendiary, but in reality the regiment passed peacefully through Market Harborough. It fought under the banner 'For the People's Freedom against all tyrants whatsoever', with soldiers drawn from Marten's tenants and those he could incite to desert other parliamentary forces. It was armed and provisioned by requisitioning the possessions of others. It was eventually recognized as part of the New Model, although it seems never to have fought as such. According to the Leveller Richard Overton the incorporation of the regiment was a means to neutralize Marten's political voice and bring the process of political reform to a halt.

After Pride's Purge on 6 December 1648 Marten and Cromwell entered the Commons together. Marten made a speech in commendation of the lieutenant-general. This was a rare piece of co-operation between the two. The Scots were convinced that he hated Cromwell even more than he hated them, so much so that he would offer his regiment to assist Charles and the Scots rather than see Cromwell rise to power. Although he later claimed the purge to be a harbinger of Cromwellian military tyranny, at the time he supported the coup. He was named a member of the high court of justice to try Charles Stuart, and despite other constitutional commitments and attendance at the discussions on the *Agreement of the People*, he nevertheless attended regularly if intermittently. He signed the death warrant of Charles I; during the signing he and Cromwell allegedly splashed each other's faces with ink.

Political and religious views Marten's political views remained unshakeable throughout his lifetime. He was always committed to a republican polity and was infamous in the early 1640s as the only person prepared to admit to such a view. He was a somewhat feckless man, starting a number of pieces in which he was to outline his political views but rarely completing them or sending them to the press. Either he got bored with writing them or political activity got in the way. Nevertheless, we can piece together a political philosophy based on two principles. Firstly, he argued that for a polity to be stable it must be in balance. This did not imply the Polybian balance between the three elements of monarchy, aristocracy, and democracy, but rather a pair of balance scales, in which the representative must always be in direct balance with those it represented. This was an expression of popular sovereignty, in which he argued that even if the Commons failed to act in the interests, or according to the wishes, of the people, the people could choose to create a 1500-member parliament to supersede a 500-member one. Secondly, he had a philosophy of the circularity of power, in which every element of the constitution must be directly represented and directly accountable to every other. Any alien element must be rigidly excluded. In particular this meant the House of Lords and the kingship. This circularity of representation was often interpreted in a nationalistic way, to describe the concept of English liberties, and thus, in Marten's political career, it was often used to pour scorn on the representatives of the kingdom

of Scotland, and their insistence that they be part of tripartite peace negotiations that included Scottish commissioners, English commissioners, and the crown.

Marten also had radical views about religion. He was accused of being an atheist, but he did make a statement which implied that he did not question whether God existed but that his viewpoint was of radical scepticism because mankind did not possess the faculties to know what or who God was. A third party called him a follower of the Stoic Epictetus. Marten's scepticism meant it was incumbent on mankind to allow total toleration of all religious viewpoints. People did not have the knowledge, or the authority that knowledge would have conveyed, to pronounce one opinion on religion more right than another. This was a viewpoint that Marten carried through his political career, arguing for liberty even for Catholics. One of the daughters from his second marriage, Mary, married the Catholic peer Thomas Parker, Lord Morley and Mounteagle. Marten also opposed the conquest of Ireland on grounds that the English could not seek religious freedom for themselves and then impose a religious settlement on others. He was constantly and vehemently hostile to the Presbyterian and Scottish covenanters' desire to impose a national church system. He supported the right of Huguenot worship in London. He also practised toleration on his own estates, being more concerned by whether the congregations accepted ministers, than by their religious views. Many radical groups, first the Levellers and later in the 1650s religious radicals such as the Quakers, met at the sign of the Mouth, in Aldersgate. He was probably present at the Levellers' meetings and, while denying being part of the Quakers' meetings there, defended their right to gather.

Commonwealth career, 1649–1654 For the first two years of the Commonwealth, Marten was at the centre of state affairs. He enjoyed life in the spotlight and in wealth and ease. During 1652 he bought Derby House, centre of the state committees, as his private London house. He received lands in recognition of his expenditure at the state's service. There was an award of £1000 a year, made on 3 July 1649, as well as lands in Eynsham, near Oxford, but the major awards consisted of the estates of Leominster Foreign, Herefordshire—a patchwork of holdings formerly part of the priory of Leominster—and Hartington, Derbyshire. The latter was a huge estate, running from Buxton in the north to Ashbourne and the Cheshire and Staffordshire borders in the south. Both estates proved difficult to manage. They were already encumbered by debts of fee-farm rents, non-payment of rents to the lord, and disputed possession, for which Marten's personal reputation, the manner by which he came by the estates, and his frequent absenteeism made him vulnerable to local royalist opponents, the most active of whom was Sir James Croft in Herefordshire. He was eventually brought down financially by the requirement to make back-payments to the new fee-farm rent farmer, Arthur Samuel. Marten attempted to alienate these lands in the 1650s to protect them from proceedings for debt and to provide for his family, but he was generally unsuccessful. He was assisted in managing his estates by a number of former Levellers, in particular John Wildman, Maximilian Petty, and William Wetton.

Marten was the author of the key constitutional changes of state. On 4 January 1649 he issued the definitive statement of Commons sovereignty on behalf of the house. He designed the new great seal and sat on the committees to abolish kingship and the Lords and to declare England to be a commonwealth. He was named to the first council of state, and was one of those who attempted to have its oath, the engagement, tightened, to include approval of retrospective actions—the regicide—as well as future government—the Commonwealth. He was a supporter of the government, pejoratively known as the Rump Parliament, which he later described as responsible for 'the best frame of lawes yett extant in the World' (University of Leeds, Marten Loder MS 93/40, fol. 4). At the time he drew on an arresting parallel to justify the perpetuation of the parliament: when Moses was found in the bulrushes, he argued, it was agreed that his own mother was the best person to care for him. Members of the Rump, the army council, and Cromwell did not agree with Marten, and fearing that the Rump designed to perpetuate its sitting, or to call fresh elections with minimal protection against the return of men committed to a monarchical restoration, Cromwell brought soldiers into the Commons chamber on 20 April 1653 and forcibly ejected the Rump. This was an action that would crystallize Marten's and Cromwell's contempt for each other. Cromwell accused Marten of drunkenness and whoredom in the speech with which he announced the dissolution of the parliament. In a series of unpublished pieces Marten railed against the ejection of the Rump, Cromwell's ambition, and the loss of republican government.

Despite Cromwell's accusation there is little evidence of Marten's womanizing. His papers contain one claim to paternity, made in 1651. His reputation for whoring seems to have been generated by the flagrant way in which he breached conventional mores by openly living with a common law wife, Mary Ward, whose brother, Job, was parliamentarian commander of the fort at Tilbury. There is evidence that they were a couple from as early as 1649, when they lavishly entertained visiting dignitaries and kept liveried servants together. They may well have been a couple from Marten's earliest time in London in 1640. If so, this was a relationship that remained constant for forty years. It was, however, adulterous, and Marten was quite open about it. Mary referred to herself, and was referred to by others, as Mary Marten. There were frequent plays on the word 'leveller' to argue that Marten's radical political stance was in fact a synonym for the seduction of women, and satires on Mary to imply his possession of a 'creature', in the same way that his regiment and his political power were bought. The couple had three daughters: Peggy, Sarah, and Henrietta (Bacon-hog).

Marten's ability to act publicly against the Cromwellian protectorate was stifled by the proceedings for debt against him. A combination of lavishly supporting the radical war effort, high living, the cost of supporting his family, investing in his brother's ambitions to be a Caribbean planter, and having been awarded lands which proved both underproductive and heavily encumbered, meant that he had amassed debts totalling approximately £35,000 by 1654. Now deprived of the legal protection of a parliamentary seat, he became prey to numerous creditors with long-standing grievances against him. His creditors sued him in the upper bench, Oliver St John issued a warrant for his arrest, and, when apprehended, he was first committed to the upper bench prison in Southwark, and then allowed to live in the area known as the Rules of Southwark, where prisoners could live on licence. There he resided with Mary Ward in the Southwark home of her sister Frances. His brother, meanwhile, continued to live on credit in Barbados, writing back to Henry expressing incredulity at his plight, and inviting Marten to join him in the Caribbean.

Trial, imprisonment, and death It was from the Rules of Southwark that Marten was recalled in 1659 to rejoin the reconstituted Rump Parliament. He did not have the power that he had formerly commanded, but he managed to secure the appointment of Edmund Ludlow as commander of the army in Ireland, and the use of Somerset House as a chapel for French protestant immigrants. At the restoration of Charles II royalists were first convinced that Marten had fled to the continent. He did, in fact, submit himself, on 20 June 1660, according to royal order. He was imprisoned first in the Tower of London, where, with other regicides, he awaited the decisions of the royal court and the parliament on their fates. At his trial in October 1660 he argued that they had spelt his name wrongly—Henry Martyn rather than Harry Marten—on the indictment and that he could not therefore be the same person who signed Charles's death warrant. He was nevertheless found guilty but famously saved from execution. This may have been because influential royalists were reluctant to create a martyr from someone of his personal notoriety. It may also have been because he was active in arguing for the lives of royalists when supporters of the high court of justice of the Commonwealth wanted retribution for war crimes that extended beyond solely the figure of Charles Stuart.

Marten was sent into internal exile, the usual fate of those who had taken an active role in the Commonwealth but had been opponents of Cromwell. He was sent first to either Holy Island or Berwick Castle. In 1662 the letters that he had written to Mary from the Tower were seized and published as *Coll. Henry Marten's Familiar Letters to his Lady of Delight*. He was transferred to Windsor Castle in May 1665, but Charles II ordered him removed from such close proximity to himself. From Windsor he was moved in 1668 to Chepstow Castle, where he remained for twelve years, in a suite of rooms in Bigod's Tower (now Marten's Tower), with liberty, at least initially, to travel around outside the castle. Mary shared his imprisonment in Chepstow, while his wife remained in the family home, Longworth Lodge, Berkshire. Their daughter Anne, who remained unmarried, looked after her. Anne died in 1671 and Margaret died, intestate, in 1679. Marten died at Chepstow on 9 September 1680, having choked while eating his supper. He was buried there in the Anglican church.

Reputation Marten's reputation, both for licentiousness and for radical politics, lived on after his death. In 1682 a pamphlet lampooned his supposed lasciviousness and applied it to his political radicalism. A character called Harvey was 'not so much for levelling the Men, as *Martin* the Women' and 'all the Women in the City are with Child by *Martin*, and so longed for Levellers' (Menippeus, *The Loyal Satirist, or, Hudibras in Prose*, 1682, 14, 18). Aphra Behn, who claimed to have met George Marten in Surinam, wrote a play called *The Younger Brother, or, The Amorous Jilt* about the patriarch Sir Henry Marten, and his two wayward sons. Her political jokes, however, placed in the mouth of the Henry Marten character, were written out, considered dated by the time the play was published in 1688. Eighteenth-century pieces about him tended to dwell on his personal life, whereas in the nineteenth-century, revivals of republican thinking dwelt on his imprisonment for his political views. A modern biographer characterizes him as a 'sceptic and a republican … a landed proprietor who took risks and was prosecuted for debt, an adulterer who practised charity, and an ideologue who preserved a sense of humour' (Barber, xi).

SARAH BARBER

Sources *A corrector of the answerer to the speech out of doores* (1646) · *Mercurius Aulicus* (19 Aug 1643) · *Mercurius Electicus* (23–30 Aug 1648) · *Mercurius Pragmaticus* (22–9 Aug 1648) · *An humble petition of thousands of well-affected inhabitants of the Citie of London and Westminster and the suburbs thereof* (1643) · *Instructions and propositions containing incouragements to all good men to subscribe for the raising of an army of ten thousand* (1643) · *An humble proposal of safety to the parliament and citie* (1643) · A. Steele Young and V. F. Snow, eds., *The private journals of the Long Parliament*, 3: *2 June to 17 September 1642* (1992) · JHC, 2–3 (1640–44) · Coll. *Henry Marten's familiar letters to his lady of delight* (1662) · *CSP dom.*, 1641–3 · BL, Add. MSS 71531–71535 · M. Menippeus, *The loyal satirist, or, Hudibras in prose* (1682) · baptism registers, Berks. RO, MF 296 · PRO, SP 16/340 · A. Behn, *The younger brother, or, The amorous jilt* (1688) · Wood, *Ath. Oxon.* · *Aubrey's Brief lives*, ed. O. L. Dick (1949); pbk edn (1992) · *An unhappie game at Scotch and English* (1646) · *The independency of England endeavoured to be maintained* (1648) · *The parliaments proceedings justified in declining a personall treaty* (1648) · *Bloody newes from the north* (1648) · NL Scot., Hamilton MS GD 1/406/1/8277 · *A word to Mr Wil Prynne* (1649) · *The memoirs of Edmund Ludlow*, ed. C. H. Firth, 2 vols. (1894), vol. 2 · *DNB* · Foster, *Alum. Oxon.* · *Members admitted to the Inner Temple, 1571–1625* [n.d.] · S. Barber, *A revolutionary rogue: Henry Marten and the English republic* (2000)
Archives Berks. RO, almanack and pocket diary · BL, parliamentary and political MSS, Add. MSS 71531–71534 · Harvard U., MSS · U. Leeds, Brotherton L., corresp. and papers · W. Yorks. AS, Leeds, papers
Likenesses P. Lely, oils, 1650–59, NPG [*see illus.*]

Marten, Sir (Clarence) Henry Kennett (1872–1948), college head, was born in Kensington, London, on 28 October 1872, the younger son of Sir Alfred George Marten (1829–1910), barrister and judge, who in 1874 became member of parliament for Cambridge borough and a QC, and his wife, Patricia Barrington, daughter of Captain Vincent Frederick Kennett of the Manor House, Dorchester-on-Thames. He was educated at Eton, where he was in the

house of Miss Evans, the last of the Eton 'dames'. He entered Balliol College, Oxford, in 1891, where A. L. Smith was his tutor. After gaining a first class in modern history in 1895 he was invited by Edmond Warre, the headmaster, to return to Eton as an assistant master to teach history. At that time the study of modern history played only a very small part in the curriculum of the school, and only in 1906 did the reform of the curriculum introduced by Edward Lyttelton, who had become headmaster in the previous year, make possible the establishment of modern history as one of the main subjects of education. Marten was the leading figure in a development which had a profound effect on the education provided in the public schools and grammar schools of the country.

Marten was a remarkable teacher. He combined a great knowledge of history, which he constantly kept up to date, with immense enthusiasm and the ability to transmit this enthusiasm to his pupils. He would always be persuading them to read the great works of historical literature, and he made them free of his splendid library, which he bequeathed to Eton, where it now constitutes the Marten Library. At the same time he insisted on clear thinking and an orderly treatment of the subject. Largely through him the study of history at Eton gained exceptional standing, with almost all boys spending at least four periods a week on it after school certificate. Yet his influence was great in wider circles than Eton, especially in the Historical Association, of which he was a founder member (1906) and the first schoolmaster president from 1929 to 1931.

With G. Townsend Warner, an assistant master at Harrow School, Marten was the author of one of the most used school textbooks of the first half of the twentieth century, *The Groundwork of British History* (1912). He collaborated on other textbooks, and in *The Teaching of History* (1938) he drew on his long experience as a schoolmaster.

From 1907 to 1927 Marten was a housemaster. In 1925 he was recommended to Lord Braybrooke, visitor of Magdalene College, Cambridge, as master to succeed A. C. Benson. The fellows did not want another Eton schoolmaster and had their own candidate, A. S. Ramsey. In the end Braybrooke appointed A. B. Ramsay, lower master at Eton, as a compromise: Marten would have been a much happier choice. As it was, Marten took on Ramsay's job, and in 1929 he was appointed vice-provost, and in 1945 provost of Eton. Although he was essentially a traditionalist and made no innovatory contribution to Eton, he added to the happiness of life and commanded great affection.

In 1938 Marten was entrusted by George VI with the historical education of the Princess Elizabeth. His teaching of English history, especially that of the constitution of this kingdom and of the British dominions, was always placed in the framework of the history of Europe, and he paid special attention to the political and constitutional history of the United States. In recognition of his services he was appointed KCVO and he was knighted by the king on the steps of the college chapel in the presence of the school on 4 March 1945. A picture of this unique ceremony by R. E. Eurich is at Eton. Marten, who was unmarried, died at the provost's lodge at Eton on 11 December 1948. His twin sister, Isabel, who had kept house for him, was a formidable figure in her own right.

R. BIRLEY, *rev.* TIM CARD

Sources personal knowledge (1959) · Eton, archives · T. Card, *Eton renewed: a history from 1860 to the present day* (1994) · *WWW* · I. Elliott, ed., *The Balliol College register, 1900–1950*, 3rd edn (privately printed, Oxford, 1953) · *CGPLA Eng. & Wales* (1949) · Venn, *Alum. Cant.*
Archives CUL, corresp. and papers | Balliol Oxf., corresp. with A. L. Smith
Likenesses R. E. Eurich, group portrait, 1945, Eton · W. Stoneman, photograph, 1945, NPG · G. Kelly, oils, Eton
Wealth at death £38,134 2s. 5d.: probate, 14 April 1949, *CGPLA Eng. & Wales*

Marten, John (*fl.* 1692–1737), surgeon, is probably one of the John Martens enrolled in the Company of Barber–Surgeons in 1692. He may have been the brother of Benjamin *Marten. John Marten's first extant work is a translation of and supplement to the *Treatise of the Safe, Internal Use of Cantharides* (1706), originally published in Latin by Joannes Groenevelt in 1698. Dedicated to William, earl of Portland, it made the internal use of cantharides (or Spanish fly) developed by Groenevelt (or Greenfield, as he is called in Marten's translation) much better known in England, and it obtained the imprimatur of the president and censors of the Royal College of Physicians of London. As the title page explains, Marten also added 'Several further and very remarkable Observations and Histories of the said Doctor, also of the Translator and others' to Groenevelt's work, which are clearly marked but almost doubling the original size of the work. While Marten claims to have received the blessings of Groenevelt for translating and supplementing his book, he was later accused by J. Spinke of having imposed himself.

According to Marten's preface, signed 'From my House in Bridg-water-Square, near Aldersgate-Street, London, a Golden Head over the Door', he had been particularly 'conversant' with the cure of 'several in the most deplorable Conditions, especially from *Venereal Causes*' and found that 'the use of Cantharides, when all other means failed' had great benefits. He therefore had approached Groenevelt, who agreed to let Marten translate and correct his book. He also thanked 'that great and learned Physitian and favourer of Learning, Dr. Edward Tyson', for suggesting some of the additions. Marten's own commentary grows in size as the original text begins to end. By pages 189–95, Marten re-emphasizes the usefulness of cantharides in treating the clap, and within another fifty pages or so degenerates into telling stories of a lascivious nature. The book ends with an advertisement for the fourth edition of Marten's own book on gonorrhoea.

This latter work, no longer extant in earlier editions, appeared in a sixth edition in 1709 (*Treatise of All the Degrees and Symptoms of the Venereal Disease, in both Sexes*), which went through additional editions thereafter. By way of an appendix it contained a 'letter' on sexual relations that veered into pornography, intended to be bound with the book but printed on a separate signature so that it could be separated if appearances warranted. The book and its appendix quickly aroused enemies. One of the chief of them, J. Spinke, published an attack on Marten titled *Quackery Unmask'd*, in which he accused Marten of the basest dishonesty; among other charges, he printed an affidavit of one 'J.C.' stating that a lawyer, Mr. Joshua Stephens, claimed to have been the real translator of the Latin work on cantharides, although Marten came into possession of his sheets. Marten or a friend rose to the defence with an anonymous *An apology for a Latin verse in commendation of Mr. Marten's Gonosologium novum proving that the same liberty of describing the diseases of the secret parts of both sexes, and their cure, (which is said by some to be obscene) has been us'd both by ancient and modern authors* (1709). But in the same year Marten was indicted in the queen's bench for 'being evil disposed and wickedly intending to corrupt the subjects of the Lady the Queene'. The indictment was eventually dismissed. But Spinke made further attacks on Marten's seventh edition in *A Short Discourse, Preliminary to the Second Edition of Quackery Unmask'd* (1711) and *Venus's Botcher, or, The Seventh Edition of Mr. Marten's (Comical) 'Treatise of the Venereal Disease'* (1711).

After these incidents Marten continued to publish, but on a safer—if also common—chronic disease related in cause, he and other practitioners thought, to venereal disease: the gout. *Attila of the Gout* was published in 1713, promising to show the reader that all previous works on the subject had been vanities, while he had developed 'an infallible Method to Cure it' in the form of a new specific. The text describes the symptoms, causes, and cures for the gout, and recommends his own specific liquor (the receipt for which is not given), concluding with letters testimonial for his remedy and an account of how previous practitioners accused of quackery had found new and effective cures. He tried to keep his remedies in the public eye with *Dishonour of the Gout* in 1721 and *Treatise of the Gout*, 4th edition, in 1738. He seems to have died at about the time he completed his last book.

HAROLD J. COOK

Sources *An apology for a Latin verse in commendation of Mr. Marten's Gonosologium novum* (1709) · J. Groenevelt, *A treatise of the safe, internal use of cantharides*, trans. J. Marten (1706) [with additions.] · J. Groenevelt, *A treatise of the safe, internal use of cantharides* (1715) · J. Spinke, *Quackery unmask'd* (1709) · J. Spinke, *Venus's botcher* (1711) · D. F. Foxon, 'Libertine literature in England, 1660–1745', *Book Collector*, 12 (1963), 21–36 · Worshipful Company of Barbers, court minute books
Likenesses G. White, line engravings, 1708 (after F. Scheffer), Wellcome L.

Marten, Maria (1801–1827). *See under* Corder, William (1804–1828).

Marth, Albert (1828–1897), astronomer, was born in Colberg, Pomerania, on 5 May 1828 of unknown parentage, and was orphaned at an early age. Initially a theology student at Berlin, he moved in 1846 to Königsberg University, where he was briefly the last pupil of F. W. Bessel, then pupil of and observatory assistant to C. A. F. Peters. Marth abandoned his PhD in early 1853 to become second assistant to J. R. Hind at George Bishop's observatory in London, a post worth £50 a year. There on 1 March 1854 he discovered the minor planet Amphitrite, and the same year he was elected a fellow of the Royal Astronomical Society (RAS). From July 1855 to January 1863 he was observer at Durham University observatory. Subservience to a difficult absentee director, an ageing 6½ inch refractor, the stipend of £80, even with accommodation and a vegetable garden, together made the position an uncertain career step. Marth could do little observing, but developed expertise as a calculator and theorist. He published orbits for comets, minor planets, the planets, and the moon.

In August 1856 Marth published in the German journal *Astronomische Nachrichten* the first part of a major work, 'Researches on satellites', in which he sought to improve on Bessel by establishing his own methods for investigating the true orbits of the satellites of Jupiter, Saturn, and Uranus. These became his speciality for the next thirty years, and the basis for all the ephemerides or annual orbit predictions he published in the *Monthly Notices of the Royal Astronomical Society* from 1870. Issued on a uniform plan, they were of great use to astronomers by encouraging observation and compelling comparison with theory.

In 1857 his intensive investigations led Marth to submit a paper to the RAS criticizing proceedings at the Royal Greenwich Observatory. After consulting John Herschel and J. C. Adams, council rejected it, and when it suffered a second rejection Marth resigned. In 1860 he published in *Astronomische Nachrichten* 'On the polar distances of the Greenwich transit circle', a lengthy and stringent criticism of the Greenwich methods and reductions. This was professional suicide. George B. Airy's reputation pivoted on having made Greenwich an exemplar by improving on Bessel's methods, and the circle was Airy's own design. Edward Holden, director of the Lick Observatory, later said that these criticisms were 'well founded in several respects, but [they] naturally made him no friends in official circles' (Holden, 203).

When William Lassell (1799–1880) took his new 48 inch reflector to Malta for 1862–5, he engaged Marth. Airy warned Lassell he saw 'malice throughout' Marth's paper, and, since he had circulated copies to the English astronomers, added, 'of his morals, I have a low opinion' (Airy to Lassell, 8 Dec 1862, CUL, RGO 6, 147, 3, 76). But Marth's skills were indispensable to Lassell, who made his employment conditional on silence. The telescope at that fine site yielded discoveries, enabling Marth to catalogue some 600 nebulae and make observations of Mars and Jupiter. Lassell's success stimulated Robert S. Newall (1812–1889) of Gateshead to order a 25 inch refractor, and in 1865 he engaged Marth, promising him a new transit instrument for his satellite observations. Marth suffered an eight-year hiatus, the transit failed to arrive, and the refractor was still incomplete in 1873, so that he was dismissed.

Marth was embittered by what he saw as a conspiracy to avoid challenging flaws in Airy's science, and he remained unemployed because Airy's withholding of patronage was virtually universally effective. However, in January 1878 he gained re-election to the RAS, where he supported attacks upon council. One member, E. B. Knobel, noted his

'sensitive nature' and 'indifferent health' (Knobel, 142). Another, Hind, found him 'stupidly prejudiced against several of the principal Fellows' (Hind to Adams, 8 May 1879, Adams papers, Box 7, St John's College, Cambridge). It was 1882 before he had a year's employment in charge of an expedition to the Cape of Good Hope to observe the transit of Venus. On his return in 1883 he became director of the remote Markree observatory in Ireland. The stipend was £200 plus accommodation, but he was required only to make meteorological observations.

Marth was an outsider by birth, education, and position, and by his criticism of Airy and the RAS council. Unmarried, he lived frugally and pursued his studies, in which he was active and accurate. He used original insights, and his work was of great use. He also published useful theoretical work on the motions of satellites, the orbits of binary stars, and instrument errors. At Markree, Marth's health began to fail, and during a visit to his native country he died suddenly, in Heidelberg on 6 August 1897, at the age of sixty-nine.   ROGER HUTCHINS

Sources E. B. K. [E. B. Knobel], *Monthly Notices of the Royal Astronomical Society*, 58 (1897–8), 139–42 • E. S. Holden, 'Albert Marth, born 1828, 1897', *Publications of the Astronomical Society of the Pacific*, 9 (1897), 202–3 • Boase, *Mod. Eng. biog.* • C. L. F. André, *L'astronomie pratique et les observatoires en Europe et en Amérique*, 1: *Angleterre* (Paris, 1874), 72 • *The Times* (13 Aug 1897), 8 • S. McKenna, 'Astronomy in Ireland from 1780', *Vistas in Astronomy*, 9 (1967), 283–96 • W. Doberck, 'The Markree observatory [pts 1–2]', *The Observatory*, 7 (1884), 283–8, 329–32 • St John Cam., J. C. Adams MSS • CUL, RGO 6

Archives RAS, letters to Royal Astronomical Society • St John Cam., J. C. Adams MSS

Martial, Richard. *See* Marshall, Richard (b. 1517, d. in or after 1575).

Martiall, John (1534–1597), religious controversialist, was born in Daylesford, Worcestershire, although when he arrived at Winchester College in 1545, aged eleven, the admission-book recorded him as a native of Defford in the same county. He went on to New College, Oxford, in 1549, and was made fellow there in 1551 and BCL on 8 July 1556. He became second master or usher at Winchester College about 1556, while Thomas Hide was headmaster. Upon Elizabeth's accession he went into exile in Louvain, and took his BA at the University of Douai in 1567. A year later he was among the first group of English Catholic exiles who formed the English College under the leadership of William Allen.

It was during his time in exile that Martiall wrote *A treatyse of the crosse gathred out of the scriptures, councelles, and auncient fathers of the primitive church* (1564). This was in part a contribution to the controversy prompted by John Jewel, bishop of Salisbury, in his 'challenge sermon', but was also a response to Elizabeth I's retention of a cross in her royal chapel. Martiall dedicated the work to Elizabeth, describing her as 'so well affectioned to the crosse … that youre Majestie have always kept it reverently in youre chappel' (fol. 1v). The tone of the work was set by the terms of the controversy started by Jewel, dwelling on the examples from scripture and the primitive church which

Martiall held supported the veneration of the cross. He stressed the merit of the cross as being more powerful and beneficial to believers than the written word: 'that which wordes could not print in their heades, the contemplation of this signe doth so printe in their mindes, that they triumph over the devil …' (fol. 116v), and pointed out that:

> every man can not reade scripture, nor understand it when he reade it: and every man can not al times so conveniently heare a good preacher, as he may se the signe of the crosse, if it might be suffred to stand.   (fol. 117r)

He denied that Catholics dwelt on signs to the exclusion of true faith, insisting that 'for answer we saye, that nothing can avayle, and profit man, unlesse he hath a stedfast faith in Christ, and faithfull belieff in the merites of his passion', but arguing that the sign of the cross was something which could strengthen such faith (fol. 20r–v).

The book was attacked by Alexander Nowell in a court sermon of March 1565, but to Nowell's dismay the queen rebuked him for his excessive language in attacking Martiall. It was James Calfhill who wrote a refutation, which led to Martiall's second work, *A Replie to M. Calfhills Blasphemous Answer Made Against the Treatise of the Crosse* (1566). In this work Martiall asked Bishop Grindal and his colleagues whether Calfhill's work reflected 'the doctrine of all your church of England', or whether it was 'the fansie only of one idle brayne' (sig. *ijr). He deplored, and listed, the abusive language Calfhill had employed, and in particular denied the charge that Catholics were subversive, comparing their work with some of the more radical protestant tracts. 'There is no blast blowen against the monstruous regiment of women. There is no libel set foorth for order of succession: there is no word uttred against dewe obedience to the soveraine' (sig. **v). The work reiterated the need for veneration of the cross, drawing a powerful comparison between secular and sacred modes of reverence:

> When we meete together we put of the cap, we bowe the knee, we humble the bodie, we offer to kisse the hand. In like manner when we receave the kinges letters, we put of our capps. When we come into the chamber of presence, and see the cloth of estate, we shewe a kinde of reverence and honour unto it, not respecting the paper and waxe, nor silken clothe, or golden chaire, but the prince that wrote it, and kinge that sate under that cloth of estate. Right so when we see the image of Christe, or any Sayncte, we put of our cappes, we make courtesy, we bowe, we cappe, we kneele, and shewe such external reverence, and honour, not because it is made of silver and gold, or curiouslye wroughte, or sette with pearle, or fynely paynted, but because it represent unto me Christ and his passion.   (sig. ***iijr–v)

There was no protestant response to this until 1580, when William Fulke attacked Martiall and Thomas Stapleton together in *T. Stapleton and Martiall* (*Two Popish Heretikes*) *Confuted*. Martiall also wrote a work entitled 'Treatise of the tonsure of the clerks', but this was left unfinished, and so never printed.

After his time in Douai, with the backing of Owen Lewis, archdeacon of Hainault, and later bishop of Cassano, Martiall became a canon of the collegiate church of St Peter at Lille in Flanders. His installation was delayed by the civil unrest in the Low Countries, but finally took place in 1579.

He served there for eighteen years, resigning the post in order to prepare himself for death, which came on 3 April 1597. He died in the arms of his friend William Gifford, later archbishop of Rheims and then dean of St Peter's Church, where Martiall was buried. He left a ring with a precious stone to adorn a piece of the true cross in the cathedral at Lille.

L. E. C. WOODING

Sources P. Milward, *Religious controversies of the Elizabethan age* (1977), nos. 64, 66 · W. Fulke, *T. Stapleton and Martiall* (*two popish heretikes*) *confuted* (1580) · Gillow, *Lit. biog. hist.*, 4.476–9 · J. Strype, *Annals of the Reformation and establishment of religion … during Queen Elizabeth's happy reign*, 1/1 (1824), 262, 493–4; 1/2 (1824), 200–01 · J. Strype, *The life and acts of Matthew Parker*, new edn, 3 vols. (1821), vol. 1, pp. 318–19; vol. 3, appx, no. xxix · T. F. Kirby, *Winchester scholars: a list of the wardens, fellows, and scholars of … Winchester College* (1888), 124 · Foster, *Alum. Oxon.* · Wood, *Ath. Oxon.*, new edn, 1.658 · J. Buxton and P. Williams, eds., *New College, Oxford, 1379–1979* (1979), 47

Martin. For this title name *see* individual entries under Martin; *see also* Faucit, Helen [Helena Martin, Lady Martin] (1814–1898); Speight, Sadie [Sadie Martin, Lady Martin] (1906–1992).

Martin family (*per. c.*1700–1832), bankers, came to prominence with **Thomas Martin** (*bap.* 1680, *d.* 1765), who was baptized at Evesham, Worcestershire, on 29 April 1680, the second and eldest surviving son of William Martin (1654–1693), coroner and mayor of the borough of Evesham, and his wife, Elizabeth (*d.* 1699), daughter of John Knight of Barrels in the parish of Wootten Wawen, Warwickshire. He had five brothers and four sisters. Together with two of his younger brothers, John [i] Martin [*see below*] and James [i] Martin [*see below*], he was to make a distinctive and important contribution to the development of the Grasshopper, one of the most famous names in English banking.

Establishment of the banking tradition The association of moneylending and the sign of the Grasshopper at 68 Lombard Street in the City of London are generally traced to Sir Thomas Gresham in the mid-sixteenth century. The contribution of the Martins in the eighteenth century was to build upon the continuous tradition of goldsmith activity at the Grasshopper, transforming it into one of the more prestigious and important of the London private banking houses. Thomas Martin left Evesham for London shortly before the end of the seventeenth century. By 1699 he was working as a clerk at the Grasshopper under Richard Smith, a distinguished goldsmith and partner in the firm, with which he was reputed to have a family connection. In this way he became the first of the Martin family to engage in the business of banking. Though he was made a partner in 1703, the entry of the Martins into banking was truly consolidated in 1711 when, on the death of the then senior partner Andrew *Stone (*d.* 1711), Thomas Martin took up the offer to buy Stone's share of the business made in his will. On payment of £9000 he became senior partner, controlling the bank virtually single-handedly until 1714, when he brought James [i] Martin into the partnership. Always the dominant partner, Thomas Martin needed all his skill and ingenuity to steer the bank through the turbulent period of the South Sea Bubble and, though he formally retired in 1726, he remained a strong influence on the bank's affairs. Thomas Martin was a man of great integrity who made significant contributions in a variety of public roles. He married Elizabeth (1691–1744), daughter of Richard Lowe of Cheshunt, Hertfordshire; they had no children. Through his wife's connections he became impropriator of the great tithes of Cheshunt. He was also MP for Wilton, Wiltshire, between 1727 and 1737. He lived in Lombard Street until 1716, when he moved to Clapham, Surrey, residing there until his death on 21 April 1765. He was buried shortly after at St Mary's Church, Cheshunt, in the same ground as his wife and younger brother William Martin (1684–1757). He died a man of immense wealth, having established the name of Martin firmly within metropolitan banking circles. He left land and property in the counties of Hertfordshire, Middlesex, and Essex, in addition to his capital in the banking house. As he died without issue, his nephew Joseph Martin [see below], second son of his brother John [i] Martin, became the chief beneficiary of his vast legacy.

From the mid-1720s the fortunes of the Grasshopper owed much to the skill and dedication of Thomas Martin's youngest brother, **James** [i] **Martin** (*bap.* 1693, *d.* 1744), baptized at Evesham on 22 October 1693. Apprenticed to his brother until becoming his partner in 1714, he became the bank's senior partner on Thomas Martin's retirement in 1726, a position he held until 1743. The bank continued to expand, providing a wide variety of personal banking services to the aristocracy and gentry. Caution was the watchword, though, and with its emphasis on private deposit banking, the style and conduct of the Grasshopper was more akin to the aristocratic West End banks than the more aggressive commercial houses of the City. Until the early 1720s James [i] Martin lived at the Three Crossed Daggers in Lombard Street, which served as the partners' City residence. About 1725 he purchased the estate and manor of Quy, Cambridgeshire, and subsequently became involved with the political life of the county. A conservator of the River Cam and a JP, he represented Cambridge in parliament between 1741 and 1744. His influence and connections secured the accounts of a number of Cambridge colleges for the Grasshopper. James [i] Martin remained a bachelor throughout his life and had no children. He died on 15 December 1744. His significance to the continuity and direction of the Martin family's involvement in the banking business in Lombard Street was to continue after his death. Having purchased the freehold to the Grasshopper some time after 1740, detailed arrangements were laid down in his will to ensure that the premises of the bank, together with his share of the capital stock, could pass to his nephew Joseph Martin, second son of his brother John [i] Martin, the only one of the first generation of Martins in the bank to have children.

John [i] **Martin** (*bap.* 1692, *d.* 1767) was baptized at Evesham on 8 July 1692. He began work at the Grasshopper about 1717, though he left in the early 1720s before securing a partnership in the business. According to the family

archives, in 1720 he married Katherine (1696–1762), daughter and heir of Joseph Jackson of Sneed Park, Gloucestershire. Together they had five sons and nine daughters. In 1723 John [i] Martin took on the lease of the estate at Overbury, Worcestershire, from the Parsons family, providing the first connection with what became the family seat. He rebuilt the main house following a severe fire in 1738. His eldest son, John [ii] Martin (1724–1794), though he did not work at the bank, received a share of the profits and spent a great deal of money improving the estate. In 1761 he married Judith (*d.* 1809), daughter and heir of William Bromley of Ham Court, Worcestershire. John [i] Martin's two other surviving sons, Joseph Martin and James [ii] Martin [*see below*], were to play key roles in deepening the family connection with the Grasshopper. Throughout his absence from Lombard Street, John [i] Martin was kept informed about the progress of the firm by James [i] Martin. On his brother's death in 1744, he returned to the capital to oversee the running of the banking house, becoming senior partner between 1744 and 1759. Despite the pressures of maintaining the Grasshopper in the front rank of London private banking houses, he still found time to become MP for Tewkesbury, in 1741–7 and 1754–61. His first wife died in 1762 and he married Anna Kinlock (*d.* 1765) in the following year. They had no children. He died on 7 March 1767 and was buried at Overbury, Worcestershire, on 25 March. With his death the extraordinary influence of the first generation of Martins in the Grasshopper came to an end. The family's position, controlling one of the City of London's important private banking houses, had been established.

Family fortunes in the later eighteenth century Joseph Martin (*bap.* 1726, *d.* 1776) was baptized on 19 January 1726 at St Martin's Church, Outwich, City of London. He was apprenticed at the Grasshopper in the early 1740s, under the tutelage of his uncle James [i] Martin. In 1746 he was brought into partnership with his father, John [i] Martin, under the conditions of his uncle's will. On his father's retirement in 1759, he became the bank's senior partner, maintaining this role until 1775, a year before his death. One of the most important achievements of his tenure at the bank was ensuring the Grasshopper's full and active participation in the formation of the London clearing house in 1773, which helped to expedite the settling of balances between bankers without the need to transfer cash. The bank also participated in the financing of various turnpike promotions and added a variety of prestigious account holders, including Sir Francis Baring and the dean and chapter of Worcester. On 6 February 1749 Joseph Martin married Eleanor (1730–1812), daughter of Sir John Torriano, British envoy at Florence. Together they had seven sons and six daughters. None of his sons followed him into the bank, though his second daughter, Eleanor (1755–1831), married John Foote, a partner in the Grasshopper. Joseph Martin lived for many years in Downing Street, Westminster, also maintaining a house at Eastwick, Surrey. An MP for both Gatton, Surrey, between 1768 and 1774, and Tewkesbury between 1774 and 1776, he was also elected sheriff of London in 1771. He died in

Downing Street in April 1776 and was buried probably at St Mary's Church, Cheshunt. He died a very wealthy man, leaving land and property in the counties of Hertfordshire, Essex, Middlesex, Surrey, Gloucestershire, Norfolk, and also the Isle of Wight.

For many years Joseph Martin had worked closely in the management of the Grasshopper with his younger brother **James** [ii] **Martin** (1738–1810) who was born on 24 May 1738 at Overbury Court, Worcestershire. Apprenticed in the mid-1750s and becoming a partner in 1760, James [ii] Martin became senior partner on Joseph's retirement in 1775, holding that position until 1807. His signal achievement was to manage the bank through the very difficult conditions associated with the early years of the Napoleonic wars. By eschewing the provision of agency links with country banks, limiting exposure to the risks of financing provincial industry and overseas trade, while concentrating on providing deposit banking for the financially secure, the Grasshopper weathered the storm better than most. He married, on 17 February 1774, Penelope (1740–1830), daughter of John Skipp of Upper Hall, Ledbury, Herefordshire, an estate she was to inherit, along with that of Whateley, in Warwickshire. Together they had three sons and four daughters. From an early age James [ii] Martin suffered from corpulence and laid out the walks in the Great Wood at Overbury in order to exercise, in the hope of relieving his condition. For much of his life in London he lived in Downing Street, next door to Pitt the younger, and the two were personal friends, though opposed in politics. Elected MP for Tewkesbury in 1776, he held the seat through successive parliaments until 1807. He died aged seventy-one on 26 January 1810 and was buried at Overbury, Worcestershire, on 3 February.

Later generations and the end of Martins Bank James [ii] Martin's eldest son, **John** [iii] **Martin** (1774–1832), born on 27 November 1774 at Ledbury, was to become part of the third generation of Martins to serve the banking house in Lombard Street. The chief beneficiary of his father's considerable estate, which included the important title to the banking house in Lombard Street, John [iii] Martin joined his father in partnership in the 1790s after an apprenticeship at the Grasshopper. On his father's retirement in 1807 he became the bank's senior partner, a position he held until 1830. These were trying times for London bankers and John [iii] Martin had the difficult task of negotiating the difficult transition from war to peace after 1815 and the financial instability that ensued, culminating in the widespread financial crisis of 1825–6. By cautious application and avoiding undue speculation, the Grasshopper came through the period relatively unscathed. The traditions laid down from the first generation of Martins in the bank of prudence, discretion, and balanced judgement, proved again of the greatest significance. On 5 March 1803 John [iii] Martin married Frances (1770–1862), daughter of Richard Stone, a partner in the Grasshopper. They had five sons and two daughters. Three of his sons, John [iv] Martin (1805–1880), James [iii] Martin (1807–1878), and Robert

Martin (1808–1897), all became partners in the Grasshopper, ensuring the close connection of the Martin family with its development into the later nineteenth century. John [iii] Martin lived in Lombard Street and Downing Street, before moving out to Camden Place, Chislehurst, in Kent. He maintained the family tradition of representing Tewkesbury in parliament, being elected MP in 1812 and holding the seat through consecutive parliaments until his death. He died on 4 January 1832 at Chislehurst, Kent, at the age of fifty-seven, and was buried at Ledbury on 13 January 1832.

The Grasshopper remained a successful private bank until the Baring crisis of 1890 demonstrated the dangers of unlimited liability. In the following year, the partners decided to seek incorporation and the business became Martin's Bank Ltd in 1891. In 1918 it amalgamated with the Bank of Liverpool, becoming the Bank of Liverpool and Martins Ltd, the title reverting to Martins Bank Ltd in 1928. In 1969 the bank merged with Barclays Bank plc, after more than four hundred years of continuous banking activity on the same site in Lombard Street.

IAIN S. BLACK

Sources priv. coll., Holland-Martin family MSS · private information (2004) · G. Chandler, *Four centuries of banking*, 1 (1964) · J. B. Martin, *The Grasshopper in Lombard Street* (1892) · F. G. Hilton-Price, *A handbook of London bankers*, 2nd edn (1890–91) · D. M. Joslin, 'London private bankers, 1720–1785', *Economic History Review*, 2nd ser., 7 (1954–5), 167–86 · will, PRO, PROB 11/908/191 [Thomas Martin] · will, PRO, PROB 11/736/290 [James [i] Martin] · will, PRO, PROB 11/927/143 [John [i] Martin] · will, PRO, PROB 11/1019/194 [Joseph Martin] · will, PRO, PROB 11/1508/94 [James [ii] Martin] · will, PRO, PROB 11/1796/102 [John [iii] Martin]
Archives priv. coll., Holland-Martin family MSS · Worcs. RO, papers
Likenesses Devis, portrait (John [iii] Martin), Tewkesbury town hall · Hudson, portrait (Joseph Martin), Overbury Court, Worcestershire · Romney, portrait (James [ii] Martin), Overbury Court, Worcestershire · J. R. Smith, portrait (James [ii] Martin), Overbury Court, Worcestershire · portrait (James [i] Martin), Overbury Court, Worcestershire
Wealth at death £300,000—incl. £113,000 left to nephew; Thomas Martin: priv. coll., Holland-Martin family MSS · approx. £35,000—James [ii] Martin: PRO, death duty registers, IR 26/156, fol. 13 · approx. £90,000—John [iii] Martin: PRO, death duty registers, IR 26/1295, fol. 49

Martin of Alnwick. See Alnwick, Martin (*d.* 1336).

Martin of Laon [Martin Scottus, Martinus Hiberniensis] (819–875), scholar, was also known as Martin Scottus and called himself Martinus Hiberniensis in the Laon annals, where he recorded his birth date and where a colleague entered his death date. The same source designated Martin as the *magister Laundunensis* ('master of Laon'). No other personal record of Martin survives and so it must be presumed that he spent his entire career as a master in the cathedral school at Laon. Nothing is known of his early intellectual formation in Ireland or of his arrival on the continent. Unlike most of his compatriots who continued to write Irish pointed minuscule script after they came to the Carolingian kingdoms, Martin mastered Carolingian minuscule, a trait suggestive of training somewhere on the continent.

From the time of Josephus Scottus at the end of the eighth century to that of Israel the Grammarian in the middle of the tenth century, the names of some forty Irish masters are recorded in European sources. As one of these, Martin of Laon's scholarly interests and teaching exemplified the Carolingian reform's emphasis on a programme of studies that exalted the liberal arts as paths to Christian wisdom.

During the third quarter of the ninth century Laon was an important political and ecclesiastical centre in the kingdom of Charles the Bald (r. 840–77). Along with nearby Rheims and Soissons, Laon served as a base for a peripatetic group of Irish masters associated with John Scottus (Eriugena), one of the most important and original scholars of the Carolingian renaissance. Martin incorporated excerpts from John's work into the teaching manuals he composed at Laon and may have known John personally.

Martin was a teacher, not an author. Evidence of his scholarly interests and teaching survives in twenty-one manuscripts that bear his notes and comments. His manuscripts reveal Martin as a collector of books, a compiler of texts, a scribe, and a supervisor of scribes. His collection consists of books primarily in biblical exegesis, the liberal arts, medicine, and Greek. Martin's significance as an early medieval master rests especially on his tutelage in Greek as evidenced by the Greek–Latin glossary and grammar he composed and partially copied (Laon, Bibliothèque Municipale, MS 444). This massive codex, acclaimed as 'the *Thesaurus linguae graecae* of its century' (Bischoff, 2.266), reflects John Scottus's interest in Greek patristic texts and the interest of Charles the Bald's court in Byzantine culture. Excerpts from both the glossary and grammar appear in manuscripts copied at other centres and attest to the influence of Martin's Greek pedagogy. Martin also compiled and partially copied a handbook for the study of the liberal arts and of Virgil (Laon, Bibliothèque Municipale, MS 468), a manuscript that remained in use at Laon for more than sixty years. Martin instructed his students in computus or time reckoning (Contreni, 'John Scottus and Bede', 111–31). His contribution to pedagogy in this highly complex and technical field can be traced in his commentary on Bede's *De temporum ratione*. As a teacher engaged in the instruction of future priests, Martin also emphasized dogmatic and pastoral matters. He annotated Laon's copy of the prescriptions of the Council of Aachen (816) regulating the lives of cathedral canons (Laon, Bibliothèque Municipale, MS 336) and put together a collection of texts which bear on the doctrine and practice of Christian life (Laon, Bibliothèque Municipale, MS 265).

Martin's collection of books passed to the Laon masters, Bernard (847–903) and Adelelm (c.860–930), his successors and probable students. Bishop Dido of Laon (c.882–95) inherited one of Martin's books and might also have studied with the Laon master. JOHN J. CONTRENI

Sources J. J. Contreni, *The cathedral school of Laon from 850 to 930: its manuscripts and masters* (1978) • A. C. Dionisotti, 'Greek grammars and dictionaries in Carolingian Europe', *The sacred nectar of the Greeks: the study of Greek in the west in the early middle ages*, ed. M. W. Herren (1988), 1–56 • 'Annales Laudunensis et sancti Vincentii Mettensis breves', ed. O. Holder-Egger, [*Supplementa tomorum I–XII, pars III*], ed. G. Waitz, MGH Scriptores [folio], 15/2 (Hanover, 1888), 1293–5 [Laon Annals] • B. Bischoff, 'Das griechische Element in der abendländischen Bildung des Mittelalters', *Mittelalterliche Studien*, 2 (1967), 246–75 • J. J. Contreni, 'The Irish contribution to the European classroom', *Carolingian learning, masters, and manuscripts* (1992), 79–90 • *Bedae venerabilis opera. Pars VI: opera didascalica*, ed. C. W. Jones, 2 (1977) • J. J. Contreni, ed., *Codex Laudunensis 468: a ninth-century guide to Virgil, Sedulius, and the liberal arts* (1984) • J. J. Contreni, 'John Scottus, Martin Hiberniensis, the liberal arts, and teaching', *Carolingian learning, masters, and manuscripts* (1992), 1–22 • J. J. Contreni, 'John Scottus and Bede', *History and eschatology in John Scottus Eriugena and his time*, ed. J. McEvoy and M. Dunne (2002), 91–140

Archives Bibliothèque Municipale, Laon, MSS 24, 37, 38, 50, 67, 80, 86, 92, 265, 273, 298, 299, 319, 336, 424, 429, 444, 464, 468 • Bibliothèque Nationale, Paris, MS latin 2024 • Deutsche Staatsbibliothek, Berlin, Phillipps MSS 1830, 1832

Martin of St Felix. *See* Woodcock, John (1603–1646).

Martin, Alexander (1739/40–1807), revolutionary army officer and politician in America, was born at Lebanon, Hunterdon county, New Jersey, the eldest son of Hugh Martin (b. c.1700) and Jane, *née* Hunter (c.1720–1807). Martin's father was originally from co. Tyrone and his mother from co. Antrim. The two families left Ireland in the late 1720s, landed at New Castle, Delaware, and a short time later settled in New Jersey where Hugh and Jane met and were married. Alexander Martin's early years are not well documented, although a brother noted that he did not speak until the age of four. His father farmed, was a justice of the peace and a Presbyterian minister, and conducted an English school. Alexander was sent to Francis Alison's academy in New London, Connecticut, and to Newark College in New Jersey; he was enrolled at the latter during the administration of Aaron Burr, when it was moved to Princeton. Martin graduated in 1756 from Nassau Hall with the baccalaureate degree; three years later he was awarded the customary master's degree, followed in 1793 by the LLD. After leaving Princeton he moved to Cumberland, Virginia, where he was a private tutor as well as a schoolmaster. After a brief trip back to his childhood home, he settled permanently in North Carolina, and in time acquired large tracts of land in Rowan and Guilford counties—particularly along the Dan River, where his first grant was for 436 acres in 1761. For his twenty-seven months of service in the American War of Independence he was granted land warrants for 2314 acres. At his death he owned over 10,000 acres.

About 1760 Martin settled in Salisbury, where he became a merchant. Soon after he was made a justice of the peace, and in 1766 he became king's attorney for Rowan county. When royal governor William Tryon visited Salisbury on 19 May 1767 en route to establish a boundary line with the Cherokee Indians, Martin was spokesman for the inhabitants of the borough and delivered a cordial address of welcome. He also was one of the governor's early supporters during the unrest that led to the 'war of the regulation', a protest of inland counties against local corruption. Though physically mistreated and 'severely whipped' by rioting regulators, Martin negotiated an agreement to refund any excess fees that had been improperly collected by local officers and to adjust other disputes between the two sides. Governor Tryon did not appreciate these efforts and eventually suppressed the regulators by force.

Martin's brother Thomas, also a graduate of Princeton and an Anglican priest who lived in Orange county, Virginia, was tutor at Montpelier to the family of James Madison, the future president of the United States. In passing between North Carolina and New Jersey, Alexander Martin became acquainted with the Madisons, leading to a family friendship that survived for many years (Martin's mother, in fact, lived with the Madison family at Montpelier for several years after her husband's death). In 1773 Martin settled his mother and siblings on his own property along the Dan River at a site that he named Danbury, in the recently created Guilford county. Subsequently, instead of dividing his time among several places of residence, he began a long and eventful political career from that base. Danbury became a place to return to from his frequent and often distant travels.

The residents of the new county must already have been acquainted with Martin, since in 1773-4 he was chosen to represent them in the colonial assembly and was re-elected to serve in the next session. During these terms, which lasted less than two months, he introduced a bill to pardon the regulators and another to require British owners of property in North Carolina to pay their just debts. In the following year he was named judge of the temporary court of oyer and terminer by Governor Josiah Martin, a distant relative, who had succeeded Tryon in 1771. This court, which lasted for only a short time, heard and determined criminal cases early in the revolutionary period.

The rapid move towards a break with Britain led to the calling of a provincial congress to act on behalf of North Carolina when an elected legislature was not possible; Martin served in two congresses in 1775. This body created an armed force in North Carolina and organized it so that it could be easily transferred for service with similar organizations from elsewhere. Martin was commissioned lieutenant-colonel of the second regiment on 1 September 1775. He remained at this rank until 10 April 1776, when he was advanced to colonel. As an officer of the continental line he saw active duty; he was one of three joint commanders who led North Carolina troops into South Carolina in December 1775 to quell an uprising of loyalists. In February at the battle of Moore's Creek Bridge, Martin helped halt loyalists in their march to Wilmington to join an expected British force. He was at Chadd's Ford in the battle of the Brandywine and at the battle of Germantown on 4 October. The defeat here ended Martin's military career. In a heavy morning fog American troops mistook each other for the enemy and exchanged fire, resulting in serious losses. Martin was charged with cowardice but was cleared by a court martial. Nevertheless, he resigned his commission on 22 November 1777 and returned home.

The state faced a bleak future. Its continental forces had been lost with the fall of Charles Town and militiamen

had left as their enlistments expired. The legislature created a board of war to assist the governor, and Martin was the most capable and efficient member in devising a programme to recruit troops and gather supplies; the board also offered encouragement to the generals. When the governor protested about the intrusion on his authority, the board for a time became a council-extraordinary. Martin continued to work, although in a less obvious manner. He was also a member of the state senate, representing Guilford county for eight terms between 1778 and 1788 and serving as speaker during five of them. No provision existed for filling a vacancy in the event of the absence of the governor, so when Governor Thomas Burke was captured by loyalists in September 1781, Martin, as speaker of the legislature, became acting governor for four months. His service to the state during these years of crisis undoubtedly contributed to his choice as governor on 20 April 1782 to succeed Burke and his re-election for two subsequent terms. Having served the permitted three one-year successive terms, he was followed by Richard Caswell for the next three years. Martin then was chosen governor for three more terms, serving from 1789 to 1792. In 1789 the University of North Carolina was chartered, and as governor Martin was chairman of the board of trustees; he continued to serve as a regular trustee for the remainder of his life. Martin's successor as governor was chosen on 11 December 1792, the same day that Martin was elected to the United States senate for service during the years 1793-9. At the end of the century, however, when he sought to return to the senate, he was denied that office. He returned home to Danbury, where his mother still lived and where he resumed the life of a distinguished countryman. Unable entirely to abandon politics, he again served his state in the senate for the terms of 1804 and 1805 in sessions that lasted just over two months.

Throughout much of his adult life Martin aspired to literary recognition. Some of his poetry, including odes on the death of several statesmen, appeared in newspapers in North Carolina and elsewhere. His most substantial piece, published in Philadelphia in 1798, was a new scene for a play by Thomas Morton, *Columbus, or, A World Discovered*. The play was produced a number of times in Philadelphia. A contemporary described him as being about 5 feet 9 or 10 inches in height, 'well formed and fine featured'.

Martin died at Danbury aged sixty-seven on 2 November 1807; his ninety-year-old mother died six days later. He was never married, but with Elizabeth Strong he had a natural son, Alexander Strong Martin, whom he acknowledged. In his will he devised both land and slaves to this son and also land to Elizabeth Strong. Martin county, created in 1774, was named in honour of royal governor Josiah Martin; after the revolutionary war when the names were changed of other counties honouring colonial governors, this name was retained, it was said, to recognize Alexander Martin. Following his death Martin's body was placed in a brick vault on his plantation, but several decades later, during a period of unusually high water on the

Dan River, the vault was flooded. The body floated out and was discovered a considerable distance away, where it was buried. The site is not now known.

WILLIAM S. POWELL

Sources C. D. Rodenbough, 'Alexander Martin', *Dictionary of North Carolina biography*, ed. W. S. Powell, 4 (1991), 222–4 • E. W. Yates, 'The public career of Alexander Martin', MA diss., University of North Carolina, 1943 • F. Nash, *Presentation of a portrait of Governor Alexander Martin to the state of North Carolina* (1909) • M. R. Williams, 'Martin, Alexander', *ANB* • R. M. Douglas, 'Martin, Alexander', *Biographical history of North Carolina*, ed. S. A. Ashe, 3 (1905), 274–80 • J. L. Cheney jun., *North Carolina government, 1585–1975: a narrative and statistical history* (1981) • W. S. Powell, J. K. Huhta, and T. J. Farnham, eds., *The regulators in North Carolina: a documentary history, 1759–1776* (1971) • R. M. Douglas, *The life and character of Governor Alexander Martin* (1908) • H. F. Rankin, *The North Carolina continentals* (1971) • J. McLachian, *Princetonians, 1748–1768* (1976) • R. Walser, 'Alexander Martin, poet', *Early American Literature*, 6 (spring 1971), 55–9 • *Roster of soldiers from North Carolina in the American revolution* (1932) • will of Alexander Martin, state archives, Raleigh, North Carolina
Likenesses oils, *c.*1793–1799, State Capitol, Raleigh, North Carolina

Martin, Alexander (1857–1946), theologian and leader of the United Free Church of Scotland, was born at Panbride, near Carnoustie, Forfarshire, on 25 November 1857, the son of the local Free Church minister, Hugh *Martin (*bap.* 1822, *d.* 1885), and his wife, Elizabeth Jane Robertson. He was educated at George Watson's College, Edinburgh, and at Edinburgh University, where he proved to be a brilliant student, winning numerous prizes and gaining first-class honours in philosophy in 1880. He then went on to study for the ministry of the Free Church of Scotland at New College, Edinburgh, where he earned further distinction. He was licensed by the Free Church Presbytery of Edinburgh in 1883, and the following year he became minister of Morningside Free Church in Edinburgh. In 1887 he married Jane Thorburn (*d.* 1948), daughter of Dr Thomas Addis, his predecessor at Morningside, with whom he had two sons and two daughters. He remained in this charge until he returned to New College as professor of apologetics and practical theology in 1897. Edinburgh University honoured him with the degree of DD in 1898 and that of LLD in 1929. He became principal of New College in 1918 and remained in that office until 1935, although he demitted his chair in 1927.

Martin was a crucial figure in the protracted negotiations which led to the union of the United Free Church of Scotland with the established church in 1929. He served as clerk to his church's union committee from its formation in 1909. His intellectual weight, administrative skill, and goodwill were all necessary to a successful outcome. He also served twice as moderator of his church, in 1920 and 1929. In the latter year he was appointed a royal chaplain and also granted the freedom of the city of Edinburgh.

Perhaps as a consequence of the public demands placed on him Martin's published output was slight, amounting to a volume of sermons, *Winning the Soul* (1897), and his Cunningham lectures which appeared as *The Finality of Jesus for Faith* (1933), in addition to a number of pamphlets. This is no way detracted from the esteem in which he was held, and his wisdom and judgement were drawn on extensively by his church, his colleagues, and his students. The change in his personal views which eventually allowed a youthful advocate of disestablishment to accept a royal chaplaincy neatly reflected the changing relationship between the presbyterian churches in this period. He died in Edinburgh on 14 June 1946.

LIONEL ALEXANDER RITCHIE

Sources *Fasti Scot.*, 9.773 • W. Ewing, ed., *Annals of the Free Church of Scotland, 1843–1900*, 1 (1914), 57 • J. A. Lamb, ed., *The fasti of the United Free Church of Scotland, 1900–1929* (1956), 581 • *WWW* • H. Watt, *New College, Edinburgh: a centenary history* (1946) • A. Muir, *John White* (1958) • *DNB*
Archives U. Edin., New Coll. L., corresp. and papers | NL Scot., corresp. with publishers • NL Wales, letters to E. O. Davies
Likenesses D. Foggie, chalk drawing, 1934, Scot. NPG • H. W. Kerr, oils, New College, Edinburgh • H. W. Kerr, oils, priv. coll.
Wealth at death £4531 17s. 8d.: confirmation, 25 July 1946, *CCI*

Martin [*formerly* Neugroschel], **Andrew** [*pseud.* Notarius] (1906–1985), lawyer, was born on 21 April 1906 in Budapest, Hungary, the only child of Louis Neugroschel (*d. c.*1943), bank manager, and his wife, Rosa Heisler (*d. c.*1933). Educated at the Lutheran College, one of Budapest's leading schools, Martin thereafter enjoyed extended and cosmopolitan university studies, spending time at Vienna, Berlin, and Paris. He received doctorates in law and political sciences from the University of Budapest and in 1940 a PhD from the London School of Economics for a comparative study of the law of trade combinations.

Martin had been admitted to the Hungarian bar in 1931, and, fluent in English, French, Italian, and German as well as his native Hungarian, he developed an international clientele. At the suggestion of a client he read for the English bar and, having acquired a home in Chislehurst, Kent, was called by the Middle Temple, of which he subsequently became a bencher, in 1940. In 1932 he married Anna Szekely (*b.* 1912), and they had one son, Peter, who became a solicitor and an authority on air law.

During the Second World War, Martin worked for the BBC, at first as a monitor but eventually writing and broadcasting, under the pseudonym Notarius, a weekly political commentary in Hungarian for the European service. Martin's easily recognizable deep voice helped make the transmissions popular and widely influential, particularly for Hungary's anti-fascist intelligentsia. After 1945 anonymity could be abandoned, and he continued to broadcast 'Andrew Martin's column' until 1965.

Martin, who formally assumed that name by deed poll in 1946 and became a naturalized British subject, resumed practice from chambers in 2 Middle Temple Lane in that year, but he rarely appeared in court, preferring rather to apply his refined and sensitive intellect to international advisory work and problems arising from the trading with the enemy and exchange control legislation. He developed a substantial, albeit highly specialized, practice and in 1952 became head of chambers in 1 Harcourt Buildings in the Temple.

Unusually for members of the bar at that time, Martin—

endowed with a remarkably retentive memory and great intellectual energy—had strong academic interests. From 1947 until 1954 he taught constitutional law and international relations at Ruskin College, Oxford; and in 1954 accepted an invitation from Southampton University to take up a part-time readership. Promoted to a chair in 1963 (which he held until 1977), he was instrumental in establishing comparative law as an obligatory component in the Southampton undergraduate curriculum.

Martin published a number of books and a stream of articles in learned journals. His talent for sustained detailed and incisive analysis is particularly evidenced by *The Legal Aspects of Disarmament* (1963) in which he forcefully refuted the then conventional view that disarmament was an unfit subject for lawyers. His most influential publication was the chapter 'The machinery of law reform' which, in collaboration with Gerald Gardiner, he contributed to their jointly-edited book, *Law Reform Now* (1963).

The Labour Party's manifesto for the 1964 election included a commitment to establish a permanent law commission responsible, as Martin had suggested, for planning and directing the reform of English law, drawing on wide comparative studies of law reform machinery. Martin personally undertook the first draft of the legislation which became the Law Commissions Act of 1965. But Gardiner, as lord chancellor in the Labour government, encountered a great deal of opposition within Whitehall in translating Martin's ambitious concept into a form congruent with the English machinery of government; and the fact that his practice at the bar had not brought Martin into close contact with many of his professional colleagues no doubt accounted for some hostile comment about the supposed predominance of 'leftish dons' such as Martin among the five founding commissioners.

Political factors may have prevented the Law Commission from carrying out the overall directive and supervisory role which Martin had envisaged; but the commission played and has continued to play, an important part in law reform in Britain, while most Commonwealth countries have set up institutions broadly similar to that for whose conception Martin must have much of the credit. Nevertheless, his initial hopes were to some extent disappointed, and, frustrated by the commission's apparent lack of progress in some areas, he did not seek an extension of his initial five-year term as a commissioner. He had taken silk in 1965 and returned to legal practice (conducting international arbitrations in England, France, and Switzerland until shortly before his death) and to writing and lecturing.

Martin was a man of distinguished appearance and cosmopolitan culture, and his sometimes rather grand manner did not conceal great personal charm. Above all, he was an idealist committed to remedying injustice both by personal intervention and by participation in institutions such as the Society of Labour Lawyers, Amnesty International, and Justice (the British branch of the international commission of jurists).

Martin died of pneumonia at University College Hospital, London, on 27 February 1985. His remains were cremated at Golders Green on 2 March. He was survived by his wife.   S. M. CRETNEY

Sources *The Times* (2 March 1985) · S. M. Cretney, 'The law commission: new dawns and false dawns', *Modern Law Review*, 59 (1996), 631–57 · personal knowledge (2004) · private information (2004) [A. Gerard] · *WWW*, 1981–90
Likenesses L. Meiner-Graf, photographs, priv. coll.
Wealth at death £311,735: probate, 26 April 1985, *CGPLA Eng. & Wales*

Martin, Anthony. *See* Marten, Anthony (c.1542–1597).

Martin, Benjamin (*bap.* 1705, *d.* 1782), lecturer on science and maker of scientific instruments, was baptized at Worplesdon, Surrey, on 1 March 1705, the third son of John Martin (*d.* 1731) of Broadstreet, who farmed near Worplesdon, and his wife, Jane. Nothing is known about his childhood; it is presumed that he spent his youth working on the land, during which period he acquired (apparently through extensive reading) knowledge of a wide range of subjects. In his late twenties he established a school at Chichester, Sussex, where (according to his advertisements) he taught almost everything from writing to astronomy. In this venture he was assisted by his marriage in 1729 to Mary (*d.* 1781), daughter of Joshua Lover, a recently deceased Chichester maltster. It was during Martin's residence at Chichester that he began to write, with the avowed intention of bringing down the price of books, especially for the benefit of those who were trying to educate themselves as he had done.

Martin's first publication *The Philosophical Grammar* (1735), consisted of an epitome of current knowledge in the various branches of natural philosophy presented in a single inexpensive volume. An enlarged second edition (1738) was reprinted six times up to 1778, and was translated into Dutch, French, and Italian. In 1737 he produced a complementary work on non-mathematical subjects, *Bibliotheca technologica*, which considered the literary arts and sciences under twenty-five headings, ranging from theology to heraldry; it was later translated into French and Italian. The *Bibliotheca* was published by subscription, and the 564 names listed show that Martin by this time was becoming well known. Other volumes written at Chichester include *Arithmetic* (1735), *Trigonometry* (1736), *Geometry* (1739), *Logarithms* (1739), and *Optics* (1740). Astronomy was presented in a large copperplate print, *Synopsis scientiae Caelestis* (1739).

Optics became a major field of interest and expertise for Martin. In 1738–9 he devised a portable compound microscope with a micrometer. Later known as drum microscopes, instruments of this pattern were produced commercially into Victorian times. Martin's own Chichester microscopes, however, made mainly of wood and cardboard, were hardly comparable with the products of professional instrument makers in London. In 1742 Martin moved to Reading, Berkshire, where he produced two quarto volumes, *Micrographia nova* (1742) and *A Course of Lectures in Natural and Experimental Philosophy* (1743). By then

Benjamin Martin (*bap.* 1705, *d.* 1782), by unknown engraver, pubd 1785

he was trying to earn a living by giving lectures and demonstrations on Newtonian experimental philosophy similar to those given in London for many years by J. T. Desaguliers FRS.

Hoping to gain support for election to fellowship of the Royal Society, he wrote to Sir Hans Sloane and other members. This distinction, he told them, would be a great help in obtaining audiences for his lectures. His manner of approach was, however, somewhat inept, and he never acquired the coveted FRS after his name.

In August 1743 Martin was lecturing in Bristol, and in 1744 he gave several courses in Bath. Early in 1745 he attempted to find audiences in London: this initial sortie into the metropolis was probably not very successful, and by September he was again lecturing in Bath, which remained his base for the next few years. In 1746 his *Essay on Electricity*, describing experiments 'as I daily shew in my Course of Philosophy', was published there. A little earlier a work on electricity by John Freke FRS had been published in London, which caused Martin some concern. However, having obtained a copy and found that (in his opinion) it was nonsense, Martin said so in the preface to his *Essay*. This naturally upset Freke, who quickly produced a second edition in which he called Martin 'an unmannerly country show-man' and deplored the practice of giving lectures for money. Martin responded at once with a supplement containing a witty and devastating attack on Freke and his theories.

In 1747 Martin produced *Philosophia Britannica* (2 vols.), a greatly expanded version of his *Lectures* (1743). An augmented three-volume edition appeared in 1759 (reprinted twice), and it was translated into German in 1772. A shorter *Plain and Familiar Introduction to the Newtonian Philosophy*, written primarily for people attending his lectures, was published in 1751 by William Owen in London; it reached a fifth edition in 1765.

After 1746 Martin spent about ten years travelling in southern England and the midlands. Although his principal occupation was lecturing on experimental philosophy, he also found time to write *Institutions of Language* (1748) and *Lingua Britannica reformata, or, A New English Dictionary* (1749). The second edition of the latter (1754) incorporated numerous topographical entries—Martin later claimed to have visited most of the principal towns of England.

Martin's most ambitious literary project was *The general magazine of arts and sciences, philosophical, philological, mathematical, and mechanical*. Designed to be published in about 120 sixpenny monthly numbers, beginning in January 1755, it was extensively advertised in London and provincial newspapers. A combination of a part-work encyclopaedia and a topical periodical, each number consisted of a few pages of five separate main works, with associated copperplates, plus a few pages of topical material, such as births and deaths, and prices of stocks. On completion of the project in 1764 the text and plates were bound into thirteen octavo volumes entitled: *The Young Gentleman and Lady's Philosophy*, *The Natural History of England*, *A Comprehensive System of Philology*, *Mathematical Institutions* (all 2 vols.), *Biographia philosophica* (1 vol.), and *Miscellaneous Correspondence* (4 vols.). Only the last had any resemblance to a periodical: the others were complete works in themselves.

In 1756 Martin abandoned travelling and settled in Fleet Street, London, near Crane Court, where the Royal Society then had its premises. Having obtained the freedom of the Goldsmiths' Company, he began to trade as an optician and instrument maker. He was now aged fifty and needed spectacles for reading. Initially for his own use, and then for general sale, he devised 'Visual Glasses', and used them for his shop sign. Unlike conventional spectacles, they had apertures partially blanked off by an annulus of horn, lenses tilted inwards, and glass tinted violet or green. Derided by established opticians, they nevertheless proved popular and were eventually copied by other traders. Martin explained their advantages in *An Essay on Visual Glasses* (1756), the first of at least thirty tracts to be published from his Fleet Street address.

Martin was assisted in his shop at first by both his wife, Mary, and daughter, Maria; the latter, who was born about 1738, became the second wife of Humphrey *Jackson FRS, chemist, in 1763. In 1757 Martin acquired the globe plates and tools of the late John Senex FRS (*d.* 1740). Globe manufacture and sale became an important part of his activities, but he also dealt in all types of scientific instruments, primarily as a retailer and wholesaler. To promote his business he issued priced catalogues of standard products, advertised frequently in the newspapers, and published descriptive tracts on individual instruments. These were novel activities at the time and were viewed with suspicion by established traders, but eventually they became the norm. In the mid-1760s, probably as a result of this aggressive marketing, he obtained substantial orders from Harvard College, Massachusetts, to replace the scientific instruments lost in a fire in 1764.

It was characteristic of Martin that he felt he could improve whatever came under his scrutiny. In 1758 he produced *New Principles of Geography and Navigation*, which contained charts based on the true spheroidal shape of the earth. In 1766 he obtained his only patent, for a new form of bilge-pump; he hoped it would be adopted by the navy, but to his disgust the Admiralty rejected it. In the same year he published *The New Art of Surveying by the Goniometer*, and in 1770 reported a new form of pendulum and escapement in *The Description and Use of a Table Clock*.

During the winters from 1756 Martin gave continuous evening lecture courses in London on experimental philosophy. He was especially active as a lecturer around the time of the expected return of Halley's comet (1758 to 1759) and the transits of Venus (1761 and 1769). However, advancing age began to curtail his lecturing—but not his writing—activities, and from about 1778 he traded as 'Benjamin Martin & Son'. The latter, Joshua Lover Martin, had been formally apprenticed to him in 1758, but apparently lacked his father's business acumen.

In January 1782 Benjamin Martin was declared bankrupt, and on 9 February he died at his home in Fleet Street, possibly as a delayed result of a suicide attempt. He was buried in St Dunstan-in-the-West, Fleet Street, on 14 February. His son made no attempt to continue the business, and is thought to have left England. Martin was one of the best known of the many popularizers of science of his day, remarkable for his successful versatility. As he died a bankrupt, all his effects were sold by auction: the sale catalogue reveals that, as one of the first true retailers in the scientific instruments trade, he held an astonishingly large and varied stock, which raised about £1000.

JOHN R. MILLBURN

Sources J. Nichols, ed., 'Brief memoirs of the late ingenious Mr Benjamin Martin, accompanied with a portrait', *GM*, 1st ser., 55 (1785), 583 · J. R. Millburn, *Benjamin Martin: author, instrument-maker, and 'country showman'* (1976) · J. R. Millburn, *Benjamin Martin: author, instrument maker and 'country showman'*, supplement (1986) · J. R. Millburn, *Retailer of the sciences: Benjamin Martin's scientific instrument catalogues, 1756–1782* (1986) · R. V. Wallis and P. J. Wallis, eds., *Biobibliography of British mathematics and its applications*, 2 (1986) · I. T.-B. van Ostade, 'Benjamin Martin the linguist', *Historiographia Linguistica*, 9 (1982), 121–33 · D. P. Wheatland, *The apparatus of science at Harvard, 1765–1800* (1968) · C. B. Waff, 'Comet Halley's first expected return: English public apprehensions, 1755–58', *Journal for the History of Astronomy*, 17 (1986), 1–37 · J. R. Millburn, 'Benjamin Martin and the Royal Society', *Notes and Records of the Royal Society*, 28 (1973–4), 15–23 · J. R. Millburn, *An annotated bibliography of Benjamin Martin*, 4 vols. (privately printed, Aylesbury, 1998) · 'Auction sales by Mr. Herring', *Morning Post, and Daily Advertiser* (5 March 1782) · 'Auction sales by Mr. Herring', *Morning Post, and Daily Advertiser* (15 March 1782) · 'Auction sales by Mr. Herring', *Morning Post, and Daily Advertiser* (20 March 1782) · parish register (baptism), Worplesdon, 1 March 1705 [1 March 1704 O.S. 12 March 1705 N.S.] · parish register (burial), St Dunstan-in-the-West, 1781 and 14 Feb 1782

Archives BL, Sloane MSS 4056 (1738): 4057 (1741)

Likenesses F. Cattini, engraving, repro. in B. Martin, *Gramatica della scienze filosofiche*, 4th edn (1769) · engraving, repro. in *Encyclopaedia Londinensis* (1816) · engraving, repro. in B. Martin, *Gramatica della scienze filosofiche* (1750) · line engraving, BM, NPG; repro. in Nichols, 'Brief memoirs' [*see illus.*]

Wealth at death bankrupt, but had 'capital more than sufficient to pay all his debts': LondG 8/12 Jan 1782; Nichols, ed. 'Brief memoirs' · five day sale of stock-in-trade (only) raised c.£1000: annotated catalogue of sale, MHS Oxf. · books, copyrights, globes, workshop tools, and personal possessions auctioned separately

Martin, Sir **Charles James** (1866–1955), physiologist and pathologist, was born at Wilmot House, Dalston, London, on 9 January 1866, the twelfth child and youngest son of Josiah Martin, actuary in the British Life Assurance Company, and his second wife, Elizabeth Mary née Lewis (1830/31–1917), whose former married name was Rothery. In his own words 'the family was a Nonconformist middle class one characteristic of the period, with a fading flavour of piety and a small revenue … the boys had to start earning their living at 15 years of age' (Chick, 173). Charles Martin was nominated for Christ's Hospital, then in the City of London, but being a delicate child went instead to a boarding-school at Hastings. When fifteen he became a junior clerk in his father's actuarial department, but against his family's wishes he decided to become a doctor. By home study and evening classes at Birkbeck College and King's College he matriculated and entered St Thomas's Hospital, where he concentrated on physiology. In 1886 he graduated BSc, gaining the gold medal in physiology and a university scholarship which took him to Leipzig to work under Karl Ludwig. After six months he returned to London as demonstrator in biology and physiology and lecturer in comparative anatomy at King's College (1887–91). He continued his medical studies at St Thomas's and qualified MRCS LSA in 1889 and MB (London) in 1890. He married, on 12 March 1891, Edith Harriett (1860–1954), daughter of Alfred Cross, architect, of Hastings; they had one daughter.

In 1891 Martin went to Australia as demonstrator in physiology at the University of Sydney; six years later he moved to Melbourne as lecturer, then in 1901 became professor of physiology, in which year he was elected FRS. While in Australia he studied the toxins and antitoxins of snake venom, developing an ingenious gelatin ultra-filter which enabled him to demonstrate two separate poisons in black snake (*Notechis pseudechis*) venom; one, a neurotoxin, passed through the filter; the other, a blood-clotting enzyme with a larger molecule, did not. Martin investigated also the metabolism and internal heat regulation of the Australian monotremes and marsupials.

Martin was a competent teacher and his vivid method of imparting knowledge made a profound impression on Australian medical education, then in its formative years. His lasting influence was recognized in 1951 by the foundation by the National Health and Medical Research Council of Australia of the Sir Charles James Martin fellowships in medical science to give young graduates experience overseas.

In 1903 Martin returned to England to become director

of the Lister Institute of Preventative Medicine, the first establishment in Britain devoted to medical research. Under his guidance the institute expanded in many directions. Very little of the original work published from the institute bore his name, but little was done without his help and inspiration; he was an unselfish director caring little where the credit went as long as the work was well done. At times he could be impatient and harshly critical, but he was also sympathetic and appreciative of any good work, including that performed by the laboratory assistants and cleaners. His personal investigations were important. The work on bubonic plague in Bombay between 1905 and 1908, by which the Indian rat flea was proved to be responsible for its spread, owed much to the plans laid at the start when Martin spent several months with the team drawn from the institute's staff and the Indian Medical Service.

Work on the internal heat regulation of man and animals, made in experiments largely on himself, was summarized in the Croonian lectures of the Royal College of Physicians delivered in 1930 and in the presidential address to the hygiene section of the Pan Pacific Congress meeting in Sydney in 1923, when the use of white labour in tropical conditions was under discussion. Other of his investigations included the mechanics of the disinfection process, heat coagulation of proteins, virus of rabbit myxomatosis, vitamins and deficiency diseases, and nutritional value of proteins. In all his work he used precise and quantitative methods, a practice unusual at the time in biological studies. In 1912 he was appointed professor of experimental pathology in London.

In 1915 Martin joined the Australian forces with the rank of lieutenant-colonel as pathologist to the 3rd Australian General Hospital on the island of Lemnos. There he improvised an efficient pathological laboratory serving 10,000 hospital beds. He found that the cause of the prevalent enteric fever was not the typhoid bacillus against which the men had been vaccinated, but the related organisms of paratyphoid A and B. Vaccination against those microbes was therefore added to the existing routine vaccination, a measure adopted later by the British Army Medical Service. While in Lemnos, Martin diagnosed as beriberi a disease among the soldiers which had baffled the physicians; he realized that the Australian soldiers' ration of white bread and tinned meat had the same vitamin deficiency as that of polished rice which caused epidemics of beriberi in Asia. He therefore caused experimental work on soldiers' rations to be started immediately at the Lister Institute. In consequence a vitamin soup cube was devised for use by the troops in the Middle East, and a division of nutrition which was active for the next thirty years was created at the institute.

After retirement in 1930 under the age limit, Martin in the next year accepted the invitation of the Australian Council of Scientific and Industrial Research to become director of its division of nutrition at the University of Adelaide where he was made professor of biochemistry and general physiology. Research was centred on protein and mineral requirements of sheep, in view of the deficiencies in certain Australian pastures.

He stayed three years and then settled at Roebuck House, Ferry Lane, Chesterton, Cambridge, but again his retirement was nominal. At the request of the Australian authorities he made an experimental study of the virus of myxomatosis and its method of spread among rabbits. The work was carried out at the Cambridge University department of experimental pathology and on the rabbit-infested island of Skokholm in Pembrokeshire; it was published in 1936. In collaboration with colleagues at the Lister Institute pellagra was produced experimentally at Cambridge in pigs fed largely on maize. The disease followed the pattern of human pellagra as seen among populations having maize as their staple food.

At the outbreak of war in 1939 Martin offered space at his home to the division of nutrition evacuated from the Lister Institute. He contributed much to its research, concerned perforce with wartime food problems. Work on the vitamin and protein value of different portions of the wheat grain enabled the authorities to decide which fractions should be included in the flour to make the most nutritious and economical national loaf.

Martin was a lover of the country and of many open-air activities; as a young man he spent vacations camping and canoeing. He was a good swimmer, fond of playing tennis, and was among the early owner–drivers of a motor car.

Martin's honours included fellowships of King's College, London (1899), the Royal College of Physicians (1913), and the Royal Society (1901), from which he received a royal medal in 1923; and honorary degrees from the universities of Sheffield, Dublin, Edinburgh, Durham, and Cambridge. He was appointed CMG in 1919 for his war service and was twice mentioned in dispatches. He was knighted in 1927. He died at his home in Chesterton on 15 February 1955. HARRIETTE CHICK, *rev.*

Sources *BMJ* (26 Feb 1955), 543–5; (5 March 1955), 608 · *The Lancet* (26 Feb 1955), 462–3, 518 · H. Chick and H. N. Drury, *Nature*, 175 (1955), 577–8 · 'Sir Charles Martin and medical research', *BMJ* (23 Aug 1952), 432–3 · W. J. O'Connor, *British physiologists, 1885–1914* (1991), 452–8 · *The Times* (17 Feb 1955) · H. Chick, *Memoirs FRS*, 2 (1956), 173–208 · b. cert. · d. cert.

Archives Australian Academy of Science, Canberra, corresp. and papers · Medical Research Council, London, corresp. and papers relating to Lister Institute | CAC Cam., corresp. with A. V. Hill · Wellcome L., corresp. with Lister Institute

Likenesses M. Lewis, oils (copy), Lister Institute of Preventive Medicine, Bushey Heath, Hertfordshire · A. J. Murch, drawing (copy), Lister Institute of Preventive Medicine, Bushey Heath, Hertfordshire

Wealth at death £23,398 8s. 6d.: probate, 19 May 1955, *CGPLA Eng. & Wales*

Martin, Claude (1735–1800), army officer in the East India Company and philanthropist, was born in the rue de la Palme, Lyons, France, on 4 January 1735, son of Fleury Martin (1708–1755), vinegar maker, and his wife, Anne Vaginay (1702–1735), butcher's daughter. At his parish school he excelled in mathematics and physics. Although apprenticed in 1749 to a local silk weaver, Martin chose to seek his fortune abroad and signed up for the army of the French

Compagnie des Indes in 1751. He arrived in Pondicherry as a 'common soldier' and rose to become bodyguard to Comte de Lally, commander-in-chief in 1758. But French influence in India was waning, and on 9 May 1760 Martin, in a pragmatic move, deserted to the British East India Company's army. In August 1761, while escorting other French deserters to augment British troops at Calcutta, his ship, the *Fateh-i-Islam* sank off the Coromandel coast. Martin was among the few survivors who eventually reached Calcutta on foot.

Commissioned ensign in 1763, Martin was promoted lieutenant in the following year, after refusing to join a body of soldiers intent on deserting. But his rapid rise received a check when he sided against the commander-in-chief, Lord Clive, during the 'white mutiny' of 1766. Officers, including Martin, who had protested about the reduction in field allowances, faced deportation from India. It was Martin's skills as a surveyor and map maker that saved him, and for the next seven years he worked in north-east India with the company's geographer James Rennell, contributing to the resulting Bengal Atlas. As a soldier, he took part in punitive raids into Bhutan, looting temples of books, pictures, relics, and wooden statues, which formed the basis of his own extraordinary collection of antiquities and curiosities.

Martin had already visited Oudh, the north Indian state which, under its rulers, the nawabs, had loosened itself from the Mughal empire. In 1775 he got himself appointed as superintendent of the nawab's arsenal in the new capital, Lucknow. He was adept at finding influential people who could promote his career, aided by flattery and gifts. In this case he solicited the help of John Bristow, the corrupt resident to the Lucknow court, who in turn went to his patron, Philip Francis, the most powerful man in British India after the governor-general, Warren Hastings. It was probably now that Martin became a freemason, allowing him to move with confidence among fellow masons occupying the highest East India Company positions. Lucknow became his permanent home, and in 1781 he completed his first house, strongly fortified and moated, on the Gumti River. During the summer he lived underground, in basements built into the river bank, moving up as the river rose during the annual monsoon. When it fell, the basements were cleared of silt for the next summer's occupation. In the rooms above, Martin established 'a perfect Musaeum' that reflected the enquiring mind of an eighteenth-century Enlightenment man. He collected natural curiosities, and commissioned paintings of birds and flowers from Indian artists. He possessed works by the Daniells, William Hodges, Johann Zoffany, and Francesco Renaldi, and appears in paintings by the last two. He bought telescopes from the astronomer royal, William Herschel, and steam engines from the Birmingham factory of Matthew Boulton and James Watt, which he used for raising water. His library contained nearly 1000 volumes, showing his scientific, architectural, botanical, and antiquarian interests, with some erotica. He never married but kept several young Indian women, including his favourite mistress, Boulone (c.1766–1844), whom he had bought when she was nine years old.

Never afraid of experimentation, in 1782 Martin successfully operated on himself for bladderstones, using an unorthodox form of lithotriptor, details of which he sent to the Company of Surgeons in London. In 1785 he built and flew the first hot air balloons in India, to the astonishment of the nawab, Asaf ud-Daula. In the arsenal he cast bells and cannon, and made fine pistols. Martin's huge fortune, which made him the richest European in eighteenth-century India, was accumulated in various ways. He owned and rented property, some of which he designed and had built himself. He traded successfully in indigo and cloth, exporting it to Europe in exchange for Spanish dollars. He lent money at 12 per cent (the company rate of interest), the largest loan being £250,000 to the nawab in 1794, which he retrieved with difficulty. He also sold European artefacts to the nawab at highly inflated prices, though his influence at the Lucknow court has been overrated.

Although retired from military duty, he volunteered to accompany Lord Cornwallis as aide-de-camp at Seringapatam, during the Third Anglo-Mysore War of 1792. His last active service was leading the nawab's army, under General Sir Robert Abercromby, against the Rohillas in 1794; he was rewarded with the rank of major-general. In the following year he began building his extraordinary palace-tomb of Constantia, south-east of Lucknow, the largest European funerary monument in India. A baroque folly, it incorporates fantastic statuary, ingenious water-cooled air-conditioning, and locally produced 'Wedgwood' decorations. News of the French Revolution influenced Martin's decision to remain in India, and he lavished money on the building. His permanent memorials are the schools he endowed, at Lucknow, Calcutta, and Lyons, each called La Martinière, and each of which celebrates as founder's day, the anniversary of his death, which occurred on 13 September 1800 at the Town House, Lucknow. His small charitable bequests are still distributed regularly to the poor at Constantia on the outskirts of Lucknow.

ROSIE LLEWELLYN-JONES

Sources R. Llewellyn-Jones, *A very ingenious man: Claude Martin in early colonial India* (1992) · R. Llewellyn-Jones, *A fatal friendship: the nawabs, the British and the city of Lucknow* (1985) · S. C. Hill, *Claude Martin* (1901) · East India Company consultations (Bengal), public; secret and military; secret and political, BL OIOC · R. Llewellyn-Jones, 'Major General Claude Martin: a French connoisseur in eighteenth-century India', *Apollo*, 145 (March 1997), 17–22 · parish register (birth), St Saturnin et St Pierre [Lyons, France] · will, BL OIOC, 1 Jan 1800 · R. Llewellyn-Jones, *A man of the Enlightenment in eighteenth-century India: the letters of Claude Martin, 1766–1800* (2003)
Archives Archives Départementales du Rhône, Lyons, France, MSS · priv. coll.
Likenesses miniature, painting on ivory, c.1760–1763, St John's Church, Calcutta, India · J. Zoffany, group portrait, oils, 1784–6 (*Colonel Mordaunt's cock-fight*), Tate collection · J. Zoffany, group portrait, oils, 1786 (*Colonel Antoine Polier and his friends at Lucknow*), Victoria Memorial Hall, Calcutta, India · F. Renaldi, portrait, c.1795, La Martinière School for Boys, Calcutta, India · G. Plare(?), portrait, watercolour, c.1799, priv. coll.
Wealth at death approx. £500,000 (forty lakhs of rupees): will, BL OIOC

Martin, David (1737–1797), portrait painter and engraver, was born on 1 April 1737 in Anstruther Easter, Fife, the first of the five children of John Martin (1699/1700–1772), the parish schoolmaster of Anstruther Easter, and his second wife, Mary Boyack (1702?–1783). He was a pupil of the portrait painter Allan Ramsay, whom he joined on a tour of Italy in 1756–7. On his return Martin became a student at the academy in St Martin's Lane, London, where he gained premiums for drawings from life in 1759, 1760, and 1761. As the principal draughtsman in Ramsay's studio in the 1760s he helped produce many of the coronation portraits of George III and Queen Charlotte.

Martin was a well-respected engraver and engraved in mezzotint Lady Frances Manners (1772; impression, British Museum) and in line William Murray, earl of Mansfield (impression, Lincoln's Inn Library), both after his own paintings; he also produced some landscape engravings. By 1770 he had his own studio and had painted his first self-portrait (National Gallery of Scotland), depicting himself with a clear fair skin and wavy ginger hair. His aquiline nose and small red lips were characteristics that dominated his later self-portraits. On 20 July 1771 he married Ann Hill (1743–1775); they had three children, all of whom died in infancy. Martin contributed works to the exhibitions of the Incorporated Society of Artists from 1765 to 1777 and was elected to the positions of treasurer, vice-president, and president between 1772 and 1777. He also exhibited portraits at the Free Society of Artists in 1767 and at the Royal Academy in 1779 and 1790.

Martin produced more than 300 portraits, including the famous painting of Benjamin Franklin (1767) which hangs in the White House, Washington. His most influential works depict members of the Scottish Enlightenment, notably the philosopher David Hume (1770, priv. coll.) and the chemist Joseph Black (1787, Scottish National Portrait Gallery). He portrayed his sitters with integrity in an honest natural style, thereby consolidating a recognizably Scottish tradition of portraiture. His female studio style is epitomized in the portrait of the Hon. Barbara Gray (1787, priv. coll.).

In 1780 Martin was admitted to the Royal Company of Archers, so signalling his return to Edinburgh. In a rare full-length portrait he painted the president of the company, Sir James Pringle of Stichill (1791–4, Royal Company of Archers, Edinburgh). In 1785 he was appointed principal painter to the prince of Wales in Scotland. Martin died on 30 December 1797 at his home, 4 St James Square, Edinburgh, and was buried on 3 January 1798 in Leith South churchyard. The contents of his home and studio were sold by auction over twenty-one days in 1799.

LUCY DIXON

Sources L. Dixon, ed., *David Martin, 1737–1797* (1997) [exhibition catalogue, Crawford Arts Centre, St Andrews, 3 Oct – 9 Nov 1997] • L. Dixon, 'David Martin, 1737–1797: a catalogue raisonné of his portraits in oils', MPhil diss., U. St Andr. • A. Smart, *Allan Ramsay: painter, essayist, and man of the Enlightenment* (1992) • D. Irwin and F. Irwin, *Scottish painters at home and abroad, 1700–1900* (1975) • D. Macmillan, *Painting in Scotland: the golden age* (1986) [exhibition catalogue, U. Edin., Talbot Rice Gallery, and Tate Gallery, London, 1986] • D. Macmillan, *Scottish art, 1460–1990* (1990) • J. C. Smith, *British mezzotinto portraits*, 4 vols. in 5 (1878–84) • H. Smailes, *The concise catalogue of the Scottish National Portrait Gallery* (1990) • *Tenth loan exhibition*, Scottish Fine Arts and Prints Club (1937) [exhibition catalogue, Royal Scot. Acad., 1937] • [J. Lloyd Williams], *National Gallery of Scotland: concise catalogue of paintings* (1997) • *The auction catalogue of David Martin's studio and house contents* (1799) [sale catalogue] • Graves, *RA exhibitors* • IGI • d. cert. • directories, Edinburgh and Leith, 1784–98

Archives NA Scot. • NG Scot. • RA • RSA • U. St Andr., muniments

Likenesses D. Martin, self-portrait, oils, *c.*1760, NG Scot. • D. Martin, self-portrait, oils, 1760–69, priv. coll. • D. Martin, self-portrait, oils, 1770–79, Scot. NPG

Wealth at death sale of books, prints, drawings, paintings from studio, and house (4 St James's Square), incl. sale from North Leigh of pleasure boat, raised £1200: *Auction catalogue*

Martin, Sir David Christie (1914–1976), scientific administrator, was born on 7 October 1914 at 44 Kidd Street, Sinclairtown, Kirkcaldy, Fife, the third of three sons (there were no daughters) of David Christie Martin (1885–1943), a local forge worker, and his wife, Helen Linton (1881–1951). He early showed an interest in science, possibly inspired by his great-uncle William Strachan, an engineer. At the suggestion of his teacher at the local primary school he went on to Kirkcaldy high school in 1927, rather than the local school attended by his brothers. He obtained the Scottish leaving certificate in the sciences, mathematics, English, and French, and was also captain of the school. In 1933 he entered Edinburgh University to study chemistry. Upon graduating with first-class honours he considered teaching but ultimately stayed on to take a PhD under J. A. V. Butler. In addition to his studies, Martin also found time to establish a social centre for students, take an active part in a variety of sports, and walk the Scottish countryside.

After obtaining his doctorate in 1939, Martin became assistant secretary to the Royal Society of Arts in London. Almost immediately he was seconded as an administrator to the Ministry of Supply where he met many influential scientists. His broad scientific background and great administrative ability were fully used in projects as diverse as studying the growth of flax and the production of new polymers and smoke screens. On 5 June 1943 he married Jean MacGaradh Wilson (*b.* 1917), whom he had met at Edinburgh University; they had no children.

After the war Martin became general secretary of the Chemical Society. However, in January 1947, Robert Robinson, president of the Royal Society, who had been with Martin at the Ministry of Supply, asked him to become assistant secretary (later called executive secretary) of the Royal Society. Martin's time at the Royal Society was extremely productive and satisfying. When he took up his position there were very few committees in the society; by the time of his death in 1976 the number was over ninety. It was on these committees that his flair for turning ideas into action became apparent. He served seven presidents and more than twenty other members of the council. His greatest achievements were his contribution to the organization of the International Geophysical Year of 1957—the important part played by Martin in establishing the laboratory at Halley Bay in the Antarctic was recognized when an ice rise there was named after him—his collaboration with Sir Cyril Hinshelwood in planning the tercentenary celebrations of the Royal Society in 1960, and the move of the Royal Society from Burlington House to its buildings in Carlton House Terrace, for which Martin had helped to raise £1 million.

Martin supported many activities outside the Royal Society, particularly those associated with making science more accessible to a wider audience; he thus anticipated later work done by the society on the public understanding of science. He made important contributions to the British Association for the Advancement of Science and one of its lectures for young scientists was named after him. He was a member (later chairman) of the BBC science consultative group. In recognition of the part he played in the tercentenary celebrations he was made a CBE in 1960; a knighthood followed in 1970. The Royal Society of Edinburgh made him a fellow in 1956 and he received honorary degrees from the universities of Edinburgh (1968) and Newcastle upon Tyne (1973).

Martin was dark and stockily built. A colleague wrote: 'I never knew him other than courteous, amiable and even under provocation without malice' (private information). It was his even temperament, his keen sense of duty, and his wide circle of friends that formed the basis for his success. He was unpretentious and treated everyone equally. Another colleague wrote: 'He saw himself very much as the servant of the Fellowship with no pretensions to policy making' (private information). After the move of the Royal Society he and his wife lived in a flat in Carlton House Terrace where they showed generous hospitality to many people associated with the society. Anyone who needed advice and reassurance had only to turn to the Martins for a sympathetic ear. He threw himself enthusiastically into the social activities of the society and the very last function he attended was a staff Christmas party. A few hours later, on 16 December 1976, he died of a heart attack at Westminster Hospital, London. He was cremated at Golders Green on 22 December 1976. He was survived by his wife.   D. E. P. HUGHES

Sources D. C. Martin, *Personal records of the FRSE* (1976) · H. Massey and H. W. Thompson, *Memoirs FRS*, 24 (1978), 391–407 · private information (2004) [J. M. Martin, K. Dunhem, I. M. Barclay, D. Chapman, J. W. Menter] · *The record of the Royal Society of London*, Royal Society (1992) · *The Times* (18 Dec 1976) · b. cert. · m. cert. · d. cert. **Archives** RS | Bodl. Oxf., file as Society for Protection of Science and Learning councillor · Bodl. Oxf., corresp. with Kurt Mendelssohn · CAC Cam., corresp. with Sir Edward Bullard · CAC Cam., corresp. with Sir James Chadwick · UCL, corresp. with J. Z. Young **Likenesses** Baron, photograph, 1970, RS **Wealth at death** £47,168: probate, 28 March 1977, *CGPLA Eng. & Wales*

Martin [*née* Eccleston]**, Dorcas, Lady Martin** (1536/7–1599), translator and bookseller, was probably the daughter of John Eccleston, grocer, of Cheapside and Tottenham, who may have moved to London from Lancashire (on her monument, Dorcas is described as the daughter of John Eccleston of Lancaster, gentleman), and his wife, Margery (*d.* 1571). She married, probably after 1552, Sir Richard *Martin (1533/4–1617), master of the mint and twice lord mayor of London, and they had five sons and one daughter. She is depicted with her husband on a silver medal of 1562, which gives her age as twenty-five. White identifies Martin as an active participant in a radical puritan circle. Martin's role in the admonition crisis appears in Archbishop Grindal's letter to Archbishop Parker which refers to her as 'the stationer for all the first impressions' of Thomas Cartwright's unlawfully published *Replie to an Answere* (1573) (Nicholson, 347–8). James Rowbotham dedicated *The Perfect Pathway to Salvation* (1590?) to her. Martin's translation of a French text, *An Instruction for Christians*, appears in the second lamp of Thomas Bentley's *Monument of Matrones* (1582) where Bentley introduces her as a 'godlie matrone and gentlewoman' (p. 221). Her translation includes prayers, psalm verses, and, notably, a catechism in which a mother questions a child.

Martin died on 1 September 1599, and was buried the following night in the south chancel of All Hallows, Tottenham.   ELAINE V. BEILIN

Sources T. Bentley, *The monument of matrones* (1582), 221–52 · M. White, 'A biographical sketch of Dorcas Martin: Elizabethan translator, stationer, and godly matron', *Sixteenth Century Journal*, 30 (1999), 775–92 · W. Nicholson, ed., *The remains of Edmund Grindal*, Parker Society, 9 (1843); repr. [1968] [Parker Society repr. 1968] · P. Collinson, 'The role of women in the English Reformation illustrated by the life and friendships of Anne Locke', *Godly people: essays on English protestantism and puritanism* (1983) · DNB · ESTC **Likenesses** Stephen of Holland, silver medal, 1562, BM; repro. in H. A. Gueter, *A guide to the exhibition of English medals*, 2nd edn (1891)

Martin, Sir Douglas Eric Holland- (1906–1977), naval officer, was born in London on 10 April 1906, the fourth of six sons (there were no daughters) of Robert Martin Holland, banker and later a director and chairman of the Southern Railway, and his wife, Eleanor Mary, daughter of George Edward Bromley-Martin, of Ham Court, Upton-on-Severn. From the early 1920s their home was Overbury Court, Tewkesbury. The family name was changed to Holland-Martin in 1923. He entered the Royal Naval College, Osborne, in 1920 and was promoted midshipman and went to sea in 1924. From then until 1939 he held a series of increasingly responsible junior appointments in which he showed great promise and that he had in abundance all the qualities required of an officer. He was an outstanding all-round games player, playing cricket for the navy between 1928 and 1933.

At the outbreak of war Holland-Martin was executive officer of the *Tartar*, based at Scapa Flow. When his captain was taken ill in October his superiors had sufficient confidence in his ability to appoint him in command, and he commanded her in North Sea operations until January 1940. Later that month he was awarded one of the earliest DSCs of the war. He was promoted to commander in 1940. Subsequently during the war he commanded *Holderness* off the east coast and in the channel, *Nubian* in the Mediterranean, and *Faulknor* in home waters as part of an international flotilla. These arduous commands were interspersed with short spells ashore, when he distinguished himself as a staff officer.

It was in *Nubian* that Holland-Martin enhanced his reputation as a dashing and effective destroyer captain. In December 1942 she joined force K in Malta to interrupt supplies to Rommel and was constantly in action for the next six months. Holland-Martin was appointed to the DSO (1943) for his skilful leadership and enterprise during this period. *Nubian* then participated in the capture of the central Mediterranean islands and the landings on Sicily and at Salerno. The latter landings won him a bar to his DSC. He left *Nubian* in December 1943.

Promoted to captain in 1946, Holland-Martin distinguished himself in a series of important posts—as naval attaché in Argentina, Paraguay, and Uruguay (1947-9); captain D4 in the *Agincourt* (1949-50); director of plans in the Admiralty (1952-3); and in command of the *Eagle* (1954). In 1951 Holland-Martin married Rosamund Mary Hornby OBE (1948), daughter of Charles Henry St John Hornby [see Hornby, (Charles Harold) St John] of Dorchester, Dorset, printer and director of W. H. Smith; they had one son and one daughter. It was a happy marriage and his stable family life contributed to the success of his career.

Promoted to rear-admiral in July 1955 Holland-Martin was flag officer flotillas, Mediterranean, for the next eighteen months, during which he trained and commanded the assault forces in the landings of the Royal Marine commandos at Port Said in November 1956. He commanded a British contribution of over 100 ships to this force, probably the last flag officer to command such a large number of British ships.

In May 1957 he was appointed deputy chief of naval personnel (officers). Five months later he was promoted to be second sea lord with the acting rank of vice-admiral and assumed responsibility for the whole of the Royal Navy's personnel at a time of great change. He was the youngest and most junior second sea lord in the history of this post and his distinguished service was rewarded by promotion to vice-admiral and his appointment as CB in January 1958. In January 1960 he was appointed flag officer air (home) and promoted to KCB. In 1961 he became admiral and took up the appointment of commander-in-chief, Mediterranean, and commander-in-chief, allied forces Mediterranean, a post he held with great distinction at a time of stress when the government was imposing reductions on the British forces there and running down the Malta base. In 1964 he was promoted to GCB. Finally in April 1964 he became commandant of the Imperial Defence College.

In 1962 Holland-Martin was a strong contender to relieve Admiral Sir Caspar John as first sea lord, but his outspoken support for a strategy which emphasized the importance of the Mediterranean at a time when oil was just being discovered in north Africa, and the British bases in Malta, Cyprus, and Gibraltar were being run down led

him to clash with his political and service masters at home. In addition he had a well voiced belief that the United Kingdom could not afford to continue with an independent nuclear deterrent, and he had seen the abandonment of the Blue Streak project as an excellent opportunity for the United Kingdom to bow out of this commitment instead of adopting the Polaris submarine programme. Once the latter had been accepted he was a strong advocate of funding any strategic nuclear deterrent force outside the normal defence budget in order that conventional forces of the service carrying out this function should not suffer, for he foresaw that funding the strategic nuclear submarine force could seriously affect the size of the conventional fleet. His outspoken support for these views probably ensured that he did not become first sea lord in the summer of 1963.

On his retirement in 1966 Holland-Martin's services were in great demand. He was a trustee of the Imperial War Museum and its vice-president and chairman (1967-77). He was chairman of the Severn region of the National Trust (1967-77) and of the governors of Malvern School (1967-76). In 1968 he was appointed chairman of the committee of inquiry into trawler safety after three trawlers had been lost with all hands in gales. His speedy and thorough inquiry gained the confidence of the industry. As a result he joined the White Fish Authority and the Herring Industry Board in 1969. In 1973-6 he was vice-admiral of the United Kingdom and lieutenant of the Admiralty. Holland-Martin died on 6 January 1977 at his home, Bell's Castle, Kemerton, Tewkesbury.   B. C. PEROWNE, *rev.*

Sources *The Times* (10 Jan 1977) · *WWW* · personal knowledge (1986) · S. W. Roskill, *The war at sea, 1939–1945*, 3 vols. in 4 (1954–61) · *CGPLA Eng. & Wales* (1977)
Archives FILM IWM FVA, actuality footage
Wealth at death £107,778: probate, 10 Feb 1977, *CGPLA Eng. & Wales*

Martin, Edward (d. 1662), college head, was born in Cambridgeshire; he was perhaps the son of Thomas Martin, baptized at Grantchester on 19 September 1591. He matriculated as a sizar from Queens' College in Easter term 1605, graduated BA in 1609, and proceeded MA in 1612. Ordained priest at Peterborough on 21 September 1617, the same year he was elected a fellow of Queens', where for some time he was a geometry lecturer. He proceeded BD in 1621. It is not clear when he first came to the attention of William Laud: he voted against the duke of Buckingham's candidacy for the chancellorship in 1626. Nevertheless, by 1628, when Laud was bishop of London, Martin was serving as his chaplain, and he acted as the licenser of a number of books in the period November 1628 to February 1632. These included, in November 1630, the notorious Arminian work *An Historicall Narration* (written by one 'J. A.'—according to William Prynne either an active Roman priest or recent convert from Catholicism, but more likely John Andrewes, author of *The Brazen Serpent*)—an act for which Martin was later criticized, and which was later raised among the charges at Laud's trial.

Elected president of Queens' College in October 1631

(and created DD by royal mandate in the same year), Martin emerged as one of the most extreme and partisan of the Laudian college heads active in the vice-chancellor's court, both demanding the release from prosecution of a series of fellows accused of maintaining crypto-Catholic doctrines (including his chaplain, Peter Hausted), and insisting on the stiffest penalties for those accused of puritanism. The college cook reported Martin as saying that 'he would rather see his son in a whore house' than let him go to the puritan lecturers in Holy Trinity Church (BL, Harley MS 7019). He was sufficiently detached from the anti-Catholicism of the time to be entrusted by Secretary of State Francis Windebank with the delicate task of playing host to the secret visit to Cambridge of the papal agent Gregorio Panzani in July 1635. He escorted Panzani around the university, and, on showing the Italian a picture of a saint 'in abito Pontificale' exclaimed with a sigh, 'when will such splendour be restored to our church!' (PRO, MS 31/9/17B, Panzani to Barberini, 15/25 July 1635). In Queens' College, Martin seems to have done his best to work such a restoration. There was an extraordinarily large sum of money spent on refurbishing and cleaning up the chapel during his first year as president. An often highly critical 1636 report on religious practice at Cambridge, commissioned by Laud, praised the arrangements in the college, while 1638 saw further alterations and renovations in the college chapel, with the altar being raised. A critical parliamentary report of 1641 noted that the chapel at Queens' and the ritual practised there 'have been much changed since Dr. Martin came in to be Master there' (BL, Harley MS 7019). He also played an important role as a proctor in the 1640 convocation. During this period Martin also accumulated local livings at a constant rate: having been made vicar of Oakington in 1626 and rector of Conington in 1630, he served as rector of Uppingham from 1631 to 1637 before proceeding to the rectories of Houghton Conquest, Bedfordshire, and Doddington.

Not surprisingly Martin proved to be a zealous royalist. In 1642 he gave £100 of his own money to the king, and also oversaw the delivery of college plate to a crown agent—actions which resulted in his arrest by Oliver Cromwell's troops and the sequestration of his property. He remained under house arrest in London, implacably opposed to the parliament (stating in a mock petition that he would 'embrace any extremity of torture and death' rather than subscribe the covenant), until his escape in 1648, but was rearrested two years later and reimprisoned. He was released shortly afterwards and spent the rest of the 1650s abroad, generally in Paris with Lord Hatton, although he was resident at Utrecht in 1656. He later described these years as full of 'nothing but Prisons, Ships, wandrings, and solitude' when he was 'very well satisfied with one Meal a day, and at night a Crust of Bread, and a Cup of any Drink' (Twigg, 143). Unlike the experience of some divines Martin's time abroad did nothing to lessen his hostility towards foreign protestants. In a series of letters written from Paris in the years 1659–60 he bitterly attacked John Cosin's conciliatory gestures towards the Huguenots at Charenton. He

particularly condemned the notion that the Church of England accepted the validity of foreign reformed ordination, and complained that by claiming that the Church of England was 'all one and the same church with the Huguenots here', men such as Cosin both enabled Roman Catholics to 'lay at our door all the Presbyterian durt, filth and prophanation', and made other English exiles in detestation of 'that accursed Genevian tyranny' turn to Rome (*Doctor Martin, Late Deane of Ely, his Opinion*, 71–6). He was most determined to crush the suggestion that foreign presbyterians could be distinguished in any way from the rebellious English presbyterians.

Such views made Martin an implacable opponent of compromise at the Restoration, when he returned as president of Queens' and applauded the college's rescue from its 'Babylonian captivity', making 'downright dishonest' claims about the college's financial mismanagement in the intervening years (Twigg, 142 and n. 13), and seizing a bequest for poor scholars to pay for repairs to the college chapel. He participated in both the Savoy conference and convocation, and was nominated dean of Ely in 1662. He never took up the post, however. Installed by proxy on 25 April he died in Cambridge three days later, and was buried in Queens' College chapel.

ANTHONY MILTON

Sources *Doctor Martin, late dean of Ely, his opinion concerning the difference betweene the Church of England and Geneva* (1662) · J. Twigg, *A history of Queens' College, Cambridge, 1448–1986* (1987) · W. G. Searle, *The history of the Queens' College of St Margaret and St Bernard in the University of Cambridge*, 2 vols., Cambridge Antiquarian RS, 9, 13 (1867–71) · CUL, MS Com Court I. 18 · BL, Harley MS 7019 · *Walker rev.*, 84–5 · Panzani to Barberini, 15/25 July 1635, PRO, MS 31/9/17B · Archivio Segreto Vaticano Nunziatura Inghilterra, Vatican City, diary of Gregorio Panzani, tom. 3a, diary, fol. 100 · A. Milton, *Catholic and Reformed: the Roman and protestant churches in English protestant thought, 1600–1640* (1995) · DNB · Venn, *Alum. Cant.* · IGI

Martin, Edward (*c*.1763–1818), mineral surveyor and civil engineer, was born at Matterdale, Cumberland, the youngest of the eight children of Joseph Martin (1712–1790) and his wife, Susanna Rumney (1717–1810). Nothing else is known of Martin's life until 1781, when John Bateman (1749–1816), the chief colliery engineer of Sir James Lowther (1736–1802) at Whitehaven, Cumberland, reported that Martin was then viewer at the nearby Whingill colliery. It seems likely that this was his earliest post; the geologist John Farey (1766–1826) later wrote that Martin 'was brought up and taught his art as a Coal-engineer in the coal district near Whitehaven' (Farey 1813, 172).

By 1787 Martin was in south Wales acting as agent to John Smith (*d*. 1797) at Gwern-llwyn-chwyth, Llansamlet. On 23 January 1788, at Llansamlet, he married Martha (1763–1844), daughter of the Swansea timber merchant Thomas Lott (*c*.1735–1808). In the mid-1790s they settled at Morriston, Glamorgan; they had at least four sons and two daughters. (This may have been his second wife; there is a record of an Edward Martin's marrying at Distington, Cumberland, in 1785.)

Martin was busy as a civil engineer by the mid-1790s. He was elected harbour trustee in 1794 and was much involved with first attempts to develop the port of Swansea. In 1803–4 he reported, with William Bevan, on how the harbour could be improved and river water there impounded for a floating harbour, and between 1805 and 1809 he was involved in improving the lighthouse on Mumbles Head. He was also active as a canal and tramroad engineer and surveyor. In 1790, by which time he was the principal Welsh colliery agent for the sixth duke of Beaufort, he had surveyed for the Swansea Canal—ultimately becoming a shareholder. With the contemporary Welsh 'canal mania' and enthusiasm for other improvements (as at Milford Haven by Charles Greville) Martin was in constant demand. Also in 1803–4, he promoted an extension to the Swansea Canal via the Oystermouth tramroad, 'using Mr [Richard] Trevethick's very ingenious machine' (*The Cambrian*, 10 March 1804).

Martin's most significant work, however, was as mining consultant. In 1797 he opened collieries in the Twrch valley. In 1799 he reported to the first marquess of Bute's agent, John Bird (1761–1840), that 'there would be Coal and Ore enough on Caerphilly Common [alone] to employ an Iron Furnace for one hundred years' (H. M. Thomas, *The Diaries of John Bird of Cardiff*, 1987, 117). In 1801 Martin reported (for Capel Hanbury-Leigh) on improving the Gnoll collieries in the Vale of Neath; in 1803 he reported on the nearby Maesmarchog stone coal (anthracite) colliery. In June 1804 he was consulted on how coal supplies for the revitalized Pontypool ironworks might be improved.

From 1804 Martin was involved as colliery-letting agent throughout south Wales. In June of that year, he took out his only patent—for making pig and cast iron from local ironstone with steam coal. It showed how aware he was of the mineral potential of the region. In 1806 he was involved in sinking a pit at Bryn-coch, the first deep pit in Wales, to about 600 feet depth. By 1809 he was operating his own coalmining partnership, the Penyvilia Vein Company at Llangyfelach, having inherited collieries on his father-in-law's death in 1808.

Martin's mineral surveying work culminated in his 'Description of the mineral bason in the counties of Monmouth, Glamorgan, Brecon, Carmarthen and Pembrokeshire', read to the Royal Society by Charles Greville on 22 May 1806. It described the distribution of the principal varieties of coal and iron strata and their lateral variation, with a sketch map showing their extent. It was widely reprinted, appearing in (for example) *The Cambrian*, on 20 July 1807, and Nicholson's *Journal of Natural Philosophy* for 1807–8. The paper also took Martin to London in April 1806, where he exchanged much geological data with John Farey (1766–1826).

Martin was working in the Llanelli coalfield from July 1806: his report contains the earliest known plan of the Llanelli syncline—he was aware of the nature of faulting in this region, a matter misunderstood by others at that time. In 1807 he took into partnership his future son-in-law, David Davies (1786–1819) of Morriston. Together they surveyed for the Pen-clawdd Canal in 1810–11 and were busy with the Kidwelly and Llanelli Canal in 1811–12. In

1811 Martin, with William Smith (1769–1839), reported on the state of the collieries at and near Nailsea for the Bristol and Taunton Canal, a work reprinted in the *Philosophical Magazine*, as by 'two eminent mineral surveyors' (38, 1811, 321).

On Martin's death on 6 May 1818 at Ynystawe, whence he had moved from Morriston, the local newspaper called him 'a man of sterling integrity and worth, eminent for his extensive knowledge of collieries' (*Cambrian*, 16 May 1818). Charles Wilkins later confirmed that Martin's 'extensive local and general mining knowledge made him indispensable in the early days of the Neath and Swansea collieries' (Wilkins, 240). Martin was buried at St John's Church, Swansea, on 16 May 1818.   H. S. TORRENS

Sources G. F. Gabb, 'Edward Martin', *Newsletter of the South West Wales Industrial Archaeology Society*, 22 (1979), 2–3 · C. Wilkins, *The south Wales coal trade and its allied industries* (1888) · S. R. Hughes, *The Brecon forest tramroads* (1990) · E. C. R. Hadfield, *The canals of south Wales and the border* (1967) · M. V. Symons, *Coal mining in the Llanelli area* (1979) · J. Davies, *Cardiff and the marquesses of Bute* (1981) · J. Bateman, 'Answers to William Walker's observations', Feb 1781, Cumbria AS, Carlisle, D/Lons/W · C. Wilkins, *The history of the iron, steel, tinplate, and other trades of Wales* (1903) · E. Martin, 'Description of the mineral bason', *PTRS*, 96 (1806), 342–7 · W. Smith and E. Martin, 'Reports on the state of the collieries at Nailsea', *Philosophical Magazine*, 38 (1811), 321–8 · W. H. Morris and G. R. Jones, 'Canals of the Gwendraeth valley, pt 2', *Carmarthenshire Antiquary*, 8 (1972), 29–44 · J. Childs, 'Landownership changes in a Glamorgan parish, 1750–1850', *Morgannwg*, 38 (1994), 42–87 · *The Cambrian* (16 May 1818) · A. W. Skempton and others, eds., *A biographical dictionary of civil engineers in Great Britain and Ireland*, 1 (2002) · parish register (burial), Swansea, St John, 16 May 1818 · parish register, Matterdale, Cumberland
Archives Glamorgan RO, Cardiff, plans and sections | NMG Wales, De la Beche MSS
Wealth at death see will, 1818, PRO PROB 11/1608

Martin, Elias (1739–1818), painter and engraver, was born in Stockholm, Sweden, and baptized there at St Gertrud Church on 8 March 1739, which was probably also the date of his birth. His parents were master joiner Olof Martin and Ulrica Haupt. He was the eldest of four brothers, one of whom was the engraver Johan Fredric Martin [*see below*]. Elias Martin was educated in his father's joinery workshop and after that by Friedrich Schultz, a master of the Stockholm painters' guild. Between 1763 and 1765 Martin was at Sveaborg Castle in Finland, where he designed ornate figureheads for warships and taught military and topographical drawing. Carl August Ehrensvärd was among his pupils and Martin was taught the techniques of engraving by Ehrensvärd's father, commandant Augustin Ehrensvärd. In 1766 Martin went to Paris where, with the help of Alexander Roslin, he began to study under Joseph Vernet at the Académie Royale de Peinture et de Sculpture. In 1768 he went to London and the following year became a student at the Royal Academy of Arts of which in 1771 he became an associate. On 31 July 1770 he married Augusta Lee (c.1753–1810) in London.

The work of English landscape painters began to influence Martin's work. Painting to order, he worked, from 1771, in watercolours, probably under the influence of Paul Sandby although in terms of style he was nearer to

J. R. Cozens and Richard Wilson. About 1772 or 1773 Martin altered his technique; rather than making outline drawings in wash which were then coloured he began to use direct juxtapositions of pigments in order to heighten the power of the colours in his paintings. The high skies and unbroken horizons of his landscape paintings are reminiscent of Canaletto's compositions. Martin was particularly interested in representing the meeting of town and country, for example in *Stockholm from Mosebacke* (*c*.1795; City Hall, Stockholm). An important watercolour of the iron bridge at Coalbrookdale under construction in 1779 shows nature juxtaposed with heavy industry and, when rediscovered in 1997, threw important light on the construction of this pioneering industrial structure (Masreilez Rooms, Stockholm).

Martin drew warm and sympathetic sketches of everyday life, and his portraits and caricatures are often very expressively rendered. However his figures, which were enlivened by his calligraphic style, were also exaggerated in their proportions, as for example in *The Two Murderers in Macbeth* (1770s; National Museum, Stockholm), and led Horace Walpole to criticize Martin's technical ability in 1779. As an engraver he worked for, among others, the print publisher John Boydell.

Martin returned to Sweden in 1780 and the following year he became a member of Konstakademien, the Swedish Royal Academy of Arts, and in 1785 professor of landscape painting there. He lived with his family at Regeringsgatan 74. Gustav III commissioned many paintings from him, for example *Gustav III's Visit to the Academy of Arts* (1782; Drottningholm Palace, Bromma).

In 1780 he planned a series of prints for wide circulation, Sweden's first *voyage pittoresque* with Swedish views presented as coloured line etchings. They were etched by his brother Johan Fredric Martin, with whom he also collaborated on the publication of a number of other paintings and drawings.

Between 1788 and 1791 Martin was again in England, resident mainly in London and Bath, but little is known of his activities during this period. Back in Sweden in the 1790s his Romantic landscapes became 'increasingly pantheistic with a sublime treatment of light and dark' (Mawer, 485), but he also did a series of paintings of folklife. Another important theme during this period was the dramatic depiction of industrial processes in furnaces and foundries. His last-known works date from 1808. In the last ten years of his life his reputation diminished considerably and he fell into ever greater obscurity. A household inventory taken after the death of his wife shows their house still to have been comfortably furnished in 1810, but Martin was later reduced to poverty, his circumstances made worse by blindness.

Martin took part in the Royal Academy's exhibitions of 1769–74, 1777, 1779–80, and 1790 and also in exhibitions arranged by the Society of Artists and the Free Society. Works by him were exhibited in the Swedish Academy of Arts exhibitions in Stockholm in 1794, 1799–1800, 1804, 1806, 1809, and 1822. From 1804 to 1809 he had permanent exhibitions in his home on Kungsbacken. Martin died at his home, Kungsbacken 19, Stockholm, on 25 January 1818.

Martin brought to Sweden the English Romantic discovery of nature and in so doing broke the French stylistic hegemony over Swedish art; it was an approach that led his paintings to be described in Swedish as landscape portraits. His work has aroused conflicting assessments, but after being almost completely forgotten for a century his work became ever more highly prized in the twentieth century. The largest collections of Martin's works are to be found in Stockholm in the National Museum and the Royal Library, in Uppsala University Library, and in the Art Museum in Gothenberg.

Johan Fredric Martin (1755–1816), copperplate-engraver and etcher, and brother of Elias Martin, was born in Stockholm and baptized there on 8 June 1755, which was probably also the date of his birth. From 1770 to 1780 Johan Fredric lived with his brother Elias in London, where he studied engraving with, among others, Francesco Bartolozzi and William Woollett. After returning to Sweden he worked on the portrait series *Swedish Gallery* (1782–3) and the etchings of his brother's landscape sketches *Swedish Views* (1805–12). His work consisted of about 300 prints, often in 'the manner of red chalk' (exhibition catalogue of the Society of Artists, 1774; Frölich, 69).

From 1785 Johan Fredric was economically and artistically independent of his brother. In 1792 he married Christina Charlotta Westerberg (*b. c*.1774). In 1815 he was appointed professor in graphic arts in the Konstakademien in Stockholm. He died on 28 September 1816 at Regeringsgatan 74, Stockholm, having taken over the house from his brother in or after 1788; he was survived by his wife.

TORSTEN WEIMARCK

Sources R. Hoppe, *Målaren Elias Martin* (1933) · H. Frölich, *Bröderna Elias och Johan Fredric Martins gravyrer* (1939) · G. Berefelt, *Svensk landskapskonst* (1965) · N. Lindhagen, *Elias Martin*, Svenska mästartecknare (1955) [Årsbok för Svenska statens konstsamlingar] · U. Cederlöf, *Svenska teckningar 1700-talet* (1982) [with Eng. summary] · P. Grate, 'Bildkonsten', in G. Alm and others, *Frihetstidens konst* (Lund, Sweden, 1997), 169–263 · P. Grate, 'Bildkonsten', in G. Alm and others, *Den gustavianska konsten* (Lund, 1998), vol. 8 of Signums svenska konsthistoria (1994–), 195–296 · J. Mawer, 'Martin, Elias', *The dictionary of art*, ed. J. Turner (1996) · IGI · M. Ahnlund, 'Two new landscapes by Elias Martin in the Nationalmuseum', *Art Bulletin of the Nationalmuseum, Stockholm*, 5 (1998), 14–15 · private information (2004) [Mikael Ahnlund]
Likenesses E. Martin, portrait, repro. in Frölich, *Bröderna Elias och Johan Fredric Martins gravyrer* · E. Martin, portrait, repro. in Hoppe, *Målaren Elias Martin*
Wealth at death 568/09 Riksdaler Banco: estate inventory, 1818

Martin, Ellis (1881–1977), artist, was born on 12 November 1881 at 11 Bayswater Terrace, Plymouth, Devon, the first of the two children of William Nicholas Martin (1849–1935), a builder and architect, and his wife, Mary Coltman, about whom nothing further is known. After primary school education in Plymouth he was educated at King's College, Wimbledon, and studied at the Slade School of Art, London. He married Mabel Verstage (*d.* 1962) of Godalming, Surrey, about 1910 and they had one child, a daughter,

Gentian, who died of tuberculosis at Midhurst Sanatorium in 1940, aged about thirty.

From about 1906 Martin worked for W. H. Smith & Son as an artist contracted to provide advertisement designs. He worked not only for the firm of Smiths, but also for several important department stores such as Selfridges and Whiteleys in London, and for such institutions as the Royal Automobile Club. He exhibited at the Royal Academy at least once, in 1916.

During the First World War Martin served with the Royal Engineers in France and was a field artist with the tank corps, producing diagrams and maps to help heavy artillery through difficult terrain. On his return he joined the Ordnance Survey in Southampton on 9 May 1919 in the wake of a government directive (*The Olivier Report*, 1914) that the Ordnance Survey should adopt a more commercial approach to the promotion and sale of its maps to the public. Prior to the war the Ordnance Survey's brief had been to produce maps almost exclusively for the use of the armed forces.

Martin's impact on the sale of Ordnance Survey maps was immediate and the remarkable change in the public perception of the Ordnance Survey was attributed directly to him (*Ordnance Survey Progress Report*, 1921). In the twenty years of his Ordnance Survey employment, Martin produced a large body of distinctive map cover designs and related advertising material which helped to establish the popular reputation and essential 'Britishness' of the Ordnance Survey map. His designs inspired every other map publisher in Britain to use artistically drawn covers for their publications, not one of which ever matched Martin's skilful work. At least one of his designs, that of a cyclist resting on a hillside, for the one-inch map series of 1919 (later redrawn to represent a hiker for the 1933 series), became an icon of the early days of the British tourist industry. They and others captured the mood of both the healthy outdoor type with rucksack and boots, and the motorist, newly awakened to the pleasures of sightseeing in his open-top tourer. The best say much about the nature of Britishness, and perhaps especially Englishness, in the inter-war years, with the landscape an integral part of that identity and the map both the means of access to it and its emblem.

Other famous cover designs included a handsome landscape of the Cairngorms (1922) which featured Douglas fir-trees drawn 'from better examples found on Southampton Common' (note from Martin, in Browne, *Map Cover Art*, 85). His finely detailed mosaic drawing for the *Map of Roman Britain* (1924) was still in use sixty-six years later when the fourth edition of the map was published in 1990.

Martin was an accomplished draughtsman and painter. His art was technical and representational, but he had an ability to instil his best work with an almost tangible sense of time and place. The work for which the Ordnance Survey employed him between the two world wars was tailor-made for his skills, and his reputation rests solidly on the corpus of atmospheric designs he produced in that period.

Martin's post was dissolved on 2 November 1940, as the Ordnance Survey resumed its military *alter ego*, abandoning maps for the general public in favour of maps for the services. He retired in 1940 to Sussex, where he died at the Homelands Nursing Home, Cowfold, Horsham, on 30 September 1977 at the age of ninety-five. When hostilities ceased in 1945 the Ordnance Survey resumed its programme of popular tourist-orientated maps, complete with pictorial covers, but map cover art never again achieved the distinction it had under Martin, and artist-drawn cover designs were finally abandoned and replaced by photographic covers. JOHN PADDY BROWNE

Sources R. P. Gossop, 'Ellis Martin', *The Newsbasket* (Aug 1912), 174–5 [house journal of W. H. Smith & Son] · J. P. Browne, 'Ellis Martin and the rise of map cover art', *Map Collector*, 35 (1986), 10–14 · J. P. Browne, *Map cover art* (1991) · b. cert. · d. cert. · D. Matless, *Landscape and Englishness* (1998)
Archives Ordnance Survey, Southampton, MSS
Likenesses photographs, priv. coll. · photographs, repro. in Browne, *Map cover art*, 66, 102
Wealth at death £18,289: probate, 8 Feb 1978, *CGPLA Eng. & Wales*

Martin [*née* Bullock], **Emma** (1811/12–1851), socialist and freethinker, was born in Bristol, the fourth child of William Bullock, a cooper, and his wife, Hannah Jones, whose family owned a tea-dealing business in the city. Emma's father died in her infancy, and a year later her mother married her second husband, John Gwyn, and the family moved into the middle-class area of Clifton.

In later years Emma wrote of the strong Christian faith of her youth 'to which a naturally sedate … and a melancholy turn of mind greatly inclined me' (Martin, *A Few Reasons*, 4). This resulted in her decision, at the age of seventeen, to join the Particular Baptists—a sternly Calvinist wing of the Baptist church then undergoing a revival. She remained in the church as a '*zealous* disciple of Jesus' (Martin, *God's Gifts*, 14) for twelve years, busy distributing evangelical tracts and collecting for the Bible Society. In 1830, at the age of eighteen, she also became the proprietor of a short-lived ladies' seminary and later a ladies' boarding-school which survived for several years; in 1835 she became the editor of the unsuccessful *Bristol Literary Magazine*. She married Isaac Luther Martin, also a Baptist, in 1831; they had three daughters. He was, however, 'a husband … whose company it was a humiliation to endure' (Holyoake, 4), and in the years after their marriage, despite all her religious and educational activities, Emma Martin became miserable and restless. She began delivering lectures on women's social status. In 1839 she attended her first Owenite socialist meeting and—astounded to hear 'so close a transcript of many of the thoughts that had passed in my mind' (Martin, *A Few Reasons*, 7)—prepared to embrace the socialist cause, only to discover that the socialists denied the divine origins of the Bible. Infuriated by this, she challenged the socialists to public debates on the validity of Christianity. Several accepted, only to find themselves in verbal combat with a very capable opponent. 'She is a lady of considerable talent', one such opponent wrote to the Owenite central board in May 1839, adding a plea that 'some able advocate of the Rational System' be sent to tackle her (*Proceedings of the Fourth Congress*, 28).

By this time, however, Emma Martin's religious beliefs were also beginning to crumble. Faced with the arguments of the freethinking Owenites—whose ideas on women's rights so strongly echoed her own—and made wretched by her personal circumstances, she felt the ground of Christian conviction begin to give way beneath her. Finally the crisis came. In the winter of 1839 Isaac Martin moved his family to London and Emma, seeing her opportunity, bolted, leaving behind not only her husband but also her church, her respectability, and the God in whom she no longer believed. She took the leap of faith and joined the socialists as a declared freethinker. Within a year she was one of the movement's best-known women adherents, lecturing, writing, and debating anti-socialists, particularly clerical ones, all over Britain. From having been a vigorous campaigner in Christ's cause, she became one of the church's most vociferous opponents, notorious for her knockabout style of free-thought polemic and for her hostility to conventional Christian views on women and marriage. It was as a patriarchal institution that the church particularly attracted her opprobrium, and it was the Owenites' commitment to non-patriarchal social institutions which won her strongest support. In 1841 the Owenite annual congress was addressed by one leading member, a man, who reminded those present that Owenism 'claimed for woman full, free and equal enjoyment of all those privileges which belonged to her as a human being' (*New Moral World*). He was followed in the speakers' list by Emma Martin, who rose to say that 'she had grown up from infancy with high thoughts and strong hopes of an improvement in the condition of her sex', but that:

> all institutions for mental improvement were confined to males, and that even the morals of the female sex were of a different stamp to those of the male. She saw no remedy for this till she saw the remedy of Socialism. When all should labour for each, and each be expected to labour for the whole, then would woman be placed in a position in which she would not sell her liberties.   (ibid.)

In the years that followed, Emma Martin's struggle to win others to this creed became inseparably bound up with her personal fight for an independent life. Any property which she would have had at the time of leaving her marriage was lost, and raising her children on the small salary paid by the Owenite central board must have been very difficult. When she went on lecture tours she usually left her daughters with friends, but this too must have had an emotional and financial cost. She did take one of her daughters with her on one occasion, but they encountered an anti-Owenite mob who began stoning them, and were forced to flee.

Emma Martin's years in Owenism coincided with the peak of the movement's ideological war against what they regarded as ignorance and error. Between 1839 and 1845 Owenites all over Britain confronted their opponents in person and in print, hammering out their message of utopian-communist ideals in the teeth of increasingly hysterical responses from political and religious conservatives. Newspaper reports of Emma's lectures described audiences of up to 3000, strongly divided in their views and expressing their opinions in raucous and sometimes violent forms. Emma's strident atheism was particularly provocative—so much so that even some of her fellow socialists objected. In 1842, angered by this lack of support from the movement, she and her fellow atheist George Jacob Holyoake set up the Anti-Persecution Union to defend freethinkers charged with blasphemy. Emma herself ended up in court on several occasions, and was forced to hide from the police on others; but unlike many militant atheists, she avoided imprisonment.

During these years Emma Martin was also one of Owenism's more prolific pamphleteers, producing tracts with titles such as *The Bible No Revelation* (1845?), *Religion Superseded* (1844?), and *Baptism a Pagan Rite* (1844)—all calculated to inflame clerical opinion. Unlike most other women Owenites she did not write pamphlets specifically on women's issues, but her style of feminist argument can be gauged from newspaper reports in the Owenite press and elsewhere. Like other campaigners for women's rights, Emma assigned great importance to the role of education in women's advancement, but in common with other socialists she also believed that only a propertyless, communal society would provide the conditions for genuine sexual equality. Appropriately for such a fierce free-thinker, she frequently took issue with scriptural representations of women (the story of the fall was a favourite target). Her language in these lectures was usually quite measured, but under provocation could become much less so. In 1844 a particularly savage confrontation between Emma Martin and the police in Manchester was reported in the Manchester press accompanied by descriptions of her as 'a humiliating spectacle of human form … and of woman's character' (Martin, *The Missionary Jubilee Panic*, 16). Emma's response was explosive:

> and what is woman's most glorious character? Is it not to kiss the hand that strikes her, to honour and obey her lord and master, and be the tame servant of the priest? To have no will of her own. To be the football of society thankful for its kicking. You know it is! Is it not dreadful when one of the sex begins to think for herself? Why others will follow the horrible example! and where will it end? … Common sense will usurp the place of spiritualism, and liberty and love will replace priestcraft. I fear I shall live to see that dreadful day! (ibid., 16–17)

By the time this episode occurred, however, Emma Martin was tiring of the battle. Before leaving on a Scottish tour in 1845 she had begun living with Joshua Hopkins (*d.* 1852), an engineer. Returning from the tour, ill and exhausted, she found that the Owenite leadership—itself weakened and divided by internal feuding—were accusing her of alienating support through her extremism. Emma Martin had had enough. She left the movement to begin training as a midwife. In 1847, the year in which her fourth daughter was born, she graduated in midwifery and, having been refused hospital positions because of her atheism, began practising privately from her home at

100 Long Acre, Covent Garden, London, where her daughters also ran a surgical bandage shop. She lectured to women in gynaecology, gave courses in midwifery, and probably offered contraceptive advice. Life was financially hard, but quiet, and her common-law union with Hopkins (who called himself Martin) seems to have been a happy one.

Emma Martin died of tuberculosis at Holly Vill, Finchley Common, Whetstone, Middlesex, on 8 October 1851. 'We have lost the most important woman … on our side', her friend Holyoake wrote (Holyoake, 2), and called for subscriptions for her gravestone for which hundreds gave, including many women who offered remembrance of 'that advocacy of women's social elevation which Mrs Martin so ably rendered' (*The Reasoner*, 12, 1852, 4). She was buried in Highgate cemetery. 'Ah!', Holyoake wrote after the quiet secular ceremony at the grave, 'what do we not owe to a woman who, like Emma Martin, takes the heroic side and teaches us … the truth of a gentler faith?' (Holyoake, 7).

BARBARA TAYLOR

Sources G. Cowie and E. Royle, 'Martin, Emma', *DLB*, vol. 6 · B. Taylor, *Eve and the new Jerusalem: socialism and feminism in the nineteenth century* (1983) · E. Royle, *Victorian infidels: the origins of the British secularist movement, 1791–1866* (1974) · E. Martin, *A few reasons for renouncing Christianity* (1850?) · E. Martin, *Religion superseded* (1844?) · E. Martin, *God's gifts and men's duties* (1843) · E. Martin, *The missionary jubilee panic* (1844) · G. J. Holyoake, *The last days of Mrs Emma Martin* (1851) · *Proceedings of the Fourth Congress of the Universal Community Society of Rational Religionists* (1839), 28 · *New Moral World* (12 June 1841) · d. cert.

Likenesses engraving, repro. in Taylor, *Eve and the new Jerusalem*, frontispiece

Martin, (Mary Anne) Frances (1829–1922), educationist and author, was born in Richmond, Surrey, where she was baptized on 4 November 1829, the daughter of Edward Curtiss Martin (*d.* 1853) and his wife, Matilda Caroline. She had an elder brother and sister. In 1849 she became one of the earliest students at Queen's College, Harley Street, London, founded by the broad-church Anglican clergyman F. D. Maurice, of whom she became a devoted follower, to improve the education of governesses. When in 1853 the council of the ladies' college at Bedford Square, London, decided to set up a school to prepare girls for the college, Frances Martin was appointed governess (or lady superintendent), assisted by her lifelong friend Jane Benson. She was a successful teacher, stimulating her pupils to produce a volume of their own poems, *Springtime among the Poets*, published in 1866. There was increasing friction, however, with the college council, who felt that the school was becoming too independent of its control, and was not carrying out the original intention of qualifying pupils to pursue higher studies at the college.

Frances Martin was among the women educationists who appeared as witnesses before the schools inquiry commission. In her evidence (21 March 1866) she affirmed her belief that women should have the opportunity to be educated to the same level as men, and particularly emphasized the importance to society of ensuring that women received moral and religious training. A member of the Church of England, she preferred the sort of denominational instruction given at Queen's College. She identified herself with those schoolmistresses who doubted whether the education of women should be conducted in the same way, or in the same subjects, as for men. She opposed the contemporary movement led by Emily Davies to admit girls to external examinations and women to university degrees, believing that this would be ultimately damaging to their best interests. Her views were not shared by the Bedford College council, especially following the death in 1866 of her friend Elisabeth Jesser Reid, the college's founder. She bitterly resented their decision in March 1868 to close the school and to concentrate on higher education, believing that 'the advocates of women's rights and women's education' were too preoccupied with the concerns of a small group of educated women: 'I should like to put a gigantic extinguisher over the existing so called colleges for ladies and all the ladies above forty interested in them' (F. Martin to A. Macmillan, 11 May 1868, BL, Add. MS 54974, fol. 39).

Remaining unmarried, and of independent financial means, Frances Martin was active in London philanthropic and publishing circles. She supported Elizabeth Gilbert's efforts to provide employment for blind people (see her 'Blind Workers and Blind Helpers', published in the *Cornhill Magazine*, May 1864) and was later Gilbert's biographer (1887; 2nd edn, 1891). In 1867 her friend the publisher Alexander Macmillan put her in editorial charge of a series of religious biographies, The Sunday Library for Household Reading, of which the first volume, F. W. Farrar's *Seekers after God*, appeared in 1868. Other contributors included Margaret Oliphant, Charlotte Yonge, R. W. Church, Thomas Hughes, and Charles Kingsley. Her own well-regarded *Angélique Arnaud, Abbess of Port Royal* (1873), based on French sources (she spent lengthy periods in France), remained until the early twentieth century the standard work in English on its subject.

From 1864 Frances Martin was involved in the Working Women's College, founded in Bloomsbury by Elizabeth Malleson as a counterpart to the Working Men's College to provide evening classes for women who had to earn their own living. When, in 1874, the college council decided to admit men she was among a minority, who included George and Amelia Tansley, Llewellyn Davies, and Sir John Lubbock, who held out for a single-sex institution, and established the College for Working Women. She was the first honorary secretary and Macmillan, who in 1879 helped to secure permanent premises at 7 Fitzroy Street, was treasurer. By 1882 there were some 200 students, mainly shopworkers, domestic servants, and women working in the tailoring trades. For a termly fee of a shilling they were offered evening classes in basic literacy and numeracy as well as vocational subjects, such as bookkeeping (she wrote to *The Times* on women as bookkeepers, 25 September 1883), and academic studies, including French and Latin. A cookery school was later added, as vocational classes leading to qualifications awarded by the Society of Arts gradually superseded the more elementary teaching. She emphasized the social aspect of the college as a meeting place for working women; it also provided opportunities for self-improvement, with a lending library, a penny bank to encourage thrift, a holiday fund, and respectable entertainments such as concerts, which she described in *Macmillan's Magazine* (October 1879, March 1884). Management of the college remained in the hands of its philanthropic backers, who hoped that the young, single women who attended would be encouraged to develop habits of prudence and forethought, and avoid some of the perils of city life. She remained as honorary secretary, and later acted as principal, until standing down in 1910.

Frances Martin died on 13 March 1922 at her home, 3 Foley Avenue, Hampstead, following what a coroner's inquest found to be an accidental fall. She was buried in Hampstead cemetery at the foot of Jane Benson's grave. Her will bequeathed £500 to the College for Working Women, which was renamed the Frances Martin College and maintained an independent existence until 1966, when it was merged with the London Working Men's College.   M. C. CURTHOYS

Sources M. J. Tuke, *A history of Bedford College for Women, 1849–1937* (1939) · letters to Alexander and George Macmillan, BL, Add. MS 54974 · *IGI* · census returns, 1881 · d. cert. · will, proved London, 4 May 1922 · *Wellesley index* · C. L. Graves, *Life and letters of Alexander Macmillan* (1910) · R. M. Harris, 'Frances Martin College', *Further Education*, 1 (Jan 1948), 225–6 · J. Purvis, *Hard lessons: the lives and education of working-class women in nineteenth-century England* (1989) · J. F. C. Harrison, *A history of the Working Men's College, 1854–1954* (1954)

Archives BL, Macmillan MSS

Wealth at death £18,873 12s. 6d.: probate, 4 May 1922, *CGPLA Eng. & Wales*

Martin, Francis (1652–1722), theologian, was born towards the end of November 1652 in Galway. He was educated first at a local school and then at home. In 1670 he became a teacher, but in 1673 Archbishop Lynch of Tuam, a relative, sent him to Louvain. He matriculated on 19 December 1673 and graduated in the arts in 1674. In 1675 he began the study of theology. He applied for the lectureship in Greek at the Collegium Trilingue in 1681, obtaining it in 1683 through the intervention of powerful anti-Jansenists in the university and the government, and retaining it until his death. Throughout his study of theology he struggled with the view of grace then prevalent in the Louvain faculty, and after his appointment as a lecturer he openly attacked it. In 1684 he obtained the licentiate in theology and became lecturer at St Martin's, a house of Augustinian canons. Complaints in 1685 and 1686 that his lectures undermined the authority of Augustine and promoted extreme claims about papal power led to opposition within the faculty to his being awarded the doctorate in theology in 1688, but the intervention of the nuncio at Brussels enabled him to take the degree.

Late in 1688 Martin wrote to the nuncio to the court of James II outlining a hypothetical scheme for the assassination of William of Orange, an abiding source of embarrassment after the letter was published in an anonymous Gallican pamphlet, *État présent de la faculté de théologie de Louvain* (Trévoux, 1701). In 1689 Martin obtained a position in Hovius College thanks to the anti-Jansenist master,

Pierre Marcelis, under whose guidance he took part in a campaign to harass and discredit suspected Jansenists at the university, among other things by bringing a malicious suit before the council of Brabant. Throughout 1691 and 1692 Martin was professor of theology at the great seminary in Malines, appointed by Archbishop Precipiano due to his stand against Jansenism. His lectures again aroused complaints, and when a thesis on Genesis in which he criticized Augustine was condemned his removal was petitioned.

Towards the end of 1692 Nicolas du Bois, ageing regius professor of scripture at Louvain, applied to have Martin deliver lectures on his behalf. The following year the governor-general acceded to the request in the face of opposition from the faculty, and Martin returned to Louvain. In 1694 Precipiano appointed him ecclesiastical censor and synodal examiner, and on du Bois's death in 1696 Martin succeeded him as regius professor by royal letters patent, subsequently becoming, again through political patronage, a regent of the faculty of theology and a canon of St Peter's in Louvain. Until 1705 he was to combat Jansenism not only in his daily lectures and his writings (of which there is no systematic bibliography), but also by using his powers in the university to block the promotions of suspected Jansenists, and his position as censor to refuse them publication, while favouring their opponents.

From 1705, growing increasingly distrustful of the Jesuits and of Molinism, and reading Pascal, Arnauld, and Dominican works on efficacious grace, Martin gradually drew closer to the Jansenists, openly aligning himself with them in 1710. Expediency may have played some role in changing his attitude. After the nadir of 1700–06, when the occupying French authorities had given full support to Archbishop Precipiano's anti-Jansenist measures, the allied victory at Ramillies (1706) inaugurated a brief period of Jansenist 'revanche' (Pirenne, 105). Martin seems to have become particularly outspoken after the death of his former patron Precipiano in 1711. In that year his former allies lodged a complaint against him in Brussels which was quashed at the intervention of the English minister, and in 1712 he propounded in his lectures theses which the then censor of books described as scandalous and which led to heated controversy. A further appeal to the Brussels internuncio to discipline Martin precipitated a dangerous dispute about secular, papal, and internal jurisdiction in the university which ended only when Martin submitted a retraction in 1713. His one constant conviction seems to have been absolute papal infallibility in doctrinal matters, so that the condemnation of Jansenism in the bull *Unigenitus* (1713) led him to abandon his support for the Jansenist party.

In 1714 the principal work of Martin's career was published, *Scutum fidei contra haereses hodiernas*, written to vindicate the Catholic faith from the attacks of John Tillotson, defending the infallibility of the church, the primacy of the pope, the sacrament of penance, transubstantiation, communion in one kind, adoration of the eucharist, the Latin liturgy, the use of images, and the invocation of saints, and denying Tillotson's charge that Catholic doctrine taught that the pope had the authority to depose secular rulers. On this last point Martin stressed that even those theologians who argued most forcefully for the opinion never claimed it was an article of faith, and commented on the irony of a whig expressing horror at the deposition of kings.

Martin approached the internuncio in 1715 with a proposal for a book supporting the debated papal bull *Unigenitus*. This was finally published in March 1720 as *Motivum juris pro bulla Unigenitus orthodoxia*. Attacking the schism threatened both by appeals against *Unigenitus* and by the 'secret machinations of the molinists' (p. 162), it was an attempt to reconcile conflicts within the church on an infallibilist basis which few would have been willing to accept. The very next year Martin published his *Brevis tractatus* expanding on his view of the papal deposing power as touched on in the *Scutum fidei* and *Motivum juris*. Martin's contacts with the earl of Sunderland, who had visited Louvain in September 1717 when secretary of state, and with the bishop of Bangor convinced him that the main obstacle to the toleration of Catholics in Britain was fear of their disloyalty arising from the papal deposing power. While maintaining that the papal primacy was instituted by Christ in St Peter, Martin showed that the power of the pope to depose secular rulers was a theological opinion rather than an article of faith, and argued strongly that it was an opinion which occasioned harm to the faithful and no good to the church. By attacking the opponents of *Unigenitus* while still fiercely opposing Molinism, and simultaneously upholding papal infallibility while denying papal authority over secular rulers, Martin was isolating himself within the university.

In the summer of 1720 Martin struck a Dominican priest during an argument and was suspended from teaching. He initiated an appeal within the university, but also sought the intervention of the council of Brabant, and returned to teaching in 1721 with his internal appeal still pending. On 4 October 1722 Martin died while undergoing surgery in the hospital of St John in Bruges, and he was buried the same month in the hospital chapel. His memorial records his ample liberality to the poor.

Martin's litigiousness, his violent temper, and his possibly opportunist shift from Molinism to Jansenism to an infallibilist opposition to both, led several contemporaries to describe him as quarrelsome, unstable, and inconsistent. His readiness to resort to civil tribunals or even political favour in university and ecclesiastical affairs, certainly in part opportunist but also foreshadowing Josephinist attitudes soon to be more widespread, was seen by some as dangerously undermining the separation of jurisdictions. When reporting Martin's death the internuncio wrote that he 'had often caused great harm to the authority of the Holy See in Flanders and had endangered the privileges of the entire University' (Giblin in *Collectanea Hibernica*, 5.104).   PAUL ARBLASTER

Sources C. Giblin, 'Catalogue of material of Irish interest in the collection *Nunziatura di Fiandra*, Vatican archives: part 4, vols. 102–22', *Collectanea Hibernica: sources for Irish history*, 5 (1962) [whole issue] • L. Ceyssens, 'François Martin (1652–1722): professeur à l'Université de Louvain', *Augustiniana*, 46 (1996), 371–404 • H. Pirenne, *Histoire de Belgique*, 5 (Brussels, 1921) • J. Lefèvre, *Documents relatifs à la juridiction des nonces et internonces des Pays-Bas pendant le régime espagnol (1596–1706)* (Brussels and Rome, 1942) • F. Martin, *Tertium juris motivum in causa Doctoris Martin contra patres Jesuitas* (1712) • F. Martin, *Scutum fidei contra haereses hodiernas, seu, Tillotsonianae concionis sub titulo strena opportuna contra papismum refutatio* (Louvain, 1714) • F. Martin, *Brevis tractatus, mutatâ priore, circa praetensam pontificis infallibilitatem, praefatione, correctior, quo sacerdotibus & pontificibus in ecclesia Christiana, nullam potestatem deponendi supremos reipublicae principes seculares competere, theologicè ac peremporiè demonstrat* ([Louvain?], 1721) • F. Claeys Bouuaert, 'Martin (François)', *Biographie nationale*, 30 (Brussels, 1959)

Martin, Frederick Joseph (1830–1883), writer, was born at Geneva, Switzerland, on 19 November 1830 and educated in Heidelberg, Germany. Nothing is known of his parents, other than the fact that his father was also called Frederick Joseph Martin. He moved to England quite young and worked as a teacher, and then from 1856 was secretary and amanuensis to Thomas Carlyle, whom he helped in his historical researches. On 17 January 1856 he married Susannah Styles (*b.* 1835), daughter of William Styles, a farmer; over the next decade they had two sons and three daughters.

Martin started a short-lived biographical magazine called *The Statesman*, in which he began an account of Carlyle's early life, but as his subject did not approve, he discontinued it. He inaugurated the *Statesman's Year-Book* in 1864, and in 1879 Benjamin Disraeli, the prime minister, struck by its usefulness, gave him a pension of £100 a year. He continued to supervise the *Year-Book* until December 1882, when he was compelled by ill health to give it up and was replaced by J. Scott Keltie. In the intervening years he had produced an enormous amount of research, including a *Life of John Clare* (1865), volume two of *The National History of England* (1873), and a variety of histories and reference books in relation to finance and commerce. He wrote largely for various papers and was an occasional contributor to *The Athenaeum*. Only a few weeks after his retirement from the *Year-Book*, Martin died at his home, 22 Lady Margaret Road, Kentish Town, London, on 27 January 1883. He was buried at Highgate cemetery on 1 February.

GORDON GOODWIN, *rev.* JESSICA HININGS

Sources Ward, *Men of the reign* • *The Times* (29 Jan 1883) • census returns, 1881 • Boase, *Mod. Eng. biog.* • m. cert. • d. cert. • *CGPLA Eng. & Wales* (1883) • private information (1893)
Archives BL, corresp. with Macmillans, Add. MS 55042 • Bodl. Oxf., corresp. and papers, Don MSS c.58–59, d.63–65 • NL Scot., corresp. and papers concerning Carlyle
Wealth at death £1962 3s. 1d.: probate, 19 Feb 1883, *CGPLA Eng. & Wales*

Martin, Sir George (1764–1847), naval officer, was the youngest son of William Martin (*d.* 1766), captain RN, and his wife, Arabella, daughter of Sir William *Rowley, admiral of the fleet. His grandfather Bennet Martin MD was a brother of William Martin, admiral of the fleet. Many members of his mother's family attained naval distinction, and by her second marriage, to Colonel Gibbs of Horsley Park, Surrey, Martin was half-brother of Major-General Sir Samuel *Gibbs. From an early age he was on the books of the yacht *Mary*, but he seems first to have gone afloat in December 1776, when he joined the *Monarch* as 'captain's servant' with his uncle Captain Joshua Rowley. On 27 July 1778 he was present in the action off Ushant, and following his uncle to the *Suffolk*, was in the battle of Grenada on 6 July 1779, and in the three actions off Martinique in April and May 1780. On 16 July 1780 he was promoted lieutenant of the *Russell*. He was afterwards with his uncle in the *Princess Royal* at Jamaica. On 9 March 1782 he was promoted to the command of the sloop *Tobago*, and on 17 March 1783 was posted into the *Preston* (50 guns). He returned to England early in 1784.

From 1789 to 1792 Martin commanded the *Porcupine* (24 guns) on the coast of Ireland, and in 1793 the *Magicienne* (32 guns) in the West Indies. In 1795 he was appointed to the *Irresistible* (74 guns), and in her took part in the battle of Cape St Vincent on 14 February 1797. At the close of the battle Nelson, whose own ship, the *Captain*, had been disabled, hoisted his broad pennant on the *Irresistible* for a few days. On 26 April two Spanish frigates, *Ninfa* and *Santa Elena*, coming home from the West Indies and ignorant of the blockade, were chased by the *Irresistible* and the frigate *Emerald* into Conil Bay. The *Santa Elena* went on shore and broke up, but the *Ninfa* was captured and became part of the British navy fleet under the name of *Hamadryad*. The skill and dash with which Martin took the ships past a dangerous reef that blocked the approach to the bay won for him the warm commendations of Lord St Vincent.

In July 1798 Martin was appointed to the *Northumberland* (74 guns), in which, on 18 February 1800, he assisted in the capture of the *Généreux*. From May 1800 he had charge of the blockade of Malta, and on 5 September received the surrender of Valletta. In 1801 he was with the fleet on the coast of Egypt under Lord Keith. In 1803 he commanded the *Colossus* in the channel, in 1804 the *Glory*, and in November 1804 was appointed to the *Barfleur*, in which he took part in the action off Cape Finisterre on 22 July 1805. On 9 November 1805 he was promoted rear-admiral. In 1806 he was second in command at Portsmouth, and in 1807 was employed on the blockade of Cadiz. He was afterwards in the Mediterranean under the orders of Lord Collingwood—for the most part on the coast of Italy or Sicily. In June 1809 he took possession of Ischia and Procida. On 23 October, with the fleet off Cape St Sebastian, he was detached in pursuit of a small squadron under Rear-Admiral Baudin. Two days later two of the pursued ships of the line ran themselves on shore not far from Cette, and on 26 October were abandoned, set fire to, and blown up. One ship of the line and one frigate got into Cette harbour; another frigate escaped.

On 31 July 1810 Martin was promoted vice-admiral, and was again employed on the coast of Sicily, and in co-operation with the army under Sir John Stuart, for which he received the order of St Januarius from the king of Naples. From 1812 to 1814 he was commander-in-chief in the Tagus, and in the summer of 1814 was knighted, when the prince regent visited the fleet at Spithead.

Martin married first, on 3 April 1804, the youngest daughter (d. 15 October 1806) of Captain John Albert *Bentinck RN, grand-niece of the duke of Portland. He married secondly, on 2 June 1815, A. Locke (d. 1 March 1842), daughter of William Locke of Norbury Park, Surrey. Apparently there were no surviving children. On 2 January 1815 he was made a KCB, and a GCB on 20 February 1821. On 19 July 1821 he attained admiral, and from 1824 to 1827 was commander-in-chief at Portsmouth, with his flag in the *Victory*. In January 1833 he was appointed rear-admiral of the United Kingdom, and vice-admiral in April 1834. He was made a GCMG in 1836, and was promoted admiral of the fleet on 9 November 1846. He died at his house in Berkeley Square, London, on 28 July 1847.

J. K. LAUGHTON, *rev.* ROGER MORRISS

Sources O'Byrne, *Naval biog. dict.* · J. Marshall, *Royal naval biography*, 1/1 (1823), 280–83 · W. James, *The naval history of Great Britain, from the declaration of war by France in 1793, to the accession of George IV*, [5th edn], 6 vols. (1859–60), vol. 4 · *The dispatches and letters of Vice-Admiral Lord Viscount Nelson*, ed. N. H. Nicolas, 7 vols. (1844–6), vol. 4 · P. Mackesy, *The war in the Mediterranean, 1803–1810* (1957) · R. Muir, *Britain and the defeat of Napoleon, 1807–1815* (1996)
Archives Suffolk RO, Ipswich, corresp. and papers | BL, letters to Lord Nelson, Add. MSS 34909–34930 · NMM, letters to Sir Thomas Foley
Likenesses Worthington & Parker, group portrait, line engraving, pubd 1803 (*Commemoration of 14 February 1797*; after R. Smirke), BM, NPG · C. Landseer, oils (after T. Lawrence), NMM

Martin, George William (1825–1881), music teacher and composer, was born in London on 8 March 1825. He began his musical studies as a chorister at St Paul's Cathedral, under William Hawes, and was one of the choirboys at Westminster Abbey for the coronation of Queen Victoria. He taught music at the Normal College for Army Schoolmasters in Chelsea, was resident music master at St John's Training College, Battersea, from 1845 to 1853, and became the first organist of Christ Church, Battersea, when it opened in 1849. In 1860 he established the National Choral Society, and subsequently for some years staged a successful series of oratorio performances at Exeter Hall. In connection with these performances he edited and published cheap editions of the oratorios and other works of the great masters then not readily accessible to the public. He was also the editor of a number of minor music periodicals. In 1864 he organized a choir of a thousand voices for the *Macbeth* music at the 300th anniversary of Shakespeare's birth. He had a special aptitude for training choirs of schoolchildren, and conducted the Metropolitan Schools Choral Society and the National Schools Choral Festival at the Crystal Palace in 1859. As a composer his talent was for the madrigal and partsong, and the publication of his prize-winning glee 'Is she not beautiful?' in 1845 marked the beginning of a successful period, during which few years passed without his winning distinction from some of the leading glee and madrigal societies in the country. 'No composer since the days of Dr Callcott has obtained so many prizes as Mr Martin', commented *The Times* in 1856. The tune 'Leominster', associated with Bonar's hymn 'A Few More Years Shall Roll', became one of his best-known compositions.

It is reported by a contemporary that, owing to intemperance, Martin sank from 'a position which at one time gave him a claim to be regarded as one of the elements of musical force in the metropolis' (*Monthly Musical Record*, 1 May 1881). He died, apparently destitute, in Bolingbroke House Hospital, Wandsworth, London, on 16 April 1881, and was buried by the parish in Brookwood cemetery, Woking. J. C. HADDEN, rev. DAVID J. GOLBY

Sources *Monthly Musical Record*, 11 (1881), 94 · *MT*, 22 (1881), 267 · B. Rainbow, 'Martin, George William', *New Grove*
Likenesses woodcut, NPG
Wealth at death destitute: *DNB*

Martin, Gregory (1542?–1582), Roman Catholic priest and biblical translator, was born at Maxfield in Guestling, Sussex. Little is known about his family and early life. Nominated in 1557 as one of the original scholars at St John's College, Oxford, by Sir Thomas White, the college's founder, Martin was an exact contemporary of Edmund Campion. Together they proceeded to the BA and MA degrees. They continued at St John's as fellows and lecturers: Campion in rhetoric (1564–70) and Martin in Greek (1564–8). In 1567 or 1568 Martin dedicated a manuscript on Greek pronunciation to Henry Fitzalan, earl of Arundel, who had visited Oxford (published in 1712 as *Gregorius Martinus ad Adolphum Mekerchum pro veteri & vera Graecarum literarum pronunciatione*). The earl's son-in-law, Thomas Howard, fourth duke of Norfolk, subsequently offered Martin a position in his household as tutor to his sons, one of whom was Philip Howard, the future earl of Arundel.

Martin resigned his St John's fellowship on 15 December 1568. Presumably religion played a role in Martin's decision: in Oxford pressure to conform to the established church was intense. There would be more freedom in the duke's household, where by word and example he encouraged the family to remain steadfast in the old faith. After the duke was arrested in 1569 as a result of the revolt of the northern earls, the household was forced to attend common prayers and services conducted by Church of England ministers. Martin fled to the continent. Before his departure, he exhorted Campion that he must not allow material worries to prevent him from following his religious convictions: 'if we two can live together, we can live for nothing; if this is too little, I have money; but if this fails, one thing remains: they that sow in tears shall reap in joy' (Gillow, *Lit. biog. hist.*, 4.485).

William Allen welcomed Martin to the recently founded English College at Douai, and Campion joined him in the summer of 1570. Together they studied theology at the new University of Douai. Both received their bachelor's degree on 21 January 1573. Martin was ordained in Brussels on 21 March 1573, and Campion departed for Rome in the spring to join the Jesuits. Martin continued his studies and was awarded a licentiate in theology on 11 January 1575. In May 1576 he started lecturing in Hebrew at the English College at Douai.

In February 1576 Allen and other English religious exiles had agreed to convert the English Hospice in Rome into a college for the education of clergy. The first group of students departed from Douai on 9 November under Martin's

direction. Enrolled as a chaplain of the hospice, Martin both taught the seminarians and devised a programme of studies for them. He remained in Rome for nearly eighteen months, a rather turbulent time as English and Welsh students clashed at the new college. Informed of Martin's arrival in Rome, Campion recommended to Robert Persons on 25 June 1577 that they try to entice Martin into the Society of Jesus: 'Do let us conspire to deliver that good soul; it is good fishing' (Simpson, 119). A week later, on 3 July 1577, Campion wrote to Martin:

> since for so many years we had in common our college, our meals, our studies, our opinions, our fortune, our degrees, our tutors, our friends, and our enemies, let us for the rest of our lives make a more close and binding union, that we may have the fruit of our friendship in heaven. (Simpson, 126)

On 28 November 1578 Persons suggested that Allen had foiled their plans: 'Mr. Marten was called away herhence by Mr. D. Allen his letters, I think they were half afrayd of him what myght becum of hym' (Hicks, 2). Allen may have had a more innocent reason for recalling Martin: an English translation of the Bible. In any case, Persons explained to William Good that the disturbances at the hospice had made Martin 'weary of Rome' (Hicks, 9). On 23 July 1578 Martin returned to the English College, recently transferred from Douai to Rheims. Oddly, no sources mention a reunion during Campion's sojourn at Rheims before his departure for England in June 1580. None the less, Martin commemorated his martyred friend with a Latin poetic eulogy first published in Allen's *A Brief Historie of the Glorious Martyrdom of xii. Reverend Priests* (1582).

In November 1578 Martin addressed a crucial problem for English Catholics in *A Treatise of Schisme*. The Elizabethan Act of Uniformity (1 Eliz. I c. 2) demanded that everyone attend services of the established church. Absentees could be punished by fines or imprisonment. Because of loyalty to their queen or fear of punishment, many Catholics considered passive attendance acceptable. The Council of Trent discussed the issue and condemned the practice. Citing scriptural and historical precedents, Martin justified Trent's decision and demonstrated, as his subtitle claimed, 'that al Catholikes ought in any wise to abstaine altogether from heretical Conventicles'. At the trial of William Carter, the work's printer, in 1584, Martin's exhortation that Catholics imitate Judith, who refused to dine with Holofernes, was interpreted as an appeal to assassinate the queen: Carter was condemned and executed.

As Martin completed this controversial manual, he embarked on an English translation of the Bible. Allen announced the project in September 1578. He, Richard Bristow, and William Reynolds were involved primarily as revisers: the work was Martin's. Between September 1578 and July 1580 Martin translated the entire Vulgate. *The New Testament of Iesus Christ* with Bristow's notes was published at Rheims in 1582. For financial reasons the Old Testament did not appear until the two volumes of *The Holie Bible* were published at Douai in 1609–10. The appearance of a Catholic Bible in English undermined traditional protestant criticism that the Roman church kept scripture out of the hands of the laity. Instead protestant theologians such as Thomas Cartwright, William Whitaker, and William Fulke attacked the credentials of the translators and denounced their work as filled with error. Despite such criticism, revised versions of Martin's translation remained extremely popular throughout the English-speaking world for nearly four hundred years.

Translating the Vulgate made Martin even more aware that theological errors could be both the cause and the effect of faulty translations. On 13 February 1579 he informed Campion that he had nearly finished a manuscript on protestant corruption and abuse of scripture. *A Discoverie of the Manifold Corruptions of the Holy Scriptures by the Heretikes of our Daies* (1582) accused protestants of doubting or denying the authority of books and passages not harmonious with their doctrine; of altering the text to justify their views; and of translating falsely to substantiate heretical ideas. The subsequent controversy involved Cartwright, Fulke, Whitaker, John Reynolds, and his Catholic brother William.

Martin worked on a third manuscript between July 1580 and April 1581. *Roma sancta* lauded the holiness and piety of contemporary Rome as evidence for the truth of Catholicism. Apparently the English College's poor finances prevented its publication. Sections were published in *A Treatyse of Christian Peregrination* (1583), along with three letters to 'heretics': a married priest; Martin's sisters, raised in heresy and married to protestants; and Thomas Whyte, warden of New College, Oxford, who dissembled his Catholic beliefs to retain his position. The epistles were reprinted as *The Love of the Soule* (1578, *vere* England, *c.*1597).

At an unspecified date Martin began to suffer from a malady of the lungs, most probably consumption. On 30 April 1582 Allen sent him to Paris to consult doctors. Apparently it was too late for medical help. He returned to Rheims on 14 September and died on 28 October. Allen preached at Martin's funeral. Martin was buried in the parish church of St Étienne. The armies of the French Revolution destroyed the church and his monument.

THOMAS M. McCOOG

Sources G. Martin, *Roma sancta*, ed. G. B. Parks (1969) • T. F. Knox and others, eds., *The first and second diaries of the English College, Douay* (1878) • G. Anstruther, *The seminary priests*, 1 (1969) • W. Kelly, ed., *Liber ruber venerabilis collegii Anglorum de urbe*, 1, Catholic RS, 37 (1940) • Foster, *Alum. Oxon.* • *The Elizabethan Jesuits: Historia missionis Anglicanae Societatis Jesu (1660) of Henry More*, ed. and trans. F. Edwards (1981) • A. F. Allison and D. M. Rogers, eds., *The contemporary printed literature of the English Counter-Reformation between 1558 and 1640*, 2 vols. (1989–94) • Gillow, *Lit. biog. hist.*, 4.484–91 • A. C. Southern, *Elizabethan recusant prose, 1559–1582* (1950) • A. Walsham, *Church papists: Catholicism, conformity and confessional polemic in early modern England* (1993) • W. H. Stevenson and H. E. Salter, *The early history of St John's College, Oxford*, OHS, new ser., 1 (1939) • R. Simpson, *Edmund Campion*, new edn (1896) • L. Hicks, ed., *Letters and memorials of Father Robert Persons*, Catholic RS, 39 (1942) • L. Pertile, 'Montaigne, Gregory Martin and Rome', *Bibliothèque d'Humanisme et Renaissance*, 50 (1998), 637–59

Archives Archivum Romanum Societatis Iesu, Rome, Fondo Gesuitico collection, letters to Edmund Campion, FG 651/636

Likenesses oils, 1573, Arundel Castle, West Sussex • oils, St John's College, Oxford

Martin, Sir Harold Brownlow Morgan (1918–1988), air force officer, was born on 27 February 1918 in Edgecliffe, Sydney, Australia, the only son and second of the three children of Joseph Harold Osborne Morgan Martin MD, medical practitioner, and his wife, Colina Elizabeth Dixon. He was educated at Randwick high school and at Lyndfield College. An accomplished horseman, he became a cadet in the Australian light horse. In 1937, intent on world travel, he left Sydney as a crew member on a liner. In 1940, in England, he joined the Royal Air Force volunteer reserve.

During his first Bomber Command tour in 455 squadron (Royal Australian Air Force) and 50 squadron (Royal Air Force), flying Hampden, Manchester, and Lancaster bombers, Martin concluded that the most effective way of penetrating enemy defences at night was to disregard regulations and to fly at low level. By questioning higher policy and refusing to allow regulations to hinder chances of success he was already showing a boldness and independence of mind which was to characterize his entire career. His first DFC came in 1942, after twenty-five sorties.

Invited to join 617 (the 'Dambuster' squadron) in March 1943, Martin made a significant contribution to its night low-level training for the actual operation. The squadron flew at night at an altitude of 150 feet all the way to its targets and released its bouncing bombs from 60 feet. Martin's bomb exploded short of the dam. He flew down the dam and over the wall three times. Despite damage to the aircraft from anti-aircraft fire, he and his crew supported the following crews and engaged the enemy's guns. The last two pilots' mines exploded successfully against the dam wall. The Möhne and Eder dams were breached, and the Sorpe Dam damaged. Martin was appointed to the DSO and this was soon followed with a bar to his DFC for his courage and resolution in a costly attack on the Dortmund and Ems Canal. He became 617's acting commander and rebuilt the squadron before handing it over, well trained, to Leonard Cheshire in 1943. He also convinced Cheshire of the feasibility of low-level night target marking, a prerequisite for accurate bombing.

In February 1944 Martin's action during an attack with 'Blockbuster' bombs on a heavily defended viaduct in southern France, for which he received a bar to his DSO, was described by Cheshire as the supreme example of inspired fearless night marking. During his last operational tour in 515 night intruder squadron, Martin again distinguished himself, gaining a second bar to his DFC (1944). He then attended the Haifa Staff College in Israel before returning to flying duties in 242 transport squadron (1946). With his war gratuity he bought a horse. In 1944 he married Wendy Lawrence, widow of Flight Lieutenant P. D. Walker, and daughter of Grenbry Outhwaite, lawyer, and Ida Rentoul, artist, of Melbourne. The marriage was very happy; the couple had two daughters.

In 1947 Martin was awarded the Britannia trophy for a record-breaking Mosquito flight (21 hrs 31 mins.) from

London to Cape Town, and the following year he received the AFC for his crucial contribution to the first jet crossing of the Atlantic, which was made by an RAF squadron. While serving in London as a squadron leader (1948–51), he began to take an interest in painting (in which he displayed a natural talent), sculpture, and archaeology, subjects he pursued most of his life. From 1952 to 1955, as a wing commander, he was air attaché in Israel, a post in which he was a success because of his diplomatic flair and grasp of the political complexities of the Middle East. This posting, extended at the Israelis' request, marked a turning point in his career, and steady progress followed.

A rewarding NATO staff post at Fontainebleau in France (1955–8) was followed by a course at the Joint Services Staff College and postings, first as group captain to signals command, and then to Cyprus, where Martin commanded the important Nicosia base. In 1963 he became an air commodore and was posted to 38 support group, where he enjoyed his contacts with the airborne forces but disagreed profoundly with the infantry over the control of the helicopter force. A course at the Imperial Defence College (1965), promotion to air vice-marshal (1967), and a return to Cyprus as the senior air staff officer prepared him for his last command appointments—air officer commanding 38 group (1967–9), then, as air marshal (1970), air officer commanding-in-chief of the RAF in Germany, and commander of the NATO second Tactical Air Force, with its force of Belgians, Dutch, Germans, and British.

Primarily because of frustration in his fight against service cuts, Martin was unhappy in his last RAF post, as air member for personnel at the Ministry of Defence (1973–4). After his retirement in 1974 he spent three years in Beirut and Athens as Middle East marketing adviser to Hawker Siddeley International, before returning to London as a consultant. He was aide-de-camp to Elizabeth II (1963–6) and was appointed CB (1968) and KCB (1971).

Martin, a vital, alert man of medium height, with powerful, humorous eyes, was universally liked and respected. He was a man of great courage who always fought unselfishly for what he believed was right. In 1985 his lifestyle became restricted when he suffered brain damage after being knocked down by a coach, but he bore his lot with fortitude and patience. He died from cancer at his home, 64 Warwick Gardens, Kensington, London, on 3 November 1988. He was survived by his wife.

FREDERICK ROSIER, rev.

Sources *The Times* (4 Nov 1988) · *Daily Telegraph* (4 Nov 1988) · P. Brickhill, *The dambusters* (1951) · R. Braddon, *Cheshire, VC* (1954) · L. Lucas, ed., *Wings of war: airmen of all nations tell their stories, 1939–1945* (1983) · personal knowledge (1996) · private information (1996)
Archives Royal Air Force Museum, Hendon, flying logs
Wealth at death £192,823: probate, 28 April 1989, *CGPLA Eng. & Wales*

Martin, Harriet Letitia (1801–1891). *See under* Martin, Richard (1754–1834).

Martin, Helen [Nell; *name in religion* Maria Gabriel] (*c*.1609–1672), Poor Clare abbess, was born in Galway city. Her family, the Martins, one of the most prominent in the city,

were one of the twelve long-established mercantile and governing families known as the tribes of Galway. As a young woman Helen (Nell) Martin entered the Poor Clare convent of Bethlehem, located on a remote section of land on Viscount Dillon's estate, near Athlone, co. Westmeath. Accounts of the community suggest the nuns came from some of the most prosperous and noble Catholic families of Ireland. Having received the habit on 24 March 1632, she was professed the following year on 25 March and took the name Maria Gabriel. During her time there she was joined by several other Galway women, notably Sister Bonaventure Browne, chronicler of the early history of the order in Ireland.

The citizens of Galway, many of whom had relatives in Bethlehem, about 1641 expressed their wish to see the Poor Clares establish themselves in the city. The decree of foundation for the Galway convent was issued by the provincial, Anthony Geoghegan, on 30 January 1642, and, following an election among the nuns who intended to travel to Galway, Sister Maria Gabriel was chosen as its first abbess. The exact location of the original convent is not known, however it is thought to have been in the vicinity of St Augustine Street and Queen Street, indicated by the placename Poor Clares' Lane, which appears on a contemporary map. She initially brought with her eleven professed sisters and two novices, though within her first year admitted a further eighteen novices.

Succeeded as abbess by Clare Anthony Kennedy in 1645, Martin's signature subsequently appears on the founding document for the Loughrea convent, co. Galway. She moved with her community to their new residence at Island Althenagh (Oileán Ealtanach), now known as Nun's Island, in 1649, and remained there until January 1653, when a Cromwellian edict was issued 'commanding all nuns of whatsoever condition, to marry or quit the kingdom'. Though most of the sisters fled to convents in Spain, she stayed in Ireland, and went into hiding with relatives in the Galway area until after the succession of Charles II, when she and a small band of nuns returned to their convent at Island Althenagh. She died in Galway, probably in the convent, on 14 January 1672, and was buried in the cemetery attached to the abbey of St Francis in Galway.

FRANCES CLARKE

Sources H. Concannon, *The Poor Clares in Ireland* (1929) · C. O'Brien, *Poor Clares, Galway, 1642–1992* (1992) · C. O'Brien, ed., *Recollections of an Irish Poor Clare in the seventeenth century* (1993) · B. Jennings, 'The abbey of St Francis, Galway', *Journal of the Galway Archaeological and Historical Society*, 22 (1946–7), 101–19 · N. Ó Muraíle, 'Aspects of the intellectual life of seventeenth century Galway', *Galway history and society: interdisciplinary essays on the history of an Irish county*, ed. G. Moran and R. Gillespie (1996), 149–211 · private information (2004) [Nun's Island Archives, Galway]
Archives Nun's Island Archives, Galway

Martin, Henry. *See* Martyn, Henry (*bap*. 1665, *d*. 1721).

Martin, Herbert Henry (1881–1954), secretary of the Lord's Day Observance Society, was born on 4 December 1881 in Norwich, the fourth of the five children of James

William Martin, boot and shoe manufacturer, and his wife, Mary Ann Blyth. He was educated at Alderman Norman's Endowed School, Norwich, a school founded for the education of Alderman Norman's male descendants, among whom Martin was included through his mother.

Martin was apprenticed to his father's trade but, having experienced conversion to Christ at the age of fourteen, he felt the urge to enter whole-time Christian service. His principals released him from his indentures, and at the early age of sixteen he became the first of the 'Wycliffe preachers' of the Protestant Truth Society founded by John Kensit. His first public address in that capacity was delivered on 17 August 1898 on the beach at Great Yarmouth. For the next twenty-five years Martin threw all his energy and religious zeal into this society's work of protest against the doctrines and practices of the Roman Catholic church and the Romeward movement in the Church of England—a task involving self-sacrifice, hardship, and some personal danger. In 1902 Martin preached on Thornbury Plain, Bristol; refusing to desist he was fined 1s. On declining payment he was imprisoned for three days in Horfield gaol, an experience he was fond of citing as an important landmark of his life's work.

During these years of travelling throughout Britain, the need for arresting the ever-growing disregard for Sunday as the divinely appointed day for rest and worship impressed itself increasingly upon Martin until it became the conviction which shaped the remainder of his career. He took up whole-time work in this cause when he joined the staff of the Imperial Alliance for the Defence of Sunday in 1923. Finding insufficient outlet there for his boundless energy and evangelistic fervour he welcomed the invitation which came in 1925 to become secretary of the Lord's Day Observance Society, which from its foundation in 1831 had always been the foremost instrument for the preservation of Sunday. Martin found the society in dire straits financially and in a state of ineffectiveness. By dint of his great organizing capacity, his unique flair for advertising and publicity, his infectious enthusiasm, and, above all, his deep spiritual conviction, he put this old society on the map and made it a power to be reckoned with in the national life. He soon gathered around him a loyal and steadily increasing staff by means of whom every part of the country was reached in the campaign to defend Sunday from secular encroachment. He revolutionized the publications of the society which, in some years, ran into millions of copies; and he exploited to the full such national occasions as the silver jubilee of George V and the coronation of George VI for the issue of special propaganda inculcating not only the observance of Sunday but also the reading of the Bible and acceptance of its teaching.

Fearing the introduction of the continental Sunday into Britain, Martin paid several visits to Paris and other European cities in order to study the subject closely, following which he wrote many articles on the theme. He travelled to Geneva in 1931 and spoke against calendar reform proposals before a League of Nations committee. In the same year he organized nationwide opposition to the legalization of the Sunday opening of cinemas. He was more successful in 1941 when his vigorous endeavours helped to bring about the rejection by the House of Commons of the Sunday opening of theatres.

A convinced churchman, Martin enjoyed fellowship with those Christians of other persuasions who shared his evangelical principles. The very nature of his activities brought upon him much unpopularity, misunderstanding, and even abuse, but his radiant buoyancy surmounted it all. Even his adversaries admired him as a clean fighter, and those who journalistically dubbed him Misery Martin knew and loved his happy, jubilant personality.

Martin married in 1903 Gertrude Elizabeth Eugene (d. 1939), daughter of John Farley, with whom he had one son. In 1942 he married Elsie Lilian, daughter of John Verdon, builder, of Kilburn, who survived her husband. In 1951 Martin retired; his powers thereafter failed rapidly and he died on 30 March 1954 at Tunbridge Wells, where he was living. H. J. W. LEGERTON, rev.

Sources *The Times* (31 March 1954) · private information (1971) · personal knowledge (1971) · *CGPLA Eng. & Wales* (1954) · P. Fryer, *Mrs Grundy: studies in English prudery* (1963), 118–24
Likenesses photograph, repro. in Fryer, *Mrs Grundy*, plate 8(a)
Wealth at death £2780 5s. 10d.: probate, 8 June 1954, *CGPLA Eng. & Wales*

Martin, Hugh (bap. 1822, d. 1885), Free Church of Scotland minister, was baptized at St Nicholas, Aberdeen, on 11 August 1822, the son of Alexander Martin and his wife, Isabella Gray. He was educated at the grammar school and Marischal College, Aberdeen, where he graduated MA in 1839. He was a distinguished student obtaining, among numerous prizes, the Gray bursary, the highest mathematical reward at Marischal College. He went on to study divinity at King's College, Aberdeen. A speech by William Cunningham at the general assembly of 1842 won him over to the cause of non-intrusion, and he was licensed as a minister of the Free Church of Scotland the following year. He served as minister at Panbride, near Carnoustie, Forfarshire, from 1844 until his removal to Free Greyfriars, Edinburgh, in 1858. On 1 September 1846 he married Elizabeth Jane Robertson, with whom he had a family; their eldest son, Alexander *Martin, was also a Free Church minister.

Martin retired from the active ministry in 1865, on grounds of ill health. From 1866 to 1868 he acted as examiner in mathematics at Edinburgh University. He also continued to write books and articles, being a frequent contributor to the *British and Foreign Evangelical Review* and the *Transactions of the London Mathematical Society*. His books included *Christ's Presence in the Gospel History* (1860), *A Study of Trilinear Co-ordinates* (1867), *The Atonement* (1870), and *The Westminster Doctrine of the Inspiration of Scripture* (1877). Together with James Begg and through the medium of a monthly periodical *The Watchword* he opposed moves to unite the Free and United Presbyterian churches. In 1872

Edinburgh University honoured him with the degree of DD. He died at home at Lasswade, near Edinburgh, on 14 June 1885.

GEORGE STRONACH, *rev.* LIONEL ALEXANDER RITCHIE

Sources private information (1893) · W. Ewing, ed., *Annals of the Free Church of Scotland, 1843–1900*, 1 (1914), 262 · m. cert. · bap. reg. Scot.

Martin, Hugh (1890–1964), ecumenical student leader and publisher, was born on 7 April 1890 in Glasgow, the son of the Revd Thomas Henry Martin, minister of the Adelaide Place Baptist Church, Glasgow, for thirty years and his wife, Clara Thorpe. His early initiation into the spirit of the ecumenical movement came in 1910 when he was a 'student observer' at the World Missionary Conference in Edinburgh, an experience which proved a permanent inspiration to him. He was educated at the Glasgow Academy, the Royal Technical College, Glasgow, and the University of Glasgow, where he won the university's Henderson biblical prize in 1913 and graduated MA with honours in the same year. He was also awarded the Baptist Union scholarship for the student with the highest percentage of marks in the Baptist Theological College of Scotland, where he studied theology (as well as at Trinity College, Glasgow) from 1909 to 1914. Placed on the Baptist ministry's probationers' list in 1914, he was transferred to the main ministerial list in 1920.

This progression would normally have led to a career in the regular Baptist ministry but Martin had become fascinated with the possibilities of work among students, and in 1914 he accepted a proposal to serve as assistant secretary of the Student Christian Movement, which was then rapidly developing, under the leadership of Tissington Tatlow, into a powerful force in the universities and colleges of Britain. This position meant that Martin was in charge of the movement's publications and their distribution in Britain and abroad, an experience which alerted him to the intricacies of publishing and helped to turn an amateur publisher into a very skilled practitioner. It also introduced him to the World's Student Christian Federation and to the friendship in their student days of many of the future church leaders of Europe and North America. Martin was treasurer of the World Federation from 1928 to 1935. He married Dorothy Priestley Greenwood on 31 July 1918, and they had two adopted sons.

Martin's skill as a committee man and as a chairman, with the ability to reconcile widely differing points of view, was seen in the preparation for the 1924 Conference on Politics, Economics, and Citizenship (COPEC), whose preparatory committee Martin chaired, with William Temple, later archbishop of Canterbury, chairing the conference itself.

The aftermath of COPEC created a new attitude to social affairs and politics in British church life, and Hugh Martin saw in it a new reading public. Taking a shrewd publishing risk, he persuaded the Student Christian Movement to establish in 1929 its publications department as a separate limited company, to be known as SCM Press. Martin and his immediate colleagues—Alex Walker, F. R. Reader, and

Kathleen Downham—forged links with authors and publishing houses in Europe and North America and built up a varied list of significant theological and sociological titles. In 1937 they brought off their chief publishing coup by establishing the Religious Book Club, which soon attained a membership of over 18,000. Each member received six books a year of a standard length at 2s. a copy. All the books were specially commissioned and dealt with many of the urgent public and theological issues of the day, notably during and after the Munich period. Martin himself wrote or edited several of the books, which illustrate his capacity for bringing groups together to discuss the content of manuscripts. One of the best of these was *Teachers' Commentary* (1932), which went into many editions.

After the outbreak of war Martin became director of the religious division in the Ministry of Information (1939–43), a post for which he was ideally suited because of his wide knowledge not only of the British churches and their leaders but of the religious situation in the countries that were now Britain's enemies. He was careful to elucidate the spiritual issues at stake in the war, and to avoid propaganda that appeared to support war aims which were unchristian. He returned to the SCM Press as managing director in 1943, and succeeded William Paton, who died in that year, as Free Church leader of the newly formed British Council of Churches.

As the war ended discussion began on the attitude of the British churches to their Christian counterparts in Europe. From such deliberations arose Christian Reconstruction in Europe (CRE) and eventually Christian Aid. Martin was on the committee of CRE and also served the Friends of Reunion (1933–43). In the early days of the British Council of Churches, during 1942, he housed the council in the SCM Press offices in Bloomsbury Street. This nursing of infant organizations was typical of Martin's practical approach to Christian co-operation and church unity. He saw the SCM Press as an instrument of debate and concern for unity, and was happy to have authors of all Christian traditions on his list. After his retirement in 1950 he served as vice-president of the British Council of Churches and in 1952–3 as moderator of the Free Church Federal Council.

Perhaps Hugh Martin's most lasting memorial is the *Baptist Hymn Book Companion* (1962), which he edited while also presiding over the revision of the Baptist *Hymn Book* (1962). He regarded this work as a tribute to the Baptists of Scotland, whose faith he had never forsaken. He was made an honorary doctor of divinity of Glasgow University in 1943 and in 1955 a Companion of Honour. He died at his home, in Lynton College Lane, East Grinstead, on 2 July 1964. His wife survived him. CECIL NORTHCOTT, *rev.*

Sources *Baptist Quarterly*, 20 (1963–4) · *Baptist handbook* (1965) · personal knowledge (2004) · private information (2004) · *The Times* (13 July 1964) · CGPLA Eng. & Wales (1964) · m. cert. · d. cert.
Wealth at death £7159: probate, 12 Oct 1964, CGPLA Eng. & Wales

Martin, James (*fl.* 1556–1588), philosopher, a native of Dunkeld, Perthshire, claimed to have begun studying philosophy at an early age, and may have been educated at Oxford. A James Martyn is listed as taking the degree of

MA on 31 March 1522, and in 1591 Andreas Libavius referred to Martin as an Oxford philosopher. He taught philosophy at the University of Paris, where in 1556 he was proctor of the German nation, which in May of the following year chose him to negotiate with the king over an unpopular tax on the university. In 1577 he was described on the title-page of his *De prima simplicium et concretorum corporum generatione … disputatio* as professor of philosophy at the University of Turin. This treatise, his major work, was dedicated to Girolamo della Rovere, archbishop of Turin. In 1588 he produced a new edition of Francisco Vallés's work of the same year, *In quartum librum Meteorologicorum Aristotelis commentaria*. The dedicatory letter (sigs. †2r–3v), addressed to Gregorio Lopez Madera, physician to Philip II of Spain, styles Martin as 'philosophiae professor ordinarius' ('ordinary professor of philosophy') at the University of Turin; and in it he refers to two other re-editions he had recently prepared for Madera: Fernando de Mena, *Commentaria in libros Galeni de sanguinis missione et purgatione* (1587), and Francisco Vallés, *De urinis, pulsibus, ac febribus compendiariae tractationes* (1588).

Martin's treatise on the primary generation of simple and compound bodies is directed against Aristotle, whose belief in the eternity of the world he maintains is both impious and inconsistent with the philosopher's own account of the infinite power of the unmoved mover. It was no doubt the anti-Aristotelian thrust of Martin's work which led Sir William Temple, the leading English proponent of the philosophical reform programme of Pierre de la Ramée, known as Ramus (1515–1572), to re-issue the treatise in Cambridge in 1584. In his prefatory letter, which gives a distinctly Ramist inflection to Martin's critique of Aristotelianism, Temple describes the Scottish philosopher as 'magno vir ingenio et exquisito judicio' ('a man of great intellect and meticulous judgement'), who argues against Aristotle with clarity (sig. ¶4r). The treatise, together with Temple's preface, was reprinted in Frankfurt in 1589. Two years later a reply was published, also in Frankfurt, by the tireless polemicist Andreas Libavius (*c*.1560–1616), professor of history and poetry at the University of Jena. In *Quaestionum physicarum controversarum inter Peripateticos et Rameos tractatus* (1591), Libavius took issue with both Temple and Martin, reserving his most contemptuous comments for the latter. Thus, adapting a phrase from Cicero, *Pro Sestio*, 72, he refers to Martin as 'ex vepreculis Taurinensibus progressa nitedula' ('a dormouse which has emerged from the thorn bushes of Turin'; sig. A7v); and he bemoans the 'stupidum Scoti ingenium' ('the dull mind of the Scot'), which has produced such a scandalously distorted picture of Aristotle's thought (pp. 28–9). Despite the polarization between Peripatetics, or Aristotelians, and Ramists indicated in his title, Libavius was aware that while Temple was a Ramist, Martin was simply an anti-Aristotelian. This distinction has been ignored, however, in modern scholarly literature, where Martin, through guilt by association with Temple, is regularly classified as a Ramist, for example, in Walter J. Ong's 1958 seminal study of Ramism. Similarly,

W. S. Howell calls Martin's treatise a 'pro-Ramist work' (Howell, 196 n. 68); and the article on Libavius in the *Dictionary of Scientific Biography* refers to Temple and Martin as 'two British disciples of Ramus' (p. 309). JILL KRAYE

Sources DNB · C. E. Du Boulay, *Historia universitatis Parisiensis*, 6 (Paris, 1673) · Emden, *Oxf.*, 4.383 · A. Libavius, *Quaestionum physicarum controversarum inter Peripateticos et Rameos tractatus* (1591) · W. J. Ong, *Ramus, method, and the decay of dialogue* (1958) · W. S. Howell, *Logic and rhetoric in England, 1500–1700* (1956) · W. Hubicki, 'Libavius, Andreas', *DSB*

Martin, James [*pseud.* Jacobus Aretius] (*fl.* 1612–1613), Latin poet, may have been the James Martin, born in Staffordshire, the son of a clergyman, who matriculated at Christ Church, Oxford, on 26 October 1604, aged sixteen. This James Martin migrated to Broadgates Hall, from where he graduated BA on 2 June 1608 and MA on 28 April 1611 (incorporated at Cambridge, 1612).

Martin's significance is as one of Oxford's most active Latin poets, at a time of very vigorous verse-writing in the university. He used the pseudonym Aretius, and appears to have been the editor of *Eidyllia* (1612), one of the collections lamenting the death of Henry, prince of Wales. He there called himself 'Germano-Britannus', which may mean no more than Anglo-Saxon: but it may indeed suggest some German origin—Wood takes Aretius to be a visiting German (Wood, *Ath. Oxon.*, new edn, 1813–20, 3.269; Wood, *Ath. Oxon.*: *Fasti*, 1.355). He is in the exotic company of Joseph Barbatus, Coptic Arab, and William Beyaert, 'Anglo-Belgicus'. Other Oxford men, listed only by initials, offer a wide selection of poetic tricks; Martin writes in sapphics, and also offers several accomplished eclogues.

Martin's other verse collection is *Primula veris* (1613), printed in London to celebrate the marriage of Princess Elizabeth and the elector palatine. It is not very clear how much is by Martin himself (perhaps most of the volume): in any case the whole is a remarkable linguistic *tour de force*. As well as Latin, Greek, and Hebrew, we find German, Italian, Czech, Russian, Polish, and 'Sarmatian'—that is, Turkish, attributed to 'Athlios Hellen' ('an unfortunate Greek'), promising that God will make 'byr ggun senín' into 'bin' ('one day for you into a thousand days'), and that a son of this happy union will smash the infidel Turks. Few Turks might read (or approve of) the sentiment, but it is a powerful expression of linguistic confidence. The book continues with an English rhapsody, French and Latin poems and chronograms, and ironic Spanish praise of the Jesuits by John Guzman. There is a long and impressive list of Martin's patrons, friends, and supporters (including Laud), and complimentary verses to him by a friend from Leiden ('philaretos': loving both virtue and Aretius), by 'Il medesimo', and by Il Cándido (a pseudonym sometimes used by Matthew Gwynne). Martin is keen to stress his sophisticated cultural and personal connections, and to praise Oxford as better than Thebes and Athens. Martin's collection may have influenced the multilingual Bathsua Reginald (later Makin) in her *Musa virginea* (1616), as well as many later university anthologies. Few at the time, or later, matched his exuberance.

On 28 May 1621 James Martin was instituted as vicar of

Preston, Lancashire. He already had connections with the town, having married Mary Southworth there on 30 May 1616; he was one of the king's preachers for Lancashire. This James Martin, probably the subject, proved a less successful clergyman. He was deprived on (perhaps unfounded) charges including simony in 1623: 'some ten years after he made bitter complaint of his treatment, alleging that his wife and son had starved to death in the street', and accusing local puritans; 'Martin seems to have been regarded as of unsound mind' (*VCH Lancashire*, 7.86). Other clergy were appointed to Preston on a temporary basis in 1623, the next official incumbent, Augustine Wildbore, being finally instituted in 1626, 'due to the deprivation of James Martin, last vicar'. The date of Martin's death is unknown.   D. K. MONEY

Sources *VCH Lancashire*, vol. 7 · Foster, *Alum. Oxon.* · Venn, *Alum. Cant.* · J. W. Binns, *Intellectual culture in Elizabethan and Jacobean England: the Latin writings of the age* (1990) · F. Madan, *Oxford literature, 1450–1640, and 1641–1650* (1912), vol. 2 of *Oxford books: a bibliography of printed works* (1895–1931); repr. (1964) · Wood, *Ath. Oxon.*, new edn · H. Fishwick, *History of the parish of Preston* (1900)

Martin, James (*bap.* 1693, *d.* 1744). *See under* Martin family (*per. c.*1700–1832).

Martin, James (1738–1810). *See under* Martin family (*per. c.*1700–1832).

Martin, Sir James (1820–1886), politician and judge in Australia, was born on 14 May 1820, at Midleton, co. Cork, Ireland, the eldest of the five children of John Martin, castle steward, of Fermoy, co. Cork, and his wife, Mary (1795–1876), the daughter of a farmer, David Hennessey, of Ballynona. The family moved to Australia in 1821, his father taking employment with Major-General Sir Thomas Brisbane, military commander at Fermoy, who had been appointed governor of New South Wales. James Martin was educated at the Commercial Academy and by other teachers in Parramatta, then at the Sydney College, which he left at the end of 1836.

Precociously talented and self-confident, Martin had by then submitted articles to *The Australian* newspaper and had come to the attention of its editor, George Robert Nichols, also a prominent lawyer. Under the latter's patronage he became acting editor of the paper in 1839 and an articled clerk to Nichols in the following year. Martin wrote for other papers as well, usually being critical of the government and promoting the causes of representative government and protectionism. He was admitted as a solicitor in 1845. In 1848 he stood successfully for the Cook and Westmoreland seat on the legislative council, but was unseated on petition. He won again in 1850.

On 20 January 1853 Martin married Isabella (1832–1909), the eldest daughter of William Long, a wine and spirits merchant of Potts Point, Sydney. They had nine sons and seven daughters. They separated in 1882.

In 1856 Martin was nominated to be attorney-general in the Cowper ministry, but this caused great controversy, as he was not a barrister. Part of the opposition grew from personal dislike of the 'vulgar fellow' (Nairn). Henry Parkes noted both Martin's 'absurd contempt for persons who did not agree with him' and 'his efforts to imitate the rich and privileged' (Parkes, 80). Martin served again as attorney-general in 1857–8, then in 1859 moved to the legislative assembly, on which he variously represented East Sydney, Orange, the Lachlan, and East Macquarie. In October 1863 he became premier, and proposed a protectionist programme. This was rejected by the council, and then by the public at the following election. Martin was again premier for two years from January 1866, and once more between December 1870 and May 1872. Under his leadership a number of measures to improve education and social welfare were passed. He was knighted in 1869.

Martin was appointed chief justice of New South Wales in 1873, once more after controversy, which 'nearly brought down the first Parkes government' (Rutledge, 207). Yet he grew to be well regarded for his abilities in this post, gaining, according to the *Sydney Morning Herald*, 'a reputation for sagacity and ability which will not soon be forgotten' (Grainger, 149). He remained chief justice until his death, from heart disease, on 4 November 1886 at his home, Clarens, in Wylde Street, Potts Point, Sydney. He was buried at St Jude's Church, Randwick, Sydney, but was reinterred alongside his wife at Waverley cemetery in 1909.   MARC BRODIE

Sources E. Grainger, *Martin of Martin Place: a biography of Sir James Martin* (1970) · M. Rutledge, 'Edward Butler and the chief justiceship, 1873', *Historical Studies: Australia and New Zealand*, 13 (1967–9), 207–22 · B. Nairn, 'Martin, Sir James', *AusDB*, vol. 5 · *Sydney Morning Herald* (5 Nov 1886), 3 · *The Times* (8 Nov 1886) · H. Parkes, *Fifty years in the making of Australian history* (1892) · J. M. Ward, *James Macarthur, colonial conservative, 1798–1867* (1981) · *DNB*

Archives Mitchell L., NSW, MSS | Mitchell L., NSW, Macarthur MSS; Parkes MSS

Likenesses T. Woolner, bronze medallion, 1854 · drawing, 1857, repro. in Grainger, *Martin of Martin Place*, facing p. 14 · E. Bell, coloured lithograph or oils, Mitchell L., NSW · photograph, repro. in Grainger, *Martin of Martin Place*, facing p. 15 · sketch, repro. in J. M. Bennet, *Portraits of chief justices of NSW, 1824–1977* (1977)

Martin, Sir James (1893–1981), ejector seat designer and manufacturer, was born on 11 September 1893 at Killinchy Woods, Crossgar, co. Down, Ireland. His father, Thomas, a farmer and inventor, died when James was two, leaving his mother, Sarah, to bring up Martin and his only sister. He had designed a three-wheel motorcar before preparing to go to university. A visit to Queen's in Belfast convinced him that he already had more practical knowledge than he was likely to learn there, so he joined his sister in London. By 1925 he was manufacturing his own vehicles in Acton, and at the same time he raced cars.

In 1929 Martin established his Martin Aircraft Company at Denham, where the business remained until his death. His goal, with the help of two boy mechanics, was a simpler and safer aircraft, then very much on aeronautical minds. Though in the next seventeen years he built five prototypes, including very fast modern fighters, he was regarded as too radical and unorthodox by the rather stuffy bureaucracies of the day. In 1934 Captain Valentine Henry Baker, a well-known flying instructor whom Martin had met some years previously, joined him in forming the Martin-Baker Aircraft Company. His experience and skill contributed to the design and development of the MB 1 and later prototypes. Their fighter, the fixed-undercarriaged MB 2 of 1937, which contained many advanced features for simplicity of construction and operation, was not ordered in 1939 in spite of laudatory reports. In 1942 the formidable MB 3 exceeded the Air Ministry's specification F.18/39, but Baker was killed in a crash of the prototype. The MB 4 was abandoned in design, but in May 1944 the first flight of the prototype of the 'magnificent' MB 5 took place. It was too late in the Second World War and none was ever ordered. The MB 5 was the last of Martin's aircraft designs to fly. He developed a single-engined jet design, the MB 6, but it never went beyond the drawing board.

After the loss of his partner and flying instructor, Martin became much concerned with how to save the lives of pilots. With the arrival of the much more expensive jet aircraft, which were entering new aerodynamic territory including very serious problems for pilots trying to bail out, Martin entered the field for which he was best known—ejector seats. In early 1944 at an Air Ministry suggestion he began work on the idea, although the concept dated back to 1940, when Martin-Baker had begun to provide the RAF with explosive balloon-cable cutters, while at the same time Martin had developed a small, simple mechanism to jettison Spitfire canopies. After tests with dummies, the first live ejection took place from a Gloster Meteor jet in 1946, and Martin was on the road to developing the world's standards in such work. Shortly after the successful test, representatives from the United States Navy visited Denham and by late 1946 had ordered ejector seats for its aircraft. In June 1947 the British followed suit and at last Martin-Baker had real production orders.

The first models simply ejected the pilot, who had then to release the seat and pull the ripcord of his parachute. Soon realizing that this was unacceptable, especially in view of data acquired on the vertical forces on the human body, by 3 September 1953 Martin had perfected the system which allowed a live ejection while the aircraft was still on the runway. In the meantime both British aircraft manufacturers and the RAF and Fleet Air Arm pilots had opposed the whole idea of ejector seats. Still not satisfied with a 12 per cent fatality rate, mainly occurring when pilots ejected close to the ground, Martin increased the explosive charge to send the seat higher and thus allow more time for the automatic opening of the parachute. He also added an explosive to jettison the canopy, further speeding up the ejection procedure. By 1966 MB seats had saved 1165 lives, and many more have been saved since.

A friendly and forthright managing director who got on well with his workforce because he was actively involved with their work and concerned to save lives, Martin lived close to his work and never took a holiday. Though not a church-goer, he frequently quoted the Bible and was generous. In 1942 he married Muriel Haines. They had two sons and two daughters, to whom he was devoted.

At the end of his work he was well honoured as one of the leaders of the second generation of British aviation entrepreneurs. He received the Wakefield gold medal of the Royal Aeronautical Society in 1951, the Laura Taber Barbour air safety award (USA) in 1958, the Cumberbatch safety trophy in 1959, and the Royal Aero Club gold medal in 1964. Among other honours he was made OBE in 1950, CBE in 1957, and knighted in 1965. He died at his home, Southlands Manor, Denham, on 5 January 1981, survived by his wife.   ROBIN HIGHAM

Sources J. Jewell, *Engineering for life: the story of Martin-Baker* (1979) · *The Times* (6 Jan 1981) · *The Times* (10 Jan 1981) · M. Ginsberg, ed., *Flight International directory of British aviation* (1981) · *Daily Telegraph* (6 Jan 1981) · B. Bedford, 'The man behind Martin-Baker: a tribute', *Flight International* (12 March 1983), 680 · P. Lewis, *The British fighter since 1912* (1974) · J. Martin, 'Ejection seats', *Journal of the Royal Aeronautical Society*, 70 (1966), 276–9 · J. Jewell, 'The life and work of Sir James Martin', *Aerospace* (May 1982), 12–21 · d. cert. · D. Hey, *The man in the hot seat* (1969) · R. Higham, 'Martin, Sir James', *DBB*
Likenesses photograph, repro. in Jewell, *Engineering for life*
Wealth at death £815,493: probate, 22 May 1981, CGPLA Eng. & Wales

Martin, Sir James Ranald (1793–1874), surgeon and medical administrator, was born on 12 May 1793, the son of the Revd Donald Martin of Kilmuir, the Isle of Skye. After the death of his mother, which occurred when he was very young, the family left for Inverness, where Martin attended school at the Royal Academy. His father and maternal grandfather desired that he should pursue a military career, but Martin showed an inclination towards medicine from an early stage and received instruction in pharmacy from two local doctors while still attending school.

In 1813 Martin left Inverness for London, where he became a student at St George's Hospital, studying under the renowned surgeon Sir Everard Home. In 1817, having become a member of the Royal College of Surgeons, he secured a position with the East India Company, and left for India in June of that year. His first appointment was at the Presidency General Hospital in Calcutta, where he treated European civilians, but in 1818 he began military service with the company's army at Fort William. Promoted to the rank of assistant surgeon, Martin soon left Calcutta for Orissa, which was in a state of revolt. Here, he served in various engagements, coping not only with the injuries of war but with high levels of sickness among the troops. Martin also became embroiled in the controversy over flogging in the army, and successfully opposed the cruelties inflicted on Indian troops by some of the more vindictive British officers.

Martin returned to Calcutta in 1819 as first assistant surgeon in the General Hospital but in 1820 resumed military duties, taking charge of the Ramgarh battalion during operations against hill tribes in northern Bengal. It was here that he contracted a fever which was to impair his health for the next ten months, but this experience led him to propose measures to prevent disease in the battalion, including the siting of camps in more elevated and 'healthy' positions. The campaign impressed on him the importance of the environment in the causation of disease and stirred a lifelong interest in medical topography.

By 1821 Martin had returned to Calcutta, where he recommended improvements to the regimental hospital and barracks, as well as other sanitary measures—most of which were adopted by the governor-general, the marquess of Hastings. But fever and arduous campaigning had taken its toll on Martin's health and he was ordered to the island of Mauritius to recuperate.

Martin returned to Calcutta in 1823 but shortly afterwards was to serve in the First Anglo-Burmese War of 1824–6. Immediately after the war Martin married the daughter of Colonel Paton CB, the quartermaster-general of the Bengal army, and settled down in Calcutta where he rapidly established the city's largest civilian practice. A further measure of his standing was his appointment in 1828 to the post of presidency surgeon; a position which he combined with his private practice and the head surgeoncy of the Native Hospital in Calcutta. It was at this institution that he developed a radical—and subsequently widely adopted—cure for hydrocephalus by the injection of diluted tincture of iodine. Martin also continued to interest himself in sanitary matters, and in 1835 won the support of the governor-general William Bentinck in his appeal for more medical topographical reports of Indian stations. Two years later Martin published his own *Medical Topography of Calcutta*, a book which marks a turning point in Anglo-Indian medicine. It was here that Martin began to turn his attention from the effects of climate on health to the sanitary condition of Indian towns. Unlike earlier writers, Martin deplored Indian sanitary habits and drew heavily on James Mill's utilitarian critique of oriental 'superstitions'. The book epitomized a new feeling among British doctors and administrators that western medicine was essential to India's civilization and progress.

Martin continued to practise in Calcutta until 1840, when his deteriorating health forced him to retire to England. He took a house in Grosvenor Street and then at Upper Brook Street, London, where he established a practice among friends and acquaintances from his time in India. He now devoted himself to devising numerous schemes for improving the health of soldiers and was employed as inspector-general of army hospitals and as president of the East India Company's medical board. He also published a series of lectures in *The Lancet* on the diseases of tropical climates and edited the seventh edition of James Johnson's widely respected work, *The Influence of Tropical Climates on European Constitutions*, published in 1856. In 1857, following the Crimean War, Martin was appointed to the royal commission inquiring into the sanitary state of the British army and, in 1859, to a similar body investigating the health of the army in India.

Martin was elected a fellow of the Royal College of Surgeons in 1845, and was made a CB in 1860 and knighted later that year. He is said to have been a handsome man, over 6 feet tall, strongly built, and with a military air and appearance. He became somewhat deaf in old age but discharged his official duties until his death from pneumonia at his home at 37 Upper Brook Street, London, on 27 November 1874.   MARK HARRISON

Sources *Medical Times and Gazette* (5 Dec 1874), 647–8 · V. G. Plarr, *Plarr's Lives of the fellows of the Royal College of Surgeons of England*, rev. D'A. Power, 2 vols. (1930) · J. R. Martin, *Notes on medical topography of Calcutta* (1837) · M. Harrison, *Public health in British India: Anglo-Indian preventive medicine, 1859–1914* (1994)
Likenesses T. H. Maguire, lithograph, 1851, Wellcome L. · E. Edwards, photograph, 1867, Wellcome L. · lithograph, 1874, Wellcome L. · E. Edwards, photograph, NPG; repro. in L. Reeve, ed., *Men of eminence* (1813)
Wealth at death under £35,000: probate, 16 Dec 1874, *CGPLA Eng. & Wales*

Martin, Johan Fredric (1755–1816). *See under* Martin, Elias (1739–1818).

Martin, John (1619–1693), Church of England clergyman, was born on 12 December 1619 in Mere, Wiltshire, the son of John Martin, a schoolmaster. He became a batteler of Trinity College, Oxford, where he matriculated in 1637, moving to Oriel College when he failed to obtain a scholarship. He graduated BA in 1640 and is recorded as having an MA by 1645. Martin was ordained by Bishop Robert Skinner of Oxford on 21 December 1645 and two days later was instituted vicar of Compton Chamberlayne, Wiltshire, by the presentation of Sir John Penruddock, who also granted him the endowed lectureship attached to the church, worth £30 a year.

As a bronze monument placed in the chancel observed (Hoare, 5.87), Martin twice paid the price for his loyalty to the Stuart monarchy. The first occasion came with the civil war and its aftermath. Ejected from his benefice in 1647 for refusing the covenant, he rented a small grazing farm in nearby Tisbury, although there is reason to believe that he was reinstated before the Restoration. Martin was suspected of involvement in the unsuccessful royalist insurrection led by Colonel John Penruddock, the son of his late patron, at Salisbury in 1654, and was briefly imprisoned. After his release he sheltered Penruddock's children and, as trustee for his estate, preserved it from sequestration. Although nothing is known of his marriage, Martin may have been the father of a son John, who was born in Tisbury at this time and who later also became a clergyman. Martin welcomed the Stuart Restoration by printing a sermon, *Hosannah: a Thanksgiving Sermon, June 28th 1660* (1660), dedicated to Bishop Brian Duppa, who had instituted him, the first of four published works. This exhibits his learning and loyalty, seeing the hand of God in the restoration of 'the cornerstone of our Church and State' (p. 32).

Martin had moderate success in his career after the Restoration, and by combining several modest benefices was able to achieve an annual income of at least £120, above the £80 considered to be the minimum for a cleric at that time. In addition to Compton Chamberlayne, in January 1661 he was instituted as rector of Melcombe Horsey, Dorset, by the presentation of Thomas Freke. Bishop Seth Ward collated Martin to the prebend of Yatesbury in Salisbury Cathedral on 22 November 1668, moving him to the more valuable prebend of Preston on 5 October 1677. Martin was also rural dean of Chalke, but refused appointment as canon residentiary of Salisbury. In October 1675 he became chaplain to Charles, earl of Nottingham. His pluralism and failure to appoint a curate led to his presentment in 1674 for non-residence in Compton Chamberlayne. The absence of further complaints suggests that thereafter he fulfilled his promise to the churchwardens to reside and was on good terms with the congregation. Martin's attention to the siting of the pulpit and his decision to bar from communion two men embroiled in a legal dispute testify to his pastoral diligence, as does his publication of *Go in Peace* (1674), a guide for young clerics visiting the sick which he dedicated to Sir George Howe, bt, whom he described as 'a Lover of the clergy'.

Martin suffered for his loyalism a second time when he lost his living in Melcombe Horsey in February 1690 and his prebendal stall in 1691 after he refused to take the oath of allegiance to William and Mary. Bishop Gilbert Burnet allowed him to retain the benefice of Compton Chamberlayne, however, and also claimed that he paid Martin from his own purse the annual income of the prebend from which he had been deprived, citing this example to disprove George Hickes's allegations that the bishop had victimized nonjurors in Salisbury diocese. Burnet recognized that Martin's behaviour resulted from his consistent record of loyalty to the Stuarts rather than from the troublesomeness which he disliked among many of the lesser clergy, reporting that Martin had said that 'he would never join the Schism with the rest of the Non-Jurors, whose Principles and Practices … he detested' (Burnet, 62–3). Burnet perhaps also approved of Martin's emphasis upon pastoral visits and collation of scriptural passages in *Go in Peace*. John Martin died on 3 November 1693 in Compton Chamberlayne, where he was buried.

DONALD A. SPAETH

Sources Wood, *Ath. Oxon.*, new edn, 4.387–90 • churchwardens' presentments, diocese of Salisbury, 1674, Wilts. & Swindon RO, D1/54/6/4, fol. 11 • G. Burnet, *Reflections upon a pamphlet, entituled, 'Some discourses upon Dr Burnet and Dr Tillotson, occasioned by the late funeral-sermon of the former upon the later'* (1696) • Foster, *Alum. Oxon.* • R. C. Hoare, *The history of modern Wiltshire*, 4 (1822), 64–5; 5 (1844), 87 • *DNB* • bishops' registers, diocese of Salisbury, Wilts. & Swindon RO, D1/1/22 • S. Ward, bishop of Salisbury, 'Liber notitiae generalis', Wilts. & Swindon RO, D1/27/1/1 • J. Ecton, *Liber valorum et decimarum* (1711) • J. Hutchins, *The history and antiquities of the county of Dorset*, 2 vols. (1774) • *A compleat collection of the works of the reverend and learned John Kettlewell, B.D.*, 2 vols. (1719) • [G. Hickes], *Some discourses upon Dr. Burnet and Dr. Tillotson, occasioned by the late funeral sermon of the former upon the latter* (1695)

Martin, John (*bap.* 1692, *d.* 1767). *See under* Martin family (*per. c.*1700–1832).

Martin, John (1741–1820), Particular Baptist minister, was born at Spalding, Lincolnshire, on 15 March 1741, the son of John Martin (*d.* 1767), publican and grazier, and Mary King (*d.* 1756). Partly self-taught, he was also educated at school in Gosberton, and afterwards at Stamford, under Dr Newark. Soon after his mother's death in 1756 he went as office boy to an attorney at Holbeach, but developed religious melancholy, and in 1760 moved to London to attend Dr John Gill's meeting-house. On 11 July 1761 he married Elizabeth Jessup (*d.* 1765), daughter of a farmer near Sleaford.

In 1763 Martin became convinced of 'the duty of believers' baptism' and published a pamphlet, suggested partly by his work in London as a watch-finisher, entitled *Mechanicus and Flavens, or, The Watch Spiritualised*. Soon afterwards he was baptized by the Revd Mr Clark in a garden at Blunham, afterwards joining the church at Gamlingay, Bedfordshire. His first charge as a minister was with the Independent congregation in Kimbolton, Huntingdonshire (1764–5), but in 1766 he was ordained to the pastorate of the Particular Baptist congregation in Shepshed, Leicestershire. Within the forward-looking Northamptonshire Association, to which Shepshed was affiliated, Martin promoted itinerancy and village preaching.

In 1773 Martin surprisingly was called to the pastorate of the deeply split church in Grafton Street, Piccadilly, London; three years earlier he had refused to preach to them because of what he took to be their shameful treatment of their ageing minister, William Anderson. He was ordained to the pastorate in March 1774 with Benjamin Wallin, Abraham Booth, and John Macgowan all sharing in the service. One of the occasional hearers during this Grafton Street pastorate was Lord George Gordon of riot fame, who failed to persuade Martin to take office in the Protestant Association. Notwithstanding a serious secession in 1776, Martin built up the remaining congregation, for whom a new chapel in Keppel Street, Bloomsbury, was built in 1795, mainly at the expense of William Ashlin, one of Martin's wealthy deacons, who had earlier seceded from the Eagle Street congregation because of dissatisfaction with the ministry of Thomas Hopkins.

Martin's approach to predestination and the freedom of the human will changed over time. In the 1770s, during his Shepshed pastorate, Andrew Fuller found him commending Jonathan Edwards and castigating the likes of John Gill and John Brine, notwithstanding the fact that he had worshipped with Gill's congregation in London in 1760. Indeed, Martin's Association letter of 1770 has been noted as a key document in concluding the period of the dominance of hyper-Calvinism, with its encouragement of all to approach Christ, among English Baptists. This evangelical stance Martin confirmed in his 1775 sermon on Romans 10: 3, published under the title *The Rock of Offence*, which argued that human failure to submit to the righteousness of God was occasioned by 'want of will and want of love' (Fuller, title-page). His arguments in this sermon were an influence prompting Andrew Fuller to move beyond traditional Calvinist categories in his thinking, while Martin appears to have moved in the opposite direction. This was especially seen in his London years, when Martin showed himself very much more conservative, in theology as in politics, and became a foremost opponent of 'Fullerism', that system of evangelical Calvinism that Fuller developed in the light of what Jonathan Edwards had achieved in the USA and which lay behind the launching of the modern missionary movement. This Martin did in a printed debate with Fuller in the years 1789–91: his *Thoughts on the Duty of Man Relative to Faith in Jesus Christ* provoked Fuller to reply in *Remarks on Mr Martin's Publication*, which took the form of five letters to a friend.

Apart from theological issues Martin easily became isolated because of his conservative political positions. First, at a meeting of the General Body of Dissenting Ministers in December 1789 he both spoke in favour of the Test and Corporation Acts and insulted a young Presbyterian minister who adopted the opposite stance. Samuel Stennett, from the chair, called upon Martin to apologize, but he refused and left the meeting. Although Martin's action caused him to lose support among his fellow dissenters, he found favour with the government. After Stennett's death in 1795, Martin in 1797 received a warrant from the government to succeed him in distributing the *regium donum*, though it was not long before he was in conflict with his fellow trustees about both process and product, a dispute that rumbled on from 1798 until 1806, when Martin's warrant was finally withdrawn. The third area of dispute was Martin's sermon, preached on a Sunday evening of January 1798 in Broad Street Chapel. There he alleged, with little sensitivity, that were the French to land in Britain many dissenters would 'unite to encourage the French and distress this country' (Ivimey, 4.77). Writing on behalf of the Baptist Board, Abraham Booth and other Baptist ministers begged Martin in vain not to publish the address, which ran to several editions. Martin not only confirmed his allegation but sought to justify his view, arguing 'That Dissenters are not less contaminated with French principles than other people appeared to be incontrovertible … can you doubt whether some of them … have wished to plant what they call the Tree of Liberty in Great Britain?' (ibid., 4.79). The managers of the evening sermon had little option but to exclude him as unfit to give further instruction under their patronage. The Baptist Board also judged Martin's castigation of his fellow dissenters untrue and 'highly calumnious' (ibid., 4.81), and expelled him from their counsels. Martin's 'exaggerated and unjust representation' (ibid., 4.81) was deemed not only unwise but unkind, and against the studied determination of the leaders of the Three Denominations to demonstrate dissenting loyalty by suggesting that many of their number were 'desirous of assisting the French Revolutionists to overthrow the monarchy and constitution of their country' (ibid., 4.81). The Baptist historian Joseph Ivimey seems to suggest that Martin's lack of judgement in part lay in failing to distinguish between dissenters' welcome to the outbreak of the revolution and what was appropriate once the revolution had developed its particular characteristics, especially when the revolutionary regime moved into conflict with neighbouring countries.

On 13 March 1798 Martin was expelled from the London Baptist Board; attempts to effect a reconciliation between Martin and his brethren as late as 1805 proved ineffectual. His sermon of 1798 led to a large secession from his chapel, but he continued to preach with unabated vigour to those remaining until April 1814, when 'a stroke of palsy' destroyed his intelligence, causing his withdrawal from the ministry. He survived a further six years until his death in London on 23 April 1820; he was buried in Bunhill Fields.   J. H. Y. BRIGGS

Sources J. Martin, *Some account of the life and writings of the Rev John Martin* (1797) • A. Fuller, *Remarks on Mr Martin's publication, entitled 'Thoughts on the duty of man relative to faith in Jesus Christ'* [n.d.] • J. Ivimey, *A history of the English Baptists*, 4 vols. (1811–30), vol. 4, esp. pp. 77–82, 342–50 • J. E. Bradley, *Religion, revolution and English radicalism* (1990) • E. F. Clipsham, 'Andrew Fuller and Fullerism: a study in evangelical Calvinism', *Baptist Quarterly*, 20 (1963–4), 214–25, esp. 223; 268–76, esp. 268 • E. A. Payne, 'Andrew Booth, 1734–1806', *Baptist Quarterly*, 26 (1975–6), 28–42 • *DNB*
Likenesses J. Linnell, etching, pubd 1813, BM, NPG

Martin, John (1774–1832). *See under* Martin family (*per. c.*1700–1832).

Martin, John (1783–1855), botanist and hand-loom weaver, was born on 17 November 1783 in Tyldesley, Lancashire, the son of a poor shopkeeper and farmer. He lived with his parents, of whom little is known, until about 1802, during which time he received some schooling and began weaving. When he was fifteen he became intensely religious, advocating voluntary poverty. None the less, when his father began losing property to creditors, Martin decided to leave home. This decision was possibly reinforced by his 'intimacy' with Betty Entwistle (d. 1825), which resulted in marriage on 18 May 1802. Three children by 1807 completed their family. In 1813 they suffered extreme poverty, forcing Martin to suspend payments to the Calvinist chapel he regularly attended. The minister's consequent contempt led Martin to abandon organized religion and turn instead to nature.

Martin subsequently structured his life around dictums from the late eighteenth-century radical text, Comte de Volney's *Law of Nature*: 'Preserve thyself, instruct thyself, moderate thyself; live for thy fellow-creatures, in order that they may live for thee'. He abstained from meat and alcohol, engaged in self-education, and supported communal efforts to acquire knowledge. His opinions on character formation, women, and marriage also suggest he was a follower of Robert Owen. However, while acknowledging that marriage had no foundation in nature, after becoming a widower in 1825 he married Alice Hurst, on 25 September 1826. She had no children and died in 1841.

Martin's study of nature was most clearly expressed in his pursuit of 'scientific botany' from 1817. A relative who belonged to the Tyldesley Botanical Society, part of the network of botanical meetings and societies established in pubs by working men, provided books from the society's library. Martin became a member in 1818 and devoted himself to studying wild plants, although he also appreciated the therapeutic effects of gardening. His botanical reputation resulted from his discoveries in and knowledge of the taxonomically challenging mosses and sedges, despite being blind in one eye following an accident while haymaking. His skill and precision were admired, although the gentleman botanist William Wilson, shocked by the disorder of Martin's cottage, dissuaded William Jackson Hooker from employing Martin as his herbarium assistant in 1831. Nevertheless, Martin continued to botanize with Wilson as well as artisans such as Richard Buxton. Fiercely independent, he showed little deference to botanical authorities when his own observation convinced him they were wrong, and refused to be defensive about his relative lack of education. The black eyepatch he wore was thought by some to heighten his intellectual appearance.

Martin remained a hand-loom weaver his entire life but from 1805 supplemented his income by serving as secretary to several friendly societies. Although continuing to labour, from 1844 he received £8 a year from Edward William Binney's fund for the relief and encouragement of scientific men in humble life. By 1851, he was living at 111 Lemon Street, Tyldesley, with his twelve-year-old grandson who was a bricklayer. He died in Tyldesley on 13 August 1855 after suffering what was probably a stroke earlier in the year. ANNE SECORD

Sources 'Death of a botanist in humble life', *Manchester Guardian* (16 Aug 1855) · 'Letter of a Lancashire botanist in humble life', *Manchester Guardian* (17 Aug 1855) · A. Secord, 'Science in the pub: artisan botanists in early nineteenth-century Lancashire', *History of Science*, 32 (1994), 269–315 · A. Secord, 'Corresponding interests: artisans and gentlemen in nineteenth-century natural history', *British Journal for the History of Science*, 27 (1994), 383–408 · W. J. Hooker, *British flora*, 2 (1833), 12 · J. B. Wood, 'New locality for *Carex axillaris*', *Phytologist*, 1 (1842), 199 · R. Buxton, *A botanical guide to the flowering plants, ferns, mosses, and algae, found indigenous within sixteen miles of Manchester* (1849), x · J. Buckley, *Chronological history of Tyldesley* (1878), 16–18 · E. W. Binney, *A few remarks respecting Mr. R. Buxton, the author of 'The Manchester Botanical Guide'* (1863), 6 · W. Wilson, letter to W. J. Hooker, 15 Oct 1831, Royal Collection, Directors' correspondence, vol. 6, letter 347 · parish register, St Mary's, Leigh, Man. CL, Manchester Archives and Local Studies, MF 418 [marriage]
Archives Man. CL, W. E. A. Axon MSS, letter [copy] · NL Wales, William Wilson corresp., letter
Wealth at death supported by charitable donations only

Martin, John (1789–1854), artist, was born on 19 July 1789 at East Land Ends, Haydon Bridge, Northumberland, the thirteenth and youngest child (only five of whom, one of them a daughter, survived childhood) of (William) Fenwick Martin, tanner, and his wife, Isabella, daughter of Richard Thompson of Lowland's End, Haydon Bridge. His brothers included Jonathan *Martin (1782–1838), arsonist, and the eccentric and self-proclaimed philosopher William *Martin (1772–1851).

Early works After apprenticeship to a coach-painter in Newcastle upon Tyne, Martin worked for a china painter, Boniface Musso, whom he accompanied to London in 1805. There he made a living painting china and glass. In 1809 he married Susan Garnett. Martin's art derived from the conventions of decorative embellishment; his subject matter, initially, was 'classical' landscape: Claudian topography with bystanders in togas. He first exhibited at the Royal Academy in 1811 (*Landscape Composition*) but first made an impact the following year with *Sadak in Search of the Waters of Oblivion* (St Louis Art Museum, Missouri), a painting remarkable for its juxtaposed incandescence and void, the combination that was to be Martin's speciality for the rest of his career.

Martin's Sadak slipping from a rocky shelf, about to plunge feet first into nothingness, thereby purging himself of memories, is a key image of the Romantic sublime. Prototype that he was, Sadak was the forerunner of other

John Martin (1789–1854), by Henry Warren, exh. RA 1839

heroes mostly destined to meet eye-catching fates, notably Cadmus the dragon slayer, Joshua in *Joshua Commanding the Sun to Stand Still* (United Grand Lodge of England, London) and the bard, last of his race, high on a mountain, cursing the English army invading Wales.

In 1817, the year of *The Bard* (Laing Art Gallery, Newcastle upon Tyne), Martin was appointed drawing master and historical landscape painter to the prince regent's daughter, Princess Charlotte, and her husband Prince Leopold of Saxe-Coburg-Saalfeld, an imposing title that could have carried some weight had the princess not died in childbirth that year. Martin looked instead to the Royal Academy for advancement or alternatively to the British Institution where, in 1817, he was awarded a £100 premium for his *Joshua*. With that encouragement, his aims as a painter were resolved: he would develop a factually spectacular epic genre involving vastness and multiplicity, with history relaxed into fiction or elaborated into legend. He began to prosper and in 1818 bought a house, 30 Allsop's Buildings, in the New Road, London.

The Fall of Babylon (priv. coll.), exhibited in 1819 at the British Institution, was a panorama painting reduced to respectable (academy-worthy) proportions. Cycloramic in its vasty architecture and wide horizons, it shows diminutive troops swarming past the Tower of Babel and across the Euphrates to the ramparts and hanging gardens of the palace where the impious Belshazzar reigns. Moments later, in *Belshazzar's Feast* (1820; priv. coll.), panic sets in as God's writing flares on the wall of the immense banqueting hall. This sequel won Martin a £200 premium at the Royal Academy exhibition of 1821. What Charles Lamb in his 'Essay on the barrenness of the imaginative faculty in the production of modern art' in *Last Essays of Elia* (1833) described as a huddle of vulgar consternation proved amazing enough to attract a paying public when it went on show in a shop in the Strand. In the accompanying leaflet biblical and archaeological sources for the composite style of architecture—part Egyptian, part Indian—were cited. Martin the showman recognized the allure of 'authenticity' while relying on the pull of crude perspectives. As the German critic G. F. Waagen said, such paintings as *Belshazzar* 'unite in a high degree the qualities which the English require above all in a work of art—effect, a powerful invention, and topographical historical truth' (G. F. Waagen, *Works of Art and Artists in England*, 1838, 2.162).

Major works As he attained the height of his celebrity, Martin did all he could to emphasize the educational value of his pictorial spectacles. As in panoramas of the battle of the Nile, ancient Rome, and ruined Pompeii, flawless workmanship and top lighting were key elements. And the larger the painting the greater its capacity to overwhelm. *The Destruction of Herculaneum and Pompeii* of 1822 was itself damaged in a flood at the Tate Gallery in 1929; the surviving fragment is sufficient to indicate that it did not have quite the impact of *Belshazzar*.

Martin was never accepted as a serious painter by the art establishment as constituted by the Royal Academy. He resolved to appeal over the academy's head, so to speak, to a broader public, and make a living by producing print versions of his successful paintings. Eventually, as John Constable remarked, Martin 'looked at the Royal Academy from the Plains of Nineveh, from the Destruction of Babylon' (Pendered, 180): vantage points attained largely on the strength of his printmaking.

Mezzotint is a medium peculiarly suited to Manichaean fantasies: the black void of the prepared plate, blackness scraped away to create forms and highlights. *Paradise Lost*, illustrated in two sets of mezzotints for the publisher Septimus Prowett in 1825–7, was ideal material for Martin, who echoed Milton's solemnity while opening out his cadences in the imagery of groves and chases bathed in silvery light and an underworld where fires tongue the darkness and bridges span nothingness and Satan's armies infest the gloom. In mezzotint Martin's vision thrived. His subjects, biblical and Miltonic, lent themselves to vast generalizations dotted with microscopic particulars. *The Seventh Plague of Egypt* (1823; Boston Museum of Fine Arts) and *The Expulsion* (c.1825; Laing Art Gallery, Newcastle upon Tyne) translated readily from text to painting to engraving.

Stressing what he conceived to be the reality underpinning myth, or revealed religion, Martin designed *The Deluge* (1826; priv. coll.; mezzotint 1828) on a basis of contemporary theory. Baron Cuvier, the geologist, visited his studio while he was working on the composition and, according to Martin, approved his presentation of the event. *The Fall of Nineveh* (1828; mezzotint 1829) was his largest and grandest Old Testament spectacular with embankments breached along the Tigris and the emperor Sardanapalus preparing a funeral pyre of Babel proportions. Martin showed the painting in the Brussels Salon in 1833. It remained unsold.

Schemes for metropolitan improvement Like Jericho, Babylon, Herculaneum, and Thebes before it, Martin's Nineveh was an awful example to Londoners of what could befall them. In the 1820s an expanding London, the new Babylon as it was often referred to, lacked infrastructure to a frightening degree. The Thames, tidal and without river walls, was both water supply and sewer. Cholera broke out in 1830. From the late 1820s onwards Martin devoted much of his time and energy to schemes for metropolitan improvement. He designed embankments to prevent the Thames flooding, to contain sewers and (grander even than anything the builders of his Nineveh had achieved) to accommodate also an underground railway system. Martin's inventive proposals included a safety lamp for coalminers, double hulls for shipping, and coastal warning lights. He proposed glazed shopping malls and uninterrupted green spaces extending from Kensington to Whitehall. Such schemes chimed in with the themes of his paintings both in relation to disasters, impending or witnessed, and in the similarities of approach: the picturesque treatment of crisis and a punctilious attention to detail.

None of Martin's schemes was given more than a polite hearing at the time, though in time virtually all of them were realized by others. Nor was his campaign for copyright protection immediately successful. His prints were pirated in Europe and the United States and while these helped spread his reputation their relative crudity encouraged the view that he was a clumsy eccentric, a view reinforced by association in 1829 when his brother Jonathan set fire to York Minster on religious grounds and was committed to Bethlem Hospital as a criminal lunatic. Another brother, William, wandered the streets of Newcastle upon Tyne selling pamphlets on subjects derived for the most part from John Martin's projects, sincerely burlesquing his ideas on safety lamps and perpetual motion machines.

Martin's plans were a distraction at a time when his sort of sublimity was going out of fashion. His mezzotint *Illustrations of the Bible* issued in parts in 1831–5 was a failure. Having cried woe as a painter and as a campaigning visionary, he was now caught up in his own destruction. His plans cost him, a friend estimated, £10,000; by 1837 he faced bankruptcy.

By all accounts lively and enthusiastic, Martin was—according to his friend Sergeant Ralph Thomas—'a deist in religion, a radical reformer in politics' (Pendered, 176). He was apt to hiss when the national anthem was played. Having lived in style for twenty years, he had to cut back. Large biblical paintings and mezzotints (*The Crucifixion*, *The Death of the First-Born*) no longer appealed; he turned to painting pretty watercolour views of the countryside around London.

Later works Yet there remained seams of progressive satisfaction. In 1834 Martin illustrated for the palaeontologist

Gideon Mantell *The Country of the Iguanadon*, realizing, from fossil bones, an artist's impression of extinct species. It served as the frontispiece to Mantell's *Wonders of Geology* (2 vols., 1838). Imagining himself, or John Martin, as 'some higher intelligence from another sphere', Mantell described looking down on earth and seeing 'winged reptiles of strange forms', then after thousands of centuries returning to see the ocean gone and dry land again appearing (Mantell, 1.455). 'Above the cliffs a beautiful city appeared; with its palaces, its temples, and its thousand edifices' (ibid.). Mantell drew on Martin as Martin drew on Mantell: what had begun with *Cadmus* and Joshua's Jericho had become a new reading of history.

The Coronation of Queen Victoria (1838; Tate Collection) was a bid by Martin to attract patrons, in the shape of the members of the nobility invited to his studio to sit for the tiny portrait heads involved. He succeeded in impressing the prince consort who, in 1840, encouraged him to return to large-scale painting by reverting to an old theme. *The Eve of the Deluge* (Royal Collection), *The Deluge* (1834; Yale U. CBA), and *The Assuaging of the Waters* (Fine Art Museums of San Francisco) restated his themes in a more richly worked manner. He also painted *Pandemonium* (1841; Forbes Collection, New York) and *The Celestial City and Rivers of Bliss* from *Paradise Lost* again, with a view to re-establishing himself as a painter first and foremost. For the rest of his life he exhibited every year at the Royal Academy.

Martin's obsessions persisted. He addressed the theme of the elimination of the human species. He had been friendly with William Godwin, father of Mary Shelley whose novel *The Last Man* prompted him to produce a drawing of the last man as a Christ figure on a headland surrounded by corpses: potential fossils. A large version (Walker Art Gallery, Liverpool), was exhibited at the Royal Academy in 1850.

In 1848 Martin moved to an apartment in Lindsay House by Battersea Bridge, a short distance downriver from 6 Davis Place, where Turner lived. There, having relinquished his directorship of the Metropolitan Sewage Manure Company—another unsuccessful venture—he planned *The Last Judgement*, a painting by himself and an engraving after it by Charles Mottram. Influenced by James Barry's *Elysium, or, The State of Final Retribution* at the Society of Arts, he planted the heads and shoulders of great artists, thinkers, and philosophers on green slopes, watching as popes, emperors, lords, and a power-mad rabble, featuring a trainload of worldly fools, slide into the pit of oblivion. He then turned to utter destruction, first with *The Destruction of Sodom and Gomorrah* (1852; Laing Art Gallery, Newcastle upon Tyne), then with one of a pair of pictures to flank *The Last Judgement: The Great Day of his Wrath* (1852), in which the cities of Sodom and Gomorrah, Babylon, Nineveh, Rome, and London have risen into the air among the exploding mountains, poised to fall into the void, snuffing out gesticulating mankind. In the other he presented his vision of paradise regained in *The Plains of Heaven* (1853; all three paintings are in the Tate Collection), where angels waft over rose bushes and lawns sloping

towards blue seas and, looming over all, the white domes of the heavenly Jerusalem.

Death and reputation Martin died at 4 Finch Road, Douglas, Isle of Man, on 17 February 1854 and was buried at Kirk Braddan cemetery, Douglas. Of his children his eldest son Alfred, who made a number of mezzotints for his father, became chief superintendent of income tax in Ireland; Charles was a portrait painter; Leopold Charles *Martin wrote a memoir of Martin and worked in the Stationery Office; Jessie Martin married Joseph Bonomi, who after her death in 1859 became curator of Sir John Soane's Museum, where another daughter, Isabella, served as his assistant.

An artist of poetic coincidence and stark contrasts, Martin invariably aimed to deluge the senses, to inspire wonder, to edify and amaze. His hold on the popular imagination was unparalleled in his day; as a showman painter—taking the sublime to the general public of the 1820s—he was both proficient and inventive. He was at best an adroit painter. As a printmaker he was altogether more formidable in that he worked in mezzotint, embellishing the imagery through successive revisions of the plate and printing with great subtlety using different mixes of inks to get the effects he wanted. His *Deluge* and his *Bridge over Chaos* are masterpieces of the medium and among the most astonishing images of the era. Martin's reputation, low when he died, declined steadily thereafter. The *Last Judgement* triptych was exhibited as a special attraction for some years and toured the United States. The paintings hung for a while in Alexandra Palace in north London. Oblivion intervened: in 1935 they were sold at auction for just under £7. *The Last Judgement* itself was cut into three strips and served as a fire screen; restored and reunited the three paintings, Martin's finale, are now in the Tate collection. Since the publication of Thomas Balston's biography of Martin in 1947 his work has been taken seriously enough for the epithet 'mad' to be dropped. Long before then, in D. W. Griffith's film *Intolerance* (1916), the mezzotint of *Belshazzar's Feast* was the basis of the enormous Babylon set. Martin's imaginative projections translated readily into cinematic terms. His epic vision was the link between panorama and cinema.

Like Milton's Adam, or Satan, the solitary protagonists of so many of his compositions, John Martin stood tall in the face of stupendous failures, not only in his enlightened schemes for urban improvement but in his determination to organize natural disasters into magnificent spectacles. First man, last man—or last woman—out of Gomorrah: in every appalling circumstance, be it eclipse or pestilence, earthquake or invasion, Martin conjured wonders out of the void.   WILLIAM FEAVER

Sources W. Feaver, *The art of John Martin* (1975) · J. D. Wees and M. Campbell, *Darkness visible: the prints of John Martin* (1986) · T. Balston, *John Martin, 1789–1854: his life and works* (1947) · J. Martin, 'Autobiographical notes', *The Athenaeum* (14 June 1834), 459 · 'A memoir of John Martin', *European Magazine and London Review*, 82 (1822), 195–7 · L. Martin, 'Reminiscences of John Martin', *Newcastle Weekly Chronicle* (Jan–April 1889) · will, PROB 11/2212, fol. 254r–v · M. L. Pendered, *John Martin: his life and times* (1923) · M. C. Stewart, *John Martin: visions of the biblical flood* (1997) [exhibition catalogue, Fine

Arts Museum of San Francisco and Yale U. CBA] · H. J. M. Hanley, M. Cooper, and S. Morris, 'The mysterious Septimus Prowett', *British Art Journal*, 2/1 (2000–01), 20–25

Likenesses C. R. Leslie, pencil, chalk, and pen-and-ink drawing, 1822, BM · W. Brockedon, chalk drawing, 1826, NPG · Sear & Co., stipple, pubd 1828, BM · H. Warren, oils, exh. RA 1839, NPG [*see illus.*] · C. Martin, drawing, 1854, Laing Art Gallery, Newcastle upon Tyne · C. Martin, portrait, 1854, Laing Art Gallery, Newcastle upon Tyne · J. Thomson, stipple (after W. Derby), BM, NPG; repro. in *European Magazine and London Review* · C. Vogel, drawing, Staatliche Kunstsammlungen, Dresden, Küpferstichkabinett · C. Wagstaff, print (after T. Wageman), BM, NPG; repro. in *Magazine of the Fine Arts*, 4 (1834)

Wealth at death under £4000: will, PRO, PROB 11/2212, fol. 254r–v

Martin, John (1789–1869), meteorologist, practised for some time as a physician in London. He is better known as editor of *An account of the natives of the Tonga Islands, in the south Pacific Ocean, with an original grammar and vocabulary of their language. Compiled and arranged from the extensive communications of Mr William Mariner, several years resident in those islands* (2 vols., 1817), reprinted in 1827 as volumes 13 and 14 of *Constable's Miscellany*. A French translation appeared in Paris in 1817; a German translation was published in Weimar in 1819 and an American edition at Boston in 1820.

William Mariner had been held in friendly captivity on the islands from 1806 until 1810. His experiences were generally corroborated by a sailor named Jeremiah Higgins, who had accompanied Mariner but who was able to leave there thirteen months before Mariner's departure.

Little is known of Martin's subsequent career. Letters he wrote to his publisher, John Murray, during the period 1815–26, preserved in the firm's archives, deal mainly with the preparation and publication of Mariner's *Tonga Islands*. By April 1823 Martin was in financial straits and declared to Murray his intention of giving a course of lectures in London on 'The inductive method of philosophy'. It is doubtful whether any lectures were given, as, in the following month, he signed the register as a witness to a marriage in Lisbon. In his letter of 20 April he wrote that friends had suggested he should sell *Tonga Islands* to Constable for their *Miscellany* and he asked Murray for his opinion. Murray must have agreed for, as already noted, this course was followed. Martin's stay in Lisbon was not a long one. In November 1825 he was committed to the Fleet prison for debt where he remained for six months. Shortly before his release he wrote to Murray thanking him for his recommendation to the Literary Fund Society for some financial help, and also for an unsolicited gift of £5. He returned to Portugal and in November 1844 he signed the minutes of a meeting of the Association of Factors, a body of British merchants.

Martin's meteorological investigations were sent, in later life, to *The Athenaeum*, which noted:

> In our own pages we have had occasion to record his labours during the last twenty years in the observation of atmospherical phenomena, especially with reference to pressure, temperature, and moisture. Martin laid down meteorological charts representing the varying aspects of months, seasons, and years from daily observation. He also

made careful observation with reference to ozone, as well as on the characteristics and circumstances affecting cholera and yellow fever. These labours are the more commendable as the work of an old man, executed in different colours with scrupulous neatness, and mostly at night after the fatigue of practice. (*The Athenaeum*, 7 Aug 1869)

In the census of May 1861 Martin was listed among the British residents in Lisbon, where he died on 8 July 1869.

GORDON GOODWIN, *rev.* DENIS J. MCCULLOCH

Sources W. Mariner, *An account of the natives of the Tonga Islands*, ed. J. Martin, 2nd edn, 2 vols. (1818) · *Johnstone's London commercial guide and street directory* (1817) · Dr Martin's letters to John Murray, London 1815–26, John Murray, London, archives · private information (2004) · Extracts from commitment books and from discharges, Kings Bench Prison, PRO, PRIS 4/37; PRIS 7/45 · *The Athenaeum* (7 Aug 1869), 181 · *N&Q*, 4th ser., 8 (1871), 305, 407

Likenesses photograph, Wellcome L.

Martin, John (1791–1855), bibliographer, was born on 16 September 1791 in London, the son of John Martin of 112 Mount Street, Grosvenor Square. He was apprenticed on 1 October 1805 to William Ginger, a Westminster bookseller, but soon afterwards turned over on 6 May 1806 to John Hatchard of Piccadilly, the publisher and bookseller with whom he served the remainder of his apprenticeship. He gained his freedom of the Stationers' Company on 6 October 1812. By 1815 he had opened his own bookshop at 23 Holles Street, Cavendish Square, but about 1819 entered into partnership with John Rodwell at 46 New Bond Street. He retired from business in 1826, but continued his bibliographical pursuits. He edited Gray's 'Bard' (1837) and Gray's 'Elegy' (1836, 1839, and 1854) with illustrations from drawings by the Hon. Mrs John Talbot, and *The Seven Ages of Shakespeare* (1840 and 1848), illustrated with wood-engravings. The production of these and other books illustrated by George Cruikshank, George Cattermole, and William Mulready was the means of introducing him to the leading artists of the day. He was a good friend of John Constable and a keen promoter of the use of original wood-engraving in book illustration. For many years, until 1845, he acted as secretary to the Artists' Benevolent Fund.

In 1834 Martin published his important and still useful *Bibliographical Catalogue of Books Privately Printed*, a second edition of which was issued in 1854. The first edition contains an account of private presses and book clubs, which Martin omitted from the second edition, but at the time of his death he was preparing a separate volume, which was to contain this portion of the first edition with additions. His correspondence of 1828–55 about privately printed books is now in the British Library.

Following the death of his wife, Elizabeth, in 1836 Martin was appointed librarian to the duke of Bedford at Woburn Abbey. For the rest of his life he lived at Froxfield, in the parish of Eversholt, near Woburn, in a house previously occupied by the writer J. H. Wiffen. Between 1845 and 1854 he visited nearly every church in Bedfordshire, and wrote a description of each in a series of articles which appeared over the pseudonym W. A. (for Woburn Abbey) in the *Bedford Times* and *Northampton Mercury*; the full text of each article is being reprinted in three volumes

953   MARTIN, JOHN

by the Bedfordshire Historical Record Society. Martin's articles promoted Tractarian ideals, drawing attention to widespread neglect and abuses in church worship and furnishings. Controversial and challenging, the series had a profound influence on churchmen in the county. Martin also played an active part in the local community, soliciting funds for a new school at Eversholt through the *Gentleman's Magazine* in April 1841.

Martin also wrote a *History and Description of Woburn and its Abbey* (1845), a shortened and rearranged version of J. D. Parry's book published in 1831. At the request of Lord John Russell he compiled an *Enquiry into the authority for a statement in Echard's History of England regarding William, Lord Russell*, which was printed for private circulation in 1852 and published in 1856. It refuted the assertion that Lord Russell opposed the mitigation of the punishment of Viscount Stafford for high treason when sheriffs Bethel and Cornish presented their petition in the House of Commons on 23 December 1680. Martin also furnished some notes to Lord John Russell's edition of the *Letters* of Rachel, Lady Russell (1853), and in 1855 he published a translation of Guizot's essay on *The Married Life of Rachel, Lady Russell*. He left unfinished an edition of the *Letters of the Earl of Chatham to his Nephew*. He was a fellow of both the Society of Antiquaries and the Linnean Society.

Martin died on 30 December 1855 at Froxfield, and was buried in Eversholt churchyard on 4 January 1856. Three of his six children survived him. His eldest son, John Edward Martin (*d.* 1893), became sub-librarian and afterwards librarian to the Inner Temple. In 1899 a stained glass window in memory of John Martin was put up by his grandchildren in the south aisle of Eversholt church.

GORDON GOODWIN, rev. CHRIS PICKFORD

Sources GM, 2nd ser., 45 (1856), 317 · *London Directory* (1814–36) · apprenticeship records, 1805–12, Stationers' Hall, London, Stationers' Company Archives · C. Pickford, ed., *Bedfordshire churches in the nineteenth century*, 1, Bedfordshire Historical RS, 73 (1994), 14–23 · census returns for Froxfield, Eversholt, Bedfordshire, 1841, 1851 · parish register (burial), Eversholt, 4 Jan 1856 · *Bedford Times* (5 Jan 1856) · IGI [London and Middlesex] · GM, 2nd ser., 1 (1834), 62–4 · will, PRO, PROB 11/2225, sig. 48 [made 6 Feb 1843, proved 21 Jan 1856] · GM, 2nd ser., 15 (1841), 381 · *The Times* (26 July 1893)

Archives BL, corresp., Add. MSS 37965–37967 | Bodl. Oxf., corresp. with Sir Thomas Phillipps · U. Edin. L., letters to David Laing · Woburn Abbey, Bedford estate MSS

Martin, John (1812–1875), Young Irelander and politician, was born at Loughorne, in the parish of Donaghmore, near Newry, co. Down, on 8 September 1812. He was the second of nine children of Samuel Martin (*d.* 1831), a gentleman farmer and linen manufacturer, and his wife, Jane, *née* Harshaw (*d.* 1847). Like his parents, he was a Presbyterian throughout his life. He was educated at Dr Henderson's school at Newry, where he first met his lifelong friend John Mitchel, and subsequently at Trinity College, Dublin, where he graduated BA in the summer of 1834. He then began to study medicine, but abandoned his course before taking a medical degree because his uncle, also called John Martin, died in 1835, leaving him a small property at Loughorne, with an annual income of £400. He returned to Loughorne and the gentleman farmer and

John Martin (1812–1875), by Henry O'Neill, pubd 1848 (after Leon Gluckman)

landlord was well liked among his tenants. In 1839 he travelled in America, and in 1841 visited the continent of Europe.

Martin became a member of the Repeal Association in 1844 and advocated a regular publication of accounts, but without effect. In 1846 he joined the secession of the Young Ireland party, and was expelled from the Repeal Association, having been refused a hearing in Conciliation Hall. He subsequently took a prominent part in the meetings of the Irish Confederation, and occasionally wrote for *The Nation*, mainly on agriculture. However, he continued to reside in Loughorne, because he was strongly attached to his area and the local community. He was a sincere, thoughtful, straightforward, and gentle person with a keen sense of humour. Together with Mitchel, he tried to convince Irish protestants of the benefits of an Irish parliament, and to recruit Ulster people into the Irish Confederation. When Mitchel established his own paper, the *United Irishman*, in February 1848 Martin became a contributor to it, although the two friends did not always hold the same political views. Three weeks after the arrest of Mitchel and the seizure of his paper Martin reoccupied his friend's offices, and on 24 June 1848 issued from them the *Irish Felon*, a 'successor to the *United Irishman*', with the avowed purpose of promoting the same principles which had been advocated in his friend's newspaper. A warrant for his arrest was issued and on 8 July Martin, who had kept out of the way until the adjournment of the commission which had been sitting in Dublin, surrendered himself to the police. From Newgate prison he wrote the letter which appeared, signed with his initials, in the fifth and last number of the *Irish Felon* (22 July 1848), in which he exhorted the people to keep their arms in spite of the proclamation, and declared that the work of overthrowing the English dominion in Ireland 'must be done at any risk, at any cost, at any sacrifice'. On 14 August he was indicted for treason at the commission court in Green Street, Dublin. He was defended by Isaac Butt QC, Sir Colman O'Loghlen, Holmes, and O'Hagan. After a trial which lasted three days Martin was found guilty, and on 19 August he was sentenced by the lord chief baron to transportation overseas for ten years. The sentence came as a shock to his local community, where he was highly respected. He was shipped off to Van Diemen's Land in the *Elphinstone*, together with Kevin Izod O'Doherty, and arrived in November 1849. O'Doherty gave him the nickname John Knox. Martin resided in the district of Bothwell, where for some time he shared a cottage with Mitchel. In 1854 a pardon, on condition of his not returning to Great Britain or Ireland, was granted to him. He settled in Paris in October 1854, and in June 1856 received an unconditional pardon. However, he refused to live in Ireland again until 1858, when the sudden death of his brother Robert and his wife, Millicent, forced him to take up residence in Kilbroney, Rostrevor, to take care of his nephews and nieces. In January 1864 he established with O'Donoghue the National League, whose object was to obtain the legislative independence of Ireland. The league only lasted until 1867. Martin took a prominent part in the funeral procession through Dublin in honour of the 'Manchester martyrs' on 8 December 1867, and delivered an address to an enormous crowd outside Glasnevin cemetery. For his share in these proceedings he was prosecuted by the government in February 1868, but owing to disagreement among the members of the jury any further attempt to obtain a conviction against him was abandoned. On 25 November 1868 he married Henrietta Mitchel (*d.* 1913), his friend's sister and the youngest daughter of the Revd John Mitchel and Mary Haslett, at Roslyn Hill Chapel, Hampstead, London. Henrietta, who had a similar political outlook, had also been involved in Young Ireland activities and had written articles for her brother's newspaper, the *United Irishman*. They had no children.

While on a visit to America in December 1869, Martin was put forward as a candidate in the nationalist interest at a by-election for County Longford. The local clergy had, however, already pledged themselves to support R. J. M. Greville Nugent, the Liberal candidate, and Martin was defeated by 1578 votes to 411. In May 1870 Martin joined the Home Government Association for Ireland, and at a by-election for County Meath in January 1871 was returned to parliament as a home-ruler by a majority of 456 votes over his Conservative opponent, G. J. Plunket. He spoke for the first time in the House of Commons in May 1871 during the debate on the second reading of the Protection of Life and Property (Ireland) Bill, when he declared that he did not 'intend to vote upon this bill nor

indeed upon any other measure which the parliament may think proper to pass in respect to the government' of his country, and contended that it was 'the inalienable right of the Irish people to be a free people, and as a free people to be bound only by laws made by the queen and a free parliament of that kingdom' (*Hansard 3*, 206.908–14, 1039–45). Martin was also involved in the formation of the Irish Home Rule League and was elected its secretary in 1874. In the same year he was again returned for County Meath at the general election in February 1874. Since he did not like to be paid for patriotic services, he resigned from his post of paid secretary, and accepted that of honorary secretary instead. He died on 29 March 1875 at Dromalane House, near Newry (the residence of Hill Irvine, Henrietta Mitchel's brother-in-law), from an attack of bronchitis caught while attending the funeral of John Mitchel. He was buried in the family plot at Donaghmore on 1 April.

Martin was a sturdy and uncompromising politician, whose sense of honour and candour earned him the affectionate nickname of Honest John Martin. His death paved the way for Charles Stewart Parnell to enter the House of Commons for the first time, as the next MP for County Meath.   G. F. R. BARKER, *rev.* BRIGITTE ANTON

Sources P. A. Sillard, *The life and letters of John Martin* (1901) · T. F. O'Sullivan, *The Young Irelanders*, 2nd edn (1945) · J. H. Cullen, *Young Ireland in exile* (1928) · history of the Harshaw family, MIC, 338/6–7, John Martin's mother · MIC, Donaghmore Presbyterian church records, Newry, Down, baptisms and marriages · J. Martin, diaries, PRO NIre. [written on board convict ship, and in Paris] · letters and documents, PRO NIre. · NL Ire., Larcom, O'Neill Daunt, William Smith O'Brien, Williams, 'Eva', K. I. O'Doherty, Mahon MSS and police reports, MS 13610 · TCD, Dillon MSS

Archives PRO NIre., corresp. and papers; diary | NL Ire., Larcom, O'Neill Daunt, William Smith O'Brien, Williams, 'Eva', K. I. O'Doherty, Mahon MSS and police reports, MS 13610 · TCD, Dillon MSS

Likenesses L. Gluckman, lithograph, pubd 1848 (after a daguerreotype), BM · L. Gluckman, lithograph, pubd 1848 (after daguerreotype), NG Ire. · H. O'Neill, engraving, pubd 1848 (after L. Gluckman), NG Ire. [*see illus.*] · group photograph, 1866 (with Father Kenyon and John Mitchel), repro. in *Templederry, my home* (1980), 18 [Fr Kenyon Community Centre souvenir booklet] · drawing, repro. in O'Sullivan, *Young Irelanders*, p. 106

Wealth at death under £450: administration, 13 July 1875, *CGPLA Ire.*

Martin, Jonathan (*c.*1705–1737), organist, was a chorister in the Chapel Royal under Dr William Croft, and studied the organ with Thomas Roseingrave. He deputized for Roseingrave at St George's, Hanover Square, and for John Weldon at the Chapel Royal, before succeeding the latter as organist on 7 May 1736; Weldon's post of composer to the Chapel Royal went to William Boyce. The only known composition by Martin is the song 'To thee, o gentle sleep' in Nicholas Rowe's *Tamerlane*. Shortly before his death he gave a concert at the Stationers' Hall, where 'though he had scarcely strength to sit upright, he played two voluntaries on the organ, showing fine invention and masterly hand' (Hawkins, 3.893). He died of consumption on 4 April 1737 and was buried in the west cloister of Westminster

Abbey. An inscription for his tomb was written by Vincent Bourne and included in Bourne's *Miscellaneous Poems* (1772).   L. M. MIDDLETON, rev. K. D. REYNOLDS

Sources *New Grove* · Grove, *Dict. mus.* (1927) · J. Hawkins, *A general history of the science and practice of music*, 5 vols. (1776)

Martin, Jonathan (1782–1838), arsonist, was born at Highside House, near Hexham, the son of (William) Fenwick Martin, a fencing master, and his wife, Isabella, *née* Thompson. John *Martin, the artist, and William *Martin were among his twelve siblings. Jonathan Martin was tongue-tied at birth; an operation in his sixth year enabled him to speak, though with some impediment. He was partly brought up by his grandmother, Ann Thompson, a woman of extreme protestant beliefs and a vivid sense of hell. As a boy he saw his sister murdered by a neighbour, Peggy Hobuck. He was sent to his uncle's farm to recover from the shock, worked with sheep, and was then apprenticed to a tanner. In 1804 he went to London and was seized by the press-gang for the navy. He served for about six years in HMS *Hercules*, seeing action at Copenhagen in 1807 and off Corunna in 1809. At this time he began to have violent and wonderful dreams. In 1810 he was paid off from the navy, resumed work as a tanner, and married for the first time. His son Richard was born in 1814. Martin was converted to Christianity; he joined the Wesleyan Methodist Connexion and became violently hostile to the Church of England. In 1817 he threatened the assassination of Edward Legge, bishop of Oxford, for which he was tried and committed to West Auckland Lunatic Asylum; he was later moved to Gateshead Asylum. He escaped from Gateshead on 17 June 1820, was recaptured, and, after going on hunger strike, again escaped on 1 July 1821. In the asylum he resumed painting (having painted intermittently since childhood); a witness at his trial in 1829 recalled his work as having 'extraordinary marks of uninstructed talent, mixed with frenzy and wildness' (Balston, *Jonathan Martin*, 30). Martin's wife died in 1821. After his escape he resumed work as a tanner and preached. The Wesleyans refused to have him back and the Primitive Methodists soon excluded him from their chapels. Even so, by his own account he converted several hundred people. At Lincoln in 1826 he published his autobiography (with further editions in 1828, 1829, and 1830). It was dictated to R. E. Leary of Lincoln and remains of much vivid interest: Martin had a sharp memory for dramatic incident. In 1828 he married again; his second wife was Maria Hudson, a woman twenty years his junior; they had no children.

The Martins settled in York and seem at this time to have been fairly prosperous. Soon after his marriage, however, Martin suffered a further breakdown, which again took an anti-clerical form. He hung threatening placards—which included his name and address—on the railings of York Minster, but the authorities did not take them seriously. On 1 February 1829 Martin attended evensong in the minster, during which he was upset by a buzzing noise from the organ. Apparently on a sudden decision, he secreted himself in the minster (the cathedral watchman had

recently been discharged), lighting a lamp in the bell-tower, which was disregarded by those who saw it. Late that night he set fire to the woodwork of the choir and escaped through a window. Next morning at about 7 a.m. smoke was seen coming from one of the doors. Only after it was discovered did the fire really take hold, the organ and the roof of the choir suddenly catching light at about 8 a.m. The fire was not brought under control until late in the afternoon and was not extinguished until the next afternoon. The roof of the central aisle was entirely destroyed from the lantern tower almost to the east window (a distance of 131 feet), as was most of the woodwork in the interior, including the organ and its screen, the tabernacle work, the stalls, galleries, bishop's throne, and the pulpit. It was one of the most spectacular consequences of arson in modern British history.

Martin was arrested near Hexham on 6 February and was tried (on a capital charge) at York Castle; Henry Brougham acted as his defending counsel, probably paid for by John Martin. On 31 March 1829 he was declared not guilty on grounds of insanity (the judge reversing the jury's original verdict). Martin was described at the time of his trial as rather stout, about 5 feet 6 inches high, with large, bushy red whiskers. He was confined in St Mary's Hospital, London, where he died on 3 June 1838. His son Richard had been brought up mainly by John Martin, and committed suicide in John Martin's house three months after his father's death.   H. C. G. MATTHEW

Sources T. Balston, *The life of Jonathan Martin … with some account of William and Richard Martin* (1945) · *The life of Jonathan Martin … written by himself* (1826) · *A full and authentic account of the trial of Jonathan Martin, with an account of the life of the lunatic* (1829) · T. Balston, *John Martin, 1789–1854* (1934) · M. L. Pendered, *John Martin, painter* (1923) · G. E. Aylmer and R. Cant, eds., *A history of York Minster* (1977) · W. Feaver, *The art of John Martin* (1975) · R. Welford, *Men of mark 'twixt Tyne and Tweed*, 3 vols. (1895)
Likenesses R. W. Brown, oils, 1829, York Minster, York · G. Cruikshank, drawing, Laing Art Gallery, Newcastle upon Tyne

Martin, Joseph (*bap.* 1726, *d.* 1776). See under Martin family (*per. c.*1700–1832).

Martin, Josiah (1685–1748), religious writer, was born on 11 June 1685 in Sussex, the son of John Martin (*d.* 1695) and his wife, Mary, *née* Rickman (1659?–1691). Martin was a member of the Peel monthly meeting of Friends. He became a good classical scholar and was spoken of by James Gough, in his 1772 translation of Madame Guyon's life, as a man whose memory was esteemed for 'learning, humility, and fervent piety'. Martin is best-known in connection with *A Letter from One of the People called Quakers to Francis de Voltaire, Occasioned by his Remarks on that People in his Letters concerning the English Nation* (1741). It was twice reprinted, in London and in Dublin, and translated into French. It was a temperate and scholarly treatise and was much in favour at the time. He edited, and contributed a long preface to, *The Archbishop of Cambray's Dissertation on Pure Love* (1735) and was one of the first of several Quakers who helped to make major works of the continental quietists available in English, thus contributing to the development of quietism in eighteenth-century English

Quakerism. His other publications included a substantial appendix to an edition of Anthony Pearson's *The Great Case of Tithes* (1730). Martin was one of a number of Quakers who, in 1736, met with Count Zinzendorf, founder of the Herrnhuter Brüdergemeinde, to discuss religious views. He also corresponded with the Dutch Quaker historian Willem Sewel about his publications.

Martin died, unmarried, on 18 February 1748, in the parish of St Andrew's, Holborn, London, and was buried in the Quaker burial-ground at Bunhill Fields. He left the proceeds of his library of 4000 volumes, sold by catalogue on 29 May 1749, to be divided among his nephews and nieces. The Quaker author Joseph Besse was his executor.

CHARLOTTE FELL-SMITH, *rev.* DAVID J. HALL

Sources 'Dictionary of Quaker biography', RS Friends, Lond. [card index] · J. Smith, ed., *A descriptive catalogue of Friends' books*, 2 (1867) · [F. de Salignac de La Mothe-Fénelon], *The archbishop of Cambray's dissertation on pure love*, 4th edn (1769) · A. N. L. Munby and L. Coral, eds., *British book sale catalogues, 1676–1800: a union list* (1977), 54 · W. I. Hull, *Willem Sewel of Amsterdam* (1933) · *Journal of the Friends' Historical Society*, 28 (1931), 80

Wealth at death legacies of £415 10s. 0d.; residue to nieces; also library of 4000 books: will, *Quakeriana*, 2 (1895), 84

Martin, Josiah (1737–1786), colonial governor, was born on 23 April 1737 in Dublin, the son of Samuel *Martin (1694/5–1776), a landowner and sugar planter in Antigua, and his second wife, Sarah (*d.* 1748), the widow of William Irish and the daughter of Edward Wyke, governor of Montserrat. He grew up in Dublin and the London area, where his education, with tutors, was managed by his half-brother Samuel, a Pelhamite MP and London agent for Antigua, Montserrat, and Nevis. His adolescence in Antigua was painful, his widowed father frequently denouncing his 'indolence' and 'mulish' disposition (BL, Add. MS 41346).

Early in the Seven Years' War Martin seized his father's approval for study at the Inner Temple as an opportunity to leave Antigua, and he then joined the 4th regiment of foot as an ensign; later he obtained a commission as lieutenant-colonel in the 22nd regiment of foot. According to his biographer, Martin became interested in colonial administration while serving in Canada. He drew on his father's espousal of efficiency, accountability, and humanitarian concerns as the basis of his new personal outlook and imperial perspective. In January 1761, while serving at Crown Point, New York, Martin married his cousin Elizabeth (Betsy) Martin (*d.* 1778), in defiance of his father's negotiations. Marriage into the New York gentry was consistent with his financial and political status, but he was disappointed in hoping for a New York political appointment. He succeeded only in keeping his wife (in his words) 'breeding sick'. Having sold his commission, he remained at a loose end until 1770, when Samuel junior's efforts obtained him the governorship of North Carolina.

Pleased to have his foot on the ladder, Martin approached this lower rung with disdain and resignation. He delayed leaving New York and conferred with William Tryon, whose transfer to New York had made the North Carolina governorship available. Martin perceived that Tryon's departure involved face-saving, both for Tryon and for his and Martin's superiors, and he sensed an opportunity to pacify his troubled new charge.

Tryon had faced the regulator movement, a backcountry farmers' insurrection against the eastern North Carolina planter élite. He had successfully led the colonial militia against the regulators, but the backcountry grievances of corrupt local government and legislative under-representation remained. Martin approached the regulators cordially and with an open mind. His challenge came from eastern leaders in the lower house, who moved to narrow the governor's field of political action. Regulator issues were in abeyance—that is, until Martin's efforts to address them raised the eastern leaders' fears that backcountry hostility towards themselves would buttress the governor's political defences. In response, eastern leaders now courted former regulators. Thus Martin unintentionally brought regulator demands to the discussions with which his colony approached the American War of Independence.

Martin was handicapped from London and outmanoeuvred by his challengers, in particular Abner Nash and Cornelius Harnett, who aimed to take control over the proceedings of the lower house and then build public support for the house's authority. Their winning tactic was a foreign attachments clause, which they added to a court bill when the law establishing the colony's courts expired in 1773. Martin's instructions forbade his concurrence. He tried to gain approval for a foreign attachments clause, but he was insecure with London following the resignation in 1772 of his patron, the earl of Hillsborough. In August 1774 the speaker of the house convened a provincial congress composed of most of the assemblymen. Under mounting pressure, Martin withdrew from his New Bern residence in late May 1775 and installed his headquarters aboard the *Cruizer*, a sloop of war in the Cape Fear river.

There Martin worked steadily until May 1776, sending emissaries into the backcountry and among the highland Scots in the upper Cape Fear valley. He received messages and visits from loyalists throughout the southern backcountry and corresponded with Native American agents and neighbouring governors. Martin pleaded with the government for troops to support a proposed loyalist uprising, and in early 1776 his London dispatch informed him that a southern campaign was in preparation, with troops and arms *en route* from Ireland for the Cape Fear river.

By the time Martin received this news, the nature of the expedition had been altered without his being informed. His loyalists observed the original timetable. Their clash with revolutionary militia at Moore's Creek Bridge on 26 February 1776 was a fiasco. Martin joined a fleet from Boston in their unsuccessful attack near Charles Town, South Carolina. Soon he was at New York, where he remained until British forces returned to Charles Town, this time successfully, in May 1780. British planners approached the southern campaign of 1780–81 on premises Martin had laid out in 1775: British troops occupying major ports and coastal areas, to be assisted by loyalists, largely in the interior, and by Native Americans. Martin accompanied the campaign's commander, Cornwallis, through the Carolinas, earning his trust and praise. Many of Martin's 1776 commissions remained active, and groups originating therein continued through 1783 in the Carolinas and East Florida.

Martin, widowed in October 1778, returned to his children at New York in 1781. His eldest child, Mary Elizabeth, remained with relatives on Long Island, but the others, Sarah, Alice, Samuel, Josiah Henry, and Augusta, had moved to London with him by 1782. Three other children had died. The family lived among sugar grandees and ranking civil servants near Grosvenor Square and Hanover Square and at an estate near Richmond, Surrey. Martin assisted loyalists who lodged compensation claims with the American loyalist claims commission. He estimated his own losses at £6500, exclusive of perquisites, and the commissioners fixed the amount of his compensation at approximately £3000. He received a governor's salary of £1000 annually during the years 1775–83. Martin died on 13 April 1786 and was buried at St George's, Hanover Square.

Martin undertook his office as governor as a stepping stone. He quickly became absorbed in colonial politics, however, and worked to reconcile the desire for greater representational and legislative integrity with imperial concerns. Once royal authority was usurped, his energetic formulation of a regional plan to displace the usurpers became the base-line of the British southern strategy.

CAROLE WATTERSON TROXLER

Sources V. O. Stumpf, *Josiah Martin: the last royal governor of North Carolina* (1986) · W. L. Saunders and W. Clark, eds., *The colonial records of North Carolina*, 30 vols. (1886–1907), vols. 8–9 · BL, Josiah Martin MSS, Add. MS 41346 · C. W. Troxler, *The loyalist experience in North Carolina* (1976) · PRO, Loyalist Claims, North Carolina, audit office 12: 34–37 · P. H. Smith, *Loyalists & redcoats: a study in British revolutionary policy* (1964) · Southern Historical Collection, Chapel Hill, North Carolina, W. A. Graham MSS · B. Tarleton, *A history of the campaigns of 1780 and 1781, in the southern provinces of North America* (1787) · H. B. Taylor, 'The foreign attachment law and the coming of the revolution in North Carolina', *North Carolina Historical Review*, 52 (1975), 21–35 · L. S. Butler, *North Carolina and the coming of the revolution, 1763–1776* (1976) · R. B. Sheridan, 'The West Indian antecedents of Josiah Martin, last royal governor of North Carolina', *North Carolina Historical Review*, 54 (1977), 253–70 · J. Schaw, *Journal of a lady of quality; being the narrative of a journey from Scotland to the West Indies, North Carolina, and Portugal, in the years 1774 to 1776*, ed. E. W. Andrews (1922) · A. R. Ekirch, '*Poor Carolina': politics and society in colonial North Carolina, 1729–1776* (1981) · J. W. Blanks, jun., 'The administration of Governor Josiah Martin in North Carolina', MA diss., University of North Carolina, 1948 · parish register, St George's, Hanover Square, London [burial]

Archives BL, Add. MS 41346 | PRO, Audit Office 12:34–37

Martin, Kenneth Laurence (1905–1984), painter and sculptor, was born on 13 April 1905 at 22 Idsworth Road, Sheffield, the son of Hugh Martin (d. 1923/4), a foreman at steel rolling mills, and his wife, Letitia, née Townsend. He studied at the Sheffield College of Art and worked in the city as a designer before moving south to London to attend the Royal College of Art in 1929. Remembering his years at the college, he observed: 'The only thing I learned at the

Royal College was when Will Rothenstein allowed me to go and copy at the National Gallery' (cited by A. Forge in *Kenneth Martin*, Yale U. CBA). He met his future wife, Mary Balmford [see Martin, Mary Adela (1907–1969)], at the Royal College of Art. The artistic and personal sympathy between them was to be of crucial importance in both their lives. They married in 1930 and had two sons, John and Paul.

Martin made abstract sculpture and paintings in a constructivist tradition which arrived late in Britain, brought by Piet Mondrian and Naum Gabo in the 1930s. He was associated with a group, which included Victor Pasmore, Mary Martin, Anthony Hill, and Adrian Heath, who established abstract art in Britain in the years immediately after the Second World War, after the insecure bridgehead erected in the 1930s by Ben Nicholson, Henry Moore, and Barbara Hepworth. The debate about abstract art, which focused on Pasmore's move from figurative to abstract painting and then to abstract construction, was carried on with great vehemence. These were heady times: constructivism was being proposed as the art of post-war reconstruction in opposition to neo-Romanticism and neo-realism. Martin admired European modernism in art, music, and architecture and can be seen as a formidable late modernist.

Martin's sculpture, in wood, brass, or aluminium, is characterized by movement, whether actual, as in the mobiles or variable pieces, or internal, within the chosen form of a piece. His mobiles often have a spiral form, derived as much from nature as from geometry, which is accentuated by movement and light. This form occurs also in his sculpture and in paintings where the movement of line, overlapping and connecting with other lines, creates web structures of surprising variety. Indeed drawing was for him the fundamental activity, constant during the time when he was mostly making sculpture, from the early 1950s, and when he returned to painting at the end of the 1960s. He devised ways of working in which chance played a part, though paradoxically his work gained in expressiveness from its basis in given systems, and his sensitive handling of materials always gave his work a personal touch. Sheffield has a tradition of working on a small scale in steel, but when he spoke of his native city it was of the Ruskin Museum and his first contacts with art, with Turner's *Liber Studiorum*, Ruskin's own drawings, and cases of crystals and stones (Martin, *Chance, Order, Change*, 5).

Martin made figurative paintings in the 1930s but these were difficult years and resources were scant. He later locked up the work of this early period and was not prepared for it to be considered again until the end of his life. After the war he taught at Camberwell School of Arts and Crafts in London with William Coldstream and Victor Pasmore. He continued to teach as a visiting lecturer at Goldsmiths' College in London until 1967 and was much valued by generations of students and fellow teachers (see, for example, W. Tucker in *Kenneth Martin*, Tate Gallery, 18).

Martin's conversion to abstraction began in a series of

paintings and drawings he made in 1948 of the railway at Chalk Farm in London in which the motif became increasingly reduced to its essential elements. He soon reversed this process and began building up complex structures from simple geometric elements. It was the start of a rigorous exploration of abstraction which one can follow in his work and in his writings over three decades. In the early 1950s painting ceased to be his main concern as he started to make three-dimensional constructions or models. He made his first mobile in 1951 and developed an impressive and original series of such works, mostly screw mobiles in which each element is rotated around a central thread. The mobile allowed him to explore the effects of movement and light on his geometric constructions; he contrived subtle effects in objects, either mobile or static, which were often made of brass and are ravishing to look at and to hold. Working in constructivism led to contacts with other artists in Europe—with, for example, François Morellet in France, Joost Baljeu in the Netherlands, Richard Lohse in Switzerland, and Gerhard von Graevenitz in Germany. And when the temporary but international movement called kinetic art became all the rage in the 1960s, he was a natural contributor; a large mobile, *Linkages* (1968, priv. coll.), greeted visitors to the survey show 'Kinetics', organized by the Hayward Gallery in London in 1970.

Martin had an exact sense of scale. Small objects could be much larger. He made a number of public sculptures, the most accessible of which is *Construction in Aluminium* (1967) outside the engineering laboratory on Trumpington Street in Cambridge. Fountains in stainless steel were made for Brixton College of Further Education, London (1961), and Gorinchem in the Netherlands (1974), the latter no longer *in situ*; and hanging constructions for the Nuffield Institute of Comparative Education, London Zoo (1967), and Victoria Plaza in London (1983), the latter sadly taken down in 1998.

In 1969 Mary Martin died during preparations for a joint Arts Council exhibition which showed each making a distinctive contribution to abstract art in Britain. The exhibition opened in Oxford in May 1970 and then toured to ten cities in the UK, including Edinburgh and Cardiff, before a final showing at the Whitechapel Art Gallery in London. Martin returned to painting at the end of 1969—in truth he had always made paintings but not as a main preoccupation in the 1950s and 1960s—and began a long series of canvases under the title Chance Order Change. These paintings resulted from drawings in which a grid was numbered at points of intersection and pairs of numbers, taken from a cup, provided a simple or complex structure of lines. But the making of the drawings and of the paintings clearly show the artist's hand. He had a special way of building up the surfaces of his paintings with white so that they absorb the light.

Martin had many exhibitions, including retrospectives at the Tate Gallery, London, in 1975 and the Yale Center for British Art, New Haven, Connecticut, in 1979, and a memorial exhibition of his later paintings at the Serpentine Gallery, London, in 1985. He gave the sixth William

Townsend memorial lecture at University College, London, in 1979 and lectured on his series Chance Order Change at the Ruskin School of Drawing in Oxford in 1982. He was made an OBE in 1971, received an honorary doctorate at the Royal College of Art in 1976 and was awarded the Midsummer prize of the City of London, also in 1976. His works are in numerous public collections, including the Tate collection; Graves Art Gallery, Sheffield; the Sainsbury Centre for Visual Arts, University of East Anglia, Norwich; the Scottish National Gallery of Modern Art, Edinburgh; the National Museum and Gallery of Wales, Cardiff; the Museum of Modern Art, New York; the Rijksmuseum Kröller–Müller, Otterlo, Netherlands; Folkwang Museum, Essen, Germany; and the Städtisches Museum Abteiberg, Mönchengladbach, Germany.

Martin was an unmistakable figure, very tall with a shock of white hair and, in his middle years at least, with a cigarette dangling precariously from his lips. Walking with him was always stimulating, even on the short journey from his studio in Eton Avenue, Belsize Park, London, to the pub on the corner. He would see things which ordinary eyes passed over. One always felt that this was the basis of his art, that seeing and making were connected, that far from being abstract his art was quite real. He died in London at the Royal Free Hospital on 18 November 1984 and was cremated on 27 November at Golders Green crematorium, London.   ANDREW DEMPSEY

Sources *Kenneth Martin*, 2 vols. (1975) [exhibition catalogue, Tate Gallery, London, 14 May – 29 June 1975] · *Kenneth Martin* (1979) [exhibition catalogue, Yale U. CBA, 18 April – 17 June 1979] · *Kenneth Martin: the late paintings* (1985) [exhibition catalogue, Serpentine Gallery, London, 29 June – 4 Aug 1985] · *Kenneth and Mary Martin* (1987) [exhibition catalogue, Annely Juda Fine Arts, London, 11 Sept – 31 Oct 1987] · K. Martin, *Chance and order: the sixth William Townsend lecture* (1979) · K. Martin, *Chance, order, change* (1983) [published to accompany an exhibition at the Leicester Polytechnic, 13–19 Jan 1983] · A. Forge and H. Lane, *Chance and order: drawings by Kenneth Martin* (1973) [exhibition catalogue, Waddington Galleries, London, 1973] · b. cert. · *The Times* (23 Nov 1984) · Mary Martin, *Kenneth Martin* (1970) [exhibition catalogue for touring exhibition by Arts Council of Great Britain, 12 May 1970 – 24 April 1971] · personal knowledge (2004)
Archives Tate collection, notes and articles
Wealth at death £170,604: probate, 18 Oct 1985, *CGPLA Eng. & Wales*

Martin, (Basil) Kingsley (1897–1969), political journalist and journal editor, was born in Ingestre Street, Hereford, on 28 July 1897, the second of four children of the Congregational minister (David) Basil Martin (b. 1858), and his wife, Charlotte Alice Turberville. His father was known locally as a man of the highest integrity who stuck fast to his Christian socialist principles, not least his belief in absolute pacifism. He attracted grudging respect but often harsh criticism, not just from the respectable burghers of Hereford but also from the elders in his own church. His was a stormy and demanding ministry, borne with good grace and fortitude, and setting an example the adult Kingsley endeavoured to match, albeit with only partial success.

The Martin family's firm principles and staunch nonconformity profoundly influenced Kingsley, which did not make for popularity in classroom or playground. His happiness at home contrasted sharply with his misery as a day boy at Hereford Cathedral school. In 1913, however, Basil Martin was appointed Unitarian minister in Finchley, so the family moved to a more congenial environment in north London. Kingsley attended Mill Hill School, free for the first time from the closed minds of the cathedral close. Relishing his new surroundings, the tyro socialist kept the First World War at a distance until the introduction of conscription in 1916. Still a sixth-former, he registered as a conscientious objector, and was soon called before a War Office tribunal. The outcome was that Martin spent the final eighteen months of the war as an orderly with the Friends' Ambulance Unit. Like so many of his generation, Martin's experiences on the western front were highly formative, reinforcing a deep strain of pacifism, and an evangelical belief in open diplomacy and global disarmament.

Martin went up to Cambridge in autumn 1919 to study history at Magdalene College. In 1920–21 he gained a first in both parts of the historical tripos, and as a result was elected to a bye-fellowship. He first chose to spend a year as a visiting scholar at Princeton. His eventual spell as a fellow at Magdalene was short-lived as in 1924 he was appointed an assistant lecturer in politics at the London School of Economics (LSE).

An appointment in the intellectual powerhouse of progressivism signalled a distinguished academic career. In fact Kingsley Martin's sojourn at the LSE lasted only three years, during which he wrote *The Triumph of Lord Palmerston* (1924) and *French Liberal Thought in the Eighteenth Century* (1929). Both books were favourably received by critics and dons alike. Martin's close friend and common room colleague Harold Laski proved a lasting influence. Indeed Martin paid tribute to his old head of department in a biographical memoir published three years after Laski's death in 1950. The maverick professor ensured his new colleague's easy entry into the higher echelons of the Labour Party, albeit at the expense of potentially valuable contacts in the trade union movement, including Ernest Bevin, scourge of so-called Hampstead intellectuals. Martin's initial failure to cultivate leading trade unionists ensured their deep suspicion of his interests and motives once his reputation had become established as a thorn in the flesh of the Labour leadership. Equally suspicious was William Beveridge, director of the LSE, with whom Martin enjoyed an increasingly uneasy relationship. Clashes between the two men became so frequent that by 1927 Martin had resolved to resign his post, and he readily accepted an opportunity to join the staff of the *Manchester Guardian*.

Writing leaders for the legendary editor–proprietor C. P. Scott would have seemed the ideal appointment for someone so firmly rooted in the nonconformist tradition, but again Martin found himself at odds with his superior. He quickly encountered difficulties in reconciling an unbridled faith in democratic socialism with the Scott family's enthusiasm for the Liberal revivalism of a rejuvenated Lloyd George. Leaders were regularly rewritten in more temperate language, or simply spiked, and after three turbulent years in Manchester Martin learned that his contract would not be renewed. At the end of a decade of sharply contrasting fortunes he returned to London in 1930 desperate to revive a flagging career.

Back in the capital, Martin's ceaseless lobbying to secure a fresh post paid off when the sickly Fabian weekly the *New Statesman* merged with its Liberal counterpart, the *Nation*, in late 1930. Having masterminded the merger of their respective papers, Arnold Bennett and John Maynard Keynes gambled on a fresh face to launch their new enterprise. Martin had already helped that year to found the *Political Quarterly*, along with Keynes and others, and was joint editor with W. A. Robson during its first year. On 1 January 1931 Martin was appointed editor of the *New Statesman and Nation*, the first issue appearing three months later. It quickly became apparent that Martin had discovered his vocation, although for the rest of his life he liked to cultivate the notion that one day he would retreat back into the less stressful ivory tower world of pure scholarship. This fantasy helped sustain him through twenty-nine years of guiding the 'Staggers and Naggers' to critical and commercial success. When, with reluctance, he handed over the editorial reins in December 1960, the paper's weekly sales had increased sixfold to 80,000, the circulation in January 1931 having stood at a mere 14,000. Advertising revenue in 1960 had grown to a remarkable £100,000 per year, ensuring a healthy return for those directors who a generation earlier had gambled on an unproven young journalist turning their paper round. As chairman until his death in 1946, Keynes applauded evidence of commercial enterprise while sensibly bowing to editorial integrity in matters of potential conflict. The Keynes–Martin partnership was not always harmonious, but it proved remarkably productive.

Kingsley Martin set out to make the *New Statesman and Nation* the flagship weekly of the left, articulating a brand of democratic socialism compatible with mainstream Labour thinking, while at the same time reserving the right to question and provoke. Thus, the paper remained loyal to Labour, but at the same time constituted a valuable forum for dissent. Indeed Martin positively relished being a perpetual critic of the Labour leadership, in or out of office. This refusal to follow a narrow party line was in many respects the key to the *New Statesman*'s success, witness its close association from the mid-fifties with the Campaign for Nuclear Disarmament, of which Martin was a founding father.

By intuition as much as logic Martin and his colleagues articulated the ideas and ideals of liberal middle-class opinion in mid-twentieth-century Britain. By the Second World War the *New Statesman* was extending its influence to anti-imperialists in Africa and Asia—most especially in India, where Martin was always held in the very highest esteem. Nationalists like Nehru applauded his good intentions, but lamented that again and again Martin proved astonishingly naïve. Forever wrestling with his conscience, whether it be in the thirties over pacifism or in the forties over continued support for the USSR, Martin reflected the doubts and dilemmas of his readers. He lived and breathed politics, and yet he would have made an appalling politician: he was impractical, and all too often he showed a lamentable lack of sound judgement and common sense. Martin was notorious for being influenced by the last person spoken to, and his editorials reflected a notorious lack of consistency, not least during the 1938 Czechoslovakian crisis when he was culpably wrong. His refusal to publish George Orwell's review article on events in Barcelona in May 1937 provided ammunition for Martin's enemies, many of whom argued that he was soft on Stalinism for too long.

Martin prided himself on encouraging the provocative and the radical, the only criterion being that the piece was stylish and well written—a requirement which extended to the back half of the paper, where literary editors such as Raymond Mortimer and V. S. Pritchett enjoyed an enviable degree of discretion. Many readers looked first to the reviews, and only later turned to the politics. Whatever their preference, they could rely on a team of regular contributors who together represented the cream of reportage, commentary, and review.

Martin's complex personality ensured that in private he was equally perplexing and contradictory, forever testing the loyalty of even his closest friends. He could be mean, petty, and rude—sometimes all at the same time—but then the next minute he could be disarmingly familiar and generous, not least when in the company of interesting and attractive women. From 7 July 1926 to 14 October 1940 he was married to Olga Walters. She left him in 1936 and sued for divorce four years later; living the life of a recluse, she died in 1964. From the mid-thirties Martin's close companion was Dorothy Woodman (1902–1970), secretary of the Union of Democratic Control. The couple were invariably as one in their political beliefs, and they shared a deep love of travelling, but in their earlier years they enjoyed what might loosely be described as an open relationship.

Martin finally agreed to vacate his Great Turnstile office in 1960, finding comfort in his South Downs garden. Always a keen chess player, he now rediscovered a passion for oil painting. Between triumphant tours of former colonies and more leisurely trips around Europe, he rewrote an earlier essay on the monarchy and began his memoirs. He completed two volumes, *Father Figures* (1966) and *Editor* (1968), the latter stoutly defending even the most contentious of his editorial decisions. Already ailing, Kingsley Martin rashly accepted an invitation to stay with the Indian ambassador in Egypt. He suffered a stroke and was rushed to the Anglo-American Hospital in Cairo, where he died of a heart attack on 16 February 1969. He donated his body for medical research. Martin's legacy was the *New Statesman*'s continued claim to be Britain's pre-eminent political weekly, but even before his untimely death that reputation was already starting to fade.

ADRIAN SMITH

Sources C. H. Rolph, *Kingsley: the life, letters and diaries of Kingsley Martin* (1973) · K. Martin, *Father figures* (1966) · K. Martin, ed., *Editor: a second volume of autobiography, 1931–1945* (1968) · M. Jones, ed., *Kingsley Martin: portrait and self-portrait* (1969) · A. Smith, *The 'New Statesman': portrait of a political weekly, 1913–1931* (1996) · E. Hyams, *The 'New Statesman': the history of the first fifty years, 1913–1963* (1963) · K. Martin, *Harold Laski: a biographical memoir* (1953) · DNB · CGPLA Eng. & Wales (1969)

Archives NYPL, Berg collection, corresp. and papers · U. Sussex, corresp. and papers | BLPES, corresp. with Violet Markham · Bodl. Oxf., corresp. with William Clark · HLRO, letters to David Lloyd George · JRL, letters to the *Manchester Guardian* · NYPL, Berg collection, Leonard Woolf papers · RIBA BAL, corresp. with Marshall Sisson · U. Sussex, corresp. as editor of the *New Statesman* · U. Sussex, corresp. with Leonard Woolf | SOUND BL NSA, 'Kingsley Martin looks back: the diarist and traveller', NP833W · BL NSA, 'Kingsley Martin looks back: the editor', NP804W · BL NSA, 'Turning point: Kingsley Martin talks to John Ellison', M870R · BL NSA, documentary recording · BL NSA, oral history interview · BL NSA, performance recording

Likenesses E. Kapp, drawing, 1956, U. Birm. · M. Ayrton, drawings · E. Kapp, drawing, *New Statesman* offices, London · D. Low, caricature pencil drawings, NPG · D. Low, drawing, *New Statesman* offices, London · Low, caricatures, repro. in *New Statesman* (1930) · Vicky, caricatures, repro. in *New Statesman* (1930) · A. Wishan, oils, *New Statesman* offices, London · photograph, Hult. Arch.

Wealth at death £37,934: probate, 30 June 1969, *CGPLA Eng. & Wales*

Martin, Leopold Charles (1817–1889), costume historian and numismatist, was born on 6 December 1817, and was baptized on 7 January 1818 at St Mary Street, St Marylebone, Middlesex, the second son of John *Martin (1789–1854), painter, and his wife, Susan. He was the godson of Leopold, later first king of the Belgians. He became an excellent French and German scholar, a skilled artist, and an authority on costume and numismatics. His wife was the sister of the artist and cartoonist Sir John Tenniel, of *Punch*. In 1836 Lord Melbourne presented him to a clerkship in the Stationery Office, which he held for many years. He died in London on 8 January 1889.

With his elder brother, Charles (1810–1906), Martin published in 1842 two volumes entitled respectively *Civil Costumes of England, from the Conquest to George III* (sixty-one plates, drawn from ancient manuscripts and tapestries, illuminated in gold and colours) and *Dresses Worn at her Majesty's bal costumé, May 1842*. He also wrote *Contributions to English Literature by the Civil Servants of the Crown and East India Company from 1794 to 1863* (1865). In conjunction with Charles Trübner he issued in 1862 an elaborate work, *The Current Gold and Silver Coins of All Countries* (2nd edn, 1863), the plates of which he drew himself. Martin was also author of the handbooks *Cardiff* and *Swansea and Gower* (1879). Shortly before he died he had begun to contribute to the *Newcastle Weekly Chronicle* a series of 'Reminiscences', about his father, the first of which appeared in the number for 5 January 1889.

GORDON GOODWIN, rev. ANNETTE PEACH

Sources Allibone, *Dict.* · Allibone, *Dict.*, suppl. · IGI · *The Athenaeum* (19 Jan 1889), 86

Martin, Sir (John) Leslie (1908–2000), architect, was born at 1 Briardene, Moston Lane, Failsworth, Manchester, on 17 August 1908, the son of Robert Martin (b. 1872), a Manchester and diocesan architect, and his wife, Emily, née Hilton.

Sir (John) Leslie Martin (1908–2000), by Philip Sayer, 1981

Education and early career Martin was educated at Manchester grammar school and studied architecture at the University of Manchester, where he was awarded an MA (1932) and a PhD (1936). Most unusually, he had entered the university directly into the third year of the course in architecture in 1926. He was awarded an honourable mention in the Royal Institute of British Architects (RIBA) Tite prize for 1929. This was followed a year later by the RIBA silver medal and the Soane medallion (the subject of which was the design of a sports club, undertaken by Martin in a somewhat neo-classical manner). While a student, Martin was strongly influenced by Samuel Alexander (1859–1938), author of *Space, Time and Deity* (1920) and former professor of philosophy at Manchester. In later life he often recalled a lecture in which Alexander observed that beauty in art is the product of human impulses and instincts and is an outgrowth from the instinct to construct—the human manifestation of what is rooted in the instincts of the bird, the beaver, and the bee. The beaver's instincts are unreflective: if it knew why it constructed its dam, and could adapt this construction for different purposes, it would be a technician. But, Alexander observed, if it could build in such a way as to consider the resulting forms for their own sakes, it would be an architect. Martin also used to recall Alexander's suggestion that the mass of architecture, with its link to practical purpose, should be the same as good prose writing, while the rest, designed

for less common purposes, might, while sharing the same language, be regarded as poetry.

In 1926 Martin met a fellow architecture student, Sadie *Speight (1906–1992), daughter of Alfred Speight, whom he married on 3 January 1935 and with whom he had two children: Susan (*b.* 1939) and Christopher, known as Kit (*b.* 1947). Years later, in his book *Buildings and Ideas, 1933–83* (1983), Martin was to write, 'My wife, Sadie Speight, has made her own very special contribution throughout the whole of my professional career' (p. vi).

For half of his working life Martin not only practised architecture but also taught it. His first teaching post, in 1930, was as an assistant lecturer and master of elementary design at the University of Manchester. In 1934, at the age of twenty-six, he was appointed head of the school of architecture in the Hull College of Art, which the RIBA was keen to expand to serve the region. Initially there were only four full-time students, but he made much of the opportunity—attracting architects such as Serge Chermayeff, Maxwell Fry, and Marcel Breuer, the mathematician Jacob Bronowski, the artist Laszlo Moholy-Nagy, and the critics Herbert Read and Morton Shand to lecture both to his students and to audiences at the city's Ferens Art Gallery, where some also exhibited. Four years after his appointment the RIBA granted the enlarged school recognition up to its intermediate examination.

It was at this time that the Martins started collecting works by Ben Nicholson and Naum Gabo, with whom Martin also edited *Circle: International Survey of Constructive Art*, published in 1937. The aim of *Circle* was to show those works of architecture, painting, and sculpture that appeared to share a common idea and spirit. Two years later, inspired by Herbert Read, Martin and his wife published *The Flat Book*, a reference book on accessible modern domestic design in its broadest sense, from building and furniture to domestic equipment and cutlery. Martin enjoyed enduring friendships with Nicholson, Barbara Hepworth, and Gabo. He often alluded to the critic Morton Shand (who introduced him to the delights of cultivating rare apple species) and to the influence of Winifred Nicholson and, in particular, her use of colour and materials.

Martin and Sadie Speight started in practice in 1933, and between 1935 and 1939 completed several conversions and small houses in the north of England. These included: extensions to a house at Brampton, Cumberland, for the art patron and collector Helen Sutherland; a house at Brampton, for another art patron, Alastair Morton of Morton Sundour and Edinburgh Weavers; the Robinson House, Ferriby, Yorkshire; and a small nursery school at Northwich (now Hartford), Cheshire. Martin later described this work as 'modest, dispersed and built for private clients who were interested in a special problem on a special site' (Martin, 202). Unusually in the modern movement, the houses were largely built of brick with some local stone: they have weathered well. The nursery school was the first example of Martin's many investigations into a type of planning and construction of general application and, with its light frame and infill walls, almost certainly influenced some post-war school design. During this period of pre-war practice Martin also designed what he claimed to be the first range of unit furniture in Britain, for Messrs Rowntree of Scarborough.

Public commissions In 1939 Martin resigned the headship at Hull and moved to London to work for the London, Midland and Scottish (LMS) railway as principal assistant architect for a modernization and development programme directed by Lord Stamp and Sir Harold Hartley. However, with the advent of war, much of his time was spent in supervising the rapid repair of railway stations and other parts of the network damaged by bombing. In parallel with this, however, research and development continued on a systematic approach to the construction of railway stations and other buildings, including the reordering of existing stations. After the war this work expanded to embrace the whole field of design within the LMS railway system, ranging from staff residences to passenger catering, and from coach livery to cutlery.

Nationalization of the railways in 1948 brought the LMS programme to a halt, and in October of that same year Martin was appointed deputy architect to the London county council (LCC). Shortly before, Herbert Morrison, Labour politician and former leader of the LCC, had asked the architect to the council, Robert Matthew, whether a permanent concert hall could be constructed on the south bank site in time for the planned opening of the Festival of Britain in May 1951. With great courage (it was a time of desperate material shortages and there was no recent precedent for constructing a building of the proposed size and complexity), Matthew replied that it could. Martin was placed in charge of the project and rapidly built up a team with Peter Moro and Edwin Williams as his principal assistants. The major challenge was how to contain a large concert hall for 3000 together with all the necessary foyer and ancillary accommodation on a very small site. He resolved this with his 'egg in a box' solution: encasing the auditorium in a heavy, enclosing structure with glazed foyers and galleries and placing this centrally over the extensive foyers, bars, and restaurants below. On its completion, J. M. Richards described the hall as 'something without precedent in this country and with very little precedent elsewhere: a modern building—modern in the sense of owing allegiance to no other age but ours—which is also monumental' (*Architectural Review*, June 1951). In 1953 Martin succeeded Matthew as architect to the council. It was during this period that the LCC architects department, involved in a huge programme of housing, schools, service buildings, and special projects, produced some of its finest work.

Educator Three years later Martin was appointed as the first professor of architecture in the University of Cambridge and head of the department of architecture. He also became a fellow of Jesus College (1957–73). Over the course of the next sixteen years Martin transformed what had been a small architecture school of little significance (without even the power to exempt its students from the RIBA final examination) into one of international standing. It became the very embodiment of the outcome of the 1958 Oxford conference which placed architectural education, supported by research, firmly in the university sector. Martin had played a major role in formulating the proposals before the conference and was responsible for drafting its final report and recommendations.

In 1967 Martin established the department's Centre for Land Use and Built Form Studies (renamed the Martin Centre in 1973) and initiated a programme of research on fundamental architectural issues. Most notably, in his work with Lionel March, he developed a strong theoretical basis for urban design—applying geometrical principles to the issue of ground coverage and building form. Martin and March summarized this work in their comparison between the pavilion form and its anti-form, the court, and demonstrated how it was possible to achieve high housing densities while at the same time providing useful space at ground level and avoiding the use of high buildings. This work flew in the face of conventional wisdom at a time when the Ministry of Housing was, through its tall building subsidy, positively encouraging the construction of local authority housing towers.

Later work In 1957, shortly after moving to Cambridge, Martin established his studio at Great Shelford, in the lower part of the King's Mill, which he and his wife converted as their family home. Here, collaborating with his associates (whom he always acknowledged), he began a series of projects, mainly in the higher-education sector, that was to last until he closed the studio in 1986. Martin regarded this work as a series of investigations into generic form and it is in this way, thematically rather than chronologically, and as a body of thought rather than a catalogue of individual buildings, that he presents it in the summary of his work, *Buildings and Ideas, 1933–83: from the Studio of Leslie Martin and his Associates* (1983).

The best-known of the Martin studio's buildings is perhaps Harvey Court, a residential court composed with stepped terraces for Gonville and Caius College in Cambridge, designed with Patrick Hodgkinson and Colin St John Wilson and completed in 1962. Other distinguished buildings include the Manor Road Library group for the University of Oxford, with Hodgkinson, Wilson, and Douglas Lanham (1964), the Kettle's Yard gallery in Cambridge, with David Owers (1970), the auditorium of the University Music School in Cambridge, with Colen Lumley (1974), and the Gallery of Modern Art for the Gulbenkian Foundation in Lisbon, with Ivor Richards (1984). In addition, the studio completed other development plans and buildings in the universities of Cambridge, Hull, Leicester, and London; the Royal Scottish Academy of Music and Drama in Glasgow; the government centre in Ta'if, Saudi Arabia, and, in 1965, a major and highly controversial development plan for Whitehall.

In addition to teaching and practising, Martin also played an important role as a competition assessor. Most notably, he was one of the team of three (with Eero Saarinen and John Ashworth) which selected Jørn Utzon's design as the winning entry in the Sydney Opera House competition. In the period of rapid university expansion in the 1960s his advice was sought by many vice-chancellors and he was instrumental in the appointment of James Stirling and James Gowan at Leicester; Chamberlin, Powell, and Bon at Leeds; and Denys Lasdun at East Anglia. He recommended Alison and Peter Smithson for the *Economist* tower commission. He was also adviser to Kuwait on the development of that city and responsible for the appointment there of Utzon, Arne Jacobsen, and Reima Pietila. He played a part in the award of the royal gold medal to Alvar Aalto in 1957, and tried—and failed—to secure a commission for him in Britain.

Martin was knighted in 1957, and held several visting professorships and honorary degrees. He was awarded the royal gold medal for architecture in 1973 and, in 1992, for the Gallery of Modern Art in Lisbon, the RIBA trustees' medal. He was a fellow of the RIBA, a member of its council (1952–8) and vice-president (1955–7), a member of the Royal Fine Arts Commission (1958–72), and consultant to the Gulbenkian Foundation, Lisbon (1959–69): he was appointed to the Portuguese order of Santiago de Espada. He died in Great Shelford on 28 July 2000, and was buried on 4 August at Gunton, Norfolk.

Critical assessment Martin's was a remarkable career. He began teaching in 1930 and completed his last building in 1990—an interval of sixty years. Having witnessed, through his architect father, the last stages of the arts and crafts movement in practice, he was thereafter always in the forefront of architectural activity. He was highly active in the emerging modern movement in the 1930s; he worked on war damage and reconstruction in the 1940s; he led the world's largest architectural office in the formative period of the welfare state, in the early 1950s; and thereafter he greatly influenced not only architecture, architectural education, and research but also the physical form of many universities in the period of expansion in the 1960s. Martin had a remarkable ability to inspire and lead. As an architect he will be best remembered for the brilliant conception and execution of the Festival Hall (which later became the first post-war building to achieve a Grade 1 listing), for the way in which he drew on precedent and tradition in developing the court form as at Harvey Court, and for the quality and clarity of works such as the Oxford library group (a compositional *tour de force*). The use of a powerful organizational principle or idea allied to a very highly developed aesthetic sense underpinned this work, but so too did a concern for materials: the 1960s and 1970s brick buildings of the 'Cambridge school' that he inspired have a modest and workmanlike quality that has worn well. However, his work was occasionally controversial. In Oxford some criticized his buildings for being 'unforgiving, bland and unsympathetic to older architecture' (*Daily Telegraph*, 1 Aug 2000). His Whitehall study provoked fierce opposition. Martin's commission for this had been a measure of the respect in which he was held for his planning and political skills. However, the sheer scale of the challenge (accommodating both a vast increase of civil servants in Whitehall and the implications of Colin Buchanan's traffic proposals for the area) together with some ill-judged publicity and the failure to convey the exploratory nature of the study (described by

Martin in *Buildings and Ideas*) inevitably led to its being remembered in an ill light.

As an educator, Martin influenced the shape of architectural education in Britain for nearly half a century and showed how the discipline could take its place in the university sector. He profoundly influenced his Cambridge students and it became a source of great pride to him that nearly thirty of these held university chairs. He made a significant contribution to architectural research, although this work has been criticized for its diagrammatic nature and for its 'failure' to recognize the true nature of cities. His powerful reflective capacity was allied to a concern for ideas, for a unifying environment and a broader culture. Above all he had a passion for quality and clarity and for principles and theory. As one of his most distinguished students, Richard MacCormac, wrote after Martin's death: 'No architect of his generation sustained a more consistent intention to relate theory to the procedure and outcome of design' (*Architectural Research Quarterly*, 4/4, 2000, 300). Martin himself summed up his position when, at the end of his introduction to *Buildings and Ideas*, he wrote (quoting from *Hamlet*) 'There is indeed a "glass of fashion". But there is also, to be discovered, a "mould of form" and it is that which has seemed to me to be the deeper and more lasting' (Martin, 11).

PETER CAROLIN

Sources J. L. Martin, *Buildings and ideas, 1933–83* (1983) · *WW* · P. Carolin and T. Dannatt, eds., *Architecture, education and research: the work of Leslie Martin: papers and selected articles* (1996) · *arq* (*Architectural Research Quarterly*), 4/4 (2000), 295–308 · *arq* (*Architectural Research Quarterly*), 5/1 (2001), 11–12 · *Dictionary of contemporary architects* (1994) · b. cert. · *The Times* (1 Aug 2000) · *Daily Telegraph* (1 Aug 2000) · *The Independent* (2 Aug 2000) · *The Guardian* (2 Aug 2000) · personal knowledge (2004) · private information (2004) [daughter; T. Dannatt] · m. cert.
Archives RIBA, drawings collection · Tate collection, transcript of interview for TV South West
Likenesses D. Haycroft, photograph, *c*.1980–1985, Jesus College, Cambridge · P. Sayer, photograph, 1981, NPG [*see illus.*]
Wealth at death £557,984—gross: probate, 10 Jan 2001, *CGPLA Eng. & Wales*

Martin, Martin (*d.* 1718), traveller and author, was probably born in Bealach, Isle of Skye, the third of the three children of Donald Martin, chamberlain of Trotternish, and Mary, daughter of Alexander, son of Donald MacDonald (Domhnall Gorm Òg) of Sleat, first baronet. The Martins of Bealach (clann Mhàrtainn a'Bhealaich) were a minor but distinguished gentry family closely associated with the local chiefs, the MacDonalds of Sleat. Martin spent much of his adolescence away from his native island at Edinburgh, where he entered the university in 1679. After graduating in 1681 he served as tutor in turn to each of the heirs of the two major Skye chiefships, Donald MacDonald of Sleat, later fifth baronet (known as Domhnall a'Chogaidh), and Roderick MacLeod of Harris (Ruairidh Òg). Following the death of the latter—'the kindest friend I had on earth' (NL Scot., MS 1389, fol. 74)—on 24 June 1695, Martin departed on clan business to the Netherlands and thence to London.

Once in London, with the support of fellow episcopalians such as George Mackenzie, Viscount Tarbat, and George Garden, Martin made contact with the virtuosi who were to prove so crucial to his future, above all David Gregory, Walter Curleton or Charleton, and Hans Sloane. For them, as well as for Robert Sibbald in Edinburgh, Martin undertook to collect curiosities from and observations concerning his native Western Isles. Despite the rather credulous nature of the 'observables', he dispatched to the Royal Society in August 1696, Martin was nevertheless voted financial encouragement to enable him further to prosecute his interests. He had also begun a degree in divinity; although he never completed his studies, it was through this that Martin was able to carry off his greatest coup, embarking 'at the Isle Essay in Harries the 29th. May, at Six in the Afternoon, 1697' (Martin, *Late Voyage*, 3) as assistant to the Revd James Campbell on a mission to pacify the recalcitrant inhabitants of the most remote island in the Hebrides.

Martin subsequently went back to London, where he published 'Several observations in the western islands of Scotland' in *Philosophical Transactions*, 19 (October 1697), and wrote up *The Late Voyage to St. Kilda*, an account published to some success in May the following year. Despite his participating in the disastrous surveying expedition under the geographer John Adair that summer—their ship eventually ran aground and had to be abandoned— Martin's star continued to rise among the virtuosi. Sloane organized a subscription on his behalf on condition that he provide 'samples of such curiosities as he finds & useful remarks he makes in his travels' (BL, Sloane MS 4068, fol. 18). This, together with a £25 grant from the Treasury, allowed Martin to make a series of more protracted journeys throughout the Hebrides. He then spent over a year in London assembling his most celebrated work, the compendious *Description of the Western Islands of Scotland*, published in July 1703. Subsequently, however, he would come to regard the book as 'the most capital error as well as the greatest Misfortune of my life' (NL Scot., MS 1389, fol. 100), which had 'abated the Career of my thoughts from so much as thinking to trouble the press any more all my days' (Bodl. Oxf., MS Ashmole 1816, fol. 336). Despite being promised £60 by the exchequer the money remained unpaid. This apparently is the reason behind Martin's rather precipitate flight back to his native Skye 'where no books nor converse are to be looked for' (ibid.). There he spent the next four years rather restlessly as tutor to Donald MacDonald, the son of his old charge. Seemingly on the very day he heard the government money was finally disbursed Martin left Skye for good 'to push his fortouns in England' (NL Scot., MS 1307, fol. 247).

Despite Martin's evident hope for a post under the new united parliament—his second article in the *Philosophical Transactions* for 1707, 'A relation of a deaf and dumb person', is something of a calling card—he was disappointed. He spent the next two years as a tutor, mainly at Leiden University with George, son of the lawyer John Mackenzie of Delvine. Building upon a long-standing interest in medicine Martin himself studied at Leiden for a short

time, having matriculated in March 1710 aged forty-one. On his return to England he began to practise as a doctor in Middlesex, where he passed the apparently unremarkable last years of his life. His final two years were taken up in an attempt to salvage the money owed by Sir Donald to his brother John Martin and lost with the forfeiture of the MacDonald estate following the 1715 rising. Martin himself, however, appears to have taken advantage of the renewed interest in the Scottish Gàidhealtachd by publishing a second edition of the *Description* in 1716, an enterprise which may have given him enough funds to finally graduate MD at Rheims in October that year. Martin died 'of an Asthma' at his lodging in Knightsbridge, London, on 9 October 1718 (NL Scot., MS 1389, fol. 159). Three days later he was buried at St Martin-in-the-Fields.

Martin's ambition to succeed as a 'British Gael' was not unusual among gentry of his generation from the Scottish Gàidhealtachd. His chosen path as collector of curiosities, natural historian, and ethnographer most certainly was. Martin ascribed his success to his 'regard of the Languadge [as a native Gael] & my Interest in those of the first rate in these places' (BL, Sloane MS 4037, fol. 127). We might add his evident energy and gifts in negotiating various clientage networks. Although his lasting value is as a chronicler of customs and beliefs even then fast disappearing, Martin himself was hardly sympathetic to them. For him their passing marked a milestone in islanders' progression to become a useful part of the British state: he was convinced that he had an important role to play in facilitating such development. Nevertheless, his naïve style, his apparent credulousness, his eagerness to relate outlandish medical observations, and above all his belief in the second sight, led to his being ridiculed by literati such as Viscount Molesworth and John Toland. Despite widespread interest in his writings, Martin himself was little more than a curiosity among the metropolitan virtuosi. His ambition for economic and social independence could only be achieved in London; yet in doing so he had forfeited his erstwhile patrons.

DOMHNALL UILLEAM STIÙBHART

Sources M. Martin, *A description of the western islands of Scotland* (1703) · M. Martin, *A late voyage to St. Kilda* (1698) · NL Scot., MS 1389, fols. 67, 73–159 · BL, Sloane MSS 4036, fols. 338, 358; 4037, fol. 127; 4039, fol. 165; 4040, fol. 384; 4044, fol. 220; 4059, fol. 314; 4068, fol. 18 · RS, LBC 11(2).160; 12.409–10; 12.334; ELM.2.17 · Bodl. Oxf., MS Ashmole 1816, fols. 326–343 · BL, Stowe MS 748, fol. 4 · PRO, PROB 11/566, fol. 108*v* · A. MacDonald and A. MacDonald, *The clan Donald*, 3 (1904), 559–60 · Leiden records, Archief Senaat en Curatoren, Actorum Facultatis Medicæ, 12, vol. 13 (6 March 1710) · matriculation roll, arts, law, and divinity, U. Edin. L., special collections division, university archives [transcribed by A. Morgan, 1933–4], p. 78 · U. Edin. L., MS Da.2.1, p. 26 · NA Scot., CC 8/8/80, fol. 196 · copy of MS list of doctors, 1550–1794, Rheims

Archives NL Scot., corresp. and papers, MS 1389 | BL, Sloane MSS, letters to Sir Hans Sloane

Wealth at death £150 owed to Martin; estate includes trunk and contents, books, and clothes: will, PRO, PROB 11/566, fol. 108*v*

Martin [*née* Balmford], **Mary Adela** (1907–1969), artist, was born on 16 January 1907 at 24 Bouverie Road West, Folkestone, Kent, only child of John Archibald Balmford (1867– 1946), pharmacist, and Sarah Hannah Balmford, *née*

Hanson (1865–1920). She attended Folkestone county school, 1915–25, and was awarded a scholarship to Goldsmiths' School of Art, London, 1925–9, and a royal exhibition to the Royal College of Art, London, 1929–32. Here she met her fellow student Kenneth Laurence *Martin (1905–1984); they married on 1 November 1930 at Kensington, London.

Four references from college tutors between 1929 and 1932 stress her dedication, thoughtfulness, and individuality as an emerging artist. However, landscape painting did not provide an income and in the early 1930s she began designing rugs. A sketch notebook from this period records that many were regularly commissioned from firms like Fortnum and Mason, as well as from architects and private clients, including the painter Duncan Grant. Her considerable abilities as a communicator—later to emerge in perceptive writing about her ideas and work—helped to secure teaching posts at London institutes between 1936 and 1940 and finally at Chelmsford School of Art. Here she taught drawing, painting, and design, subsequently becoming head of the weaving department until 1943. When she resumed painting in 1948—following four years dedicated to bringing up two young sons—her work was informed by current ideas in pictorial construction and measurement. While her earlier influences had been Serge Diaghilev's Ballets Russes, and the critical writings of Roger Fry and Clive Bell, now she became immersed in the geometrical theories of Matila Ghyka and Jay Hambidge, and the writings of D'Arcy Thompson, the biologist. Rapidly becoming dissatisfied with paint as a medium for precise mathematical development, the desire to use real space and real materials led to her first relief: *Columbarium* (carved plaster, 1951; priv. coll.). The next relief was constructed: *Spiral Movement* (oil on wood, 1951; Tate collection). From then onwards all her work was non-representational and constructed.

Mary Martin's work and contribution to the development of post-war British constructivism are significant. In 1950 or 1951, together with a group of like-minded artists—including Kenneth Martin, Victor Pasmore, Adrian Heath, and Anthony Hill, who had all renounced figurative art—she began participating in small exhibitions of the new abstract, constructed art. Traditional artists and galleries were often so hostile that she was physically barred from submitting an abstract construction to one gallery. But she began writing increasingly perceptive statements about the nature of her work and its social relevance and began exploring the possibility of collaboration with architects, who were excited by her inventive ideas.

Mary Martin's first major exhibition, with Kenneth Martin, was held at the Heffer Gallery, Cambridge, in 1954, where she showed ten reliefs. The same year, the book *Nine Abstract Artists* by Lawrence Alloway contained the first critical assessment of her contribution and her own first published statement. Strong international connections were fostered; she exchanged several letters with Charles Biederman (b. 1906), the American structurist,

carefully distinguishing her own making process of 'nuclear building' from his 'abstracting'. The Dutch journal *Structure* published four articles by her between 1961 and 1963, while perhaps her most cogent article, 'Reflections', was included in *DATA (directions in art, theory and aesthetics)*, edited by Anthony Hill (1968). She was involved in nine architectural projects and commissions: the first in 1956 with John Weeks, the architect, the second with Kenneth Martin for the exhibition 'This is tomorrow' (Whitechapel Art Gallery, London). The Musgrave Park Hospital, Belfast, commission followed, with a free-standing brick and stainless-steel two-sided wall: *The Waterfall* (1957). Her final commission, completed in 1969, is the 60 foot long *Wall Construction* for the University of Stirling. Here incoming top natural light is continually absorbed, fragmented, and reflected by the angled aluminium plates.

During the nineteen years of her mature professional life, Mary Martin made over sixty reliefs and constructions. Although these may be divided into perhaps six generic groups, the best-known are those that utilize the diagonally cut half-cube, usually faced with stainless steel. Limited, applied colour was introduced to some works which she referred to as 'positive' (white), 'negative' (black), or 'neutral' (red). The ordering of elements was sometimes according to overlapping golden-mean rectangles, whose thicknesses of material were frequently determined by successive Fibonacci numbers; other works were built around developments from pendulum permutations. Her philosophical concern was always with what was possible between the outer, front face of the relief and the wall surface on which it hung.

Her two most important and best-known works are probably *Black Relief* (1957; Tate collection), consisting of thin, stacked layers of wood—their thicknesses identified by brilliant red or ochre—faced with black 'perspex' and geometrically organized in squares and rectangles, and *Cross* (1969; Walker Art Gallery, Liverpool), consisting of stainless steel-faced half-cubes, permutated in cross-formation on black 'formica', and with which she won first prize (jointly with Richard Hamilton) in the John Moores competition, 1969. Her work finally received the highest acclamation possible from her peers.

Mary Martin died of cancer at the age of sixty-two, in Hampstead General Hospital, London, on 9 October 1969 and was cremated on 14 October at Golders Green crematorium. Exhibitions of her work have been held since, including a retrospective at the Tate Gallery in 1984. Although her output was relatively small, she nevertheless produced a body of remarkable works at a significant point in the development of British abstract constructed art.   SUSAN TEBBY

Sources Mary Martin estate archives, priv. coll. · M. Compton and others, *Mary Martin* (1984) [exhibition catalogue, Tate Gallery, London, 3 Oct – 25 Nov 1984] · L. Alloway, *Nine abstract artists* (1954), 3, 13–14, 33–43 · G. Rickey, *Constructivism: origins and evolution*, rev. edn (1995), 61, 98, 121 · W. Rotzler, *Constructive concepts* (1977), 165, 167, 168, 170, 204, 232, 280 · A. Hill, ed., *DATA (directions in art, theory and aesthetics)* (1968), 95–6 · *Mary Martin, Kenneth Martin* (1970) [exhibition catalogue for touring exhibition by Arts Council of

Great Britain, 12 May 1970 – 24 April 1971] • M. Martin, 'Art, architecture and technology', *Structure*, 4th ser., 1 (1961), 16 • M. Martin, 'Art and philosophy', *Structure*, 4th ser., 2 (1962), 45 • M. Martin, 'Pro-art and anti-art', *Structure*, 5th ser., 1 (1962), 19 • M. Martin, 'On construction', *Structure*, 5th ser., 2 (1963), 37 • M. Martin, 'A personal recollection', *View* [Goldsmiths' School of Art] (1966) • private information (2004) • personal knowledge (2004) • b. cert. • m. cert. • d. cert.

Archives Arts Council of England • priv. coll., estate archives • Royal Albert Memorial Museum, Exeter • Tate collection, works and material relating to subject • Ulster Museum, Belfast • University of East Anglia • Walker Art Gallery, Liverpool

Likenesses K. Martin, pastel, *c*.1934, NPG • A. Flowers, photograph, 1956, repro. in Compton and others, *Mary Martin*; priv. coll. • J. Maltby, photograph, 1960, repro. in Compton and others, *Mary Martin*; priv. coll. • photograph, *c*.1965, repro. in Compton and others, *Mary Martin*; priv. coll.

Wealth at death £6349: administration, 31 Dec 1969, *CGPLA Eng. & Wales*

Martin, Mary Ann, Lady Martin (1817–1884). *See under* Martin, Sir William (1807–1880).

Martin, Mary Letitia (1815–1850), philanthropist, was born on 28 August 1815 at Ballinahinch Castle, co. Galway, the only child of Thomas Barnewall Martin (1786–1847), MP for the county, and his wife, Julia Kirwan. Richard *Martin (1754–1834), the well-known philanthropist and founder of the RSPCA, nicknamed 'Humanity Martin', was her grandfather. Mary Martin followed the family philanthropical tradition, devoting herself to improving the condition of her father's tenantry and earning the popular title of the Princess of Connemara. During the great famine, when the tenants were unable to pay rent, the Martins spent large sums on food and clothing for them, and gave continuous work to several hundred labourers.

For Mary Martin's sake her father ill-advisedly broke the entail, mortgaged his large estates to the extent of £200,000 to the Law Life Assurance Society, and further burdened himself with the debts of his father and grandfather, liabilities dating as far back as 1775. When he died on 23 April 1847 the heavily charged estates passed to Mary. On 14 September 1847 she married her cousin, Arthur Gonne Bell of Brookside, co. Mayo, who assumed by royal licence the surname and arms of Martin. Around the time of her marriage she borrowed further large sums of money, with which to relieve her tenantry, both from private sources and from the Law Life Assurance Company; when she was unable to pay the instalments of her father's mortgages, the society insisted on the observance of the bond. The property was among the first brought into the encumbered estates court. Out of an estate of nearly 200,000 acres not a single rood remained to Mary Martin. She retired to Fontaine L'Evêque in Belgium, and attempted to support herself by her writing, publishing *Julia Howard, a Romance* (1850), which is believed to contain much autobiographical material as well as information on the workings of the penal laws. It is set in the 1740s in the west of Ireland, where Julia Howard, the niece of a member of parliament, buys up an estate and engages in philanthropy. The hero, through no fault of his own, loses his estates, and becomes a soldier of fortune. Mary Martin

also published *St Etienne: a Tale of the Vendeam War* (1845) set in Napoleonic times, and contributed to the *Encyclopédie des Gens du Monde* and other French periodicals. While emigrating to America she was prematurely confined on board ship, and died on 7 November 1850, only ten days after reaching New York. Her husband survived until 1883.   ELIZABETH LEE, *rev.* MARIA LUDDY

Sources Burke, *Gen. Ire.* • S. J. Brown, *Ireland in fiction* (1916) • A. E. S. Martin, *Genealogy of the family of Martin* (1890) • S. Lynam, *Humanity Dick Martin: 'king of Connemara', 1754–1834* (1975), 280–88 • M. Edgeworth, *Tour in Connemara and the Martins of Ballinahinch* (1950)

Martin, Matthew (1748–1838), natural historian and philanthropist, born in Somerset, was at first engaged in trade at Exeter. He married on 9 July 1773; his wife, Penelope, died on 9 August 1827. An early interest in natural history led Martin to publish at Exeter *The Aurelian's Vade-Mecum* (1785), listing those plants on which caterpillars fed, 'aurelian' being the Latin term for a chrysalis, and *Observations on Marine Vermes, Insects, &c* (1786). He had been a member of the Bath Philosophical Society, but moved to London and was living at Half Moon Street, Piccadilly, in 1794 when he was elected fellow of the Royal Society.

In 1796 Martin began inquiring into the circumstances of beggars in the metropolis, encouraging several of these unfortunates to explain their circumstances to him. He became secretary to the Society for Bettering the Condition and Improving the Comforts of the Poor, founded in December 1796, and lived above its offices at 3 Parliament Street. Martin proposed a systematic inquiry into the nature and extent of begging in London, and in 1800 obtained a grant of £1000 from the Treasury. His report was published in 1803 as *Letter to Lord Pelham on the State of Mendicity in the Metropolis* and reissued by the society in 1811. The institution in January 1805 of the Bath Society for the Investigation and Relief of Occasional Distress was partly due to his efforts. Martin appears to have undertaken a further inquiry, supported partly by a government grant and partly by contributions raised by his 'Appeal to public benevolence for the relief of beggars'.

Probably about 1826 Martin obtained the post of secretary to a commission for adjusting San Domingo claims, set up to deal with the claims of merchants disadvantaged by the independence of Haiti from France, and he settled in a house adjoining Poets' Corner, near Westminster Abbey. He then retired to Blackwater Park, Charlton, Kent, which was probably where he died, on 20 November 1838, survived by three sons and two daughters.

     [ANON.], *rev.* ANITA MCCONNELL

Sources *GM*, 2nd ser., 11 (1839), 104 • *GM*, 1st ser., 97/2 (1827), 282 • T. Bernard, 'Extract from an account of a chimney-sweeper's boy, with observations and a proposal for the relief of chimney sweepers', *The reports of the Society for Bettering the Condition and Increasing the Comforts of the Poor*, 1 (1798), 146–56 • 'Regulations adopted by the society', *The reports of the Society for Bettering the Condition and Increasing the Comforts of the Poor*, 1 (1798), 267–71 • will, PRO, PROB 11/1904 sig. 768

Archives BL, letters to Lord Spencer

Likenesses J. Sconler, miniature, 1770, V&A

Wealth at death under £6000: PRO, death duty registers, IR 26/1492, no. 821; will, PRO, PROB 11/1904, sig. 768

Martin, Paul Augustus (1864–1944), photographer, was born on 16 April 1864 in Herbeuville, France, to a local farming family, his father, Jean Baptiste Martin, being a mill and vineyard owner. When his childhood home was destroyed in 1869 by the hostilities of the Franco-Prussian War, his family was forced to relocate in Paris, but in turn they were trapped there during the siege and the brutal commune of 1871. Having barely survived, the family fled to London in 1872, where they settled in without further difficulty. After attending St Mark's College in Chelsea, Martin studied at the École Gosserez at Châlons-sur-Marne, France, from 1878. In 1880 he was apprenticed to the London wood-engraver M. Douet and did so well that he stayed with him for six years. In 1886 he moved to the Fleet Street firm of R. and E. Taylor. The public had a voracious appetite for the woodcuts filling the popular press and for some years Martin was a skilled practitioner in this active industry.

When he was ten years old Martin had purchased a packet of materials to 'make your own photographs', and he produced simple cyanotypes of leaves and other objects by contact. By 1884 he was able to afford a camera and began practising as one of the new wave of amateur photographers. In the first decades of photography most of the sensitive materials had to be made by the photographer himself, often immediately before use. An already costly hobby was made prohibitively expensive to most working people simply because they did not have sufficient leisure time to practise it. With the widespread introduction of packaged factory-made plates and paper in the 1880s, it became possible to take photographs in odd moments and on the occasional bank holiday. Martin's early work was generally a record of outings he had taken with friends, and he became active in the camera clubs and in amateur exhibitions.

In 1892 Martin acquired one of the new breed of so-called 'detective' cameras. Most of these were novelties, inspired by literature and disguised in various ways. His bulky Facile plate camera was wrapped in paper to look like a parcel of books. Held under an arm, it permitted the taking of candid 'snap-shots' (a term applied by Sir John Herschel) with relatively short exposures. Martin's world was that of the working person and it was to this world that he turned for subjects. He was never a voyeur, but by not calling particular attention to the act of photographing he was able to inject real life into his images. Many of his pictures were taken while running errands in the Fleet Street area. Others were taken on bank holidays, in the public parks, and on excursions.

Martin's mechanical ingenuity greatly improved his simple camera and allowed him to photograph under conditions previously thought impossible. In 1896 he was awarded the royal medal by the Royal Photographic Society for his series of London by Gaslight photographs (now in the collection of the Royal Photographic Society at the National Museum of Photography, Film and Television, Bradford). Taken at dusk with a mixture of twilight and the novel new gas-lighting, the series presented an image of urban life previously unrecorded by photography. A measure of its impact at the time is the fact that his night views beat out another new type of imaging introduced in 1896—the Röntgen rays. He was invited to show his work at the exhibitions of the pioneering art-photography group the Linked Ring Brotherhood (though he was never a member), and he supplied images to the Eastman Kodak Company to use in their advertising. He was in constant demand as a speaker and a judge to camera clubs and exhibited widely.

Even as Martin's reputation in the world of amateur photography was growing ever greater, his hobby was beginning to undermine his livelihood. The demand for woodcuts began to shrink near the end of the century as photomechanical processes became more common. He declined George Davison's offer in 1899 to join the Kodak firm as he had heard that their prospects were 'none too rosy', a decision he was later to regret bitterly. He had already completed arrangements to enter into partnership with H. G. Dorrett, a fellow amateur, and left woodengraving to set up as a photographer to supply the press. In this highly competitive and rapidly evolving area he was never successful, and the firm eventually did most of its trade in making lowly photographic buttons.

Martin married Clara Emily Ackary (b. 1867/8) on 20 October 1900; they had two sons. He continued to photograph for exhibition, often during family holiday trips, but more and more came to recognize just how special his 1890s work with the Facile camera had been. In retirement he once again became an active lecturer: with his enormous moustache and ample supply of lantern-slides depicting the end of the century, he was widely known. Although he had never been successful as a press photographer, he now found he had a steady demand from publishers wanting accurate and lively views of days gone by. In 1937 Beaumont Newhall included his work in his pioneering photohistorical exhibition 'Photography, 1839–1937'. In 1939 his work was featured in the 'Centenary of photography' exhibition at the Victoria and Albert Museum in London. That same year he published his autobiography, *Victorian Snapshots*.

With the advent of the Second World War Martin lost his opportunity to appear before camera clubs. His death at 55 Hosack Road, Balham, London, on 7 July 1944 went unnoticed in the press; he was buried in Morden cemetery, London, on 12 July. The turmoil of the blitz very nearly destroyed his photographic legacy; however, nearly a thousand of his lantern-slides and press-prints were rescued from commercial files by Helmut and Alison Gernsheim and are now at the University of Texas at Austin. The photographic historian Brian Coe discovered the remains of Martin's work for Kodak sitting in a barrel ready for silver recycling: these now form part of the Kodak Collection in the National Museum of Photography, Film and Television at Bradford. Meticulously kept personal albums, mostly of platinum prints, were preserved by his family and are now in the Victoria and Albert Museum. Quite by chance the contents of an auctioned tea trolley yielded many of his exhibition negatives and prints and they are now preserved in the archives of the Royal Photographic Society, held at the National Museum of Photography, Film and Television. Although he was not a social documentarian by intent, Martin's photographs are among the finest records of late nineteenth-century society, and particularly urban working-class life. He had lived and worked in England most of his life but never obtained citizenship.　　　　　　　　　　　LARRY J. SCHAAF

Sources B. Jay, *Victorian candid camera: Paul Martin, 1864–1944* (1973) · R. Flukinger, L. Schaaf, and S. Meacham, *Paul Martin: Victorian photographer* (1977) · P. Martin, *Victorian snapshots* (1939) · P. Martin, 'A diary of events personal and general … 1869 to 1944', unpubd MS, University of New Mexico · d. cert. · m. cert.
Archives National Museum of Photography, Film and Television, Bradford, Royal Photographic Society collection · University of New Mexico, MSS and photographs · V&A | National Museum of Photography, Film and Television, Bradford, Kodak collection · U. Texas, Gernsheim collection
Likenesses photograph, 1895, U. Texas · K. Hutton, photograph, 1942, U. Texas
Wealth at death £4713 0s. 1d.: probate, 11 Nov 1944, CGPLA Eng. & Wales

Martin, Percy (1871–1958), engineer and motor vehicle manufacturer, was born in Columbus, Ohio, USA, on 19 June 1871. He graduated as a mechanical engineer (in electrical engineering) at Ohio State University, Columbus, in 1892. His involvement in the British motor industry, which occupied the greater part of his working life, began with a chance meeting in London in 1901 while on holiday in England after working as an engineer in Milan and Berlin for General Electric, the dominant American company in the developing worldwide electrical industry. Martin met H. F. L. Orcutt, who had been asked by the chairman of Daimler, the motor manufacturers, to look for a successor to J. S. Critchley as works manager at Coventry. After an interview, Martin was appointed in October 1901, continuing with Daimler and the amalgamated Daimler/BSA group until his retirement in 1934. He became a naturalized British citizen.

Despite the involvement of the financier H. J. Lawson in its origins, Daimler had already gained the cachet of royal patronage, but it needed technical and managerial skill to consolidate its position. As an engineer/businessman, Martin's contribution to Daimler was immediate: within a year of his appointment a more rational model policy had been adopted and he had designed and built new 12 and 22 hp cars. Managerial control over design, operations, and materials was combined with improved incentive payments, notably the contentious premium bonus system. This was seen by Martin as the carrot rather than the stick to move productive effort along lines laid down by management (Lewchuk, 140–42).

Martin's long-term career with Daimler was associated with two major technical developments, based on acquired technical rights: the Silent Knight engine, marketed in 1909, and the fluid flywheel, based on the Föttinger hydraulic coupling, and introduced in 1930. The Silent Knight was a sliding- or sleeve-valve engine, developed by F. W. Lanchester from the designs of Charles

Y. Knight of Wisconsin. Daimler acquired exclusive manufacturing rights in the UK, with permission to export. The advantages of smoother and quieter operation than the poppet-valve engine remained until overtaken by engine design and fuel improvements in the early 1930s. Silent Knight was, however, a more expensive engine to build, and opinions differ as to whether Daimler merged with the Birmingham Small Arms Company (BSA) in 1910 from a position of strength or weakness. On balance, Martin's appointment as managing director of the reconstituted Daimler concern and as one of three Daimler directors on the BSA board suggest that his skills and value to the new group were fully recognized. The BSA had been founded in 1861 and had added cycle components, cycles, and motor cycles to its range of products, but its diversification into car manufacture, from 1907, had proved disappointing. It is therefore certain that Daimler had something to offer BSA as car (and subsequently commercial vehicle) manufacturers. That the BSA group remained something of an agglomeration, rather than becoming an integrated structure, can hardly be laid at Martin's door.

Martin's experience came into its own during the First World War, when the group's factories were devoted to military production, in particular staff cars, lorries, tank and aero-engines, and aeroplanes. In addition, Martin was made deputy controller of petrol engine supply at the Ministry of Munitions in February 1917 and given a seat on the Air Board. Also in February he was appointed controller of mechanical transport, a position he held until departmental reorganization in November.

In the early post-war period Martin entered into what has been described as a 'reckless deal' with George Holt Thomas, the aviation pioneer, to acquire his Airco group, which included the engine manufacturer Peter Hooker. This acquisition, at the outset of a period of recession, involved unwarranted expenditure and expansion. From 1926 to 1929 Daimler and the commercial vehicle manufacturers AEC were involved in a joint venture, the Associated Daimler Company, but it did not live up to Martin's hopes, AEC proving the dominant partner. Meanwhile, in 1927, Martin had approached Louis Coatalen to propose a merger between Sunbeam and Daimler, but this came to nothing. However, the acquisition by the BSA group of the ailing Lanchester Motor Company at the end of 1930 was rightly seen as industrial rationalization and may be regarded as the culmination of Martin's links with the remarkable Lanchester brothers.

Towards the end of his career Martin was closely involved in the development and introduction of the Daimler fluid flywheel, having acquired manufacturing rights in the Föttinger hydraulic coupling in 1929. The introduction of the epicyclic (Wilson) gearbox in conjunction with the fluid flywheel is credited to Martin, who apparently was particularly proud of his part in the development of this technical improvement. He was chairman of Daimler from January 1934 to October 1935, having retained his seat on the board after retirement. Changes at Daimler, probably overdue, followed Martin's retirement;

these included the establishment of a separate bus division, Transport Vehicles (Daimler) Ltd, in 1936 and extensive development of the works, to speed production, in 1937–8.

Martin married, in July 1902, a fellow American, Alice Helen Heublein (d. July 1958) of Hartford, Connecticut, whom he had met in Berlin while she was on holiday. They had a son, John, and a daughter, Helen. Like a number of other midland industrialists, Martin settled in Kenilworth, where he bought Spring Farm, later extended by the purchase of the adjoining Camp Farm. He died, following a heart attack, at The Spring, Kenilworth, on 10 November 1958. His son subsequently pursued a business career in the USA and his daughter, who did not marry, managed The Spring estate after her father's death and became a great benefactor of the nearby University of Warwick.   RICHARD A. STOREY

Sources St J. C. Nixon, *Daimler, 1896–1946* (1946) · J. Prioleau, *Forty years of progress* (1936) · B. E. Smith, *The Daimler tradition* (1972) · J. B. Rae, *The American automobile: a brief history* (1965) · A. Bird and F. Hutton Stott, *Lanchester motor cars* (1965) · *Coventry Evening Telegraph* (11 Nov 1958) · *Coventry Evening Telegraph* (17 Nov 1958) · *Coventry Evening Telegraph* (16 Feb 1959) · *Coventry Standard* (23 Dec 1954) · private information (2004) · R. Storey, 'Martin, Percy', *DBB* · W. Lewchuk, *American technology and the British vehicle industry* (1987) · D. Thoms and T. Donnelly, *The motor car industry in Coventry since the 1890s* (1985) · J. Wood, *Wheels of misfortune: the rise and fall of the British motor industry* (1988) · R. P. T. Davenport-Hines, *Dudley Docker: the life and times of a trade warrior* (1984) · Lord Montagu and D. Burgess-Wise, *Daimler century* (1995) · d. cert.
Archives Coventry City RO, Daimler minute books · Museum of British Road Transport, Coventry, presentation album on retirement
Wealth at death £63,054 13s. 11d.: probate, 29 Jan 1959, *CGPLA Eng. & Wales*

Martin, Peter John (1786–1860), doctor and geologist, was born on 26 March 1786 in Pulborough, Sussex, the son of Peter Patrick Martin (1750–1840) of Edinburgh, who had set up in medical practice in Pulborough in 1774 and married Mary Backshell in 1778. The second-born in a family of nine children, Martin had five sisters and three brothers. Thomas (1779–1867), the eldest son, together with his father, were largely responsible for Peter Martin's early education. When Thomas entered medical practice in Reigate, Surrey, Martin moved with him, prior to taking up his own studies in medicine at the united hospitals of Guy's and St Thomas's in London and later, from 1805 to 1807, at the University of Edinburgh medical school. After completing his studies (MRCS 1813) Martin joined his father in practice in Pulborough, where he married his cousin, Mary Watson of Dunbar, in 1821. A family of four daughters and one son were born between 1822 and 1831; the son, Robert (1827–1891), became a physician at St Bartholomew's.

Martin was reputed to have gained his interest in geology during his residency in Edinburgh, where he became partial to the 'Huttonian theory'. In any event, once he had joined his father in practice, he began to study the land around his native Pulborough. Between 1829 and 1857 he contributed several papers to the Geological Society of London (of which he was elected a fellow in 1833)

and to the *Philosophical Magazine*. His most important publication was, however, produced privately in 1828—*A geological memoir on a part of western Sussex with some observations upon chalk-basins, the Weald-denudation and outliers-by-protrusion*. This thin quarto volume brought Martin into a county already investigated by other eminent geologists, including William Henry Fitton (whom Martin acknowledged in his preface) and in particular Gideon Mantell (1790–1852), the 'wizard of the Weald' and discoverer of the dinosaur *Iguanodon*. It was a thinly disguised 'attack' (Martin to John Hawkins, 26 May 1828, London, Geological Society Archives) on Mantell in Martin's book which attracted some attention from contemporaries such as the Wernerian John Hawkins (1761?–1841), who regarded Martin as 'a sort of heaven inspired geologist' (Hawkins to Mantell c.1832, in Steer). Yet Martin's work was also criticized for relying too heavily on the works of others, particularly Mantell's 1822 *South Downs* and later publications.

Mantell himself hoped to chastise 'the over-weening vanity and dogmatism' (Mantell to Hawkins, 3 Jan 1832, Hawkins MSS, W. Sussex RO) which he unearthed in Martin's book. Ironically, one of Martin's lasting achievements was the coining of the term 'Wealden', describing certain strata in Sussex which Mantell had first determined as being of freshwater origin. In later years, as evidenced in Mantell's own journal, the two men became friendly despite these early quarrels, often exchanging visits, specimens, and letters. Ultimately however, Martin's own writings refer to the Huttonian school of thought for explanations of Wealden geology too frequently to be regarded as seminal by modern workers. His strengths as a geologist stemmed from his detailed and accurate local observations, rather than grander deductions and theories.

Martin's interests extended far beyond geology. He contributed papers on tumuli and Roman roads to the *Sussex Archaeological Collections*, and on gardening to the *Gardeners' Chronicle* (mostly between 1841 and 1845 and often under the initials 'P. P.'), as well as lecturing on literature to the Philosophical and Literary Society of Chichester (1833–4). He was a capable musician and was noted by obituarists as having great powers of memory and knowledge of the arts, and a delightful style of conversation. As a doctor, Martin was very popular and with a career spanning over forty years was much sought after for consultations and opinions. He published one medical paper, 'Case of hereditary ichthyosis', in the *Transactions of the Medical and Chirurgical Society* in 1818. He died at Pulborough on 13 May 1860.   JOHN A. COOPER

Sources *GM*, 3rd ser., 9 (1860), 198–201 · *BMJ* (26 May 1860) · Boase, *Mod. Eng. biog.* · F. W. Steer, ed., *I am, my dear sir … A selection of letters written mainly to and by John Hawkins* (1959) · D. T. Moore, J. C. Thackray, and D. L. Morgan, 'A short history of the museum of the Geological Society of London, 1807–1911', *Bulletin of the British Museum (Natural History)* [Historical Series], 19 (1991), 51–160 · parish records, Pulborough, W. Sussex RO · private information (2004) [Duncan Rabagliati, descendant] · d. cert. · P. Martin, letter to J. Hawkins, 26 May 1828, GS Lond. · W. Sussex RO, Hawkins papers

Archives BGS, fossils · GS Lond., corresp. · W. Sussex RO, corresp. | NL NZ, letters to Gideon Algernon Mantell
Wealth at death under £6000: probate, 24 Aug 1860, *CGPLA Eng. & Wales*

Martin, Sir Richard (1533/4–1617), goldsmith, whose early life is obscure, was sworn free of the Goldsmiths' Company of London in 1555. He subsequently took no fewer than forty apprentices and served four times as prime warden of the company. His standing as one of the most important goldsmiths of his day is further evidenced by his appointment both to the office of warden of the mint, and as a supplier to Queen Elizabeth I, to whom, he claimed in 1593, he was accustomed to purvey annually 'above £1000 worth of plate and chains of gold … and sometimes thrice so much' (Collier, 181).

The occasion of Martin's going to the mint, which was in 1572, and not, as has commonly been stated, in 1559–60, was the reorganization of the administration there, consequent upon the demise of his fellow goldsmith Thomas Stanley. The system of direct management, which had operated since the start of the open debasement of the coinage in 1544, was replaced by the more traditional arrangements, whereby the master worker took responsibility for the production of coins at the correct weight and standard, and a number of royal officials, of whom the warden was the most senior, provided a control mechanism. It was the warden who formally accounted to the crown for production, and it was to the wardenship that Martin was appointed. The master worker, with whom he should have been able to deal harmoniously, was another goldsmith, John Lonyson, but, in the event, their relationship was marked only by discord.

The point at issue was the exploitation of the remedy, or working tolerance, which allowed coin marginally deficient in weight or fineness nevertheless to pass current. Traditionally, far from being seen as a device to facilitate the manufacture of substandard coin, the remedy had been regarded simply as a safeguard to protect the master worker, in case, by sheer chance, his coins proved to be deficient. To Martin all this was perfectly clear, whereas to Lonyson it certainly was not. As it happened, Lonyson's indenture had not been as tightly drawn as it should have been, and thus, to him, so long as his coins were passed standard at the trial of the pyx, not only had he fulfilled his legal obligation, but he might pocket as profit all that arose from his coins' falling short of the prescribed standards, while still remaining within the remedies. When a detailed government inquiry found that technically Lonyson was correct, order was only restored by his being given higher coining allowances, which were to be paid for by officially reducing both the fineness and weight of all gold and silver coins made. Lonyson had won; but so too had Martin for, in addition to Lonyson's now being controlled in the extent to which he might benefit from the coinage above the levels set in his indenture, from September 1578 Lonyson was permitted to coin only by a series of short-term commissions, issued jointly to Martin and himself. In 1582 Martin completed his triumph when,

Sir Richard Martin (1533/4–1617), by Steven Corneliszoon van Herwijck, 1562

on Lonyson's death, he himself secured the office of master worker.

Despite the absurdity of a situation in which Martin in one capacity was allowed to be the official check on what he did in another, Martin continued to hold both his offices until 1599, and during that time was instrumental in stilling one of the most important debates the mint has ever known: namely, how the sterling standard was to be defined. Both Martin and his opponent, Thomas Keeling, assay master at Goldsmiths' Hall, were agreed that sterling was 11 oz 2 dwt fine and that, when tested by fire assay, approximately 2 dwt of silver, would drain away with the impurities into the cupel, giving a result which implied that silver was 2 dwt less than it actually was. What they were not agreed upon, however, was the figure from which the 2 dwt should be deducted: was it, as Martin said, from 11 oz 2 dwt of fine silver put in at the melting, and which would give an assay result of around 11 oz, or was it, as Keeling claimed, from 11 oz 4 dwt of fine silver which would result after the assay in a standard of 11 oz 2 dwt? Between 1583 and 1586 the debate, through words and practical demonstration, was intense, but in the end it was Martin's view that prevailed.

In addition to trading as a goldsmith, and holding office at the mint, Martin owned a salt works, and became in 1568 a founder member of the Society of Mineral and Battery Works, from which he obtained leases on the wire works at Tintern, as well as, for a time, on the battery works themselves. It is said that in 1596 he owned, with two of his sons, Nathaniel and Richard, over one-third of all the paid-up shares in the society, of which two years previously he had become, with his son-in-law, Sir Julius Caesar, joint governor. Martin also had an interest in overseas trade, being mentioned in the charters of the Levant Company, as well as appearing as a founder member of the Turkey Company, and being three (possibly four) times governor of the Russia Company. The surviving portion of a double-entry journal for 1581 not only dispels doubts which have been expressed as to whether he actually did trade in merchandise, but shows clearly that he was also a moneylender.

An alderman from 1578, sheriff in 1581, and lord mayor in 1589 (the year in which he was knighted) and 1594, Martin was, at the height of his influence, possibly the most active of all London's senior aldermen, not least through his being comptroller-general of hospitals from 1594 to 1602. In the latter year, however, he was declared bankrupt, and degraded from the aldermanry. Temporarily imprisoned, he was forced to sell for £10,200 his principal residence in Tottenham, his great messuage in Milk Street in the City of London, together with other property and leases in town and country. Martin found his position all the harder to bear because of yet another serious dispute at the mint, this time with Sir Thomas Knyvet, to whom he had relinquished the wardenship in 1599. In the course of a spirited defence designed to show, but in the end failing to substantiate, that he did not, as Knyvet alleged, owe the crown £8382, Martin produced a significant treatise on assaying which he dedicated to James I in 1603/4.

Martin's first wife, whom he married before 1562, was Dorcas Ecclestone (1536/7–1599) [see Martin, Dorcas], daughter of Sir John Ecclestone of Lancashire. A second marriage took place before 1616, when the younger Richard Martin bequeathed to his father and his lady £3 each for a ring; and it was this Lady Martin, Elizabeth, formerly Bourne (d. 1627), sister of John Cottesford, goldsmith of London, who was able on Sir Richard's death successfully to claim payments in respect of his mint office. By the first marriage there were five sons and one daughter, Dorcas, who took as her second husband Sir Julius Caesar, master of the rolls. Two of the sons, Nathaniel and Richard, were associated with Martin at the mint, where Nathaniel was clerk from 1589 to 1594 and Richard was deputy master worker from 1588 to 1598 and then joint master worker from 1598 to 1607. Another son, Captain John Martin (d. 1632), was a member of the council of Jamestown, Virginia. Sir Richard Martin died in July 1617, and was buried in Tottenham, where his first wife, Dorcas, had been interred in 1599. C. E. CHALLIS

Sources C. E. Challis, The Tudor coinage (1978) · C. E. Challis, ed., A new history of the royal mint (1992) · C. E. Challis, ed., The history of the Goldsmiths' company, 1509–1696 [forthcoming] · A. B. Beaven, ed., The aldermen of the City of London, temp. Henry III–[1912], 2 vols. (1908–13) · R. G. Lang, 'London's aldermen in business, 1600–1625', Guildhall Miscellany, 3 (1969–71), 242–64 · DNB · J. P. Collier, ed., The Egerton papers, CS, 12 (1840), 181 · S. Van Herwijck, portrait medal, 1562, BM
Archives BL, Harley MSS, mint papers · CUL, treatise on reorganization of the mint · LUL, treatise on the mint | BL, Add. and Lansdowne MSS · CLRO, remembrancia and repertories · Goldsmiths' Hall, London, court minute books and apprentice books · PRO, state MSS domestic, accounts various and memoranda rolls in the exchequer
Likenesses S. C. van Herwijck, silver medal, 1562 (his wife on the reverse), BM [see illus.] · B. Wright, line engraving, 1600, BM

Wealth at death declared bankrupt, 1602; owed crown £8382; sold property for £10,200, 1602; but wealth exceeded this; widow received money and goods totalling £103 from mint office

Martin, Richard (1570–1618), barrister and politician, was born at Otterton, Devon, the son of William Martin of Otterton and Anne, daughter of Richard Parker of Sussex. He matriculated at Pembroke College, Oxford, as a commoner in 1585, and made his mark as a debater although he left without taking his degree. He entered the Middle Temple in 1590, but was temporarily expelled after leading a riotous Lord of Misrule festival in February 1591. Martin became part of the Mitre circle of poets and wits whose members included Ben Jonson, Fulke Greville, John Selden, John Hoskins, Arthur Ingram, and Lionel Cranfield, whose close friend and attorney he became. His mercurial temperament was suggested by an incident in February 1598 in which he was assaulted with a cudgel by Sir John Davies, who had earlier prefaced his 'Orchestra' with a dedicatory sonnet to him.

Martin was elected MP for Barnstaple, Devon, in 1601, through the patronage of Robert Chichester. He made his maiden address on 10 November, was active in the debates against monopolists, and won attention by chiding Serjeant John Hele for suggesting that subsidies belonged to the monarch by right. On 8 December he was appointed to the committee for privileges. In 1602 he was called to the bar, and in 1603 he gave a speech of welcome on James I's accession at Stamford Hill which, published with the king's assent, earned him the sobriquet of London Oracle. Returned again to parliament in 1604 for Christchurch, Hampshire, possibly through the patronage of Sir Robert Cecil, he soon emerged as one of the half-dozen leaders of the House of Commons and a frequent spokesman in conferences with the Lords. In 1604 he took a prominent part in the Goodwin–Fortescue election dispute, served as a member of the committee that framed the apology and satisfaction that defended the Commons' privileges, and sharply objected to the speaker's forwarding petitions or bills to the king without the assent of the house. Martin remained similarly active throughout the four sessions of James's first parliament. He was prominent in the debates on the Anglo-Scottish union, supporting Sir Edwin Sandys's brief for a perfect union, and in 1607 he defended John Hare, who had denounced the abuses of purveyance; he joined Hoskins in attacking John Cowell's The Interpreter for casting aspersions on the common law and the subject's liberties. In 1610 he assailed what he called 'an arbitrary, unlimited, and transcendent power to levy impositions' (Gardiner, 88), and chaired the committee that dealt with this issue. That same year he offered a bill to deprive ministers who exalted prerogative beyond its proper bounds and 'tread upon the neck of the law' (E. R. Foster, 2.328). In November he chaired the important debates over the adoption of the great contract.

Despite the seeming popularity of many of his positions Martin retained his connections with Salisbury, and was praised by Lord Treasurer Sackville for his short and apt

Richard Martin (1570–1618), by Simon de Passe, 1620

answers in conference. He kept up his academic associations, and in September 1611 took part in a philosophical feast at Brasenose College, Oxford. In February 1613 he organized the masque in honour of the marriage of Frederick V, elector palatine, and Princess Elizabeth at the Middle Temple.

The London gossip John Chamberlain reported in 1614 that Martin was growing rich from his legal practice and was unwilling to jeopardize it by standing for parliament again; Francis Bacon also noted that 'Martin hath money in his purse'. He did appear before the House of Commons in May as counsel for the Virginia Company, which he had represented since 1612. Departing from his brief, however, he lectured the Commons on their slow proceedings and disorderly carriage, was censured by the house, and was forced to recant his remarks. This episode, too, does not appear to have done Martin lasting damage although the company's leading projectors, the earl of Southampton and the lords Sheffield and De La Warr, were furious with him. In 1616 he was Lent reader of the Middle Temple, and James commended him at Cranfield's suit to succeed Sir Anthony Benn as recorder of London in 1618. Installed on 1 October, he died some time between 31 October and 7 November 1618 and was buried in the Temple Church. His will was executed by the mayor of Exeter, and

contained small bequests to the parish church of Otterton as well as to that of Culliton-Raleigh, Devon, where his country residence was located.

Martin never married, although he was rumoured to be the father of a daughter by Lady Lake. His untimely death aborted a career still in the ascendant. He was admired by many of the leading figures of his time, and Ben Jonson dedicated his 'Poetaster' to him. Anthony Wood reports that Martin was a poet in his own right, although only a single verse epistle, to Sir Henry Wootton, appears to survive. His career should be seen in the context of the group of Middle Temple reformers, including Sandys, Hoskins, and James Whitelocke, that formed the core of the parliamentary opposition in the first two decades of the seventeenth century. The hundred he owned in Virginia still bears his name. It was the site of a massacre of colonists by local Indians in 1622.   ROBERT ZALLER

Sources *CSP dom.*, 1611–18, 72, 125, 234, 589, 591, 595 · E. R. Foster, ed., *Proceedings in parliament, 1610*, 2 vols. (1966) · Foster, *Alum. Oxon.* · M. Jansson, ed., *Proceedings in parliament, 1614 (House of Commons)* (1988) · *The letters of John Chamberlain*, ed. N. E. McClure, 2 vols. (1939) · J. Nichols, *The progresses, processions, and magnificent festivities of King James I, his royal consort, family and court*, 4 vols. (1828) · W. Notestein, *The House of Commons, 1604–1610* (1971) · T. K. Rabb, *Jacobean gentleman: Sir Edwin Sandys, 1561–1629* (1998) · *The parliamentary diary of Robert Bowyer, 1606–1607*, ed. D. H. Willson (1931) · Wood, *Ath. Oxon.*, new edn · S. R. Gardiner, ed., *Parliamentary debates in 1610*, CS, 81 (1862) · S. D'Ewes, ed., *The journals of all the parliaments during the reign of Queen Elizabeth, both of the House of Lords and House of Commons* (1682) · HoP, *Commons, 1558–1603*
Archives HLRO
Likenesses S. de Passe, line engraving, 1620, AM Oxf., BM [*see illus.*]

Martin, Richard (1754–1834), animal welfare campaigner and social reformer, was born in February 1754, probably in Dublin, the eldest son of Robert Martin (1714–1794), landowner, of Dangan in Galway and his first wife, Bridget Barnewall (*d.* 1762), third daughter of John Barnewall, styled eleventh Baron Trimleston, and his wife, Mary. Both his parents' families were of Catholic Anglo-Norman descent and he was the first family member to be brought up as a protestant—a device planned by his father to entitle Richard Martin to enter parliament to fight for Catholic emancipation. He was sent to Harrow School where a senior master, Samuel Parr, criticized 'wanton barbarity' to animals, an attitude already impressed upon Martin by his mother. He matriculated at Trinity College, Cambridge, in 1773, was admitted to Lincoln's Inn in February 1776, and in June entered the Irish House of Commons where he sat until 1783 as member for Jamestown, co. Leitrim, and from 1798 to 1800 for Lanesborough in the same county. In 1781 he was called to the Irish bar and in the same year, he conducted his only case, that against George Robert FitzGerald, 'Fighting FitzGerald', who was convicted of unlawfully imprisoning his own father. FitzGerald, a notorious madcap, had already earned Martin's contempt for shooting a wolfhound belonging to Lord Altamont. Martin, friend of both dog and owner, eventually challenged FitzGerald to a duel with pistols in which both participants were slightly wounded. This was not Martin's only duel, and at least one was to prove fatal for his adversary.

On the death of his father in 1794, Martin came into property which covered a third of co. Galway, some 200,000 acres of which were bog, mountain, and moorland in Connemara. He took up residence at Ballynahinch Castle, Connemara, at about this time, visiting Dublin, London, and Paris to pursue his political interest in parliamentary reform. In 1801 he was elected to the parliament in London as member for co. Galway which he continued to represent until 1826, speaking up for Catholic emancipation, opposing slavery, introducing a bill in 1821 to secure defence counsel for those on capital charges, and sharing with Sir James Mackintosh a campaign to abolish the death penalty for forgery. In Ireland, too, Martin was known for his humanitarian concerns, urging the pardoning of rebels, interceding on behalf of young men and women in trouble with their parents or the authorities, and for taking into his house and feeding the poor and hungry. So renowned was he for his philanthropy that the prince regent nicknamed him 'Humanity Martin', an epithet which became popularized as 'Humanity Dick'.

Martin is best remembered for his robust championing of the protection of animals. On 18 May 1821 he published a bill proposing to make it an offence to 'wantonly beat, abuse or ill-treat' any 'horse, cow, ox, heifer, steer, sheep or other cattle' belonging to another person. This bill, amended to include mares, geldings, mules, and asses, passed through the Commons on 1 June but was defeated in the House of Lords. Undismayed, Martin reintroduced his bill and, with the help of Lord Erskine in the Lords, it received royal assent on 22 July 1822. This act, known as Martin's Act, was the first national parliamentary legislation in the world to penalize cruelty to animals. His repeated attempts to introduce further legislation to protect cats, dogs, and animals in slaughterhouses, and to ban dogfighting and bull-baiting, all failed. But Martin vigorously enforced his act, bringing horse dealers, drovers, and carters before the magistrates, often paying their fines out of his own pocket. On 16 June 1824 Martin, with William Wilberforce, Thomas Fowell Buxton, and other reformers, established the body which eventually flourished as the Royal Society for the Prevention of Cruelty to Animals (RSPCA), after a precarious early period in which Martin had to rescue its first secretary, Arthur Broome, from debtors' prison. Martin was among the first to propose that the society should employ inspectors.

Besides his concern for the welfare of horses and farm animals, Martin also denounced vivisection as 'too revolting to be palliated by any excuse' (Greenwood, 82). He denied that he attacked the cruel sports of the poor while ignoring those of the rich, asserting that he was 'equally anxious to meddle with both when he found them opposed to the dictates of humanity' (Hansard 2, 24 Feb 1825, col. 657). When he was once asked why he took so much trouble to defend animals, Martin allegedly retorted: 'Sir, an ox cannot hold a pistol!'

Martin was described as 'a short, thick-set man, with evidence in look and manner, even in step and action, of indomitable resolution' (Fairholme and Pain, 47). His niece, Harriet Martin, recalled his 'large-hearted sympathy with suffering of whatsoever kind' (ibid., 47–8). In parliament, it was said, his sense of humour disarmed the opposition—'he holds the House by the very test of the human race, laughter, and while their sides shake, their opposition is shaken and falls down at the very same instant'. Yet, he could be formidable—'he lets drive at the House like a bullet, and the flag of truce is instantly flung out upon both sides' (ibid., 27–8). It was undoubtedly this combination of warmth, wit, and manly ebullience which enabled Martin to win some of his battles for reform. Anecdotes abound to testify to both his compassion and his pride. It was said that widows and children on his Irish estates would pray for his deliverance, that he had stopped a journey to investigate the reasons for a child's crying, and had comforted a shy girl at a grand function; yet he would also imprison malefactors and debt collectors at Ballynahinch. He was a friend of George IV but, typically, stood up for the estranged Queen Caroline. When the king asked him who would win a Galway election, Martin reputedly replied 'The survivor, Sire!'

Martin was twice married. He married first, on 8 February 1777, Elizabeth (d. c.1795), daughter of George Vesey of Lucan, co. Dublin, with whom he had two surviving sons, Thomas Barnewall (1786–1847) [see below] and St George (1788–1800), and a daughter, Letitia (d. 1858). Martin was deserted by his first wife in 1791. On 5 June 1796 he married Harriet (d. 1846), author, the second daughter of Hugh Evans and widow of Captain Robert Hesketh; they had a son, Richard (b. 1797), who emigrated to Canada in 1833, and three daughters who never married, Harriet Letitia (1801–1891) [see below], Georgina (b. 1806), and Mary (b. 1810). Harriet Martin published at least two works after her marriage to Martin, Helen of Glenross (1802) and Remarks on John Kemble's Performance of Hamlet and Richard III (1802).

Martin enjoyed the theatre and an active social life. He neither drank to excess nor gambled, yet his generosity with money so compounded his inherited debts that eventually he was forced to flee to France to escape his creditors. He died at 6 rue de l'Ecu, Boulogne, on 6 January 1834, his last thoughts being on the care of his family and his dog. Martin's grave was damaged in an air raid in September 1944 and his remains were re-interred in Boulogne's eastern cemetery in 1972, marked by a plaque paid for by the RSPCA.

Martin's son **Thomas Barnewall Martin** (1786–1847), politician and landowner, was born on 4 October 1786 at Ballynahinch Castle, co. Galway. He was member of parliament for Galway from 1832 until his death of 'famine fever', caught when visiting his tenants in the Clifden workhouse, on 23 April 1847. The Law Life Assurance Society subsequently took possession of the Martin estates and sold them. His half-sister **Harriet Letitia Martin** (1801–1891), author, was born in London on 5 July 1801. She travelled extensively in Europe and America and while staying with John Banim and his wife in Paris, she wrote a story entitled *Canvassing*. This was published in 1835 and she went on to publish a novel, *The Changeling, a Tale of the Year '47*, in 1848. She died in Dublin on 12 January 1891.

RICHARD D. RYDER

Sources S. Lynam, *Humanity Dick Martin: 'king of Connemara', 1754–1834* (1975) · E. G. Fairholme and W. Pain, *A century of work for animals: the history of the R.S.P.C.A., 1824–1924* (1924) · R. D. Ryder, *Animal revolution: changing attitudes towards speciesism* (1989), 83–92 · *The Times* (17 June 1824) · G. Greenwood, *Animal World* [RSPCA] (July 1925), 82 [R. Martin, letter to L. Gompertz, 16 April 1832] · *Hansard* 2, cols. 657–8 · S. C. Hall, *Retrospect of a long life, from 1815 to 1883*, 2 vols. (1883) · RSPCA Archives, London · *DNB* · *IGI* · P. J. Jupp, 'Martin, Richard', HoP, *Commons, 1790–1820*
Archives L. Cong., debates in the Irish House of Commons · NL Ire., Lord Lieutenants' Union corresp. · priv. coll., RSPCA MSS · priv. coll., London Corporation Repertories · PRO, Home Office files, series 100/101 | BL, letter-book of first marquess of Buckingham · BL, Cornwallis MSS · BL, letters to Lord Hardwicke, Add. MSS 35729–35739, *passim* · BL, Law Hedges' journal · BL, Liverpool MSS · BL, corresp. with Sir Robert Peel, Add. MSS 40221–40397, *passim* · BL, Wickham MSS · NA Ire., Westmorland MSS · NL Ire., Bellew MSS · NL Ire., D'Arcy MSS · NL Ire., French MSS · NL Ire., Gormanston MSS · NL Ire., Heron MSS · NL Ire., Teeling MSS · priv. coll., Erskine MSS · priv. coll., Kilmaine MSS · priv. coll., Martin MSS · PRO NIre., Ballyglunnin MSS · PRO NIre., corresp. with Lord Castlereagh · PRO NIre., Maggs MSS
Likenesses S. Drummond, lithograph, BM · possibly by E. Landseer, pen-and-ink sketch, AM Oxf. · oils, Royal Society for the Protection of Animals, London
Wealth at death died in debt: Lynam, *Humanity*; *DNB*

Martin, Robert Montgomery (1800x02–1868), author and civil servant, was born while his family were living at 106 Great Britain (afterwards Parnell) Street, Dublin, the younger son of law agent John Martin (*d.* 1808) of Augher, co. Tyrone, and Mary Hawkins of Dublin. His father's family were 'loyal' Ulster, Anglican protestants, his mother's well-to-do tradespeople. His life was dominated by a self-appointed task—the study of the British empire, which Martin saw in terms of a vast free-trade area of new territories in allegiance to the British crown. The early death of his father leaving him without support, Martin—the better to pursue his imperial concerns—trained as a doctor, and then served in Ceylon and with the Owen expedition on the east coast of Africa (1820–24) as an assistant surgeon and naturalist; in 1826 he arrived in Sydney, New South Wales, where he unsuccessfully sought official employment, before settling as a surgeon in Parramatta. He moved to Calcutta in 1828 once again as a surgeon, but his fortuitous rescue of Dwarkanath Tagore brought him into contact with Hindu reformers of the Brahmo Samaj, particularly Ram Mohan Roy, with whom he established, and for a short time edited, the *Bengal Herald* (1829).

After returning to Ireland in 1830 Martin became associated with Daniel O'Connell and edited the repealist *Irishman*, but by 1833 the protestant Martin had turned pro-union, publishing his *Ireland as it Was, Is, and Ought to Be*. The overseas empire was, however, always in his mind, as evidenced in a lifetime of publication: in 1834–5 came his pioneering, five-volume *History of the British Colonies*, followed by such related works as *Statistics of the Colonies of the British Empire* (1839). In 1833 Martin published *Taxation of the British Empire*; this was followed by studies of the poor

laws and the hand-loom weavers. Influenced by his friend Edward S. Cayley MP, with whom he edited the *Agricultural and Industrial Magazine* (1834–5), Martin was active in organizations concerned with economic and social reform, particularly the Central Agricultural Society, whose journal, *The Agriculturist*, he co-edited in 1836. Consistent with the principles of the Birmingham school, he advocated the establishment of colonial banks which would forge the financial links of empire—in the case of the proposed Bank of Asia in defiance of Indian government policies (1840–43). Martin opposed repeal of the corn laws and stood unsuccessfully as protectionist candidate in the 1846 by-election at Bridport, Dorset.

Martin's writings, though drawing on official sources, were influenced by his practical Christianity and by his association with leading intellectuals. He was a founder member of the Statistical Society of London (1834), the Colonial Society (1837), and the East India Association (1867). He opposed duelling, suttee, and slavery, advocated the abolition of flogging, and was active in the work of the Aborigines Protection Society.

Martin sought patronage, but his contribution was questioned, particularly by the formidable Sir James Stephen, the permanent under-secretary of the colonial department. Naïvely he allowed interviews with William IV and Princess Victoria (1832) to feed his expectations. It was his work on Ireland and his assumed financial literacy which, in 1844, eventually led the colonial secretary, Edward G. Stanley, to appoint Martin treasurer of Hong Kong. By then Martin, with his background as a publicist, was temperamentally unqualified for a civil service position. His tenure was brief and controversial. Concluding that Hong Kong was unsuitable as a base for British operations in the East, Martin left his post in 1845 to present his views to the government. This was considered an act of resignation, a view which Martin contested, unsuccessfully, for three years, while publishing his own views in his *British Position and Prospects in China* (1846) and *China: Political, Commercial and Social* (2 vols., 1847).

Martin's Irish background and Indian experiences brought him into contact with Marquess Wellesley, whose correspondence he edited (1836). Martin subsequently embarked on a biography, which was never completed, of Arthur Wellesley, first duke of Wellington; however, as a virtual private secretary to the second duke, he devoted some twelve years to collecting and collating material for the authoritative *Supplementary Despatches … [of the] Duke of Wellington* (15 vols., 1858–72). Martin was concurrently publishing materials relevant to his activities in the promotion of colonial steamship, mining, and banking ventures, as well as updated editions of his earlier works. He continued, unsuccessfully, to propose projects to the colonial and foreign departments. His work with the second duke of Wellington had, however, provided him with financial security, and in 1861 he was able to withdraw to Sutton, Surrey, where he served as justice of the peace from 1863 to 1868.

In 1826 Martin had married Jane Avis Frances Keith (*b. c.*1808); the marriage was dissolved (10 Vict. c. 72) in 1847, thus enabling him to marry Eliza Barron [see Phillips, Eliza (1822/3–1916)], his solicitor's niece, on 11 November the same year. As Martin was then in debt, his success in obtaining a private act of parliament must be ascribed to 'access' in the broadest sense rather than to wealth. Martin died at Wellesley Lodge, Reigate Road, Sutton on 6 September 1868, and was buried at Sutton parish church.

At a time when some questioned the value of the empire, Martin was its spokesman. He favoured a reformed colonial policy and, as a proprietor of the East India Company (1838–43), debated both at India House and through journal articles. But his lack of financial backing and his tendency to rush to judgement were factors minimizing his effectiveness; the former led him to seek *ex post facto* official recompense for activities freely entered into, the latter lost him support at key moments. Martin, however, had a ready pen and his importance lies primarily in his chronicling of empire and his exposition of political and social issues, particularly in the context of non-Ricardian economics. The very diversity of his activities and writings—267 printed works and 580 surviving unpublished letters and memoranda—underlines his significance. FRANK H. H. KING

Sources F. H. H. King, *Survey our empire! Robert Montgomery Martin (1801?–1868), a bio-bibliography* (1979) · A. Seymour, 'Robert Montgomery Martin: an introduction', in R. M. Martin, *History of the British colonies: possessions in Europe*, 5: *Gibraltar* (1835); facs. edn (1998), i–xiv · m. cert.
Archives BL, Peel MSS, Add. MSS 40408–40611 · LPL, Blomfield MSS · Lpool RO, Stanley MSS · NL Scot., Letters from Sir Archibald Alison · NRA Scotland, Correspondence with Sir Thomas Makdougall-Brisbane · Strathclyde Regional Archives, Glasgow, Sir William Stirling Maxwell MSS · [F. H. H. King, *Survey our Empire! Robert Montgomery Martin (1801?–1868), a bio-bibliography* (1979)]
Wealth at death under £3000: probate, 22 Sept 1868, *CGPLA Eng. & Wales*

Martin, Roger (1526/7–1615), recusant and memoirist, was born between 3 August 1526 and 3 August 1527. He was the eldest son of Richard Martin, esquire (d. c.1573), and his first wife, Anne (d. 1528), daughter of Thomas Eden of London. The Martin family allegedly originated in Dorset, but had lived in Long Melford, Suffolk, from the late fourteenth century; their 'coming up was by cloth making' (MacCulloch, *Chorography*, 97) and by the acquisition of land in Suffolk and Essex. Their principal home was at the southern end of the town at Melford Place, opposite their chapel of St James. In 1484 Roger's great-grandfather, the merchant clothier Richard Martin, had completed a chantry chapel in Melford church; his initials and merchant's mark were placed above it on the exterior of the chancel. His armigerous grandfather (and godfather), another Roger Martin, was clearly a major influence; in his will of 1535 he left to 'little Roger' assets including valuable tableware, an Essex manor, and £100. At that time Roger was being educated by Edward Tyrrell, a local chantry priest and schoolteacher. In 1546 Roger, like his grandfather before him, was admitted to Lincoln's Inn.

During Edward VI's reign Melford church was purged to conform to the new protestantism. Still in his early twenties, Roger Martin was dismayed when liturgical features provided by earlier generations were sold or destroyed. He was more than a reproachful bystander, however, for as a principal inhabitant who was also churchwarden during Queen Mary's reign and beyond (1553–9) he acted as scribe, commenting on the accounts of other churchwardens, correcting faulty arithmetic, compiling memoranda on legacies, debts, and church lands, listing church goods, and annotating parochial accounts long after he left office, even as late as 1580. He showed considerable legal acumen, quoting earlier wills, rentals, and charters, making an index and numerous cross-references, and arguing that the wishes of testators and donors should always be observed. To him the events of Edward's reign were 'the spoyle of Melford churche', during which precious objects were 'scateryd abrode and delyveryd to certen lyght persons' (black book, fols. 25r, 56v). When churchwarden in Mary's reign, he expunged 'vayn scrybylyng upon the churche walles' and 'scrypture upon the roodelofte' (ibid., fol. 38v); in these years he also bought or re-introduced such Catholic furnishings as censer, holy water sprinkler, and the high rood. In 1557–8 he and his fellow churchwarden Richard Clopton spent the large sum of £51, mainly on repairs to the church and church-house.

Martin is best known, however, for writing 'The state of Melford church … as I did know it'. In this brief but unique document he lovingly describes the church as it was in his youth: for example its images and tabernacles, and its dramatic processions on Palm Sunday. He mentions religious objects salvaged and removed to his house, including a reredos, and expresses the hope that 'my heires will repaire, and restore [them] again, one day' (Dymond and Paine, 2). The original document, written some time during Elizabeth I's reign, was destroyed c.1692, but had previously been copied, probably incompletely, by a local schoolmaster named Jonathan Moor. This copy gave rise to four versions printed between 1825 and 1873 which, though imperfect, have been widely quoted. Moor's transcription was rediscovered in the Norfolk Record Office in 1990 and published two years later.

Martin spent his last decades branded as a popish recusant who refused the rites and sermons of the established church. Between 1578 and 1580 he suffered two periods of imprisonment in Ipswich and Norwich. Conditions were not totally bad: in Norwich, for example, Martin and four other Catholic gentlemen shared a heated room and table for their meals. In 1590 he found himself with other prominent recusants in Wisbech Castle. He was released in 1595, but had to give a bond for his returning to custody if necessary. Other penalties were purely financial. In 1581 he was fined nearly £200 and when in 1585 he was required to supply a horse for the queen's service, he complained that his whole income was not above £200 and that he was already £200 in debt. After two more convictions in 1587 two of his manors were seized and leased by the crown. Finally, from 1599 until 1614 Martin was regularly presented in the consistory court at Norwich. His household was said to contain known or suspected priests, such as Gregory Gunnes and Henry Foster, and travellers and messengers who 'are holden to be very daungerous by flitting and removing from one recusant to another' (returns of papists, Norfolk RO, DN/DIS 9/1a, fol. 49r). Thus for some thirty-five years he had to endure surveillance, imprisonment, and substantial loss of income. Supported, however, by strong religious and social ties, he and his family retained their faith and genteel status, and were certainly not reduced to abject poverty.

Martin married twice and had ten children. He and his first wife, Ursula, daughter of Sir Thomas Jermyn of Rushbrook, had four sons and two daughters; she died in 1562. His second wife was Margaret, daughter of Walter Bowles of Pembrokeshire, with whom he had two sons and two daughters. After her death in 1578 Martin remained a widower for thirty-seven years. He died in Long Melford, probably at Melford Place, on 3 August 1615, aged eighty-eight, and was buried on the 7th in the Martins' ancestral chapel in Melford church under a brass depicting him and his two wives; his will does not survive. The Martin family lived on in Melford for several more generations and in 1667 became baronets.   DAVID DYMOND

Sources Black Book of Melford, Suffolk RO, FL 509/1/15 · R. Martin, 'The state of Melford church … as I did know it', Norfolk RO, COL 8/3/1–10, T 129E; Suffolk RO, J 726 [microfilm] · D. Dymond and C. Paine, *The spoil of Melford church: the Reformation in a Suffolk parish*, 2nd edn (1992) · W. Hervey, *The visitation of Suffolk, 1561*, ed. J. Corder, 1, Harleian Society, new ser., 2 (1981), 17–20 · J. J. Howard, ed., *Visitation of Suffolke, 1561*, 1 (1866), 207–30 · will, PRO, PROB 11/29, sig. 10 [Roger Martin, grandfather] · will, PRO, PROB 11/12, sig. 4 [Richard Martin, great-grandfather] · returns of papists, Norfolk RO, DN/DIS 9/1a · J. Strype, *Annals of the Reformation and establishment of religion … during Queen Elizabeth's happy reign*, 2nd edn, 2 (1725), 293–4, appx, pp. 62–4; 3 (1725), appx, pp. 140–42 · will, PRO, PROB 11/19, sig. 12 [Lawrence Martin, great-uncle] · *Lincoln's Inn*, vol. 1 (1896), 22, 25 · V. B. Redstone, 'Chapels, chantries and gilds in Suffolk', *Proceedings of the Suffolk Institute of Archaeology and History*, 12 (1906), 34–5 · D. MacCulloch, ed., 'Henry Chitting's Suffolk collections', *Proceedings of the Suffolk Institute of Archaeology and History*, 34 (1977–80), 103–28, esp. 121 · D. N. J. MacCulloch, *The chorography of Suffolk*, Suffolk Records Society, 19 (1976), 96–7 · *APC, 1577–8*, 310–13; *1578–80*, 47–8; *1597–8*, 588–9; *1590*, 10 · *CSP dom.*, *1581–90*, 279, 322; *1595–7*, 151 · H. Bowler, *Recusants in the exchequer pipe rolls, 1581–1592*, ed. T. J. McCann, Catholic RS, 71 (1986), 117–18 · *Miscellanea, XII*, Catholic RS, 22 (1921), 107, 121 · H. Bowler, ed., *Recusant roll no. 2 (1593–1594)*, Catholic RS, 57 (1965), 158–9 · H. Bowler, ed., *Recusant roll no. 3 (1594–1595) and recusant roll no. 4 (1595–1596)*, Catholic RS, 61 (1970), 89, 223 · H. Foley, ed., *Records of the English province of the Society of Jesus*, 6 (1880), 728, 731 · G. Anstruther, *The seminary priests*, 1 (1969), 367 · E. Farrer, *East Anglian miscellany* (1930), 62, 64–7, 69–74, 78–89 · C. Paine, 'The rebuilding of Long Melford church', *Long Melford: the last 2000 years*, ed. E. Wigmore (2000), 24–30 · W. Parker, *The history of Long Melford* (1873), 70–75, 124–6 · E. L. Conder, *Church of the Holy Trinity, Long Melford, Suffolk* (1887), 31–2, 71–3 · GEC, *Baronetage*, 4.41–2 · M. M. C. Calthrop, ed., *Recusant roll no. 1, 1592–3*, Catholic RS, 18 (1916), 112, 311

Archives Norfolk RO, Colman collection, late seventeenth-century transcript · Suffolk RO, Bury St Edmunds, Black Book of Melford

Likenesses monumental brass, 1615, Long Melford church; repro. in Conder, *Church of the Holy Trinity*, pl. xiii

Martin, Sadie. *See* Speight, Sadie (1906–1992).

Martin, Samuel (1694/5–1776), plantation owner, was born in Antigua, the eldest son of Captain Samuel Martin (*d*. 1697) and his wife, Lydia, daughter of Colonel Thomas of Antigua, sugar plantation owners based in what was later known as Greencastle, in New Division, Antigua. He claimed descent from a general serving under William the Conqueror, and from an ancestor who had participated in the conquest of Ireland in the reign of Elizabeth I. His grandfather, a royalist, had moved to the West Indies, following the confiscation of his land in Ireland by Cromwell's army. Martin's father, it is believed, had moved to Antigua from Surinam in 1667. By 1697, when his slaves murdered him, the plantation consisted of more than 500 acres.

Details of Martin's early life are very sketchy. Following the death of his father he was sent to live with relatives in Ireland, the estate in Antigua being managed by members of his family and friends. He was educated at Mr Biby's school in Caddington, Hertfordshire. At the age of sixteen he went to Trinity College, Cambridge, where he was admitted on 17 April 1711, but he does not appear to have taken a degree. Shortly afterwards he married Frances Yeamans, daughter of John Yeamans, attorney-general of the Leeward Islands; their son, Samuel, was born in Antigua on 1 September 1714. During the next thirty years the family lived mainly in Antigua, interspersed with spells in England between 1716 and 1718. Martin returned to England in 1728 but very little is known about his activities over the next twenty years, with the exception that, following the death of his first wife, he married Sarah (*d*. 1747/8), widow of William Irish of Montserrat and daughter of Edward Wyke, lieutenant-governor of Montserrat. Their first son, Henry, was born in 1733 at Shroton, Dorset. It is probable that they lived, at least for part of the time, on Martin's family's estates in Ireland, while the plantation was looked after by a series of managers, aided by his brother Josiah, who was a member of the island's privy council.

On his return to Antigua, to remedy the deterioration in the fortunes of the plantation, Martin embarked on a rigorous policy of reconstruction. This rapidly established his reputation as a leading member of the island's community. He was speaker of the island's assembly from 1750 to 1763 and colonel of its militia; the diarist Janet Schaw described him as the 'loved and revered father of Antigua' (Sheridan, 'West Indian antecedents', 258), a title won as much for his economic as his political activity. Although he helped to pioneer improvements at most of the key stages in sugar-making and rum distillation his interests focused mainly on the non-manufacturing side of production. He was a firm advocate of crop rotation followed by marling, in order to improve soil fertility. He was also instrumental in developing more effective systems of drainage and utilizing windmills rather than animals for crushing the cane.

By the standards of his contemporaries Martin was an enlightened slave owner. He advocated the provision of adequate supplies of food, clothing, shelter, and medical facilities for slaves, and ground for the cultivation of their own food. This was not simply an altruistic response but motivated by mercenary considerations, since he appreciated the financial benefits to be derived from a healthy, well-trained, and productive labour force that was able to reproduce itself. In order to maximize the profitability of the undertaking his programme focused mainly on the training and direction of black slaves. Unlike his compatriots he was also prepared to work alongside his slaves in the fields, clearly illustrating that he 'did not conform to the stereotyped image of the planter as a leisured gentleman who sipped Madeira and rum punch amidst a harem of Mulatto concubines' (Sheridan, 'Samuel Martin', 137). Nevertheless he still defended the principles of slavery.

Martin's progressive methods were detailed in his *Essay upon Plantership*. It is not clear when it was first issued but the third, extensively revised edition was published in 1756 and was followed by a fourth edition, published in London in 1765. The fifth edition, of 1773, contained a preface, 'On the management of negroes'; further reprints followed. Martin also issued diplomas to the substantial numbers of young Englishmen and Scotsmen who sought their fortunes in the West Indies and had received training from him in plantation administration.

Martin might be regarded as Antigua's leading and most progressive planter in the 1730s. The improvements that he advocated were adopted primarily in Antigua, where the industry was already beginning to experience long-term secular decline due to a multitude of factors that included soil exhaustion, the spread of crop diseases, severe drought, and the growing tendency towards absentee ownership. As a result production costs in Antigua were considerably higher than in other parts of the British empire, such as the Ceded Islands and Jamaica. During his own lifetime he had succeeded in making sugar production a moderately profitable enterprise on his own estates. Martin died in 1776, probably on his estate of Greencastle, Antigua. His legacy was rather short-lived since his innovations were not immediately adopted outside Antigua and his descendants continued as absentee owners for several generations before the estate was sold in the nineteenth century.

Three of his sons, however, became prominent in public life. Samuel (1714–1788), educated at Trinity College, Cambridge, and the Inner Temple, became MP for Camelford (1747–68) and for Hastings (1768–74); he is probably best remembered for the duel that he fought with Wilkes in 1763, having called him a 'cowardly scoundrel' (Valentine, 585). Henry (1733–1794) succeeded his half-brother in Antigua; he became comptroller of the navy and MP for Southampton, in 1790, and was created baronet in 1791. Martin's third son, Josiah *Martin (1737–1786), pursued a career in the army before becoming governor of North Carolina at the outbreak of the American War of Independence.   JOHN MARTIN

Sources R. B. Sheridan, 'Samuel Martin, innovating sugar planter of Antigua, 1750–1776', *Agricultural History*, 24 (1960), 126–39 · A. Valentine, *The British establishment, 1760–1784: an eighteenth-century biographical dictionary*, 2 vols. (1970) · R. B. Sheridan, 'The West Indian antecedents of Josiah Martin, last royal governor of North Carolina', *North Carolina Historical Review*, 54 (1977), 253–70 · Venn, *Alum. Cant.* · L. S. Butler, 'Martin, Samuel', *ANB* · F. W. Pitman, 'The settlement and financing of British West India plantations in the eighteenth century', *Essays in colonial history presented to Charles Mclean by his students* (New Haven, 1931) · F. W. Pitman, *The development of the British West Indies, 1700–1763* (New Haven, 1917) · N. Deerr, *The history of sugar*, 2 vols. (1949–50) · S. Martin, 'An essay upon plantership', ed. A. Young, *Annals of agriculture and other useful arts* (1792) · D. R. Fisher, 'Martin, Henry I', HoP, *Commons, 1790–1820* · L. B. Namier, 'Martin, Samuel', HoP, *Commons, 1754–90* · GEC, *Baronetage*, 5.269

Archives BL, papers, Add. MSS 41346–41353, 41474 | BL, Josiah Martin papers
Wealth at death see will, PRO, PROB 11/1031, sig. 227, mentioned in Venn, *Alum. Cant.*, 152

Martin, Sir Samuel (1801–1883), judge, was the son of Samuel Martin of Culmore, Newtownlimavady, co. Londonderry. He graduated BA at Trinity College, Dublin, in 1821 (MA in 1832) and received an honorary LLD on 2 September 1857. In May 1821 he entered Gray's Inn, and in 1826 the Middle Temple, where he was called to the bar on 29 January 1830, after practising for the previous two years as a special pleader. He was a pupil of Sir Frederick Pollock, afterwards lord chief baron of the exchequer, and subsequently became close friends with him on the northern circuit, where he rapidly acquired an extensive commercial practice. In Easter term 1843 Martin was made queen's counsel, and on 28 August 1838 he married Frances (Fanny) Homera (d. 1874), eldest daughter of Sir Frederick Pollock. They had one daughter, Frances Arabella, (d. 1903), who later married Sir Edward Macnaghten.

In 1847 Martin entered parliament as Liberal MP for Pontefract, and made his maiden speech on the Crown and Government Security Bill of 1848. On 6 November 1850 he succeeded Baron Rolfe in the court of exchequer. He was created serjeant-at-law the following day, and was knighted on 13 November. He was a judge of unusual strength. Though adept in the refinements of special pleading and the intricate procedure of the time, he was not a pedantic stickler for forms, and tried to prevent their being used unfairly. His knowledge of business and quick mastery of the essential points made his judgments terse and precise. As a criminal judge he did not shrink from imposing heavy sentences, but his natural kindness often led him to find mitigation. Increasing deafness led Martin to retire early from the bench on 26 January 1874. On 2 February he took the privy council oath but his deafness meant he took no part in the proceedings of the judicial committee.

Martin was a keen horseman and was said to have been a good judge of horses; in 1874 he was elected an honorary member of the Jockey Club. He died at his rooms, 132 Piccadilly, on 9 January 1883.   J. M. RIGG, rev. HUGH MOONEY

Sources *The Times* (10 Jan 1883) · *Annual Register* (1883), pt 2, p. 120 · *Solicitors' Journal*, 18 (1873–4), 247–8 · *Law Times* (20 Jan 1883), 218 · E. Foss, *Biographia juridica: a biographical dictionary of the judges of England ... 1066–1870* (1870) · J. Haydn, *The book of dignities: containing rolls of the official personages of the British empire* (1851), 413 · *Life of John, Lord Campbell, lord high chancellor of Great Britain*, ed. Mrs Hardcastle, 2 (1881), 330 · W. Ballantine, *Some experiences of a barrister's life*, new edn (1890), 223, 247 · W. Ballantine, *The old world and the* new (1884), 210 · *Hansard 3* (1848), 98.244, 347, 426; (1849), 104.582; (1850), 110.136–8

Archives BL, legal notes, Add. MS 43646

Likenesses W. Walker, mezzotint, pubd 1853 (after H. W. Phillips), BM · wood-engraving (after photograph by London Stereoscopic Co.), NPG; repro. in *ILN* (20 Jan 1883)

Wealth at death £34,944 2s. 3d.: probate, 19 March 1883, *CGPLA Eng. & Wales*

Martin, Samuel (1817–1878), Congregational minister, was born on 28 April 1817 at Woolwich, the son of William Martin, shipwright, and his wife, Mary Pool (d. 1829). His mother died when he was twelve years old and that left a lasting impression upon him. He received his early education from Thomas James, the minister of Salem Chapel, Woolwich, and later at the school conducted by the Revd Richard Cecil at Turvey, Bedfordshire. In 1829 he joined a firm of architects in the City of London but abandoned his training there and entered the Western College, Exeter, in October 1836. His ambition to serve the London Missionary Society in India was thwarted when the society decided in 1839 that he was not strong enough physically for the work. In 1839 he was ordained at Highbury Chapel, Cheltenham, and on 2 October of the same year he married Mary (d. 1880), the daughter of John Trice of Tunbridge Wells. They had at least three sons. In July 1842 he moved to Westminster Chapel, London, the new church built by the Metropolitan Chapel Building Association the previous year. His ministry there was extremely successful and in 1863 the chapel had to be pulled down and a new one, capable of seating up to 3000 people, was opened in 1865. In 1862 he was chairman of the Congregational Union of England and Wales. His last years were dogged by ill health and in 1876 Henry Oliver joined him as co-pastor. He delivered his last sermon in June 1877 and died on 5 July 1878 at 19 Belgrave Road, Pimlico, London. He was buried at Abney Park cemetery, London, on 10 July after services conducted by his fellow congregationalist J. C. Harrison and by A. P. Stanley, the dean of Westminster.

Samuel Martin made Westminster Chapel one of the foremost nonconformist preaching stations in London, although his preaching style was quiet and simple with no dramatic rhetorical flourishes. He had modified the strict Calvinism of his father and propounded an evangelicalism that was both practical and devotional and which centred on God's universal beneficent rule. His numerous publications exemplify the way in which the horizons of evangelicalism were broadening during the Victorian era. Many of these were lectures delivered at meetings of the Young Men's Christian Association (YMCA) and reveal his concern for young people. These covered a large number of topics, such as history in *Anglo-Saxon Christianity* (1862), morals in *Gambling* (1856), politics in *Christianity, Pure Socialism* (1851), science in *Michael Faraday* (1867), and economics in his twelve lectures, *Money* (1850). He was one of the first vice-presidents of the YMCA, and his lectures attracted a wide audience among the shop assistants of West End stores. Above all he was a gifted and attractive pastor, sensitive to people's needs and predicaments, and radiating a warm sympathy with all who sought his ministrations.

R. TUDUR JONES

Sources DNB · *Congregational Year Book* (1879), 330–32 · D. M. Lewis, ed., *The Blackwell dictionary of evangelical biography, 1730–1860*, 2 vols. (1995) · C. Binfield, *George Williams and the YMCA: a study in Victorian social attitudes* (1973) · m. cert. · *CGPLA Eng. & Wales* (1878) · IGI

Archives DWL

Likenesses C. Baugniet, lithograph, BM, NPG · J. Cochran, stipple (after H. Room), BM, NPG · Elliott & Fry, carte-de-visite, NPG · D. J. Pound, stipple and line engraving (after photograph by W. G. Smith), NPG · oils, Congregational Centre, Castle Gate, Nottingham

Wealth at death under £8000: probate, 13 Aug 1878, *CGPLA Eng. & Wales*

Martin, Sarah (1791–1843), prison visitor, was born in June 1791 at Caister on the Norfolk coast. She was an only child and her father, a local tradesman, and her mother both died in her infancy. She was brought up by her widowed grandmother, a glove maker, and attended Caister village school. From the age of twelve Sarah Martin read well-known classics obtained from a local library; from the age of fourteen she walked to work at Great Yarmouth, 3 miles away, as a dressmaker, an occupation which maintained her for most of her life. At the age of nineteen she heard a sermon at a Church of England meeting-house in Yarmouth and, though previously having a deep distrust of religion, she became a dedicated convert, and by 1811 had learned much of the Bible by heart. In 1826 her grandmother died, leaving her about £250, which produced an income of £10–12 per year. Sarah Martin left Caister to live with a poor widow in Great Yarmouth. From 1811 she had been teaching in the local Sunday school and reading the Bible in the local poor-house infirmary.

Great Yarmouth borough gaol and house of correction was severely criticized by James Neild in his 1812 survey of English prisons. The prison, which consisted of seven underground dungeons and a day-room, was filthy, disease-ridden, and infested with vermin. The poorly fed prisoners were unsupervised and allowed to tyrannize over each other; the prison lacked heating and medical care, and the regime indulged those with funds in gambling, drunkenness, and vice, eschewing any of the protective or rehabilitative programmes which, following the work of John Howard in the late eighteenth century, had become received wisdom in prison government.

From 1810 Sarah Martin had reflected on the prison which she passed daily on her way to work. In August 1819, however, she heard that a woman had been committed there for cruelty to her child and she visited her. The meeting was painful, for the woman was very distressed at injuring her own child, but Martin persevered in her visits and began to meet the male prisoners also. They were at first contemptuous towards her, but her regular visits became accepted by staff and prisoners as well as by the borough councillors of Great Yarmouth who, embarrassed by James Neild's revelations, were initially most reluctant to allow her access. She was to continue work at the prison until her death a quarter of a century later.

Sarah Martin's methods involved a combination of biblical instruction, personal friendship, and practical aid. She was a persistent visitor of individual prisoners, with whom she would talk about their own human needs, the evil of crime, and the consolations of religion, building up many deep and abiding relationships. She would make contact with prisoners' families outside, either by visits or correspondence, to prepare for release, and she would fund prisoners, from her own income or later charitable donations, who had no food or resources to get them home. This was at times problematic: as Great Yarmouth was a seaport, families would arrive from far away searching for their menfolk, or released prisoners who were sailors would need a great deal of help to get a vessel to take them home. Sarah Martin aimed to appeal to the heart of the prisoner and was frank in her expectation that promises to desist from criminality would be kept after release, on occasion making simple contracts with prisoners to that effect. On every Sunday she held at least one collective religious service in the prison at which Bible reading and a sermon were a major element. In addition she taught selected prisoners to read and write using children's books and religious literature which she obtained from the Society For Promoting Christian Knowledge. In particular she taught them to memorize scripture as she had memorized it as a young woman. She also taught women prisoners her own needlework skills and provided useful work, such as bookbinding or making of bone spoons, for the men: the articles thus made were sold and the profit given to each prisoner on discharge. Martin would also find work for prisoners on release. Finally she would visit or correspond with former prisoners. Central to all her methods was constant reference to the Christian faith.

In 1824 the council extended the prison adding improved accommodation above ground. Sarah increased her attendance until, by the late 1830s, she was at the prison every day. Up to 1838 Sarah depended on her own trade and local donations to resource this work; she refused all offers of finance from the borough until 1841, when £12 a year was granted her. She also received funds from Elizabeth Fry's British Ladies' Society. By now her work was becoming well known, as the inspector of prisons appointed under the 1835 Prison Act for the north and east, Captain William John Williams, had viewed her activities with astonishment and recorded her progress in detail: these reports were published as part of the annual reports of the prison inspectors. By this time she was receiving assistance from the Hon. Revd Pellew, chaplain to the borough; just after her death a prison chaplain and schoolmaster were appointed.

Sarah Martin's theology—inseparable from her mission—emphasized three tenets. Firstly she insisted that there was an inseparable connection between sin and sorrow, arguing that vice and crime, however alluring, invariably led to sorrow and pain. Secondly she insisted on a similar indissoluble connection between goodness and happiness. Thirdly she urged with great passion that by the sacrifice of Christ on the cross atonement and redemption were available to all and that by faith in Christ even those most sunk in sin could find peace and salvation. All were lost to the temptation of sin, she argued, unless they turned to Christ to be reborn spiritually and thus delivered from the wrath of God. She believed most strongly that where love and charitable bonds failed, the malice and corruption of Satan instantly entered in.

Sarah Martin provided an unyielding and dedicated model of the prison missionary, persisting in visiting those who rebuffed her or fell back on old ways. She believed that even the most hardened would soften when shown love and compassion in the context of Christian consolation, and was especially attentive to the women and children in prison. Her innermost beliefs were revealed in her religious poetry, which emphasized the all-protecting offer of life eternal to the faithful and the demonic snares of Satan awaiting all who reject their Saviour. A persistent theme in her poetry is the suffering of sin and the importance of the missionary rescuer.

Towards the end of her life Sarah Martin also superintended a school for pauper children and set up classes for factory women on two nights a week in St Nicholas' Church, Great Yarmouth. She became ill in the winter of 1842, although she continued to visit the prison until April 1843. Thereafter she suffered intense agony and did not leave her sickbed, consoling herself writing appropriate poetry. This, with other verse, was published after her death as *Selections from the Poetical Remains of Miss S. Martin* (1845). She died on 15 October 1843 at Great Yarmouth and was buried at Caister by the side of her grandmother.

Sarah Martin is difficult to classify. She was plainly closely in tune with the Quaker and Anglican evangelical approach to the reform and the consolation of prisoners represented by Elizabeth Fry and the London-based Prison Discipline Society, and yet she was far from the wealthy banking network of Mrs Fry's family and friends. She began her work at about the same time as Elizabeth Fry and cannot be regarded as a mere imitator. She did not move on any national stage, for she was intensely bound to Caister and Great Yarmouth and never ventured more than a few miles from them. Of humble birth, she left no mission or movement. She was remembered, however, for the depth of her faith and for the genuine unostentatious love she held for prisoners and other neglected groups. A woman of great feeling, she appears to have had a remarkable capacity for entering into the sufferings of others. Practical and energetic, she wanted prisoners to be busy learning new skills and active rather than slothful and despairing.   BILL FORSYTHE

Sources G. Mogridge, *Sarah Martin: the prison visitor of Great Yarmouth* (1872) • C. Barber, *A brief sketch of the life of the late Sarah Martin* (1844) • C. L. Balfour, *A sketch of Sarah Martin* (1854) • [J. Bruce], *EdinR*, 85 (1847), 320–40 • J. M. Denew, 'Introductory notice', in *Selections from the poetical remains of Miss S. Martin* (1845) • 'Inspectors of prisons … northern and eastern district', *Parl. papers* (1835–43) [reports 1–8] • W. J. Forsythe, *The reform of prisoners, 1830–1900* (1987) • J. Neild, *The state of the prisons* (1812)

Archives Norfolk RO, notes written to keeper of Great Yarmouth gaol • Tolhouse Museum, Great Yarmouth, journals and account books

Martin, Susannah (*d.* 1692). *See under* Salem witches and their accusers (*act.* 1692).

Martin, Sir Theodore (1816–1909), lawyer and biographer, born at Edinburgh on 16 September 1816, was the only son in a family of ten children of a well-to-do Edinburgh solicitor, James Martin, who was for some years private secretary to Andrew, Lord Rutherfurd. His grandfather, also Theodore Martin, was ground officer on the estate of Cairnbulg, near Fraserburgh, Aberdeenshire; and his mother, Mary, was the daughter of James Reid, a shipowner of Fraserburgh.

Early life and writings Martin attended the Royal High School in Edinburgh, under Dr Adam, and then Edinburgh University (1830–33), of which he was created an honorary LLD in 1875. At university a love of literature was awakened in him by the lectures of James Pillans, professor of humanity. He studied German and interested himself in music and the stage.

Martin's earliest literary venture was editing the journal *Dramatic Review* with W. H. Logan. He translated the work of François Rabelais and contributed to the *Carlton Chronicle* and was then invited by William Tait to contribute to *Tait's Edinburgh Magazine*. He attracted the attention of W. E. Aytoun with his humorous pieces written under the pseudonym of Bon Gaultier (from Rabelais), in particular with his satire on the fashionable novel in the style of Harrison Ainsworth's *Dick Turpin* entitled 'Flowers of Hemp, or, The Newgate Garland'. Aytoun had been three years senior to Martin at university and, at his request, the naturalist Edward Forbes introduced the two men, and 'a kind of Beaumont and Fletcher partnership', as Martin called it, was the result. From 1842 to 1844 they collaborated on a series of humorous pieces for *Tait's* and *Fraser's* magazines composed of poems, parodies in prose (including a set of prize novels earlier than William Thackeray's 1847 'Prize Novels' in *Punch*), and a series of humorous colloquies in the fashion of John Wilson's *Noctes Ambrosianae* called 'Bon Gaultier and his Friends'. Most of the verse was collected into *Bon Gaultier's Ballads* (1845), which achieved immense popularity and reached a sixteenth edition in 1903. The poems parodied the leading verse of the day, including Tennyson's 'Locksley Hall' in 'The Lay of the Lovelorn' and Elizabeth Barrett Browning in 'The Rhyme of Sir Lancelot Bogle'. Other targets included Thomas Moore and Leigh Hunt, and some of the poems posed as competition exercises for the poet laureateship vacated by Robert Southey's death in 1843. Martin and Aytoun also worked together on a series of translations which appeared in *Blackwood's Edinburgh Magazine* in 1843–4 and were published as *Poems and Ballads of Goethe* (1858).

Legal and parliamentary activities Martin was bred to the law and devoted most of his life to his legal work. He practised as a solicitor in Edinburgh until June 1846, when he moved to London, thus ending his literary partnership with Aytoun. In 1847 he joined Hugh Innes Cameron as a parliamentary solicitor to form the firm Cameron and Martin. When Cameron left the firm in 1854, Martin conducted it single-handedly for eight years until joined by William Leslie in 1862. Leslie died in 1897 but the firm was known as Martin and Leslie until 1907, when it became

Sir Theodore Martin (1816–1909), by Rudolph Lehmann, 1873

known as Martin & Co. Martin's parliamentary business in London was extensive, profitable, and important. Among the earliest private bills which he prepared and piloted through parliamentary committees were those dealing with the Shrewsbury and Chester Railway and the River Dee Navigation, which familiarized him with north Wales, where he eventually bought a country residence. He also carried the bill for the extension to London of the Manchester, Sheffield, and Lincolnshire Railway. During 1879 he was closely engaged in negotiating the merger of all the London water companies under a public trust; but the measure was dropped during the last days of Lord Beaconsfield's ministry. Martin's parliamentary work was his main occupation during his lifetime, and he conducted it with unsparing energy and much ability.

Dramatic work and marriage Martin's early enthusiasm for the drama developed steadily. Edmund Kean was one of his first theatrical heroes. On a visit to London in 1840 he first saw Helen *Faucit (1814–1898) act, and after seeing her performance of Rosalind in Shakespeare's *As You Like It* at Glasgow in December 1843 he wrote some 'prophetic lines', in which he fancied himself Orlando. In July 1846 he extolled her powers in an article, 'Acting as one of the fine arts', in the *Dublin University Magazine*. In the same year he translated *Kong Renés datter*, a Danish romantic drama by Henrik Hertz, which she produced in 1849.

Helen Faucit's fascination grew on Martin, who is said to have followed her from place to place until he made her his wife (E. M. Sellar, *Recollections and Impressions*, 1907, 37). They were married on 25 August 1851 in the old church of St Nicholas at Brighton and spent their wedding tour in

Italy. After their return in November she resumed her acting career, which continued practically until 1871. In April 1852 she appeared at Manchester in Martin's adaptation of *Adrienne Lecouvreur*. In the same year they bought their London house, 31 Onslow Square, where Thackeray was their near neighbour and where they formed the centre of a large and cultivated social circle. This remained Martin's London residence until the end of his life, though he was almost driven out of it at the last by the noise of passing motor omnibuses, a nuisance which, in 1906, he denounced in *The Times*. The summer and autumn of 1861 were spent in Denbighshire at Bryntysilio, on the banks of the River Dee, about 2 miles above Llangollen. In 1865 he bought the house and adjoining grounds, both of which were considerably enlarged as the years went on. Bryntysilio remained the favourite country residence of Martin and his wife. He associated himself effectively with the industrial activities of the locality and took a great interest in Welsh music. His marriage to Helen Faucit was a happy one, though childless.

Later writings and translations After his marriage Martin's literary activity increased and his reputation widened. In 1859 he was one of the umpires for the prize offered by the Crystal Palace Company at the Burns centenary festival. His literary energies were chiefly divided between essays on the stage for periodicals, and translations from Latin, German, and Italian, with occasional adaptations for the theatre. In *Fraser's Magazine* (February 1858, December 1863, January 1865) he lamented the decay of the English drama, subsequently arguing in 'The drama in England', a paper on the Kembles (*Quarterly Review*, January 1872), that a cardinal necessity for the recovery of the English stage was the presence of a governing mind in control of a national theatre. To the *Quarterly Review* he also contributed biographical essays on David Garrick (July 1868) and William Charles Macready (November 1872). Most of his writings on the drama he collected for private circulation as *Essays on the Drama* (1874). He also wrote on the actress Rachel in *Blackwood's Edinburgh Magazine* (September 1882), while in *Shakespeare or Bacon?* (reprinted in 1888 from *Blackwood's Edinburgh Magazine*) he sought to dispel the 'Baconian' delusion. The essays on Garrick, Macready, the Kembles, and Rachel, with a vindication of Baron Stockmar (*Quarterly Review*, October 1882), reappeared in *Monographs* (1906).

Martin was a versatile translator. In 1854 and 1857 he published, from the original Danish or from the German, English versions of Adam Gottlob Oehlenschläger's romantic dramas *Aladdin* and *Correggio*. In 1860 he printed his translation of the *Odes* of Horace, which, like all Martin's versions of Latin poetry, is more fluent than scholarly. This was subsequently incorporated in *The Works of Horace* (2 vols., 1882) with the tasteful, rather than learned, monograph on the Roman poet which he had contributed in 1870 to Collins's Ancient Classics for English Readers series, and the substance of two lectures, 'Horace and his friends', delivered at the Edinburgh Philosophical Institution in October 1881. His other translations include *The Poems of Catullus*, with an introduction and notes (1861),

and books i–vi (1896) of Virgil's *Aeneid*. In 1862 he published his translation of Dante's *Vita nuova*, which he dedicated in a charming sonnet to his 'own true wife'.

German poetry occupied Martin's energies with more marked success. In November 1850 he had a translation of Goethe's *Prometheus* printed in the *Dublin University Magazine*, and in 1865 he published a version of the *First Part of 'Faust'*; the *Second Part* was published in 1886. The *First Part* went through many reprints and reached a ninth edition in 1910; a second, revised edition of the *Second Part* came out in the same year. A translation of Heine's poetry, published as *Poems and Ballads of Heinrich Heine*, appeared in 1878, and in 1889 *The Song of the Bell, and other Translations from Schiller, Goethe, Uhland and Others*, an anthology of German lyric poetry, was published. Martin did not shirk any metrical or other difficulty, but there is a lack of precision and finish in the execution. A spirited translation of Friedrich Halm's (Baron von Münch-Bellinghausen's) *Der Fechter von Ravenna* (1854), an essentially theatrical type of German romantic drama, was printed, as *The Gladiator of Ravenna*, for private circulation. It was reprinted in 1894 with *Madonna pia* (founded on the marquis de Belloy's *La malaria* of 1853), *Kong Renés datter*, and *The Camp*. Martin also translated the poems of Giacomo Leopardi in 1904.

Biography of Prince Albert In 1866 Martin began work on the project which was to secure his lasting fame, *The Life of His Royal Highness the Prince Consort*. By that year Queen Victoria's passion for memorializing her late husband culminated in her determination to commission a continuation of his biography begun by her private secretary, General Charles Grey, as *The Early Years of the Prince Consort*. Neither Grey nor the queen's other literary assistant, Sir Arthur Helps, were in a position to take on the *Life*, and Helps recommended Martin. The queen interviewed him on 14 November 1866 and, finding him 'very pleasing, clever, quiet, and *sympathique*' (*Letters of Queen Victoria*, 2nd ser., 1.372), engaged him to write the biography. Despite apparently extracting from the queen a promise that he should have a free hand as to both the time and the manner in which the work was to be carried out (T. Martin, *Queen Victoria as I Knew Her*, 1908, 19), he was obliged to work under the close supervision of the queen: she selected the documents for his use and intervened widely in the manuscript. Her children were initially hostile to the enterprise. In 1874, before the publication of the first volume, Victoria wrote to her eldest daughter to reassure her that 'He is most careful, and so refined, honourable and discreet that he would hurt no one's feelings if possible' (Fulford, 4.143); by 1877 the crown princess was offering to send him material from the Berlin archives. The biography ran eventually to five volumes, published in 1875, 1876, 1877, 1879, and 1880. Each volume was generally well received, to the queen's delight, though the one of 1877, covering the years of the Crimean War, provoked controversy over the constitutional right of the crown to intervene in matters of foreign policy. It was extensively reviewed, giving rise to an interesting critique from W. E. Gladstone which was reprinted in volume 1 of his *Gleanings of Past Years* (1879). Martin's *Life* is a goldmine of letters and papers and is less adulatory in tone than might be expected; its relative under-use by historians is a comment less on its content than on the absence of an index. A digest of it was published as Martin's memoir of the prince consort in the *Dictionary of National Biography*.

Martin was rewarded for his services with the CB in 1878 and the KCB in 1880. His wife had been admitted to court circles in 1878, and he became one of the queen's confidential, if unofficial, servants: in 1898 she sent him on a mission to the press to persuade them to alter their anti-German tone (*Letters of Queen Victoria*, 3rd ser., 3.224–5).

Martin followed up *The Life of … the Prince Consort* with a second effort in political biography, *A Life of Lord Lyndhurst* (1883), at the request of Lyndhurst's family. It is an attempt to correct the harsh impression given of Lyndhurst by Lord Campbell in the supplement (1869) to *The Lives of the Lord Chancellors*. Martin's refutation wearies by its length but he paints a successful portrait, though it excited enormous controversy.

The final years In 1881 Martin was elected lord rector of St Andrews University, and in October he delivered his inaugural address on education. During that year and the following one some time was spent in Italy. In 1887 he and his wife made a final journey abroad to the Riviera. Up to that time, when Lady Martin's health began to fail, both of them had continued their social activities in London and Wales. In 1896, on his eightieth birthday, Queen Victoria sent Martin the insignia of KCVO. Lady Martin died at Bryntysilio on 31 October 1898, and thereafter Martin devoted himself to her biography, which appeared in 1900. In 1901 he issued for private circulation *Queen Victoria as I Knew Her*, which was published in 1908. He continued to write until near the end of his life. His last contribution to *Blackwood's Magazine* was a 1907 article on Dante's 'Paolo e Francesca'.

For many years Martin had been an active worker for the Royal Literary Fund, becoming a member of the fund in 1855, an auditor in 1862, a member of the general committee in 1868, and registrar in 1871. He resigned the office of registrar and his seat on the committee in 1907, but was re-elected to the committee the next month. In succession to James Orchard Halliwell-Phillipps he became a trustee of Shakespeare's birthplace on 6 May 1889, and he retained the office until his death. He was a frequent visitor to Stratford upon Avon, and in 1900 he placed in the church of the Holy Trinity a marble pulpit to the memory of his wife, designed by G. F. Bodley, though his earlier wish to place a monument to her there had caused a public outcry. In 1906 he celebrated his ninetieth birthday at Bryntysilio. He died there on 18 August 1909 and was buried on the 21st alongside his wife in Brompton cemetery, London. A. W. WARD, rev. SAYONI BASU

Sources *The Times* (19 Aug 1909) • C. Knight, ed., *The English cyclopaedia: biography*, 6 vols. (1856–8) [suppl. (1872)] • *The Scotsman* (19 Aug 1909) • L. C. Sanders, *Celebrations of the century* (1887) • A. T. C. Pratt, ed., *People of the period: being a collection of the biographies of upwards of six thousand living celebrities*, 2 (1897) • *Men and women of the time* (1899) • Irving, *Scots.* • *The letters of Queen Victoria*, ed. A. C. Benson, Lord Esher [R. B. Brett], and G. E. Buckle, 9 vols. (1907–32), 2nd ser., vol. 1, p. 372; 3rd ser., vol. 3, pp. 224–5 • *Darling child: private correspondence of Queen Victoria and the crown princess of Prussia, 1871–1878*, ed. R. Fulford (1976)

Archives NL Scot., corresp. and papers • NRA, corresp. and literary papers | BL, letters received relating to biography of Prince Albert • BL, corresp. with W. E. Gladstone • Bodl. Oxf., letters received relating to biography of Prince Albert • Bodl. Oxf., letters to Benjamin Disraeli • Bodl. Oxf., letters to George Smith • NL Scot., letters to A. and C. Black • NL Scot., letters to J. S. Blackie • NL Scot., corresp. with Blackwoods • NL Scot., letters to John Hill Burton • NL Scot., letters to Robert Horn • NL Scot., incl. corresp. with Sir John McNiell • NL Wales, letters to George Stovin Venables • Royal Arch., papers relating to biography of Prince Albert incl. letters from Queen Victoria • U. Durham L., letters to General Charles Grey

Likenesses R. Lehmann, crayon drawing, 1873, BM [*see illus.*] • R. Herdman, oils, 1876, NPG • J. Archer, oils, 1878, Blackwood & Sons, Edinburgh • J. Archer, oils, 1881, Scot. NPG • Lock & Whitfield, woodburytype photograph, 1881, NPG • J. Mordecai, oils, 1907, priv. coll. • F. M. Bennett, oils, 1908, NPG • R. Cholmondeley, oils, Scot. NPG • F. Dixon, oils, priv. coll. • T. Duncan, oils (aged ten), Scot. NPG • R. Herdman, oils, priv. coll. • Walery, photograph, NPG • L. Ward, watercolour, repro. in *VF* (7 July 1877) • J. & C. Watkins, cartes-de-visite, NPG • photograph, NPG

Wealth at death £157,706 12s. 11d.: probate, 25 Nov 1909, CGPLA Eng. & Wales

Martin [Martyn], **Thomas** (1520/21–1592/3), civil lawyer and polemicist, the son of John Martin of Cerne, Dorset, was educated at Winchester (admitted 1533, aged twelve) and New College, Oxford, of which he became a fellow in 1540, and subsequently (*c.*1550) at Bourges University in France. Martin's engagement in anti-evangelical polemic in the reign of Mary I created the opportunity for protestant propagandists such as John Ponet and John Bale to blacken his reputation, and it is to them that allegations of Martin's scandalous lifestyle, academic improprieties, and vacillating views on such controversial issues as clerical celibacy at Bourges can be traced. At the accession of Queen Mary he returned to England from studies in Paris and entered the service of the new lord chancellor, Stephen Gardiner, for whom he became an active administrator, first as an official in the archdeaconry of Berkshire and subsequently as chancellor of the diocese of Winchester. Although Martin originally sat in the parliament of 1553 as MP for the borough of Saltash, Cornwall, Gardiner's patronage ensured that he was subsequently returned as member for the Wiltshire borough of Hindon. After Gardiner's death in 1555, the warden of Winchester, John White, helped him secure the Wiltshire seat of Ludgershall. He also enjoyed an active diplomatic career, narrowly failing to become ambassador to France in 1556, but none the less engaging in negotiations with Philip II over the projected marriage of Princess Elizabeth and over trading relations between the Merchant Adventurers and the Netherlands. It was, however, Martin's rapid advancement in the law that most distinguished his career. Having graduated DCL at Oxford in 1555, he became master of requests by 1556, and master in chancery by 1557. He held the protonotaryship of chancery (1557–60), but lost the office at the accession of Elizabeth despite his willingness to swear the oath of supremacy.

Martin's enthusiasm for Marian policy found particular expression in his *Traictise Declarying … that the Pretensed*

Marriage of Priests … is No Mariage (published in May 1554), a defence of the regime's reintroduction of clerical celibacy in which Gardiner himself probably also had a hand. Although Ponet, one of the great apologists for clerical marriage, replied from exile, Martin's work proved sufficiently popular for Robert Caley to seek a monopoly of printing it in 1558, although when Ponet's response was posthumously published in 1566 Martin declined to prolong the exchange.

Martin's career in royal service reached its apogee in September 1555, when he was entrusted by the council with the prosecution of heretics, ultimately serving alongside Bishop Brooks of Gloucester and his fellow civil lawyers John Story and David Lewis as royal proctor at the trial of Archbishop Thomas Cranmer. Accounts of the trial reveal the shrewdness of Martin's opening address on the relationship between the secular and ecclesiastical power, a strategy that exposed one of Cranmer's points of weakness. He was equally ruthless in pressing the archbishop on whether all oaths, good or bad, ought to be obeyed; on his changing belief on the eucharist; and on the history of the supreme headship of the church, issues over which he succeeded in flustering the otherwise dignified Cranmer. That Martin provided the real teeth of the prosecution is implied both by Cranmer's choice of him as a conduit for a letter of appeal to the queen (subsequently published in Emden in 1556) and by her consultation of him as to whether she should even read it. Such zeal in the Catholic cause rendered him obnoxious to the protestant party, and accounts for his disappearance from public office under Elizabeth. Although he remained a Catholic, Martin none the less continued to work as a civil lawyer into the 1590s, being frequently involved in appeals from the prerogative court of Canterbury and the courts of admiralty and arches.

Martin was twice married; first, by January 1555, to Mary, daughter of John Roys of London, with whom he had two sons and one daughter; and second, some time after 1565, to Margery, widow of William Denton of Southwark, with whom he had one daughter. His estates in Steeple Mordern, Cambridgeshire, Fenstanton, Huntingdonshire, and London were subject to litigation in requests shortly before his death. He was still alive in March 1592. Thomas, his son and the executor of his will (proved 7 August 1593), subsequently sued his stepmother and half-sister in chancery to obtain the administration of his estate.   STEVE HINDLE

Sources HoP, *Commons, 1509–58*, 2.578–80 · T. Martin, *A traictise declarying and plainly provyng that the pretensed marriage of priests … is no mariage* (1554) · PRO, SP 11/5/8, 27, 34, 202; 11/9/30 · PRO, PROB 11/82, sig. 60 · Foster, *Alum. Oxon., 1500–1714*, 3.980 · Emden, *Oxf.*, 4.384 · D. MacCulloch, *Thomas Cranmer: a life* (1996), 391, 573–81 · C. Haigh, *English reformations: religion, politics, and society under the Tudors* (1993), 227–8

Archives NRA · PRO, SP 11/5/8, 27, 34, 202

Martin, Thomas (*bap.* 1680, *d.* 1765). *See under* Martin family (*per. c.*1700–1832).

Martin, Thomas (1697–1771), antiquary, was born on 8 March 1697 in the Free School House of the Suffolk parish

Thomas Martin (1697–1771), by Peter Spendelowe Lamborn, pubd 1779 (after Thomas Bardwell, 1748)

of St Mary's, adjoining the Norfolk town of Thetford. He was the seventh of nine children of William Martin (*c.*1650–1721), rector of Great Livermere in Suffolk, and curate of St Mary's, and his wife, Elizabeth Burrough, the only daughter of Thomas Burrough of Bury St Edmunds. He was educated at the free school, where for some time he was the only scholar and left to his own devices. He hoped to study at Cambridge, but about 1715 he was placed against his wishes as an articled clerk with his elder brother Robert, a Thetford attorney.

From an early age Martin was fascinated by the antiquities of his locality and kept notebooks of his visits. When only twelve or thirteen years old he was recommended to Peter Le Neve, Norroy king of arms and president of the Society of Antiquaries, as the most knowledgeable person to act as a guide to the antiquities of the town. The subsequent friendship between the young man and the elderly antiquary was to have a far-reaching effect on the direction of Norfolk historiography for the remainder of the century. Martin was admitted a fellow of the Society of Antiquaries about 1719 on Le Neve's recommendation and remained an enthusiastic and influential member until his death.

About 1721 or 1722 Martin achieved a degree of financial independence by marrying a widow, Sarah Cropley (*d.* 1731), the daughter of John Tyrell or Thorold; their first child was born in Thetford in 1722. Soon afterwards the couple moved to Palgrave, in Suffolk, where he practised as an attorney. They had eight children, two of whom died young. Sarah died on 15 November 1731, ten days after giving birth to twins.

Throughout his life Martin was a compulsive collector of books and manuscripts, and a great compiler of catalogues. According to Sir John Cullum's preface to Martin's *History of … Thetford*, he was also a 'skilful and indefatigable' antiquary and 'had the happiest use of his pen, copying, as well as tracing, with dispatch and exactness, the different writing of every aera, and tricking arms, seals, &c, with great neatness'. In September 1724 Eton College paid him £30 for setting the muniment room in order and compiling a digest of records. This was followed by a brief tour into Wales, but thereafter he seems to have spent most of his time in East Anglia.

Peter Le Neve died in 1729, having appointed Martin, together with Thomas Tanner, chancellor of Norwich, and his young widow, Frances (*née* Beeston), as executors of a complex and idiosyncratic will. Over the next two years Martin spent much time at Le Neve's former home in Great Whitchingham helping the widow to isolate the latter's enormous collection of Norfolk and Suffolk materials from his other book and manuscript collections, which were to be auctioned. Le Neve's Norfolk collection was described by Richard Gough as 'the greatest fund of antiquities for his native county that ever was collected for any single one in the kingdom' (Gough, 2.2). It was intended by the collector to be deposited after his death in an unspecified public repository in Norwich. However, the appointment of Tanner to the see of St Asaph in December 1731, followed by Martin's marriage to Frances Le Neve in January 1732, meant that the terms of the will were never carried out. The couple soon afterwards moved with the collection to Martin's home in Palgrave.

Martin's malversation in respect of the Le Neve manuscripts dismayed Tanner and other members of the Norfolk antiquarian community, such as Benjamin Mackerell, but no one was willing to contest the issue. After Tanner's death in 1735 the matter was quietly forgotten, but it was doubtless why he decided to leave his own manuscripts to the Bodleian Library rather than combine them with Le Neve's collection, as originally intended. Soon afterwards Martin appears to have acquired and relished the seemingly ironic sobriquet Honest Tom, which he retained for the remainder of his life.

Martin and his second wife had eight children, four of whom did not survive infancy, before Frances died in 1751. Martin continued to enjoy rude good health until old age, in spite of the many colourful accounts of his inordinate drinking bouts and boisterous conduct while under the influence of alcohol. Yet his company was always sought, and his friendship valued, by far more sober and respectable men. However, his continuing obsession with collecting historical antiquities of all kinds, coupled with an increasing neglect of his profession and his dissipated habits, ultimately took their toll of his fortune. By 1762 he was forced to dispose of some of his substantial book and coin collections to meet the increasing demands of his creditors, and this process continued throughout the last decade of his life.

Martin partially redeemed his illegitimate custody of the Le Neve collections by his willingness to make them available to interested scholars, or to provide visitors and correspondents with the benefit of his substantial knowledge and assistance. Thus he was an important figure in the compilation and production of several historical works relating to East Anglia and his assistance is frequently noted. He played a crucial role throughout the prolonged and complex gestation of Francis Blomefield's *History of Norfolk* between 1731 and 1775, although he did not live to see it completed. He had encouraged Blomefield to undertake the task and put at his disposal all the Le Neve materials. After Blomefield's death in 1752, Martin purchased many of the author's manuscripts, including the priceless Paston letters, and assisted his widow to dispose of the unsold copies of his history. He then encouraged Charles Parkin to complete the work. Following Parkin's death, he persuaded the King's Lynn bookseller William Whittingham to publish the work and recruited the young antiquary John Fenn to see it through the press.

Martin never published any work during his lifetime in spite of repeated stated intentions of doing so. The history of Thetford bearing his name was compiled after his death from his notes, largely by a Mr Davis, a dissenting minister in Diss. Proposals for this work were issued in 1774 by John Worth, a chemist, who purchased many of Martin's collections. Five sheets were printed in Norwich before Worth's own death brought an end to the project.

Martin died on 7 March 1771, and was buried in the porch of Palgrave church. He still retained a large and valuable collection of printed books and manuscripts at his death, which were disposed of in a complex series of public auctions and private sales. The collection was utterly and irrevocably dispersed within five years of his death. In spite of his disreputable past and dissolute character, Martin was esteemed by the new generation of East Anglian antiquaries. In 1772 John Ives wrote and privately printed *A Pastoral Elegy on the Death of Thomas Martin* and paid for an engraved portrait of him. Richard Gough purchased Martin's notes relating to Thetford together with the manuscript by Davis, which he further revised before publishing it in 1779, together with a memoir by Sir John Cullum and Ives's portrait. John Fenn read an account of Martin's life to the Society of Antiquaries in November 1780 and later left money for a monument to him in Palgrave church.

DAVID STOKER

Sources J. Fenn, 'Memoirs of the life of Thomas Martin, Gent.', *Norfolk Archaeology*, 15 (1903–4), 233–66 • D. Stoker, 'The ill-gotten library of "Honest Tom" Martin', *Property of a gentleman: the formation, organisation and dispersal of the private library, 1620–1920*, St Paul's Bibliographies (1991), 90–112 • Nichols, *Lit. anecdotes*, 5.384–8; 6.97; 9.413–39 • T. Martin, *The history of the town of Thetford*, ed. R. Gough (1779), 284–5 • J. Cullum, preface, in T. Martin, *The history of the town of Thetford*, ed. R. Gough (1779), xi–xviii • *The correspondence of the Reverend Francis Blomefield, 1705–52*, ed. D. Stoker, Norfolk RS, 55 (1992) • D. Stoker, 'Benjamin Mackerell, antiquary, librarian, and plagiarist', *Norfolk Archaeology*, 42 (1994–7), 1–12 • R. G. [R. Gough], *British topography*, [new edn], 2 vols. (1780) • *Letters between Rev. James Granger … and many of the most eminent literary men of his time*, ed. J. P. Malcolm (1805), 102–3 • D. Stoker, 'Mr Parkin's magpie, the other Mr Whittingham, and the fate of Great Yarmouth', *The Library*, 6th ser., 12 (1990), 121–31 · D. Stoker, '"Innumerable letters of good consequence in history": the discovery and first publication of the Paston letters', *The Library*, 6th ser., 17 (1995), 107–55 · P. Strong and F. Strong, 'The last will and codicils of Henry V', *EngHR*, 96 (1981), 79–102 · P. Grinke, 'John Ives and the library of "Honest" Tom Martin', *The warden's meeting* (1977), 39–42 · Vertue, *Note books*, 5.119 · Nichols, *Illustrations*, 3.608; 5.167–8

Archives BL, papers relating to Dunwich, Add. MS 34653 · BL, historical collections, Add. MSS 24318–24319, 27402 · Bodl. Oxf., corresp. and papers · Bodl. Oxf., Norfolk and Suffolk collections · Bodl. Oxf., notebook of journey from Eton to Wales · CUL, commonplace book mainly relating to scientific subjects · CUL, notes on Cambridgeshire churches · Essex RO, Chelmsford, Essex church notes · Norfolk RO, corresp., notebooks, papers and MSS relating to Norfolk topography, genealogy, and history · Norfolk RO, notebook · Suffolk RO, Ipswich, account book · Suffolk RO, Ipswich, historical notes and papers relating to parishes of Dunwich and Eye · Suffolk RO, Ipswich, notes relating to parish of Palgrave · Suffolk RO, Ipswich, notes relating to Suffolk religious houses · Suffolk RO, Bury St Edmunds, Suffolk church notes, incl. notes by other antiquaries · Suffolk RO, Bury St Edmunds, Suffolk monumental inscriptions | BL, copy of Gough's *Anecdotes of British topography* with Martin's copious MS notes and additions · Bodl. Oxf., copy of John Kirby's *Suffolk traveller* with MS notes and additions by subject (and other antiquaries) · Bodl. Oxf., copy of Benjamin Mackerell's *History of King's Lynn* with MS notes and additions by subject · Norfolk RO, Castle Museum deposit · Norfolk RO, Colman MSS · Norfolk RO, Duleep Singh MSS · Norfolk RO, Norfolk and Norwich Archaeological Society deposit · Suffolk RO, Ipswich, collections for a history of Norfolk and Suffolk made by Peter le Neve with MS additions by subject

Likenesses T. Bardwell, portrait, 1748, priv. coll. · P. Audinet, engraving, *c.*1771, repro. in Nichols, *Illustrations*, 3.608 · T. Cook, etching (after J. Fenn), BM, NPG; repro. in J. Ames, *Typographical antiquities*, ed. T. F. Dibdin and W. Herbert, 4 vols. (1810–19), vol. 2, p. 304 · P. S. Lamborn, etching (after T. Bardwell, 1748), AM Oxf., BM, NPG; repro. in Martin, *The history of the town of Thetford*, frontispiece [*see illus.*]

Wealth at death insolvent: Fenn, 'Memoirs'

Martin, Thomas [Tommy] (1916–1987), boxer, was born at 8 Northfield Cottages, Reading, on 22 January 1916, the eldest child of Stephen Martin, licensed hawker, who was of Jamaican origin, and his wife, Annie, *née* Shank. At fourteen Martin began work as a waterboy on a fairground boxing booth. His first professional contest occurred in 1933, though like many boxers of the period he combined his professional career with appearances on a travelling boxing booth. He lost only three out of twenty-five contests in his first full year as a professional in 1936. Among his victims were Paul Schaeffer, a highly regarded Canadian fighter, and Tommy Henderson, the reigning Scottish light-heavyweight champion. By 1937 Martin's reputation as a formidable middleweight meant that, even at this early stage of his career, some of the country's leading boxers would not meet him. He was therefore forced to box as a heavyweight, using hidden weights in his pockets at weigh-ins so as not to reveal to his opponents his true stature.

Martin embarked on a short Caribbean tour in the second half of 1937 before returning to top the bill at a 2000-seat sell-out appearance in Deptford, where his family had settled in 1917. By the end of 1938 Martin had boxed in Jersey, France, Italy, Austria, and Yugoslavia, while he

had also met some of the country's top boxers, including the Welsh heavyweight Jimmy Wilde, Frank Hough, Tom Reddington, and Jack Hyams.

A short tour of Australia followed before Martin returned to Britain late in 1938. Here he continued where he had left off by beating a number of leading heavyweights. In November 1939 he outpointed the future British heavyweight champion Jack London, who outweighed him by over 3 stone. By this time Martin's growing reputation meant that calls were now made for him to be allowed to challenge Jock McAvoy for the British heavyweight title. However, owing to the colour bar operated by the British Boxing Board of Control, black boxers could not contest British titles and even though McAvoy was quite prepared to meet him for the title, Martin was not allowed to fight for the championship. The situation was raised in parliament by Martin's local MP, Walter Green, who noted the detrimental effect such a ban might have on non-white colonial servicemen, and calling for 'such discrimination against British-born subjects solely on colour grounds' to be discouraged (*Hansard 5C*, 373, 31 July 1941, 1548–9). However, both the British Boxing Board of Control and secretary of state Herbert Morrison decided that the matter would not be discussed until the war was over, with Morrison referring to 'differences of opinion on the question whether spectacular fights between opponents of different colours ought to be encouraged', rather than prejudice against 'coloured boxers', as the reason for the boxing board's rule on contestants for British titles (ibid., 1549).

Early in 1941 Martin embarked on yet another foreign boxing tour, this time to America. Here, a victory over the highly rated Leroy Hynes meant that Martin, along with Tommy Farr, became one of only two British heavyweights ranked in the world's top ten during the 1940s. In 1941 he returned to Britain, where he joined the ARP and then the RAF. However, his career was by now in decline: he lost to Jack London in a return, to Freddie Mills, the future world champion, and to Al Robinson, and he retired in February 1942.

Martin was injured while serving with the RAF, but later joined the merchant navy. It was reported that, after being torpedoed and ending up in Montreal, he went temporarily blind. It was also reported that he saw service with the Canadian mounties, before eye problems again resurfaced, and he underwent treatment in the USA. He married Norma Blue in New York in April 1946, and became an American citizen. After training to be a physiotherapist, he opened a gymnasium in Hollywood, before finally becoming a prison governor in the American Virgin Islands.

One among only a handful of highly talented black British boxers active before the Second World War, Martin was unique in that his career also overlapped with the start of the conflict. The war saw calls for the colour bar to be repealed at their most vociferous. Many opponents of the ban cited Martin's boxing and service records as the main reason for its removal, stressing that while black men were prepared to fight for Britain in the war they were not allowed to fight for their national title in a boxing ring because of their colour. The ban was finally lifted in 1947, by which time Martin was retired and already an American citizen. He died in the American Virgin Islands on 14 October 1987.

GARY SHAW

Sources R. Olver, *Boxing News* (24 Aug 1984), 10–11 • G. Shaw, 'The rise and fall of the colour bar in British boxing, 1911–1947', *2000 British Society of Sports History conference* [Liverpool 2000] [2000] • b. cert.

Martin, Sir Thomas Acquin (1850–1906), engineer and industrialist, born at Four Oaks, Sutton Coldfield, near Birmingham, on 6 March 1850, was the son of Patrick William Martin, leather manufacturer, of Birmingham, and his wife, Mary Anne, *née* Bridges. After education at the Birmingham Oratory School, Edgbaston, he entered the engineering firm of Walsh Lovett in Birmingham. He married, on 2 April 1869 at Birmingham, Sarah Ann, daughter of John Humphrey Harrby of Hoarwithy, Herefordshire. They had a daughter and five sons, four of whom entered their father's business.

In 1874 Martin went to Calcutta to open a branch of Walsh Lovett. Displaying exceptional business capacity, he soon founded the firm of Martin & Co., Clive Street, Calcutta, and Laurence Pountney Hill, London, which played an important part in the industrialization of India. In 1889 the firm took over the management of the Bengal Iron and Steel Company, which inaugurated iron production at Burrakur on a capitalized basis, permitting, for the first time, competition with imported products. An output of 9000 tons of pig iron was produced annually. The firm also pioneered the construction of light railways along district roads in India, to serve as feeders of the main lines. It built and managed the Howrah–Amta, Howrah–Sheakhala, Bukhtiarpur–Bihar, Barasat–Basirhat, Shahdara (Delhi)–Saharanpur, and Arrah–Sasaram light railways, which had a total length of 300 miles. Many jute mills in Bengal were constructed by the firm, and up to Martin's death in 1906 it had the management of the Arathoon jute mills, Calcutta. Three large collieries in Bengal, and the Hooghly Docking and Engineering Company, were also under its control. The Tansa duct works, providing Bombay with a constant water supply from a lake 40 miles distant, was engineered by the firm, as was the supply of water to the suburbs of Calcutta, and of a large number of Indian provincial towns, including Allahabad, Benares, Cawnpore, Lucknow, Agra, and Srinagar (Kashmir). With Edward Thornton as principal architect, it erected chiefs' palaces and important public buildings in various parts of India, particularly in Calcutta, where it acted as contractor for the All-India Victoria Memorial Hall.

Early in 1887 Martin was appointed agent-general by Abdur Rahman Khan, amir of Afghanistan, and he sent to Kabul Salter Pyne, the first European to reside there for any length of time since the Second Anglo-Afghan War of 1878–80. Pyne, on behalf of Martin's firm, built an arsenal, a mint, and various factories and workshops for the amir, subsequently introducing, as state monopolies, a number of modern industries.

Martin was frequently consulted by the amir on questions of policy, and he and his agents were often able to render political service to Great Britain. Abdur Rahman selected him to be chief of the staff of Prince Nasrullah Khan, his second son, on the prince's mission to England in 1895. In August, during the visit, Martin was knighted. Though the amir's main objective in arranging the visit—the opening of direct diplomatic relations with Great Britain—was not achieved, he retained the fullest confidence in Martin. On his return to Kabul, Nasrullah Khan was accompanied by Martin's younger brother Frank, who succeeded Pyne as engineer-in-chief.

A man of genial manner and generous disposition, Martin was a close student of human nature. He proved his common sense and catholicity of temper by admitting into partnership, in 1889, an able Bengali, R. N. Mukherji. Broken in health by severe toil in a tropical climate, Martin spent much of his later life in Europe. He died at his home, Binstead House, Ryde, Isle of Wight, on 29 April 1906 and was buried in Ryde cemetery. He was survived by his wife.

F. H. BROWN, rev. IAN ST JOHN

Sources *The Times* (1–14 May 1906) • *The Englishman* (17 Feb 1912) [Calcutta] • *Birmingham Daily Post* (2 May 1906) • *The life of Abdur Rahman, amir of Afghanistan*, ed. and trans. M. Khan, 2 vols. (1900) • J. A. Gray, *At the court of the ameer* (1895) • Admn. report, Indian railways for 1910, 1910 • E. Balfour, *Cyclopaedia of India and of eastern and southern Asia* (1905) • F. A. Martin, *Under the absolute amir* (1907) • V. Chirol, *Indian unrest* (1910) • private information (1912) • *DNB* • CGPLA Eng. & Wales (1907)
Likenesses oils, 1912 (after miniature), Martin & Co., Calcutta
Wealth at death £7128 0s. 1d.: probate, 30 Oct 1907, CGPLA Eng. & Wales

Martin, Thomas Barnewall (1786–1847). *See under* Martin, Richard (1754–1834).

Martin, Sir Thomas Byam (1773–1854), naval officer, born at Ashtead House, Surrey, on 25 July 1773, was the third surviving son of Sir Henry Martin, baronet (*d.* 1794), for many years naval commissioner at Portsmouth and afterwards comptroller of the navy, and his wife, Eliza Anne Gillman, *née* Parker, of Hilbrook, co. Cork. His father's half-brother, Samuel Martin (*d.* 1789), was treasurer to the dowager princess of Wales. Thomas was educated privately at Freshford, near Bath (1780), Southampton grammar school (1781), and Mr Coles's boarding-school in Guildford (1782–5). Through the influence of Henry Martin, and in accordance with the irregular custom of the day, Thomas, before he was eight, was entered on the books of the *Canada* (Captain William Cornwallis) in 1780–81; in 1782, of the *Foudroyant* (Captain Sir John Jervis); and in 1783, of the *Orpheus* (Captain George Campbell). He entered the Royal Naval Academy at Portsmouth in August 1785. He first went afloat in April 1786, as 'captain's servant' on the *Pegasus*, with Prince William Henry (afterwards William IV), whom in March 1788 he followed to the *Andromeda*. He was afterwards for a few months in the *Southampton*, and on 22 November 1790 he was promoted lieutenant of the *Canada*. Despite his powerful patronage he still served afloat for four years before receiving his commission. For the next two years (from 1790/91) he

Sir Thomas Byam Martin (1773–1854), by Henry Robinson (after George Richmond, 1849)

served in the *Inconstant* and the *Juno*; and on 22 May 1793 he was promoted to command the *Tisiphone*, fitting out for the Mediterranean, where, on 5 November 1793, he was posted to the frigate *Modeste* which had been seized at Genoa by Admiral Gell only the month before.

In 1795 Martin was appointed to the *Santa Margarita*, employed on the coast of Ireland, where he captured many privateers, and on 8 June 1796 he took the *Tamise*, a prize from the English two years before. She had now a heavier armament and more numerous crew; but against superior discipline, seamanship, and gun-training she was powerless and could kill only two and wound three on the *Santa Margarita*, while she herself lost thirty-two killed and nineteen wounded, several mortally.

In 1797 Martin commanded the *Tamar* in the West Indies and in five months captured nine privateers with an aggregate of 58 guns and 519 men. In 1798 he returned to England in command of the *Dictator*; he was then appointed to the *Fisgard*, a powerful frigate captured from the French only the year before. On 20 October, off Brest, he fell in with, and after a sharp action captured, the *Immortalité*, sailing homeward from the destruction of Bompard's squadron on the coast of Ireland. In addition to her complement, the *Immortalité* had on board 250 soldiers, and her loss was consequently very great. Otherwise the two frigates were nearly equal in force, and the *Fisgard's* victory was considered one of the most brilliant frigate actions of the war. In 1798 Martin married Catherine, daughter of Captain Robert Fanshawe, for many years naval commissioner at Plymouth. They had three daughters and three sons, the eldest of whom was Sir William

Fanshawe *Martin, baronet (1801–1895). Their second son, Sir Henry Byam Martin, died an admiral in 1865; and the third, Lieutenant-Colonel Robert Fanshawe Martin, died in 1846.

For the next two years the *Fisgard* was employed actively off the coast of France under the orders of Sir John Warren and, in company with different ships of the squadron, captured or destroyed several warships, privateers, coasting craft, and batteries. From 1803 to 1805 Martin commanded the line-of-battle ship *Impétueux* in the channel and on 24 November 1804 helped save many lives from the wreck of HMS *Venerable* in Tor Bay, Devon. In 1807 he commanded the line-of-battle ship *Prince of Wales*, also in the channel, and in 1808 the *Implacable* in the Baltic. On 26 August 1808, while attached to the Swedish fleet under the immediate orders of Sir Samuel Hood in the *Centaur*, he brought to action the Russian ship *Sewolod* and had a large share in her capture. In his official letter Hood assigned much of the credit to Martin, and Gustaf IV Adolf, the king of Sweden, conferred on him the cross of the order of the Sword. He was again in the Baltic in 1809. On 1 August 1811 he was promoted rear-admiral, and in 1812, with his flag in the *Aboukir*, he took part in the defence of Riga against the French army under Davoust. He was afterwards second in command at Plymouth until 1814. In September 1813 he was sent on a mission to Wellington's headquarters in Spain to resolve the difficulties then arising in the transport service. He did this to the satisfaction of all concerned.

On 2 January 1815 Martin was made a KCB and on 11 November was appointed deputy comptroller of the navy. On 24 February 1816 he became comptroller and held the office until 2 November 1831. Chosen by Lord Melville for his combination of administrative ability and sea experience, Martin dominated the post-war policy of the navy during his long term in office. On his advice the fleet was reconstructed around a nucleus of large and very powerful new ships, while maintaining a high level of skilled labour in the royal dockyards, to meet any sudden emergency. He worked closely with the naval architect and structural engineer, Sir Robert Seppings, to improve the quality and durability of British warships. Although his office was normally considered apolitical Martin was a tory, and he became closely identified with government policy at a time when naval policy became a political question. The whig reform ministry of 1830 took office committed to making large savings on defence spending in order to fund other aspects of their political programme. Bolstered by his long service and high rank Martin publicly criticized government policy in the House of Commons, though his office made him a member of the ministry. Unable to control him, or even remove him from his government seat, Sir James Graham and Earl Grey secured the consent of Martin's old shipmate, Prince William Henry (now William IV), to dismiss him on grounds of insubordination. The Navy Board was abolished the following year.

From 1818 to 1831 Martin sat in parliament as member for Plymouth. On 12 August 1819 he was made vice-admiral, a GCB on 3 March 1830, admiral on 22 July 1830, vice-admiral of the United Kingdom in 1847, and admiral of the fleet on 13 October 1849. After his dismissal as comptroller of the navy he was twice offered command of the Mediterranean Fleet, but his wife's ill health and his large pension were always against a return to active service in peacetime. Frequently called on to advise the government, he was still serving the state in 1854, outlining the strategy for naval operations in the Baltic and reporting on Lord Cochrane's plan to use poison gas. He died at the admiral-superintendent's house in Portsmouth on 21 October 1854. Sir William Hotham recorded that:

> his capacities for business and thorough knowledge of the state of the navy marked him as a fit man to be at the head of its civil department. He added to a strong understanding and quick perception great personal application and activity, and transacted arduous business without any trouble to himself and satisfactorily to others; exceedingly amiable in his family and much beloved by those who knew him well. (Hotham MSS)

During his long and distinguished career Martin formed the views that directed his policy after 1815. Although a natural, and political, conservative, he never opposed the development of new technology, but merely required new technologies to demonstrate their advantages. He was the last and most able comptroller of the navy. In a period of retrenchment he reconstructed the fleet, providing a sound base for British diplomacy and deterrence, modernized the infrastructure, and provided sound guidance in the early years of naval technical development. His working relationship with Melville and Seppings forms a high point in the history of British naval administration.

J. K. LAUGHTON, rev. ANDREW LAMBERT

Sources BL, Martin MSS · A. D. Lambert, *The last sailing battlefleet: maintaining naval mastery, 1815–1850* (1991) · *Letters and papers of Admiral of the Fleet Sir Thos. Byam Martin, GCB*, ed. R. V. Hamilton, 3 vols., Navy RS, 12, 19, 24 (1898–1903) · U. Hull, Brynmor Jones L., Hotham MSS, DDHO · P. A. Symonds and D. R. Fisher, 'Martin, Sir Thomas Byam', HoP, *Commons* · Boase, *Mod. Eng. biog.*
Archives BL, corresp. and papers, Add. MSS 41346–41475 | Duke U., Perkins L., corresp. with Lord Melville · NA Scot., letters to Lord Melville · NL Scot., letters to Sir Thomas Cochrane · NMM, Seppings MSS
Likenesses G. Richmond, oils, 1849, repro. in Hamilton, ed., *Letters and papers*, vol. 2, frontispiece · T. W. Mackay, oils, 1852; formerly United Service Club, London · H. Robinson, engraving (after G. Richmond, 1849), AM Oxf. [*see illus.*]

Martin, Violet Florence [*pseud.* Martin Ross] (1862–1915), novelist, was born on 11 June 1862 at Ross House, co. Galway, the last of the ten children of landlord James Martin (1804–1872), a journalist, and his wife, Anna Selina Fox (1822–1906). The Martins were a Norman family, of a branch that had been so long in Ireland that it had no inhibitions about marrying into the native Irish aristocracy. One of the 'tribes of Galway', the Martins had been royalist and Catholic until Violet Martin's great-grandfather had turned protestant in order to marry an O'Hara. The O'Haras had been a great native Irish Catholic family, parts of which had turned protestant. As a result

Violet Florence Martin (1862–1915), by Edith Somerville, 1886

Violet Martin was connected to an Irish-speaking Catholic Ireland that was closed off from her cousin and colleague Edith *Somerville (1858–1949), with whom she wrote novels, as Somerville and Ross, on the religious and social complexities of Irish life. Their families were alike, though, in that failure of rents affected them in the same way, and Violet's father had to make an income from journalism. As her mother's last child Violet was brought up as a pet, indulged by her elder sisters and her brothers.

Violet left Ross and moved to Dublin with her mother when her brother Robert, unable to keep up the place, leased out Ross for fifteen years in 1872 after their father's death. To earn a living Robert wrote theatrical pieces and comic Irish songs and was known by the title of one of these, 'Ballyhooly'. At Ross during the first decade of her life Violet absorbed an understanding of the nuances of spoken Irish that always distinguished her from her writing partner. The understanding informs her essays with a depth of sympathy unique in the Anglo-Irish writing of the period. By the late 1890s when Somerville and Ross were learning Irish systematically in classes using the textbooks of the Society for the Preservation of the Irish Language and O'Growney's three-volume primer, Irish was in general decline in the country, prompting the artificial respiration of the revivalists.

In Dublin, Violet Martin was educated at Alexandra College. She had a prodigious memory for recitation and retained lengths of quotation from Shakespeare, Milton, and other heavyweights from her Alexandra days, and also biblical quotations from her Dublin Sunday school drilling, including the Psalms. In this basic literary grounding she differed from her partner: the Somervilles' governesses never lasted long enough at Drishane House (Castletownshend, co. Cork) to plant any serious literary interests, and in its leisure Drishane tended to sensational novels. Like Edith Somerville, Violet Martin had tribes of cousins, and spent an inordinate amount of time visiting or being visited. This was an easily available form of free entertainment for a class heading for bankruptcy. She was very attached to her eldest sister, Edith Dawson, whose home she often visited, being a devoted aunt to her nephews and nieces.

Fully aware of the embarrassed financial state of her family Edith Somerville had vowed to support herself by her late teens. Violet Martin, too, began to see the attraction of an independent income, possibly through a keen appreciation of the miserable life of her stay-at-home sister Selina. Her early attempts at journalism, political articles, show an obvious gift but are in patches quite stiff and wordy. Her brother Robert, whose colleagues in London were helpful to Martin in placing her work, called her 'our little Carlyle'.

After meeting Edith Somerville in a throng of cousins at Castletownshend in January 1886, Violet Martin went out of her way to write amusingly to Edith, who shortly afterwards left for Paris, to study at Colarossi's studio. There were already two Violets established in the cousinage and quite quickly Violet Martin became 'Martin'. Only persistence on Martin's part made their relationship a live issue, as Edith did not have time to answer Martin's letters. In the way of fiction writers, Edith breezily glosses over these negative points in her romantic account of their friendship in her contribution to their *Irish Memories*, and ignores the facts of Martin's leading role in, and manipulation of, the outset of their literary career together, as though it were an instant mutual decision. It is a sore point with surviving relatives whether she would have been so fulsome in praising Martin had she realized what the biographer Maurice Collis would make of her words. But whatever stories they later told each other and others about their joining forces, it is clear that Martin had the stronger will, and whatever accommodation they made to one another they had a working system that was profoundly satisfying and successful.

In 1888 Martin and her mother returned to Ross, and decided to keep it going between them, helped by subscriptions from Robert, the heir, who spent his holidays with them. Although Martin was small and slight, her appearance was misleading—the independence and strength of will necessary in this undertaking was impressive. It was she who cut down the brambles, bracken, and undergrowth that had choked the gardens at Ross and replanted them, and she who restored and painted the interior of the great house. Of necessity the women who remained on Irish estates running them in the absence of their male relatives came into contact with, and relied on, some of those men of the Irish middle classes who were coming into power. It is in its minute portraits of the intermingled personalities of the two classes in Ireland, the one moving up, the other down, that the writing of Somerville and Ross has abiding worth and interest. Cheerfully mercenary, they turned into literature the events of their daily lives, and of their friends and relatives Martin wrote:

> Let us take Carbery and grind its bones to make our bread—
> Cut, my dear! It would be new life to me to cut it—and we
> will serve it up to the spectator so that its own mother
> wouldn't know it!

Martin wrote this in a letter to Edith after the success of their first novel, *An Irish Cousin* from 1889. Today this novel is little known but it is a well constructed 'shocker' influenced by Lefanu's *Uncle Silas*, and remarkable for its inclusion of exactly rendered dialect speech. Martin was an admirer of Maria Edgeworth, who pioneered the technique of taking tracts of verbatim Irish dialect into her novels—Scott emulating Edgeworth in this with Scots. In Drishane, Somerville and Ross could read the letters between Maria and her beloved Nancy Crampton (the wife of Charles Kendal Bushe) who was their common great-grandmother. They began to formulate a better novel, while still earning enough to get by. Bread-and-butter income came from writing up tours for journals like the *Lady's Pictorial* while serious intent was reserved for their novel *The Real Charlotte*, which fermented behind the scenes for three years. It appeared in 1894 to mixed reviews, some of which were depressing. Although they knew that this novel was a peak in their creative output, mystifyingly it was some years before the common reader agreed with them. Nonplussed, they cast about in the meantime for a more popular and financially productive line.

When Martin was invalided after a hunting fall in 1898, Somerville and Ross had to produce something for their agent J. B. Pinker at high speed, to a horribly imminent deadline. The series of light-hearted stories, *Some Experiences of an Irish RM*, grew from the nucleus of a resident magistrate with myopia—a myopia physical and mental, a fall guy who was at sea in Ireland. The chief running joke was provided by the catastrophes consequent on his extreme short sight and frequent loss of pince-nez, compounded by his English slowness on the uptake. Set against him were two creations, of the Irish earth earthy, to tie him in knots for the honour of Ireland: Slipper and Flurry Knox. In the extremity of an approaching deadline Martin and Edith fell on their letters to each other of the late 1880s and used them as a quarry. The germ of the RM Major Yeates seems likely to have sprung from Martin: his horse the Quaker is a repaint of her borrowed mount with the West Carbery hounds and the entire Martin family bore the disability of extreme myopia, and pince-nez, like a heraldic charge—as a distinction indicative of their gentle blood, like writing illegibly. *Some Experiences of an Irish*

RM published by Longmans in 1899 made them famous and better paid.

Martin had a subtle sense of humour and could be overcome by fits of unstoppable laughter during which speech was impossible and the only solution, should the situation be delicate, was to remove her from the scene. Delicately feminine in appearance, she particularly enjoyed meeting people who had thought, from her pen-name, that she was a man. Her nickname among their group of independent women friends was Mr Ross. She met W. B. Yeats at her cousin Augusta Gregory's and from her letters to Edith describing their meeting comes the revelation that Martin recognized in Yeats his similarly keen sense of humour and through it was able to connect with him. Like Martin, Yeats was well armoured with a façade of reserved refinement, but they instantly responded generously to one another. He later helped with critical recognition of *The Real Charlotte*, and, surprisingly, was an admirer of Major Yeates, once he had been assured that he was no relation.

From the time that they began to write together in 1888, Somerville and Ross relied heavily on the excellent Irish postal system, Somerville being based at her home in co. Cork and Ross at her home in co. Galway. Their work was often perfected in drafts passing back and forth through the post, and in passing round the family to approved readers for comments. It was not until the death of Mrs Martin in February 1906 that Martin moved to Castletownshend. Even so she was often away visiting her family, and deliberately arranged to be away at times like harvesting when the running of the Drishane farm, a co-operative venture shared by the Somerville sisters, prevented any chance of writing work.

In 1908 both writers attended the mass women's suffrage rally in Hyde Park where they had been so impressed by the speeches of Mrs Pethick-Lawrence and Christabel Pankhurst that they decided to join the movement and become active campaigners for the cause. As suffragists Edith and Martin were president and vice-president of the Munster Women's Franchise League, and were in office when the war broke out in 1914. Up until then, in the cause of suffrage, nationalist and unionist women had peacefully joined forces, but when a fund was used to purchase an ambulance for the front, this caused a split, the nationalists breaking away under Mary MacSwiney, the sister of the lord mayor of Cork. The last published writing by Somerville and Ross was a pamphlet for the Conservative and Unionist Women's Suffrage Society, *With Thanks for the Kind Enquiries*, an account of the aid sent to the front by Irish women suffragists.

Martin was never fully fit from the time of her fall in 1898, and various journeys were taken to spa towns for relief, but it was thought later by doctors that all the while a brain tumour was spreading. In early December 1915 she suddenly collapsed, was taken to the Glen Vera Nursing Home in Cork, and died there on 21 December. She was buried at St Barrahane's, Castletownshend, on 23 December. Memorial tributes were fulsome in praise of her writing and Somerville and Ross was kept alive as a literary firm for some time by the efforts of the surviving partner.

Though some Irish critics, notably Frank O'Connor even before Edith Somerville's death in 1949, have tried to rehabilitate them in their home country, since the separation of Ireland and Britain their reputation has been adrift in the space between. The recent critical attention paid to *The Silver Fox* by Declan Kiberd in his study *Irish Classics* (2000) may signal renewed interest.

GIFFORD LEWIS

Sources V. F. Martin, diaries, Queen's University, Belfast · E. A. Œ. Somerville, correspondence with M. Ross, NYPL, Humanities and Social Sciences Library, Berg collection · review scrapbooks, Coghill family papers · E. Œ. Somerville and V. F. Martin, *Irish memories* (1917) · Munster Womens Franchise League papers, Queen's University, Belfast, special collections · letters to or from Violet Martin, Drishane, Castletownshend, co. Cork, E. Œ. Somerville archives, section 6 · G. Lewis, *Somerville and Ross: the world of the Irish RM* (1985) · *The selected letters of Somerville and Ross*, ed. G. Lewis (1989) **Archives** NRA, priv. coll., corresp. · Queen's University, Belfast, corresp., notebooks, and commonplace books · TCD, corresp. | BL, corresp. with Society of Authors, Add. MS 56814 · Drishane, Castletownshend, co. Cork, E. Œ. Somerville archives · NYPL, Berg collection · TCD, letters to William Meredith · Sourden, Rothes, Fife, Coghill family papers **Likenesses** E. A. Œ. Somerville, oils on panel, 1886, NPG [*see illus.*] · H. Coghill, photograph, *c.*1891 (with E. A. Œ. Somerville), repro. in Lewis, ed., *Selected letters* **Wealth at death** £228 13*s.* 0*d.*: probate, Ireland, 1916

Martin, William (*c.*1696–1756), naval officer, appears to have been the eldest son of Tutchen Martin (*d.* 1702) of Stepney and his wife, Bennet Garsh, or Gage, although another account states that his father was Commodore George Martin (*d.* 1724). Confusion also exists as to his early service, but he seems to have entered the navy as a volunteer per order, or king's letter boy, on 26 August 1708 on the *Dragon*. When the *Dragon* went to Newfoundland in May 1710 Martin was put on shore at Plymouth 'for his health'. He appears to have taken passage to the Mediterranean in the *Ranelagh* almost immediately, for on 30 July 1710 he was promoted second lieutenant of the *Resolution* by Sir John Norris. On 4 January 1712 he was appointed by Sir John Jennings, also in the Mediterranean, to the *Superbe*, in which he continued until July 1714. Between 1715 and 1718 he transferred from the *Cumberland*, flagship of Sir John Norris in the Baltic, to the *Rupert*; and to the *Cumberland*, again with Norris. On 9 October 1718 he was promoted captain in the *Cumberland*, and took post from that date. On 9 February 1720 he was appointed to the *Blandford*, which between 1720 and 1721 was attached to the Baltic fleet under Norris, and was afterwards employed in American waters in the suppression of piracy. On 16 August 1726 he married Mary Atkins of Twell, Gloucestershire; they had no children.

From 1727 to 1732 Martin commanded the *Advice* in the fleet supporting Gibraltar and then in the channel, under Sir Charles Wager; and later the *Sunderland* on the home station, at Lisbon, or in the Mediterranean (1733–7). In May 1738 he was appointed to the *Ipswich*, one of the fleet in the Mediterranean under Rear-Admiral Nicholas Haddock. In January 1741 he hoisted a broad pennant in command of a detached squadron off Cadiz, and in July 1742 was sent by Admiral Thomas Mathews to enforce the neutrality of

Naples. With three ships of the line, two frigates, and four bomb-vessels he sailed into Naples Bay on the afternoon of 9 August, and sending his flag captain Merrick De Langle, on shore, requested an immediate and categorical answer to his demands. The Neapolitans attempted to make conditions, and De Langle returned to the ship with their deputy. Martin replied that he was sent 'as an officer to act, not a minister to treat', and desired De Langle to insist on a prompt answer. Martin's force was small, but superior to any the Neapolitans could raise against it, and they yielded to the pressure put on them.

Martin was subsequently employed in protecting Tuscany from any attempt on the part of the Spaniards, and in February 1743 was sent to Genoa to require the destruction of Spanish magazines. He was later involved in the sinking of a Spanish ship of the line, the *San Isidro* at Ajaccio.

Towards the end of the year Martin returned to England, and on 7 December he was promoted to the rank of rear-admiral. In February 1744 he commanded in the Channel Fleet under Sir John Norris, and on 19 June 1744 he was advanced to vice-admiral, and was second in command in the fleet which went to Lisbon under Sir John Balchen. Balchen during this period asked Martin to report on the state of the contract hospitals; the report was so critical that it strongly influenced the decision to establish medical centres solely for the navy. On Balchen's death Martin was appointed to the chief command, which he held during 1745. In December he and his squadron were sent to the Downs under Admiral Edward Vernon, and on Vernon's dismissal he succeeded to the command. Following the collapse of the Jacobite threat he took the squadron back to its usual station, and commanded the principal fleet, until in July 1746 he sought and was granted leave to retire for health reasons. He had served almost continuously since 1738, and had already warned the Admiralty that he needed a respite.

During this command Martin conducted his squadron diligently and carefully. However, owing to the lack of a settled policy, the Admiralty's practice of reacting to any information received by ordering the squadron hither and thither to meet the need, and its necessary visits to port to replenish its provisions, a number of French squadrons was able to make their departure. No blame for the escapes was laid on him, and the ample notice he gave of his wish to retire seems to dispel the suggestion that he was piqued by George Anson's assumption of the command, although he might have been irked by public criticism. On 15 July 1747 he was promoted admiral of the blue. Charnock described him as a handsome and learned man who spoke several languages with ease, and who, when in command, was said to live in 'the greatest splendour, maintaining his rank in the highest style' (J. Charnock, *Biographia navalis*, 6 vols., 1794–8, 4.69). He retired to Twickenham where he died on 17 September 1756 'being about sixty years old' (ibid.).

J. K. LAUGHTON, *rev.* A. W. H. PEARSALL

Sources H. W. Richmond, *The navy in the war of 1739–48*, 3 vols. (1920) · R. Beatson, *Naval and military memoirs of Great Britain*, 3 vols. (1790) · *The letters of Horace Walpole, earl of Orford*, ed. P. Cunningham, 1 (1857); repr. (1891) · Burke, *Gen. GB* · *DNB* · logs, PRO, ADM 51/222, 427 · muster books, PRO, ADM 36/2838, 2840 · pay book, PRO, ADM 33/276 · letters to admiralty, PRO, ADM 1/2098 · journal, PRO, ADM 50/64 · Commission and warrant books, PRO, ADM 6/13
Archives PRO, ADM MSS
Wealth at death property in Stepney

Martin, William (*b.* 1753, *d.* in or after 1836), painter, was born in August 1753 and baptized on 15 August in the parish of St Peter Mancroft, Norwich, the son of William Martin and his wife, Margaret. He displayed an early aptitude for painting, and in 1766 was awarded a gold palette for a historical painting by the Society of Arts. He entered the Royal Academy Schools on 15 October 1772 and began exhibiting there in 1775. His address in that year was given as that of G. B. Cipriani RA, and it is possible that he lodged there until as late as 1791. He showed at the Royal Academy up to 1816, and his output was a mixture of historical subjects and portraits. His practice did occasionally extend to landscapes, for which he won a premium in 1780. About 1800 he was engaged on decorative paintings at Windsor Castle for George III, exhibiting three small, related sketches at the Royal Academy in that year. In 1807 he moved to Marylebone and in 1810 appeared credited as 'Historical Painter to His Majesty'.

His contributions to the Royal Academy ended after 1816, although he continued sending works to the British Institution until 1831. He was still in correspondence with a Norwich patron, James Bennett, until 1836; it is assumed that he died, unmarried about this time. His ties to his home city remained strong. In 1787 he presented *The Death of Lady Jane Grey* and *The Death of Queen Eleanor* (engraved F. Bartolozzi RA) to the corporation of Norwich and they both hang in St Andrew's Hall there. Bartolozzi also engraved his *Imogen's Chamber. The Barons Swearing the Charter of Liberties at Bury St. Edmunds* (engraved W. Ward) is in the University of Oxford collection; *A Cottage Interior* (engraved C. Turner) is in Norwich Castle Museum.

TINA FISKE

Sources artist's file, archive material, Courtauld Inst., Witt Library · B. Stewart and M. Cutten, *The dictionary of portrait painters in Britain up to 1920* (1997) · Waterhouse, *18c painters* · T. Fawcett, 'Eighteenth-century art in Norwich', *Walpole Society*, 46 (1976–8), 71–90 · S. C. Hutchison, 'The Royal Academy Schools, 1768–1830', *Walpole Society*, 38 (1960–62), 123–91, esp. 138 · Graves, *RA exhibitors* · Graves, *Brit. Inst.* · *A catalogue of the portraits and paintings in St. Andrews Hall and other public buildings*, City of Norwich (1905) · *Catalogue of pictures, drawings, etchings and bronzes in the picture gallery of the Norwich Castle Museum*, Norwich Castle Museum, 3rd edn (1904) · *Summary catalogue of paintings in the Ashmolean Museum*, Ashmolean Museum (1980) · A. Cox-Johnson, *Handlist of painters, sculptors and architects associated with St. Marylebone, 1760–1960* (1963) · *IGI*
Archives Norfolk RO, letters to James Bennett of Norwich

Martin, William (*d.* 1815), typefounder, was probably born in Birmingham, the son of a local printer whose family originally came from Scotland. It is likely that William began work at John Baskerville's type foundry at Easy Hill, Birmingham, where his brother, Robert, was Baskerville's foreman. In London from about 1787, Martin was employed by the bookseller and publisher George Nicol, in whose house on Pall Mall he developed his types for seven years before moving to his own foundry in Duke Street, St James's, Piccadilly.

During his time with Nicol, as well as after, when he worked principally for William Bulmer at the Shakspeare Press, Martin aimed to produce a type uniting 'utility, elegance and beauty' (preface to Bulmer's edition of *The Poems of Goldsmith and Parnell*, 1795) superior to that of rival British presses, and a competitor to continental designs. Martin and Nicol achieved their ambition with a type that confounded the experts in a hoax known as the Bodoni Hum in which connoisseurs mistook Bulmer's printing and Martin's types to be a product of the leading typefounder Bodoni. An integral contributor to the success of Bulmer's Shakspeare Press, Martin was rightfully acclaimed for his work on the magnificent volumes printed by John Boydell, among them *The Poetical Works of John Milton* (3 vols., 1794–7), *An History of the River Thames* (2 vols., 1794–6), and *The Dramatic Works of Shakespeare* (9 vols., completed 1802).

In their design Martin's types drew on Baskerville, but were influenced more significantly by Bodoni. He adapted to the transition from the old to the modern face, discarded the long 's', and created his own individual style by ameliorating the rotundity of the old face and the angularity of the modern, thereby making the result more pleasing to the eye. His romans, which appeared in Thomas Frognall Dibdin's three works *Typographical Antiquities*, *Bibliotheca Spenceriana*, and *Bibliographical Decameron*, were admired for their clarity as were his italics, though these were criticized also for being too calligraphic. However, it was Martin's orientals and greeks that evidenced his outstanding talent. It was through his oriental face design that he gained the title 'oriental type founder and printer to the East India Company' in 1803. Though widely praised, his greek characters, exhibited in Musaeus's *The Loves of Hero and Leander* (1797), none the less divide critics, who maintain either that his work makes the text easier to read or that the faces are 'cramped' (Reed, 326).

Aside from William Bulmer, John McCreery of Liverpool was probably the first publisher to use the Martin types, in his poem *The Press* (1803); they also appear in *A Specimen of the Improved Types of G. R. Harris* (1807). A 'man whose modesty was equal to his talents' and one who would 'listen to every hint of improvement' (Nicol, 3), William Martin died in London in 1815. His foundry, which had been supported by the Shakspeare Press, was continued for a short time by William Bulmer, but was merged with that of Henry Caslon in 1817.   VIVIENNE W. PAINTING

Sources T. B. Reed, *A history of the old English letter foundries*, rev. A. F. Johnson (1952) • P. C. G. Isaac, 'William Bulmer (1757–1830): fine printer', *Archaeologia Aeliana*, 5th ser., 16 (1988), 223–37 • J. R. Barker, 'John McCreery: a radical printer, 1768–1832', *The Library*, 5th ser., 16 (1961), 81–103 • F. E. Pardoe, *John Baskerville of Birmingham, letter-founder and printer* (1975) • T. C. Hansard, *Typographia: an historical sketch of the origin and progress of the art of printing* (1825) • W. B. Todd, *Dictionary of printers, London and vicinity, 1800–1840* (1972) • G. Nicol, 'Papers on the Shakespeare Gallery', 7 June 1791, St Bride's printing library, London, 39802

Martin, William (1767–1810), naturalist and actor, was born at Mansfield, Nottinghamshire, the son of Joseph Martin, a hosier, and Ann Mallatratt (c.1746–1819), both from Mansfield. About 1769 he and his mother were abandoned; Joseph Martin moved to Ireland as an actor, adopted the name Booth, and, after extraordinary new careers as portrait painter, inventor (of the polygraphic process for copying oil paintings), and patentee (of new methods of making cloth and linen), died in London in 1797. Martin's mother, forced to support herself and son, likewise chose an acting career, and tried to educate her son at the best schools available to her itinerant lifestyle and straitened circumstances.

William Martin took to the stage aged five. About 1778, he took drawing and writing lessons from James Bolton (1735–1799) of Stannary, near Halifax. Bolton took great interest in, and published much on, natural history. He proved a crucial influence on Martin. In 1782 Martin settled with Stanton's company of actors in the Peak District of Derbyshire where, in 1785, he first met fellow naturalist White Watson (1760–1835). Martin's first scientific publication, on ants, appeared in 1788. Although he continued to dabble in zoology, some time before 1789—inspired by the geologist Abraham Mills FRS (c.1750–1828)—he started to study the fossil and mineral riches of the Peak District. In May 1789 he issued the prospectus of a joint work with Watson, which he would engrave, on the minerals, spars, and fossils of Derbyshire. But their collaboration proved impossible when Watson, who was to contribute the minerals, failed to deliver. The first five parts, of an intended fourteen, of Martin's own *Figures and Descriptions of Petrifactions … in Derbyshire*, appeared between 1794 and 1796, with all text and most of the drawing, etching, and colouring of the twenty-nine plates by him. These were the first coloured illustrations of British fossils and Martin was elected fellow of the Linnean Society in 1796, when his paper on fossil brachiopods was also read.

On 17 April 1797, at Stoke-on-Trent, Martin married Mrs Mary Adams, 'an unfortunate but interesting young widow … and actress' (Hull, 560). Martin's full-time acting career was soon part-exchanged for a new career as writing-master, from 1798 at Burton upon Trent, then from 1800 in Buxton, and finally from 1805 at Macclesfield, also at the King's School there. In 1800 Martin was sending fossils and minerals to James Sowerby (1757–1822), who illustrated many of them. In the same year, he bought a fourth share in the Buxton theatre (where he continued acting in their midsummer season until 1809).

Martin's book *Outlines … of Extraneous Fossils*, the first systematic study of general palaeontology and of fossilization in English, was published in April 1809. Its publication led to Martin's election as corresponding member of the Manchester Literary and Philosophical Society and, in June, honorary membership of the Geological Society of London. The book also inspired John Farey (1766–1826) to visit Martin at Macclesfield in April 1809. Farey offered to collaborate in preparing a detailed geological map, in an attempt to improve the stratigraphic knowledge of Derbyshire fossils. However, their second meeting (intended for September 1809 at Sir Joseph Banks's house at Overton) had to be abandoned, as Martin was seriously ill with consumption. Nevertheless, Martin's second book, dedicated to Banks, *Petrificata Derbiensia*, was published in August 1809. It completed his earlier work and described the Carboniferous limestone and other fossils of Derbyshire, and was illustrated with his own engravings. Owing to his illness, the intended second volume, on fossils (especially plants) from coal strata, never appeared. Martin died on 31 May 1810 at Back Street, Macclesfield, leaving no provision for his widow, six young children, or his aged mother. He was buried on 3 June at Christ Church, Macclesfield. Subscriptions were made to support his dependants, one of whom was William Charles Linnaeus *Martin (1798–1864). Martin was honoured with the brachiopod genus *Martinia* named after him in 1844, as was one of the most characteristic Derbyshire fossil corals, *Lithostrotion martini*, in 1851.   H. S. TORRENS

Sources J. Hull, 'An account of the life and writings of the late Mr William Martin FLS', *Monthly Magazine*, 32 (1812), 556–65 · J. Challinor, 'The beginning of scientific palaeontology in Britain', *Annals of Science*, 6 (1948–50), 46–53 · R. McCoola, *Theatre in the hills* (1994) · J. Feather, 'John Walter and the Logographic Press', *Publishing History*, 1 (1997), 92–109 · *Journal of the House of Commons*, 47 (1792), 499, 559–60, 626, 680, 721–2, 763, 1075, 1090 [Mr Booth's petition] · 'Joseph Booth', *Monthly Magazine*, 26/2 (1808–9), 315–16, 516–18 · J. Edmondson, *James Bolton of Halifax* (1995) · W. Martin, 'Formicae', *GM*, 1st ser., 58 (1788), 975–8, pl. 3 · H. M. Muir-Wood, 'The Brachiopoda of Martin's *Petrificata Derbiensia*', *Annals and Magazine of Natural History*, 12th ser., 4 (1951), pp. 97–118, pls. 3–6 · W. Martin, 'On the localities of certain reliquia, or extraneous fossils, found in Derbyshire', *Philosophical Magazine*, 39 (1812), 81–5 · J. Farey, *General view of the agriculture and minerals of Derbyshire* (1811), xxi · J. Farey, 'On the importance of knowing and accurately discriminating fossil-shells', *Philosophical Magazine*, 53 (1819), 112–32 · 'advertisement', *Derby Mercury* (4 June 1789) · 'Literary intelligence', *GM*, 1st ser., 79 (1809), 727
Archives Derbys. RO, Matlock, Watson MSS · Devizes Museum, Wiltshire, Cunnington MSS · Liverpool Central Library, Roscoe MSS · University of Bristol, J. Sowerby MSS

Martin, William (1772–1851), eccentric and self-proclaimed philosopher, was born on 21 June 1772 at the Twohouse, Haltwhistle, Northumberland, the eldest of four sons of (William) Fenwick Martin (d. 1813) and his wife, Isabella (d. 1813), daughter of Richard Thompson, a farmer. The second son, Richard, a quartermaster in the guards, served through the Peninsular War and was present at Waterloo. The youngest sons were Jonathan *Martin (1782–1838), arsonist, and John *Martin (1789–1854), artist. There was one daughter, Ann. William's early years were spent with his maternal grandparents near Haydon Bridge, and he accompanied them when they moved in 1775 to a farm in Kintyre. When his grandparents died he went to live with his father, then foreman of a tannery at Ayr. In 1782 father and son returned to Northumberland. Martin is next heard of working in a ropery at Howdon Dock, and in the following year he joined the Northumberland militia at Durham. Discharged in 1805 Martin, an able mechanic, was granted a patent for improvements to shoes, and began taking an interest in perpetual motion

William Martin (1772–1851), by George Patten, *c*.1821

machines. He ridiculed the colliers of the north-east because they were still running their wagons on wooden rails, rather than on iron rails as in the midlands, not understanding that the local cost of iron was uneconomically high.

In 1808 Martin went to London where he exhibited his Eureka perpetual motion machine, which was apparently simply a pendulum driven by a concealed current of air. In the following year he returned to his modest trade of rope making, and in 1810 to the militia. In Ireland with his regiment he learned the elements of line engraving. Apart from his quackery and noisy absurdities Martin's skill brought him in 1814 the Isis silver medal of the Society of Arts for his spring weighing machine with circular dial and index. In the same year he married, describing his wife only as 'an inoffensive woman, respected by rich and poor, and a celebrated dressmaker' (W. Martin, *Philosopher's Life*, 1833, 33). They settled first at Newcastle upon Tyne, then at Wallsend, where, supported by her earnings, he was able to concentrate on his multifarious inventions until her death on 16 January 1832.

He founded the Martinean Society, based on opposition to the Royal Society, and particularly hostile to the Newtonian theory of gravitation, against which he harboured a growing antagonism, which ultimately embraced all men of science. Styling himself 'anti-newtonian', Martin began giving lectures, first in the Newcastle district and from 1830 throughout England. Throughout these years his voice was heard at many meetings, ranting against scientists in general. He was inevitably drawn to the annual gatherings of the British Association for the Advancement of Science, the butt of his polemic *The defeat of the eighth scientific meeting of the British Association of Asses, which we may properly call the rich folks' hopping, or the false philosophers in an uproar* (1838). Newton remained his chief hate, but Herschel, Faraday, Sedgwick, and Lardner attracted his wrath. Declaring himself a staunch supporter of the Church of England he also denounced papists, bishops, Puseyites, Unitarians, and all those he considered to have left the true path. In a torrent of pamphlets he heaped abuse on impostors, false philosophers, and those who had converted his inventions to their own gain, continuing the while to work on further mechanical projects. In 1835 he proposed a new form of miners' safety lamp, and when it was rejected because of its fragility and uncertain performance he denounced the discoveries of George Stevenson and Humphry Davy in these fields as dishonest, claiming that they had stolen his ideas. Martin was a familiar figure in and around Newcastle: J. B. Langhorne described him as 'a stout, portly man, perfectly cracked but harmless. He used to strut about wearing the Society of Arts medal round his neck' (*N&Q*, 134). From 1849 Martin lived with his brother John at Chelsea, where he died on 9 February 1851.

THOMAS SECCOMBE, rev. ANITA MCCONNELL

Sources T. Balston, *The life of Jonathan Martin … with some account of William and Richard Martin* (1945) • M. A. Richardson, ed., *The local historian's table book … historical division*, 5 vols. (1841–6), vol. 3, pp. 137–9; vol. 4, pp. 279, 366 • *GM*, 2nd ser., 35 (1851), 327–8 • *GM*, 2nd ser., 41 (1854), 433 • J. Sykes, *Local records, or, Historical register of remarkable events, which have occurred in Northumberland and Durham*, 2 (1833) • J. Latimer, *Local records, or, Historical register of remarkable events which have occurred in Northumberland and Durham … 1832–57* (1857) • H. Dircks, *Perpetuum mobile, or, A history of the search for self-motive power, from the 13th to the 19th century* (1870) [2nd series] • *N&Q*, 4th ser., 12 (1873), 48, 133–4, 252–3, 278 • R. L. Galloway, *Annals of coal mining and the coal trade*, 2nd ser. (1904), 159, 315; repr. (1971)
Likenesses G. Patten, miniature, *c*.1821, NPG [*see illus.*] • Collard, line engraving (after H. P. Parker), NPG • Lambert, engraving (after H. P. Parker) • engravings, Laing Art Gallery, Newcastle

Martin, William [*pseud.* Peter Parley] (**1801–1867**), children's writer, was born at Woodbridge, Suffolk, the son of Jane Martin, an unmarried laundress who worked for officers of the garrison stationed at Woodbridge during the Napoleonic wars. Reputedly, his father was Sir Benjamin Blomfield. After attending a dame-school at Woodbridge, in 1815 he became an assistant to Thomas Howe, a woollen draper at Battersea, Surrey. Howe's wife was a close friend of Elizabeth Fry, the Quaker social reformer, and under the guidance of these two women Martin improved his education sufficiently to obtain the post of master in a school at Uxbridge. He remained there until 1836, when he returned to Woodbridge and earned his living by delivering lectures and writing.

After beginning by producing articles for magazines, Martin began to undertake more substantial books for purchase by schools and parents. He wrote *The Christian Philosopher* (1832), *Every Boy's Arithmetic* (1833), with J. T.

Crossley, edited the *Educational Magazine* (1835), which was 'short-lived and uninteresting' (Darton, 223), *The Parlour Book, or, Familiar Conversations, on Science and the Arts* (1835?), *The Book of Sports, Athletic Exercises, and Amusements* (1837?), and *The Moral and Intellectual School Book* (1838). He more famously took on the pseudonym used by Samuel Griswold Goodrich of New England, whose first Peter Parley book, *Tales of Peter Parley about America*, appeared in 1827, and which was followed by a series of similar, highly successful tales at the rate of five or six volumes a year. Darton notes that 'in thirty years over 7,000,000 copies of some 116 *genuine* Parleys were sold' and that Goodrich was therefore eminently 'worth pirating' by English authors and publishers (ibid., 227). Martin was one of several English 'Peter Parleys' to take up the idea of short, explanatory, and entertaining narratives for the school and home tutoring market. Others were the writer George Mogridge (*Sergeant Bell and his Raree-Show*, 1839) and the publishers Thomas Tegg, Charles Tilt, Edward Lacey, and Samuel Clark. Martin, however, was regarded by Goodrich in his memoirs as the most successful—or troublesome. Martin wrote *Peter Parley's Tales for Boys and Girls at Home and Abroad* (*c*.1835) and produced many numbers of *Peter Parley's Magazine* for the publishers Darton and Clark, who began this as a monthly publication in 1839, and then bound it up in a gift book at Christmas as *Peter Parley's Annual: a Christmas and New Year's Present for Young People* (1840). The magazine ceased publication in 1863, while the annual continued until 1892 under different editors and various imprints. Other Parley titles attributed to Martin include *Peter Parley's Tales for Youth* (*c*.1844) and *Peter Parley's Tales about Kings & Queens* (1848).

Martin also continued with educational publishing, editing the *British Annals of Education* (1844) and producing several successful schoolbooks, among which were *The Intellectual Expositor and Vocabulary* (1851), *Intellectual Reading Book* (1851), and *The Intellectual Grammar* (1852). He used another pseudonym, Old Chatty Cheerful, for *The Boy's Own Annual* (1861) and a series of Household Tracts for the People with titles that included *Household Management, or, How to Make Home Comfortable* (1861); *How to Rise in the World to Respectability, Independence and Usefulness* (1861), and *Men who have fallen from wealth, fame and respectability, to poverty, shame and degradation, from a want of principle* (1861). His range and versatility in writing and editing popular works for adults and young people gave him the reputation of 'a very capable, all-round hack' (Darton, 224). He was also considered to have been a man of dissipated habits and loose morals in his later years, giving his friends some anxiety. He died at his home, Holly Lodge, Woodbridge, Suffolk, on 22 October 1867, and was buried in the cemetery there. He married three times, and was survived by his third wife, Harriet Agnes, and two sons.

MARGARET KINNELL EVANS

Sources BL cat. • F. J. Harvey Darton, *Children's books in England: five centuries of social life*, rev. B. Alderson, 3rd edn (1982) • J. St John, *The Osborne collection of early children's books, 1476–1910: a catalogue*, 2 vols. (1958–75) • Boase, *Mod. Eng. biog.* • private information (1893) [V. B.

Redstone; J. Loder] • *The Bookseller* (9 Oct 1889), 989 • *The Bookseller* (8 Nov 1889), 1204 • *DNB*

Wealth at death under £600: probate, 28 Nov 1867, *CGPLA Eng. & Wales*

Martin, Sir William (1807–1880), judge in New Zealand, the son of Henry Martin, a manufacturer, and his wife, Mary, was born in Birmingham and baptized there on 22 May 1807. He attended King Edward VI's Grammar School, Birmingham, and in 1825 matriculated from St John's College, Cambridge, whence in 1829 he graduated as twenty-sixth wrangler and fourth classic and took the second chancellor's medal. In 1831 he was elected fellow of his college and in 1832 proceeded MA and was admitted at Lincoln's Inn; he was called to the bar in 1836. Having resigned his fellowship in 1838 he went to London to practise law.

At college Martin had been a close friend of George Augustus Selwyn, who was to become the first bishop of New Zealand, and at Selwyn's prompting he accepted the office of chief justice of New Zealand in January 1841. On 3 April 1841 he married Mary Ann Parker [*see below*] at St Ethelburga, Bishopsgate, London, where her father was rector; however, Martin sailed alone for New Zealand only three days later.

In New Zealand, Martin's first task was to impress on the Maori their rights and responsibilities under British law, to which they were subject after the treaty of Waitangi. This he managed more effectively than he did his second task, the setting up of a system of courts and procedures for the new colony. His ideas for these closely followed British practice and were over-complex for a young colony.

Martin worked closely with Selwyn in setting up schools and establishing a scheme for church administration. He and Selwyn consistently defended the rights of the Maori, particularly in 1847 when they protested against certain clauses in the proposed new constitution which they felt broke faith with the Maori.

Always in poor health, Martin returned with his wife to England in August 1855 on leave. He spent the winter of 1856–7 in Italy and in 1857 resigned his post. That same year an honorary DCL was conferred on him by the University of Oxford and the New Zealand government granted him a pension. In 1860 he was knighted.

In 1859 the Martins returned to New Zealand and settled in Auckland. Martin's poor health prevented his accepting a seat in 1860 on the new council for native affairs, but his interest in the Maori continued and he did his utmost to prevent war with the Maori in the 1860s. His pamphlet *The Taranaki question* (1860) defended the stand taken by Wiremu Kingi Te Rangitake at Waitara, and later works argued for a respect for the Maori based on the principles of the treaty of Waitangi. Martin protested against the Native Lands Act of 1865 and in 1871 helped to draft amendments to it.

In 1874 the Martins left New Zealand for the last time. They went first to Lichfield to live in the bishop's palace, where Selwyn was bishop, and later moved to Torquay. An able linguist, who knew Hebrew, Arabic, and Melanesian and Polynesian dialects, Martin published *Inquiries Concerning the Structure of the Semitic Languages* (2 vols., 1876–8). He died at Matlock Terrace, Torquay, on 18 November 1880.

Martin was praised for his ability and integrity even by those who disagreed with his views. Those views and his works all sprang from his deep Christian faith.

Martin's wife, **Mary Ann Martin** [*née* Parker], Lady Martin (1817–1884), mission worker, shared this faith. She was born on 5 July 1817, the daughter of William and Ann Parker. Although she was an invalid throughout her life, this did not stop her acquiring a good education, being cheerful and enterprising, marrying Martin, and joining him in New Zealand in 1842, the year after his arrival there. She settled at Taurarua (Judges Bay, Auckland) and busied herself in setting up a hospital for the Maori, running classes for them and for Europeans, and with religious work. With Sarah Selwyn and Caroline Abraham, she was known as one of the 'three graces' who followed George Selwyn. She was convinced of the need to enlighten the Maori, but treated them with deep respect, regard, and liking, and was privately very critical of European ignorance of their customs. Having returned to England with her husband in 1874 she died on 2 January 1884 in Torquay. Her experiences are described in her book *Our Maoris* (1884).   ELIZABETH BAIGENT

Sources G. P. Barton, 'Martin, William, 1807–1880', *DNZB*, vol. 1 • G. Lennard, *Sir William Martin* (1961) • R. Dalziel, 'Martin, Mary Ann, 1817–1884', *DNZB*, vol. 1 • Venn, *Alum. Cant.* • *CGPLA Eng. & Wales* (1881)

Archives BL, letters to Sir Richard Owen and Lady Owen, Add. MS 39954

Likenesses J. Dickson, lithograph, pubd 1842 (after J. Carpenter), BM

Wealth at death under £4000: probate, 12 Jan 1881, *CGPLA Eng. & Wales*

Martin, William Charles Linnaeus (1798–1864), writer on natural history, was baptized on 23 February 1798, at Burton upon Trent, Staffordshire, the son of William *Martin (1767–1810), the naturalist, and his wife, Mary, an actress whose former married name was Adams. From October 1830 to 1838 he was superintendent of the museum at the Zoological Society of London.

Martin's earliest works were *A Natural History of Quadrupeds*, of which only 544 pages were issued in 1840, *A General Introduction to the Natural History of Mammiferous Animals* (1841), *The History of the Dog* (1845), and *The History of the Horse* (1845). These were followed, between 1847 and 1858, by a series of works on fish, poultry, cattle, pigs, and sheep, which appeared either separately or as volumes in the *Farmer's Library*, *Books for the Country*, and *The Country House*. In 1857 the writer Samuel Sidney edited and rewrote Martin's *The Pig*.

Martin was also author of a number of ornithological works: *An Introduction to the Study of Birds ... with a Particular Notice of the Birds Mentioned in Scripture* (1850), and *A General History of Humming-Birds ... with ... Reference to the Collection of J. Gould* (1852). He also edited a fourth edition of Robert Mudie's *Feathered Tribes of the British Islands* (1854) for Henry George Bohn's *Illustrated Library* and, in conjunction with

Francis Trevelyan Buckland and others, contributed papers to *Birds and Bird Life* (1863). Forty-five papers were also read by Martin before the Zoological Society, and appeared in its *Proceedings*.

Martin died on 15 February 1864, at his home, 10 Dacre Park Terrace, Lee, in Kent. He was survived by his wife, Mary Jane.   B. B. WOODWARD, *rev.* YOLANDA FOOTE

Sources *GM*, 3rd ser., 16 (1864), 536 · private information (1893) [P. L. Sclater] · Allibone, *Dict.* · *CGPLA Eng. & Wales* (1864)
Wealth at death under £100: probate, 6 Dec 1864, *CGPLA Eng. & Wales*

Martin, Sir William Fanshawe, fourth baronet (1801–1895), naval officer, son of Sir Thomas Byam *Martin (1773–1854) and his wife, Catherine, daughter of Captain Robert Fanshawe RN, was born on 5 December 1801. He entered the navy in June 1813, served under his father's flag off the Scheldt, and in January 1816 was appointed to the *Alceste*, then going to China with Lord Amherst. After his return he was in the yacht *Prince Regent* with Sir Edward Hamilton, and in the frigate *Glasgow* with Captain Anthony Maitland in the Mediterranean. On 15 December 1820 he was promoted lieutenant of the *Forte*, and a few months later was moved into the *Aurora*, going out to the South American station, where, on 8 February 1823, he was promoted commander of the sloop *Fly*. In her he rendered valuable assistance to the British merchants at Callao in a time of civil war, and was afterwards known in the navy as Fly Martin. He attained post rank on 5 June 1824. From 1826 to 1831 Martin commanded the frigate *Samarang* (28 guns) in the Mediterranean. On 25 July 1827, he married Anne Best (*d.* 1836), daughter of the Hon. William *Best, the first Baron Wynford. They had two sons who died young, and two daughters. On 21 May 1838 he married Sophia Elizabeth (*d.* 12 Nov 1874), daughter of Robert Hurt of Wirksworth; they had five daughters and one son, Richard Byam Martin, who succeeded to the baronetcy. Up to 1831 Martin's career was driven by the powerful position filled by his father, thereafter he spent the 1830s on half pay while the whigs held office. The ill health of his first wife, who died on 1 April 1836, and the care of his children also kept him from the sea until he had remarried.

In 1844 and 1845 Martin was flag captain at Sheerness, and in 1845–6 he commanded ships in the squadrons of evolution, demonstrating his strong antipathy towards those designed by Sir William Symonds. From 1849 to 1852 he was commodore in command of the Lisbon squadron, where he carried out a series of trials that demonstrated the suitability of the screw propeller as an auxiliary source of power in large sailing ships, which led directly to the decision to build an all-steam navy, taken in 1852. On 28 May 1853 he was promoted to the rank of rear-admiral. From 1853 until his promotion to vice-admiral on 13 February 1858, he was superintendent of Portsmouth Dockyard, an appointment that reflected the esteem in which his father was still held. Here he demonstrated great ability, having to administer the largest dockyard at a critical period, meeting the twin demands of the Crimean War and the Anglo-French naval race. Between

March 1858 and June 1859 he was senior naval lord in Lord Derby's second ministry, a post that recognized both his standing in the service and his strong tory politics. Although he refused to take a seat in the House of Commons, Martin dominated the board, especially in the all too frequent absence of the first lord, Sir John Pakington. He stopped Pakington's scheme to remove naval patronage from the board to the first lord's private office, by threatening to resign. An advocate of heavier artillery, Martin led the discussions that culminated in the order for the first British seagoing ironclad, HMS *Warrior*, part of a reconstruction of the navy to reflect the experience of the Crimean War and the strategic impact of new technology. In 1860 he was appointed to the command of the Mediterranean station, primarily to develop steam tactics, an area where the prime minister, Lord Palmerston, believed that the navy was falling behind the French. His systems of evolution, practised on a small scale, and then tried at sea, were meant to train the officers of the fleet to understand the limitations of their equipment, and ensure that they could execute the relatively simple manoeuvres required in battle with speed and precision. He held this post for three years, and in that time effected a major reform of naval discipline. Many of the ships of his fleet were manned by 'bounty' men and were bordering on mutiny. Martin none the less made the fleet into an excellent fighting force. His insistence on obedience was not always agreeable to captains and commanders, but if not loved, he was feared, and the work was done.

On 28 June 1861 Martin was made KCB, and on 14 November 1863 became an admiral; on the death of his cousin, Sir Henry Martin, third baronet, he succeeded to the baronetcy on 4 December 1863. From 1866 to 1869 he was commander-in-chief at Plymouth. In April 1870 he was retired under the scheme introduced by Hugh Childers. On 24 May 1873 he was made a GCB, and in September 1878 appointed rear-admiral of the United Kingdom. In 1879 he published a small pamphlet, *Cyprus as a Naval Station and a Place of Arms*, an exposition of Mediterranean strategy. In his later years he resided mainly at Upton Grey, near Winchfield, Hampshire, and he died there on 24 March 1895.

After a career made by his father, and from whom he took his politics, his professional ideas, and much else, Martin proved a worthy beneficiary of his rapid advancement. Although a bitter partisan of the tory party Martin was a thorough professional, who earned the respect of all who served with him. One of the most important flag officers of the era, he was a critical architect of the thoroughly professional service.

J. K. LAUGHTON, *rev.* ANDREW LAMBERT

Sources BL, Martin MSS · personal knowledge (1901) · A. D. Lambert, *The last sailing battlefleet: maintaining naval mastery, 1815–1850* (1991) · A. D. Lambert, *Battleships in transition* (1984) · J. H. Briggs, *Naval administrations, 1827 to 1892: the experience of 65 years*, ed. Lady Briggs (1897) · Mrs F. Egerton, *Admiral of the fleet: Sir Geoffrey Phipps Hornby, a biography* (1896) · C. I. Hamilton, *Anglo-French naval rivalry, 1840–1870* (1993) · S. Sandler, *The emergence of the modern capital ship* (1979) · *Letters and papers of Admiral of the Fleet Sir Thos. Byam Martin,*

GCB, ed. R. V. Hamilton, 3, Navy RS, 19 (1901) · E. Rasor, *Reform in the Royal Navy* (1976) · Burke, *Peerage*

Archives BL, corresp. and papers, Add. MSS 41408–41462 · NMM, letter-books, LBK/18–19 | BL, letters to Sir Charles Napier, Add. MSS 40033, 40043–40045 · Bucks. RLSS, Somerset MSS

Wealth at death £103,935 2s. 8d.: resworn probate, 1896, *CGPLA Eng. & Wales* (1895)

Martin, William Keble (1877–1969), botanical artist, was born on 9 July 1877 at Radley, near Oxford, the sixth child in the family of five sons and four daughters of the Revd Charles Martin, warden of St Peter's College, Radley, and his wife, Dora, younger daughter of George *Moberly, bishop of Salisbury, and sister of R. C. Moberly. George Moberly was an intimate friend of John Keble, originator of the Oxford Movement.

In 1891 the family moved to Dartington and Keble Martin was sent to Marlborough College, where he remained until 1895. In 1896 he went up to Christ Church, Oxford. Among his tutors were S. H. Vines and A. W. Church. Keble Martin became especially interested in mosses, and made the acquaintance of the botanist George Claridge Druce. He obtained a pass degree in Greek philosophy, botany, and church history in 1899. Keble Martin then attended Cuddesdon Theological College, and was ordained in 1902. From 1902 to 1909 he was a curate, successively, at Beeston, Ashbourne, and Lancaster. In 1909 he became vicar of Wath upon Dearne, near Rotherham, Yorkshire, being married the same year to Violet (d. 1963), daughter of Henry Chaworth-Musters, of Colwick Hall, Nottingham. They had two sons, one of whom died at the age of two, and three daughters.

Throughout these years Keble Martin devoted his spare time to the study of flowers. He became adept at drawing the plants which he observed, while simultaneously cataloguing them precisely. He preferred the wild flower to the cultivated, assembling related plants together on plates in order to portray an example of each species. He was interested in colour contrast, delighting in the depiction of pale flowers against their dark foliage. Together with Gordon T. Fraser, he edited the *Flora of Devon* (1939) for the botanical section of the Devonshire Association, of which he had become a member in 1930.

In the winter of 1917 Keble Martin volunteered to go overseas as a temporary chaplain to the armed forces, and was assigned to the 34th Northumberland Fusiliers in France. In 1920 he published *A History of the Ancient Parish of Wath-upon-Dearne*. In 1921 he became rector of Haccombe and Coffinswell, near Torquay. He now found more time for his flower studies and drawings, but was also an assiduous parish priest. He designed a new church at Milber, which was later built according to his plan, with three diverging naves before the altar.

When Keble Martin's flower plates were exhibited at the International Botanical Congress held in Cambridge in 1930, he gained recognition as a botanist of note. He had already, in 1928, been elected a fellow of the Linnean Society. A move to Great Torrington, north Devon, in 1934 left him with little time for botany, though he sometimes managed to attend meetings of the Linnean Society in London, where his drawings were exhibited. His attitude was then, as it had been formerly, that

> If some of our members fancy that modern science is not compatible with the Christian faith, it may be of some help to them to be assured that this is not at all the case. These two aspects of truth complete one another. We speak of natural law, let us call it the trustworthiness of nature, mercifully provided for us.

During the Second World War, Keble Martin continued his parochial work at Torrington and, in 1943, moved to the benefice of Combe in Teignhead with Milber. He was anxious to have a parish which would be less exacting than Torrington, and also to see that his plans for a church at Milber were implemented. He achieved both these objects with the move. However, Keble Martin was ageing and Milber was hilly and so, in 1949, he resigned his benefice and retired to Gidleigh, near Chagford. He continued to work part-time for neighbouring churches, replacing clergy who were absent or ill.

Keble Martin's wife had a stroke in 1957 and a heart attack in 1960; she died in 1963. In 1960 his eldest daughter died of leukaemia. He was encouraged during this difficult time by the possibility that his coloured drawings of flowers, by now numbering almost 1500, might be published. An appeal was launched with the support of several well-known botanists and the encouragement of the duke of Edinburgh, who wrote an introduction to the book. It was published as *The Concise British Flora in Colour* in 1965 and became a best-seller. Exeter University awarded Keble Martin an honorary DSc in 1966 and in December of that year the Post Office asked him to submit designs for postage stamps. Four stamps with his designs were issued in 1967.

Keble Martin married, secondly, in 1965, Florence (Flora) Lewis, a widow. He then busied himself with writing his autobiography, *Over the Hills* (1968). He died at his home, Broadymead, Woodbury, near Exeter, on 26 November 1969.

C. S. NICHOLLS, *rev.*

Sources W. Keble Martin, *Over the hills* (1968) · *The Times* (28 Nov 1969) · Desmond, *Botanists*, rev. edn · *CGPLA Eng. & Wales* (1970)

Wealth at death £1955: probate, 9 April 1970, *CGPLA Eng. & Wales*

PICTURE CREDITS

Macqueen, Robert, Lord Braxfield (1722–1799)—Scottish National Portrait Gallery

Macrae, (John) Duncan Graham (1905–1967)—Scottish National Portrait Gallery

Macray, William Dunn (1826–1916)—© Bodleian Library, University of Oxford

Macready, William Charles (1793–1873)—© National Portrait Gallery, London

MacSwiney, Terence James (1879–1920)—National Gallery of Ireland

McTaggart, John McTaggart Ellis (1866–1925)—The Master and Fellows, Trinity College, Cambridge

McTaggart, William (1835–1910)—National Gallery of Scotland

McTavish, Simon (1750–1804)—National Archives of Canada / C-000164

MacWhirter, John (1837–1911)—© National Portrait Gallery, London

Madan, Falconer (1851–1935)—© Bodleian Library, University of Oxford

Madan, Spencer (1729–1813)—reproduced by kind permission of the Bishop of Peterborough; photograph: The Paul Mellon Centre for Studies in British Art

Madden, Sir Charles Edward (1862–1935)—© National Portrait Gallery, London

Madden, Sir Frederic (1801–1873)—© National Portrait Gallery, London

Maddox, Isaac (1697–1759)—by kind permission of the Bishop of Worcester and the Church Commissioners; photograph: The Paul Mellon Centre for Studies in British Art

Madge, Charles Henry (1912–1996)—© National Portrait Gallery, London

Madison, James (1751–1836)—Bowdoin College Museum of Art, Brunswick, Maine, Bequest of the Honorable James Bowdoin III

Madocks, William Alexander (1773–1828)—© National Portrait Gallery, London

Maffey, John Loader, first Baron Rugby (1877–1969)—The de László Foundation; collection National Portrait Gallery, London

Magee, John (1750?–1809)—photograph reproduced with the kind permission of the Trustees of the National Museums & Galleries of Northern Ireland

Magee, William (1766–1831)—by kind permission of the Board of Trinity College Dublin

Magee, William Connor (1821–1891)—© National Portrait Gallery, London

Maginn, William (1794–1842)—© National Portrait Gallery, London

Magniac, Hollingworth (1786–1867)—HSBC Holdings plc

Magnus Maximus (d. 388)—© Copyright The British Museum

Magnus, Katie, Lady Magnus (1844–1924)—courtesy of Jewish Museum, London

Magnus, Sir Philip, first baronet (1842–1933)—© National Portrait Gallery, London

Magnússon, Eiríkur (1833–1913)—National Museum of Iceland

Magrath, John Richard (1839–1930)—© National Portrait Gallery, London

Maguire, James Rochfort (1855–1925)—© National Portrait Gallery, London

Mahaffy, Sir John Pentland (1839–1919)—© National Portrait Gallery, London

Mahler, Kurt (1903–1988)—© National Portrait Gallery, London

Mahomed, Deen (1759–1851)—Wellcome Library, London

Mahony, Francis Sylvester (1804–1866)—V&A Images, The Victoria and Albert Museum

Mainauduc, John Boniot de (c.1750–1797)—© National Portrait Gallery, London

Maine, Sir Henry James Sumner (1822–1888)—Collection Trinity Hall, Cambridge; photograph D. J. Scott, Cambridge, 1933

Mair, Lucy Philip (1901–1986)—© Lotte Meitner-Graf

Mair, Dame Sarah Elizabeth Siddons (1846–1941)—from St George's School for Girls, Edinburgh, Archive

Maitland, Agnes Catherine (1849–1906)—The Mistress and Fellows, Girton College, Cambridge

Maitland, Frederic William (1850–1906)—© National Portrait Gallery, London

Maitland, James, eighth earl of Lauderdale (1759–1839)—Scottish National Portrait Gallery

Maitland, John, first Lord Maitland of Thirlestane (1543–1595)—© National Portrait Gallery, London

Maitland, John, duke of Lauderdale (1616–1682)—Scottish National Portrait Gallery

Maitland, Sir Thomas (1760–1824)—in the collection of the Thirlestane Castle Trust; photograph courtesy the Scottish National Portrait Gallery

Maitland, William, of Lethington (1525x30–1573)—in the collection of Thirlestane Castle Trust

Makarios III (1913–1977)—Getty Images – Chris Ware

Makin, Bathsua (b. 1600, d. in or after 1675)—© National Portrait Gallery, London

Makins, Roger Mellor, first Baron Sherfield (1904–1996)—© National Portrait Gallery, London

Malan, Daniël François (1874–1959)—Getty Images – Merlyn Severn

Malcolm, Sir Dougal Orme (1877–1955)—© National Portrait Gallery, London

Malcolm, Hugh Gordon (1917–1942)—The Imperial War Museum, London

Malcolm, Lavinia (1847/8–1920)—courtesy Dollar Museum Trust

Malcolm, Sir Neill (1869–1953)—© National Portrait Gallery, London

Malcolm, Sir Pulteney (1768–1838)—Scottish National Portrait Gallery

Malcolm, Sarah (c.1710–1733)—National Gallery of Scotland

Malet, Sir Charles Warre, first baronet (1753–1815)—photograph by courtesy Sotheby's Picture Library, London

Malet, Sir Edward Baldwin, fourth baronet (1837–1908)—Getty Images – Hulton Archive

Malibran, Maria Felicia (1808–1836)—© Photo RMN – Bulloz

Malinowski, Bronisław Kasper (1884–1942)—© National Portrait Gallery, London

Mallet, Sir Louis (1823–1890)—The British Library

Mallock, William Hurrell (1849–1923)—© National Portrait Gallery, London

Mallon, James Joseph (1874–1961)—Toynbee Hall, London; photograph National Portrait Gallery, London

Mallory, George Herbert Leigh (1886–1924)—© National Portrait Gallery, London

Malone, Edmond (1741–1812)—© National Portrait Gallery, London

Maltby, Edward (1770–1859)—by kind permission of the Lord Bishop of Durham and the Church Commissioners of England. Photograph: Photographic Survey, Courtauld Institute of Art, London

Malthus, (Thomas) Robert (1766–1834)—by kind permission of the Master and Council of Haileybury; photograph National Portrait Gallery, London

Man, Felix Hans (1893–1985)—© Roger George Clark; collection National Portrait Gallery, London

Manby, George William (1765–1854)—© The Royal Society

Mangnall, Richmal (1769–1820)—© National Portrait Gallery, London

Manley, Michael Norman (1924–1997)—Getty Images – Neil Libbert

Manley, Norman Washington (1893–1969)—Getty Images – George Freston

Mann, Cathleen Sabine (1896–1959)—photograph by courtesy Sotheby's Picture Library, London

Mann, Sir Horatio, second baronet (1744–1814)—Marylebone Cricket Club, London / Bridgeman Art Library

Mann, Jean (1889–1964)—© National Portrait Gallery, London

Mann, Thomas (1856–1941)—Getty Images – Hulton Archive

Manners, John, marquess of Granby (1721–1770)—Bequest of John Ringling, Collection of the John and Mable Ringling Museum of Art, the State Art Museum of Florida

Manners, John James Robert, seventh duke of Rutland (1818–1906)—© National Portrait Gallery, London

Manners, Mary Isabella, duchess of Rutland (1756–1831)—© National Portrait Gallery, London

Manners, (Marion Margaret) Violet, duchess of Rutland (1856–1937)—© National Portrait Gallery, London

Mannheim, Karl (1893–1947)—© National Portrait Gallery, London

Mannin, Ethel Edith (1900–1984)—© Estate of Paul Tanqueray; collection National Portrait Gallery, London

Manning, Henry Edward (1808–1892)—© National Portrait Gallery, London

Manning, Dame (Elizabeth) Leah (1886–1977)—© National Portrait Gallery, London

Manning, Thomas (1772–1840)—courtesy Royal Asiatic Society, London

Mannix, Daniel (1864–1963)—courtesy of the National Library of Ireland

Mannock, Edward (1887–1918)—© reserved / courtesy of the Trustees of the Royal Air Force Museum

Mansbridge, Albert (1876–1952)—© National Portrait Gallery, London

Mansel, Henry Longueville (1820–1871)—© National Portrait Gallery, London

Mansell, Sir Robert (1570/71–1652)—© National Museums and Galleries of Wales

Mansergh, James (1834–1905)—courtesy of the Institution of Civil Engineers Archives

Mansergh, (Philip) Nicholas Seton (1910–1991)—© National Portrait Gallery, London

Manson, Sir Patrick (1844–1922)—© National Portrait Gallery, London

Mant, Richard (1776–1848)—© National Portrait Gallery, London

Manton, Sidnie Milana (1902–1979)—Godfrey Argent Studios / Royal Society

Manton, Thomas (bap. 1620, d. 1677)—© National Portrait Gallery, London

Mantovani, Annunzio Paolo (1905–1980)—V&A Images, The Victoria and Albert Museum; collection National Portrait Gallery, London

Manwood, Sir Roger (1524/5–1592)—© Crown copyright. NMR

Maples, Chauncy (1852–1895)—© National Portrait Gallery, London

Maplethorpe, Cyril Wheatley (1898–1983)—Museum of the Royal Pharmaceutical Society of Great Britain

Mappin, Sir Frederick Thorpe, first baronet (1821–1910)—© National Portrait Gallery, London

Mar, Norman René del (1919–1994)—© Derek Allen; collection National Portrait Gallery, London

Mara, Gertrud Elisabeth (1749–1833)—© National Portrait Gallery, London

Marcet, Jane Haldimand (1769–1858)—Edgar Fahs Smith Collection, University of Pennsylvania Library

Marchant, Nathaniel (1738/9–1816)—by courtesy of the Trustees of Sir John Soane's Museum

Marconi, Guglielmo (1874–1937)—Getty Images - Hulton Archive

Mare, Thomas de la (*c*.1309–1396)—reproduced by courtesy of H. M. Stutchfield, F.S.A., Hon. Secretary of the Monumental Brass Society

Mare, Walter John de la (1873–1956)—© National Portrait Gallery, London

Marett, Robert Ranulph (1866–1943)—The Rector and Scholars of Exeter College, Oxford / Estate of Henry Lamb

Margaret [of Anjou] (1430–1482)—V&A Images, The Victoria and Albert Museum

Margoliouth, David Samuel (1858–1940)—© National Portrait Gallery, London

Margoliouth, Moses (1815–1881)—© National Portrait Gallery, London

Marjoribanks, Edward, second Baron Tweedmouth (1849–1909)—© National Portrait Gallery, London

Markby, Sir William (1829–1914)—© National Portrait Gallery, London

Markham, Sir Albert Hastings (1841–1918)—© National Portrait Gallery, London

Markham, Beryl (1902–1986)—Getty Images - Hulton Archive

Markham, Sir Clements Robert (1830–1916)—© National Portrait Gallery, London

Markham, Violet Rosa (1872–1959)—© reserved

Markham, William (*bap.* 1719, *d.* 1807)—© National Portrait Gallery, London

Markievicz, Constance Georgine, Countess Markievicz in the Polish nobility (1868–1927)—courtesy of the National Library of Ireland

Marks, Michael (1859–1907)—Marks & Spencer Company Archive

Marks, Simon, first Baron Marks (1888–1964)—Estate of the Artist; collection unknown; photograph Courtauld Institute of Art, London

Marochetti, (Pietro) Carlo Giovanni Battista, Baron Marochetti in the nobility of Sardinia (1805–1867)—© National Portrait Gallery, London

Marot, Daniel (1661–1752)—© National Portrait Gallery, London

Marples, (Alfred) Ernest, Baron Marples (1907–1978)—© National Portrait Gallery, London

Marquand, Hilary Adair (1901–1972)—© National Portrait Gallery, London

Marquis, Frederick James, first earl of Woolton (1883–1964)—© National Portrait Gallery, London

Marrant, John (1755–1791)—Ashmolean Museum, Oxford

Marriott, Sir John Arthur Ransome (1859–1945)—© National Portrait Gallery, London

Marryat, Frederick (1792–1848)—© National Portrait Gallery, London

Marryat, Thomas (1730–1792)—Ashmolean Museum, Oxford

Marsden, Sir Ernest (1889–1970)—© National Portrait Gallery, London

Marsden, Kate (1859–1931)—The Royal Geographical Society, London

Marsden, Samuel (1765–1838)—Alexander Turnbull Library, National Library of New Zealand, Te Puna Matauranga o Aotearoa (A-039-038)

Marsden, William (1754–1836)—© National Portrait Gallery, London

Marsden, William (1796–1867)—Royal Marsden Hospital; photograph National Portrait Gallery, London

Marsh, Sir Henry, first baronet (1790–1860)—© National Portrait Gallery, London

Marsh, Herbert (1757–1839)—by permission of the Master and Fellows of St John's College, Cambridge

Marsh, Narcissus (1638–1713)—The Rector and Scholars of Exeter College, Oxford

Marsh, Dame (Edith) Ngaio (1895–1982)—Alexander Turnbull Library, National Library of New Zealand, Te Puna Matauranga o Aotearoa / New Zealand Freelance Collection (F-46800-1/2)

Marshal, William (I), fourth earl of Pembroke (*c*.1146–1219)—Temple Church, London / Bridgeman Art Library

Marshall, Alfred (1842–1924)—by courtesy of the Estate of Sir William Rothenstein; collection St John's College, Cambridge

Marshall, Arthur Calder- (1908–1992)—© National Portrait Gallery, London

Marshall, Sir Guy Anstruther Knox (1871–1959)—© National Portrait Gallery, London

Marshall, John (1765–1845)—The University of Leeds Art Collection

Marshall, Thomas Humphrey (1893–1981)—© National Portrait Gallery, London

Marshall, Walter Charles, Baron Marshall of Goring (1932–1996)—Godfrey Argent Studios / Royal Society

Marshall, Sir William Raine (1865–1939)—The Imperial War Museum, London

Marsham, Sir John, first baronet (1602–1685)—© National Portrait Gallery, London

Marson, Una Maud Victoria (1905–1965)—BBC Picture Archives

Martel, Sir Giffard Le Quesne (1889–1958)—© National Portrait Gallery, London

Marten, Henry (1601/2–1680)—© National Portrait Gallery, London

Martin, Benjamin (*bap.* 1705, *d.* 1782)—© National Portrait Gallery, London

Martin, John (1789–1854)—© National Portrait Gallery, London

Martin, John (1812–1875)—by courtesy of the National Gallery of Ireland

Martin, Sir (John) Leslie (1908–2000)—© Philip Sayer; collection National Portrait Gallery, London

Martin, Sir Richard (1533/4–1617)—© Copyright The British Museum

Martin, Richard (1570–1618)—© National Portrait Gallery, London

Martin, Sir Theodore (1816–1909)—© Copyright The British Museum

Martin, Thomas (1697–1771)—Ashmolean Museum, Oxford

Martin, Sir Thomas Byam (1773–1854)—Ashmolean Museum, Oxford

Martin, Violet Florence (1862–1915)—© Estate of Edith Somerville; collection National Portrait Gallery, London

Martin, William (1772–1851)—© National Portrait Gallery, London

Oxford dictionary of
national biography